KV-316-173

STAFFORDSHIRE LIBRARIES
3 8014 02663 5943

AUSTRALIA
The Law Book Company
Brisbane • Sydney • Melbourne • Perth

CANADA
Carswell
Ottawa • Toronto • Calgary • Montreal • Vancouver

Agents:
Steimatzky's Agency Ltd., Tel Aviv
N.M. Tripathi (Private) Ltd., Bombay
Eastern Law House (Private) Ltd., Calcutta
M.P.P. House, Bangalore
Universal Book Traders, Delhi
Aditya Books, Delhi
MacMillan Shuppan KK, Tokyo
Pakistan Law House, Karachi, Lahore

Current Law

YEAR BOOK
1995

VOLUME TWO

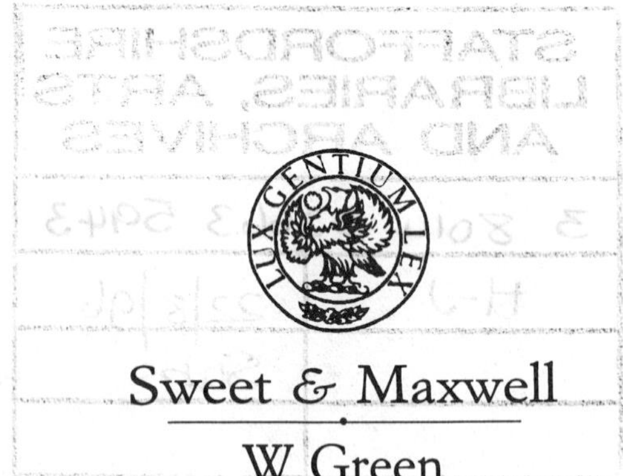

Sweet & Maxwell
W Green

Current Law

YEAR BOOK 1995

Being a Comprehensive Statement of the Law of 1995

SWEET & MAXWELL EDITORIAL TEAM

Sarah Andrews, Melanie Bhagat, Ala Kuzmicki, Sophie Lowe, Ceri Pickering

W. GREEN EDITORIAL TEAM

Janie Brash, Charlotte Hall, Peter Nicholson

Editors

English and Commonwealth Law

MARGARET AUSTIN, LL.M.
NICHOLAS BAATZ, M.A., B.C.L., *Barrister*
CATHERINE BARNARD, B.A., LL.M.
CHRISTOPHER BUTLER, LL.B., *Barrister*
IAN FERRIER, M.A., *Barrister*
SHAUN FERRIS, B.A., *Barrister*
NICHOLAS GASKELL, LL.B., *Barrister*
IAN GOLDSWORTHY, Q.C.
GEOFFREY HARDING, Ph.D, *Solicitor, Wilde Sapte*
ALASTAIR HUDSON, LL.B., LL.M., *Barrister*
CHARLES JOSEPH, B.A., *Barrister, FCI Arb*
SIMON LOFTHOUSE, *Barrister*
ANN McALLISTER, B.A., LL.M., *Barrister*
SIOBHAN McGRATH, B.A., *Barrister*
PETER MANTLE, *Barrister*
VANESSA MIDDLETON LL.B., *Solicitor, Davenport Lyons*
ALEXANDRA MILLBROOK, B.A., *Barrister*
ALISON MORLEY, LL.B., *Barrister*
JULIE O'MALLEY, LL.B., *Barrister*
ANTHONY PITTS, *Barrister*
CHARLES SCOTT, LL.B., *Barrister*
ISOBEL SINCLAIR, LL.B., *Solicitor, Norton Rose*
HELEN TATE, LL.B., *Barrister*
JOHN TATE, LL.B., *Barrister*

English and Commonwealth Law (cont.)

WILLIAM UPTON, M.A., LL.M., *Barrister*
WILLIAM VANDYCK, B.A., *Barrister*
ROBERT WEBB, Q.C., LL.B.
GORDON WIGNALL, M.A., *Barrister*

European Communities:

ALISON GREEN, LL.M., *Barrister*
CONOR QUIGLEY, LL.B., *Barrister*

Northern Ireland:

RALPH ERSKINE, LL.B., *Barrister*

Scotland:

MALCOLM THOMSON, Q.C., LL.B.

Damages Awards

PETER MANTLE, *Barrister*
DAVID KEMP, Q.B., B.A., *Barrister*

Articles

SIMON LOFTHOUSE, *Barrister*
ALISON GREEN, LL.M., *Barrister*

LONDON • HONG KONG • DUBLIN • OXFORD • EDINBURGH

Sweet & Maxwell
W. Green
1996

The Mode of Citation

of the Current Law Year Book

is, *e.g.:*

[1995] 2 C.L.Y. 1282

The 1995 Year Book is published in two volumes.

ISBN: This volume only: 0–421–57750–9
with volume 1 and Citators: 0–421–57770–3

Published in 1996 by
Sweet & Maxwell Limited of
100 Avenue Road, Swiss Cottage, London NW3 3PF
Typeset by LBJ Enterprises Limited of Aldermaston and Chilcompton
Printed by The Bath Press, Bath.

No natural forests were destroyed to make this product;
farmed timber was used and then replanted.

PREFACE

This volume completes 48 years of Current Law publishing. It supersedes the issues of *Current Law Monthly Digest* for 1995 and covers the law from January 1 to December 31 of that year.

Citators

The *Case Citator*, the *Legislation Citator* and the *Statutory Instrument Citator* are contained in separate volumes, issued with this volume.

The new *Current Law Citators* cover cases, statutes and now statutory instruments, during the years 1989–95. There are permanent bound volumes covering cases during the period 1947–76 and 1977–88, and statutes during 1947–71 and 1972–88. Separate volumes were published in the *Scottish Current Law* series covering the years 1948–76 and 1977–88 (cases) and 1948–71 and 1972–88 (statutes).

The present volume contains a table of cases digested and reported in 1995, the usual tables covering 1995 statutory instruments, although the table showing their effect on the orders of earlier years has been superseded by the *Statutory Instruments Citator*, and is therefore no longer included in the Year Book, and tables of Northern Ireland Statutory Rules and Orders.

Books and Articles

Indexes of the books and articles published in 1995 are included at the back of this volume. The full title, reference and the name of the author are given in each case and both indexes are arranged under *Current Law* headings. Scottish books are classified separately under "Scotland" but articles in Scottish journals, which may deal with subjects of wider interest, are amalgamated with the U.K. list.

Index

The subject-matter index in this volume follows the new improved format introduced at the beginning of 1991 in the monthly digest and has been compiled by Nigel Smith and Chantal Hamill. The 30-year Index from 1947–76 may be found in the 1976 *Current Law Year Book.* The Scottish Index for the years 1972–86 may be found in the Scottish 1986 *Year Book.* Scottish material prior to 1972 can be found in the *Scottish Current Law Year Book Master Volumes*, published in 1956, 1961, 1966 and 1971.

Statutes

54 Acts received the Royal Assent during the year. A complete list of Statutes appears under the title Statutes and Orders.

Cases

The number of cases digested exceeds 3,500. This figure does not include the short reports showing what damages have been awarded in cases of injury or death. These decisions have been collected and edited by Mr David Kemp. The *Quantum* of Damages Table at the front of this volume provides a guide to the personal injury decisions reported in 1995.

The Year Book again includes a selection of cases of persuasive force from the courts of the Commonwealth and from the English county courts.

Jurisdictions

The text of the *Current Law Year Book* is divided into three sections, covering respectively U.K., England and Wales and E.U. (which includes material applicable to Great Britain or the U.K. as a whole); Northern Ireland; and Scotland. Coverage of European Union cases takes the form of digests of all European Court of Justice decisions, created by reference to the European Court of Justice transcripts. Coverage of English and European journals dealing with the law of the European Communities and the national law of European states is now contained in *European Current Law*, which began publication of monthly digests in January 1992 and which publishes its own Year Book.

Northern Ireland

All Northern Irish Acts and Orders and the cases reported from the courts of Northern Ireland have been digested, together with a selection of the cases reported from the courts of the Republic of Ireland. This work has been carried out by our editor in Northern Ireland, Mr T.R. Erskine.

Scotland

The Scottish text is prepared by the W. Green editorial team in Edinburgh in the same manner as the Sweet & Maxwell *Current Law* team working on the England & Wales/U.K. text in London. Case digests are prepared by our case editor in Scotland, Malcolm Thomson, Q.C. Users should note that the *Current Law Year Book* does not repeat the references to cases noted in *Green's Weekly Digest* which appear in the Scottish section of *Current Law Monthly Digest*. *Green's Weekly Digest* is purely a précis of recent judgments of the Scottish courts; cases of legal significance will be digested in *Current Law* through their appearance in one of the series of law reports proper.

Cases *"ex relatione"*

We welcome short reports of cases submitted by members of both branches of the legal profession. They are noted as *"Ex rel. A.B., Barrister"* or *"Ex rel. C.D., Solicitors"*, as the case may be. These reports, we believe, are of considerable value to the profession, since the contributor can properly be regarded as having first-hand knowledge of the facts. Unfortunately, occasional instances have been brought to our notice in which reports of this kind have been misleading or even incorrect. We are grateful to those who bring such matters to our attention and we seek to correct the report in a later issue or in the *Current Law Year Book.* We must stress, however, that we are entirely dependent on the contributor for the accuracy of his or her report. It is impracticable for us independently to check the facts stated to us.

The General Editor thanks those who have pointed out errors and those who have sent in notes of interesting cases.

May 1996

CONTENTS

VOLUME 1

THE LAW OF 1995 DIGESTED UNDER TITLES:

Note: Italicised entries refer to Scotland only.

VOLUME 2

MINORS

3360. Accomodation—judicial review—application made by "child in need" to be accommodated—child already placed with new family—local authority refusing to accomodate child—whether child should be accommodated under the Children Act—whether fulfilling duties under the 1989 Act in past sufficient

[Children Act 1989 (c.41), ss.17, 20(3).]

T applied for judicial review of the decision of the Director of Social Services not to provide her with accommodation under the Children Act 1989, s.20(3), which would have the effect of providing her carers with a fostering allowance and ongoing support from the local authority after she reached the age of 18, on the grounds that her welfare was not likely to be seriously prejudiced if accomodation were not provided.

Held, allowing T's application, that the director had erred in considering only the past and not the future when determining whether T's welfare would be prejudiced by the failure to provide accommodation, and had not considered the likelihood of the local authority exercising its powers and duties under s.17 of the 1989 Act in the future (*R. v. Hillingdon London Borough Council, ex p. Puhlhofer* [1986] C.L.Y. 1619 considered).

T. (ACCOMODATION BY LOCAL AUTHORITY) *Re* [1995] 1 F.L.R. 159, Johnson J.

3361. Adoption—application by foster-parents supported by local authority—marriage breakdown due to affair by foster-father—foster-mother continuing the application—application opposed by local authority and guardians *ad litem*—whether court should grant adoption orders

F and M were foster-parents who fostered four children from two families. The children from B family, two boys with mental and physical disabilities, aged 15 and 13 and a girl aged 11, were placed with F and M in 1983. A, a girl aged nine, born to unmarried parents with drink and drug problems was taken into care by the local authority and placed with F and M in 1987. A's mother died in 1990 and A was directed to live with F and M with a view to adoption in wardships proceedings. F and M were approved as adoptive parents and issued proceedings to adopt the children which the guardians *ad litem* supported. The father of the B children refused to give his consent. A's grandmother and father wished to have continued contact. In 1992 F had an affair with another woman. M colluded with F in keeping the affair secret from social workers. The affair was subsequently reported to the local authority and A's father applied for a residence order after being told of allegations of sexual abuse made against F by his adult son which subsequently proved to be untrue. F and M's marriage broke down and F went to live with the other woman. M continued with the adoption proceedings as sole applicant but the application was opposed by the local authority and guardians *ad litem*. A's father relapsed to drugs and his application for a residence order was withdrawn. The local authority had no plans to remove the children from M's long-term care but the family would continue to obtain support under a case order.

Held, granting the adoption, that as far as the B children were concerned it was a clear case since they had known no other family for the past 11 years and there was no concerns about the actual care given. The father had had no contact for five years and since there was no likelihood of future contact a reasonable man would consent to the adoption, therefore his consent could be dispensed with. In relation to A there had been considerable delay in the application and it was time for a decision. It was decided an adoption order was in her best interests despite the upheaval in the home as she looked on M as her mother and the other children as brothers and sisters.

B. AND S. (MINORS) (ADOPTION), *Re* [1995] 1 F.C.R. 486, Ewbank J.

3362. Adoption—application by unmarried foster-parents—requirement that application be made by one person—whether court having jurisdiction to make order in favour of one person and to grant joint residence order

[Adoption Act 1976 (c.36), s.14; Children Act 1989 (c.41), s.11(4).]

The case concerned the court's jurisdiction to make orders in respect of a five-year-old child who had been living with unmarried foster-parents who wished to adopt him. It was accepted that the couple, who had lived together for more than twenty years, were well able to provide for the child's needs but under s.14 of the Adoption Act 1976 only one person, apart from a married couple, could apply for an adoption order.

Held, that an adoption order would be made in favour of the foster-father and, given the circumstances of the case, a joint residence order in favour of both partners would be appropriate. The court had jurisdiction to make such an order under s.11(4) of the Children Act 1989.

A.B. (A MINOR) (ADOPTION: UNMARRIED COUPLE), *Re*, *The Times*, August 10, 1995, Cazalet J.

3363. Adoption—application to remove child from care of foster-parent—local authority seeking other prospective adopters—foster-parent applying to adopt child—local authority seeking to serve notice for removal of child—whether application "related to welfare of the child"—whether welfare of child first consideration

An application for leave to issue a notice to remove a child from foster-parents was a decision relating to the adoption of a child and the need to safeguard and promote the welfare of the child was the paramount consideration.

C was placed with a foster-mother, B. The local authority care plan envisaged that C would be adopted and A, potential adopters, were introduced to C. Before C was due to move permanently B served a notice of intention to apply to adopt C on the local authority. The local authority then applied under s.30 of the Adoption Act 1976 for leave to issue a notice for C's removal on B. The judge granted the application and B applied with the support of the guardian *ad litem*.

Held, allowing the appeal, that the application was one which related to the child's adoption and the interests of C were the first consideration. Whilst the local authority care plan was to be given considerable weight so too should the foster-parent's intention to adopt and the attitude of the guardian *ad litem*. Where the foster-parent's application was genuine and had a reasonable prospect of success leave to issue a notice to remove the child should be refused (*S. v. Huddersfield Borough Council* [1974] C.L.Y. 2361, *B. (Minors) (Termination of Contract; Paramount Consideration), Re* [1993] C.L.Y. 2771 applied; *P. (An Infant) (Adoption Parental Consent), Re* [1977] C.L.Y. 1919 distinguished).

C. (A MINOR) (ADOPTION NOTICE: LOCAL AUTHORITY), *Re* [1994] 1 W.L.R. 1220, C.A.

3364. Adoption—application to remove natural father as party to proceedings—meaning of "parent"—statutory interpretation

[Adoption Rules 1984 (S.I. 1984 No. 265), r.15; Adoption Act 1976 (c.36), s.72; Children Act 1989 (c.41), Sched. 10.]

The prospective adopters of C appealed against the dismissal of their application that C's natural father, unmarried and without parental responsibility, be removed as a party to the adoption proceedings which were governed by r.15 of the Adoption Rules 1984.

Held, allowing the appeal, that under s.72(1) of the Adoption Act 1976, as amended by para. 30 of Sched. 10 of the Children Act 1989, the word "parent" meant any parent with parental responsibility for the child under the 1989 Act. Rule 2(2) of the Adoption (Amendment) Rules 1991 further provided that words or phrases contained therein were to have the same meaning as they bore in the 1976 Act, unless a contrary intention appeared. It therefore followed that the definition contained in the 1976 Act directly applied to r.15 of the 1984 Rules. The matter was directed to be further considered in the county court.

C. (MINOR) (ADOPTION: PARTIES), *Re*, *The Times*, June 1, 1995, C.A.

3365. Adoption—conditions—imposition of condition by court—adoptive parents Jehovah's Witnesses—condition requiring undertaking not to withhold consent to blood transfusion for child without court order—whether condition appropriate

[Adoption Act 1976 (c.36), s.12.]

It was rarely appropriate for a court to impose a condition on the making of an adoption order that was against the wishes of the adoptive parents.

Mr and Mrs H, practising Jehovah's Witnesses, sought to adopt E. The judge expressed concern that they might withhold consent to a blood transfusion for E at some time in the future because of their religious beliefs, and imposed a condition upon the adoption order requiring an undertaking from Mr and Mrs H not to withhold such consent without an application to the court. Mr and Mrs H appealed against the order.

Held, allowing the appeal, that it was not desirable to impose conditions against the wishes of the adoptive parents, particularly where the condition had a continuing effect. A condition that was resented by the parents would risk undermining their relationship with the child. It would also be difficult to supervise and enforce because of the undesirability of placing the adopters in contempt of court (*C. (A Minor) (Adoption: Conditions), Re* [1988] C.L.Y. 2302 applied).

S. (A MINOR) (ADOPTION ORDER: CONDITIONS), *Re* [1995] 2 All E.R. 122, C.A.

3366. Adoption—contact—contact order and freeing order made—procedure for subsequent adoption and contact hearings—whether parent's consent properly dispensed with where contact order made—whether freeing order properly made where contact order also made

[Adoption Act 1976 (c.36), ss.12(3), 16(2)(b), 18(5), 19; Children Act 1989 (c.41), s.8.]

Following the Children Act 1989, continuing contact between the child and his birth family was not incompatible with an order freeing the child for adoption.

A was born in 1990 and M and F separated shortly afterwards. A was later placed with foster-parents and, in November 1991, was the subject of an uncontested care order. The local authority applied to free A for adoption, and for leave to terminate contact between A and her parents. Both M and F applied for contact with a view to A's rehabilitation to M. The applications were heard together in September 1992. The guardian *ad litem* recommended that A be freed for adoption, but also that A's contact with M and new family was beneficial and should be continued, if possible, after adoption. The judge found that there was no prospect of rehabilitation, that adoption was in A's best interests and so dispensed with M and F's agreement to adoption. A freeing order was made, as was an order for M to have monthly contact until A's adoption, the local authority having not opposed such contact.

Held, dismissing M's appeal, that (1) the judge's finding that adoption was in A's best interests was unchallenged, and adoption would be in her best interests even if there were no post-adoption contact; (2) since the 1989 Act, a judge could free the child for adoption but at the same time preserve contact between the child and the birth family pending adoption. M would retain the right to respond to any application by the local authority to vary the existing contact order, or could apply herself for variation. The hypothetical reasonable parent would recognise that A should be adopted and that she would retain the right to be heard on the question of contact. The court could not therefore properly interfere with the judge's finding that M was unreasonably withholding her consent to adoption (*Southwark London Borough Council v. H.* [1985] C.L.Y. 2191, *E. (Minors) (Adoption: Parental Agreement), Re* [1991] C.L.Y. 2495, *C. (Minors) (Adoption), Re* [1992] C.L.Y. 3012 distinguished); and (3) a freeing order extinguished the birth parents' parental responsibility and they became former parents with no right to apply for an order under s.8 of the Children Act 1989.

[*Per curiam*: Whilst infrequent contact with the birth family up to or three times a year might be acceptable after a freeing order, monthly contact would seem incompatible with the likely views of prospective adopters, and had evidently inhibited the search for a suitable adoptive family for A. Where contact was ordered to continue post-freeing, there should be judicial continuity, and if possible the same judge should hear the adoption application as would hear any application affecting the birth parent's contact.]

R. (A MINOR) (ADOPTION: CONTACT ORDER), *Re* [1994] 1 F.C.R. 104, C.A.

3367. Adoption—contact—freeing for adoption order—variation of contact order—whether jurisdiction to vary—whether family proceedings were still continuing

A father of three children applied for an extension of time in order to appeal against an order varying the contact element of an order freeing his children for adoption. Under the terms of the original order the parents were allowed contact with the children 12 times a year, but the order was varied to reduce the contact to three times a year.

Held, allowing the application, that an application was concluded on the making of a contact order so that family proceedings within the meaning of s.8(3) of the Children Act 1989 were no longer continuing, and therefore a judge did not have jurisdiction to vary the order under s.10. Nevertheless the court would exercise its powers to vary the order to allow contact three times a year pending further consideration by the High Court.

C. (MINORS) (CONTACT: JURISDICTION), *Re The Times*, February 15, 1995, C.A.

3368. Adoption—contact—leave to apply for—informal contact arrangements with adoptive parents—not carried out by adoptive parents—no reasons given—whether appropriate for court to investigate—procedure for leave applications

T appealed against an order dismissing her application for leave to commence contact proceedings in respect of her half-brothers and sisters who had been adopted. There had been an informal agreement with the adoptive parents that they would send the appellant annual progress reports but this did not happen. T argued that the consensual nature of adoption was under threat if the adoptive parents could resile from informal agreements without giving reasons and without the courts being able to enquire into the matter.

Held, allowing the appeal, that there was no evidence that contact would be too disruptive to the children and reasons should be given by the adoptive parents.

[*Per curiam*: In applications for leave to apply for direct or indirect contact with children who had been adopted, the aim was to avoid unnecessary disturbance to the adoptive parents whilst ensuring that the court had as much information as possible to enable it to determine the application. The appropriate procedure was, therefore, to notify the local authority of the application where the authority was the adoption agency but, since an application for leave was not the substantive application, it was not always necessary to bring in the Official Solicitor as respondent nor to transfer proceedings to the Family Division of the High Court, although this might be appropriate in certain cases.]

T. (MINORS) (ADOPTED CHILDREN: CONTACT), *Re* (FC 95/6083/F), July 28, 1995, C.A.

3369. Adoption—contact—leave to apply for—whether natural parents entitled to bring application

[Children Act 1989 (c.41), ss.8, 10(9).]

At the first stage of a split adoption hearing the judge dispensed with the natural parents' consent on the grounds that it was being unreasonably withheld. An assurance was given through the social worker that photographs and news about schooling would be forthcoming. The second stage of the hearing took place nine weeks later when the natural parents were not present and an adoption order was made without any conditions and without mentioning the photographs and reports. None were subsequently sent. Three years later, the natural parents applied for leave to make a contact application to enforce the assurance which they had originally been given.

Held, that the unfairness to the natural parents was real but leave to make the application would not be given because the adopters were opposed to contact. The correct procedure would have been to apply to amend the order to appeal on the grounds that the original adoption order was flawed, unfair and deficient (*C. (A Minor) (Adopted Child: Contact), Re* [1993] C.L.Y. 2763, *C. (A Minor) (Adoption Order; Conditions), Re* [1988] C.L.Y. 2302, *D. (A Minor) (Adoption Order: Conditions), Re* [1992] C.L.Y. 3008 referred to).

[*Per curiam*: the case illustrates the pitfalls of split hearings of contested county court adoption applications.]

E. (ADOPTED CHILD: CONTACT: LEAVE), *Re* [1995] 1 F.L.R. 57, Thorpe J.

3370. Adoption—contact order—access to adopted child—whether order necessary where access already provided on informal basis

It was unnecessary to bind adoptive parents to permit natural parental access to the adopted child where there had been ready and willing agreement to continuing and open access.

T. (A MINOR) (CONTACT ORDER), *Re*, *The Times*, January 13, 1995, C.A.

3371. Adoption—foster-parents applying for adoption—local authority seeking leave to serve notice of intention to remove child—whether court should grant leave

[Adoption Act 1976 (c.36), ss.6, 22, 30, 31, 32, Sched. 2; Children Act 1989 (c.41).]

Notwithstanding that the child was in care and that, therefore, the court had no power to review the local authority care plan, it was for the court to decide whether or not the child should be removed from the prospective adopters, applying the test set out in s.6 of the Adoption Act 1976.

P was now 21 months old. She had been with the foster-parents since birth. P was made the subject of a care order when five months old, with the local authority care plan being to place her for adoption by a black family. In December 1993 the foster-parents gave notice to the local authority of their intention to adopt, and issued their adoption application. The applicants were a white couple in their forties, and had an adopted daughter of mixed race who was now aged 12. The local authority wished to implement its care plan and continue the search for a same race placement. It therefore sought the leave of the court to serve notice of their intention to remove P from the applicants, as required by ss.30 and 31 of the Adoption Act 1976. It indicated that, as there was no adoptive placement immediately available, that, if granted leave, the notice would not be served straight away, but that the foster-parents could continue looking after P until a new placement was identified.

Held, dismissing the application, that (1) once the foster-parents had served notice of their intention to apply for adoption, in accordance with s.22 of the Adoption Act 1976, then the provisions of ss.30 and 31 came into play, and the local authority needed the leave of the court to serve notice of intention to remove P from the applicants. Parliament had considered and amended ss.22, 30 and 31 in passing the Children Act 1989, but had not taken that opportunity to prevent or restrict or limit foster-parents from giving notice or applying for an adoption order. The submission that the court should be very slow to interfere with the local authority care plan when considering its application must fail, and the application would be determined in accordance with the provisions of the Adoption Act 1976; (2) the decision was for the court, and the court should not delegate the decision to the local authority or grant leave on the basis that the local authority would decide to serve the notice at a time and in circumstances which were unknown; (3) the decision whether or not to grant leave was governed by s.6 of the Adoption Act 1976, with the child's welfare the first consideration; and (4) on the facts, it would be wrong to grant leave to the authority to serve a notice, as it would be very detrimental to disrupt P's attachment to the foster-parents without there first being a full inquiry by the guardian *ad litem*.

P. (A MINOR) (REMOVAL OF CHILD FOR ADOPTION), *Re* [1994] 2 F.C.R. 537, Miss Mary Hogg, Q.C. sitting as a High Court judge.

3372. Adoption—freeing for adoption—local authority seeking freeing order—mother having legitimate sense of grievance against local authority—mother resisting freeing application and applying for contact—judge dispensing with mother's agreement and making freeing order—whether judge plainly wrong

[Adoption Act 1976 (c.36), ss.6, 16(2), 18; Children Act 1989 (c.41), ss.8, 34.]

The judge was not plainly wrong in finding that a parent with concerns over her child's placement with a lesbian, and with a legitimate sense of grievance against the local authority, was unreasonably withholding her consent to a freeing order.

E, now aged 12, was born to parents who had a chaotic and violent relationship. When she was aged two and a half, she was taken into care. E last lived with M when the child was aged three. There followed a series of unsuccessful foster placements, while M continued to seek E's rehabilitation to her and the discharge of the care order. Eventually E was placed with A, a lesbian single woman, who was an experienced social worker and who showed a strong commitment to E. A wished to care for E on a long-term basis, possibly with a view to adoption. The local authority applied for a freeing order, which was opposed by M, whose application for contact was heard at the same time. The court made a freeing order, finding that M was unreasonably withholding her consent, and dismissed M's contact application.

Held, dismissing M's appeal, that (1) the court would only interfere with the decision of the court below if it had misdirected itself in law or was plainly wrong (*G. v. G. (Minors: Custody Appeal)* [1985] C.L.Y. 2594 applied); (2) no challenge was made to the finding that adoption was in the best interests of the child, and the judge had correctly identified that as a separate and distinct issue. Looking at his judgment as a whole, the judge had applied the correct objective test, and had approached the case from the point of view of the hypothetical reasonable parent (*D. (A Minor) (Adoption: Freeing Order), Re* [1991] C.L.Y. 2499 applied); (3) the judge had carefully considered the possible impact on E of being brought up by a lesbian, and his findings on this issue could not be faulted (*D. (An Infant) (Adoption: Parent's Consent), Re* [1976] C.L.Y. 1751, *C. v. C. (A Minor) (Custody Appeal)* [1991] C.L.Y. 2548, *B. v. B. (Minors) (Custody, Care and Control)* [1991] C.L.Y. 2547 considered); (4) although the judge had found that M had had a legitimate grievance against the local authority, he had found that the reasonable parent would recognise that the overwhelming advantages of adoption for E would outweigh that sense of grievance. His decision could not be faulted, and the court agreed with his findings (*B. (A Minor) (Adoption: Parental Agreement), Re* [1991] C.L.Y. 2494, *E. (Minors) (Adoption: Parental Agreement), Re* [1991] C.L.Y. 2495 considered); and (5) as to the decision on contact, the judge had had before him an abundance of evidence that any order for contact would be disastrous. Nothing should be done which might jeopardise E's placement.

E. (ADOPTION: FREEING ORDER), *Re* [1995] 1 F.L.R. 382, C.A.

3373. Adoption—freeing for adoption—mother refusing to agree to adoption—judge finding that there should be contact between mother and children post-adoption—judge dispensing with mother's agreement—whether order appropriate in circumstances—proper course to be followed

[Adoption Act 1976 (c.36), s.16(2).]

A local authority applied for a freeing order in respect of twins. M refused to consent. The judge found that adoption would promote the welfare of the children but that they would benefit from continuing contact with M post-adoption and so made the order sought, dispensed with the M's consent under the Adoption Act 1976, s.16(2) but directed the local authority, as the adoption agency, to seek prospective adopters who would accept continuing contact. He also directed that he should hear the adoption application and would allow M to be heard on the adoption application.

Held, M's appeal allowed, that the judge had sought to make contact a pre-condition of adoption but he could not guarantee that there would be an adoption order with contact. If there was no continuing contact, then M would not be unreasonable in withholding her agreement. The judge should have refused to dispense with M's consent and put over the question of contact until the hearing of the adoption application.

P. (MINORS) (ADOPTION: FREEING ORDER), *Re* [1994] 2 F.C.R. 1306, C.A.

3374. Adoption—guardian *ad litem* report—child promised confidentiality—mother seeking disclosure—whether wrong to promise confidentiality

[Adoption Rules 1984 (S.I. 1984 No. 265), r.53(2).]

The report of a guardian *ad litem* in adoption proceedings is presumed confidential unless the party seeking disclosure can show good reason. A promise of confidentially is a promise that might not be kept if the court orders disclosure.

Following divorce the two children of the family remained with the father. Contact with the mother became very infrequent. The father remarried and the new wife applied to adopt the children. The guardian *ad litem* prepared a report which contained in part the childrens' wishes and feelings; this information had been given on a promise of confidentiality. The mother applied to inspect the report. The judge refused, saying that the promise of confidentiality was to be honoured.

Held, dismissing the appeal, that there was a presumption that the information in a report by a guardian was confidential; the onus was on the party seeking disclosure to show good reason. The court would only interfere if the judge had erred in approach or was plainly wrong (*S. (A Minor) (Adoption Application) (Disclosure of Information), Re* [1994] C.L.Y. 3086 applied).

[*Per curiam*: A guardian *ad litem* must realise that by making a promise of confidentiality, he is making a promise he might not be able to keep. The question of disclosure was a matter for the court.]

D. (MINORS) (ADOPTION REPORTS: CONFIDENTIALITY), *Re* [1995] 1 W.L.R. 356, C.A.

3375. Adoption—illegal private placement—whether court having jurisdiction retrospectively to authorise illegal private placement—whether illegal private placement a bar to the court making an adoption order

[Adoption Act 1976 (c.36), ss.6, 11, 12, 13, 22, 24, 57; Children (Allocation of Proceedings) Order 1991 (S.I. 1991 No. 1677), art. 12.]

Although the court had no power retrospectively to authorise an illegal private adoption placement, the court was not barred from making an adoption order in such a case, which should be heard in the High Court.

G had been placed for adoption in contravention of s.11 of the Adoption Act 1976. An application to adopt G was made to a county court, and the judge refused to transfer the case to the High Court. G's guardian *ad litem* appealed against the refusal to transfer the case.

Held, allowing the appeal and transferring the case to the High Court, that (1) no court had power retrospectively to authorise a placement in breach of s.11 (*Adoption Application (Non-Patrial: Breach of Procedures), Re* [1993] C.L.Y. 2766 applied; *S. (Arrangements for Adoption), Re* [1985] F.L.R. 579 considered; *Z.H.H. (Adoption Application), Re* [1993] C.L.Y. 2755 distinguished); (2) however, unlike in the case of an application following illegal payments in contravention of s.57, there was no bar to the court making an adoption order following an illegal placement; (3) since only the High Court had power to authorise a placement which would otherwise be in breach of s.11, where a breach of s.11 had occurred, the case should be heard in the High Court; and (4) the proper course was for the county court to transfer the case under Art. 12 of the Children (Allocation of Proceedings) Order, which replaced the previous Practice Directions.

G. (ADOPTION: ILLEGAL PLACEMENT), *Re* [1995] 1 F.L.R. 403, C.A.

3376. Adoption—jurisdiction to set aside—child of Arab parents adopted by Jewish family—child's subsequent application to set aside adoption order

The court had no power to set aside an adoption order that had been properly made.

B was born to Arab parents and placed with and adopted by a Jewish couple, and was raised as a Jew. Some years later B discovered that his parents were Arab and applied for an order nullifying the adoption order. The application was refused because of a lack of jurisdiction.

Held, dismissing B's appeal, that the court had no jurisdiction to make an order nullifying the adoption order which had been regularly made because of a mistake by the parties as to race or ethnic origin. To allow such an application would undermine the adoption system which regarded adoption orders as being made for life. Such orders could only be set aside where there had been a denial of natural justice (*M. (Minors) (Adoption), Re* [1991] C.L.Y. 2498 distinguished; *J. and J. v. C.'s Tutor* [1948] S.C. 636 considered).

B. (ADOPTION ORDER: JURISDICTION TO SET ASIDE), *Re* [1995] 3 All E.R. 333, C.A.

3377. Adoption—report—natural father unaware of child's existence—whether report should include father's views about the adoption application—whether practicable to ascertain father's views

[Adoption Rules 1984 (S.I. 1984 No. 265), r.4(4), Sched. 2.]

Where an unmarried father did not know of the existence of his child who was the subject of an adoption application, and where it would be detrimental to the child were the father made aware of the child's existence, it would not be practicable to ascertain his wishes for inclusion in the Schedule 2 report.

By the time of P's birth, the relationship between M and F had long since broken down. F had not married M and was unaware of P's existence. M placed P with the local authority for adoption shortly after the birth. P's carers applied for adoption. The local authority compiling the Schedule 2 report for the court were required to set out the views of each natural parent in relation to the proposed adoption, so far as was practicable. Directions were sought as to whether it was practicable to discover F's views.

Held, that (1) although the Adoption Act 1976 defined a parent as a parent with parental responsibility, it was clear that the reference to each natural parent in r.4(4) of the Adoption Rules 1984 included a reference to the unmarried father; (2) when considering whether a course of action was "practicable", it was permissible to look at the outcome. If F's becoming aware of P's existence would be detrimental to P, the court would hold that it was not practicable to ascertain his views (*Owen v. Crown House Engineering* [1973] C.L.Y. 1146 applied); and (3) F knew of the existence of P's brother, and if, as was likely, contact between F and P's brother continued, F would become aware of P's existence sooner or later. It was in P's interests to face up to the matter now, and the court directed the necessary information to be ascertained and placed in the Schedule 2 report.

P. (ADOPTION) (NATURAL FATHER'S RIGHTS), *Re* [1994] 1 F.L.R. 771, Ewbank J.

3378. Adoption—sexual abuse allegations—placement for adoption—reliability of evidence—witness not available for cross-examination—no social worker present at interview to determine reliability—whether evidence to be relied on

[Children and Young Persons Act 1969 (c.54).]

A mother and father appealed against a decision to remove their twin girls from their home and place them for adoption in the light of the father's previous convictions under the Children and Young Persons Act 1969 and subsequent allegations of sexual abuse. The ground for appeal concerned evidence given by a teenage girl, in the form of a written statement to the police, alleging ill-treatment and indecent exposure against the father. It was held that she could not be cross-examined, because she had been sexually abused by another man and was not up to discussing her allegations. Added to this there was no video evidence to record how the child looked on giving evidence and no social worker present to describe what sort of child she was.

Held, allowing the appeal, that, although the judge was generally cautious about evidence, he should have directed himself with extreme care and given reasons why he believed the evidence of the girl was credible. The case was remitted to the High Court for retrial.

W. (MINORS), *Re* (95/5739/F; 95/0390/F; 95/0391/F), July 19, 1995, C.A.

3379. Allocation of proceedings

CHILDREN (ALLOCATION OF PROCEEDINGS) (AMENDMENT) ORDER 1995 (No. 1649), made under the Children Act 1989, Sched. 11, Pt. 1; operative on October 2, 1995.

3380. Best interests of child—medical treatment—revocation of reporting restriction to raise money for medical treatment. See R. v. CAMBRIDGE AND HUNTINGDON HEALTH AUTHORITY, *ex p.* B. (NO. 2), §4203.

3381. Care—contact—costs—termination of contact between parents and children in care—justices refusing application—finely balanced case—whether local authority should pay father's costs

[Children Act 1989 (c.41), ss.8, 34; Family Proceedings Courts (Children Act 1989) Rules 1991 (S.I. 1991 No. 1395), r.22.]

Although it is not a presumption, it is unusual to make orders for costs in children proceedings, and where a local authority has acted reasonably in a finely balanced case, it should not be penalised in costs.

M and F had two children, J now aged 14, and B now aged 12. Both children had been in care since 1987. The local authority applied for leave to terminate contact between the children and their parents pursuant to s.34(4) of the Children Act 1989. In relation to J, the application was unopposed; but in relation to B, the parents and B himself (then aged 11), opposed the termination of contact. The guardian *ad litem*'s report stated that she supported the application, but that the case was finely balanced and before expressing her concluded view she would wish to hear the evidence at the hearing. She confirmed her provisional view in her evidence, but after a four-day hearing the justices refused the application, and ordered that there be direct contact twice a year. F applied for his costs, and the justices ordered the local authority to pay £1,200 towards F's costs. The local authority appealed.

Held, allowing the appeal, that (1) r.22 of the Family Proceedings Courts (Children Act 1989) Rules 1991 gave no guidance as to the justices' discretion in the matter of costs; (2) however, although it was not a presumption, it was unusual to order costs in children cases, unless a party's conduct had been reprehensible and his or her stance in the proceedings had been beyond the band of what was reasonable (*Gojkovic v. Gojkovic (No. 2)* [1992] C.L.Y. 2090, *Hillingdon London Borough Council v. H.* [1992] C.L.Y. 2114, *Sutton London Borough Council v. Davis (No. 2)* [1994] C.L.Y. 3597 applied; and (3) the local authority's conduct had not been unreasonable, in the light of the finely balanced nature of the case and the guardian *ad litem*'s support for the application. As a matter of public policy, a local authority carrying out its statutory duties in bringing the application should not be penalised in costs where the justices formed a different view to that of the authority. The appeal would be allowed.

M. (LOCAL AUTHORITY'S COSTS), *Re* [1995] 1 FLR 533, Cazalet J.

3382. Care—contact—grandparents—leave of court to apply for contact—relevant considerations

[Children Act 1989 (c.41), s.34.]

Grandparents, who did not fall into the special category of persons who could apply for contact orders as of right under s.34(1) of the Children Act 1989, were required to seek the leave of the court to apply for contact with their grandchildren who had been placed in care with the local authority. Relevant considerations for the court, in deciding whether leave should be granted, would be the nature of the contact desired, the importance to the child of the connection with the grandparent, the child's need for stability and the wishes of the parents and local authority. The court must weigh up the merits of the case, guarding against frivolous or vexatious applications and those obviously doomed to failure.

M. (MINORS IN CARE) (CONTACT: GRANDMOTHER'S APPLICATION), *Re*, *The Times*, April 21, 1995, C.A.

3383. Care—juvenile offenders—whether local government liable to pay compensation to victims

[Children and Young Persons Act 1933 (c.12), s.55.]

Where a local authority had done all that it reasonably could to prevent young people who were in its care, or for whom it had provided accommodation, from committing crimes, it would be unjust to make an order under s.55 of the Children and Young Persons Act 1933, as amended, requiring the authority to pay compensation to the victims.

D. v. D.P.P., *The Independent*, April 4, 1995, D.C.

3384. Care—local authority home—decision to move child to home against wishes—whether amenable to judicial review. See R. v. KINGSTON-UPON-THAMES ROYAL BOROUGH, *ex p.* T., §67.

3385. Care—short-term care

CHILDREN (SHORT-TERM PLACEMENTS) (MISCELLANEOUS AMENDMENTS) REGULATIONS 1995 (No. 2015) [£1·10], made under the Children Act 1989, Sched. 6, para. 10(1)(a)(2)(f)(l); amend S.I. 1991 Nos. 890, 893, 895, 910; operative on August 25, 1995; reg. 2(3) of these Regulations amends the Foster Placement (Children) Regulations 1991 making it clear that the prohibition on voluntary organisations placing a child outside the British Isles applies to cases where the voluntary organisation acts on behalf of a local authority as well as to cases where it is itself responsible for the child; amend the provisions relating to short-term periods of care for children.

3386. Care order—appeal—court declining to make care order—court making interim care order pending hearing of appeal—whether interim care order should be continued

[Children Act 1989 (c.41), s.40.]

Where an appeal against a refusal to make a care order was not obviously hopeless, the Court of Appeal would preserve the status quo and continue an interim care order until the full hearing of the appeal.

The local authority brought care proceedings in respect of a young girl, making serious allegations against M and the stepfather S. At the time of the hearing the child was living with a foster-parent, having contact twice a week with M and S. After a five-week hearing ending on July 22, 1993 the judge made a residence order in favour of M. The local authority appealed with the support of the guardian *ad litem*, and the judge made an interim care order under s.40 of the Children Act 1989 pending appeal. The interim care order was made to last until August 1993 for the Court of Appeal to consider whether it should be continued. The substantive appeal was listed for September 1993.

Held, continuing the interim care order pending appeal, that (1) following the practice of the Court of Appeal to be very cautious in child cases, the appeal was not a hopeless one, and consequently it was not for the court to prejudge the outcome of the full appeal hearing (*G. v. G. (Minors: Custody Appeal)* [1985] C.L.Y. 2594 considered); (2) pending the full appeal hearing, contact would be increased to prepare the child for the probable imminent move.

M. (A MINOR) (APPEAL: INTERIM CARE ORDER) (NO. 1), *Re* [1994] 1 FLR 54, C.A.

3387. Care order—application to discharge—leave to withdraw application and apply for contact—whether action hopeless—whether solicitors to pay costs. See O. (A MINOR) (WASTED COSTS APPLICATION), *Re*, §4034.

3388. Care order—assessment—interim care order—whether jurisdiction to make interim residence order in favour of parents at same time to enable assessment to take place in home

[Children Act 1989 (c.41), ss.31, 38(6).]

M appealed against an interim care order made in respect of her son A, aged two. At birth A was placed on the Child Protection Register and, after an incident of violence, an emergency protection order was made. Following assessment of the parents A was returned to M, but his behaviour and health deteriorated. M also failed to attend an important case review during which a supervision order was rejected because there was evidence that A required protection from his father. M failed to give satisfactory reasons for non-attendance. An interim care order was made. M challenged the fact that the judge declined, when making the interim care order, to exercise his power under the Children Act 1989, s.38(6), to make an interim order of residence in her favour. M argued that there was a general and specific power allowing the judge to order that the child could live at home whilst assessment under s.38 took place.

Held, dismissing the appeal, that when a court made an interim care order it gave complete control to the local authority and had no power to impose a residential condition. The judge had power to order an assessment under s.38(6). If it was appropriate that the assessment be made while the child was living at home, the judge was to decide whether to make an interim residence order subject to supervision. If the conditions for the making of a care order existed in terms of s.31, then the interim care order was the only path available.

L. (A MINOR), *Re*, May 22, 1995, C.A.

3389. Care order—care plan—care order in best interests of children—court unhappy with local authority care plan—whether court should make full care order or a further interim care order

[Family Law Reform Act 1969 (c.46), s.7(2); Children Act 1989 (c.41), ss.1, 31, 38.]

Where the court was satisfied that the threshold criteria were made out and the local authority care plan, even if untested and inchoate, was the only practical course for the child, the court should make a final care order.

The local authority sought final care orders in respect of four of M's children. The judge found that the threshold criteria in s.31 of the Children Act 1989 were made out, and that the children's welfare required the making of care orders and their removal from M's care. The local authority's care plan had changed shortly before the hearing, and now proposed three different foster placements for the children, even though little preparation had been done and no final match had been made between the children and the foster-parents. The guardian *ad litem* opposed final care orders but suggested further interim care orders until the care plan was clarified.

Held, making final care orders, that (1) the care plan should accord with the relevant Department of Health guidance. The court was obliged to scrutinise the care plan, and if not satisfied that the plan was in the best interests of the child, it might refuse to make a care order (*Manchester City Council v. F. (Note)* [1993] 1 FLR 419 considered); (2) under the Children Act 1989, the High Court no longer had any power to monitor care orders, and once a care order had been made the court had no say in the administrative arrangements for the child unless there was an application before the court (*B. (Minors) (Termination of Contact: Paramount Consideration), Re* [1993] C.L.Y. 2771 considered); (3) the court should only pass responsibility over to the local authority by way of final care order when all the facts are as clearly known as can be hoped. The use of s.38 to make a further interim care order after a "final" hearing should be sparing in the extreme and designed for a specific purpose. The court should be alert to the danger of using an interim care order as a way of exercising the now defunct jurisdiction to supervise and monitor care orders (*C. v. Solihull Metropolitan Borough Council* [1993] C.L.Y. 2770, *Hounslow London Borough Council v. A.* [1993] C.L.Y. 2772, *C. (A Minor) (Interim Care Order), Re* [1993] C.L.Y. 2779, *G. (Minors) (Interim Care Orders), Re* [1993] C.L.Y. 2780 considered); and (4) on the facts, final care orders represented the only practical course of action for the children.

J. (MINORS) (CARE: CARE PLAN), *Re* [1994] 1 FLR 253, Wall J.

3390. Care order—care plan—care plan for child to remain in care of parents—whether care order or supervision order the correct order to make

[Children Act 1989 (c.41), ss.23(4)(5), 31, Sched. 3; Placement of Children with Parents etc. Regulations 1991 (S.I. 1991 No. 893).]

It was not wrong to make a care order as opposed to a supervision order where the local authority, if granted a care order, planned for the child to remain in her parents' care, and where serious concerns existed as to the likely future standard of parenting.

T was the fifth child of M and F. Her four elder siblings had all been taken into care and placed for adoption. They had been subjected to massive neglect. M and F had been hostile to help from the local authority. M had failed to protect the children from members of the extended family who were potential sexual abusers. The parenting deficiencies only manifested themselves when the children were older than T. The local authority commenced care proceedings when T was one month old. T was made the subject of an interim supervision order and a family assessment was carried out. When T was six months old, a full care order was made. M and F appealed.

Held, dismissing the appeal, that (1) the Children Act 1989, s.23(4)(5), and the Placement of Children with Parents etc. Regulations 1991 envisaged that local authorities could place children with their parents even after a full care order had been made. It was not wrong in law to make a care order where such a placement was planned (*M. v. Westminster City Council* [1984] C.L.Y. 2206 considered); (2) the nature of a supervision order was to help and assist a child and the directions which might be attached under Sched. 3 were limited. It did not confer parental responsibility on the local authority, and any conditions attached could not be enforced in themselves by the court, but breaches were merely evidence to assist the court's decision in further proceedings (*Croydon London Borough Council v. A. (No. 3)* [1993] C.L.Y. 2871 considered); and (3) on the facts, a supervision order would not begin to address the parents' problems. The decision to make a care order rather than a supervision order was not plainly wrong (*G. v. G. (Minors: Custody Appeal)* [1985] C.L.Y. 2594 applied; *C. v. Solihull Metropolitan Borough Council* [1993] C.L.Y. 2770 distinguished).

T. (A MINOR) (CARE OR SUPERVISION ORDER), *Re* [1994] 1 FLR 103, C.A.

3391. Care order—care plan—challenged as inchoate—whether care plan in best interests of child—whether appropriate to make interim care order to supervise local authority's execution of care plan

[Family Law Reform Act 1969 (c.46), s.7(2); Children Act 1989 (c.41), ss.1, 31, 37, 38; Family Proceedings Courts (Children Act 1989) Rules 1991 (S.I. 1991 No. 1395), r.28.]

Where the local authority care plan was inchoate but nevertheless in the best interests of the children, it was wrong to make interim care orders in an attempt to supervise the implementation of the care plan.

M had four children. The local authority commenced care proceedings, intending that the children remain with M. However, shortly before the final hearing, the local authority received further information and planned to remove the children if full care orders were granted. Their care plan was only produced on the second day of hearing. The guardian *ad litem* argued that the care plan was untested and inchoate, and submitted that interim care orders should be made and a final decision postponed until the evidence was complete.

Held, granting full care orders, that (1) the threshold criteria were satisfied and it was in the best interests of the children that they be removed from M (*M. (A Minor) (Care Order: Threshold Conditions), Re* [1994] 1 F.C.R. 849 considered); (2) once the court had made a full care order, it had no power to supervise or monitor the administrative arrangements made by the local authority for the child, and the involvement of the guardian *ad litem* must also end (*B. (Minors) (Termination of Contact: Paramount Consideration), Re* [1993] C.L.Y. 2771, *Kent County Council v. C.* [1993] C.L.Y. 2782 applied); (3) the care plan was an extremely important document, and should accord with the relevant Department of Health guidance. The care plan would be subjected to rigorous scrutiny in every case, and wherever possible, evidence in support of the care plan should be available (*Manchester City Council v. F.* [1993] 1 F.C.R. 1000 considered); (4) the court should only pass responsibility over to the local authority when all the facts were as clearly known as could be hoped. If the court was not satisfied about material aspects of the care plan, or was not satisfied that the care plan was in the best interests of the child, the court could refuse to make a care order (*A. (A Minor) (Care Proceedings), Re* [1993] 1 F.C.R. 164, *C. (A Minor) (Care Proceedings), Re* [1992] 2 F.C.R. 341

considered); (5) the making of interim care orders in cases listed as, and intended to be, the final hearing, where the court had heard all the available evidence, needed to be approached with great caution, and the court should be alert to the danger of using an interim care order as a means of exercising the now defunct supervisory role of the court. The uncritical use of the power to make interim care orders, with consensual extensions possible by an administrative rather than a judicial process, was to be discouraged. The court should also be mindful of the need to avoid delay (*G. (A Minor) (Interim Care Order), Re* [1993] 2 F.C.R. 557 considered); and (6) on the facts, despite the fact that the care plan was necessarily inchoate in the circumstances, it was appropriate, and represented the only practical course of action for the children.

R. (MINORS) (CARE PROCEEDINGS: CARE PLAN), *Re* [1994] 2 F.C.R. 136, Wall J.

3392. Care order—care plan—local authority seeking care order with a view to adoption—parents seeking supervision orders—whether court has power to direct local authority as to implementation of care plan—whether court has power to impose residence conditions on care plan

The court was prohibited from making directions as to the implementation of, and imposing conditions on, a local authority's care plan.

The local authority applied for a care order on a baby whose seven sisters were in care. The judge made an interim care order and directed the local authority to carry out an assessment while the child was living at home with the parents. At the final hearing it was common ground that the parents' care of the child was excellent. The parents conceded that the threshold criteria were satisfied but argued that a supervision order was appropriate. The local authority sought a care order with a view to adoption with the guardian *ad litem*'s support. The judge made a supervision order for 12 months with conditions which were not specified in the order. The local authority appealed and indicated that if a care order were made then they would remove the child from his parents for adoption. The guardian supported the parents' view that a supervision order was appropriate.

Held, dismissing the appeal, that conditions attached to a supervision order should be specified in the order. No conditions could be attached to a care order made once the criteria in the Children Act 1989, s.31(2), had been satisfied. It was the duty of the court to scrutinise the care plan and it could refuse to make a care order if it disagreed with the care plan. The court was prohibited by the Children Act 1989, s.100(2)(a), from imposing its own concept of welfare on to the manner in which a care order was implemented.

T. (A MINOR) (CARE ORDER: CONDITIONS), *Re* [1994] 2 FLR 423, C.A.

3393. Care order—conflicting interests of children—child applying to revoke care order—half-sister applying to be freed for adoption—which child's interests to have priority

The interests of a child applying to revoke a care order prevailed over the interests of her half-sister applying to be freed for adoption.

S. (MINORS) (PROCEEDINGS: CONFLICTING INTERESTS), *Re*, *The Times*, December 29, 1994, Wall J.

3394. Care order—contact—application by local authority to terminate contact to facilitate adoption placement—whether judge applying correct test in giving leave to terminate contact

[Children Act 1989 (c.41), ss.31, 34(1)(4).]

An application by a local authority for leave to terminate contact with children in care should be refused if the benefits of contact outweighed the disadvantages of disrupting any of the local authority's long-term plans which were inconsistent with such contact.

The local authority brought care proceedings in respect of two boys, now aged five and four. The parents consented to a care order, but the local authority care plan was for adoption and they sought an order under s.34(4) of the 1989 Act allowing them to refuse contact between the boys and their parents. The local authority stated that none of the adopters on their books would accept open adoption. The guardian *ad litem* and his expert stated that contact would be of benefit and the parents were unlikely to undermine a new placement. The judge granted the local authority leave to terminate contact, on the basis that he could only refuse the application if the local authority were acting capriciously.

Held, allowing the appeal and remitting the matter for hearing by a High Court judge, that (1) s.34 of the Children Act 1989 places a heavy emphasis on the presumption of continuing parental contact; (2) the judge had applied the wrong test. The courts had no power to review the care plan of the local authority, the care plan must command the greatest respect from the court, and contact must not be allowed to destabilise the arrangements for the child. However, it was the court which had to decide the question of contact with the interests of the child as the paramount consideration. If the benefits of contact outweighed the disadvantages of disrupting any of the local authority's long-term plans inconsistent with such contact, the s.34(4) application must be refused (*B. (Minors) (Termination of Contact: Paramount Consideration), Re* [1993] C.L.Y. 2771 applied; *West Glamorgan County Council v. P.* [1993] 1 FLR 407 overruled); and (3) on the facts, the grant of leave to terminate contact had been premature. Given the guardian *ad litem*'s strong support for face-to-face contact, the local authority should have attempted to find prospective open adopters.

E. (A MINOR) (CARE ORDER: CONTACT), *Re* [1994] 1 FLR 146, C.A.

3395. Care order—contact—child in care wishing to see her siblings—whether order could be made requiring parents to permit contact between child in care and her siblings

[Children Act 1989 (c.41), ss.1, 8, 9(1), 34(2)(3), Sched. 2, para. 15.]

A child in care could not obtain an order requiring her parents to allow her contact with her siblings under s.34(2) of the Children Act 1989.

K was 16 and had become beyond her parents' control. In May 1993 she left home and was accommodated by the local authority. The parents wanted nothing more to do with her and refused to allow her to see her two sisters and two brothers aged between 14 and five. K wanted to see her siblings, especially her 12-year-old sister. In November 1993, the final hearing of the application for a care order came on. At the hearing K applied through her solicitor for an order under s.34(2) of the Children Act 1989 permitting her to have contact with the other four children. The case was adjourned to January 1994. The guardian *ad litem* contended that the court could under s.34(2) compel the parents to allow K to see her siblings. All parties understood the application to be for an order requiring the parents to comply with whatever contact between the children was deemed appropriate. The magistrates made a care order (against which there was no appeal) and four orders under s.34(2) that K should have supervised contact with each of her siblings. However, in drafting the order the clerk followed the wording of s.34(2) and the orders provided that the local authority should permit such contact. The parents appealed against those orders. K's legal advisers soon realised that those orders were ineffective to achieve contact, and K obtained leave from a judge of the High Court to apply for a s.8 contact order providing for contact between her and her siblings. The substantive application was listed to be heard with the appeal against the s.34(2) orders.

Held, allowing the appeal, that (1) all the parties and the magistrates had misunderstood the nature of an order under s.34(2). The misunderstanding was the belief that an order under s.34(2) could oblige any person named in the order or, if such person was a minor, could oblige the person with whom he or she lived, to have or permit the contact provided for. Unless the local authority itself was applying for a s.34(2) order, the court's jurisdiction should only be used where the local authority was adopting a stance in respect of contact between the child in care and another person which was suggested by the child or that person to be inappropriate. The compulsory effect of a s.34(2) order, providing for the contact which was to be allowed between the child in care and the named person, attached only to the local authority (*Birmingham City Council v. H. (No. 3) (A Minor)* [1994] 1 F.C.R. 896 considered); (2) on K's s.8 application, it was the welfare of each individual sibling that was paramount (*Birmingham City Council v. H. (No. 3) (A Minor)* [1994] applied); (3) the four siblings had indicated that they did not wish to see K. As a result, K's s.8 application was dismissed on the basis that K might send cards, letters and postcards to her siblings; and (4) there was no need for a s.34(2) order requiring the local authority to permit contact between K and her siblings, as the local authority had a duty to promote contact. The court would not make an otiose order.

F. (A MINOR) (CONTACT: CHILD IN CARE), *Re* [1994] 2 F.C.R. 1354, Wilson J.

3396. Care order—contact—continuing relationship—mother suffering from Munchausen's syndrome by proxy—mother living apart from children's fathers—fathers offering to care for children—whether care orders should be made—whether contact between mother and children should cease

[Children Act 1989 (c.41), ss.1, 31, 34.]

It was not appropriate to terminate all contact between a child and his mother, who suffered from Munchausen's syndrome by proxy, where there was a continuing relationship between mother and child, and where there were positive aspects of contact.

M had given birth to three children in 1986, 1988, 1990. The girl born in February 1988 had died in July 1988. The two boys had different fathers. The elder boy had been admitted to hospital suffering from dehydration with a concentration of sodium. A second post-mortem on the dead girl concluded that it was 95 per cent probable that M had injected her with salt, thus causing her death. The younger boy had also been admitted to hospital following an injection of some harmful substance. M was diagnosed as suffering from Munchausen's syndrome by proxy. The local authority sought care orders in respect of both boys with a view to their eventual placement with their respective fathers. M accepted that she could not have the boys living with her, but sought contact with them. The local authority sought the termination of all contact with either boy, but the guardian *ad litem* disagreed.

Held, that (1) it was conceded by all parties that the threshold criteria for making care orders were satisfied. The boys' welfare demanded that care orders be made, though in due course they might be discharged and residence orders made in favour of the fathers; (2) M's contact with the younger boy would be of no benefit to him and would render him at risk of emotional harm. M's contact would be terminated (*B. (Minors) (Termination of Contact: Paramount Consideration), Re* [1993] C.L.Y. 2771); and (3) the elder boy had a continuing relationship with M. Despite the dangers posed by a person with M's condition, there were positive aspects of past contact, and he would no doubt retain strong memories of M. The local authority were obliged to afford M reasonable contact under s.34, and it was unnecessary to make any order for contact.

[*Per curiam*: The local authority should not act in an adversarial manner, but should present its case in a balanced way and not fail to refer to factors which were unhelpful to its case.]

B. (MINORS) (CARE PROCEEDINGS), *Re* [1994] 1 F.C.R. 471, Hollings J.

3397. Care order—contact—prohibition on applications—father convicted of manslaughter of mother—father applying for contact on release from prison—whether order should be made prohibiting any further application for contact without leave of court

[Children Act 1989 (c.41), ss.1, 34, 91(14).]

In extreme circumstances, the court would make an order under s.91(14) of the Children Act 1989, barring future applications without leave of the court, notwithstanding the absence of a history of repeated or near-vexatious applications.

In 1988, M died as a result of a violent assault by F, witnessed by the three children. The children were taken into care, and F was convicted of manslaughter. On his release, F applied for a contact order; the local authority applied for an order permitting the refusal of contact between F and the children, and for an order under s.91(14) of the Children Act 1989 barring F from making any further application for contact without leave. The experts were united in their view that the children would suffer intense psychological distress if they were to have contact with F.

Held, dismissing F's contact application, that (1) his application was hopeless, and blind to the children's needs: an order would be made that there be no contact between F and the children without leave of the court; (2) although the court had power under s.34(2) of the 1989 Act to make an order specifically prohibiting contact, it was not necessary to consider the local authority's application for such an order in the light of the dismissal of F's application (*Kent County Council v. C.* [1993] C.L.Y. 2782 considered); and (3) an order under s.91(14) was exceptional and should only be made with a clear evidential basis. In earlier cases involving applications for orders under s.91(14), there had been a history of repeated and near-vexatious applications to the court. Despite the absence of such a history in this case, in the extreme circumstances the children needed to be protected from the risk of unnecessary continuing disturbance by repeated or revived litigation. Accordingly, F would be prohibited from making any further application for contact without leave of the court (*H. (Child Orders: Restricting Applications), Re* [1992] C.L.Y. 2990, *F. v. Kent County Council* [1994] 2 C.L. 351 considered).

Y. (CHILD ORDERS: RESTRICTING APPLICATIONS), *Re* [1994] 2 F.L.R. 699, Thorpe J.

3398. Care order—contact—whether judge could allow contact to be reviewed by court after care order made

[Children Act 1989 (c.41), ss.31, 33(3), 34, 91(1).]

A court making a care order cannot review the implementation of the local authority care plan and where the nature and extent of contact is an integral part of the care plan, it is not for the court to determine precisely what contact is reasonable.

M and F had two children, now aged two-and-a-half years and 14 months respectively. The younger child was found to have sustained serious non-accidental injuries and a care order was made in respect of him. The local authority care plan was for a progressive rehabilitation of the child to M. The judge also made an order providing for reasonable contact between the child and his parents. The order provided for the issue of contact to be adjourned, and in August 1993, an order was made further adjourning the matter to September 1993. The local authority appealed against the August adjournment, contending that the judge was attempting to review the implementation of the care plan.

Held, allowing the appeal, that (1) once the child was the subject of a care order, the court had no continuing role in the child's future welfare. Although the courts had the power to determine reasonable contact and could in theory impose contact at odds with the care plan, where the nature and extent of contact was an integral part of the care plan, it was not open to the court to decide precisely what contact was reasonable (*B. (Minors) (Termination of Contact: Paramount Consideration), Re* [1993] C.L.Y. 2771 applied; *A. v. Liverpool City Council* [1981] C.L.Y. 1796 not followed); (2) here the sole dispute between the parents and the local authority was the timing of the rehabilitation. That dispute related plainly to the implementation of the care plan and it was unreal to regard it as a dispute over contact. The judge's proposed reconsideration of contact would lead him to stray into the forbidden territory of supervising the administration of the local authority's arrangements for rehabilitation. The adjournment of the question of parental contact was without jurisdiction; (3) the order for reasonable contact with the parents was otiose, given the duty on the local authority under s.34(1) to afford reasonable parental contact, in the absence of any order to the contrary; and (4) s.34 related mainly to the position arising subsequent to the making of a care order, and it would be extremely rare for the court to exercise its power under s.34(5) to make orders for contact under its own motion, simultaneously with making a care order.

S. (A MINOR) (CARE: CONTACT ORDER), *Re* [1994] 2 F.L.R. 222, C.A.

3399. Care order—placement outside jurisdiction—mother applying for residence order—local authority applying for leave to place children with family living outside jurisdiction—whether court should approve application

[Children Act 1989 (c.41), Sched. 2, para. 19(3)(5).]

A local authority applied to place two children in their care with members of their maternal family in the U.S. under the Children Act 1989, Sched. 2, para. 19. It was clear from medical evidence adduced by M that she was unable to undertake the care of the children. M did not consent to the application but indicated that if her application for a residence order failed then she would accept the placement in the U.S.

Held, dismissing M's application and granting the local authority's application, that M's application must fail in the light of her medical evidence. It was manifestly in the children's interests to live outside the jurisdiction, where arrangements for their reception and welfare had been made and where the persons who had parental responsibility had given their consent, while the children were too young to give consent, it followed that the requirements of para. 19(3) were satisfied.

G. (MINORS) (CARE: LEAVE TO PLACE OUTSIDE JURISDICTION), *Re* [1994] 2 FLR 301, Thorpe J.

3400. Care order—sexual abuse—appeal against order—whether judge erred in exercise of discretion in making care order—video evidence—whether preferable for statements to police and social workers to be video-taped

After lengthy care proceedings involving 10 children from an extended family, where a picture emerged of long-standing, serious and persistent sexual abuse with disgusting features, the father of a 12-year-old boy appealed against a care order made on the grounds that it was not in the best interests of the boy to return home, because, while the father could be criticised, he had not been found to have abused the boy.

Held, dismissing the appeal, that the judge had been plainly right because the father had not accepted the seriousness of the events. It would have been preferable for the statements made by the boy to the police and social workers to have been recorded on videotape to enable the court to view the questions and answers, gestures, body movements, vocal inflection and intonation.

W. (A MINOR) (CARE ORDER), *Re* [1994] Fam.Law 11, C.A.

3401. Care order—threshold criteria—agreement between parties—agreement—dispute over factual basis—extent of court's investigative duty

[Children Act 1989 (c.41), s.31.]

A court making a care order where the parties agreed it should be made, should nevertheless satisfy itself by relevant evidence as to the proper factual basis for the making of the order.

A local authority applied for a care order in respect of an eight-year-old boy. All the parties were in agreement about the care order but the factual basis was in dispute. The local authority wanted the court to make specific findings of fact as to the father's abuse of the boy in various ways, while the father argued that this was unnecessary. The authority wanted to put in statements made by the father to the police in a criminal trial, which had been ruled inadmissible at trial resulting in his acquittal.

Held, on a preliminary issue on the above question, that the court should make a proper inquiry so as to be satisfied as to the correct basis for making the care order, and the local authority should present relevant material evidence. However, an investigation of the criminal allegations against the father was unnecessary and would extend the cost and length of the hearing; the authority therefore could not produce the statements in evidence (*Devon County Council v. S.* [1992] C.L.Y. 3026 distinguished).

G. (A MINOR) (CARE ORDER: THRESHOLD CONDITIONS), *Re; sub nom.* G. (A MINOR) (CARE PROCEEDINGS), *Re; sub nom* HACKNEY LONDON BOROUGH v. G. [1994] 3 W.L.R. 1211, Wall J.

3402. Care order—threshold criteria—agreement by parties that conditions satisfied—whether magistrates entitled to make findings of fact regarding conditions

[Children Act 1989 (c.41), s.31.]

Where, in proceedings involving a local authority's application for a care order, the parties were agreed that the threshold conditions in s.31 of the Children Act 1989 had been satisfied, magistrates should still make findings of fact on how those conditions had been met.

C. (A MINOR), *Re, The Independent,* August 7, 1995, Douglas Brown J.

3403. Care order—threshold criteria—mother unable to care for child—aunt's application for residence order heard along with local authority's application for care order—whether threshold criteria met

[Children Act 1989 (c.41), ss.1(3), 3, 17(1)(b), 31(2).]

If, at the date of the hearing, a suitable family member is willing and able to give the child care to a reasonable parental standard, the threshold criteria for making a care or supervision order cannot be satisfied, and there is no requirement to determine the family member's application for a residence order before consideration of the threshold criteria.

M was the mother of a 14-month-old child. M was unable to care for the child adequately, and interim care orders were made placing the child in short-term foster care. C, M's aunt, wished to care for the child but the local authority decided, after conducting an assessment of C, that adoption would be in the child's best interests. C applied for a residence order and the local authority sought a full care order with leave to terminate M's contact. After hearing the applications together, the judge dismissed C's application and granted those of the local authority.

Held, allowing C's appeal, that it was not sufficient to show that the person(s) with parental responsibility could not provide the required degree of care for the child. If, at the time of the hearing, there was a suitable family member who was willing and able to give the child care to a reasonable parental standard, the threshold criteria for a care or supervision order were not met. In such circumstances, the court was not bound to decide the residence order application independently of, and prior to, any consideration of the threshold criteria. In most cases, the applications should be heard together (*M. (A Minor) (Care Order: Threshold Conditions), Re* [1994] 9 C.L. 288 applied).

OLDHAM METROPOLITAN BOROUGH COUNCIL v. E. [1994] 1 F.L.R. 568, C.A.

3404. Care order—threshold criteria—orphans—accommodated by local authority—no signifcant harm currently—authority submitting that there was a risk of future signifcant harm—whether care orders should be made

[Children Act 1989 (c.41), ss.20, 22, 23, 24, 31, 100.]

Where orphans accommodated by the local authority had settled and well-managed lives, there was no risk of significant harm to them and thus the threshold criteria for care orders had not been established.

D were aged five and six; their parents cohabited, and did not marry. Their mother died suddenly and their father subsequently declined any responsibility. Following the breakdown of placements within the extended family, the local authority accommodated the children. M children were aged 16 and 15: their mother had died shortly after their birth, and their father died when they were aged 14 and 13. They too were now accommodated by the local authority. There was no person with parental responsibility for any of the four children, and the local authority applied for care orders for all four. The local authority conceded that none of the children was currently suffering from significant harm, but submitted that there was a risk of future significant harm if the local authority were not fully empowered, by means of care orders, to deal with crises or emergencies. The guardian *ad litem* opposed the making of care orders.

Held, dismissing the application, that ss.20, and 22 to 24 of the Children Act 1989 provided a comprehensive and specific set of duties to meet the needs of orphaned children. Section 31 of the 1989 Act was designed to protect families from invasive care orders unless there was a manifest need evidenced by a perceptible risk of significant harm. Although the local authority was not seeking to invade in these cases, s.31 must be construed sensibly and realistically. The children's lives were well-settled and managed, and the threshold criteria had not been established (*Newham London Borough Council v. A.G.* [1993] C.L.Y. 2781 considered).

[*Per curiam*: If there was some shortcoming in the statutory framework, it was not for the court to remedy the deficiency by a strained construction of the s.31 threshold criteria.]

BIRMINGHAM CITY COUNCIL v. D.; BIRMINGHAM CITY COUNCIL v. M. [1994] 2 F.L.R. 502, Thorpe J.

3405. Care order—threshold criteria—residence order—grandparents' application heard together with care proceedings—whether threshold criteria met—whether magistrates wrong to make care orders

[Children Act 1989 (c.41), s.31.]

There was no evidence to justify a finding that the threshold criteria for a care order were satisfied where the children's grandparents were enjoying successful staying contact with the children, in the absence of any other evidence of likely significant harm from the grandparents.

M had three children; the first had been taken into care and adopted at an early age. In March 1990 M married H, and two months later gave birth to K, now aged three. In 1991 M gave birth to G, now aged two, following a relationship with another man. M had a spell in prison for offences related to drug abuse and two months following her release the local authority commenced care proceedings in respect of both children, who were removed from M. M's parents had staying contact and were assessed as potential carers, but the local authority abandoned the assessment as it considered that they would be unable to protect the children during M's contact. By November 1993 the local authority had a care order in respect of K. M's mother applied for a residence order in respect of both children, which was heard by the magistrates together with the application for a care order in respect of G. The local authority care plan was for adoption. The guardian *ad litem* recommended that G be placed with M's parents. The magistrates made a care order. The children, through the guardian *ad litem*, appealed, and contact with M's parents was ordered pending appeal.

Held, allowing the appeal and granting M's mother a residence order in respect of both children, that (1) the magistrates had applied the correct test, but had come to the untenable finding that the children would be likely to suffer significant harm in the grandparents' care. Staying contact had been successful, and that was a pointer, at the very least, to the fact that full-time care might also be successful (*M. (A Minor) (Care Order: Threshold Conditions), Re* [1994] 3 C.L. 276 (C.A., later overruled by H.L.) applied); (2) the magistrates had failed to give convincing reasons for departing from the recommendation of the guardian *ad litem* and had not balanced the perceived demerits of the grandparents with the risks inherent in placing the children for adoption. Adoption was in reality a course of last resort.

H. (A MINOR) (CARE OR RESIDENCE ORDER), *Re* [1994] 2 F.L.R. 80, Hollis J.

3406. Care order—threshold criteria—serious allegations of ill-treatment rejected by court—threshold criteria met on other grounds—whether judge applying correct test in deciding what order should be made—whether judge correct to grant residence order to mother

[Children Act 1989 (c.41), s.31.]

The primary facts of past harm had to be proved to establish the threshold criteria on a balance of probabilities but the more serious the allegation, the more convincing the evidence required.

The local authority brought care proceedings in respect of a six-year-old girl, who had been admitted to hospital underweight, emaciated, severely dehydrated and with multiple bruising on her body. She suffered renal failure and a duodenal haematoma. The local authority contended that this had been caused by punching whereas the mother and her partner alleged it had been caused by a fall. The judge found the threshold criteria met on the grounds that the mother had failed to seek medical assistance at an earlier stage and that there were cumulative concerns about the child's welfare. However he declined to make a care order but to give the mother and her partner a chance as parents he made a residence order to the mother on condition that she continued to live with her partner's parents.

Held, dismissing the local authority's and the guardian *ad litem's* appeals, that the judge had correctly directed himself that the local authority had to prove their case on the balance of probabilities, the more serious the allegation, the more convincing the evidence required to find it proved, and was entitled to find that the local authority had not made out their case on the more serious allegations (*M. (A Minor) (Appeal No. 2)),* [1995] 1 C.L. 252 *Re H. v. H. (Minors) (Child Abuse: Access)* [1989] C.L.Y. 2442, *K. v. K. (Child Cases: Evidence)* [1989] F.C.R. 356, *Newham London Borough Council v. AG* [1993] C.L.Y. 2781, *W. (Minors) (Wardship): Evidence), Re* [1990] C.L.Y. 3200 referred to).

M. (A MINOR) (CARE PROCEEDINGS: APPEAL), *Re* [1995] 1 F.C.R. 417, C.A.

3407. Care order—welfare of minor—order sought in respect of child of minor mother—whether welfare of baby or welfare of mother paramount

[Children Act 1989 (c.41), ss.1(1), 31, 34, 105(1).]

Where a local authority seeks a care order in relation to a child whose mother herself is still a minor, the court is required to determine the application for a care order with the infant child's welfare as the paramount consideration.

M had been made the subject of a care order at the age of 15, and was then engaged in prostitution, drug abuse and a series of criminal offences. In 1991 M was detained in secure accommodation. The local authority considered that M's egocentric nature would pose a danger to any child she might have. M subsequently gave birth to L while still under the age of 18 herself. The local authority applied for a final care order in respect of L, which was granted.

Held, dismissing M's appeal, that in determining whether the welfare of the infant or that of the child-mother was paramount, the correct approach was to identify which child was the subject of the application and which child it was whose welfare was directly involved. Here, no question relating to M's upbringing arose, and the judge had rightly held L's welfare as the paramount consideration (*Birmingham City Council v. H. (A Minor)* [1994] 3 C.L. 282 applied). It was plain that L was at risk of significant harm from M's neglect of her in pursuit of her own desires, and from some physical abuse likely to occur when M could no longer tolerate the frustration created by the normal demands of a young baby. There was no need for the judge to have made explicit findings as to the type of harm envisaged. Although the court should consider the threshold criteria first and go on to consider the welfare of the child in reaching a decision whether or not to make a care order, in this case it was inevitable there could be no easy demarcation of this two-stage process. Having decided that time did not permit an attempt at rehabilitation and consequent assessment, the judge was not plainly wrong in refusing to make an interim care order; he was plainly right to make a care order (*Humberside County Council v. B.* [1993] C.L.Y. 2778 considered).

F. v. LEEDS CITY COUNCIL [1994] 2 F.L.R. 60, C.A.

3408. Care order—welfare test—two half-sisters in care—father of elder child seeking residence order and revocation of care order—local authority applying for orders freeing both children for adoption—whose interests paramount

[Adoption Act 1976 (c.36), s.6; Children Act 1989 (c.41), ss.1(1), 39; Family Proceedings Rules 1991 (S.I. 1991 No. 1247), r.4.11.]

In proceedings under the Children Act 1989, where the interests of two or more children were in conflict, then the court should reach a decision based on a balancing exercise; but where the application under the 1989 Act related to only one child and other applications involving other children were under the Adoption Act 1976, then the paramountcy principle applied only to that child.

T was aged six and E nearly four. M had married F1, the father of T, but later divorced him and married his brother, F2, the father of E. F2 had physically and sexually abused E. Both children were made the subject of care orders. The local authority care plan was for the half-sisters to be placed for adoption together. F1 applied for a revocation of the care order in relation to T, although he felt unable to offer E a home. The local authority's applications for freeing orders in relation to both T and E were heard at the same time. F1 claimed that it was in T's best interests to live with him, whereas the local authority's case was that T and E's best interests, and especially E's, were served by their being adopted by the same family.

Held, revoking the care order and making a residence order in favour of F1 in relation to T, but freeing E for adoption, that (1) the test for the revocation of a care order was the welfare test in s.1(1) of the Children Act 1989, and it was for the person seeking revocation to show the child's welfare required the care order to be revoked; (2) where two children were the subject of the same application under the Children Act 1989, it was not possible to treat either child's welfare as paramount, but their interests must be balanced so as to produce the outcome of least detriment to both children (*Birmingham City Council v. H. (No. 2)* [1994] C.L.Y. 3180, *F. (Contact: Child in Care), Re* [1995] 1 FLR 510 applied); and (3) only T was the subject of the application to revoke the care order. A balancing exercise could only be undertaken if there were before the court another application in which E's welfare was paramount. However, the application to free E for adoption was governed by s.6 of the Adoption Act 1976, which provided for E's welfare to be the first, but not the paramount, consideration. Whilst it was highly unsatisfactory that the test should hinge on the vagaries of procedure, the court was bound to treat T's welfare as paramount, and it was not open to perform the balancing exercise described above. The care order in respect of T would be revoked and there would be a residence order in favour of F1. E would be freed for adoption. The same result would have been achieved had the balancing exercise been necessary.

T. AND E. (PROCEEDINGS: CONFLICTING INTERESTS), *Re* [1995] 1 FLR 581, Wall J.

3409. Care proceedings—adjournment—reduction of contact—*ex parte* application to adjourn—whether exceptional circumstances proved—whether legal representitives should be present at hearing

The local authority applied to reduce contact to two children in their care. Before the case was heard and when all parties and their representatives were in the court precincts, the local authority applied *ex parte* to adjourn the hearing to enable an investigation of allegations of sexual abuse to be carried out without the knowledge of the parents. The justices granted the adjournment.

Held, allowing the parents' appeal, that an *ex parte* application to adjourn should only be made in exceptional circumstances and where the best interests of the children justified the course. Even then the representatives, subject to an undertaking not to pass on information to their clients or subject to the court's directions, should be present at the hearing of such an application.

B. (MINORS) (CARE: PROCEDURE), *Re* [1994] Fam.Law 72, Bracewell J.

3410. Care proceedings—contested care proceedings—whether use by local authorities of solicitors within legal department appropriate

The use by local authorities of solicitors employed within the council's legal department to represent them in contested care proceedings was a growing practice which was to be regretted, since employed solicitors did not have the experience that specialist local counsel had in this field and their position made it more difficult for them to advise the authority with detachment.

B. (MINORS) (LOCAL AUTHORITIES: REPRESENTATION), *Re*, *The Times*, May 19, 1995, C.A.

3411. Care proceedings—criminal trial—order in which proceedings should be heard—whether delay allowable

[Children Act 1989 (c.41), s.1.]

In a case as serious as murder, it was preferable for the trial to be dealt with first and the care proceedings to follow unless there were exceptional reasons for requiring the child's long-term future to be settled without delay.

The parents of a small boy were charged with the murder of his sister. The local authority commenced care proceedings which were due to be heard after the Crown Court trial. The trial had to be postponed. The care judge refused to vacate the care hearing.

Held, allowing the appeal, that in a case as serious as murder, it was preferable for the criminal trial to be concluded first and the care proceedings to follow unless there were exceptional circumstances requiring the child's long-term future to be decided without delay.

S. (CARE ORDER: CRIMINAL PROCEEDINGS), *Re* [1995] 1 F.L.R. 151, C.A.

3412. Care proceedings—disclosure—documents in care proceedings to defence in criminal trial—confidentiality—conflict with public interest

Leave of the family court was needed before documents in care proceedings could be disclosed to the defence in a criminal trial in which the child was a witness. In deciding whether leave should be granted, the court must carefully weigh the public interest in making available relevant information against the importance of preserving confidentiality in care proceedings. Relevant factors to be considered would include the importance of the information, the purpose for which it was needed and the seriousness of the offence charged.

A. (A MINOR) (CARE PROCEEDINGS: DISCLOSURE), *Re*, *The Independent*, October 23, 1995 (C.S.), C.A.

3413. Care proceedings—disclosure—inconsistent statements made by mother in care proceedings—father charged with rape—whether court should give leave for disclosure of statements in care proceedings for use in criminal proceedings

[Children Act 1989 (c.41), s.98(2).]

Two children were found to have been sexually abused and the question was whether F was the perpetrator. The evidence against him was contained in two inconsistent statements by M which the judge in care proceedings had found could not be relied upon. F was charged with rape as a result of M's statements. F sought disclosure of M's statements, a transcript of her oral evidence in the care proceedings and transcripts of video interviews with the children under the Family Proceedings Rules 1991, r.4.23, for use in the course of his defence.

Held, granting leave, that the principles which had previously applied in wardship cases in deciding whether to grant leave were equally applicable in Children Act cases. It was greatly in the interests of the children and justice that F had a fair trial and that there should be no impediments to a fair trial and balancing the need for a fair trial with the importance of confidentiality in Children Act proceedings disclosure should be ordered. M could not rely upon the the Children Act 1989, s.98(2), which was applicable only to an accused in criminal proceedings and not to a witness. Leave would also be given in relation to the video transcripts because the children were unlikely to be involved in the criminal proceedings and there could be no detriment to them if leave were granted. The Children Act documents would be disclosed to F's counsel in the criminal proceedings, who should be able to satisfy himself that nothing material to the father's defence had been overlooked.

K. (MINORS) (CARE PROCEEDINGS: DISCLOSURE), *Re* [1994] 2 F.C.R 805, Booth J.

3414. Care proceedings—disclosure—medical reports—privilege—whether legal professional privilege attached to a report ordered to be filed with the court

A two-year-old girl (E) was admitted to hospital after consuming a quantity of methadone which, according to the child's mother, had been left carelessly in a beaker in the kitchen. Interim care orders were made in respect of E and her brother, who were placed with foster-parents. A medical report on the circumstances surrounding E's admission to hospital and treatment was commissioned by E's mother and filed with the court in care proceedings. As the result of a request by the police authority to be joined as a party to proceedings and to have medical reports made available so that it could investigate whether a criminal offence might have been committed, the court ordered disclosure of the report. The mother appealed against the court's decision, arguing, first, that legal professional privilege attached to the report and, secondly, that her privilege against self-incrimination would be infringed.

Held, dismissing the appeal, that it was doubtful whether legal professional privilege could be said to attach to a report which had been ordered to be filed with the court and made available to all parties, but even if it did the court had a discretion to override it in the interests of the child (*Oxfordshire County Council v. M.* [1994] 6 C.L. 289 considered). As for the second argument, the mother had voluntarily commissioned the report and made no claim as to privilege when it was filed with the court. The order for disclosure could not be criticised as being unreasonable.

L. (MINORS: DISCLOSURE OF REPORTS), *Re*, *The Independent*, March 29, 1995, C.A.

3415. Care proceedings—disclosure—video of police interview with children—subpoena *duces tecum*

A subpoena *duces tecum* was the appropriate procedure for a parent in care proceedings to require the police to disclose copies of videos of police interviews with some of his children during the course of criminal proceedings where these interviews could be important in care proceedings concerning his other children. The police were required to disclose copies to the parent and the local authorities concerned.

M. (MINORS) (CARE PROCEEDINGS: POLICE VIDEOS), *Re*, *The Times*, July 7, 1995, Sir Stephen Brown.

3416. Care proceedings—evidence—none before court—interim care order—application opposed by parents—no evidence before court—magistrates making interim care orders—whether wrong to make orders in absence of evidence

[Children Act 1989 (c.41), ss.38, 94; R.S.C., Ord. 55, rr.1, 7(2); Children (Admissibility of Hearsay Evidence) Order 1991 (S.I. 1991 No. 1115); Family Proceedings Rules 1991 (S.I. 1991 No. 1247), rr.1.3, 4.22; Family Proceedings Courts (Children Act 1989) Rules 1991 (S.I. 1991 No. 1395 (L.17)), rr.17, 21.]

Any order on an opposed application, made without any evidence filed in accordance with the rules, was fatally flawed and must be set aside.

M and F had two children, aged seven and five. The local authority commenced care proceedings, and sought interim care orders. At the first hearing before the magistrates, no statements of evidence had been filed under r.17 of the Family Proceedings Courts (Children Act 1989) Rules 1991, and the magistrates refused to admit written statements or hear oral evidence. The magistrates made interim care orders having heard submissions only.

Held, allowing the appeal, but making interim care orders pending reconsideration by the magistrates, that (1) r.17 of the Rules provided that statements of evidence and documents relied on should be filed before the hearing, and r.21 required the magistrates to read the evidence filed under r.17. The magistrates had made a fundamental error in making orders on an opposed application without any evidence at all before them, and the orders would be set aside (*R. v. Croydon Juvenile Court, ex p. N.* [1987] C.L.Y. 2462, *R. v. Birmingham City Juvenile Court, ex p. Birmingham City Council* [1988] C.L.Y. 2316, *Hampshire County Council v. S.* [1993] C.L.Y. 2829 considered); (2) by virtue of R.S.C., Ord. 55, r.1, Ord. 55 applied to any appeal to the High Court from any tribunal, and the court therefore had power to admit further evidence under Ord. 55, r.7(2); and (3) the appeal constituted "any proceedings on an application for a care order" within s.38 of the Children Act 1989, and so the court had power to make interim care orders on appeal. On the facts, interim care orders would be made.

S. v. MERTON LONDON BOROUGH [1994] 1 F.C.R. 186, Ward J.

3417. Care proceedings—evidence—oral evidence—interim care order—magistrates deciding not to hear evidence from father—whether material irregularity

[Children Act 1989 (c.41), s.38(1).]

Where the court considering an application for an interim care order heard oral evidence from one side, it was wholly inappropriate not to hear oral evidence from the other, and advocates for all parties had a duty to advise the magistrates of their fundamental error.

On a local authority's application to the magistrates for interim care orders, the magistrates heard evidence from a social worker. Having heard from F's advocate, the magistrates decided not to hear evidence from F, and made the interim care orders. F appealed.

Held, allowing the appeal but granting interim care orders until a hearing before a different Bench, that (1) the refusal to hear F was a material irregularity and plainly wrong, as was the procedure taken in making the decision and the refusal to give reasons for the decision; (2) if the magistrates were in the process of making, or were about to make, a decision which was procedurally plainly wrong, all advocates had a duty to act non-adversarially and advise the magistrates that they were about to make a fundamental error; (3) although an appeal against an interim order is an unusual course, it was justified here as F could not be sure that the bench would not exclude his evidence again at the next hearing (*G. (Minors: Costs), Re* [1993] Fam.Law 621 considered); and (4) there was no need for four parties funded by the taxpayer to be represented by counsel on an appeal where there was general agreement that the appeal would have to be allowed. In future, the court might disallow costs where there had been unnecessary representation.

F. (A MINOR) (CARE ORDER: PROCEDURE), *Re* [1994] 1 FLR 240, Wall J.

3418. Care proceedings—expert evidence—absence of specific directions sought from court—court not informed that mother wished to call six experts—whether generalised orders could be made—whether nature of evidence adduced and identity of expert matter for party or court

The court should take a proactive role and maintain a tight grip on children's cases.

A local authority applied for care order on a boy on the grounds that M was suffering from Munchausen's Syndrome by Proxy. Leave was granted for the child to be examined by a paediatrician for the local authority and the guardian *ad litem*, for disclosure of the child's medical records and those of his brother to all parties and for M's records to be disclosed to a paediatrician instructed by the guardian. A s.37 assessment was ordered on one child and an assessment of M and children either as a unit or individually. A series of interim care orders were made by consent. M applied for interim defined contact and for leave to disclose medical records to an expert of her choice. Later M applied to amend her application from "expert" to "experts". The judge was not told that M intended to instruct six experts. The final hearing had to be adjourned because of the unavailability of the guardian's paediatrician. Five reports on behalf of M were served two days before the hearing, the sixth and seventh on the first and second days of the hearing.

Held, that the court should take a proactive role and was under a duty to maintain a tight grip on conduct in children's cases. The court should give directions which should not be delegated to the parties and set a timetable for a case which was otherwise in grave danger of drift. Generalised orders granting leave to disclose papers to experts should never be granted. When applying for leave there was a positive duty to put all relevant information before the court, including the identity of the expert or the area of expertise and advocates should consider at an early stage the issues in the case to which expert medical evidence might be relevant and should be able to justify the need for expert medical evidence on the court's enquiry. When granting leave the court should, where possible, give further directions as to the timescale, disclosure of reports, discussions between experts and filing of further statements. If further directions cannot be given at the time of grant of leave then a further directions hearing should be fixed. Time estimates should be considered in advance in the light of the number of expert witnesses and the likely length of their evidence.

G. (MINORS) (EXPERT WITNESSES), *Re* [1994] 2 FLR 291, Wall J.

3419. Care proceedings—expert evidence—child abuse—duties of expert witnesses—guidance for expert witnesses

The court underlined the duty of an expert witness to be objective, impartial and not to mislead by omission.

A was born in August 1992. In November 1992, M and F took him to hospital following a seizure. A was subsequently found to have multiple fractures to the ribs, both arms, and brain damage. Care proceedings were commenced. The clinical paediatrician and two forensic consultant radiologists gave evidence that the injuries were non-accidental. M and F instructed a Dr P, who stated in his report that the fractures were almost certainly due to some temporary form of brittle bone disease. His report made no mention of the brain damage. The judge found that A had suffered multiple non-accidental injuries whilst in the care of M and F. He then adjourned into open court to give a judgment as to the role of medical experts in cases of alleged child abuse.

Held, that (1) the role of the expert was to form an assessment and express his opinion within the particular area of his expertise. The role of the judge was to decide particular issues in individual cases. It was not for the judge to become involved in medical controversy except in the extremely rare case where such a controversy is itself an issue which needs to be resolved by the judge in order to decide the case; (2) the court was, therefore, not usually a suitable forum in which an expert should advance untested hypotheses. However, there would sometimes be cases where there was genuine disagreement on a medical issue, or where it was necessary for a party to advance a particular hypothesis to explain a given set of facts. In such cases, the judge would have to decide the issue; (3) where an expert did advance a hypothesis he owed a very heavy duty to explain to the court that what he was advancing was a hypothesis, that it was controversial, and to place before the court all the material which contradicted the hypothesis. He should also disclose all his material to the other experts in the case; (4) a misleading opinion from an expert was likely to instil false hope in parents, and was also likely to reinforce parental denial of abuse, rendering rehabilitation of the child to the parents more complex and less likely. In short, both the parents and the child were ill-served by a misleading opinion; (5) an expert witness should be independent, objective, and non-partisan. He should never assume the role of advocate. He should state the facts or assumptions on which his opinion is based, and should not omit material facts inconsistent with his opinion (*National Justice Compania Naviera SA v. Prudential Assurance Co.* [1993] 2 Lloyds Rep. 68, *J. (Child Abuse: Expert Evidence, Re* [1991] F.C.R. 193, considered); and (6) Dr P failed in his duty to the court in that he had misled by omission to a very serious extent in failing to deal with the brain damage. In failing to disclose the controversial nature of his research, he lacked objectivity and omitted factors which did not support his opinion. Further, given his evidence in other cases where findings were made by the court of non-accidental injuries, but where he had continued to record such cases as involving brittle bone disease, there was a considerable doubt as to the validity of his research data.

[*Per curiam*: Unless a report from Dr P complied with the above guidelines, his evidence in any case involving the alleged non-accidental injury of infants in the first year of life should be treated with the greatest caution and reserve.]

A.B. (A MINOR) (MEDICAL ISSUES), *Re* [1995] 1 F.C.R. 280, Wall J.

3420. Care proceedings—expert evidence—guidelines for directions to be given when seeking expert evidence in child cases—procedure to be followed by experts in presenting evidence—duty of local authority to disclose all relevant information

(1) In child cases generalised orders for giving leave for expert evidence should never be made; the expert or area of expertise should be identified. There was a positive duty to place all relevant information before the court and the court had a positive duty to inquire into the information. The court should give directions if granting leave for papers to be shown to a particular expert or set a date for directions to be given.

(2) If a number of experts where instructed; each expert should be expressly required to hold discussions with other experts in the same field and then set

out in writing prior to the trial the areas of agreement or dispute. The letter of instruction to each expert should be disclosed to the other parties.

(3) Any party proposing to apply for leave to instruct an expert should give the other parties and the court written explanation of the area of expertise of the proposed expert and reasons as to why the court should grant leave.

(4) Directions should be given to ensure that an expert knew that he was expected to prepare a joint document with the other experts setting at areas of agreement and disagreement. Reports should be served by a specified date and a timetable stated.

(5) A local authority who brought case proceedings had a duty to disclose all relevant information in their possession or power, excluding that protected by public interest immunity including documents which might modify or cast doubt on their case. If relevant documents appeared to be protected by public interest immunity the local authority should draw the attention of the parties are the guardian *ad litem* and invite application to court.

(6) In all cases it was particularly important that no local authority should draw the guardian *ad litem's* attention to any matters of concern within the documents. The guardian *ad litem* should seek the court's directions if he came across relevant documents and the local authority refused to disclose.

C. (CHILD CASES: EVIDENCE AND DISCLOSURE), *Re*, [1995] 2 F.C.R. 97 Cazalet J.

3421. Care proceedings—expert evidence—pre-trial review—all experts agreeing that children's welfare required care orders and long-term alternative placements—whether parents having right to contest result and seek contact orders after pre-trial review—role of Legal Aid Board

[Children Act 1989 (c.41), s.34(4).]

Important expert reports in care proceedings should be available before the pre-trial review, and where all experts were agreed that rehabilitation was not feasible, the matter should be referred to the Legal Aid Board to allow the Board to consider whether it was prepared to continue to finance the litigation.

Three children were accommodated by the local authority. An assessment was made which was adverse to any rehabilitation, and proceedings were commenced seeking care orders and the termination of parental contact. All the experts, including the one instructed on behalf of the parents, recommended care orders and long-term alternative placement. The parents contested the applications by challenging the local authority's general presentation and the conclusions reached by the local authority witnesses and in the assessment.

Held, making care orders and giving leave to terminate contact, that (1) there could be no doubt that the statutory threshold criteria had been met, and that the children's welfare compelled the making of care orders; (2) the search for a new placement for these three disturbed children would be difficult enough, without the added disadvantages of having to accommodate parental contact. Any advantage to the children from parental contact did not begin to outweigh those disadvantages: the children's welfare dictated a termination of contact pursuant to s.34(4) of the Children Act 1989 (*B. (Minors) (Termination of Contact: Paramount Consideration), Re* [1993] C.L.Y. 2771 applied); (3) the unanimity of professional opinion, available before the pre-trial review, prompted very little forensic reaction at the pre-trial review. Where all experts (including the parents' expert) were agreed that rehabilitation could be eliminated and that alternative long-term placements should be found, the litigation should not be allowed to proceed just as though the parents' expert had been favourable to their case. In such circumstances, the parents' legal team were under a duty to refer the matter to the Legal Aid Board to give the Board the opportunity to review the degree to which it is prepared to continue to finance the litigation; and (4) influential reports should be available before the pre-trial review, and at the pre-trial review advocates had a duty to draw the court's attention to the reality that there was only one possible forensic conclusion. The court would thereby be enabled, not to preclude the parents' need to put their case before the court through oral evidence, but to keep that need within reasonable bounds.

N. (CONTESTED CARE APPLICATION), *Re* [1994] 2 F.L.R. 992, Thorpe J.

3422. Care proceedings—expert evidence—video interviews—guidance and observations on expert witnesses and video interviews

The court gave guidelines on the use of video interviews and in relation to expert witnesses.

After a case lasting 14 days, with estimated costs of over half a million pounds, the judge made the following observations:

(1) Video interviews: the police and the hospital had refused to release the video tapes of interviews with the child. Consequently, a number of experts, as well as the barristers and solicitors for the parties, had had to travel to the police station and the hospital to view the interviews. Some of the experts had had to give their opinion on the basis of transcripts alone. It was to be hoped that the practice of the police and of hospitals would change so that copies of tapes could be made to allow viewing for the purposes of court proceedings. A solicitor would usually be justified in seeking a copy, the copy to be made at the solicitor's expense, and the cost would ordinarily be a proper legal aid disbursement. The solicitor should give a written undertaking not to copy or release the tape, except temporarily to counsel or to an expert. If the hospital or police force unreasonably declined to make a copy available, then the court could order the production of the tape for copying, with the possibility of costs being awarded against the hospital or police force;

(2) Expert witnesses: the court would direct the experts to meet in order to attempt to reach agreement or to narrow the issues. It would be good practice for a solicitor for one of the parties, usually the guardian *ad litem*'s solicitor, to be responsible for seeking to convene a meeting of experts.

R. (CHILD ABUSE: VIDEO EVIDENCE), *Re* [1995] 1 F.L.R. 451, Johnson J.

3423. Care proceedings—HIV test of child—procedure to be followed

[Children Act 1989 (c.41), s.38(6).]

Where in care proceedings a direction is sought for the child to be tested for HIV, the question should be transferred for hearing by a High Court judge.

M and F's child was the subject of an interim care order. At a directions hearing, a direction was sought for the child to be HIV tested. The district judge made the direction, and M and F appealed. The judge adjourned the hearing for evidence to be filed in support of the direction, and on seeing this evidence, M and F withdrew their appeal.

Held, that the decision whether to order a child be tested for HIV was one which gave rise to a whole range of emotional, psychological and practical problems, and needed consideration of the policy factors bearing on the decision. Until there was an established body of principles governing the decision, the question should be heard by a High Court judge and proceedings transferred if necessary. This was also the view of the President of the Family Division.

HIV TESTS (NOTE), *Re* [1994] 2 F.L.R. 116, Singer J.

3424. Care proceedings—interim supervision order agreed—child of family sustaining non-accidental injury prior to final hearing—local authority and guardian seeking interim care order—whether interim supervision or interim care order should be made—whether justices' reasons adequate

M had two children, C, born in 1989, and A, born in 1991, who had hearing and communication difficulties and was dependent on his brother. A had been accommodated by the local authority on 13 occasions, frequently accompanied by C. Care proceedings were commenced which had proceeded by way of interim supervision orders. In November 1993, M moved in with a man whose two children had been on the Child Protection Register. In January 1994, M admitted causing bruising and scratching to C and both children's physical condition and behaviour had deteriorated. At the hearing in January 1994 when all parties believed a supervision order would be made by consent, the guardian *ad litem* and local authority sought an interim care order. The justices dismissed the application for an interim care order and made an interim supervision order.

Held, allowing the guardian's and local authority's appeals, that the making of an interim supervision order indicated that the justices had found the threshold criteria satisfied, although it was inconsistent with their finding that A was at risk in M's boyfriend's household. It was far from clear that the justices had treated the children's welfare as the paramount consideration when deciding the order to make in the light of the considerable evidence that A was at risk of emotional and physical harm if left in the care of M. The justices should have expressly indicated what evidence they had accepted and what they had rejected.

LEICESTERSHIRE COUNTY COUNCIL v. G. [1994] 2 FLR 329, Stuart-White J.

3425. Care proceedings—interim supervision order imposed—child aged five months—child suffering significant harm—whether interim care order to be substituted

[Children Act 1989 (c.41), ss.1, 31, 39, Sched. 3, para. 3.]

K was now five months old, and was the fourth of M's children by four different fathers. The eldest had been freed for adoption, and the next two were the subject of interim care orders. When K was born in February 1993, the local authority obtained an unopposed interim supervision order. In May 1993 M's mother dropped K in the street, though no lasting injuries were sustained. The local authority obtained an *ex parte* order converting the interim supervision order into an interim care order. At an *inter partes* hearing the next day the interim care order was confirmed, but was to be reviewed in June at a hearing fixed in relation to the two elder children. K was placed with foster-parents who lived some distance away, making daily contact with M virtually impossible. In June there was no judge available for the hearing that had been fixed, and the next date given was in August. M appealed against the *inter partes* interim care order made in May. The Court of Appeal decided that the appeal was unnecessary, and that what was required was a review on the merits of the interim care order.

Held, that notwithstanding M's long-term problems, which would need to be considered at the final hearing, K's present welfare required her return to M. On M's undertaking not to allow her mother to have contact with K, an interim supervision order would be substituted, and a condition imposed that M attend a day centre twice a week.

C. (A MINOR) (INTERIM CARE), *Re* [1994] 1 F.C.R. 447, Balcombe L.J. sitting as a judge of the Family Division.

3426. Care proceedings—local authority care plan—objection to plan by child—legal representation of child—whether child to be represented by separate solicitor

S, the second of seven children who were the subject of care proceedings, objected to the care plan proposed by the local authority. The guardian *ad litem* and the solicitor representing the children made an application that S be represented by a different solicitor, but the judge refused on the ground that the proceedings were at a late stage and such a move would cause the hearing to be postponed. He urged the children's solicitor to use his skill to represent both S and her siblings to the best of his ability.

Held, allowing the guardian *ad litem's* appeal, that an advocate would find it impossible in care proceedings to put forward the local authority's plan whilst simultaneously acting for a child who was resisting that plan.

P. (MINORS) (REPRESENTATION), *Re*, *The Times*, November 16, 1995, C.A.

3427. Care proceedings—non-compliance with rules—interim supervision order agreed—at subsequent directions hearing local authority seeking interim care order without notice—procedural irregularity—court making interim care orders—whether orders valid

[Children Act 1989 (c.41), ss.1, 31, 33, 35, 38, 44, 45; Family Proceedings Rules 1991 (S.I. 1991 No. 1247), rr.4.14, 4.16.]

An interim care order made without notice of the change in the nature of the local authority's application, and with no oral evidence or cross-examination, was fatally flawed and would be set aside.

W was born in March 1993 to M, then aged 16. F was in his thirties. In September 1993, the local authority initiated care proceedings. On November 2, 1993 the court made an interim supervision order and accepted a series of undertakings from M. The matter was listed to come back before the court at a directions hearing on November 29, 1993. On that date, without any notice to M, and without M's personal attendance, the local authority applied for an interim care order. The judge refused an application for an adjournment made on M's behalf, and refused to allow M's counsel to cross-examine the social worker involved. The judge made an interim care order to last until December 22, 1993, on which date it was continued until February 11, 1994. On December 31, 1993, the local authority obtained an *ex parte* emergency protection order, expressed to last until January 19, 1994, and, purportedly in pursuance of that order, removed W and placed him with foster-parents. M appealed against the interim care orders of November 29 and December 22.

Held, allowing the appeal, that (1) the order of November 29, 1993 was tainted by non-compliance with the rules: under the Family Proceedings Rules 1991, r.4.14(5), in a non-urgent case, two clear days' notice was required of any change in the nature of the order sought. Further, M should have been present, under r.4.16; (2) the court was required to permit evidence and cross-examination relevant to the change of circumstances and the question why a different order was being sought. The November order, and the December order which had been made as a continuation of the November order and again made without the court hearing any evidence, were therefore flawed and would be set aside (*Hampshire County Council v. S.* [1993] C.L.Y. 2829 applied); (3) however, the court was satisfied that there were grounds for making a short interim care order, which would last until a hearing in the county court in a few days' time.

[*Per curiam*: (1) Where the threshold criteria were satisfied, it was only if a supervision order appeared unlikely to be sufficient to obviate the risk of significant harm that the court should go on to make a care order; (2) the emergency protection order was probably invalid, there being no power to make such an order to last in excess of eight days, and was also unnecessary, since a valid interim care order allowed the local authority to remove the child.]

W. (A MINOR) (INTERIM CARE ORDER), *Re* [1994] 2 F.L.R. 892, C.A.

3428. Care proceedings—residence order—application by aunt in respect of niece—care proceedings in respect of nephew in family proceedings court—aunt applying to be joined as party in care proceedings—whether proceedings concerning siblings should be consolidated—whether aunt should be joined as party to care proceedings

[Children Act 1989 (c.41), ss.7, 8, 10(9), 37, 41.]

Proceedings relating to siblings should be heard by the same tribunal wherever possible, and where separate proceedings were instituted in different courts the proceedings should be consolidated at an early stage.

M and F had separated and their children, a boy aged six, and a girl aged four, remained with M. The boy was accommodated by the local authority, and care proceedings were later commenced in the magistrates' court in relation to him. The local authority planned to rehabilitate the boy with M, and a hearing was fixed for July 1994 for the magistrates to approve the boy's return to M. By 1993, M's sister had taken over from M in looking after the girl, and she had applied for a residence order in relation to the girl in the county court. The aunt and M and F agreed that the two sets of proceedings should be consolidated and that the care proceedings in relation to the boy be transferred to the county court. The magistrates refused the transfer, and this was upheld by a district judge. In April 1994, the aunt applied to be joined as a party to the care proceedings in the magistrates' court, with a view to its transfer to the county court and consolidation. The magistrates refused to join the aunt, who appealed.

Held, dismissing the appeal, that (1) wherever possible, proceedings relating to siblings should be heard by the same tribunal. One court should deal with a family. One court should hear all the evidence, and one court should make all the decisions. The parties and the courts had a duty to consider at an early stage how the disposal of each child's case could be most effectively managed. Where separate proceedings in different courts were instituted in relation to siblings, then as a general rule every effort should be made at the earliest possible stage for the proceedings to be consolidated; (2) in deciding whether or not to grant leave to the aunt to become a party to the care proceedings, s.10(9) of the Children Act 1989 did not directly apply, as she was not seeking a s.8 order, and her application was procedural only. However, the underlying thinking behind s.10(9) was applicable, and the proper test to be applied was whether an order for consolidation and transfer was necessary for the proper determination of the proceedings relating to each child, taking into account the matters listed in s.10(9) (*G. v. Kirklees Metropolitan Borough Council* [1993] 1 F.L.R. 805, *North Yorkshire County Council v. G.* [1993] 2 F.L.R. 732 considered); (3) the demarcation of proceedings into public law proceedings, with a guardian *ad litem* for the child, and private law proceedings, with no guardian, gave rise to particular difficulties in cases such as this. The aunt's strongest argument for consolidation was that in her residence application in relation to the girl in the county court, she would not have access to the material available to the magistrates in the care proceedings relating to boy. However, in a private law case where a local authority had been involved and evidence from the authority was relevant, the proper course would be for an application to be made to the court hearing the private law proceedings for a report under s.7 of the Children Act 1989 which the local authority was obliged to provide; (4) although the guardian *ad litem*'s report was confidential to the care proceedings, there was no objection to the report being made available in the private law proceedings. If two courts have to deal with different sets of proceedings concerning siblings, the guardian's report should be made available in both sets of proceedings; and (5) on the facts, there was no real issue before the magistrates to decide, and no real issue in which the aunt had a specific interest. Considering all the circumstances, including the risk of delay if the aunt were joined and the proceedings transferred, the magistrates had not been plainly wrong to refuse a transfer.

W. v. WAKEFIELD CITY COUNCIL [1994] 2 F.C.R. 564, Wall J.

3429. Care proceedings—"specified proceedings"—investigation by local authority into child's circumstances following direction by court—guardian *ad litem* appointed in "specified proceedings"—local authority deciding not to seek public law order—whether proceedings no longer "specified"—whether guardian could continue to act

[Children Act 1989 (c.41), ss.37, 41; Family Proceedings Rules 1991 (S.I. 1991 No. 1247), rr.4.10–4.11, 9.2A, 9.5.]

Proceedings ceased to be "specified proceedings" where a local authority, having carried out an investigation pursuant to a direction under s.37 of the 1989 Act, decided not apply for a public law order.

The parents of a 14-year-old girl, who had gone to live with her boyfriend at his parents' address, applied for, *inter alia*, a residence order. A direction was given under the Children Act 1989, s.37(1), to the local authority and a guardian *ad litem* was appointed under s.41 for the girl, who also applied for leave to apply for a residence order, although this was not proceeded with. One year later the local authority had not completed their investigation although they had indicated that they did not intend to apply for a public law order in respect of the girl. The guardian was critical of the local authority's investigation and sought guidance as to her continuing involvement given the local authority's decision not to apply for a care or supervision order.

Held, confirming the continued involvement of the guardian *ad litem*, that (1) proceedings ceased to be "specified proceedings" once a local authority had decided not to apply for a care or supervision order after the completion of an investigation under s.37(1); and (2) however, the court would exercise its discretion to retain the guardian *ad litem* under the Family Proceedings Rules 1991, r.9.5, in the girl's best interests, until the local authority had completed their investigation and a final resolution could be ordered or sanctioned by the court, and with the consent of the guardian *ad litem* who could be funded as an expert under the girl's legal aid certificate. The girl did not object to the continuing involvement of the guardian so the reappointment would not contravene the provisions of r.9.2A(4)-(6) of the 1991 Rules (*D.H. (A Minor) (Child Abuse), Re* [1995] 7 C.L. 380; *Essex County Council v. B.* [1994] C.L.Y. 1813; *M. (Minors) (Care Proceedings: Child's Wishes), Re* [1995] 7 C.L. 389; *Nottinghamshire County Council v. P.* [1993] C.L.Y. 2860; *S. (A Minor) (Independent Representation), Re* [1993] C.L.Y. 2845 referred to).

CE (SECTION 37 DIRECTION), *Re* [1995] 1 F.L.R. 26, Wall J.

3430. Child abduction—acquiescence—wrongful removal by mother—whether father's inactivity constituted acquiescence—whether court could inquire into applicant's actual state of mind

[Hague Convention on the Civil Aspects of International Child Abduction 1980, Arts. 12, 13.]

In deciding whether a parent has acquiesced to the wrongful removal of his child, it is appropriate in some cases for the court to enquire into the requesting parent's state of mind, notwithstanding that acquiescence is to be assessed from an objective survey of the circumstances.

M and F had emigrated to Australia, where they had three children aged nine, eight and four. Following the breakdown of the marriage, M wrongfully removed the boys to England. Eight months later, F applied for their return to Australia under the Hague Convention. The judge held that F's inactivity was due to erroneous legal advice and so F had not acquiesced to the removal. The judge also held that the eldest boy's objections to a return were not such as to justify him declining to order a return and ordered the return of the boys.

Held, dismissing the appeal, that (1) when considering whether a child was sufficiently mature for his objections to a return to be considered, the court was not restricted to a general appraisal of the child's capacity to form and express views which bore the hallmark of maturity. The court could, and often should, assess the child's maturity in the light of how he answered the question whether he objected to a return (*S. v. S. (Child Abduction) (Child's Views), Re* [1993] C.L.Y. 2796, *B. v. K. (Child Abduction)* [1994] 11 C.L. 433 considered); (2) the test for determining whether a parent had acquiesced to a removal was whether he had conducted himself in a way which would be inconsistent with him later seeking the summary return of the children (*A.Z. (A Minor) (Abduction: Acquiescence), Re* [1994] 3 C.L. 277 applied, *Kammin's Ballrooms Co. v. Zenith Investments (Torquay)* [1970] C.L.Y. 1525 considered); (3) acquiesence was primarily to be established by inference drawn from an objective survey of the acts and omissions of the aggrieved parent, but this did not exclude an element of subjective analysis. There would be occasions when the court will need to consider private motives and other influences affecting the aggrieved parent, relevant to the issue of acquiescence, but known only to him alone. However, the court should be careful not to give undue emphasis to such subjective elements, which were inherently less reliable than inferences drawn from overt acts and omissions viewed through the eyes of an outside observer (*A. (Minors) (Abduction: Custody Rights), Re* [1992] C.L.Y. 3051, *W. v. W. (Child Abduction: Acquiescence)* [1994] 6 C.L. 291 considered); and (4) the judge had not erred in considering the fact that erroneous advice had been given to F nor in his conclusion that F had not acquiesced to the removal.

S. (MINORS) (ABDUCTION: ACQUIESCENCE), *Re* [1994] 1 F.L.R. 819, C.A.

3431. Child abduction—children's views—consent order for return—children objecting to return—whether children should be joined as parties

[Child Abduction and Custody Act 1985 (c.60), Sched. 1; Hague Convention on the Civil Aspects of International Child Abduction 1980, Art. 13; Family Proceedings Rules 1991 (S.I. 1991 No. 1247), r.6.5.]

Where there was an application under the Hague Convention for the return of a child to his country of habitual residence and the child objected to being returned, only in exceptional circumstances should the child be joined as a party to the proceedings.

M and F were married in Australia in 1976 and their two sons were born there. The sons were aged 11 and nearly 10 when M and F separated in 1986 and M came to England. In 1988 the court in Australia awarded custody of the boys to F. In April 1993 M wrongfully removed the boys from Australia to England. F applied under the Hague Convention for the return of the boys, and after negotiations a consent order was made for their return. Both boys objected to being returned to F and the elder tried to commit suicide. At the airport both boys were very upset and the elder one created such a scene that the captain refused to take off with the boys on board. The boys were returned to M and applied to be joined as parties to the proceedings, but the application was refused. The boys appealed against this refusal and M appealed against the consent order.

Held, dismissing the boys' appeal but allowing M's appeal, that (1) the court had a discretion under Art. 13 to refuse the return of the children where it found that they objected to being returned and had attained an age and degree of maturity at which it was appropriate to take account of their views. Once the court was put on inquiry as to whether the children were of a sufficient degree of maturity, a solution would ordinarily be best achieved by inviting the court welfare officer to assess the children's maturity and to report their views to the court. Only in exceptional circumstances would it be necessary for the children to be joined as parties to the proceedings and separately represented and on the facts separate representation was unnecessary (*L. v. L. (Minors) (Separate Representation)* [1995] 1 C.L. 272 considered); (2) the boys' objections had not been put before the judge who made the consent order for return. In the light of the fundamental change of circumstances now that such evidence was available, the consent order would be set aside. Since there was insufficient evidence for the court to exercise its own discretion under Art. 13, the matter would be remitted to a High Court judge (*P. v. P. (Minors) (Child Abduction)* [1992] C.L.Y. 3055 applied; *R. (A Minor: Abduction), Re* [1992] C.L.Y. 3048, *S. v. S. (Child Abduction) (Child's Views)* [1993] C.L.Y. 2796 considered); and (3) it was artificial to say that where a child objected to a return to a parent but not to a return to the requesting state, the child's objections were irrelevant. The court is not precluded under Art. 13 from considering the objections of a child to returning to a parent *(C. v.*

C. (Minor: Abduction: Rights of Custody Abroad) [1989] C.L.Y. 2437 considered; *B. v. K. (Child Abduction)* [1994] C.L. 433 disapproved).

M. (A MINOR) (CHILD ABDUCTION), *Re* [1994] 1 F.L.R. 391, C.A.

3432. Child abduction—emotional harm—children living with mother in U.K.—father living in U.S. applying for change in custody arrangements—whether in children's best interests to move from U.K. to U.S.—whether father demonstrated compelling reasons to move children—whether father's religious beliefs compatible with children's welfare

After their parents' divorce, the children lived with M in the U.K. while F remained in the U.S., where they had been born. F retained the children after a contact visit and applied for a variation of the custody arrangements.

Held, that there was a risk of emotional harm to the children if they were uprooted and moved to the U.S. F was a born-again fundamentalist Christian, who had planned to move the children to a school which mirrored his beliefs, but it was more likely, without commenting on F's religion, that the children would be better equipped to deal with the harsh realities of life if they were educated within a more liberal tradition. F had not demonstrated any compelling reasons to remove the children from M with whom they had lived all their lives.

H. v. H. (MINORS) (FORUM CONVENIENS) (NO. 3) [1994] Fam.Law 13, H.H.J. Wilson.

3433. Child abduction—foreign order—breach of restraining order of foreign court—child not in jurisdiction—whether English court has power to make interim orders before child's arrival in jurisdiction

[Child Abduction and Custody Act 1985 (c.60), s.5, Sched. 1, arts. 7, 8, 11.]

An English court may make interim orders in respect of a child who had not yet arrived in the U.K. but was expected to do so.

Following their separation the mother, a U.S. national, and the father, an Iraqi national, were granted joint custody of their son. The Superior Court of California ordered that the boy should not be removed from California without the consent of both parents or the leave of the court. In breach of this order the father removed the boy to Iraq. The Californian court ordered the father to return the child to his mother. The father agreed to bring the boy to the U.K. to discuss the situation with the mother. Prior to the father's arrival the mother applied for an order that the child be returned to her pending an *inter partes* hearing.

Held, granting the relief sought, that since the power to make the interim orders undoubtedly existed under s.5 of the Child Abduction and Custody Act 1985 if the child had just arrived in the U.K., it would be extraordinary if that power did not exist in respect of a child who was very likely to arrive in the U.K.

N. (CHILD ABDUCTION: JURISDICTION), *Re* [1995] 5–6 FLR 96, Wilson J.

3434. Child abduction—foreign order—recognition and enforcement—father having temporary care bringing children to England—order of French court ordering return of children—mother seeking return under Hague Convention—whether court should order return

[Hague Convention on the Civil Aspects of International Child Abduction 1980, Arts. 3, 5, 12, 13.]

Where a foreign court had made an order for the return of children to its jurisdiction, the interests of comity required the English court to uphold the judgment of the foreign court, and to uphold its findings of fact.

M and F were French and had lived together in France. They were not married and had two children, now aged six and four. They separated in 1991 and F took over the care of the children and applied to the court for parental authority. Three days before the final hearing F came to England with the children. M visited the children in England and kept in contact by post. The French court found that F had removed the children without M's consent, refused F's application and ordered the return of the children to France. M applied in England for a return of the children under the Hague Convention.

Held, granting M's application, that (1) although M had conceded interim care to F and F's application for parental authority had been pending, M alone had parental authority under French law and F's removal of the children was wrongful within Arts. 3 and 5 of the Convention; (2) despite evidence adduced which suggested that M had consented to the removal, the question of prior consent had been litigated to a conclusion in the French court, which had found that M had not consented to the removal; (3) M's conduct in visiting and contacting the children was necessary in order to preserve her relationship with them and did not amount to acquiescence within Art. 13 (*A. (Minors) (Abduction: Custody Rights), Re* [1992] Fam. 106 applied); (4) the court was therefore bound to order the return of the children forthwith under Art. 12; and (5) even had F established a defence within Art. 13, the court would still have exercised its discretion under Art. 13 to return the children, as the children's welfare required their return to the locality and extended family where they belonged, and the court was required to uphold the decision of the French court in the interests of comity.

R. (MINORS) (ABDUCTION), *Re* [1994] 1 FLR 190, Thorpe J.

3435. Child abduction—foreign order—recognition and enforcement—mother obtaining *ex parte* interim residence order in England—father obtaining order for sole custody in Dublin—whether court should refuse enforcement of Irish order

[Child Abduction and Custody Act 1985 (c.37), ss.15, 16, Sched. 2; European Convention on the Recognition and Enforcement of Decisions Concerning Custody of Children 1980, Arts. 7, 10.]

The court can refuse to recognise an Irish order for sole custody where it is incompatible with an *ex parte* interim residence order which is unlimited in time.

M and F lived in Ireland. M brought their two children to England and in July 1992 F applied to the Dublin court for custody of the children and an order for their return to Ireland. In August 1992 M applied to the court in England and obtained *ex parte* interim residence orders on October 2, 1992. The Dublin court granted sole custody to F on October 27, 1992 and declared that M had unlawfully removed the children from Ireland. F applied for enforcement of the Dublin court order under Art. 7 of the European Convention.

Held, dismissing the application, that although under Art. 7 of the European Convention decisions relating to custody made in one contracting state must ordinarily be recognised and enforced in other contracting states, the court had a discretion to refuse recognition and enforcement under Art. 10(1). The Dublin court order for sole custody was plainly incompatible with the English residence order, which was not limited in time. The fact that the English order might properly be termed an interim order was entirely irrelevant to whether the orders were incompatible. The English order was clearly a decision given pursuant to proceedings begun before the request for recognition and enforcement of the Dublin order, as the request was only made in November 1992. As the children had been in England for some 18 months, a refusal of recognition and enforcement would be in accordance with their welfare.

M. (CHILD ABDUCTION) (EUROPEAN CONVENTION), *Re* [1994] 1 F.L.R. 551, Rattee J.

3436. Child abduction—grave risk to child alleged—whether child must be returned

A mother appealed against an order to return her child, whom she had wrongly removed, back to the U.S. The question was whether the mother had breached the father's custody rights under the Hague Convention on Civil

Aspects of International Child Abduction 1980 which provided that a child should not be returned if likely to be placed at grave risk and in an intolerable situation and, if she had, whether Art. 13 applied.

Held, allowing the appeal, that the judge at first instance had found that the child had been wrongfully removed from the father and that no case under Art. 13 had been made out. It was contrary to the principles behind the Convention that a child should be secretly abducted from the parent who had been granted custody of the child. It was very difficult to establish a grave risk to the child under Art. 13, and if the case could not be decided by affidavits the child would be returned in order for the court of the child's habitual residence to hear the case. However, in the instant case, the evidence provided by the mother should be considered as being true since the consequences to the child would be very grave if that evidence was accurate. This was an exceptional situation and a case under Art. 13 had been made out.

F. (A MINOR) (CHILD ABDUCTION: RISK IF RETURNED), *Re*, *The Times*, February 15, 1995, C.A.

3437. Child abduction—habitual residence—declaration on the child's habitual residence requested—whether English court entitled to make such a declaration

[Hague Convention on the Civil Aspects of International Child Abduction 1980, Art. 15; Child Abudction and Custody Act 1985 (c.60), s.8.]

A mother who had removed her child from the jurisdiction of England and Wales to California appealed against the making of a declaration that such removal was wrongful under the Hague Convention on the Civil Aspects of International Child Abduction 1980. The declaration was made following a request under s.8 of the Child Abduction and Custody Act 1985 and Art. 15 of the Hague Convention by the father, on the advice of the Official Solicitor acting on behalf of the Lord Chancellor's Department as the central authority of the U.K.

Held, dismissing the appeal, that the court had jurisdiction to hear such an application under Art. 15 and it was for the court to decide whether they should make the declaration as requested. In the instant case the central authority of the U.S. was faced with an English residence order and a complicated matrimonial history and requested the help of the English court before putting the application to the U.S. courts. In a situation such as this, where the requesting state had not made a decision on the habitual residence, it would be better for the English court to make a declaration assuming that the habitual residence was in England. The request for a declaration meant that the court would have to consider issues that would be decided in another jurisdiction, but the issues were technically different. The English court would have to decide whether the child was habitually resident in England according to English law and the Californian court would have to decide the issue according to Californian law. The court should not disbar itself from granting such declarations since Parliament had given it jurisdiction to do so.

P. (A MINOR) (CHILD ABDUCTION: DECLARATION), *Re*, *The Times*, February 16, 1995, C.A.

3438. Child abduction—habitual residence—father agreeing to mother moving to England with child—mother taking child back to Canada to attempt reconciliation but removing child back to England two months later—whether removal to England wrongful—whether child habitually resident in Canada at time of removal

[Child Abduction and Custody Act 1985 (c.60); Hague Convention on the Civil Aspects of International Child Abduction 1980, Arts. 3, 13, 15.]

For an order for the return of a child to be made under the Hague Convention, the child must be habitually resident in the requesting state immediately prior to the wrongful removal or retention.

A was born in 1991 in Canada. M and F, A's parents, separated in 1992, and A remained with M. In December 1992, following legal advice, M and F executed an agreement under seal, which gave M interim custody, and by which F consented to M and A returning to live in England. The agreement was to expire on the signing of a final separation agreement or on seven days' written notice by either party. M took A to England in December 1992 with the intention of settling here, but returned with A at the end of the month in order to attempt a reconciliation. This was unsuccessful and M and A returned to England on March 8, 1993 without F's knowledge or consent. On the same day F gave written notice of termination of the December 1992 agreement. F thereafter applied for A's return under the Hague Convention.

Held, dismissing the application, that (1) A was not habitually resident in Canada immediately before his removal to Engand on March 8, 1993, and thus his removal was not wrongful under the Convention. On leaving Canada in December 1992, A, then in the sole custody of M, ceased to be habitually resident in Canada. On returning to Canada for the short period of the attempted reconciliation, M did not form a settled intention to return to Canada, and thus neither M, nor A, still in M's sole custody, became habitually resident in Canada again (*J. (A Minor) (Abduction: Custody Rights), Re* [1990] C.L.Y. 3151 applied); (2) in any event F had acquiesced in M's removal of A (*S. (Minors) (Abduction: Acquiescence), Re* [1994] 1 F.L.R. 819 applied).

[*Per curiam*: M raised the matter of A's habitual residence for the first time at the hearing itself. If a specific defence under the Hague Convention was to be raised, it was desirable that it should appear in the affidavits, or that notice be given of it.]

B. (CHILD ABDUCTION: HABITUAL RESIDENCE), *Re* [1994] 2 F.L.R. 915, Ewbank J.

3439. Child abduction—habitual residence—removal of children from naval base

[Hague Convention on the Civil Aspects of International Child Abduction 1980, Art. 4.]

Where the mother of three children had wrongfully removed them from a U.S. naval base in a non-Convention country in which the father had a service posting, the habitual residence of the children under Art. 4 of the Hague Convention on the Civil Aspects of International Child Abduction 1980 was not the U.S., but the country to which the father had been posted.

A. (MINORS), *Re*, *The Independent*, October 16, 1995 (C.S.), Cazalet J.

3440. Child abduction—joinder of child—judge ordering return to Ireland—child objecting to return—child joined as party to proceedings and appealing judge's order—whether joinder appropriate—whether court required to consider new evidence as to child's objections

[Hague Convention on the Civil Aspects of International Child Abduction 1980, Art. 13.]

Although the child should only be joined as a party to proceedings under the Hague Convention in exceptional circumstances, where the dispute is between the child and his mother and not between the parents and where the child's representation is the only avenue by which the court can consider his objections to a return, it will be appropriate for the child to be joined.

N was now 13. Following M and F's separation in 1986, N stayed with M in Ireland and F returned to England. In 1992, N ran away and was taken to hospital, where he was found to have non-accidental injuries which he said had been caused by M's partner. He said he had suffered physical abuse for seven years and he had considered suicide. Although a place of safety order was made, N remained at home and M began a series of proceedings in order to establish control over him, ultimately seeking N's detainment in a secure unit. In the autumn of 1993, N ran away eight times and eventually F responded to his pleas by bringing him to England. N was placed in a children's home. M applied under the Hague Convention for his return to Ireland. The court ordered his return to Ireland on the basis that he would not return to M until a decision of the Irish court. N ran away from the home and refused to return until the order for his return to Ireland was stayed. F was not legally aided nor represented, and did not appeal against the order for return. N's application to be joined as a party to the proceedings was granted and he obtained leave to appeal against the order for return. N appealed against the order for return; M appealed against the order joining N as a party.

Held, allowing N's appeal, that a child should only be made a party to Hague Convention proceedings in exceptional cases. However, the present case was exceptional, in that N had been in serious dispute with M for the previous two years, and given that F had not appealed the order for return, the only way for the court to consider N's objections to return was by N's own representation (*M. (A Minor) (Child Abduction), Re* [1995] 7 C.L. 372 applied). There was a large quantity of evidence in support of N's allegations regarding M and her partner. N was now 13, and the court was satisfied that he had sufficient maturity for his views to be considered under Art. 13. He had valid objections to a return, and the court was therefore entitled to exercise its discretion under Art. 13 to refuse a return.

M. (A MINOR) (ABDUCTION: CHILD'S OBJECTIONS), *Re* [1994] 2 F.L.R. 126, C.A.

3441. Child abduction—jurisdiction—child not yet physically present within U.K.—Hague Convention—whether jurisdiction to make order

[Child Abduction and Custody Act 1985 (c.60), s.5; Hague Convention on the Civil Aspects of International Child Abduction 1980, Arts. 7, 8, 11.]

On an application under the Hague Convention for the return of a child wrongfully removed from a contracting state, the court had jurisdiction to make orders in respect of the child notwithstanding the fact that the child was not yet physically present in the jurisdiction.

A was aged two years and eight months. His parents lived in California, and on the breakdown of their marriage they reached an agreement (recorded in a court order) that A should live with M, and have contact with F, but that A should not be removed from California save by agreement or by leave of the court. Following a contact weekend, F, who was an Iraqi national, removed A to Iraq. F wished to discuss matters with M in England. M informed the U.S. Central Authority, which made a request under the Hague Convention to the U.K. Central Authority to take all possible steps to assist in A's return to M in California. Before the parents' imminent meeting in London, to which F was likely to bring A, M applied *ex parte* for an order authorising the tipstaff to collect A from F and to return him to M's care.

Held, granting the application, that nothing in s.5 of the Child Abduction and Custody Act 1985 prevented the powers of the court from being exercised in respect of a child not yet physically present in the jurisdiction. The language of both the 1985 Act and the Hague Convention was noticeably wide, and the court was under a duty to co-operate with all contracting states in making orders to secure the return of wrongfully removed children. On the facts, that duty could only be discharged by making orders for A's initial restoration to M's care on his anticipated arrival in the U.K.

A. v. A (ABDUCTION: JURISDICTION) [1995] 1 F.L.R. 341, Wilson J.

3442. Child abduction—non-Convention country—children removed from Italy by mother—father seeking return of children—concerns expressed regarding adequacy of provision for mother on return to Italy—undertakings given—whether validity of undertakings questionable in light of fresh evidence

The principles applicable in cases under the Hague Convention should prima facie be applied in non-Convention cases and the court was entitled to assume that undertakings given in this jurisdiction would be treated seriously by judges in another country.

The mother who was English and the father who was Italian lived in Italy and had two children. Their relationship broke down and the mother applied for custody of the children. She was living in a hotel while the children lived with their father. When the mother was told that the custody application had little prospect of success, she took the children to England without the father's consent and applied for a residence order. The father filed an answer in the English proceedings but sought the peremptory return of the children which was granted on the father giving certain undertakings, although the judge expressed some concern at the practical arrangements for the children in Italy. At the hearing of the mother's appeal, she sought to adduce further evidence that the arrangements made in Italy were inadequate.

Held, dismissing the appeal, that (1) the principles applicable in Hague Convention cases should prima facie be applied to non-Convention cases. Judges in one country were entitled to assume that undertakings would be regarded seriously by judges in another jurisdiction; (2) there had been sufficient material before the judge to be satisfied that a return order would be in the best interests of the children and the mother's new evidence merely reinforced that view (*D. v. D. (Child Abduction: Non-Convention Country)* [1995] 1 C.L. 261, *Ladd v. Marshall* [1954] C.L.Y. 2507, *S. (Minors) (Abduction), Re* [1994] C.L.Y. 3157 referred to).

[*Per curiam*: the principles upon which the courts act in non-Convention cases are: (1) normally, the best interests of the children are secured by having their future determined in the jurisdiction of their habitual residence; (2) the essence of the jurisdiction to grant a peremptory return order was that the judge should act urgently; and (3) it is assumed that facilities such as rights of representation would be secured as well within one state's jurisdiction as within another.]

M. (ABDUCTION: NON-CONVENTION COUNTRY), *Re* [1995] 1 F.L.R. 89, C.A.

3443. Child abduction—non-Convention country—mother removing child from South Africa to Britain—Hague Convention inapplicable—removal not in breach of rights of custody—father bringing wardship proceedings seeking return of child to South Africa—principles to be applied—whether court should order return of child

[Child Abduction and Custody Act 1985 (c.60), Sched. 1; Hague Convention on Civil Aspects of International Child Abduction 1980, Arts. 3, 4, 12, 13.]

In a non-Convention case, it was appropriate to apply the general principles of the Hague Convention, namely that it was in the interests of children not to be abducted from one country to another, and that any decision as to their future was best taken in the jurisdiction of their habitual residence, although the court could have regard to wider aspects of the child's welfare.

F was a British national and a citizen of South Africa. His family divided their time equally between South Africa and the Isle of Man. M was British and her family lived in the Isle of Man. M and F married in 1989 on the Isle of Man. S was born there in 1990. In 1993, the three of them went to live in South Africa, buying a house and registering S for entry into a school. Later in 1993 F left the family home and commenced proceedings for divorce and custody. In November 1993, M was granted sole interim custody, with access to F. In 1994 M brought S to England. F applied in wardship for S's summary return to South Africa (the Hague Convention not applying as South Africa was not a party).

Held, granting the application, that (1) the general principles of the Hague Convention were equally applicable in non-Convention cases. They were that it was in the interests of children that they should not be abducted from one country to another, and that it was usually in the best interests of children for their future to be decided by the jurisdiction in which they had been habitually resident. However, in non-Convention cases the wardship court retained the discretion to consider the wider aspects of the children's welfare (*L. (Minors) (Wardship: Abduction), Re* [1974] C.L.Y. 2417, *R. (Minors) (Wardship: Jurisdiction), Re* (1981) 2 F.L.R. 416, *F. (A Minor) (Adbuction), Re* [1991] C.L.Y. 2526, *S.*

(Minors) (Adbuction), Re [1993] 2 F.C.R. 499, *D. v. D. (Child Abduction)* [1994] 1 F.C.R. 654 applied); (2) had this been a Convention case, the application would have failed as the removal was not in breach of F's rights of custody, as M had been granted sole interim custody; however (3) M and F had chosen South Africa as their home and S's home for the foreseeable future; M had brought S to England, and not to the family's historical home in the Isle of Man; and there were divorce and custody proceedings in South Africa. In the circumstances, the court would order S's summary return.

S. v. S. (CHILD ABDUCTION: NON-CONVENTION COUNTRY) [1995] 1 F.C.R. 188, Hollis J.

3444. Child abduction—non-Convention country—wardship—whether Convention principles applying to non-Convention cases

[Hague Convention on the Civil Aspects of International Child Abduction 1980, Arts. 8, 13; Family Proceedings Rules 1991 (S.I. 1991 No. 1247), r.6.3.]

The court was not required in a non-Convention case to apply the provisions of the Hague Convention to the letter but should decide the case in accordance with the general principles of the Convention whilst retaining the discretion to consider the wider aspects of the child's welfare.

M was English and F was Greek. They were married and had two children, N now aged seven, and E, aged three. In December 1991 F removed the children to Greece. In May 1992 M went to Greece and made an application for the children's return. A consent order was drawn up, providing that M was to have care of the children on condition that she did not remove the children from Greece without F's written consent. In August 1992 M removed the children to England without such consent. F brought wardship proceedings in England seeking an order for the children's summary return. Although it was a non-Convention case, the judge applied the Hague Convention almost literally, and found that the children had been habitually resident in Greece, that their removal was wrongful, and there was no defence within Art. 13 to an order for return, which he duly made. M appealed. By the time of the appeal hearing three months later M was five months' pregnant and stated that she would not return with the children.

Held, allowing the appeal, that (1) it was proper to apply the general principles of the Hague Convention in a non-Convention case. It was in the interests of children that their parents should not abduct them from one country to another, and any decision relating to the upbringing of children was best decided in the jurisdiction in which they had hitherto been habitually resident. However, the court retained the discretion to consider the wider aspects of the children's welfare (*G. v. G. (Minors) (Abduction)* [1992] C.L.Y. 3046, *F. (A Minor) (Abduction: Jurisdiction), Re* [1991] C.L.Y. 2526 applied; *H. (Minors) (Abduction: Custody Rights), Re; S. (Minors) (Abduction: Custody Rights), Re* [1991] C.L.Y. 2528 considered); (2) the judge had directed himself properly in accordance with the general principles of the Convention and his findings could not be challenged. His order for summary return was fully justified at the time; and (3) M's pregnancy changed the position. The return of the children without M would not be in their best interests. Whilst the court deprecated M's conduct, the children's welfare now required a hearing on the merits by an English court at the earliest opportunity.

D. v. D. (CHILD ABDUCTION: NON-CONVENTION COUNTRY) [1994] 1 FLR 137, C.A.

3445. Child abduction—non-Convention country—whether Convention principles applying to non-Convention cases—whether Pakistan inappropriate forum

[Children Act 1989 (c.41), s.1(1); Hague Convention on the Civil Aspects of International Child Abduction 1980.]

The general principles of the Hague Convention would be applied in non-Convention cases provided that the courts of the country of the children's habitual residence applied principles which were acceptable to the English courts as being appropriate.

M and F were both Muslims born in Pakistan. They married in England, and thereafter lived in Pakistan with their three children. In November 1992 M took the younger two children to England without F's knowledge or consent. F sought the children's summary return to Pakistan. The judge ordered their return. M appealed, contending that Pakistan did not apply the same system of law for child welfare decisions as that applied in England.

Held, dismissing the appeal, that (1) the court must apply the general philosophy of the Hague Convention in non-Convention cases. It was in the interests of children not to be abducted from one country to another, and any decision as to their upbringing was best decided in the jurisdiction in which they had hitherto been habitually resident, provided that the courts of that jurisdiction applied principles acceptable to the English courts as appropriate (*L. (Minors) (Wardship: Jurisdiction), Re* [1974] C.L.Y. 2417, *R. (Minors) (Wardship: Jurisdiction), Re* (1981) FLR 416, *G. v. G. (Minors) (Abduction)* [1992] C.L.Y. 3046, *F. (A Minor) (Abduction: Jurisdiction), Re* [1991] C.L.Y. 2526 applied); (2) prima facie the children's future should be decided in Pakistan. The courts in Pakistan would try to give effect to the children's welfare from the Muslim point of view. The differences between English and Pakistani law were not such as to render the Pakistani court an inappropriate forum.

S. (MINORS) (ABDUCTION), *Re* [1994] 1 FLR 297, C.A.

3446. Child abduction—peremptory order for return of children—application for adjournment to assemble evidence—assumption of fair hearing in another jurisdiction—whether principle of international comity could be departed from

The mother of two boys, who was a British citizen married to a citizen of Dubai, appealed against a peremptory order requiring her to return her children to Dubai. On making one of her annual visits to her family in England she filed for divorce and obtained an interim residence order in respect of the children. After making undertakings to the court, the father obtained a peremptory order for their return to Dubai, their country of habitual residence, the court refusing the mother's application for an adjournment to enable her to assemble evidence to show that she would be disadvantaged if the case was heard in Dubai.

Held, dismissing the appeal, that English courts assumed that a fair hearing would be provided in another jurisdiction and that the foreign court would take account of the proceedings in the English courts. The principle of international comity would only be departed from if exceptional circumstances could be shown.

M. (MINORS) (ABDUCTION: PEREMPTORY RETURN ORDER), *Re*, *The Times*, November 20, 1995, C.A.

3447. Child abduction—rights of custody—child living in Australia—father agreeing to removal of child for six months—mother failing to return child—father applying for child to be returned under Hague Convention—whether father had "rights of custody" within terms of Convention at date of removal—whether father's consent to removal obtained by deception a valid consent—whether English court having jurisdiction to make Convention order

"Rights" in the Hague Convention sense included the inchoate rights of those carrying out parental duties and functions although those rights had not been recognised formally in law.

M, who was British, and F, who was Australian, never married and had one child who was born in Australia. They separated and later M became addicted to heroin and travelled to England, leaving the child in the care of F and the maternal grandmother. The grandmother wished to travel with the child to England. F would only agree to the child leaving Australia for six months and the grandmother signed a minute of a consent order, including a provision that the child could be removed from Australia to travel. M indicated that she had also signed the consent order. When the child arrived in England M issued wardship proceedings, notice of which reached F after the Australian court had approved the consent order. M failed to return the child and F applied for his immediate return. The judge ordered the child's immediate return.

Held, dismissing M's appeal, that the Hague Convention was to be construed broadly, without attributing to its terms their specialist meaning within domestic law. "Rights of custody" enlarged upon, but was not necessarily synonymous with, the connotation of "custody". "Rights" could include the inchoate rights of those carrying out duties and enjoying privileges of custodial or parental character, while not recognised or enshrined in law and it was a matter for the court to determine on the facts of each case. It was unlikely that a court would find a consent to be valid when it had been founded on a calculated and deliberate fraud by the absconding parent.

B. (A MINOR) (ABDUCTION), *Re* [1994] 2 FLR 249, C.A.

3448. Child abduction—rights of custody—whether removal of child by mother from USA without father's consent was in breach of father's rights of custody—whether exceptional circumstances warranting refusal to order child's return to USA

[Child Abduction and Custody Act 1985 (c.60), Sched. 1, Arts. 3, 13(b); Convention on the Civil Aspects of International Child Abduction, Art. 3.]

It is for the English court to determine whether the rights of the parent under Colorado law are "rights of custody" for the purposes of Art. 3 of the Convention on the Civil Aspects of International Child Abduction.

M, a British citizen, married F, an American citizen, in Colorado in 1987. In 1990 their son, C, was born. In June 1994 M applied to the Adams county court for a temporary restraining order requiring F to leave the matrimonial home. The order did not prohibit M from leaving the jurisdiction with the child. M arrived in the U.K. with the child in July 1994. F successfully applied under the Child Abduction and Custody Act 1985 for an order that M be required to return to the USA with the child. The court was supplied with expert evidence that the law of Colorado recognised both parents' rights to the custody of their child. M filed affidavits alleging that F had behaved violently towards her, her mother and towards C, and that such violence had had a very serious impact on C's behaviour.

Held, allowing M's appeal, that (1) "rights of custody" under the Convention are broader than an order of the court and parents have rights in respect of their children without the need to have them declared by the court (*B. (A Minor) (Abduction), Re* [1995] 4 C.L. 317 considered). It is repugnant to the philosophy of the Convention for one parent unilaterally, secretly and with full knowledge that it is against the wishes of the other parent who possesses "rights of custody" to remove the child from the jurisdiction of the child's habitual residence. Both F and M enjoyed rights of custody under Colorado law and by her removal of the child M wrongfully breached F's rights, contrary to art. 3 of the Convention; (2) a very high standard is required to establish under Art. 13(b) of the Convention that there is a grave risk that the child's return would expose the child to physical or psychological harm or otherwise place the child in an intolerable situation, so that the court should not order the child's return. On the extreme facts of this case, in particular the likelihood that the child would be returning to the same situation as that which had a very serious effect on him before his removal, and the fact that F had not responded to M's specific allegations of violence despite having the opportunity to do so, that standard was satisfied.

F. (A MINOR), *Re* [1995] 3 W.L.R. 339, C.A.

3449. Child abduction—stay of domestic proceedings—habitual residence in France—stay of proceedings in England—whether stay should be ordered where close family connection with England

[Family Proceedings Rules 1991 (S.I. 1991 No. 1247), r.6.11; Hague Convention on the Civil Aspects of International Child Abduction 1980.]

In exceptional cases, the court will allow proceedings relating to the children's upbringing to continue in England despite the fact that the conditions for the return of the children under the Hague Convention were satisfied.

Following their marriage in England in 1983, M and F had a somewhat nomadic life. In 1992, F and the two children settled in France with M staying in England. The children went to local schools and F started a business. In July 1993 M wrongfully removed the children to England but soon returned them to F in France. In August 1993 M indicated her wish for divorce, but in September 1993 M and F agreed that the whole family would move to England on a temporary basis in order to avert the breakdown of the marriage. The family moved to F's mother's house, but within five days M had filed a divorce petition and obtained an *ex parte* order preventing the children's removal from the jurisdiction. Under great pressure, F reluctantly agreed to let M leave with the children. M's application for an interim residence order was adjourned to be heard together with F's application for the return of the children to France under the Hague Convention.

Held, that (1) F was entitled to an order for return under the Hague Convention. The children had remained habitually resident in France, and M's unilateral action in issuing proceedings was quite inconsistent with the agreement that the stay in England was to be temporary. F had thereupon retracted his consent to the children's temporary residence in England. M's failure to accept F's withdrawal of consent amounted to a wrongful retention under the Hague Convention (*S. (Minors) (Convention on the International Aspects of International Child Abduction: Wrongful Retention), Re* [1994] 4 C.L. 427 applied); (2) the ordinary consequence of ordering the return of children under the Hague Convention was that an investigation of the merits of the case would be conducted in the jurisdiction of the requesting state. However, the facts were quite exceptional; the family's connection with England was much stronger than with France. As everything pointed to a merits hearing in England, M's applications under the Children Act 1989 would be allowed to proceed and any stay that might have been achieved would be removed.

H. v. H. (CHILD ABDUCTION: STAY OF DOMESTIC PROCEEDINGS) [1994] 1 F.L.R. 530, Thorpe J.

3450. Child abduction—undertakings—father seeking return of children to Greece—father offering undertakings to English court—mother stating situation would be intolerable if children were to return—whether court could take into account father's undertakings—whether undertakings to English court enforceable in another jurisdiction—whether English court should investigate legal procedures of co-signatory to Convention

It was permissible and, in some cases, obligatory for the English court to investigate and form a value judgement upon legal procedures of a co-signatory to the Hague Convention to evaluate the effect of undertakings.

F was Greek and M English. They married in 1987 and lived in a financially secure and comfortable lifestyle until M removed the children to England where she obtained an *ex parte* interim residence order and a prohibited steps order. F sought the return of the children under the Hague Convention and offered undertakings. M argued that the return of the children would expose them to an intolerable situation and that there were factors in the Greek legal system which would force the reunification of the family and rendered nugatory F's undertakings.

Held, that although the undertakings offered by F were not enforceable in Greece, the court was satisfied that the return of the children without the protection of the undertakings would place them in an intolerable situation. It was permissible for the English court to investigate and form a value judgement upon the legal procedures of a co-signatory to the Convention. The practice of accepting undertakings had been expressly approved by the Court of Appeal in appropriate cases and the court could influence the outcome as to whether there should be a return by extracting undertakings.

O. (CHILD ABDUCTION: UNDERTAKINGS), *Re* [1994] 2 FLR 349, Singer J.

3451. Child abduction and custody

CHILD ABDUCTION AND CUSTODY (PARTIES TO CONVENTIONS) (AMENDMENT) ORDER 1995 (No. 264) [£1·10], made under the Child Abduction and Custody Act 1985 (c.60), s.13; operative on March 1, 1995; amends S.I. 1986 No. 1159 so as to add Malta to the list of contracting states on the European Convention on Child custody.

CHILD ABDUCTION AND CUSTODY (PARTIES TO CONVENTIONS) (AMENDMENT) (NO. 2) ORDER 1995 (NO. 1031) [£1·10], made under the Child Abduction and Custody Act 1985 (c.60), s.2; operative on May 1, 1995; amends the 1993 Convention so as to to specify that Italy is a contracting state to the Convention.

CHILD ABDUCTION AND CUSTODY (PARTIES TO CONVENTIONS) (AMENDMENT) (NO. 3) ORDER 1995 (No. 1295) [£1·10], made under the Child Abduction and Custody Act 1985 (c.60), s.13; substitutes a new Sched. 2 in S.I. 1986 No. 1159.

CHILD ABDUCTION AND CUSTODY (PARTIES TO CONVENTIONS) (AMENDMENT) (NO. 4) ORDER 1995 (No. 1616), made under the Child Abduction and Custody Act 1985, s.2; operative on July 1, 1995; amends the Child Abduction and Custody (Parties to Conventions) Order 1993 in order to specify that Zimbabwe is a Contracting State to the Convention on the Civil Aspects of International Child Abduction, The Hague, October 25, 1980.

3452. Child abuse—breach of statutory duty—negligence—whether breach of statutory duties by local authority actionable in private law claim for damages—whether local authorities vicariously liable for acts of employed professionals

[Children and Young Persons Act 1969 (c.54), ss.1, 2; Child Care Act 1980 (c.5), ss.1, 2(1), 18; Children Act 1989 (c.41), ss.17, 31; Education Act 1944 (7 & 8 Geo. 6, c.31), ss.8, 33(2), 34(1); Education Act 1981 (c.60), ss.2, 4, 5, 7.]

In cases involving Acts establishing a framework for the promotion of the social welfare of the community, it would require exceptionally clear language to show a parliamentary intention that those responsible for carrying out such difficult and sensitive duties should be liable in damages if they fail to discharge their statutory obligations.

In the first of two cases concerning allegations of child abuse (the Bedfordshire case), five children claimed that they had suffered parental abuse and neglect over a period of five years. They claimed that the local authority, despite being fully aware of such abuse, had failed in its duty under s.17(1) of the Children Act 1989 to safeguard their welfare and had failed to apply for a care order under s.31 of the Act of 1989. In the second of the two cases (the Newham case), an order was made for the removal of a child from her mother on the erroneous assumption that the mother's boyfriend was sexually abusing the child. The mother and the child claimed that the psychiatrist and social worker employed by the local authority had failed to investigate the facts with proper care, thereby causing injury to the plaintiffs. In both cases the defendant local authorities succeeded at first instance in having the plaintiffs' claims struck out as disclosing no cause of action. The Court of Appeal dismissed the plaintiffs' appeals.

In three further cases (the education cases) various plaintiffs brought claims against their local education authorities (LEAs) alleging failures in performance of the LEAs' statutory duties under the Education Acts of 1944 and 1981. In one case (the Hampshire case) the plaintiff's claim was based solely on the alleged vicarious liability of the LEA for the failure of the headmaster and others to refer the plaintiff for an assessment of his special educational needs under s.5 of the Act of 1981. In the other cases (the Dorset case and the

Bromley case) the plaintiffs claimed that the LEA had negligently failed to make proper provision for their special educational needs, contrary to the duties of the LEA under ss.2 and 7 of the Act of 1981, in addition to claims for vicarious liability. In each of the education cases the plaintiffs' claims were struck out at first instance for disclosing no reasonable cause of action. The plaintiffs' appeals were allowed in part by the Court of Appeal.

Held, dismissing the plaintiffs' appeals in the child abuse cases and the LEAs' appeals in the education cases, that (1) although a breach of a statutory duty does not by itself give rise to a private law cause of action, one will arise if it can be shown that the statutory duty was imposed for the protection of a limited class of the public, and Parliament intended members of that class to have a private right of action for breach of that duty. If the statute does provide some other means of enforcing that duty that will generally indicate that a private right of action does not lie, but the presence of such other means of enforcement will not necessarily be decisive (*Cutler v. Wandsworth Stadium* [1947–51] C.L.Y. 4241, *Lonrho v. Shell Petroleum Co. (No. 2)* [1980] C.L.Y. 2135 considered); (2) in order to found a cause of action flowing from the careless exercise of statutory powers or duties, the plaintiff has to show that the circumstances are such as to raise a duty of care at common law. The mere assertion of the careless exercise of a statutory power or duty is not sufficient (*Geddis v. Proprietors of Bann Reservoir* (1878) 3 App. Cas. 430, *Home Office v. Dorset Yacht Co.* [1970] C.L.Y. 1849 considered); (3) if the decisions complained of fall within the ambit of a statutory discretion they cannot be actionable in common law. If the decision complained of is so unreasonable that it falls outside the ambit of the discretion conferred, there is no *a priori* reason for excluding all common law liability. However, if the factors relevant to the exercise of the discretion include matters of policy, the court cannot adjudicate on such policy matters and accordingly a common law duty of care in relation to the taking of decisions involving policy matters cannot exist. If the complaint alleges carelessness not in the taking of a discretionary decision to do some act, but in the practical manner in which that act has been performed, the question whether a common law duty of care exists is to be determined according to the usual principles within the context of the statutory framework (*Anns v. Merton London Borough Council* [1977] C.L.Y. 2030, *Rowling v. Takaro Properties* [1988] C.L.Y. 2441, *Hill v. Chief Constable of West Yorkshire* [1989] A.C. 53 applied); (4) the duty imposed on local authorities under s.17 of the Children Act of 1989 is a general duty pointing to an issue of peculiar sensitivity: the decision whether to split the family in order to protect the child. It is impossible to construe such a provision as demonstrating an intention that even where there is no carelessness by the authority it should be liable in damages if a court subsequently decided that the removal or failure to remove a child was a breach of that duty; (5) although in the child abuse cases the plaintiffs' complaints concerned the manner in which the local authorities exercised their duties to safeguard the welfare of children under s.17 of the Act of 1989 and did not involve considerations of policy, it was not just and reasonable to superimpose a common law duty of care on the authorities in addition to their statutory duties to protect children. A common law duty of care would cut across the whole statutory system for the protection of children at risk. Local authorities may adopt a more cautious approach to their duties, and a substantive complaints procedure already existed (*Caparo Industries v. Dickman* [1990] C.L.Y. 3266 considered); (6) the social workers and the psychiatrists were retained by the local authority to advise the local authority, not the plaintiffs, and did not assume any professional duty of care to the plaintiffs. The local authorities could not be vicariously liable for their actions; (7) in the education cases, it was not just and reasonable to impose on a LEA a duty of care to exercise the statutory discretion involved in operating the special needs machinery of the Education Act 1981. If a common law duty were held to exist there was a real risk that it might encourage hopeless and vexatious cases. As in the child abuse cases, the courts should hesitate long before imposing a common law duty of care in the exercise of statutory powers for social welfare purposes; (8) where a LEA offered psychological advice to the public in exercise of a statutory power, it comes under a duty to exercise care in its conduct; and (9) a headmaster, psychologist or adviser employed by a LEA is under a duty of care in providing advice to parents and children. The position was quite different from that of the doctor and social worker in the child abuse cases, since there was no potential conflict between the professional's duty to the plaintiffs and his duty to the LEA.

X. (MINORS) v. BEDFORDSHIRE COUNTY COUNCIL [1995] 3 W.L.R. 152, H.L.

3453. Child support

CHILD SUPPORT (COMPENSATION FOR RECIPIENTS OF FAMILY CREDIT AND DISABILITY WORKING ALLOWANCE) REGULATION 1995 (No. 3263) [£1·55], made under the Child Support Act 1991, s.54, and the Child Support Act 1995, ss.24, 27(2). In force: January 23, 1996.

CHILD SUPPORT (MISCELLANEOUS AMENDMENTS) REGULATIONS 1995 (No. 123), made under Child Support Act 1991 (c.48); amend S.I. 1992 Nos. 1812, 1813, 2645; operative on February 16, 1995; impose an obligation on employers to provide information about alleged absent parents who deny parentage in relation to child support; amend the 1992 Reg.

CHILD SUPPORT (MISCELLANEOUS AMENDMENTS) (NO.2) REGULATIONS 1995 (No. 3261), made under the Child Support Act 1991 ss.12(2)(3), 14(1)(1A)(3), 16, 17, 18, 32(1), 41(2), 41B(3)(6), 42(1), 46(5)(11), 51, 52, 54, 56(3), Sched. 1, paras. 5(1)(2), 6(2), 8, 11 and Child Support Act 1995 s.18(7). Amends S.I. 1992 No. 1812, 1813, 1815, 1816, 1989, 2645; 1993 584; 1994 227; 1995 1045. operative on December 18, 1995 for regs.1, 23, 48, 56 and January 22, 1996 for remainder; [£5·60. Various Regulations), made under the the Child Support Act 1991 are amended by these Regulations. The Child Support (Arrears, Interest and Adjustment of Maintenance Assessments) Regulations 1992 are amended to provide for circumstances where a parent must reimburse the Secretary of State for overpayments of maintenance paid to an absent parent. The Child Support (Information, Evidence and Disclosure) Regulations 1992 are amended so they apply to the provision of information on reviews, to set the time within which information must be supplied, to extend the circumstances in which information can be given and to make provision for the Secretary of State to disclose information to child support officers to give information to each other. The Child Support (Maintenance Arrangements and Jurisdiction) Regulations 1992 are amended so that applications for maintenance assessments are allowed even when a court order exists and a court has no power to vary or enforce that order. The Child Support (Maintenance Assessment Procedure) Regulations 1992 are amended and additional Regulations relating to lapsing of appeals, dates of new assessments and reduced benefit directions are added. The Child Support (Maintenance Assessments and Special Cases) Regulations 1992 are amended to make furthor provision relating to definitions for the purposes of reviews and to make provision for the adjusting of existing maintonance assessments.

CHILD SUPPORT (MISCELLANEOUS AMENDMENTS) (NO.3) REGULATIONS 1995 (No. 3265), made under the Child Support Act 1991 ss.51, 54; amends S.I. 1992 No. 1813, 1815; 1995 3261. This SI has been made in consequence of a defect in S.I. 1995 No. 3261 and is being sent free of charge to all known recipients of that SI. operative on January 22, 1996; [65p]. These Regulations amend provisions made by the Child Support (Miscellaneous Amendments) (No.2) Regulations 1995. Regulation 32B of the Child Support (Maintenance Assessment Procedure) Regulations 1992 is moved so that it precedes Regulation 32A and mistaken references in Regulation 2 of the Child Support (Maintenance Assessments and Special Cases) Regulations 1992 and Regulation 57 of the Child Support (Miscellaneous Amendments) (No.2) Regulations 1995 are corrected.

3454. Child support—appeals—delays—press notice

The Council on Tribunals (the statutory watchdog on tribunal performance and procedures) has issued a press notice entitled "Child Support Appeals: A Pattern of Serious Delays is Developing". It calls for steps to be taken to reduce the delays in the hearing of child support appeals. For further information contact Mr P. Harris at the Council on Tribunals, 22 Kingsway, London, WC2B 6LE. Telephone 071 936 7292.

3455. Child support—Commissioners

CHILD SUPPORT COMMISSIONERS (PROCEDURE) (AMENDMENT) REGULATIONS 1995 (No. 2907), made under the Child Support Act 1991 ss.22(3), 24(6)(7), 25(2)(3)(5), Sched. 4, para. 4A; amends S.I. 1992 No. 2640. operative on December 4, 1995; [65p]. The Child Support Commissioners (Procedure) Regulations 1992 are amended so that certain functions of Commissioners can be performed by nominated officers and to provide for Commissioners to consider decisions made by nominated officers.

3456. Child support—contribution notice—child accommodated by local authority —whether contribution notice must specify the standard contribution for all children looked after by local authority—whether magistrates should consider child's needs and local authority expenditure in determining father's contribution

[Children Act 1989 (c.41), s.92(2), Sched. 1, para. 4, Sched. 2, Pt. III, paras. 21(6), 22, 23; Social Security Act 1986 (c.50), ss.24, 25, 26(3); Child Support Act 1991 (c.48); Family Proceedings Courts (Children Act 1989) Rules 1991 (S.I. 1991 No. 1395), rr.1(2), 21(6).]

In assessing the liability of a parent to contribute to the cost of a local authority looking after his child, the court should determine the liability simply by comparing his income and expenses, and there was no first call on his income towards maintaining the child.

The local authority agreed to accommodate E, who was 15. The local authority served a notice requiring F to contribute £96·47 per week towards the cost of looking after E, pursuant to Sched. 2, Pt. III, of the Children Act 1989. F was only prepared to offer £50 per week, so the local authority applied to the magistrates for a contribution order. F was ordered to pay £96·47 per week. F appealed.

Held, allowing the appeal, that (1) the Family Proceedings Courts (Children Act 1989) Rules 1991 applied to the application, and by r.21(6), the magistrates were required to state their findings and reasons. Their failure to do so was a fundamental irregularity, and in the absence of sufficient evidence on which the court could exercise its own discretion, the matter would be remitted for rehearing; (2) para. 22(4) of Sched. 2, Pt. III, of the Children Act 1989 provided that the local authority might specify in a contribution notice a standard weekly sum determined by the authority for all the children it looked after. The authority's failure to specify such a figure in the contribution notice was not fatal to the validity of the notice as para. 22(4) was permissive only and not mandatory; and (3) Sched. 2, Pt. III defined a parent's obligation to contribute as one to be made with due regard only to the contributor's means, and contained no requirement for the court to have regard to the child's needs or the local authority's expenditure on the child. The court therefore had to compare F's income and expenses, and provided the expenses were reasonable, it was not open to the court to state that F should set aside income in order to contribute to the local authority before meeting his reasonable expenses.

C. (A MINOR) (CONTRIBUTION NOTICE), *Re* [1994] 1 FLR 111, Ward J.

3457. Child support—deduction from earnings order—breach of duty—failure to take account of welfare of child affected by decision—whether judicial review the appropriate remedy for payer. See B. v. SECRETARY OF STATE FOR SOCIAL SECURITY, §10.

3458. Child support—disputed paternity—court's power to give directions for use of blood tests—test to be applied

[Family Law Reform Act 1969 (c.46), s.20; Child Support Act 1991 (c.48), s.27.]

In proceedings under s.27 of the Child Support Act 1991 for the determination of paternity, the court had power to direct the use of blood tests.

E was now 16. M sought child maintenance for E from F through the Child Support Agency, but F denied that he was E's father. M therefore made an application to the court under s.27 of the Child Support Act 1991 to determine E's paternity. M sought a direction under s.20 of the Family Law Reform Act 1969 for the use of blood tests. E himself had signed a form of consent to the direction sought. F opposed the direction.

Held, granting the application, that (1) proceedings under s.27 were civil proceedings, and hence the court had jurisdiction under s.20 to direct the use of blood tests to determine paternity; (2) the court should direct a blood test, unless satisfied that it would be against E's interests to do so. There was no evidence that it would be against E's best interests to direct a blood test, and the direction would be made (*S. v. S.; W. v. Official Solicitor* [1972] A.C. 24 applied); and (3) there was no need to join E as a party to the proceedings (*Practice Direction* [1975] 1 W.L.R. 81 considered).

E. (CHILD SUPPORT: BLOOD TESTS), *Re* [1995] 1 F.C.R. 245, Stuart-White J.

3459. Child support—maintenance order—mother seeking revocation to apply for child support assessment—whether order should be revoked

[Matrimonial Causes Act 1973 (c.18), ss.25, 31; Child Support Act 1991 (c.48), s.8(3); Child Support Act 1991 (Commencement No. 3 and Transitional Provisions) Order 1992 (S.I. 1992 No. 2644).]

Where an existing child maintenance order is in force, the court will not ordinarily revoke the order to allow a parent to apply for an assessment from the Child Support Agency during the transitional period.

M and F divorced in 1985 and M had care of the three children of the family. In 1986 F was ordered to pay child maintenance of £41 per month per child. In April 1993, the Child Support Agency wrote to M stating that M would be eligible to apply for a child support assessment if the court order were revoked. The district judge granted M's application to revoke the order and F appealed.

Held, allowing the appeal, that (1) s.8(3) of the Child Support Act removed the courts' powers to make, revive or vary an order for child maintenance. However, under para. 2 of the transitional provisions, where there was an existing maintenance order a parent with care not in receipt of benefit was not permitted to apply to the Agency during the transitional period and para. 5 allowed an existing order to be varied during the transitional period; (2) the court's powers to vary or revoke a maintenance order derived from s.31 of the Matrimonial Causes Act 1973, and the factors set out in s.25 of the Act must be taken into account on variation or revocation; (3) accordingly, the court was obliged to regard the child's welfare as the first consideration on an application to revoke the order for child maintenance. Although an assessment under the Child Support Act 1991 was likely to be higher than a court order under the Matrimonial Causes Act 1973, all the factors in s.25 of the 1973 Act had to be considered and it did not follow that the child's welfare required the revocation of the order; and (4) the scheme of the transitional provisions was that existing orders should continue until the end of the transitional period in 1996. Although there might be particular reasons justifying revocation in an individual case, in the generality of cases the appropriate course was to apply to vary the order under the 1973 Act.

B. v. M. (CHILD SUPPORT: REVOCATION OF ORDER) [1994] 1 F.L.R. 342, H.H.J. Bryant.

3460. Child support—Mareva injunction—whether available in support. See DEPARTMENT OF SOCIAL SECURITY v. BUTLER (FCE/95/6034/D), §4174.

3461. Child Support Act 1995 (c.34)

This Act amends the mechanism of the Child Support Act 1991 (c.48) in connection with the assessment, collection and enforcement of payments of child support maintenance and other maintenance, and introduces a child maintenance bonus.

The Act received Royal Assent on July 19, 1995.

3462. Child Support Act 1995—commencement

CHILD SUPPORT ACT 1995 (COMMENCEMENT NO. 1) ORDER 1995 (No. 2302 (C.46)) [£1·10], made under the Child Support Act 1995, s.30(4); bringing into force various provisions of the Act on September 4, 1995 and October 1, 1995.

CHILD SUPPORT ACT 1995 (COMMENCEMENT NO.2) ORDER 1995 (No. 3262 (C.76)), made under the Child Support Act 1995 s.30(4). operative on bringing into operation various provisions of the Act on December 18, 1995, January 22, 1996; [£1·10]. Provisions of the Child Support Act 1995 brought into force by this order on December 18, 1995 are s.16, relating to lapse of appeals to child support appeal tribunals, s.17, relating to determination of questions other than by Child Support Commissioners and paragraph 18 or Sched. 3 and s.30(5) as far as it relates to paragraph 18, relating to expenses. Provisions of the same Act brought into force by this Order on January 22, 1996 are s.9, in respect of insertion of s.28I(4) into the Child Support Act 1991, s.11, relating to reviews and interim maintenance assessments, the remainder of s.13 relating to reviews on change of circumstance, s.14, relating to cancellation of maintenance assessments on review and s.15, relating to reviews at instigation of child support officers.

3463. Child support and income support. See SOCIAL SECURITY, §4578.

3464. Child-minder—registration—duty of local authority—whether right of action. See T. (A MINOR) v. SURREY (COUNTY COUNCIL), §3647.

3465. Children Act Advisory Committee—report

The third annual report of the Children Act Advisory Committee was published on January 26, 1995. It covers areas including the issue of delay in the High Court and county courts, the replacement of individual application forms with one application per family and best practice for the judiciary when ordering court welfare reports. It also reports on the introduction of National Standards for Probation Service Family Court Welfare Work and follows the development of the new Family Court Forums which have been set up to replace the Family Court Services Committees. Guidance for courts in the context of ordering expert witness reports is also contained in the report. Copies are available from Chris Miles, Family Policy Division, 5th Floor,

Trevelyan House, 30 Great Peter Street, London, SW1P 2BY. Telephone 0171 210 8704.

3466. **Children panel—whether membership relevant to costs—whether exceptional circumstance in relation to bill of costs.** See CHILDREN ACT 1989 (TAXATION OF COSTS), *Re*, §4019.

3467. **Children's hearings—grounds for referral—member of the same household as person committing offence—relevance of admission of grounds for referral in relation to another child.** See M. v. KENNEDY, §5517.

3468. **Contact—appeal—principles to be applied on appeal to High Court—relevance of racial issues to contact**

[Children Act 1989 (c.41), s.94.]

The High Court, when hearing an appeal under s.94 of the Children Act 1989, should not interfere with the justices' decision unless it was plainly wrong.

S was now aged seven and was of mixed race. M and F were not married, and after they separated, F had sporadic contact with S. Following F's contact application, a consent order was made which, however, proved ineffective. F made a further application, seeking a parental responsibility order; M, who had re-married, sought the discharge of the consent order for contact. The justices discharged the consent order, and F appealed. The judge criticised a number of aspects of the justices' handling of the case, but dismissed the appeal. F appealed to the Court of Appeal, contending that the judge on appeal was free to look at the matter entirely afresh and exercise his or her own discretion.

Held, allowing the appeal, that when hearing an appeal from the justices under s.94 of the Children Act 1989 the High Court should not interfere with the justices' decision unless it was plainly wrong (*G. v. G. (Minors: Custody Appeal)* [1985] C.L.Y. 2594 applied). Applying that test, neither the justices nor the judge had dealt with the issue of race and the welfare officer's concerns as to S's confusion about her racial identity had not been addressed. Accordingly, the appeal would be allowed and the matter remitted to the Family Division.

M. (SECTION 94 APPEALS), *Re* [1995] 1 FLR 546, C.A.

3469. **Contact—appeal from magistrate's decision—where particular care to be taken in assessing magistrate's balancing exercise**

Where magistrates disagreed with the conclusions of a court welfare officer without giving reasons, or without dealing with important factors, or without giving clear reasoning on crucial aspects of their decision, an appellate court would be justified in looking with particular care at the usual balancing exercise.

M. (A MINOR) (CONTACT ORDER), *Re*, *The Times*, December 21, 1994, C.A.

3470. **Contact—child of 17 seeking contact with his father—child seeking disclosure of father's address from Child Support Agency—procedure to be adopted—whether court should order disclosure**

[Family Law Act 1986 (c.55), s.1; Children Act 1989 (c.41), s.8; Child Support Act 1991 (c.48), ss.14, 50(6); Child Support (Information, Evidence and Disclosure) Regulations 1992 (S.I. 1992 No. 1812).]

The court had no power under s.50(6) of the Child Support Act 1991 to order the Secretary of State to disclose information held by the Child Support Agency, but could request the disclosure of the whereabouts of a party to proceedings under the applicable Practice Direction.

C was aged 17 and made an application for contact with F, whom he had not seen for many years and whose whereabouts were unknown. C believed that the Child Support Agency knew of F's whereabouts, and C obtained an *ex parte* order under s.50(6) of the Child Support Act 1991 granting leave to the Secretary of State to provide the information sought. The Secretary of State applied to have the order set aside.

Held, granting the application and setting aside the order, that (1) information held by the Child Support Agency was confidential and it was an offence to disclose such information. There were numerous exceptions to this prohibition, including one in s.50(6)(d) allowing disclosure for the purpose of instituting any proceedings before the court. However, s.50(6) merely provided a defence to criminal proceedings and did not confer any general power to allow disclosure. The regulations made under the 1991 Act allowed disclosure limited to proceedings under the 1991 Act or the Benefit Acts, and did not include disclosure for the purpose of proceedings under the Children Act 1989; (2) however, there was an arrangement under which the court could request disclosure of addresses held by government departments, which included tracing the whereabouts of a person in cases where certain orders, including s.8 orders, were being sought. The court would therefore request the Secretary of State to disclose to C's solicitors F's address if known to him (*Registrar's Direction (Disclosure of Addresses)* [1988] 1 W.L.R. 648 applied).

C. (A MINOR) (DISCLOSURE OF ADDRESS), Re, [1995] 1 F.C.R. 202, Ewbank J.

3471. Contact—child refusing to see step-mother—whether hearing to determine cause in child's best interests

F, who had remarried, maintained contact with his three children. His eight-year-old daughter suddenly refused to see his wife although she still wanted to see F. F wanted the issue to be determined by a trial which would investigate what had occurred between his wife and daughter. The judge decided it was not in the child's best interests at that time and that it would be best to leave the matter over some months. F appealed against this decision.

Held, allowing the appeal, that an order should be made that the child should be joined as a party to the hearing and should be represented by the Official Solicitor as her guardian *ad litem*.

W. (A MINOR), *Re* (CCFMI 94/1360/F), November 25, 1994, C.A.

3472. Contact—consent order—circumstances in which Court of Appeal would entertain appeal against consent order—judicial conduct—whether apparent failure to appreciate issue involved and threat that party could be ordered to pay costs inappropriate

F applied for contact after an absence of some years from C's life. M was prepared to agree contact provided F's identity was not disclosed, which was not acceptable to F. At the hearing the judge indicated that there appeared to be no issue as to contact save for the mechanics. He observed that the parents were under a duty to ensure that C retained contact with them both, that it appeared that F was committed and had a great deal to offer C and that there was no reason why contact should not start immediately. He warned M that there was a serious risk of *inter partes* costs being awarded against her. M consented to a contact order.

Held, M's appeal allowed and remitting the case for rehearing, where criticism was made of the judge, that the appropriate procedure was to appeal to the Court of Appeal rather than bring fresh proceedings to determine in what circumstances consent had been given. There was a real issue as to contact after F's long absence from C's life and the judge had appeared to misunderstand the issue or had decided against M without hearing essential evidence from her and the welfare officer. The judge's remarks on costs had led the mother to believe that he had already made up his mind that she was being unreasonable and she had formed the conclusion that there was no point in pursuing her case.

R. (A MINOR) (CONSENT ORDER: APPEAL), *Re* [1994] 2 F.C.R. 1251, C.A.

3473. Contact—*ex parte* order made—difficulties over contact—notice to show cause issued—matter resolved by the time case appealed—whether abuse of appeal process to bring unnecessary appeal using civil legal aid funds. See S. v. S. (ABUSE OF PROCESS OF APPEAL), §3101.

3474. Contact—grandparent—leave to apply granted—approach to grant of order

[Children Act 1989 (c.41), s.10(9).]

A grandparent had to apply under the Children Act 1989, s.10(9), for leave to apply for a contact order under s.8 of the Act, but there was no presumption that, once leave had been given, a grandparent was entitled to have contact with a child of the family unless cogent reasons were given. The approach to be followed was not that followed for a natural parent.

A. (A MINOR) (CONTACT APPLICATION: GRANDPARENT), *Re*, *The Times*, March 6, 1995, C.A.

3475. Contact—hearing—application by father—delay in proceedings—application dismissed without hearing oral evidence—whether court entitled to dismiss application without full hearing

C's parents separated in 1989 very shortly after C's birth. F saw C he left the area to look for work in the summer of 1992. F made an application for contact and there were various delays, largely attributable to F's failure to contact the court welfare officer. The magistrates at a directions hearing refused F's application to adjourn and considered the case on the written statements alone. They dismissed F's application for contact and ordered that no further application should be made without the leave of the court.

Held, allowing F's appeal and remitting the case for rehearing, that despite the long delays F's application was not so hopeless that it should be dismissed without a full hearing and the magistrates should have heard all the evidence before reaching their conclusion.

M. (A MINOR) (CONTACT), *Re* [1994] 2 F.C.R. 968, Hollis J.

3476. Contact—indirect contact order—conditions—whether appropriate and in the best interest of the child—whether court has jurisdiction to decide conditions of indirect contact order

[Children Act 1989 (c.41), ss.8, 11.]

The mother of a three-year-old child who was separated from the father, and implacably opposed to any direct or indirect contact with him, appealed against a county court judge's order that the father should have indirect contact with the child, which was to take the form of the mother sending photographs of the child every three months, reporting on progress at nursery school and on any illnesses suffered and passing on to the child cards and presents sent by the father. The mother argued that the court had no jurisdiction to attach such conditions to the order.

Held, dismissing the appeal, that it was for the court to decide whether indirect contact was appropriate and in the best interests of the child in a situation where direct contact with the non-custodial parent was not possible at that time, and the court had ample powers under ss.8(1) and 11(7) of the Children Act 1989 to make the orders necessary to facilitate such contact. Disagreeing with the judgment of Wall J. in *M. (A Minor) (Contact: Conditions), Re*, the court held that the mother's reluctance to cooperate did not defeat the court's power to make the order. It was entirely reasonable that the mother should be required to read the father's letters to the child and provide progress reports. (*M. (A Minor) (Contact: Conditions), Re.* [1993] C.L.Y. 2827 considered)

O. (A MINOR) (CONTACT: IMPOSITION OF CONDITIONS), *Re*, *The Times*, March 17, 1995, C.A.

3477. Contact—indirect contact order—order for contact by post—whether jurisdiction to impose condition that mother read out father's letters to child—whether jurisdiction to order mother to write progress reports to father

[Children Act 1989 (c.41), ss.8, 11(7).]

The court should not attach a condition to a contact order requiring a mother to read to the child correspondence from the father without the mother's consent, and there was no power to attach a condition requiring the mother to write progress reports on the child to the father.

M and F, who had never married, separated in 1991 when their child was aged one. F applied for a contact order, and interim orders were made. In January 1993 F was sentenced to three years' imprisonment. In May 1993 the magistrates ordered indirect contact by post, which M had to read to the child, and directed M to write three-monthly progress reports on the child to F. M appealed.

Held, allowing the appeal, that (1) the magistrates had failed to make clear findings of fact, to address their minds fully to the range of options open to them, and to give clear reasons for their decision; (2) cogent reasons should be given for denying contact. No court should deprive a child of contact with a natural parent unless wholly satisfied that it was in the child's interest that there should be no contact, and that was a conclusion the court should be slow to reach. The same principles applied whether the decision was for contact to cease or to recommence (*R. (A Minor) (Contact), Re* [1993] 2 FLR 762, *H. (Minors) (Access), Re* [1992] C.L.Y. 2999, *K.D. (A Minor), Re* [1988] C.L.Y. 2294, *M. v. M. (Child: Access)* [1973] C.L.Y. 2160, *B. (Minors: Bizarre Behaviour) (Access), Re* [1992] C.L.Y. 2993 followed; *Starling v. Starling* [1983] C.L.Y. 2418, *F. (A Minor) (Access), Re* [1993] C.L.Y. 2748 considered); (3) on the facts, the magistrates were right to order indirect contact by post; (4) there was no power by way of a contact order under s.8 or by way of a condition under s.11(7) of the 1989 Act to order M to write progress reports on the child to F (*W. v. B.* [1991] C.L.Y. 2474 considered); (5) there was, however, jurisdiction under s.11(7) to direct a residential parent to keep the other parent informed of the child's whereabouts as a necessary condition of contact taking place; and (6) whilst there might be jurisdiction to order a mother to read to the child correspondence from the father, it should only be exercised if the mother is prepared to consent to it, and would always be subject to the mother's right to censor material which in her judgment was unsuitable for the child to hear (*D. (A Minor) (Adoption Order: Conditions), Re* [1992] C.L.Y. 3008 considered).

M. (A MINOR) (CONTACT: CONDITIONS), *Re* [1994] 1 FLR 272, Wall J.

3478. Contact—interim order—mother refusing to comply—father applying for enforcement of order—whether justices' reasons adequate—whether justices wrong to refuse direct contact

[Children Act 1989 (c.41), s.1(3).]

The court would dismiss an appeal against a magistrates' court's refusal of face-to-face contact where the decision was not plainly wrong, even though the magistrates had failed to give adequate reasons for their decision.

J was nearly four years old when F's application for contact came on for final hearing before the magistrates. M and F never married and separated just before J's birth. M alleged that F was very violent towards her both during the relationship and afterwards. F's contact with J was sporadic and problematic. In February 1993 F applied for contact. F had supervised contact organised by the welfare officer, but two further contact sessions were cancelled by M following her allegation that she had received intimidatory telephone calls

from F. In August 1993 the justices made an interim order for fortnightly supervised contact for two hours on each occasion, to last for three months. M wished to appeal against this order, and this delayed implementation of the order. M refused to co-operate and F applied to enforce the August order. In January 1994, the justices ordered there to be three occasions of supervised contact, a further welfare report and a one-day final hearing in March. At the final hearing, the justices refused to make any order for direct contact between F and J, merely stating that the grounds for the application had not been proved and the application was dismissed.

Held, dismissing F's appeal, that (1) justices had a duty to give full reasons for interim orders just as for full orders. If justices decided (for good reason) that they could not make findings of fact when making an interim order and deliberately refrained from detailed investigation as part of the overall strategy of reaching a final conclusion only on the final hearing, that process itself constituted a reasoning process which should be explained on making the interim order; (2) in August 1993 the justices had heard a good deal of evidence, but failed to make findings as to many disputed facts, including M's allegations of violence which were a major reason for M's refusal to co-operate with contact. Further, in offering F a chance to prove himself and ordering interim supervised contact, the justices had departed from the recommendation of the court welfare officer without giving reasons for doing so. The reasons were inadequate, and had legal aid been granted to M to appeal, the court would have felt constrained to allow the appeal; and (3) however, at the March hearing, the justices had given full reasons and had properly directed themselves. Despite F's sense of grievance, the justices had applied the right test and it could not be said that their decision that direct contact was not in J's best interests was plainly wrong.

F. v. R. (CONTACT: JUSTICES' REASONS) [1995] 1 FLR 227, Wall J.

3479. Contact—interim order—parents agreeing interim contact prior to hearing—welfare officer recommending interim order—magistrates refusing to make interim order—whether interim order offended against delay principle

An interim order providing for a monitored programme of contact did not offend against the delay principle.

F applied for contact with, and parental responsibility for, his daughter aged three-and-a-half years. The welfare officer recommended an order for contact to underline a tentative agreement reached by the parents just before the hearing, which provided for a programme of monitored contact with the welfare officer supervising the first visit and a review in four months time. The magistrates rejected the proposals and suggested that there should be a final order either by consent or after a full hearing or F's application should be withdrawn because of the delay in concluding the proceedings.

Held, allowing F's appeal, that an order providing for a monitored programme to reintroduce contact was not detrimental to the child's interests and did not offend against the principle of delay in the Children Act 1989, s.1(2).

B. (A MINOR) (CONTACT: INTERIM ORDER), *Re* [1994] 2 FLR 269, Ewbank J.

3480. Contact—interim order—principle of contact in dispute—whether justices right to make order without assistance of court welfare report and without hearing oral evidence

[Family Proceedings Courts (Children Act 1989) Rules 1991 (S.I. 1991 No. 1395), r.21(5)(6).]

There are few circumstances where an order for interim contact should be made, where the principle of contact is genuinely in dispute, without the court hearing oral evidence and/or having the advice of an expert or a welfare officer as to the likely effect of contact on the child.

L was now six years old. His parents had had a brief relationship around the time of his birth, but never married. F had not seen L for at least two years. M alleged that F had been violent to her in the past and she had obtained an injunction from the county court. F applied for contact and parental responsibility. M's answer asserted that she was only willing for contact to take place in supervised circumstances at a family centre. Following a further alleged incident of threatened violence, M's attitude to contact hardened. The parties' statements revealed a substantial number of issues between the parties. At the interim hearing, the court welfare officer did not attend, not having been allocated in time. M sought an adjournment, but this was refused. The justices made an interim order for contact at a contact centre, without hearing oral evidence. The justices' reasons stated that they had come to no conclusion as to the parties' credibility, that they had considered all aspects of the welfare checklist and found no cogent reasons to deny contact.

Held, allowing M's appeal, that (1) it was unacceptable for the court to state that it had considered all aspects of the welfare checklist, without further particularisation, unless it has elsewhere in its reasons dealt with the checklist items in detail (*H. (A Minor) (Care Proceedings: Child's Wishes), Re* [1994] C.L.Y. 3135, *D.B. and C.B. (Minors), Re* [1994] C.L.Y. 3209, *R. v. Oxfordshire County Council (Secure Accommodation Order)* [1992] C.L.Y. 3129 considered); (2) the justices' reasons were wholly inadequate. The obvious question which they had to ask themselves was whether it was in the interests of this child in the particular circumstances of this case for there to be an order for interim contact to his father pending a full investigation and a final hearing. The justices nowhere asked themselves that question; (3) no court should deprive a child of contact to a natural parent unless wholly satisfied that it was in the interests of the child that contact should cease, and that was a conclusion at which a court should be extremely slow to arrive. There must be cogent reasons to deny contact (*M. (A Minor) (Contact: Conditions), Re* [1995] 1 C.L. 266 applied); (4) it was perfectly possible for interim contact orders to be made where the principle of contact was in dispute, even without hearing oral evidence, provided the court was satisfied that contact was genuinely in the best interests of the child, and that the interim order did not prejudge the issue; (5) apart from cases in which previously satisfactory contact has been arbitrarily terminated by the residential parent, it was very difficult to envisage circumstances where an interim contact order could properly be made in a case where the principle of contact was genuinely in dispute and where there were substantial and unresolved factual issues, without the court hearing oral evidence and/or having the advice of an expert or court welfare officer as to the likely effect of contact on the child; (6) the procedure before the justices had been flawed. They should have adjudicated on M's application for an adjournment, bearing in mind that they were entitled to refuse an adjournment if the delay in obtaining a report from the welfare officer was too substantial; (7) justices were masters of their own procedure. If the parties both wished to proceed without there being oral evidence but the justices considered that they could not properly do so, they should decline to follow the parties' suggested approach. The guidance given by the courts to justices relating to interim applications applied equally to both public law and private law cases (*Hampshire County Council v. S.* [1993] C.L.Y. 2829 considered); and (8) on the facts, the order would be set aside. It would be wrong for the appeal court to make any order on the same material as was before the court below. A further interim hearing, which had already been fixed, should go ahead with the welfare officer to attend, and should be heard by a different bench.

D. (CONTACT: INTERIM ORDER), *Re* [1995] 1 FLR 495, Wall J.

3481. Contact—jurisdiction—expert evidence—whether power to order local authority to obtain psychiatric report

[Children Act 1989 (c.41), s.7; R.S.C., Ord. 40.]

A court hearing a contact application had no power under s.7 of the Children Act 1989 to order a local authority to obtain a report from a child psychiatrist.

The court could invite the parties to the proceedings to instruct an expert to give evidence about the child's emotional wellbeing or it could invoke R.S.C., Ord. 40, on the appointment of experts, but s.7 gave a local authority a discretion, over which the court had no control, as to whether to appoint a child psychiatrist.

K. (A MINOR) (CONTACT: PSYCHIATRIC REPORT), *Re*, *The Times*, April 13, 1995, C.A.

3482. Contact—leave to remove child from jurisdiction—father's contact with children breaking down—mother seeking leave to remove children permanently from jurisdiction—proposal not soundly based—whether leave should be granted—whether move would in fact increase father's chances of contact

[Children Act 1989 (c.41), s.1(3).]

In considering whether or not to grant leave to a parent to remove the children permanently from the jurisdiction, there was no requirement that the parent's proposal be reasonable before granting leave.

M and F had two children, now aged 12 and 10. M and F separated in 1988, the children stayed with M, and F was granted reasonable contact. In 1991, M remarried, and in 1992 the children's contact with F broke down. M and her new husband proposed to move to France with the children, and so M applied for leave to remove the children permanently from the jurisdiction. The judge found that M's proposal was not well planned nor soundly based. He further found that to refuse leave would lead to the children feeling seething resentment, but that the move to France would in fact improve F's chances of having genuine contact. The judge granted leave and F appealed.

Held, dismissing F's appeal, that (1) where a parent sought leave to remove the children permanently from the jurisdiction, the reasonableness and the practicalities of the proposal were matters to which the court had to give considerable weight. However, there was no rule that where a proposal was not considered reasonable, that was a conclusive reason for refusing leave (*Poel v. Poel* [1970] C.L.Y. 777, *Nash v. Nash* [1973] C.L.Y. 887, *Moodey v. Field* (unrep.) C.A.T., February 13, 1981, *Chamberlain v. De La Mare* [1983] C.L.Y. 2447, *Belton v. Belton* [1988] C.L.Y. 2340, *F. (A Minor), Re* [1988] C.L.Y. 2359, *Tyler v. Tyler* [1990] C.L.Y. 3106, *K. v. K. (Removal of Child from Jurisdiction)* [1992] 2 F.C.R. 161 considered); (2) this was an unusual case, in that the normal assumption that the father had a close relationship with the children did not apply. Given the judge's finding that F would see substantially more of the children if the move were sanctioned, his decision to sanction the move was not plainly wrong.

B. (MINORS) (REMOVAL FROM JURISDICTION), *Re* [1994] 2 F.C.R. 309, C.A.

3483. Contact—leave to remove child from jurisdiction—mother applying for leave to remove children permanently from jurisdiction—mother having sensible plans for children—whether leave should be granted

[Children Act 1989 (c.41).]

Where the parent looking after a child made a reasonable proposal to move permanently to another jurisdiction, the court would sanction that proposal unless it was clearly against the child's interests, and this principle had remained unaltered following the commencement of the Children Act 1989.

M was American and was born and raised in Pittsburgh. M had come to Britain and cohabited with F for 10 years. M had two daughters, aged 12 and nine. It later transpired that F was the father of neither child. M had obtained a residence order, and M now sought leave to remove the children permanently from the jurisdiction.

Held, granting M's application, that (1) if the parent with whom the children lived proposed to move with the children to another country, and the proposal was a reasonable one, leave should only be refused if it was clearly shown that the move would be against the interests of the children. The principle remained unaltered after the commencement of the Children Act 1989 (*Poel v. Poel* [1970] C.L.Y. 777, *M. (Minors) (Removal from Jurisdiction), Re* [1992] 1 F.C.R. 422 applied; *N. v. B. (Children: Orders as to Residence)* [1993] 1 F.C.R. 231 considered); (2) M did not have to show that she had a contract to buy a specific home. She had sensible plans well under way for both the home and the children's school, and she had the financial capacity to carry out the plans. The children knew Pittsburgh, and knew M's family there. Their relationship with F was at a low ebb. M's proposal was reasonable, and the move was not against the interests of the girls.

W. (MINORS) (REMOVAL FROM JURISDICTION), *Re* [1994] 1 F.C.R. 842, Thorpe J.

3483a. Contact—leave to remove child from jurisdiction—principles to be applied in determining whether to grant leave

[Children Act 1989 (c.41), s.1(3).]

The Children Act 1989 has not altered the test for deciding whether to grant leave to remove a child permanently from the jurisdiction.

H was born in England. F was English; M Swedish. M removed H from the family home in England and took H to Sweden. A reconciliation failed, and F obtained an *ex parte* residence order and an order from the Swedish court for H's return to England under the Hague Convention. M returned to the family home, pending the adjudication of the residence applications. The judge granted a residence order in favour of M and gave her leave to remove H permanently from the jurisdiction. F appealed, contending that the earlier authorities on the question of leave to remove had been overturned by the Children Act 1989.

Held, dismissing the appeal, that the Children Act 1989 had not altered the underlying factors to be considered, nor the test to be applied when deciding whether or not a parent should be given leave to remove a child permanently from the jurisdiction. The 1989 Act merely emphasised that the s.1(3) checklist must be applied when considering the child's welfare. The judge had applied the correct test and taken all relevant factors into account, and his decision was not plainly wrong (*Poel v. Poel* [1970] C.L.Y. 777, *M. v. A. (Wardship: Removal from Jurisdiction)* [1994] C.L.Y. 3281 applied).

H. v. H. (RESIDENCE ORDER: LEAVE TO REMOVE FROM JURISDICTION) (NOTE) [1995] 1 FLR 529, C.A.

3484. Contact—leave to remove child from jurisdiction—residence order in favour of mother—contact order in favour of father—mother and child moving to the Netherlands—mother repudiating contact order—father applying for residence order and definition or determination of specific contact dates—mother applying to Dutch court for variation—whether court should enforce or vary contact orders—whether court should grant discretionary stay

[Family Law Act 1986 (c.55), ss.1, 2, 3, 5(2).]

S was born in 1990 to unmarried parents who later separated. F sought a residence order. M sought to take S out of the jurisdiction to The Netherlands. The court granted parental responsibility to F and a residence order to M giving her leave to remove S permanently from the jurisdiction and providing for contact by F. The specific contact dates were to be agreed between M and F default of which, determined by the court. The order also provided that M should deliver and collect S from F. M and F agreed contact dates. In 1994, due to financial difficulties, M asked F to share S's travelling costs. When S returned from visiting F in England he was seen by a doctor as M thought he was showing signs of disturbance due to the contact. M informed F and subsequently repudiated the contact order. F applied for a residence order and for the contact provisions to be recognised in the Netherlands. M issued proceedings in the Netherlands to vary contact. F's application was amended to seek, alternatively, the definition or dissemination of specific contact dates.

Held, that (1) F's application for residence was an excessive reaction due to M's provocation. The fundamental questions as to S's upbringing and future had been decided and there had been no fundamental development; (2) the court had jurisdiction under ss.1 to 3 of the Family Law Act 1986, unless F's application was under s.8 of the Childrens Act 1989, because under s.2(2) of the 1986 Act jurisdiction would be excluded unless S was present in England and Wales; (3) F's application for S had left the jurisdiction was a free-standing one for a s.8 order and consequently the court had no jurisdiction; (4) the court returned jurisdiction in respect of continuing orders the terms of which required variation or discharge and since it remained, *a fortiori* the court had jurisdiction to entertain F's application for definition or determination of specific contact dates; and (5) F's application would not be stayed and orders would be made defining contact. Section 5(2) of the 1986 Act imported a statutory discretion which reinforced the common law discretion to stay proceedings. A court shall consider the welfare of the child in determining the most appropriate forum but it was not a paramount consideration. A choice between jurisdictions was not a question in respect of the upbringing of a child with s.1(1)(a) of the 1989 Act (*Spiliada Maritime Corp. v. Consulex; Spiliada, The* [1987] C.L.Y. 3135).

S. (A MINOR) (CONTACT: JURISDICTION), *Re* [1995] 2 F.C.R. 162, Thorpe J.

3485. Contact—mother applying for contact—18 months since last contact—children expressing wish not to see mother—judge concluding that forcing contact in the short-term would cause long-term emotional damage—whether judge correct to refuse contact

[Children Act (c.41), s.1(3).]

The court had to consider whether the fundamental emotional need of a child to have a relationship with both parents was outweighed by the depth of harm that a child might suffer by virtue of a contact order.

The parties were married in 1982 and had two children. They separated in 1989 and the children remained with the father. Difficulties with contact arose and in 1991 the court welfare officer recommended that contact with the mother should be stopped. The mother accepted the recommendation and contact ceased in January 1992. In July 1993 the mother applied for contact. A second court welfare officer noted that indirect contact had not been successful and that contact would have an adverse effect on the children both in the short- and long-term. The judge refused to make a contact order.

Held, dismissing the mother's appeal, that the court had to consider whether the fundamental emotional need of a child to have an enduring relationship with both parents was outweighed by the depth of harm that a child might suffer by virtue of a contact order. The judge was entitled to form the view that the risk of distress to the children outweighed the strong presumption in favour of contact, with which view the mother had concurred in 1992 (*B. (Minors: Access), Re* [1991] C.L.Y. 2472, *H. (Minors) (Access), Re* [1992] C.L.Y. 2999, *W. (A Minor) (Contact), Re* [1995] 7 C.L. 381 referred to).

M. (MINORS) (CONTACT), *Re* [1995] 1 F.C.R. 753.

3486. Contact—mother refusing contact—father applying for contact—child not aware of father—child regarding mother's fiancé as father—court making contact order not only with father but also with father's mother—whether court applying correct principles

[Children Act 1989 (c.41), s.10(1).]

A child living with her mother should have contact with her father, unless there were cogent reasons for the child to be denied such contact.

H was aged nearly four, and was born in November 1989. M and F separated in August 1990, and in subsequent divorce proceedings the decree absolute was made in May 1991. F had contact until M decided that it should cease in March 1992. F applied for a contact order. H regarded M's fiancé as her father. The court welfare officer recommended a limited programme of supervised contact in order for her to be able to see H and F together. The judge made an order in line with this recommendation, although he had declined to order the welfare officer to attend the hearing. The judge also added provision for H to see F's mother first, with a gradual introduction to F, despite there being no application for contact by or in favour of F's mother.

Held, dismissing M's appeal, that (1) in general, it was in the interests of both parent and child that they should have contact with each other, unless there were cogent reasons to the contrary (*H. (Minors) (Access), Re* [1992] C.L.Y. 2999, *R. (A Minor) (Contact), Re* [1994] 10 C.L. 335 applied; *S.M. (A Minor) (Natural Father: Access), Re* [1992] C.L.Y. 3000 distinguished); (2) the court welfare officer's report was very full, and there was nothing that she could have added in oral evidence, particularly as she had never had the opportunity of seeing H and F together; (3) the judge had applied the correct principles and his decision was not plainly wrong (*G. v. G. (Minors: Custody Appeal)* [1985] C.L.Y. 2594 applied); and (4) the court had a complete discretion to make an order of its own motion under s.10(1)(b) of the Children Act 1989. The use of the grandmother as a catalyst in smoothing F's contact was very sensible and could not be faulted.

[*Per curiam*: (1) The case of *S.M. (A Minor) (Natural Father: Access), Re* [1992] C.L.Y. 3000 was distinguishable on the basis that, in that case, the father had been an unmarried father. However, this was not a fundamental distinction; most important of all, it was a high watermark case where the general presumption in favour of contact was rebutted on the special facts of the case; (2) M intended to disobey any order for contact made or upheld by the court. That was not a very attractive argument against contact and M's attitude was a very irresponsible one.]

H. (CONTACT: PRINCIPLES), *Re* [1994] 2 F.L.R. 969, C.A.

3487. Contact—mother refusing contact after meeting second husband—mother stating contact not in child's best interests—mother stating that she would disobey any order made—whether "no order" presumption applicable

An order for contact should be made if the interests of the child so demanded despite a mother's avowal to disobey the order.

The parties married in 1988 but separated in 1989. Contact was a source of continual problems. F had an order for reasonable contact which M never sought to vary or discharge. After she met her second husband, M made a deliberate endeavour to terminate contact and it became clear that she was teaching the child to regard her second husband as the natural father. The judge refused to make an order for contact under the Children Act 1989, s.1(5), on F's application, on the grounds that it would destabilise the child. M had stated that if an order were made, she would disobey it.

Held, allowing F's appeal, that contact was the right of the child and save in exceptional circumstances the judge had a duty to make an order in the face of a mother's obduracy. The judge had abdicated his responsibilities by making no order.

W. (A MINOR) (CONTACT), *Re* [1994] 2 FLR 441, C.A.

3488. Contact—mother stopping contact—father applying for contact after one year—welfare officer recommending contact—mother's psychiatrist recommending no contact—court welfare officer revising opinion and recommending indirect contact—whether justices right to order contact in light of evidence

M and F never married and separated when their child was 12 months' old in 1989. Access continued until terminated by M in 1991. In 1992 F sought contact and was abusive towards M, who consequently suffered from depression and anxiety and had to receive treatment. F applied for contact which was recommended by the court welfare officer. M's psychiatrist recommended in a report that contact would have an adverse effect on M's mental health and the welfare officer revised his recommendation to indirect contact. The justices ordered direct contact on the grounds that M was a stronger personality than the psychiatrist had stated and would be able to put the child's interests above her own fears and concerns.

Held, dismissing M's appeal, that the psychiatrist had not been asked to provide an independent report on what was in the child's best interests but had been instructed by M. The justices were entitled to reach the conclusions they did on the evidence before them that the likelihood that M would suffer a depressive illness was a possibility not a prognosis and that it was in the child's best interests to be aware of his paternal, racial and cultural background. The court welfare officer had revised his opinion after M's expert's evidence and the justices were entitled to reject the evidence provided they gave reasons for so doing.

P. (A MINOR) (CONTACT), *Re* [1994] 2 FLR 374, Booth J.

3489. Contact—mother terminating contact with father—father having no physical contact—whether judge wrong not to make contact order—whether leave to appeal required

[Supreme Court Act 1981 (c.54), s.18(1)(h)(ii); Children Act 1989 (c.41), s.8(1).]

Where a parent appeals against an order which denies him any physical contact with the child but permits only indirect contact, no leave to appeal is required.

M and F were divorced after a short marriage and had one son, C, aged 10. M remarried in 1988 and after F had smacked the child during contact, M cut off contact in 1991. F applied for a contact order. In 1992 the welfare officer stated that M was very anxious about contact and felt that contact was not in C's best interests, stating that C was aware of M's anxieties and feelings. In 1992 the court adjourned the hearing for two months to allow M to reconsider her attitude to contact, but in January 1993 she was still implacably hostile to F and to F having contact. The court made no order on F's contact application save allowing F to send letters and presents.

Held, that s.18(1)(h)(ii) of the Supreme Court Act 1981 (now R.S.C., Ord. 59, r.1B(1)(f)(ii)(iii)) provided that leave to appeal was required except where an applicant for contact with a child was refused all contact. The section contemplated direct or physical contact, and no leave to appeal was required against an order which permitted indirect contact only (*Allette v. Allette* [1987] C.L.Y. 2438 applied). The principles that it was the right of the child to have contact with the parent with whom he did not reside, and that very cogent reasons were required for denying the child this right, were well established. There were strong policy reasons for saying that a recalcitrant parent should not be allowed to frustrate what the court considered the child's welfare required. It had been open to the judge to make a contact order, and it was difficult to see that M could successfully have appealed had he done so. However, the judge's decision that contact was not in C's best interests was not plainly wrong and could not be interfered with (*G. v. G. (Minors: Custody Appeal)* [1985] C.L.Y. 2594 applied).

J. (A MINOR) (CONTACT), *Re* [1994] 1 F.L.R. 729, C.A.

3490. Contact—non-biological father—mother living with partner who was not the father of child—mother and partner holding themselves out to be parents of child—relationship ending and mother living with another man—whether former partner to have contact with child

R underwent a gender-reassignment operation and lived with A, although not in a sexual sense. A had a brief affair with another man and gave birth to a daughter. A and R held themselves out to be the child's parents and R was registered on the birth and baptismal certificates as the father. After their separation, A started living with another man and stopped contact to R, who applied for, and was granted, contact.

Held, dismissing A's appeal, that notwithstanding the lack of a blood tie and the lapse of time since the child had seen R, it was in her interests to have contact with R and the judge had taken account of all relevant considerations.
R. (A MINOR) (CONTACT), *Re* [1994] Fam.Law 187, C.A.

3491. Contact—oral evidence—application for contact decided on written evidence and submissions only—whether judge wrong not to hear oral evidence

[Children Act 1989 (c.41), ss.9(6), 34, 91(14), Sched. 14, para. 5.]

A judge hearing proceedings under the Children Act 1989 has a broad discretion to determine the court's procedure, and is not always obliged to hold a full hearing, nor to permit the parties to call and cross-examine any witnesses they choose.

M and F had two daughters, P, aged 17, and D, aged 12. Following M and F's separation in 1983, the girls remained with M and were joined in 1985 by S, M's new partner, by whom she had five children. P left home in 1990, alleging that S had physically and sexually abused her. S was prosecuted but acquitted of the charges. In 1991 P and D were made the subject of care orders and contact with M and S was to be at the local authority's discretion. Contact did take place, but was stopped following D making allegations of abuse by S. S applied for an order defining contact with both girls. The district judge referred the matter to a High Court judge for consideration as to whether the application should proceed to a full hearing or be dismissed. The judge dismissed the application and discharged the earlier contact order, but heard no oral evidence, deciding the case on submissions and written evidence.

Held, dismissing the appeal, that (1) the court had the power to determine a case without oral evidence where a parent, whose access had previously been terminated in wardship proceedings, was fortuitously now able to apply for contact following the implementation of the Children Act 1989 and where the prospects of the application succeeding were so remote it would be wrong to allow the application to proceed. However, the facts here were far removed from that situation, and the judge had been wrong to adopt that approach (*Cheshire County Council v. M.* [1994] 2 C.L. 352 distinguished); (2) however, even outside this limited category of cases, the judge had a discretion to determine the court's procedure and to decide the case on written evidence and submissions. The court was not required to permit the parties to call or cross-examine any witnesses they chose (*A. and W. (Minors) (Residence Orders: Leave to Apply), Re* [1992] C.L.Y. 3123, *W. v. Ealing London Borough Council* [1994] 10 C.L. 336 considered; *H. (Child Orders: Restricting Applications), Re* [1992] C.L.Y. 2990, *F. v. Kent County Council* [1994] 2 C.L. 351 distinguished); (3) in exercising this discretion, the court must consider (a) whether there was sufficient written evidence upon which to make a decision; (b) whether the proposed oral evidence or cross-examination was likely to affect the outcome of proceedings; (c) the welfare of the child and the effect thereon of further litigation; (d) whether a full hearing would result in delay detrimental to the child's welfare; (e) the application's prospects of success; and (f) whether a full hearing was required by the justice of the case; and (4) the judge had erred, but the court had sufficient information to exercise this discretion itself. It would be wrong to impose contact against the wishes of a girl of P's age, and given D's wishes S would have no prospects of success if the matter were to proceed to a full oral hearing. The judge had adopted the correct procedure, albeit for the wrong reasons.
B. (MINORS) CONTACT), *Re* [1994] 2 F.L.R. 1, C.A.

3492. Contact—oral evidence—grandmother's application—conflicting written statements—whether magistrates entitled to hear oral evidence to decided disputed facts

[Children Act 1989 (c.41), s.10(2)(9).]

On an application for leave to apply for a contact order, where there is a stark factual issue between the parties, the court should hear oral evidence and form a broad view of the merits of the substantive application.

H and W had four children aged between eleven and two. G, W's mother, applied for leave to apply for a contact order. H and W both opposed the grant of leave. G's solicitor put before the court a letter in which G stated that she had had regular contact until March 1994, she was genuinely interested in their welfare, and that they had enjoyed their contact with her. H and W had signed a statement to the effect that G had interfered in W's life, that she swore in the children's presence and belittled W to them, and that they considered any future contact would be upsetting and of no benefit to the children. No oral evidence was adduced. The justices refused leave, on the basis that the application would be disruptive to the settled family unit, would cause distress to H and W and would interfere with the smooth running of family life.

Held, allowing G's appeal and remitting the matter to a fresh bench, that (1) on an application for leave to apply for a s.8 order, the court must consider the factors set out in s.10(9) of the Children Act 1989, and also consider the overall merits of the substantive application and whether it had a reasonable prospect of success; (2) the justices should have heard sufficient oral evidence to form a view on the disputed facts as to the merits of the application and as to any risk that there might be of the proposed application disrupting the children's lives to such an extent that they would be harmed by it. The extent of the evidence and cross-examination was a matter for the justices, but it could not be wrong to allow cross-examination which went to the merits (*G. v. Kirklees Metropolitan Borough Council* [1994] C.L.Y. 3257, *A. (A Minor) (Residence Order: Leave to Apply), Re* [1994] C.L.Y. 3125 considered).

F. AND R. (SECTION 8 ORDER: GRANDPARENT'S APPLICATION), *Re* [1995] 1 FLR 524, Cazalet J.

3493. Contact—private law proceedings—joinder of local authority—local authority not applying for care or supervision order—whether local authority should be joined as a party to the contact proceedings

[Children Act 1989 (c.41), ss.8, 37; Family Proceedings Courts (Children Act 1989) Rules 1991 (S.I. 1991 No. 1395), r.7.]

A local authority could not apply for private law orders under s.8 of the Children Act 1989, and it was wrong for a local authority to be joined as a party to private law proceedings.

M and F had never married and had three children, aged between eight and five. F was convicted of indecent assault upon the 13-year-old daughter of the woman with whom he was cohabiting and he was sentenced to 18 months' imprisonment. Shortly before F's release, M applied for a number of s.8 orders. The local authority was directed to investigate under s.37 of the Children Act 1989, and F subsequently applied for limited supervised contact. The local authority took the view that F's attitude to his previous offence was such that he was a serious risk to the children, and that as there was no mileage in long-term unsupervised contact, there was little purpose in ordering short-term supervised contact. It decided not to apply for a care or supervision order, but at an *inter partes* directions hearing, the local authority was joined as a party to the father's contact application. At the final hearing, the local authority opposed the making of a contact order. M herself did not oppose limited supervised contact, and sought leave to withdraw her s.8 applications. The justices dismissed F's contact application.

Held, dismissing F's appeal, that (1) although the justices had a discretion under r.7 of the Family Proceedings Courts (Children Act 1989) Rules 1991 to allow any person to be joined as a party to private law proceedings, it was inconsistent with the scheme of the Children Act 1989 for a local authority to be joined as a party. The local authority's duties under s.37 were fully set out and did not include advocating any point of view in relation to the private law proceedings which gave rise to the s.37 investigation. Local authorities were precluded from applying for a residence or contact order, and there was little difference between that and inviting the court to make a different s.8 order to the one proposed by other parties (*Nottinghamshire County Council v. P.* [1993] C.L.Y. 2860 considered); (2) however, the local authority's participation as a party had not affected the outcome of the proceedings, as the same information would still have been available to them. It had been open to the justices to make the findings that they had on the evidence, and it could not be said that their decision was plainly wrong (*G. v. G. (Minors: Custody Appeal)* [1985] C.L.Y. 2594 applied).

F. v. CAMBRIDGESHIRE COUNTY COUNCIL [1995] 1 FLR 516, Stuart-White J.

3494. Contact—prohibited steps order—father seeking reinstatement of contact—seeking to instruct child psychologist—mother applying for father's parental responsibility order to be rescinded—prohibited steps order—change of surname—order under statute—whether justified

[Children Act 1989 (c.41), s.91(14).]

F was the father of two boys, J and A. He was not married to M but lived with her for several years. F applied for contact with the children to be reinstated and for a child psychologist to be instructed in respect of M. M applied for leave to change the boys' surnames to the name of her new husband, for a prohibited steps order to prevent the father visiting the boys' school and to rescind the parental responsibility order granted to F. An order made preventing F making further application without leave of the court for a period of three years under the Children Act 1989, s.91(14), was also at issue. There was much bitterness between the parties which had had an adverse effect on the children. J had refused to see his father and the father had become obsessive about his right to see the children.

Held, dismissing the appeal save as to the s.91(14) order where the appeal was allowed with liberty to the mother to be heard, that (1) the reinstatement of contact would be harmful to the children in the foreseeable future; (2) the children had already been through enough and a child psychologist would be of no value, particularly as there was no real prospect of contact with F; (3) M had sought to protect her new family, the children themselves wished to take the name of their stepfather and there was no reason for the court to intervene; (4) a prohibited steps order was justified as it would frustrate the order for no direct contact if indirect contact were to be allowed through the school; (5) the parental responsibility order would be rescinded in this very unusual case. Within the definition of parental responsibility in the 1989 Act, the father had no constructive or positive role to play; and (6) it was premature to make a s.91(14) order and this would be set aside.

S. (MINORS), *Re* (CCFMI 94/1097/F), May 1, 1995, C.A.

3495. Contact—sexual abuse—father's application for contact coinciding with investigation of child abuse allegations—guidance as to role of court and necessary directions for speedy and effective trial

[Children Act 1989 (c.41), ss.7, 11, 32, 98; R.S.C., Ord. 38, r.13; C.C.R., Ord. 20, r.12; Family Proceedings Rules 1991 (S.I. 1991 No. 1247), rr.4.14, 4.15; Family Proceedings Courts (Children Act 1989) Rules 1991 (S.I. 1991 No. 1395), rr.14, 15.]

The court gave important guidance as to the procedure to be adopted in cases involving allegations of child sexual abuse, and in cases where there was a joint local authority and police investigation continuing alongside private law proceedings.

F made an application for contact to see his children (A and B) in May 1992. The parties agreed at court in July 1992 that F should have contact subject to the approval of the local authority. Subsequently, M withdrew her consent to that arrangement, and the local authority and police made a joint investigation of allegations that F had abused the children. F was not told what was going on until September 1992, when he was arrested and interviewed by the police. In August 1992, the local authority, without the knowledge of the court or of F, referred A to Great Ormond Street Hospital. Directions were made by correspondence between the parties and the court, and a court welfare officer was ordered to report, but she was hampered by the fact that the hospital's assessment was continuing. The worker in charge of the assessment opposed any contact between A and F while the assessment was continuing. Eventually, F appealed against the district judge's directions, and the circuit judge gave directions for an interim hearing in December 1992. The interim hearing was vacated owing to the continuing assessment at the hospital. The welfare officer reported in March 1993. In March 1993, the judge ordered that A be permitted to attend a therapy group for sexually abused children. A final hearing was fixed for four days in June 1993, but the time estimate was woefully short; the judge made orders for interim contact, starting with the paternal grandparents, leading on to supervised contact with F. The final hearing was adjourned to be heard by a High Court judge over 10 days, and the hearing took place in March 1994. The judge gave an earlier judgment dealing with the substantive issues, and gave a further judgment in open court dealing with procedural matters.

Held, that (1) F's application was issued in May 1992 and was heard in March 1994. The delay was unacceptable. The court had a duty to be proactive in setting a timetable under s.11 of the Children Act 1989 in order to avoid delay (*G. (Minors) (Expert Witnesses), Re* [1995] 4 C.L. 312, *M.D. and T.D. (Minors) (Time Estimates), Re, (Note)* [1995] 4 C.L. 186 considered); (2) where a welfare officer was asked to report, the court should not leave the hearing to be set down on the first open date after receipt of the report, but should provide a deadline for the filing of the report and fix a date accordingly (*M.D. and T.D. (Minors) (Time Estimates), Re, (Note)* [1995] 4 C.L. 186 applied); (3) when asking a welfare officer to report, the court should do so in the context of its duty under s.11, and should analyse and give expression to the issues which the welfare officer was being asked to cover. The court should also consider what further directions were required; (4) where there were private law proceedings running in tandem with a local authority investigation the court must act as a co-ordinating agency. In general, the court had no power to direct the course of a local authority's child protection procedures, but the court could and should ensure that the investigation was co-ordinated and ran in tandem with the private law proceedings; (5) it was bad practice for directions in difficult child cases to be sought and given in writing and without the attendance of the parties. Directions appointments were important occasions. The court should appraise itself of the issues and keep a tight grip on a case; normally this could only be done by a hearing attended by both parties and their representatives so that the court could make its own assessment of the specific directions necessary to ensure a speedy resolution. While it was appreciated that courts had busy and lengthy lists, if the court took a tight grip at an early stage, substantial savings in time and costs would be achieved at later stages. At the initial hearing, the court should give comprehensive directions and set a timetable, including the fixing of a provisional hearing date. Practitioners should direct their minds at the earliest possible opportunity to all the possible ramifications of the case, so that directions could be given sooner rather than later; (6) it was not necessary that every case involving an allegation of child sexual abuse be transferred to the High Court; (7) in cases involving contested allegations of child sexual abuse, the circuit judge (preferably the one who would ultimately try the case) should hear the directions appointments, and not the district judge; (8) the principal weapon in the court's armoury to ensure co-ordination of local authority investigations with private law proceedings was the power to order a s.7 report. The court could impose a deadline for the filing of such a report. Usually it would take the form of a statement by the responsible social worker; in urgent cases, it might consist of a letter from the local authority legal department; (9) it might also be appropriate for the author of a s.7 report to give oral evidence. In private law proceedings a local authority must be perceived to be neutral and bipartisan. It should not give evidence on behalf of either party. A social worker should be called at the invitation of the court and be cross-examined by both parties. In the unlikely event that the local authority did not make the social worker available, the court could issue a witness summons for his or her attendance; (10) the court had jurisdiction to compel discovery of material held by the police or the local authority which had been obtained in the course of their child protection investigation, on the parties offering suitable undertakings as to the use of the material. The practice ought to be that such material be made available, although the local authority or the police might of course wish to raise matters of public interest immunity (*Norwich Pharmacal Co. v. Customs and Excise Commissioners* [1973] C.L.Y. 2643 considered); and (11) the court had no power over the police's criminal investigation. However, the court hearing the private law proceedings should be kept aware at every stage of the current state of the criminal investigation and/or prosecution. Where the court was concerned about delay, the most the court could do was to make it clear to the police, through the local authority, that the court was awaiting the outcome of the criminal investigation, that the sooner a decision whether or not to prosecute was taken the better for the family and that the court would be reconsidering the matter at a further directions appointment (on a specified date) when it would expect to know the police's decision.

[*Per curiam*: Unless there was clear evidence of significant disturbance in a child apparently arising from sexual abuse against a background of marital breakdown, therapy in a group for abused children should not be provided before a court has decided the question of abuse.]

A. AND B. (MINORS) (NO. 2), *Re* [1995] 1 F.L.R. 351, Wall J.

3496. Contact—sexual abuse—interviewing techniques—investigation of sexual abuse allegations—role of guardian *ad litem*

[Children Act 1989 (c.41), ss.1(2), 16.]

The court made important observations on the conduct of cases involving child sexual abuse allegations, and on the investigation of such allegations.

M and F separated in 1989 and had two boys, C born in 1986, and A born in 1987. In 1989 it was agreed that F would have visiting contact during the day, which was to develop into staying contact, although in fact no staying contact took place. In June 1990, on returning from contact, A indicated that he had been sexually abused by F. The next week both A and C made similar indications. Subsequently, in June and July, C was interviewed on four occasions, and A on three occasions, the interviews all lasting at least one hour. F was arrested but denied all the allegations, and was subsequently released and informed that no charges would be made. By November 1990, M was convinced that F had abused the boys, while F was convinced that M had failed to protect them from abuse or had connived in abuse. In January 1991, F applied for contact. A child psychiatrist, K, was jointly instructed by M and F, and he concluded that the interviews were wholly unreliable, and recommended there be supervised contact. The guardian *ad litem*, who did not see K's report until the morning of the trial, had written in her report that she considered that C had been exposed to an inappropriate sexual experience, and that A had experienced at least physical abuse. The matter came on for hearing in November 1993.

Held, that (1) the court did not believe that the boys had been sexually abused. It was highly likely that an innocent act on F's part, holding A up so that he avoided urinating over his clothes and holding his penis in order to direct the flow of his urine, had been distorted and expanded by misunderstanding and inappropriate interviewing into an allegation of abuse. Neither party was guilty of any sexual abuse (*H. (A Minor) (Child Abuse: Evidence), Re; K. v. K.* [1990] C.L.Y. 3185 applied); (2) there should be supervised contact between F and C, and reasonable contact between F and A, but no such contact with A should be arranged save by agreement between the parties in consultation with the supervising officer and the Official Solicitor; and (3) there would be a family assistance order, with the local authority to make an officer available to supervise the contact and the officer should not have had any previous involvement in the case (*Leeds City Council v. C.* [1993] C.L.Y. 2826 considered).

[*Per curiam*: (1) The interviews were in flagrant breach of a number of guidelines laid down in the Cleveland Report. There appeared to be an unfortunate tendency amongst those charged with the difficult task of investigating child sexual abuse to concentrate all their efforts on extracting information from the child, without attempting to fit any allegations made into the factual circumstances from which they arise. Incompetent interviewing was a further abuse in the name of child protection on a child who may or may not have suffered the evil of abuse. Further, the interview itself was valueless as evidence and it would frequently render impossible the task of the court in deciding whether or not there had been abuse. It was bad practice for the alleged perpetrator to be kept in total ignorance of what was happening to his child, as it fostered a growing sense of grievance and rendered subsequent co-operation with social services very difficult; (2) the guardian *ad litem* had been extremely unwise to venture an opinion on the likelihood of sexual abuse having occurred. The issue of whether or not abuse had occurred was one for the court, not the guardian *ad litem*, to decide; it was not the function of the guardian *ad litem* to adopt a judicial role. The report should be limited to factual observations and assessments within his or her professional expertise as a social worker. Any recommendations contained in the report should be based on alternative premises, namely whether a finding of abuse is to be made or not. In addition, the analysis of interviews with children is a highly specialised skill which should only be undertaken by an expert in the field, not by the guardian *ad litem*, who should seek such expert advice. Where, as here, there was an expert jointly instructed by the parties, the guardian should be given the opportunity of taking over the instruction of the expert, or if that is inappropriate, of instructing his or her own expert; (3) it was astonishing that F's solicitors had not disclosed K's report to the guardian *ad litem*, who saw the report for the first time on the morning of the hearing. Privilege did not apply to reports of this nature, and the court had power to override the privilege (*Oxfordshire County Council v. M.* [1994] 6 C.L. 289 considered); (4) the delay in this case was unacceptable and inexcusable. The parties' advisers have a duty in children's cases to ensure that a case does not drift and is determined with a minimum of delay. The Official Solicitor, or any other independent guardian *ad litem* acting in the case, should regularly review the file, and if the case was not making satisfactory progress, should take out a directions appointment to ensure such progress is made; and (5) directions appointments are not formalities, but should be used to ensure the case is tightly timetabled and speedily resolved. Directions should be drawn up precisely. Where further directions are likely to be needed, the court should fix a date for the next directions hearing. In difficult cases likely to be heard by a judge, the district judge should direct that a directions appointment be heard by a judge.

B. v. B. (CHILD ABUSE: CONTACT) [1994] 2 F.L.R. 713, Wall J.

3497. Contact—stepfather—whether any presumption that stepfather should continue to have contact—whether judge wrong to order contact

[Children Act 1989 (c.41), s.1.]

There was no presumption that a stepfather should be allowed contact with his stepchild.

H and W married but separated shortly afterwards. W's relationship with another man soon broke down and H, fully aware that W was pregnant by her former lover, accepted her back. H attended the child's birth, and acted as the child's father. The child was registered in H's name. When the child was six months old, W left again and soon after resumed her relationship with F. When H discovered this he made a serious assault on W. Nevertheless, H had regular weekly staying contact with the child for a further eight months, until H and W were finally divorced. W thereupon stopped H's contact. H's application for contact was resisted by W and F on the ground that contact would be disruptive to their relationship. However, the welfare officer reported that there was a close bond between H and the child, and that he had continued regularly to see and maintain the child even after separation. The judge ordered that H should have contact.

Held, dismissing W's appeal, that (1) there was no presumption that a stepfather should continue a relationship with a stepchild. However, there were cases where there were people in the life of a child who did not have a biological relationship with the child, but who nevertheless were very important to the child. The judge had not approached the case on the basis of any presumption in favour of H having contact; (2) H represented the early stability in the child's life, and could continue to do much good for the child in the future, provided that he recognised that he was not the child's father, and that he had to adapt his relationship to the child to that of a minor figure. In this unusual case, the judge had balanced all the factors and his decision was not plainly wrong.

H. (A MINOR) (CONTACT), *Re* [1994] 2 F.C.R. 419, C.A.

3498. Contact—written reasons—reasons for decision given orally and not recorded in writing at time of decision—whether decision vitiated by procedural irregularity

[Children Act 1989 (c.41), s.41(3); Family Proceedings Rules 1991 (S.I. 1991 No. 1247), r.9.2A; Family Proceedings Courts (Children Act 1989) Rules 1991 (S.I. 1991 No. 1395), rr.14(1)(d), 21(5)(6)(7); Guardians Ad Litem and Reporting Officers (Panels) Regulations 1991 (S.I. 1991 No. 2051).]

Where magistrates have not given sufficient written reasons for their decision as required by rules of court, this vitiates their decision which must therefore be set aside and the defect cannot be rectified by written reasons later supplied to the appellate court.

W was now eight and lived with M and her stepfather. Following M's allegation in 1990 that F had sexually abused W during a period of staying contact, M stopped all contact. F was not prosecuted and in 1992 he applied for a contact order. The magistrates ordered separate representation for W and appointed a solicitor for her. Interim supervised contact was ordered and the reasons given orally. At a further hearing, the magistrates saw W in private and decided that no order for contact should be made, again giving their reasons orally. F appealed, relying on the magistrates' failure to record their reasons in writing as required by the rules.

Held, allowing the appeal and remitting the matter to a county court judge, that had the rules been complied with, it was unlikely that their decision could have been upset on appeal. However, r.21(5) of the Family Proceedings Courts (Children Act 1989) Rules 1991 required the magistrates to record their findings of fact and reasons in writing before announcing their decision. The rules were mandatory, and applied to all decisions, including interim proceedings; supplying the reasons in writing at a later stage could not rectify the defect. The magistrates' reasons were inadequate and the procedural irregularity vitiated their decision, which must be set aside (*W. v. Hertfordshire County Council* [1993] C.L.Y. 2777 applied; *G. v. G. (Minors: Custody Appeal)* [1985] C.L.Y. 2594, *R. v. Oxfordshire County Council (Secure Accommodation Order)* [1992] C.L.Y. 3129, *Hillingdon London Borough Council v. H.* [1992] C.L.Y. 2114, *S. v. S. (Minors: Periodical Payments)* [1993] C.L.Y. 2841, *S. v. Oxfordshire County Council* [1994] 2 C.L. 346 considered).

W. (A MINOR) (CONTACT), *Re* [1994] 1 F.L.R. 843, Wall J.

3499. Contempt—documents used in Children Act proceedings—medical reports—publication by newspapers—whether contempt of court. See OFFICIAL SOLICITOR v. NEWS GROUP NEWSPAPERS, §3959.

3500. Costs—family proceedings—whether to be awarded against Legal Aid Board—cases involving children—whether principles different to other areas of civil law. See KELLER v. KELLER AND LEGAL AID BOARD, §3971.

3501/2. Costs—termination of contact—care proceedings—termination of contact—justices refusing application—finely balanced case—whether local authority should pay costs. See M. (LOCAL AUTHORITY'S COSTS), *Re*, §3381.

3503. Court welfare officer—recommendation—decision of judge not to follow recommendation—requirement to provide reasons for dissent

In child cases, a judge who decided not to follow the court welfare officer's recommendation was not required to state in specific terms why he dissented from the recommendation provided the reasons he gave for his decision were a sound basis for the exercise of his discretion.

V. (A MINOR), *Re*, *The Independent*, July 24, 1995, C.A.

3504. Court welfare officer—recommendations—departure from

If magistrates in the Family Proceedings Court deciding Children Act 1989 applications decided to depart from the court welfare officer's recommendations, as they were perfectly entitled to do, they must give clear reasons for doing so.

L. (A MINOR), *Re*, *The Independent*, April 24, 1995, Connell J.

3505. Court welfare officer—recommendations—not followed—whether judge obliged to give reasons for departing from recommendations

A mother appealed against a decision restricting contact with her four-year-old child to four times a year. The appeal was on the grounds that the judge failed to pay sufficient attention to a welfare officer's report recommending regular contact and gave no reasons for this failure. A successful period of supervised contact was also ignored.

Held, allowing the appeal, that the judge misdirected himself by failing to take into account the welfare officer's report. He had looked at possible future psychological consequences of contact by considering matters on which he had no evidence. Reasons must be given when departing from the recommendations of a welfare officer. A rehearing before a different judge was ordered.

D. (A MINOR), *Re* (LTA 95/5554/E), July 18, 1995, C.A.

3506. Court welfare officer—report—whether appeal lay against order that report be prepared

A judge had a discretion to order a court welfare officer to prepare a report on a child. An appeal from such an order should not have been brought.

W. (A MINOR) (WELFARE REPORTS: APPEALS), *Re*, *The Times*, January 25, 1995, C.A.

3507. Disabled child—care-hours provision—reduction in hours—whether under duty to assess child under Chronically Sick and Disabled Persons Act—whether request necessary for duty to arise—whether need for schooling justified reduction in care-hours. See R. v. BEXLEY LONDON BOROUGH COUNCIL, *ex p.* B., §3225.

3508. Evidence—bundles—guidelines on use of video evidence

Wall J. has issued guidance on the preparation of bundles for use in children's cases and on the procedure governing the adducing of videotaped material.

Wall J. issued 15 directions for guidance as to the preparation of bundles for use in children's cases, and the procedure to be adopted where videotaped material is to be used, the most important of which are: (1) bundles should be prepared in consultation with counsel and with the advisers for the other parties; (2) bundles should be presented in a chronological sequence and with pages individually paginated; (3) wherever possible the chronology prepared by the applicant should cross-refer to the relevant page in the relevant bundle; (4) there should always be a witness bundle; (5) where videos of interviews with children formed part of the evidence, the parties should attempt to agree on the manner in which they were to be used, or a directions appointment should be taken out; and (6) where a challenge was made to the interviewing technique or there was a dispute as to the interpretation of what was said, transcripts should be obtained and placed in a separate bundle.

B. v. B. (COURT BUNDLES: VIDEO EVIDENCE) [1994] 1 F.L.R. 323, Wall J.

3509. Family proceedings—appeals—duty of legal advisers—merits of case

It was important in family proceedings for legal advisers to take a detached view of the merits of cases rather than be carried along by the wishes of parents who were often in a highly emotional state, so that appeals were not brought in hopeless cases where the inevitable result was a waste of public funds and emotional harm to the children involved.

N. (MINORS) (RESIDENCE), *Re*, *The Times*, April 6, 1995, C.A.

3510. Family proceedings—disclosure—social workers—minor's injuries—whether oral admissions made to social worker and documents could be disclosed without leave of court. See G. (MINOR) (SOCIAL WORKER: DISCLOSURE), *Re*, §2315.

3511. Family proceedings—time estimates—hearings before High Court judge—procedure to be adopted

A hearing with a time estimate of three days ran for seven days. The judge was authorised by the President to issue the following guidance:

1. Time estimates should include provision for judicial reading and time for delivery of an *ex tempore* judgment.

2. Solicitors and counsel should consult with each other to see if the time estimate could be agreed by all parties as part of the co-operative process to ensure a case is properly prepared for trial.

3. Counsel should think realistically about cross-examination of important witnesses and a realistic calculation of likely length with each witness should be made.

4. Sufficient time should be set aside for expert medical evidence.

5. No time estimate can be accurate if time-limits are not observed.

6. Directions hearings are not formalities and, where possible, counsel who will have conduct of the substantive hearing should be briefed for the directions hearing and should take every opportunity to discuss time estimates.

7. Where estimated length of trial is discussed in court, legal representatives and judges should consider the following: (i) the documents to be read and length of time to read; (ii) the likely length of opening; (iii) the likely length of oral evidence; (iv) the length of time which points of law or procedure may take to argue; (v) the number and length of closing speeches; and (vi) the time likely to be taken for an *ex tempore* judgment.

8. If a case overruns its time estimate due to negligent or incompetent estimation of time, the court should consider sanctions against those responsible, including making wasted costs orders.

M.D. AND T.D. (MINORS) (TIME ESTIMATES) (NOTE), *Re* [1994] 2 FLR 336, Wall J.

3512. Financial provision—property adjustment order—for benefit of child—whether order should be made for outright transfer of property to child. See A. v. A. (A MINOR: FINANCIAL PROVISION), §2355.

3513. Fostering—application for re-registration as foster carer—pornographic video shown to child in care—children main consideration—whether application right to be refused

C appealed against the refusal of his application for judicial review of the decision of the local authority's Fostering Panel not to re–register him as a foster carer. Relations between C and the department had deteriorated following the department's investigations into an allegation that C had shown a child in his care a pornographic video. The chairwoman of the panel had written to C stating that, although C had given a clear account of the incident, there was some concern that he had not accepted that his actions were inappropriate. C thereafter made numerous complaints against the department. The decision which was the subject of C's judicial review application was taken at a meeting to which C was invited. The chairwoman, who had been the subject of many of C's complaints, did not attend and the meeting was chaired by the area general manager, with three departmental team managers and two family placement team social workers present. The decision not to re-register C was taken after talking to him and then deliberating after he had left. C's complaint centred on the fact that the participants included people against whom he had registered complaints and who were not members of the panel. He contended that the decision was consequently unfair and in breach of natural justice.

Held, dismissing the appeal, that the fact that some members already had knowledge which might predispose them to reaching a certain conclusion did not necessarily mean that they could not reach a decision which was fair. Each case had to be considered in its context, taking account of the nature of the decision-making body and of the decision which had to be reached. Where decisions involved the care of children, their interest had to be the main consideration and it was apparent that the panel had considered very carefully the question of C's continuing registration and that the contribution of the social workers was relevant to the discussion. On the facts of the case, the composition of the panel did not render the decision unfair and there was no breach of natural justice.

R. v. AVON COUNTY COUNCIL, *ex p.* CRABTREE, *The Independent*, November 29, 1995, C.A.

3514. Guardian *ad litem*—care proceedings—adoption—case record—whether guardian *ad litem* having right to see case record

[Children Act 1989 (c.41), s.42; Family Proceedings Rules 1991 (S.I. 1991 No. 1247), r.4.11.]

A guardian *ad litem* appointed for the child in care proceedings is entitled to disclosure of the local authority's case record relating to the prospective adopters.

A was born in 1989. M committed suicide in 1991 and F was unable to care for A. After a few months with M's mother, A was placed with a short-term foster-parent. The local authority applied for a care order and interim care orders were made. The local authority planned for A to be adopted. It showed the case record of one set of prospective adopters to A's guardian *ad litem*, following which it was agreed that they were not suitable. A further set of prospective adopters was found, and this time approved by the local authority's adoption panel as a match for the child. One month later the final hearing of the care proceedings took place, but the local authority had not shown the case record of the approved adopters to the guardian. The judge held that the guardian had no right to see the case record, and made a care order.

Held, allowing the appeal, that (1) s.42 of the Children Act 1989 entitled the guardian *ad litem* to examine and take copies of all records of, or held by, the local authority which were compiled in connection with any functions which stood referred to its social services committee, and which related to the child. Such records were admissible in evidence. The case record was prepared by the local authority in the exercise of its functions as an adoption agency, a function which stood referred to the social services committee; (2) the guardian *ad litem* could only perform the duties imposed on him by r.4.11 of the Family Proceedings Rules 1991 if he had access to the case record. Section 42 therefore entitled him to see the records and to include information derived therefrom in his report. By the explicit provision in s.42(3), the right of access to the records prevailed over any claims of confidentiality, privilege, or public interest immunity, though the guardian *ad litem* would be fully conscious that the identity of the prospective adopters would very often be required to kept confidential (*Adoption Application, Re* [1990] C.L.Y. 3127, *S. (A Minor) (Adoption Application) (Disclosure of Information), Re* [1994] 6 C.L. 288 distinguished; *R. v. North Yorkshire County Council, ex p. M.* [1989] C.L.Y. 2430, *Manchester City Council v. F.* [1994] 2 C.L. 349 considered); (3) while in the majority of cases it was most unlikely that the court would refuse to make a care order on account of the suitability or otherwise of the local authority's proposed placement, the court was not a rubber stamp and always had the right to refuse a care order (*B. (Minors) (Termination of Contact: Paramount Consideration), Re* [1993] C.L.Y. 2771 applied; *W. (A Minor) (Wardship: Restrictions on Publication), Re* [1992] C.L.Y. 3146, *Cheshire County Council v. M.* [1994] 2 C.L. 352, *E. (A Minor) (Care Order: Contact), Re* [1995] 1 C.L. 256 considered); and (4) the judge had therefore been wrong to make a care order without the benefit of a report from the guardian *ad litem* about the effect on A's interests of the making of a care order, and of the placement with the prospective adopters.

T. (A MINOR) (GUARDIAN *AD LITEM*: CASE RECORD), *Re* [1994] 1 F.L.R. 632, C.A.

3515. Guardian *ad litem*—care proceedings—child giving instructions to own solicitor conflicting with those of guardian *ad litem*—procedure to be adopted in such circumstances—presentation of medical evidence at hearing

[Children Act 1989 (c.41), s.41; Family Proceedings Rules 1991 (S.I. 1991 No. 1247), rr.4.11, 4.12; Family Proceedings Courts (Children Act 1989) Rules 1991 (S.I. 1991 No. 1395), rr.11, 12.]

Where it appeared to the guardian *ad litem* appointed for the child in public law proceedings that the child was instructing the solicitor appointed for him directly, or intended to conduct the proceedings on his own behalf, the guardian should inform the court of this and seek directions as to representation.

Care proceedings were brought in respect of R, a boy aged 12, and E, his sister, aged 4. Although the court was informed at an early stage that R was separately represented, no directions were sought from the court for the separate representation of his guardian *ad litem*. R wished to return home and to remain with his sister, but the guardian considered that care orders were necessary and the siblings might have to be separated. The judge heard evidence from three paediatricians and a psychiatrist. One of the paediatricians gave evidence which differed from his earlier report. In the light of this evidence and having seen the paediatrician's notes for the first time, the other experts changed their opinions on the issue of the sexual abuse of E, thereby transforming the case. The judge found that E had been sexually abused by a member of her family and made care orders in respect of both children, which meant that they would be separated.

Held, that (1) care proceedings were specified proceedings within s.41 of the Children Act 1989, and the court had a duty to appoint a guardian *ad litem* for the child unless satisfied that one was not required to safeguard the child's interests. Where there was no conflict between the child and his guardian, the guardian would usually appoint a solicitor for the child under r.4.11(2) of the Family Proceedings Rules 1991; (2) r.4.11(3) required the guardian to inform the court if the child was instructing his solicitor direct, or intended to conduct, and was capable of conducting, the proceedings on his own behalf.

The guardian should inform the court at a directions hearing, to allow the court to consider the question of representation and, if appropriate, to grant leave for the guardian to be represented. The guardian should be alert to the possibility of a conflict between himself and the child from the outset, and steps should be taken to resolve the conflict well before the final hearing; (3) the solicitor must represent the child in accordance with the guardian's instructions, unless the solicitor considered that the child was capable of giving instructions on his behalf, in which case the solicitor must accept the child's instructions (*H. (A Minor) (Care Proceedings: Child's Wishes), Re* [1994] 2 C.L. 348 considered); (4) it was important that the court was so informed as there might be an issue about the capacity of the child to give coherent and consistent instructions, which the court would be able to resolve, possibly with the help of expert evidence. Where a solicitor was representing a child in accordance with the child's instructions, the child should not be in court nor should he give evidence, although the judge might agree to see him; and (6) medical experts should be fully instructed. The papers sent to the expert with the letter of instruction should be carefully selected, the letter of instruction should list the papers sent, and should always be disclosed and included in the bundle (*Oxfordshire County Council v. M.* [1994] 6 C.L. 289 considered). Doctors with clinical experience of the child outside the context of the proceedings should review their notes before writing their report and should ensure that all their clinical material was available to the other experts and the court. Experts should be kept up to date with developments and should be invited to confer before trial in order to reach agreement or limit the issues. The legal advisers should co-operate in ensuring that experts were available and could give evidence in a logical sequence.

M. (MINORS) CARE PROCEEDINGS: CHILD'S WISHES), *Re* [1994] 1 F.L.R. 749, Wall J.

3516. Guardian *ad litem*—disclosure of admission of mother to social services department and police—whether admission confidential—whether leave of court required for disclosure—whether guardian *ad litem*'s appointment to be terminated

[Family Proceedings Rules 1991 (S.I. 1991 No. 1247 (L.20)), r.4.10(9).]

The confidentiality enjoyed by a report by a guardian *ad litem* extends to information collected by the guardian for the purpose of preparing the report and such confidentiality is that of the court and not of the guardian *ad litem*.

In care proceedings instituted by the council relating to a baby admitted to hospital with head and chest injuries which were diagnosed as non-accidental, M admitted to the guardian *ad litem* that she had caused the injuries. The police were informed by the Duty Welfare Officer and the guardian *ad litem* was interviewed in order to obtain a witness statement attesting to the admission made to her. The Crown Prosecution Service sought to rely on the admission in pending criminal proceedings. M applied under r.4.10(9) of the 1991 Rules for the termination of the guardian *ad litem's* appointment on the ground that she could not co-operate with her.

Held, granting the application, that (1) the confidentiality enjoyed by a report by a guardian *ad litem* extended to information collected by the guardian for the purpose of preparing the report and such confidentiality was that of the court and not of the guardian; (2) since M's admissions had been spoken in confidence, the police had been wrong to try to make use of them, and the guardian had been wrong to make a witness statement without the prior leave of the court for the disclosure to be made (*F., Re* [1977] C.L.Y. 1965, *Brown v. Matthews* [1990] C.L.Y. 2248, *X, Y and Z (Minors) (Wardship: Disclosure of Material), Re* [1992] C.L.Y. 3137 applied).

OXFORDSHIRE COUNTY COUNCIL v. P. [1995] 2 W.L.R. 543, Ward J.

3517. Guardian *ad litem*—Official Solicitor as guardian—explanatory leaflets

The Lord Chancellor's Department has published three leaflets explaining the work of the Official Solicitor. *The Official Solicitor and Me*, aimed at children under 10, explains why the Official Solicitor has become involved in the court proceedings. *What it Means to Have the Official Solicitor Acting as Your Guardian "ad litem"*, for older childrem, explains various legal terms, how the Official Solicitor will help and the procedures that will be followed. *The Official Solicitor as Guardian "ad litem" of Your Child* is for parents, relatives and other adults, such as foster-parents and teachers, who are involved in court proceedings concerning the future of a child. Copies of the leaflets are available from the Head of Administration, Official Solicitor's Office, telephone 0171 911 7151.

3518. Guardian *ad litem*—report

The Department of Health has issued a press release entitled *SSI Report on Guardian ad Litem Service Published* (95/425), published on September 1, 1995. The findings of the report confirm that work is achieved within set time-scales by competent and skilled guardians *ad litem*. Appraisals had proved effective and panels were competently managed. Areas needing further work were highlighted as use of research evidence and expert witnesses in the court setting, work planning, ensuring consistency in the writing of court reports and retention and storage of records relevant to a guardian *ad litem* enquiry.

3519. Hours of employment—press release. See EMPLOYMENT, §2009.

3520. Housing—local authority accommodation—child with special needs—offers of accommodation rejected by carers—whether local authority in breach of housing duties—whether judicial review to be granted where other remedies available. See R. v. BRENT LONDON BOROUGH COUNCIL, *ex p.* S., §68.

3521. Housing—unborn child—unintentionally homeless person—whether a "person who might be reasonably expected to reside" with homeless person. See R. v. NEWHAM LONDON BOROUGH COUNCIL, *ex p.* DADA, §2580.

3522. Interview—of child victim—child in care—father charged with rape—whether child's welfare the overriding consideration. See M. (MINORS: INTERVIEW), *Re*, §1142.

3523. Jurisdiction—forum—citizens of U.S.—parents divorced in U.S. court—mother obtained *ex parte* orders for interim residence and prohibited steps in England—father made applications in U.S.—whether proceedings should take place in England or U.S.

The parents were U.S. citizens and were married in 1984. C was born in Texas in 1988. In 1990 the family were posted to England with the U.S. Air Force. They separated and C and F returned to America. By a marital settlement agreement they made detailed arrangements for shared physical custody of C. Whilst C was in her care in England, M obtained *ex parte* an interim residence order and a prohibited steps' order preventing F from removing C from the jurisdiction. The orders were served on F but M took no further steps. F took proceedings in the U.S. The High Court restored M's applications of its own motion and the issue was where the C's future should be decided.

Held, staying M's application for residence and discharging the prohibited steps' order, that the reality of the situation was that this was an American family, whose affairs had been dealt with in America and were only in England as a result of the posting with the Air Force. Both M and F would encounter similar obstacles of inconvenience and expense in conducting the litigation in America and England respectively.

M. v. B. (CHILD: JURISDICTION) [1994] 2 F.C.R. 899, Thorpe J.

3524. Jurisdiction—forum—custody proceedings commenced in Scottish court—mother removing child from father's care and moving to England—whether Scottish or English courts appropriate forum to decide future upbringing of child and welfare of child

[Family Law Act 1986 (c.55), s.15(1).]

An interim residence order was no different in principle from a residence order.

The parents were of Scottish origin. After their separation the child remained with the mother and had contact with the father. In 1992 the father assumed care for the child and issued custody proceedings in Scotland. The mother removed the child to England without the father's consent. He obtained an *ex parte* residence order, which could not be enforced because the mother's whereabouts were unknown. The mother obtained an *ex parte* interim residence order in England. The father registered the Scottish order in England and sought its enforcement and a declaration that the English High Court should decline jurisdiction in favour of the Scottish court. The mother sought a stay of the Scottish order.

Held, dismissing the father's applications, that an interim residence order was no different in principle from a residence order. Therefore the existing Scottish order ceased to have effect because it made provision for any matter for which the same or different provision is made by the order of the other court in the U.K. under the Family Law Act 1986, s.15(1) (*T. v. T. (Custody: Jurisdiction*) [1992] C.L.Y. 3088 referred to.)

S. v. S. (CUSTODY: JURISDICTION) [1995] 1 F.L.R. 155, Bracewell J.

3525. Maintenance—periodical payments—appeal from decision of justices—practice—methods of appeal

[Domestic Proceedings and Magistrates' Courts Act 1978 (c.22), ss.20, 29; Magistrates' Courts Act 1980 (c.43), ss.95, 111; Children Act 1989 (c.41), s.94; Family Proceedings Rules 1991 (S.I. 1991 No. 1247), rr.4.22, 8.2.]

An appeal brought under s.94 of the Children Act 1989 against orders made in proceedings under the Domestic Proceedings and Magistrates' Courts Act 1978 will be dismissed for want of jurisdiction.

F was liable to pay child maintenance under orders made under the Domestic Proceedings and Magistrates' Courts Act 1978. In 1993, F made an application under s.20 of the 1978 Act for a downward variation of the order. In 1994 F was summoned to appear before the justices in respect of arrears that had accrued. The justices refused to remit the arrears, made a suspended warrant of committal to prison in respect of the arrears and refused F's application for a variation. F sought to appeal against the orders under s.94 of the Children Act 1989.

Held, dismissing the appeal, that (1) the only method of challenging the justices' refusal to remit arrears under s.95 of the Magistrates' Courts Act 1980 was by way of case stated under s.111 of the 1980 Act (*Berry v. Berry* [1986] C.L.Y. 2094 applied); (2) F was out of time for stating a case and there was no method of extending time; (3) there was no right of appeal under the Magistrates' Courts Act 1980 against a committal or suspended committal to prison; (4) the maintenance order was not made under the Children Act 1989 and there were no proceedings at first instance under the 1989 Act. The power to remit arrears on appeal under s.94(8) therefore did not apply, and thus the court had no power to entertain the appeal in respect of the refusal to remit the arrears; (5) as for the refusal to vary the order, there was a route of appeal under s.29(1) of the Domestic Proceedings and Magistrates' Courts Act 1978. Again, the order was not made under the Children Act 1989, nor was the application to vary made under the 1989. The route of appeal under s.94 of the 1989 Act was therefore not available in respect of the refusal to vary the order. There was no jurisdiction to entertain the appeal against any of the orders, and the appeal would be dismissed (*S. v. S. (Children: Financial Provision)* [1994] C.L.Y. 3241 distinguished).

P. v. P. (PERIODICAL PAYMENTS: APPEALS) [1995] 1 FLR 563, Bracewell J.

3526. Maintenance order—appeal against lump sum order—evidence on which order based not known at appeal—whether justices must specify evidence used in making order—appeals procedure—whether variation of maintenance order more expeditious

[Children Act 1989 (c.41), Sched. 1.]

The putative father appealed against dismissal of his appeal from a lump sum order of £1,000 made in the Family Proceedings Court in respect of his son. He claimed that there was no finding by the appeal judge as to exactly which documents the magistrates had before them. By omitting to make this finding the appeal judge was unable to establish whether there was sufficient information to entitle the magistrates to make the order without granting an adjournment. He further submitted that the appeal judge had tacitly acknowledged that there were matters which the magistrates needed to investigate further.

Held, allowing the appeal and remitting the matter to the magistrates, that (1) if the question of which documents were before the magistrates was incapable of being resolved, then remission was clearly required; (2) by one means or another the father's true financial position had to be known to achieve fairness.

[*Per curiam*: (1) It was a pity that there was no provision, in the standard form of reasons to be stated by magistrates, for them to set out the documentary material on which they had relied, so that a subsequent court could ascertain the material on which an order was based; (2) the Children Act 1989 contained wide provisions for the making of maintenance orders in respect of children of unmarried parents. In particular there were wide powers of variation contained in Scheds. 1(4)(5) and 6. Although in this case an appeal was inevitable, in the general run of cases it would be advisable to consider whether a variation application would be a better option.]

D. (A MINOR), *Re* (LTA 94/6672/F), April 6, 1995, C.A.

3527. Maintenance order—arrears—justices deciding not to remit arrears—whether discretion exercised correctly—whether arrears should be remitted

In considering whether to enforce arrears of maintenance, the starting point was that arrears over one year old are not enforced unless there were special circumstances.

M and F had two children. Following their separation, M obtained an order that F pay child maintenance; however, F soon lost his job and, although there were times when he had work and could have paid child maintenance, arrears began to accrue. M issued proceedings to enforce the maintenance order. When the justices heard the application the arrears were then £4,100 and F was at that stage unemployed. F was ordered to pay off the arrears at the rate of £10 per week, on top of the existing order. The justices stated that they had exercised their discretion not to remit the arrears outstanding.

Held, allowing F's appeal, that (1) the starting point was that arrears over one year old were not enforced unless there were special circumstances; (2) the justices appeared to have fallen into error in considering they had a discretion to remit the arrears rather than discretion to enforce them (*Russell v. Russell* [1986] C.L.Y. 1095 applied); and (3) the court would therefore exercise its own discretion. Whatever might be said as to F's fault in allowing the arrears to accrue, an order to pay off the arrears in instalments could only be properly made if there was evidence that F could now properly pay that amount. There was no such evidence, and so the arrears would be remitted, and the order to pay £10 per week towards the arrears would be discharged.

B. v. C. (ENFORCEMENT: ARREARS) [1995] 1 FLR 467, Johnson J.

3528. Non-molestation injunction—*ex parte* injunctive relief obtained against minor with no means—whether injunction should be renewed *inter partes* against minor defendant—circumstances in which relief should be granted

P had been granted an *ex parte* non-molestation injunction and order restraining D, a 16-year-old girl from entering, visiting, approaching or loitering within 200 yards of his address. The orders were served on the girl at her grandmother's address.

Held, discharging the injunction, that the orders were unenforceable, since D was too young to be sent to prison, was unemployed, had no means and no guardian *ad litem* had been appointed. A minor defendant should be protected by a guardian *ad litem* because an injunction was the most immediate and gravest from of relief available from the county court.

P. (A MINOR) (INJUNCTION), *Re* [1994] Fam.Law 131, H.H.J. Harris

3529. Ouster order—whether order could be made where no application is made. See M. (MINORS) (DISCLOSURE OF EVIDENCE), *Re*, §3562.

3530. Parental responsibility—applications for—whether relevant to consider status to be conferred

[Children Act 1989 (c.41), s.4.]

It was important to remember, in applications for parental responsibility orders under s.4 of the Children Act 1989, that such orders conferred status on a father which involved more than the mere giving of powers and duties.

S. (A MINOR) (PARENTAL RESPONSIBILITY), *Re*, *The Times*, February 22, 1995, C.A.

3531. Parental responsibility—contact—order made in favour of father—whether court should grant order where acrimony between parents

[Family Law Reform Act 1987 (c. 42), s.4(1); Children Act 1989 (c.41), ss.1(5), 2(8), 4(1)(a), 13(1), 94.]

The fear that a parental responsibility order would be used by the father to interfere in the mother's day-to-day care of the child was a misunderstanding as to the nature of such an order and was no reason to deny the father a parental responsibility order.

M and F had never married and had a five-year-old daughter. Their short period of cohabitation had ended acrimoniously but F had obtained orders for extensive contact. At one stage, M was working and F looked after the child for over half the week. When this arrangement was stopped, acrimony reappeared and F applied to the magistrates for residence, contact and parental responsibility orders. His application for a residence order was dismissed but an order was made providing for staying contact on alternate weekends and for further contact during school holidays. F appealed against the refusal to make a parental responsibility order.

Held, allowing the appeal, that the magistrates had been wrong to refuse an order on the basis that the acrimony would lead to F questioning aspects of the child's upbringing unnecessarily. A parental responsibility order gave F no right to interfere in the day-to-day care of the child or to override the mother. F had shown great love and concern for the child, had looked after her extensively at one stage in the past, and would play a major role in her life with the benefit of the contact order; the magistrates were plainly wrong to place so much weight on the spectre of F's misuse of the proposed order at the expense of his substantial role in the child's life. It was overwhelmingly in the child's best interests for a parental responsibility order to be made (*H.*

(Minors) (Local Authority: Parental Rights) (No. 3), Re [1991] C.L.Y. 2500 applied; *C. (Minors) (Parental Rights), Re* [1992] C.L.Y. 3113, *H. (A Minor) (Parental Responsibility), Re* [1993] C.L.Y. 2832 considered).

P. (A MINOR) (PARENTAL RESPONSIBILITY ORDER), *Re* [1994] 1 F.L.R. 578, Wilson J.

3532. Parental responsibility—contact—principles to be applied on application for parental responsibility order—blood tests—father seeking direction for blood tests to determine paternity of younger child—no application before court relating to younger child—whether jurisdiction to direct use of blood tests

[Family Law Reform Act 1969 (c.46), ss.20, 21; Children Act 1989 (c.41), ss.1(1)(5), 4, 13(1).]

Where a father had shown a sufficient degree of attachment and commitment to his child, it was prima facie in the interests of the child that a parental responsibility order be made. There was no jurisdiction to make a free-standing direction for the use of blood tests.

M and F started a relationship in 1985 but neither married nor cohabited. C was born in 1987, and F had had regular contact with her since birth. At the time of the application F had visiting contact every other weekend. There was another child, a boy, H, born in 1990, whose paternity was unclear: his father might have been F or another man with whom M had had a relationship. F had had no contact with H since H's birth. F applied for staying contact with C, a parental responsibility order in respect of C and an order adding C's name to his passport. M opposed these applications and sought a reduction in contact, and a prohibited steps order preventing F from taking C out of the jurisdiction. F also sought a direction for blood tests to determine H's paternity. The judge ordered a reduction of contact and refused staying contact. The judge made no order on the passport application, but granted the prohibited steps order sought by M. He refused to make a parental responsibility order or a direction for blood tests. F appealed against all the orders made or refused, and sought to adduce fresh evidence.

Held, allowing the appeal in part, that (1) leave to adduce fresh evidence would be refused, as it was all material which could have been adduced in the court below (*Ladd v. Marshall* [1954] C.L.Y. 2507 applied); (2) although the judge had departed from the welfare officer's recommendations on contact, he had given his reasons for so doing, and there was no basis on which the court could say that the order reducing contact and refusing staying contact was plainly wrong (*G. v. G. (Minors: Custody Appeal)* [1985] C.L.Y. 2594); (3) the judge was plainly entitled, having regard to s.1(5) of the Children Act 1989, to make no order on the application relating to the passport. However, he should have reached the same conclusion on the application for a prohibited steps order, as there was insufficient evidence to justify such an order; (4) where a father had shown the degree of attachment and commitment to his child that F had shown to C through regular contact and financial support, it was prima facie in the child's interests that a parental responsibility order be made. There was nothing to indicate to the contrary, and the order would be made (*H. (Minors) (Local Authority: Parental Rights (No. 3)), Re* [1991] C.L.Y. 2500, *C. (Minors) (Parental Rights), Re* [1992] C.L.Y. 3113, *H. (A Minor) (Parental Responsibility), Re* [1993] C.L.Y. 2832 considered); and (5) a direction for the use of blood tests to determine paternity could only be made in civil proceedings in which paternity fell to be determined. F had made no application in relation to H: there were no such civil proceedings before the court. There was no power to make a free-standing direction for the use of blood tests, and the judge had been right to refuse to make the direction.

[*Per curiam*: (1) In any event, had there beem jurisdiction to make a direction for the use of blood tests, the direction should be refused as M did not consent to the taking of a sample from H (*S. v. McC; W. v. W.* [1970] C.L.Y. 762, *F. (A Minor) (Blood Tests: Paternity Rights), Re* [1993] C.L.Y. 2857 considered); (2) the court would assume that the grant or refusal of a parental responsibility order was governed by the paramountcy principle in s.1(1) of the Children Act 1989.]

E. (PARENTAL RESPONSIBILITY: BLOOD TESTS), *Re* [1995] 1 F.L.R. 392, C.A.

3533. Parental responsibility—criteria to be considered when making order

[Children Act 1989 (c.41), ss.1–3, 4(1), 33(3)(5), 91(14).]

A father's lack of insight into his child's needs, his awkwardness and his inability to get on with social workers responsible for the child were no reasons in themselves for denying the father a parental responsibility order under s.4 of the Children Act 1989.

M and F were unmarried and had a six-year-old daughter. F had regular contact with the child, who was in care. M had had problems with alcohol and drugs. The judge ordered that the child remain in care, that contact between her and F be at the local authority's discretion, but refused to grant F a parental responsibility order.

Held, allowing F's appeal, that (1) where a father had shown a degree of commitment to the child, where there was a degree of attachment between father and child and where the father's reasons for applying for an order were not demonstrably wrong or improper, prima facie it would be in the interests of the child to make a parental responsibility order, though the above criteria were not exhaustive (*H. (Minors) (Local Authority: Parental Rights) (No. 3), Re* [1991] C.L.Y. 2500 applied; *D. v. Hereford and Worcester County Council* [1991] C.L.Y. 2508 considered); (2) even assuming that F had shown a lack of insight into his child's needs, that he was awkward, difficult and unable to get on with the social workers, this would not be a reason in itself to refuse a parental responsibility order; and (3) as it was clearly in the child's interests for F to be given a proper part to play in her life and to acquire *locus standi*, a parental responsibility order would be made.

G. (A MINOR) (PARENTAL RESPONSIBILITY ORDER), *Re* [1994] 1 F.L.R. 504, C.A.

3534. Paternity—blood test—consent—whether court should give direction where mother was unlikely to comply

[Family Law Reform Act 1969 (c.46), s.20, 21; Children Act 1989 (c.41), s.4.]

A court has power to direct the use of blood tests for determining paternity notwithstanding that the mother of the child indicates that she does not intend to comply with the direction.

H and W married in 1992, but W soon left H for a new partner. S was conceived within the disputed period of time and was now five months old. Both H and W's new partner believed themselves to be S's father. H applied for contact with S. W disputed whether S was H's child. H applied for a direction for the use of blood tests to determine S's paternity. W indicated that she did not intend to consent on S's behalf for a blood sample to be taken.

Held, granting the application, that (1) the scheme of the Family Law Reform Act 1969 envisaged that a direction for the use of blood tests may be given with which a party might not comply and such non-compliance would not be unlawful. Consequently M's announced prospective non-compliance was no bar to the court making a direction, although it was a factor to be weighed in the court's discretion; (2) in principle, in the absence of cogent reasons to the contrary, it was better to resolve doubt rather than uphold it. H had parental responsibility, and it was not in S's long-term interests for the allocation of parental responsibility to remain unresolved; and (3) S's long-term interests were best served by her knowing the truth but also by the adults founding their lives together on a fact rather than a wish. Accordingly, the discretion would be exercised to direct the use of blood tests (*S. (An Infant) v. S.; W. v. Official Solicitor* [1970] C.L.Y. 762 applied; *F. (A Minor) (Blood Tests: Paternity*

Rights), Re [1993] C.L.Y. 2857, *R. (A Minor) (Contact), Re* [1994] 10 C.L. 335 distinguished).

G. (A MINOR) (BLOOD TEST), *Re* [1994] 1 F.L.R. 495, M. Horowitz, Q.C.

3535. Paternity—blood test—contact sought by possible father—mother adamantly refusing to allow child to be tested—whether direction for blood tests should be made

[Family Law Reform Act 1969 (c.46), ss.20, 21, 23; Family Law Reform Act 1987 (c.42), s.23.]

The court should decline to exercise its discretion to make a direction for the use of blood tests under s.20 of the Family Law Reform Act 1969 where the mother was adamant that she would not comply with any direction given by the court.

C was aged 22 months at the time of the hearing. B, C's mother, had had a sexual relationship with both F, and her husband, at the time of C's conception. B induced each man to believe that he was C's father. When C was aged 10 months, B stopped F seeing the child, and so F applied for a contact order and a parental responsibility order. There was great hostility between the parties, and B was adamant that she would not comply with any direction for blood tests and that she would never allow F to have contact. F applied for a direction for the use of blood tests to determine C's paternity.

Held, dismissing the application, that (1) where the court made a direction for blood tests under s.20 of the Family Law Reform Act 1969, s.21 provided that if a party refused to undergo a test, or if a person having care and control of the child refused to allow a sample of the child's blood to be taken, the refusal was not a contempt and the sample could not be taken. The section reinforced the rights of individuals not to undergo medical testing or treatment without their consent (*T. (Consent to Medical Treatment) (Adult Patient), Re* [1992] C.L.Y. 2918, *C. (Adult: Refusal of Treatment), Re* [1994] 7 C.L. 288, *O. (A Minor) (Medical Treatment), Re* [1993] C.L.Y. 2853, *R. (A Minor) (Blood Transfusion), Re* [1994] 1 C.L. 274 considered); (2) the power to direct a blood test under s.20 was discretionary. In general, the court ought to permit a blood test of a young child to be taken, unless satisfied that it would be against the child's interests (*S. v. McC.; W. v. W.* [1970] C.L.Y. 762 applied); (3) however, the mother's adamant refusal to permit the child to undergo a blood test was determinative: the court should not exercise its discretion to direct a blood test in the face of such a refusal (*S. v. McC.; W. v. W.* [1970] C.L.Y. 762, *F. (A Minor) (Blood Tests: Paternity Rights), Re* [1993] C.L.Y. 2857 considered; *G. (A Minor) (Blood Test), Re* [1994] 1 F.L.R. 495 distinguished); (4) where a direction was made, and a party failed to comply with the direction, the power to draw adverse inferences against that party, in determining the question of paternity, was at large (*A. (A Minor) (Paternity: Refusal of Blood Test), Re* [1994] 2 F.L.R. 463 applied); (5) even where a party had been adamant that she would not comply with any direction for blood tests, and the court had refused to make a direction on that basis, it was still open to the other party to argue on the substantive applications that an adverse inference should be drawn on account of the refusal; and (6) if (3) above were incorrect, it was necessary to consider the other factors. F was unlikely to succeed in his application for contact, though this was less certain in the case of his application for a parental responsibility order. Balancing all the factors, the court would decline to direct blood tests in its discretion (*H. (A Minor) (Parental Responsibility), Re* [1993] C.L.Y. 2832 considered).

C.B. (A MINOR) (BLOOD TESTS), *Re* [1994] 2 F.L.R. 762, Wall J.

3536. Paternity—blood test—evidence—mother having sexual intercourse with three men at time of conception—proceedings against just one man—refusal to undergo blood tests—whether inference of paternity could be drawn in light of refusal to test

M gave birth to a child in April 1989. She commenced proceedings in the county court to establish that R, one of three men with whom she had been having sexual intercourse at the time of conception, was the father. R denied paternity and contended that it would be unjust to single him out from the other men as the putative father when it was not proposed to subject them to the same risk. The judge found that R knew that he could be the father, which was why he refused the blood test, but could not draw the inference from the refusal to submit to testing that he was the father of the child.

Held, allowing M's appeal, that genetic testing could now establish certainty as to paternity and any man who doubted whether he was the father could put his mind at rest by submitting to a test. Against the background of scientific advance, if a father refused to submit to a test to establish paternity, the inference that he was the father was inescapable in the absence of very clear and cogent reasons why he should not be tested. R had no such excuse and the inference had to be drawn that he was the father.

G.W. (A MINOR) (BLOOD TESTS), *Re* [1994] 2 F.C.R. 908, C.A.

3537. Paternity—blood test—husband and grandmother applying for blood tests—whether discretion should be exercised to carry out tests despite wife's non-consent

[Family Law Reform Act 1969 (c.46), ss.20, 21.]

H and W married in August 1992. There was a dispute as to the date of separation, W contending that it took place in early September, whilst H argued that the date was in November 1992. W gave birth to a child in April 1993 and declared that her new partner was its father. F and his mother applied for directions under the Family Law Reform Act 1969, s.20, for blood tests to resolve the question of paternity.

Held, that the discretion to order blood tests would be exercised in favour of the father and the grandmother, even though W indicated that she would not consent to the taking of blood samples. H would have parental responsibility for the child by operation of the presumption of legitimacy and it was not beneficial for the child in the long term for the issue of parental responsibility to remain unresolved and to reassert itself at a time when it might cause greater distress to those involved. M's lack of consent was not conclusive and merely a factor to be borne in mind (*W. v. W.* [1972] A.C. 24, *F. (A Minor) (Blood Tests: Paternity Rights), Re* [1993] C.L.Y. 2857 applied).

C.G. (A MINOR) (BLOOD TESTS), *Re* [1994] 2 F.C.R. 889, Michael Horowitz, Q.C. sitting as a deputy judge.

3538. Paternity—maintenance—respondent denying paternity—respondent not present nor represented at hearing—putative father applying for judicial review—whether court should grant judicial review

[Children Act 1989 (c.41), s.94.]

It is only in exceptional circumstances that the court will exercise its discretion to grant judicial review of a decision of the justices where an appeal against the decision lies under s.94 of the Children Act 1989.

M gave birth to twins and applied to the justices for child maintenance against B, whose solicitors filed an answer denying that he was the father. B went to work in Greece for some months, and his solicitors wrote to the court and to M's solicitors seeking an adjournment for the purpose of DNA tests to be carried out. B had made an application for legal aid for such tests, which had not yet been granted or denied. The justices, despite opposition from M's solicitors, adjourned the case for two weeks. B's solicitors wrote to the court and informed them that B was willing to return to the U.K. for the purpose of the DNA tests, but that legal aid for the tests had still not been granted. It was implicit that B sought an adjournment. The justices decided to hear the application and ordered B to pay £25 per week. B sought judicial review of the justices' decision.

Held, dismissing B's application, that (1) the fact that B had a right of appeal under s.94(1) of the Children Act 1989 and had not pursued that alternative remedy could not of itself be sufficient to oust the jurisdiction of the court to exercise its discretion as to whether judicial relief should be granted (*R. v. I.R.C., ex p. Preston* [1985] C.L.Y. 1782, *R. v. Deputy Governor of Parkhurst Prison, ex p. Leech; R. v. Deputy Governor of Long Lartin Prison, ex p. Prevot* [1988] C.L.Y. 2976 considered); (2) only in exceptional circumstances should the court exercise its discretion to grant judicial review where an adequate alternative remedy existed. There was nothing exceptional on the facts to justify B's failure to use the s.94 appeal route. That alone was sufficient to dismiss the application (*R. v. Bradford Justices, ex p. Wilkinson* [1990] C.L.Y. 1007 considered); and (3) had it been necessary for the court to decide on the merits, given M's production of a letter from B in which he had (at an earlier date) accepted paternity, the court could not say that no reasonable bench would have refused an adjournment.

R. v. HIGH PEAK MAGISTRATES' COURT, *ex p.* B. [1995] 1 FLR 568, Cazalet J.

3539. Periodical payments orders—made under repealed Act—whether possible now to vary or discharge orders

[Guardianship of Minors Act 1971 (c.3), s.11B; Interpretation Act 1978 (c.30), s.16; Children Act 1989 (c.41), s.94, Scheds. 1, 14.]

Orders made under the Guardianship of Minors Act 1971 continue in force notwithstanding the repeal of the 1971 Act, and the court retains power to vary orders made under the 1971 Act.

Justices made an order under s.11B of the Guardianship of Minors Act 1971 for F to pay to M £10 per week for each of their three children. In 1991, the whole of the 1971 Act was repealed by the Children Act 1989. In 1992, the justices made a consent order varying the maintenance order. F's application for further variation was dismissed and he was ordered to pay accrued arrears. F wished to appeal, and on counsel's advice, notice of appeal was issued purportedly under s.94 of the Children Act 1989. After counsel expressed concern as to whether this was the correct method of appeal, the effect of the 1971 Act's repeal and the absence of any specific transitional provisions in the Children Act 1989 allowing variation of orders made under the now repealed 1971 Act, a second appeal by way of notice of motion was filed. M did not oppose the appeal.

Held, allowing the appeal, that (1) orders made under the Guardianship of Minors Act 1971 continued in force despite the Act's repeal, and the ability to apply for variation and revocation was also preserved, by virtue of s.16(1) of the Interpretation Act 1978 (*Debtor, A (No. 490 of 1935), Re* [1936] Ch. 237, *Aitken v. South Hams District Council* [1994] C.L.Y. 3408 applied); (2) the correct method of appeal was by way of notice of motion, and not under s.94 of the Children Act 1989.

B. v. B. (PERIODICAL PAYMENTS: TRANSITIONAL PROVISIONS) [1995] 1 FLR 459, Douglas Brown J.

3540. Prohibited steps order—education—father having custody of child—father arranging for child to attend boarding school offering special form of care—father not informing mother—mother applying *ex parte* for prohibited steps order to prevent child being sent to the school—application refused—whether Court of Appeal should interfere with judge's decision

The Court of Appeal should only interfere with a judge's decision if it was so clearly wrong that it should overturn the decision.

The parties divorced in 1987. F was granted custody of the two children, a boy aged nine and a girl aged six in divorce proceedings. The boy suffered learning difficulties at school and became very troublesome. F arranged for the child to attend a boarding school offering special care. F did not inform M. M applied *ex parte* for a prohibited steps order to prevent F sending the child to the school. The judge refused the application. M appealed. The judge indicated that the issue could be heard *inter partes* 10 days later. M indicated that she would apply for an interim residence order for both children at the hearing and this would be prejudiced if the child started attending the boarding school.

Held, dismissing M's appeal, that the Court of Appeal should only interfere with the judge's decision if it was so clearly wrong that it should overturn the decision. M should have been consulted as she had parental responsibility. The refusal of M's application would have a major effect on her application for an interim residence order. But the judge had to regard the child's welfare as the major consideration and there was no material to suggest that F had not looked after them perfectly well. There was a strong argument that the judge made the right, or at least the least wrong, order.

G. (PARENTAL RESPONSIBILITY: EDUCATION), *Re* [1995] 2 F.C.R. 53, C.A.

3541. Prohibited steps order—sexual abuse—by mother's partner—supervision orders with conditions made in respect of mother's other children and care order in respect of abused child—whether jurisdiction to make prohibited steps order against mother—whether jurisdiction to make prohibited steps order against non-party—whether conditions to be attached to supervision order

[Children Act 1989 (c.41), ss.8, 9(5)(a).]

A prohibited steps order against a person who is not a party to care proceedings, requiring him not to have or to seek contact with the child concerned, will not contravene s.9(5) of the Children Act 1989.

The youngest of six children, S, was found to have been sexually abused by J, the mother's then partner. In proceedings brought by the local authority, a care order was made in respect of S, supervision orders for the other children were made subject to the condition that there should be no contact between any of the children and J, and a prohibited steps order under s.8 of the 1989 Act was made against the mother to prevent contact between J and the children. The judge held, however, that he had no jurisdiction to make a prohibited steps order against J because he was not a party to the family proceedings.

Held, allowing the guardian *ad litem*'s appeal, that (1) since a prohibited steps order against the mother had the same result as a contact order requiring her not to allow contact with J, it contravened s.9(5)(a) of the 1989 Act; (2) there was no power under the 1989 Act to attach conditions to a supervision order and accordingly, the judge had no power to make either order; (3) a prohibited steps order against J which required him not to have or to seek contact with the children would not contravene s.9(5); and (4) where the court made an order under s.8 of the 1989 Act against a person who was not a party to the proceedings, it would normally give leave under that section or under s.11(7)(d) to apply to vary or discharge it (*Nottinghamshire County Council v. P.* [1993] C.L.Y. 2860 considered).

H. (MINORS) (PROHIBITED STEPS ORDER), *Re* [1995] 1 W.L.R. 667, C.A.

3542. Prohibited steps order—sexual abuse by father—ouster—whether local authority could apply for exclusion order under inherent jurisdiction of court

[Children Act 1989 (c.41), ss.31, 34, 38, 100.]

A local authority is able to invoke the inherent jurisdiction of the High Court with respect to children to obtain an order excluding from the family home a father who presents a risk to the children.

M and F had four children, aged six to 13. The children had a half-sister S, aged 16, who left home and made allegations of sexual abuse against F. The family proceedings court found that S had been abused over a prolonged period by F and that the four younger children were at risk of significant harm. The court made supervision orders and a prohibited steps order that F should have no contact with the children save as permitted and supervised by the local authority. Following the Court of Appeal's doubt in another case as to whether a prohibited steps order could be used to oust a father from the home, the local authority applied for care orders and for orders under s.34(4) of the Children Act 1989 granting leave to refuse contact between F and the children. The local authority later discovered that F had been living in the family home since the original supervision orders had been made and it applied for an order excluding F from the family home under the inherent jurisdiction of the High Court.

Held, granting the application, that (1) the inherent jurisdiction of the High Court with respect to children could only be invoked by a local authority if there was no other route open under the Children Act 1989; (2) an interim care order, which would allow the children's removal from the home should M not co-operate and allow the children contact with F, was not in the best interests of the children; (3) s.34 of the Act was designed to promote reasonable contact between a child in care and his parents. It was not appropriate for use as a method of obtaining an ouster order against a father in circumstances such as these (*Nottinghamshire County Council v. P.* [1993] C.L.Y. 2860 distinguished); and (4) since there was no other route open to the local authority, and the other criteria laid down in s.100 were satisfied, an order excluding F from the family home would be made under the inherent jurisdiction of the High Court with respect to children.

S. (MINORS) (INHERENT JURISDICTION: OUSTER), *Re* [1994] 1 F.L.R. 623, Connell J.

3543. Prohibited steps order—surname—unmarried parents—informal adoption of step-father's name—father prohibited steps order to prevent use seeking—whether to be granted

After a relationship of about seven years, the parties, who never married, separated, having had two children. The children's birth certificates recorded their surname as that of the father, G. In 1990, when the children were aged four and six, they informally adopted the mother's boyfriend's surname, A, and in the same year their mother had the first of her children by A. The mother and her boyfriend subsequently married in 1992. The surname of the two older children was not changed by deed poll. On all official documents, such as their passports, medical and dental records, the children were known as G. At school the children were known as A. At their father's house, they used the name G. The father had also subsequently married and had other children. There was no parental responsibility order in favour of the father, although he had had contact over the years with the children, and had applied in 1992, *inter alia*, for parental responsibility. The mother had persistently objected to the father having parental responsibility. The father asked for a prohibited steps order to prevent the mother changing the children's surname and a specific issue order concerning what name the children were to use. The mother challenged the court's jurisdiction to make any such orders at all. There were other matters concerning contact also in dispute.

Held, that a parental responsibility order would be made in the father's favour. The court had jurisdiction to make the order requested by the father, and in any event this case was not one where there had been any formal change of surname, only an informal change in daily use. The approach to be adopted was to have regard to the welfare of the children, and in doing so, account had to be taken of the use of the name A at school, and the significance that might be given to the change of the name from that of the father, to that of the step-father. The surname was important, as it indicated a contact and relationship with the father. The court welfare officer noted that school records for the children recorded their names officially as either G(A) or A(G), and that the children did not appear to be overly bothered which surname was used, but had indicated there might be some embarrassment at school were they to change their name from A to G. She recommended that it might be less confusing for the children if their names were hyphenated. The judge ordered that the mother was prohibited from affecting a change in the children's surname, and it was ordered that the children should be known as and use the name G-A (hyphenated) henceforth (*T. (Otherwise H.) (An Infant), Re* [1962] C.L.Y. 1945, *D. v. B. (Surname: Birth Registration)* [1978] C.L.Y. 2026, W. v. A. [1980] C.L.Y. 1808 considered; *F. (Child: Surname), Re* [1994] C.L.Y. 3207 applied).

G. v. A., March 24, 1995, Mr Recorder Lowther, Hitchin County Ct. [*Ex rel.* Ruth Blair, Barrister, 2 King's Bench Walk, instructed by Alistair Meldrum & Co., Enfield.]

3544. Reporting restrictions—child's father a paedophile—television programme dealing with detection and arrest—injunction sought by child's mother to restrain broadcast of material identifying father—whether court's jurisdiction could be invoked

The parental jurisdiction of the court can only be used to restrain publication of matters relating to matters affecting the care of the children in question but does not extend to protecting children from publicity not directed at them or those who care for them.

A television company proposed to broadcast a documentary about the detection and arrest of a convicted paedophile who was S's father. S's mother was concerned that the film would identify her and S and sought an order that the film should be broadcast only if the father's face was obscured. The television company had already agreed to edit out all scenes showing S, the mother or the house and road in which they lived. Kirkwood J. granted the injunction.

Held, allowing the television company's appeal, that the television company was entitled to publish the programme in full and no further conditions should have been imposed on the broadcast. The exercise of the court's parental jurisdiction was not appropriate in such cases (*X. (Wardship: Jurisdiction), Re* [1975] C.L.Y. 2203, *M. and N. (Minors), Re* [1990] C.L.Y. 3190 applied; *F. (A Minor) (Publication of Information), Re* [1976] C.L.Y. 1805, *C. (A Minor) (Wardship: Medical Treatment) (No. 2), Re* [1989] C.L.Y. 2497, *W. (A Minor) (Wardship: Restrictions on Publication), Re* [1992] C.L.Y. 3146 considered).

R. v. CENTRAL INDEPENDENT TELEVISION [1994] 3 W.L.R. 20, C.A.

3545. Reporting restrictions—injunction—abduction of ward by father—injunction in wardship proceedings prohibiting report of criminal trial of father—whether ward a "person in respect of whom" criminal proceedings taken

[Children and Young Persons Act 1933 (23 & 24 Geo. 5, c.12), s.39.]

A judge conducting a criminal trial has power under s.39 of the Children and Young Persons Act 1933 to restrain reports of proceedings which involve a ward of the court and it is better for such a judge to consider whether to make such an order than for the order to be made by a judge in wardship proceedings.

F removed the ward from M to whom care and custody had been granted in wardship proceedings. He was arrested and charged with the ward's abduction and committed for trial. An order was made in the wardship proceedings restraining publication of any material relating to the ward. F applied for the order to be lifted so as to allow publication of reports of his trial. The judge concluded that the publicity that would be generated thereby would be detrimental to the ward's welfare and that any order under s.39 of the Children and Young Persons Act 1933 made by the trial judge would not give as much protection as an order made in wardship proceedings. An order was made prohibiting publication of any material relating to the ward.

Held, allowing F's appeal, that the ward was plainly "a person in respect of whom" the criminal proceedings had been taken and that, as a general principle it was better for any restraint of reports of public proceedings to be imposed to the extent necessary to protect the proper administration of justice. Accordingly it was for the trial judge to consider whether it was necessary to restrict reporting of F's trial (*Att.-Gen. v. Leveller Magazine* [1979] C.L.Y. 2120, *Mohamed Arif (An Infant), Re* [1968] C.L.Y. 257 considered).

R. (A MINOR) (WARDSHIP: RESTRICTIONS ON PUBLICATION), *Re* [1994] 3 W.L.R. 36, C.A.

3546. Reporting restrictions—judge's discretion to make order and hear representations from persons with legitimate interest—procedure to be followed when making order restricting reporting

[Children and Young Persons Act 1933 (c.12), s.39(1).]

There is no statutory authority which limits the persons from whom the court is entitled to receive representations when considering the making of an order under s.39 of the Children and Young Persons Act 1993.

At a preliminary hearing in connection with the trial of two defendants charged with the manslaughter of one of their children and cruelty to three others, an order was made under s.39 of the 1933 Act that no report of the trial should include particulars calculated to lead to the identification of the children concerned. The order was renewed at the commencement of the trial despite written and oral representations to the judge made by a court journalist as to the terms and effect of the order. The judge also heard representations in support of the order on behalf of the local authority which had care of the surviving children. There had been initial confusion as to the scope of the original order and the judge made it clear that the terms of his order related specifically to the children who were alive but expressed the view that reporting the names of the defendants and the deceased child was calculated to lead to the identification of the children who were protected by the order. Two journalists appealed under s.159 of the Criminal Justice Act 1988.

Held, dismissing the appeal, that (1) there was no statutory authority which limited the persons from whom the court is entitled to receive representations when considering the making of an order under s.39 of the 1933 Act; (2) the judge had complete discretion to allow representations to be made to him by those parties whom he considered had a legitimate interest; and (3) the judge was required to weigh the public interest in the full reporting of a crime, including the identification of the defendant, against the need to protect the victim from further harm (*R. v. Southwark Crown Court, ex p. Godwin; R. v. Same, ex p. The Daily Telegraph; R. v. Same, ex p. MGN; R. v. Same, ex p. Associated Newspapers; R. v. Same, ex p. Newspaper Publishing; sub nom. Godwin, Re* [1992] C.L.Y. 970 applied; *R v. Central Independent Television* [1994] 1 C.L. 269 considered).

[*Per curiam*: An order under s.39 of the 1933 Act should clearly identify the relevant child or children to which it relates; a written copy of the order should be drawn as soon as possible and made available in the court office.]

CROOK, *Re* [1995] 1 W.L.R. 139, C.A.

3547. Residence—appeal—test to be applied by appellate court

An appellate court should not interfere with the decision of the court below unless it was plainly wrong.

M and F married in July 1988 and had three daughters, aged five, four, and 16 months respectively. The family lived in North Wales but in March 1994 M left with the children to go and live in Kent. The court welfare officer stated that M had not appreciated the possibly devastating effect of the move to Kent for the children. In the welfare officer's view, F would put the children's needs first, whereas M gave great importance to a new relationship with a new man. The welfare officer recommended that there be a residence order to F in respect of all three children. The judge found the case to be a difficult one but made an order in line with the welfare officer's recommendations.

Held, dismissing M's appeal, that an appellate court should not interfere with the decision of the court below unless it was plainly wrong. The judge had taken into account all the relevant factors, and although the decision might have gone either way, the judge's approach could not be faulted.

D. (MINORS) APPEAL), *Re* [1995] 1 F.C.R. 301, C.A.

3548. Residence—application by child—whether court should grant leave to apply for residence order

[Children Act 1989 (c.41), ss.1, 8, 10(8)(9), 12(2), 23(6)(b), 39, 41(6); Family Proceedings Rules 1991 (S.I. 1991 No. 1247), r.4.3.]

Even where the child applying for leave to apply for a residence order had sufficient understanding to make the application, the court still had a discretion whether or not to grant leave.

S was aged 14, currently living in a children's home, having been in care for eight years. S wished to live with a long-standing friend, Mrs B, who supported S's application for a residence order. The previous year Mrs B had been rejected as a foster carer by the local authority, who were now reassessing her suitability. The authority took a neutral stance, but M opposed the application for leave.

Held, granting leave to S to apply for a residence order, that (1) even where the child had sufficient understanding to make the application for a s.8 order, the court still had a discretion whether or not to grant leave. In determining the leave application, no issue arose as to the child's upbringing, and the child's welfare was not the paramount consideration. The checklist of matters in s.10(9) applied only where the applicant for leave was not the child concerned (*A. and W. (Minors) (Residence Order: Leave to Apply), Re* [1992] C.L.Y. 3123 considered); (2) while the rules permitted an application for leave to be made *ex parte*, where the applicant was the child the application should be on notice to all those with parental responsibility; (3) the court should have regard to the prospects of success of the substantive application and should not grant leave where the substantive application was doomed to fail (*F. v. S. (Adoption: Ward)* [1973] C.L.Y. 2163 considered); (4) although a residence order could not be made in favour of the child herself, the Children Act 1989 gave the child the ability to seek any s.8 order, and it would be wrong to require the applicant to be the person in whose favour the proposed residence order was to be made. The court would take into account the fact that Mrs B would be unlikely to succeed if she applied for leave to apply for a residence order; (5) whilst the fact that the local authority was bound under s.23(6)(b) to consider Mrs B as a potential carer for S was a relevant matter for the court to take into account in deciding whether to grant leave, it was no bar to the grant of leave; and (6) it would be wrong to require S to apply for the discharge of the care order under s.39(1).

S.C. (A MINOR) (LEAVE TO SEEK RESIDENCE ORDER), *Re* [1994] 1 FLR 96, Booth J.

3549. Residence—application by child—whether court should grant leave to apply for section 8 order

[Children Act 1989 (c.41), ss.1, 8, 10.]

The court would not grant leave to a child to apply for a residence order where there was no question of any order of the court being enforced by physical force, nor would it grant leave to a child to apply for a specific issue order over an unimportant matter such as a short foreign holiday.

C, who was aged nearly 15, fell out with her parents, stayed for the holiday at a friend's house, and refused to return when the holiday ended. C applied for leave to apply for a residence order to allow her to live away from her parents and for a specific issue order that she be allowed to go on a two-week holiday to Bulgaria. C's parents opposed the applications.

Held, refusing leave to apply for a specific issue order and adjourning the application for leave to apply for a residence order generally with liberty to restore, that (1) C had been given statutory rights to seek the intervention of the court under the Children Act 1989, and the court should not seek to impede the exercise of those rights. The child's welfare was the paramount consideration in deciding whether to grant leave; (2) as to leave to apply for a residence order, there was no question of anyone seeking to enforce any order of the court by physical means. Applying the no order principle in s.1(5) of the Children Act 1989, there might be disadvantages in enshrining in a court order a state of affairs which ought better to be resolved by discussion between C and her parents; and (3) as to leave to apply for the specific issue order, this was not the kind of issue that Parliament had envisaged being litigated when it allowed children to apply for leave to apply for s.8 orders. The jurisdiction should be reserved for important matters. To grant leave would be interpreted as though the court would be willing to intervene in any case where a child was in disagreement with its parents. It would be interpreted by C as the achievement of some advantage over her parents in a situation where she should be dealing directly with her parents and not seeking the intervention of the court.

C. (A MINOR) (LEAVE TO SEEK SECTION 8 ORDERS), *Re* [1994] 1 FLR 26, Johnson J.

3550. Residence—children's views—representation of children—whether judge right to order children to be represented by solicitor from child care panel without joining children as parties

[R.S.C., Ord. 80, r.2; Family Proceedings Rules 1991 (S.I. 1991 No. 1247), rr.1.3, 2.57, 9.2, 9.2A, 9.5; Children Act 1989 (c.41), Pt. IV; Adoption Rules 1984 (S.I. 1984 No. 265), r.15; Hague Convention on the Civil Aspects of International Child Abduction 1980, Art. 21.]

Where separate representation for children was required in private law family proceedings in the High Court, the children should be joined as parties to the proceedings.

M and F were Australian and had three children. They were due to return to Australia in 1994. M and F separated in 1992, the children remaining with F, and M having only limited contact. M applied for interim contact. At the hearing, the court welfare officer indicated that she was unable adequately to reflect the children's views to the court. The judge directed, *inter alia*, that the children should be represented by a solicitor on the child care panel, without joining the children as parties to the proceedings. F opposed the separate representation of the children and appealed against that part of the order.

Held, that (1) although the technical point as to whether the children must be joined as parties would be left open, where separate representation for children was required in family proceedings in the High Court the children should be joined as parties for practical reasons; (2) there were funding difficulties in inviting a panel guardian *ad litem* or a solicitor from the child care panel to act as guardian *ad litem* in private law proceedings, and the court should normally invite the Official Solicitor to act on behalf of the child. However, since arrangements had been put in place, there was no reason why the court should now appoint the Official Solicitor as guardian *ad litem* instead; and (3) the decision to order separate representation was clearly right in the circumstances.

[*Per curiam*: The ordinary rule under R.S.C., Ord. 80, r.2, that where a child is to be represented by a guardian *ad litem* he must be joined as a party applied equally in family proceedings.]

L. v. L. (MINORS) (SEPARATE REPRESENTATION) [1994] 1 FLR 156, C.A.

3551. Residence—*ex parte* application—oral application for leave to apply made by relative—whether court should grant leave

[Children Act 1989 (c.41), ss.1, 10(9); Family Proceedings Courts (Children Act 1989) Rules 1991 (S.I. 1991 No. 1395), r.3.]

The fact that an applicant for leave to apply for a residence order had failed to file a written request as required by the Family Proceedings Courts (Children Act 1989) Rules 1991 did not invalidate the grant of leave or the substantive order made.

C was the cousin of the father of two boys and was the only person able to look after them when M went into hospital. Three days later, M requested the boys' return as she planned to return to her alcoholic husband, the boys' stepfather. The boys did not wish to go with their mother. C made an oral *ex parte* application to the magistrates for leave to apply for a residence order, and thereafter for a residence order. Leave was granted, along with an interim residence order lasting five weeks. M appealed.

Held, that (1) although the Family Proceedings Courts (Children Act 1989) Rules 1991, r.3, required an applicant for leave to file a written request, an order made without such a request having been made was not automatically invalid. The court would not set aside the order and the grant of leave on the merits, as the magistrates had acted properly in an emergency situation; (2) it was wrong in the circumstances to grant an interim residence order of five weeks' duration. The application needed to be determined quickly, and as there was an imminent hearing of M's contact application, the interim residence order should be reconsidered on that occasion.

O. (MINORS) (LEAVE TO SEEK RESIDENCE ORDER), *Re* [1994] 1 FLR 172, Ewbank J.

3552. Residence—father violent—mother dead—residence order granted in favour of uncle rather than father—whether breach of child's right to upbringing by natural parents

An appeal was made by a father against a refusal of his application for a residence order. The case concerned a three-year-old girl whose mother died when she was two. The relationship between the child's parents was violent and the mother did not allow the father to see the child for the last three months of her life because of his violence and drunkenness. The child's grandmother and the maternal uncle and his wife applied for residence orders. The local authority also applied for a supervision order in case a residence order was granted in favour of the father which they opposed. The father's application for a parental responsibility order was granted. The residence order was granted in favour of the child's uncle. The father argued that the most important factor to be considered was that the child should be brought up by a natural parent.

Held, dismissing the appeal, that the judge below correctly determined in the face of persuasive evidence, that the father was not a suitable person to have care of the child, and it was in the child's best interests for the residence order to be granted to the maternal uncle (*K. (A Minor) (Ward: Care and Control), Re* [1990] C.L.Y. 3138, *K. (A Minor) (Wardship: Adoption), Re* [1991] C.L.Y. 2485, *K.D. (A Minor) (Ward: Termination of Access), Re* [1988] C.L.Y 2294 considered).

K. (A MINOR), *Re*, December 15, 1994, C.A.

3553. Residence—foster-parents seeking leave to apply—child accommodated by local authority at request of natural parents—child placed with foster-parents—foster-parents seeking leave to apply for residence order with consent of local authority—natural parents objecting—whether local authority could or should consent

C was accommodated by a local authority because her natural parents were unable to care for her. She was placed with foster-parents who later sought leave to apply for a residence order with the consent of the local authority. The natural parents opposed the application on the grounds that the local authority was merely accommodating the child and could not give a valid consent because they did not have parental responsibility; or if they could give consent, they should not do so as both the accommodating social services local authority and adoption agency had responsibility for the child.

Held, granting leave to the foster-parents, that the consent required was that of the local authority accomodating the child, which had been given. The local authority had consented in its role as accommodating social services authority and not in its role as an adoption agency.

P. (A MINOR) (LEAVE TO APPLY: FOSTER PARENTS), *Re* [1994] 2 F.C.R. 1093, Hale J.

3554. Residence—foster-parents seeking leave to apply—local authority consent—relevance of authority's role as adoption agency—whether court should grant leave—wardship—other proceedings existing to determine child's welfare—whether any additional advantage in child remaining a ward of court

[Adoption Act 1976 (c.36), s.6; Children Act 1989 (c.41), ss.1(1), 8, 9(2)(3), 10(5)(9), 22(1), 23(2)(3), 105(1).]

Where a child accommodated by a local authority was in the care of foster-parents, the foster-parents might apply for leave for an order under s.8 of the Children Act 1989, provided they had the consent of the local authority, whether or not that local authority was also acting as an adoption agency in relation to the child.

N, a girl born in 1990, suffered from Down's Syndrome and additional respiratory problems. In 1991 she was placed with foster-parents. M and F were Orthodox Jews, and the foster agreement stipulated that N was to be brought up in accordance with this religion. In May 1992, M and F decided that N should be adopted by an Orthodox Jewish family, but the first prospective adopters were unacceptable to them and the foster-parents were not acceptable because they were not Orthodox Jews. A second prospective adoptive family was found by the local authority, whereupon the foster-parents initiated wardship proceedings, and subsequently applied for leave to apply for a residence order. The application was heard together with the parents' application to discharge the wardship.

Held, granting both applications, that (1) local authority foster-parents could only apply for leave to apply for a s.8 order with the consent of the local authority. The "local authority" for this purpose meant the local social services authority accommodating the child. That consent having been given, the foster-parents were clearly entitled to apply for leave, despite the parents' submission to the contrary; (2) in answer to the parents' submission that the local authority should not have consented because of its dual role as both the accommodating local social services authority and an adoption agency, its role as an adoption agency played no part in its giving of consent. Any challenge to the giving of consent had to be by way of judicial review (*D.M. (A Minor) (Wardship: Jurisdiction), Re* [1987] C.L.Y. 2518 applied; *A. v. Liverpool City Council* [1981] C.L.Y. 1796, *A. and W. (Minors) (Residence Orders: Leave to Apply), Re* [1992] C.L.Y. 3123, *B. (Minors) (Termination of Contact: Paramount Consideration), Re* [1993] C.L.Y. 2771 considered); (3) in considering whether to grant leave to the foster-parents, the child's welfare was not the paramount consideration, though undoubtedly relevant, and the court must also bear in mind the prospects of success of the substantive application (*A. and W. (Minors) (Residence Order: Leave to Apply), Re* [1992] C.L.Y. 3123, *S.C. (A Minor) (Leave to Seek Residence Order), Re* [1994] 1 F.L.R. 96 applied); (4) s.10(9)(c) required the court to consider the disruption that the proposed application might cause in the child's life. This had two aspects: on the one hand, the foster-parents' application would not disrupt N's present placement with them, but on the other hand, it would disrupt the long-term plans for N's adoption by a family acceptable to her parents; (5) weighing all the factors, it was an appropriate case for the foster-parents to be given leave to apply for a residence order; and (6) given that the case would stay in the High Court, and the Official Solicitor would remain involved, there was no advantage in N remaining a ward of court. The court could deal with this exceptional and difficult case in the same way under the Children Act 1989 as under the wardship jurisdiction. The wardship would therefore be discharged.

[*Per curiam*: Had the court not granted the foster-parents leave to apply for a residence order, it would have been a bold decision, to say the least, to allow them to proceed in the wardship proceedings.]

C. v. SALFORD CITY COUNCIL [1994] 2 F.L.R. 926, Hale J.

3555. Residence—interim residence order—mother given care and control—mother arrested and sectioned for neglect—interim order made in favour of father—whether order valid

[Mental Health Act 1983 (c.20), s.4; Children Act 1989 (c.41), s.1.]

The mother of T, an eight-year-old boy, appealed against an interim residence order in favour of his father after T was removed from her care under a police protection order. Following his parents' divorce a joint custody order with care and control to the mother was made. T had lived with his mother until concerns were expressed about her ability to care for him and provide for his educational welfare as he had missed an entire school term and required help for dyslexia. Following the mother's failure to respond to requests from social services, the educational welfare services and T's father went to visit T, the police arrested the mother for neglect under s.1 of the Children Act 1989 and she was sectioned under s.4 of the Mental Health Act 1983. The mother received no psychiatric treatment and was released as a bed could not be found. She argued that she was wrongly sectioned under the 1983 Act and that the father was acting maliciously.

Held, dismissing the appeal, that (1) it was not the practice of the Court of Appeal to interfere with an interim residence order and the safety and well-being of T required that he should live with his father until a full hearing was arranged; (2) directions were made under the inherent jurisdiction of the court in the terms of the Children Act 1989, that the Official Solicitor be appointed to act as T's legal representative, for court welfare officer's report to be obtained and for a consultant child psychiatrist to assess T's needs and evaluate the adverse effect on him of being removed from his mother; and (3) the matter was transferred to the Principal Registry of the Family Division so that the issue of T's future was decided as quickly as possible.

S. (A MINOR), *Re* (95/0039/F; 94/0040/F) March 13, 1995, C.A.

3556. Residence—reasons—magistrates making order in favour of father—whether magistrates' reasons sufficient—whether magistrates having jurisdiction to hear application for stay pending appeal

[Children Act 1989 (c.41), ss.11(7), 94.]

In children cases, magistrates should conduct a reasoned balancing act of the factors supporting each party's case and should give reasons sufficient to assess whether the conclusion could be supported or was plainly wrong.

M and F, who were not married, separated two years ago. Their child was now three. The child stayed with F from Monday to Thursday, and with M for the rest of the week. M subsequently married another man and became pregnant. The child developed signs of anxiety and stress. Both M and F applied for a residence order. The magistrates made a residence order in favour of F. M appealed and, pending appeal, applied to both the magistrates and to the High Court for a stay of the order which was refused.

Held, allowing the appeal, that the magistrates had failed to set out in their reasons any of the agreed facts or any findings that they might have made. This was an important decision which required the magistrates to express reasons which would make sense and which would justify their decision to both parents. The reasons should be sufficient to assess whether their decision could be supported, or was plainly wrong. The magistrates had taken into account only one factor, but there should have been a reasoned balancing act of the factors on either side. The reasons did not add up to any cogent explanation why this child should live long-term with F.

J. (A MINOR) (RESIDENCE), *Re* [1994] 1 F.L.R. 369, Singer J.

3557. Residence—relevant considerations—mother appealing against outcome of order—whether judge entitled to take into account financial disadvantage of child living with mother

The mother of a three-year-old child appealed against the making of a residence order whereby the child would live with his father during the week and with his mother most weekends. She argued that the judge should not have taken into consideration the likely financial effect of her giving up work to become a full-time carer and the subsequent CSA assessment of the father's income.

Held, dismissing the application, that in considering an application for a residence order, the judge was entitled to look at all aspects of the case, including financial considerations.

R. (A MINOR) (RESIDENCE ORDER: FINANCIAL CONSIDERATIONS), *Re*, *The Times*, May 10, 1995, C.A.

3558. Residence—residence order—granted with prohibited steps orders—care order refused on failure to meet threshold criteria—whether jurisdiction to make prohibited steps orders—whether criteria met

[Children Act 1989 (c.41), s.31.]

A residence order was granted to the grandparents of F and an application for a care order by the local authority failed on the basis of not meeting the threshold criteria under the Children Act 1989, s.31. The judge also made prohibited steps orders as between mother, father, grandparents and child. The guardian *ad litem* appealed and the mother cross-appealed.

Held, allowing the appeal and the cross-appeal in part, that the court below had no jurisdiction to make prohibited steps orders and these were set aside. The residence order was set aside and a care order substituted, the s.31 criteria having been met given the violent background of the father. The mother was to have indirect access subject to an undertaking not to seek contact without the concurrence of local authority or until a further order and the grandparents were to continue to care for the child.

F. (A MINOR), *Re* (94/6637/F; 94/7325/F; 94/0986/F), January 30, 1995, C.A.

3559. Residence—sexual abuse—mother alleging sexual abuse of children by father—justices finding no evidence of sexual abuse and granting residence to mother and contact to father—whether mother estopped from renewing her allegations of sexual abuse

The court's duty to inquire into all the facts relating to a child's circumstances and its duty to place the child's welfare as its paramount consideration means that, where necessary in the interests of justice, the court in a children's case can refuse to be bound by a previous finding which would otherwise give rise to an estoppel *per rem judicatam*.

A was aged seven and B aged five. M and F never married. F issued an application for custody in a magistrates' court. M made a cross-application. M alleged that F had sexually abused the children and had been violent to her; F said that A's inappropriate sexual knowledge was due to M's coaching. The justices found that A did have inappropriate knowledge but that there was no evidence that it had resulted from her contact with F. They made no other findings as to the disputed matters, and made a residence order in favour of M, and granted contact to F. Contact broke down, and F applied to the High Court for a residence order. F sought to argue that the court should not entertain any inquiry into whether A and B. had been sexually abused, on the basis that M was estopped from raising that issue by the justices' finding.

Held, that (1) for an estoppel *per rem judicatam* to arise, the same issue must have been decided in proceedings between the same parties in a judgment of a court of competent jurisdiction, which was final and conclusive, and which was adjudicated on the merits (*DSW Silo- und Verwaltungsgesellschaft mbH v. Owners of the Sennar; Sennar (No. 2), The* [1985] C.L.Y. 1291 applied); (2) fresh evidence was admissible to show that the judgment of the earlier court was wrong; (3) the Children Act 1989 created a unified jurisdiction between all the courts. For the purpose of issue estoppel, a magistrates' court was a court of competent jurisdiction whose finding could give rise to an estoppel (*Hayward v. Hayward (orse. Prestwood)* [1961] C.L.Y. 2838 doubted); (4) the doctrine of issue estoppel was based on the public interest in certainty and finality of litigation, and to prevent hardship to a litigant having to defend the same allegation twice. In child care cases, however, there was a countervailing public interest for the court to protect children, to regard their welfare as paramount, and to inquire into the statutory checklist items. Whilst the court should not be slow to use the rule of evidence of issue *per rem judicatam* where appropriate, the court had a duty to inquire into the truth, and where necessary in the interests of justice, the court could refuse to be bound by a rule of estoppel; and (5) F was not, in reality, vexed by having the issue of sexual abuse reventilated when his case was that A's inappropriate knowledge was due to M's disgraceful conduct in planting the ideas in A's head. In the absence of clear findings by the justices on all the matters in dispute, the court would hear all the evidence.

K. v. P. (CHILDREN ACT PROCEEDINGS: ESTOPPEL) [1995] 1 FLR 248, Ward J.

3560. Residence—shared residence order—father applying for shared residence order—parents never cohabiting—whether order should be made

[Children Act 1989 (c.41), ss.1(1)(3), 3(1), 4(1), 11(4).]

Although the court has power to make a shared residence order, such an order should be made rarely and only in exceptional circumstances.

M and F had never married and had not cohabited for any appreciable time. They had one child, a boy aged 14. For seven years from the age of five the child lived with M, and had staying contact with F on alternate weekends and half of the school holidays. In 1990, this arrangement changed when F moved away, though occasional contact was maintained. In March 1991 M cut off contact and F applied for residence or, alternatively, contact. Interim contact orders to F broke down and in October 1991 F applied for a shared residence order. In March 1992 the court made a residence order in favour of M, a parental responsibility order in favour of F and provided for weekly visiting contact, subject to the child's wishes. F appealed against the refusal of a shared residence order.

Held, dismissing the appeal, that although it had previously been held that it was not open to the court to make a joint care and control order, it was clear, under s.11(4) of the Children Act 1989, that the court was now empowered to make a shared residence order in favour of two people who were not living together (*Riley v. Riley* [1987] C.L.Y. 2489 not followed). However, almost invariably the circumstances would require that a child should make his settled home with one parent. The judge had considered all the relevant factors and had acted entirely properly in not making a shared residence order. The child needed a settled home and should not pass to and fro between M and F, especially in the light of the differences between them (*P. (Minors) (Wardship: Care and Control), Re* [1992] C.L.Y. 3148 considered).

H. (A MINOR) (SHARED RESIDENCE ORDER), *Re* [1994] 1 F.L.R. 717, C.A.

3561. Residence—shared residence order—whether shared residence order to be made

[Children Act 1989 (c.41), ss.8, 11(4).]

Whilst there was no need for exceptional circumstances before the court could make a residence order sharing the care of a child between two parents living apart, there would have to be some positive benefit to the child in departing from the usual residence order in favour of one parent.

M and F were married and had two children. They separated in 1991, the children living with M. In early 1992, F obtained an order for staying contact, which was later varied to share the care of the children during the school holidays equally between M and F. The children spent one-third of the year with F. F now applied for a shared residence order, while M sought a continuation of the present arrangements. The judge made a shared residence order.

Held, dismissing M's appeal, that the courts had disapproved of orders for joint care and control prior to the Children Act 1989. However, s.11(4) specifically contemplated that a child might have a residence with more than one person and the courts' earlier disapproval of such arrangements could no longer be regarded as good law (*Riley v. Riley* [1987] C.L.Y. 2489 not followed). However, the views expressed in *Riley*, that a child should have one settled home and that competing homes could lead to confusion, were still of some weight. There was no requirement of exceptional circumstances before a shared residence order could be made. The usual order would still be for residence to one parent with contact to the other parent. There would have to be demonstrated some positive benefit for the child in departing from the conventional order, and consequently a shared residence order would be an unusual order. The decision to make a shared residence order was a matter for the discretion of the judge and on the facts, the judge's decision was not plainly wrong (*G. v. G. (Minors: Custody Appeal)* [1985] C.L.Y. 2594 applied; *H. (A Minor) (Shared Residence Order), Re* [1995] 7 C.L. 398 considered).

A. v. A. (MINORS) (SHARED RESIDENCE ORDER) [1994] 1 F.L.R. 669, C.A.

3562. Residence proceedings—confidential evidence—whether discretion to withhold should be exercised—whether ouster order could be made where no application before court

[Matrimonial Homes Act 1983 (c.19), s.1(3).]

For the court to consider evidence which was withheld from a party to the proceedings, it must be shown that real harm would ensue to the children were the evidence to be disclosed to that party.

M commenced divorce proceedings against F in 1992 after a 15-year marriage. Concerns were raised as to M's mental stability, and the two children of the family were placed on the child protection register. F applied for a residence order, proposing to remain in the family home, though he did not apply to exclude M. The welfare officer's report contained a confidential addendum setting out the children's views and anxieties, which was given to the court but not disclosed to either M or F or their legal advisers. M sought disclosure of the addendum but the judge refused its disclosure, made a residence order in favour of F and ordered that M should leave the family home in the interests of the children.

Held, dismissing the appeal, that (1) the correct test to apply in deciding that evidence should be withheld from a party to the proceedings was whether real harm would ensue from the disclosure. The judge had erred in refusing disclosure on the less stringent test of whether there was a risk of significant harm, and there was no need for the addendum to have remained confidential (*Official Solicitor v. K.* [1963] C.L.Y. 1807 applied; *C. (A Minor: Irregularity of Practice), Re* [1992] C.L.Y. 3003, *B. (A Minor) (Disclosure of Evidence), Re* [1993] C.L.Y. 2747, *G. (Minors) (Welfare Report: Disclosure), Re* [1994] 11 C.L. 464 considered); (2) the court would exercise its own discretion on the issue of residence. The balance was overwhelmingly in favour of making a residence order in favour of F; (3) the judge had failed to take account of all the factors in s.1(3) of the Matrimonial Homes Act 1983 relevant to the decision to make an ouster order, and had wrongly concentrated solely on the needs of the children. Although the ouster application was not specifically dealt with in cross-examination at first instance, the same issues had been raised by the residence application. The court would therefore exercise its own discretion, and in the extreme circumstances of this case the needs of the children were determinative even when set in balance with the other factors. Since an application for an ouster order had now been filed, the order would be confirmed (*Richards v. Richards* [1983] C.L.Y. 1861, *Gibson v. Austin* [1993] C.L.Y. 1926 applied; *Shipp v. Shipp* [1988] C.L.Y. 1667, *Whitlock v. Whitlock* [1988] 1658 considered).

M. (MINORS) (DISCLOSURE OF EVIDENCE), *Re* [1994] 1 F.L.R. 760, C.A.

3563. Section 91(14) order—applications to be made only with leave of court—residence and contact orders at issue—*ex parte* applications for leave—followed by *inter partes* hearings—appropriate procedure—whether order justified

[Children Act 1989 (c.41), s.91(14).]

In a case concerning a boy, aged five, F made an application for leave to appeal out of time an order made in November 1994, and for leave to adduce fresh evidence. At the November 1994 hearing, F's application for a residence order had been dismissed, and contact was further defined. In addition, the trial judge made various other orders, including a second order under the Children Act 1989, s.91(14), that F was not to make any further applications without leave of the court. There had been a previous contested residence application which was heard and adjudicated upon in March 1993; there had also been a two-day application concerning various issues of contact in October 1993, after which the trial judge had not only dismissed F's six applications then before the court, and made a defined contact order, but also made the first order under s.91(14) against F. The court had operated the s.91(14) order in such a way that F went *ex parte* to get leave to issue his further applications, and thereafter the applications were served on M, and *inter partes* hearings took place. Not only had there been various applications and hearings *ex parte* and *inter partes* since the first s.91(14) order was made, but there had been various applications and hearings since the 1994 s.91(14) order was made.

Held, dismissing F's application for leave to appeal out of time and for leave to adduce further evidence, and making a number of comments concerning s.91(14) of the Children Act 1989, that the history of this case demonstrated that it was an entirely proper case for the s.91(14) order, and that this was so at the end of 1993. One difficulty in making such an order is that unless the situation as to precise contact arrangements is spelt out, the case may need to come back to court. It is most undesirable for applications for leave, especially, in cases such as this to be made *ex parte*. It is more satisfactory if applications for leave are *inter partes* to establish if there is a genuine need, and so that the court is assisted *inter partes* as necessary if there is not a genuine need. It might be that there was a further need for definition of the contact order in this case. It is desirable that if an order under s.91(14) is made, leave is not granted lightly, and should generally be granted *inter partes*, where there was a clear need for further orders. An obvious way needs to be found to mark the existence of such orders so that they are drawn to the attention of those deciding whether to grant leave.

N. (A MINOR) (SECTION 91(14) OF THE CHILDREN ACT 1989), *Re*, October 5, 1995, C.A. [*Ex rel.* Ruth Blair, Barrister, 2 King's Bench Walk, instructed by Kosky Seal & Co., Solicitors.]

3564. Secure accommodation

CHILDREN (SECURE ACCOMMODATION) AMENDMENT REGULATIONS 1995 (No. 1398) [£1·10], made under the Children Act 1989 (c.41), ss.25(2), 26(2), 104(4), Sched. 5, para. 7(1)(2)(ff)(g)(3), Sched. 6, para. 10(1)(2)(f)(jj)(l)(3); operative on June 23, 1995; amend S.I. 1991 No.1505 in connection with the extension of provision of secure accommodation provided for by the Criminal Justice and Public Order Act 1994.

3565. Secure accommodation—"beyond parental control"—time at which extent of parental control should be assessed—whether criteria for secure accommodation subject to paramountcy principle

[Children Act 1989 (c.41), ss.1(1), 25(1)(4), 31(2), 38(2).]

The expression "beyond parental control' describes a state of affairs existing at any time and there is no need to show that the child is beyond parental control at the time of the hearing.

S was 13 and had lived with M since her parents had separated when she was seven months old. She had developed a wayward, uncontrollable and disturbed disposition and was periodically violent. She was accommodated by the local authority, which subsequently sought an interim care order and an order authorising S to be detained in secure accommodation. The local authority relied on the "beyond parental control" limb of the threshold criteria for a care order in s.31 of the Children Act 1989. The stipendiary magistrate made both orders.

Held, dismissing the appeal, that it was plain that the expression "the harm or likelihood of harm is attributable to the child's being beyond parental control" was capable of describing a state of affairs in the past, in the present, or in the future, according to the context in which it fell to be applied. There was no need to show that the child was beyond parental control at the time of the hearing. It followed that, although S had been looked after by the local authority for three months by the time of the magistrate's decision, S was at all times material to the magistrate's consideration beyond parental control. There were no grounds on which the orders could be set aside (*M. (A Minor) (Care Order: Threshold Conditions), Re* [1994] C.L.Y. 3141 distinguished; *M. v. Westminster City Council* [1984] C.L.Y. 2206, *D. (A Minor), Re* [1987] C.L.Y. 2437, *Northamptonshire County Council v. S.* [1993] C.L.Y. 2769, *Newham London Borough Council v. A.G.* [1992] C.L.Y. 3029 considered).

M. v. BIRMINGHAM CITY COUNCIL [1994] 2 F.L.R. 141, Stuart-White J.

3566. Secure accommodation—child remanded on bail with conditions of residence as directed by local authority—justices making secure accommodation order—whether jurisdiction to make secure accommodation order where child bailed to local authority accommodation

[Bail Act 1976 (c.63); Children Act 1989 (c.41), ss.20(1), 22(1)(6), 25(1); Children (Secure Accommodation) Regulations 1991 (S.I. 1991 No. 1505), reg. 6.]

The court had power to make a secure accommodation order where a child had been remanded on bail in criminal proceedings, and where a condition of that bail was that she comply with directions of the local authority as to her residence.

C, aged 14, suffered from isolated symptoms of a psychiatric disorder. In June 1994 she was arrested for allegedly stabbing a fellow pupil at school. She was granted bail by the magistrates; one of the bail conditions was that she comply with directions of the local authority as to her residence. She was placed in a children's home. A week later, bail was extended on the same terms. However, on the same day, the local authority placed her in a secure unit, and two days later the family proceedings court made a secure accommodation order for three months. C appealed, contending there was no jurisdiction to make such an order.

Held, dismissing the appeal, that s.25 of the Children Act 1989 permitted the court to make a secure accommodation order in respect of a child being looked after by the local authority. Although the Children (Secure Accommodation) Regulations 1991 made express provision for children remanded to local authority accommodation, they made no provision for children looked after by the local authority pursuant to a remand on bail. It was clear that C was being looked after by the local authority, albeit pursuant to conditions of bail rather than on a voluntary basis. It would be strange if the court had no power to make a secure accommodation order merely because the child had been bailed rather than remanded to local authority accommodation.

[*Per curiam*: It would have been better, as the Children Act 1989 was supposed to be a comprehensive statute, had the Act spelt out the powers over bailed children.]

C. (SECURE ACCOMMODATION: BAIL), *Re* [1994] 2 F.L.R. 922, Hollis J.

3567. Secure accommodation—duration—justices making interim order lasting one month and a further order for three months at adjourned hearing—whether duration of order valid

[Children Act 1989 (c.41), s.25; Family Proceedings Courts (Children Act 1989) Rules 1991 (S.I. 1991 No. 1395), r.4; Children (Secure Accommodation) Regulations 1991 (S.I. 1991 No. 1505), regs. 10, 11, 12, 13.]

A secure accommodation order may be made for an initial period of at most three months, so that where an interim order had been made for one month, a further order may only be made for a further two months.

C was 15 years old, and it was agreed by all parties that the criteria for a secure accommodation order were satisfied. In February 1994, the justices made an interim secure accommodation order for one month, and adjourned the case for the guardian *ad litem* to complete his inquiries. At the adjourned hearing in March 1994, the justices made a secure accommodation order for a further three months.

Held, allowing C's appeal, that a secure accommodation order restricted the liberty of a child, and the provisions governing its duration must be strictly construed. Although the court had the express power to adjourn an application for a secure accommodation order, the regulations were clear: subject to exceptions which did not apply here, the maximum initial duration of a secure accommodation order was three months. If Parliament had intended to allow a court to adjourn for one month, and then ignore that period when imposing the maximum term allowed, the Regulations would have so stated unequivocally. At the adjourned hearing, the court was still seised of the original application, pursuant to which a term of no more than three months could be imposed. The term of three further months was therefore unlawful (*R. v. Oxfordshire County Council (Secure Accommodation Order)* [1992] C.L.Y. 3129, *Hereford and Worcester County Council v. S.* [1994] 2 F.L.R. 360 considered).

C. v. HUMBERSIDE COUNTY COUNCIL [1994] 2 F.L.R. 759, Bracewell J.

3568. Secure accommodation—serious offences charged—child remanded in care of local authority—application for secure accommodation order—criteria to be applied by the court—consideration of the welfare of the child—whether appellate court should interfere with decision

[Children Act 1989 (c.41), s.25; Children (Secure Accommodation) Regulations 1991 (S.I. 1991 No. 1505) reg. 6.]

A 14-year-old boy (AE) was remanded in the care of the local authority after being charged with serious offences including arson with intent to endanger life. The local authority applied for a secure accommodation order on the basis that AE had absconded from local authority care 31 times, had committed further offences, and that he was a risk to himself and others. The magistrates granted an order for 21 days on the basis that it was the minimum period required for an assessment and psychiatric treatment. AE appealed, arguing that the magistrates had erred in that they were under a duty not only to satisfy themselves as to the criteria set out in s.25 of the Children Act 1989 but also to consider the welfare of the child in accordance with s.1 of the Act.

Held, dismissing AE's appeal, that applications by local authorities to use secure accommodation in relation to a child remanded in the care of the local authority in criminal proceedings were governed by s.25 of the Children Act 1989 as modified by reg. 6 of the Children (Secure Accommodation) Regulations 1991. The Family Proceedings Courts (Children Act 1989) Rules 1991 did not apply and therefore there was no provision for the appointment of a guardian *ad litem* nor was there a requirement for the magistrates to give their reasons. The magistrates had, however, given some reasons and it was clear that the hearing went beyond the mere question of whether the criteria in s.25 of the Act could be established and into matters relating to AE's welfare. The magistrates had not erred in their approach and therefore the appellate court should not interfere with the decision.

A.E. v. STAFFORDSHIRE COUNTY COUNCIL [1995] 2 F.C.R. 84, Kirkwood J.

3569. Secure accommodation—welfare of child—whether welfare of child paramount consideration—whether court required to adjourn for report from guardian *ad litem*

[Children Act 1989 (c.41), ss.1(1), 25.]

In exceptional cases the court can make a secure accommodation order without adjourning for a report from the guardian *ad litem*.

A 14-year-old boy accommodated by the local authority had been behaving in a difficult and disruptive manner. The authority under s.25 of the 1989 Act applied to keep him in secure accommodation. The guardian *ad litem*, appointed by the court, asked for time to prepare a report in order to offer informed recommendations. The court refused his request and made a three-month order. The judge dismissed an appeal.

Held, dismissing the appeal, that s.1 of the Children Act 1989 (welfare of the child being the paramount consideration), did not apply to an application under s.25. The local authority had a power to place the child in such accommodation if he was likely to injure others. A guardian *ad litem* had therefore to adapt his general duties to the specific requirements of the application. The court would normally allow a report to be prepared before making such an order, in exceptional cases the court had the power to make the order without waiting for input from the guardian (*Hereford and Worcester County Council v. S.* [1994] C.L.Y. 3269 not followed).

M. (A MINOR) (SECURE ACCOMMODATION ORDER), *Re* [1995] 2 W.L.R. 302, C.A.

3570. Secure accommodation—youth court remanding boy into care of local authority—whether application to be made to remanding court. See LIVERPOOL CITY COUNCIL v. B., §1202.

3571. Sexual abuse—admissibility—video recordings of child witness—child subsequently giving more innocent explanation—whether recording should have been admitted. See R. v. HAWKINS (STEPHEN ARTHUR) (94/5793/X4), §946.

3572. Sexual abuse—interview of child victim—Cleveland Guidelines—reliability of evidence in criminal context—whether Guidelines applicable to criminal matters—whether evidence admissible. See R. v. DUNPHY (JOHN), §910.

3573. Sexual abuse—reliability of child sex abuse victim—victim having before made allegations of sexual misconduct—whether judge should have advised jury as to how to deal with the evidence of previous allegations. See R. v. COOPER (EDGAR ROY) (94/2670/Z3), §1095.

3574. Sexual abuse—standard of proof—whether standard lower than balance of probabilities where only one likely perpetrator

[Children Act 1989 (c.41), s.91(14), Sched. 14.]

Where there was only one possible perpetrator of sexual abuse of children, the standard of proof for determining whether any abuse had occurred was a standard commensurate with the serious nature of the issues involved.

M and F had four children all aged below 10, who were the subject of care orders. M visited them every week at their children's home, but F had not had contact since being charged with physically and indecently assaulting the children. F was acquitted of all charges and sought a residence order, or alternatively contact with the children if they were to remain in care. M was not living with F and was unable to look after the children. The local authority maintained that the children should remain in care and made allegations against both parents of physical and emotional neglect and physical and sexual abuse, especially against F. The allegations were denied. The judge found that the children had been sexually abused and that, in the absence of any other candidate, F was the perpetrator. The judge ordered the children should remain in care and that there should be no contact between the children and any member of their biological family.

Held, dismissing F's appeal, that (1) ordinarily, the standard of proof required for finding that abuse had occurred was the balance of probabilities. However, the standard of proof for finding that any particular individual had sexually abused a child was a standard commensurate with the seriousness of the allegation, although proof beyond reasonable doubt was not required. The judge was wrong to apply a two-stage approach, namely, first whether any abuse had occurred and secondly, whether F was the perpetrator (*Bater v. Bater* (1951) C.L.C. 2847, *H. (A Minor), Re; K. v. K.* [1990] C.L.Y. 3185, *McB. (A Minor), Re* (1993) unrep. applied; *G. (A Minor) (Child Abuse: Standard of Proof), Re* [1987] C.L.Y. 2474 considered); (2) the judge's decision to refuse F contact with the children had not depended solely on the findings as to sexual abuse. The order was fully justified whether or not the findings could stand and the appeal would be dismissed.

W. (MINORS) (SEXUAL ABUSE: STANDARD OF PROOF), *Re* [1994] 1 F.L.R. 419, C.A.

3575. Specific issue order—application by mother and children to live in housing association house without ex-cohabitee—whether court has power to oust ex-cohabitee where no violence alleged

[Children Act 1989 (c.41), ss.3, 8, 15, Sched. 1, para. 1.]

A and B were a cohabiting couple living in a two-bedroom housing association house where they held a joint tenancy. In September 1992, A left B and went with their children to live with her parents. In March 1993 A applied for a specific issue order that she be allowed to live in the house without B. At trial the judge refused to grant the relief because it was outside his powers to do so.

Held, dismissing A's appeal, that where a right of occupation would be interfered with, the question where a child should live was not suitable for determination on an application for a specific issue order since it would in substance be an ouster order (*Ainsbury v. Millington* [1987] C.L.Y. 2886 considered).

F. (MINORS), *Re* (1993) (1994) 26 H.L.R. 354, C.A.

3576. Specific issue order—child in need—requiring local authority to exercise its powers and duties—whether appropriate—whether child in need

It was for a local authority to decide whether a child was in need and it was not appropriate for a court to make a specific issue order requiring the local authority to exercise its powers and duties under Pt. III of the Children Act 1989. J could only challenge the local authority's view that he was not a child in need by applying for judicial review of its decision in the Queen's Bench Divisional Court.

J. (A MINOR) (SPECIFIC ISSUE ORDER), *Re*, *The Times*, February 21, 1995, Wall J.

3577. Supervision order—application to extend—whether jurisdiction to make interim care order on application to extend supervision order

[Children Act 1989 (c.41), ss.31(2)(5)(b), 35, Sched. 3, para. 6.]

The court has no jurisdiction to make an interim care order on an application to extend an existing supervision order.

An 11-year-old girl, living with her mother, was placed under a 12-month supervision order. Within the time period social workers applied for an extension of the order under s.35 of the Act. The guardian *ad litem* recommended a care order in place of the supervision order. The mother and the local authority resisted the recommendation. The family proceedings court ruled that they had no jurisdiction to make a care order on an application to extend a supervision order. The judge allowed an appeal.

Held, allowing the mother's appeal, that an application to extend a supervision order was not an "application for a supervision order" within s.31(5)(b) of the Act. There was no jurisdiction, on an application to extend an order, to replace it with an interim care order.

A. (A MINOR) (SUPERVISION ORDER: EXTENSION), *Re* [1995] 1 W.L.R. 482, C.A.

3578. Supervision order—child protection—child victim of Munchausen's syndrome by proxy—whether mother should have supervised contact—whether supervision order could be made to effect supervision of contact by local authority—whether covert video surveillance evidence admissible

[Children Act 1989 (c.41), ss.1(2)(5), 8, 9(5)(a), 11(7), 16, 31(1)(2).]

In serious cases where child protection issues are involved, it is permissible for the court to effect supervision of contact by the local authority by means of a supervision order.

M and F were married and had one child, D, aged nearly two. G, M's mother, took a large part in D's daily life and he had a strong bond with her. In January 1993 when he was nearly one, D was admitted to hospital with a respiratory tract infection. On the next two days, D stopped breathing while alone with M in the hospital cubicle. It was suspected that M was suffering from Munchausen's syndrome by proxy. M and D were transferred to a specialist unit, where covert video surveillance was used. M was not told of the surveillance and F was not asked for his permission. The video recorded two further assaults on D and M was arrested. M at first denied involvement but later pleaded guilty to a charge of cruelty and was sentenced to three years' probation with a condition of psychiatric treatment. In March 1993, G obtained an order for bi-monthly contact, supervised by F, which was successful. The local authority commenced care proceedings, and D was returned to F in July 1993 under interim care orders. In August the court ordered that M have contact for one hour every two weeks supervised by the local authority. In December at the final hearing it was agreed that a residence order should be made in favour of F. The local authority sought the termination of all contact between D and M and her side of the family. F and the guardian *ad litem* could see no benefit to D from contact with M.

Held, that (1) it was important that M did not become a frightening fantasy figure for D. Limited contact supervised by the local authority would be in his best interests and there would be six contact periods of up to two hours in the next 12 months while M underwent further assessment and treatment; (2) G was an important figure in D's life, and there was no reason why her contact should not continue as before; (3) if M's contact with D was not supervised, there was a likelihood of significant harm. The care referred to in s.31(2)(b)(i) of the Children Act 1989 included not only the care given by the parent with whom the child was living, but the care given by a parent during contact. Accordingly, the likelihood of significant harm was attributable to the care likely to be given by M and the threshold criteria for a supervision order were met; (4) the court could not make supervision by a local authority a condition of contact under s.11(7) of the Children Act 1989, nor could it be achieved by means of a specific issue order (*Leeds City Council v. C.* [1993] C.L.Y. 2826 applied); (5) while supervision of contact by the local authority would usually be effected by a family assistance order, it was appropriate to make a supervision order in more serious cases where there was an element of child protection involved. A supervision order would therefore be made. While it was generally undesirable for contact to be supervised over a lengthy period of time, it was appropriate here (*Leeds City Council v. C.* [1993] C.L.Y. 2826 distinguished; *M. (A Minor) (Care Order: Threshold Conditions), Re* [1994] 9 C.L. 288, *Nottinghamshire County Council v. P.* [1993] C.L.Y. 2860, *C. v. Solihull Metropolitan Borough Council* [1993] C.L.Y. 2770, *Hounslow London Borough Council v. A.* [1993] C.L.Y. 2772 considered); (6) evidence produced by covert video surveillance was generally admissible. Even if evidence had been unlawfully or improperly obtained, it would be admissible in proceedings concerning a child where the welfare of the child plainly required the discovery of the true manner in which the child had been abused (*I.T.C. Film Distributors v. Video Exchange* [1982] C.L.Y. 1335, *R. v. Smurthwaite; R. v. Gill* [1994] 6 C.L. 79, *R. v. Bailey; Same v. Smith* [1993] C.L.Y. 668, *R. v. Jones (M.A.)* [1994] 11 C.L. 160 considered); and (7) if the doctor considered that covert video surveillance was essential for the treatment of his minor patient, he was entitled to undertake it without parental consent, provided that he was satisfied that there was no risk of any serious harm to the patient (*B. (A Minor) (Wardship: Sterilisation), Re* [1988] C.L.Y. 2533, *F. v. West Berkshire Health Authority* [1989] C.L.Y. 3044, *J. (A Minor) (Consent to Medical Treatment), Re* [1992] C.L.Y. 2919, *J. (A Minor) (Wardship: Medical Treatment), Re* [1991] C.L.Y. 2588 considered).

D.H. (A MINOR) (CHILD ABUSE), *Re* [1994] 1 F.L.R. 679, Wall J.

3579. Supervision order—duration—parties agreed on supervision order to last for six months—justices making supervision order for 12 months—whether power to make supervision order for less than 12 months

[Children Act 1989 (c.41), s.31, Sched. 3, Pt. II, para. 6(1).]

A supervision order may be made for any period not exceeding 12 months.

R was aged 11, and had a brother W, aged 13. Care proceedings were initiated by the local authority in respect of both boys, and interim supervision orders were made. At the hearing of the local authority's applications, the guardian *ad litem* and R's social worker both recommended there be a six-month supervision order in respect of R. R's mother did not dissent from this course. The justices held that a 12-month supervision order was necessary and made an order of that duration. All parties appealed.

Held, allowing the appeal and substituting a six-month supervision order, that Sched. 3, Pt. II, para. 6(1) of the Children Act 1989 provided that a supervision order should cease to have effect at the end of a period of 12 months beginning with the date of the order. This might mean that the order must endure for 12 months, or that it may be made for a maximum of 12 months. The court should resolve the ambiguity by favouring the construction likely to be of practical advantage, *i.e.*, that 12 months was a maximum period (*Devon County Council v. S.* [1993] C.L.Y. 2873 considered).

M. v. WARWICKSHIRE COUNTY COUNCIL [1994] 2 F.L.R. 593, Thorpe J.

3580. Supervision order—interim care orders sought by local authority—magistrates granting interim supervision orders with condition of residence—enforceability—whether magistrates wrong to make interim supervision orders

[Children Act 1989 (c.41), ss.31, 38, Sched. 3.]

Following a serious injury to one of M and F's three children, the local authority sought interim care orders as the best way of ensuring the children went to a family assessment centre. The magistrates were anxious that the children should go there, but following F's agreement to go to the centre with the children they made interim supervision orders and ordered that the children comply with directions given by the supervisor as to the place of residence. The local authority were concerned about enforcement, and brought the matter back before the magistrates who confirmed the order and provided that the supervisor's power to give directions as to a place of residence should commence on the date on which the family was supposed to go to the centre. The magistrates stated that if the parents failed to go on that date, the local authority could take any action within the terms of the order, "including foster care". The local authority appealed against the refusal to make an interim care order.

Held, dismissing the appeal, that (1) although the court's powers to attach conditions to a supervision order under Sched. 3 to the Children Act 1989 included the power to require the children to comply with the supervisor's directions as to their residence, there was no method by which the direction could be enforced. The local authority could only bring the matter back to court under s.35 or seek a variation of the supervision order; (2) consequently the only order which would have given the local authority the power to remove the children from M and F, and place them in foster care, was an interim care order; (3) though the magistrates had erred, there was no point in interfering with the order as the family had gone to the assessment centre on the appointment date and the order had worked satisfactorily so far; and (4) when the matter came back before the magistrates, they should take care to consider all the relevant criteria (*R. v. Oxfordshire County Council (Secure Accommodation Order)* [1992] C.L.Y. 3129 considered).

R. AND G. (MINORS) (INTERIM CARE OR SUPERVISION ORDERS), *Re* [1994] 1 F.L.R. 793, Ewbank J.

3581. Supervision order—requirements contained in supervision order—mother, father and guardian *ad litem* seeking a court order for the local authority to direct the father to attend a course of treatment—whether court had power so to order

[Children Act 1989 (c.41), Sched. 3, paras. 2–5.]

Under a supervision order, it was solely a matter for the local authority to give directions to the father or any other responsible person, and the court had no power to order the local authority to give any such directions.

Care proceedings were brought in respect of two children, S and A, who lived with M. F, who was having contact with the children, had been convicted and jailed for a sexual offence against his stepchild, but he was now anxious to have some treatment for his problems. All parties agreed that there should be supervision orders in respect of S and A. M, F, and the guardian *ad litem* sought an order from the court that the local authority direct F to attend a particular course of treatment. The local authority opposed the order, contending there was no power to make it.

Held, refusing the order sought, that any requirements as to the treatment of the supervised child were a matter for the court under paras. 2, 4 and 5 of Sched. 3 to the Children Act 1989. In contrast, para. 3 of Sched. 3 provided that a supervision order could order a responsible person to comply with any directions given by the supervisor. Under para. 3, the directions to be complied with were solely a matter for the supervisor, and the court had no power to order the local authority to give such directions.

H. (SUPERVISION ORDER), *Re* [1994] 2 F.L.R. 979, Bracewell J.

3582. Surname—change of surname by deed poll—Practice Direction

This Practice Direction was issued by the Lord Chancellor's Department on behalf of the Senior Master of the Queen's Bench Division on December 20, 1994.

1(a) Where a person has, by any order of the High Court, County Court or Family Proceedings Court, been given parental responsibility for a child and applies to the Central Office, Filing Department, for the enrolment of a Deed Poll to change the surname (family name) of such child who is under the age of 18 years (unless, in the case of a female, she is married below that age), the application must be supported by the production of the consent in writing or every other person having parental responsibility.

(b) In the absence of such consent, the application will be adjourned generally unless and until leave is given to change the surname of such child in the proceedings in which the said order was made and such leave is produced to the Central Office.

2(a) Where an application is made to the Central Office, Filing Department, by a person who has not been given parental responsibility of the child by any order of the High Court, County Court or Family Proceedings Court for the enrolment of a Deed Poll to change the surname of such child who is under the age of 18 years (unless, in the case of a female, she is married below that age), leave of the Court to enrol such Deed will be granted if the consent in writing of every person having parental responsibility is produced or if the person (or, if more than one, persons) having parental responsibility is dead or overseas or despite the exercise of reasonable diligence it has not been possible to find him or her for other good reason.

(b) In cases of doubt the Senior Master or, in his absence, the Practice Master will refer the matter to the Master of the Rolls.

(c) In the absence of any of the conditions specified above the Senior Master or the Master of the Rolls, as the case may be, may refer the matter to the Official Solicitor for investigation and report.

3 These directions are issued with the approval of the Master of the Rolls.

4 The *Practice Direction (Minor: Change of Surname)* dated 24 May 1976 [1977] 1 W.L.R. 1065 is hereby revoked and the *Practice Direction (Change by Deed Poll of Surname of Child)* dated 11 April 1994 is hereby revised by the addition of the words "Family Proceedings Court" in paragraphs 1(a) and 2(a).

PRACTICE DIRECTION (Q.B.D.) (CHANGE BY DEED POLL OF SURNAME OF CHILD) (Ord. 63, r.10), December 20, 1995.

3583. Tobacco—sale of cigarettes to under-age child—defence of reasonable precautions and exercise of due diligence—whether precautions acceptable. See HEREFORD AND WORCESTER COUNTY COUNCIL v. T & S STORES, §1292.

3584. Wardship—jurisdiction—protection of children—order prohibiting non-relative from contacting children

[Children Act 1989 (c.41), s.100.]

The court's inherent jurisdiction could be invoked to protect children who were thought to be at risk from their mother's husband even though he was not their father.

Y was married to the mother of nine children. He had a history of sexual offences but the mother did not perceive him as a risk to her children. The local authority did perceive him as a risk on the basis that he had paedophiliac tendencies. The local authority applied in wardship proceedings for leave to invoke the inherent jurisdiction of the court. The district judge refused to grant the application on the basis that there was no jurisdiction to do so and the local authority could take care proceedings.

Held, allowing the local authority's appeal, that s.100 of the Children Act 1989 did not apply because the local authority was not seeking to have protective powers bestowed upon it but was inviting the court to exercise such powers. A care order could do more harm than good by interfering with the mother's parental role. If the court's powers were not exercised there were grounds to believe that the children would suffer harm and so leave to invoke the court's inherent jurisdiction would be granted (*Nottinghamshire County Council v. P.* [1993] C.L.Y. 2860 considered).

DEVON COUNTY COUNCIL v. S. [1995] 1 All E.R. 243, Thorpe J.

MORTGAGES

3585. Breach of trust—solicitors—transfer of advance by solicitors—breach of building society's instructions—whether solicitors liable to repay—whether solicitors held advance on trust. See BRISTOL & WEST BUILDING SOCIETY v. A. KRAMER & CO., §4686.

3586. Constructive notice—charge over matrimonial home as security for loan to company—husband and wife—creditor's duty to satisfy himself that wife entered into obligation freely with knowledge of true facts—certificate from company solicitor that he had advised wife—whether creditor entitled to assume that independent advice given to wife—whether presumption of undue influence existed. See BANCO EXTERIOR INTERNACIONAL v. MANN, §2443.

3587. Constructive notice—misrepresentation—man and woman in long-standing relationship—woman persuaded to sign charge over her home in favour of bank by man—charge over home as security for loan—constructive notice—creditor's duty to satisfy himself that woman entered into obligation freely with knowledge of true facts—man's solicitor affirming to bank that he had advised woman—whether creditor entitled to assume that independent advice given to woman—whether presumption of undue influence existed. See MASSEY v. MIDLAND BANK, §2446.

3588. Constructive notice—misrepresentation—surety—charge on matrimonial home—induced by husband's misrepresentation—whether enforceable against wife by bank—whether enforceable in part. See TSB BANK v. CAMFIELD (KEVIN ANTHONY) (CCRTF 94/0231/E), §2447.

3589. Constructive notice—undue influence—by husband—wife signed certificate stating she had been advised by solicitor—whether bank entitled to rely on certificate. See MIDLAND BANK v. SERTER, §2450.

3590. Constructive notice—undue influence—whether bank entitled to rely on certificate—whether mortgage should be set aside. See BANK OF BARODA v. RAYAREL, §2452.

3591. Forfeiture—relief—underleases—relief against forfeiture available to a mortgagee by subdemise—whether available retrospectively—whether mesne profits to be paid off—whether service charge rent. See SINCLAIR GARDENS INVESTMENTS (KENSINGTON) v. WALSH (PATRICK), FOLAN (BRIDIE) AND BRISTOL & WEST BUILDING SOCIETY (CCRFT 93/1371/E; 94/0082/E; 94/0084/E; QBENI 94/0210E), §2992.

3592. Interest relief—extra-statutory tax concession. See REVENUE AND FINANCE, §4347.

3593. Mortgage indemnities—recognised bodies

MORTGAGE INDEMNITIES (RECOGNISED BODIES) ORDER 1995 (No. 210), made under the Housing Act 1985 (c.68), s.444(1); operative on February 20, 1995; specifies 13 additional bodies as recognised bodies for the purposes of the Housing Act 1985, ss.442 and 443.

MORTGAGE INDEMNITIES (RECOGNISED BODIES) (NO. 2) ORDER 1995 (No. 2053) [65p], made under Housing Act 1985, s.444(1); operative on August 21, 1995; specifies four additional bodies as recognised bodies for the purposes of ss.442 and 443 of the Housing Act 1985.

3594. Mortgagor protection—mortgagee obtaining collateral advantage—whether equity will intervene

[Aus.] Equity will not intervene to protect a mortgagor merely because a mortgagee obtains a collateral advantage, but will do so if there has been unconscionable conduct by the mortgagee as, for example, more readily found in the case of a necessitous borrower.

MODULAR DESIGN GROUP PTY. (IN LIQUIDATION), *Re* [1995] A.L.M.D. 2716, Sup. Ct., NSW.

3595. Possession—failure to pay capital element—whether arguable defence—whether judge wrong not to exercise discretion to set aside earlier order

An order for possession to the building society was made in respect of B's home for his failure to pay the capital element of his mortgage. The judge refused to set aside the order and B sought leave to appeal against this decision, contending that the judge was wrong not to exercise his discretion to set aside the earlier order.

Held, allowing the appeal, that B put forward an arguable defence that until he was asked to pay a sum of £900, he was unaware that he was under any liability to make repayment of capital until the end of the mortgage period, which had been entered into as an endowment mortgage. The trial judge had, on perusal of the papers, found no arguable defence or considered the possibility of suspension of the possession order. These matters ought to be addressed and accordingly B was granted leave to appeal, with an extension of time in respect of the possession order.

ABBEY NATIONAL v. BUXTON (LTA 94/6817/E) (LTA 94/6817/E), October 27, 1994, C.A.

3596. Possession—order for possession made—joint loan to husband and wife—enforcement of security—whether wife had signed agreement because of misrepresentation—whether order should be set aside

Finality in litigation takes precedence over prejudice to the losing party.

P successfully brought an action to recover properties from a husband and wife which had been offered as security for a loan. The wife subsequently sought to argue that she had signed the loan agreement only because of her husband's misrepresentation, and consequently any order for possession against her should be set aside.

Held, that the principle of finality in litigation was an important one, and would not be set aside. These allegations should have been brought in the lower court, not once the case had finally been decided against her.

WOODEL v. B.M. SAMUELS FINANCE GROUP [1995] 69 P. & C.R. 311, C.A.

3597. Possession—repeat application—hard circumstances—no prospect of mortgagor reducing arrears—whether order should be made

[Administration of Justice Act 1970 (c.31), s.36.]

B bought a new house with an NHBC guarantee, which proved to have structural problems, causing trouble when B tried to sell in 1990. Negotiations with NHBC were begun. AN, the mortgagees, took proceedings for possession on B's defaulting on repayments, but agreed to suspend possession provided that money was paid at once and that there was to be a six-month review. When a consent order was drawn up for the approval of a judge the latter provision was mistakenly omitted and this was not noticed by AN. When the matter came to the judge in 1991 the order differed from the draft agreement in that it was an N31 order containing no order for monetary judgment, it specified a date for possession but provided that possession would only be given with leave of the court, the order was not expressed to be a consent order and B was not present. An application to vary the order on the grounds that the arrears were increasing greatly was refused in 1992. A further application in 1994 to gain a variation of the order or possession under the Administration of Justice Act 1970, s.36 was dismissed at first instance, as the judge considered that he had no jurisdiction where the application was in the same terms as the 1992 application.

Held, allowing the appeal and making an order for possession, that the judge below did have jurisdiction although he could reject what amounted to a repeat application if it was an abuse of process. However, the court could not suspend an order for possession under s.36, however hard the circumstances, if there was no prospect of the mortgagor reducing the arrears. Negotiations with NHBC were still not concluded and were unlikely to cover the debt. The 1991 arrangement was intended only to be temporary and it could not have been contemplated that AN would take less than the full monthly outgoings indefinitely.

ABBEY NATIONAL MORTGAGES v. BERNARD [1995] NPC 118, C.A.

3598. Possession—series of suspensions—entitlement to relief—whether shown that mortgagee able to pay arrears within a reasonable period

[Administration of Justice Act 1970 (c.31), s.36.]

M obtained a mortgage from AN on March 4, 1993. He was advanced £59,375, with initial monthly payments of £345·08. Immediately he began to default. On July 13, 1993, AN issued proceedings for recovery. An order for possession was made, but set aside on September 20, on M's application advising that M would be able to pay the arrears as he was now in receipt of the necessary income. He issued a cheque to AN, which was dishonoured. AN again sought possession. On January 19, 1994, a further suspended order for possession was granted, as M again insisted he could pay. He failed to do so and AN applied for a warrant for possesion. On April 28, 1994, M applied for the warrant to be suspended again, as the property was now being sold for a sum in excess of the amount owed. He was ordered to pay £1,000 within 14 days, but failed to do so. The warrant for possession was due to be executed on August 15, 1994, but on August 9, M made an application to have this further stayed, paid £1,000 in cash to AN, offered to pay £175 per month to settle the arrears, and offered to continue making the repayments. He failed to make the repayments, and paid nothing further towards the arrears. The warrant for possession was further listed to take place on November 14. M made a further application which was heard on November 11, 1994, and the warrant for possession was suspended with a new date for execution to be fixed in one month's time. It was also ordered that he make no further applications to suspend the warrant for possession in any circumstances. He made a further payment of £560 towards the arrears, but no other payments of any kind were made. M appealed to the judge against the order. At the next hearing on May 22, 1995, AN's solicitors did not appear, but M was ordered to pay AN the sum of £1,000 before May 26, when the matter would be further heard. M did not pay, and did not attend the subsequent hearing, and his appeal was dismissed. The warrant for possession was due to be executed on July 12 at 12 noon. M then sought leave to appeal against the judge's order, and if leave were granted, sought a stay of execution of the warrant for possession.

Held, that M's application was dismissed. M was ordered to pay AN's costs of the application, to be taxed if not agreed. The Court stated that "it seems to be clear that [M], having failed to comply with the conditions on which the suspension of possession is granted is not in a position to complain about the orders and warrants for possession made. His record on payment is deplorable. Only about £1,500 has ever been paid. The grounds for a successful appeal are quite hopeless. The district judge at first instance was fully entitled to order as he did". This was clearly a case where the Administration of Justice Act 1970, s.36, needed to be applied. A mortgagor must be able to show that he is able to pay mortgage arrears within a reasonable period before being entitled to relief under s.36(2) of the 1970 Act. It was clear that M would not have been able to make the mortgage repayments or pay the arrears within a reasonable period of time, especially given his record on payment. Costs were awarded to AN.

ABBEY NATIONAL v. MEWTON, July 12, 1995, C.A. [*Ex rel.* Trobridges, Solicitors, Plymouth.]

3599. Power of sale—property purchased by mortgagor from local authority—mortgagor challenging validity of local authority sale after possession order granted—property sold by mortgagee in advance of date given to mortgagor—jurisdiction of court to interfere with sale

[Administration of Justice Act 1970 (c.31), s.36; C.C.R., Ord. 37.]

D purchased the lease of a flat from Westminster Council and secured an advance from NP by a mortgage on the flat. D defaulted on the mortgage payments and a suspended order for possession was made under the Administration of Justice Act 1970, s.36. D further defaulted on instalments and let the flat, in breach of the terms of the mortgage. A warrant for possession was issued and executed giving vacant possession to NP. D then applied under C.C.R., Ord. 37, to have the orders set aside, on the grounds that the lease had been granted by the City of Westminster Council pursuant to a "designated sales policy", which was the subject of proceedings by the District Auditor, and if this policy was found to be unlawful he would have the right to surrender the lease to the council and recover the premium paid for it. NP contracted to sell the flat and through a breakdown of communications completed the sale ahead of the date communicated to D's solicitors. At the hearing the judge found that NP's conduct had been reprehensible and set aside the earlier orders. He also ordered that D be readmitted to the property and that the Chief Land Registrar be restrained from registering the title of the purchaser. NP appealed.

Held, allowing the appeal and setting aside the order, that (1) it was inappropriate to grant an injunction against the Chief Land Registrar who had not been notified of the application and was not represented; (2) the order seriously affected the rights of the purchaser obtaining legal estate in the property; (3) the order required D to be readmitted to the flat and this was no longer in NP's power; (4) D had brought the application at a time when he had no longer any right to redeem the mortgage. In those circumstances, there was no jurisdiction to prevent NP from completing the sale to the purchaser and there was no jurisdiction under the 1970 Act, s.36, to stay or suspend an order for possession once it had been executed; and (5) this was not the case of an *ultra vires* transfer. The lease was a valid lease, within the power of the Westminster Council to grant, and it did not cease to be valid because it was granted (if this was found to be the case) pursuant to an unlawful decision of the council.

NATIONAL PROVINCIAL BUILDING SOCIETY v. AHMED (CCRTF 94/1635/E), May 5, 1995, C.A.

3600. Power of sale—sale of farm with quota—whether free to exercise choice to sell both together where exercised in good faith—advice of surveyor—whether surveyor negligent

E, who had a charge over a farm owned by H which had a large milk quota, appointed a receiver and sold the farm and quota. H claimed that more money could have been obtained had the quota been sold separately.

Held, that (1) E, provided it exercised its powers in good faith, was free to exercise those powers as it chose, and was not under a duty to H to sell the quota separately (*Tse Kwong Lam v. Wong Chit Sen* [1983] C.L.Y. 2484, *China & South Seas Bank v. Tan Soon Gin* [1990] C.L.Y. 2440, *Downsview Nominees v. First City Corp.* [1993] C.L.Y. 2881 followed); (2) a surveyor who advised a mortgagee in the lawful exercise of a power of sale, was not liable to the mortgagor on the grounds that the sale was at an undervalue. E owed H a duty to take reasonable care to obtain a proper price and there was no need to place its advisor under a like duty.

HUISH v. ELLIS [1995] N.P.C. 3, H.H.J. Raymond Jack, Q.C.

3601. Priority—purchaser's mortgagee—priority over charging order of creditors—whether subrogation to rights of former mortgagee

B's judgment creditors appealed against a ruling that the mortgagee, Abbey National Plc (AN) who financed the purchase of B's former house, took priority to their charging order. B granted a legal charge over the property to the Halifax Building Society (H) and subsequently contracted to sell the house. The purchaser's solicitor, D, also acted for the intended mortgagee AN. AN sent D the purchase moneys on terms that they must be used only to complete the purchase and otherwise returned. D paid B's solicitors who paid H. D became bankrupt. Subsequently the creditors obtained a charging order.

Held, dismissing the appeal, that AN, the purchaser's mortgagee, was entitled to a charge in priority to the judgment creditors by reason of subrogation to the rights of the former mortgagee whose legal charge had been discharged. The payment that discharged the legal charge could be traced back to AN's payment because a fiduciary relationship existed between AN and their solicitors D. D held the purchase money in trust for AN because AN's intention had always been to retain a beneficial interest in the money until a legal mortgage was granted (*Agip (Africa) v. Jackson* [1992] C.L.Y. 2039 considered).

BOSCAWEN v. BAJWA, *The Times*, April 25, 1995, C.A.

3602. Professional negligence—solicitor—acting for both lenders and purchasers—solicitors hearing of information suggesting the property might have been overvalued—whether solicitors should have told the lenders. See MORTGAGE EXPRESS v. BOWERMAN & PARTNERS (A FIRM), §3696.

3603. Professional negligence—survey—measure of damages—money lent solely because of negligent valuation—whether loss due to fall in property market recoverable. See BANQUE BRUXELLES LAMBERT SA v. EAGLE STAR INSURANCE CO., §1834.

3604. Redemption—notice period—request for title deeds and redemption statement—whether effective notice

A legal charge incorporated a term requiring P mortgagors to give "either one month's written notice to the [mortgagee, D] or pay an administrative fee of one month's interest in lieu of such notice" (Condition 18). On October 5, 1994, P's solicitors wrote to D stating that they were instructed in connection with the sale of the property and asking for the title deeds, and for a redemption statement calculated to October 30, 1994, together with the daily rate of interest. On October 11, 1994, D sent P's solicitors a redemption statement, with the daily interest rate. Completion of the sale and redemption of the mortgage took place on December 2, 1994. D charged P one month's interest, on the basis that the necessary one month's notice had not been given. P paid the sum "under protest" and then sued D to recover the money paid.

Held, dismissing P's action for recovery of the money, that Condition 18 required unconditional notice to be given. Ps' solicitors' letter of October 5 simply gave notice of intention to redeem the mortgage conditional upon the sale proceeding (which it might not have done) and therefore was, as a matter of contruction, insufficient to constitute notice in accordance with the Condition.

JENKIN & JENKIN v. HOUSEHOLD MORTGAGE CORP., October 6, 1995, Deputy District Judge Crick, High Wycombe County Ct. [*Ex rel.* Nicholas Yell, Barrister, No. 1 Sergeants' Inn, Fleet St.]

3605. Subrogation—lender subrogated to a previous lender whose loan only enforceable by means of a previous subrogation—whether mortgage to be aside

L ensured that W, who owned the matrimonial home, obtained independent legal advice before L lent money to H backed by a charge on the property, which was registered. Subsequently B lent money to H, partly to pay off L and partly to cover a builder's debt, but did not require that W should obtain legal advice as she had already done so. Consequently, W did not realise she was putting the home at risk again. A further loan to H with the property as security was made by CP, on H and a female accomplice forging a transfer into the joint names of H and W and executing a charge in favour of CP. .W knew nothing of this. The money owed to B was paid off by CP. On default by H, CP sought repayment of the debt. The judge at first instance held that W had no contractual liability and ordered the charge to be vacated. Further, because B had failed to explain matters to W she was bound only by the builder's debt, but B was entitled to subrogation on L's debts. CP should be subrogated to B in respect of that sum which would be secured by a new security by way of deposit of the land certificate. He ordered W to pay 35 per cent of CP's costs. W appealed against costs, argued that subrogation was inappropriate, and that B's charge should not have been set aside in part only where she had had no independent advice.

Held, that the judge was not right to set aside B's mortgage on terms that a new charge was created (*TSB Bank v. Camfield,* [1994] 12 C.L. 72 followed). However, although CP was not entitled to be subrogated to B's charge, as there was actual consent by W to L's charge, CP could step into B's shoes in respect of L's debt and was entitled to be subrogated to L's charge and should be registered as proprietor of L's charge. Order for costs to remain unchanged.

CASTLE PHILLIPS FINANCE v. PIDDINGTON [1994] NPC 155, C.A.

3606. Summary judgment—adjournment—failure properly to register the mortgagee's charge—registered as equitable charge—whether solicitor liable in restitution to mortgagor. See BRISTOL AND WEST BUILDING SOCIETY v. BRANDON, §4227.

3607. Taxable person—receiver—income of mortgaged property—VAT money collected—whether receiver to be treated as taxable person—whether appointment of receiver meant firm had gone into receivership. See SARGENT v. CUSTOMS AND EXCISE COMMISSIONERS, §5106.

3608. Valuation report—surveyor—professional negligence—proceedings not issued within limitation period—whether statute barred. See HEATHCOTE AND HEATHCOTE v. DAVID MARKS & CO., §3712.

NATIONAL HEALTH

3609. Dental charges

NATIONAL HEALTH SERVICE (DENTAL CHARGES) AMENDMENT REGULATIONS 1995 (No. 444) [65p], made under the National Health Service Act

1977 (c.49), s.79A, Sched. 12, para. 3(2); operative on April 1, 1995; further amend S.I. 1989 No. 394 so as to increase the maximum charge payable by a patient for dental treatment and appliances to £300.

3610. Dentistry—fees—meaning of "unexpected hazard"—remuneration dependent on whether "unexpected hazard" occurred—whether standard rule applicable or individual case facts relevant—whether reasons adequate

W applied for judicial review of the decision of the Dental Practice Board concerning fees due to him for the provision of general dental services. W acted as the anaesthetist during a dental operation when the patient suffered a laryngeal spasm. The question was whether a laryngeal spasm was an "unexpected hazard" within the meaning of the Statement of Dental Remuneration. The referees decided that it was not and therefore W was not entitled to £28, the sum prescribed in the Statement. The reason given by the referees was that they had not been provided with any evidence that a laryngeal spasm was an unexpected hazard. There was expert evidence on both sides. W contended that the referees had only considered the general question as to whether laryngeal spasm was an unexpected hazard, whereas each individual case must be considered separately. He also submitted that the referees failed to give adequate reasons for their decisions in that they had not expressed a view of the meaning of "unexpected hazard".

Held, allowing the application, that (1) the referees said that they had been offered no evidence on the question as to whether laryngeal spasm was an unexpected hazard when they clearly had; (2) the Board accepted that it had adopted a restrictive approach so as to limit claims; (3) the particular case should always be considered as well as the general point; and (4) the reasons given here were neither proper nor adequate (*Save Britain's Heritage v. Secretary of State for the Environment and Number 1 Poultry & City Index Property Investment Trust* [1991] C.L.Y. 3494 followed).

R. v. NORTH YORKSHIRE FAMILY HEALTH SERVICE AUTHORITY, *ex p.* WHITE (CO/1598/93), December 16, 1994, Dyson J.

3611. District health authorities

NATIONAL HEALTH SERVICE (DETERMINATION OF DISTRICTS) ORDER 1995 (No. 562) [£1·55], made under the National Health Service Act 1977 (c.49), ss.8(1)(2)(4), 126(4); operative on April 1, 1995; abolishes the districts of Chester, Chichester, East Surrey, Mid Downs, Mid Surrey, North West Surrey, South and East Cheshire, South West Surrey and Worthing and establishes new districts.

NATIONAL HEALTH SERVICE (DETERMINATION OF DISTRICTS) (NO. 2) ORDER 1995 (No. 533) [£1·10], made under the National Health Service Act 1977 (c.49), ss.8(1)(2)(4), 126(3)(4); operative on April 1, 1995; abolishes the districts of East Dyfed and Pembrokeshire and establishes a new district of Dyfed.

NATIONAL HEALTH SERVICE (DISTRICT HEALTH AUTHORITIES) ORDER 1995 (No. 563) [£1·10], made under the National Health Service Act 1977 (c.49), ss.8(1)(b)(1A)(c), 126(3); operative on April 1, 1995; abolishes the specified health authorities and establishes the new specified health authorities in their place.

NATIONAL HEALTH SERVICE (DISTRICT HEALTH AUTHORITIES) (NO. 2) ORDER 1995 (No. 534) [£1·10], made under the National Health Service Act 1977 (c.49), ss.8(1)(b)(1A)(c), 126(3) and the Welsh Language Act 1993 (c.38), s.25(2); operative on April 1, 1995; abolishes the East Dyfed and Pembrokeshire Health Authorities and establishes the new Dyfed Health Authority.

3612. Employees—injury benefits

NATIONAL HEALTH SERVICE (INJURY BENEFITS) REGULATIONS 1995 (No. 866) [£3·70], made under the Superannuation Act 1972 (c.11), ss.10(1)–(3),

12(1)(2), Sched. 3; operative on April 13, 1995; revoke and replace S.I. 1974 No. 1547, as amended, and provide for the payment of injury benefits in certain circumstances to persons who suffer injury in the course of their employment in the NHS.

3613. Family Health Services

FAMILY HEALTH SERVICES APPEAL AUTHORITY (ESTABLISHMENT AND CONSTITUTION) ORDER 1995 (No. 621) [£1·10], made under the National Health Service Act 1977 (c.49), ss.11(1)(2)(4), 126(4), Sched. 5, para. 9(7)(b); operative on April 1, 1995; provides for the establishment and constitution of a special health authority (the Family Health Services Appeal Authority) to exercise certain appellate and other functions of the Secretary of State formerly exercised on her behalf by the Northern and Yorkshire Regional Health Authority.

FAMILY HEALTH SERVICES APPEAL AUTHORITY REGULATIONS 1995 (No. 622) [£1·95], made under the National Health Service Act 1977 (c.49), ss.13, 16, 17, 18, 42, 126(4), Sched. 5, paras. 12, 16; operative on April 1, 1995; revoke S.I. 1992 No. 660, amend S.I. 1994 No. 682 and provide for the appointment and tenure of office of members of that authority.

NATIONAL HEALTH COMMISSIONER (FAMILY HEALTH SERVICES APPEAL AUTHORITY) ORDER 1995 (No. 753) [65p], made under the Health Service Commissioners Act 1993 (c.46), s.2(5); operative on April 17, 1995; provides that the Family Health Service Appeal Authority is a Special Health Authority which is subject to investigation by the Health Service Commissioner.

NATIONAL HEALTH SERVICE (FUNCTIONS OF FAMILY HEALTH SERVICES AUTHORITIES) (PRESCRIBING INCENTIVE SCHEMES) REGULATIONS 1995 (No. 692) [£1·10], made under the National Health Service Act 1977 (c.49), ss.15(1)(b), 126(4); operative on April 1, 1995; confer a new statutory function on Family Health Services Authorities to establish and operate schemes to make payments to GP practices in their localities which contain their prescribing costs.

3614. Fund-holding practices

NATIONAL HEALTH SERVICE (FUND-HOLDING PRACTICES) AMENDMENT REGULATIONS 1995 (No. 693) [£1·95], made under the National Health Service Act 1977 (c.49), s.126(4)(5) and the National Health Service and Community Care Act 1990 (c.19), ss.14(6), 15(7); operative on April 1, 1995; amend S.I. 1993 No. 567, the principal change being the creation of two levels of fund-holding practice, namely community fund-holding practices (minimum of 3,000 patients) and standard fund-holding practices (minimum of 5,000 patients), existing fund-holders automatically becoming standard fund-holding practices.

NATIONAL HEALTH SERVICE (FUND-HOLDING PRACTICES) (FUNCTIONS OF FAMILY HEALTH SERVICES AUTHORITIES) REGULATIONS 1995 (No. 3280 made under National Health Service Act 1977 s.126(4)(5) and National Health Service and Community Care Act 1990 ss.14(6), 15(7), 17(1)(2); amends S.I. 1993 No. 567. operative on January 9, 1996; [£1·10]. These Regulations transfer certain functions relating to fund-holding practices to Family Health Services Authorities (FHSAs) from Regional Health Authorities (RHAs) and in Wales from the Secretary of State by an amendment to the National Health Service (Fund-holding Practices) Regulations 1993. Applications for recognition as fund holding practices must now be sent to the FHSA who will forward them to RHAs with recommendations on the suitability of the practice to have fund holding status. The FHSA has been given the responsibility to gather information relevant to the RHA's determination of sums allotted to fund-holding practices and to propose an allotted sum for each practice.

3615. General dental services

NATIONAL HEALTH SERVICE (GENERAL DENTAL SERVICES) AMENDMENT REGULATIONS 1995 (No. 3092) [£1·10], made under the National Health

Service Act 1977, ss.15(1), 35(1), 36(1), 49E, 126(4); amend S.I. 1992 No. 66. In force: December 21, 1995; make provisions relating to dentists who have been suspended from the provision of general dental services or have been declared not fit to be engaged in the provision of those services by the NHS Tribunal. Provision is also made to enable Family Health Services Authorities to transfer to another dentist and to transfer back if the suspended dentist is reinstated.

3616. General medical services

NATIONAL HEALTH SERVICE (GENERAL MEDICAL SERVICES) AMENDMENT REGULATIONS 1995 (No. 80) [£1·55], made under the National Health Service Act 1977 (c.49), ss.15(1), 29, 33(2A)(a), 126(4); operative on February 6, 1995; amend S.I. 1992 No. 635 in connection with practice vacancies and doctors' terms of service.

NATIONAL HEALTH SERVICE (GENERAL MEDICAL SERVICES) AMENDMENT (NO. 2) REGULATIONS 1995 (No. 3093) [£1·10], made under the National Health Service Act 1977, ss.15(1), 29, 30(1), 49E, 126(4). In force: December 21, 1995 for regs. 1–6 and January 1, 1996 for reg. 7; amend S.I. 1992 No. 635 which regulates the terms on which general medical services are provided under the National Health Service Act 1977. Provision is made for cases where general medical practitioners are suspended or disqualified from providing medical services by the NHS Tribunal. Regulation 3 affords protection to suspended doctors from removal from the medical list where they have not provided general medical services for six months. Regulation 4 requires temporary arrangements to be made for the provision of general medical services to a suspended doctor's patients by the Family Health Services Authority, and reg. 5 provides for payments to be made to suspended doctors. Doctors' terms of service are amended by reg. 6 to stop a doctor engaging a suspended or disqualified doctor as a deputy or assistant. Regulation 7 adds "Temazepam Soft Gelatin Gel-Filled Capsules" to this list of drugs which may not be prescribed by GPs.

3617. General ophthalmic services

NATIONAL HEALTH SERVICE (GENERAL OPHTHALMIC SERVICES) AMENDMENT REGULATIONS (No. 558) [£1·10], made under the National Health Service Act 1977 (c.49), ss.38, 126(4); operative on April 1, 1995; further amend S.I. 1986 No. 975 so as to include a definition of Disability Working Allowance and to extend free sight tests to persons in receipt of that allowance who have capital resources of £8,000 or less.

3618. Health authorities—judicial review—formal complaints procedure—whether reasonable not to use procedures where complainant contemplating litigation. See R. v. CANTERBURY AND THANET DISTRICT HEALTH AUTHORITY; SOUTH EAST THAMES REGIONAL HEALTH AUTHORITY, *ex p.* F. AND W., §40.

3619. Health Authorities Act 1995 (c.17)

This Act reforms the administrative structure of the National Health Service by abolishing the eight Regional Health Authorities and replacing District Health Authorities and Family Health Services Authorities and Health Authorities.

The Act received Royal Assent on June 28, 1995.

3620. Health authority—administrative decision-making—treatment for 10-year-old girl—refusal to fund further treatment—whether local authority's refusal lawful

On an application for judicial review relating to medical treatment the court's only function is to consider the lawfulness of the decision and not to decide on the effectiveness of the treatment or the merits of conflicting medical opinions.

The patient, a 10-year-old girl, was diagnosed as suffering from leukaemia. After treatment she suffered a relapse and the doctors were of the opinion that no further remedial treatment should be given. B's father sought further medical advice and obtained opinions that a bone marrow transplant was possible. The treatment, in two stages, would cost £75,000 with only a 10 to 20 per cent chance of success. B requested the health authority to allocate funds for the treatment and the authority refused. B's father applied for judicial review of the decision. The judge refused to make an order of mandamus compelling the authority to provide funds but made an order of certorari quashing the decision to refuse to provide funds.

Held, allowing the health authority's appeal, that the question for the court was whether the decision was lawful. It was not for the court to decide between conflicting medical opinions or how to spend the health authority's budget. On the facts of the case the authority had proceeded correctly and the decision could not be said to have been unlawful.

R. v. CAMBRIDGE DISTRICT HEALTH AUTHORITY, *ex p.* B. [1995] 2 All E.R. 129, C.A.

3621. Health authority—budgets—funding—misapplication of funds—facilitator posts paid for from cash limited funds set aside for payment of general practitioner costs—whether Secretary of State to investigate further after resignation of those responsible

[National Health Service Act 1977 (c.49); National Health Service (General Medical and Pharmaceutical Services) Regulations 1974 (S.I. 1974 No. 160).]

The Manchester Health Services Authority (M) used cash limited funds set aside for the reimbursement of general practice staff costs and rents, and premises improvement grants, for the appointment of eight facilitators. Three of the facilitators (all dental) were attached, without the general practitioners' knowledge, to general practices which did not provide dental services. The Manchester Local Medical Committee applied for judicial review of the decision of the Secretary of State not to take action on requests made by the LMC to investigate the use of the budget to fund the facilitator posts, or, alternatively, to hold an inquiry into the abuse of power. The Chairman and Chief Executive had resigned when the misapplication of funds came to light.

Held, dismissing the application but granting a declaration that the payments were unlawful, that (1) in terms of the National Health Service Act 1977, the National Health Service (General Medical and Pharmaceutical Services) Regulations 1974 and guidance circulars and letters issued by the Secretary of State for Health, the use of funds for the provision of general medical services was strictly regulated. The use of this money for the appointment of facilitators was unlawful. However, once that error had been discovered and admitted to, and the appropriate action taken, there was no further point in continuing to investigate or inquire into the matter; (2) the declaration of illegality was made to ensure that M would not be guilty of the same error a second time.

R. v. SECRETARY OF STATE FOR HEALTH, *ex p.* MANCHESTER LOCAL MEDICAL COMMITTEE (CO/3306/93; CO/189/94), March 28, 1995, Collins J.

3622. Health authority—medical records—access to—whether patient having right of access—whether health authority acted in patient's best interests

[Convention for the Protection of Human Rights and Fundamental Freedoms (1953) (Cmd. 8969), Art. 8.]

A health authority, as the owner of a patient's medical records, can deny a patient access to them if it is in the patient's best interests to do so.

A, who had a background of psychological problems, had repeatedly requested access to his medical records, all of which had been made before 1991 and were not subject to the Access to Health Records Act 1990 or the

Data Protection Act 1984. Voluntary disclosure of the records was refused by the health authorities. In proceedings for judicial review the judge held that A had no right of access to his medical records at common law and that a refusal to disclose them did not constitute a breach of the provisions of Art. 8 of the Convention.

Held, dismissing A's appeal, that (1) a health authority, as the owner of the patient's medical records, may deny the patient access to them if it is in his best interests to do so; (2) since the court was satisfied that the respondent health authorities had done all that was necessary to comply with their duties to A, the judge in the exercise of his discretion had been entitled to refuse the relief sought (*Sidaway v. Board of Governors of the Bethlem Royal Hospital and the Maudsley Hospital* [1985] C.L.Y. 2318 considered).

R. v. MID-GLAMORGAN FAMILY HEALTH SERVICES AUTHORITY, *ex p.* MARTIN [1995] 1 W.L.R. 110, C.A.

3623. Health service trusts—change of name

Orders made under the National Health Service Act 1977, s.126(3)(4), and the National Health Service and Community Care Act 1990, s.5(1), changing the name of the specified National Health service trusts:

S.I. 1995 Nos. 918 (Llandough Hospital and Community) [65p]; 968 (East Surrey Healthcare) [65p]; 1235 (Bexley Community Health) [65p]; 2379 (East Surrey Priority Care National Health Service Trust) [£1·10].

3624. Health service trusts—dissolution

Orders made under the National Health Service Act 1977 (c.49), s.126(3); and the National Health Service and Community Care Act 1990 (c.19), s.5(1), Sched. 2, para. 29(1), dissolving the specified health service trusts:

S.I. 1995 Nos. 477 (Broadgreen Hospital) [65p]; 478 (Fosse Health, Leicestershire Community) [65p]; 479 (Royal Liverpool University Hospital) [65p]; 480 (St. James's University Hospital) [65p]; 481 (Weybourne Community) [65p]; 792 (Homewood) [65p]; 801 (United Leeds Teaching Hospitals) [65p]; 846 (Wolverly) [65p].

3625. Health service trusts—establishment

Orders made under the National Health Service Act 1977 (c.49), s.126(3) and the National Health Service and Community Care Act 1990 (c.19), s.5(1) amending the constitution of the specified National Health Service trusts:

S.I. 1995 Nos. 88 (Princess Royal Hospital) [65p]; 91 (Royal Hull Hospital) [65p]; 92 (Cumbria Ambulance Service) [65p]; 99 (Teddington Memorial Hospital: amending S.I. 1993 No. 123) [65p]; 117 (North Hampshire Hospitals); 141 (West Wales) [£1·10]; 142 (Cardiff) [£1·10]; 143 (University Dental Hospital) [£1·10]; 769 (Glan-y-Môr) [£1·10]; 770 (University Hospital of Wales Healthcare) [£1·10]; 842 (Newham Community Health Services) [£1·10]; 843 (City and Hackney Community Services) [£1·10]; 844 (University Hospital Birmingham) [£1·10]; 845 (Royal Orthopaedic Hospital) [£1·10]; 847 (Tower Hamlets Healthcare) [£1·10]; 848 (Surrey Heartlands) [£1·10]; 996 (Robert Jones and Agnes Hunt Orthopaedic and District Hospital) [65p]; 1311 (Durham County Ambulance); 1469 (Calderdale Healthcare); 1709 (Royal Orthopaedic Hospital); 2697 (Kent Ambulance); 2797 (Gwent Community Health).

3626. Health service trusts—originating capital debt

NATIONAL HEALTH SERVICE TRUSTS (ORIGINATING CAPITAL DEBT) ORDER 1995 (No. 407) [£1·95p], made under the National Health Service and Community Care Act 1990 (c.19), s.9(1)(4); operative on March 15, 1995; determines the amount of originating debt of NHS trusts established on April 1, 1993.

NATIONAL HEALTH SERVICE TRUSTS (ORIGINATING CAPITAL DEBT) AMENDMENT ORDER 1995 (No. 791) [£1·95], made under the National Health

Service Act 1977 (c.49), s.126(3) and the National Health Service and Community Care Act 1990 (c.19), s.9(1)(4); operative on March 15, 1995; amends S.I. 1995 No. 407 (and re-issues it in its amended form) so as to correct amounts specified in the earlier Order in relation to the North Durham Acute Hospitals NHS Trust.

NATIONAL HEALTH SERVICE TRUSTS (ORIGINATING CAPITAL DEBT) (WALES) ORDER 1995 (No. 394) [65p], made under the National Health Service and Community Care Act 1990 (c.19), s.9(1)(4); operative on March 3, 1995; determines the amount of originating debt of NHS trusts in Wales established on April 1, 1993.

NATIONAL HEALTH SERVICE TRUSTS (ORIGINATING CAPITAL DEBT) (WALES) (NO. 2) ORDER 1995 (No. 2783) [65p], made under the National Health Service and Community Care Act 1990, s.9(1)(4); operative on November 10, 1995; determines the amount of capital debt of NHS Trusts established under the National Health Service and Community Care Act 1990 with an operational date of April 1, 1994 and provides also for the splitting of the originating capital debts into loan and public dividend capital.

3627. Health service trusts—transfer of property

Orders made under the National Health Service Act 1977 (c.49), s.92(1), transferring property formerly held by the specified health authority to the specified National Health Service trusts:

S.I. 1995 Nos. 2 (Plymouth) [65p]; 82 (City Hospitals Sunderland) [65p]; 83 (Derbyshire Royal Infirmary) [65p]; 84 (North Tyneside Health Care) [65p]; 85 (Southport and Formby Community Health Services) [65p]; 86 (West Lancashire) [65p]; 87 (Wrightington Hospital) [65p]; 89 (Priority Healthcare Wearside 1995) [65p]; 90 (Pilgrim Health) [65p]; 301 (Brent and Harrow Health); 324 (Nottingham City Hospital) [65p]; 341 (Carlisle Hospitals) [65p]; 342 (Guild Community Healthcare) [65p]; 343 (Hounslow and Spelthorne Community and Mental Health) [65p]; 344 (Lancashire Ambulance Service) [65p]; 345 (Preston Acute Hospitals) [65p]; 346 (Richmond, Twickenham and Roehampton Healthcare) [65p]; 347 (St. Albans and Hemel Hempstead) [65p]; 348 (Trafford Healthcare) [65p]; 378 (Bolton Hospitals) [65p]; 379 (Burton Hospitals) [65p]; 380 (Central Nottinghamshire Healthcare) [65p]; 381 (Community Healthcare Bolton) [65p]; 382 (East Surrey Learning Disability and Mental Health Service) [65p]; 383 (Greenwich Healthcare) [65p]; 384 (King's Mill Centre for Health Care Services) [65p]; 385 (Lincoln Hospitals) [65p]; 386 (Premier Health) [65p]; 387 (Surrey Ambulance Service) [65p]; 473 (Glan Clwyd District General Hospital) [65p]; 474 (Gofal Cymuned Clwydian Community Care); 475 (Wrexham Maelor Hospital) [65p]; 502 (Carmarthen and District Hospital) [65p]; 503 (Derwen) [65p]; 504 (Ceredigion and Mid Wales) [65p]; 505 (Llanelli Dinefwr) [65p]; 564 (United Leeds Teaching Hospitals) [65p]; 565 (Wolverley) [65p]; 567 (Gwynedd Health Authority to North Wales Ambulance [65p]; 568 (Gwynedd Health Authority to Gwynedd Hospitals [65p]; 569 (Gwynedd Health Authority to Gwynedd Community [65p]; 932 (Portsmouth Hospitals) [65p]; 933 (Portsmouth Health Care) [65p]; 934 (Hereford Hospitals) [65p]; 935 (Dartford and Gravesham) [65p]; 937 (Winchester and Eastleigh Healthcare) [65p]; 938 (Stoke Mandeville Hospital) [65p]; 1088 (South and East Wales Ambulance) [65p]; 1089 (Morriston Hospital) [65p]; 1090 (Nevill Hall and District) [65p]; 1107 (East Glamorgan); (North Wales Ambulance) [65p]; 1123 (Special Trustees for the Royal Free Hospital) [65p]; 1124 (Camden and Islington Community Health Services) [65p]; 1125 (Whittington Hospital) [65p]; 1126 (Special Trustees for the Middlesex Hospital) [65p]; 1127 (North Yorkshire Health Authority) [65p]; 1128 (Royal London Homoeopathic Hospital) [65p]; 1129 (University College Hospital) 65p]; 1232 (Glan Hanfren) [65p]; 1233 (Powys Health Care) [65p]; 1234 (South and East Wales Ambulance) [65p]; 1242 (North East Worcestershire Community Health Care) [65p]; 1243 (Mancunian Community Health) [65p]; 1244 (Wirral Community Healthcare) [65p]; 1245 (Havering Hospitals) [65p]; 1246 (BHB Community Health Care) [65p];

1247 (Haringey Health Care) [65p]; 1248 (South Durham Health Care) [65p]; 1249 (Dewsbury Health Care) [65p]; 1259 (Westcountry Ambulance Services) [65p]; 1260 (Bishop Auckland Hospital) [65p]; 1261 (Darlington Memorial Hospital) [65p]; 1262 (Worthing and Southlands Hospitals) [65p]; 1263 (Mid Essex Community and Mental Health) [65p]; 1264 (New Possibilities) [65p]; 1265 (Salisbury Health Care) [65p]; 1588 (Walsgrave Hospitals); 1589 (Kettering General Hospital); 1590 (Tavistock and Portman); 1602 (East Wiltshire); 1603 (Rockingham Forest); 1604 (Swindon and Marlborough); 1657 (Dudley Priority); 1731 (Mancunian Community Health); 1732 (South Manchester University Hospitals); 1733 (Tameside and Glossop); 1734 (Tameside and Glossop); 1735 (Gloucestershire); 1736 (North Manchester Healthcare); 1766 (South Kent Community Healthcare); 1767 (South Kent Hospitals); 1768 (Birmingham Heartlands Hospital); 1910 (West Kent Health Authority); 1911 (Kent Ambulance); 1912 (Mid Kent Healthcare); 1913 (North Kent); 1914 (Royal Victoria Infirmary and Associated Hospitals); 1462 (Northampton Community Healthcare) [65p]; 1463 (Northampton General Hospital) [65p]; 1464 (Royal Wolverhampton Hospitals) [65p]; 1465 (Norfolk and Norwich Health Care) [65p]; 1466 (Leicestershire Ambulance and Paramedic Service) [65p]; 1467 (Alexandra Health Care) [65p]; 1468 (Derbyshire Ambulance Service) [65p]; 1489 (Norwich Community Health Partnership) [65p]; 1490 (Norfolk Mental Health Care) [65p]; 1491 (Leicestershire Mental Health Service) [65p]; 1492 (Bury Health Care) [65p]; 1493 (Cumbria Ambulance Service) [65p]; 1494 (North Lakeland Healthcare) [65p]; 1534 (West Yorkshire Metropolitan Ambulance Service) [65p]; 1991 (Dudley Group of Hospitals); 1992 (Furness Hospitals); 1993 (Severn Community and Mental Health); 1994 (South Cumbria Community and Mental Health); 1995 (Westmorland Hospitals National Health Service Trust); 2129 (Central Manchester Healthcare); 2149 (Greater Manchester Ambulance Service); 2150 (Warwickshire Ambulance Service); 2322 (Northern Birmingham Community Health); 2323 (Northern Birmingham Mental Health); 2324 (South Warwickshire Mental Health); 2325 (Fosse Health, Leicestershire Community); 2326 (Worcester Royal Infirmary); 2327 (City Hospital); 2377 (West Herts Community Health) [65]; 2378 (Mount Vernon and Watford Hospitals) [65p]; 2411 (Rhondha Health Care) [65p]; 2434 (West Midlands Ambulance Service); 2435 (Mental Health Services of Salford); 2457 (Northern and Yorkshire Region) [65p]; 2459 (National Blood Authority) [65p]; 2491 Mid Glamorgan Ambulance National Health Service Trust) [65p]; 2492 (Velindre Hospital National Health Service Trust) [65p]; 2493 (Cardiff Community Healthcare National Health Service Trust) [65p]; 2494 (University Dental Hospital National Health Service Trust) [65p]; 2495 (Llandough Hospital and Community National Health Service Trust) [65p]; 2496 (South and East Wales Ambulance National Health Service Trust) [65p]; 2497 (George Eliot Hospital) [65p]; 2581 (Surrey Heartlands National Health Service Trust) 65p]; 2691 (Cheshire Community Healthcare National Health Service Trust) [65p]; 2698 (West Cheshire National Health Service Trust) [65p]; 2749 (North Worcestershire); 2781 (Manchester); 2811 (West Glamorgan); 2875 (Manchester); 2958 (Stockport Healthcare); 2959 (Stockport Acute Services); 3028 (National Blood Authority); 3182 (Sussex Ambulance Service); 3256 (Hinchingbrooke Health Care); 3257 (Kent and Sussex Weald); 3258 (Mid-Kent Healthcare); 3259 (Weald of Kent Community); 3260 (Queen Victoria Hospital); 3285 (Sandwell Healthcare).

3628. Litigation—special health authority to help administration of claims—press release

The Department of Health has issued a press release entitled *New NHS Litigation Authority established*, published on October 30, 1995. The new authority, which has been set up as a Special Health Authority, will assist with the administration of the Clinical Negligence Scheme for Trusts (established to help NHS trusts in England with clinical negligence). The Authority will be responsible for ensuring that patients' claims are dealt with sensitively and fairly and will receive advice on general policy issues from a policy steering group consisting of representatives of the Scheme.

3629. Litigation Authority

NATIONAL HEALTH SERVICE LITIGATION AUTHORITY (ESTABLISHMENT AND CONSTITUTION) ORDER 1995 (No. 2800) [65p], made under the National Health Service Act 1977, s.11(1)(2)(4), Sched. 5, para. 9(7)(b); operative on November 20, 1995; provides for the establishment and constitution of the National Health Service Litigation Authority which will exercise functions in connection with the establishment and the administration of the scheme for meeting liabilities of health service bodies to third parties for loss, damage or injury arising out of the exercise by those bodies of their functions.

NATIONAL HEALTH SERVICE LITIGATION AUTHORITY REGULATIONS 1995 (No. 2801) [£1·95], made under the National Health Service Act 1977, ss.16, 126(4), Sched. 5, paras. 12, 16; operative on November 20, 1995; make provision regarding the membership and procedure of the National Health Service Litigation Authority.

3630. Medical treatment—complaint—parent of minor patient acting on minor's behalf—patient attaining majority opposed to complaint—whether jurisdiction to hear

[National Health Service (Service Committees and Tribunal) Regulations 1974 (S.I. 1974 No. 000), reg. 6(3).]

A parent who complains about the medical treatment of an infant patient is not entitled to insist that the complaint proceed contrary to the wishes of the patient once the patient has attained majority.

Doctor A prescribed a drug to a patient, W, who was then aged 17. F, who was the father of W, initiated a complaint in respect of the prescription without W's consent. W turned 18 and a question arose as to whether F had the proper standing to make a complaint on W's behalf. A applied for judicial review to quash a decision of the Secretary of State for Health that she had jurisdiction to deal with the complaint.

Held, granting the application, that there was nothing in reg. 6(3) of the National Health Service (Service Committees and Tribunal) Regulations 1974 to prevent the initiation of a complaint by a parent on behalf of a minor merely because the minor did not support the complaint. But, ignoring incapacity by reason of sickness or infirmity, once the patient attains majority the person who initiated the original complaint is not entitled to insist that it proceed contrary to the patient's wishes.

R. v. SECRETARY OF STATE FOR HEALTH, ex p. BARRATT [1994] 5 Med L.R. 235, Judge J.

3631. National Blood Authority

HEALTH SERVICE COMMISSIONER FOR ENGLAND (NATIONAL BLOOD AUTHORITY) ORDER 1994 (No. 2954) [65p], made under the Health Service Commissioners Act 1993 (c.46), s.2(5); operative on January 1, 1995; designates the said Authority as a body subject to review by the Commissioner.

3632. National Health Service (Amendment) Act 1995 (c.31)

This Act, *inter alia*, makes provisions regarding the disqualification of practitioners under s.46 of the National Health Service Act 1977 (c.49), amends the rules regarding the constitution of the tribunal under that section, and makes corresponding provisions for Scotland.

The Act received Royal Assent on July 19, 1995.

3633. National Health Service (Amendment) Act 1995—commencement

NATIONAL HEALTH SERVICE (AMENDMENT) ACT 1995 (COMMENCEMENT NO. 1 AND SAVING) ORDER 1995 (No. 3090 (C.70)) [£1·10], made under the

National Health Service (Amendment) Act 1995, s.14(3)(4); brings into force on December 21, 1995 certain provisions of the National Health Service (Amendment) Act 1995 which amend the National Health Service Act 1977 relating to the powers of the National Health Service Tribunal: s.1, relating to disqualified practitioners and the engagement in provision of services by others; s.2, relating to interim suspension of practitioners; s.3, relating to appeals against disqualification and the removal of the right to appeal to the Secretary of State; s.4, relating to the removal of disqualification; s.5, relating to the procedure relating to disqualification; s.6, relating to the constitution of the tribunal; s.14(2), relating to repeals, so far as it relates to the provisions of the Schedule brought into force by this Order.

3634. National Health Service trust—professional review report commissioned by Regional Health Authority—whether findings of report to be disclosed to plaintiff in negligence action. See MERCER v. ST. HELENS & KNOWSLEY HOSPITALS NHS TRUST AND NORTH WEST REGIONAL HEALTH AUTHORITY, §4124.

3635. Nurses, midwives and health visitors—registration

NURSES, MIDWIVES AND HEALTH VISITORS (PERIODIC REGISTRATION) AMENDMENT RULES APPROVAL ORDER 1995 (No. 967) [£2·40], made under the Nurses, Midwives and Health Visitors Act 1979 (c.36), s.22(4); operative on April 1, 1995; introduces a continuing education requirement as part of the renewal of registration requirements.

3636. Optical charges and payments

NATIONAL HEALTH SERVICE (OPTICAL CHARGES AND PAYMENTS) AMENDMENT REGULATIONS 1995 (No. 34) [65p], made under the National Health Service Act 1977 (c.49), s.126(4), Sched. 12, para. 2A; operative on February 1, 1995; amend S.I. 1989 No. 396.

NATIONAL HEALTH SERVICE (OPTICAL CHARGES AND PAYMENTS) AMENDMENT (NO. 2) REGULATIONS 1995 (No. 691) [£1·95], made under the National Health Service Act 1977 (c.49), s.126(4), Sched. 12, para. 2A; operative on April 1, 1995; further amend S.I. 1989 No. 396 in respect of payments to be made by vouchers for certain costs incurred in connection with the supply, replacement and repair of optical appliances.

NATIONAL HEALTH SERVICE (OPTICAL CHARGES AND PAYMENTS) AMENDMENT (NO. 3) REGULATIONS 1995 (No. 2307) [65p], made under the National Health Service Act 1977 s.126(4), Sched. 12, para. 2A; amend S.I. 1989 No. 396; operative on October 1, 1995.

3637. Pension scheme

NATIONAL HEALTH SERVICE PENSION SCHEME REGULATIONS 1995 (No. 300) [£8·10], made under the Superannuation Act 1972 (c.11), ss.10(1)–(3), 12(1)(2), Sched. 3; operative on March 6, 1995; consolidate with amendments S.I. 1980 No. 362, as amended, and make provision for the superannuation of persons employed in the NHS.

3638. Pharmaceutical services

NATIONAL HEALTH SERVICE (PHARMACEUTICAL SERVICES) AMENDMENT REGULATIONS 1995 (No. 644) [£1·55], made under the National Health Service Act 1977 (c.49), ss.41, 42, 43, 126(4); operative on April 1, 1995; amend S.I. 1992 No. 662 in respect of advice which may be provided by pharmacists, requirements in connection with additional professional services; the determining authority for remuneration for specified pharmaceutical services, and terms of service and fair wages for staff.

3639. Prescription charges

NATIONAL HEALTH SERVICE (CHARGES FOR DRUGS AND APPLIANCES) AMENDMENT REGULATIONS 1995 (No. 643) [£1·10], made under the National Health Service Act 1977 (c.49), ss.77, 126(4); operative on April 1, 1995; amend S.I. 1989 No. 419 so as to increase charges provided for therein.

NATIONAL HEALTH SERVICE (CHARGES FOR DRUGS AND APPLIANCES) AMENDMENT (NO. 2) REGULATIONS 1995 (No. 2737) [65p], made under the National Health Service Act 1977, ss.77, 83A(1), 126(4); operative on October 20, 1995; amend S.I. 1989 No. 419 by exempting all persons who have attained the age of 60 years from paying charges for drugs and appliances supplied by doctors and chemists providing pharmaceutical services, and by health authorities and NHS trusts to outpatients; made in order to comply with Council Dir. 79/7 on the progressive implementation of the principle of equal treatment in matters of social security.

3640. Prescription charges—age criteria—sex discrimination—contrary to E.C. Equal Treatment Directive—press release

The Department of Health has issued a press release entitled *Exemption from prescription charges to be equalised for men and women from tomorrow* (Press Release 95/491), published on October 19, 1995. Gerald Malone, Minister for Health, has announced the equalisation of the age of exemption from prescription charges for men and women to 60 in a statement to the House of Commons today. The announcement follows the ECJ ruling that regulations governing prescription charge age exemption arrangements are not consistent with Council Dir. 79/7/EEC, which provides for the equal treatment of men and women in matters of social security. The case was brought by Cyril Richardson who was required to pay prescription charges at the age of 64, when his wife, aged 62, had been exempt from charges from the age of 60. Mr Richardson argued that he had suffered discrimination contrary to the EC Directive on equal treatment and his case was referred by the High Court to the ECJ for a ruling.

3641. Prescription charges—different exemptions for women and men—whether sex discrimination—application to ECJ for preliminary ruling—proportionality—European Community

[Council Directive 79/7; National Health Service (Charges for Drugs and Appliances) Regulations 1989 (S.I. 1989 No. 419).]

R, aged 64, contended, in an application for judicial review, that, as a result of reg. 6(1) of the National Health Service (Charges for Drugs and Appliances) Regulations 1989 which exempted women over 60 years and men over 65 years from prescription charges, he had suffered discrimination contrary to Council Dir. 79/7. The Secretary of State argued that prescription charges did not fall within the scope of the Directive and the Queen's Bench Divisional Court sought a preliminary ruling from the ECJ on (i) whether reg. 6(1) was covered by Art. 3(1) of the Directive (ii) if so, whether the permitted derogation in Art. 7(1)(a) applied and (iii) in the event of the provision in reg. 6(1) being found to be contrary to the Directive, whether persons affected could rely on the direct effect of the Directive to bring claims for damages in respect of periods prior to the date of the ECJ's judgment.

Held, that (1) being part of a statutory scheme and affording protection against the risk of sickness, reg. 6(1) fulfilled the conditions laid down in Art. 3(1) and fell within the scope of Dir. 79/7; (2) Art. 7(1)(a) permitted forms of discrimination which were necessarily and objectively linked to the difference in retirement age set by a Member State for the purpose of granting retirement pensions, but the discrimination underlying reg. 6(1) was not objectively necessary, either to avoid disturbing the financial equilibrium of the social security system or to ensure coherence between the retirement pension system and other benefit schemes (*Thomas v. Chief Adjudication*

Officer [1993] E.C.R. I–1247 considered); and (3) there was no justification for restricting the effect of the present ruling regarding time. Thus, the direct effect of the Directive could be relied upon to support claims for damages for periods prior to the date of the judgment.

R. v. SECRETARY OF STATE FOR THE HEALTH DEPARTMENT, *ex p.* RICHARDSON (C–137/94), *The Times*, October 27, 1995, ECJ.

3642. Service committees and tribunals

NATIONAL HEALTH SERVICE (SERVICE COMMITTEES AND TRIBUNAL) AMENDMENT REGULATIONS 1995 (No. 3091) [£1·95], made under the National Health Service Act 1977, ss.49, 49C(2), 126(4). In force: December 21, 1995; amend S.I. 1992 No. 664 in order to implement the provisions of the National Health Service (Amendment) Act 1995, which amended the provisions of the National Health Service Act 1977 and provided the National Health Service Tribunal with the power to suspend doctors, dentists, pharmacists, opthalmic medical practitioners and opticians from providing their respective services. Part II provides for the appointment of a deputy chairman of the Tribunal and makes other amendments relating to officers of the Tribunal. Part III abolishes the right to appeal against Tribunal decisions to the Secretary of State. The procedure relating to applications for interim suspension and continuation of suspension pending appeal is set out in Pt. IV along with provision for the Chairman or his Deputy to carry out the functions of the Tribunal which relate to suspension applications. Provision is made for the chairman of the Tribunal to give practice directions and determine Tribunal procedure in Pt. V along with amendments relating to costs, evidence, witnesses and referrals to professional bodies.

3643. Travelling expenses

NATIONAL HEALTH SERVICE (TRAVELLING EXPENSES AND REMISSION OF CHARGES) AMENDMENT REGULATIONS 1995 (No. 642) [£1·10], made under the National Health Service Act 1977 (c.49), ss.83A, 126(4), 128(1); operative on April 1, 1995; further amend S.I. 1988 No. 551.

NATIONAL HEALTH SERVICE (TRAVELLING EXPENSES AND REMISSION OF CHARGES) AMENDMENT (NO. 2) REGULATIONS 1995 (No. 2352) [65p], made under the National Health Service Act 1977, ss.83A, 126(4), 128(1); amend S.I. 1988 No. 551; operative on October 2, 1995.

NEGLIGENCE

3644. Automatism—hypoglycaemia—definition of voluntary control—whether total loss of voluntary control—whether gradual loss of control sufficient for automatism

CG instructed solicitors in the recovery of damages occasioned to their vehicle arising from a road traffic accident on July 23, 1990, on the approach to the Dartford Tunnel, which had involved eight vehicles. The claim was for less than £4,000 net of interest. AE alleged that their driver, R, who was a diabetic, was suffering from an attack of hypoglycaemia which had begun without warning and which could not reasonably have been foreseen or guarded against. The defence was that of automatism, that R was not responsible in law for what happened, because he had no voluntary control over his actions. A number of witnesses gave evidence of erratic driving on R's part, who was described in evidence as apparently unaware of other traffic. In order to establish the defence of automatism, it had to be established that a total destruction of voluntary control had taken place:

evidence of impairment, to however severe an extent, was insufficient. Evidence was given that the regime R was under to control his diabetes was changed, so that he was given human, rather than animal, insulin. In two episodes following the change, R experienced a collapse, and in a third episode, wandered briefly in a dazed condition. Evidence was given that the classic accompanying symptoms of a hypoglycaemic attack, dizziness, headache, sweating, blurring of vision, which warn of the onset of an attack, and often provide diabetics with the opportunity to take some preventative action, may not have taken place in this case because R had been on insulin for a long time, and his body was used to the fluctuation of the sugar level. R did go to his doctors, who tested him for epilepsy, but who failed to give any advice relevant to hypoglycaemia. R tested his blood sugar on the morning in question, gave himself more breakfast because he found it to be low, and then set off to Southend, travelling anti-clockwise round the M25, having no intention to travel through the Dartford Tunnel. He had no recollection of anything after the M11. His apparent ability to remember and discuss things immediately after the accident was not necessarily inconsistent with a hypoglycaemic attack, as the effect of the insulin he had taken earlier in the day would be wearing off.

Held, reviewing the relevant authorities, that it was accepted that the individual afflicted by hypoglycaemia is unaware of what is happening, and as a result is unable to do anything about it. The result of this is that he is disabled effectively from making any conscious decision which stops him driving in a manner which leads to disaster but, nonetheless, the courts, having looked at the driving and having seen that he has been able to undertake manoeuvres of various kinds, said that there cannot have been a complete absence of voluntary control. In one sense of course there had been a loss of voluntary control, because the individual is not able voluntarily to stop doing what he is doing, namely continuing to drive, but that is not the legal definition. One would suspect that the legal definition would require the driver to run off the road, totally fail to steer around any obstacle or to take any necessary avoiding measures. Although there is a degree of artificiality in an approach which distinguishes between gradual onset of a condition and sudden, it being equally impossible in both cases for the individual to act on it, the recorder suggested that the defence of automatism could not be raised where there was gradual loss of control, even if, at the time of the accident itself, there was a total loss of control, but held in this case that total loss of control had not occurred at the time of the accident, as R was still capable of swerving to avoid traffic.

CHELSEA GIRL v. ALPHA OMEGA ELECTRICAL SERVICES, May 9, 1994, Mr Recorder Collins, Q.C., Mayors and City of London County Court. [*Ex rel.* Putsmans, Solicitors, Birmingham.]

3645. Bank—duty of care—loan advice—loan to renovate and sell house—house sold at loss—whether damages available

V brought an action in negligence against LB for failing to advise them against a business venture undertaken with the assistance of a bank loan. In 1988 they approached LB for a loan to buy an old house to renovate and sell. The bank manager viewed the figures they produced, accompanied them to help them find suitable property and eventually approved the loan. However, the renovation cost more than expected, the property market fell disastrously and they sold the house in 1990 for a considerable loss.

Held, that if borrowers asking for a loan to finance a transaction specifically sought advice on the prudence of the transaction, the bank owed them a duty of care in respect of advice given. The evidence in the instant case established that such a duty of care arose. The duty of care was violated because the bank manager should have taken account of their existing debts, insufficient income and lack of business experience and advised them not to proceed. To borrow more than the house was worth on a bridging loan was clearly not prudent when, even relying on a steep rise in property values, the projected profit was relatively modest. V was awarded damages based on the loss on sale of the property.

VERITY v. LLOYDS BANK, *The Independent*, September 19, 1995, Taylor J.

3646. Carriage by sea—negligent stowage—leakage of dangerous chemicals—whether distributors liable

The charterer of a ship which carried drums of dangerous chemicals, namely hydrochloric acid and sodium hypochlorite, shipped by T, which subsequently leaked as a result of damage to the containers, was able to bring an action in tort against the distributors of the substances alleging negligent stowage, since it was arguable that they should have taken preventive steps to neutralise the danger.

LOSINJSKA PLOVIDBA v. TRANSCO OVERSEAS, *The Times*, July 18, 1995, Mance J.

3647. Child-minder—statutory duty of local authority to maintain register—local authority deciding not to suspend or deregister child-minder under investigation—infant seriously injured while in child-minder's care—whether local authority having duty to take reasonable care in exercising its statutory obligations to register and deregister child-minders—whether local authority liable for negligent misstatement

[Nurseries and Childminders Regulation Act 1948 (c.53), s.5.]

There is, prima facie, no statutory duty under the Nurseries and Child-minders Regulation Act 1948 nor any common law duty owed by local authorities to take reasonable care in the exercise of their obligation to register or deregister child-minders.

T suffered a serious non-accidental injury while in the care of a registered child-minder, W. T's mother, prior to engaging W, had contacted the local authority's nursery and child-minding adviser, B, who confirmed that W was registered as a child-minder under the 1948 Act and told her that there was no reason why T could not safely be left in W's care. In fact, B was aware that less than three months earlier another child in W's care had been seriously injured, probably through violent shaking, although it remained unresolved whether or not W had caused the injury. As a result of his injuries T, suing by his mother, claimed damages for personal injuries against, *inter alia*, the local authority for breach of statutory duty in failing to cancel W's registration pursuant to s.5 of the 1948 Act, breach of a common law duty of care in failing to cancel the registration and negligent misstatement.

Held, giving judgment for T against the local authority on the ground of negligent misstatement, that (1) while the purpose of the 1948 Act was clearly to ensure that only those persons who were fit to look after children under five should be registered as child-minders and that a person could not be so fit when there was an unresolved question about a non-accidental injury suffered by a child who had been in that person's care, a failure by the local authority to meet its implied obligations under the Act to suspend the child-minder's registration pending further investigations did not confer a private law right of action for statutory breach of duty on a child who had been injured while in the care of the minder as this had not been expressly imposed in the statute; (2) the issues of breach of statutory duty and common law negligence in respect of the exercise of power by a local authority under the 1948 Act ran on parallel lines and, as such, there was no common law duty owed by local authorities to take reasonable care in the exercise of their obligations to register or de-register child-minders; but (3) if the local authority knew or ought to have appreciated that there was a significant risk in placing a child in the care of a particular child-minder, yet still informed a parent that there was no reason why a child should not be placed in that person's care, it might be liable for negligent misstatement so that, on the facts, it was clear that there was a significant risk to any infant placed in W's care and, in the circumstances, the local authority was liable for negligent misstatement.

T. (A MINOR) v. SURREY COUNTY COUNCIL [1994] 4 All E.R. 577, Scott-Baker J.

3648. Civil aviation authority—certification that plane safe—whether duty to owner of aircraft

P, owner of an aircraft which crashed a month after it was certified airworthy by C, sued C for negligence, claiming that they owed him a duty of care. P's case was dismissed.

Held, dismissing P's appeal, that C had the responsibility of supervising aircraft owners not in their own interest but in the interests of the general public. C could not therefore owe the owners a duty of care to inspect their aircraft thoroughly, because to maintain the planes in a safe condition was primarily the owner's responsibility. They could not call on the supervisory authority to protect them from their own mistakes (*Marc Rich & Co. AG v. Bishop Rock Marine Co.* [1994] 12 C.L. 633, *Yuen Kun Yu v. Att.-Gen. of Hong Kong* [1988] A.C. 175, *Mariola Marine Corp. v. Lloyd's Register of Shipping* [1991] C.L.Y. 2668, *Murphy v. Brentwood District Council* [1991] C.L.Y. 2661 considered).

PHILCOX v. CIVIL AVIATION AUTHORITY, *The Times*, June 8, 1995, C.A.

3649. Coastguard—whether duty of care owed to mariner

The coastguard owed no duty of care to a mariner in its watching, listening or rescue co-ordination activities.

SKINNER v. SECRETARY OF STATE FOR TRANSPORT, *The Times*, January 3, 1995, Gareth Edwards, Q.C. sitting as a deputy judge.

3650. Contributory negligence—breach of contract—strict performance building contract—failure by plaintiff to prevent defendant from committing breaches—whether contributory negligence defence applicable. See DAMAGES, §1571.

3651. Contributory negligence—sport—unsupervised gymnastic activity—spinal injury—contributory negligence finding—appropriate degree of supervision—degree of responsibility to be assumed by young athlete

[Law Reform (Contributory Negligence Act) 1945 (c.28), s.1(1).]

F suffered serious and permanent spinal injury when he failed to perform a successful forward somersault in the activities hall at the Bedford Youth House. B provided these premises which offered facilities and services for young people between 18 and 25 years. B appealed against a decision that they were liable to F in negligence. B alleged that the accident occurred because F had placed landing gym mats too close to a wall and had attempted a dangerous gymnastic exercise without assistance, knowing the potential risks. They contended that the judge below was wrong to conclude that the unsupervised provision of the gym mats was the cause of F's accident. F cross-appealed against the finding of contributory negligence to the extent of two-thirds. F contended that he had not been given proper instruction or supervision at the Youth House or been warned of the risks both of performing such a manoeuvre and of placing landing mats close to a wall. F submitted that his conduct did not amount to fault within the Law Reform (Contributory Negligence) Act 1945, s.1(1).

Held, dismissing both the appeal and the cross-appeal, that (1) the court accepted the contention that the lack of supervision and accessibility of the gym mats could not be the basis of primary liability. The mere foreseeability of the injury and B's failure to prevent it were insufficient to establish liability (*Sutherland Shire Council v. Heyman* [1985] C.L.Y. 2274 approved); (2)

however, the findings of negligence were not restricted to that point. B were liable in negligence because a youth worker employed by them had assumed the task of teaching F to do forward somersaults and thereon assumed a duty to make him aware of the risks and dangers. B provided no warnings of the dangers, either verbal or written, and compounded that failure by allowing unsupervised access to the gym mats; and (3) F had to bear a substantial part of the blame for the accident, since the risks were obvious to a reasonably intelligent person. F was an intelligent accomplished athlete. He was aware of what could happen if he over-rotated when attempting the somersault. On the evidence, it was apparent that the extra effort given to impress his audience caused him to land against the wall.

FOWLES v. BEDFORDSHIRE COUNTY COUNCIL (QBENF 93/1384/C), May 17, 1995, C.A.

3652. Crown Prosecution Service—alleged carelessness and delay in prosecution of case—whether duty of care—whether CPS immune from liability

In the absence of some voluntary assumption of responsibility to a particular defendant, the CPS is immune from actions for negligence.

Ps in two cases were arrested, charged and held in custody. After 22 and 85 days in detention respectively, the CPS discontinued proceedings. Both Ps brought actions in negligence claiming, in one case, unreasonable delay in obtaining and communicating the results of forensic tests and in the second, unreasonable delay in concluding the case was bound to fail. The claims were struck out as showing no cause of action.

Held, dismissing the appeals, that there was no general duty of care owed by the CPS in its conduct of a prosecution. The relationship of the parties was not sufficiently proximate to establish the duty, and in any event it was contrary to public policy to impose such a duty (*Hill v. Chief Constable of West Yorkshire* [1988] C.L.Y. 2435 applied; *Welsh v. Chief Constable of the Merseyside Police* [1993] C.L.Y. 2943 distinguished).

ELGUZOULI-DAF v. COMMISSIONER OF POLICE OF THE METROPOLIS; McBREARTY v. MINISTRY OF DEFENCE [1995] 2 W.L.R. 173, C.A.

3653. Debenture trust deed—secure advance to company—directors of company furnishing reporting certificates to trustee pursuant to deed—certificates allegedly prepared negligently—whether directors acting as company's agents—whether company vicariously liable for directors' negligence—whether company and directors joint tortfeasors—trustee releasing company from liability—whether directors thereby released. See NEW ZEALAND GUARDIAN TRUST v. BROOKS, §2199.

3654. Director—negligence—breach of duty—signing unread insurance form—compensation to company—misfeasance summons—whether relief should be granted. See D'JAN OF LONDON, *Re*; COPP v. D'JAN, §595.

3655. Discovery—medical records—personal injury action—repetitive strain injury—limitation that records to go to medical advisers only—whether legal advisers entitled to see records. See BAKER v. PAPER SACKS, §4119.

3656. Discovery—medical records—personal injury action—whether entitled to require disclosure to legal as well as medical advisers. See HIPWOOD v. GLOUCESTER HEALTH AUTHORITY, §4120.

3657. Education authority—statutory duties—children with special educational needs—failure properly to assess and provide for needs—whether action in negligence for breach of common law duty of care. See E. (A MINOR) v. DORSET COUNTY COUNCIL; CHRISTMAS v. HAMPSHIRE COUNTY COUNCIL; KEATING v. BROMLEY LONDON BOROUGH COUNCIL, §1927.

3658. Employer—duty of care—repetitive strain injury—known risk of teno-synovitis—whether employer's breach of duty to warn of known risk relevant to claim of repetitve strain injury

An employer owes a duty to employees engaged in work with a known risk of an injury with a definable pathology to warn and educate as to the risk of that injury. Breach of that duty will enable an employee to recover damages for abnormal pain, even though the employee's condition has no definable pathology.

P and others were employed by D in repetitive work with a known risk of teno-synovitis. Although P did not suffer from teno-synovitis, she alleged that she suffered from repetitive strain injury (RSI) causing pain and sued D for damages for personal injury. D denied negligence, and disputed whether P suffered from a category of physical injury which could be said medically to exist. D argued that RSI involved no physical, diagnosable conditions other than the simple aches and pains of life.

Held, finding in favour of P, that (1) it had been clear that certain of D's work processes were likely to cause clinically diagnosable disorders, such as teno-synovitis, in a minority of workers. D had a duty, as employer, to take reasonable and proportionate steps to reduce this potential harm. This duty included a duty to warn employees of the risks and consequences of teno-synovitis so that the employees could make a choice whether to undertake work involving a risk of that harm, and so that they would bring any symptoms of that condition to the attention of a doctor at the first opportunity. There was no duty to warn of RSI, the very existence of which as a clinical condition was in dispute. There was also a duty to ensure an effective system of job rotation to combat the repetitiveness of tasks in areas where there was a greater risk of physical harm. D was found to have been in breach of these duties; (2) P, while not suffering from a recognised clinical condition such as teno-synovitis, had more than likely felt pain over and above the ordinary aches and pains of life. The wider, diffuse condition of RSI had neither been proven to exist nor been ruled out. It was likely that this abnormal pain was consequent on the work performed by P. P could recover in respect of this abnormal pain to the extent that it had been suffered as a consequence of D's breach of duty, albeit that the foreseeable risk giving rise to that duty was the risk of teno-synovitis rather than of abnormal pain with no definable pathology.

MOUNTENAY (HAZZARD) v. BERNARD MATTHEWS [1994] 5 Med L.R. 293, H.H.J. Mellor.

3659. Employer—duty to take reasonable care for health and safety of employee—duty to provide a safe system of work—whether duty extends to risk of psychiatric illness

An employer's duty to take reasonable care to provide his employee with a safe system of work and take reasonable steps to prevent him from risks which are reasonably foreseeable extended to risks of psychiatric illness.

W, who was responsible for four teams of social services fieldworkers employed by the NCC, suffered a mental breakdown in November 1986 and was forced to spend four months away from work. This breakdown followed a lengthy period over which W's work pressures increased significantly and, despite repeated attempts to do so, he had not persuaded the NCC either to increase staff or provide guidance as to work distribution or prioritisation. Upon his return he was offered no additional support from the NCC and by September 16, 1987 he was advised to go on sick leave and suffered a second mental breakdown. He was dismissed on the grounds of permanent ill-health in February 1988 and brought an action for damages against the NCC for breach of their duty of care to take reasonable steps to avoid exposing him to a health-endangering workload.

Held, upholding W's claim for damages, that (1) there is no logical reason why the risk of psychiatric damage should be excluded from the scope of an employer's duty to provide his employee with a reasonably safe system of work and to take reasonable steps to protect him from risks which are reasonably foreseeable (*Bolton v. Stone* [1947–51] C.L.C. 6789 considered). Once a duty of care has been established the standard of care required for the performance of that duty must be measured against the yardstick of reasonable conduct on the part of a person in the position of that person who owes the duty (*Glasgow Corporation v. Muir* [1943] A.C. 448, *Paris v. Stepney Borough Council* [1947–51] C.L.C. 6587 considered), and the practicability of the remedial measures must clearly take into account the resources and facilities of the person or body owing the duty of care (*British Railways Board v. Herrington* [1972] C.L.Y. 2344 considered). The duty does not extend to negligible risks but only to materially substantial risks. Although the evidence established that prior to W's first breakdown it was reasonably foreseeable that W might sustain a mental breakdown of some sort in consequence of his work, it was not reasonably foreseeable to the NCC that the workload to which he was exposed gave rise to a material risk of mental illness, in the sense that the risk to which W was exposed was higher than that which would ordinarily affect a social services middle manager in his position; (2) when W returned to work after his first illness it was reasonably foreseeable to the NCC that if he was again exposed to the same workload as he had been handling at the time of his first breakdown without substantial back-up there was a sizeable risk that he would again succumb to mental illness and that such illness would be likely to end his career; and (3) in deciding whether it was reasonable for the NCC to take action to alleviate that risk regard must be had to the acute staffing problems then experienced by the NCC. However, it was wrong to say that, in the context of a contract of employment between a statutory body and an employee, the statutory body could rely on considerations of policy both to justify a decision which caused damage or injury to the employee, and to prevent the court from evaluating the reasonableness of the body's conduct (*Anns v. Merton London Borough Council* [1977] C.L.Y. 2030, *Lavis v. Kent County Council* [1993] C.L.Y. 2949 considered). Having regard to the size of the risk of a repetition of W's mental illness and the likely gravity of that illness, the standard of care expected of a reasonable local authority required that the NCC take measures to ensure that W's workload was permanently reduced, either through additional assistance or restructuring of the social services.

WALKER v. NORTHUMBERLAND COUNTY COUNCIL [1995] IRLR 35, Colman J.

3660. *Ex turpi causa*—excessive violence—trespasser shot—whether damages available—whether doctrine of *ex turpi causa non oritur actio* applicable

[Occupier's Liability Act 1984 (c.3), s.1.]

N appealed against an award of damages in a personal injury action brought by R, who was shot at close range by N when trespassing on N's allotment. N, who had been asleep in his shed when he was woken by R trying to break in, had poked his shotgun through a hole in the shed door and fired. The judge awarded damages on the basis that N had used violence in excess of the reasonable limits allowed by lawful self-defence and was negligent by reference to the standard of care to be expected of a reasonable man who found himself in such a situation. N challenged the finding that he was negligent and also contended that he had a complete defence under the rule that no cause of action might be founded on an illegal or immoral act.

Held, dismissing the appeal, that the finding of negligence was justified on the facts. As regards the doctrine of *ex turpi causa non oritur actio*, there was a public interest which required that someone engaging in illegal conduct should not benefit from his crime, but different considerations applied in cases arising in tort than in cases arising in a property or contract context (*Tinsley v. Milligan* [1993] C.L.Y. 1839 considered). Old common law authorities and the Law Commission report *Liability for Damage or Injury to*

Trespassers (Cmnd. 6428) acknowledged the existence of some duty towards trespassers and N could not rely on the doctrine to relieve him of liability.

REVILL v. NEWBERRY, *The Times*, November 3, 1995, C.A.

3661. Foreseeability—damage to property—nuisance and negligence—claim against council—trees causing subsidence—cracks in house—whether damage by trees foreseeable

[Highways Act 1980 (c.66), s.96.]

P claimed damages in nuisance and negligence against the local council for cracks in his house resulting from trees, causing subsidence to the property by drying out the soil which was of medium shrinkability.

Held, allowing the claim, that the council's knowledge about the type of soil in the locality, shown by its advice to property owners, meant that the risk of damage caused by tree roots was foreseeable and therefore the council, which was responsible for the trees in question, could be held liable in nuisance and negligence. P's claim for breach of statutory duty was, however, denied because the trees had not been planted pursuant to the council's powers under s.96 of the Highways Act 1980.

PATERSON v. HUMBERSIDE COUNTY COUNCIL, *The Times*, April 19, 1995, D.C.

3662. Girl Guide camp—appropriate level of supervision

P, then aged 11, attended her first Girl Guide camp, and burnt her leg whilst cooking sausages. P claimed against the Guide Association, complaining of the first aid treatment she received and of the level of instruction and supervision. The complaint relating to first aid was abandoned, with the Guiders congratulated by the judge upon their prompt first aid treatment. The judge found that P had received instruction. As to supervision, the court considered P's age, her previous experience and the extent of her training and instruction. The judge commented that a Guide Camp should be an enjoyable experience for all, and was also to teach and inform the young and to encourage a level of responsibility in the young. The court accepted that there was good supervision throughout. A stifling supervision would have had the effect of discouraging all initiative. P's claim failed and her action was dismissed.

LEONARD v. GIRL GUIDE ASSOCIATION, May 25, 1995, District Judge N. Vincent, Truro County Ct. [*Ex rel.* Robin Challans, Cann & Hallett, Solicitors, Exeter.]

3663. Highway authority—condition of highway—mud dropped by heavy vehicles—failure to prevent—whether breach of duty of care

[Highways Act 1980 (c.66), s.58(1).]

Where a highway became dangerously slippery because it was covered in mud, and the highway authority had done nothing other than have it swept once a week, the highway authority cannot claim to have taken all reasonable precautions to keep the road from becoming dangerous.

P fell from his motorcycle because the road on which he was travelling was slippery with wet mud, which had accumulated from heavy lorries passing to and from a nearby building site. P claimed that the highway authority had failed in its duty to maintain the road. The council relied on the Highways Act 1980, s.58(1), as a defence, arguing that they had taken all reasonable precautions.

Held, dismissing the defence, that merely to have the road swept once a week did not consititute taking all reasonable precautions.

MISELL v. ESSEX COUNTY COUNCIL (1995) 93 L.G.R. 108, Colman J.

3664. Highway authority—failure to maintain highway—duty to inspect pavements—personal injury resulting from defective paving slab—statutory defence of regular system of inspections—whether adequacy of authority's general system relevant if inspection of accident site established

[Highways Act 1980 (c.66), s.58.]

On May 17, 1992, P was walking along a paved footpath near her home, holding her young son's hand. P walked towards a set of five low steps. The steps were made up of paving slabs supported on bricks, and were open to view as there was grass verging on either side. One of the steps had fallen forward to rest upon the slabs below, the supporting bricks having been removed. The fallen flagstone created a raised defect of one inch when descending the staircase, and the front edge of the step had sunk by approximately three inches. As P descended the steps, she tripped and fell, sustaining injuries to her knee, shoulder and neck. D authority relied upon the statutory defence pursuant to the Highways Act 1980, s.58. D authority's highway inspector gave evidence that the section of the footpath had been inspected on three occasions in the 16 months prior to P's accident and the highway reports for each such inspection were produced. The inspection report dated January 5, 1991 revealed a defect in the steps; this was subsequently repaired and did not appear on the two further inspection reports prior to the accident.

Held, that there was a regular system in the area, which was being carried out properly. It had been submitted on P's behalf that there were only five highway inspectors working for the authority, and that this could not be sufficient to cover the authority's highways adequately. However, the judge held that it was necessary only to determine whether the area in which a plaintiff's accident occurred was inspected regularly, and found that it was. The judge concluded that the statutory defence was made out, and dismissed P's claim. The judge also commented that had P's claim succeeded, he would have reduced any damages awarded by two-thirds, for contributory negligence

ALLEN v. NEWCASTLE CITY COUNCIL, June 29, 1995, Mr Recorder Hirst, Newcastle-upon-Tyne County Ct. [*Ex rel.* Simon Wood, Barrister and Andrew McMurchie, Solicitor, Crutes, Newcastle-upon-Tyne.]

3665. Letting agent—advice to prospective landlord—possession of house required at expiry of short-term lease—advice related only to landlord seeking personal occupation—whether breach of duty of care

[Rent Act 1977 (c.42), Sched. 15.]

Where a landlord, who wishes to let premises and regain vacant possession at a later stage, approaches a letting agent to draft a lease, the letting agent has a duty to explain the exact basis upon which possession may be obtained under the proposed lease.

P wished to let a flat until such time as it might be sold, and approached D, a firm of letting agents. On D's advice, P signed a lease notifying the tenant that P was an owner-occupier and that the letting was under Case 11 to Sched. 15 of the Rent Act 1977, which provides that the court will order possession in favour of an owner-occupier landlord who intends to resume occupancy. P then attempted to recover possession of the premises, but the possession proceedings were not argued on the Case 11 basis, as P had no intention of personally resuming possession. P failed to recover possession and argued that D had been in breach of their duty to exercise reasonable skill and care in relation to the letting.

Held, giving judgment for P, that P had made it clear that it was important that possession should be recovered at the expiry of the term. D had failed to explain that if P wished to obtain possession on the Case 11 ground they would have to resume possession. This failure was a breach of the duty of care owed to P.

HELLINGS v. PARKER BRESLIN ESTATES [1994] EGCS 128, Sir Mervyn Davies, sitting as a judge of the Chancery Division.

3666. Limitation of actions—negligent valuation—date of accrual of cause of action—whether date of valuation or date of loss. See FIRST NATIONAL COMMERCIAL BANK v. HUMBERTS, §3172.

3667. Local authority—building regulation inspections—purchaser told final inspection carried out—purchaser discovered departures from regulations—whether local authority liable for negligent misstatement

A purchaser who had been told on inquiry that a final inspection had taken place under the building regulations and who subsequently found, on completion of purchase, that departures from the regulations had taken place, sought to make the local authority liable for negligent misstatement. The judge struck out the claim.

Held, dismissing the appeal, that the authority did not take on a special duty of care under *Hedley Byrne v. Heller* as no specific relationship of proximity could be established by the correspondence, nor was any assumption of responsibility assumed in the answer (*Hedley Byrne v. Heller* [1963] C.L.Y. 2416, *Murphy v. Brentwood* [1991] C.L.Y. 2661, *Henderson v. Merrett* [1994] C.L.Y. 3362, *Caparo Industries v. Dickman* [1990] C.L.Y. 3266 considered).

KING v. NORTH CORNWALL DISTRICT COUNCIL [1995] NPC 21, C.A.

3668. Local authority—duty to keep premises secure—tenants of council rehoused but not all belongings moved at once—house boarded up badly—house entered through defectively boarded window and ransacked—whether local authority liable for losses resulting from third party's wrongdoing

P was a tenant of D council. She and her family had been subjected to, *inter alia*, racially motivated harassment, which had on one occasion resulted in a window of her council house being smashed and on another occasion a door panel being broken. D knew about the problems experienced by P. These problems were not unusual for the area. P asked to be re-housed, and this was arranged. Not all her belongings could be removed at once. Some of her belongings remained in the council house. D knew this. The ground floor windows of the house were boarded up by D. The technique used for boarding up was found to be satisfactory, but the standard of workmanship was not. A gap was left between a board and the sill of one window which would have allowed, and in fact did allow, prising instruments to be used more readily to prise the board away and gain access to the house. About one week after boarding up, the house was burgled. Entry was gained through the defectively boarded window. The house was ransacked and a large number of P's goods were destroyed or stolen. P brought an action in negligence against D, contending that D owed her a duty of care to take reasonable care to ensure that the house was secure.

Held, dismissing P's claim, that although there were special circumstances in which a defendant might be liable to a plaintiff for injuries which resulted from a third party's deliberate wrongdoing (such as a contractual relationship between the plaintiff and the defendant, or control by the defendant over the third party), no such special relationship existed here. Accordingly, D did not owe P a duty of care. Application of the tests for the existence of a duty of care laid down in *Caparo v. Dickman* produced the same result (*Caparo v. Dickman* [1990] C.L.Y. 3266, *Smith v. Littlewoods Organisation* [1987] C.L.Y. 2597 applied).

REED v. DONCASTER METROPOLITAN BOROUGH COUNCIL, March 9, 1995, H.H.J. Mettyear, Doncaster County Ct. [*Ex rel.* Charles Foster, Barrister, 11 King's Bench Walk.]

3669. Medical negligence—anaesthetist—administration of epidural during labour—resultant paralysis—whether negligent injection of toxic substance

P, a pregnant mother, was given an epidural to ease her labour pains. P experienced severe pain in her legs and bottom and suffered total paralysis in the saddle area. P sued D, alleging that a toxic substance was administered to her during the epidural. D argued that P's condition had been caused by fibrocartilaginous embolism or spontaneous infarction.

Held, that the anaesthetist had been negligent. The positive defences advanced by D were inconsistent with the evidence. Although a safe procedure to ensure the administration of the correct drug was in place, the judge was not satisfied that the anaesthetist had followed it. There was no direct evidence that a toxic substance had been administered, but the evidence of the pain felt by the plaintiff was consistent with the thesis that there had been some human error.

RITCHIE v. CHICHESTER HEALTH AUTHORITY [1994] 5 Med LR 187, H.H.J. Anthony Thompson, Q.C.

3670. Medical negligence—anaesthetist failing to intubate patient—whether procedure adopted one which no reasonably competent health authority would adopt—whether anaesthetist negligent

Unless a medical procedure adopted by a health authority is patently unsafe or against common practice a court should not find that its adoption was negligent.

P was injected with anaesthetic and paralysing drugs during an operation. The anaesthetist made an attempt to intubate P which failed. Following the procedure laid down by D, the health authority, he did not re-attempt intubation, but allowed P to wake up. P suffered panic and distress upon waking, as the paralysing drugs had not worn off. P claimed that the failure to intubate was negligent and that the procedure was such that no reasonable authority would have adopted it. D argued that although the procedure involved the risk of transient terror it avoided the risk of far greater injury by hypoxia.

Held, dismissing P's claim, that (1) the failure to intubate was not negligent; (2) the procedure had been adopted by D with knowledge of the risks and disadvantages which might occur. The court would not interfere and find that this was a decision which no reasonable authority would have adopted.

EARLY v. NEWHAM HEALTH AUTHORITY [1994] 5 Med LR 214, Mr Patrick Bennett, Q.C. sitting as a deputy judge.

3671. Medical negligence—date of knowledge—delay in giving treatment—whether statement of delay sufficient to fix plaintiff with knowledge. See COLEGROVE v. SMYTH, §3168.

3672. Medical negligence—date of knowledge—failure to operate resulting in loss of use of hand—whether knowledge that hospital treatment had not worked imbued plaintiff with relevant knowledge. See SMITH (MICHAEL JOHN) v. WEST LANCASHIRE HEALTH AUTHORITY (CCRTF 94/1240/C), §3169.

3673. Medical negligence—date of knowledge—plaintiff unaware defendant's acts or omissions arguably negligent—whether such knowledge necessary to start time running against the plaintiff. See DOBBIE v. MEDWAY HEALTH AUTHORITY, §3171.

3674. Medical negligence—discovery—public interest immunity—independent professional review report—whether findings available to plaintiff in negligence claim. See MERCER v. ST. HELENS & KNOWSLEY HOSPITALS NHS TRUST AND NORTH WEST REGIONAL HEALTH AUTHORITY, §4124.

3675. Medical negligence—failure to examine—delivery by forceps—baby too high in pelvis—whether registrar's failure to examine patient at first-hand negligent—whether midwife's failure to abdominally palpate patient negligent

A doctor who failed to gain first-hand knowledge of a patient, and left the case to be managed by midwives, was negligent in attempting to deliver the patient's baby by forceps when the baby was too high in the patient's pelvis.

P sued D in respect of injuries he received during birth. An examination of his mother, upon admission to hospital, had revealed that the baby's head was unusually high. This was reported to the acting registrar, who did not examine the patient but instructed that she be left for a few hours. The baby made a little more progress in descent. When the acting registrar was eventually called he examined the patient and attempted to deliver the baby by forceps.

Held, upholding P's claim, that (1) the acting registrar had been negligent in failing to examine the patient, given the warning sign that the baby's head was high. He deprived himself of any first-hand knowledge of the patient and left the case to be managed by the midwives; (2) the midwife had been negligent in failing to abdominally palpate the patient and merely relying on vaginal examinations; and (3) the acting registrar was negligent in attempting to extract the baby by Kielland's forceps at a time when it was too high in the mother's pelvis. This negligence at least materially contributed to, if it did not solely cause, P's injuries.

PARRY v. NORTH WEST SURREY HEALTH AUTHORITY [1994] 5 Med L.R. 259, H.H.J. Curtis.

3676. Medical negligence—general practitioner's examination of patient failing to reveal cause of illness—whether negligent in failing to verify diagnosis

A general practitioner will be negligent if, in reliance upon his initial examination, he fails to take proper professional care in verifying his diagnosis of the patient in circumstances where the initial examination may not have discovered the true cause of the patient's illness.

D, a general practitioner, was called out to see the deceased on June 26, 1987. The deceased complained of a pain in his chest, which he attributed to heavy lifting work, and of a cold and diarrhoea. D examined the deceased and diagnosed him as suffering from a suspected pulled muscle and viral gastroenteritis. On June 28, 1987 the deceased died as a result of acute pneumococcal pneumonia which D had failed to diagnose. The deceased's wife, P, sued D and a preliminary issue arose as to whether D had been negligent in his examination of the deceased or in making provisions for a follow up examination.

Held, finding in favour of P, that there had been no confirmatory signs of pneumonia in the deceased, and D had conducted the examination without negligence. However D had erred in unequivocally attributing the chest pain to muscle strain. D was negligent in failing to recognise the uncertainties attending his diagnosis and he should have borne in mind the possibility that the chest pain might be pleural. D should have arranged for the deceased to be examined again within 24 hours, at which time the symptoms of pneumonia would have been apparent.

BOVA v. SPRING [1994] 5 Med LR 120, Sedley J.

3677. Medical negligence—midwife—patient with history of caesarian section—midwife absent for few minutes—whether constant attendance required

There is no need for a midwife to be in constant supervision of the labour of a patient who has a history of giving birth by caesarean section.

P was born with cerebral palsy brought on by hypoxia caused by severe prolonged foetal bradycardia shortly before delivery by caesarean section. P's mother had previously given birth by caesarean section, and P argued that her labour should have been monitored with particular care and that a midwife should have been in constant attendance throughout. The midwife had been absent for some nine minutes during which bradycardia had been in progress. P sued alleging negligence.

Held, dismissing P's claim, that the midwife's absence from the room for nine minutes had not been negligent. The midwife's continuous presence was not medically essential from the point of view of avoiding any risk that might arise from trial of scar. Even if the absence had been negligent, P would have been unable to prove that an additional nine minutes of bradycardia had materially increased her disability.

JAMES v. CAMBERWELL HEALTH AUTHORITY [1994] 5 Med L.R. 253, H.H.J. Fawcus.

3678. Medical negligence—paralysis after operation—*res ipsa loquitur*—possible non-negligent cause of injury—whether possible to rely on maxim in such circumstances

P cannot rely upon the maxim *res ipsa loquitur* to create a presumption of negligence where there is no evidence of negligence and a possible non-negligent cause of the injury.

P suffered paralysis from C6 downwards some 12 to 18 hours after a sagittal split osteotomy which rendered her permanently tetraplegic. P could not point to any particular traumatic incident, but relied on the maxim *res ipsa loquitur*, arguing that the only possible explanation for the catastrophe was that her neck had suffered hypertension and shearing stress during the operation. D argued that there was no evidence of hyper tension or shearing stress, and contended that the tetraplegia could have been the result of the rare condition of fibro-cartilaginous embolism (FCE). This phenomena could only be proved following an autopsy.

Held, dismissing P's claim, that it was inappropriate to apply the *res ipsa loquitur* maxim here. P had to show that her condition was caused by the negligent infliction of a traumatic injury, and her case would fail if it were equally likely that her tetraplegia was caused by FCE. It was not acceptable that hypertension or the application of shearing force could have taken place without being observed by those in the operating theatre. The evidence which suggested that there had been negligence was equivocal. FCE was a more probable cause of her tetraplegia than negligence during surgery.

HOWARD v. WESSEX REGIONAL HEALTH AUTHORITY [1994] 5 Med LR 57, Morland J.

3679. Medical negligence—test—practice accepted by responsible body of doctors—whether small group sufficient

D appealed against the dismissal of her medical negligence claim, on the grounds that the wrong test was applied to determine whether the surgeon's actions were negligent.

Held, dismissing the appeal, that *Bolam v. Friern Hospital Management Committee* established that a doctor who acted according to practices accepted by a responsible body of doctors was not negligent. The court was entitled to find that this requirement was satisfied even where the number of specialist doctors who would accept the doctor's practices was small. In this context a body of doctors which could not be described as "substantial" might nevertheless be "responsible" (*Bolam v. Friern Hospital Management Committee* [1957] C.L.Y. 2431 applied; *Hills v. Potter* [1984] C.L.Y. 2322 considered).

DEFREITAS v. O'BRIEN, *The Times*, February 16, 1995, C.A.

3680. Medical negligence—unsuccessful sterilisation—risk of failure—whether warning sufficiently clear and comprehensive

L agreed to be sterilised during the birth of her third child by Caesarian section. She alleged that she was not informed of any risk of failure before the operation and the consent form she signed made no reference to such risk. A post-operative warning was given, however, L subsequently became pregnant. On a preliminary issue of liability, the court found in favour of L, and W appealed.

Held, dismissing the appeal, that a sufficiently clear and comprehensive warning as to the risk of failure must be given and reasonable steps taken to ensure it was understood. The warning given after the operation was inappropriate as to both timing and conditions. At no time was an effective warning made to L or her husband.

LYBERT v. WARRINGTON HEALTH AUTHORITY, *The Times*, May 17, 1995, C.A.

3681. Navy—duty to prevent employee becoming drunk—liability for employee's death or injury due to drunkenness—employee's widow suing employer for damages—whether employer owing duty of care to employee to prevent drunkenness and injury or death caused thereby—Naval regulations imposing duty on officers to discourage drunkenness and to take appropriate action to prevent injury or fatality—whether and to what extent employer liable for employee's death—whether and to what extent employee himself liable

[Queen's Regulations for the Royal Navy 1967, art. 1810.]

P was the widow and executrix of the deceased who had been a naval airman who died after becoming so drunk at a naval base that he passed into a coma and asphyxiated on his own vomit. The deceased's commanding officer was charged with an offence under Naval regulations imposing a duty on officers to discourage drunkenness and to take appropriate action to prevent injury or fatality. P brought an action suing the Navy in negligence of the basis that it owed a duty of care to the serviceman. There was evidence adduced of widespread laxity in the enforcement of regulations requiring the control of heavy drinking. It was alleged that the Navy had failed to impose discipline and that it had failed to provide adequate medical care for the deceased. The trial judge equated the Queen's regulations with safety regulations in factories in deciding for P but also finding that the deceased had been guilty of contributory negligence.

Held, allowing the appeal in part, that (1) the judge had been wrong to equate the Queen's regulations with safety codes in factories because the purpose of the regulations was to preserve discipline and good order in the Navy and was in no sense intended to create standards or give advice with reference to reasonable care for the safety of men when drinking off-duty. The regulations could not therefore be invoked directly in deciding whether a duty of care was owed and whether the defendant was in breach of it; (2) the mere existence of regulatory or public duties does not of itself create a special relationship imposing a duty of care in law for the safety of others. The characteristic which distinguished those special relationships was the element of reliance, expressed or implied in the relationship, which the party to whom the duty was owed was entitled to place on the other party to make provision for his safety. New duties to take care for others should be developed incrementally and by analogy with established categories. It was neither justified nor reasonable to blame one adult for another adult's lack of self-control. No one was better placed to judge the amount which he could consume than the individual himself. Therefore the deceased was the only person responsible at law for his collapse (*Home Office v. Dorset Yacht Co.* [1970] C.L.Y. 1849, *Anns v. Merton London Borough Council* [1977] C.L.Y. 2030 considered); and (3) however, once the deceased had collapsed and was no longer capable of looking after himself, it was accepted that the defendant's care for him had been inadequate. The defendant had a duty of care towards the deceased and was liable for damages to that extent. The deceased's contributory negligence should be raised to two-thirds in these circumstances.

BARRETT v. MINISTRY OF DEFENCE [1995] 3 All E.R. 87, C.A.

3682. Nervous shock—foreseeability of risk—primary victim—whether sufficient that a defendant should have reasonably foreseen that a plaintiff might suffer personal injury as a result of his negligence

Once it is established that D is under a duty of care to avoid causing personal injury to P, it is unnecessary to ask whether D should have reasonably foreseen injury by shock and instead it is sufficient to ask whether

D should have reasonably foreseen that P might suffer personal injury as a result of D's negligence.

P was involved in an accident with a car driven by D. P suffered no physical injury but had previously suffered from myalgic encephalomyelitis (ME). P claimed that as a result of the accident his condition had worsened and brought an action against D, claiming damages for personal injuries caused by D's negligence. The trial judge found for P and awarded him damages. The Court of Appeal allowed an appeal by D on the ground that injury by nervous shock to P was not reasonably foreseeable by D.

Held, allowing P's appeal (by a three to two majority), that in cases of nervous shock it is essential to distinguish between primary and secondary victims. Where P is a primary victim and it is established that D was under a duty of care to avoid causing personal injury to P, it is enough to ask whether D should have reasonably foreseen that P might suffer personal injury as a result of D's negligence. It was unnecessary to ask, as a separate question, whether D should have foreseen injury by shock (*Bourhill v. Young* [1943] A.C. 92, *King v. Phillips* [1953] C.L.Y. 964, *Overseas Tankship (U.K.) v. MOAS Dock & Engineering Co. (The Wagon Mound)* [1961] C.L.Y. 2343, *Alcock v. Chief Constable of South Yorkshire Police*; Jones v. Wright [1992] C.L.Y. 3250 considered). In the absence of agreement between the parties the case went back to the Court of Appeal on the issue of causation.

PAGE v. SMITH [1995] 2 W.L.R. 644, H.L.

3683. Personal injury—animals—attack by cows—foreseeability of attack—whether lack of fencing negligent

P was attacked by a suckler herd of Charolais cows whilst walking his dogs on leads down a public road. The road, which ran through D's farmland, had gates at either end. Motorists and other users of the road had to open these to pass, closing them behind them. At some time no more than three weeks prior to the attack on P, the daughter-in-law of D's farm manager had been chased and badly frightened by the same herd of cows while walking her dogs. She reported the incident to D's farm manager. P suffered severe injuries which, but for the intervention of a passerby, might well have proved fatal.

Held, that D, and in particular D's farm manager, were negligent in keeping the herd in a field from which the gated road was not fenced off after the first incident. If a human being is attached to a dog, as P was, then if it is foreseeable that cows would attack the dog, then it is foreseeable that a human attached to the dog is likely to get hurt. Judgment for P was given in the agreed sum of £45,794·86.

BIRCH v. MILLS, January 20, 1995, H.H.J. Durman, Birmingham County Ct. [*Ex rel.* Michael J. Harrison, Barrister, 2 Temple Gardens.]

3684. Personal injury—expert evidence

The Court of Appeal heard the defendant's objections to experts' evidence in a claim for personal injuries suffered in a road accident, and substituted its findings on contributory negligence for those of the trial court. In the instant case the court had wrongly permitted the experts to draw conclusions from the facts which it was the judge's task to draw, *e.g.* that the driver was grossly negligent. Their assertions were inadmissible and irrelevant. Regret was expressed at the tendency for numerous experts to be instructed in road accident claims, which only served to increase the length and costs of the trial. In such claims, it was the exception not the rule that experts should be required. The court should ensure that if unnecessary experts were called in legal aid cases this was brought to the attention of the taxing master.

LIDDELL v. MIDDLETON, *The Times*, July 17, 1995, C.A.

3685. Personal injury—liability under statute—plaintiff injured by Border collie—whether dog's characteristics to be compared with dogs generally or the breed of dog—whether actual knowledge by keeper of abnormal characteristics required. See HUNT v. WALLIS, §320.

3686. Police—individual in custody—relevant information not passed to CPS—whether breach of duty of care

On October 27, 1990 two men robbed a British Gas showroom. One of the robbers carried a double-barrelled shotgun. Two women had fleeting glimpses of the gunman at different stages of the robbery. A, a police officer on a motor bike, chased the getaway car. The gunman ran from the car towards A and tried to fire at the front wheel of the bike but the gun failed to discharge. A later gave a detailed description of the gunman. On January 24, 1991 P was arrested on suspicion of armed robbery. On January 25, 1991, an identification parade was held at a police station. The two women identified P as the gunman. The showroom security guards identified non-suspects and A failed to identify anyone. P was charged with robbery and firearms offences. On January 26, 1991 P appeared before the magistrates' court where bail was refused on the grounds that the court believed P would fail to surrender and would commit offences whilst on bail. The court cited the strength of the identification evidence against P in support of its refusal. On January 31, and February 4, 1991 bail was further refused for the same reasons. On February 25, 1991 A attended the offices of the Robbery Squad in order to sign an additional statement relating to the robbery. While he was there he saw a colour photograph and immediately recognised it as being of the gunman. He told an officer involved in the robbery inquiry that he was positive of this identification. The photograph was *not* of P. A was not asked and did not make a statement relating to this identification until May 8, 1991. On March 4 and 11, 1991 P appeared before the magistrates and was remanded in custody on identical grounds. On March 13, 1991 P appeared once again before the court and the CPS maintained the objection to bail, telling the court that P was the man who had pointed the gun at A. Despite this objection P was granted bail. Neither the CPS nor P's solicitor were notified of the positive identification until or after May 8, 1991. P sued D in negligence alleging that as a result of the failure promptly to inform the CPS or P's solicitor of A's identification of another man on February 25, 1991, his period of time in custody on remand was foreseeably and wrongfully prolonged. D accepted that A's identification of February 25, 1991 was relevant to the issue of P's bail, that the failure to pass on the information was careless and that this caused P to spend additional time in custody but applied to strike out P's claim on the basis that D owed no duty of care to the P.

Held, dismissing the application to strike out, that (1) applying the three-stage test established in *Caparo Industries v. Dickman* [1990] C.L.Y. 3266, it was not seriously in dispute that extended detention was a reasonably foreseeable consequence of the omission to pass on the information which was of crucial relevance to the issue of P's bail. Accordingly, P had established both that the damage he suffered was reasonably foreseeable and that the relationship between P and D was sufficiently proximate; (2) the public policy grounds which influenced the decisions in *Hill v. Chief Constable of West Yorkshire* [1988] 2 All E.R. 238 and *Osman v. Ferguson* [1993] 4 All E.R. 344 were distinguishable from the facts of the instant case which concerned a man in custody, not a free member of the public. The mischief upon which the public policy decision in *Hill* was based does not apply. This case raised issues of personal liberty. In all the circumstances it would be fair, just and reasonable to impose the duty contended for by P. The police owe a duty of care to a person held in custody promptly to pass on to the CPS information which reasonably foreseeably would have a substantial impact on a determination of whether that person continues to be held in custody.

WHITE (MICHAEL) v. CHIEF CONSTABLE OF MERSEYSIDE, December 20, 1994; Hedley J.; Liverpool County Ct. [*Ex rel. Tim Owen, Barrister*].

3687. Police—whether police owing duty of care to individual detained in custody

L was arrested by Kent police on suspicion of stealing a boat. He was held in custody and brought a claim in negligence against the Chief Constable, stating that a duty of care was owed to secure the vessel and its contents in L's absence and that the Chief Constable, his servants or agents, negligently failed to take reasonable steps to ensure this. L claimed that a large number of items were stolen or damaged and the boat eventually became a total loss. The Chief Constable appealed to have the action struck out because the particulars of the claim did not disclose a cause of action.

Held, dismissing the appeal, that the submission by the Chief Constable that the police owed no duty of care to L because there was not a sufficient relationship of proximity and that otherwise the police would owe a duty to a very wide class of people, could not be upheld. It was clear to the judge that the matter should go to trial, as the facts may be crucial in determining the existence of a duty of care.

LERVOLD (HAROLD) v. CHIEF CONSTABLE OF KENT (CCRTI 94/0131/F) (CCRTI 94/0131/F), November 9, 1994, C.A.

3688. Prison officer—escorting segregated prisoner to visiting area—prisoner attacked by other prisoners—whether choice of route negligent—whether officer should have followed prisoner rather than led

P was a segregated prisoner at a category C establishment. He was escorted by a single officer, with another segregated inmate, to the visiting area along a non-segregated corridor, in which were about 20 other prisoners. P was attacked by some of those prisoners while walking along the corridor, and claimed damages for both physical and psychological injuries.

Held, that the prison officer had been negligent, first in choosing to take the segregated prisoners down a corridor when it was unsafe to do so, and where there was an alternative, safer, route and, secondly, in the manner in which he led the prisoners down the corridor, namely by leading, rather than following, them.

BURT v. HOME OFFICE, June 27, 1995, H.H.J. Hyam, Norwich County Ct. [*Ex rel*. John Whitting, Barrister, 1 Crown Office Row, Temple.]

3689. Professional negligence—architect or engineer—whether concurrent duties of care in negligence owed to the employer with whom there is a contract

W engaged HLM as architects and Webb as engineers for the construction of hospital buildings. W employed a contractor ARC under the JCT 1980 standard form of contract. W commenced proceedings against HLM and Webb on the basis that it had suffered payments of loss and expense to ARC, and being unable to claim liquidated damages from ARC, as a result of negligent extensions of time granted by HLM, W also sought to claim with reference to periods of delay caused by HLM and Webb.

Held, allowing the application, that where there is a contractual relationship between a person and someone professing special skills for which professional qualifications are necessary, and where the contract depends upon the exercise of these skills, the principles in *Hedley Byrne v. Heller* apply. There may be a concurrent duty to take reasonable care to prevent or avoid economic loss. There is nothing unfair or unreasonable in architects and engineers being liable for economic loss over a longer period than they would be under their contracts where the damage arising under the contract arises at a later date. Both HLM and Webb owed W a tortious duty to take reasonable care and to avoid economic loss (*Hedley Byrne & Co. v. Heller & Partners* [1963] C.L.Y. 2416, *Tai Hing Cotton Mill. v. Liu Chong Hing Bank* [19884] C.L.Y.171, *Midland Bank Trust Co. v. Hett, Stubbs and Kemp* [1978] C.L.Y. 2822, *Sutherland Shire Council v. Heyman* [1986] C.L.Y. 2274, *Junior Books v. Veitchi* [1982] C.L.Y. 766, *Ross v. Caunters* [1979] C.L.Y. 2570, *Scally v.*

Southern Health and Social Services Board [1992] C.L.Y. 1917, *White v. Jones* [1993] C.L.Y. 2990 considered).

WESSEX REGIONAL HEALTH AUTHORITY v. HLM DESIGN [1994] 10 Const. L.J. 165, Fox-Andrews J.

3690. Professional negligence—architects—meaning of "fails to proceed regularly and diligently". See WEST FAULKNER ASSOCIATES v. LONDON BOROUGH OF NEWHAM, §490.

3691. Professional negligence—auditors—claim that audited accounts contained inaccuracies—whether negligence caused or allowed companies to incur losses—whether auditors knew of reliance to be placed on accounts

P1 was a company in liquidation, P2 was a company which owned all the shares in P1, and P3 was a company which acquired all the shares in P2. The claim was that the audited accounts of P1 and P2 for the years 1985 to 1989 contained substantial inaccuracies and that, in not noticing the inaccuracies, D, a firm of accountants, were negligent and in breach of duties in contract and tort owed to P1 and P2 and in tort to P3, resulting in loss and damage. It was held at first instance that neither P1 nor P2 could recover damages for incurring an obligation to repay sums advanced by P3, or for trading losses as a result of relying on D's negligent auditing and continuing to trade when they would otherwise not have done so. Further, P3's claim in tort for loss resulting from making loans to, and buying shares in, P2 would be struck out as there was no reasonable cause of action.

Held, dismissing the appeal and cross-appeal, that (1) the acceptance of a loan could not be described as a loss causing damage. The use to which the loan was put could cause a loss, but this was not what was pleaded, and if it were, it would be difficult to attribute such a loss to D; (2) D's breach of duty made it possible for P1 and P2 to incur trading losses but it did not "cause" those losses in the legal sense; (3) P3's claim in tort for losses caused by reliance on D's representations should not be struck out because it was clear that the 1986 accounts were prepared not only for audit purposes but also to fix the price at which P3 was to buy the shares in P2. Further evidence was required on this issue (*Caparo Industries v. Dickman* [1990] C.L.Y. 3266, *Morgan Crucible v. Hill Samuel Bank* [1991] C.L.Y. 2653 considered); and (4) P3's claims for loss as a result of making loans to P2 and as a result of buying further shares in P2 did not state that D was aware of the reliance to be placed by P3 on the audited accounts. Therefore the pleaded facts did not establish a duty of care on D in either issue (*Caparo Industries v. Dickman* [1990] C.L.Y. 3266 applied).

GALOO v. BRIGHT GRAHAME MURRAY [1994] BCC 319, C.A.

3692. Professional negligence—auditors—local authority—payments by officers—whether auditors owing statutory or common law duty of care to officers—whether auditors owing statutory duty or duty of care to local authority

[Local Government Finance Act 1982 (c.32), s.15.]

W council brought an action against former officers for breach of contract and fiduciary duty in respect of procurement of payments by W without proper authority. The officers brought third-party proceedings against employees of the Audit Commission who had audited W's accounts in accordance with Pt. III of the Local Government Finance Act 1982 and allegedly advised them on the payments, alleging breach of statutory duty under s.15 of the 1982 Act, and negligence. The auditors applied to set aside or strike out the proceedings on the basis that they owed no statutory or common law duty to the officers. The judge concurred, but allowed the third-party notices to stand in part, holding that the auditors owed a statutory duty to W, breach of which might give the officers a right of contribution. Both the auditors and officers appealed.

Held, dismissing the appeal, that (1) Parliament was to be taken to have intended that local authorities had a cause of action against auditors for a breach of statutory duty, particularly the duty under s.15; (2) allowing the officers' appeal, as W arguably had a case in negligence, the parts of the officers' pleadings in respect of the same should not be struck out; and (3) in respect of reports under s.15(3) of the 1982 Act, since Parliament intended that district auditors should be able to criticise local authority officers without fear of an action for negligence by that officer, the auditors owed no duty of care to the officers in respect of such reports.

WEST WILTSHIRE DISTRICT COUNCIL v. GARLAND AND COND [1995] 2 W.L.R. 439, C.A.

3693. Professional negligence—divorce petition—financial relief—whether correct computation of damages. See SHARPLES v. COOLE & HADDOCK (A FIRM), §1832.

3694. Professional negligence—estate agent—whether liable where loss due to collapse of property prices—whether entitled to counterclaim for peremptory termination of a retainer. See CANDLE SERVICES v. WARREN REID MEADOWCROFT, §173.

3695. Professional negligence—Lloyd's Names—whether members' agents owing a duty of care. See AIKEN v. STEWART WRIGHTSON MEMBERS AGENCY, §2906.

3696. Professional negligence—solicitor—acting for both lenders and purchasers—solicitors hearing of information suggesting the property might have been overvalued—whether solicitors should have told the lenders

B&P, solicitors, cross-appealed against a Chancery Division ruling that they were liable in negligence to their mortgagee clients (ME) for failing to disclose information which suggested that the property might have been overvalued. B&P, acting for both ME and the purchaser in a conveyancing transaction, learned of two recent sales of the property at a much lower price, and informed the purchaser but not ME. The court found that if B&P had informed ME a second valuation would have been arranged and the mortgage offer would have been withdrawn. The issue of damages had been decided in the solicitor's favour, but the decision was reversed in *Banque Bruxelles Lambert SA v. Eagle Star Insurance Co.* [1995] 8 C.L. 217.

Held, dismissing the cross-appeal, that the information was not confidential either to the purchaser or to the mortgagee, but was relevant to both. As such both clients should have been informed and, although the case did not involve a conflict of interest, if B&P had represented only the lenders instead of the lenders and purchasers jointly, it was hard to imagine that the lenders would not have been told. B&P were not instructed to investigate and advise whether accepting the mortgage was a good commercial decision, but where in the course of investigating title they came across information which was not confidential and which was relevant for the mortgagee because it cast doubt on the valuation, the mortgagee had every right to expect that their solicitor would inform them accordingly.

MORTGAGE EXPRESS v. BOWERMAN & PARTNERS (A FIRM), *The Times*, August 1, 1995, C.A.

3697. Professional negligence—solicitor—bank intending to advance money to customer—solicitor employed to draft necessary documents and advise bank—bank suffering loss—whether solicitor negligent—whether negligence was cause of loss

The bank had instructed the defendant solicitors to prepare documentation with reference to an overdraft of £3.5 million in favour of F&S Ltd. F&S became unable to pay under bills of exchange tendered as part of the overdraft arrangement through insolvency. The bank took an insurance policy owned by F&S Ltd as part of the security for the overdraft. When the bank sought to claim under the policy, the insurance company refused payment on the basis that the loss did not fall within the insurance the policy. The bank claimed damages from the solicitors on the basis that they were negligent in failing to ensure that the insurance policy provided adequate security for the loan.

Held, that (1) the bank had not established that it was inadequately advised about the effect of the assignment of a policy or the significance of breaches of the policy terms by the insured; (2) the solicitors were negligent in failing to point out that there was a serious mismatch between the insurance cover and the duration of the facility which had not been remedied in the drafting of the facility agreement; and (3) the bank had failed to prove that it would not have entered into the facility agreement without the security or that the facility agreement would not have been in substantially the same terms had the security not been present.

COUNTY NATWEST v. PINSENT & CO. [1994] 3 Bank L.R. 4, Hobhouse J.

3698. Professional negligence—solicitor—breach of Code of Practice—whether provisions mandatory

A client suing her former solicitor did not necessarily prove negligence on the solicitor's part by establishing that the solicitor breached the Law Society's Guide to Professional Conduct of Solicitors. The Guide set out a code of proper and accepted practice, but its provisions were not mandatory. Negligence would continue to be determined according to the principles established in *Donoghue v. Stevenson* ([1932] A.C. 562).

JOHNSON v. BINGLEY, *The Times*, February 28, 1995, B.A. Hynter, Q.C.

3699. Professional negligence—solicitor—civil action against former solicitors for damages for negligence in conduct of criminal defence—whether civil action an abuse of process of court—whether plaintiff having had full opportunity to put forward case—whether new evidence entirely changing aspect of criminal case—whether plaintiff's claim sustainable in law—whether collateral attack on final decision of court

P was convicted of aggravated burglary and sentenced to seven years. His conviction was upheld by the Court of Appeal. P brought a civil action against his former solicitors for damages for negligence in the conduct of his defence. The district judge struck the matter out as an abuse of the process of the court. The plaintiff appealed to a judge in chambers as to whether he had had full opportunity to put forward his case. The judge ordered a trial of the preliminary issue on whether the plaintiff's claim was sustainable in law.

Held, dismissing the application, that a plaintiff's claim for damages against his former solicitors was prima facie an abuse of the process of the court in that it amounted to the initiation of proceedings for the purposes of mounting an attack on the final decision of a criminal court of competent jurisdiction. As such it was contrary to public policy and unsustainable in law unless, at the very least, new and reliable evidence was available which entirely changed the aspect of the criminal case. Where the applicant had had a full opportunity to contest the original criminal claim and was unable to produce new and reliable evidence that the conviction was wrong, the interests of the administration of justice required the court to apply the rigour of the public policy rule and strike out his claim. On these facts, the plaintiff had failed to provide the court with such evidence and therefore his case was not sustainable in law and should not be allowed to proceed (*Hunter v. Chief Constable of the West Midlands Police* [1982] C.L.Y. 2382 applied).

SMITH v. LINSKILLS (A FIRM) [1995] 3 All E.R. 226, Potter J.

3700. Professional negligence—solicitor—costs of litigation—successful client inadequately protected—whether solicitors acting with proper skill and care

R, on the advice of his solicitors, M, accepted a personal guarantee from A, a director of F, with whom he was involved in litigation, as security for costs. A owned a house. On F losing the action and appealing, R again sought a guarantee for costs and was again advised by M to accept A's guarantee. As there was a succession of charges against A's house R was unable to recover his judgment and costs. The judge, entering judgment on R's counterclaim, found that M should have insisted on a caution on the register.

Held, dismissing the appeal, that M had not acted with proper skill and care in advising R to accept A's offer to renew the guarantee just before the appeal without any inquiry as to the value of the equity or the extent of the beneficial interest.

MARTIN BOSTON & CO. v. ROBERTS [1995] NPC 28, C.A.

3701. Professional negligence—solicitor—failure to implement testator's instructions—whether liable in damages to disappointed beneficiaries—whether duty of care

A solicitor drawing up a will can be liable to an intended beneficiary if his negligence foreseeably deprives that beneficiary of a legacy.

The testator sent a letter to his solicitors giving instructions for a will to be prepared, including a gift of £9,000 to J. The letter was received in July but had not been acted upon by September when the testator died. J sought damages against the solicitors for negligence. The judge dismissed the claim on the basis that the solicitors owed no duty of care to J. The Court of Appeal allowed the appeal, holding that a solicitor's breach of duty in failing to draw up a will rendered him liable to a disappointed prospective beneficiary. The solicitors appealed to the House of Lords.

Held, dismissing the appeal, that where a solicitor accepted instructions to draw up a will and, as a result of negligence, an intended beneficiary was foreseeably deprived of a legacy, the solicitor was liable for the loss. The solicitor's responsibility to his client should be extended in law to an intended beneficiary who was reasonably foreseeably deprived of his legacy. The solicitor could be said to be in a special relationship with those intended to benefit (*Hedley Byrne & Co. v. Heller & Partners* [1963] C.L.Y. 2416, *Linden Gardens Trust v. Lenesta Sludge Disposals* [1993] C.L.Y. 303, *Nocton v. Lord Ashburton* [1914–15] All E.R. 45, *Caparo Industries v. Dickman* [1990] C.L.Y. 3266, *Henderson v. Merrett Syndicates; Hallam-Eames v. Same; Huges v. Same; Arbuthnott v. Feltrim Underwriting Agencies: Deeny v. Gooda Walker (in Liq.)* [1994] 12 C.L. 636 applied; *Robertson v. Fleming* [1861] 4 Macq 167, *Ross v. Caunters* [1979] C.L.Y. 2570 doubted).

WHITE v. JONES [1995] 1 All E.R. 691, H.L.

3702. Professional negligence—solicitor—failure to make proper inquiries during conveyance—highway affecting property—whether solicitor negligent

[Land Compensation Act 1973 (c.26).]

P wished to purchase a flat and engaged D, a solicitor, to act for her. D failed to make the inquiries which would have unveiled the plans for a major new highway in front of the property. P purchased the flat for £115,000. P was put to great inconvenience once the construction of the road started, being forced to move out of the premises, and sued D for negligence.

Held, that (1) the failure to make inquiries was clearly negligent; (2) damages for the diminution in the capital value of the property would be calculated by taking the difference between the price paid and the market value of the property, assuming that there would have been a market for the property for either an investor or an adventurous private purchaser who would have needed a real incentive to buy. Damages for this head were assessed at £32,000 which included interest; (3) no deduction would be made in respect of P's claim under the Land Compensation Act 1973, given its speculative nature; and (4) damages for the serious effect to her quality of life would be assessed at £6,000 plus interest

FARAGHER v. GERBER [1994] EGCS 122, H.H.J. Lachs sitting as a deputy judge.

3703. Professional negligence—solicitor—negligent legal advice—pre-trial and trial—solicitor sued on basis of counsel's advice—counsel immune from suit—settlement advised—subsequent deterioration in condition—whether abuse of process to sue solicitor

Although solicitors do not share the same immunity from action as barristers, it is vexatious and an abuse of process to sue solicitors in respect of legal advice to settle given at the court door when the solicitors had instructed counsel who did have immunity in respect of such advice.

P instructed D1, a firm of solicitors, to claim damages in respect of the injuries he had received in a road accident. D2 was engaged as counsel and D3 as a medical expert. D3 prepared a report in conjunction with the medical expert of the party then being sued by P. This report discussed an operation for the amelioration of P's condition, and concluded that the operation had a good chance of success. In reliance on this report D1 and D2 advised P to enter into a court door settlement. P later had the operation, but it was unsuccessful and worsened his condition. P sued D3 alleging that the medical report had been overly optimistic regarding the possibility of a successful operation, and that this negligent advice had induced P to enter into a disadvantageous settlement. P sued D1 and D2 alleging negligent legal advice, arguing that they had failed to advise him not to settle once and for all until operation had been carried. out.

Held, striking out P's pleadings, that (1) D3 had immunity from suit as a witness whose medical report had been prepared for trial. P's argument that there was no immunity as the report had a dual purpose of giving medical advice to P in addition to advising as to evidence was rejected. The preparation of the report could be said to be pre-trial work so intimately connected with the conduct of the case in Court that it was a preliminary decision affecting the way the case would be conducted when it came to hearing (*Palmer v. Durnford Ford* [1992] C.L.Y. 3499 considered); (2) neither D1 nor D2 could be said to be negligent in having failed to amend P's pleadings to claim provisional damages, as neither had been instructed that a deterioration in P's condition was a possible consequence of the operation. D2 had immunity in respect of the advice given at the court door as this was an activity intimately connected with the court proceedings. P argued that D1 could have no immunity in respect of the advice they had given as they had not acted as advocates. But D1 had instructed counsel, so that the matters complained of were no longer their responsibility. D1 had no separate identity from D2 in respect of the advice given. To refuse D1 immunity would be to outflank the immunity granted to D2.

LANDALL v. DENNIS FAULKNER & ALSOP [1994] 5 Med L.R. 268, Holland J.

3704. Professional negligence—solicitor—option to purchase shares—exchange of contract contrary to instructions—damages—date at which damages to be assessed

Where an option has been granted through the negligence of solicitors, the date on which to assess the loss will be the date of the accrual of the cause of action.

A entered into negotiations for the sale of shares to E, in the form of an option to purchase to be granted to E. A instructed his solicitor, B, not to exchange contracts on this deal without referring back to him. B's colleague, unaware of this instruction, exchanged contracts. The question arose as to what date was to be used in assessing damages: the date of exchange of contracts or the date when the option was actually exercised.

Held, that the date to be taken into account was that of exchange of contracts, and therefore losses incurred by A in repurchasing the option from E two years later, were not recoverable from B.
AMERENA v. BARLING [1995] 69 P. & C.R. 252, C.A.

3705. Professional negligence—surveyor—defective valuation—lender relying on valuation—whether lender contributorily negligent—whether valuer liable for losses attributable to collapse of the property market

Where a negligent valuation has induced a lender to make a loan and to incur losses, and these losses include losses attributable to the collapse of the property market, the defendant is liable for these losses.

P lent £21 million secured on a property which had been valued by D at £30·5 million. The borrower defaulted on the loan and P sold the property for £3·1 million, and sued D for damages. D argued that P had not relied on the valuation in deciding to make the loan, and that P had been contributorily negligent by making a loan for 90 per cent of the purchase price without determining the accuracy of the valuation.

Held, that P had indeed relied on the valuation, but had been 20 per cent contributorily negligent. D's valuation had caused P loss, and this loss included that attributable to the collapse in the property market (*Banque Bruxelles Lambert SA v. Eagle Star Insurance Co.* [1995] 1 C.L. 294 applied).
NYCKLEN FINANCE CO. v. STUMPBROOK CONTINUATION [1994] 33 EG 93, H.H.J. Fawcus, sitting as a deputy judge.

3706. Professional negligence—surveyor—defective valuation—whether purchasers suffering loss—whether damages for discomfort and mental suffering recoverable

There is no distinction between "no transaction" cases and "successful transaction" cases in an action for damages in tort, and the duty to exercise reasonable care is the same in tort as in contract.

P purchased a house, valued by D at £37,000, for £42,000 in June 1988. The valuation turned out to have been defective, and the house was worth only £32,000 in June, and by August 1988, £37,000. P argued that they would not have gone ahead with the purchase had they been aware of the defects. D argued that there had been no loss, as by the time the house was purchased in August 1988, it was worth the sum for which it had been valued, albeit three months earlier.

Held, giving judgment for P and awarding damages for physical inconvenience, discomfort and mental suffering, that they had paid too much for the property in reliance on D's negligent valuation (*Watts v. Morrow* [1992] C.L.Y. 1548 applied).
SHAW v. HALIFAX (S.W.) [1994] 26 EG 142, Graham Jones sitting as Official Referee.

3707. Professional negligence—surveyor—duties of surveyors in making a valuation report—damages—value of house with serious defect—general damages for worry leading to unemployment and repossession

P bought a property for £56,000 in 1986, with a building society loan of £40,000, in reliance on a valuation report prepared by the D without obtaining a more detailed survey. P sought to sell the property. A potential purchaser withdrew after having a survey carried out over the property. It transpired that a heavy concrete purlin had been mispositioned in the roof space. P1 became depressed by this discovery, leading to his dismissal from work. P fell into arrears with their mortgage and were evicted. The property was sold at auction for £29,000. P claimed £37,364·65 and general damages for inconvenience and distress.

Held, allowing the application, that the surveyor was negligent in failing to spot and report the purlin and the gap left by its mispositioning. Further, the surveyor ought to have been on notice as to the type of construction which would be acceptable to building societies as representing suitable security. Ps' loss was the difference between the value of the property in 1986 had it been in the condition represented by D, and the actual value of the property in 1986. Worry leading to loss of employment and repossession of the property is such a common result in this kind of case that it ought to have been reasonably foreseeable to D. General damages were therefore awarded in the amount of £6,000.

EZEKIEL (DAVID AND MARGIE) v. IAN McDADE [1994] 10 Const. L.J. 122, Bowser J.

3708. Professional negligence—surveyor—failure to take account of comparable rents in locality—whether negligent

A valuer who values the rental value of a property without taking into account comparable rents in the locality is negligent.

B, a bank, lent money to S secured by a charge over a property, which had been valued by P, who also estimated the rental value. S then defaulted on the loan, and B sold the property for considerably less than its valuation price. B brought an action against P for negligence.

Held, giving judgment for B, that P had been negligent in making the valuation, in that he had failed to take account of comparable rents.

UNITED BANK OF KUWAIT v. PRUDENTIAL PROPERTY SERVICES [1994] 30 EG 103, Gage J.

3709. Professional negligence—surveyor—introduction fee paid on understanding that floor areas correctly stated—whether surveyor liable for loss of value and costs

H agreed to pay an introduction fee to B, a firm of surveyors, who had given H details of properties offered for sale by another agent, on condition that B would give an "assurance" that the floor areas were correct. B replied that an inspection had been carried out and the areas were correct, although this was not the case.

Held, that B was under a duty to check the floor areas given in the agent's particulars as a result of the undertaking to do so, which established a liability in negligence for loss of value and legal costs.

HUNT v. BEASLEY DRAKE [1995] NPC 35, H.H.J. David Smith, Q.C.

3710. Professional negligence—surveyor—measure of damages—money lent solely because of negligent valuation—whether loss due to fall in property market recoverable. See BANQUE BRUXELLES LAMBERT SA v. EAGLE STAR INSURANCE CO., §1834.

3711. Professional negligence—surveyor—mortgage valuation—prospect of planning permission for property—whether hope value to be included

In February 1988 C contracted to buy property for which it had proposals for development and applied to P for a loan of £370,000. D provided a valuation for P which stated that the open market value of the property was £595,000. As was its policy, P provided a loan based on 70 per cent of the purchase price, and took a mortgage as security. C failed to pay interest to P and the property was sold in 1991 for £220,000. P claimed that D had negligently valued the property. D asserted that in making the valuation it had been assumed that planning permission would be granted for the proposed development.

Held, dismissing P's claim, that (1) the open market value of freehold property must necessarily include such additional amount prospective purchasers would pay for the property with planning permission if there was hope of such permission; (2) the ISVA/RCIS guidance notes for mortgage valuations were not appropriate for valuing property not intended for residential use by individuals. The RCIS "Guidance Notes on the Valuation of Assets (2nd ed.)" were a guide to the meaning of open market value for mortgage purposes; and (3) the figures in D's valuation were not outside the range of figures which a competent valuer, using the residual method, might adopt.

ALLIED TRUST BANK v. EDWARD SYMMONS & PARTNERS [1994] 22 EG 116, Mr C. Clarke, Q.C. sitting as a deputy judge.

3712. Professional negligence—surveyor—mortgage valuation report—proceeding not issued within limitation period—date of knowledge—whether proceedings statute barred

[Limitation Act 1980 (c.58), s.14A.]

In early 1983 D inspected and prepared a mortgage valuation report upon a property subsequently purchased by P. It was later found that there was settlement at the property but no mention has been made of this in the report. A writ was not issued until December 1989 and so the claim was prima facie statute barred but P sought to rely upon s.14A of the 1980 Act. In 1985 P were aware that the property had a major structural defect and had obtained a report from another firm of surveyors stating that it was assumed defects were apparent at the time of D's inspection and that these defects should have been brought to the attention of the building society.

Held, that P were fixed with the knowledge of their solicitors and in 1985 had sufficient information to justify embarking upon the preliminaries to the issue of a writ, and as such they had sufficient knowledge at this time for the purposes of s.14A of the 1980 Act. P had attempted to argue that they did not have knowledge of the identity of D until 1988 as the report did not disclose the identity of the surveyor. However, the court decided that P could not rely upon this as a simple enquiry would have revealed the appropriate identity of D. The claim was therefore statute barred.

HEATHCOTE AND HEATHCOTE v. DAVID MARKS & CO., December 13, 1994; Buckley J.; Manchester District Registry [*Ex rel. James Chapman & Co., Solicitors*]

3713. Professional negligence—surveyor—mortgagee's power of sale—whether free to exercise as chooses where exercised in good faith—advice of surveyor—whether surveyor negligent. See HUISH v. ELLIS, §3600.

3714. Professional negligence—surveyor—rent review—whether in valuing restaurant properties valuer entitled to rely on adjoining retail comparables

The defendant was appointed by the RICS to give a rent valuation on a restaurant property under a rent review clause. The plaintiff, the tenant of the property, claimed that the defendant had been negligent in taking into account comparables other than restaurants.

Held, dismissing the appeal, that a valuer is not negligent because another valuer would have reached a different conclusion. Other uses of the property are not irrelevant even though letting as a restaurant may require a landlord to let at a discount and even though the valuation supplied by the plaintiff·s valuer did have the support of a respectable body of professional opinion (*Bolam v. Friern Hospital Management Committee* [1957] C.L.Y. 2431 referred to).

ZUBAIDA v. HARGREAVES [1995] 9 EG 320, C.A.

3715. Professional negligence—surveyor for classification society—negligent ship survey—physical damage—proximity—whether classification society surveyor owed duty of care to cargo owner. See MARC RICH & CO A.G. v. BISHOP ROCK MARINE CO., BETHMARINE CO. AND NIPPON KAIJI KYOKAI, NICHOLAS H., THE, §4519.

3716. Professional negligence—valuer—fall in property market—whether negligent over-valuation of property

A valuation of land by a professional valuer is not negligent if the valuation lies within the proper bracket of valuation.

B wished to remortgage property and applied to P for a loan. P appointed D to value the property, which D valued at £155,000. B defaulted on the mortgage and the property was sold for £75,000. P contended that the proper valuation was £120,000, and claimed damages for negligent over-valuation.

Held, dismissing P's claim, that (1) D had not been negligent as the valuation lay within the proper bracket of valuation; (2) if there had been negligence on the part of D, the fact that P's solicitors had evidence that B was an unsatisfactory borrower would not amount to contributory negligence on the part of P, as it was not the role of P's solicitors to disclose this information to P so that P could be taken to have notice of the fact.

AXA EQUITY & LAW HOME LOANS v. GOLDSACK & FREEMAN [1994] 23 EG 130, Marr Johnson J.

3717. Professional negligence—valuer—latent damages provisions—limitation period—writ one day out of time—effect. See SPENCER-WARD v. HUMBERTS, §3167.

3718. Professional negligence—valuer—report confidential to building society—whether mortgagor entitled to rely on valuation in action for damages against building society

[Administration of Justice Act 1970 (c.31), s.36.]

A building society will not be liable for a negligent property valuation where the society's conditions indicate that it does not assume responsibility for the report.

D purchased property with the aid of a mortgage provided by P. P obtained an order for possession upon D falling into arrears. D applied to the county court for leave to appeal out of time against the possession order, arguing that D would be able to pay off the arrears within a reasonable time as a result of a claim against P for damages arising from a negligent valuation report. Leave to appeal out of time being refused.

Held, dismissing D's appeal, that D failed to satisfy the test indicated in s.36 of the Administration of Justice Act 1970 of showing that the arrears would be paid within a reasonable time. The cross-action against P would not succeed unless P could be said to have assumed responsibility for the valuation report. Such an assumption was negatived by the wording of P's general conditions, which provided that the valuer's report was confidential and that P accepted no responsibility for the workmanship, construction or condition of the property (*Smith v. Bush (Eric S.)* [1989] C.L.Y. 2566 applied).

TIPTON & COSELEY BUILDING SOCIETY v. COLLINS [1994] EGCS 120, C.A.

3719. Professional negligence—valuer—turnover valuation of restaurant for purposes of loan—restaurant closed down—whether valuation negligent

In December 1989 and May 1990 P made loans to the owner of a restaurant which were secured as second charges on the property. The loans were made in reliance on the audited and management accounts of the restaurant and a valuation made by D, a firm of valuers. D recorded that the turnover for 1989 was likely to be in excess of £1 million with net profitability of £330,000. The restaurant later closed and was sold for £475,000 as a result of which P lost the sums advanced and interest. P claimed £650,000 plus interest, alleging that they had relied on D's valuation which was negligent. D counterclaimed, alleging contributory negligence.

Held, dismissing the claim, that (1) D's valuation should have been based on the guidance notes prepared by the assets valuation standards committee of the RICS because the property was to be used as security for a loan; (2) D's valuation was one which a competent valuer, using proper care and skill, could properly have reached. P knew that the valuation depended on current turnover and profitability and relied on the management accounts. D had not been negligent; and (3) had D been negligent then, in considering the counterclaim for contributory negligence, as P had more information available to him affecting the valuation than D had, P would have been very likely to have been found contributorily negligent for relying on the valuation without giving D the accounts information for comment.

CRANE HEATH SECURITIES v. YORK MONTAGUE [1994] 21 EG 124, Jacob J.

3720. Professional negligence—valuer—unusual property—value collapsing in recession—whether correct value on evidence—contributory negligence

A property, unusual in that it was a grade 2 listed building comprising three buildings merged into one, was valued in 1990 by M, a valuer, at £400,000, on the strength of which C lent the prospective buyer £300,000. C argued that had the correct valuation been made it would not, as the judge accepted, have lent that sum. The property was eventually sold for £120,000 in 1993 on the borrower's insolvency, the value having collapsed in the recession. M adduced evidence to support his original valuation. The judge found that the market had risen in 1989 by some 40 per cent.

Held, that, on the evidence, the valuation was not negligent, although perhaps a little high, as it was within the 10 per cent margin accepted by C. A 15 per cent margin would have been acceptable in this case because of the uniqueness of the property. Had there been negligence the judge would have found that there had been contributory negligence on the part of C, who should have asked further questions of the borrower, since his income had shown wild fluctuations.

CREDIT AGRICOLE PERSONAL FINANCE v. MURRAY [1995] NPC 33, H.H.J. John Baker.

3721. Professional negligence—valuer—valuation—liability for loss due to excessive valuation

C valued a property at £350,000 for the purpose of security for a loan. Based on that valuation, S took out a mortgage of £175,000 in respect of her husband's business. In her statement of claim she argued that C were liable for any subsequent loss in the husband's business due to the excessive valuation. C appealed against the reinstatement of S's claim.

Held, allowing the appeal, that the statement of claim struck out. The statement of claim disclosed no cause of action as the acceptance of a loan was not a loss causing damage nor one which should have been foreseen by C.

SADDINGTON v. COLLEYS PROFESSIONAL SERVICES, *The Times*, June 22, 1995, C.A.

3722. Repetitive strain injury—medical evidence of conditions caused by repetitive work—lack of advice for employees—no job rotation—whether valid claim

M suffered various injuries as a result of having to carry out tasks that involved repetitive use of her hands. For many years she had carried out work that involved testing motors. This involved a lot of lifting, twisting and turning. In September 1990 she began the work about which the complaint was made. She was testing heavier motors, each weighing in excess of 6lb. The work she did was unrelenting; she was required to test 130 an hour and was under considerable pressure to do this. M contended that this relentless work, involving gripping, twisting, turning and lifting, caused various conditions. M had dormant osteoarthritis in both her thumbs, which manifested itself after this work began, and she also suffered from carpal tunnel syndrome and de Quervain's tenosynovitis. M's expert contended that all three conditions were caused by the work in question.

Held, that M's expert's evidence was accepted in preference to that given by the employer's, A's, doctor, who contended that none of them were caused by work. The judge found that A were negligent. There was knowledge that work of this nature would give rise to a foreseeable risk of injury. In spite of this, no advice had been given as to how to approach work of this nature and what action to take in the event of pain, or indeed about the consequences of failing to act when there had been pain. Furthermore, the judge found that A were negligent in failing to introduce the system of job rotation. M was awarded damages of £8,500 for pain and suffering. Loss of earnings to date of trial were £27,531·47 and an award of future earnings of £6,618 was made.

MITCHELL v. ATCO, July 5, 1995, Mr Assistant Recorder Hawkesworth, Norwich County Ct. [*Ex rel.* Robin Thompson & Partners, Solicitors, London.]

3723. Repetitive strain injury—whether medical evidence established injury—whether tasks sufficiently repetitive—whether employers negligent

L was 49 when she began work at C's premises. She was employed in the production of quilts, which involved a variety of tasks, including the use of overlock and panel stitch sewing machines. She developed puffiness and pins and needles in her hands, and some swelling on the back of one hand. The G.P. diagnosed tenosynovitis. L's expert stated that the only symptom L suffered from when he saw her, was swelling, and he had not noted pain or crepitis. L was later diagnosed as suffering from carpal tunnel syndrome, and underwent operations. L's expert agreed that there was little evidence that carpal tunnel syndrome was caused by her work, but stated that the work had caused tenosynovitis, which led to carpal tunnel syndrome.

Held, that L failed to establish either foreseeability or medical causation and C's medical evidence was preferred. It was found that L did not have tenosynovitis which led to carpal tunnel syndrome, but rather that L had suffered from carpal tunnel syndrome from the outset. The carpal tunnel syndrome did not arise from the employment, but had simply been revealed by the work at C's premises, which was repetitive, but which had not caused the condition. Furthermore, it was found that C had not been negligent in relation to L's work. L's work was not the sort which would lead to a repetitive strain injury, as it was found that the work had to be repetitive in the sense of at least once a minute, whereas L was only handling a quilt every three to five minutes. After L had first complained to C's supervisor that she was encountering difficulties, she was moved on to a different job. If liability had been established, a figure of £5,250 general damages would have been awarded.

LADDS v. COLOROLL (IN LIQUIDATION), August 14, 1995, H.H.J. Heath, Lincoln County Ct. [*Ex rel.* Langleys, Solicitors, Lincoln.]

3724. Road traffic accident—car park—whether "road"—whether involvement of Motor Insurers' Bureau justified

[Road Traffic Act 1988 (c.52), s.192(1).]

A road traffic accident occurred on May 3, 1992 in the car park of a rest-home. Proceedings were issued in January 1994, and a notice was given to the Motor Insurers' Bureau (MIB), who subsequently instructed solicitors on July 5, 1994. The MIB was joined as second defendant. The MIB argued that they could have no liability for P's claim, as the locus of the accident did not constitute a road within the definition of the Road Traffic Act 1988, s.192(1). P's solicitors subsequently discontinued the action as against the MIB, but refused to pay costs in the arbitration. An application was lodged, asking for costs of the proceedings, including the costs of the application to be paid by P in any event.

Held, that the locus could never had constituted a road within the definition of s.192(1), and P's solicitor's conduct had been unreasonable in involving the MIB. P's solicitors were ordered to pay assessed costs.

SEVERN TRENT WATER v. WILLIAMS AND THE MOTOR INSURERS' BUREAU, March 8, 1995, District Judge Rhodes, Watford County Ct. [*Ex rel.* Weightman Rutherfords, Solicitors, Liverpool.]

3725. Road traffic accident—insurer known—Motor Insurers' Bureau contacted anyway—whether solicitors to pay costs of unnecessary involvement

P was a passenger involved in a road traffic accident on April 13, 1993. Notice of issue of proceedings was given to the Motor Insurers' Bureau (MIB) on June 23, 1994, in spite of the fact that the Eagle Star Insurance Company had confirmed they were the relevant insurer for the driver of the vehicle almost 12 months before the issue of proceedings.

Held, that it was unreasonable for P's solicitors to have involved the MIB. P and/or her solicitors were to pay the MIB's costs of, and incidental to, the action, to be taxed on Scale 1 if not agreed. If the costs were not paid by P within 28 days, P's solicitors were to show cause why they should not pay the MIB's costs.

MILLS v. TONER AND THE MOTOR INSURERS' BUREAU, January 1, 1995, District Judge Johnson, Liverpool County Ct. [*Ex rel.* Weightman Rutherfords, Solicitors, Liverpool.]

3726. Road traffic accident—knowingly accepting lift from drunk driver—personal injuries—measure of damages—contributory negligence—motor insurance—whether able to claim against Motor Insurers' Bureau

C was travelling as a passenger in a car with his brother L, the owner, driving. Both had been drinking heavily and the car collided with a lamp post, causing C to sustain severe head injuries. L had no insurance and was unemployed, so the MIB was contacted as any judgment against him was unlikely to be satisfied. The judge ordered damages to C be reduced by one third due to his bearing some responsibility for the damage and rejected his claim that the MIB was liable to satisfy the judgment obtained against his brother, as no notice had been given of the bringing of proceedings within seven days of their commencement.

Held, dismissing C's appeal, that (1) the decision to reduce damages by one third because C was at fault was upheld. The judge based his view on what was just and equitable on the facts and found the blameworthiness of C was to the greatest extent possible short of direct participation with the driver; (2) C failed to give notice of the bringing of proceedings to the MIB as required by its agreement with the Secretary of State. Two letters were sent from C to the MIB concerning the claim for damages but it was held that these did not amount to sufficient notice within the meaning of the agreement. Notice should have been given when the writ was issued; and (3) the evidence showed C knew or had reason to believe that no insurance policy was in force and was a user of the vehicle within cl. 6(i)(c)(ii) of the MIB Agreement 1972. As a passenger C came within the definition of user of a vehicle for the purpose of the agreement as there was evidence he was engaged in a joint venture to use the vehicle to get home and this purpose continued notwithstanding the amount he subsequently drank before allowing himself to be carried in the vehicle. Therefore the MIB had no liability to C (*Brown v. Roberts* [1963] C.L.Y. 3071, *B. (A Minor) v. Knight* [1982] C.L.Y 2756 distinguished).

STINTON (CHRISTOPHER BRIAN) v. THE MOTOR INSURERS' BUREAU (QBENF 93/0141/C) (QBENF 93/0141/C), November 11, 1994, C.A.

3727. Road traffic accident—Motor Insurers' Bureau—property damage excess not exceeded—whether Bureau involved unnecessarily—costs

A road traffic accident occurred on July 18, 1993. Proceedings were issued on May 4, 1994, and notice was given to the Motor Insurers' Bureau (MIB), which subsequently instructed solicitors, and was joined as second defendant. The MIB felt that it did not have to make a payment to P since the claim did not appear to exceed the MIB £175 property damage excess. P's solicitors were put on notice. They refused to concede this point, and the matter proceeded to arbitration on October 17, 1994.

Held, that P's solicitors had been unreasonable in involving the MIB unnecessarily. They need never have contacted the MIB. Costs were awarded against P's solicitors personally, to be taxed on Scale 1 if not agreed.

MASTIN v. BLANCHARD AND MOTOR INSURERS' BUREAU, October 17, 1994, District Judge Reeves, Mold County Ct. [*Ex rel.* Weightman Rutherfords, Solicitors.]

3728. Road traffic accident—Motor Insurers' Bureau—whether proper enquiries made as to identity of defendant's insurers—whether Bureau involved unnecessarily

Proceedings were issued concerning a road traffic accident, and the matter was subsequently referred to solicitors on behalf of the Motor Insurers' Bureau (MIB). *Inter alia*, the MIB contended that no reasonable enquiries had been made to identify D's insurers prior to notifying the MIB, which should not simply be used as a post box.

Held, that P's solicitors had involved the MIB unnecessarily. It was incumbent on the plaintiff's solicitors to make proper enquiries as regards the identity of an insurer for a prospective defendant before involving the MIB. P was ordered to pay the costs of the action on Scale 1, to be taxed if not agreed.

GRANADA U.K. RENTAL & RETAIL v. SPN FAREWAY AND MOTOR INSURERS' BUREAU, April 7, 1995, District Judge Urquart, Wigan County Ct. [*Ex rel.* Weightman Rutherfords, Solicitors.]

3729. Road traffic accident—standard of care—personal injury—road accident—defendant being overtaken—whether defendant negligent in continuing at a steady speed when room for overtaking obviously running out

Where one driver creates a dangerous situation by attempting to overtake another when room for overtaking is running out and then persists in trying to complete the manoeuvre, the other driver is not negligent in continuing to drive at a steady speed instead of slowing down.

P sued D for damages for personal injuries sustained in a road accident, claiming D was negligent. Both P and D were driving in the same direction along a dual carriageway when P, who was in the offside lane, attempted to overtake D, who was in the nearside lane. P was unable to complete her manoeuvre before the dual carriageway narrowed to a single file, two-lane road and she collided with oncoming traffic driving properly in the other direction. P's primary case was that she had started to overtake at a point when she had enough room to complete the manoeuvre but that D had deliberately accelerated and decelerated, preventing her from either overtaking or falling in behind him. At the trial of the issue of liability, the judge found that P had attempted to overtake at a point when, in order for the cars to reach the single carriageway section in single file, D would either have to accelerate and P drop behind or P would have to accelerate and D slow down so that P could get ahead. Further, that when she realised this dilemma, P had continued to accelerate in the belief that D would slow down and she would get ahead. The judge rejected P's primary case that D had deliberately prevented P from overtaking or falling in behind him, but held that D had been negligent in holding a steady speed rather than slowing down. D was held 25 per cent responsible and P 75 per cent responsible.

Held, allowing D's appeal, that (1) having rejected P's primary case, which in essence was that D had created the dangerous situation by deliberately altering his speed rather than driving at a steady pace, the judge should have been slow to find that D was negligent because he continued to drive at a steady pace instead of slowing down; (2) the evidence indicated that P had created the dangerous situation by attempting to overtake at a late stage and then persisted in it by choosing the obviously dangerous course of trying to accelerate and complete the manoeuvre. The ordinary reasonable driver cannot be expected to anticipate that the following driver will drive dangerously and to extricate that driver from the dangerous situation which that driver creates. That places too high a duty on the reasonable driver. The onus on the driver in D's situation was to drive normally at a proper speed and on a proper course. D could not be held negligent, therefore, for continuing to drive at a steady pace rather than slowing down.

SMITH v. CRIBBEN [1994] P.I.Q.R. P218, C.A.

3730. Shipping—negligence of surveyor employed by classification society—damage suffered by cargo owners—whether classification society owed duty of care to cargo owners

It would not be fair, just or reasonable to impose a duty of care on classification societies so that they would have unlimited liability in negligence to shipowners and cargo owners.

In the course of a voyage the vessel Nicholas H developed a crack in its hull. The shipowners requested their classification society, NKK, to perform a survey of the damage. D, an employee of NKK, carried out the survey and at first recommended that the vessel put in to dry dock for permanent repairs, but after protests from the shipowners over the costs of such an action changed his mind and recommended temporary repairs only. Shortly afterwards the ship sank as a result of the crack and the entire cargo, valued at U.S. $6 million, was lost. MR, the cargo owners, recovered U.S. $500,000 from the shipowners, which represented the extent of the shipowners liability having regard to the tonnage limitation applicable to the vessel, and sued NKK for the balance. Their claim succeeded at first instance but this decision was reversed by the Court of Appeal.

Held, dismissing MR's appeal, that (1) whatever the nature of the harm suffered by the plaintiff, it was necessary to consider the matter not only by inquiring about foreseeability but also by considering the nature of the relationship between the parties, and to be satisfied in all the circumstances that it was fair, just and reasonable to impose a duty of care (*Home Office v. Dorset Yacht Co.* [1970] C.L.Y. 1849 applied); (2) although there was a sufficient degree of proximity in this case to fulfil that requirement for the existence of a duty of care, it would be unfair, unjust and unreasonable to impose a duty of care on NKK as against the shipowners who would ultimately have to bear the consequence of holding classification societies liable, such consequences being at variance with the bargain between shipowners and cargo owners based on an internationally agreed contractual structure; and (3) it would also be unjust, unfair and unreasonable towards classification societies because they act for the collective welfare and would not have the benefit of any limitation provisions.

MARC RICH & CO. AG v. BISHOP ROCK MARINE CO. [1995] 3 W.L.R. 227, H.L.

3731. Statutory duty—breach—whether evidence of negligence—whether separate cause of action

[Aus.] A breach of statutory duty may by itself give rise to a separate cause of action, and also be evidence of negligence in common law.

DILLON v. AYRES [1995] A.L.M.D. 3569, Sup Ct. NT.

3732. Summary judgment—personal injury—plaintiff pleading *res ipsa loquitur*—alternative explanation for accident not pleaded in defence—whether general denial of negligence sufficient for issue to be tried. See BERGIN v. DAVID WICKES TELEVISION, §4230.

3733. Television interference and depositing of dust due to road construction—whether cause of action. See HUNTER v. CANARY WHARF, §3743.

3734. Vaccine manufacturer—safety tests on batches of vaccine—whether vaccine manufacturer or doctor prescribing vaccine negligent—Ireland

The manufacturer of a vaccine which arguably carries a risk of severe injury has a high duty to take care when carrying out safety tests on individual batches of the vaccine.

P was given an injection containing a pertussis component, and later suffered post-pertussis vaccinal encephalopathy (PPVE). P sued W, the manufacturers of the vaccine. The High Court held that the pertussis component in the vaccine could cause PPVE. In addition it was held that W had been negligent in releasing the batch of the vaccine administered to P as, whilst passing certain tests, the batch failed to pass a mandatory national test and failed an optional test carried out at W's initiative. The High Court also held that P had failed to show that the PPVE had been caused by the vaccine, as there was an insufficient temporal connection between the administration of the vaccine and the onset of PPVE. The court rejected the evidence on behalf of P that the symptoms occurred eight hours after the vaccination, preferring the evidence of the family doctor that P's mother did not complain about P's condition until some two-and-a-half months later. P appealed, and W applied to vary the finding of negligence in the judgment, arguing that the tests which had been failed were unreliable.

Held, allowing P's appeal and dismissing W's application, that (1) as there was a considerable body of scientific opinion that the vaccine could cause a serious reaction, W had a duty to exercise a high degree of care when testing it. Merely to comply with minimum national requirements in testing the vaccine, or to rely on the point of view that the risks involved were not great would not necessarily be enough to discharge the duty of care. There was insufficient evidence to impugn the validity of the tests, and W had been negligent in releasing the vaccine; (2) the trial judge erred in rejecting the evidence of P's mother as to when the first fit took place. Given that this evidence was prima facie credible, it was not displaced by the fact that the family doctor had not recorded any complaints by the mother until two-and-a-half months after the injection. A new trial was ordered on the issue of damages.

BEST v. WELLCOME FOUNDATION, O'KEEFE, THE SOUTHERN HEALTH BOARD, THE MINISTER FOR HEALTH FOR IRELAND, ATT.-GEN. [1994] 5 Med LR 81, Irish Supreme Court.

3735. Vicarious liability—excessive use of violence—liability of employer for acts of club doormen—whether acting in course of employment—responsibility of manager to restrain doormen

V visited a nightclub owned by S and, having been refused entry, kicked the door of the premises, breaking the glass. He was pursued into the car park of the premises by two doormen, P and M, and the manager and was attacked. P was convicted of causing grievous bodily harm with intent. V appealed against the dismissal of a claim for damages for personal injury. The issues subject to appeal were that S was vicariously liable for the acts of the three men and that the manager was in breach of a duty of care to V in failing to control and supervise the doormen and enforce S's rules.

Held, allowing the appeal, that (1) the conduct of the assailants was a reaction to the damage to the door for the protection of S's property and was not a private quarrel unrelated to the employee's duties (*Keppel Bus Co. v. Sa'ad Bin Ahmad* [1974] C.L.Y. 1231, *Daniels v. Whetstone Entertainments and Allender* [1962] C.L.Y. 1140 distinguished); (2) it was an unauthorised act which was within the province of their proper duty generally to preserve the integrity of the club. Although it was an unlawful and unauthorised manner of carrying out their duty, this was not a frolic of their own but an act for which the employer must be held vicariously liable (*Harrison v. Michelin Tyre Co.* [1985] C.L.Y. 1281 applied); and (3) it was the duty of the manager of such an establishment to exercise proper control over employees to prevent unwarranted assaults on customers.

VASEY v. SURREY FREE INNS (CCRTF 94/1184/C), May 5, 1995, C.A.

NUISANCE

3736. Disrepair of adjoining house—property allowed to become derelict—damp—vermin—draughts—distress and annoyance—*quantum*. See SMITH v. NIXON, §1642.

3737. Eviction—nuisance—local authority housing—press release. See HOUSING, §2532.

3738. Foreseeability—damage to property—nuisance and negligence—claim against council—trees causing subsidence—cracks in house—whether damage by trees foreseeable. See PATERSON v. HUMBERSIDE COUNTY COUNCIL, §3661.

3739. Infestation—whether landlord liable for infestation of cockroaches

A landlord who was not in occupation of adjoining premises, nor who as owner could be said to have the necessary degree of control over adjoining premises, could not be held liable in nuisance for an infestation of cockroaches.

A was the tenant on an estate owned by a housing association. A's flat was in a block of three, each of which had its own entrance and in respect of which there were no common parts. Soon after moving in, A discovered that the flat was infested by cockroaches. Other tenants on the estate also suffered from infestation. In 1990 the local authority served an abatement notice on the association. As a result, it was decided to treat the entire area of infestation, as opposed to the piecemeal approach previously adopted. The treatment was successful and A suffered no further infestation. The association took proceedings against A for arrears of rent. She counterclaimed for damages in respect of the infestation, alleging nuisance, negligence and breach of an implied term. At the trial the judge found that A had suffered damage for a period of six years but that there was no evidence on which he could make a finding as to the origin of the infestation. Further, there was no evidence that the infestation had occurred as a result of any breach of the plaintiff's repairing obligations. He dismissed A's counterclaim.

Held, dismissing A's appeal, that there were no premises of which the association could be said to be occupier for the purposes of the law of nuisance; nor could it be liable as owner, since, first, it was not proved, and the judge was not prepared to infer, that the cockroaches entered the flat from property owned by the association and, second, the association had nothing like the degree of control over the remainder of the estate that would be required for the principle to operate. The claim in nuisance could therefore not be sustained (*Wringe v. Cohen* [1940] K.B. 229, considered).

HABINTEG HOUSING ASSOCIATION v. JAMES (1994) 27 H.L.R. 299, C.A.

3740. Smell—pig housing units erected in close proximity to neighbouring dwellings pursuant to planning permission—whether grant of planning permission constituting defence to action in nuisance

P bought a farmhouse and outbuildings on land adjacent to D's pig farm.

Both P's property and the farmland were formerly in common ownership. There were two means of access to P's property, one of which ("the south entrance") could only be reached by crossing a part of D's land but there was no express right of way and D took the view that P were not entitled to use it and blocked it off with a wall. D also applied for and, despite P's objections, obtained planning permission to build two pig housing units on their land, one of which was only a few metres away from one of P's outbuildings which was used as a holiday cottage. In proceedings, P obtained damages against D for obstructing a right of way to their property with the new wall and for nuisance in the form of smell from the pigs in the housing units, and injunctions requiring D to demolish the wall and restraining them from keeping pigs in the housing units. On D's appeal P contended for an implied grant in their conveyance of an easement of necessity entitling them to a right of way over D's land. D argued that no such right was intended and, as regards the nuisance, contended that since they had obtained planning permission for the pig housing units, any smell emanating therefrom could not amount to a nuisance in law.

Held, allowing the appeal in part, that (1) the class of easements implied in favour of a grantee included easements necessary to the reasonable enjoyment of the property granted and which had been and were at the time of the grant used by the owners of the entirety for the benefit of the part granted but that, on the facts, the south entrance to P's property was not necessary for its reasonable enjoyment since the other entrance would do just as well and it followed that P acquired no right of way through the south entrance (*Wheeldon v. Burrows* [1874–80] All E.R. Rep. 669, *Sovmots Investments v. Secretary of State for the Environment; Brompton Securities v. Same* [1977] C.L.Y. 333 considered); (2) unlike Parliament, a planning authority had no jurisdiction to authorise a nuisance save insofar as it had a statutory power to permit a change in the character of a neighbourhood and the nuisance was such that it inevitably resulted from the authorised use; and (3) in the present case, the planning permission granted was not a strategic planning decision affected by considerations of public interest but amounted only to a change of use of a small piece of land for the benefit of P and to the detriment of the objectors in the quiet enjoyment of their house and as such it followed that the judge was entitled to conclude that the planning consents did not prevent P from succeeding in their claim in nuisance (*Allen v. Gulf Oil Refining* [1981] C.L.Y. 2003 considered).

WHEELER v. J.J. SAUNDERS [1995] 2 All E.R. 697, C.A.

3741. Statutory nuisance—appeals

STATUTORY NUISANCE (APPEALS) REGULATIONS 1995 (No. 2644) [£1·10], made under the Environmental Protection Act 1990, Sched. 3, para. 1(4); revoke S.I. 1990 Nos. 2276, 2483; operative on November 8, 1995; make provision for appeals to magistrates' courts against notices served under s.80 and s.80A of the EPA 1990; reg. 2 sets out grounds on which such appeals may be made, prescribes procedures to be followed, and the action which the court may take to give effect to its decision on appeal; reg. 3 prescribes cases in which an abatement notice is to be suspended pending the abandonment of, or a decision by a magistrates' court on appeal.

3742. Statutory nuisance—liability for recurrence of nuisance—statutory defences available

[Environmental Protection Act 1990 (c.43), s.82; Public Health Act 1936 (c.49).]

C, a council tenant, brought a complaint against H council under Pt. II of the Environmental Protection Act 1990 that he was a person aggrieved by the existence of a statutory nuisance because there was a problem of condensation, dampness and mould in his flat. At the time of the hearing the problem had abated but the magistrate had to ask whether it was likely to recur. H had tried to install electric convector heaters in the flat but had been refused entry because C wished to have gas-fired central heating installed on grounds of cost. The magistrate found that if the nuisance was likely to recur, recurrence would be attributable to C's action in preventing the installation of the heaters and, therefore, H was not liable. C appealed by way of case stated against this decision, arguing that the defence relied on by H, of not being the person by whose "act, default or sufferance" the nuisance arose or continued, was not available under s.82 of the Act.

Held, dismissing the appeal, that *Warner v. Lambeth London Borough Council*, decided under the Public Health Act 1936 which was replaced by ss.79 to 82 of the 1990 Act, found that it was open to a person against whom proceedings were brought to rely on the defence advanced by H. The schemes of both Acts were similar and there was no reason why the defence should not be open to H for determination by the magistrate (*Warner v. Lambeth London Borough Council* [1984] C.L.Y. 1663 considered).

CARR v. HACKNEY LONDON BOROUGH COUNCIL, *The Times*, March 9, 1995, McKinnon J.

3743. Television interference and depositing of dust due to road construction—whether cause of action

H and a number of other plaintiffs living in East London brought two actions claiming damages for nuisance and negligence. First, they claimed damages in nuisance from C in respect of interference with reception of television broadcasts due to the presence of Canary Wharf Tower. Secondly, they claimed damages in nuisance and negligence against London Docklands Development Corporation in respect of the depositing of dust on their properties due to the construction of the Limehouse Link Road. Both the plaintiffs and defendants appealed against findings on preliminary issues.

Held, that occupation of a property as a home enabled an occupier to sue in private nuisance. It was not necessary to have a right of exclusive possession of the property. In the first action, the plaintiffs' appeal was dismissed and the defendant's cross-appeal allowed. The presence of a building in the line of sight to a television transmitter was not actionable as an interference with the use and enjoyment of land, and interference with television reception was not capable of constituting either a private or public nuisance. In the second action, the defendants' appeal was dismissed and the plaintiffs' cross-appeal allowed. The deposit of excess dust on the plaintiffs' homes was capable of founding an action in negligence. Whether it did was dependent upon proof of physical damage, such proof being dependent on circumstances and evidence. Both parties were given leave to appeal to the House of Lords.

HUNTER v. CANARY WHARF, *The Times*, October 13, 1995, C.A.

PARLIAMENT

3744. Occupational pensions—Members of Parliament

PARLIAMENTARY PENSIONS (AMENDMENT) REGULATIONS 1995 (No. 2867) [£1·55], made under the Parliamentary and Other Pensions Act 1987, s.2(1)(4); operative on December 1, 1995; amend S.I. 1993 No. 3253, improving the accrual rate for service as a Member of Parliament before June 20, 1983 from sixtieths to fiftieths for Members in service on April 1, 1995 and changing the provisions relating to gratuities payable in respect of MPs and the holders of ministerial and other offices who die in service on or after that date. There are a number of consequential amendments arising from the improvement in the accrual rate. The amount of the death in service gratuity which may be paid under the scheme in respect of any participant in service on or after April 1, 1995, is to be increased to three times an MP's salary at the time of death. A scheme member may nominate more than one person to receive the gratuity, and the persons nominated may include any institution or trust; have effect from April 1, 1995.

3745. Parliamentary Commissioner

PARLIAMENTARY COMMISSIONER ORDER 1995 (No. 1615), made under the Parliamentary Commissioner Act 1967, s.4(2); operative July 31, 1995; adds the Arts Council of England, the Arts Council of Wales, the Biotechnology and Biological Sciences Research Council, the Council for the Central Laboratory of the Research Councils, the Occupational Pensions Board and other organisations to the list of departments and authorities which are subject to investigation by the Parliamentary Commissioner for Administration.

PARTNERSHIP

3746. Dissolution of partnership—undistributed assets—unequal contributions by partners to acquisition of assets—defendant carrying on business after dissolution of partnership—sale of assets—plaintiff claiming equal share

P and D entered into a partnership and bought a newsagent's business. D contributed capital of £23,000 and P £4,500. It was agreed that P would provide most of the labour since D had provided most of the capital. P then left voluntarily and the partnership came to an end. D continued trading and acquired the freehold of the premises for £80,000. Some time later he sold the premises and other partnership assets at a profit. P then sought a half share of the profits.

Held, ordering accounts to be taken and an inquiry carried out, that given the unequal financial contributions of the partners, the fact that P voluntarily terminated the partnership and the fact that the increased value of the premises was due to D's efforts and expenditure, rather than external forces, the profits were not to be shared equally. The profits of the disposal of the assets were to be distributed according to the capital contributions made by the parties with an allowance in D's favour to take account of the fact that he had continued the business after P had left and taking into account D's contribution of £80,000 to acquire the freehold (*Manley v. Sartori* [1927] 1 Ch. 157, *Thompson's Trustee in Bankruptcy v. Heaton* [1974] C.L.Y. 2740 applied; *Sobell v. Boston* [1975] C.L.Y. 2478 considered; *Barclays Bank Trust Co. v. Bluff* [1981] C.L.Y. 2016, *Chandroutie v. Gajahar* [1987] C.L.Y. 2767 distinguished).

POPAT v. SHONCHHATRA [1995] 1 W.L.R. 908, Mr David Neuberger, Q.C.

3747. Unpaid partnership debt—creditors' rights—right to present petition against partner without seeking winding up

S appealed against a decision upholding her bankruptcy arising from a debt owed to Customs and Excise by a partnership between S and another. S argued that a creditor could not enforce a partnership debt by means of an individual bankruptcy order unless the petition was combined with a winding up petition or a judgment had been made against the partnership.

Held, that art. 15(3) of the Insolvent Partnerships Order 1986 dispensed with both the requirement for the winding-up petition and the partnership judgment. As stated in Lindley & Banks on Partnership (17th ed, 1995, p. 808, para. 27–48), if a partnership debt was unpaid, the creditors had the right to present a petition against any of the partners without seeking to wind up the partnership.

SCHOOLER v. CUSTOMS AND EXCISE COMMISSIONERS, *The Times*, August 9, 1995, C.A.

PATENTS AND DESIGNS

3748. Amendment—action settled—whether court having jurisdiction to allow amendment of patent

P applied to amend a patent which had been in issue in litigation between the parties. The parties settled the main action on the basis that the action would be settled on the terms set out in a Tomlin schedule after the conclusion of the amendment proceedings. When the motion to amend first came before the judge, the issue of jurisdiction to allow amendment was raised. The judge invited the Comptroller to consider the amendments and the question of jurisdiction. The Comptroller replied stating that he would not wish to argue that the court did not have jurisdiction to consider the proposed amendments, so long as a Tomlin order was outstanding.

Held, allowing the amendment, that the amendment of patents should only be permitted in actions where the parties have in effect settled their dispute where: (a) amendments are not substantial in amount or effect; (b) there is no apparent matter of controversy; and (c) no matter of public interest arises. If none of these matters exists, the court should allow patents to be amended (*Congoleum Industries Inc. v. Armstrong Cork Co.* [1977] C.L.Y. 2170 followed; *Lever Bros.* (1955) 72 R.P.C. 198, *Critchley Bros. v. Engelman & Buckham* [1971] C.L.Y. 8608 referred to).

IMPERIAL CHEMICAL INDUSTRIES v. RAM BATHROOMS AND ROHM GmbH [1994] F.S.R. 181, Patents Ct.

3749. Amendment—discretion of hearing officer—whether prior evidence required

An applicant for amendment of a patent must provide evidence for the hearing officer to consider before deciding whether or not to exercise his discretion.

A brought revocation proceedings against R, the patentee. The patent included process claims and apparatus claims. R offered to amend the patent by deleting the apparatus claims, but without admitting invalidity. R later withdrew this offer, but subsequently applied to delete the apparatus claims. At the hearing, no arguments were considered on these claims. At a subsequent hearing following an interim decision at the initial hearing, the hearing officer found in R's favour without considering any evidence on the point.

Held, allowing A's appeal, that R's conduct in offering to delete, then reinstating and defending, and subsequently applying to delete the apparatus claims again, required explanation and evidence, and not merely argument, before the hearing officer could decide whether or not to exercise the discretion.

COAL INDUSTRY (PATENTS)'S PATENT [1994] R.P.C. 661, Jacob J.

3750. Amendment—partial invalidity—discretion—whether specification framed with reasonable skill and knowledge

[Patents Act 1977 (c.37), ss.62, 63, 75, 76.]

There is a material difference between deletion of claims and validation by reformulation; the courts are more likely to allow the former than the latter. At the trial of the action the judge held that the majority of the claims of the patent in suit were valid and infringed. He also found that certain groups of claims were invalid for insufficiency. P applied to amend the patent by deleting the invalid claims. D opposed the amendments and contended that the court should not exercise its discretion in favour of P. They also argued that the specification of the patent had not been framed with reasonable skill and knowledge.

Held, allowing the amendment, that (1) there was a material difference between deletion of claims and validation by reformulation. P were seeking the former which the courts were generally more likely to allow. On the facts, there was no reason to prevent the Ps from amending (*Van der Lely (C.) NV v. Bamfords* [1964] C.L.Y. 2766 applied); and (2) the specification of a patent was framed with reasonable skill and knowledge if it was in a form which a person with reasonable skill in drafting patent specifications and knowledge of the law and practice could produce with the patentee's knowledge of the invention. The specification of the patent in suit was one which a competent and properly instructed patent agent could have produced (*Hallen Co. v. Brabantia (U.K.)* [1992] C.L.Y. 3318 considered).

CHIRON CORP. v. ORGANON TEKNIKA (NO. 7); CHIRON CORP. v. MUREX DIAGNOSTICS (NO. 7) [1994] F.S.R. 458, Aldous J.

3751. Amendment—partially invalid patent—plaintiffs amending by deletion of invalid claims—defendants alleging valid claims not sought to be amended not supported by description—whether a proper ground for opposing amendment

[Patents Act 1977 (c.37), ss.14, 72, 74–76, 130; Patents Act 1949 (c.87), s.32; European Patent Convention, Arts. 83, 84, 138.]

Under the Patents Act 1977 there is a difference between what may be a ground for rejecting a specification or curtailing a specification in the Patent Office before grant and what may be a ground for revocation of a patent after grant.

At the trial the judge held that the majority of claims of the patent in suit were valid and infringed. He also found certain groups of claims relating to a vaccine to be invalid for insufficiency; as the specification did not disclose how to produce the vaccine in a manner clear and complete enough to be performed by a person skilled in the art. P applied to delete the claims which had been held invalid. D opposed the amendments sought, arguing that in considering the exercise of his discretion to allow amendments under s.75 of the 1977 Act the judge should require P to submit to a drastic curtailment of claim 1, and consequently of all claims dependent on claim 1, so that those claims were fairly based on the body of the specification. The background to the application was that under the 1977 Act it was not a ground of objection to the validity of a patent and for claiming revocation in an infringement action that the claim was not fairly based on the specification. The judge struck out D's pleas but granted D leave to appeal.

Held, dismissing the appeal, that (1) under the Patents Act 1977 there is a difference between what may be a ground for rejecting a specification or curtailing a specification in the Patent Office before grant and what may be a ground for revocation of a patent after grant; (2) on examination of a patent specification before grant it is a requirement that the claims in the specification must define the matter for which protection is sought, be clear and concise and be supported by the description. Lack of support is not a ground for revocation of a patent after grant (*Genentech's Patent* [1990] C.L.Y. 3472 referred to); and (3) if there is to be an amendment in this sort of case, there must be some nexus between the amendment that is sought and what has made the amendment necessary. What P wanted to delete followed naturally from the judge's ruling that certain claims were invalid; D was simply looking for a procedural opportunity to put forward a claim for an unrelated amendment which was outside the purview of the action.

CHIRON CORP. v. ORGANON TEKNIKA (NO. 11) [1995] F.S.R. 589, C.A.

3752. Amendment—plaintiffs seeking to amend by deletion of invalid claims—defendants in infringement action opposing amendment—whether valid claims which were not sought to be amended were not supported by description—whether amendment should only be allowed if subject matter of invalid claims disclaimed from principal claims—whether practice of European Patent Office relevant

[Patents Act 1977 (c.37), ss.14, 72, 74–76, 130; Patents Act 1949 (c.87), s.30; European Patent Convention, Art. 102; R.S.C., Ord. 18, r.19.]

At the trial the judge held that the main claims of the patent in suit, relating to the Hepatitis C Virus (HCV), were valid and infringed. He also held that certain groups of claims concerning vaccines and the growth of HCV *in vitro* were invalid for insufficiency. P applied to amend the patent in suit to meet the judgment by deleting the claims which had been found to be invalid. D opposed amendment and submitted a statement of objections. P applied to strike out the statement or part of it.

Held, striking out parts of the statement of objections, that (1) the principles applicable to the exercise of the discretion to allow amendments under the Patents Act 1949 are also applicable to the exercise of discretion under s.75 of the 1977 Act. Under these principles there was a significant difference between an amendment seeking to validate an invalid claim and one which amounted to deletion of an invalid claim (*Smith Kline & French Laboratories v. Evans Medical* [1990] C.L.Y. 3460, *Van der Lely (C.) N.V. v. Bamfords* [1964] C.L.Y. 2766 considered); (2) P's argument that s.74 of the 1977 Act barred an opponent from raising lack of support in amendment proceedings was rejected. As the pleading in the present case stood, D was not putting in issue the validity of the valid claims; (3) when considering the allowability of an amendment, the court must consider matters relating to the cause and effect of the amendment, the reason why it is sought, when and how that need arose and the general conduct of the patentee in relation to those matters. It was not necessary to consider matters having no nexus with the amendment sought or the cause for it. In the present case there was no nexus between the alleged lack of support for the valid claims and the requirement to delete the invalid claims. There would be no justice in requiring the amendment of valid claims because other claims were being deleted; (4) D's plea that the patentee should disclaim HCV vaccines and tissue culture systems from the valid claims as a condition of amendment being allowed was based on a misconception. The valid claims did not claim an invention of an HCV vaccine or a method of growing HCV in tissue culture. The fact that D might need to use the invention of claim 1 to make an HCV vaccine or grow HCV in tissue culture was irrelevant; and (5) although the European Patent Office would have come to the same conclusion this was not directly relevant. Jurisdiction under the European Patent Convention was not exactly the same as that given by the Patents Act 1977. Further, the fact that ss.75 and 76 of the Act are not mentioned in s.130(7) of the Act suggests that the question of amendment is left to the decision of the national courts (*The General Electric Co. (T–427/88)* [1991] E.P.O.R. 486 referred to).

CHIRON CORP. v. ORGANON TEKNIKA (NO. 5); SAME v. MUREX DIAGNOSTICS (NO. 5) [1994] F.S.R. 258, Patents Ct.

3753. Application—eggshells as oral medicament for treating ulcers—Swiss-type claim—whether claim supported by description

[Patents Act 1977 (c.37), s.14(5)(c).]

The application in suit related, amongst other things, to the use of eggshells as a medicament for the treatment of ulcers. Documents cited during examination in the Patent Office referred to the use of eggshells for treating ulcers but not in an oral medicament. A Japanese specification, which was also cited, described the oral administration of eggshells to reduce nutritional deficiencies responsible for a number of ailments but not for the treatment of ulcers. The applicant sought to introduce a Swiss-type claim to the use of eggshells in the preparation of an oral medicament for the treatment of ulcers. In the Patent Office the hearing officer found that the description did not provide the necessary support for the claim under s.14(5)(c). A appealed to the Patents Court, appearing in person.

Held, dismissing the appeal, that where the novelty of an invention resides not in the composition of the medicament itself but in the particular treatment to which it was directed, a clear indication that such a treatment has been tried and tested is essential to provide the necessary support for the claim.

There was not the requisite support for A's claim which would be refused under s.14(5)(c).

McMANUS'S APPLICATION [1994] F.S.R. 558, Patents Ct.

3754. Application—international patent—delay in filing—postal problems

[Patents Rules 1990 (S.I. 1990 No. 2384), r.97; Patents Co-operation Treaty, Arts. 11(1), 48(1), r.82.2(a).]

The international application in suit had been filed in the U.K. Patent Office as receiving office under the Patent Co-operation Treaty (PCT) claiming priority from earlier U.K. applications filed on December 16, 1992. The 1993 application was posted on December 15, 1993. In the normal course of post the 1993 application would have been received at the Patent Office on December 16, 1993, with the result that it would have been received within a year of filing the 1992 application. In those circumstances priority from the 1992 application could be claimed. However, the package was damaged and the application was delayed in the post with the result that it was not received until December 17, 1993. The applicant contended that the application should be accorded a filing date of December 16 under r.97 of the Patents Rules 1990 as the date on which it would have been received in the normal course of post. The applicant also argued that the delay should be excused under Art. 48.1 and r.82.2 of the PCT on the grounds that there had been an interruption in the mail. The hearing officer in the Patent Office rejected these arguments and the applicant applied for judicial review of the decision.

Held, refusing the application, that (1) the PCT and its rules contain a complete code for filing international applications. Article 11 requires the Patent Office to give the application the international filing date of the day of receipt. Although Art. 48 provides for delay in meeting certain time-limits only Art. 48.1 applies to delays which would affect applications in other Member States; (2) the Regs. relevant to Art. 48.1 are contained in r.82.2. This rule relates only to interruptions in the postal service, not to mistakes or variations occurring when the service was being supplied. Delay due to damage to a package is nothing like interruption of the service on account of war, strike or natural calamity; (3) r.97 of the Patents Rules 1990 did not apply to an international application filed in the U.K. Patent Office as receiving office. The jurisdiction of the Patent Office when so acting came from the PCT, which was a complete code, and the Office must apply the rules, regulations and conditions laid down in the Treaty.

ARCHIBALD KENRICK & SONS'S INTERNATIONAL APPLICATION [1994] R.P.C. 635, Aldous J.

3755. Application—threats relating to a pending patent application—conditional threats—whether "person aggrieved"

[Patents Act 1977 (c.37), ss.69, 70; R.S.C., Ord. 14A, Ord. 18, r.19.]

D1 was a firm of solicitors acting for D2, a Danish research institute. P was the managing director and controlling force behind I Ltd, which was involved in the treatment of liquid waste. The action concerned alleged threats contained in a series of letters written by D1 on behalf of D2 to P, I Ltd and to a customer of I Ltd. These letters referred to a pending application for a European Patent for a process of waste disposal and gave notice that D2 intended to take action to restrain infringements of its rights. D1 applied to strike out the statement of claim on the grounds that it disclosed no reasonable cause of action.

Held, dismissing the application, that (1) threats of proceedings in respect of acts done between publication and grant of a patent are actionable within s.70(1) of the Patents Act 1977, but may be justified under s.70(2) where the acts, if done, would constitute an infringement of a patent (*Ellis & Sons v. Pogson* (1923) 40 R.P.C. 179 referred to); (2) a conditional threat, *i.e.* a threat to sue once the patent is granted, can amount to a threat within the meaning of s.70 and is actionable; (3) the threatening letter to the customer should be read through the eyes of the reasonable and normal recipient. The wording of the threats was vague and the threatener should not be given the benefit of the doubt. The threats were in respect of all and any infringements of the patent, and were not limited merely to the process. Accordingly, D1 could not avail itself of the defence given by s.70(4); and (4) P was a "person aggrieved". The entire correspondence containing the intimidating course of action was to be read as a whole. The course of conduct was aimed at P, his company, I Ltd, and its customers. P would be likely to suffer damage in his personal capacity due to his intimate involvement with the direction and work of the company (*Reymes-Cole v. Elite Hosiery Co.* [1961] C.L.Y. 6519 distinguished; *C. Evans & Sons v. Spriteband* [1985] F.S.R. 367, *Prudential Assurance Co. v. Newman Industries (No. 2)* [1982] C.L.Y. 331 referred to).

BRAIN (PATRICK JOHN) v. INGLEDEW BROWN BENNISON AND GARRET (A FIRM) [1995] F.S.R. 552, Jacob J.

3756. Construction—ambiguity—matters to which court should have regard—whether evidence of meaning admissible—whether drawing of evidence from different sources permissible

[Patents Act 1949 (c.87), s.32(1)(c)(f)(i); Civil Evidence Act 1972 (c.30), s.3.]

The Court must adopt a purposive construction and not a literal one.

P sued D for infringement of its patent relating to a process for repairing the lining of furnaces. D counterclaimed for revocation. P argued that the process involved two stages, first the projection of solid particles against a surface and secondly, the burning of the particles when they arrived at the surface, but not before. D contended that the claim included the burning of particles before they arrived at the surface. The trial judge found the patent valid and infringed, and D appealed.

Held, allowing the appeal, that (1) the interpretation of a patent is a question of law for the judge to decide and evidence of what a patent means is not admissible, nor is evidence of what the patentee intended it to mean; (2) the court should have regard to the surrounding circumstances at the date of publication; (3) the court should admit evidence of the meaning of technical terms; (4) the whole document should be read together, but if a claim is in clear language, the monopoly sought cannot be extended or cut down by reference to the rest of the specification; (5) the court must adopt a purposive construction (*Catnic Components v. Hills & Rutter* [1982] R.P.C. 183 followed; *Fothergill v. Monarch Airlines* [1980] C.L.Y. 128, *Schuler (L.) AG v. Wickman Machine Tool Sales* [1973] C.L.Y. 396 referred to); (6) subsequent conduct is not available as an aid to interpretation (*Schuler v. Wickman Machine Tool Sales* [1973] C.L.Y. 396 applied); (7) a claim must not be construed with an eye on prior material, in order to avoid its effect (*Molins v. Industrial Machinery Co.* [1938] 55 R.P.C. 31 applied); (8) the patent was not limited in the way contended by P, since there was material in the specification suggesting that particles could burn before they reached the surface; (9) on the question of ambiguity: if P's interpretation of the claim had not been rejected, it was very arguable that the claim was not sufficiently and clearly defined; (10) on anticipation: it is not permissible to draw information from different sources to arrive at composite knowledge; (11) (*per* Peter Gibson L.J.) guidance may be obtained from a subordinate claim on the true construction of the antecedent claim; (12) (*per* Peter Gibson L.J. and Waite L.J.) to establish anticipation, all that is required is to see whether, if the teaching in the prior document is carried out, that action would inevitably constitute an infringement (*The General Tire & Rubber Co. v. Firestone Tyre and Rubber Co.* [1975] C.L.Y. 2503 applied); (13) (*per* Peter Gibson L.J. and Waite L.J.) it is not necessary that the prior art be equal in practical utility or disclose the same invention in all respects; (14) on obviousness: the rule that expert opinion cannot be allowed on the issue which the court has to decide (in this case obviousness) was abrogated by s.3 of the Civil Evidence Act 1972; and (15) identifying the inventive step must be done by looking at the patent alone.

GLAVERBEL SA v. BRITISH COAL CORP. [1995] F.S.R. 254, C.A.

3757. Construction—inventive step—whether Protocol on Interpretation of Art. 69 should be applied—considerations to apply when deciding on obviousness

[Patent Act 1977 (c.37), s.125, European Patent Convention, Art. 69; Protocol on Interpretation of Art. 69 of the European Patent Convention.]

Construction of patent specifications should be based on the Protocol on Interpretation of Art. 69 of the European Patent Convention and not the *Catnic* tests.

P was the proprietor of two patents, called the Uniax and Biax patents, which related to methods for producing stretched plastic nets used in civil engineering. Both patents required the use of a starting material which was "substantially uniplanar", meaning that it was symmetrical about the median plane. The Uniax patent involved stretching the starting material in one direction, and the Biax in two directions at right angles to each other. P alleged that D's "TT" and "LBO" nets, infringed both patents. D claimed that its nets were produced from starting material which was not "substantially uniplanar". The prior art consisted of two processes for producing the starting material, called the strand-extruding process and the flat sheet process, both of which suffered from defects when stretched. P's contended inventive step was that nets produced from a uniplanar starting material of a minimum thickness, and having a substantially regular pattern of holes, had strong junctions without suffering from the defects of the prior art. The judge at first instance found both patents to be invalid on the ground of obviousness and P appealed.

Held, finding both patents valid, and that D's TT net infringed the Uniax patent, that (1) in construing the claims of a patent, the Protocol on Interpretation of Art. 69 of the European Patent Convention should be applied and not the tests set out in *Catnic Components v. Hill & Smith* [1981] C.L.Y. 2042 which was decided before the Patents Act 1977 came into force; (2) in applying the Protocol, the approach of the German courts should be followed, namely that the scope and content of the claims must be determined by applying the meaning which a person skilled in the art would attribute to the wording of the claims; (3) in this case a skilled man would consider departures from uniplanetary at either the edge of the starting material or on a part of the starting material which was not intended to be stretched as immaterial and would accordingly conclude that the starting material was still "substantially uniplanar"; (4) in considering whether an invention is obvious, the principles laid out in *Mölnlycke AB v. Procter & Gamble* [1991] C.L.Y. 2694 should be applied. These are: (i) the criterion for deciding whether the invention involved an "inventive step" is wholly objective and is defined in s.3 of the Patents Act 1977 as being whether the step in question was obvious to a person skilled in the art, having regard to any matter which forms part of the state of the art; (ii) the test is qualitative, not quantitative; (iii) what was included in the state of the art at the priority date and the question of obviousness are questions of fact; (iv) assessment of obviousness with hindsight must be avoided; (v) the burden of proof in showing no inventive step was involved is on those attaching the validity of the patent; (vi) the four steps laid down in *Windsurfing International v. Tabur Marine* [1985] R.P.C. 59 continue to provide assistance. These are (a) identifying the inventive step; (b) imputing the common general knowledge in the art at the priority date to the normally skilled but unimaginative addressee in the art; (iii) identifying any differences between the cited prior art and the invention; and (iv) asking whether, without knowledge of the invention, those differences constitute obvious steps to the skilled man or whether they require any degree of invention; (5) in this case, the inventive concept constituted a combination of features, there was a multiplicity of possible starting points in the prior art, and each of the relevant features of the prior art were interdependent, so that changing one of the features invalidated the teaching of the prior art in respect to others. The correct question was whether it would have been obvious to a man skilled in the art at the priority date to select the combination of features used in P's patents; (6) it would not have been obvious to the skilled man to use a uniplanar starting material of sufficient thickness, of either the extruded strand or flat-sheet type. Accordingly, both patents were valid; (7) D's TT nets were "substantially uniplanar" within the meaning of that expression in the Uniax patent (though not the similar expression in the Biax patent) and therefore infringed the Uniax patent; and (8) D's LBO nets were not uniplanar, and it would not have been obvious to the skilled man that when D's starting materials for the LBO net were stretched they would behave like uniplanar starting materials. Accordingly, the LBO nets did not infringe either of P's patents.

PLG RESEARCH v. ARDON INTL. [1995] F.S.R. 116, C.A.

3758. Construction—petition for revocation and declaration of non-infringement—purposive construction—whether *Catnic* principles apply to Patents Act 1977

[Patents Act 1949 (c.87), s.32(1)(f)(i); Patents Act 1977 (c.37) ss.60, 72(1)(a)(c)(d), 125, 130(7); European Patent Convention, Art. 69; Protocol on the Interpretation of Art. 69.]

The "purposive" construction set out in *Catnic* sits squarely within the guidelines of the European Patent Convention Protocol.

R was the proprietor of a U.K. patent, granted under the 1949 Act (the Forrer patent) and a European Patent (the Oliff patent), granted since the 1977 Act. The patents related to cartons used for packaging cans and bottles, and to blanks for the formation of such cartons. P petitioned for revocation of the patents and declarations that P's blanks did not infringe R's patents.

Held, finding the patents valid and infringed, that (1) on the construction of the Forrer Patent: the purpose of a claim was to give protection to the patentee whilst giving a reasonable degree of certainty to the public. Prior to 1977, a claim was construed literally and if there was no textual infringement, the Court would then consider whether the infringement took the substance or "pith and marrow" of the claim (*C. Van der Lely N.V. v. Bamfords* [1963] C.L.Y. 2628, *Rodi & Weinberger AG v. Henry Showell* [1969] C.L.Y. 2911, *Dere & Co. v. Harrison McGregor & Guest* [1965] R.P.C. 183 referred to); (2) the ambit of the monopoly set out in the Forrer claim had to be determined according to Lord Diplock's "purposive" construction in *Catnic Components v. Hill & Smith* [1981] C.L.Y. 2042 and using the three questions laid out in *Improver Corp. v. Remington Consumer Products*, namely (i) does the variant have a material effect on the way the invention works, (ii) if no, would this have been obvious at the date of publication to a reader skilled in the art, (iii) if yes, would that reader nevertheless have understood from the language of the claim that the patentee intended that strict compliance with the primary meaning was an essential requirement of the invention; (3) construction of the Oliff Patent: the Protocol states that Art. 69 of the European Patent Convention should be interpreted between the two extremes of strict, literal construction and use of the claims merely as a guideline. "Purposive" construction as suggested by Lord Diplock in *Catnic* fits squarely within the guidance of the Protocol, and the Patents Court is bound to use this approach (*Improver Corp. v. Remington Consumer Products* [1991] C.L.Y. 2698, *Anchor Building Products v. Redland Roof Tiles* [1991] C.L.Y. 2958, *Strix v. Otter Controls* [1992] C.L.Y. 3290, *A.C. Edwards v. Acme Signs and Displays* [1993] C.L.Y. 3028, *Southco Inc. v. Dzus Fastener (Europe)* [1993] R.P.C. 3040, *Optical Coating Laboratory v. Pilkington Pty* [1993] F.S.R. 310, *Speciality Products Inc. v. Murpro Montasser* [1994] F.S.R. 99 followed; *PLG Research v. Ardon Int.* [1995] F.S.R. 116 distinguished); (4) on the infringement of Forrer Patents: the variants would not have been considered by a skilled reader to have been intended as an essential requirement of the invention and therefore P's blanks infringed the Forrer patent; (5) on the validity of the Forrer Patent: the inventive concept was a blank which overcame the disadvantages of the prior art. Whilst the individual features of the invention were not new, it was the way they acted in combination which mattered. There were substantial differences to the prior art. The modifications to the prior art were not obvious. Accordingly, the attack based on obviousness failed (*Windsurfing International Inc. v. Tabur Marine (GB)* [1985] R.P.C. 59 applied; *Non-Drip Measure Co. v. Strangers* [1943] 60 R.P.C. 142, *Technograph Printed Circuits v. Mills and Rockley (Electronics)* [1972] R.P.C. 346 referred to; (6) the question of whether a claim is fairly based is a matter of construction upon a comparison between the claim and the specification. To confine the specification to "end-loading" blanks would be unfair on the patentee as it would allow the invention to be used in, for example, a "wrap-around" system without infringement. Accordingly, the attack based on lack of fair basis failed (*Insituform Technical Services v. Inliner U.K.* [1993] C.L.Y. 3035 applied; *British United Shoe Machinery Co. v. A. Fussell & Sons* [1908] 25 R.P.C. 631 referred to); (7) on the infringement of Oliff Patent: P's blanks infringed the Oliff patent; (8) on the validity of Oliff Patent: without the benefit of hindsight, the Oliff patent involved an inventive step and therefore the attack based on obviousness failed; (9) the claim when purposively construed was clear and therefore the attack based on insufficiency failed; and (10) a patentee may amend his claim by the addition of limitations but he cannot for the first time describe an invention which was not described explicitly or implicitly in the application. Here, the amendments to R's claim did not extend the disclosures and therefore the attack based on added matter failed (*A.C. Edwards v. Acme Signs and Displays* [1993] C.L.Y. 3028 followed).

ASSIDOMAN MULTIPACK (FORMERLY MULTIPACK WRAPAROUND SYSTEMS) v. THE MEAD CORP [1995] F.S.R. 225, Aldous J.

3759. Council Regulation—creation of supplementary protection certificate challenged—whether a reservation by States to regulate substantive patent law to exclusion of Community—European Community

Spain sought the annulment of Council Reg. (EEC) 1768/92 concerning the creation of a supplementary protection certificate for medicinal products. Its central argument was that, in the allocation of powers between the Community and the Member States, the latter had not surrendered their sovereignty in industrial property matters, so that the Community had no power to regulate substantive patent law.

Held, that neither Arts. 222 EC nor 36 EC reserve a power to regulate substantive patent law to the Member States to the exclusion of any Community action in the matter. The Regulation was validly adopted on the basis of Art. 100A of the E.C. Treaty which permits legislation to be adopted for the functioning of the internal market.

SPAIN v. GREECE (C–350/92), July 13, 1995, ECJ.

3760. Defence—amendment of defence—defence struck out in first action—whether defence can be raised in second action—whether *res judicata*. See CHIRON CORP. v. MUREX DIAGNOSTICS (NO. 9), §4193.

3761. Designs—convention countries

DESIGNS (CONVENTION COUNTRIES) (AMENDMENT) ORDER 1995 (No. 2988) [£1·10], made under the Registered Designs Act 1949, ss.13(1), 37(5); amends S.I. 1994 No. 3219. In force: December 15, 1995 for arts. 1, 2(a), 3(a)(i)(b), December 25, 1995 for arts. 2(b), 3(a)(ii) and January 1, 1996 for arts. 2(c), 3(a)(iii); amends the list of convention countries for the purposes of all the provisions of the Registered Designs Act 1949. Albania, Costa Rica, Peru, Saint Kitts and Nevis, Saint Lucia, Saint Vincent and the Grenadines, Singapore, Turkmenistan, Venezuela and Azerbaijan, listed in Pts. 1 and 2 of the

Schedule have acceded to the International Convention for the Protection of Industrial Property (the Paris Convention) (Cmnd. 4431) since the last Order was made. Antigua and Barbuda, Bahrain, Belize, Bolivia, Botswana, Brunei Darussalam, Colombia, Djibouti, Dominica, Guatemala, Jamaica, Kuwait, Macau, Maldives, Mozambique, Myanmar, Namibia, Nicaragua, Sierra Leone and Thailand, listed in part 3 of the Schedule, are not party to the Paris Convention but are party to the Agreement Establishing the World Trade Organisation (including the Agreement on Trade-Related Aspects of Intellectual Property Rights (Cm. 2556–59, 2561–69, 2571–74)).

3762. Fees

PATENTS (FEES) RULES 1995 (No. 2164) [£1·95], made under the Patents Act 1977, s.123(1)(2)(3), Sched. 4, para. 14 and S.I. 1988 No. 93; revoke S.I. 1992 No. 616; operative on September 4, 1995.

3763. Infringement—appeal—relating solely to costs—whether court having jurisdiction to hear appeal. See PROUT v. BRITISH GAS, §3919.

3764. Infringement—discontinuance of proceedings—leave to withdraw allegations of infringement in respect of certain patents—terms of withdrawal

[R.S.C., Ord. 21, r.3.]

A defendant should not be deprived of an advantage by the discontinuance of proceedings.

P applied for leave to withdraw claims of infringement in respect of two out of four patents in issue. P was prepared to undertake not to bring further proceedings in respect of the actual acts of infringement which had occured to date. D submitted that leave to withdraw should only be given on P's undertaking not to bring proceedings for infringement of the two patents by any act of D in relation to one of D's products.

Held, refusing P leave to withdraw, that (1) it is for the court to say whether an action should be discontinued and upon what terms (*Fox v. Star Newspaper Co.* [1898] 1 Q.B. 636 referred to); (2) the court has a complete discretion and must exercise it upon the facts and taking into account the practice in the Patents County Court that normally some undertaking is required; (3) P must not be compelled to litigate against its will and the defendant should not be deprived of an advantage or in any way prejudiced; (4) if leave to withdraw was granted on P's terms, P would be free to allege infringement of the two patents in respect of D's future acts, thereby starting the action all over again; (5) it could be of interest to third parties as to whether a product of the type in question infringed any of the patents; and (6) accordingly, to allow P's application would be to deprive D of an advantage and deprive the public of resolution of an issue which has been raised.

ALBRIGHT & WILSON v. S.B. CHEMICALS [1994] R.P.C. 608, Aldous J.

3765. Infringement—discovery—multinational group of companies—whether shareholder control sufficient to infer assistance to primary infringer or common design. See UNILEVER v. CHEFARO PROPRIETARIES, §4130.

3766. Infringement—infringement of valid patent—injunctions—whether injunction should be granted—whether damages should be awarded in lieu of an injunction—whether injunction to be stayed pending appeal

[Supreme Court Act 1981 (c.54), s.50.]

P commenced patent infringement actions against D1 and D2 in 1992. The patent was found to be valid and infringed but D1 and D2 had a defence under the Patents Act 1977 due to the terms of certain agreements. P amended the agreements and commenced further proceedings against D1 and D2. D1 and

D2 consented to an Order 14 judgment but the matter of injunctions was stood over. D1 and D2 argued that the injunctions should be limited in two ways. First, the injunctions should exclude exploitation of D2's serotyping assay and secondly, the injunctions should exclude research and development trials. D1 and D2 also claimed that the injunctions should be stayed pending appeal.

Held, granting the injunctions sought by P and refusing the request for a stay, that (1) the court has power under s.50 of the Supreme Court Act 1981 to refuse to award an injunction and to award damages instead. This includes power to award a restricted injunction and damages as compensation for the restriction. In exercising its discretion under s.50, the court can take into account the interests of third parties but those interests should not prevail over private interests (*Wrotham Park Estate Co. v. Parkside Homes* [1974] C.L.Y. 3130, *Miller v. Jackson* [1977] C.L.Y. 2146, *Kennaway v. Thompson* [1980] C.L.Y. 2007 considered); (2) in most cases the approach suggested in the case of *Shelfer v. City of London Electric Lighting Co.* should be sufficient to decide whether damages should be granted instead of an injunction (*Shelfer v. City of London Electric Lighting Co.* [1895] 1 Ch. 287 followed); (3) the interests of the public will normally be protected by the provisions of the Patents Act 1977 which contains safeguards. It is a good working rule that an injunction will be granted to prevent continued infringement of a patent, even though that would have the effect of enforcing a monopoly, thereby restricting competition and maintaining prices. Something more must be established to persuade the court to depart from the *Shelfer* guidelines; (4) the *Shelfer* guidelines assume that the court will have evidence before it to be able to estimate the compensation, conclude that it was adequate and small and that the defendant was able to pay it. There was no such evidence before the court in this case. The suggestion that the court should refuse the injunction and order there to be an inquiry as to the amount of compensation could not be accepted; (5) the injunctions would not be limited to exclude the matters requested by D1 and D2. The public interest was properly protected by the provisions of the Patents Act 1977; and (6) the purpose of granting a stay of a final injunction pending appeal after a judgment on the merits is to prevent injustice should the appeal succeed. On balance, on the facts of this case, the balance of the risk of doing an injustice meant that the injunctions should not be stayed (*Minnesota Mining and Manufacturing Co. v. Johnson & Johnson* [1977] C.L.Y. 2320 applied).

CHIRON CORP. v. ORGANON TEKNIKA (NO. 10); CHIRON CORP. v. MUREX DIAGNOSTICS (NO. 10) [1995] F.S.R. 325, Aldous J.

3767. Infringement—pleadings—amendment—abuse of dominant position defence—test for Hepatitis C virus—application to strike out defence—test to be applied when considering matters relating to control of proceedings—whether effect on trade between Member States

[R.S.C., Ord. 18, r.19; Treaty of Rome, Art. 86.]

The patent in suit related to test kits for detecting antibodies to the Hepatitis C virus. P alleged infringement by D. D pleaded a Euro defence based on Art. 86 of the Treaty of Rome, alleging that P had abused their dominant position in the market for such test kits. P applied to strike out that pleading under R.S.C., Ord. 18, r.19. At the same hearing D applied to amend its defence so as to allege that P had a dominant position in two further markets. At first instance the judge held that although P had good arguments on lack of a dominant position and absence of abuse the position was not clear enough to merit striking out. However, the judge also held that there was no arguable case that there was an effect on trade between Member States. The amendments were refused and the judge ordered that the part of D's defence based on Art. 86 should be struck out. D appealed.

Held, dismissing the appeal, that (1) matters relating to the control of the conduct of the proceedings are matters within the province of the judge at first instance. The test, in considering whether or not to allow the appeal, was to ask whether the judge was plainly wrong in striking out that part of the defence originally pleaded and refusing to allow the amendment sought by D (*Ashmore v. Corp. of Lloyd's* [1992] C.L.Y. 3624 applied); (2) although P had a strong case on the facts that they were not in a dominant position in the market of Hepatitis kits, the judge was not plainly wrong in refusing to strike out the defence on this ground; (3) the judge at first instance concluded that it was speculation that D's kits would save lives if used instead of or as well as P's kits. The judge was not plainly wrong in holding that such speculation was not sufficient to turn refusal to licence, which was not itself an abuse under Art. 86, into such an abuse; (4) the judge was right to examine each head of abuse separately. It was not the proper approach to consider whether there was an overall pattern of abuse; (5) although P had a strong case that they had not abused their dominant position by charging excessive prices for their kits, the judge was not plainly wrong in refusing to strike out the defence on this ground; (6) the judge was not plainly wrong in his conclusion that there was a sufficient nexus between the alleged abuse and the relief sought to allow the pleading to stand (*Imperial Chemical Industries v. Berk Pharmaceuticals* [1981] C.L.Y. 2788, *British Leyland Motor Corp. v. Armstrong Patents Co.* [1964] C.L.Y. 432 referred to); and (7) the judge was right to hold that the alleged abuse of charging unfair prices for the kits did not affect trade between Member States and to strike out the Euro defence for that reason. The nexus alleged must be between the abuse (high prices) and interstate trade. It is not sufficient to plead a nexus between the injunction sought by way of remedy for infringement of the patent and interstate trade (*Volvo (A.B.) v. Erik Veng (U.K.) (238/87)* [1989] 4 C.M.L.R. 122 referred to).

[Per Staughton L.J.: (1) no more weight should be given to the decision of the judge at first instance than is appropriate on any other question of law. A judge is not justified in striking out all or part of a defence unless the defence cannot succeed. The court must decide for itself whether the judge at first instance was right to strike out all or part of a defence; (2) even if it were shown that P had a dominant position in a relevant market and was abusing that position so as to affect trade between Member States, that would not lead to the conclusion that a national court should not enforce P's patent. To refuse relief to the proprietor of a patent against an infringer as a remedy for abuses such as were alleged could be altogether lacking in proportionality. It might also give rise to a fluctuating situation whereby a patent was sometimes enforceable and sometimes not.]

CHIRON CORP. v. MUREX DIAGNOSTICS (NO. 2) [1994] F.S.R. 187, C.A.

3768. Infringement—pleadings—amendment of pleadings—whether conditional pleadings allowed

Conditional pleadings are not allowable in patent proceedings.

P sought to amend its pleading by adding a second patent to the claim which it would only seek to rely on if the first patent was held to be invalid.

Held, refusing P's application to amend in this way, that whilst it was permissible to plead an allegation of infringement in the alternative, it is not permissible to plead an allegation of infringement dependent on a particular condition arising.

BELOIT TECHNOLOGIES v. VALMET PAPER MACHINERY [1994] R.P.C. 664, Aldous J.

3769. Infringement—pleadings—amendments relating to fresh allegations of prior user—dates to be inserted in *See v. Scott-Paine* Order

In a patent infringement action, D applied to re-amend its particulars of objections so as to introduce two further allegations of prior user. The proposed amendments were not objected to, but a dispute arose as to the relevant date to be inserted into the *See v. Scott-Paine* order which the parties accepted should be made.

Held, that (1) the dates relevant to the fresh allegations would be those of the original particulars of objection. In relation to the second allegation, the date would be that closest to the date when the information relating to the second alleged prior use came to D's attention. It would not be right to penalise a defendant who sought to rely on a prior use which came to his attention by chance in circumstances where it could not be suggested that he should have found out at an earlier date (*Williamson v. Moldline* [1987] C.L.Y. 2794 followed).

LA BAIGUE MAGIGLO v. MULTIGLOW FIRES; SAME v. ORS [1994] R.P.C. 295, Patents Ct.

3770. Infringement—pleadings—form and construction of *See v. Scott-Paine* orders

In an action for patent infringement D was given leave to amend its defence and counterclaim and a *See v. Scott-Paine* order was made. The parties disputed the wording of the order. D contended that the order should say that upon election by P to discontinue and submit to an order for revocation of the patent the award of costs to P should be qualified by the words "in so far as such costs have been incurred by reason of the failure [of D] to deliver its defence and counterclaim in the form now sought to be amended". D argued that unless these qualifying words were included, a patentee, when presented with amendments to the particulars of objections, could use them as a vehicle to withdraw from the action on favourable terms as to costs whereas in fact it would have maintained the action, even if the new grounds of objection had been pleaded sooner.

Held, refusing to include the qualifying words, that (1) the words used in *See v. Scott-Paine* qualified the costs of the counterclaim only, not the costs of the action; (2) as the costs of the counterclaim for revocation in modern actions are of little consequence compared with the costs of the action, the form of words used in *Williamson v. Moldline*, in which the qualifying words were omitted, was appropriate (*Williamson v. Moldline* [1987] C.L.Y. 2794, *Norprint v. S.P.J. Labels and Labelply* [1979] C.L.Y. 2055, *See v. Scott-Paine* (1933) 50 R.P.C. 56 referred to); and (3) it was not appropriate to leave to the district judge the question whether the plaintiff would certainly, would probably, or might have abandoned the claim had the particulars of objection been delivered originally in their amended form.

VESTAR INC. v. LIPOSOME TECHNOLOGY INC. [1995] F.S.R. 391, Patents County Ct.

3771. Infringement—pleadings—*See v. Scott-Paine* order—whether to allow amendment to defence and particulars of objections

In a patent infringement action, D sought to amend its defence and particulars of objections. P resisted the amendments on the basis of exercise of discretion. Alternatively, if amendment was allowed, P argued that they should only be allowed on condition that the trial date be vacated and that the order should contain a *See v. Scott-Paine* order. The amendments to the defence related primarily to supplementing D's defence under s.64 of the Patent Act 1977. The amendments to the particulars of objections concerned amending an allegation of prior user and the introduction by amendment of new pleas of insufficiency and obviousness. The trial was fixed for 11 weeks time.

Held, that (1) the amendments to supplement the s.64 defence were embarrassing. It was not enough to give particulars by referring generally to documents disclosed in the list of documents. If properly pleaded the amendments would be allowed; (2) as to the particulars of objections, the proposed amendment to the prior user plea would be likely to impose a heavy burden on P who was not a large international company with substantial resources. However, in view of the public interest in having invalid patents revoked and valid patents upheld, the amendments would in principle be allowed. The trial date would be vacated and a *See v. Scott-Paine* order made; (3) the new plea of insufficiency was not properly particularised and would not be allowed in the form pleaded; (4) the fresh plea of obviousness would be allowed, again subject to a *See v. Scott-Paine* order being made; and (5) the *See v. Scott-Paine* order would be in the standard form. A defendant who seeks to amend is seeking an indulgence, particularly so in this case where D was seeking to raise matters which in the main and perhaps completely had been within its knowledge for a long time. D should elect first and decide whether they wished the amendments to be allowed and if they did then the normal consequences would apply.

INSTANCE v. DENNY BROS. PRINTING [1994] F.S.R. 396, Patents Ct.

3772. Infringement—security for costs—legal expenses insurance—application before close of pleadings—whether oppressive

[Companies Act 1985 (c.6), s.726(1); Third Parties (Rights Against Insurers) Act 1930 (c.25), s.1.]

An application for security for costs in the Patents County Court could be considered oppressive if it was made before close of pleadings.

In a patent infringement action, D applied for security for costs of £20,000. P had legal expenses insurance providing £100,000 of cover for the action. There was evidence that the insurers had accepted a claim in respect of the action under the policy and had made a provision of £20,000 for D's costs.

Held, dismissing the application, that (1) there was no basis for holding that P would be unable to find £20,000 if necessary; (2) moreover, D was protected by P's legal expenses insurance pursuant to s.1(1)(b) of the Third Parties (Rights Against Insurers) Act 1930; and (3) in any event, the application was premature as it was made before close of pleadings and before the merits had been considered in the course of the preliminary consideration.

AIRMUSCLE v. SPITTING IMAGE PRODUCTIONS [1994] R.P.C. 604, Patents County Court.

3773. Infringement—threats of infringement—interlocutory injunction—*ex parte* order—delay in bringing motion to hearing—whether inexcusable and inordinate delay

[Patents Act 1977 (c.37), s.72.]

A plaintiff who has obtained interlocutory relief is under a duty to apply to the court for the earliest appropriate hearing date.

In an action to restrain threats of patent infringement, P initially obtained *ex parte* relief on January 29, 1993. At the *inter partes* hearing about a week later, the motion was stood over to come on as a motion by order not earlier than March 22, 1993 and a programme for the filing of evidence was established. No evidence in reply was served until November 11, 1993 and no attempt was made by P to fix the hearing of the motion until the end of October 1993.

Held, refusing interlocutory relief, that (1) a plaintiff who has obtained interlocutory relief pending hearing of a motion cannot sit back and allow the matter simply to drift. He is under an obligation to apply to the court for the earliest appropriate date for the hearing of the motion; (2) orders which have been made *ex parte* should only be made for a limited period until the matter can be fully considered by the court. There was thus a particular duty upon a party obtaining *ex parte* relief to push proceedings forward to hearing. Save in exceptional circumstances, the court should therefore dismiss a motion with the consequence that the *ex parte* order lapses, where there is inexcusable and inordinate delay by the plaintiff. The facts in the case showed such delay. It was therefore not appropriate to grant interlocutory relief on this motion.

[*Per curiam*: The Patents Court was not merely a forum for deciding matters in disputes as and when the parties wish. Orders of the Patents Court very often affect the public and therefore the court will take steps to ensure and encourage speedy and effective resolution of disputes.]

HONG KONG TOY CENTRE v. TOMY U.K. [1994] F.S.R. 593, Aldous J.

3774. Infringement—threats of legal proceedings—malicious falsehood—whether interlocutory injunction available where defendant contends that statements true

[Patents Act 1977 (c.37), s.70.]

The case concerned a boot for horses' hooves which had originally been designed by a U.S. company, L, which had obtained patent protection for the boot in the USA in 1970 under the name "Easyboot". In 1972 D obtained a sample of Easyboot from Germany and went on to obtain a U.K. patent in respect of the boot as first importers. From 1974 to 1977 D sold L's boots in the U.K. In 1977 this arrangement ceased and D decided to manufacture and sell a similar boot in the U.K. under the name "Equiboot". This name was registered as a trade mark. P1 was an American company formed in January 1994 which bought L and all the rights to Easyboot. P2 was P1's U.K. distributor. In August 1994 P2 began a marketing campaign in the U.K. to sell the Easyboot and issued a leaflet which included the words "From the inventors of Equiboot – the new generation Easyboot". D responded by issuing a letter to customers stating that there was no association between P1 and the Equiboot and that D was taking legal action to protect its name. D also placed an advertisement in *Horse and Hound* which included the following "Equiboot. The Original – And Still The Best! – Beware of Imitations. Ask For Equiboot By Name." The Ps commenced an action and sought interlocutory relief for threats of legal proceedings for patent infringement and malicious falsehood. D maintained that there had been no threat and they would justify the statements sought to be restrained at trial.

Held, refusing to grant interlocutory relief, that (1) there was no serious issue to be tried relating to threats. The threat to take legal proceedings in the letter was made to protect D's name and reputation. Nothing was said about a patent and no connection could be made between the threat and a statement that D was the original patentee of Equiboot; (2) the normal principles applicable to interlocutory injunctions do not apply where the defendant contends that the alleged defamatory statements are true. In this case the interlocutory injunction sought based in malicious falsehood was inappropriate as the statements made may be capable of being justified at trial (*Bestobell Paints v. Bigg* [1975] F.S.R. 421, *Kaye v. Robertson* [1991] F.S.R. 62 considered).

[*Per curiam*: D may legally be the inventor of the Equiboot and not just the patentee. Until the passing of the Patents Act 1977, the law considered an inventor to be not only a person who devised an article, but also a person who introduced the article into the U.K. (*Plimpton v. Malcolmson* (1876) 3 Ch.D. 531 referred to).

EASYCARE v. BRYAN LAWRENCE [1995] F.S.R. 597, Aldous J.

3775. Infringement—validity—chemical composition—acid metabolite—whether part of process disclosed as specification of invention

[Patents Act 1977 (c.37), s.60(2).]

MD, a pharmaceutical company, appealed against the dismissal of their claim to patent the acid metabolite which was created in the livers of people taking the drug terfenadine, as invalid. In 1972 MD had successfully patented the anti-histamine drug terfenadine. The patent expired in 1992 and other companies, including N, began producing terfenadine. MD claimed their monopoly in terfenadine continued on the basis of a later patent obtained to protect the acid metabolite, which MD had discovered was a by-product of terfenadine. MD brought the action against N and others under s.60(2) of the Patents Act 1977 for infringement of the acid metabolite patent.

Held, dismissing the appeal, that a chemical composition could only be judged to be part of the state of the art if it was part of a process which has been disclosed as a specification of an invention. The composition of acid metabolite was therefore not new because it was already part of the 1972 patent for terfenadine, even though it was not appreciated at the time the patent was granted. If the specifications of the patent were followed then the production of acid metabolite was inevitable and therefore it was not novel, which was the main precondition for the grant of a patent.

MERRELL DOW PHARMACEUTICALS v. HN NORTON & CO., *The Times*, October 27, 1995, H.L.

3776. Infringement—validity—genetic engineering—Hepatitis B virus—sufficiency—whether patent invalid for lack of inventiveness

[Patents Act 1977 (c.37), ss.1, 72.]

B sued M, claiming that M had infringed their patent of the application of genetic engineering techniques on genetic material from the Hepatitis B virus. The judge upheld the validity of the patent in suit and the infringement and said that the statutory requirement of sufficiency was satisfied by disclosing how to make a single embodiment of the invention. M appealed on the ground that the patent was invalid as it lacked inventiveness and there was insufficient disclosure.

Held, allowing the appeal, that unless the description in the patent specification, taken together with other relevant evidence, disclosed an invention within the meaning of ss.1(1) and 72(1)(a) of the Patents Act 1977, the patent was invalid. The determination of sufficiency within the meaning of s.72(1)(c) depended on the interaction between the description in the specification and the claim, with reference to the state of the art at the time of the application.

BIOGEN INC. v. MEDEVA (HANF 93/1659/B) (CHANF 93/1659/B), October 27, 1994, C.A.

3777. Infringement—validity—Hepatitis C virus—whether method for identifying virus obvious—significance of research by others—insufficiency—whether more than one claim in the inventions—whether capable of industrial application

[Patents Act 1977 (c.37), ss.1–4, 14, 44, 60, 67, 72, 125, 130.]

P was the proprietor of a patent relating to the Hepatitis C virus (HCV). There were two infringement actions which were heard together. In 1987 scientists employed by P identified a clone of the causative agent of HCV. P had previously tried numerous techniques to identify the agent, which had been unsuccessful. The successful method was expression screening. The infected samples used by P as a starting material in the successful experiments were samples of plasma from a chimpanzee. The patent in suit contained claims, *inter alia*, to immunologically reactive HCV polypeptides, test kits for *in vitro* testing for HCV, methods for performing such tests, vaccines for HCV and methods for propagating the virus in tissue culture. The matters in dispute were infringement and validity including obviousness, insufficiency and whether the patent was non-patentable as a discovery and/or not capable of industrial application. The construction of two exclusive licences made by P with O and A and the relevance of s.44 of the Patents Act 1977 were also in issue.

Held, finding that D had a good defence to the action, that (1) the patent contemplated that carriers such as gelatine would be used in test kits. The polypeptides in question, to be useful for test kits, had to be isolated from other polypeptides found in the body. The skilled person would know that gelatine would not interfere with the action of an HCV polypeptide. Therefore, the polypeptides in Ds' kits were in a substantially isolated form and claim 1 was infringed by Ds' kits (*Catnic Components v. Hill & Smith* [1983] C.L.Y. 2776, *Southco Inc. v. Dzus Fastener Europe* [1993] C.L.Y. 3040 applied); (2) the patent was not obvious. The fact that a defendant's case involves reconstructing the factual background at the priority date does not mean that the invention in question was not obvious. The court must consider that what may seem obvious once the answer is known may have been far from obvious without the knowledge of the answer (*John-Manville Corporation's Patent* [1967] C.L.Y. 2975 considered); (3) the length of time in achieving a result can never be determinative. A person can work for years and miss the obvious. That logic cannot be applied where the prior art relied on is recent; (4) in assessing obviousness the court has to assume the mantle of the skilled person and impute to him what was common general knowledge. To decide what knowledge a person skilled in the art would have had it was necessary to look at relevant papers and articles (*Windsurfing International Inc. v. Tabur Marine (Great Britain)* [1985] R.P.C. 59 applied); (5) the identification of the sequence of HCV was not obvious in November 1987. Ds' arguments were based on unacceptable hindsight. It was significant that everything needed to make the patent had been available since 1984, but no one had succeeded until 1987, despite the number of people trying and the great incentives offered; (6) lack of availability of starting material of the kind possessed by P would not have prevented anyone else from trying expression screening if they otherwise would have done so; (7) Ds' submission that certain claims were invalid as discoveries was untenable. Many inventions that are patented arise from a discovery, but a technical contribution to the known art is needed to make the discovery patentable. Here the claims were concerned with a technical aspect of the discovery, being limited to products, kits and methods of testing (*Merrill Lynch's Application* [1989] C.L.Y. 3279 applied; *Genentech Inc.'s Patent* [1990] C.L.Y. 3472 considered); (8) s.4(1) of the Patents Act 1977 provides that inventions are to be taken to be capable of industrial application if they can be made in any kind of industry. There was no evidence that anything falling within any of the claims could not be made and Ds' submissions as to industrial application failed; (9) the test kits claimed in the patent were capable of being used for diagnosis of HCV in humans, but were not practised on the body. Ds' submissions in relation to s.4(2) and method of treatment therefore also failed; (10) as to sufficiency, it is correct that if a claim relates to more than one invention, each invention must be capable of performance by the skilled person if the specification is not to be insufficient. Here the invention was based on the discovery of the sequence of HCV. Claim 1 claimed a new class of chemicals whose relation to one another was set out in the patent. If the Ds were right, claim 1 would relate to hundreds or thousands of inventions. That could not be right. The claims of the patent claimed only one inventive concept and one invention; (11) Ds' real complaint was that the claims of the patent were not properly supported by the description. Section 72(1)(c) of the 1977 Act, governing revocation for insufficiency, could not be manipulated in the way the Ds wished. It was important that the effect of the section be the same as that of its equivalents in other European countries (*Mentor Corp. v. Hollister Inc.* [1992] C.L.Y. 3317, *Mölnycke A.B. v. Proctor and Gamble (No. 5)* [1992] F.S.R. 549 followed); (12) the description in the patent relating to vaccines was insufficient. P had spent excessive years of effort on their vaccine programme without discovering a practical vaccine which would be effective against the strain from which P cloned HCV; (13) P had attempted to undertake tissue culture work since 1988 but their success had been partial. Even assuming P had had the success which P claimed, the time and work needed to achieve success exceeded that required by law and the specification was also insufficient in relation to tissue cultures; and (14) the second licence agreement did not offend s.44(1)(c) but the first licence agreement did offend s.44(1)(b). At the date when the first licence agreement with O was made the patent in suit had been applied for. A waiver subsequently entered into by P and O was not effective to avoid the section. Accordingly Ds had a defence to the action under s.44 by virtue of the agreement between P and O (*Tool Metal Manufacture Co. v. Tungsten Electric Co.* [1955] 2 All E.R. 657 applied).

CHIRON CORP. v. ORGANON TEKNIKA (NO. 3); SAME v. MUREX DIAGNOSTICS (NO. 3) [1994] F.S.R. 202, Patents County Ct.

3778. Infringement—validity—obviousness—disposable nappy fastenings—criterion for deciding whether obvious—registration of exclusive licence—whether entry on register of notice of application amounting to registration of licence

[Patents Act 1977 (c.37), ss.2(2), 3, 68.]

P1 brought an action seeking an injunction and damages against D for infringement of a patent that concerned a method by which a nappy was fastened to the waist of a baby. At trial, D denied infringement and attacked the validity of the patent on the grounds of obviousness, insufficiency and added matter. A further issue concerned an exclusive licence granted to P2 by P1 which, due to Patent Office practice at the time, was not registered within six months on the grounds that a revocation application was pending. The licence was finally registered after determination of the revocation application in favour of P1, more than six months later. At trial, D contended that the registrar had no power to refuse registration and that it would have been practicable to register the licence within six months. The trial judge held that the patent was valid and had been infringed. It was also held that the exclusive licence had been registered as soon as practicable. P was awarded indemnity costs from the date of the certificate of contested validity. D appealed on the issues of obviousness, added matter, registration of the exclusive licence and indemnity costs.

Held, dismissing the appeal, that (1) under the Patents Act 1977, the criteria for deciding whether or not the claimed invention involved an inventive step was wholly objective and required a qualitative and not a quantitative test. The court was required to make a finding of fact as to what was, at the priority date, included in the state of the art and to find again as a fact, having regard to the state of the art, whether the alleged inventive step would have been obvious to a skilled person. Application of the statutory criterion would almost invariably require an expert witness to provide primary evidence. The importance attached to secondary evidence, for example contemporaneous events and commercial success, would vary case by case. The "clear and unmistakable" test was not part of the statutory criterion of obviousness and should not be used (*General Tire & Rubber Co. v. Firestone Tire & Rubber Co.* [1975] C.L.Y. 2503 applied; *Hallen Company (U.K.) v. Brabantia* [1992] C.L.Y. 3318 distinguished); (2) although formulated with reference to the Patents Act 1949, the analysis in *Windsurfing International v. Tabur Marine* [1985] R.P.C. 59 continued to provide assistance; (3) the essential difference between earlier state of the art "target tapes" and the patent in suit was the idea of "DFS" (Dedicated Fastening Surface). It would not have been obvious to a skilled man with knowledge of the state of the art to adopt the DFS solution which was a genuinely different concept and idea. Where the subject matter of a patent was an idea, the inventive step involved an act of insight, rather than mere development and application of existing ideas. D had not satisfied the court that DFS was obvious. The patent was a technical innovation; (4) deletion of references in the specification did not amount to disclosing subject-matter beyond that which was already disclosed in the application; (5) the purpose of s.33(4) of the Patents Act 1977 was simply to secure priority, but was not a substitute for registration; (6) the equitable doctrine of "relating back" had no application to a statutory scheme for registration of patents. To allow such application would introduce unwelcome uncertainty to the Act and Rules; and (7) the word "practicable" should be interpreted in the context of the particular statutory provision in which it appeared and in this case required the applicant to take all steps which a reasonable applicant acting on competent advice would take in the circumstances. In the present case, the applicant had received advice from an experienced patent agent who had done all he reasonably could to obtain registration.

MÖLNLYCKE A.B. v. PROCTOR & GAMBLE (NO. 5) [1994] R.P.C. 49, C.A.

3779. Infringement—validity—obviousness—pregnancy testing device—whether obvious—whether damages to be awarded in respect of period before patent granted

[Patents Act 1977 (c.37), ss.3, 14(5), 69(3), 125(1).]

It is for a defendant to bring himself within the exception contained in s.69(3) of the Patents Act 1977.

P was the proprietor of a patent for an analytical device to be used as a home pregnancy test. P brought proceedings against D for infringement of P's patent by D's own home pregnancy test, and D counterclaimed for revocation on the ground of obviousness over the prior art. D also argued that damages should not be awarded in respect of the period before the patent was granted pursuant to s.69(3) of the 1977 Act. In addition, separate proceedings were afoot under which D sought a declaration of non-infringement of a new product of D's.

Held, finding the patent valid and infringed, and rejecting D's submission under s.69(3), that (1) whilst P's requirements for its patent were the same as had been required prior to 1987, no one had recorded all these requirements as P had, and the existing tests were all far from the desired product according to these requirements. The magnitude of the problems with the existing products was important in relation to the way in which the skilled man would read the patent and how he would appreciate its inventive step, and in deciding the question of obviousness; (2) the test for obviousness is that set out in statute and none other. In operating that test the *Windsurfing* logical structure is helpful. The test is one of overall fact. Inferences from secondary evidence are irrelevant (*Mölnycke A.B. v. Procter & Gamble* [1995] 1 C.L. 292, *Windsurfing International v. Tabur Marine (Great Britain)* [1985] R.P.C. 59 applied); (3) it is the "inventive concept" of the claim in question which must be considered, not some generalised concept to be derived from the specification as a whole; (4) although the differences between the patent and the prior art were very small, they amounted to a great deal so far as a practical test was concerned. To arrive at these small differences was not obvious but rather required a flash of insight that all the long-desired objectives could be achieved in one go by a simple adaptation of the prior art; (5) there was enough in the circumstances of the case for commercial success to be of some support to non-obviousness, even though the prior art was only nine months before the date of the patent (*Salford Electrical v. BSH Industries*, June 10, 1993, Patents Court considered); (6) s.69(3) of the 1977 Act provides for an exception to the general rule that the patentee is entitled to damages. It is therefore for D to bring himself within the exception. The court must consider whether or not it would have been reasonable to expect that a patent would be granted conferring protection from such an act. This must be reached by consideration of the specification of the A specification as a whole, and not merely the claims of that specification. The question is objective and therefore does not depend on the knowledge or expectation of a particular defendant. So it is for D to show that it would not have been reasonable to expect that P would get a valid claim covering what he does (*Genentech's Patent* [1990] C.L.Y. 3472 referred to); and (7) it was appropriate to grant P a general injunction qualified by a proviso allowing D to sell their new product until further order (*Minnesota Mining & Manufacturing Co. v. Johnson & Johnson* [1976] C.L.Y. 2034 followed).

[*Per curiam*: It would make sense in many cases for the patentee to indicate which claims really matter at an early stage, particularly where the patent contains a large number of claims, for instance at the stage of the defence to counterclaim.]

UNILEVER v. CHEFARO PROPRIETARIES [1994] R.P.C. 567, Patents Ct.

3780. Infringement—validity—partial invalidity—amendment—damages for infringement—whether plaintiff to have damages only from the date of judgment

[Patents and Designs Act 1907 (c.29), s.32A; Patents Act 1949 (c.87), s.62(3); Patents Act 1977 (c.37), s.63.]

In a patent infringement action, certain claims of one of the patents in suit had been found to be infringed, but one of the claims had been found to be invalid. D did not contest that the specification had been framed in good faith and with reasonable skill and knowledge. The question remaining, therefore, was the date from which damages should be reckoned under s.63 of the Patents Act 1977. D submitted that the inquiry as to damages should run only from the date of judgment, while P submitted that damages should be paid in respect of all infringements occurring within the six years before the date of the writ. There was also the question of whether orders for evidence in the inquiry would be limited to the date of expiry of the last patent.

Held, that (1) there was no fetter upon the discretion given by s.63(2) of the Patents Act 1977. If it had been the law in 1919 that a patent with an invalid claim was invalid until amended, then that was no longer the law. The court had power to grant relief in respect of a partially valid patent without requiring amendment. It was for the court to decide upon the facts of each case the date from which damages would be reckoned (*J. & S. Eyres v. John Grundy* (1939) 56 R.P.C. 253, *Page v. Brent Toy Products* (1950) 67 R.P.C. 4, *Leggatt v. Hood's Original Darts Accessories* [1957–51] C.L.C. 7107, *Van der Lely (C.) NV v. Bamfords* [1964] C.L.Y. 2766, *David Kahn v. Conway Stewart & Co.* [1972] F.S.R. 620, *Hallen Co. v. Brabantia (U.K.)* [1992] C.L.Y. 3318 considered); (2) in exercising its discretion under s.63(2), the court would primarily look to see whether the partial invalidity of the patent had had an effect upon the defendant. The court would be concerned to see that any action or inaction of the plaintiff should not unfairly prejudice the defendant. There could be cases where it would be unconscionable to allow the plaintiff to recover damages prior to the date of judgment or the date when the patent was amended. However, an unmeritorious defendant should not be able to avoid paying damages for infringement unless there was strong evidence to require that conclusion; (3) the court would also consider the position of the public, which would normally be safeguarded by requiring amendment and imposing conditions as to the date when the damages should be reckoned. It did not follow that a defendant who had infringed with full knowledge should have the benefit of conditions imposed for members of the public (*Page v. Brent Toy Products* (1950) 67 R.P.C. 4 applied); (4) in the present case there were no grounds for depriving P of any damages. The appropriate date from which damages should be reckoned was the date of first infringement; and (5) orders for the evidence of infringement in the inquiry would be limited to the date of expiry of the last patent, with liberty to apply at any time for orders for discovery (*Helitune v. Stewart Hughes* [1995] 8 C.L. referred to).

GERBER GARMENT TECHNOLOGY v. LECTRA SYSTEMS [1994] F.S.R. 471, Aldous J.

3781. Infringement—validity—patent held to be valid in previous action—whether validity *res judicata*—whether parts of defence alleging invalidity to be struck out

[R.S.C., Ord. 18, r.19.]

Where a defendant has raised invalidity in an earlier action, and the patent has been held to be valid, the validity of the patent is *res judicata* between the parties and the defendant cannot relitigate. Previous actions between the parties resulted in certain claims of the patent in suit being held to be valid and infringed. However, the judge held that a licence agreement between P afforded D a defence under s.44 of the Patents Act 1977. In the earlier actions D had counterclaimed for revocation of the patent in suit on the ground of lack of novelty and obviousness. They relied, amongst other things, on prior art relating to proteins of a particular virus. At the trial D withdrew their reliance on this prior art at the end of P's case. P removed the offending provision from the licence agreement but failed to have their pleadings amended to reflect this deletion prior to the order being drawn up. As a result P issued fresh proceedings for patent infringement. D served defences alleging that the patent was invalid and relied upon the prior art which they had ceased to rely on at the earlier trial. P applied to strike out this part of the defence and claimed that the allegations were *res judicata*.

Held, striking out the parts of the defence alleging invalidity, that (1) cause of action estoppel was a complete bar to a matter being relitigated save where the earlier judgment did not decide points because they were not raised. However, it was open to the court not to apply the doctrine of issue estoppel where special circumstances existed whether or not the issue was raised and decided in the earlier case (*Arnold v. National Westminster Bank* [1991] C.L.Y. 1736 applied); (2) the cause of action raised by D in the earlier actions was that the patent was invalid. Accordingly the validity of the patent was *res judicata* between the parties. D could not relitigate (*Shoe Machinery Co. v. Cutlan (No. 2)* (1896) 13 R.P.C. 141, *Parmenter v. Malthouse Joinery* [1994] C.L.Y. 3746 considered); and (3) even if the judge was wrong to hold that cause of action estoppel applied, in any event the circumstances could not be termed "special circumstances" such as to allow the allegations to be raised again.

CHIRON CORP. v. ORGANON TEKNIKA (NO. 6); CHIRON CORP. v. MUREX DIAGNOSTICS (NO. 6) [1994] F.S.R. 448, Aldous J.

3782. Infringement—whether reasonable person would assess claim as infringement

A patent claim must be in terms such as to allow a reasonable person, competent in the art, to work out what would constitute an infringement and whether the patent itself could be invalidated by prior use (*Glaverbell SA v. British Coal Corp.* [1995] R.P.R. 255 considered).

SMOOTHYSIGNS v. METRO PRODUCTS (ACCESSORIES AND LEISURE), *The Times*, August 4, 1995, D.C.

3783. Interlocutory injunction—patent concerning helicopter rotor blader—cross-undertaking—inquiry as to damages—striking out of pleading—abuse of process—access to confidential exhibit—whether specific discovery essential—whether alleged damage too remote. See HELITUNE v. STEWART HUGHES, §4156.

3784. Legislation—drafting departure from wording of European Patent Convention—whether appropriate

[Patents Act 1977 (c.37), s.6.]

The parliamentary draughtsman should not have departed from the wording of the European Patent Convention 1973 when implementing it in the Patent Act 1977, particularly s.6(1). Although the wording of the Convention was obscure, the draughtsman's efforts to clarify the point gave rise only to further complications and costs.

BELOIT TECHNOLOGIES v. VALMET PAPER MACHINERY (No. 2), *The Times*, May 12, 1995, Jacob J.

3785. Patent licensing—European Communities

Commission Regulation (EC) 70/95 of January 17, 1995 amending Reg.

(EEC) 2349/84 on the application of Art. 85(3) E.C. to certain categories of patent licensing (O.J. L12/13).

3786. Patent licensing agreements—European Community

Commission Regulation (EC) 2132/95 of September 7, 1995 amending Reg. 2349/84 on the application of Art. 85(3) of the Treaty to certain categories of patent licensing agreements (O.J. L214/6).

3787. Patents—convention countries

PATENTS (CONVENTION COUNTRIES) ORDER 1994 (No. 3220) [£1·55], made under the Patents Act 1977 (c.37), ss.90(1), 124(3); operative on January 13, 1995; declares the countries specified in Sched. 1 to be convention countries for the purposes of s.5 of the 1977 Act.

PATENTS (CONVENTION COUNTRIES) (AMENDMENT) ORDER 1995 (No. 2989) [£1·10], made under the Patents Act 1977, ss.90(1), 124(3); amends S.I. 1994 No. 3220. In force: December 15, 1995 for arts. 1, 2(a), 3(a), December 25, 1995 for arts. 2(b), 3(b), and January 1, 1996 for arts. 2(c), 3(c); specified Albania, Antigua and Barbuda, Bahrain, Belize, Bolivia, Botswana, Brunei Darussalam, Columbia, Costa Rica, Djibouti, Dominica, Guatemala, Jamaica, Kuwait, Macau, Maldives, Mozambique, Myanmar, Namibia, Nicaragua, Peru, Saint Kitts and Nevis, Saint Lucia, Saint Vincent and the Grenadines, Sierra Leone, Singapore, Thailand, Turkmenistan and Venuzuela as Convention countries for the purposes of s.5 of the Patents Act 1977.

3788. Patents County Court—transfer of action to High Court—costs—whether judicial discretion to be interfered with. See MENTOR CORP. v. COLOR-PLAST A/S, §4237.

3789. Patents rules

PATENTS RULES 1995 (No. 2093) [£11·30], made under the Patents Act 1977; revoke S.I. 1990 No. 2384, S.I. 1992 No. 1142, S.I. 1993 No. 2423; operative on September 4, 1995; consolidate, with modifications, the Patents Rules 1990 as amended.

3790. Pleadings—amendment—patent infringement—whether plaintiff able to amend agreement offending statute—whether court having jurisdiction to amend pleadings after judgment

[Patents Act 1977 (c.37), s.44; R.S.C., Ord. 20, r.5.]

At the trial the judge held that certain claims of the patent in suit were valid and infringed, but found that Ds had a defence under s.44 of the Patents Act 1977 because of a licence agreement made between P and O. After judgment but before any order was made, P and O amended the offending agreement. P claimed that the agreement as amended did not contravene s.44 and sought to amend their pleadings to rely upon that modification to contend that after the date of amendment Ds had infringed and intended to infringe the patent and because of the amending agreement no defence arose under s.44. P submitted that the court ought, in the exercise of its discretion, to allow the amendments sought, since that would be the cheapest, quickest and most convenient way to decide the issue of whether the amended agreement contravened s.44. P also relied on the fact that one of the Ds was refusing to accept service of fresh proceedings. Ds contended that the court had no jurisdiction to permit the amendment sought by P, arguing that after judgment had been given the cause of action merged with the judgment. Ds further argued that P had had no cause of action at the trial.

Held, refusing leave to amend the pleadings, that (1) Ord. 20, r.5, was wide enough to cover a case where amendment is sought after judgment but before an order is drawn up; (2) it was not the case that P had no cause of action at the date of the writ. A distinction should be drawn between a case where a party has no right upon which he could litigate at the date of the writ and adding a new cause of action arising subsequent to the writ. The finding at trial had been that Ds had a defence to the action, not that P had no cause of action (*Roban Jig & Tool Co. and Elkadart v. Taylor* [1979] C.L.Y. 363, *Vax Appliances v. Hoover* [1991] C.L.Y. 2704 considered); (3) the position would have been different if the order had been drawn up and the court was *functus officio* except as to carrying out the provisions of the order (*Mölnlycke A.B. v. Proctor and Gamble (No. 6)* [1993] C.L.Y. 3172 distinguished); and (4) although the court did have jurisdiction to allow the amendments, leave to amend would be refused in the exercise of the court's discretion. P had been fully aware of the issues concerning s.44 and had chosen to fight the action on the basis of the agreements as they stood. If fresh proceedings would cause any delay this was P's fault. Ds should have every opportunity to take such points of objection as they wished in a fresh action rather than being swept into dealing with matters sought to be raised by amendment after judgment.

CHIRON CORP. v. ORGANON TEKNIKA (NO. 4); SAME v. MUREX DIAGNOSTICS (NO. 4) [1994] F.S.R. 252, Patents Ct.

3791. Preliminary ruling—judgment already given by Court of Appeal—whether Court of Appeal *functus officio*—whether House of Lords acting adminstratively or judicially in refusing leave to appeal. See CHIRON CORP. v. MUREX DIAGNOSTICS (NO. 8), §4201.

3792. Registered design—infringement—whether proper proprietor of commissioned design. See BREVILLE EUROPE v. THORN EMI DOMESTIC APPLIANCES, §857.

3793. Registered design—parts for motorvehicles—applications to register design refused—whether vehicle parts "articles"—whether dependent on appearance of another article of which intended to form integral part—whether excluded from registration

[Registered Designs Act 1949 (c.88), ss.1(1)(b)(ii), 44(1) (as amended and substituted by Copyright, Designs and Patents Act 1988 (c.48), ss.265, 272, Sched. 4).]

An "article" within the meaning of s.44(1) of the Registered Designs Act 1949 Act must have an independent life as an article of commerce and not merely be an adjunct of some larger article of which it forms part.

A made numerous applications for the registration of various motorvehicle components, such as door panels, steering wheels, seats, bonnet tops and fuel covers, pursuant to s.1 of the 1949 Act, as amended and substituted by the 1988 Act. All the applications were rejected by the registrar, and later the superintendent examiner, on the ground that the designs were excluded by s.1(1)(b)(ii) of the 1949 Act. An appeal to the Registered Designs Appeal Tribunal was dismissed in respect of the majority of applications on the ground that vehicle parts forming part of and contributing to the overall shape and appearance of the vehicle were not articles of commerce but formed part of the complete vehicle and were not registrable under the definition of "article" in s.44(1) of the 1949 Act. A's application for judicial review of that decision was dismissed by the Divisional Court.

Held, dismissing A's appeal, that (1) for a spare part to qualify as an "article" within the meaning of s.44(1) of the 1949 Act it must have an independent life as an article of commerce and not be merely an adjunct of some larger article of which it formed part; (2) accordingly, since A's components had not been shown to have been conceived as items of commerce on their own the Appeal Tribunal had correctly concluded that they were not registrable and the

Divisional Court rightly upheld that conclusion (*Sifam Electrical Instrument Co. v. Sangamo Weston* [1971] C.L.Y. 1877 applied).

R. v. REGISTERED DESIGNS APPEAL TRIBUNAL, *ex p.* FORD MOTOR CO. [1995] 1 W.L.R. 18, H.L.

3794. Registered designs

REGISTERED DESIGNS (FEES) RULES 1995 (No. 2165) [£1·10], made under the Registered Designs Act 1949, ss.36, 40, 44(1) and S.I. 1988 No. 93; operative on September 4, 1995; revoke and replace the 1992 Rules, aligning fees in respect of several matters with fees for corresponding matters under the Patents (Fees) Rules 1995 (S.I. 1995 No. 2164) with effect from September 4, 1995.

REGISTERED DESIGNS (FEES) (NO. 2) RULES 1995 (No. 2913) [£1·10], made under the Registered Designs Act 1949, ss.36, 40, 44(1). In force: December 4, 1995; revoke and replace S.I. 1995 No. 2165. Fees in respect of several matters have been further aligned with fees prescribed for corresponding matters under the Patents (Fees) Rules 1995 (S.I. 1995 No. 2164). Provision is made for applying on Form 9A to extend the period of protection into a fourth and fifth-year period, the fees being £310 and £450 respectively. The additional fee payable in respect of extra time for making application to extend the period of protection is increased from £18 to £24 for each extra month up to a maximum of six months. The fee, when applying on Form 19A for settlement of the terms of a licence of right, is £50.

REGISTERED DESIGNS RULES 1995 (No. 2912) [£6·75], made under the Registered Designs Act 1949, ss.1(5), 3(1)(4)(6), 5(2), 6(6), 8(3), 8A(1)(3), 11(1), 17(1)(5)(6), 18(1), 19(1)(2), 20(3)(4), 22(2), 29, 30(1)(3), 31, 32(1), 36(1)(1A), 39(1), 44(1); revoke S.I. 1990 No. 1456. In force: December 4, 1995; consolidate, with amendments, S.I. 1989 No. 1105. Provisions relating to the address for service to be provided by applicants for registration and by persons concerned in any proceedings have been revised together with the procedure to be followed by applicants when responding to objections made to an application by the registrar. The provision concerning time-limits for completing applications is revised to refer to applications for registration of a design excluded from an earlier application, as are provisions for applications for the registration by title by any person becoming entitled amongst other things by assignment, transmission or operation of law. Requests to alter or correct a person's address or address for service in the register, or on an application or other document, are revised to require that the relevant entry be identified in the register, application or document.

3795. Restoration—inability to pay renewal fee because of shortage of funds—whether proprietor took reasonable care to pay

[Patents Act 1977 (c.37), s.28(3); European Patent Convention, Art. 122(1).]

The renewal fee of the applicant's patent was not paid by the due date nor was it paid during the six months' period of grace allowed under the Patents Act 1977. This was because the proprietor's assets, including the patent, had been placed as security under the United States Bankruptcy Code and there were no funds from which the fee could be paid. When funds became available after the six-month period the proprietor applied for restoration of the patent under s.28 of the Patents Act 1977, which required the proprietor to have taken reasonable care to see that the renewal fee was paid in time. The Patent Office took the view that shortage of funds was not an acceptable ground for restoration. The proprietor appealed to the Patents Court, arguing that lack of funds to pay the renewal fee was not conclusive against restoration of the patent. He also argued that guidance as to the proper construction of s.28(3) could be obtained from decisions of the European Patent Office under Art. 122(1) of the European Patent Convention.

Held, dismissing the appeal, that (1) the fact that a renewal fee was not paid because of lack of funds was not conclusive against restoration. A proprietor was not required to keep himself in a financial position to pay renewal fees at all times by s.28(3). It was sufficient that he took reasonable care to see the fee was paid. Each case will depend on its facts. If the failure to pay is due to lack of funds the patentee must establish reasonable care before there can be restoration. That may require seeking financial assistance and in appropriate cases taking reasonable care to avoid impecuniosity (*EDF's Patents* [1992] R.P.C. 205, *Halpern and Ward's Patent*, January 26, 1993, Patents County Court, unrep., *Radakovic, Svatopluk/Re-establishment of rights (Decision J22/88)* [1990] Official Journal EPO 244 considered); (2) a party who intended to pay a renewal fee, but could not do so, must establish that he had taken reasonable care to pay. That required him to establish that his inability to pay had not resulted from any lack of reasonable care. Where the circumstances surrounding the impecuniosity of the proprietor were complicated, as in this case, the onus to discharge would be heavy; (3) the applicant did not discharge the onus on him and would not be given leave to file further evidence. It was incumbent on the proprietor, having contended that s.28(3) enabled restoration, to come before the court with all the evidence that he would wish to put. There was a public interest in hearing the matter speedily and having it finally resolved; and (4) s.28(3) did not have to be construed to have the same effect as Art. 122 of the European Patent Convention. It used different words and imposed materially different timing constraints. In addition, Art. 122 appeared to be directed to applications and patents which were proceeding in the European Patent Office and not to patents generally (*Jade, The* [1976] 1 All E.R. 920 referred to).

AMENT'S APPLICATION [1994] R.P.C. 647, Patents Court.

3796. Restoration—non-payment of renewal fees—proprietor relying on licensee to pay renewal fees—whether proprietor had taken reasonable care

[Patents Act 1977 (c.37), s.28(3)(a).]

It is not reasonable for a proprietor to rely on a licencee to pay renewal fees without checking and, if necessary, ensuring that the fee was paid.

A, the proprietor of a patent, applied for restoration of the patent following a failure to pay renewal fees by the due date or within the six months period of grace thereafter. A's patent agents had written to A on four occasions reminding A that the fees were due. During this period A was negotiating a licence with W in respect of the patents and following the grant of the licence, W became responsible for paying renewal fees. Shortly before the six-month period expired, A faxed W reminding W that it should pay the renewal fees, but did not check that the payments had been made by W. W failed to pay the renewal fees. The hearing officer held that A had failed to take reasonable care, as required by s.28(3)(a) of the Patents Act 1977 to ensure that the fees were paid.

Held, dismissing A's appeal, that (1) when a patentee knows, after a series of reminders, that a fee has not been paid and the final date is approaching, it is not reasonable to leave the matter in the hands of a licencee who has failed to pay in the past without checking and, if necessary, ensuring that the fee is paid; (2) the words "reasonable care" do not need explanation. The standard is that required of the particular patentee acting reasonably in ensuring that the fee is paid.

CONTINENTAL MANUFACTURING & SALES' PATENT [1994] R.P.C. 535, Aldous J.

3797. Revocation—dried baker's yeast—fair basis—obviousness—whether too wide

[Patents Act 1949 (c.87), s.32(1)(f)(i).]

A claim for an article patented for a special purpose is not too wide merely because the article might be used by someone else for a different purpose.

A applied for revocation of R's patent in respect of baker's yeast on the grounds of lack of fair basis and obviousness. A claimed that R's claims were not fairly based because they claimed that every baker's yeast was capable of fermenting sweetened dough by whatever process and from whatever yeast strain. A also claimed that R's gas release claims were arbitrary and unexplained, and that the patent was too wide.

Held, dismissing the application, that (1) no question of law arises in deciding fair basis, and the words are ordinary words of the English language; (2) there was ample teaching in the specification to reject the complaint of lack of fair basis; (3) there was no evidence to suggest that R's gas release claims were arbitrary; (4) an article may be patented for a special purpose even though someone may think of using it for a different purpose; and (5) R's claims were not obvious.

LESAFFRE'S PATENT [1994] R.P.C. 521, C.A.

3798. Supplementary Protection Certificate—licences of right—whether certificate limited by previous endorsement of patent

[Patents Act 1977 (c.37), s.46(3)(a), Sched. 1, para. 4(2)(c); Council Regulation (EEC) 1768/92, Art. 5; Patents (Supplementary Protection for Medicinal Products) Rules 1992 (S.I. 1992 No. 3162), r.5.]

A Supplementary Protection Certificate has the same rights as those which existed under the basic patent.

A Supplementary Protection Certificate (SPC) had been entered into force following the expiry of the basic patent. R applied for the settlement of terms of a licence of right. A argued that the Comptroller had no jurisdiction to settle the terms because the SPC was not subject to licences of right. The Comptroller disagreed and refused to stay the proceedings or refer the matter to the ECJ.

Held, dismissing A's appeal, that (1) an SPC gave no more nor no less rights than those which existed under the basic patent and therefore the Comptroller did have jurisdiction to grant terms for a licence of right; (2) the fact that R had had a licence did not prevent it from applying for a licence of right; and (3) the construction of Art. 5 of Council Reg. (EEC) 1768/92 was *acte clair*.

RESEARCH CORP.'S SUPPLEMENTARY PROTECTION CERTIFICATE [1994] R.P.C. 667, Aldous J.

3799. Validity—wind-shear warning system—declaration of non-infringement sought—whether patents valid

[Patents Act 1949 (c.87), ss. 22(1), 32(1)(i); Patents Act 1977 (c.37), s.71.]

D had two patents relating to wind-shear detection systems for use in aircraft. P had a system which it claimed differed in material respects. P challenged the validity of D's patents and sought a declaration of non-infringement.

Held, finding the patents valid and not infringed, that (1) the specifications in suit were to be construed as of their date of publication (*Willemijn Houdstermaatschappij B.V. v. Madge Networks* [1993] C.L.Y. 3031 followed); (2) it did not follow, as P alleged, that the claims in issue claimed all ways of achieving a result. All that was contended was that certain obvious variants on the claimed means were covered by the claim. Application of the principles set out in the *Catnic* decision offered the necessary safeguard against unfairness to the public, so it was not necessary to consider fair basis separately from construction (*International Business Machines' Corps' Application* [1981] C.L.Y. 2064, *Catnic Components v. Hill and Smith* [1981] C.L.Y. 2024 considered); (3) P was right to say that resolving inertial acceleration along the airmass flight path is materially different from resolving inertial acceleration along the horizontal axis—this was a material difference between the two systems; (4) D's attempt to establish that there is a downdraft drift angle (delta) signal, within the meaning of the patent claims, in the signals of P's system failed. This was a further material difference between the systems of P and D; (5) in relation to variants, the three relevant questions were set out in the *Improver* case. The first was, did the variant have a material effect on the way in which the invention works? There were material effects resulting from the variants in this case and the D did not therefore pass this hurdle (*Improver Corp. v. Remington Consumer Products* [1991] C.L.Y. 2698 followed); (6) even assuming that the findings relied on in considering the first question were wrong, D failed on the second question. It would not have been obvious to the skilled man at the date of publication that the variant would not have a material effect; and (7) assuming that the findings on both the first and second questions were wrong, the third remained. The claims of the patent in suit were in one sense very basic: they had a strictly limited number of required means for generating and processing signals. It was difficult to see how the notional skilled reader, reading the claims at their publication date and taking into account the inventive concepts and described embodiments, could fail to regard the specified means as other than essential and strict compliance with them the intention of the patentee.

SUNDSTRAND CORP. v. SAFE FLIGHT INSTRUMENT CORP. [1994] F.S.R. 599, Patents County Ct.

PENSIONS AND SUPERANNUATION

3800. Civil service pensions

PENSIONS INCREASE (CIVIL SERVICE COMPENSATION SCHEME 1994) REGULATIONS 1995 (No. 1680), made under the Pensions (Increase) Act 1971, s.5(2)(4); operative on July 25, 1995; apply the provisions of the 1971 Act to any pensions payable under the Civil Service Compensation Scheme 1994.

PENSIONS INCREASE (CIVIL SERVICE SUPPLEMENTARY (EARNINGS CAP) PENSION SCHEME 1994) REGULATIONS 1995 (No. 1683), made under the Pensions (Increase) Act 1971, s.5(2)(4); operative on July 25, 1995; apply the provisions of the 1971 Act to any pensions payable under the Civil Service Supplementary (Earnings Cap) Pensions Scheme 1994 (being a superannuation scheme made under s.1 of the Superannuation Act 1972). Section 5(4) of the 1971 Act confers power to provide for increases to take effect retrospectively. Regulation 4 permits increases in respect of any pension beginning on or after March 2, 1992.

3801. Civil service superannuation

SUPERANNUATION (ADMISSION TO THE PRINCIPAL CIVIL SERVICE PENSION SCHEME) ORDER 1995 (No. 1293) [£1·10], made under the Superannuation Act 1972 (c.11), s.1(5)(8); operative on June 6, 1995; adds specified employments to the list of employments and offices in Sched. 1 to the 1972 Act so that the Civil Service pension schemes may apply to them.

3802. Coal industry

INDUSTRY-WIDE COAL STAFF SUPERANNUATION SCHEME REGULATIONS 1994 (No. 2973) [£10·35], made under the Coal Industry Act 1994 (c.21), s.22, Sched. 5, paras. 3(1)(6), 5(1)(2); operative on December 15, 1994; provide for the establishment of new pension schemes that must satisfy the terms of a trust deed set out in the Regulations.

INDUSTRY-WIDE MINEWORKERS' PENSION SCHEME REGULATIONS 1994 (No. 2974) [£8·70], made under the Coal Industry Act 1994 (c.21), s.22, Sched. 5, paras. 3(1)(6), 5(1)(2); operative on December 15, 1994; provide for the establishment of new pension schemes that must satisfy the terms of a trust deed set out in the Regulations.

3803. Commutation

PENSIONS COMMUTATION (AMENDMENT) REGULATIONS 1995 (No. 2648) [£1·10], made under the Pensions Commutation Act 1871, ss.4, 7;

operative on December 1, 1995; amend S.I. 1968 No. 1163 by substituting in the Schedule of those Regulations new tables giving rates to be used in calculating the capital sum to be paid in commutation of a pension or a portion of a pension.

3804. Company pension scheme—surplus fund—employees belonging to company pension scheme—company's scheme in substantial actuarial surplus—part of company sold and employees transferred to purchaser's employment—employees joining purchaser's pension scheme—company's pension scheme giving trustee discretion to transfer to purchaser's scheme such assets as it deemed appropriate—trustee transferring amount equal only to past service reserve of transferring employees, leaving surplus in company's scheme—plaintiff employees seeking disclosure of documents indicating reasons for trustee's decision—whether trustee of pension fund required to give reasons for exercise of discretion

Where a discretion is entrusted to a trustee by the relevant trust instrument, the trustee is not required to give reasons for the exercise of that discretion and, in the absence of any evidence of impropriety, the court will not interfere.

P were members of and contributed to a company pension scheme ("the existing scheme"). The division of the company in which they worked was sold to CMP and P were transferred into CMP's employment. Pending the setting up of its own pension scheme, CMP was admitted temporarily as a participating company into the existing scheme. Notwithstanding the fact that in the years preceding the transfer the employers had as a result of the fund being in surplus enjoyed a "contributions holiday", when the CMP scheme was set up the trustee of the existing scheme, in accordance with the terms of the trust deed, determined to transfer to the CMP scheme an amount equal only to the past service reserve of the transferring employees, leaving the whole of the surplus in the existing scheme. P asked the trustee to disclose all the trust documents in its possession which indicated or might indicate the reasons for the trustee's determination. The trustee refused and P issued a summons seeking disclosure.

Held, dismissing the summons, that where a discretion was entrusted to a trustee by the relevant trust instrument, the trustee was not required to give reasons for the exercise of that discretion and, in the absence of any evidence of impropriety, the court would not interfere since, in general, the principles applicable to private trusts as a matter of trust law applied equally to pension schemes.

WILSON v. LAW DEBENTURE TRUST [1995] 2 All E.R. 337, Rattee J.

3805. Company pension scheme—surplus fund—enhanced payments to those taking redundancy—obligation to pay into scheme by instalments a sum equal to cost of providing enhanced benefits—power to amend scheme—preclusion of payments of money to employer—whether employer could use surplus to discharge obligation to pay instalments

A contractual obligation to pay into a pension scheme amounts equal to the cost of providing enhanced benefits under the scheme is a real disposable asset of the scheme and any use of a surplus under the scheme to reduce or discharge that obligation will constitute a payment to the employer.

P established a pension scheme with D as its sole trustee. By cl. 45(1)(ii), P had the power to amend the scheme subject to a proviso prohibiting payment of moneys of the scheme to the employers. After a reduction of the workforce it was agreed that P would pay the cost of enhanced benefits under the scheme for those taking voluntary redundancy by instalments. At 1993 the outstanding instalments stood at £100 million. P sought to set off these instalments against an actuarial surplus in the scheme of £989 million and applied for approval of an amendment of the scheme under cl. 45(1)(ii). P argued that there was no difference between a reduction in its obligation to pay standard contributions at the expense of the surplus and such a set off, that there was an implied right to set the obligation to pay instalments off against the surplus which was applicable for P's benefit, and that the amendment did not involve a payment to P, the employer, since the surplus and the benefit of the instalments were not real figures representing disposable assets.

Held, disallowing the proposed amendment, that where P was under an obligation to make payments of sums required to meet the costs of enhanced benefits, then any payment to P out of the scheme of an equivalent amount was prohibited as a payment to the employer. The instalments were a real not just an actuarial asset, representing an actual obligation. The obligation to pay instalments already existed and any release of that obligation was a payment out of the scheme. P was not entitled to use the surplus to discharge or reduce its obligation to pay instalments.

BRITISH COAL CORP. v. BRITISH COAL STAFF SUPERANNUATION SCHEME TRUSTEES [1995] 1 All E.R. 912, Vinelott J.

3806. European Members of Parliament

EUROPEAN PARLIAMENTARY (UNITED KINGDOM REPRESENTATIVES) PENSIONS (ADDITIONAL VOLUNTARY CONTRIBUTIONS SCHEME) (NO. 2) ORDER 1995 (No. 739) [£2·40], made under the European Parliament (Pay and Pensions) Act 1979 (c.50), s.4(1)–(3); operative on April 4, 1995; makes provisions for members of the pension scheme for U.K. representatives of the European Parliament to pay additional voluntary contributions towards their pensions.

3807. Fair trial—civil proceedings—reversionary pension—unreasonable length of proceedings—whether violation of rights. See MASSA v. ITALY (NO. 14399/88), §2629.

3808. Guaranteed minimum increase

GUARANTEED MINIMUM PENSIONS INCREASE ORDER 1995 (No. 515) [65p], made under the Pension Schemes Act (c.48), s.109(4); operative on April 6, 1995; specifies 2·2 per cent for the purposes of s.109(2)(3) of the 1993 Act.

3809. Income-related benefits. See SOCIAL SECURITY, §4616.

3810. Increase

PENSIONS INCREASE (PENSION SCHEME FOR MR ALLAN DAVID GREEN) REGULATIONS 1995 (No. 1682), made under the Pensions (Increase) Act 1971, s.5(2)(4); operative on July 25, 1955; apply the provisions of the 1971 Act to any pension payable under the Pension Scheme for Mr Allan David Green.

PENSIONS INCREASE (PENSION SCHEMES FOR MR DEREK COMPTON LEWIS) REGULATIONS 1995 (No. 1681), made under the Pensions (Increase) Act 1971, s.5(2); operative on July 25, 1995; apply the provisions of the 1971 to any pension payable under the Pension Schemes for Mr Derek Compton Lewis.

PENSIONS INCREASE (REVIEW) ORDER 1995 (No. 708) [£1·10], made under the Social Security Pensions Act 1975 (c.5), s.59(1)(2)(5)(5ZA); operative on April 10, 1995; sets out the amounts by which the rates of public service pensions are to be increased.

3811. Inland Revenue—receipts of commission—insurance and personal pension schemes—taxation implications—revised Statement of Practice. See REVENUE AND FINANCE, §4367.

3812. Insurance companies—pension business. See INSURANCE, §2892.

3813. Judicial pensions

JUDICIAL PENSIONS (MISCELLANEOUS) REGULATIONS 1995 (No. 632) [£1·95], made under the Judicial Pensions and Retirement Act 1993 (c.8), ss.1(2)–(4), 2(7)(e), 3(4)(5); operative on March 31, 1995; make miscellaneous provision in relation to matters arising under the 1993 Act.

JUDICIAL PENSIONS (GUARANTEED MINIMUM PENSION ETC.) ORDER 1995 (No. 2647) [£1.10], made under the Pension Schemes Act 1993, s.141; operative on November 1, 1995, modifies the judicial pensions scheme in order to enable it to meet the contracting-out requirements laid down by the 1993 Act.

JUDICIAL PENSIONS (QUALIFYING JUDICIAL OFFICES ETC.) (CITY OF LONDON) ORDER 1995 (No. 633) [£1·95], made under the Judicial Pensions and Retirement Act 1993 (c.8), ss.1(8), 21(2), 29(4); operative on March 31, 1995; amends Sched. 1 to the 1993 Act by adding the offices of Recorder of London and Common Serjeant to the list of judicial offices which may be qualifying offices for the purposes of the new pension arrangements contained in Pt. 1 of the said Act.

3814. Judicial pensions—appeals

JUDICIAL PENSIONS (APPEALS) REGULATIONS 1995 (No. 635) [£1·10], made under the Pension Schemes Act 1993 (c.48), s.20(4), the Judicial Pensions Act 1981 (c.20), s.32A(4), the Sheriffs' Pensions (Scotland) Act 1961 (c.42), s.9A(3), the Superannuation Act 1972 (c.11), s.13(6), the Parliamentary Commissioner Act 1967 (c.13), Sched. 1, para. 4, the Parliamentary Commissioner Act (Northern Ireland) 1969 (c.10 (N.I.)), Sched. 1A, para. 4, the National Health Service Act 1977 (c.49), s.107, the National Health Service (Scotland) Act 1978 (c.29), s.91 and S.I. 1987 No. 460; operative on March 31, 1995; make provision as to the manner in which, and the time within which, appeals under s.20 of the 1993 Act are to be brought.

3815. Judicial pensions—benefits

JUDICIAL PENSIONS (ADDITIONAL BENEFITS FOR DISREGARDED EARNINGS) REGULATIONS 1995 (No. 640) [£1·10], made under the Judicial Pensions and Retirement Act 1993 (c.8), s.9(5); operative on March 31, 1995; provide for the regulation of payments of benefit under s.19 of the 1993 Act.

JUDICIAL PENSIONS (PRESERVATION OF BENEFITS) ORDER 1995 (No. 634) [£1·10], made under the Pension Schemes Act 1993 (c.48), s.141, and the Pension Schemes (Northern Ireland) Act 1993 (c.49), s.137; operative on March 31, 1995; provides for reduced pensions and derivative benefits to be preserved and become payable in the case of a member of the pensions scheme established under the 1993 Act who ceases to hold office before normal retirement age.

3816. Judicial pensions—contributions

JUDICIAL PENSIONS (ADDITIONAL VOLUNTARY CONTRIBUTIONS) REGULATIONS 1995 (No. 639) [£4·70], made under the Judicial Pensions and Retirement Act 1993 (c.8), s.10, 12(2), 23, 29(3)(4), Sched. 2, and the Judicial Pensions Act 1981 (c.20), s.32A; operative on March 31, 1995; make provision for the payment of additional voluntary contributions towards pensions payable under the 1993 Act.

JUDICIAL PENSIONS (CONTRIBUTIONS) REGULATIONS 1995 (No. 638) [£1·95], made under the Judicial Pensions and Retirement Act 1993 (c.8), s.9; operative on March 31, 1995; prescribe contributions to be made towards surviving spouses' and childrens' pensions payable under the 1993 Act.

JUDICIAL PENSIONS (CONTRIBUTIONS) (AMENDMENT) REGULATIONS 1995 (No. 2961) [£1·55], made under the Judicial Pensions and Retirement Act 1993, s.9. In force: December 11, 1995; correct errors in S.I. 1995 No. 638 and provide that the refund provisions of reg. 8(8) apply to office holders to whom the pension scheme applies by virtue of s.1(1)(d) of the Judicial Pensions and Retirement Act 1993 as well as to those by virtue of s.1(1)(b) of that Act.

3817. Judicial pensions—General Commissioners

RETIREMENT AGE OF GENERAL COMMISSIONERS ORDER 1995 (No. 3192) [65p], made under Judicial Pensions and Retirement Act 1993, ss.26(9),

29(3)(4). In force: January 1, 1996; adds the office of General Commissioner to the list of judicial offices in respect of which there is a maximum retirement age of 70 years contained in Sched. 5 of the Judicial Pensions and Retirement Act 1993. The new retirement age of 70 years will apply to persons appointed to the post for divisions in England and Wales, Scotland and Northern Ireland on or after January 1, 1996. Sections of the 1993 Act relating to the authorisation of the continuing in office of a General Commissioner until the age of 75 by the Secretary of State for Scotland are disapplied. The previous retirement age of 75 years made under the Taxes Management Act 1970, s.2(7), will continue to apply to those Commissioners appointed on or before December 31, 1995.

3818. Judicial pensions—transfers

JUDICIAL PENSIONS (TRANSFER OF ACCRUED BENEFITS) REGULATIONS 1995 (No. 637) [£3·20], made under the Judicial Pensions and Retirement Act 1993 (c.8), s.23, Sched. 2; operative on March 31, 1995; make provision in relation to the transfer of benefits between non-judicial pension schemes and schemes constituted under the 1993 Act.

JUDICIAL PENSIONS (TRANSFERS BETWEEN JUDICIAL PENSION SCHEMES) REGULATIONS 1995 (No. 636) [£2·80], made under the Judicial Pensions and Retirement Act 1993 (c.8), ss.12, 29; operative on March 31, 1995; provide for the valuation of benefits transferred between existing judicial pension schemes and that constituted under the 1993 Act.

3819. Judicial Pensions and Retirement Act 1993—commencement

JUDICIAL PENSIONS AND RETIREMENT ACT 1993 (COMMENCEMENT) ORDER 1995 (No. 631 (C.15)) [65p], made under the Judicial Pensions and Retirement Act 1993 (c.8), s.31(2); brings all provisions of the 1993 Act into force on March 31, 1995.

3820. Judicial review—Security and Investment Board—pension transfer and opt-out penalty—SIB guidance—whether Board exceeded powers. See R. v. SECURITIES AND INVESTMENTS BOARD, *ex p.* INDEPENDENT FINANCIAL ADVISERS ASSOCIATION, §153.

3821. Local government. See LOCAL GOVERNMENT, §3260.

3822. Occupational and personal pension schemes

OCCUPATIONAL AND PERSONAL PENSION SCHEMES (LEVY) REGULATIONS 1995 (No. 524) [£1·55], made under the Pension Schemes Act (c.48), ss.175(1)(2)(4), 181(1), 182(2)(3); operative on April 1, 1995; revoke and replace S.I. 1990 No. 2277 and make provision for a levy to meet the cost of the Pensions Ombudsman.

OCCUPATIONAL AND PERSONAL PENSION SCHEMES (MISCELLANEOUS AMENDMENTS) REGULATIONS 1995 (No. 35) [£1·55], made under the Pension Schemes Act 1993 (c.48), ss.9(3)(5), 19(4), 23(1), 26, 29(3), 31(1), 73(1), 113(1)(3), 162, 181, 182(2)(3); operative on February 7, 1995; revoke S.I. 1976 No. 598 and amends S.I. 1984 No. 380, S.I. 1985 No. 1929, S.I. 1987 Nos. 1101, 1110, and 1117, S.I. 1988 No. 137 and S.I. 1991 No. 167.

OCCUPATIONAL AND PERSONAL PENSION SCHEMES (MISCELLANEOUS AMENDMENTS) (NO. 2) REGULATIONS 1995 (No. 3067) [65p], made under the Pension Schemes Act 1993, ss.73(1)(2)(4), 113(1)(3), 153(1)(2), 181(1), 182(1)–(3). In force: February 1, 1996; make miscellaneous amendments to parts of S.I. 1991 No. 167 relating to the securing of short service benefit by an insurance policy or annuity contract and add to S.I. 1987 No. 1110 a new Regulation placing an obligation on trustees or managers of personal pension schemes to inform members within three months if they do not receive payments of contributions on due dates. The report of the Occupational Pensions Board on the draft of these Regulations which was referred to them is contained in Cm. 3052.

3823. Occupational pension schemes

OCCUPATIONAL PENSION SCHEMES (EQUAL ACCESS TO MEMBERSHIP) AMENDMENT REGULATIONS 1995 (No. 1215) [£1·10], made under the European Communities Act 1972 (c.68), s.2(2), and the Pension Schemes Act 1993 (c.48), ss.118(4), 153(3), 181(1), 182(2); operative on May 31, 1995; modify the equal access requirements of s.118 of the 1993 Act and amend S.I. 1976 No. 142 in order to implement Art. 119 of the Treaty establishing the EEC.

OCCUPATIONAL PENSION SCHEMES (EQUAL TREATMENT) REGULATIONS 1995 (No. 3183) [£1·95], made under the Pensions Act 1995, ss.63(5), 64(2)(3), 66(4), 124(1). 174(2)(3); revoke S.I. 1976 No. 142. In force: January 1, 1996; implement the requirements of Art. 119 of the Treaty of Rome concerning equal pay for men and women by supplementing requirements for equal treatment relating to occupational pension schemes provided in ss.62 and 66 of the Pensions Act 1995. Regulation 2 provides that the Equal Pay Act 1970 will have effect, subject to certain modifications, in relation to an equal treatment rule. Provision that courts and tribunals may not make financial awards for claims relating to breach of equal treatment rules is made by reg. 3 and the employers are given the right to appear before a tribunal by reg. 4. Regulations 5 and 6 give courts and tribunals the power to make declarations on the applicant's equal treatment rights and to obtain any additional information from employers. Provision is made for financial awards to pensioner members in respect of any breach of equal treatment rule in reg. 7 and employers are required to provide any additional resources required. Permitted exemptions to an equal treatment rule are provided for under regs. 13 to 15.

3824. Occupational pensions

OCCUPATIONAL PENSIONS (REVALUATION) ORDER 1995 (No. 3021) [65p], made under the Pension Schemes Act 1993, Sched. 3, para. 2(1). In force: January 1, 1996; specifies the revaluation percentage for the revaluation of benefits under occupational pension schemes for each revaluation period specified in s.2 of the Order.

3825. Occupational pensions—Members of Parliament. See PARLIAMENT, §3744.

3826. Occupational pensions—Prime Minister. See CONSTITUTIONAL LAW, §716.

3827. Occupational pensions—sex discrimination—equal pay—retirement ages differing according to sex—equalisation—European Community. See VAN DEN AKKER v. STICHTING SHELL PENSIOENFONDS (C–28/93), §1997.

3828. Occupational pensions—sex discrimination—equal pay—retirement ages differing according to sex—whether discriminatory—European Community. See SMITH v. AVDEL SYSTEMS (C–408/92), §1998.

3829. Occupational pensions—sex discrimination—equal pay—use of actuarial factors differing according to sex—limitation of the effects in time of the *Barber* judgment—European Community. See COLOROLL PENSION TRUSTEES v. RUSSELL (C–200/91), §2001.

3830. Occupational pensions—sex discrimination—equal treatment—married man's civil servant pension lower than that for women—whether discrimi-

natory—European Community. See BESTUUR VAN HET ALGEMEEN BURGERLIJK PENSIOENFONDS v. BEUNE (C–7/93), §1996.

3831. Occupational pensions—sex discrimination—right to join scheme—equal pay—limitation of the effects in time of the *Barber* judgment—European Community. See VROEGE v. NCIV INSTITUUT VOOR VOLKSHUISVESTING BV AND STICHTING PENSIOENFONDS NCIV (C–57/93), §2000.

3832. Occupational pensions—sex discrimination—right to join scheme—equal pay for men and women—limitation of the effects in time of the *Barber* judgment—European Community. See FISSCHER v. VOORHUIS HENELO BV AND STICHTING BEDRIJFSPENSIOENFONDS VOOR DE DETAILHANDEL, §1999.

3833. Ombudsman

PERSONAL AND OCCUPATIONAL PENSION SCHEMES (PENSIONS OMBUDSMAN) (PROCEDURE) RULES 1995 (No. 1053) [£1·95], made under the Pensions Schemes Act 1993 (c.48), s.149(2)(3); operative on May 10, 1995; make provision as to the procedure to be followed when there has been a complaint or dispute relating to a personal or occupational pension scheme that is referred to the Pensions Ombudsman under the 1993 Act.

3834. Ombudsman—jurisdiction—pension funds with both trustees and managers—maladministration alleged against managers—whether jurisdiction to consider allegations where there were also trustees of the fund—whether ombudsman entitled to rely on own knowledge that certain companies managed funds

[Pension Scheme Act 1993 (c.48), ss.146(1), 151(4).]

Two preliminary issues were raised in two appeals under the Pension Scheme Act 1993, s.151(4). Both appellants were the successors or alleged successors to insurance companies which had arranged insurance policies for insured occupational pension schemes which had been funded and established under trusts. The pensions ombudsman had found them each guilty of maladministration and they appealed. The first issue concerned the construction of s.146(1) of the Act. Both appellants contended that the phrase "trustees or managers" meant "trustees or, if there were no trustees, the managers". If the appellants were correct in that assertion the ombudsman did not have jurisdiction to investigate allegations of maladministration. The second issue was whether there was sufficient evidence to find that the insurance companies to which the day-to-day running of the schemes had been delegated by the trustees were managers.

Held, that (1) the pensions ombudsman had jurisdiction under the 1993 Act, s.146(1), to investigate complaints about pension scheme managers, whether or not the pension schemes concerned also had trustees. The words "trustees or managers" in s.146(1) must be given their ordinary meaning, because otherwise members would be denied access to a cheap method of dispute resolution by excluding those who often bore the greatest responsibility for pension scheme maladministration; (2) it was not sufficient for the ombudsman to rely on his own knowledge of the role of insurance companies in relation to pension schemes (in the same way as Rent Assessment Committees use their knowledge of rent levels). However, there was sufficient material on which the ombudsman could rely, including reference to the fact that the insurance company was a manager, which had not been denied in correspondence.

CENTURY LIFE v. PENSIONS OMBUDSMAN (CO/1128/94; CO/3553/94), May 12, 1995, Dyson J.

3835. Overseas service

OVERSEAS SERVICE (PENSIONS SUPPLEMENT) REGULATIONS 1995 (No.

238) [£5·60], made under the Pensions (Increase) Act 1971 (c.56), ss.11, 11A, 12, 13(2)(4); operative on March 1, 1995; revoke and replace S.I. 1977 No. 320 and provide for the payment of pension supplements to or in respect of certain officers who have served governments, authorities or institutions of overseas territories.

3836. Pension fund—action by members of scheme concerning administration of scheme—application for pre-emptive costs order—costs to be paid out of pension fund—whether jurisdiction to make order

[Supreme Court Act 1981 (c.54), s.51.]

The court has jurisdiction under s.51 of the Supreme Court Act 1981 to make a pre-emptive costs order providing for any costs incurred by or ordered against a party to an action concerning the administration of a pension fund to be met out of the fund.

In an action against the trustees of the pension fund, P obtained an order for costs providing that any costs incurred by P or ordered against him would be met by the pension fund itself. The defendants appealed, contending that there was no jurisdiction to make such an order.

Held, dismissing the appeal, that the position was analogous to that of a minority shareholder bringing a derivative action, as a person who had given consideration for a limited interest in a fund alleging injury to the fund as a whole and obtaining a pre-emptive costs order indemnifying him against costs from the fund (*Wallersteiner v. Moir (No. 2)* [1975] C.L.Y. 2602 applied).

McDONALD v. HORN [1995] 1 All E.R. 961, C.A.

3837. Pension fund rules—ill health termination—whether employee entitled to early pension

H was dismissed at the age of 45 years on the grounds of ill health. She was a member of the building society's pension scheme which provided that an early pension could be granted when a member retired due to incapacity. The trustees of the scheme rejected her claim for an early pension on the basis that dismissal did not qualify as "retirement", and "incapacity" meant permanent incapacity. The High Court dismissed H's claim and she appealed.

Held, allowing H's appeal in part, that the High Court had not erred in finding that "incapacity" should be construed as permanent incapacity. A member must therefore prove that future employment was impossible due to physical or mental incapacity. The High Court had erred, however, in finding that there could not be a "retirement" under the scheme when an employee was dismissed. The manner in which the employment terminated was irrelevant for these purposes.

HARRIS v. SHUTTLEWORTH [1994] IRLR 547, C.A.

3838. Pensions Act 1995 (c.26)

The Act received Royal Assent on July 19, 1995.

3839. Pensions Act 1995—commencement

PENSIONS ACT 1995 (COMMENCEMENT NO. 1) ORDER 1995 (No. 2548) [65p], made under the Pensions Act 1995, s.180(1); operative on October 2, 1995; brings into force ss.90, 156, 169, 172, Sched. 6, para. 6 of the Act.

PENSIONS ACT 1995 (COMMENCEMENT NO. 2) ORDER 1995 (No. 3104 (C.71)) [65p], made under the Pensions Act 1995, s.180(1); brings into force various provisions of the Act on December 4, 1995 and January 1, 1996; provides for ss.90, 156, 169, 172, 173 (part), 174 (part), 175 (part) and Sched. 6, para. 1 to come into force on October 2, 1995.

3840. Pensions appeal tribunal—rehearing—leave—war pension—disability—applicant arguing deafness resulting from military service—new evidence—whether rehearing should be ordered

B, aged 81, applied for leave to appeal for a rehearing by a tribunal of a claim for a disability pension originally rejected in 1959. B claimed the deterioration of his hearing was due to a bomb dropped by the RAF while he was a prisoner of war in Tobruk in 1942. The appeal was based on new evidence of an audiologist stating that he had no doubt that the deafness was caused by "military factors". The Secretary of State refused to grant leave to appeal.

Held, allowing the application, that there was an error in law on the part of the tribunal. It is usually the job of the Secretary of State to decide whether a claim should be reheard, but the court should judge each case on its facts. A rehearing would be undesirable unless new evidence was so strong that the tribunal would be unable to disregard it. The new medical report was considered strong enough. The initial refusal by the Secretary of State to grant leave to appeal amounted to a prejudging of the evidence. The matter was remitted for rehearing.

BROWN v. SECRETARY OF STATE FOR SOCIAL SECURITY (PA/03/95), July 21, 1995, Macpherson J.

3841. Pensions tribunal—allowing appeal—Secretary of State's notice sent to wrong office—whether Secretary of State entitled to extension of time to appeal

T applied for a pension on the basis that her husband's death had been hastened by his service on Christmas Island, where nuclear tests were being conducted. This was rejected by the Secretary of State, and the Pensions Tribunal allowed T's appeal. The Secretary of State wished to appeal against this, but because the notice had been sent to the wrong office, was unable to do so within the time-limit. The Secretary of State applied for an extension of time.

Held, granting the application for an extension, but dismissing the appeal, that there was an acceptable excuse for the delay, but on the substance of the case it was held that T had discharged the onus of proof necessary to show that her husband's death had been precipitated by his exposure to radiation on Christmas Island.

SECRETARY OF STATE FOR SECURITY v. TITMUS [1994] C.O.D. 266, D.C.

3842. Personal equity plans

PERSONAL EQUITY PLANS (AMENDMENT) REGULATIONS 1995 (No. 1539), made under the Income and Corporation Taxes Act 1988, s.333, and the Taxation of Chargeable Gains Act 1992, s.151; operative on July 6, 1995; amend the 1989 Regulations and extend the range of investments which may be held under general plans to preference shares and convertible preference shares of companies incorporated in Member States of the EU and to bonds and convertible bonds of companies incorporated in the U.K.

PERSONAL EQUITY PLAN (AMENDMENT NO.2) REGULATIONS 1995 (No. 3287 made under Income and Corporation Taxes Act 1988, ss.333,333A and Taxation of Chargeable Gains Act 1992 s.151. operative on January 9, 1996; [£1·10]. These Regulations amend the Personal Equity Plan Regulations 1989 (the principal Regulations) in relation to the qualifications for plan managers. They provide that a European institution within the meaning of the Banking Co-ordination (Second Council Directive) Regulations 1992, which may carry on home-regulated investment business in the UK in accordance with those Regulations, or a person who is authorised under s.31 Financial Services Act 1986, must appoint a tax representative for the purpose of discharging the duties of a plan manager under the principal Regulations, or make other arrangements with the Inland Revenue Commissioners for the discharge of those duties, if it does not have a branch or business establishment in the UK through which it intends to carry out the functions of a plan manager. The amendments also provide for the termination of the appointment of a tax representative, set out the powers and liabilities of such representatives and make consequential amendments to the principal Regulations.

3843. Personal injuries

PERSONAL INJURIES (CIVILIANS) AMENDMENT SCHEME 1995 (No. 445)

[£1·95], made under the Personal Injuries (Emergency Provisions) Act 1939 (c.82), ss.1, 2; operative on April 10, 1995; further amends S.I. 1983 No. 686.

3844. Personal pension schemes

PERSONAL PENSION SCHEMES (APPROPRIATE SCHEMES) AMENDMENT REGULATIONS 1995 (No. 1612), made under the Pension Schemes Act 1993, ss.9(5)(a), 181(1), 182(2); amend S.I. 1988 No. 137; operative on July 19, 1995.

3845. Redundancy and premature retirement—compensation. See LOCAL GOVERNMENT, §3268.

3846. Retirement—local authorities' discretion to award extra years' pension credit for workers retiring early—whether discretion open to challenge

[Local Government Compensation for Premature Retirement Regulations 1982 (S.I. 1982 No. 1009), reg. 5.]

J applied for early retirement and accepted a package including credit for two years' additional benefit. He then claimed that he was entitled to 10 years' additional benefit under a further scheme "Pers 43/1" adopted by the council on February 1, 1984 and sought a declaration to enforce his rights under this scheme. The Recorder dismissed his claim and J appealed.

Held, dismissing the appeal, that (1) although the scheme was mandatory in tone, it had to be read subject to reg. 5 of the Local Government Compensation for Premature Retirement Regulations 1982 which gave a discretion to credit an eligible person with a period of service not exceeding 10 years; (2) reg. 5 did not create a binding 10-year credit as this would be a fetter upon the exercise of the local authority which was clearly not intended by Parliament. Thus the local authority had a discretion to grant J anything from zero to 10 years but was perfectly entitled to give him enhanced credit of two years and no more; and (3) J also suggested that the court had to take into account the rights he had in relation to redundancy but as this factor did not form part of the Recorder's judgment it could not be raised at this stage.

JONES v. MID GLAMORGAN COUNTY COUNCIL (CCRTF 91/1544/C) (CCRTF 91/1544/C), November 17, 1994, C.A.

3847. Retirement annuities—exemption from tax in respect of qualifying premiums—taxpayer receiving income from Lloyd's syndicates as external name—taxpayer paying qualifying premium under annuity contract out of income received from syndicates—whether taxpayer entitled to retirement annuity relief—whether premium paid out of relevant earnings—whether income received from syndicates immediately derived from the carrying on by him of his trade. See KOENIGSBERGER v. MELLOR, §2789.

3848. Retirement benefits schemes

RETIREMENT BENEFITS SCHEMES (INDEXATION OF EARNINGS CAP) ORDER 1994 (No. 3009) [65p], made under the Income and Corporation Taxes Act 1988 (c.1), s.590C(6); specifies the earnings cap for the year 1995–1996 for the purposes of s.590C of the 1988 Act, as £78,600.

RETIREMENT BENEFITS SCHEMES (INDEXATION OF EARNINGS CAP) ORDER 1995 (No. 3034) [65p], made under the Income and Corporation Taxes Act 1988, s.590C(6). In force: April 6, 1996; specifies the earnings cap, for the purposes of s.590C of the Income and Corporation Taxes Act 1988 for the year of assessment 1996/7 to be £82,200. This figure is also the figure for the premitted maximum or allowable maximum for 1996–97 for the purposes of the following sections of the Act: ss.590B, 592, 594, 599, 640A, 646A and for the purposes of para. 20 and, by para. 22, for the purposes of para. 21 of Sched. 6 to the Finance Act 1989.

RETIREMENT BENEFITS SCHEMES (INFORMATION POWERS) REGU-

LATIONS 1995 (No. 3103) [£2·40], made under the Income and Corporation Taxes Act 1988, s.605(1A)(1B)(1D)(1E). In force: January 1, 1996; make provision for the furnishing of information and documents in connection with retirement benefit schemes to the Inland Revenue commissioners ("the Board"). Part II deals with the information to be given by retirement benefit schemes without the service of a notice requiring that information. Part III deals with particulars and documents relating to approved schemes, relevant statutory schemes and certain annuity contracts. Part IV deals with inspections of records of approved schemes, relevant statutory schemes and annuity contracts by the Board and the retention of records relating to such schemes by prescribed persons.

3849. Revaluation of earnings factors. See SOCIAL SECURITY, §4637.

3850. Service pensions—disablement and death. See ARMED FORCES, §365.

3851. Sex discrimination—old-age pension—increase for dependent spouse in respect of one pension—corresponding reduction by another Member State—European Community

A Dutch national was employed in the Netherlands for 37 years and then worked in Belgium for eight years. His spouse was not employed. He was awarded a Dutch pension on the basis of 100 per cent of his net minimum salary, 50 per cent on account of his being a married person and 50 per cent on account of the fact that his spouse had not then reached the age of 65. He also had a Belgian pension calculated at the household rate. When his spouse did reach the age of 65, she was granted a Dutch pension on the basis of 50 per cent of the net minimum salary, but her husband's pension was equally reduced. However, her husband's Belgian pension was then recalculated at a single rate on the ground that his spouse now had an income.

Held, that Community law, in particular Arts. 48 and 51 E.C. and Art. 4(1) of Dir. 79/7 on the progressive implementation of the principle of equal treatment for men and women in matters of social security, does not preclude national legislation which provides for the right to a pension at the household rate where the worker's spouse has ceased all gainful employment and is not in receipt of a retirement pension or equivalent benefit, but which applies only the less favourable single rate where the worker's spouse is in receipt of a retirement pension or equivalent benefit. Where, for the purpose of applying a provision of its domestic law, a national court has to characterise a social security benefit awarded under the statutory scheme of another Member State, it should interpret its own legislation in the light of the aims of Arts. 48 to 51 E.C. and, as far as is at all possible, prevent its interpretation from being such as to discourage a migrant worker from actually exercising his right to freedom of movement.

VAN MUNSTER v. RIJKSDIENST VOOR PENSIOENEN (C–165/91), October 5, 1994, ECJ.

3852. Teachers' superannuation—additional voluntary contributions. See EDUCATION, §1945.

3853. War pensions. See ARMED FORCES, §366.

PETROLEUM

3854. Emissions—European Community

European Parliament and Council Dir. 94/63/EC of December 20, 1994 on the control of volatile organic compound (VOC) emissions resulting from the storage of petrol and its distribution from terminals to service stations (O.J. L365/24).

3855. Hydrocarbons—licensing

HYDROCARBONS LICENSING DIRECTIVE REGULATIONS 1995 (No. 1434) [£1·10], made under the European Communities Act 1972 (c.68), s.2(2); operative on June 30, 1995; make provision in relation to the conditions for the granting and using authorisations for the prospection, exploration and production of hydrocarbons.

3856. Petroleum revenue tax—losses carried back—basis on which interest to be calculated

[Oil Taxation Act 1975 (c.22), Sched. 2, para. 17.]

Legislation should be construed in a manner fairly susceptible of achieving the result which Parliament must have intended.

Ps were participators in the Piper Oilfield in the United Kingdom sector of the North Sea. In July 1988 a tragic accident occurred which substantially destroyed the Piper field production facilities. Major redevelopment was required to bring the field back into production in February 1993. Each P incurred allowable losses which it sought to relieve by making claims to be carried backwards and set against assessable profits accruing in earlier chargeable periods. The Revenue disputed the interest payable in respect of these claims.

Held, allowing Ps' appeals in part, that (1) a loss from one period could not be relieved against profits of two periods; (2) a loss in two periods could not be relieved against profits of one period; and (3) an amendment to the statute could not affect rights which had already accrued.

[*Per Curiam*: Petroleum revenue tax was prospectively abolished by Finance Act 1993, s.185].

ELF ENTERPRISE CALEDONIA v. I.R.C. [1994] S.T.C. 785, Sir Donald Nicholls, V.-C.

3857. Production

PETROLEUM (PRODUCTION) (LANDWARD AREAS) REGULATIONS 1995 (No. 1436) [£5·60], made under the Petroleum (Production) Act 1934 (c.36), s.6(1); operative on June 30, 1995; partially implement Council Dir. 94/22/EEC on the conditions for granting and using authorisations for the prospection, exploration and production of hydrocarbons.

PETROLEUM (PRODUCTION) (SEAWARD AREAS) (AMENDMENT) REGULATIONS 1995 (No. 1435) [£1·55], made under the Petroleum (Production) Act 1934 (c.36), s.6; operative on June 30, 1995; partially implement Council Dir. 94/22/EEC on the conditions for granting and using authorisations for the prospection, exploration and production of hydrocarbons by amending S.I. 1988 No. 1213.

POLICE

3858. Complaints procedure—dismissal of constable—whether complainant entitled to documentation of appeal

A person whose complaint led to the dismissal of a police constable had no right to documents emanating from the constable's appeal.

R. v. SECRETARY OF STATE FOR THE HOME DEPARTMENT, *ex p.* GOSWELL, *The Times*, December 31, 1994, Brooke J.

3859. Confiscation powers—press release. See CRIMINAL SENTENCING, §1337.

3860. Defences—driving without due care and attention—car in pursuit of potential robbers—whether defence of necessity available. See D.P.P. v. HARRIS (NIGEL), §4407.

3861. Disciplinary proceedings—dismissal of probationer without disciplinary proceedings—whether breach of duty of fairness

It was a breach of the duty of fairness to dispense with the services of a probationary police officer without disciplinary proceedings in which he could disprove the allegations.

The services of C, a probationary constable, were dispensed with following alleged incidents involving procedural impropriety. C maintained that the evidence against him was fabricated by other officers who had conspired together, and sought judicial review of the decision to dismiss him. He obtained a declaration that the Chief Constable had acted unlawfully in withholding a report from him, but his claim that it was irrational of the Chief Constable not to hold a disciplinary hearing was rejected, and he appealed.

Held, allowing the appeal, that given the conflict of evidence, it was both irrational and unfair not to hold a disciplinary hearing and to give C the opportunity to prove himself innocent of the matters considered worthy of disciplinary proceedings.

R. v. CHIEF CONSTABLE OF THE WEST MIDLANDS POLICE, *ex p.* CARROLL (1995) 7 Admin. L.R. 45, C.A.

3862. Disciplinary proceedings—police appeal tribunal—whether Home Secretary obliged to accept factual findings

The Home Secretary is not obliged to accept the factual findings of an appeal tribunal set up by him under the Police Act 1964.

B and others were police officers involved in a pub brawl whilst off duty. Charges were brought under the police Discipline Code. The disciplinary tribunal recommended that the officers be dismissed and the officers appealed to the Secretary of State. An appeal tribunal was appointed under the Police Act 1964 for a rehearing of the charges; it found them not proved and recommended that the appeals be allowed. The Home Secretary felt that on all the evidence the charges were proved and decided to dismiss the officers, who sought to challenge that decision on the basis that he was obliged to accept the appeal tribunal's findings.

Held, dismissing the appeals, that (1) the function of an appeal tribunal set up under the Police Act 1964 was to conduct an inquiry and report to the Home Secretary; that did not preclude him from disagreeing with their conclusion; (2) on the evidence, the Home Secretary had been entitled to draw different inferences from the statements to those drawn by the tribunal.

R. v. SECRETARY OF STATE FOR THE HOME DEPARTMENT, *ex p.* BARR (1995) 7 Admin. L.R. 157, C.A.

3863. Discipline

POLICE (DISCIPLINE) (AMENDMENT) REGULATIONS 1995 (No. 1475) [65p], made under the Police and Criminal Evidence Act 1984 (c.60), s.101, and the Police Act 1964 (c.48), s.33; operative on July 10, 1995; amend S.I. 1985 No. 518 so that the hearing of a discipline charge may be delegated by a Chief Constable to an assistant chief constable.

POLICE (DISCIPLINE) (AMENDMENT NO. 2) REGULATIONS 1995 (No. 2517) [65p], made under the Police Act 1964, s.33 and the Police and Criminal Evidence Act 1984, s.101; operative on November 1, 1995, amend S.I. 1985 No. 518; give officers of the rank of commander in the Metropolitan Police Force appointed by the Commissioner rights to exercise the same disciplinary functions as deputy assistant commissioners.

3864. Duty of care—individual in custody—relevant information not passed to CPS—whether breach of duty of care. See WHITE (MICHAEL) v. CHIEF CONSTABLE OF MERSEYSIDE, §3686.

3865. Duty of care—individual in custody—whether police owing duty of care to individual detained in custody. See LERVOLD (HAROLD) v. CHIEF CONSTABLE OF KENT (CCRTI 94/0131/F), §3687.

3866. Equipment—disposal of seized equipment

POLICE (DISPOSAL OF SOUND EQUIPMENT) REGULATIONS 1995 (No. 722), made under Criminal Justice and Public Order Act 1994 (c.33); operative on April 10, 1995; provide for the disposal of equipment seized under s.63 of the 1994 Act which relates to raves.

3867. Judicial review—Chief Constable—insufficient resources to attend protests against livestock exports—Chief Constable only allowing exporters' lorries through two days a week—whether contravening EEC rules on restriction of exports—whether Chief Constable's decision unreasonable. See R. v. CHIEF CONSTABLE OF SUSSEX, *ex p.* INTERNATIONAL TRADER'S FERRY, §9.

3868. Legal advice at station—police circular excluding solicitor's clerk—clerk having been arrested for attempting to pervert the course of justice—whether police having acted in good faith

H was a solicitor's clerk who was the subject of a circular sent by a Deputy Chief Constable which stated that he was to be refused access to police stations to advise and attend detained persons. H applied for judicial review of the circular.

Held, dismissing the application, that the fact that H had been arrested for attempting to pervert the course of justice was a relevant consideration, and on the facts before the court the Deputy Chief Constable had not acted in bad faith.

R. v. CHIEF CONSTABLE OF LEICESTERSHIRE, *ex p.* HENNING [1994] C.O.D. 256, D.C.

3869. Ministry of Defence police—police committee

MINISTRY OF DEFENCE POLICE (POLICE COMMITTEE) REGULATIONS 1995 (No. 939) [65p], made under the Ministry of Defence Police Act 1987 (c.4), s.1(5); operative on May 1, 1995; revoke S.I. 1988 No. 1098.

3870. Motorvehicles—removal and disposal

POLICE (RETENTION AND DISPOSAL OF VEHICLES) REGULATIONS 1995 (No. 723), made under Criminal Justice and Public Order Act 1994 (c.33), s.67(3); operative April 10, 1995; provide for the retention, safe keeping, disposal and destruction of vehicles seized.

3871. Police and Criminal Evidence Act 1984—codes of practice. See CRIMINAL EVIDENCE AND PROCEDURE, §1189.

3872. Police and Magistrates' Courts Act 1994—commencement. See CRIMINAL EVIDENCE AND PROCEDURE, §1190.

3873. Police areas

POLICE AREAS (WALES) ORDER 1995 (No. 2864) [£1·10], made under the Police Act 1964, ss.21A, 21C; operative on December 11, 1995 for arts. 1 and

4 and April 1, 1996 for remainder of Order, in accordance with art. 1(2); amends police areas in Wales to take account of the reorganisation of local government in Wales under the Local Government (Wales) Act 1994. Police areas in Sched. 1A to the Police Act 1964 are described by reference to local government areas. Art. 3 of this Order ensures that, notwithstanding the changes to their areas, the existing police authorities continue to exist. The Order also makes transitional provisions relating to the budget and policing plan for the 1996–97 financial year, makes transfers of property consequential on the changes to police areas and transfers certain civilian staff from the South Wales police authority to Gwent police authority.

3874. Police federation

POLICE FEDERATION (AMENDMENT) REGULATIONS 1995 (No. 2768) [£1·10], made under the Police Act 1964, s.44; amend S.I. 1969 No. 1787, S.I. 1971 No. 1498, S.I. 1973 No. 706; operative on November 15, 1995; amend the Police Federation Regulations 1969 so that men and women can vote in the elections held under those Regulations, thereby removing present restrictions where only men or only women could vote in certain elections. Restrictions are also removed from the sex qualifications of persons to be elected.

3875. Powers of entry—entry to private premises without warrant—where reasonable belief in breach of the peace—whether lawful

The police are entitled to enter private premises without a warrant when they have reasonable grounds for believing a breach of the peace is likely to occur.

The plaintiff, W, divorced from H, was ordered by the county court to deliver up H's furniture and effects. H, before the expiry of the time-limit, went to the house with police officers and removed the items. W returned before their departure and insisted that the items be put back; the police insisted that H should be allowed to drive away. W brought proceedings against the police, claiming damages for trespass and breach of duty. The judge dismissed the claim on the ground that the police were carrying out their duty to prevent a breach of the peace.

Held, dismissing W's appeal, that the police had power to enter private premises without a warrant to prevent a breach of the peace if they had reasonable grounds for believing one was likely to occur. The facts of this case were such as to provide the police officers with a lawful excuse for entering the property (*Thomas v. Lawkins* [1935] All E.R. 655 considered).

McLEOD v. COMMISSIONER OF POLICE OF THE METROPOLIS [1994] 4 All E.R. 553, C.A.

3876. Public interest immunity—complaints against police—reports of investigating officers—whether a class to which public interest immunity attached—whether disclosure necessary. See TAYLOR v. ANDERTON (POLICE COMPLAINTS AUTHORITY INTERVENING), §4123.

3877. Regulations

POLICE REGULATIONS 1995 (No. 215), [£7·35], made under the Police Act 1964 (c.48), s.33; operative on March 8, 1995; consolidate with amendments S.I. 1987 No. 851.

POLICE (AMENDMENT) REGULATIONS 1995 (No. 547) [£1·95], made under the Police Act 1964 (c.48), s.33; operative except for reg. 13 on April 1, 1995, reg. 13 operative on April 13, 1995; amend S.I. 1995 No. 215.

POLICE (AMENDMENT NO. 2) REGULATIONS 1995 (No. 2020) [£1.95], made under the Police Act 1964, s.33; amend S.I. 1995 No. 215; make provision for the rank of assistant commissioner in the City of London force and other provisions in respect of pay.

3878. Trespass—by police—search outside powers—*quantum*. See HARRISON AND HOPE v. CHIEF CONSTABLE OF POLICE FOR GREATER MANCHESTER, §1846.

POST OFFICE

3879. National Savings—stock register

NATIONAL SAVINGS STOCK REGISTER (AMENDMENT) REGULATIONS 1994 (No. 3277) [£1·10], made under the National Debt Act 1972 (c.65), s.3; operative on February 1, 1995; amend S.I. 1976 No. 2012 so as to alter the rates of commission due to the Director of Savings when stock on the Register is bought or sold through him.

PRACTICE (CIVIL)

3880. Abuse of process—amendments to pleadings—striking out—refusal of leave to re-amend statement of claim—whether appellate court to re-examine striking out of action

A applied for leave to appeal against the striking out of his action for restitution of commission against D's personal representatives. Before his death D was managing director of National Trade Services in which A, an Iraqi businessman, became the major shareholder. The amended statement of claim asserted that D fraudulently converted and misappropriated commissions to the company. However, A asserted in his oral evidence that in fact the commission had been due not to the company but to A himself. The judge refused leave to re-amend the statement of claim and struck out the action as an abuse of process.

Held, granting leave to appeal, that (1) it was right to allow the appellate court to re-examine whether the judge was right to strike out the action at that stage in the proceedings and whether to allow the claims to be re-amended; (2) since A intended to apply to adduce further evidence on Iraqi law which was not presented at first instance, the Court of Appeal should hear the application.

AL-HILO (JA'FAR MOHAMMED ABDUL MUHSIN) AND NATIONAL TRADE SERVICES CO. v. DANIEL (SIMON) (LTA 94/7041/B), March 30, 1995, C.A.

3881. Abuse of process—application in bankruptcy proceedings—applicant not trustee in bankruptcy or creditor—whether court having jurisdiction to strike out

[R.S.C., Ord. 18, r.19.]

The provisions of R.S.C., Ord. 18, r.19, have no application to interlocutory processes or summonses brought under the Insolvency Rules 1986.

P made an application in pending bankruptcy proceedings. The trustee in bankruptcy, on the ground that the application disclosed no maintainable case, sought an order that it be struck out pursuant to R.S.C., Ord. 18, r.19, or alternatively pursuant to the inherent jurisdiction of the court.

Held, that the court had an inherent jurisdiction to stay all proceedings which were frivolous, vexatious or an abuse of its process and, where an affidavit in support of an application in pending bankruptcy proceedings disclosed no maintainable case, an order could be made striking out the application.

PORT v. AUGER; *sub nom.* PORT (A BANKRUPT) (NO. 56 OF 1987), *Re*; PORT v. AUGER [1994] 1 W.L.R. 862, Harman J.

3882. Abuse of process—benzodiazepine group action—cost-benefit analysis—costs to defendant out of all proportion to benefit to plaintiffs—whether court having power to strike out

[R.S.C., Ord. 18, r.19; Legal Aid Act 1988 (c.34), ss.15, 17.]

In a group action for personal injuries, the court has an inherent power to strike out, as vexatious and an abuse of process, claims in which the irrecoverable costs likely to be incurred by the defendant are out of all proportion to any benefit that the plaintiffs are likely to obtain if successful.

P, users of benzodiazepine drugs and most of whom were legally aided, began a group action against the manufacturers (D1). In the alternative, in a small number of cases, they sued the prescribers of the drugs (D2). The claims against D2 would only be pursued if the claims against D1 failed. Any damages which P might recover against D2 would be consumed by legal aid charges for the costs of the unsuccessful claims against D1. The costs likely to be incurred by D2 were astronomical and the effect of s.17 of the Legal Aid Act 1988 was that, win or lose, they would be irrecoverable. D2 applied to strike out the claims against them on the grounds that they were vexatious and an abuse of process. Kennedy J. granted the application on the grounds that D2's irrecoverable costs were out of all proportion to any benefits which P might obtain from the litigation.

Held, dismissing P's appeal, that (1) the court has an inherent power to strike out proceedings on the grounds that they are vexatious and an abuse of process, where they involve serious injustice to the other party (*Hunter v. Chief Constable of the West Midlands* [1982] C.L.Y. 2382 referred to); (2) in most cases it will be inappropriate for the court to undertake a cost-benefit analysis of the kind entered into by the judge, but here the irrecoverable costs likely to be incurred by D2 were astronomical whereas the benefit to P was at best extremely modest and in all probability nothing. That involved great injustice to D2. The judge was therefore right to strike out the claims against D2 on the grounds that the benefit to P was out of all proportion to the irrecoverable costs of D2 (*Joyce v. Sengupta* [1993] C.L.Y. 3097 considered).

[*Per curiam*: In these appeals the Court was concerned only with group litigation. The question whether, and if so, to what extent, these principles apply to non-group litigation may have to be considered hereafter.]

A.B. v. JOHN WYETH & BROTHER [1994] P.I.Q.R. P109, C.A.

3883. Abuse of process—champerty—statutory exemption of liquidators—whether to be extended—whether action to be stayed on basis of champertous arrangement. See GROVEWOOD v. JAMES CAPEL & CO., §2824.

3884. Abuse of process—declaration of trust—action in relation to equitable interests in land—no equity left in house because of mortgage arrears—whether action an abuse of process—whether amendments for declarations of beneficial interest to be permitted

[C.C.R., Ord. 13, r.5(2).]

T appealed against the striking-out of her claim that she had a beneficial interest in a property in the name of her former cohabitee's girlfriend. T and D occupied a property which was in D's name but financed by pooled resources and, after the parties separated, D discharged the original mortgage and borrowed further sums in relation to the property he shared with his new girlfriend. A deed of trust was made for that property acknowledging D's contribution. This was later revoked and the property declared to be the girlfriend's absolutely. The mortgage fell into arrears and possession was sought. D argued an order for sale was pointless because there was no equity to divide with T as the mortgage arrears exceeded the value of the property. This had led to T's claim being subsequently struck out as an abuse of process. T appealed on the grounds that the court lacked the jurisdiction to strike out, as the procedural formalities in C.C.R., Ord. 13, r.5, had not been complied with, namely that written notice had not been given. She also submitted that it was wrong to dismiss the action at such a late stage in the trial and her counsel now sought to make amendments to the original application for a declaration of a beneficial interest, so that if the appeal was allowed, the case could be remitted to the county court.

Held, allowing the appeal, that (1) the court had the power to waive the requirement for written notice under C.C.R., Ord. 50, r.4, which provided that the court could authorise notice to be given orally and had the power to abridge the usual two-day notice period. No objection had been made against this waiver at the time; (2) the discretion of the judge below in striking out T's claim could not be criticised as it was exercised in relation to control of proceedings; and (3) there was, however a justiciable issue in the proposed amendment seeking a declaration of trust which was worthy of consideration. The matter was to be heard in the county court to proceed on the amendment of pleadings in T's claim.

THOMPSON (DEBORAH ANNE) v. DIXON (GRAHAM) (CCRTI 94/0685/F), February 2, 1995, C.A.

3885. Abuse of process—delay—appeal court ordered retrial of libel case in light of additional evidence—fresh evidence to show that new witness had lied at trial—plaintiff pleading lack of finance to explain delay—whether public interest in discovering truth

G sued the defendant for publishing an article alleging that G had admitted that he had been treated for AIDS. At trial G asserted that he was not a homosexual and therefore it was improbable that he had been treated for AIDS. The jury found in G's favour and on May 18, 1988 awarded him £20,750 damages against N and M. N and M appealed on the ground that they had fresh evidence that would show that G had lied at trial. The Court of Appeal were impressed by the evidence of a witness (H) who claimed that he had had sex with G a number of times and had been told by G that he had AIDS. On May 24, 1989, a retrial was ordered. G did not issue a summons for directions for the retrial until July 13, 1993. N and M had issued a summons to strike out for want of prosecution on April 14, 1992. They argued that G was guilty of inordinate and inexcusable delay between May 24, 1989 and April 14, 1992 which was likely to cause serious prejudice to the defendants. G argued that the delay was due to lack of finance and the fact that he was reasonably involved over a period of time in gathering evidence to rebut M and N's fresh evidence. G appealed against the striking out of his action.

Held, allowing the appeal, that the judge had properly exercised his discretion with respect to G's excuses for delay. G's lack of finance was no excuse. G had in his possession in March 1989 evidence that H had retracted his evidence. He had no justification for delaying as long as he did on grounds that he was awaiting further and better restrictive evidence from H. On the issue of the prejudice caused by the delay the judge had erred in not giving sufficient weight to the public interest in seeing that all parties and their witnesses declare the truth before the court. H was an influential witness who had retracted his evidence, claiming that M and N had bribed him, before going on to retract the retraction. There was a suspicion that there had been a conspiracy by one of the parties to pervert the course of justice in which a solicitor or solicitors were involved. This was an exceptional case where justice demanded that these issues be properly explored at trial.

GILBERTHORPE v. HAWKINS, NEWS GROUP NEWSPAPERS, MIRROR GROUP NEWSPAPERS AND GLOUCESTERSHIRE NEWSPAPERS (QBENI 94/0156/E), March 15, 1995, C.A.

3886. Abuse of process—delay—company directors' disqualification proceedings—whether to be struck out for want of prosecution. See OFFICIAL RECEIVER v. B., §590.

3887. Abuse of process—delay—personal injuries action—whether plaintiff's delay prejudicing defendant in relation to liability

S brought an action for damages for personal injuries sustained in a collision with C's lorry. S had to leave his job as lieutenant in the Royal Navy after failing to make a complete recovery. Both the facts relating to liability and *quantum* were disputed on many points. S issued a writ just short of the limitation period and his solicitors were slow to assemble details relating to damages. His claim for damages was struck out for want of prosecution nearly eight years after the accident, on the ground that his failure to present his claim properly had led to prejudice to C in relation to damages. S appealed.

Held, dismissing the appeal, that (1) there had been a period of inordinate and inexcusable delay on the part of S in conducting his case and the judge was right to strike out the claim due to prejudice; (2) the basis of the decision should not have been prejudice in relation to damages but that the delay caused substantial prejudice to the defendants as to liability. The memory of critical witnesses would continue to fade during the period of delay which would create problems which could seriously prejudice C (*Allen v. McAlpine (Sir Alfred) & Sons; Bostic v. Bermondsey & Southwark Hospital Management Committee; Sternberg v. Hammond* [1968] C.L.Y. 3104, *Gratrix v. Phoenix Walters*, unrep. cited).

SHRIMPTON v. CHEGWYN (QBENI 93/0165/E) (QBENI 93/0165/E), November 8, 1994, C.A.

3888. Abuse of process—delay—want of prosecution—appeal from arbitral award—whether necessary to establish prejudice

[Arbitration Act 1979 (C.42), s.1(3)(b).]

T made an application under s.1(3)(b) of the Arbitration Act 1979 for leave to appeal from an arbitrator's award made in relation to a rent review dispute. The application was made within the 21 days required by R.S.C., Ord. 73, r.5, but, due to a combination of T's dilatoriness, errors in court administration and accommodation of the convenience of counsel, the hearing of the application was delayed for almost 18 months. An application by L to strike out T's proceedings for want of prosecution was granted by the judge.

Held, allowing T's appeal, that (1) the court's inherent power to strike out appeals to the High Court from awards of arbitrators was not limited to cases where the delay occasioned by one party was such as to cause serious prejudice to the other, but was exercisable whenever there had been a failure to conduct and prosecute the appeal with all deliberate speed; (2) it was incumbent on an applicant for leave to appeal under the 1979 Act to use all reasonable endeavours to achieve a hearing as soon as practicable; but (3) it would be unjust in the circumstances, when uncertainties in the law existed and where the delay was partly caused by an administrative error of court staff, to strike out the application (*Birkett v. James* [1977] C.L.Y. 2410 distinguished).

SECRETARY OF STATE FOR THE ENVIRONMENT v. EUSTON CENTRE INVESTMENTS [1994] 3 W.L.R. 1081, C.A.

3889. Abuse of process—delay—want of prosecution—counterclaim—jurisdiction to dismiss counterclaim for want of prosecution—whether claim should be dismissed at same time

The court has the power to dismiss a counterclaim for want of prosecution both under its inherent jurisdiction and under the Rules of the Supreme Court. A counterclaim is treated as if it were an independent action whereby the rules applying to the main action also applied to the counterclaim. It did not automatically follow that the dismissal of the counterclaim for want of prosecution would lead to the dismissal of the claim in the absence of any application by the defendant and in the present case such a course was not appropriate because the claim and counterclaim were separate entities (*Allen v. McAlpine* [1968] C.L.Y. 3104 applied; *Zimmer Orthopaedic v. Zimmer Manufacturing Co.* [1968] C.L.Y. 3114 considered).

OWEN (TRADING AS MAX OWEN ASSOCIATES) v. PUGH [1995] 3 All E.R. 345, Otton J.

3890. Abuse of process—delay—want of prosecution—whether delay inexcusable—expert evidence—whether need to obtain satisfactory explanation

P started a business for the supply of spectacle frames and lenses and as he was not a qualified optician, he had to get prescriptions from other opticians. P ceased trading after 18 months and brought a claim against T for conspiring to injure his business, by delaying the supply of prescriptions and persuading other opticians to do the same. He claimed for loss of profits and issued a writ three years after the cessation of business. There was also delay in pleadings and discovery. The judge dismissed the action for want of prosecution and held that the delay was manifestly inordinate and inexcusable, giving rise to serious prejudice to T. P appealed against the decision that the delay was inexcusable.

Held, dismissing the appeal, that (1) the judge's decision was well within his discretion and he had made no error of principle as to the question of inexcusability; (2) P submitted that the delay was excusable because it was effectively caused by the death of one counsel and the need for expert evidence of forensic accountants by his successor, but it was perfectly obvious from the outset that such expert evidence was necessary if P's claim was to succeed and the claim should have been evaluated at an earlier stage. T had no idea how *quantum* was formulated and a writ should not have been issued until financial advice had been received. The accountants' advice should have been obtained in the initial stages and it was inexcusable for the progress of the action to be delayed and it had given rise to serious prejudice to T (*Trill v. Sacker* [1993] C.L.Y. 3336 cited).

PRIESTNELL v. TRYBUCHOWSKI (QBENI 94/0803/E), September 8, 1994, C.A.

3891. Abuse of process—delay—whether financial prejudice caused

G appealed against an order striking out his personal injury claim for want of prosecution. S sought to show that G's inordinate and inexcusable delay in proceeding with the claim had caused them financial prejudice, but G contended that, before prejudice could be found to exist, S must account for the value to them of retaining the sum which was due to G in damages and which, but for the delay, they would not have had.

Held, allowing the appeal, that S could not prove financial prejudice to a degree necessitating the striking out of G's claim purely by reference to the liabilities caused by the delay (*Hayes v. Bowman* [1989] C.L.Y. 2963 approved as authority for the principle that the prejudice to S had to be set against the benefit they had gained by retaining the sum required to pay G's damages during the delay period).

GAHAN v. SZERELMEY (U.K.), *The Times*, November 16, 1995, C.A.

3892. Abuse of process—interest on damages—proceedings brought solely for payment of interest on agreed damages—summary judgment for agreed sum awarded—whether statutory interest payable

D collided with P in a road traffic accident caused by D's negligence. On

April 5, 1994, P's insurers paid the uninsured losses in full, £1,566·31, having earlier settled the claim for the repairs through a "knock for knock" agreement between the insurers. D's insurers stated that they were not prepared to pay interest on the uninsured losses, as the matter would be settled prior to the issue of proceedings. P did not accept this, and on July 6, 1994 therefore returned D's cheque in settlement. On September 23, 1994, P issued proceedings, in effect solely for the interest. On March 27, 1995, P applied for summary judgment under C.C.R., Ord. 9, r.14, in the sum of £1,566·31, plus interest and costs.

Held, granting summary judgment in respect of the uninsured losses, that interest on damages only falls when proceedings are properly issued. Statutory interest is only payable once the summons has been stamped by the court office. As a payment was made prior to the commencement of proceedings, P was not entitled to any interest. He ought to have accepted the offer and settlement when it was made, and was unreasonable in rejecting D's insurers' cheque. P was not awarded his costs.

A.C. INTERNATIONAL v. HEALTHCARE PRODUCTIONS, June 8, 1995, District Judge Caward, Hitchin County Ct. [*Ex rel.* Prettys Solicitors.]

3893. Abuse of process—issue of warrant for possession—over six years since order for possession made—whether leave required

[C.C.R. 1981, Ord. 26, r.5.]

W was granted a secure tenancy by H council in 1982 but, after she failed to pay rent when due, the council in 1985 obtained an order for possession. This order was suspended on condition that she clear her rent arrears and pay the current rent. W failed, however, to clear the arrears and a warrant for possession was issued in 1986. There followed various applications to stay execution of the order, culminating in the issue by the county court office of a new warrant for possession in May 1994, which was followed by a further warrant in April 1995, which was executed. W applied to set aside the execution, arguing that the warrant was defective because, under C.C.R., Ord. 26, r.5, leave of the court must first be obtained in cases where more than six years had elapsed since the making of the order for possession and the order had not been removed.

Held, allowing the appeal, that the requirement of leave, allowing the court to take into consideration any changed circumstances since the original order, was not just a formality and the issue of a warrant without such leave was an abuse of process.

HACKNEY LONDON BOROUGH COUNCIL v. WHITE, *The Times*, May 17, 1995, C.A.

3894. Abuse of process—litigation of same issue—alleged negligent underwriting of insurance claims—institution of further proceedings for breach of duty—whether abuse of process—whether litigation brought upon same subject matter

BMA appealed against the refusal to strike out B's action as an abuse of process in the course of the Lloyd's litigation concerning the alleged negligent underwriting of insurance claims by members' agents and managing agents. B, a member of the Gooda Walker action group, who had successfully prosecuted their claim, had instituted further proceedings claiming damages for breach of duty with regard to portfolio selection. BMA argued that the new proceedings were contrary to the rule in *Henderson v. Henderson* (1843) 3 Hare 100, which held that when litigation was brought upon the same subject matter the whole case should be brought before the court, not just certain aspects of it.

Held, dismissing the appeal, that it was a rule of public policy that claims should be conducted expeditiously and economically and that a defendant should not be oppressed by a number of actions on the same issue. However, B's new claim was not an abuse of process as it raised a new issue which would not have been decided in previous proceedings and did not cause BMA to suffer any prejudice.

BARROW v. BANKSIDE MEMBERS AGENCY, *The Times*, November 10, 1995, C.A.

3895. Abuse of process—negligent legal advice—pre-trial and trial—solicitor sued on basis of counsel's advice—counsel immune from suit—settlement advised—subsequent deterioration in condition—whether abuse of process to sue solicitor. See LANDALL v. DENNIS FAULKNER & ALSOP, §3703.

3896. Abuse of process—no cause of action—writ issued by bankrupt—whether writ could be validated by subsequent reassignment of causes of action

[R.S.C., Ord. 18, r.19.]

L was adjudged bankrupt, causing a statutory assignment of all causes of action to his trustee. He issued a writ and G applied to strike out the proceedings under R.S.C., Ord. 18, r.19, on the basis that there was no cause of action vested in L at the time of issue. L's action was struck out as being frivolous, vexatious and otherwise an abuse of the court process. L sought leave to appeal.

Held, dismissing the application, that despite a subsequent equitable reassignment of causes of action to L there was no title in L when the writ was issued. His subsequent acquisition of title provided no ground to appeal and it was absurd to issue a writ when no cause of action was vested.

LOUGHRIDGE (THOMAS) v. GO GAS CO. (LTA 94/6607/E) (LTA 94/6607/E), December 1, 1994, C.A.

3897. Abuse of process—overstatement of claim in order to avoid reference to arbitration—whether abuse of process

[C.C.R., Ord. 19, rr.3, 4.]

It is an abuse of process under C.C.R., Ord. 19, rr.3 and 4 for a plaintiff to overstate his claim in order to avoid having the matter automatically referred to arbitration.

A number of employees who were bringing minor personal injuries claims against their employers did not want their cases referred to arbitration, because of the rules relating to costs, the effects these rules would have on trade union assistance, and the chances of their obtaining out of court settlements. The claimants, in an attempt to avoid the automatic reference of their cases to arbitration intentionally overstated the amounts of their claim. The employers argued that this was abuse of process.

Held, that the arbitration procedure is intended to improve access to justice, and the overstating of a claim in order to avoid arbitration will be regarded by the court as an abuse of process.

AFZAL v. FORD MOTOR CO. [1994] 4 All E.R. 720, C.A.

3898. Abuse of process—premature issue of proceedings—inadequate opportunity to settle—whether claim to be struck out

P's solicitors sent a letter before action dated August 15, 1994 to D's insurers notifying of their instructions to pursue a claim against D, arising out of a road traffic accident which occurred on August 5, 1994. This letter asked for confirmation that the insurers would be indemnifying D, it also asked for an admission of liability, concession of interest to be paid on all heads of damage and agreement to pay reasonable costs and disbursements. D's insurers responded quickly by letter of August 18, 1994 and requested, *inter alia*, details of negligence alleged against D and documentary evidence in support of P's claim. By a letter of September 14, 1994 P's solicitors responded giving brief details of negligence and advising that full details of P's claim were at that time being collated. By a letter of October 5, 1994 sent by D's insurance brokers to the insurers, the insurers were provided with a copy of a county court summons issued by P's solicitors on September 29, 1994. At that time the insurers had been provided with no further documentation or details of P's claim. A defence was immediately drawn up by the insurers, admitting negligence but pleading specifically that P had never seen fit to disclose documentation to support her claim. Following signature by the relevant officer of D company, the defence was filed with the court. By a letter of November 14, 1994, P's solicitors finally provided D's insurers with documentation to support P's special damage claim. This was over a month after proceedings had been issued. An application was made to the court for P's claim to be struck out as an abuse of process and/or for a stay of the proceedings until further court order. A costs order was also sought against P.

Held, that P's claim should be struck out as an abuse of process, since no adequate opportunity had been afforded to the insurers to settle the matter. Costs were awarded to the insurers on scale 1 and the matter was certified fit for counsel.

MOUNTFORD v. EVANS GROUP, January 11, 1995; District Judge Reeves; Mold County Ct. [*Ex rel. Hill Dickinson Davis Campbell, Solicitors*].

3899. Abuse of process—premature issue of proceedings—insufficient opportunity for insurers to compromise action—plaintiff's solicitors failure to answer enquiries—whether claim should be struck out

On December 20, 1994, P was involved in a road traffic accident. On January 16, 1995, P's solicitors wrote a letter before action to D. On January 25, 1995, D's insurers wrote to P's solicitors requesting details of P's insurance and VAT status. P's solicitors did not answer that letter. On March 22, 1995, D's insurers, not having received a response to their letter, telephoned P's solicitors, but were unable to speak with the solicitor who was dealing with P's claim, and were informed that their telephone call would be returned the following day. The telephone call was not returned. On May 10, 1995, D's insurers wrote to P's solicitors, querying whether P intended to pursue the claim. P's solicitors did not respond to that letter, and on May 19, 1995, county court proceedings were issued. P's claim was confined to a claim for personal injuries. D's solicitors applied to strike out the proceedings on the basis that they were precipitous, and that D's insurers had not been afforded any or any reasonable opportunity to compromise the claim. The district judge dismissed that application. D's solicitors appealed to the circuit judge.

Held, that (1) the precipitous issue of proceedings was capable of amounting to an abuse of process; (2) on the facts of the case, because D's insurers had never requested details of P's claim, the issue of proceedings was not precipitous and therefore not an abuse of process.

CALVERT v. SHARPLES, September 18, 1995, H.H.J. Holt, Blackpool County Ct. [*Ex rel.* David Kenny, Barrister, 15 Winckley Square, Preston.]

3900. Abuse of process—premature issue of proceedings—no reply received from insurers—whether premature issue of proceedings

P's unattended motor car was involved in a road traffic accident on February 19, 1995. P's son witnessed the incident, and took the details of the van which was responsible. He telephoned D, the company which owned the van, who denied all liability. P instructed solicitors, who wrote a letter before action to D company on April 10, 1995, requesting that they pass the letter to their insurance company. No reply or acknowledgment had been received from either D, or their insurance company, and three weeks later on May 1, 1995, proceedings were issued. D, through their insurance company, filed a defence, denying negligence, on May 15, 1995, and at the same time made an application that P's case be struck out or stayed, on the ground that issue of proceedings had been premature and constituted an abuse of process. The deputy district judge allowed this application on July 27, 1995, and P appealed to the circuit judge.

Held, that it could not be right that P's solicitors could not issue proceedings until they heard from D's insurance company. There was no obligation or duty whatsoever to get in touch with any insurance company unless of course, not uncommonly, P required the protection of the Road Traffic Act 1988, s.152, but that did not affect the issue in this case. As it happened, eight months had passed since the incident, and apparently D had still not provided a statement from their driver. The judge observed that in two of the cases cited by D, the insurance companies had managed to respond within three days and nine days of letters before action. The judge referred to the judgment in *Parkinson & Parkinson v. Maritime Housing Association*, in which it was said "it was the courts' concern to deal with cases speedily and plaintiffs should not be struck out for acting speedily". In the instant case the line of authorities cited by D could not assist, because this was not one of those cases where the defendant could say that if only they had known of the details of the claim, they would have paid up. They had disputed, and continued to dispute, liability. D had personally denied liability, had received a letter before action and had not even acknowledged receipt of it to P's solicitors. Either D themselves, or their insurance company, must have delayed because it was over three weeks between the letter before action, and any acknowledgement, which in fact came first from D's insurance company, on May 2, 1995, by which time proceedings had already been issued. It was important to remember that this was an action against D, and not against the insurance company. P's appeal was allowed, the stay was lifted, and D were ordered to pay the costs below, and of this appeal, on scale 1. The judge noted that this was a case properly limited by P to £1,000, and on the filing of a defence the case was referred to arbitration. All the costs now were the responsibility of D. This was not a case in which there was any abuse by P's solicitors (*Curran v. Curran* [1995] 12 C.L. 428, *Calvert v. Sharples* [1995] 10 C.L. 669, *Parkinson & Parkinson v. Maritime Housing Association* [1995] 11 C.L. 592, *Baker v. Southern Water* [1995] 9 C.L. 397, *Mountford v. Evans Group* [1995] 3 C.L. 416, *Chennels v. Ashton* [1995] 3 C.L. 417, *Cave v. Jones (Warrington)* [1995] 3 C.L. 418, *Cluley v. Viatha* [1994] C.L.Y. 3595, *Bartlett v. Nixon* [1994] C.L.Y. 3594 considered).

GREAVES v. WILLIAM BARKER BUILDING MERCHANTS, October 31, 1995, H.H.J. Morgan, Birkenhead County Ct. [*Ex rel.* Michael J. Pickavance, Barrister.]

3901. Abuse of process—premature issue of proceedings—no reply received from insurers—whether solicitors acted reasonably in issuing proceedings

Following a road traffic accident on November 12, 1994, P solicitors (P being D's daughter) wrote to D's insurance company on February 3, 1995, requesting that they confirm indemnity and admit liability. D's insurance company failed to reply. P's solicitors issued proceedings on February 23, 1995, having heard nothing from the insurance company. D's solicitors issued an application to strike out P's summons, on the basis that P's solicitors had acted unreasonably by the premature issue of proceedings without giving D's solicitors a satisfactory opportunity to settle the claim and that the claim was therefore an abuse of process.

Held, that P's solicitors had acted reasonably, they had corresponded with D's insurance company, and received no reply. P's solicitors waited for three weeks and then issued proceedings. There was no abuse (*Bartlett v. Nixon* [1994] C.L.Y. 3594, *Cluley v. Viatha* [1994] C.L.Y. 3595, *Chennels v. Ashton* [1995] 3 C.L. 417, *Mountford v. Evans Group* [1995] 3 C.L. 416, *Belnavis v. Ali*, unrep. considered).

CURRAN v. CURRAN, May 26, 1995, Deputy District Judge Grosscurth, Birkenhead County Ct.

3902. Abuse of process—premature issue of proceedings—offer in open correspondence—not accepted—whether sufficient opportunity to settle—whether proceedings to be stayed

Following a road traffic accident on December 15, 1994, P's solicitors wrote a letter before action to D on the same day. The letter made it clear that if liability was not admitted, proceedings would be issued. It did not state a time-limit for the admission to be made. On January 10, 1995, D insurers wrote requesting full details of P's claim but not admitting liability. On January 30, P issued proceedings and gave notice to D. On February 6, D wrote making an offer to settle. P's solicitors then warned that they were applying for an assessment of damages. On April 3, D issued their application to stay but did not file any defence. D's solicitors then issued an application to stay the proceedings, and sought costs, on the ground that P had issued proceedings prematurely and not afforded D an opportunity to settle the claim without recourse to litigation.

Held, that P was entitled to issue proceedings. An offer had been made in open correspondence which P had not accepted. D had had time to assess the claim and had still not admitted liability. P's actions could be taken into account when the costs of the action were considered. Any application such as this should be made with expedition.

ENNIS v. COULTON, May 9, 1995, District Judge Berkson, Liverpool County Ct. [*Ex rel.* Kennan, Bell & Co., Solicitors, Merseyside.]

3903. Abuse of process—premature issue of proceedings—whether claim to be struck out

Following a road traffic accident, P's solicitors wrote to D's insurers on October 18, 1994 requesting that they confirm indemnity, admit liability, concede that interest would be paid on all heads of damages and further agree to bear reasonable costs and disbursements. The insurers responded quickly and by a letter of October 27, 1994 wrote to request full details of the negligence alleged together with documentation in support of P's claim. P's solicitors wrote by letter of November 2, 1994, providing a copy of an engineer's report relating to P's vehicle. It later transpired that a county court summons had also been issued that day against D. D's insurers passed the matter to be dealt with by solicitors and an immediate application was lodged to strike out P's claim as an abuse of process or, in the alternative, to stay the proceedings until further court order.

Held, that P's claim would be struck out, as the premature proceedings had been an abuse of process. Costs were awarded against P on scale 1 to be taxed if not agreed and the matter was certified fit for counsel.

CHENNELS v. ASHTON, January 11, 1995; District Judge Reeves; Mold County Ct. [*Ex rel. Hill Dickinson Davis Campbell, Solicitors*].

3904. Abuse of process—premature issue of proceedings—whether insurers given enough time to settle

On April 24, 1995, P2 was involved in a road traffic accident while driving a car owned by her husband, P1. On the same day, Ps' solicitors sent a letter before action to D, and gave notice to D's insurers that proceedings would be issued within seven days, unless it was confirmed whether or not liability was in dispute. Notwithstanding P1's fully comprehensive insurance, D's insurers sent Ps' solicitors details of their claims management scheme by a letter dated May 4, 1995, which contained the phrase "It is not our intention to contest primary liability". Ps' solicitors had no further contact with D's insurance company, and, the appropriate papers having been sent to the court on June 29, 1995, proceedings were issued on July 12, incorporating a claim for P1's lost excess, and P2's personal injuries and loss of earnings. On July 24, D's solicitors sent P's solicitors a fully pleaded defence admitting liability and putting *quantum* in issue. On July 27, 1995, P's solicitors served a list of documents and documentation in support of the various heads of claim. P's statements were sent to D's solicitors on August 23, and on August 25, a hearing date, September 28, was received for the trial of *quantum*. On September 6, D's solicitors issued an application for an order that the action be struck out, or stayed, as abuse of process for being issued too early. In support, D's solicitors cited three cases, *Mountford v. Evans Group*, *Chennels v. Ashton* and *Cave v. Jones (Warrington)*.

Held, the district judge noting that these cases were not binding on her, that there had been correspondence between the insurance company and P's solicitors, and proceedings had not been issued until two months after the letter before action, which had intimated a seven-day period. She held that it was the court's concern to deal with cases speedily, and P should not be struck out for acting speedily. To a certain extent D's solicitors were arguing the matter on the basis of convenience for their insurance company, and the court received such applications from defendants time and time again for their insurance company's benefit. D could have settled the claim in the time available. P were awarded the costs of the application in any event (*Mountford v. Evans Group* [1995] 3 C.L. 416, *Chennels v. Ashton* [1995] 3 C.L. 417, *Cave v. Jones (Warrington)* [1995] 3 C.L. 418 considered).

PARKINSON & PARKINSON v. MARITIME HOUSING ASSOCIATION, September 19, 1995, District Judge Johnson, Birkenhead County Ct. [*Ex rel.* Michael W. Halsall, Solicitors, Merseyside.]

3905. Abuse of process—premature issue of proceedings—whether proceedings to be stayed—whether costs to be ordered

P was involved in a road traffic accident on September 5, 1994. P's solicitors wrote a letter before action to D dated September 20, 1994 and thereafter to D's insurers dated October 27, 1994, advising that they were only instructed to claim for personal injury. By a letter dated November 10, 1994, P's solicitors wrote to D's insurers stating that they awaited offers with regards to the claim within the next 14 days and in the event that an offer was not received within that time period, they proposed proceedings without further recourse. P's solicitors then issued proceedings on November 11, 1994. D's solicitors issued an application to stay the action on the grounds that the proceedings had been issued prematurely, reference being made to P's solicitors' letter dated November 10, 1994. The application asked for the costs of the proceedings, including the costs of the application to be paid by P in any event.

Held, that the court had an inherent jurisdiction to stay proceedings and that the proceedings had been issued prematurely. The proceedings were ordered to be stayed until a further order of the court was made and P was ordered to pay the costs of proceedings to include the costs of the application in any event (*Cluley v. Vaitha* [1994] 7 C.L. 361, *Barlett v. Nixon* [1994] 9 C.L. 338 distinguished).

CAVE v. JONES (WARRINGTON), January 25, 1995; Deputy District Judge Grosscurth; Birkenhead County Ct. [*Ex rel. Hill Dickinson Davis Campbell, Solicitors*].

3906. Abuse of process—premature issue of proceedings—whether sufficient time allowed—whether action abuse of process

P suffered an injury at work on August 22, 1994. P's solicitors sent a letter before action on November 30, 1994. D, in replying, made no admissions. By a letter dated April 6, 1995, D invited P's solicitors to forward medical evidence, and suggested a discussion, although no admissions were made. Proceedings were commenced on April 11, 1995. In their defence, D admitted negligence but put causation, loss and damage in issue. An application was made to the court for P's claim to be struck out as an abuse of process, and/or for a stay of proceedings until further court order, on the grounds that no reasonable opportunity had been afforded to D to settle the case.

Held, dismissing the action, that it was against public policy to prevent a plaintiff bringing his claim within the time-limits and no abuse of process was discernable. This decision is being appealed (*Mountford v. Evans Group* [1995]

3 C.L. 416, *Chennels v. Ashton* [1995] 3 C.L. 417, *Cave v. Jones (Warrington)* [1995] 3 C.L. 418 considered.

BAKER v. SOUTHERN WATER, August 29, 1995, District Judge Samuels, Mayor and City of London County Ct. [*Ex rel.* Christopher Goddard, Barrister, Devereux Chambers, London.]

3907. Abuse of process—public or private law claim—interconnection with BT system—charges and costs—challenge by way of originating summons—whether judicial review matter—whether statutory nature of charges necessarily a public law matter

M, a licensed telecommunications operator, proceeded by way of originating summons against the Director General of Telecommunications (D), contending that, in setting the charges for interconnection with the BT system pursuant to his powers under the agreement, he had misinterpreted the charging and costs structure in the agreement. D and BT argued that any challenge as to how the charges were set was governed by public law and therefore could only be raised by way of judicial review under R.S.C., Ord. 53. The C.A. struck out the summons.

Held, allowing the appeal, that courts must adopt a flexible approach to the precise limits of private law and public law. The overriding question was whether proceedings other than judicial review proceedings amounted to an abuse of process. Although by granting an operator's licence D performed a statutory function, nevertheless his action might lead to disputes that were outside the scope of administrative law. The dispute concerning interconnection charges was a dispute between two operators which in substance was contractual, even though it could also be described as a dispute in licence terms. Procedure by way of originating summons in the commercial court was equally and perhaps more appropriate than procedure by way of judicial review (*Roy v. Kensington and Chelsea and Westminster Family Practitioner Committee* [1992] C.L.Y. 30, *O'Reilly v. Mackman* [1983] C.L.Y. 2603 considered).

MERCURY COMMUNICATIONS v. DIRECTOR GENERAL OF TELECOMMUNICATIONS, *The Times*, February 10, 1995, H.L.

3908. Abuse of process—striking out—circumstances in which striking out not appropriate

[Aus.] An application to strike out should be reserved for the plainest of cases. A strike-out application should not be granted unless the action is so manifestly groundless that it does not warrant argument. Moreover, where there are complex questions of law to be determined, it is as well that the matter go to full trial for one can never be sure whether some piece of evidence might be of great significance in interpreting the facts to which the law is to be applied.

EXECUTOR TRUSTEE AUST. v. PEAT MARWICK HUNGERFORDS [1995] A.L.M.D. 2766, Sup. Ct., S.A.

3909. Abuse of process—ulterior motive—maintenance of action—defamation—whether abuse of process

The facts of the case were extremely complicated and involved the republication of a libel against B and her employer, C, by a rival company. Judgment was given ordering B's action to be struck out as an abuse of process.

Held, that the important issue was the decision to strike out a long drawn out action of this type just before it came to trial. The alleged libel was an extremely serious one and the judge's reasons for striking out the action must be examined. In *Lonrho v. Fayed (No. 5)*, Stuart-Smith J. stated that an action can be struck ouit if it is pursued for ulterior motives. C had shown that they intended to seek the ruin of the rival company and their support of B's action was part of that campaign. The trial judge felt that, although B had a good case, the case was of small value and had been brought for an ulterior motive. C were paying for the action and therefore it was their motives which were relevant. In any case, B must have colluded with C. However, there was no evidence at all to support the latter contention. As for the first point, the fact that a party is motivated by malice could not be taken into account. Such an innovation would result in the court's having to delve into a minefield of confused motives and intentions. Therefore an abuse would only occur if the proceedings themselves were not properly constituted. In this case, even if B could be seen to have the motives of C, this was not a clear and obvious case where the action should be struck out. It must also be understood that champerty was unlawful but maintenance was not (*Lonrho v. Fayed (No. 5)* [1993] C.L.Y. 2580, *Champtaloup v. Thomas* [1976] 2 N.S.W.L.R. 264 considered.)

BROXTON (FIONA) v. McCLELLAND (ARDEN C.) (LTA 95/5065/E), January 31, 1995, C.A.

3910. Adjournment—financial provision application—restoration of case—whether party adverse can restore the case

[R.S.C., Ord. 32, r.4.]

H and W divorced in 1990 after a marriage lasting 20 years. At that time both parties received income support and H faced outstanding liabilities of £500,000, incurred when his property development company foundered in the recession. In 1992 W applied for financial relief and her application was adjourned generally with liberty to restore. H did not appeal at the time but sought leave to restore the application in 1994. That application was refused and H appealed.

Held, dismissing the appeal, that (1) it could not be right that H seek to restore W's application: the restoration of a case was essentially a matter for the person who brought it; (2) although there was no direct authority on the matter the court had regard to R.S.C., Ord. 32, r.4, which provided that if a hearing of a summons was adjourned generally the party by whom the summons was taken out may restore it to the list. There was no suggestion of the party adverse being able to restore the matter and the same principle was to be applied to the application for financial relief.

HAWTHORNE v. HAWTHORNE (LTA 94/6840/F), November 30, 1994, C.A.

3911. Administration—examination and production of documents—*ex parte* application—jurisdiction of court to order examination by U.S. attorney. See MAXWELL COMMUNICATIONS CORP. (NO. 3), *Re*, §2814.

3912. Admissibility—hearsay evidence—application to rectify Trade Mark Register—whether rules of admissibility apply. See ST. TRUDO TRADE MARK, §4947.

3913. Advocates—court dress

The requirements of *Practice Direction (Court Dress)* [1994] 1 W.L.R. 1056 of July 19, 1994 are reaffirmed: Queen's Counsel wear a short wig and silk (or stuff) gown over a court coat; junior counsel wear a short wig and stuff gown with bands; solicitors wear a black stuff gown with bands but no wig.

The direction was made by the Lord Chancellor after consultation with the Heads of Divisions and applies throughout the Supreme Court (including the Crown Court) and in county courts.

PRACTICE DIRECTION (COURT DRESS) (NO. 2) [1995] 1 W.L.R. 6488.

3914. Affidavits—marking of exhibits to affidavits—addition to existing practice direction

The practice direction relating to the marking of exhibits to affidavits, given on July 21, 1993, [1983] 1 W.L.R. 922, is amended by the addition of a new requirement (iv): "the identifying initials and number of each exhibit to the affidavit"; by renumbering requirement (iv) as (v) and adding "EWJ 3, 4 and 5" to the end of the example given.

PRACTICE DIRECTION (SUP.CT.) (EVIDENCE: DOCUMENTS) [1995] 1 W.L.R. 510, Lord Taylor of Gosforth C.J.

3915. Anton Piller order—risk of incrimination—proceedings for infringement of a trade mark or passing off—whether risk of incrimination excuses obligation to comply with order

[Supreme Court Act 1981 (c.54), s.72.]

P applied for the discharge of part of an Anton Piller order which required him to allow the search of his premises and to provide documents and information in an action, in which P was the 16th defendant, for infringement brought by C against a large-scale criminal organisation which produced and sold counterfeit Coca-Cola. P asserted that if he provided the information he would be incriminated in criminal proceedings and expose himself to the risk of violence from other members of the organisation.

Held, dismissing the application, under s.72 of the Supreme Court Act 1981 if an order was made in proceedings for infringement of a trademark or passing off, the risk of incrimination in related proceedings did not excuse a person from being required to comply with the order. Although it was accepted that there was a real risk of physical violence to P, it was not a sufficient ground for discharging the Anton Piller order as his interests were outweighed by those of C, who had a pressing need for the information. Furthermore, the public interest required that a tortfeasor should not be exempted from the obligation to disclose information by pleading risk to himself as it was important that the fraud should be suppressed and the men in the organisation identified.

COCA-COLA CO. v. GILBEY, *The Independent*, October 10, 1995, Lightman J.

3916. Appeal—absence of parties—possession order in respect of mortgage arrears—application for setting aside of order—notice of proceedings—lack of prospect of success

[C.C.R., Ord. 37, r.2.]

A appealed against the refusal to set aside a judgment given against him whereby a possession order was granted in respect of his mortgage arrears. He had applied under C.C.R., Ord. 37, r.2, to have the order set aside on the grounds that he did not have notice of the proceedings and was absent throughout.

Held, dismissing the appeal, that although A had missed the commencement of proceedings through no fault of his own, his absence continued after he had become aware of proceedings and he had made no attempt to apply for a rehearing. He had ignored an opportunity to be heard and had no explanation for his staying away and his absence was therefore deliberate. Furthermore, a retrial would involve a rehearing of matters of fact which had already been investigated and would prejudice the mortgagee who could not be protected against the financial consequences if the judgment was set aside. The court was entitled to take into account the fact that A's defence lacked any real prospect of success (*Shocked v. Goldschmidt* [1994] C.L.Y. 1023 applied).

NATIONAL COUNTIES BUILDING SOCIETY v. ANTONELLI, *The Independent*, November 30, 1995, C.A.

3917. Appeal—case stated—whether certain questions to be added to case stated

[R.S.C., Ord. 61, rr.3, 4.]

Where a question was identified, and potentially arguable and relevant, it should be included in the case stated.

The compensating authority sought to appeal from a decision of the tribunal. In the preparation of the case stated the tribunal refused to accede to a request from the authority that certain questions be included in the case stated for the Court of Appeal.

Held, that if the questions were identified and potentially arguable and relevant they should be included in the case stated. In this matter they should be included, but the whole case would have to be remitted to the tribunal since when the appeal came to be heard it would be necessary for the Court of Appeal to know what was the evidence and what findings on it had been made in connection with the issues which would now be included in the case stated (*Stokes v. Cambridge Corp.* [1962] C.L.Y. 402, *Pointe Gourde Quarrying and Transport v. Subintendent of Crown Lands* [1947] A.C. 565, *Tersons v. Stevenage Development Corp.* [1964] C.L.Y. 125 considered).

OZANNE v. HERTFORDSHIRE COUNTY COUNCIL [1995] 35 RVR 40, C.A.

3918. Appeal—costs—interest—whether interest may be awarded on costs for periods prior to or following a direction to pay costs. See BROADWAY VIDEO (WHOLESALE) v. CUSTOMS AND EXCISE COMMISSIONERS, §5010.

3919. Appeal—costs—relating solely to costs—patent infringement action—whether court having jurisdiction to hear the appeal

[Supreme Court Act 1981 (c.54), s.18(1)(f).]

The service of a notice limited to an appeal to the Court of Appeal on the question of costs falls foul of s.18(1)(f) of the Supreme Court Act 1981.

P brought proceedings in the Patents County Court against D for misuse of confidential information and patent infringement. At the end of the hearing, but before judgment was given, submissions on the question of costs were made. At that time the judge made it clear that the parties could come back and make applications relating to costs. Subsequently the judge delivered a written judgment with P winning on the issue of breach of confidential information but losing on the issue of infringement. The judge made no order as to costs. The judgment and the proposed order were sent to both parties under the cover of a letter which invited comments on the proposed order. P made no further representations but D made further submissions as to costs. The court replied to both parties that the judge had considered the order further but had made no amendments. Following that order D appealed, challenging various of the judge's decisions, including the decision as to costs. By way of reply to that notice P gave a notice challenging solely the judge's decision on costs. The issue before the Court of Appeal was whether by serving a notice limited to the question of costs P fell foul of s.18(1)(f) of the Supreme Court Act 1981, which denies the Court of Appeal jurisdiction to hear an appeal relating solely to costs.

Held, dismissing P's application that (1) there was no material upon which the judge could be said to have either failed to exercise a discretion or to have failed to exercise it judicially (*Scherer v. Counting Instruments* [1986] C.L.Y. 2572 referred to); (2) P had no grounds upon which he could circumvent the clear language of s.18(1)(f).

[*Per curiam*: If the circumstances had been such as to deny the plaintiff a fair opportunity to make his submissions on costs in knowledge of what the final outcome of the hearing was then the case would have fallen into the category of cases in which the court had jurisdiction to hear an appeal on costs. If this procedure as to the making of submissions on costs is continued it should be made clear to the parties that they have a full right to be heard to make representations on the issue of costs. Further, an indication should be given in the written judgment as to why no costs order was considered appropriate.]

PROUT v. BRITISH GAS [1994] F.S.R. 160, C.A.

3920. Appeal—expedition—whether inhibition of development as creative artist relevant

P, known professionally as George Michael, sought expedition of the hearing of an appeal against the finding that his recording contract with S was not a restraint of trade breaching Art. 85 of the Treaty of Rome 1957 and that P was bound by it. P contended that his development as a creative artist was inhibited so long as the litigation remained unresolved and suggested that his career was blighted by enforced inactivity.

Held, dismissing the application, that (1) a number of guidelines have been laid down with regard to expedition applications and grounds which would allow expedition included where a party might lose his livelihood, business or home or suffer irreparable loss or hardship. Other situations may include cases where an appeal would otherwise become futile or where there would be serious detriment to public administration or public interest (*Unilever v. Chefaro Proprietaries* [1995] 2 C.L. 235 followed); (2) P's application came nowhere near satisfying the criteria which the court required before it would grant expedition. The effect of expediting an appeal would be to cause postponement or cancellation of other fixtures from the list and in the present case it would be unthinkable to impose those consequences on other litigants.

PANAYIOUTOU (GEORGIOS) v. SONY MUSIC ENTERTAINMENT (U.K.) (FC3 94/7090/B), January 12, 1995, C.A.

3921. Appeal—family proceedings—duty of legal advisers—merits of case. See N. (MINORS) (RESIDENCE), *Re*, §3509.

3922. Appeal—fresh evidence—personal injury action—fresh evidence suggesting fabrication of evidence by plaintiff—grounds upon which fresh evidence will be admitted before the Court of Appeal

[R.S.C., Ord. 59, r.10(2).]

Fresh evidence suggesting fabrication of evidence by the plaintiff at trial will be admitted before the Court of Appeal on "special grounds" where the evidence became available by chance, is highly relevant and is apparently credible.

P claimed damages for personal injuries from his employer, D. At the trial of the action, P gave evidence that he had sustained the injuries in the course of his employment when he slipped descending from a mechanical digger which had a step missing. D was held liable and damages were ordered to be assessed. After the trial, D pursued third party proceedings against DC, the firm which owned the machine and said to be responsible for all repairs to it. DC informed D that one its employees, C, who was previously unaware of the proceedings, recalled a conversation during which P stated that he sustained the injuries whilst canoeing and that he was going to fabricate a claim against D. Fifteen months after the trial, D was allowed to appeal out of time against the judgment and applied to adduce C's new evidence.

Held, allowing the appeal and ordering a retrial, that (1) fresh evidence will be admitted before the Court of Appeal where "special grounds" exist. This requires three conditions to be satisfied. First, that the fresh evidence could not have been obtained with reasonable diligence for use at trial; second, that the evidence, if given, would probably have an important influence on the result of the case, though it need not be decisive; and third, that the evidence must be apparently credible, though it need not be incontrovertible (*Ladd v. Marshall* [1954] C.L.Y. 2507 applied); (2) in the instant case, these conditions were satisfied because the fresh evidence had only become available through chance, it would plainly be significant or highly relevant at trial and, on the face of it, C's evidence was credible, although it was plainly not incontrovertible. The only satisfactory way in which the evidence should be received was on a retrial, where C's evidence could be subjected to cross-examination; and (3) (*per* Staughton L.J.) delay is not mentioned as part of the *Ladd v. Marshall* test but it is obviously relevant. Here, the delay was insufficient to mean that the fresh evidence should be rejected.

LATTIMER v. CUMBRIA COUNTY COUNCIL [1994] P.I.Q.R. P395, C.A.

3923. Appeal—inadmissible petitions—contempt of court—cause titles—practice direction

The following practice direction was issued by the Clerk of the Parliaments on February 13, 1995. The following amendments to the Practice Directions applicable to Civil Appeals (the Blue Book) and the Practice Directions applicable to Criminal Appeals (the Red Book) have been agreed with effect from the date of this notice.

Inadmissible petitions

Blue Book, after direction 1.4, insert the following new direction: *"Admissibility of petitions*

"Petitions are not admissible for presentation if they fall into one of the following categories: (a) petitions for leave to appeal to the House of Lords from a refusal by the Court of Appeal to grant leave to appeal to that court from a judgment of a lower court, or from any other preliminary decision of the Court of Appeal in respect of a case in which leave to appeal to the Court of Appeal was not granted; (b) petitions for leave to appeal to the House of Lords against a refusal by the Court of Appeal or a Divisional Court of the Queen's Bench Division to grant an *ex parte* application for leave to apply for judicial review under R.S.C., Ord. 53; (c) petitions for leave to appeal to the House of Lords barred by para. 13(4) of Sched. 11, or by para. 7(4) of Sched. 22, to the Housing Act 1985; (d) petitions for leave to appeal to the House of Lords brought by a petitioner in respect of whom the High Court has made an order under s.42 of the Supreme Court Act 1981 (restriction of vexatious proceedings) unless leave to present such a petition has been granted by the High Court or a judge thereof pursuant to that section; (e) petitions for leave to appeal from a decision of the Court of Appeal on any appeal from a county court in any probate proceedings; (f) petitions for leave to appeal from a decision of the Court of Appeal on an appeal from a decision of the High Court on a question of law under Pt. III of the Representation of the People Act 1983. Inadmissible petitions will not be accepted for presentation to the House. Where there is doubt as to the admissibility of a petition, it may, at the direction of the Principal Clerk, be accepted for presentation to the House so that its admissibility may be decided by an Appeal Committee."

Blue Book, direction 4.5, omit the entire direction.

Blue Book, direction 4.6, at the beginning insert:

"Where appropriate, the Appeal Committee will first consider whether a petition is admissible."

Contempt of court

Red Book, direction 1.1, at the end, insert:

"In cases involving criminal contempt of court, an appeal lies to the House of Lords at the instance of the defendant and, in respect of an application for committal or attachment, at the instance of the applicant from any decision of the Court of Appeal (Criminal Division), the Courts Martial Appeal Court or a Divisional Court of the Queen's Bench Division."

Red Book, direction 2.3, now reads: "A certificate is not required in contempt of court cases where the decision of the court below was not a decision on appeal."

Blue Book, after direction 1.4, insert the following new direction:

"Contempt of court cases

"In cases involving civil contempt of court, an appeal may be brought under s.13 of the Administration of Justice Act 1960. Leave to appeal is required and an application for such leave must first be made to the court below. If that application is refused, a petition for leave to appeal may be presented to the House of Lords. Where the decision of the court below is a decision on appeal under the same section of the same Act, leave to appeal to the House of Lords will only be granted if the court below certifies that a point of law of general public importance is involved in that decision and if it appears to that court or to the House, as the case may be, that the point is one that ought to be considered by the House. Where the court below refuses to grant the certificate required, a petition for leave to appeal will not be accepted for presentation to the House."

Blue Book, after direction 2.1, insert the following new direction:

"A petition for leave to appeal in a case involving civil contempt of court must be lodged in the Judicial Office within 14 days beginning from the date of the refusal of such leave by the court below. The application to the court must itself be made within 14 days beginning from the date of the decision of that court from which leave to appeal is sought."

Cause titles

Blue Book, direction 3.3, at the end, insert:

"The names of the parties to the original action who are not parties to the petition to the House should still be included in the title and the names of all parties should be given in the same order as in the title used in the court below."

Blue Book, direction 3.3, and Red Book, direction 5.4 (omitting the sentence in brackets), at the end, insert:

"In any petition concerning minors or where in the courts below the title used has been such as to conceal the identity of one or more parties to the action, this fact should be clearly drawn to the attention of the Judicial Office at the time the petition is lodged, so that the title adopted in the House of Lords may take due account of the need to protect the identity of the minors or parties in question. (Petitions involving minors are normally given a title of the form *In re X*, where X is the initial letter of the child's surname.)"

Blue Book, direction 10.3, at the end, insert:

"The names of the parties to the original action who are not parties to the appeal to the House should still be included in the title and the names of all parties should be given in the same order as in the title used in the court below."

Blue Book, after direction 10.3, and Red Book, after direction 12.3 (omitting the sentence in brackets), insert the following new direction:

"Appeals involving minors

"In any appeal concerning minors or where in the courts below the title used has been such as to conceal the identity of one or more parties to the action, this fact should be clearly drawn to the attention of the Judicial Office at the time the appeal is lodged, so that the title adopted in the House of Lords may take due account of the need to protect the identity of the minors or parties in question. (Appeals involving minors are normally given a title of the form *In re X*, where X is the initial letter of the child's surname.)

"In any appeal concerning minors, parties should also consider whether it would be appropriate for the House to make an order under s.39 of the Children and Young Persons Act 1933 and should, in any event, inform the Judicial Office if such an order has been made by a court below. A request for such an order should be made in writing, preferably on behalf of the parties to the appeal, as soon as possible after the appeal has been presented and not later than two weeks before the commencement of the hearing."

PRACTICE DIRECTION (H.L.) (AMENDMENTS TO PROCEDURE) [1995] 1 W.L.R. 422, H.L.

3924. Appeal—leave to appeal—action involving land—dispute as to whether a lease granted to plaintiff—whether action for possession of land—whether leave to appeal required—test to be applied

[County Court Appeals Order 1991 (S.I. 1991 No. 1877); C.C.R., Ord. 59, r.1(b).]

M entered into negotiations with N regarding the lease of a flat. A dispute arose as to whether or not N had agreed to grant a lease of the flat to M. M claimed that he was entitled to possession of the premises pursuant to the terms of a written or oral agreement with N and asked for an order for specific performance of this contract. N argued that any discussions had been subject to contract and there had never been any concluded legal agreement. The trial judge decided that all negotiations had been subject to contract and an order was made dismissing M's action. M served a notice of appeal repeating his claims in the action and the question arose as to whether leave to appeal was required.

Held, that leave to appeal was required. Under C.C.R., Ord. 59, r.1(b), leave to appeal is required for "(d) orders which include the giving or refusing of possession of land". The correct approach was to look at the face of the proceedings to see whether or not they included the giving or refusing of possession of land. It was not appropriate to analyse or investigate the precise issues raised at the trial. Furthermore, it was relevant to look at the notice of appeal to see what the appellant was asking for from the Court of Appeal. On the face of the proceedings the case came within Ord. 59, r.1(b) and leave to appeal was required.

MOLAVA v. RAHIM, April 10, 1995, C.A.

3925. Appeal—leave to appeal—challenge to grant of leave—strict test

Since the requirement of leave to appeal served as a filter mechanism, saving both time and expense, applications to the full Court of Appeal to set aside the grant of leave must satisfy the strict test laid down in *Iran Nabuvat, The* [1990] C.L.Y. 3735. Thus, an applicant seeking to challenge the grant of leave must show either that there were facts not revealed to the single Lord Justice hearing the application for leave or that a statutory provision or legal authority had been overlooked. In the absence of such elements, the granting of leave should be deemed conclusive. To allow a lesser threshold would run the risk of undermining the purpose of the requirement of leave.

FIRST TOKYO INDEX TRUST v. MORGAN STANLEY TRUST CO., *The Times*, October 6, 1995, C.A.

3926. Appeal—leave to appeal—from Official Referee on a question of fact—principles upon which leave will be granted by the Court of Appeal

Disputes arose over the terms of a property sale contract between companies in the Virgin group and a third-party purchaser. The Virgin companies sought to sue their solicitors and their surveyors. The matter was heard by the Official Referee. The parties sought to appeal to the Court of Appeal on matters of fact.

Held, granting the leave to appeal, that the test for grant of leave to appeal to the Court of Appeal from an Official Referee on questions of fact should be whether the ground of appeal which it is sought to argue has a reasonable prospect of success. All three parties' appeals on the specific factual issues passed the applicable test on these facts (*Iran Nabuvat, The* [1990] C.L.Y. 3735, *Hoskisson v. Moodie Homes* [1990] C.L.Y. 3730, *Decon Engineering Co v. James Howden & Co.* [1993] C.L.Y. 3112 considered).

VIRGIN GROUP v. DE MORGAN GROUP [1994] 10 Const. L.J. 247, C.A.

3927. Appeal—leave to appeal—negligence action—judicial decision-making—whether specified issues to be tried in advance—trial judge's powers

T applied for leave to appeal against Lightman J.'s decision to order that specified issues raised in a negligence action brought by T against the second defendant should be tried in advance of the trial of other issues between the parties. The judge had concluded that, if such issues were tried first and decided against T, the action as a whole must fail and further costs would be avoided.

Held, granting leave to appeal and dismissing the appeal, that it was appropriate that leave should be granted because, although the issue was on one level a simple matter of procedural practice, it raised the issue of the way in which the Court of Appeal should approach the trial judge's exercise of his powers. This type of decision certainly fell within the procedural decision making ambit of the judge and the Court of Appeal would be reluctant to interfere unless the trial judge had erred in his decision. No ground existed to interfere with the decision in the instant case as it was an appropriate order to make and all relevant factors had been considered.

THERMAWEAR v. LINTON, *The Times*, October 20, 1995, C.A.

3928. Appeal—leave to appeal—practice and procedure—unreasonable exercise of discretion—whether leave to appeal justified

[Aus.] A manifestly unreasonable exercise of discretion by a primary judge, even in a matter of practice and procedure, is sufficient to attract leave to appeal and to authorise the Court of Appeal to set aside the order under appeal, redetermine the matter itself or remit it to the primary forum for reconsideration.

GARRARD (t/a ARTHUR ANDERSON & CO.) v. EMAIL FURNITURE PTY. [1994] A.L.M.D. 3805, Sup. Ct., NSW.

3929. Appeal—new issues of fact and law raised by court after close of argument—*force majeure*—whether duty to allow submissions on propriety of considering new issues

[H.K.] Where the court seeks to introduce a new legal issue on appeal, it should ensure that the parties have an opportunity to deal with it, in accordance with the principles which apply if a party wishes to raise a new point.

The sellers agreed to sell a quantity of cotton seed expellers, originating in the Henan province of China, to the buyers. The contract contained a *force majeure* clause providing that the sellers had to furnish the buyers with a certificate attesting any such event. The sellers did not deliver the whole contract quantity and sought to rely on the *force majeure* clause. They provided a certificate from the appropriate trade council stating that there had been drought in Henan with heavy losses and reduction of cotton. The buyers denied that the *force majeure* clause applied to the facts of the case, or that the certificate issued complied with the terms of the contract. At trial the deputy judge gave judgment for the sellers holding that there was an oral collateral contract that the goods would originate in Henan, that the sellers' failure to deliver the full amount of goods was due to a cause beyond their control within the meaning of the *force majeure* clause and that the certificate complied with the requirements of the clause. On the buyers' appeal, the Court of Appeal of Hong Kong held that the certificate tendered by the sellers was insufficient for the purposes of the *force majeure* clause. Additionally, and without the issue having been raised or argued by either party, the Court held that, at the time of contracting, the sellers had known of the risk that the buyers would not receive the goods due to *force majeure* and that, in such circumstances, the clause was not in law effective to excuse the under-delivery.

Held, allowing the appeal, that (1) the principles which inhibited parties from raising new points on appeal applied equally where it was the court which sought to introduce the new legal issue and that before taking a new matter into account, the court should ensure that the parties were given an opportunity to deal with it; (2) on the rare occasions when an appellate court found it proper to consider introducing an entirely new question of law and fact the first step was to have the propriety of doing so thoroughly explored by adversarial means; (3) accordingly, the question of the sellers' knowledge of possible *force majeure* conditions should not have been taken into account nor formed a ground of decision (*Owners and Freight Owners of the Tasmania v. Smith* (1890) 15 App.Cas. 223, *Esso Petroleum Co. v. Southport Corporation* [1956] C.L.Y. 6056 applied); and (4) since the requirement in the *force majeure* clause for a certificate was additional to the onus on the sellers to prove by evidence each of the requirements of the clause, the *force majeure* clause was to be construed as requiring the certificate to attest only as to the existence of the *force majeure* event.

HOECHEONG PRODUCTS CO. v. CARGILL HONG KONG [1995] 1 W.L.R. 404, P.C.

3930. Appeal—point not taken below—possibility of further evidence—whether possible to speculate on course of conduct at trial

[Aus.] It is always difficult for counsel, and almost impossible for judges, to say with any certainty how a case would have been conducted if a point not relied on below had been taken at the original hearing. The court must pay great attention to what counsel say about the matter.

WINGATE MARKETING PTY. v. LEVI STRAUSS & CO. [1994] A.L.M.D. 3809, Fed. Ct. of Aus.

3931. Appeal—proper law issues—interval between consideration of questions of proper law and factual issues—whether 28 days sufficient—whether appeal to House of Lords on proper law likely

M brought an action to recover 10.6 million shares or their value from parties with whom those shares had been lodged as security. An issue before the trial judge was whether the defendants were on notice of the title claim by M when the shares were lodged with them. This involved issues of fact, but also of law as to whether the law of England or the law of New York applied. The judge held that the law of New York applied, thus imposing less stringent obligations on the defendants. M appealed and directions were subsequently given that the proper law issues would be heard first and would be followed 28 days after the close of arguments with the factual issues. All parties agreed that the proper law issues needed to be heard first but challenged the order on the grounds that the 28-day interval was too short to prepare for such a considerable undertaking, and in the light of the fact that there might be an appeal to the House of Lords on the proper law issue.

Held, varying the order to the extent of removing the provision that the factual issues should follow 28 days after the close of arguments in relation to the proper law appeal, that considering the unusual nature of the case, the eventuality of an appeal to the House of Lords on the proper law issues should be considered. The amount of preparation for a hearing of the factual issues should not be underestimated.

MACMILLAN v. BISHOPSGATE INVESTMENT TRUST (FC3 95/5832/B; FC3 95/5833/B; FC3 95/5834/B), May 22, 1995, C.A.

3932. Appeal—time-limit—application for extension of time—no reason given for delay—whether discretion should be exercised

[R.S.C., Ord. 58, rr.1, 3.]

Where the applicant placed no material before the court to explain why there had been a delay in seeking to appeal, there was no material upon which the court could exercise its discretion and, accordingly, an application for an extension of time would inevitably fail (*Ratnam v. Cumarasamy* [1965] C.L.Y. 3066 approved; *Revici v. Prentice Hall* [1969] C.L.Y. 2782, *Costellow v. Somerset County Council* [1993] C.L.Y. 3338, *Regalbourne v. East Lindsey District Council* [1994] 12 C.L. 738 considered).

SAVILL v. SOUTHEND HEALTH AUTHORITY, *The Times*, December 28, 1994, C.A.

3933. Appeal—time-limit—extension—leave to appeal out of time—factors to be taken into account

[R.S.C., Ord. 10, r.1(2)(3); Ord. 3, r.5.]

It is in the discretion of the court to grant or refuse an extension of time in which to appeal, but in exercising the discretion certain factors will usually be taken into account and it is wrong to ignore the fact that the delay was short and caused no prejudice whatsoever to the respondent.

P obtained a default judgment against D1 for damages for personal injuries sustained in a road accident. D2, who was obliged to meet any unsatisfied judgment obtained by P against D1, applied to have the judgment set aside on grounds of irregularity. The judgment was set aside on August 31, 1993. P had seven days in which to appeal. Her solicitor, S, returned from holiday on September 6 and sent instructions to counsel on September 9. Unknown to S, counsel was on holiday until September 27. On his return, counsel sent a draft notice of appeal on September 28 to S, who applied that day for leave to appeal out of time. The judge refused the application, referring to remarks of Lord Denning M.R. in *Revici v. Prentice Hall*. The judge was not referred to the decision in *Costellow v. Somerset County Council*, in which the Court of Appeal gave guidance on the exercise of the discretion to extend time.

Held, allowing P's appeal against the refusal to extend time, that (1) the factors which the court will usually take into account when deciding whether to grant an extension of time for an appeal are: (a) the length of the delay, (b) the reasons for the delay, (c) the chances of the appeal succeeding if an extension of time for appealing is allowed, and (d) the degree of prejudice to the potential respondent if the application is granted; (2) in the instant case, the judge was misled by the dicta in *Revici* and had adopted an over-strict approach which was out of line with the *Costellow* guidelines. He had erred in the exercise of his discretion; and (3) exercising the discretion afresh in the light of the four factors mentioned and the *Costellow* guidelines, the appeal would be allowed and leave to appeal out of time granted. The period of delay was only three weeks; although S's delay did not absolve him of criticism, it occurred during the long vacation, his mistake was genuine and he acted promptly once he was aware of it; P had a reasonably arguable case on an appeal and there was no prejudice to D2. The fact that P could sue S, her legal adviser, in negligence was a relevant but not necessarily a determinative factor (*Costellow v. Somerset County Council* [1993] C.L.Y. 3338, *Revici v. Prentice Hall* [1969] C.L.Y. 2782 considered).

WOODHOUSE v. MCDONALD YOUNG AND THE MOTOR INSURERS' BUREAU [1994] P.I.Q.R. P446, C.A.

3934. Appeal—time-limit—extension—service of county court summons—failure of court to serve summons in time—plaintiff incorrectly informed by court that summons served—whether there is a discretion to extend time—whether strong reasons against exercise of discretion

[C.C.R., Ord. 13, r.4; Ord. 37, r.5.]

Where the failure to serve a county court summons within the period required for service is due entirely to the fault of the court, there is discretion to extend the period for service under C.C.R., Ord. 13, r.4 and Ord. 37, r.5 and there must be strong reasons before the court will refuse to exercise the discretion in the applicant's favour.

Three days before the expiry of the limitation period for P's personal injury action, his solicitors, S, issued a summons on his behalf in the county court. The court was obliged to effect service of the summons but failed to do so. A month later, S telephoned the court and were told, incorrectly, that the summons had been served. Default judgment was entered against D some months later. Shortly after, D became aware of the proceedings and indicated that the summons had never been served. P was granted an extension of the period for service and duly served the summons. On D's application, the district judge set aside the service. P's appeal was dismissed.

Held, allowing P's appeal, that (1) in exceptional circumstances and where the interests of justice so require, the court has discretion to extend the period for service of a county court summons under C.C.R., Ord. 13, r.4, and Ord. 37, r.5; (2) before the court will exercise the discretion by extending the period for service, the applicant had to show that there was a good reason for such an extension and provide a satisfactory explanation for the failure to apply during the period of the original validity; (3) in the instant case the judge had erred in refusing to entertain P's application by not attaching any real significance to the fact that the failure to serve in due time was entirely the fault of the court and that it was not unreasonable for S to assume service had been duly effected. No criticism could be made of S and apart from being deprived of a limitation defence, which was not decisive, there was no other prejudice to D; and (4) exercising the discretion afresh, the court's error provided good reason for an extension and a satisfactory explanation for failure to apply during the period of the original validity. Where the failure to satisfy the period for service was entirely the court's fault, some strong reason would have to be shown before an extension of the period would be refused (*Singh v. Dupont Harper Foundries* [1994] 1 W.L.R. 769, *Ward-Lee v. Linehan* [1993] C.L.Y. 3311 applied; *Barr v. Barr* [1994] P.I.Q.R. 45 considered).

KELLIHER v. E.H. SAVILL ENGINEERING [1994] P.I.Q.R. P387, C.A.

3935. Appeal—time-limit—extension of time for appeal—Community law point bringing earlier decision into question—whether time-limits to apply to appeal against earlier decision. See SETIYA v. EAST YORKSHIRE HEALTH AUTHORITY, §1987

3936. Appeal—trustee unwilling to pursue litigation—whether bankrupt competent to pursue—legal representation—bankrupt's father—whether bankrupt could represent him. See DIXON v. WORDSWORTH (FC3 92/5594/E; LTA 92/6461/C), §419.

3937. Assignment of action—unliquidated damages claims in tort and contract—non-personal actions—whether assignment contrary to public policy

[Aus.] Provided the action is not of a personal nature and that the assignee has a genuine commercial interest, both an action for unliquidated damages in tort and an action for unliquidated damages for breach of contract are capable of assignment and the assignment will not be contrary to public policy. Nor will the assignment offend either the law of maintenance or champerty.

SOUTH AUSTRALIAN MANAGEMENT CORP. v. SHEAHAN [1995] A.L.M.D. 3577, Sup. Ct., S.A.

3938. Bias—allegation of judicial bias—test to be applied—"reasonable man"

The trial judge hearing a trial had previously acted for one of the defendants in unrelated proceedings. This was brought to the parties' attention at the outset and no objections were made. A week into the trial the defendant objected to the judge and sought his replacement, alleging bias against the defendant by the judge. The judge refused the application that he should retire from the case.

Held, dismissing the application for leave to appeal, that the defendant's earlier failure to object to the judge was relevant. It was for the court to determine what a reasonable man would think looking at what the judge had done (*Vakauta v. Kelly* [1988] 13 NSWLR 502 applied).

ARAB MONETARY FUND v. HASHIM (1994) 6 Admin L.R. 348, C.A.

3939. Care proceedings—disclosure—medical reports—privilege—whether legal professional privilege attached to a report ordered to be filed with the court. See L. (MINORS: DISCLOSURE OF REPORTS), *Re*, §3414.

3940. Case management—Chancery Division—procedure—practice direction

The following Practice Direction was issued by Sir Richard Scott, V.-C. on April 25, 1995:

1. The provisions of the Chancery Guide shall apply to litigation in the Chancery Division of the High Court of Justice.

2. In the case of any inconsistency between the provisions of the Chancery Guide and the provisions of any previous direction (including *Practice Direction (Civil Litigation: Case Management)* [1995] 1 W.L.R. 508) the provisions of the Chancery Guide shall prevail.

3. The provisions of the Chancery Guide are subject to any subsequent practice direction that may be made.

PRACTICE DIRECTION (CH.D.) (PROCEDURE AND CASE MANAGEMENT) [1995] 1 W.L.R. 785, Sir Richard Scott, V.-C.

3941. Case management—importance of reducing costs and delay—moves to speed up civil litigation

Failure by practitioners to conduct cases economically will result in appropriate orders for costs, including wasted costs orders.

The court will exercise its discretion to limit discovery, the length of oral submissions, the time allowed for the examination and cross-examination of witnesses, the issues on which it wishes to be addressed and reading allowed from documents and authorities.

Unless otherwise ordered, witness statements shall stand as witness in chief.

Facts, not evidence, are to be pleaded, in accordance with R.S.C., Ord. 18, r.7. In advance of trial, parties should use their best endeavours to decide which are the best issues and it is their duty to reduce the amount of expert evidence.

R.S.C., Ord. 34, r.10(2)(a) to (c) with reference to the trial bundle will be strictly enforced.

In cases estimated to last for more than 10 days, a pre-trial review should be applied for or in default may be appointed by the court. It should be conducted between eight and four weeks before the trial by the trial judge and should be attended by the advocates who will conduct the trial.

A completed check-list in the form set out in the Practice Direction must be lodged with the court two months before the trial.

A skeleton argument must be lodged with the court three days before the trial, concisely summarising each party's submissions in relation to each of the issues and citing the main authorities.

The opening speech should be succinct.

This direction applies to all lists in the Queen's Bench and Chancery Divisions.

PRACTICE NOTE (D.C.) (CIVIL LITIGATION, CASE MANAGEMENT) [1995] 1 All E.R. 385.

3942. Case management—pre-trial checklist—practice direction

The Lord Chief Justice has issued a Practice Direction on behalf of the Senior Master, Queen's Bench Division. The following pre-trial checklist form shall be added to the Queen's Bench Masters' Practice Forms.

No. PF77

Pre-Trial Check List Form

[SHORT TITLE AND NUMBER OF ACTION]

DATE OF TRIAL:

PARTY LODGING CHECKLIST:

NAME OF SOLICITOR:

NAME(S) OF COUNSEL FOR TRIAL (if known):

SETTING DOWN

1. Has the Action been set down?

PLEADINGS

2. (a) Do you intend to make any amendment to your pleading?

(b) If so, when?

INTERROGATORIES

3. (a) Are any interrogatories outstanding?
(b) If so, when served and upon whom?
EVIDENCE
4. (a) Have all orders in relations to expert, factual and hearsay evidence been complied with? If not, specify what remains outstanding.
(b) Do you intend to serve/seek leave to serve any further report or statement? If so, when and what report or statement?
(c) Have all other orders in relation to oral evidence been complied with?
(d) Do you require any further leave or orders in relation to evidence? If so, please specify and say when you will apply.
5. (a) What witnesses of fact do you intend to call? [LIST NAMES]
(b) What expert witnesses do you intend to call? [LIST NAMES]
(c) Will any witness require any interpreter? If so, which?
DOCUMENTS
6. (a) Have all orders in relation to discovery been complied with?
(b) If not, what orders are outstanding?
(c) Do you intend to apply for any further orders relating to discovery?
(d) If so, what and when?
7. Will you not later than seven days before trial have prepared agreed paginated bundles of fully legible documents for the use of counsel and the Court?
PRE-TRIAL REVIEW
8. (a) Has a pre-trial review been ordered?
(b) If so, when is it to take place?
(c) If not, would it be useful to have one?
LENGTH OF TRIAL
9. What are counsels' estimates of the minimum and maximum lengths of the trial? [The answer to question 9 should ordinarily be supported by an estimate of length signed by the counsel to be instructed.]
ALTERNATIVE DISPUTE RESOLUTION (ADR) (See the Practice Direction dated 10.12.93)
10. Have you or Counsel discussed with your client(s) the possibility of attempting to resolve this dispute (or particular issues) by ADR?
11. Might some form of ADR procedure assist to resolve or narrow the issues in this case?
12. Have you or your client(s) explored with the other parties the possibility of resolving this dispute (or particular issues) by ADR?
[SIGNATURE OF THE SOLICITOR—DATE]
NOTE: This check list must be lodged not later than two months before the date of hearing with copies to the other parties.
PRACTICE DIRECTION (Q.B.D.) (PRE-TRIAL CHECKLIST) (CIVIL LITIGATION: CASE MANAGEMENT), March 14, 1995.

3943/4. Chancery business in the northern area—long vacation 1995

During the long vacation His Honour Judge Kolbert (sitting as a judge of the High Court) will sit at the Courts of Justice, Crown Square, Manchester on August 10; at the Law Courts, Quayside, Newcastle upon Tyne on September 12 and 21; at the Courthouse, 1 Oxford Row, Leeds, on September 28.

His Honour Judge Maddocks (sitting as a judge of the High Court) will sit at the Queen Elizabeth II Law Courts, Derby Square, Liverpool on August 11 and 14 and September 22; and at the Courts of Justice, Crown Square, Manchester on August 15.

His Honour Judge Howarth (sitting as a judge of the High Court) will sit at the Courts of Justice, Crown Square, Manchester on September 8 and 28.

Their Honours Judges Kolbert, Maddocks, Gilliland, Q.C. and Howarth will also sit on such other days as may be necessary for the purpose of hearing those applications that require to be immediately or promptly heard and are within their jurisdiction, which according to the practice in the Chancery Division are usually heard in Court or by the judge in Chambers personally.

Papers for use in Court

The following papers must be lodged in the District Registry in which the case is proceeding by 1 p.m. three days before the day on which the application is to be made:

(a) a Certificate of Counsel that the case requires to be immediately or promptly heard and stating concisely the reasons; (b) two copies of the Notice of Motion bearing the District Registry Seal; and (c) two copies of the writ and of the pleadings (if any); and (d) office copy affidavits in support and in answer (if any).

If the case is proceeding in the Manchester District Registry, the papers (which need only include one copy of (b) and (c) above) may be lodged at that Registry by 1 p.m. two days prior to the day on which the application is to be made.

In cases of great urgency the papers may be sent direct by post to the Listing Officer (Chancery Division), Manchester District Registry, The Courts of Justice, Crown Square, Manchester, M3 3FL.

Solicitors should apply to the Clerk in Court for the return of their papers immediately after the application has been disposed of.

Applications to the vacation judge direct

When the vacation judge is not sitting application may be made to him personally, but only cases of *extreme* urgency. His address must first be obtained from the officer in charge of his list at the Manchester District Registry and the judge is not to be telephoned except after reference to that officer, unless the Registry is closed when the need first appears.

Application may also be made of the judge by letter for an Order to which counsel may consider the applicant entitled. It must be accompanied by counsel's brief, office copy affidavits in support and a minute on a separate sheet of paper signed by counsel and also an envelope, sufficiently stamped, capable of receiving the papers and addressed to "The Chief Clerk, Manchester County Court, The Courts of Justice, Crown Square, Manchester, M3 3FL" to whom the papers will be returned.

3945. Civil courts

CIVIL COURTS (AMENDMENT) ORDER 1995 (No. 1897) [65p], made under the County Courts Act 1984, s.2(1); operative on October 27, 1995, arts. 3(b), 4(b), September 29, 1995 for remaining provisions; amends the 1983 Order so as to close the county courts at Wisbech and Market Drayton.

CIVIL COURTS (AMENDMENT) (NO.2) ORDER 1995 (No. 3173 (L.21) made under County Courts Act 1984 s.2(1); amends S.I. 1983 No. 713. In force: December 29, 1995 for all provisions except arts.3(f), 4(c), January 2, 1996 for arts.3(f), 4(c); [£1·10]. The Civil Courts Order 1983 is amended to close the County Courts at Bargoed, Barry, Cardigan, Llandrindod Wells and Otley and to transfer the County Court at Brentwood to Basildon.

3946. Conditional fees

CONDITIONAL FEE AGREEMENTS ORDER 1995 (No. 1674), made under the Courts and Legal Services Act 1990, s.58; operative on July 5, 1995; provides that a conditional fee agreement which relates to specified proceedings shall not be unenforceable by reason only of its being a conditional fee agreement.

CONDITIONAL FEE AGREEMENTS REGULATIONS 1995 (No. 1675), made under the Courts and Legal Services Act 1990, s.58; operative on July 5, 1995; prescribe the requirements with which an agreement between a client and his legal representative must comply so as to enable it to be a conditional fee agreement under Courts and Legal Services Act 1990, s.58.

3947. Consent order—settlement—negotiations as to disposal of action by consent order incorporating undertakings—wording of order not agreed—whether agreement legally binding

Notwithstanding that agreement as to settlement terms has been reached in principle, the parties to an action must agree with the wording of a consent order before they can be irrevocably bound.

P brought an action alleging passing off and trade mark infringement against D. Negotiations were entered into by the parties' solicitors with a view to settling the action by way of a consent order incorporating undertakings. During the course of four telephone conversations the solicitors reached agreement in principle on the terms of settlement. However, they were subsequently unable to agree the wording of the order. D alleged that the parties had reached a legally binding agreement and sought an order that all further proceedings be stayed.

Held, dismissing the motion, that (1) it was not impossible for there to have been a legally binding agreement before the actual wording of the order was agreed. However, the whole object of the negotiations was to arrive at a form of order which could be presented to the court as agreed. In these circumstances the onus is on the person who contends that a contract has been concluded before the wording of the order is agreed to show that the parties intended to enter into a binding agreement; (2) neither party is in a position to bring the matter before the court for a consent order to be made until he can show the form of consent order that the court is being asked to make. In such a case there is a presumption that the meeting of minds of the parties had to be a meeting of minds on the precise wording of the order; and (3) on the facts, the parties were not *ad idem* on the substance of the agreement. Even if they had been *ad idem*, neither party would have been irrevocably bound until the wording was agreed (*Donwin Productions v. EMI Films* [1984] C.L.Y. 365, *Edwards v. Skyways* [1964] C.L.Y. 589, *Pagnan SpA v. Feed Products* [1988] C.L.Y. 427, *Perry v. Suffields* [1916] 2 Ch. 187 referred to).

DALGETY FOODS HOLLAND BV v. DEB-ITS [1994] F.S.R. 125, Edward Nugee, Q.C. sitting as a deputy judge.

3948. Consent order—slip rule—financial provision on divorce—draft consent order—incorrect date—whether capable of amendment under slip rule. See POUNDS v. POUNDS, §2337.

3949. Contempt—breach of licence—premises licensed for public music and dancing—breach of terms of order—no reference to terms of order as varied in notice of motion or committal order—whether fatal to committal

[Licensing Act 1964 (c.26), s.182.]

L appealed against an order to activate a suspended sentence of 84 days' imprisonment for contempt of court. L was in breach of an order preventing the use of his premises for public music and dancing and was given a suspended sentence. L then applied for and was granted a variation of the order which provided that if the provision of music was within the Licensing Act 1964, s.182, then the order would not be breached. L committed further breaches of the order and was committed to 84 days' imprisonment. He raised the claim that there was no reference to the order as varied in the notice of motion or the committal order, that the terms of the order were not set out and that the breaches were not adequately particularised.

Held, dismissing the appeal, that (1) it was not suggested by L that the variation provided an excuse for the alleged breaches, or led him to believe there was no breach of the order. This was a purely technical omission of no practical significance; (2) there was no stringent requirement for the terms to be set out and it was plain that L was in no doubt of what he was said to have done wrong; (3) the breaches that L committed were set out in the notice of motion and were stated with unmistakable clarity.

Obiter dicta: the court must constantly bear in mind that no person is to be deprived of his liberty if there is any question of an unfair procedure being adopted. On the other hand, there is a public interest in the enforcement of orders by the court since parties in whose favour the order was made should not be deprived of the protection which they were intended to have.

WALTHAM FOREST LONDON BOROUGH COUNCIL v. LOIZOU (FC3 95/5990/F), May 22, 1995, C.A.

3950. Contempt—breach of Mareva injunctions—undertaking not to dispose of lump sum—financial provision proceedings—whether imprisonment correct sentence—whether any mitigating circumstances

R applied for bail pending an appeal against a sentence of six months' imprisonment. R was in breach of an undertaking not to dispose of more than one-half of the monies to be received on termination of his employment with the police force on grounds of ill health. It was intended that the funds be available to R's wife in financial provision proceedings. R received a lump sum of £37,250 and spent it. The court considered the application as the substantive appeal.

Held, allowing the appeal, that there were highly exceptional factors in this case which had to be taken into account. R was a police officer who had attended the Hillsborough disaster and had suffered from depression as a result. His marriage had failed and he cared for the three children. The children had clearly suffered from the deterioration in their father's health and the breakdown of the marriage and their father's imprisonment would increase the stress. Imprisonment was the correct punishment but the term would be reduced to three months.

ROBINSON v. ROBINSON (FC2 95/5721/F), April 12, 1995, C.A.

3951. Contempt—breach of order not to contact employers—video tape of parties engaged in sexual activity—appropriate period of detention—whether possible to purge

J undertook not to communicate with any person connected with M's employment. The judge found that J had sent a video tape to someone connected with M's employers, which recorded the parties engaged in sexual activity. The breach was flagrant and substantial, meant to cause the greatest possible embarrassment to M. An immediate prison sentence of 28 days was imposed.

Held, dismissing J's application to purge the contempt, with an apology, that he should not be released. The sentence imposed was as lenient as possible. J had behaved in an inappropriate and gross way and there were material inaccuracies in his affidavit.

MAYELL v. JACKSON, April 6, 1995, H.H.J. M. Cotterill, Exeter County Ct. [*Ex rel.* Crosse & Crosse, Solicitors, Exeter.]

3952. Contempt—breach of order not to use or threaten violence—inaccuracies in committal order—sentencing began before mitigation by defendant's counsel—whether invalidated order—whether sentence of 12 months' imprisonment excessive

F and M cohabited during the 1980's and separated sometime after the birth of their son in 1992. Following two injunctions against F, and an incident of assault occasioning actual bodily harm, F was committed for 14 days for breaches of an order that the parties should not communicate. However, despite further threatened violence, the parties' relationship improved. In March 1995 the injunctions and contempt proceedings arising from them were discharged by F's undertaking, *inter alia*, not to use or threaten violence to M. However, that day F assaulted M in two separate incidents and made a threatening phone call two days later. F was committed for contempt and sentenced to 12 months' imprisonment. He appealed on the grounds that the committal was defective, the evidence did not justify certain findings of violence, there was no opportunity to mitigate and there was no allocation of penalties to the four points of contempt found proved.

Held, dismissing the appeal, that (1) the fact that the committal order was inaccurate in a large number of respects did not undermine the validity of the order; (2) the particulars of violence proved were not in any way inadequate as a result of the manner in which they were described; (3) although the judge was at fault in going straight to the passing of sentence without giving defence counsel an opportunity to mitigate, he remedied that error by giving defence counsel time to receive instructions and present mitigation; and (4) it was apparent that the judge concluded that a sentence of 12 months' was appropriate and intended that to be a concurrent penalty on each of the four contempts.

NARING v. DHAMI (CCRTF 95/0593/F), May 22, 1995, C.A.

3953. Contempt—breach of order prohibiting natural parents from harassing adoptive parents—whether prison sentence appropriate

H and W appealed against an order committing them to prison for a year for contempt. They had breached orders forbidding them from making allegations about the care being provided for their former children by their adoptive parents. H and W alleged that the letters containing the allegations had been written by a social worker with the intent of framing them. The trial judge concluded that both parents were responsible for writing and sending the letters.

Held, dismissing the appeal, that the trial judge was right to take a very serious view of the contempt. The parents had denied that they had committed the breaches, had expressed no regret and made no promises that they would not repeat them. The breaches were flagrant and persistent and seriously disturbed the adoption process. Furthermore, they had falsely accused innocent parties and tried to affect the judgment of social workers, police and county court judges. The sentences were completely appropriate and the court fully approved them.

O. (MINORS), *Re* (FAFMF 94/1664/F), January 13, 1995, C.A.

3954. Contempt—breach of undertaking not to use violence on wife—committal to prison pending further consideration

[Contempt of Court Act 1981 (c.49), s.14; Criminal Justice Act 1967 (c.80), ss.67, 104.]

D had been found guilty of contempt for a breach of an undertaking given on September 6, 1995 not to use violence against his wife, nor to communicate with her in any way. On October 5 he was committed to prison, with a direction for a further consideration of sentence on October 20. D appealed, arguing that the indefinite form of the sentence was contrary to s.14(1) of the Contempt of Court Act 1981.

Held, allowing the appeal, that it was accepted that cases arose where the victim of a contemnor's actions needed protection from further acts, but it could be difficult to determine an appropriate sentence. The sentence had to be effective enough to protect the victim, but the order made should allow the contemnor to purge his contempt. Taking advice from the Official Solicitor, it was held that (1) the original sentence was bad and inconsistent with s.14(1) of the 1981 Act; (2) having made an error in the original committal, the judge had no power to consider the sentence further at a future date; (3) the wording used at first instance had the effect of deleting the part of the original order allowing D to purge his contempt, a right he should not have been deprived of (*Vaughan v. Vaughan* [1973] C.L.Y. 935 considered). It was also accepted that remanding D into custody when finding him guilty of contempt, before sentencing him, meant that he would effectively serve part of his sentence twice as, pursuant to ss.67 and 104 of the Criminal Justice Act 1967, time spent in custody in contempt cases was not deductible from the final sentence. The alternative method would have been to order D's release at a future specified date, while leaving his right to purge the contempt intact (*Yager v. Musa* [1961] C.L.Y. 6871 considered). As this had not been done, the original order was quashed and D's release ordered. A six-month suspended sentence was substituted, suspended until the date of decree absolute in divorce proceedings between D and his wife.

DELANEY v. DELANEY, *The Times*, November 2, 1995, C.A.

3955. Contempt—divorce—financial provision for wife and son—whether sentence excessive

H, a former soldier, appealed against a sentence of nine months' imprisonment for contempt of court in matrimonial proceedings. H had spent the entire £20,000 gratuity he received on leaving the army in breach of an injunction obtained by H's wife. None of the money was spent for the benefit of his wife and son. The trial judge ruled that the contempt was flagrant and about as bad as could be imagined.

Held, dismissing the appeal, that despite H's previous good character and army service, the sentence was not excessive. H had taken no notice of the court order whatsoever but had committed a substantial breach and deprived W of any chance of a lump sum.

HUDSON v. HUDSON, *The Times*, March 23, 1995, C.A.

3956. Contempt—jurisdiction—industrial tribunal—attempting to persuade witness to withdraw evidence—whether contempt jurisdiction extending to industrial tribunal

[Contempt of Court Act 1981, s.19; R.S.C., Ord. 52, r.1(2).]

The Queen's Bench Divisional Court has jurisdiction under R.S.C., Ord. 52, r.1(2)(a)(iii), to punish for contempt of court in connection with industrial tribunal proceedings.

S presented a complaint to an industrial tribunal that he had been constructively and unfairly dismissed from his position as a solicitor's clerk with PG. PG applied to the Queen's Bench Divisional court for an order committing S to prison for contempt of court on the grounds that he had sought to persuade potential witnesses in the tribunal proceedings to retract statements which suggested that S had received unauthorised payments from clients during the period of his employment. The question was whether an industrial tribunal was an "inferior court" for the purposes of R.S.C., Ord. 52, r.1(2)(a)(iii).

Held, granting PG's application, that an industrial tribunal had many of the characteristics of a court of law, it was a body which discharged judicial rather than administrative functions as part of the judicial system and it fulfilled the definition of a court in s.19 of the Contempt of Court Act 1981 as "any tribunal or body exercising the judicial power of the State". An industrial tribunal was therefore an "inferior court" within the meaning of R.S.C., Ord. 52, r.1(2)(a)(iii), and the Queen's Bench Divisional Court had jurisdiction to entertain the application (*Att.-Gen. v. B.B.C.* [1980] C.L.Y. 2119 applied).

PEACH GREY & CO. (A FIRM) v. SOMMERS [1995] 2 All E.R. 513, D.C.

3957. Contempt—matrimonial property—not to be removed—breach of order protecting matrimonial property—whether imprisonment appropriate

P appealed against an order committing him to prison for 14 days for breach of an undertaking to leave the matrimonial home and not to remove any property from it.

Held, dismissing the appeal, that the judge had concluded beyond reasonable doubt that P had removed articles from the house, rather than that a burglary had taken place. P was given the opportunity at committal to return the items removed, but he only produced some of them. The sentence was correctly imposed.

POSEY v. POSEY (CO-970-93), January 27, 1995, C.A.

3958. Contempt—reporting restrictions—postponement of publication—postponement of newspaper reporting of civil proceedings—overlap of issues and material between civil actions and criminal trials pending and imminent—factors to be taken into account by court when considering whether to order postponement of reporting—whether "substantial" risk of prejudice to administration of justice in criminal trials—whether postponement order "necessary" for avoiding substantial risk of prejudice. See MGN PENSION TRUSTEES v. BANK OF AMERICA NATIONAL TRUST AND SAVINGS ASSOCIATION, §1011.

3959. Contempt—reporting restrictions—publication of medical reports used in Children Act proceedings—whether public interest in publishing the information should be weighed against the interference with administration of justice

[Administration of Justice Act 1960 (c.65), s.12; European Convention for the Protection of Human Rights and Fundamental Freedoms 1985, Art. 10.]

Where there is a charge of contempt of court based on the publication of information relating to family proceedings heard in private, it is not necessary to find some threat to or interference with the administration of justice.

Shortly after Beverley Allitt's conviction for murder, H contacted *The Sun* newspaper and told them that his ex-wife W also suffered from Munchausen's syndrome by proxy and had continued to work as an auxiliary nurse in a hospital. H showed reporters documents relating to the contested proceedings for custody of his child. *The Sun* published the story, quoting at length from the medical reports filed in the proceedings. The Official Solicitor brought proceedings for contempt of court under s.12(1) of the Administration of Justice Act 1960, for publication of information relating to proceedings heard in private, against the publisher and editor of *The Sun*.

Held, finding the charge of contempt to be made out and fining each respondent, that (1) it was clear that the prohibition in s.12(1) extended not only to the information given to the judge at the actual hearing but also to documents such as confidential medical reports. The respondents had therefore published "information relating to proceedings" within s.12(1) (*F. A Minor) (Publication of Information), Re* [1976] C.L.Y. 2119 applied; *Scott v. Scott* [1913] A.C. 417 considered); (2) the *mens rea* required for a contempt under s.12(1) was made out on the facts. The respondents had known that the information related to proceedings concerned with the upbringing of a child and that the proceedings were private proceedings. It was not necessary to prove that the respondents knew that publication was forbidden by law; (3) in contempt proceedings under s.12, it was not necessary to find that a threat to or interference with the administration of justice. Section 12(4) did not require the court to take into account the public interest in publication, and in any event there was no need to publish extensive extracts from the medical reports (*Att.-Gen. v. Times Newspapers* [1973] C.L.Y. 2618 distinguished); and (4) in so far as Art. 10 of the European Convention on Human Rights was relevant, the restriction on freedom of expression made by s.72(1) was lawful under the Convention (*Linghans v. Austria* (1986) 8 E.H.R.R. 407 applied).

OFFICIAL SOLICITOR v. NEWS GROUP NEWSPAPERS [1994] 2 F.L.R. 174, Connell J.

3960. Contempt—reporting restrictions—substantial risk of serious prejudice to fair trial—accused charged with murder—respondents broadcasting or publishing details of accused's previous conviction for murder—criminal proceedings commenced nine months later—whether broadcast or publication creating substantial risk of serious prejudice to trial. See ATT.-GEN. v. INDEPENDENT TELEVISION NEWS, §1012.

3961. Contempt—witness refusing to testify—general principles—guidelines on sentencing

M refused to give evidence at a trial. The accused had been charged with hurling a rock at a police car, causing very serious injuries to a police officer. M and two other witnesses gave statements identifying the accused as the thrower of the rock. M refused to give evidence through fear. He was a family man of good character save only for a short custodial sentence for failure to pay a fine six years previously. He was sentenced to 12 months' imprisonment.

Held, allowing M's appeal, that M's sentence should be reduced to three months' imprisonment. The following general principles applied: (1) an immediate custodial sentence was the only appropriate sentence for those interfering with justice, save in exceptional circumstances, albeit a moderate sentence would usually be enough to mark the gravity of the matter and stiffen the resolve of other witnesses; (2) there was no rule that interference with jurors was more serious than a refusal to give evidence, the circumstances of each case being all important; (3) although regard should be had to the maximum of three months' imprisonment for failure to comply with a witness order, a longer sentence was appropriate for a blatant contempt; and (4) the contempt is best dealt with at the end of the trial or the Crown's case, and the contemnor must be given opportunity to give evidence as to his reasons. The principal matters affecting sentence were: the gravity of the offence being tried; the effect on the trial; the contemnor's reasons; whether there was a defiance to the judge; sentences in similar cases; the contemnor's antecedents; whether a special deterrent is necessary, for example at the beginning of a series of trials where witnesses are being threatened or becoming disaffected.

R. v. MONTGOMERY [1995] 2 All E.R. 28, C.A.

3962. Costs—application under the Highways Act—application withdrawn without requirement of leave—whether council entitled to costs

[Highways Act 1980 (c.66); R.S.C., Ord. 94, r.2(2)(b).]

K lodged an application challenging the Secretary of State's decision to approve two side roads orders made under the Highways Act 1980. The application was made out of time, and had not been served on the local authority, C, as required by R.S.C., Ord. 94, r.2(2)(b). C sought to be joined to the proceedings and to have the notice of motion struck out, with an order for costs. K then withdrew the application, by a consent order, and submitted that as the proceedings were withdrawn without any requirement of the leave of court, there was no application to which C could be joined so as to recover its costs.

Held, awarding the council its costs, that even if the application to which C wished to be joined no longer existed, the court had jurisdiction to award the council the costs of the motion.

ESTATE OF KINGSLEY v. SECRETARY OF STATE FOR TRANSPORT [1994] C.O.D. 358, D.C.

3963. Costs—assessment—remuneration due to receivers

[R.S.C., Ord. 30, r.3; Ord. 62, r.7.]

The receivers of E appealed against a preliminary ruling requiring remuneration due to them from the plaintiffs to be assessed by a taxing officer on the standard basis. They alleged that the judge did not have jurisdiction to make such an order, as under R.S.C., Ord. 62, r.7(2) receivers' remuneration should not be taxed.

Held, dismissing the appeal, that under an amendment to Ord. 30, r.3, made by the Rules of the Supreme Court (Amendment) Order 1992, the court had jurisdiction to choose whether to order payments made to receivers appointed by the High Court to be assessed by a master in the Chancery Division or, alternatively, by the taxing officer on either the standard or the indemnity basis. The amendments introduced by the 1992 Order must take precedence over Ord. 62, r.7(2).

ALLIANCE & LEICESTER BUILDING SOCIETY v. EDGESTOP (NO. 2), *The Times*, May 24, 1995, C.A.

3964. Costs—automatic striking-out—partial admission—solicitors failed to realise case struck out—whether both solicitors responsible

[C.C.R., Ord. 17, r.11(1)(b).]

P's action was struck out under C.C.R., Ord. 17, r.11, on September 15, 1993. Neither P's nor D's solicitors appreciated that fact and both went on carrying out various steps in the action until September 27, 1994, when D's solicitors first took the point. P submitted that the case did not fall within the automatic directions by virtue of C.C.R., Ord. 17, r.11(1)(6), on partial admission.

Held, that the case was automatically struck out. On the question of costs the district judge awarded the costs of the action up to the date of the payment in accordance with the partial admission to P, the costs of the action to the date of automatic striking-out to D, no order for costs between the automatic striking-out of the action and the date when D first realised that the action had been struck out, and P to pay D's costs thereafter. Counsel's submissions on behalf of P that in so far as P's solicitors were responsible for not appreciating the fact that the action had been automatically struck out, D's solicitors were also responsible for not appreciating the point and both went on regardless, and that in the circumstances P should not be penalised in costs for a default on behalf of D or his solicitors were accepted.

TRETHOWANS (BUILDERS) v. OSMAN, December 20, 1994; District Judge D. White; Truro County Ct. [*Ex rel. E. M. Treneer, Barrister, Preston Goldburn, Solicitors*.]

3965. Costs—champerty—non-party maintaining unsuccessful party's action—whether court having power to award costs against non-party

Although maintenance and champerty are no longer tortious or criminal, the law of maintenance and champerty is preserved for the purposes of considering whether a contract is illegal.

P, a domiciled Scotsman, brought an action in the High Court in England against D for damages in negligence. He had no means of financing litigation and retained the services of a company, Q, which had been established in Scotland for the purpose of handling personal injury claims on a contingency fee basis. On the trial of a preliminary issue the judge's decision that D owed P a duty of care was reversed by the Court of Appeal, which awarded D costs. D applied by summons for an order that Q pay their costs.

Held, granting the order sought, that (1) although maintenance and champerty were no longer tortious or criminal, the law of maintenance and champerty was preserved for the purposes of considering whether any contract was illegal; (2) in determining whether a party had sufficient interest in maintaining an action to save such maintenance from contractual illegality, a highly relevant consideration was whether there was a business context such as insurance or trade union activity; and (3) Q's policy not to accept liability for a successful adverse party's costs rendered its contract with P illegal independently of the illegality which arose from the champertous nature of the agreement (dicta of Lord Denning M.R. in *Hill v. Archbold* [1967] C.L.Y. 3776 applied).

McFARLANE v. E.E. CALEDONIA (NO. 2) [1995] 1 W.L.R. 366, Longmore J.

3966. Costs—counterclaim for delivery charge and collection expenses—plaintiff agreeing to provide credit note for delivery charge before issue of proceedings—whether success of counterclaim for delivery charge justified costs—whether defence without merit

[C.C.R., Ord. 19, r.14(2).]

P received confirmation of an order from D on May 1, 1995, for three steel bollards at a total contract price of £522·13. It was P's usual practice to open a credit line and then to factor its debts. In this instance the parties agreed that D would be permitted to pay by cheque. This was at D's request. P received a cheque from D on May 18, 1995, drawn in P's favour. D then contacted P claiming that the goods were required urgently and requesting that they be permitted to collect them first thing on May 19, 1995. P consented to this request, despite the fact that the cheque would not yet have cleared, and D collected the goods at 7.00 a.m. on May 19, 1995. The cheque was presented for payment and returned unpaid. Although D had notice of the dishonour on June 6, 1995, they failed to pay the sum due. P issued a summons on June 12 1995, for £525·45, including interest. D then served its defence and counterclaim, admitting the amount of £400·38, but counterclaiming the amount of £121·75. D alleged that P had failed to deliver the goods by the agreed date and that D had consequently had to collect the goods from P. The counterclaim consisted of a credit note (£35·75) which D alleged P had failed to issue in respect of the delivery charge included in the contract price, and the sum of £86, being the amount in respect of the expense incurred by D in collecting the goods. Before issuing proceedings, P offered to issue D with a credit note in respect of the delivery charge, and the £35·75 was therefore never in dispute.

Held, that although the counterclaim in respect of the £35·75 delivery charge succeeded, the defence was totally without merit. Therefore P were awarded judgment for £486·88 plus interest, costs as endorsed on summons and £235 in respect of costs assessed pursuant to C.C.R., Ord. 19, r.14(2).

STREETSCENE v. C. MCADAMS, August 15, 1995, Deputy District Judge Taylor, Sheffield County Ct. [*Ex rel.* G. Yates, Hartley Linfoot & Whitlam, Sheffield.]

3967. Costs—default judgment—defendant's failure to file defence—damages less than £1,000—whether entitled to taxed costs

P claimed unliquidated damages for less than £1,000 and interlocutory judgment for damages to be assessed with costs was entered, D having failed to file a defence to the claim.

Held, that, in spite of the authorities cited, and the arguments raised by D's solicitors, P was entitled to his taxed costs on County Court Scale 1. C.C.R., Ord. 38, r.2, was mandatory and, even if there was a discretion to award costs other than taxed costs in a case where interlocutory judgment had been entered, there was nothing upon which the court could exercise its discretion to stray from the rules.

DIMOND v. GENERAL COMMUNICATIONS, September 27, 1994, Cardiff County Ct. [*Ex rel.* Philip Bradley, Solicitor, Dolmans, Cardiff.]

3968. Costs—discontinuance—order granting leave to discontinue without order as to costs—whether jurisdiction not to make costs order in favour of defendant

[R.S.C., Ord. 21, r.3.]

S sought leave to appeal against an order granting leave to B to discontinue proceedings against S which made no order as to costs. S argued that *Stratford v. Lindley* established the principle that the court should exercise its discretion under R.S.C., Ord. 21, r.3, without coming to any view on the merits of the plaintiff's case. S also relied on *Barretts & Baird (Wholesale) v. Institute of Professional Civil Servants* as establishing that the plaintiff should pay the defendant's costs on discontinuance.

Held, dismissing the application, that Ord. 21, r.3 gave the court wide discretion as to who should bear the costs in the case. In this instance the court below had exercised that discretion impeccably (*Stratford v. Lindley (No.*

2) [1969] C.L.Y. 2816, *Barretts & Baird (Wholesale) v. Institute of Professional Civil Servants* [1987] C.L.Y. 3769 considered).

BRITANNIA LIFE ASSOCIATION OF SCOTLAND v. SMITH (LTA 95/5225/B), June 8, 1995, C.A.

3969. Costs—discretion not to award—no order made as plaintiff legally aided—whether relevant matter

[Legal Aid Act 1988 (c.34), s.31.]

K applied for a mandatory injunction requiring L council to repair her heating system and carry out other outstanding repairs. A penal notice was not ordered because L agreed to do the work but a question arose as to costs. K was in receipt of legal aid and the judge decided there was no order to be made as to costs, as K was legally aided and would not have to pay costs.

Held, allowing K's appeal, that the judge had taken into account a matter wholly unconnected with the cause of the action as to costs and irrelevant to the exercise of his discretion. Under s.31(1) of the Legal Aid Act 1988 the rights conferred upon a person under the Act shall not affect the rights or liabilities of other parties, or the principles upon which the court's discretion is normally exercised. There was no basis upon which K could be deprived finally of her costs of the application as she had been successful (*Scherer v. Counting Instruments* [1986] C.L.Y. 2572 cited).

KNIGHT (LOLA ELAINE) v. LAMBETH LONDON BOROUGH COUNCIL (CCRTI 94/0330/E), November 28, 1994, C.A.

3970. Costs—disqualification of director—director seeking leave to act as a director—whether Secretary of State entitled to costs on an indemnity basis. See DICETRADE, *Re*; SECRETARY OF STATE FOR TRADE AND INDUSTRY v. WORTH, §583.

3971. Costs—family proceedings—whether to be awarded against Legal Aid Board—cases involving children—whether principles different to other areas of civil law

[Legal Aid Act 1988 (c.34), s.18(4)(a).]

Since the usual order in children's cases was for no order for costs, in order to make a costs order against the Legal Aid Board it was necessary to show that the legally aided party would, unusually, have had to pay the unassisted party's costs.

H and W had two children and were married in 1979. W issued divorce proceedings, and there were cross applications for care and control of the children. H ws legally aided, W was not. The judge made an interim order for care and control to H, with access to W. At the second hearing on the question both parties remained in the family home, although it was agreed that it should be sold and the judge granted care and control to W. A consent order was made in the ancillary relief proceedings for the sale of the family home and its division with two-thirds to W, one-third to H. H's share was eaten up by his legal aid charge, but W was able to purchase a new home with her capital, together with a mortgage. W sought a costs order against the Legal Aid Board in respect of the hearings. The judge dismissed her application on the ground that, under s.18(4)(a) of the Legal Aid Act 1988, no costs order would have been made against H apart from the 1988 Act.

Held, dismissing W's appeal, that (1) the words "apart from this Act" in s.18(4)(a) of the Legal Aid Act 1988 required the court to envisage a situation where the other party had not had the benefit of legal aid, did not have the protection against liability for costs provided by s.17 and would himself have a considerable burden in respect of his own costs; (2) it was unusual to order costs in children cases, though an order for costs remained in the court's discretion, and might well be made where a party had been unreasonable in his conduct of litigation, reprehensible in his conduct generally, or where there was a marked disparity in the parties' income (*Gojkovic v. Gojkovic (No. 2)* [1992] C.L.Y. 2090, *Sutton London Borough Council v. Davis (No. 2)* [1994] C.L.Y. 3597 considered); and (3) both the 1989 and the 1990 decisions were finely balanced. The only asset of the parties was the family home, which would have to be sold and replaced by two new households, and so neither could be said to have abundant means. Apart from the 1988 Act, no order would have been made against H.

KELLER v. KELLER AND LEGAL AID BOARD [1995] 1 FLR 259, C.A.

3972. Costs—fixed costs—claim for over £1,000—acceptance of lower payment-in—whether plaintiff to receive costs

P was a police driver who in February 1993 sustained a minor "whiplash" type injury as a result of a collision with a stolen vehicle he was pursuing. His principal complaints were completely resolved within two weeks but he did not resume sports for three months. There was no time off work. The Domestic Regulations Insurer offered £750 to settle. P's solicitors indicated that they were minded to accept the offer so long as their costs were also met, failing which they would commence proceedings. The defence rejected the request and proceedings limited to £3,000 were thereafter issued. A defence was entered and this was followed by an application that the proceedings should stand referred to arbitration. The judge felt the claim for damages in excess of £1,000 was borderline but not unsustainable and, therefore, refused the application. Two weeks after the judge's refusal the defence made a payment in of £800 which, very shortly afterwards, and before any further steps in the action had been taken by P, was accepted. An order for payment out of court and costs on scale 1 was sought.

Held, that *inter alia*, P and his solicitors had clearly decided that they would accept a payment-in below £1,000 before the defence request to have the proceedings stand referred to arbitration, and in the circumstances they would only be allowed to recover the issue fee whilst being ordered to pay those of D's costs incurred after the payment-in, including those of the final hearing, on scale 1.

HORNER v. WHITE, January 12, 1995; District Judge Southcombe; Clerkenwell County Ct. [*Ex rel. Pip Punwar, Barrister*].

3973. Costs—fixed costs—claims brought together—damages arising from road traffic accident—claim for over £1,000 arbitration level—whether claims should have been valued separately

Proceedings were commenced in the county court on behalf of P1 and P2, claiming damages arising from a road traffic accident on February 9, 1993. P2 was travelling as a passenger in P1's vehicle when a collision occurred with a car driven by D. P1's claim was limited to £680 special damages together with an unliquidated claim for general damages by way of inconvenience. P2's claim included, in addition to special damages, a claim for personal injury. P1 and P2 had the benefit of legal expense insurance and D was represented through his motor insurers. Following unsuccessful negotiations, proceedings were commenced limiting both Ps' damages to £25,000. A defence admitting negligence but disputing *quantum* was served, following which P1's claim was settled for £680 on the proviso that the question of costs in relation to P1's claim would be determined at the conclusion of P2's claim. At the assessment of damages hearing in relation to P2's claim on April 11, 1995, P2 recovered £6,088·96 by way of damages and interest thereon. D then applied for an order in respect of P1's costs that P1 be entitled to recover only the fixed costs of the action on the basis that his claim had no reasonable expectation of exceeding the £1,000 arbitration level. D relied upon *Haile v. West*. P1 relied on *Wright and Wright v. Holman*.

Held, that the case in question was not analogous with *Haile* but the question is one of reasonableness. Once it has been accepted, as it was in this case, that P1 could bring his claim with P2, then he should get (most likely modest in any event) his costs on scale 1. Once P2 had properly joined P1 in her action then there were not three scales available in the county court which included a notional scale for costs of cases valued at less than £1,000, but only the two standard county court scales known as scales 1 and 2 (*Haile v. West* [1939] 4 All E.R. 339; *Wright and Wright v. Holman* [1994] 9 C.L. 339 considered).

SMITH AND SMITH v. BISHOP, April 11, 1995; Luton County Ct. [*Ex rel.* Claire Thompson, Barrister].

3974. Costs—fixed costs—engineer's report—premature issue of application—plaintiff conceding that not entitled to fixed costs and issue fee—issue of summons before provision of full details of plaintiff's claim—whether entitled to engineer's fee

P commenced proceedings against D for damages arising out of a road traffic accident in November 1993. The claims for costs of repairs and loss of use were agreed between P and D following issue of the proceedings. P's solicitors claimed fixed costs of £33, along with the issue fee of £60 and £58·16 in respect of an engineer's fee. P's solicitors then conceded that they would not be entitled to their fixed costs and issue fee on the basis that they had issued prematurely before providing D with full details of their client's claim, despite a number of requests. P's solicitors still argued, however, that they were entitled to the engineer's fee. D's solicitors argued that the engineer's fee was part of P's solicitors claim for costs and if P's solicitors were conceding that they were not entitled to their fixed costs or issue fee, the same must be said for the engineer's fee.

Held, that the engineer's fee formed part of the costs of the action and because P's solicitors were conceding that they were not entitled to their fixed costs or the issue fee, they were not entitled to recover the engineer's fee of £58·16 either.

SMITH v. STREET, November 7, 1994, Birkenhead County Ct. [*Ex rel.* Irwin Mitchell, Solicitors, Birmingham.]

3975. Costs—fixed costs—interlocutory judgment—damages to be assessed—whether reasonable expectation of recovering more than £1,000—whether costs on scale 1 followed failure to file defence

Following a road traffic accident, P issued a claim limited to £1,000. Despite having denied liability in pre-action correspondence, D's representatives failed to file a defence, and interlocutory judgment was entered pursuant to C.C.R., Ord. 9, r.6. On the date fixed for assessment of damages, the *quantum* of P's claim was agreed at the door of the court in the sum of £780·92 (inclusive of interest), and the sole issue left was whether or not P was entitled to costs on Scale one.

Held, that, although the court had some sympathy with D, the rules were clear. No defence had been filed, and in the absence of any grounds for criticising P's conduct of the litigation, P was entitled to have his costs taxed on scale 1 if not agreed, rather than fixed costs.

THOMAS v. RHODES COACHES, March 22, 1995, District Judge Reeves, Mold County Ct. [*Ex rel.* Bartlett & Son, Solicitors, Wrexham.]

3976. Costs—fixed costs—interlocutory judgment—payment into court—whether entitled to costs on scale 1—whether case to be dealt with as if referred to arbitration

P's car was damaged when D's vehicle collided with it. P commenced proceedings in the county court for damages not exceeding £1,000. P subsequently entered interlocutory judgment for damages to be assessed. However, prior to the assessment of damages hearing, a payment into court was made of £430 in full and final settlement, which P accepted. P contended that he was entitled to his costs on scale 1 due to the fact that interlocutory judgment had been entered and therefore the proceedings had not been referred to arbitration. D asked the court to deal with the matter as if it had been referred to arbitration.

Held, that where there is an interlocutory judgment, and a payment into court accepted, P is entitled to costs on scale 1.

SMITH v. CITY OF SALFORD, March 28, 1995, District Judge Brazier, Stockport County Ct. [*Ex rel.* J. Keith Park & Co., Solicitors, Merseyside.]

3977. Costs—fixed costs—interlocutory judgment—whether scale costs to be awarded

P was involved in a road traffic accident in September 1994. Proceedings limited to £1,000 were issued in February 1995. No defence was filed. At assessment, the deputy district judge awarded £242 in respect of repairs, with £10 out of pocket expenses.

Held, on the question of P's entitlement to scale costs, that no defence had been filed, and therefore the case was not automatically referred to arbitration. Interlocutory judgment had been entered for damages to be assessed, and costs. There was no suggestion that P's solicitors had attempted to play the rules, and scale costs would be awarded.

CROFT v. PHILIPS, April 21, 1995, Deputy District Judge Kitto, Redditch County Ct. [*Ex rel.* Nicky Marshall, Barrister, Pall Mall Chambers, Stoke-on-Trent.]

3978. Costs—fixed costs—payment into court—entitlement costs—whether plaintiff genuinely expected award to exceed £1,000

[C.C.R., Ord. 19, r.4; C.C.R., Ord. 11, r.5.]

P sustained a whiplash injury to the neck in a road traffic collision. P issued proceedings limited to £5,000 and indicated that the case was suitable for trial. P claimed special damages of £104 and general damages in respect of the injury. P's medical evidence was that the injury had exacerbated pre-existing cervical lordosis, though the period of exacerbation was not clear from the report. D paid into court £685 and, upon P's death from unconnected causes, that sum was accepted by P's estate. D applied to the court for an order that costs should be allowed under C.C.R., Ord. 19, r.4 rather than under Ord. 11, r.5 and that they therefore be restricted to costs on the summons. That application was made on the basis that at the time of issue of proceedings, P had no reasonable expectation of recovering more than £1,000 and that that was demonstrated by the acceptance of £685. P contended that costs should be recovered on the standard basis pursuant to Ord. 11, r.5, as whiplash injuries were notoriously difficult to value, and as on the basis of authorities, P could reasonably have thought that her injuries came within the £10,000 to £15,000 bracket. P argued that the acceptance of the payment into court was of no significance given the circumstances of that acceptance.

Held, that the only evidence upon which the court could rely in seeking to decide whether P had a reasonable expectation of recovering more than £1,000 was the medical report. On that basis, P did not have such a reasonable expectation of recovering the £807 necessary to push the claim over £1,000. Accordingly, P had abused the process of the court. Proceedings should have been referred to arbitration and P would recover only the costs on the summons under Ord. 19, r.4. Further, P should pay D's costs of the application (*Afzal v. Ford Motor Co.* [1994] C.L.Y. 3776 considered).

WALD v. JONES, July 10, 1995, Deputy District Judge Kirkham, Hull County Ct. [*Ex rel.* Paul Greaney, Barrister.]

3979. Costs—fixed costs—payment into court—limited damages awarded—whether fixed costs to be awarded

P was a 27-year-old toolmaker who suffered injuries to his finger in the course of his employment with D. He was not wearing gloves and his wound required seven stitches. When P's claim was issued it was claimed to be worth more than £1,000 and less than £3,000. Ds paid £400 into court with allegations of contributory negligence. In view of the nature of these allegations P shortly afterwards accepted D's increased offer of £600. An order to stay was made by consent in July 1992 to enable P to receive his damages but leaving the question of costs to be decided after an appeal which was pending in the Romford County Court in the case of *Afzal*. When, a year later, the case of *Afzal* was still not resolved but was pending in the Court of Appeal, P sought and was granted an order for his costs of the action on county court scale 1 to be taxed failing agreement.

Held, that D's appeal would be dismissed, thereby allowing P to recover his costs on county court scale 1.

GOMMERSALL v. FORD MOTOR COMPANY, November 11, 1994; H.H.J. Paynter-Reece; Romford County Ct. [*Ex rel. Robin Thompson and Partners, Solicitors*].

3980. Costs—fixed costs—payment into court—reasonable expectations—liability admitted in defence—application for fixed costs by defendant—whether reasonable expectations as to level of costs

P accepted a payment into court in the sum of £700 in a personal injury action where damages had been limited to £3,000. P had sustained relatively minor injury to his shin resulting in some discolouration and general bruising. P had taken two days' holiday allowance away from work and had largely recovered after two weeks. Liability had been admitted in the defence and D applied for an order that P be allowed fixed costs only.

Held, allowing P's appeal and upholding the district judge's view that P's solicitors had a reasonable expectation that damages might exceed £1,000 and should therefore be entitled to costs on county court scale 1. In reaching this view, although it was accepted that the appropriate bracket for pain and suffering based on the medical report was £600–£850, P's solicitors had nonetheless pleaded a claim for the value of loss of holiday entitlement and placed this reasonably in the sum of £200. It was held that P's solicitors had a reasonable and genuine expectation that damages might exceed £1,000 irrespective that P accepted a payment of £700.

SINGH v. GOODYEAR, October, 1994; Wolverhampton County Ct. [*Ex rel. Rowley Ashworth, Solicitors*].

3981. Costs—fixed costs—payment into court—under £1,000—two payments—one before commencement of action for value of vehicle—one to cover damages for personal injury—whether payments should be considered together—whether within small claims limit

[C.C.R., Ord. 11, r.3(5).]

P was involved in a road traffic accident. Liability was not disputed and £360 was paid to him by D's insurers for the agreed value of his vehicle. He then issued proceedings limited to £2,000, claiming damages for personal injury and the £360 for the vehicle. D filed a defence and applied to have the claim referred to arbitration under C.C.R., Ord. 19, r.3 on the ground that *quantum* would not exceed £1,000. Before the application was heard, P amended his claim to include a sum of £180 for loss of use. D's application failed because the district judge said that he did not have the power to assess the value of the injury (this was before the decision in *Afzal v. Ford Motor Co.*). D then paid £750 into court which was accepted by D in time. P applied for an order that D should pay P's costs to be taxed on scale 1 pursuant to Ord. 11, r.3(5) of C.C.R., notwithstanding that P had accepted less than £1,000.

Held, rejecting P's appeal against the failure of this application, that the £360 paid before issue of proceedings did not properly form part of P's claim at the commencement of the action, it was no longer in issue and its inclusion might be construed as an over-estimation of the claim's value. The claim for loss of use which was added later could not have been within the minds of those who formulated the claim and should not form part of the damages that P could reasonably have expected to recover at the date of issue. P could not have had reasonable expectation that the claim's value would have exceeded £1,000.

TATTER AND TATTER v. SINGH, February 10, 1995, H.H.J. Wilcox, Birmingham County Ct. [*Ex rel*. Buller Jeffries, Solicitors, Birmingham.]

3982. Costs—fixed costs—payment into court—whether reasonable expectation of obtaining more than £1,000—whether payment near limit suggested reasonable expectation

P sustained an injury to his neck and shoulder, necessitating a two-week absence from work. After fairly lengthy correspondence, D indicated that liability would not be in dispute, but refused to confirm that they would pay costs. Following commencement of proceedings, a payment into court of £875 was accepted. D refused to pay costs on the grounds that P did not have reasonable expectation of obtaining more than £1,000 and that proceedings should not have been commenced in the first place. D appealed against the district judge's decision that costs should be paid on Scale 1.

Held, dismissing the appeal, that the payment into court of £875 was so close to the figure of £1,000 that it was an indication that the case was reasonably valued at over £1,000. He further held that D had allowed several hundred pounds worth of costs to have been incurred by P prior to accepting liability. It was for D to decide what to do in these circumstances regarding payment of P's reasonable costs before issue and where P is at the mercy of D. The court noted that it was not surprising that proceedings were issued and that until the question of costs was answered by D, this type of litigation would continue.

RAMAGE v. VAUXHALL MOTORS, April 10, 1995, Wandsworth County Ct. [*Ex rel*. Peter Carson, Solicitor, Rowley Ashworth, Leeds.]

3983. Costs—fixed costs—premature issue of proceedings—road traffic litigation—whether proceedings issued before insurers given opportunity to settle claim

On July 12, 1994, P's solicitors wrote a letter before action to D intimating a claim arising from a road traffic accident on June 30, 1994. A copy of the letter was sent to D's road traffic insurers seeking confirmation within 14 days that indemnity would be granted, that liability was not in dispute, that interest would be paid on all heads of damages and that reasonable costs and disbursements would be met. The letter further stated that if confirmation was given the letter was formal notice under the Road Traffic Act to commence proceedings against D. On July 20, 1994 D's insurers replied requesting details as to why D was being held responsible for the accident and requesting details of the claim with supporting documentation. Without further correspondence P's solicitors issued proceedings on July 28, 1994 limiting damages to £1,000. Negligence was not in dispute and D's insurers wished to settle the claim. After an extension of time a defence admitting negligence was sent on September 2, 1994 to the Mold County Court. Judgment in default was entered on September 2, 1994. As soon as information and documentation was provided by P's solicitors as to the items claimed an offer was made to settle P's claim in the sum of £335·90. This offer was accepted; however, P's solicitors sought costs on scale 1. The action proceeded to an assessment of damages hearing on the costs point only. At the assessment of damages hearing the judge felt that proceedings had been issued prematurely without giving D's insurers adequate opportunity to settle the claim.

Held, that P would be awarded the agreed sum of £335·90. However, P's costs of the action were disallowed save for £33 fixed costs which the judge felt P's solicitors would have been entitled to in any event. An order was made that P pay D's costs of the assessment of damages hearing in any event to be taxed if not agreed on scale 1. A certificate for counsel was granted.

ROSE v. PITMAN, November 2, 1994; District Judge Reeves; Mold County Ct. [*Ex rel. Wendy J. Sanders, Solicitor*].

3984. Costs—fixed costs—premature issue of proceedings—whether defendant given adequate opportunity to respond

On November 2, 1994, P's solicitors wrote a letter before action to D's insurers, intimating a claim arising from a road traffic accident on October 12, 1994. That letter sought confirmation within 14 days that liability would not be in dispute, that they would be granting their insured indemnity, that interest would be paid on all heads of damage and that they would be responsible for P's solicitors' costs and disbursements. The letter further stated that if confirmation was not given, the letter was formal notice under the Road Traffic Act to commence proceedings against D. On November 10, 1994, D's insurers replied, confirming their interest, and requesting details of P's claim with documentary evidence in support and advice as to P's VAT status. P's solicitors replied on November 28, 1994, enclosing a copy of the accident repair invoice evidencing P's policy excess. They also stated that P's claim included sums for sundry expenses and inconvenience, and suggested that they would be prepared to settle for a total of £100, together with fixed costs of £33. On December 1, 1994, D's insurers replied confirming that they would pay P's policy excess of £50. They also requested detailed and where appropriate documentary evidence to support the claim for sundry expenses and inconvenience. Without further correspondence, P's solicitors issued proceedings on January 3, 1995, limiting damages to £1,000. Negligence was not in dispute, and D's insurers wished to settle the claim. Solicitors instructed by D's insurers filed a defence admitting liability and at the same time wrote to P's solicitors stating that D's insurers were prepared to pay £125 in full and final settlement of P's claim, but that they were not prepared to pay costs, either the issue fee or fixed costs as proceedings had been issued prematurely. The £125 was accepted as an interim payment, and the matter proceeded to an arbitration hearing. The only issue to be decided was the question of P's solicitors' costs.

Held, that proceedings had been issued prematurely without giving D's insurers adequate opportunity to settle the claim (*Rose v. Pitman* [1995] 1 C.L. 314 considered).

ROCKETT v. ROTHERHAM HEALTH SERVICE TRUST, April 26, 1995, District Judge Reeve, Mold County Ct. [*Ex rel.* Richard West of Gepp & Sons, Solicitors, Chelmsford.]

3985. Costs—fixed costs—unreasonable conduct in arbitration proceedings—unmeritorious defence—whether plaintiff entitled to costs

[C.C.R., Ord. 19, r.4(2)(c).]

P claimed damages totalling £821·32 as a result of a road traffic accident. D denied any involvement in the accident. At the arbitration hearing D's evidence was entirely discounted and judgment was awarded to P. P applied for costs on scale 1 rather than fixed costs and contended that as D's evidence was palpably false this amounted to unreasonable conduct for the purposes of Ord. 19, r.4(2)(c).

Held, that in circumstances where D had plainly and simply lied in relation to his involvement in the accident thus engendering the proceedings, the court would exercise its discretion under Ord. 19, r.4(2)(c), and costs were awarded to P on scale 1.

WRIGHT v. RYDER, March 24, 1995; D.D.J. Healey; Bodmin County Ct. [*Ex rel.* Nigel Partridge, Lyons Davidson, Solicitors].

3986. Costs—indemnity costs—defendant—refusal of plaintiff's to settle Calderbank offer—whether costs to be awarded

A defendant in an action for personal injuries who refused a plaintiff's offer to settle which was contained in a *Calderbank* letter, could in principle be awarded indemnity costs when the plaintiff was then awarded damages in excess of the offer made. In the instant case the offer had been made only six days before the start of the trial, and the defendants were therefore not given sufficient time to evaluate it or to respond and should be indemnified accordingly (*Calderbank v. Calderbank* [1975] C.L.Y. 963).

McDONNELL v. WOODHOUSE & JONES, *The Times*, May 25, 1995, Waterhouse J.

3987. Costs—interest—costs greater than damages awarded—costs and damages exceeding £5,000—whether interest payable on costs

[County Courts (Interest on Judgments) Order 1991 (S.I. 1991 No. 1184 (L.12)).]

P had been awarded judgment in a personal injury action which had begun in the High Court and had been transferred to the county court. P was awarded damages of £3,045 and costs of £15,000 representing High Court costs up to a specified date and county court costs thereafter. Costs were eventually settled at £11,750 but P applied for an order that he was entitled to interest on those costs under the County Courts (Interest on Judgments Debts) Order 1991. D submitted that interest should not be payable on the county court costs.

Held, that the costs were far greater than the damages in this case and the issue was therefore an important one. The County Courts (Interests on Judgment Debts) Order 1991 defines "judgment debt" as a debt under a relevant judgment, and "relevant judgment" as a judgment or order of a county court for the payment of a sum of money of not less than £5,000. The meaning of "sum of money" is not clear but in the court's opinion any sum of money which is part of a judgment debt (and that includes costs) will carry interest until paid from the date of the relevant judgment. An order for costs will therefore carry interest from the day of judgment (*Hunt v. Douglas (R.M.) (Roofing)* [1987] C.L.Y. 2793 applied).

EVANS (LYNDON) v. GWENT COUNTY COUNCIL, April 8, 1994; H.H.J. Pitchford; Gwent County Ct. [*Ex rel. Robin Thompson and Partners, Solicitors*].

3988. Costs—interim certificate—petition to wind up company—*locus standi* of petitioner. See TOTTENHAM HOTSPUR v. EDENNOTE, §2863.

3989. Costs—interlocutory applications—whether judge limited as to amount of award

[C.C.R. 1981, Ord. 38, r.19.]

Following dismissal of her claim for damages M sought leave to appeal against an award of costs of £400 to the defendants. M argued that as the award was made in relation to an interlocutory application, the judge was limited to award £95 in terms of C.C.R., Ord. 38, r.19.

Held, refusing the application, that there was no merit in M's complaint. The judge correctly applied Ord. 38, r.19.1 and Appendix C thereto, to the case before him.

MCLEOD (SALLY) v. WOLSEY HALL OXFORD AND MIDDLESEX UNIVERSITY AND COMMON PROFESSIONAL EXAMINATION BOARD (LTA 94/569/F), February 1, 1995, C.A.

3990. Costs—judgment debts—set-off—whether creditor entitled to set off costs award against debt. See BROOKES v. HARRIS, §3108.

3991. Costs—judicial review—application to have respondent committed for contempt—costs of responding to such an application—whether wasted costs order appropriate. See R. v. LIVERPOOL CITY COUNCIL, *ex p.* MAY, §134.

3992. Costs—magistrates' court—whether litigant has an automatic right of appeal against costs order

[Control of Pollution Act 1974 (c.40).]

A notice was served on W in respect of a refuse tip operated by them, and they appealed. The case was settled between the parties' lawyers and it was agreed that the appeal would be postponed for six months to allow remedial work to be carried out. The parties agreed that costs should be paid as the court would decide, but following the court's decision on costs W disagreed, and appealed. The issue to be decided in the High Court was whether an appeal was unavailable because of the settlement agreement.

Held, that although the costs order was incidental to the Control of Pollution Act 1974, there was no right of appeal against the magistrates' decision in these circumstances.

R. v. CANTERBURY CROWN COURT, *ex p.* KENT COUNTY COUNCIL [1994] Env.L.R. D3, D.C.

3993. Costs—nil contribution by legally-aided party—relevance to costs issue

H was allowed judgment in the sum of £10,500 in an action against C. He was acting as a litigant in person and in deciding the matter of costs was not asked by the judge to make submissions in regard to C's solicitor's response. C was legally aided with a nil contribution and the judge decided not to make an order against him, nor to make an order as to costs. H sought leave to appeal, claiming that he had costs of £3,000 to be met.

Held, granting leave, that there was no reason in principle why a judge should refuse to make an order on the basis that the legally-aided party had a nil contribution. The judge should have invited H to make submissions on the matter if he wished to do so.

HORNBY v. CRIPPS (LTA 94/5749/C), January 13, 1995, C.A.

3994. Costs—non-party—costs of Official Solicitor—whether judge right to order non-party to pay costs of the Official Solicitor

[Supreme Court Act 1981 (c.54), s.18(1)(f).]

Where an application had been made by a person following independent legal advice, and that application was dismissed as misconceived and unnecessary, it was wrong to make an order for costs against another person not party to the proceedings.

The health authority set up a committee to review the legality of medical treatment for children, and its draft report recommended the institution of proceedings under the Children Act 1989 in cases of doubt. The hospital, having received the draft report, took its own legal advice which was to the same effect. Shortly afterwards, prompted by the report, the hospital brought proceedings in respect of the medical treatment of three children. The Official Solicitor was appointed as the children's guardian *ad litem*. The judge dismissed the hospital's applications as misconceived and unnecessary, and ordered the health authority to pay one half of the Official Solicitor's costs. The health authority appealed, with leave of the judge, against the order for costs.

Held, allowing the appeal, that (1) the Court of Appeal would only interfere with the judge's discretion as to costs where it was plainly wrong or where there was an error of law (*Findlay v. Railway Executive* [1947–1951] C.L.C. 7595, *Alltrans Express v. CVA Holdings* [1984] C.L.Y. 2601 applied); (2) an order for costs against a non-party was always exceptional and should not be made unless the non-party is so closely connected with, or responsible for, the proceedings as to make it just to saddle him with the liability for the costs (*Aiden Shipping Co. v. Interbulk; Vimeria, The* [1986] C.L.Y. 2606, *Symphony Group v. Hodgson* [1993] C.L.Y. 3153 applied); (3) since the hospital had taken its own legal advice and did not inform or consult the health authority before making the applications, it was plainly wrong to make any order for costs against the health authority; and (4) since the Official Solicitor was entitled to a contribution towards his costs, the hospital would be ordered to pay half his costs (*Eady v. Elsdon* [1901] 2 K.B. 460, *P.C. (An Infant), Re* [1961] C.L.Y. 4366,

G. (Official Solicitor's Costs), Re [1982] 3 FLR 340, *H. (A Minor), Re*, October 30, 1986, unrep. considered).

NORTHAMPTON HEALTH AUTHORITY v. THE OFFICIAL SOLICITOR AND THE GOVERNORS OF ST. ANDREWS HOSPITAL [1994] 1 FLR 162, C.A.

3995. Costs—non-party—witness—husband seeking order for costs against accountant who gave evidence for wife in ancillary relief proceedings—procedure to be adopted on application for costs against witness—whether court should make order for costs against the witness

[R.S.C., Ord. 15, r.6.]

Costs orders against persons who were not parties to the proceedings were exceptional, and a forensic accountant who had given evidence for the wife in ancillary relief proceedings should not be ordered to pay the husband's costs.

In ancillary relief proceedings, the judge made criticisms of the forensic accountant who gave evidence for W. H sought to join the accountant as a second respondent to the proceedings for the determination of an application that he be ordered to pay H's costs or such part thereof as might be just. H further sought leave to serve points of claim to form the basis of pleadings in the costs application.

Held, dismissing the application, that (1) the determination of an application for costs against a stranger should ordinarily be by summary procedure. Further, a costs order against a non-party would always be exceptional and an application for such an order should be treated with considerable caution (*Symphony Group v. Hodgson* [1993] 3 W.L.R. 830 applied); (2) the proper procedure was to arrange a hearing at which the non-party could attend and to indicate in solicitor correspondence particulars of how the application would be put. It was unnecessary and undesirable to join the potential payer as a party; and (3) ordinarily, witnesses in civil proceedings enjoyed immunity from any form of civil action in respect of their evidence. In any event, the principal causative factor of the wasteful presentation of W's case was W's unshakeable and unfounded conviction that H had concealed assets.

[*Per curiam*: Forensic accountants make a very important contribution in the field of ancillary relief. The readiness to continue to make this contribution should not be shaken by the risk that if this evidence was critically received they might be ordered to pay part of the litigation costs.]

S. v. S. (APPLICATION FOR COSTS AGAINST WITNESS) [1995] 1 F.C.R. 185, Thorpe J.

3996. Costs—notice of discontinuance—legal aid certificate discharged—whether plaintiff entitled to status of assisted party. See BARKER v. RYE, §3105.

3997. Costs—payment into court—automatic striking-out—payment out of court to D on dismissal of P's application for reinstatement of action—payment back into court following P's successful appeal—whether D entitled to protection of payment in court for entire period

P sustained a broken finger on his dominant hand in a road traffic accident in June 1991. He brought an action seeking general damages in respect of this injury and special damages in respect of commission which he claimed he had lost whilst unable to work. D made payment into court on March 18, 1993 which took into account the claimed loss of commission. P's action was automatically struck out. D then discovered evidence which cast very significant doubt upon the veracity of P's claim for loss of commission. P applied for the reinstatement of his action and D cross-applied for the money in court to be reduced in the event that the action was reinstated. The applications were heard on May 20, 1994: P's application was dismissed by the district judge who also ordered payment out to D of all money in court. On appeal on June 28, 1994, however, the action was reinstated. On August 9, 1994 D made a renewed payment into court, but in a reduced figure: it took no account of the claimed loss of commission. P accepted the renewed payment in within 21 days of August 9, 1994 and asserted that the normal costs consequences should follow. D contended that the money had been paid out of court only because of the default of P and that it would therefore be right to disregard the fact that there had been a period when there was no money in court. D invited the court to award her her costs from March 18, 1993, the date of the original payment into court.

Held, that the money was paid out of court only because P allowed his action to be automatically struck out; had it not been for this default there would have been a reduction of the money in court but no total withdrawal. D should not be prejudiced by P's default. D was entitled to the protection of a payment into court for the whole of the period from March 18, 1993. P had not accepted D's payment into court within 21 days of March 18, and had therefore to pay D's costs from that date (*Garner v. Cleggs* [1983] C.L.Y. 3023 considered).

ASHTON v. CHARMAN, January 20, 1995; District Judge Brown; Croydon County Ct. [*Ex rel. Paul Greaney, Barrister*].

3998. Costs—payment into court—consent order for interlocutory judgment with damages to be assessed and costs—award less than payment into court—whether entitled to costs

P's Porsche was damaged in a road traffic accident, and he hired a replacement Porsche at a total cost of £4,875, whilst repairs were being carried out. Proceedings were issued on March 20, 1995, and a defence was filed admitting negligence, but disputing *quantum*. On April 4, 1995, D made a payment into court. D then consented to the interlocutory judgment, with damages to be assessed, and costs, and on May 5, 1995, the court sealed the consent order. At the assessment of damages hearing, P failed to beat the payment in but the district judge held that P was entitled to the costs of the action up to and including the assessment of damages hearing, notwithstanding the payment into court. The word "costs" in the consent order was construed to mean the costs of the action. The consent order overruled the normal rule that D was entitled to costs from the date of the payment in.

Held, on D's appeal, that the correct construction of the word "costs" in the consent order should be "such costs as are ordered by the person assessing the damages". There were no grounds for the proposition that those words overrode the payment in, and there was never any intention that this should be the case. D's appeal was allowed, and P was ordered to pay D's costs from April 4, 1995.

WINTER v. VAN DER POOL, September 27, 1995, H.H.J. Quentin Edwards, Q.C., Central London County Ct. [*Ex rel.* Browne Jacobson, Solicitors, London.]

3999. Costs—payment into court—failure to allow adequate opportunity to settle—whether premature issue of proceedings—whether absolute right to tax bill of costs following acceptance of payment into court

Following a road traffic accident on January 9, 1995, P's solicitors sent a letter before action dated January 19, 1995, together with a s.152 notice (under the Road Traffic Act 1988) to D's insurers. By letter dated January 24, 1995, D's insurers requested details. Proceedings were issued on January 30, 1995. D made a payment into court on February 17, 1995, which was thereafter accepted on February 21, 1995. On March 7, 1995, D's solicitors issued an application that P's solicitors' costs in the action be disallowed on the grounds that they issued prematurely and failed to allow D's insurers sufficient time to deal with their client's claim.

Held, that a plaintiff has an absolute right to tax his bill of costs following acceptance of payment into court. D's application was dismissed, and P was given leave to lodge a bill of costs for taxation within 14 days. Costs were awarded to P, to be taxed on scale 1 if not agreed (*Stafford Knight and Co. v. Conway* [1970] C.L.Y. 401 followed).

SINGLETON v. JACKSON, June 8, 1995, Deputy District Judge Levin, Birkenhead County Ct. [*Ex rel.* Michael W. Halsall, Solicitors, Merseyside.]

4000. Costs—payment into court—failure to allow adequate opportunity to settle—whether premature issue of proceedings—whether relevant to costs

[C.C.R., Ord. 11, r.3(5).]

Following a road traffic accident on July 22, 1994, P's solicitors wrote to D by letter, dated January 6, 1995, and this letter was passed to D insurers, who wrote to P's solicitors on January 16, 1995, requesting documentation in support of P's claim. By letter dated January 18, 1995, P's solicitors provided this documentation. On January 25, 1995, P's solicitors issued proceedings. D filed a defence on February 16, 1995, and a payment into court was made on February 20, 1995. On February 27, 1995, a notice of acceptance of the payment into court was filed by P's solicitor. D's solicitors issued an application to debar P from taxing his costs, on the grounds that P had acted unreasonably in failing to provide D with an adequate opportunity to settle this matter without the issue of proceedings.

Held, that the court was not persuaded that it had discretion to negate the rules regarding notice of acceptance, specifically C.C.R., Ord. 11, r.3(5). The deputy district judge found that this was not an application as to whether there was an abuse of process of the court, it was an application as to whether P was entitled to costs. The court would not go behind the rules and the application was ill-conceived in its present form. Following acceptance of payment into court, the plaintiff has an absolute right to lodge a bill for taxation. The action was dismissed and P awarded his costs (*Bartlett v. Nixon* [1994] C.L.Y. 3594 considered).

CORLESS v. CORNER, May 31, 1995, Deputy District Judge Grosscurth, Birkenhead County Ct. [*Ex rel.* Michael W. Halsall, Solicitors, Merseyside.]

4001. Costs—payment into court—notice of acceptance—entitlement to taxed costs—whether discretion in court to limit costs recoverable by plaintiff

[C.C.R., Ord. 11, r.3(5).]

D's car collided with the rear of P's car, causing substantial damage to it. P obtained an engineer's report on the cost of repairs and the value of the vehicle. Having regard to the extent of the damage, P was, under the terms of his insurance policy, entitled to have his car replaced with a new car. Prior to the commencement of the proceedings D's insurers requested a copy of the engineer's report which P's insurers refused to supply. By that time P's car had been disposed of by salvage. D's insurers failed to admit liability and failed to make any offers in settlement of P's claim. P commenced proceedings, seeking to recover £19,000 based on the cost of providing a replacement car. D filed a defence admitting negligence but denying causation and *quantum* and continued to request sight of the engineer's report. P claimed to have supplied a copy of the report with its letter before action but D's insurers claimed not to have received it. Four-and-a-half months after the commencement of the proceedings D paid £16,050 into court. P accepted the sum paid into court within 21 days and thereupon became entitled under C.C.R., Ord. 11, r.3(5), to lodge a bill of costs for taxation. D issued an application seeking an order to restrict P's costs to those stated on the summons in lieu of costs taxed on scale 2, on the grounds that if P's insurers had supplied the engineer's report when asked to do so D could have paid into court within two weeks of the commencement of the proceedings and thereby limited its exposure to costs to those stated on the face of the summons and that P was guilty of some unfair conduct in forcing D to defend the action with no evidence concerning P's car or its value, the damage caused and the likely cost of its repair. D's application was dismissed by the district judge. D appealed to the circuit judge who found in D's favour on the factual matters in dispute concerning the provision of the engineer's report and allowed the appeal.

Held, allowing P's appeal, that P's claim was not for a debt or liquidated demand. In consequence, under C.C.R., Ord. 11, r.3(5), P was entitled as of right to lodge a bill of costs for taxation. The Court did not have any discretion to interfere with that right and had no power to make an order limiting P's costs to those stated on the summons (*Stafford Knight & Co. v. Conway* [1970] C.L.Y. 401 followed).

MEDISURE MARKETING AND MANAGEMENT v. WOOLVEN, November 9, 1994, C.A., [*Ex rel. Charles E. Scott, Barrister*].

4002. Costs—payment into court—same amount as offer made before proceedings began—whether P's costs to be limited

[C.C.R. Ord. 11, r.5.]

P was involved in a road traffic accident on August 22, 1994, and suffered a whiplash injury for six to eight months. A letter before action was written on December 20, 1994, and appropriate notice given under the Road Traffic Act 1988, s.152, to D's insurers. On January 10, 1995, P's solicitors requested an admission of liability. On February 20, D's insurers offered £1,000 general damages. On February 22, this was rejected. On March 24, P's solicitors requested an increased offer, but the insurers stated that they thought £1,000 was fairly reasonable, and if proceedings were issued in the case, they would make a payment in of that sum and refer the court to *Calderbank*. Proceedings were instituted on April 12, and on May 12, a payment of £1,000 was made into court. Upon further consideration, P decided to accept the payment into court (in view of the risks of litigation) and a notice of acceptance was filed on May 17. D's solicitors issued an application asking the court to limit P's costs up to the date of the original offer of March 29, and thereafter the costs to be D's. P's solicitors relied upon C.C.R., Ord. 11, r.3(5), and the case of *Stafford Knight & Co. v. Conway*, which confers an absolute right to lodge a bill of costs to taxation if a notice of acceptance has been filed.

Held, dismissing D's application, that there was an absolute right to taxed costs following a notice of acceptance. The matter was one to be dealt with on taxation. D's subsequent appeal against this decision was dismissed (*Stafford Knight & Co. v. Conway* [1970] C.L.Y. 401 considered).

HUGHES v. VOSE, August 11, 1995, District Judge Richardson, Birkenhead County Ct. [*Ex rel.* Michael W. Halsall, Solicitors.]

4003. Costs—payment into court of costs on summons—whether representing costs of action—whether additional costs recoverable

[County Courts Act 1984 (c.28), s.138(2).]

D, in accordance with the County Courts Act 1984, s.138(2), paid into court the rent in arrears, and the costs on the summons being £111, that is £65 court fee and £56 solicitors' costs, suggesting that by reason of this payment, the action ceased. However, and as is very often the case, P had incurred considerably more costs than £111. The argument therefore focused on what costs P was entitled to recover under the Act.

Held, that the costs of the action meant the entire costs of the action, and not just the court fee and solicitors' costs.

MELVIEW PROPERTIES v. PERSONAL REPRESENTATIVES OF DR KLINGER (DEC'D), October 12, Recorder Hill-Smith,Central London Ct. [*Ex rel.* Steven Woolf, Hardwicke Building, Lincoln's Inn.]

4004. Costs—personal injury action—two defendants—plaintiff successful against one defendant but not the other—unsuccessful defendant not blaming successful defendant—whether unsuccessful defendant should be ordered to pay successful defendant's costs

In some circumstances, an unsuccessful defendant in a personal injury action may be ordered to pay a successful defendant's costs, even though the unsuccessful defendant has at no time sought to blame the other for the injury.

P attended the casualty department of one of D1's hospitals with a foot complaint and was treated by a doctor, M, who was under a contract of service with D1. Nearly a week later, P was seen by her own G.P., D2. Two days later she was admitted to another of D1's hospitals and treated by medical staff there. Her leg was eventually amputated. P claimed damages for personal injury against D1, alleging negligence by M, and against D2 for his own negligence. At no time did D2 seek to hold M responsible for P's injury but at a late stage he did seek to blame the medical staff who had treated P at the second hospital. P adopted these allegations and amended her claim against D1 accordingly. P succeeded in her action against D2 but was unsuccessful against D1, both with regard to the allegations against M and the allegations against the staff at the second hospital. Judge J. ordered D2 to pay D1's costs save in so far as they related to the allegations against M, on the ground that D2 had never sought to blame M. P appealed against the order that she should pay that part of D1's costs relating to the allegations of negligence by M.

Held, allowing P's appeal, that (1) in relation to costs, the court had a general discretion to do what, in all the circumstances of the case, it thought was right; (2) where a plaintiff sued two defendants and succeeded against only one of them, the fact that the unsuccessful defendant had at no time sought to blame the other, successful defendant was a very weighty consideration in deciding whether to order the unsuccessful defendant to pay the other's costs but it was not conclusive. By treating it as conclusive, the judge had failed to exercise his discretion at all; and (3) exercising the discretion afresh, all the other factors weighed in favour of ordering D2 to pay the whole of D1's costs. As far as P was concerned, she was suing various persons all within the umbrella of the NHS. It was reasonable for P to sue D1 in respect of M. More importantly, it was inappropriate to make an order which benefited P in respect of one of the issues on which she had failed against D1 (the allegations of negligence by staff at the second hospital) but not in respect of the other (the allegation of negligence by M). P should not be penalised for bringing D1 into the action at the outset and for making no more extensive allegations than if she had simply adopted those made by D2 (*Scherer v. Counting Instruments* [1986] C.L.Y. 2572 applied; *Hong v. A. & R. Brown* [1948] 1 K.B. 515, *Elgindata (No. 2), Re* [1993] C.L.Y. 3144 considered).

[*Per curiam*: The facts of the case were unusual and it was doubtful whether it would be possible to apply them by analogy, save very rarely.]

GERDES-HARDY v. WESSEX REGIONAL HEALTH AUTHORITY [1994] P.I.Q.R. P368, C.A.

4005. Costs—registration as child-minder—application—applicant on legal aid—successful appeal to be registered as child-minder—justices ordering local authority to pay costs—whether entitled to make order

[Family Proceedings Courts (Children Act 1989) Rules 1991 (S.I. 1991 No. 1395), r.22(1).]

Where justices are hearing proceedings under the Children Act 1989 relating to the registration of a child-minder, they are entitled to exercise their discretion to award costs.

Following the legally-aided applicant's successful appeal to the justices to be registered as a child-minder, the justices, at an adjourned hearing, ordered the local authority to pay her costs of £15,712. The local authority appealed the order of costs.

Held, dismissing the appeal, that (1) the proceedings did not relate to a child but to the applicant's fitness to be registered as a childminder so that it was open to the justices to use their discretion on the question of costs; (2) it had been reasonable for the justices to make a specific order as to costs on the ample material available to them.

[*Per curiam*: There is an urgent need for reform of procedures in relation to the quantification of costs in civil proceedings in the magistrates' court.]

SUTTON LONDON BOROUGH COUNCIL v. DAVIS (NO. 2) [1994] 1 W.L.R. 1317, Wilson J.

4006. Costs—reserved costs—family proceedings—not requested at conclusion of original hearing—whether jurisdiction to award subsequently

The Family Division had jurisdiction to award reserved costs, which should have been, but were not, requested at the conclusion of the original hearing, in a supplementary order to the original costs order (*British Natural Premium Provident Association v. Bywater* [1897] 2 Ch. 531, *Cobbold v. Garrett* [1929] W.N. 16 considered).

S. v. S. (FAMILY PROCEEDINGS: RESERVED COSTS ORDERS), *The Times*, February 23, 1995, Michael Horowitz, Q.C.

4007. Costs—security for costs—bankrupt given financial help by mother—jurisdiction of court

[R.S.C., Ord. 23.]

H appealed against a decision allowing C's appeal against an order that he provide security for H's costs in a libel action against H, in default of which the proceedings would be stayed. C became bankrupt soon after proceedings began and C's mother gave an undertaking to pay H's costs. H sought to argue that R.S.C., Ord. 23, was not exhaustive as to the circumstances in which an order for security for costs might be made and that the court had an inherent jurisdiction to make use of orders to guard against the abuse of maintenance.

Held, dismissing the appeal, that it was clear from the wording of Ord. 23 that it was intended to be exhaustive as to the circumstances in which a court could require security for costs. There was nothing to justify the making of an order where a family member sought to give financial help to someone in C's position.

CONDLIFFE v. HISLOP, *The Times*, November 3, 1995, C.A.

4008. Costs—security for costs—counterclaim—founded on same facts—whether to grant stay of proceedings—whether defendant had contumeliously failed to comply with previous order

P applied for a permanent stay of a counterclaim during arbitration proceedings. The claims were substantial and founded on the same facts.

Held, dismissing the application, that where claims were based on the same facts, an order for security of costs should be for the full amount of the costs and not just for P's increased costs in defending the counterclaim. A temporary order for a stay already existed and an order for a permanent stay would deprive a defendant of his claim. Such an order should not be made unless the defendant had contumeliously failed to comply with a previous order or if there was absolutely no chance that an application to lift the stay would succeed.

PETROMIN v. SECNAV MARINE, *The Times*, March 9, 1995, Coleman J.

4009. Costs—security for costs—counterclaim—substantial claimants—claim based on same body of facts—whether plaintiff to be secured for full costs or merely counterclaim

Where both parties were substantial claimants founding their claims on the same body of facts, as in the instant case, the plaintiff was entitled to be secured in respect of costs no less fully than if he were merely defendant to the claim advanced in the counterclaim and not also plaintiff in the action. Therefore, any order for security of costs was to be for the full amount of those costs and not merely for the amount by which the plaintiff's costs were increased in defending the counterclaim. In deciding whether to grant the permanent stay of a counterclaim, the defendants having failed, contrary to the court's order, to provide security for the plaintiff's costs of the counterclaim, it was important to give appropriate weight to the fact that an order would absolutely deprive the claimant of his claim.

PRETOMIN v. SECNAV MARINE, *The Times*, March 9, 1995, Colman J.

4010. Costs—security for costs—counterclaim—whether security for costs should be given by a counterclaiming defendant

D had been engaged to develop a site and engaged Ps as construction managers for the development. D agreed to pay Ps all costs reasonably incurred together with a management fee of £1·2 million. Difficulties arose and D refused to make any further instalment payments of the management fee. The contract was terminated and Ps claimed prime costs and fees of about £1 million. D counterclaimed damages for breach of contract and expense and financing charges totalling £15 million. Ps sought an order for security for costs which they were granted. D sought leave to appeal against this order.

Held, dismissing the application for leave to appeal, that whether security for costs should be ordered to be given by a counterclaiming defendant is a matter of discretion (*New Fenix v. General Accident* [1911] K.B. 619 applied). The court must consider whether the defendant is in such a character of plaintiff in the counterclaim that it ought to be ordered to give security because it has taken up the position of plaintiff irrespective of the defence to the original action. The court can make such an order even in the absence of exceptional circumstances. The Official Referee had not erred in his discretion to an extent which should cause the Court of Appeal to review it.

L/M PARTNERSHIP v. CIRCLE PARTNERSHIP [1993] 9 Const. L.J 196, C.A.

4011. Costs—security for costs—joinder as plaintiff—court powers to impose conditions upon joinder—whether defendant protected against costs which cannot be paid by plaintiff

S, a director of E, appealed against an order that he pay £5,000 into court as security for costs in order to be joined as a plaintiff in addition to E in its action against C. The company had been sold to him after the commencement of the action. C cross-appealed that the joinder should be set aside. The proceedings had been stayed when E had not complied with an order for security for costs. C claimed that the transaction by which the business was sold to S was a sham, intended to frustrate the court's order for security and circumvent the rule that companies could not claim legal aid.

Held, allowing the appeal in part, that the condition on the joinder be set aside and the cross-appeal dismissed. The county court, whilst having no jurisdiction to order a personal plaintiff to pay security for costs, did have power to impose conditions upon joinder. This included security for costs and the basis for the order was that C should be in the same position with regard to S as it was with E. However, E's action had been stayed and S was a personal plaintiff. The law offered a defendant no protection against costs which could not be paid by impoverished personal plaintiffs. There was no justification for the contention that S's action was a sham. He had exposed himself to the extent of his personal liability and he should not be penalised for that. Nor would the fact that he was eligible for legal aid, and the company was not, be a sufficient reason to refuse joinder. It was for the Legal Aid Board to enquire into the circumstances of any claim and to determine whether the grant of legal aid would be unreasonable.

EUROCROSS SALES v. CORNHILL INSURANCE, *The Times*, September 5, 1995, C.A.

4012. Costs—security for costs—"nominal plaintiff"—whether plaintiff was being deliberately duplicitous

[R.S.C., Ord. 23, r.1.]

T appealed against the refusal of his application that E provide security for costs under R.S.C., Ord. 23, r.1.

Held, dismissing the appeal, that Ord. 23, r.1 provided that a "nominal plaintiff" could be asked to provide security for costs. However, it must be proved that the plaintiff was being deliberately duplicitous and acting for the benefit of someone else before he could be regarded as a nominal plaintiff. This was not so in the instant case.

C.A. ENVIS v. THAKKAR, *The Times*, May 2, 1995, Kennedy L.J.

4013. Costs—security for costs—Northern Ireland plaintiff—enforceability of judgment—whether security for costs to be ordered automatically

[R.S.C., Ord. 23, r.1(1)(a).]

The court has jurisdiction to make an order for security for costs against a company incorporated in Northern Ireland.

D, a company incorporated and resident in Northern Ireland, appealed against an order to provide security for costs for the second defendant, K. The first defendant, KB, had been dissolved in Austria in 1991.

Held, allowing the appeal, that *Raeburn v. Andrews* established that security for costs should be ordered against plaintiffs from Northern Ireland because judgments were not enforceable against them, but this did not apply after the Judgments Extension Act 1868, which made judgments enforceable in England also enforceable in any other part of the U.K. The court had a discretion as to whether to order security for costs and here decided to refrain on the grounds that D had a strong claim and financial problems (*Raeburn v. Andrews* (1874) L.R. 9 Q.B. 118 considered).

DYNASPAN (U.K.), *Re*; DYNASPAN (U.K.) v. KATZENBERGER BAUKONSTRUKTIONEN (H.) GmbH & CO. KG [1995] 1 BCLC 536, Robert Walker J.

4014. Costs—security for costs—ordinarily resident out of the jurisdiction—test of ordinary residence

[R.S.C., Ord. 23, r.1(1)(a).]

A plaintiff is ordinarily resident outside the jurisdiction if the central control and management of the company actually abides and is exercised overseas.

P, a travel company, incorporated in Jersey, petitioned the court for relief under s.459 of the Companies Act 1985. D applied for an order pursuant to R.S.C., Ord. 23, that P give security for costs on the ground that P was ordinarily resident out of the jurisdiction.

Held, making the order, that P was ordinarily resident outside the jurisdiction of the central control and management of the company actually abides and is exercised overseas (*Unit Construction Co. v. Bullock* [1959] C.L.Y. 1519 applied).

LITTLE OLYMPIAN EACH WAYS, *Re* [1994] 4 All E.R. 561, Lindsay J.

4015. Costs—small claims—costs awarded on grounds of unreasonable conduct by plaintiff—leave to apply out of time to set aside award—whether arbitrator had jurisdiction to order taxation—whether judge had discretion as to amount of costs awarded

[C.C.R., Ord. 19, r.4(2)(c), C.C.R., Ord. 38, r.19.]

P and D were involved in a dispute over alleged defective workmanship in respect of a swimming pool installed by P at D's home. P sued for £953, being the balance of money allegedly due in respect of the works, plus interest, and pursuant to C.C.R., Ord. 19, the proceedings were referred to arbitration. D was successful and was awarded the costs of the action under C.C.R., Ord. 19, r.4(2)(c), on the grounds of unreasonable conduct by P, to be taxed on Scale 1 if not agreed. The costs were taxed and certified in the sum of £1,389·58, but before payment P argued that costs directed under C.C.R., Ord. 19, r.4(2)(c), on the grounds of unreasonable conduct" shall not be taxed but the amount to be allowed shall be specified by the arbitrator or district judge", per C.C.R., Ord. 19, r.4(5). P did not seek to disturb the finding that there had been unreasonable conduct but applied for leave to apply out of time on the ground that the arbitrator had no jurisdiction to order taxation. The judge appointed himself arbitrator (following *Leung v. Garbutt*), and heard argument as to the quantification of costs. P's counsel submitted that C.C.R., Ord. 38, r.19, dealing with assessed costs, applied to C.C.R., Ord. 19, r.4(2)(c), and the maximum which might be awarded was the figure set out in Appendix C, in this case, £488.

Held, on P's application to set aside the award in part, that leave would be granted and the award of taxed costs was contrary to C.C.R., Ord. 19, r. 4(5) and must be set aside. Rejecting P's submissions, C.C.R., Ord. 38, r.19, had no application and that there was a complete discretion as to the amount of costs which might be specified on the ground of unreasonable conduct. This was because (1) the award of costs in these circumstances was a punitive measure; (2) prior to the introduction of C.C.R., Ord. 19, r.4(5) in 1992, costs awarded for unreasonable conduct could be taxed; (3) there was no reason to suppose that the amendment was intended to impose the Appendix C limit; (4) C.C.R., Ord. 19 is a self-contained code and there was no reason to import elements of the main body of the rules; and (5) C.C.R., Ord. 38, r.19 was itself not exhaustive. Accordingly, D's costs of the arbitration were ordered in the sum of £1,389·58. P was further ordered to pay D's costs of the application to set aside the award, on Scale 1 (*Leung v. Garbett* [1980] C.L.Y. 411 followed).

FRONDA v. JACKSON, January 24, 1995; H.H.J. Goodman; Croydon County Ct. [*Ex rel. Philip Rainey, Barrister*].

4016. Costs—solicitors' liability—adjournment hearing—second hearing—client out of country—booking date after trial set down—solicitors failing to apply for adjournment before client left—correspondence to obtain consent from plaintiff—whether solicitors to pay costs

Following a pre-trial review, an action was set down for trial on June 28, 1995, with a time estimate of one day. On May 22, D's solicitors advised that D would be unavailable in June, since he would be out of the country visiting relatives Although these arrangements had been made months before, they had not been brought to the attention of the district judge at the pre-trial review. D's solicitors could not provide dates at that stage, but advised that they would do so as soon as the information was available from their client. P agreed to their request for an adjournment of the trial. On July 13 the matter was relisted for hearing on September 8. P wrote on July 20, confirming the trial date. On August 3, P received a letter from D's solicitors stating "our client has made arrangements to spend two weeks in Spain commencing on September 2, 1995" and requesting a further adjournment of the trial. In a letter of August 8, P asked whether or not D had known of this arrangement when the trial was relisted, and if so, whether his solicitors had also known of it. P indicated that they would not consent to a second adjournment and wished D to explain his position to the district judge. On August 15, P were provided with a copy of D's booking confirmation, dated July 30. D's solicitors advised that "if you persist in your refusal to an adjournment, we will be forced to draw this specifically to the Court's attention on the question of costs". P, noting that the date of issue of D's holiday booking form was well after notification of the trial date, requested an explanation from D's solicitors as to why the holiday had been booked to conflict with the trial date. On August 29, P received a letter from D's solicitors, stating "our instructions are that our client did not, in fact, book the holiday which will clash with the adjourned hearing of this matter on September 8. The arrangements were made without our client's knowledge by members of his family. The holiday was given to our client in view of his poor health. We have requested written confirmation of this from our client and will forward the same to you as soon as we are in receipt of it". On August 29, P confirmed that they were still not agreeing to an adjournment. D's solicitors had not, in fact, yet made an application to adjourn. P had asked for D's supporting documents, for the bundle, on a number of occasions, without success. They were now advised that the papers were with counsel. P lodged the trial bundles with the court and served a copy on D's solicitors. On September 1, 1995, P delivered their brief to counsel, with a copy of the trial bundle. On September 4, D's solicitors telephoned P and advised that their application to break the fixture would be heard on September 6. A letter from D's brother was produced, explaining why he had booked the holiday for D, even though the matter was listed for trial. D's solicitors confirmed to the court that D was already abroad, and would not be able to attend the September 8 hearing. Their application relied on *Joyce v. King*: "if it is clear that it will not be possible for a litigant to obtain justice without an adjournment then, regardless of inconvenience, an adjournment should be granted". P advised the court of their consistent opposition to the adjournment since August 8, and submitted that an application for adjournment should have been made earlier.

Held, that the only merit in D's application was that D, as the sole witness for the defence, could not be heard if he were not in the country, and, if the case proceeded to trial, judgment would almost inevitably be entered against him. The judge indicated that the situation could have been avoided if, as soon as D's solicitors became aware that P were not consenting to an adjournment, they had made an application to take the matter out of the list. The correspondence did not excuse this failure. Because of the risk of injustice to D, the judge was obliged to grant the application, but he did so only because D was already abroad. D's solicitors were ordered to pay P's costs of the application, and the costs of trial thrown away, to be taxed on Scale 1 if not agreed (*Joyce v. King*, *The Times*, July 13, 1987 cited).

TROBRIDGES v. WALKER, September 6, 1995, H.H.J. J.E. Previte, Q.C., Plymouth County Ct. [*Ex rel.* H. Davies, Trobridges, Solicitors, Plymouth.]

4017. Costs—solicitors' liability—case automatically struck out—without prejudice offer rejected after case struck out—whether solicitors liable to pay costs personally

P was involved in a road accident on March 22, 1991, and issued proceedings against D on November 19, 1992. A defence was filed on December 17, 1992, together with a request for further and better particulars of the particulars of claim. The automatic directions began to run on January 1, 1993. An application was issued on April 1993, to force P to give replies to the request for further and better particulars, and those replies were then made available by P's solicitors on June 3. P's solicitors served their list of documents on June 21. A request was made to P's solicitors to supply copies of P's wage slips in support of his claim for loss of earnings on September 2; a substantive reply to the enquiry was not made available until February 8, 1994. A "without prejudice" offer was made to P, with a view to settling the claim on March 3, which was rejected by P on May 23, 1994, by which time P's claim had been automatically struck out. P's solicitors did not respond to the question of the striking out until April 28, 1995. D's solicitors issued an application for the costs of the action to be paid by P's solicitors, P's solicitors issued a cross-application, asking for the case to be reinstated.

Held, that the application to reinstate the case would be dismissed, on the grounds that P's solicitors had not shown that they had dealt with the case with reasonable diligence. P was ordered to pay D's costs of the application, and of the action, on scale 2, subject to a means test under the Legal Aid Act 1988. It was further provided that P's solicitors were to show cause, on application to be made within one month of the date of the order, why they should not be personally liable for D's costs. P's solicitors made no attempt to do this, and by a further order the court confirmed that P's solicitors were to pay D's costs personally on Scale 2.

HAUGHTON v. R. & V. HANNAH & SONS, May 16 and August 2, 1995, District Judge Pomfret, Southport County Ct. [*Ex rel.* Hill Dickinson Davis Campbell, Solicitors, Liverpool.]

4018. Costs—solicitors' liability—striking out of claim—legally aided client whose legal aid status not notified to defendant—whether solicitors personally liable for costs

[C.C.R., Ord. 17, r.11(9).]

P was employed by D company, and was involved in an accident which occurred on June 12, 1992 at D's premises. A county court summons was issued against D on July 22, 1993, and a defence was filed to the action on September 3, 1993, resulting in a form N450 being issued, with automatic directions to run from September 13, 1993. Thereafter D's solicitors issued interlocutory applications on November 24, 1993, May 17, September 1 and October 25, 1994, attempting to obtain: replies from P to a request for further and better particulars; the filing of a list of documents; copies of documents in P's list; and an agreed date for exchange of witness statements, respectively. P was ordered to pay the costs of each interlocutory application, in any event. The 15 months to set the action down for trial, in accordance with C.C.R., Ord. 17, r.11(9), expired on December 27, 1994. P's solicitors issued an application on April 11, 1995 for the court to order that the action be set down for trial on the first available day, with a time estimate of one day. D's solicitors, arguing that the case had been struck out, issued a cross-application, asking the court to order that P's solicitors pay the costs of the action, including the costs of the application, personally. P's solicitors, in responding to the application in relation to costs, advised that their client was legally aided, which was the first notification that D's solicitors had received of P's legal aid status. A notice of issue of legal aid, dated May 18, 1995, was forwarded to D's solicitors, which confirmed that P had been legally aided since February 4, 1993. The court confirmed that no notice of issue of legal aid, or any legal aid certificate had been lodged with the court. P's solicitors then issued an application to have the claim reinstated and served an affidavit in support. The hearing of P's application to reinstate and D's application for costs came before the district judge on May 24, who adjourned both applications to enable P's solicitors to serve D's solicitors with their chronology of events. On June 12, P's application to reinstate the action was refused on the grounds that P's solicitors had not dealt with the case with reasonable diligence. In the costs application, which had been reserved to a later date, the district judge held that P's solicitors' conduct of the case fell below the standard required by a reasonable firm of solicitors. D had been prejudiced by not being advised of P's legally aided status whilst the action was being pursued. Accordingly, the court ordered that P's solicitors were to pay the costs of the action, including the costs of the application, personally, such costs to be taxed on an indemnity basis on scale 2 if not agreed.

HOLDEN v. ABER BUILDING SUPPLIES, July 20, 1995, District Judge R.A. Hoffman, Wrexham County Ct. [*Ex rel.* Hill Dickinson Davis Campbell, Solicitors.]

4019. Costs—taxation of costs—care proceedings—guidance on submission of bill of costs—whether solicitor from children panel appearing as advocate in itself an "exceptional circumstance" for the purposes of allowing larger amount

[Matrimonial Causes Act 1973 (c.18), s.50; Matrimonial and Family Proceedings Act 1984 (c.42), ss.40(1), 46(3), Sched. 3; Matrimonial and Family Proceedings Act 1984 (Commencement No. 5) Order 1991 (S.I. 1991 No. 1211); R.S.C., Ord. 62, r.12; C.C.R., Ord. 38; Civil Legal Aid (General) Regulations 1989 (S.I. 1989 No. 339), reg. 107(3)(b); Matrimonial Causes

(Costs) Rules 1988 (S.I. 1988 No. 1328), r.10, Sched. 1, para. 1(2)(4)(a), Sched. 2; Family Proceedings (Costs) Rules 1991 (S.I. 1991 No. 1832), r.2(2); Legal Aid in Family Proceedings (Remuneration) Regulations 1991 (S.I. 1991 No. 2038), regs. 3(1)(2)(4)(c)(7), 7, Scheds. 1, 2.]

A solicitor-advocate's membership of the Law Society's Children Panel was in itself an exceptional circumstance in care proceedings, giving a discretion to the taxing officer to allow a larger amount of costs than that specified in the relevant costs regulations.

A solicitor who was a member of the Law Society's Children Panel had acted for the stepfather of a child in care proceedings. He appeared as an advocate throughout the proceedings, including the final hearing, which lasted for six days (having been set down for 10 days). In total, there were five respondents to the local authority application, and the local authority was represented by leading counsel. The stepfather was a difficult client in that he was volatile and aggressive. Following the hearing, at which an interim care order was made, the solicitor submitted a bill of costs to be taxed under Sched. 1 to the Legal Aid in Family Proceedings (Remuneration) Regulations 1991 (the 1991 Regulations). The solicitor sought a mark-up for care and attention in respect of certain items. The district judge taxed the bill, and reviewed the matter following the solicitor's objections, and did not allow the mark-up in relation to all items. The solicitor sought a further review by the judge and assessors.

Held, that (1) the amounts allowed were set out in Sched. 1 to the 1991 Regulations. The taxing officer could allow a larger amount than the prescribed amount where it was reasonable, having regard to the matters set out in reg. 3(4)(c) of the 1991 Regulations; (2) no legal definition could be given for the words "exceptional circumstances of the case" in reg. 3(4)(c)(iii), nor was one necessary. The courts were well used to dealing with these words and taxing officers were well able to recognise exceptional circumstances; (3) the words "exceptional circumstances of the case" must mean the circumstances of the particular case at whatever level of court it is heard. It was only if the case affected the work done by the lawyers in a qualitative or quantitative sense that it became reasonable for the taxing officer to exercise the discretion to allow a larger amount; (4) on the true construction of reg. 3(4)(c)(iii) of the 1991 Regulations, membership of the Law Society's Children Panel in care proceedings was in itself an exceptional circumstance giving the taxing officer a discretion to allow a larger amount. It remained in the discretion of the taxing officer as to whether a larger amount should be given in any particular part of the bill in question; (5) some factors would not in themselves constitute exceptional circumstances justifying a larger hourly rate, but could justify the taxing officer allowing as reasonable more than the usual number of hours, at the prescribed hourly rate; (6) the mere appearance of a solicitor as an advocate did not constitute exceptional circumstances. However, the solicitor was a member of the Children's Panel, and the exceptional circumstance which therefore existed was unaffected by the fact that he was acting for the stepfather and not for the child. Looking at the specific features of the case, it was a heavy case, and certain features constituted exceptional circumstances; (7) the discretion to allow a larger amount was to be exercised in accordance with reg. 3(7) of the 1991 Regulations, which incorporated the "seven pillars" familiar to taxing officers; (8) the power to include an allowance for general care and conduct conferred by para. 1(4)(a) of Sched. 1 to the Matrimonial Causes (Costs) Rules 1988 had no application to taxations under the 1991 Regulations; (9) the starting point in the exercise of the taxing officer's discretion was the fixed rates prescribed by the 1991 Regulations. The district judge must keep in mind the controlling yardstick that numbers of solicitors are carrying out work, not within the exceptional circumstances range, but at the prescribed rates (*Freeman v. Freeman* unreported), February 21, 1992, Eastham J. distinguished); (10) it was well established that, in general, a solicitor's remuneration consisted of two elements, first an hourly rate representing the broad average direct cost of the work and secondly, a percentage mark-up for care and conduct (*R. v. Wilkinson* [1981] C.L.Y. 525, *Lloyds Bank v. Eastwood* [1974] C.L.Y. 2927, *Leopold Lazarus v. Secretary of State for Trade and Industry* [1976] C.L.Y. 2129 applied); (11) the 1991 Regulations contain only a figure for an hourly rate, which must be presumed to be inclusive of care and control. However, the taxing officer is entitled, when exercising his discretion to allow a larger amount, to have regard to the broad average direct cost and the mark-up approach. The court was not bound by such an approach, but it formed part of the fund of knowledge which the taxing officer employs when exercising his discretion (*Johnson v. Reed Corrugated Cases* [1992] C.L.Y. 3447, *Brush v. Bower Cotton & Bower (A Firm)* [1993] C.L.Y. 3169 considered; *B., Re* (unreported), March 21, 1986, Master Hirst, *R. v. Dunwoodie* [1978] C.L.Y. 536 distinguished); and (12) the court therefore substituted its own assessment as to what items would be allowed a larger amount, and the extent of the uplift in each case.

[*Per curiam*: (1) Factors which might well raise an exceptional circumstance included: innate difficulties of communication with the client, conflict of detailed expert evidence, a hearing in excess of two days without counsel, and where the child has instructed his own solicitor, conflict between the guardian *ad litem* and the child; (2) where an hourly rate was sought in excess of the specified amount, that had to be stated and an explanation provided of how it was calculated. The bill of costs should also identify and justify the specific areas of activity in respect of which the larger amount was claimed.]

CHILDREN ACT 1989 (TAXATION OF COSTS), *Re* [1994] 2 F.L.R. 934, Cazalet J.

4020. Costs—taxation of costs—counsel—seeking higher figure than prescribed rate—requirement that items requiring exercise of discretion are clearly identified

[Legal Aid in Family Proceedings (Remuneration) Regulations 1991 (S.I. 1991 No. 2038), Sched. 1.]

Where, in relation to taxation of costs in Sched. 1 to the Legal Aid in Family Proceedings (Remuneration) Regulations 1991, counsel sought a higher figure than the prescribed rate for particular items of work, those items requiring an exercise of discretion by taxing officers should be clearly identified.

H. (A MINOR: TAXATION OF COUNSEL'S COSTS), *Re*, *The Independent*, August 14, 1995, Cazalet J.

4021. Costs—taxation of costs—exceptional circumstances—whether solicitor entitled to uplift of fees to reflect exceptional circumstances of case—whether appropriate to grant declaration

[Criminal and Care Proceedings (Costs) Regulations 1989 (S.I. 1989 No. 343), Sched. 1, para. 3(b).]

A question was raised by the applicant under Legal Aid in Criminal and Care Proceedings (Costs) Regulations 1989, Sched. 1, para. 3(b), to determine the proper test of "exceptional" within the phrase "the appropriate authority may allow fees at more than the relevant basic rate . . . taking into account all the relevant circumstances of the case . . . (b) exceptional circumstances". The solicitor sought to uplift his fees to reflect the exceptional circumstances of case. The committee found that a case would only have exceptional circumstances if it were "unusual or extraordinary" and that an uplift would not be appropriate on these facts.

Held, allowing the application, that the words "taking into account all the relevant circumstances" were unrestricted. The primary responsibility for considering the question of exceptional circumstances was on the original taxing officer. The interpretation that a case would only have exceptional circumstances if it were "unusual or extraordinary" would mean that a murder case or complex fraud would only qualify for an uplift if they were even more complicated than normal murders or complex frauds. Rare cases would never qualify for an uplift because there could be no comparisons with other cases. The decision of the committee would therefore be quashed.

R. v. LEGAL AID BOARD, *ex p.* R.M. BROUDIE & CO. [1994] C.O.D. 435, D.C.

4022. Costs—taxation of costs—interlocutory judgment—whether plaintiff entitled to lodge bill of costs to be taxed

[C.C.R., Ord. 11, r.2(3)(a).]

P's claim arose from a damage-only road traffic accident which occurred on July 12, 1992. Proceedings were issued in the Reading County Court on July 20, 1994 and P claimed for costs of repairs to his motorvehicle in the sum of £1,944·47, and interest. P brought his claim on a default summons in the form N1, and upon the summons, claimed the costs for repairs plus interest, the court fee in the sum of £65·00 and "to be taxed" in the section for solicitors costs. D did not file a defence or enter an admission, and on September 6, 1994, judgment in default was entered against D for the damages claimed in the particulars of claim, interest, and the £65·00 court fee. D instructed solicitors, who made payment of the judgment sum by letter of October 6, 1994. P issued an application seeking an order for costs on scale 1, based on C.C.R., Ord. 11, r.2(3)(a). D argued that as P's claim was a liquidated demand as per C.C.R., Ord. 1, r.10, P erred in law in claiming costs to be taxed on the summons when he should have sought fixed costs pursuant to C.C.R., Ord. 38, r.18, which affords the defendant the opportunity to pay the sum claimed plus the costs of the summons under C.C.R., Ord. 11, r.2(2). Having entered those fixed costs on the summons, P was only entitled to fixed costs on entering default judgment pursuant to Appendix B, Pt. 2, of C.C.R., Ord. 38.

Held, that P was not entitled to costs to be taxed upon entry of a default judgment in the circumstances and P's application was dismissed with assessed costs.

HUGHES (MICHAEL DAVID) v. JONES (STEPHEN) December 2, 1994; District Judge Burgess; Reading County Ct. [*Ex rel. Cole and Cole, Solicitors*].

4023. Costs—taxation of costs—parents separately represented in wardship proceedings—no conflict of interest—whether costs should be reduced despite authorisation of Legal Aid Board. See B. AND H. (MINORS) (COSTS: LEGAL AID), *Re*, §3112.

4024. Costs—taxation of costs—solicitor's hourly expense rates—contentious business—City firm used—taxing master using previous awards as basis of assessment—whether other material showing level of costs actually incurred in area relevant

Taxing masters should have regard to general levels of costs actually incurred in the area at the relevant time rather than relying solely on the figures that they have usually awarded in the past.

P, a firm of accountants, instructed a firm of City solicitors to act for them to recover fees which had been withheld by D, who alleged negligence against P. Summary judgment was obtained and on taxation P's solicitors claimed costs including £140 per hour for the work of a partner and £80 per hour for an assistant solicitor. The taxing officer reduced the rates to £100 and £75 per hour. Both sides sought a review and at the review the taxing master reduced the rates to £90 and £70 per hour, based on the rates he had awarded in the past. He ignored the information contained in a review of hourly costs by area which showed that a City solicitors hourly costs were £171 for a partner and £101 for an assistant solicitor. P applied for a review of the decision.

Held, increasing the rates to the amounts claimed, that the taxing officer's task was to determine the broad average direct costs of the work done by solicitors in the relevant area of work at the relevant time. If it was reasonable for P to instruct a City firm then the fact that other solicitors could have done the work more cheaply was irrelevant. When considering the appropriate level of costs a taxing officer should not rely solely on awards he had made in the past as these would tend to be out of date. All relevant information should be used. Here the use of the City solicitors by P was reasonable and the rates sought, by comparison with those charged by others in the same area, were also reasonable (*Company, A (No. 004081 of 1989), Re* [1995] 6 C.L. 310 followed).

KPMG PEAT MARWICK McLINTOCK v. HLT GROUP [1995] 2 All E.R. 180, Auld J.

4025. Costs—taxation of costs—solicitors' hourly expense rates—*inter partes* taxation—evidence from properly—conducted expense rate surveys—central London law societies survey—whether evidence to be taken into account in assessing the broad average direct costs for the area concerned

[C.C.R., Ord. 38, r.24(4).]

On taxation and on a reconsideration of P's bill of costs, the district judge refused to allow expense rates claimed therein, and declined to adopt material contained in the January 1993 edition of *Writ*, a publication of the London Solicitors Litigation Association which contained comparative data based upon a survey conducted in the City of London and City of Westminster and Holborn areas showing various average expense rates for categories of fee earners in those areas. The district judge distinguished the case of *A Company, Re* (July 26, 1993, unreported) and found that reference therein to the survey was confined to the facts of that case and was *obiter dictum*. The district judge allowed expense rates for a partner of P's solicitors firm carrying out work in the City of London at £70·00 and £50·00 for a trainee solicitor in the same firm. P appealed the decision by way of review pursuant to C.C.R., Ord. 38, r.24(4).

Held, allowing P's appeal and refusing to distinguish the case of *A Company, Re* on it's facts, that reference therein to the survey was neither confined to the particular facts of that case, nor, was it *obiter dictum*. Further, applying the decision of *KPMG Peat Marwick (A Firm) v. The HLT Group*. and finding that it was reasonable for P to instruct a City of London firm, the district judge ought to have had regard to the results contained in the survey. The district judge was wrong not to allow the expense rates claimed by P's solicitors. P's solicitors were entitled to the rates claimed, £140·00 for a partner and £60·00 for a trainee. (*A Company, Re*. July 26, 1993, unrep., *KPMG Peat Marwick (A Firm) v. The HLT Group*, March 14, 1994, unrep., applied).

NSP CATALOGUE HOLDINGS PLC v. TRUEBELL MARKETING PLC AND COMPARE LTD, November 15, 1994, H.H.J. Hallgarten, Q.C.; Central London County Ct. [*Ex rel. Nicholas Bacon, Barrister*].

4026. Costs—taxation of costs—split trial—taxation before conclusion of proceedings—whether costs of liability trial to be taxed before *quantum* hearing

[R.S.C., Ord. 62, r.8(2).]

In an action for damages for personal injuries, where the issues of liability and *quantum* were ordered to be tried separately, the plaintiff was granted leave to tax his bill forthwith without having to wait for the conclusion of the action, as the hearing on *quantum* would not have been listed for many months.

BLACKMAN v. PRYOR, June 28, 1994, Ognall J.

4027. Costs—taxation of costs—trust property proceedings—trustees joined as defendants—offer by trustees to submit to decision of court—trustees appearing by leading and junior counsel—order for trustees' costs to be paid on indemnity basis—whether sums properly allowed—counsel's fees

P was the defendant to an action brought by a company. P brought a counterclaim alleging a breach of an agreement to sell him shares. P joined the trustees in whose names the shares were registered as defendants. The trustees did not plead to the counterclaim and offered in their defences to submit to whatever order was made by the court. Their solicitor informed P's solicitor that the trustees intended to appear at trial by leading and junior counsel and no response or objection was received. In subsequent negotiations the trustees' solicitor suggested that it was senseless for the trustees to attend the trial given that they had agreed to act as directed by the court but no response was received, save from P's solicitor, who suggested that there be cross-examination of the trustees on the question of breach of trust and fraud on a power. The trustees attended the trial which was due to last 20 days with leading and junior counsel but leading counsel was released at the opening of the trial with the judge indicating that leading counsel would be given notice of any application affecting him. Two weeks later the matter was settled and P was ordered to pay the trustees' costs on an indemnity basis. Leading counsel for the trustees appeared at the hearing to mention the settlement at a fee of £1,500. The costs were taxed at £86,284. P sought a review of the taxation.

Held, disallowing the fee of £1,500, but allowing the other items of costs as taxed, that where costs on an indemnity basis are ordered there are two questions. The first is whether the expenditure fell within the meaning of the phrase "all costs" as set out in R.S.C., Ord. 62, r.12(2). The second question was whether it could be shown beyond reasonable doubt that the amount was unreasonable or that it had been unreasonably incurred. Here it could not be said that the fees of both counsel were unreasonable or unreasonably incurred, given the estimated length of the trial and the possible allegations and issues to be confronted by the trustees. The fee for leading counsel attending the settlement hearing was unreasonably incurred and one would not ordinarily expect leading counsel to attend such a hearing. That item would be disallowed.

COMPANY, A (NO. 004081 OF 1989), *Re* [1995] 2 All E.R. 155, Lindsay J.

4028. Costs—wasted costs order—acting without actual authority—patent agent—whether personally liable

[Copyright Designs and Patents Act 1988 (c.48), s.292(1); Supreme Court Act 1981 (c.54), s.51(6); The Supreme Court Practice 1993, Vol. 2, para. 3874.]

A solicitor or patent agent may be liable for wasted costs incurred as a result of continuing to act without actual authority.

P brought an action for infringement of patent against D. S, a patent agent, represented D in the action. At the end of March, one of the officers of D authorised S to discuss the proceedings with one of D's financial backers who subsequently told S that they, and not the officers of D, were running the company. P took three further expensive steps in the action. S subsequently (incorrectly) believed that D had been wound up and applied to be removed from the record. D's defence was subsequently struck out and P entered judgment and applied for an order that S's firm pay part of the costs of the action.

Held, ordering S's firm to pay all P's costs incurred from April 15, that (1) s.292 of the Copyright Designs and Patents Act 1988 gives a registered patent agent the power to do, in connection with patent infringement actions, anything which a solicitor might do, and is subject to the same liability if he acts without authority. If a solicitor acts without authority, even if he does not know that he has no authority, or believes he has authority, it is likely that he will be personally liable for the costs of proceedings taken by him without authority, as summarised in para. 3874 of Vol. 2 of *Supreme Court Practice 1993*. In addition, under s.51(6) of the Supreme Court Act 1981, the Court may make a "wasted costs order" against a legal or other representative; (2) up to the end of March, S had at least implied authority from one of the officers of D; (3) authorisation to S to discuss the litigation with a third party, who was not an officer, employee or shareholder of D, was not delegation of power by a proper officer to the third party to give further instructions in the action.

Accordingly, from at the latest April 15, S had no authority to take further steps in the action, even if he believed that the third party could give him authority (*Ridehalgh v. Horsefield; Allen v. Unigate Dairies; Roberts v. Coverite (Asphalters); Philex v. Golban; Watson v. Watson; Antonelli v. Wade Gery Farr (A Firm)* [1994] C.L.Y. 3263 applied); and (4) it is not open to a solicitor to assume that he has or continues to have instructions. S was under a duty to obtain written confirmation of authority to act from the backer or other confirmation of the backer's status as a proper officer, as well as to check D's ability to pay the continuing costs of the action. Such a duty is owed by a solicitor not merely to himself, but also to the court and his opponent.

BELL FRUIT MANUFACTURING CO. v. TWIN FALCON [1995] F.S.R. 144, Ford J.

4029. Costs—wasted costs order—adjournment sought by counsel—earlier case overran—whether order justified—whether behaviour unreasonable

A barrister (B) appealed against a wasted costs order made by a Crown Court judge when B requested a last-minute adjournment of a case in which he was to act for the defence. The defendant was mentally disabled and could not be expected to be represented by another barrister, having placed trust in B. However, B was acting in another Crown Court trial, expected to last two days and end immediately before the instant case, and the first case overran.

Held, allowing the appeal, that a wasted costs order was justified only where the legal adviser acted unreasonably. B was over-optimistic to expect no delay in a trial due to end immediately before his next case began, but such conduct did not amount to unreasonable behaviour. The judge should not impose so draconian a penalty without taking account of the daily demands of practice and the difficulties associated with time estimates.

BARRISTER (WASTED COSTS ORDER NO. 4 OF 1993), *Re*, *The Times*, April 21, 1995, C.A.

4030. Costs—wasted costs order—ancillary relief—counsel failing to reassess claim following further information—whether court should make wasted costs order against wife's advisers

[Supreme Court Act 1981 (c.54), s.51.]

Counsel has a duty to reassess any earlier advice in the light of further information, even where not specifically instructed to advise further, and failure to do so can lead to a wasted costs order against him.

H and W started cohabiting in 1980 and married in 1987. Following their separation, W commenced divorce proceedings in 1990. H's income was then £200,000 pa. The parties jointly owned the matrimonial home and an investment property with a combined equity of £160,000. W instructed solicitors and was represented by R. At an early stage, R had an informal telephone conference with a barrister B, who advised that the pre-marital cohabitation could be significant if W had made important contributions during that period. By December 1990, W had found out that H and his new partner had bought a large London property. B, believing that H was a wealthy young man, advised in conference that W should accept no less than £200,000 in settlement of her claims; however, R discovered that H's large London property was heavily charged to the bank and had little or negative equity. This information was passed to B, who was instructed to settle W's affidavit of means. He completed this in April 1991, and thereupon W made her application for ancillary relief. In his affidavit, H stated that he now had no income, and pointed out that the London property had no equity. In July 1991 R, suspecting that H had hidden assets, served a lengthy questionnaire on H's solicitors and she advised W that she should seek 100 per cent of the equity in the two properties, amounting to £160,000, on the basis of her contributions during her 10-year relationship with H. Following an interlocutory application later that month, B gave an informal indication that W should seek a lump sum of £100,000 to £150,000, without having had an opportunity properly to peruse the papers. W became legally aided in March 1992. A new barrister, S, was instructed in June 1992. He advised in conference in that month that W should offer to accept £154,000. However, W's advisers soon tried to get W to accept a lower figure. Four days before the hearing in June 1992 W offered to accept £123,000 but this was rejected. At the time of the hearing, the parties, net assets amounted to £30,000. The district judge ordered H to pay W a lump sum of £20,000. H,s costs exceeded £70,000, and W's private costs exceeded £60,000. H applied for a wasted costs order against R, and sought the balance of his costs from the Legal Aid Board. W also applied for a wasted costs order against R. The Legal Aid Board sought an order against R for W's legal aid costs to be disallowed. R joined B as a respondent to the applications.

Held, allowing the applications in part, that (1) there had been a massive waste of costs in W's application for ancillary relief. Whilst in some cases it might be possible to identify the specific costs which had been wasted and to charge them to the lawyers concerned, the present more complicated case had to be approached in a different way. While applications for wasted costs orders should ordinarily be heard summarily, the complexity of this case and the multitude of claims militated against such an approach; (2) the test for the court in an application under s.51 of the Supreme Court Act 1981 for a wasted costs order must be judged from the respondent legal adviser's point of view, without the distortion of hindsight. The court had to consider what a reasonable solicitor would do; if the conduct permitted of a reasonable explanation, it might be regarded as optimistic and as reflecting on the adviser's judgment, without being unreasonable (*Ridehalgh v. Horsefield*; *Allen v. Unigate Dairies*; *Roberts v. Coverite (Asphalters)*; *Philex v Golban*; *Watson v. Watson*; *Antonelli v. Wade Gery Farr (A Firm)* [1994] C.L.Y. 3623 applied); (3) a solicitor was entitled to rely on the advice of counsel properly instructed but should not do so blindly (*Locke v. Camberwell Health Authority* [1992] C.L.Y. 4087 applied); (4) although W's application for ancillary relief was only filed in April 1991, liability for costs could precede that date, as the date would depend on the facts of the case. W's costs ran from August 1990, and H's from October 1990 (*Frankenburg v. Famous Lasky Film Service* [1931] 1 Ch. 428, *Gibson's Settlement Trusts, Re; Mellors v. Gibson* [1981] C.L.Y. 2136 applied); (5) although B was not instructed to reassess the correct figure for the lump sum award when asked to settle W's affidavit of means, the new information should have alerted him to the need for reassessment. Counsel was required to warn his solicitor that circumstances had changed, and to reconsider his previous views. However, counsel's liability under the wasted costs litigation arose only on October 1, 1991, and by that date the effects of B's failure to correct his original opinion had been spent. Therefore no order would be made against B (*Fozal v. Gofur* [1993] C.L.Y. 3174 applied); (6) the questionnaire drafted by R was far too detailed and long, given that it should have been realised that H was not a wealthy man and it had led to considerable unnecessary expense (*Evans v. Evans* [1990] C.L.Y. 229 considered); and (7) R's advice in March 1992 that W should have all the equity in the two properties was fanciful and unreasonable and led to vast waste. R was wrong to say that the advice given in the initial informal telephone conference about cohabitation was fundamental to the future conduct of the case; and (8) there had been no wasted costs before February 1991. From then until March 1992, the judge apportioned responsibility for the wasted costs between R for the most part and W to a much smaller extent. From March 1992 onwards, 80 per cent of the costs had been wasted, for which R was solely responsible; accordingly, H should have a proportion of his costs from February 1991 paid by R on an indemnity basis, with the balance of his costs arising since W had been legally aided paid by the Legal Aid Board on an indemnity basis. R should pay a proportion of W's costs incurred before she became legally aided paid, and 80 per cent of W's legal aid costs would be disallowed.

C. v. C. (WASTED COSTS ORDER) [1994] 2 F.L.R. 34, Ewbank J.

4031. Costs—wasted costs order—application—whether trial judge or another judge could hear an application

The question at issue in this case was whether applications for wasted costs against legal advisers in a case involving cross-petitions under the Companies Act 1985, and which had been dismissed after 165 days of litigation, could be heard by the trial judge or whether they should proceed before another judge.

Held, that the applications ought not to proceed, as a hearing by the trial judge would involve serious unfairness to the legal advisers and a rehearing in front of another judge would be horrendous. The conduct of judges should not become the subject of litigation.

FREUDIANA HOLDINGS, *Re* [1994] NPC 89, Jonathan Parker J.

4032. Costs—wasted costs order—failure to serve a Legal Aid Certificate prior to trial—whether wasted costs order appropriate

[Civil Legal Aid (General) Regulations 1989 (S.I. 1989 No. 339), reg. 50.]

P were legally aided and brought an action against the installer of their central heating system. D paid £1,500 into court, about half P's claim. D subsequently obtained a grant of legal aid. D's solicitor did not notify P as was mandatorily required by reg. 50 of the Civil Legal Aid (General) Regulations 1989, until the day before trial.

Held, applying the three-part test set out in *Ridehalgh v. Horsefield* ([1994] 9 C.L. 341), that (1) in the circumstances it was negligent of D's solicitor not to serve notice of issue (*Roberts v. Coverite* [1994] 3 W.L.R. 462 distinguished); (2) on the evidence the breach caused P's loss because there was affidavit evidence before the court to the effect that had P known that they were dealing with a legally aided defendant and the implications thereof, they would have taken the payment into court. It was inconceivable that D would not have permitted this, in the circumstances; and (3) it was just to make an order in the circumstances, given that not to do so would deprive P of the fruits of their victory by operation of the legal aid charge on their own costs from the date that D became legally aided to the date of the trial.

NORTH AND NORTH v. RATCLIFFE, November 4, 1994, District Judge Butler; Burton-Upon-Trent County Ct. [*Ex rel. David Evans, Barrister.*]

4033. Costs—wasted costs order—interlocutory application—whether order can be made before completion of action

A wasted costs order will not normally be made before the completion of an action, as it is necessary to look at the advice given in the context of the case as a whole, before determining whether the advice given was such that no reasonable legal advisor would have given it.

D applied for discovery at a time in an action when discovery would not normally have been applied for. The judge dismissed the application as wholly misconceived, and ordered that D pay P's costs, but that such an order could not be enforced without the permission of the court, as D was legally-aided. P applied for a wasted costs order against D's lawyers.

Held, such an application could only generally be made after the trial, as it would only then be apparent whether the advice given had been so unreasonable as to merit it. On the facts here there was no evidence that the advice to apply for discovery was so erroneous that a wasted costs order should be made.

FILMLAB SYSTEMS INTERNATIONAL v. PENNINGTON [1994] 4 All E.R. 673, D.C.

4034. Costs—wasted costs order—mother advised to apply to discharge care order—mother subsequently seeking to leave to withdraw application and apply for contact—whether mother's solicitors should pay costs of supposedly hopeless application

[Children Act 1989 (c.41), ss.34, 91(14); R.S.C., Ord. 80, r.2.]

A legal adviser should not be made to pay any wasted costs where, although he or she advised the making of an application with little prospect of success, that application was not improper or manifestly inappropriate.

L was born in 1989. In 1993 the local authority sought a care order. M was suffering from a mental illness, and the Official Solicitor was acting as her guardian *ad litem*. Before the hearing, M instructed a new firm of solicitors, who took the view that she was capable of giving instructions. Owing to a misunderstanding between M's new solicitors, the Official Solicitor's representative and the Official Solicitor's agents, M was advised not to attend the final hearing of the application for a care order. At the final hearing in January 1994, the court refused an application for an adjournment made on M's behalf and made a care order. Advised by her new solicitors, in February 1994, M issued an application to discharge the care order. At the hearing of that application in May 1994, the court indicated that a discharge was unlikely. M thereupon sought leave to withdraw the application for a discharge, and sought directions in her application for contact with L in care. The local authority submitted that leave to withdraw should only be given on condition that M's solicitors pay the costs thrown away, and submitted that any application by M should have been made through a next friend.

Held, granting leave to withdraw the application for discharge of the care order, that (1) M had been advised by her solicitors to make an application which, whilst having little prospect of success, was nonetheless not necessarily an improper one. In the light of the difficult and complex situation the solicitor found herself in, it would not be appropriate to make a wasted costs order (*Ridehalgh v. Horsefield; Allen v. Unigate Dairies; Roberts v. Coverite (Asphalters); Philex v. Golban; Watson v. Watson; Antonelli v. Wade Gerry Farr (A Firm)* [1994] 9 C.L. 341, *Watson v. Watson (Wasted Costs Order)* [1995] 3 C.L. 619 applied); (2) M's solicitors had considered whether or not M had had capacity to give instructions. Only if that issue had been ignored would the court have been minded to make a wasted costs order, and so it would not be a condition of leave to withdraw that M's solicitors pay the costs thrown away; and (3) M's application for contact was not an abuse, nor was it frivolous or vexatious. The application should be allowed to proceed and directions were given (*W. v. Ealing London Borough Council* [1993] C.L.Y. 2757 considered).

O. (A MINOR) (WASTED COSTS APPLICATION), *Re* [1994] 2 F.L.R. 842, Connell J.

4035. Costs—wasted costs order—notice given to Motor Insurers' Bureau—property damage excess not exceeded—whether Bureau involved unnecessarily. See MASTIN v. BLANCHARD AND MOTOR INSURERS' BUREAU, §3727.

4036. Costs—wasted costs order—unreasonable conduct—listing responsibilities of the proper officer of the court—whether solicitors to check progress with listing office

[C.C.R., Ord. 13, r.3(2), Ord. 19, rr.3(1), 4(2)(c).]

In the course of proceedings referred automatically to arbitration under C.C.R., Ord. 19, r.3(1), P's solicitors wrote to the Clerk to the Court requesting that the date fixed for hearing be vacated as being unsuitable for P. D's solicitors were not "copied in" on this correspondence. The Clerk to the Court acknowledged that the date was unsuitable and undertook to relist the matter. The hearing was not relisted and neither P's nor D's solicitors were ever notified by the Clerk of a relisted date. D, a witness, and D's solicitor attended on the pre-arranged hearing date, and subsequently claimed costs of the whole proceedings as between party and party from P. The district judge found that there had been unreasonable conduct in relation to the proceedings, pursuant to Ord. 19, r.4(2)(c), on the part of P in not contacting the listing office again prior to the date originally fixed to check that the hearing had been vacated. P appealed.

Held, allowing the appeal, that there was no unreasonable conduct on the part of P within the meaning of Ord. 19, r.4(2)(c), since P was entitled to rely on the undertaking of the listing office to relist the matter, and was under no duty to supervise the responsibilities of the proper officer of the court with respect to listing and notification of adjournment under C.C.R., Ord. 13, r.3(2), notwithstanding that P's solicitors had failed to comply with the rules of best practice in not copying D's solicitors in on the correspondence with the court.

SCHWARCZ v. GRAY AND GRAY, November 18, 1994; H.H.J. Marr-Johnson; Clerkenwell County Ct. [*Ex rel. Tom Skinner, Barrister*].

4037. Counterclaims—remedies—joinder—availability of remedy to subsidiary company

[R.S.C., Ord. 15, r.6.]

Where a defendant company had a remedy against the plaintiff for malicious prosecution and abuse of process in an asset-freezing action, the same remedy was available to a subsidiary company belonging to the defendant and the subsidiary was entitled to be joined as a party to the defendant's counterclaim. There was nothing in the wording of R.S.C., Ord. 15, r.6, or its forerunner, which restricted "matters in dispute" to only the plaintiff's claim and not the counterclaim.

BALKANBANK v. TAHER (NO. 4), *The Times*, April 14, 1995, Clarke J.

4038. County court—fees

COUNTY COURT FEES (AMENDMENT) ORDER 1995 (No. 2627 (L.11)) [£1·55], made under the County Courts Act 1984, s.128; operative on October 30, 1995; amends S.I. 1982 No. 1706 by removing exemption from payment of court fees from those receiving income support and civil legal aid, setting a flat fee of £65·00 on non-money claims, replacing the 10 pence per pound plaint fee scale with fee bands, replacing with fee bands the current 15 pence per pound fee scale on issue of warrants of execution, replacing the scale of fees payable on issue of warrants of delivery and possession with a flat fee of £80·00, abolishing the additional fee payable for a warrant of delivery or possession where the recovery of money is also sought, replacing with a flat fee of £50·00 the current fee of 10 pence per pound payable on an attachment of earnings application, increasing fees paid on dividends, increasing fees for copies of documents to £1·00 per page, increasing the fee on issue of a debtor's petition in bankruptcy by £5·00 to £25·00, increasing the fee for issuing a creditor's petition in bankruptcy by £5·00 to £55·00, increasing the fee for issuing any other petition under the Companies or Insolvency Acts by £5·00 to £55·00, increasing the fee on the hearing of an application under the Companies or Insolvency Acts before a district judge by £5·00 to £20·00 and abolishing the fee payable on the hearing of a public examination.

4039. County court—forms

COUNTY COURT (FORMS) (AMENDMENT) RULES 1995 (No. 970) [£1·10], operative on April 30, 1995; amend S.I. 1982 No. 586.

COUNTY COURT (FORMS) (AMENDMENT (NO. 2) RULES 1995 (No. 1583 (L.7)), made under the County Courts Act 1984, s.75; operative on August 24, 1995; amend the County Court (Forms) Rules 1982 by inserting forms for use in proceedings for interim possession orders.

COUNTY COURT (FORMS) (AMENDMENT NO.3) RULES 1995 (No. 2839 (L.16)), made under the County Courts Act 1984 s.75; amends S.I. 1982 No. 586. In force: January 8, 1996; [£5·10]. New forms of summons and of defence, taking into account the increase in the small claims limit to £3,000, are substituted into the County Court (Forms) Rules 1982 along with a new Form N92, application for administration order. An outdated note on the notices of hearing in arbitration is also revised along with other miscellaneous amendments.

COUNTY COURT (FORMS) (AMENDMENT NO.4) RULES 1995 (No. 3278 (L.19)), made under the County Courts Act 1984 s.75; amends S.I. 1982 No. 586. In force: January 8, 1996; [65p]. Corrections are made to the new forms of summons and one of the forms of defence, introduced by the County Court

(Forms) (Amendment No.3) Rules 1995 as a result of the raising of the small claims limit, by amending the County Court (Forms) Rules 1982.

4040. County court—remedies

COUNTY COURT REMEDIES (AMENDMENT) REGULATIONS 1995 (No. 206 (L.2)) [65p], made under the County Courts Act 1984 (c.28), s.38; operative on February 1, 1995; provide that, where proceedings are to be or are included in the Central London County Court Business List, a circuit judge nominated by the senior presiding judge may grant a Mareva injunction.

4041. County court—rules

COUNTY COURT (AMENDMENT) RULES 1995 (No. 969) [65p], operative on April 30, 1995; amend S.I. 1981 No. 1687 so as to change the procedure to be followed where a warrant of execution is issued in one court and sent to another court for execution.

COUNTY COURT (AMENDMENT (NO. 2) RULES 1995 (No. 1582 (L.6)), made under the County Courts Act 1984, s.75; amend S.I. 1981 No. 1687; operative on August 24, 1995; effect a procedure for obtaining interim possession orders in summary proceedings and empower the district judges to make possession order.

COUNTY COURT (AMENDMENT NO. 3) RULES 1995 (No. 2838 (L.15)) [£1·55], made under the County Courts Act 1984, s.75. In force: December 1, 1995 for all provisions except rr.2–5; January 8, 1996 for rr.2–5; amend S.I. 1981 No. 1687 by the increase of the small claims limit, except for personal injury actions, to £3,000; amend the small claims procedure; provide for taxation of costs where a conditional fee agreement has been made; revise cost provisions and increase allowances for witnesses and fixed costs along with further miscellaneous amendments.

COUNTY COURT (AMENDMENT NO.4) RULES 1995 (No. 3277 (L.18)), made under the County Courts Act 1984 s.75; amends S.I. 1981 No. 1687; 1995 2838. In force: January 8, 1996 for rule 5, January 29, 1996 for all provisions except rule 5; [65p]. Amendments are made to the County Court Rules 1981 and the County Court (Amendment No.3) Rules 1995 by these Rules. Rule 2 enables litigants to recover a sum not exceeding £260·00 for legal advice obtained for making or defending claims for injunctions, orders for specific performance or other similar relief in proceedings referred automatically to arbitration under the small claims procedure. Rule 3 increases the limit on fees paid for the services of an expert in small claims to £200·00. Rule 4 clarifies the point that applications to set aside awards made in the absence of parties are to be made to the court rather than the awarding arbitrator. Rule 5 inserts the transitional provision that "nothing in rules 2 to 5 shall apply to proceedings issued beforeJanuary 8, 1996" into the 1995 Amendment No.3 Rules.

4042. County court—striking out—admission—no judgment applied for within time-limit—whether to be extended

[C.C.R., Ord. 9, r.10.]

P was injured in a road traffic accident on April 26, 1992. Proceedings were issued in June 1993, and a defence admitting negligence but denying *quantum* was entered on August 31, 1993. The automatic directions timetable began to run on September 15, 1993. On P's solicitor's application for an extension of time in which to request a trial date, D's solicitors successfully argued that P's claim was automatically struck out pursuant to Ord. 9, r.10, which provides that where proceedings have been issued and an admission has been entered, but no judgment has been applied for within 12 months, P's case shall be struck out and that there is not discretion to extend the 12-month period.

Held, that P's claim should be struck out and that the costs of the entire action should be D's in any event.

MOLONEY v. COLEMAN, November 29, 1994; District Judge Somerville; Reading County Ct. [*Ex rel. Cole and Cole, Solicitors*].

4043. County court—striking out—admission relating to negligence but not damage—no judgment applied for—whether case struck out

[C.C.R., Ord. 9, r.10.]

P was injured in a road traffic accident on May 22, 1993. Proceedings were issued in January 1994, and a defence admitting negligence but denying that P had suffered the "alleged injury, loss and damage pleaded" was delivered on February 2, 1994. The case was subject to automatic directions. On P's application for an extension of time in which to request a trial date in May 1995, D's solicitors argued that P's claim was struck out pursuant to Ord. 9, r.10 on the basis that proceedings had been issued, an admission had been entered but no judgment had been applied for within 12 months. The district judge rejected D's submissions. D appealed to the judge in chambers.

Held, that P was not entitled to enter judgment unless and until D had admitted negligence and damage. D's admission was only as to negligence and not as to damage. In the circumstances, P's claim was not struck out under Ord. 9, r.10 and the appeal was dismissed

HAYES v. COLYER, June 12, 1995, H.H.J. McKinney, Bournemouth County Ct. [*Ex rel*. Mark Stephen Lomas, Barrister, 3, Paper Buildings.]

4044. County court—striking out—automatic directions—abuse of process—failure to comply with automatic directions for discovery and disclosure of evidence—whether action in bad faith or wilful disregard of rules

[C.C.R., Ord. 17, r.11.]

MF appealed in an action for personal injuries against the refusal of its application to set aside as an abuse of process A's request for a hearing date within 15 months of the close of pleadings. The county court had given a date for a pre-trial review and MF argued that, in belatedly requesting a hearing date outside the date upon which pleadings were deemed to be closed, but within 15 months of that date, A had failed to comply with the automatic directions for discovery and disclosure of evidence under C.C.R., Ord. 17, r.11, and that her action should therefore be struck out.

Held, dismissing the appeal, that although A had failed to comply with the automatic directions, whose aim was to stamp out delay, the conduct of her action was not an abuse of process under Ord. 17, r.11, as she had not acted in bad faith or shown wilful disregard of the rules, but had proceeded within the 15-month time-limit applicable in almost every case. The court recommended the adoption of the practice of the Central London County Court in personal injury cases, whereby the court assumed control on receipt of the defence by allocating a date for trial and a timetable and issuing to the parties a listing information form. The court would then step in by fixing a date for a pre-trial review if the forms were not returned, thus removing unnecessary delay and the obstructive striking-out procedure.

ASHWORTH v. MCKAY FOODS, *The Times*, November 16, 1995, C.A.

4045. County court—striking out—automatic directions—admission—no judgment applied within the time-limit—whether defence amounting to admission

[C.C.R., Ord. 9, r.10.]

P was injured in a road traffic accident on October 16, 1993. Proceedings were issued in December 1993, and a defence was entered on January 10, 1994. The defence admitted "that the said accident was caused by D's negligent driving" but, "denied that P suffered the loss or damage pleaded". On P's application for an extension of the time in which to request a trial date,

D's solicitors argued that P's claim was automatically struck out pursuant to Ord. 9, r.10, which provides that where an admission had been entered, but no judgment applied for within 12 months, P's case shall be struck out and there is no discretion to extend the 12-month period. The district judge held that the case had not been struck out under that rule.

Held, on D's appeal, that P's claim had not been struck out under Ord. 9, r.10, as the defence did not amount to an admission under the rule.

GEORGE v. CARNEY, April 25, 1995; H.H.J. Tibber; Edmonton County Ct. [*Ex rel. Edwin Buckett, Barrister*].

4046. County court—striking out—automatic directions—application for judgment in default of defence—whether completion of N9 form constituting a defence—whether directions order made during currency of automatic directions timetable affecting timetable

[C.C.R., Ord. 17, r.11.]

P allegedly victim of Ds' medical negligence, issued a summons on November 5, 1992 containing a general endorsement that: "Plaintiff's claim arises out of the Defendants' negligence whilst treating her . . . between August and November 1989". On the same day P obtained an order granting leave to serve the summons without a medical report. On November 20, 1992 D completed the N9 "Form for Replying to a Summons" in similar short form stating: "A fully pleaded Defence will follow in due course once a fully pleaded Particulars of Claim is served". A notice that automatic directions applied was issued on December 3, 1992. The Ord. 17 timetable commenced on December 17, 1992 and the 15-month period provided by Ord. 17, r.9, expired on March 17, 1994. On February 11, 1993 an order was made extending the time in which P was to file a medical report to April 5, 1993. P subsequently filed a medical report within time. Upon P's application dated October 7, 1993 for further directions an order was made on January 19, 1994 that: "a fully pleaded Particulars of Claim" be served within three months and a defence within three months thereafter. P served the particulars of claim on April 19, 1994. No defence was subsequently received. Upon P's application for judgment in default of defence, D contended that since no further direction as to the automatic directions timetable had been given on January 19, 1994, the original timetable applied and that accordingly P's claim was struck out.

Held, on P's application for a declaration that the action was not struck out; (1) the completion of the N9 "Form for Replying to a Summons" was a defence within Ord. 9, r.17, and hence the automatic timetable did indeed commence on December 17, 1992; (2) however, the Order of January 19, 1994 was a direction within Ord. 17, r.11(2)(b), and that therefore automatic directions took effect subject to the order of January 19, 1994; to hold otherwise would be to hold that at the time of the making of the order of December 19, 1994 the court was setting a time for the filing of the fully pleaded defence after the expiry of the Ord. 17 timetable. Although the Order of January 19, 1994 was silent as to further directions, common sense dictated that its purpose must have been to create a new timetable which was to come into effect upon the service of the full defence; alternatively (3) if the court was wrong, the application of P of October 17, 1993 on which no order was made included an application that "the action be set down for trial with a time estimate of two days". Although no order was made, such a request was a satisfactory discharge of P's obligation under Ord. 17, r.11(3)(d) and (9). Accordingly the action was not struck out. D would be ordered to serve a defence within 14 days and automatic directions would be ordered to apply from 14 days after the filing of the defence.

RAWLINS (GILLIAN MARY) v. WALSALL HEALTH AUTHORITY, February 27, 1995; District Judge Hearne; Walsall County Ct. [*Ex rel. Philip Goddard, Barrister*].

4047. County court—striking out—automatic directions—consolidated actions—relevant timetable

P issued two sets of proceedings against the same three defendants for sums due as guarantors of a lease. The first action was commenced in the High Court and transferred to Bournemouth County Court by order dated June 21, 1993. By C.C.R., Ord. 17, r.11, the automatic directions timetable in the first action commenced on July 5, 1993. The second action was commenced in the Bournemouth County Court on April 7, 1994, and a defence was filed on April 13, 1994. In respect of the second action, a notice of automatic directions was issued by the court dated April 19, 1994. The two actions were consolidated by consent order dated July 22, 1994. No application was made to set down the consolidated action for trial until March 28, 1995. The district judge ordered that, despite the order for consolidation, the first action was struck out automatically pursuant to C.C.R., Ord. 17, r.11(9), after 15 months, that is, on October 5, 1994. He declared that the second action remained in existence. The judge allowed P's appeal; the effect of consolidation was to create one new action from two old actions. The district judge was wrong to bring Ord. 17, r.11, into play in the way in which he had. There was no specific provision in the C.C.R. setting out the effect of consolidation on the automatic directions timetable. A common sense approach should be adopted, in accordance with the principles set out in the C.A. decisions of *Rastin v. British Steel* and *Gardner v. Southwark London Borough Council*. Where there has been consolidation, in the absence of any unconscionable conduct, a fresh automatic directions timetable should commence from the date of consolidation. The consolidated action was not, therefore, struck out (*Rastin v. British Steel*; *Todd v. Evans; Adams v. Geest; Byrne v. Webber; Donaldson v. Canavan; Ayres v. British Steel* [1994] C.L.Y. 3635, *Gardner v. Southwark London Borough Council* April 19, 1994, C.A. unreported, considered).

G.A. PROPERTY SERVICES v. BAKER, BLAKE & WILLIAMS, August 30, 1995, H.H.J. Hooton, Bournemouth County Ct. [*Ex rel.* James Stuart, Barrister, Lamb Chambers, instructing solicitors MacLeish, Littlestone, Cowan & Kemp.]

4048. County court—striking out—automatic directions—counterclaim—application to reinstate—whether counterclaim could be pursued—whether claim pursued with reasonable diligence

[C.C.R., Ord. 17, r.11(9).]

P were involved in a road traffic accident with D, as a result of which they sustained personal injuries, and both vehicles were damaged. A summons was issued, and D entered a defence and counterclaim for the cost of repairs to her vehicle. P's claim was struck out under C.C.R., Ord. 17, r.11(9). D applied for costs, and that her own claim be set down for trial. The district judge granted D's applications, relying upon Ord. 21, r.4(2), refusing P's cross-application for reinstatement.

Held, that P's claims should remain struck out, and D should be allowed to proceed with her counterclaim. The district judge had properly directed herself in finding that P had failed to prosecute their claims reasonably diligently. This was evidenced by a period in excess of five months during which P's solicitors had failed to respond to a request for the exchange of witness statements, which was explained as being due to the absence of an employee from P's solicitors' offices. The circuit judge made no finding as to whether or not Ord. 21, r.4(3) conferred upon him any discretion to dismiss D's counterclaim but concluded in any event that the refusal to reinstate P's claims did not deprive D from pursuing her counterclaim. P's remedy was as against their solicitors.

BOURNE AND BOURNE v. CURRIE, April 10, 1995, H.H.J. O'Brien, Brentwood County Ct. [*Ex rel.* Nigel S. Brockley, Barrister, Bracton Chambers, instructed by Budd Martin Burrett, Solicitors, Colchester.]

4049. County court—striking out—automatic directions—defence and counterclaim amended—whether claim automatically struck out

P sued D for breach of contract. A defence and counterclaim were delivered on June 30, 1993. The particulars of claim were subsequently amended, pursuant to an order of the court. An amended defence and counterclaim were delivered on July 22, 1994. On May 26, 1995, D applied to the deputy district judge for his costs, on the basis that P's claim had been automatically struck out. D argued that pleadings had closed on July 28, 1993 (28 days after the delivery of the defence and counterclaim), that the 15-month period during which P could have applied for a hearing date had expired on October 27, 1994, and that P's action had been automatically struck out, P having failed to apply for a hearing date within that period. P contended that the pleadings closed on August 19, 1994 (28 days after the delivery of the amended defence and counterclaim), that the 15-month period did not expire until November 18, 1995, and that the action had therefore not been automatically struck out. The deputy district judge accepted P's submissions and dismissed D's application.

Held, that in considering when pleadings closed for the purposes of C.C.R., Ord. 17, r.11(9), the relevant pleading was the last pleading, and therefore the automatic directions timetable did not begin to run until 28 days after the delivery of the amended defence and counterclaim. Accordingly P's action had not been automatically struck out, and D's appeal would be dismissed (*Rastin v. British Steel; Todd v. Evans; Adams v. Geest; Byrne v. Webber; Donaldson v. Canavan; Ayres v. British Steel* [1994] C.L.Y. 3635 considered).

UNICAR (LEEDS) v. MACASKILL, June 12, 1995, H.H.J. Walker, Doncaster County Ct. [*Ex rel.* Paul Greaney, Barrister.]

4050. County court—striking out—automatic directions—defence filed late—forms issued in lieu of pre-trial review—whether automatic directions triggered despite lateness of defence—whether forms superseded automatic directions

[C.C.R., Ord 9, r.2(6); Ord. 17, r.11(11)(a).]

P claimed damages for personal injury. Proceedings were issued on April 14, 1993 and a defence was filed dated May 21, 1993. On June 29, 1993, the court sent the parties a form stating that the matter had been given preliminary consideration and that the following orders were to stand as having been made on a pre-trial review, unless either party sought to apply otherwise. The order provided, *inter alia*, that "This action be heard on a date and at a venue to be fixed when both parties file certificates of readiness with time estimate. Liberty to apply for further directions." An identical form was sent out by the court dated August 3, 1993. P did not apply to set the matter down until November 2, 1994, after D had made application for his costs of the action on the basis that P's claim had been struck out. On appeal P argued that (i) because the defence had not been served within 14 days of the summons, as required by C.C.R., Ord. 9, r.2(6), pleadings had never closed in accordance with Ord. 17, r.11(11)(a), and thus the automatic directions did not apply and (ii) in the alternative the effect of the forms was to supersede the setting down provisions contained within Ord. 17.

Held, that, while acknowledging the superficial attraction of the first argument, such a construction would exclude a great many cases from the ambit of Ord. 17, and could lead to a temptation for defendants deliberately to delay filing defences. The latter argument was rejected because the form sent out by the court was to be regarded as an administrative matter and thus not sufficient to oust the requirements of Ord. 17. P's claim was accordingly struck out automatically in September 1994.

VARSANI v. DAVY, October 17, 1995, H.H.J. Lowe, Willesden County Ct. [*Ex rel.* Richard Wilkinson, Barrister, 1 Temple Gardens, instructed by Cole & Cole, Solicitors.]

4051. County court—striking out—automatic directions—defence filed with court—no copy sent to plaintiff's solicitors—no form N450 served—whether pleadings closed

[C.C.R., Ord. 17, r.11(11)(a).]

P's claim for personal injury was one to which the automatic directions applied. A defence was served on the court and sent to P's solicitors by D's solicitors on October 13, 1992. The court did not send a copy of the defence to P's solicitors, nor was a copy of Form N450 ever sent to either party. The issue for the judge was the interpretation of C.C.R., Ord. 17, r.11(11)(a) as to the date for closure of pleadings. P argued that automatic directions did not apply until the court itself had sent a copy of the defence to P's solicitors in accordance with Ord. 9, r.2(7) and that accordingly in the present case pleadings had never closed. P relied on the decisions in *Rennie v. Elemeta Industries* and *Polius v. United Biscuits (U.K.)*.

Held, upholding the decision of the district judge, that the contrary line of authority expressed in *Massey v. Stockport Metropolitan Borough Council* and *Mulhern v. Martin* was to be preferred. Order 9, r.2(7) was concerned purely with administration by the court office and pleadings closed in accordance with Ord. 9, r.2(6), 14 days after delivery to the court of a defence. Accordingly, the matter had been automatically struck out on January 26, 1994 (*Rennie v. Elemeta Industries*, unrep. (November 14, 1994, H.H.J. Simpson); *Polius v. United Biscuits (U.K.)*, unrep. (June 1, 1994, H.H.J. Lowe); *Massey v. Stockport Metropolitan Borough Council*, unrep. (January 13, 1995, H.H.J. Hardy); and *Mulhern v. Martin*, unrep. (March 17, 1995, H.H.J. Mettyear) considered).

HERRING v. CHURWELL METALS, June 26, 1995, H.H.J. Marr-Johnson, Clerkenwell County Ct. [*Ex rel.* Richard Wilkinson, Barrister, 1 Temple Gardens, instructed by Greenwoods, Solicitors.]

4052. County court—striking out—automatic directions—defence filed with court but not sent by court to solicitors—defence sent by defendant's solicitors to plaintiffs—whether automatic directions triggered—whether plaintiff's request for hearing date a valid request

[C.C.R., Ord. 9, rr.2, 10; Ord. 17, r.11; Ord. 37, r.5.]

P issued proceedings against D out of Southampton County Court. D's solicitor sent a copy of the defence to P's solicitor, and filed two copies of the defence in the court. The court officer did not send a copy of the defence to P's solicitor and did not issue form N450. Towards the end of the 15-month period, P's solicitor lodged a brief request to fix a date for the trial. D applied for a declaration that P's claim had been automatically struck out on the basis that the request for a hearing date was a sham, not a valid request and not in accordance with C.C.R., Ord. 17, r.11(8). P, on enquiry, discovered that the court had not sent a copy of the defence to his solicitors, in accordance with Ord. 9, r.2(7), and therefore applied for an order/declaration that the automatic directions timetable had never been triggered. D made further application that if indeed the court had not properly delivered the defence in accordance with Ord. 9, r.2, then the matter should be declared to be automatically struck out under Ord. 9, r.10.

Held, that the arguments in *Polius v. United Biscuits*, relied on by P, were preferred to those in *Mulhern v. Martin*, relied on by D. Order 17, r.11, referred to the whole of Ord. 9, r.2, and compliance with Ord. 17, r.11(11)(a), required satisfying Ord. 9, r.2(7), and not simply Ord. 9, r.2(6), as D had contended. The consequences of breach of the automatic directions were severe, and in his view one should not impose severe consequences without spelling out precisely what would lead up to them. The district judge's view was that it was a cold matter of construction of Ord. 17, r.11. He did not consider it appropriate to apply Ord. 37, r.5, and thereby retrospectively start the automatic directions timetable. He found that P did not fall foul of Ord. 9, r.10, construing the word "delivered" in Ord. 9, r.10, differently to the word "delivery" in Ord. 17, r.11(11)(a). If this was wrong, he would exercise the inherent jurisdiction of the court and treat any failure to enter judgment under Ord. 9, r.10, as an irregularity. The issue as to whether or not the application to fix was valid or a sham was not one which the district judge had to decide, but he indicated that had that been an issue before him, then he would have been in favour of P, *i.e.* that the mere sending of the letter requesting a fixture sufficed, notwithstanding that Ord. 17, r.11(8) had not been complied with (*Polius v. United Biscuits* and *Mulhern v. Martin* considered).

McDERMOTT v. SHARP, May 24, 1995, District Judge Simons, Trowbridge County Ct. [*Ex rel* Francis Goddard, of Morris Goddard & Ward, Solicitors, Devizes.]

4053. County court—striking out—automatic directions—defence served but not filed—whether automatic directions apply—whether claim should be struck out

[R.S.C., Ord. 9, r.10.]

A summons claiming, *inter alia*, damages in conversion from D2 was issued on August 27, 1993. D2 served a defence on October 27, 1993 but did not file the defence of the court. D1 was a company in liquidation and took no active part in the proceedings. In October 1994, P served a request for further and better particulars of the defence. On February 17, 1995 P's solicitor asked the court office to confirm that the claim had been struck out under the automatic directions (no trial date having been requested within 15 months of close of pleadings) or, in the alternative, if the automatic directions did not run by virtue of the fact that the defence had not been filed, that the action was struck out under R.S.C., Ord. 9. r.10, no defence having been delivered and no judgment having been entered with in 12 months of the summons. The point was considered by the district judge as the preliminary point at a hearing on April 21, 1995 convened to hear P's application for an order in respect of the further and better particulars of the defence.

Held, that the automatic directions did not apply since no defence had been delivered because no defence had been filed. However, if no defence had been filed then because no judgment had been entered within 12 months of service of summons the claim was automatically struck out under R.S.C., Ord. 9, r.10.

U.S. LEASING v. McKENNA CORPORATION AND PETER McKENNA, April 25, 1995; Longley J.; Central London County Ct. [*Ex rel. Cole and Cole, Solicitors*].

4054. County court—striking out—automatic directions—directions—court's directions requiring certificate of readiness and time estimate—whether supplanted automatic directions

P claimed damages for professional negligence from her former solicitors and commenced proceedings on September 9, 1992. D filed a "holding defence" on October 20, 1992, and subsequently filed a fully pleaded defence on March 23, 1993, in order to stave off summary judgment. On the same day the deputy district judge gave directions, including a direction that witness statements should be exchanged within 28 days and a direction that "this action be listed for hearing by a judge . . . upon receipt of a certificate of readiness and time estimate from either party giving seven days' notice to the other party". The case not having been listed within 15 months of close of pleadings, the district judge declared on February 24, 1995, that the action was automatically struck out.

Held, allowing P's appeal, that the directions given by the court on March 23, 1993, could only be read as supplanting the automatic directions in Ord. 17, r.11. On one view, the direction as to listing was open-ended; but on another view, it was not, for it gave either party the option of bringing the case to trial. When such a direction had been given, no defendant could be heard to complain that the case had not been listed, because he was given the power to list the case himself. The judge preferred the decisions in *Bird (Annie) v. Initial Contract Services* and *Nelson & Guy v. Infil Housing Co-op*, which held that the displacement of the automatic directions did not have to be express. He further considered it relevant, though not decisive, that P's solicitor had believed that the automatic directions had been displaced (*Bird (Annie) v.*

Initial Contract Services [1994] C.L.Y. 3648, *Nelson & Guy v. Infil Housing Co-op* [1994] C.L.Y. 3645 considered).

RATCLIFFE v. PAGE & CO., May 4, 1995, H.H.J. Pollard, Lincoln County Ct. [*Ex rel*. Jonathan Watt-Pringle, Barrister.]

4055. County court—striking out—automatic directions—directions—*ex parte* order relating to money paid into court—whether pre-trial review amounting to new directions

P issued proceedings seeking damages and an injunction resulting from D's occupation of an adjoining property. The court, when issuing the fixed date summons, listed the matter for a pre-trial review. At the pre-trial review orders were made for discovery, inspection, exchange of witness statements and experts' reports and for the matter to be set down on a certificate of readiness of either party. No application was made for a hearing date within 15 months of the defence and D contended that the matter had been struck out. They obtained an *ex parte* order from a district judge that the monies they had previously paid into court should be paid out to them. P applied for a declaration that the matter had not been struck out. That was on the basis that as the matter had been listed for a pre-trial review and that Ord. 17, r.11 did not apply by virtue of Ord. 17, rr.11(2)(a) and the matter was governed instead by Ord. 17, rr.1–10. As a secondary point they contended that if the matter was not excluded from Ord. 17, r.11, the directions actually given varied the automatic directions.

Held, that the matter had not been struck out under both heads. D then sought an order that they should have leave to pay the monies previously paid out of court back into court and that the payment in should be treated as having been effective from the date it was originally made. That was opposed. The district judge made an order directing D to pay the money back into court within 14 days and not to be paid out without leave. On the question of costs the district judge felt that although D had started the ball rolling by asking the court to conclude the matter had been struck out, he felt that a series of administrative and judicial acts had contributed to the position and therefore made an order for P's costs in the case.

GREEN AND GREEN v. EIC (EXETER), April 6, 1995, H.H.J. Cotterall, Exeter County Ct. [*Ex rel. Crosse and Crosse, Solicitors*].

4056. County court—striking out—automatic directions—directions—pre-trial review—certificate of readiness required by order—new open-ended timetable—subsequent delay—plaintiff acting in person—whether automatic directions still relevant

P began an action for damage for breach of a grant-aided building contract. Acting in person on November 16, 1993, she issued her summons endorsed with particulars of claim in the sum of £4,065. On December 1, 1993, D in person served his defence. On December 9, 1993, the court served a notice that automatic directions applied (form N450). In early January 1994, P filed a listing notice indicating (erroneously) that the case was ready for trial, but no application to set down was included. The court referred the matter to a district judge who ordered a pre-trial review pursuant to C.C.R., Ord. 17, r.10. The pre-trial review took place on March 28, 1994. P was still acting in person, but D was now represented by solicitors. The district judge set a new timetable for the future progress of the action and exchange of documents, including Scott schedules, meeting of experts etc. Paragraph 8 of the order stated "Trial date to be fixed on filing of certificate of readiness by the parties with a time estimate". The order was silent on the issue of the automatic directions, and the new timetable was open-ended, providing no date by which a certificate of readiness had to be filed. P instructed solicitors on April 26, 1994, who requested and were granted by D's solicitors a general extension of time with regard to serving P's list of documents. P's solicitors proceeded to take detailed instructions and instructed P's surveyor to re-inspect and provide a detailed report and prepare a Scott schedule. Counsel drafted amended particulars of claim to include the local authority as second defendant. P's solicitors pressed the surveyor for his report. In late 1994, D's solicitors began to complain about P's delay and issued a request for further and better particulars of P's original claim. By February 1995, D's solicitors were complaining of prejudice to D. On February 15, 1995, P applied to the court for leave to join the local authority as second defendant, and to amend the particulars of claim in accordance with the draft submitted. P did not make application to the proper officer to fix a date by March 23, 1995, which was the date on which the action would have been struck out if the automatic directions still applied. On March 28, 1995, D applied for a declaration that P's claim had been struck out pursuant to the automatic directions.

Held, dismissing D's application, that it was quite clear that if the order of March 28, 1994 said the action was to be set down on filing a certificate of readiness, it was an order which superseded Ord. 17, r.11(3), and by r.11(2)(b), the automatic directions were subject to that.

GRAHAM v. BLAYNEY, June 2, 1995, District Judge Davies, Bow County Ct. [*Ex rel*. Geoffrey Mott, Barrister.]

4057. County court—striking out—automatic directions—directions—pre-trial review—joint certificates of readiness ordered—whether automatic directions superseded

[C.C.R., Ord. 17, r.11.]

P brought proceedings against D, for trespass arising out of a boundary dispute, by summons and particulars of claim on May 14, 1992. The matter was listed for pre-trial review on June 12, 1992, when directions were given by the district judge concerning the filing of the defence, the exchange of witness statements, the filing of expert evidence and in particular directing that the matter be set down for trial on the filing of joint certificates of readiness. A defence was filed on July 14, 1992. On October 31, 1994, on P's application, the district judge ordered D to serve witness statements within 14 days. The district judge also ordered that the trial be listed on the first open date after November 30, 1994, time estimate one-and-a-half days. On April 28, 1995, D, relying upon *Daw v. Tilcon* and *Cooper v. The Post Office*, contended that, as the district judge had not expressly excluded the operation of automatic directions at either pre-trial review, they should be taken as being included in the directions given by the district judge or as remaining untouched. In other words, D contended that the obligation to request a hearing date remained upon P and that the directions given by the district judge were merely supplementary to the automatic directions and did not displace them. The deputy district judge dismissed D's application for a declaration that the action had been struck out automatically on October 30, 1993. At the appeal, P, relying on *Nelson and Guy v. Infill Housing Co-op.*, contended that C.C.R., Ord. 17, r.11(4)(a), preserved the district judge's right to give whatever directions he thought fit (including an order that a pre-trial review be held, or that a date be fixed for a final hearing), and that r.11(2)(b) provided that such directions given by a district judge in a case to which automatic directions applied, superseded those automatic directions. P further contended that the exception in r.11(2)(a) specifically indicated that automatic directions would be superseded by directions given in a pre-trial review. P contrasted r.11(2)(a) as it appeared in the 1995 edition of the *Green Book*, with the version of the rule in the 1990 edition, where that exception did not appear, and where r.11(2)(a) was not linked to r.11(4)(a). P argued that the inclusion of the exception must mean that any directions given at a pre-trial review should take precedence over automatic directions, otherwise the exception would have no meaning. The judge dismissed D's appeal. The directions given on June 12, 1992 and October 31, 1994, set a new timetable. It was clear under Ord. 17, r.11(4) that the court could, if it wished, alter the automatic directions and provide something different. This amounted to nothing more than returning to the old method, which had existed in all such cases before the advent of automatic directions, of obtaining the consent of both parties, before the trial was set down, to a timetable set down by the court. The automatic directions would be superseded by the district judge's directions and the matter could be set down for trial after the 15-month timetable had expired (*Daw v. Tilcon* [1995] 1 C.L. 322, *Cooper v. Post Office* (unrep.), *Nelson & Guy v. Infill Housing Co-op.; Rastin v. British Steel; Todd v. Evans; Adams v. Geest; Byrne v. Webber; Donaldson v. Canavan; Ayres v. British Steel* [1994] C.L.Y. 3635 considered).

HILL v. GARCIA, July 13, 1995, H.H.J. Harrison Hall, Coventry County Ct. [*Ex rel.* Robin Arwel Lewis, Barrister, Priory Chambers.]

4058. County court—striking out—automatic directions—directions—standard form—whether directions issued by the court set open-ended timetable

[C.C.R., Ord. 17, r.11(9).]

In November 1991 the court gave directions on one of their standard forms. The directions included a provision that "The case be adjourned generally. Liberty to parties to apply for a hearing when advocates on each side have advised on evidence and all parties lodge a certificate of readiness". In November 1994 a deputy district judge declared that the action had been automatically struck out on February 17, 1993, pursuant to Ord. 17, r.11(9).

Held, allowing the appeal, that (1) on their true construction the court's directions had established an open-ended timetable which imposed no obligation on the plaintiff to request a trial date by a certain time; (2) in providing that the "case be adjourned generally" the court's directions had not fixed a time for the hearing of the action: the parties had liberty to apply for this purpose; and (3) both parties had to sign the certificate of readiness before the action could be set down. This consensual approach made artificial any attempt to read the court's directions as subject to the automatic strike-out provision which imposed a sanction on one party only (*Nelson v. Infil Housing Co-op.; Rastin v. British Steel; Todd v. Evans; Adams v. Geest; Byrne v. Webber; Donaldson v. Canavan; Ayres v. British Steel* [1994] 5 C.L. 303, *Bird (Annie) v. Initial Contract Services* [1994] 12 C.L. 680 considered).

McGUIRE AND McGUIRE v. LAMBETH LONDON BOROUGH COUNCIL, February 13, 1995; H.H.J. Collins; Wandsworth County Ct. [*Ex rel. Jon Holbrook, Barrister*].

4059. County court—striking out—automatic directions—directions—standard form—whether directions issued by the court setting new timeable and replacing automatic direction

[C.C.R., Ord. 17, r.11.]

P suffered a back injury after falling from a ladder at work on February 22, 1990. Proceedings were issued on February 18, 1993 only a few days within the limitation period. D's solicitors asked for an extension of time for serving the defence which was granted by P's solicitors. The defence was in fact not served in time but was posted to the court on June 7, 1993 with a covering letter asking for "further and better particulars." P agreed that the effective date of service was June 9, 1993 and that therefore pleadings closed on June 23, 1993. The last date for setting down in accordance with the Rules was therefore September 23, 1993. The Edmonton County Court sent to both parties a notice headed "Automatic Direction". It was properly sealed by the court but was headed with the date June 21, being that the date under the notice from which the timetable was to begin. Under the notice the last date for setting down was October 5, 1993. P's solicitors began to get anxious as to the timetable and wrote a letter to D's solicitors on August 6, 1993. There was a telephone exchange and P's solicitors at that stage made it clear that they believed the final date was Otober 5, 1994. An application for an extension of the timetable was made by P's solcitors but the court could only give a hearing date in November, after the expiry of the timetable and the application was abandoned. On September 29, 1994 P's solicitors wrote to the Court making an application to set down in accordance with Ord. 17, r.11(3). The Court confirmed the application and set the case down to be heard in March 1994. On January 4, 1994 D made an application for a declaration that the case was struck out under Ord. 17, r.11. The district judge decided that the case was struck out on September 23, 1994 and ordered P's solicitors to show cause why they should not pay all the costs of the action. P appealed and in the alternative applied for reinstatement. The issue before the judge was whether the notice sent out by the Court was a further or different direction in accordance with Ord. 17, r.11(14)(a). The district judge said it was not on the assumption that the notice was sent out as an administrative matter, did not have judicial impact and was not therefore a direction.

Held, allowing the appeal, that (1) the Form N450 was, on proper construction "further or different directions" within the meaning of Ord. 17, r.11(4)(a), and therefore the case had not been struck out under the rules and the request to set down had been a proper one; (2) P's solicitor was therefore entitled to take the date for the commencement of the timetable from the Form N450 which was a sealed document, couched in directive terms which provided steps that both parties were to comply with. The judge had regard for the position of a potential litigant in person who had been sent the document. If looked at without the trappings of law it was a direction telling the parties what to do and would have been considered as binding (Bird (Annie) v. Inial Contract Services [1994[12 C.L. 68; *Nelson and Guy v. Infil Housing Co-op; Rastin v. British Steel; Todd v. Evans; Adams v. Geest; Byrne v. Webber; Donaldson v. Canavan; Ayres v. British Steel; Rastin v. British Steel* [1994] 3 C.L. 331; *Todd v. Evans; Adams v. Geest; Byrne v. Webber; Donaldson v. Canavan; Ayres v. British Steel* considered.)

MORLEY v. JEWSON LTD, January 31, 1995; H.H.J. Quentin Edwards Q.C., Central London County Ct. [*Ex rel. Charles Hale, Barrister.*]

4060. County court—striking out—automatic directions—directions—standard form—whether the court's directions override automatic direction

[C.C.R., Ord. 17, r.11.]

Proceedings for an industrial deafness claim, were served on May 7, 1993. D by first-class post served a defence on Friday July 2, 1993 both on P's solicitors and by lodging a copy at court. Automatic directions applied and the notice issued by the court stipulated July 22, 1993 as the date when the timetable was to commence. P's solicitors took that date as the starting point and calculated that the matter had to be set down no later that 15 months and 14 days thereafter, namely, no later than November 5, 1994. On October 17, 1994, at a hearing to extend the timetable by six months, the district judge agreed with D that the matter had been struck out, as no request for a trial date had been made within 14 days of delivery of defence, namely by October 16, 1994. On appeal, D contended that this was the correct decision based on Ord. 17, r.11, that pleadings were deemed to be closed 14 days after delivery of defence irrespective of the court's own timetable.

Held, allowing the appeal that (1) P's solicitors were entitled to rely on the court's own notice. There was no ambiguity about the date which clearly set out that the timetable began 14 days thereafter. The judge considered the position of a plaintiff acting in person who did not have detailed knowledge of the provisions of County Court Rules. That person would be entitled to rely upon the date set out by the court and it would be illogical for there to be a different rule for P acting in person and those who have legal representatives; (2) that the defence had in any event not been delivered on July 2, 1993 but merely sent by post. Delivery must be the date of arrival at the county court. In this case the defence was served on a Friday and was date stamped received by the court on Monday July 5, 1993. Even on D's own argument therefore, the timetable did not expire until October 19, 1994 and the district judge was wrong to have held that the matter had been struck out on October 17, 1994.

BAILEY v. J. DIXON (DONCASCTER), November 8, 1994, Leeds County Ct.

4061. County court—striking out—automatic directions—directions appointment—case to be set down for hearing upon joint certificate of readiness—whether direction supplanting automatic directions

[C.C.R., Ord. 17, r.11(9).]

In 1992 P began a High Court action to recover money due under a contract for building work. The defence was served on January 15, 1993 and the case was transferred to the county court by an order dated June 29, 1993. Pursuant to C.C.R., Ord. 17, r.11(9), the action was liable to be struck out on October 13, 1994. On October 19, 1993, P requested a directions appointment. The fixed date was vacated by agreement; on August 15, 1994, the directions appointment was reinstated and the district judge gave directions giving both parties leave to call an additional expert each and providing for the case to be set down for hearing upon a joint certificate of readiness with an agreed time estimate. P's solicitor continued to conduct the litigation in the belief that the requirement to request a trial date within 15 months of close of pleadings had been supplanted by the district judge's direction. On application by D, the district judge considered whether the action was automatically struck out.

Held, that the action was not automatically struck out. The automatic directions had been supplanted so as to create an open-ended timetable. The judge held that it was permissible for the court to consider the nature and stage of the proceedings in order to ascertain the true intention of the district judge in giving directions. It was clear that the district judge here thought that the matter was not ready for trial. Accordingly, it was his intention to create an open-ended timetable, therefore the action was not struck out. In deciding whether the failure to comply with the automatic directions was excusable, the fact that P's solicitor believed that the direction of August 15, 1994, had replaced the automatic direction could be taken into account. Although P could be criticised, there had been no significant failure, and reinstatement would have been justified, had the appeal succeeded (*Rastin v. British Steel* [1994] C.L.Y. 3635, *Nelson and Guy v. Infil Housing Co-op; Rastin v. British Steel; Tood v. Evans; Adams v. Geest, Byrne v. Webber; Donaldson v. Canavan; Ayrers v. British Steel* [1994] C.L.Y. 3645, *Daw v. Tilcon* [1995] 1 C.L. 322 considered).

BANGAR (t/a BSB BUILDERS) v. SINGH AND KAUR, June 21, 1995, H.H.J. O'Rorke, Nottingham C.C. [*Ex rel.* Sean Hale, Barrister, St. Mary's Chambers, Nottingham.]

4062. County court—striking out—automatic directions—directions by consent—whether overriding automatic directions

[C.C.R., Ord. 17, r.11.]

P began a county court action against three defendants for damages. The automatic directions in C.C.R., Ord. 17, r.11, applied. The last defence was received by the court in January 1992. Accordingly, pursuant to Ord. 17, r.11(9), the action was liable to be automatically struck out in April 1993. On January 24, 1992 certain directions were given by consent including the following: "action be listed for hearing on receipt of a certificate of readiness from all parties together with an agreed estimate of time". All parties continued to conduct the litigation until well after April 1993. However, in October 1994, the district judge declared that the action had, in fact, been automatically struck out in April 1993, no request having been made by P for a hearing date before then. P appealed on the ground that the direction given on January 24, 1992 had replaced or varied the automatic direction, creating, in effect, an open-ended timetable.

Held, dismissing the appeal, that (1) the direction on January 24, 1992 did not replace or vary the obligation to request a hearing date set out in Ord. 17, r.11(3)(d). The direction did not create an open-ended timetable, but rather was a supplementary or further direction. Pursuant to Ord. 17, r.11(2)(b), it was to be read subject to the automatic directions; (2) in the absence of an express provision inserted in the direction to that effect, it could not be inferred from the direction that the intention of the parties was to seek to override the automatic directions (*Nelson & Guy v. Infil Housing Co-op* [1994] 5 C.L. 303 compared).

DAW v. TILCON, November 23, 1994; H.H.J. Grenfell; Bradford County Ct. [*Ex rel. Andrew T.A. Dallas, Barrister*].

4063. County court—striking out—automatic directions—directions issued in third party action—whether superseded automatic directions in main action—no form N450 sent out—whether timetable triggered—whether reasonable diligence justifying reinstatement

[C.C.R., Ord. 17, r.11(9).]

P's action against D was automatically struck out, no application to set down having been made within the 15 months provided by C.C.R., Ord. 17, r.11(9). D applied to have monies paid out of court, and for costs in the action. P applied to reinstate the action following the C.A.'s decision in *Rastin*. P alleged that no form N450 had been received by P's solicitors, and that directions which had been issued in a third party action supervened the automatic directions in the main action, arguing that therefore the action was not struck out.

Held, dismissing P's application to reinstate the action, that form N450 is for information purposes only, it is not a formal notice of the court. Third party directions had no bearing on a direction in the main action (the point was abandoned by P during the hearing and this was praised by the judge). In deciding whether the failure to comply with the automatic directions was excusable, having regard to the threshold test of reasonable diligence, as set out in *Rastin*, P had failed to comply with the automatic directions for discovery, exchange of witness statements and setting down. As far as the court was concerned P had taken no steps in the action between witness statements on December 31, 1993 and making an application to reinstate on February 28, 1995, over one year later (*Nelson & Guy v. Infill Housing Co-op.; Rastin v. British Steel; Todd v. Evans; Adams v. Geest; Byrne v. Webber; Donaldson v. Canavan; Ayres v. British Steel* [1994] C.L.Y. 3635 considered).

WATTS v. HASTINGS, March 16, 1995, District Judge Trent, Barnet County Ct. [*Ex rel.* Emily Formby, Barrister.]

4064. County court—striking out—automatic directions—extension—order made by consent to extend time-limit—failure to request hearing date—whether case prosecuted with reasonable diligence

[C.C.R., Ord. 17, r. 11(3)(d).]

In a personal injury action to which the automatic directions applied, P was obliged by C.C.R., Ord. 17, r.11(3)(d), to request a hearing date by August 3, 1993. The automatic striking out date under r.11(9) was May 3, 1994. On January 12, 1994 an order was made by consent in these terms: "Upon the parties agreeing terms and by consent it is ordered that there be an extension of three months from the end of the 15 months timetable within which to request a hearing date". Just before August 3, 1994, P's solicitors applied for a further extension. That application was not heard until after August 3, 1994 when the District Judge ruled that P's claim had already been automatically struck out. P appealed to the judge arguing that the effect of the three-month extension was to extend the six-month period for requesting a hearing date to August 3, 1994, and P therefore had a further nine months before the case was automatically struck out.

Held, dismissing the appeal, that the effect of the order was retrospectively to extend the original six-month period by three months, so the automatic striking-out date, nine months later, was on August 3, 1994. Although P's solicitors had applied for a further extension before the strike-out date, they had not requested a hearing date, so the case was struck out. Because P had not prosecuted the case with reasonable diligence the application to reinstate was refused.

BLACKMAN v. MYSON GROUP PLC, November 2, 1994; H.H.J. Sumner; Wandsworth County Ct. [*Ex rel. Nicholas Vineall, Barrister*].

4065. County court—striking out—automatic directions—extension of time for setting down—whether County Court Rules further extend time for nine months

[C.C.R., Ord. 17, r.11(9).]

In December 1993, the court approved an extension of time for setting down P's action by six months from January 1994. In September 1994 D applied for directions on the counterclaim consequent to P's claim being "automatically struck out". P relied upon Ord. 17, r.11(9), and contended that it had the effect of adding a further nine months to any extension of the time for setting down approved by the court.

Held, that Ord. 17, r.11(9), requires P to request a hearing date within 15 months of the day on which pleadings were deemed to be closed or within nine months of the expiry of any period fixed by the court for making such request. The wording was clear and unequivocal and P's claim was not automatically struck out. D was ordered to pay P the costs of the application.

STENTIFORD-CROOK v. GARDINER, July 24, 1994; District Judge Meredith; Torquay County Ct. [*Ex rel. Nigel Partridge, Lyons Davidson, Solicitor*].

4066. County court—striking out—automatic directions—filing two or more defences—whether each defence triggering a new timetable

[C.C.R., Ord. 17, r.11.]

The issue determined in this matter was when, where two or more defendants file a defence several months apart, the timetable in respect of Ord. 17, r.11(9) commences. The district judge concluded that the timetable commenced 14 days after delivery of the first defence. The district judge considered two questions: (a) how pleadings are deemed to re-open each time a defendant files a defence and whether each defence triggers a new timetable and (b) whether time runs indefinitely if one defendant does not file a defence.

Held, that the time must run from the first defence as to conclude otherwise would remove the teeth of Ord. 17, r.11, and would abdicate the role of the court in management of litigation as implied in the case of *Rastin*. There is nothing in Ord. 17, r.11, which makes any provision for substituting one set of automatic directions for another unless the court specifically orders otherwise by way of an Order. An Order can only be made by the matter coming before a district judge and not by the issue of a further N450 as considered in the case of *Bird (Annie) v. Initial Contract Services*. Regard was had to the Law Society *Gazette* of November 9, 1994 and the proposals concerning clarification of the rule. The close of pleadings therefore occurred 14 days after the filing of the first defence. In this matter the case was struck out. No appeal has been issued (*Rastin v. British Steel; Todd v. Evans; Adams v. Geest, Byrne v. Webber; Donaldson v. Canavan; Ayres v. British Steel* [1994] 3 C.L. 331, *Bird (Annie) v. Initial Contract Services* [1994] 12 C.L. 680 considered).

GRIST (C.) v. STC AND THE FORESTRY COMMISSION, February 16, 1995; District Judge A.T. North; Pontypridd County Ct. [*Ex rel. Howard Palser and Partners, Solicitors*].

4067. County court—striking out—automatic directions—form N450—actual date of court's receipt of defence—different to date on form N450—which date to apply to timetable

P received form N450 from the court, telling him that the automatic directions began 14–28 days after the "above date", which was January 4, 1994. Unbeknown to P, the court had in fact received the defence, not on January 4, 1994, but on December 20, 1993. P requested a hearing date within the time-limit, on a timetable beginning on January 4, 1994, but outside the time-limit on a timetable beginning on December 20, 1993. The district judge held that the case was struck out.

Held, allowing P's appeal, that although form N450 was merely a practice form, and had no other status than as a notification to the parties that the automatic directions applied, the date given as the date of receipt of the defence in form N450 was crucial to the timetable. Form N450 did not in itself constitute directions. However, the timetable begins 14 days after delivery of the defence at the court office (or 28 days if it includes a counterclaim). Only the court can know the date on which the defence was delivered to the court office. If the court volunteers this information, whether by way of N450 or in any other way, that will be deemed to be the date on which the defence was delivered, even though the defence may in fact have been delivered on a different date. It would make the striking-out provisions even more draconian than they are if a plaintiff who makes enquiries or receives a voluntary notification from the court as to the date of delivery of the defence should find, too late, that a different date applies. If this was wrong, the appeal would in any case be allowed. Both D and P were sent the form N450, and D was therefore well aware which date the court was using as the date of delivery, and therefore the date of commencement of the timetable. Nevertheless, D did not raise, either with the court or P, the fact that the date on the N450 was wrong. This did not prevent them from subsequently seeking to rely on the earlier, correct date. D was estopped by its conduct from denying that the true date of delivery of the defence was the date on the form N450.

JACOBS v. GENEVA INDUSTRIES, October 17, 1995, H.H.J. Viljoen, Watford County Ct. [*Ex rel.* Sam Neaman, Barrister, 4 Paper Buildings, Temple.]

4068. County court—striking out—automatic directions—form N450—commencement of timetable—date of receipt of defence by court—whether the sending of form N450 constituted direction

[C.C.R., Ord. 17, r.11.]

A road traffic accident took place on December 1, 1989 and the summons was taken out on November 26, 1992. A defence dated December 9, 1992 was received by the court on December 14, 1992 and a copy of it was sent to P's solicitor but it did not bear any legible date of receipt. Correspondence showed that P's solicitors had the defence by December 21, 1992. The Court did not send out any automatic directions. On September 10, 1993 P's solicitor wrote to the court asking whether automatic directions applied and, if they did, asking what the date for commencement of the timetable was, In that letter he also stated that P was not ready and might need more time. The letter was put before a district judge, who instructed the clerk to reply to the effect that automatic directions applied from the date of receipt of the defence by the court and that the sending of any information was a courtesy aimed primarily at the litigant in person. In error the clerk sent a copy of N450 in the form set out in the County Court Rules and inserted the date September 21, 1993 in the box for the start of the timetable. This was accompanied by a compliments slip saying that automatic directions applied as per the attached document. The compliments slip was dated September 24, 1993. P's solicitor took this as a new start date given as a direction by the Court for the purposes of Ord. 17, r.11(2) and (4). On the basis of this date the case would be automatically struck out under Ord. 17, r.11(9), on January 4, 1995. An application to set down was made in December 1994 and at the court's direction the case was listed for a pre-trial review. At that hearing the court raised the question of whether the case was struck out, the order of September 1993 being of no effect. On the full hearing of the point on February 12, 1995 counsel for the MIB acting as an interested party (the defendant not appearing or being represented) argued that the sending of an N450 was not a giving of directions for the purpose of Ord. 17 if performed in an administrative capacity by a clerk. Such an order only varied the timetable if it was performed as a judicial act within s.27 of the County Courts Act 1984. P argued that in this case the solicitor, having written to the Chief Clerk of the Court, and knowing that such a letter would normally go before a district judge for an answer, must be entitled to rely upon it as an order.

Held, that the agreed facts proved that it had gone before a district judge who had considered the matter and indicated what reply to give. The reply was therefore given in a judicial capacity as the clerk was acting under the direction of the district judge even if the gave the wrong information in the form of an incorrectly drawn order. The judge had a power to correct the clerk's error under Ord. 15, r.5 (the Slip Rule), but declined to do so on the basis that it would be inequitable to do so P having relied upon it (*Moore v. Buchanan; Buchanan v. Moore-Pataleena; Moore v. Buchanan (Married Woman); sub nom. Moore v. Buchanan; sub nom. Moore v. Buchanan; Buchanan v. Moore-Pataleena [1967] C.L.Y. 3149 followed). The case was therefore not stuck out (Nelson and Guy v. Infil Housing Co-op; Rastin v. British Steel; Todd v. Evans; Adams v. Geest; Byrne v. Webber; Donaldson v. Caraven; Ayres v. British Steel* [1994] 4 C.L. 303 distinguished; *Bird (Annie) v. Initial Contract Services* [1994] 12 C.L. 680 not followed).

[*Per curiam*: A Form N450 is normally sent out without judicial consideration, so in those circumstances any date inserted in the document other than the actual date of receipt of the Defence by the court is of no effect. A prudent plaintiff will therefore presume that the date of receipt by the court is that on the Defence, or at latest the next working day. Where a defendant sends a copy of the Defence to the plaintiff with the common courtesy letter saying "we are today sending a copy of the Defence to the Court", then the next working day should be assumed to be the date from which the timetable is calculated. The automatic directions timetable can only be varied by the court acting within s.37 of the 1984 Act.]

CASSANDRO v. NEMBHARD, February 13, 1995; H.H.J. Burford; Aldershot and Farnham County Ct. sitting at Southampton. [*Ex rel. Steven Weddle, Barrister*].

4069. County court—striking out—automatic directions—form N450—second N450 amending first—amended form giving wrong delivery of defence date—whether affected timetable—whether case to be reinstated

P's claim arose out of a road traffic accident on December 11, 1991. Proceedings were issued in the Leeds County Court on December 8, 1992, and a defence was served by D's advisors, received by P's advisors on January 13, 1993. The form N450 Notice of Automatic Direction was not issued until November 1993, and then only following an enquiry to the court by P's advisors. The form N450 exhibited the date January 13, 1993 as the date the defence was received. Following a further enquiry by P's advisors to the court a second copy of form N450 was sent to P's advisors with the word "amended" placed in the top right hand corner and with the date January 13, 1993 crossed out and replaced with the date November 11, 1993. In November 1994 P's advisors issued an application seeking leave to file and serve amended particulars of claim. At the hearing of the application on December 15, 1994, the district judge held that the action had been automatically struck out on P's failure to request a trial date pursuant to Ord. 17, r.11(9). P's advisors issued an application to reinstate the action, which was refused on the grounds that the action had not been prosecuted with reasonable diligence. P sought to appeal that decision, and applied for leave to appeal the decision of December 15 out of time. In support of the appeal, P argued that the court timetable began 14 days after November 11, 1993, the date shown on the amended form N450. P also submitted that the amendment to the N450 itself constituted a different direction within the meaning of Ord. 17, r.2(b).

Held, that the court was satisfied that the defence had been delivered to the court in January 1993, when a copy had been supplied by D's advisors to P's advisors. The amendment of the form N450 was not a direction given by the court, since it was highly likely that the amendment was made by an executive or administrative officer of the court rather than a circuit judge or district judge. Further, the court timetable begins 14 days after actual delivery of the defence to the court, and not from the date specified in the form N450. If no form N450 were issued, then it could not be argued that the timetable never commenced. Therefore, the district judge was right to find in December 1994 that the action was struck out. However, P and her advisors had in all the circumstances pursued the action with reasonable diligence and their failure to comply with the rules excusable. The action was therefore reinstated.

KIRKHAM v. COOPER (t/a CARPET AND CURTAINS CENTRE), April 20, 1995, H.H.J. Bush, Leeds County Ct. [*Ex rel.* Simon Bass, Nelson & Co., Solicitors, Leeds.]

4070. County court—striking out—automatic directions—form N450—subsequent transfer to another court—new form N450 issued—which dates to be followed

[C.C.R., Ord. 17, r.11(9).]

P issued proceedings in Blackburn County Court on November 1, 1993. A defence and counterclaim were served on November 18, 1993. The court then issued automatic directions on form N450 on December 2, 1993. There was no automatic transfer to D's home court at that time. On February 3, 1994, P served a reply and defence to the counterclaim. Blackburn County Court then realised that the matter should have been transferred earlier to Thanet County Court on the filing of the defence. By order of February 16, 1994, the court transferred the action to Thanet County Court, and further purported to make an order "that the automatic directions issued on December 2, 1993 be and are hereby dismissed". Thanet County Court gave notice of transfer on February 22, and on March 10, 1994 issued a second form N450. The pleadings were deemed closed 28 days after service of the defence and counterclaim, and under the Blackburn timetable, the action would be automatically struck out on March 30, 1995. Under the Thanet timetable, the action would be automatically struck out on July 7, 1995. On July 3, 1995, P's solicitors wrote to Thanet with a request that the action be set down for trial.

Held, on an application by D for an order that the action had already been automatically struck out, that P should have followed the Blackburn timetable, and the action was struck out on March 30, 1995. P must abide by the rules, and pleadings were deemed to have closed 28 days after the delivery of the defence and counterclaim. Under Ord. 17, r.11(9), a request must be made to set down within 15 months of the day on which pleadings are deemed to be closed. Although P had relied upon the Thanet timetable, it being the only one in existence, questions arose as to what happened if the date given in the Thanet timetable was not the actual date from which time ran, as provided by the rules. Because form N450 is not an order in itself, not a judicial act, and only provides a warning to P as to the automatic striking out provisions, the form cannot overrule or change the meaning of the rules. It was important for a plaintiff to calculate the dates from the rules and not necessarily from form N450. As to the counterclaim, this had not been automatically struck out, but by reason of the parties consenting to the district judge considering the future of the counterclaim, despite no cross-application having been issued by P, it was held that the counterclaim should be struck out for want of prosecution, but without prejudice to the right to serve any counterclaim in any fresh proceedings commenced by P.

JOINTLINK v. ST. CRISPINS, September 26, 1995, District Judge Hawthorne, Thanet County Ct. [*Ex rel.* Walmsley & Barnes, Solicitors, Margate.]

4071. County court—striking out—automatic directions—form N450—whether action struck out for failure to request fixture of date for hearing—court issuing a form N450—whether setting new timetable—whether constituting new directions

[C.C.R., Ord. 17, r.11.]

By default summons issued on September 11, 1992 P commenced proceedings in Guildford County Court for the balance due for construction of a hard tennis court at D's property. D, then acting in person, filed defences alleging bad workmanship and counterclaiming damages. The action was transferred to Reigate County Court and a notice of transfer issued by that court giving a new case number. Reigate also issued a document headed "Notes for guidance on automatic directions" in the form prescribed by form N450 (1990) showing (correctly) the "Date defence received" as September 25, 1992, so that, for the purposes of Ord. 17, r.11, pleadings were deemed to be closed on October 23, 1992: Ord. 17, r.11(11)(a). On October 22, 1992 P served a reply and defence to counterclaim. D then instructed solicitors. On January 27, 1993 an order was made, by consent, transferring the action back to Guildford County Court. On or about February 2, 1993 Guildford issued a document headed "Notice that automatic directions apply" in the revised (1992) form N450. This stated "these notes tell you what you must do and the timetable you must follow. If you want to change any of these directions you must apply to the court. The timetable begins 14 days after the date given above, or 28 days if a counterclaim was filed with the defence". The date given on the form against the printed word "Date" was "2.2.93". Nothing on the revised form indicated the date on which the defence was received. P's solicitor, who had not received a copy of the "Reigate directions", deposed that she regarded the Guildford document as setting the timetable so that the 15-month time-limit for requesting a date for the hearing expired on June 2, 1994. On May 6, 1994 P's solicitor applied for a date accordingly. D's solicitors (who had not received the "Guildford directions") contended that the action had been struck out automatically on January 24, 1994 pursuant to Ord. 17, r.11(9). They applied for a declaration to that effect and an order for costs. D indicated that they intended to proceed with their counterclaim. P issued a cross-application for a declaration that the action had not been struck out on the basis that the document issued by Guildford County Court replaced the automatic directions, alternatively for reinstatement. On August 3, 1994 the district judge granted Ds' application and refused to exercise his discretion to reinstate the action. He held that the issue of the Guildford document was simply an administrative exercise by the court to inform the parties that automatic directions applied and that P's solicitor was not entitled to rely upon it as giving different directions.

Held, allowing P's appeal, that (1) the Guildford document constituted "further or different directions" within the meaning of Ord. 17, r.11(4)(a). It set out in direct form what was to be done and it was not possible to construe it as other than the court giving directions of its own motion for the conduct of the action, even though the date "2.2.93" may have been written in error; (2) however, if that decision was wrong, it was appropriate to order reinstatement. Although there were periods of delay which might be criticised, overall there had been no significant failure to conduct the case with expedition. The failure by P's solicitor to apply for a date until May 6, 1994 was excusable: she was entitled to rely on the Guildford document as indicating that the time-limit expired on June 2, 1994. Further, it was clearly in the interests of justice that the claim, which was not statute-barred, should be tried with the counterclaim

(*Rastin v. British Steel; Todd v. Evans; Adams v. Geest; Byrne v. Webber; Donaldson v. Canavan; Ayres v. British Steel.* [1994] 3 C.L. 331 considered).

McINTOSH AND PARTNERS v. DUDLEY, February 8, 1995; H.H.J. Slot; Guildford County Ct. [*Ex rel. David Lamming, Barrister*].

4072. County court—striking out—automatic directions—form N450—wrong date on form—effect on automatic directions—request for hearing date—whether valid

[C.C.R., Ord. 17, r.11(8).]

The summons was issued in September 1993, and the defence was dated October 7, 1993 and filed on October 8. Accordingly, close of pleadings took place on October 22, 1993, and in normal circumstances the case would be struck out 15 months thereafter on January 22, 1995. It was conceded by P that if the sole criterion for deciding when the 15-month period starts to run is close of pleadings, then the action was struck out on January 22. A form N450 was sent to P, stating that a defence had been received. There was a box on the form marked "Date" which should have had the date of delivery of the defence. Unfortunately, the date entered on the form N450 was November 16, 1993. A request for trial was made within 15 months of November 30, on February 3, 1995. P claimed that the 15-month period started from November 30, arguing that as the plaintiff can have no knowledge of the date of filing of the defence, it has to rely on form N450, and that litigants in person, unlikely to appreciate the subtleties of form N450 would be trapped if not able to rely on the date given on the from. There were no Court of Appeal decisions.

Held, that form N450 could not override the clear meaning of the rules. Form N450 was clearly stated to be notes for guidance. It could not vary the automatic directions rule in which the 15-month period ran from close of pleadings unless there was a local practice direction or specific order of the court to the contrary. The judge also accepted D's submission that the action be regarded as struck out because no valid request for trial had been made, the request having been made by way of letter dated February 3, 1995, which was in breach of Ord. 17, r.11(8) (which the judge held was to be read in conjunction with Ord. 17, r.11(3)(d)), as it did not contain any details of the number of witnesses to be called, or estimated length of time. Further, the letter of February 3, which stated that the case was ready for trial was, in the judge's view, a sham, as the case was not ready for trial because none of the automatic directions had been complied with.

GREAT YARMOUTH CEILINGS v. GRINT DRYLINING (FREETHORPE), May 24, 1995, H.H.J. Barham, Norwich County Ct. [*Ex rel.* Philip Kerridge, Rogers and Norton, Solicitors, Norwich.]

4073. County court—striking out—automatic directions—hearing date—extension of time allowed for setting down—appropriate test

P applied for an extension of the time allowed for setting down. D opposed the extension on the grounds that there had been three identifiable periods of significant delay in progressing the action.

Held, that the principles enunciated in *Rastin v. British Steel* applied to a prospective application for an extension of time in the same way as to a retrospective application. The court was to be guided by those principles in the exercise of its discretion, save that in a retrospective application, P has an additional and substantial hurdle to get over if he has allowed the time for setting down to expire, there then being clear evidence of a failure to comply with the timetable. Insofar as this case was a prospective application, that hurdle did not have to be surmounted, and approval of P's application could be considered in a less draconian fashion.

PIROUET v. DAIRY CREST, June 28, 1995, District Judge Ewing, Holywell County Ct. [*Ex rel.* Walker, Smith & Way, Solicitors, Wrexham.]

4074. County court—striking out—automatic directions—hearing date—failure to obtain consent—no application to district judge—whether application valid

[C.C.R., Ord. 17, r.11(9).]

P2 was injured in a road accident allegedly caused by D's negligence, while driving P1's car. The summons was issued on October 18, 1993, claiming special damages for P1 in relation to the car hire charges, and general damages for P2's whiplash injury. A defence was filed on November 9, 1993, denying liability, and was served together with a request for further and better particulars of claim. Automatic directions were issued on November 10, 1993, the timetable commencing on November 24, 1993. Ps' solicitors sent only three letters to D's solicitors between November 9, 1992 and March 28, 1995. The first, dated November 25, 1993, included Ps' list of documents, the second, dated December 17, 1993, included Ps' CRU certificate and the third, dated March 2, 1995, included the further and better particulars, an up-to-date medical report, photographs and sketch plan of the *locus in quo* and additional documents to be added to discovery. The letter also informed D's solicitors that a hearing date had been applied for. That request had been filed on February 16, 1995, that is eight days before the case was to be automatically struck out. The court thereupon entered the case in the warned list, commencing April 3, 1995. D applied for a declaration that the action was in fact struck out under C.C.R., Ord. 17, r.11(9), in that, notwithstanding the request for a hearing date, no valid request had been made in compliance with Ord. 17, r.11(3)(d) and (8). Any request for a hearing date after six months from the close of pleadings had to be made with the consent of the other parties or on an application to a district judge, following from the word "shall" in Ord. 17, r.11(3)(d). The request failed to comply with Ord. 17, r.11(8) in that no attempt was made by Ps' solicitors to agree either the estimated length of the hearing, or the number of witnesses to be called. The request, being invalid, should be disregarded, and in the absence of a valid request, the action was automatically struck out. On March 31, 1995, the district judge declared that the action was struck out because the request was invalid and ordered P to pay D's costs of the action.

Held, dismissing D's appeal, that the reference in Ord. 17, r.11(9) to a request for a hearing date must mean a request complying with both Ord. 17, r.11(3)(d) and Ord. 17, r.11(8). Whilst no authorities were cited as to the interpretation of these precise rules, it was clear that their main purpose was to bring litigation to trial without unnecessary delay. A request for a hearing date and automatic striking out rules are central to that purpose. It was open to a plaintiff who did not know how many witnesses were to be called by the defendant to apply for a time extension. The time given by the rules to elicit such information had been described by the C.A. as generous. The action was struck out.

PRIESTLEY & PRIESTLEY v. WEYMAN, June 22, 1995, H.H.J. Morgan, Barnet County Ct. [*Ex rel.* J.I.Farquharson, Barrister, Exeter.]

4075. County court—striking out—automatic directions—hearing date—plaintiff had failed to make proper discovery—no proper co-operation with defence team—whether application a valid one—whether action struck out

[C.C.R., Ord. 17, r.11.]

P began proceedings in January 1991, alleging various breaches by D of a contract to effect insurance cover on P's behalf. P's action would have been struck out automatically under C.C.R., Ord. 17, r.11(9) on May 16, 1995, but P applied, shortly before that date, for the action to be set down, notwithstanding his failure to disclose expert evidence on which he said he intended to rely, to exchange witness statements or to agree sketch plans. He had not given proper discovery and had made no attempt to agree with D either the length of the trial or the number of witnesses to be called. The district judge ordered that the action should be set down for trial but that no hearing date should be allocated for three months to enable outstanding interlocutory applications to be completed. D appealed on the grounds that the application to set down was an abuse of the process of the court, which ought to have been refused.

Held, that P had blatantly failed to comply with the automatic directions regarding the preparatory steps, but that he had complied in essence with Ord. 17, r.11(3)(d), in applying for a date for the hearing to be fixed. His failures were matters of detail which did not invalidate an otherwise correct application to set down. Accordingly, D's appeal would be dismissed, but P's claim would be stayed and the stay not lifted until he had complied with the requirement to give proper discovery and had provided D with witness statements, expert reports, sketch plans, photographs and any other evidence on which he intended to rely at trial.

EVANS v. BRISTOL & WEST BUILDING SOCIETY, June 14, 1995, H.H.J. Bradbury, Ipswich County Ct. [*Ex rel.* Michael Lane, Barrister, East Anglian Chambers.]

4076. County court—striking out—automatic directions—hearing date—trial date requested within timetable—fee for setting down not paid—whether case struck out—whether automatic directions required setting down within 15 months—whether request without fee sufficient

[C.C.R., Ord. 17, r.11; County Court Fees (Amendment) Order 1994 (S.I. 1994 No. 1936 (L.9)).]

P's personal injury action was subject to automatic striking out, pursuant to C.C.R., Ord. 17, r.11(9) on September 9, 1994. On September 8, 1994, P's solicitors sent a fax to the court requesting a trial date, but did not send or pay the setting down fee prescribed in the County Court Fees (Amendment) Order 1994 (S.I. 1994 No. 1936 (L.9)). On September 12, 1994, the court wrote to P's solicitors stating that the case would not be set down until the setting down fee was paid. On September 29, the fee was paid. D issued a summons for a declaration that the action was automatically struck out, as no proper request for a trial date had been made, pursuant to Ord. 17, r.11, by September 9. The court held that a request for a trial date was made within the meaning of Ord. 17, r.11(3)(d) and (9), even if the action could not be set down because of the failure to pay the setting down fee. Accordingly, the action did not stand struck out. Had it been the intention of the rules to provide for automatic striking out if the action was not set down within 15 months of the close of pleadings, Ord. 17, r.11, sub-rules (3)(d) and (9) would have been amended by the County Court Fees (Amendment) Order 1994, which introduced a setting down fee in the county court, to provide expressly for striking out on failure to pay.

GUMBLEY v. BARMBY, March 8, 1995, H.H.J. Tetlow, Manchester County Ct. [*Ex rel.* Richard Bradley, Oriel Chambers, Liverpool.]

4077. County court—striking out—automatic directions—hearing date—whether request for trial date sufficient

[C.C.R., Ord. 17, r.11(1A)(3)(d)(9).]

The parties were involved in a road traffic accident on July 17, 1988. An action was commenced in the Queen's Bench Division on March 7, 1990. On January 14, 1992, P applied to set down for trial but soon thereafter on D's suggestion, and by consent, the matter was transferred to the Mayor's and City of London County Court. In his Notice of Transfer of Proceedings Before Judgment dated May 20, 1992 the district judge indicated that automatic directions would apply "pursuant" to C.C.R., Ord. 17, r.11(1A). On April 26, 1993, P wrote to the court requesting a date for the hearing of an application to set down. Before the application was due to be heard the parties jointly wrote to the court requesting that the date fixed for the application be vacated. On reading the parties' written application the district judge struck out the application to set down. On June 8, 1994, P wrote to the court requesting a trial date. On June 27, 1994, D applied for an order that the action stand struck out pursuant to Ord. 17, r.11(9). On July 21, 1994, the district judge heard the application and held that the letter of June 8, 1994 was sufficient a request to comply with Ord. 17, r.11(3)(d) and (9). The application was dismissed. D appealed.

Held, dismissing the appeal, that the written application of April 26, 1993 had been struck out and was, therefore, of no effect. However, because the action had been commenced prior to October 1, 1990 (see note to Ord. 17, r.11), automatic directions did not apply; notwithstanding the indication of the district judge and the conduct of the parties. Leave to appeal to the court of Appeal was subsequently refused by both the single judge and, most recently, the full court.

GLEED v. MILTON KEYNES BOROUGH COUNCIL, September 5, 1994; H.H.J. Byrt, Q.C.; Central London County Ct) [*Ex rel. Pip Punwar, Barrister*].

4078. County court—striking out—automatic directions—interlocutory consent judgment—damages to be assessed plus costs—whether overriding automatic directions

An application was made by D to strike out P's claim under the 15-month rule, albeit that interlocutory judgment had been obtained by consent with damage to be assessed plus costs. D's appeal was dismissed ([1994] C.L.Y. 3642) and D appealed.

Held, that those responsible for drafting the automatic directions had in their contemplation that when an interlocutory judgment was obtained, the court would provide further directions under C.C.R., Ord. 17, r.11(4)(a), supplanting the usual automatic directions contained in Ord. 17, r.11(3). Had the deputy district judge's order regarding damages to be assessed not been made, then this might not have constituted a further and different direction, in which case the outcome of the appeal might have been different.

JOBBINS v. ARTHUR, December 5, 1994, H.H.J. Smith, Bristol County Ct. [*Ex rel.* Lyons Rounsfell, Solicitors, Bristol.]

4079. County court—striking out—automatic directions—notice of appeal outside limitation period—whether delay would prejudice a fair trial

P sought to appeal against the decision of the district judge striking out their claim, given on February 3, 1995. Notice of appeal had not been served within the prescribed time-limit and leave was therefore sought from the judge for leave for the appeal to proceed. Order 58, r.1, as amended by Ord. 58, r.3, allows seven days for the notice of appeal to be issued and a further five days for service; immediately following the decision of the district judge there was a change of solicitors and the notice was issued on the last day, *i.e.* February 14, 1995. P's new solicitors contacted the Court Office, stating that the notice had been issued but there would be a delay while the matter was referred to a judge for listing. The judge interpreted this as a listing difficulty. The sealed notice was not sent back by the court to P's solicitors until February 27, 1995, for a return date on February 18, 1995. At that time P's solicitors were not concerned with the time for service of the notice of appeal as they had misread the rules and relied on the notes in the *White Book*. The judge stated that those notes are misleading. On February 17, 1995 P's solicitor sent draft notice of appeal and draft supporting affidavits to D1 and D2 and these were received on February 21, 1995, the last day for service of the sealed notice. No application was made for an extension of time for service. P's solicitors had filed an affidavit admitting he was labouring under a misapprehension as to the effect of the rules. The judge found that it was impossible for P's solicitors to have complied with the rules as the court itself retained a sealed copy for a period of several weeks coupled with the misunderstanding the solicitor was labouring under the delay was considered to be explained and understandable. Discretion was therefore exercised to enable the appeal to proceed. P's claim was based on a spraying operation which occurred on July 21, 1989. Proceedings were issued at the very end of the limitation period and not served until the very end of the four-month period of validity. D complained in particular of four periods of delay: (1) delay in service of the writ; (2) delay in the service of the statement of claim which was outside the period prescribed by the rules; (3) a period of 11 months in serving the list of documents; and (4) a period of six months in failing to file notice of change of solicitors. P sought to argue that there was delay on the part of Ds and in particular to a period from April 1993 to the end of 1994 when D2 failed to respond to a request for further and better particulars of the defence. The judge found that there was inordinate and inexcusable delay. The judge dismissed the suggestion that D2 were estopped from striking out the claim because of a delay in dealing with the further and better particulars. He said this is a factor which he bore in mind in reaching his decision but at the end of the day it was so insignificant when viewed at the extent of the delay of which he found P guilty.

Held, dismissing P's appeal, that this case was unlikely to be tried until seven years after the incident. He found that the passage of time seemed to have worked a serious prejudice against there being a fair trial of the issue. In particular he was concerned that the two spraying operatives would only be likely to be able to describe how they ordinarily carried out their work and even if they had any recollection of working on D1's farm the prospects of them adding to their evidence in a constructive and credible way through cross-examination and re-examination was extremely poor. P was ordered to pay D's costs of the action and of the appeal.

WILSON v. GREED AND AGRI-CHEMICALS, April 18, 1995; H.H.J. O'Malley sitting as High Court judge; Exeter District Registry [*Ex rel. Crosse and Crosse, Solicitors*].

4080. County court—striking out—automatic directions—reinstatement—admission of liability—whether setting down provisions apply

[C.C.R., Ord. 17, r.11.]

Both Ps brought claims for damages for personal injury and other consequential losses arising out of a road traffic accident which occurred on July 27, 1991. Proceedings were issued on July 10, 1992 and on August 7, 1992 a defence was filed admitting liability but disputing *quantum*. On November 24, 1992 and December 4, 1992 payments into court were made in an attempt to settle P1 and P2's claims respectively. No procedural steps were taken thereafter until November 8, 1993 when notice of change was filed by Ps' new solicitors. No application was made to set the matter down for trial within the 15-month time period prescribed by Ord. 17, r.11, and accordingly the matter was struck out automatically. An application to set the matter down for trial was apparently made by Ps' solicitors only a matter of a couple of weeks after the claim had been struck out. Ps' solicitors applied for the action to be reinstated before a district judge and their application was successful. D appealed against that decision and the appeal was heard on November 1, 1994. The appeal was successful and the action was confirmed as being struck out. It was argued on behalf of Ds that in order to have the action reinstated, Ps had to satisfy the court that overall that case had been conducted with reasonable diligence and that the failure to set the matter down within the time prescribed by the rules was excusable. Ps' solicitors maintained that the reason for their failure to set the matter down in time was that their understanding of the rules was that if an admission of liability had been made in the case, setting down provisions did not apply.

Held, that the failure to set the matter down within the prescribed time-limit was not excusable since the reason put forward by Ps' solicitors for their failure did not amount to an "excuse". The judge found that ignorance or misunderstanding of the rules did not make Ps' actions excusable, that the case had effectively gone to sleep and that therefore the action should not be reinstated.

WILLIAMS AND WILLIAMS v. PARKER, November 1, 1994; H.H.J. Owen, Manchester County Ct. [*Ex rel.* James Chapman & Co., Solicitors].

4081. County court—striking out—automatic directions—reinstatement—delay—wrongful dismissal claim—whether plaintiff showing due diligence in pursuing claim

[C.C.R., Ord. 17, r.11.]

P started work as an assistant solicitor with T in early 1989 and claimed that, subject to satisfactory performance, he was told that he would be made an equity partner on February 1, 1991. T denied that a contractual promise had been made. Instead of partnership P was given notice terminating his employment and he commenced proceedings in the county court and parallel proceedings in the Industrial Tribunal and the Employment Appeal Tribunal for wrongful dismissal. P successfully applied to have his action reinstated, after it was struck out under C.C.R., Ord. 17, r.11. T then sought leave to appeal against this decision.

Held, allowing the application, that under Ord. 17, r.11, a plaintiff should request a hearing date within six months of the close of pleading and an action would automatically be struck out if the plaintiff had not done so within nine months. Delay had been caused over the filing of documents and P had also delayed his application for reinstatement. A guiding principle on reinstatement of actions was that the plaintiff must show he is innocent of any significant failure to conduct his case with expedition and that he prosecuted his case with reasonable diligence (*Rastin v. British Steel* [1994] 8 C.L. 316, *Hoskins v. Wiggins Teape (U.K.)*, unrep. cited). Such expedition had not been shown by P and so T was granted leave to appeal against the reinstatement.

HAWKES v. TREASURES & RIVER WYATT (LTA 94/5930/F; LTA 94/5931/F) (LTA 94/5930/F; LTA 94/5931/F), October 20, 1994, C.A.

4082. County court—striking out—automatic directions—reinstatement—extension—new strike-out date incorrectly entered on computerised diary system—whether reinstatement on basis of reasonable diligence justified

On June 1, 1994, the court approved an application by consent for an extension of the automatic timetable providing for striking out of P's claim within 15 months, by a further three months. P's solicitors incorrectly entered the new strike out date on their computerised diary system as December 13, 1994, rather than November 13, as it should have been. P applied to set her case down on November 14, 1994, the day after her case was struck out. D applied for the matter not to be listed, as they were awaiting their own medical evidence upon P. On the hearing of that application, P was notified that her case had been struck out. P applied to have her case reinstated, and this was granted by the district judge.

Held, rejecting D's appeal, that P had conducted her case with reasonable diligence and the failure to set down was excusable as it was entirely technical in nature and a prospective application to extend the timetable would inevitably have been granted. As liability was not in dispute and D were awaiting their own medical evidence no hardship had been caused to D at all. D was ordered to pay P's cost of the appeal.

O'DELL v. WEAVER, March 21, 1995, H.H.J. Tyrer, Milton Keynes County Ct. [*Ex rel.* Fennemores, Solicitors, Milton Keynes.]

4083. County court—striking out—automatic directions—reinstatement—failure to apply for hearing date—action automatically struck out—application to reinstate—threshold conditions for reinstatement—whether failure to apply due to oversight of legal representative excusable

[C.C.R., Ord. 17, r.11.]

Before the court will consider where the balance of justice lies, an applicant for the reinstatement of an action automatically struck out under C.C.R., Ord. 17, r.11, must first show that he has conducted his case with reasonable diligence and that the failure to comply with the rule is excusable. Failure to comply which is the result of an oversight by the applicant's legal representative will not ordinarily be regarded as excusable.

P began a personal injury action against D which was transferred to the county court in July 1991. Due to an oversight by his solicitors, S, P failed to apply for a hearing date within the time-limits prescribed by C.C.R., Ord. 17, r.11, and the action was automatically struck out in November 1992. However, before and after that date there was activity on both sides. In November 1991 counsel was instructed to prepare a schedule of special damage although, despite requests by D, one was never prepared. In January 1992, D made an offer to settle on the basis of 25 per cent contributory negligence, which P rejected in July 1992. After the automatic striking out, S instructed a doctor to prepare a new medical report and D made a payment into court in satisfaction of P's claim. In March 1993, D learned that P had not applied for a hearing date and sought confirmation from the court that the action had automatically been struck out. Before receiving an answer, D consented to a payment out to P of part of the sum standing in court. When they received confirmation, D informed P, who applied to reinstate the action. The district judge refused P's application but the county court judge, delivering his judgment before the Court of Appeal in *Rastin v. British Steel* balanced the parties' conflicting interests and reinstated the action.

Held, allowing D's appeal, that (1) the Court of Appeal decision in *Rastin* established that before an action which has been automatically struck out will be reinstated, two conditions must be satisfied. An applicant must first show that he has, save in his failure to comply with r.11(3)(d) and (4), prosecuted his case with at least reasonable diligence. Second, that his failure to comply with the rule was excusable. Only if those two threshold conditions were satisfied was it open to the court to enter into a general consideration of the relative positions of the parties and the balance of justice between them; (2) regarding the second condition, what the Court of Appeal had in mind in *Rastin* was that, once an applicant had satisfied the first condition, the court will be more likely to regard his failure to comply with the rule as excusable if he can show that the application was in fact a formality because the court would have been bound, or almost bound, to grant an application for an extension had it been made prospectively. The court would be more likely to regard a failure to comply with the time-limit as excusable if the failure was of a technical (a reference essentially to the mere passage of time: *per* Simon Brown L.J.) nature. But it was unlikely that a failure to comply would be regarded as excusable because someone acting for the applicant forgot to comply, or was ill, or too busy, or a letter was mislaid in the post. What the court had in mind was a broad and simple test to be applied by the trial judge: "In all the circumstances, was the failure to comply with the setting down rule excusable?"; and (3) in the instant case, P failed to satisfy either of the threshold conditions. P had delayed in preparing the schedule of special damage, in deciding whether to accept or reject D's offers and in obtaining new medical evidence, so that although there had been activity, very little had been done to advance the action and P failed to show that the case was prosecuted with at least reasonable expedition. P also failed to satisfy the second condition since the only excuse tendered for the failure to comply was that it was the result of an oversight, which will not ordinarily be regarded as excusable, in the absence of other favourable considerations. It was therefore unnecessary to decide where the interests of justice lay by balancing the interests of P against those of D, although the conduct of D in making offers and consenting to the interim payment would have been relevant to that exercise (*Rastin v. British Steel* [1994] 1 W.L.R. 732 applied and explained).

HOSKINS v. WIGGINS TEAPE (U.K.) [1994] P.I.Q.R. P377, C.A.

4084. County court—striking out—automatic directions—reinstatement—failure to set down—application to reinstate—relation between automatic striking-out provision and power to extend time—whether time to be extended twice

[C.C.R., Ord. 17, r.11(4)(9).]

P, a minor, suffered injuries while riding an all-terrain vehicle owned by D. Proceedings commenced in January 1992 in accordance with the automatic directions. Delay in answering the interrogatories lead to the action being automatically struck out in default of setting down. Application to reinstate was issued and was granted on August 31, 1993 by an order which extended the time for setting down to December 31, 1993. The order did not contain an express provision as to default within this extended period but it was assumed that in such an event the action would once again be struck out. P made a further application to extend time for setting down at the beginning of December 1993. This application was eventually heard, after adjournments, on April 5, 1994, when it was dismissed as being an application to reinstate retrospectively. Although the application had been made within the extended time-limit, the judge considered that P's solicitors should have ensured that it was heard within that period also. P applied on April 7, 1994 to reinstate the action and D cross-applied to dismiss the application as an abuse of process. Both applications were heard in August 1994 by the same judge who had dismissed the application on April 5, 1994, and he accepted P's submission that the wording of the order made on August 31, 1993 read in conjunction with C.C.R., Ord. 17, r.11(9), meant that the action was not automatically struck out until nine months after the four-month extension, *i.e.* September 1994. There was, in his opinion, no need to reinstate the action as it was still "live". D then sought evidence of the intention of the judge who had made the original order of August 31, 1993 who indicated that it had never been his intention for the action to remain live after December 31, 1993 when the extension ran out. D appealed and applied for an amending order pursuant to C.C.R., Ord. 15, r.5, (the "slip rule") to add the words "and in default P's action be struck out" to the original order.

Held, allowing D's appeal, that (1) although the court would not ordinarily amend an order to include a provision for striking-out, if it was necessary the words could be added under the slip rule; (2) however, in this case there was no necessity to amend the order because both parties had known that the judge's intention in granting the order of August 31, 1993 was that in default of setting down within the prescribed four-month limit the action would be struck out once again on December 31, 1993; and (3) P's application to reinstate would be dismissed.

SMITH v. WALKER WHEELS, November 1, 1994; H.H.J. Stephenson; Newcastle-upon-Tyne County Ct. [*Ex rel. Crutes, Solicitors*].

4085. County court—striking out—automatic directions—reinstatement—whether delay excusable

[C.C.R., Ord. 17, r.11.]

An application was made by B for leave to appeal against a decision to extend time for an application for a hearing date in a personal injury action. C.C.R., Ord. 17, r.11, provided that, after pleading had been closed, the plaintiff should request a date for a hearing within six months. Guidance was laid out in *Rastin v. British Steel* on the exercise of the court's jurisdiction to extend time for an action after it had been deemed to be struck out. The plaintiff must prove that he had prosecuted the case with reasonable diligence and the failure to comply with the rule must be excusable. In the instance case, V's solicitors had misunderstood bona fide, the effect of an order extending time for an application for a trial date.

Held, dismissing the application, that the primary point for consideration was whether the delay was excusable. The trial judge believed that it was. There had been a misunderstanding about the effect of the order in May and that misunderstanding was understandable. There was also a discussion as to whether the judge should have taken the view that the action was prosecuted with due diligence. However, the county court judge had assessed the point properly and there were no grounds for appeal against his decision (*Rastin v.*

British Steel; Todd v. Evans; Adams v. Geest; Byrne v. Webber; Donaldson v. Canavan; Ayres v. British Steel [1994] 8 C.L. 316 considered).

VALLELY (JOHN GERRARD) v. BRITISH RAILWAYS BOARD (LTA 94/5697/F), December 19, 1994, C.A.

4086. County court—striking out—automatic directions—stay of proceedings ordered pending plaintiff's filing of statement explaining special damages claim—whether automatic directions timetable suspended or continuing

[C.C.R., Ord. 6, r.1(5); Ord. 17, r.11.]

P was injured while in D's employment and claimed damages in a negligence action, in which it was alleged that D failed to provide a safe system of work. P's solicitors wrote to D on October 17, 1989, February 1, 1990, and on April 19, 1990. On May 4, 1990, D responded to the letters for the first time by denying liability. P issued proceedings on September 30, 1992, the last day of the three-year limitation period, but did not issue a medical report with the proceedings, nor a schedule of special damages, as required by C.C.R., Ord. 6, r.1(5). P was granted leave to issue proceedings, but an order was made that the action be stayed pending the filing of a medical report, with the provision that P's action was to be dismissed if the medical reports were not filed within four months' time. P filed his reports within the time. On October 22, 1992, D filed his defence as a bare denial and pleadings closed 14 days later, on November 6, 1992. On February 8, 1993, D applied for a stay of proceedings pending the filing by P of a statement explaining his claim for special damages, which was granted on March 16, 1993. On March 22, 1994, P provided details of his claim for special damages when he filed his amended particulars of claim, thereby lifting the stay which had been made in March 1993. On January 25, 1994, an order was made to extend the time before which the action would automatically be struck out, pursuant to Ord. 17, r.11(9), so that the action would not be struck out until February 25, 1995, rather than on May 25, 1994. On July 6, 1994, P applied for an order to extend time in which to request a date for trial, which application was only heard on March 23, 1995, nearly a month after the case should have been automatically struck out. The district judge held that the Form N9 bland denial could constitute a defence and had triggered the operation of the automatic directions. He also held that the order of March 16, which ordered a stay until P provided details of his claim for special damages, did not suspend the operation of the automatic directions. P appealed against the district judge's decision that the case was automatically struck out.

Held, considering the nature of the order staying the action, that it was an order, in effect, made against a plaintiff who had failed to comply with the rules then in operation. This was not an order staying the action in effect for all purposes until such time as P took the trouble to file his schedule of special damages. The judge then considered the application for reinstatement of the action. The claim was only made on the last day of the primary limitation period. There had been a delay of one year between the order staying proceedings until P supplied details of his special damages and the provision of those details (£150 of special damages). In addition the case began with a failure to observe the provisions of Ord. 17, because the medical report was not filed with the pleadings. It was really difficult to see how a case as simple as this had taken so long. There had been an utter failure by P to pursue his action with anything nearing reasonable diligence.

HOGG v. STOCKTON PLANT, June 12, 1995, H.H.J. Cartlidge, Sunderland County Ct. [*Ex rel.* Jacksons, Solicitors, Middlesbrough.]

4087. County court—striking out—automatic directions—summary judgment—damages to be assessed—directions that medical reports and special damages be agreed—interim payment and payment into court—whether case struck out for failure to apply for trial date

[C.C.R., Ord. 9, r.3(6); C.C.R., Ord. 17, r.11(1)(o).]

P issued proceedings for personal injuries arising out of a road traffic accident on October 21, 1992. D issued a full defence on December 9, 1992, but admitted liability in open correspondence and made an interim payment of £4,000. P applied for, and by consent obtained, summary judgment, with damages to be assessed, on February 23, 1993. On the same day the district judge also ordered that (i) medical reports be agreed if possible, and in default both parties to be at liberty to call two medical witnesses, the substance of whose reports were to have been disclosed, and (ii) special damages be agreed if possible. Attempts were made to settle the matter, and a payment into court was made in December 1994. In April 1995, D wrote to the court contending that the action had been struck out for failure to apply for a trial date in April 1994. The district judge ruled that the action had not been struck out.

Held, rejecting D's appeal, that (1) construing C.C.R., Ord. 17, r.11(1)(o) and Ord. 9, r.3(6), where summary judgment was obtained after admissions, the automatic directions do not apply, and the action was therefore not struck out (*Jobbins v. Arthur* [1994] C.L.Y. 3642, *Egerton Jones v. Busby* [1994] C.L.Y. 3646 considered and applied); (2) if the above decision had not been made in P's favour, then the judge would not have construed the directions given by the district judge on February 23, 1993 as being "further directions" which superseded the automatic directions, because they did not address the question of a timetable (*Nelson and Guy v. Infil Housing Co-op.; Rastin v. British Steel; Todd v. Evans; Adams v. Geest; Byrne v. Webber; Donaldson v. Canavan; Ayres v. British Steel* [1994] C.L.Y. 3645, *Bird (Annie) v. Initial Contract Services* [1994] C.L.Y. 3648 considered and distinguished).

SIMPSON v. WILSON-LIM, September 11, 1995, H.H.J. Wiggs, Poole County Ct. [*Ex rel*. Guy Opperman, Barrister, 3 Paper Buildings.]

4088. County court—striking out—automatic directions—transfer of action—applicable timetable

Following a road traffic accident, proceedings were issued in Southampton on July 17, 1992, claiming damages for loss of use, insurance excess, cost of hiring an alternative vehicle and miscellaneous expenses. A defence was filed, dated August 18, 1992. The court issued a notice to the parties, signed by the district judges, stating that the action was one to which automatic directions pursuant to C.C.R., Ord. 17, r.11 applied; accordingly, no pre-trial review would be held. The court further issued a form entitled "Notes for Guidance on Automatic Directions (Order 17, rule 11)" which stated that the defence had been received by the court on September 7, 1992, and which set out the relevant directions pursuant to the rules. An order to transfer the case to the Oxford County Court was made on October 12, 1993. County court form N450 was issued by the Oxford County Court, dated November 10, 1993. Liability was conceded by D in February 1994, and the action was eventually listed for assessment of damages on February 15, 1995. At trial, D questioned the jurisdiction of the court to entertain P's claim, upon the basis that the action had been struck out, pursuant to the automatic directions, in December 1993. It was established that no direction had been given to the court office by a district judge to issue a further form N450 to vary the timetable; nor was there any local practice direction in existence whereby the proper officer was required or authorised to send out a further form N450 upon transfer of a case from another county court.

Held, that no officer of the court other than a district judge or judge had authority to give directions varying the timetable laid down in the rules. The form N450 issued by the court did not effect any variation to the timetable laid down by the rules and therefore the action had been struck out in December 1993 (*Bird (Annie) v. Initial Contract Services* [1994] C.L.Y. 3648 considered).

TURNER v. C.I. STROUD, February 15, 1995, H.H.J. Wilson-Melor, Q.C., Oxford County Ct. [*Ex rel.* Justin Mort, Barrister, 2 Temple Gardens.]

4089. County court—striking out—automatic directions—transfer of action—further automatic directions issued—case struck out—whether second directions superseding first

P's claim arose out of a road traffic accident on August 15, 1991. Proceedings were issued in the Reading County Court in January 1993, and Reading County Court issued automatic directions which began to apply with effect from February 5, 1993. Initially, D were separately represented, but an agreement as to liability was reached and an admission of negligence was filed with the court on November 25, 1993. In October 1993, the matter was transferred to Cardiff County Court which issued another set of automatic directions on October 6, 1993. On June 5, 1994, P's case was automatically struck out under the first set of automatic directions, issued by Reading County Court. P's solicitors had been a little late serving their List of Documents in accordance with the first set of automatic directions, and had completely failed to agree a date for the exchange of medical expert evidence. In addition, notwithstanding the fact that an admission of negligence was entered in November 1993, P's solicitors had failed to apply for judgment to be entered. In addition, in 1994 the only correspondence from P's solicitors was dated January 1994, and there was no further correspondence until September 1994 by which time the case had already been struck out. It then took P's solicitors a further two months to apply for reinstatement of the claim. On P's solicitor's application to reinstate, they sought to argue that the automatic directions issued by Cardiff County Court in October 1993 superseded the automatic directions issued by Reading County Court in February 1993, and the automatic directions issued by Cardiff County Court provided the timetable under which the case would automatically be struck out, and that timetable had not yet expired.

Held, that this submission would be rejected by the district judge, taking into account the delays that had occurred throughout P's claim should remain struck out and the costs of the entire action should be D's in any event.

WILLIAMS (S.) v. GLOBE COACHES AND P. A. EVANS, November 25, 1994; District Judge Wynn Rees; Cardiff County Ct. [*Ex rel. Cole and Cole, Solicitors*].

4090. County court—striking out—automatic directions—transferred actions—jurisdiction—applicability of automatic directions to action commenced in High Court before October 1, 1990 and transferred to a county court after July 1, 1991—whether direction given in county court disapplied provision of County Court Rules for automatic striking out—whether order declaring that action automatically struck out made without jurisdiction

[County Courts Act 1984 (c.28) ss.40, 75(1), 75(2)(4), 147; C.C.R. 1981 (S.I. 1981 No. 1687 (L.20)), as amended, Ord. 16, r.6(1A), and Ord. 17, r.11(2)(b)(3)(d)(4)(a)(9); County Court (Amendment No. 4) Rules 1989 (S.I. 1989 No. 2426 (L.19)), rr.13, 14; County Court (Amendment No. 3) Rules 1990 (S.I. 1990 No. 1764 (L.17)), rr.14, 17; County Court (Amendment No. 2) Rules 1991 (S.I. 1991 No. 1126 (L.10)), rr.23, 24; County Court (Amendment No. 3) Rules 1991 (S.I. 1991 No. 1328 (L.14)), r.19; County Court (Amendment No. 4) Rules 1991 (S.I. 1991 No. 1882 (L.28)), r.7.]

On January 24, 1989 Ps began proceedings against D in the High Court for damages for personal injuries. A dispute as to validity of service of writ was resolved by an order of December 4, 1990 and interim payments made by D. Pleadings closed in the High Court on January 31, 1991. In August 1992 an agreement was made between parties' solicitors for a general extension of time for taking any further procedural action on either side, terminable on 28 days' notice. Payments were made into court in respect of claims of each P in

1992 and 1993. On February 2, 1990 Ord. 17, r.11, (automatic directions) was brought into operation by S.I. 1989 No. 2426, r.13. Applications were excluded in respect of "proceedings commenced" before February 2, 1990 (S.I. 1989 No. 2426, r.14). On October 1, 1990 a new Ord. 17, r.11, including present r.11(9) (actions automatically struck out if hearing date not requested within specified periods), was substituted by S.I. 1990 No. 1764, r.14. Application of the new rule was excluded in respect of "proceedings commenced" before October 1, 1990 (S.I. 1990 No. 1764, r.17). With effect from July 1, 1991 a new C.C.R., Ord. 17, r.11(1A) was introduced by S.I. 1991 No. 1328, r.19. The object of the new r.11(1A) was to make it clear that automatic directions apply to cases transferred down from the High Court. With effect from September 16, 1991, Ord. 16, r.6(1A), was amended by S.I. 1991 No. 1882, r.7, by adding a provision that, where proceedings are transferred down from the High Court, for the purposes of Ord. 17, r.11, the pleadings should be deemed to be closed 14 days after the date of transfer. On April 8, 1993 an order was made for the transfer of the action to Oxford County Court. On May 7, 1993 notice of the transfer was given by the court to the parties' solicitors. P1, P2 and P3 successfully applied for further interim payments. On hearing of those applications on August 20, 1993, D applied for directions as to further conduct of action. An order was made requiring Ps to take certain steps and directing that action be listed for trial on certificates of readiness for trial being given to the court by both sides. Neither side gave certificate of readiness, made any application to court or requested the court to fix a hearing date. On August 16, 1994 an order was made *ex parte* declaring that action automatically struck out due to a failure to request a hearing date. On October 17, 1994 the district judge set aside that order on the grounds that the proceedings had been commenced before October 1, 1990 and that, by virtue of Ord. 17, r.11(9), did not apply. D appealed under Ord. 13, r.1(10).

Held, dismissing the appeal and refusing leave to appeal to the Court of Appeal, that the order of August 16, 1994 was made without jurisdiction and was rightly set aside on three grounds: (1) by virtue of s.75 of the 1984 Act, there was power to make rules regulating the conduct of actions proceeding in a county court, which had been commenced in the High Court and transferred to a county court, and by virtue of s.75(2) to exclude or limit the application of such rules to such actions. The words "proceedings commenced" in S.I. 1990 No. 1764, r.17, were not limited to proceedings commenced in a county court, but extended to proceedings begun in the High Court and transferred to a county court. Where an action is transferred from the High Court to a county court, the High Court ceases to have any jurisdiction in respect of the action and the action is treated for all purposes as if it had been commenced in a county court, subject only to the appellate jurisdiction of the High Court in respect of the order for transfer provided for by s.40(5) of the 1984 Act. Accordingly, Ord. 17, r.11, did not apply to the action; (2) If the first ground was wrong and D was correct in contending that Ord. 17, r.11, applied to proceedings transferred from the High Court only on the coming into operation of S.I. 1991 No. 1328, r.19. It was common ground that Ord. 17, r.11(9), did not apply to actions commenced in a county court before October 1, 1990. By Ord. 17, r.11(1A), Ord. 17, r.11 applies to transferred actions "as it applies to actions commenced in a county court". Ord. 17, r.11, therefore, does not apply to actions commenced in the High Court before October 1, 1990; and (3) (If the second ground was wrong) Ord. 17, r.11(4)(a), gave the court power to give directions differing from the automatic directions specified in Ord. 17, r.11(3), including, but not limited to, an order fixing a date for the hearing. By virtue of Ord. 17, r.11(2)(b), where the court gave such directions, the automatic directions provided for in r.11(3) took effect subject to such directions. The court had power to disapply or modify Ord. 17, r.11(3)(d), which required the plaintiff to request the fixing of a hearing date. If the court dispenses with the requirement to make such a request, Ord. 17, r.11(9) was also disapplied. The order of August 20, 1993 that action be listed for trial on certificates of readiness by both parties disapplied Ord. 17, rr.11(3)(d) and 11(9) (*Hall v. British Gas*, June 3, 1994, unreported, *Moody v. Steward* (1870) L.R.6 Exch. 35, *D'Errico v. Samuel* [1896] 1 Q.B. 163, *Buckley and Beach v. National Electric Theatres* [1913] 2 K.B. 277 followed).

WALTERS v. NEWTON, February 2, 1994; H.H.J. Irvine; Oxford County Ct. [*Ex rel. Derrick Turriff, Barrister*].

4091. County court—striking out—default summons—failure to serve defence or apply for default judgment—result of agreement between parties to extend time for service of defence—court's jurisdiction to retrospectively extend time

[C.C.R., Ord. 9, r.10.]

In this and two other cases involving claims for damages for personal injury the issue concerned the operation of C.C.R., Ord. 9, r.10, where the parties had agreed that there should be an extension of time (terminable on notice) for delivery of defence. Order 9, r.10, provided that where 12 months had expired from the date of service of a default summons if, *inter alia*, no admission, defence or counterclaim had been delivered, the action would be struck out.

Held, that the court's ordinary power of retrospective extension of time under Ord. 13, r.4(2), was excluded in respect of Ord. 9, r.10. The court's power of prospective extension under Ord. 13, r.4(1), was not necessarily so excluded. The lack of specificity in Ord. 9, r.4, left a doubt whether it was intended to apply to agreements reached between the parties before expiry of the 12-month period. That doubt must be resolved in favour of the plaintiffs; (2) if this construction of Ord. 9, r.10, was wrong, Ord. 37, r.5 would not have saved the plaintiffs, because there was no requirement to enter judgment. Estoppel, waiver, election and acquiescence would have been of no assistance to the plaintiffs.

LOVELL v. PORTER (CCRTI 94/0754/F; CCRTI 94/1461/F; CCRTI /94/1531/F), May 26, 1995, C.A.

4092. County court—striking out—default summons—relevance of further steps

[C.C.R., Ord. 9, r.10.]

In a default action for personal injuries, if, at the end of 12 months from the date of service of a default summons, no admission, defence or counterclaim had been delivered and no judgment entered, the claim would be automatically struck out under C.C.R., Ord. 9, r.10, even if further steps were taken after the 12-month period had expired, as the rule was mandatory.

WEBSTER v. ELLISON CIRCLIPS, *The Independent*, June 21, 1995, C.A.

4093. County court—striking out—reinstatement of action—court order not complied with—default not due to neglect or a deliberate flout of order—whether court having jurisdiction to reinstate

Where the terms of a court order had not been complied with and the reasons for default were other than neglect or a deliberate flouting of the order, the court had an inherent jurisdiction to decide whether to reinstate an action previously struck out by considering the reasons or excuses put forward for the default and its causes and effects.

HOGG v. AGGARWAL, *The Times*, August 1, 1995, Sedley J.

4094. Court administration—fees—press release

The Court Service has issued a press release entitled *Revision of court fees and exemption rules* (Press Notice 240/95), published on October 13, 1995. Three amendment orders concerning fees and exemption rules for family proceedings and in the county court and Supreme Court come into force on October 30, 1995. Not all fees have been changed but the overall increase reflects the fact that many fees have remained unchanged for several years. Income from fees falls short of the cost of administering civil courts by around £100 million, the balance being made up from general taxation. The Lord Chancellor's objective is to move toward civil courts' costs being met by court users through fees. Full details of the fee changes are attached to the press release.

4095. Court of Appeal—citation of law reports—use of unreported judgments—lists of authorities—practice direction

This practice direction was issued by Sir Thomas Bingham M.R. on June 22, 1995:

When authority is cited, whether in written or oral submissions, the following practice should in general be followed.

If a case is reported in the official Law Reports published by the Incorporated Council of Law Reporting for England and Wales, that report should be cited. These are the most authoritative reports; they contain a summary of argument; and they are the most readily available.

If a case is not (or not yet) reported in the official Law Reports, but is reported in the Weekly Law Reports or the All England Law Reports, that report should be cited.

If a case is not cited in any of these series of reports, a report in any of the authoritative specialist series of reports may be cited. Such reports may not be readily available: photstat copies of the leading authorities or the relevant parts of such authorities should be annexed to written submissions; and it is helpful if photostat copies of the less frequently used series are made available in court.

It is recognised that occasions arise when one report is fuller than another, or when there are discrepancies between reports. On such occasions, the practice outlined above need not be followed. It is always helpful if alternative references are given.

Where a reserved written judgment has not been reported, reference should be made to the official transcript (if this is available) and not to the handed-down text of the judgment. Counsel are reminded that lists of authorities, including textbooks, to which they wish to refer should be delivered to the Head Usher's office not later than 5.30 p.m. on the working day before the day when the hearing of the application or appeal is due to commence: see *The Supreme Court Practice 1991*, vol. 1, p. 884. Counsel should also seek confirmation that an adequate number of copies are available for the use of the court and, if this is not the case, should themselves provide an appropriate number of photocopies.

This Practice Direction supersedes paragraph 5 of *Practice Direction (C.A.) (Presentation of Argument)* [1989] 1 W.L.R. 281, and also *Practice Direction (C.A.) (Law Reports: Citation)* [1991] 1 W.L.R. 1.

PRACTICE DIRECTION (C.A.) (CITATION OF AUTHORITY) [1995] 1 W.L.R. 1096.

4096. Court of Appeal—judgments—written reserved judgments handed down without being read aloud—advance copies—practice direction

This practice direction was issed by Sir Thomas Bingham M.R. on June 22, 1995:

When the court reserves judgment, it has become the general practice in recent years for the written judgment to be handed down without, as in the past, being read aloud. In this way, much time is saved for the court, for practitioners and for litigants. Unless the court otherwise orders, copies of the written judgment are made available to the parties' legal advisers on the afternoon before judgment is due to be pronounced on condition that the contents are not communicated to the parties themselves until one hour before the listed time for pronouncement of judgment. Delivery to legal advisers is made to enable them to consider the judgment and decide what consequential orders they should seek. The condition is imposed to prevent the outcome of the case being publicly reported before judgment is given, since the judgment is confidential until then.

The court may order earlier delivery to parties' legal advisers if it appears that they might, with more time, be able to agree the orders consequential on the judgment and so obviate the need for the cost of a further attendance in court. If, for any reason, a party's legal advisers have special grounds for seeking a relaxation of the usual condition restricting disclosure to the party itself, a request for relaxation of the condition may be made informally through the clerk to the presiding Lord Justice. A copy of the written judgment will be made available to any party who is not legally represented at the same time as to legal advisers. It must be treated as confidential until judgment is given.

When the court hands down its written judgment, it will pronounce judgment in open court. Copies of the written judgment will then be made available to recognised law reporters and representatives of the media. In cases of particular interest to the media, it is helpful if requests for copies can be intimated to the presiding Lord Justice's clerk in advance of judgment, so that the likely demand for copies can be accurately estimated.

If any member of the public (not being a party to the case, or a law reporter, or a representative of the media) wishes to read the written judgment of the court on the occasion when it is handed down, a copy will be made available for him or her to read and note in court on request made to the associate or clerk to the presiding Lord Justice. The copy must not be removed from the court and must be handed back after reading. The object is to ensure that such a person is in no worse a position than if the judgment had been read aloud in full. Copies of the judgment can be ordered from the official shorthand writers on payment of the appropriate fee.

Anyone who is supplied with a copy of the handed-down judgment, or who reads it in court, will be bound by any direction which the court may have given in a child case under s.39 of the Children and Young Persons Act 1933, or any other form of restriction on disclosure, or reporting, of information in the judgment.

PRACTICE DIRECTION (C.A.) (HANDED DOWN JUDGMENTS) [1995] 1 W.L.R. 1055, C.A.

4097. Court of Appeal—maximum number of judges

MAXIMUM NUMBER OF JUDGES ORDER 1994 (No. 3217) [65p], made under the Administration of Justice Act 1968 (c.5), s.1(2), and the Supreme Court Act 1981 (c.54), s.2(4); operative on December 15, 1994; amends the 1968 Act by increasing the number of Lords of Appeal in Ordinary to 12 and amends the 1981 Act so as to increase the number of ordinary judges of the Court of Appeal to 32.

4098. Court users survey—Crown Court and county court

The Court Service has published a report of the first national, independent survey to measure customer satisfaction with the Crown and county courts in England and Wales. Court users, including witnesses, jurors, plaintiffs and lawyers, were asked what standards of service they expected from the courts, and how well the courts were meeting the standards in the *Courts Charter*. The report is available from the Charter Branch, the Court Service, Room 6.54, Southside, 105 Victoria Street, London, SW1E 6QT. Telephone 0171 210 1791.

4099. Courts and Legal Services Act 1990—commencement

COURTS AND LEGAL SERVICES ACT 1990 (COMMENCEMENT NO. 10) ORDER 1995 (No. 641 (C.16)) [65p], made under the Courts and Legal Services Act 1990 (c.41), s.124(3); brings s.82 of the 1990 Act into force on March 6, 1995.

4100. Damages—provisional damages—addition to existing practice direction

The following is added to *Practice Direction (Provisional Damages: Procedure)* of [1985] 1 W.L.R. 961: "9A. In any case in which the Court of Appeal allows an appeal from the whole or part of a judgment for provisional damages all the provisions of Part A of this practice direction still apply, both as to the judgment at first instance and, *mutatis mutandis*, the judgment and directions of the Court of Appeal".

PRACTICE DIRECTION (Q.B.D.) (PROVISIONAL DAMAGES: AMENDED PROCEDURE) [1995] 1 W.L.R. 507, Lord Taylor of Gosforth C.J.

4101. Declaration—application by local authority to prevent family of patient accommodated by local authority from contacting her—whether jurisdiction to grant declaratory relief—extent of court's powers to grant declaration

P was aged 20 years and had a learning disability. She was accommodated by the local authority, who applied for declarations that P's family should be prevented from contacting her, removing or attempting to remove her from the accommodation and from attempting to persuade her to return home to them.

Held, refusing the applications, that the court could only grant declaratory relief to protect a legal right. The local authority was endeavouring to protect the patient by preventing her from associating with her family and there was no power to grant declaratory relief which would interfere with the right of freedom of association enjoyed by P. Declaratory relief can only be granted to protect a legal right.

CAMBRIDGESHIRE COUNTY COUNCIL v. R. [1994] 2 F.C.R. 973, Hale J.

4102. Declaration—capacity—disabled persons—residence—court's jurisdiction to allow disabled person to make own decision

Where a difficult question arose as to the right of an 18-year-old physically handicapped young man to decide where he wanted to live in view of the risk of interference from his over-protective mother, it was just and reasonable for the court to exercise its jurisdiction to make a declaration that the son had a right to make his own decision on the matter.

V. (HANDICAPPED ADULT: RIGHT TO DECIDE RESIDENCE), *Re*, *The Independent*, August 14, 1995, D.C.

4103. Declaration—interim declaration—whether court could make interim declaration

There is no such concept known to law as an interim declaration.

F was aged 37 and suffering from anoxeria nervosa. She was detained under the Mental Health Act in a hospital owned by the applicant health service trust. F was in a critical condition and might well die if she did not eat. The trust obtained an order *ex parte* which declared naso-gastric feeding against F's consent to be lawful, and which set a return date. On the return date, F sought the discharge of the order on the basis that the court had no power to grant an interim declaration. The judge held that the declaration had been a final declaration, rightly made, and directed that F's application to set aside the *ex parte* order should be heard as soon as possible.

Held, allowing the appeal and discharging the order, that in the light of the clear provision in the order setting a return date the order could not be regarded as a final order. Since there was no such concept known to law as an interim declaration, the judge had had no jurisdiction to make the order which should have been set aside (*F. v. West Berkshire Health Authority* [1989] C.L.Y. 3044, *S. (Adult: Refusal of Treatment), Re* [1993] C.L.Y. 2706, *Camden London Borough Council v. R. (A Minor) (Blood Transfusion)* [1994] 1 C.L. 274 considered).

RIVERSIDE MENTAL HEALTH NATIONAL HEALTH SERVICE TRUST v. FOX [1994] 1 F.L.R. 614, C.A.

4104. Declaration—mentally handicapped adult—right of access to parents—mother seeking declaration that she should have regular access—whether court had jurisdiction to make declaration governing access to mentally handicapped adult

[Mental Health Act 1959 (c.72); R.S.C., Ord. 15, r.16.]

A mentally incapacitated adult had a right of access to his or her parents at common law, and the court had jurisdiction to declare that such access was necessary in his or her best interests.

C was now aged 23 and was severely mentally handicapped. M and F had now divorced, and F continued to run the registered home where C lived. M complained that she had been prevented from having access to C. M sought a declaration that it was necessary in the best interests of C that she should have regular access to C. A preliminary issue was taken as to whether the High Court had jurisdiction to make the declaration.

Held, that (1) following the Mental Health Act 1959, the High Court had no *parens patriae* jurisdiction over the person of a mentally incapacitated adult; (2) a child had the right of access to his parent, and to deprive a child of such access was to deprive the child of an important contribution to his or her emotional development (*M. v. M. (Child: Access)* [1973] C.L.Y. 2160, *K.D. (A Minor), Re* [1988] C.L.Y. 2294, *H. (Minors) (Access), Re* [1992] C.L.Y. 2999 considered); (3) although access itself was not *per se* a tortious act, if contrary to her will or contrary to her best interests if she could not express her will, C was being denied access to M, and her freedom was being interfered with, that in itself was a tortious act. C had a right of access to her parents; (4) the declaratory jurisdiction was not confined to questions of the medical treatment of mentally incapacitated adults, but included any question where the lawfulness of a particular act was in issue (*F. (Mental Patient: Sterilisation), Re* [1990] 2 A.C. 1, *T. (Consent to Medical Treatment) (Adult Patient), Re* [1992] C.L.Y. 2918, *Airedale National Health Service Trust v. Bland* [1993] C.L.Y. 2712, *A., Re* [1992] C.L.Y. 2956, *J. (A Minor) (Wardship: Medical Treatment), Re* [1991] C.L.Y. 2588, *J. (A Minor) (Child in Care) (Medical Treatment), Re* [1992] C.L.Y. 2954/5, *R. (A Minor) (Wardship: Consent to Treatment), Re* [1992] C.L.Y. 3135 considered); and (5) accordingly, the High Court had jurisdiction under Ord. 15, r.16, to make the declaration sought.

C. (ADULT PATIENT) (ACCESS: JURISDICTION), *Re* [1994] 1 F.C.R. 705, Eastham J.

4105. Declaration—Norwegian citizen residing with applicant in U.K.—incapacitated by stroke—family in Norway seeking to remove patient to Norway—applicant seeking injunction to restrain move and declaration that move unlawful—jurisdiction—*locus standi*

S was a Norwegian national who lived with P in England. S suffered a major stroke and his family wished to transfer him back to Norway. P sought a declaration that such a move was unlawful as it was not in S's best interests.

Held, granting the relief sought, that where a person is present within the jurisdiction but is incapable of giving his consent to a proposed course of action that affects his rights, the court has jurisdiction, by reason of his presence within the jurisdiction, to declare whether that course of action is lawful as being in his best interests. The court would not in such cases insist on the demonstration of a specific legal right by the party making the application for relief where that applicant had a specific and legitimate interest in the matter. Given P's assumption of the duty of caring for S, it was demonstrable that she had a sufficient interest to maintain the proceedings (*Gillick v. West Norfolk and Wisbech Area Health Authority and the D.H.S.S.* [1985] C.L.Y. 2230, *T. (Consent to Medical Treatement) (Adult Patient), Re* [1992] C.L.Y. 2918 considered).

S. (HOSPITAL PATIENT: COURT'S JURISDICTION), *Re* [1995] 3 All E.R. 290, C.A.

4106. Default judgments—automatic—failure to acknowledge writ—difficulty of enforcement in foreign court

[R.S.C., Ords. 13, 19.]

BB served a writ on K and other defendants which they failed to acknowledge. Following expiry of the time for acknowledgment, BB sought to enter a default judgment against K. The court was required to determine whether, as requested by BB, the claim should proceed to trial without the presence of the defendant, or whether, as was usual, the judgment should be obtained through the automatic method under R.S.C., Ord. 13, r.1.

Held, that although BB could have been expected to enter an automatic default judgment, the fact that K was beyond the jurisdiction of the court could make such a judgment difficult to enforce in a foreign court, as no judicial investigation had taken place before the judgment was issued. Order 13 did not oust the inherent jurisdiction of the court to proceed to trial of the claim where acknowledgement of service had not occurred within the time allowed (*Austin v. Wildig* [1969] C.L.Y. 2929 and Note 19/7/6 of the Supreme Court Practice 1995 considered). Order 19 allowed a full trial and there was no reason why the court should not exercise its jurisdiction in this way if B could not obtain the relief sought by way of an Ord. 13, r.1, default judgment.

BERLINER BANK v. KARAGEORGIS, *The Times*, November 27, 1995, Colman J.

4107. Defences—admissibility—commencement of proceedings

Where a defendant intended to rely on the defence of no or part consideration which addressed issues of both fact and law, the arguments should be clearly set out at the commencement of proceedings and not raised first in counsel's closing address.

TRAMP LEASING v. SANDERS, *The Times*, April 18, 1995, C.A.

4108. Disclosure—legal professional privilege—allegation of transaction at undervalue—whether legal advice sought or given to effect an inquiry was privileged. See BARCLAYS BANK v. EUSTICE, §2835.

4109. Discovery—computer files—breach of confidentiality claim—alleged copying of information from database—whether jurisdiction to order disclosure—whether information on the files is property or information

[R.S.C., Ord. 24, r.7; Ord 29, r.2(1).]

P and D carried on competing businesses, in each case selling computer peripherals and consumables by telephone to end users in the U.K. P sued D for an account of profits made by D by the alleged misuse of valuable and confidential information relating to the customers of P's business. Former employees of P's, now working for D were said to have copied the information from P's computer database, in breach of terms as to confidentiality in their contracts of employment. D were said to have used the information, in the knowledge that it had been wrongly copied from P's computer database. D denied that there had been any copying, and insisted that it had no computer database itself, although it admitted that it used computers for word processing of invoices, etc. After pleadings and exchange of lists of documents and witness statements, P applied for disclosure, either under R.S.C., Ord. 24, r.7, or Ord. 29, r.2(1), or under the court's inherent power, of D's computer files containing information relating to the identity of, requirements of, and purchases by D's potential and actual customers, so that they might be inspected by an independent expert in information technology (with suitable safeguards to protect the confidentiality of the information), for the purpose of comparing them with P's computer database to see if there had been copying. D objected that the court had no jurisdiction to order disclosure of the information contained in its computer files, because the information (as opposed to the file) was neither a "document" that should be disclosed under Ord. 24, r.7, nor "property" which could be inspected under Ord. 29, r.2(1), and the court should not use its inherent power to expand the ambit of those Rules.

Held, ordering disclosure, that (1) the computer files and the information they contained were relevant "documents" which were discoverable under Ord. 24, r.7(2), or alternatively they were "property" that could be inspected under Ord. 29, r.2(1). The issue was not what the information was, but whether it had been copied (*Huddlestone v. Control Risks Information Services* [1987] C.L.Y. 2988 applied); (2) alternatively, the court had inherent power to fill any lacuna in the Rules; here the lacuna arose because Ords. 24 and 29 did not yet deal expressly with modern information technology. It would be strange if the court had an inherent power to order disclosure by way of Anton Piller order, but not on the hearing of an interlocutory summons seeking this relief. On the facts, disclosure should be ordered, subject to the safeguards suggested (*CHC Software Care v. Hopkins & Wood* [1993] C.L.Y. 3348 applied).

C. v. P.B.P., October 31, 1995; H.H.J. Malcolm Lee, Q.C., designated Circuit Mercantile Judge sitting as a High Court Judge; Birmingham District Registry, Mercantile List (Birmingham); in Chambers, reported by leave of the Judge. [*Ex rel.* Peter Susman, Barrister, New Court Chambers, Temple.]

4110. Discovery—contempt—civil action—breach of orders made by Director General of Fair Trading—unused material—whether analogous to criminal case—whether full common law duty of disclosure to apply

R was an accessory respondent, together with other individual accessory respondents and corporate respondents, in an action for contempt brought by the Director General of Fair Trading. The allegation was that the respondents were in contempt of court by breaching, and aiding and abetting the breach of, orders made by the Director General in 1978 and 1979 which restrained companies in the ready-mixed concrete business from engaging in restrictive practices. R sought to impose the common law duty of disclosure on the Director General of Fair Trading, in the contempt proceedings. The information sought was within the ambit of unused material which a prosecutor would have to disclose, and included, for example, tape recordings of interviews with Office of Fair Trading witnesses and prior drafts of witness statements and affidavits. Some of these items would, in civil discovery, be protected by legal privilege. It was argued by R that, notwithstanding whether aiding and abetting a contempt of court is technically a civil or criminal contempt (a matter which is open to some debate), the proceedings were so analogous to criminal proceedings (considering, *inter alia*, the potential sanction) that the duty to disclose unused material should apply.

Held, that the summons sought by R would be granted, on the basis that discovery of documents in these proceedings should be approached more by analogy with the criminal than the civil practice. Therefore, the Director General should disclose, *inter alia*, the draft statements being sought, just as a criminal prosecutor would have to, to comply with his duty to disclose unused material.

DIRECTOR GENERAL OF FAIR TRADING v. REID, December 20, 1994, Buckley J., Restrictive Practices Court. [*Ex rel.* Justin Cole, Barrister, 5 Paper Buildings. R represented by Jonathan Caplan, Q.C., instructing solicitors Travers Smith Braithwaite.]

4111. Discovery—documents held by Legal Aid Board—whether privileged. See R. v. LEGAL AID BOARD, *ex p.* LONDON DOCKLANDS DEVELOPMENT CORP., §3121.

4112. Discovery—environmental report—applicant requiring different report to be disclosed—no evidence of further report—whether leave to apply for judicial review to be granted

T sought discovery of documents from the council relating to toxic compounds coming from News International's print works at Wapping. However, since Popplewell J. refused the initial application, the council had produced a report and it seemed T had received what she wanted. However, T claimed that this was not the report that she required. She was trying to see a report written by the South East Institute of Public Health which, she claimed, differed materially from the report which had been given to her. The South East Institute denied that a separate report existed.

Held, refusing the application, that T's real complaint was that the Institute's survey was not adequate and the council should have commissioned a more thorough survey. The council had provided the report that the applicant asked for and was entitled to under the Environmental Protection Information Regulations 1992. There was no evidence that there was another report in existence.

TOWER HAMLETS LONDON BOROUGH COUNCIL, *ex p.* TILLY, *Re* (FC3 94/7021/D), December 15, 1994, C.A.

4113. Discovery—holiday photographs—damages sought for disappointing holiday—photographs taken by plaintiff's family—whether court had jurisdiction to order disclosure of photographs

P booked a holiday with D holiday company, for herself, her husband, mother and three other members of her family. She issued proceedings against D on behalf of the whole party, claiming that the holiday was worthless and that the group had suffered distress and disappointment. D applied for an order for specific disclosure of the party's holiday photographs. P said that she had taken no photographs. Other members of her family had taken photographs but, she argued, they were not parties to the action and the court could not therefore order them to disclose the photographs.

Held, on appeal from the decision of the district judge, that the photographs were plainly relevant in view of the allegation that the holiday was worthless and distress and disappointment were suffered. Holiday claims are cases calling for special treatment. The other members of the party were not third parties unconnected with the claim, but were members of P's family on whose behalf the claim was brought by her. It would take the most compelling evidence to satisfy a court that the photographs were not within the possession, custody or power (with the emphasis on the word "power") of P. It was therefore appropriate, as a first step, to order that P swear an affidavit concerning the photographs (*Woodar Investment Development v. Wimpey Construction U.K.* [1980] C.L.Y. 2792 considered).

HENLEY v. COSMOSAIR, January 9, 1995, Brighton County Ct. [*Ex rel.* Mason Bond, Solicitors, Leeds.]

4114. Discovery—legal professional privilege—communications between legal adviser and client—legal advisers giving advice on own and as part of team of advisers—advice on business transaction—non-legal advisers sued in negligence—whether documents from legal advisers privileged—whether privilege waived

P bought three insurance companies. Before the sale P had engaged a number of professional advisers who provided advice as a team and individually. After the sale P found itself heavily exposed to losses and sued its non-legal advisers. P's accountants, one of those sued, sought discovery of the documents passing between P and P's solicitors on the grounds that the solicitors had not given only legal advice but had given more general commercial advice on the transaction as part of the team of advisers. They also contended that as all of the advisers were part of the same team, the advice of one part of that team could not be privileged. Finally, they argued that by suing their non-legal advisers P had waived their claim to privilege.

Held, dismissing the application, that a solicitor's professional duties were not restricted to advice on matters of law or construction, but included advice on the commercial wisdom of entering a particular transaction in respect of which legal advice had been sought. Such advice was privileged, as was the case in the present instance. The duty of confidence owed to P by its legal advisers was qualified to the extent that the solicitors could have decided to disclose communications passing between them and P to the non-legal advisers. This was a matter for the solicitors' professional judgement at the time. Where the communications were not disclosed the duty of confidence remained and the communications remained privileged. Legal professional privilege was not waived merely by suing non-legal advisers (*Anderson v. Bank of British Columbia* [1876] 2 Ch. D. 644, *Balabel v. Air India* [1988] C.L.Y. 1594, *Lillicrap v. Nalder* [1993] C.L.Y. 3226 applied; *Hearn v. Rhay* [1975] 68 FRD 574 considered).

NEDERLANDSE REASSURANTIE GROEP HOLDING NV v. BACON & WOODROW [1995] 1 All E.R. 976, Colman J.

4115. Discovery—legal professional privilege—medical report making reference to letters from plaintiff solicitors—whether specific discovery order to be granted.

In his personal injury action, D disclosed and relied on a medical report from a consultant orthopaedic surgeon, which referred to letters from P's solicitors. D applied for specific discovery of these letters. D's application was dismissed by the district judge, who held that D had failed to show an unequivocal act of waiver of privilege by P (*Booth v. Warrington Health Authority* [1993] C.L.Y. 3230 applied).

BATES v. TREND ALUMINIUM PRODUCTS, June 6, 1995, Deputy District Judge Killin, Norwich County Ct. [*Ex rel.* Anthony J. Bate, Barrister, East Anglian Chambers, Norwich.]

4116. Discovery—legal professional privilege—solicitor's professional indemnity policy—assured solicitor sued for negligence—solicitors appointed to act for assured—communications between assured, solicitors and counsel—whether communications privileged—whether privilege waived

P, a solicitor, was insured under a professional indemnity policy with D. There was an exclusion under the policy in respect of dishonesty or fraud and cl. 8(c) provided that D could require solicitors' reports to be submitted directly to it. A claim was made against P, which he referred to D. D consented to its brokers appointing RPC as solicitors. After negotiations, D repudiated liability under the policy and RPC ceased to act on P's behalf. In arbitration proceedings under the policy, D pleaded dishonesty by P. D asked for discovery of RPC's file for the period when they were acting for P, including communications between P and RPC and instructions to counsel. The judge ruled that the documents were privileged and D appealed. It was accepted that the documents were privileged against anyone other than D.

Held, allowing D's appeal, that (1) the effect of cl. 8 was that any communication which RPC received from P or third parties concerning the subject matter of the claim was to be disclosable to D; (2) in particular, D was entitled to reports as to everything which RPC had learned about the claim and was not limited to matters relevant to the claim against P as opposed to the liability of D; and (3) D was entitled to demand reports on whatever transpired in the course of RPC's retainer, even when the demands were made after the termination of the retainer.

BROWN (ALISTAIR GRAHAM JOHN) v. GUARDIAN ROYAL EXCHANGE ASSURANCE [1994] 2 Lloyd's Rep. 325, C.A.

4117. Discovery—legal professional privilege—suspicion of fraud—whether discovery to be ordered

Discovery would not be ordered on a mere suspicion that the documents might amount to evidence of fraud. The presumption that documents were protected by legal professional privilege would not readily be displaced.

ROYSCOTT SPA LEASING v. LOVETT, *The Independent*, January 23, 1995, C.A.

4118. Discovery—medical notes—stay of proceedings—personal injuries action—medical experts—refusing access to full medical notes—whether court has the power to order a stay of proceedings

P claimed for personal injuries and various items of special damage. D's solicitors requested facilities for a medical examination and sent a form of authority to P's solicitors to allow their expert access to the full notes. P agreed to the examination but refused to allow access to GPs notes other than those which were directly connected to the accident. It was argued that D's expert was only entitled to see relevant notes and, as P's expert had indicated in his report there was no significant past history, which meant disclosure was limited to notes relating to the accident itself.

Held, that it was for the medical experts to determine whether or not there was information of any relevance contained within the GPs notes and that accordingly it was only fair to allow D's expert access to the full notes. P having refused such access, the court had the power to stay the proceedings. P's solicitors consented to access in order to avoid a stay.

WICKHAM v. DWYER, January 1, 1995; Sonnex J.; Reading County Ct. [*Ex rel. Cole and Cole, Solicitors*].

4119. Discovery—medical records—personal injury action—repetitive strain injury—limitation that records to go to medical advisers only—whether legal advisers entitled to see records

P claimed damages for an upper limb disorder due to repetitive work. D instructed their own medical expert to examine P. D requested disclosure of P's medical records. P consented to full disclosure of all medical records, subject to the limitation that the records go to D's medical expert only, and not to D's legal advisers. D did not accept this limitation and issued an application for non-party discovery against the G.P. and other holders of the records. P submitted to the district judge that the appropriate procedure involved the records being delivered to D's medical expert only, who could refer to and copy only those extracts which he considered to be relevant. P relied upon *Dunn v. British Coal Corp.* and *Elliott v. MEM*. P also submitted that D had to show that an order was necessary, as R.S.C., Ord. 24, r.8, is imported into the C.C.R. for the purposes of non-party discovery applications. D sought to rely upon an obiter comment in *Elliott*. The district judge accepted that P's limitation was appropriate in the circumstances.

Held, that this decision should be upheld (*Dunn v. British Coal Corp.* [1993] C.L.Y. 3223, *Elliott v. MEM.*, March 1993, C.A., unrep. considered).

BAKER v. PAPER SACKS, December 14, 1994, H.H.J. Paynter Reece, Romford County Ct. [*Ex rel.* Doug Christie, Robin Thompson & Partners, Solicitors, Ilford.]

4120. Discovery—medical records—personal injury action—whether entitled to require disclosure to legal as well as medical advisers

[County Courts Act 1984 (c.28), s.53.]

Where damages and loss of future earnings were claimed in personal injury cases, the defendants were entitled, under s.53 of the County Courts Act 1984, to have the plaintiff's medical records disclosed to both their medical and legal advisers, not just to their medical advisers as decided in *Dunn v. British Coal Board* (*Dunn v. British Coal Board* [1993] C.L.Y. 3223 considered).

HIPWOOD v. GLOUCESTER HEALTH AUTHORITY, *The Times*, February 21, 1995, C.A.

4121. Discovery—mistake—discovery carried out under pressure of time and without due care—privileged documents mistakenly disclosed and then inspected and copied by the other party—whether disclosure result of obvious mistake—whether mistake had to be obvious to hypothetical reasonable solicitor or to actual recipient before other party could be restrained from using documents—whether injunction should be granted to prevent other party making use of documents

P brought an action against D for trade mark infringement and passing off. Similarly actions were being brought concurrently in the U.S. Agreement had been reached that documents discovered in the U.K. would be used in the U.S. litigation and vice versa. An order for discovery was made in the U.S. which made discovery in the U.K. more urgent. D was therefore under some pressure to disclose documents. P's solicitors found documentation in the documents disclosed to them relating to fees for D's solicitors, counsel and U.S. attorneys. Also among the documents were legal opinions advising on P's claims and the strategy to be adopted. Despite the fact that D might have been able to claim privilege with reference to these documents, P decided that, in the circumstances, they were entitled to make use of the documents in the U.S. litigation and informed D's solicitors that they intended to do so. D sought an injunction restraining use of the documents and ordering their return on the basis that they were privileged and disclosed by reason of a mistake that would have been obvious to the hypothetical reasonable solicitor.

Held, granting the motion, that (1) although the party giving discovery was under a duty to ensure that only documents in respect of which no privilege was claimed were disclosed to the other side, if privileged documents were in fact disclosed and then inspected, the court had a discretion under its equitable jurisdiction to grant an injunction preventing the other party from making use of those documents. In the absence of fraud, the general rule is that an injunction should be granted only if disclosure of the documents occurred as the result of an obvious mistake which would have been obvious to the hypothetically reasonable solicitor. The court therefore had to decide on the balance of probabilities whether the reasonable solicitor would have realised that privilege had not been waived and that a mistake had been made. This decision would take into account the extent of the claim to privilege in the list of documents, the complexity of the discovery, the way in which it had been carried out and the surrounding circumstances. Where discovery had been carried out under a tight timetable without due care and where there were a substantial number of documents involved, a reasonable solicitor would realise that a mistake had been made. On the facts, the documents were privileged documents and there was no reason why the defendant should have waived privilege (*Derby and Co. v. Weldon (No. 8)* [1991] C.L.Y. 2861 applied); (2) in deciding whether or not a document was privileged, the correct approach was to look at the substance and the reality of the document, the circumstances in which it came into existence and its purpose. Where a document was privileged, it was not necessary to decide whether or not that would have been obvious to the reasonable solicitor. It was merely necessary to consider whether the reasonable solicitor would have realised that it had been disclosed by mistake. On these facts, it was obvious that the documents in question were privileged (*Duncan, Re; Garfield v. Fay* [1968] C.L.Y. 3096, *Great Atlantic Insurance Co. v. Home Insurance Co.* [1981] C.L.Y. 2185 applied).

INTERNATIONAL BUSINESS MACHINES CORP. v. PHOENIX INTERNATIONAL (COMPUTERS) [1995] 1 All E.R. 413, Aldous J.

4122. Discovery—originating summons proceedings—insurance documents—terms of cover available to agents—whether financial particulars legally relevant to case

[R.S.C., Ord. 5, r.4; R.S.C., Ord. 24; Third Party (Rights Against Insurers) Act 1930 (c.25).]

The errors and omissions underwriters of a large number of managing and members' agents at Lloyd's issued an originating summons in the course of litigation proceedings with their respective Names. A number of second defendants in the action were granted an order for disclosure by the E&O underwriters of policies or certificates of insurance for the subject matter of questions posed in the originating summons namely the level of cover provided to the agents. Disclosure of notifications or purported notifications by the agents of claims by Names was refused. The E&O underwriters appealed against the first part of the order on the grounds that the details in issue had no bearing on the resolution of any of the questions in the originating summons, since the answer to those questions would be the same irrespective of the limits or amounts concerned. The fact that it was important for the Names to know what funds were available did not mean that the information related to issues that the court was asked to resolve.

Held, allowing the appeal, that (1) there was no automatic discovery in originating summons proceedings, the applicant for discovery had to show that the documents called for related to matters in question and that disclosure was necessary either for disposing fairly of the cause or matter or for saving costs. However, any parts of a document which were not relevant may be deleted or covered up, (*Dolling-Baker v. Merrett* [1990] C.L.Y. 2865, *GE Capital Corporate Finance Group v. Bankers Trust Co* (1990) (unrep.) followed); (2) the disclosure of the information in question would be calculated to dispose fairly of the matter and would save costs, but it was clearly the law that only documents relating to matters in question were disclosable and the information did not relate to those questions; and (3) the contention that discovery was necessary as one of the matters in question posed by underwriters was incorrect because the same point could be made in any case where there was doubt as to the funds of the opposing party in litigation and the law clearly stated otherwise. The funds available were relevant to whether the Names will recover but not relevant to the originating summons (*Bekhor (A.J.) & Co. v. Bilton* [1981] C.L.Y. 2159 followed).

COX v. BANKSIDE MEMBERS AGENCY (LTA 94/6391/B; LTA 94/7098/B; LTA 94/7124/B), November 29, 1994, C.A.

4123. Discovery—public interest immunity—complaints against police—reports of investigating officers—whether a class to which public interest immunity attached—whether disclosure necessary

[Supreme Court Act 1981 (c.54), s.69(1)(3).]

The reports of investigating officers into complaints against police form a class to which public interest immunity attaches. The decision whether to order production is to be reserved for the trial judge.

In 1987 P was charged with offences of dishonesty in respect of his business affairs. In 1990 he was acquitted and began an action for, *inter alia*, malicious prosecution. P's pleadings were wide-ranging and lengthy; the list of documents produced by D contained reports prepared by investigating officers into police conduct. D asserted a class claim to public interest immunity and declined to produce them for inspection. P applied for their production and sought trial by jury. The judge ordered trial by judge alone and rejected the claim to immunity.

Held, that (1) refusing P's appeal, the trial was clearly more suitable for a judge alone; (2) granting D's appeal, the reports of investigating officers fell into a class to which public interest immunity attached; however, the question of whether to order production or not was reserved for the trial judge to make the usual balancing act decision (*R. v. Chief Constable of West Midlands Police, ex p. Wiley* [1995] 1 A.C. 274 considered).

TAYLOR v. CHIEF CONSTABLE OF GREATER MANCHESTER; *sub nom.* TAYLOR v. ANDERTON (POLICE COMPLAINTS AUTHORITY INTERVENING) [1995] 1 W.L.R. 447, C.A.

4124. Discovery—public interest immunity—medical negligence claim—independent professional review report—whether findings available to plaintiff in negligence claim

In the course of treatment by an area health authority National Health Service trust, P made various complaints to the hospital management which in due course led to the setting up of an independent professional review. Two independent consultants from other areas conducted the review and it was common ground that in the course thereof they would have not only the medical notes available but also evidence, both written and oral, from various medical staff involved in the treatment as well as from P. The independent professional review was conducted pursuant to the instructions of the regional health authority (who held the report and relevant documents). P applied for a copy of the documentation leading up to the report and the report itself. It was noted that (not uncommonly) the same firm of solicitors was acting for the regional health authority and the area health authority National Health Service trust, although that did not form an express part of the judgment. The regional health authority opposed discovery upon the basis of public interest immunity, *i.e.* opposed discovery of the entire documentation. In the course of argument, and by analogy, the cases of *Campbell v. Tameside Metropolitan Council*, *R. v. Chief Constable of the West Midlands, ex p.* Wiley and *Kaufmann v. Credit Lyonnais* were referred to by P.

Held, upholding P's application, that there was no basis shown for public interest immunity upon the basis of the class of documents, albeit, as P conceded, that the specific contents of any individual document might be eligible for public interest immunity (*Campbell v. Tameside Metropolitan Council* [1982] C.L.Y. 2467, *R. v. Chief Constable of the West Midlands, ex p. Wiley* [1994] C.L.Y. 3677, *Kaufmann v. Credit Lyonnais, The Times*, February 1, 1995 considered).

MERCER v. ST. HELENS & KNOWSLEY HOSPITALS NHS TRUST AND NORTH WEST REGIONAL HEALTH AUTHORITY, May 5, 1995, Deputy District Judge Freeman, St. Helens County Ct. [*Ex rel.* Christopher Limb, Barrister, Young Street Chambers, Manchester.]

4125. Discovery—relevance—production of documents—party blanking out passages on grounds of irrelevance—application for order to inspect entire documents—whether irrelevant passages may be omitted—test of relevance—grounds on which courts will disregard claim to irrelevance

P brought proceedings against a number of parties as a result of a management buy-out conducted by a syndicate (of which P was a member) which failed. P, a firm of accountants, sued D4 for negligence and misrepresentation in a document on which P claimed to have relied. P's solicitors served its list of documents for discovery with some passages blanked out from some documents which the plaintiff asserted were irrelevant to the proceedings. D4 obtained an order to permit them to inspect the complete documents on the basis that it would assist their defence.

Held, allowing P's appeal, that it is well established that a party is entitled to seal up or cover up parts of a disclosed document on the ground of irrelevance just as it could withhold an entire document on the ground of irrelevance, provided that the irrelevant part could be covered without destroying the sense of the rest or making it misleading. Therefore, there is no distinction to be made between documents which are wholly irrelevant and documents which are partly irrelevant. The test for relevance is not whether it is at least potentially relevant but whether it was not unreasonable to suppose that the passages contained information which may either directly or indirectly enable the defendant either to advance his own case or damage the P's case. On the facts, the blanked out parts referred to transactions with which P was involved and there was no reason to suppose that such material could support the defence (*Cie Financiere et Commerciale du Pacifique v. Peruvian Guano Co.* (1882) 11 Q.B.D. 55 applied; *Great Atlantic Insurance Co. v. Home Insurance Co.* [1981] C.L.Y. 2522 distinguished).

GE CAPITAL CORPORATE FINANCE GROUP v. BANKERS TRUST CO. [1995] 2 All E.R. 993, C.A.

4126. Discovery—simultaneous discovery agreed—expert evidence—medical negligence claim—medical evidence—leave to adduce further evidence sought—whether would involve undue delay in trial

The action was a claim for damages for medical negligence. The infant plaintiff sustained an injury to his left shoulder during delivery, in February

1987, due to alleged improper delivery techniques and lack of appropriate medical assistance. An order was made, by consent, for a mutual and simultaneous exchange of medical or expert evidence, limited to three witnesses per party. Only disclosed reports could be adduced in evidence and exchange was to take place by a specified date. There were postponements of the material date by consent, but ultimately the plaintiff disclosed two medical reports and the defendants disclosed one. The defendants sought leave to serve two further reports of a consultant and a midwife. The plaintiff argued that a further postponement of the trial would have a prejudicial effect. The defendants appealed against an order dismissing their application for leave to adduce expert evidence out of time.

Held, allowing the appeal and giving leave to the defendants to adduce further evidence (the plaintiff was also given the opportunity to adduce further evidence in response), that (1) it was in the interests of justice to allow the case to be judged on all the evidence which may be material for the judge's decision; (2) in the light of the plaintiff's delay in commencing proceedings, although further delay would result in some prejudice to the plaintiff, an indulgence could be allowed to the defendants.

S. (A MINOR), *Re* (93 59492), April 12, 1995, C.A.

4127. Discovery—simultaneous exchange—expert evidence—debarral clause for party not disclosing simultaneously sought—whether to be granted

P appealed the deputy district judge's dismissal of P's application for an order seeking a simultaneous exchange of engineering evidence in a personal injury action, with a debarral clause for any party not disclosing engineering evidence. The argument turned on the question of how the courts should interpret the automatic directions provided in the action, pursuant to C.C.R., Ord. 17, r.11. It was argued by D that, since the directions indicated that a party "may not" be able to use the evidence at trial, it was not an actual debarral, and that accordingly the order should not be made. P argued that the footnote to R.S.C., Ord. 38, r.35, which sets out the machinery in relation to the pre-trial disclosure of expert evidence, specifies that it should not operate so as to allow one party to over-reach any other party by obtaining the disclosure of the other party's expert evidence before the trial, without, at the same time, disclosing their own expert evidence to that party, with the penalty of being precluded from calling such expert evidence at the civil trial. It was stressed on P's behalf that the correspondence had given D's solicitors ample opportunity to indicate whether or not they were going to seek to rely upon any expert engineering evidence, and that they had failed to answer this question.

Held, allowing P's appeal, that the parties must, within 14 days exchange any engineering evidence upon which they would rely in the case, and also that the parties be debarred from calling any engineering evidence other than that disclosed in accordance with the first part of the order.

ROWBOTHAM v. J. LYONS & CO., May 16, 1995, H.H.J. Cotton, Barnsley County Ct. [*Ex rel.* Whittles, Solicitors.]

4128. Discovery—simultaneous exchange of witness statements—failure to exchange simultaneously—principles on which court's discretion to allow witnesses to be called should be exercised

[C.C.R., Ord. 17, r.11; Ord. 20, r.12A.]

A party failing to comply with C.C.R., Ord. 20, r.12A, Ord. 17, r.11(4)(c) requiring simultaneous exchange of witness statements and disclosing witness statements late, must explain and excuse his default on affidavit if seeking the exercise of the court's discretion to allow him to adduce oral evidence at trial from the witnesses whose statements had been disclosed late. P and D's solicitors in a personal injuries action had agreed a date for the exchange of witness statements. D's solicitor exchanged one witness statement in compliance with the agreement but three months after the agreed date served five more witness statements. All were witnesses who were still in the employment of D and whose existence and importance to the issues in the action should have been appreciated prior to the date for exchange of witness statements. The deputy district judge refused D's application for leave to adduce oral evidence from the five witnesses whose statements had been disclosed late. No affidavit evidence was adduced by D's solicitor on the appeal from the deputy district judge's order.

Held, dismissing D's appeal, that the provisions of Ord. 20, r.12A, incorporated in the automatic directions procedures under Ord. 17, r.11, were introduced in order to achieve openhandedness in personal injury litigation. Order 17, r.11(4)(c), specifying simultaneous exchange was designed, as a matter of justice, to ensure that witnesses making statements were untrammelled by what was to be said by witnesses on the other side, so that they would neither consciously nor unconsciously alter their evidence. It might be a proper reason for the exercise of the court's discretion, under Ord. 20, r.12A(10), to allow oral evidence to be called even though witness statements had not been served simultaneously, that matters had emerged in exchanged witness statements which could not have been foreseen by a party, or if a relevant witness had proved difficult to trace or was abroad. However, a party at mercy must in general provide, by affidavit, some explanation or excuse to enable the court to exercise its discretion in their favour. Draconian penalties were imposed on plaintiffs who failed to comply with the requirements of the automatic directions for seeking trial dates and, by analogy, the court should demonstrate that the rules in relation to simultaneity of exchange were to be obeyed.

TAYLOR v. REMPLOY, January 18, 1995; Norman Francis sitting as a Deputy County Court Judge; Cardiff County Ct. [*Ex rel. Neil Bidder, Barrister*].

4129. Discovery—split trial—copyright infringement—whether plaintiff entitled to discovery of documents as to *quantum* before trial

[R.S.C., Ord. 24, rr.1, 2, 3, 8.]

P, who was legally aided, sued D for damages for infringement of copyright in a musical work. He alleged that D had composed theme music which reproduced, or was an adaptation of, the whole or a substantial part of his musical work. The parties agreed to a split trial, liability being determined before an inquiry as to damages. P sought discovery on the issue of *quantum* of damages. He argued that he needed to make an accurate assessment of his claim for three reasons. First, so that he could assess the merits of prosecuting his claim. Secondly, so that the legal aid authorities could make an informed decision as to whether to continue to support his claim. Thirdly, so to make an informed response to any offer of settlement. The master ordered discovery on the issue of *quantum*. D appealed to the judge, providing affidavit evidence which gave an outline indication of the damages which P might recover from them. The evidence showed that the discovery as ordered would be a substantial exercise producing a disruptive effect on D's business.

Held, allowing the appeal, that (1) each party is obliged to make discovery of documents relevant to all issues in the trial in the action, whether or not there is to be a split trial. However, the court only had jurisdiction to enforce that obligation to the extent that discovery was necessary for disposing fairly of the cause or matter or for saving of costs. The burden of proof in each case is upon the party alleging lack of necessity. The court had a discretion to order discovery relating to any matter in issue in the pleadings, including an issue relating to the inquiry as to damages, which might not ultimately arise for determination. In this case discovery would be refused (*Ventouris v. Mountain* [1992] C.L.Y. 3479 applied *Hazeltine Corporation v. B.B.C.* [1979] C.L.Y. 2039 distinguished); (2) in all ordinary cases in which liability and *quantum* were to be tried separately, the court would exercise its discretion to limit discovery to the issue of liability (*Buchanon-Michaelson v. Rubenstein* [1965] C.L.Y. 3104 followed); (3) the interest of the plaintiff in knowing the value of his claim did not on its own justify an order for discovery of documents relevant to *quantum*. The interest of P in making a meaningful report to the legal aid authorities did not justify an order for the discovery sought. A legally aided litigant for this purpose cannot be in a different position from any other litigant (*Saxton, Re; Johnson v. Saxton* [1962] C.L.Y. 2442 applied).

[*Per curiam*: The likely inability of the applicant for discovery on the issue of *quantum* to meet any adverse order for the additional costs of such discovery might also be a relevant consideration. However, it was unnecessary to consider this factor in the present case.]

BALDOCK v. ADDISON [1995] 1 All E.R. 437, Lightman J.

4130. Discovery—third party—patent infringement—pregnancy testing device—multi-national group of companies—whether shareholder control sufficient to infer assistance to primary infringer or common design

[C.C.R., Ord. 8, r.2(1), Ord. 9, r.12; R.S.C., Ord. 11, r.1., Ord. 12, r.8.]

A person not shown to be arguably liable in any action could not be made a party to proceedings simply in order to obtain discovery.

The patent in suit related to a pregnancy testing device. D1, the alleged primary infringer, counterclaimed for revocation of the patent on the grounds of obviousness. D2 was the ultimate holding company of D1 and had been joined in the proceedings for the purpose of obtaining discovery. A director of D1 and a director of D2 both served on the board of an indirect holding company of D1. The judge in the Patents County Court had refused to set aside service of the summons of the case on D2, holding that there were issues on control of D1 which in the interest of justice should be considered further in the course of the proceedings. D2 appealed to the Court of Appeal.

Held, allowing the appeal and setting aside service on D2, that (1) a person or body not shown to be arguably liable in any action could not be made a party to proceedings simply in order to obtain discovery. What must be shown was a good arguable case, that there were facts from which an inference could clearly and properly be drawn that the party sought to be added had assisted the infringement or that there had been a common design relating to acts which constituted infringement; (2) the mere fact that D2 could override by financial and voting control decisions made by D1, and that various directors were common to group companies, was not sufficient to enable the court to say that there was a good arguable case from which the inference of control and thus either of assistance or of common design by D2 could be inferred (*Mölnlycke A.B. v. Proctor & Gamble (No. 4)* [1992] C.L.Y. 3285, *Norwich Pharmacal Co. v. Customs and Excise Commissioners* [1974] C.L.Y. 2643, *Unilever v. Gilette U.K.* [1989] C.L.Y. 2805 referred to).

[*Per curiam*: When validity of a patent is challenged on the ground of obviousness it is standard practice to ask for discovery of the research and development which went into the defendant's product. However, the rules of discovery in patent actions are not altogether adequate to deal with multinational groups of companies. Whether discovery could be obtained against the group company which had done the research and development depended upon the plaintiff discovering which company had done it and whether an arguable case could be shown for joining that company as a defendant, although the plaintiff would usually have no interest in obtaining a final judgment against the additional defendant.]

UNILEVER v. CHEFARO PROPRIETARIES [1994] F.S.R. 135, C.A.

4131. Discovery—use of documents disclosed on discovery—documents disclosed by bank pursuant to court order

Where a bank produced documents pursuant to a court order the information contained in them could be used by the plaintiff to extend the claim by an amended pleading and to institute proceedings overseas (*Bankers Trust Co. v. Shapira* [1980] C.L.Y. 2136, *Norwich Pharmacal v. Customs and Excise Com-*

missioners [1973] C.L.Y. 2643, *Morton-Norwich Products v. Intercen D.C. (No. 2)* [1981] C.L.Y. 2043 considered).

MOHAMED OMAR v. CHIIKO AIKAWA OMAR, *The Times*, December 27, 1994, Jacob J.

4132. Discovery—video evidence—personal injury action of malingering—whether video to be disclosed

An application was made for leave to appeal against a decision allowing M to present video evidence in a forthcoming personal injury action without first disclosing it to L. The purpose of the evidence was to try and prove that L was a malingerer. M argued against this by maintaining that, if L were given the opportunity of seeing the evidence, then he would, in bad faith, seek to find ways of explaining it away.

Held, granting leave to appeal, allowing the appeal and ordering M to disclose the video evidence, that having considered *McGuinness v. Kellogg Company of Great Britain, Digby v. Essex County Council* and *Khan v. Armaguard*, the court concluded that the principle of openness as expounded by Rose L.J. in *Khan* applied. This was an ordinary case of the defendant trying to show that the plaintiff was trying to conceal the true nature of his injuries. There were no special reasons for ordering non-disclosure and the judge below misdirected himself in this regard (*McGuinness v. Kellogg Company of Great Britain* [1988] C.L.Y. 2827, *Digby v. Essex County Council* [1994] P.I.Q.R. P53; *Khan v. Armaguard* [1994] 3 C.L. 339 considered).

LIBBY-MILLS (TIMOTHY WILLIAM) v. METROPOLITAN POLICE COMMISSIONER, December 7, 1994, C.A.

4133. Distraint—fees

DISTRAINT BY COLLECTORS (FEES, COSTS AND CHARGES) (AMENDMENT) REGULATIONS 1995 (No. 2151) [65p], made under the Taxes Management Act 1970, s.61(6); operative on September 8, 1995; amend S.I. 1994 No. 236, making new provision with respect to the fees chargeable on or in connection with the levying of distress where a visit is made to premises, and with respect to the costs and charges recoverable where distress has been levied, and the goods are subsequently sold.

4134. Expert evidence—admissibility—road traffic expert's report—no measurable facts from accident site—whether evidence should be included

Two Ps were knocked down whilst crossing a road. Neither had a recollection of anything after they stepped off the kerb. At the trial they sought to rely on the opinion of a road traffic expert whose report did not rely on any measurable features from the accident site but consisted of a commentary on the statements which had been exchanged and an opinion as to the inferences to be drawn. On a preliminary point anticipated by the judge it was argued by D that only the court could approach the evidence in this way and would at least do so on the whole of the evidence rather than statements, that only an expert witness who had applied principles within his expertise to measurable facts could give evidence of what was likely to have occurred, and that assessing the reliability of witnesses on the basis of statements was outside the competence of such an expert.

Held, in excluding the evidence, that this was a classic case where the judge had to assess what occurred, no expert principles had been applied to matters outside the court's experience and it was not the function of an expert to deal with such issues (it was not expert evidence). *Hinds v. London Transport* [1979] C.L.Y. 1726 referred to:

[*Per curiam*: The judge further criticised the view of certain solicitors that they were entitled to surround the court with information which they put in as expert evidence on issues which were within the court's function.]

BELL AND TREACY v. HARLEY, November 28, 1993; H.H.J. Sheerin; Cambridge County Ct. [*Ex rel. Simon Livesey, Barrister*].

4134a. Expert evidence—control by court—desirability of limiting accountants' evidence—duration—whether court has power to fix timetable for the presentation of evidence.

The court ruled in an interlocutory judgment in an action in the Queen's Bench Division for damages, that the court had both the power and the duty to achieve finality in its proceedings by placing a fair and realistic limit on the examination, cross-evaluation, and re-examination of the witnesses to be called before it. The limits were not cast in bronze, might not be reached and, if they were reached in circumstances in which it was apparent that fairness required them to be extended, the Court would retain the power to extend them. However, such extensions would only be granted where something unforeseen made it necessary to do so.

VERNON v. BOSLEY [1995] 2 F.C.R. 78, Sedley J.

4135. Expert evidence—control by court—whether court having power to prevent unnecessary expert evidence being called

[R.S.C., Ord. 38, r.4.]

Where there was no need for expert evidence in the case the Court should have, but did not have, the power to limit the number of experts or prevent such evidence being called.

RAWLINSON v. WESTBROOK, *The Times*, January 25, 1995, C.A.

4136. Expert evidence—duty of care

Where an expert witness gave evidence in support of a claim, he had a responsibility to take the matter seriously and not to include in his statement anything which he did not know to be true or which he had not made the effort to find out.

AUTOSPIN (OIL SEALS) v. BEEHIVE SPINNING, *The Times*, August 9, 1995, Laddie J.

4137. Expert evidence—notice not given—leave to call refused—whether adjournment to be granted

M, a firm of architects, had undertaken some work for G, which G argued had been charged at an excessive and unreasonable rate in terms of hours worked. The judge ordered that M should recover a total of just over £1,000 in unpaid fees. G was refused leave to call two expert witnesses to give evidence that the hours charged were excessive. Both parties acted in person. G applied for leave to appeal and an extension of time.

Held, refusing leave to appeal, that (1) the judge acted correctly by refusing leave to call witnesses, because no statement from G's experts had been produced in advance. In order to call an expert in rebuttal M would have applied for an adjournment and this would have led to an escalation in costs which would have eaten up the contested sum of £1,000. M had a right to be protected against incurring such additional costs; (2) further adjournment could only lead to the same result so the application for adjournment was dismissed.

WILLIAM MILLER & ASSOCIATES v. GUPTA (LTA 93/6732/C) (LTA 93/6732/C), October 21, 1994, C.A.

4138. Expert evidence—personal injury. See LIDDELL v. MIDDLETON, §3684.

4139. *Hansard*—Construction of statutes—use of *Hansard*—procedure for service of extracts

A party wishing to cite *Hansard* as an aid to construction of a statute in final or interlocutory hearings must, unless otherwise directed, serve the extract and a summary of the argument involved on all other parties at least five clear days before the hearing.

PRACTICE DIRECTION (SUP. CT.) (HANSARD EXTRACTS) [1995] 1 All E.R. 234.

4140. Infringement—computer software—plaintiff's right to inquiry as to damages where infringement slight—defendant's right to inquiry as to damages on plaintiff's cross-undertaking—appropriate costs order where only minor infringement established. See JOHN RICHARDSON COMPUTERS v. FLANDERS (NO. 2), §855.

4141. Injunction—agreement subject to Florida law and London arbitration—dispute about whether claim settled—proceedings commenced in Florida to enforce settlement—application to grant injunction restraining foreign proceedings—whether jurisdiction to make order—whether interim or final relief sought

[Arbitration Act 1950 (c.27), s.12(6); R.S.C., Ord. 73, r.7.]

P engaged D, a Florida corporation, as a consultant to a Liberian corporation operating a shipyard in Mexico. The agreement was subject to Florida law, but subject to London arbitration. Disputes were referred to arbitration and a further dispute occurred about whether the claim had been settled. D commenced proceedings in Florida to enforce the alleged settlement. P applied under R.S.C., Ord. 73, r.7, for a summons to be served in Florida restraining D from proceeding there and damages for breach of the arbitration agreement. The basis of jurisdiction was alleged to be the powers under the Arbitration Act 1950, s.12(6). D was not represented in court, but its U.S. lawyer faxed an affidavit, which was in effect a legal brief, applying to set aside the summons. P invited the court to treat the fax as a proper submission.

Held, that (1) the court cannot normally receive faxed written submissions from overseas lawyers, but in the exceptional circumstances of the case they would be treated as written submissions in support of an application to set aside service; (2) the granting of leave under Ord. 73, r.7, is subject to the same considerations as that under R.S.C., Ord. 11, r.4(2); (3) there was no jurisdiction to make the order under the Arbitration Act 1950, s.12(6) as P was seeking a final injunction, not interlocutory relief, nor was there a claim for relief in respect of an existing or anticipated reference; (4) it would not be possible to amend the application to seek interim relief as that would not be sustained by the issue in the existing or anticipated reference, but a claim to preserve the status quo until an award had been made in a reference independent of the alleged breach of the arbitration agreement; and (5) in any event, given that the U.S. was a party to the New York Convention, and that a jurisdictional challenge was underway in Florida, it would not be appropriate to grant an injunction at this stage.

SOKANA INDUSTRIES v. FREYRE & CO. [1994] 2 Lloyd's Rep. 57, Colman J.

4142. Injunction—breach of restrictive covenant—house built with access to private roadway in breach—no interim relief sought—whether damages in lieu appropriate

Where a house was built in a private cul de sac in breach of a restrictive covenant, damages in lieu of injunctive relief may be an appropriate remedy.

P bought a house as part of a development of similar houses, served by a private road cul de sac. Each plot was conveyed subject to covenants not to use any part of the unbuilt land save as a garden, and to keep the relevant portion of the road in repair. In 1987 Ds bought a house some distance from P. They bought a piece of land with no access to the road and obtained planning permission to build a house. P threatened to obtain an injunction but made no application in fact. When the building was almost completed, P applied for an injunction. The judge found that the proposed user was a breach of covenant, but that in all the circumstances it would be oppressive to grant the injunction and awarded a modest sum in compensation for breach.

Held, dismissing the appeal, that having regard to the history of the matter and P's failure to seek interlocutory injunctive relief, and since restrictive covenants were not to be regarded as absolute or perpetually inviolable, the grant of an injunction would be oppressive. The judge had approached the question of compensation correctly (*Leeds Industrial Cooperative Society v. Slack* [1924] A.C. 851 applied; dicta in *Anchor Brewhouse Development v. Berkley House (Docklands) Developments* [1988] C.L.Y. 3606 disapproved).

JAGGARD v. SAWYER [1995] 1 W.L.R. 269, C.A.

4143. Injunction—county court—warrant for possession already granted—whether jurisdiction to grant injunction restraining dealing with land in question

A lessor obtained and executed an order for possession of warehouse premises. The lessee applied unsuccessfully to a county court judge to have the warrant set aside. The lessee then applied for leave to appeal to the C.A. against this refusal. He also applied to the county court for an injunction to restrain the landlord from leasing or otherwise dealing with the land pending the appeal.

Held, that, under the County Courts Act 1984, s.38, the county court has the power to grant injunctions "in any proceedings". In this case the "proceedings" had already been terminated. The jurisdiction of the county court came to an end once judgment was given. The county court had an express power to grant a stay of execution pending appeal, but an injunction following execution went further. There was no jurisdiction to grant such an order.

COLVIA MANAGEMENT v. GANESH, June 6, 1995, H.H.J. Burkett-Baker, Q.C., Ilford County Ct. [*Ex rel.* Mark Loveday, Barrister, Chambers of Alan Tyrrell, Q.C.]

4144. Injunction—demands on bank guarantors—action for fraudulent misrepresentation—whether injunction necessary

The sellers (W) of a business appealed against an order granting an injunction to restrain them from making demands on bank guarantors of letters of credit, performance bonds and guarantees. Before the second and third instalments were paid, the buyers (T) brought an action for fraudulent misrepresentation. The third instalment was secured by a performance guarantee. T claimed that W knew that a major customer of the business intended to stop using the business and had failed to disclose that information. The relief sought was an injunction against W and it was agreed that there were no authorities on that point.

Held, dismissing the appeal, that on the evidence the buyers had satisfied the court that, for the purposes of the injunction, they had an arguable case at full trial that fraud was a reasonable inference of the sellers' behaviour. The judge had not made any errors which would justify interference with his decision.

THEMEHELP v. WEST, *The Times*, May 2, 1995, Waite L.J.

4145. Injunction—*ex parte* injunction—domestic dispute—breach—committal order defective—whether to be rectified

N appealed against a suspended committal order for breach of an *ex parte* injunction restraining her from causing L any physical or mental harm for a period of 11 months.

Held, allowing the appeal and discharging the order, that (1) the granting of *ex parte* injunctions in domestic and family disputes was normally undesirable and in any event should not be granted for such a long period. The committal order was defective but such orders were not normally rectified unless there were exceptional circumstances (*M. v. P. (Contempt of Court: Committal Order); Butler v. Butler* [1993] C.L.Y. 3132 distinguished); (2) the sentence of three months' imprisonment for the sort of breaches which occurred in this case was excessive. A 14-day sentence would have been long enough; and (3) to suspend the sentence for a whole year was equally excessive, six months would have been sufficient. If the court therefore chose to rectify the order, it would have been to adjust the sentence accordingly. However, there was no point in so doing since the period of six months had passed. Hoffmann L.J. observed that *ex parte* orders should only be made in limited circumstances, where the defendant could not be contacted or there was reason to believe the defendant would take action to defeat the order (*First Express, Re* [1992] C.L.Y. 2530 considered). Furthermore Nottingham County Court should examine the manner in which such orders are made to ensure there is no unnecessary expenditure of public money.

LOSEBY v. NEWMAN (FC 394/5169/F), June 21, 1994, C.A.

4146. Injunction—exclusion of alleged troublemakers from shopping centre—whether public right of way—whether any licence revocable. See CIN PROPERTIES v. RAWLINS (MARTIN), §4560.

4147. Injunction—jurisdiction—restraint from harassment—imprisonment following breach—appeal—whether court having power to restrain person from entering exclusion zone

[C.C.R., Ord. 13, r.6.]

A appealed against a decision committing him to prison for breach of an injunction restraining him from harassing B or coming within 250 yards of her home. A argued that there was no power to impose the injunction and referred to the commentary on C.C.R., Ord. 13, r.6, in the *County Court Practice 1995,* p. 237, which stated that there was no common law power to restrain a person from entering an exclusion zone. It was argued for A that this view was supported by other authorities.

Held, dismissing the appeal, that the length of sentence was varied but the injunction which included the exclusion zone was reimposed. The court's power to grant injunctions was not limited only to restraining orders which were tortious. A Mareva injunction, for instance, restrained conduct which was not in itself unlawful. There were two conflicting principles at stake: the interest of the defendant and his liberty had to be respected up to the point where his conduct affected the rights of the plaintiff, but the plaintiff also had rights which the court must protect. Respect for the law would suffer if people could not be protected by it. In situations where the defendant might intimidate or harass the plaintiff if he came near her home, it was proper to impose an exclusion zone.

BURRIS v. AZADANI, *The Times*, August 9, 1995, C.A.

4148. Injunction—patent infringement—whether damages should be awarded in lieu of an injunction—whether injunction to be stayed pending appeal. See CHIRON CORP. v. ORGANON TEKNIKA (NO. 10); CHIRON CORP. v. MUREX DIAGNOSTICS (NO. 10), §3766.

4149. Injunction—revival of foreign action—*forum conveniens*—whether stay of proceedings to be granted

APT had originally commenced proceedings in New York against APT (UK) Ltd, a company controlled by A, with A joined as co-defendant. However, APT discontinued the action against A personally, proceeding solely against the company in New York, and instead commenced an action against him in England. APT sought to stay the English proceedings and A applied for an injunction to restrain APT from reviving the action against him in New York.

Held, dismissing APT's application and granting A's injunction, that whilst accepting that plaintiffs could stay their own proceedings, it was usual to require that, once commenced, actions were either brought to trial or properly discontinued. A was English and resident here, therefore U.K. jurisdiction was the *forum conveniens* (*Société Nationale Industrielle Aerospatiale v. Lee Jui Kak* [1987] C.L.Y. 3024 distinguished). The English proceedings would not be stayed. The potential injustice of allowing APT to proceed against A in both jurisdictions had to be considered alongside whether APT would be deprived of legitimate juridical advantage by an injunction. The court held that if, having refused to stay the English proceedings, it then refused to restrain the New York proceedings, A would have the substantial disadvantage of having to fight on two fronts, whereas APT would only face one front. As such the U.S. action should be stayed.

ADVANCED PORTFOLIO TECHNOLOGIES v. AINSWORTH, *The Times*, November 15, 1995, D.C.

4150. Interest—equitable jurisdiction—claim for interest only—pawnbroker withholding surplus money after selling pawned articles—fiduciary relationship between pawnbroker and pawnor—claim for interest on withheld monies—whether claim maintainable in absence of debt or damages claim. See MATHEW (THOMAS) v. T. M. SUTTON, §2203.

4151. Interest—restitution—when cause of action arose—whether simple or compound interest payable

[Supreme Court Act 1981 (c.54), s.35(a).]

A shipbuilding yard agreed to construct a ship for a shipowner, with financing provided by D, a bank. The shipowner ran into financial difficulties and P was anxious to take over the contract. It deposited £600,000 in 1981 with D as a token of future intent and the sum was payable only on successful conclusion of refinancing negotiations. Negotiations broke down in 1986 and P successfully sued for the return of the sum. It was agreed that statutory interest was payable under the Supreme Court Act 1981, s.35(a) from the cause of action to the date of judgment. The judge held that the payment was conditional and that compound interest should be awarded as the payments were held on constructive trust. D appealed and the questions arose: (a) whether the sum was payable only on successful conclusion of refinancing negotiations, or outright; (b) whether P was entitled to compound interest under the court's equitable jurisdiction; (c) at which date the cause of action arose; (d) the basis on which the calculation should be made; and (e) if the payments were conditional, but simple interest only was allowable, the date from which such interest should run.

Held, allowing the appeal in part, that (1) the payments were conditional and not outright; (2) it was impossible to find any trust relationship as there was no intention that D should become a fiduciary in respect of the payments, nor would it be unconscionable if D were not so treated (*Barclays Bank v. Quistclose Investments* [1968] C.L.Y. 459 distinguished); (3) nor was there an intention that the funds should be kept for a particular purpose (as opposed to becoming the general property of D) and it followed that only simple interest could be awarded; and (4) P's cause of action for the restitution of the payment arose when the negotiations finally failed and not from when the payment was made and simple interest ran from that date in 1986 (*West Deutsche Landesbank Girocentrale v. Islington London Borough Council* [1994] C.L.Y. 3911 distinguished).

GUARDIAN OCEAN CARGOES, TRANSORIENT SHIP CARGOES, MIDDLE EAST AGENTS S.A.L. AND MED LINE SA v. BANCO DO BRASIL (NOS. 1 AND 3) [1994 2 Lloyd's L.R. 152, C.A.

4152. Interim damages—discretion of judge. See CAMPFIL v. BARCLAYS BANK, §1612.

4153. Interim relief—reference to the European Court of Justice—validity of regulation—conditions for interim relief—European Community

[Treaty of Rome 1957, Art. 189.]

Where a national court had referred to the ECJ for a preliminary ruling the question of the validity of an E.C. Regulation which formed the basis of a national administrative measure, Art. 189 of the Treaty of Rome 1957 was to be interpreted as not precluding that court from granting interim relief for the benefit of the person seeking protection. The conditions governing the grant of such interim relief were that the court must have serious concerns about the validity of the Community Act, the interim relief must be necessary to avoid irreparable damage to the party seeking relief, the court must take account of the Community interest and it must observe any ruling of the ECJ or CFI on the lawfulness of the Regulation concerned.

ATLANTA FRUCHTHANDELSGESELLSCHAFT mbH v. BUNDESAMT FUR ERNAHRUNG UND FORSTWIRTSCHAFT (C–465/93), *The Times*, November 29, 1995, ECJ.

4154. Interlocutory consent order—moneys held in special account until judgment—whether plaintiff entitled by stay or further order to restrain release of moneys

A schedule to an interlocutory consent order providing that P's solicitor would countersign withdrawal instructions relating to a special account did not necessarily confer upon P a right of veto upon release of the moneys held in that account.

In a copyright infringement action relating to computer programs D1 and D2 agreed pursuant to an interlocutory consent order to pay a percentage of the proceeds of continuing sales into a special account in the name of D2. In the order D1 and D2 undertook not to withdraw money from the account without P's consent or leave of the court until judgment in the action or further order in the meantime. A schedule to the order provided that any withdrawal from the account required the countersignature of P's solicitor. At trial P succeeded in establishing only minor infringements. An inquiry as to damages in favour of P and an inquiry as to damages in favour of D on P's cross-undertaking were ordered. P intended to appeal. After judgment, P's solicitor refused to countersign the withdrawal of moneys by D2 from the special account. D1 and D2 sought an order for the release of the money. It was held that as a matter of construction of the order, the provision requiring countersignature by P's solicitor was administrative and that the substantive restraint was contained in the undertaking not to withdraw any moneys until judgment. It was implicit in the order that at the time of judgment the court was entitled as a matter of discretion to impose such further restraints on the moneys as appeared justified. The judge ordered that out of the £80,000 in the account, £60,000 be released to D1 and D2 and the sum of £20,000 be retained pending the determination of P's inquiry as to damages. P appealed against this decision.

Held, dismissing the appeal, that (1) as a matter of construction the provision relating to the countersignature of P's solicitor was not a free-standing provision conferring a right of veto upon release. It was simply a mechanism for policing the terms of the substantive undertaking; (2) the fate of the fund depended on the proper construction of the order and undertakings embodied in it. A literal reading of the order would lead to the conclusion that on judgment, whether in favour of P or D, the fund was removable by D. However, on judgment it was for the judge to decide how the fund was to be dealt with. The decision was one calling for an exercise of judicial discretion; (3) reliance on a case relating to a stay of execution pending appeal was rejected. The fund was D's property. That was a critical distinction in relation to a case dealing with a stay on judgment (*Quantel v. Spaceward Microsystems (No. 2)* [1990] R.P.C. 147 distinguished); and (4) what P was asking for in effect was security for damages which it hoped to win at appeal. This would, if granted, be equivalent to granting a post-judgment Mareva injunction without any evidence of dissipation. It was impossible to say that the judge's exercise of his discretion was plainly wrong. Accordingly P's applications were dismissed.

JOHN RICHARDSON COMPUTERS v. FLANDERS (NO. 3) [1994] F.S.R. 153, C.A.

4155. Interlocutory injunction—admissibility of evidence—affidavit in support—affidavit based on DTI inspectors' report—whether entitled to rely on report in affidavit

[R.S.C., Ord. 41, r.5(2).]

An applicant for an interlocutory injunction is entitled to rely, in his supporting affidavit, on intermediate sources of information such as a DTI inspector's report.

P concluded a number of reinsurance contracts with D. In due course actions were brought against D claiming that the contracts were illegal and void. At one stage of the interlocutory proceedings P sought injunctions, supported by affidavits that relied largely on the contents of a Department of Trade report into the conduct of D. D sought to strike out the affidavits as inadmissible on the basis that the DTI report did not meet the requirements of an affidavit.

Held, refusing the application, that the power of the court to grant an interlocutory injunction should be flexible and not fettered by technical rules of admissibility that might apply at trial. It did not follow that intermediate sources of information ought not to be referred or relied on, with the applicant compelled solely to rely on original sources. P were therefore entitled to rely on the DTI report in their affidavit.

DEUTSCHE RUCKVERSICHERUNG AG v. WALBROOK INSURANCE CO.; GROUP JOSIRE (FORMERLY KNOWN AS GROUP JOSI REASSURANCE SA) v. SAME [1994] 4 All E.R. 181, Phillips J.

4156. Interlocutory injunction—damages—patent concerning helicopter rotor blader—cross-undertaking—inquiry as to damages—striking out of pleading—abuse of process—access to confidential exhibit—whether specific discovery essential—whether alleged damage too remote

[R.S.C., Ord. 24, rr.5, 8.]

In an action for infringement of P's patent, D had been restrained by interlocutory injunction from making, using or offering for disposal a system for monitoring the performance of helicopter rotor blades. At the trial the judge held that the patent was invalid and revoked it, and he directed that there should be an inquiry as to damages. In the inquiry D alleged that the injunction had prevented it from completing the development of a component of its device which could only be tested by use in a complete system. P also applied to strike out this pleading on the ground that any loss following from this effect was too remote to be recovered and that the pleading was an abuse of process as it was inconsistent with statements made on behalf of D earlier in the proceedings. P applied for an order to permit its technical director to examine a notebook belonging to D's development engineer, which was an exhibit to an affidavit. Due to the confidential nature of the exhibit, access to it had been restricted to P's legal advisors, although D had suggested that P instruct an independent expert to examine it. P relied on the general principle that a party to litigation should be allowed to know the facts disclosed in the course of the litigation. P also sought specific discovery of certain classes of documents.

Held, refusing to strike out the pleading or permit access by the director to the exhibit, but allowing limited discovery, that (1) although the injunction did not specifically prevent the development of the component, it was at least possible that D would be able to satisfy the judge conducting the inquiry that the impossibility of carrying out such development in the absence of a complete system was a natural and inevitable consequence of the injunction; (2) in relation to abuse of process, the facts which D was alleged now to be contradicting were not relevant at the trial and were not explored. D's present claim did not therefore represent an attack on a previously decided issue, nor could it be said to be a manifest sham. To regard it as an abuse of process would be tantamount to saying that a party who had put forward one version of relevant facts might never be allowed to put forward a different version, even if the discrepancy were explained; (3) a notebook recording the results of tests carried out in the course of development of D's new product was likely to contain important trade secrets. There might be serious prejudice to D if these became known to P's technical director, even without any deliberate impropriety. P's interests would adequately be served if there was disclosure to an independent expert (*Warner-Lambert Co. v. Glaxo Laboratories* [1975] C.L.Y. 2505, *Roussel Uclaf v. I.C.I.* [1991] C.L.Y. 2693 considered); (4) D's manufacturing costs could be ascertained without production of the specifications sought, and specific discovery of them was not necessary for disposing fairly of the inquiry as to damages; (5) as D had stated that it had no further documents showing the prices charged by it, and there was nothing to suggest that this statement was wrong, there was no sufficient basis for ordering specific discovery of such documents; and (6) a limited order for discovery would be made in respect of documents showing the purchase price paid by D to a supplier for a particular component.

HELITUNE v. STEWART HUGHES [1994] F.S.R. 422, Ferris J.

4157. Interlocutory injunction—declaratory relief sought—non-contractual relationship—whether court having jurisdiction to grant injunction when the only relief sought is a declaration that a course of action is unlawful

The court had power to grant an injunction where the only relief sought was a declaration that an arrangement was unlawful and in restraint of trade; the action for such a declaration amounted to a cause of action giving the court jurisdiction to grant an interlocutory injunction.

D passed a resolution preventing Welsh football clubs from playing in a league organised by the English Football Association, but the applicants wished to continue playing in that league. D imposed sanctions by prohibiting the clubs from playing their home games in Wales, causing a loss of revenue to the clubs. The clubs sought a declaration that the decision preventing them playing their home games at their own grounds was void as being in unreasonable restraint of trade and they also sought an interlocutory injunction to allow them to play their home games in Wales. D contended that there was no jurisdiction to grant such an injunction where the only relief claimed was a declaration in respect of a non-contractual relationship, since any injunction would depend upon the grant of the declaration.

Held, granting the injunction, that although a contract or arrangement in unreasonable restraint of trade was merely void and unenforceable rather than creating a wrong, the right of an injured party to bring proceedings for a declaration was a cause of action upon which a jurisdiction to grant an interlocutory injunction could be based. On the facts the injunction would be granted (*Veracruz Transportation Inc. v. VC Shipping Co. Inc.; Veracruz, The* [1992] 1 Lloyd's Rep. 353, *Siskina (Cargo owners) v. Distos Sia Naviera SA; Siskina, The* [1977] C.L.Y. 2344 considered).

NEWPORT ASSOCIATION FOOTBALL CLUB v. FOOTBALL ASSOCIATION OF WALES [1995] 2 All E.R. 87, Jacob J.

4158. Interlocutory injunction—early discovery—copyright infringement—pantomime lyrics and music—lyrics non-infringing—whether form of relief misconceived

If a plaintiff has a cause of action then he can sue upon that cause of action and lead evidence in support. It is not the function of the court to see whether or not he has a cause of action. P brought an action alleging that the copyright in respect of a pantomime entitled "Peter Pan the British Musical" was infringed by another pantomime, "Peter Pan, the Return". By this interlocutory application they sought an order preventing the showing of the pantomime unless D allowed the solicitors acting for P to inspect the script, lyrics, music and stage directions relating to the proposed production. D exhibited the script of their pantomime to an affidavit prior to the hearing. P were also given access to the lyrics of the production. It was therefore common ground before the hearing that neither the script nor the lyrics infringed the copyright of P.

Held, refusing the application, that (1) the form of injunction sought could not be granted by the court as it encompassed within it acts which were manifestly lawful. The court cannot impose a precondition of production of documents as a condition of a defendant conducting lawful acts; (2) if a plaintiff has a cause of action then he can sue upon that cause of action and lead evidence in support. It is not the function of the court to allow a plaintiff to see whether he has a cause of action. The form of relief sought was misconceived; and (3) although the court had a discretion to order discovery, this was not a case in which early discovery would be appropriate since P had not as yet put forward any evidence to suggest that they had a right which was being infringed (*R.H.M. Foods v. Bovril* [1982] C.L.Y. 2511 considered).

CHATER AND CHATER PRODUCTIONS v. ROSE [1994] F.S.R. 491, Jacob J.

4159. Interlocutory injunction—reference to the European Court of Justice—whether in view of its duration stay should be discharged

N applied for the discharge of a stay, imposed by the Divisional Court, on the granting to it of a product licence. The matter had been referred to the European Court of Justice which, N claimed, would mean the final determination might be as much as two years in the future.

Held, dismissing the application, that the Court had imposed a suspension which would endure until the final outcome of the proceedings which had been referred to the European Court of Justice. The questions to be asked were whether there was a serious issue to be tried, and when this was answered positively, whether damages would be an adequate remedy. Considering the consequences of lifting or retaining the stay, and how these would be affected depending on the eventual outcome of the matter, the court held that the least injustice would be done by dismissing the application to remove the stay.

SCOTIA PHARMACEUTICALS INTERNATIONAL v. SECRETARY OF STATE FOR HEALTH AND NORGINE [1994] C.O.D. 241, D.C.

4160. Interrogatories—injury sustained whilst working on construction site—interrogatories served without an order—whether proper use

[R.S.C., Ord. 26, r.3(i); C.C.R., Ord. 15, r.11(1).]

P commenced proceedings against D1 and D2 for damages in respect of an injury he sustained whilst at work on a construction site. Following the service of a defence by D1, but before discovery, P served on D1 eight short interrogatories without order pursuant to the provisions of R.S.C., Ord. 26, r.3(i), and C.C.R., Ord. 15, r.11(i). At the hearing of an application for the withdrawal of the interrogatories D1 did not dispute the legitimacy of the questions asked but argued that, in the light of the observations of Colman J. in *Det Danske Hedeselskabet v. KDM International*, the interrogatories were premature because the answers could be expected to emerge in due course from discovery and the exchange of witness statements.

Held, dismissing the application, that the court was bound by the provisions of Ord. 26. *Det Danske* was a decision that appeared to turn on its own particular facts, namely the increased use of oppressively long interrogatories by parties appearing before the Commercial Courts. P had been right to serve interrogatories rather than a request for further and better particulars. Whether or not P continued or discontinued his action against D1 depended on the answers given to the interrogatories. If P was forced to wait until after discovery before being able to properly consider discontinuance costs would be needlessly incurred by all parties and P stood to be more heavily damnified in costs as a result thereof. In all the circumstances interrogatories were necessary both for fairly disposing of the matter and for the saving of costs. D1 was to pay P's costs of the application in any event (*Det Danske Hedeselskabet v. KDM International*, May 28, 1993, unrep. considered).

JONES v. SWIFT STRUCTURES, April 19, 1995; Deputy District Judge Perry; Romford County Ct. [*Ex rel.* Pip Punwar, Barrister].

4161. Interrogatories—prior to witness statement—application to set aside—whether interrogatories were premature

P had tripped at the Ds' premises. Interrogatories were served on the Ds who sought to set them aside, *inter alia*, on the ground that they were premature prior to the exchange of witness statements.

Held, that whilst two of the interrogatories were disallowed, the balance was not premature. It was not necessary to await the exchange of witness statements before asking questions which were relevant and the answers to which may support the P's claim or assist in defeating the Ds' defence.

NAILOR v. FOLEY LODGE HOTELS, January 27, 1995; District Judge Catlin; Reading County Ct. [*Ex rel. Simon Livesey, Barrister*].

4162. Joinder of parties—addition or substitution of National Health Service trust as a party

[R.S.C., Ord. 15, r.7(2).]

Y health authority engaged PTP as architects for the design and construction of hospital buildings. Y employed F under a JCT standard form of contract to construct the buildings. In September 1992, Y issued a writ against F and PTP alleging defects in the buildings. F alleged that there was a final certificate which provided a complete defence. Therefore, Y pleaded negligent issue of the final certificate against PTP. Under the National Health Service and Community Care Act 1990, the Secretary of State transferred the appropriate liabilities to an NHS trust. Y applied to join the trust as a party to the proceedings under R.S.C., Ord. 15, r.7(2).

Held, allowing the application, that Y could apply under Ord. 15 on the basis that this situation fell within r.7(2); an order under Ord. 15, r.7 did not remove the original party from the proceedings; and the fact that Y might have claims itself which it wished to pursue did not preclude an order under r.7. The purpose of s.35 of the Limitation Act 1950 was to prevent the joinder of a party such that a claim could be pursued which would otherwise have been statute barred. Y's claim was not such a claim (*Linden Garden Trust v. Lenesta Sludge Disposals* [1993] C.L.Y. 303, *Toprak Energi Sanayi AS v. Sale Tilney Technology* [1994] C.L.Y. 3798 considered).

YORKSHIRE REGIONAL HEALTH AUTHORITY v. AMEC BUILDING [1994] 10 Const. L.J. 336, Lloyd J.

4163. Judgment—interpretation—whether inconsistency—sentence to be interpreted in context of judgment as whole

When a party appealed against judgment on the grounds of inconsistency and pointed out apparent conflict between a sentence in the judgment and the ultimate conclusion, the court should interpret the sentence not like part of a statute but in the context of the judgment as a whole and against the background of the facts.

CLARKE v. SMITH, *The Independent* (C.S.), September 4, 1995, C.A.

4164. Judgment—setting aside—defendants failing to comply with debarring order—whether hearing to establish whether document complies with order

Ds consented to the debarring order. They were required to answer further and better particulars within a certain period. They served a document that purported to comply. However, a number of particulars were not answered adequately. P entered judgment. Ds applied to have judgment set aside.

Held, that while Ds were under an obligation to comply fully with the order where there is a question as to the effectiveness of a document, failing which a penalty will ensue, there should be a hearing as to whether the document complies with the order. Accordingly, before P can enter judgment an application should be issued on notice so that this point can be argued before the court.

LATTIMORE v. DEPARTMENT OF TRANSPORT, March 9, 1995; District Judge Karet; Watford County Ct. [*Ex rel.* Robin Thompson & Partners, Solicitors].

4165. Judgment debt—debtor declared bankrupt while appeal against judgment debt pending—leave sought to appeal out of time—criteria for granting leave. See DEBTOR, A (NO. 799 of 1994), *Re, ex p.* COBBS PROPERTY SERVICES, §411.

4166. Jurisdiction—High Court and county courts

HIGH COURT AND COUNTY COURTS JURISDICTION (AMENDMENT) ORDER 1995 (No. 205 (L.1)) [65p], made under the Courts and Legal Services Act 1990 (c.41), s.1; operative on February 1, 1995; provides that where the High Court or a county court is considering whether to transfer proceedings to or from the Central London County Court Business List, it will not be presumed that the action should be tried in the High Court unless the value of the action exceeds £200,000 and that judgments given in proceedings arising out of the Consumer Credit Act 1974 (c.39) shall only be enforced in the county court, whatever enforcement method is chosen.

4167. Lands Tribunal—practice direction. See PRACTICE DIRECTION NO. 1 OF 1994, §4288.

4168. Lloyds litigation—*in camera*—confidential information—whether hearing in open court would be commercially damaging

An application for the substantive hearing to be heard *in camera* because of privileged and confidential information contained in the evidence was denied. Open hearings in all Lloyd's litigation were of fundamental importance. The court would exercise its inherent jurisdiction where appropriate to give directions with a view to avoiding unnecessary reference to information which could be commercially damaging, provided that such directions would not interfere with the parties arguing their cases to their best advantage. Applications relating to sensitive information should be made at least six weeks in advance.

HALLAM-EAMES v. MERRETT SYNDICATES (NO. 2), *The Times*, June 16, 1995, Cresswell J.

4169. Lloyd's litigation—to be commenced in Commercial Court

In order to facilitate the efficient and effective case management of all litigation involving the Lloyd's insurance market, all cases must in future be commenced in the Commercial Court of the Queen's Bench Division.

DEENY v. LITTLEJOHN & CO., *The Times*, February 23, 1995, Cresswell J.

4170. Lloyd's Names—litigation—moratorium—general moratorium on all Names—whether contrary to principle of right of access to courts

If some Lloyd's Names wished to defer the start of their group actions in order to allow time to consider any settlement offer made by Lloyd's, the court would try to assist by revising the timetable where practicable. However, it was contrary to the principle of the right of access to the courts for all to try to impose a general moratorium on all Names cases regardless of the wishes of individual groups.

LLOYD'S LITIGATION: MORATORIUM APPLICATION, *Re*, *The Times*, August 10, 1995, Cresswell J.

4171. Magistrates' courts—amalgamations. See CRIMINAL EVIDENCE AND PROCEDURE, §1180.

4172. Magistrates' courts—inspections—annual report—press release. See CRIMINAL EVIDENCE AND PROCEDURE, §1184.

4173. Mareva and Anton Piller injunctions—standard forms to be used unless there is a good reason—procedure to be adopted on application

Guidance and standard forms were issued for the grant of *ex parte* Mareva injunctions and Anton Piller orders. The forms of order provided should be used except when the judge hearing a particular application considered that there was a good reason for adopting a different form.

PRACTICE DIRECTION (*EX PARTE* MAREVA INJUNCTIONS AND ANTON PILLER ORDERS) [1994] 1 W.L.R. 1233

4174. Mareva injunction—child support claim—statutory proceedings before magistrates—DSS seeking interlocutory injunction to prevent disposal of earnings before liability order obtained—whether having jurisdiction to do so

[Child Support Act 1991 (c.48); Supreme Court Act 1981 (c.54), s.37.]

The DSS made a renewed application for a Mareva injunction to prevent B from disposing of his assets before the DSS could obtain a liability order from magistrates for the collection of maintenance. B was in arrears totalling £4,000 under a maintenance assessment by the CSA. He accepted he could be liable for £2,000, but had appealed against the assessment. The DSS relied on the general principle that the court had power to grant an injunction when fairness demanded that it should do so and contended that the High Court had power to grant interlocutory relief by virtue of the provisions of the Supreme Court Act 1981, s.37.

Held, dismissing the application, that the issues had to be considered in relation to the Child Support Act 1991 which governed the DSS's power to enforce collection of maintenance and to bring proceedings to obtain liability orders. The 1991 Act gave the Secretary of State power to make a deduction from earnings order before a liability order was made, but gave no ancillary or supportive jurisdiction to the High Court. For this reason, and for reasons of policy, it would not be desirable for the court to grant Mareva injunctions in support of statutory proceedings before magistrates' courts.

DEPARTMENT OF SOCIAL SECURITY v. BUTLER (FCE/95/6034/D), July 21, 1995, C.A.

4175. Mareva injunction—contempt by corporation—breach of order—circumstances in which corporation guilty of contempt—whether conduct constituted contempt—whether intention of alter ego relevant—whether assets should be sequestered. See Z BANK v. D1, §577.

4176. Mareva injunction—damages—court discretion to order assessment—whether court to enquire into circumstances in which case was discontinued

The terms of a Mareva injunction granted against L, a chartered accountant who was charged with forgery and deception as a result of his involvement with forged bonds, included an undertaking by G to abide by an order as to damages suffered by L as a result of the injunction. L was acquitted of the criminal charges and civil proceedings were started, but G issued a summons for leave to discontinue these when, in view of L's financial situation, it became clear that they were unlikely to recover any more money but could face considerable costs if they continued the case. L, however, issued a summons for an inquiry into damages sustained by him by reason of the Mareva injunction and that he should be allowed to enter judgment against G for the amount of the damages. L now appealed against the dismissal of his application for an inquiry.

Held, dismissing the appeal, that in exercising its discretion to order an assessment as to damages under an undertaking, the court should enquire into the circumstances in which the case was discontinued. The instant case was not one in which the Mareva injunction was wrongly obtained or maintained and G would be fully justified in continuing their action if they chose to do so. No inquiry as to damages was therefore necessary in the interests of justice, and equity did not require the undertaking to be enforced.

GOLDMAN SACHS INTERNATIONAL v. LYONS, *The Times*, February 28, 1995, C.A.

4177. Mareva injunction—disclosure—injunction applying to assets within jurisdiction—whether jurisdiction to order disclosure of assets worldwide

[Arbitration Act 1950 (14 Geo. 6, c.27), ss.12(6)(f), 26; Supreme Court Act 1981 (c.54), s.37(1).]

The court has jurisdiction, in respect of a Mareva injunction granted in respect of arbitration awards limited to assets within the jurisdiction, to order disclosure of assets worldwide.

In April 1994 the owners of a chartered ship obtained a Mareva injunction under the Arbitration Act 1950 to enable enforcement of awards. The injunction was confined to assets within the jurisdiction, but the court order required disclosure of information on worldwide assets. The charterers applied to vary the order.

Held, dismissing the application, that the court had jurisdiction to order disclosure of assets which, in appropriate cases, included assets outside the jurisdiction (*Orwell Steel (Erection and Fabrication) v. Asphalt and Tarmac (U.K.)* [1984] C.L.Y. 2645 applied; *Derby and Co. v. Weldon (Nos. 3 and 4)* [1989] C.L.Y. 3027 distinguished).

GIDRXSLME SHIPPING CO. v. TANTOMAR-TRANSPORTES MARITIMOS LDA [1995] 1 W.L.R. 299, Colman J.

4178. Mareva injunction—expiry—divorce proceedings—failure to continue interim injunction—whether could be corrected under slip rule—whether husband in contempt

[Matrimonial Causes Act 1973 (c.18), s.37(2)(a); C.C.R., Ord. 15, r.5; Ord. 29, r.1(3).]

The slip rule could not be used to reactivate a Mareva injunction which had expired through oversight.

In divorce proceedings, W made an *ex parte* application for an injunction under s.37 of the Matrimonial Causes Act 1973 restraining H from disposing of his assets. The district judge made the order to last until an *inter partes* hearing. On the return date, further interlocutory orders were made, but the injunction was not continued in force. More than two weeks later, W's advisers realised the oversight and wrote by facsimile to the court, pointing out that there had been no continuation and seeking an amendment of the order made on the return date under the slip rule to provide for the injunction's continuation. A district judge purported to make this amendment. H later disposed of £17,800, and W obtained a further *ex parte* injunction restraining disposal of assets. When the matter came before the judge, he considered that the earlier order had remained in force throughout and found H in contempt, imposed a suspended committal order, and set aside the disposition of £17,800.

Held, allowing the appeal and quashing the committal order, that (1) the extension of the order without hearing from H was entirely inappropriate in the circumstances, and could not be saved by reference to the slip rule in Ord. 15, r.5. While the court would not permit technical infringement of the rules to defeat the ends of justice, the slip rule should not be used where there was a failure to comply with a requirement relating to injunctions imposing serious restrictions upon the activities of litigants (*Clarke v. Clarke* [1991] C.L.Y. 2801 applied); (2) the injunction had ceased to have effect on the return date, and the purported amendment under the slip rule was ineffective. There was therefore no order of which H could be in breach; (3) in any event, the judge had turned the return date of an *ex parte* injunction into a committal hearing. There had been no compliance with the mandatory requirements relating to committal hearings laid down in Ord. 29, r.1(3), and the committal order should be quashed for this reason too; and (4) the order setting aside of the disposition of £17,800 was made without prior notice and was equally seriously flawed and should be set aside.

LANGLEY v. LANGLEY [1994] 1 F.L.R. 383, C.A.

4179. Mareva injunction—foreign jurisdictions—territorial jurisdiction of Hong Kong courts—service of process

[R.S.C., Ord. 11, r.1 (Hong Kong).]

MB appealed against an order of the Court of Appeal of Hong Kong affirming the setting aside of an order granting an *ex parte* Mareva injunction against L, who was in custody in Monaco. Proceedings instigated by MB were in progress in Monaco and an order attaching L's assets had been granted there, but the Monaco court ruled it had no jurisdiction to attach L's assets in Hong Kong. The issues to be decided by the Privy Council were of the territorial jurisdiction of the Hong Kong courts pursuant to the Hong Kong R.S.C., Ord. 11, r.1.

Held, dismissing the appeal, that although Ord. 11 r.1(m), provided that a writ could be served outside the jurisdiction where "the claim is brought to enforce any judgment", if proceedings outside the jurisdiction were still in progress or pending the court was not entitled to allow a writ for a Mareva injunction freezing assets within the jurisdiction of a foreigner who was outside the jurisdiction. Moreover, having regard to the purposes of Ord. 11, r.1(b), it was clear that extraterritorial jurisdiction could not be founded merely on the presence of assets within the jurisdiction.

MERCEDES-BENZ AG v. LEIDUCK, *The Times*, August 11, 1995, P.C.

4180. Mareva injunction—injunction in Ireland—worldwide injunction in English court—counterclaim—Irish injunction discharged—whether English court having jurisdiction to hear counterclaim

[Civil Jurisdiction and Judgments Act 1982 (c.27), s.25; R.S.C., Ord. 28, r.7.]

English courts have jurisdiction to hear a counterclaim brought by a defendant as a result of a worldwide Mareva injunction granted to the plaintiff in England in aid of proceedings brought by the plaintiff in another jurisdiction.

P brought an action in Ireland alleging fraud against D and P obtained Mareva injunctions in Ireland and England in aid of those proceedings. Following judgment in Ireland the injunctions were discharged subject to the question of enforcement of the cross-undertakings as to damages given by P. On P's application to strike out D's counterclaim for want of jurisdiction the judge held that the English courts did not have jurisdiction to deal with the counterclaims because R.S.C., Ord. 28, r.7(1), was confined to proceedings where the plaintiff had sought some substantial relief from the court.

Held, allowing D's appeal, that there was no reason for drawing a distinction within R.S.C., Ord. 28, r.7(1), between the grant of interim relief under s.25 of the Civil Jurisdiction and Judgments Act 1982 and the grant of final relief. The court had jurisdiction to deal with a counterclaim in both cases. To hold otherwise would prevent the defendant from counterclaiming for ancillary relief in actions where the plaintiff sought only interim relief which would be unjust (*Republic of Liberia v. Gulf Oceanic* [1985] C.L.Y. 2612, *Metal Scrap Trade Corp. v. Kate Shipping Co.* [1990] C.L.Y. 362, *Channel Tunnel Group and France Manche SA v. Balfour Beatty Construction* [1993] C.L.Y. 151 applied.)

BALKANBANK v. TAHER (NO. 3) [1995] 1 W.L.R. 1067, C.A.

4181. Mareva injunction—insurance companies—reinsurance agreement—likelihood of enforcement elsewhere

O applied to have set aside an order granting a Mareva injunction in favour of S. Both parties were insurance companies who, by a reinsurance agreement in 1969, participated in the joint payment of claims. In 1990 O stopped paying these claims. Mareva relief was granted to S to prevent O removing their assets out of the U.K. in order to defeat any award S might obtain.

Held, dismissing the application, that it was not disputed by either party that O wished to remove their assets from the U.K., but O's argument that any awards or judgments obtained by S could be enforced in Singapore, where they had a substantial business, was rejected. The court was prepared to continue the injunction because if O's assets were removed then S's claim and costs would probably not be met in full.

STRONGHOLD INSURANCE CO. v. OVERSEAS UNION INSURANCE, *Lloyds List*, October 26, 1995 (I.D.), D.C.

4182. Mareva injunction—to preserve status quo and property—nature of evidence required

[Aus.] A plaintiff claiming a Mareva injunction is not required to show that the purpose of the defendant's disposition of assets, occurring or apprehended, is to prevent recovery of the amount of any judgment which might be obtained. On the contrary, a proper basis for granting such an injunction arises where the plaintiff shows that there is a danger of dissipation of assets by the defendant which is likely to prevent such recovery.

NORTHCORP v. AUMAN PROPERTIES (AUSTRALIA) PTY. [1995] A.L.M.D. 2390, Sup. Ct., Queensland.

4183. Mareva injunction—undertaking as to damages—causation—principles on which damages to be assessed—whether loss caused by issue of injunction—whether loss within contemplation of plaintiff. See THARROS SHIPPING CO. v. BIAS SHIPPING, §1636.

4184. Mareva injunction—worldwide pre-trial injunction—plaintiff obtaining interim relief in aid of substantive action proceeding in Irish court—court discharging injunction by consent on failure of Irish action and directing an inquiry into damages—defendants seeking to advance counterclaims in respect of losses sustained by reason of injunction—whether court having jurisdiction to entertain counterclaims in respect of claim for interim relief—whether originating summons seeking Mareva relief an "action" for purposes of procedural rules—whether court retaining discretion to order plaintiff to pay damages to defendants

[Civil Jurisdiction and Judgments Act 1982 (c.27), s.25, Sched. 1, art. 24; R.S.C., Ord. 28, r.7(1).]

An application for interim relief under s.25 of the Civil Jurisdiction and Judgments Act 1982 is not an "action" begun by originating summons within the meaning of R.S.C., Ord. 28, r.7.

In the course of proceedings issued in Ireland alleging fraud in respect of a joint venture agreement, P obtained a Mareva injunction restraining D from dealing with their assets within the jurisdiction of the Irish court and subsequently issued an originating summons in the English court seeking worldwide Mareva relief as against D, which was granted pursuant to s.25 of and Sched. 1 to the 1982 Act. At the trial of the substantive Irish action, the court rejected P's principal allegation of fraud and discharged the Irish injunction. Shortly thereafter the English court made a consent order discharging the worldwide Mareva injunction and directed that there be an inquiry into the damages sustained by D by reason of the English injunction which P ought to pay. D claimed that they had suffered catastrophic losses and sought to advance various counterclaims against P under R.S.C., Ord. 28, r.7(1). By an application to the court pursuant to Ord. 12, r.8 P contended that the court had no jurisdiction to entertain D's counterclaims on the ground that an application under s.25 of the 1982 Act was not an "action" within the meaning of Ord. 28, r.7(1). D claimed that the court no longer had a discretion whether to award damages to them because it had already exercised its discretion in making the earlier consent order.

Held, striking out D's counterclaims, that (1) an application for interim relief under s.25 of the 1982 Act was not an "action" begun by originating summons within the meaning of R.S.C. Ord. 28, r.7 which, on its true construction, limited the availability of a counterclaim to those actions where the plaintiff claimed substantive relief and thereby submitted to the jurisdiction of the court in respect of any claim which the defendant might wish to advance on the merits (*Channel Tunnel Group and France Manche S.A. v. Balfour Beatty Construction* [1993] C.L.Y. 151 considered); (2) an undertaking in damages was given to the court, not the defendant, and it was for the court to decide whether it was appropriate to order the plaintiff to pay damages in any particular case; and (3) the question whether the court had exercised its discretion to order a plaintiff to pay damages to the defendant in respect of losses sustained as a result of a Mareva injunction would clearly depend on the facts of the particular case and on the facts here the court had not yet exercised its discretion (*Norwest Holst Civil Engineering v. Polysius*, *The Times*, July 23, 1987 and *Financiera Avenida v. Shiblaq* [1991] C.L.Y. 2914 considered).

BALKANBANK v. TAHER [1994] 4 All E.R. 239, C.A.

4185. Order—review of order—trespass by defendants—building of sewer without permission—order to reinstate land as far as "reasonably practicable"—whether financial consideration relevant—whether court has jurisdiction to review order

A court order to reinstate land as far as "reasonably practicable" includes financial considerations of the cost of any works relative to the value of the land.

P owned a stretch of land incorporating a disused railway embankment for which he had planning permission for residential development. He planned to sell the land for about £50,000. D trespassed on the land to lay a sewer causing serious damage to it and to trees and fencing on the land. P was awarded compensatory damages and the judge ordered restoration of the site, including the replanting of trees "so far as reasonably practicable". The cost of works contemplated by the parties was in the order of £12,000 but the scheme as drawn up by P's expert would have cost over £200,000. D applied to set aside the scheme as unreasonable.

Held, granting the order, that the phrase "reasonably practicable" included financial considerations: it meant having regard to what was reasonable in relation to the value of the site. The court had jurisdiction to review the order, and would vary it (dictum in *Christel v. Christel* [1951] 2 K.B. 725 applied).

JORDAN v. NORFOLK COUNTY COUNCIL [1994] 1 W.L.R. 1353, Sir Donald Nicholls, V.-C.

4186. Parties—change in identity of claimant—whether existing proceedings should be allowed to continue—whether affected by expiry of limitation period

[R.S.C., Ord. 15, r.7.]

IC was an Italian company which had merged into another, Cereol Italia Srl, which argued that the court had inherent jurisdiction to allow it to take over an action against the defendants brought by IC.

Held, that R.S.C., Ord. 15, r.7, addressed the circumstances where there was a change in the identity of the claimant which could not have been foreseen when proceedings were issued. In these situations, any existing proceedings should be allowed to continue even if the limitation period had expired, provided that the action was originally started within time. The rationale behind limitation periods did not apply to this type of case (*Toprak Enerji Sanayi AS v. Sale Tilney Technology* [1994] C.L.Y. 3798 distinguished).

INDUSTRIE CHIMICHE ITALIA CENTRALE v. ALEXANDER G. TSAVLIRIS & SONS MARITIME CO., *The Times*, August 8, 1995, Mance J.

4187. Penal notices—request to court to endorse penal notice on order—whether appropriate to include named party

M sought mandamus requiring the chief clerk and the district judge to endorse a penal notice on an order to which the Borough of Lambeth had consented. The clerk of court had declined to endorse a penal notice, addressed to the Director of Housing, without the leave of the judge, who refused to allow the endorsement without the express consent of Lambeth Council. He was also concerned whether it was right to name an individual officer on the notice.

Held, granting the application, that it was appropriate in the present case to use form N.77 adapted to include a named individual and directing the penal notice to them.

R. v. WANDSWORTH COUNTY COURT, *ex p.* MUNN [1994] C.O.D. 283, D.C.

4188. Personal injuries—interim payment—minor—settlement not possible until surgery performed in future—interim payment of almost all damages sought to ensure higher interest than that awarded by court—whether appropriate. See CADYWOULD v. CLARKE, §1647.

4189. Pleadings—amendment—change in law—reinstatement of abandoned part of claim—expiry of limitation period—whether to be allowed

The judge has jurisdiction to allow amendments to pleadings resulting from the plaintiff's mistake and it is his duty to ensure that procedural technicalities do not defeat claims with potential merit.

D and P entered into a contract for work to be performed on a bungalow which, within two years of construction, required rebuilding due to subsidence. P claimed breach of duty and breach of contract but later abandoned his claim in contract under the house purchaser's agreement and his amended statement of claim relied solely on a claim for economic loss. Subsequently there was a change in the course of the law which disallowed a claim for economic loss. An application was therefore made to reinstate the claim for breach of contract. D argued that the reamendment of the pleadings raised a new course of action outside the limitation period and was a matter of discretion.

Held, that if the sequence of the amendment was altered so that amendment of the further and better particulars were first allowed as a matter of discretion, then the reamendment of the statement of claim could follow as a further matter of discretion. The judge had jurisdiction to allow an amendment to a statement of claim where that resulted from a mistake and had not given rise to an estoppel or prejudice. It was appropriate in the circumstances to allow the alteration in the sequence of the amendments to avoid prejudice to D. It was the duty of the court to ensure that the procedural technicalities did not defeat potential substantial merits. If P's amendments were allowed, D's summons for striking out must necessarily fail.

BURTON v. MBC (BUILDERS-ASHINGDON) (1995) 69 P.& C.R. 496, C.A.

4190. Pleadings—amendment—formulation of claim—causation and loss—whether judge could give direction

A judge could not require a party to formulate its claim as to causation and loss by a particular method.

GMTC TOOLS AND EQUIPMENT v. YUASA WARWICK MACHINERY (FORMERLY WARWICK MACHINE TOOLS), *The Times*, January 3, 1995, C.A.

4191. Pleadings—amendment—limitation period—claim for damages in negligence—application to amend made before expiry of period—hearing date after expiry—whether leave to amend to be granted

[Limitation Act 1980 (c.58), s.35(1)(3); R.S.C., Ord. 20, r.5(5).]

The provisions of s.35(3) of the Limitation Act 1980 clearly indicate that the relevant date for expiry of the limitation period, where leave is sought to amend, is the date at which the actual amendment is made.

In July 1992 P sought leave to amend their statement of claim in an action for damages against D, consulting engineers. In particular they sought to add claims for negligent misstatements set out in reports dated December 1985 and August 1987. The judge refused the application holding, *inter alia*, that the relevant date for the expiry of the limitation period was the date the court actually gave leave to amend.

Held, dismissing the appeal, that the provisions of s.35(3) of the 1980 Act made clear that the relevant date for expiry was the date the amendment was actually made. It mattered not that the limitation period had not expired at the date when the application for leave to amend was made (dictum in *Bank of America National Trust and Savings Association v. Chrisman; Keyriaki, The* [1994] C.L. 390 applied; *Kennett v. Brown* [1988] C.L.Y. 2162 overruled).

WELSH DEVELOPMENT AGENCY v. REDPATH DORMAN LONG [1994] 4 All E.R. 10, C.A.

4192. Pleadings—amendment—patent infringement—whether to allow amendment to defence and particulars of objections. See INSTANCE v. DENNY BROS. PRINTING, §3771.

4193. Pleadings—amendment of defence—defence struck out in first action—whether defence can be raised in second action—whether *res judicata*

[Treaty of Rome, Art. 86; R.S.C., Ord. 14.]

In an action commenced in 1992, P brought an action against D for patent infringement. D denied infringement and pleaded a Euro-defence under Art. 86 of the Treaty of Rome. The Euro–defence was struck out. At the trial of the action, the patent was found to have been infringed but it was held that D had a defence under the Patents Act 1977, as certain of P's agreements contained offending clauses. P removed the clauses and commenced a second action against D. Again D denied infringement and pleaded the Euro-defence. D then decided to omit the Euro-defence under Art. 86 and served an amended defence. P applied for summary judgment to which D consented subject to certain questions being stood over. D then applied to amend its defence to include the Euro-defence.

Held, dismissing the application and refusing leave to amend, that (1) the Art. 86 defences in the first and second actions were the same and it would be an abuse of process to allow D to plead it. The doctrine of *res judicata* applied; (2) the doctrine of *res judicata* also applied to allegations concerning the Treaty of Rome; (3) the decision to strike out the Art. 86 defence in the first action implied that it would not be arguable before the European Court of Justice and was therefore *acte clair*; (4) the court was not *functus officio*. On a strict reading of the Order made at the Ord. 14 hearing, the court had power to allow amendment of the pleadings to include further claims; and (5) had the matter not been *res judicata* the court would in any event have exercised its discretion against allowing the amendment.

CHIRON CORP. v. MUREX DIAGNOSTICS (NO. 9) [1995] F.S.R. 318, Aldous J.

4194. Pleadings—amendment of points of claim—unfair prejudice petition—application to strike out—whether reasonable cause of action disclosed—whether rules of pleading applying to points of claim

[R.S.C., Ord. 18, r.19.]

The court should require late amendments of pleadings to be fully particularised.

After eight days of the hearing of a petition under s.459 of the Companies Act 1985 the petitioner obtained leave to amend the petition. When the amended points of claim were delivered the respondent applied to strike out the petition and amended points of claim under R.S.C., Ord. 18, r.19, and the inherent jurisdiction of the court. The petitioner argued that Ord. 18 did not apply to a petition.

Held, striking out parts of the amended points of claim, that although a petition was not a pleading the points of claim were to be treated as a pleading to which the rules of court applied. The court should require late amendments to be fully particularised and it should be careful to ensure that oppression was not caused by allowing the parties to raise facts which gave rise to a grievance but which did not constitute conduct of the affairs of the company and could not found a petition.

UNISOFT GROUP (NO. 3), *Re* [1994] 1 BCLC 609, Harman J.

4195. Pleadings—amendment to name of respondent—substitution of party—enforcement of unfair dismissal award—claim against temple owned by unincorporated association registered as charity—trustees to be identified as respondent rather than temple—whether jurisdiction to make amendment

In 1989, S, a Hindu priest, issued an originating application in the industrial tribunal claiming unfair dismissal. The respondents were "D, R, B and P as trustees of the Hindu temple". In 1993, after protracted proceedings, S was awarded £10,150 against "The Hindu Temple". D, R, B and P were part of an "ad hoc" committee in effective control of the Hindu Cultural Society Slough, at the time of S's employment and its termination. They were not validly appointed. The Hindu Cultural Society Slough is an unincorporated association, registered as a charity, which owns the Hindu Temple, Slough. In 1994, S sought to enforce the award in the county court, pursuant to the Employment Protection (Consolidation) Act 1978, Sched. 9, para. 7 and C.C.R., Ord. 25, r.12. S applied to amend the name of the respondent from "The Hindu Temple" to "The Trustees and the Executive Committee Members for the time being of the Hindu Cultural Society Slough (alternatively known as the Hindu Temple)". The relevant persons were identified by a Schedule and were validly appointed officers of the Society. D, R, B and P were not listed in the Schedule. A deputy district judge allowed the amendment substituting the new respondents, who then appealed.

Held, that (1) the deputy district judge had no power to allow the amendment as the county court only had jurisdiction to enforce the recovery of the award as if payable under an order of the court; and (2) even if there was a power to amend pursuant to C.C.R., Ord. 15, r.1, then that power could only be exercised after judgment or final decree, and where the effect was to substitute a new party, if there had been a genuine mistake and the defendant well knew who was intended to be sued by the plaintiff. This condition was a long way from being fulfilled in this situation as there were genuine difficulties as to the liability of the current trustees and committee members (*Singh v. Atombrook* [1989] C.L.Y. 2885 considered).

SHARMA v. TRUSTEES AND THE EXECUTIVE COMMITTEE MEMBERS FOR THE TIME BEING OF THE HINDU CULTURAL SOCIETY SLOUGH (aka THE HINDU TEMPLE), May 5, 1995, H.H.J. Hague, Q.C., Slough County Ct. [*Ex rel.* Bernard Lo, Barrister.]

4196. Pleadings—patent infringement—amendment of pleadings—whether conditional pleadings allowed. See BELOIT TECHNOLOGIES v. VALMET PAPER MACHINERY, §3768.

4197. Pleadings—personal injury claims—pre-action inspection—whether case sufficiently pleaded

P suffered a tennis elbow type injury allegedly by reason of the repetitive nature of her work for D on a bottling and capping line at their factory. A claim was intimated by letter in general terms as aforesaid and inspection facilities sought to allow an engineer to visit the relevant part of the factory and to report on the production line. The application was opposed on the basis that P's case was not presently put or "pleaded" with particularity and inspection prior to the case being put with particularity amounted to a "fishing" expedition.

Held, that P's application would be granted. P indicated sufficiently the broad nature of the allegations to be made. P was in possession of a full legal aid certificate and the court was satisfied that proceedings would be issued in any event. If proceedings were going to be issued, then it was likely that at some stage there would be an inspection and if that inspection took place then it would be at a later stage when considerable costs had been incurred on both sides impinging on the public purse. Referring to the *Roper* case, it was indicated that since 1980 there was a new approach in the courts of openness and "cards on the table" (*Roper v. Slack and Parr* [1981] C.L.Y. 2165 relied upon).

PARKER v. ICAL, November 23, 1994; Deputy District Judge Brooks; Bolton County Ct. [*Ex rel. Christopher Limb, Barrister*].

4198. Pleadings—purpose of pleadings in litigation

Pleadings were to enable the other party to know the case to meet. They were not for the purpose of delay or games-playing.

TRUST SECURITIES HOLDINGS v. SIR ROBERT MCALPINE, *The Times*, December 21, 1994, C.A.

4199. Pleadings—substitution of party—expiry of limitation period—whether constituting new claim—whether court having jurisdiction to allow substitution

[Limitation Act 1980 (c.58), s.35(2); R.S.C., Ord. 15, r.7.]

The second defendant (PTP) appealed against the decision to allow Y health authority to substitute, under R.S.C., Ord. 15, r.7, a health trust as plaintiffs after the relevant limitation period had expired. PTP claimed that the substitution constituted a new claim under s.35(2) of the Limitation Act 1980 and therefore the court did not have jurisdiction to allow substitution.

Held, dismissing the appeal, that the substitution of the trust did not constitute the making of a new claim within the meaning of s.35(2), and the section had no bearing on the court's discretion to order substitution in the circumstances provided for by Ord. 15, r.7 (*Toprak Enerji Sanayi AS v. Sale Tilney Technology* [1994] C.L.Y. 3798 not followed).

YORKSHIRE REGIONAL HEALTH AUTHORITY v. FAIRCLOUGH BUILDING, *The Times*, November 16, 1995, C.A.

4200. Precedent—previous court's decision on question of fact—principles of law assumed—whether court bound

The court was not bound by a previous court's decision on a question of fact, nor by a principle of law which was only assumed in the previous proceedings.

R. v. SECRETARY OF STATE FOR THE HOME DEPARTMENT, *ex p.* KUET, *The Independent*, February 20, 1995, C.A.

4201. Preliminary ruling—judgment already given by Court of Appeal—whether Court of Appeal *functus officio*—whether House of Lords acting adminstratively or judicially in refusing leave to appeal

[Treaty of Rome, Arts. 86, 177; Patents Act 1977 (c.37), s.44.]

The essence of a preliminary ruling is that it must precede the judgment of the referring court. Once the domestic court has given judgment and its order has been drawn up it is *functus officio* and has no power to make a reference under Art. 177.

P brought an action for patent infringement against D. P applied to strike out certain paragraphs of the defence relating to Art. 86 Treaty of Rome. D sought leave to amend its Art. 86 pleading. No application was made by D for a reference under Art. 177. The High Court struck out the Euro-defence and refused leave to amend. D appealed to the Court of Appeal which upheld the judge's decision and refused leave to appeal to the House of Lords. D applied to the Court of Appeal for a reference to the European Court of Justice under Art. 177. This application was adjourned until D had petitioned the House of Lords for leave to appeal and had been refused. D then renewed its application to the Court of Appeal for an Art. 177 reference. P contended that the Court of Appeal was *functus officio* as it had already given judgment and had no jurisdiction to make a preliminary reference under Art. 177.

Held, refusing D's application, that (1) Art. 177 confers on the European Court of Justice jurisdiction to give preliminary rulings. The essence of a preliminary ruling is that it must precede the judgment of the referring court. Once the domestic court has given judgment and its order has been drawn up it is *functus officio* and has no power to make a reference under Art. 177. The Court of Appeal was therefore *functus officio* and could not make the reference (*Magnavision v. General Optical Council* [1987] 2 C.M.L.R. 262, *Fratelli Pardini v. Ministero del Commercio con l'Estero* [1988] E.C.R. 2041 applied); (2) where there is no right to apply to the House of Lords for leave to appeal from a decision of the Court of Appeal on a refusal by the Court of Appeal for leave to appeal against the decision of the court below, then the Court of Appeal will be the court of last resort. Where, on a refusal by the Court of Appeal to grant leave to appeal there is a right to apply to the House of Lords for such leave, then the House of Lords is the court of last resort (*Bulmer (H.P.) v. Bollinger* [1974] C.L.Y. 1471 referred to); (3) in granting or refusing leave to appeal the House of Lords is acting in its judicial capacity not an administrative capacity; and (4) if the House of Lords had considered that a reference was necessary it could have granted leave to appeal. The House of Lords had declined to do this and it was not for the Court of Appeal to review that decision.

CHIRON CORP. v. MUREX DIAGNOSTICS (NO. 8) [1995] F.S.R. 309, C.A.

4202. Professional negligence—surveyors—mortgage valuation report—proceedings not issued within limitation period—whether statute barred. See HEATHCOTE AND HEATHCOTE v. DAVID MARKS & CO., §3712.

4203. Reporting restrictions—application for revocation of orders—disclosure of identity of child—whether permissible to raise funds for medical treatment—whether in best interests interests of child

[Children and Young Persons Act 1933 (c.12), s.39.]

B, the father of a child suffering from a serious illness who was refused NHS funding for medical treatment, applied for the revocation of orders laying down reporting restrictions under s.39 of the Children and Young Persons Act

1933, preventing the disclosure of her identity. B argued that, as he wanted to raise money to fund further treatment, publicity was no longer harmful to his daughter, who was now aware of the nature of her illness, and the reporting restrictions might jeopardise an exclusive publishing agreement with a national newspaper which had agreed to help fund the child's future treatment.

Held, allowing the application, that the court had a duty to protect the best interests of the child and although the necessity to court publicity for financial gain was regrettable, the maintenance of reporting restrictions could not be justified if their consequences could result in the denial of potentially life-saving treatment.

R. v. CAMBRIDGE AND HUNTINGDON HEALTH AUTHORITY, *ex p.* B. (NO. 2), *The Times*, October 27, 1995, C.A.

4204. Reporting restrictions—proceedings concerning children—judge's discretion to make order and hear representations from persons with legitimate interest—procedure to be followed when making order restricting reporting. See CROOK, *Re*, §3546.

4205. *Res judicata*—local authority housing—illness of minor as result of disrepair—whether *res judicata*—whether minor and mother-tenant single party

[C.C.R., Ord. 10, r.10.]

C, a minor with Down's Syndrome, appealed against a decision refusing a claim for damages against H council. The claim arose as a result of illness suffered due to disrepair of the council home C shared with the rest of the family. C's claim was refused under the principle of *res judicata* as C's mother, in her role as tenant, had already reached a settlement in the same matter.

Held, allowing the appeal, that although it was in the public interest to have a single action wherever possible, there was no justification for extending the doctrine of *res judicata* as applied in *Yat Tung Investment & Co. v. Dao Heng Bank* [1975] C.L.Y. 211 and *Talbot v. Berkshire County Council* [1993] C.L.Y. 1851 to the present case. H's argument that the nexus between the mother and C meant they should be treated as a single party could not be upheld, as to follow it would create the paradoxical situation that C's claim was barred, but separate actions by older siblings could go ahead. However, separate actions were to be avoided where possible, and local authorities faced with claims by a tenant should enquire if other members of the household were likely to advance their own claims.

[*Per curiam*: The practice of claims brought by a tenant being settled in judgments given for their entire family should cease. Where disabled persons were involved, the practice risked subverting C.C.R., Ord. 10, r.10, which existed to safeguard their interests. In addition it also ran the risk of tempting poorer claimants to sacrifice the long-term interests of their dependants for short-term gain.]

C. (A MINOR) v. HACKNEY LONDON BOROUGH COUNCIL, *The Times*, November 10, 1995, C.A.

4206. Service—notice of trial listing—not less than 21 days' notice required—whether Saturday a day of service

[C.C.R., Ord. 17, r.11(10).]

D were applying to have a trial listing removed from the list. The basis of their application was that the listing officer had not given "not less than 21 days' notice" to every party, as required under C.C.R., Ord. 17, r.11(10). The trial was listed to start on June 12, 1995. Although it was accepted that the listing officer had sent out the notice by first class post on May 18, D's solicitors maintained that they did not receive it on May 19. A weekend then intervened and the first working day thereafter (when the notice was first seen) was May 22. The judge agreed that for the purpose of assessing the relevant period, Ord. 1, r.9(2) applied. Accordingly, the trial start date was to be discounted. P did not support D's application, and contended that, since it was accepted that the notice was sent first class on May 18, it was proper to assume that if not received by D on May 19, it would have been received on May 20, which was a Saturday. P contended that, in this case, Saturday could be a day of service.

Held, that, applying Ord. 7, r.1 and the notes thereto in the County Court Practice, Saturday could not be a day of service. It was accepted that the first working day that the notice was received was May 22. The judge, again applying Ord. 1, r.9(2) again discounted that day. Accordingly, he accepted D's assertion that they had not had "not less than 21 days' notice", there being just 20 days' notice. However, he accepted P's other submission that he had power to abridge time under Ord. 13, r.4. In this case it was agreed that D's dates of unavailability that had been lodged on May 11 had not excluded the trial dates. Furthermore, D's only stated difficulty was not linked to difficulty in that regard, but that they perceived a difficulty in now effecting a payment into court. The judge found that with pleadings having been long since closed, and evidence exchanged, this was not a good reason. Further, that the breach of Ord. 17, r.11(10) was small. He therefore found no merit in D's application. Accordingly, he abridged time for the notice of trial and dismissed D's application with costs. D was refused leave to appeal to the C.A.

MAPLE v. GRIBBLE BOOTH & TAYLOR, May 26, 1995, H.H.J. MacIntosh, Exeter County Ct. [*Ex rel.* Crosse & Crosse, Solicitors, Exeter.]

4207. Service—notices by post—deeming provisions in articles of association—effect of non-delivery. See THUNDERCREST, *Re*, §608.

4208. Service—notices on landlords—address at which notices may be served by tenant—whether company's registered office sufficient—whether necessary to specify that address one on which notices may be served. See KNOLLDOWNE PROPERTIES v. BROMLEY & COGGER, §3002.

4209. Service—out of jurisdiction—letter of credit issued by Indian bank with no London branch—payable in London—jurisdiction. See BANK OF BARODA v. VYSYA BANK, §398.

4210. Service—writ—out of jurisdiction—whether service outside jurisdiction appropriate

[R.S.C., Ord. 11, r.1(1).]

CN, a U.S. insurance company, issued a summons to set aside an order giving DR leave to serve proceedings out of the jurisdiction. DR was a successor in title to certain reinsurance business undertaken by a company which had subsequently gone into liquidation, and leave to serve by way of a writ that a reinsurance contract with CN was void and unenforceable had been granted on the ground that the claim fell within the terms of the R.S.C., Ord. 11, r.1(1)(d).

Held, that although DR had shown that it had a good arguable case that its claim came within Ord. 11, r.1(1)(d), service outside the jurisdiction was inappropriate as the circumstances surrounding the contested agreements were more strongly connected with England than the U.S. and, furthermore, concurrent proceedings were taking place in New York. Service of the writ was accordingly set aside.

DR INSURANCE CO. v. CENTRAL NATIONAL INSURANCE CO. OF OMAHA, *Lloyd's List*, November 2, 1995 (I.D.), D.C.

4211. Service—writ—personal representatives—order appointing representatives not made or served within writ's lifetime—limitation period expired—whether extension of writ to be granted or discretion to waive service requirements

P was a passenger in a car which was involved in a collision. D, the driver of the car, died in the collision. P claimed damages against the estate. D's solicitors wrote to P's solicitors explaining that in order for P to pursue a personal injury claim, P must issue a writ and then apply for an order that personal representatives of D be made party to the proceedings, under R.S.C., Ord. 15, r.6A. D's solicitors advised that two partners of their firm would be prepared to represent the estate for these purposes. Subsequently, the names of two partners were given to D's solicitors. D's solicitors confirmed that they had made an application *ex parte* for an order that the two partners be named as D's representatives, and made an application for a service of the schedule of special damages to be served 56 days after service of the writ. In fact, service of the writ was not effected within the four-month period. About 14 months later, just a few days before the limitation period was due to expire, another writ was issued, precisely the same as the first, but for its date of issue. D's solicitors acknowledged service of the new writ, and issued a summons to strike it out as an abuse of process. No order pursuant to Ord. 15, r.6A, had been made, and no copy Order was therefore served with the writ. In fact the application had been made within the validity of the writ, but by an error of the court, had not been made. P's solicitors had proceeded on the basis that the order had been made. The district judge, in part responsible for the error, refused to strike out the writ as an abuse of process on February 9, 1994, and made the order under Ord. 15, r.6A(4)(a) appointing the two partners as D's representatives. The application under Ord. 15, r.6A had been made within the validity of the writ, but the order was made over three months after the time for service of that writ had expired without having been extended. On February 21, the district judge made an *ex parte* order extending the 1993 writ for four months, which meant that it would expire on February 27. In fact the lifetime of the 1993 writ and the limitation period had expired. D applied to set aside this order, which was granted. P appealed, arguing that the order appointing the named partners as D's representatives regularised the earlier procedural deficiencies, or that any irregularities should be corrected under Ord. 2, r.1, or that under Ord. 6, r.8 the facts revealed a good reason justifying an extension of the 1993 writ.

Held, that (1) failure to serve the order appointing the representatives meant that the representatives did not become parties to the action and could not be regularised by a subsequent order; (2) it was not appropriate to exercise the court's discretion to waive the service requirements. P's solicitors had perpetrated a long train of errors, while D's solicitors had behaved perfectly properly throughout, in particular they had not been lulling P into inactivity. D would obviously suffer prejudice if the judge were to exercise his discretion under Ord. 2, r.1 (*Foster v. Turnbull*, May 15, 1990, C.A., unrep., *Chappell v. Cooper* [1980] C.L.Y. 1676 considered); and (3) although the court had been in error in unjustifiably raising a query about the validity of the papers, and had failed to raise this with P's solicitors, P were at fault in a number of ways, in particular failing to serve copies of the order and the writ on the new parties. No good reason had been shown for their failure to pursue the court's failure to issue the order (*Singh (Joginder) v. Duport Harper Foundries* [1994] C.L.Y. 3827, *Kelliher v. Savill Engineering* [1994] C.L.Y. 3766 considered).

WEBB v. PERSONAL REPRESENTATIVES OF WHATLEY (DEC'D), September 26, 1994, H.H.J. Grabiner sitting as a High Court judge. [*Ex rel.* Bunkers, Solicitors, Hove.]

4212. Set-off—carriage charges—domestic carriage by land—whether set-off allowed in such cases

D were retailers who engaged P, carriers, to transport and deliver Christmas hampers. P's claim was, in the main, their carriage charges for effecting those deliveries. D did not dispute P's claim, but sought to set off cross-claims for short delivery and other breaches of contract against P's claim. P contended that their claim was for freight charges and that the law was that there could be no deduction by way of abatement or set-off from such charges. D accepted that this was the case in shipping cases, and in international freight cases, but argued that the rule should not apply to charges for domestic carriage by land. The only case referred to which dealt with domestic carriage by land was *A.S. Jones v. Burton Gold Medal Biscuits*, in which the rule preventing set-off had been applied.

Held, that left to itself the court would have decided that the rule preventing set-off did not apply to domestic carriage by land, and it was not bound by the first instance decision of *A.S. Jones*. However, that case was indistinguishable from the instant case, and it would not be right to depart from it at first instance (*A.S. Jones v. Burton Gold Medal Biscuits*, April 11, 1984, Nolan J., unrep. considered).

UNITED CARRIERS v. HERITAGE FOOD GROUP, *The Times*, March 8, 1995, May J.

4213. Set-off—charterparty dispute—mandatory stay—whether plaintiff entitled to set-off

[Arbitration Act 1975 (c.3).]

A defendant's claim for hire at a stipulated rate is a claim for a liquidated debt which can be set off against a plaintiff's claim.

P and D fell into disputes over a time charterparty. One dispute was resolved by arbitration, and D agreed to pay a certain sum to P. The second dispute also went to arbitration, but remained in part unresolved, with the parties disagreeing over how many days the vessel was off-hire. D sought to retain part of the sum owing to P as set-off for their claims relating to the period when the vessel was off-hire. P issued a writ seeking payment, and D claimed the right of set-off. The judge gave judgment for P.

Held, dismissing D's appeal, that D's claim in the second dispute was capable of giving rise to set-off, but because D's claim was subject to a mandatory stay under the Arbitration Act 1975 they were not entitled to leave to defend.

AECTRA REFINING AND MANUFACTURING v. EXMAR [1994] 1 W.L.R. 1634, C.A.

4214. Set-off—common law—whether sums due on other contracts between the same parties can be set off as mutual debts

D contracted to construct petrol stations throughout England and Wales. D subcontracted the work to P. Nine such contracts were entered into between P and D on September 28, 1989. P carried out the bulk of the work in most instances but did not complete it in every case. On September 4, 1990 an administrative receiver was appointed by P's bank. P was wound up by the court on December 5, 1990. The administrative receiver commenced proceedings to recover sums owed with reference to work performed at a particular petrol station. D raised set-off of amounts due under different contracts, specifically equitable set-off, set-off of mutual debts at common law and sought to rely on the insolvency rules. D appealed against the judge's dismissal of all three counts of set-off.

Held, dismissing the appeal, that at common law D can only set off money demands which can be ascertained readily and without difficulty (*Stooke v. Taylor* [1880] 5 QBD 569). D's claims were based on estimated valuations the accuracy of which could only be ascertained by litigation or arbitration. The claims were therefore not valid claims for set-off at common law (*Hanak v. Green* [1958] C.L.Y. 2734, *Axel Johnson Petroleum AB v. M.G. Mineral Group* [1992] C.L.Y. 3617 considered).

HARGREAVES v. ACTION 2000 [1993] 9 Const. L.J. 193, C.A.

4215. Small claims—arbitration reference—£1,000 limit—whether reasonable prospect of recovering more—appeal against referral to arbitration—whether appeal reasonable

P was a fitter in D's factory. He suffered a fairly severe contusion injury to the back of his right hand when a spanner broke in his hand. He had no time off work. The bruising and swelling cleared up in one week, although the hand continued to be painful and tender for a further week. He could not do the gardening for four weeks. In eight to 10 weeks the residual aches and pains had resolved, however, at the date of his medical report, 10 months after the accident, P's wrist continued to ache on lifting anything heavy. This problem was expected to resolve in a few more months, with no future problems and no permanent disability. P claimed damages in respect of his injury limited to £3,000. Special damages of £11·75 were claimed. The district judge decided, following the decision of the C.A. in *Afzal v. Ford*, that P had no reasonable prospect of recovering more than £1,000, and the case was automatically referred for arbitration pursuant to C.C.R., Ord. 19, r.3. P appealed to the judge against the decision of the district judge.

Held, dismissing the appeal, that P had no reasonable expectation of recovering over £1,000. The judge said it was clear from Afzal v. Ford that the courts should discourage interlocutory applications in small cases. P should have accepted the district judge's decision. The appeal constituted unreasonable conduct under Ord. 19, r.4(2)(c) and D were awarded their costs of the appeal (*Afzal v. Ford Motor Co.* [1994] C.L.Y. 3776 considered).

RAJARATNAM v. FORD MOTOR CO., June 1, 1995, H.H.J. Platt, Romford County Ct. [*Ex rel.* Toby Gee, Barrister, One Paper Buildings.]

4216. Small claims—arbitration reference—false imprisonment—very short period of detention—£1,000 limit—whether claim likely to exceed limit—whether right to trial by jury relevant—whether referral to arbitration appropriate

[County Courts Act 1984 (c.28), s.66; C.C.R., Ord. 19, r.3.]

P claimed damages, including aggravated and exemplary damages, against D for false imprisonment and trespass. The period of detention relied upon was very short. P issued proceedings claiming damages limited to £5,000. D successfully applied to the district judge for an order that the case be referred to arbitration on the basis that the damages, if awarded, would not exceed £1,000. P appealed, submitting not only that any damages received would be likely to exceed £1,000, but also that, in any event, it was wrong to refer the case to arbitration. They argued that claims involving allegations of false imprisonment, which would normally carry the right to trial by jury, were in a special category, and were not, for example, comparable with claims considered in *Afzal v. Ford Motor Co.* P further argued that the fact that they would lose legal aid and would, if the matter proceeded to arbitration, have to conduct the case in person (including cross-examining police officers and making submissions as to law) were relevant factors.

Held, that the district judge had not been wrong to conclude that the level of damages involved would not exceed £1,000. However, having referred to the County Courts Act 1984, s.66 and to C.C.R., Ord. 19, r.3, he held that it was relevant to consider that if the matter was referred to arbitration, P would lose their right to trial by jury, given by s.66, which he regarded as important. The subject matter of the claim and the other relevant circumstances meant that it was inappropriate for the matter to proceed by way of arbitration and accordingly the appeal was allowed, and the matter ordered to proceed by way of trial by jury (*Afzal v. Ford Motor Co.* [1995] 5 C.L. 382 considered).

DUFFUS AND DUFFUS v. CHIEF CONSTABLE OF DERBYSHIRE, March 14, 1995, H.H.J. Styler, Derby County Ct. [*Ex rel.* Mark Rogers, Barrister, 50 High Pavement, Nottingham.]

4217. Small claims—arbitration reference—health and safety at work—complexity of case—default judgment set aside—whether reference to arbitration to be rescinded

[C.C.R., Ord. 19, r.2(iv)(a).]

On February 9, 1993, P sustained injury at work whilst lifting a base plate off a pallet with a crane, when an eye belt came out of its threaded hole and, still attached to the wire strop, it shot across the pallet striking P on the shoulder. Fortunately, P sustained relatively minor injuries, namely discomfort in the left arm and shoulder for several weeks and a minor scar on the shoulder. No permanent disability from the injury was anticipated. P was off work for one week and for the following two weeks upon his return was unable to work above shoulder height. Liability having been disputed, P was left with no option but to commence court proceedings. It was felt there were no reasonable prospects of obtaining greater than £1,000, therefore proceedings were issued limiting the claim to £1,000. D failed to lodge a defence within the requisite period, and on the fifteenth day, judgment was entered for damages to be assessed plus costs on Scale 1. D successfully applied to have judgment set aside, but P's solicitors counter-appealed that, should judgment be set aside and D be granted leave to file a defence, the reference to arbitration should then be rescinded.

Held, allowing P's application, and rescinding the reference to arbitration, that this was a case falling within the provisions of C.C.R. Ord. 19, r.2(iv)(a), namely that it involved a difficult question of law or a question of fact of exceptional complexity. In reaching this decision, the district judge took note of the fact that the pleaded case was sufficiently complex to take it out of the norm of Factories Act cases. There were a wide ranging set of allegations pleaded, including reference to the construction of a crane, the strength and maintenance of a crane and matters of instruction of P as to safety. The district judge further found that the absence of adequate discovery would be a serious fetter to P in this case. Having considered the rules, and the decision in *Afzal v. Ford Motor Co.* the district judge rescinded the reference to arbitration, with the costs of the application to P on Scale 1 (*Afzal v. Ford Motor Co.* [1994] C.L.Y. 3776 applied).

BROOKE v. BRITISH AEROSPACE, June 1, 1995, Deputy District Judge Furness, Leeds County Ct. [*Ex rel.* Peter Carson, Rowley Ashworth, Solicitors, Leeds.]

4218. Small claims—arbitration reference—health and safety at work—whether too complicated to refer to arbitration

[C.C.R., Ord. 19, r.9(2)(b).]

P, aged 22, was employed as a spot welder, and suffered a 2cm laceration to the tip of his left index finger on his non-dominant hand, whilst operating an allegedly defective electronic welding machine. Sutures were inserted; he did not lose any time off work, but was placed on light duties for two weeks. The medical evidence was agreed and it was accepted that, six months after the accident, the tip of his finger was still extremely tender if banged or knocked, he suffered a tingling discomfort in cold weather, and he still found it difficult to pick up objects between his left thumb and index finger because of the tenderness felt. There was a 2cm scar, minimal tissue deformity on the site of the scar and, although there was still some scope for improvement at the date of the medical examinations seven months after the accident, the residual symptoms were expected to be permanent. No special damages were claimed. The particulars of claim limited the claim to £3,000, and relied upon breaches of the Factories Act 1961, s.14 and of the Provision and Use of Work Equipment Regulations 1992, the Personal Protective Equipment at Work Regulations 1992, and the Management of Health and Safety at Work Regulations 1992. D applied, pursuant to C.C.R., Ord. 19, r.9(2)(b) to refer the matter to arbitration, on the basis that P had no reasonable prospect of recovering damages exceeding £1,000.

Held, that there were reasonable prospects of P recovering more than £1,000 at trial. Further, regardless of the question of *quantum*, P's claim involved difficult questions of law, and questions of fact of exceptional complexity. P's solicitor had commissioned an expert report in relation to the machine, which had been significantly modified since the accident. It would be inappropriate for P to conduct his case on the basis of the regulations and the Factories Act, without representation. Accordingly, the court decided, pursuant to Ord. 19, r.3, that the matter should proceed by trial in open court (*Afzal v. Ford Motor Co.* [1994] C.L.Y. 3776 considered).

FRAIL v. L.D.V., September 1, 1995, District Judge Singleton, Birmingham County Ct. [*Ex rel.* Nicholas Xydias, Barrister, 5 Fountain Court, Birmingham.]

4219. Small claims—arbitration reference—hire charges disputed—payment of lower sum returned—whether matter to be referred to arbitration

Following a road traffic accident on November 9, 1994, P's solicitors wrote a letter before action dated November 14, 1994. By letter dated November 17, D confirmed that they were insured for third party liability, and stated that they did not propose to raise an issue as to liability. P was claiming repairs, hire charges and miscellaneous expenses. By letter dated January 4, 1995, D confirmed that they would pay the repairs in full, but did not accept the hire account as given and offered only two days' hire. D sent P a cheque for the repair account together with two days' hire. That cheque was returned by P as unacceptable on January 9, 1995. By letter dated January 12, 1995, D informed P's solicitors that the cheque did not have any conditions attached with regards to acceptance, and returned the cheque. On January 19, P's solicitors returned the cheque, informed D that P's instructions were to pursue a claim for the entire amount of the hire charges, gave notice pursuant to the Road Traffic Act 1988, s.152, and enclosed a copy of the particulars of claim. On February 1, 1995, D's solicitors came on the record as acting for D, enclosing a defence filed that day, and giving notice of their intention to issue an application alleging that P's proceedings were an abuse of process. On February 13, 1995, P's solicitors wrote to the court to set the matter down for hearing, enclosing the appropriate fee. The matter was listed for May 4, 1995. On March 3, D's solicitors served P's solicitors with an application for the matter to be referred to arbitration on the grounds that (a) it had always been admitted that the damages to the vehicle should be paid, (b) D paid to P a sum for repairs to the car and therefore the only matter in issue related to hire which was a figure below £1,000, and (c) the most suitable venue for disposal of the action was arbitration. The district judge felt that it was curious that there was no allegation in the defence that the matter should be referred to arbitration, and further noted that if the hire charge was allowed in full, the claim was probably worth over £1,000. The deputy district judge took into account that the matter was listed for an assessment on May 4, and refused the application and gave P his costs of the application.

Held, on D's appeal, that if P were awarded the full amount of the hire charge the claim would exceed £1,000, and the deputy district judge had been correct in dismissing D's application. The application to refer the case to arbitration had been made too late, after assessment had been given and contrary to the guidelines laid down (*Afzal v. Ford Motor Co.* [1994] C.L.Y. 3776, *Hoptroff v. TNT Express (U.K.)* [1994] C.L.Y. 3775 considered).

DODD v. TNT EXPRESS (U.K.), June 23, 1995, Recorder Bulmer, Q.C., Birkenhead County Ct. [*Ex rel.* Michael W. Halsall, Solicitors, Merseyside.]

4220. Small claims—arbitration reference—whether reasonable expectation of recovering more than £1,000—relevance of other awards

P's claim was in respect of personal injury sustained in an accident at D's factory. Proceedings were issued on January 12, 1995, in which P claimed damages not exceeding £3,000. D pleaded in their defence that P had no reasonable expectation of recovering more than £1,000, and that the claim should accordingly be automatically referred for arbitration. The district judge formed his own view of the amount involved, in accordance with the procedure suggested by the C.A. in *Afzal v. Ford Motor Co.*, and referred the case for arbitration. P applied for an order rescinding the arbitration reference pursuant to C.C.R., Ord. 19, r.3. P sought to rely on *Bacarese v. Strong & Fisher* (Halsbury's Abridgment 1990, para. 773) in which the plaintiff's discomfort after an accident, less serious than P's injury, resolved after a few days and she was awarded £900.

Held, that *Bacarese* was an exceptional award, and that he would not take it into account in deciding whether P had a reasonable expectation of recovering over £1,000. P had no such reasonable expectation, and the appeal was dismissed. Further, the application constituted unreasonable conduct under C.C.R., Ord. 19, r.4(2)(c), and D were given the costs of the application (*Afzal v. Ford Motor Co.* [1994] C.L.Y. 3776 applied; *Bacarese v. Strong & Fisher* (Halsbury's Abridgment 1990, para. 773) distinguished).

GIRLING v. FORD MOTOR CO., June 7, 1995, Deputy District Judge Perry, Romford County Ct. [*Ex rel.* Toby Gee, One Paper Buildings.]

4221. Small claims—jurisdiction—district judge—breach of landlord and tenant legislation—whether district judge having power to grant specific performance

[C.C.R. 1981, Ord. 13, r.6, Ord. 19, r.3; Landlord and Tenant Act 1985 (c.70), s.11.]

J and another appealed against decisions that their claims for specific performance and damages against their landlord L council for breach of a repairing obligation under s.11 of the Landlord and Tenant Act 1985 could be determined by the district judge within his jurisdiction for small claims arbitration.

Held, dismissing the appeal, that a district judge could exercise all the powers of a High Court judge, including the power to grant specific performance and other injunctive relief, as confirmed by C.C.R., Ord. 13, r.6(2). The judges below had not misapplied *Afzal v. Ford Motor Co.* as requiring all small claims under s.11 to be automatically referred to arbitration. Automatic referral could be rescinded under Ord. 19, r.3(2), but the final decision lay with the district judge as to whether it would be unreasonable to proceed to arbitration, having regard to the subject-matter and circumstances of the parties. The small claims arbitration procedure would be the norm in most s.11 claims as they were relatively simple. A claimant's lack of representation could not form a ground for ordering trial in court as the burden upon the tenant could be reduced with the benefit of expert evidence. However, trial could be ordered if, despite the small sum involved, justice could not be served to an unrepresented claimant (*Afzal v. Ford Motor Co.* [1994] 6 C.L. 360 considered).

JOYCE v. LIVERPOOL CITY COUNCIL; WYNNE v. SAME [1995] 3 All E.R. 110, C.A.

4222. Stay of proceedings—personal injuries action—matter set down for trial—application for stay pending defence's medical examination of plaintiff—whether stay to be granted

Following a motorcycle accident in July 1990, P suffered injuries to the lower left leg. Medical evidence was obtained in the form of two consultant orthopaedic surgeons' reports which were served when proceedings were instituted in July 1993. Following an unsuccessful attempt to negotiate a settlement, and the rejection of D's payment in June 1994, D requested their own medical examination of P. P's solicitors refused, on grounds of delay, to consent and set the matter down for trial. D then applied for a stay of P's claim unless and until P released his medical notes and attended an examination by D's expert. At the hearing of the application it was accepted by P's representative that there was a disparity between the expert's report and P's personal interpretation of his injuries.

Held, that D's application for a stay, and that request for a medical examination would be refused, with costs to P, upon the court being assured that the only medical evidence P intended to rely upon was the two pre-existing reports. The court took the view that the trial judge was likely to rely upon the expert's views, in favour of the lay client. Adjudication was rejected (*Farrow v. Davies* [1994] 6 C.L. 85 considered).

HOLLOWAY v. FUDIO, November 25, 1994; District Judge Edwards; Southampton County Ct. [*Ex rel. Guy Opperman, Barrister*].

4223. Stay of proceedings—personal injuries action—psychiatric examination—refusal to allow friend to be present—appeal—whether judge's decision reasonable

W appealed against a county court judge's decision that her action for personal injuries against A council be stayed until after she had undergone a psychiatric examination by a consultant psychiatrist. W, a nervous person, had wished to have a companion with her throughout the examination but the psychiatrist had refused to allow this. The judge accepted that her request to take her friend along was reasonable in view of her nervousness, but viewed her insistence on having her friend present throughout the examination as unreasonable.

Held, dismissing the appeal, that there was no basis on which to conclude that the judge erred in reaching this decision.

WHITEHEAD v. AVON COUNTY COUNCIL, *The Times*, May 3, 1995, C.A.

4224. Stay of proceedings—professional inquiry—whether to be stayed pending civil action. See R. v. CHANCE, *ex p.* SMITH, §147.

4225. Subpoena—expert witness—*ex parte* application to set-aside—made by third party for whom expert had already agreed to appear at another trial—whether jurisdiction to entertain application

P subpoenaed an expert employment consultant to give evidence in a personal injury action taking place in Durham. Unknown to P, the employment consultant had previously agreed to appear at another hearing in Cambridge. Two days before the date of hearing, the plaintiff in the Cambridge action applied *ex parte* in the Durham action for an order that the subpoena be set aside. That order was made, not to be enforced until P, in the Durham action, had the opportunity of making representations. The following day there was a hearing at which both plaintiffs made representations.

Held, restoring the subpoena, that the court does not have jurisdiction to hear an application to set a subpoena aside from a person who is neither a party to the action, nor the subpoenaed witness himself.

KELLY v. DURHAM COUNTY COUNCIL, April 27, 1995, H.H.J. Carr sitting as a judge of the High Ct. [*Ex rel.* Nicholas Hill, Barrister, 6 Park Square, Leeds.]

4226. Subpoena *duces tecum*—application to set aside subpoena—non-party required to produce documents on a date prior to main trial date—absence of authority for new practice compelling early production of documents—whether subpoena defective—whether interlocutory practice flawed

The interlocutory practice of calling for the production of documents specified in a subpoena *duces tecum* on a date prior to the date of the intended trial is not flawed.

In an action claiming damages for professional negligence the plaintiff issued a subpoena *duces tecum* against J, a non-party. J applied to set aside the subpoena on the ground, *inter alia*, that it was defective in that it called for the production of documents on a date other than the day fixed for the main trial and that there was no warrant in the Rules of the Supreme Court for that practice.

Held, dismissing the application, that the court had a wide measure of control over the manner in which a trial would be conducted, including the manner in which it would receive evidence. Consequently the interlocutory practice which had developed of calling for the production of documents specified in a subpoena *duces tecum* on a date prior to the date of the intended trial was not flawed if it could be done conveniently and without injustice (dictum of Donaldson M.R. in *Williams v. Barclays Bank* [1987] C.L.Y. 1674 applied).

KHANNA v. LOVELL WHITE DURRANT (A FIRM) [1994] 4 All E.R. 267, Sir Donald Nicholls, V.-C.

4227. Summary judgment—adjournment—failure properly to register the mortgagee's charge—registered as equitable charge—whether solicitor liable in restitution to mortgagor

[R.S.C., Ord. 14.]

B appealed against a decision adjourning their application for summary judgment. A solicitor had failed properly to register the mortgagee's charge which as a result was registered as an equitable rather than a legal charge.

Held, allowing the appeal, that it was a term of the trust that the charge be effected by the solicitor and therefore he was liable in restitution to the mortgagor. There could be no objection to more than one application for summary judgment under R.S.C. Ord. 14, if the second claim was founded on a different factual or legal basis.

BRISTOL AND WEST BUILDING SOCIETY v. BRANDON, *The Times*, March 9, 1995, Coleman J.

4228. Summary judgment—affidavit—source of deponent's information not clear—whether fatal to summary judgment

B bank were awarded summary judgment for £55,105·25 in respect of two unrecovered loans. D appealed on the ground, *inter alia*, that the affidavit in support of the bank's application was defective because it did not identify the source of the deponent's information or belief. The point had not been taken below by D, who was then acting in person, and the Court of Appeal allowed B to put in a second affidavit which B contended cured the defects in the first one.

Held, that the defence and counterclaim (pleaded by D whilst acting in person) were not arguable, but allowed D's appeal on the ground that neither affidavit made clear from which source the deponent (B's solicitor) had received particular information. Because Ord. 14 proceedings deprive a defendant of his opportunity to defend a plaintiff's claim and, in particular, the opportunity of hearing and cross-examining the plaintiff's witnesses, it is all the more necessary that the technical requirements of an affidavit in support of the application should be observed so that a defendant and the court can assess whether the information or belief as to material matters on which the plaintiff's claim is based were derived directly or indirectly from persons who could be expected to have the necessary knowledge or be the keepers of necessary documents.

BARCLAYS BANK v. PIPER, May 24, 1995, C.A. [*Ex rel.* Nicholas Stanton, Barrister, 169 Temple Chambers, Temple.]

4229. Summary judgment—late application—no real defence to action—whether delay fatal to application for summary judgment

[R.S.C., Ord. 14.]

Where there was no defence to a claim or the defendants could not show that there was an issue in dispute, delay in itself was not fatal to a late application for summary judgment under R.S.C., Ord. 14. Such an application was commendable as it saved the costs and time of a full trial.

BRINKS v. ABU-SALEH, *The Times*, January 30, 1995, Jacob J.

4230. Summary judgment—personal injury—plaintiff pleading *res ipsa loquitur*—alternative explanation for accident not pleaded in defence—whether general denial of negligence sufficient for issue to be tried

[R.S.C., Ord. 14, rr.1, 4.]

Where *res ipsa loquitur* applies, summary judgment under R.S.C., Ord. 14, r.4, will not be refused because theoretical possibilities negativing the inference of negligence exist if the pleaded defence only comprises a general denial of negligence rather than an explanation to the contrary.

P, an actor, was injured during filming when a sledge on which he was being carried overturned. The sledge was under the sole management and control of D. On the evidence, there was nothing wrong with the sledge. P sued for damages for personal injury. In his statement of claim he relied on the maxim *res ipsa loquitur*. D filed a defence denying liability and asserting the occurrence was a true accident but without seeking to provide an alternative explanation. P applied for summary judgment which was granted by the Master. Buckley J. allowed D's appeal on the ground that, although *res ipsa loquitur* applied, there were possibilities negativing the inference of negligence, namely culpability by independent contractors or pure accident.

Held, allowing P's appeal, that (1) "*res ipsa loquitur*" is a convenient label for a group of situations in which an unexplained accident is, as a matter of common sense, the basis for an inference of negligence. On the facts, this was a case in which one could truly say that in the ordinary course of things the accident would not have happened without negligence (*Scott v. London and St. Katherine Docks Co.* (1865) 3 H. & C. 596 referred to); (2) the defence did not seek to provide an explanation negativing the inference of negligence by attributing its cause to independent contractors or to an unforeseen external agency such as a specific, unforeseen, unavoidable and fortuitous occurrence. There was no arguable defence and no issue to be tried. R.S.C., Ord. 14 requires a defendant to show cause and the possibilities referred to by the judge were pure theoretical hypothesis (*Lady Anne Tennant v. Associated Newspapers Group* [1979] C.L.Y. 359 considered).

BERGIN v. DAVID WICKES TELEVISION [1994] P.I.Q.R. P167, C.A.

4231. Supreme court—fees

SUPREME COURT FEES (AMENDMENT) ORDER 1995 (No. 2629 (L.13)) [£1·10], made under the Supreme Court Act 1981, s.130, the Insolvency Act 1986, ss.414, 415 and the Finance Act 1990, s.128; operative on October 30, 1995; amends S.I. 1980 No. 821 by removing exemption from payment of court fees from those receiving income support and civil legal aid and increasing fees for issue of writs, originating summons, motions, petitions, cross-appeals to the High Court, respondent's appeal to the High Court, applications for garnishee orders, charging orders or receivers, applications to examine judgment debtors before officers in the court, appointment of Commercial Court judges as arbitrators, appointment of official receivers as arbitrators, judge arbitrators per day after the first day, official referee arbitrators per day after first day, appeals to the Court of Appeal, applications to the Court of Appeal, applications to a judge to review a taxing officer's decision, issue of companies' winding-up petitions, issue of bankruptcy petions (debtor or creditor), issue of any other petition under the Company or Insolveny Acts and cross-appeals or respondent's notices under the Company or Insolvency Acts. In addition fees payable on obtaining copies of documents are replaced with a single fee, the fee payable on the hearing of a public examination is revoked, search fees are now charged at £5·00 per file rather than £5·00 per hour and a new fee for personal searches of bankruptcy and companies records is introduced.

4232. Supreme Court Procedure Committee—Annual Report 1994

The Supreme Court Procedure Committee which provides a forum for suggestions for practice improvements to be considered has published its twelfth annual report. Copies are available from Ian Johnson at the Lord Chancellor's Department, Southside, Room 4.05, 105 Victoria Street, London, SW1E 6QT. Telephone 0171 210 2108.

4233. Supreme Court Rules

RULES OF THE SUPREME COURT (AMENDMENT) 1995 (No. 2206 (L.9)) [£4·70], made under the Supreme Court Act 1981, ss.18, 51, 84; operative on

December 1, 1995 for rr.52 and 53, October 1, 1995 for the remainder; amend S.I. 1965 No. 1776 as follows: Pt. 1 amends the rules relating to revenue appeals; Pt. 2 imposes a requirement to seek leave to appeal in certain proceedings and clarifies the meaning of "order" for the purposes of that requirement; Pt. 3 introduces a new rule for the taxation of fees arising under a conditional fee agreement between a solicitor and his client; Pt. 4 amends Ord. 115 to take account of the Drug Trafficking Act 1994 to update relevant statutory references, insert new provisions relating to the making of confiscation orders against defendants who have died or absconded and amend the provisions of Ord. 115 dealing with the recovery of property under the 1994 Act; and Pt. 5 makes miscellaneous amendments.

RULES OF THE SUPREME COURT (AMENDMENT NO. 2) 1995 (No. 2897 (L.17)) [£1·10], made under the Supreme Court Act 1981, s.84. In force: December 1, 1995; amend S.I. 1965 No. 1776 by the increase of costs allowed to a litigant in person and the fixed costs recoverable, correct an error in an earlier 1995 amendment and assign appeals on a point of law from the Pensions Ombudsman to the Chancery Division and the imposition of a leave requirement on any appeal from the Chancery Division.

RULES OF THE SUPREME COURT (AMENDMENT NO.3) 1995 (No. 3316 (L.20)), made under the Supreme Court Act 1981 s.85; amends S.I. 1965 No. 1776. In force: January 15, 1996; [£1·95. Various amendments are made to the Rules of the Supreme Court 1965 by these Rules. A new Order 100 is substituted which makes provision for proceedings and service of documents under the Trade Marks Act 1994 and the Olympic Symbol etc. (Protection) Act 1995. Miscellaneous amendments are made to Order 104 which relates to patents proceedings including provision for the serving documents. Rule 8 provides for a praecipe for caveat against release to be filed in Admiralty proceedings when the Admiralty Registry is closed and fresh provisions relating to limitation actions are substituted for Order 75, rule 38 by Rule 9. Provisions of Order 115 are extended so as to apply to Northern Ireland confiscation orders by Rule 10 and Rule 11 makes consequential amendments to Order 115 resulting from the provisions of the Proceeds of Crime Act 1996.

4234. Third party proceedings—contribution—development costs—restitution—damages

[Civil Liability (Contribution Act) 1978 (c.47), ss.1, 6.]

C made an agreement with N council and F to develop a shopping centre, with F and C sharing the development costs. H were the development consultants appointed by F and part of their responsibility was to authorise F's share of the costs claimed by C. Part of the claims made by C included notional interest amounting to over £6·5 million. F sought repayment of most of that sum on the ground that it did not constitute part of the development costs and that litigation was eventually settled. Thereafter F claimed damages from H equalling the amount of the wrongly paid interest. H then issued third party proceedings against the developers, claiming contribution under the Civil Liability (Contribution) Act 1978. H now appealed against an order striking out their third-party claims as disclosing no cause of action.

Held, allowing the appeal, that the issue turned on the construction of s.1 of the 1978 Act and whether a claim by F against the developers would be a claim for the same damage alleged by F against H, so that H could claim a contribution against the developers. Despite the difference between a claim for restitution and a claim for damages, each could be a claim for damages under ss.1(1) and 6(1). The last words of s.6(1), "whatever the legal basis of his liability," made it clear that the liability was not confined to actions arising out of a breach of duty. Accordingly, on the assumption that the developers were liable to F for part or all of the interest, s.1(1) of the Act applied.

FRIENDS' PROVIDENT LIFE OFFICE v. HILLIER PARKER MAY & ROWDEN, *The Times*, April 15, C.A.

4235. Third party proceedings—place of trial—proceedings for damages for breach of covenant—Crown joined as third party on claim for indemnity—whether proceedings "civil proceedings . . . against Crown"—whether third party proceedings against Crown required to take place in London

[Crown Proceedings Act 1947 (c.44), s.19(2); R.S.C., Ord. 77, rr.1(2), 9(1), 13(1).]

Third party proceedings against the Crown are "civil proceedings . . . against the Crown" for the purposes of R.S.C., Ord. 77, r.13(1).

In an action begun by writ in the Newcastle-upon-Tyne District Registry, the Secretary of State for the Environment was joined as third party. The judge directed that the action and third party proceedings be heard in Newcastle. The Secretary of State appealed against that direction.

Held, allowing the appeal, that third party proceedings against the Crown were "civil proceedings . . . against the Crown" for the purposes of R.S.C., Ord. 77, r.13(1) and accordingly the trial of those proceedings should be heard in London.

ST. MARTIN'S PROPERTY INVESTMENT v. PHILIPS ELECTRONICS (U.K.); SECRETARY OF STATE FOR THE ENVIRONMENT (THIRD PARTY) [1994] 3 W.L.R. 1074, Rattee J.

4236. Transfer of action—date of transfer—automatic directions—when transfer effective

The proceedings were commenced in the District Registry on September 26, 1990. On April 29, 1993 an order was made that the action be transferred to the county court. The order was not sealed until June 17, 1993. On August 10, 1993 the parties were sent a letter advising that the action had now been transferred to the county court and allocated a county court number. P did not apply for a hearing date until November 7, 1994. D applied to the court for a declaration that the matter had been struck out under C.C.R., Ord. 17, r.11, as no hearing date had been requested within 15 months of the transfer.

Held, that the date of transfer was neither when the order was made or when it received the court seal, but when the court had written on August 10, advising that the matter had been transferred to the county court and a Plaint number allocated to it. The decision was based on the notes on p. 270 of the Green Book, under the heading "Procedure for Transfer".

KWICKSERVE v. JONES AND JONES, February 9, 1995; H.H.J. Hume-Jones; Exeter County Ct. [*Ex rel. Crosse & Crosse, Solicitors*].

4237. Transfer of action—from Patents County Court to High Court—patent infringement—costs—whether judicial discretion to be interfered with

An order made by a judge to transfer or not to transfer an action from the Patents County Court to the High Court is an order made in the exercise of a judicial discretion and the grounds on which the Court of Appeal can interfere with such an order are limited.

The appellants, M, were the owners of the patent in issue in infringement proceedings. M issued a writ against the respondents, C, commencing infringement proceedings in the High Court. M had also commenced infringement proceedings against H founded on the same patent in respect of two designs. In this action M was successful as to the first design but not the second design. H appealed. In the meantime C issued a summons in the county court seeking a declaration that their design (which was similar to the second non-infringing design in the case in which judgment had been given) did not infringe M's patent. M applied to have this action transferred to the

High Court to be heard with M's infringement action against C. The county court judge refused M's application and M appealed. Prior to the hearing of M's appeal the Court of Appeal upheld the decision in the action between M and H. Furthermore, M's action against C in the High Court was settled. These events resulted in M and C agreeing that the remaining county court action for the declaration should be transferred to the High Court. However, the parties were unable to agree as to costs. C argued that it should have the costs of the appeal because the order which the judge made refusing transfer was one which he was right to make in the sense that it was an order that the judge was entitled to make in the exercise of discretion.

Held, ordering that M should bear the costs of the appeal, that an order made by a judge to transfer or not to transfer an action from the Patents County Court to the High Court is an order made in the exercise of a judicial discretion and the grounds on which the Court of Appeal can interfere with such an order are limited. There was nothing to which the judge failed to direct his attention that he should have taken into account and nothing that he ought not to have taken into account. M's appeal ought to have failed and the costs of the appeal ought to be paid by M to C.

MENTOR CORP. v. COLORPLAST A/S [1994] F.S.R. 175, C.A.

4238. Transfer of action—Lloyds litigation—whether to be brought in Chancery Division—circumstances justifying transfer of action

In the absence of special circumstances requiring transfer to another division, there was no reason why the Lloyds syndicate litigation could not be held in the Chancery Division. The courts did not encourage applications to transfer cases from one division to another.

DEENY v. LITTLEJOHN; SAME v. WALKER, *The Times*, January 19, 1995, Arden J.

4239. Tribunals—annual report of the Council on Tribunals

The Council on Tribunals has published its Annual Report 1993–1994 which describes aspects of the Council's work during the year August 1, 1993 to July 31, 1994 including the advice on proposals for new tribunals and other appeal procedures. The report is published by HMSO priced £14·00.

4240. Undertakings—no express liberty to apply—no change in circumstances—whether liberty to apply implied

The court will not compel a defendant to contest a motion if he is prepared to give undertakings whilst reserving the possibility of applying later to discharge them.

P built a robot which he used to take photographs of the inside of the Great Pyramid of Cheops, and incorporated these photographs into a film. D was given a copy of P's film during negotiations between P and D relating to a documentary. D used P's film in a programme without P's consent. P brought proceedings for infringement of copyright and D gave undertakings not to sell or reproduce the programme until judgment or further order. No express liberty-to-apply clause was included in the undertakings but D applied for the undertakings to be varied or discharged, claiming to have obtained evidence that P did not own the copyright in the film, relying on an implied liberty to apply. There had been no change in circumstances from those which existed at the time the undertakings were given. P contended that D was not entitled to make the application.

Held, disallowing P's motion to strike out D's application, that (1) with interlocutory applications just as much as final trials, the court is concerned to achieve a just degree of finality. On the other hand, if an undertaking is given or an interlocutory injunction is granted by consent where the parties envisaged that under the liberty to apply an application could be made to vary the injunction or undertakings, even if there is no change in circumstances the court will give effect to that intention. This applies equally whether the liberty to apply is express or implied (*Chanel v. F.W. Woolworth & Co.* [1981] C.L.Y. 2126, *Butt v. Butt* [1987] C.L.Y. 3031 referred to); (2) the court will not seek to compel a defendant to contest an interlocutory motion when the defendant is prepared to give an undertaking as sought, whilst reserving the possibility of applying later to discharge it. Here, D granted undertakings not to sell or reproduce the programme whilst it sought evidence and D was entitled to apply under an implied liberty to discharge or vary those undertakings without the need to show changed circumstances.

GANTENBRINK v. B.B.C. [1995] F.S.R. 162, Sir Donald Nicholls, V.-C.

4241. "Unless" order—repeated and persistent failures to comply with orders—extension of time—whether extension should be granted

P failed to comply with various orders including, eventually, an "unless" order for specific discovery. D entered judgement in default. An extension of time was later granted by the judge.

Held, allowing D's appeal, that (1) it is important that breaches of "unless" orders should not be incautiously condoned or overlooked; (2) a defaulter would only escape the consequences of judgment against it if it could show both that there was no intention to ignore or flout the order and that failure to obey was due to extraneous circumstances, and it was open to the court to consider whether the failure was contumacious (*Costellow v. Somerset County Council* [1993] C.L.Y. 3338 considered); (2) the combination of repeated and persistent failures to comply with peremptory orders, the absence of any credible excuse and the prejudice caused to the D meant that the action should be dismissed.

CARIBBEAN GENERAL INSURANCE v. FRIZZELL INSURANCE BROKERS [1994] 2 Lloyd's Rep. 32, C.A.

4242. Vexatious litigant—"civil proceedings"—refusal of *ex parte* applications for leave to commence proceedings and for leave to move for judicial review—whether judicial review "civil proceedings"—whether leave to commence proceedings necessary—whether applications renewable to Court of Appeal

[Supreme Court Act 1981 (c.54), s.42(1A)(3)(4) (as amended by the Prosecution of Offences Act 1985 (c.23), s.24); R.S.C., Ord. 59, r.14(3).]

A, a vexatious litigant subject to a civil proceedings order under s.42(1) of the Supreme Court Act 1981, as amended, issued a series of applications under s.42(3) for, *inter alia,* leave to continue proceedings and to move for judicial review of administrative decisions of the Legal Aid Board. The applications were refused and A sought to challenge the refusals on the ground that he was enabled by R.S.C., Ord. 59, r.14(3), to renew his applications for leave to the Court of Appeal. The Court of Appeal was asked whether it had jurisdiction to entertain the renewed applications and whether judicial review proceedings were "civil proceedings" within the meaning of s.42(1A) of the 1981 Act as amended.

Held, declining jurisdiction, that (1) Ord. 59, r.14(3), was to be read subject to s.42(3) and (4) of the 1981 Act which clearly intended that any decision of the High Court to give or refuse leave should be final; (2) s.42 plainly embraced all court proceedings and thus, a vexatious litigant seeking judicial review was required to obtain leave under s.42(3) in addition to leave to move; and (3) further, having regard to s.42(4), no procedure existed or should arise in relation to applications under s.42 comparable with the settled practice to entertain renewed applications for leave to move for judicial review under Ord. 59, r.14(3).

EWING (NO. 2), *ex p.* [1994] 1 W.L.R. 1553, C.A.

4243. Vexatious litigants—standard of proof

[Supreme Court Act 1981 (c.54), s.42.]

The civil standard of proof was to be used in applications for civil proceedings orders against vexatious litigants under s.42 of the Supreme Court Act 1981 (*R. v. Secretary of State for the Home Department, ex p. Khawaja* [1983] C.L.Y. 1908 followed).

ATT.-GEN. v. HAYWARD, *The Times*, November 20, 1995, C.A.

4244. Witnesses—order of appearance—no representation at trial—appellant unable to call witnesses in order—whether leave to appeal against damages to be granted

N, a hotelier sought leave to appeal against an order, awarding damages for repudiation of a contract to a carpenter, K, who had agreed to make and supply wardrobes for his hotel. N contended that because he had no representation at the trial he was unable to call the witnesses he required and in the order most beneficial to his case.

Held, refusing the application, that the judge had accepted the evidence of K and his expert witnesses on what were essentially questions of fact. There was no substance in the appeal. N and his witnesses gave their evidence and this was adequately considered by the court.

KITE (KEITH WILLIAM) v. NASSER (PRINCE M.) (94/6590/F), February 2, 1995, C.A.

4245. Writ—late amendment—whether permissible—whether cause of action time barred at date of amendment—whether judge should have exercised discretion against amendment

Lessees of a block of flats in London issued a writ in March 1987, which was served in March 1988, alleging negligence and breach of statutory duty in the development of, or design, or construction, of the flats. In March 1993 an amendment of the writ was allowed so as to include a claim expressly based on breach of warranty, which had been given by the council in respect of defects which might appear. Relevant defects had appeared in the 1980s but there had been no reply to surveyors' letters until February 1987.

Held, that (1) the judge was right to allow the amendment where the claim under the warranty arose out of design and construction, *i.e.* substantially the same facts as the original cause of action; (2) the council was liable only when it did not make good or defray the cost of repairs and on the facts this liability did not arise before the end of March 1987, it being unreal to say there was a breach of warranty where discussions were still proceeding, so that the relevant period of limitation (six years) had not expired at the date of the amendment in March 1993; and (3) the court would not interfere with the exercise of the judge's discretion as there was no material consideration which was decisive against amendment and joinder of new parties.

VINCENT v. BROMLEY LONDON BOROUGH COUNCIL [1994] N.P.C. 149, C.A.

4246. Writ—specific performance of contract for sale of land—action against Crown

[Crown Proceedings Act 1947 (c.44).]

Where a writ had been issued out of the High Court initiating an action for specific performance of a contract for the sale of land, the action was a civil proceeding against the Crown falling within ss.21 and 23(2) of the Crown Proceedings Act 1947.

FIRGLEN v. SECRETARY OF STATE FOR THE ENVIRONMENT, *The Times*, November 16, 1995, D.C.

4247. Writ—validity—writ served outside period of validity—extension refused—irregularity not waived—whether jurisdiction to make order that writ treated as served later

H issued a writ against TR on July 8, 1992, claiming damages in contract and tort. The writ was, however, not regularly served during the period of its validity and the claim in contract became time-barred before TR was aware of the proceedings. An application under R.S.C., Ord. 6, r.8, to extend the validity of the writ was refused, and the judge also refused to waive the irregularity under Ord. 2, r.1. The judge did, however, make an order that the writ be treated as issued and served on November 9, 1992, the date when the proceedings had come to the attention of one of TR's partners. TR argued that the judge had no jurisdiction to make such a direction.

Held, allowing the appeal, that to treat a writ as being issued months later than its actual date of issue was not permissible, since to do so might affect the rights not only of the parties themselves, but also of third parties. No adequate explanation had been given for failure to serve within the writ's validity and no good reason had been shown to justify extending its validity beyond the limitation period. There was, therefore, no authority under the R.S.C. for the judge to make the order he had made, and his discretion had accordingly been exercised in an impermissible way (*Kleinwort Benson v. Barbrak* [1987] C.L.Y. 3125 considered).

HARRISON v. TOUCHE ROSS, *The Times*, February 14, 1995, C.A.

4248. Writ—validity period—service after expiry justified under foreign procedural law—whether service valid—concurrent writ—whether four or six month period of validity of writ—whether validity of writ should be extended—whether concurrent writ validly served

[R.S.C., Ord. 6, r. 8(1); R.S.C., Ord. 11 r. (1)(2); Civil Jurisdiction and Judgments Act 1982.]

P issued a writ on March 5, 1993 against D within the one-year Hague Rules time bar, but did not serve it immediately as it doubted if security could be obtained. P then learned that D's ship might be arrested and applied to serve the writ in Greece where D was domiciled. The writ was served on July 5, 1993, as July 4 was a Sunday. It was not possible to effect service on a Sunday in Greek law, which extended time to the next working day. D applied to set aside the writ on the basis that it had been served after its validity had expired. P applied for time for service to be extended under R.S.C., Ord. 6, r. 8. P obtained a concurrent writ on July 2 which was served in Cyprus where D was registered.

Held, that (1) under R.S.C., Ord. 6, r. 8(1) the writ was valid for four months as no leave to serve out the jurisdiction was required in the case of a Convention country for the purposes of the Civil Jurisdiction and Judgments Act 1982 and R.S.C., Ord. 11(1)(2); (2) under English law (the *lex fori*) the period for service therefore expired on July 4 and there was no authority for the proposition that where the local procedural law prescribes a different period for the validity of a writ or similar originating process this can override the English time requirements; (3) in order to obtain an extension of time where the writ has ceased to be valid and the Hague Rules time bar has expired, P must show a good reason for an extension of time where the writ has ceased to be valid and the Hague Rules time bar has expired, P must show a good reason for an extension and a satisfactory explanation for the failure to apply for an extension before expiry (*Myrto (No. 3) The*, [1987] A.C. 597 applied); (4) the failure to issue a writ until the end of the Hague Rules period did not provide a sound basis for the extension requested; and (5) although Cyprus was not a Convention country the validity of the concurrent writ was not six months, but four months, as with the original writ, and there was no power to grant leave for such service in Cyprus, as where a writ can be served under R.S.C., Ord. 11, r. 1(2), it must be so served and the plaintiff does not have the option of seeking leave to serve elsewhere under Ord. 11, r. 1(1).

ABDULLAH ALI ALMUNAJEM SONS CO. v. RECOURSE SHIPPING CO.; REEFER CREOULE, THE [1994] 2 Lloyd's Rep. 584, Saville J.

4249. Writ of *fieri facias*—voluntary arrangement—whether execution creditor is secured creditor. See PECK v. CRAIGHEAD, §2847.

PRESS

4250. Trials—press coverage—sensational and exclusive—effect on jury—whether risk of prejudice to defendant. See R. v. TAYLOR (MICHELLE ANN) AND TAYLOR (LISA JANE), §1101.

PRISONS

4251. Life imprisonment—"technical lifer"—early release—whether plea of diminished responsibility ought to have been considered

P, who was convicted of murder and transferred to Broadmoor, applied for judicial review of the decision of the Secretary of State refusing to treat him as a "technical lifer", that is a person who, although sentenced to life imprisonment, is detained under a hospital order. Had he been so treated he would have had a better chance of an early release. He argued that his failure to plead diminished responsibility was a result of his mental illness.

Held, granting the application, that this was an unusual case, and the possibility of a plea of diminished responsibility ought to have been investigated.

R. v. SECRETARY OF STATE FOR THE HOME DEPARTMENT, *ex p.* PILDITCH [1994] C.O.D. 352, D.C.

4252. Parole—discretionary life prisoner—whether safety of public limited to U.K. public. See R. v. PAROLE BOARD, *ex p.* WHITE, §116.

4253. Parole—Discretionary Lifer Panel—procedural impropriety—observations on who should represent Secretary of State before Parole Board—observations on affidavit evidence in judicial review proceedings

[Criminal Justice Act 1991 (c.53), ss.32, 34; Parole Board Rules 1992.]

G had been convicted in 1983 of the murder of his wife and the rape of his daughter. The conviction for murder was reduced to manslaughter on the grounds of diminished responsibility on appeal. By virtue of Criminal Justice Act 1991, s.34(3), the respondent Board had a duty to direct the release of a discretionary life prisoner as soon as the relevant part of the sentence has been served. Under s.34(4) the respondent has no such duty to give a direction unless it was satisfied that it is no longer necessary to incarcerate the prisoner for the protection of the public. The Discretionary Life Panel was convened on June 15, 1993 for an oral hearing at which Mr Tanner, the Lifer Liaison Officer, gave evidence representing the Secretary of State. The respondent identified a number of areas of concern including the prisoner's relationship with his fiancée and his attitude to drink and drugs. The respondent determined not to release G. G challenged the decision on grounds of irrationality and procedural impropriety.

Held, granting the application, that the role played by Mr Tanner did not give rise to unfairness on the basis that he had been able to explain his own views and the views of the Secretary of State. The Parole Board Rules gave the Secretary of State wide power to appoint persons represent his views. There had been no unfairness on the ground that "probing" questions had been asked because G had been represented by a solicitor. There was clearly evidence before the Panel on which it could reach the decision it did. The Panel was not obliged to accept the reports which favoured release. However, there might have been a misunderstanding by the Panel on what G had said about drugs and steroids in particular. For that reason the respondent's decision would be quashed.

[*Per curiam*: In future cases there should be a note of the proceedings before the panel, such as a county court judge would produce. The note should be produced on the grant of leave in judicial review proceedings].

R. v. PAROLE BOARD, *ex p.* GITTENS [1994] C.O.D. 441, D.C.

4254. Parole—life sentence—misunderstanding of evidence by the Board—whether case should be remitted

G was sentenced to life imprisonment for manslaughter and when his case came up for parole the Board were not convinced that he was no longer a danger to the public, because he had failed to recognise his alcoholism and the need to avoid intoxication while under stress. He applied for judicial review of the decision.

Held, granting the application, that there had been a misunderstanding by the Board of some of the evidence given by G with regard to drugs which he had been taking at the time of the incident. In a case such as this, which was finely balanced, that misunderstanding was sufficient to quash the decision and the case would be remitted for reconsideration.

R. v. PAROLE BOAD, *ex p.* GITTENS [1994] C.O.D. 351, D.C.

4255. Parole—Parole Board's decision—whether gives rise to legitimate expectation—whether Home Secretary's decision not to accept Board's recommendation unreasonable

[Criminal Justice Act 1991 (c.53), ss.32, 34.]

E had been sentenced to a discretionary life sentence for various offences. E came before the Discretionary Lifer Panel under the Criminal Justice Act 1991, s.34(4). The Panel recommended that, rather than release E, he should be transferred to a category D prison to test his behaviour in open conditions. The Home Secretary rejected this recommendation. E challenged this decision on the basis that the Secretary of State's decision had been unreasonable in the light of the Panel's recommendations.

Held, refusing the application, that the Panel was not a body with a fact-finding role. Once it had decided that E should not be released on licence, its role was purely advisory in accordance with s.32 in contrast to its directive role under s.34. Further, no legitimate expectation had been caused by the Panel hearing. It could not be said that the Home Secretary's decision was so outrageous as to be in defiance of logic or acceptance of moral standards that no sensible person could have arrived at the decision (*Council of Civil Service Unions v. Minister for the Civil Service* [1985] C.L.Y. 12, *R. v. Home Secretary, ex p. Sakala*, *The Times*, January, 26, 1994 considered).

R. v. SECRETARY OF STATE FOR THE HOME DEPARTMENT, *ex p.* EDWARDS [1994] C.O.D. 443, D.C.

4256. Parole—prisoner serving life sentence transferred to mental hospital—Secretary of State refusing to certify for review or refer case to parole board—whether "life prisoner" if detained in mental hospital—whether right to consideration for release on licence

[Mental Health Act 1983 (c.20), s.50(1); Criminal Justice Act 1991 (c.53), ss.34, 35(2), Sched. 12, para. 9.]

The right to a hearing for life prisoners before a Parole Board under the terms of the Criminal Justice Act 1991 was conferred on those who were subject only to the provisions of that Act and not on mental patients for whom the provisions of the Mental Health Act 1983 applied.

The applicants in the first case were serving discretionary life sentences and the applicant in the second case had been ordered to be detained at Her Majesty's pleasure, having been convicted at the age of 17 of murder. All had been transferred to mental hospitals by order of the Secretary of State under s.47 of the Mental Health Act 1983 and a restriction direction had been made in each case so that they were liable to be detained until the Secretary of State consented to their discharge. The applicants in both cases were informed that the Secretary of State did not intend to certify them as life prisoners eligible for review by the Parole Board for release on licence. They sought judicial review of those decisions. The Divisional Court declared that the discretionary life prisoners were life prisoners for the purpose of para. 9 of Sched. 12 to the Criminal Justice Act 1991 and a decision not to certify them as such was unlawful. It also declared that the applicant in the second case was a life prisoner for the purposes of s.35(2) of the 1991 Act and that the Secretary of State could seek the recommendation of the Parole Board before exercising his power under s.50 of the 1983 Act. The Secretary of State appealed.

Held, allowing the appeals, that although all of the applicants were existing life prisoners under the 1991 Act consideration of their discharge remained subject to the provisions of the 1983 Act and the procedures laid down in that Act.

R. v. SECRETARY OF STATE FOR THE HOME DEPARTMENT, *ex p.* H.; R. v. SAME, *ex p.* HICKEY; *sub nom.* R. v. SECRETARY OF STATE FOR THE HOME DEPARTMENT, *ex p.* T. [1994] 3 W.L.R. 1110, C.A.

4257. Parole—refusal of prisoner to admit guilt—application for certiorari and mandamus—whether admission of guilt necessary consideration

Z, a prisoner convicted of arson, applied for orders of certiorari and mandamus in respect of the decisions of the Secretary of State and Parole Board to refuse him parole because he continued to deny that he was guilty of the offence.

Held, allowing the appeal, that the decision was quashed and the Parole Board required to reconsider its decision. In the majority of cases a prisoner should not be refused parole solely because he continued to refuse to admit his guilt. Each case must be decided on its own facts but, in general, if the prisoner was not a persistent offender and the facts did not indicate a probability of reoffending, less weight should be attached to his attitude then to the offence.

R. v. SECRETARY OF STATE FOR THE HOME DEPARTMENT AND THE GOVERNOR OF FRANKLAND PRISON, *ex p.* ZULFIKAR; SAME AND THE PAROLE BOARD, *ex p.* SAME, *The Times*, July 26, 1995, D.C.

4258. Parole—refusal to order immediate release of prisoner on licence—redetention—recommendations of Parole Board—whether correct test applied. See R. v. PAROLE BOARD, *ex p.* WATSON, §117.

4259. Prison officer—dismissal—improper relationships with prisoners—whether matter of public law. See R. v. SECRETARY OF STATE FOR THE HOME DEPARTMENT, *ex p.* MOORE, §42.

4260. Prison officer—escorting segregated prisoner to visiting area—prisoner attacked by other prisoners—whether choice of route negligent—whether officer should have followed prisoner rather than led. See BURT v. HOME OFFICE, §3688.

4261. Prison rules

PRISONS (AMENDMENT) RULES 1995 (No. 983) [£1·10], made under the

Prison Act 1952 (c.52), s.47; operative on April 25, 1995; amend S.I. 1964 No. 388 in relation to unconvicted prisoners.

PRISON (AMENDMENT) (NO. 2) RULES 1995 (No. 1598), made under the Prison Act 1952, s.47; operative on July 17, 1995; amend S.I. 1964 No. 388 to require more detailed provision in relation to the systems of privileges for prisoners; make certain exceptions to the rights of unconvicted prisoners to wear their own clothes.

4262. Prisoner—transfer to different prison—lack of reasons for transferral—judicial review—whether denial of natural justice. See R. v. SECRETARY OF STATE FOR THE HOME DEPARTMENT, *ex p.* PARRY (FC3 94/5261/D), §43.

4263. Prisoners—Home Office research bulletin

The Home Office Research and Statistics Department has published a special edition research bulletin No. 36 1994, (ISSN 0962–0478) on different aspects of the prison service. The articles contained in the bulletin are concerned with four main themes: maintaining order, control and discipline and a safe environment; providing decent conditions for prisoners and meeting their needs, including health care; providing positive regimes which help prisoners address their offending behaviour and allowing them as full and responsible life as possible; and helping prisoners prepare for their return to the community. Available from the Home Office Research and Planning Unit, 50 Queen Anne's Gate, London, SW1H 9AT.

4264. Prisoners (Return to Custody) Act 1995 (c.16)

This Act creates a summary offence of remaining unlawfully at large, without reasonable excuse, after being temporarily released from a prison, remand centre or young offender institution. Provision is made for the police to enter and search premises without a warrant for the purpose of arresting persons unlawfully at large.

The Act received Royal Assent on June 28, 1995.

4265. Prisoners (Return to Custody) Act 1995—commencement

PRISONERS (RETURN TO CUSTODY) ACT 1995 (COMMENCEMENT) ORDER 1995 (No. 2021 (C.41)) [65p], made under the Prisoners (Return to Custody) Act 1995, s.3(2), brings into force on September 5, 1995 the Prisoners (Return to Custody) Act 1995.

4266. Prisoner's rights—refusal to receive nutrition—hunger strike—prisoner with full mental capacity refusing nutrition—Home Secretary seeking declaration that he might lawfully observed and abide by prisoner's refusal to receive nutrition—whether declaration should be granted

A prisoner of sound mind had the right to refuse nutrition, and the court would grant a declaration that the Home Secretary might lawfully abide by the prisoner's refusal.

D was on hunger strike in prison. D suffered from personality disorder, but all the experts agreed that he was of sound mind and capacity. The Home Secretary brought a summons seeking a declaration that he might lawfully abide by D's refusal of nutrition, and that he might lawfully abstain from providing hydration and nutrition for so long as D retained the capacity to refuse the same.

Held, granting the declarations sought, that (1) every person's body was inviolate against any form of physical molestation (*F. (Sterilisation: Mental Patient), Re* [1989] C.L.Y. 3044 applied); (2) a patient's wishes must be respected, so that he was entitled to refuse treatment which his doctors believed to be in his best interests (*T. (An Adult) (Consent to Medical*

Treatment), Re [1992] C.L.Y. 2918, *Airedale National Health Service Trust v. Bland* [1993] C.L.Y. 2712 applied); (3) a patient who was entitled to consent to treatment which might or would have the effect of prolonging his life, who refused so to consent and who died as a result, did not commit suicide, nor did his doctor aid or abet suicide in complying with the patient's wishes (*Airedale National Health Service Trust v. Bland* [1993] C.L.Y. 2712 applied); (4) the presumption of capacity to consent or refuse to medical treatment might be rebutted by evidence of mental incapacity or other circumstances (*T. (An Adult) (Consent to Medical Treatment), Re* [1992] C.L.Y. 2918, *C. (Refusal of Medical Treatment), Re* [1994] 1 F.L.R. 31 considered); (5) the defendant's right of self-determination was not diminished by his status as a detained prisoner (*R. v. Deputy Governor of Parkhurst, ex p. Leech* [1988] C.L.Y. 2976 applied); (6) in the absence of any countervailing interest of the state in protecting innocent third parties or preserving internal order and discipline within the jail, there was a plain case for the declarations sought (*S. (An Adult: Refusal of Treatment), Re* [1993] C.L.Y. 2706, *Caulk, Re* (1984) 480 A. 2d. 93, *Thor v. Superior Court* (1993) 885 P. 2d. 375 considered; *Leigh v. Gladstone* (1909) 26 T.L.R. 139 disapproved).

SECRETARY OF STATE FOR THE HOME DEPARTMENT v. ROBB [1995] 1 F.L.R. 412, Thorpe J.

4267. Prisoners' rights—visitors—denial of physical contact to high risk prisoners—judicial review. See R. v. SECRETARY OF STATE FOR THE HOME DEPARTMENT, *ex p.* O'DHUIBHIR, §45.

4268. Release date—set-off period—time spent in police custody—effect of concurrent sentences. See R. v. GOVERNOR OF STYAL PRISON, *ex p.* MOONEY, §1473.

4269. Remission—terrorist offences—Northern Ireland—press release

The Northern Ireland Office has issued a press release entitled *Northern Ireland (Remission of Sentences) Bill published* (Press Notice L75/95), published on October 26, 1995. The Bill allows for the release of prisoners serving fixed term sentences of five years or more to be released under licence halfway through their sentences, subject, in the case of those convicted of scheduled offences, to recall on licence from the halfway to the two-thirds point if their liberty presents a risk to the safety of others or if they are likely to commit further offences. Remission for this category of offender was reduced to one third in 1989.

4270. Young offender institution

YOUNG OFFENDER INSTITUTION (AMENDMENT) RULES 1995 (No. 984) [£1·10], made under the Prison Act 1952 (c.52), s.47; operative on April 25, 1995; amend S.I. 1988 No. 1422 so as to change the procedure for the temporary release of inmates and so as to increase the power of governors in relation to disciplinary offences.

YOUNG OFFENDER INSTITUTION (AMENDMENT) (NO. 2) RULES 1995 (No. 1599), made under the Prison Act 1952, s.47; operative on July 17 1995; amend S.I. 1988 No. 1422 to make more detailed provision relating to the systems of privileges for inmates of young offender institutions.

4271. Young offender institutions—training

The Prison Service has issued a press release entitled *Home Secretary Announces High Intensity Training for Young Offenders* (30N/95), published on September 18, 1995. A new high intensity training regime for young offenders has been unveiled by Home Secretary Michael Howard. It is aimed at breaking the cycle of re-offending by young criminals and involves a rigorous 16-hour day discipline and hard work as its foundation.

PUBLIC ENTERTAINMENTS AND RECREATION

4272. Activity Centres (Young Persons' Safety) Act 1995 (c.15)

This Act provides for the regulation of persons providing facilities where adventure activities are engaged in by young persons under the age of 18, including the imposition of safety or licensing requirements.

The Act shall come into force on August 28, 1995.

4273. Cycle racing on highways. See ROAD TRAFFIC, §4394.

4274. Film industry—European Convention

EUROPEAN CONVENTION ON CINEMATOGRAPHIC CO-PRODUCTION (AMENDMENT) ORDER 1995 (No. 1298) [65p], made under the Films Act 1985 (c.21), Sched. 1, para. 4(5); operative on June 7, 1995; amends S.I. 1994 No. 1065 by adding Slovakia to the Schedule thereto.

EUROPEAN CONVENTION ON CINEMATOGRAPHIC CO-PRODUCTION (AMENDMENT) (NO. 2) ORDER 1995 (No. 1963) [65p], made under the Films Act 1985, Sched. 1, para. 4(5); amends S.I. 1994 No. 1065; operative on August 16, 1995.

EUROPEAN CONVENTION ON CINEMATOGRAPHIC CO-PRODUCTION (AMENDMENT) (NO. 3) ORDER 1995 (No. 2730) [65p], made under the Films Act 1985, Sched. 1, para. 4(5); operative on November 8, 1995, amends S.I. 1994 No. 1065; inserts "Republic of Finland" in the appropriate place in the Schedule.

4275. Football

FOOTBALL SPECTATORS (SEATING) ORDER 1995 (No. 1706), made under the Football Spectators Act 1989, s.11(1)-(3); operative on July 31, 1995; directs the Football Licensing Authority to include in any licence to admit spectators to any football grounds listed in Sched. 1, a condition imposing requirements specified in Sched. 2 as respects the seating of spectators at designated football matches at those premises.

4276. National parks—Wales

NATIONAL PARK AUTHORITIES (LEVIES) (WALES) REGULATIONS 1995 (No. 3019), made under the Local Government Finance Act 1988 ss.74, 140(4), 143(1)(2) and Environment Act 1995 s.71(3)(6). operative on December 21, 1995; [£1·95. Provision is made by these Regulations for National Park authorities and National Parks in Wales to issue levies for the purpose of meeting their expenses in respect of financial years beginning on or after April 1, 1996 to billing authorities. Provision for the issue of levies is included in Regulation 4 and the apportionment of levies between councils is provided for in Regulation 5 and the Schedule. Regulation 6 stipulates the maximum amount of levies and the issuing of substituted levies is covered by Regulation 7. Regulations 8 and 9 are concerned with the payment of levies and interest thereon and Regulation 10 provides for a council to anticipate a levy which may be issued to it.

NATIONAL PARKS AUTHORITIES (WALES) ORDER 1995 (No. 2803) [£4·15], made under the Town and Country Planning Act 1990, s.4A(1), the Welsh Language Act 1993, s.25(2), the Local Government (Wales) Act 1994, s.54(1)(2)(e) and the Environment Act 1995, ss.63(1)(2), 64(7)(8), 75(3)–(7), Sched. 7, para. 1(2), 2(1)–(3). National Park Authorities are established on November 23, 1995 for the three existing National Parks in Wales, the Brecon Beacons National Park, the Pembrokeshire Coast National Park and the Snowdonia National Park and each Authority is given an English and a Welsh Name. Each National Park authority will, on April 1, 1996, become, *inter alia*, the local planning authority and hazardous substances authority for its own National Park, taking the place of those Councils for those Welsh county and county boroughs any part of whose area lies within that National Park. Provision is also made for the first and subsequent appointment of members to each authority, resignation of members and filling of vacancies, notices of appointment of members and meetings and proceedings of an authority. One third of the members will be appointed by the Secretary of State for Wales, and the remaining two thirds will be appointed by the constituent Welsh county and county borough councils.

4277. Sports facilities—safety

SAFETY OF SPORTS GROUNDS (DESIGNATION) ORDER 1995 (No. 1990) [65p], made under the Safety of Sports Grounds Act 1975, ss.1(1), 18(2); amends S.I. 1985 No. 1064, S.I. 1986 No. 1296; operative on August 25, 1995; designates the Cellnet Riverside Stadium, Middlesbrough, Cleveland as a sports ground requiring a safety certificate under the Safety of Sports Grounds Act 1975.

PUBLIC HEALTH

4278. AIDS—European Community

European Parliament and Council Decision 1729/95/EC of June 19, 1995 on the extension of the Europe against AIDS programme (O.J. L168/1).

4279. Blood safety—self-sufficiency—European Community

E.C. Council Resolution of June 2, 1995 on blood safety and self-sufficiency in the Community ([1995] O.J. C164/1).

4280. Dangerous substances—European Community

Commission Decision of September 14, 1994 concerning the prohibition of PCP notified by Germany (O.J. L316/43).

Directive 94/48/EC of the European Parliament and of the Council of December 7, 1994 relating to restrictions on the marketing and use of certain dangerous substances and preparations (O.J. L331/7).

4281. Genetically modified micro-organisms—contained use—European Community

Commission Directive 94/51/EC of November 7, 1994 adapting to technical progress Dir. 90/219/EEC on the contained use of genetically modified micro-organisms (O.J. L297/27).

4282. Home and leisure accidents—European Community

Council Decision 95/184/EC of May 22, 1995 amending Decision 3/92/94/EC introducing a Community system of information on home and leisure accidents (O.J. L120/36).

4283. Ships and aircraft

PUBLIC HEALTH (SHIPS AND AIRCRAFT) (ISLE OF MAN) (REVOCATION) ORDER 1995 (No. 267) [65p], made under the Public Health (Control of

Disease) Act 1984 (c.22), s.76; operative on March 1, 1995; revokes S.I. 1982 Nos. 1671 and 1672.

4284. Vaccine damage—payments

VACCINE DAMAGE PAYMENTS (SPECIFIED DISEASE) ORDER 1995 (No. 1164) [65p], made under the Vaccine Damage Payments Act 1979 (c.17), s.1(2)(i); operative on May 31, 1995; adds Haemophilus type b infection (Hib) to the list of diseases in respect of which payments can be made under the 1979 Act.

RATING AND VALUATION

4285. Former enterprise zones

VALUATION FOR RATING (FORMER ENTERPRISE ZONES) REGULATIONS 1995 (No. 213) [65p], made under the Local Government Finance Act 1988 (c.41), Sched. 6, para. 2(8); operative on April 1, 1995; provide that the existence of an enterprise zone is to be disregarded for the purpose of making an assessment in relation to that part of a hereditament that is situated within a former enterprise zone.

4286/7. Lands Tribunal—appeal by way of case stated—whether tribunal is required when requested to include questions in case stated which raise points of law

A decision of a Lands Tribunal, concerning acquisition of land in connection with road improvements, was made. The tribunal was requested to include in the case stated questions which raised points of law. The applicant contended that these questions must be included unless they were considered by the tribunal to be irrelevant or unarguable. The three questions were (a) whether the tribunal erred in law in assuming that planning permission had been granted for development of the land; (b) whether the tribunal erred in law in concluding the number of houses which which would have had direct access to the distributor road; and (c) whether the tribunal erred in law with reference to the remission of the case stated from the Court of Appeal.

Held, allowing the application, that the questions raised relevant and arguable legal questions and therefore should be included by the tribunal in the case stated.

HERTFORDSHIRE COUNTY COUNCIL v. ROTHSCHILD TRUST (C.I.) [1994] 48 EG 125, C.A.

4288. Lands Tribunal—practice direction

[Lands Tribunal Act 1949 (c. 42), s. 3(4).]

The provisions of s.3(4) of the Lands Tribunal Act 1949 restrict the right of appeal from a decision of the tribunal to "any person aggrieved by the decision as being erroneous in point of law".

A proposed appellant who requires a tribunal to prepare a case stated for the Court of Appeal may set out the grounds for the appeal in the application to the tribunal. where no grounds of appeal are so set out, the applicant will be invited to set out those grounds of appeal within 14 days of the application. It is the duty of the applicant to define the questions of law which it seeks to raise. A question of law which is stated in vague or general terms will not be accepted. The tribunal will decline to state a case if no grounds of appeal are produced or if, in the opinion of the tribunal, those grounds disclose no point of law. The decision of the tribunal will in all cases contain a statement of the evidence given and the tribunal's findings of fact. A copy of the decision will

be appended to the case stated. No appeal will lie without leave in respect of the tribunal's award of costs; which is wholly a matter of its discretion.
PRACTICE DIRECTION NO. 1 OF 1994 49 EG 119, Lands Tribunal.

4289. Lands Tribunal decision

The rateable value of premises in West Yorkshire used as offices and at the extreme end of a secondary shopping area was assessed at £3,150.
APPEAL OF CHILTON-MERRYWEATHER (V.O.), *Re* (RA/488/1992) [1994] RA 417, Lands Tribunal.

4290. Lands Tribunal decision

The r.v.s of workshops and warehouses in South Humberside were reduced by 35 per cent and 17.5 per cent respectively to allow for the discharge from neighbouring premises of a substance known as petro-chemical coke.
APPEALS OF DAWSON, *Re* (V.O.) (RA/801-806/1992) [1995] 35 RVR 29, Lands Tribunal.

4291. Lands Tribunal decision

A warehouse, office and premises in Bristol were assessed at £62,000 rv made up as to 6,288 square metres of warehouse at £8·75 psm and 317 square metres of office space at £22·08 psm.
CLARK v. ROGERS (V.O.) (RA/94/1993) [1994] RA 169, Lands Tribunal.

4292. Lands Tribunal decision

A superstore in West Yorkshire was assessed at £234,000 r.v. having been reduced, *inter alia*, because the ratepayer was only a hypothetical tenant.
CO-OPERATIVE RETAIL SERVICES v. OATES (VO) (RA/336/1993) [1995] RA 151, Lands Tribunal.

4293. Lands Tribunal decision

A composite hereditament comprising a shop and residential accommodation in Bradford was assessed at £2,700 r.v.
CORBETT (V.O.) v. FERDINAND (RA/404/1992) [1995] RA 1, Lands Tribunal.

4294. Lands Tribunal decision

An air-conditioning system in a shop unit in West London was to be taken into account in ascertaining the rateable value of the premises and the appropriate decapitalisation figure was six per cent as provided by the statutory regulations.
DOROTHY PERKINS RETAIL v. CASEY (V.O.) (RA/148/1992) [1994] RA 391, Lands Tribunal.

4295. Lands Tribunal decision

The compensation to be paid in respect of delay and expense incurred under a building contract caused by a refusal to consent to the lopping of a tree under a preservation order was assessed at £5,115.
FACTORSET v. SELBY DISTRICT COUNCIL (REF/174/1993) [1995] 35 RVR 49, Lands Tribunal.

4296. Lands Tribunal decision

It is permissible to advance expert evidence as to the value of a lease even where the claimant's lease is not capable of assignment.
GOODERAM v. DEPARTMENT OF TRANSPORT (REF/106/1993) [1995] 35 RVR 12, Lands Tribunal.

4297. Lands Tribunal decision

A swimming pool in a sports centre was not part of a single hereditament and so fell to be assessed separately.

GREEN (V.O.) v. BARNET LONDON BOROUGH COUNCIL [1994] R.A. 235.

4298. Lands Tribunal decision

A railway booking office was assessed to rates since it was akin to a shop in position and was used mainly as office premises.

HALLIDAY (V.O.) v. BRITISH RAILWAYS BOARD (RA/613/1992) [1994] R.A. 297.

4299. Lands Tribunal decision

The gross value for shop units was reduced, *inter alia*, by the application of a disability allowance to values assessed by zoning, to allow for irregular shaped floor area.

MARKS AND SPENCER v. COX (V.O.) (LVC/207–209/1991) [1994] R.A. 258.

4300. Lands Tribunal decision

A restaurant and premises in Bromley was assessed at £24,000 r.v. taking into account its location and lack of amenity.

MARKS (TRUSTEE OF T.N. MARKS DECEASED) v. GROSE (V.O.) (RA/471/1993) [1995] RA 49, Lands Tribunal.

4301. Lands Tribunal decision

The r.v. of a group of agricultural buildings in Pinner, Middlesex, was reduced to £12,350.

McPHAIL v. SAUL (RA/186/93) [1995] RA 39, Lands Tribunal.

4302. Lands Tribunal decision

The right to utilise the side wall of a building for advertising purposes in Canterbury was rateable and correctly assessed at £1,000 r.v.

O'BRIEN v. SECKER (V.O.) (RA/423/1993) [1995] RA 13, Lands Tribunal.

4303. Lands Tribunal decision

Pipelines carrying to storage tanks the product of an enterprise drilling for oil were not rateable.

OTTEWELL (V.O.) v. BP EXPLORATION OPERATING CO. (RA/639-644/1992) [1995] RA 22, Lands Tribunal.

4304. Lands Tribunal decision

The assessment of a shop and premises, including a sub post office, was confirmed at £5,400 rv calculated on the basis of £125 psm for Zone A but making a discount of 75 per cent for the post office counter.

PATEL v. BROADWAY (V.O.) (RA/146/1992) [1994] RA 223, Lands Tribunal.

4305. Lands Tribunal decision

A modern purpose-built visitor centre in Plymouth was assessed at £103,000 r.v., using the contractor's basis where no other method of assessment could be used.

PLYMOUTH CITY COUNCIL v. HOARE (VO) [1995] RA 69, Lands Tribunal.

4306. Lands Tribunal decision

A purpose-built conference hall and leisure centre in Plymouth was

assessed at £627,750 r.v. on the contractor's basis since there was no question of profitability, rental evidence or comparables.
PLYMOUTH CITY COUNCIL v. HOARE (VO) (NO. 2) [1995] RA 92, Lands Tribunal.

4307. Lands Tribunal decision

A leisure centre in South Hams comprising principally swimming pools and squash courts was assessed at £68,000 r.v. using the contractor's basis where there was no question of profitability, rental evidence or comparables.
SOUTH HAMS DISTRICT COUNCIL v. HOARE (VO) [1995] RA 116, Lands Tribunal.

4308. Lands Tribunal decision

The zone A rateable value of a shop in London E6 was reduced from £500 per square mile to £475 per square mile. The valuation officer had criticised the rents of the appeal hereditaments as evidence on a number of grounds. The tribunal concluded that the rents of the appeal property and the immediately adjoining shops were at the lower end of the band of values present in value negotiations, but reduced the assessment slightly to better reflect the rental evidence.
SPECIALEYES v. FELGATE (V.O.) (RA/387/1992) [1994] RA 338.

4309. Lands Tribunal decision

The Zone A value of shop premises in Welwyn Garden City was reduced from £350 psm to £325 psm where it was not in a peak trading location.
THOMAS COOK GROUP v. HALLIDAY (V.O.) (RA/499/1992) [1994] RA 137, Lands Tribunal.

4310. Lands Tribunal decision

A swimming pool in Tavistock was assessed at £96,500 r.v. using the contractor's basis where there was no question of profitability, rental evidence or comparables.
WEST DEVON DISTRICT COUNCIL v. HOARE (VO) [1995] RA 132, Lands Tribunal.

4311. Leasehold enfranchisement—cost of surveyor in connection with a reference to a leasehold valuation tribunal—whether recoverable from the tenant. See COVENT GARDEN GROUP v. NAIVA, §3021.

4312. Leasehold enfranchisement—valuation—freehold block of 10 flats—factors to be considered—price to be paid in accordance with statute. See TRERYN HEIGHTS, GODALMING, *Re*, §3026.

4313. Non-domestic rating—alteration of lists and appeals

NON-DOMESTIC RATING (ALTERATION OF LISTS AND APPEALS) (AMENDMENT) REGULATIONS 1995 (No. 609) [£1·95], made under the Local Government Finance Act 1988 (c.41), ss.55(2)–(6), 143(1)(2); operative on March 31, 1995; amend S.I. 1993 No. 291.

4314. Non-domestic rating—chargeable amounts

NON-DOMESTIC RATING (CHARGEABLE AMOUNTS) (AMENDMENT) REGULATIONS 1995 (No. 961) [£5·60], made under the Local Government Finance Act 1988 (c.41), ss.58, 143(1); operative on March 31, 1995; amend S.I. 1994 No. 3279.

NON-DOMESTIC RATING (CHARGEABLE AMOUNTS) (AMENDMENT NO. 2) REGULATIONS 1995 (No. 1678), made under the Local Government Finance Act 1988, ss.58, 143(1)(2); operative on July 4, 1995.

NON-DOMESTIC RATING (CHARGEABLE AMOUNTS) (AMENDMENT NO.3) REGULATIONS 1995 (No. 3322), made under the Local Government Finance Act 1988 ss.58, 143(1)(2); amends S.I. 1994 No. 3279. operative on December 20, 1995; [65p]. The Non-Domestic Rating (Chargeable Amount) Regulations 1994, relating to chargeable amounts payable by non-domestic ratepayers, are amended by these Regulations. Figures prescribed in Regulations 8, 23 and 31 for the calculation of the appropriate fraction used in calculating maximum and annual changes in rates bills are reduced. In Regulation 8(2)(a) the figure 110 is replaced with 107.5, in 8(2)(b) the figure 107.5 is replaced with 105, in 8(2)(c) the figure 105 is replaced with 102.5, in 23(2)(a) the figure 110 is replaced with 107.5 and in 31(2)(a) the figure 110 is replaced with 107.5.

4315. Non-domestic rating—contributions

NON-DOMESTIC RATING CONTRIBUTIONS (ENGLAND) (AMENDMENT) REGULATIONS 1995 (No. 3181) [£1·10], made under the Local Government Finance Act 1988, ss.140(4), 143(1)(2), Sched. 8, paras. 4, 6; amend S.I. 1992 No. 3082. In force: December 31, 1995; amend the rules for calculating the payment of non-domestic rating contributions contained in the Non-Domestic Rating Contributions (England) Regulations 1992. Certain figures used in calculating contributions and provisional amounts are altered and provision is made in relation to areas ceasing to be enterprise zones.

NON-DOMESTIC RATING CONTRIBUTIONS (WALES) (AMENDMENT) REGULATIONS 1995 (No. 3235), made under the Local Government Finance Act 1988 ss.140(4), 143(1)(2), Sched. 8, paras. 4, 6; amends S.I. 1992 No. 3238. operative on December 31, 1995; [65p]. Various technical amendments are made to the Non-Domestic Rating Contributions (Wales) Regulations 1992 relating to calculations of provisional amounts paid during the year, final calculations and payments made after year end of non-domestic rating contributions by billing authorities under Part II of Sched. 8 to the Local Government Finance Act 1988. The amendments take effect from the financial year beginning on or after April 1, 1996.

4316. Non-domestic rating—Cornish tinner—whether exempt from liability to pay rates

[General Rate Act 1967 (c.9), s.104; Local Government Finance Act 1988 (c.41); Stannaries Court (Abolition) Act 1896 (c.45); Non-Domestic Rating (Collection and Enforcement) (Local Lists) Regulations 1989 (S.I. 1989 No. 1056), regs. 16, 17.]

A Cornish tinner is not exempted from the payment of rates by virtue of his occupation.

T was assessed to rates on a property used for a business. He was a party in the business which was a form of unincorporated association. In due course the local magistrates' court made a liability order in respect of unpaid rates. T appealed, seeking to argue that the lands of the Duchy of Cornwall were not part of the U.K. for the purposes of the legislation, that if they were he was exempted from the rating legislation by virtue of his status as a tinner, and that even if that were not the case the case against him had to be dealt with by a county court.

Held, that on a true construction of the legislation the lands of the Duchy of Cornwall were plainly part of the U.K. The intention of Parliament was that everyone otherwise liable to non-domestic rates should pay them, including tinners, and the question of non-domestic rates could only be dealt with in the magistrates' court since when the Stannaries Court was abolished only those matters which the county court in 1896 could deal with were transferred to it. This did not include non-domestic rates (*R. v. East Powder Justices, ex p.*

Lampshire [1979] C.L.Y. 1776, *Secretary of State for Trade and Industry v. Trull*, March 30, 1992, Millett J., unrep., considered).

TRULL v. RESTORMEL BOROUGH COUNCIL [1994] 34 R.V.R. 122, Latham J.

4317. Non-domestic rating—council tax—demand notices

COUNCIL TAX AND NON-DOMESTIC RATING (DEMAND NOTICES) (ENGLAND) AMENDMENT REGULATIONS 1995 (No. 121) [£1·10], made under the Local Government Finance Act 1988 (c.41), s.143(1)(2), Sched. 2, paras. 1, 2(2)(ga)(h) and the Local Government Finance Act 1992 (c.14), s.113(1)(2), Sched. 2, paras. 2(4)(j), 14(1); operative on February 15, 1995; amend S.I. 1993 No. 191 to take account of the establishment of new police authorities and the re-valuation of hereditaments for non-domestic rating in 1995.

4318. Non-domestic rating—demand notices

NON-DOMESTIC RATING (DEMAND NOTICES) (WALES) (AMENDMENT) REGULATIONS 1995 (No. 284) [£1·10], made under the Local Government Finance Act 1988 (c.41), ss.140(4), 143(1)(2), 146(6), Sched. 9, paras. 1, 2(2), 6A(1) and the Welsh Language Act 1993 (c.38), s.26(3); operative on March 2, 1995; amend S.I. 1993 No. 252 to reflect the establishment of the new police authorities.

4319. Non-domestic rating—distress for rates—levy of distress—dispute as to ownership—whether magistrates' court obliged to hear and determine dispute

[Magistrates' Courts Act 1980 (c.43), ss.9, 53; Police (Property) Act 1897 (c.30); Criminal Justice Act 1972 (c.71); Non-Domestic Rating (Collection and Enforcement) (Local Lists) Regulations 1989 (S.I. 1989 No. 1056), regs. 12, 14, 15.]

Magistrates are not obliged to hear and determine potentially complex matters in connection with a dispute as to the ownership of goods the subject of a walking possession agreement resulting from a levy of distress for rates.

A liability order for unpaid rates was made against a subsidiary company of H&B. The bailiff entered the property twice in October 1991 and purportedly entered into a walking possession agreement or agreements in respect of certain valuable items. H&B claimed that the items had previously been sold to it by the subsidiary. H&B laid a complaint in the magistrates' court, but when the matter came before the justices they declined to hear the complaint on the grounds that the matter was a complex one both as to the law and factually, and, *inter alia*, on the ground that it would be a case where discovery was appropriate and they had no power to order discovery.

Held, that the justices were correct not to hear the complaint. There were more appropriate civil remedies available in the county court and in the High Court (*Harrington, Re* [1984] 1 A.C. 743, *R. v. Horsham Justices, ex p. Richards* [1985] C.L.Y. 517, *R. v. Kneeshaw* [1974] C.L.Y. 534, *Lyons (Raymond) & Co. v. Metropolitan Police Commissioner* [1975] C.L.Y. 2574 considered).

R. v. BASILDON JUSTICES, *ex p.* HOLDING AND BARNES [1994] RA 157, Schiemann J.

4320. Non-domestic rating—late notification of alteration in list—liability order sought in magistrates' court—whether validity of entry in list capable of challenge before magistrate

[Local Government Finance Act 1988 (c.41), ss.41, 43, 45, 55; Non-Domestic Rating (Collection and Enforcement) (Local Lists) Regulations 1989 (S.I. 1989 No. 1056), regs. 3, 4, 12, 23; Non-Domestic Rating (Alteration of Lists and Appeals) Regulations 1990 (S.I. 1990 No. 582), regs. 4, 8, 9, 16.]

An entry in a valuation list is not capable of challenge in a magistrates' court.

The valuation officer omitted the relevant premises from the valuation list. After some months the error was realised and an entry was made. Rs were not notified of the new entry, but instead were told (wrongly) that the relevant entry had in fact been deleted from the list. Nearly two years later the authority began proceedings for a liability order for unpaid rates. After the issue of proceedings the valuation officer notified Rs of the further error and said that the time for an appeal against the entry would be extended. The magistrate refused to make a liability order on the basis that the rate was not due since no notice of the alteration in the list had been served within six weeks of the alteration. The authority appealed.

Held, that the liability order should have been made because reg. 23 of the 1989 Regulations made it plain that any matter which could found an appeal under s.55 of the 1988 Act was inadmissible as a defence to a liability order, and accordingly the magistrate was not entitled to accept the challenge to the entry in the list which was something appealable under s.55 (*China v. Harrow U.D.C.* [1953] C.L.Y. 2065, *County and Nimbus Estates v. Ealing London Borough Council* [1978] C.L.Y. 2469, *Kates v. Jeffery* [1914] 3 K.B. 160, *Mansel v. Itchen Overseers* [1906] 1 K.B. 160, *Pebmarsh Grain v. Braintree District Council* [1980] RA 236, *R. v. Thames Magistrates' Court, ex p. Christie* [1979] RA 231, *R. v. Valuation Officer, ex p. High Park Investments* [1987] C.L.Y. 3183, *Shillito v. Hinchcliffe* [1922] 2 K.B. 236, *Westminster (Mayor of) v. Army and Navy Auxiliary Co-operative Supply* [1902] 2 K.B. 125 considered).

HACKNEY LONDON BOROUGH COUNCIL v. MOTT AND FAIRMAN [1994] RA 381, Auld J.

4321. Non-domestic rating—occupation of part of hereditament—whether liable for the whole—whether regulations intended to impose such liability

[Non-Domestic Rating (Collection and Enforcement) (Miscellaneous Provisions) Regulations 1990 (S.I. 1990 No. 105), reg. 3; Local Government Finance Act 1988 (c.41), s.50.]

F appealed by way of case stated against a decision that he was liable for non-domestic rates on Ford Quarry. F worked from offices on the site from which he controlled several companies, all of which used the site. The question was whether the fact that F occupied part of a hereditament meant that a liability order for the whole could be served on him under the Non-Domestic Rating (Collection and Enforcement) (Miscellaneous Provisions) Regulations 1990.

Held, allowing the appeal, that the Regulations did not change the way occupation was determined under s.50 of the Local Government Finance Act 1988, as had been contended by BBC. The Regulations were not intended to impose upon an occupier of part of a hereditament liability to pay non-domestic rates on the whole property.

FORD v. BURNLEY BOROUGH COUNCIL, *The Times*, March 6, 1995, Pill J.

4322. Non-domestic rating—police authorities

NON-DOMESTIC RATING (POLICE AUTHORITIES) ORDER 1995, (No. 1679), made under the Local Government Finance Act 1988, s.64(7a)(7b)(7c); operative on July 7, 1995.

4323. Non-domestic rating—storage—bus depot—whether overnight parking of buses at a depot storage—whether liability avoided

[Non-Domestic Rating (Unoccupied Property) Regulations 1989 (S.I. 1989 No. 2261), reg. 2.]

B council appealed by way of case stated against a decision that the transport company, L, were not liable to pay non-domestic rates on their bus depot, where buses were parked overnight for everyday use.

Held, allowing the appeal, that the daily parking of buses could not be described as "storage" within the terms of reg. 2(5) of the Non-Domestic

Rating (Unoccupied Property) Regulations 1989 and, therefore, L were liable to pay a non-domestic rate.

BARNET LONDON BOROUGH COUNCIL v. LONDON TRANSPORT PROPERTY, *The Times*, May 11, 1995, Harrison J.

4324. Non-domestic rating—unoccupied property

NON-DOMESTIC RATING (UNOCCUPIED PROPERTY) (AMENDMENT) REGULATIONS 1995 (No. 549) [65p], made under the Local Government Finance Act 1988 (c.41), s.45(1)(d)(9); operative on April 1, 1995; amend S.I. 1989 No. 2261 so as to increase to £1,500 the rateable value of an unoccupied non-domestic hereditament for the purposes of exemption from non-domestic rates.

4325. Purchase notices—requisite number of tenants—whether tribunal entitled to consider identity of property going to validity of purchase notice—determination of reduction in consideration attributable to the grant of a lease and to costs of carrying out works specified in statutory notices of repair. See SAGA PROPERTIES v. PALMEIRA, §3048.

4326. Rateable values—electricity supply industry

ELECTRICITY SUPPLY INDUSTRY (RATEABLE VALUES) (AMENDMENT) ORDER 1995 (No. 962) [£1·10], made under the Local Government Finance Act 1988 (c.41), ss.140(4), 143(1)(2), Sched. 6, paras. 3(2); operative on April 1, 1995; amends S.I. 1994 No. 3282.

4327. Valuation and community charge tribunal

VALUATION AND COMMUNITY CHARGE TRIBUNALS (AMENDMENT) (ENGLAND) REGULATIONS 1995 (No. 363) [£1·10], made under the Local Government Finance Act 1988 (c.41), ss.55, 140(4), 143(1)(2), Sched. 11, paras. 1, 3(2), 5, 8 and the Local Government Finance Act 1992 (c.14), s.24; operative on March 10, 1995; amend S.I. 1989 No. 439 in relation to the composition of the said tribunals.

4328. Valuation list—council tax—maisonette accessible only through shop below—whether to be shown in valuation list—"composite hereditament"—bias—member of tribunal a member of county council—whether possibility of bias

[Local Government Finance Act 1992 (c.14), ss.1, 3, 21–24; Local Government Finance Act 1988 (c.41), ss.64, 66; Council Tax (Alteration of Lists and Appeals) Regulations 1993 (S.I. 1993 No. 290), regs. 23, 32; Council Tax (Contents of Valuation Lists) Regulations 1992 (S.I. 1992 No. 553), reg. 2; Council Tax (Situation and Valuation of Dwellings) Regulations 1992 (S.I. 1992 No. 550), reg. 7; Council Tax (Chargeable Dwellings) Order 1992 (S.I. 1992 No. 549), art. 2.]

W sought to challenge the inclusion on the valuation list of a maisonette above a shop. The dwelling could only be reached through the shop. In addition he claimed that part of the dwelling was used for the purposes of the shop below, such as storage. He also claimed that a member of the tribunal was biased since he was a member of the local county council.

Held, that the appeal was misconceived since the questions of means of access and usage had no bearing on the inclusion of the dwelling in the list if the dwelling was a composite hereditament, *i.e.* so long as at least one room was used exclusively for the purposes of a dwelling. Furthermore, since the local county council was not the billing authority, the council member was expressly entitled to sit as a tribunal member by reg. 23 of the Council Tax (Alteration of Lists and Appeals) Regulations.

WILLIAMS v. BRISTOL DISTRICT VALUATION OFFICER AND AVON VALUATION TRIBUNAL [1995] RA 189, Collins J.

4329. Valuation tribunals

VALUATION TRIBUNALS (WALES) REGULATIONS 1995 (No. 3056), made under the Local Government Finance Act 1988 ss.140(4), 143(1)(2), Sched. 11, paras. 1, 3 to 8, 11, 12, 14 to 16; amends S.I. 1989 No. 439. operative on January 1, 1996 for regs.1-14 and April 1, 1996 for remainder; [£4·70. New valuation tribunals for Wales are established and provision is made for determining appeals relating to community charge and council tax. Provision for the establishment of the tribunals on April 1, 1996 is contained in Parts II and III with Regulation 2 establishing four tribunals covering areas detailed in Sched. 1 and Regulations 3 and 4 providing for members of tribunals, their appointment and their duration of membership. Chairmen and presidents are dealt with in Regulations 5 and 6 with Regulations 7 and 8 providing for disqualification of membership and allowances payable to members respectively. Staffing, administration, accommodation and equipment are covered in Regulations 9 to 12. Procedures for appeals relating to council tax and community charges are provided in Parts V and VI and Part VII amends the Valuation and Community Charge Tribunals Regulations 1989 by disapplying them in relation to the newly established tribunals.

REGISTRATION OF BIRTHS, DEATHS AND MARRIAGES

4330. Births and deaths—Welsh language

REGISTRATION OF BIRTHS AND DEATHS (WELSH LANGUAGE) (AMENDMENT) REGULATIONS 1995 (No. 818) [£1·95], made under the Births and Deaths Registration Act 1953 (c.20), ss.5, 9(5), 10(1), 10A(1), 11(1)(b), 39, as extended by the Welsh Language Act 1993 (c.38), s.26(3); operative on April 1, 1995; make minor amendments to S.I. 1987 No. 2089.

4331. Births, deaths and marriages

REGISTRATION OF BIRTHS, DEATHS AND MARRIAGES (MISCELLANEOUS AMENDMENTS) REGULATIONS 1995 (No. 744) [65p], made under the Marriage Act 1949 (c.76), ss.55(1), 74(b) and the Registration Service Act 1953 (c.37), ss.6(2), 20(d); operative on April 1, 1995; amend S.I. 1968 No. 2049 and S.I. 1986 No. 1442 so as to provide for the relevant particulars of a marriage on approved premises to be entered by the registrar in the form of attestation of marriage, and also to remove the age restrictions on appointment to a registration office.

4332. Fees

REGISTRATION OF BIRTHS, DEATHS AND MARRIAGES (FEES) ORDER 1995 (No. 3162), made under the Public Expenditure Act 1968 s.5(1)(2), Sched. 3, paras. 1, 2; revokes S.I. 1994 No. 3257. operative on April 1, 1996; [£1·55]. Fees payable under Acts relating to the registration of births, deaths and marriages and associated matters from April 1, 1996 are specified in the Schedule to this Order.

4333. Marriage—approved premises

MARRIAGE (APPROVED PREMISES) REGULATIONS 1995 (No. 510) [£2·80], made under the Marriage Act 1949 (c.76), ss.46A, 46B(2), 51(1A)(b); operative on April 1, 1995; supplement the Marriage Act 1994 which permit civil marriages to take place on approved premises by setting out the application procedure, criteria for approval and requirements for registers of approved premises.

4334. Public record office

PUBLIC RECORD OFFICE (FEES) REGULATIONS 1995 (No. 991) [£1·55], made under the Public Records Act 1958 (c.51), s.2(5); operative on May 1, 1995; revoke and replace S.I. 1994 No. 2353.

RESTITUTION

4335. Interest—restitution—when cause of action arose—whether simple or compound interest payable. See GUARDIAN OCEAN CARGOES, TRANS-ORIENT SHIP CARGOES, MIDDLE EAST AGENTS S.A.L. AND MED LINE SA v. BANCO DO BRASIL (NOS. 1 AND 3), §4151.

4336. Interest-rate swap agreement—between bankers and local authority—agreements *ultra vires* and void *ab initio*—whether bankers entitled to recover payments made

[Limitation Act 1980 (c.58), ss.5, 29(5).]

Where plaintiff bankers had made payments to local authorities under interest swap agreements which were subsequently ruled *ultra vires* and void, they were entitled, in principle, to recover payments made.

Over a period of years in the 1980s, P bankers entered into five interest swap contracts with D local authority. P also entered into parallel hedging transactions to offset their liabilities. In 1991 the House of Lords ruled that such transactions were *ultra vires* and void *ab initio*. P began an action claiming restitution of over £1·6 million as money paid under the contracts.

Held, that P were entitled to restitution in respect of those contracts (treating them separately) which allowed for restoration to the pre-existing position and which were not time-barred. The fact that P had followed a hedging strategy in parallel to the interest swap transactions was irrelevant to the recognition of a restitutionary remedy *in personam* (dicta in *Footman Bower & Co., Re* [1961] C.L.Y. 5024, *Lipkin Gorman v. Karpnale* [1991] C.L.Y. 502 applied).

KLEINWORT BENSON v. SOUTH TYNESIDE METROPOLITAN BOROUGH COUNCIL [1994] 4 All E.R. 972, Hobhouse J.

4336A. Interest-rate swap agreement—recovery of money paid—defence of change of position—interest rate swap agreement entered into between local authority and bankers—agreement *ultra vires* local authorities and void—whether local authority entitled to recover net sum paid to bankers under agreement—whether bank had been unjustly enriched by receipt of money—whether any relevant change of position by bank precluding local authority from recovering sum paid—whether defence of change of position confined to changes which had taken place after receipt of money

P had entered into an interest swap agreement with the D. D was aware that the Audit Commission had expressed concern over the power of local authorities to enter into interest swap agreements. The agreement required payments of interest calculated by reference to a notional amount of money. The bank entered into hedging transactions to cover its exposure under the agreement. On August 3, 1988 the bank made the first payment under the transaction and on February 3, 1989, the local authority paid the first instalment under the agreement to the bank. In February 1989, the swaps market became aware that litigation had commenced concerning the capacity of local authorities to enter into interest rate swap agreements. Pending a final decision in that action, P made no further payments under the agreement. P brought an action against D contending that it was entitled to the repayment of the money had and received and that D had no defence on the basis that it had suffered no change of position as a result of receiving the money. D contended that the overall position had to be considered and that it had made an overall net loss having entered into the swap agreement and the resulting hedging agreements in good faith.

Held, that (1) P (as net payer under the interest rate swap agreement) was prima facie entitled to recover the net payment made to D as money had and received, being either money in equity or on the basis that there was no consideration for the payments in that both law and equity treated D as having been unjustly enriched. The fact that D made a loss on the transaction as a whole or had entered into agreements which proved to be void was immaterial. Even if P were entitled to recover sums only at common law, the position would be the same because P would be entitled to recover the net sums paid as money had and received on the basis that there was no consideration for the payment and that it was P's money which was being paid to D; (2) if a net payee under a swap agreement could demonstrate that it had altered its position in good faith after the receipt of money from the net payer it might be able to rely on the defence of change of position. What it could not do was rely on the supposed validity of the change of position because the transaction was void *ab initio*. If the change of position defence was based on the validity of the interest rate swap agreement which was in fact void, the result was that neither events before or after payment could be taken into account. Therefore, D's reliance on the effectiveness of the contract and its protective strategy could not afford D any defence of change of position. D had therefore been unjustly enriched by the receipt of P's money (*Hazell v. Hammersmith and Fulham London Borough Council* [1991] C.L.Y. 2420, *Lipkin Gorman v. Karpnale* [1991] C.L.Y. 502, *Westdeutsche Landesbank Girozentrale v. Islington London Borough Council* [1994] C.L.Y. 3911 referred to).

SOUTH TYNESIDE METROPOLITAN BOROUGH COUNCIL v. SVENSKA INTERNATIONAL [1995] 1 All E.R. 545, Clarke J.

4337. Interest-rate swap agreements—*ultra vires*—application for restitution—determination of jurisdiction—interpretation of national legislation by European Court—whether jurisdiction to give ruling—European Community

[Brussels Convention; Civil Jurisdiction and Judgments Act 1982.]

The parties had entered into a series of interest-rate swap contracts which were subsequently declared *ultra vires* by the House of Lords. P then sued in England for restitution of the money paid in performance of those contracts. D challenged the jurisdiction of the English court, arguing that the action had to be brought before the courts of the place of D's domicile in Scotland. P countered that the claim was either in matters relating to a contract or to tort, delict or quasi-delict and thus that the English courts had jurisdiction. This was to be determined by reference to the Civil Jurisdiction and Judgments Act 1982, which implemented the Brussels Convention and also, in similar terms, provided for the allocation of jurisdiction as between English and Scottish courts. The European Court of Justice was asked to interpret the relevant provisions relating to this issue since they were identical to the provisions determining jurisdiction under the Brussels Convention.

Held, that the European Court of Justice has no jurisdiction to give a preliminary ruling in this case. There were certain differences between the Convention, on the one hand, and provisions of the Act and, in particular, the Act does not specifically allow the national courts to decide disputes internal to the U.K. by applying absolutely and unconditionally the interpretation of the Convention.

KLEINWORT BENSON v. CITY OF GLASGOW DISTRICT COUNCIL (C–346/93), March 28, 1995, ECJ.

REVENUE AND FINANCE

4338. Appropriation Act 1995 (c.19)

The Act received Royal Assent on July 19, 1995.

4339. Budgetary and financial affairs—European Community

Council Regulation (EC) 3320/94 of December 22, 1994 on the consolidation of the existing Community legislation on the definition of the ECU following the entry into force of the Treaty on European Union (O.J. L350/27).

Council Regulation (E.C.) 2687/94 of October 31, 1994 on Community financial contributions to the International Fund for Ireland (O.J. L286/5).

Council Regulation (E.C.,Euratom) 2728/94 of December 31, 1994 establishing a Guarantee Fund for external actions (O.J. L293/1).

Council Decision 94/728/EC,Euratom of December 31, 1994 on the system of the European Communities' own resources (O.J. L293/9).

Council Decision 94/729/EC of December 31, 1994 on budgetary discipline (O.J. L293/14).

4340. Capital movements—exporting money—national legislation requiring prior authorisation—whether Directive precluded transaction—whether Directive rendered contrary national rules inapplicable—European Community

D were prosecuted for exporting substantial amounts of money from Spain without having obtained the required authorisation in accordance with Spanish legislation. That legislation provided that the export of coins, banknotes and bank cheques was subject to a prior declaration when the amount exceeded PTAs 1 million and was subject to prior administrative authorisation when the amount exceeded PTAs 5 million.

Held, that Arts. 30 and 59 EC were not relevant, but that Dir. 88/361/EEC precluded the export of coins, notes and cheques being made conditional on prior authorisation but, by contrast, did not preclude a transaction of that nature being made conditional on a prior declaration. This was directly effective and could be relied on before national courts to render inapplicable contrary national rules.

CRIMINAL PROCEEDINGS AGAINST BORDESSA (C-358/93 AND C-416/93), February 23, 1995, ECJ.

4341. Codes of practice—press release

The Inland Revenue has published a supplement to the Practitioners Series booklet IR131. The supplement updates existing Statements of Practice and includes new ones published between January 1, 1994 and June 30, 1995. It is available free of charge from tax offices and the Public Enquiry Room, West Wing, Somerset House, Strand, London WC2R 1LB.

4342. Consolidated Fund (No. 2) Act 1994 (c.41)

This Act makes provision for the application of £1,276,707,000 from the Consolidated Fund for the service of the year ending March 31, 1995 and for the application of £95,397,951,000 for the service of the year ending on March 31, 1996.

The Act received Royal Assent on December 16, 1994.

4343. Consolidated Fund Act 1995 (c.2)

This Act makes provision for the allocation of £167,222,897·35 out of the Consolidated Fund for the service of the year ending March 31, 1994 and of £1,171,475,000 for the year ending March 31, 1995.

The Act received Royal Assent on March 23, 1995.

4344. Contractual savings schemes

FINANCE ACT 1995 (CONTRACTUAL SAVINGS SCHEMES) (APPOINTED DAY) ORDER 1995 (No. 1778 (C.35)) [65p], made under the Finance Act 1995, s.65, Sched. 12, para. 4(3); brings into operation various provisions of the 1995

Act on July 31, 1995; appoints July 31, 1995 as the day from which the amendments to s.326 of ICTA 1988 made by paras. 4 and 5 of Sched. 12 to the Finance Act 1995 will apply to new contractual savings schemes certified under s.326 of the 1988 Act by the Treasury.

4345. Exchange gains and losses—Inland Revenue statement of practice and explanatory document

The Inland Revenue has published an explanatory document entitled *Exchange Gains and Losses and Financial Instruments: Explanatory Statement*. This document includes a statement of practice entitled "Application of foreign exchange and financial instruments legislation to partnerships which include companies". The explanatory document sets out the Inland Revenue's views on aspects of the legislation in the Finance Acts 1993, 1994 and the Finance Bill 1995. Copies are available priced £4·00 each (post free) from the Reference Library, New Wing, Somerset House, London, WC2R 1LB. Cheques to be made payable to Inland Revenue.

4346. Extra-statutory concession—interest payable in the U.K.

The Inland Revenue has published an extra-statutory concession enabling, in certain circumstances, interest payable outside the U.K. to be treated as interest payable in the U.K. in relation to the Taxes Acts. It is attached to Statement of Practice 1/95, which sets out the Revenue's interpretation of the phrase "interest payable in the United Kingdom". Enquiries to the Inland Revenue Public Enquiry Room, West Wing, Somerset House, London, WC2R 1LB.

4347. Extra-statutory concession—mortgage interest relief

The Inland Revenue has published an extra-statutory concession allowing relief for interest on a loan to buy a property which is used for both residential and business purposes, in part under the provisions relating to mortgage interest and in part as a deduction in computing business profits.

The Inland Revenue has also published a revised version of extra-statutory concession A27, *Mortgage Interest Relief: Temporary absence from mortgaged property*. It has been amended to take account of the changes to the rules for taxing income from property made by the Finance Act 1995. Enquiries to the Inland Revenue Public Enquiry Room, West Wing, Somerset House, London, WC2R 1LB.

4348. Finance Act 1993—appointed day

FINANCE ACT 1993, SECTION 11, (APPOINTED DAY) ORDER 1995 (No. 2715 (C.55)) [65p], made under the Finance Act 1993, s.11; appoints December 1, 1995 as the day on which s.11 of the Finance Act 1993 comes into force. Section 11 adds s.6A to the Hydrocarbon Oil Duties Act 1979. Section 6A charges a duty of excise on the setting aside for a chargeable use of, or on the chargeable use of any non-hydrocarbon oil liquid, comprised in s.6A, which is respectively for use or used as fuel for an engine, motor or other machinery ("substitute fuel") or as an additive or extender for any such substitute fuel or for any hydrocarbon oil, such as diesel fuel, charged with duty by the 1979 Act. Section 6A enables the Treasury to make an order prescribing the rate of excise duty which shall apply on any such setting aside or chargeable use. Section 11 repeals provisions of the 1979 Act relating to petrol substitutes and power methylated spirits, and amends other provisions mentioned in subs. (3), and amends the Excise Duties (Surcharges or Rebates) Act 1979.

4349. Finance Act 1994—appointed day

FINANCE ACT 1994, SECTION 105, (APPOINTED DAY) ORDER 1995 (No. 3125 (C.72)), made under the Finance Act 1994 s.105(5). operative on bringing into force s.105(3) and s.105(4)(b) of the Act on January 1, 1996; [65p]. This Order appoints January 1, 1996 as the day that the Finance Act 1994 s.105(3), s.105(4)(b) and the Retirement Benefits Schemes (Information Powers) Regulations 1995,), made under the those sections, come into force. The new provisions introduced by these sections and regulations relate to the Inland Revenue Commissioners' powers to make regulations relating to information and documents connected with retirement benefits schemes.

4350. Finance Act 1995 (c.4)

This Act grants certain duties, alters other duties and amends the law relating to the National Debt and the Public Revenue, as well as making further provision in connection with finance. Part I deals with duties of excise, Part II with VAT and insurance premium tax, Part III with income tax, corporation tax and capital gains tax, Part IV with petroleum revenue tax and Part V with stamp duty.

The Act received Royal Assent on May 1, 1995.

4351. Finance Act 1995—appointed day

FINANCE ACT 1995, SECTION 20, (APPOINTED DAY) ORDER 1995 (No. 2892 (C.61)) [65p], made under the Finance Act 1995, s.20; brings into operation s.20 of the 1995 Act on December 1, 1995; this section amends the Customs and Excise Management Act 1979 by inserting s.137A, which provides for the recovery of overpaid excise duty.

FINANCE ACT 1995, SECTION 24, (APPOINTED DAY) ORDER 1995 (No. 1374 (C.28)) [65p], made under the Finance Act 1995 (c.4), s.24(2); appoints June 1, 1995 as the day on which the Value Added Tax Act 1994 (c.23), s.32, shall be revoked.

FINANCE ACT 1995, SECTION 63(2), (APPOINTED DAY) ORDER 1995 (No. 3236), made under the Finance Act 1995 s.63(5). operative on January 1, 1996; [65p]. This Order relating to TESSAs opened after January 1, 1996 applies to the Finance Act 1995 s.63(2) which made amendments to ICTA 1988 s.326A(4) by adding relevant European institutions to the list of societies and institutions with which TESSAs may be held. A relevant European institution is one authorised within the meaning of the Banking Co-ordination (Second Council Directive) Regulations 1992 as amended.

FINANCE ACT 1995, SECTION 82, (APPOINTED DAY) ORDER 1995 (No. 2933 (C.63)) [65p], made under the Finance Act 1995, s.82(4). provides for manufactured interest on gilt-edged securities to have effect in relation to any payments made on or after January 2, 1996.

4352. Financial markets and insolvency

FINANCIAL MARKETS AND INSOLVENCY (MONEY MARKET) REGULATIONS 1995 (No. 2049) [£2·80], made under the Companies Act 1989, ss.171, 176, 181, 185, 186; operative on August 15, 1995; apply the provisions of Pt. VII of the Companies Act 1989, with modifications, to certain aspects of the settlement arrangements in relation to the money markets provided by persons admitted to a list maintained by the Bank of England under s.171 of the 1989 Act.

4353. Financial services—discovery—restricted information—whether action for breach of statutory duty

[Financial Services Act 1986 (c.60), ss.179, 187(3).]

Section 179 of the Financial Services Act 1986 does not confer a personal cause of action upon those whose consent is required for the disclosure of restricted information where there has been disclosure without their consent.

P2 made a substantial loan from pension funds of which it was a trustee to P1 in respect of which the beneficiaries of the pension funds brought an action against Ps. The Securities and Investment Board (SIB) appointed investigators to conduct an investigation into P2. The investigators sought and obtained information from the auditors of the funds, and the SIB disclosed to the auditors certain information obtained by the SIB in the course of its investigation. Ps sought damages from the SIB on the grounds that it had wrongfully disclosed restricted information contrary to s.179 of the 1986 Act and but for such disclosure Ps would have reached a settlement of the beneficiaries' action upon terms which did not require either of them to make any payment to the fund.

Held, striking out the action, that (1) s.179 of the 1986 Act did not confer a personal cause of action upon those whose consent was required for the disclosure of restricted information where there had been disclosure without their consent; (2) the disclosure of non-restricted information by the SIB to assist the beneficiaries in the course of their litigation accorded with its express role under the 1986 Act, which was to protect the interests of investors and customers of financial services; and (3) on the facts, the disclosures complained of did not constitute restricted information and accordingly the claim would be struck out in its entirety since there was no personal cause of action, no mala fides and no disclosure in contravention of the 1986 Act.

MELTON MEDES v. SECURITIES AND INVESTMENTS BOARD [1995] 2 W.L.R. 247, Lightman J.

4354. Financial services—European regulated markets

FINANCIAL SERVICES ACT 1986 (EUROPEAN REGULATED MARKETS) (EXEMPTION) ORDER 1995 (No. 3273), made under the Financial Services Act 1986 s.46 In force: January 1, 1996; [65p] This Order makes provision for an exemption from the scope of the authorisation requirement imposed by Part I of the Financial Services Act 1986. The exemption is needed because Art.15.4 of Council Directive 93/22/EEC on investment services in the securities field has the effect that an EEA State must allow a market of the kind described in the Order to place within the territory of the State the facilities necessary to enable investment firms from that State to become members of the market or to have access to it. The exemption has the effect that a person may, without having to obtain authorisation under the Financial Services Act, provide within the UK trading facilities constituting a market which operates without any requirement for a person dealing on the market to have a physical presence either in the EEA State from which the trading facilities are provided or on any physical floor that the market may have, provided that the market appears on a list drawn up by another EEA State pursuant to the provisions of Art.16 of Directive 93/22.

4355. Financial services—exemptions

FINANCIAL SERVICES ACT 1986 (MISCELLANEOUS EXEMPTIONS) ORDER 1995 (No. 202) [65p], made under the Financial Services Act 1986 (c.60), s.46; operative on February 22, 1995; provides that the Commonwealth Development Corporation and the Church of Ireland Trustee shall be exempt from the 1986 Act for specified purposes.

4356. Financial services—investment advertisements

FINANCIAL SERVICES ACT 1986 (INVESTMENT ADVERTISEMENTS) (EXEMPTIONS) ORDER 1995 (No. 1266) [£3·20], made under the Financial Services Act 1986 (c.60), ss.58(3)(a)–(c)(4), 205A; operative on June 19, 1995; amends and adds to the various restrictions on advertising imposed by s.57 of the 1986 Act.

FINANCIAL SERVICES ACT 1986 (INVESTMENT ADVERTISEMENTS) (EXEMPTIONS) (NO. 2) ORDER 1995 (No. 1536) [£3·20], made under the Financial Services Act 1986 (c.60), ss.58(3)(d), 205A; operative on June 19,

1995; consolidates, amends and adds to the various exemptions from the restrictions on advertising imposed by s.57 of the 1986 Act.

4357. Financial services—investment services

FINANCIAL SERVICES ACT 1986 (INVESTMENT SERVICES) (EXTENSION OF SCOPE OF ACT) ORDER 1995 No. 3271), made under the Financial Services Act 1986 ss.2, 205A. operative on January 1, 1996; [£1·55]. In order to give effect to provisions of Council Directive 93/22, the Investment Services Directive, this Order amends the scope of the Financial Services Act 1986. Articles 3 and 4 add certain instruments to the investments within Part I of Sched. 1 of the 1986 Act which relates to shares in industrial and provident societies and bills of exchange. Article 5 extends the definition of activities which constitute the carrying on of investment business and the definition of "investment business" as it relates to Part II of Sched. 1 of the 1986 Act to cover the provision of all investment services to which the EC Directive applies.

4358. Financial services—investors' compensation scheme—home income plans—misleading advice—compensation—judicial review of assessment policy

[Financial Services Act 1986 (c.60), s.54.]

ICS appealed against a Court of Appeal decision allowing B's application for judicial review of ICS's policy in relation to the assessment of compensation. B and others were purchasers of home income plans on which they had lost money as a result of misleading advice given by financial advisers who had subsequently gone into liquidation. ICS claimed they were entitled to deduct from any compensation sums already received and spent under the home income plan, and also to cap to £500 the amount recoverable for adviser's fees paid out in attempts to mitigate the loss.

Held, allowing the appeal, that r.2.04 of the Financial Services (Compensation of Investors) Rules 1990, made by the SIB under s.54 of the Financial Services Act 1986, provided that the claims which could be compensated were for property held and those arising from other simple transactions. Applications for compensation relating to any other claims would only be met when the ICS thought that it was fair and reasonable to do so. The investors claim that they should receive the same amount of money they would have received in any action against their advisers had they not gone into liquidation, including amounts already received and spent, could not be sustained because ICS had discretion under the Rules to disallow sums already received by the investors and therefore the decision could not be said to be one which no reasonable authority could have reached. The result might be unfortunate but the courts could not interfere.

R. v. INVESTORS COMPENSATION SCHEME, *ex p.* BOWDEN, *The Times*, July 18, 1995, H.L.

4359. Financial services—investors' compensation scheme—self-regulating organisation—contributions for default of non-members—whether lawful—judicial review

[Financial Services Act 1986 (c.60), s.54.]

SLAS applied for judicial review of the rules of the SIB's Investors' Compensation Scheme, under which members of the Personal Investment Authority, a self-regulating organisation, could be required to make contributions towards the costs of compensating for the default of non-members. SLAS, a member of the PIA, submitted that the rules were unlawful under s.54(3)(b) of the Financial Services Act 1986.

Held, dismissing the application, that the purpose of s.54(3)(b) was to ensure that the contributions from existing members of a self-regulating organisation were sufficient to discharge its liabilities. Section 54 did not allocate liability, but legitimised the method by which the self-regulating organisation chose to do so under the rules of the compensation scheme.

R. v. SECURITIES AND INVESTMENTS BOARD, *ex p.* SUN LIFE ASSURANCE SOCIETY, *The Independent*, October 5, 1995, Sedley J.

4360. Financial services—professional standards

The Securities and Investments Board (SIB) has issued a press release entitled *SIB Publishes Standards of regulation for self-regulating organisations and recognised professional bodies* (Press Release PN/SIB/035/95), published on September 14, 1995. Copies of Guidance Release 3/95, *Standards of Regulation for Self Regulating Organisations and Standards of Regulation for Recognised Professional Bodies* are available from SIB Publications, price £5·00.

4361. Financial Services Act 1986—commencement

FINANCIAL SERVICES ACT 1986 (COMMENCEMENT) (NO. 13) ORDER 1995 (No. 1538 (C.33)), made under the Financial Services Act 1986, s.211(1); brings into operation various provisions of the 1986 Act on June 19, 1995; brings in s.212(3) of and Sched. 17 to the Financial Services Act 1986, which repeals Pt. III of and Sched. 3 to the Companies Act 1985.

4362. Government trading funds

BUYING AGENCY TRADING FUND (EXTENSION) ORDER 1995 (No. 1665), made under the Government Trading Funds Act 1973, ss.1, 2(1), 2A, 6(1); operative on July 1, 1995.

DEFENCE EVALUATION AND RESEARCH AGENCY TRADING FUND ORDER 1995 (No. 650) [£1·10], made under the Government Trading Funds Act 1973 (c.63), ss.1(1), 2, 2A(1), 6(1); operative on April 1, 1995; amends S.I. 1993 No. 380 so as to extend the operations of the former Defence Research Agency Trading Fund (now renamed the Defence Evaluation and Research Agency Trading Fund) and to provide for additional assets to be appropriated to the fund.

4363. Inland Revenue—financial trader status—Statement of Practice

The Inland Revenue has published a new Statement of Practice SP3/95, setting out the guidelines which the Board of Inland Revenue will use in deciding whether a company should be approved as a financial trader for the purposes of s.177(1) of the Finance Act 1994. Enquiries to the Inland Revenue Public Enquiry Room, West Wing, Somerset House, London, WC2R 1LB.

4364. Inland Revenue—interest payable in the U.K.—Statement of Practice

A revised statement of practice entitled "Interest Payable in the U.K." (C.5) has been issued by the Inland Revenue. It sets out the Inland Revenue's interpretation of interest payable in the U.K. in relation to ss.337(3), 338(1)(3)(b) and 349(2)(3)(a) of the Taxes Acts. Inland Revenue statements of practice are available free of charge from any Tax Enquiry Centre or Tax Office, or may be obtained from the Inland Revenue Public Enquiry Room, West Wing, Somerset House, Strand, London, WC2R 1LB.

4365. Inland Revenue—legal entitlement and administrative practices—revised Statement of Practice

The Inland Revenue has issued a revised Statement of Practice SP6/95, which explains the circumstances in which overpayments of tax are not repaid automatically. It supersedes an existing Statement of Practice SP1/80. Enquiries to the Inland Revenue, Public Enquiry Room, West Wing, Somerset House, London, WC2R 1LB.

4366. Inland Revenue—long-term insurance—computations of profit for tax purposes—Statement of Practice

The Inland Revenue has published a Statement of Practice SP4/95 on the measurement of the taxable trading profit from life insurance business, and other forms of long-term insurance. Enquiries to the Inland Revenue Public Enquiry Room, West Wing, Somerset House, London, WC2R 1LB.

4367. Inland Revenue—receipts of commission—insurance and personal pension schemes—taxation implications—revised Statement of Practice

The Inland Revenue has published a Statement of Practice SP5/95 about the taxation implications of receipts of commission on the sale of any insurance policies, life annuity contracts, capital redemption policies and personal pension schemes. This replaces Statement of Practice 3/79. Enquiries to the Public Enquiry Room, West Wing, Somerset House, London, WC2R 1LB.

4368. Inland Revenue—tax credit relief—list of admissible and inadmissible taxes

The Inland Revenue has published a booklet IR146, *Double Taxation Relief—Admissible and Inadmissible Taxes*. It contains a full list of foreign taxes whose admissibility for tax credit relief the Inland Revenue have considered up to December 31, 1994. Copies of the booklet are available from The Public Enquiries Room, West Wing, Somerset House, London, WC2R 1LB.

4369. Inland Revenue—venture capital trusts—Statement of Practice

The Inland Revenue has issued a press release entitled *News on Venture Capital Trusts*, published on September 14, 1995. The Government is to relax the rules on capital trusts which prevent the trusts from controlling the companies in which they invest. The Inland Revenue is to issue guidance on various technical issues, and has published two new statements of practice (SP7/95 and SP8/95) and revised texts of two other statements of practice (SP2/94 and SP3/94) which are appended to the press release and are also available from the Inland Revenue Public Enquiry Room, West Wing, Somerset House, London, WC2R 1LB.

4370. Interest rates

TAXES (INTEREST RATE) (AMENDMENT) REGULATIONS 1995 (No. 2436) [65p], made under the Finance Act 1989, s.178; amend S.I. 1989 No. 1297; operative on October 6, 1995; reduce the official rate of interest for the purposes of taxation of beneficial loans made to employees from eight per cent to 7.75 per cent per annum from October 6, 1995.

4371. Investment services

INVESTMENT SERVICES REGULATIONS 1995 (No. 3275), made under the European Communities Act 1972 s.2(2). Amends 1974 c.39; 1986 c.60 operative on January 1, 1996 for all regs except regs 27 and 31, and January 1, 1997 for regs 27 and 31; [£7·45. These Regulations give effect to provisions of Council Directive 93/22/EEC on investment services in the securities field and Council Directive 93/6/EEC on the capital adequacy of investment firms and credit institutions. Part I of the Regulations defines various words and expressions for the purposes of the Regulations. Part II deals with recognition in the UK of European investment firms. Part III makes provision for the implementation of certain decisions by the Council or Commission of the European Communities. Part IV deals with recognition in other EEA states of UK investment firms. Part V amends the Financial Services Act 1986. Part VI amends the Consumer Credit Act 1974. Part VII introduces new requirements obliging persons who wish to acquire or increase holdings in UK authorised investment firms in excess of specified sizes to notify the relevant regulators before doing so.

4372. Lloyd's underwriters

LLOYD'S UNDERWRITERS (SPECIAL RESERVE FUNDS) REGULATIONS 1995 (No. 353) [£1·55], made under the Finance Act 1993 (c.34), ss.182(1)(c)(4), 184(1)(3), Sched. 20, paras. 3(2), 4(8), 5(10), 6(1)(3), 11(5); operative on March 9, 1995; make provision in relation to the special reserve funds of non-corporate underwriting members of Lloyd's.

LLOYD'S UNDERWRITERS (SPECIAL RESERVE FUNDS) (AMENDMENT) REGULATIONS 1995 (No. 1185) [£1·10], made under the Finance Act 1993 (c.34), s.182(1)(c)(4); operative on May 23, 1995; amend S.I. 1995 No. 353.

LLOYD'S UNDERWRITERS (TAX) (1992–93 TO 1996–97) REGULATIONS 1995 (No. 352) [£1·95], made under the Finance Act 1993 (c.34), ss.182(1)(3)(4), 184(1)(3) and the Taxation of Chargeable Gains Act 1992 (c.12), s.209(2)(6); operative on March 9, 1995; make provision for the assessment and collection of tax charged on non-corporate underwriting members of Lloyd's for the years of assessment 1992–93 to 1996–97 in accordance with s.171 of the 1993 Act.

LLOYD'S UNDERWRITERS (TAX) REGULATIONS 1995 (No. 351) [£2·80], made under the Finance Act 1993 (c.34), ss.179(2), 179A(3)(b), 182(1)(4)(5), 184(1)(3) and the Finance Act 1994 (c.9), ss.227(2), 229(a), 230(1)(3); operative on March 9, 1995; make provision for the taxation of underwriting members of Lloyd's.

4373. Motorvehicle taxation—imports—whether discriminatory internal taxation—whether prohibited by Community law—European Community

P sought reimbursement of the motorvehicle tax charged to him when he imported a second-hand car into Portugal from Belgium. The tax was levied in Portugal on motorvehicles imported new or second-hand, or assembled or manufactured in Portugal, and which been duly registered. P argued that the tax on imported second-hand vehicles was either an import duty or discriminatory internal taxation prohibited by the E.C. Treaty.

Held, that a motorvehicle tax applied without distinction to vehicles assembled or manufactured in a Member State and to both new and imported second-hand vehicles is not a customs duty or charge having equivalent effect within the meaning of Arts. 9 and 12 EC. However, it is incompatible with Art. 95 EC for a Member State to charge on second-hand cars from other Member States a tax which, calculated without taking the vehicle's actual depreciation into account, exceeds the residual tax incorporated in the value of similar second-hand motorvehicles already registered in the national territory.

FAZENDA PUBLICA v. NUNES TADEU (C–345/93), March 9, 1995, ECJ, Fifth Chamber.

4374. Premium savings bonds

PREMIUM SAVINGS BONDS (AMENDMENT) REGULATIONS 1995 (No. 1002) [65p], made under the National Debt Act 1972 (c.65), s.11; operative on May 1, 1995; revoke reg. 6 of S.I. 1972 No. 765.

4375. Profits tax—taxpayer objecting to assessments—whether commissioner determining objections "within a reasonable time"—whether commissioner deprived of jurisdiction

[Inland Revenue Ordinance (Laws of Hong Kong, 1993 rev. c.112), ss.14, 64(1)(2).]

[H.K.] Having regard to the provisions of the Inland Revenue Ordinance (Laws of Hong Kong, 1993 rev. c.112) as a whole, even where the deputy commissioner failed to make a determination within a reasonable time, nevertheless his failure would not render his determinations void.

In 1986 notices of assessment demands for profits tax under s.14 of the Inland Revenue Ordinance were made on the taxpayer as agent for the company. Notices of objection were given by the taxpayer. A determination was made, from which the taxpayer appealed. Shortly before the hearing two further determinations were made so as to enable all the assessments to be considered simultaneously. The taxpayer applied for certiorari to quash the determinations since they had not been made within a reasonable time as required by s.64(2). The judge quashed them and the Court of Appeal reversed the decision.

Held, dismissing the appeal to the Judicial Committee, that whether a determination had been made by the commissioner within a reasonable time was a question of fact and here there were satisfactory explanations. In any event, even if the commissioner had so failed, his failure would not have deprived him of jurisdiction or have rendered his determination void (*London and Clydeside Estates v. Aberdeen District Council* [1980] C.L.Y. 315 applied; *Cullimore v. Lyme Regis Corp.* [1981] C.L.Y. 8042 distinguished).

WANG v. COMMISSIONER OF INLAND REVENUE [1994] 1 W.L.R. 1286, P.C.

4376. Prohibition—financial intermediaries offering investment in off-market commodities futures—via unsolicited telephone calls—whether restriction on freedom to provide services. See ALPINE INVESTMENTS BV v. MINISTER VAN FINANCIEN (C–384/93), §641.

4377. Regulatory bodies—LAUTRO—rule amendment on eligible employees' indebtedness—whether rule unreasonable and irrational

LAUTRO amended its rules so that no member company could employ a person who owed another member company in excess of £1,000. This was challenged by the applicant for judicial review who argued that the rule was wholly unreasonable, and had illogical consequences.

Held, dismissing the application, that indebtedness on the part of an employee in an investment business could affect his business competence, and this rule was designed to mitigate the mischief of an employee in debt selling policies because of their commission value to him, rather than because of their suitability to the purchaser's circumstances.

R. v. LIFE ASSURANCE AND UNIT TRUST REGULATORY ORGANISATION, *ex p.* KENDALL [1994] C.O.D. 169, D.C.

4378. Returns—automatic penalties—extra-statutory concession

The Inland Revenue has issued a press release entitled *Automatic Penalties for Late Company and Employers' and Contractors' End-of-year Returns: Extra-statutory Concession*, published on September 14, 1995. A booklet containing details of extra-statutory concessions is available free from the Inland Revenue Public Enquiry Room, West Wing, Somerset House, WC2R 1LB.

4379. Revenue collection—statistics

Tho Chartorod Instituted of Public Finance and Accountancy has published *Revenue Collection Statistics: 1993–94 Actuals* (SIS Ref. 42.95). It is the fourth in a series of statistics describing the levies made by local authorities following the Government's introduction of the community charge and the national non-domestic rate in April 1990. For further information, telephone 0181 667 1144. Price £80·00 to non-SIS subscribers. ISSN 0966–0836.

4379a. Savings—tax treatment of interest—guide. See BUILDING SOCIETIES, §517.

4380. Securities—sale and repurchase

SALE AND REPURCHASE OF SECURITES (MODIFICATION OF ENACTMENTS) REGULATIONS 1995 (No. 3220) [£1.10], made under the Income and

Corporation Taxes Act 1988, s.737E(1)(2)(4); operative on January 2, 1996; modify provisions dealings with tax treatment of transactions involving the sale and purchase of securities.

4381. Tax reforms—substitute return forms

Advance copies of the major 1995 Return forms are now available for professional bodies and software houses who wish to produce substitute forms. A specimen copy of each return form and an information sheet "Tax Returns: Guidelines for Production of Substitute Forms" can be obtained from Inland Revenue, Corporate Communications Office, 6th Floor (KB), North West Wing, Bush House, London, WC2B 4PP. Applications for approval of substitute 1995 Return forms should be sent to Room 9/3A at the same address.

4382. Tax reliefs

MANUFACTURED PAYMENTS AND TRANSFER OF SECURITIES (TAX RELIEF) REGULATIONS 1995 (No. 3036) [65p], made under the Income and Corporation Taxes Act 1988, ss.730A(7), 737D(1). In force: January 2, 1996; make provision for payments of manufactured dividends, manufactured interest and manufactured overseas dividends made to certain pension schemes and funds to be exempt from income tax, and manufactured payments made to insurance companies who are carrying on pensions business are exempt from corporation tax. Similar provision is also made in relation to payments of interest under the part of ICTA 1988 dealing with the treatment of price differential on the sale and repurchase of securities where payment is made to pension schemes, funds and insurance companies.

4383. TESSAS

TAX-EXEMPT SPECIAL SAVINGS ACCOUNT (AMENDMENT) REGULATIONS 1995 (No. 1929), made under the Income and Corporation Taxes Act 1988, s.326C(1)(1A); amends S.I. 1990 No. 2361; operative on August 11, 1995.

TAX-EXEMPT SPECIAL SAVINGS ACCOUNT (RELEVANT EUROPEAN INSTITUTIONS) REGULATIONS 1995 (No. 3239), made under the Income and Corporation Taxes Act 1988 ss.326C(1)(1A), 326D; amends S.I. 1990 No. 2361. operative on January 2, 1996; [£1·10]. These Regulations provide that European authorised institutions wihtin the meaning of the Banking Co-ordination (Second Council Directive) Regulations 1992 (S.I. 1992 No. 3218, amended by S.I. 1993 No. 3225 and 1995 1217) which may accept deposits in the UK in accordance with those Regulations and which operate tax-exempt special savings accounts, must appoint tax representatives for the purposes of discharging the duties of the institution under the Tax-exempt Special Savings Account Regulations 1990 or make other arrangements with the Inland Revenue Commissioners for the discharge of those duties. They also amend the 1990 Regulations so as to add relevant European institutions to the societies and institutions which may operate accounts and make further amendments which are consequential on that addition.

4384. Uncertificated securities

UNCERTIFICATED SECURITIES REGULATIONS 1995 (No. 3272), made under the Companies Act 1989 s.207 and Transfer of Functions (Financial Services) Order 1992; revokes S.I. 1992 No. 225. operative on December 19, 1995; [£6·30. The legal framework underlying the operation of a computer based system and set of procedures used to transfer of title to a unit of a security without written instruments or evidencing by certificate and the criteria which the Operator, the person around which the system centres, are set out in these Regulations. Part I sets out the purposes and definitions of the Regulations, Part II makes provisions regarding the Operator, his approval by the Treasury, compliance and supervision, Part III sets out conditions on which issuers are able to allow securities issued to become participating issues, the keeping of registers of securities by participating issuers, conversions and new issues and dematerialised instructions are dealt with in Part V. Part IV covers miscellaneous and supplemental provisions including breaches of statutory duty and the liability of officers. The Schedules include requirements for approval of a person as Operator, the prevention of restrictive practices and adaptations with respect to Northern Ireland.

4385. Vocational training

VOCATIONAL TRAINING (PUBLIC FINANCIAL ASSISTANCE AND DISENTITLEMENT TO TAX RELIEF) (AMENDMENT) REGULATIONS 1995 (No. 3274), made under the Finance Act 1991 s.32(1) operative on January 8, 1996; [65p]. These Regulations update the Vocational Training (Public Financial Assistance and Disentitlement to Tax Relief) Regulations 1992 by adding new types of public financial assistance, extending existing types to cover locally named schemes within the same type, and removing a type (Training Credits Scheme) that has been replaced.

ROAD TRAFFIC

4386. Automatism—hypoglycaemia—definition of voluntary control—whether total loss of voluntary control—whether gradual loss of control sufficient for automatism. See CHELSEA GIRL v. ALPHA OMEGA ELECTRICAL SERVICES, §3644.

4387. Careless driving—causing death by—influence of drink or drugs—whether sentencing guidelines for drink driving cases relevant to drug case. See R. v. JORDAN, §1315.

4388. Careless driving—causing death having consumed excess alcohol—whether sentence excessive. See R. v. DEERY, §1319.

4389. Careless driving—compensation order—meaning of word "payable"—whether amount must be immediately owing—whether magistrates' power to award compensation limited to amount unrecoverable from Motor Insurers' Bureau. See D.P.P. v. SCOTT, §1327.

4390. Causing death by dangerous driving—jury directions—police officer attempting to stop stolen motorcycle. See R. v. WALLINGTON, §1053.

4391. Causing death by dangerous driving—sentencing—good character. See R. v. MARTON (DOUGLAS JOHN) (94/6872/Y3), §1346.

4392. Construction and use

ROAD VEHICLES (CONSTRUCTION AND USE) (AMENDMENT) REGULATIONS 1995 (No. 551) [£2·80], made under the Road Traffic Act 1988 (c.52), s.41(1)(2)(5); operative on April 1, 1995; further amend S.I. 1986 No. 1078 in relation to brakes and tyres.

ROAD VEHICLES (CONSTRUCTION AND USE) (AMENDMENT) (NO. 2) REGULATIONS 1995 (No. 737) [65p], made under the Road Traffic Act 1988 (c.52), s.41(1)(2)(5); operative on March 31, 1995; amend S.I. 1995 No. 551 in relation to brakes and tyres in order to correct an error.

ROAD VEHICLES (CONSTRUCTION AND USE) (AMENDMENT) (NO. 3) REGULATIONS 1995 (No. 1201) [65p], made under the Road Traffic Act 1988 (c.52), s.41(1)(2)(5); operative on June 1, 1995; further amend S.I. 1986 No. 1078.

ROAD VEHICLES (CONSTRUCTION AND USE) (AMENDMENT) (NO. 4)

REGULATIONS 1995 (No. 1458), made under Road Traffic Act 1988, s.41(1)(2)(5), amend S.I. 1986 No. 1078; require certain goods vehicles to be fitted with speed limiters, exempt a vehicle when it is used on a road in circumstances similar to those that attracting the exemption under the Vehicle Excise and Registration Act 1994, Sched. 2, para. 21.

ROAD VEHICLES (CONSTRUCTION AND USE) (AMENDMENT) (NO. 5) REGULATIONS 1995 (No. 2210) [£2·40], made under the Road Traffic Act 1988, s.41(1)(2)(5); amend S.I. 1986 No. 1078; operative on September 25, 1995 for the purposes of reg. 3(4)(5)(5), January 1, 1996 for all other purposes; amend reg. 61 of the 1986 Regulations to introduce compulsory compliance with emission limits from vehicles with spark ignition engines first used on or after January 1, 1997 as set by Council Dir. 94/12 and provision for other vehicles whenever first used to comply with those limits as an alternative to existing requirements.

ROAD VEHICLES (CONSTRUCTION AND USE) (AMENDMENT) (NO. 6) REGULATIONS 1995 (No. 3051) [£1·10], made under the Road Traffic Act 1988, s.41(1)(2)(5). In force: January 1, 1996; amend S.I. 1986 No. 1078 by increasing the maximum overall width of motor vehicles, various agricultural trailers and vehicles and trailers drawn by motor vehicles with a maximum gross weight exceeding 3500kg from 2.5m to 2.55m with the exception of locomotives which are not agricultural vehicles and refrigerated vehicles which are already subject to a maximum overall width of 2.75 and 2.6m respectively. The definition of "overall width" in the 1986 Regulations is also amended so that guidewheels fitted to a bus can be disregarded provided they do not project more than 75mm beyond the side of the bus.

4393. Costs—appeal against conviction on the grounds of inconsistency allowed—costs refused—whether should be allowed. See R. v. SHEFFIELD CROWN COURT, *ex p.* AUBREY (CO2712/93), §1015.

4394. Cycle racing on highways

CYCLE RACING ON HIGHWAYS (AMENDMENT) REGULATIONS 1995 (No. 3241 made under Road Traffic Act 1988 s.31(2)(3); amends S.I. 1960 No. 250. In force: January 26, 1996; [65p]. These Regulations increase the maximum number of competitiors from 60 to 80 for "bicycle races" held and conducted under the "standard conditions" of the Cycle Racing on Highways Regulations 1960.

4395. Dangerous driving—causing death by—excess alcohol—mitigating factors and remorse of defendants no reason for not imposing adequate sentence. See R. v. RAYNER (ATT.-GEN.'S REFERENCE (NO. 24 OF 1994)); R. v. WING (ATT.-GEN.'S REFERENCE (NO. 32 OF 1994)), §1344.

4396. Disqualification from driving—excess alcohol—medical emergency—necessity of risk of serious injury. See D.P.P. v. WHITTLE, §1348.

4397. Disqualification from driving—excess alcohol—special reasons for not disqualifying—friends of motorist injured—motorist trying to find ambulance and taxi—driving friends to hospital—whether constituting special reasons. See D.P.P. v. UPCHURCH, §1349.

4398. Disqualification from driving—excess alcohol—special reasons for not disqualifying—threat by woman to accuse of rape—whether personal crisis amounting to emergency. See D.P.P. v. ENSTON, §1352.

4399. Disqualification from driving—excess alcohol—special reasons for not disqualifying—no intention to drive—attempts to find alternative transport—need to return home because of threats of violence made against baby and babysitter—whether constituting special reasons. See D.P.P. v. KNIGHT (NOTE–1988), §1350.

4400. Disqualification from driving—removal of disqualification order—legal aid refused—judicial review—whether application is "criminal proceedings". See R. v. LIVERPOOL CROWN COURT, *ex p.* McCANN, §3114.

4401. Disqualification from driving—term—failure to provide specimen at police station—plea to offence of failing to provide specimen for roadside test—whether plea to incompetent offence. See R. v. MOORE (FRANK), §1353.

4402. Drivers' records—exemption—breakdown vehicle. See FORGAN v. HAMILTON, §6293.

4403. Driving instruction

MOTOR CARS (DRIVING INSTRUCTION) (AMENDMENT) REGULATIONS 1995 (No. 1218), made under the Road Traffic Act 1988, ss.125(3), 127(2), 132(2), 141 and S.I. 1988 No. 643; amend S.I. 1989 No. 2057; operative on May 29, 1995.

4404. Driving licences

MOTOR VEHICLES (DRIVING LICENCES) (AMENDMENT) REGULATIONS 1995 (No. 1200) [£1·10], made under the Road Traffic Act 1988 (c.52), ss.89(3)(4)(b), 105(1)(3), 108(1), 192(1); operative on May 29, 1995; amend S.I. 1987 No. 1378 so as to increase the fees for ordinary driving tests, London taxi driver tests and extended driving tests.

MOTOR VEHICLES (DRIVING LICENCES) (AMENDMENT) (NO. 2) REGULATIONS 1995 (No. 2076) [65p], made under the Road Traffic Act 1988, ss.89(3)(6)(7), 105(1)(2)(3), 108(1), 192(3); amend S.I. 1987 No. 1378; operative on August 15, 1995; contain a minor amendment consequential upon the substitution of two new exemptions from the provisions of the Motor Vehicles (Driving Licences) (Large Goods and Passenger Carrying Vehicles) Regulations 1990.

4405. Driving licences—disqualification—driving without insurance. See DOCHERTY v. NORMAND, §6308.

4406. Driving licences—large goods and passenger-carrying vehicles

MOTOR VEHICLES (DRIVING LICENCES) (LARGE GOODS AND PASSENGER-CARRYING VEHICLES) (AMENDMENT) REGULATIONS 1995 (No. 1162) [65p], made under the Road Traffic Act 1988 (c.52), ss.91(b), 105(1)(3), 108(1), 192(1); operative on May 29, 1995; amend S.I. 1990 No. 2612 so that 10 days' notice must be given of the cancellation of a driving test in order for the fee to be repaid.

MOTOR VEHICLES (DRIVING LICENCES) (LARGE GOODS AND PASSENGER CARRYING VEHICLES) (AMENDMENT NO. 2) REGULATIONS 1995 (No. 2075) [65p], made under the Road Traffic Act 1988, ss.105(1)(2)(3), 108(1); amend S.I. 1990 No. 2612; operative on August 15, 1995.

4407. Driving offences—driving without due care and attention—necessity—police officer in pursuit of vehicle under surveillance—whether defence of necessity available

[Road Traffic Act 1988 (c.52), s.5; Traffic Signs Regulations and General Directions 1981 (S.I. 1981 No. 859), reg. 34.]

The defence of necessity does not override the circumstances in which a police car may proceed through a red traffic light as set out in reg. 34 of the Traffic Signs Regulations and General Directions 1981.

D was a plain clothes police officer in an unmarked police car who was pursuing a car containing individuals who were thought likely to commit an armed robbery that day at an unknown location. The putative robbers' car passed through a green traffic light at a junction. D arrived when the light had changed to red. He proceeded to cross the junction after momentarily checking it was safe. As he crossed he collided with a car travelling through the junction on the green light. D could not see the car because it was shielded from view by a line of traffic which was stationary in a filter lane. D was prosecuted for careless driving and was acquitted on the ground that the defence of necessity was open to him, as it had been necessary for him to cross the junction in order to ensure that the armed robbery would, if it took place, be foiled.

Held, allowing the prosecutor's appeal, that the defence of necessity was not available to D as reg. 34 of the Traffic Signs Regulations and General Directions 1981 made express provision for the circumstances in which a police car could pass through a red light. In any event D should have moved forward carefully so as to ensure he had a clear view before moving across the junction. Had he done so the accident would have been avoided. From an objective standpoint D had failed to act reasonably or proportionately in order to avoid the threat of death or serious injury to other motorists. Even if the defence of necessity had been open to D it would have failed in any event (*R. v. Denton* [1988] C.L.Y. 3137, *R. v. Martin (Brian)* [1989] C.L.Y. 860 considered).

D.P.P. v. HARRIS (NIGEL) [1995] RTR 100, D.C.

4408. Driving offences—failure to comply with drivers' rest periods—derogation—whether permissible

[Council Regulation 3820/85.]

B was convicted of offences involving the infringement of Arts. 6 and 7 of Council Reg. 3820/85. B and his employer had anticipated that he would not be able to comply with the Regulation in relation to drivers' rest periods because of the nature of his load. B argued that Art. 12 allowed derogations from Arts. 6 and 7. The question referred to the ECJ was whether a driver was entitled to the benefit of Art. 12 if the need to depart from the conditions laid down in Arts. 6 and 7 was known before his journey began.

Held, that Art. 12 could not be relied on where the reasons for derogation were known prior to the commencement of the journey. Articles 6 and 7 could only be departed from if unexpected circumstances arose during the journey and protection was only afforded to a driver in such circumstances.

CRIMINAL PROCEEDINGS AGAINST BIRD (C–235/94), *The Times*, November 29, 1995, ECJ.

4409. Driving tests

The Department of Transport (DoT) has issued a press release entitled *New Measures Ahead for Start of Theory Test* (Press Notice No. 268), published on August 31, 1995. Provisions to cut down on waiting time for driving tests when the new theory part of the tests come into operation on July 1, 1996 have been announced by Transport Minister. The new test, consisting of 35 road safety questions must be taken by all prospective drivers, and the normal arrangements will be that candidates must pass this section before progressing to the on-road practical test.

4410. Excess alcohol—being in charge of vehicle—wheel clamp applied to vehicle—whether any likelihood of motorist driving vehicle—whether application of clamp "damage to vehicle"

[Road Traffic Act 1988 (c.52), s.5(2)(3).]

The application of a wheel clamp to a vehicle does not constitute damage to the vehicle within the meaning of s.5(3) of the Road Traffic Act 1988.

D's vehicle was fitted with a wheel clamp and payment of £35 was required for the release of the clamp, which D refused to pay. He attempted to remove the clamp with a hammer and was found and arrested by a police officer. He was found to have consumed excess alcohol and was charged and convicted with an offence of being in charge of a vehicle under s.5 of the Road Traffic Act 1988. He appealed to the Crown Court arguing that the presence of the wheel clamp meant that there was no likelihood that he would drive the vehicle whilst his breath alcohol exceeded the prescribed limit. The prosecutor argued that the application of the clamp amounted to damage to the vehicle which, under s.5(3), should be disregarded. The Crown Court found that D intended to remove the clamp and, had he done so, would have driven and so his appeal was dismissed.

Held, allowing D's appeal, that since D refused to pay the release fee there was little likelihood of the clamp being released and so little likelihood of D driving. Accordingly the defence under s.5(2) should succeed unless it was right that the clamp amounted to damage to the vehicle but it could not sensibly be said that the application of a clamp amounted to "damage" within the meaning of s.5(3) (*D.P.P. v. Watkins* [1989] C.L.Y. 3259 applied).

DRAKE v. D.P.P. [1994] RTR 411, D.C.

4411. Excess alcohol—blood specimen—medical reason—correct procedures—whether application for order of certiorari to quash conviction admissible

C and M applied for orders of certiorari to quash their convictions on charges of driving with excess alcohol, to which they had pleaded guilty, on the basis that the police had not observed the procedure prescribed in *D.P.P. v. Warren* ([1993] C.L.Y. 3788) when taking samples from the applicants for analysis.

Held, dismissing the application, that the court's jurisdiction to grant certiorari would only be exercised in cases where the prosecution's conduct could be said to be analogous to fraud (*R. v. Burton upon Trent Justices, ex p. Woolley* [1994] C.L.Y. 3974, *R. v. Cheshire Justices, ex p. Sinnott* [1994] C.L.Y. 3972 considered). Here there was merely a procedural error and the applicants had undoubtedly pleaded guilty because they recognised that they had consumed excess alcohol.

R. v. DOLGELLAU JUSTICES, *ex p.* CARTLEDGE; R. v. PENRITH JUSTICES, *ex p.* MARKS, *The Times*, August 4, 1995, D.C.

4412. Excess alcohol—blood specimen—medical reason—police forms—whether deficient by way of failure to specify grounds for objection

[Road Traffic Act 1988 (c.52), ss.5, 8.]

B appealed by way of case stated against his conviction for drink driving pursuant to s.5 of the Road Traffic Act 1988, on the grounds that the police proforma he was given was deficient as it failed to specify that any objection to giving a blood sample should be on medical grounds in accordance with s.8(2) of the Act.

Held, dismissing the appeal, that the guidelines laid down in *D.P.P. v. Warren* [1993] C.L.Y. 3788 were not to be interpreted strictly. The option in s.8(2) had been given correctly so as to enable B to make an informed choice as to whether to object, thus meeting the requirements of justice.

BALDWIN v. D.P.P., *The Times*, May 13, 1995, D.C.

4413. Excess alcohol—blood specimen—medical reason—sample taken in hospital after accident—whether asked about medical reason—whether failure to follow proper procedure

[Road Traffic Act 1988 (c.52), ss.5(1)(a), 9.]

Where a person in hospital is required to provide a specimen, the police officer has no obligation to inform the driver why a breath specimen cannot be taken and, although the officer must ask whether there is any reason why a blood specimen should not be taken, there is no obligation to ask specifically whether there is any such reason based on medical grounds.

W, a motorist, was at a hospital following a crash. He refused to provide specimens of breath because of his injuries. The sergeant then said that he would require a specimen of blood or urine and asked W if there were any matters he would like the sergeant to take into account in deciding which specimen should be taken. The sergeant then took a specimen of blood which indicated an excess alcohol level. W pleaded guilty to driving with excess alcohol. He sought an order of certiorari to quash his conviction upon being informed by the prosecution that the procedure for obtaining the blood specimen was flawed in that the officer had not asked if there was any reason why a blood specimen should not be taken.

Held, dismissing the application, that where a requirement to provide a specimen was made of a driver at a hospital there was no obligation to inform him why a specimen of breath could not be taken nor to ask him specifically whether there were any medical grounds not to take a specimen of blood. The requirements of s.9 of the Road Traffic Act 1988 were met by asking the motorist whether there was any reason a specimen of blood should not be taken from him. That gave the motorist the opportunity to raise any objection to providing a specimen of blood. On the facts all of the relevant requirements had been met and the evidence of the blood specimen would have been admissible. Even if they had not been met the case was not one where the court could grant an order of certiorari since the conduct of the prosecution could not be said to have been conduct analogous to a fraud (*D.P.P. v. Warren* [1992] C.L.Y. 3788, *R. v. Secretary of State for the Home Department, ex p. Al-Mehdawi* [1990] C.L.Y. 66 considered; *D.P.P. v. Duffy* [1994] RTR 241 not followed; *R. v. Kingston-upon-Thames Justices, ex p. Khanna* [1986] C.L.Y. 2942, *R. v. Bolton Magistrates' Court, ex p. Scally* [1991] C.L.Y. 3108 distinguished).

R. v. BURTON UPON TRENT JUSTICES, *ex p.* WOOLLEY [1995] RTR 139, C.A.

4414. Excess alcohol—blood specimen—medical reason—whether tablets capable of being medical reason—whether officer obliged to enquire further

[Road Traffic Act 1988 (c.52), s.7.]

When a police officer asked a drink driving suspect whether there was any medical reason why he should not give a blood specimen pursuant to s.7 of the Road Traffic Act 1988 and the suspect replied that he took tablets, the officer should not have dismissed the answer out of hand. The suspect's medication could be a sufficient medical reason for not providing a blood specimen and therefore the officer should have asked further questions, considered the matter properly and asked a doctor if in doubt.

WADE v. D.P.P., *The Times*, February 14, 1995, D.C.

4415. Excess alcohol—blood specimen—police duty to supply on driver's request—sample taken but custody officer unable to find it later—accused leaving police station without sample—whether duty to supply fulfilled

[Road Traffic Offenders Act 1988 (c.52), s.15(5).]

J appealed against conviction for a drink driving offence on the grounds that he asked for part of the blood specimen he had given but contrary to s.15(5) of the Road Traffic Offenders Act 1988 the police failed to supply it to him. Immediately after giving the specimen J asked for part and the police divided the specimen, labelled both containers and gave one to J to hold. Then because J was detained for further questioning they put J's container in the fridge for him. J asserted that when he was eventually released he asked for his container but had to leave without it because the custody officer could not find it. The magistrates did not believe him.

Held, dismissing the appeal, that (1) by dividing the blood specimen, labelling the containers, giving one to the suspect and entering the matter in the custody record, the police fulfilled their statutory duty to supply part of the specimen as requested. To ensure that the suspect did not leave the station without his container was not required of the police (*R. v. Jones (Colin)* [1974] C.L.Y. 3290, *R. v. Sharp* [1968] C.LY. 3443 considered); (2) evidence of the alcohol level in the police sample was not rendered inadmissible if the suspect requested part but failed to take the trouble to collect it when he left. On the evidence the magistrates were entitled to find that J had done so.

JOHNSON (ANTHONY HAROLD) v. D.P.P. (CO 1241/94), October 13, 1994, D.C.

4416. Excess alcohol—breath specimen—admissibility—inaccuracy of computer printout

[Police and Criminal Evidence Act 1984 (c.60), s.69.]

A printout from a Lion Intoximeter which showed that the alcohol reading had been reduced to allow for acetone was admissible on drink driving charges, notwithstanding s.69 of the Police and Criminal Evidence Act 1984, because no impropriety was involved. Any inaccuracy was in the defendant's favour.

ASHTON v. D.P.P., *The Times*, July 14, 1995, D.C.

4417. Excess alcohol—breath specimen—admissibility—intoximeter mistakenly believed to be incorrect—refusal to submit blood sample—whether conviction on basis of breath specimen possible

[Road Traffic Act 1988 (c.52), s.5(1)(a).]

H appealed against his conviction under s.5(1)(a) of the Road Traffic Act 1988 for driving whilst over the prescribed alcohol limit, after providing positive samples of breath. However, the intoximeter was mistakenly believed to be calibrating incorrectly and H was requested to give a blood sample, which he refused to do. H was convicted on the evidence of the intoximeter.

Held, dismissing the appeal, that H's breath specimen could still be produced as evidence because the intoximeter was working correctly and giving an accurate reading. Even though blood alcohol test procedures had been initiated, the breath test was still admissible because it had not been replaced by a blood or urine sample (*D.P.P. v. Winstanley* [1993] C.L.Y. 3485 considered).

HAGUE v. D.P.P., *The Times*, November 14, 1995, D.C.

4418. Excess alcohol—breath specimen—admissibility—no evidence adduced that Lion Intoximeter working reliably—whether prosecution could rely upon presumption that machine functioning reliably

[Police and Criminal Evidence Act 1984 (c.60), Sched. 3, paras. 8, 9; Road Traffic Act 1988 (c.52), s.5(1).]

Evidence is required that a Lion Intoximeter machine is working properly and it is not open to the prosecution to seek to rely upon a presumption that the machine was functioning correctly and reliably.

G was charged with driving with excess alcohol. In convicting him, the magistrates relied on a printout from a Lion Intoximeter but no evidence was adduced that the Intoximeter was working or that the printout was reliable. G applied for judicial review of the magistrates' decision to convict.

Held, allowing the application, that the prosecutor could not rely on the presumption that the device was working normally. The justices did not have the evidence on which to convict and therefore the conviction should be set aside (*R. v. Shephard (Hilda)* [1992] C.L.Y. 722 applied).

R. v. MEDWAY MAGISTRATES' COURT, *ex p.* GODDARD [1995] RTR 206, D.C.

4419. Excess alcohol—breath specimen—admissibility—substitution of blood or urine sample—whether defendant's inability to understand options relevant

[Road Traffic Act 1988 (c.52), ss.7(4), 8(2).]

The D.P.P. appealed against B's acquittal on a drink driving charge. B had provided a positive breath sample which was low enough to allow him to elect to provide, under s.8(2) of the Road Traffic Act 1988, a sample of blood or urine in its place. However, partly because of the alcohol he had consumed, B was unable to understand the options open to him. He claimed that his right under ss.7(4) and 8(2) of the Act to substitute a blood or urine sample for his breath sample had been denied.

Held, allowing the appeal, that since B's inability to understand the offer to replace the breath sample was, at least partly, attributable to his state of intoxication, he could not claim that the breath specimen was inadmissible. The case was remitted to the justices.

D.P.P. v. BERRY, *The Times*, November 7, 1995, D.C.

4420. Excess alcohol—breath specimen—failure to provide—alleged bronchitis attack—police surgeon finding that suspect was fit—whether procedure should have been restarted

[Road Traffic Act 1988 (c.52), s.7(1)(a).]

The D.P.P. appealed by way of case stated against the dismissal of a case against S, who had been charged under s.7 of the Road Traffic Act 1988, with an offence of failing to provide a specimen of breath, on suspicion of driving with excess alcohol. A police officer had asked him to breathe into an intoximeter and warned him that failure to do so may result in prosecution. S agreed but then failed to provide any specimen, claiming that he had an attack of bronchitis, a claim which the police sergeant believed was false. The procedure was halted so that a police surgeon could be called, who then pronounced S fit. S was then charged with failing to provide a specimen but the magistrates held that S had no case to answer, finding that the police sergeant should have restarted the procedure.

Held, allowing the appeal, that (1) the justices were wrong to decide that S had not failed to provide a sample of breath and the police procedure should have been restarted; (2) under s.7(1)(a) of the 1988 Act, a person was guilty of an offence if he failed to produce a specimen without reasonable excuse, when required. The section was quite clear and S had not raised any defence of reasonable excuse; and (3) the case was to be remitted to the magistrates for rehearing.

D.P.P. v. SHUKER (THOMAS JOHN) (CO 2822/94), March 7, 1995, Balcombe J.

4421. Excess alcohol—breath specimen—failure to provide—change of mind—whether refusal

[Road Traffic Act 1988 (c.52), s.7.]

S appealed by way of case stated against his conviction under s.7 of the Road Traffic Act 1988 of the offence of refusing to provide a specimen of breath. He had said "no" when asked to provide a specimen but within five seconds had said he wanted to change his mind.

Held, allowing the appeal, that in considering whether there was a refusal the justices should have had regard to all S's words and conduct and not ignored his words after the initial withholding of consent as refusal was a matter of fact and degree (*R. v. McAllister* [1974] C.L.Y. 3284 considered).

SMYTH v. D.P.P., *The Times*, June 21, 1995, D.C.

4422. Excess alcohol—breath specimen—failure to provide—defendant in accident suffering chest injuries—whether reasonable excuse for failing to provide specimen—whether magistrates' decision perverse

D was involved in a road traffic accident at 1.00 a.m. when he lost control of his car. He was taken to hospital by ambulance. Before departing from the scene of the accident he was asked to provide a specimen of breath for analysis by an Alcolmeter. The test was positive. After treatment at the hospital D was discharged with his arm in a sling and taken to the police station. He was asked to provide a specimen of breath for analysis by an Intoximeter machine which he did so with no apparent difficulty. He was twice asked to provide a second specimen but on each occasion, although he put the mouthpiece to his mouth, no breath entered the machine. Three hours later he was able to supply a specimen for analysis by an Alcolmeter. D was prosecuted for failing to supply a specimen of breath for analysis contrary to s.7(6) of the Road Traffic Act 1988. D contended that he was unable to do so as a result of pain caused by his injuries. D put before the court without objection from the prosecutor a report prepared by a consultant orthopaedic surgeon based on information received from D stating that it was not reasonable to expect D to supply a specimen of breath given the raised air pressure he would have needed to generate to breath into the Intoximeter machine. There was also before the court an agreed statement from a director of Lion Laboratories stating that the Intoximeter was as easy to breath into as an Alcolmeter. D was acquitted.

Held, allowing the prosecutor's appeal, that the decision of the justices was perverse. They had failed to give any consideration to the evidence concerning the ease with which the Intoximeter could be used, the fact that D had apparently provided samples without difficulty before and they had ignored the fact that there was no objective evidence of the physical condition D claimed to be in at the time he was asked to provide a second specimen.

R. v. RADFORD [1995] RTR 86, D.C.

4423. Excess alcohol—breath specimen—failure to provide—failure of Lion Intoximeter—appeal by way of case stated—matters included in case stated—whether procedure followed relevant

[Road Traffic Act 1988 (c.52), s.7(6).]

C applied to amend a case stated arising from a charge of failing to provide a breath specimen contrary to s.7(6) of the Road Traffic Act 1988. She had been asked four times to blow into a Lion Intoximeter and only one attempt had been made successfully before the machine aborted. C submitted that the intoximeter was not an accurate device and sought amendment of the case stated to include what procedure was carried out and for the justices to attach their notes of evidence.

Held, allowing the application, that the matters in issue were necessary to determine the case properly and amendment was granted.

CHADBURN (LORRAINE) v. D.P.P. (CO 3803/94), March 8, 1995, Balcombe L.J.

4424. Excess alcohol—breath specimen—failure to provide—failure of police officer to provide information—whether reasonable excuse

A police officer administering a breath test for a drink driving offence was not required to tell the suspect that a Lion Intoximeter had a three-minute cycle, therefore failure to give the information did not amount to a reasonable excuse for the suspect to fail to provide a specimen.

D.P.P. v. COYLE, *The Times*, July 17, 1995, D.C.

4425. Excess alcohol—breath specimen—failure to provide—whether charge including all possible types of specimen bad for duplicity

[Police and Criminal Evidence Act 1984 (c.60), s.78; Road Traffic Act 1988 (c.52), s.7.]

W appealed against conviction for refusing to give a breath specimen under the Road Traffic Act 1988 on the grounds that he was not warned at the roadside that refusal to give the specimen would be an offence, he had been taking medication and the charge was bad for duplicity.

Held, dismissing the appeal, that (1) the magistrates' decision not to exercise their discretion under s.78 of the Police and Criminal Evidence Act

1984 to exclude the evidence was upheld. A warning was not necessary in these circumstances as distinct from those stipulated in s.7 of the 1988 Act; (2) the magistrates were entitled to find on the evidence that W had not taken the medication which he asserted would have affected any breath specimen so he did not have a reasonable excuse for refusing to give a specimen; and (3) the charge "that you having been required to provide a specimen of breath/ blood/urine for analysis pursuant to s.7 of the Road Traffic Act 1988 failed without reasonable excuse to do so" was not bad for duplicity (*D.P.P. v. Butterworth* [1994] 9 C.L. 384 considered; *Williams v. D.P.P* [1991] R.T.R. 214, *Wyllie v. Crown Prosecution Service*, unrep. distinguished). A single offence of refusing to give a specimen was established by s.7(6) of the 1988 Act, whether that specimen was breath, blood or urine might be charged following a single investigation, but only if the defendant refused to give a specimen on separate and distinct occasions.

WORSLEY (TREVOR JAMES) v. D.P.P. (CO–1679–92), November 11, 1994, D.C.

4426. Excess alcohol—causing death by dangerous driving—evidence of alcohol consumption—whether admissible

[Road Traffic Act 1988 (c.52), ss.1, 2A.]

The fact that a driver was adversely affected by drink is a circumstance relevant to the issue whether he was driving dangerously.

A was charged with causing death by dangerous driving. At trial the prosecution were given leave to adduce evidence of A's consumption of alcohol prior to the accident, based mainly on a witness statement indicating that A had drunk five or six pints of lager. In the event, the evidence of alcohol consumption went no further than that A had been seen with a glass in his hand and had been drinking. A did not give evidence. The judge, in summing up, reminded the jury of the evidence given about A's alcohol consumption but did not warn them not to take it into account. A was convicted.

Held, allowing the appeal, that (1) on a prosecution for dangerous driving the fact that a driver was adversely affected by drink was a circumstance relevant to the issue whether he was driving dangerously; (2) in order for evidence of alcohol consumption to be admissible it had to show that the amount of drink consumed was such as would adversely affect a driver or that the driver was in fact affected; (3) in view of the content of the witness statement the evidence of alcohol consumption had been properly admitted but since the evidence given established no more than that A had had a glass in his hand and had consumed alcohol, the judge should have warned the jury against taking A's drinking into account; and (4) the failure to do so was a material misdirection or non-direction and, as it could not be said that the jury would have convicted if the drink element had been effectively withdrawn from their consideration, the conviction would be quashed (*R. v. McBride* [1961] C.L.Y. 1714, *R. v. Thorpe* [1972] C.L.Y. 2992 applied; *R. v. Lawrence* [1981] C.L.Y. 2382, *R. v. Peters (Anthony Raymond)* [1993] C.L.Y. 3530 distinguished).

R. v. WOODWARD (TERENCE) [1995] 1 W.L.R. 375, C.A.

4427. Excess alcohol—causing death by reckless driving—whether evidence of excess alcohol admissible

In a trial for causing death by driving without due care and attention after having consumed alcohol above the prescribed limit, evidence that the driver had consumed alcohol in excess of the limit was admissible, even though the only issue in question at the trial related to whether the car was driven without due care and attention (*R. v. McBride* [1961] C.L.Y. 1714 followed).

R. v. MILLINGTON, *The Times*, May 12, 1995, C.A.

4428. Excess alcohol—"consumption"—alcohol absorbed by means of injection—whether consumption included injection

[Road Traffic Act 1988 (c.52), s.5.]

The word "consume" in s.5 of the Road Traffic Act 1988 is not restricted to drinking but can cover other means of ingestion of alcohol, including injection.

J was charged with driving having consumed alcohol in excess of the legal limit. J had been injected with a pain killer Kenalog which contained an aqueous solution of 1.5 per cent alcohol. The magistrate found that "consumimg" in s.5(1) of the Road Traffic Act 1988 did not include the injection and J was acquitted.

Held, allowing the D.P.P.'s appeal, that Parliament's purpose in passing the relevant provisions of the Road Traffic Act was to deter those with alcohol in their bodies from driving and, in that context, the word "consume" in s.5 included the introduction of alcohol into the body by way of an injection of a pain killer that contained alcohol. The word "consume" was not restricted to drinking but could cover other means including the introduction of alcohol by injection.

D.P.P. v. JOHNSON (DAVID) [1995] R.T.R. 9, D.C.

4429. Excess alcohol—driver parked at roadside—voluntary confession that he had driven to location—breath test then caution—whether confession admissible. See WHELEHAN v. D.P.P., §1000.

4430. Excess alcohol—duress—offenders driving due to fear—whether subjective or objective test

[Road Traffic Act 1988 (c.52), s.5(1)(a).]

D and P were charged separately with driving with excess alcohol, contrary to s.5(1)(a) of the Road Traffic Act 1988 but in each case the magistrates dismissed the charges on the basis that the defence of duress had been proved. In D's case, the magistrates found that he had been suffering from stress and anxiety when he accepted an invitation to go for a meal with a male acquaintance. On returning to the man's flat, D become the subject of an unwelcome sexual advance and, fearing for his life, ran from the flat and drove away. Applying a subjective test, the magistrates considered it more likely than not that events had caused D to lose complete control of his will. In P's case, the magistrates found that she was frightened of men. She had formed a relationship with a man, but at a party she had a row with him and he made unspecified threats against her. She ran to her house but decided to hide in her car. After five minutes or so, she drove 200 yards before being stopped. The D.P.P. appealed by way of case stated.

Held, allowing both appeals and remitting to the magistrates with a direction to convict, that the defence of duress, although subjective, had objective elements, namely whether there was good cause to fear that death or serious injury would occur unless the respondent acted as he had done and whether a sober person of reasonable firmness, sharing the respondent's characteristics, would have responded in the same way. In D's case, there was no finding that he had been in fear of his life or serious injury at the moment he drove off or that he continued to be frightened during the two miles he drove before being stopped. Nor had the magistrates considered whether there was good cause for D's fear or whether there It was necessary for him to continue driving as far as he did. In P's case, the magistrates had wrongly applied a subjective test and were also wrong to consider whether the distance driven was reasonable rather than necessary. They should have considered whether there was good cause for her to fear, which there was not (*R. v. Graham* [1982] C.L.Y. 556, *R. v. Howe* [1987] C.L.Y. 800, *D.P.P v. Bell* [1992] C.L.Y. 3783 considered).

D.P.P v. DAVIS; SAME v. PITTAWAY [1994] Crim.L.R. 600, D.C.

4431. Excess alcohol—public place—car park of members club—whether public place

[Road Traffic Act 1988, s.4.]

The car park of a bona fide member's club was not a public place for the purposes of s.4 of the Road Traffic Act 1988.

H was convicted of being unfit in charge of a motor vehicle in a public place, contrary to s.4(2) of the Road Traffic Act 1988. His car was parked in the car park of a community centre, easily accessible to the public. The centre was a members club, membership of which was obtained by the nomination of an existing member. The justices found that the car park was a public place. H appealed.

Held, allowing the appeal, that H used the car park as a member of a bona fide club, which was not of such a size it was indistinguishable from the public at large in the locality. Thus, the car park was not a public place (*D.P.P. v. Vivier* [1992] C.L.Y. 3813; *Sandy v. Martin* [1974] C.L.Y. 3317; *Bowman v. D.P.P.* [1992] C.L.Y. 3812; *Pugh v. Knipe* [1972] C.L.Y. 3040; *Severn View Social Club and Institute v. Chepstow (Monmouthshire) Justices* [1968] C.L.Y. 382; *Panama v. Piccadilly v. Newberry* [1962] C.L.Y. 2537; *D.P.P. v. Cartman* (1992) unreported considered).

HOWELL v. D.P.P. (1994) 158 J.P.

4432. Goods vehicle—access permits—breach of conditions—requirement that permit holder minimise use of restricted roads

[Greater London (Restriction of Goods Vehicles) Traffic Order 1985; Road Traffic Regulation Act 1984 (c.27), s.8.]

TNT's conviction for breaching conditions attached to goods vehicle access permits granted under the Greater London (Restriction of Goods Vehicles) Traffic Order 1985, contrary to s.8 of the Road Traffic Regulation Act 1984, was upheld. A condition that the permit holder should minimise use of restricted roads required the holder to stay off such roads until as near as possible to the stopping place and take the shortest practicable route to the next stopping place. Commercial considerations, such as time saved by delivery vans when using restricted roads, did not affect practicability (*Post Office v. Richmond upon Thames London Borough Council* [1995] RTR 28 followed).

TNT EXPRESS (U.K.) v. RICHMOND UPON THAMES LONDON BOROUGH COUNCIL, *The Times*, June 27, 1995, Waller J.

4433. Goods vehicle—constructed with boiler to carry molten asphalt—whether licence tax chargeable at basic duty—whether constructed primarily to carry loads—whether exempt from regulations

[Goods Vehicle (Plating and Testing) Regulations 1988 (S.I. 1988 No. 1478).]

D owned a rigid two axle vehicle to which a boiler fitted with burners and stirrers was fitted. The vehicle was used to carry molten asphalt for laying floors and to keep the asphalt molten. The vehicle displayed an excise licence indicating duty paid at the basic rate for a heavy goods vehicle. D was charged with using the vehicle without a goods vehicle test certificate and for not having paid the higher rate of duty chargeable on the vehicle. The justices found that the vehicle was exempt from the Goods Vehicle (Plating and Testing) Regulations 1986 because it amounted to moveable plant or equipment specially designed for an engineering purpose and not constructed to carry a load. They dismissed the informations and the prosecutor appealed.

Held, allowing the appeal, that the first question to be asked is whether the vehicle was constructed to carry a load. If that was its primary purpose then the Regulations applied. Only if that question was answered in the negative was it necessary to consider the question of whether the vehicle was especially designed for engineering operations. In this case the vehicle was designed to carry a load, namely asphalt and the fact that it also had a secondary purpose, keeping the asphalt in a molten state, did not change its primary purpose. Accordingly the justices had erred in law in holding that the Regulations did not apply to the vehicle.

D.P.P. v. DERBYSHIRE [1994] RTR 351, D.C.

4434. Goods vehicle—operator breaking conditions of access permit—whether giving rise to possibility of criminal offence

[Road Traffic Regulation Act 1984 (c.27), s.8(1).]

Where a goods vehicle operator breaks the conditions of his access permit, he can be charged with a criminal offence despite the existence of an administrative procedure for the revocation of the permit on breach of a condition.

D operated goods vehicles in excess of 16.5 tonnes gross weight. The vehicles were subject to restrictions relating to prescribed streets and times as provided by the Greater London (Restrictions of Goods Vehicles) Traffic Order 1985. RLBC had issued permits for the vehicles under art. 5 exempting the vehicles from the terms of the Order. Condition 5 of the Conditions Normally Considered for Attachment to a Permit applied, requiring D to ensure that the use of the vehicles on the roads in questions and at the times to which the permit related was essential and such use was kept to a minimum. In three cases it was found that D's vehicles had used restricted streets to a destination that could have been reached without using those streets but involving a longer journey and greater costs. D was convicted of contravening s.8 of the Road Traffic Regulation Act 1984 by reason of the failure to comply with Condition 5.

Held, dismissing D's appeal, that since it was not essential for D's vehicles to use the restricted route to reach the destination there had been a breach of Condition 5. In consequence there had been an offence. The fact that there existed a procedure for the council to give D notice and thereafter to revoke D's permits did not preclude the existence of an offence.

POST OFFICE v. RICHMOND UPON THAMES LONDON BOROUGH COUNCIL [1995] R.T.R. 28, D.C.

4435. Goods vehicles—international road haulage

GOODS VEHICLES (INTERNATIONAL ROAD HAULAGE PERMITS) (REVOCATION) REGULATIONS 1995 (No. 1290) [65p], made under the International Road Haulage Permits Act 1975 (c.46), s.1(1) and the European Communities Act 1972 (c.68), s.2(2); operative on June 12, 1995; revoke S.I. 1975 No. 2234 and reg. 13 of S.I. 1992 No. 3077.

4436. Goods vehicles—licensing of operators

GOODS VEHICLES (LICENSING OF OPERATORS) (FEES) REGULATIONS 1995 (No. 3000) [£1·55], made under the Goods Vehicles (Licensing of Operators) Act 1995, ss.45(1), 57(1), 58(1). In force: January 1, 1996; impose a new fee structure for goods vehicles operators' licences, qualifications and fees. A new fee with application for licence costing £160 is introduced. The fee for the issue of a licence is increased to £250 from £185 and the fee for issue of a publishable variation is changed slightly to a fee with application for publishable variation and decreased to £160 from £185. New fees for issue of interim licences and continuation in force of licences are introduced costing £42 and £250 respectively. The additional fee for motor vehicles specified on the licence is now £7 per motor vehicle per quarter if paid five-yearly in advance and £8·50 per motor vehicle per quarter if paid annually in advance. Additional fees for motor vehicles specified on an interim licence remain unchanged at £10 per vehicle.

GOODS VEHICLES (LICENSING OF OPERATORS) REGULATIONS 1995 (No. 2869) [£4·15], made under the Goods Vehicles (Licensing of Operators) Act 1995, ss.2, 5(3)(8), 8(3)(4)(5), 10, 11(2), 12(2)(3)(6)(7), 14(5), 17(2), 18(3), 19(9)(10), 23(2), 30(1)(4), 31(5), 33, 34(1), 35(3), 36(2)(3), 46(1)(2), 47, 48(2)(3)(4),

57(1)(2)(3)(4)(5)(7)(8)(9), Sched. 4, paras. 1, 3 and the European Communities Act 1972, s.2(2); revoke S.I. 1984 Nos. 176, 666, 1391, S.I. 1987 Nos. 841, 2170, S.I. 1988 No. 2128, S.I. 1990 Nos. 1849, 2640, S.I. 1991 Nos. 1969, 2239, S.I. 1992 No. 2319, S.I. 1993 No. 301, S.I. 1994 No. 1209, S.I. 1995 No. 1488; operative on January 1, 1996; include new provisions consequent on the prospective changes to the goods vehicle operator licensing system made by Chap. III of Pt. I of the Deregulation and Contracting Out Act 1994 which were included in the consolidating 1995 Act, including continuous licensing and review of operating centres, and for partnerships; prescribe matters relating to applications for licences; prescribe matters relating to objections and representations; contain provisions about operating centres; prescribe various matters relating to inquiries held by a traffic commissioner under s.35 of the 1995 Act; prescribe matters relating to the content, publication and availability of statements (known as "Applications and Decisions") by a traffic commissioner, and relating to the provision of reasons for his decisions.

GOODS VEHICLES (OPERATORS' LICENCES, QUALIFICATIONS AND FEES) (AMENDMENT) REGULATIONS 1995 (No. 1488), made under the Transport Act 1968, ss.60(2)(b), 89(1), 91(1); amend S.I. 1984 No. 176; operative on July 1, 1995.

4436a. Goods vehicles—plating and testing

GOODS VEHICLES (PLATING AND TESTING) (AMENDMENT) REGULATIONS 1995 (No. 1456), made under the Road Traffic Act 1988, ss.49, 51(1); operative on July 1, 1995, amends S.I. 1988 No. 1478; creates an exemption from the requirement to undergo examinations for plating and annual tests.

4437. Goods Vehicles (Licensing of Operators) Act 1995 (c.23)

This Act consolidates provisions, regarding the licensing of operators of specified goods vehicles, from the Transport Act 1968 (c.73) and other related Acts and Statutory Instruments.

The Act received Royal Assent on July 19, 1995.

4438. Goods Vehicles (Licensing of Operators) Act 1995—commencement

GOODS VEHICLES (LICENSING OF OPERATORS) ACT 1995 (COMMENCEMENT AND TRANSITIONAL PROVISIONS) ORDER 1995 (No. 2181 (C.44)) [£1·95], made under the Goods Vehicles (Licensing of Operators) Act 1995, s.61; operative on bringing into operation various provisions of the 1995 Act on January 1, 1996; brings into force on January 1, 1996 all the provisions of the Goods Vehicles (Licensing of Operators) Act 1995 other than s.50 and Sched. 5.

4439. Motor cycle noise

MOTOR CYCLE SILENCER AND EXHAUST SYSTEMS REGULATIONS 1995 (No. 2370) [£1·55], made under the Motor Cycle Noise Act 1987, s.1; relate to E.C. Dir. 78/1015 concerning motorcycle silencers and exhaust systems; operative on August 1, 1996.

4440. Motor Cycle Noise Act 1987—commencement

MOTOR CYCLE NOISE ACT 1987 (COMMENCEMENT) ORDER 1995 (No. 2367 (C.47)) [65p], made under the Motor Cycle Noise Act 1987, s.2(3); brings the Motor Cycle Noise Act 1987 into force on August 1, 1996.

4441. Motor insurance—refusal to indemnify for third party claim—accident on beach car park—whether "road". See MCGURK AND DALE v. COSTER (ON BEHALF OF MITRE INSURANCE ASSOCIATION), §2912.

4442. Motor Insurers' Bureau—passenger knowingly accepting lift from drunk driver—personal injuries—whether passenger a "person using the vehicle". See STINTON (CHRISTOPHER BRIAN) v. THE MOTOR INSURERS' BUREAU (QBENF 93/0141/C), §3726.

4443. Motorvehicles—approximation of laws—European Community

Commission Directive 94/53/EC of November 15, 1994 amending Dir. 78/316/EEC on the approximation of the laws of the Member States relating to the interior fittings of motorvehicles (O.J. L299/26).

4444. Motorvehicles—authorisation of special types

MOTOR VEHICLES (AUTHORISATION OF SPECIAL TYPES) (AMENDMENT) ORDER 1995 (No. 3052) [65p], made under the Road Traffic Act 1988, s.44. In force: January 1, 1996; amends S.I. 1979 No. 1198 by increasing the maximum permitted overall width of vehicles constructed or adapted for use as grass cutters or hedge trimmers and which are authorised for use on roads from 2.5 metres to 2.55 metres. As a consequence of amendments made to the Road Vehicles (Construction and Use) Regulations 1986, the same amendments are made for the purposes of agricultural motor vehicles, agricultural trailers, agricultural trailed appliances, and agricultural motor vehicles towing off-set agricultural trailers.

4445. Motorvehicles—designation of approval marks

MOTOR VEHICLES (DESIGNATION OF APPROVAL MARKS) (AMENDMENT) REGULATIONS 1995 (No. 3342), made under the Road Traffic Act 1988 s.80(1); Amends S.I. 1979 No. 1088. operative on February 5, 1996; [65p]. A new item 7D, a marking relating to centre mounted stop lamps, is prescribed by these Regulations and inserted into the Motor Vehicles (Designation of Approval Marks) Regulations 1979 as a result of amendments made and incorporated into the second revision of ECE Regulation 7.

4446. Motorvehicles—maximums—European Community

Directive 95/1/EC of the European Parliament and of the Council of February 2, 1995 on the maximum design speed, maximum torque and maximum net engine power of two-or three-wheel motorvehicles (O.J. L52/1).

4447. Motorvehicles—technical standards—European Community

Commission Directive 95/48/EC of September 20, 1995 adapting to technical progress Council Dir. 91/21/EEC relating to the masses and dimensions of motorvehicles of category M1 (O.J. L233/73).

4448. Motorvehicles—tests

MOTOR VEHICLES (TESTS) (AMENDMENT) REGULATIONS 1995 (No. 1457), made under the Road Traffic Act 1988, ss.45, 46, 47; operative on July 1, 1995, amend S.I. 1981 No. 1694; introduce a provision exempting a vehicle when it is used on a road in circumstances similar to those that previously attracted the exemption from duty under the Vehicle Excise Registration Act 1994, Sched. 2, para. 21.

MOTOR VEHICLES (TESTS) (AMENDMENT) (NO. 2) REGULATIONS 1995 (No. 2438) [£1·10], made under the Road Traffic Act 1988, ss. 45, 46 and S.I. 1988 No. 643; amend S.I. 1981 No. 1694; operative on October 9, 1995;

further amend the Motor Vehicle (Tests) Regulations 1981 which provide for certain motorvehicles to undertake a MOT.

4449. Motorway traffic

MOTORWAY TRAFFIC (ENGLAND AND WALES) (AMENDMENT) REGULATIONS 1995 (No. 158) [65p], made under the Road Traffic Regulation Act 1984 (c.27), s.17(2)(3); operative on January 1, 1996; further amend S.I. 1982 No. 1163 so as to prohibit buses from using the outside lane on motorways which have three or more carriageways.

4450. Off-road events

MOTOR VEHICLES (OFF ROAD EVENTS) REGULATIONS 1995 (No. 1371) [65p], made under the Road Traffic Act 1988 (c.52), s.13A; operative on June 15, 1995; re-enact S.I. 1992 No. 1370 as amended.

4451. Parking—controlled parking zone—lack of consultation—judicial review—whether decision valid. See R. v. CAMDEN LONDON BOROUGH COUNCIL, *ex p.* CRAN, §84.

4452. Parking—illegal parking—whether judicial review to be granted for the purpose of allowing an illegal activity. See R. v. HEREFORD AND WORCESTER COUNTY COUNCIL, *ex p.* SMITH (TOMMY), §73.

4453. Parking enforcement outside London—guidance

The Department of Transport and the Welsh Office have published a Local Authority Circular 1/95 (Welsh Office Circular 26/95) entitled *Guidance on Decriminalised Parking Enforcement Outside London*, giving guidance on three main areas: (1) to inform local authorities outside London of the scope for them to set up and operate a decriminalised parking enforcement regime under the provisions of the Road Traffic Act 1991; (2) to advise them on how to apply to the Secretary of State for the necessary powers; and (3) to advise them on how to set up and operate an effective and efficient decriminalised enforcement regime. Available from HMSO, price £13·00, ISBN 0–11–551703–0.

4454. Public service vehicles

PUBLIC SERVICE VEHICLES (CONDITIONS OF FITNESS, EQUIPMENT, USE AND CERTIFICATION) (AMENDMENT) REGULATIONS 1995 (No. 305) [£1·10], made under the Road Traffic Act 1988 (c.52), s.41(1)(5), and the European Communities Act 1972 (c.68), s.2(2); operative on March 14, 1995; further amend S.I. 1981 No. 257 in relation to the carriage of fire extinguishers by public service vehicles.

4455. Public service vehicles. See TRANSPORT, §4994.

4456. Public service vehicles—licences. See TRANSPORT, §4995.

4457. Registration marks—sale

SALE OF REGISTRATION MARKS REGULATIONS 1995 (No. 2880) [£1·55], made under the Vehicle Excise and Registration Act 1994, ss.27, 57(2); revoke S.I. 1989 No. 1938, S.I. 1993 No. 986, S.I. 1994 No. 2977; operative on December 18, 1995; revoke all previous regulations relating to the sale of rights relating to registration marks and the schemes made under them and make a new scheme providing for registration marks to which s.27 of the

Vehicle Excise and Registration Act 1994 applies to be assigned to vehicles registered in the names of, or the nominees of, persons who have acquired rights under the scheme to have marks so assigned. The revoked schemes, however, continue to apply to unexercised rights granted before these Regulations come into force. The main change introduced by these Regulations is that the new scheme enables a right to be acquired to assign a registration mark to a vehicle registered in the Northern Ireland register of mechanically propelled vehicles.

4458. Road traffic accident—car park—whether "road"—whether involvement of Motor Insurers' Bureau justified. See SEVERN TRENT WATER v. WILLIAMS AND THE MOTOR INSURERS' BUREAU, §3724.

4459. Road traffic accident—insurer known—Motor Insurers' Bureau contacted anyway—whether solicitors to pay costs of unnecessary involvement. See MILLS v. TONER AND THE MOTOR INSURERS' BUREAU, §3725.

4460. Road traffic accident—Motor Insurers' Bureau—whether proper enquiries made as to identity of defendant's insurers—whether Bureau involved unnecessarily. See GRANADA U.K. RENTAL & RETAIL v. SPN FAREWAY AND MOTOR INSURERS' BUREAU, §3728.

4461. Road traffic accidents—payments for treatment

ROAD TRAFFIC ACCIDENTS (PAYMENTS FOR TREATMENT) ORDER 1995 (No. 889), made under Public Expenditure and Receipts Act 1968 (c.14); operative on April 17, 1995; increases amounts payable under Road Traffic Act 1988 (c.52), s.157(2) and 158(2); s.157 provides for payments for hospital treatment of traffic casualties to be made by an owner or insurer of a vehicle the use of which gave rise to the injuries, and s.158 for payments to be made, by the person using such a vehicle, for emergency treatment.

4462. Road Traffic Act 1991—amendment

ROAD TRAFFIC ACT 1991 (AMENDMENT OF SECTION 76(3)) ORDER 1995 (No. 1437) [65p], made under the Road Traffic Act 1991 (c.40), s.76(4); operative on July 3, 1995; amends s.76(3) of the 1991 Act.

4463. Road Traffic (New Drivers) Act 1995 (c.13)

This Act provides for the revocation of the driving licences of new drivers who accumulate six or more points on their licences within a probationary period lasting for two years after the driver first becomes a qualified driver. A driver whose licence has thus been revoked must pass a further test to regain the entitlement to drive.

The Act received Royal Assent on June 28, 1995.

4464. Road vehicles—registration and licensing

ROAD VEHICLES (REGISTRATION AND LICENSING) (AMENDMENT) REGULATIONS 1995 (No. 1470), made under the Vehicle Excise and Registration Act 1994, ss.22(1)(e)(2)(3), 57(1)(2)(3)(5), Sched. 4, para. 7(7); operative on July 1, 1995, amend S.I. 1971 No. 450; make amendments as a result of the Vehicle Excise and Registration Act 1994, s.7.

4464a. Roadside check. See NORMAND v. McKELLAR, §6314.

4465. Special parking areas

ROAD TRAFFIC (SPECIAL PARKING AREA) (LONDON BOROUGH OF

CROYDON) (AMENDMENT) ORDER 1995 (No. 2930) [£1·95], made under the Road Traffic Act 1991, ss.76(1), 77(6). In force: December 14, 1995; amends S.I. 1994 No. 1490, which lists the roads excluded from the special parking area designated by that Order.

ROAD TRAFFIC (SPECIAL PARKING AREA) (LONDON BOROUGH OF MERTON) (AMENDMENT) ORDER 1995 (No. 680) [£1·95], made under the Road Traffic Act 1991, ss.76(1), 77(6); operative on March 31, 1995.

ROAD TRAFFIC (SPECIAL PARKING AREA) (LONDON BOROUGH OF REDBRIDGE) (AMENDMENT) ORDER 1995 (No. 616) [£1·10], made under the Road Traffic Act 1991 (c.40), ss.76(1), 77(6); operative on March 31, 1995; amends S.I. 1994 No. 1509 by excluding from the special parking area certain areas which are to be transferred to the county of Essex in accordance with local government boundary changes.

ROAD TRAFFIC (SPECIAL PARKING AREAS) (LONDON BOROUGH OF REDBRIDGE) (AMENDMENT NO. 2) ORDER 1995 (No. 1335) [£1·10], made under the Road Traffic Act 1991 (c.40), ss.76(1), 77(6); operative on June 16, 1995; adds to the special parking area designated in S.I. 1994 No. 1509.

ROAD TRAFFIC (SPECIAL PARKING AREA) (LONDON BOROUGH OF SUTTON) (AMENDMENT) ORDER 1995 (No. 618) [£1·10], made under the Road Traffic Act 1991 (c.40), ss.76(1), 77(6); operative on March 31, 1995; amends S.I. 1994 No. 1507 by excluding from the special parking area certain areas which are to be transferred to the county of Surrey in accordance with local government boundary changes.

ROAD TRAFFIC (SPECIAL PARKING AREAS) (LONDON BOROUGH OF SUTTON) (AMENDMENT NO. 2) ORDER 1995 (No. 1334) [£1·10], made under the Road Traffic Act 1991 (c.40), ss.76(1), 77(6); operative on June 16, 1995; adds to the special parking area designated in S.I. 1994 No. 1507.

ROAD TRAFFIC (SPECIAL PARKING AREA) (ROYAL BOROUGH OF KINGSTON UPON THAMES) (AMENDMENT) ORDER 1995 (No. 617) [£1·10], made under the Road Traffic Act 1991 (c.40), ss.76(1), 77(6); operative on March 31, 1995; amends S.I. 1994 No. 1497 by excluding from the special parking area certain areas which are to be transferred to the county of Surrey in accordance with local government boundary changes.

ROAD TRAFFIC (SPECIAL PARKING AREAS) (ROYAL BOROUGH OF KINGSTON UPON THAMES) (AMENDMENT NO. 2) ORDER 1995 (No. 1333) [£1·10], made under the Road Traffic Act 1991 (c.40), ss.76(1), 77(6); operative on June 16, 1995; adds to the special parking area designated in S.I. 1994 No. 1497.

ROAD TRAFFIC (SPECIAL PARKING AREAS) (LONDON BOROUGH OF LAMBETH) (AMENDMENT) ORDER 1995 (No. 679) [£4·15], made under the Road Traffic Act 1991, ss.76(1), 77(6); operative on March 31, 1995.

4466. Standard of care—personal injury—road accident—defendant being overtaken—whether defendant negligent in continuing at a steady speed when room for overtaking obviously running out. See SMITH v. CRIBBEN, §3729.

4467. Tachograph—drivers driving in excess of permitted hours—transport manager responsible for checking records and warning offending drivers—repeated contraventions—whether "permitted" by transport manager

A transport manager who only issued repeated and ineffectual written warnings in the face of repeated contraventions of the regulations relating to drivers' hours was held to have permitted breaches of the regulations by failing to take more effective action.

L was the transport manager whose duties included the issue and collection of tachograph charts. He inspected the results of the analysis of the charts and interviewed any drivers found to have offended against the regulations. The analysis was then signed and used as a warning. It was found that the drivers had consistently contravened the regulations dealing with driving hours over a three-month period. L was convicted of permitting breaches of the regulations because he had knowledge of the offences committed before those set out in the information and there was an inference that he knew about the subject offences or had turned a blind eye to them. L appealed.

Held, dismissing the appeal, that the fact that L had done all he could to discourage the offences because he had power only to warn the drivers was not of itself sufficient. L could have done more by progressing to disciplinary action against the drivers.

LIGHT v. D.P.P. [1994] RTR 396, D.C.

4468. Tachograph—exception—weight of vehicle—"permissible maximum weight"—meaning

[Road Traffic Act 1988 (c.52), s.108; EEC Reg. 3820/85, art. 4.]

For the purposes of tachograph requirements, the "permissible maximum weight" of a van and its trailer is the combined gross laden weight, and the van's train weight is irrelevant.

D was the operator of a van which was stopped by the police whilst towing a single axle trailer. The van was not fitted with a tachograph. According to the plate fixed to the van its gross laden weight was 2.6 tonnes. The trailer's gross laden weight was 0.9 tonnes. The van's maximum train weight was 4.6 tonnes. D was prosecuted and convicted of an offence of using the vehicle on the road without a tachograph. Under Council Reg. 3820/85, a tachograph was not required to be fitted if the "permissible maximum weight" of the vehicle including any trailer or semi-trailer did not exceed 3.5 tonnes. D appealed by way of case stated contending that the maximum permissible weight of the van and its trailer was 3.5 tonnes so that no tachograph was required.

Held, allowing D's appeal, that by virtue of s.108 of the Road Traffic Act 1988 the expression "permissible maximum weight" meant the gross laden weight of the van plus the gross laden weight of the trailer, *i.e.* 3.5 tonnes. The maximum train weight was a different weight definition from that with which the court was concerned and was of no relevance to the issue before it.

SMALL v. D.P.P. [1995] RTR 95, D.C.

4469. Tachograph—failure to record working time—after driving worked in yard—whether time spent not driving to be recorded—whether rest period

[Transport Act 1968 (c.73), s.95.]

The prosecutor appealed against a ruling that H, an HGV driver, was not guilty of failing to record working time on his tachograph as required by Art. 15 of Council Reg. 3821/85 on recording equipment on road transport. After a day's driving, he stayed at his employer's premises and worked in the yard for five hours, which he did not record. The magistrate ruled that because he had finished driving and did not intend to drive until the following day and because he worked overtime voluntarily rather than at his employer's request, the time he spent amounted to a rest period under the Regulation and did not have to be recorded.

Held, allowing the appeal, that (1) in the context of the Regulation, the words "daily working period" and "rest period" must be construed according to their ordinary natural meaning. If a driver worked overtime after driving, that overtime period formed part of his daily working period and must therefore be recorded; (2) the mischief which the Transport Act 1968, s.95, and Council Reg. 3821/85 were intended to prevent was the risk of accidents casued by drivers who were fatigued by excessive hours of work, whatever form the work might take; and (3) even if a driver volunteered to do overtime, once he had volunteered, he was not free to do as he wished with his time, so the time was not spent resting and must be recorded.

PRIME v. HOSKING (CO 2703/94), December 12, 1994, D.C.

4470. Tachograph—public service vehicle—journey without passengers—whether record required. See R. W. APPLEBY v. VEHICLE INSPECTORATE, §4993.

4471. Traffic order

HOUNSLOW (VARIOUS ROADS) TRAFFIC ORDER 1969 (VARIATION)

ORDER 1995 (No. 3159) [65p], made under the Road Traffic Regulation Act 1984 s.6(1)(3), Sched. 9, Pt. IV. In force: December 9, 1995; adds art. 9A to the Hounslow (Various Roads) Traffic Order 1969 stating that subject to the provisions of that Order, vehicles exceeding 6 feet 6 inches in width are prohibited from proceeding on the flyover or slip road.

4472. Traffic signs

TRAFFIC SIGNS (AMENDMENT) REGULATIONS AND GENERAL DIRECTIONS 1995 (No. 3107) [£1·55], made under the Road Traffic Regulation Act 1984, ss.64(1)(2)(3), 65(1); amend S.I. 1994 No. 1519. In force: January 5, 1996; introduce a wider definition of the term "tourist attraction", prescribe the new tourist facility signs and make provision regarding the permitted variants and illumination of those signs by amending the Traffic Signs Regulations 1994. The Traffic Signs Directions 1994 are also amended in order to include the new signs among those not permitted to be placed on motorways.

TRAFFIC SIGNS GENERAL (AMENDMENT) DIRECTIONS 1995 (No. 2769) [£1·10], made under the Road Traffic Regulation Act 1984, s.65(1); amend S.I. 1994 No. 1519; operative on November 10, 1995; make amendments in relation to the placing of traffic signs indicating speed limits at junctions between roads with differing speed limits. Other minor amendments to the Traffic Signs General Directions 1994 are also made.

4473. Type approval

MOTOR CYCLE (EC TYPE APPROVAL) REGULATIONS 1995 (No. 1513) [£2·40], made under the European Communities Act 1972 (c.68), s.2(2); operative on July 10, 1995; implement Council Dir. 92/61/EEC on E.C. type approval for motorcycles.

MOTOR VEHICLES (EC TYPE APPROVAL) (AMENDMENT) REGULATIONS 1995 (No. 2328) [65p], made under the European Communities Act 1972, s.2(2); operative on October 1, 1995; amend S.I. 1992 No. 3107.

MOTOR VEHICLES (TYPE APPROVAL FOR GOODS VEHICLES) (GREAT BRITAIN) (AMENDMENT) REGULATIONS 1995 (No. 1323) [£2·80], made under the Road Traffic Act 1988 (c.52), ss. 54(1), 61; operative on June 12, 1995; further amend S.I. 1982 No. 1271 in relation to exhaust and noise emissions.

MOTOR VEHICLES (TYPE APPROVAL) (GREAT BRITAIN) (AMENDMENT) REGULATIONS 1995 (No. 1322) [£1·55], made under the Road Traffic Act 1988 (c.52), ss.54(1), 61, 63; operative on June 12, 1995; further amend S.I. 1984 No. 981 in relation to exhaust and noise emissions.

MOTOR VEHICLES (TYPE APPROVAL MARKS) (FEES) REGULATIONS 1995 (No. 925) [£7·35], made under the Road Traffic Act 1988 (c.52), s.6(1)(2), the Finance Act 1973 (c.51), s.56(1)(2), S.I. 1988 No. 643 and the Finance Act 1990 (c.29), s.128; operative on April 24, 1995; revoke and replace with modifications S.I. 1994 No. 1265.

4473a. Vehicle excise—design weight certificate

VEHICLE EXCISE (DESIGN WEIGHT CERTIFICATE) REGULATIONS 1995 (No. 1455), made under Vehicle Excise and Registration Act 1994, ss.57, 61A; operative on July 1, 1995; make provision for the issue of design weight certificates.

4474. Vehicle excise duty

VEHICLE EXCISE DUTY (DESIGNATION OF SMALL ISLANDS) ORDER 1995 (No. 1397) [£1·10], made under the Vehicle Excise and Registration Act 1994 (c.22), Sched. 1, para. 18(4); operative on July 1, 1995; designates specified islands as small islands for the purposes of Sched. 1, para. 18, to the 1994 Act.

4475. Vehicle excise duty—enforcement—cars—press release

The Department of Transport has issued a press release entitled *Sir George Young gives car tax dodgers the "boot"* (Press Notice 323), published on October 11, 1995. The Secretary of State for Transport has announced that untaxed vehicles will be wheel-clamped, in a pilot project to operate initially in the London Borough of Kensington and Chelsea and other parts of the capital. Drivers will be required to pay a fee of £68 for declamping and £135 plus storage costs if the vehicle is impounded and to produce a VED licence or pay £100 as surety for obtaining one before the vehicle will be released. The new powers will focus on serious offenders rather than those whose licence may have slipped off the screen or whose licences are out of date by only a few days; details will be checked against DVLA records before clamping action is taken. The scheme is to be extended to other parts of the country by the end of 1996. A background note on the measure is attached to the press release.

4476. Vehicle excise duty—requirement of delivering excise licence—notice—proof

[Customs and Excise Management Act 1979 (c.2), s.102.]

The DoT appealed by way of case stated against a decision quashing L's conviction, under s.102(3) of the Customs and Excise Management Act 1979, of failing to deliver up an excise licence after the cheque used to pay the duty was dishonoured.

Held, allowing the appeal, that it was necessary to prove L had in fact received notice of the requirement to deliver up the excise licence in order to establish an offence. The prosecution needed only to prove that such notice had been sent by registered mail or recorded delivery to the address given when L had applied for the licence, as laid down in s.102(2).

DEPARTMENT OF TRANSPORT v. LADD, *The Times*, May 29, 1995, D.C.

4477. Vehicle licence—unlicensed car—assessment of amount payable on conviction—effect of compounding previous offence

D pleaded guilty to keeping an unlicensed car for a period beginning in March 1991. He sent a cheque to compound that offence in February 1992. He was then prosecuted for failing to pay the duty in respect of a further period between February and April 1992. The prosecutor argued that he should pay the full amount of the penalty due, calculated from March 1991 to April 1992, despite his earlier payment, which, it was argued, did not constitute a payment of the duty due, but merely a compounding of the offence. The justices held that the compounding of the proceedings for the offence in February was a full settlement in lieu of prosecution.

Held, dismissing the appeal, that the prosecutor had accepted the sum paid to compound the offence, and if the Department of Transport wished to make it clear that compounding an offence did not include the payment of the duty which had gone unpaid, they should make this clear.

SECRETARY OF STATE FOR TRANSPORT v. DAVIS [1994] C.O.D. 76, D.C.

4478. Vehicle parking

HYDE PARK AND THE REGENT'S PARK (VEHICLE PARKING) REGULATIONS 1995 (No. 993) [£1·10], made under the Parks Regulation (Amendment) Act 1926 (c.36), s.2(1) and the Road Traffic Regulation Act 1984 (c.27), s.62; operative on April 3, 1995; revoke and replace S.I. 1994 No. 432.

4479. Volunteer drivers—motor mileage allowances—explanatory leaflet

The Inland Revenue have published a new leaflet (IR122) entitled *Volunteer Drivers* in response to requests for an easy to understand explanation of when a profit occurs and how that profit is calculated. Enquiries to the Inland Revenue Public Enquiries Room, West Wing, Somerset House, London, WC2R 1LB.

SALE OF GOODS

4480. Agency agreement—damages—implied terms—whether difference between disclosed and undisclosed principal

[Sale of Goods Act 1979 (c.54), s.14.]

Section 14(5) of the Sale of Goods Act 1979 applies to any sale by an agent, whether the principal is disclosed or undisclosed.

T instructed a firm to sell a boat on his behalf under a brokerage and agency agreement. The boat was sold to B who knew that it was sold under a brokerage scheme but thought that it was owned by the firm. B did not know the name of the owner nor the fact that the owner was not selling in the course of a business. B discovered defects in the boat rendering it unseaworthy and brought proceedings for breaches of s.14 of the Sale of Goods Act 1979. The sheriff held that the firm had sold the boat in the course of their business and assoilzied T. On appeal the sheriff principal granted a decree in favour of B. T's appeal to the Court of Session was dismissed.

Held, dismissing T's appeal, that s.14 enabled an action to be brought for a breach of an implied term against an undisclosed principal himself and not just the agent action for the principal. As it had not been brought to B's notice that T was not selling in the course of a business B was entitled to succeed in his action.

BOYTER v. THOMSON [1995] 3 W.L.R. 36, H.L.

4481. Auction—painting a forgery—whether sale to be set aside. See DE BALKANY v. CHRISTIE MANSON & WOODS, §2456.

4482. Conditions and warranties—standard form—whether condition fair and reasonable—whether practicable to give notice of defect within prescribed time-limit. See KNIGHT MACHINERY (HOLDINGS) v. RENNIE, §6320.

4483. Contract of sale—incorporation of charterparty demurrage clause—notice of readiness—minor discrepancies in references to marks on cargo—whether charter in existence at relevant date—whether notice of readiness to be given by master or seller—whether notice of readiness given before or after tender of documents—whether documents could be rejected for discrepancies. See GILL & DUFFUS SA v. RIONDA FUTURES, §4521.

4484. Contract of sale—incorporation of charterparty terms—incorporation of time-bar clause. See OK PETROLEUM AB v. VITOL ENERGY SA, §4522.

4485. GAFTA 100—discharging costs from ship's hold to rail for seller's account—bill of lading allocating costs of loading and discharge between carrier and merchant—whether bill of lading a conforming bill for the purposes of GAFTA 100

S sold a cargo of soya bean meal to B on the GAFTA 100 form, cl. 16 of which provided that the cost of discharge from ship's hold to ship's rail was for S's account and from the ship's rail overboard for B's account. By the time the ship discharged, nobody had put the silo operator in funds. B was obliged to pay all the costs, including those from ship's hold to rail and claimed these costs from S. The bill of lading issued by the carrier provided in cl. 20(2) that loading and discharging should be effected by stevedores appointed by the carrier, "the merchant paying the actual cost of such operations directly to the stevedores". However, cl. 20(3)(e) provided that the merchant should pay all "inward expenses" charged after the goods have passed the ship's rail, while cl. 20(3)(b) provided that the merchant should pay the expenses of loading as far as the ship's rail. The question was whether the bill of lading was a conforming bill for the purposes of GAFTA 100. The arbitrators found that the effect of the bill was to make the receivers jointly and severally liable to pay directly to the stevedores the entire cost of discharging. S appealed.

Held, allowing the appeal, that (1) "inward expenses" in cl. 20(3)(e) could refer to the costs of discharging a cargo; (2) cl. 20(3)(b) clearly provided that the merchant was to pay as far as the ship's rail and, in the absence of express agreement, the merchant was not liable for loading expenses beyond that point; (3) it followed that cl. 20(3) provided for the incidence of the costs of loading and discharge expenses to be apportioned between the merchant and the carrier on the basis that loading was to be paid for by the merchant as far as the ship's rail and discharging was to be paid for after the goods had passed the ship's rail; (4) it was not the intention of the parties that the merchant should pay for the cost of loading after the ship's rail or for the costs of discharging before the ship's rail and it was accordingly necessary to construe cl. 20(2) in such a way as not to conflict with cl. 20(3); and (5) cl. 20(2) merely provided that even though the carrier might appoint the stevedore, the relevant part of the actual costs for which the merchant had agreed to be liable must be paid directly to the stevedore, even where that agreement appeared in a booking note and not in the bill itself.

CEVAL INTERNATIONAL v. CEFETRA BV [1994] 1 Lloyd's Rep. 651, Longmore J.

4486. Leasing agreement—agency—finance/leasing company—whether a supplier agent of leasing company. See J.D. WILLIAMS & CO. (t/a WILLIAMS LEASING) v. McCAULEY, PARSONS AND JONES, §2458.

4487. Leasing agreement—agency—supplier making representations—whether acting as agent for owner of goods—whether distinction between leasing agreement and hire-purchase agreement. See WOODCHESTER EQUIPMENT (LEASING) v. BRITISH ASSOCIATION OF CANNED AND PRESERVED FOODS IMPORTERS AND DISTRIBUTORS, §2459.

4488. Retention of title—subcontractor bought from manufacturer subject to retention clause—subcontractor installing equipment without retaining title—whether manufacturer entitled to reclaim from premises at which installed—whether equipment annexed to property as fixture. See AIRCOOL INSTALLATIONS v. BRITISH TELECOMMUNICATIONS, §821.

4489. Sale of Goods (Amendment) Act 1995 (c.28)

This Act alters the law relating to the rights of a purchaser of unascertained goods forming part of an identified bulk to give effect to the recommendation of the Law Commission and the Scottish Law Commission in their report *Sale of Goods Forming Part of a Bulk* (Law Com. No. 215 and Scot. Law Com. No. 145).

The Act received Royal Assent on July 19, 1995.

4490. Title—assignment—equipment lease—only one assignment registered as a charge on book debts—whether unregistered assignment of lease unenforceable by assignee—whether option agreement between lessor and lessee binding

[Companies Act 1985 (c.6), ss.395, 396(1)(e).]

The assignment of an equipment lease is binding on the lessee notwithstanding an option to terminate between the original lessor and the lessee, provided the assignment has been registered as a charge on book debts.

A leased computer equipment to C and then assigned the rents payable to O. Under an option agreement between A and C, C had the right to terminate the leases without penalty before the full period of the leases had expired. In the case of one lease the assignment was registered as a charge on book debts but in the case of a second lease it was not. O sued C for compensation for C's refusal to pay the rents due under the leases.

Held, dismissing the action in relation to the non-registered assignment but not the registered assignment and directing an enquiry as to damages in respect of the latter, that (1) the non-registration of the assignment avoided it as between A and O and prevented O from recovering rent from C; (2) the rights created by the lease whose assignment was registered bound C for the full term of the lease since the option agreement was binding only between A and C.

ORION FINANCE v. CROWN FINANCIAL MANAGEMENT [1994] 2 BCLC 607, Vinelott J.

4491. Title—documents of title—original invoices from suppliers of cars—cars assigned by hire company to finance company—then sold to another finance company—whether hire company sellers in possession—whether invoices documents of title—whether assignments of hire cars under block discounting policy charge on book debts

A motor hire company, S, entered into a block discounting agreement in the Consumer Credit Trade Association standard form, and, pursuant to this agreement, assigned a number of motor cars and the benefits of the hire agreements of those cars which S had entered into with individual hirers, to A, a finance company. Soon after, S sold the same cars to D, another finance company, for lease back. Before agreeing to purchase the cars, D required S to produce the original invoices from the suppliers of the cars which, together with proof that the suppliers had been paid, D treated as documents of title to the cars. A had not required S to hand over the original invoices. D claimed title passed to them, as S were sellers in possession.

Held, that the invoices, even with proof of payment, were not documents of title. Further, S were not in constructive possession of the cars, which remained in the hands of the individual hirers. Further, although A had agreed to extend facilities up to £100,000 to S, the assignments under the block discounting policy were not to be treated as a charge on book debts, but as true assignments which did not therefore require registration under the Companies Act, s.395.

ANGLO-IRISH ASSET FINANCE v. D.S.G. FINANCIAL SERVICES, July 27, 1995, H.H.J. Gower, Q.C. sitting as a deputy judge. [*Ex rel.* Edward Bailey, Barrister, 5 Bell Yard, London.]

4492. Title—wine merchant—receivership—whether goods held in storage for customers property of company or customers

[Sale of Goods Act 1979 (c.54), s.16.]

Even where property has not been allocated to each individual customer, where customers have paid for wine, and left it with the seller for storage, on the seller going into receivership the wine is to be regarded as being the property of the customer who has paid for it, and not of the seller.

A wine merchant sold wine to customers, who left the wine with him for storage purposes, and drew it out at will. The wine merchant separated the stock from his general trading stock. On the wine merchant's receivership the receiver applied to the court for directions as to who owned the wine. The customers argued that under the Sale of Goods Act 1979, s.16, the goods had been ascertained by being set aside from the trading stock, and so belonged to them.

Held, giving directions, that (1) the wine stocks were the property of the customers who had paid for them. The fact that the wine had been set aside in a bonded warehouse as non-trading stock was sufficient to show that the goods had been ascertained; (2) a contract of sale did not create equitable rights, so no trust existed nor any interest based on estoppel or specific performance.

ELLIS, SON AND VIDLER, *Re sum nom.* STAPYLTON FLETCHER, *Re*; ELLIS, SEN AND VIDLER, *Re* [1994] BCC 532, H.H.J. Paul Baker, Q.C.

4493. Tobacco—sale of cigarettes to under-age child—defence of reasonable precautions and exercise of due diligence—whether precautions acceptable. See HEREFORD AND WORCESTER COUNTY COUNCIL v. T & S STORES, §1292.

SEA AND SEASHORE

4494. Offshore installations

OFFSHORE INSTALLATIONS (SAFETY ZONES) ORDER 1995 (No. 494), made under the Petroleum Act 1987, s.22(1)(2); operative on April 1, 1995.

OFFSHORE INSTALLATIONS (SAFETY ZONES) (NO. 2) ORDER 1995 (No. 1567), made under the Petroleum Act 1987, s.22(1)(2); operative on June 21, 1995.

OFFSHORE INSTALLATIONS (SAFETY ZONES) (NO. 3) ORDER 1995 (No. 1575), made under the Petroleum Act 1987, s.22(1)(2); revokes S.I. 1995 No. 1567.

OFFSHORE INSTALLATIONS (SAFETY ZONES) (NO. 4) ORDER 1995 (No. 1956), made under the Petroleum Act 1987, s.22(1)(2); operative on August 10,

OFFSHORE INSTALLATIONS (SAFETY ZONES) (NO. 5) ORDER 1995 (No.

OFFSHORE INSTALLATIONS (SAFETY ZONES) (NO. 5) ORDER 1995 (No. 2363) [£1·10], made under the Petroleum Act 1987, s.22(1)(2); operative on September 25, 1995.

OFFSHORE INSTALLATIONS (SAFETY ZONES) (NO. 6) ORDER 1995 (No. 2795) [65p], made under the Petroleum Act 1987, s.22(1)(2); operative on November 15, 1995; establishes safety zones with a radius of 500m from a specified point around installations specified in the Schedule and stationed in specified waters. Vessels are prohibited from entering or remaining in these safety zones except with the consent of the Health and Safety Executive or in accordance with the Offshore Installations (Safety Zones) Regulations 1987.

4495. Offshore installations—emergency response

OFFSHORE INSTALLATIONS (PREVENTION OF FIRE AND EXPLOSION, AND EMERGENCY RESPONSE) REGULATIONS 1995 (No. 743) [£2·80], made under the Health and Safety at Work etc. Act 1974 (c.37), ss.15(1)–(3)(a)(5)(b), 82(3)(a), Sched. 3, paras. 1(2), 6, 8, 9, 11–13(1)(3), 14, 15(1), 16, 18, 20; operative on June 20, 1995; provide for the protection of persons on offshore oil and gas installations from fire and explosion and for securing an effective emergency response.

4496. Offshore installations—management and administration

OFFSHORE INSTALLATIONS AND PIPELINE WORKS (MANAGEMENT AND ADMINISTRATION) REGULATIONS 1995 (No. 738) [£3·20], made under the Health and Safety at Work etc. Act 1974 (c.37), ss.15(1)–(3)(a)(5)(b), 82(3)(a), Sched. 3, paras. 6, 14, 15(1), 16; operative on June 20, 1995 save for reg. 23(2) which is operative on June 20, 1997; contain requirements for the management and administration of offshore oil and gas installations for purposes of health and safety and give effect to specified provisions of Council Dirs. 89/391/EEC and 92/91/EEC.

4497. Offshore installations—oilwells and pipelines

HEALTH AND SAFETY AT WORK ETC ACT 1974 (APPLICATION OUTSIDE GREAT BRITAIN) ORDER 1995 (No. 263), made under Health and Safety at

Work etc. Act 1974 (c.37), s.84; revokes S.I. 1989 No. 840; operative on March 15, 1995; revokes the 1989 Order and re-enacts its provisions with modifications where provisions relate to oilwells and pipelines within territorial waters; inserts new provisions relating to legal proceedings.

SHIPPING AND MARINE INSURANCE

4498/9. Arbitrator—jurisdiction—settlement agreement reached under arbitration—subsequent claim of duress—whether settlement agreement terminated jurisdiction of arbitrator. See CHIMIMPORT v. G D'ALESIO SAS; PAOLA D'ALESIO, THE, §339.

4500. Bill of lading—carrier's liabilities—address—whether Hague Rules limited liability—pre-loading

[Carriage of Goods by Sea Act 1991 (Australia).]

When a bill of lading was issued by the carriers TTA in respect of carriage of a crate of agricultural spare parts from Sydney to Hamburg and thence inland to a place in France, the letters CFS were inserted into the "Place of Acceptance" and "Place of Delivery" boxes. The shipper delivered the crate to the container depot in Sydney for consolidation into the intended container for loading, but when the container was discharged and deconsolidated the crate did not outturn. The shipper brought an action for damages arising out of the contract.

Held, that the shipper was entitled to the amount claimed. The bill of lading could not take effect as a combined transport bill since the letters CFS were not an address and there was, on the face of it, nothing to indicate any intention other than port-to-port shipment. As the goods were never loaded into the intended container, the amended Hague Rules under s.10 of the Australian Carriage of Goods by Sea Act 1991, which only applied from the time of loading onto the ship, did not apply to limit the carrier's liability. Carriers wishing to limit their liability in respect of pre-loading loss must make appropriate provision in the contract of carriage.

NEW HOLLAND AUSTRALIA PTY. v. TTA AUSTRALIA PTY.; RESOLUTION BAY, THE, *Lloyd's List*, September 27, 1995, Sup. Ct. (NSW).

4501. Bill of lading—charterparty—incorporation of charterparty terms into bill—fixture made orally to include Centrocon London arbitration clause—recap telex mistakenly referred to Synacomex form with arbitration in Paris—Centrocon arbitration clause incorporated—whether Synacomex form incorporated

On July 23, 1990, U concluded with C a contract of affreightment for six to 12 voyages on the Synacomex 1974 form, with arbitration in Paris. C needed to obtain a vessel to perform this contract, and at short notice, conducted over the telephone a fixture of P's vessel on March 7, 1991. It was agreed to apply the terms of a previous charter, which was on the Synacomex 1990 form with a Centrocon London arbitration clause. A recap telex of March 7, 1991, however, mistakenly referred to the 1974 form. After the casualty, C sent to P for a signature a copy of the 1990 form, with the typed Centrocon clause. The charterparty was never signed or returned until 1993. C nominated the H to U and simply stated that the charterparty was the "Synacomex". The bill of lading dated March 8, 1991 provided for freight "as per C/p . . . in accordance with the charterparty dated . . . [left blank], all the terms, conditions and exceptions of which charterparty, including the arbitration clause, are incorporated herewith". The main issue was whether the bill of lading incorporated the fixture agreed on July 23, 1990, March 7, 1991 and, if the latter, whether it included the Centrocon arbitration clause.

Held, that (1) an incorporation clause in a bill of lading is incapable of incorporating a charterparty whose terms have not been reduced into writing by the time the bill of lading is issued; (2) an oral contract, evidenced only by a recap telex, did not qualify for this purpose. The only exceptional case where extrinsic evidence may be relevant is where the bill of lading leaves blank the identify of the charterparty (*San Nicholas, The* [1976] 1 Lloyd's Rep. 8, considered); (3) alternatively, on its true construction, the bill of lading did not incorporate an oral agreement for London arbitration which, at the date of the bill of lading, was not evidenced by any document at all; (4) accordingly, the March 7, 1991 fixture was not incorporated, nor was any London arbitration clause; (5) (obiter) if a formal charterparty has been executed in sufficient time to be sent or shown to the bill of lading holder when it first demands to be shown a copy, (and if the date on the charterparty is earlier than that on the bill of lading), there was no reason why the court should go behind the date that appeared on the charterparty or investigate whether the charterparty was executed before or after the bill of lading was issued; (6) (*obiter*) alternatively, a contract of affreightment could fall within the definition of charterparty in the bill of lading and it was more likely that the parties intended to incorporate the July 23, 1990 contract as the bill was more apt to refer to an instrument in writing than to an oral contract and the reference to freight was more appropriate to the contract of affreightment; and (7) (*obiter*) if the March 7, 1991 contract with the Centrocon clause had been incorporated it was doubtful if sufficient notice had been given to the shipper or indorsee of the existence of the clause (*Interfoto Picture Library v. Stiletto Visual Programmes* [1987] C.L.Y. 445 considered).

PARTENREEDEREI M/S HEIDBERG AND VEGA REEDEREI FRIEDRICH DAUBER v. GROSVENOR GRAIN AND FEED CO., UNION NATIONALE DES COOPERATIVES AGRICOLE DE CEREALES AND ASSURANCES MUTUELLES AGRICOLES; HEIDBERG, THE [1994] 2 Lloyd's Rep. 287, H.H.J. Diamond, Q.C.

4502. Bill of lading—charterparty bill—incorporation of charterparty arbitration clause—clause referred to disputes between "owner and charterer"—whether clause incorporated—whether permissible to manipulate clause to apply to shipper

[Arbitration Act 1975 (c.3), s.1.]

Shippers of a cargo of steel claimed for damage caused while it was being carried in D's ship under a charterparty bill of lading which contained a clause on the reverse stating "all terms and conditions . . . and arbitration clause of the charterparty as dated overleaf are . . . incorporated". On the face of the bill, there was an additional clause which stated that the conditions of the charterparty were incorporated in the bill of lading "and have precedence if there is a conflict, English Law and jurisdiction applies". The relevant charterparty clause provided that disputes between "the Owners and Charterers" should be subject to London arbitration. The question was whether this clause was incorporated into the bill of lading so as to cover disputes between the shippers and D.

Held, that (1) the arbitration clause could not be incorporated unless it was expressly referred to in the bill (*Federal Bulk Carriers v. C. Itoh & Co.; Federal Bulker, The* [1989] C.L.Y. 3346 applied) and the reference in the clause in question was such a reference; (2) although it was not possible to manipulate the arbitration clause so as to read "shipper" for "charterer" where there were general words of incorporation (*Miramar Maritime Corporation v. Holborn Oil Trading; Miramar, The* [1984] C.L.Y. 3156), here there were specific words of incorporation and it was possible to manipulate the clause so as to make its incorporation effective (*Ouinoussin Pride, The* [1991] 1 Lloyd's Rep. 126, followed; *Navigazione Alta Italia Spa v. Svenske Petroleum AB; Nai Matteini, The* [1988] 1 Lloyd's Rep. 452 not followed); (3) the reference to "English Law and jurisdiction" was not inconsistent with such a finding, but could be explained by reference to the supervisory jurisdiction of the court over arbitrations; and (4) the arbitration clause so incorporated was still an arbitration agreement for the purposes of the Arbitration Act 1975, s.1.

DAVAL ACIERS D'USINOR ET DE SACILOR v. ARMARE Srl; NERANO, THE [1994] 2 Lloyd's Rep. 50, Clarke J.

4503. Bill of lading—discharging costs—whether carrier or receiver liable for costs between ship's hold and rail. See CEVAL INTERNATIONAL v. CEFETRA BV, §4485.

4504. Bill of lading—Haulage Rules Art. III r.6—time bar—Himalaya clause—whether "suit was brought" within Art. III r.6—whether plaintiff entitled to bring fresh action when claim dismissed for want of prosecution—whether agents and port authority protected by Himalaya clause

[Hague Rules, Art. III, r. 6.]

P claimed as cargo owners against D1–3 for damage to cargo carried by D1 under bills of lading subject to the Hague Rules. D2 was the carrier's general agent at the port of discharge and D3 was the owner of the port. The cargo was discharged on January 24, 1988 and the one-year time bar under the Hague Rules, Art. III, r. 6, operated "unless suit is brought" within one year after delivery. Extensions were granted until October 1990. The writ was issued in March 1990 and served in October 1990. There was delay of between 19–24 months between D's further and better particulars of points of defence and P's next steps, although there had been negotiations to achieve without prejudice agreements. D1–3 applied in 1993 for the claims to be dismissed for want of prosecution. P issued new writs in 1993. P argued that it would be wrong to dismiss the claims at a time when it would still be possible to issue a writ within the six year time bar of the Limitation Act 1980 and that D2 and D3 were not parties to the bill of lading and so not entitled to rely on the one year time bar. D2 and D3 claimed to rely on the Himalaya clause in the bill of lading.

Held, that (1) the delay was inordinate, inexcusable and caused serious prejudice to D1–3, and there was no reason why negotiations which are not making progress cannot be pursued simultaneously with the advancement of the litigation; (2) the words "unless suit is brought" mean that the action must be a proper or competent one (*The Nordglimt* [1988] Q.B. 183 applied); (3) to permit fresh proceedings to be brought after the initial proceedings have been dismissed for want of prosecution would be to defeat the purpose of the rule; (4) earlier proceedings cannot be relied on as having been brought within one year if they have been dismissed for want of prosecution and it followed that P's action against D1 would be dismissed; and (5) although there were doubts as to the extent to which D2 and D3 could rely on the Himalaya clause in the bill of lading the court would dismiss the claims against them in the first action in view of the prejudice suffered.

FORT STERLING v. SOUTH ATLANTIC CARGO SHIPPING N.V.; FINNROSE, THE [1994] 2 Lloyd's Rep. 559, Rix J.

4505. Bill of lading—liability of carrier—exclusion clause—whether term "carrier" encompasses subcontractors and agents

H claimed damages against R in respect of confectionery being shipped from Sydney to Singapore which was found to be damaged on arrival. R had subcontracted the carriage to another company (RCL). A bill of lading was issued which contained a clause limiting the carrier's liability for loss of or damage to goods to where the unsuitability or defective condition of the container was due to "want of due diligence on the part of the carrier". While the confectionery was being loaded the container was punctured as a result of the loading crane being operated negligently. On arrival at Singapore the cargo was found to have been affected by moisture penetration and was considered not fit to be sold. R, relying on the exclusion clause in the bill of lading, argued that it was not negligent because it had subcontracted the loading to RCL, a reputable organisation.

Held, that the term "carrier" in the exclusion clause encompassed sub-contractors or agents, and R could not avoid liability if such subcontractors failed to show due diligence. H was entitled to full damages against R.

HARPERS TRADING (SINGAPORE) PTE v. RFL INTERNATIONAL; PLANETA, THE, *Lloyd's List*, August 16, 1995, Sup.Ct. (NSW).

4506. Bill of lading—misdelivery—delivery of cargo without production of a bill of lading—delivery to port authority—whether carrier liable—whether exemption clause covered the misdelivery—whether delivery in accordance with customs, practice and procedure of port

P was the holder of a bill of lading indorsed to it in blank. The bill contained a clause under which the carrier was "in no case responsible for loss or damage to cargo . . . after discharging" and incorporated "all terms and conditions, liberties and exceptions" of a charterparty. The charterparty provided in cl. 46 that if bills of lading were unavailable at discharge, the carrier would agree to discharge against production of a bank guarantee. It also provided in cl. 14 that stevedores were to be appointed by shippers/receivers and in cl. 23 that demurrage was to be settled between owners and "charterers" (in substitution for "receivers" on the standard printed form of bill). P sold the cargo to F, on terms that title did not pass until payment. F, in turn, had sold it to BMH (the notify party on the bill). BMH paid F, but F failed to open a letter of credit in P's favour. The cargo was shipped on FIOST terms and BMH arranged for the port authority, CSP, to discharge the cargo to it in Russia. The discharge took place without production of a bill of lading and the cargo owner, P, sued the carrier for the loss of the cargo. The question was whether it was a breach of the contract of carriage for the shipowner to discharge cargo without production of a bill. The carrier also argued that it had complied with its delivery obligation because it had (i) delivered in accordance with the practice, custom and law of the port, and/or (ii) it delivered to P's agent and so P could not recover damages. It also argued that there would in any event have been detention and demurrage costs.

Held, that (1) subject to the particular terms of the contract concerned, a master is not entitled to deliver goods otherwise than against an original bill of lading unless it is proved to his reasonable satisfaction both that the person seeking the goods is entitled to possession of them and that there is some reasonable explanation of what has happened to the bill of lading. The existence of the express indemnity in cl. 46, which was effectively incorporated into the bill, contemplated that there would be liability if there was delivery without production of the bill ; (2) in order to cater for circumstances where a bill of lading is lost or stolen it is necessary to imply a term that the master must deliver cargo without production of an original bill in circumstances where it is proved to his reasonable satisfaction both that the person seeking delivery of the goods is entitled to possession and what has become of the bills of lading; (3) the carrier had made no enquiries of CSP to see how they were entitled to delivery or what had happened to the bills of lading and was accordingly liable; (4) the loss arose from delivery without production of the bill because discharge would not have begun if the master had asked for the original bill; (5) accordingly, as P's loss arose on discharge and not after it, the words in the bill were neither intended, nor apt, to exclude liability for discharge without production of a bill; (6) there was a distinction between law and custom which, if strictly proved, would protect the carrier and "practice". A custom must be reasonable, certain, consistent with the contract, universally acquiesced in and not contrary to law; (7) although CSP had in practice a monopoly over discharging, CSP was not P's agent and there was no legal requirement of Russian law that there should be delivery without a bill; (8) nor could it be said that, under the FIOST clause which was incorporated into the bill of lading, CSP was in English law the agent of P. Accordingly, delivery was not made to P, or its representatives, and P was entitled to recover substantial damages; (9) the carrier could set off sums which the cargo owner would have been obliged to incur, *e.g.* where expense would have been incurred if the master had refused to deliver the cargo; and (10) it was not possible to manipulate the word "charterers" in cl. 23 to cover P, as the deletion and express reference elsewhere to "charterers" showed an intention that it was only to be the charterers and not the receivers (*i.e.* P) who were to be responsible for demurrage.

SA SUCRE EXPORT v. NORTHERN RIVER SHIPPING; SORMOVSKIY 3068, THE [1994] 2 Lloyd's Rep. 266, Clarke J.

4507. Bill of lading—non-delivery of cargo—measure of damages—mitigation—currency of loss—whether damages to be assessed in US dollars

A carrier was liable for breach of a bill of lading undertaking to deliver a cargo of oil belonging to P. The question was whether the damages and interest were to be assessed in US dollars or Ghanaian cedis. P was a Ghanaian Government Department and was shipper and consignee for a Ghanaian coastal voyage. It had borne the cost of refining the cargo in cedis, the currency in which it carried on business and in which all its books were kept. P had intended to sell the cargo in cedis to Ghanaian companies. If P had to buy oil from abroad it would remit cedis to the State Bank, which would purchase dollars (in which oil was transacted internationally), although there was no evidence that the cargo in question was so replaced. The nearest available market to Ghana for replacement oil was in Italy where oil would have had to be bought in dollars. Between the date of breach, 1982, and the date of trial, 1991, the cedi declined dramatically against the US$ from 2.75 cedis/$1 to 375 cedis/$1. The judge held that, although cedis were the currency of loss, in order to provide *restitutio in integrum* the award had to be made in dollars on the basis of the price of importing oil. The Court of Appeal allowed the appeal and held that the loss fell to be measured in cedis. P appealed.

Held, dismissing the appeal, that (1) the award of damages is to be assessed at the date of breach and no account is to be taken of fluctuations in the relevant currency between the date of breach and the date of judgment. Delay between the breach and judgment dates is compensated by the award of interest; (2) damages had to be calculated in the currency in which P felt the loss, which was the cedi (*Services Europe Atlantique Sud (SEAS) of Paris v. Stockholms Rederiaktiebolag Svea of Stockholm, Folias, The* [1979] A.C. 685, applied); (3) (obiter) when ascertaining the replacement value of a cargo which has not been delivered by a carrier, it does not follow that the currency in which such replacement cargo would have been bought on the market constitutes the currency in which the cargo owner felt its loss; (4) in any event, even if P had purchased a cargo in dollars, it would have expected cedis to acquire the dollars from the State Bank (Folias, The, applied) and, accordingly, the loss fell to be measured in cedis.

ATTORNEY-GENERAL OF THE REPUBLIC OF GHANA AND GHANA NATIONAL PETROLEUM CORPORATION v. TEXACO OVERSEAS TANKSHIPS, TEXACO MELBOURNE, THE [1994] 1 Lloyd's Rep. 473, H.L.

4508. Charterparty—bareboat charterparty—condition on redelivery—repairs to generator—vessel subject to Class condition—whether generator should be replaced—whether shipowner entitled to replacement cost or nominal damages—whether shipowner entitled to "cost of cure"

C bareboat chartered the R from S, under which there were obligations to ensure that all repairs were to be effected so as not to diminish the value of the vessel and that the vessel was redelivered with clean Class Certificates. A dispute arose as to the condition of a generator which had been repaired by C.

The vessel was not fully in Class unless the repair had lasted for two years. The arbitrator decided that, although it was difficult to say that the value of the R had been diminished, as the Class condition would not be lifted without a replacement generator, S was entitled to its replacement cost. C claimed that S was only entitled to nominal damages.

Held, that (1) where a contract makes specific provision for the condition or attributes of a vessel on redelivery, the shipowner would not necessarily be able to recover the cost of remedying a failure to comply with the provision; (2) such a cost would only be recoverable if it represented reasonable expenditure and recovery on a "cost of cure" basis will not be allowed if that cost is disproportionate to the financial consequences of the deficiency (*Sealace Shipping Co. v. Oceanvoice; Alecos M., The* [1991] C.L.Y. 3194 applied; *Ruxley Electronics and Construction v. Forsyth; Laddingford Enclosures v. Same* [1994] C.L.Y. 1439 distinguished); (3) the arbitrator had erred by allowing S to recover the cost of whatever steps were necessary to remove the Class qualification, regardless of how unreasonable it was to take such steps or incur such costs; and (4) the matter would be remitted so that the arbitrator could consider whether the replacement was reasonable or, if not, whether S had suffered any lesser prejudice.

CHANNEL ISLAND FERRIES v. CENARGO NAVIGATION; ROZEL, THE [1994] 2 Lloyd's Rep. 161, Phillips J.

4509. Charterparty—bareboat charterparty—repudiation by charterer—measure of damages—mitigation—vessel in damaged condition on redelivery—vessel not repaired but laid up—whether shipowner acted reasonably in not repairing vessel—whether charterer discharged burden of showing failure to mitigate—whether shipowner entitled to lost profits from lost chance of sale to charterer—whether shipowner entitled to repositioning expenses after wrongful redelivery

C wrongly repudiated a bareboat charterparty with S by a premature redelivery of S's vessel, which was in a defective condition for which C was responsible. The vessel on redelivery would have required $1 million repairs in order to enable her to trade, but S decided not to undertake the repairs because the market would only have brought in $4000–5000 per day and the operating costs were about $4500 per day. S laid up the vessel, seeking to sell her and awaiting an improvement in the market which did not occur. S accepted the repudiation and claimed (i) damages representing the hire payable for the remaining nine months of the charter, (ii) damages for loss of profits as a result of the inability to sell the vessel to C under a purchase option in the charterparty, (iii) additional expenses incurred in taking the vessel from the United Kingdom to Greece for lay-up. C claimed that S had failed to mitigate its loss by seeking to recharter the vessel at the market rate.

Held, that (1) S had displaced any prima facie measure of loss because there was no market for rechartering the vessel in her unrepaired state and S had acted reasonably in declining to repair an old vessel; (2) the burden was accordingly on C to show that S had behaved unreasonably and in any event C failed to discharge that burden; (3) there was no claim for the lost profits on completion of the charter as, if the option to buy had been exercised by C, S would have received less than the sound value of the vessel, and if the option had not been exercised S would in any event be entitled to a sum representing the diminution in value of the vessel by reason of its defective condition; (4) although S might have expected to bear the costs of crewing the vessel after redelivery in accordance with the charterparty, C's breach in redelivering a sound vessel had deprived S of the opportunity of trading the vessel immediately and so the extra costs of crewing and repositioning were recoverable; and (5) S was, exceptionally, entitled to its costs on an indemnity basis as C had persisted in an unsustainable allegation of fraud, which was based on the evidence of an unqualified expert.

THARROS SHIPPING CO. AND DEN NORSKE BANK v. BIAS SHIPPING, BULK SHIPPING A.G. AND BULK OIL A.G. BULK SHIPPING A.G. AND BULK OIL A.G. v. THARROS SHIPPING CO. AND DEN NORSKE BANK AND THEODORE HALKEDIS, GRIPARION (NO. 2), THE [1994] 2 Lloyd's Rep. 533, Rix J.

4510. Charterparty—time charter—breach by shipowner—damages—charterer hiring substitute vessel—charterer making profit on sale of bunkers—whether charterer should give credit for profit in damages claim

S time-chartered its vessel to C. Owing to a breach by S, C had to charter a replacement vessel and claimed damages. The arbitrators did not take into account a profit which C made when it sold the bunkers remaining on board the substitute vessel on its redelivery to the substitute owners. S appealed, contending that the profit should be taken into account.

Held, dismissing the appeal, that (1) it was not necessary to embark on a two-stage process by asking whether the substitute fixture was a consequence of the breach and then by asking whether the profit arose out of the substitute fixture (*British Westinghouse Co. v. Underground Electric Rys.* [1912] A.C. 673 considered); (2) the question was whether any profit or loss arose out of, or was sufficiently closely connected with, the breach to require it to be brought into account in assessing damages; (3) in order to form a common-sense judgement of the sufficiency of the causal nexus between the breach and the profit it was necessary to take into account all the circumstances, including the nature and effects of the breach, the nature of the profit, the manner in which it occurred and any intervening or collateral factors which played a part in its occurrence; and (4) the substitute charter was not the cause of the profit and its performance was merely the occasion in respect of which C was able to make a collateral windfall profit and the arbitrators were entitled to find that the profit was not a consequence of the breach.

FAMOSA SHIPPING CO. v. ARMADA BULK CARRIERS; FANIS, THE [1994] 1 Lloyd's Rep. 633, Mance J.

4511. Charterparty—time charter—NYPE form—charterers' orders to load cargo—master refusing to exceed classification society super-stability limits—no evidence that ship would be made unsafe—whether master entitled to refuse order—whether shipowner liable for failing to load cargo

S time-chartered its vessel to C on the NYPE form to carry zinc concentrates. Under cl. 7 the whole of the vessel's holds was to be at C's disposal, but "not more than she can reasonably stow and carry". At a stage in loading, the vessel was still above her marks, but the master declined to load any more cargo as he correctly calculated that to do so would involve a breach of a rule imposed by the vessel's classification society concerning super-stability. This rule was only operated by the particular classification society. There was no finding that the actual loading requested would have made the ship unseaworthy and C claimed damages in respect of the cargo shut out. The arbitrator rejected the claim and C appealed.

Held, dismissing the appeal, that (1) neither the use of the word "can" in cl. 7, nor the fact that cl. 7 related to the vessel's capacity and the quantity of cargo she could load, meant that the word "reasonably" must necessarily be restricted by reference to considerations of physical safety or seaworthiness; (2) cl. 7 embraced the possibility that there could be other relevant considerations making it reasonable not to load, having regard to the joint interests of owners and charterers; (3) a vessel could not reasonably be expected to stow or carry cargo in conditions not permitted by her stability data and there was no reason why class rules laid down for the vessel should not be treated similarly, at least where their existence was in general terms in the contemplation of the parties and their general function was to ensure the vessel's safe operation in the interests of owners and charterers; and (4) the fact that no other classification society had a similar rule was immaterial in view of the fact that the rule was neither irrational or unreasonable.

FURNESS WITHY (AUSTRALIA) PTY. v. BLACK SEA SHIPPING CO.; ROMAN KARMEN, THE [1994] 1 Lloyd's Rep. 644, Mance J.

4512. Charterparty—time-charter—redelivery—vessel ordered on illegitimate last voyage—vessel redelivered late—whether legitimacy of voyage established at date order given—whether charterers in repudiatory breach

In determining the date for judging the validity of the charterers' order for the final voyage it is necessary to ascertain the intention of the parties from the terms of the charterparty itself.

By the terms of a time charterparty in the New York Produce Exchange form the owner chartered the vessel to the charterers for a maximum of 70 days. The vessel was delivered off Antwerp on January 8, 1988 and proceeded in ballast to South America where she performed two voyages. On February 9, 1988, before completion of the second voyage, the master was instructed by the charterers to proceed to an additional port, Palua, to load a cargo for Fos in Italy. At that time redelivery in accordance with the charterparty could reasonably have been expected but the ship was held up and it became impossible to redeliver her within the stipulated period. The vessel nevertheless proceeded to Palua on February 25 on which date the owners informed the charterers that they declined to perform the voyage to Fos and requested the charterers to give revised orders for the final voyage. No such orders were given and a dispute arose. A without-prejudice agreement was entered into and the vessel performed her voyage and was eventually redelivered eight days late. The dispute which concerned validity of the charterers' order to proceed to Palua was referred to arbitration. The arbitrator found in favour of the owners and his award was upheld by Evans J. On appeal by the charterers the Court of Appeal allowed the appeal and remitted the matter to the arbitrator for reconsideration.

Held, allowing the appeal, that (1) in determining the date for judging the validity of the charterers' order for the final voyage it was necessary to ascertain the intention of the parties from the terms of the charterparty itself and, accordingly, the correct date for ascertainment was February 25, 1988, by which date an order originally permissible had become illegitimate; (2) although timely redelivery was not a term of the contract, breach of which would amount to repudiation, the fact that the charterers had no intention of giving valid orders to enable the vessel to be redelivered within the stipulated time constituted an anticipatory breach which enabled the owners to treat the contract as ended (*Alma Shipping Corporation of Monrovia v. Mantovani; Dione, The* [1974] C.L.Y. 3561, *Motor Oil Hellas (Corinth) Refineries SA v. Shipping Corporation of India; Kanchenjunga, The* [1991] C.L.Y. 3227, *Batis Maritime Corp. v. Petroleos del Mediterraneo SA; Batis, The* [1991] C.L.Y. 3226 considered).

TORVALD KLAVENESS A/S v. ARNI MARITIME CORP. [1994] 1 W.L.R. 1465, H.L.

4513. Charterparty—towage—jurisdiction over charterers—ownership of fuel—fraudulent misrepresentation by charterers—whether owners of barge entitled to rescind—whether attachment over tugboat confirmed

The owners (BB) of the barge Boss applied to the court to confirm an attachment over the tugboat Tigr and bunkers full of fuel contained therein. BB had attached the Tigr and fuel *ad fundandem vel confirmandem jurisdictionem*, intending to commence proceedings *in personam* against the owners and charterers of Tigr for damage which allegedly occurred when Boss was being towed and became grounded on rocks. The towage contract included an exemption clause but BB asserted that they had validly rescinded the contract for misrepresentation which the charterers made about Tigr's pulling power.

Held, granting the application, that the fuel which the charterers provided and paid for belonged to them because the agreement between the owners and charterers made no specific provision that it should not. The court therefore had jurisdiction over the charterers as owners of the fuel which was attached. BB had established a prima facie case that the charterers made fraudulent misrepresentations and that Boss went aground because Tigr did not have the capacity they claimed. Tigr's owners authorised the exemption clause in the contract made on their behalf by the charterers when they made Tigr available and commenced the tow. Therefore BB was entitled to rescind both the contract with the charterers and the contract with the owners contained in the Himalaya clause, and the attachment of the tug and the fuel was confirmed.

TIGR, THE, *Lloyd's List*, September 19, 1995 (I.D.), Sup. Ct. (SA).

4514. Charterparty—voyage charter—breach by charterer—dangerous cargo—detention—shipowner undertaking substitute voyage—freight actually earning higher than typical hire rates—mitigation—whether benefit to be taken into account by arbitrator—whether award to be remitted

[Arbitration Act 1950 (c.27), s.22; Arbitration Act 1979 (c.42), s.1(2).]

C breached a charterparty with S by shipping dangerous cargo on S's vessel. S's vessel was detained, but S managed to obtain a substitute fixture at a freight rate which was higher than typical hire rates. The arbitrator awarded damages against C and recorded that it was common ground between the parties that C was not entitled to the benefit of the higher freight actually earned on the substitute voyage. It was agreed that this was a misunderstanding which merited a remittal to the arbitrator under the Arbitration Act 1950, s.22. C appealed asking for a lesser sum to be substituted, taking into account the benefit gained, or for the appeal to be remitted under s.22.

Held, remitting the award, that (1) it was not possible to find an error of law which gave the court jurisdiction under the Arbitration Act 1979, s.1, as the arbitrator had expressly stated that the parties were agreed; (2) in any event, there was no obligation to take such benefits into account (*Fanis, The* [1994] 1 Lloyd's Rep. 633 followed), and it could not therefore be said that the arbitrator would necessarily have decided the case in C's favour; and (3) the case would be remitted to the arbitrator in order for the benefit issues to be considered.

MARC RICH A.G. v. BEOGRADSKA PLOVIDBA; AVALA, THE [1994] 2 Lloyd's Rep. 363, Tuckey J.

4515. Charterparty—voyage charter—demurrage—frustration—"Voywar 1963" war risks clause giving "liberty to comply" with orders of belligerents—Iraqi invasion of Kuwait—shipowner ordered to discharge cargo to Iraqis—whether charterparty frustrated—whether clause protected against breach only—whether clause covered frustrating event—whether demurrage payable

On July 7, 1990, S chartered its vessel to C to carry a cargo to Kuwait. The vessel arrived on July 31 and commenced discharge, but on August 2, Iraq invaded Kuwait. The Iraqis ordered the cargo to be discharged on August 10, in C's name. Discharge commenced on August 11 and was completed on September 1. The Iraqis seized all the cargo as it was discharged. S claimed demurrage. C claimed that the charterparty was frustrated on August 10/11. The "Voywar 1963" war risks clause in the charterparty gave S "liberty to comply" with the orders of belligerents. C argued that although the clause protected an owner from being in breach it did not provide that the doing of the act was due performance. The arbitrator found that it was only the actual seisure of the cargo from August 11 which could have frustrated the charterparty but that, as the clause provided an alternative mode of performance, there was no frustration. C appealed.

Held, dismissing the appeal, that (1) the commercial judgement of the arbitrator would not be interfered with; (2) in any event, although it was possible in delay cases for a risk to be covered by an express provision but for the contract to be frustrated when that risk materialises in some overwhelming form, where the clause in question covers some event not merely in a minor form, but also in a major form, it is difficult to argue that the parties have not made such specific provision for the event in question as to exclude the operation of the doctrine of frustration (*Evia (No. 2), The* [1981] 2 Lloyd's Rep. 613 distinguished); (3) the words "liberty to comply" indicated that the charterparty was not to be frustrated where the liberty was being carried out, although the result may be different, *e.g.* where an indefinite delay was concerned; and (4) the doctrine of frustration did not operate where the cargo was discharged without a frustrating delay at the contractual port of destination in compliance with the orders of a belligerent power which stole the cargo, or where the shipowner was carrying out the agreed adventure under an express liberty in the charterparty.

KUWAIT SUPPLY CO. v. OYSTER MARINE MANAGEMENT; SAFEER, THE [1994] 1 Lloyd's Rep. 637, Rix J.

4516. Charterparty—voyage charter—negotiations by telephone and telex—allegation that fixture "subject details"—allegation that recap telex not reflecting oral agreement—minor details in charterparty form remaining to be agreed—whether fixture "subject details"—whether fixture concluded

C entered negotiations with S for S to charter its ship to C for the carriage of a cargo of wheat to Bangladesh. C sent a telex proposing terms, including "otherwise Synacomex terms". There was a telephone conversation whose terms were disputed. S claimed only to have agreed "subject details", but C denied that there had been any such qualification. C sent a recap telex which made no reference to the phrase, but included two matters which S later disputed. It stated that it was S's responsibility to have the vessel accepted by the receivers and also incorporated the Synacomex strike clause. It later became clear that there might be significant delays in Bangladesh and S claimed that no fixture had been agreed. The issues were (i) whether there was a consensus, but "subject details", (ii) if there was no express reference to "subject details", were there important terms still to be agreed between the parties, or had a concluded agreement been reached? It was accepted that if the words had been used there could be no binding agreement.

Held, that (1) there was a binding contract as there was no express mention of the words "subject details" in the telephone conversation; (2) the words concerning S's responsibility were consistent with the expectations of the parties at the time and were expressly agreed; (3) there had also been express mention of the strike clause, as there would have been no need to refer to it otherwise, given the general agreement to Synacomex terms; and (4) although there were blanks in the Synacomex form which needed to be filled in and a number of clauses in which specific choices would have to be made, it was not suggested that these would have presented any difficulty. The Court would be slow not to uphold what was intended to be a binding bargain just because there were minor matters in relation to which there would be no difficulty at all to be ironed out once the formal charterparty was drawn up.

GRANIT S.A. v. BENSHIP INTERNATIONAL [1994] 2 Lloyd's Rep. 526, Waller J.

4517. Charterparty—voyage charter—safe port—vessel damaged by fender as a result of third vessel passing—plaintiff injured by wrongs of charterer and passing vessel—contribution—whether berth unsafe—whether charterer liable to shipowner—whether contribution payable by passing vessel to charterer—whether necessary to foresee actual loss

[Civil Liability (Contribution) Act 1978 (c.47).]

P voyage chartered the vessel X to D2. While mooring at a berth, the X was passed by D1's vessel, the Y. The interaction between the vessels caused the

X to collide with the quay and she was holed by a fender consisting of truck tyres around a metal shaft. It was accepted that it was negligent to attempt to pass until the X was securely moored. There was a dispute between D2 and P as to whether the pilot of the X signalled to the Y that the X was alongside the berth and that the Y could pass. P claimed against D2 in tort and against D1 for breach of the safe port obligation in the charter. D1 claimed that (a) D's pilot had authorised the passing and (b) the loss was too remote. The judge found against D1 and D2 and they appealed.

Held, dismissing the appeal, that (1) the pilot of the X did not signal she was alongside and that the Y could pass. Accordingly, the Y was negligently passing; (2) the true test of remoteness was whether it was foreseeable that, as a result of the Y's negligence, the X would suffer hull damage, and it was unnecessary to foresee that the hull would be holed by the penetration of a fender which was supposed to protect the vessel rather than harm it; (3) by reason of the design of the fender the berth was unsafe despite ordinary prudence and skilful navigation (*Eastern City, The* [1958] 2 Lloyd's Rep. 127, *Evia (No. 2), The* [1982] 1 Lloyd's Rep. 334 applied); (4) despite the negligence of the pilot, there was no break in the chain of causation as both this and the unsafety were effective causes of the accident; and (5) accordingly, both D1 and D2 were liable for the whole of P's damages and the judge's apportionment of contribution between them was correct, namely one third as to D2 and two thirds as to D1.

PREKOOKEANSKA PLOVIDBA v. FELSTAR SHIPPING CORP. AND SETRAMAR Srl AND STC SCANTRADE A.B. (THIRD PARTY); CARNIVAL, THE [1994] 2 Lloyd's Rep. 14, C.A.

4518. Charterparty—voyage charter—"Worldfood" charterparty—commencement of laytime—notice of readiness—notice given in good faith but vessel in fact unready—whether notice a nullity—whether laytime commenced but subject to deduction

C chartered a vessel from S under the "Worldfood" voyage charterparty, as used by the U.N.'s World Food Programme. Clause 8 provided that before tendering (NOR) the master should ensure that all holds were clean and in all respects suitable to receive the cargo to the shipper's satisfaction. Clause 9 provided that if the vessel was found to be unready after berthing the actual time lost was not to count as laytime. The vessel arrived at the loadport on August 10/11 when NOR was given. As there were no berths available, she waited at the anchorage. On August 28, the master was ordered to remove insect infestation, of which he had been unaware. On September 7 the vessel shifted to a vacant berth. On September 8 an inspection revealed that the infestation was still present and the holds were fumigated. By September 9 the vessel was fit. Loading commenced on September 10. A dispute arose as to when laytime commenced and the questions were: (i) whether the NOR was a nullity as the vessel was not ready, so that laytime commenced on September 10, or (ii) whether laytime commenced, but was subject to a deduction for time lost. The arbitrators found for S on the basis of (ii) and C appealed.

Held, dismissing C's appeal, that (1) in construing the laytime cl. 9, there was a strong presumption that there was to be consistency between the treatment of physical unreadiness and free pratique; (2) cl. 8 imposed the same duties as at common law, namely to ensure that the holds were fit to receive cargo before giving NOR; and (3) the effect of cll. 8 and 9 was to require C to pay for waiting time at the anchorage when they had not provided a berth, but that S would bear the risk of delay if the vessel caused delay after arrival at the berth because she was unready (*Linardos, The* [1994] 2 Lloyd's Rep. 28 followed).

UNITED NATIONS FOOD AND AGRICULTURE ORGANISATION, WORLD FOOD PROGRAMME v. CASPIAN NAVIGATION; JAY GANESH, THE [1994] 2 Lloyd's Rep. 358, Colman J.

4519. Classification society—negligence—duty of care—whether surveyor owed duty of care to cargo owner. See MARC RICH & CO A.G. v. BISHOP ROCK MARINE CO., BETHMARINE CO. AND NIPPON KAIJI KYOKAI, NICHOLAS H., THE, §3730

4520. Collision—apportionment of liability—whether vessels equally to blame

The general cargo ship, H, and the Liberian VLCC, S, collided in the North Sea in circumstances where each vessel was partly to blame. The bow of the S struck the port side of the H in conditions of visibility reduced by fog. Disputes arose as to respective speeds and headings and the question arose as to the apportionment of liability.

Held, that (1) both vessels were keeping a poor lookout and proceeding too fast; (2) both failed to take positive early helm action to avoid a "close quarters" situation; (3) S failed to alter course and H made a number of small alterations of course which caused the vessels to approach each other on collision courses; and (4) but for the actions of the H there would have been no collision and, taking into account both blameworthiness and causative potency, liability would be apportioned 60 per cent to H and 40 per cent to S.

SKYRON AND HEL, THE [1994] 2 Lloyd's Rep. 254, Clarke J.

4521. Contract of sale—incorporation of charterparty demurrage clause—notice of readiness—minor discrepancies in references to marks on cargo—whether charter in existence at relevant date—whether notice of readiness to be given by master or seller—whether notice of readiness given before or after tender of documents—whether documents could be rejected for discrepancies

D provided a guarantee to P in respect of the obligations of buyers under a cif sale contract of bagged suger, dated May 8. The sale contract was for cargo already shipped under "April" bills of lading and provided for demurrage "as per C/P" to be for the buyer's account and settled every 15 days. A charterparty dated May 12 was eventually agreed between P's suppliers and the shipowner which provided for demurrage at £5,000 per day. There was a standard agreement between the shipowner and the suppliers which stipulated rates of demurrage for particular ports. P's sale contract from the suppliers provided for demurrage at £2,000 per day. The vessel's discharge was delayed while the shipowner exercised a lien for general average, but the master still served a notice of readiness. The buyers refused tender of documents on the grounds of various minor discrepancies and failed to meet an arbitration award in respect of demurrage incurred and P claimed on the guarantee at the £5,000 rate.

Held, that (1) D was liable since the expression "as per C/P" referred to the charterparty pursuant to which the cargo was being carried under the bills of lading referred to in the sale contract; (2) provided that the charterparty was a genuine commercial arrangement it did not matter that it had not been drawn up at the date of the sale contract or that it depended on a standing arrangement; (3) where a shipowner is lawfully and reasonably exercising a lien it can nevertheless serve a valid notice of readiness and the vessel could therefore be legally and physically ready to discharge; (4) on a true construction the sale contract was not one of indemnity in respect of P's obligations, but contained a separate scheme of liability whereby demurrage was ascertained and paid by the buyers every 15 days; (5) the notice of readiness under the sale contract was to be given by the master and not by P;

(6) it was immaterial that the notice was tendered before or after P tendered the documents to the buyers and the liability of the buyers was accordingly for £5,000 per day; (7) there was a good tender of documents, even though some of the documents provided a more detailed description of shipping marks in the cargo than others; (8) although the phytosanitary certificate did not contain all the details of other documents it complied with the Refined Sugar Association rules as it was issued by the appropriate authority and referred to the relevant goods; and (9) in any event the delay in discharge was not caused by any inadequacy in documents.

GILL & DUFFUS SA v. RIONDA FUTURES [1994] 2 Lloyd's Rep. 67, Clarke J.

4522. Contract of sale—incorporation of charterparty terms—incorporation of time-bar clause

In determining a preliminary issue as to whether a claim under a contract of sale which necessitated the chartering of two vessels was time-barred, the same rules of construction were to be applied as to the case of incorporation of charterparty terms into the bill of lading. The time-bar clause could not be incorporated into the contract for sale as it did not form part of the substantive provisions relating to demurrage but was ancillary to them and the wording of incorporation could not be construed so widely.

OK PETROLEUM AB v. VITOL ENERGY SA, *The Times*, May 29, 1995, Colman J.

4523. Cristal contract—claims—jurisdiction—whether jurisdiction of courts could be excluded

C, the administrator of the Cristal Contract (the international agreement entitled the Contract Regarding a Supplement to Tanker Liability for Oil Pollution) and the associated compensation fund, appealed against a ruling that any determination made by them as to the validity of claims was open to review by an English court, even though a clause of the contract specified that C should be the "sole judge" in accordance with the contract terms. C argued that they had exclusive jurisdiction to determine whether or not the time-limit for the plaintiff's claim had expired.

Held, allowing the appeal, that there were many circumstances in which the jurisdiction of the High Court might be restricted, including where the parties to a contract incorporated a term to exclude a right of challenge by the courts. Although it was a general rule of common law that to oust the jurisdiction of the courts completely was contrary to public policy, questions of fact were to be treated differently from questions of law. Given the nature of the international agreement and the functions of C under the contract, it was right that C's decision was final and binding on matters of fact and was not reviewable, provided that C acted fairly and not perversely in making any determination.

WEST OF ENGLAND SHIP OWNERS MUTUAL INSURANCE ASSOCIATION (LUXEMBOURG) v. CRISTAL, *The Times*, October 26, 1995, C.A.

4524. Forum—*forum non conveniens*—same issues already determined by Bulgarian court—*lis alibi pendens*—whether Bulgaria most appropriate forum—whether *Spilada* principles to be applied differently where *lis alibi pendens*. See VARNA (NO. 2), THE, §696.

4525. Harbour—Blyth Harbour Act 1986

BLYTH HARBOUR ACT 1986 (AMENDMENT) ORDER 1995 (No. 2645) [65p], made under the Coal Industry Act 1994, s.67(2)(3); operative on November 10, 1995; makes provision for the appointment of certain commissioners under the Blyth Harbour Act 1986, following a re-organisation of the coal industry under the Coal Industry Act 1994.

4526. Harbour revision

BRISTOL CITY DOCKS HARBOUR REVISION ORDER 1995 (No. 421) [£1·10], made under the Harbours Act 1964 (c.40), s.14(7); operative on March 8,

1995; authorises the construction of a footbridge and a landing stage in the St. Augustine's Reach part of Bristol Docks.

BRISTOL CITY DOCKS (NO. 2) HARBOUR REVISION ORDER 1995 (No. 422) [£1·10], made under the Harbours Act 1964 (c.40), s.14(7); operative on March 8, 1995; authorises the construction of a pedestrian walkway and pontoons in a specified part of the said Docks.

PORTSMOUTH (CAMBER DOCK) HARBOUR REVISION ORDER 1995 (No. 1063) [£2·40], made under the Harbours Act 1964 (c.40), s.14(7); operative on April 13, 1995; provides for the construction of a new quay in Portsmouth Harbour.

4527. Hovercraft

HOVERCRAFT (APPLICATION OF ENACTMENTS) (AMENDMENT) ORDER 1995 (No. 1299) [65p], made under the Hovercraft Act 1968 (c.59), operative on May 17, 1995; amends S.I. 1972 No. 971.

4528. International standards—safety, pollution and working conditions—European Community

Council Directive 95/21/EC of June 19, 1995 concerning the enforcement, in respect of shipping using Community ports and sailing in the waters under the jurisdiction of the Member States, of international standards for ship safety, pollution prevention and shipboard living and working conditions (port state control) (O.J. L157/1).

4529. Jurisdiction—Brussels Convention—*lis pendens*—related actions—effect of the International Convention relating to the arrest of seagoing ships—European Community. See OWNERS OF CARGO LATELY LADEN ON BOARD TATRY v. OWNERS OF MACIEJ RATAJ; TATRY, THE (C–406/92), §704.

4530. Marine insurance—contract terms—accident outside trading units

[Aus.] A, mortgagees of the fishing vessel Northern L, claimed under the marine insurance policy issued by C when the vessel caught fire and sank. C denied liability on the grounds that the accident took place outside the trading limits stipulated by the policy and no notice had been given that the vessel was travelling outside the limits.

Held, that the institute fishing vessel clause, to the effect that if notice was given the assured would be covered notwithstanding any breach of warranty of locality, and a clause to the effect that breach of warranty clauses were held covered with or without notice, must be read together. Their effect was that, although the accident occurred outside the stipulated trading limits and the underwriters had not been notified, nevertheless the assured was covered providing the duty of utmost good faith was not breached. The term "warranty as to locality" included warranties about the vessel's location both at commencement and during the period of cover and applied to the trading limits provision.

AUSTRALIA & NEW ZEALAND BANKING GROUP v. COMPAGNIE D'ASSURANCES MARITIMES AERIENNES ET TERRESTRES; NORTHERN L, THE, *Lloyd's List*, June 1, 1995, Sup. Ct. Vic.

4531. Marine insurance—contract terms—latent defect in welds—whether damage caused to actual vessel

PEP claimed the costs of repairs to its accommodation platform against the defendant underwriters (S). The platform suffered fatigue cracking in its legs as a result of fatigue stress in the welds which joined the legs to the columns.

Held, that PEP's policy contained an Inchmaree clause providing cover for damage caused to the vessel by latent defects, boilers bursting or shafts breaking, and a claim would only be paid if damage had been caused to the actual vessel, which the welds themselves were not part of. Accordingly, although PEP had established that the welds were defective and this was a latent defect, these had not caused damage to the actual vessel and therefore the cost of repairs was not covered by the policy.

PROMET ENGINEERING PTE v. STURGE; NUKILA, THE, *Lloyd's List*, November 15, 1995 (I.D.), Comm. Ct.

4532. Marine insurance—damages—whether cost of towage deducted—disbursements

[Marine Insurance Act 1909 (Australia), s.22.]

F, owner of the dredger Coral which sank in calm seas while being towed to purchasers in India, sued CIG under the unvalued marine insurance policy. F was obliged by the contract to deliver Coral to be scrapped, and towage was arranged as the vessel was not capable of sailing under her own steam. F claimed the full contractual sale price but the lower court held that the cost of towage must be deducted. F appealed.

Held, allowing the appeal, that under s.22 of the Marine Insurance Act 1909 (Australia) the insurable value of a ship which could not make the insured voyage except under tow was not reduced by towage costs, because the policy contemplated a voyage under tow. Towage costs were in the nature of disbursements required to make the ship fit for the voyage, analogous to money advanced for the crew's wages.

FRANKE v. CIG GENERAL INSURANCE; CORAL, THE, *Lloyd's List*, May 17, 1995, C.A.

4533. Marine insurance—lead underwriter clause—Lloyd's Underwriters' Agreement (General Marine Business) 1983—misrepresentation and non-disclosure—whether 1983 agreement binding—whether lead underwriter acted as agent—whether continuing duty of disclosure

P chartered a barge which it intended to beach while discharging. P's brokers obtained insurance quotations to cover possible liabilities to the barge owner in respect of beaching damage. The brokers then obtained a slip which was subject to the approval by the Salvage Association (SA) of the beaching arrangements, and which contained a wide LU clause allowing lead underwriters to bind following underwriters. This first slip was signed by a leading underwriter and D, as following underwriters. The SA was unable to approve the arrangements. The broker returned to the lead underwriter, indicating that it was urgent for cover to be arranged as the barge was about to sail and that he had mistakenly omitted the Institute War Clauses (cargo) from the slip. The lead underwriter agreed to cover the risk and scratched the SA fax accordingly. The barge sailed and the broker later prepared a second slip. To the SA subject was added "T.B.A. L/U Only" [To Be Agreed Leading Underwriter only]. The second slip was signed by D. P became liable to the barge owner and claimed against D who alleged misrepresentation and non-disclosure.

Held, that (1) the SA subject was a contingent condition of the contract and not a promissory condition and was binding on each following underwriter; (2) the Lloyd's Underwriters' Agreement (General Marine Business) 1983 did not bind P as it was not substituted for the LU clause; (3) a leading underwriter is the agent of the following underwriters and a principal can in general authorise an agent to waive a contingent condition; (4) the leading underwriter did have the actual authority of the following underwriters, under the particular LU clause used, to waive even a contingent condition; (5) although the leading underwriter believed that he was scratching only for his own syndicate, the effect of the LU clause was that he had dispensed with the SA subject for D; (6) the removal of the SA subject was a material increase in the risk and constituted a material non-disclosure which entitled D to avoid the second slip; (7) there was also a material non-disclosure in that the second slip was broked on the basis that it was the same as before except for the changed war clauses; and (8) although the policy was based on the second slip, that was not sufficient to create a continuing duty of disclosure after the first slip and D were liable to P on the basis of the first slip (*Black King Shipping Corp. v. Massie; Litsion Pride, The* [1985] C.L.Y. 3208 considered).

ROADWORKS (1952) v. J.R. CHARMAN [1994] 2 Lloyd's Rep. 99, H.H.J. Kershaw, Q.C.

4534. Marine insurance—perils of the sea—proof—unexplained loss—water entering hull after contact with external object—whether unascertainable accident—whether assured can recover for total loss

The vessel M was on a voyage off the Spanish coast when a "bump" was felt aboard and seawater flooded into the engine room, from whence it spread to No. 4 hold. The vessel became a total loss and the owners claimed under their policy on the basis of a loss by a peril of the sea. They alleged (1) that there had been a collision with an unidentified object, probably a container; or (2) that as the vessel was seaworthy, and if the ingress of water was unexplained, her loss was to be presumed and/or inferred to have been caused by perils of the sea; or (3) that the loss was by unspecified perils of the sea as inferred from the elimination of all other possible causes. The judge found that the ingress of water caused by collision with a container was so improbable as to be virtually impossible and dismissed the claim. The owners appealed.

Held, dismissing the appeal, that (1) the judge was entitled to find that a collision with a container was improbable and it would be ridiculous to hold that there had been a collision with some other unknown object; (2) the burden of proof was on the owners to establish a peril of the sea and it was not possible to argue that if a ship was seaworthy when she set out and was lost, the loss must be from a peril of the sea unless the underwriter affirmatively established that it was due to some other cause; (3) any presumption as to the cause of loss which applied when a ship was lost with all hands, and no trace, could not apply in the present case where a number of specific perils of the sea, *e.g.* collision or uncharted reefs, had been eliminated; (4) the ingress of water had not been caused by unseaworthiness and, although the underwriters had not set up a positive case of scuttling, they were entitled to put the owners to proof; and (5) the judge was not bound to accept that on a balance of probabilities the vessel was lost by an unascertainable peril of the sea, as the only possible explanation for the type of damage suffered had already been rejected (*Rhesa Shipping Co. SA v. Herbert David Edmunds; Popi M, The* [1985] C.L.Y. 3207 applied).

LAMB HEAD SHIPPING CO. v. JENNINGS; MAREL, THE [1994] 1 Lloyd's Rep. 624, C.A.

4535. Marine insurance—reinsurance—non-disclosure of misappropriated premiums—whether agent having duty to disclose dishonesty—whether contract avoidable

[Marine Insurance Act 1906 (c.41), ss.18(1), 19.]

Certain reinsurers, including 24 insurance companies and 62 Lloyd's syndicates, with whom PCW had arranged, through brokers, contracts of reinsurance on behalf of its syndicates, argued that they could avoid those contracts through non-disclosure of the fact that certain people in PCW had misappropriated premiums received for the benefit of the Names on the PCW syndicates. The reinsurers appealed against a ruling by Waller J. on a preliminary issue and contended that under s.19 of the Marine Insurance Act 1906 an agent to insure must disclose such dishonesty as a "material circumstance".

Held, dismissing the appeal, that since the dishonesty of an agent was not something which "ought to be known" by the principal under s.18(1) of the 1906 Act or which was to be imputed to the principal (*Re Hampshire Land* [1896] 2 Ch. 743, *Belmont Finance Corp. v. Williams Furniture* [1979] Ch. 250

considered), there was no reason why the same principle could not apply to a case where the principal's rights were affected if the agent did not disclose the fraud to a third party.

PCW SYNDICATES v. PCW REINSURERS, *The Independent*, September 8, 1995, C.A.

4536. Marine insurance—storage—cargo damage—cargo stored in warehouse other than warehouse named in policy—whether liability excluded

Cargo belonging to CT was damaged whilst in a warehouse owned by SGS Services. The cargo was insured with B under a memorandum to a policy which provided that it would be covered for 60 days storage in SGS Services, Energiweg 1, Spijkenisse, Netherlands. CT claimed under the policy, but B denied liability on the ground that the cargo had been stored in a warehouse in Rotterdam, its discharge port, rather than at the address on the memorandum, which was the only warehouse for which the insurance was valid.

Held, that there was evidence that the address given in the memorandum was merely the administration office address for the trading company, and commercial good sense dictated that the memorandum indicated the company with whom the cargo would be stored, not the specific warehouse. For insurance purposes the identity of the warehouseman was generally more important than where the warehouse itself was located. Had the insurers intended that the cargo should be covered in only one warehouse, its name should have been noted in the memorandum before the name of the storage company. The cargo clearly fell within the terms of the insurance as agreed by the parties.

CECOM TRADE BV v. BISHOP, *Lloyd's List*, October 19, 1995 (I.D.), D.C.

4537. Marine insurance—warranty of seaworthiness—whether mixed policy

[Marine Insurance Act 1906 (c.41), s.39.]

LI, insurer to KY, appealed against a ruling of the Singapore court of first instance that KY were entitled to claim under their marine policy for the loss of their ship the "Pab". KY owned another ship insured by LI under a time policy which specified geographical limitations, *i.e.* the trading area of the Far East and Pacific. KY purchased the "Pab" in Brazil and arranged with LI for insurance by means of an endorsement to the policy. The words "including one delivery voyage from Montevideo to the trading area" were added to the clause on the limits of the trading area. LI submitted that the effect was to change the policy from a time policy to a mixed policy under which a warranty of seaworthiness, which admittedly the "Pab" could not meet, was implied.

Held, dismissing the appeal, that a warranty of seaworthiness would be implied under s.39 of the Marine Insurance Act 1906 if the policy was mixed, *i.e.* if the ship was insured both for a specified period and for a voyage from one port to another. The reference to a voyage which was added to the clause specifying the limits of the trading area should not be interpreted as changing the policy from a time policy to a mixed policy with an implied warranty of seaworthiness. The addition only modified the trading limits covered.

LOMBARD INSURANCE CO. v. KIN YUEN CO.; PAB, THE, *Lloyds List*, July 25, 1995, C.A.

4538. Merchant shipping—certification of deck and marine engineer officers

MERCHANT SHIPPING (CERTIFICATION OF DECK AND MARINE ENGINEER OFFICERS) (AMENDMENT) REGULATIONS 1995 (No. 1429) [£1·95], made under the Merchant Shipping Act 1970 (c.36), ss.43, 99(2) and the European Communities Act 1972 (c.68), s.2(2); operative on August 1, 1995; amend S.I. 1985 No. 1306, S.I. 1986 No. 1935 and S.I. 1991 No. 824 so as to recognise foreign certificates of competence issued by certain authorities abroad.

4539. Merchant shipping—employment of young persons

MERCHANT SHIPPING (EMPLOYMENT OF YOUNG PERSONS) REGULATIONS 1995 (No. 972) [£1·10], made under the Merchant Shipping Act 1970 (c.36), s.51(2)(3), and the Merchant Shipping (Registration, etc.) Act 1993 (c.22), Sched. 4, para. 5; operative on May 1, 1995; prescribe the circumstances and conditions under which children and young persons may be employed in a ship.

4540. Merchant shipping—fees

MERCHANT SHIPPING (FEES) REGULATIONS 1995 (No. 1893) [£3·70], made under the Merchant Shipping (Safety Convention) Act 1949, s.33(2) and the Merchant Shipping (Registration, etc) Act 1993, Sched. 4, para. 79; revoke S.I. 1991 Nos. 784, 1404, S.I. 1993 Nos. 1340, 1676, S.I. 1994 No. 502; operative on August 1, 1995; prescribe changes in some of the rates charged and introduce new fees in respect of tonnage measurement, radio surveys, Certificates of Equivalent Competency and the administration of marine examinations.

4541. Merchant shipping—hours of work

MERCHANT SHIPPING (HOURS OF WORK) REGULATIONS 1995 (No. 157) [£1·10], made under the Merchant Shipping Act 1979 (c.39), ss.21(1)(a)(3)(6), 22(1); operative on February 28, 1995; give effect in part to the Merchant Shipping (Minimum Standards) Convention 1976, requiring that safety standards regarding hours of work be established.

4542. Merchant shipping—light dues

MERCHANT SHIPPING (LIGHT DUES) (AMENDMENT) REGULATIONS 1995 (No. 525) [65p], made under the Merchant Shipping (Mercantile Marine Fund) Act 1898 (c.44), s.5(2); operative on April 1, 1995; amend S.I. 1990 No. 364 so as to remove light dues from Ro-Ro vessels whose liability for the dues is assessed by reference to a tonnage certificate issued in accordance with the International Convention on Tonnage Measurement of Ships 1969.

4543. Merchant shipping—medical treatment

MERCHANT SHIPPING AND FISHING VESSELS (MEDICAL STORES) REGULATIONS 1995 (No. 1802), made under the European Communities Act 1972, s.2(2) and the Merchant Shipping Act 1979, ss.21(1)(a)(3)(4)(6), 22(1) and the Medicines Act 1968, s.103(3); amend S.I. 1986 No. 144; revoke S.I. 1988 No. 1116 1547; operative on August 1, 1995; implement Council Dir. 92/29 on the minimum safety and health requirements for improved medical treatment on board vessels.

MERCHANT SHIPPING (SHIPS' DOCTORS) REGULATIONS 1995 (No. 1803), made under the Merchant Shipping Act 1979, ss.21(1)(a)(3)(6), 22(1); revoke S.I. 1981 No. 1065; operative on August 1, 1995; replace the 1981 Regulations and implement Council Dir. 92/29.

4544. Merchant shipping—officer nationality

MERCHANT SHIPPING (OFFICER NATIONALITY) REGULATIONS 1995 (No. 1427), made under the Merchant Shipping Act 1970, ss.43, 92; operative on August 1, 1995; require that certain descriptions of U.K. ships serving a strategic function (*i.e.* cruise ships, fishing vessels, product tankers and ro-ro ships) carry as master persons who are Commonwealth citizens or nationals of other EEA States or NATO States.

4545. Merchant shipping—port state control

MERCHANT SHIPPING (PORT STATE CONTROL) REGULATIONS 1995 (No. 3128), made under the European Communities Act 1972, s.2(2), the Merchant Shipping Act 1979, ss.21(a)(b)(c)(3)(4)(6), 22(1)(3), the Merchant Shipping (Prevention of Oil Pollution) Order 1983 and the Merchant Shipping (Prevention and Control of Pollution) Order 1987. In force: January 1, 1996; implement Council Dir. 92/21 which is concerned with the enforcment of international standards for ship safety, pollution prevention and living and working conditions on-board ship, in respect of shipping using Community ports and sailing in waters under the jurisdiction of Member States. Part I deals specifically with the implementation of the EC legislation covering interpretation and application, designation of a competent authority, inspection commitments and procedures, the expanded inspection of ships, reports of inspections, rectification of deficiencies and detention notices, rights to appeal, compensation, follow up inspections, the professional profiles of inspectors, reports from pilots and port authorities, publication of detentions, reimbursement of costs and offences. Parts II and III contain related provisions which are not concerned with the implementation of the Directive. Part II deals with rights of appeal and compensation with respect to detained ships and Part III implements the new Chap. XI of the Safety of Life at Sea Convention 1974 (SOLAS) which deals with the inspection of familiarity of the crew with essential procedures and operations related to safety.

4545a. Merchant shipping—reporting requirements

MERCHANT SHIPPING (REPORTING REQUIREMENTS FOR SHIPS CARRYING DANGEROUS OR POLLUTING GOODS) REGULATIONS 1995 (No. 2498) [£1·95], made under the European Communities Act 1972, s.2(2) and S.I. 1990 No. 2595, art. 3, and the Merchant Shipping Act 1979, ss.21(1)(a)(b)(3)-(6), 22(1); operative on October 31, 1995, revoke S.I. 1981 No. 1077, S.I. 1982 No. 1637, S.I. 1994 No. 3245; implement Council Directive 93/75 relating to vessels using Community ports whilst carrying dangerous or polluting goods.

4546. Merchant shipping—seamen's documents

MERCHANT SHIPPING (SEAMEN'S DOCUMENTS) (AMENDMENT) REGULATIONS 1995 (No. 1900), made under Merchant Shipping Act 1970, s.71; operative on September 1, 1995; amend S.I. 1987 No. 408 to remove the requirement that a discharge book contains the seaman's National Insurance number.

4547. Merchant shipping—survey and certification

MERCHANT SHIPPING (SURVEY AND CERTIFICATION) REGULATIONS 1995 (No. 1210) [£3·20], made under the Merchant Shipping Act 1979 (c.39), ss.21(1)(a)–(c)(3)–(6), 22(1)(3); operative on June 1, 1995; revoke and replace requirements for the survey and certification of passenger ships and cargo ships previously contained in specified Acts and instruments.

4548. Merchant Shipping Act 1970—commencement

MERCHANT SHIPPING ACT 1970 (COMMENCEMENT NO. 11) ORDER 1995 (No. 965 (C.24)) [£1·55], made under the Merchant Shipping Act 1970 (c.36), s.101(4); brings into force on May 1, 1995 ss.51, 100(3) (part), Sched. 5 (part).

MERCHANT SHIPPING ACT 1970 (COMMENCEMENT NO. 12) ORDER 1995 (No. 1426 (C.30)) [£1·55], made under the Merchant Shipping Act 1970 (c.36), s.101(4); brings into force on August 1, 1995, s.100(3) (part), Sched. 5 (part) which revoke the Aliens Restriction (Amendment) Act 1919 (c.92), s.5.

4549. Merchant Shipping Act 1995 (c.21)

This Act consolidates provisions affecting merchant shipping from, *inter alia*, the Merchant Shipping Acts 1894 to 1994.

The Act received Royal Assent on July 19, 1995.

4550. Port authorities

DUNDEE PORT AUTHORITY TRANSFER SCHEME 1995 CONFIRMATION ORDER 1995 (No. 3023) [£1·95], made under the Ports Act 1991, s.9(6)(7);

revokes S.I. 1992 No. 1435; confirms the Dundee Port Authority Transfer Scheme 1995, made by the Dundee Port Authority under the Ports Act 1991 s.9, as modified by the Secretary of State for Transport. The Scheme takes effect on November 24, 1994 and on that date all property, rights and liabilities of the Authority, except as stated in para. 2(a) of the Scheme, and all functions conferred or imposed on the Authority by any local statutory provision are transferred to the successor company specified in para. 3 of the Scheme.

4551. Protection of wrecks

PROTECTION OF WRECKS (DESIGNATION NO. 1) ORDER 1995 (No. 2654) [65p], made under the Protection of Wrecks Act 1973, ss.1(1)(2)(4), 3(2); revokes S.I. 1991 No. 2746; operative on November 20, 1995; designates an area off the Smalls Reef, Dyfed, round the site of what is thought to be the wreck of a vessel which is of historical and archaeological importance, as a restricted area for the purposes of the Protection of Wrecks Act 1973.

4552. Sale of ship—classification—obligation to notify buyers of matters affecting ship's class—time of commencement of obligation—whether obligation to notify beginning after date of contract

A contract to sell the Niobe was made under the Norwegian Saleform 1983 (NSF), clause 11 of which states "the vessel . . . shall be delivered . . . as she is at the time of inspection, fair wear and tear accepted. However . . . the seller shall notify the classification society of any matters coming to their knowledge . . . which would lead to the withdrawal of the vessel's class". The buyers (N) had a number of objections to the vessel's condition on delivery. It was argued for the buyers that the sellers (T) were under a duty to notify the classification society of any matters affecting the ship's class whenever those matters came to light. The Court of Appeal ruled that the obligation to notify only began after the date of the contract, not prior to the contract, and did not include the time between the survey and the contract, or the contract and delivery.

Held, allowing the appeal, that the sensible commercial construction of the clause should be that put forward by the buyers. It could not be right to allow the sellers to conceal defects coming to their attention either before or after the last special survey. The obligations under the contract were surely intended to exist alongside obligations to the society. There was no inherent contradiction in that. Therefore the obligation owed by the sellers under cl. 11 was to notify the society of any defects coming to their knowledge at any time after the last relevant survey and before delivery.

NIOBE MARITIME CORP. v. TRADAX OCEAN TRANSPORTATION SA; NIOBE, THE, *The Times*, April 3, 1995, H.L.

4553. Sale of ship—Saleform 1987—vessel to be delivered "with present class free of recommendations"—classification society recommendation—whether proper "recommendation" made—whether recommendation communicated—whether buyer had agreed to pay for repairs

S agreed to sell a vessel to B on the Saleform 1987. The contract provided that the vessel should be delivered "with present class free of recommendations". It was expected that some work would be required by B after delivery in order to obtain a regular special survey and S agreed that a surveyor could begin inspections before delivery. B agreed to pay for all work ordered by them. The classification society surveyor who was allowed on board noted that steelwork repairs were needed and informed his head office by telephone of the fact that he would make a recommendation accordingly. A note of the conversation and a brief report was then put on the vessel's file. B claimed damages on the basis that on delivery the vessel had defective steelwork that needed repairing. S denied breach and claimed that B either agreed to pay for extra work, or waived any rights.

Held, that (1) a requirement made by a classification society surveyor that a specified course of action must be taken as a condition of the vessel remaining in class was a "recommendation" within the Saleform contract and it was not necessary for there to be any more formal recommendation; (2) the communication of a requirement by a surveyor to his head office was sufficient communication to constitute the making of a "recommendation", but in any event the requirement had been communicated to S before delivery; (3) the express agreement that B would pay for all work ordered by them implicitly extended to cover any work ordered pursuant to the recommendations made by the surveyor as a result of inspection for completing the special survey; (4) even though the work was consequent on a recommendation, it was work for which B had agreed to pay and B was not able to recover damages; and (5) (*obiter*) B had not waived any rights at the completion meeting, but had any damages been awarded they would have been reduced by one third to reflect betterment, as more work was carried out than required.

K/S STAMAR v. SEABOW SHIPPING; ANDREAS P, THE [1994] 2 Lloyd's Rep. 183 Phillips J.

4554. Salvage services—total loss—salve value of hull and equipment—fair payment for services

L and others claimed payment for salvage services rendered to the yacht Yolaine in October 1991. The yacht keeled over after being anchored off Portlock Wier and her hull was penetrated by a boulder. The equipment on board amounted to £3,000. The hole was patched up and the yacht pumped out as a result of salvage services rendered to the yacht. The yacht had been in significant danger and it was likely that she would have been a total loss without the salvage services. The issue was therefore what would constitute fair payment for the services.

Held, that, as the effect of the services rendered was to salve both the hull and equipment, it was appropriate to take the salved value of both at the time the services terminated. However, because some of the yacht's equipment had been removed before other services were rendered, it was important to take into account the value of this equipment in assessing the amount of salvage remuneration.

LEY v. DELAISSE, *Lloyd's List*, May 10, 1995, D.C

4555/6. Seafarers—training—European Community

Council Directive 94/58/EC of November 22, 1994 on the minimum level of training of seafarers (O.J. L319/28).

4557. Ship inspection and survey organisations—European Community

Council Directive 94/57/EC of November 21, 1994 on common standards for ship inspection and survey organisations and for the relevant activities of maritime administration (O.J. L319/20).

4558. Shipping and Trading Interests (Protection) Act 1995 (c.22)

This Act consolidates various provisions from the Merchant Shipping Act 1974 (c.43), the Merchant Shipping Act 1979 (c.39), the Criminal Justice Act 1982 (c.48), the Merchant Shipping Act 1988 (c.12), and the Merchant Shipping (Registration, etc) Act 1993 (c.22) for the protection of shipping and trading interests.

The Act received Royal Assent on July 19, 1995.

4559. Value added tax. See VALUE ADDED TAX, §5081.

SHOPS, MARKETS AND FAIRS

4560. Shopping centre—lessors seeking injunction to exclude alleged troublemakers—whether public right of way—whether any licence revocable

[Highways Act 1980 (c.66), s.35; Highways Act 1971 (c.41), s.18; Race Relations Act 1976 (c.74), s.20.]

CIN, lessees of the Swangate shopping centre (the Centre) appealed against a preliminary ruling in their action for injunctions to exclude from there certain youths alleged to be troublemakers. The pedestrian malls of the Centre were not dedicated to the public as highways or as walkways under the Highways Act 1980, s.35. The county court, however, ruled that members of the public had an equitable licence to enter, but that the licence was revocable for good reason. The respondents had counterclaimed for declaratory and injunctive relief and damages, including damages for unlawful discrimination. In the appeal, the questions were whether there was: (a) dedication of the walkways as a highway, (b) a walkways agreement, (c) an equitable licence, or (d) a public right to use the malls not covered by any of these heads.

Held, allowing the appeal and remitting the case, that (1) there was no dedication, as only the freeholder could make an effective dedication and the freeholder was not party to the proceedings; (2) there was no statutory walkways agreement, the clause within the lease governing the walkways did not fall within the Highways Act 1971, s.18, and there was no evidence, *i.e.* bye laws or land charges, that the parties intended to dedicate the walkways as footpaths; (3) the court found no representation or acquiescence by CIN which might be relied upon by the public as an irrevocable licence to use the walkway as a public right of way. It was doubtful whether the principles stated in *Crabb v. Arun District Council* and *Williams v. Staite* could confer rights upon the public at large. There was no need for the courts to intervene to reconsider the interests of shopping centre proprietors and members of the public where the statutory framework provided therefor was not invoked (*Crabb v. Arun District Council* [1975] C.L.Y. 1191, *Williams v. Staite* [1978] C.L.Y. 2487 considered); and (4) subject only to the issue under the Race Relations Act 1976, s.20, the shopping centre lessees had the right at any time to determine any licence the respondents may have had to enter the Centre.

CIN PROPERTIES v. RAWLINS (MARTIN), February 1, 1995, C.A.

4561. Sunday trading—local authority's enforcement policy—whether discriminatory against large retailers—whether unlawful

[Shops Act 1950 (14 Geo. 6, c.28).]

The council sought injunctions against T for trading on a Sunday in contravention of the Shops Act 1950. T sought judicial review of the decision on the grounds that the council had allowed Sunday trading by small retailers so long as they did not advertise or no complaints were received. T argued that the policy adopted by the council meant that large retailers were discriminated against.

Held, dismissing the application, that in determining how to enforce the 1950 Act a council was entitled to take into account the limited resources available to it and the impracticability of taking proceedings against all retailers or none at all. The policy was a fair and sensible one.

R. v. KIRKLEES METROPOLITAN BOROUGH COUNCIL, *ex p.* TESCO STORES (1994) 92 L.G.R. 279, D.C.

4562. Sunday trading—retail video outlet—whether "shop"

[Shops Act 1950 (14 Geo. 6, c.28), s.74.]

R, convicted of contravening the provisions of the Shops Act 1950 relating to Sunday trading, submitted that its retail video outlet was not a shop within the meaning of the Act on the basis of a decision in the High Court of Judiciary in Scotland, *Boyd v. Bell*, which had not been brought to the attention of the Court of Appeal in *Lewis v. Rogers*, a case indistinguishable from this case.

Held, that a video retail outlet was a shop within the Act. The court was not prepared to speculate on whether the Court of Appeal would have decided

differently if it had had the benefit of reading the Scottish case (*Boyd v. Bell* [1974] C.L.Y. 3654 considered; *Lewis v. Rogers* [1985] C.L.Y. 3238 followed).
RITZ VIDEO [1995] N.P.C. 12, C.A.

4563. Sunday trading—rulings on validity of legislation pending in the European Court of Justice—successive informations laid on a weekly basis in interim—application to stay hearing of summonses as abuse of process

[Shops Act 1950 (14 Geo. 6, c.28).]

The council laid informations against a company for contraventions of the Shops Act by trading on Sundays. The results of a reference to the ECJ was pending and the company applied to the justices for a stay of all summonses on the ground that to prosecute for every Sunday on which it traded until the resolution of that case was oppressive and an abuse of the process. The justices refused and the company applied for judicial review.

Held, dismissing the application, that the justices had been entitled to regard the council as having acted properly in the exercise of their power.

(*Per* Sedley J.: where a domestic statute is arguably in conflict with a Directive made under the Treaty of Rome the operation of the statute is not suspended and remains in force.)

R. v. LINCOLN CITY COUNCIL, *ex p.* WICKES BUILDING SUPPLIES (1994) 92 L.G.R. 215, D.C.

SOCIAL SECURITY

4564. Adjudication

SOCIAL SECURITY (ADJUDICATION) REGULATIONS 1995 (No. 1801), made under the Social Security Administration Act 1992; amend S.I. 1987 No. 335, S.I. 1988 No. 1725, S.I. 1991 Nos. 706, 2284, S.I. 1992 No. 247, S.I. 1993 Nos. 861, 1985, S.I. 1995 No. 829; revoke S.I. 1986 No. 2218, S.I. 1987 Nos. 1424, 1970, S.I. 1989 No. 1689, S.I. 1990 No. 603, S.I. 1991 Nos. 1950, 2889, S.I. 1994 Nos. 1082, 2686; operative on August 10, 1995; revoke the 1986 Adjudication Regulations and re-enact their provisions, taking account of the consolidation effected by the Social Security Contributions and Benefits Act 1992 and the Social Security Administration Act 1992 and the changes made by the Social Security (Incapacity for Work) Act 1994. These Regulations relate to the determination of claims and questions under the 1992 Acts.

4565. Adjudication—judicial review—funeral payment—return of body to Bangladesh—whether regulations could be challenged on grounds of race discrimination. See R. v. SECRETARY OF STATE FOR SOCIAL SECURITY, *ex p.* NESSA, §156.

4566. Appeal—Commissioners' decision—whether court has jurisdiction to grant leave to appeal

[Social Security Administration Act 1992 (c.5), ss.23(1)(9), 24(1).]

Where a social security commissioner refused leave to appeal to him from a decision of a Social Security Appeal Tribunal, as required by the Social Security Administration Act 1992, ss.23(1)(9) and 24(1), the Court of Appeal had no jurisdiction to entertain an application for leave to appeal from that refusal.

KUGANATHAN v. CHIEF ADJUDICATION OFFICER, *The Times*, March 1, 1995, C.A.

4567. Attendance allowance—accommodation—persons suffering from illness—no arrangements made by local authority—whether entitlement to payment of attendance allowance

[Social Security (Attendance Allowance) (No. 2) Regulations 1975 (S.I. 1975 No. 598), reg. 4(1)(c).]

Where a local authority had the power to make arrangements for the provision of residential accommodation for persons suffering from illness and to pay some or all of the costs of providing such accommodation but they had not in fact made any such arrangements, those persons were nevertheless entitled to payment of attendance allowance within the terms of reg. 4(1)(c) of the Social Security (Attendance Allowance) (No. 2) Regulations 1975.

CHIEF ADJUDICATION OFFICER v. KENYON, *The Times*, November 14, 1995, C.A.

4568. Attendance allowance—retired claimant absent from U.K.—claimant resident in E.C. Member State—whether entitled to allowance

C, a retired British national who had lived in Spain since 1985, claimed attendance allowance on September 3, 1988. The adjudication officer decided that attendance allowance was not payable because C was not present in the U.K. This decision was confirmed by a Social Security Appeal Tribunal who also decided that E.C. legislation was not relevant because C had retired from employment.

Held, that (1) a retired person who had previously worked in a Member State remained with the scope of E.C. Reg. 1408/71; (2) attendance allowance is an "invalidity benefit" for the purposes of Art. 10 of E.C. Reg. 1408/71; and (3) Art. 10 of E.C. Reg. 1408/71 applies to a situation where a person already has a benefit which is subsequently forfeited when that person goes to another Member State. It does not apply where there is no initial entitlement to benefit (*Social Security Decision No. R(A) 4/75* and *Social Security Decision No. R(S) 9/81* affirmed).

SOCIAL SECURITY DECISION NO. R(A) 2/94.

4569. Attendance allowance and disability allowance

SOCIAL SECURITY (ATTENDANCE AND DISABILITY LIVING ALLOWANCES) AMENDMENT REGULATIONS 1995 (No. 2162) [£1·10], made under the Social Security Contributions and Benefits Act 1992, ss.67(2), 72(8); amend S.I. 1991 Nos. 2740, 2890; operative on September 14, 1995; amend the 1991 Regulations to insert references to the corresponding legislation having effect in Scotland.

4570. Benefits

SOCIAL SECURITY (UNEMPLOYMENT, SICKNESS AND INVALIDITY BENEFIT) AMENDMENT REGULATIONS 1995 (No. 2192) [65p], made under the Social Security Contributions and Benefits Act 1992, ss.25A(1)(a)(3)(a), 175(1)(3); amend S.I. 1983 No. 1598; operative on September 25, 1995.

SOCIAL SECURITY (UNEMPLOYMENT, SICKNESS AND INVALIDITY BENEFIT) AMENDMENT (NO. 2) REGULATIONS 1995 (No. 3152) [£1·10], made under the Social Security Contributions and Benefits Act 1992, ss.25A(1)(a)(ii), 122(1). In force: January 1, 1996; amend S.I. 1983 No. 1598 by making provisions to treat Venture Trust trainees as available for, and actively seeking, employment up to a period of five weeks in a year.

4571. Benefits—reduced eligibility for foreign nationals—press release

The Department of Social Security has issued a press release entitled *Peter Lilley proposes new controls on benefits to persons from abroad* (Press Release 95/128), published on October 11, 1995. The Secretary of State for Social Security has announced proposed regulations to prevent abuse of the system by foreign nationals. Asylum seekers who do not claim asylum until after their arrival would not be entitled to benefit, while those who claim at the point of entry but whose claim is refused would become ineligible for benefit from the time of refusal. Changes are also proposed in relation to sponsored immigrants and other foreign persons who claim non-contributory benefits.

4572. Benefits—students

SOCIAL SECURITY BENEFITS (MISCELLANEOUS AMENDMENTS) REGULATIONS 1995 (No. 1742), made under the Social Security Contributions and Benefits Act 1992, ss.25A(3)(a), 123(1), 130(2)(4), 136(3)(5), 137(1), 175(3)–(5); amend S.I. 1983 No. 1598, S.I. 1987 Nos. 1967, 1971, 1973, S.I. 1991 No. 2887, S.I. 1992 No. 1814, operative in accordance with reg. 1(1).

4573. Benefits—temporary absence from dwelling

HOUSING BENEFIT, COUNCIL TAX BENEFIT AND INCOME SUPPORT (AMENDMENTS) REGULATIONS 1995 (No. 625) [£2·80], made under the Social Security Contributions and Benefits Act 1992 (c.4), ss.123(1)(d)(e), 131(11), 135(1), 137(1)(2)(h)(i), 175(1)(3)–(6) and the Social Security Administration Act 1992 (c.5), ss.5(1)(k), 6(1)(l); operative for regs. 1, 3, 4, 6 and 7 on April 1, 1995, for reg. 2 on either April 1, 1995 or April 3, 1995 (dependent on intervals when rent is payable), and for reg. 5 on April 10, 1995; amend S.I. 1987 Nos. 1967 and 1987 No. 1971 and S.I. 1992 No. 1814 in connection with a person's temporary absence from a dwelling normally occupied as his home.

4574. Benefits—up-rating

SOCIAL SECURITY BENEFITS UP-RATING ORDER 1995 (No. 559), made under Social Security Administration Act 1992 (c.5) and Social Security (Incapacity for Work) Act 1994 (c.18); Pt. II relates to non-income related benefits and increases the rates and amounts of various benefits; specifies earnings limits for child dependancy increases; specifies the weekly rate of statutory sick pay; specifies the lower rate of statutory maternity pay; increases the rates of disability living allowance; increases the weekly rates of child benefit and one parent benefit; increases the weekly rates of long-term incapacity benefit; Pt. III relates to family credit, disability working allowance, income support, housing benefit and council tax benefit.

SOCIAL SECURITY BENEFITS UP-RATING REGULATIONS 1995 (No. 580), made under Social Security Contributions and Benefits Act 1992 (c.4) and Social Security Administration Act 1992 (c.5); amend S.I. 1977 No. 343, S.I. 1982 No. 1408, S.I. 1983 No. 1598, S.I. 1994 No. 2946; revoke S.I. 1994 No. 559; operative on 10 April, 1995 for all except reg. 7; April 13, 1995 for reg. 7.

4575. Benefits received after an accident—injured person unemployed before and after accident—how to avoid undercompensation. See HASSALL v. SECRETARY OF STATE FOR SOCIAL SECURITY, §1645.

4576. Canada

SOCIAL SECURITY (CANADA) ORDER 1995 (No. 2699) [£1·95], made under the Social Security Administration Act 1992, s.179(1)(a)(2); revokes S.I. 1959 No. 2216, S.I. 1962 No. 173, S.I. 1973 No. 763, S.I. 1977 No. 1873; operative on December 1, 1995; gives effect to the consolidated arrangements contained in letters exchanged between the Governments of the U.K. and Canada by making provision for the modification of the Social Security Administration Act 1992 and the Social Security Contributions and Benefits Act 1992 and Regulations made thereunder. The provisions relate to child benefit, unemployment benefit and retirement pensions.

4577. Child support—compensation. See MINORS, §3453.

4578. Child support and income support

CHILD SUPPORT AND INCOME SUPPORT (AMENDMENT) REGULATIONS 1995 (No. 1045) [£6·10], made under the Child Support Act 1991 (c.48), ss.8(11), 10(1), 12(2)(3), 14(1)(3), 16(1), 17(4), 18(11), 21(2), 29(2), 32, 41(3), 42, 43(1), 46(11), 47, 51, 52, 54, 57, Sched. 1, paras. 4(3), 5(1)(2), 6(2)(4)(5), 7(1), 8, 9(a), 11 and the Social Security Contributions and Benefits Act 1992 (c.4), ss.135(1), 137(1), 175(1)(3)(4); operative on April 18, 1995, save for regs. 1 and 58 which are operative on April 13, 1995; make amendments to various regulations made under the 1991 Act which relate to the operation of the Child Support Agency and the manner in which child support maintenance assessments and orders are made.

4579. Claims and payments

SOCIAL SECURITY (CLAIMS AND PAYMENTS) AMENDMENT REGULATIONS 1995 (No. 3055) [65p], made under the Social Security Administration Act 1992, ss.15A(2)(b), 189(1); amend S.I. 1987 No. 1968. In force: April 1, 1996. The fee stated in para. 7 to Sched. 9A of the Social Security (Claims and Payments) Regulations 1987 which qualifying lenders pay for the purpose of defraying administrative expenses incurred by the Secretary of State in making payments in respect of mortgage interest direct to qualifying lenders is reduced from 80 pence to 77 pence.

4580. Community care grant—reintegration after period in hostel for single pregnant women—whether hostel providing institutional or residential care

A applied for judicial review of a decision refusing her a community care grant. Such grants are payable where a person has been in institutional or residential care, and the grant will help them establish themselves in the community. A had been resident in a hostel for single pregnant women, and the case depended on whether the hostel provided institutional or residential care.

Held, dismissing the application, that even if A had received care and support in the hostel, the hostel was not established to provide institutional care (*R. v. Social Fund Inspector and Secretary of State for Social Services, ex p. Healey* [1991] C.L.Y. 68 considered).

R. v. SOCIAL FUND INSPECTOR, *ex p.* IBRAHIM [1994] C.O.D. 260, D.C.

4581. Contractors—employment status—self-employment—national insurance—press release. See BUILDING AND CONSTRUCTION, §500.

4582. Contributions

SOCIAL SECURITY (CONTRIBUTIONS) AMENDMENT REGULATIONS 1995 (No. 514) [65p], made under the Social Security Contributions and Benefits Act 1992 (c.4), ss.117(1), 175(1)–(3); operative on April 6, 1995; amend S.I. 1979 No. 591 so as to reduce the Class 2 contributions payable by share fishermen.

SOCIAL SECURITY (CONTRIBUTIONS) AMENDMENT (NO. 2) REGULATIONS 1995 (No. 714) [65p], made under the Social Security Contributions and Benefits Act 1992 (c.4), ss.5, 116(2)(a), 119, 175(1)–(3) and the Social Security Contributions and Benefits (Northern Ireland) Act 1992 (c.7), s.116(2)(a); operative on April 6, 1995; further amend S.I. 1979 No. 591.

SOCIAL SECURITY (CONTRIBUTIONS) AMENDMENT (NO. 3) REGULATIONS 1995 (No. 730), made under Social Security Contributions and Benefits Act 1992 (c.4); operative on April 6, 1995; further amend S.I. 1979 No. 591; reg. 2 revokes reg. 70; reg. 3 amends regs. 26A, 27A and 27B.

SOCIAL SECURITY (CONTRIBUTIONS) AMENDMENT (NO. 4) REGULATIONS 1995 (No. 1003) [65p], made under the Social Security Contributions and Benefits Act 1992 (c.4), ss.3(2)(3), 122(1), 175(1)–(3); operative on April 6, 1995; further amend S.I. 1979 No. 591.

SOCIAL SECURITY (CONTRIBUTIONS) AMENDMENT (NO. 5) REGULATIONS 1995 (No. 1570), made under the Social Security Contributions and Benefits

Act 1992, ss.3(2)(3), 122(1), 175(1)-(3); amend S.I. 1979 No. 591; operative on July 18, 1995.

SOCIAL SECURITY (CONTRIBUTIONS) (RE-RATING AND NATIONAL INSURANCE FUND PAYMENTS) ORDER 1995 (No. 561) [£1·10], made under the Social Security Administration Act 1992 (c.5), ss.141(4)(5), 142(2), 145(2), 189(1)(3) and the Social Security Act 1993 (c.3), s.2(2)(8); operative on April 6, 1995; increases contributions and the upper and lower wages levels for contributions.

4583. Contributions—determination of applicable legislation—whether subject to legislation of Member State in which plaintiff resident—European Community

A dispute arose concerning the payment of social security contributions in the case of a Danish worker, residing in Denmark and employed exclusively by an undertaking situated in Germany, but who in the course of his employment relationship regularly, for several hours each week and for a period not limited to 12 months, partly pursued his activity in Denmark.

Held, that Article 14(2)(b)(i) of Reg. 1408/71 on social security schemes, which provides that a person normally employed in the territory of two or more Member States is to be subject to the legislation of the Member State in whose territory he resides, if he pursues his activity partly in that territory, applies in this situation.

CALLE GRENSHOF ANDRESEN GmbH v. ALLGEMEINE ORTSKRANKENSKASSE FÜR DEN KREIS SCHLESWIG-FLENSBURG (C–425/93), February 16, 1995, ECJ, Second Chamber.

4584. Contributions—subcontractor failing to make contribution—determination of applicable legislation—whether E.C. law precluding national legislation—whether main contractor liable—European Community

A Dutch company, which had carried out insulation work in Belgium as a subcontractor for a Belgian company, became insolvent as a result of financial difficulties. During the liquidation, it became apparent that it had not paid its social security contributions to the competent body. Under Belgian legislation, the main contractor was liable to pay the contributions. The question arose as to whether Community law applied to this situation.

Held, that Council Reg. 1408/71 did not preclude national legislation which made a main contractor liable for social security contributions left unpaid by a defaulting sub-contractor.

RHEINHOLD & MAHLANV v. BESTUUR VAN DE BEDRIJFSVERENIGING VOOR DE METAALNIJVERHEID (C–327/92), May 18, 1995, ECJ, Sixth Chamber.

4584a. Credits

SOCIAL SECURITY (CREDITS) AMENDMENT REGULATIONS 1995 (No. 2558) [65p], made under the Social Security Contributions and Benefits Act 1992, ss.22(5), 122(1), 175(1)-(3); operative on November 1, 1995, amend S.I. 1975 No. 556; provide for a person to be credited equal to the lower earnings limit in respect of weeks for which family credit is paid.

4585. Disability living allowance—whether extends to deaf person

[Social Security Contributions and Benefits Act 1992 (c.4), s.72(1)(b)(i).]

A social security commissioner was right to decide that, for the purposes of determining entitlement to disability living allowance under s.72(1)(b)(i) of the Social Security Contributions and Benefits Act 1992, "frequent attention . . . in connection with . . . bodily functions" included attention which was reasonably required to enable the claimant, a deaf person, to carry on, as far as possible, a normal social life. There was nothing in the legislation to suggest that only attention which was essential to maintain life was reasonably required.

SECRETARY OF STATE FOR SOCIAL SECURITY v. FAIREY, *The Times*, June 22, 1995, C.A.

4586. Disability working allowance and income support

DISABILITY WORKING ALLOWANCE AND INCOME SUPPORT (GENERAL) AMENDMENT REGULATIONS 1995 (No. 482) [£2·40], made under the Social Security Contributions and Benefits Act 1992 (c.4), ss.124(1)(d)(i)(3), 129(2B)(b)(c)(8), 135(1), 137(1), 175(1)(3)(4) and the Social Security (Incapacity for Work) Act 1994 (c.18), s.12(1); operative on April 13, 1995, save for arts. 1, 3 and 4 which are operative on April 11, 1995; amend S.I. 1991 No. 2887 and S.I. 1987 No. 1967 as a consequence of the coming into force of the 1994 Act.

4586a. Family credit

SOCIAL SECURITY (EFFECT OF FAMILY CREIDT ON EARNINGS FACTORS) REGULATIONS 1995 (No. 2559) [65p], made under the Social Security Contributions and Benefits Act 1992, ss.45A, 122(1), 175(1)-(3); operative on November 1, 1995, make provision in a case where family credit is paid to one of a married or unmarried couple, as to which member of the couple s.45A of the 1992 Act applies to.

4587. Free movement of persons—cumulation of benefits—payment of benefit as Italian national by Italy and as unfit for work by Belgium—Italian payments based on insurance system—whether overpayment of benefits

The defendant had been paid invalidity benefits by the Belgian authorities on the ground that he was unfit for work. Since he was an Italian national and was also insured in Italy, the Italian social security board also had paid him a benefit. When the Belgian authorities realised the double payment, they commenced proceedings to recover the perceived overpayment. The defendant challenged the amount of overpayment and argued that the Belgian rules were incompatible with Reg. (EEC) 1408/71.

Held, that an invalidity benefit of the nature of the Italian benefit in question was not an independent benefit within the meaning of Art. 46(1) of Reg. (EEC) 1408/71 in as much as it was calculated in accordance with the system of aggregation of insurance periods and apportionment of benefits. Article 12(2) of the Regulation does not preclude the application of a national rule against overlapping benefits where a migrant worker receives in one Member State benefits intended to compensate for loss of income as a result of incapacity for work due to sickness, and in another Member State an invalidity benefit calculated by aggregating insurance periods and apportioning benefits, increased by a pension supplement intended to guarantee the worker the minimum national pension. For the purposes of applying national rules against overlapping of benefits, it is for the national court to classify the benefits in question in accordance with the applicable national legislation, taking into account the rules relating to conflict of laws, since the E.C. rules are not relevant.

UNION NATIONALE DES MUTUALITES SOCIALISTES v. DEL GROSSO (C–325/93), April 6, 1995, ECJ, Second Chamber.

4588. Free movement of persons—migrant workers—unemployment benefits—agreement to claim benefit from state in which neither resident nor working—whether entitled to claim benefits from state in which last worked and in which resident—European Community

[EEC Reg. 1408/71, Art. 71.]

The applicant worked and lived in the Netherlands from 1980. In 1988, he moved to Belgium for a temporary period, but declared that he wished to remain subject to Netherlands social security. Accordingly, the Belgian and Netherlands authorities agreed that Netherlands social security legislation should continue to be applied to him for the period of his employment in Belgium. In 1990, he was dismissed from his employment and was paid severance compensation from the Netherlands. He then sought unemployment benefit in Belgium but this was refused on the ground that only Netherlands legislation applied to him.

Held, that Art. 71(1)(b)(ii) of Council Reg. (EEC) 1408/71 on the application of social security schemes to employed persons, to self-employed persons and to members of their families moving within the Community, applied to unemployed persons who during their last employment resided in the Member State where they worked, even where the competent authorities had agreed that the employed person is to remain under the social security legislation of another State. This applies even where the agreement came into being when the employed person was already working and residing in the territory of one and the same Member State.

RIJKSDIENST VOOR ARBEIDSVOORZIENING v. VAN GEESTEL (C–454/93), June 29, 1995, ECJ, Sixth Chamber.

4589. Free movement of persons—sickness benefits—worker resident in a Member State other than the competent State—whether entitled to benefits in kind for members of the worker's family in the State of residence—European Community

[EEC Reg. 1408/71, Art. 19.]

D was employed in France and affiliated to the local sickness insurance fund in Metz concerning her children's entitlement to benefits in kind. She was married to a German national and the whole family lived together in Germany. A dispute arose with the German social security authorities relating to entitlement to sickness benefits.

Held, that Art. 19(2) of Council Reg. (EEC) 1408/71 on the application of social security schemes to employed persons, to self-employed persons and to members of their families moving within the Community, is to be understood as meaning that when a worker resides with the members of his family in the territory of a Member State other than the Member State in which he works, under whose legislation he is insured by virtue of that Regulation, the conditions for entitlement to sickness benefits in kind for members of that person's family are also governed by the legislation of the State in which that person works, in so far as the members of his family are not entitled to those benefits under the legislation of their State of residence.

DELAVANT v. ALLGEMEINE ORTSKRANKENKASSE FÜR DAS SAARLAND (C–451/93), June 8, 1995, ECJ, Sixth Chamber.

4590. Free movement of persons—social security schemes—application of schemes to persons moving within the Community—validity of provision—European Community

Two questions were referred on the validity of point 4 of Annex VI, section I (now J) of Reg. 1408/71 on the application of social security schemes to persons moving within the Community, as codified by Reg. 2001/83. The national court asked first whether that provision could restrict the scope of Art. 45(4) of the Regulation inasmuch as it introduced a new factor, the status of the employed person when the incapacity arises, in order to determine under which Netherlands legislation (WAO or AAW) the right to benefits may be acquired. Secondly, it considered the question of whether it was lawful for that provision to introduce, by referring to Netherlands legislation, an additional condition such as the receipt of certain amount of income from work during the year prior to the commencement of the incapacity for work, in view of the fact that such a condition was not required for the application of the national legislation to which the employee was to be regarded as still subject for the purposes of Art. 45(4) of the Regulation.

Held, as to the first question, that Arts. 48 to 51 of the Treaty were intended to ensure that workers did not lose social security advantages granted to them by the legislation of a Member State as a result of exercising their right to freedom of movement. That was not the case as regards the provision in question. A person who had worked exclusively in the Netherlands and had ceased to work before the materialisation of the insured risk was in the same situation as a person who avails himself of the right to freedom of movement and who was previously subject to a scheme based on the progressive constitution of rights. As regards the second question, Art. 51 and Reg. 1408/71 provided only for the aggregation of insurance periods completed in different Member States and did not regulate the conditions under which those insurance periods were constituted. Community law did not preclude the national legislature from altering the conditions for granting benefits for incapacity, provided that the new requirements did not give rise to discrimination between Community workers. The income requirement laid down by the Netherlands legislature as a condition for entitlement to AAW benefits was thus compatible with Community law. The questions therefore raised no factor affecting the validity of the provision.

BESTUUR VAN DE NIEUWE ALGEMENE BEDRIJFSVERENIGING v. DRAKE (C–12/93), September 20, 1994, ECJ.

4591. Home energy efficiency grants

HOME ENERGY EFFICIENCY GRANTS (AMENDMENT) REGULATIONS 1995 (No. 49) [65p], made under the Social Security Act 1990 (c.27), s.15; operative on February 9, 1995; amend S.I. 1992 No. 483 so as to extend the definition of householder and to omit a requirement concerning repayment where work was not carried out or did not comply with specified standards.

4592. Housing and council tax benefit. See HOUSING, §2586.

4593. Housing and council tax benefits—local government changes. See LOCAL GOVERNMENT, §3196.

4594. Housing benefit. See HOUSING, §2590.

4595. Housing benefit—agreement to pay rent—long-standing friendship—no tenancy agreement—no steps taken to recover rent—whether commercial or non-commercial arrangement. See R. v. POOLE BOROUGH COUNCIL, *ex p.* ROSS (CO–3127–93), §2591.

4596. Housing benefit—applications for judicial review—whether Secretary of State entitled to notice. See R. v. LIVERPOOL CITY COUNCIL, *ex p.* MULDOON; R. v. RENT OFFICER SERVICE, *ex p.* KELLY, §2592.

4597. Housing benefit—eligible rent—whether reduction possible on ground that rent unreasonably high—wide interpretation of "rent" to include service charges. See R. v. EAST YORKSHIRE BOROUGH OF BEVERLEY HOUSING BENEFITS REVIEW BOARD, *ex p.* HARE, §2594.

4598. Housing benefit—Housing Benefit Review Board—whether landlord entitled to appeal to Housing Benefit Review Board as to assessment of housing benefit—*locus standi*—whether sufficient interest. See R. v. STOKE CITY COUNCIL, *ex p.* HIGHGATE PROJECTS, §2598.

4599. Housing benefit—Housing Benefits Review Board—secretary to Board informing applicant of Board's decision—whether notification complied with Housing Benefit regulations—whether applicant disentitled to benefit. See R. v. SOLIHULL METROPOLITAN BOROUGH COUNCIL HOUSING BENEFITS REVIEW BOARD *ex p.* L. SIMPSON, §2599.

4600. Housing benefit and council tax benefit—permitted totals. See HOUSING, §2586.

4601. Incapacity benefit

SOCIAL SECURITY (INCAPACITY BENEFIT) (CONSEQUENTIAL AND TRANSITIONAL AMENDMENTS AND SAVINGS) REGULATIONS 1995 (No. 829) [£3·70], made under the Social Security Contributions and Benefits Act 1992 (c.4), s.86A(1), and the Social Security (Incapacity for Work) Act 1994 (c.18), s.12(1); operative on April 13, 1995; make general consequential amendments and transitional provisions due to the replacement of sickness benefit and invalidity benefit by incapacity benefit.

SOCIAL SECURITY (INCAPACITY BENEFIT) (TRANSITIONAL) REGULATIONS 1995 (No. 310) [£4·15], made under the Social Security (Incapacity for Work) Act 1994 (c.18), ss.4(12), 12(1); operative on April 13, 1995; make transitional provisions in relation to the transition to incapacity benefit from sickness benefit and invalidity benefit.

4602. Incapacity for work

SOCIAL SECURITY (INCAPACITY FOR WORK) (GENERAL) REGULATIONS 1995 (No. 311) [£3·70], made under the Social Security Administration Act 1992 (c.5), s.61A, and the Social Security Contributions and Benefits Act 1992 (c.4), ss.171C, 171D, 171E, 171G(2)–(4); operative on April 15, 1995; make provision in relation to determinations as to capacity to work for the purposes of the Social Security Contributions and Benefits Act 1992.

SOCIAL SECURITY (INCAPACITY FOR WORK) MISCELLANEOUS AMENDMENTS REGULATIONS 1995 (No. 987) [£1·55], made under the Social Security (Incapacity for Work) Act 1994 (c.18), ss.4, 7, 12, the Social Security Contributions and Benefits Act 1992 (c.4), ss.171A, 171C, 171D, 171E, and the Social Security Administration Act 1992 (c.5), ss.59, 61A, Sched. 3; operative on April 3, 1995, save for reg. 4 which is operative on April 13, 1995; make miscellaneous amendments to S.I. 1995 Nos. 310 and 311 and S.I. 1976 No. 615.

4603. Income support

INCOME SUPPORT (GENERAL) AMENDMENT AND TRANSITIONAL REGULATIONS 1995 (No. 2287) [£1·10], made under the Social Security Contributions and Benefits Act 1992 s.135(1), 137(1), 175(1)(3)–(5); operative on October 2, 1995; amend the standard rate of interest applicable to a loan which qualifies for income support under Sched. 3 of S.I. 1987 No. 1967 from 8.35 per cent to 8.39 per cent.

INCOME SUPPORT (GENERAL) AMENDMENT REGULATIONS 1995 (No. 3320 made under Social Security Contributions and Benefits Act 1992 ss.135(1), 137(1), 175(1)(3) to (5); amends S.I. 1987 No. 1967. operative on January 1, 1996; [65p]. The standard rate of interest applicable to loans qualifying for income support under Sched. 3 of the Income Support (General) Regulations 1987 is lowered from 8.39 per cent to 8.00 per cent.

SOCIAL SECURITY (INCOME SUPPORT AND CLAIMS AND PAYMENTS) AMENDMENT REGULATIONS 1995 (No. 1613), made under the Social Security Contributions and Benefits Act 1992, ss.135(1), 136(5)(b), 137(1), 175(1)(3)–(5) and the Social Security Administration Act 1992, ss.5(1)(p), 15A(2), 189(1)(4), 191.

SOCIAL SECURITY (INCOME SUPPORT, CLAIMS AND PAYMENTS AND

ADJUDICATION) AMENDMENT REGULATIONS 1995 (No. 2927) [£1·55], made under the Social Security Contributions and Benefits Act 1992, ss.123(1)(a), 135(1), 136(5)(b), 137(1)(2)(h), 175(1)(3)(4) and the Social Security Administration Act 1992, ss.5(1)(p), 27(1)(a), 189(1)(4)(5), 191. In force: December 12, 1995; make miscellaneous amendments to the S.I. 1995 No. 1801, S.I. 1987 No. 1968 and S.I. 1987 No. 1967. Regulation 2 limits the occasions when reductions in the capital outstanding on a loan are considered to be relevant changes of circumstances for the purposes of review of decisions. It also makes similar provision relating to changes in the rate of interest which affect the amount of income of the claimant which is disregarded. Regulations 5 and 6 amend Scheds. 3 and 9 respectively of the Income Support Regulations, widening the definition of a disabled person for the purposes of Sched. 3; correcting a rule on temporary absence to cover those who have to leave their home because of violence from non-family members; providing for when the eligible capital outstanding on a loan shall be determined; providing that a claim must be made within 12 weeks from the end of a previous claim for housing costs; omitting the provision whereby the amount of a remortgage entered into after October 2, 1995 shall, subject to certain conditions, be new housing costs; and providing that carers and lone parents may, in certain circumstances, be treated as entitled to income support even if their income and/or capital exceeds certain thresholds.

4604. Income support—capital—establishing whether property constitutes capital affecting entitlement to income support—onus of proving that requirements for entitlement are not satisfied

When applying for income support from July 26, 1988 C stated that he owned property in addition to that occupied as his home. It transpired that he owned an unoccupied residential property and a tenanted shop. C had a mortgage which had been taken over by his bank. He was in dispute with the bank over a further loan of £120,000 taken out to purchase a farm. On May 3, 1988 the bank had obtained a judgment against C in respect of £31,458 and had obtained charging orders against both properties to enforce the judgment. The bank held the deeds to both properties and had registered notice of deposit of the land certificates with H.M. Land Registry as security against the further loan. The adjudication officer did not accept that the deposit of land certificates constituted an "incumbrance" against the properties and disallowed the claim on the grounds that C's capital exceeded the prescribed amount, *i.e.* £6,000. On November 10, 1988 C put both properties up for sale and as a result an award of income support was made. On appeal the adjudication officer's decision for the period to November 9, 1988 was upheld. C appealed to the commissioner.

Held, upholding C's appeal, that (1) it was perverse of the tribunal to accept valuations of the properties produced by the district valuer disregarding the offer prices as "wholly unrealistic" on an associated appeal heard the same day but to accept the offer prices of the properties as the market value in this appeal; (2) although notice of deposit of the land certificates is not itself an "incumbrance" it serves as a caution at the Land Registry and is notice that the certificates are held as security for money. The notice of deposit in this case were clear evidence that incumbrances were secured on the properties; (3) although the onus of proving entitlement rests with C that onus does not absolve the statutory authorities from investigating and ascertaining the facts; (4) in order to decide whether property constitutes capital which will affect entitlement to income support it is necessary for the adjudicating authorities to establish: (a) the date of claim, (b) who has legal title and who is the beneficial owner(s) at the date of claim if there is no caution or restriction on the land register it is probable that the registered proprietor of the land is also the beneficial owner, (c) who is in occupation of the property and the nature of that occupation. Such findings are essential in order to determine whether the property can be disregarded under provisions in Sched. 10, and if necessary for a proper valuation to be made, (d) the market value of C's (and or his or her partner's) interest in the property at the date of claim. "Market value" is the price which would be obtained between a willing buyer and willing seller without regard to any incumbrances secured on the property, (e) whether a sale would involve expenses. In the case of land, expenses would be involved and so 10 per cent should be deducted from the "market value", (f) the amount of any incumbrances secured on the property. Capital is subject to an incumbrance if a creditor has a secured right to resort to it (or prevents its disposal) until satisfaction of his debt in preference to that of any unsecured debtor: the amount of any incumbrances must only be deducted once. If it is secured on two or more properties the value of each falls to be taken into account, their value should be aggregated and the incumbrance deducted from the total and all sums secured by incumbrances held by different incumbrancers must be aggregated when secured on the same property or properties and (g) the period in issue. On a fresh claim this will usually be from the date of claim down to the date on which the statutory authority gives its decision. If the situation is fluid the claim must be looked at week by week and findings as to the position in weeks subsequent to the date of claim should also be made on each of the points on which findings have been made in respect of the date of claim.

SOCIAL SECURITY DECISION NO. R(IS) 21/93.

4605. Income support—capital—interest in property—beneficial entitlement in possession—valuation—whether interest subject to tenancy in favour of another a capital asset

[Income Support (General) Regulations 1987 (S.I. 1987 No. 1967), regs. 49(a), 52.]

Under regs. 52 and 49(a) of the Income Support (General) Regulations 1987, concerning the calculation of a claimant's capital for income support purposes, a person's interest in a house to which he was beneficially entitled in possession was to be calculated as if he, with others, was entitled to the whole beneficial interest in the property in an equal share and then this beneficial interest was to be valued at its current market value. Further, an interest in property which was subject to a tenancy in favour of another person was a reversionary interest under reg. 46 of the Regulations and would not be treated as a capital asset.

CHIEF ADJUDICATION OFFICER v. PALFREY, *The Times*, February 17, 1995, C.A.

4606. Income support—capital—interest in property—whether for sale—onus of proving that requirements for entitlement are not satisfied

[Income Support (General) Regulations 1987 (S.I. 1987 No. 1967), reg. 49, Sched. 10, para. 26.]

When applying for income support C stated that he owned two properties in addition to that occupied as his home. On August 9, 1988 an adjudication officer disallowed the claim on the basis that the capital value of the properties calculated under Income Support (General) Regulations 1987, reg. 49, exceeded the prescribed amount, *i.e.* £6,000. C appealed to a Social Security Appeal Tribunal. On November 10, 1988, before the appeal was heard, the Department received confirmation that both properties had been put up for sale. On the basis that the value of both properties could be disregarded under para. 26 of Sched. 10 the adjudication officer made an award of income support from that date. Following receipt of information which indicated that both properties had been withdrawn from sale, the adjudication officer decided that C was not entitled to income support from December 7, 1988. That decision was upheld by appeal tribunal and C appealed to the commissioner.

Held, allowing C's appeal, setting aside the tribunal's decision and remitting the case to another tribunal, that (1) the tribunal should establish the exact terms of the award, in particular whether it was for an indefinite or fixed period; (2) it should make specific findings with regard to entitlement for days subsequent to the date of claim in respect of which there had been an award; and (3) as regards all such days the onus of proving that the requirements for entitlement are no longer satisfied, and from what date, rests with the adjudication officer.

SOCIAL SECURITY DECISION NO. R(IS) 20/93.

4607. Income support—capital—person's standing in company the same as that of a sole owner or partner—value of shareholding—whether benefit overpaid

[Income Support (General) Regulations 1987 (S.I. 1987 No. 1967), reg. 51.]

On October 9, 1990 the adjudication officer revised the award of supplementary benefit/income support for the period January 26, 1985 to September 18, 1989 and determined that there had been an overpayment of benefit recoverable from C. This was because he had failed to disclose that his wife had capital assets in excess of £6,000. On appeal the tribunal upheld the decision of the adjudication officer, finding that C's wife held 99 per cent of the shares in a private limited company which had assets that included a freehold property worth over £20,000. C appealed to the commissioner.

Held, allowing C's appeal, that (1) C's wife was in a position analogous to that of a sole owner or partner in the business and consequently reg. 51(4) of the Income Support (General) Regulations 1987 applied; (2) she was to be treated as possessing 99 per cent of the capital of the company. This capital should have been disregarded as she was undertaking activities in the course of the business of the company throughout the relevant period: she held the post of director and was engaged in other administrative work on its behalf; (3) the amount of capital she was to be treated as possessing was her proportionate share of the net value of the company after liabilities had been taken into account; and (4) it was not the value of any individual items making up the companies capital that was relevant, rather it was the net worth of the company that mattered. It was therefore irrelevant that the company possessed a freehold in excess of £20,000. The net worth of the total assets was far below the statutory limit for the purposes of claiming income support.

SOCIAL SECURITY DECISION NO. R(IS) 13/93.

4608. Income support—conditions of entitlement—ancillary school worker—whether engaged in remunerative work

[Income Support (General) Regulations 1987 (S.I. 1987 No. 1967), reg. 5(2)(b)(i).]

C's wife, whose hours of work fluctuated, worked as a school receptionist for an average of fractionally over 24 hours a week in term time. Her contract of employment which commenced in June 1990 prescribed that she would be paid for the hours worked in term time only and that the school holidays would be unpaid. Following a claim on January 7, 1992, C was refused income support on the grounds that his wife was engaged in remunerative work within the meaning of reg. 5(2)(b)(i) of the Income Support (General) Regulations 1987. On appeal the tribunal upheld the adjudication officer's decision averaging the hours over the eight-week period ending on January 2, 1992. C appealed to the commissioner.

Held, allowing the appeal, that (1) the hours of work fluctuated over a recognisable cycle which was a one-year period of 52 weeks; (2) because there was a continuing contract of employment which made specific provision for school holidays, these holidays fell within the meaning of the words "where the cycle involves periods in which the person does no work" in reg. 5(2)(b)(i) and not under "any other absences", the school holidays therefore fell to be taken into account when averaging out the number of hours over the yearly cycle.

SOCIAL SECURITY DECISION NO. R(IS) 15/94.

4609. Income support—housing costs—previously rented accommodation—house purchased with a mortgage—whether restricted housing costs can be reduced in line with reduced interest rates—whether regard to be had to rent changes since date of purchase

On October 30, 1989, whilst in receipt of income support, C purchased her home which had previously been rented from the local authority. Interest payable on the loan of £14,385 used to purchase the home was calculated under para. 7(4) of Sched. 3 to the Income Support (General) Regulations 1987 to be £28·01. The adjudication officer restricted this amount under para. 10(1) of Sched. 3 to £14·65, the amount of the eligible rent immediately before the date of purchase. The housing costs payable were increased as the interest rate on the loan increased until on March 1, 1990 they were £18·60. When interest rates fell, the housing costs were reduced until, on August 1, 1991, they were £11·44. C appealed to the Social Security Appeal Tribunal which upheld the adjudication officer's decision to reduce the amount of housing costs payable. C appealed to a Social Security Commissioner.

Held, that (1) there is no provision in para. 10(1) of Sched. 3 to the Income Support (General) Regulations 1987 to reduce the restricted housing costs on a reduction to the interest rate; (2) when the eligible interest calculated under para. 7(4) of Sched. 3 falls below the restricted amount, then the amount payable will be the eligible interest; and (3) no regard should be had to any changes to the rent that may have taken place after the date of purchase.

SOCIAL SECURITY DECISION NO. R(IS) 8/94.

4610. Income support—housing costs—responsibility for housing costs—grandmother claiming house left to grandson—whether grandmother responsible for housing costs

On May 19, 1989 C's daughter acquired an interest in the home now occupied by C and her grandson. C's daughter acquired her interest in the home by way of a deposit of £24,000 and a mortgage of £34,250. Both the mortgage and the home were in the sole name of the daughter. C, her daughter and grandson moved into the home together from their previous home which they had also shared. On May 16, 1991, C's daughter died. C remained in the home and on May 30, 1991 made a claim for income support for herself and her grandson. On the claim for income support she stated that the home had been left to her grandson. The award of income support did not include housing costs. Correspondence followed between the Social Security Department, the mortgagor and C's solicitor. An impasse was reached when the mortgagor required as a condition of transferring the mortgage into C's name, an undertaking from the Social Security Department that all the interest due on the loan would be paid as an eligible housing cost. On January 7, 1992 the adjudication officer issued a decision that no housing costs would be paid. C appealed to a Social Security Appeal Tribunal who upheld the adjudication officer's decision. C appealed to a Social Security Commissioner.

Held, that (1) the term partner in para. 3(a)(b) of Sched. 3 to the Income Support (General) Regulations 1987 has the same meaning as in reg. 2(1); (2) para. 3(1) of Sched. 3 is a deeming regulation and lays down the circumstances under which a person who is not legally liable for repayment of a loan can be treated as responsible for payment of those costs with regard to income support; and (3) there is no doubt that C's daughter's estate was liable for the repayments on the loan. An incorporeal person, or the estate of a deceased person, can be liable for debts just as a corporeal person may be. C can therefore be treated as responsible for the housing costs under para. 3(1)(b) of Sched. 3.

SOCIAL SECURITY DECISION NO. R(IS) 12/94.

4611. Income support—immigrant with leave to remain—parents in refugee camp unable to finance journey to U.K.—whether parents available to support during education

[Immigration Act 1971 (c.77), s.3; Income Support (General) Regulations 1987 (S.I. 1987 No. 1967), reg. 13(2).]

C, a Somalian national, came to the U.K. on January 28, 1988 to study English, supported by his family in Somalia. He was sponsored by a family friend in the U.K. with whom he stayed until November 1988 when he moved to Sheffield. He claimed income support in November 1988 because his family's assets had been frozen following the outbreak of war in Somalia. His family had fled to Ethiopia and were last known to be in a refugee camp. He was paid income support as a "person from abroad". On March 8, 1990 the adjudication officer determined that C, who was by then 17 years old and had been granted further leave to remain in the U.K., was not entitled to benefit because he was to be treated as engaged in relevant education and was not estranged from his parents. Visas had been issued authorising his parents to enter the U.K. but they were unable to finance the journey. On appeal, the tribunal upheld the adjudication officer's decision. C appealed to the commissioner.

Held, that (1) in the context of reg. 13(2)(d) and (e) of the Income Support (General) Regulations, a sponsor is not the same as a person acting in the place of a parent; (2) the "physical or moral danger" and "serious risk to his physical or mental health referred to in para. (d)(ii) of reg. 13(2) need not emanate from C's parents; and (3) subject to certain exceptions, all persons who are not British citizens are prohibited from entering Great Britain for the purposes of reg. 13(2)(e)(iii) "unless given leave to do so" under the provisions of s.3 of the Immigration Act 1971.

SOCIAL SECURITY DECISION NO. R(IS) 9/94.

4612. Income support—income—payment to miner's widow in lieu of concessionary coal—whether voluntary payment—whether income for purposes of assessing income support

C, whose late husband had been a miner, received a cash payment of £6·92 per week from the National Coal Board. This payment was in lieu of concessionary coal and was made pursuant to an agreement between British Coal and the National Union of Mineworkers. The adjudication officer decided that this income fell to be taken into account in full in the calculation of C's income support. C appealed to a Social Security Appeal Tribunal, the point at issue being whether the weekly payment was "voluntary" and could therefore be disregarded. Upholding the adjudication officer's decision, the tribunal decided that the payment was not voluntary because it was legally enforceable. C appealed to the Social Security Commissioner. The commissioner decided that the tribunal's decision was erroneous in point of law. The tribunal had reached the right conclusion on the basis of an incorrect interpretation of the law.

Held, that (1) the question whether a payment of cash in lieu of concessionary coal of the type received by C was "voluntary" was considered in the context of the Housing Benefit (General) Regulations 1987 and the Community Charge Benefit (General) Regulations 1989 in *R. v. Doncaster Metropolitan Borough Council, ex p. Boulton* and it was held there that such a payment was not voluntary; (2) in that judgment, Laws J. said that the word "voluntary" in the context of housing benefit and community charge benefit legislation denoted the obtaining or giving of something without anything being obtained in return; (3) the provision allowing for a partial disregard to apply to "voluntary" payments was not at all concerned with the question whether or not the payer had entered upon legal obligations; it was concerned with cases where a person or body, outside the state, had shouldered some part of the burden of providing relief to persons living in the kind of economic circumstances which will allow the payment of an income-related benefit, without receiving anything in return; (4) the national agreement (under which cash payments in lieu of concessionary coal are made) was entered into by British Coal in the interests of good labour relations so as to better secure the willing services of its employees. British Coal therefore made the agreement in the expectation of improved industrial relations and efficiency being obtained in return. This legitimate and proper purpose was far removed from the purpose of benevolence which lies behind the term "voluntary" in the regulations; and (5) the payment in lieu of concessionary coal in this case was not voluntary. The principle enunciated by Laws J. in *R. v. Doncaster Metropolitan Borough Council, ex p. Boulton* [1993] C.L.Y. 3678 in relation to the Housing Benefit and Community Charge Benefit Regulations applies equally to the interpretation of para. 15 of Sched. 9 to the Income Support (General) Regulations 1987.

SOCIAL SECURITY DECISION NO. R(IS) 4/94.

4613. Income support—misrepresentation—claimant mentally incapable—failure to disclose savings—whether overpayment recoverable

[Social Security Act 1986 (c.50), s.53.]

S, an elderly resident in a nursing home was mentally incapable of understanding her affairs. Her claim for income support was completed by somebody in the nursing home and failed to disclose her substantial savings. S had signed the claim and the Secretary of State for Social Security successfully claimed repayment of the overpaid benefits under s.53(1) of the Social Security Act 1986, on the grounds of misrepresentation. This decision was subsequently set aside and the Chief Adjudication Officer appealed.

Held, allowing the appeal, that under s.53(1) of the 1986 Act overpayment was recoverable where the claimant had fraudulently or otherwise failed to disclose or had misrepresented a material fact. The section was also applicable to innocent as well as fraudulent non-disclosure. It was no defence that S was mentally incapacitated, nor could the responsibility for repayment lie with the nursing home. S was the only person able to make the claim, which she did by signing the form, and it made no difference that she was not aware of any misrepresentation.

CHIEF ADJUDICATION OFFICER v. SHERRIFF, *The Times*, May 10, 1995, C.A.

4614. Income support—students—temporary withdrawal from courses—intercalated period—whether still students—whether entitled to income support

C appealed against a decision of the social security commissioner that students who temporarily withdrew from courses qualified for income support. The students could not take out loans or qualify for awards because they were not attending a course and therefore they applied for income support. The question was whether they were still students during the period they were away from their studies. The Income Support (General) Regulations 1987 provided that anyone attending a full-time course should be treated as still attending it through any period of vacation until the end of the course or until the course was abandoned. The students argued that the intercalated period could not classify as vacation because they were not attending a course.

Held, dismissing the appeal, that students were normally entitled to both grants and loans, but there was no such entitlement when they were not attending courses, regardless of the reason. Therefore if a student was ineligible for social security benefits when not attending courses there would be a section of society that was reduced to destitution. A person could not be classed as a student when he no longer attended a course due to an intercalated period.

CHIEF ADJUDICATION OFFICER v. CLARKE, *The Independent*, February 15, 1995, C.A.

4615. Income support and child support. See SOCIAL SECURITY, §4578.

4616. Income-related benefits

INCOME-RELATED BENEFITS SCHEMES AMENDMENT (NO. 2) REGULATIONS 1995 (No. 2792) [£1·55], made under the Social Security Contributions and Benefits Act 1992, ss.123(1), 136(5)(b), 137(1), 175(1) and the Social Security Administration Act 1992, ss.134(8)(b), 139(6)(b), 189(1), 191(1); amend S.I. 1987 Nos. 1967, 1971, 1973, S.I. 1991 No. 2887, S.I. 1992 No. 1814; operative on October 28, 1995; secure uniformity of treatment of pensions payable to women in respect of their being, or having been, widows of members of the Royal Navy, Army or Royal Air Force in respect of council tax benefit, disability working allowance, family credit, housing benefit and income support. Local authorities are empowered to modify their council tax benefit and housing benefit schemes so as to disregard pensions payable to these women.

INCOME-RELATED BENEFITS SCHEMES AND SOCIAL SECURITY (CLAIMS AND PAYMENTS) (MISCELLANEOUS AMENDMENTS) REGULATIONS 1995 (No. 2303) [£3·70], made under the Social Security Contributions and Benefits Act 1992, ss.123(1), 124(1)(d), 129(3), 130(2)(4), 135(1), 136(1)(3)–(5), 137(1)(2)(b)(d)(h)(i)(l), 175(1)(3)–(6), the Social Security Administration Act 1992, ss.5(1)(h)(i)(o), 6(1)(h)(i), 189; amend S.I. 1987 Nos. 1967, 1968, 1971, 1973, S.I. 1991 No. 2887, S.I. 1992 No. 1814, S.I. 1995 Nos. 482, 626; operative on October 2, 1995 and October 3, 1995.

INCOME-RELATED BENEFITS SCHEMES (MISCELLANEOUS AMENDMENTS) REGULATIONS 1995 (No. 516) [£2·40], made under the Social Security Contributions and Benefits Act 1992 (c.4), ss.123(1)(a)–(c), 128(5), 129(4)(8), 135(1), 136(3)(5)(a)(b), 137(1)(2)(c)(d)(i), 175(1)(3)(4); operative on April 10, 1995, save for regs. 2–16 which are operative on April 11, 1995; make miscellaneous amendments to S.I. 1991 No. 2887 and S.I. 1987 Nos. 1967 and 1973.

INCOME-RELATED BENEFITS SCHEMES (MISCELLANEOUS AMENDMENTS) (NO. 2) REGULATIONS 1995 (No. 1339) [£1·10], made under the Social Security Contributions and Benefits Act 1992 (c.4), ss.123(1)(b)–(e), 128(5), 129(8), 136(3)(5)(b), 137(1)(2)(c)(d), 175(1)(3)(4); operative on July 17, 1995; provide for the increase in income related benefits.

INCOME-RELATED BENEFITS SCHEMES (WIDOWS' ETC. PENSIONS DISREGARDS) AMENDMENT REGULATIONS 1995 (No. 3282), made under the Social Security Contributions and Benefits Act 1992, ss.123(1), 136(5)(a)(b), 137(1), 175(1) and Social Security Administration Act 1992, ss.134(8)(b), 139(6)(b), 189(1), 191(1). Amends S.I. 1987 No. 1967,1971,1973; 1991 2887; 1992 1814; 1995 2792. operative on December 20, 1995; [£1·10]. These Regulations, made in consequence with defects in S.I. 1995 No. 2792, ensure that the first £10·00 of pensions paid to soldiers' widows under the Pensions and Yeomanry Pay Act 1884 are disregarded for the purpose of income related benefits under the Council Tax Benefit (General) Regulations 1992, the Disability Working Allowance (General) Regulations 1991, the Family Credit (General) Regulations 1987, the Housing Benefit (General) Regulations 1987, the Income Support (General) Regulations 1987 and the Income-related Benefits Schemes Amendment (No.2) Regulations 1995. Local authorities may make modifications to their housing benefit and council tax benefit schemes in order to take these provisions into account. A correction is also made to a cross-reference in the Disability Working Allowance (General) Regulations 1991.

4617. Income-related benefits—requirement of habitual residence—whether judicial review to be granted

[Income Related Benefits Schemes (Miscellaneous) (No. 3) S.I. 1994 (S.I. 1994 No. 1801).]

S and others applied for judicial review of the Secretary of State's introduction, under the Income Related Benefits Schemes (Miscellaneous Amendments) (No. 3) Regulations 1994, of the requirement of habitual residence in the U.K. as a condition of eligibility for income-related benefits such as income support, housing benefit, and council tax benefit.

Held, dismissing the application, that the Secretary of State was acting within his powers when, by making the Regulations which amended the schemes under the Social Security Contributions and Benefits Act 1992, he qualified applicants' entitlement by reference to a residence test. Further, E.C. law on freedom of movement and rights of residence within the European Union did not confer automatic entitlement to welfare benefits (*Centre Public D'Aide Social de Courcelles v. Lebon* [1988] E.C.R. 2811, *Brown v. Secretary of State for Scotland* [1988] E.C.R. 3205 considered).

R. v. SECRETARY OF STATE FOR SOCIAL SERVICES, *ex p.* SARWAR, *The Independent*, April 12, 1995, D.C.

4618. Industrial injuries benefit—dependent children

SOCIAL SECURITY (INDUSTRIAL INJURIES) (DEPENDENCY) (PERMITTED EARNINGS LIMITS) ORDER 1995 (No. 581), made under the Social Security Contributions and Benefits Act 1992 (c.4); operative on April 10, 1995; where a disablement pension with unemployability supplement is increased in respect of a child and the beneficiary is one of two persons who are spouses residing together or an unmarried couple, the 1992 Act provides that the interest shall not be payable in respect of the first child if the other person's earnings are £120 a week or more and in respect of a further child for each complete £16 where the earnings exceed £120.

4619. Injury benefit—National Health Service employees. See NATIONAL HEALTH, §3612.

4620. Invalid care allowance

SOCIAL SECURITY (INVALID CARE ALLOWANCE) AMENDMENT REGULATIONS 1995 (No. 2935) [65p], made under the Social Security Contributions and Benefits Act 1992, ss.70(8), 175. In force: December 12, 1995; reg. 2 revokes reg. 8(2)(b) of the S.I. 1976 No. 409 which provided that a person's earnings for the purpose of reg. 8(1) of the 1976 Regulations are to be disregarded for any week throughout which he is absent from his employment with his employer's authority.

4621. Invalid care allowance—two severely disabled sons—not possible to care for both at once—whether number of hours of caring could be aggregated

C had two severely disabled sons who normally lived in residential accommodation, but came to stay with her from time to time at her home. Because of their extreme disabilities, it was not possible for C to have both of her sons at home at the same time, and so they stayed with her separately. Normally, neither of them stayed for more than 35 hours in any week. However, there were occasions when their separate stays when added together, totalled more than 35 hours in a week. The Social Security Appeals Tribunal on a reference by the adjudication officer, decided that care for each of two severely disabled persons cannot be aggregated in respect of the number of hours in any benefit week to satisfy the conditions of caring for at least 35 hours in a benefit week: reg. 4(1) of the Social Security (Invalid Care Allowance) Regulations 1976.

Held, allowing C's appeal, that (1) the Interpretations Act 1889 and 1978 authorise a process of selective pluralising of the wording of s.37(1) of the Social Security Act 1975, and reg. 4(1) of the Social Security (Invalid Care Allowance) Regulations 1976; (2) where a claimant cares for two or more severely disabled persons, the test is whether he is, or is likely to be, caring for those persons for at least 35 hours a week. The crucial consideration is the overall length of time for which the carer is engaged in caring; and (3) however many persons a claimant may be caring for, only one allowance will be payable. As it is the length of caring, rather than the number of persons cared for which determines entitlement, it is only reasonable that entitlement to *one* allowance will also arise on the basis of the total length of caring for a number of persons.
SOCIAL SECURITY DECISION NO. R(G) 3/93.

4622. Invalidity benefit—incapacity for normal occupation—consideration of alternative forms of work—whether onus of proof on claimant or adjudication officer—whether detailed job specifications required

C, a 54-year-old factory worker, had been receiving invalidity benefit since December 1, 1990 due to back pain. Medical reports by divisional medical officers of the Benefits Agency Medical Service indicated that C was incapable of her normal occupation, but capable of work within certain limits. The adjudication officer reviewed the indefinite award of invalidity benefit and disallowed benefit from, and including, April 22, 1992. The Social Security Appeal Tribunal upheld the adjudication officer's decision and C appealed to a commissioner.

Held, that (1) an award under reg. 17(1) of the Social Security (Claims and Payments) Regulations 1987 can only be terminated on review under para. 4 of the regulation if the requirements for entitlement are shown not to be satisfied. The onus of proof in such circumstances rests with the adjudication officer; (2) appeal tribunals are well-qualified to judge in a common sense manner the questions of whether or not persons are incapable of work which they can be reasonably expected to do. The tribunal may properly conclude, using its own knowledge and expertise, that suitable employment exists which a claimant can reasonably be expected to do without any need for detailed job specifications; (3) except where it may be properly concluded from common knowledge that suitable employment exists of which C must have been capable, the appeal tribunal is assisted if the adjudication officer provides alternative job descriptions for which C was capable at the material time; and (4) such alternative job descriptions should be up-to-date and briefly describe the various tasks involved: they should not contain technical phraseology or be exceedingly detailed.
SOCIAL SECURITY DECISION NO. R(S) 4/94.

4623. Invalidity benefit—increase of benefit for adult dependant—weekly or daily benefit and the effect of trade disputes on entitlement—whether benefit overpaid

[Social Security Act 1975 (c.14), ss.45, 49A(ii); Social Security Benefit (Dependency) Regulations 1977 (S.I. 1977 No. 343), reg. 8(2)(6).]

C had received invalidity benefit (IVB), including an increase for his wife continuously since April 19, 1982. He was therefore entitled to the benefit of the transitional protection applying to the "tapered" earnings rule for determining the amount of increase payable (reg. 8(6) of the Social Security Benefit (Dependency) Regulations 1977). On July 4, 1989 his wife's trade union called a strike and she was involved in one-day strikes on July 4, 1989, July 11, 1989, July 18, 1989 and July 20, 1989. This came to light when C notified his local office in October 1989 of an increase in his wife's wages. As a result the adjudication officer reviewed the award of an increase of IVB and decided that there was no entitlement to the increase for July 4, 1989, July 11, 1989, July

18, 1989 and July 20, 1989. As a break in entitlement caused C to lose the right to have the "tapered" earnings rule applied, the adjudication officer also decided that no increase was payable from and including July 5, 1989 due to the fact that the earnings of the claimant's wife in the previous week exceeded the limit permitted by the "all or nothing" earnings rule (reg. 8(2) of the Social Security Benefit (Dependency) Regulations 1977) and had continued to do so. The revised decision resulted in an overpayment of benefit from July 4, 1989 to March 3, 1990. The adjudication officer determined that the overpayment from July 4, 1989 to October 22, 1989 was recoverable from C on the grounds that he failed to disclose a material fact. C appealed.

Held, that (1) increase of benefit under s.45 of the Social Security Act 1975 (now s.83 of the Social Security Contributions and Benefits Act 1992) is a daily benefit; (2) under s.49A(ii) of the Social Security Act 1975 (now s.91 of the Social Security Contributions and Benefits Act 1992) there is no title to an increase for an adult dependant where that dependant is involved in a trade dispute and either has been or would have been disqualified for unemployment benefit were they otherwise entitled. The use of the word "otherwise" is to cover all those dependants participating in trade disputes whatever their actual position as to entitlement to unemployment benefit.

SOCIAL SECURITY DECISION NO. R(S) 6/94.

4624. Invalidity benefit—rate reduced in accordance with State retirement pension—determination of pensionable age—whether sex discrimination—EEC law

[Council Directive 79/7, Art. 7(1)(a); Social Security Contributions and Benefits Act 1992 (c.4).]

G and others, for reasons of ill health, ceased employment before they reached pensionable age. They received invalidity pension at the full rate until they reached pensionable age but, in accordance with the provisions of s.33 of the Social Security Contributions and Benefits Act 1992, after reaching pensionable age they received a reduced amount equivalent to the state retirement pension they would have received if they had not elected to continue receiving invalidity pension. The rate of invalidity pension for women was thus restricted to the rate of state retirement pension from the age of 60, whereas for men the relevant age was 65. Under s.34 of the Act women are entitled to invalidity allowance, which is paid in addition to invalidity pension to people who are more than five years under pensionable age when they first become incapable of work, only if they are over 55 on leaving work, whereas the relevant age for men in the same position is 60. The Court of Appeal referred to the ECJ for a preliminary ruling the question of whether ss.33 and 34 were lawful under Art. 7(1)(a) of Council Dir. 79/7.

Held, that the forms of discrimination were objectively and necessarily linked to the difference in pensionable age which a Member State had a right to set under Art. 7(1)(a), and the derogation in Art. 7(1)(a) extended to the differences between the rates of invalidity pension payable to men and women on reaching pensionable age. It also extended to the different ages of entitlement to invalidity allowance paid under s.34.

GRAHAM v. SECRETARY OF STATE FOR SOCIAL SECURITY, *The Times*, September 25, 1995, ECJ.

4625. Invalidity pension—migrant workers—increase in invalidity pension—application of national rule prohibiting overlapping of benefits—European Community

An Italian national resident in Italy received invalidity pensions from the competent institutions in Belgium and Italy. The application of the Belgian anti-overlapping rules involved a reduction of the Belgian pension to take account of the Italian one. In 1990, the pensioner started to receive an additional new benefit in Italy, the family unit allowance, which replaced all other family benefits for most people. The Belgian authority took the view that the allowance was an integral part of the pension and re-examined his rights to the Belgian pension, applying Art. 51(2) of Reg. 1408/71 on the application of social security schemes to persons moving within the Community, as codified by Reg. 2001/83.

Held, that Art. 51 related only to benefits governed by Chap. 3 of Title III of Reg. 1408/71 which applies to old-age and death pensions, that is to say, to survivors' and invalidity pensions. Furthermore, Art. 51(2) of the Regulation did not suggest that the recalculation should be the consequence of anything other than an alteration in the method of determining, or the rules for calculating, the benefits governed by that chapter. It followed that when the rules for calculating other kinds of benefit were altered, Art. 51 ought not apply. The family unit allowance is a family benefit within the meaning of Art. 1(u)(i) of the Regulation. Accordingly, it falls within the scope of Chap. 7 of Title II of the Regulation and its award did not give rise to the application of Art. 51 nor authorised the recalculation of the Belgian pension.

BETTACCINI v. FONDS NATIONAL DE RETRAITE DES OUVRIERS MINEURS (C-301/93), September 22, 1994, ECJ, Second Chamber.

4626. Invalidity pension—whether remuneration last received by the worker in another Member State to be taken into account—European Community

A dispute arose concerning the calculation of an invalidity pension in France. A question was referred asking the court whether the last sentence of Art. 46(2)(a) of Reg. 1408/71 on the application of social security schemes to employed persons, to self-employed persons and to members of their families moving within the Community, as codified by Reg. 2001/83, was to be interpreted as meaning that where the amount of the invalidity benefit under a Member State's legislation depends on the remuneration received by the worker at the time when the invalidity occurred, and the worker in question was not at that time subject to the social security scheme of that State because he was working in another Member State, the competent institution must calculate the theoretical amount of the benefit on the basis of the remuneration last received by the worker in the other Member State.

Held, that the Regulation must be interpreted in the light of Art. 51 E.C. The objective set out in Art. 51(a) entailed that migrant workers were not to lose their right to social security benefits or have the amount of those benefits reduced because they had exercised the right to freedom of movement conferred on them by the Treaty. It followed that in situations as in the main proceedings Art. 46(2)(a) of the Regulation required that account be taken, for the purposes of calculating the theoretical amount of the benefit, of the remuneration received by the worker at the time when he became incapacitated in a Member State other than that under whose legislation the theoretical amount was calculated.

REICHLING v. INSTITUT NATIONAL D'ASSURANCE MALADIE INVALIDITÉ (INAMI) (C-406/93), August 9, 1994, ECJ, Sixth Chamber.

4627. Jobseekers Act 1995 (c.18)

This Act introduces the jobseekers' allowance as a replacement for unemployment benefit and income support for the unemployed. Provision is also made for the promotion of the employment of the unemployed and for the assistance of persons without settled way of life.

The Act received Royal Assent on June 28, 1995.

4628. Jobseekers Act 1995—commencement

JOBSEEKERS ACT 1995 (COMMENCEMENT NO. 1) ORDER 1995 (No. 3228 (C.75)) [£1·10], made under the Jobseekers Act 1995, s.41(2)(3); brings into force various provisions of the Act on December 12, 1995, January 1, 1996, April 1, 1996, April 6, 1996; Provisions of the Jobseekers Act 1995 authorising the making of Regulations are brought into force on 12 December, 1995 by this Order. Further provision is made for s.29 of the same Act, relating to the making of pilot schemes, to enter into force on January 1, 1996, for s.28, relating to expediated claims for housing benefit and council tax benefit and exchange of information between authorities, to enter into force on 1 April, 1996, for s.27, s.34(3) and s.34(7), relating to deductions made by employers on the employment of the long-term unemployed and s.33 and s.34, relating to inspection and offences, to enter into force on 6 April, 1996 and for provisions relating to resettlement places, inclusive of s.30, to come into force on April 1, 1996.

4629. Jobseeker's allowance

JOBSEEKER'S ALLOWANCE (TRANSITIONAL PROVISIONS) REGULATIONS 1995 (No. 3276), made under the Jobseekers Act 1995 ss.35(1), 36(2) to (5), 40. In force: October 7, 1996; [£3·20. These Regulations provide for continuity between, on the one hand, unemployment benefit and income support for those who are required to be available for and actively seeking employment and, on the other hand, a jobseeker's allowance. They contain provisions for awards of income support made to those required to be available for and actively seeking employment to be terminated and replaced by awards of a jobseeker's allowance; for continuity between unemployment benefit and a jobseeker's allowance; setting out the conditions a claimant needs to satisfy for an award of a jobseeker's allowance arising under these Regulations to continue; and for transitional protection to be given for a limited period to persons formerly entitled to unemployment benefit or income support.

4630. Maternity pay

STATUTORY MATERNITY PAY (COMPENSATION OF EMPLOYERS) AMENDMENT REGULATIONS 1995 (No. 566) [65p], made under the Social Security Contributions and Benefits Act 1992 (c.4), ss.167(1)(c), 171(1), 175(1)–(3); operative on April 6, 1995; amend S.I. 1994 No. 1882 so as to increase to five per cent the additional amount of statutory maternity pay a small employer may recover.

4631. Model forms—European Community

Commission Decision 95/353/EC No. 155 of July 6, 1994 on the model forms necessary for the application of Council Regs. (EEC) 1408/71 and 574/72 (O.J. L209/1).

4632. National assistance

NATIONAL ASSISTANCE (ASSESSMENT OF RESOURCES) (AMENDMENT) REGULATIONS 1995 (No. 858) [£1·10], made under the National Assistance Act 1948 (c.29), s.22(5); operative on April 13, 1995; amend S.I. 1992 No. 2977.

NATIONAL ASSISTANCE (ASSESSMENT OF RESOURCES) (AMENDMENT NO. 2) REGULATIONS 1995 (No. 3054) [65p], made under the National Assistance Act 1948, s.22(5) and the Social Work (Scotland) Act 1968, s.87(3). In force: December 20, 1995; replace provisions for property to be disregarded in S.I. 1992 No. 2977 for the purpose of reflecting a change in the Income Support (General) Regulations 1987.

NATIONAL ASSISTANCE (SUMS FOR PERSONAL REQUIREMENTS) REGULATIONS 1995 (No. 443) [65p], made under the National Assistance Act 1948 (c.29), s.22(4); operative on April 10, 1995; replace and revoke S.I. 1994 No. 826 and prescribe the sums that local authorities are to assume that residents in accommodation provided under the 1948 Act, the Social Work (Scotland) Act 1968 and the Mental Health (Scotland) Act 1984 will require for their personal requirements.

4633. Overpayment—prevention—severe disability premium and invalid care allowance—whether amount recoverable

[Social Security Act 1986 (c.50), s.27(2)(4); Income Support (General) Regulations 1987 (S.I. 1987 No. 1967), Sched. 2, para. 13(2)(a); Social Security (Payments on Account, Overpayments and Recovery) Regulations 1987 (S.I. 1987 No. 491), reg. 8(2).]

C, a widow, lived alone and her daughter was her appointee. From March 16, 1989 a severe disability premium was included in her award of income support. On July 12, 1990 the appointee informed the local office that she was receiving invalid care allowance in respect of caring for C. Arrears of invalid care allowance from March 20, 1989 were paid to the appointee on July 16, 1990. The adjudication officer reviewed the award of income support. He decided that income support of £1,679·50 (later amended to £1,781·60) would not have been paid if the invalid care allowance had been paid on time. The amount overpaid was held to be recoverable from C under s.27 of the Social Security Act 1986. On appeal by C the tribunal confirmed the adjudication officer's decision. C appealed to the commissioner.

Held, dismissing C's appeal, that (1) s.27 of the Social Security Act 1986 is not restricted in its operation to cases where the prescribed payment, referred to in subs. (2)(a) of s.27, and the amount ("the relevant amount") referred to in subs. (2)(b), have been paid to the same person, or where the prescribed payment is paid to a member of the claimant's family whose resources and requirements are aggregated with those of the claimant; (2) in reg. 8(2) of the Social Security (Payments on Account, Overpayments and Recovery) Regulations 1987 the words "taken into account" should be given a wide interpretation, and in the context include "take notice of"; (3) the words "in the case of an amount" in s.27(4)(a) of the Social Security Act 1986 refer to a payment by way of income support; and (4) one condition for treating a claimant as a severely disabled person set out in para. 13(2)(a)(iii) of Sched. 2 to the Income Support (General) Regulations 1987, is that "an invalid care allowance under section 27 of the Social Security Act is not in payment to anyone in respect of caring for him". The meaning of the words "in payment" is not limited to timeous payment but includes payment in arrears.

SOCIAL SECURITY DECISION NO. R(IS) 14/94.

4634. Reciprocal agreements

SOCIAL SECURITY (RECIPROCAL AGREEMENTS) ORDER 1995 (No. 767) [£1·55], made under the Social Security Administration Act 1992 (c.5), s.179(1)(b)(2); operative on April 13, 1995; provides for social security legislation to be modified to take account of changes made by the Social Security (Incapacity for Work) Act 1994 introducing incapacity benefit in relation to specified Orders in Council which give effect to reciprocal agreements between the U.K. and other countries relating to social security matters.

4635. Recoupment

SOCIAL SECURITY (RECOUPMENT) (PROLONGATION OF PERIOD FOR FURNISHING OF CERTIFICATE OF TOTAL BENEFIT) ORDER 1995 (No. 1152) [65p], made under the Social Security Administration Act 1992 (c.5), s.96(4); operative on April 27, 1995; provides that the period of three months shall be substituted for the time-limit specified in s.96(1)(c).

4636. Retirement benefit

SOCIAL SECURITY (GRADUATED RETIREMENT BENEFIT) AMENDMENT REGULATIONS 1995 (No. 2606) [£1·10], made under the Social Security Contributions and Benefits Act 1992, ss.62(1), 175(1)–(3) and the Social Security Administration Act 1992, ss.150(11), 155(7), 189(1)(3)(4); operative on November 1, 1995; reg. 2 amends S.I. 1978 No. 393 by substituting a new reg.

2 providing for annual up-rating of GRB and for additional GRB derived from the contributions of a deceased spouse to be included in the sum to be uprated; reg. 3 amends s.36(7) of the National Insurance Act 1965 to limit the circumstances in which a person is treated as entitled to a retirement pension for the purpose of enabling him to receive GRB on its own.

4637. Revaluation of earnings factors

SOCIAL SECURITY REVALUATION OF EARNINGS FACTORS ORDER 1995 (No. 1070) [£1·10], made under the Social Security Administration Act 1992 (c.5), s.148(3)(4); operative on May 11, 1995; provides for the revaluation of earnings factors for the purposes of Pt. III of the Pensions Schemes Act 1993 for specified tax years.

4638. Severe disablement allowance—severely disabled woman living with parents—whether entitled

[Income Support (General) Regulations 1987 (S.I. 1987 No. 1967); Social Security Act 1975 (c.14), s.104.]

B was severely disabled. She lived with her parents and received income support. She did not receive severe disability premium and the decision of an adjudication officer not to award the premium in 1988 was challenged. Two other claimants in similar positions, T and C, were granted severe disability premium payments after an appeal to the Social Security Commissioner. B then applied for review of her benefits. She succeeded in her claim before the Social Security Appeal Tribunal (SSAT) but that decision was overturned by the same Social Security Commissioner. She therefore appealed against his decision. The appeal turned on whether B was entitled to seek a review of the 1988 decision not to award her severe disability premium and whether she would have been entitled to such an award had she challenged the decision when it was first made.

Held, allowing the appeal, that (1) s.104 of the Social Security Act 1975 stated that any decision of an adjudication officer may be reviewed by an adjudication officer or by a SSAT. The original decision of the adjudication officer was erroneous in law and therefore could be appealed; (2) in answer to the question whether B was entitled to a severe disability premium, the court was required to decide whether she satisfied the criterion set down in reg. 13(2)(a)(ii) of the 1987 Regulations. Did B have "non-dependents aged 18 or over residing with her"? This was a question of ownership of the property not the relationship between the parties. In this case it was apparent that B resided with her parents who were tenants of the property they all occupied; and (3) the court considered in detail the question whether B would be entitled to the premium because her parents jointly occupied the property in terms of reg. 3(c) of the 1987 Regulations. The Court found the judgment of Hoffmann J. in *Fullwood v. Chesterfield Borough Council* persuasive, that the phrase "jointly occupies" denoted some form of legal relationship between occupiers. Thus, no such relationship existed in this case and reg. 3(c) did not apply (*Fullwood v. Chesterfield Borough Council* [1994] 9 C.L. 218 considered).

BATE (ANNE MARIE) v. CHIEF ADJUDICATION OFFICER (93/0820/B), November 30, 1995, C.A.

4639. Sex discrimination—severe disablement allowance—time-limit in entitlement—loss of entitlement to non-contributory invalidity pension because of condition imposed on cohabiting or married women—Community Directive providing for equal treatment of men and women in payments of social security—not transposed into national law—limit on arrears of benefits claimable—whether authority entitled to rely on time-limit

[Social Security Act 1975 (c.14), s.165A; Council Directive (EEC) 79/7.]

A rule of national law that merely limited the period in respect of which arrears of social security benefits were payable, prior to the bringing of a claim, was not precluded from application by Community law, even where the directive upon which the claim was based had not been transposed into national law.

J was awarded a non-contributory invalidity pension, but payment was stopped in 1982 when she began cohabiting with a man, because she could not satisfy the additional condition imposed on cohabiting women that they should be incapable of performing household duties. In 1984 the pension was abolished and replaced by the severe disablement allowance payable to both sexes on the same terms. The regulations allowed those who could have claimed the old pension to benefit from the new allowance. J made a claim in 1987 on the grounds that she should have been entitled to the old pension because the additional condition offended against Art. 4 of Council Dir. (EEC) 79/7, which applied the principle of equal treatment for men and women in social security matters. The claim was rejected and J appealed to the Social Security Commissioners who referred the matter to the Court of Justice. The Court ruled that the condition was discriminatory to females and incompatible with Art. 4. The Social Security Commissioners awarded J disablement allowance from 1986 but refused any payments before that date because s.165A of the 1975 Act imposed a 12-month maximum period for any arrears claim. J appealed to the Court of Appeal on the basis that the authorities could not rely on the time-limit when the Directive's provisions had not been transposed into national law, with the effect that the full extent of individuals' rights could not be ascertained. The case was referred to the Court of Justice for a ruling on whether it was compatible with Community law to apply to a claim based on the direct effect of Dir. 79/7 a rule of national law limiting the period over which arrears could be claimed, where the Directive had not been transposed into national law.

Held, that Community law did not preclude the application of a rule limiting the period over which arrears could be claimed. The wording of the rule indicated that it applied generally and so actions based on Community law were not subject to less favourable conditions that those applying to similar domestic actions. The rule was not a bar to proceedings, it merely imposed a limit on the period over which arrears were payable (*Steenhorst-Neerings v. Bestuur van de Bedrijfsvereniging voor Detailhandel, Ambachten en Huisvrouwen (C–338/91)* [1993] ECR I-5475 applied; *Emmott v. Minister for Social Welfare (C–208/90)* [1992] ECR I-4269 distinguished).

JOHNSON v. CHIEF ADJUDICATION OFFICER (NO. 2) [1995] 2 All E.R. (E.C.) 258, ECJ.

4640. Sickness benefit—unemployed worker—leave to seek work in another E.C. State for limited period—hospitalised in that State—staying beyond authorised period—whether entitled to sickness payments from State in which registered unemployed—European Community

After working in Germany as a building labourer, P, an Italian national, registered as unemployed in Germany and received unemployment benefit. He was authorised to go to Italy for a period of three months in order to seek employment there. While in Italy, he fell ill and was hospitalised. At the end of the three-month period, he applied for German cash sickness benefits. The German fund rejected his application in respect of the period after the three months expired. After his illness, P returned to Germany. He sought payment of the benefits for the extended period in Italy.

Held, that Art. 25(4) of Council Reg. (EEC) 1408/71 on the application of social security schemes to employed persons, to self-employed persons and to members of their families requires the competent institution to decide on a request for the extension of the period in respect of which sickness benefits are payable even though that request has not been made expressly by the unemployed person but may be inferred from an application for cash sickness benefits. In ascertaining whether there is a case of *force majeure* within the meaning of Art. 25(4) of the Regulation, the competent institution must conduct an appraisal of the circumstances of the case in order to determine whether the unemployed person may reasonably be required to return to the competent State, regard being had not only to the risks that his state of health may significantly deteriorate or his chances of recovery diminish as a result of the return journey, but also to the severity of the ordeal which he would thereby be enforced to endure.

PERROTTA v. ALLGEMEINE ORTSKRANKENKASSE MUNCHEN (C–391/93), July 13, 1995, ECJ, First Chamber.

4641. Social fund—cold weather payments

SOCIAL FUND COLD WEATHER PAYMENTS (GENERAL) AMENDMENT REGULATIONS 1995 (No. 2620) [£1.55], made under the Social Security Contributions and Benefits Act 1992, ss.138(2)(4), 175(1)(3)(4); operative on November 1, 1995, amend S.I. 1988 No. 1724; increases the prescribed amount payable for each period of cold weather.

4642. Social fund—maternity and funeral expenses

SOCIAL FUND MATERNITY AND FUNERAL EXPENSES (GENERAL) AMENDMENT REGULATIONS 1995 (No. 1229) [£1·10], made under the Social Security Contributions and Benefits Act 1992 (c.4), ss.138(1)(4), 175(1)(3)(4); operative on June 5, 1995; amend S.I. 1987 No. 481 by further specifying who may be entitled to a payment from the social fund by way of funeral expenses.

4642a. Social fund—payment—social security directions—whether classification of medical item correct—whether inspector using discretion correctly. See R. v. SOCIAL FUND INSPECTOR, *ex p.* CONNICK, §155.

4643. Social fund—repairs to central heating system—not minor repairs—whether payment from fund excluded as a "repairs and improvements" exception—whether provision of heating referred to installation or to any subsequent restoration of heating

[Income Support (General) Regulations 1987 (S.I. 1987 No. 1967), Sched. 3; Social Security Administration Act 1992 (c.5).]

The social fund officer refused to award T a payment from the social fund for the cost of repairs to her central heating system. This decision was sustained by the social fund review officer and social fund inspector. T then applied for judicial review. Although it was accepted that the repairs were not minor repairs in terms of the social fund directions issued under the Social Security Administration Act 1992, T submitted that the repairs did not fall within the exceptions under "repairs and improvements" set down in the Income Support (General) Regulations 1987, Sched. 3, para. 8(h), because that subparagraph referred to "provision for heating". T argued that "provision" meant "first time installation".

Held, dismissing the application, that the interpretation submitted by T was not accepted. The meaning of "provision" was to provide heating and a repairer would provide heating by repairing the system.

R. v. SOCIAL FUND INSPECTOR, *ex p.* TUCKWOOD (CO 3807–94), April 27, 1995, Popplewell J.

4644. Social fund inspector—review of officer's decision—whether law in force at time of review or time of decision to be applied

[Social Security Administration Act 1992 (c.5), s.66.]

Under s.66(4) of the Social Security Administration Act 1992, a social fund inspector who was reviewing the decision of a social fund officer on a claim for a community care grant was required to apply the law in force at the time of the review and not the law in force when the social fund officer made the decision under review.

R. v. SOCIAL FUND INSPECTOR, *ex p.* LEDICOTT, *The Times*, May 24, 1995, Sedley J.

4645. State benefits—guide for trade unionists

The Labour Research Department has published a booklet entitled *State*

Benefits 1995—a guide for trade unionists. The booklet provides claimants and their advisers with a guide to state benefits, covering the full range of both means-tested and non-means-tested benefits, explaining the qualification rules, how to claim the benefit and giving the new rate effective from April 1995. Available from the Labour Research Department, 78 Blackfriars Road, London, SE1 8HF, price £2·65 (or £10·00 for non-labour movement bodies).

4646. Statutory sick pay. See EMPLOYMENT, §2057.

4647. Statutory sick pay—maternity pay—press release. See EMPLOYMENT, §2058.

4648. Unemployment benefit—ineligible period—terminal payment—wages not paid for the whole of the notice period—whether disentitlement should only apply to days for which salary received

C's employment terminated on December 31, 1989 and he received a sum of £20,000. His contract of employment entitled him to six months' notice of termination. That notice was given to him on December 15, 1989. The local adjudication officer decided that C had received compensation as defined in reg. 7(6) of the Social Security (Unemployment, Sickness and Invalidity Benefit) Regulations 1983, and was not entitled to unemployment benefit from January 1, 1990 to April 10, 1990. A forward disallowance was also imposed for the period April 11, 1990 to June 15, 1990. The Social Security Appeal Tribunal upheld the disentitlement. It was common ground that the £20,000 paid, less appropriate deductions, was less than six months' salary. The majority found that the ineligible period was six months (the due date), because the employer represented that the money paid included a payment in lieu of notice. The dissenting member considered the effect of reg. 7(1)(d)(5) and (6) was that where C had received less than normal salary for the period of notice, disentitlement should only apply to those days for which the salary had been received, not for the full period of notice.

Held, allowing C's appeal and remitting the case to another tribunal for re-hearing, that (1) it was not clear that the employer represented that the money paid included a payment in lieu of notice. If the tribunal to whom this case was remitted found that the employer had not so represented, they would need to determine the amount which was left to rank as compensation after deduction of the relevant items in reg. 7(6)(a)–(f), so that they could calculate the "standard date"; (2) the dissenting member's view was not correct. In calculating the "due date" it was not relevant to take into account the fact that salary had not been paid for the whole of the contractual period of notice.

SOCIAL SECURITY DECISION NO. R(U) 1/94.

4649. Vocational training. See REVENUE AND FINANCE, §4385.

4650. Welfare food—dried milk

WELFARE FOOD (AMENDMENT) REGULATIONS 1995 (No. 1143) [£1·10], made under the Social Security Act 1988 (c.7), s.13(3)(4), and the Social Security Contributions and Benefits Act 1992 (c.4), 175(2)–(5); operative on May 22, 1995; amend S.I. 1988 No. 536 in relation to dried milk.

4651. Widow' pension—polygamy—administrative decision-making—whether benefit to be split between two wives

A decision of the Department of Health and Social Security in 1991 to the effect that M's husband had been married both to M and to his second wife and that, therefore, the state widow's pension should be split between both women, was not perverse or irrational, despite the fact that a social security appeal tribunal found that there had been no marriage ceremony between the deceased husband and his second wife. The statutory rules governing entitlement to a state pension and to a pension under the National Health Service Superannuation Scheme required no special interpretation of "widowhood" and the same issues fell to be considered under both schemes. The DHSS was, however, entitled to depart from the view of the tribunal, provided it had properly considered all the material before it.

R. v. DEPARTMENT OF HEALTH, *ex p.* MISRA, *The Times*, April 15, 1995, Latham J.

4652. Widow's benefit and retirement pensions

SOCIAL SECURITY (WIDOW'S BENEFIT AND RETIREMENT PENSIONS) AMENDMENT REGULATIONS 1995 (No. 74) [65p], made under the Social Security Contributions and Benefits Act 1992 (c.4), ss.121(1)(a), 175(1)(3); operative on February 10, 1995; amend S.I. 1979 No. 642 by providing for a voidable marriage in respect of which a decree absolute of nullity of marriage has been granted before August 1, 1971 to be treated as if it was a valid marriage terminated by divorce at the date of annulment.

4653. Workers' compensation

PNEUMOCONIOSIS ETC. (WORKERS' COMPENSATION) (PAYMENT OF CLAIMS) (AMENDMENT) REGULATIONS 1995 (No. 1514) [£1·95], made under the Pneumoconiosis etc. (Workers' Compensation) Act 1979 (c.41), ss.1, 7; operative on July 1, 1995; amend S.I. 1988 No. 668 so as to increase the payments made thereunder.

4654. Workmen's compensation

WORKMEN'S COMPENSATION (SUPPLEMENTATION) (AMENDMENT) SCHEME 1995 (No. 746) [£1·10], made under the Social Security Contributions and Benefit Act 1992 (c.4), Sched. 8, para. 2 and the Social Security Administration Act 1992 (c.5), Sched. 9, para. 1; operative on April 12, 1995; further amends S.I. 1982 No. 1489.

SOLICITORS

4655. Breach of trust—solicitors holding funds on trust for mortgagee—funds paid away to stranger in breach of trust—whether same loss would have been suffered in no breach—whether mortgagee entitled to summary judgment and order for restitution. See TARGET HOLDINGS v. REDFERNS (A FIRM), §2195.

4656. Care proceedings—contested care proceedings—whether use by local authorities of solicitors within legal department appropriate. See B. (MINORS) (LOCAL AUTHORITIES: REPRESENTATION), *Re*, §3410.

4657. Commissioners for oaths

COMMISSIONERS FOR OATHS (PRESCRIBED BODIES) REGULATIONS 1995 (No. 1676), made under the Courts and Legal Services Act 1990, ss.113(1), 119(1); operative on July 31, 1995; recognise the Institute of Legal Executives as a prescribed body for the purposes of Courts and Legal Services

Act 1990, s.113 and thus allow members of that institution to act as commissioners for oaths.

4658. Conflict of interest—former partner of solicitor's firm representing plaintiffs acting for opponent—whether risk of prejudice

Three plaintiff companies applied for an injunction to stop a former partner of a solicitor's firm acting for an opponent in patent proceedings in the U.K. and abroad. His former firm had acted for one of the plaintiffs in the proceedings and, when he moved to his new firm, one of the defendants wanted him to act as their solicitor. He had not been involved in the litigation in his former firm but he did work in the intellectual property department. The former partner claimed that he possessed no confidential information on the case and therefore there was no risk of prejudice. The plaintiffs contended that he might not recall that he had heard relevant information but that once he started work on the case, he might recall such information. They claimed that they only had to show that there was a risk that such information had been received by the former partner.

Held, refusing the injunction, that it was for the former partner to show that there was no real risk that he was in possession of confidential information. In the instant case, that had been done to the court's satisfaction. The plaintiffs had only established that there was a possibility of information being communicated to the former partner and after hearing his evidence the court was satisfied that there was no real risk of prejudice.

A FIRM OF SOLICITORS, *Re*, *The Times*, May 9, 1995, Lightman J.

4659. Conflict of interest—mortgages—solicitors acting for both borrower and lender—whether mortgagee having constructive knowledge of misrepresentation

In applying to BNP Mortgages (now HMS) for a further mortgage secured on his house, Mr S stated that the purpose of the loan was to buy shares in the family business. His real intention was, however, to pay off the first mortgage and use the balance to repay his business debts and to pay his solicitors (RZ) for their services in this and the earlier transactions. In granting the loan, BNP asked RZ to act as its solicitor, so RZ was acting for both borrower and lender in the transaction. When S defaulted on the loan, BNP sought and was granted an order for possession of the house. Mrs S appealed on the basis that, under the principles of *Barclays Bank v. O'Brien* [1994] 1 A.C. 180 and *CIBC Mortgages v. Pitt* [1994] 1 A.C. 200, BNP was under a duty to ensure that her agreement to the mortgage transaction, which would in reality not bring her any personal financial benefit, had been properly obtained. RZ's knowledge of the true purpose of the loan could, she argued, be imputed to BNP because RZ, acting as BNP's agent in the mortgage transaction, had a duty to communicate its knowledge to BNP.

Held, dismissing the appeal, that a conflict of interest arose as soon as RZ was told the true purpose of the loan in that RZ had a prima facie duty to communicate its knowledge to BNP but this conflicted with its duty to Mr and Mrs S not to disclose such information without their consent. In this situation, notwithstanding RZ's position as agent of BNP in the transaction, RZ's knowledge of the true purpose of the loan could not be imputed to BNP. BNP, therefore, could not be said to have had constructive notice of the misrepresentation and was entitled to an order for possession.

HALIFAX MORTGAGE SERVICES (FORMERLY BNP MORTGAGES) v. STEPSKY, *The Times*, June 27, 1995, Edward Nugee Q.C.

4660. Contempt—insulting comments—whether solicitor entitled to advice prior to being taken into custody

W, a solicitor, applied for judicial review of the order of the magistrates that he be taken into custody and detained until the rising of the court. W had been overheard commenting that "any delay is a result of the ridiculous listing of the Clerk of the Court".

Held, granting the application, that although it could not be said that no reasonable Bench would have found the remark wilfully insulting, W should have been given the opportunity to obtain advice before the contempt issue was decided (*Balogh v. St. Albans Crown Court* [1974] C.L.Y. 2912, *Bodden v. Commissioner of Police of the Metropolis* [1990] C.L.Y. 880, *R. v. Jordan* (1888) 36 W.R. 797 considered).

R. v. TAMWORTH MAGISTRATES' COURT, *ex p.* WALSH [1994] C.O.D. 277, D.C.

4661. Conveyancing—transfer of funds on behalf of clients—bank charges recharged to clients—VAT—whether liable for output tax. See SHUTTLEWORTH & CO. v. CUSTOMS AND EXCISE COMMISSIONERS, §5091.

4662. Costs—duty to comply with statutory regulations—extension of funds—private retainer. See JOYCE v. KAMMAC (1988), §3111.

4663. Costs—solicitors' liability—adjournment hearing—second hearing—client out of country—booking date after trial set down—solicitors failing to apply for adjournment before client left—correspondence to obtain consent from plaintiff—whether solicitors to pay costs. See TROBRIDGES v. WALKER, §4016.

4664. Costs—solicitors' liability—case automatically struck out—without prejudice offer rejected after case struck out—whether solicitors liable to pay costs personally. See HAUGHTON v. R. & V. HANNAH & SONS, §4017.

4665. Costs—solicitors' liability—striking out of claim—legally aided client whose legal aid status not notified to defendant—whether solicitors personally liable for costs. See HOLDEN v. ABER BUILDING SUPPLIES, §4018.

4666. Law Society—disciplinary procedures—assumption of control of solicitor's client funds—application for withdrawal of prohibition notice

[Solicitors Act 1974 (c.47), Sched. 1, para. 6(4).]

The Law Society had powers under para. 6 of Sched. 1 to the Solicitors Act 1974 to assume control of a solicitor's client funds by passing a resolution. Paragraph 6(4) provided for the solicitor to apply to the High Court, within eight days of receiving a prohibition notice, for the notice to be withdrawn but the court had no implied power to extend the eight-day time-limit.

SOLICITOR, *Re*, *The Independent* (C.S.), September 4, 1995, Walker J.

4667. Law Society—disclosure—records—powers of Law Society—whether dishonesty

[Solicitors Act 1974 (c.47), Sched. 1.]

The Law Society applied for an order under Sched. 1 to the Solicitors Act 1974 that a solicitor should produce any documents in his or his firm's possession connected to his practice or any trust controlled by him.

Held, allowing the application, that although the solicitor admitted making false entries in his records, these had caused no financial loss to anyone and he argued that the Law Society had no reason to suspect dishonesty so as to enable it to exercise its powers under Sched. 1. That argument could not be accepted by the court. The word "dishonesty" should be wide enough to cover the circumstances in this case.

SOLICITOR, A (NO. S2700 OF 1995), *Re*, *The Times*, July 11, 1995, Blackburne J.

4668. Law Society—practising certificate—renewal—conditions imposed—whether disciplinary matters capable of being delegated to assistant director

[Solicitors Act 1974 (c.47), s.79(1).]

The Law Society's powers under the Solicitors Act 1974, s.79(1), allow the delegation of disciplinary matters to an assistant director.

C, a solicitor, practised under a restricted practising certificate from 1981. In 1991 a tribunal found over 30 charges of professional neglect or misconduct proved and suspended him for three months. In 1992, an assistant director of the Solicitors Complaints Bureau decided that the applicant should be granted a practising certificate but subject to a more stringent condition that had been imposed earlier, namely that he should practise only in approved employment. C challenged the decision on the basis that although s.79(1) of the Solicitors Act 1974 permitted discharge of the council's functions to individuals, there had been no proper delegation to the assistant director as there had been no consideration of his suitability, that there should have been an oral hearing and C ought to have been warned of the possible restriction.

Held, dismissing the application, that (1) the delegation was proper having regard to practical reality: it was the status of the official that determined whether power was properly delegated to him; (2) procedural fairness did not require an oral hearing in this case; and (3) the restriction ought to have been in C's mind in any event, having regard to his disciplinary record.

R. v. SOLICITORS COMPLAINTS BUREAU, *ex p.* CURTIN (1994) 6 Admin. L.R. 657, C.A.

4669. Law Society—professional conduct—dealing with complaint—whether Law Society owing duty of care to investigate complaints promptly and properly

W complained that H, a partner in a law firm, wrongly acted for both sides when arranging a series of loans for W, on the security of W's home, and that H failed to disclose that H's husband was a director of one of the lenders. H's firm acted for the lenders in issuing court proceedings and obtained possession of the cottage for them. W wrote to the Law Society, complaining about H on a number of occasions. The Law Society initially replied that H owed no duty to third parties, and after W pointed out that she was their client, not a third party, they referred her to the court. Eventually the Law Society concluded that it had been unwise for H's firm to act for the lenders, and that the failure to disclose H's husband's interest in the lenders was conduct unbefitting a solicitor, and issued a formal rebuke. W sought damages from the Law Society, arguing that as a result of the Law Society's incompetence and delay, she lost the chance of avoiding repossession of her home and suffered anxiety and distress.

Held, that if there were a duty owed to W by the Society, it did not include a duty to provide peace of mind or freedom from distress. Even though the Society appeared not to have lived up to the standards reasonably to be expected of it, there was no prospect of establishing that its failure properly or timeously to investigate her complaints could have any sounding in damages. The loss W suffered was not directly caused by the Law Society's incompetence and delay.

WOOD v. LAW SOCIETY, *The Times*, March 2, 1995, C.A.

4670. Law Society—professional conduct—intervention notice—whether solicitor entitled to be given particulars of suspected dishonesty

[Solicitors Act 1974 (c.47), Sched. 1.]

G, a sole practitioner, appealed against a refusal to order the withdrawal of a Law Society intervention notice which stated that there was reason to suspect he had acted dishonestly. The notice resolved to vest his clients' funds in the Law Society and refer G to a disciplinary tribunal. G argued that a solicitor served with a notice of intervention under the Solicitors Act 1974 had the right to be given particulars of the suspected dishonesty and reasons for it contemporaneously with the notice, and that otherwise the notice was invalid and had to be withdrawn. He also sought the withdrawal of a second notice which notified him of failure to comply with the Solicitors Accounts Rules 1991.

Held, dismissing the appeal, that there was no requirement that a solicitor be given particulars of suspected dishonesty at the time a notice of intervention was given nor any requirement that principles of natural justice be considered. The essential feature of the statutory procedure was that any action could be taken swiftly, enabling the Law Society to act on any possible misconduct and the solicitors in question to respond quickly by seeking to suspend that course of action, (*Yogarajah v. Law Society* (unrep.) followed). Under para. 6 of Sched. 1 to the 1974 Act, G could apply to the High Court and he would then have the opportunity of hearing the case against him. The same reasoning also applied to the second intervention notice.

GILES v. LAW SOCIETY, *The Times*, October 20, 1995, C.A.

4671. Legal practice course—grant—student claiming insufficient salary in prospect as criminal legal aid solicitor—whether entitled to grant. See R. v. WARWICKSHIRE COUNTY COUNCIL, *ex p.* WILLIAMS, §1883.

4672. Legal professional privilege—solicitor's professional indemnity policy—assured solicitor sued for negligence—solicitors appointed to act for assured—communications between assured, solicitors and counsel—whether communications privileged—whether privilege waived. See BROWN (ALISTAIR GRAHAM JOHN) v. GUARDIAN ROYAL EXCHANGE ASSURANCE, §4116.

4673. Professional conduct—privileged documents—documents read—fairness and justice

In the course of acting for Norwich Union Fire Insurance Society (NU), N, a solicitor with M, received seven files containing privileged information which had been sent in error by A's counsel. Relying on para. 16.07 of *The Guide to Professional Conduct of Solicitors* (6th ed. 1993), N, once he realised that the documents were privileged, ceased reading them and sought further instructions from NU, who instructed N to read all the files and then return them to A. Subsequently M offered undertakings to A not to make use of information derived from the files, but refused a request to stop acting for NU in the action. A applied for an injunction restraining M from acting as NU's solicitors.

Held, allowing the application, that M had been able to gain an accurate perception of the view of A's advisers as to the merits of his claim, and to allow them to take advantage of such information would be contrary to the requirements of fairness and justice. Parties must be free to communicate with their legal advisers without fearing that such privileged information may be used by the opposing side (*Ridehalgh v. Horsefield* [1994] C.L.Y. 3623 considered).

[*Per curiam*: Paragraph 16.07 of the Guide to Professional Conduct contained an apparent anomaly in that it required a solicitor in the same position as N to stop reading, inform the other side and then return the documents, whilst also advising that, before returning the documents, a solicitor should consider whether to seek instructions from his client about the matter.]

ABLITT v. MILLS & REEVE, *The Times*, October 25, 1995, Blackburne J.

4674. Professional negligence—solicitor—bank intending to advance money to customer—solicitor employed to draft necessary documents and advise bank—bank suffering loss—whether solicitor negligent—whether negligence was cause of loss. See COUNTY NATWEST v. PINSENT & CO., §3697.

4675. Professional negligence—solicitor—civil action against former solicitors for damages for negligence in conduct of criminal defence—whether civil action an abuse of process of court—whether plaintiff having had full opportunity to put forward case—whether new evidence entirely changing aspect of criminal case—whether plaintiff's claim sustainable in law—whether collateral attack on final decision of court. See SMITH v. LINSKILLS (A FIRM), §3699.

4676. Professional negligence—solicitor—costs of litigation—successful client inadequately protected—whether solicitors acting with proper skill and care. See MARTIN BOSTON & CO. v. ROBERTS, §3700.

4677. Professional negligence—solicitor—failure to make proper inquiries during conveyance—highway affecting property—whether solicitor negligent. See FARAGHER v. GERBER, §3702.

4678. Professional negligence—solicitor—negligent legal advice—pre-trial and trial—solicitor sued on basis of counsel's advice—counsel immune from suit—settlement advised—subsequent deterioration in condition—whether abuse of process to sue solicitor. See LANDALL v. DENNIS FAULKNER & ALSOP, §3703.

4679. Professional negligence—solicitor—option to purchase shares—exchange of contract contrary to instructions—damages—date at which damages to be assessed. See AMERENA v. BARLING, §3704.

4680. Professional negligence—solicitor—wills—failure to implement testator's instructions—whether liable in damages to disappointed beneficiaries. See WHITE v. JONES, §3701.

4681. Professional negligence—solicitors acting for both lenders and purchasers—solicitors hearing of information suggesting the property might have been overvalued—whether solicitors should have told the lenders. See MORTGAGE EXPRESS v. BOWERMAN & PARTNERS (A FIRM), §3696.

4682. Professional negligence—whether breach of Code of Practice sufficient—provisions not mandatory. See JOHNSON v. BINGLEY, §3698.

4683. Removal from record—fees unpaid—whether leave to appeal to be granted

[C.C.R., Ord. 37, r.2, Ord. 50, r.5.]

The judge ordered that C's solicitor should be removed from the record under C.C.R., Ord. 50, r.5, on the grounds that the solicitor's bills had not been paid. C applied for leave to appeal against the order and to raise the point that she received short notice of the applications that the solicitors were making.

Held, dismissing the appeal, that the latter was not a point on which to grant leave to appeal unless the order given was plainly wrong. This was clearly an appropriate order. C had asked the county court to reconsider the order, pursuant to Ord. 37, r.2, yet the court did not seem to have had these provisions in mind. It remained that the judge's order was correct. This was not a suitable case to give leave to appeal as it was inevitable that the solicitor would cease to act for C.

BARCLAYS BANK v. CURTIS (JANICE MAUREEN) (94/5689/F) (94/5689/F), October 27, 1994, C.A.

4684. Road traffic accident—insurer known—Motor Insurers Bureau contacted anyway—whether solicitors to pay costs of unnecessary involvement. See MILLS v. TONER AND THE MOTOR INSURERS' BUREAU, §3725.

4685. Summary judgment—adjournment—failure properly to register the mortgagee's charge—registered as equitable charge—whether solicitor liable in restitution to mortgagor. See BRISTOL AND WEST BUILDING SOCIETY v. BRANDON, §4227.

4686. Transfer of advance by solicitors—breach of instructions of building society—whether solicitors liable to repay—whether solicitors held advance on trust

Where solicitors were in breach of their instructions to inform a building society of matters which might prejudice the society's security or matters which were at variance with the society's offer of advance, they were liable to repay the advance; the advance was held by them on a trust to apply in accordance with the society's instructions.

BRISTOL & WEST BUILDING SOCIETY v. A. KRAMER & CO., *The Independent*, January 26, 1995, Blackburne J.

4687. Wrongful dismissal—assistant solicitor—automatic directions—reinstatement. See HAWKES v. TREASURES & RIVER WYATT (LTA 94/5930/F; LTA 94/5931/F), §4081.

STAMP DUTIES

4688. Sale of land—deed of agreement—liability of purchaser to stamp duty—whether agreement a conveyance on sale of equitable interest

[Stamp Act 1891 (c.39), s.54.]

Where a company entered a deed of agreement to purchase land which the vendors held as nominees for the purchaser, a company owned by the vendors, and the land was subsequently sold to a third party, the purchaser was liable to stamp duty because the agreement was a conveyance on sale of an equitable interest under s.54 of the Stamp Act 1891 and was completed on the date of the deed's execution.

PETER BONE v. I.R.C., *The Independent* (C.S.), September 4, 1995, Vinelott J.

4689. Stamp duty reserve tax—stock lending—reliefs

The Inland Revenue has issued a press release entitled *Stock Lending: Stamp Duty Reserve Tax*, published on October 2, 1995. The Revenue has published three extra-statutory concessions providing relief from stamp duty reserve tax on certain stock lending transactions. The text of the concessions is attached to the press release.

4690. Stamp duty reserve tax—Tradepoint

STAMP DUTY RESERVE TAX (TRADEPOINT) REGULATIONS 1995 (No. 2051) [£1·10], made under the Finance Act 1991, ss.116(3)(4), 117; operative on

August 25, 1995; exempt from stamp duty reserve tax certain agreements to transfer equity securities made in the course of trading in those securities on Tradepoint.

STATUTES AND ORDERS

4691. Retrospectivity—statutory instrument removing limit on compensation for sex discrimination—correct approach. See HARVEY v. INSTITUTE OF MOTOR INDUSTRY, §2038.

4692. Royal Assents

Activity Centres (Young Persons' Safety) Act 1995 (c.15), §4272
Agricultural Tenancies Act 1995 (c.8), §197
Appropriation Act 1995 (c.19), §4338
Atomic Energy Authority Act 1995 (c.37), §367
Building Societies (Joint Account Holders) Act 1995 (c.5), §509
Carers (Recognition and Services) Act 1995 (c.12), §3195
Charities (Amendment) Act 1995 (c.48), §547
Child Support Act 1995 (c.34), §3461
Children (Scotland) Act 1995 (c.36), §5514
Civil Evidence Act 1995 (c.38), §2274
Civil Evidence (Family Mediation) Scotland Act 1995 (c.6), §5922
Commonwealth Development Corporation Act 1995 (c.9), §439
Consolidated Fund Act 1995 (c.2), §4342
Consolidated Fund (No. 2) Act 1994 (c.41), §4343
Criminal Appeal Act 1995 (c.35), §1020
Criminal Injuries Compensation Act 1995 (c.53), §1592
Criminal Justice (Scotland) Act 1995 (c.20), §5593
Criminal Law (Consolidation) (Scotland) Act 1995 (c.39), §5758
Criminal Procedure (Consequential Provisions) (Scotland) Act 1995 (c.40), §5595
Criminal Procedure (Scotland) Act 1995 (c.46), §5596
Crown Agents Act 1995 (c.24), §1516
Disability Discrimination Act 1995 (c.50), §1982
Environment Act 1995 (c.25), §2138
European Communities (Finance) Act 1995 (c.1), §2250
Finance Act 1995 (c.4), §4350
Gas Act 1995 (c.45), §2486
Geneva Conventions (Amendment) Act 1995 (c.27), §2941
Goods Vehicle (Licensing of Operators) Act 1995 (c.23), §4437
Health Authorities Act 1995 (c.17), §3619
Home Energy Conservation Act 1995 (c.10), §2539
Insurance Companies (Reserves) Act 1995 (c.29), §2893
Jobseekers Act 1995 (c.18), §4627
Land Registers (Scotland) Act 1995 (c.14), §5995
Landlord and Tenant (Covenants) Act 1995 (c.30), §2999
Law Reform (Succession) Act 1995 (c.41), §5148
Licensing (Sunday Hours) Act 1995 (c.33), §3143
Medical (Professional Performance) Act 1995 (c.51), §3316
Mental Health (Patients in the Community) Act 1995 (c.52), §3343
Merchant Shipping Act 1995 (c.21), §4549
National Health Service (Amendment) Act 1995 (c.31), §3632
Northern Ireland (Remission of Sentences) Act 1995 (c.47), §5207
Olympic Symbol etc. (Protection) Act 1995 (c.32), §2929
Pensions Act 1995 (c.26), §3838

Prisoners (Return to Custody) Act 1995 (c.16), §4264
Private International Law (Miscellaneous Provisions) Act 1995 (c.42), §2943
Proceeds of Crime Act 1995 (c.11), §1454
Proceeds of Crime (Scotland) Act 1995 (c.43), §5784
Requirements of Writing (Scotland) Act 1995 (c.7), §5589
Road Traffic (New Drivers) Act 1995 (c.13), §4463
Sale of Goods (Amendment) Act 1995 (c.28), §4489
Shipping and Trading Interests (Protection) Act 1995 (c.22), §4558
South Africa Act 1995 (c.3), §475
Statute Law (Repeals) Act 1995 (c.44), §4693
Town and Country Planning (Cost of Inquiries etc.) Act 1995 (c.49), §4885

4693. Statute Law (Repeals) Act 1995 (c.44)

This Act seeks to reform statutory law by repealing certain enactments that are considered unnecessary.

The Act received Royal Assent on November 8, 1995.

TELECOMMUNICATIONS

4694. Abuse of dominant position—copyright—television listings—whether refusal to supply weekly television listings materials abuse. See RADIO TELEFIS EIREANN v. INDEPENDENT TELEVISION PUBLICATIONS, §618.

4695. Broadcasting—local radio licences

BROADCASTING (RESTRICTIONS ON THE HOLDING OF LICENCES) (AMENDMENT) ORDER 1995 (No. 1924), made under the Broadcasting Act 1990, Sched. 2, Pt. III, para. 2(3)(a)(b)(4); operative on July 221, 1995.

4696. Broadcasting—share ownership

BROADCASTING (INDEPENDENT PRODUCTIONS) (AMENDMENT) ORDER 1995 (No. 1925), made under the Broadcasting Act 1990, s.16(5); amends S.I. 1991 No. 1408; operative on July 21, 1995.

4697. Broadcasting Complaints Commission—jurisdiction to hear complaint. See R. v. BROADCASTING COMPLAINTS COMMISSION, *ex p.* BRITISH BROADCASTING CORP., §6.

4698. Broadcasting Complaints Commission—television documentary—matter in public domain—whether infringement of privacy. See R. v. BROADCASTING COMPLAINTS COMMISSION, *ex p.* GRANADA TELEVISION, §7.

4699. Broadcasting Complaints Commission—whose complaints to be heard. See R. v. BROADCASTING COMPLAINTS COMMISSION, *ex p.* CHANNEL FOUR TELEVISION CORPORATION, §5.

4700. BT system—interconnection—charges and costs—challenge by way of originating summons—whether judicial review matter—whether statutory nature of charges necessarily a public law matter. See MERCURY COMMUNICATIONS v. DIRECTOR GENERAL OF TELECOMMUNICATIONS, §3907.

4701. CB radio—quality control

WIRELESS TELEGRAPHY (CITIZENS' BAND AND AMATEUR APPARATUS) (VARIOUS PROVISIONS) (AMENDMENT) ORDER 1995 (No. 2588) [£1·10], made under the Wireless Telegraphy Act 1967, ss.7(2), 13(4) and the Telecommunications Act 1984, ss.84, 85(1); operative on October 27, 1995; amends S.I. 1988 No. 1215 which restricts the manufacture, sale, hire, offer or advertisment for sale or hire, custody and control and import of certain CB radios and the manufacture of certain amateur radio apparatus.

4702. Conservation area—telecommunications equipment—relay stations—permission refused on basis of alternative sites—whether relevant. See BRITISH BROADCASTING CORP., VODAPHONE, ORANGE PERSONAL COMMUNICATIONS AND MERCURY PERSONAL COMMUNICATIONS v. SECRETARY OF STATE FOR THE ENVIRONMENT AND BRISTOL CITY COUNCIL (CO/798/95), §4773.

4703. E.C. Directive—telecommunications—failure to implement—open network provision for leased lines—whether publication of general conditions sufficient—European Community

The European Commission sought a declaration that Luxembourg had failed to adopt the necessary measures so as to comply with Council Dir. 92/44/EEC on the application of open network provision to leased lines. This Directive contains rules ensuring that users have access to information on leased line offerings, rules on the supply conditions which must be published, on users' rights in the event of termination of services, and on compliance with essential requirements in relation to conditions for access and usage. Luxembourg argued that access to the services in question and the conditions under which they are to be supplied was governed by the General Conditions for Telecommunications Services, published by the postal and telecommunications undertaking. It acknowledged, however, that the legislation on Telecommunications Services was only at a draft stage.

Held, that in order to ensure that directives are fully applied in law and in fact, Member States must provide a precise legal framework in the field in question, by adopting rules of law capable of creating a situation which is sufficiently precise, clear and transparent to allow individuals to know their rights and rely on them before the national courts. This was not satisfied by merely publishing a list of general conditions.

E.C. COMMISSION v. LUXEMBOURG (C–220/94), June 15, 1995, ECJ, Fifth Chamber.

4704. European Community—legislation relating to telecommunications required—open network provision to leased lines—failure to implement Directive—whether failure to implement Directive justified by internal legal problems—European Community. See E.C. COMMISSION v. GREECE (C–259/94), §2249.

4705. Foreign satellite service—proscription

FOREIGN SATELLITE SERVICE PROSCRIPTION ORDER 1995 (No. 2917) [65p], made under the Broadcasting Act 1990, ss.177, 178. In force: December 5, 1995; proscribes the foreign satellite service known as XXX TV Erotica, formerly known as TV Erotica, for the purposes of s.178 of the Broadcasting Act 1990. Section 178 provides that various acts in support of a proscribed service shall be criminal offences.

4706. Freedom to provide services—national legislation designed to maintain a pluralist, non-commercial broadcasting network—European Community

TV10, a company governed by Luxembourg law which was a commercial broadcasting organisation established in Luxembourg, supplied radio and television programmes into the Netherlands. It obtained authorisation from the

Luxembourg authorities to transmit its programmes via the Astra satellite, which directed them to Netherlands territory. However, the day-to-day management of TV10 was largely in the hands of Netherlands nationals and its programmes were intended to be transmitted by cable networks primarily in Luxembourg and the Netherlands. The Netherlands authorities concluded that the company had established itself in Luxembourg in order to escape the Netherlands legislation applied to domestic associations. Accordingly, it held that TV10 could not be regarded as a foreign broadcaster within the meaning of Dutch legislation and that its programmes could therefore not be transmitted by cable in the Netherlands. The central question was whether this constituted a case of establishment or freedom to provide services.

Held, that the concept of provision of services referred to in Arts. 59 and 60 EEC covers the transmission via cable network operators established in one Member State of television programmes supplied by a broadcasting body established in another Member State, even if that body established itself there in order to avoid the legislation applicable in the receiving State to domestic broadcasters. The provisions of the Treaty are to be interpreted as not precluding a Member State from treating as a domestic broadcaster a broadcasting body constituted under the law of another Member State, and established in that State, but whose activities are wholly or principally directed towards the territory of the first Member State, if that broadcasting body was established there in order to enable it to avoid the rules which would be applicable to it if it were established within the first State.

TV10 SA v. COMMISSARIAT VOOR DE MEDIA (C–23/93), October 5, 1994, ECJ, Fifth Chamber.

4707. Licence charges

WIRELESS TELEGRAPHY (LICENCE CHANGES) REGULATIONS 1995 (No. 1331) [£3·70], made under the Wireless Telegraphy Act 1949 (c.54), s.2(1) and S.I. 1988 No. 93, art. 8; operative on July 1, 1995; provide for fees to be paid in relation to wireless telegraphy licences granted under s.1 of the 1949 Act.

WIRELESS TELEGRAPHY (LICENCE CHARGES) (AMENDMENT) REGULATIONS 1995 (No. 244) [£1·10], made under the Wireless Telegraphy Act 1949 (c.54), s.2(1), operative on April 1, 1995; amend S.I 1991 No. 542.

4708. Pan-European integrated digital network—European Community

Commission Decision 94/796/EC of November 18, 1994 on a common technical regulation for the pan-European integrated services digital network (ISDN) primary rate access (O.J. L329/1).

Commission Decision 94/797/EC of November 18, 1994 on a common technical regulation for the pan-European integrated services digital network (ISDN) basic access (O.J. L329/14).

4709. Public telecommunications systems

Orders made under the Telecommunications Act 1984 (c.12), s.9, designating the specified telecommunication systems as public telecommunications systems:

S.I. 1995 Nos. 182 (AT&T Communications (U.K.) Ltd) [65p]; 941 (Liberty Communications Limited systems) [65p]; 1375 (Mercury Personal Communications Limited) [65p]; 2750 (Orange Personal Communications Services Ltd) [65p].

4710. Radio Authority—company proposing takeover which would exceed restrictions on holding licences—Radio Authority approving scheme—whether authority entitled to come to that conclusion

[Broadcasting Act 1990 (c.42), Sched. 2, Pt. I, para. 1(3)(b); Broadcasting (Restrictions on the Holding of Licenses) Order 1991 (S.I. 1991 No. 1176), arts. 11(5), 12(4).]

The court will not interfere with the a decision of the Radio Authority on the question of number of licences held unless the decision is tainted by illegality.

E effectively held three licences to broadcast. E planned to take over T which effectively held five licences. Since this would exceed the permitted level of six licences, E devised a scheme to create a new company owned equally by E and its bankers, which would hold some licences. E applied to the Radio Authority for a decision as to whether this was satisfactory. The authority decided that if the scheme went ahead E would not be regarded as holding too many licences. Other parties made objections and sought judicial review of the Authority's decision.

Held, dismissing the applications, that the Radio Authority was charged with the factual evaluation of control, and the court would not interfere unless the Authority's action was legally tainted. There was material before the Authority upon which it was legally permissible to come to the conclusion that it had reached.

R. v. RADIO AUTHORITY, *ex p.* GUARDIAN MEDIA GROUP; R. v. RADIO AUTHORITY, *ex p.* TRANS WORLD COMMUNICATIONS [1995] 1 W.L.R. 334, Schiemann J.

4711. Registers

TELECOMMUNICATIONS (REGISTERS) ORDER 1995 (No. 232) [65p], made under the Telecommunications Act 1984 (c.12), ss.19(4)(5), 21(3), 23(4); operative on March 1, 1995; prescribes the hours during which the registers kept under the 1984 Act are to be kept open for public inspection and the fees payable for the supply of copies of the register.

4712. Satellite broadcasting rights—licences—cross-territory broadcasting—whether licences required for both territories—country where question of infringement to be decided. See SATELLITE TELEVISION BROADCASTING, *Re*, §868.

4713. Satellite communications—EEC law

SATELLITE COMMUNICATIONS SERVICES REGULATIONS 1995 (No. 1947) [£1·95], made under the European Communities Act 1972, s.2(2); implement E.C. Dir. 94/46; amend E.C. Dirs. 88/301, 90/388; operative on August 14, 1995; implement Commission Dir. 94/46 which provides for the removal of special and exclusive rights in respect of fixed satellite communication services, other than public voice telephony, between the U.K. and other Member States and members of the EEA and of the market for satellite Earth station equipment by amending Dirs. 88/301 and 90/388.

4714. Short range devices

WIRELESS TELEGRAPHY (SHORT RANGE DEVICES) (EXEMPTION) (AMENDMENT) REGULATIONS 1995 (No. 1081) [£1 10], made under the Wireless Telegraphy Act 1949 (c.54), ss.1(1), 3(1)(a)(b), and the Telecommunications Act 1984 (c.12), s.84(1)(b); operative on May 10, 1995; amend S.I. 1993 No. 1591 so as to extend the categories of telemetry and telecommand apparatus exempted by those regulations to include medical and biological telemetry devices and databuoy telemetry devices.

4715. Television licence fees

WIRELESS TELEGRAPHY (TELEVISION LICENCE FEES) (AMENDMENT) REGULATIONS 1995 (No. 655) [£1·10], made under the Wireless Telegraphy Act 1949 (c.54), s.2 (as extended); operative on April 1, 1995; amend S.I. 1991 No. 436 so as to raise to £28·50 the fee for a monochrome television licence, and to £86·50 the fee for a colour television licence and so as to increase the issue fee and instalments of specified instalment licences.

4716. Terminal equipment

TELECOMMUNICATIONS TERMINAL EQUIPMENT (AMENDMENT) REGULATIONS 1995 (No. 144) [£7·35], made under the European Communities Act 1972 (c.68), s.2(2); operative on January 30, 1995; correct errors and defects in S.I. 1992 No. 2423 and S.I. 1994 No. 3129.

4717. Terminal equipment—failure to implement E.C. law on mutual recognition of their conformity—whether breach of obligation—European Community

The Commission sought a declaration that, by failing to implement Council Dir. 91/263 on the approximation of the laws of the Member States concerning telecommunications terminal equipment, including the mutual recognition of their conformity, Belgium was in breach of its obligations under the Directive and under Art. 189 E.C.

Held, that Belgium was in breach of its obligations and the declaration was accordingly granted.

E.C. COMMISSION v. BELGIUM (C–218/94), May 4, 1995, ECJ, Sixth Chamber.

4718. Transmission right—unauthorised programme decoders—whether requirement of specific design for unauthorised use—whether a restriction on trade between Member States. See BRITISH SKY BROADCASTING GROUP v. LYONS (DAVID), §870.

4719. Video recordings

VIDEO RECORDINGS (LABELLING) (AMENDMENT) REGULATIONS 1995 (No. 2550) [65p], made under the Video Recordings Act 1984, s.8; operative on November 1, 1995; amend S.I. 1985 No. 911 by introducing a new explanatory statement indicating those works which the authority responsible for video classification consider to be particularly suitable for children and by providing that labels on recordings of new video works will contain the unique title assigned to them on classification.

VIDEO RECORDINGS (REVIEW OF DETERMINATIONS) ORDER 1995 (No. 2551) [£1·10], made under the Video Recordings Act 1984, s.4B; operative on November 1, 1995; provides that video works which were classified before November 3, 1994 may have their classification certificates renewed and that the classifying authority may issue a certificate specifying a different age restriction or refuse to classify the work altogether. A decision to withdraw a work's classification would take effect after two weeks and a decision to change the classification of a work would take effect after three months.

4720. Wireless telegraphy

WIRELESS TELEGRAPHY (ISLE OF MAN) ORDER 1995 (No. 268) [£1·55], made under the Wireless Telegraphy Act 1949 (c.54), s.20(3), the Marine, Etc., Broadcasting (Offences) Act 1967 (c.41), s.10, the Wireless Telegraphy Act 1967 (c.72), s.13(4), the Telecommunications Act 1984 (c.12), s.108, and the Broadcasting Act 1990 (c.42), s.204(6); operative on March 8, 1995; extends specified provisions of the 1984 and the 1990 Acts to the Isle of Man and amends S.I. 1981 No. 1113 so as to revoke the extension of the Wireless Telegraphy Act 1967, s.7, to the Isle of Man.

TORT

4721. Breach of confidence—police use of suspect's photograph—whether defence of public interest

When police reasonably used a suspect's photograph to prevent or detect crime they had a public interest defence against any action for breach of confidence in respect of the photograph.

HELLEWELL v. CHIEF CONSTABLE OF DERBYSHIRE, *The Times*, January 13, 1995, Laws J.

4722. Conversion—car stolen—repairs—travelling expenses—loss of use—exemplary damages—diminution in value—*quantum*. See CLARKE v. SEAMAN, §1581.

4723. Damages—remoteness—plaintiff injured by wrongs of contractual party and tortfeasor—whether necessary to foresee actual loss. See PREKOOKEANSKA PLOVIDBA v. FELSTAR SHIPPING CORP. AND SETRAMAR Srl AND STC SCANTRADE A.B. (THIRD PARTY); CARNIVAL, THE, §4517.

4724. Double actionability—foreign tort—proper law of tort to be applied—exceptions to general rule—tort not actionable under *lex fori*—actionable under *lex loci delicti*—whether party can exclude *lex fori* and rely upon *lex loci delicti*

[H.K.] In exceptional cases where a tort is committed in a foreign country and is not actionable in this country but is actionable in the foreign country, it would be possible to depart from the rule of double actionability.

Following the discovery of defects in the buildings on a construction project in Saudi Arabia governed by contracts under Saudi Arabian law the respondents, including a consortium known as PCG, commenced proceedings against insurers in Hong Kong claiming an indemnity. The insurers counterclaimed against PCG, alleging that it was their default and negligence that had caused the damage and, if the insurers were liable to the rest of the respondents, they were entitled to an indemnity from PCG. PCG sought to strike out the counterclaim as, under Hong Kong law, there could be no subrogated claim until the insurers had indemnified the rest of the respondents which had not been done. The insurers sought to amend their counterclaim alleging that the law of Saudi Arabia applied, under which the claim could be brought. The judge and the Hong Kong Court of Appeal refused the insurers application to amend since the *lex loci* did not allow such a claim to be made. The insurers appealed.

Held, allowing the appeal, that the usual rule was that an act done in a foreign country was actionable in England only if it was actionable as a tort in England and under the law of the foreign country. That rule was not inflexible and it was possible to depart from it on clear grounds to avoid injustice. The exception could be applied to enable a party to rely upon the *lex loci delicti* where the claim was not actionable under the *lex fori* (*Chaplin v. Boys* [1969] C.L.Y. 469 considered; *Adhiguna Meranti, The* [1988] C.L.Y. 395 overruled).

RED SEA INSURANCE CO. v. BOUYGUES SA [1994] 3 All E.R. 749, P.C.

4725. False imprisonment—reference to arbitration. See DUFFUS AND DUFFUS v. CHIEF CONSTABLE OF DERBYSHIRE, §4216.

4726. False imprisonment—service in armed forces—whether capable of amounting to unlawful imprisonment

Although, in theory, compelling a person to serve in the armed forces could amount to unlawful imprisonment, in the instant case P was clearly lawfully committed to serve as a soldier.

PRITCHARD v. MINISTRY OF DEFENCE, *The Times*, January 27, 1995, H.H.J. Previte, Q.C. sitting as a deputy judge.

4727. False imprisonment—wrongful detention—detention of a minor in police detention room—*quantum*. See AGOHA v. CHIEF CONSTABLE OF MERSEYSIDE, §1598.

4728. Malicious prosecution—informers—false complaint—whether false complaint liable in damages

W made false and malicious allegations of indecent exposure against M, a next door neighbour with whom she had long had an acrimonious relationship. Charges were brought but dropped before the trial as the CPS offered no evidence. M was subsequently awarded damages against W for malicious prosecution. W successfully appealed but M appealed against the ruling.

Held, allowing the appeal, that there was no English precedent on the issue but Commonwealth cases, including *Pandit Gaya Parshad Tewari v. Sardar Bhagat Singh*, established that if a person made a false complaint and influenced the police to help them have an innocent person prosecuted, they should not escape liability merely because technically they were not the prosecutor. If a person knowingly made a false complaint and the facts on which the prosecution was based were only within the complainant's own knowledge, the police had no real discretion as to whether to prosecute and the complainant was in substance the one responsible for the prosecution. Such a person should not escape liability for setting the prosecution in motion. Arguments based on public policy against liability for complainants were rejected because genuine complainants had no reason to fear malicious prosecution proceedings, even if they were mistaken in their allegations (*Pandit Gaya Parshad Tewari v. Sardar Bhagat Singh* (1908) 24 T.L.R. 884 considered).

MARTIN v. WATSON, *The Times*, July 14, 1995, H.L.

4729. Misconduct in a public office—local government officers—whether offence restricted to Crown servants or to officers with public function. See R. v. BOWDEN (TERENCE) (93/6974/X2), §165.

4730. Misfeasance in public office—claim that Home Secretary reckless in failing to discharge public duty—whether intent to injure plaintiff an essential ingredient of tort

Intent to injure the plaintiff is an essential ingredient in the tort of misfeasance in public office and must be pleaded in a statement of claim.

P, a citizen of New Zealand, had been arrested in South Africa and was placed on a flight to New Zealand. The flight stopped off in London where P was wanted on charges under the Theft Act 1978. P was arrested and committed for trial. P applied for judicial review claiming that he had been detained in England as a result of an avoidance of the South African extradition procedure. He also sought discovery of documents relating to his removal and detention. Discovery was refused as the Secretary of State for the Home Department had signed a certificate claiming public interest immunity, and the Divisional Court felt that it did not have jurisdiction to examine the circumstances surrounding P's presence in the country, given that he was a defendant in criminal proceedings. The House of Lords reversed the Divisional Court's decision and remitted the case to the Divisional Court, where the Court allowed disclosure of the documents, having regard to their importance in the administration of justice, even though the documents were entitled prima facie to public interest immunity. P then brought a claim for damages against, amongst others, the Secretary of State for the Home Department. P argued that, in not considering whether the public interest in non-disclosure was outweighed by the public interest in proper administration of justice, the Secretary of State had been negligent and committed an act of misfeasance. The Secretary of State applied for the statement of claim to be struck out, saying that so far as it concerned him it disclosed no cause of action or was frivolous, vexatious or an abuse of process.

Held, allowing the application, that (1) intent to injure P was an essential ingredient of the tort of misfeasance in public office, and that as no such intent had been pleaded, the statement of claim contained no cause of action (*Dunlop v. Woollahra Municipal Council* [1981] C.L.Y. 1846, *Bourgoin S.A. v. Ministry of Agriculture, Fisheries and Food* [1986] C.L.Y. 1437 and dictum of Slade J. in *Jones v. Swansea City Council* [1991] C.L.Y. 3411 applied); (2) even if the Secretary of State had been under such a duty it was a public duty and, as such, imposing a private law duty of care in favour of a private litigant wanting to see the documents in question could not be said to be fair, just or reasonable; and (3) in any event, P's claim was bound to fail on the facts (*Caparo Industries v. Dickman* [1990] C.L.Y. 3266 applied).

BENNETT v. COMMISSIONER OF POLICE OF THE METROPOLIS [1995] 1 W.L.R. 488, Rattee J.

4731. Occupiers' liability—visitor slipping on algae—personal injury—whether occupiers' liability

[Occupiers' Liability Act 1957 (c.31), s.2.]

W council appealed against a decision that they were negligent and in breach of the duty of care under s.2(2) of the Occupiers' Liability Act 1957 owed to S, who was injured after slipping on algae at the Cobb, Lyme Regis.

Held, allowing the appeal, that S was a visitor who was well able to assess the danger and knew that the algae might be slippery. The judge was wrong to make a finding against W as owners and occupiers of the Cobb as S would probably not have been affected by any warning notice displayed. The judge's award of damages was set aside accordingly.

STAPLES v. WEST DORSET DISTRICT COUNCIL, *The Times*, April 28, 1995, C.A.

4732. Passing off—common field of activity—likelihood of confusion—nature of business—defendant engaged in Far East trade—plaintiff engaged in high quality trade in England—whether any comparison or likelihood of confusion

In a passing off case it is important to consider all the circumstances, particularly the nature of the goods dealt in by both parties, to see whether there is a real likelihood of deception.

P was the well-known store in Piccadilly, Fortnum & Mason, which alleged passing off against a company incorporated in 1988 under the shelf name of Fortnam Limited. P sought interlocutory relief. D admitted that P had an outstanding reputation in its name, but disputed the exact extent of P's trade. D carried on business as an importer of low-priced goods from Hong Kong and China and then as an exporter of those goods to Europe. D did not apply its name to the goods themselves and there was no direct connection between the goods and the name.

Held, refusing relief, that (1) passing off cases turn on individual fact. It was important to consider all the circumstances, in particular a comparison between the goods in which P and D deal and the nature of the trade in order to decide whether there is a real likelihood of deception; (2) on the evidence it was most unlikely that any customer of D would buy D's goods in the belief that he was acquiring the goods of P. D's trade was primarily wholesale and largely overseas and P's was in England and was retail (*Ewing v. Buttercup Margarine Co.* [1917] 2 Ch. 1, *Financial Times v. Evening Standard* [1991] C.L.Y.

3419, *Lego System Aktieselskab v. Lego M. Lemelstrich* [1983] C.L.Y. 3786, *Lyngstad v. Anabas Products* [1977] C.L.Y. 413, *Wombles v. Wombles Skips* [1975] C.L.Y. 448 referred to).

FORTNUM & MASON v. FORTNAM [1994] F.S.R. 438, Harman J.

4733. Passing off—counterfeit razors—whether innocence a defence. See GILLETTE U.K. v. EDENWEST, §4936.

4734. Passing off—interlocutory injunction—Pot Noodle food snacks—whether expert evidence admissible to show likelihood of confusion—whether evidence from members of the public admissible

In passing off cases, where the goods were of a kind not normally sold to the general public, expert evidence was admissible.

P manufactured a range of hot snack meals known as the "Golden Wonder Pot Noodle" range. Since the launch of the range in 1977 the products had been sold in identical containers made of white polypropylene covered by a foil lid with an angled band of vertical ribbing around the top. D1 was the distributor of "Nissin Cup Noodles" in the U.K. P sought an injunction to restrain D from importing, advertising and supplying "Nissin Cup Noodles" which it alleged were being passed off as P's product. D2 had been selling "Cup Noodles" in Japan since 1971 and had expanded its operations to 80 countries around the world. In 1991, shortly after joint venture negotiations with P collapsed, D2 decided to build a manufacturing plant to serve the whole of Europe. For the European market, D2 decided to change its packaging from polystyrene to polypropylene. D2 argued that this meant that it had to add ribbing around the top, as polypropylene was less heat-resistant. On legal advice, D2 wrote to P in October 1992 saying that it intended to market "Cup Noodles" in the U.K. and enclosing a sample of the packaging. P did not object to this in its reply. P adduced evidence of confusion from marketing experts and members of the public. D argued that the evidence of the experts was inadmissible by its nature and that the evidence of the public should not be admitted in view of the circumstances in which it was obtained and the pro forma nature of the affidavits.

Held, refusing an injunction, that (1) P had established a considerable reputation in its "Pot Noodle" range and the get up had become distinctive of those products. However, the court found it surprising that members of the public would be likely to confuse the get up of the "Nissin Cup Noodle" with that of the "Pot Noodle". The surface graphics were quite different and the ribbing, when looked at closely, was also different; (2) there was no absolute rule against admitting expert evidence directed to the question whether the matter complained of was calculated to deceive. In cases where the goods were of a kind not normally sold to the general public, evidence of persons accustomed to dealing in that market was admissible. Where the goods were sold to the public, expert evidence may be admissible if the judge, as an ordinary shopper, was not able to assess the likelihood of confusion. As the present case concerned a straightforward food product the evidence of marketing experts was inadmissible (*A.G. Spalding and Brother v. A.W. Gamage* (1915) 32 R.P.C. 273, *Ballantine (George) & Son v. Ballantyne Stewart & Co.* [1959] C.L.Y. 3331, *General Electric Co. (of U.S.A.) v. General Electric Co.;* sub nom. *GE Trade Mark* [1972] C.L.Y. 3435, *Sodastream v. Thorn Cascade Co.* [1982] C.L.Y. 2300, *Guccio Gucci SpA v. Paolo Gucci* [1992] C.L.Y. 4437 and *Taittinger v. Allbev* [1993] C.L.Y. 3627 considered); (3) although the affidavit evidence of the public was admissible, the circumstances in which it was obtained were such that little weight could be attached to it. However, it could not be said that there was no serious issue to be tried; and (4) the balance of convenience did not favour the grant of an injunction. Any adjustments to D2's production processes would involve serious dislocation. Furthermore there was no convincing explanation for P's inaction following receipt of the letter from D2 in October 1992. P had ignored this warning, and in the meantime, D2 had expended time, trouble and expense launching "Cup Noodles" in its new container. This was a factor which weighed heavily in the exercise of the discretion (*Films Rover International v. Cannon Film Sales* [1987] C.L.Y. 465, *R. v. Secretary of State for Transport, ex p. Factortame (No. 2)* [1991] C.L.Y. 4032 applied).

DALGETY SPILLERS FOODS v. FOOD BROKERS [1994] F.S.R. 504, Blackburne J.

4735. Passing off—interlocutory injunction—reusable adhesive tack—whether confusion at point of sale—whether confusion after sale might influence subsequent purchase

There can be no evidence of confusion in the colour of a product if the colour of the product cannot be seen until the packaging is removed.

P had sold blue reusable adhesive tack under the trade mark BLU-TACK since 1972. D began selling a similarly blue coloured reusable adhesive tack in 1993. P sought an interlocutory injunction against D for passing off, relying solely on the colour of the tack.

Held, refusing grant of the injunction, that although P had established a reputation in its blue coloured tack and in the name BLU-TACK, since it was not possible to see the colour of D's tack until the packaging was removed there could be no possibility of confusion at the point of sale. The consumer would only discover the colour of D's product after purchase, at which point confusion was immaterial unless the consumer mistakenly purchased D's product in the belief, because of his recollection that the product was blue, that it was BLU-TACK. There was no evidence that any such confusion had arisen either in respect of one of the rival blue products on the market, or in respect of D's product during the five months prior to P's application being heard (*Reckitt and Colman Products v. Borden* [1990] C.L.Y. 3465, *Hoffman-La Roche (F.) & Co. A.G. v. D.D.S.A. Pharmaceuticals* [1965] C.L.Y. 2952, *Sodastream v. Thorn Cascade Co.* [1982] C.L.Y. 2300 distinguished).

BOSTICK v. SELLOTAPE G.B. [1994] R.P.C. 556, Blackburne J.

4736. Passing off—interlocutory injunction—whether logo confusingly similar—whether serious issue to be tried

P was an Irish statutory body established to promote the export of Irish foods. P had adopted a logo including the words "food Ireland", intended to convey an image of Ireland as a source of natural food products. It consisted of a symbol representing the sun rising over a valley of green hills leading down to the sea. The logo was used extensively in Ireland and abroad in displays featuring Irish food. P sought an interlocutory injunction to prevent D using a logo incorporating the words "Waterford foods", which P alleged was confusingly similar and would lead to the belief that D's products were promoted by P. D's logo was described as a yellow sun above a blue and green valley. D argued that the alleged acts of passing off would take place outside the jurisdiction and, in the absence of proof that they were actionable in the jurisdiction where they would be committed, could not be enjoined by an Irish court. D further argued that P had no reputation in the logo and would suffer no injury if confusion arose; that there was in any event no similarity between the logos and that therefore, there was no serious issue to be tried. P contended that the fact that passing off might occur in other jurisdictions was not fatal to obtaining relief in Ireland; that the damage they would suffer would be in the performance of their statutory duties and that the probability of confusion was demonstrated by evidence from their marketing and design experts.

Held, refusing injunctive relief, that (1) in passing off actions the court has jurisdiction to grant relief even though the actual passing off takes place in other jurisdictions in certain circumstances. Both parties being incorporated under Irish law, it was reasonable to determine their rights and duties under Irish law. There was sufficient evidence to establish that a cause of action was available in the U.K. Both limbs of the test in *Philliips v. Eyre*, as refined, were satisfied and the Irish court therefore had jurisdiction (*Phillips v. Eyre* (1870) L.R. 6 Q.B. 1, *Chaplin v. Boys* [1969] C.L.Y. 469 considered); (2) however, a defendant is not to be injuncted, even at the interlocutory stage, unless evidence is adduced as to the law in the jurisdictions where the tortious acts are alleged to have been committed. Accordingly, P had to establish that there was a serious issue to be tried (*Dunhill (Alfred) v. Sunoptic SA and Dunhill (C.)* [1979] C.L.Y. 2694 considered); (3) there was no evidence that the logo was known in connection with P or any business in which they were engaged. The logo promoted Irish foods, not those of D. P had failed to adduce any independent evidence as to the risk of confusion. It was D's competitors in the U.K. export market who were primarily affected by the alleged similarity between the logos but there was no evidence that they shared P's concerns; and (4) applying the common sense test of first impressions when comparing the logos, the probability of any significant confusion was remote (*Laura Ashley v. Coloroll* [1987] C.L.Y. 3751 referred to).

AN BORD TRACHTALA v. WATERFORD FOODS [1994] F.S.R. 316, Keane J., High Court of Ireland.

4737. Passing off—trade mark infringement—IBM memory cards—reworking—whether misrepresented. See INTERNATIONAL BUSINESS MACHINES CORP. v. PHOENIX INTERNATIONAL (COMPUTERS), §4938.

4738. Passing off—unintended deception harming reputation and goodwill—order restraining use

The use, by D, of a name of a high degree of similarity in form and meaning to that of B could amount to an unintended deception which might harm the reputation and goodwill enjoyed by B. An order would, therefore, be made restraining D from continuing to use that name.

BRITISH DIABETIC ASSOCIATION v. DIABETIC SOCIETY, *The Times*, October 23, 1995, Robert Walker J.

4739. Passing off—wheelchair cushions—whether an action lies in the absence of deception

The essence of an action of passing off is deception, and where there is no evidence that a manufacturer will deceive prospective purchasers of its product into thinking it is the product of a rival, the action will be dismissed.

H brought an action against W, alleging that W was passing off its goods, wheelchair cushions, as the goods of H. H produced the cushions originally, and W began to sell a cheaper, copied version of the product. The cushions were only purchased by health care professionals.

Held, dismissing the action, that the purchasers were unlikely to be deceived into thinking that W's product was actually made by H, and therefore W was not passing off its goods as H's to the purchasing health professionals.

HODGKINSON & CORBY v. WARDS MOBILITY SERVICES [1994] 1 W.L.R. 1564, Jacob J.

4740. Tort and delict—choice of law—Law Commission Report

The Law Commission and the Scottish Law Commission have published *Private International Law: Choice of Law in Tort and Delict* (Law Com. No. 193 and Scot. Law Com. No. 129). Available from HMSO, price £8·00.

TOWN AND COUNTRY PLANNING

4741. Advertisements—control—display outside restaurant—goods sold in restaurant—whether deemed consent

[Town and Country Planning (Control of Advertisements) Regulations 1992 (S.I. 1992 No. 666), reg. 6, Sched. 3, Class 5.]

When considering whether an advertisement displayed on business premises has deemed consent, it is necessary only that the goods advertised are sold on those premises and it is irrelevant that the goods are unrelated to the principal business carried on on the premises.

V was a poster advertising company that erected poster advertisements for, *inter alia*, cigars and cigarettes on the flank wall of a restaurant. The restaurant did stock both products for sale therein but the advertisements made no obvious connection between the product and the fact that they were on sale in the restaurant. V was prosecuted for displaying an advertisement without planning consent. V was acquitted on the basis that, as the goods referred to in each advertisement were sold within the restaurant, the advertisement enjoyed the benefit of a deemed consent under Class 5 of Sched. 3 to, and reg. 6 of the Town and Country Planning (Control of Advertisements) Regulations 1992.

Held, dismissing the prosecutor's appeal, that the advertisements fell within Class 5 of Sched. 3. The words "goods sold" in Class 5 were general words apt to refer to branded goods as well as generic goods.

BERRIDGE v. VISION POSTERS [1995] 159 J.P. 218, D.C.

4742. Agricultural building—extension of existing buildings and use—possible environmental health nuisance—whether a material consideration—whether agreement required—whether development likely to lead to unacceptable noise levels

[Town and Country Planning Act 1990 (c.8), s.78, 106; Circular 16/91; P.P.G. 7.]

E council refused permission for, *inter alia*, the extension of a stock building, to provide for an additional 50 sheep and 50 goats, 70m from the nearest residential property. As an agricultural extension, it was appropriate development in the Green Belt, and accorded with most of the development plan policies. E argued that it was likely to harm the living conditions of nearby properties by reason of the increased noise, smells and flies. Despite complaints about the current use, it had not been possible to establish that a statutory nuisance had been caused. G refused to enter into a s.106 agreement to regulate the use, including the storage of manure and refuse, pest control and the disposal of carcasses.

Held, dismissing the appeal, that (1) the changes to agricultural permitted development rights to give local authorities control over livestock units within 400m of houses indicated that matters such as smell and noise, although within the scope of environment protection legislation, can be legitimate planning considerations; (2) the prevention of further problems could only be achieved by other legal powers after they had caused significant further harm to interests of acknowledged importance; (3) the proposed extension would be likely to harm the living conditions of nearby properties by reason of the increased smells and flies; (4) in the absence of the s.106 agreement, the harm would be unacceptable, as it could not reasonably be mitigated by planning conditions and the operation of other environmental powers; and (5) the proposal would be unlikely to lead to unacceptable or uncontrollable levels of noise.

EPPING FOREST DISTRICT COUNCIL v. GREYS MILKING SHEEP (Refs: T/APP/J1535/A/94/232621/P5 and /235371/P5) (1994) 9 P.A.D. 754.

4743. Agricultural building—permitted development rights—whether barn reasonably necessary—whether economic viability a prerequisite to permitted development rights

[Town and Country Planning Act 1990 (c.8), s.174; Town and Country Planning General Development Order 1988 (S.I. 1988 No. 1813), Class A, Sched. 2, Pt. 6.]

R appealed against an enforcement notice against his steel-clad barn, alleging that its erection constituted permitted development. The barn was reasonably necessary for the purpose of storing hay crops from the 28-acre agricultural unit. The council argued that a distinction should be made between a common undertaking in one agricultural unit and the present co-operation between two owners, and challenged whether a barn, or one of this size, was reasonably necessary on financial and economic considerations.

Held, allowing the appeal, that (1) the commercial viability of an agricultural unit is not a prerequisite to permitted development rights; (2) as a matter of fact and degree, and on the balance of probabilities, the land had been in use for the purposes of agriculture for the purposes of trade or business and comprised both owners' holdings; and (3) the building was reasonably necessary for, and was designed for, the purposes of the agricultural activities which might reasonably be expected to be conducted on the unit (*Clarke v. Secretary of State for the Environment and Melton Borough Council* [1993] C.L.Y. 3813 followed; *Broughton v. Secretary of State for the Environment and Chester District Council* [1992] C.L.Y. 4319 considered).

MAIDSTONE DISTRICT COUNCIL v. O'NEILL (Ref: T/APP/C/93/U2335/630325) (1994) 9 P.A.D. 747.

4744. Agricultural holding—notice to quit—Case B—planning permission sought by landlord and tenant—landlord transferring interest in property—whether landlords estopped from serving notice to quit relying on planning permission—whether notice served following severance of reversion valid. See JOHN v. GEORGE, §186.

4745. Agricultural land—applicant wishing to site caravan on farm land for purposes of livery business—inspector recommending conditional permission—refusal by Secretary of State—whether grounds to quash decision

A applied for planning permission to site a caravan on agricultural land for the purposes of a livery business. Permission was refused on the ground that the caravan was a breach of structure plan and local plan policies because it was a permanent dwelling. The inspector recommended that permission be granted subject to conditions. However, the Secretary of State decided that the caravan would be contrary to the policies identified and refused permission.

Held, that the Secretary of State's decision would not be quashed as, having taken into account all the evidence, it was up to the Secretary of State to use his judgement. The Secretary of State accepted that there might be circumstances where the livery stables required an attendant to live on or nearby, thus justifying the provision of accommodation. However, A lived at the farmhouse on the premises and there was no evidence to show that he was unsuitably placed to tend the horses. The Secretary of State had taken into account all material evidence and there had not been any breach of natural justice.

BUCKNEY v. SECRETARY OF STATE FOR THE ENVIRONMENT [1994] EGCS 72, Mr Nigel MacLeod, Q.C.

4746. Agricultural land—caravan site licence—whether necessary for purposes of agriculture—whether financial test appropriate—whether would cause demonstrable harm rather than harm

[Planning Policy Guidance 1 (PPG 1); Planning Policy Guidance 7 (PPG 7).]

F applied to quash the decision of an inspector, appointed by the Secretary of State, dismissing his appeal against the refusal of C council to grant planning permission to site a residential caravan on his land for an agricultural worker for a period of two years. The grounds for the application were that, first, the inspector misdirected himself when considering "harm" on the impact on the area, rather than "demonstrable harm" as referred to in PPG1. Secondly, it was perverse for the inspector to conclude that F had failed to establish sufficient agricultural need to outweigh the visual objections, because he took into account immaterial considerations, namely the availability of accommodation in a nearby village. Thirdly, the inspector misapplied the functional and financial tests under the Annexe to PPG7, as a financial test was inappropriate.

Held, dismissing the application, that (1) there was no evidence to suggest that the inspector did not have "demonstrable harm" in mind when using the term "harm"; (2) the inspector followed the advice in PPG7 and although the caravan would have been convenient, it was not an essential functional requirement and thus the inspector's decision was not perverse. Alternative accommodation was a material consideration and the weight given to it was a matter for the inspector's discretion; and (3) the financial test was appropriate as it provided evidence of whether the agricultural enterprise was likely to be sustained for a reasonable time. Application of the test depended on the facts of each case and in this case the inspector was entitled to apply it.

FOSTER v. SECRETARY OF STATE FOR THE ENVIRONMENT AND CREWE AND NANTWICH BOROUGH COUNCIL (CO/1294/955), August 2, 1995, R Purchas Q.C.

4747. Agricultural land—mobile home—installation on open agricultural land without planning permission—local plan policy supported grant of temporary permission for a caravan to enable agricultural enterprise to become viable—whether inspector applied correct test as to viability

L installed a mobile home on open agricultural land without planning permission as part of a calf-rearing business. W council issued an enforcement notice against the installation of the mobile home and L appealed against the enforcement notice. The policy behind the local plan supported the grant of a temporary permission for a caravan to enable an agricultural enterprise to become viable and the issue therefore arose as to whether the enterprise was or could become viable. The inspector sought to assess the enterprise's viability on the basis of whether the enterprise would generate enough profit to support a full-time agricultural worker. L argued that the inspector had not applied the correct test.

Held, that the calculation of profit of the enterprise showed an apparent misunderstanding of the financial evidence which was sufficient to create a flaw in the inspector's reasoning. The onus of persuading the inspector of the viability and sustainability of the enterprise was on L. The inspector was justified in using the full-time worker test to determine whether the enterprise was sustainable on the basis of the information as then understood.

LOMAS v. SECRETARY OF STATE FOR THE ENVIRONMENT AND WYRE FOREST DISTRICT COUNCIL (1995) 69 P. & C.R. 622, Jeremy Sullivan, Q.C.

4748. Appeal—application for approval of reserved matters—whether section applying to such an application—whether inspector redetermined principles of development established by the outline planning permission

[Town and Country Planning Act 1990 (c.8), ss.54A, 78.]

The applicants had been granted outline planning permission for residential development on land at Kew Gardens within the area of the council. There were two schemes submitted to the council. The council failed to reach a determination within the required time with reference to the first scheme and refused permission for the second scheme. The developers appealed under s.78 of the Town and Country Planning Act 1990 to the Secretary of State.

Held, dismissing the application, that s.54A of the Town and Country Planning Act 1990 applied to an appeal against refusal of reserved matters. When the Secretary of State made his determination of a s.78 appeal, he had to have regard to the provisions of the development plan and to act in accordance with s.54A. The appeal decision was a determination under the planning Acts. The development plan was a material consideration and it was trite law that regard must be had to all material considerations and therefore s.54A applied.

ST. GEORGE DEVELOPMENTS v. SECRETARY OF STATE FOR THE ENVIRONMENT [1994] 3 P.L.R. 33, Mr Nigel Macleod, Q.C. sitting as a deputy judge.

4749. Appeal—burden of proof—development plan policy—single dwelling-house converted to two flats—enforcement notice—whether inspector wrongly cast onus of proof on local planning authority to uphold the development plan

[Town and Country Planning Act 1990 (c.8), s.54A.]

D converted a single dwelling-house into two flats, extending the property and adding a second bathroom. N council issued an enforcement notice in respect of the unauthorised change of use on the basis that the change of use from a dwelling-house to flats was contrary to the local plan. D appealed and the appointed inspector found that there had not been enough information provided by D for N to decide that the conversion was contrary to its local plan. N appealed, arguing that the inspector had wrongly applied s.54A of the Town and Country Planning Act 1990 in casting the onus of proof on the local planning authority to uphold the development plan.

Held, dismissing the application, that the inspector had not incorrectly applied s.54A and had not placed the burden of supporting the development plan upon N. The inspector had reviewed the material considerations, in particular the existing housing stock and need for small family houses in the area, and had concluded that the representations submitted by N were not sufficient to rebut the conclusions he had formed upon the material considerations which he had identified. The statutory test under s.54A for rebuttal of the presumption in favour of the development plan was met if there were "material considerations which indicate otherwise" and the further guidance in PPG 1 could not change the text in s.54A nor put a gloss on the statute.

NEWHAM LONDON BOROUGH COUNCIL v. SECRETARY OF STATE FOR THE ENVIRONMENT AND DANIEL (1995) 70 P. & C.R. 288, Malcolm Spence, Q.C.

4750. Appeal—consistency—appeals against refusal and enforcement notices—heard by two inspectors—conflicting decisions—whether desirability of consistency taken into account

W bought agricultural land to extend the gardens of residential property and applied for retrospective planning permission for a change of use. Permission was refused and enforcement notices were later served. W appealed against the refusal of permission and against the enforcement notices. The appeals proceeded independently by way of written submissions. The inspector dealing with the first appeal dismissed it. The inspector dealing with the appeal against the enforcement notices allowed the appeal. His decision was challenged by the council.

Held, dismissing the applications, that the inspector had made it plain that the earlier decision was "material" but that he disagreed with it. It was plain that the interests in securing consistency of decision making had been taken into account. The disagreement was partly on subjective visual matters, the reasons for which could be shortly stated.

AYLESBURY VALE DISTRICT COUNCIL v. SECRETARY OF STATE FOR THE ENVIRONMENT AND WOODRUFF (1994) 68 P. & C.R. 276, Jeremy Sullivan, Q.C. sitting as a deputy judge.

4751. Appeal—consistency—hotel—failure to consider local plan inspector's recommendation—relevance of council's response to recommendation—whether decision flawed

[Town and Country Planning Act 1990 (c.8), s.288; Town and Country Planning Development Plan Regulations 1991 (S.I. 1991 No. 2794), reg. 16(4).]

R applied for planning permission to erect a hotel on a site which had been recommended for hotel use by the local plan inspector. However, his recommendations conflicted with the borough local plan which encouraged residential development in the area. The local planning authority had not accepted the local plan inspector's recommendation and proposed to modify the policy to residential use. The inspector refused R planning permission finding that the proposed site was in a predominantly residential area and that the local plan inspector's recommendation was not a material consideration (*Jeantwill v. Secretary of State for the Environment* [1991] C.L.Y. 4184 followed). R applied to quash the decision on the grounds that it was wrong to regard the local plan inspector's recommendations as immaterial and to say that the council had rejected the recommendation entirely when it had only rejected it in part.

Held, allowing the application, that (1) the local plan inspector's conclusions were a most material consideration which a later inspector would be bound to take into account. He might wish to disagree with those conclusions but this ought to be supported by reasons (*Bath Society v. Secretary of State for the Environment* [1991] C.L.Y. 4148 cited); (2) the council was obliged to give notice of any proposed modification to uses by reg. 16(4) of the Town and Country Planning Development Plan Regulations 1991 and to invite objections in respect of it. Thus, there was still the opportunity for R to seek to persuade the council to accept the local plan inspector's recommendation. The policy position was not settled and the conclusions of the local plan inspector should not have been brushed aside (*Jeantwill v. Secretary of State for the Environment* [1994] 3 C.L. 429 distinguished); and (3) the council had accepted certain elements of the recommendations relating to small-scale commercial use which was at odds with its contention that housing was a priority need. This was arguably an important shift of policy and should have been considered.

RAVEBUILD v. SECRETARY OF STATE FOR THE ENVIRONMENT (CO/2675/94), November 21, 1994, Jeremy Sullivan, Q.C.

4752. Appeal—costs—award of costs against council—whether decision rational—whether proper test applied

The proper test for an award of costs on a planning appeal is that set out in Circular 2/87, para. 5 (now Circular 8/93), namely that unreasonable conduct has caused the party making the application to incur expense unnecessarily.

At an appeal to the Secretary of State the council put forward reasons for refusing planning permission. The inspector, in his decision, rejected all but one of the reasons and awarded the applicant the costs of refuting the other reasons advanced by the council. The council applied to quash the award of costs.

Held, granting the application and remitting the matter back to the Secretary of State, that the proper test for an award of costs was whether the unreasonable conduct of the authority had caused the other party to incur unnecessary costs. A failure to adduce evidence substantiating a reason for refusing permission could be a basis for an award of costs but such a result did not follow as a matter of course. "Unreasonable" in the context of this test bore its ordinary meaning. The inspector had to give clear and intelligible reasons for his decision and he had failed to do so. That raised a substantial doubt as to whether his decision was proper and the matter would be remitted.

R. v. SECRETARY OF STATE FOR THE ENVIRONMENT, *ex p.* NORTH NORFOLK DISTRICT COUNCIL [1994] 2 PLR 78, Auld J.

4753. Appeal—costs—multiple representation in planning appeals—whether each party entitled to separate orders for costs

The Secretary of State for the Environment, a developer and a development corporation appealed (conjoined) for costs following a successful appeal to the House of Lords.

Held, that (1) the Secretary of State should normally be entitled to the whole of his costs when successful in defending his decision, and should not be required to share his award of costs by apportionment (*Wychavon District Council v. Secretary of State for the Environment and Velcourt* [1995] 8 C.L. 617 disapproved); (2) a developer will not normally be entitled to his costs unless he can show there was a separate issue on which he was entitled to be heard, namely an issue not covered by counsel for the Secretary of State, or unless he has an interest which requires separate representation; (3) a second set of costs is more likely to be awarded at first instance than in the Court of Appeal or House of Lords; (4) an award of a third set of costs will rarely be justified; and (5) in this case both the Secretary of State and the developer were entitled to the whole of their costs because the scale of the development and the importance of the outcome for the developers was exceptional, and the case raised difficult questions of principle arising out of a change in Government policy between the date of application and the final decision.

BOLTON METROPOLITAN DISTRICT COUNCIL v. SECRETARY OF STATE FOR THE ENVIRONMENT; SAME v. MANCHESTER SHIP CANAL CO.; SAME v. TRAFFORD PARK DEVELOPMENT CORP. [1995] 1 W.L.R. 1176, H.L.

4754. Appeal—costs—unsuccessful appeal against grant of planning permission—whether Secretary of State should be awarded costs of appeal

A decision by a judge not to award costs to the Secretary of State where he has successfully defended an appeal is plainly wrong. A district council appealed against the grant of planning permission, and lost. Costs were awarded against them to the second respondent, a commercial enterprise, but not to the first respondent, the Secretary of State. The Secretary of State appealed.

Held, allowing the appeal, that the decision was plainly wrong, as the Secretary of State had a duty to appear to support his decision, and had won on all points of law.

WYCHAVON DISTRICT COUNCIL v. SECRETARY OF STATE FOR THE ENVIRONMENT [1995] 69 P. & C.R. 394, C.A.

4755. Appeal—costs—whether successful defendants entitled to costs—court discretion

The House of Lords was required to determine whether the successful defendants in a planning appeal were all entitled to costs. The Secretary of State defended his decision to allow costs for all the appellants: the Secretary of State himself, the developer Manchester Ship Canal Co. (MSC) and Trafford Park Development Corp. (TPD), who had been separately represented at the appeal.

Held, that there were no rules on issues of costs which remained within the court's discretion in each case. The Secretary of State, having successfully defended a decision to grant planning permission, would normally be entitled to costs in full without any apportionment. Developers would not be entitled to costs unless they showed a specific issue or interest, apart from being developers, which required separate representation. Although a second set of costs might well be awarded in the court of first instance, the Court of Appeal and House of Lords would be less likely to award them, and a third set of costs would rarely be awarded. In the instant case, the Secretary of State was awarded costs in full, TPD were denied costs, and MSC were awarded costs because of unusual features, *i.e.* the Secretary of State was called upon to justify a wider change of policy on out of town shopping centres, the development was exceptionally large and important and it was unusual for neighbouring authorities to oppose planning permission (*Waverley Borough Council v. Secretary of State for the Environment* [1988] 3 P.L.R. 101,

Wychavon District Council v. Secretary of State for the Environment, The Independent, October 24, 1994 considered).

BOLTON METROPOLITAN BOROUGH COUNCIL v. SECRETARY OF STATE FOR THE ENVIRONMENT (NO. 2), *The Times*, July 17, 1995, H.L.

4756. Appeal—enforcement notice—extension of compliance time granted to allow negotiations to proceed—whether council's refusal to negotiate invalidated decision

[Town and Country Planning Act 1990 (c.8), s.106.]

A undertook the restoration of a listed house situated in an area of outstanding natural beauty. An enforcement notice was issued requiring the demolition of a neighbouring building which A had erected for storage purposes. A's appeal against the notice was dismissed, although the inspector varied the notice to extend the compliance period from three to six months in order that the parties involved might discuss a solution to the problems arising from the need for storage. A appealed against the inspector's decision to uphold the notice, arguing that it had been ineffective in its purpose as the local planning authority had refused to enter into negotiations regarding the need for storage.

Held, dismissing A's appeal, that the failure of the envisaged discussions did not affect the legal validity of the inspector's decision, which had to be judged as at the date of the decision. It was clear that the inspector had decided that the particular building should not receive planning permission, and the possibility of temporary planning permission had been rejected in the High Court. A's argument that the inspector should have deferred his decision so as to allow the parties time to enter into an agreement under s.106 of the Town and Country Planning Act 1990 could not be sustained. In the circumstances it would not have been proper to coerce the parties into entering a s.106 agreement.

PINNEGAR v. SECRETARY OF STATE FOR THE ENVIRONMENT [1994] EGCS 165, C.A.

4757. Appeal—inspector's decision—whether invalid for failing to take into account an E.C. Directive—whether local authority able to rely on Directive

An appellant local authority argued that a decision of a planning inspector should be overturned because it failed to take into account E.C. Council Dir. 85/337.

Held, dismissing the appeal, that the local authority was not an individual for the purposes of Community law as it was an emanation of the state, and could not therefore rely on an unimplemented Directive against the respondents.

WYCHAVON DISTRICT COUNCIL v. SECRETARY OF STATE FOR THE ENVIRONMENT AND VELCOURT [1994] C.O.D. 205, D.C.

4758. Appeal—procedure—conservation area decision—misdirection as to appeal procedure pursuant to s.288 of the Town and Country Planning Act 1990—error corrected—applicant ignored correction—application to strike out proceedings—whether court having jurisdiction

[Planning (Listed Buildings and Conservation Areas) Act 1990 (c.9), s.39; Town and Country Planning Act 1990 (c.8), s.288.]

A sought to appeal against a decision of the Fenland District Council under s.39 of the Planning (Listed Buildings and Conservation Areas) Act 1990. By an administrative error, A was directed to the wrong method of appeal by the District Council. As a result of the misdirection, A erroneously appealed pursuant to s.288 of the Town and Country Planning Act 1990. The Treasury Solicitor, on behalf of the Secretary of State, corrected this error in time and undertook to A that no point on effluxion of time would be taken against him should he seek to appeal. There was no response from A to this information. Therefore, the Secretary of State applied to have A·s appeal struck out.

Held, allowing the application, that there was no right of appeal under s.288 of the Town and Country Planning Act 1990. There was a requirement of leave to appeal under the correct method, s.65 of the Town and Country Planning Act 1990, which had not been obtained. Therefore, the appeal was struck out.

O·BRIEN v. SECRETARY OF STATE FOR THE ENVIRONMENT AND FENLAND DISTRICT COUNCIL [1994] 68 P & CR 314.

4759. Appeal—reasons—expansion of existing site—applicant contending that refusal would jeopardise business—whether this issue dealt with

A's proposal to extend their premises was refused outline planning permission. The main issue was whether the likely impact of the proposal on the appearance of the landscape was to be weighed against its economic advantages and the inspector decided that the proposal would have an adverse impact on the attractive rural area which was serious enough to outweigh the commercial considerations of enabling the business to grow. A appealed on the ground that the inspector had failed to deal with the central issue that their business would be in jeopardy unless the expansion was allowed.

Held, refusing A's application, that the case of *Hope* stated that the question was whether the reasons were adequate in the circumstances of a particular case. The inspector had identified the main issue and carried out the necessary balancing exercise. The reasons were clear and intelligible and the inspector was not required to spell out all the considerations (*Hope v. Secretary of State for the Environment* [1976] C.L.Y. 2725 applied).

RICHARD READ (TRANSPORT) v. SECRETARY OF STATE FOR THE ENVIRONMENT [1994] EGCS 85, Mr Roy Vandermeer, Q.C.

4760. Appeal—reasons—shopping centre—administrative decision—requirement of sufficient reasons for conclusions on controversial issues—whether reasons were adequate

The Secretary of State appealed against the Court of Appeal's decision in favour of a consortium of district councils who opposed the grant of planning permission for a shopping centre and sports complex which M intended to build at Trafford Park. The Secretary of State granted planning permission following two public inquiries. After the first inquiry he issued an interim decision letter in favour of the project but subject to concerns about motorway traffic problems. Following a change in motorway building plans a second inquiry was held on the specific issue of motorway congestion, and the Secretary of State accepted the inspector's recommendation and granted planning permission. B and other district councils complained that in the decision the need for urban regeneration (particularly the development's effect on other shopping centres), and the alternative option of reserving the Trafford Park site for high technology industrial development, were not taken properly into account.

Held, allowing the appeal, that the Secretary of State's planning decisions had to include reasons in sufficient detail to show what conclusion had been reached on the principal controversial issues. They did not have to refer to every material consideration, however insignificant, or deal with every argument, however peripheral (*Hope v. Secretary of State for the Environment* (1975) C.L.Y. 3358 followed). In the instant case, the Secretary of State had dealt with the issue of urban regeneration and the reasons he gave, although not very full and badly expressed, were adequate. The question concerning whether to reopen a full public inquiry because the balance of advantage had shifted since the interim decision, was for the Secretary of State's judgment. The suggestion about industrial use was not disregarded altogether but did not need to be dealt with in greater detail.

BOLTON METROPOLITAN DISTRICT COUNCIL v. SECRETARY OF STATE FOR THE ENVIRONMENT, *The Times*, May 25, 1995, H.L.

4761. Appeals

TOWN AND COUNTRY PLANNING (DETERMINATION OF APPEALS BY

APPOINTED PERSONS) (PRESCRIBED CLASSES) (AMENDMENT) REGULATIONS 1995 (No. 2259) [65p], made under the Town and Country Planning Act 1990, ss.333, 336. Sched. 6, para. 1; amend S.I. 1981 No. 804; operative on October 2, 1995.

4762. Building regulations—procedural changes. See BUILDING AND CONSTRUCTION, §497.

4763. Byway—reclassification—classifying byway as open to all traffic—term "private carriage road" used in inclosure award—whether construction of inclosure award prevents reclassification

[Wildlife and Countryside Act 1981 (c.69), s.54.]

D applied to quash a Reclassification Order, confirmed by the Secretary of State for the Environment, which classified a track between two Cambridgeshire villages as a byway open to all traffic under s.54(3) of the Wildlife and Countryside Act 1981.

Held, allowing the application that the Order could be quashed as, upon the proper construction of the relevant inclosure award, a deliberate distinction had been made between private carriage roads and public routes giving equal rights to vehicular traffic which subsequent use did not destroy.

DUNLOP v. SECRETARY OF STATE FOR THE ENVIRONMENT, *The Times*, May 5, 1995, D.C.

4764. Caravan—panels bolted together on a concrete base—whether a caravan

[Caravan Sites and Control of Development Act 1960 (c.62), s.29(1).]

A mobile home consisting of four units bolted together is not a caravan.

C had permission to site a caravan for human habitation on their smallholding. This they replaced with a mobile home, built from four units which were bolted together, resting on a concrete base. The mobile home had no wheels or subframe. Planning permission to retain it was refused, and the case was remitted to the High Court to determine whether the structure was a caravan. The Secretary of State decided it was not, and C appealed.

Held, that the Secretary of State was entitled to find within the terms of the Caravan Sites and Control of Development Act 1960, s.29(1), that the mobile home was not a caravan, as it did not possess the quality of mobility, and could not have been towed away by a trailer or single vehicle.

CARTER v. SECRETARY OF STATE FOR THE ENVIRONMENT [1994] 29 EG 124, C.A.

4765. Change of use—bureau de change—enforcement notices—whether class A1 or class A2 use—whether change material

The use of shop premises as a bureau de change should be classified as class A2 use.

P operated two shops as bureaux de change. Enforcement notices were served alleging change of use from class A1 to class A2 without planning permission. P's appeal against the enforcement notices was dismissed and they applied for leave to appeal.

Held, refusing leave to appeal, that there was no arguable point of law on which it could be suggested that the inspector's decision was wrong. A bureau de change was a financial institution providing financial services within the meaning of class A2 of the Town and Country Planning (Use Classes) Order 1987. There was a change of use class from A1 to A2 which required planning permission unless it did not produce a material difference. The issue of materiality was a question of fact which should not be challenged unless there was no evidence on which the inspector could have formed such a conclusion.

PALISADE INVESTMENTS v. SECRETARY OF STATE FOR THE ENVIRONMENT AND KENSINGTON AND CHELSEA ROYAL BOROUGH COUNCIL (1995) 69 P. & C.R. 638, C.A.

4766. Change of use—landlord's consent—proposed on terms that lease should include landlord's break clause—whether a "fine" within s.19(3) of the Landlord and Tenant Act 1927—whether change of use involved structural alterations and s.19(3) inapplicable. See BARCLAYS BANK v. DAEJAN INVESTMENTS (GROVE HALL), §2971.

4767. Change of use—material considerations—proposed conversion of bedsits into self-contained flats—refusal of permission—whether council's multiple-occupation policy a material consideration

Material considerations are not confined to strict questions of amenity or environmental impact and the need for housing in a particular area is a material consideration.

M applied for permission to change the use of a house from multiple occupancy (with 20 bedsits) to seven self-contained flats. At the appeal the inspector refused permission, accepting the council's policy in favour of providing all forms of accommodation and restricting the number of more expensive properties in the area. The decision was quashed by the judge and the Secretary of State appealed.

Held, allowing the appeal, that material considerations were not limited to strict questions of amenity or environmental impact but included matters that served a planning purpose which related to the character of the land. The need for housing within a particular area was a material consideration. The proposed change amounted to a change in the character of the land.

MITCHELL v. SECRETARY OF STATE FOR THE ENVIRONMENT [1994] 2 PLR 23, C.A.

4768. Change of use—material considerations—unitary development plans requiring disabled access—addition of steps to premises hindering disabled access—whether failure to consider material consideration

An application was made for the change of use of premises. The council refused planning permission because, *inter alia*, the change of use involved adding steps to the front of the premises, which would exacerbate access problems for those with restricted mobility and thus be contrary to the policies of the unitary development plan. On appeal the inspector decided that the council's reason for refusal could not be sustained; although the effect on the disabled should be taken into account under the unitary development plan, more recent advice in PPG 1 pointed out that in this context planning control was limited and should not be used to secure objectives achievable under other legislation. Here the new steps could be considered under other legislation. The council applied to have the inspector's decision quashed on the ground that he had overlooked a material consideration.

Held, quashing the inspector's decision, that the inspector had erred in thinking that PPG 1 absolved him from considering the policies of the unitary development plan. Although PPG 1 stated that planning grounds were not to accomplish objectives achievable under other legislation, this advice applied where it was sought to achieve objectives outside the planning process. In this case, disabled persons' needs were to be taken into account as specified in policy form in the unitary development plan.

RICHMOND UPON THAMES LONDON BOROUGH COUNCIL v. SECRETARY OF STATE FOR THE ENVIRONMENT [1994] EGCS 123, Mr M.R.K. Gray, Q.C. sitting as a deputy judge.

4769. Change of use—part of site—failure to consider established use of part of site—whether present use of land could rely on past use rights

Established use on one area of land cannot bring about an established use on another area of land.

K owned land that was divided into three parts. The site had originally been occupied by a gas company but that use ceased and from 1964 one part of the site came to be used for repair and manufacture for quarrying, metal recovery and the coal industry. The council served an enforcement notice. K's appeal to the Secretary of State was dismissed. K appealed to the High Court, contending that the question of the established use of the site had not been properly addressed.

Held, allowing the appeal, that although an established use on one part of a site could not bring about an established use on the other parts of the site it was incumbent on the inspector to consider whether there was an immune use on a part of the site. The failure to do so amounted to a failure to have regard to a material consideration and the matter would be remitted (*Mansi v. Elstree Rural District Council* [1964] C.L.Y. 3580 applied).

JOHN KENNELLY SALES v. SECRETARY OF STATE FOR THE ENVIRONMENT [1994] 1 PLR 10, Mr Malcolm Spence, Q.C. sitting as a deputy judge.

4770. Change of use—reversion to previous use—industrial land used as agricultural land—reversion to industrial use—whether planning permission required

Where the change of use of industrial land to agricultural does not involve development of the land, the subsequent reversion to industrial use will require planning permission.

Land was originally used industrially and in 1972 was put into cultivation. In 1988 A sought to change it back to industrial use. The planning inspector held that this constituted a change of use for which permission was necessary. A appealed, contending that the former industrial use had never been supplanted.

Held, dismissing the appeal, that the change of use to agricultural was lawful even without permission and the continued use of the land as agricultural land meant that the original industrial use was supplanted. Any new industrial use therefore required permission (*Cynon Valley Borough Council v. Secretary of State for Wales and Oi Mee Lan* [1987] C.L.Y. 3710, *Pioneer Aggregates (U.K.) v. Secretary of State for the Environment* [1984] C.L.Y. 3415, *West Oxfordshire District Council v. Secretary of State for the Environment and Coles* [1988] C.L.Y. 3517, *White v. Secretary of State for the Environment* [1989] C.L.Y. 3569, *Young v. Secretary of State for the Environment* [1983] C.L.Y. 3676 considered).

J.L. ENGINEERING AND JOHN LENNIW v. SECRETARY OF STATE FOR THE ENVIRONMENT AND WARRINGTON BOROUGH COUNCIL (1994) 67 P. & C.R. 354, D.C.

4771. Change of use—use classes—solicitors' offices—services—whether solicitors' offices coming within category

[Town and Country Planning (Use Classes) Order 1987 (S.I. 1987 No. 764).]

K, a solicitor, appealed against the upholding of the dismissal of his appeal against the local planning authority's refusal to grant planning permission for change of use from a shop to a solicitor's office within Class A2 of the Town and Country Planning (Use Classes) Order 1987.

Held, allowing the appeal, that Class A2 required services to be provided "principally for visiting members of the public" and, although some solicitor's offices would definitely not fall within this category because their services were provided almost entirely by way of telephones and correspondence, it was quite feasible that a solicitor wishing to offer advice along the lines of a Citizens' Advice Bureau or a Law Centre, albeit on a profit basis, would fall within Class A2. The existence of an appointments system did not preclude a solicitor's office from qualifying under A2. The difficulties of administering those solicitors who chose to run an A2 office were for the local authority to deal with and should not be a bar to a grant of planning permission.

KALRA v. SECRETARY OF STATE FOR THE ENVIRONMENT, *The Times*, November 13, 1995, C.A.

4772. Conservation area—demolition of bridges—whether replacement structures a material consideration

[Listed Buildings and Conservation Areas Act 1990 (c.9), s.74.]

C was refused permission to demolish and replace two bridges located in a conservation area on the grounds that the replacement structures would not preserve or enhance the character of the area. C appealed arguing that the replacement structure was not a relevant consideration when deciding whether to give consent under s.74 of the Listed Buildings and Conservation Areas Act 1990.

Held, dismissing the appeal, that the nature or appearance of the replacement structures was a relevant matter to be taken into account.

KENT COUNTY COUNCIL v. SECRETARY OF STATE FOR THE ENVIRONMENT AND CANTERBURY CITY COUNCIL [1995] 68 P. & C.R. 520, Mr Gerald Moriarty, Q.C. sitting as a deputy judge.

4773. Conservation area—telecommunications equipment—relay stations—permission refused on basis of alternative sites—whether relevant

[Town and Country Planning Act 1990 (c.8), s.288.]

The BBC and others applied under the Town and Country Planning Act 1990, s.288, to quash a decision of an inspector appointed by the Secretary of State dismissing an appeal against refusal of planning permission within a conservation area for the addition of telecommunications code power operators' equipment at an existing relay station. It was argued that the inspector erred in law by taking into account whether alternative sites could be used. This was an immaterial consideration. He also concluded that the BBC failed to give sufficient consideration to alternative sites. It was further argued that the inspector's decision that increased traffic produced by the site would cause demonstrable harm was perverse.

Held, dismissing the application, that (1) whether a consideration was material should be decided on the facts of the case. It was material that the BBC should have considered alternative sites. The need for avoiding proliferation of sites (which the BBC argued would occur if this site could not be used), did not outweigh the harm caused by allowing permission on the site; (2) the decision was not perverse as it was a matter of fact and degree for the judgment of the inspector on consideration of the evidence of the respondent and representations of local residents.

BRITISH BROADCASTING CORP., VODAPHONE, ORANGE PERSONAL COMMUNICATIONS AND MERCURY PERSONAL COMMUNICATIONS v. SECRETARY OF STATE FOR THE ENVIRONMENT AND BRISTOL CITY COUNCIL (CO/798/95), August 18, 1995, R. Purchas, Q.C.

4774. Crown land applications

TOWN AND COUNTRY PLANNING (CROWN LAND APPLICATIONS) REGULATIONS 1995 (No. 1139) [£1·10], made under the Town and Country Planning

Act 1990 (c.8), ss.299(5), 333(1); operative on June 3, 1995; modify the 1990 Act and S.I. 1995 No. 419 in their application to Crown land.

4775. Development—affordable housing—no site-specific policy making provision for affordable housing—whether need for affordable housing a material consideration capable of outweighing presumption in favour of development in accordance with statutory plan—whether inspector justified in refusing permission

An application had been made by the applicant for planning permission to construct housing near Truro. Outline permission had been granted in 1989. That permission had lapsed but a fresh application was made while the permission was still valid. The district council accepted the principle of the residential development but introduced a requirement that the land be used for "affordable housing". On appeal, the inspector appointed by the Secretary of State considered whether the permission should make provision for affordable housing. The applicant appealed the inspector's decision that the proposal did not contain adequate provision for affordable housing.

Held, dismissing the application, that it was the policy of the Secretary of State to encourage local planning authorities to have regard to the provision of affordable housing. Therefore, the need to provide affordable housing was a consideration which the inspector was justified in bearing in mind in reaching his decision. The inspector had considered all the relevant policies and had decided that the proposal did not contain sufficient provision for affordable housing. The fact that a consideration was located outside the statutory scheme did not mean that it was incapable of having great weight. It was a matter for the inspector's planning judgement even where that extra-statutory factor made unacceptable a proposal which would otherwise have been acceptable. It was not in accordance with this principle that each case should be decided on its own merits (*Mitchell v. Secretary of State for the Environment* [1994] 69 P. & C.R. 60 referred to).

ECC CONSTRUCTION v. SECRETARY OF STATE [1994] 69 P. & C.R. 51, Gerald Moriarty, Q.C. sitting as a deputy judge.

4776. Development—agricultural land—erection of glasshouse—whether sufficient consideration of agricultural unit

L wished to erect a glasshouse on land near his farm and applied to the local authority with details of the building for determination of whether prior approval would be required. The G.D.O. would permit the development if, *inter alia*, it was on land comprised in an agricultural unit and not within 25m of a classified road. L's application was initially rejected on the ground that the building would be within 25m of a road, but when this was shown not to be the case the authority required no further details. P, the owner of adjacent land, sought judicial review on the ground that the authority had failed to give proper consideration to the issue of whether the land was within an agricultural unit. When the glasshouse was erected it was smaller than the specifications given to the council and P also applied for judicial review of the council's decision not to take enforcement action.

Held, granting the applications for judicial review, that the authority had only given cursory attention to the issue of whether the land was "agricultural land", despite a plain legislative intention to the contrary. A planning authority must usually make a detailed inquiry when seeking to determine whether land is comprised within an agricultural unit. As the initial determination was flawed, the premise upon which the decision not to take enforcement action proceeded was falsely based.

R. v. SEVENOAKS DISTRICT COUNCIL, *ex p.* PALLEY [1994] EGCS 148, Tucker J.

4777. Development—competing retail sites for out-of-town superstore—offer to find road—whether a material consideration—whether inspector applying correct policy test

The Secretary of State was not wrong to exclude an offer by a developer to fund a road link to a proposed out-of-town superstore as a material consideration.

Of the three retails stores' applications for permission to build superstores the local planning inquiry report favoured T's application. T had offered to provide funding for a road link. The inspector took account of the offer although it had only a tenuous link to the proposed development and it would have been unreasonable for the council to have made the offer a condition of the development. The Secretary of State disagreed with the inspector and refused T's application, holding that T's offer failed to meet the requirements of Circular 16/91 because the proposed funding was not related in scale or size to the proposed development. The road link was not so directly related to the development site that it was required before they could go ahead and, because the offer did not satisfy the terms of the Circular, it could not amount to a reason for granting or refusing an application. The High Court quashed the decision-holding that the offer of funding was a material factor that should have been taken into account by the Secretary of State.

Held, allowing the Secretary of State's appeal, that the Secretary of State had not erred in excluding the offer as a material consideration. The offer was not for a planning purpose and was not connected to the proposed development site. If the planning benefits were off-site as in the present case then the degree of connection with the land was a factor that determined the materiality of the offer. Furthermore the weight to be given to a particular consideration was a matter for the Secretary of State. Having considered the offer the Secretary of State was entitled to attach no weight to it (*R. v. Plymouth City Council, ex p. Plymouth and South Devon Co-operative Society* [1993] C.L.Y. 3936 followed).

TESCO v. SECRETARY OF STATE FOR THE ENVIRONMENT AND WEST OXFORDSHIRE DISTRICT COUNCIL AND TARMAC PROVINCIAL PROPERTIES (1994) 68 P.& C.R. 219, C.A.

4778. Development—contrary to development plan—approach when considering plan and proposed development—development plan requirements overtaken by events—whether departure from plan must be spelled out

[Town and Country Planning Act 1990 (c.8), s.54A.]

An inspector was not required expressly to spell out any departure from a development plan where it was obvious that the development plan had been overtaken by events.

The inspector allowed L's appeal and granted permission for the development of the land for use as a petrol station. He stated that the land use requirements of the original statutory development plan had been overtaken by events and that there was no overriding land use objection to the development even though the plan did not include a petrol station. The council sought to have the decision quashed on the grounds that the inspector had failed properly to apply s.54A of the 1990 Act.

Held, dismissing the application, that it was evident from the outset that the appeal scheme did not conform with the requirements of the development plan but the inspector had concluded that the land use proposals in the plan had been overtaken by events and he was entitled to reach such a decision. He had given reasons why he did not regard any conflict between the appeal proposals and the plan as determinative of the appeal. Although it should be made clear in a decision whether the proposal was being treated as being in compliance with the development plan there was no requirement that such indication had to be spelled out in express terms (*St. Albans District Council v. Secretary of State for the Environment and Allied Breweries* [1993] C.L.Y. 3945 applied).

SPELTHORNE BOROUGH COUNCIL v. SECRETARY OF STATE FOR THE

ENVIRONMENT (1994) 68 P. & C.R. 211, Mr David Keene, Q.C. sitting as a deputy judge.

4779. Development—council rejected recommendation in proposed modifications to plan—whether adequate reasons—council's decision not to hold a further inquiry—whether unreasonable—whether breach of legitimate expectation

[Town and Country (Structure and Local Plans) Regulations 1982 (S.I. 1982 No. 555), regs. 29, 31.]

A owned land which was identified in the local plan as a site for future housing development, to be phased in over time. Following a local planning inquiry, the inspector recommended bringing forward development of the site. R2 council rejected the inspector's recommendation in proposed modifications to plan which did not bring forward the development of As' land. R2 refused to re-open the inquiry and gave their reasons as being "other factors have been taken into account". The matter went before the Planning and Development Committee which recommended that there be a second inquiry but then withdrew that recommendation. The issue arose whether R2 had given adequate reasons and whether there was a breach of As' legitimate expectation that there would be a second inquiry.

Held, dismissing the application, that the reasons given by R2 were adequate and intelligible, since there was cross-reference to a number of background documents. However they could be criticised for lack of clarity. The resolution of April 1993 did give rise to legitimate expectations by means of an express promise that there would be a second inquiry. The second decision not hold an inquiry was therefore invalid because it did not give objectors an opportunity to be heard before the overturning of the earlier resolution. Notwithstanding the breach of legitimate expectation, A had not suffered any substantial prejudice as their objections had been made in writing and had been considered (*British Railways Board v. Slough Borough Council* [1994] C.L.Y. 4349, *Council of Civil Service Unions v. Minister for the Civil Service* [1985] C.L.Y. 12 referred to).

PELHAM HOMES v. SECRETARY OF STATE FOR THE ENVIRONMENT AND RUNNYMEDE BOROUGH COUNCIL [1994] 69 P. & C.R. 64, David Widdicombe, Q.C. sitting as a deputy judge.

4780. Development—drive-through restaurant—refusal on highway grounds—council adapted roundabout analysis programme ARCADY—little weight—costs not awarded

[Town and Country Planning Act 1990 (c.8), s.78.]

M appealed against the non-determination of an application for a drive-through restaurant. The council argued that there would be unacceptable congestion on the adjacent roundabout unless it was signalised, relying on the results from adapting the ARCADY analysis programme for the whole roundabout and a higher percentage of new trips than M accepted.

Held, allowing the appeal, that (1) the development would not materially prejudice the free flow of traffic; (2) the percentage of new trips did not matter, since the maximum flow would be only 120 vehicles on a roundabout where the flow was 5,000 vehicles and the maximum delay would be 0.5 seconds per vehicle at peak flows; (3) it would not be safe to attach significant weight to the ARCADY results, due to the cumulative effect of the assumptions made; (4) signalisation was almost certain to occur in any event; and (5) costs were not awarded, as the council had not acted unreasonably in using ARCADY, and had provided substantial evidence at the inquiry.

HOUNSLOW LONDON BOROUGH COUNCIL v. MCDONALDS RESTAURANTS (Ref: T/APP/F5540/A/93/23041P5) (1994) 9 P.A.D. 598.

4781. Development—gliding club—harm to rural character of locality

[Town and Country Planning Act 1990 (c.8), s.78.]

E applied to develop existing permitted facilities at a gliding airfield in the countryside, to add buildings and change the use of land to include gliding with light aircraft support.

Held, dismissing the appeal, that (1) the introduction of substantial built structures would cause demonstrable harm to the rural character and appearance of the locality, contrary to development plan policy; (2) the significant intensification of flying activity would cause unacceptable levels of noise and disturbance to local residents and would affect the positive recreational value of the countryside; and (3) the level of occupiers' privacy would not be significantly reduced.

BRAINTREE DISTRICT COUNCIL v. ESSEX GLIDING CLUB (Ref: T/APP/Z1510/A/93/431692/P5) (1994) 9 P.A.D. 646.

4782. Development—land informally used as open space—permission for development granted—presumption in favour of development—whether onus of proof on those objecting to development

Paragraph 15 of PPG 1 (1988) envisaged a presumption in favour of development and not in favour of the developer and so it was wrong to impose an onus of proof on those objecting to a development.

The borough council, C, sought to buy a piece of land from the county council, D, with a view to making it available for public use. The land was already informally used as open space by the general public. No agreement could be reached and D sold the land to B subject to the grant of planning permission. The inspector granted B planning permission, allowing the appeal from the refusal of C. C sought to have the decision quashed but the deputy judge held that the inspector's finding that the land would not be put to use as public open space if the development was refused could not be challenged.

Held, allowing C's appeal, that it would be wrong to place a burden of proof on objectors to a proposed development and that was not what was envisaged by para. 15 of PPG 1. The inspector's decision could not be challenged on that point but he had erred in failing fully to deal with the use of the land if the permission was not granted. He had ignored the *de facto* use of the land as public open space which was a material matter.

CHRISTCHURCH BOROUGH COUNCIL v. SECRETARY OF STATE FOR THE ENVIRONMENT (1993) (1994) 68 P. & C.R. 116, C.A.

4783. Development—material considerations—applications for development of motorists' service area—rival sites—whether planning merits of other applications a material consideration—criteria for materiality

Failure by the inspector to take into consideration other possible sites for a motor service area was a failure to consider material matters.

E sought permission to develop his land as a motorists' service area, there being an acknowledged need for one such area along the A47 trunk road. Six other applications had been made for similar permissions in respect of different sites. All applications were refused. E appealed to the Secretary of State and elected for a public inquiry. R also appealed but elected the written representations procedure. Requests to consider all of the appeals together or to have them all considered by the same inspector were rejected. R's appeal was allowed but E applied to quash the decision on the basis that the inspector had failed to take into account the merits of the rival applications which were material matters. The High Court granted E's application, quashed the decision and remitted the matter to the Secretary of State who appealed.

Held, dismissing the appeal, that the other possible sites and the applications in respect of those sites were material considerations and should have been taken into account. Had that been done a different decision may have been given.

SECRETARY OF STATE FOR THE ENVIRONMENT v. EDWARDS; *sub nom.* EDWARDS (P.G.) v. SECRETARY OF STATE FOR THE ENVIRONMENT AND ROADSIDE DEVELOPMENTS AND BRECKLAND DISTRICT COUNCIL (1994) 1 PLR 62, C.A.

4784. Development—material considerations—out-of-town superstore—link road—developer's offer of full funding for link road—whether a material consideration—whether sufficient weight given to consideration

[Town and Country Planning Act 1990 (c.8), ss.70(2), 106 (as substituted by the Planning and Compensation Act 1991 (c.34), s.12).]

If a planning obligation has some connection with a proposed development it is a "material consideration" when considering whether planning permission should be granted and regard must be had to it. The weight that the material consideration should be given is a question of planning judgement within the exclusive providence of the local planning authority or Secretary of State.

Two developers, T and P, applied for planning permission to build superstores outside the town centre. P's application was not determined within the statutory period. On P's appeal to the Secretary of State for the Environment, T's application was called in also. The inspector had recommended that the council should negotiate the funding of a link road with T and P. T later offered to fund the link road fully and entered into an agreement with the council to do so under s.106 of the Town and Country Planning Act 1990. The inspector recommended that T's application be granted and P's be dismissed. The Secretary of State issued a decision letter dismissing the inspector's recommendations and T's application and allowed P's appeal. T applied to the High Court where the deputy judge quashed the Secretary of State's letter, saying that the Secretary of State had not treated T's planning obligation to fund the road as a material consideration. The Court of Appeal allowed P's appeal.

Held, dismissing T's appeal, that a planning obligation under s.106 of the Town and Country Planning Act 1990 was a "material consideration" within the meaning of s.70(2) of the Town and Country Planning Act 1990. Here, although the link between the road and the development was slight, it was relevant. However, it could not be said that the Secretary of State had failed to have regard to the planning obligation or had treated it as immaterial, but had merely declined to give it any, or significant, weight. It was entirely for the decision-maker to attribute to the relevant considerations such weight as he thought fit, and the court would not interfere unless the decision-maker had acted unreasonably in the *Wednesbury* sense (*Hall & Co. v. Shoreham-by-Sea Urban District Council* [1964] C.L.Y. 3600, *Newbury District Council v. Secretary of State for the Environment* [1980] C.L.Y. 2667, *R. v. Plymouth City Council, ex p. Plymouth and South Devon Co-operative Society* [1993] C.L.Y. 3936 considered).

TESCO STORES v. SECRETARY OF STATE FOR THE ENVIRONMENT [1995] 1 W.L.R. 759, H.L.

4785. Development—open-cast coal mine—refusal—World Heritage Site—Hadrian's Wall military zone—inspector recommending granting permission—Secretary of State disagreeing and reaching different decision—adequate reasons—whether finding of fact

[Town and Country Planning (Inquiries Procedure) Rules 1988 (S.I. 1988 No. 944.]

C sought permission to carry out open-cast coal mining at a site that lay within an area of great landscape value and was visible from the line of Hadrian's Wall, a scheduled ancient monument as well as being within the curtilage of a World Heritage Site. The principal objection at the public inquiry was the visual impact of the mine and the inspector concluded that the mine would be visible but that the intrusion would be minimal and he recommended that the appeal should be allowed. The Secretary of State disagreed on the ground that insufficient weight had been given to the impact of the proposal on the setting of Hadrian's Wall. He dismissed the appeal. C challenged the decision.

Held, dismissing the application, that the Secretary of State had given clear and adequate reasons for disagreeing with his inspector. That disagreement was not on a question of fact but on a matter of opinion. It was accepted that the mine was visible, the disagreement lay in the impact that resulted from that. Where there was such a disagreement of opinion it was permissible for the reasons to be shortly stated. There had been no breach of the procedural rules laid down in the Town and Country Planning (Inquiries Procedure) Rules 1988 by reason of the fact that the parties had not been given an opportunity to make further representations because the finding of opinion made by the Secretary of State was outside the scope of the rule in question.

COAL CONTRACTORS v. SECRETARY OF STATE FOR THE ENVIRONMENT AND NORTHUMBERLAND COUNTY COUNCIL (1994) 68 P. & C.R. 285, Mr David Keene, Q.C. sitting as a deputy judge.

4786. Development—out-of-town superstore—whether site adjacent to town centre to be given priority—whether decision made on a misunderstanding of planning policy

Where there is a prospect of a development which will meet a priority need, the authority is justified in refusing planning permission to a rival enterprise.

T applied for permission to build a superstore outside Gloucester. The Gloucestershire Structure Plan had identified a different site within the city as appropriate for such a store, and S, a supermarket company, intended to build one there. S stated that it would pull out if T were given permission to proceed. The Structure Plan gave priority to meeting retail needs in Gloucester. T appealed against the refusal of permission.

Held, dismissing the appeal, that the Structure Plan allowed priority to be given to the proposed development by S, and this was sufficient grounds for refusing T permission.

CARTER COMMERCIAL DEVELOPMENTS v. SECRETARY OF STATE FOR THE ENVIRONMENT [1995] 69 P. & C.R. 359, Latham J.

4787. Development—permitted development—proposed development within prohibited distance from main road—whether within permitted development exemptions

Where the General Development Order does not specifically grant permission, the matter is entirely open for the planning authority to consider all the issues that arise in making its decision.

P appealed against the refusal of planning permission for a large poultry house which was within 25 metres away from a road, arguing that the GDO created a presumption in favour of the development, despite the fact that exceptions were made (from the general presumption in favour of development) for buildings within that distance from a road.

Held, dismissing the appeal, that there was no need to try to look at the reasoning behind the 25-metre exclusion; the building was not within a category of development permitted by the GDO.

PEACOCK v. SECRETARY OF STATE FOR THE ENVIRONMENT [1995] 69 P. & C.R. 388, C.A.

4788. Development—repair—derelict building—enforcement notice against reconstruction—whether works of renovation or repair—whether existing use rights abandoned

A bought a derelict bungalow which had not been occupied for 30 years and started working on it. An enforcement notice was issued against A and he contended that the work was renovation or repair, not rebuilding, as the council saw it. The council also decided that there had been virtual abandonment of the residential use of the site and that A could not be allowed to pre-empt any decision on planning permission. The inspector refused A's appeal against the enforcement notice and stated that A's reliance on the exemption from the definition of development contained in the Town and Country Planning Act 1990, s.55(2)(a) could not succeed, as the work being done on the bungalow was reconstruction and was therefore beyond the scope of the section.

Held, dismissing A's appeal, that (1) it was irrelevant to the decision under s.55 whether or not the building was a dwelling-house; (2) the inspector was under no obligation to consider the GDO principles involved as it was not his role to see whether A's case could be improved by applying different considerations.

HUGHES v. SECRETARY OF STATE FOR THE ENVIRONMENT [1994] EGCS 86, Mr Malcolm Spence, Q.C.

4789. Development—residential development—proposal not in accordance with development plan—whether planning authority applied the correct test in granting permission—whether decision to grant permission was flawed on the ground of bias or otherwise unlawful

[Town and Country Planning Act 1990 (c.8), s.54A.]

S objected to planning permission being granted to P for residential development of land adjoining S's land. S also owned two alternative potential sites for residential development. SDC granted planning permission to P for residential housing development in 1992 partially on the basis that they considered that there might be a need for extra housing. This proposal was not in accordance with the local development plan. SDC made a second award of planning permission for residential development and a northern access road in 1994. S brought an action for judicial review to challenge the grant of planning permission on the grounds that the planning authority had not applied the correct test in granting permission consistently with s.54A of the Town and Country Planning Act 1990, it ought to have considered the need for further housing and the decision to grant permission was flawed on the ground of bias or otherwise unlawful.

Held, that (1) the 1994 decision had not been shown to be unlawful or otherwise susceptible to judicial review. However, the 1992 decision had been reached upon a materially inadequate consideration of the need for the proposed housing in conflict with the terms of the development plan. The question of the need for housing was a planning judgement and there was a rational basis upon which the decision that there was a need for more housing could have been reached in 1994. SDC had been properly advised about the effect of s.54A and the planning officer's report had identified the need for the proposed housing as being an exceptional circumstance under HSG 5. The case for bias was without foundation. It was no criticism of the planning officer's report that the words of that report lead to the conclusion which it propounded. The 1994 decision was not otherwise unlawful. The questions raised against the planning permission were of planning judgement; (2) the 1992 decisions could not stand because the meeting on the planning application failed to consider critical terms of the development plan. The planning report did not give proper consideration to the question whether there was a need for the residential development. It was not sufficient that the meeting had experience of the issues surrounding local development where there was no evidence of discussion relating to the requirement of the extra housing. It was not possible therefore that the committee had understood the objections to the development.

R. v. SELBY DISTRICT COUNCIL, *ex p.* SAMUEL SMITH OLD BREWERY (1995) 70 P. & C.R. 250, May J.

4790. Development—residential development—unilateral undertaking—establishment of nature conservation area—visual amenity—whether harm caused to an ecological unit

[Town and Country Planning Act 1990 (c.8), s.78.]

W applied for residential development on 3.78 hectares and offered a unilateral undertaking to provide a nature conservation area with a detailed scheme of management on 1.37 hectares. The appeal site was part of an ecological unit of some 13 hectares, and was seen as part of a green wedge, providing visual relief from the built-up urban surroundings.

Held, dismissing the appeal, that (1) the scale and location of the proposals would have a serious detrimental effect on the visual amenities of the locality; (2) the site was a "green field site" of notable environmental quality and value to the local community; (3) the harm was not outweighed by the desirability of providing housing within existing urban areas or the potential benefits of the undertaking; (4) the positive nature conservation benefits of the undertaking were not assured as there was a lack of a defined and enforceable commitment of resources to a definite time schedule; however (5), the development would not have unduly harmed the ecological interest of the locality nor have reduced the overall size of the unit below any important ecological threshold.

WORCESTER CITY COUNCIL v. WORCESTER CONSOLIDATED MUNICIPAL CHARITY (Ref: T/APP/D1835/A/94/234623/P2) (1994) 9 P.A.D. 723.

4791. Development—wind turbines—renewable energy issue—balance with the need to protect the countryside—effects on visual and residential amenity—effect of combined proposals—whether turbines would dominate outlook unacceptably

[Town and Country Planning Act 1990 (c.8), s.78.]

The council refused W's proposals to erect two wind farms and associated development of nine wind turbines and 14 turbines respectively, near to each other on high, exposed ground. Although the landscape had neither local or national protection status, it was of high quality, visually unspoiled by high silos or tall masts. W held contracts under the Second Non-Fossil Fuel Obligation Order (NFFO) for the two proposals.

Held, dismissing the appeal, that (1) the protection of the countryside must be carefully weighed against the need to develop renewable energy; (2) neither proposal was in accordance with the development plan, but the renewable energy issue was an important material consideration; (3) the merits of the NFFO policy were not open to question having been settled by the making of the Order; (4) although wind turbines generated only small amounts of electricity, any contribution to reducing CO_2 emissions was of significance and benefit; (5) whilst the greatest importance should be attached to the need to reduce emissions, W's proposals were amongst many measures which would help in achieving that national policy aim; (6) both proposals in combination would have an effect greater than the sum of the parts; (7) the visual effects of both wind farms would cause unacceptable harm to the attractive local landscape and affect middle distance views; (8) although each turbine was sensitively designed, Groups of nine, 14 or 23 such machines lose those qualities as the eye becomes confused by the number, size and insistent movement; (9) the turbines' presence would unacceptably dominate the outlook of nearby properties and would seriously harm residential amenity; (10) there was a risk of sleep disturbance at nearby houses, as there would be significant increase in noise levels could be expected; and (11) since the turbines would provide employment and could attract visitors, the effect on the local tourist economy was finely-balanced.

NORTH DEVON DISTRICT COUNCIL v. WEST COAST WIND FARMS (Refs: T/APP/X1118/A/93/231441–2/P6) (1994) 9 P.A.D. 822.

4792. Development corporations

BRISTOL DEVELOPMENT CORPORATION (AREA AND CONSTITUTION) ORDER 1995 (No. 3269), made under the Local Government, Planning and Land Act 1980 ss.134, 135, Sched. 26, para. 1. operative on January 1, 1996; [65p]. The Bristol Development Corporation (Area and Constitution) Order 1988, which designated the Bristol urban development area and established the Bristol Development Corporation, is revoked by this Order. Articles 2 and 3 are revoked from January 1, 1996 and the remainder from April 1, 1996.

BRISTOL DEVELOPMENT CORPORATION (DISSOLUTION) ORDER 1995 (No. 3323), made under the Local Government, Planning and Land Act 1980 s.166. In force: January 1, 1996; [65p]. The Bristol Development Corporation will cease to act on January 1, 1996 except for the winding up of its affairs and preparing its final accounts and will be dissolved on April 1, 1996.

BRISTOL DEVELOPMENT CORPORATION (PLANNING FUNCTIONS) ORDER 1995 (No. 2899) [65p], made under the Local Government, Planning and Land Act 1980, ss.148(2), 149(1)(3)(11) and the Town and Country Planning Act 1990, ss.59, 333(7); revokes S.I. 1989 Nos. 93, 2205; operative on December 18, 1995; makes transitional provisions in connection with the transfer of planning functions from the Bristol Development Corporation to the councils of the City of Bristol and the County of Avon.

BRISTOL DEVELOPMENT CORPORATION (TRANSFER OF PROPERTY, RIGHTS AND LIABILITIES) ORDER 1995 (No. 2900) [65p], made under the Local Government, Planning and Land Act 1980, s.165A; operative on December 19, 1995; transfers to the Secretary of State any residual property, rights and liabilities of the Bristol Development Corporation. It is proposed that the Bristol Development Corporation will be dissolved on April 1, 1996.

LEEDS DEVELOPMENT CORPORATION (AREA AND CONSTITUTION) ORDER 1995 (No. 916) [65p], made under the Local Government, Planning and Land Act 1980 (c.65), ss.134, 135, Sched. 26, para. 1; operative on April 1, 1995; revokes S.I. 1988 No. 1145.

LEEDS DEVELOPMENT CORPORATION (DISSOLUTION) ORDER 1995 (No. 966) [65p], made under the Local Government, Planning and Land Act 1980 (c.65), s.166; operative on April 1, 1995; dissolves the said Corporation.

LEEDS DEVELOPMENT CORPORATION (PLANNING FUNCTIONS) ORDER 1995 (No. 389) [£1·10], made under the Local Government, Planning and Land Act 1980 (c.65), ss.148(2), 149(1)(3)(11) and the Town and Country Planning Act 1990 (c.8), ss.59, 333(4)(7); operative on March 30, 1995; revokes S.I. 1988 No. 1551 and S.I. 1989 No. 2206 and makes transitional provisions in connection with the transfer of planning functions from the Leeds Development Corporation to the Leeds City Council.

LEEDS DEVELOPMENT CORPORATION (TRANSFER OF PROPERTY, RIGHTS AND LIABILITIES) ORDER 1995 (No. 390) [65p], made under the Local Government, Planning and Land Act 1980 (c.65), s.165A; operative on March 31, 1995; vests in the Secretary of State any residual property, rights or liabilities of the Leeds Development Corporation.

LONDON DOCKLANDS DEVELOPMENT CORPORATION (ALTERATION OF BOUNDARIES) ORDER 1995 (No. 3098) [£1·95], made under the Local Government, Planning and Land Act 1980, s.134(3A)(5). In force: December 31, 1995; removes an area of the London Borough of Newham comprising approximately 324.5 hectares from the London Docklands urban development area and contains transitional provisions concerning powers, liability for compensation and planning functions of the development corporation in that area. The council of the London Borough of Newham becomes the local planning authority for the excluded area. A map showing the excluded area is attached.

4793. Enforcement notice—appeal—costs—consent as to siting of crusher—further consent relating to works—challenge as to effect of second consent on first—whether Secretary of State entitled to costs

R sought leave to appeal against a decision of the planning inspectorate that a concrete crushing machine could only be sited within a prescribed area of land. A consent was obtained in 1984 which permitted the siting of the crusher on the land for use only in connection with the backfilling of quarry land. A further consent in 1985 permitted the siting of a spoil heap in connection with the crusher and the re-exportation of the crushed material from the site. R argued that the 1985 consent allowed him to locate the crusher outside the site.

Held, dismissing the application for leave, that (1) the 1985 consent was ancillary to the 1984 consent and so the restriction in the 1984 consent limiting the crusher's use to the prescribed area remained. The inspector's finding was not fundamentally flawed; (2) costs would be awarded in favour of the Secretary of State because the application amounted to an opposed *ex parte* hearing and the Minister's participation was appropriate and necessary (*R. v. Secretary of State for Wales, ex p. Rozhon* [1994] C.L.Y. 3558 considered).

RANDALL v. SECRETARY OF STATE FOR THE ENVIRONMENT AND BUCKINGHAMSHIRE COUNTY COUNCIL (CO/1721/93), April 3, 1995, Sedley J.

4794. Enforcement notice—appeal—jurisdiction to grant leave to appeal

[Supreme Court Act 1981 (c.54), s.1(1); Town and Country Planning Act 1990 (c.8), s.289(6).]

H applied for leave to appeal from the High Court's refusal to grant leave, as required by s.289(6) of the Town and Country Planning Act 1990 as amended, against a decision of the Secretary of State on an enforcement notice appeal.

Held, dismissing the application, that there was nothing in s.289(6) of the 1990 Act as amended, or in s.1(1) of the Supreme Court Act 1981, which gave the Court of Appeal jurisdiction (*Bland v. Chief Supplementary Benefit Officer* [1983] C.L.Y. 3482, *Geogas SA v. Trimmo Gas* [1991] C.L.Y. 3505 considered).

HUGGETT v. SECRETARY OF STATE FOR THE ENVIRONMENT; WENDY FAIR MARKETS v. SAME; BELLO v. SAME, *The Times*, March 1, 1995, C.A.

4795. Enforcement notice—appeal—unauthorised use—individual enforcement notices served on buildings within a complex of former farm buildings—whether inspector committing an error of law in treating the separate sites as forming a composite application

[Town and Country Planning Act 1990 (c.8), ss.174, 177.]

Where a planning inspector hears appeals against individual enforcement notices relating to separate sites on the same piece of land, he should consider each individually and not treat them as a composite application for planning permission.

B and others occupied buildings within a complex of former farm buildings. Each building was served with an individual enforcement notice requiring the cessation of unauthorised commercial use. B and the other occupiers appealed, arguing that the inspector had committed an error of law in treating the separate sites as forming a composite application rather than treating them on their individual merits.

Held, that the inspector had fallen into an error of law in treating the five separate sites together and had not applied ss.174 and 177 of the Town and Country Planning Act 1990 correctly. The wording of those provisions provided a plain duty on an inspector considering separate appeals against enforcement notices to treat each one as a deemed application for planning permission and to treat each application individually and on its planning merits. Had the inspector dealt with each application individually, he would have been entitled to take into account that a precedent might be set for other applications by allowing any individual permission and that the cumulative effect was that each application should be refused. However, it was not sufficient to treat the applications as a composite application and then to consider them individually as an afterthought. Each case should be considered on its merits in the first place.

BRUSCHWEILLER v. SECRETARY OF STATE FOR THE ENVIRONMENT AND CHELMSFORD BOROUGH COUNCIL (1995) 70 P. & C.R. 150, R.M.K. Gray, Q.C.

4796. Enforcement notice—appeal—unauthorised window—removal required—appeal by way of written representations—new issue raised by inspector in dismissing the appeal—whether breach of natural justice

[Town and Country Planning (Appeals) (Written Representations Procedure) Regulations 1987 (S.I. 1987 No. 701), reg. 9.]

Town and Country Planning (Appeals) (Written Representations Procedure) Regulations 1987, reg. 9, does not define the matters that the Secretary of State can lawfully take into account when determining an appeal by written representations.

A block of flats was erected and included a dormer window on one flat contrary to the terms of the planning permission. G bought the flat and was then served with an enforcement notice requiring the removal of the window. He appealed by way of written representations to the Secretary of State and offered to install a fixed window with frosted glass. The inspector dismissed the appeal and held that the proposed condition offered by G would be unenforceable. G sought to quash the decision, arguing that there had been a breach of natural justice and a breach of reg. 9 of the 1987 Regulations by raising a new issue that G had not been given the opportunity to address. The High Court dismissed the application.

Held, dismissing G's appeal, that reg. 9 gave the Secretary of State the authority to determine an appeal taking into account only written representations and supporting documents. The regulation did not define the matters that he could lawfully take into account. There had been no breach of the principles of natural justice because the issue was the intrusiveness of the window and the inspector's decision on this issue was a proper one. He was entitled to have regard to the question of enforcement when considering the proposed condition.

GEHA v. SECRETARY OF STATE FOR THE ENVIRONMENT (1993) (1994) 68 P. & C.R. 139, C.A.

4797. Enforcement notice—appeal procedure—supporting documents not filed until a later date—whether appeal made

[R.S.C., Ord. 94, r.12(2)(c).]

The local authority issued an enforcement notice against W who sought to appeal. The application form for leave to appeal was lodged within the 28-day period together with the draft originating motion but the affidavit verifying the facts was not sworn until some six weeks later. W argued that the application had been "made" within the 28-day period.

Held, refusing W's application for leave to appeal, that there was no authority for the proper construction of the "making" of an application under R.S.C., Ord. 94, r.12(2)(c). However, it was not simply filling in a form but required certain steps, including service, in order to constitute an application. Therefore, the application was not "made" within 28 days because of its discrepancies.

WENMAN v. SECRETARY OF STATE FOR THE ENVIRONMENT [1994] EGCS 100, Mr David Keene, Q.C.

4798. Enforcement notice—estoppel—caravans on site—letter from planning officer stating that no permission needed—whether s.53 determination—whether authority estopped from issuing enforcement notice

[Town and Country Planning Act 1971 (c.78), s.53.]

A owned land occupied by caravans. The local planning authority issued an enforcement notice alleging breach of planning control by use of land without planning permission as a caravan site. A appealed, relying on a letter from the planning authority's enforcement officer which had been written before A purchased the land. The letter stated that it had been agreed that planning permission would not be required for the stationing of caravans on the land. The inspector allowed A's appeal on the ground that the letter amounted to a determination within s.53 of the Town and Country Planning Act 1971 which estopped the authority from issuing an enforcement notice. The authority appealed.

Held, dismissing the appeal, that the inspector had been entitled to conclude that the planning authority had delegated the power to make the s.53 determination to its officer, and that the decision could not be revoked.

EAST LINDSEY DISTRICT COUNCIL v. SECRETARY OF STATE FOR THE ENVIRONMENT [1994] EGCS 119, Nigel Macleod, Q.C., sitting as a deputy judge.

4799. Enforcement notice—failure to comply—compensation order—necessity to establish or quantify loss, damage or personal injury arising from offence

[Town and Country Planning Act 1990 (c.8), s.179(1).]

B pleaded guilty to non-compliance with an enforcement notice contrary to the Town and Country Planning Act 1990, s.179(1). He failed to demolish two extensions to his house which had been erected without planning consent. B was sentenced to pay compensation to six of the occupiers of adjacent properties in the amount of £300 each, and ordered to pay £1,700 towards the prosecution's costs.

Held, that there was no evidence that four of the neighbours had suffered any loss. One neighbour was alleged to have suffered a loss of privacy, but no one was living in B's house during the relevant period. Another neighbour might have suffered some loss of light but there no evidence on which the loss of light could be quantified. This was not a simple straightforward case where the amount of compensation could be readily ascertained; compensation orders were not appropriate and they would be quashed in view of B's financial circumstances. A conditional discharge was substituted. The order for costs would remain (*R. v. Donovan* (1981) 3 Cr.App.R.(S.) 192 considered).

R. v. BRISCOE [1994] 15 Cr.App.R.(S.) 699, C.A.

4800. Enforcement notice—failure to comply—whether notice effective—judicial review

[Town and Country Planning Act 1990 (c.8), s.179.]

W was charged with not complying with an enforcement notice within the required period under the Town and Country Planning Act 1990, s.179(2) of which stated that an owner of land who was in breach of an enforcement notice would be guilty of an offence. W appealed against conviction and challenged the issue of the notice on the ground of perversity, irrelevant matters and bad faith.

Held, dismissing the appeal, that so long as the enforcement notice was not defective, it would remain an enforcement notice until it was quashed. A criminal court did not have the power to quash an enforcement notice and the decision to issue it could not be challenged on the grounds of perversity under the *Wednesbury* principle (*Wednesbury Corp. v. Associated Provincial Picture Houses* [1948] 1 K.B. 223). W should ask for the adjournment of the trial in order to apply for judicial review of the decision to issue the notice. The time-limit in such a case would normally be extended.

R. v. WICKS, *The Times*, April 19, 1995, C.A.

4801. Enforcement notice—limitation period—replacement notices issued after implementation of 10-year limitation period—whether replacement notices related to breaches since 1963 or to breaches within 10-year limitation period

[Town and Country Planning Act 1990 (c.8), s.171B.]

H council issued enforcement notices relating to land used principally for industrial purposes which was being used without authorisation for car-breaking, the sale of spare parts and associated storage. Part of the land was used for car-breaking from a date after the end of 1963 but more than 10 years before the issue of the original enforcement notices in 1992. The enforcement notices were withdrawn and replacement notices issued in August 1993 under s.171B(4) of the Town and Country Planning Act 1990. The issue arose as to whether the replacement enforcement notices were governed by the 1963 limitation period or by the 10-year limitation period under s.171B(3).

Held, remitting the case to the Secretary of State, that as from July 27, 1992, enforcement notices could only be issued on the basis of the 10-year limitation period proposed by s.171B(3). A distinction must be made between a breach of planning control and the limitation period applying to an enforcement action in respect of such a breach. The breach of planning control alleged under the "second bite" enforcement notice issued under s.171B(4) must be the same breach as that alleged in the previous defective notice. However, it could not be a change of use since 1963 because this would be contrary to the express provisions of s.171B(3).

WILLIAM BOYER (TRANSPORT) v. SECRETARY OF STATE FOR THE ENVIRONMENT AND HOUNSLOW LONDON BOROUGH COUNCIL (1995) 69 P. & C.R. 630, Jeremy Sullivan, Q.C.

4802. Enforcement notice—service—use of land in contravention of—whether necessary to prove service—whether offence requires *mens rea*

[Town and Country Planning Act 1971 (c.78), s.89(5).]

A were charged with using land in breach of agreement notices, contrary to s.89(5) of Town and Country Planning Act 1971. The notices had been issued in 1979 in respect of business activities being carried on there unlawfully by others, including the owner of the land. In 1990, a site inspection revealed A carrying on business in breach of the enforcement notices. At trial, A submitted that the enforcement notice should have been served on the owner of the land under s.87 and there was no evidence that it had and that the offence under s.89(5) required proof of *mens rea* and proof of knowledge of the enforcement notice was not established by an entry on the land charges register. The judge having rejected the submissions, A changed their pleas to guilty and appealed.

Held, dismissing the appeals, that (1) s.243(1) precluded the questioning of the validity of an enforcement notice except by way of an appeal under s.88(1). Failure to serve a notice did not render it a nullity (*McDaid v. Clydebank District Council* [1984] C.L.Y. 3422 distinguished; *R. v. Mayor of London Borough of Greenwich, ex p. Patel* [1986] C.L.Y. 3271 applied); (2) the presumption that proof of *mens rea* was required could be displaced. Section 243(2) provided an opportunity to challenge an enforcement notice by those who did not know it had been served and demonstrated that s.89(5) was an absolute offence which did not require proof of knowledge or *mens rea* (*Brend v. Wood* (1946) 175 LT 306, *Gammon v. Att.-Gen. of Hong Kong* [1984] C.L.Y. 951, *Sweet v. Parsley* [1969] C.L.Y. 2210, *Wrekin District Council v. Shah* [1985] C.L.Y. 1608 considered).

R. v. COLLETT; SAME v. FURMINGER; SAME v. NAZARI; SAME v. POPE; SAME v. BANDARI [1994] Crim.L.R. 607, C.A.

4803. Enterprise zones

DEARNE VALLEY ENTERPRISE ZONES (DESIGNATION) ORDER 1995 (No. 2624) [£1·55], made under the Local Government, Planning and Land Act 1980, Sched. 32, para. 5; operative on November 3, 1995; designates six areas, three in Barnsley, two in Rotherham and one in Doncaster, which have been subject to enterprise zone schemes as enterprise zones for a period of 10 years.

EAST DURHAM ENTERPRISE ZONES (DESIGNATION) ORDER 1995 (No. 2812) [£1·95], made under the Local Government, Planning and Land Act 1980, Sched. 32, para. 5; operative on November 29, 1995; designates six zones located in the district of Easington, which have been subject to enterprise zone schemes, as enterprise zones. The designation is effective for 10 years. Maps are attached.

EAST MIDLANDS ENTERPRISE ZONES (ASHFIELD) (DESIGNATION) ORDER 1995 (No. 2758) [£1·10], made under the Local Government, Planning and Land Act 1980, Sched. 32, para. 5; operative on November 21, 1995; designates an area located between the M1 and the A611 in Ashfield which has been the subject of the East Midlands Enterprise Zone No. 7 Scheme as an enterprise zone. The designation will have effect for 10 years. A plan of the enterprise zone area is attached to the S.I.

EAST MIDLANDS ENTERPRISE ZONES (BASSETLAW) (DESIGNATION) ORDER 1995 (No. 2738) [£1.10], made under the Local Government, Planning and Land Act 1980, Sched. 32, para. 5; operative on November 16, 1995, designates an area as an enterprise zone.

EAST MIDLANDS ENTERPRISE ZONES (MANSFIELD) (DESIGNATION) ORDER 1995 (No. 2260) [£1.10], made under the Local Government, Planning and Land Act 1980, Sched. 32, para. 5; operative on September 22, 1995, designates an area as an enterprise zone

EAST MIDLANDS ENTERPRISE ZONES (NORTH EAST DERBYSHIRE) (DESIGNATION) ORDER 1995 (No. 2625) [£1·10], made under the Local Government, Planning and Land Act 1980, Sched. 32, para. 5; operative on November 3, 1995; designates three areas in the Holmewood area of North East Derbyshire, which have been the subject of three enterprise zone schemes adopted by the North East Derbyshire District Council, as enterprise zones.

4804. Environmental assessment

TOWN AND COUNTRY PLANNING (ENVIRONMENTAL ASSESSMENT AND PLANNING AND PERMITTED DEVELOPMENT) REGULATIONS 1995 (No. 417) [£1·55], made under the European Communities Act 1972 (c.68), s.2(2); operative on June 3, 1995; further implement Council Dir. 85/337/EEC.

TOWN AND COUNTRY PLANNING (ENVIRONMENTAL ASSESSMENT AND UNAUTHORISED DEVELOPMENT) REGULATIONS 1995 (No. 2258) [£2·40], made under the European Communities Act 1972, s.2(2); implement provisions of Dir. 85/337; operative on October 2, 1995.

4805. Established use certificate—clay pigeon shooting—shooting five days a week—whether certificate justified—whether residents having sufficient interest for judicial review. See R. v. SHEFFIELD CITY COUNCIL, *ex p.* POWER, §139.

4806. Established use certificate—possible concurrent use—not investigated—whether certificate validly made

The local authority issued an established use certificate for clay pigeon shooting on land where the evidence suggested that shooting had taken place on the land on Sundays and during the week. The evidence did not show that shooting took place every day and there was no inquiry as to any other uses to which the land was put. The applicants sought judicial review of the decision to grant a certificate.

Held, allowing the application and quashing the certificate, that a certificate issued in terms that were wider than the existing use of the land was, in effect, a grant of planning permission. In a case of an application for an established use certificate only the applicant was allowed to make representations. Since judicial review was the only course by which others could challenge such a decision it was right that they should be treated as having *locus standi*. The certificate as issued was unlimited in frequency and character. The local authority, to issue such a certificate, must have been satisfied that there was no other established use of the land. That question had never been considered and the authority could not have been satisfied that the shooting was anything more than an occasional use.

R. v. SHEFFIELD CITY COUNCIL, *ex p.* RUSSELL (1994) 68 P. & C.R. 331, Turner J.

4807. Established use certificate—refusal—temporary permission—whether use lawful

[Town and Country Planning Act 1990 (c.8), ss.191, 192.]

B's land had been used for the repair, maintenance and storage of motorvehicles from before 1964 and this use was carried on without planning permission until 1987 when B was granted temporary planning permission for two years. He tried to obtain permanent permission but this was refused and an enforcement notice was issued for the use to be discontinued. Under ss.191 and 192 of the Town and Country Planning Act 1990 there is immunity from an enforcement notice if there is an established use of the land but the council refused to grant an existing use certificate as s.191 did not apply. B appealed.

Held, dismissing the appeal, that (1) the use of the land did constitute an established use up to the time B applied for planning permission. If B had applied instead for an established use certificate, that would have been granted; (2) the granting of temporary planning permission changed the use of the land into lawful use so the established use no longer existed and s.191 no longer applied; and (3) the decision in *Bolivian and General Tin Trust v. Secretary of State for the Environment* ([1972] C.L.Y. 3328) would not be overruled.

BAILEY (ALAN CHARLES) v. SECRETARY OF STATE FOR THE ENVIRONMENT (QBCOF 93/0405/D), December 15, 1994, C.A.

4808. Footpaths—order reclassifying roads as public footpaths—confirmation by Secretary of State—whether suitability of routes should be considered

[Wildlife and Countryside Act 1981 (c.69), s.54, Sched. 15; Circular 2/93.]

S council submitted an order to the Secretary of State for the Environment for his confirmation, to reclassify certain roads used as public footpaths (RUPPs) as bridleways. An inspector was appointed to determine the matter, who held an inquiry. S had consulted the parish council, which supported the proposals, and could confirm that there were no local objections.

Held, confirming the order without modification, that there was clear evidence of use by horses. There was not sufficient evidence of vehicular use to reclassify them as bridleways open to all traffic (BOATs). The sole purpose of reclassification was to establish precisely the rights that existed, and not the suitability or amenity of the routes (Circular 2/93, Annex B applied).

SHROPSHIRE COUNTY COUNCIL'S RECLASSIFICATION ORDER (Ref: FPS/A 3200/8/7) (1994) 9 P.A.D. 843.

4809. Footpaths and rights of way—definitive map—refusal to direct modifications—addition of public footpath and by-way—whether right of way exists or reasonably alleged to exist—evidential tests

[Wildlife and Countryside Act 1981 (c.69), s.53(c)(i).]

B and N applied to their respective county councils for orders to modify the definitive maps and statements of by-ways, public paths and rights of way. The councils decided not to make an order and B and N appealed to the Secretary of State. He dismissed their appeals on the basis that sufficient evidence had not been provided. B and N sought judicial review to quash the decision.

Held, allowing the application and quashing the decision, that under the terms of the Wildlife and Countryside Act 1981, s.53(c)(i), the test to be applied was whether the evidence produced established either that a right of way existed or that it was reasonable to allege that a right of way existed. The first test required proof on a balance of probability but the second test was satisfied if it could be shown that a reasonable person could reasonably allege a right of way existed. The evidence required to satisfy the second test was less than that required to prove that a right of way did exist and the Secretary of State had not considered properly the second test.

R. v. SECRETARY OF STATE FOR THE ENVIRONMENT, *ex p.* BAGSHAW AND NORTON [1995] 68 P.& C.R. 402, Owen J.

4810. General development—consolidation

The Department of the Environment and the Welsh Office have published Circular 9/95 (Welsh Office, 29/95) entitled *General Development Order Consolidation 1995* which describes the main changes being introduced to the permitted development and procedural provisions, and some minor changes affecting the meaning of the existing provisions. It also gives advice on certain other permitted development rights and procedural matters. Available from HMSO, price £6·25. ISBN 0–11–753102–2.

4811. General development order

TOWN AND COUNTRY PLANNING GENERAL DEVELOPMENT (AMENDMENT) ORDER 1995 (No. 298) [£1·10], made under the Town and Country Planning Act 1990 (c.8), ss.59, 60, 61(1), 333(7); operative on March 9, 1995; amends S.I. 1988 No. 1813.

4812. General development procedure

TOWN AND COUNTRY PLANNING (GENERAL DEVELOPMENT PROCEDURE) ORDER 1995 (No. 419) [£6·10], made under the Town and Country Planning Act 1990 (c.8), ss.59, 61(1), 71, 73(3), 74, 77(4), 78, 79(4), 188, 193, 196(4), 333(7), Sched. 1, paras. 5, 6, 7(6), 8(6) and the Coal Industry Act 1994 (c.21), s.54; operative on June 3, 1995; consolidates with amendments the procedural provisions of S.I. 1988 No. 1813, as amended.

TOWN AND COUNTRY PLANNING (GENERAL DEVELOPMENT PROCEDURE) (WELSH FORMS) ORDER 1995 (No. 3336), made under the Town and Country Planning Act 1990 ss.59, 65, 74, 77(4), 79(4), 193 as extended by Welsh Language Act 1993 s.26(3). operative on February 14, 1996; [£3·70. Welsh versions of forms contained in the Town and Country Planning (General Development Procedure) Order 1995 Sched. 1 to 4 are prescribed by this Order. The forms, which may be used in respect of land in Wales, are set out in the Schedules 1 to 4 of this Order. Part 1 of Sched. 1 contains a letter from local planning authorities to be sent to applicants on receipt of applications for planning permission or certificate of lawful use or development. Part 2 of Sched. 1 contains notification to be sent to applicants when planning permission has been refused by a local planning authority or when a local authority has granted planning permission subject to conditions. Notices of applications or appeals for planning permission to be published by applicants in newspapers or served on owners or tenants are contained in Part 1 or Sched. 2 and Part 2 of Sched. 2 sets out certificates for use with applications and appeals for planning permission relating to ownership of land and notice to be given to agricultural tenants. Sched. 3 contains notices to publicise applications for planning permission issued by the local planning authority and a certificate of lawful use or development is contained in Sched. 4.

4813. General permitted development

TOWN AND COUNTRY PLANNING (GENERAL PERMITTED DEVELOPMENT) ORDER 1995 (No. 418) [£8·10], made under the Town and Country Planning

Act 1990 (c.8), ss.59, 60, 61, 74, 333(7) and the Coal Industry Act 1994 (c.21), s.54; operative on June 3, 1995; consolidates with amendments the permitted development provisions of S.I. 1988 No. 1813, as amended.

4814. Green Belt—agricultural use—land and buildings formerly in agricultural use—unauthorised use for storage of scaffolding—whether re-use of redundant buildings appropriate—use of adjacent land

A group of buildings and a yard, previously in agricultural use, had fallen into disuse before being occupied for storage of scaffolding and building materials. C issued enforcement notices. On appeal the inspector quashed the notices and granted permission for the use of the yard and buildings for non-agricultural purposes.

Held, allowing C's appeal, that although the re-use of redundant buildings and adjacent land was an appropriate use in Green Belt land, that did not apply to the surrounding open land which also used for storage. That storage was more visible than storage within the buildings and the inspector had failed to consider whether it was appropriate to a rural area.

BROMLEY LONDON BOROUGH COUNCIL v. SECRETARY OF STATE FOR THE ENVIRONMENT [1995] 68 P. & C.R. 493, Mr Malcolm Spence, Q.C. sitting as a deputy judge.

4815. Green Belt—boundaries—objection to proposal to include site—whether burden of proof on objector—whether extension of boundaries of Green Belt requires exceptional circumstances—whether inspector giving proper consideration to material issues raised by objector

[Town and Country Planning Act 1990 (c.8), s.287.]

R council had proposed that the whole of the land owned by S should be included in the Green Belt and that the western part of the land should be designated for cemetery use. S objected and R altered the draft plan. S sought to object to the modifications. The inspector found for R and, in effect, reinstated the original proposals. R refused S's request for a second inquiry. S appealed under s.287 of the Town and Country Planning Act 1990.

Held, allowing the application, that there was no burden of proof resting upon those who objected to a proposed Green Belt notation to justify exclusion from it. On the contrary it is for the body promoting the alteration to apply Government policy. It was not necessary that the inspector should find that exceptional circumstances existed before altering the Green Belt policy However, the inspector must give adequate reasons to apply or depart from it. If the inspector had approached the matter correctly, there would have been a realistic prospect that the matter would not have been included in the Green Belt. Where the inspector disagreed with an objector about the issues, the objector was entitled to a tolerably clear report upon those issues even if the objector himself agreed with the council (*Carpets of Worth v. Wyre Forest District Council* [1991] C.L.Y. 3483, *Laing Homes v. Avon County Council* [1994] C.L.Y. 4384 referred to).

SWAN HILL DEVELOPMENTS v. SOUTHEND-ON-SEA BOROUGH COUNCIL [1994] 3 P.L.R 14, Mr Malcolm Spence, Q.C. sitting as a deputy judge.

4816. Green Belt—cemetery—whether visual harm—whether psychological effect relevant

[Town and Country Planning Act 1990 (c.8), s.78.]

A appealed against the refusal of permission for a cemetery in the Green Belt on a site near to school grounds and houses. There was no dispute that such a use was appropriate in the Green Belt.

Held, dismissing the appeal, that (1) although it was consistent in principle with the function of the Green Belt, the development would be visually harmful; (2) the development would be on a vulnerable site on the edge of open countryside, and it would further erode the character and appearance of the locality and the Green Belt; but (3) the use would not have an unacceptable psychological effect on either the residents or schoolchildren; and (4) it was not a valid planning objection that certain categories of the community should be protected against exposure to the obvious associations with death.

WALSALL METROPOLITAN BOROUGH COUNCIL v. WEST MIDLANDS CO-OPERATIVE SOCIETY (Ref:T/APP/V4630/A/93/229927/P7) (1994) 9 P.A.D. 677.

4817. Green Belt—change of use—mixed residential and office use—individual working from home with one part-time member of staff—very special circumstances—whether personal and temporary permission granted

[Town and Country Planning Act 1990 (c.8), s.174.]

G appealed against an enforcement notice alleging a change of use at G's home in the Green Belt from residential to a mixed residential and office use. G worked from home with one part-time member of staff. G's presence was a significant factor in minimising the risk of serious deterioration in his wife's mental health.

Held, allowing the appeal, and granting a temporary, personal permission, that (1) as a matter of fact and degree a change of use had occurred; (2) this was not an appropriate development in the Green Belt; but (3) there were very special circumstances sufficient to outweigh the very small harm to the objectives of Green Belt policy; (4) the use was very modest and was not likely to have any significant effect on the locality's character and appearance; and (5) weight could be given to the policy to encourage small businesses and to G's personal circumstances.

THREE RIVERS DISTRICT COUNCIL v. GREENSHIELDS (Ref:T/APP/C/92/P1490/622002) (1994) 9 P.A.D. 577.

4818. Green Belt—extensive grounds—application for meeting hall—application refused by Secretary of State on grounds of visual impairment of Green Belt land—Secretary of State satisfied that proposal was an "institution in extensive grounds"—whether decision illogical

H applied for planning permission for the construction of a meeting hall on Green Belt land. The Secretary of State refused the application after deciding first that the proposal was an institution in extensive grounds of the character which was permissible for the purposes of PPG 2, para. 13, and secondly that the visual amenity of the Green Belt would be injured by the proposal.

Held, allowing H's appeal and quashing the decision of the Secretary of State, that the decision was illogical and unacceptable in so far as the Secretary of State concluded that the proposal would not harm the openness of the Green Belt and then concluded that there would be a detriment to the appearance and character of the Green Belt. The Secretary of State adopted the wrong approach in considering whether the Green Belt would be harmed by the development as opposed to whether interests of acknowledged importance other than the preservation of the Green Belt itself would be harmed.

HARROW MEETING ROOM TRUST TRUSTEES v. SECRETARY OF STATE FOR THE ENVIRONMENT [1994] EGCS 59, Nigel Macleod, Q.C. sitting as a deputy judge.

4819. Green Belt—outdoor sport—whether referring to public sport only and not covering domestic tennis court—consideration of planning merits

The Green Belt outdoor sports exception is not limited to public sports.

H owned a strip of wooded land which lay within the Green Belt on which he built a private tennis court. B council refused his application for planning permission for the change of use from woodland to residential garden including a tennis court; the inspector dismissed H's appeal, relying upon PPG

2 which permitted the use of Green Belt land for outdoor sports, which he interpreted as public outdoor sports only.

Held, that the inspector had erred in law by implying that the exception with reference to outdoor sports centres in PPG 2 was intended to be restricted to public sports. There was no indication in the guidance that a distinction should be made between the approach to public and private sports and there was no justification for adding this qualification to the statutory guidance. However, on the facts the error was not material. The inspector had concluded that the development was harmful to the surroundings, would set a precedent with even more harmful consequences and was in conflict with the development plan. A development which caused demonstrable harm to the Green Belt therefore had to be refused.

HOUGHTON v. SECRETARY OF STATE FOR THE ENVIRONMENT AND BROMLEY LONDON BOROUGH COUNCIL (1995) 70 P. & C.R. 178, Malcolm Spence, Q.C.

4820. Green Belt—residential development—immediate benefits found to be insufficient—whether failure to take account of local plan

A applied for residential development in the Green Belt. The inspector stated that the main issue was whether the site should be developed for all the accompanying immediate benefits or whether it should be retained for possible long-term development needs, in line with the local plan. He concluded that the permanence of the Green Belt in the medium to long term was of overriding weight.

Held, refusing the application to quash the inspector's decision, that (1) the whole basis of the phasing policy would be seriously undermined if the decision was quashed; (2) the inspector did not misapply the local plans or take into account irrelevant considerations. The decision had been reached after having carried out the required balancing exercise.

PELHAM HOMES v. SECRETARY OF STATE FOR THE ENVIRONMENT [1994] EGCS 102, Mr David Widdicombe, Q.C.

4821. Green Belt—waste deposit—recycling—whether immune—whether immunity a very special circumstance

[Town and Country Planning Act 1990 (c.8), s.174.]

The council issued an enforcement notice alleging a material change of use of land in the Green Belt by the deposit, recovery and recycling of waste and the associated erection of buildings. F alleged that the use was immune from enforcement, as it had continued for over 10 years. F accepted that the buildings were in breach of planning control.

Held, allowing the appeal, and granting planning permission for the buildings, that (1) on the balance of probabilities, the use had been continuous for over 10 years; (2) very special circumstances would be needed to grant permission for the building in the Green Belt; (3) the immunity of the use from enforcement was a circumstance of great importance; and (4) the building was not very prominent, facilitated the recycling use and involved the removal of other decrepit buildings.

SURREY COUNTY COUNCIL v. FOSS (Ref:T/APP/C/93/B3600/629193) (1994) 9 P.A.D. 670.

4822. Gypsies—caravan site—local plan policy restricting further gypsy caravan sites—Green Belt—whether racial discrimination—whether a fetter on discretion

[Race Relations Act 1976 (c.74), s.1(1).]

A local plan policy not to make further provision for gypsy caravan sites within an area did not contravene the Race Relations Act 1976 nor did it treat gypsies less advantageously than other ethnic minority groups.

S, a Romany gypsy, moved on to a site in Surrey within the catchment area of R. The area had been designated an area with sufficient sites for gypsies. Planning permission had been refused for a mobile home on the site on the basis that it was on Green Belt land and because it contradicted the local plan which did not intend to provide for further gypsy caravan sites. R obtained an injunction to exclude S from the land and commenced committal proceedings. S applied for judicial review, arguing that a local plan policy which restricted further gypsy caravan sites was an illegal contravention of the Race Relations Act 1976 or was a fetter on R's discretion to refuse the application.

Held, dismissing the application, that there was no reason for judicial review. R had a duty to formulate a local plan policy and to take into account all material factors. The local plan policy did not offend against the Race Relations Act 1976 because the reference to "gypsy" was that used in the Caravan Sites Act 1968 and did not discriminate against gypsies as an ethnic minority. Further, the policy did not accord to gypsies a treatment less advantageous than to other ethnic groups; rather, it moved from treating gypsies as a distinct ethnic group to being treated in the same way as other ethnic groups. The designation under the Caravan Sites Act 1968 raised a presumption against what would be an inappropriate development within the Green Belt. This applied equally to gypsies as to other ethnic minorities and therefore did not offend against the Race Relations Act 1976.

R. v. RUNNYMEDE BOROUGH COUNCIL, *ex p.* SMITH (1995) 70 P. & C.R. 244, Owen J.

4823. Gypsies—caravans—enforcement notice—failure of local authority to provide site—whether breach of statutory duty is relevant factor in committal proceedings

[Caravan Sites Act 1968 (c.52), s.6.]

The failure of a local authority to provide caravan sites as required by the Caravan Sites Act 1968, s.6(1), is a relevant factor to be taken into consideration when deciding whether to make a committal order against a defendant who has parked a caravan site on land without permission, and refuses to remove it.

D1, a gypsy, purchased land and placed caravans on it for himself and his family (D2). He applied for planning permission, which was refused, and was served with an injunction requiring that he cease to use the land for those purposes. D1 ignored the injunction, and D1 and D2 refused offers of housing made by the authority. Orders were made committing D1 and D2 to prison. They appealed.

Held, that the failure of the authority to provide a caravan site, as it was statutorily required to do, was a relevant factor and in the circumstances D2 would not be imprisoned; D1, however, had been primarily responsible for the defiance of the law, and would be sent to prison (*Mole Valley District Council v. Smith; Reigate and Banstead Borough Council v. Brown* [1992] C.L.Y. 4263, *Guildford Borough Council v. Smith* [1994] C.L.Y. 4360 considered).

WAVERLEY BOROUGH COUNCIL v. MARNEY [1995] 93 L.G.R. 86, C.A.

4824. Gypsies—decision to evict—whether local authority took duties to children into account

[Caravan Sites Act 1968 (c.52), s.6; Children Act 1989 (c.41), s.17.]

In deciding to evict gypsies, a local authority had given sufficient consideration to their duties to the children living on the site.

A group of travellers occupied an unauthorised caravan site from 1993. As a result of a growing number of complaints, the council visited the site on several occasions. The council was told that there were children on the site only at weekends. At the time the council were in breach of their statutory duty under s.6 of the Caravan Sites Act 1968. In July 1994 the council decided to bring possession proceedings against the travellers. In August 1994 a further visit to the site was made and the council officer was informed that there were 10 children on the site, six of whom were of school age but none of whom were enrolled at any school. The officer asked if anyone was disabled or had health problems but was not informed of any such children. The council also had the comments of the director of social services that there was no known need for social services involvement. The council confirmed their decision that possession proceedings should be pursued. The travellers sought judicial review of the decision and produced evidence that one of the children on the site had a clubfoot, another had been profoundly affected by the death of his sister in a traffic accident and another was asthmatic.

Held, dismissing the travellers' application, that on the evidence the council were aware of their obligations under the Children Act 1989 and they took into account the likely consequences for the children if eviction took place.

R. v. AVON COUNTY COUNCIL, *ex p.* HILLS (1995) 27 H.L.R. 411, Harrison J.

4825. Gypsies—duty to provide site—whether decision not to do so perverse

The respondent council sought possession of land on which the applicant gypsies had parked their caravans. The council was under a duty to provide a site for use by such people and had failed to do so. The applicants applied for judicial review of this decision.

Held, dismissing the application, that the applicants had *locus standi* to be heard, but the decision of the authority, when considered in the light of all the circumstances, was not perverse (*R. v. Brent London Borough Council, ex p. MacDonagh* [1990] C.L.Y. 2467 considered).

R. v. BATH CITY COUNCIL, *ex p.* NANKERVIS AND WILSON [1994] C.O.D. 271, D.C.

4826. Gypsies—occupation of local authority land without authorisation—occupiers claiming to be gypsies—whether travelling for purposes of obtaining livelihood necessary—whether for council to determine whether occupiers were gypsies—whether issue to be decided by court as precedent fact

[Caravan Sites Act 1968 (c.52), ss.6 (as amended by the Local Government Act 1985 (c.51), s.16, Sched. 8, para. 11), 16.]

For the purposes of the Caravan Sites Act 1968 there should be some recognisable connection between the travelling of those claiming to be gypsies and the means they make or seek their livelihood.

Unauthorised occupiers of council land claimed that they were gypsies and that, pursuant to s.6 of the 1968 Act, the council had a duty to provide them with adequate accommodation. Following a decision by the council that they were not gypsies, the occupiers applied for judicial review, contending that the council had misconstrued the definition of "gipsies" in s.16 of the 1968 Act. The applications were dismissed. The occupiers appealed against that decision.

Held, dismissing the appeals, that (1) when construed in the context of the 1968 Act as a whole, the definition of "gipsies" in s.16 imported the requirement that there should be some recognisable connection between the travelling of those claiming to be gypsies and the means whereby they made or sought their livelihood so that those who led a wandering life with their homes merely according to fancy and unconnected to their means of livelihood fell outside that definition; (2) it was a matter for the council concerned to determine whether persons were gypsies for the purposes of the 1968 Act; and (3) since the council had applied the correct test and there was no challenge to the decision on the grounds of unreasonableness, it was not for the court on an application for judicial review to determine as a precedent fact whether the occupiers were gypsies (*R. v. Oldham Metropolitan Borough Council, ex p. Garlick; R. v. Bexley London Borough Council, ex p. Bentum; R. v. Tower Hamlets London Borough Council, ex p. Begum*

(Ferdous) [1993] C.L.Y. 2041 applied; *Mills v. Cooper* [1967] C.L.Y. 1784 considered; *R. v. Secretary of State for the Home Department, ex p. Khera; R. v. Secretary of State for the Home Department, ex p. Khawaja* [1983] C.L.Y. 1908 distinguished).

R. v. SOUTH HAMS DISTRICT COUNCIL, *ex p.* GIBB; SAME v. GLOUCESTERSHIRE COUNTY COUNCIL, *ex p.* DAVIES; SAME v. DORSET COUNTY COUNCIL *ex p.* ROLLS [1994] 3 W.L.R. 1151, C.A.

4827. Gypsies—permission for gypsy site—county council decision—bias—whether procedural fairness

W parish council applied for certiorari to quash a decision of the county council granting planning permission for a gypsy site. The reason for the application was that members of the council who had proposed the site were also on the planning subcommittee.

Held, dismissing the application, that the fact that some council members' functions overlapped did not automatically mean that a decision was wrongly made or that the members had closed minds. There was no evidence of procedural unfairness or of a breach of natural justice.

R. v. HEREFORD AND WORCESTER COUNTY COUNCIL, *ex p.* WELLINGTON PARISH COUNCIL, *The Times*, April 9, 1995, D.C.

4828. Land compensation—certificates of alternative development—appeal procedure—failure by Minister to comply with—whether certificates to stand

[Land Compensation Act 1961 (c.33), s.17, s.18; Land Compensation Development Order 1974.]

A owned land which the Transport department proposed to acquire for a bypass. A applied for certificates of alternative development under s.17 of the Land Compensation Act 1961. The certificates were granted on the grounds that planning permission would have been granted were it not for the bypass proposal. The Secretary of State for Transport appealed under s.18 of the 1961 Act to the Secretary of State for the Environment against the grant of the certificates. The Transport Secretary failed, however, to follow the notice requirements of the Land Compensation Development Order 1974. The Environment Secretary purported to grant an extension of time for the service of the required notice, although there was no power to do so. By a later decision on the merits it was decided that the certificates should not have been granted. A challenged the decision to hear the appeals. The Environment Secretary argued that A had not suffered prejudice and that, if the certificate stood, the Lands Tribunal in assessing compensation would have difficulty in assuming that the certificates were correct when the decision on the merits indicated that they were not.

Held, giving judgment for A, that the Transport Secretary's appeal against the certificates should have been treated as withdrawn for failure to comply with the required procedure. As a result the decision on the merits could not stand and A's certificates were valid. The circumstances of this case were not sufficiently exceptional to justify the court exercising its discretion to uphold an invalid decision and refuse relief to A.

WARD v. SECRETARY OF STATE FOR THE ENVIRONMENT [1994] EGCS 164, Harrison J.

4829. Land compensation—depreciation caused by public works—freehold interest subject to tenancy—whether tenancy to be disregarded if "temporary"

[Land Compensation Act 1973 (c.26), s.4(4)(a); Rent Act 1977 (c.42), Sched. 15.]

A's house was affected by the M25 motorway and he claimed compensation in March 1988. The value of the property and the reduction in the notional value were agreed but the issue was what reduction, if any, should be made for the fact that the property was subject to a tenancy. A argued that there should be no reduction because the tenancies were such as to enable A to regain possession under Case 11 of Pt. II to Sched. 15 of the Rent Act 1977 and that the tenants had been chosen from those who only required temporary accommodation so that A could regain possession without difficulty. He argued that a potential purchaser would not therefore reduce any bid for the property.

Held, reducing the notional value of the property by 25 per cent, that s.4(4)(a) of the 1973 Act made it plain that the nature of the interest to be valued must be taken to be that which subsisted at the date that the claim was submitted. Any rights A had under the Rent Acts were personal and could not have been assigned to a purchaser (*Bwllfa & Merthyr Dare Steam Collieries v. Pontypridd Waterworks* [1903] A.C. 426, *Waterworth v. Bolton Metropolitan District Council* [1979] C.L.Y. 306 considered).

ALLEN v. DEPARTMENT OF TRANSPORT (1994) 68 P. & C.R. 347, Lands Tribunal.

4829a. Land compensation—depreciation in value attributed to bypass—whether two valuers necessary—burden of proof—whether evidence of settlements and awards nationally relevant—whether any depreciation in value—whether subject property benefited by bypass

[Land Compensation Act 1973 (c.26), Pt. I.]

The subject property was located between 210 metres and 260 metres from a newly constructed bypass. The bypass construction meant that the subject property was now located in a cul-de-sac. The claimant sought compensation under Land Compensation Act 1973. The claimant's surveyor did not have local knowledge. The claimant contended that the 1973 Act required only depreciation in value of the subject property and not necessarily proof of the comparative open market values before and after the bypass was constructed. Similarly, the claimant contended that there was therefore no requirement for specifically local evidence.

Held, that it is not necessary under Land Compensation Act 1973 for the claimant to give direct evidence of the value of his property before and after the construction works are performed. The open market value may be required where the depreciation is expressed as a percentage change in the value. There is no requirement for there to be more than one valuer. It would be most useful to the tribunal, however, were a local surveyor to give evidence. Depreciation can be calculated as a percentage reduction in value, or by taking part of the reduction as being due to the physical factors identified, or by a spot figure identified by the valuer based on his own experience (*English Exporters (London) v. Eldonwall* [1973] C.L.Y. 1902, *Fallows v. Gateshead Metropolitan Borough Council* [1993] 66 P & CR 460, *Land Securities v. Westminster City Council* [1993] C.L.Y. 2525, *W. Clibbett v. Avon County Council* [1976] 1 EG 171 referred to).

HALLOWS v. WELSH OFFICE [1995] 21 EG 126, Lands Tribunal.

4830. Land compensation—public works—depreciation—footbridge at end of cul de sac replaced by road bridge creating through road—whether compensation payable

[Land Compensation Act 1973 (c.26), s.9.]

The subject property was on a road that ended as a cul de sac at a footbridge over a river. Under a traffic management scheme the footbridge was replaced by a road bridge and the carriageway was widened. On a preliminary issue as to whether the claimants were entitled to compensation for the depreciation caused by the increase in traffic, the council argued that the loss had been caused by a creation of a new road over the footbridge, not an alteration to an existing highway and so was not covered by the Act.

Held, that compensation was payable. Section 9 of the Act took effect if the carriageway of a highway was altered. The road here had been altered. The physical factors giving rise to the compensation were caused by the use of the altered carriageway and the source of those factors were situated on the altered length of carriageway and so compensation was payable.

WILLIAMSON AND WILLIAMSON v. CUMBRIA COUNTY COUNCIL (1994) 68 P. & C.R. 367, Lands Tribunal.

4831. Listed building—alteration of whole building—whether removal of chimney breasts and consequential alterations demolition or alterations—whether compensation payable for refusal of consent

[Planning (Listed Buildings and Conservation Areas) Act 1990 (c.9), ss.8 and 27.]

The Secretary of State refused permission for building work to be done to a Grade II listed building to remove internal chimney breasts and extending the adjoining floors into the space created. The respondents claimed compensation under s.27 of the Planning (Listed Buildings and Conservation Areas) Act 1990 on the grounds that permission had been refused for alterations to a listed building. At a hearing of a preliminary issue, it was contended by the council that the application had been for demolition and not for alterations and therefore no compensation was payable under the 1990 Act.

Held, allowing the council's appeal, that under the 1990 Act demolition and alteration were mutually exclusive concepts. For the purposes of the 1990 Act, the term "building" includes part of a building. The removal of part of a building must constitute its demolition within s.8 of the 1990 Act.

SHIMIZU (U.K.) v. WESTMINSTER CITY COUNCIL [1995] 23 EG 118, C.A.

4832. Listed building—change of use—temporary permission for office use—restoration of residential use—whether inspector should have considered effect of reversion on architectural features

[Planning (Listed Buildings and Conservation Areas) Act 1990 (c.9), s.66(1).]

An inspector must, under the Planning (Listed Buildings and Conservation Areas) Act 1990, s.66(1), consider the effects of a proposed change of use on a listed building.

H owned a building which had been granted temporary permission for use as an office. When this permission expired the local authority issued a notice requiring its residential use to be restored. H argued that it was a listed building, and that permission ought to be granted to continue its office use and for works to be carried out to enhance its architectural features. The inspector, in making his decision, failed to consider the effects of reversion to residential use on the special qualities of the building.

Held, allowing H's appeal, that the inspector had a statutory duty to consider whether the historic and architectural features of the building would be seriously affected by the authority's proposals to convert it to residential use.

HEATHERINGTON (U.K.) v. SECRETARY OF STATE FOR THE ENVIRONMENT [1995] 69 P. & C.R. 374, David Keene, Q.C. sitting as a deputy judge.

4833. Listed building—conditional consent—removal of condition sought—allowed on grounds of ill health—inspector upholding condition—whether merits of earlier permission dealt with

A owned a listed residential property and were granted listed building consent in 1990 to make an opening in party walls between two ground-floor rooms which they wanted to use as a single unit due to ill health and inability to use stairs. The consent was subject to a condition that the opening should be permitted for five years or for as long as occupied by A, whichever was the longer. A sought to have this condition removed. A similar listed building consent had been granted in 1989 for an opening between two rear rooms but that consent was unconditional. The inspector found that the condition was reasonable in that it balanced a compassionate concern for A's physical needs with the long-term protection of a listed building.

Held, quashing the inspector's decision, that (1) the principal question was the approach to be taken to the fact that the principle the inspector was propounding could be breached by the 1989 permission and the approach to be followed was clearly set in the *Snowden* case; (2) the inspector had omitted the essential step of asking himself the question as to whether he needed to weigh the merits of allowing the appeal against the merits or demerits of a possible implementation of the 1989 permission (*Snowden v. Secretary of State for the Environment and Bradford City Metropolitan Council* [1981] C.L.Y. 2663 applied).

GWINNELL v. SECRETARY OF STATE FOR THE ENVIRONMENT [1994] EGCS 81, Mr Nigel MacLeod, Q.C.

4834. Listed building—development in grounds—semi-derelict building—development scheme helpful in funding restoration—whether benefit outweighed harm

Outline planning permission was refused for development in the grounds of a semi-derelict Grade II listed priory. A scheme approved in August 1991 to rebuild the priory was not financially viable on its own. However, the present development scheme would help to fund the restoration. The inspector nonetheless decided that the present scheme would cause more harm to the character of the area and the setting of the priory than would be outweighed by the benefit of restoring the priority.

Held, dismissing the appeal, that although Circular 8/87 stated that every effort should be made to preserve Grade II listed buildings, that did not justify any degree of harm overriding other planning objectives; (2) the inspector had carried out the required balancing exercise and the court could find no inconsistencies in his findings; and (3) further, the proposed development would weaken the objection to coalescence along the A120.

WORSTED INVESTMENTS v. SECRETARY OF STATE FOR THE ENVIRONMENT [1994] EGCS 66, Mr David Keene, Q.C.

4835. Malvern Hills Act 1995 (c.iii)

This Act confers additional powers upon the Malvern Hills Conservators in relation to the lands commonly known as the Malvern Hills; these powers relate, *inter alia*, to the provision of facilities for the public, the disposal of land, the control of finances and the management of the land.

The Act received Royal Assent on June 28, 1995.

4836. Minerals

TOWN AND COUNTRY PLANNING (MINERALS) REGULATIONS 1995 (No. 2863) [£1·10], made under the Town and Country Planning Act 1990, ss.315(1), 333(1), 336(1); revoke S.I. 1971 No. 756; operative on November 3, 1995, modify certain provisions of the Town and Country Planning Act 1990 as they apply to development consisting of winning and working of minerals or involving the depositing of mineral waste.

4837. Permitted development—advice on implementation

The Department of the Environment and the Welsh Office have published Circular 3/95 (Welsh Office, 12/95) entitled *Permitted Development and Environmental Assessment* explaining the provisions of paras. (10) to (12) of art. 3 of the Town and Country Planning (General Permitted Development) Order 1995 (S.I. 1995 No. 418) and the Town and Country Planning (Environmental Assessment and Permitted Development) Regulations 1995 (S.I. 1995

No. 417); and giving advice on their implementation. Available from HMSO, price £3·00. ISBN 0-11-753078-6.

4838. Planning authority—landowner seeking advice—duty of care—whether authority negligent in failing to advise an application for determination—whether plaintiff relied on advice

P was the owner of land and buildings which had been occupied since 1965 by a boat repair business. In December 1989 P sought the advice of D's planning department on the availability of planning permission for proposals made by T following an offer to buy the property. On the advice of D's planning department, P made an application for planning permission on January 26, 1990, which was refused on April 26, 1990. On further advice from the planning department P applied for a certificate under s.53 of the Town and Country Planning Act 1971, which obviated the necessity for planning permission to be granted. T withdrew his interest. P claimed damages based on D's failure to advise P that an application could have been made under s.53.

Held, dismissing the claim, that D did not owe a duty of care to P. The relationship between the parties was not one of reliance nor was it a relationship equivalent to contract (*Spring v. Guardian Assurance* [1994] C.L.Y. 1918 applied). A person seeking advice or guidance from a local authority about a planning application does not place a *Hedley Byrne v. Heller* duty on the local authority. There were no special circumstances in the present case to deviate from that general rule. On the evidence there was no reason why D should have thought that P would rely on its advice or that P did rely on its advice. Even if there had been a duty of care, D's officers had not been negligent because advice as to the possibility of a s.53 application would not have resolved P's question as to planning permission (*Banque Bruxelles Lambert SA v. Eagle Star Insurance Co.* [1994] C.L.Y. 3379, *Hedley Byrne and Co. v. Heller and Partners* [1963] C.L.Y. 2416, *Henderson v. Merrett Syndicates* [1994] C.L.Y. 3362 considered).

TIDMAN v. READING BOROUGH COUNCIL [1994] 3 P.L.R. 72, Buxton J.

4839. Planning control

RAIL CROSSING EXTINGUISHMENT AND DIVERSION ORDERS, THE PUBLIC PATH ORDERS AND THE DEFINITIVE MAPS AND STATEMENTS (AMENDMENT) REGULATIONS 1995 (No. 451) [£1·95], made under the Highways Act 1980, the Wildlife and Countryside Act 1981, and the Town and Country Planning Act 1990, ss.259(4), 333, Sched. 14, para. 1(2)(b)(v); amend S.I. 1993 Nos. 9, 10, 11 and 12; made in consequence of defects in S.I. 1993 No. 9, 10 and 11; operative on March 29, 1995.

4840. Planning control—breach—injunctions granted to prevent breaches—whether jurisdiction to grant mandatory injunctions—whether structures including fibreglass fish "incidental to enjoyment of dwelling-house as such"

[Town and Country Planning Act 1990 (c.8), ss.55(2)(d), 187B.]

The county court has jurisdiction under s.187B of the Town and Country Planning Act 1990 to grant a mandatory injunction preventing anticipated breaches of planning control.

A and B, a father and son, lived at a house in a residential area. The house was registered in B's name. A erected a fibreglass fish on the roof of the house without planning permission. The refusal of A's retrospective application for planning consent was the subject of an appeal to the Secretary of State but A continued to place other items on the property without consent including a replica Spitfire aeroplane. The council sought and obtained injunctions against both A and B requiring them to remove the Spitfire and restraining them from causing or permitting any structural alterations (other than the fish) to be affixed to the building in breach of planning controls. A and B appealed to the Court of Appeal, contending that the court had no power to grant a mandatory injunction, merely negative ones. It was also argued that the placing of the Spitfire fell within the meaning of "the use of any land within the curtilage of a dwelling-house for any purpose incidental to the enjoyment of the dwelling-house as such" and did not amount to a development.

Held, dismissing the appeal, that s.187B was drawn on the assumption that an actual as well as an intended breach of planning control could be prevented and the word "restrain" had to be given a wide meaning, extending not just to anticipated breaches of planning control but actual breaches as well. The concept of what is "incidental to the enjoyment of the dwelling-house as such" involved an element of objective reasonableness and was not a matter solely at the whim of the individual owner or occupier.

CROYDON LONDON BOROUGH COUNCIL v. GLADDEN [1994] 1 PLR 30, C.A.

4841. Planning control—breach—interlocutory injunctions granted—discharge—whether court having power to grant injunctions

[Town and Country Planning Act 1990 (c.8), s.187B.]

The courts have power to grant interlocutory injunctions under s.187B of the Town and Country Planning Act 1990 to prevent anticipated as well as actual breaches of planning control.

H applied for and was refused planning permission to instigate a change of use of his land and to convert an agricultural building into a residence. At the time of the refusals of the applications H was already using the land for the new use and had started to convert the building into a residence. The council, having commenced enforcement proceedings in the past, applied for and was granted injunctions to stop H from continuing the use of the land and from permitting the buildings to be occupied. The injunctions were set aside by the High Court on H's application on an undertaking to prosecute appeals against the refusals.

Held, granting the council's appeals, that the powers conferred by s.187B were wide and not limited by previous restrictions such as applied in *City of London Corp. v. Bovis Construction*. Where there had been an actual breach that power was not limited to the grant of an injunction at trial and an injunction could be granted at an interlocutory stage. The court was not confined to a preservation of the status quo at the interlocutory stage (*City of London Corp. v. Bovis Construction* [1989] C.L.Y. 3133, *East Hampshire District Council v. Davies* [1991] C.L.Y. 3463 distinguished).

RUNNYMEDE BOROUGH COUNCIL v. HARWOOD; *sub nom* HARWOOD v. RUNNYMEDE BOROUGH COUNCIL [1994] 1 PLR 22, C.A.

4842. Planning control—breach—planning contravention notice procedure—when to be deployed

[Town and Country Planning Act 1990 (c.8), s.171C.]

The planning contravention notice procedure under s.171C of the Town and Country Planning Act 1990 could not be deployed unless it appeared that a breach of planning control might have taken place.

R. v. TEIGNBRIDGE DISTRICT COUNCIL, *ex p.* TEIGNMOUTH QUAY COMPANY, *The Times*, December 31, 1994, Judge J.

4843. Planning controls over demolition

The Department of the Environment and the Welsh Office have published Circular 10/95 (Welsh Office 31/95) entitled *Planning Contols over Demolition* giving guidance on planning controls over the demolition of certain buildings. This reflects changes in the scope of "development" and to permitted development rights introduced as part of the general development order consolidation. Available from HMSO, price £3·00. ISBN 0–11–753114–6.

4844. Planning inquiry—costs—late withdrawal of developer's appeal—whether reasonable to award costs to local planning authorities

L withdrew its appeal on the day fixed for the inquiry into L's proposals for the development of its land. The Secretary of State awarded the four local planning authorities their costs of attending the inquiry on the grounds that L's late withdrawal of the appeal and its failure to withdraw at an earlier stage was unreasonable. He held that L's position had depended upon the decision on whether to modify the Suffolk Structure Plan amendment which had been approved by the Secretary of State by letters in May 1992. He held that it was sufficient for L to have one month to consider its position at which time it should have withdrawn its appeal. L sought to quash the decision on costs.

Held, dismissing the application, that it was not possible to hold that the inspector or the Secretary of State had acted unreasonably. The meaning of the May 1992 letter was unambiguous. More then one set of costs would be awarded to the respondents on the application as they all had a legitimate justification for appearing in court to oppose the application.

LANDMATCH v. SECRETARY OF STATE FOR THE ENVIRONMENT AND EAST CAMBRIDGESHIRE DISTRICT COUNCIL (1994) 68 P. & C.R. 160, Mr Malcolm Spence, Q.C. sitting as a deputy judge.

4845. Planning inquiry—legitimate expectations to have proposals considered—applicant informed that proposals to be considered at inquiry—inspector ruling that proposals outside scope of inquiry—whether breach of natural justice

E applied for judicial review of orders made under the A34 Trunk Road (A34/M4 Junction 13 Improvement) Side Roads Order 1993 under the provisions of the Highways Act 1980, Sched. 2. The first ground for review was that the Secretary of State made the orders without considering E's proposals and therefore had not taken into account a material consideration. The second ground was that E had been given assurances that his proposals would be considered and therefore his legitimate expectations were not fulfilled. The public were invited to comment on the junction scheme and E sent a letter with his proposals. He sent a copy of his suggestions to his M.P. The Minister for Roads sent a reply to E and to his M.P. saying that his suggestion would be given careful consideration. Later, the Secretary of State wrote to E telling him that he could comment on the draft orders for the scheme and E made further submissions. A public inquiry was opened and E prepared a case to present to it and gave his evidence. However, after the inquiry, the inspector decided that E's proposals were outside the scope of the inquiry and irrelevant and immaterial to his conclusions.

Held, allowing the application, that (1) the inspector should have given findings of fact and reasons before concluding that E's proposals were outside the ambit of the inquiry; (2) in failing to fulfil his quasi-judicial function the inspector was in breach of the Highways Inquiry Procedure Rules 1976, r.15; and (3) E had not been allowed to meet the Secretary of State's case properly and the inspector was in breach of natural justice. The Secretary of State's decision was fundamentally flawed and *ultra vires* (*Bushell v. Secretary of State for the Environment* [1980] C.L.Y. 1337, *Binney and Anscomb v. Secretary of State for Transport* [1985] C.L.Y. 1601, *Prest v. Secretary of State for Wales* (1973) 81 L.R.G. 193, *R. v. Immigration Appeal Tribunal, ex p. Khan (Mahmud)* [1983] C.L.Y. 1919, *Levy v. Marrrable & Co.* [1984] C.L.Y. 1239 followed).

R. v. SECRETARY OF STATE FOR TRANSPORT, *ex p.* ELLISON (CO/2844/93), December 14, 1994, Potts J.

4846. Planning inquiry—legitimate public expectation—proposed development partially in accordance with development plan—public expectation as to how decisions made—whether material consideration

[Town and Country Planning Act 1990 (c.8), s.54A.]

While there is a legitimate public expectation that planning decisions will be made in accordance with PPG 1, there is no legitimate expectation that a particular application will necessarily be determined purely by reference to the relevant plan.

On a public inquiry it was decided that the proposed development would accord with some of the development plan policies but would seriously conflict with other parts of the development plan. The Secretary of State indicated that the plan provided the basis for consistent decision and that to allow the development would remove the certainty that the public were entitled to expect in determining what type of development was to be permitted. The applicants sought to quash the decision arguing that there had been a failure to comply with the terms of PPG 1 of 1992 which stated that where material policies in the plan pulled in different directions the appeal should be determined on its merits.

Held, allowing the application, that there was a legitimate public expectation that any planning decision would be arrived at in accordance with the guidance in PPG 1 but there was no expectation that any application will be determined solely by reference to the relevant development plan. The general consideration relied upon by the Secretary of State was not a material consideration relating to the use of the land, it related only to the way in which the decision was to be reached.

TRUSTEES OF THE VISCOUNT FOLKESTONE 1963 SETTLEMENT (LOUP) v. SECRETARY OF STATE FOR THE ENVIRONMENT (1994) 68 P. & C.R. 241, Mr Gerald Moriarty, Q.C. sitting as a deputy judge.

4847. Planning inspector—bias—whether new evidence admitted in breach of natural justice—right to cross-examine refused—whether appropriate to cross-examine someone with quasi-judicial function

Although cross-examination of a person holding quasi-judicial office is not normally desirable, it should be allowed where there is a conflict in affidavit evidence which would otherwise lead to an inference of improper behaviour.

J appealed against the refusal of planning permission to alter the use of land. J claimed to have heard a discussion between the inspector and the council's barrister concerning evidence not presented at the appeal. J alleged bias on the part of the inspector. J's affidavit and that of the inspector were in direct contradiction. The issue arose whether the dispute could be resolved on the affidavits or whether the inspector should attend for cross-examination to eliminate possibility of fabrication.

Held, allowing the appeal, that while the principle was clear that the cross-examination of witnesses would be allowed when the justice of the case required, the question whether there was to be a cross-examination was one for the exercise by the judge of his discretion and was a discretion with which the Court of Appeal would not interfere unless the judge misdirected himself. Where two affidavits on their face showed a difference which was not attributable to a difference of recollection and there was a possibility that one or other was being deliberately untruthful, cross-examination of a person holding quasi-judicial office should be allowed to explain evidence which would otherwise lead to an inference of improper behaviour on the part of that person.

JONES v. SECRETARY OF STATE FOR WALES (1995) 70 P. & C.R. 211, C.A.

4848. Planning obligation—additional infrastructure required to support proposed development—agreement between council and developers for apportionment of cost between developers—whether policy requiring contribution from developers lawful

[Town and Country Planning Act 1990 (c.8), s.106.]

Where residential development makes additional infrastructure necessary or desirable, a council's policy that requires major developers to contribute to the cost of such infrastructure is lawful and does not amount to the imposition of an illegitimate planning levy.

The council had decided to make s.106 agreements with developers of a proposed development in order to fund the cost of the infrastructure required to support the proposed development. The contributions were calculated according to the enhanced land value. CH withdrew from the group of developers involved. Subsequently CH's application for planning permission was rejected. The appeal against that refusal failed. CH sought judicial review of the policy expressed in the draft local plan, of the s.106 agreements and of any planning permissions that took account of such agreements on the grounds that the council had acted illegally in introducing a form of land tax in return for a grant of planning permission. The judge dismissed the application and CH appealed.

Held, dismissing the appeal, that the policy requiring the developers to contribute to the cost of the additional infrastructure relating to the development was lawful. It was not an illegal planning levy and did not amount to a sale of planning consent. The judge had been right to dismiss CH's application.

R. v. SOUTH NORTHAMPTONSHIRE DISTRICT COUNCIL, *ex p.* CREST HOMES (1995) 93 L.G.R. 205, C.A.

4849. Planning obligation—permission for "warehouse club" with exclusion for retail use—whether warehouse club use amounted to retail use—whether statute capable of restraining retail use

[Town and Country Planning Act 1990 (c.8), s.106.]

C operated a "warehouse club" offering goods packaged in bulk quantities to business users and those in a defined employment group who paid a subscription to C. The council granted planning permission to C for the erection of a warehouse club on land upon which, under the local plan, retail use was excluded. The permission was subject to a s.106 agreement binding C and its successors in title by which any extension of use into retail use as described in class A1 of the Town and Country Planning (Use Classes) Order 1987 would constitute development and require fresh permission. The applicants sought judicial review to quash the grant of planning permission.

Held, dismissing the applications, that the sale of goods largely in bulk to a restricted class of customer did not amount to retail use within class A1. Since the agreement was designed to protect any extension of the use to retail and since the agreement was capable of being enforced, the council had not acted unreasonably in granting permission whilst opposing development into retail use (*Lewis v. Rogers* [1985] C.L.Y. 3238 considered).

T. v. THURROCK BOROUGH COUNCIL, *ex p.* TESCO STORES (1994) 92 L.G.R. 321, Schiemann J.

4850. Planning obligation—s.106 agreement—whether improper to grant permission before terms of agreement known—whether notice of terms of agreement should be given to objectors

Where a s.106 agreement is merely regulatory of how premises are to be occupied or used there is no requirement (except in exceptional cases) to bring the terms of the agreement to the notice of objectors.

The council granted planning permission to S subject to their entering a s.106 agreement confining occupancy of the proposed building to a certain type of occupier. D, who objected to the proposed development, applied unsuccessfully for judicial review, arguing that the grant of permission before the terms of the s.106 agreement was known was improper and because the terms of the agreement had not been passed on to D. D sought leave to appeal against the refusal of their application.

Held, dismissing the appeal, that there was no requirement for the council to tell D of the terms of the s.106 agreement and the council's decision would have been no different if the terms of the agreement were known to them before granting permission.

DANIEL DAVIES & CO. v. SOUTHWARK LONDON BOROUGH COUNCIL [1994] 1 PLR 45, C.A.

4851. Planning obligation—unilateral undertaking—Area of Outstanding Natural Beauty—proposed golf course—purpose of development to raise funds to pay for repairs to listed buildings—unilateral undertaking to use revenue for repairs—whether a planning obligation

A unilateral undertaking to use revenue from a golf course to repair listed buildings was a s.106 obligation as it required specified operations to be carried out on the land.

E applied for planning permission to develop a golf course on land situated within a designated area of outstanding natural beauty. The purpose of the development was to raise funds to pay for necessary repairs to listed buildings on another part of the land. E offered a unilateral undertaking to be made under s.106 to achieve that purpose. At E's appeal against the deemed refusal of the application the inspector decided that the proposals would cause harm to the area of outstanding natural beauty but that the harm would not be excessive and the benefit in the raising of revenue to repair the buildings outweighed the disadvantages. Permission was granted and the council applied to quash the decision on the basis that the undertaking was a nullity because it could not be enforced because it did not define what repairs were to be performed and it did not constitute a planning obligation under s.106.

Held, dismissing the application, that the undertaking contained provisions which required specified operations to be carried out on land as envisaged by s.106(1)(b). The inspector was entitled to conclude that the undertaking would ensure that the funds raised from the proposal would be used mainly to secure the repair of the buildings. The undertaking also required E to deliver a schedule of specified works within a set time which would specify the operations for the purposes of s.106(1)(b).

SOUTH OXFORDSHIRE DISTRICT COUNCIL v. SECRETARY OF STATE FOR THE ENVIRONMENT [1994] 1 PLR 72, Sir Graham Eyre, Q.C. sitting as a deputy judge.

4852. Planning permission—building—erection of mosque—conditions restricting gatherings or acts of worship to inside the building and preventing occupation prior to completion of the building works—breach of condition notice—judicial review—whether steel and concrete frame clad with corrugated sheeting was a "building"—whether holding a short-lived religious ceremony was "occupation"

A was a nominee of a charitable trust which administered the property of the Dawoodi Bohra Muslim community in the U.K. In October 1987, R granted outline planning permission to the trust for the erection of a mosque together with dwelling-houses and associated community facilities. One condition was that "no religious or ceremonial gatherings or acts of worship shall take place within the site except within the buildings". A further condition was imposed when full planning permission was granted in November 1988 that no part of the development was to be occupied until all the construction had been satisfactorily completed. By August 1992, the construction had been partially completed but the mosque had not been roofed completely. On August 19, 1,500 people met for five hours to conduct an act of religious worship on the site. The council served a breach of condition notice on January 27, 1993, alleging breaches of both conditions.

Held, allowing the application, that the gathering took place within the building. The structure constituted a building even though it had not been completely roofed. The community was not occupying the building at the material time even though it was using the building for short-lived ceremony for their own religious purposes (*Moir v. Williams* [1892] 1 Q.B. 264 referred to).

R. v. EALING LONDON BOROUGH COUNCIL, *ex p.* ZAINUDDAIN [1994] 3 P.L.R. 1, Tucker J.

4853. Planning permission—challenge to grant by potential rival developer—whether having *locus standi* to commence judicial review proceedings

If the commercial interests of a person may be affected by a decision in a way not common to the general public then that person may have *locus standi* to commence proceedings for judicial review of that decision.

Outline planning permission was granted to B to develop retail premises. S owned land and planned to develop its own retail premises but had not applied for planning permission. S sought to challenge the decision to grant B permission questioning whether S had *locus standi*.

Held, dismissing the application, that S did have *locus standi* and could bring an application. S's commercial interests were so affected by the decision that they were entitled to bring the proceedings to challenge the decision.

R. v. CANTERBURY CITY COUNCIL, *ex p.* SPRINGIMAGE (1994) 68 P. & C.R. 171, Mr David Keene, Q.C. sitting as a deputy judge.

4854. Planning permission—condition—entitlement of inspector to substitute condition prohibiting occupation until works carried out

Where, following an application for planning permission for a development, a local authority had imposed a condition for water attenuation and storage works to be carried out in order to prevent local flooding which had not been undertaken, it was open to a planning inspector to substitute a condition prohibiting occupation of the development until such works were carried out, as the substitution was not contrary to the Water Industry Act 1991, nor was any duplication involved.

WE BLACK v. SECRETARY OF STATE FOR THE ENVIRONMENT, *The Times*, November 27, 1995, D.C.

4855. Planning permission—condition—limiting opening hours of restaurant—whether reasonable—whether to be construed strictly

A condition attached to a planning permission for use of premises as a restaurant provided that use should only take place between the hours of 0800 and 2200 Monday to Saturday and between the hours of 0930 and 2100 on Sunday. It was admitted that customers were consuming food after these hours but that food was not being served.

Held, that outside the permitted hours there could be no preparation or serving of food, no presence of customers for whatever reason and no cleaning or tidying up. The condition was not unreasonable in a residential neighbourhood (*Newbury District Council v. Secretary of State for the Environment* [1980] C.L.Y. 2667 followed).

REES v. SECRETARY OF STATE AND CHILTERN DISTRICT COUNCIL [1994] NPC 125, Mr M. Spence, Q.C. sitting as a deputy judge.

4856. Planning permission—condition—occupancy restriction—whether condition applied to building not authorised by that permission

An outline planning permission granted permission to erect a garage and a dwelling in connection with agriculture at a specific location. The construction was carried out 90 feet to the west of the precise location. The issue was whether a condition as to occupancy in the planning permission could be enforced with reference to a building which was not the subject of the planning permission.

Held, allowing the appeal, that where a development is carried out in breach of planning controls and is not implementing any planning permission granted, it cannot be subject to conditions set out in that planning permission. The case of *Kerrier District Council v. Secretary of State for the Environment and Brewer* [1981] C.L.Y. 2727 was wrongly decided.

HANDOLL v. WARNER GOODMAN & STREAT [1995] 25 EG 157, C.A.

4857. Planning permission—condition—occupation restriction—enforcement notice—validity—served four years after breach of occupancy condition—whether condition relating to building operations

[Town and Country Planning Act 1990 (c.8), s.172(4).]

Planning permission was granted for the building of a house subject to a condition that occupation of the house was limited to a person employed in agriculture. Occupation commenced in 1986 and in 1991 an enforcement notice alleging a breach of the condition was served. The inspector held that the lapse of a period of over four years from the date of the breach rendered service of the notice out of time under s.172(4) of the 1990 Act and allowed the occupants' appeal. The council's appeal to the High Court was dismissed and the council appealed.

Held, allowing the appeal, that the condition related exclusively to occupancy and did not relate to a building operation. Section 172(4) did not apply (*Harvey v. Secretary of State for Wales* [1990] C.L.Y. 4379 distinguished; *Peacock Homes v. Secretary of State for the Environment* [1984] C.L.Y. 3431 considered).

NEWBURY DISTRICT COUNCIL v. MARSH (1994) 92 L.G.R. 195, C.A.

4858. Planning permission—condition—removal—consideration of planning circumstances existing at time of application necessary

[Town and Country Planning Act 1990 (c.8), ss.73, 73A.]

R sought planning permission for five years for the use of land and buildings as livery stables in January 1978. Permission was granted with a condition that there be a person employed locally in agriculture or forestry who occupied the property as trainer/manager at the hackney stables. In 1979 R then sought a second planning permission without the occupation condition. This was granted in 1984 subject to a requirement that occupation be limited to either of R. R appealed against the refusal of permission without the condition. The inspector found that the condition had not been appropriately imposed and should be removed. S council appealed on the basis that the inspector had erred in law with reference to ss.73 and 73A of the Town and Country Planning Act 1990.

Held, allowing the first two grounds of the application, that the inspector was correct to accept that the condition was valid until found to serve a useful purpose no longer. Although the application was made under s.73, the inspector had proceeded under s.73A(2)(c) which relates to the development carried out without compliance with a condition. On the facts there was no breach of condition because R2 had remained in occupation of the property. However, there was no significant difference between ss.73 and 73A in relation to the main issue. The inspector was entitled to consider whether the condition was appropriately imposed on the merits in 1984. The inspector should have gone on to consider the current need for such a condition. The question under ss.73 and 73A should be whether the particular condition is justified in the circumstances existing at the time of the determination of the appeal (*Hanily v. Minister of Local Government and Planning* [1952] C.L.Y. 512,

Mouchell Superannuation Fund Trustees v. Oxfordshire County Council [1992] C.L.Y. 4346 referred to).

SEVENOAKS DISTRICT COUNCIL v. SECRETARY OF STATE FOR THE ENVIRONMENT AND GEER [1994] 69 P. & C.R. 87, Gerald Moriarty, Q.C. sitting as a deputy judge.

4859. Planning permission—conditions—circular

The Department of the Environment (11/95) and the Welsh Office (35/95) have issued a circular giving advice about the use of planning conditions. The circular brings the references in DoE Circular 1/85 (Welsh Office 1/85) up to date and incorporates additional policy guidance issued since 1985, for example, in Planning Policy Guidance Notes. Published by HMSO, price £6·50.

4860. Planning permission—curtilage of property—whether right test applied

[Town and Country Planning Act 1990 (c.8), s.174(2).]

M was the owner of a Grade II listed building and constructed a swimming pool and tennis court on an open grassed area which formed part of his property. The planning inspector upheld an enforcement notice by the council that the pool, tennis court and associated shed were constructed without planning permission because the site fell outside the curtilage of the property. He restricted curtilage to a small area inconsistent with the 12 acres contested in the appeal. He also considered a retaining wall following a boundary on an ordnance survey map to be a clear line of demarcation historically associated with the property, a former rectory. M applied to have the decision set aside, after an unsuccessful appeal under s.174(2) of the Town and Country Planning Act 1990, on the ground that the inspector fell into error on a number of points, that he equated "curtilage" with "garden", that he wrongly relied on the existence of enclosure and that he overlooked the purpose of the retaining wall in the context of the historic relationship between the land and dwelling.

Held, dismissing the application, that (1) there was no rigid definition to curtilage but there were three identifiable characteristics: curtilage was constrained to a small area about a building, an intimate association with the land within the curtilage was required to make the considered land part and parcel of it and it was not necessary for there to be any physical enclosure of the land within the curtilage but the considered land must be part of the enclosure with the house (*Methuen-Campbell v. Walkers* [1979] C.L.Y. 1607, *Dyer v. Dorset County Council* [1989] 1 Q.B. 346 considered); there was no error in the inspector's approach or evidence to show he felt constrained to equate "curtilage" with "garden". The use of the word "garden" merely reflected the way in which the case had been argued; and (3) M argued that in approaching the matter of enclosure the inspector had overlooked that the meaning of enclosure could be satisfied without any physical enclosure being present. However, there was no indication that the inspector had failed to apply the correct concept, nor that he placed particular reliance upon enclosure in reaching his decision; and (4) the inspector did not fall into error in his use of historical associations in relying on the boundary line of glebe land associated with the former rectory. M argued that the property now fulfilled a different purpose as a family house with a larger curtilage. The inspector did not make an error of law in looking at the function of the eighteenth century property, but regarded the relevance of curtilage in the present day. The inspector paid considerable attention to the visual aspect which showed a clear demarcation line of the retaining wall which separated the formal garden and orchard with the more open meadow. The coincidence with the old boundary could rightly be used in the decision and was consistent with it.

McALPINE (DAVID) v. SECRETARY OF STATE FOR THE ENVIRONMENT (CO/3417/93), November 14, 1994, Nigel MacLeod, Q.C.

4861. Planning permission—landfill quarries—risk of munitions in mine shaft—non-disclosure of information—judicial review sought—subsequent disclosure—whether costs of application recoverable. See R. v. BRITISH COAL CORP., *ex p.* IBSTOCK, §132.

4862. Planning permission—limited permission recommended by inspector—refusal of permission by Secretary of State—gypsy caravans—whether any remedy by way of judicial review

[Town and Country Planning Act 1990 (c.8), s.285.]

The council had statutory responsibility for providing sites for gypsy caravans in their area and their travellers' subcommittee decided to bring possession proceedings against A, who were travellers with caravans set up on land which was no longer being used for its original purpose. The inspector recommended that limited planning permission be granted but the Secretary of State refused permission. A applied for leave to move for judicial review, having argued that that was their only potential remedy.

Held, refusing the application, that (1) the court did not find it necessary to pursue whether the judge in the lower court was correct or whether A's argument was correct; (2) the Secretary of State had given planning reasons as to why he did not accept the inspector's conclusions and had carried out the proper balancing exercise.

R. v. AVON COUNTY COUNCIL, *ex p.* VALENTINE [1994] EGCS 71, C.A.

4863. Planning permission—"local centre"—whether superstore or retail park included in definition

Since the term "local centre" implied a development of shops which sold mainly convenience goods and attracted people from the local area, it would be irrational to allow provision of a superstore or retail park where planning permission was granted for a local centre.

BRAINTREE DISTRICT COUNCIL v. SECRETARY OF STATE FOR THE ENVIRONMENT, *The Times*, October 9, 1995, D.C.

4864/5. Planning permission—minerals

The Department of the Environment has issued a press release entitled *Minister Urges Partnership Between Industry and Local Authorities to Modernise Old Quarries* (News Release 483), published on October 4, 1995. The Government published guidance to local authorities, landowners and minerals operatives in England and Wales on how old mineral permissions should be reviewed and modernised. *Minerals Planning Guidance: Environment Act 1995: Review of Mineral Planning Permissions*, ISBN 0–11–753175–8, is available from HMSO bookshops at £15·00.

4866. Planning permission—outline permission—condition—dwelling-house to be constructed next to listed barn—barn subsequently destroyed—whether outline permission capable of implementation

Outline planning permission was valid and capable of being implemented despite the destruction of a listed barn.

B owned land on which was located a listed barn. B applied for outline planning permission to erect dwellings on the land and submitted drawings and plans showing houses erected next to the barn to form a courtyard. Outline permission was granted subject to conditions, one of which required the development to be carried out in accordance with the plans. B later applied for approval of matters that had been reserved for further consideration and submitted a second set of plans and drawings and approval was granted subject to the same condition as had been applied to the earlier grant of approval. The barn was demolished in a gale and the question was whether the outline planning permission remained effective because the works described therein could not be carried out in their entirety. B sought a declaration that the permission was valid and capable of implementation. B's application was dismissed on the grounds that the condition requiring the development to be carried out in accordance with the approved plans referred to the first set of plans lodged and so the house had to be built with the barn which was no longer possible.

Held, allowing B's appeal, that the term "submitted and approved plans" in the condition referred to the second set of plans. The first condition had the effect of ensuring that further details were submitted for approval and that the works were carried out in accordance with those detailed plans.

BURHILL ESTATES CO. v. WOKING BOROUGH COUNCIL [1994] 1 PLR 51, C.A.

4867. Planning permission—outline permission—regard only to be given to the permission, not merits of proposal

S council appealed against the dismissal of its application for judicial review, in which it had sought a declaration that a developer's proposal to increase the floor space for new buildings by 45 per cent fell outside the outline planning permission previously granted. S contended that the general rule in *Miller-Mead v. Minister of Housing and Local Government*, that in continuing a planning permission regard was only to be paid to the permission and not to the actual merits of the proposal, should be overlooked. They argued that the planning authority lacked the jurisdiction to grant permission for the increased floor space.

Held, dismissing the appeal, that the planning permission was clear and unambiguous and enlargement of the site was not of itself invalid. The matter depended upon the extent to which applications could be considered in determining the scope of the planning permission which had been granted. The permission had not sufficiently incorporated the application so that the floor area could not subsequently be reduced on a full hearing of the appeal and it was too late to challenge the validity of the planning authority's jurisdiction. The developers' appeal should he heard on its merits having regard to local planning policies (*Miller-Meed v. Minister of Housing and Local Government* [1963] C.L.Y. 3406).

R. v. SECRETARY OF STATE FOR THE ENVIRONMENT, *ex p.* SLOUGH BOROUGH COUNCIL, *The Times*, May 24, 1995, C.A.

4868. Planning permission—outline permission—reserved matters to be submitted for approval—expiry of time within which reserved matters to be submitted—application to extend time-limits—whether valid

[Town and Country Planning Act 1990 (c.8), s.73.]

An application to extend the time within which reserved matters in an outline planning permission are to be submitted can be made under s.73 of the Town and Country Planning Act 1990 after the expiry of the relevant time-limit.

W was granted outline planning permission to develop the site subject to various conditions, one of which was the submission of various reserved matters for approval within two years. W submitted details of the reserved matters after the expiry of the time-limit and then applied to the council under s.73 of the 1990 Act to amend the condition imposing the time-limit. W obtained a letter from the Secretary of State for the Environment stating that an application under s.73 could be made at any time prior to the expiry of the period for commencing the development because s.73(4) was a definitive statement of the extent to which an application under s.73 could be precluded on time grounds and there was no preclusion where the time for submitting details of reserved matters had expired but the time for beginning the development had not expired. The council applied to set aside the decision because the outline permission had lapsed under the terms of its conditions and any application under s.73 depended on the existence of a valid planning permission.

Held, dismissing the application, that it was plain from the section that the only restrictions upon the exercise of s.73 were those contained in s.73(4). An application under s.73 could be made after the time for an application for approval of reserved matters had expired where that time-limit was different from the one stated in s.73(4).

R. v. SECRETARY OF STATE FOR THE ENVIRONMENT, *ex p.* CORBY BOROUGH COUNCIL [1994] 1 PLR 38, Pill J.

4869. Planning permission—outline permission—two planning permissions in respect of same site—retail development and non-retail development—s.106 agreement to carry out two developments simultaneously—one permission allowed to lapse—effect of lapse of permission

Where two outline planning permissions were granted, one in respect of retail and one non-retail development, there was an implied term that the developer would take all reasonable steps to carry out the development.

B applied for planning permission to develop the Elstree Studios site to build a retail development and to build a new studio complex. Outline planning permission was granted subject to conditions requiring approval of certain reserved matters within three years. B and the council entered into a s.106 agreement under which B agreed to proceed with both developments simultaneously. The retail development was completed but the non-retail development did not proceed and the outline planning permission was allowed to lapse. B argued that their obligations under the s.106 agreement could no longer be performed because they depended on the continued existence of the outline planning permission. The council applied for an injunction restraining B from pulling down the remaining buildings at the site. B sought a determination of the issue under R.S.C., Ord. 14A.

Held, granting the injunction and dismissing B's application, that there was a serious issue to be tried. Having regard to the objective of the parties it was necessary to imply into the agreement a term that B would take all steps necessary to enable them to carry out the non-retail development (including making a fresh application for planning consent). Alternatively it was arguable that B should not be allowed to profit from its own self-induced frustration of the agreement.

HERTSMERE BOROUGH COUNCIL v. BRENT WALKER GROUP [1994] 1 PLR 1, Jacob J.

4870. Planning permission—part of site—development of land—small portion not built on reserved for railway station—railway plans abandoned—whether vacant plot could be developed

A small portion of land, which had permission for development, was left vacant because it was reserved by the Government for a railway station. On the railway plans falling through, C, who had subsequently bought the small plot, was refused permission to develop it. He sought judicial review of this decision.

Held, that land which formed part of a planning application, but which was not to be built upon and which was therefore taken into account in assessing site density, could not later be sold off separately and treated as a site for the purposes of a subsequent planning application. Further, the use of the land so as to utilise its site coverage and plot ratio potential for purposes of the original development was not inconsistent with its reservation for the purposes of a railway and C erred in arguing that a development site could not include an area so reserved.

CINAT v. ATT.-GEN. OF HONG KONG [1994] N.P.C. 145, P.C.

4871. Planning permission—renewal—unadopted unitary development plan—whether renewal should normally be granted—whether emerging unitary development plan a material change

The emerging policies of an unadopted unitary development plan should be taken into account when considering an application for the renewal of planning permission.

A bought the garden of a house for which planning permission for the erection of another house had been granted previously. This planning permission was subject to the condition that work should start before the end of a five year period. A failed to commence work within time and made an application for the renewal of the permission. This was refused after a public inquiry. A appealed, arguing that an unimplemented planning permission should normally be renewed unless there were material changes in the planning circumstances.

Held, dismissing the appeal, that there had been a material change in planning policy as a result of an emerging unitary development plan regarding the density of the developments within towns. This plan had been promoted since the original grant of planning permission, although it had not yet been adopted. The inspector had been correct to take into account the emerging policy considerations of the unadopted unitary development plan.

NAWAR v. SECRETARY OF STATE FOR THE ENVIRONMENT [1994] EGCS 132, Mr R.M.K. Gray, Q.C., sitting as a deputy judge.

4872. Planning permission—Secretary of State's call-in of application—refusal to call in competing proposal

[Town and Country Planning Act 1990 (c.8), s.288.]

C applied for planning permission to develop a supermarket. H also applied for permission to develop a supermarket on a different site. H had selected M to develop the site and granted M an option to purchase. H's application was "called-in" for determination by the Secretary of State. The council requested that C's application should also be called in and a joint inquiry held but this application was refused by the Secretary of State who did not give any reasons for the refusal. Thereafter C was granted planning permission. The council and M (H's chosen developer) applied separately under s.288 of the Town and Country Planning Act 1990 to quash the decision to grant planning permission. C argued that M had no *locus standi*. The council also applied by way of judicial review to quash the Secretary of State's decision to refuse to call in C's application.

Held, granting the application, that (1) where all of the facts pointed to one result and a different result had been given the court could infer that there were no valid reasons for such a result. Although the guidelines on the recovery of jurisdiction were not binding, where a case prima facie fell within one of the guidelines so that a call-in was indicated the court was entitled to expect the Secretary of State to give reasons for not following the guideline and taking a different course. In the absence of any given reasons the court could infer that there were no valid reasons; (2) M had *locus standi* to challenge a decision under s.288 of the Town and Country Planning Act 1990 as a "person aggrieved".

MORBAINE v. SECRETARY OF STATE FOR THE ENVIRONMENT AND SOUTH NORTHAMPTON DISTRICT COUNCIL [1995] 68 P. & C.R. 525, Mr David Widdicombe, Q.C. sitting as a deputy judge.

4873. Planning permission—Secretary of State's call-in of application—refusal to call in competing proposal—failure to give reasons for refusal—whether obligation to give reasons—challenge by rival developer with option to purchase—*locus standi*

[Town and Country Planning Act 1990 (c.8), s.288.]

C applied for planning permission to build a retail food store on land on the outskirts of Towcester. At the same time, S was proposing a local plan under which a retail food store would be erected on a site known as TR1 outside Towcester. M applied to S to build a retail food store on site TR1. C appealed to the Secretary of State against S's failure to determine its application and an inquiry was convened. The decision was taken not to call in the second application. S applied for judicial review of the Secretary of State's failure to call in C's application, and S and M brought proceedings under s.288 of the Town and Country Planning Act 1990 to challenge the inspector's decision to grant planning permission to C. The High Court judge quashed the Secretary of State's decision and upheld the s.288 challenges.

Held, allowing the appeals, that the guidelines relating to the recovery of jurisdiction in planning matters by the Secretary of State did not include an "unofficial guideline" for call-in where two proposals could be considered as potential alternatives. In any event, by stating that normal procedures should apply and that further delay in deciding C's application would be unacceptable, the Secretary of State had given adequate reasons for not calling in C's appeal. Further, where an application was made under s.288 that an appeal ought to be heard by the Secretary of State rather than an inspector, the "challenge" to the inspector's power to hear the appeal must at least amount to a clear submission that if the inspector were to go on to determine the appeal he would be acting unlawfully because the decision not to call it in was invalid. Consideration of a retail shopping development among existing shopping amenities must be conducted within an examination of all the planning factors, including the environmental factors, and not simply in terms of size and supplies alone. The inspector had not prejudged M's application either by deciding on the question of accommodating C's application or by granting planning permission to C and thereby increasing the likelihood that the TR1 development would have to be abandoned. PPG 1 did not lay down a rule that as soon as a proposal was found to be contrary to an emerging local plan it must, as a normal course, be turned down on the grounds of prematurity.

SOUTH NORTHAMPTONSHIRE DISTRICT COUNCIL v. SECRETARY OF STATE FOR THE ENVIRONMENT; MORBAINE v. SECRETARY OF STATE FOR THE ENVIRONMENT (1995) 70 P. & C.R. 224, C.A.

4874. Planning permission—Secretary of State's call-in of application—two applications for supermarket developments—joint inquiry refused—whether Secretary of State having to give reasons for decision

Two firms of developers, C and M, applied for planning permission for supermarkets on sites in Towcester. M's application was called in for determination by the Secretary of State but the council's request for the Secretary of State also to call in C's application and hold a joint inquiry was refused, the Secretary of State stating that there was insufficient reason to delay consideration of C's application. This refusal was quashed by a decision of the High Court which concluded that the case came within unofficial guidelines for call in where two proposals for development could be considered as potential alternatives. In such cases, the court held, the Secretary of State should have given reasons for not calling in the application and, in the absence of these reasons, the court would conclude that there were no valid reasons for the decision.

Held, allowing the appeal, that the judge had erred in requiring reasons to be given for the Secretary of State's decision. There was no obligation for the Secretary of State to provide reasons but in this case he had in fact done so in his letter of refusal. Further, there was no evidence from the case cited as being authority for the unofficial guideline referred to by the judge, *R. v. Secretary of State for the Environment, ex p. Allied London Property Developments* (unreported), that such a guideline existed. Instead, the case had emphasised the importance of dealing with planning applications expeditiously.

R. v. SECRETARY OF STATE FOR THE ENVIRONMENT, *ex p.* SOUTH NORTHAMPTONSHIRE DISTRICT COUNCIL, *The Times*, March 9, 1995, C.A.

4875. Planning restrictions—persistent breaches of planning control—interlocutory injunctions granted—whether balance of convenience test applicable—whether injunction too vague to be permissible—whether structure for purpose incidental to enjoyment of a dwelling house

[Town and Country Planning Act 1990 (c.8), s.187B.]

Injunctions were awarded against the appellant, H, under Town and Country Planning Act 1990, s.187B, restraining him from moving into occupation of certain buildings on green belt land and from storing motorvehicles on Green Belt land. H had been fined for contravention of planning restrictions on previous occasions. The injunctions were discharged on the giving of undertakings by H. The local authority appealed against the discharge of the injunctions. Injunctions were awarded against the appellants, JG and GG, following their deliberate policy of erecting bizarre structures on the roof of their suburban house without planning permission. JG had indicated to the local authority and in a newspaper interview that he would replace any structure with another structure when he was made to take it down. JG and GG appealed against the injunctions for potential breaches of planning regulations.

Held, that (1) with reference to H, the American Cyanamid test did not apply to Town and Country Planning Act 1990, s.187B because it would have the effect of awarding temporary planning permission, where that had been refused by the planning authority, once the injunctions were discharged. The injunctions were therefore restored; (2) with reference to JG and GG, the Town and Country Planning Act 1990, s.187B permits the granting of injunctions to deal with intended breaches of planning control as well as actual breaches. Nor was the injunction too vague to be permissible, relating as it did to structures on the exterior of JG and GG's property.

[*Per curiam*: the concept of what was incidental to the enjoyment of a residential property was considered. The erection of a children's "wendy house" or a fountain would be incidental to the enjoyment of a residential property. The erection of a replica spitfire aircraft on the roof of a suburban house did not fulfil such a function].

HARWOOD v. RUNNYMEDE BOROUGH COUNCIL; LONDON BOROUGH OF CROYDON v. GLADDEN [1994] 68 P & CR 300.

4876. Public right of way—shopping centre walkways—whether public had right to use—whether equitable licence to use—whether any such licence revocable. See CIN PROPERTIES v. RAWLINS (MARTIN), §4560.

4877. Public rights of way—amendments and advice—public path orders

The Department of the Environment has published Circular 7/95 entitled *Public Rights of Way: Amendment Regulations and Advice on Public Path Orders*, describing the provisions contained in the Rail Crossing Extinguishment and Diversion Orders, the Public Path Orders and the Definitive Maps and Statements (Amendment) Regulations 1995 (S.I. 1995 No. 451). The Circular also provides further guidance on procedures concerned with modifying the rights of way network, in particular the use of combined powers to create, extinguish or divert public rights of way. Available from HMSO, price £1·50, ISBN 0–11–753101–4.

4878. Purchase notice—validity—relating only to part of land in respect of which planning permission refused—whether tribunal having jurisdiction to determine compensation

[Town and Country Planning Act 1990 (c.8), s.137.]

C, who had purchased a disused railway cutting, obtained planning permission in 1988 to fill in a part of the land and to build two houses on it. In 1990 an application to develop the whole of the land was refused. C therefore served a purchase notice on the council under s.137 of the Town and Country Planning Act 1990 requiring it to purchase that part of the land which was not covered by planning permission and sought compensation. The council contended that the purchase notice was invalid because it did not relate to the whole of the land over which planning permission had been refused. Therefore, it contended that the tribunal did not have jurisdiction to hear the appeal.

Held, that a proper construction of s.137 of the 1990 Act required that the whole of the land in respect of which planning permission has been refused must be referred to in the purchase notice. This notice was invalid and the tribunal had no jurisdiction to decide on compensation. There was no order as to costs on the grounds that the council's conduct was found to have resulted in delay, additional costs and wasted hearing dates (*Smart & Courteney Dale v. Dover Regional District Council* [1972] C.L.Y. 3353, *Wain v. Secretary of State for the Environment* [1982] C.L.Y. 3196 considered).

COOK AND WOODHAM v. WINCHESTER CITY COUNCIL [1994] 69 P. & C.R. 99, Lands Tribunal.

4879. Quarrying—order to prevent resumption of quarrying—evidence

[Town and Country Planning Act 1990 (c.8), Sched. 9, para. 3.]

M appealed against a refusal to allow judicial review of a decision of the Secretary of State for Wales declining to confirm an order made by M to prevent the resumption of quarrying of minerals at Ewenny Quarry, where quarrying had ceased in 1961. M had relied upon para. 3 of Sched. 9 of the Town and Country Planning Act 1990, as amended, by which a mineral planning authority could ban, by order, the resumption of quarry working if the quarry had not been worked for at least two years and if there was little possibility of resumption of working to any substantial extent.

Held, dismissing the appeal, that after the making of the order there was evidence of revived interest in the quarry, but M contended that the Secretary of State for Wales should only have taken notice of the evidence available at the time the order was made and not of subsequent developments. If that were not so, then a landlord could take steps to resume working before the order was confirmed. However, if the Secretary of State could not consider new evidence he would be ignoring reality, and the court concluded that he could therefore not be limited as to which evidence he could consider.

R. v. SECRETARY OF STATE FOR WALES, *ex p.* MID-GLAMORGAN COUNTY COUNCIL, *The Times*, February 10, 1995, C.A.

4880. Restrictive covenant—agreement regulating form of refuse to be deposited in landfill site—applicant sought to vary agreement—local authority refused unless consideration provided by applicant—whether such refusal lawful—local authority required by statute to obtain best reasonable consideration for any disposal of land acquired for planning purposes—whether relaxation of contractual rights a "disposal" of land

[Town and Country Planning Act 1990 (c.8), s.233.]

B owned land in Essex and sought planning permission for the working of clay forming a part of the land and for the refilling of that part of the site. The county council, as mineral and waste disposals authority, sought the views of the local borough council, T. T indicated that they would object to proposals for refilling the site otherwise than by high density baling. B submitted plans that were acceptable to T and granted T an option to acquire the land for future development. The option was structured by means of a lease and an underlease. Both leases contained covenants requiring B to use high density baling only. B sought to be released from this obligation.

Held, dismissing the appeal, that the issue between the parties was whether the agreement between them and the variation sought by B would amount to a disposal of land under Town and Country Planning Act 1990, s.233. However, a "disposal" of land, as defined in s.336 of the 1990 Act, involved not merely the contractual relaxation of rights but an altogether more fundamental surrender of proprietorial rights. As such, s.233 did not apply to the variation sought by B.

R. v. THURROCK BOROUGH COUNCIL, *ex p.* BLUE CIRCLE INDUSTRIES [1994] 69 P. & C.R. 79, C.A.

4881. Restrictive covenant—discharge or modification—restriction that "granny annexe" not be used as independent dwelling unit—whether conferring practical benefit

[Town and Country Planning Act 1971 (c.78), s.52.]

A store was converted into a "granny annexe" on the applicants entering into a s.52 covenant that the annexe would not be used as an independent dwelling unit. Planning permission was later obtained for use of the annexe as an independent dwelling and the applicants sought to discharge the covenant, arguing that it conferred no benefit on the council, the only objector. The council argued that a release of the covenant would undermine its ability to control development.

Held, modifying the restriction to permit occupation as an independent dwelling subject to a condition restricting further development, that the use of the annexe as an independent dwelling would not affect the locality any more than its existing use and there was no practical benefit secured by the covenant. The decision to permit such occupation could not therefore be said to undermine the authority's policy aims of preventing obtrusive development. The fact that planning permission had been granted for the proposed use was a relevant but not overriding factor because the planning regime was separate from the restrictive covenant regime.

WILLIAMSON'S APPLICATION, *Re* (1994) 68 P. & C.R. 384, Lands Tribunal.

4882. Rural areas—environmental protection—planning policy—press release

The Secretaries of State for Environment and for Agriculture have launched a White Paper, *Rural England: A Nation Committed to a Living Countryside*, which provides a comprehensive review of rural policy and sets out how sustainable development can be implemented in the countryside. The White Paper focuses on the need for a thriving countryside and includes a number of measures to strengthen rural businesses, improve housing and protect the environment. These include a rate relief scheme for general stores and post offices; exempting villages of less than 3,000 from the proposed housing purchase grant scheme in order to encourage development of affordable housing; consultation on new powers for parish councils in crime prevention and community transport; a Rural Charter Initiative to ensure rural areas have adequate services; expansion of the Countryside Stewardship scheme; and consultation on a new Rural Business Use Class to encourage new businesses while reducing uncontrolled expansion. The White Paper is published by HMSO, Command No. 3016, ISBN 0 10 130162 6, £18·90. A summary will be available free of charge from DoE, Publications Despatch Centre, Blackhorse Road, London, SE99 6TT. Telephone: 0181 691 9191.

4883. Structure plan—alteration—Secretary of State's failure to give reasons—discretion to grant relief—whether Secretary of state obliged to give reasons for decision—whether substantial prejudice by decision

[Town and Country Planning Act 1990 (c.8), ss.35(10), 35A(7).]

The wording of s.35A(7) of the Town and Country Planning Act 1990 does not absolve the Secretary of State from giving reasons for a decision for approving a plan and rejecting objections to the plan.

The Secretary of State called in the local plan alteration and then approved the plan. L had objected to the plan but no mention was made in the Secretary of State's approval letter of those objections and no reasons were given for rejecting them. L sought to quash the approval of the plan and the Secretary of State argued that the wording of s.35A(7) of the 1990 Act meant that he was not required to state the reasons for his decision to an objector, merely to "give the authority" a statement of his reasons.

Held, dismissing the application, that the wording in the Act did not absolve the Secretary of State from giving a statement of his reasons, they merely indicated the procedural requirement that the reasons must be given to the local authority who must pass them on to the objector. The failure to give reasons made the approval of the plan defective but in this case L had not suffered substantial prejudice by the decision and the court would not exercise its discretion to grant relief.

LANDMATCH v. SECRETARY OF STATE FOR THE ENVIRONMENT AND SUFFOLK COUNTY COUNCIL AND FOREST HEALTH DISTRICT COUNCIL; *sub nom*. LANDMATCH v. SECRETARY OF STATE FOR THE ENVIRONMENT; R. v. SAME, *ex p.* LANDMATCH (1993) (1994) 68 P. & C.R. 149, Mr Malcolm Spence, Q.C. sitting as a deputy judge.

4884. Structure plan—modifications—Secretary of State—approval of modifications to structure plan—extent of duty to give reasons

[Town and Country Planning Act 1990 (c.8), s.35 (subsequently replaced); Town and Country Planning (Structure and Local Plans) Regulations 1982 (S.I. 1982, No. 555), regs. 21, 22.]

The Secretary of State decided to hold an examination in public into the replacement structure plan submitted in February 1990 by Cheshire County Council. There was a conflict regarding Chester between those seeking to provide more houses and jobs in the city and those seeking to preserve its historic buildings and sites and its Green Belt. The Greater Chester Local plan, which had been the subject of an inquiry in 1988, contained proposals for the deletion of land from the Green Belt in three areas of the city and a holding direction was put on this plan to enable the Secretary of State to reach a decision on both plans after the examination in public. As a result, issues relating to land released from the Green Belt for housing were considered in more detail than usual for structure plan purposes. The final decision was challenged on the ground that there had been a failure to give adequate and intelligible reasons for modification of the housing policy from land for 7,800 dwellings to 6,100 dwellings. The Secretary of State was under a statutory duty to give reasons.

Held, that the alleged deficiency of reasons would only be a ground for quashing the decision if the applicants had been substantially prejudiced by the Secretary of State's failure to explain why he had rejected their particular arguments, where he had explained his reasons for not releasing more Green Belt land. This was not a planning application but the approval of a structure plan and the Secretary of State was entitled to take account of the whole picture and was not required to give detailed consideration to one site.

ALFRED McALPINE HOMES (NORTH) v. SECRETARY OF STATE FOR THE ENVIRONMENT [1994] N.P.C. 138, C.A.

4885. Town and Country Planning (Cost of Inquiries etc.) Act 1995 (c.49)

The Secretary of State may recover payments from local authorities in respect of administrative costs of certain local inquiries and other hearings relating to Town and Country Planning.

The Act received the Royal Assent on November 8, 1995.

4886. Tree preservation order—conservation area—inspector dealt with application to fell trees as development—whether appropriate—whether failure to mention matters equivalent to failure to consider them

[Planning (Listed Buildings and Conservation Areas) Act 1990 (c.9), s.72.]

S applied to quash a decision of the Secretary of State dismissing an appeal against I council's decision to refuse consent for the felling of a tree in their garden which was damaging a wall. The grounds for the appeal were, first, that the inspector wrongly took Policy ENVA of the Unitary Development Plan into account as a material consideration when there was no formal requirement to apply it. Secondly, the inspector misconstrued the policy. On his interpretation all felling was prevented. This would be an unlawful fetter on the council. Finally, there was an error in the inspector's approach to his duty under the Planning (Listed Buildings and Conservation Areas) Act 1990, s.72, by regarding a tree felling order as development, in which case no tree would ever be removed. In addition, certain matters were not taken into account, as the inspector failed to refer to and analyse the characteristics of the conservation area and have regard to its planning history.

Held, dismissing the appeal, that (1) the inspector was entitled to bear Policy ENVA in mind, and construed it correctly to mean that trees should not be felled unless necessary and in those cases they should be replaced. The inspector correctly approached his duty under s.72; (2) an inference could not be made that the inspector failed to consider matters just because there was no specific reference to them (*Bolton Metropolitan District Council v. Secretary of State for the Environment* [1995] 7 C.L. 528 followed).

SHERWOOD v. SECRETARY OF STATE FOR THE ENVIRONMENT AND ISLINGTON LONDON BOROUGH COUNCIL (CO/1075/95), August 16, 1995, R. Purchas, Q.C.

4887. Tree preservation order—modification of area—powers of planning authorities

[Town and Country Planning Act 1990 (c.8), s.199(1).]

E, a landowner, appealed against the dismissal of his application to quash a tree preservation order made by W council in respect of a site over which there was concern for visual amenity. The planning authority had modified the original "area" order to include woodland comprising a greater mixture of broadleaved trees and E argued that, following *Britnell v. Secretary of State for Social Security*, the extended order was unlawful as the power to modify a tree preservation order under s.199(1) of the Town and Country Planning Act 1990 should be construed more narrowly.

Held, allowing the appeal, that the change from an area order to a "woodland" order was unlawful as it was outside the scope of s.199(1), since the proposed modifications would affect new trees not covered by the original designation and would create an entirely different order (*Britnell v. Secretary of State for Social Security* [1991] 1 W.L.R. 198 considered).

EVANS v. WAVERLEY BOROUGH COUNCIL, *The Times*, July 18, 1995, C.A.

4888. Use classes

TOWN AND COUNTRY PLANNING (USE CLASSES) (AMENDMENT) ORDER 1995 (No. 297) [65p], made under the Town and Country Planning Act 1990 (c.8), ss.55(2)(f), 333(7); operative on March 9, 1995; amends S.I. 1987 No. 764.

TRADE AND INDUSTRY

4889. Authorisation of exports—Serbia and Montenegro—European Community

Council Regulation (EC) 1380/95 of June 12, 1995 amending Reg. (EEC) 990/93 with a view to authorising the export of certain goods to Serbia and Montenegro ([1995] O.J. L138/1).

4890. Co-operation agreement—Yemen Arab Republic—European Community

Council Decision 95/67/EC on the conclusion of an Agreement amending the Co-operation Agreement between the European Economic Community and the Yemen Arab Republic (O.J. L 57/77).

4891. Commercial policy—former Yugoslav Republic of Macedonia—serious international tension constituting a threat of war—interim measures—European Community

The European Commission brought an action under Art. 225 EC for a declaration that Greece had made improper use of the powers provided for in Art. 224 EC in order to justify the unilateral measures it had adopted which prohibited trade, in particular via the port of Thessalonica, in products originating in, coming from or destined for the former Yugoslav Republic of Macedonia and imports into Greece of products originating in or coming from that Republic, and that by doing so it had infringed Art. 113 EC and Community legislation relating to international trade. The European Commission also sought interim measures requiring Greece to suspend its measures.

Held, that the Commission had shown that its arguments were sufficiently pertinent and serious to establish a prima facie case justifying interim measures, but nevertheless the necessary evidence of the existence of imminent harm had not been established. Accordingly, the application for interim measures was dismissed.

E.C. COMMISSION v. GREECE (C–120/94R), June 29, 1994, ECJ.

4892. Common commercial policy—renewal and maintenance—European Community

Council Decision 95/133/EC of April 19, 1995 authorising the automatic renewal or maintenance in force of provisions governing matters covered by the common commercial policy contained in the friendship, trade and navigation treaties and trade agreements concluded between Member States and third countries (O.J. L89/30).

4893. Corporation Agreement—partnership and development—Sri Lanka—European Community

Council Decision 95/129/EC of March 27, 1995 concerning the conclusion of the Corporation Agreement between the European Community and the Democratic Socialist Republic of Sri Lanka on Partnership and Development (O.J. L85/32).

4894. Department of Trade and Industry—fees

DEPARTMENT OF TRADE AND INDUSTRY (FEES) (AMENDMENT) ORDER 1995 (No. 1294) [£1·55], made under the Finance (No. 2) Act 1987 (c.51), s.102(5); operative on May 11, 1995; amends S.I. 1988 No. 93 by specifying for the purposes of the 1987 Act functions and matters which are to be taken into account in determining fees in respect of the Secretary of State's functions in relation to insurance companies and members of Lloyds.

4895. Department of Trade and Industry—inspectors' report—affairs and membership

The Department of Trade and Industry has published the inspectors' report into the affairs and membership of James Ferguson Holdings plc and the affairs of Barlow Clowes Gilt Managers Limited. Enquiries telephone 0171 215 5000.

4896. Dumped imports—protection—European Community

Council Regulation (EC) 1251/95 of May 29, 1995 amending Reg. (EC) 3283/94 on protection against dumped imports from countries not members of the European Community ([1995] O.J. L122/1).

4897. EEC–Austria Free Trade Agreement—ECJ ruling—concept of originating product—methods of administrative co-operation—European Community

The European Court of Justice was asked to rule on the meaning of certain provisions of the EEC–Austria Free Trade Agreement.

Held, that it is permissible to dispense with production of the documents mentioned in Title II of Protocol 3 to the EEC–Austria Agreement in the version contained in Council Reg. (EEC) 1598/88 concerning the declaration of the concept of "originating products" and methods of administrative co-operation, where the origin of the goods in issue has been established beyond doubt on the basis of objective evidence which could not have been manipulated or falsified by those involved, where both the importer and the exporter concerned took the steps necessary to obtain the documents referred to in the Protocol, and where it was for reasons beyond their control, such as anti-competitive conduct by other persons concerned contrary both to the objective and the terms of the Agreement, that it was impossible for them to produce those documents.

BONAPHARMA ARZNGIMITTEL GmbH v. HAUPTZOLLAMT KREFELD (C-334/93), February 23, 1995, ECJ, Fifth Chamber.

4898. E.C. Directives—machinery—failure to implement—imminent changes to Directive—European Community

The European Commission sought a declaration that, by failing to adopt the necessary national implementing legislation, Italy had failed to fulfil its E.C. Treaty obligations. Italy had not yet implemented Dir. 89/392/EEC on the approximation of the laws of the Member States relating to machinery or Dir. 91/368/EEC which amended Dir. 89/392/EEC. However, Italy argued that those Directives were in the process of being amended by the Council of Ministers, and that it would be appropriate for Italy to implement the Directives once amended accordingly.

Held, that Italy was in breach of its Treaty obligations. The fact that the Community was in the process of possibly amending the legislation did not release Italy from its obligation to comply with present Community law.

E.C. COMMISSION v. ITALY (C-182/94), June 1, 1995, ECJ, Fifth Chamber.

4899. Export credits—investment guarantees

EXPORT AND INVESTMENT GUARANTEES (LIMIT ON FOREIGN CURRENCY COMMITMENTS) ORDER 1995 (No. 1988), made under Export and Investment Guarantees Act 1991, s.6(4)(a); operative on July 27, 1995; increases the limit of the amount of the aggregate foreign currency commitments of the Secretary of State from 15,000 million special drawing rights to 20,000 million special drawing rights to accommodate prospective future business.

4900. Export refunds

EXPORT REFUNDS (ADMINISTRATIVE PENALTIES) (RATE OF INTEREST) REGULATIONS 1995 (No. 2861) [65p], made under the European Communities Act 1972, s.2(2). In force: December 1, 1995; reg. 2 specifies the rate of interest to be applied in the calculation of any interest payable pursuant to Art. 11 of Commission Reg. 3665/87 laying down common detailed rules for the application of the system of export refunds on agricultural products, which was amended as regards the recovery of amounts unduly paid and sanctions by Commission Reg. 2945/94. Article 11(1) provides for the payment of interest on the amount payable in certain circumstances by an exporter who has requested a refund in excess of that applicable, and Art. 11(3) provides for the payment of interest on the amount to be reimbursed by an exporter to whom an export refund has been unduly paid. The rate of interest so specified is one percentage point over the sterling three-month London interbank offered rate. In the case of interest specified in Art. 11(1), interest is charged for the period beginning 30 days after the date of receipt of the payment demand and ending on the day preceding the date of payment; and in the case of interest specified in Art. 11(3), interest is charged for the period between the date of payment of the export refund and the date of reimbursement.

4901. Exports—European Community

Council Regulation (EC) 3287/94 of December 22, 1994 on pre-shipment inspections for exports from the Community (O.J. L349/79).

4902. Exports—export licences—failure to obtain export licences—goods for military and civil purposes—security—application to ECJ for preliminary ruling—principle of proportionality—European Community

[EEC Treaty 1957, Art. 113; Council Regulation 2603/69.]

L was charged with having delivered to Iraq machinery and chemical products, being goods which could be used for both military and civil purposes, without the export licences which were necessary for such goods under German law. The German court sought a preliminary ruling from the ECJ on the application of Art. 113 of the Treaty of Rome 1957 and rts. 1 and 11 of Council Reg. 2603/69 as amended.

Held, that Art. 113 was to be interpreted as meaning that German rules governing such exports fell within its scope and that the Community had exclusive competence, except where it gave Member States specific authorisa. Whilst Art. 1 of Council Reg. 2603/69 prohibited the application of quantitative restrictions to products exported from the European Union to non-member countries, Art. 11 provided an exception in circumstances where public security was a consideration. In such circumstances the principle of proportionality would not preclude a Member State imposing a requirement that an applicant must prove that the goods would be used solely for civil purposes, or refusing a licence if the goods could objectively be used for a military purpose. Neither did E.C. law preclude Member States from imposing criminal penalties in respect of breaches of licensing procedure.

CRIMINAL PROCEEDINGS AGAINST LEIFER (C–83/94), *The Times*, November 2, 1995, ECJ.

4903. External trade—products originating in the overseas countries and territories—derogations—European Community

The Netherlands sought the annulment of a Commission decision refusing a derogation from the definition of concept of originating product in respect of certain pre-recorded video cassettes. Goods are to be considered as originat ing products in the overseas countries and territories if they are either wholly obtained or sufficiently worked or processed there.

Held, that the Commission had been wrong to refuse the derogation sought. The Commission had wrongly delayed in making its decision. The decision was therefore annulled.

NETHERLANDS v. E.C. COMMISSION (C–430/92), October 26, 1994, ECJ, Sixth Chamber.

4904. Free movement of goods—imported medicinal products not authorised in state of import—prohibition of advertising—European Community

As it was permitted to do under national law, a company imported into Germany medicinal products which had not been authorised by the German authorities. It advertised these in German publications aimed for professionals in the health sector. A German competitor applied for a court order that the importing company cease the advertising on the ground that it was prohibited under the law on advertising in the health sector.

Held, that as the relevant national law applied solely to foreign medicinal products, it must fall within the scope of Art. 30 EEC. As the prohibition on advertising may restrict imports of medicinal products into Germany, it is a measure having equivalent effect to a quantitative restriction on imports. However, the health and life of humans rank foremost among the interests protected by Art. 36 and it is for the Member States to decide what degree of protection to ensure. Nevertheless, national rules or practices having, or likely to have, a restrictive effect on the importation of pharmaceutical products are compatible with the Treaty only to the extent that they are necessary for the effective protection of health and life of humans. In this case, in the absence of harmonisation or mutual recognition, Member States are permitted to prohibit entirely the marketing in their territory of medicinal products which have not been authorised by the competent national authorities. The prohibition of advertising had the purpose of ensuring that the general requirement of national authorisation under German law was not systematically circumvented by manufacturers obtaining authorisation for their medicinal products in a Member State imposing fewer requirements and importing them into Germany on the basis of orders encouraged by an advertising campaign. It was therefore necessary for the effectiveness of the national authorisation scheme. Consequently it was justified on public health grounds under Art. 36.

LUCIEN ORTSCHEIT GmbH v. EURIM-PHARM ARZNEIMITTEL GmbH (C–320/93), November 10, 1994, ECJ, Fifth Chamber.

4905. Free movement of goods—motorvehicles—roadworthiness tests—MOT tests—whether requirement that garage established in national state invalid—European Community

S was convicted of driving a motorvehicle without a valid test certificate. On appeal, the question arose whether Community law precluded national legislation by virtue of which test certificates for vehicles registered in that State could not be issued by garages established in another Member State.

Held, that neither the provisions of the EEC Treaty relating to the free movement of goods services or competition, to the freedom to provide services and to competition, nor those of Council Dir. 77/143/EEC on the approximation of the laws of the Member States relating to roadworthiness tests of motorvehicles and their trailers, preclude national legislation which does not permit test certificates of cars registered in that State to be issued by garages established in another Member State. It was true that this requirement might lead the owners of cars to dispense with the services of garages established abroad and to forego the opportunity to purchase there any spare parts which might be required, because it was practical and less expensive to have maintenance and repairs undertaken in a garage which, when servicing or repairing the vehicle, could also carry out the periodic test free of charge. Requirements of that kind could be justified, however, by reasons of road safety, which constituted overriding reasons relating to the public interest.

CRIMINAL PROCEEDINGS AGAINST VAN SCHAIK (C–55/93), October 5, 1994, ECJ, Fifth Chamber.

4906. Free movement of goods—obscene publications—definition of obscene material—confiscation of material by customs and excise—whether public morality affecting right to free movement of goods

The applicant was a member of a pressure group aiming to reform the U.K.'s obscenity laws. He applied for judicial review of the court's decision not to state a case for the opinion of the High Court. He had returned to the U.K. from the Netherlands and had six sexually explicit videos seized by Customs and Excise officers. He argued that, *inter alia*, this was contrary to Art. 30 of the Treaty of Rome which allows the free movement of goods.

Held, dismissing the application, that Art. 36 of the Treaty of Rome allows for derogations from the right to free movement of goods on grounds of public morality (*R. v. Bow Street Magistrates' Court, ex p. Noncyp* [1990] 1 Q.B. 123, *R. v. Waterfield* [1975] C.L.Y. 740 considered).

R. v. UXBRIDGE JUSTICES, *ex p.* WEBB [1994] C.O.D. 24, D.C.

4907. Free movement of goods—quantitative restrictions—prohibition of products sold at a loss—whether equal application of legislation to domestic products and those of other member states—EEC law

[Treaty of Rome 1957, Art. 30.]

Where a law of a Member State prohibited traders from offering for sale products at a loss and provided that sales which yielded only a very low profit margin were to be treated as sales at a loss, Art. 30 of the Treaty of Rome 1957 did not apply so long as the provisions applied equally to the marketing of products from other Member States as to domestic products (*Keck, Re* [1993] E.C.R. I–6077 applied).

GROUPEMENT NATIONAL DES NEGOCIANTS EN POMMES DE TERRE DE BELGIQUE v. ITM BELGIUM SA, *The Times*, September 25, 1995, ECJ.

4908. Free movement of persons—doctors—medical specialities—training periods—remuneration—European Community. See E.C. COMMISSION v. SPAIN (C–277/93), §3313.

4909. Freedom to provide services—liberalisation of capital movements—loan for construction of dwelling—interest rate subsidy—requirement that obtained from credit institution—incompatible with EEC law—European Community

[Treaty of Rome 1957.]

A Member State's rule which provided that, in order to qualify for an interest rate subsidy for dependent children, a loan for the construction of a dwelling must have been obtained from a credit institution approved in that Member State, was incompatible with provisions in the Treaty of Rome 1957 on freedom to provide services and liberalisation of capital movements.

SVENSSON v. MINISTRE DU LOGEMENT DE L'URBANISME (C–484/93), *The Times*, November 29, 1995, ECJ.

4910. Imports—European Community

Council Regulation (EC) 3283/94 of December 22, 1994 on protection against dumped imports from countries not members of the European Community (O.J. L349/1).

Council Regulation (EC) 3284/94 of December 22, 1994 on protection against subsidised imports from countries not members of the European Community (O.J. L349/22).

Council Regulation (EC) 3285/94 of December 22, 1994 on the common rules for imports and repealing Reg. (EC) 528/94 (O.J. L349/53).

4911. Imports—plants originating in another Member State—requirement of authorisation—whether failure of a Member State to fulfil its obligations—European Community

Italy required prior authorisation for all imports of plants susceptible to fire blight. The Commission sought a declaration that Italy had thus failed to fulfil its obligations under Art. 11 of Dir. 77/93/EEC on protective measures against the introduction of harmful organisms of plants, as amended by Dir. 88/572 and Dir. 89/439, and Art. 30 of the Treaty in conjunction with Art. 10(1) of Reg.

234/68 on the establishment of a common organisation of the market in live plants. It argued that the Directive was designed to remove the obstacles to intra-Community trade in plants, while reorganising the Member States' plant-health inspections. The Directive provided that the examination of plants was to be conducted in the State of origin and specified the inspections which might be carried out in the State of destination. These inspections were limited by the provisions of Art. 11(1) and (3) of the Directive, from which it followed that the earliest that the inspections could take place was at the border. The requirement of authorisation prior to the introduction of plants from other Member States into Italy did not feature among the protective measures authorised for the State of destination.

Held, that the Directive introduced a consistent and exhaustive set of measures capable of being implemented to ensure the protection of plants within the Community. Where a directive harmonised measures to ensure the protection of animal and human health and establish Community procedures to ensure compliance, recourse to Art. 36 EEC was no longer justified. The same solution applied where a directive harmonised the measures necessary for the protection of plants.

E.C. COMMISSION v. ITALY (C–294/92), September 20, 1994, ECJ.

4912. Imports—textiles from Taiwan—value of goods for customs purposes—inclusion of charges for "own" quotas issued free of charge—no separate declaration of quota charges excluded from customs value—whether charges to be included in valuation—European Community

Women's clothing manufactured in Hong Kong and Taiwan was imported into the Community. The Customs Audit Office for the Düsseldorf tax region found that the quota charges invoiced by the exporter had not been included in the declaration of the customs value and that it was impossible to establish whether the sums paid related to the use of the exporter's own quotas or in the acquisition of a third party's export quotas. The quota charges from Taiwan had not been declared. The Principal Customs Office, Essen, considered that the charges ought to be included in the valuation for customs and sent the importer a revised demand.

Held, that it followed from the combined provisions of Art. 3(1) and (3)(a) of Reg. 1224/80 on the valuation of goods for customs purposes, as amended by Reg. 3193/80, that the customs value included all payments made or to be made by the seller as a condition of the sale of imported goods by the buyer to the seller or by the buyer to a third party to satisfy an obligation of the seller. Quotas allocated free of charge, as in this case, could have a commercial value for the seller but entailed no charges for him. Amounts invoiced in respect of those quotas constituted a disguised element of the price so are to be included in the customs value of goods. Importers could not be required to indicate separately charges for third party quotas and charges for own quotas as the Regulation was silent on the matter. However, a buyer who wished to exclude quota charges from customs value must establish that they were third party quotas or own quotas granted to the exporter against payment.

KLAUS THIERSCHMIDT GmbH v. HAUPTZOLLAMT ESSEN (C–340/93), August 9, 1994, ECJ, Fifth Chamber.

4913. Industrial training

S.I. 1995 Nos. 25 (construction board—levy) [£1·55]; 26 (engineering construction—levy) [£1·55].

4914. International trade—European Community

Council Decision 94/798/EC of December 8, 1994 accepting, on behalf of the Community, Annexes E.7 and F.4 to the International Convention on the Simplification and Harmonisation of Customs Procedures (O.J. L331/11).

Council Decision 94/882/EC of December 19, 1994 concerning the conclusion of a Co-operation Agreement between the European Community and the Republic of South Africa (O.J. L341/61).

Council Regulation (EC) 3286/94 of December 22, 1994 laying down Community procedures in the field of the common commercial policy in order to ensure the exercise of the Community's rights under international trade rules, in particular those established under the auspices of the World Trade Organisation (O.J. L349/71).

Council Regulation (EC) 356/95 of February 20, 1995 amending Reg. (EC) 3268/94 laying down Community procedures in the field of the common commercial policy in order to ensure the exercise of the Community's rights under international trade rules, in particular those established under the auspices of the World Trade Organisation (O.J. L41/3).

4915. Iron and steel—ECSC Treaty—steel quota which may be produced and delivered in the Common Market—European Community

F brought an appeal against the judgment of the Court of First Instance of June 5, 1992 in which that court refused to annul the Commission's decision imposing a fine on the applicant for exceeding its steel quotas. It also sought to reduce the amount of that fine.

Held, that the Commission had acted properly and the appeal was dismissed. In respect of the reduction of the fine, where questions of law were being decided in the context of an appeal, it was not for the ECJ to substitute, on grounds of fairness, its own appraisal for that of the Court of First Instance adjudicating, in the exercise of its unlimited jurisdiction, on the amount of a fine imposed on an undertaking by reason of its infringement of Community law.

FINANZIARIA FINSIDER SpA v. E.C. COMMISSION (C–320/92 P), December 15, 1994, ECJ.

4916. Monopolies and Mergers Commission investigation—judicial review—whether rule in agreements "attributable" to monopoly—whether against public interest. See R. v. MONOPOLIES AND MERGERS COMMISSION, *ex p.* NATIONAL HOUSE BUILDING COUNCIL, §166.

4917. Packaging—European Community

European Parliament and Council Dir. 94/62/EC of December 20, 1994 on packaging and packaging waste (O.J. L365/10).

4918. Precious metals—lack of hallmark—whether sale to be banned—European Community

H was prosecuted in the Netherlands for having had in her possession or having traded gold and silver rings not bearing the hallmark required by the Waartborgwet 1986 Law.

Held, that the market for articles of precious metal was the subject of differing national rules on quality. Legislation which required additional hallmarking of articles of precious metal imported from other Member States, in which they are lawfully traded and hallmarked, rendered the imports more difficult and costly. However, the requirement that an importer cause to be affixed a hallmark indicating the quantity of precious metal used was in principle of such a nature as to ensure effective protection for consumers and to promote fair trading. Accordingly, Art. 30 does not preclude national rules prohibiting the sale of articles of precious metal not bearing a hallmark under those rules, provided that those articles do not bear a hallmark in accordance with the legislation of the Member State of exportation containing information which is equivalent to that provided by the hallmarks required by the rules of the Member State of importation and which is intelligible to consumers.

Where national rules require the hallmark to be affixed by an independent body, the marketing of articles of precious metal imported from other Member States may not be prohibited if those articles have in fact been hallmarked by an independent body in the Member State of exportation. However, Art. 30 precludes the application of national rules which prohibit the marketing of articles of precious metal which do not indicate the date of their manufacture, where those articles have been lawfully marketed without that indication in other Member States from which they have been imported.

NEELTJE v. HOUTWIPPER (C–293/93), September 15, 1994, ECJ, Fifth Chamber.

4919. Restrictive trade practices—price-fixing—construction industry—Commission fine—action for annulment—whether rules of Association of Building Contractors in contravention of E.C. law—European Community. See VERENIGING VAN SAMENWERKENDE PRIJSREGELENDE ORGANISATIES IN DE BOUWNIJVERHEID v. E.C. COMMISSION (T–29/92), §652.

4920. Sanctions—prohibition exports—validity of national legislation—whether reference to ECJ necessary

[Council Regulation 1432/92; Council Regulation 990/93; Customs and Excise Management Act 1979 (c.2); Criminal Appeal Act 1968 (c.19), s.32(1); Serbia and Montenegro (United Nations Sanctions) Order 1992 (S.I. 1992 No. 1302).]

The court was required to determine joined appeals against conviction for evading the prohibition on exporting goods to Serbia. The questions for the court to consider were whether the Serbia and Montenegro (United States Sanctions) Order 1992 and Council Regs. 1432/92 and 990/93 were valid, and if so whether the sanctions could be effectively enforced by penalties.

Held, dismissing the appeal, that no reference to the ECJ was required to determine that both the E.C. Regulations and 1992 Order were valid. Effective statutory mechanisms existed in the U.K. to enforce the sanctions with penalties pursuant to the Customs and Excise Management Act 1979. If the particulars of the offences as charged specified the Order instead of the Regulations, or vice versa, the court was nevertheless entitled to convict, applying the proviso in s.32(1) of the Criminal Appeal Act 1968 (*R. v. Ayres* [1984] C.L.Y. 538 followed).

R. v. SEARLE, *The Times*, February 27, 1995, C.A.

4921. Social policy—European Social Fund—training programme—reduction in financial assistance—whether breach of duty to the state—European Community

The applicant, a Portuguese company, applied for assistance from the European Social Fund in respect of a projected training programme. It received an advance of 50 per cent. On completion of the training programme, a claim for final payment was made. The Portuguese authorities then carried out an accounting analysis of the claim and decided to reduce the amount payable. This amount was confirmed by the Commission and the applicant sought the annulment of this Commission decision.

Held, that the Commission had acted unlawfully in reducing the assistance initially granted to the applicant. The decision was not properly reasoned and was therefore in breach of the duty to state reasons imposed by Art. 190 of the Treaty.

EUGENIO BRANCO v. E.C. COMMISSION (T–85/94) January 12, 1995, CFI, Third Chamber.

4922. State aids—European Community

Commission Decision 95/253/EC of January 17, 1995 on aid awarded by the French Government to Allied Signal Fibers Europe SA (O.J. L159/21).

Commission Decision 95/282/EC of July 17, 1995 on Finnish State aid for seeds (O.J. L173/58).

4923. State aids—incompatible with Common Market—Commission decision ordering recovery—non-implementation—whether objective difficulties amounted to defence—European Community

In Decision 90/224/EEC of May 24, 1989, the European Commission found that aid granted by the Italian Government to two companies was incompatible with the Common Market, contrary to Art. 92(1) EEC. The Italian Government was ordered to abolish the aid and recover it from the recipient undertakings within two months. The European Court of Justice rejected an application for annulment of that decision. Without contesting its obligation to comply with the decision, Italy referred to objective difficulties hampering implementation arising from the procedure for winding up the companies.

Held, that the only defence available to a Member State is to plead that it was absolutely impossible for it to implement the decision properly. However, a Member State which, in giving effect to a Commission decision, encounters unforeseen and unforeseeable difficulties or becomes aware of consequences overlooked by the Commission, must submit those problems to the Commission for consideration, together with proposals for suitable amendments to the decision in question. In such cases, the Commission and the Member State must, pursuant to the principle of co-operation, work together in good faith with a view to overcoming the difficulties whilst fully observing the Treaty provisions. Since Italy had not taken such a stance, it was in breach of its Treaty obligations (*Italy v. E.C. Commission (C–261/89)* [1991] ECR I–4437).

E.C. COMMISSION v. ITALY (C–349/93), February 23, 1995, ECJ, Sixth Chamber.

4924. State aids—letter initiating the investigation procedure—suspension of aid—whether part of general aid scheme or new aid—European Community

Italy sought the annulment of the Commission's decision to initiate the procedure provided for in Art. 93(2) E.C. against the grant of aid by Italy to Italgrani. The Commission was of the view that the aid was not permitted by Art. 92(3) E.C. Italy objected to the aid as being classified as new aid, since the Commission had already been notified of and had approved a general scheme for aid in the Mezzogiorno. Italy said that the aid was no more than a specific implementation of that general scheme.

Held, that the Commission's decision was partially unlawful. Once a general aid scheme had been notified to the Commission, individual implementing measures did not need to be notified, since the Commission would only appraise them in the same manner as the general scheme.

ITALY v. E.C. COMMISSION (C–47/91), October 5, 1994, ECJ.

4925. State aids—shipbuilding—whether aid development assistance—general principles of Community law—European Community

Germany sought the annulment of a Commission Decision concerning proposed aid by Germany to the Chinese shipping company Cosco for the construction of container vessels. Under Dir. 90/684, aid related to shipbuilding granted as development assistance could be deemed to be compatible with the Common Market if it complied with certain OECD rules. Germany had decided to grant aid in respect of three container vessels which were to be built in Bremen and Wismar. However, the Commission decided that the aid could not be considered as genuine development aid and ruled that it was not compatible with the Common Market.

Held, that the Commission had acted lawfully. The aid could not be regarded as genuine development aid. There had been no breach by the

Commission of the principles of legal certainty and the protection of legitimate expectations.

GERMANY v. E.C. COMMISSION (C-400/92), October 5, 1994, ECJ.

4926. Statistics

STATISTICS OF TRADE (CUSTOMS AND EXCISE) (AMENDMENT) REGULATIONS 1994 (No. 2914) [65p], made under the European Communities Act 1972 (c.68), s.2(2); operative on January 1, 1995; amend S.I. 1993 No. 3015 by increasing the thresholds in reg. 3 to £150,000.

STATISTICS OF TRADE (CUSTOMS AND EXCISE) (AMENDMENT) REGULATIONS 1995 (No. 2946) [65p], made under the European Communities Act 1972, s.2(2); amend S.I. 1992 No. 2790; revoke S.I. 1994 No. 2914. In force: January 1, 1996; change the assimilation threshold set for trade in goods despatched, or goods received, in reg. 3(1) of the 1992 Regulations from £150,000 to £160,000.

4927. Subsidised imports—protection—European Community

Council Regulation (EC) 1252/95 of May 29, 1995 amending Reg. (EC) 3284/94 on protection against subsidised imports from countries not members of the European Community ([1995] O.J. L122/2).

4928. Tariff quotas—European Community

Council Regulation (EC) 3361/94 of December 29, 1994 opening tariff quotas with respect to Austria, Finland and Sweden (O.J. L356/5).

4929. Technical progress—European Community

Commission Directive 94/68/EC of December 16, 1994 adapting to technical progress Dir. 78/318/EEC on windscreen wipers and washer systems of motorvehicles (O.J. L354/1).

Commission Directive 94/78/EC of December 21, 1994 adapting to technical progress Dir. 78/549/EEC as regards the wheel guards of motorvehicles (O.J. L354/10).

4930. Trade agreement—textile products—European Community

Council Decision 95/131/EC of February 20, 1995 on the provisional application of certain Agreements between the European Community and third countries on trade in textile products (O.J. L94/1).

4931. Uruguay Round—European Community

Council Regulation (EC) 3288/94 of December 22, 1994 amending Reg. (EC) 40/94 on the Community trade mark for the implementation of the agreements concluded in the framework of the Uruguay Round (O.J. L349/83).

Council Regulation (EC) 3290/94 of December 22, 1994 on the adjustments and transitional arrangements required in the agriculture sector in order to implement the agreements concluded during the Uruguay Round (O.J. L349/105).

Council Decision 94/800/EC of December 22, 1994 concerning the conclusion on behalf of the European Community, as regards matters within its competence, of the agreements reached in the Uruguay Round multilateral negotiations (1986–1994) (O.J. L336/1).

TRADE MARKS AND TRADE NAMES

4932. Anton Piller order—proceedings for infringement of a trade mark or passing off—risk of incrimination—whether risk of incrimination excuses obligation to comply with order. See COCA-COLA CO. v. GILBEY, §3915.

4933. Birmingham Assay Office Act 1995 (c.vi)

This Act, *inter alia*, increases the range of activities which may be undertaken by the Birmingham Assay Office to include the analysis of materials and articles of any kind. Section 16 of the Hallmarking Act 1973 (c.43) is amended retrospectively to validate the making of the Birmingham Assay Office Order 1989 (S.I. 1989 No. 900).

The Act received Royal Assent on July 19, 1995.

4934. Community trade mark

COMMUNITY TRADE MARK (FEES) REGULATIONS 1995 (No. 3175), made under the Trade Marks Act 1994 s.52. operative on January 1, 1996; [65p]. These Regulations provide that a fee of GPB 15.00 may be charged by the registrar of trade marks when applications for Community trade marks are filed at the Patent Office.

4935. Counterfeit and pirated goods

COUNTERFEIT AND PIRATED GOODS (CONSEQUENTIAL PROVISIONS) REGULATIONS 1995 (No. 1447) [£1·10], made under the European Communities Act 1972 (c.68), s.2(2); operative on July 1, 1995; make provision consequential on Council Reg. (EC) 3295/94 which provides for the prohibition of the release for free circulation of counterfeit and pirated goods.

TRADE MARKS (EC MEASURES RELATING TO COUNTERFEIT GOODS) REGULATIONS 1995 (No. 1444) [65p], made under the European Communities Act 1972 (c.68), s.2(2); operative on July 1, 1995; amend Trade Marks Act 1994, s.89(3) so as to give effect to Council Reg. (EC) 3295/94 which provides for the prohibition of the release for free circulation, export, re-export or entry for a suspensive procedure of counterfeit and pirated goods.

4936. Infringement—counterfeit razors—whether innocence a defence

[R.S.C., Ord. 14.]

D purchased in Italy and resold in the U.K., counterfeit razors. P sued for infringement of the registered trade mark and passing off and, having obtained interlocutory relief, applied for summary judgment under R.S.C., Ord. 14. D disputed that the goods were counterfeit and, if they were, that he had ever dealt in them. In the alternative, D contended that as an innocent dealer, no order for an inquiry as to damages should be made. P accepted that D had been unaware of the fact that the goods were counterfeit, but that such innocence was irrelevant.

Held, giving judgment for P and ordering an inquiry as to damages for infringement of trade mark and passing off, that (1) it was not shown that there was any issue or question in dispute that ought to be tried, or that for some other reason there ought to be a trial of P's claims and P was thus entitled to injunctive relief; (2) it was well settled law that the innocence on the part of the infringer was no defence to a claim to damages (*Henry Heath v. Frederick Gorringe* (1924) 41 R.P.C. 457 followed; *Slazenger v. Spalding* [1910] 1 Ch. 257 not followed; *Ellen v. Slack* (1880) 24 Sol J. 290 distinguished); and (3) there was no good reason why, if damages were recoverable from the innocent infringer of a registered trade mark, they should not be recoverable for innocent passing off (*A.G. Spalding v. A. W. Gamage* (1915) R.P.C. 273 followed).

GILLETTE U.K. v. EDENWEST [1994] R.P.C. 279, Blackburne J.

4937. Infringement—eye-drops—interlocutory injunction—whether unregistered trade mark confusingly similar to registered trade mark—whether registration should be rectified having regard to non-use in the U.K.

[Trade Marks Act 1938 (c.22), ss.4, 12(2), 26, 31, 68(2)(b).]

P owned a number of trade mark registrations having the suffix -CROM. One of these was VICROM which was used only in respect of eye-drops exported to New Zealand. D applied for rectification of the register in respect of the mark VICROM and launched a similar product under the name EYE-CROM. D argued that P's mark would be pronounced "vic-rom" and not "vi-crom" and was not confusingly similar to EYE-CROM. D contended that the registration of VICROM should be expunged for non-use under s.26(1)(b) and also that the registration should be limited under s.26(2), having regard to its use in the export trade only. P sought an interlocutory injunction restraining D from advertising, selling or supplying pharmaceutical products under the name EYE-CROM.

Held, granting the injunction, that (1) VICROM and EYE-CROM were confusingly similar in sound (*Saville Perfumery v. June Perfect and F.W. Woolworth & Co.* (1941) 58 R.P.C. 147 and *Aristoc v. Rysta* (1945) 62 R.P.C. 65 followed); (2) registration might be expunged under s.26(1)(b) in the absence of use on goods of the registration but not in the absence of use only in particular locations. Section 31 deemed VICROM to have been used in relation to goods for which it had been used for export. The allegation of invalidity based on s.26(1)(b) therefore failed (*South Metropolitan Gas Co.'s Trade Mark* (1933) 50 R.P.C. 321 followed); (3) the argument that the registration of VICROM should be limited under s.26(2) could not succeed. D"s mark did not qualify for registration under s.12(2), s.31 deemed export use to be use in the U.K. and no application had been made to limit the registration to particular export markets; (4) use of the mark EYE-CROM infringed the registration of VICROM; there was no serious defence to be tried; (5) there was no serious risk of injustice to D if the injunction were granted (*Patel v. Smith (W.H.) (Eziot)* [1987] C.L.Y. 3039, *R. v. Secretary of State for Transport, ex p. Factortame (No. 2)* [1991] C.L.Y. 4032 referred to); and (6) as to the further allegation that the use of EYE-CROM infringed the registration of P's trade mark OPTICROM, there was a serious issue to be tried.

FISONS v. NORTON HEALTHCARE [1994] F.S.R. 745, Aldous J.

4938. Infringement—IBM computer memory cards—cards allegedly reworked—defences—whether misrepresentation

[R.S.C., Ord. 14A; Ord. 15, r.5; Ord. 18, r.19; Ord. 19, r.7; Ord. 27, r.3; Trade Marks Act 1938 (c.22), s.4(3); Treaty of Rome, Arts. 85, 86.]

P, a large manufacturer and supplier of computer equipment and a proprietor of the U.K. trade mark "IBM", complained that D had supplied "reworked" memory cards as IBM manufactured cards. P used the term "reworked" memory to describe memory that had been manufactured by a third party independently of IBM, but using IBM components. P asserted that sale of such "reworked" cards under a description containing the words "IBM manufactured" amounted to trade mark infringement and passing off. P also provided a maintenance service in respect of its computers which D alleged to be a powerful factor in the decision to purchase a particular computer. D claimed that P had been refusing service for its computers where they had been modified by the installation of non-IBM parts with the object of causing customers to buy modifications and spare parts from P itself and not from independent competitors. D pleaded defences of "no misrepresentation", acquiescence, the statutory defence under s.4(3) of the Trade Marks Act 1938 and a "Euro-defence", alleging infringement of Arts. 85 and 86 of the Treaty of Rome. D counterclaimed infringement of Arts. 85 and 86 of the Treaty of Rome arising respectively from P's withdrawal of maintenance services, and the provision for such withdrawal in the maintenance agreements. D meanwhile submitted a complaint to the Commission. Interim measures were refused but the investigation was still in progress. D served a notice of motion to stay proceedings until final determination by the Commission and P then served a notice of motion seeking an order that D's defence and counterclaim be struck out pursuant to Ord. 14, r.19. The latter was subsequently amended to seek judgment pursuant to Ord. 14A; Ord. 19, r.7; Ord. 27, r.3 or Ord. 15, r.5. The issue which P wished the court to decide under Ord. 14A was (1) whether D's description of its memory cards as being "IBM manufactured" amounted to a misrepresentation and/or (2) whether D's memory cards were goods to which P had applied, or consented to the use of, the trade mark "IBM" pursuant to s.4(3) of the Trade Marks Act 1938.

Held, striking out the Euro-defence but not the remainder of the defences or counterclaim, staying the counterclaim pending disposal of D's complaint to the Commission or further order, and refusing a stay of action pending disposal of D's complaint to the Commission, that (1) the "no misrepresentation" defence could not be struck out because there were real issues of importance to be tried (*Erven Warninck Besloten Vennootschap v. Townend (J.) & Sons (Hull)* [1979] C.L.Y. 2690 applied; *Burberrys v. J.C. Cording & Co.* (1909) 26 R.P.C. 693, *G.H. Gledhill & Sons v. British Perforated Toilet Paper Company* (1911) 28 R.P.C. 429, *Diehl K.G.'s Application, Re* [1969] C.L.Y. 3566 referred to). The issue could not be determined under Ord. 14A since the question was one of a more general nature involving fact rather than law, namely whether certain of the essential ingredients of the tort of passing off were established; (2) the defence of acquiescence would not be struck out since the facts alleged, if proved, might be capable of establishing acquiescence (*Habib Bank v. Habib Bank AG Zurich* [1982] C.L.Y. 3262 applied; *Taylor Fashions v. Liverpool Victoria Friendly Society; Old and Campbell v. Same* [1979] C.L.Y. 1619, *Wenlock v. Maloney* [1965] C.L.Y. 3282 referred to). It was not the function of the court on an application to strike out pursuant to Ord. 18, r.19, to embark upon a detailed process of weighing evidence; (3) the statutory defence under s.4(3) of the Trade Marks Act 1938 would not be struck out since the provisions of s.4(3) were complex and technical and could not be applied with any precision to any given situation until the relevant facts had been found at trial, and similarly the issue could not be determined under Ord. 14A because it involved consideration of substantial matters of fact; (4) the "Euro-defences" under Arts. 85 and 86 would be struck out. There must be some nexus between the infringement of the intellectual property right complained of and the abuse. If D succeeded in its case that "IBM manufactured" meant no more than manufactured either by IBM, or by someone else from IBM parts to IBM specifications, then D would not need its Euro-defence. Such a defence would only be relevant if it was held that IBM's case on misrepresentation was correct. In that event it would be no defence to the claim of passing off for D to show that P was bound, as a result of the application of Art. 86, to maintain the reworked memory it manufactured (*Imperial Chemicals Industries v. Berk Pharmaceuticals* [1981] C.L.Y. 2788 considered); (5) the counterclaim would not be struck out. There was no need for a nexus between the claim and the counterclaim and the latter raised issues, such as P's maintenance policy throughout the E.C., which went wider than issues raised by P's claim. Any decision by the Commission or the European Court of Justice would authoritatively determine the counterclaim. The counterclaim should thus proceed independently of P's claim and would be stayed until conclusion of D's complaint to the Commission; and (6) the action would not be stayed since a party who had properly commenced an action over which the English courts had jurisdiction had a right to proceed to trial. The Commission and the European Court of Justice did not have jurisdiction to deal with claims of passing off or trade mark infringement.

INTERNATIONAL BUSINESS MACHINES CORP. v. PHOENIX INTERNATIONAL (COMPUTERS) [1994] R.P.C. 251, Ferris J.

4939. Infringement—passing off—interlocutory injunction—balance of convenience—whether "apparatus for use with computers"—whether plaintiffs on notice when told of intentions in confidence—whether defendants entitled to costs

[Trade Marks Act 1938 (c.22), ss.7, 11.]

P was the supplier of high-performance computers known as work-stations. In February 1993 P launched a range of products under the name INDIGO which P had registered as a trade mark as of February 5, 1991 in a class including "computers and apparatus for use with computers". P claimed to have between three and five per cent of the top end of the pre-press market and had ambitions to expand further into this field. P did not make printers. D was a member of a group called the Indigo group. The group intended to exhibit a new digital printing press (the "E-Print") at a trade fair in September 1993. P commenced proceedings for infringement of registered trade mark and passing off and applied for an interlocutory injunction to restrain D from marketing the E-Print under the mark INDIGO, in particular at the trade fair.

Held, refusing the injunction, that (1) there was a triable issue as to whether P or D had first used the mark INDIGO. P's case that such market activity that there was before the priority date was on a confidential basis and was too spasmodic to constitute continuous use for the purposes of s.7 of the 1938 Act was arguable; (2) P's case on trade mark infringement was significantly more likely to fail than to succeed. It was the goods to be sold and not the constituent parts that were in issue. The E-Print was a printer and was not converted into a computer by the versatility of its operation. Marks of sourced articles such as the work-station which was a part of the E-Print would not be removed by D. If the monitor and the keyboard were to be regarded as separate articles of commerce, their separate source would be identified. This does not convert the rest of E-Print into apparatus for use with a computer, it remains a printing press; (3) a confidential intimation of an intention to infringe a trade mark or to engage in passing off was not any the less notice of that intention because it was confidential. At most the confidence would fetter communications to the outside world. It would not effectively impede the taking of steps to restrain the intended torts; (4) P's case on passing off raised a triable issue in relation to the date when D started to use the mark INDIGO; (5) damages would not be an adequate remedy for either side, but the prospective loss to P if the injunction was refused was far more uncertain than D's loss if it were granted. D had continued with its preparations for the trade fair and with only three weeks before the fair it was too late for D to reorganise its stand. Furthermore it was the fault of P that the matter had only just come before the court. The injunction would not therefore be granted (*Management Publications v. Blenheim Exhibitions Group* [1992] C.L.Y. 4141 applied); and (6) in deciding whether or not to order P to pay D's costs in any event there were two questions to be answered. Would it be unfair for D to have the costs of the motion even if they lost at trial and was the launch of the motion justified? In the present case it would be unfair for D to have its costs even if it lost at trial and the motion was justified. The order would therefore be D's costs in the cause.

SILICON GRAPHICS v. INDIGO GRAPHIC SYSTEMS (U.K.) [1994] F.S.R. 403, Knox J.

4940. Infringement—two trade marks with overlapping specifications of goods—mark to come into use in U.K.—whether one mark invalid—whether bona fide intention to use—whether likelihood of confusion—whether court must presuppose that mark is in use or will come into use

[Trade Marks Act 1938 (c.22), ss.12(2), 21(1), 26(1)(a)(b), 32; Trade Marks Act 1994 (c.26), ss.7(3), 10(2).]

Section 10 of the Trade Marks Act 1994 presupposes that the plaintiff's mark is in use or will come into use.

P, part of a cosmetic group of companies, was the registered proprietor of two marks, ORIGINS, which were associated and were registered, *inter alia*, for the same goods, men's clothing. P had not used either mark, but neither mark had been registered for more than five years. P used the mark in the U.S. for cosmetics and clothing, and intended to do so shortly in the U.K. D opened two men's clothes shops under the name "Origin Clothing Limited", and sold goods with the label ORIGIN. P issued a summons for summary judgment and D counterclaimed for rectification.

Held, granting summary judgment, that (1) a defendant is not prevented from serving a defence and counterclaim after being served with an Ord. 14

summons (*Hobson v. Monks* [1884] W.N.8 referred to); (2) s.10 of the Trade Marks Act 1994 presupposes that P's mark is in use or will come into use. A court must assume a plaintiff's mark is used in a normal and fair manner in relation to the goods for which it was registered and must then assess a likelihood of confusion in relation to the way the defendant uses its mark, discounting external added matter or circumstances. On this basis D's mark was confusingly similar to P's marks; (3) there is no provision in the Trade Marks Act 1938 which prevents the registration of a mark twice for the same goods by the same proprietor; (4) there was bona fide intention by P to use its marks; and (5) honest concurrent use under s.12(3) of the 1938 Act is not a defence. D had not made an application for registration but had D done so the period and amount of use was so little it was wholly improbable that such an application would have succeeded.

[*Per curiam*: Concurrence under s.7 of the 1984 Act in respect of honest concurrent use may be concurrence of the applicant's user with the registration of the other proprietor and/or its use, so that use of both marks is not essential (*L'Amy Trade Mark* [1938] R.P.C. 137 doubted).]

ORIGINS NATURAL RESOURCES INC. v. ORIGIN CLOTHING [1995] F.S.R. 280, Jacob J.

4941. Licensing—permission granted by registered proprietor of mark—whether licensee entitled to sue for infringement

If the registered proprietor of a trade mark granted a person permission to use it, the proprietor's licensee was not entitled to sue that person for infringement.

NORTHERN & SHELL v. CONDE NAST, *The Independent*, February 13, 1995, Jacob J.

4942. Priorities

TRADE MARKS (CLAIMS TO PRIORITY FROM RELEVANT COUNTRIES) (AMENDMENT) ORDER 1995 (No. 2997) [£1·10], made under the Trade Marks Act 1994, s.36(1)(2); amends S.I. 1994 No. 2803. In force: January 1, 1996; specifies Antigua and Barbuda, Bahrain, Belize, Bolivia, Botswana, Brunei Darussalam, Columbia, Djibouti, Dominica, Ecuador, Guatemala, Hong Kong, India, Jamaica, Kuwait, Macau, Maldives, Mozambique, Myanmar, Namibia, Nicaragua, Pakistan, Sierra Leone and Thailand as countries in which an application for registration of a trade mark conferred priority in respect of an application for the registration of a trade mark in the UK. Claims to priority must be made within six months from the date of filing the application in the relevant country.

4943. Registration—service mark—airline services—whether CLUB a generic word signifying business class air travel—whether distinctive—whether substantial evidence of use sufficient to overcome objections to registration

[Trade Marks Act 1938 (c.22), ss.9, 10.]

The word CLUB has become a generic term for business class travel facilities.

A, an airline company, applied to register the mark CLUB in respect of airline services, accepting that the mark was not, prima facie, registrable but relying on substantial use and evidence of actions taken to prevent competitors from using the mark.

Held, refusing the application, that (1) the mark was descriptive of airline services offered to clubs or club facilities provided by airlines. There was evidence of a widespread understanding of the descriptive significance of the word in the airline industry; (2) the mark had become a generic term for business class air travel and was, therefore, not distinctive. It is not possible to claim exclusive rights to a word which has become part of the common currency of the trade (*TARZAN Trade Mark* [1970] C.L.Y. 2859 referred to); (3) whilst the mark had generated substantial revenue for A and had achieved a high degree of factual distinctiveness, distinctiveness in fact is not conclusive for the purposes of registration (*Electrix's Application* [1958] C.L.Y. 3426 referred to); and (4) the substantial evidence of use was insufficient to overcome the objections to registration.

CLUB TRADE MARK [1994] R.P.C. 527, Trade Mark Registry.

4944. Registration—service mark—conflicting applications—extension of time—whether extension applying equally to both parties

[Trade Marks Act (Cap. 332) ss.22, 23, 24, 62, 78; Trade Marks Rules, r.29; Supreme Court of Judicature Act (Cap. 322), s.7 of First Schedule; R.S.C., Ord. 53, Ord. 87, r.2(4)(5).]

[Singapore] An extension of time applied for by one party in respect of conflicting trade mark applications applies equally to all parties involved.

A and B both lodged conflicting applications for service marks on the same day. Eighteen months later, the registrar served a notice refusing to register the marks until the rights had been determined by the High Court or agreed between A and B. A and B had three months in which to respond. B applied for, and was granted, an extension but A did not and failed to respond in time. A subsequently applied to the registrar for an extension but this was refused, despite B consenting to an extension, and A's application was removed from the record. A applied *ex parte* for an order of certiorari to restore its application and for time to apply to the court pursuant to s.24 of the Trade Marks Act (Cap. 332), which provided that such an application was to be determined by the court.

Held, granting A the relief sought, that (1) r.29 of the Trade Mark Rules, which stated that if the registrar objected to an application, the application would be deemed to have been withdrawn unless the applicant responded within two months, did not apply because the registrar did not object to the application; (2) instead, the registrar decided to make a referral to the court under s.24 of the Trade Marks Act, and therefore r.2(4) and (5) of R.S.C., Ord. 87 applied, under which the registrar could not take sides but must treat both sides equally. Consequently, an extension given to B should equally have applied to A, and only one party need make the application for an extension; and (3) the registrar acted improperly by failing to maintain judicial impartiality and prejudicially affected A by depriving A of a benefit which was within its legitimate expectation.

VENICE SIMPLON ORIENT EXPRESS INC.'S APPLICATIONS [1995] F.S.R. 103, High Court of the Republic of Singapore, Selvam J.

4945. Registration—trade mark—headshawls—proprietorship of trade mark—whether Arabic name label a trade mark

[Trade Marks Act 1938 (c.22), ss.2, 10, 11, 17, 22, 26(2), 28, 31, 68; Trade Marks Act 1875 (c.22); Patents, Designs and Trade Marks Act 1883 (c.57), ss.62(1), 71, 75; Trade Marks Act 1905 (c.15), ss.12(1), 20, 42.]

A, trading as J.L. & Sons, applied for registration of a trade mark in Arabic characters in respect of headshawls. The history of the mark was that J.L. & Sons came into the ownership of A. Through a series of corporate restructures, A was entirely separated from the new owners of J.L. & Sons. From the 1930s, headshawls were shipped from India to Saudi Arabia. They gained a high reputation and became known as "Bassam" headshawls. From 1965 these were shipped directly from England to the firm of Alajlan in Saudi Arabia. To combat counterfeit, Alajlan supplied A with a stamp to use on all production. Alajlan were registered proprietors of the mark in Saudi Arabia. Alajlan did not trade in the U.K. and it was with their consent that A applied for registration in the U.K. Registration was opposed on the grounds that (1) the trade mark was not a trade mark within the meaning of the Trade Marks Act 1938; (2) Alajlan were the true owners of the mark and A exercised no genuine control over J.L. & Sons and being entirely separated from them meant that the mark did not indicate a genuine connection between A and the goods; (3) the essential feature of the mark was AL BASSAM which was a common surname not capable of distinguishing A's goods; (4) the mark was likely to cause confusion; and (5) the scope of the applications should be limited to goods for export to Saudi Arabia and other specified countries in accordance with actual usage. The Registrar allowed the applications and found that (1) the mark was a device and could be a label or a ticket (2) Alajlan and A judged it in their interests to secure registration of the mark and the applications should be in A's name trading as J.L. & Sons (*Ullmann & Co. v. Cesar Leuba* [1908] A.C. 448, *J. Defries & Sons and Helios Mfg Co. v. Electric and Ordinance Accessories Co.* (1906) 23 R.P.C. 341 distinguished; *SABATIER (K) Trade Mark* [1993] R.P.C. 97 referred to); (3) A chose J.L. & Sons to trade under the mark and it was immaterial if they were not subject to higher control in respect of quality (*RADIATION Trade Mark* (1930) 47 R.P.C. 37, *General Electric Co. (of U.S.A.) v. General Electric Co.* [1972] C.L.Y. 3435, *Revlon v. Cripps & Lee* [1980] C.L.Y. 2728 referred to); (4) AL BASSAM had two possible meanings, one of which was a surname. In accordance with published Registry practice, the mark qualified for Part B registration (*W & G Trade Mark* (1913) 30 R.P.C. 660, *SFD Trade Mark* [1975] R.P.C. 607, *SWALLOW Raincoats' Application* [1947-1951] C.L.C. 10359, *CANNON Trade Mark* [1980] C.L.Y. 2723, *WACKER-CHEMIE GmbH's Application, Re* [1957] C.L.Y. 3575, *DIAMOND T Trade Mark* (1921) 38 R.P.C. 373, *I CAN'T BELIEVE IT'S YOGHURT Trade Mark* [1992] R.P.C. 533 referred to); (5) s.31 of the Trade Marks Act 1938 provided that use in the course of export served to substantiate any purpose material under the Act. There was therefore no reason to limit the scope of the applications (*F. Reddaway & Co.'s Application* (1927) 44 R.P.C. 27, *Glenforres etc Co.'s Application (Whiteley's)* (1934) 51 R.P.C. 326, *Anheuser-Busch Inc. v. Budejovicky Budvar Narodni Podnik* [1984] C.L.Y. 3528 referred to). O appealed to the High Court on the grounds that A was not entitled to be the registered proprietor, that the mark did not qualify for Part B registration and that the applications should be refused unless limited to exports to Saudi Arabia and neighbouring countries.

Held, dismissing the appeal, that (1) s.17 of the Trade Marks Act 1938 set out primarily how an applicant must apply and provided the claim was bona fide, then neither the Registrar nor the court was under a duty to look into the validity of the claim and any conflicts between rival claimants should be dealt with under ss.11 and 12 of the Trade Marks Act 1938 (*General Electric Co. (of U.S.A.) v. General Electric Co.* [1972] C.L.Y. 3435, *A.G. Spalding & Bros v. A.W. Gamage* (1915) 32 R.P.C. 273, *Vitamins Application* [1956] R.P.C. 1, *Cheryl Playthings, Re; sub nom. RAWHIDE Trade Mark* [1962] C.L.Y. 3051, *GENETTE Trade Mark* [1968] C.L.Y. 3928 considered; dictum of Whitford J. in *KARO STEP Trade Mark* [1977] C.L.Y. 3061 not followed); (2) A was responsible for production of the goods and it was their use which was deemed by s.31 to constitute use. Alajlan had not used the mark in the U.K. and had no business there, therefore they had no proprietary rights over the trade mark in the U.K. Whether A held any rights on trust for Alajlan, was not relevant; (3) there was no reason why a mark which would be registrable when the U.K. position was considered, should be refused registration under s.10 of the Trade Marks Act 1938 because of events in another country; (4) the name AL BASSAM whilst fairly common in Saudi Arabia, was little known in the U.K. and there was no reason to conclude that Part B registration would impinge upon the needs of any honest trader in the U.K.; and (5) no limitation should be placed upon the use of the mark as it had been used by A for 17 years and so qualified for registration under the Trade Marks Act 1938.

AL BASSAM TRADE MARK [1994] R.P.C. 315, Aldous J.

4946. Registration—trade mark—opposition—non-alcoholic drinks—whether mark capable of distinguishing—descriptiveness—whether mark deceptive

[Trade Marks Act 1938 (c.22), ss.9, 10, 11, 12(1).]

The application for the registration of the trade mark JOCKEY in respect of low calorie non-alcoholic drinks was opposed on the grounds that JOCKEY on soft drinks describes drinks for jockeys, and hence is not a distinctive mark, neither is it capable of distinguishing the applicants' goods. Further grounds of opposition were that the mark would be deceptive if used in relation to drinks other than for jockeys and that it was deceptive and confusing having regard to the opponent's trade mark, JOKER. The opponents filed evidence of the volume of sales in the U.K. of non-alcoholic drinks under their trade mark JOKER but gave no information as to the manner of use of the mark. No evidence was given as to the public's perception of the mark in relation to the goods. No evidence was filed by the applicants.

Held, allowing the application, that (1) the opponent's argument that there were drinks especially adapted for jockeys required evidence to support it. If the opponents believed that members of the public would see a connection between a range of low calorie drinks and sportsmen, they should have conducted a survey to confirm this. There was no evidence that the public would see any connection between goods sold under the mark and jockeys. There was therefore no inherent deception under ss.9, 10 and 11; (2) JOCKEY and JOKER were very well known English words. Their pronunciation was different and they differed visually. The images which they conjured up were very different. Confusion between them was unlikely and therefore the remaining grounds of opposition under ss.11 and 12(1) also failed (*Smith Haydon and Co.'s Application* (1946) 63 R.P.C. 97, *Berlei (U.K.) v. Bali Brassiere Co.* [1969] C.L.Y. 3565, *Pianotist Co.'s Application* (1906) R.P.C. 774 followed).

JOCKEY TRADE MARK, *Re* [1994] F.S.R. 269, Trade Marks Registry.

4947. Registration—trade mark—rectification—hearsay evidence—whether rules of admissibility apply on applications before Registrar

[Trade Marks Act 1938 (c.22), ss.1, 17, 18(5)(6), 25, 26, 27(4), 32, 33, 40, 50, 54, 55; Civil Evidence Act 1968 (c.64), ss.1, 2, 18; Trade Marks and Service Marks Rules 1986 (S.I. 1986 No. 1319), rr.49–52, 82, 83; Trade Marks Act 1994 (c.26), ss.64, 105, Sched. 3, para. 18; R.S.C., Ord. 38, rr.1, 2, 21(1)(4), Ord. 41, r.5.]

Rules as to the admissibility of hearsay evidence in civil proceedings apply in applications before the Registrar.

R was the registered proprietor of two trade marks, both ST. TRUDO, in respect of alcoholic and other beverages. A applied to rectify the register on the basis that A was the true proprietor of the marks. The main evidence was contained in two statutory declarations made by A's financial manager. These contained details of commercial discussions between A and R in respect of the marks of which he had no personal involvement and in respect of which he had failed to disclose any other means of knowledge. R applied to strike out those parts of the declarations on the ground that they were inadmissible as hearsay. The registrar rejected R's submission that he was unable to receive hearsay evidence, and R appealed.

Held, granting R's application and striking out those parts, that (1) s.1 of the Civil Evidence Act 1968, which governs the admissibility of hearsay evidence, applies "in any civil proceedings", which are defined in s.18 of that Act as including any proceedings in relation to which the strict laws of evidence apply. The registrar was bound by the strict laws of evidence; (2) a deponent must confine his evidence to what he can prove within his own knowledge, as required by Ord. 41, r.5. This applies equally to applications before the registrar as it does on an appeal. If it were not so, different material would be receivable in evidence by the registrar from what is receivable by the court on appeal from him; accordingly, (3) hearsay evidence could not properly be given before the registrar and such evidence could not be entertained on appeal except in accordance with the 1968 Act, so that first-hand hearsay may be included in a statutory declaration, but second-hand or more remote hearsay may not be included by any means.

ST. TRUDO TRADE MARK [1995] F.S.R. 345, Ferris J.

4948. Registration—trade mark—rectification—meaning of "person aggrieved"—whether infringement of copyright a ground for rectification of register—whether alternative remedy prevents person from being a "person aggrieved"

[Trade Marks Act (Cap 332), ss.11, 15(1), 38, 39(1)(a); Copyright Act 1911 (c.46), s.5.]

[Singapore] The fact that an applicant for rectification of the register has an alternative remedy does not prevent them from being a "person aggrieved".

A commissioned the design of a corporate logo under the name AUVI and subsequently used it extensively in respect of hi-fi equipment. R became the registered proprietor of a separate logo trade mark under the name AUVI in respect of hi-fi equipment. The two logos were virtually identical. A sought rectification of R's trade mark. R sought leave to amend its trade mark.

Held, ordering the removal of the mark from the register, that (1) R had copied A's logo; (2) there was no evidence that A's logo resembled any ordinary typeface, and accordingly A's logo was an artistic work which enjoyed copyright protection. Simplicity alone does not prevent a work from acquiring copyright (*British Northrop v. Texteam Blackburn* [1973] C.L.Y. 422, *KARO STEP Trade Mark* [1977] R.P.C. 255 referred to); (3) if a person in the same trade as the registered proprietor of the mark in question is prevented from lawfully doing something which he would otherwise have been able to do had the mark not been registered, then that person is a "person aggrieved" (*OSCAR Trade Mark* [1979] R.P.C. 173, *KARO STEP Trade Mark* [1977] R.P.C. 255, *Ritz Hotel v. Charles of the Ritz* [1990] C.L.Y. 4527, *Powell's Trade Mark* [1894] A.C. 8, *DAIQUIRI RUM Trade Mark* [1969] C.L.Y. 3561, *Lever Bros v. Sunniwite Products* C.L.C. 10350, *WELLS FARGO Trade Mark* [1977] C.L.Y. 3065, *CONSORT Trade Mark* [1980] C.L.Y. 2731, *Arnold Palmer, Re* [1987] 2 M.L.J. 681 considered); (4) the fact that A had an alternative remedy for infringement of copyright did not prevent A from being a person aggrieved; (5) since A were legal owners of the copyright at the date proceedings were issued, they were entitled to apply for rectification; A's delay of 14 months was no bar to the application; and (6) R's mark would not be varied because it would involve a change which substantially affected the identity of the mark.

AUVI TRADE MARK [1995] F.S.R. 288, Chao Hick Tin J., High Court of Singapore.

4949. Registration—trade mark—software for financial management—whether mark distinctive—whether descriptive and laudatory

[Trade Marks Act 1938 (c.22), ss.9, 10.]

The fact that alternative words were available for use by traders is no answer to criticism of a mark.

A's application for registration of the mark PROFITMAKER in respect of financial computer software was refused.

Held, dismissing the appeal, that (1) the hearing officer was correct to conclude that the mark would indicate that the goods to which the mark was applied would be profitable, and that accordingly the mark was descriptive and laudatory, and did not qualify for Part A registration; (2) in considering registration under Part B, the hearing officer correctly concluded that it was highly likely that other traders in the relevant market would wish to use the word PROFITMAKER (*TORQ-SET Trade Mark* [1959] R.P.C. 344 followed); and (3) the fact that traders have a number of alternative ways of describing a product which will make profit is no answer to the criticism of the mark.

PROFITMAKER Trade Mark [1994] R.P.C. 613, Mr Hugh Laddie, Q.C.

4950. Sheffield Assay Office Act 1995 (c.v)

This Act, *inter alia*, increases the range of activities which may be undertaken by the Sheffield Assay Office to include the analysis of materials and articles of any kind. Section 16 of the Hallmarking Act 1973 (c.43) is amended retrospectively to validate the making of the Sheffield Assay Office Order 1978 (S.I. 1978 No. 639).

The Act received Royal Assent on July 19, 1995.

TRADE UNIONS

4951. Amalgamation—ballot—entitlement to vote—definition of "member"—whether a "limited member" is a member entitled to vote in an amalgamation ballot

[Trade Union and Labour Relations Act 1992 (c.52), ss.1, 50, 100B.]

Where union rules create more than one class of member, it is necessary, in determining which class is entitled to vote in a ballot for the transfer of engagements, to examine the relationship between each class of members and the union, and the right of that class to participate in the main purposes of the union.

The NUM (Yorkshire Area), a union in its own right and a constituent part of the NUM, proposed to transfer its engagements to the NUM. Under the union's rules limited members were not entitled to vote. A ballot was carried out amongst the full members of the union and resulted in approval for the proposed transfer. M, a limited member of the union, lodged an objection with the Certification Officer, claiming that an instrument of transfer should not be registered, since not all "members" had been accorded entitlement to vote in the ballot, contrary to s.100B of the Trade Union and Labour Relations Act 1992. The Certification Officer upheld this objection.

Held, allowing the union's appeal, that as there was no definition of "member" in the Act of 1992, the scope of s.100B depended on its interpretation in the context of the scheme and purposes both of the group of sections relating to the transfer of engagements and of the 1992 Act as a whole. A helpful approach was to ask how the language of the section would be understood by those to whom the section was addressed and whose affairs were intended to be affected by it. The phrase "members of a trade union" was expressive of a constitutional relationship between individuals and the organisation to which they belonged, and that relationship was to be determined prima facie by the rules of the union as the body of members, although the rule book might not always be determinative of membership for the purposes of the Act of 1992. Where there were more than one class of members and there were significant differences between those different classes, it may become clear that, as in this case, the rights of one class to participate in the principal purposes of the union were not substantial and they should not be regarded as "members" under s.100B of the Act of 1992.

NATIONAL UNION OF MINEWORKERS (YORKSHIRE AREA) v. MILLWARD [1995] IRLR 411, E.A.T.

4952. Certification officer—fees

CERTIFICATION OFFICER (AMENDMENT OF FEES) REGULATIONS 1995 (No. 483) [£1·10], made under the Trade Union and Labour Relations (Consolidation) Act 1992 (c.52), ss.108, 293; operative on April 1, 1995; alter fees payable to the Certification Officer in relation to Trade Unions and Employers' Associations.

4953. Contract of employment—breach of contract—post as trade union official abolished—whether entitled to a declaration that union's decision null and void

M was elected to become a full-time officer of the union. Before he took up this position, the union was reorganised for financial reasons and M was informed that he would not be required as a full-time officer. He sought a declaration that the union's decision was null and void.

Held, dismissing the application, that M was not entitled to any remedy over and above his right to damages for breach of contract. The union was not required to comply with the rules of natural justice by consulting with him before repudiating his contract. M had the same remedies against the union as he would have against any other prospective employer.

MEACHAM v. AMALGAMATED ENGINEERING AND ELECTRICAL UNION [1994] IRLR 218, Graeme Hamilton, Q.C. sitting as a deputy judge.

4954. Discrimination on basis of union activity—action short of dismissal—purpose of action taken—whether insistence on full-time trade union official having managerial experience before promotion was "for the purpose" of preventing him from continuing with full-time union activities. See DEPARTMENT OF TRANSPORT v. GALLACHER, §1989.

4955. Discrimination on basis of union activity—redundancy selection criteria—trade union official—working on particular task to enable him to spend half of day on union business—those doing that task made redundant—whether selection discriminatory—whether unfair dismissal. See O'DEA v. ISC CHEMICALS (EATRF 94/0722/B), §2104.

4956. Discrimination on basis of union activity—selection for redundancy—trade union activities—inadmissible reason—selection based on employee's contribution—employee working predominantly for union—employer permitting employee's non-compliance with agreed division of time between employer's business and union work—whether selection for redundancy based on trade union activities. See DUNDON v. GPT, §2106.

4957. Industrial action—ballots—notice of ballot—whether notice of ballot complied with statutory requirements

[Trade union and Labour Relations (Consolidation) Act 1992 (c.52), ss.219, 226(1)(b), 226A(1)(a)(2)(c), 234A(1)(3)(a).]

The college employed 872 lecturers, 288 of whom were members of the union. Union dues were deducted directly from the salaries of 109 of those members. The union gave notice to the college of a ballot of and strike action by "all our members employed by your institution". The High Court granted the college an injunction restraining strike action on the ground that the notice given by the union did not fulfil the requirements of ss.226A and 234A in that it did not enable the college to identify the employees involved. The union appealed.

Held, dismissing the appeal, that the notice given to the college did not provide adequate information to enable it to identify the relevant employees. Consequently, the union did not enjoy immunity from tortious liability. The union must specify a category of employees or provide names of individuals so that they could be readily identified. The union's description was not sufficiently precise.

BLACKPOOL AND THE FYLDE COLLEGE v. NATIONAL ASSOCIATION OF TEACHERS IN FURTHER AND HIGHER EDUCATION [1994] IRLR 227, C.A.

4958. Industrial action—ballots—tort immunities—whether majority achieved in ballot

[Trade Union Act 1984 (c.49), ss.10(1)(3), 11(4).]

P was in dispute with its employees over pay. The union conducted a ballot of 2,642 employees. 1,265 voted in favour of strike action, 1,225 voted against and 147 abstained. In answer to a separate question, 1,059 voted in favour of action short of a strike, 1,156 against action short of a strike and 427 abstained. The union called a strike. P contended that there was not a majority in favour of strike action and brought proceedings for inducement of breach of contract. The High Court dismissed this application.

Held, dismissing P's appeal, that the High Court had not erred in finding that the two questions on the ballot paper should be treated separately. The ballot votes of 1,265 employees in favour of strike action and 1,225 against amounted to a majority under s.10 of the Trade Union Act 1984, notwithstanding that 2,642 employees had taken part in the overall voting process.

WEST MIDLANDS TRAVEL v. TRANSPORT AND GENERAL WORKERS' UNION [1994] IRLR 578, C.A.

4959. Industrial action—ballots—tort immunity—statutory interpretation

[Trade Union and Labour Relations (Consolidation) Act 1992 (c.52), ss.219, 226.]

N, contending that immunity from suit conferred by s.219 of the Trade Union and Labour Relations (Consolidation) Act 1992, as amended, should be preserved, appealed against an order restraining it from inducing a large number of new members, who had joined the union after a ballot on strike action had taken place, to take part in industrial action. LU sought to argue that statutory immunity should not be preserved, as new members had not been balloted and were recruited solely to maximise the effects of the action.

Held, allowing the appeal, that under the 1992 Act immunity was protected where, as here, the action contemplated had majority support and was intended to be taken in furtherance of a legitimate trade dispute. To retain immunity, under s.226, the ballot had to show support for collective industrial action. This was distinct from the participation of particular individuals in action, as even those voting against might choose to participate. Nothing in the Act prevented the union including in the collective action those who were not members at the time the ballot was held, even though their participation was induced to increase the effectiveness of the intended action.

LONDON UNDERGROUND v. NATIONAL UNION OF RAILWAYMEN, MARITIME AND TRANSPORT STAFF, *The Times,* October 9, 1995, C.A.

4960. Redundancy—consultation procedures—trade unions—press release. See EMPLOYMENT, §2032.

4961. Trade unions—refusal of employment on grounds of trade union membership—whether "membership" including "activities". See HARRISON v. KENT COUNTY COUNCIL, §2060.

4962. Union elections—election of general president—irregularities—whether power to declare ballot invalid after receiving scrutineer's report and declaring result

[Trade Union and Labour Relations (Consolidation) Act 1992 (c.52), ss.46, 48, 52.]

Unless expressly empowered by its rules to do so, a trade union has no power to cancel an election after the independent scrutineer has reported to the union expressing satisfaction as to the statutory matters, and once the result of the election has been declared.

D stood as one of eight candidates for the office of General President of the GPMU. In possible contravention of r.9(2) of the GPMU rules, which prohibited the publication of any material other than a 400-word statement in the union journal, D was quoted in a newspaper article commenting on an anonymous statement which made disparaging remarks about another candidate, W. Following the return of the ballot papers the union received the certification of USBS, the independent scrutineer, that the statutory requirements had been complied with, and shortly after announced D as the successful candidate. W complained that D's actions contravened r.9(2). The union appointed the general manager of USBS, H, to investigate the allegations. H reported that D's actions contravened r.9(2), that the ballot should be set aside and a fresh election held. GPMU accepted this report. D challenged the union's authority to order a new election.

Held, allowing D's claim, that (1) the power to cancel an election after the result has become known and published was one which, if capable of being lawful, would require careful drafting so as to avoid potential abuse of the electoral system and a corruption of the legislative controls contained in the Trade Union and Labour Relations (Consolidation) Act 1992. There was no such provision in the GPMU rules (*Heatons Transport (St Helens) v. TGWU* [1972] C.L.Y. 3452, *British Actors' Equity Association v. Goring* [1978] C.L.Y. 3003 considered; *Jacques v. AUEW* [1987] C.L.Y. 3768 applied); (2) there was no power in the union rules to delegate to H any decisions about the interpretation of those rules; and (3) in deciding to cancel the result of the ballot the union council had acted unfairly in not providing an opportunity for D to be heard.

[*Per curiam*: Even if the union had the power to cancel the election following the declaration of the result, in doing so the council had acted unreasonably since D's actions could not be construed as a breach of r.9(2).]

DOUGLAS v. GPMU [1995] IRLR 426, Morison J.

TRANSPORT

4963. Aid—trans-European networks—European Community

Council Regulation (EC) 2236/95 of September 18, 1995 laying down general rules for the granting of Community financial aid in the field of trans-European networks (O.J. L228/1).

4964. Air transport—Paris—European Community

Commission Decision 95/259/EC of March 14, 1995 on a procedure relating to the application Council Reg. (EEC) 2408/92—French traffic distribution rules for the airport system of Paris (O.J. L162/25).

4965. Animal health. See ANIMALS, §293.

4966. Assessment of environmental effects

TRANSPORT AND WORKS (ASSESSMENT OF ENVIRONMENTAL EFFECTS) REGULATIONS 1995 (No. 1541) [£1·10], made under the European Communities Act 1972 (c.68), s.2(2); operative on August 1, 1995; amend s.14 of the 1992 Act so as implement Arts. 8, 9 of Council Dir. 85/337/EEC.

4967. Bell's Bridge Order Confirmation Act 1995 (c.iv)

This Act makes the necessary provisions to authorise Scottish Enterprise to turn Bell's Bridge (over the river Clyde) into a permanent footbridge. The Act confirms the Provisional Order to like effect which was made under the Private Legislation Procedure (Scotland) Act 1936 (c.52).

The Act received Royal Assent on July 19, 1995.

4968. Bridges

BIRMINGHAM CITY COUNCIL (BIRMINGHAM AND FAZELEY CANAL BRIDGE) SCHEME 1994 CONFIRMATION INSTRUMENT 1995 (No. 1301)

[£3·20], made under the Highways Act 1980, s.106(3); operative on the date on which the notice that it has been confirmed is first published in accordance with the Highways Act 1980, Sched. 2, para. 1; authorises Birmingham City Council to construct over the navigable waters of the Birmingham and Fazeley Canal the bridge specified in the Schedule to this Scheme.

WOLVERHAMPTON BOROUGH COUNCIL (WEDNESFIELD WAY) (BRIDGE OVER THE WYRLEY AND ESSINGTON CANAL) SCHEME 1994 CONFIRMATION INSTRUMENT 1995 (No. 1357) [£1·55], made under the Highways Act 1980, ss.106(3), 108(4); operative on the date on which notice that it has been confirmed is first published in accordance with the Highways Act 1980 Sched. 2, para. 1; authorises the Council to construct over the Wyrley and Essington Canal the bridge specified in the Schedule to this Scheme as part of the highway which they are proposing to construct, and contains plans and specifications of the bridge.

COUNTY COUNCIL OF CLWYD (RIVER DEE ESTUARY BRIDGE) (VARIATION) SCHEME 1995 CONFIRMATION INSTRUMENT 1995 (No. 3126), made under the Highways Act 1980 s.106(3). operative on On the date on which notice that it has been confirmed is first published in accord. with para. 1 of Sched. 1 to the Highways Act 1980; [£3·20. The County Council of Clwyd (River Dee Estuary Bridge) (Variation) Scheme is confirmed without modification by this Statutory Instrument. The scheme is set out in the Schedule and a plan entitled Deeside Road Link —River Crossing (A548 Shotton —Connah's Quay Bypass) attached.

COUNTY COUNCIL OF NORFOLK (RECONSTRUCTION OF WELNEY SUSPENSION BRIDGE) SCHEME 1994 CONFIRMATION INSTRUMENT 1995 (No. 1805) [£1·10].

BOROUGH OF TRAFFORD (EASTERN SPINE CANAL BRIDGE) SCHEME 1993 CONFIRMATION INSTRUMENT 1995 (No. 33)[£2·40].

BOROUGH OF TRAFFORD (5063) TRAFFORD/WHITE CITY GYRATORY SYSTEM CANAL BRIDGES) SCHEME 1993 CONFIRMATION INSTRUMENT 1995 (No. 38) [£2·40].

COUNTY COUNCIL OF HUMBERSIDE (RIVER HILL BRIDGE) SCHEME 1994 CONFIRMATION INSTRUMENT 1995 (No. 748) [£3·70].

KENT COUNTY COUNCIL (HALE STREET MEDWAY BRIDGE) SCHEME 1994 CONFIRMATION INSTRUMENT 1995 (No. 1594).

SOMERSET COUNTY COUNCIL (BRIDGEWATER NORTHERN DISTRIBUTOR ROAD BRIDGE) SCHEME 1992 CONFIRMATION INSTRUMENT 1995 (No. 270) [£1·10].

SEVERN BRIDGE (AMENDMENT) REGULATIONS 1995 (No. 1677).

COUNTY COUNCIL OF STAFFORDSHIRE (TRENT AND MERSEY CANAL) BRIDGE SCHEME 1994 CONFIRMATION INSTRUMENT 1995 (No. 2956) [£2·40], made under the Highways Act 1980, s.106(3); will become operative on the date on which notice that it has been confirmed is first published; confirms the County Council of Staffordshire (Trent and Mersey Canal) Bridge Scheme 1994, with modifications. The Scheme is set out in the Schedule to the Instrument.

COUNTY COUNCIL OF THE ROYAL COUNTY OF BERKSHIRE (A329(M) LODDON BRIDGE CONNECTING ROAD) SPECIAL ROAD SCHEME 1995 CONFIRMATION INSTRUMENT 1995 (No. 2201) [£1·95], made under the Highways Act 1980, s.16; operative on on the date on which notice that it has been confirmed in accordance with para. 1 of Sched. 2 to the Highways Act 1980.

4969. Bridges—Severn Bridge speed limit

M4 MOTORWAY (SEVERN BRIDGE) (SPEED LIMIT) REGULATIONS 1995 (No. 2168) [65p], made under the Road Traffic Regulation Act 1984, s.17(2)(3); operative on October 1, 1995.

4970. Bridges—Severn Bridge tolls

SEVERN BRIDGES TOLLS ORDER 1995 (No. 3254), made under the Severn

Bridges Act 1992 s.9(2)(b); revokes S.I. 1994 No. 3158. operative on January 1, 1996; [65p]. This Order fixes the tolls for 1996 payable for motor cars, motor caravans, goods vehicles and buses travelling from east to west using the Severn Bridge. Calculations of increases in tolls have been based on the percentage increase in the Retail Prices Index between March 1989 and September 1995. The charge for Category 1 vehicles, motor cars and motor caravans, is £3·80, for Category 2 vehicles, small goods vehicles and small buses is £7·70 and for Category 3 vehicles, other goods vehicles and buses, the charge is £11·50.

4971. Dartford–Thurrock crossing

DARTFORD–THURROCK CROSSING (AMENDMENT) REGULATIONS 1995 (No. 2060) [£1·10], made under the Dartford–Thurrock Crossing Act 1988, ss.25(1)(2), 26, 44(3), 46(1); amend S.I. 1994 No. 2031; operative on September 1, 1995.

DARTFORD–THURROCK CROSSING TOLLS ORDER 1995 (No. 2059) [£1·10], made under the Dartford–Thurrock Crossing Act 1988, s.17(4); operative on September 1, 1995.

4971a. European Community Directive—European Parliament objection—consultation in adoption of E.C. legislation—Directive relating to taxes and tolls on roads and certain infrastructures—whether changes to directive changed nature of legislation—European Community. See EUROPEAN PARLIAMENT v. COUNCIL OF THE EUROPEAN UNION (C–21/94), §2247.

4972. Fees

DEPARTMENT OF TRANSPORT (FEES) (AMENDMENT) ORDER 1995 (No. 1684), made under the Finance (No. 2) Act 1987, s.102(5); operative on July 1, 1995, amends S.I. 1988 No. 643; further amends the 1988 Order by substituting a new Table III and Table VI in Sched. 1.

4973. Freedom to provide services—maritime transport—charges imposed on embarkation and disembarkation—not imposed where transport between national ports—whether France in breach—European Community

The Commission sought a declaration that France had infringed Art. 59 E.C. by imposing certain charges in respect of maritime transport.

Held, that by maintaining in force a system for levying charges on the disembarkation and embarkation of passengers in the case of vessels using port installations situated on its continental or island territory and arriving from ports situated in another Member State or travelling to them, whereas in the case of passenger transport between two ports situated on national territory those charges are levied only on embarkation for departure from the continental or island port, and by applying higher rates of charges when passengers arrive from or embark for ports in another Member State than when they travel to a port situated on the national territory, France was in breach of its obligations under Reg. (EEC) 4055/86, applying the principle of freedom to provide services to maritime transport.

E.C. COMMISSION v. FRANCE (C–381/93), October 5, 1994, ECJ.

4974. Highway—dedication—obstruction of highway—prescription

The principle that the law would not countenance the creation of rights based on long user which was prohibited by public statute applied equally to claims to presumed dedication of a highway as it did to claims to easements by prescription.

ROBINSON v. ADAIR, *The Times*, March 2, 1995, D.C.

4975. Highway—dedication—uninterrupted use by public—whether presumption of intention to dedicate—whether onus of rebuttal on landowner

[Highways Act 1960 (c.66), s.31.]

D removed a barrier which had been erected by P across land being used by the public. The county court held that the land belonged to P and that it was not subject to a public right of way.

Held, allowing D's appeal, that, under s.31 of the Highways Act 1980, 20 years of uninterrupted use by the public of a piece of land gave rise to a presumption of an intention to dedicate the land as a highway. The onus of rebutting the presumption lay with the landowner, and the court would be slow to infer an unexpressed intention not to dedicate in the absence of overt acts of interference with the public user.

WARD v. DURHAM COUNTY COUNCIL [1994] EGCS 39, C.A.

4976. Highway—obstruction—meaning of obstruction

[Highways Act 1980 (c.66), s.149(1).]

The local authority appealed against a decision of the justices dismissing a complaint against a trader who had failed to comply with a notice requiring him to cease from obstructing a pavement contrary to the Highways Act 1980, s.149(1). The facts showed that about a third of the pavement was obstructed, but the justices did not consider this sufficient obstruction to constitute a nuisance.

Held, allowing the appeal, that no reasonable Bench could have reached that decision. Obstruction is caused where the pavement is made difficult to pass by reason of an obstacle, and it could not be said that there was no obstruction in this case (*Haydon v. Kent County Council* [1978] C.L.Y. 1547, *Jacobs v. London County Council* [1947–51] C.L.C. 6751 considered).

CORNWALL COUNTY COUNCIL v. BLEWETT [1994] C.O.D. 46, D.C.

4977. Highway—stopping up order—diversion to old road resulting in old and new roads running parallel—old road terminating in cul de sac—whether old road unnecessary—whether old road replaced or supplemented by new highway

[Highways Act 1980 (c.66), s.116.]

A road was diverted so that part of the original road was parallel to the new diverted section. The original road thereby became a cul de sac and ended in the side of a cutting through which the new road passed. Magistrates refused an order to stop up the old road under the Highways Act 1980, s.116. H council appealed successfully to the Crown Court. W then appealed by way of case stated, arguing that the old road was still necessary, not unnecessary in terms of s.116(1)(a) of the 1980 Act.

Held, allowing the appeal, that the Crown Court had adopted the wrong approach. They should have taken the view that two roads existed and then gone on to see whether the old road was necessary. In fact they treated the case as one where an existing road was being replaced by a new one. As the court had no local knowledge, it was impossible for it to say that the same decision would have been reached had the correct approach been adopted. "Unnecessary" in the context of s.116(1)(a) meant unnecessary for the purposes of use as a highway, *i.e.* passing and repassing (*Ramblers Association v. Kent County Council* [1991] C.L.Y. 3557 followed).

WESTLEY v. HERTFORDSHIRE COUNTY COUNCIL (CO/2517/94), March 29, 1995, Collins J.

4978. Highway—whether obstruction by motorvehicle

[Highways Act 1980 (c.66), s.137; Road Vehicles (Construction and Use) Regulations 1986 (S.I. 1986 No. 1078), reg. 103; Removal and Disposal of Vehicles Regulations 1986 (S.I. 1986 No. 183).]

In determining whether a vehicle left on a road was an obstruction under reg. 3 of the Removal and Disposal of Vehicles Regulations 1986, a wide interpretation should be given to the words "obstruction to persons using the road" to include persons who might be expected to be using the road. It was wrong to adopt in this context the meaning given to "obstruction" in s.137 of the Highways Act 1980 and reg. 103 of the Road Vehicles (Construction and Use) Regulations 1986 which required a reasonable use of the highway.

CAREY v. CHIEF CONSTABLE OF AVON AND SOMERSET, *The Times*, April 7, 1995, C.A.

4979. Highway authority—failure to maintain highway—duty to inspect pavements—personal injury resulting from defective paving slab—statutory defence of regular system of inspections—whether adequacy of authority's general system relevant if inspection of accident site established. See ALLEN v. NEWCASTLE CITY COUNCIL, §3664.

4980. Highway maintenance—land registration—agreement to maintain highway—whether overriding rights—whether "public rights". See OVERSEAS INVESTMENT SERVICES v. SIMCOBUILD CONSTRUCTION, §823.

4981. Highways—caravan parking illegally—whether judicial review to be granted for the purpose of allowing an illegal activity. See R. v. HEREFORD AND WORCESTER COUNTY COUNCIL, *ex p.* SMITH (TOMMY), §73.

4982. Highways—inquiries procedure

HIGHWAYS (INQUIRIES PROCEDURE) RULES 1994 (No. 3263) [£3·20], made under the Tribunals and Inquiries Act 1992 (c.53), s.9; operative on January 10, 1995; regulate the procedure to be followed in England and Wales in respect of public local inquiries which are held in connection with schemes or orders proposed to be made under the Highways Act 1980, Pt. II.

4983. Inland waterway transport—European Community scrapping premiums—available financial resources—European Community

T sued the Dutch Minister of Transport in a dispute concerning the rejection of an application for scrapping the premium for a pusher craft on the ground that the financial resources in the Netherlands account for this type of vessel were not sufficient to cover the premium. This premium was available pursuant to Reg. (EEC) 1101/89 on structural improvements in inland waterway transport. This Regulation sought to bring about a substantial reduction in structural overcapacity in inland waterway transport and provided for a scrapping scheme.

Held, that the Regulation did not require that a valid application for a scrapping premium must be accepted if the aggregate financial resources available to the funds of the Member States concerned were sufficient. An application must be refused when the financial resources required to cover it exceed the budget provided for in the Regulation, notwithstanding the fact that funds for other types of vessel are not exhausted.

TIERLINCK v. MINISTER VAN VERKEER EN WATERSTAAT (C–414/93), June 1, 1995, ECJ, Fifth Chamber.

4984. Light railways

FOXFIELD LIGHT RAILWAY ORDER 1995 (No. 1236) [£1·95], made under the Light Railways Act 1896 (c.48), ss.7, 10–12, 18 and the Transport Act 1968 (c.73), s.121(4); operative on May 4, 1995; provides for the operation of the said light railway.

LOW MOOR TRAMWAY LIGHT RAILWAY ORDER 1995 (No. 2501) [£1·55], made under the Light Railways Act 1896, ss.7, 10, 11, 12, 18 and Transport Act 1968, s.121(4); operative on September 21, 1995; provides for the construction and operation of the said light railway.

NORTHAMPTON AND LAMPORT LIGHT RAILWAY ORDER 1995 (No. 1300)

[£1·95], made under the Light Railways Act 1896 (c.48), ss.7, 10–12, 18 and the Transport Act 1968 (c.73), s.121(4); operative on May 10, 1995; provides for the operation of the said light railway.

OSWESTRY LIGHT RAILWAY ORDER 1995 (No. 2142) [£1·10], made under the Light Railways Act 1896, ss.7, 10 to 12, 18; operative on July 29, 1995; empowers the Cambrian Railways Society Ltd to work the railway as a light railway under the 1868 Act and in accordance with the provisions of the Order.

WELSH HIGHLAND RAILWAY (TRANSFER) LIGHT RAILWAY ORDER 1995 (No. 861) [65p], made under the Light Railway Act 1896 (c.48), ss.7, 9–12, 24; operative on March 15, 1995; makes provision in relation to the operation of the said light railway.

4985. Light rapid transport

GREATER MANCHESTER (LIGHT RAPID TRANSIT SYSTEM) (LAND ACQUISITION) ORDER 1995 (No. 2383) [£1·10], made under the Transport and Works Act 1992, ss.1, 5; operative on September 26, 1995; confers fresh powers of compulsory acquisition on Greater Manchester Passenger Transport Executive for the purposes of the Greater Manchester (Light Rapid Transit System) Act 1990.

4986. London cabs—fare increase. See LONDON, §3287.

4987. Motorvehicle taxation—imports—whether discriminatory internal taxation—whether prohibited by Community law—European Community. See FAZENDA PUBLICA v. NUNES TADEU (C–345/93), §4373.

4988. Passenger Transport Authority

GREATER MANCHESTER PASSENGER TRANSPORT AUTHORITY (INCREASE IN NUMBER OF MEMBERS) ORDER 1995 (No. 1522) [65p], made under the Local Government Act 1985 (c.51), ss.29(2), 103(1); operative on July 19, 1995; alters the composition of the Greater Manchester Passenger Transport Authority.

4989. Passenger transport executives

PASSENGER TRANSPORT EXECUTIVES (CAPITAL FINANCE) (AMENDMENT) ORDER 1995 (No. 1431) [65p], made under the Local Government and Housing Act 1989 (c.42), s.39(5)–(7); operative on June 30, 1995; amends S.I. 1990 No. 720.

4990. Penalty fares

LONDON REGIONAL TRANSPORT (PENALTY FARES) ACT 1992 (ACTIVATING NO. 2) ORDER 1995 (No. 1071) [65p], made under the London Regional Transport (Penalty Fares) Act 1992 (c.xvi), s.3(4); operative on April 30, 1995; brings into force the provisions of the 1992 Act relating to penalty fares in relation to specified bus services in London.

4991. Priority route—London

LONDON PRIORITY ROUTE (AMENDMENT) ORDER 1995 (No. 1130) [£1·10], made under the Road Traffic Act 1991 (c.40), s.50(1); operative on June 1, 1995; amends S.I. 1992 No. 1372 so as to alter the priority route network for London.

4992. Public service transport

SECTION 19 MINIBUS (DESIGNATED BODIES) (AMENDMENT) ORDER 1995 (No. 1540) [£1·10], made under the Transport Act 1985 (c.67), s.19(7); operative on July 17, 1995; amends S.I. 1987 No. 1229.

4993. Public service vehicle—tachograph record—journey from depot to docks without passengers—whether tachograph record required for journey—operating company wholly owned by another company—whether owning company was the driver's employer

D1 owned H, a company that organised coach trips to the continent. D2 was the driver of an empty coach that was taken to the docks for embarkation. At the docks he was asked to produce a tachograph record but was unable to do so because he had not been issued with one. The justices convicted D1 of failing to issue a tachograph record and D2 of failing to produce tachograph records. Both defendants appealed.

Held, allowing D1's appeal and dismissing D2's appeal, that the responsibility for the supply of tachograph records lay with the employer. It did not follow from the fact that one company wholly owned another that the holding company was the employer. The driver might be employed by the subsidiary company and the justices had erred in assuming that D1 was the employer simply because it wholly owned H. It was not right to split up a journey to the continent into two sections, one of positioning before passengers were collected and the other of actually carrying passengers. The justices had been right to decide that a tachograph was required for the journey taking the empty coach to the docks.

R. W. APPLEBY v. VEHICLE INSPECTORATE [1994] RTR 380, D.C.

4994. Public service vehicles

PUBLIC SERVICE VEHICLES (CONDITIONS OF FITNESS, EQUIPMENT, USE AND CERTIFICATION) (AMENDMENT) REGULATIONS 1993 (No. 3012) [65p], made under the Public Passenger Vehicles Act 1981 (c.14), ss.10(1), 52(1)(a), 60; operative on January 2, 1994; amend S.I. 1981 No. 257 so as to prescribe new fees.

PUBLIC SERVICE VEHICLES (CONDUCT OF DRIVERS, INSPECTORS, CONDUCTORS AND PASSENGERS) (AMENDMENT) REGULATIONS 1995 (No. 186) [65p], made under the Public Passenger Vehicles Act 1981 (c.14), ss.25(1), 60(2); operative on March 1, 1995; amend S.I. 1990 No. 1020 so that passengers on a public service vehicle are not prohibited by those regulations from speaking to the driver when the vehicle is not in motion.

PUBLIC SERVICE VEHICLES (LOST PROPERTY) (AMENDMENT) REGULATIONS 1995 (No. 185) [£1·10], made under the Public Passenger Vehicles Act 1981 (c.14), s.60(1); operative on March 1, 1995; modify the definition of the relevant vehicles in S.I. 1978 No. 1684.

4995. Public service vehicles—licences

PUBLIC SERVICE VEHICLES (OPERATORS' LICENCES) (FEES) REGULATIONS 1995 (No. 2909) [£1·55], made under the Public Passenger Vehicles Act 1981, ss.52, 60(1)(e). In force: January 1, 1996; replace the provisions in regs. 19 and 20 of the Public Service Vehicles (Operators' Licences) Regulations 1986, which have been revoked by the Public Service Vehicles (Operators' Licences) Regulations 1995, and impose a new fee structure. Regulation 3 and the Schedule set out the fees for operators' licences and discs, and when they shall be payable. Regulation 4 provides that fees paid for discs which are unused shall be refundable in specified circumstances.

PUBLIC SERVICE VEHICLES (OPERATORS' LICENCES) REGULATIONS 1995 (No. 2908) [£2·80], made under the Public Passenger Vehicles Act 1981, ss.14A(2), 16(1A)(3)(4), 18(1)(3), 49A(2)(3), 57(3), 59, 60, 81(1), 82(1) and the Transport Act 1985, s.27(1)(3); revoke S.I. 1986 No. 1668; S.I. 1990 No. 1852;

S.I. 1993 No. 2753; S.I. 1995 No. 689. In force: January 1, 1996; consolidate with modifications the Public Service Vehicles (Operators' Licences) Regulations 1986. They include new provisions consequent on the changes made by Chap. IV of the Deregulation and Contracting Out Act 1994, including the expiry of discs, the election to pay for discs annually and the manner in which notices are to be given. The provisions dealing with fees are now contained in the Public Service Vehicles (Operators' Licences) (Fees) Regulations 1995 (S.I. 1995 No. 2909).

PUBLIC SERVICE VEHICLES (OPERATORS' LICENCES) (AMENDMENT) REGULATIONS 1995 (No. 689) [65p], made under the Public Passenger Vehicles Act 1981 (c.14), ss.14A(2), 59, 60; operative on April 1, 1995; amend S.I. 1986 No. 1668 so as to prescribe the time within which, and manner in which, an objection to the grant of a public service vehicle operator's licence must be made, and so as to require a copy of the objection to be sent to the applicant.

4996. Rail crossings. See TOWN AND COUNTRY PLANNING, §4838.

4997. Railway—infrastructure—capacity and fees—European Community

Council Directive 95/19/EC of June 19, 1995 on the allocation of railway infrastructure capacity and the charging of infrastructure fees ([1995] O.J. L143/75).

4998. Railway undertakings—licensing—European Community

Council Directive 95/18/EC of June 19, 1995 on the licensing of railway undertakings ([1995] O.J. L143/70).

4999. Railways

CHINNOR AND PRINCES RISBOROUGH RAILWAY (EXTENSION) ORDER 1995 (No. 2458) [£1·95], made under the Transport and Works Act 1992, ss.1, 5, Sched. 1, paras. 1, 2, 15, 16, 17; operative on October 9, 1995; authorises the transfer of part of the former Thame branch railway line adjacent to its convergence with the Chinnor & Princes Risborough Railway in Buckinghamshire.

FORGE LANE, HORBURY LEVEL CROSSING ORDER 1995 (No. 2952) [£1·55], made under the Transport and Works Act 1992, ss.1, 5, Sched. 1, paras. 1, 2. In force: November 20, 1995; authorises the construction and operation of a new level crossing and the operation of an existing level crossing at Forge Lane, Horbury, near Wakefield, to form part of the Bombardier Prorail Ltd railway undertaking.

GREAT CENTRAL (NOTTINGHAM) RAILWAY ORDER 1995 (No. 2143) [£2·40], made under the Transport and Works Act 1992, ss.1, 5; operative on June 29, 1995; authorises the maintenance and operation of an existing railway in the parishes of Ruddington and East Leake in the borough of Rushcliffe, Nottinghamshire and the construction of a new railway within the former Ministry of Defence Ordnance Depot in the parish of Ruddington.

HEATHROW EXPRESS RAILWAY (TRANSFER) ORDER 1995 (No. 1332) [£1·10], made under the Transport and Works Act 1992 (c.42), s.6; operative on June 7, 1995; provides for the transfer of the functions and property of Heathrow Airport Ltd granted under the Heathrow Express Railways Acts 1991 to any other person who may construct the works and exercise the powers of the company under the 1991 Acts.

RAILTRACK (SWINEDYKE LEVEL CROSSING) ORDER 1995 (No. 3188), made under the Transport and Works Act 1992 ss.1, 5, Sched. 1, paras. 1, 4. operative on December 27, 1995; [£1·10]. The status of the level crossing of Southorpe Lane, Northorpe, Lincolnshire by the railway between Gainsborough Central and Kirton Lindsey stations is reduced to a public footpath crossing with private accommodation road from its present status of public vehicular crossing.

TRAFFORD PARK RAILWAY ORDER 1995 (No. 2446) [£2·40], made under the Transport and Works Act 1992, ss.1, 5, Sched. 1, paras. 1, 2, 16, 17; operative on September 12, 1995.

5000. Railways—Marylebone diesel depot

BRITISH RAILWAYS (MARYLEBONE DIESEL DEPOT) ORDER 1995 (No. 1228) [£1·10], made under the Transport and Works Act 1992 (c.42), ss.1, 5; operative on May 22, 1995; removes restrictions on the use of the land which comprises the site of the former Marylebone Diesel Depot.

5001. Railways—safety cases

The Health and Safety Executive (HSE) has issued a press release entitled *Health and Safety Commission Reaffirm Commitment to Railway Safety* (C44:95), published on August 23, 1995. The HSE has reviewed railway safety with the Chief Inspecting Officer of Railways, concluding that railways are undergoing fundamental reorganisation and restructuring. Following HSC recommendations in January 1993, all of which were accepted by the Government, three pieces of legislation were introduced in 1994, Railways (Safety Case) Regulations, Railways (Safety Critical Work) Regulations and Carriage of Dangerous Goods by Rail Regulations.

5002. Railways pensions

RAILWAYS PENSIONS (SUBSTITUTION AND MISCELLANEOUS PROVISIONS) ORDER 1995 (No. 430) [£4·15], made under the Transport Act 1980 (c.34), ss.52B, 52D(4)(5); operative on March 12, 1995; ends the liability of the Secretary of State to make payments under s.52(1) of the 1980 Act in respect of two sections of the Railways Pension Scheme and makes provision for payments to be made in substitution for that liability.

5003. Rapid transit highway—private contract—awarded for completion of rapid transit highway—whether breach of obligations under Community law whether derogation from Directive justified—European Community

The Commission sought a declaration that Italy was in breach of its obligations under Community law in that the provincial administration of Ascoli Piceno had awarded a private contract relating to the completion of part of a section of rapid transit highway.

Held, that Italy was liable since the provisions of Council Dir. 71/305 had not been fully complied with. In particular, Art. 9 of the Directive, which provided for a derogation when, for technical or artistic reasons or for reasons connected with the protection of exclusive rights, the works may only be carried out by a particular contractor, was an exception which had to be interpreted strictly. The burden of proving the existence of exceptional circumstances justifying a derogation lies on the person seeking to rely on those circumstances. This had not been satisfied in this case.

E.C. COMMISSION v. ITALY (C–57/94), May 18, 1995, ECJ.

5004. Special roads

S.I. 1995 Nos. 231 (M1—A1 Link Road/East Leeds Radial) [£3·20]; 426 (M1—A1 Belle Island to Bramham Crossroads and connecting roads) [£2·40]; 1094 (M25—Junctions 10 to 15—variable speed limits) [£1·55]; 3266 (Mancunian Way A635(M) and A57(M) Mancunian Way Slip Roads [£1·10]; 3270 (M27 Ower–Chilworth Section) [65p].

5005. Street works

STREET WORKS (REGISTERS, NOTICES, DIRECTIONS AND DESIGNATIONS) (AMENDMENT) REGULATIONS 1995 (No. 990) [65p], made under the

New Roads and Street Works Act 1991 (c.22), ss.53(1)–(3)(6), 104(1); operative on July 1, 1995; create new requirements about the way street authorities keep street works registers.

STREET WORKS (REGISTERS, NOTICES, DIRECTIONS AND DESIGNATIONS) (AMENDMENT NO. 2) REGULATIONS 1995 (No. 1154) [£1·10], made under the New Roads and Street Works Act 1991 (c.22), s.64(1)(2); operative on May 26, 1995; amend S.I. 1992 No. 2985.

STREET WORKS (REGISTERS, NOTICES, DIRECTIONS AND DESIGNATIONS) (AMENDMENT NO. 3) REGULATIONS 1995 (No. 2128) [£1·10], made under the New Roads and Street Works Act 1991, ss.64(1)(2), 104(1); amend S.I. 1992 No. 2985; revoke S.I. 1995 No. 1154; operative on September 11, 1995; amend the criteria for designating streets as traffic-sensitive pursuant to s.64 of the New Roads and Street Works Act 1991.

5006. Transport policies and programme submissions—guidance to local authorities

The Department of Transport has published Local Authority Circular 2/95 entitled *Transport Policies and Programme Submissions for 1996–1997* giving guidance to local authorities on drawing up their transport policies and programmes and explains how the Transport Supplementary Grant and other capital funding mechanisms for local transport infrastructure will operate in 1996–1997. It replaces Circular 2/94. Available from HMSO, price £4·85. ISBN 0–11–551739–1.

5007. Trunk roads

S.I. 1994 Nos. 3004 (A1 Haringey-amending S.I. 1993 No. 896) [65p]; 3005 (A1 Haringey-amending S.I. 1993 No. 897) [65p]; 3006 (Islington-amending S.I. 1993 No. 891 [65p]; 3007 (A1 Islington-amending S.I. 1993 No. 895 [65p].

S.I. 1995 Nos. 5 (Chester-Bangor (A55)) [65p]; 17 (A23 (Brighton Road, Croydon)) [65p]; 124 (A205 (Richmond and Wandsworth)) [65p]; 125 (A205 (Hounslow)) [65p]; 126 (A205 (Hounslow)) [65p]; 203 (A11 (Thetford Bypass)) [65p]; 219 (Cardiff-Glan Conwy) [65p]; 220 (Chester-Bangor) [65p]; 231 (M1–A1) [65p]; 296 (A3 (Kingston Bypass)) [65p]; 299 (A638 (King Royd Lane)) [65p]; 320 (A3 (Malden Way)) [65p]; 335 (A3 (Wandsworth)) [65p]; 336 (A3 (Merton)) [65p]; 337 (A3 (Kingston upon Thames)) [65p]; 338 (A3 (Merton)) [65p]; 339 (A3 (Kingston upon Thames)) [65p]; 405 (A63 (South Cave)) [65p]; 406 (A63 (Welton)) [65p]; 425 (A64 Bramham Crossroads) [65p]; 432 (A65 (Chelker Bends)) [65p]; 433 (A15 (Brigg and Redbourne Bypass)) [65p]; 485 (A5 (Priorslee)) [65p]; 745 (Cardiff-Glan Conwy) [65p]; 819 (A638) [65p]; 870 (A312 (The Parkway, Hounslow)) [65p]; 1009 (A5) [65p]; 1048 (A61 (Tankersly Roundabout)) [65p]; 1144 (A23 (Streatham High Road)) [65p]; 1153 (A19) [65p]; 1158 (A4 (Great West Road, Hounslow) [65p]; 1165 (A1 (Islington)) [65p]; 1166 (A1 (Islington)); 1413 (A41) [65p]; 1593 (A3 (Kingston Vale)) [65p]; (A312 (The Parkway, Hounslow)) [65p]; 1658 (B1003/A57) [65p]; 1692 (A12 (Redbridge)) [65p]; (A316 (Hounslow)) [65p]; 1694 (A316 (Richmond)) [65p]; 1695 (A12 (Redbridge)) [65p]; 1696 (A4100 (Redbridge)) [65p]; 1697 (A316 (Richmond)) [65p]; 1698 (A316 (Hounslow)) [65p]; 1699 A406 (Newham and Barking and Dagenham)) [65p]; 1700 (A13 (Barking and Dagenham)) [65p]; 1701 (A13 (Newham)) [65p]; 1702 (A10 (Haringey)) [65p] 1703 (A13 (Havering)) [65p]; 1946 (A30 (Kennards House)); 2067 (A43 (Whitfield turn)) [65p]; 2068 (A43 (Whifield Turn)) [65p]; 2124 (London Fishguard Road) [65p]; 2146 (Dolgellau to South of Birkenhead) [65p]; 2182 (A650 (Crossflatts)) [65p]; 2215 (A12 (Eastern Avenue, Redbridge)) [65p]; 2216 (A3 (Beverly Way, Merton)) [65p]; 2245 (A13 (Tower Hamlets)) [65p]; 2246 (A406 (Enfield)) [65p]; 2443 (A20 (Greenwich)) [65p]; 2444 (A2 (Bexley)) [65p]; 2445 (A20 (Bexley and Bromley)) [65p]; 2448 (Glanusk Park (Crickhowell-Llyswen [65p]; 2454 (London South Circular [65p]; 2519 (A2 (Bexley)) [65p]; (A2 (Greenwich)) [65p]; 2521 (A10 (Enfield)) [65p;] 2523 (A12 (Redbridge and Barking and Dagenham)) [65p]; 2524 (A13 (Barking and Dagenham and Newham)) [65p]; 2525 (A13 (Havering)) [65p]; 2526 (A13

(Newham)) [65p]; 2527 (A20 (Bexley and Bromley)) [65p]; 2528 (A20 (Greenwich)) [65p]; 2530 (A102 (Tower Hamlets)) [65p] 2532 (A406 (Enfield)) [65p]; 2533 (A406 (Redbridge)); 2534 (A406 (Newham, Redbridge and Barking and Dagenham)) [65p] 2535 (A406 (Waltham Forest)) [65p]; 2536 (A1400 (Redbridge)) [65p]; 2685 (A23 (Croydon)) [65p]; 2686 (A23 (Croydon)) [65p]; 2687 (A23 (Croydon)) [65p]; 2688 (A205 (Richmond)) [65p]; 2689 (A23 (Croydon)) [65p]; 2744 (A205 (Richmond and Wandsworth)) [65p]; 2746 (A205 (Upper Richmond Road West)) [65p]; 2879 (A3 (Robin Hood Way)) [65p]; 2965 (A30 (Great South West Road, Hounslow)) [65p]; 2966 (A41 (Baker Street)) [65p]; 2967 (A501 (Fitzroy Street)) [65p]; 3058 (A102 (Blackwall Tunnel)) [65p]; 3100 (A12 (Colchester Road, Havering)) [65p]; 3139 (A40 (Ealing)) [65p]; 3142 (A406 (Brent)) [65p]; 3143 (A406 (Brent)) [65p]; 3164 (A40 (Hillingdon)) [65p]; (3168 (A501 (Euston Road and Osnaburgh Street)) [65p].

TRESPASS

5008. Police—search outside powers—*quantum of damages*. See HARRISON AND HOPE v. CHIEF CONSTABLE OF POLICE FOR GREATER MANCHESTER, §1846.

VALUE ADDED TAX

5009. Appeal—costs—contingency fee—whether tribunal entitled to award costs in case taken on contingency fee basis

[Value Added Tax Tribunals Rules 1986 (S.I. 1986 No. 590), r.29.]

An award for costs cannot be made in the absence of a liability to pay his adviser's fee by the appellant.

R, through his company P, represented V at an appeal before a tribunal on the basis that he would charge him only the amount awarded for costs. The appeal was successful and costs were awarded. Customs and Excise appealed the award.

Held, allowing the appeal, that costs may only be awarded on an indemnity basis (*Customs and Excise Commissioners v. Ross* [1990] C.L.Y. 4630 applied).

CUSTOMS AND EXCISE COMMISSIONERS v. VAZ, PORTCULLIS (VAT CONSULTANCY), INTERVENING [1995] S.T.C. 14, Macpherson of Cluny J.

5010. Appeal—costs—interest—whether interest may be awarded on costs for periods prior to or following a direction to pay costs

[Value Added Tax Tribunals Rules 1986 (S.I. 1986 No. 590), r.29.]

By analogy with the Rules of the Supreme Court, the Tribunal may not in a direction award interest on costs incurred before the date of the direction; nor is there an entitlement to award interest on costs following the direction since the tribunal is not a court.

In deciding an appeal, the tribunal had directed, *inter alia*, that Customs and Excise should pay the appellants' interest on their costs from the date on which they were paid until the date of reimbursement at a rate to be agreed or directed by the tribunal in default of agreement; or so far as the appellants had not paid the costs and incurred a liability to interest on them at ordinary commercial rates, the amount of that interest. Customs and Excise applied to the tribunal to vary the direction by omitting any reference to interest on costs.

Held, granting the application, that (1) interest on costs could not run in respect of periods prior to the date of the direction (*Hunt v. Douglas (R.M.)*

Roofing [1989] C.L.Y. 2935 applied); (2) there was no jurisdiction to award interest on costs from the date of a direction until the date of payment (*Nader v. Customs and Excise Commissioners* [1994] C.L.Y. 4557 applied).

BROADWAY VIDEO (WHOLESALE) v. CUSTOMS AND EXCISE COMMISSIONERS [1994] VATTR 271, London Tribunal.

5011. Appeal—discretionary powers—commissioner's decision to assess—whether tribunal having supervisory jurisdiction over commissioner's discretion to assess

[Value Added Tax Act 1983 (c.55), s.40(1)(o)(p).]

The appellants had defaulted in payment of VAT between April 1990 and April 1992 as a result of difficulties caused by the recession. VAT Central Unit issued default surcharges on the basis of centrally-held computer information without reference to the local VAT office. The appellants contended that their position under the recession constituted a reasonable excuse and, in the alternative, that the surcharges had been issued automatically despite the fact that they were discretionary and therefore were invalid. The tribunal dismissed the appeal on the basis that, while the appellants' reasons were capable of constituting a reasonable excuse, they had invested large amounts of money in capital expenditure during this period. The tribunal considered that it had jurisdiction to review the probity of issuing the surcharges under the Value Added Tax Act 1983, s.40(1). The tribunal found that the commissioners should have exercised their discretion rather than issuing surcharges automatically but that the surcharges would have imposed in any event.

Held, dismissing the appeals, that the supervisory jurisdiction of the tribunal with reference to any of the headings in the Value Added Tax Act 1983, s.40, depended on the wording of the particular paragraphs. Such jurisdiction would therefore either be expressly provided for or would follow by necessary implication. While the right to surcharge, the decision to assess to surcharge and the amount of such surcharge were all linked issues, s.40(1) dealt with them separately. Therefore, there was no right of appeal against the decision to assess to surcharge taken by the commissioners. Where there was a liability to surcharge, it was at the discretion of the commissioners to assess for it. The tribunal had no implicit powers to review the commissioners' decision. The commissioners were entitled to adopt the position that once liability to surcharge had arisen, they were at liberty to assess for it unless there was some special reason not to do so. However, the tribunal's decision that the commissioners had failed to exercise their powers represented a finding of fact which should not be interfered with. Having reached that finding of fact, the tribunal was entitled to dismiss the appeal on the basis that surcharges would have been raised in any event (*Customs and Excise Commissioners v. Corbitt (J.H.) Numismatists* [1980] C.L.Y. 2780, *Van Boeckel v. Customs and Excise Commissioners* [1981] C.L.Y. 2839 referred to).

DOLLAR LAND (FELTHAM) v. CUSTOMS AND EXCISE COMMISSIONERS [1995] S.T.C. 414, Judge J.

5012. Appeal—discretionary powers—whether wrong approach adopted by tribunal

[Value Added Tax Act 1983 (c.55), s.40(1)(n).]

CEC appealed against a ruling that the VAT tribunal had adopted the wrong approach when allowing an appeal under s.40(1)(n) of the Value Added Tax Act 1983 against CEC's decision to require security for VAT.

Held, dismissing the appeal, that in s.40 appeals against discretionary CEC decisions, such as a decision to require a trader to provide security, the VAT tribunal's role was appellate rather than supervisory. The principles of reasonableness established in *Associated Provincial Picture Houses v. Wednesbury Corp.* [1948] C.L.Y. 8107 were not relevant. If the tribunal decided that CEC made the wrong decision, the appeal should be allowed. The tribunal's task was not to substitute its own discretion if it considered the decision of CEC was flawed.

JOHN DEE v. CUSTOMS AND EXCISE COMMISSIONERS, *The Times*, July 20, 1995, C.A.

5013. Appeal—evidence—mobile home unit—whether supply included work necessary for the development of site as a permanent park for residential caravans and hence partly zero-rated

The VAT tribunal found that the cost of the provision of brickwork and the installation of services peculiar to a specific site were attributable to a sale of a mobile home rather than to the periodic payment for occupancy of the site. It was argued that the tribunal had reached its decision in the absence of vital documents relating to the agreement to supply the site and to the construction of the brickwork around the site. This had not been the primary issue before the tribunal and therefore all the contractual documents had not been produced before the tribunal.

Held, that it would be inappropriate for the court to quash the decision of the tribunal in the light of the uncertainty over the existence of the documentation, and that the matter should be referred to the tribunal for redetermination with reference to all the appropriate documents (*Stonecliff Caravan Park v. Customs and Excise Commisioners* (MAN/91/1667), unrep. considered).

CUSTOMS AND EXCISE COMMISSIONERS v. BARRATT [1995] S.T.C. 661, Potts, J.

5014. Appeal—extra-statutory concession—whether tribunal entitled to take into account non-application of extra-statutory concession

[Value Added Tax Act 1994 (c.23), s.83.]

On an appeal the tribunal may consider the application of an extra-statutory concession, albeit not the reasonableness of the concession itself.

S built a boat for C and issued invoices not including VAT because it was understood that the boat was intended for export. Ultimately it was arrested for non-payment of a debt owed by C to a creditor who had a charge on the boat. Customs and Excise assessed S to tax on the basis that the export of the boat had not followed the terms of the relevant extra-statutory concession.

Held, allowing S's appeal, that the decision in relation to the concession was unreasonable and had taken irrelevant considerations into account.

SHEPHERD v. CUSTOMS AND EXCISE COMMISSIONERS [1994] VATTR 47, London Tribunal.

5015. Appeal—hearing in absence of party—no power in tribunal to hear in absence—whether power to hear oral application forthwith limited to hearing of which valid notice given

[Value Added Tax Tribunal Rules 1986 (S.I. 1986 No. 590), rr.4, 23(2), 26(2).]

On November 9, 1993 A appealed against an assessment to tax. The Commissioners applied under r.6 of the Value Added Tax Tribunals Rules 1986 for the appeal to be dismissed because it could not be entertained by reason of s.40(3) of the Value Added Tax Act 1983. The application was noted to be heard on January 13, 1994. A made a hardship application and applied for the hearing on January 13 to be vacated. The commissioners served a notice on January 4, 1994 withdrawing their earlier application. However, they sought to oppose the hardship application and made a r.6 application. Prior to this, A's accountant was notified in a conversation with a member of the tribunal staff that the January 13 hearing would be adjourned and that he need not attend. However, on January 13, the chairman of the tribunal heard the application in A's absence and dismissed the appeal. A sought to have this direction set aside.

Held, allowing the application, that Value Added Tax Tribunal Rules 1986, r.26(2), empowered the tribunal to consider an application which was called on for hearing. The notice of the hearing for January 13 related to an application which had been withdrawn and therefore there was no application on January 13 to which r.26(2) could apply. The Value Added Tax Tribunal Rules 1986, r.23(2), providing for an application made at a hearing to be heard forthwith, only applied where there was a valid hearing of which 14 day's notice had been given. This did not apply to the January 13 hearing because the only application notified for hearing on that day had been withdrawn. The direction issued as a result of the hearing on January 13 must therefore be withdrawn as being *ultra vires*.

CUMHUR AKAR v. CUSTOMS AND EXCISE COMMISSIONERS [1994] V.A.T.T.R. 176, London Tribunal.

5016. Appeal—jurisdiction—whether decisions to deregister and to assess reviewable by tribunal

[Value Added Tax Act 1994 (c.23), s.73, Sched. 1, para. 13.]

A decision to deregister is reviewable as the exercise of a discretion, but not a decision to assess, which is the exercise of an enabling power.

AB applied for VAT registration as a breeder of racehorses. She was voluntarily registered but later deregistered and assessed to tax on disallowed input tax. She appealed and later applied to amend her grounds of appeal to two points, *i.e.* she had at all times carried on a business of horse breeding and that the decision to assess her retrospectively was an unreasonable exercise of the discretion regarding assessments. The tribunal heard as a preliminary point whether it had jurisdiction to review decisions taken by the Customs and Excise to deregister her and assess her.

Held, allowing the appeal in part, that the decision to deregister but not the decision to assess was reviewable.

BROOKES v. CUSTOMS AND EXCISE COMMISSIONS [1994] VATTR 35, London Tribunal.

5017. Appeal—re-assessment—"best judgment" basis—two-stage process

The supervisory jurisdiction of a VAT tribunal hearing an appeal against a tax assessment had to be conducted objectively on a "best judgment" basis. This required a two-stage process. First, as a question of fact, the tribunal had to decide what information the commissioners had used to make the assessment. Secondly, as a value judgment, it had to decide how the commissioners had arrived at the assessed figure, by re-assessing figures used in their computation. The supervisory function of the VAT tribunal called for a reasonable standard to be employed in the re-assessment process.

GEORGIOU v. CUSTOMS AND EXCISE COMMISSIONERS, *The Times*, October 19, 1995, D.C.

5018. Appeal—refusal by commissioners to repay interest on assessed tax paid on account—tribunal's jurisdiction to entertain appeal—whether "the amount of any . . . interest"

[Value Added Tax Act 1983 (c.55), s.40(1)(p).]

The taxpayer partnership had been assessed to value added tax on June 25, 1991 and also to two serious misdeclaration penalties totalling £1,009·80 and default interest of £328·48. The taxpayer wrote to the commissioners on November 27, 1991 to ascertain whether or not interest was continuing to run, so that it could pay any interest on a without prejudice basis. On December 2, 1991, the taxpayer made payment to the commissioners by cheque in the sum of £528·14, which was intended to represent interest on the tax assessed. The commissioners offset part of the misdeclaration penalties and the whole of the default interest of £328·48. Following the submission of a repayment return, the commissioners repaid the amounts of the misdeclaration penalties of an aggregate £1,009·80. The taxpayer appealed, claiming repayment of the £528·14 interest it had paid. The commissioners sought to strike out the appeal on the basis that the tribunal had no jurisdiction to hear it under s.40(1)(p) of the 1983 Act.

Held, refusing the application, that s.40(1)(p) provided for an appeal against a decision of the commissioners with respect to "an amount of any . . . interest . . . specified in an assessment under s.20 Finance Act 1985". It followed therefore that s.40(1)(p) was broad enough to encompass the present appeal against the commissioner's refusal to pay interest. The payment made by the taxpayer was a voluntary payment which was made with an implied term that if it were not due, it would be returned. For the commissioners to refuse to return it would be an unjust enrichment at the taxpayer's expense.

RMSG v. CUSTOMS AND EXCISE COMMISSIONERS [1994] V.A.T.T.R. 167, London Tribunal.

5019. Appeal—refusal to refer question to European Court—judicial review advised as appropriate—alternative statutory route not advised—ruling that judicial review not appropriate—whether leave to be granted for appeal out of time

[Tribunals and Inquiries Act 1992 (c.53), s.11; Treaty of Rome 1957, Art. 177.]

C appealed against the refusal of an application for extension of time to lodge a notice of appeal under the Tribunals and Inquiries Act 1992, s.11, and a refusal of leave to move for judicial review. The case involved a decision of the London VAT and Duties Tribunal not to refer a question on input tax to the European Court of Justice for a ruling under the Treaty of Rome 1957, Art. 177. Counsel advised C to challenge the refusal by way of judicial review and the tribunal also believed this to be the appropriate route. Leave was given to apply for judicial review and at the same time use of s.11 of the 1992 Act was discounted as a means of appeal. At the application it was held that judicial review was inappropriate, as s.11 provided a specific statutory procedure to be used for appeal. C was by that stage out of time to appeal against the tribunal's decision under s.11 and an application for an extension of time was dismissed.

Held, allowing the appeal for an extension of time and dismissing the application for leave to move for judicial review that, as s.11 was the appropriate procedure, judicial review was inappropriate. It was undesirable to allow C to use another route after having already been unsuccessful once, but it was understandable that they chose the incorrect route. As they had not behaved mischievously they should be allowed another attempt.

R. v. LONDON VALUE ADDED TAX AND DUTIES TRIBUNAL, *ex p.* CONOCO (LTA 95/5861/D; LTA96/6060/D), July 19, 1995, C.A.

5020. Appeal—resumed in taxpayer's absence—whether tribunal should have adjourned resumed hearing

S, a sole trader, had been assessed to VAT on purchases of furniture, which S claimed were his own property. At a first hearing of a tribunal S had failed to explain mistakes in his trading accounts with reference to those assessments. Documents had been produced at this hearing which had not been shown to the commissioners throughout the course of correspondence. S had been given notice of a further hearing of the tribunal in this matter. S wrote to the tribunal explaining that he would be unable to attend, that he would send documents requested from him and that he understood that the hearing might proceed without him. S did not request an adjournment as he had been informed he was able to do by either of two letters or a telephone call. The issue before the court was whether an adjournment ought to have been permitted.

Held, dismissing S's application, that the tribunal was correct not to have granted an adjournment because S had not requested an adjournment and, alternatively, no ground was advanced why there should be an adjournment given that the issue could not have turned on any evidence which S had not already given at the first hearing. The applicant cannot attack the finding of fact of a tribunal where there was evidence to support that finding before it. The applicant had no right of appeal against a pure finding of fact to the High Court. Further there was no explanation tendered by S as to the mistake which had been made in the trading accounts in any event (*Edwards (Inspector of Taxes) v. Bairstow* [1956] A.C. 14, *Rose v. Humbles (Inspector of Taxes)* [1972] C.L.Y. 1702 referred to).

SANDLEY v. CUSTOMS AND EXCISE COMMISSIONERS [1995] STC 230, Turner J.

5021. Appeal—right of audience—accountant—whether accountant had to hold current membership of incorporated society of accountants at time of hearing before being permitted to represent taxpayer

[Taxes Management Act 1970 (c.9), s.50(5).]

The taxpayer had sought to appeal against various assessments to income tax and to capital gains tax. The general commissioners had refused to hear representations on the taxpayer's behalf from an accountant, F. The reason for the refusal was that F's membership of an incorporated society of accountants had been suspended in the wake of convictions for criminal offences relating to falsification of documents. The taxpayer argued that under the Taxes Management Act 1970, s.50(5), the general commissioners were required to hear any accountant and that, in any event, the general commissioners should have exercised their discretion to hear F on the taxpayer's behalf.

Held, that s.50(5) required that the commissioners were required to hear any accountant, meaning an accountant who has not been suspended or expelled from an incorporated society of accountants. The requirement of continued membership was implicit in the subsection. Therefore, the general commissioners were not required to hear F.

CASSELL v. CRUTCHFIELD [1995] STC 663, Blackburne J.

5022. Assessment—based on till grand total memory—duty of assessing officer to consider "all material"—standard of judgement required—whether reduction made to commissioners' "best judgement"

[Value Added Tax Act 1983 (c.55), para. 4(1)(2)(6)(9).]

The taxpayer carried on the business of a take-away food shop. The shop sold hot food which was standard-rated and cold food which was zero-rated. The taxpayer admitted by a letter under-declaration of tax as a result of removing cash from tills and not recording all purchases. In May 1990, the taxpayer was assessed to value added tax in the sum of £61,902. In November 1990, after a review, the assessment was reduced to £56,444. A penalty notice of assessment under s.13 of the Finance Act 1985 was issued for dishonest evasion with a five per cent reduction for co-operation. A appealed on the basis that the assessments and the review were not carried out to the "best judgement" of the commissioners. Further, he contended that the assessments were excessive and that the reduction for co-operation ought to have been 50 per cent. The tribunal ordered the commissioners to serve a supplementary list of documents under their control. This list was to be verified by affidavit. A was dissatisfied by the affidavit and appealed against it also.

Held, allowing the appeal in part, that under the 1983 Act, para. 4(1)(2)(6)(9), the burden of proof was on A to establish that the assessment and review had not been carried out in the "best judgement" of the commissioners. For this purpose the relevant judgement was the judgement of the assessing officer who should consider all the relevant material obtained during the course of the inquiry by officers. The judgement required of the assessing officer was not that of an expert in law or accountancy. An arithmetical error does not vitiate an assessment unless the result it produces which a competent officer should have realised was unreasonable. On these facts, the assessment was made to the officer's "best judgement". When the commissioners are confirming or reducing an assessment, it is not necessary that the commissioners exercise their best judgement. Despite the fact that the commissioners had exercised the best of their judgement, on the facts before the tribunal, the assessment should be reduced further. The penalty levied under s.13 of the Finance Act 1985 should be reduced to 75 per cent. The tribunal found that the commissioners had failed to comply with the direction for the discovery of documents. However, such failure had not been wilfully disobedient and therefore no penalty would be imposed (*Van Boeckel v. Customs and Excise Commisioners* [1981] C.L.Y. 2839, *Seto v. Customs and Excise Commissioners* [1981] STC 698 referred to).

MARIOS CHIPPERY v. CUSTOMS AND EXCISE COMMISSIONERS [1994] V.A.T.T.R. 125, Manchester Tribunal.

5023. Assessment—global assessment—notice—whether sufficient details

[Value Added Tax Act 1983 (c.55).]

H appealed against a ruling that a global assessment of his under-declared VAT spanning several accounting periods, was validly made and notified under the Value Added Tax Act 1983. The notice giving the assessment did not show the amount due for each period but three schedules accompanying the letter of notification contained details which clarified how the sums were made up and would enable an assessment for each period to be calculated.

Held, dismissing the appeal, that a global tax assessment of VAT was permissible in circumstances where separate assessments could have been calculated (*Customs and Excise Commissioners v. Le Rififi* [1995] 10 C.L. 856 followed). Sufficient notice had been given as the schedules containing details of the assessment were to be treated as part of the notice (*International Language Centres v. Customs and Excise Commissioners* [1983] S.T.C. 394 considered).

HOUSE v. CUSTOMS AND EXCISE COMMISSIONERS, *The Times*, October 20, 1995, C.A.

5024. Assessment—global assessment rather than assessments for each accounting period—whether permissible—whether right to levy entire penalty on company or one director

[Value Added Tax Act 1994 (c.23), ss.61, 76.]

The requirement in the Act to assess penalties by reference to accounting periods is mandatory.

The Customs and Excise assessed a penalty of £65,304 on B on the grounds of his dishonest conduct as a director of AO Ltd for the period from May 1, 1986 to October 31, 1990.

Held, allowing B's appeal, that (1) the assessment was invalid because it was in a global amount rather than for each accounting period (*Don Pasquale (A Firm) v. Customs and Excise Commissioners* [1991] C.L.Y 3632 distinguished); (2) even if the assessment were valid the imposition of the entire penalty on one director was unjust.

BASSIMEH v. CUSTOMS AND EXCISE COMMISSIONERS [1994] VATTR 7, London Tribunal.

5025. Assessment—input tax—limitation period—whether deduction permissible

[Value Added Tax Act 1983 (c.55), Sched. 7.]

The commissioners appealed against a VAT Tribunal ruling that an assessment of input tax due from C was time-barred under para. 4(2) of Sched. 7 to the Value Added Tax Act 1983. C was allowed a deduction for input tax on a payment to terminate a hotel management agreement on condition that repayment would be made to the commissioners if the payment was subsequently determined not to be consideration for a taxable supply. The payment was made in the accounting period ending March 1991 and the input VAT was claimed in the accounting period ending June 1991.

Held, dismissing the appeal, that the limitation period for input VAT assessment ran not from the period in which the taxpayer made the claim to deduct input VAT, but from the earlier period when the payment on which input VAT was recovered was made by the taxpayer. In the context of the limitation provisions, input VAT was for the period when the taxpayer paid it, not for subsequent periods when the taxpayer claimed to recover it from the commissioners or when the commissioners allowed recovery.

CUSTOMS AND EXCISE COMMISSIONERS v. CROYDON HOTEL AND LEISURE COMPANY, *The Times*, June 1, 1995, Popplewell J.

5026. Assessment—limitation period—actual knowledge that VAT returns incorrect

[Value Added Tax Act 1983 (c.55), Sched. 7, para. 4(5).]

For the purposes of para. 4(5) of Sched. 7 to the Value Added Tax Act 1983 the limitation period for corrective VAT assessments started to run only when the commissioners had actual knowledge that VAT returns contained errors. The court rejected the taxpayer's argument that the limitation period started to run at an earlier time by reason of the commissioner's constructive knowledge, *i.e.* the customs officer who checked the return ought to have noticed the mistake. The matter was remitted to the VAT tribunal.

CUSTOMS AND EXCISE COMMISSIONERS v. POST OFFICE, *The Independent*, June 19, 1995, Potts J.

5027. Assessment—separate assessments—in default of proper returns by taxpayer—assessment in prescribed form covering a number of periods including a period which was out of time—whether single assessment—whether assessment out of time

The commissioners assessed the company to VAT in default of proper returns. The commissioners issued the assessment on three sheets of form VAT 191, which was structured to permit assessments to be made by reference to different accounting methods for different accounting periods. The taxpayer argued that one of the assessments was made more than six years after the assessment period and was therefore out of time. The taxpayer argued further that *Don Pasquale (A Firm) v. Customs and Excise Commissioners* ([1991] C.L.Y. 3632), a decision of the Court of Appeal, bound the tribunal and the High Court to interpret the assessments on the form VAT 191 as being a single assessment and therefore all out of time.

Held, allowing the appeal, that the doctrine of precedent requires that the legal principle on which the court decided be followed. A subsequent court was not bound by the interpretation placed on a specific instrument. The form VAT 191 was not intended to form a single assessment. The facts of the previous Court of Appeal decision are indistinguishable from the instant case but the court is not bound by the doctrine of precedent to follow that decision. The form constituted 24 separate assessments and not one global assessment. Therefore only the first assessment was out of time (*Ashville Investments v. Elmer Contractors* [1989] Q.B. 488, *Grange (S.J.) v. Customs and Excise Commissioners* [1979] C.L.Y. 2740, *International Language Centres v. Customs and Excise Commissioners* [1983] C.L.Y. 3841 referred to).

CUSTOMS AND EXCISE COMMISSIONERS v. LE RIFFI [1995] STC 103, C.A.

5028. Assessment—transfer of business without notification—nil returns made by taxpayer—whether jurisdiction point may be raised at hearing—whether nil returns correct where taxpayer was still registered but had ceased trading

[Value Added Tax Tribunals Rules 1986 (S.1.1986, No. 590), r.6 (1).]

Where a business is transferred without notification to the Customs and Excise, the transferor remains liable to make returns, but is not accountable for tax due from the transferred business.

C carried on business as a retailer. He transferred the business to a company, but did not advise the Customs and Excise of the change and continued to submit VAT returns in his own name. Later the company was put into liquidation and C recommenced business through another company. He applied for this company to be registered. This was done and C's registration was cancelled. In the meantime assessments to VAT were raised on him in respect of periods for which he had made no return. C ultimately submitted nil returns and appealed against the assessments. At the hearing the Customs and Excise submitted as a preliminary point that the tribunal had no jurisdiction to hear the appeal since returns had not been made at the time the assessments were raised.

Held, allowing the appeal, that (1) the jurisdiction point could not be taken without prior notice; (2) although C was liable to make returns, he had made no supplies and accordingly the nil returns were correct; and (3) where a business is transferred without notification to the Customs and Excise, the transferor remains liable to make returns, but is not accountable for tax due from the transferred business.

CADMAN v. CUSTOMS AND EXCISE COMMISSIONERS [1994] VATTR 296, Manchester Tribunal.

5029. Buildings and land

VALUE ADDED TAX (BUILDINGS AND LAND) ORDER 1994 (No. 3013) [65p], made under the Value Added Tax Act 1994 (c.23), s.51; operative on November 30, 1994; amends Sched. 10 to the 1994 Act.

VALUE ADDED TAX (BUILDINGS AND LAND) ORDER 1995 (No. 279) [£1·55], made under the Value Added Tax Act 1994 (c.23), s.51; operative on March 1, 1995; amends Sched. 10 to the 1994 Act.

VALUE ADDED TAX (CONSTRUCTION OF BUILDINGS) ORDER 1995 (No. 280) [£1·55], made under the Value Added Tax Act 1994 (c.23), ss.30(4), 96(9); operative on March 1, 1995; substitutes a new Group 5 of Sched. 8 to the 1994 Act.

VALUE ADDED TAX (LAND) ORDER 1995 (No. 282), made under Value Added Tax Act 1994 (c.23), s.31(2); operative on March 1, 1995; amends Group 1 of Sched. 9 (land) to the 1994 Act which exempts, with a number of exceptions, the grant of interest in or right over land; provides a revised definition of grant pertaining to the surrender of an interest.

VALUE ADDED TAX (PROTECTED BUILDINGS) ORDER 1995 (No. 283) [£1·10], made under the Value Added Tax Act 1994 (c.23), ss.30(4), 96(9); operative on March 1, 1995; substitutes a new Group 6 of Sched. 8 to the 1994 Act.

5030. Cars

VALUE ADDED TAX (CARS) (AMENDMENT) ORDER 1995 (No. 1269) [£1·10], made under the Value Added Tax Act 1994 (c.23), ss.5(3)(5), 11(4), 43(2), 50A; operative on June 1, 1995; amends S.I. 1992 No. 3122 in relation to the operation of the margin scheme in relation to motorcars.

VALUE ADDED TAX (CARS) (AMENDMENT) (NO. 2) ORDER 1995 (No. 1667), made under the Value Added Tax 1994, ss.5(3)(5), 43(2), 50A; amends S.I. 1992 No. 3122; revokes S.I. 1993 No. 2951; operative on August 1, 1995; art. 3 of S.I. 1992 No. 3122 amends art. 4 of the principal Order which provides for supplies of cars that have been subject to input tax restriction to be treated as neither a supply of goods nor a supply of services.

5031. Consideration for fuel

VALUE ADDED TAX (INCREASE OF CONSIDERATION FOR FUEL) ORDER 1995 (No. 3040) [65p], made under the Value Added Tax Act 1994, s.57(4). In force: April 6, 1996; amends Table A of s.57(3) of the Value Added Tax Act 1994 by increasing the fixed scales used as the basis for charging VAT on road fuel provided by businesses for private motoring by five per cent. The increase will affect taxable persons from their prescribed accounting periods beginning on or after April 6, 1996.

5032. Derogation—United Kingdom—European Community

Council Decision 95/252/EC of June 29, 1995 authorising the United Kingdom to apply a measure of derogation from Arts. 6 and 17 of the Sixth Council Directive (77/388/EEC) on the harmonisation of the laws of the Member States relating to turnover taxes (O.J. L159/19).

5033. EEC law—press release

HM Customs and Excise has issued a press release entitled *Business Brief* (24/95), published on November 6, 1995. Draft Finance Bill provisions on the implementation of the Second VAT Simplification Directive have been sent to members of the Joint VAT Consultative Committee and other interested parties for urgent consultation. Copies of the draft legislation may be obtained from Mrs Alison Duffy, HMCE, VAT Policy Directorate, International Division, 4th Floor East, New King's Beam House, 22 Upper Ground, London, SE1 9PJ.

5034. Electronic funds transfer

Customs and Excise have issued a press release entitled *Changes to VAT Accounting* (45/95), published on September 21, 1995. Customs and Excise are to introduce changes to the VAT Annual Accounting Scheme on April 1, 1996. Prior to that date all repayments of VAT will be made by electronic means and businesses will be encouraged to pay their VAT electronically.

5035. Environment Agency. See VALUE ADDED TAX, §5075.

5036. Exemption—betting, gaming and lotteries—hire of chip sorting machines for use in casino—whether supply of machines an exempt supply—whether provision of facilities for playing games of chance

[Value Added Tax Act 1983 (c.55), Sched. 6, Group 4, item 1.]

The company operated a casino, in which it had installed chip sorting machines at the roulette table to make the croupiers more efficient. The company argued that the payment of hire charges for the machines were not liable to VAT because they were exempt as the provision of facilities for the playing of games of chance under the Value Added Tax Act 1983, Sched. 6, Group 4, item 1. The commissioners argued that the machines were not used in the playing of the game of chance.

Held, allowing the appeal, that the meaning of the phrase "the provision of any facilities for . . . the playing of any games of chance" was not clear and therefore should be construed in the light of the wording and purpose of the Sixth Directive. The exemption in art. 13(B) was designed to exclude "gambling" from the ambit of VAT and did not require Member States to exempt the supply of gambling equipment to those who used it for gambling. Therefore, the supply of chip sorting machines or roulette wheels was excluded from the ambit of the exemption.

CUSTOMS AND EXCISE COMMISSIONERS v. ANNABEL'S CASINO [1995] STC 225, Schiemann J.

5037. Exemption—body allocating grants from funds supplied by Parliament—whether making taxable supplies—whether supplies exempt even if taxable—whether a public authority

[Value Added Tax Act 1994 (c.23), Sched. 9. Group 5, Items 1, 5; E.C. Council Directive 77/388, Arts. 4 (5), 13B(d).]

In disbursing monies supplied by Parliament, a body incorporated by Royal Charter is not engaged in making supplies for consideration, but is engaged in activities as a public authority.

The AC was a body incorporated by Royal Charter, whose main activity was the distribution of a parliamentary grant to arts organisations. It also carried out some commercial activities on which it accounted for VAT and reclaimed some input tax. It contended that it was entitled also to reclaim input tax relating to supplies made to the recipients of grants and to the Department of National Heritage. The Customs and Excise decided that these supplies were exempt and there was no entitlement to input tax in respect of them.

Held, dismissing the appeal, that (1) in exercising its grant-making function, the AC was not making supplies for a consideration in the course of furtherance of a business (*National Water Council v. Customs and Excise Commissioners* [1978] C.L.Y. 3031 applied); (2) the grant-making activity was not otherwise exempt from VAT; and (3) the AC was a body governed by public law engaging in activities as a public authority and was not a taxable person in respect of them (*Foster v. British Gas* [1991] C.L.Y. 1673 applied).

ARTS COUNCIL OF GREAT BRITAIN v. CUSTOMS AND EXCISE COMMISSIONERS [1994] VATTR 313, London Tribunal.

5038. Exemption—business purposes—repairs and refurbishment of two houses in Cathedral cloisters—vergers required to reside in houses for better performance of their Cathedral duties—whether moneys expended on repairs for purposes of business carried on by Dean and Chapter

[Value Added Tax Act 1983 (c.55), s.14.]

In 1991 A carried out repair works on two houses situated in the Cathedral cloisters with the intention that the Head Verger and the Dean's Verger should occupy the houses for the better performance of their duties. After the completion of the works, the houses were opened to the public for 28 days a year for which an admission charge was levied. VAT was levied on the admission charge. A were commencing a programme of commercial activities to make money by charging for entry to parts of the Cathedral buildings and by commencing certain retail activities. The vergers were responsible for the proper supervision of the Cathedral and those parts of the Cathedral for which the public were charged for access. A contended that an allowance should have allowed against input tax for the cost of repair of the houses. The commissioners had disallowed the expenditure on the grounds that it was incurred with reference to domestic accommodation for a non-business use.

Held, allowing the appeal, that the vergers lived in the houses as a result of their contracts of service and that the accommodation in these houses was of benefit to A because it facilitated the advancement of As' aims and purposes for the Cathedral. These purposes were partly business and partly non-business and therefore an apportionment should be made of 50/50 between the two types of purposes allowing half of the expenditure for input tax.

DEAN AND CHAPTER OF HEREFORD CATHEDRAL v. CUSTOMS AND EXCISE COMMISSIONERS [1994] V.A.T.T.R. 159, London Tribunal.

5039. Exemption—company making taxable and exempt supplies—legal services in connection with disputes as to amounts payable by insurer under contracts to provide taxable supplies of insurance services—whether legal services used wholly or exclusively in making taxable supplies of insurance

[Value Added Tax (General) Regulations 1985 (S.I. 1985 No. 886), reg. 30.]

The company made exempt and taxable supplies of insurance and had reached an agreement with the commissioners as to the calculation of amounts of input tax. The company incurred legal expenses in relation to the interpretation of treaties of insurance to provide taxable supplies of reinsurance. In each case the company entered into litigation to limit the amount of its liability. The company sought to bring the amount of the legal fees into the calculation of input tax. The commissioners contended that the supplies of legal services were not connected with taxable supplies but rather occurred as a result of them. The company contended that the legal expenses in challenging the validity of the contract had been used wholly or exclusively in the making of taxable supplies: Value Added Tax (General) Regulations 1985, reg. 30.

Held, dismissing the appeal, that legal or other services obtained by the reinsurer in determining its liability were causally connected with the making of payments under reinsurance contracts when they were made. The legal services had been wholly or exclusively used in making taxable supplies within the meaning of reg. 30 (*Card Protection Plan v. Customs and Excise Commissioners* [1994] C.L.Y. 4608, *National Transit Insurance v. Customs and Excise Commissioners* [1975] C.L.Y. 3499 referred to).

CUSTOMS AND EXCISE COMMISSIONERS v. DEUTSCHE RUCK U.K. REINSURANCE CO. [1995] S.T.C. 495, Auld J.

5040. Exemption—EEC law—supply of services—medicines and hospital services

[Sixth Council Dir. 77/388, Art. 13A; Value Added Tax Act 1994 (c.23), Sched. 8.]

Medicines and services such as nursing and the provision of accommodation provided to patients during the course of in-house hospital treatment were exempt supplies for VAT purposes under Art. 13A(1) of the Sixth Council Dir. 77/388 and the relevant U.K. legislation. No input VAT was therefore recoverable on a separate supply of zero-rated goods in respect of the drugs or any prostheses supplied during surgical care pursuant to items 1 or 2, Group 12 of Sched. 8 to the Value Added Tax Act 1994.

CUSTOMS AND EXCISE COMMISSIONERS v. WELLINGTON PRIVATE HOSPITAL, *The Independent*, May 30, 1995, Jowitt J.

5041. Exemption—gambling—whether compatible with Directive

R was alleged to have failed to account for VAT due on takings from gaming machines installed in public houses and elsewhere.

Held, dismissing R's appeal against the trial judge's ruling that the Value Added Tax Act 1983, Sched. 6, group 4, note 1(d) was not incompatible with the Sixth Council Directive (77/388/EC), that (1) Art. 13B(f) of the Directive included betting, lotteries and other gambling as being subject to VAT, subject to conditions and limitations laid down by each Member State, within a list of exemptions; (2) the limitation under para. (f) entitled the Member State to restrict, but not extend, the scope of an exemption; and (3) the proviso in note 1 of group 4 of Sched. 6 to the 1983 Act, which excluded the provision of a gaming machine from the exemption, was thus not incompatible with the E.C. Directive.

R. v. RYAN [1994] Crim. L.R. 858, C.A.

5042. Exemption—land—property used as principal private residence—lease precluded occupation of the property for one month of the year—whether lease taxable as holiday accommodation—whether U.K. entitled to exclude lease from exemption for private residences

[Value Added Tax Act 1994 (c.23), Sched. 9, Group 1, Item 1(e), Notes (11), (13), Sched. 8, group 5, Note (13); E.C. Council Directive 77/388, Art. 13B(b)(1).]

Where Community law allows exclusions from exemptions, the exercise of that power must be objectively justifiable where it produces an apparently arbitrary and discriminatory result.

Mr and Mrs A jointly leased a lodge in a marina and used it as their principal place of residence. Under the terms of the lease, they were precluded from occupying the lodge in February. Customs and Excise issued a decision that the rent and service charge were taxable at the standard rate since the lodge was holiday accommodation. Mrs A appealed, contending that since the lodge was her principal place of residence, it could not in any relevant sense be described as holiday accommodation.

Held, allowing Mrs A's appeal, that although the U.K. legislation excluded her lease from exemption, that exclusion constituted inequality of treatment compared with other leases of homes and so was incompatible with Community law (*European Coal and Steel Community v. Liquidator of Ferriere Sant Anna Spa* [1983] C.L.Y. 1456 applied).

ASHWORTH v. CUSTOMS AND EXCISE COMMISSIONERS [1994] VATTR 275, London Tribunal.

5043. Exemption—partial—hotelier—part of building used as private residence—apportionment—application to ECJ for preliminary ruling—European Community law

[Sixth Council Directive 77/388.]

The ECJ was requested to give a preliminary ruling in a hotelier's appeal against the German tax authorities. A contended that on the sale of his hotel the part of the building which he had used as his own private residence was VAT exempt. The German authorities, however, asserted that the building was an indivisible supply because under German law it was registered as a single item.

Held, that the extent of property rights transferred by a transaction was a question of national law, but the preconditions for a supply of goods were governed by the Sixth Council Dir. 77/388, because the legislative objective was to base the common system for VAT on a uniform definition of taxable transactions. If a taxable person sold property used partly for business and partly for private purposes, he was not acting in the capacity of a taxable person within the meaning of Art. 2(1) in respect of the part of the property which he had chosen to reserve for his private use. A taxable person was entitled to choose, at the time he acquired an asset, to keep part for his own use rather than assign the entire asset to the business and to exclude that part from the VAT system. Apportionment would be based not on floorspace but on proportions of private-to-business use in the year of acquisition. The trader had to demonstrate an intention to keep the part among his private assets throughout his ownership. There would be no right to deduct input VAT under Art. 17(2)(a) and no adjustment of the input VAT deduction under Art. 20(2) in respect of the reserved part.

FINANZAMT UELZEN v. ARMBRECHT (C–291/92), *The Times*, October 26, 1995, ECJ.

5044. Exemption—premises—whether separate supplies of land and fire control equipment to be treated as one

[EEC Sixth Directive (77/388), Art. 13B(b)(3).]

Notwithstanding English land law, supplies of land and equipment may be treated as two supplies where that is the economic reality of the transaction.

A operated an aquarium. It entered into a contract with T to install fire control and alarm systems and with SL to sell its lease. A claimed input tax on the installation of the fire equipment. Customs and Excise disallowed it on the basis that there was a single exempt supply of the premises including the equipment.

Held, allowing A's appeal, that there were, on the facts, two supplies.

AQUARIUM ENTERTAINMENTS v. CUSTOMS AND EXCISE COMMISSIONERS [1994] VATTR 61, London Tribunal.

5045. Exemption—services supplied to building society by security firm loading and unloading cash machines and transporting the cash—whether exempt as dealing in money

[Value Added Tax Act 1994 (c.23), Sched. 9, Group 5.]

For the exemption to apply, there must be a dealing with the money as money and not in a way similar to any other goods.

N, a building society, had services supplied to it by S, a security firm, in loading and unloading its automatic telling machines dispensing cash, and transporting the cash to and from the machines. Customs and Excise decided that none of the services supplied by S to N were exempt from VAT. N appealed, contending that the services were exempt in all or part as a dealing in money.

Held, dismissing the appeal, that there was no dealing with money as money (*Williams & Glyn's Bank v. Commissioners, The* [1975] C.L.Y 3504 applied; *Barclays Bank v. Customs and Excise Commissioners* [1988] VATTR 23 distinguished).

NATIONWIDE ANGLIA BUILDING SOCIETY v. CUSTOMS AND EXCISE COMMISSIONERS [1994] VATTR 30, London Tribunal.

5046. Exemption—supply of services in connection with exempt transaction—professional services relating to sale of shares—whether deduction of input tax allowable—European Community

The appellant was a holding company providing services to a group of trading companies producing goods for use in the furniture industry. It sold the shares which it held in a company in order to raise capital to pay certain debts. In its VAT return, it sought to deduct the VAT paid for professional services relating to the sale of the shares. The commissioners of Customs and Excise refused to allow the deduction on the ground that the sale of shares was an exempt transaction.

Held, that Art. 17 of the Sixth VAT Directive required that, except in the cases expressly provided for, where a taxable person supplies services to another taxable person who uses them for an exempt transaction, the latter person is not entitled to deduct the input of VAT paid, even if the ultimate purpose of the transaction is the carrying out of a taxable transaction.

BLP GROUP v. CUSTOMS AND EXCISE COMMISSIONERS (C–4/94), April 6, 1995, ECJ, Fifth Chamber.

5047. Exemption—video poker machines—whether Member State could exclude gaming machines from exemption—whether reference to Court of Justice required for clarification—whether exclusion from exemption on provision of a gaming machine extending to payment in or proceeds from machine

[Value Added Tax Act 1983 (c.55), Sched. 6, Group 4, note (1)(d); EEC Directive 77/388, art. 13B(f).]

A owned and controlled video poker machines in public houses. The machines did not pay out winnings, rather they were gambled further on the machine or the winnings were collected from the bar. The commissioners contended that the machines were gaming machines and that A was supplying gaming services, therefore excluding its exemption under Group 4. It was also argued that the exclusion of gaming machines from exemption was a permitted limitation under EEC Dir. 77/388. A sought a reference of a question to the European Court of Justice as to the permissibility of the limitation, despite a previous decision by the Court of Appeal to that effect. A further contended that the winnings paid out should be deducted from the value of the supply.

Held, dismissing the appeal, that while a reference could be made under art. 177 of the Treaty of Rome by a court despite a decision of a superior court on that point of law, the point of law at issue in this case was so obvious that there was no need for such a question to be referred. Article 13B(f) of the Sixth Directive established beyond question that the imposition of VAT on gaming machines was permissible in certain Member States. The word "provision" in note 1(d) to Group 4 means something different from "supply". It must be construed to mean "provision to players" and therefore the tribunal was correct to conclude that providing gaming machines to make a supply of gaming services was excluded from exemption (*B.L.P. Group v. Customs and*

Excise Commissioners [1994] C.L.Y. 4552, *Bulmer (H.P.) v. Bollinger (J.) SA* [1974] C.L.Y. 1471, *R. v. Ryan* [1994] STC 446 referred to).

FEEHAN v. CUSTOMS AND EXCISE COMMISSIONERS [1995] STC 75, Hidden J.

5048. Exemption—YMCA operating club providing sporting and leisure facilities—club open to members of all ages on payment of subscriptions—whether services supplied to members "closely linked to . . . welfare work"

[EEC Sixth Directive, Art. 13A.1(g).]

A was the representative member of a VAT group of companies which operated a club providing recreational facilities in return for membership fees. A was a charitable organisation which provided a very broad range of recreational facilities in return for a range of membership fees. People who were financially disadvantaged were permitted to use the facilities at a reduced rate or even at no membership fee. The facilities were also available in some circumstances to school groups and "disadvantaged" groups (the latter category including a college for the mentally handicapped). The aim in charging membership fees was to cover costs. A contended that the supplies it made were exempt from VAT under the EEC Sixth Directive, Art. 13A.1(g), on the basis that the supplies were "closely linked to welfare and social security work".

Held, dismissing the appeal, that the exemption for supplies "closely linked to welfare and social security work" under the EEC Sixth Directive, Art. 13A.1(g) required provision for the needy, whether poor or handicapped. The facilities provided did not have any connection with such welfare work (*Yoga for Health Foundation v. Customs and Excise Commissioners* [1984] C.L.Y. 3584 distinguished).

[*Per curiam*: The fact that Art. 13A.1(g) provided for specific exemption from VAT under specific conditions indicated that it was not intended to have broad effect.]

CENTRAL YMCA v. COMMISSIONERS OF CUSTOMS AND EXCISE [1994] V.A.T.T.R. 146, London Tribunal.

5049. Finance Act 1995—appointed day. See REVENUE AND FINANCE, §4350.

5050. Fraud—fraudulently evading VAT—length of sentence. See R. v. DAYAN (ABRAHAM), §1388.

5051. Fraudulent evasion—defendant failing to make returns or to pay assessments in full—whether necessary to prove intention to make permanent default

[Value Added Tax Act 1983 (c.55), s.39(1).]

For the purposes of s.39(1) of the Value Added Tax Act 1983 it is unnecessary to prove an intention to make permanent default.

D was managing director of a company registered for value added tax. He failed to file returns or to pay the assessments made. When interviewed by Customs and Excise inspectors he admitted failing to submit his VAT returns but denied any intention to defraud the commissioners. He was subsequently convicted of being knowingly concerned in the fraudulent evasion of value added tax, the judge having directed the jury that "evasion" in s.39(1) of the 1983 Act meant a deliberate non-payment when a payment was due. D appealed on the question whether it was necessary also to prove an intention to make permanent default.

Held, dismissing the appeal, that it was unnecessary to prove an intention to make permanent default since no words to that effect appeared in s.39(1) of the 1983 Act and there was no reason why they should be implied (*D.P.P. v.*

Turner [1973] C.L.Y. 579 applied; *R. v. Allen (Christopher)* [1985] C.L.Y. 890 distinguished).

R. v. DEALY [1995] 1 W.L.R. 658, C.A.

5052. Imported goods relief

VALUE ADDED TAX (IMPORTED GOODS) RELIEF (AMENDMENT) ORDER 1995 (No. 3222) [65p], made under the Value Tax Act 1994, s.37(1); amends S.I. 1984 No. 746. In force: January 1, 1996. The maximum value for relief from VAT on final importations of certain goods, where the consignments are of low value, is raised from £15 to £18 by an amendment made to the Value Added Tax (Imported Goods) Relief Order 1984.

5053. Input tax

VALUE ADDED TAX (INPUT TAX) (AMENDMENT) ORDER 1995 (No. 281) [£1·15], made under the Value Added Tax Act 1994 (c.23), s.25(7); operative on March 1, 1995; amends S.I. 1992 No. 3222 in connection with construction of buildings in order to maintain the parity of treatment between speculative and contract builders.

VALUE ADDED TAX (INPUT TAX) (AMENDMENT) (NO. 2) ORDER 1995 (No. 1267) [£1·10], made under the Value Added Tax Act 1994 (c.23), s.25(7); operative on June 1, 1995; amends S.I. 1992 No. 3222 in relation to the operation of the margin scheme.

VALUE ADDED TAX (INPUT TAX) (AMENDMENT) (NO. 3) ORDER 1995 (No. 1666) [£1·10], made under the Value Added Tax Act 1994, s.25(7); amends S.I. 1992 No. 3222; revokes S.I. 1993 No. 2954; supersedes S.I. 1995 No. 1666 (same number) previously published on July 17, 1995; operative on August 1, 1995; further amends the 1992 input tax Order to enable VAT charged on the supply, acquisition from another Member State or importation of cars to be recovered as input tax in a broader range of circumstances and to introduce a new 50 per cent input tax recovery restriction on leasing charges where there is any private use of the car.

5054. Input tax—alterations—local authority—apportionment

[Value Added Tax Act 1994 (c.23), s.33.]

Under s.33(1) of the Value Added Tax Act 1994 the input VAT which H council was entitled to recover on the cost of rebuilding the fire-damaged Alexandra Palace must be apportioned. Although H had a statutory duty to rebuild the Palace, which was used as a public amenity, the building was also to be used commercially as a conference centre and therefore only the proportion of input VAT reflecting its non-commercial use could be recovered.

HARINGEY LONDON BOROUGH COUNCIL v. CUSTOMS AND EXCISE COMMISSIONERS, *The Independent*, June 19, 1995, Dyson J.

5055. Input tax—apportionment—building and development—whether entitlement to input VAT on sites for future development

A builder and developer who made both taxable and non-taxable supplies and who calculated apportionment input VAT attributable to taxable supplies in accord with reg. 30(1)(d) of the Value Added Tax (General) Regulations 1985 (which were replaced in 1992) was not entitled to include input VAT paid during 1990–91 on sites acquired for potential future development. To attribute such input VAT to taxable supplies would result in a distorted calculation.

CUSTOMS AND EXCISE COMMISSIONERS v. DENNIS RYE, *The Independent*, August 21, 1995, McCullough J.

5056. Input tax—attribution of input tax—construction of buildings for new engineering faculty—basis of apportionment—whether permissible to take into account later taxable supplies in making apportionment

[Value Added Tax Act 1983 (c.55); Value Added Tax (General) Regulations 1985 (S.I. 1985 No. 886), reg. 30; E.C. Council Directive 77/388, Arts. 17, 20(1).]

The college commissioned the construction of engineering buildings. The two buildings were completed in July 1990 and June 1991 respectively. As a result of changes in VAT legislation, the construction work was not zero-rated from April 1, 1989 and did not attract relief under the capital goods scheme until April 1, 1990. The college sought, and received, the approval of the commissioners to enter into a sale and lease-back arrangement to obtain relief for the intervening period. In April 1992 the college entered into sale and leaseback arrangements with a wholly-owned subsidiary company. The elections were made for the waiver of exemption for the leases. The college sought to introduce a time apportionment for input tax purposes of 93 per cent with reference to the first building and 97 per cent with reference to the second. The commissioners contended that the time apportionment was inappropriate on the basis that a deduction could not be allowed for a use which could not have been intended at the time when the input tax was incurred. The tribunal held that the attribution made by the commissioners had been a provisional attribution under Value Added Tax (General) Regulations 1985, reg. 30, but that as events developed the use of the buildings did not conform to the basis of the provisional attribution. A final attribution on a fair and reasonable basis should have been made to take account of the successive uses of the buildings.

Held, allowing the appeal, that there was no general power in s.15(3) of the Value Added Tax Act 1983 to do what was fair and reasonable where the regulations were considered to be less than comprehensive. The regulations were the means of providing a fair and reasonable attribution and were intended to be comprehensive. That there was no provision to transform a provisional deduction was not problematical, rather at the end of the longer period if there was no change to the provisional deduction, then the status of the provisional deduction remained. Outside the period, there was nothing which enabled a further adjustment to be made and therefore the right provided by the provisional deduction became absolute. The general objectives of the Sixth Directive were not the only consideration to be taken into account when interpreting the U.K. legislation on value added tax. There must be limits to the flexible approach to such interpretation. Tribunals were not at liberty to interpret Art. 20 of the Sixth Directive so as to achieve what was considered to be a fair and reasonable result. The doctrine of direct effect depended upon establishing that the provisions of a directive appeared to be unconditional and precise. The terms of Art. 20 did not produce such an unconditional and precise result. Rather they were to be filled out and refined by Member States as part of the development of a coherent tax scheme (*Rompelman (D.A.) and Rompelman-van Deelen (A.E.) v. Minister van Financien (case 268/830)* [1985] C.L.Y. 1499 referred to).

CUSTOMS AND EXCISE COMMISSIONERS v. UNIVERSITY OF WALES COLLEGE, CARDIFF [1995] S.T.C. 611, Carnwath J.

5057. Input tax—capital goods—whether the capital goods rules apply following acquisition of goods for private use—criteria for determining whether goods are acquired for business use

[E.C. Council Directive 77/388, Art. 20.]

The taxpayer worked as an employed and a self-employed tax consultant. He sought to bring his car into his trade as a self-employed at its commencement. He sought to declare input tax on a proportion of the purchase price of the car under the German rules enacting Council Dir. 77/388, Art. 20. The German rules placed a restriction on the availability of deduction at a minimum of 10 per cent business use out of the total use. The Finanzamt contended that the taxpayer was to be regarded as having purchased the car initially solely for his private use and therefore was not entitled to make adjustments when the car was subsequently brought into the business.

Held, that the existence of a right to deduct was to be determined solely by reference to the capacity in which the person was acting at the time that the right to deduct arose. To the extent that a taxable person used the supplies for the purposes of his taxable transactions he was entitled to deduct the VAT with reference to those supplies. However, where the supplies were used for private purposes, no right of deduction arose. Article 20(2) of the Sixth Directive could not change non-deductible expenditure into deductible expenditure. Where a person acquired goods for the purposes of an economic activity within the meaning of Art. 4, he did so as a taxable person, even if the goods were not immediately used for a taxable supply. Therefore Art. 20(2) includes the use of goods for a taxable supply where that use is not immediate but does involve allocation to an economic activity within Art. 4. Whether goods have been allocated to an economic activity within Art. 4 is a matter of fact, which must be decided with reference to all the circumstances of the case, including the nature of the goods concerned and the period between the acquisition and use in the economic activity. The adjustment provisions in Art. 20(2) have no bearing on the decision whether or not the goods were used for the purposes of the economic activity. The taxable person has the right to deduct input tax with reference to those goods no matter how small the business use. An administrative rule restricting the amount of deduction available was a derogation from Art. 17.

LENNARTZ v. FINANZAMT MUNCHEN III (C–97/90) [1995] S.T.C. 514, ECJ, Sixth Chamber.

5058. Input tax—deduction—whether Customs and Excise reasonably entitled to refuse without production of invoices

[Value Added Tax (General) Regulations 1985 (S.I. 1985 No. 886), regs. 12(1), 62(1).]

Customs and Excise are entitled to exercise their discretion not to allow the deduction of input tax in the absence of a satisfactory explanation for the absence of invoices.

K was in business as a wholesale and retail supplier of jewellery. He was arrested at Dover and charged with smuggling gold and Krugerrands, to which he pleaded guilty. Customs and Excise subsequently assessed him to VAT, without allowing any deduction for input tax. K appealed, contending that Customs and Excise had previously removed the relevant invoices. The tribunal dismissed his appeal.

Held, dismissing K's appeal, that in the circumstances the decision of the tribunal was one to which it was manifestly entitled to come.

KOHANZAD v. CUSTOMS AND EXCISE COMMISSIONERS [1994] S.T.C. 967, Schiemann J.

5059. Input tax—disallowance of input tax—professional fees incurred in connection with disposal of shares in subsidiary—purpose of sale to pay company's debts—whether input tax paid on services deductible

[E.C. Council Directive 67/227, Art. 2; E.C. Council Directive 77/388, Art. 17(2).]

BLP disposed of shares held by it in a German subsidiary company. In disposing of the shares, BLP incurred VAT on professional fees which it sought to deduct as input tax. The commissioners refused to accept the deduction on the basis that the disposal was an exempt transaction within Council Dir. 77/388, Art. 17(2). BLP contended that the purpose of the sale was to raise funds to pay off debts which had arisen directly from taxable transactions and that the professional fees should have been considered to be "for the purposes of its taxable transactions" under Art. 17. This question was referred to the European Court of Justice.

Held, that the right to deduct under Art. 17(2) arose only in respect of goods and services which had a direct and immediate link with taxable transactions: the ultimate aim pursued by the person was irrelevant. Article 17 should be interpreted to mean that where a taxable person supplies services to another taxable person who used them for an exempt transaction, the latter person was not entitled to deduct the input VAT paid, even if the ultimate purpose of the transaction was the performance of a taxable transaction.

BLP GROUP v. CUSTOMS AND EXCISE COMMISSIONERS [1995] S.T.C. 424, ECJ, Fifth Chamber.

5060. Input tax—exclusion of credit—provision of hospitality to customers predominant purpose in construction and use of chalets—whether input tax incurred on chalets should be wholly excluded—whether input tax could be apportioned to reflect business purpose of chalets

[Value Added Tax (Special Provisions) Order 1981 (S.I. 1981 No. 1741), art. 9(1).]

A designed and manufactured electronic equipment which was exhibited at airshows in the U.K. and abroad. A sought to introduce input tax suffered on the cost of construction of hospitality chalets used at the airshows. The commissioners argued that the chalets were used for the purpose of business entertainment. A contended that the hospitality chalets were used also for a business purpose and therefore sought an apportionment of that expenditure. The commissioners refused such an apportionment under the Value Added Tax (Special Provisions) Order 1981, art. 9(1), on the basis that the chalets were used for the purpose of business entertainment.

Held, dismissing the appeal, that where there is a supply which is used for both business entertainment and partly for business purposes, the taxpayer was entitled to an apportionment of the tax between the entertainment and other business uses. To deny A a deduction would be to deny it the basic right of deduction under Council Dir. 77/388. Further, under the Value Added Tax (Special Provisions) Order 1981, art. 9 was susceptible of a number of meanings and therefore it was capable of allowing an apportionment between entertainment and non-entertainment uses. Article 17 of the Sixth Directive provided for a right of deduction and para. (2) necessitated an apportionment where the relevant supply was for a combination of purposes. Article 17 is the overriding legislative provision requiring that an apportionment on the facts of the instant case (*National Water Council v. Customs and Excise Commissioners* [1978] C.L.Y. 3031 referred to).

THORN EMI v. CUSTOMS AND EXCISE COMMISSIONERS [1995] STC 674, C.A.

5061. Input tax—exclusion of credit—transfer of business as a going concern—company in financial difficulties selling equipment and stock to taxpayer company—whether transfer of part of a business as a going concern

[Value Added Tax (Special Provisions) Order 1981 (S.I. 1981 No. 1741), art. 12(1).]

P was the sole shareholder of I Ltd. P was also the sole shareholder of P Ltd which was incorporated on Aril 7, 1992 to purchase stock and equipment from I. At the outset, P Ltd's business was conducted from I's premises. Between 20 and 30 per cent of P Ltd's customers were former customers of I. The commissioners disallowed P Ltd's claim for deduction of input with reference to the purchase of stock and equipment from I on the basis that it constituted transfer of I's business as a going concern.

Held, dismissing the appeal, that in determining whether there had been a transfer of a business or part of a business as a going concern, the proper approach was to take a broad view of the circumstances as a whole. The intention of the transferor and transferee were facts which the tribunal was entitled to take into account when adopting that approach. On the facts of the instant case the tribunal had not misused evidence of P's intention, nor were the facts found by the tribunal perverse (*Customs and Excise Commissioners v. Dearwood* [1986] C.L.Y. 3487, *Kemmir v. Frizell* [1968] 1 All E.R. 414 referred to).

CUSTOMS AND EXCISE COMMISSIONERS v. PADGLADE [1995] S.T.C. 602, Schiemann J.

5062. Input tax—press release

HM Customs and Excise issued a press release entitled *Business Brief*

(21/95), published on October 8, 1995. Topics covered are: input tax on cars let before August 1, 1995; successful High Court challenge by Next Plc and Grattan Plc of Customs' interpretation of the law relating to the 1991 VAT rate change; reclaiming of VAT incurred on business entertainment; and details of new VAT publications.

5063. Input tax—refund—national rules exempting traders from requirement to make returns—depriving them of opportunity to claim refunds of VAT paid but not due—whether in breach of Community law—European Community

A challenge was made to the Greek system of VAT as it applied to petroleum products in that it was not possible to deduct input tax on a substantial amount of the VAT payable.

Held, that Arts. 2, 11 and 17 of the Sixth Directive precluded national rules which made the importation of finished petroleum products subject to VAT calculated on the basis of a basic price different from that provided for in Art. 11 and which, by exempting traders in the petroleum sector from the obligation to submit returns, deprived them of the right to deduct VAT charged directly on transactions relating to inputs. Article 13 precluded an exemption from VAT on services in respect of the transport and storage of petroleum products that are connected with the transport of these products from a first destination to another named destination. A taxable person may claim, with retroactive effect from the date on which the arrangements at issue came into force, a refund of VAT paid without being due, by following the procedural rules laid down by the domestic legal system of the Member State concerned, provided that those rules are not less favourable than those relating to similar, domestic actions nor framed in a way such as to render virtually impossible the exercise of rights conferred by Community law.

BP SUPERGAS ANONIMOS v. GREECE (C–62/93), July 6, 1995, Sixth Chamber, ECJ.

5064. Interest—prescribed rate

VALUE ADDED TAX ACT 1994 (INTEREST ON TAX) (PRESCRIBED RATE) ORDER 1995 (No. 521) [65p], made under the Value Added Tax Act 1994 (c.23), s.74(6); operative on March 6, 1995; increases to seven per cent the prescribed rate of interest on VAT recovered or recoverable by assessment.

5065. Magisterial law—mode of trial—VAT—summary trial—whether appropriate procedure in charge under Value Added Tax Act. See R. v. NORTHAMPTON MAGISTRATES, *ex p.* CUSTOMS AND EXCISE COMMISSIONERS, §1176.

5066. Output tax—retail scheme—whether tax chargeable on gross amount charged to customers or set amount received from finance company under undisclosed credit transaction

[Value Added Tax Act 1994 (c.23), Sched. 11, para. 6; Value Added Tax (Supplies by Retailers) Regulations 1972 (S.I. 1972 No. 1148), reg. 2(1); Customs and Excise Notice 727, para. 14.]

The retail scheme makes an explicit distinction between credit arrangements where a separate charge for credit is disclosed to the customer and where it is not.

P sold furniture as a retail trader. It accounted for VAT using Retail Scheme A, under which the unit of measurement of its output VAT was the aggregate amount of the "daily gross takings" for the period. Some customers bought goods on "interest-free" credit arranged through a finance company. The finance company paid P a discounted amount based on the interest it would have charged the customer. P issued the customer with an invoice charging the published price. Customs and Excise assessed P on the total which the customer agreed to pay to the finance company. P appealed, contending that VAT was payable on the lesser sum which it received from the finance company. The tribunal dismissed the appeal.

Held, dismissing P's appeal, that in cases of undisclosed credit transactions, tax is payable on the full amount payable by the customer.

PRIMBACK v. CUSTOMS AND EXCISE COMMISSIONERS [1994] S.T.C. 957, May J.

5067. Overpayment—tax allegedly overpaid by mistake—whether commissioners precluded from repaying tax—whether unjust enrichment a defence to claim for repayment

[Finance Act 1989 (c.26), s.24(3).]

A carried on the business of operating a computer skills correspondence course. Students were charged a market rate fee for tuition. The manuals supplied were zero-rated. The question arose as to the VAT treatment of the remainder of the fees paid by the students. A paid for the professional bodies' membership and examination fees for students, and also reimbursed students' accommodation expenses when the course required them to attend residential courses. A contended that VAT paid with reference to these items should not be standard-rated but should be treated as disbursement costs. The commissioners contended that there was a single standard-rated supply, which was paid into a single bank account. The commissioners further contended that A was not entitled to repayment of tax because of unjust enrichment. The tribunal considered the availability of a defence of unjust enrichment.

Held, dismissing the appeal, that to succeed in a defence of unjust enrichment under the Finance Act 1989, s.24(3), the commissioners had to show that tax which was not due was passed on by the trader. The fact that the tax was disclosed on an invoice could not be conclusive of the matter. It was necessary to consider the market forces operating on the students and the fact that it had not been demonstrated that the tax had been passed on to the students (*Amministrazione della Finanze dello Stato v. San Giorgio SpA (No. 199/82)* [1985] C.L.Y. 1433 applied).

COMPUTEACH INTERNATIONAL v. CUSTOMS AND EXCISE COMMISSIONERS [1994] V.A.T.T.R. 237, Manchester Tribunal.

5068. Payments on account

VALUE ADDED TAX (PAYMENTS ON ACCOUNT) (AMENDMENT) ORDER 1995 (No. 291) [£1·15], made under the Value Added Tax Act 1994 (c.23), s.28; operative on March 2, 1995; amends S.I. 1993 No. 2001.

5069. Penalty—belated notification—anxiety—whether reasonable excuse for failure—no commercial advantage—whether penalty should be mitigated

[Value Added Tax Act 1994 (c.23), ss.67(1)(a), 70.]

In deciding whether to mitigate a penalty, the tribunal should consider the amount of the penalty in relation to the level of culpability.

C was a director of HK Ltd which provided advertising and marketing services to W Ltd, HK became insolvent and C started to provide the same services for W as HK had done. He also made an individual voluntary arrangement with his creditors and later engaged the supervisor of his arrangement as his accountant. The accountant told him that he must register at once. He did so in September 1993. The Customs and Excise concluded that he should have done so in July 1992 and assessed him to a penalty of £1,902. C appealed, contending that the complexity and nature of the supplies involved and the emotional pressures due to insolvency problems provided a reasonable excuse for the default, and alternatively asked for mitigation.

Held, allowing the appeal in part, that (1) reasonable excuse had not been established since C must have known that the supplies were taxable and was clearly able to conduct his business effectively; (2) the penalty should be mitigated by 30 per cent because C did not attempt to conceal the fact that he had registered late and obtained no competitive advantage from his conduct (*Jordan v. Customs and Excise Commissioners* [1995] 11 C.L. 805 applied).

COHEN v. CUSTOMS AND EXCISE COMMISSIONERS [1994] VATTR 290, London Tribunal.

5070. Penalty—belated notification—pressure of work and anxiety—whether reasonable excuse for failure—whether culpable—whether penalty should be mitigated

[Value Added Tax Act 1994 (c.23), ss.67(1)(a), 70.]

Mitigation of a penalty does not require exceptional circumstances and depends essentially on the extent of the taxpayer's blame for the defaults.

J worked in the petrochemicals industry as a construction materials co-ordinator on a self-employed basis. His turnover increased to the extent that he should have registered for VAT within 30 days at the end of November 1992, but did not do so until January 1994. The Customs and Excise assessed a penalty of £2,108, being 20 per cent of his net tax liability for that period. J appealed, contending that he had a reasonable excuse on grounds of pressure of work, anxiety regarding the poor performance of a wine bar business in which he was a partner and the need to find a home near his work for his wife, who had become pregnant. He also applied for mitigation of the penalty.

Held, allowing the appeal in part, that (1) in view of J's experience of VAT in the wine bar business he did not have a reasonable excuse for his default; (2) the fact that he went through the registration threshold progressively and corrected the situation as soon as he became aware of it merited a reduction in the penalty of 40 per cent.

JORDAN v. CUSTOMS AND EXCISE COMMISSIONERS [1994] VATTR 286, London Tribunal.

5071. Penalty—evasion—conduct involving dishonesty—failure to register—whether tax evaded—amount of tax evaded

[Finance Act 1985 (c.54), s.13(1)(3).]

The company was not registered for value added tax and made no returns. The commissioners imposed a penalty on the director of the company and the person responsible for the failure to register for evasion of tax by dishonest omission under the Finance Act 1985, s.13(1). The company argued that because it was not registered for VAT it could not have made false claims for input tax nor any understatements of output tax. The company sought to argue further that the definition in the Finance Act 1985, s.13(3), provided an exhaustive definition of the words "amount of tax evaded" in s.13(1).

Held, allowing the appeal, that a failure to register or to make any returns constituted acts of omission for the purposes of tax evasion under the Finance Act 1985, s.13(1). The definition of "the amount of tax evaded" was not exhaustive of the circumstances giving rise to the imposition of a penalty under s.13(1). Therefore, the company's failure to register was an omission which gave rise to a penalty (*Brister v. Customs and Excise Commissioners* (LON/92/750), unrep. referred to).

CUSTOMS AND EXCISE COMMISSIONERS v. STEVENSON [1995] STC 667, Buxton, J.

5072. Penalty—whether dishonest conduct can be inferred where an application for registration was refused and no returns were made

[Value Added Tax Act 1994 (c.23), ss.60(3), 69(9).]

Where conflicting interpretations of a statute arise, the more lenient construction should apply where a penalty is involved.

S was assessed to a penalty as a director of TB and D Ltd for evasion of VAT. He appealed, contending that since the company had been refused registration, no false claim for credit for input tax or false understatement of output tax had taken place, and accordingly a penalty was not exigible on the terms of the statute. Customs and Excise contended that the words in the statute were for clarification and not determinative of the offence.

Held, allowing the appeal, that despite difficulties in accepting S's construction of the statute, an interpretation which avoided a penalty should be adopted where possible (*Customs and Excise Commissioners v. P & O Steam Navigation Co.* [1994] C.L.Y. 4591 applied).

STEVENSON v. CUSTOMS AND EXCISE COMMISSIONERS [1994] VATTR 25, London Tribunal.

5073. Penalty notice—directors—validity of notice—specifying total penalty rather than amount attributable to each director—consideration of culpability

[Finance Act 1986 (c.41), s.14.]

A penalty notice for VAT default issued under s.14 of the Finance Act 1986 against a director was valid although the notice specified only the total penalty rather than the amounts attributable to each period of default. Prima facie a director had joint liability for the entire penalty, but evidence adduced by the director that he was less culpable than other directors should be taken into account by the Commissioners of Customs and Excise when deciding how much to require him to pay.

CUSTOMS AND EXCISE COMMISSIONERS v. BESSIMEH, *The Independent,* August 28, 1995, D.C.

5074. Pharmaceutical goods

VALUE ADDED TAX (PHARMACEUTICAL GOODS) ORDER 1995 (No. 652) [65p], made under the Value Added Tax Act 1994 (c.23), ss.30(4), 96(9); operative on April 1, 1995; amends Group 12 of Sched. 8 to the 1994 Act by adding a provision relating to goods supplied by doctors authorised to provide pharmaceutical services on behalf of the NHS.

5075. Refund

VALUE ADDED TAX (REFUND OF TAX) ORDER 1995 (No. 1978) [65p], made under the Value Added Tax Act 1994, s.33(3); operative on August 18, 1995; entitles the Environment Agency to claim refunds of VAT on supplies, or acquisition or importations by it if those supplies, acquisitions or importations are not for the purposes of any business carried on by it.

VALUE ADDED TAX (REFUND OF TAX) (NO. 2) ORDER 1995 (No. 2999) [65p], made under the Value Added Tax Act 1994, s.33(3). In force: December 15, 1995. National Park authorities which were established under the Environment Act 1995, s.63, and fire authorities constituted by a combination scheme, made under the the Fire Services Act 1947, s.6, are to be entitled to claim refunds of VAT under the Value Added Tax Act 1994, s.33, on supplies to, or acquisitions and importations by them which are not for the purposes their business.

5076. Registration—application made in error—whether registration effective

[Value Added Tax Act 1994 (c.23), Sched. 1, paras. 5, 13.]

A duly executed application for registration is binding on the person making it.

YL purchased the assets of a fish and chip shop on June 11, 1992 and commenced business on June 24. His accountant forwarded in error a request for registration to the Customs and Excise and the business was duly registered as from June 11. When the error was discovered, the Customs and Excise cancelled the registration with effect from August 17, the date when they first received notification of the error. YL appealed, contending that the registration was ineffective.

Held, allowing the appeal in part, that the Customs and Excise had acted properly in registering the business and later cancelling the registration, but that the correct date of registration was June 24.

YING LUONG (A PARTNERSHIP) v. CUSTOMS AND EXCISE COMMISSIONERS [1994] VATTR 349, Manchester Tribunal.

5077. Registration—failure to register—requirement to make return for period prior to registration date—return period exceeding 12 months—whether invalid

[Value Added Tax (General) Regulations 1985 (S.I. 1985 No. 886), reg. 58(1)(c); E.C. Council Directive 77/388, Art. 22.]

B commenced trading in 1974 and registered for VAT in November 1987. On a control visit, a Customs and Excise officer discovered that B should have been registered for VAT in 1976. The commissioners directed the business to make a return for the period 1976 to 1987. No return was submitted. The matter came before the VAT tribunal. B argued that under E.C. Council Directive 77/388, Art. 22, a return could not be required for a period of longer than one year. Further, B contended that even if the commissioners were able to require a return for a period of 12-and-a-half years under the Value Added Tax (General) Regulations 1985, reg. 58(1)(c), such a provision was *ultra vires* the statutory provisions. The tribunal found for the commissioners. B appealed further that under Value Added Tax (General) Regulations 1975, reg. 51, there was an obligation to furnish a return on "every registered person" and not on "every person who . . . was or is required to be registered".

Held, dismissing the appeal, that under s.4(1) of the Finance Act 1972, every person was a taxable person who "is or is required to be registered". Section 31(1) of the Act empowered the commissioners to demand that a return be made by a "taxable person" who had not made a return. Therefore reg. 51 could not be relied upon to confer protection on those people who ought to have been registered but had not. B had failed to make returns for the 12-and-a-half years period and therefore the commissioners were empowered to demand returns for those periods. The preamble and Art. 22(4) of the Sixth Directive clearly provided that mechanisms of payment of tax with reference to periods of not longer than one year were designed to ensure regular flows of tax income. They were not intended to prevent or inhibit the collection of tax from those who continued to trade without paying tax. Further, the words "may impose other obligations" in Art. 22(8) of the Sixth Directive could be interpreted to enable the demand for returns in special circumstances where the commissioners deemed such obligations to be "necessary for the correct levying and collection of the tax". The tribunal had found that on these facts, it was "necessary" for the period of the return to be extended (*Customs and Excise Commissioners v. Le Rififi* [1995] S.T.C. 103, *Don Pasquale (A Firm) v. Customs and Excise Commissioners* [1991] C.L.Y. 3632, *Grange (S.J.) v. Customs and Excise Commissioners* [1979] C.L.Y. 2740 referred to).

BJELLICA v. CUSTOMS AND EXCISE COMMISSIONERS [1995] S.T.C. 329, C.A.

5078. Registration limits increase

VALUE ADDED TAX (INCREASE OF REGISTRATION LIMITS) ORDER 1994 (No. 2905) [65p], made under the Value Added Tax Act 1994 (c.23), Sched. 1, para. 15, Sched. 3, para. 9; operative on November 30, 1994, save for art. 3 which is operative on January 1, 1995; increases the VAT registration limits for taxable supplies and acquisitions from other Member States to £46,000 and increases the limit for cancellation of registration in respect of taxable supplies and in respect of acquisitions to, respectively, £44,000 and £46,000.

VALUE ADDED TAX (INCREASE OF REGISTRATION LIMITS) ORDER 1995 (No. 3037) [65p], made under the Value Added Tax Act 1994, Sched. 1, para. 15, Sched. 3, para. 9. In force: November 29, 1995 for arts.1, 2 and January 1, 1996 for art. 3. The VAT registration limits for taxable supplies from other

Member States are increased from £46,000 to £47,000 with effect from November 29, 1995 and the VAT registration limits for taxable acquisitions from other member states are increased by the same amount from January 1, 1996. The limit for cancellation of registration in the case of taxable supplies is increased from £44,000 to £45,000 with effect from November 29, 1995 and the limit for cancellation of registration in the case of taxable acquisitions is increased by the same amount from January 1, 1995.

5079. Regulations

VALUE ADDED TAX REGULATIONS 1995 (No. 2518) [£11·30], made under the Value Added Tax Act 1994, ss.3(4), 6(14), 7(9), 8(4), 12(3), 14(3), 16(1)(2), 18(5)(5A), 24(3)(4)(6), 25(1)(4)(6), 26(1)(3)(4), 28(3)(4)(5), 30(8), 35(2), 36(5), 37(3)(4), 38, 39(1), 40(3), 46(2)(4), 48(3)(b)(4)(6), 49(2)(3), 52, 54(1)(2)(3)(6), 58, 79(3), 80(6), 88(3)(5), 92(4), 93(1)(2), 95(5), 97(1), Sched. 1, para. 17, Sched. 2, para. 9, Sched. 3, para. 10, Sched. 7, paras. 2(1)(2), Sched. 11, paras. 2(1)(2)(3)(4)(5)(6)(7)(8)(9)(10)(11)(12), 5(4)(9), 6(1)(2), 7(1); revokes S.I. 1972 No. 1148, S.I. 1973 No. 293, S.I. 1975 No. 274, S.I. 1979 No. 224, S.I. 1980 No. 1537, S.I. 1985 Nos. 886, 1650, S.I. 1986 Nos. 71, 305, 335, S.I. 1987 Nos. 150, 510, 1427, 1712, 1916, 2015, S.I. 1988 Nos. 886, 1343, 2083, 2108, 2217, S.I. 1989 Nos. 1132, 1302, 2248, 2255, 2256, 2259, 2355, S.I. 1990 Nos. 420, 1943, S.I. 1991 Nos. 371, 691, 1332, 1532, S.I. 1992 Nos. 644, 645, 1844, 3096, 3097, 3099, 3100, 3101, 3102, 3103, S.I. 1993 Nos. 119, 761, 762, 764, 856, 1222, 1223, 1224, 1639, 1941, 3027, 3028, S.I. 1994 Nos. 803, 3015, S.I. 1995 Nos. 152, 913, 1069, 1280; cover the registration and provisions for special cases, VAT invoices and other invoicing requirements, E.C. sales statements, accounting, payment and records, payments on account, annual accounting, cash accounting, supplies by retailers, trading stamps, time of supply and time of acquisition, valuation of acquisitions, place of supply, input tax and partial exemption, adjustments to the deduction of input tax on capital items, importations, exportations and removals, new means of transport, the old bad debt relief scheme, the new bad debt relief scheme, repayments to Community traders, repayments to third country traders, repayment supplement, refunds to "do it yourself" builders, flat-rate scheme for farmers, distress and diligence.

VALUE ADDED TAX (AMENDMENT) REGULATIONS 1995 (No. 3147), made under the Value Added Tax 1994 ss.26(1)(3), 30(8), Sched. 11, para. 2(1); amends S.I. 1995 No. 2518. operative on January 1, 1996; [65p]. Amendments are made by these Regulations to the Value Added Tax Regulations 1995. Regulation 3 makes provisions so that a person providing a VAT invoice which relates to the leasing of motor cars must state on the invoice whether the vehicle is qualified under the Value Added Tax (Input Tax) Order 1992. Regulations 4 and 5 correct and upate cross-references in the 1995 Regulations, the Value Added Tax Act 1994 and the Value Added Tax (Protected Buildings) Order 1995. Regulation 6 extends the time limit for the exportation of goods by overseas visitors as a consequence of an amendment made to Council Directive 77/388, "the 6th VAT Directive", by Council Directive 95/7, "the 2nd VAT Simplification Directive".

VALUE ADDED TAX (GENERAL) (AMENDMENT) REGULATIONS 1994 (No. 3015) [£1·10], made under the Value Added Tax Act 1994 (c.23), s.26(1)(3)(4); operative on December 1, 1994; further amend S.I. 1985 No. 886.

VALUE ADDED TAX (GENERAL) (AMENDMENT) REGULATIONS 1995 (No. 152) [£1·10], made under the Value Added Tax Act 1994 (c.23), s.93(1)(2), Sched. 11, para. 2(1); operative on February 15, 1995; further amend S.I. 1985 No. 886.

VALUE ADDED TAX (GENERAL) (AMENDMENT) (NO. 2) REGULATIONS 1995 (No. 913) [65p], made under the Value Added Tax Act 1994 (c.23), s.37(3); operative on the date that the Finance Act 1995 comes into force; amend S.I. 1985 No. 886 in relation to the importation of works of art and certain motor cars.

VALUE ADDED TAX (GENERAL) (AMENDMENT) (NO. 3) REGULATIONS

1995 (No. 1069) [65p], made under the Value Added Tax Act 1994 (c.23), s.26(1), Sched. 11, para. 2(10)(a); operative on the same day that the Finance Bill 1995 is passed; further amend S.I. 1985 No. 886 to provide special rules for dealing with VAT which might be chargeable on supplies within a group.

VALUE ADDED TAX (GENERAL) (AMENDMENT) (NO. 4) REGULATIONS 1995 (No. 1280) [65p], made under the Value Added Tax Act 1994 (c.23), s.30(8); operative on June 1, 1995; further amend S.I. 1985 No. 886 in connection with the margin scheme.

5080. Reliefs—community care—press release

HM Customs and Excise has issued a press release entitled *VAT relief for homecare extended* (News Release 48/95), published on October 9, 1995. Commercial concerns providing homecare services for elderly and disabled people may now be able to do so without charging VAT to their clients. Customs and Excise will shortly hold discussions with representatives of the homecare service industry to ensure that the details of these changes are agreed and can be implemented as soon as possible.

5081. Ships and aircraft

VALUE ADDED TAX (SHIPS AND AIRCRAFT) ORDER 1995 (No. 3039) [£1·10], made under the Value Added Tax Act 1994, s.30(4). In force: June 1, 1996; varies Group 8 of Sched. 8 to the Value Added Tax Act 1994, made partly as a consequence of amendments made to Art. 5 of Council Dir. 77/388 and partly to give statutory effect to the zero-rating of certain supplies of parts and equipment for zero-rated ships and aircraft. New items 1 and 2, which maintain zero-rating for the modification and conversion of qualifying ships and aircraft and notes (1) and (7) are amended as a result, new items 2(a) and 2(b) are introduced in order to extend zero-rating to supplies of certain parts and equipment for such ships and aircraft and item 10 is amended to extend zero-rating to the making of arrangements for the supply or parts and equipment under new items 2(a) and 2(b). A new Note, A1, defining "qualifying ships" and "qualifying aircraft" for the purposed of Group 8 is introduced and a new Note (2(a)) excludes certain supplies of parts and equipment to Government departments from zero-rating under the new items 2(a) and 2(b). Note (2) is amended in order to provide zero-rating for the letting on hire of goods zero-rated under the new items 2(a) and 2(b).

5082. Special provisions

VALUE ADDED TAX (SPECIAL PROVISIONS) (AMENDMENT) ORDER 1995 (No. 957) [65p], made under the Value Added Tax Act 1994 (c.23), ss.32(1)–(6), 37(1); operative on the date the Finance Act 1995 comes into force; amend S.I. 1992 No. 3129 so as to remove the relief from VAT on the importation of certain antiques, works of art and collectors' pieces.

VALUE ADDED TAX (SPECIAL PROVISIONS) ORDER 1995 (No. 1268) [£2·40], made under the Value Added Tax Act 1994 (c.23), ss.5(3)(5), 11(4), 43(2), 50A; operative on June 1, 1995; revokes and re-enacts with amendments S.I. 1983 No. 1088, S.I. 1992 No. 3129 and S.I. 1995 No. 957 which provide for the calculation of VAT by reference to the profit margin on certain goods.

VALUE ADDED TAX (SPECIAL PROVISIONS) ORDER 1995 (AMENDMENT) ORDER 1995 (No. 1385) [65p], made under the Value Added Tax Act 1994 (c.23), s.5(3); operative on June 1, 1995; corrects an error in S.I. 1995 No. 1268.

5083. Supply—goods—change in rate of value added tax—requirement to account for value added tax at new rate from date of change—whether schemes altered time of supply from date of delivery to date of receipt of payment—whether *ultra vires*

The taxpayer company was a retailer of goods by mail order and used a retail scheme to determine its liability to output tax. The taxpayer used the standard method of assessment which meant that credit sales were not included in the taxable amount until payment had been received. On April 1, 1991 the standard rate of value added tax was raised from 15 per cent to 17.5 per cent. As a result, the Customs and Excise commissioners assessed the taxpayer to additional value added tax on its credit sales on the basis that when a change in rate occurred during a retailer's tax period Appendix C of Customs and Excise Notice 727 required that the calculation of output tax for that period be performed in two parts, the first part, in respect of the beginning of the period to the day before the date of the change, using the old value added tax fraction, the second part, in respect of the date of change to the end of the period, using the new value added tax fraction. The taxpayer appealed against the assessment on the basis that the retail schemes did not affect the time of supply but only the value of the supply, and that the time of supply of the goods was the date of their delivery; and further that the retail schemes, which had been introduced with the aim of simplifying the procedure for charging value added tax, were *ultra vires* because they imposed an increase in the amount of tax due at the final consumption in contravention of Art. 27(1)of the Sixth Directive.

Held, that the Customs and Excise Notice 727 was concerned with the value of supplies rather than the time of supplies. The retail schemes simplified the quantification of the value of goods. While the value of the supplies was based on the amounts received during a prescribed accounting period, the time of supply remains unaltered for the purpose of ascertaining liability to value added tax. Therefore, if there were a change in the rate during an accounting period, the calculation of the amount of tax followed the procedure set out in Appendix C without altering the time of supply. Article 27 provides, in effect, that whatever measures are taken to simplify procedures, they must have no more than a negligible effect on the tax due at the final consumption stage. The question of whether or not the effect was negligible was a matter of fact for the tribunal. The effect of the change on the taxpayer as participants in the retail schemes was not trivial. Therefore, there was no basis on which to interfere with the finding of fact of the tribunal that the effect of the change was not negligible (*G.U.S. Merchandise Corp. v. Customs an Excise Commisioners* [1982] C.L.Y. 3336 considered).

CUSTOMS AND EXCISE COMMISSIONERS v. NEXT [1995] STC 651, Judge J.

5084. Supply—goods—consideration—goods supplied free of charge to persons introducing potential customers to suppliers—consideration corresponding to price paid by supplier for goods—whether distinct from taxable amount of goods bought by new customer—European Community

[EEC Sixth Directive, Art. 11A(1)(a).]

A question was referred to the European Court of Justice under Art. 177 of the Treaty of Rome by the VAT Tribunal.

Held, allowing the appeals, that EEC Sixth Directive, Art. 11A(1)(a), with reference to the harmonisation of turnover taxes, should be interpreted to mean that the taxable amount in respect of an article supplied without extra charge to a person who is introduced as a new customer, is distinct from the taxable amount in respect of the goods bought from the supplier by the new customer and corresponds to the price paid for that article.

EMPIRE STORES v. CUSTOMS AND EXCISE COMMISSIONERS [1994] V.A.T.T.R. 145, Manchester Tribunal.

5085. Supply—goods—consideration—half proceeds of sale donation to charity—whether full proceeds of sale chargeable to tax

[Value Added Tax Act 1994 (c.23), ss.5(2)(a), 19; E.C. Council Directive 77/388, Art. 11.]

The consideration for a supply is the amount obtained by the supplier from the purchaser.

P was an artist. She exhibited a painting at a charitable event on terms that half the proceeds of sale were to go to charity and half to herself. The painting was sold for £13,000 and P received £6,500, on which she accounted for VAT. Customs and Excise assessed her to tax on the basis that she had made a supply of goods for a consideration of £13,000. P appealed, contending that it was the purchaser and not P who made the donation to charity.

Held, allowing P's appeal, that the consideration for the supply was the amount which she actually received.

PATRICK v. CUSTOMS AND EXCISE COMMISSIONERS [1994] VATTR 247, London Tribunal.

5086. Supply—goods—determination of value—company selling goods through non-taxable persons—discount allowed for agents own purchases—special method for determining gross takings—whether variation of retail scheme H or separate agreement—whether company entitled to resile from agreed method

GUS was a representative company for VAT purposes of a group which sold goods by mail order. GUS sold through agents who were non-taxable persons. The agents made a reduction of 10 per cent for their own purchases and received a 10 per cent commission for goods sold to third parties. GUS had used a modified form of retail scheme H to take account of these payments. However, a review showed that the approach was mistaken and sought to recover previous overpayments in their returns. The commissioners agreed to the use of the revised percentage for future periods but did not accept that it could be applied retrospectively. GUS appealed. The commissioners argued that GUS had adopted a modified version of retail scheme H and that the correspondence as a whole indicated an agreement from which GUS could not resile without the consent of the commissioners.

Held, dismissing the appeals, that the commissioners had a specific statutory power to adopt any retail scheme by agreement with the retailer and also had the authority to adopt binding, free-standing agreements. Whether such an agreement had been entered into was a question of fact which could be answered by examining the correspondence which had been entered into. The correspondence read as a whole indicated such a binding agreement when GUS entered its first return taking advantage of the newly determined percentage. Therefore, GUS was precluded from altering the basis of assessment without the agreement of the commissioners.

G.U.S. MERCHANDISE CORP. v. CUSTOMS AND EXCISE COMMISSIONERS (NO. 2) [1995] STC 279, C.A.

5087. Supply—goods—retail schemes—eligibility to use retail scheme—whether supplies to value added tax registered customers retail sales

The society was a retailer of food and funeral services which also carried on the business of a motor dealership. It sold motor cars and spare parts to customers who were registered for VAT and to customers who were not registered for VAT. The society used retail scheme B to account for its output tax. The commissioners refused to accept this method of calculation on the basis that para. 1 of Customs and Excise Notice 727 required that all supplies to other VAT registered traders were excluded from the retail schemes. The taxpayer contended that it was irrelevant whether the supply was to a VAT registered retailer or not and further that the Customs and Excise Notice 727 did not have statutory effect.

Held, dismissing the appeal, that the whole of para. 1 was intended to have statutory force and effect; there was no part of it which contained mere advice or recommendations. It clearly required that the supplies to other VAT registered businesses should be accounted for outside the retail schemes

(*GUS Merchandise v. Customs and Excise Commissioners* [1982] C.L.Y. 3336 referred to).

OXFORD, SWINDON AND GLOUCESTER CO-OPERATIVE SOCIETY v. CUSTOMS AND EXCISE COMMISSIONERS [1995] S.T.C. 583, Dyson J.

5088. Supply—goods and services—fuel card—whether appellant purchases goods or services which are standard-rated and resupplies them to its customers or whether appellant makes exempt supplies of financial services

[Value Added Tax Act 1983 (c.55), Sched. 6, Group 5, items 1, 2, 5 and Note (4).]

A was the representative member of a VAT group. The group comprised Overdrive, OFIS, and Dialcard. Each of these subsidiary companies operated card schemes relating to the provision of motor fuel and motor-related goods and services. Each scheme was governed by an agreement between the group company and the merchant and another agreement between the group company and the customer. The merchant was usually a petrol station selling motor fuel and the customer was usually a large company with numerous employees. The Overdrive and Dialcard schemes provided that the cardholder purchased fuel as the agent of Overdrive or Dialcard. The property in the fuel passed, under the agreement, from the merchant to Overdrive or Dialcard on the signing of a supply voucher. Overdrive or Dialcard then sold the fuel to the cardholder. The cardholder was expressed to the Overdrive or Dialcard's agent in the purchasing of supplies. Under the Overdrive "bunkerfuel" scheme, Overdrive purchased diesel oil which was delivered to an Overdrive tank at a specified merchant's site. The oil was mixed with other oil belonging to the merchant. The merchant then invoiced Overdrive for the oil: Overdrive then paid the invoice. The cardholder filled his vehicle at the merchant's site and signed a supply voucher. The merchant then sent the supply vouchers to Overdrive. Overdrive made no payment to the merchant at this point. Rather, Overdrive sent invoices to its customers for the bunkerfuel. It was common ground that the merchant and Overdrive were co-owners of the fuel when it was mixed in the tank. Under the Overdrive "pre-purchase" scheme, the agreement provided that when a cardholder filled its vehicle with fuel, the merchant sold the fuel to Overdrive with the cardholder acting as Overdrive's agent. Overdrive then sold the fuel to the consumer. The OFIS scheme provided that the cardholder purchased fuel as the agent of OFIS. The property in the fuel passed, under the agreement, from the merchant to OFIS on the signing of a supply voucher and the presentation of the card to the merchant, OFIS then sold the fuel to the cardholder. The cardholder was expressed to the OFIS's agent in the purchasing of supplies. A contended that the cards were agency cards and not credit cards and therefore the cards were used to purchase goods and not simply as a means of facilitating payment. Therefore, the supply to the customers was a taxable supply.

Held, allowing the appeal in part, that under the Overdrive and Dialcard schemes, the property in the fuel passed at the pump from the merchant to the cardholder who was under a personal liability to pay for it. Therefore, there was a supply, whatever happened on the signing of the voucher and that the agreements did not have the effect of providing that the only supply was between Overdrive or Dialcard and the merchant. Under the bunkerfuel scheme, the property in the oil delivered passed to Overdrive which therefore had a right as tenant in common to the appropriate proportion of fuel in the merchant's tank. The cardholder was entitled to take delivery of the fuel on the condition that the transaction was governed by the bunkerfuel agreements. The fuel remained the property of Overdrive and the merchant until the cardholder signed the supply voucher. On signing there was an appropriation of part of Overdrive's property and there was a taxable supply from Overdrive to the cardholder. The analysis was the same for the pre-purchase scheme as for the bunkerfuel scheme except that the oil was purchased by Overdrive from the merchant and not an oil company. There was therefore a taxable supply by Overdrive to the cardholder. Under the OFIS scheme, there was a taxable supply of goods and services to customer as provided in the agreements (*Customs and Excise Commissioners v. Diners Club* [1989] C.L.Y. 3739 applied; *R. v. Department of Social Security, ex p. Overdrive Credit Card* [1991] C.L.Y. 3347 considered).

HARPUR GROUP v. CUSTOMS AND EXCISE COMMISSIONERS [1994] V.A.T.T.R. 180, London Tribunal.

5089. Supply—services—agency providing temporary nursing staff—whether supplying nursing services as principal

[Value Added Tax Act 1983 (c.55), Group 7, Sched. 6.]

Reed carried on the business of supplying temporary nurses to hospitals. Reed nurses were self-employed. Reed retained a high degree of control over their activities, paid nurses according to an hourly rate and deducted income tax and national insurance contributions. The commissioners decided that Reed were supplying nursing services as principal and were therefore making exempt supplies under Group 7, Sched. 6 of the Value Added Tax Act 1983. In October 1990, the commissioners issued assessments claiming payment of input tax which Reed had deducted with reference to the provision of nurses to hospitals. Reed contended that it had acted as a recruitment agency supplying nursing staff. The tribunal found that Reed was a recruitment agency. In reaching its decision, the tribunal relied both on the contracts and on an overall view of the facts, in particular that Reed had supplied the nurses who in turn had supplied their services to the hospitals.

Held, dismissing the appeal, that where there is a contract for the supply of goods or services between two parties, the contract is conclusive of the issue of supply for VAT purposes. Where there are three or more parties involved, the contract might not be conclusive for the purposes of VAT. Where the issue remains undecided, it is a matter of fact for the tribunal. In the instant case, the contractual obligations were conclusive of the parties' private law obligations but were not conclusive of the VAT obligations. On these facts, the tribunal relied both on the contracts and on an overall view of the facts, in particular that Reed had supplied the nurses who in turn had supplied their services to the hospitals. Therefore, there was no basis on which the tribunal's decision could be challenged (*Associated Provincial Picture Houses v. Wednesbury Corporation* [1947–51] C.L.Y. 8107, *Customs and Excise Commissioners v. MacHenrys (Hairdressers)* [1993] C.L.Y. 4100, *Customs and Excise Commissioners v. Music and Video Exchange* [1992] C.L.Y. 4551, *R. v. Spens* [1991] C.L.Y. 716 referred to).

CUSTOMS AND EXCISE COMMISSIONERS v. REED PERSONNEL SERVICES [1995] S.T.C. 588, Laws J.

5090. Supply—services—air travel—limousine service to and from airport at request of "Upper Class" passengers—whether separate supply

[Value Added Tax Act 1983 (c.55), s.3(2).]

VAA appealed from the VAT tribunal's ruling that transport by limousine between home and airport, which VAA provided at no extra charge at the request of its "Upper Class" passengers, was a separate supply from the supply of air travel. If the supplies were separate under s.3(2) of the Value Added Tax Act 1983 the air travel would be zero-rated but the limousine travel would be standard-rated. VAA argued that the air travel and limousine travel were a single supply because both were supplied under a single contract for international transport. Alternatively the limousine travel was incidental or integral to the supply of air transport.

Held, allowing the appeal, that, although passengers often did not request limousine travel until a considerable time after the flight had been booked, because both were provided for one irreducible and indivisible price they were nevertheless provided under a single indivisible contract and must therefore be treated as one single supply. If necessary the court would have held the limousine travel was integral to the air travel.

VIRGIN ATLANTIC AIRWAYS v. CUSTOMS AND EXCISE COMMISSIONERS, *The Times*, February 16, 1995, Turner J.

5091. Supply—services—bank charges on transfer of funds by solicitor on behalf of client—recharged to client—whether liable for output tax

Transfers of funds in connection with conveyancing transactions are part of the overall service provided by a solicitor to his client and a solicitor had to account for output tax on bank charges arising from such transfers, billed to the client.

S were a firm of solicitors performing conveyancing transactions for clients. They paid bank fees for completion monies transmitted by the Clearing Houses Automated Payments Service (CHAPS) and billed these as separate items on the completion account rendered to clients. Customs and Excise instructed them to account for output tax on these items.

Held, dismissing S's appeal, that the CHAPS fees charged to the client were liable to output tax (*Rowe and Maw v. Customs and Excise Commissioners* [1975] C.L.Y. 3502 applied).

SHUTTLEWORTH & CO. v. CUSTOMS AND EXCISE COMMISSIONERS [1994] VATTR 355, London Tribunal.

5092. Supply—services—discount cards—company distributing cards direct or through intermediaries to public entitling bearer to restaurant benefits—whether consideration for cards to be disregarded to value added tax purposes at all stages of supply

[Value Added Tax Act 1983 (c.55), Sched. 4, para. 6.]

G produced and distributed discount cards which were purchased by the public directly or through W. The cards entitled the holder to a complimentary main course meal and a bottle of wine at specific restaurants on a given number of occasions. G and W claimed that the amounts received on the sale of the cards should be disregarded for the purposes of VAT at all stages during the supply under Value Added Tax Act 1983, Sched. 4, para. 6, as a right to receive goods or services for the amount stated on a voucher. The commissioners considered that the cards did not fall within para. 6 because they had no face value.

Held, allowing the commissioners' appeal, that the cards did not grant any right to receive goods or services. The card granted a discount which was an expectation and not a right. Therefore, the card did not constitute a right to receive goods or services. Discount cards were not vouchers of the kind contemplated by para. 6. Therefore, the cards in this case did not apply at any stage to the supply of the cards and therefore the supplies were subject to VAT.

CUSTOMS AND EXCISE COMMISSIONERS v. GRANTON MARKETING [1995] S.T.C. 510, Tucker J.

5093. Supply—services—dispensing optician fitting and supplying spectacles—whether separate supply of dispensing services or single supply of spectacles—whether services exempt or part of a single standard-rated supply of goods

[E.C. Council Directive 77/388, Art. 13A(1)(c); Value Added Tax Act 1983 (c.55), Sched. 6, Group 7, item 1(b).]

L carried on business as opticians, employing both ophthalmic opticians to carry out eye tests and dispensing opticians to fit spectacles. The commissioners accepted that the services of ophthalmic opticians were exempt supplies separate from the supply of spectacles. However, the commissioners issued a decision in September 1992 which opined that the supply of spectacles by L was a single, standard-rated supply of goods to which the dispensing opticians' services were merely ancillary. L contended that the dispensing opticians' services were a separate, exempt supply of services.

Held, dismissing the commissioners' appeals, that there were two separate supplies: one of spectacles and one of dispensing optician's services. The history of Value Added Tax Act 1983, Sched. 6, Group 7, item 1(b) suggested that it was intended that the services of dispensing opticians were to be exempted (*British Railways Board v. Customs and Excise Commissioners* [1977] C.L.Y. 3133, *Card Protection Plan v. Customs and Excise Commissioners* [1994] C.L.Y. 4608, *E.C. Commission v. United kingdom (No. 353/85)* [1988] C.L.Y. 1574 referred to).

CUSTOMS AND EXCISE COMMISSIONERS v. LEIGHTONS [1995] S.T.C. 458, McCullough J.

5094. Supply—services—foreign exchange—press release

HM Customs and Excise has issued a press release entitled *Business Brief* (22/95), published on October 13, 1995. Customs and Excise is to appeal against a VAT Tribunal decision that forex transactions are supplies for consideration. The Tribunal did not determine the value of the consideration and the Chairman said that if either party wished this matter to be resolved, he would refer it to the ECJ. Customs and Excise considers this decision to be unsatisfactory and has decided to appeal in the High Court rather than seek a reference by the tribunal to the ECJ. Until the question is resolved, Customs will continue to regard forex transactions as being outside the scope of VAT. Customs wishes to determine the effect of the revised VAT exemption for education, which has been in place for more than a year. Comments should be sent to Peter Kershaw, HMCE, VAT4C, 4th Floor, New King's Beam House, 22 Upper Ground, London, SE1 9PJ.

5095. Supply—services—overpayments by customers credited to next account in default of request for repayment—overpayments accounted for at time of receipt only if expressly deliberate otherwise accounted for at time of next quarter's invoice—whether overpayments payments in respect of future supplies—whether all overpayments should be accounted for at time of receipt—whether overpayments consideration for future supplies of services

[Value Added Tax (General) Regulations 1985 (S.I. 1985 No. 693), reg. 23(1)(a).]

BT supplied continuous telecommunications services to its customers. Customers were billed by a quarterly invoice. On some occasions customers would unintentionally pay more than was stated on the invoice. Where there was no request for a refund or explanation of the overpayment, BT would offset the surplus against the invoice for the following quarter. BT did not account for output tax on such overpayments. The commissioners sought to charge output tax on the amount of the surplus payments from the date of receipt of the payment by BT on the basis that the overpayments constituted payments received "in respect of" continuous supplies of services within the meaning of Value Added Tax (General) Regulations 1985, reg. 23(1)(a). The tribunal held that the payments were made to BT under mistake and that crediting a mistaken payment to a customer's account did not constitute consideration. The commissioners contended that the overpayments were payments for future services.

Held, dismissing the appeal, that a payment in respect of services was not made unless both supplier and customer agreed to treat it as such. The supplier had no right to appropriate the mistaken payment to be a payment for future supplies on a unilateral basis. Such right to appropriate could only arise in circumstances where there were mutual debts owed. A payment made in respect of continuous supplies constituted consideration. However, where a payment was made under mistake of fact, it could not constitute such consideration unless the payer agreed to allocate the mistaken payment to any particular future supply. There could only be an implied term that any overpayment would be credited to the customer's next invoice with reference to a particular course of dealing with a specific customer. Where there was no communication with the customer as to the reason for the overpayment where the customer agreed to such a course in the future, there could be no such implied term. The evidence before the tribunal was that most such payments were accidental but it did not have evidence as to all the overpayments. Therefore it was mistaken to discharge the assessment with reference to all the payments. Deliberate overpayments fell within Value Added Tax (General) Regulations 1985, reg. 23(1)(a), and therefore should have been accounted for at the time of receipt (*Apple and Pear Development Council v. Customs and Excise Commissioners* [1988] C.L.Y. 1572, *Cheall v. APEX* [1982] C.L.Y. 3286, *Customs and Excise Commissioners v. Faith Construction* [1989] C.L.Y. 3770, *New Zealand Shipping Co. v. Societe des Ateliers et Chantiers de France* [1919] A.C. 1 referred to).

CUSTOMS AND EXCISE COMMISSIONERS v. BRITISH TELECOM [1995] S.T.C. 239, Dyson J.

5096. Supply—services—payment by lessor to trustees of maintenance fund—whether consideration for supply of services—whether exempt as part of supply of interest in land

[Value Added Tax Act 1994 (c.23), s.4, Sched. 9, Group 1, item 1.]

Payments made to a maintenance fund by a lessor and not by tenants are made pursuant to contract and not as between beneficiaries under a trust and their trustees and are not part of the supply of an interest in land to the tenants.

N was a block of luxury flats. The entire building was leased to NG. Some flats were held on long sub-leases and managed by the trustees of NM. Others were managed directly by NG, which made payments to NM as a service charge. After a voluntary disclosure by the trustees, Customs and Excise raised assessments for VAT and default interest in respect of the payments. The tribunal dismissed the trustees' appeal.

Held, dismissing their appeal, that the payments were properly chargeable to tax as consideration for a supply of services.

NELL GWYNN HOUSE MAINTENANCE FUND TRUSTEES v. CUSTOMS AND EXCISE COMMISSIONERS [1994] S.T.C. 995, Popplewell J.

5097. Supply—services—place of supply—whether satellite television supplied where received

[EEC Sixth Directive (77/388), Art. 9.2(c); Value Added Tax Act 1983 (c.55), Sched. 5, Group 9, item 3; Value Added Tax (Place of Supply of Services) Order 1992 (S.I 1992 No. 3121), reg. 15.]

The place of supply of satellite television is where it is physically transmitted rather than where it is received.

BSB supplied satellite television to subscribers, *inter alia*, in Ireland and the Channel Islands. The Customs and Excise decided that the supplies were liable to VAT as a supply of television broadcasting. BSB appealed, contending that the supply was of entertainment.

Held, dismissing the appeal, that (1) the supply was in principle one of entertainment but could be one of broadcasting as well; (2) the type of entertainment services provided by BSB were not within the scope of the Sixth Directive, which deals with the case of the supplier of the services moving between countries.

BRITISH SKY BROADCASTING v. CUSTOMS AND EXCISE COMMISSIONERS [1994] VATTR 1, London Tribunal.

5098. Supply—services—supply of single service or of separate services—supply of limousine service to and from airport in the course of transport by air at no extra charge—whether limousine service integral or incidental to supply of air transport

[Value Added Tax Act 1983 (c.55), Sched. 5, Group 10, item 4.]

Both appellants operated international airline flights. Passengers travelling to the U.K. on the appellants' flights were entitled to a number of choices of transfer on arrival in the U.K. One such option was the provision of a limousine service for those travelling on first class flights. The flight ticket made no mention of the appellants' obligation to provide the limousine service. A small charge was levied only in circumstances where the limousine was required to travel outside the home counties area. The commissioners contended that the limousine service constituted a separate standard-rated supply from the provision of the airline flight. The appellants contended that the provision of the limousine and the international flight constituted a single zero-rated supply under the Value Added Tax Act 1983, Sched. 5, Group 10, item 4 and that the word "place" in item 4 referred to the place to which the customer was travelling and not simply to the airport.

Held, allowing the appeal, that while there was no doubt that the main purpose of the contract was the provision of a passenger flight, the transport by way of limousine was subsidiary to the main purpose of the contract and was part of one indivisible supply made by the appellants. The passenger had made one payment for transportation to a destination. The term "place" in item 4 must have a broader meaning than simply "airport". Therefore, "place" in this context must mean the home of the customer. The question of whether the supply of a limousine on request at no extra charge was part of one indivisible contract is a question which must be considered on a common sense basis. It would be unrealistic to split the provision of the limousine from the flight (*Aer Lingus v. Customs and Excise Commissioners* [1992] 5 VATTR 438, *British Airways v. Customs and Excise Commissioners* [1990] S.T.C. 643, *British Railways Board v. Customs and Excise Commissioners* [1977] 2 All E.R. 873 referred to).

VIRGIN ATLANTIC AIRWAYS v. CUSTOMS AND EXCISE COMMISSIONERS [1995] S.T.C. 341, Turner J.

5099. Supply—services—time of supply—advance booking of theatre tickets—proceeds expressed to be held by theatre in trust for ticket holders until performance—whether payments received in respect of future supplies

[Value Added Tax Act 1983 (c.55), s.5(1).]

R ran the Richmond Theatre, selling tickets in advance for performances at the theatre. In accordance with its standard terms, R sought to create a trust of any money paid for tickets such that R did not become the beneficial owner of the money until the performance had taken place. However, R further provided that it was not accountable for any interest with reference to the money. The commissioners assessed R to value added tax from the time when it received money for advance tickets.

Held, the standard terms conferred on R the ability to use the money for its own purposes and therefore did not confer of the customer any proprietary interest in the money. The money was paid and received as consideration for the ticket and therefore R should account for the tax at the date of receipt of the money under Value Added Tax Act 1983, s.5(1) (*Space Investments v. Canadian Imperial Bank of Commerce* [1986] C.L.Y. 285 applied). The question of whether a supply was made and the question whether or not the customer retained any equitable interest in the money were conceptually different. Despite the purported retention of an equitable interest by the customer, when the transaction was considered in the round the customer tendered consideration for the tickets in advance. Therefore, even if the terms and conditions did create a trust, the customer had still made an advance payment in respect of a supply which gave rise to a liability for output tax at the time of the payment.

CUSTOMS AND EXCISE COMMISSIONERS v. RICHMOND THEATRE MANAGEMENT [1995] S.T.C. 257, Dyson J.

5100. Supply—services—time of supply—services supplied through agent acting in own name—supply treated both as supply to agent and supply by agent—whether supply by agent to be treated as having taken place at time of supply to agent

[Value Added Tax Act 1983 (c.55), s.32(4); Value Added Tax (General) Regulations 1985 (S.I. 1985 No. 886), reg. 26.]

The borough, as the agent for a finance company, paid builders on invoices rendered during the course of certain building contracts. The borough claimed the payments as its input tax credit in the accounting periods in which the payments were made. However, the borough did not make good the amounts or pay output tax until later periods. The commissioners contended that under the Value Added Tax Act 1983, s.32(4), the supply from the contractor to the borough and the supply from the borough to the finance company could be treated as taking place at the same time. The borough appealed and argued further that the supply from the borough to the finance company was a supply in the course of construction of a building under the Value Added Tax (General) Regulations 1985, reg. 26.

Held, dismissing the appeal, that the Value Added Tax Act 1983, s.32(4), deemed what would have been a single supply to be two simultaneous supplies. The deemed supply by the agent to the principal is treated as having taken place at the time of the actual supply to the agent. Therefore, on the facts of the instant cases, the supply of the services to the borough was deemed to be simultaneous with the supply from the borough to the finance company. The supply from the borough to the finance company was a deemed supply and therefore Value Added Tax (General) Regulations 1985, reg. 26, had no application.

METROPOLITAN BOROUGH OF WIRRAL v. CUSTOMS AND EXCISE COMMISSIONERS [1995] S.T.C. 597, Potts J.

5101. Supply—services—tour operators' margin scheme—depreciation of vehicles—commissioners' power to challenge method of calculation—depreciation based on actual cost not future replacement cost—whether general expenses attributable to in-house supply only to be included in calculations of overheads

[Value Added Tax (Tour Operators) Order 1987 (S.I. 1987 No. 806), art. 7.]

A were in the business of tour operators and of owning and operating tour buses. The former undertaking was subject to the Value Added Tax (Tour Operators) Order 1987. A made in-house supplies of transport for tours operated by themselves. Under VAT Leaflet 709/5/88 this was subject to special calculation. After prolonged discussion between A and the commissioners, agreement was reached as to the form of calculation to be used. By a letter, the commissioners sought to withdraw from the agreement and substitute an alternative method of calculating depreciation which was not to be based on replacement cost of a bus or coach. A appealed that this was an unfair and perverse act on the part of the commissioners.

Held, allowing the appeal in part, that the commissioners were entitled under the Value Added Tax (Tour Operators) Order 1987, art. 7, to direct A as to the manner in which calculations were to be made. This had been done in VAT Leaflet 709/5/88. The reference to "the cost to you" in the leaflet was to the actual cost incurred and not to possible future cost. General overheads such as repairs and accountancy expenses were not items to be included in this part of the formula. Rather it should be limited to costs directly related to the tour operations and to some proportion of the indirect cost of in-house supplies of transport such as garage facilities (*Jenny Braden Holidays v. Customs and Excise Commissioners* [1993] Decision No. 10892 referred to).

WHITTLE RA, DL AND GA (t/a GO WHITTLE) v. CUSTOMS AND EXCISE COMMISSIONERS [1994] V.A.T.T.R. 202, Manchester Tribunal.

5102. Supply—services—tour operators margin scheme—place of supply—facilities for tours in the U.K.—invoice to tour operator and not tourist—whether supplies for the "benefit of tourists"—whether supplies made in the U.K.

A organised tours for Japanese tourists in London, taking its instructions from its Tokyo office. A organised hotel accommodation, covered restaurant bookings, theatre tickets and a tour guide for the tourists. The theatre tickets were transmitted to Tokyo and distributed to the tour operator. All of these items were invoiced to A and the tourists were issued with vouchers from A, by the tour guide, for these services. A would then invoice the tour operator in a currency which could be other than sterling. The commissioners were of the view that A was making supplies of hotel accommodation and restaurant meals in the U.K., that the tour guides were supplies of a cultural, educational or entertainment nature within art. 5(4) of the Value Added Tax (Tour Operators) Order 1987, and that the supplies of theatre tickets were supplies of entertainment services performed in the U.K.

Held, allowing the appeal in part, that the expression "for the benefit of travellers" in the Value Added Tax (Tour Operators) Order 1987 covered supplies by wholesale providers of travel services to retail providers and therefore covered A's provision to the tour operator. A's services did not constitute "designated travel services" within art. 3 of the Value Added Tax (Tour Operators) Order 1987 because A did not make supplies to the tour operator in its capacity as a "tour operator in a member state of the E.C. in which it had established its business or had a fixed establishment". On the basis that A had rights over the hotel accommodation, and that it made those rights available to the tour operator in return for the global fee paid by the tour operator to A, A was making a supply of accommodation within the Value Added Tax (Tour Operators) Order 1987, art. 5(5). Similarly, A made supplies of restaurant meals to the tour operator under art. 4 and of sight-seeing tours under art. 5(4). However, it did not make supplies of theatre tickets in the U.K. (*Independent Coach Travel (Wholesaling) v. Customs and Excise Commissioners* [1994] C.L.Y. 4614 applied).

GULLIVER'S TRAVEL AGENCY v. CUSTOMS AND EXCISE COMMISSIONERS [1994] V.A.T.T.R. 210, London Tribunal.

5103. Supply—transfer of business as going concern—transfer of all food and non-food stock—transfer of business operating Retail Scheme B since its registration in 1973—whether stock taken over to be treated by difference-accounting method

[Value Added Tax (Special Provisions) Order 1981 (S.I. 1981 No. 741), art. 12A.]

A carried on the business of food retailers. It used Retail Scheme B to account for VAT on sales of food and non-food which were aggregated on its calculations. A took over the food and non-food retailing of South Midlands Co-operative Society. A continued its business as an amalgam of its previous business together with the South Midlands business. The stock acquired from South Midlands was added to that sold by A and subsequently sold in the ordinary course of A's business. A continued to use Retail Scheme B to calculate its VAT. The commissioners assessed A to VAT of £176,091 on the basis that South Midlands had not used Retail Scheme B for food and therefore the food received from South Midlands should not have been treated as goods for resale for the purpose of Retail Scheme B calculations.

Held, allowing the appeal, that (1) under the Value Added Tax (Special Provisions) Order 1981, art. 12, A was to be treated as the successor to the business of South Midlands but the provision did not imply that A was required to follow the trading practices and accounting methods of its predecessor; (2) the stock of food taken over from South Midlands consisted of goods received for resale in the tax period but they were not goods which A had had in stock when it began to use Retail Scheme B because it had already been using the Scheme when the stock was taken over. Therefore the assessment was incorrect (*G.U.S. Merchandise Corp. v. Customs and Excise Commisioners* [1982] C.L.Y. 3336 referred to).

CO-OPERATIVE WHOLESALE SOCIETY v. CUSTOMS AND EXCISE COMMISSIONERS [1994] V.A.T.T.R 228, Manchester Tribunal.

5104. Supply of services

VALUE ADDED TAX (PLACE OF SUPPLY OF SERVICES) (AMENDMENT) ORDER 1995 (No. 3038) [65p], made under the Value Added Tax Act 1994, s.7(11); amends S.I. 1992 No. 3121. In force: January 1, 1996. Articles 4 and 5 amend the 1992 Order as a consequence of the amendment of Art. 28(b) of Council Dir. 77/388 (the Sixth VAT Directive) by Council Dir. 95/7 (the Second VAT Simplification Directive) resulting in the moving of the place of supply of valuations of, or work on, goods, to the customer's Member State from the place where the services are physically performed. Article 6 removes the requirement for business customers from another Member State to have a VAT registration number in that Member State for certain services to be treated as supplied where the customer belongs. In addition, references to provisions of the Value Added Tax Act 1994 have been substituted for those of the Value Added Tax Act 1983.

VALUE ADDED TAX (SUPPLY OF SERVICES) (AMENDMENT) ORDER 1995 (No. 1668) [65p], made under the Value Added Tax Act 1994, s.5(4); amends S.I. 1993 No. 1507); supersedes S.I. 1995 No. 1668 (same number) previously published on July 17, 1995; operative on August 1, 1995; art. 6A excludes from the scope of the charge to tax imposed by art. 3 of the principal Order, the use by a taxable person of a motor car which has been let to him on hire for private purposes, or for purposes other than those of his business, if the leasing charge has been subject to a 50 per cent restriction on input tax recovery.

5105. Tax free shops

VALUE ADDED TAX (TAX FREE SHOPS) ORDER 1995 (No. 3041) [65p], made under the Value Added Tax Act 1994, ss.30(4), 96(9). In force: January 1, 1996; increases with reference to Art. 28K of Council Dir. 77/388, the value of goods, other than wines, spirits, perfume and toilet water and tobacco products, that can be supplied at tax rate of zero in a tax free shop to a person travelling to a destination in another Member State, from £71·00 to £75·00.

5106. Taxable person—receiver—income of mortgaged property—VAT money collected—whether receiver to be treated as taxable person—whether appointment of receiver meant firm had gone into receivership

[Law of Property Act 1925 (c.20), s.109(8) Value Added Tax (General) Regulations 1985 (S.I. 1985 No. 886, reg. 11).]

S, receiver of the income of mortgaged property, appealed against orders relating to the disposal of VAT monies gathered by him. Section 109(8) of the Law of Property Act 1925 provided that all money collected by the receiver should be applied to discharge all outgoings affecting other mortgaged property. The State Bank of Australia had appointed S under the provisions of three charges for recovery of loans made to Lontrex Properties. The bank ordered S to pay the VAT part of the rents gathered by him to them. The Customs and Excise Commissioners contended that they could treat the receiver as a taxable person directly liable for the VAT under reg. 11 of the Value Added Tax (General) Regulations 1985. The receiver sought directions under s.35 of the Insolvency Act 1986.

Held, that the question to consider was whether the appointment of a receiver over Lontrex meant that it had gone into receivership. Regulation 11 applied when a taxable person had become so incapacitated that it could no longer carry on a business. Receivership meant that the company's business was taken out of the hands of the directors and put into the hands of receivers, which had not occurred in this situation. In theory, a receiver had discretion under s.109(8) but in reality had to account to the commissioners for VAT, since failure to do so would mean that Lontrex would have committed a criminal offence. If the commissioners took an action for unpaid VAT against Lontrex it could mean that the company would be wound up. The receiver must therefore account to the commissioners for the VAT.

SARGENT v. CUSTOMS AND EXCISE COMMISSIONERS, *The Times*, February 23, 1995, C.A.

5107. Tour operators

VALUE ADDED TAX (TOUR OPERATORS) (AMENDMENT) ORDER 1995 (No. 1495), made under the Value Added Tax Act 1994 (c.23), 53(1)(2); operative on January 1, 1996; amends S.I. 1987 No. 1806 and S.I. 1990 No. 751.

5108. Tour operators—press release

HM Customs and Excise has issued a press release entitled *Tour operators benefit from VAT review* (Press Release 50/95), published on October 24, 1994 From January 1, 1996, tour operators will in some cases be able to alleviate the effects of a change in VAT on travel and holidays in the EU. The changes will cover the areas of agency arrangements, changes to the treatment of supplies between businesses and the treatment of some transport as "in-house" and will ensure that the U.K. meets its E.C. obligations but will not penalise smaller tour operators. Revised guidance on the Tour Operators' Margin Scheme (TOMS), incorporating the changes, will be issued in late November or early December. A detailed briefing note is attached to the press release.

5109. Trading stamps

VALUE ADDED TAX (TRADING STAMPS) REGULATIONS 1995 (No. 3043) [65p], made under the Value Added Tax Act 1994, s.52; amend S.I. 1995 No. 2518. In force: June 1, 1996. Part X of the Value Added Tax Regulations 1995, which makes special provision for the valuation, for VAT purposes, of goods supplied under trading stamp schemes, is revoked by these Regulations. This means that trading stamps will have the same VAT treatment as any other discount voucher and the VAT law relating to promotion schemes involving trading stamps will be simplified.

VALUE ADDED TAX (TREATMENT OF TRANSACTIONS) (TRADING STAMPS) ORDER 1995 (No. 3042), made under the Value Added Tax Act 1994 s.5(3); revokes S.I. 1973 No. 325. operative on June 1, 1996; [65p]. This Order revokes the Value Added Tax (Treatment of Transactions) (No.1) Order 1973 which will mean that trading stamps will be subject to the same VAT treatment as other discount vouchers and simplifies the application of VAT laws to promotion schemes.

5110. Transitional measures—European Community

Council Directive 94/76/EC of December 22, 1994 amending the Sixth VAT Directive 77/388/EEC by the introduction of transitional measures applicable, in the context of the enlargement of the European Union on January 1, 1995, as regards value added tax (O.J. L 365/53).

5111. Transport

VALUE ADDED TAX (TRANSPORT) ORDER 1994 (No. 3014) [65p], made under the Value Added Tax Act 1994 (c.23), ss.30(4), 96(9); operative on April 1, 1994; varies Sched. 8, Group 8, to the 1994 Act.

VALUE ADDED TAX (TRANSPORT) ORDER 1995 (No. 653) [65p], made under the Value Added Tax Act 1994 (c.23), s.30(4); operative on April 1, 1995; amends the 1994 Act so as to provide for zero-rating of air navigation services when supplied in respect of certain zero-rated aircraft, or when received by specified persons for business purposes.

5112. Treatment of transactions

VALUE ADDED TAX (TREATMENT OF TRANSACTIONS) ORDER 1995 (No. 958) [65p], made under the Value Added Tax Act 1994 (c.23), s.5(3); operative on the date the Finance Act 1995 comes into force; relieves from VAT certain transactions relating to the temporary importations of second-hand goods and works of art.

5113. Zero-rating—books—whether philatelic collectors' items constituted books

[Value Added Tax Act 1994 (c.23), Sched. 8, Group 3, Item 1.]

Philatelic goods qualify for relief as books where any stamps included are a minor element in the composite item.

S traded in various goods originally sold by British post offices which had become collectors' items. These included descriptive folders and booklets which originally included stamps, and books of pre-decimal and decimal stamps. Customs and Excise decided that the goods did not qualify for zero-rating as books, etc.

Held, allowing S's appeal in part, that the items other than the books of stamps qualified for zero-rating.

SCHUSMAN v. CUSTOMS AND EXCISE COMMISSIONERS [1994] VATTR 120, London Tribunal.

5114. Zero-rating—charities—charity providing care and medical treatment for handicapped persons—construction of soft games room designed solely for the therapy of the handicapped—whether services supplied in construction zero-rated—whether installation of observation windows the supply of medical equipment designed solely for use in medical diagnosis or treatment handicapped persons

[Value Added Tax Act 1983 (c.55), Sched. 5, Group 16, item 5, note (4).]

The centre was a charity providing assessment, treatment and residential care for children and adults suffering from epilepsy. The centre appealed against a decision of the commissioners that the provision of a soft games area in the recreational unit and in installing observation windows were not zero-rated.

Held, allowing the commissioners' appeal, that the tribunal failed to ask itself what were the supplies made in the construction of the games area: clearly none of supplies in question could have been brought within the items set out in Group 16 and therefore could not qualify for zero-rating. In deciding whether the supply of observation windows was a supply of "relevant goods" within the Value Added Tax Act 1983, Sched. 5, Group 16, item 5, note (4), the test was twofold: whether the goods were medical and whether they had been supplied for use in medical diagnosis or treatment. The observation windows could not be considered to be medical equipment even if they were used in the treatment of epilepsy (*Clinical Computing v. Customs and Excise Commissioners* [1983] C.L.Y. 3880, *I.R.C. v. Barclay Curle* [1969] C.L.Y. 1659, *Lancer U.K. v. Customs and Excise Commissioners* [1987] C.L.Y. 3864 referred to).

CUSTOMS AND EXCISE COMMISSIONERS v. DAVID LEWIS CENTRE [1995] S.T.C. 485, Owen J.

5115. Zero-rating—construction—redevelopment involving demolition of building apart from concrete frame—whether new building or reconstruction of existing building

[Value Added Tax Act 1983 (c.55), Sched. 5, Group 8, Note (1A).]

The fact that part of an old structure is retained does not itself prevent the end result from being a new building.

MH had a long lease of a light industrial building with three storeys plus basement. It carried out a redevelopment of the building to an office block with four floors plus basement. The existing reinforced concrete frame was re-used, but the external fabric of the building and all internal walls, lift, stairs and services were replaced. MH claimed input tax on the cost of the development, but this was denied by the Customs and Excise on the grounds that the work constituted the conversion, reconstruction, alteration or enlargement of an existing building, so that a sale would not be zero-rated

Held, allowing MH's appeal, that considered as a totality the work was so extensive, that the building was essentially new (*Customs and Excise Commissioners v. London Diocesan Fund* [1993] C.L.Y. 4107 applied).

MARCHDAY HOLDINGS v. CUSTOMS AND EXCISE COMMISSIONERS [1994] VATTR 253, London Tribunal.

5116. Zero-rating—diaries and address books—whether "books" or "booklets"

[Value Added Tax Act 1983 (c.55), Sched. 5, Group 3, item 1.]

The company traded as a general printer, producing diaries and address books. The company contended that they were physically complete and therefore "booklets" within item 1, Group 3, Sched. 5 of the Value Added Tax Act 1983. The commissioners contended that, because the diaries and address books were designed primarily to be written in and not read, they were not eligible to be zero-rated as "books" or "booklets".

Held, allowing the appeal, that the ordinary meaning of the word "book" or "booklet" was an object which had the characteristics of being read or looked at. A blank diary or address book was not, in this ordinary sense, a book. Therefore, the items did not fall to be zero-rated (*Brutus v. Cozens* [1972] C.L.Y. 706, *John Pimblett and Sons v. Customs and Excise Commissioners* [1988] STC 358, *Maughan (Surveyor of Taxes) v. Free Church of Scotland* [1893] 3 T.C. 207 referred to).

CUSTOMS AND EXCISE COMMISSIONERS v. COLOUR OFFSET [1995] STC 85, May J.

5117. Zero-rating—press release

HM Customs and Excise has issued a press release entitled *Business Brief* (Business Brief 23/95), published on October 24, 1995. Customs and Excise is issuing new guidance on the zero-rating of incontinence products. The operation of VAT for supplies of such products to commercial nursing homes and NHS Trusts is clarified. In the light of responses to a consultation document, Ministers have decided to take up the option in the Second VAT Simplification Directive to retain the current zero-rating of process work on materials which leads to the production of zero-rated goods. The situation with regard to tax treatment of fees charged under the Building Act 1984 is clarified. Because building control services associated with non-domestic construction can be supplied only by local authorities, they are outside the scope of VAT. Guidance will be issued shortly on how traders not registered for VAT may submit claims for repayment of tax charged.

5118. Zero-rating—protected building—alterations to building in curtilage of listed building—whether two buildings can constitute one dwelling

[Value Added Tax Act 1994 (c.23), Sched. 8, Group 6, Item 2, Note (1).]

A separate building within the curtilage of and appurtenant to a protected building may be part of the entity constituting a dwelling.

H owned and occupied a listed building. Nine feet away from the main buildings was another listed building, also owned and occupied by H. He pulled down a wooden structure attached to the second building and replaced it with a brick building for use as a billiards room. Although physically separate, the main building and the second building were connected underground by shared services. The Customs and Excise ruled that the building works did not qualify for zero-rating as approved alterations to a protected building.

Held, allowing H's appeal, that the two buildings together formed one dwelling (*Lewis (Inspector of Taxes) v. Rook* [1992] C.L.Y. 348 applied).

HARDY v. CUSTOMS AND EXCISE COMMISSIONERS [1994] VATTR 302, Manchester Tribunal.

5119. Zero-rating—protected building—construction of new building connected to protected building by covered walkway and brick wall—whether a building separate from a protected building—whether construction constituting an alteration of protected building

[Value Added Tax Act 1983 (c.55), Sched. 5, Group 8A, item 2, note (6A).]

A owned a listed farmhouse and obtained planning permission and listed building consent to replace a barn with a building to house a swimming pool. The building was connected to the house by a covered walkway. A claimed that the building works fell to be zero-rated under Value Added Tax Act 1983, Sched. 5, Group 8A, item 2 on the basis that the works were done to a protected building under an approved scheme. The commissioners argued that the building was separate from the listed farmhouse, by reference to note (6A). The tribunal relied on the dictionary definition of the word "separate" and on the opinion of the local planning officer. The commissioners appealed, contending that the tribunal had not directed itself properly as to the legal meaning of the term "separate" in this context.

Held, dismissing the commissioners' appeal, that while no words can replace the words of a statute, a dictionary definition can assist to understand the various possible contexts in which a word may be used. There was no evidence that the tribunal has substituted another meaning of the word for that used in the statute. The tribunal had not misdirected itself by concluding that the opinion of the planning officer was of some persuasive effect. Therefore, the tribunal had not acted unreasonably or perversely in reaching its decision (*Brutus v. Cozens* [1973] A.C. 854 referred to).

CUSTOMS AND EXCISE COMMISSIONERS v. ARBIB [1995] S.T.C. 490, Latham J.

5120. Zero-rating—protected building—whether redecoration scheme constituted alteration

[Value Added Tax Act 1994 (c.23), s.30, Sched. 8, Group 6, item 2, note (6)(a).]

A scheme of repair and redecoration does not constitute an alteration of a building.

St. A's church, a listed building, underwent a redecoration scheme which included filling in cracks in stone and plasterwork and reproducing as far as possible earlier paintwork. The Customs and Excise decided that this work was repair and maintenance and not an alteration of the building. St. A's appealed.

Held, dismissing the appeal, that the work did not constitute an alteration of the building.

ST. ANNE'S CATHOLIC CHURCH v. CUSTOMS AND EXCISE COMMISSIONERS [1994] VATTR 102, London Tribunal.

5121. Zero-rating—reconstruction of concert hall in music academy—whether for relevant charitable purposes—whether for public purposes

[Value Added Tax Act 1994 (c.23), Sched. 8, Group 6, item 2, notes (1), (3); EEC Sixth Directive (77/388), Art. 4.5.]

The activities of a school of music cannot be described as being of a non-business or of a public character.

RAM, a school of music which was a registered charity, carried out reconstruction work on its concert hall. Customs and Excise refused a certificate for zero-rating on the ground that the building was not intended for use solely otherwise than in the course or furtherance of a business.

Held, dismissing RAM's appeal, that (1) RAM's activities were of a business character (*Customs and Excise Commissioners v. Morrison's Academy Boarding Houses Association* [1977] C.L.Y. 3128 applied); (2) RAM did not engage in its educational activities as a public authority.

ROYAL ACADEMY OF MUSIC v. CUSTOMS AND EXCISE COMMISSIONERS [1994] VATTR 105, London Tribunal.

5122. Zero-rating—construction work—whether "work on a new building" or only "conversion of existing building"

A "before and after" test had to be applied to determine whether, for VAT zero-rating purposes, construction work was work on a new building, or whether it was only conversion, alteration, reconstruction or enlargement of an existing building.

CUSTOMS AND EXCISE COMMISSIONERS v. MARCHDAY HOLDINGS, *The Independent*, July 31, 1995, D.C.

WATER AND WATERWORKS

5123. Barrage—London Borough of Barking

BARKING BARRAGE ORDER 1995 (No. 519) [£6·75], made under the Transport and Works Act 1992 (c.42), ss.3, 5; operative on March 7, 1995; empowers the borough to construct a semi-tidal barrage across the River Roding.

5124. British Waterways Act 1995 (c.i)

The British Waterways Board was established by the Transport Act 1962. In order to fulfil its remit, powers to enter land and repair or maintain, or carry out other operations with respect to, the inland waterways owned or managed by them, further provision should be made for the regulation and management by the Board of the inland waterways. This Act, therefore, amends or repeals certain statutory provisions relating to the Board.

The Act received Royal Assent on January 16, 1995.

5125. Drainage—sewage flooding into home—allegations of negligence and nuisance—council acting as agents for statutory undertakers—whether agents liable

D acted as agents for the statutory undertakers, Thames Water Authority. P's house was flooded with sewage on six occasions between 1987 and 1992. Insurers declined to insure the property against flood damage following the incidents. P alleged that D were responsible, either directly or as agents, for the drainage of the area, as well as for all watercourses and also alleged negligence in D failing to maintain capacity in the drainage system as well as nuisance.

Held, dismissing P's claim, that (1) the body statutorily responsible under the Public Health Act 1936 was Thames Water Authority and not D; (2) a statutory body could not put forward as a defence that they had taken all reasonable steps by delegating their functions to a local authority; and (3) there was no evidence that D had carried out any of the functions delegated to them without reasonable regard and care for the interests of all those who might have been affected by their actions.

KING v. HARROW LONDON BOROUGH COUNCIL [1994] EGCS 76, H.H.J. Humphrey Lloyd, Q.C.

5126. Effluent—taking a sample for analysis—whether necessary to notify occupier of land

[Water Act 1989 (c.15), s.148(1).]

It is not necessary that an occupier of land be notified of the intention to have a sample of effluent analysed before the sample is divided into parts for analysis.

The Attorney-General referred to the court the questions of whether the notification to an occupier of land of the intention to divide a sample of effluent for analysis purposes must precede the taking of the sample, and what the meaning of the phrase "there and then" in s.148(1) of the Water Act 1989 was.

Held, that there was no necessity that the notification to the occupier precede the division of the sample for analysis; and the phrase "there and then" meant that the sample must be divided for analysis at or near the site where it is taken, on the occasion on which it is taken (*Copol Clothing v. Hindmarch (Inspector of Taxes)* [1984] C.L.Y. 452 referred to).

ATT.-GEN'S REFERENCE (NO. 2 OF 1994) [1994] 1 W.L.R. 1579, C.A.

5127. Hartlepools water company

HARTLEPOOLS WATER COMPANY (CONSTITUTION AND REGULATION) ORDER 1995 (No. 79) [£1·10], made under the Statutory Water Companies Act 1991 (c.58), ss.12(1), 14; operative on February 14, 1995; revokes S.I. 1987 No. 1597, S.I. 1988 No. 1592, revokes in part S.I. 1986 No. 401 and approves a proposal by the water company that a memorandum and articles of association should have effect in place of provisions contained in the water company's local orders.

5128. Internal drainage boards

AMALGAMATION OF THE HOLME COMMON, RIVER BURN AND STIFFKEY RIVER INTERNAL DRAINAGE BOARDS ORDER 1995 (No. 1325) [£1·55], made under the Land Drainage Act 1991 (c.59), s.3(5)(7); operative on May 12, 1995; confirms a scheme for the amalgamation of the said internal drainage boards.

RECONSTITUTION OF THE BUCKINGHAM INTERNAL DRAINAGE BOARD ORDER 1994 (No. 2851) [£1·10], made under the Land Drainage Act 1991 (c.59), s.3(5)(7); operative on November 1, 1994; confirms a scheme for the reconstitution of the said Board.

5129. Pipelines—Wales

DWR CYMRU CYFYNGEDIG (PIPELAYING AND OTHER WORKS) (CODE OF PRACTICE) ORDER 1995 (No. 1556), made under the Water Industry Act 1991, s.182(2).

5130. Water companies—procurement practices

The Office of Water Services (OFWAT) has issued a press release entitled *OFWAT Begins Checks on Water Company Procurement Practices* (News Release PN 25/95), published on September 22, 1995. OFWAT is to begin a series of checks on water company accounts to ensure that regulated business is kept separate from other companies within the group and that no cross-subsidy is taking place. Findings will be announced in OFWAT's Annual Report to Parliament in June 1996.

5131. Water pollution—causing noxious or polluting matter to enter controlled waters—absolute offence—engineering company having oil tank on site—vandals damaging sight gauge on oil tank—oil leaking into nearby brook—whether company having "caused" polluting matter to enter brook—whether act of vandals reasonably foreseeable in view of earlier minor incidents of vandalism—whether justices entitled to dismiss information against company

[Water Act 1989 (c.15), s.107(1)(a).]

R was a company which operated a light engineering works and stored heating oil on site in a tank adjacent to a surface drain, which led to a controlled water course (the brook). The works were shut down over Christmas and during this time the release mechanism which controlled the flow of oil from the tank was vandalised and the brook was polluted with oil which leaked from the tank. The National Rivers Authority (NRA) brought an information against R, charging the company with having caused polluting matter to enter controlled waters contrary to s.107(1)(a) of the 1989 Act. The justices dismissed the information on the grounds that although the s.107(1)(a) offence was prima facie an absolute one, R had not "caused" the oil to enter controlled waters, since the oil leak was the result of an intervention by a third party and the vandalism involved was not reasonably foreseeable because it was out of all proportion to earlier, more minor, incidents.

Held, dismissing the NRA's appeal, that (1) although foreseeability would be relevant to any inquiry into whether a party "knowingly permitted" polluting matter to enter into controlled waters for the purposes of s.107(1)(a) of the 1989 Act, it was of less significance, although still a factor, when considering who or what "caused" the resulting pollution; (2) on the facts found, it was open to the justices to find that the vandals had "caused" the escape of the oil and not R (dictum of Lord Wilberforce and of Lord Salmon in *Alphacell v. Woodward* [1972] C.L.Y. 3549 applied; *National Rivers Authority v. Yorkshire Water Services* [1995] 3 C.L. 576 considered).

NATIONAL RIVERS AUTHORITY v. WRIGHT ENGINEERING CO. [1994] 4 All E.R. 281, D.C.

5132. Water pollution—causing polluting matter to enter river—cement washed into river during building operations carried out by company—employees admitting liability—employees not exercising controlling mind of company—whether company liable for acts of junior employees

[Water Resources Act 1991 (c.57), s.85.]

A company will be criminally liable under s.85 of the Water Resources Act 1991 where the pollution results solely from the acts or omissions of its employees acting within the course and scope of their employment, regardless of whether those employees can be said to be exercising the controlling mind and will of the company.

R was a company engaged in building houses on a residential development. During the construction of a water feature on site a nearby stream, which was a controlled water within the meaning of s.104 of the 1991 Act, became polluted when cement was allowed to be washed into it. On subsequent investigation by the National Rivers Authority (NRA) R's site agent and site manager both accepted responsibility. An information was brought against R, alleging that it had caused polluting matter to enter controlled waters contrary to s.85 of the 1991 Act. The justices held that there was no case to answer and dismissed the information on the ground that the NRA had failed to show that the company itself was liable because neither the site agent nor the site manager were of sufficient seniority within the company to enable them to be categorised as persons whose acts were the acts of the company.

Held, allowing NRA's appeal, that (1) the question in all cases where a company was prosecuted under s.85 of the 1991 Act was whether as a matter of common sense the company, by some active operation or chain of operations carried out under its essential control, caused the pollution of controlled water; (2) a company would accordingly be criminally liable for causing pollution which resulted solely from the acts or omissions of its employees acting within the course and scope of their employment, regardless of whether they could be said to be exercising the controlling mind and will of the company; and (3) on the facts it was immaterial that those in R's head office had no direct part in determining the precise construction which allowed the cement to wash into the stream, since those immediately responsible on site were R's employees and acting apparently within the scope of that employment (dictum of Lord Wilberforce, of Viscount Dilhorne and of Lord Salmon in *Alphacell v. Woodward* [1972] C.L.Y. 3549 applied; *Tesco Supermarkets v. Nattrass* [1971] C.L.Y. 10538 distinguished).

NATIONAL RIVERS AUTHORITY v. ALFRED McALPINE HOMES EAST [1994] 4 All E.R. 286, D.C.

5133. Water pollution—"causing" pollution to enter controlled waters—whether questions properly admitted in evidence

[Water Resources Act 1991 (c.57), ss.85(1), 209(1); Salmon and Fresh Water Fisheries Act 1975 (c.51), s.4(1).]

C was convicted of causing polluted matter to enter controlled waters and of causing damage to fish by a poisonous discharge, even though the spillage was from a defective pipe and after its discovery C's conduct was exemplary. The questions at issue were whether C had "caused" the pollution and whether readings taken from a machine, which indicated that C had exceeded requirements as to the composition and volume of trade effluent which it was enabled to discharge under a consent, were properly admitted in evidence under the Water Resources Act 1991, s.209.

Held, that the Recorder's decision, that the question as to whether C had caused the pollution was one of fact to be left to the jury and that the readings should be admitted in evidence, was correct (*Alphacell v. Woodward* [1972] C.L.Y. 3549 considered).

C.P.C. (U.K.) [1994] NPC 112, C.A.

5134. Water pollution—controlled waters—river bed—stirring up of material—whether pollution

[Water Resources Act 1991 (c.57), s.85.]

NRA appealed by way of case stated against B's acquittal of causing polluting matter to enter controlled waters. B was performing work on a river which involved driving diggers along the river bed which resulted in mud and silt being stirred up, causing severe discolouration of the water.

Held, dismissing the appeal, that controlled waters included the river bed but no offence been committed under s.85 of the Water Resources Act 1991 as B had not introduced a pollutant to the river but had merely stirred up existing matter. A question of fact existed as to whether certain matter was a pollutant and this was to be decided on the merits of each case.

NATIONAL RIVERS AUTHORITY v. BIFFA WASTE SERVICES, *The Times*, November 21, 1995, D.C.

5135. Water pollution—effluent discharged under licence—exceeding licence conditions—whether more than one person can commit offence

[Water Act 1989 (c.15), s.107.]

The Attorney-General referred questions to the court arising from the acquittal of a commercial trade effluent disposal licensee, a sewage undertaker and the borough council for causing polluted matter to enter controlled waters contrary to the Water Act 1989, s.107. The company discharged effluent under licence to the sewerage system. The sewage undertaker was responsible for the system but contracted out day-to-day management to the borough council. On the days when the pollution occurred, the company was discharging effluent in greater volume and concentration than the licence conditions permitted, the council allowed part of the pumping station to become blocked and each of these factors contributed to the pollution.

Held, that (1) the offence of causing polluting matter to enter controlled waters contrary to s.107 of the Act could be committed by more than one person each responsible for separate acts which contributed to the pollution entering the waters. Whether the defendant's action was a cause of pollution of the waters was a question of fact in each case. "Cause" must be interpreted by reference to its plain common sense meaning. Some active participation was required, but not necessarily knowledge. There might be circumstances in which both the organisation which ran a sewerage system and the organisation which discharged matter to the system were liable for causing pollution by their separate actions (*Alphacell v. Woodward* [1972] C.L.Y. 3549, *National Rivers Authority v. Yorkshire Water Services* [1994] 3 C.L. 579 considered); (2) a sewerage organisation's failure to maintain an efficient pumping system, in breach of statutory duty or negligently, amounted to a positive act or chain of operations which could cause pollution and attract criminal liability.

ATT.-GEN.'S REFERENCE (NO. 1 OF 1994), *Re* (94/0097/S1), January 19, 1995, C.A.

5136. Water pollution—pollution of controlled waters—breach of condition attached to consent—whether defendant liable if no positive act of discharge committed

[Water Resources Act 1991, ss.85, 88, Sched. 10.]

A criminal offence is committed under s.85(6) of the Water Resources Act 1991 where breaches of the conditions of a consent occur, whether or not the defendant performed an act causing the breach.

TW had the benefit of a consent granted by the National Rivers Authority allowing them the use of an outfall into the river Test. It was a condition of the consent that any effluent discharged would contain no traces of oil or grease. TW were convicted of 4 offences under s.85(6) of the Water Resources Act 1991 for contravening the condition. TW appealed by way of case stated on the basis that the company did not in fact discharge effluent containing oil and grease into the river.

Held, dismissing the appeal, that compliance with a condition attached to a consent was a positive obligation. The appellant was under a duty to ensure that the effluent discharged contained no traces of oil or grease, and as a lawfully applicable condition, failure to do so was a criminal offence, whether or not there was an act of discharge (*Alphacell v. Woodward* [1972] C.L.Y. 3549 applied).

TAYLOR WOODROW PROPERTY MANAGEMENT v. NATIONAL RIVERS AUTHORITY (1994) 158 J.P. 1101, C.A.

5137. Water pollution—sewage undertaker—whether liable for discharge by an unknown person

[Water Act 1989 (c.15), ss.107(1)(a), 108.]

The defence in s.108 of the Water Act 1989 is available to a sewage undertaker where pollution has been caused through a discharge into its sewers, by an unknown person.

A sewage undertaker, Y, was convicted of having allowed polluted matter (iso-octanol) to enter controlled waters, contrary to the Water Act 1989, s.107(1)(a). Y had granted permission to its industrial customers to discharge trade effluent into its sewers on the basis that they did not discharge iso-octanol, and an unidentified customer had discharged the iso-octanol without Y's knowledge. The court allowed Y's appeal, but made no finding as to whether Y had caused the pollution. NRA appealed. The Divisional Court upheld NRA's appeal, and Y appealed to the House of Lords. The House of Lords held that the questions to be determined were whether the only reasonable conclusion to be reached was that Y had been guilty of allowing the pollution, contrary to s.107(1)(a), and whether the statutory defence in s.108(7) was available in relation to a charge under this section.

Held, allowing Y's appeal, that the circumstances in which the pollution occurred did not preclude a finding that Y had caused the pollution contrary to s.107(1)(a), but that the defence in s.108(7) could apply in such circumstances.

NATIONAL RIVERS AUTHORITY v. YORKSHIRE WATER SERVICES [1994] 3 W.L.R. 1202, H.L.

WEIGHTS AND MEASURES

5138. Guernsey and Alderney

WEIGHTS AND MEASURES (GUERNSEY AND ALDERNEY) ORDER 1995 (No. 1011) [65p], made under the Weights and Measures Act 1985 (c.72), ss.11(16), 94(2); operative on June 1, 1995; provides that weighing and measuring equipment stamped in accordance with Guernsey or Alderney weights and measures legislation may be used for trade in Great Britain and declares that Guernsey and Alderney are designated countries for the purposes of specified provisions of the 1985 Act.

5139. Measuring equipment

MEASURING EQUIPMENT (CAPACITY MEASURES AND TESTING EQUIPMENT) REGULATIONS 1995 (No. 735) [£2·80], made under the Weights and Measures Act 1985 (c.72), ss.5(9), 10(1)(b), 11(1)(4)(7), 15(1)(2), 86(1), 94(1); operative on April 10, 1995; prescribe certain dry and liquid capacity measures for trade use.

MEASURING EQUIPMENT (LIQUID FUEL AND LUBRICANTS) REGULATIONS 1995 (No. 1014) [£3·20], made under the Weights and Measures Act 1985 (c.72), ss.11(1)(4), 12(12), 15(1), 86(1), 94(1); operative on May 4, 1995; replace with amendments S.I. 1988 No. 128 and take account of International Recommendation R117 issued by the International Organisation for Legal Metrology.

MEASURING EQUIPMENT (LIQUID FUEL DELIVERED FROM ROAD TANKERS) (AMENDMENT) REGULATIONS 1995 (No. 3117), made under the Weights and Measures Act 1985 ss.11(1)(4), 12(12), 15(1), 86(1), 94(1); amends S.I. 1983 No. 1390. operative on December 29, 1995; [£1·10]. The Measuring Equipment (Liquid Fuel Delivered from Road Tankers) Regulations 1983 are amended by the withdrawal of the requirement that dipstick measuring systems incorporated in bottom loaded compartments be made in accordance with a pattern holding a pattern approval certificate and the provision for acceptance of test results for measuring equipment imported from member states of the EU or parties to the EEAA. The Regulations refer to EN 45001 (BS 7501) which may be obtained from BSI or HMSO.

5140. Measuring instruments

MEASURING INSTRUMENTS (EC REQUIREMENTS) (ELECTRICAL ENERGY METERS) REGULATIONS 1995 (No. 2607) [£2.40], made under the European Communities Act 1972, s.2(2); operative on November 1, 1995, revoke S.I. 1980 No. 886; implement the obligations of the U.K. under Council Directive 76/891, as amended by Council Directive 82/621.

MEASURING INSTRUMENTS (EEC REQUIREMENTS) (FEES) (AMENDMENT) REGULATIONS 1995 (No. 1376) [£1·10], made under the Finance Act 1973 (c.51), s.56(1)(2); operative on July 1, 1995; amend fees payable in connection with services undertaken by the DTI in relation to weighting instruments.

5141. Units of measurement

UNITS OF MEASUREMENT REGULATIONS 1995 (No. 1804) [£1·55], made under the European Communities Act 1972, s.2(2); amend S.I. 1994 No. 2867; operative on October 1, 1995; implement Council Dirs. 71/354 and 80/181 which provide for the phasing out of the use of imperial units of measurement, with certain exceptions permitting the continued use of imperial units until respectively, December 31, 1999, and beyond that date.

5142. Weighing instruments

NON-AUTOMATIC WEIGHING INSTRUMENTS (EEC REQUIREMENTS) REGULATIONS 1995 (No. 1907) [£6·10], made under the European Communities Act 1992, s.2(2), and the Weights and Measures Act 1985; revoke S.I. 1992 No. 1579; operative on September 1, 1995; implement Council Dir. 90/384 (as amended by Dir. 93/68) on the harmonisation of the laws of Member States relating to non-automatic weighing instruments.

5143. Weighing machines

NON-AUTOMATIC WEIGHING MACHINES AND NON-AUTOMATIC WEIGHING INSTRUMENTS (AMENDMENT) REGULATIONS 1995 (No. 428) [£1·10], made under the European Communities Act 1972 (c.68), s.2(2), and the Weights and Measures Act 1985 (c.72), ss.15(1), 86(1); operative on March 27, 1995; amend S.I. 1988 No. 876 and S.I 1992 No. 1579.

WILLS AND SUCCESSION

5144. Condition—charitable gift—gift conditional upon care of pets—no pets at time of death—whether gift still capable of passing

[Administration of Justice Act 1982 (c.53), s.21.]

T made a will in 1974 leaving half his estate to N and the remaining half to C, conditional on the latter caring for any of his domestic pets. If C did not agree to this then the residue would pass to N. At the time of making his will T owned one dog which predeceased him and was never replaced. N, relying on *Re Brown's Will* (1881) 18 Ch.D. 61, claimed C could not fulfil T's condition and therefore could not take the gift, in which case N would be entitled to the entire estate.

Held, that the condition imposed by T's will was impossible to fulfil and should be deemed as spent. As such C were entitled to their share of the gift absolutely. Clause 3 of the will must be construed as requiring C to care for T's pets but if T had no pets the gift should still pass, as, if not construed in this manner, it would be deemed ambiguous and s.21 of the Administration of Justice Act 1982 would apply, allowing extrinsic evidence of T's intention to be admitted. T had clearly stated his intention and only if his request that any animals be looked after by C was refused would the gift fail and the residue fall to N. C had not refused, they merely could not fulfil the request, and therefore the estate would be divided equally between the two charities.

WATSON v. NATIONAL CHILDREN'S HOME, *The Times*, October 31, 1995, Colyer J.

5145. Executor de son tort—characteristics—tenant renting part of property of deceased—death of landlord—whether tenant by his actions becoming an executor de son tort and constructive trustee—whether tenant entitled to property

A tenant who has not acted in any way as an executor will not become an executor de son tort, or be liable as a constructive trustee for property (part of which the tenant is renting) which is left vacant after the owner's death.

P and her mother left P's father in 1953, and there was no further contact between them. The father owned a property, part of which he let to J, a tenant. When the father died in 1971, without a will, J continued to occupy the property, but took no steps to install himself as executor, other than to burn some rubbish and clean the vacant part of the premises into which he then moved. In 1983 he contacted solicitors, who traced P. P claimed that she was entitled to the property absolutely, subject only to J's weekly tenancy. J counterclaimed that he was entitled to the property. The court found that J had acted as an executor de son tort, and therefore time could not run in his favour, as he was a trustee, and time can not run in favour of a trustee against his beneficiary in such circumstances.

Held, allowing J's appeal, that J had not done anything which could be regarded as characteristic of an executor. He had not therefore become a constructive trustee, and was under no obligation to seek out and notify P of her father's death. J was therefore entitled to the property.
POLLARD v. JACKSON (1994) 67 P. & C.R. 327, C.A.

5146. Family provision—application six years out of time—whether leave to apply out of time should be granted

[Inheritance (Provision for Family and Dependants) Act 1975 (c.63).]

Where there is no prejudice to the other beneficiaries, the court will in exceptional circumstances grant leave to apply for financial provision out of a deceased person's estate under the Inheritance (Provision for Family and Dependants) Act 1975, despite the fact that the statutory time-limit has long expired.

W was now aged 90. Her husband's will provided for W to occupy the former matrimonial home and have the benefit of the income from the will trust investments for life and thereafter the estate devolved to his nephews and nieces. Probate was granted in 1987, but in 1993, following a dramatic fall in interest rates, W found herself with not enough to live on. W applied for leave to apply out of time for financial provision out of the deceased's estate. The district judge granted leave, and the trustees appealed.

Held, dismissing the appeal, that where the statutory time-limit of six months had been grossly exceeded, the burden on the applicant to prove sufficient grounds for its extension was a heavy one but the burden had been discharged in the exceptional circumstances of the case. W had had no independent advice as to the implications of the will at the time of her husband's death, there was no prejudice to the other beneficiaries and the application had only been necessary owing to events outside W's control (*Salmon, (Dec'd), Re; Coard v. National Westminster Bank* [1980] C.L.Y. 2818 considered).
STOCK v. BROWN [1994] 1 F.L.R. 840, Thorpe J.

5147. Family provision—reasonable financial provision—deceased's failure to support son in infancy—son growing up with own income providing comfortable standard of living—no provision made for son on father's death—whether a failure to make reasonable financial provision

[Inheritance (Provision for Family and Dependants) Act 1975 (c.63), ss.1(1), 2(1), 3(1).]

A failure by a father to provide for an infant during the infant's childhood could not be used to found a claim for provision from the deceased father's estate when the infant had become an adult.

P was the only child of J and his wife. The parents separated and P was brought up by his mother and stepfather. J made no financial provision for P's upbringing and died with an estate of £300,000 leaving the substantial residue to three charities but making no provision for P. P was married with a house and mortgage and owned two companies, the income from which provided P and his family with a comfortable standard of living. P applied for reasonable financial provision to be made for him out of J's estate. The judge found that there had been no good reason for J's failure to support P in his childhood and that it had been unreasonable for J to have made no provision for P's maintenance and awarded P £30,000 from the estate.

Held, allowing the residuary legatees' appeal, that on an application for financial provision the court had to ask whether it would be reasonable for the applicant to receive a sum for his maintenance. Where the applicant was an adult capable of earning his own living some special circumstance such as a moral obligation of the deceased towards the applicant had to be established before such provision would be made. Such special circumstances were limited to matters that were still operative at the date of the deceased's death and did not include a moral failure to support the applicant during childhood which had no lasting effect on P (*Coventry (Dec'd), Re; Coventry v. Coventry* [1979] C.L.Y. 2807 applied).

JENNINGS (DEC'D), *Re* [1994] 3 W.L.R. 67, C.A.

5148. Law Reform (Succession) Act 1995 (c.41)

This Act introduces rules relating to the distribution of estates on intestacy, and amends the Wills Act 1837 (c.26) and the Children Act 1989 (c.41) respectively, to alter the effect on a will of the testator's divorce or the annulment of his marriage.

The Act received the Royal Assent on November 8, 1995.

5149. Wills—incorporation of standard forms and clauses in wills—practice direction

The following Practice Direction was issued by Gerald Angel, Senior District Judge, on April 10, 1995:

Rule 14(3) of the Non-Contentious Probate Rules 1987 makes provision for the production to the Court of any document which is incorporated in a will. This provision extends to the incorporation of standard will forms and clauses, other than statutory will forms.

As from the date of this Direction when application is made to admit to proof a will which incorporates standard forms or clauses as contained in a published document, production of that document will not be required in any individual case, unless otherwise directed, if the published document containing the standard forms or clauses (together with as many copies as may be required) has been previously lodged with the Senior District Judge and accepted by him as sufficient lodgment for the purposes of this Direction.

PRACTICE DIRECTION (FAM.D.) (INCORPORATION OF STANDARD FORMS AND CLAUSES IN WILLS), April 10, 1995.

NORTHERN IRELAND

ADMINISTRATIVE LAW

5150. Public Record Office

PUBLIC USE OF THE RECORDS (AMENDMENT) RULES (NORTHERN IRELAND) 1995 (No. 123) [£1·10], made under the Public Records Act (Northern Ireland) 1923 (c.20), s.9; operative on April 3, 1995; increase fees charged by the Public Record Office.

5151. Transfer of functions

DEPARTMENTS (TRANSFER OF FUNCTIONS) ORDER (NORTHERN IRELAND) 1995 (No. 96) [£1·10], made under the Ministries Act (Northern Ireland) 1944 (c.14), s.4; operative on April 1, 1995; transfers to the Department of Health and Social Services certain functions of the Department of Education relating to social activities.

AGRICULTURE

5152. Agricultural marketing

AGRICULTURAL MARKETING ORDER PART II (CERTIFICATION OF CESSATION OF EFFECT IN RELATION TO MILK) (NORTHERN IRELAND) ORDER 1995 (No. 103) [65p], made under S.I. 1993 No. 2665 (N.I. 10), art. 23(3); operative on March 20, 1995; certifies March 1, 1995, as the day on which Part II of the 1993 S.I. (except art. 26) ceased to have effect in relation to milk.

5153. Agriculture (Conservation Grants) (Northern Ireland) Order 1995

AGRICULTURE (CONSERVATION GRANTS) (NORTHERN IRELAND) ORDER 1995 (No. 3212 (NI.21)), made under the Northern Ireland Act 1974 Sched. 1, para. 1. In force: February 14, 1996; [£1·10]. Powers to make Regulations for making grants to those conserving or enhancing the countryside or promoting the enjoyment of the countryside are conferred on the Department of Agriculture in order to correspond with the Environment Act 1995 s.98.

5154. Apple orchards—grubbing up

APPLE ORCHARD GRUBBING UP (AMENDMENT) REGULATIONS (NORTHERN IRELAND) 1995 (No. 15) [65p], made under the European Communities Act 1972 (c.68), s.2(2); operative on January 19, 1995; amend the 1991 (No. 157) Regulations to take account of Commission Reg. 3149/94/EC.

5155. Arable areas—payments

ARABLE AREAS PAYMENTS REGULATIONS (NORTHERN IRELAND) 1995 (No. 381) [£5·70], made under the European Communities Act 1972 (c.68), s.2(2); operative on November 6, 1995; provide for payments to producers of certain arable crops; revoke the 1994 (Nos. 181, 405) Regulations.

5156. Cattle—artificial insemination

ARTIFICIAL INSEMINATION OF CATTLE (ASSISTANCE) (REVOCATION) SCHEME (NORTHERN IRELAND) 1995 (No. 54) [65p], made under the Agriculture (Temporary Assistance) Act (Northern Ireland) 1954 (c.31), ss.1(1), 2(1); operative on April 1, 1995; revokes the 1989 (No. 2) Scheme.

5157. Eggs—marketing standards

EGGS (MARKETING STANDARDS) REGULATIONS (NORTHERN IRELAND) 1995 (No. 382) [£1·95], made under the European Communities Act 1972 (c.68), s.2(2); operative on November 6, 1995; replace, with amendments, and revoke, the 1987 (No. 407) and 1991 (No. 470) Regulations.

5158. Environmentally sensitive areas

Order made under S.I. 1987 No. 458 (N.I. 3), art. 3(1), relating to environmentally sensitive areas:
S.R. 1995 No. 179 (Sperrins) [£1·10].

5159. Farms and conservation grants

FARMS AND CONSERVATION GRANT (AMENDMENT) SCHEME (NORTHERN IRELAND) 1995 (No. 187) [£1·10], made under S.I. 1987 No. 166 (N.I. 1), art. 16(1)(2); operative on May 31, 1995; amends the 1989 (No. 38) Scheme.

FARM AND CONSERVATION GRANT (AMENDMENT) (NO.2) SCHEME (NORTHERN IRELAND) 1995 SR 1995 463), made under the S.I. 1987 No. 166 (NI.1), art.16(1)(2); amends SR 1989 38. operative on January 30, 1996; [65p]. This Scheme amends the 1989 Scheme (SR 1989 38).

5160. Feedingstuffs

FEEDING STUFFS REGULATIONS (NORTHERN IRELAND) 1995 (No. 451) [£11·90], made under the Agriculture Act 1970, ss.66(1), 68(1)(1A)(3), 69(1)(6)(7), 70(1), 73(3), 74(1), 74A, 84, 86 and the European Communities Act 1972, s.2(2); revoke S.R. 1992 No. 270; S.R. 1993 No. 349; S.R. 1994 Nos. 123, 502. In force: January 15, 1996; implement specified Council and Commission Directives in relation to animal feedingstuffs.

5161. Fees

DEPARTMENT OF AGRICULTURE (FEES) (REVOCATION) ORDER (NORTHERN IRELAND) 1995 (No. 202) [65p], made under S.I. 1988 No. 929 (N.I. 8), art. 3; operative on July 1, 1995; revokes the 1991 (No. 40) Order.

5162. Fertilisers

FERTILISERS (AMENDMENT) REGULATIONS (NORTHERN IRELAND) 1995 (No. 49) [£5·20], made under the Agriculture Act 1970 (c.40), ss.66(1), 68(1)–(3), 69(1)(3)(6)(7), 70(1), 74(1), 74A(1)(2)(4), 84, 86(1)–(3)(9); operative on April 3, 1995; amend the 1992 (No. 187) Regulations to implement Commission Dir. 93/69/EEC.

5163. Game meat

LARGE FARMED GAME MEAT (PRODUCTION AND MARKETING) REGULATIONS (NORTHERN IRELAND) 1995 (No. 454) [£1·10], made under the European Communities Act 1972, s.2(2). In force: January 8, 1996; implement

Council Dir. 91/495 in relation to the production and marketing of large farmed game meat (but do not apply to rabbits or birds or their meat).

5164. Habitat improvement

HABITAT IMPROVEMENT REGULATIONS (NORTHERN IRELAND) 1995 (No. 134) [£3·70], made under the European Communities Act 1972 (c.68), s.2(2); operative on May 1, 1995; authorise aid to farmers who undertake to withdraw land from agricultural production for environmental purposes or to use environmental farming practices.

5165. Hill livestock—compensatory allowances

HILL LIVESTOCK (COMPENSATORY ALLOWANCES) (AMENDMENT) REGULATIONS (NORTHERN IRELAND) 1995 (No. 22) [£1·55], made under the European Communities Act 1972 (c.68), s.2(2); operative on January 31, 1995; amend the 1994 (No. 417) Regulations.

HILL LIVESTOCK (COMPENSATORY ALLOWANCES) (AMENDMENT) (NO. 2) REGULATIONS (NORTHERN IRELAND) 1995 (No. 245) [£1·10], made under the European Communities Act 1972 (c.68), s.2(2); operative on July 1, 1995; amend the 1994 (No. 417) Regulations.

HILL LIVESTOCK (COMPENSATORY ALLOWANCES) (AMENDMENT) (NO. 3) REGULATIONS (NORTHERN IRELAND) 1995 (No. 404) [£1·10], made under the European Communities Act 1972, s.2(2); amend S.R. 1994 No. 417. In force: November 15, 1995.

5166. Marketing development

MARKETING DEVELOPMENT SCHEME (NORTHERN IRELAND) 1995 (No. 27) [£1·95], made under S.I. 1993 No. 2665 (N.I. 10), art. 26(1)–(3); operative on March 8, 1995; authorises the payment of grants for carrying out approved proposals in connection with marketing agricultural, horticultural and related produce.

MARKETING DEVELOPMENT SCHEME (SPECIFICATION OF ACTIVITIES) ORDER (NORTHERN IRELAND) 1995 (No. 28) [65p], made under S.I. 1993 No. 2665 (N.I. 10), arts. 26(2)(c), 30(b); operative on March 8, 1995; specifies activities for the purposes of the 1993 Order.

5167. Milk Marketing Board

MILK MARKETING BOARD (RESIDUARY FUNCTIONS) REGULATIONS (NORTHERN IRELAND) 1995 (No. 25) [£4·70], made under S.I. 1993 No. 2665 (N.I. 10), art. 17(2)(3)(6); operative on March 1, 1995; deal with the Milk Marketing Board's constitution and enable the Board to wind up its affairs.

5168. Milk marketing scheme—revocation

MILK MARKETING SCHEME (CERTIFICATION OF REVOCATION) ORDER (NORTHERN IRELAND) 1995 (No. 104) [65p], made under S.I. 1993 No. 2665 (N.I. 10), art. 4(5); operative on March 20, 1995; certifies the revocation of the Milk Marketing Scheme (Northern Ireland) 1989 as having occurred on March 1, 1995.

5169. Moorland—livestock extensification

MOORLAND (LIVESTOCK EXTENSIFICATION) REGULATIONS (NORTHERN IRELAND) 1995 (No. 239) [£3·20], made under the European Communities Act 1972 (c.68), s.2(2); operative on July 10, 1995; authorise payments to farmers who reduce their flocks of ewes.

5170. Organic farming aid

ORGANIC FARMING AID REGULATIONS (NORTHERN IRELAND) 1995 (No. 116) [£2·40], made under the European Communities Act 1972 (c.68), s.2(2);

operative on April 24, 1995; authorise aid to farmers who undertake to introduce organic farming methods.

5171. Pesticides

PESTICIDES (MAXIMUM RESIDUE LEVELS IN CROPS, FOOD AND FEEDING STUFFS) (EEC LIMITS) REGULATIONS (NORTHERN IRELAND) 1995 (No. 33) [£6·35], made under the European Communities Act 1972 (c.68), s.2(2); operative on April 24, 1995; implement Council Dirs. 90/642/EEC and 93/58/EEC by specifying maximum limits for pesticide residues in certain products.

PESTICIDES (MAXIMUM RESIDUE LEVELS IN CROPS, FOOD AND FEED STUFFS) (EEC LIMITS) (AMENDMENT) REGULATIONS (NORTHERN IRELAND) 1995 (No. 461) [£4·15], made under the European Communities Act 1972, s.2(2); amend S.R. & O. (N.I.) 1995 No. 33. In force: February 14, 1996; implement the provisions of Dirs. 94/29 and 94/30.

PESTICIDES (MAXIMUM RESIDUE LEVELS IN CROPS, FOOD AND FEEDING STUFFS) (NATIONAL LIMITS) REGULATIONS (NORTHERN IRELAND) 1995 (No. 32) [£5·70], made under the Food and Environment Protection Act 1985 (c.48), ss.16(2)(k)(l)(15), 24(3); operative on April 24, 1995; specify the maximum amount of pesticide residues which may be left in certain crops, food and feedingstuffs which are not the subject of European Union Council Directives and revoke the 1988 (No. 313) Regulations.

5172. Pig production development—levy

PIG PRODUCTION DEVELOPMENT (LEVY) (AMENDMENT) ORDER (NORTHERN IRELAND) 1995 (No. 141) [65p], made under the Pig Production Development Act (Northern Ireland) 1964 (c.25), s.5(1)–(3); operative on May 1, 1995; increases to 21p the levy payable on slaughtered or exported pigs and revokes the 1990 (No. 4) Order. $$9

5173. Plant health

PLANT HEALTH (AMENDMENT) ORDER (NORTHERN IRELAND) 1995 (No. 250) [£3·70], made under the Plant Health Act (Northern Ireland) 1967 (c.28), ss.2, 3(1), 3A, 3B(1), 4(1); operative on June 14, 1995; amends the 1993 (No. 256) Order to implement Commission Dirs. 93/106, 110/EC and 95/4/EC.

PLANT HEALTH (AMENDMENT NO.2) ORDER (NORTHERN IRELAND) 1995 SR 1995 494), made under the Plant Health Act (Northern Ireland) 1967 ss.2, 3(1), 3A, 3B(1), 4(1); amends SR 1993 256; 1995 250. operative on February 1, 1996; [£4·70. This Order amends SR 1993 256 to implement Commission Directives 95/40 and 95/41.

5174. Plant health—potatoes

PLANT HEALTH (AMENDMENT) (POTATOES) ORDER (NORTHERN IRELAND) 1995 (No. 164) [65p], made under the Plant Health Act (Northern Ireland) 1967 (c.28), ss.2, 3(1), 3A, 3B(1), 4(1); operative on May 17, 1995; amends the 1993 (No. 256) Order.

5175. Plant material marketing

MARKETING OF FRUIT PLANT MATERIAL REGULATIONS (NORTHERN IRELAND) 1995 (No. 416) [£2·80], made under the European Communities Act 1972 (c.68), s.2(2); operative on December 11, 1995; implement Council Dir. 92/34/EEC and Commission Dirs. 93/48, 64 and 79/EEC on the marketing of fruit plant propagating material and fruit plants intended for fruit production.

MARKETING OF ORNAMENTAL PLANT MATERIAL REGULATIONS (NORTHERN IRELAND) 1995 (No. 414) [£2·40], made under the European Communities Act 1972 (c.68), s.2(2); operative on December 11, 1995; implement Council Dir. 91/682/EEC and Commission Dirs. 93/49, 63 and 78/

EEC on the marketing of ornamental plant propagating material and ornamental plants.

MARKETING OF VEGETABLE PLANT MATERIAL REGULATIONS (NORTHERN IRELAND) 1995 (No. 415) [£2·80], made under the European Communities Act 1972 (c.68), s.2(2); operative on December 11, 1995; implement Council Dir. 92/33/EEC and Commission Dirs. 93/61 and 62/EEC on the marketing of vegetable plant propagating and planting material other than seed.

5176. Plant protection

PLANT PROTECTION PRODUCTS (FEES) REGULATIONS (NORTHERN IRELAND) 1995 (No. 372) [£1·95], made under the Finance Act 1973 (c.51), s.56(1)(2)(5) and S.I. 1991 No. 764 (N.I. 8), art. 3(1)(2)(4); operative on November 6, 1995; prescribe fees to be paid to the Department of Agriculture in connection with services provided in pursuance of obligations under Council Dir. 91/414/EEC, as amended, in relation to placing plant protection products on the market.

PLANT PROTECTION PRODUCTS REGULATIONS (NORTHERN IRELAND) 1995 (No. 371) [£4·70], made under the European Communities Act 1972 (c.68), s.2(2); operative on November 6, 1995; implement Council Dir. 91/414/EEC and Commission Dirs. 93/71/EEC and 94/37/EEC in relation to placing plant protection products on the market.

5177. Potatoes

POTATOES ORIGINATING IN THE NETHERLANDS (NOTIFICATION) ORDER (NORTHERN IRELAND) 1995 (No. 438) [£1·10], made under the Plant Health Act (Northern Ireland) 1967, ss.2, 3(1), 3B(1), 4(1). In force: November 29, 1995; impose notification requirements as respects potatoes grown in the Netherlands.

5178. Poultry, etc. meat—hygiene

POULTRY MEAT, FARMED GAME BIRD MEAT AND RABBIT MEAT (HYGIENE AND INSPECTION) REGULATIONS (NORTHERN IRELAND) 1995 (No. 396) [£7·65], made under the European Communities Act 1972 (c.68), s.2(2); operative on November 17, 1995; implement Council Dirs. 71/118/EEC and 91/495/EEC and, in part, Council Dir. 91/494/EEC on health problems affecting the production and marketing of fresh poultry meat, farmed game bird meat and rabbit meat; revoke the 1994 (No. 346) Regulations.

5179. Seed potatoes

SEED POTATOES (CROP FEES) REGULATIONS (NORTHERN IRELAND) 1995 (No. 148) [£1·10], made under the Seeds Act (Northern Ireland) 1965 (c.22), s.1; operative on May 8, 1995; increase fees for the certification of seed potato crops and revoke the 1994 (No. 128) Regulations.

SEED POTATOES (TUBER AND LABEL FEES) (AMENDMENT) REGULATIONS (NORTHERN IRELAND) 1995 (No. 334) [65p], made under the Seeds Act (Northern Ireland) 1965 (c.22), s.1(1)(2)(2A); operative on September 25, 1995; increase fees under the 1982 (No. 236) Regulations; revoke the 1994 (No. 386) Regulations.

5180. Seeds

CEREAL SEEDS (AMENDMENT) REGULATIONS (NORTHERN IRELAND) 1995 (No. 366) [£1·10], made under the Seeds Act (Northern Ireland) 1965 (c.22), ss.1(1)(2A), 2; operative on October 24, 1995; amend the 1994 (No. 254) Regulations.

5181. Sheep annual premium

SHEEP ANNUAL PREMIUM (AMENDMENT) REGULATIONS (NORTHERN IRELAND) 1995 (No. 403) [£1·10], made under the European Communities Act

1972, s.2(2); amend S.R. 1992 No. 476. In force: November 15, 1995; amend the application period for sheep annual premium.

5182. Suckler cow premium

SUCKLER COW PREMIUM (AMENDMENT) REGULATIONS (NORTHERN IRELAND) 1995 (No. 246) [£1·55], made under the European Communities Act 1972 (c.68), s.2(2); operative on July 1, 1995; amend the 1993 (No. 280) Regulations.

ANIMALS

5183. Animal health—diseases

BOVINE LEUCOSIS ORDER (NORTHERN IRELAND) 1995 (No. 369) [£1·95], made under S.I. 1981 No. 1115 (N.I. 22), arts. 5(1), 10(6), 12(1), 14(b)–(d)(f)(h), 19(e)(h)(i)(k), 44(b), 60(1); operative on October 30, 1995; provides for the control of bovine leucosis; revokes the 1977 (No. 33) Order.

BOVINE LEUCOSIS SCHEME ORDER (NORTHERN IRELAND) 1995 (No. 370) [£1·95], made under S.I. 1981 No. 1115 (N.I. 22), art. 8(1)(2); operative on October 30, 1995; provides for the prevention and control of enzootic bovine leucosis.

BOVINE SPONGIFORM ENCEPHALOPATHY ORDER (NORTHERN IRELAND) 1995 (No. 274) [£2·80], made under S.I. 1981 No. 1115 (N.I. 22), arts. 2(3), 5(1), 10(6), 18(7), 19(e)(f)(k), 44, 60(1); operative on August 1, 1995; replaces, with amendments, and revokes, the 1988 (No. 422), 1989 (No. 49) and 1992 (No. 214) Orders.

DISEASES OF ANIMALS (FEEDINGSTUFFS) (AMENDMENT) ORDER (NORTHERN IRELAND) 1995 (No. 43) [£1·10], made under S.I. 1981 No. 1115 (N.I. 22), arts. 2(3), 5(1), 19(e)(f)(k), 32, 44, 60(1); operative on March 27, 1995; amends the 1992 (No. 215) Regulations.

DISEASES OF ANIMALS (MODIFICATION) ORDER (NORTHERN IRELAND) 1995 (No. 44) [£1·10], made under S.I. 1981 No. 1115 (N.I. 22), arts. 2(3), 16(2); operative on April 17, 1995; amends the 1981 S.I. by adding certain diseases to it.

DISEASES OF ANIMALS (MODIFICATION NO. 2) ORDER (NORTHERN IRELAND) 1995 (No. 273) [£1·10], made under S.I. 1981 No. 1115 (N.I. 22), art. 16(2); operative on August 1, 1995; amends the 1981 S.I. as respects cattle slaughtered in connection with bovine spongiform encephalopathy.

DISEASES OF ANIMALS (MODIFICATION) (NO. 3) ORDER (NORTHERN IRELAND) 1995 (No. 368) [£1·10], made under S.I. 1981 No. 1115 (N.I. 22), art. 16(2); operative on October 30, 1995; modifies Sched. 2 to the 1981 S.I. in relation to bovine leucosis.

SPECIFIED DISEASES (NOTIFICATION AND MOVEMENT RESTRICTIONS) (AMENDMENT) ORDER (NORTHERN IRELAND) 1995 (No. 82) [£1·95], made under S.I. 1981 No. 1115 (N.I. 22), arts. 2(3), 5(1), 10(6), 12(1), 14, 19(e)(f)(k), 60(1); operative on April 3, 1995; amends the 1991 (No. 455) Order.

5184. Carcases—landing

LANDING OF CARCASES AND ANIMAL PRODUCTS (AMENDMENT) ORDER (NORTHERN IRELAND) 1995 (No. 315) [65p], made under S.I. 1981 No. 1115 (N.I. 22), arts. 24(1), 60(1); operative on September 6, 1995; amends the 1985 (No. 161) Order and revokes the 1993 (No. 486) Order.

5185. Game birds—preservation

GAME BIRDS PRESERVATION ORDER (NORTHERN IRELAND) 1995 (No. 252) [65p], made under the Game Preservation Act (Northern Ireland) 1928 (c.25), ss.7C(1), 7F; operative on August 11, 1995; prohibits, subject to exemptions, the killing of certain game birds during the normal open season for game birds and restricts dealing in certain game birds.

5186. Import and export

ANIMALS AND ANIMAL PRODUCTS (IMPORT AND EXPORT) (IDENTIFICATION) ORDER (NORTHERN IRELAND) 1995 (No. 256) [65p], made under S.I. 1981 No. 1115 (N.I. 2), arts. 5(1)(b), 60(1); operative on July 17, 1995; authorises the identification or marking of animals detained under the 1995 (No. 52) Regulations.

ANIMALS AND ANIMAL PRODUCTS (IMPORT AND EXPORT) REGULATIONS (NORTHERN IRELAND) 1995 (No. 52) [£5·20], made under the European Communities Act 1972 (c.68), s.2(2); operative on April 10, 1995; replace, with amendments, and revoke the 1993 (No. 305) Regulations.

5187. Poultry disease

DISEASES OF POULTRY ORDER (NORTHERN IRELAND) 1995 (No. 465) [£3·20], made under S.I. 1981 No. 1115 (N.I. 22), arts. 2(3), 5(1), 10(6), 12(1), 14, 18(7), 19(e)(f)(g)(h)(i)(k), 44, 46(7A), 60(1); revokes S.R. & O. (N.I.) 1949 No. 192; S.R. & O. (N.I.) 1964 No. 199; S.R. & O. (N.I.) 1973 Nos. 477, 478; amends S.R. & O. (N.I.) 1983 No. 406. In force: January 15, 1996; implements, with S.R. & O. (N.I.) 1995 No. 464, the requirements of Dirs. 92/40/EEC and 92/66/EEC.

DISEASES OF POULTRY SCHEME ORDER (NORTHERN IRELAND) 1995 (No. 464) [£1·95], made under S.I. 1981 No. 1115 (N.I. 22), art. 8(1)(2). In force: January 15, 1996; implements, with S.R. & O. (N.I.) 1995 No. 465, Dirs. 92/40/EEC and 92/66/EEC.

5188. Racing pigeons

RACING PIGEONS (VACCINATION) REGULATIONS (NORTHERN IRELAND) 1995 (No. 168) [65p], made under the European Communities Act 1972 (c.68), s.2(2); operative on May 29, 1995; require racing pigeons entered in pigeon shows or races to have been vaccinated against Newcastle disease.

5189. Welfare

WELFARE OF ANIMALS REGULATIONS (NORTHERN IRELAND) 1995 (No. 172) [£3·70], made under the Welfare of Animals Act (Northern Ireland) 1972 (c.7), s.2(1) and the European Communities Act 1972 (c.68), s.2(2); operative on May 24, 1995 (part) and May 24, 1996 (remainder); replace, with amendments, and revoke, the 1987 (No. 360), 1989 (No. 4) and 1991 (No. 407) Regulations.

WELFARE OF ANIMALS (SCHEDULED OPERATIONS) (AMENDMENT) ORDER (NORTHERN IRELAND) 1995 (No. 173) [65p], made under the Welfare of Animals Act (Northern Ireland) 1972 (c.7), s.14(3); operative on June 12, 1995; amends Schedule 1 to the 1972 Act as respects the age at which certain operations may be performed without an anaesthetic.

5190. Wildlife

WILDLIFE (1995 ORDER) (COMMENCEMENT) ORDER (NORTHERN IRELAND) 1995 (No. 322 (C.6)) [65p], made under S.I. 1995 No. 761 (N.I. 6), art. 1; brings arts. 3 and 4 of the 1995 S.I. into operation on August 15 and September 15, 1995, respectively.

5191. Wildlife (Amendment) (Northern Ireland) Order 1995 (S.I. 1995 No. 761 (N.I. 6))

This Order repeals certain exceptions to the protection of wild birds in Pt. II of the Wildlife (Northern Ireland) Order 1985 and permits general licences to be issued to kill wild birds. The Order comes into operation on days to be appointed.

ARMED FORCES

5192. Sex discrimination

SEX DISCRIMINATION (NORTHERN IRELAND) ORDER 1976 (APPLICATION TO ARMED FORCES ETC) REGULATIONS 1995 (No. 318) [65p], made under the European Communities Act 1972 (c.68), s.2(2); operative on September 14, 1995; amends S.I. 1976 No. 1042 (N.I. 15) to meet obligations under Council Dir. 76/207/EEC in relation to the armed forces of the Crown.

ATOMIC ENERGY

5193. Radioactive substances—metrication

RADIOACTIVE SUBSTANCES (METRICATION) ORDER (NORTHERN IRELAND) 1995 (No. 297) [£1·55], made under the Radioactive Substances Act 1993 (c.12), ss.8(6)–(8), 11(1)(3), 15(2)(3); operative on September 1, 1995; amends the 1962 (Nos. 242, 244, 248, 249, 250), 1963 (Nos. 219, 222) and 1967 (No. 313) Orders.

AVIATION

5194. Airports—economic regulation

AIRPORTS (1994 ORDER) (COMMENCEMENT) ORDER (NORTHERN IRELAND) 1995 (No. 294 (C.4)) [65p], made under S.I. 1994 No. 426 (N.I. 1), art. 1(2); brings the 1994 S.I. into operation on September 1, 1995.

COMPANY LAW

5195. Audit exemption

COMPANIES (1986 ORDER) (AUDIT EXEMPTION) REGULATIONS (NORTHERN IRELAND) 1995 (No. 128) [£2·80], made under S.I. 1986 No. 1032 (N.I. 6), art. 265(1)(3); operative on May 1, 1995; exempt small companies which satisfy certain conditions from having their annual accounts audited.

5196. Fees

COMPANIES (FEES) REGULATIONS (NORTHERN IRELAND) 1995 (No. 312) [£1·55], made under S.I. 1986 No. 1032 (N.I. 6), art. 657(1)(a); operative on October 2, 1995; specify fees for the purposes of the 1986 S.I.

COMPANIES (FEES) (AMENDMENT) REGULATIONS (NORTHERN IRELAND) 1995 (No. 384) [65p], made under S.I. 1986 No. 1032 (N.I. 6), art. 657(1)(a);

operative on November 16, 1995; prescribe the fee for an application under art. 603A of the 1986 S.I.

COMPANIES (INSPECTORS' REPORTS AND RECORDS INSPECTION) (FEES) REGULATIONS (NORTHERN IRELAND) 1995 (No. 313) [£1·10], made under S.I. 1986 No. 1032 (N.I. 6), arts. 430(3), 675(1)(4), 681(1) and S.I. 1989 No. 2404 (N.I. 18), art. 21(4); operative on October 2, 1995; replace with amendments, and revoke, the 1987 (No. 258) Regulations.

5197. Forms

COMPANIES (FORMS) REGULATIONS (NORTHERN IRELAND) 1995 (No. 383) [£1·55], made under S.I. 1986 No. 1032 (N.I. 6), arts. 603A(2), 603D(4); operative on November 16, 1995; prescribe forms for the purposes of arts. 603A(2) and 603D(4) of the 1986 S.I.

CONSUMER PROTECTION

5198. Price indications—resale of tickets

PRICE INDICATIONS (RESALE OF TICKETS) REGULATIONS (NORTHERN IRELAND) 1995 (No. 258) [£1·55], made under S.I. 1987 No. 2049 (N.I. 20), art. 19; operative on July 24, 1995; require resellers of entertainment tickets to give specified price information to consumers.

5199. Price marking

PRICE MARKING (AMENDMENT) ORDER (NORTHERN IRELAND) 1995 (No. 231) [£2·40], made under the Prices Act 1974 (c.24), s.4; operative on July 3, 1995; amends the 1992 (No. 59) Order.

CONVEYANCING AND REAL PROPERTY

5200. Land registration

COMPULSORY REGISTRATION OF TITLE ORDER (NORTHERN IRELAND) 1995 (No. 412) [£1·10], made under the Land Registration Act (Northern Ireland) 1970 (c.18), s.25(1); operative on June 1, 1996; declares part of the Ards local government area to be a compulsory registration area under the 1970 Act.

5201. Registration of deeds—fees

REGISTRATION OF DEEDS (FEES) ORDER (NORTHERN IRELAND) 1995 (No. 317) [£1·55], made under the Registration of Deeds Act (Northern Ireland) 1970 (c.25), s.16(1); operative on October 2, 1995; increases fees for documents lodged in the registry of deeds and for other matters done in the registry; revokes the 1991 (No. 4) Order.

CRIMINAL EVIDENCE AND PROCEDURE

5202. Children's Evidence (Northern Ireland) Order 1995 (S.I. 1995 No. 757 (N.I. 3))

This Order makes further provision with respect to children as witnesses, sets out a procedure for transferring certain offences involving children direct to the Crown Court without committal proceedings and provides for testimony from child witnesses by video recordings. The Order comes into operation on days to be appointed.

5203. Confiscation orders

CRIMINAL JUSTICE (CONFISCATION) (ENFORCEMENT OF CONFISCATION ORDERS MADE IN ENGLAND AND WALES OR SCOTLAND) ORDER (NORTHERN IRELAND) 1995 (No. 411) [£1·10], made under S.I. 1990 No. 2588 (N.I. 17), art. 26; operative on December 12, 1995; provides for the enforcement of certain confiscation orders made in England and Wales or Scotland.

5204. Customs and Excise

POLICE AND CRIMINAL EVIDENCE (APPLICATION TO CUSTOMS AND EXCISE) (AMENDMENT) ORDER (NORTHERN IRELAND) 1995 SR 1995 456), made under the S.I. 1989 No. 1341 (NI.12), art.85(1); amends SR 1989 465. operative on January 1, 1996; [65p]. This Order confers powers of arrest on officers of Customs and Excise in respect of certain arrestable offences.

5205. Petty sessions districts

PETTY SESSIONS DISTRICTS (AMENDMENT) ORDER (NORTHERN IRELAND) 1995 (No. 5) [65p], made under S.I. 1981 No. 1675 (N.I. 26), art. 11(2); operative on January 16, 1995; amends the 1994 (No. 470) Order.

CRIMINAL LAW

5206. Drug offences

MISUSE OF DRUGS (AMENDMENT) REGULATIONS (NORTHERN IRELAND) 1995 (No. 305) [65p], made under the Misuse of Drugs Act 1971 (c.38), ss.7, 10, 31; operative on September 1, 1995; amend the 1986 (No. 52) and 1987 (No. 68) Regulations.

MISUSE OF DRUGS (AMENDMENT) (NO.2) REGULATIONS (NORTHERN IRELAND) 1995 SR 1995 480), made under the Misuse of Drugs Act 197 ss.7,10,31; amends SR 1986 52. operative on January 15, 1996; [£1·10]. These regulaions amend SR 1986 52.

MISUSE OF DRUGS (DESIGNATION) (VARIATION) ORDER (NORTHERN IRELAND) 1995 (No. 306) [65p], made under the Misuse of Drugs Act 1971 (c.38), s.7(4)(5); operative on September 1, 1995; amends the 1987 (No. 66) Order.

CRIMINAL SENTENCING

5207. Northern Ireland (Remission of Sentences) Act 1995 (c.47)

This Act allows the release on licence of persons serving sentences under s.14 Norther Ireland (Emergency Provisions) Act 1991 (c.24).

The Act received Royal Assent on November 8, 1995.

5208. Northern Ireland Remission of Sentences Act 1995 —commencement

NORTHERN IRELAND (REMISSION OF SENTENCES) ACT 1995 (COMMENCEMENT) ORDER 1995 (No. 2945 (C.64)) [65p], made under the Northern

Ireland (Remission of Sentences) Act 1995, s.2; brings the Act into force on November 17, 1995.

EDUCATION

5209. Curriculum

CURRICULUM (PROGRAMME OF STUDY AND ATTAINMENT TARGETS IN ART AND DESIGN) ORDER (NORTHERN IRELAND) 1995 (No. 203) [£1·10], made under S.I. 1989 No. 2406 (N.I. 20), art. 7(1)(a)(5); operative on August 1, 1995; specifies a programme of study and attainment targets for art and design and revokes the 1993 (No. 344) Order.

CURRICULUM (PROGRAMME OF STUDY AND ATTAINMENT TARGETS IN MUSIC) ORDER (NORTHERN IRELAND) 1995 (No. 205) [£1·10], made under S.I. 1989 No. 2406 (N.I. 20), art. 7(1)(a)(5); operative on August 1, 1995; specifies a programme of study and attainment targets for music and revokes the 1993 (No. 342) Order.

CURRICULUM (PROGRAMME OF STUDY AND ATTAINMENT TARGET IN TECHNOLOGY AND DESIGN) ORDER (NORTHERN IRELAND) 1995 (No. 206) [£1·10], made under S.I. 1989 No. 2406 (N.I. 20), art. 7(1)(a)(5); operative on August 1, 1995; specifies a programme of study and attainment targets for technology and design and revokes the 1993 (No. 343) Order.

CURRICULUM (PROGRAMMES OF STUDY AND ATTAINMENT TARGETS IN FRENCH, GERMAN, ITALIAN, SPANISH AND IRISH) ORDER (NORTHERN IRELAND) 1995 (No. 224) [£1·10], made under S.I. 1989 No. 2406 (N.I. 20), art. 7(1)(a)(5); operative on August 1, 1995; specifies programmes of study and attainment targets for French, German, Italian, Spanish and Irish and revokes the 1992 (No. 289) Order.

5210. Curriculum—exceptions

CURRICULUM (ENGLISH AND MATHEMATICS) (EXCEPTIONS) REGULATIONS (NORTHERN IRELAND) 1995 (No. 251) [65p]; made under S.I. 1989 No. 2406 (N.I. 20), art. 15(b); operative on August 1, 1995; set out an exception for some pupils as respects English or Mathematics in year 12.

5211. Education reform—1989 Order—commencement

EDUCATION REFORM (1989 ORDER) (COMMENCEMENT ORDER NO. 5) (AMENDMENT) ORDER (NORTHERN IRELAND) 1995 (No. 204 (C.2)) [£1·95], made under S.I. 1989 No. 2406 (N.I. 20), art. 1(3)(4); revokes the 1993 (No. 346) Order and part of the 1992 (No. 5) Order so as to cancel the introduction from August 1, 1995, of technology and design, art and design, music and French, German, Italian, Spanish or Irish as compulsory contributory subjects at key stage 4. It brings art. 6(1)(2) of, and Sched. 2 to, the 1989 S.I. into operation on August 1, 1995, for technology and design, art and design, music and French, German, Italian, Spanish or Irish as compulsory contributory subjects at key stage 3 and arts. 5(5) and 11(1)(e) into operation on August 1, 1995, for pupils in key stage 3.

5212. Grammar schools—charges

GRAMMAR SCHOOLS (CHARGES) (AMENDMENT) REGULATIONS (NORTHERN IRELAND) 1995 (No. 277) [65p], made under S.I. 1989 No. 2406 (N.I. 20), art. 132(2)(3); operative on September 1, 1995; amend the 1992 (No. 171) Regulations.

5213. Pupils' achievements—information

EDUCATION (INDIVIDUAL PUPILS' ACHIEVEMENTS) (INFORMATION) REGULATIONS (NORTHERN IRELAND) 1995 (No. 323) [£3·20], made under S.I.

1986 No. 594 (N.I. 3), arts. 17A(1)(2)(2A), 134(1) and S.I 1989 No. 2406 (N.I. 20), art. 31(2)(3); operative on September 12, 1995 (part), August 1, 1996 (part) and August 1, 1997 (remainder); replace with amendments, and revoke, the 1991 (No. 351) Regulations.

5214. Schools—suspension and expulsion of pupils

SCHOOLS (SUSPENSION AND EXPULSION OF PUPILS) REGULATIONS (NORTHERN IRELAND) 1995 (No. 99) [£1·10], made under S.I. 1986 No. 594 (N.I. 3), arts. 49(4), 134(1); operative on September 1, 1995; replace, with amendments, and revoke the 1985 (No. 202) Regulations.

5215. Secondary schools—admissions criteria

SECONDARY SCHOOLS (ADMISSIONS CRITERIA) REGULATIONS (NORTHERN IRELAND) 1995 (No. 303) [£1·10], made under S.I. 1989 No. 2406 (N.I. 20), art. 38(6); operative on September 4, 1995; replace, with amendments, and revoke, the 1994 (No. 342) Regulations; require, *inter alia*, grant-aided schools to draw up admission criteria for prospective pupils.

5216. Student loans

EDUCATION (STUDENT LOANS) REGULATIONS (NORTHERN IRELAND) 1995 (No. 279) [£3·20], made under S.I. 1990 No. 1506 (N.I. 11), art. 3(2), Sched. 2, paras. 1(1)(3)(4), 2(1), 3(4); operative on August 1, 1994; revoke, and replace with amendments, the 1994 (No. 230) Regulations.

5217. Students awards

STUDENTS AWARDS REGULATIONS (NORTHERN IRELAND) 1995 (No. 1) [£6·35], made under S.I. 1986 No. 594 (N.I. 3), arts. 50(1)(2), 134(1); operative on February 1, 1995; replace with amendments and revoke the 1993 (No. 439) Regulations on mandatory awards to students.

ELECTION LAW

5218. Parliamentary constitutencies

PARLIAMENTARY CONSTITUENCIES (NORTHERN IRELAND) ORDER 1995 (No. 2992) [£1·95], made under the Parliamentary Constituencies Act 1986, s.4 and Northern Ireland Constitution Act 1973, s.28(5). In force in accordance with art. 1(2); gives effect to the recommendations of the Boundary Commission for Northern Ireland in its report dated June 20, 1995. The report sets out proposals for parliamentary constituencies in Northern Ireland following a review of representation in the House of Commons of Northern Ireland. Article 3(1) amends s.1(1) of the Northern Ireland Assembly Act 1973 so that any future Northern Ireland Assembly shall consist of 90 members and art. 3(2) amends the Schedule to that Act by setting out new constituencies and the number of members to be returned for each.

EMPLOYMENT

5219. Employers' liability—compulsory insurance

EMPLOYERS' LIABILITY (COMPULSORY INSURANCE) GENERAL (AMENDMENT) REGULATIONS (NORTHERN IRELAND) 1995 (No. 50) [65p], made under S.I. 1972 No. 963 (N.I. 6), arts. 5(2), 10(1); operative on March 27, 1995; amend the 1975 (No. 231) Regulations as respects the limit of compulsory insurance.

5220. Employment protection—increase of limits

EMPLOYMENT PROTECTION (INCREASE OF LIMITS) ORDER (NORTHERN IRELAND) 1995 (No. 342) [£1·95], made under the Contracts of Employment and Redundancy Payments Act (Northern Ireland) 1965 (c.19), Sched. 3, para. 5(5), S.I. 1976 No. 1043 (N.I. 16), arts. 34(7), 35(5), 37(2), 37A(7), 70, 80(3) and S.I. 1976 No. 2147 (N.I. 28), arts. 5(5), 63(4); operative on September 27, 1995; increases various limits and amounts under the 1965 Act and the 1976 S.Is.

5221. Employment protection—part-time employees

EMPLOYMENT PROTECTION (PART-TIME EMPLOYEES) REGULATIONS (NORTHERN IRELAND) 1995 (No. 46) [£1·10], made under the European Communities Act 1972 (c.68), s.2(2); operative on March 19, 1995; give effect to Council Dirs. 75/117/EEC and 76/207/EEC as respects the employment rights of part-time employees.

5222. Fair employment—public authorities

FAIR EMPLOYMENT (SPECIFICATION OF PUBLIC AUTHORITIES) (AMENDMENT) ORDER (NORTHERN IRELAND) 1995 (No. 10) [£1·55], made under the Fair Employment (Northern Ireland) Act 1989 (c.32), s.25(1)(2); operative on February 1, 1995; specifies various bodies as public authorities for the purposes of Pt. II of the 1989 Act.

FAIR EMPLOYMENT (SPECIFICATION OF PUBLIC AUTHORITIES) (AMENDMENT NO. 2) ORDER (NORTHERN IRELAND) 1995 (No. 430) [£1·55], made under the Fair Employment (Northern Ireland) Act 1989, s.25(1)(2); amends S.R. 1989 No. 475. In force: January 1, 1996.

5223. Fair Employment (Amendment) (Northern Ireland) Order 1995 (S.I. 1995 No. 758 (N.I. 4))

This Order removes the limit of £35,000 on amounts awarded by the Fair Employment Tribunal under s.26 of the Fair Employment (Northern Ireland) Act 1976 and deals with interest on amounts awarded under s.26. The Order came into operation on May 16, 1995.

5224. Fair employment tribunal—remedies

FAIR EMPLOYMENT TRIBUNAL (REMEDIES) ORDER (NORTHERN IRELAND) 1995 (No. 240) [£1·55], made under the Fair Employment (Northern Ireland) Act 1976 (c.25), s.26(6A)(7), S.I. 1976 No. 1043 (N.I. 16), art. 61(3)(5)(6), and the Fair Employment (Northern Ireland) Act 1989 (c.32), s.6(3); operative on July 17, 1995; deals with interest on awards under s.26(1)(b) of the 1976 Act.

5225. Redundancies and transfer of undertakings

COLLECTIVE REDUNDANCIES AND TRANSFER OF UNDERTAKINGS (AMENDMENT) REGULATIONS (NORTHERN IRELAND) 1995 (No. 417) [£2·40], made under the European Communities Act 1972 (c.68), s.2(2); operative on December 3, 1995; ensure that, where there are to be redundancies or a transfer of an undertaking, the arrangements under legislation for consultation by the employer comply with Council Dirs. 77/187 and 75/129.

5226. Sex discrimination—lone parents—special treatment

SEX DISCRIMINATION (SPECIAL TREATMENT OF LONE PARENTS) ORDER (NORTHERN IRELAND) 1995 (No. 216) [65p], made under S.I. 1990 No. 246

(N.I. 2), art. 10(1)(3); operative on June 21, 1995; applies art. 10 of the 1990 S.I. to certain special treatment afforded to lone parents as respects jobskills.

ENVIRONMENTAL LAW

5227. Batteries and accumulators—dangerous substances

BATTERIES AND ACCUMULATORS (CONTAINING DANGEROUS SUBSTANCES) REGULATIONS (NORTHERN IRELAND) 1995 (No. 122) [£2·80], made under the European Communities Act 1972 (c.68), s.2(2); operative on April 26, 1995; implement Council Dir. 91/157/EEC and Commission Dir. 93/86/EEC on batteries and accumulators containing more than specified levels of mercury, cadmium or lead.

5228. Dog fouling

DOG FOULING (PRESCRIPTION OF PLACES) REGULATIONS (NORTHERN IRELAND) 1995 (No. 236) [65p], made under S.I. 1994 No. 1896 (N.I. 10), art. 4(1); operative on July 7, 1995; prescribe places where it is an offence for persons to permit a dog in their charge to deposit its excrement.

5229. Genetically modified organisms—release

GENETICALLY MODIFIED ORGANISMS (DELIBERATE RELEASE) (AMENDMENT) REGULATIONS (NORTHERN IRELAND) 1995 (No. 413) [£3·20], made under the European Communities Act 1972 (c.68), s.2(2) and S.I. 1991 No. 1714 (N.I. 19), arts. 8(1)(4)(5)(7), 19(1)(4); operative on December 8, 1995; implement Commission Dir. 94/15/EC on the deliberate release into the environment of genetically modified organisms.

5230. Home Energy Conservation Act 1995—commencement

HOME ENERGY CONSERVATION ACT 1995 (COMMENCEMENT) ORDER (NORTHERN IRELAND) 1995 SR 1995 455 (C.9)), made under the Home Energy Conservation Act 1995 ss.8(2), 9(2)(3). operative on bringing into operation various provisions of this Act on January 1, 1996, April 1, 1996; [65p]. This Order brings ss.3(1), 4(1)(2) of the 1995 Act into operation on January 1, 1996 and the remainder into operation on April 1, 1996.

5231. Litter

LITTER CONTROL AREAS (FORM OF DESIGNATION ORDER) REGULATIONS (NORTHERN IRELAND) 1995 (No. 238) [£1·10], made under S.I. 1994 No. 1896 (N.I. 10), art. 10(7); operative on July 7, 1995; set out the form of orders designating land as litter control areas.

LITTER CONTROL AREAS ORDER (NORTHERN IRELAND) 1995 (No. 237) [£1·10], made under S.I. 1994 No. 1896 (N.I. 10), art. 10(1)(2); operative on July 7, 1995; specifies descriptions of land which may be designated by district councils as litter control areas.

LITTER (DOG FAECES) ORDER (NORTHERN IRELAND) 1995 (No. 235) [65p], made under S.I. 1994 No. 1896 (N.I. 10), art. 2(7); operative on July 7, 1995; applies arts. 7–9 of the 1994 S.I. to dog faeces on certain land.

LITTER (DESIGNATION OF ROADS) (AMENDMENT) ORDER (NORTHERN IRELAND) 1995 (No. 18) [65p], made under S.I. 1994 No. 1896 (N.I. 10), art. 2(5); operative on February 27, 1995; designates part of the M3 for the purposes of the 1994 Order.

LITTER (FIXED PENALTY NOTICES) REGULATIONS (NORTHERN IRELAND) 1995 (No. 17) [£1·10]; made under S.I. 1994 No. 1896 (N.I. 10), art. 6(5);

operative on February 27, 1995; prescribe a form of notice under art. 6(5) of the 1994 Order and revoke the 1994 (No. 352) Regulations.

LITTER (NON-RELEVANT LAND) ORDER (NORTHERN IRELAND) 1995 (No. 184) [65p], made under S.I. 1994 No. 1896 (N.I. 10), art. 2(3); operative on June 30, 1995; designates certain tidal land as land which is not relevant for the purposes of the S.I. (S.I. 1994 No. 1896, (N.I. 10)).

5232. Natural habitats

CONSERVATION (NATURAL HABITATS, ETC.) REGULATIONS (NORTHERN IRELAND) 1995 (No. 380) [£6·35], made under the European Communities Act 1972 (c.68), s.2(2); operative on November 13, 1995; implement Council Dir. 92/43/EEC on the conservation of natural habitats, wild fauna and flora.

5233. Street litter—control notices

STREET LITTER (CONTROL NOTICES) ORDER (NORTHERN IRELAND) 1995 (No. 42) [£1·10], made under S.I. 1994 No. 1896 (N.I. 10), art. 14(1)(2); operative on March 31, 1995; specifies descriptions of premises and land in respect of which street litter control notices may be issued.

FAMILY LAW

5234. Polygamous Marriages (Northern Ireland) Order 1995

POLYGAMOUS MARRIAGES (NORTHERN IRELAND) ORDER 1995 (No. 3211 (NI.20)), made under the Northern Ireland Act 1974 Sched. 1, para. 1; amends 1992 c.7; S.I. 1978 No. NI 15; 1984 NI 14; 1989 NI 4. operative on February 14, 1996; [£1·55]. This Order makes the provision that a potentially polygamous marriage entered into by unmarried parties outside Northern Ireland shall be void if either party is domiciled in Northern Ireland. The Order is made to correspond with Part II of the Private International Law (Miscellaneous Provisions) Act 1995.

FIRE SERVICE

5235. Factory, office and shop premises

FIRE SERVICES (NON-CERTIFICATED FACTORY, OFFICE AND SHOP PREMISES) (REVOCATION) REGULATIONS (NORTHERN IRELAND) 1995 (No. 34) [65p], made under S.I. 1984 No. 1821 (N.I. 11), arts. 34(1)(3)(4), 52(1)(b); operative on March 13, 1995; revoke the 1986 (No. 352) Regulations.

FIREARMS AND EXPLOSIVES

5236. Prescribed forms

FIREARMS (PRESCRIBED FORMS) REGULATIONS (NORTHERN IRELAND) 1995 (No. 247) [£5·70], made under S.I. 1981 No. 155 (N.I. 2), arts. 10(2), 14(1), 15(1)(2), 16, 27(1)(2), 28(6), 34(1)(3)(5), 42(1), 58(1)(a)(1A); operative on July 3,

1995; replace, with amendments, and revoke, the 1981 (No. 132) and 1986 (No. 268) Regulations.

FISH AND FISHERIES

5237. Angling

FOYLE AREA (ANGLING) REGULATIONS 1995 (No. 196) [£2·80], made under the Foyle Fisheries Act 1952 (Rep. of Ir. No. 5), s.13(1), and the Foyle Fisheries Act (Northern Ireland) 1952 (c.5), s.13(1); operative on June 1, 1995; specify permitted methods of angling in certain waters in the Foyle Area and revoke the 1990 (No. 262) Regulations.

5238. Eel fishing

EEL FISHING (LICENCE DUTIES) REGULATIONS (NORTHERN IRELAND) 1995 SR 1995 489), made under the Fisheries Act (Northern Ireland) 1966 ss.15(1), 19(1); revokes SR 1994 438. operative on January 1, 1996; [£1·10]. These Regulations increase duties on licences for fishing engines for taking eels and revoke SR 1994 438.

5239. Fish health

FISH HEALTH (AMENDMENT) REGULATIONS (NORTHERN IRELAND) 1995 (No. 174) [£3·20], made under the European Communities Act 1972 (c.68), s.2(2); operative on May 24, 1995; amend the 1993 (No. 306) Regulations so as to implement Commission Decisions 93/44, 55 and 169/EEC and Council Dir. 93/54/EEC.

5240. Fishing engines

FOYLE AREA (LICENSING OF FISHING ENGINES) (AMENDMENT) REGULATIONS 1995 (No. 459) [£1·55], made under the Foyle Fisheries Act 1952, s.13(1)(2) and the Foyle Fisheries Act (Northern Ireland) 1952, s.13(1)(2); amend S.R. & O. (N.I.) 1976 No. 362; revoke S.R. & O. (N.I.) 1993 No. 481. In force: January 9, 1996; increase licence fees for nets and game fishing in the Foyle area.

5241. Fishing vessels—decommissioning

FISHING VESSELS (DECOMMISSIONING) SCHEME (NORTHERN IRELAND) 1995 (No. 391) [£2·40], made under S.I. 1987 No. 166 (N.I. 1), art. 17(1)(2); operative on November 13, 1995; provides for the payment of grants towards decommissioning, by scrapping, vessels which have predominately fished for nephrops in 1994.

5242. Grants

FISHERIES AND AQUACULTURE STRUCTURES (GRANTS) REGULATIONS (NORTHERN IRELAND) 1995 (No. 385) [£2·80], made under the European Communities Act 1972 (c.68), s.2(2); operative on November 6, 1995; provide for the payment of grants in respect of certain investments or projects relating to aquaculture and fisheries.

FOOD AND DRUGS

5243. Animals, meat and meat products

ANIMALS, MEAT AND MEAT PRODUCTS (EXAMINATION FOR RESIDUES AND MAXIMUM RESIDUE LIMITS) (AMENDMENT) REGULATIONS

(NORTHERN IRELAND) 1995 (No. 97) [£2·40], made under S.I. 1991 No. 762 (N.I. 7), arts. 15(1)(a)(b)(f)(3), 16(1), 25(1)(2)(a)(b)(3), 26(3), 32, 47(2), 48(2), Sched. 1, paras. 3, 7; operative on April 15, 1995; amend the 1992 (No. 39) Regulations and implement Council Reg. 2377/90/EEC in relation to maximum residue limits of veterinary medicinal products in foodstuffs of animal origin.

5244. Bovine offal

BOVINE OFFAL (PROHIBITION) (AMENDMENT) REGULATIONS (NORTHERN IRELAND) 1995 (No. 136) [£1·10], made under S.I. 1989 No. 846 (N.I. 6), arts. 15(1)(2), 72(1)(4); operative on April 28, 1995; amend the 1990 (No. 30) Regulations.

SPECIFIED BOVINE OFFAL ORDER (NORTHERN IRELAND) 1995 (No. 458) [£3·20], made under S.I. 1981 No. 1115 (N.I. 22), arts. 2(3), 5(1), 19(b)(e)(f)(k), 29(1)(2), 32, 44, 46(7A), 60(1); revokes S.R. & O. (N.I.) 1992 No. 215. In force: December 21, 1995; implements measures relating to bovine offal, bovine spongiform encephelopathy, and disposal of animal waste: Decision 94/474, which repealed Decisions 89/469 and 90/200; Dir. 90/667, which amended Dir 90/425; Decision 92/562 and Decision 94/382.

5245. Bovine offal—food safety. See FOOD AND DRUGS, §2409.

5246. Dairy products—hygiene

DAIRY PRODUCTS (HYGIENE) REGULATIONS (NORTHERN IRELAND) 1995 (No. 201) [£6·95]; made under the European Communities Act 1972 (c.68), s.2(2), and S.I. 1991 No. 762 (N.I. 7), arts. 15(1)–(3), 16(1)(2), 17(2), 18, 25, 26(3), 27(2), 30(9), 32(1)(2), 47(2), 48(2), Sched. 1, paras. 4(b), 5, 6(1)(a), 7(1); operative on July 1, 1995; implement Council Dir. 92/46/EEC in relation to health rules for the production and marketing of raw milk, heat-treated milk and milk-based products, and amend the 1977 (No. 8) Regulations, and revoke the 1966 (No. 204), 1980 (No. 436), 1981 (No. 233), 1983 (No. 336), 1987 (No. 229), 1988 (Nos. 420, 436), 1990 (No. 13) and 1991 (Nos. 151, 526) Regulations and the 1992 (No. 302) Order.

5247. Extraction solvents

EXTRACTION SOLVENTS IN FOOD (AMENDMENT) REGULATIONS (NORTHERN IRELAND) 1995 (No. 263) [65p], made under S.I. 1991 No. 762 (N.I. 7), arts. 15(1)(a)(c), 16(1), 25(1)(a)(3), 47(2); operative on August 7, 1995; amend the 1993 (No. 330) Regulations.

5248. Food safety—fishery products

FOOD SAFETY (FISHERY PRODUCTS) (IMPORT CONDITIONS AND MISCELLANEOUS AMENDMENTS) REGULATIONS (NORTHERN IRELAND) 1995 (No. 113) [£4·70], made under the European Communities Act 1972 (c.68), s.2(2) and S.I. 1991 No. 762 (N.I. 7), arts. 15(1)(3), 16(1), 25(3), 26(3), 47(2), 48(2), Sched. 1, paras. 2, 5(1)(2), 6(1), 7(1); operative on May 1, 1995; specify conditions for importing fishery products.

5249. Food safety—general hygiene

FOOD SAFETY (GENERAL FOOD HYGIENE) REGULATIONS (NORTHERN IRELAND) 1995 (No. 360) [£3·70], made under the European Communities Act 1972 (c.68), s.2(2) and S.I. 1991 No. 762 (N.I. 7), arts. 15(1), 16(1), 25(1)(3), 26(3), 47(2); operative on October 23, 1995; implement Council Dir. 93/43/EEC on the hygiene of foodstuffs.

5250. Food safety—shellfish

FOOD SAFETY (LIVE BIVALVE MOLLUSCS AND OTHER SHELLFISH) (IMPORT CONDITIONS AND MISCELLANEOUS AMENDMENTS) REGU-

LATIONS (NORTHERN IRELAND) 1995 (No. 112) [£3·70], made under the European Communities Act 1972 (c.68), s.2(2) and S.I. 1991 No. 762 (N.I. 7), arts. 15(1)(3), 16(1), 25(3), 26(3), 47(2), 48(2), Sched. 1, paras. 2(2), 5(1)(2), 6(1), 7(1); operative on May 1, 1995; specify conditions for importing live bivalve molluscs and other shellfish.

5251. Food safety—temperature control

FOOD SAFETY (TEMPERATURE CONTROL) REGULATIONS (NORTHERN IRELAND) 1995 (No. 377) [£2·80], made under S.I. 1991 No. 762 (N.I. 7), arts. 15(1), 16(1), 25(1)(3), 26(3), 47(2); operative on November 20, 1995; replace, with amendments, and revoke, the 1964 (No. 129), 1990 (No. 301) and 1991 (No. 383) Regulations.

5252. Fruit juices

FRUIT JUICES AND FRUIT NECTARS (AMENDMENT) REGULATIONS (NORTHERN IRELAND) 1995 (No. 106) [65p], made under S.I. 1991 No. 762 (N.I. 7), arts. 15(1)(a)(c)(e), 16(1); operative on May 1, 1995; amend the definition of "fruit nectar" in the 1977 (No. 182) Regulations.

5253. Infant formula and follow-on formula

INFANT FORMULA AND FOLLOW-ON FORMULA REGULATIONS (NORTHERN IRELAND) 1995 (No. 85) [£4·15], made under the European Communities Act 1972 (c.68), s.2(2) and S.I. 1991 No. 762 (N.I. 7), arts. 15(1)(a)(b)(e)(f), 16(1), 25(1)(3), 26(3), 47(2); operative on April 17, 1995; implement Commission Dirs. 91/321/EEC and 92/52/EEC on infant formulae and follow-on formulae (certain foods for infants and young children).

5254. Meat—hygiene

MEAT (HYGIENE, INSPECTION AND EXAMINATIONS FOR RESIDUES) (CHARGES) REGULATIONS (NORTHERN IRELAND) 1995 (No. 431) [£2·80], made under the European Communities Act 1972, s.2(2); amend S.R. 1992 No. 39; S.R. 1995 No. 396; revoke S.R. 1991 No. 6. In force: December 19, 1995 for reg. 12 (with reg. 11 so far as may be necessary to enable the Department or a district council to exercise the power conferred by reg. 12) and January 7, 1996 for remainder. These Regulations implement Council Dir. 85/73 in relation to fees for health inspections of certain meat.

5255. Mechanically recovered meat

MECHANICALLY RECOVERED MEAT REGULATIONS (NORTHERN IRELAND) 1995 SR 1995 470), made under the S.I. 1989 No. 846 (NI.6), arts 15(1)(2)(i). In force: December 18, 1995; [£1·10]. These Regulations impose restrictions on the use of the vertebral column of bovine animals and require premises on which meat is recovered by mechanical means from bovine animals to be registered.

5256. Plastic materials—contact with food

PLASTIC MATERIALS AND ARTICLES IN CONTACT WITH FOOD (AMENDMENT) REGULATIONS (NORTHERN IRELAND) 1995 (No. 107) [£4·70], made under the European Communities Act 1972 (c.68), s.2(2) and S.I. 1991 No. 762 (N.I. 7), arts. 15(2), 16(1), 25(1)(a)(3), 26(3), 32, 47(2); operative on May 1, 1995; amend the 1993 (No. 173) Regulations and implement Commission Dirs. 93/8/EEC and 93/9/EEC relating to plastic materials and articles intended to come into contact with foodstuffs.

5257. Spirit drinks

SPIRIT DRINKS (AMENDMENT) REGULATIONS (NORTHERN IRELAND) 1995 (No. 105) [£1·95], made under the European Communities Act 1972 (c.68), s.2(2) and S.I. 1991 No. 762 (N.I. 7), art. 16(2); operative on May 1, 1995; amend the 1990 (No. 219) Regulations by making provision for the enforcement and execution of certain provisions.

5258. Welfare foods

WELFARE FOODS (AMENDMENT) REGULATIONS (NORTHERN IRELAND) 1995 (No. 211) [65p], made under S.I. 1988 No. 594 (N.I. 2), art. 13(3)(4); operative on June 26, 1995; amend the 1988 (No. 137) Regulations.

GAMING AND WAGERING

5259. Bingo

GAMING (BINGO) (AMENDMENT) REGULATIONS (NORTHERN IRELAND) 1995 (No. 344) [65p], made under S.I. 1985 No. 1204 (N.I. 11), art. 76(2); operative on October 26, 1995; increase a maximum charge under the 1987 (No. 8) Regulations; revoke the 1992 (No. 42) Regulations.

5260. Fees

BETTING, GAMING, LOTTERIES AND AMUSEMENTS WITH PRIZES (VARIATION OF FEES AND MONETARY LIMITS) ORDER (NORTHERN IRELAND) 1995 (No. 343) [£1·55], made under S.I. 1985 No. 1204 (N.I. 11), arts. 2(2), 37(2)(5), 75(2), 76(5), 77(4), 111(8), 115(9), 126(15), 128(3), 136(15), 154(7); increases fees and amounts relating to betting, gaming, lotteries and amusements with prizes.

5261. Horse racing—charges on bookmakers

HORSE RACING (CHARGES ON BOOKMAKERS) ORDER (NORTHERN IRELAND) 1995 (No. 198) [65p], made under S.I. 1990 No. 1508 (N.I. 12), art. 9(1); operative on July 1, 1995; increases charges payable by bookmakers under art. 9 of the 1990 S.I. and revokes the 1994 (No. 189) Order.

5262. Variation of monetary limits

GAMING (VARIATION OF MONETARY LIMITS) ORDER (NORTHERN IRELAND) 1995 (No. 442) [£1·10], made under S.I. 1985 No. 204 (N.I. 11), arts. 106(3), 108(16); amends S.I. 1985 No. 1204 (N.I. 11); S.R. 1987 No. 186; S.R. 1990 No. 238; revokes S.R. 1993 No. 88. In force: January 15, 1996; increases certain monetary limits under S.I. 1995 No. 1204.

HEALTH AND SAFETY AT WORK

5263. Borehold sites and operations

BOREHOLE SITES AND OPERATIONS REGULATIONS (NORTHERN IRELAND) 1995 SR 1995 491), made under the S.I. 1978 No. 1039 (NI.9), arts.17(1)(2)(4)(5)(6), 55(2), Sched. 3, paras. 1(1)(2), 5, 7, 8, 10, 11, 13, 14(1), 15, 17, 20(b). operative on March 11, 1996; [£3·20. Gives effect to provisions of Dir 92/91 (OJ L348, 28 November, 1992).

5264. Chemicals—hazard information and packaging

CHEMICALS (HAZARD INFORMATION AND PACKAGING FOR SUPPLY) REGULATIONS (NORTHERN IRELAND) 1995 (No. 60) [£7·65], made under the

European Communities Act 1972 (c.68), s.2(2) and S.I. 1978 No. 1039 (N.I. 9), arts. 17(1)–(6), 54(1)(4), 55(2), Sched. 3, paras. 1(1)(4)(5), 2, 14, 15; operative on March 31, 1995; replace with amendments, and revoke, the 1993 (No. 412) Regulations and revoke the 1986 (No. 758), 1990 (No. 1736) and 1993 (No. 1546) Regulations.

5265. Construction—design and management

CONSTRUCTION (DESIGN AND MANAGEMENT) REGULATIONS (NORTHERN IRELAND) 1995 (No. 209) [£4·15]; made under S.I. 1978 No. 1039 (N.I. 9), arts. 17(1)–(4)(6), 20(2), 43(2), 55(2), Sched. 3, paras. 1(1), 5(1), 13, 14(1), 15, 19, 20; operative on June 26, 1995; implement most of Council Dir. 92/57/EEC in relation to requirements at temporary or mobile construction sites.

5266. Dangerous goods—carriage by road and rail

CARRIAGE OF DANGEROUS GOODS BY ROAD AND RAIL (CLASSIFICATION, PACKAGING AND LABELLING) REGULATIONS (NORTHERN IRELAND) 1995 (No. 47) [£6·95], made under S.I. 1978 No. 1039 (N.I. 9), arts. 17(1)–(6), 20(2), 54(1)(4), 55(2), Sched. 3, paras. 1(1)–(4), 2, 3(1), 5, 11, 13–15; operative on March 30, 1995; deal with the classification, packaging and labelling of dangerous goods for carriage by road or rail.

5267. Electrical equipment—explosive atmospheres

ELECTRICAL EQUIPMENT FOR EXPLOSIVE ATMOSPHERES (CERTIFICATION) REGULATIONS (NORTHERN IRELAND) 1995 (No. 275) [£1·55]; made under the European Communities Act 1972 (c.68), s.2(2); operative on August 21, 1995; amend the 1990 (No. 284) Regulations to implement Commission Dirs. 94/26 and 44/EEC in relation to electrical equipment for use in potentially explosive atmospheres.

5268. Explosives—harbour areas

EXPLOSIVES IN HARBOUR AREAS REGULATIONS (NORTHERN IRELAND) 1995 (No. 87) [£5·70], made under S.I. 1978 No. 1039 (N.I. 9), arts. 17(1)–(5)(6)(a)(b), 40(2)(4)(6), 54(1)(3), 55(2), Sched. 3, paras. 1(1)–(4), 2, 3, 5, 6, 8, 10, 11, 12(1), 13, 14(1), 15, 17(a), 19, 20(a)–(c), 21; operative on April 17, 1995; control the carriage, loading, unloading and storage of explosives in harbours and harbour areas; revoke the 1977 (No. 890) Regulations.

5269. Gas safety—installation and use

GAS SAFETY (INSTALLATION AND USE) REGULATIONS (NORTHERN IRELAND) 1995 (No. 3) [£4·15]; made under S.I. 1978 No. 1039 (N.I. 9), arts. 17(1)(2)(4)–(6), 55(2), Sched. 3, paras. 1(1)–(3), 11, 15, 19; operative on February 20, 1995 (part), January 20, 1996 (part) and September 1, 1996 (remainder); impose requirements as to the installation and use of gas fittings.

5270. Mines

MINES MISCELLANEOUS HEALTH AND SAFETY PROVISIONS REGULATIONS (NORTHERN IRELAND) 1995 (No. 379) [£1·95], made under S.I. 1978 No. 1039 (N.I. 9), arts. 17(1)–(4), 55(2), Sched. 3, paras. 1(1)(2), 7, 8, 10, 11, 13, 15, 17(a), 20(b); operative on December 31, 1995; implement, in relation to mines, Council Dir. 92/104/EEC on the health and safety of workers in surface and underground mineral extracting industries and contain other provisions about mines.

5271. Mines and quarries

MINES AND QUARRIES (TIPS AND TIPPING PLANS) REGULATIONS (NORTHERN IRELAND) 1995 (No. 296) [£4·70], made under S.I. 1978 No. 1039

(N.I. 9), arts. 17(1)–(5), 55(2), Sched. 3, paras. 1(1)(c), 5(1), 13, 14(1), 15, 17(a), 19, 20; operative on September 1, 1995; set out requirements notably as to the provision of information relating to tips and the drainage, maintenance and inspection of tips in mines and quarries.

5272. Offshore installations and pipelines

OFFSHORE INSTALLATIONS (PREVENTION OF FIRE AND EXPLOSION, AND EMERGENCY RESPONSE) REGULATIONS (NORTHERN IRELAND) 1995 (No. 345) [£3·20], made under S.I. 1978 No. 1039 (N.I. 9), arts. 17(1)–(3)(5), 55(2), Sched. 3, paras. 1(2), 7, 8, 10, 11, 12(1)(3), 13, 14(1), 15, 17, 19; operative on October 9, 1995; contain requirements for the protection of persons on offshore oil and gas installations from fire and explosion and for securing effective response in emergencies; revoke S.I. 1976 No. 1542, S.I. 1977 No. 486 and S.I. 1978 No. 611 and the 1994 (No. 239) Regulations.

OFFSHORE INSTALLATIONS AND PIPELINE WORKS (MANAGEMENT AND ADMINISTRATION) REGULATIONS (NORTHERN IRELAND) 1995 (No. 340) [£3·20], made under S.I. 1978 No. 1039 (N.I. 9), arts. 17(1)–(3)(5), 55(2), Sched. 3, paras. 5, 13, 14(1) 15; operative on October 9, 1995 (part) and June 20, 1997 (remainder); implement certain provisions of Council Dirs. 92/91/EEC, on the safety and health protection of workers in the mineral-extracting industries through drilling, and 89/391/EEC, on improvements in the safety and health of workers.

5273. Quarries

QUARRIES MISCELLANEOUS HEALTH AND SAFETY PROVISIONS REGULATIONS (NORTHERN IRELAND) 1995 (No. 378) [£2·80]; made under S.I. 1978 No. 1039 (N.I. 9), arts. 17(1)–(3), 55(2), Sched. 3, paras. 1(1)(2), 7, 8, 10, 11, 13, 14(1), 15, 17, 20(b); operative on December 31, 1995 (part) and October 5, 1998 (remainder); implement, in relation to quarries and mines above ground, Council Dirs. 92/91 and 104/EEC on the health and safety of workers in surface and underground mineral extracting industries and contain other provisions about quarries.

5274. Substances hazardous to health

CONTROL OF SUBSTANCES HAZARDOUS TO HEALTH REGULATIONS (NORTHERN IRELAND) 1995 (No. 51) [£5·70]; made under S.I. 1978 No. 1039 (N.I. 9), arts. 2(5), 17(1)–(6), 55(2), Sched. 3, paras. 1(1)(2), 2(1), 5(1), 7, 8, 10, 12(1)(3), 13, 14(1), 15; operative on March 30, 1995; impose duties on employers and employees in relation to exposure to substances hazardous to health; revoke the 1982 (No. 273), 1990 (No. 374), 1992 (No. 61) and 1993 (No. 41) Regulations.

5275. Work equipment

PROVISION AND USE OF WORK EQUIPMENT (AMENDMENT) REGULATIONS (NORTHERN IRELAND) 1995 (No. 26) [£1·10]; made under S.I. 1978 No. 1039 (N.I. 9), art. 17(1)(2), Sched. 3, para. 1(1) (3); operative on March 13, 1995; update references to European Union directives in the 1993 (No. 19) Regulations.

HOUSING

5276. Housing benefit

HOUSING BENEFIT (GENERAL) (AMENDMENT) REGULATIONS (NORTHERN IRELAND) 1995 (No. 64) [£1·10], made under the Social Security Contributions and Benefits (Northern Ireland) Act 1992 (c.7), ss.122(1)(d), 132(1)(3)(4)(d), 171(5) and the Social Security Administration (Northern Ireland) Act 1992 (c.8), ss.5(1)(e), 61(3), 73(1); operative on March 6, 1995; amend the 1987 (No. 461) Regulations.

HOUSING BENEFIT (GENERAL) (AMENDMENT NO. 2) REGULATIONS (NORTHERN IRELAND) 1995 (No. 84) [£1·95], made under the Social Security Contributions and Benefits (Northern Ireland) Act 1992 (c.7), ss.122(1)(d), 129(4), 131(1), 132(3)(4)(b); operative on April 1, 1995 (part) and April 3, 1995 (remainder); amend the 1987 (No. 461) Regulations as respects patients, non-dependant deductions, applicable amounts and sums to be disregarded.

HOUSING BENEFIT (GENERAL) (AMENDMENT NO. 3) REGULATIONS (NORTHERN IRELAND) 1995 (No. 89) [£1·55], made under the Social Security Contributions and Benefits (Northern Ireland) Act 1992 (c.7), ss.122(1)(d), 131(1), 132(1)(3)(4)(a)(b), 133(2)(d)(i)(h)(l), 171(5) and the Social Security Administration (Northern Ireland) Act 1992 (c.8), s.5(1)(l)(p); operative on April 1, 1995 (part) and April 3, 1995 (remainder); amend the 1987 (No. 461) Regulations.

HOUSING BENEFIT (MISCELLANEOUS AMENDMENTS) REGULATIONS (NORTHERN IRELAND) 1995 (No. 129) [£2·80], made under the Social Security Contributions and Benefits (Northern Ireland) Act 1992 (c.7), ss.122(1)(d), 129(2)(4), 131(1), 132(3)(4)(a)(b), the Social Security Administration (Northern Ireland) Act 1992 (c.8), s.120(1)(2) and S.I. 1992 No. 1898 (N.I. 12), art. 14(1); operative on various dates in April, 1995; amend the 1987 (No. 461) and 1988 (No. 118) Regulations.

HOUSING BENEFIT AND INCOME SUPPORT (GENERAL) (AMENDMENT) REGULATIONS (NORTHERN IRELAND) 1995 (No. 101) [£1·95], made under the Social Security Contributions and Benefits (Northern Ireland) Act 1992 (c.7), ss.122(1)(a)(d), 131(1), 133(2)(h)(i), 171(5); operative on April 1, 1995 (part), April 3, 1995 (part) and April 10, 1995 (remainder); amend the 1987 (Nos. 459 and 461) Regulations as respects a person's temporary absence from home.

5277. Repairs—grants

REPAIRS GRANTS (APPROPRIATE PERCENTAGE) ORDER (NORTHERN IRELAND) 1995 (No. 284) [£1·10], made under S.I. 1992 No. 1725 (N.I. 15), art. 74(3), Sched. 3, para. 4(3); operative on September 4, 1995; amends percentages in para. 4(2) of Sched. 3 to the 1992 S.I.

5278. Replacement grants

HOUSING (REPLACEMENT GRANT) (AMENDMENT) REGULATIONS (NORTHERN IRELAND) 1995 (No. 242) [£1·10], made under S.I. 1992 No. 1725 (N.I. 15), art. 73; operative on July 21, 1995; amend the 1992 (No. 378) Regulations.

5279. Secure tenancies

SECURE TENANCIES (ABANDONED PROPERTY) ORDER (NORTHERN IRELAND) 1995 (No. 299) [£1·10], made under S.I. 1983 No. 1118 (N.I. 15), art. 41(6); operative on September 5, 1995; sets out the procedure to be followed by landlords in relation to property found in houses repossessed under the 1983 S.I.

INDUSTRIAL AND FRIENDLY SOCIETIES

5280. Credit unions—authorised investments

CREDIT UNIONS (AUTHORISED INVESTMENTS) REGULATIONS (NORTHERN IRELAND) 1995 (No. 31) [£1·55], made under S.I. 1985 No. 1205

(N.I. 12), art. 33(1); operative on March 21, 1995; specify authorised investments for credit unions and revoke the 1986 (No. 129) Regulations.

INSOLVENCY

5281. Partnerships

INSOLVENT PARTNERSHIPS ORDER (NORTHERN IRELAND) 1995 (No. 225) [£12·90], made under S.I. 1989 No. 2404 (N.I. 18), art. 24(1) and S.I. 1989 No. 2405 (N.I. 19), art. 364; operative on September 1, 1995; replaces, with amendments, and revokes, the 1991 (No. 361) Order.

5282. Rules

INSOLVENCY (AMENDMENT) RULES (NORTHERN IRELAND) 1995 (No. 291) [£1·10], made under the Registration of Deeds Act (Northern Ireland) 1970 (c.25), s.19(3) and S.I. 1989 No. 2405 (N.I. 19), art. 359; operative on October 1, 1995; amend the 1991 (No. 364) Rules.

LANDLORD AND TENANT

5283. Lands Tribunal decision

A applied under art. 5 of the Property (Northern Ireland) Order 1978 for the extinguishment of a covenant in a fee farm grant dated March 4, 1952, prohibiting the erection of more than one additional house on the premises granted.

Held, that the covenant should be modified to allow the erection of three additional houses on condition that they complied with planning permission already granted.

FARQUHARSON'S APPLICATION, *Re* (R/1/1994), Lands Tribunal.

5284. Lands Tribunal decision

A applied under art. 5 of the Property (Northern Ireland) Order 1978 for the modification of a covenant in a sub-fee farm grant of October 2, 1935, prohibiting the use of the premises for the sale of intoxicating liquor.

Held, that the covenant should be modified to permit the sale of intoxicating liquor for consumption off the premises, in view of (1) the purposes of the covenant; (2) the change in the character of the neighbourhood; (3) the lack of benefits secured to the objectors; and (4) the unreasonable impediment imposed by the covenant on the proposed change of use.

ANDREWS v. DAVIS (R/17/1994), Lands Tribunal.

5285. Lands Tribunal decision

B applied under art. 5 of the Property (Northern Ireland) Order 1978 for the extinguishment of covenants in leases of 1899 and 1903 and an underlease of 1944, all of which prohibited the use of the premises for the purposes of any trade or business.

Held, that the covenant in the underlease should be extinguished and that the covenants in the other leases should be extinguished in so far as they affected the premises demised by the underlease.

BELL v. NIXON (R/11/1994), Lands Tribunal.

5286. Lands Tribunal decision

M applied under art. 5 of the Property (Northern Ireland) Order 1978 for the effective extinguishment of a covenant in a lease of December 22, 1947, requiring the use of the premises as a public house.

Held, that the application should be granted, in view of (1) the purposes of the covenant; (2) the change in the character of the neighbourhood from residential to commercial use and its neglect and decline; (3) the dissolution of the company originally entitled to the benefit of the covenant; (4) the unreasonable impediment imposed by the covenant on the proposed change of use.

McKEE v. O'CALLAGHAN (R/13/1993), Lands Tribunal.

5287. Lands Tribunal decision

[Leasehold (Enlargement and Extension) Act (Northern Ireland) 1971 (c.7), s.24.]

R applied under s.24 of the Leasehold (Enlargement and Extension) Act (Northern Ireland) 1971 to acquire the freehold of premises. The Tribunal was asked to decide, as a preliminary point, whether the lease under which B occupied a dwelling was granted "by reason of" the 1971 Act.

Held, that since the dominant cause of the grant of the lease was the 1971 Act, it was granted "by reason of" that Act.

BELL v. KER (R/16/1994), Lands Tribunal.

5288. Lands Tribunal decision

[Leasehold (Enlargement and Extension) Act (Northern Ireland) 1971 (c.7), s.24.]

A applied under s.24 of the Leasehold (Enlargement and Extension) Act (Northern Ireland) 1971 to acquire the freehold of premises.

Held, allowing the application, that the registrar should be appointed to execute the conveyance, since the person required to convey it was unknown or could not be ascertained.

ERWIN AND ERWIN, *Re* (R/6/1993), Lands Tribunal.

5289. Rent—registered rents—increase

REGISTERED RENTS (INCREASE) ORDER (NORTHERN IRELAND) 1995 (No. 29) [65p], made under S.I. 1978 No. 1050 (N.I. 20), art. 33(2); operative on March 6, 1995; increases rents registered under Pt. V of the 1978 Order by 7.25 per cent.

LEGAL AID

5290. Criminal proceedings—costs

LEGAL AID IN CRIMINAL PROCEEDINGS (COSTS) (AMENDMENT) RULES (NORTHERN IRELAND) 1995 (No. 243) [£1·95], made under S.I. 1981 No. 228 (N.I. 8), art. 36(3); operative on June 29, 1995; amend the 1992 (No. 314) Rules by increasing the remuneration for certain work and altering the date after which certain work may be remunerated at discretionary rates.

5291. Financial conditions

LEGAL AID (FINANCIAL CONDITIONS) REGULATIONS (NORTHERN IRELAND) 1995 (No. 77) [£1·10], made under S.I. 1981 No. 228 (N.I. 8), arts. 9(2), 12(2), 22, 27; operative on April 10, 1995; increase certain limits of eligibility for legal aid; revoke the 1994 (No. 97) Regulations.

5292. Legal advice and assistance

LEGAL ADVICE AND ASSISTANCE (AMENDMENT) REGULATIONS (NORTHERN IRELAND) 1995 (No. 76) [£1·10], made under S.I. 1981 No. 228

(N.I. 8), arts. 7(2), 22, 27; operative on April 10, 1995; amend the scale of contributions in the 1981 (No. 366) Regulations and revoke the 1994 (No. 98) Regulations.

LEGAL ADVICE AND ASSISTANCE (FINANCIAL CONDITIONS) REGULATIONS (NORTHERN IRELAND) 1995 (No. 75) [65p], made under S.I. 1981 No. 228 (N.I. 8), arts. 3(2), 7(3), 22, 27; operative on April 10, 1995; increase certain limits of eligibility for legal advice and assistance and revoke the 1994 (No. 96) Regulations.

LITERARY AND SCIENTIFIC INSTITUTIONS

5293. Arts Council

ARTS COUNCIL (1995 ORDER) (COMMENCEMENT) ORDER (NORTHERN IRELAND) 1995 (No. 304 (C.5)) [65p], made under S.I. 1995 No. 1623 (N.I. 8), art. 1(2); brings the 1995 S.I. into operation on September 1, 1995.

5294. Constitution and functions of Art Council

Arts Council (Northern Ireland) Order 1995 (S.I. 1995 No. 1623 (N.I. 8)). This Order sets out the constitution and functions of the Arts Council for Northern Ireland. The Order comes into operation on a day to be appointed.

5295. Constitution and functions of governors of Observatory

Armagh Observatory and Planetarium (Northern Ireland) Order 1995 (S.I. 1995 No. 1622 (N.I. 7)). This Order sets out the constitution and functions of the Governors of the Armagh Observatory and Planetarium. The Order came into operation on August 29, 1995.

LOCAL GOVERNMENT

5296. Change of name

Order made under the Local Government Act (Northern Ireland) 1972 (c.9), s.51(1):

S.R. 1995 No. 325 (change of name—Armagh district council) [65p].

5297. Defined activities—exemptions

LOCAL GOVERNMENT (DEFINED ACTIVITIES) (EXEMPTIONS) ORDER (NORTHERN IRELAND) 1995 (No. 364) [£1·10], made under S.I. 1992 No. 810 (N.I. 6), arts. 4(8), 16(3); operative on November 1, 1995, specifies situations in which work will not be treated as falling within a defined activity for the purposes of art. 4(8) of the 1992 S.I.; revokes the 1992 (No. 520) Order.

5298. Designated area

Order made under S.I. 1989 No. 490 (N.I. 2):

Art. 3(2)(5): S.R. 1995 No. 30 (alteration of Laganside designated area) [65p].

5299. Economic development

PROMOTION OF ECONOMIC DEVELOPMENT (INCREASE OF FINANCIAL LIMIT) ORDER (NORTHERN IRELAND) 1995 (No. 45) [65p], made under S.I.

1992 No. 810 (N.I. 6), art. 28(4); operative on April 1, 1995; increases a financial limit in art. 28(1) of the 1992 S.I.

5300. Functional work

LOCAL GOVERNMENT (COMPETITION IN FUNCTIONAL WORK) REGULATIONS (NORTHERN IRELAND) 1995 (No. 362) [£1·55], made under S.I. 1992 No. 810 (N.I. 6), art. 7(3)(4); operative on November 1, 1995; describe the nature of the work which certain councils may not carry out unless conditions designed to ensure competition are fulfilled.

LOCAL GOVERNMENT (SPECIFIED PERIODS FOR FUNCTIONAL WORK) REGULATIONS (NORTHERN IRELAND) 1995 (No. 363) [£1·10], made under S.I. 1992 No. 810 (N.I. 6), art. 9(1); operative on November 1, 1995; specify periods during which functional work falling within certain defined activities must be carried out.

5301. General grant

LOCAL GOVERNMENT (GENERAL GRANT) ORDER (NORTHERN IRELAND) 1995 (No. 177) [65p], made under S.I. 1972 No. 1999 (N.I. 22), Sched. 1, Pt. I, para. 3(1); operative on June 21, 1995; specifies districts to be taken into account in calculating a rate product when computing the resources element of a grant to district councils.

5302. Local Government (Miscellaneous Provisions) (Northern Ireland) Order 1995 (S.I. 1995 No. 759 (N.I. 5))

This Order makes miscellaneous amendments of the law relating to district councils, including the naming of streets, the vacation of the office of councillor because of non-attendance, the appointment of council officers, the investment of council funds and the sealing of contracts by councils. The Order comes into operation on days to be appointed.

MEDICINE

5303. Dental charges

DENTAL CHARGES (AMENDMENT) REGULATIONS (NORTHERN IRELAND) 1995 (No. 83) [£1·10], made under S.I. 1972 No. 1265 (N.I. 14), arts. 98, 106, Sched. 15; operative on April 1, 1995; increase the maximum charge for dental treatment.

5304. Dental services

GENERAL DENTAL SERVICES (AMENDMENT) REGULATIONS (NORTHERN IRELAND) 1995 SR 1995 488), made under the S.I. 1972 No. 1265 (NI.14), arts.61(1)(2)(2AA), 106, 107(6), Sched. 1, para. 8E; amends SR 1993 326. operative on December 21, 1995; [£1·55]. These regulations amend SR 1993 326.

5305. Drugs and appliances—charges

CHARGES FOR DRUGS AND APPLIANCES (AMENDMENT) REGULATIONS (NORTHERN IRELAND) 1995 (No. 135) [£1·10], made under S.I. 1972 No. 1265 (N.I. 14), arts. 98, 106, Sched. 15; operative on April 1, 1995; amend the 1973 (No. 419) Regulations.

CHARGES FOR DRUGS AND APPLIANCES (AMENDMENT NO. 2) REGULATIONS (NORTHERN IRELAND) 1995 (No. 402) [£1·10], made under S.I. 1972

No. 1265 (N.I. 14), arts. 98, 106, Sched. 15; operative on October 20, 1995 (part) and November 1, 1995 (remainder); amend the 1973 (No. 419) Regulations.

5306. Medical and pharmaceutical services

GENERAL MEDICAL AND PHARMACEUTICAL SERVICES (AMENDMENT) REGULATIONS (NORTHERN IRELAND) 1995 (No. 56) [£1·55], made under S.I. 1972 No. 1265 (N. I. 14), arts. 56, 106, 107(6); operative on March 30, 1995; amend the 1973 (No. 421) Regulations as respects doctors' terms of service.

GENERAL MEDICAL AND PHARMACEUTICAL SERVICES (AMENDMENT NO. 2) REGULATIONS (NORTHERN IRELAND) 1995 (No. 126) [£1·20], made under S.I. 1972 No. 1265 (N.I. 14); arts. 63, 106, 107(6); operative on April 1, 1995; amend the 1973 (No. 421) Regulations.

GENERAL MEDICAL AND PHARMACEUTICAL SERVICES (AMENDMENT NO. 3) REGULATIONS (NORTHERN IRELAND). 1995 SR 1995 487 S.I. 1972 No. 1265 (NI.14), arts.56,63(1)(2),106,107(6), Sched. 11, pt.1, para. 8E; amends SR&O (NI) 1973 421. operative on December 21, 1995, for regs. 1 to 7, January 1, 1996 for reg.8; [£1·95. These Regulations amend SR&O (NI) 1973 421.

MINORS

5307. Adopted persons—birth records

ADOPTED PERSONS (BIRTH RECORDS) REGULATIONS (NORTHERN IRELAND) 1995 SR 1995 484), made under the S.I. 1987 (No. 2203 (NI.22), art.54A(3)(5). In force: February 19, 1996; [65p]. These Regulations prescribe forms for adopted persons seeking information.

5308. Adopted persons—contact register

ADOPTED PERSONS (CONTACT REGISTER) (FEES) REGULATIONS (NORTHERN IRELAND) 1995 SR 1995 485), made under the S.I. 1987 No. 2203 (NI.22), art.54(1)(2). operative on February 19, 1996; [£1·95. These Regulations prescribe fees for entries in the adoption contact register.

5309. Child support

CHILD SUPPORT (1995 ORDER) (COMMENCEMENT NO. 1) ORDER (NORTHERN IRELAND) 1995 (No. 428 (C.8)) [£1·10], made under the Northern Ireland Act 1974, Sched. 1, para. 2(1) and S.I. 1995 No. 2702 (N.I.13), art.1(3); brings into force on November 16, 1995 arts. 1, 2, 6(1)(5) (for a specified purpose), 12–15, 16 (part), 17, 18, 19(1)(2)(b)(c)(3)(4), 20 and Sched. 3 (part) to S.I. 1995 No. 2702; brings into force on November 16, 1995 arts. 1, 2, 6(1)(5) (for a specified purpose) 12–15, 16 (part), 17, 18, 19(1)(2)(b)(c)(3)(4), 20 and Sched. 3 (part) to S.I. 1995 No. 2702.

CHILD SUPPORT (MISCELLANEOUS AMENDMENTS) REGULATIONS (NORTHERN IRELAND) 1995 (No. 19) [£1·55], made under S.I. 1991 No. 2628 (N.I. 23), arts. 16(1), 18(5), 47, 48, Sched. 1, para. 11; operative on February 16, 1995; amend the 1992 (Nos. 339, 340 and 466) Regulations.

CHILD SUPPORT (MISCELLANEOUS AMENDMENTS NO.2) REGULATIONS (NORTHERN IRELAND) 1995 SR 1995 475), made under the S.I. 1991 No. 2628 (NI.23), arts.14(2)(3), 16(1)(1A)(3), 18, 19(4)(6), 20(8)(11), 32(1)(2), 38(2), 38B(3)(6), 39, 43(5)(11), 47, 48, 49(2)(3), Sched. 1, paras. 5(1)(2), 6(2), 8, 11 and S.I. 1995 No. 2702 (NI.13), art.12(6). Amends SR 1992 339, 341, 342, 390, 466; 1993 117; 1994 37; 1995 162. operative on December 18, 1995, January 22, 1996; £5·70. These Regulations amend various regulations), made under the the Child Support (Northern Ireland) Order 1991.

5310. Child support and income support

CHILD SUPPORT AND INCOME SUPPORT (AMENDMENT) REGULATIONS (NORTHERN IRELAND) 1995 (No. 162) [£6·95], made under S.I. 1991 No. 2628 (N.I. 23), arts. 10(11), 12(1), 14(2)(3), 16(1)(3), 18(1), 19(4), 20(11), 23(2)(3), 29(2)(3), 32, 38(3), 39, 40(1), 43(11), 44, 47, 48, 50(2), Sched. 1, paras. 4(3), 5(1)(2), 6(2)(4)(5), 7(1), 8, 9(a), 11 and the Social Security Contributions and Benefits (Northern Ireland) Act 1992 (c.7), s.131(1); operative on April 13, 1995 (part) and April 18, 1995 (remainder); amend the 1987 (No. 459), 1992 (Nos. 339, 340, 341, 342, 390 and 466), 1993 (Nos. 50 and 73) and 1994 (No. 37) Regulations.

5311. Child Support (Northern Ireland) Order 1995 (S.I. 1995 No. 2702 (N.I. 13))

This Order amends the Child Support (Northern Ireland) Order 1991 to improve the provision for the assessment, collection and enforcement of payments for child support maintenance. It also introduces a system of departure directions to allow the amount of child support maintenance payments to be varied in some cases. The Order comes into operation on days to be appointed.

5312. Children

CHILDREN (NORTHERN IRELAND CONSEQUENTIAL AMENDMENTS) ORDER 1995 (No. 756) [£1·95], made under the Northern Ireland Constitution Act 1973 (c.36), s.38(2) and the Northern Ireland Act 1974 (c.28), Sched. 1, para. 1(7); operative on days to be appointed; makes miscellaneous amendments which are consequential on S.I. 1995 No. 755.

5313. Children—1995 Order—commencement

CHILDREN (1995 ORDER) (COMMENCEMENT NO. 1) ORDER (NORTHERN IRELAND) 1995 (No. 248 (C.3)) [65p], made under S.I. 1995 No. 755 (N.I. 2), art. 1(2); brings arts. 1, 2, 155–157, 183, 184(1) (part) (2), 185 (part) of, and Scheds. 8 (part), 9 (part), 10 (part) to, the 1995 S.I. into operation on July 1, 1995.

5314. Children (Northern Ireland) Order 1995 (S.I. 1995 No. 755 (N.I. 2))

This Order replaces certain provisions of the Children and Young Persons Act (Northern Ireland) 1968 and amends the law relating to illegitimacy and guardianship. Part II makes the welfare of a child the paramount consideration in certain proceedings, Pt. III provides for various orders with respect to children in family proceedings, Pt. IV imposes duties on health and personal services boards and trusts towards certain children and their families, Pt. V deals with care and supervision orders and Pt. VI with child assessment orders and orders for the emergency protection of children. Parts VII to IX regulate homes provided for children by boards, trusts and others, Pts. X and XI relate to private arrangements for fostering, child-minding and day care for children under 12. Part XII restricts the employment of children and performances involving children, Pt. XIII deals with the Department of Health and Social Services' supervisory functions, Pt. XIV provides for parents not being married to each other to have no effect in law on certain relationships, Pt. XV for the appointment of guardians and Pt. XV for jurisdiction and procedure. The Order comes into operation on days to be appointed.

NATIONAL HEALTH

5315. Assessment of resources

HEALTH AND PERSONAL SOCIAL SERVICES (ASSESSMENT OF RESOURCES) (AMENDMENT) REGULATIONS (NORTHERN IRELAND) 1995

(No. 286) [£1·10], made under S.I. 1972 No. 1265 (N.I. 14), arts. 36(6), 99(5); operative on September 4, 1995; amend the 1993 (No. 127) Regulations.

5316. Health and personal social services

HEALTH AND PERSONAL SOCIAL SERVICES (AMENDMENT) (1995 ORDER) (COMMENCEMENT NO.1) ORDER (NORTHERN IRELAND) SR 1995 486 (C.12); made under S.I. 1995 No. 2704 (NI.14), art.1 and Northern Ireland Act 1974, Sched. 1, para. 2(1). operative on bringing into operation various provisions of S.I. 1995 2704 (NI.14) on December 20, 1995; [£1·10]. This Order brings arts. 3 (Part), 4 (part), 5-7 of S.I. 1995 No. 2704 into operation on December 20, 1995.

5317. Health and Personal Social Services (Amendment) (Northern Ireland) Order 1995 (S.I. 1995 No. 2704 (N.I. 14))

This Order amends the law relating to the disqualification, for health service purposes, of certain practitioners. The Order comes into operation on days to be appointed.

5318. Health and social services agency—establishment

Order made under S.I. 1990 No. 247 (N.I. 3):
Art. 3(1)(2)(4)(6): S.R. 1995 No. 397 (guardian *ad litem*) [65p].

5319. Health and social services trusts—dissolution

Orders made under S.I. 1991 No. 194 (N.I. 1):
Art. 10(1) (with Sched. 3, para. 23(2)): S.R. 1995 Nos. 142 (Eastern Ambulance Service HSS Trust; revokes the 1992 (No. 493) Order); 351 (Armagh and Dungannon) [£1·55].

5320. Health and social services trusts—establishment

Order made under S.I. 1991 No. 194 (N.I. 1):
Art. 10(1) (with Sched. 3, paras. 1, 3-6(2)(d)): S.R. 1995 Nos. 6 (Causeway) [£1·95]; 143 (Northern Ireland Ambulance HSS Trust) [£1·10]; 421 (United Hospitals) [£1·10]; 422 (Altnagelvin hospital) [£1·10]; 423 (Foyle) [£1·55].

5321. Health and social services trusts—originating capital debt

Orders made under S.I. 1991 No. 194 (N.I. 1):
Art. 14(1)(4): S.R. 1995 Nos. 124 (Green Park HSS Trust) [65p]; 144 (HSS Trusts) [£1·10].

5322. Ophthalmic services

GENERAL OPHTHALMIC SERVICES (AMENDMENT) REGULATIONS (NORTHERN IRELAND) 1995 (No. 115) [£1·10], made under S.I. 1972 No. 1265 (N.I. 14), arts. 62, 106, 107(6); operative on April 1, 1995; amend the 1986 (No. 163) Regulations to take account of disability working allowance.

5323. Optical charges

OPTICAL CHARGES AND PAYMENTS (AMENDMENT) REGULATIONS (NORTHERN IRELAND) 1995 (No. 16) [65p], made under S.I. 1972 No. 1265 (N.I. 14), arts. 98, 106, Sched. 15; operative on February 1, 1995; increase an amount in the 1989 (No. 114) Regulations.

OPTICAL CHARGES AND PAYMENTS (AMENDMENT NO. 2) REGULATIONS (NORTHERN IRELAND) 1995 (No. 114) [£1·95], made under S.I. 1972 No. 1265 (N.I. 14), arts. 98, 106, Sched. 15; operative on April 1, 1995; amend the 1989 (No. 114) Regulations.

OPTICAL CHARGES AND PAYMENTS (AMENDMENT NO. 3) REGULATIONS

(NORTHERN IRELAND) 1995 (No. 358) [65p], made under S.I. 1972 No. 1265 (N.I. 14), arts. 98, 106, Sched. 15; operative on October 1, 1995; amend the 1989 (No. 114) Regulations.

5324. Superannuation

HEALTH AND PERSONAL SOCIAL SERVICES (SUPERANNUATION) REGULATIONS (NORTHERN IRELAND) 1995 (No. 95) [£9·00], made under S.I. 1972 No. 1073 (N.I. 10), arts. 12, 14, Sched. 3; operative on April 1, 1995; consolidate with amendments, and revoke, the 1983 (Nos. 152 and 178), 1984 (No. 336), 1988 (No. 271), 1990 (No. 62) and 1994 (No. 203) Regulations.

5325. Travelling expenses and remission of charges

TRAVELLING EXPENSES AND REMISSION OF CHARGES (AMENDMENT) REGULATIONS (NORTHERN IRELAND) 1995 (No. 138) [£1·95], made under S.I. 1972 No. 1265 (N.I. 14), arts. 45, 98, 106, 107(6), Sched. 15, para. 1(b); operative on April 1, 1995; amend the 1989 (No. 348) Regulations.

TRAVELLING EXPENSES AND REMISSION OF CHARGES (AMENDMENT NO. 2) REGULATIONS (NORTHERN IRELAND) 1995 (No. 361) [£1·10], made under S.I. 1972 No. 1265 (N.I. 14), arts. 45, 98, 106, 107(6); operative on October 2, 1995; amend the 1989 (No. 348) Regulations.

PENSIONS AND SUPERANNUATION

5326. Increase

GUARANTEED MINIMUM PENSIONS INCREASE ORDER (NORTHERN IRELAND) 1995 (No. 62) [65p], made under the Pension Schemes (Northern Ireland) Act 1993 (c.49), s.105; operative on April 6, 1995; specifies 2.2 per cent as the increase for that part of guaranteed minimum pensions attributable to earnings factors for 1988–1989 and subsequent tax years and payable by occupational pension schemes.

PENSIONS INCREASE (REVIEW) ORDER (NORTHERN IRELAND) 1995 (No. 39) [£1·95], made under S.I. 1975 No. 1503 (N.I. 15), art. 69(1)(2)(5)(5ZA); operative on April 10, 1995; increases public service pensions.

5327. Judicial pensions—1991 Order—commencement

JUDICIAL PENSIONS (1991 ORDER) (COMMENCEMENT NO. 3) ORDER (NORTHERN IRELAND) 1995 (No. 188 (C.1)) [65p], made under S.I. 1991 No. 2631 (N.I. 24), art. 1(2); brings art. 6 of the 1991 S.I. into operation on June 1, 1995.

5328. Judicial pensions—additional voluntary contributions

JUDICIAL PENSIONS (ADDITIONAL VOLUNTARY CONTRIBUTIONS) REGULATIONS (NORTHERN IRELAND) 1995 (No. 189) [£4·15], made under the County Courts Act (Northern Ireland) 1959 (c.25), s.127A, the Resident Magistrates' Pensions Act (Northern Ireland) 1960 (c.2), s.9A, and the Judicial Pensions Act (Northern Ireland) 1960 (c.20), s.11A; operative on June 1, 1995; provide for the payment by members of existing judicial pension schemes of additional voluntary contributions.

JUDICIAL PENSIONS (ADDITIONAL VOLUNTARY CONTRIBUTIONS) (NO. 2) REGULATIONS (NORTHERN IRELAND) 1995 (No. 255) [£3·70], made under the Judicial Pensions Act (Northern Ireland) 1951 (c.20), s.11A; operative on July 23, 1995; provide for the payment by the holders of certain judicial offices of additional voluntary contributions.

5329. Judicial pensions—appeals

JUDICIAL PENSIONS (APPEALS) REGULATIONS (NORTHERN IRELAND) 1995 (No. 210) [£1·10], made under the County Courts Act (Northern Ireland) 1959 (c.25), s.132A(4), the Resident Magistrates' Pensions Act (Northern Ireland) 1960 (c.2), s.21A(4), and the Social Security (Northern Ireland) Act 1975 (c.15), Sched. 10, para. 7B(4); operative on June 21, 1995; provide for the manner in which, and time within which, certain appeals against decisions of administrators of various judicial and other pension schemes are to be brought.

5330. Judicial pensions—guaranteed minimum pension

JUDICIAL PENSIONS (GUARANTEED MINIMUM PENSION) ORDER (NORTHERN IRELAND) 1995 (No. 389) [£1·95], made under the Pension Schemes (Northern Ireland) Act 1993 (c.49), s.137; operative on November 1, 1995; modifies the pension scheme in Pt. 1 of the Judicial Pensions and Retirement Act 1993.

5331. Judicial pensions—preservation of benefits

JUDICIAL PENSIONS (PRESERVATION OF BENEFITS) ORDER (NORTHERN IRELAND) 1995 (No. 388) [£1·95], made under the Pension Schemes (Northern Ireland) Act 1993 (c.49), s.137; operative on November 1, 1995; provides, as respects certain holders of specified judicial offices, for reduced pension benefits to be preserved if they cease to hold office before reaching normal pension age.

5332. Occupational and personal pension schemes

OCCUPATIONAL AND PERSONAL PENSION SCHEMES (MISCELLANEOUS AMENDMENTS) REGULATIONS (NORTHERN IRELAND) 1995 (No. 7) [£1·95], made under the Pension Schemes (Northern Ireland) Act 1993 (c.49), ss.5(3)(5), 15(4), 19(1), 22, 25(3), 27(1), 35, 69(1), 109(1)(3), 158, Sched. 1, para. 8; operative on February 7, 1995; make miscellaneous amendments to the 1985 (Nos. 259 and 356), 1987 (Nos. 279, 288 and 295), 1988 (No. 34) and 1991 (No. 37) Regulations and revoke the 1976 (No. 139) and 1991 (No. 462) Regulations.

OCCUPATIONAL AND PERSONAL PENSION SCHEMES (MISCELLANEOUS AMENDMENTS NO. 2) REGULATIONS (NORTHERN IRELAND) 1995 (No. 441) [£1·10], made under the Pension Schemes (Northern Ireland) Act 1993, ss.69(1)(2)(4), 109(1)(3), 149(1)(2); amend S.R. 1987 No. 288; S.R. 1991 No. 37; S.R. 1994 No. 300. In force: February 1, 1996.

5333. Occupational and personal pension schemes—levy

OCCUPATIONAL AND PERSONAL PENSION SCHEMES (LEVY) REGULATIONS (NORTHERN IRELAND) 1995 (No. 65) [£1·95], made under the Pension Schemes (Northern Ireland) Act 1993 (c.49), s.170(1)(2)(4); operative on April 1, 1995; replace with amendments, and revoke, the 1990 (No. 423) Regulations.

5334. Occupational and personal pension schemes—Ombudsman

PERSONAL AND OCCUPATIONAL PENSION SCHEMES (PENSIONS OMBUDSMAN) (PROCEDURE) RULES (NORTHERN IRELAND) 1995 (No. 167) [£1·95], made under the Pension Schemes (Northern Ireland) Act 1993 (c.49), s.145(2)–(4); operative on May 10, 1995; set out the procedure to be followed where a complaint or dispute is referred to the Pensions Ombudsman.

5335. Occupational pension schemes—equal access

OCCUPATIONAL PENSION SCHEMES (EQUAL ACCESS TO MEMBERSHIP) (AMENDMENT) REGULATIONS (NORTHERN IRELAND) 1995 (No. 183) [£1·10], made under the European Communities Act 1972 (c.68), s.2(2) and the Pension Schemes (Northern Ireland) Act 1993 (c.49), ss.114(4), 149(3); operative on May 31, 1995; amend the 1976 (No. 238) Regulations so as to extend equal access requirements.

5336. Occupational pensions—revaluation

OCCUPATIONAL PENSIONS (REVALUATION) ORDER (NORTHERN IRELAND) 1995 (No. 435) [65p], made under the Pension Schemes (Northern Ireland) Act 1993, Sched. 2, para. 2(1). In force: January 1, 1996; specifies the revaluation percentages for benefits under occupational pension schemes.

5337. Pensions (Nothern Ireland) Order 1995

PENSIONS (NORTHERN IRELAND) ORDER 1995 (No. 3213 (NI.22)), made under the Northern Ireland Act 1974 Sched. 1, para. 1; amends 1959 c.25 (NI); 1960 c.2 (NI); 1964 c.29 (NI); 1969 c.7 (NI); 1971 c.35 (NI); 1975 c.15 (NI); 1981 c.20; 1988 c.1; 1992 c.5, 7, 8; 1993 c.8, 49; 1995 c.26. Amends S.I. 1976 No. NI 15, 16; 1978 NI 15; 1986 NI 6; 1989 NI 13, 19, 1994 NI 12; 1995 15. operative on in accordance with art.1; [£17·10]. The law relating to occupational pensions, state pensions and personal pensions in Northern Ireland is amended by this Order which is made to correspond with the provisions of the Pensions Act 1995. Part II of the Order relates to occupational pensions, covering supervision by the authority, member-nominated trustees and directors, independent trustees, functions of trustees and managers, employee trustees, advisors, the resolution of disputes, equal treatment, indexation, minimum funding requirements, the modification of schemes, winding up, the compensation system and money purchase schemes. Part III relates to state pensions and Part IV relates to the certification of pension schemes and effects on members' state scheme rights and duties.

5338. Personal pension schemes

PERSONAL PENSION SCHEMES (APPROPRIATE SCHEMES) (AMENDMENT) REGULATIONS (NORTHERN IRELAND) 1995 (No. 266) [65p], made under the Pension Schemes (Northern Ireland) Act 1993 (c.49), s.5(5)(a); operative on July 19, 1995; amend the 1988 (No. 34) Regulations.

POLICE

5339. Police (Amendment) (Northern Ireland) Order 1995 (No. 2993 (N.I. 17))

POLICE (AMENDMENT) (NORTHERN IRELAND) ORDER 1995 (No. 2993 (N.I. 17)) [£6·10], made under the Northern Ireland Act 1974, Sched. 1, para. 1; S.R. & O. (N.I.) 1977 No. 2; S.R. & O. (N.I.) 1987 No. 10; S.R. & O. (N.I.) 1989 No. 12. In force on days to be appointed under art. 1(2); Provisions of the Police and Criminal Evidence (Northern Ireland) Order 1989 relating to police powers in the investigation of crime are amended by Pt. II of this Order and provisions of the Police (Northern Ireland) Order 1987 relating to complaints against the police are amended by Pt. IV. New provisions for regulations relating to the conduct, efficiency and discipline of members of the RUC and RUC reserve are made by Pt. III.

5340. R.U.C.

ROYAL ULSTER CONSTABULARY (AMENDMENT) REGULATIONS 1995 (No. 117) [£2·40], made under the Police Act (Northern Ireland) 1970 (c.9), s.25; operative on April 1, 1995; amend the 1984 (No. 62) Regulations.

ROYAL ULSTER CONSTABULARY (AMENDMENT NO. 2) REGULATIONS 1995 (No. 400) [£1·55], made under the Police Act (Northern Ireland) 1970 (c.9), s.25; operative on November 24, 1995; amend the 1984 (No. 62) Regulations as respects ranks, pay and allowances.

ROYAL ULSTER CONSTABULARY (PROMOTION) REGULATIONS 1995 (No. 120) [£2·80], made under the Police Act (Northern Ireland) 1970 (c.9), s.25; operative on May 1, 1995; replace with amendments, and revoke, the 1981 (No. 19), 1983 (No. 113), 1985 (Nos. 42 and 337), 1992 (No. 243) and 1993 (No. 339) Regulations.

5341. R.U.C. and R.U.C. Reserve

ROYAL ULSTER CONSTABULARY AND ROYAL ULSTER CONSTABULARY RESERVE (FULL-TIME) (TEMPORARY PROVISIONS) REGULATIONS 1995 (No. 137) [65p], made under the Police Act (Northern Ireland) 1970 (c.9), ss.25, 26; operative on April 30, 1995; move the early May public holiday to the second Monday in May 1995.

5342. R.U.C. Reserve

ROYAL ULSTER CONSTABULARY RESERVE (FULL-TIME) (APPOINTMENT AND CONDITIONS OF SERVICE) (AMENDMENT) REGULATIONS 1995 (No. 118) [£1·10], made under the Police Act (Northern Ireland) 1970 (c.9), s.26; operative on April 13, 1995; amend the 1988 (No. 36) Regulations.

ROYAL ULSTER CONSTABULARY RESERVE (FULL-TIME) (APPOINTMENT AND CONDITIONS OF SERVICE) (AMENDMENT NO. 2) REGULATIONS 1995 (No. 339) [65p], made under the Police Act (Northern Ireland) 1970 (c.9), s.26; operative on October 1, 1995; amend the 1988 (No. 36) Regulations.

ROYAL ULSTER CONSTABULARY RESERVE (FULL-TIME) (APPOINTMENT AND CONDITIONS OF SERVICE) (AMENDMENT NO. 3) REGULATIONS 1995 (No. 401) [65p], made under the Police Act (Northern Ireland) 1970 (c.9), s.26; operative on November 24, 1995; amend the 1988 (No. 36) Regulations as respects an allowance.

ROYAL ULSTER CONSTABULARY RESERVE (PART-TIME) (APPOINTMENT AND CONDITIONS OF SERVICE) (AMENDMENT) REGULATIONS 1995 (No. 119) [65p], made under the Police Act (Northern Ireland) 1970 (c.9), s.26; operative on April 13, 1995; amend the 1988 (No. 35) Regulations.

PRACTICE (CIVIL)

5343/4. Costs—security for costs—Northern Ireland plaintiff—enforceability of judgment—whether security for costs to be ordered automatically. See DYNASPAN (U.K.), *Re*; DYNASPAN (U.K.) v. KATZENBERGER BAUKONSTRUKTIONEN (U.) GmbH & CO. KG, §4013.

5345. County court divisions

COUNTY COURT DIVISIONS (AMENDMENT) ORDER (NORTHERN IRELAND) 1995 (No. 5) [65p], made under S.I. 1980 No. 397 (N.I. 3), art. 3(1); operative on January 16, 1995; amends the 1994 (No. 471) Order.

5346. County court rules

COUNTY COURT (AMENDMENT) RULES (NORTHERN IRELAND) 1995 (No. 48) [£4·15], made under S.I. 1980 No. 397 (N.I. 3), art. 46; operative on March 20, 1995; amend County Court Rules as respects Ord. 51, parental orders under s.30 of the Human Fertilisation and Embryology Act 1990 and applications for access to health records.

COUNTY COURT (AMENDMENT NO. 2) RULES (NORTHERN IRELAND) 1995 (No. 151) [£5·20], made under S.I. 1980 No. 397 (N.I. 3), art. 47; operative on September 1, 1995; amend the 1981 (No. 225) Rules as respects the entry of cases for hearing, notices of intention to defend, the compulsory exchange of medical and other expert evidence, a single judgment default procedure, the service of civil bills and other documents by first class post and other matters.

COUNTY COURT (AMENDMENT NO. 3) RULES (NORTHERN IRELAND) 1995 (No. 282) [£3·20], made under S.I. 1980 No. 397 (N.I. 3), art. 47; operative on August 31, 1995 (pt.) and September 1, 1995 (remainder); amend the 1981 (No. 225) Rules.

5347. County courts—fees

COUNTY COURT FEES (AMENDMENT) ORDER (NORTHERN IRELAND) 1995 (No. 221) [£1·95], made under the Judicature (Northern Ireland) Act 1978 (c.23), s.116(1); operative on June 1, 1995; increases fees for county court proceedings.

COUNTY COURT FEES (AMENDMENT NO. 2) ORDER (NORTHERN IRELAND) 1995 (No. 290) [65p], made under the Judicature (Northern Ireland) Act 1978 (c.23), s.116(1); operative on September 1, 1995; amends the 1994 (No. 280) Order.

5348. Judgments enforcement—fees

JUDGMENTS ENFORCEMENT FEES (AMENDMENT) ORDER (NORTHERN IRELAND) 1995 (No. 217) [65p], made under the Judicature (Northern Ireland) Act 1978 (c.23), s.116(1); operative on June 1, 1995; increases the fee for a search in the register of judgments.

5349. Magistrates' courts—fees

MAGISTRATES' COURTS FEES (AMENDMENT) ORDER (NORTHERN IRELAND) 1995 (No. 222) [£1·95], made under the Judicature (Northern Ireland) Act 1978 (c.23), s.116(1); operative on June 1, 1995; increases some fees for proceedings in magistrates' courts.

5350. Matrimonial proceedings—fees

MATRIMONIAL CAUSES FEES (AMENDMENT) ORDER (NORTHERN IRELAND) 1995 (No. 218) [£1·55], made under the Judicature (Northern Ireland) Act 1978 (c.23), s.116(1); operative on June 1, 1995; increases the majority of fees for matrimonial proceedings in the High Court or divorce county courts.

5351. Rules of the Supreme Court

RULES OF THE SUPREME COURT (NORTHERN IRELAND) (AMENDMENT) 1995 (No. 2) [£4·15], made under the Judicature (Northern Ireland) Act 1978 (c.23), s.55; operative on February 2, 1995; amend the 1980 (No. 346) Rules as respects certain appeals, proceedings relating to minors, arrangements for obtaining certain parental orders, applications for access to medical records and expenses in criminal proceedings in the Court of Appeal.

5352. Supreme Court—fees

SUPREME COURT FEES (AMENDMENT) ORDER (NORTHERN IRELAND) 1995 (No. 220) [£3·20], made under the Judicature (Northern Ireland) Act 1978 (c.23), s.116(1); operative on June 1, 1995; increases the majority of fees payable in the Supreme Court.

5353. Supreme Court—non-contentious probate—fees

SUPREME COURT (NON-CONTENTIOUS PROBATE) FEES (AMENDMENT) ORDER (NORTHERN IRELAND) 1995 (No. 219) [£1·95], made under the

Judicature (Northern Ireland) Act 1978 (c.23), s.116(1); operative on June 1, 1995; increases some fees in non-contentious probate proceedings.

5354. Tribunals

TRIBUNAL REGULATIONS (NORTHERN IRELAND) 1995 SR 1995 493), made under the S.I. 1972 No. 1265 (NI.14), arts.65,89,106, Sched. 11. operative on December 21, 1995; [£3·70. These Regulations replace, with amendments, and revoke SR 1973 411.

PRISONS

5355. Remission—terrorist offences—press release. See PRISONS, §4269.

5356. Rules

PRISON AND YOUNG OFFENDERS CENTRE RULES (NORTHERN IRELAND) 1995 (No. 8) [£6·35], made under the Prison Act (Northern Ireland) 1953 (c.18), s.13; operative on March 1, 1995; deal with the treatment and discipline of prisoners, including inmates in young offenders centres, the duties of prison staff and the functions of prison visitors and revoke the 1982 (Nos. 169 and 170) and 1983 (Nos. 248 and 249) Rules.

PRISON AND YOUNG OFFENDERS CENTRE (AMENDMENT) RULES (NORTHERN IRELAND) 1995 (No. 264) [£1·10], made under the Prison Act (Northern Ireland) 1953 (c.18), s.18, as extended by the Treatment of Offenders Act (Northern Ireland) 1968 (c.19), s.2; operative on August 1, 1995; amend the 1995 (No. 8) Rules.

PUBLIC ENTERTAINMENTS AND RECREATION

5357. Film exhibitions

CINEMATOGRAPH (SAFETY) (AMENDMENT) REGULATIONS (NORTHERN IRELAND) 1995 (No. 192) [£1·10], made under S.I. 1991 No. 1462 (N.I. 12), art. 6(1)(2); operative on June 12, 1995; amend the 1965 (No. 129) Regulations by, in particular, extending them to all film exhibitions.

RATING AND VALUATION

5358. Lands Tribunal decision

Premises occupied by N were used to produce a newspaper and for other purposes. N appealed against C's refusal to distinguish the premises as primarily industrial.

Held, that in producing a newspaper an article was being made, so that the newspaper business carried on was primarily industrial.

NEWTOWNARDS CHRONICLE v. COMMISSIONER OF VALUATION FOR NORTHERN IRELAND (VR/4/1992), Lands Tribunal.

5359. Lands Tribunal decision

Premises occupied by R were used to process potatoes and other vegetables for sale. R appealed against C's refusal to distinguish the premises as industrial.

Held, that only the processing of potatoes, which involved washing and grading them and removing waste, was an adaptation for sale, so that part of the net annual value should be distinguished as industrial.

ROBINSON (TRADING AS ROBIPAK) v. COMMISSIONER OF VALUATION FOR NORTHERN IRELAND (VR/4/1992), Lands Tribunal.

5360. New valuation list

NEW VALUATION LIST ORDER (NORTHERN IRELAND) 1995 (No. 57) [65p], made under S.I. 1977 No. 2157 (N.I. 28), art. 45(1); operative on April 1, 1995; specifies 1996 as a year in which a new valuation list is be issued for rating purposes.

NEW VALUATION LIST (TIME AND CLASS OF HEREDITAMENTS) ORDER (NORTHERN IRELAND) 1995 (No. 58) [65p], made under S.I. 1977 No. 2157 (N.I. 28), art. 39A; operative on April 1, 1995; specifies hereditaments in relation to a new valuation list and April 1, 1995, as the date by reference to which their net annual values are to be ascertained.

5361. Regional rate

RATES (REGIONAL RATE) ORDER (NORTHERN IRELAND) 1995 (No. 55) [65p]; made under S.I. 1977 No. 2157 (N.I. 28), arts. 2(2), 7(1), 27(4); operative on April 1, 1995; fixes the regional rate for the year ending March 31, 1996 and the amount by which it is reduced for dwelling-houses.

REGISTRATION OF BIRTHS, DEATHS AND MARRIAGES

5362. Fees

BIRTHS, DEATHS AND MARRIAGES (FEES) ORDER (NORTHERN IRELAND) 1995 (No. 208) [£1·95], made under the Registration of Births, Deaths and Marriages (Fees, Etc.) Act (Northern Ireland) 1955 (c.29), s.1(1)(2), and S.I. 1976 No. 1041 (N.I. 14), art. 47(1)(2); operative on August 1, 1995; specifies fees payable under enactments for the registration of births, deaths and marriages and revokes the 1992 (No. 217) Order.

REVENUE AND FINANCE

5363. Appropriation (Northern Ireland) Order 1995 (S.I. 1995 No. 754 (N.I. 1))

This Order authorises the issue out of the Consolidated Fund of sums for the years ending March 31, 1995 and 1996 and of sums on account, appropriates those sums and deals with the application of sums as appropriations in aid. The Order came into operation on March 15, 1995.

5364. Appropriation (No. 2) (Northern Ireland) Order 1995 (S.I. 1995 No. 1969 (N.I. 11))

This Order authorises the issue out of the Consolidated Fund of further sums for the year ended March 31, 1995 and that ending March 31, 1996 and appropriates those sums and deals with the application of sums as appropriations in aid. The Order came into operation on July 26, 1995.

5365. Consolidated Fund—loans

NORTHERN IRELAND (LOANS) (INCREASE OF LIMIT) ORDER 1995 (No. 675) [65p], made under the Northern Ireland (Loans) Act 1975 (c.83), s.1(5), and the Northern Ireland (Loans) Act 1985 (c.76), s.1(2); operative on March 31, 1995; increases to £2,000 million the aggregate amount outstanding by way of principal in respect of certain loans.

5366. Lands Tribunal—salaries

LANDS TRIBUNAL (SALARIES) ORDER (NORTHERN IRELAND) 1995 (No. 145) [65p], made under the Lands Tribunal and Compensation Act (Northern Ireland) 1964 (c.29), s.2(5); operative on May 26, 1995; increases the salaries of members of the Lands Tribunal; revokes the 1994 (No. 157) Order.

5367. Parliamentary Commissioner and Commissioner for Complaints—salaries

SALARIES (PARLIAMENTARY COMMISSIONER AND COMMISSIONER FOR COMPLAINTS) ORDER (NORTHERN IRELAND) 1995 (No. 386) [65p], made under S.I. 1973 No. 1086 (N.I. 14), art. 4(2); operative on November 20, 1995; increases the salaries of the Parliamentary Commissioner and Commissioner for Complaints; revokes the 1994 (No. 400) Order.

5368. Public expenditure—Northern Ireland

FINANCIAL PROVISIONS (NORTHERN IRELAND) ORDER 1995 (No. 2991 (N.I. 16)) [£1·95], made under the Northern Ireland Act 1974, Sched. 1, para. 1; amends S.R. & O. (N.I.) 1973 No. 16; S.R. & O. (N.I.) 1993 No. 5. In force: January 24, 1996; contains various miscellaneous financial provisions; makes provision for the Department of Finance and Personnel to amend or repeal provisions requiring a statutory body or Northern Ireland Department to obtain the consent of the Department to exercise its functions. The Financial Provisions (Northern Ireland) Order 1993 is amended in relation to the reserves, public dividend capital and borrowing limits of trading funds. Time-limits for the preparation and audit of certain accounts under the Exchequer and Financial Provisions Act (Northern Ireland) 1950 are extended. The requirement that a loan made to Enterprise Ulster must be repaid within the same financial year is removed from the Enterprise Ulster (Northern Ireland) Order 1973.

ROAD TRAFFIC

5369. Accidents—payments for treatment

ROAD TRAFFIC ACCIDENTS (PAYMENTS FOR TREATMENT) ORDER (NORTHERN IRELAND) 1995 (No. 139) [65p], made under the Public Expenditure and Receipts Act (Northern Ireland) 1968 (c.8), s.5, Sched. 3; operative on May 11, 1995; increases the maximum amount to be paid by insurers or owners of motorvehicles for hospital in-patient treatment of certain road traffic casualties.

5370. Disabled persons—badges

DISABLED PERSONS (BADGES FOR MOTOR VEHICLES) (AMENDMENT) REGULATIONS (NORTHERN IRELAND) 1995 (No. 332) [65p], made under the Chronically Sick and Disabled Persons (Northern Ireland) Act 1978 (c.53), s.14; operative on October 2, 1995; amend the 1993 (No. 202) Regulations.

5371. Driving instruction—fees

MOTOR CARS (DRIVING INSTRUCTION) (FEES) (AMENDMENT) REGULATIONS (NORTHERN IRELAND) 1995 (No. 154) [£1·10], made under S.I. 1981

No. 154 (N.I. 1), arts. 132(2)(a)(d), 135(2)(a), 218(1); operative on May 22, 1995; increase various fees under the 1991 (No. 373) Regulations and revoke the 1993 (No. 391) and 1994 (No. 408) Regulations.

5372. Driving licences

MOTOR VEHICLES (DRIVING LICENCES) (AMENDMENT) REGULATIONS (NORTHERN IRELAND) 1995 (No. 152) [£1·10], made under S.I. 1981 No. 154 (N.I. 1), arts. 5(3)(4), 218(1); operative on May 22, 1995; amend the 1994 (No. 365) Regulations.

MOTOR VEHICLES (DRIVING LICENCES) (LARGE GOODS AND PASSENGER-CARRYING VEHICLES) (TEST FEES) (AMENDMENT) REGULATIONS (NORTHERN IRELAND) 1995 (No. 156) [65p], made under S.I. 1981 No. 154 (N.I. 1), arts. 5(4), 218(1); operative on May 22, 1995; increase the fee for a driving test for large goods or passenger-carrying vehicles and revoke the 1991 (No. 280) Regulations.

5373. Goods vehicles—certification—fees

GOODS VEHICLES (CERTIFICATION) (FEES) (AMENDMENT) REGULATIONS (NORTHERN IRELAND) 1995 (No. 155) [£1·10], made under S.I. 1981 No. 154 (N.I. 1), arts. 54(1), 58(1), 218(1); operative on May 22, 1995; increase various fees under the 1990 (No. 224) Regulations.

5374. Goods vehicles—testing

GOODS VEHICLES (TESTING) REGULATIONS (NORTHERN IRELAND) 1995 (No. 450) [£4·70], made under S.I. 1995 No. 2994 (N.I. 18), arts. 65(1)(2)(5), 66(3), 67, 69(5), 72(3), 108(1)(2), 110(2); revoke S.R. 1990 No. 224; S.R. 1991 No. 355; S.R. 1993 Nos. 78, 424; S.R. 1994 Nos. 54, 410; S.R. 1995 No. 155. In force: January 24, 1996; make fresh provision for the testing of goods vehicles.

5375. Motorvehicle testing

MOTOR VEHICLE TESTING REGULATIONS (NORTHERN IRELAND) 1995 S.R. 1995 No. 448 [£3·70], made under S.I. 1995 No. 2994 (N.I. 18), arts. 61(2)(6), 62, 63(5)(6)(7), 72(1)(2), 75(8), 81(8)(9), 110(2); revokes S.R. 1982 No. 383; S.R. 1987 No. 351; S.R. 1989 No. 234; S.R. 1993 Nos. 94, 77; S.R. 1994 Nos. 409, 411; S.R. 1995 Nos. 157, 158. In force: January 24, 1996; make fresh provision for the testing of goods vehicles, except goods vehicles and public service vehicles.

5376. Motorvehicle testing—fees

MOTOR VEHICLE TESTING (FEES) (AMENDMENT) REGULATIONS (NORTHERN IRELAND) 1995 (No. 157) [£1·10], made under S.I. 1981 No. 154 (N.I. 1), arts. 33(2)(6), 35(3), 36(4), 218(1); operative on May 22, 1995; increase various fees under the 1989 (No. 234) Regulations.

5377. Motorvehicles—construction and use

MOTOR VEHICLES (CONSTRUCTION AND USE) (AMENDMENT) REGULATIONS (NORTHERN IRELAND) 1995 (No. 94) [£2·80], made under the European Communities Act 1972 (c.68), s.2(2) and S.I. 1981 No. 154 (N.I. 1), arts. 28(1), 218(1); operative on May 1, 1995; amend the 1989 (No. 299) Regulations.

5378. Motorvehicles—taxi drivers' licences—fees

MOTOR VEHICLES (TAXI DRIVERS' LICENCES) (FEES) (AMENDMENT) REGULATIONS (NORTHERN IRELAND) 1995 (No. 153) [65p], made under S.I.

1981 No. 154 (N.I. 1), arts. 79A(2), 218(1); operative on May 22, 1995; increase two fees under the 1991 (No. 454) Regulations.

5379. Motorvehicles—type approval

MOTOR VEHICLES (TYPE APPROVAL) (AMENDMENT) REGULATIONS (NORTHERN IRELAND) 1995 (No. 38) [£4·15], made under S.I. 1981 No. 154 (N.I. 1), arts. 31A(1), 31D(1), 218(1); operative on April 1, 1995; amend the 1985 (No. 294) Regulations and revoke the 1990 (No. 312) Regulations.

5380. Noise insulation

NOISE INSULATION REGULATIONS (NORTHERN IRELAND) 1995 (No. 409) [£4·15], made under S.I. 1973 No. 1896 (N.I. 21), art. 22; operative on December 7, 1995; provide for the insulation of buildings against noise caused, or expected to be caused, by traffic using new roads and certain altered roads.

5381. Orders

Orders made under S.I. 1981 No. 154 (N.I.1):

Art 21(1) S.R. 1995 Nos 111 (one-way traffic—Londonderry) [65p]; 121 (urban clearways—Belfast) [65p]; 130 (control of traffic—Belfast) [65p]; 194 (one-way traffic—Belfast) [65p]; 200 (control of traffic—Belfast) [£1.10]; 212 (one-way traffic—Carrickfergus) [£1.10]; 213 (one-way traffic—Londonderry) [65p]; 241 (control of traffic—Enniskillen [£1.10]; 285 (one-way traffic—Boylan Road, Glenlough, Ballymoney) [65p]; 287 (one-way traffic—Londonderry) [65p]; 289 (bus lanes—Ormeau Road, Belfast) [£1.10]; 292 (one-way traffic—Portadown) [65p]; 307 (one-way traffic—Enniskillen) [65p]; 311 (control of traffic—Belfast—No. 2 [£1.10]; 316 (one-way traffic—Coleraine) [65p]; 319 (one-way traffic—Limavady) [65p]; 326 (control of traffic—Belfast—No. 3) [£1.10]; 327 (control of traffic—Belfast—No. 4) [65p]; 328 (urban clearways—Belfast—No. 2) [65p]; 336 (control of traffic—Hillsborough [65p]; 352 (one way traffic—Killyreagh) [65p]; 390 (urban clearways—Belfast) [65p]; 393 (one-way traffic—Belfast) [65p]; 407 (one-way traffic—Portadown [65p]; 408 (control of traffic—Newry) [65p]; 418 (one-way traffic—Castlederg) [65p]; 419 (one-way traffic—Castlederg [£1.10]; 425 (control of traffic—Galgorm, Ballymena) [£1.10]; 427 (Control of traffic—Bangor [65p].

Art. 22(1) S.R. 1995 Nos 9 (traffic weight restriction—Hannahstown Hill, Belfast) [65p]; 14 (traffic weight restriction—Bog Road, Forkhill) [65p]; 195 traffic weight restriction—Corramore Road, Plumbridge) [£1.10]; 197 (traffic weight restriction—Davagh Road, Greencastle); 207 (traffic weight restriction—Barnaghs Road, Carrickmore [£1.10]; 375 (traffic weight restriction—Shankbridge, Ballymena) [£1.10]; 394 (traffic weight restriction—Newry) [£1.10]; 452 (traffic weight restriction—McRory's Road, Newtownhamilton) [£1.10].

Art. 50(4)(a) S.R. 1995 No. 365 (speed limits) [£1.95].

Art. 50(4)(c) S.R. 1995 No. 309 (restricted roads) [£1.10].

Art. 51(1) S.R. 1995 No. 288 (temporary speed limit—Sydenham by-pass, route A2, Belfast—continuation) [65p].

Art. 51(4) S.R. 1995 No. 90 (temporary speed limit—Sydenham by-pass, route A2, Belfast) [65p].

Art. 51(5) S.R. 1995 No. 147 (experimental speed limit, M3—indefinite continuation) [65p].

Art. 104(1)(c) S.R. 1995 Nos 20 (parking places on roads) [£1.10]; 176; parking places on roads) [£1.10]; 308 (parking places on roads) [£1.55]; 398 (parking places on roads) [£1.55]; 499 (parking places on roads) [£1.95].

Art. 105(1) S.R. 1995 Nos 21 (off-street parking) [£1.95]; 497 (off-street parking);

Arts. 107(1), 109(2), 111(1)(2) S.R. No. 331 (on-street parking) [£1.10].

5382. Private passenger vehicles—certification—fees

LARGE PRIVATE PASSENGER VEHICLES (CERTIFICATION) (FEES) (AMEND-

MENT) REGULATIONS (NORTHERN IRELAND) 1995 (No. 158) [65p], made under S.I. 1981 No. 154 (N.I. 1), arts. 67(3), 69, 218(1); operative on May 22, 1995; increase fees for inspecting large private passenger vehicles.

5383. Public service vehicles—licence fees

PUBLIC SERVICE VEHICLES (LICENCE FEES) (AMENDMENT) REGULATIONS (NORTHERN IRELAND) 1995 (No. 159) [£1·10], made under S.I. 1981 No. 154 (N.I. 1), arts. 61(1), 66(1), 218(1); operative on May 22, 1995; increase various fees under the 1985 (No. 123) Regulations; revoke the 1986 (No. 229), 1988 (No. 352), 1991 (No. 101) and 1994 (No. 407) Regulations.

5384. Road traffic offences

ROAD TRAFFIC (NORTHERN IRELAND) ORDER 1995 (No. 2994 (N.I. 18)) [£11·30], made under the Northern Ireland Act 1974, Sched. 1, para. 1; amends S.R. & O. (N.I.) 1933 No. 42; S.R. & O. (N.I.) 1993 No. 42; S.R. & O. (N.I.) 1981 No. 4; S.R. & O. (N.I.) 1984 No. 15; S.R. & O. (N.I.) 1985 No. 6; S.R. & O. (N.I.) 1989 No. 12; S.R. & O. (N.I.) 1991 No. 3; S.R. & O. (N.I.) 1992 No. 2; S.R. & O. (N.I.) 1993 No. 15; S.R. & O. (N.I.) 1994 No. 15; revokes S.R. & O. (N.I.) 1982 No. 3; S.R. & O. (N.I.) 1983 No. 3; S.R. & O. (N.I.) 1989 No. 5. In force in accordance with art. 1(2)(3); sets out the main road safety provisions for Northern Ireland. This includes making provision for offences of causing death or grievous bodily injury by dangerous driving, dangerous driving, careless and inconsiderate driving and causing death or grievous bodily injury by careless driving whilst under the influence of drink or drugs which is contained in Part II of the Order along with protective measures, cycling offences and restrictions in the interests of safety. Part III deals with the construction and use of vehicles and equipment, making offences of using motor vehicles or trailers in a condition which may cause injury, and empowers the Department of Transport to make regulations relating to the use and construction and testing of vehicles. Miscellaneous amendments are made to the Road Traffic (Northern Ireland) Order 1981 relating to the extension of its enforcement provisions to include offences under this Order.

5385. Road vehicles—lighting

ROAD VEHICLES LIGHTING REGULATIONS (NORTHERN IRELAND) 1995 (No. 449) [£10·90], made under the European Communities Act 1972, s.2(2), and S.I. 1995 No. 2994 (N.I. 18), arts. 55(1)(2)(4)(6), 59(1)(3), 110(2); revoke S.R. & O. 1968 No. 93; S.R. & O. 1969 No. 214; S.R. & O. 1971 No. 72; S.R. 1979 Nos. 65, 389; S.R. 1983 Nos. 129, 162; S.R. 1988 No. 292; S.R. 1990 No. 182; S.R. 1991 No. 543. In force: January 24, 1996; implements provisions of Dirs. 75/756, 80/233, 83/276, 84/8, 89 278 and 91/663.

5386. Roads—traffic calming

TRAFFIC CALMING REGULATIONS (NORTHERN IRELAND) 1995 (No. 302) [£1·10], made under S.I. 1993 No. 3160 (N.I. 15), art. 65(4); operative on September 11, 1995; provide for the construction and maintenance of traffic calming works.

5387. Street Works (Northern Ireland) Order 1995

STREET WORKS (NORTHERN IRELAND) ORDER 1995 (No. 3210 (NI 19) made under Northern Ireland Act 1974 Sched. 1, para. 1; amends 1847 c.34; 1958 c.30; 1970 c.18 NI; 1972 c.2 NI; 1984 c.12; 1991 c.22; 1977 NI 7; 1981 NI 1; 1991 NI 11; 1992 NI 1; 1993 NI 15; 1994 NI 1. operative on on days to be appointed under art.1(2); [£8·10]. Supersedes Draft SI ISBN 0 11 54918 X issued 16 November, 1995. This Order makes new provision to facilitate the coordination and control of street works in Northern Ireland and to make statutory undertakers and other undertakers of work more accountable for their street works. The Order makes it an offence to place apparatus in a street or to break up a street without a statutory right or a street works licence. The Department of the Environment is required to establish a register of street works; the execution of street works is restricted for 12 months in a street which has been the subject of substantial road works; certain categories of street are subject to special controls; undertakers of works must adopt appropriate safety standards and employ properly qualified supervisors and operatives; undertakers must reinstate streets after completion of works; penalties are imposed on undertakers for unreasonably prolonged works; and they must provide compensation for damage or loss caused by their street works.

5388. Traffic signs

TRAFFIC SIGNS (AMENDMENT) REGULATIONS (NORTHERN IRELAND) 1995 (No. 232) [£3·20], made under S.I. 1981 No. 154 (N.I. 1), art. 27; operative on July 14, 1995; amend the 1979 (No. 386) Regulations.

TRAFFIC SIGNS (AMENDMENT NO. 2) REGULATIONS (NORTHERN IRELAND) 1995 (No. 399) [65p], made under S.I. 1981 No. 154 (N.I. 1), art. 27; operative on November 29, 1995; amend the 1979 (No. 386) Regulations.

SALE OF GOODS

5389. Price indications—resale of tickets. See NORTHERN IRELAND: CONSUMER PROTECTION, §5198.

5390/1. Price marking. See NORTHERN IRELAND: CONSUMER PROTECTION, §5199.

SEA AND SEASHORE

5392. Deposits—exemptions

DEPOSITS IN THE SEA (EXEMPTIONS) ORDER (NORTHERN IRELAND) 1995 (No. 234) [£1·10], made under the Food and Environment Protection Act 1985 (c.48), ss.7(1)(2), 25(3); operative on July 7, 1995; exempts specified operations from the licensing requirements of the 1985 Act.

SHIPPING AND MARINE INSURANCE

5393. Harbours and docks—order

Order made under the Harbours Act (Northern Ireland) 1970 (c.1), s.1(1):

S.R. 1995 No. 185 (Belfast harbour—variation of limits; revokes the 1993 (No. 204) Order) [65p].

5394. Port orders

Ports (Amendment) (Northern Ireland) Order 1995 (S.I. 1995 No. 1627 (N.I. 10)). This Order enables Departments to reconsider the amount of the levy assessed under art. 16 of S.I. 1994 No. 2809 (N.I. 16). The Order came into operation on August 29, 1995.

SOCIAL SECURITY

5395. Adjudication

SOCIAL SECURITY (ADJUDICATION) REGULATIONS (NORTHERN IRELAND) 1995 (No. 293) [£6·35], made under the Social Security Administration (Northern Ireland) Act 1992 (c.8), ss.15(3), 18(3)(b), 20(2)(4), 21(9)(10), 23(3), 24(3), 25(1), 28, 29(3), 30(8), 31(1)(2), 32(4), 33(10), 43(2), 44(2)(3), 45(3)(7)(9), 46(3)(4), 48(6), 53(1), 56, 57, 59(1)–(3), 60, 68(1), 139, 165(6), Sched. 3, Sched. 7, para. 2; operative on August 25, 1995; consolidate, and revoke, the 1987 (No. 466), 1989 (No. 397), 1990 (No. 119), 1991 (No. 406), 1992 (No. 36) and 1994 (Nos. 21, 150, 396) Regulations.

5396. Attendance allowance and disability living allowance

SOCIAL SECURITY (ATTENDANCE ALLOWANCE AND DISABILITY LIVING ALLOWANCE) (AMENDMENT) REGULATIONS (NORTHERN IRELAND) 1995 (No. 59) [£1·10], made under the Social Security Contributions and Benefits (Northern Ireland) Act 1992 (c.7), ss.67(2), 72(8) and the Social Security Administration (Northern Ireland) Act 1992 (c.8), s.71(1); operative on March 3, 1995; amend the 1992 (No. 20) Regulations in relation to preserved rights.

5397. Benefits

SOCIAL SECURITY BENEFITS (MISCELLANEOUS AMENDMENTS) REGULATIONS (NORTHERN IRELAND) 1995 (No. 280) [£1·10], made under the Social Security Contributions and Benefits (Northern Ireland) Act 1992 (c.7), ss.25A(3)(a), 122(1), 129(2)(4), 132(3)(4)(b), 171(5); operative on various dates between August 1, 1995 and September 5, 1995; amend the 1987 (Nos. 459, 461, 463) and 1992 (No. 78) Regulations and revoke the 1994 (No. 233) Regulations.

5398. Benefits—up-rating

SOCIAL SECURITY BENEFITS UP-RATING ORDER (NORTHERN IRELAND) 1995 (No. 71) [£6·35], made under the Social Security Administration (Northern Ireland) Act 1992 (c.8), s.132 and S.I. 1994 No. 1898 (N.I. 12), art. 4(6); operative on various dates between April 1 and 13, 1995; increases the rates and amounts of certain social security benefits and other sums and revokes the 1994 (No. 74) Order.

SOCIAL SECURITY BENEFITS UP-RATING REGULATIONS (NORTHERN IRELAND) 1995 (No. 72) [£1·00], made under the Social Security Contributions and Benefits (Northern Ireland) Act 1992 (c.7), ss.30E(1), 57(1)(a)(ii), 90(b), 113(1)(a), Sched. 7, para. 2(3) and the Social Security Administration (Northern Ireland) Act 1992 (c.8), s.135(3); operative on April 10, 1995 (part) and April 13, 1995 (remainder); qualify the application of s.135(3) of the Administration Act, apply a disqualification in the 1978 (No. 114) Regulations and amend the 1977 (No. 74), 1984 (Nos. 92 and 245) and 1994 (No. 461) Regulations; revoke the 1994 (No. 75) Regulations.

5399. Canada

SOCIAL SECURITY (CANADA) ORDER (NORTHERN IRELAND) 1995 (No. 405) [£2·80], made under the Social Security Administration (Northern Ireland) Act 1992 (c.8), s.155(1)(2); operative on December 1, 1995; modifies Northern

Ireland social security legislation to give effect to an agreement with Canada; revokes the 1960 (No. 15), 1962 (No. 10), 1973 (No. 370) and 1977 (No. 336) Orders.

5400. Child support and income support. See NORTHERN IRELAND: MINORS, §5310.

5401. Claims and payments

SOCIAL SECURITY (CLAIMS AND PAYMENTS) (AMENDMENT) REGULATIONS (NORTHERN IRELAND) 1995 (No. 439) [65p], made under the Social Security Administration (Northern Ireland) Act 1992, s.13A(2)(b); amend S.R. 1987 No. 465; revoke S.R. 1994 No. 457. In force: April 1, 1996.

5402. Contributions

SOCIAL SECURITY CONTRIBUTIONS (AMENDMENT) REGULATIONS (NORTHERN IRELAND) 1995 (No. 61) [65p]; made under the Social Security Contributions and Benefits (Northern Ireland) Act 1992 (c.7), s.117(1); operative on April 6, 1995; amend the 1979 (No. 186) Regulations by increasing the rate of Class 2 contributions by share fishermen.

SOCIAL SECURITY (CONTRIBUTIONS) (AMENDMENT NO. 2) REGULATIONS (NORTHERN IRELAND) 1995 (No. 88) [65p], made under the Social Security Contributions and Benefits (Northern Ireland) Act 1992 (c.7), ss.5, 119; operative on April 6, 1995; amend the 1979 (No. 186) Regulations by increasing certain amounts and decreasing the weekly rate of Class 2 contributions by volunteer development workers; revoke the 1994 (No. 78) Regulations.

SOCIAL SECURITY (CONTRIBUTIONS) (AMENDMENT NO. 3) REGULATIONS (NORTHERN IRELAND) 1995 (No. 91) [£1·10], made under the Social Security Contributions and Benefits (Northern Ireland) Act 1992 (c.7), s.17(3)(6), Sched. 1, para. 6(1); operative on April 6, 1995; amend the 1979 (No. 186) Regulations.

SOCIAL SECURITY (CONTRIBUTIONS) (AMENDMENT NO. 4) REGULATIONS (NORTHERN IRELAND) 1995 (No. 146) [£1·10], made under the Social Security Contributions and Benefits (Northern Ireland) Act 1992 (c.7), s.3(2)(3); operative on April 6, 1995; amend the 1979 (No. 186) Regulations.

SOCIAL SECURITY (CONTRIBUTIONS) (AMENDMENT NO. 5) REGULATIONS (NORTHERN IRELAND) 1995 (No. 257) [65p], made under the Social Security Contributions and Benefits (Northern Ireland) Act 1992 (c.7), s.3(2)(3); operative on July 18, 1995; amend the 1979 (No. 186) Regulations.

SOCIAL SECURITY (CONTRIBUTIONS) (RE-RATING AND NORTHERN IRELAND NATIONAL INSURANCE FUND PAYMENTS) ORDER (NORTHERN IRELAND) 1995 (No. 79) [£1·10], made under the Social Security Administration (Northern Ireland) Act 1992 (c.8), s.129 and S.I. 1993 No. 592 (N.I. 2), art. 4(3); operative on April 6, 1995; increases amounts of certain weekly earnings and contributions and reduces certain percentage rates relating to social security.

5403. Disability working allowance and income support

DISABILITY WORKING ALLOWANCE AND INCOME SUPPORT (GENERAL) (AMENDMENT) REGULATIONS (NORTHERN IRELAND) 1995 (No. 67) [£2·80], made under the Social Security Contributions and Benefits (Northern Ireland) Act 1992 (c.7), ss.122(1)(a)(c), 123(1)(d)(i)(3), 128(2B)(b)(c)(8), 131(1) and S.I. 1994 No. 1898 (N.I. 12), art. 14(1); operative on April 11, 1995 (part) and April 13, 1995 (remainder); amend the 1987 (No. 459) and 1992 (No. 78) Regulations.

5404. Incapacity benefit

SOCIAL SECURITY (INCAPACITY BENEFIT) (CONSEQUENTIAL AND TRANSITIONAL AMENDMENTS AND SAVINGS) REGULATIONS (NORTHERN IRE-

LAND) 1995 (No. 150) [£4·15], made under the Social Security Contributions and Benefits (Northern Ireland) Act 1992 (c.7), ss.86A(1), 113(1)(b), 121(3), the Social Security Administration (Northern Ireland) Act 1992 (c.8), s.5(1)(o), 59(1) and S.I. 1994 No. 1898 (N.I. 12), art. 14(1); operative on April 13, 1995; amend various social security regulations and contain transitional provisions consequential on the replacement of sickness benefit and invalidity benefit by incapacity benefit; revoke the 1986 (No. 82) Regulations.

SOCIAL SECURITY (INCAPACITY BENEFIT) (TRANSITIONAL) REGULATIONS (NORTHERN IRELAND) 1995 (No. 35) [£4·70], made under S.I. 1994 No. 1898 (N.I. 12), arts. 6, 9, 14(1); operative on April 13, 1995; deal with the transition to incapacity benefit from sickness benefit and invalidity benefit.

5405. Incapacity for work

SOCIAL SECURITY (INCAPACITY FOR WORK) (GENERAL) REGULATIONS (NORTHERN IRELAND) 1995 (No. 41) [£4·15], made under the Social Security Contributions and Benefits (Northern Ireland) Act 1992 (c.7), ss.167A–E and the Social Security Administration (Northern Ireland) Act 1992 (c.8), s.59A; operative on April 13, 1995; relate to determinations as to capacity for work for the purposes of the Social Security Contributions and Benefits (Northern Ireland) Act 1992.

SOCIAL SECURITY (INCAPACITY FOR WORK) (MISCELLANEOUS AMENDMENTS) REGULATIONS (NORTHERN IRELAND) 1995 (No. 149) [£1·95], made under the Social Security Contributions and Benefits (Northern Ireland) Act 1992 (c.7), ss.167A, 167C(3), 167D, 167E, the Social Security Administration (Northern Ireland) Act 1992 (c.8), s.57(1), 59A, Sched. 3, para. 4 and S.I. 1994 No. 1898 (N.I. 12), arts. 6, 9, 14(1); operative on April 7, 1995 (part) and April 13, 1995 (remainder); amend the 1976 (No. 175) and 1995 (Nos. 35 and 41) Regulations.

5406. Income support

INCOME SUPPORT (GENERAL) (AMENDMENT AND TRANSITIONAL) REGULATIONS (NORTHERN IRELAND) 1995 (No. 350) [£1·10], made under the Social Security Contributions and Benefits (Northern Ireland) Act 1992 (c.7); ss.122(1)(a), 131(1); operative on October 2, 1995; amend the 1987 (No. 459) and 1995 (No. 301) Regulations.

INCOME SUPPORT (GENERAL) (AMENDMENT) REGULATIONS (NORTHERN IRELAND) 1995 SR 1995 492), made under the Social Security Contributions and Benefits (Northern Ireland) Act 1992 ss.122(1)(a), 131(1); amend SR 1987 459. operative on In accord. with reg.1(1)(2); [£1·10]. These Regulations amend SR 1987 459.

SOCIAL SECURITY (INCOME SUPPORT AND ADJUDICATION) (AMENDMENT) REGULATIONS (NORTHERN IRELAND) 1995 (No. 434) [£1·95], made under the Social Security Contributions and Benefits (Northern Ireland) Act 1992, ss.122(1)(a), 131(1), 132(4)(b), 133(2)(h) and the Social Security Administration (Northern Ireland) Act 1992, s.25(1)(a); amend S.R. 1987 No. 459; S.R. 1995 No. 293. In force: December 12, 1995.

SOCIAL SECURITY (INCOME SUPPORT AND CLAIMS AND PAYMENTS) (AMENDMENT) REGULATIONS (NORTHERN IRELAND) 1995 (No. 301) [£5·20], made under the Social Security Contributions and Benefits (Northern Ireland) Act 1992 (c.7), ss.122(1)(a), 131(1), 132(4)(b), 133(2)(h)–(j), 171(5) and the Social Security Administration (Northern Ireland) Act 1992 (c.8), ss.5(1)(q), 13A(2); operative at the beginning of a claimant's first benefit week on or after October 2, 1995; amend the 1987 (Nos. 459, 465) Regulations.

5407. Income-related benefits

INCOME-RELATED BENEFITS AND SOCIAL SECURITY (CLAIMS AND PAYMENTS) (MISCELLANEOUS AMENDMENTS) REGULATIONS (NORTHERN IRELAND) 1995 (No. 367) [£5·70], made under the Social Security Contributions and Benefits (Northern Ireland) Act 1992 (c.7), ss.122(1), 123(1)(d)(i), 128(3), 131(1), 132(1)(3)(4)(a)(b), 133(2)(b)(d)(ii), 171(5) and the Social Security Administration (Northern Ireland) Act 1992 (c.8), s.5(1)(h)(j); operative on October 2, 1995 (part) and October 3, 1995 (remainder); amend the 1987 (Nos. 459, 461, 463, 465), 1992 (No. 78) and 1995 (No. 129) Regulations.

INCOME-RELATED BENEFITS (MISCELLANEOUS AMENDMENTS) REGULATIONS (NORTHERN IRELAND) 1995 (No. 86) [£2·80], made under the Social Security Contributions and Benefits (Northern Ireland) Act 1992 (c.7); ss.122(1)(a)–(c), 127(5), 128(4)(8), 131(1), 132(3)(4)(a)(b), 133(2)(c)(d)(i); operative on April 10, 1995 (part) and April 11, 1995 (remainder); amend the 1987 (Nos. 459 and 463) and 1992 (No. 78) Regulations.

INCOME-RELATED BENEFITS (MISCELLANEOUS AMENDMENTS NO. 2) REGULATIONS (NORTHERN IRELAND) 1995 (No. 223) [£1·95], made under the Social Security Contributions and Benefits (Northern Ireland) Act 1992 (c.7), ss.122(1)(b)–(d), 127(5), 128(8), 132(3)(4)(b), 133(2)(c)(d)(i); operative on July 17, 1995 (part), July 18, 1985 (part) and the day following the expiration of certain awards; amend the 1987 (Nos. 461, 463) and 1992 (No. 78) Regulations.

INCOME-RELATED BENEFITS (MISCELLANEOUS AMENDMENTS NO. 3) REGULATIONS (NORTHERN IRELAND) 1995 (No. 410) [£1·55], made under the Social Security Contributions and Benefits (Northern Ireland) Act 1992 (c.7); ss.122(1), 132(4)(a)(b); operative on October 28, 1995; amend the 1987 (Nos. 459, 461 and 463) and 1992 (No. 78) Regulations in relation to the treatment in respect of certain benefits of pensions payable to women in respect of their being, or having been, widows of members of the armed forces.

INCOME-RELATED BENEFITS (WIDOWS' ETC. PENSIONS DISREGARDS) (AMENDMENT) REGULATIONS (NORTHERN IRELAND) 1995 (No. 481) [£1·10], made under the Social Security Contributions and Benefits (Northern Ireland) Act 1992, ss.122(1), 132(4)(a); amend S.R. & O. (N.I.) 1987 Nos. 459, 461, 463; S.R. & O. (N.I.) 1992 No. 78. In force: December 20, 1995; correct errors in S.R. & O. (N.I.) 1995 No. 410.

5408. Industrial injuries—permitted earnings

SOCIAL SECURITY (INDUSTRIAL INJURIES) (DEPENDENCY) (PERMITTED EARNINGS LIMITS) ORDER (NORTHERN IRELAND) 1995 (No. 73) [65p]; made under the Social Security Contributions and Benefits (Northern Ireland) Act 1992 (c.7), Sched. 7, para. 4(5); operative on April 10, 1995; increases amounts in para. 4(4) of Sched. 7 to the Act.

5409. Invalid care allowance

SOCIAL SECURITY (INVALID CARE ALLOWANCE) (AMENDMENT) REGULATIONS (NORTHERN IRELAND) 1995 (No. 429) [65p], made under the Social Security Contributions and Benefits (Northern Ireland) Act 1992, s.70(8); amend S.R. 1976 No. 99. In force: December 12, 1995.

5410. Jobseekers (Northern Ireland) Order 1995 (S.I. 1995 No. 2705 (N.I. 15))

This Order introduces the jobseeker's allowance, which replaces unemployment benefit and income support for unemployed people. It also makes provision to promote the employment of the unemployed. The Order comes into operation on days to be appointed.

5411. Pneumoconiosis—compensation

PNEUMOCONIOSIS, ETC. (WORKMEN'S COMPENSATION) CLAIMS (AMENDMENT) REGULATIONS (NORTHERN IRELAND) 1995 (No. 338) [£1·95], made under S.I. 1979 No. 925 (N.I. 9), arts. 3(3), 4(3), 11(1)(4); operative on October 15, 1995; amend the 1988 (No. 242) Regulations.

5412. Reciprocal agreements

SOCIAL SECURITY (RECIPROCAL AGREEMENTS) ORDER (NORTHERN IRELAND) 1995 (No. 110) [£1·95], made under the Social Security Administration

(Northern Ireland) Act 1992 (c.8), s.155(1)(b)(2); operative on April 13, 1995; modifies social security legislation, to take account of incapacity benefit, in relation to certain orders providing for reciprocity with other countries.

5413. Revaluation of earnings factors

SOCIAL SECURITY REVALUATION OF EARNINGS FACTORS ORDER (NORTHERN IRELAND) 1995 (No. 169) [£1·10], made under the Social Security Administration (Northern Ireland) Act 1992 (c.8), s.130; operative on May 17, 1995; revalues earnings factors.

5414. Social fund—cold weather payments

SOCIAL FUND (COLD WEATHER PAYMENTS) (GENERAL) (AMENDMENT) REGULATIONS (NORTHERN IRELAND) 1995 (No. 387) [65p], made under the Social Security Contributions and Benefits (Northern Ireland) Act 1992 (c.7), s.134(2); operative on November 1, 1994; increase the amount payable for each period of cold weather; revoke the 1994 (No. 383) Regulations.

5415. Social fund—funeral expenses

SOCIAL FUND (MATERNITY AND FUNERAL EXPENSES) (GENERAL) (AMENDMENT) REGULATIONS (NORTHERN IRELAND) 1995 (No. 190) [£1·55], made under the Social Security Contributions and Benefits (Northern Ireland) Act 1992 (c.7), s.134(1)(a); operative on June 5, 1995; amend the 1987 Regulations (No. 150) by specifying who may be entitled to payments from the social fund for funeral expenses.

5416. Statutory maternity pay

STATUTORY MATERNITY PAY (COMPENSATION OF EMPLOYERS) (AMENDMENT) REGULATIONS (NORTHERN IRELAND) 1995 (No. 74) [65p], made under the Social Security Contributions and Benefits (Northern Ireland) Act 1992 (c.7), s.163(1)(c); operative on April 6, 1995; amend the 1994 (No. 271) Regulations.

5417. Statutory sick pay

STATUTORY SICK PAY PERCENTAGE THRESHOLD ORDER (NORTHERN IRELAND) 1995 (No. 69) [£1·95]; made under the Social Security Contributions and Benefits (Northern Ireland) Act 1992 (c.7), s.155A(1)(2); operative on April 6, 1995; enables employers to recover payments of statutory sick pay in excess of 13 per cent of their liability for Class 1 contributions payments in any income tax month.

STATUTORY SICK PAY PERCENTAGE THRESHOLD ORDER 1995 (CONSEQUENTIAL) REGULATIONS (NORTHERN IRELAND) 1995 (No. 70) [£1·10]; made under the Social Security Contributions and Benefits (Northern Ireland) Act 1992 (c.7), ss.155A(4), 159(5); operative on April 6, 1995; effect savings, and amend the 1982 (No. 263) Regulations, consequentially to the 1995 (No. 69) Order.

5418. Unemployment, sickness and invalidity benefit

SOCIAL SECURITY (UNEMPLOYMENT, SICKNESS AND INVALIDITY BENEFIT) (AMENDMENT) REGULATIONS (NORTHERN IRELAND) 1995 (No. 341) [65p], made under the Social Security Contributions and Benefits (Northern Ireland) Act 1992 (c.7), s.25A(1)(a)(3)(a); operative on September 25, 1995; amend the 1984 (No. 245) Regulations.

5419. Widow's benefit and retirement pensions

SOCIAL SECURITY (WIDOW'S BENEFIT AND RETIREMENT PENSIONS) (AMENDMENT) REGULATIONS (NORTHERN IRELAND) 1995 (No. 13) [65p];

made under the Social Security Contributions and Benefits (Northern Ireland) Act 1992 (c.7), s.120(1)(a); operative on February 10, 1995; amend the 1979 (No. 243) Regulations as respects certain voidable marriages.

5420. Workmen's compensation

WORKMEN'S COMPENSATION (SUPPLEMENTATION) (AMENDMENT) REGULATIONS (NORTHERN IRELAND) 1995 (No. 102) [£1·55], made under the Social Security Contributions and Benefits (Northern Ireland) Act 1992 (c.7), s.171(4), Sched. 8, para. 2; operative on April 12, 1995; amend the 1983 (No. 101) Regulations by adjusting the lower rates of lesser incapacity allowance and revoke the 1994 (No. 83) Regulations.

TOWN AND COUNTRY PLANNING

5421. Environmental assessment

PLANNING (ENVIRONMENTAL ASSESSMENT AND PERMITTED DEVELOPMENT) REGULATIONS (NORTHERN IRELAND) 1995 (No. 357) [£1·10], made under the European Communities Act 1972 (c.68), s.2(2); operative on October 16, 1995; further implement Council Dir. 85/337/EEC on the assessment of the effects of certain public and private projects on the environment.

5422. Fees

PLANNING (FEES) REGULATIONS (NORTHERN IRELAND) 1995 (No. 78) [£3·70], made under S.I. 1991 No. 1220 (N.I. 11), arts. 127, 129(1); operative on April 3, 1995; replace with amendments, and revoke, the 1992 (No. 97), 1993 (No. 81) and 1994 (No. 58) Regulations.

5423. General development

PLANNING (GENERAL DEVELOPMENT) (AMENDMENT) ORDER (NORTHERN IRELAND) 1995 (No. 356) [65p], made under S.I. 1991 No. 1220 (N.I. 11), art. 13; operative on October 16, 1995; amends the 1993 (No. 278) Order.

PLANNING (GENERAL DEVELOPMENT) (AMENDMENT NO. 2) ORDER (NORTHERN IRELAND) 1995 (No. 424) [£1·10], made under S.I. 1991 No. 1220 (N.I. 11), art. 13; operative on December 18, 1995; amends the 1993 (No. 278) Order as respects close circuit television cameras to be used for security purposes.

5424. Historical monuments

HISTORIC MONUMENTS AND ARCHAEOLOGICAL OBJECTS (NORTHERN IRELAND) ORDER 1995 (S.I. 1995 No. 1625 (N.I. 9)) [£6·75], provides for the protection of historic monuments and archaeological objects. The Order came into operation on August 29, 1995.

5425. Industrial enterprise fund

INDUSTRIAL ENTERPRISE FUND (WINDING UP) ORDER (NORTHERN IRELAND) 1995 (No. 453) [65p], made under S.I. 1982 No. 1083 (N.I. 15), art. 26(3). In force: February 1, 1996; winds up the Industrial Enterprise Fund.

TRADE AND INDUSTRY

5426. Industrial training—levy

Order made under S.I. 1984 No. 1159 (N.I. 9):
Arts. 23(2)(3), 24(3)(4): S.R. 1995 No. 283 (construction industry) [£1·95].

TRADE UNIONS

5427. Certification officer—fees

CERTIFICATION OFFICER (FEES) REGULATIONS (NORTHERN IRELAND) 1995 (No. 133) [£1·10], made under S.I. 1992 No. 807 (N.I. 5), arts. 5(4), 6(2), 80(1); operative on April 30, 1995; set out fees payable to the certification officer under the 1992 S.I.

5428. Trade Union and Industrial Relations—1995 Order—commencement

TRADE UNION AND INDUSTRIAL RELATIONS (1995 ORDER) (COMMENCEMENT AND TRANSITIONAL PROVISIONS) ORDER (NORTHERN IRELAND) 1995 (No. 354 (C.7)) [65p], made under S.I. 1995 No. 1980 (N.I. 12), art. 1(2), Sched. 3, para. 1; brings the 1995 S.I. into operation on October 1, 1995, except for arts. 140, 150(4), Sched. 4 (part) which come into operation on April 1, 1996 and arts. 35, 36, 150(3) (part), Sched. 3, para. 3 which come into operation on August 30, 1996.

5429. Trade Union and Industrial Relations (Northern Ireland) Order 1995 (S.I. 1995 No. 1980 (N.I. 12))

This Order amends and largely restates the law relating to trade unions and industrial relations. The Order comes into operation on days to be appointed.

TRANSPORT

5430. Orders

ROADS (SPEED LIMIT) (NO. 3) ORDER (NORTHERN IRELAND) 1995 (No. 432) [£1·95], made under S.I. 1981 No. 154 (N.I. 1), art. 50(4)(c); amends S.R. & O. (N.I.) 1969 No. 250; S.R. & O. (N.I.) 1972 No. 89; S.R. 1976 No. 182; S.R. 1981 No. 207; S.R. 1982 No. 131; S.R. 1984 No. 126; S.R. 1985 No. 106; S.R. 1987 No. 164; S.R. 1989 Nos. 108, 256; S.R. 1992 No. 498; S.R. 1994 No. 153. In force: January 4, 1996.

5431. Public service vehicles

PUBLIC SERVICE VEHICLES (AMENDMENT) REGULATIONS (NORTHERN IRELAND) 1995 (No. 446) [£1·10], made under S.I. 1981 No. 154 (N.I. 1), arts. 61(1), 66(1), 80, 218(1); amend S.R. 1985 No. 123. In force: January 24, 1996.

PUBLIC SERVICE VEHICLES (CONDITIONS OF FITNESS, EQUIPMENT AND USE) REGULATIONS (NORTHERN IRELAND) 1995 (No. 447) [£6·35], made under S.I. 1981 No. 154 (N.I. 1), arts. 66(1), 218(1) and S.I. 1995 No. 2994 (N.I. 18), arts. 55(1)(2)(4)(6), 110(2); revoke S.R. & O. (N.I.) 1960 No. 91; S.R. & O. (N.I.) 1967 No. 224; S.R. & O. (N.I.) 1969 No. 63; S.R. 1988 No. 335; S.R. 1994 No. 435. In force: January 24, 1996; replace, with amendments, and revoke

S.R. & O. (N.I.) 1960 No. 91, S.R. & O. (N.I.) 1967 No. 224, S.R. & O. (N.I.) 1969 No. 63, S.R. 1988 No. 335 and S.R. 1994 No. 435.

WATER AND WATERWORKS

5432. Asbestos

CONTROL OF ASBESTOS IN WATER REGULATIONS (NORTHERN IRELAND) 1995 (No. 93) [£1·10], made under the European Communities Act 1972 (c.68), s.2(2); operative on May 1, 1995; implement Council Dir. 87/217/EEC on the prevention and reduction of pollution by asbestos, in relation to asbestos emissions into the aquatic environment.

5433. Surface waters—classification

SURFACE WATERS (CLASSIFICATION) REGULATIONS (NORTHERN IRELAND) 1995 (No. 11) [65p], made under the Water Act (Northern Ireland) 1972 (c.5), s.4B; operative on March 1, 1995; set out criteria for classifying water quality in waterways.

5434. Urban waste water—treatment

URBAN WASTE WATER TREATMENT REGULATIONS (NORTHERN IRELAND) 1995 (No. 12) [£3·70], made under the European Communities Act 1972 (c.68), s.2(2); operative on March 1, 1995; implement Council Dir. 91/271/EEC on urban waste water treatment.

WEIGHTS AND MEASURES

5435. Metrication

WEIGHTS AND MEASURES (METRICATION) (AMENDMENT) ORDER (NORTHERN IRELAND) 1995 (No. 227) [£1·55], made under S.I. 1981 No. 231 (N.I. 10), arts. 6(4), 19(2)(3); operative on July 3, 1995; amends the 1981 S.I.

WEIGHTS AND MEASURES (METRICATION AMENDMENTS) REGULATIONS (NORTHERN IRELAND) 1995 (No. 228) [£3·20], made under S.I. 1981 No. 231 (N.I. 10), arts. 8(1), 9(1)–(4), 10(6), 13(1)(2); operative on July 3, 1995; amend the 1984 (Nos. 117, 188), 1985 (No. 319), 1986 (Nos. 308, 311), 1987 (No. 310), 1989 (No. 109), 1991 (No. 200) and 1993 (No. 441) Regulations.

WEIGHTS AND MEASURES (METRICATION) (MISCELLANEOUS GOODS) (AMENDMENT) ORDER (NORTHERN IRELAND) 1995 (No. 230) [£1·10], made under S.I. 1981 No. 231 (N.I. 10), art. 19(2)(3)(7); operative on July 3, 1995; amends the 1989 (Nos. 69, 164) Orders.

5436. Packaged goods and quantity marking

WEIGHTS AND MEASURES (PACKAGED GOODS AND QUANTITY MARKING AND ABBREVIATION OF UNITS) (AMENDMENT) REGULATIONS (NORTHERN IRELAND) 1995 (No. 229) [£1·95], made under S.I. 1981 No. 231 (N.I. 10), arts. 13(1)(g), 19(6)(a)(d), 30, 31, 37, 38; operative on July 3, 1995; amend the 1990 (No. 410) and 1991 (No. 320) Regulations.

5437. Units of measurement

UNITS OF MEASUREMENT REGULATIONS (NORTHERN IRELAND) 1995 (No. 226) [£1·10], made under the European Communities Act 1972 (c.68), s.2(2); operative on July 3, 1995; amend S.I. 1980 No. 1070, the 1981 S.I., the Weights and Measures Act 1985 and S.I. 1986 No. 1082.

SCOTLAND

ADMINISTRATIVE LAW

5438. Judicial review—competency—argument not put to board. See ANDREW v. CITY OF GLASGOW DISTRICT COUNCIL, §6426.

5439. Judicial review—competency—availability of alternative remedy. See ALAGON v. SECRETARY OF STATE FOR THE HOME DEPARTMENT, §6024.

5440. Judicial review—competency—scope of supervisory jurisdiction of Court of Session—decision of courts of Church of Scotland. See LOGAN v. PRESBYTERY OF DUMBARTON, §5889.

5441. Judicial review—competency—scope of supervisory jurisdiction of Court of Session—statutory discretion formerly exercised under royal prerogative

[Criminal Procedure (Scotland) Act 1975 (c.21), s.263.]

Section 263 of the Criminal Procedure (Scotland) Act 1975 provides that the Secretary of State may, on the consideration of any conviction or sentence passed (other than sentence of death), refer the whole case to the High Court which is to hear and determine the referral as if it were an appeal, regardless of whether an appeal against such conviction or sentence has previously been decided by the High Court or the person convicted has petitioned for the exercise of Her Majesty's mercy. The petitioner was convicted on four charges of possessing and passing on counterfeit banknotes, and thereafter applied for judicial review of the Secretary of State's subsequent refusal to refer his case back to the High Court. The charges arose out of two meetings at which the petitioner had given counterfeit banknotes to a detective sergeant who had not disclosed that he was such. The petitioner's objections at the trial to the tape recordings of these meetings being placed before the jury were rejected, and a direction given by the trial judge that regard should be had as to whether they were fairly obtained or not and further that if the petitioner's contention, that he knew all along that the detective sergeant was a police officer, were not to be accepted, then he should not be convicted. The petitioner's request to the Secretary of State that his case be referred back to the High Court was based on evidence consisting of a taped phone conversation between himself and a prisoner at H.M. Prison, Glenochil, prior to the meetings which had given rise to the charges on which he had been convicted. The petitioner claimed this tape showed that he had been aware of the police involvement and that the Crown had deliberately withheld this evidence at the trial thus depriving him of an integral part of his defence. He further claimed that the Crown had deliberately excised from the judicial examination parts which would have supported his defence. The Secretary of State in his letter refusing the request for a referral replied that there was no evidence that the officers at the petitioner's trial had any knowledge of the tape in question at the time of the trial and that the tape in any case did not show that the petitioner had been "tipped off" regarding the police involvement. The petitioner sought review of this decision, arguing that the Secretary of State had not had regard to the grounds of the application, as he was bound to, but rather had reached his decision upon a misconception of the ground on which the application was based. Counsel for the respondent argued that the petition was incompetent in that the matter was entirely one for the Secretary of State's discretion and, being closely connected with the royal prerogative, as such was not subject to the supervisory jurisdiction of the Court of Session. Further, the respondent had in any event dealt appropriately with the petitioner's application.

Held, that (1) the power contained in s.263 met the characteristics of a "jurisdiction" or "power to decide" and, being conferred by statute, its exercise was prima facie subject to the supervisory jurisdiction of the Court of Session; (2) no procedural impropriety being alleged, the petition effectively challenged the substantive merits of the Secretary of State's decision, the Secretary of State having answered the allegations advanced by the petitioner in his application to him, and was therefore incompetent; and petition dismissed. (*West v. Secretary of State for Scotland* [1992] C.L.Y. 5191, followed; *Leitch v. Secretary of State for Scotland* [1982] C.L.Y. 3591; [1983] C.L.Y. 4862, distinguished; *Moore v. Secretary of State for Scotland* [1984] C.L.Y. 4502, discussed.)

McDONALD v. SECRETARY OF STATE FOR SCOTLAND (O.H.), 1996 S.L.T. 16.

5442. Judicial review—competency—scope of supervisory jurisdiction of Court of Session

A student was not permitted by a university to complete a diploma course, the student having failed to pay the fees. He petitioned for judicial review of the decision to exclude him, for declarator that the decision had been illegal and for damages. The university argued that its relationship with the student was one of contract, that judicial review was incompetent and that the student, having been in breach of contract by reason of his non-payment of the fees, could not enforce any rights under the contract. Having held that the former student was in breach and that the application had to be refused, the court then considered the question of competency.

Held, that although membership of a university could produce situations where judicial review was appropriate whether or not it involved a tripartite relationship, the issue in this case being a purely contractual one, judicial review was incompetent; and petition dismissed.

JOOBEEN v. UNIVERSITY OF STIRLING (O.H.), 1995 S.L.T. 120.

5443. Judicial review—competency—scope of supervisory jurisdiction of Court of Session

B, the chief executive of C, a district council, sought reduction, suspension and interdict by judicial review of a motion by C to suspend B from duty and temporarily assume A in B's place pending an investigation into internal auditors' reports. At a first hearing C argued that (1) B's petition was incompetent and (2) alternatively it should not be granted as C had acted *intra vires*. At debate on issue (1) C founded upon *West v. Secretary of State for Scotland* [1992] C.L.Y. 5191 as imposing a rule that contractual rights and obligations such as those between employer and employee were not amenable to judicial review. B argued that in order to reconcile the rule with *Watt v. Strathclyde Regional Council* [1992] C.L.Y. 5704, Parliament was the third party to the relationship between B and C as it exercised statutory restraint over C in Sched. 7 to the Local Government (Scotland) Act 1973. Alternatively, the tripartite concept dealt primarily with the situation where a private employer conferred jurisdiction on an independent quasi-judicial body, distinguishing it from actings in the public sector, and in any event a tripartite relationship was not essential where there had been an excess of power in the discharge of an administrative function. Where a public authority made an administrative decision by *ultra vires* means and which prejudiced an employee, judicial review was available. C had the statutory restraint of Sched. 7 to the 1973 Act but had exceeded C's power (*Guthrie v. Miller* (1827) 5 S. 711). B's status was almost a position of public office (*Malloch v. Aberdeen Corporation* [1971] C.L.Y. 12835) as opposed to a mere employee.

Held, petition dismissed as incompetent. Judicial review was available where a tripartite relationship existed and, in principle, not where contractual rights or obligations could be enforced. That applied both in the public and private sectors. The supervisory jurisdiction was available only in absence of other remedies (*Watt* distinguished). Considerations of statutory restraint were relevant to the exercise of a discretion but B's case was not attacking C's discretion but the legality of the procedure followed. B's status was irrelevant for so long as he remained an employee subject to an employment contract and without any statutory protection as a public officer. C had exercised a power available in terms of B's employment contract and not a statutory grant. B had a remedy under employment legislation and as B had already prepared a summons claiming an ordinary remedy it was conceivable that such a claim could be formulated. Priority should be given to ordinary remedies in contracts with public as well as private bodies.

BLAIR v. LOCHABER DISTRICT COUNCIL (O.H.), 1995 S.L.T. 407.

5444. Judicial review—jurisdiction. See McDONALD v. SECRETARY OF STATE FOR SCOTLAND, §6055.

5445. Judicial review—local government—competitive tendering. See ETTRICK AND LAUDERDALE DISTRICT COUNCIL v. SECRETARY OF STATE FOR SCOTLAND, §6109.

5446. Judicial review—natural justice—investigation into sheriff's fitness for office

[Sheriff Courts (Scotland) Act 1971 (c.58), s.12(2) and (3).]

Section 12(1) of the Sheriff Courts (Scotland) Act 1971 provides that an investigation may be undertaken by the Lord President and the Lord Justice Clerk into a sheriff's fitness for office and for a report thereon to be made to the Secretary of State for Scotland. Under s.12(2) the Secretary of State may make an order removing a sheriff from office if the report is to the effect that the sheriff is unfit for office by reason of, *inter alia*, "inability". A former sheriff sought judicial review of an order made by the Secretary of State removing him from office following upon a report of an investigation carried out by the Lord President and the Lord Justice-Clerk ("the senior judges"). The investigation had been undertaken at the request of the Secretary of State and took the form of a general investigation into the sheriff's conduct since 1980. Particular examples of the sheriff's conduct were identified and investigated in detail. Statements were taken from a number of persons with experience of his conduct. At the completion of their preliminary inquiries the senior judges provided the sheriff with a list of the cases relevant to his conduct which they were to investigate together with short details of each case and appended documentation where appropriate. He was invited to answer a number of questions and make observations. Following the sheriff's written response the senior judges interviewed a number of persons before interviewing the sheriff. Thereafter the senior judges submitted their report to the Secretary of State. The report was to the effect that the sheriff was unfit for office "by reason of inability", in particular that the sheriff's conduct was improper and that it stemmed from a defect in character which rendered him unable to perform the judicial functions of a sheriff according to the standard which was essential for the proper administration of justice. The sheriff sought reduction of the order and the report on four grounds, namely, that (i) the report proceeded upon a misinterpretation of the word "inability" which the sheriff submitted should be restricted to meaning incapacity through physical or mental illness or disability from performing judicial functions; (ii) the report was not in the form and substance required by s.12(1), and was therefore a nullity, in that the senior judges had failed to carry out an administrative inquiry and had made no decision but merely reached the view that there was a statable case for the sheriff's removal; (iii) there had been a failure to comply with the requirements of natural justice in that the sheriff should have been told who had spoken both for and against him, been informed what evidence had been rejected and for what reasons, been given copies of all the witnesses' statements, have had the opportunity to examine the relevant court processes, and been informed of the senior judges' preliminary conclusions; and (iv) in conducting their inquiry the senior judges had not acted rationally, having failed to investigate the factual background in certain instances and having rejected the sheriff's explanations and justifications.

Held, that (1) "inability" in s.12 of the 1971 Act should be construed in its ordinary wider sense as including a want of ability as this was consistent with the history of its use as compared with the use of the expression "disability", and because otherwise there would be no statutory provision to cover those cases in which for reasons other than illness or disability a sheriff was unable properly to perform his judicial functions; (2) although the senior judges were required to conduct an investigation and prepare a report which it would be reasonable to expect would be influential, the decision to remove the sheriff lay exclusively with the Secretary of State and accordingly the sheriff's attack on the report was entirely misconceived; (3) as no rules were laid down by statute as to the procedure to be followed, the senior judges were the masters of their own procedure subject only to the requirement to act fairly which, in the circumstances, they had done, and the sheriff had not averred fault or circumstances relevant to infer that the senior judges were required as a matter of fairness to do more than they had done to give him notice of the case which he had to meet; (4) the sheriff's averments in regard to lack of rationality were wholly irrelevant as they contained nothing which would suggest that the senior judges came to a wrong or unreasonable conclusion, and in any event it was no part of proceedings for judicial review to embark on a review of the merits of the conclusions to which an inquiry or investigation had come; and petition dismissed. *Observed*, that the question whether the requirements of natural justice had been met by the procedure adopted in any given case had to depend to a great extent on the case's own facts and circumstances.

STEWART v. SECRETARY OF STATE FOR SCOTLAND (O.H.), 1995 S.L.T. 895.

5447. Judicial review—procedural impropriety—approval by Secretary of State of proposed chief executive of insurance company. See BUCHANAN v. SECRETARY OF STATE FOR TRADE AND INDUSTRY, §6033.

5448. Judicial review—procedure—board reaching correct decision but error in reasoning. See ANDREW v. CITY OF GLASGOW DISTRICT COUNCIL, §6426.

5449. Judicial review—reasons for decision. See SAFEWAY STORES v. NATIONAL APPEAL PANEL, §6148.

5450. Judicial review—statutory instrument—whether *ultra vires*. See EAST KILBRIDE DISTRICT COUNCIL v. SECRETARY OF STATE FOR SCOTLAND, §6105.

5451. Judicial review—unreasonableness. See LADBROKE RACING (STRATHCLYDE) v. WILLIAM HILL (SCOTLAND), §5974; STRATHCLYDE PHARMACEUTICALS v. ARGYLL AND CLYDE HEALTH BOARD, §6147.

5452. Judicial review—unreasonableness—Boundary Commission recommendations. See GALLIE v. BOUNDARY COMMISSION FOR SCOTLAND, §5905.

5453. Judicial review—unreasonableness—refusal of legal aid. See McTEAR v. SCOTTISH LEGAL AID BOARD, §6092.

5454. Judicial review—whether challenge barred by tacit acquiescence

A motor vehicle trader, who had been on the chief constable's list of contractors approved for the purpose of removing vehicles including abandoned vehicles, was removed from the list in May 1990 following discovery of a stolen car on his premises. In September 1990 he was acquitted of any offence in relation to the car but in October 1990 he was refused reinstatement to the list. A petition for judicial review of the decision to remove the contractor from the list was presented in October 1992 and, in May 1993 was amended to bring under review instead the decision to refuse reinstatement.

Held, that not only had there been no breach by the chief constable of his duties in relation to the list but also the inordinate delay in seeking judicial review amounted to *mora*, taciturnity and acquiescence; and prayer of petition refused.

ATHERTON v. STRATHCLYDE REGIONAL COUNCIL (O.H.), 1995 S.L.T. 557.

5455. Natural justice—refusal to allow cross-examination

In terms of the Food Safety Act 1990, s.9, an authorised officer of a food authority has power to inspect any food intended for human consumption and, if it appears to him that any such food fails to comply with food safety requirements, to seize the food and remove it in order to have it dealt with by a justice of the peace. The person in charge of the food may attend before the justice of the peace and is entitled to be heard and to call witnesses. The justice of the peace is empowered to make certain orders in relation to the food on the basis of such evidence as he considers appropriate in the circumstances. A hearing in terms of s.9 of the 1990 Act took place before a justice of the peace on February 24, 1995 in relation to 44 batches of Lanark Blue cheese produced by the petitioner and which were allegedly contaminated with listeria monocytogenes and unfit for human consumption. At the hearing the petitioner was represented by senior counsel and the food authority by a solicitor, neither of whom was allowed by the justice to cross examine the other's witnesses, any questions having to be put through the justice. Senior counsel declined to put any questions in this way. On March 3, 1995 the justice issued a decision ordering that the cheese should be disposed of or destroyed. The petitioner sought judicial review of the justice's decision. The Lord Ordinary reduced the decision and held that the justice was under a duty to exercise his powers in terms of the Act in accordance with the principles of natural justice, especially as she was obliged by the statute to reach her decision on the basis of evidence: there had been a denial of natural justice because the petitioner's counsel was denied the opportunity, by cross-examining the other side's witnesses, of testing the strength of their evidence. The food authority and their authorised officer reclaimed and argued, *inter alia* that the justice was acting in an administrative capacity only and that her only duty was to act fairly. She was not bound to act in accordance with the principles of natural justice, as she was not being required to decide an issue between the parties, and in proceedings which were administrative in character it was not unfair for her to insist that all questions to witness should be put through her.

Held, that (1) the principles of natural justice and the duty to act fairly were both expressions of the same concept, and in view of the nature of the proceedings the justice was under a duty to have regard to the principles of natural justice; (2) the circumstances required the justice to allow cross-examination if the proceedings were to be fair and whether or not to allow cross-examination was not a matter for the justice's discretion; (3) as there was a difference of opinion between experts on points which were crucial to a sound determination of the questions which the justice had to decide and the petitioner had been denied the opportunity to test the strength of the food authority's experts, the prejudice which resulted from the refusal to allow cross-examination was self evident; and reclaiming motion refused. *Opinion*, that it was not necessary to aver prejudice to make a relevant case of breach of natural justice. (*Cigaro (Glasgow) v. City of Glasgow District Licensing Board* [1983] C.L.Y. 4431, commented on).

ERRINGTON v. WILSON, 1995 S.L.T. 1193.

5456. Natural justice—voluntary association. See BROWN v. EXECUTIVE COMMITTEE OF THE EDINBURGH DISTRICT LABOUR PARTY, §5542.

5457. Statutory corporation—*ultra vires*—power to sell land. See PIGGINS & RIX v. MONTROSE PORT AUTHORITY, §6406.

5458. Voluntary association—disciplinary committee—competency of review. See BROWN v. EXECUTIVE COMMITTEE OF THE EDINBURGH DISTRICT LABOUR PARTY, §5542.

5459. Voluntary association—natural justice. See BROWN v. EXECUTIVE COMMITTEE OF THE EDINBURGH DISTRICT LABOUR PARTY, §5542.

AGENCY

5460. Principal and agent—constitution of agency—son acting as "personal representative" of deceased father

The son of a deceased taxpayer undertook, in a letter which had been prepared by the Inland Revenue, to pay £20,000 in respect of the deceased's tax liabilities. The offer was made by the son as the "personal representative" of the deceased. In an action of payment founded on the letter the defender argued that in signing the letter he did not accept personal liability but was acting in a representative capacity. He further argued that the offer contained in the letter was ambiguous and should be construed in his favour. The Lord Ordinary granted summary decree. The defender reclaimed.

Held, that (1) the relationship of father and son did not *per se* give rise to a contract of agency, nor could a relationship of agent and principal be created after the death of the putative principal; (2) the use of the term "personal representative" was purely descriptive and did not signify the existence of a relationship of or akin to agency; (3) the terms of the offer were not ambiguous; and reclaiming motion refused.

ADVOCATE (LORD) v. CHUNG, 1995 S.L.T. 65.

5461. Principal and agent—liability of agent for disclosed principal

Opinion, that solicitors who instructed a custody report on behalf of a legally aided client had acted as agents for a disclosed principal and were not personally liable for the fees of the reporter.

CATTO v. LINDSAY & KIRK (Sh.Ct.), 1995 S.C.L.R. 541.

5462. Principal and agent—liability of agent for disclosed principal—whether personal liability for undertaking. See DIGBY BROWN & CO v. LYALL, §6434.

AGRICULTURE

5463. Agricultural holdings—arbitration—powers of arbiter

[Agricultural Holdings (Scotland) Act 1991 (c.55), s.60(1).]

Held, where an arbiter had been appointed by the Secretary of State for Scotland under s.60(1) of the 1991 Act to determine the claims, questions and differences which had arisen between the landlords and tenant of an agricultural holding, that the arbiter had jurisdiction to determine the tenant's claim for damages or compensation arising from certain alleged failures of the landlords.

HILL v. WILDFOWL TRUST (HOLDINGS) (Sh.Ct.), 1995 S.C.L.R. 778.

5464. Agricultural holdings—notice to quit—consent to operation—application dismissed—expenses—appeal. See FANE v. MURRAY, §5940.

5465. Agricultural holdings—notice to quit—consent to operation—competency of application to Scottish Land Court

[Agricultural Holdings (Scotland) Act 1991 (c.55), ss.21(3) and 24(1).]

The landlord of an agricultural holding served a notice to quit on the tenants of the holding who thereafter served a counter notice on the landlord. The landlord then applied to the Scottish Land Court for consent to the operation of the notice to quit. The initial form of application to the court did not specify the ground or grounds on which the landlord sought the court's consent to the operation of his notice to quit. Furthermore the notice to quit detailed a removal date of May 28, which was inconsistent with the lease particulars set out in the notice.

Held, that (1) the specification by the landlord applicant in his initial form of application to the court of the matters as to which he sought to satisfy the court was a statutory requirement; (2) the notice to quit *ex facie* failed to give a period of notice which complied with the provisions of s.21(3) of the Agricultural Holdings (Scotland) Act 1991; and tenant's plea to the competency of the application sustained and application dismissed.

O'DONNELL v. HEATH, 1995 S.L.T. (Land Ct.) 15.

5466. Agricultural holdings—notice to quit—validity. See O'DONNELL v. HEATH, §5465.

5467. Agricultural holdings—rent properly payable—arbitration—appeal against award of arbiter

[Agricultural Holdings (Scotland) Act 1991 (c.55), s.61(2); Scottish Land Court Act 1993 (c.45), Sched. 1, para. 13(1).]

The tenant of an agricultural holding appealed against the award of an arbiter appointed by the Secretary of State for Scotland to fix the rent for his holding. The tenant's grounds of appeal were *inter alia* that the amount of the award fixed by the arbiter was excessive; and that the whole or part of the total expenses of the arbitration had not been awarded in favour of the tenant. The tenant did not suggest how the arbiter might have erred in making his award, but referred the court to the evidence and founded on what was described as the court's inherent right of review of arbiter's awards.

Held, that (1) the court would regard an award appealed against as valid and correct until the appellant showed cause why it should be altered, and the existence of a power to ascertain facts by such mode of enquiry as the court deemed appropriate did not relieve an appellant of the burden of showing cause why the arbiter's award was wrong, either in fact or law and (2) the appeal on the question of expenses should be refused as the arbiter had not exercised his discretion improperly in disposing of the expenses as he did.

MACIVER v. BROADLAND PROPERTIES ESTATES, 1995 S.L.T. (Land Ct.) 9.

5468. Agricultural workers—wages—farm manager—whether a "grieve"

[Agricultural Wages (Scotland) Act 1949 (c.30), s.4; Scottish Agricultural Wages Board Order No. 38, Sched. 1, section c, para. 1.]

T, a company which owned a farm, appealed against conviction under s.4(1)(a) and (b) of the Agricultural Wages (Scotland) Act 1949 for failing to pay an employee (M) the appropriate minimum wages and holiday pay due to a grieve under the order. T was run by I, a consultant physician. M's duties involved the day to day running of the farm, with one to three employed or self employed assistants. I stayed at the farm most weekends and exercised close supervision of the general policy of running it, took decisions regarding the provision of all major items of equipment and ran the farm's finances. M did his duties on a "hands on" basis, but did not have responsibility for policy or financial matters apart from limited selling and purchasing powers. He gave I general advice on agricultural matters. The sheriff held on the foregoing evidence that M "was more akin to a grieve than a farm manager", given his hands-on work and his lack of financial control. T argued that this was insufficient to establish the matter beyond reasonable doubt. The Crown argued that it was a matter of fact in each case and that M was doing what a traditional grieve would do.

Held, appeal allowed. As mechanisation had increased, the number of employees on farms had fallen and the number of grieves had decreased. Farmers and managers themselves had become working farmers and working managers; that did not necessarily change a manager's status or job description to that of grieve. A grieve customarily reported to and received instructions from the employer or his representative, who might be a farm manager. He was not qualified to run a farm. Here however M gave I general advice on farming matters, which was a function of a manager and not of a grieve.

TEVIOT SCIENTIFIC PUBLICATIONS v. McLEOD, 1995 S.C.C.R. 188.

5469. Agriculture holdings—garden centres

[Agricultural Holdings (Scotland) Act 1949 (c.75), ss.1 and 93(1); Agricultural Holdings (Scotland) Act 1991 (c.55), ss.1 and 85(1).]

A sought declarator that a lease granted to B was not an agricultural holding within s.1 of the 1949 and 1991 Acts. A let to B 80 acres in 1984 for 25 years. Under the lease B were to use the subjects primarily for their business of seedsmen and nurserymen, and the wholesale and retail sale of garden products; A averred that the predominant use was such sale, and not as a market garden. B averred that the land was predominantly used for the planting and propagation of young trees and their subsequent sale. B sought dismissal, arguing that the definition of agriculture included horticulture, seed growing and nursery grounds (s.93(1) of the 1949 Act; s.85(1) of the 1991 Act; *MacEwen and Law, Joint Applicants* [1986] C.L.Y. 3917). The concept of retail sale did not render the subjects non-agricultural. Where there was mixed use the test was whether the tenancy, as a whole, was agricultural (Gill, *Agricultural Holdings* (2nd ed.), para. 199; *Howkins v. Jardine* [1951] 1 K.B. 614; *Short v. Greeves* [1988] C.L.Y. 67). The existence of a rent review clause in commercial terms with provision for arbitration did not negative an intention of agricultural use; the statutory provisions overrode it so far as inconsistent. A argued that B had a commercial lease of a garden centre and not of agricultural land.

Held, proof before answer allowed. The statutory definition would have to be applied to the facts. Thereafter A and B's intention would be relevant only to the issue of whether the use was lawful under the lease. The scope of B's operations was in B's memorandum of association and a narrow construction should not be placed on the "business of seedsmen and nurserymen" (*Short v. Greeves, supra*). The references to market gardens and nursery grounds in s.93(1) of the 1949 Act were distinct and were treated as so in ss.65–67 of the 1949 Act. The inconsistent clauses only demonstrated that A and B might not have consciously had in mind the creation of an agricultural tenancy but did not negative the possibility. A would require to establish that B's use was not agricultural as a whole (*Howkins v. Jardine*). *Observed*, that much would depend on the relationship between the use of the subjects for propogation and use for the sale of natural or man-made products, including the nature and extent of the sale of bought-in products.

ABERDEEN DISTRICT COUNCIL, CITY OF v. BEN REID AND CO., *The Times*, October 6, 1995.

5469a Cattle. See ANIMALS, §5473.

5470. Hill Farming. See SCOTLAND: AGRICULTURE, §5471.

5471. Livestock extensification

HEATHER MOORLAND (LIVESTOCK EXTENSIFICATION) (SCOTLAND) REGULATIONS 1995 (No. 891) [£2·80], made under the European Communities Act 1972 (c.68), s.2(2); operative on April 24, 1995; provide for the payment of aid to farmers who undertake to reduce the proportion of sheep per forage area, thereby pursuing agricultural methods compatible with the requirements of the protection of the environment and the maintenance of the countryside.

5472. Potatoes

SEED POTATOES ORIGINATING IN THE NETHERLANDS (NOTIFICATION) (SCOTLAND) ORDER 1995 (No. 2874) [65p], made under the Plant Health Act 1967 (c.8), s.3 (as amended by the European Communities Act 1972 (c.68) s.4(1) and Sched. 4 and the Criminal Justice Act 1982 (c.48) s.42); operative on November 7, 1995; requires persons who have or had in their possession, or who know of the presence in Scotland of seed potatoes grown in 1995 in the Netherlands, to notify the Secretary of State; non-compliance with this order without reasonable excuse will lead to a summary conviction or a fine.

ANIMALS

5473. Cattle

ARTIFICIAL INSEMINATION OF CATTLE (ANIMAL HEALTH) (SCOTLAND) AMENDMENT REGULATIONS 1995 (No. 2556) [£1·55], made under the Animal Health and Welfare Act 1984 (c.40), ss.10(1) and (2); operative October 23, 1995; clarify the requirements for trade in both deep-frozen and fresh bovine semen.

[S.I. 1985 No. 1857 amended.]

WARBLE FLY (SCOTLAND) AMENDMENT ORDER 1995 (No. 2042) [£1·10], made under the Animal Health Act 1981 (c.22) ss.1, 8(1), 15(4) and 86(1); operative on September 1, 1995; provides a veterinary inspector with power to serve a notice on a cattle owner where, after examination, the cattle are found to be infested by warble fly.

[S.I. 1982 No. 207 amended.]

5474. Dogs—dangerous dogs—dangerously out of control in a public place—person in charge of dog

[Dangerous Dogs Act 1991 (c.65), s.3(1) and (2).]

Section 3(1) of the 1991 Act provides that if a dog is dangerously out of control in a public place, the owner and, if different, "the person for the time being in charge of the dog" is guilty of an offence. Subsection (2) provides that where the accused is the owner of such a dog but was not at the material time in charge of it, it shall be a defence for the accused to prove that "the dog was at the material time in the charge of a person whom he reasonably believed to be a fit and proper person to be in charge of it". An accused person who was the owner of a dog was tried on summary complaint for a contravention of s.3(1)(*a*) of the 1991 Act. He had left the dog in the care, custody and control of a woman, B, from whom he had separated. On the day of the offence he went to B's house and saw his dog in a playing field to the rear of the house. As he went to retrieve the dog it bit a girl. The accused brought the dog under control and reported the incident to B. The sheriff considered that it was inequitable to conclude that the accused had charge of the dog at the time of the incident but he also held that the dog was not in B's charge. The accused relied on the defence in s.3(2) but the sheriff rejected the defence on the ground that the accused had resumed responsibility for the dog when he saw it in the park although the sheriff accepted that the accused had reasonably believed that B was a fit and proper person to be in charge of the dog. The accused was convicted and appealed.

Held, that (1) the fact that a dog was dangerously out of control in a public place did not mean that no person was in charge of it; (2) the owner had responsibility for the dog unless he could prove his defence under s.3(2) and then the responsibility for keeping the dog under control rested with that other person; (3) at the material time B was still in charge of the dog and it was still her responsibility to keep it under control; and appeal allowed and conviction quashed.

SWINLAY v. CROWE, 1995 S.L.T. 34.

5475. Dogs—dangerous dogs—dangerously out of control in a public place—person in charge of dog

[Dangerous Dogs Act 1991 (c.65), ss.3(1)(*b*) and 10(3).]

T appealed against conviction of allowing a boxer dog to be dangerously out of control in a public place. T's dog had approached two children in a playpark, barked and jumped at them, then bit one on the foot, the other on the leg and the first one on the leg and then on the arm before T caught it. It had not previously bitten anyone. The sheriff held that while the dog was not dangerously out of control within s.10(3) at the outset of the incident, it was so by the end, following *Normand v. Lucas*, 1993 G.W.D. 15–975.

Held, appeal allowed. In contrast to *Normand v. Lucas*, this was a single incident with no appreciable interval and no stage before the end at which there were grounds for reasonable apprehension that the dog would injure someone.

TIERNEY v. VALENTINE, 1995 S.L.T. 564.

5476. Wild birds protection—taking of eggs—sentence. See FORSYTH v. CARDLE, §5835.

ARBITRATION

Agricultural holdings. See AGRICULTURE.

5477. Arbiter—scope of jurisdiction. See ERDC CONSTRUCTION v. H.M. LOVE & CO., §5479.

5478. Arbitration clause—construction. See TAYMECH v. TRAFALGAR HOUSE CONSTRUCTION (REGIONS), §5487.

5479. Submission—deed of submission—construction—scope of arbiter's jurisdiction

A company was appointed by an architect on behalf of the owners to carry out work to a tenement building under a common repairs scheme. After the work had finished the company claimed that because of failures on the part of the architect they were entitled to certain sums in addition to the agreed contract price. The owners disputed that it was competent for the company to seek payment of any sums where that claim was based on *quantum meruit*, and the dispute was referred to arbitration. The arbiter issued proposed findings that it was competent for the claimants to claim on the basis of *quantum meruit*. At the request of the owners the arbiter stated a case for the opinion of the Court of Session, on the question of whether the *quantum meruit* claim was competent. Before the Inner House the owners argued that the *quantum meruit* claim was incompetent on various grounds: first, that the arbiter's jurisdiction to deal with the dispute had to be determined solely by the joint deed of appointment which had superseded the general submission to arbitration contained in the initial contract between the parties for the building work, and as the joint deed did not contain any reference to a claim by the company on the basis of *quantum meruit* the arbiter therefore had power to deal only with claims based on the contract itself; secondly, that the claim based on *quantum meruit* had only been advanced for the first time before the arbiter, and the arbiter could not deal with such a claim without there being a prior dispute between the parties in relation to a claim on *quantum meruit*; thirdly, that the company could claim *quantum meruit* only if they had repudiated the initial contract, and there were no averments that they had done so. The company argued that the owners, in failing to take a plea of no jurisdiction in the closed record of the arbitration, had waived their right to object to any claim based on *quantum meruit*, founding on the case of *Halliburton Manufacturing & Service v. Bingham Blades & Partners* [1984] C.L.Y. 3721. They also argued that it was not necessary for them to have repudiated the contract in order to have a claim based on *quantum meruit*, and that it was open to them to claim under the contract itself and to claim as an alternative that they were entitled to repudiate and claim on the basis of *quantum meruit*.

Held, that (1) when seeking to ascertain the scope of reference to the arbiter, regard had to be had both to the initial contract and to the joint deed of appointment; (2) so read the deed was widely expressed and entitled the arbiter to consider all claims which the company put before him; there was no suggestion that the company had rescinded the contract, and (*per* the Lord Justice Clerk (Ross) and Lord Wylie) in a situation of material breach the contractors had to elect between affirming the contract and claiming damages, and repudiating the contract and claiming *quantum meruit*, and the company having elected to receive payment under the contract could not claim *quantum meruit*; (*per* Lord McCluskey) while it was not necessarily the case that an election had to be made before completion of the works, or perhaps even before a claim was brought, the company did not explicitly plead either option but were attempting both to accept payment under the contract in part and to advance a claim *quantum meruit* in respect of all works done, including those paid for under the contract, which was prohibited on the authorities; and questions answered accordingly. *Opinion*, that the rule of practice applied in the *Halliburton* case did not necessarily apply in an arbitration where the arbiter had complete control over his own procedure, and the arbiter was entitled to find, as he did, that the owners had not waived their right to object to the competency of the *quantum meruit* claim. *Morrison-Knudsen Co. Inc. v. British Columbian Hydro and Power Authority* (1978) 85 D.L.R. (3rd) 186, followed.

ERDC CONSTRUCTION v. H.M. LOVE & CO., 1995 S.L.T. 254.

AVIATION

Carriage by air. See CARRIERS.

International carriage by air. See CARRIERS.

BANKING

5480. Negotiable instrument—instrument induced by fraudulent misrepresentation—whether enforceable. See UNIVERSAL IMPORT EXPORT v. BANK OF SCOTLAND, §5579.

BANKRUPTCY

5481. Sequestration—failure to disclose assets and liabilities—whether offence not to disclose liabilities of partnership not sequestrated

[Bankruptcy (Scotland) Act 1985 (c.66), s.19(2)(b).]

Held, that a bankrupt was not guilty of a failure to disclose his assets and liabilities under s.19(2)(b) of the 1985 Act in respect of certain liabilities of a partnership of which he was a partner but which had not itself been sequestrated.

HEYWOOD v. SCRIMGEOUR (Sh.Ct.), 1995 S.C.C.R. 644.

5482. Sequestration—powers of trustee—disposal of debtor's family home

[Bankruptcy (Scotland) Act 1985 (c.66), s.40.]

In the sequestration of a debtor's estates, the debtor's spouse having refused consent to the sale of the family home, the permanent trustee applied to the court for authority to sell the property in accordance with the terms of s.40 of the 1985 Act. The debtor's spouse and their three children opposed the application, contending that it would be detrimental to the health of both the debtor and his spouse to move out of the family home which they had occupied for 26 years and that one of the children was still dependent upon them.

Held, that while it would plainly have been in the interests of the creditors for the house to be sold, since the stress involved for the debtor in moving from the family home would be considerable with potentially fatal results and such a move would be materially detrimental to the health of the debtor's spouse, in the circumstances authority to sell the house should be refused; and application refused.

GOURLAY'S TR. v. GOURLAY, 1995 S.L.T. (Sh.Ct.) 7.

5483. Sequestration—procedure—appeal to sheriff principal—competency

In an action by P for the sequestration of B, where B had objected to the court's jurisdiction, answers were allowed and a hearing fixed. The hearing did not proceed. After a debate on the relevancy of P's averments, a preliminary proof on jurisdiction was fixed. P appealed. B challenged the competency of the appeal since it related to a sequestration process. P argued that the authorities against such appeals related to sequestration and post-sequestration procedure, not to pre-sequestration procedure which was simply summary application procedure.

Held, appeal dismissed as incompetent. The appeal provisions of the Sheriff Court Acts were not applicable to sequestration (Goudy, *Bankruptcy* (4th ed.), p. 444; Dobie, *Sheriff Court Practice*, p. 391). The structure and purpose of the Bankruptcy (Scotland) Act 1985 did not admit of appeal prior to sequestration being awarded. *Opinion*, that sequestration procedure should proceed without delay upon documents produced by the petitioning creditor, as the main purpose was to preserve the debtor's estate. The need for answers arose only very rarely and only when elaborate inquiry was essential before the decision to grant or refuse sequestration could be addressed. An aggrieved debtor should pursue recall procedure or an action of reduction in the event that issues such as jurisdiction required to be tried (*Scottish Milk Marketing Board v. Wood*, 1936 S.L.T. 470).

PAGANELLI PROPERTIES (GLASGOW) v. BIBA, 1995 S.L.T. (Sh.Ct.) 70.

5484. Sequestration—procedure—order that bankrupt provide trustee with list of assets and liabilities—competency of appeal to sheriff principal

[Bankruptcy (Scotland) Act 1985 (c.66), s.64; Sheriff Courts (Scotland) Act 1907 (c.51), ss.27 and 28.]

Section 64(1) of the Bankruptcy (Scotland) Act 1985 provides that a bankrupt is obliged to take every practicable step necessary to enable the trustee in bankruptcy to perform his functions. Section 64(2)(b) further provides that if the bankrupt fails to comply with the section the sheriff may order him to do so. A sheriff ordered a bankrupt in terms of s.64(2)(b) to provide a list of her assets and liabilities. The bankrupt appealed to the sheriff principal against the order. The sheriff principal, founding on *Accountant in Bankruptcy v. Allans of Gillock* [1991] C.L.Y. 4423, dismissed the appeal as incompetent on the basis that the 1985 Act made no provision for a right of appeal against a s.64(2)(b) order. The bankrupt further appealed to the Court of Session, arguing that (1) the sheriff's interlocutor was a judicial and not an administrative one and therefore was subject to appeal in terms of the provisions contained in ss.27 and 28 of the Sheriff Courts (Scotland) Act 1907; (2) the sheriff's judgment was a final one in respect that it disposed of the whole of the merits of the summary application which had been made by the trustee and therefore was subject to appeal in terms of ss.27 and 28 of the 1907 Act; (3) the 1985 Act by inference allowed an appeal against such an order; and (4) in any event an appeal to the Court of Session was competent to allow that court to rectify an incompetent decision of the sheriff.

Held, that (1) the sheriff's decision was clearly not incompetent and therefore no question of the Court of Session exercising its supervisory jurisdiction arose; (2) it was clear that in granting the order the sheriff was acting in a judicial capacity and the rights of appeal against such a decision were governed by ss.27 and 28 of the Sheriff Courts (Scotland) Act 1907; (3) there was no necessary implication to be drawn from the 1985 Act that the legislature intended to remove the rights of appeal under the 1907 Act but (4) the sheriff's order was not a final judgment in terms of s.27 of the Sheriff Courts (Scotland) Act 1907 as it did not dispose of the whole subject matter of the cause, that is, the sequestration proceedings, and accordingly appeal was only possible with leave of the sheriff which had not been given; and appeal dismissed. (Dicta in *Accountant in Bankruptcy v. Allans of Gillock* 1991 S.L.T. 765, disapproved.) *Opinion reserved*, on question of whether the Court of Session had power in the exercise of its pre-eminent jurisdiction to rectify an incompetent decision of the sheriff in an appeal from the sheriff principal.

INGLE'S TR. v. INGLE, (I.H.), 1996 S.L.T. 26.

5485. Undischarged bankrupt—title to sue

T sought warrant to cite Y, a building society, and a firm of sheriff officers in an action for interdict and interim interdict against the enforcement of a decree in favour of Y for the repossession of heritable subjects, by T's summary ejection therefrom. T wished to remain in the property until the sale was completed. He claimed that the property would sell better if occupied and that ejection was unreasonable. T was an undischarged bankrupt and his trustee had declined to raise proceedings. Y challenged T's title to sue and claimed that if interdict was granted T might refuse to co-operate with the sale, incurring further loss to his creditors. Warrant to cite and interim interdict were refused by the sheriff. T appealed.

Held, appeal refused. An undischarged bankrupt had no title to sue in proceedings where the trustee had not consented and the litigation might compete with the creditors or the trustee (*Dickson v. United Dominions Trust* [1987] C.L.Y. 4913). *Opinion*, that interim interdict would in any event have been refused: *Gordaviran v. Clydesdale Bank* [1994] C.L.Y. 5912, would have been followed despite a submission for T that that decision did not take account of dicta in *Armstrong, Petr.* [1988] C.L.Y. 4356, since the effect of these dicta was to be read restrictively (*Halifax Building Society v. Gupta* [1994] C.L.Y. 5913). A decree lawfully granted in one court should not be the subject of some sort of supervision of another court before it could be enforced.

THOMSON v. YORKSHIRE BUILDING SOCIETY (Sh.Ct.), 1994 S.C.L.R. 1014.

BUILDING AND CONSTRUCTION

5486. Building contract—breach of contract—loss—overdraft interest incurred as result of delay in payment—relevancy

A counterclaim was presented by the defenders, main contractors, for damages said to arise from the admitted failure of the pursuers properly to carry out their subcontract work by using non-waterproof and inadequate materials. The employers' architect had accordingly declined to issue a certificate certifying payment to the defenders. The defenders claimed that as a result of the delays they had suffered a loss in incurring charges to finance their business consisting of overdraft interest. The sheriff dismissed the counterclaim. The defenders appealed.

Held, that (1) the defenders had been occasioned loss by the pursuer's breach of contract, which loss was clearly foreseeable and was within the reasonable contemplation of parties at the time the contract was made; (2) interest being sought not as a general damage but as the measure of actual loss, which loss was clearly foreseeable and arose naturally from the pursuers' breach of contract, the claim was relevant; and appeal allowed and proof before answer in the counterclaim allowed.

NELSON (W.M.) CLADDING v. MURRAY WILLIAMSON (BUILDERS), 1995 S.L.T. (Sh.Ct.) 86.

5487. Building contract—construction—arbitration clause

Clause 18 of a subcontract provided, *inter alia*, that (1) if a dispute arose in connection with the subcontract it was to be referred to arbitration, but (2) if a dispute arose in connection with the main contract and the contractor was of the opinion that such dispute touched or concerned the subcontract works, then the contractor might require that any dispute under the subcontract be referred to the arbitrator to whom the dispute under the main contract was referred. An action for payment of sums allegedly due in terms of the subcontract between the contractor and the subcontractor having been sisted for arbitration, the subcontractor called upon the contractor to refer the dispute to arbitration in terms of cl. 18. The contractor declined to do so and the subcontractor raised an action seeking an order ordaining the contractor to comply with cl. 18(1). The contractor argued that a dispute had arisen in connection with the main contract which was the subject of Court of Session proceedings in which the contractor sought declarator that an agreement for the completion and settlement of contracts had been concluded, that the contractor was of the opinion that that dispute "touched or concerned the subcontract works" because, the subcontract being a pay as paid contract, no payment was due to the subcontractor until the action in connection with the main contract was resolved, and that in terms of cl. 18(3) the contractor had, by notice, abrogated the provisions of cl. 18(1).

Held, that (1) in considering whether or not there was justification for the view that "the contractor is of the opinion that such dispute touches or concerns the subcontract works", cl. 18 had to be looked at as a whole; (2) the point of contact between the main dispute and the subcontract dispute had to be some matter which would have a material bearing on the decision on both disputes; (3) on the pleadings, while the dispute between the contractor and the employer might have a bearing on whether the pursuers were entitled to immediate payment, it did not "touch or concern the subcontract works" and there was therefore no material connection, or if there was it had not been properly averred by the contractor; and that the contractor had not shown that it was entitled to abrogate the proposed arbitration under cl. 18(1). *Opinion*, that it was regrettable that a clause in a standard form contract should be so drafted as to cause the parties to the contract such difficulty in identifying the proper procedure for resolving disputes between them. Insofar as there was any logic behind cl. 18 there should, so far as possible, be an avoidance of unnecessary duplication of either arbitration or litigation when matters in dispute between the employers and contractors on the one hand and contractors and subcontractors on the other hand had some common origin.

TAYMECH v. TRAFALGAR HOUSE CONSTRUCTION (REGIONS) (O.H.), 1995 S.L.T. 1003.

5488. Building contract—construction—incorporation of conditions of main contract into subcontract—indemnity clause

A contractor was engaged by a gas supply company to carry out boring operations under a road surface to provide a tunnel to carry gas pipes. The main contract between them was subject to the general conditions of contract of the British Gas Corporation. Those conditions included a provision requiring the contractor to indemnify the employer in certain circumstances. The contractor intimated by letter to its subcontractor that the subcontract conditions were as the contract general conditions and that no variation would be allowed. These contractual terms were accepted by the subcontractor. The contractor sought to recover from the subcontractor sums equivalent to losses which the contractor had previously paid to the gas supply company in respect of a gas pipe fracture. The contractor alleged that these losses had been caused by the negligence of sub-subcontractors responsible for excavation. The subcontractor disputed that the indemnity provision had been effectively incorporated into the subcontract.

Held, that (1) the general conditions were specifically apt to govern the contract between the contractor and employer and could not be properly adapted to govern the relationship between contractor and subcontractor other than by specific words, which the court could not supply; (2) while the general words used in the subcontract showed the parties' intention that the subcontractors should be bound to perform their subcontract in such a way as not to put the contractors in breach of contract with the employer, the words used were not apt to incorporate an indemnity clause making the subcontractors responsible for the negligence of the sub-subcontractors and liable to relieve the contractor of his contractual obligation to indemnify the employer; and action dismissed. (*Brightside Kilpatrick Engineering Services v. Mitchell*

Construction (1973) [1976] C.L.Y. 208, and *Goodwins Jardine & Co v. Charles Brand & Son* (1905) 7 F. 995, followed.)

COMOREX v. COSTELLOE TUNNELLING (LONDON) (O.H.), 1995 S.L.T. 1217.

5489. Building contract—construction—"storm"—"bursting or overflowing of water tanks, apparatus or pipes"

[JCT Standard Form of Building Contract (1980) Private Edition with Quantities, cl. 22C.]

The occupiers of a building suffered serious damage as a result of water penetration during roof works. They sought to recover damages from the builders with whom they had a contract governed by the JCT conditions, cl. 22C of which puts the employer and not the contractor at risk where damage is suffered from a variety of causes including "storm" and "bursting or overflowing of water tanks, apparatus or pipes". The water damage was the result of heavy rainfall.

Held, that although rain alone could amount to "storm" there was insufficient evidence to establish rain severe enough to amount to "storm"; that the escape of water from the gutters was not within the exception; and decree of damages pronounced. *Opinion*, that the exception for "bursting or overflowing of water . . . pipes" related to water supply pipes and not to drains.

NIMMO (WILLIAM) & CO. v. RUSSELL CONSTRUCTION (O.H.), 1995 S.L.T. 1281.

5490. Building contract—implied term—business efficacy—consequences of delay

[Prescription and Limitation (Scotland) Act 1973 (c.52), s.6(1).]

Specialist subcontractors linked into a fixed-price contract to do certain work for the main subcontractor in a building contract. The contract was contained within various documents, one of which was the tender of the specialist subcontractors. Said document provided that the specialist subcontractors could extend the date of completion and be paid over and above the contract price where a delay was not due to their fault. The contract was to be performed between January 1985 and July 1986. In the event work commenced in June 1985 and was not completed until May 1987. The specialist subcontractors raised an action suing, first, for payment in respect of extra works and, second, for damages arising from the delay. It was agreed that there should be a proof before answer on the claim for extras but the defenders argued that the claim based on delay was irrelevant. The pursuers had initially relied upon one of their standard conditions of contract but at procedure roll it had been held that those conditions had been superseded by the defenders' contract conditions which had no such provision. In March 1993, more than five years after the work had been completed, the pursuers amended their pleadings to contend that there were two implied terms in the contract, the first term being concerned with entitlement to payment of extra costs if delay not caused by them caused the original contract period to be extended, and the second term relating to the pursuers being given access to the site to carry out the work within the contract period. A claim for damages was based upon an alleged breach of that condition. At a further procedure roll hearing the defenders argued that the contract was not subject to the allegedly implied terms and in any event that any right to recover damages for breach of the second implied term had prescribed. They contended that terms could be implied only (i) if they were terms to which the parties would inevitably have agreed; (ii) if the contract would not work without them; or (iii) if they were required to find out what the contract really was. They contended that the first implied term was not necessary to make the contract work and would not necessarily have been acceptable to both parties to the contract; and that the second implied term tried to impose an obligation on the defenders which they could not have fulfilled and generally, that both implied terms were not necessary for business efficacy or were not terms which it would be said must have been within the contemplation of the parties when the contract was entered into. The pursuers argued in particular that the length of the contract period was a material factor in pricing the job when it was a fixed-price contract and that accordingly it was necessary to provide for the consequences of delay not caused by them since, if no such provision was implied, the contract could be grossly extended without a remedy being available to them.

Held, that, although it might be necessary to imply into a contract terms relating to delay, the implied terms contended for here sought to impose obligations arising from delays over which the defenders had no control and were therefore terms which the defenders could not have intended to accept; and action dismissed so far as laid upon the alleged implied terms. *Opinion,* that the claim for breach of the second implied term had not prescribed since the claim for damages for breach of the contract was another aspect of the contractual obligation to make payment arising out of delay and accordingly a relevant claim under the basic obligation had been made by the action, thus interrupting the running of the prescriptive period.

DUCTFORM VENTILATION (FIFE) v. ANDREWS-WEATHERFOIL (O.H.), 1995 S.L.T. 88.

5491. Building contract—variation—defective materials—employer holding contractor responsible but instructing continued performance of work with defective materials

[I.C.E. Conditions of Contract (5th ed.) c.11, 13(3) and 51(1).]

A local authority engaged contractors to construct an underground sewer. The contract was governed by the I.C.E. Conditions of Contract (5th ed.). Clause 13(1) obliged the contractors to adhere to the engineer's instructions and directions. Clause 13(3) entitled them to reimbursement of any costs caused by unforeseeable disruption to their arrangements and methods of construction arising from an instruction or direction, and deemed any variation required by an instruction or direction to have been given pursuant to cl. 51. Clause 51(1) provided, that "variations" included "changes in quality, form and character". Clause 361.9 provided that certain prefabricated tunnel segments should be capable of withstanding a variety of specified forces without cracking. The engineer approved certain segments which the contractors proposed to use. While the tunnel was under construction, cracks occurred in the segments. The contractors asked the engineer to consider reimbursing their costs arising out of the cracking. The engineer wrote in reply, saying that "the cracked segments were acceptable subject always to the requirement to make them reasonably watertight". The claim for payment was taken to an arbiter, who found that the contractors were not responsible for the cracking, and that they were entitled to payment for the variation of the contract. The authority appealed by way of stated case, seeking the opinion of the court on, *inter alia*, the question whether the contract had been varied in terms of cl. 51. They argued that the acceptance by the engineer of defective materials was not an order to vary the contract, but a concession to the contractors. A variation had to be expressly ordered; the letter contained no such order. The context of the letter was that the engineer had held the contractors responsible for the cracking, but had been prepared as a concession to accept the segments if they were repaired. The contractors contended that the letter was couched as a concession only because of an assumption by the engineer that had proved to be mistaken. The substitution of repaired segments instead of segments that met the specification had been required only because the design approved by the engineer had proved to be inadequate.

Held, that since in his letter the engineer had accepted cracked segments which had been made reasonably watertight in place of segments which complied with the specification, the letter constituted a variation of the contract in terms of cl. 51; and question answered in the affirmative. *Per* the Lord Justice Clerk (Ross): The letter was also an instruction or direction requiring a variation in terms of cl. 13(3), and was therefore to be deemed a variation in terms of cl. 51.

SHANKS & McEWAN (CONTRACTORS) v. STRATHCLYDE REGIONAL COUNCIL, 1995 S.L.T. 172.

5492. Building operations—whether windowcleaning a "building operation"

[Factories Act 1961 (c.34), s.176(1); Construction (Working Places) Regulations 1996 (S.I. 1996 No. 94), reg. 2.]

E, a window cleaner, sought damages from his employer (T), after he fell from his ladder while cleaning the windows of a house, averring both a common law case and that his work was a building operation within the meaning of the 1966 Regulations. T sought dismissal of the latter case. E argued that his work fell within the definition of "building operation" in s.176(1) of the Factories Act, applied to reg. 2 of the 1966 Regulations, in that it constituted "maintenance", "maintained" being defined as "maintained in an efficient state, in efficient working order, and in good repair". Window cleaning involved both the external cleaning of the structure and the maintenance of it, and was on either basis a building operation in that (1) a building would be incomplete if its windows were not glazed, and the glazed windows were therefore part of the structure; and (2) without such cleaning the building would cease to be in good repair.

Held, statutory case dismissed. (1) The case law indicated that there was a distinction between glass forming part of the structure of the building and glass inserted in a window. The ordinary action of window cleaning was quite distinct from the processes for the external cleansing of structures (*Lavender v. Diamints* [1949] C.L.Y. 3973); on the other hand the cleaning of a glass roof supported by rafters would constitute a building operation (*Bowie v. Great International Plate Glass Insurance Cleaning Co., The Times*, May 14, 1981). The present case clearly fell outwith the regulations. (2) The definition of "building operation" impliedly excluded from the scope of "maintenance" any external cleaning that was not cleaning of the structure.

EDIE v. EDIE (O.H.), *The Scotsman*, September 20, 1995.

5493. Building regulations

BUILDING (PROCEDURE) (SCOTLAND) AMENDMENT REGULATIONS 1995 (No. 1572) [£1·55], made under the Building (Scotland) Act 1959 (c.24), ss.2(4) (as substituted by the Local Government (Scotland) Act 1973 (c.65) Sched. 15), 4(8) (as substituted by the Building (Scotland) Act 1970 (c.38), s.2), 4A (as added by the Building (Scotland) Act 1970 (c.38), s.2), 6(2) (as amended by the Building (Scotland) Act 1970 (c.38), Sched. 1), 6(3A) (as added by the Health and Safety at Work etc. Act 1974 (c.37), Sched. 7), 6A(7) (as added the Building (Scotland) Act (c.38), s.4), 6B(3) (as added by the Building (Scotland) Act (c.38), s.4), 20 (as substituted by the Housing (Scotland) Act 1986 (c.65), s.19(6)), 24(1)(b), 29(1) and Sched. 3; operative on July 24, 1995; further amend the Building (Procedure) (Scotland) Regulations 1981, increase the building control fees and make minor amendments to reflect recent changes in the building standards regulations.

[S.I. 1981 No. 1499 amended. S.I. 1991 No. 1528 revoked.]

5494. Building regulations—fees. See BUILDING AND CONSTRUCTION, §5493.

5495. Surveyor—negligence–contributory negligence by building society. See LEEDS PERMANENT BUILDING SOCIETY v. WALKER FRASER & STEELE, §6153.

CAPITAL TAXATION

5496. Inheritance tax

INHERITANCE TAX (DELIVERY OF ACCOUNTS) (SCOTLAND) REGULATIONS 1995 (No. 1459) [65p], made under the Inheritance Tax Act 1984 (c.51);

operative on July 1, 1995; increase from £125,000 to £145,000, for deaths on or after April 6, 1995, the limit of value of a deceased's estate below which the delivery of an account for the purpose of inheritance tax is dispensed with.
[S.I. 1981 No. 881 amended.]

5497. Inheritance tax—variation of testamentary provisions—application of curator *bonis*. See B.'s CURATOR BONIS, §6464.

CARRIERS

5498. Carriage by air—claim against carrier at common law—whether covered by items of Warsaw Convention. See ABNETT v. BRITISH AIRWAYS, §5499.

5499. International carriage—damages claim against carrier at common law—competency

[Carriage by Air Act 1961 (c.27), s.1(1) and (2) and Sched. 1]

A, a passenger on an aircraft detained in Kuwait where it had stopped over at the time of the Iraqi invasion, and who had then been detained in Kuwait for about a month, reclaimed against the Lord Ordinary's decision that her action against the airline (B) at common law was excluded by the terms of the Convention in Sched. 1 to the 1961 Act. A argued that the Convention did not exclude common law rights of action which could not be brought within the terms of Arts. 17, 18 and 19: see Art. 24, and that a substantial weight of American authority supported this interpretation.

Held, reclaiming motion refused. It was advisable to have in mind the purposes behind the enactment of the Warsaw Convention in 1929: to achieve a uniformity of law and procedure applicable to aviation claims; to limit the liability of air carriers in order to promote the development of the industry; and to give the passenger a right of action in certain circumstances in which he might otherwise find it difficult to prove a claim. The terms of s.1(1) of the 1961 Act demonstrated that the (amended) Convention was intended to regulate all the rights and liabilities of carriers and passengers to which the Convention applied, and to read it as allowing other rights and liabilities where it did not apply would strike at the very purpose of uniformity which it was intended to achieve. It appeared that American courts had to rely on the terms of the Convention alone and that their decisions were of limited assistance. The decisions contained dicta supporting each side and the point had not yet been ruled on by the Supreme Court. Regarding the provisions of the Convention itself, the all embracing terms of Art. 1(1) and heading and terms of Chap. 3 indicated the intention to lay down a comprehensive code on liability. *Sidhu v. British Airways*, C.A., January 27, 1995, unreported, was followed in its reasoning (including its comments on the American decisions) and its result.

ABNETT v. BRITISH AIRWAYS, 1995 S.C.L.R. 654.

CHARITIES

5500. Accounts

CHARITIES (EXEMPTION FROM ACCOUNTING REQUIREMENTS) (SCOTLAND) AMENDMENT REGULATIONS 1995 (No. 645) [65p], made under the Law Reform (Miscellaneous Provisions) (Scotland) Act 1990 (c.40), s.4(4)(*b*); operative on March 31, 1995; amend the Charities (Exemption from Accounting Requirements) (Scotland) Regulations 1993 so as to extend the class of Scottish charitable statutory corporation from one which is established by statute whose accounts are required to be examined and certified by the Comptroller and Auditor General, to one which is established by Statute or Royal Charter whose accounts are required to be examined and certified by the Comptroller and Auditor General, thereby extending the exemption of classes of recognised bodies.

[S.I. 1993 No. 1624 amended.]

5501. Charitable purposes—winding up of trust fund—whether income applicable to charitable purposes only. See MUIR (WILLIAM) (BOND 9) EMPLOYEES' SHARE SCHEME TRS. v. I.R.C., §6027.

5502. Dormant accounts

CHARITIES (DORMANT ACCOUNTS) (SCOTLAND) REGULATIONS 1995 (No. 2056) [£1·55], made under the Law Reform (Miscellaneous Provisions) (Scotland) Act 1990 (c.40), s.12(10); operative on September 1, 1995; provide the procedure to be followed by the Scottish charities nominee in dealing with dormant accounts of Scottish charities.

Income Tax. See INCOME TAX.

5503. Rates—relief—charitable purposes—social club with bar facilities. See COALBURN MINERS' WELFARE AND CHARITABLE SOCIETY v. STRATHCLYDE REGIONAL COUNCIL, §6251.

CHILDREN AND YOUNG PERSONS

5504. Access. See F. v. F., §5528.

5505. Access—best interests of child

M appealed against the sheriff's award to F of access to C, a child of M and F's relationship now aged almost five. F had lived with M for the first three years of C's life but following separation had had no contact with C. C had chronic asthma and attacks could occur at any time. The sheriff found it would be in C's best interest to have contact with F in an interlocutor of January 17, 1994 but made no detailed order for access in the hope that in a period of continuation M and F would arrange access between them, and in particular that M would give F information on how to care for C in the event of an asthma attack. M refused to co-operate with F. F advised the court on April 29, 1994 that he had consulted his doctor (D) and D was satisfied that F was able to operate C's nebuhaler and recognise the onset of an attack. The sheriff then made a detailed order.

Held, appeal allowed and case remitted to the sheriff. The sheriff was entitled to conclude that access was in C's interest. However having found as a precondition of access that F should receive adequate instruction on how to look after C in an asthmatic attack, the sheriff should not have been ready to accept F's claim that D had given the necessary instruction without any other independent confirmation. It was essential to minimise risk to C's health and access should not commence until the sheriff was satisfied on reliable information. Accordingly the detailed access order should be recalled and the case remitted for a further hearing on F's ability to cope. *Observed*, that while there were difficulties involved in referring to a family conciliation service in the face of opposition such as M's, it might be appropriate at the present stage for an experienced mediator to help reassure M and help her address the practical arrangements.

HARRIS v. MARTIN, 1995 S.C.L.R. 580.

5506. Access—best interests of child—standard of proof

[Law Reform (Parent and Child) (Scotland) Act 1986 (c.9), ss.2(1)(b) and 3(2).]

Held, in proceedings by way of minute to vary to nil an award of access in favour of a father to his two children, that his parental rights conferred by s.2(1) of the 1986 were subject to the provisions, *inter alia*, of s.3(2) of that Act and that s.3(2) did not prescribe a higher standard of proof in such proceedings than the balance of probabilities.

GREIG v. GREIG (Sh.Ct.), 1995 S.C.L.R. 789.

5507. Adoption—application by natural father with award of custody to adopt child after death of natural mother—whether appropriate

[Adoption (Scotland) Act 1978 (c.28), s.6.]

The father and mother of a child were not married. After the death of the mother, the father was awarded custody of the child and the maternal grandmother was awarded access each weekend. The father then sought to adopt the child and his application was opposed by the grandmother.

Held, that it had not been proved that an adoption order would be more likely than the existing custody order to safeguard and promote the welfare of the child; and application refused.

H. v. M. (Sh. Ct.), 1995 S.C.L.R. 401.

5508. Adoption—freeing for adoption—effect of order—rights of mother

[Law Reform (Parent and Child) (Scotland) Act 1986 (c.9), ss.3(1) and 9(1)(b); Adoption (Scotland) Act 1978 (c.28), s.18(1) and (5); Children Act 1975 (c.72), s.47(2).]

Section 18(5) of the Adoption (Scotland) Act 1978 provides that on the making of an order declaring a child free for adoption under that section the parental rights and duties relating to the child vest in the adoption agency. Section 3(1) of the Law Reform (Parent and Child) (Scotland) Act 1986 provides that "Any person claiming interest may make an application to the court for an order relating to parental rights". Section 9(1)(b) of the 1986 Act provides that "Nothing in this Act shall . . . affect the law relating to adoption of children." A local authority obtained an order under s.18 of the 1978 Act, freeing two illegitimate children for adoption. The order vested the parental rights relating to the children in the local authority, and the children were then placed with prospective adoptive parents. The natural mother of the children presented a petition to the Court of Session under s.3 of the 1986 Act, seeking an order relating to parental rights in respect of the children, namely an order for custody of, which failing access to, the children. The local authority opposed the petition and challenged the competency of the proceedings. The Lord Ordinary repelled that plea and a reclaiming motion was refused. In the House of Lords it was accepted on behalf of the mother that if the law were as stated in *Beagley v. Beagley* [1984] C.L.Y. 4266, and *Borders Regional Council v. M.* [1986] C.L.Y. 3629, a parent whose rights had been divested under s.18 of the 1978 Act could not apply for custody or access. It was maintained, however, that the position had been altered by s.3(1) which was unqualified in its terms as to who might apply for an order relating to parental rights; the link of a divested mother together with her concern for the best interests of her children gave her sufficient interest for the purposes of the subsection. It was further argued that an order made under s.3(1) in favour of a parent divested under s.18 of the 1978 Act would not affect the law relating to adoption within the meaning of s.9(1)(b) of the 1986 Act.

Held, that s.3(1) had to be construed in a manner which did not alter existing adoption law, namely in a manner which conferred on divested parents neither rights in relation to their natural children of which Parliament in the Act of 1978 had specifically provided that they should be divested, nor rights the exercise of which would effectively cut across the procedure and effect of adoption, and that s.9(1)(b) was a complete answer to the mother's contention; and appeal allowed. *Opinion*, that the majority in the Second Division had been correct to conclude that a divested parent was "a person other than a parent . . . or guardian" for the purposes of s.47(2) of the Children Act 1975.

D. v. GRAMPIAN REGIONAL COUNCIL (H.L.), 1995 S.L.T. 519.

5509. Adoption—overseas

ADOPTION (DESIGNATION OF OVERSEAS ADOPTIONS) (VARIATION) (SCOTLAND) ORDER 1995 (No. 1614) [65p], made under the Adoption (Scotland) Act 1978 (c.28), ss.60(4) and 65(2); operative July 10, 1995; includes China among those countries whose adoptions are designated in the Adoption (Designation of Overseas Adoptions) Order 1973 and therefore are to be recognised in Scotland.

[S.I. 1973 No. 19 amended.]

5510. Aliment—backdating—special cause

[Family Law (Scotland) Act 1985, s.3(1)(c)(ii).]

The Family Law (Scotland) Act 1985, s.3(1)(*c*)(ii) gives the court power to backdate an award of aliment "on special cause shown", to a date prior to the bringing of the action. In a consistorial cause the amount of aliment which a father was to pay for his children and the backdating of any such award were in dispute. The sheriff awarded a weekly sum backdated to a date prior to the raising of the actions founding on the fact that the defender had not paid. The defender appealed to the sheriff principal.

Held, that special cause to backdate an award had to mean something more than, as in the present case, the usual refusal to pay; and appeal allowed accordingly.

ADAMSON v. ADAMSON, 1995 S.L.T. (Sh.Ct.) 45.

5511. Aliment—child alimented by mother's husband in mistaken belief that he was child's father—whether accepted as a child of his family

[Family Law (Scotland) Act 1985 (c.37), s.1(1).]

During the subsistence of a marriage the wife gave birth to a child, of whom the husband suspected that he was not the father but was unable to prove it. On divorce the wife obtained awards of custody and aliment in respect of the child. The wife later consented to DNA testing which established that her former husband was not the child's father.

Held, that the former husband was under no obligation to aliment the child because he had never accepted the child into his family in the knowledge that he was not in fact the child's father.

WATSON v. WATSON (Sh.Ct.), 1994 S.C.L.R. 1097.

5512. Aliment—enforcement of foreign maintenance order—change of circumstances

[Maintenance Orders (Reciprocal Enforcement) Act 1972 (c.18), ss.7(2) and 8(8).]

Held, in an application under s.7 of the 1972 Act for confirmation of a provisional order for payment of aliment of £300 per month made in Canada against a father who was then working, that the order should be confirmed to the extent only if ordering payment of £2·50 per week with effect from the date of the interlocutor as the father was by then unemployed.

McINTYRE v. McINTYRE (Sh.Ct.), 1995 S.C.L.R. 765.

5513. Child neglect. See M. v. ORR, §5790; M. v. NORMAND, §5791.

Children in care of local authorities. See LOCAL GOVERNMENT.

5514. Children (Scotland) Act 1995 (c.36)

This Act reforms the Law of Scotland relating to children, to the adoption of children and to young persons who as children have been looked after by a local authority; makes new provision regarding the relationship between parent and child and guardian and child and makes provision regarding children's residential establishments.

The Act received Royal Assent on July 19, 1995.

5515. Children (Scotland) Act 1995 (c.36)—commencement

CHILDREN (SCOTLAND) ACT 1995 (COMMENCEMENT No. 1) ORDER 1995 (No. 2787) (C.57) [£1·10], made under the Children (Scotland) Act 1995 (c.36), s.105(1); brings into force ss.1(1)–(3), 15, 35, 37, 99, 103, 104, 105(4) and (5), Sched. 4, paras. 12, 13, 18(1) and (2), 40(b), 45 and 53(1) and (3), on November 1, 1995 and in Sched. 5, the repeal undernoted.

[Registration of Births, Deaths and Marriages (Scotland) Act 1965 (c.49), s.43, partly repealed.]

5516. Children's hearings—grounds for referral—amendment by Court—competency

[Social Work (Scotland) Act 1968 (c.49) s.32(2)(d).]

S, the father of a child (J) born on April 6, 1988, appealed a sheriff's decision to find grounds for referral in terms of s.32(2)(d) of the 1968 Act established. The sheriff rejected two allegations that S had used lewd, indecent and libidinous practices and behaviour towards J, but held that a third "that in October 1990, or thereabouts, in Berlin, [S] engaged in sexual activity with [J] by requiring her to wash his erect penis" had been proved subject to an amendment deleting the words up to "Berlin" and substituting "that on occasions since October 1990 or thereabouts, in Berlin and elsewhere, the exact date and exact locus being unknown". S argued that (1) s.32(2)(d) did not apply as the alleged offence was not one of those mentioned in Sched. 1 to the Criminal Procedure (Scotland) Act 1975, because it had been committed outwith the jurisdiction of the Scottish courts (*Merrin v. S.* [1987] C.L.Y. 4003); (2) the court had to determine before J's hearsay evidence was admitted whether or not she knew the difference between truth or lies; the sheriff had not been entitled to use later evidence to support her conclusion that J did appreciate the difference, and on the basis of her interview with J, the sheriff had not been entitled to accept J as an admissible witness; (3) the sheriff had not been entitled to amend the grounds for referral; and (4) on the evidence the grounds were not made out. The reporter and J's mother argued that, if the sheriff's approach had been wrong, the case should be remitted to her in order that she could approach the matter in the correct manner.

Held, appeal allowed. (1) In s.32(2)(d) "offence" was to be construed as "conduct amounting to any offence", there being no requirement that the offence had to be one which could be prosecuted in Scotland. Many families travelled outwith Scotland from time to time and it would be a serious gap in the 1968 Act, which was intended to provide for children who needed compulsory measures of care, if J, who would be in just as much need of protection wherever the alleged conduct had occurred, were not protected because the conduct had occurred outside Scotland. There was no reason to construe the section in such a restricted way, given the purpose of the Act; that proceedings under the Act were civil proceedings *sui generis*; that s.32(2)(d) was concerned with the conduct toward J and there was no requirement to establish the identity of any offender or the date and place of the offence; that hearsay evidence was admissible; that there was no need for corroboration; and that proof was on the balance of probabilities. (2) While the sheriff had referred to other evidence supporting her "initial impression" as to

J's admissibility, it was clear that she had reached a conclusion after the interview that J was an admissible witness, which she was entitled to do, because, while J had initially indicated that she did not know what it was to tell the truth, she had shown through examples that she did understand to some extent the difference between lying and telling the truth. (3) While a sheriff was entitled to delete part of the grounds of referral which had not been made out, she had not been entitled to amend the grounds of her own accord by substituting a new allegation (*McGregor v. D.* [1977] C.L.Y. 3239). (*Opinion, per* Lord Weir, that while it would be undesirable for reasons of fairness for evidence to be led which was at variance with the grounds of referral, it would be very unfortunate if a case failed because of a minor inconsistency, and a sheriff had to have some latitude, depending on the character and extent of the inconsistency and the degree of prejudice, to find the grounds established, notwithstanding any inconsistency.) (4) There was no basis for the conclusion that S had acted in the manner described while in a bath. S had stated that he and J had bathed together, but J's hearsay evidence did not suggest that S had required her to touch his private parts, and S's expert, whom the sheriff had found the most helpful, stated that J's warmth towards S, her lack of fear and her lack of sexualised behaviour were inconsistent with earlier sexual abuse. Further the sheriff's failure to say whether or not she believed S's evidence indicated that there was no sound factual basis for her findings. (5) Given that there had been extensive adjustments proposed to the stated case, which had given the sheriff ample opportunity to make her position clear, that 11 months had elapsed since the case was signed, and that only some of the evidence had been taken down in shorthand, it was doubtful that the sheriff could provide any useful additional information and the case would be remitted to the sheriff in order for her to dismiss the application and discharge the referral.

S. v. KENNEDY, *The Scotsman*, November 29, 1995.

5517. Children's hearings—grounds for referral—grounds accepted—parents subsequently denying that grounds accepted—procedure

[Social Work (Scotland) Act 1968 (c.49), s.49(1); Act of Sederunt (Social Work) (Sheriff Court Procedure) Rules 1971 (S.I. 1971 No. 92), r. 14(2).]

A reporter referred two children to a children's hearing on the grounds provided by s.32(2)(c) to (dd) of the 1968 Act. When their cases came before the hearing for the first time, it was noted by the reporter that the children's mother and stepfather accepted the grounds of referral, subject to certain amendments to the annexed statement of facts. On that occasion, the cases were continued for reports. After a second continuation, the hearing decided that the children were in need of compulsory measures of care and made supervision requirements. The children's mother and stepfather then presented petitions to the *nobile officium* seeking an order for an application to the sheriff for a finding as to whether the grounds of referral were established. The stepfather submitted that he had not accepted the grounds in s.32(2)(d) and (dd). The mother submitted that the amendments had amounted to a material departure from the original statement of facts, and that her acceptance of the amendments could not be construed as acceptance of the grounds themselves. Both petitioners contended that at the first sitting the hearing should therefore have directed the reporter to apply to the sheriff for a determination of whether the grounds were established. They submitted that application to the *nobile officium* was competent, because no appeal to the sheriff had been competent against what had occurred at that sitting, since it had been merely a procedural step and not a decision within the meaning of s.49(1) of the 1968 Act. The couple also had a third child of their own. The stepfather submitted that, because he could not challenge the grounds derived from s.32(2)(d) and (dd), he was deemed to be an offender in terms of Sched. 1 to the Criminal Procedure (Scotland) Act 1975. He contended that his position was thereby prejudiced, because his supposed acceptance of the offence would, at any subsequent hearing for the referral of the third child, be sufficient proof that she was a member of the same household as such an offender, in terms of s.32(2)(dd).

Held, that (1) it could be inferred from s.50(1) of the 1968 Act and rule 14(2) of the Act of Sederunt (Social Work) (Sheriff Court Procedure) Rules 1971 that an appeal to the sheriff could be taken against a decision of a children's hearing on the ground of an alleged irregularity occurring at any stage of the proceedings leading to the decision; (2) the petitions were therefore incompetent because, although the petitioners were correct that no appeal could have been taken at the time of the first sitting of the hearing, the matters raised in the petitions could have been the subject of an appeal once the hearing had decided that compulsory measures were needed, because at that stage there was a decision in terms of s.49(1); and petitions dismissed. *Observed*, that (1) the court could not assume that the petitioners' averments were true, as it would have needed to do before it could have granted the petitions, and that the proper process in which to resolve the dispute of fact as to whether the petitioners had or had not accepted the grounds of referral was an appeal to the sheriff under s.49(1); (2) the stepfather's position had not in fact been prejudiced by what had taken place, because, unlike a sheriff's determination that grounds of referral had been established, a parent's acceptance of such grounds in respect of one child was not sufficient proof of the facts in a subsequent referral of another child on the same grounds. *H. v. McGregor* [1973] C.L.Y. 3542 applied; *McGregor v. H.* [1983] C.L.Y. 3981, distinguished.

M. v. KENNEDY, 1995 S.L.T. 123.

5518. Children's hearings—grounds for referral—grounds not established on re-hearing—order regulating return of children to families after long absence—*nobile officium*

[Social Work (Scotland) Act 1968 (c.49), s.42.]

Six families whose children had been removed from their care under the Social Work (Scotland) Act 1968, s.42, petitioned the *nobile officium* to be allowed to lead additional evidence that had not been led at the original hearing before the sheriff, which evidence could have been available or could reasonably have been made available at the time of the hearing. Having remitted the case to the sheriff to reconsider, the court considered his report.

Held, that in the light of this new evidence the sheriff's new recommendations were to be given effect; the original grounds of proof were not now met and therefore the children must be returned to their families as soon as practicable; and that it was competent for the court in exercise of the *nobile officium* to regulate the children's re-integration having regard to their best interests.

L. PETRS., *The Times*, April 21, 1995.

5519. Children's hearings—grounds for referral—member of the same household as person committing offence—relevance of admission of grounds for referral in relation to another child. See M. v. KENNEDY, §5517.

5520. Children's hearings—grounds for referral—proof of—competency of interim orders following proof. See P. v. KENNEDY, §5524.

5521. Children's hearings—grounds for referral—proof of—lack of parental care—regime necessary to deal with children's disturbed behaviour

[Social Work (Scotland) Act 1968 (c. 49), s.32(2)(c).]

By s.32(1) and (2)(c) of the Social Work (Scotland) Act 1968 a child may be in need of compulsory measures of care if "lack of parental care is likely to cause him unnecessary suffering or seriously to impair his health or development". A reporter to a children's hearing applied to the sheriff for a finding whether grounds of referral relating to two adopted children had been established. The sheriff found that, as a result of experiences prior to their adoption, the children were disturbed. He found that, for the protection of other children, the adopted children required to be closely supervised by their adoptive parents; but also that the degree of supervision necessary was impairing their emotional development. He further found that the adoptive parents were acting responsibly in what they thought were the best interests of the children, that they had sought and followed professional advice about the children's problems, and that, given the resources available to them they were looking after the children as best they could. At the same time, he found that there was a lack of parental care inasmuch as the children's development was being impaired. He held that the grounds had been established. The adoptive parents appealed.

Held, that (1) s.32(2)(c) applied where a child was likely to be harmed because it was being deprived, by the act or omission of its parent, of the care that was reasonably to be expected of a reasonable parent; (2) neither a failure to attain perfection or success in parental care, nor the absence of some care that might be provided by others, constituted a lack of parental care falling within the terms of s.32(2)(c); (3) since the sheriff had found the parental supervision which was impairing the children's development, and which was thus giving rise to the alleged lack of parental care, to be necessary, and that also the parents were prepared to adjust it on professional advice, he had erred in law in holding that the criterion in s.32(2)(c) had been met; (4) in any event the sheriff had erred by failing to take material considerations into account, namely (i) the identification of the impairment that he had found was being caused, (ii) the establishing of any causal link between the parents' regime and any lack of care, (iii) the question of prospective parental care, and (iv) the individual circumstances of each child; and appeal allowed. *Finlayson, Applicant* [1990] C.L.Y 4753, distinguished; *M. v. McGregor* [1981] C.L.Y. 2951, followed. *Observed*, that in a case in which, through no fault of their own, parents were or had been rendered (for example by accident or illness) incapable of caring properly for their children, the criteria in s.32(2)(c) might be met, even though no blame attached to the parents.

D. v. KELLY, 1995 S.L.T. 1220.

5522. Children's hearings—grounds for referral—proof of—procedure—presence in court of parent of child witness—child not the subject of the grounds for referral

[Social Work (Scotland) Act 1968 (c.49), ss.30(1) and (2) and 94(1); Act of Sederunt (Social Work) (Sheriff Court Procedure Rules) 1971 (S.I. 1971 No. 92), ss.2(1) and (2) and 8(4).]

Held, that throughout the 1971 Rules the expression "the child" referred to the child who was the subject of the ground of referral, and that the sheriff had not been entitled under rule 8(4) to exclude from court the guardian of a child who was giving evidence in the course of a hearing under s.42 of the 1968 Act and who was not the subject of the ground of referral in dispute.

T. v. WATSON, 1995 S.L.T. 1062.

5523. Children's hearings—grounds for referral—proof of—restrictions of proof. See P. v. KENNEDY, §5524.

5524. Children's hearings—procedure—application to sheriff—motion to restrict proof—powers of sheriff

[Act of Sederunt (Social Work) (Sheriff Court Procedure Rules) 1971 (S.I. 1971 No. 92), r.8.]

Two children were referred to a children's hearing on various grounds including that they were members of the same household as a person who had committed a sexual offence. The grounds of referral were not accepted by the children's mother. The reporter was directed to apply to the sheriff for a finding as to whether or not the grounds of referral were established. The father was on petition on charges of alleged rape, lewd and libidinous conduct and a contravention of the Sexual Offences (Scotland) Act 1976 in respect of incidents not involving the children subject to the hearing. Prior to the hearing the father's agent moved the sheriff to exclude the evidence of four named witnesses who were the complainers in the petition, on the grounds that the "rehearsal" of their evidence at the hearing would be prejudicial to the conduct of the father's trial. The sheriff refused the motion as incompetent. The father appealed by stated case, arguing, *inter alia*, that in the circumstances the referral proceedings were not necessary for the children's protection in advance of the trial.

Held, that (1) the sheriff had no power *ab ante* to restrict the evidence which a reporter sought to present to the court in support of grounds of referral; (2) criminal proceedings did not take precedence over referral proceedings in respect of children arising out of the same circumstances; and appeal refused. (*McGregor v. D* [1977] C.L.Y. 3239, and *Ferguson v. P* [1989] C.L.Y. 3904 followed.) *Observed*, that (1) there was no interim period in the referral proceedings which came to an end when the criminal trial was concluded, the result of the trial would not affect the arrangements made for the case and welfare of the children; (2) a sheriff had no power to make interim orders for the care and welfare of the children under referral pending his decision on an application by a reporter or a subsequent appeal; (3) the purposes of bail conditions and of the welfare provisions of the 1968 Act were entirely different, and the former did not make adequate provision for children the subject of referral proceedings; and (4) it was unnecessary for the sheriff to state that she was satisfied to the criminal standard of proof that the grounds of referral had been established.

P. v. KENNEDY, 1995 S.L.T. 476.

5525. Children's hearings—supervision requirement—disputed matter left to discretion of social work department—whether "condition"—validity

[Social Work (Scotland) Act 1968 (c.49), s.44(1), Children's Hearing (Scotland) Rules 1986 (S.I. 1986 No. 2291), ss.9(3) and 24 and Form 10A.]

K, a reporter, appealed against a sheriff's decision to allow an appeal by M and W, parents of P, in respect of a children's hearing decision. P was in foster care and M and W had supervised access. The hearing had concluded that a previous supervision requirement should continue and that P should continue to reside with foster parents. In relation to a request for access by M and W, the hearing imposed no condition within s.44(1) of the 1968 Act and form 10A of the 1986 Rules, but decided that access was to remain at the discretion of the social work department. The sheriff held that the hearing had erred in that they had not been entitled to divest themselves of responsibility for deciding on access, and in not making their reasons clear as to whether the long term intention to free P for adoption had been a material consideration in making their decision, as it would have been outwith the social work department's powers to terminate access for this reason. A children's hearing subsequently convened by K in terms of s.49(5)(b) had varied the order to specify the access to be allowed and in this respect the issue was no longer live for W and M, but the court agreed to hear the appeal given that the sheriff's decision had wider implications (*Humphries v. S.* [1986] C.L.Y. 3635; *Sloan v. B.* [1991] C.L.Y. 4461).

Held, that the hearing was entitled under s.44(1) to leave matters such as access to the discretion of the social work department (Lord Marnoch dissenting as to whether this was so in the present case). Section 44(1) of the 1968 Act left the children's hearing free to impose what "conditions" they felt appropriate (*Sloan v. B.*), subject to the requirements of s.44. The children's hearing had not imposed a "condition" within the meaning of s.44(1) of the 1968 Act, which related (*per* the Lord President (Hope) and Lord Mayfield) to conditions referred to in rule 24 and form 10A of the 1986 Rules, and set out in the relevant part of the form. A supervision requirement was a discretionary power vested in the local authority in relation to a variety of matters, including who should come into contact with the child and under what conditions (*D. v. Strathclyde Regional Council* [1985] C.L.Y. 3751), and a parent could not use a common law action to obtain access to such a child. It was competent for a children's hearing to impose a "condition" regarding access (*Kennedy v. A.* [1986] C.L.Y. 3636), but they were not required by law to decide on access even if there was a dispute between the parents and the social work department. *D. v. Strathclyde Regional Council* [1991] C.L.Y. 4463 could be distinguished (*per* the Lord President and Lord Mayfield) in that in this case the children's hearing had not made it a "condition" of the supervision requirement that access was to remain at the discretion of the social work department. If a "condition" was imposed it had to be clear and unambiguous (*D. v. Strathclyde Regional Council* (1991)). The reasons given by the children's hearing were satisfactory (*per* the Lord President and Lord Mayfield) in that they contained a clear statement of the material considerations to which they had regard and were intelligible to the persons to whom they were addressed (*H. v. Kennedy*, 1992 G.W.D. 6–270). M and W's history of access and the fact that P had not been adversely affected had been recorded at the hearing. They also, by using the word "remain", inferred that the status quo, whereby access had been exercised once a month, would be unaltered for the time being. There was, in the circumstances, no need for there to be a reference to the long term plan for P. Observed, that the sheriff ought not to have criticised the Social Work Services Group circular no. SW11/1986 which had been issued to complement and clarify the code of practice laid down by the Secretary of State, where he had not been addressed about the circular and had not read the code of practice. *Opinion*, that it was unnecessary for K to have obtempered the sheriff's interlocutor meantime, despite the lack of provision for this situation in s.51(1), as an appeal sisted execution of the decree (*Macleay v. Macdonald*, 1928 S.L.T. 463) and there was no express provision to the contrary in the 1968 Act. Care should be taken not to act upon a decision in a way which would cause difficulty should the appeal be allowed. *Per* Lord Marnoch (dissenting in part): In substance the hearing had imposed a condition. In the absence of a "condition" the parent of a child under a supervision requirement had no right to obtain access to the child (*D. v. Strathclyde Regional Council* [1985] C.L.Y. 3731). Given the background it was plainly necessary for the hearing to deal with the question of access and their decision had to be read in that light as well as the statutory context. The case of *D. v. Strathclyde* (1991) was indistinguishable and correctly decided.

KENNEDY v. M., 1995 S.L.T. 717.

5526. Children's hearings—supervision requirement—whether lapsed—effect of appeal

[Social Work (Scotland) Act 1968 (c.49), ss.47(1) and 48(3).]

X and Y, of whom T was the father, were referred to the children's panel (P) in January 1991. T had had custody and lived with D, their mother. When T was accused of an offence which did not involve the children, a supervision requirement was made and X and Y were directed to reside with foster carers. Following a review X and Y were to have access to T and D. D then obtained legal custody. At a subsequent review in November 1993 P made provision for unsupervised access to T to be facilitated by the social work department instead of as directed by them. On D's appeal the sheriff discharged the referral on the ground that a supervision requirement could not be made or continued for the purpose of enabling unsupervised access. The reporter and safeguarder appealed to the Court of Session. On appeal D argued that the court could not hear the merits of the appeal as the supervision requirement had, as a matter of law, lapsed and could not be revived. If the need for supervision disappeared the process came to a stop (ss.47(1) and 48(3) of the

1968 Act). A "requirement" had to be reviewed annually or else it came to an end. The requirement of November 1993 had remained in force notwithstanding D's appeal, as it had not been suspended under s.49(8). On the sheriff's decision the referrals had been discharged but the effect of the present appeal was to suspend the discharge (*Kennedy v. M.* [1995] C.L.Y. 5525; *Macleay v. Macdonald*, 1928 S.L.T. 463). As there had been no subsequent review in November 1994 the requirement had fallen and the appeal should be refused. The reporter argued that proceedings in children's hearings were *sui generis* and the rule in *Macleay* did not apply.

Held, appeals refused as incompetent. D's argument was correct. Supervision requirements, once made, continued until variation, discharge or lapse. As no review had taken place within one year the requirement had lapsed. *Kennedy v. M.* was directly in point. *Observed*, that Kearney on *Children's Hearings and the Sheriff Court*, pp.366–367 was inconsistent with *Kennedy, supra* and it was illogical to suggest that an appeal against the sheriff's decision would reinstate the requirement.

STIRLING v. D., 1995 S.L.T. 1089.

5527. Custody—best interests of child—foster parents. See R. v. R., §6107.

5528. Custody—best interests of child—whether formal award should be made

[Law Reform (Parent and Child) (Scotland) Act 1986 (c.9), s.3(2).]

W raised an action against H for custody of A, a child of their marriage aged four. W and H had separated on November 20, 1992 and A had been in W's *de facto* custody every since. H counterclaimed for access and for interdict against causing A to be known by the surname of W's cohabitee (C), by whom W had another child in January 1994. On one occasion there had been a disagreement over A's care; W's father had intervened and had assaulted H unjustifiably. W then insisted on H having his mother present when residential access took place. W complained that H had obsessional behaviour and argued against the amount of access to be granted to H and the granting of residential access. H and W were agreed that W should have the day to day care of A but H argued against a custody order as being unnecessary and a restriction of his parental rights (*Potter v. Potter* [1993] C.L.Y. 4795).

Held, custody awarded to W; access on a residential and non-residential basis granted but preferably to be as agreed between H and W; interdict refused. (1) As there had been disputes there should be no doubt over who had day to day control over A (*Macdonald v. Macdonald* [1993] C.L.Y. 4793 followed). H and W could not be relied upon to work things out for themselves and it was in the best interests of A that custody be awarded to W. Had there been no bitterness and difficulty between H and W it might well have been appropriate to make no order. (2) Access during the week was undesirable as it was important A's weekly routine remained the same as A got older. Access should be at weekends only, once non-residential and once residential in each month, plus one week at Christmas and two weeks during the summer holidays; however, H and W should be flexible over access in light of A's wishes and how access worked in practice. As there was no evidence that H's behaviour would harm A, access should be unsupervised. (3) There was no authority as to the proposition that the parent of a child was entitled to regulate the name of his child and it had not been shown that this was a right falling within the definition of "parental rights". It was doubtful if civil courts had any authority to deal with this (*Forlong, Petr.* (1880) 7 R. 910). In any event interdict was inappropriate as it was available only where alleged actings violated H's rights, which calling a child by a different name could not be said to do. *Opinion*, that interdict would still have been refused as on the evidence it was in A's best interests that his name remain as that of C, as W was to marry C and A was known by his name at nursery school, the health centre and his future primary school.

F. v. F. (Sh.Ct.), 1995 S.C.L.R. 189.

5529. Custody—delivery—illegitimate child removed by father

Held, where the father of an illegitimate child who had for some time been

living with the child's mother left her taking the child with him, that the mother's motion for interim custody and delivery of the child should have been granted pending the production of a report.
HADDOW v. MOFFAT (Sh.Ct.), 1995 S.C.L.R. 793.

5530. Custody—international child abduction—both parents guardians of child and having joint rights of custody under Australian law

[Child Abduction and Custody Act 1985 (c.60), Sched. 1, arts. 3, 4, 5 and 21.]
The father and mother of a child resided in Australia where, by statute, each parent of a child is a guardian of the child and both parents have joint custody, subject to any court order in force. Following the parents' separation in 1992, the child resided with the mother. The father enjoyed substantial access, including residential access, and was to an extent involved in the child's dental and health care. In about May 1994 the mother decided to return to Scotland with the child and asked the father for his consent to the child's removal. The father refused to consent, but the mother, having concealed her preparations for doing so, removed the child to Scotland on August 12, 1994. The father presented a petition to the Court of Session under the Child Abduction and Custody Act 1985, seeking an order for the return of the child to Australia. The mother argued that, prior to her departure with the child in August 1994, she was the only party exercising rights of custody as defined in art. 5 of Sched. 1 to the Act, that the father exercised only rights of access as defined in art. 5 and that his refusal of her request for consent to the removal had been no more than an expression of those rights in that he would cease to enjoy those rights in Australia upon the child's departure: his refusal was not based upon any right as a guardian accorded to him by Australian law to determine the child's place of residence.

Held, that (1) although the care and control exercised by the father could conveniently be referred to as "access", in the absence of any court order making a distinction between custody and access his entitlement arose only from the joint rights of custody provided by Australian law; (2) having exercised his right as a guardian under Australian law to refuse a change of residence, and not having abandoned that decision, the father was continuing to exercise his joint right of custody at the date of the child's removal, and the removal of the child from Australia was accordingly unlawful; and order for return of the child pronounced.
McKIVER v. McKIVER (O.H.), 1995 S.L.T. 790.

5531. Custody—international child abduction—child objecting to return

[Child Abduction and Custody Act 1985 (c.60), Sched. 1, art. 13.]
M petitioned for the return of her daughter C, aged 13, from Scotland to Ireland. M and D, C's father, had separated in 1994 and D left Ireland to come to Scotland. C had remained with M. In 1995 C left Ireland with the help of her aunt A, to come to live with D in Scotland. D accepted that M had rights of custody but argued that an exception should be made in that C objected to being returned (art. 13 of Sched. 1 to the 1985 Act). C claimed that M and her new boyfriend B were frequently drunk and did not care about the children. She had been unhappy at home and was not doing well as school. She was much happier with D and was doing well at school. A psychologist gave supporting evidence giving her opinion, based on an interview with C. D's evidence indicated that he had not had any previous indication of C's unhappiness during visits to Ireland but was happy to look after her in Scotland. M's witnesses all contradicted C's account. D argued that having established C's objection to being returned, the court had only to be satisfied that C was of sufficient age and maturity to have her views taken into account.

Held, petition granted. While C's objection was genuine, she had exaggerated her unhappiness and there was not sufficient substance in C's objection to justify departing from the aim of the 1985 Act. The exception should only be used where the circumstances were exceptional (*Urness v. Minto* [1994] C.L.Y. 5439; *S. v. S.* [1992] C.L.Y. 2796).

MARSHALL v. MARSHALL, *The Scotsman*, October 4, 1995.

5532. Custody—international child abduction—petition brought outwith time limit for mandatory return of child—whether acquiescence in wrongful retention of child

[Child Abduction and Custody Act 1985 (c.60), Sched. 1, arts. 12 and 13.]

The Child Abduction and Custody Act 1985, by incorporation of the Convention on the Civil Aspects of International Child Abduction, provides remedies where a child is wrongfully removed or retained from the country where he or she was habitually resident before the removal. The court of the requested state is not bound to order the return of the child if it is established that the petitioning parent had consented to or acquiesced in the removal or retention. Where the petition has not been brought within one year of the retention, the court has a discretion not to order the return of the child, if it is demonstrated that the child is now settled in its new environment. In July 1992 a husband and wife living in Canada came to Scotland, with their daughter then aged 10 months, to visit the wife's parents for two weeks. The husband returned to Canada after that period, the intention being that the mother and child should remain in Scotland for a further week. Thereafter the mother telephoned the father, advising that she did not intend to return with the child. The father frequently wrote to and telephoned the mother. He contacted an organisation called Child Find. He attended a solicitor and obtained an award of interim custody in the Canadian court. Thereafter he learned about the Hague Convention and instructed his solicitor to petition in terms thereof. The solicitor delayed at various points. The father was eventually given proper advice at the Attorney General's office in Canada and a petition was served on the mother in May 1994. At a proof before the Lord Ordinary, the mother argued that there had been acquiescence on the part of the father, and, further, that the child was now settled in her new environment. The Lord Ordinary held that there was no acquiescence and, even if there had been, he would have exercised his discretion in favour of ordering return of the child. He also held that the mother had not demonstrated that the child was now settled in her new environment and that accordingly art. 12 applied, making an order for return mandatory. The mother reclaimed.

Held, that (1) while acquiescence might be active or passive and might be inferred from unexplained activity, no such inference could necessarily be drawn where apparent inactivity was explained and that explanation was accepted, and the Lord Ordinary was entitled to hold that acquiescence was not the proper inference to be drawn in this case; (2) on the issue of settlement the proper question was not a balancing exercise between the interests of the child and the Convention but whether the child was settled in her new environment that the court would be justified in disregarding an otherwise mandatory requirement to have the child returned; (3) since the child's emotional security and stability were provided principally by her mother, who would go with the child if an order were made for her return, the mother had failed to demonstrate that such settlement had been established; and reclaiming motion refused.

SOUCIE v. SOUCIE, 1995 S.L.T. 414.

5533. Custody—international child abduction—rights of custody

[Child Abduction and Custody Act 1985 (c.60), Sched. 1, arts. 3, 4 and 5.]

The 1985 Act gives the force of law in the United Kingdom to the Convention on the Civil Aspects of International Child Abduction. The Convention provides in art. 3 that removal or retention of a child is wrongful where it breaches rights of custody which existed under the law of the state in which the child had been habitually resident and which were actually being exercised or would have been so exercised but for the child's removal or retention.

Article 5 provides that rights of custody include rights relating to the care of the person of the child and, in particular, the right to determine the child's place of residence; and that rights of access include the right to take a child for a limited period of time to a place other than the child's habitual residence. The mother and father of a child divorced in 1987 in Texas. The mother was appointed "managing conservator" of the child and the father "possessory conservator". These corresponded broadly with awards of custody and of access respectively. The domicile and/or legal residence of the child was to be determined at the sole discretion of the mother. Each conservator required to give 30 days' notice, where possible, of intention to change place of residence. The mother, who was of Scottish origin, came to Scotland in 1993 with the child on a return ticket having advised the father that she intended to visit her relatives for the summer vacation. Shortly thereafter she informed him that she intended to remain there. The father argued that the removal and retention of the child were "wrongful" because they breached rights of custody vested, first, in himself, and secondly, in the court in Texas. He argued that, when she originally left the U.S., the mother had already formed an intention of changing residence, and had thus removed the child in breach of the notice requirements. He further argued that the provisions for notice on change of residence gave him a role which amounted to a right, along with the mother, to determine the child's place of residence if a change of residence to a place outwith the jurisdiction of the court in Texas was intended and that, accordingly, he must be regarded as having "rights of custody"; and that the removal or retention had breached his "rights relating to the care of the person of the child", including "permanent rights", conferred by the Texas Family Code, at all times to have access to the child's records and rights of consultation with doctors, and thus had breached his rights of custody by virtue of art. 5(a) of the Convention. He also argued that once the court in Texas had invoked its jurisdiction in relation to custody, that court had the right to determine the child's place of residence and continued to do so even after an exercise of that right and, accordingly, also had "rights of custody".

Held, that (1) since it was not established that the mother had intended to remove the child permanently when she left the U.S. the obligation on her had been to give the required notice on the day she finally made up her mind; (2) the existence of a right to apply for modification of existing orders or to invoke the power of the court in Texas to maintain the status quo pending modification, and the possibility that that court might act upon it, did not in any way derogate from the mother's existing sole discretion, or produce any joint right to determine the child's place of residence; (3) the expression "rights relating to the care of the person of the child", although wide in its scope, could not be so construed as to cover the potential and concomitant rights of a parent who enjoyed access rights, at times when the child was not in that parent's actual care, whether by virtue of the access award or simply *de facto* and, in any event, the "permanent rights" were not breached by the removal and retention; (4) accordingly the removal and retention had not breached any rights of custody attributed to the father and (5) since a court had no apparent power or right, *ex proprio motu*, to make any determination as to place of residence when it had already made orders dealing with these matters and conferred rights upon others, without holding matters over for its own future determination, and without any requirement that its authority or permission be obtained as a prerequisite for any future determination, the court in Texas had no rights of custody, nor could the removal or retention be seen as constituting a breach of any such rights; and petition dismissed. (*C. v. C. (Minor: Abduction: Rights of Custody Abroad)* [1989] C.L.Y. 2437 and *B. v. B. (Child Abduction: Custody Rights)* [1993] C.L.Y. 2789, distinguished.) *Doubted*, whether a court had any rights of custody in relation to a child. (*B. v. B.*, considered.)

SEROKA v. BELLAH (O.H.), 1995 S.L.T. 204.

5534. Custody—international child abduction—"rights of custody"

[Child Abduction and Custody Act 1985 (c.60), Sched. 1, arts. 3, 5, 12, 14, 15 and 21.]

The Child Abduction and Custody Act 1985, which incorporates as a Schedule the Convention on the Civil Aspects of International Child Abduction, provides certain remedies where a child is "wrongfully removed or retained" in terms of art. 3, outwith the country where the child is "habitually resident" immediately before the removal or retention. For removal or retention to be wrongful, the removal or retention has to be in breach of the rights of custody, joint or sole, attributed to a person by the law of the state in which the child was habitually resident. The father and mother of a child resided in Ibiza, where the Spanish Civil Code provided that each parent had equal parental rights of *patria potestas* over the child. Following their separation, they entered into a binding agreement under Spanish law whereby the mother had actual care and control of the child and the father had access. The agreement expressly preserved the parties' joint rights of *patria potestas*. On December 6, 1993, the mother removed the child to Scotland without the father's consent. The father presented a petition to the Court of Session under the 1985 Act, seeking an order for the return of the child to Spain. The mother argued that the agreement, which provided that the mother could change her domicile, and by implication that of the child, contained no express provision entitling the father to withhold consent to the removal of the child from Ibiza. The father's rights were only of access, and his share of the *patria potestas* amounted only to nebulous general parental rights stopping short of "rights of custody" under the Hague Convention. Custody therefore belonged exclusively to the mother, and the removal was accordingly not unlawful.

Held, that (1) where the rights conferred on parents might be shared in many different ways on a separation, the rights enjoyed by a parent should be considered as a whole in determining whether they amounted to rights of custody; (2) while a right of access might not amount to "rights of custody", the right of the father to access taken with the general supervisory rights of the *patria potestas* and the implicit agreement that the child's residence should not be changed from Ibiza without the father's agreement amounted to rights of custody for the purposes of the Hague Convention and the removal of the child from Ibiza was accordingly wrongful; and petition granted. *Opinion reserved*, on whether under art. 15 the approach of the courts of the requesting state or that of the state to which the request was made should prevail if there was a difference between them as to the interpretation of the expression "rights of custody".

BORDERA v. BORDERA (O.H.), 1995 S.L.T. 1176.

5535. Custody—order for educational expenses. See MACDONALD v. MACDONALD, §5876.

5536. Custody—procedure—reports—whether necessary to obtain report prior to interim hearing. See R. v. R., §6107.

Jurisdiction. See JURISDICTION.

5537. Parental rights—choice of name for child—whether parental right. See F. v. F., §5528.

5538. Parental rights—effect of order freeing child for adoption. See D. v. GRAMPIAN REGIONAL COUNCIL, §5508.

5539. Paternity, declarator of—procedure—motion requesting executrix of alleged father to provide bodily sample for testing—competency

[Law Reform (Miscellaneous Provisions) (Scotland) Act 1990 (c40), s.70.]

Section 70 of the Law Reform (Miscellaneous Provisions) (Scotland) Act 1990 permits the court, in any civil proceedings to request "a party to the proceedings" to provide a sample of blood or other body fluid or body tissue for analysis. A mother sought declarator that a soldier who was killed before her child was born was born was the father of the child. She brought an action against the soldier's executrix, who was his mother. The sheriff refused as incompetent a motion asking the court to request the defender to provide a sample of blood for analysis. The pursuer appealed to the sheriff principal.

Held, that the soldier's executrix, as defender to the action, was a party to the proceedings and there was no unfairness in requesting her to provide a sample; and appeal allowed.

MACKAY v. MURPHY, 1995 S.L.T. (Sh.Ct.) 30.

5540. Paternity, evidence of—power to request "a party to the proceedings" to provide bodily sample. See MACKAY v. MURPHY, §5539.

CIVIL LIBERTIES

Immigration. See IMMIGRATION.

CLUBS AND ASSOCIATIONS

5541. Members' clubs—rates—relief—charitable purposes—social club with bar facilities. See COALBURN MINERS' WELFARE AND CHARITABLE SOCIETY v. STRATHCLYDE REGIONAL COUNCIL, §6251.

5542. Voluntary association—disciplinary committee—possibility of bias

Nine councillors of the City of Edinburgh District Council who were members of the council Labour Party group petitioned for suspension and interdict in respect of disciplinary proceedings brought against them which could have led to the withdrawal of the group whip and their subsequent ineligibility to stand for election as Labour candidates. Following a council meeting on December 2, 1993 a special meeting of the Edinburgh District Labour Party and its executive committee had been convened and on December 6, had passed a motion which was highly critical of the conduct of the nine councillors relating to the same matters which thereafter became subject to the disciplinary proceedings, which were to culminate in a hearing before the disciplinary authority on January 11, 1994. Under the rules of Edinburgh District Council Labour group the disciplinary authority was a specially convened joint meeting of the Labour group and the executive committee of the Edinburgh District Labour Party. The first ground on which suspension and interdict were sought was that the motion that had been passed on December 6, had been passed on a majority of 60 to one by individuals who included members of the disciplinary authority and that the motion disclosed a basis for a reasonable apprehension of something so prejudicial to a fair and impartial investigation of the questions to be decided by the disciplinary authority as to amount to a denial of natural justice. The second ground was that the nine councillors had not acted in a manner that had laid them open to competent disciplinary proceedings. The respondents argued that it was not competent for the courts to interfere in the internal affairs of a voluntary association, especially where, as here, there were appeal procedures provided, and also argued that, even if the disciplinary proceedings were without merit, that was no reason to prevent the members of the hearing from exercising their quasi-judicial authority fairly and so deciding.

Held, that (1) although the court would only interfere in the proceedings of a voluntary association in extraordinary circumstances, where, as here, there was an apprehension of a denial of natural justice averred in that the behaviour of members of the disciplinary body in supporting the motion on December 6, was calculated to create in the mind of a reasonable man a suspicion concerning their impartiality, thus disqualifying the members who had so acted even although in fact no bias exists and thereby invalidating the decision of the whole body, the petitioners had made out a prima facie case; (2) the existence of an appeal procedure was not a bar to the court's exercise of its powers; (3) the balance of convenience favoured the petitioners; and interim interdict and interim suspension pronounced.

BROWN v. EXECUTIVE COMMITTEE OF THE EDINBURGH DISTRICT LABOUR PARTY (O.H.), 1995 S.L.T. 985.

COMPANY LAW

5543. Action by company—caution for expenses—consequences of failure to find caution. See METRIC MODULES INTERNATIONAL v. LAUGHTON CONSTRUCTION CO, §5929.

5544. Directors—disqualification—leave to remain director of another company. See SECRETARY OF STATE FOR TRADE AND INDUSTRY v. BROWN, §5546; SECRETARY OF STATE FOR TRADE AND INDUSTRY v. PALFREMAN, §5547.

5545. Directors—disqualification—notice of intention to apply for order—less than required period of notice given—whether requirement mandatory or directory

[Company Directors Disqualification Act 1986 (c.46), ss.6(1), 7(2) and 16(1).]

The Secretary of State for Trade and Industry applied to Glasgow Sheriff Court on March 10, 1994 for disqualification orders against two directors. Notice of his intention to do so had been given less than 10 days earlier as required under s.16(1). The directors sought to have the applications dismissed as incompetent on the basis that the 10 day period of notice was mandatory and that the proceedings were accordingly a nullity.

Held, the 10 day notice requirement was discretionary rather than mandatory and that failure to comply with it did not invalidate the applications; and plea to competency repelled.

SECRETARY OF STATE FOR TRADE AND INDUSTRY v. LOVAT (Sh.Ct.), 1995 S.C.L.R. 180.

5546. Directors—disqualification—period of disqualification

[Company Directors Disqualification Act 1986 (c.46), ss.1 and 6(1) and (4).]

The Company Directors Disqualification Act 1986 provides for the disqualification of a person from being a director of a company without the leave of the court in circumstances including the company having become insolvent. The minimum period of disqualification is two years and the maximum 15 years where the disqualification is on that ground. The Secretary of State for Trade and Industry petitioned the court for the disqualification of a director of a company under s.6 of the 1986 Act in that the company of which he was a director had become insolvent as a result of non-payment of sums of income tax deducted from employees' earnings. The director had been responsible for sales. Another director of the company, who had been responsible for the company's financial affairs, had previously been disqualified for a period of three years. It was admitted by the respondent director that he had been in breach of his duty to make inquiries into the running of the financial affairs of the company and compliance with the Companies Acts, and that a disqualification order was appropriate. It was argued that his conduct had been less blameworthy than that of the other director who had been the senior of the two in terms of age and experience, the respondent director having been first employed by the company under the direction of the other director. It was also submitted that his responsibility in respect of the company's insolvency was as a consequence of a failure to attempt to rectify the company's position rather than from any active role in the creation of that position. It was submitted that he should not be disqualified from continuing to be a director of another company since (1) there were adequate safeguards to secure its proper management in that there were two independent directors, one of whom held a balancing shareholding, and proper accounting arrangements, and (2) his expert knowledge of the market in which the company operated made it desirable that he remain involved in company policy as a director. It was argued for the Secretary of State that the court, in deciding whether or not to allow the director to remain as director of the new company, should have regard to a salary increase which the directors of the new company had awarded themselves in 1992 after the company had made a loss in 1991 and to a breach of the limit prescribed under the Companies Act 1985 for loan accounts.

Held, that (1) since the director must have been fully aware of the problems of the first company it was as much his responsibility as that of the other director to see that proper control was maintained over company finances and that a three year disqualification was appropriate; but (2) the director's salary had not risen since the increase in 1992 and in that time the new company's profitability had substantially improved, and the breach of the loan limit was not a material one and in any event it had occurred by virtue of an accounting practice which had been discontinued, whereas it was in the company's interests to have the director's expertise in its management, leave should be granted to that effect; and orders pronounced accordingly.

SECRETARY OF STATE FOR TRADE AND INDUSTRY v. BROWN (O.H.), 1995 SL.T. 550.

5547. Directors—disqualification—period of disqualification

[Company Directors Disqualification Act 1986 (c.46), ss.1(1) and 6(1).]

The 1986 Act empowers the court to grant orders, called disqualification orders, against directors of a company which has become insolvent. If an order is granted the person disqualified may not be a director of, or otherwise involved in, the management of a company without the leave of the court, for the duration of the order. The Secretary of State for Trade and Industry having petitioned for a disqualification order in respect of a director of a company, the parties entered into a joint minute agreeing that the respondent had been director of a company which had become insolvent, it having been put into liquidation at the instance of the Inland Revenue, and that the insolvency had been because of the company's failure to pay income tax, national insurance and value added tax. The company had been one of three of which the directors had all been members of the same family. The parties agreed in suggesting to the court that a disqualification period of three years was appropriate. It was argued for the respondent that, notwithstanding any disqualification order, he should be given leave to continue to hold directorships of the two associated companies in respect of which there was no complaint and which employed a large number of people.

Held, that (1) a three-year disqualification period was appropriate, the behaviour being at a low level of seriousness; but (2) the respondent would be allowed to remain director of the other two companies on the condition that a nominated solicitor be appointed to and remain on their boards as a director independent of the family, it being competent for the court to impose conditions when granting leave and there being no indication that the circumstances which had led to the non-payment of taxes in respect of the insolvent company applied to the other two companies; and disqualification order pronounced and leave granted accordingly. (*Re Chartmore* [1991] C.L.Y. 399, commented on and followed.)

SECRETARY OF STATE FOR TRADE AND INDUSTRY v. PALFREMAN (O.H.), 1995 S.L.T. 156.

5548. Directors—disqualification—taking part in management of company when undischarged bankrupt. See DREW v. H.M. ADVOCATE, §5730.

5549. Floating charges—receiver appointed—effect of—disposition granted and delivered by company but not yet recorded

[Real Rights Act 1693 (c.13); Companies Act 1985 (c.6), s.462(1); Insolvency Act 1986 (c.45), s.53(7).]

Section 462(1) of the Companies Act 1985 provides that a company may create a floating charge "over all or any part of the property (including uncalled capital) which may from time to time be comprised in its property and undertaking". Section 53(7) of the Insolvency Act 1986 provides that: "On the appointment of a receiver under this section, the floating charge by virtue of which he was appointed attaches to the property then subject to the charge; and such attachment has effect as if the charge was a fixed security over the property to which it has attached." A company granted a floating charge which bore to be over "the whole of the property . . . which is or may be from time to time . . . comprised in our property and undertaking". The company were the heritable proprietors of certain subjects. They concluded missives for the sale of the subjects. The purchasers paid the price and the company delivered to them an executed disposition. The following day, before the disposition had been recorded, the holder of the floating charge appointed joint receivers of the property of the company. The disposition was subsequently recorded, together with a standard security in favour of creditors of the purchasers. The receivers brought an action against the purchasers and their creditors (the first and second defenders respectively). They sought declarator that the floating charge had attached to the subjects, that it operated as if it were a fixed security having priority over the standard security, and that they were entitled to take possession of the subjects and sell or otherwise dispose of them. The second defenders argued that, on a proper construction of the word "property" in s.462(1) of the 1985 Act, the subjects had ceased to be the property of the company when the disposition had been delivered. They contended that the holder of a delivered but unrecorded disposition had a right beyond that of an ordinary personal right against the seller, which, although not a complete real right, was a right of property. They argued that the rule that, until such a conveyance was recorded, a third party could acquire a real right of ownership through a further grant by the granter, was founded on the policy that third parties should be entitled to rely on the faith of the register, and not upon a right of property remaining in the granter. Although in the present case the company had been the infeft proprietors, the cases of heritage held by the infeft proprietor in trust, or held by a creditor infeft upon a conveyance granted in security yet *ex facie* absolute, showed that the true or beneficial ownership of heritage might be vested in someone other than the infeft proprietor. Accordingly, the phrase "property and undertaking" should be construed to exclude subjects which were not available for use for the commercial purposes of the company because, in the present case, they had been granted irrevocably to the purchasers. In the alternative, the second defenders argued that the effect of delivery of the disposition and receipt of the price had been to render the company the constructive trustees of the subjects, which they then held for behoof of the first defenders. The Lord Ordinary granted decree *de plano* in favour of the pursuers. The second defenders reclaimed.

Held, that (1) there was no such thing as a right lying between a personal right on the one hand and a real right on the other, and no such thing as a real right which was imperfect, incomplete or inchoate (*Mitchell v. Ferguson* (1781) Mor. 10296, explained and followed; *Young v. Leith* (1844) 6 D. 370; (1847) 9 D. 932, followed); (2) only one real right of ownership was recognised in any one thing at any one time; (3) (*per* the Lord President and Lord Sutherland) the example of a trust was no exception, for there the right of property was vested in the infeft trustee, the beneficial interest being only a personal right; (*per* Lord Coulsfield) although in Scotland a trust was generally assumed to involve a distinction between legal and beneficial ownership, the treatment of a trustee's right of ownership as merely an apparent title was to be distinguished as an established exception to the general rules (*Heritable Reversionary Co. v. Millar* (1892) 19 R.(H.L.) 43, distinguished); (4) a real right of ownership, and hence the property, in heritage was conveyed to a grantee only upon the recording of the grant, and so long as it remained unrecorded, the delivery of a conveyance neither divested the granter of, nor constituted in the grantee, any right of property, but merely constituted in the grantee an ordinary personal right against the granter (*Young v. Leith* and dicta of Lord Cameron in *Gibson v. Hunter Homes Designs* [1976] C.L.Y. 3188, followed; dicta in *James Grant & Co. v. Moran* [1948] C.L.Y. 4438, 4440, 4655 and *Thomas v. Inland Revenue* [1953] C.L.Y. 4057, disapproved; dicta in *Bowman v. Wright* (1877) 4 R. 322, *Embassy Picture House (Troon) v. Cammo Developments* [1970] C.L.Y. 3280, *Gibson* (*per* the Lord President), *Lombardi's Tr. v. Lombardi* [1982] C.L.Y. 3852, *Leeds Permanent Building Society v. Aitken, Malone & Mackay* [1986] C.L.Y. 4437, *Macdonald v. Scott's Exrs.* [1981] C.L.Y. 3522, and *Margrie Holdings v. Commissioners of Customs and Excise* [1990] C.L.Y. 5957 (*per* the Lord President), not followed); (5) since a purposive interpretation of the 1985 and 1986 Acts revealed an intention to give companies the widest scope for creating floating charges over their property, and to enable a floating charge to attach all property of the company which could be the subject of a "fixed security" in terms of s.70(1), there were no grounds for restricting the ordinary meaning of the statutory language to exclude the subjects of an unrecorded conveyance; (6) a constructive trust was created only by surrounding circumstances, and not by the mere fact of the delivery or constructive delivery of property to a purchaser under a contract of sale (*Stevenson v. Wilson* (1907) 14 S.L.T. 743, distinguished; *Gibson* and dicta in *Heritable Reversionary Co., Bank of Scotland v. Liquidators of Hutchison Main & Co.*, 1914 1 S.L.T. 111 and *National Bank of Scotland Glasgow Nominees v. Adamson*, 1932 S.L.T. 492, followed); and reclaiming motion refused. Authorities reviewed. *Observed*, that (1) in determining whether the holder of an unrecorded disposition had a right of property, different principles applied in cases concerned with matters such as jurisdiction or taxation, rather than pure questions of property law (dicta in *Fraser v. Fraser and Hibbert* (1870) 8 M. 400 (*per* the Lord President), approved); and (2) (*per* the Lord President (Hope) the result of the case was unsatisfactory, but that was the consequence of the introduction by Parliament of the concept of a floating charge, which was alien to the law, and was a matter which could be corrected only by Parliament.

SHARP v. THOMSON, 1995 S.L.T. 837.

5550. Insurance company—approval of proposed chief executive—procedure—fairness. See BUCHANAN v. SECRETARY OF STATE FOR TRADE AND INDUSTRY, §6033.

5551. Receiver—effect of appointment—heritable property. See SHARP v. THOMSON, §5549.

5552. Register of companies—application for restoration of company—company struck off register as not carrying on business or in operation

[Companies Act 1985 (c.6), ss.652(1) and 653(2).]

M appealed a sheriff's decision to refuse his petition for an order in terms of s.653 of the 1985 Act for a company (R), struck off in November 1993 under s.652, to be restored to the register of companies. M held 99 of the 100 shares in R, which had been incorporated in 1985, and was a guarantor for R in a lease granted by C in 1988 of subjects, which were operated as a snooker centre. In September 1989, a company (S), of which M was an employee, had entered into an agreement with R, under which S bought the whole fittings and fixtures and stock within the centre, undertook the management of the centre and received all the profits. S had not been incorporated by the date of the agreement and no steps were taken to ratify the contract, but M had continued to operate the centre on his own behalf. C had raised an action against R for irritancy of the lease and payment of rent arrears, which R had defended on the grounds that C had failed to keep the subjects in a good state of repair: this action had been sisted. C had raised a further action against M for recovery of the subjects, in which M had consented to decree passing. M argued that (1) the holding of a lease showed that R was "carrying on business" as at November 1993; and (2) C were opposing the petition simply to provide a way out of their action against R; and, given that there had been no objection by the registrar of companies or the Lord Advocate, and that M, as guarantor, would be greatly prejudiced if R were not restored to the register, it was just that R be so restored.

Held, appeal refused. (1) Whether M had been "carrying on business or in operation" at the time of striking off was a question of fact for the sheriff. The words had to be given a normal and reasonable meaning and the mere holding of a right in heritable property was not sufficient. (2) Whether restoration was nevertheless "just" within s.653(2) was a matter for the sheriff and M had not made out any ground for the exercise of his discretion to be reviewed. The prejudice M might suffer as guarantor was irrelevant because his title to raise the petition was as a member of R and it was purely fortuitous that he was also a guarantor.

McSHANE v. COMET GROUP (Sh.Ct.), 1994 S.C.L.R. 1077.

5553. Register of companies—striking company off register—company not carrying on business or in operation. See McSHANE v. COMET GROUP, §5552.

5554. Winding up—gratuitous alienations—discharge by creditor of standard security—whether discharges alienations involving discharge of company's rights

[Insolvency Act 1986 (c.45), s.242.]

Section 242 of the Insolvency Act 1986 provides that where any claim or right of a company has been discharged by an alienation made within two years of the commencement of winding up, the alienation may be challenged by the liquidator, and that upon such challenge decree of reduction shall be pronounced unless any person seeking to uphold the alienation establishes that it was made for adequate consideration. The liquidator of a company sought to reduce discharges of two standard securities as gratuitous alienations under s.242 of the 1986 Act. The granters of the standard securities averred that no sums had been advanced to them by the company, and that the securities had been granted at the request of a former director of the company who had advanced them certain sums. They argued that as no sums had been due by them to the company, the discharges did not involve the discharge of any claim or right by the company in terms of s.242(2)(a), and in any event the discharges had been made for adequate consideration. It was argued for the liquidator that the terms of the securities showed that the company had a right to payment of the sums therein specified, whether or not any sums had been advanced and whatever sums had been advanced, and that the company had rights in security distinguishable from the claims for payment, the discharge of which constituted alienations.

Held, that (1) on a reasonable construction of the standard securities no right to payment arose until advances had been made; (2) even if there were

distinguishable rights in security, the worth of such rights and the adequacy of consideration for their discharge were distinct questions, and it was open to the defenders to establish that discharges for no money were made for adequate consideration, and proof before answer allowed.
RANKIN v. MEEK (O.H.), 1995 S.L.T. 526.

5555. Winding up—liquidator—powers—inquiry into company's dealings—production of documents and examination on oath—jurisdiction

[Insolvency Act 1986 (c.45), ss.236(2) and (3), 237(3) and 426(5).]

Section 236(2) of the Insolvency Act 1986 provides that the court may on the application of, *inter alia*, a liquidator of a company summon to appear "any person" known or suspected to have in his possession any property of the company or supposed to be indebted to the company or whom the court thinks capable of giving information concerning the promotion, formation, business, dealings, affairs or property of the company. Section 236(3) provides that the court may require any such person to produce any books, papers or other records in his possession or under his control relating to the company. By s.237(3) the court may order "any person", who if within the jurisdiction of the court would be liable to be summoned before it under s.236, to deliver property of the company or to be examined within or outwith the United Kingdom. Section 426 provides, *inter alia*, for co-operation and assistance between courts exercising jurisdiction in relation to insolvency in any other part of the United Kingdom "or any other relevant country or territory". Liquidators of a company sought orders against a firm of accountants, and certain individual partners and employees of the firm, for production of documents and examination on oath of the individuals. In this latter regard they also sought authorisation and approval of letters of request for examination of, *inter alios*, a former employee of the firm who lived in New York. The former employee argued that it would be incompetent to grant orders against him because he was not subject to the jurisdiction of the court. The firm had formerly acted as auditors and financial advisers to the company, which just prior to winding up had suffered an enormous loss of investment assets through improper and unauthorised dealings. The liquidators sought the orders in exercise of their duty to investigate as fully as possible the conduct of the affairs of the company, the circumstances of sale and disposal of assets and the prospects of recovery of assets, including possible claims against third parties one of whom was the firm of accountants. The making of the orders was opposed by the accountants and the individuals concerned on the grounds of oppression and unreasonableness. There had already been a demonstrably substantial amount of co-operation which, they undertook, would continue on the liquidators giving a clear indication as to the topics upon which and the areas about which they wished to examine. This was necessary both to save the firm's time and resources in ascertaining what information was required from over 50 files, and to avoid the hazard of exposing individuals to a general examination particularly where the liquidators were intent on determining whether there was a potential claim.

Held, that (1) the meaning of "any person" in s.236(2) of the Insolvency Act 1986 was not confined to persons resident in the jurisdiction of the court or who had been personally served with the petition within the jurisdiction, but extended to any person whether within the United Kingdom or not, and accordingly the court had jurisdiction in respect of the individual in New York where there was provision to seek the co-operation of the court there (*Re Tucker* [1993] C.L.Y. 2345, not followed); (2) the liquidators had demonstrated prima facie grounds for consideration by the court of their application for the exercise of the extraordinary powers given to the court by ss.236 and 237 of the Insolvency Act 1986, and the present was such an exceptional case that despite the degree of co-operation already shown by the respondents there were insufficient countervailing considerations to weigh against making an order for production of documents, which was less oppressive than an order for oral examination; (3) the order for production should be limited at that stage to the firm of accountants alone, and not the individual partners and employees, and limited also to the documents set out under the specific heads, all of which bore upon matters which the liquidators properly required to investigate; (4) it was unnecessary at that stage to pronounce orders for oral examination against the individual respondents since material for any oral examination might only appear after the order for production against the firm was satisfied, but this was without prejudice to the petitioners' right to seek such an order if co-operation was not forthcoming to any reasonably stated requirements; and case put out by order to settle the terms of the introduction to the calls and of the undertakings required. (*Re British and Commonwealth Holdings (Nos. 1 and 2)* [1992] C.L.Y. 2317 followed.)

McISAAC AND WILSON, PETRS. (O.H.), 1995 S.L.T. 498.

5556. Winding up—liquidator—resignation during course of liquidation—whether entitled to seek exoneration and discharge

[Companies Act 1948 (c.38), s.242.]

In 1976 a provisional liquidator was appointed to a company. Subsequently he was nominated and appointed official liquidator. The liquidation proved long and complex. Having ingathered the assets, the liquidator presented a note to the court seeking to resign as liquidator in that the liquidation would still take some time. A former director opposed the note on various grounds, which were rejected by the Lord Ordinary, who pronounced interlocutors, *inter alia*, authorising the liquidator to resign and remitting for reports with respect to considering an exoneration and discharge. The former director reclaimed, arguing, *inter alia*, that a liquidator who resigned during the course of a liquidation was not entitled to exoneration and discharge.

Held, that although there was no express statutory provision for a liquidator who had resigned to be exonered and discharged by the court, the power to exoner and discharge a liquidator who had resigned had to be implied; and reclaiming motion refused.

BROWN v. DICKSON, 1995 S.L.T. 354.

COMPULSORY PURCHASE

5557. Compulsory purchase order—confirmation by Secretary of State—material change of circumstances

P, the owners of certain land, appealed against a compulsory purchase order by C, a regional council, confirmed by S, the Secretary of State. C's order was made pursuant to their powers to relieve or prevent congestion by providing a public car park under ss.32 and 40 of the Road Traffic Act 1984 and their preliminary designs for the land incorporated a footbridge over a dual carriageway to provide pedestrian access to a proposed new shopping complex. Following a public local inquiry the reporter (R) concluded that (1) the car parking facilities were necessary as there was a projected shortfall of parking spaces in the area by the year 2000; (2) none of the alternative sites proposed were comparable to the appeal site and that two named sites had major planning, ownership and environmental difficulties; and (3) P's offer of a long lease of the land to C was not in the wider interests of the purpose of the order. R further concluded that for the car park to operate effectively, the proposed footbridge should be provided simultaneously with the opening of the car park. P thereafter sought to reopen the public local inquiry because of further developments, which S refused following correspondence with the parties. S confirmed R's report except for the recommendation as to timing, as R had no power to determine when the transfer would take place once the order was confirmed. P argued that the order should be quashed on the grounds that (1) there had been a material change of circumstances since the close of the inquiry as the two named sites might now become available; (2) C had changed their strategy for dealing with the car parking problems from town centre parking to park and ride facilities; (3) S, in deciding not to accept R's recommendation about the pedestrian footbridge, had failed to comply with rule 9(2) of the Compulsory Purchase by Public Authorities (Inquiries Procedure) (Scotland) Rules 1976; (4) the appeal site was not required for car parking in view of the Stirling Initiative document which indicated that C intended to use part of the site for commercial development; and (5) the order was not necessary as C's aim to use the appeal site for car parking could be achieved by a long lease.

Held, appeal refused. (1) P's grounds of appeal did not refer to the alternative sites and therefore the issue was not properly raised. In any event, the sites referred to on appeal were not the same as those discussed at the initial inquiry, and even if they were developed there would still be a shortfall in parking. (2) S did not act unfairly in refusing to reopen the inquiry as the proposed park and ride facilities introduced by C were a supplement to, not a substitute for, the car parks at the appeal site. (3) P's argument regarding the footbridge was also not properly raised. In any event S was not disagreeing with R on his findings or because of the receipt of any new evidence but because of the competency of delaying the transfer of land once C confirmed the order. (4) There was no evidence that C had agreed to the Initiative document or adopted it as part of their planning policy and therefore no evidence that they intended to use the area in part for commercial development. A subsequent document published by C restated their original position. (5) R was entitled to take the view that even if a long lease could be negotiated, it would create insecurity in the long term as to what would happen to the car park once its term expired, especially as P's subjects formed only part of the proposed car park area.

STIRLING PLANT (HIRE AND SALES) v. CENTRAL REGIONAL COUNCIL, *The Times*, February 9, 1995.

5558. Possession—obtaining possession following compulsory purchase order. See GLASGOW AIRPORT v. CHALK, §6396.

CONFLICT OF LAWS

5559. Comity—interdict—interim interdict—restraint of foreign proceedings. See SHELL U.K. EXPLORATION AND PRODUCTION v. INNES, §6052.

Custody of child—international child abduction. See CHILDREN AND YOUNG PERSONS.

5560. Procedure—interim orders—injunction obtained in England on basis not available under Scots law. See G. v. CALEDONIAN NEWSPAPERS, §6203.

CONSTITUTIONAL LAW

5561. Crown—immunity. See WOOD v. LORD ADVOCATE, §6386.

5562. Crown—immunity—award of expenses against Crown—Crown not party to action. See MEEKISON v. UNIROYAL ENGLEBERT TYRES, §5936.

5563. Public expenditure—whether authorised—EC Agreement on Social Policy. See MONCKTON v. LORD ADVOCATE, §5916.

CONSUMER CREDIT

5564. Conditional sale agreement—connected lender liability—purchase of second-hand car—whether conditional sale agreement caught by extension of liability under statute—whether creditor liable under other grounds

[Consumer Credit Act 1974 (c.39), ss.11(1)(a), 12(a), 75; Sale of Goods Act 1979 (c.54), s.14.]

Section 75 of the Consumer Credit Act 1974 extends liability to a creditor where the actual offender is a third party. The section does not apply in the case of a conditional sale agreement where the creditor as a contracting party for the supply may be treated as a supplier and be liable for any breach of contract.

P entered into a conditional sale agreement with a finance company (D) for the purchase of a second-hand car previously sold to D by a dealer. The car was rejected by P as it was alleged to be suffering from defects which D was unable to correct. P, pleading that the car was not of merchantable quality, brought actions against both the dealer and D. The Sheriff found for P on the basis that D was liable to P under s.75.

Held, dismissing D's appeal, that although the Sheriff had made an error in holding that s.75 applied, D was nevertheless liable for breach of contract under the conditional sale agreement between P and D.

RENTON v. HENDERSONS GARAGE (NAIRN) AND UNITED DOMINIONS TRUST [1994] CCLR 29, Sheriff Principal D.J. Risk, Q.C.

5565. Debtor-creditor-supplier agreement—liability of creditor for breaches by supplier

[Consumer Credit Act 1974 (c.39), s.75(1).]

Held, in an action of payment by a finance company against a debtor, that the latter was entitled to plead as a defence to the claim that the goods in question had been defective and that he had been entitled to reject them and to treat the contract of sale as repudiated.

FORWARD TRUST v. HORNSBY (Sh.Ct.), 1995 S.C.L.R. 574.

CONTRACT

5566. Agreement—requirement for registration under Restrictive Trade Practices Act 1976. See MACKIE & DEWAR v. DIRECTOR GENERAL OF FAIR TRADING, §6456.

5567. Breach of contract—claim based on *quantum meruit*. See ERDC CONSTRUCTION v. H.M. LOVE & CO., §5479.

Breach of contract—damages. See DAMAGES.

5568. Breach of contract—remedy—*actio quanti minoris*—competency

A appealed the sheriff principal's decision ([1993] C.L.Y. 4876) to allow F's appeal against a sheriff's decision and to dismiss A's action in respect of loss and damage which A averred they had sustained following the purchase from F of a sandwich bar business. A alleged that F was in breach of a warranty that accounts of the business were true and accurate and that F had made fraudulent and negligent misrepresentations in respect of the accuracy of the accounts. The sheriff principal had held that as the claim for breach of warranty was truly an *actio quanti minoris* it was incompetent and that A's case based on misrepresentation was irrelevant because the warranty could not be regarded as a representation inducing A to enter the contract. Before the appeal was heard A amended to incorporate averments concerning misrepresentations by F in the prior communings. A argued that the rule prohibiting the *actio quanti minoris* did not apply because (1) the contract was a mixed one for the sale of a business and the lease of a shop and the claim of damages related to the higher price paid for the business and the higher rental agreed on the basis of the business's profitability; (2) the action was based on breach of a warranty, which being a guarantee as to a state of affairs was analogous to warrandice of title; (3) A and F had agreed that an action of damages would be open to A: this could be seen from the use of the words "the vendor warrants" in a number of clauses which were clearly not material and the non-supersession clause, which continued the warranties in full force and effect; (4) there had been fraud by F, in that F had represented the accounts to A as accurate at a meeting before missives were entered into, although F, who had been running the business himself, had to have known that aspects of the accounts were false, F having later conceded that the accounts were "not precise"; and (5) matters were no longer entire, as A had only discovered the breach of warranty following a commission and diligence about six months after A had taken over the business, by which time the turnover had increased, and the stock lines and nature of the business had changed. F argued, *inter alia*, that A's averments of fraudulent misrepresentation did not show F's responsibility for the accounts, which had been prepared by an accountant and were marked "subject to audit".

Held, appeal allowed, A's averments anent breach of warranty excluded from probation (Lord Osborne dissenting) and *quoad ultra* proof before allowed. (1) *Per* the Lord Justice Clerk (Ross) and Lord Morison: The opening paragraph of A's offer had referred first to the purchase of the contents and business and A were referred to throughout as "the purchaser" and F as "the vendor". The ancillary agreement for a lease of the subjects in which the business was carried on could not alter the character of the contract, which remained one of sale and, in any event, there was no authority for any exception in relation to composite contracts. *Per* Lord Osborne (dissenting): The prohibition against the *actio quanti minoris* was a peculiarity of the non-statutory law of sale, which unnecessarily and undesirably restricted the range of remedies available to a dissatisfied purchaser, had no positive value in modern commercial conditions and was of questionable ancestry ("The History of the *Actio Quanti Minoris* in Scotland", 1991 J.R. 190). As there was no direct authority requiring the prohibition to be applied to a contract such as the present, which was truly a composite one (the element of lease being of equal importance to the element of sale), there was no justification for its application. (2) While the words "the vendor warrants" showed that the provision was a material term, the words did not alter the meaning of the clause which was merely a term of the contract and they did not create an exception to the prohibition. There was no analogy with warrandice, which did not provide a remedy based merely on loss attributable to a property being worth less than that which had been warranted (*Clark v. Lindale Homes* [1994] 7 C.L. 696). (3) The non-supersession clause related only to the delivery of the lease and had no bearing in relation to the sale of the business, and there was no implication from it or the other warranties that A were entitled to benefit from the *actio quanti minoris.* (4) While, if there had been fraud, A would have had a remedy based on delict, the *actio quanti minoris* was still incompetent as it was based on a breach of the terms of the contract and it was irrelevant that A was induced fraudulently to enter the contract (*Bryson & Co. v. Bryson,*

1916 1 S.L.T. 361 and *Smith v. Sim* [1955] C.L.Y. 3224, followed; *Widdowson v. Hunter* [1989] C.L.Y. 4428, disapproved). (5) While there was an exception to the prohibition where matters were not entire, A had not given sufficient specification regarding the change in the business. Restitution could still have taken place, although some of the stock had been used up, as the business remained a sandwich bar and had not been fundamentally altered (*McCormick & Co. v. F. E. Rittmeyer & Co.* (1869) 7 M. 854, followed; *Bald v. Scott* (1847) 10 D. 289, distinguished). (6) Although the sheriff principal had been correct to dismiss the action, A's amendments meant that they had now averred sufficient for proof on their cases of fraudulent and negligent misrepresentation. The averment concerning F's concession regarding the accounts made after conclusion of missives was relevant as it could infer previous knowledge of the falsity of the accounts.

FORTUNE v. FRASER, 1995 S.C.L.R. 121.

Building contracts. See BUILDING AND CONSTRUCTION.

5569. Conditions and warranties—limitation of liability—"time related costs"

Management contractors in the construction of a concert hall raised an action against a construction company employed as subcontractors. The contract was constituted by the contractors' printed form of subcontract and five letters passing between the parties. In terms of one of those letters it was agreed that damages "in respect of time related costs" should be subject to a limit of £100,000. About six months after the subcontractors commenced work, the contractors determined the contract on the basis of the subcontractors' alleged failure to proceed diligently with the contract, and sought damages of £2,741,000 for breach of contract. The subcontractors contended that any damages due fell within the limitation of liability agreement and were thus limited to £100,000. The Lord Ordinary accepted this contention and restricted any damages to be awarded to the figure of £100,000. The First Division took the contrary view and construed the limitation clause as applying only to costs related "to the consequences for the [subcontractors] in damages of late completion of the subcontract works". The subcontractors appealed, arguing, *inter alia*, that a "time related cost" was a cost which was incurred having some relationship to time, in contrast to a cost which had some relationship to failure in specification, and that a failure to proceed with due diligence was a breach involving delay and hence a time related cost.

Held, that a clause limiting liability required to state clearly and unambiguously the scope of the limitation and would be construed with a degree of strictness, albeit not to the same extent as an exclusion or indemnity clause, and that the subcontractors had wholly failed to show that the limitation clause was so framed as to cover damages flowing from a repudiatory breach on their part leading to termination and hence non-performance of the subcontract; and appeal dismissed. (*Ailsa Craig Fishing Co. v. Malvern Fishing Co.* [1981] C.L.Y. 2994; [1982] C.L.Y. 3501, applied.)

BOVIS CONSTRUCTION (SCOTLAND) v. WHATLINGS CONSTRUCTION (H.L.), 1995 S.L.T. 1339.

5570. Construction—exclusion of liability clause—hire—transfer of liability for third party claims

A widow sought damages from her late husband's employers arising from his death following an accident at work involving a forklift truck. The employers had hired the truck from its owners, who were convened as a third party. Clause 5(*b*) of the contract of hire provided that the hirer would "take all reasonable steps to keep himself acquainted with the state and condition of the plant. If such plant be continued at work or in use in an unsafe and unsatisfactory state, the hirer shall be solely responsible for any damage, loss or accidents whether directly or indirectly arising therefrom". Clause 8 provided that the hirer would alone be responsible for all claims arising in connection with the operation of plant operated by drivers supplied by the owner. Clause 9 provided that the hirer would be responsible for expenses arising from a breakdown and all loss and damage incurred by the owners through the hirer's negligence or misuse while the plant was idle due to such a breakdown. Clause 13 provided: "(*a*) . . . nothing in this clause affects the operation of Clauses 5, 8 and 9", and "(*b*) . . . the hirer shall fully and completely indemnify the owner in respect of all claims by any person whatsoever for injury to person or property caused by or in connection with or arising out of the use of the plant". At procedure roll debate the owners sought dismissal of the action against them on the ground that cl. 5(*b*) entailed that all liability had been transferred to the hirers, it being accepted that c.13(*b*) alone was not sufficient to transfer liability to the hirer where the owners were themselves at fault.

Held, that (1) the construction of cl. 5(*b*) was not affected by any anterior fault on the part of the owners and was habile to give an exclusion of liability to the owners (*U.S.A. v. Arc Construction and H.S. Ices Hire*, Hobhouse J, Queen's Bench Division May 8, 1991, unreported, followed); (2) on consideration of the pursuer's averments, upon which the third party founded, it could not be decided before proof whether cl. 5(*b*) applied as it was not clear that the truck had been "continued at work or in use" since it was not in use at the time, it having been found to have a fault that was being investigated, or that the hirers had been aware that the truck was in an unsafe or unsatisfactory state; and proof before answer allowed.

CAMERON v. McDERMOTTS (SCOTLAND) (O.H.) 1995 S.L.T. 542.

5571. Construction—indemnity—negligence

A man injured in an accident on an oil rig sued his employers and the owners of the oil rig and the concession in which it operated. The rig owners settled with the pursuer and sought to be indemnified by the employers in terms of a cl. 2.3 incorporated into a contract between them, which bound the employers to indemnify the owners from "all . . . causes of action in respect of death or of injury to personnel provided by [the employers] howsoever caused". Clause 2.4 bound the owners to indemnify the employers from "all . . . causes of action in respect of death or of injury to [the owners'] employees howsoever caused". The Lord Ordinary upheld the owners' claim to be indemnified. The employers reclaimed, arguing that cl. 2.3 did not require to be construed as covering negligence by the owners.

Held, that (1) on a proper construction of cl. 2.3, all that was required to bring the indemnity into play was loss, injury and damage caused to some extent by the owners' breach of statutory duty, which was conceded, and that it was irrelevant whether the breach was a negligent one; (2) there was no content for cl. 2.3 of sufficient substance to displace its prima facie application to the owners' own negligence; (3) cll. 2.3 and 2.4 were to be read as reciprocal, having the effect of allocating total liability for injury and death in respect of the workforce of each of the defenders to that workforce's employer regardless of fault; and reclaiming motion refused. *Opinion*, that the reciprocity argument might succeed even if the condition did not meet the third test in *Canada Steamship Lines v. R.* [1952] C.L.Y. 610.

NELSON v. ATLANTIC POWER AND GAS, 1995 S.L.T. 102.

5572. Construction—indemnity–negligence. See COMOREX v. COSTELLOE TUNNELLING (LONDON), §5488.

5573. Construction—mutuality of obligations—right of set off. See COMMON SERVICES AGENCY v. PURDIE AND KIRKPATRICK; EUROCOPY (SCOTLAND) v. LOTHIAN HEALTH BOARD, §5577.

5574. Construction—offer made by "personal representative" of deceased taxpayer—whether offer ambiguous—whether personal liability created. See ADVOCATE (LORD) v. CHUNG, §5460.

5575. Construction—payment on occurrence of a stipulated event—whether enforceable

Held, that an agreement which provided for a fixed payment to be made to a selling agent on the event of a sale even where the agent had not been involved in finding or introducing the purchaser was enforceable.

HART (CHRIS) (BUSINESS SALES) v. DUNCAN (Sh.Ct.), 1994 S.C.L.R. 1104.

5576. Construction—transfer of liability

H sued L, having been injured at work by reason of a defective vehicle belonging to K, the third party, but hired to L at the material time. The contract of hire provided for insurance of the vehicle by L, including provision for L to pay K the amount of any excess on the insurance, and also made L "responsible for all third party claims howsoever arising". At debate between L and K it was agreed that H's claim was that of a "third party" and that L had insured the vehicle at the time. Neither sought to aver that the clause was one of indemnity. K argued that the clause transferred risk (*Scottish Special Housing Association v. Wimpey Construction UK* [1986] C.L.Y. 3613) and that the words should be construed for what they plainly meant, whatever the consequences. L claimed that the clause was merely administrative, determining who should handle the claim and did not specifically cut down L's rights of subrogation or any common law rights of relief.

Held, L's claim against K dismissed. Contracts of a commercial nature should be given their intended meaning (*Stephen (Forth) v. Riley UK* [1976] C.L.Y. 2978). It was always in the hands of an insured by lawful contract to limit the extent to which there might be subrogation of rights. Even if the consequences raised diminished the rights of L or their insurers, that did not affect the construction of the clause provided it could be given a clear and specific meaning. L's construction of the language of the clause would have to include additional wording in order to meet their point. The general law admitted the efficiency of such a contractual arrangement if the relevant words submitted to it.

HALLIDAY v. LYALL AND SCOTT (O.H.), 1995 S.L.T. 192.

5577. Construction—whether contract for hire of photocopier or for sale of paper supplied

In two actions the suppliers of photocopiers argued that the contract between the parties was one of hire. The users of the photocopiers argued that the contract was one for the purchase of an agreed minimum number of sheets of paper. At debate both sheriffs construed the contract as one of hire. The users of the photocopiers appealed to the sheriff principal, who issued a joint note.

Held, that the contracts were of hire, with the cost of that hire being determined by reference to the amount of use made of the copiers but subject to an agreed minimum cost; and appeals refused, except in relation to the restriction of proof in one case by the sheriff to the matter of set off.

COMMON SERVICES AGENCY v. PURDIE AND KIRKPATRICK; EUROCOPY (SCOTLAND) v. LOTHIAN HEALTH BOARD, 1995 S.L.T. (Sh.Ct.) 34.

5578. Construction—whether contract for hire of photocopier or for sale of paper supplied—commercial purpose of contract

Suppliers of photocopiers provided a machine to a health board. The copier itself was provided free but the health board undertook to purchase a minimum amount of blank A4 photocopy paper from the suppliers who also had a monopoly in the supply of parts and requisites. Following a dispute about payment the suppliers raised an action in the sheriff court for payment of sums due under the contract. The sheriff and, on appeal, the sheriff principal rejected the health board's argument that the contract was not a contract of hire but rather a contract for supply of A4 paper, and that thus the supplier's averments were irrelevant. The health board appealed to the Court of Session, maintaining their argument that in the absence of the use of the word "hire" in the contract and there being no hire charges for the copier, the contract was not one of hire, that the suppliers were seeking payment based on the number of copies made according to the copier's meter rather than on the amount of A4 paper supplied and that the pursuers' pleadings were irrelevant.

Held, that (1) common sense dictated that the contract be regarded in accordance with its commercial purpose; (2) prima facie the contract was one for hire of equipment, having all the essential elements of a contract for the location of corporeal moveables; (3) the fact that charges were related to volume of copies made, with a monthly minimum, was not inconsistent with the contract being one of hire of a photocopier; (4) although some of the pursuers' averments referred to charges due on the basis of copies made rather than on the basis of the contractually agreed monthly volume, they ought to be given the opportunity of proving that they were entitled to payment of the sums claimed; and appeal refused.

EUROCOPY (SCOTLAND) v. LOTHIAN HEALTH BOARD, 1995 S.L.T. 1356.

Consumer Credit. See CONSUMER CREDIT.

Employment. See EMPLOYMENT.

5579. Enforceability—contract involving negotiable instrument—contract induced by fraudulent misrepresentation of third party

A company sold goods to another company. As payment for the goods the buyers delivered a bank draft to the sellers, in which the sellers were named as payees. Unknown to the sellers and the bank, the funds which had been lodged with the bank on behalf of the buyers to cover the bank draft had been obtained by the fraud of the buyers. The lodging of the funds was part of a fraudulent scheme by the buyers to attempt to disguise the fact that the funds had been obtained by fraud. On presentation of the draft by the sellers to the bank, the bank refused to make payment having discovered that the buyers had obtained the funds fraudulently. The sellers raised an action for payment against the bank. The Lord Ordinary held that the fraud of the buyers did not affect the bank's obligations to the sellers, and that the bank was contractually obliged to make payment to the payee. The bank relaimed. Before the Inner House the parties were agreed that under s.5 of the Bills of Exchange Act 1882 the sellers were entitled to treat the bank draft, which was drawn by the bank upon itself, as a bill of exchange or a promissory note as their option, and that it contained a contractual undertaking by the bank to the sellers to pay the sum specified therein. The bank contended that they were not obliged to pay, as (1) the issuing of the draft was induced by the fraudulent misrepresentations of a third party (the buyers) to the effect that the funds on the faith of which the draft had been issued were truly the property of the buyers, and that although the general rule of contract law was that error induced by the fraud of a third party left a contractual relationship unaffected, there was an exception in the case of a negotiable instrument; and (2) the payment designed to be effected by the draft was so tainted by illegality, and so contrary to public conscience, as constituting part of a fraudulent scheme involving embezzlement and money laundering, as to be unenforceable by the court. The bank further contended that the sellers required to aver and prove that they had given full value for the draft.

Held, that (1) the general principle that error induced by the fraudulent misrepresentation of a third party left a contractual relationship unaffected contained no exception in relation to contracts constituted by negotiable instruments; (2) there was no principle that any payment representing the proceeds of serious crime was, regardless of the innocence of the immediate parties to the contract, illegal and unenforceable; (3) no illegality attached to the contract underlying the issue of the bank draft, the sellers' agreement to accept the draft in settlement of an existing debt, and the bank having been issued to settle that debt, had been given for full value; and reclaiming motion refused. (*R. E. Jones Ltd v. Waring & Gillow* [1926] A.C. 670, and *G. M. Scott (Willowbank Cooperage) v. York Trailer Co.* [1969] C.L.Y. 3954, considered; dicta in *Thackwell v. Barclays Bank* [1986] C.L.Y. 158, not followed.) *Per* Lord Morison: Where a party averred a genuine commercial contract in respect of which consideration was agreed at arms length and appeared *ex facie* not to be unreasonable in amount, the onus of proving that they had received some gratuitous benefit from their contract should lie with the party asserting that.

UNIVERSAL IMPORT EXPORT v. BANK OF SCOTLAND, 1995 S.L.T. 1318.

5580. Error—induced by fraudulent misrepresentation of third party. See UNIVERSAL IMPORT EXPORT v. BANK OF SCOTLAND, §5579.

5581. Implied term—business efficacy. See DUCTFORM VENTILATION (FIFE) v. ANDREWS-WEATHERFOIL, §5490.

Insurance. See INSURANCE.

Lease. See LANDLORD AND TENANT.

5582. Lease—implied term—whether sufficiently specific. See THOMSON v. THOMAS MUIR (WASTE MANAGEMENT), §6061.

Partnership. See PARTNERSHIP.

Prescription. See PRESCRIPTION.

5583. Quasi-contract—recompense—*quantum lucratus*. See MORGAN GUARANTY TRUST CO. OF NEW YORK v. LOTHIAN REGIONAL COUNCIL, §5586.

5584. Quasi-contract—recompense—title to sue

Having settled the claims of two occupants of a car during a collision, an insurance company sought to recover from the uninsured driver of the other car involved the amount which it had paid. When the case came before the sheriff for debate the defender sought dismissal of the action, submitting that he had not been unjustly enriched since the third parties could have pursued an action against him and the pursuers had not obtained an assignation of the third parties' rights against him. The insurance company submitted that it had a right of recovery based upon recompense rather than restitution.

Held, that (1) the payments by the insurance company to the third parties did not discharge the defender's liability to the third parties; (2) it was not the defender but the third parties who, having been indemnified by the pursuers and yet continuing to have a right of raising an action against the defender, had been enriched; and defender's plea to the relevancy sustained and action dismissed.

NORWICH UNION FIRE INSURANCE SOCIETY v. ROSS, 1995 S.L.T. (Sh.Ct.) 103.

5585. Quasi-contract—repetition—error of law. See MORGAN GUARANTY TRUST CO. OF NEW YORK v. LOTHIAN REGIONAL COUNCIL, §6118.

5586. Quasi-contract—restitution—error of law

On July 16, 1987 a local authority entered into an interest rate and currency exchange agreement (a "swap agreement") with a merchant bank. The agreement was to subsist until July 17, 1992. In terms of the agreement each party agreed to pay to the other, on a specified date or dates, an amount calculated by reference to the interest which would have accrued over a given period on the same notional principal sum, on the assumption that different interest rates applied in each case. Prior to October 17, 1989, the bank had made net payments to the local authority of £368,104·52. Following upon the decision of the divisional court in England in *Hazell v. Hammersmith and Fulham London Borough Council* [1991] C.L.Y. 2420, that such "swap agreements" were *ultra vires* local authorities and unlawful, no further payments were made by either party after October 17, 1989. The bank sought repayment of the sums paid to the local authority. The Lord Ordinary, having held that such agreements were *ultra vires* local authorities in Scotland, dealt with the question of the remedies which were available to the bank to recover the moneys paid. He found that the decisions of *Glasgow Corporation v. Lord Advocate* and *Taylor v. Wilson's Trs.* were binding upon him and were authority for the view that an error of law in the interpretation of a public general statute as to the contractual capacity of the local authority rendered the *condictio indebiti* inapplicable and undermined the bank's right to a remedy in general. Before a court of five judges, on the assumption that it was *ultra vires* the local authority to enter into the agreement, it was argued for the bank that those cases had been wrongly decided and that error of law was not a bar to an action of repetition under the *condictio indebiti*, and, in the alternative, that the remedy of recompense was available.

Held, that (1) the appropriate remedy for the recovery of money paid or property transferred under an obligation which was void but was erroneously thought to be valid, was an action of repetition under the *condictio indebiti* and not a claim based on recompense; (2) a payment not due might be recovered under the *condictio indebiti* irrespective of whether the mistake under which it was paid was one of fact or of law, and that the error of law rule had no sound foundation in principle; (3) the essentials of the *condictio indebiti* were that the sum which the pursuer paid was not due and that he had made the payment in error, and these matters had to be the subject of averment by the pursuer to show a prima facie entitlement to the remedy; (4) it was not part of the law of Scotland that the error had to be shown to be excusable, although the nature of the error and the question whether it could have been avoided might play a part in the decision as to where the equities might lie where that point was raised in answer to the pursuer's claim, it being for the defender to raise the issues which might lead to a decision that the remedy should be refused on grounds of equity; (5) the pursuers' averments were sufficient to show that they were prima facie entitled to their remedy, and the defenders had not made any averments to show that it would be inequitable for the pursuers, to recover the sum paid; and reclaiming motion allowed, decree granted *de plano* and case remitted to the Outer House for consideration of the question of interest. (*Stirling v. Earl of Lauderdale* (1733) Mor. 2930, approved; *Glasgow Corporation v. Lord Advocate* [1959] C.L.Y. 3974, and *Taylor v. Wilson's Trs.* [1974] C.L.Y. 4104, overruled. Authorities reviewed.)

MORGAN GUARANTY TRUST CO. OF NEW YORK v. LOTHIAN REGIONAL COUNCIL, 1995 S.L.T. 299.

5587. Rectification. See HUEWIND v. CLYDESDALE BANK, §5980.

5588. Rectification—misdescription of grantor—different company in same group—intention—relevancy

[Law Reform (Miscellaneous Provisions) (Scotland) Act 1985 (c.73), s.8(1)(*b*).]

The Law Reform (Miscellaneous Provisions) (Scotland) Act 1985, s.8, provides that where the court is satisfied that a document transferring a right failed to express accurately the intention of the grantor, it may order the document to be rectified in order to give effect to that intention. Two companies, Goldberg and Brunswick (which was controlled by Goldberg), held accounts with a bank. Operations on the accounts over a certain limit required the signatures of authorised signatories of Brunswick. On July 31, 1989 the treasurer of Goldberg issued oral instructions to the bank to transfer such a sum from Brunswick's account into Goldberg's account, this being a loan from Brunswick to Goldberg. The bank duly reflected this transfer on its records. The authorised director and the company secretary of Brunswick, who were also director and company secretary respectively of Goldberg, executed a letter, dated July 31, 1989 and received by the bank on August 3, 1989, which purported to be an instruction to the bank to transfer the sum into the account of Goldberg. The letter was written on the headed notepaper of Goldberg and purported to be signed on its behalf. The bank petitioned the court to rectify the letter by substituting the name of Brunswick for that of Goldberg. Brunswick and its liquidator opposed the petition on the grounds that the letter was in effect an *ex post facto* ratification of the transfer which had already taken place, and was not the document which was intended to create, transfer, vary or renounce a right within the scope of s.8(1)(*b*); that the grantor of the letter was Goldberg, and s.8(1) did not allow for the rectification of errors relating to the identify or description of the grantor; and that the petitioner's averments were irrelevant in that they did not seek to explain why the signatories signed on behalf of Goldberg if they had actually intended to sign on behalf of Brunswick. At procedure roll, the Lord Ordinary rejected the respondents' submission that the case did not fall within s.8(1)(*b*) of the Act, and he repelled the respondents' plea to the competency. He decided that the argument on relevancy raised a question of fact about which the petitioners had to be allowed to lead evidence, and accordingly allowed a proof before answer. The respondents reclaimed, presenting the arguments on the scope of s.8(1)(*b*) as questions of relevancy.

Held, that (1) the document as rectified would have been effective to transfer the *ius crediti* in the sum in the bank account and was one to which s.8(1)(*b*) applied; (2) the error averred by the petitioners to have arisen in this case was one which could be corrected under s.8(1)(*b*) of the 1985 Act; (3) the petitioners had to be allowed an opportunity to lead evidence as to the intention of the persons who signed the document, as the existence or otherwise of the given intention was a question of fact for which a concluded view could not be formed without having heard the evidence; and reclaiming motion refused. Observations, per the Lord President (Hope), on the phrase "the grantor of the document" s.8(1)(*b*) of the 1985 Act.

BANK OF SCOTLAND v. BRUNSWICK DEVELOPMENTS (1987), 1995 S.L.T. 689.

5589. Requirements of Writing (Scotland) Act 1995 (c.7)

This Act reforms the law of Scotland with regard to the requirement of writing for certain matters and the formal validity of contractual and other documents. It also abolishes any rule of law restricting the proof of any matter to writ or oath and abolishes the procedure of reference to oath. The Act received Royal Assent on May 1, 1995.

5590. Restrictive covenant—reasonableness—disclosure of confidential information

A company's former employee went to work for a competitor. The company was granted interim interdict against the former employee on the basis that she had acted in breach of certain provisions of a code of professional conduct, which formed part of her contract of employment and which purported to apply in the event of "termination of employment by either party for whatever reason". The interdict prohibited the defender from, *inter alia* (1) divulging any confidential information concerning the company's customers, suppliers or current or future business interests; and (2) approaching or soliciting any actual or prospective customers of the company for a period of 12 months following the termination of her employment. The defender sought recall of the interim interdicts on the basis that the company had failed to make out a prima facie case. She argued that the whole covenant was too wide because it purported to apply irrespective of the reason for termination of her contract; and that the prohibition in the code on divulging confidential information, being the foundation for the first interim interdict, was wider than would be implied by law, was wholly unspecific and gave no clear indication as to what was covered by the prohibition, having regard further to the fact that it was unlimited in time. In relation to the second interim interdict, the defender argued that it was too wide in that it had no geographical restriction and attempted to protect the company in respect of future business contacts with whom she had never dealt. The company argued that this interdict was a necessary extension of the first interdict in order to secure that that interdict was effective. It would prevent unwitting as well as deliberate use of such information for the benefit of the competitor. It was suggested that the defender could avoid such unwitting use by making a suitable inquiry on an approach to a prospective customer. The company submitted further that the interdict was equally supportable at common law, subject to appropriate amendment tying the prohibition to competition with them and restricting it to those who were customers at the time of the termination of employment.

Held, that (1) the whole covenant was not too wide as the phraseology in the code did not require to be read as extending to unlawful termination (*Lux Traffic Controls v. Healey* [1994] C.L.Y. 5502, distinguished); (2) it was reasonably clear from the code that the phrase "the Company's current/future business interests" related to the kind of information which would be derived from existing documents to which the defender was privy, such as sale and market research plans and records, and which reflected legitimate business interests which the company was prima facie entitled to protect against competition, and accordingly, accepting the company's averments *pro veritate*, the terms of the restriction contained in the first interim interdict were not so wide as to be unreasonable; but (3) as the company had failed to aver that the defender knew or was likely to know existing customers, or how she could determine who was a prospective customer at the date of the termination of her employment, and standing that the restriction contained in the covenant would cover any situation in connection with the sale of goods or products wholly unrelated to those supplied by the company, it was wholly unjustifiable as protection for the company's legitimate business interests and wholly unreasonable in extent, and accordingly the company had failed to set out even a weak prima facie case; and (4) even a restricted interdict, if it were open to the company to ally an interdict against competition based on an implied obligation at common law together with the covenanted prohibition upon divulging confidential information, would still be too wide in its extent; and second interim interdict recalled.

ARAMARK v. SOMMERVILLE (O.H.), 1995 S.L.T. 749.

5591. Sale—of business—*actio quanti minoris*—whether competent. See FORTUNE v. FRASER, §5568.

Sale of goods. See SALE OF GOODS.

Sale of heritage. See HERITABLE PROPERTY AND CONVEYANCING.

5592. Unfair contract terms—standard form—whether condition fair and reasonable—whether practicable to give notice of defect within prescribed time limit. See KNIGHT MACHINERY (HOLDINGS) v. RENNIE, §6320.

CRIMINAL EVIDENCE AND PROCEDURE

5593. Criminal Justice (Scotland) Act 1995 (c.20)

This Act amends the criminal justice system of Scotland in respect of criminal proceedings, the investigation of offences, the sentences and other disposals, legal and relating to certain appeals and the treatment of offenders; the Act also amends the Law of Scotland in relation to confiscation of the proceeds of, and forfeiture of property used in crime and provides for the preparation of jury lists for criminal and civil trials.

The Act Received Royal Assent on July 19, 1995.

5594. Criminal Justice (Scotland) Act 1995 (c.20)—commencement

CRIMINAL JUSTICE (SCOTLAND) ACT 1995 (COMMENCEMENT NO. 1, TRANSITIONAL PROVISIONS AND SAVINGS) ORDER 1995 (c.45) (No. 2295) [£1·10], made under the Criminal Justice (Scotland) Act 1995 (c.20); brings into force on September 26, 1995 the following provisions of the said Act: s.22(1), (3), (4), (7) and (9), ss.35, 42, 43 and 65, s.117(1) and (2) and s.118, para. 87 of Sched. 6 and makes transitional and savings provisions in respect of ss.35, 42 and 65 of the Act.

5595. Criminal Procedure (Consequential Provisions) (Scotland) Act 1995 (c.40)

This Act gives effect to the consolidation of enactments in the Criminal Procedure (Scotland) Act 1995 (c.46), the Proceeds of Crime (Scotland) Act 1995 (c.43) and the Criminal Law (Consolidation) (Scotland) Act 1995 (c.39).

The Act received Royal Assent on November 8, 1995.

5596. Criminal Procedure (Scotland) Act 1995 (c.46)

This Act seeks to consolidate several areas of Scottish criminal procedure.

The Act received Royal Assent on November 8, 1995.

5597. Evidence—admissibility—answers by accused to police questions—inducement by police. See HARLEY v. H.M. ADVOCATE, §5729.

5598. Evidence—admissibility—evidence irregularly obtained—search without warrant

E appealed against conviction on a charge under s.5(b)(i) of the Wireless Telegraphy Act 1949, challenging the sheriff's decision to allow evidence of two police officers of the finding of a radar detection device in E's car. E had been seen travelling at speed but when the police officers directed their radar gun at the vehicle, E immediately braked. E was then observed by the officers with what appeared to be a radar detection device on the dashboard. The device was seen to flash red lights when the radar gun was directed at it. E was then stopped. The device was no longer visible but there were two velcro strips where it had been seen and the cigarette lighter socket was empty. E was unco-operative but the police searched the glove compartment and removed the device. E argued that the police had carried out an irregular search without a search warrant and without having obtained E's consent or arresting him.

Held, appeal refused. In circumstances of such urgency the absence of a search warrant could be excused. To have obtained a warrant would have given E time to dispose of the device which the police had justifiable reason to believe was in the car. There was no indication that the police had acted in bad faith as arresting E for obstruction would not have excused the necessity for justification of the search. The question was one of fact and degree weighing up the nature of the irregularity as against the public interest.

EDGLEY v. BARBOUR, 1995 S.L.T. 711.

5599. Evidence—admissibility—evidence of crime not charged

Held, in the course of a trial where the accused were charged with being concerned in the supply of drugs, that it was incompetent to leak evidence of the actual supply of drugs to a witness on a particular occasion as this would have been evidence of a crime not libelled.

ADVOCATE, H.M. v. CORMACK, 1995 S.C.C.R. 477.

5600. Evidence—admissibility—forensic report—service on accused. See DUFFY v. NORMAND, §5621.

5601. Evidence—admissibility—identification—no identification parade held prior to trial

D appealed against conviction of rape and breach of ss.2 and 5 of the Firearms Act 1968 on the grounds that the trial judge erred in admitting evidence by the complainer (C) whereby she identified D as he sat in the dock, as no identification parade had been held prior to the trial and, since the court was cleared before C gaver her evidence, there was only one person she could identify as the assailant.

Held, appeal refused. C. was properly asked to make express identification of D in court (*Bruce v. H.M. Advocate* 1936 J.C. 93). An identification parade was not required in Scotland. The trial judge had put D's criticism of the evidence to the jury, and it was for them to determine the relaibility of the evidence. Even if the jury had not accepted it, there would still have been ample evidence linking D to the offence.

DUDLEY v. H.M. ADVOCATE, 1995 S.C.C.R. 52.

5602. Evidence—admissibility—line of evidence outwith libel

An accused person was tried on indictment for assaulting his 10 week old daughter to the danger of her life. There was evidence that she had sustained fractured ribs at least two weeks before the alleged assault. Objection was taken to the line of evidence about the fractures as being outwith the terms of the charge but the trial judge repelled the objection on the basis of an assurance from the advocate depute that the evidence was only to be used as background medical history. One Crown witness, a paediatrician, stated that he had diagnosed non-accidental injury because of several factors including the previous rib fractures but in re-examination he accepted that he made the same diagnosis even when leaving the rib fractures out of account. The advocate depute did not suggest to the jury that the rib fractures had been caused by the accused. The accused was convicted and appealed, contending that the trial judge had erred in repelling the objection and that the evidence was prejudicial to the accused because it implicity suggested to the jury that he had caused the previous rib fractures.

Held, that (1) in view of the assurance from the advocate depute, although it was an incomplete statement of the use which might be made of the evidence of previous rib fractures, the trial judge was right to repel the objection; (2) after the advocate depute's address there was no material risk of the jury's being misled into considering that the rib fractures were sustained in any way other than by accident and accordingly the leading of the evidence was not prejudicial to the accused; and appeal refused. *Observed,* that if the trial judge had been alerted to the possibility of the line of the paediatrician's evidence implying that the rib fractures were non-accidental, it was doubtful whether he would have repelled the objection.

KLEIN v. H.M. ADVOCATE, 1995 S.L.T. 1034.

5603. Evidence—admissibility—measurement of object. See NORMAND v. WALKER, §5688.

5604. Evidence—admissibility—psychologist's report on likely behaviour at interview—accused not giving evidence

B appealed against conviction for murder on the grounds that the judge had erred in sustaining *in hoc statu* a Crown objection to the leading of evidence of

S, a clinical psychologist, whose report suggested that B's score, in accordance with the Gudjonsson Scales of Suggestibility, indicated vulnerability in an interview situation if it was suggested that his responses required to be changed. During a police interview, B had denied being at the locus altogether but had gone on to admit to being there and to stabbing X after a detective had warned B during a break in the interview that he was doing himself no favours by denying his presence. The objection was on the ground that it was not proposed to have B give evidence, which would result in irremediable prejudice to the Crown. B submitted that, by the exclusion of S's evidence, the jury had been precluded from considering B's mental state and vulnerability at the time of the police interview (*R. v. Ward (Judith Theresa)* [1993] C.L.Y. 723). B would have been exposed to disadvantages in cross examination if he had given evidence.

Held, appeal refused. The judge had been right to sustain the objection *in hoc statu*. English authority might depend on rules of law or practice with which the court was not familiar. There had been no proper basis laid in the Crown case for the leading of evidence that B was suffering from a mental illness or personality disorder that would render his statement to police inadmissible (*cf. Advocate, H.M. v. Gilgannon*, [1983] C.L.Y. 4089; *Higgins v. H.M. Advocate* [1993] C.L.Y. 4887, 5026, 5031). The question was whether B was under such pressure and emotional stress at the interview that it affected his responses: this depended on the evidence of those present at the interview. Had B given evidence that he had been affected by the factors referred to in S's report then the situation would have been altered but, as there was no evidence from B or from the police present at the interview that B's statement had been influenced by these factors, it was not for the jury to speculate as to B's vulnerability (*Boyne v. H.M. Advocate* [1980] C.L.Y. 2972).

BLAGOJEVIC v. H.M. ADVOCATE, 1995 S.C.C.R. 570.

5605. Evidence—admissibility—roadside check. See NORMAND v. McKELLAR, §6314.

5606. Evidence—admissibility—search without warrant. See GAVIN v. NORMAND, §5746.

5607. Evidence—admissibility—statement by accused

Held, on B's appeal against conviction for reset on the basis that an incriminating statement made to police by B had been unfairly obtained and so was inadmissible, the sheriff having found that B was threatened with arrest and custody if he did not co-operate, that the appeal would be allowed since the sheriff had given no reason why he thought it not unfair to allow B's statement in evidence and, in finding that there was insufficient impropriety or pressurisation to justify exclusion of the various statements made by B, had inverted the burden of proof, the burden being with the Crown to establish that any statements were made voluntarily and fairly; further, the fact that B decided to make a statement which would incriminate him on a charge of reset rather than housebreaking was irrelevant if the statement was extracted by way of pressure.

BLACK v. ANNAN, 1995 S.C.C.R. 273.

5608. Evidence—admissibility—statement by accused

Held, where an accused had made a statement when the police were suspicious of him because of discrepancies between an earlier statement made by him and the statements of other witnesses and after a warrant had been obtained to search his house, but he had not been cautioned, that the question of whether a caution should have been given fell to be determined as part of the more general test of fairness which, in the absence of exceptional circumstances, was a matter for the jury in the light of the whole evidence and appropriate directions in law given in the charge; and objection to admissibility of the statement repelled.

ADVOCATE (H.M.) v. MIDDLER, 1994 S.C.C.R. 838.

5609. Evidence—admissibility—whether a search—whether evidence irregularly obtained

Held, where an accused's car had been driven to a police station following his arrest on a drink-driving charge, that a police constable, who opened the car door and looked inside the car, had carried out a search without having had the power to do so, and accordingly that evidence of what he had found within the car was inadmissible.

GRAHAM v. ORR, 1995 S.C.C.R. 30.

5610. Evidence—admissibility—whether evidence irregularly obtained

[Misuse of Drugs Act 1971 (c.38), s.23(2).]

An accused person was tried on summary complaint for a contravention of s.5(2) of the Misuse of Drugs Act 1971. At about 1 a.m. on the date of his arrest, two police officers, who approximately two months earlier had received information that the accused was involved in the possession and supply of controlled drugs, saw the accused in the street, for the first time since they had received that information, and detained him in order to search him. The accused was found to be in possession of a quantity of cannabis resin. Objection was taken to the search on the ground that the police had no reasonable grounds for suspecting that the accused had drugs because the officers' information was too old. The sheriff repelled the objection. The accused was convicted and appealed by stated case. The sheriff made no finding that the police had reasonable grounds for suspecting that the accused was in possession of controlled drugs or that the police believed that they had such grounds.

Held, that in the absence of evidence which could show a sound basis for the police having reasonable grounds for suspicion, they were not entitled to search the accused; and appeal allowed and conviction quashed. *Observed*, that there was no question that if any specific period of time had elapsed, that disabled the police from acting upon information they received.

IRELAND v. RUSSELL, 1995 S.L.T. 1348.

5611. Evidence—children—live television link—identification evidence. See BROTHERSTON v. H.M. ADVOCATE, §5716.

5612. Evidence—corroboration—assault. See McGRORY v. H.M. ADVOCATE, §5630.

5613. Evidence—corroboration—identification. See MURPHY v. H.M. ADVOCATE, §5625.

5614. Evidence—corroboration—identification

W appealed against conviction of driving while disqualified on the grounds that there was insufficient evidence to corroborate his identity as the driver of the car which collided with a vehicle driven by B. B had identified W as the driver at the time of the collision but her passenger, H, could only say that the driver was male. In response to police injuries, W had stated either X or his daughter, D, were the drivers of the car on the date of accident, X denied that he had ever driven W's car, although he had been asked by W to be nominated as a driver in insurance documents. The sheriff, after concluding that W was not telling the truth, found that the undisputed fact that W was the registered keeper of the car provided sufficient corroboration for B's evidence, W argued that the fact that he was the registered keeper of the car was insufficient on is own to corroborate B's evidence, and his false statement to the police could not provide corroboration of his identity as it was simply a false denial which was a worthless piece of evidence (*Fisher v. Guild* [1991] C.L.Y. 4574).

Held, appeal refused. While the fact of W being the registered keeper was insufficient on its own, by combining W's demonstrably false statement that someone else was driving the car with the fact that he was the registered keeper of it, there was sufficient evidence from which it could be inferred that W was deliberately seeking to avoid detection and to corroborate B's clear identification of W (*Fisher*, distinguished).

WINTER v. HEYWOOD, 1995 S.L.T. 586.

5615. Evidence—corroboration—indecent assault

An accused person was tried on a summary complaint with indecent assault. The complainer gave evidence that in the early hours of the morning she was awakened by the accused's kneeling at the end of her bed. He had uncovered her nakedness and was running his hand over her buttocks and between her thighs. She told the accused to leave. He left the room but remained in the house. The complainer was aware of his presence as she could hear his heavy breathing. The accused was later found by the police hiding under the stairs. There was evidence that the complainer was distressed after the incident when she telephoned a friend who telephoned the police. The sheriff found that the complainer's distress was unequivocally caused by the sexual attack on her and the accused's continued presence in her house. He repelled a submission of no case to answer. No defence evidence was led and the accused was convicted. He appealed arguing that the complainer's distress was incapable of corroborating her evidence.

Held, that the sheriff's finding linked the accused's presence in the complainer's house to the previous sexual attack upon her and, as it was clear that the sheriff was satisfied that without the sexual attack upon her, her distress would not have been present, the complainer's evidence was corroborated by the evidence of her distress; and appeal refused.

MacLEAN v. McCLORY, 1995 S.L.T. 1316.

5616. Evidence—corroboration—*Moorov* doctrine

An accused person was tried on an indictment libelling two offences of lewd, indecent and libidinous practices and behaviour towards two boys (charges 1 and 2) and one charge of sodomy (charge 3) in respect of the complainer on charge 2. All charges were alleged to have taken place at the same loci. The complainer on charge 1 was aged between 10 and 12 years when the conduct occurred on numerous occasions between spring 1988 and March 1990. The complainer on charge 2 was aged 12 years when the conduct occurred on numerous occasions between December 1991 and August 1992. The complainer on charge 1 spoke to being offered money by the accused to induce him to permit the indecent behaviour to take place but the complainer on charge 2 spoke to being indecently assaulted and not being a willing participant. The mother of the complainer on charge 2, contrary to her son's evidence, said that he had only come in contact with the accused in the summer of 1992. At the close of the Crown case the accused was acquitted on charge 3. In charging the jury the sheriff directed that they could look at the evidence led on charge 3 in relation to charge 2. The accused was convicted and appealed on the grounds of misdirection and that the *Moorov* rule was inapplicable as the offences were not sufficiently related in time and character.

Held, that (1) the essential element in charges 1 and 2 was that the accused had behaved indecently towards (and in effect indecently assaulted) a 12 year old boy, and the similarities in character and circumstances were such that provided that there was not too great a period of time between the two charges, it was open to the jury to conclude that the conduct constituted one course of conduct; (2) even on the mother's evidence the interval between the charges was two years and three months which was not such as to exclude application of the *Moorov* rule; (3) there was no misdirection in saying that the evidence on charge 3 was available in respect of charge 2; and appeal refused. (*Coffey v. Houston* [1992] C.L.Y. 5375, applied.)

SMITH v. H.M. ADVOCATE, 1995 S.L.T. 583.

5617. Evidence—corroboration—*Moorov* doctrine

Held, on R's appeal against conviction of presenting a double barrelled shotgun at the driver of an ice cream van, forcing him to drive round various streets, robbing him of money and cigarettes and asking to be let off near a certain street, on the grounds that the *Moorov* doctrine (1930 S.L.T. 596) could not be applied using a charge on which there was sufficient evidence, that of holding up assistants in a grocer's shop using a single barrelled shotgun, robbing them of money and cigarettes, abducting a nearby motorist and forcing him to drive to the same street, that where the case was one which fell into the "open country" described in *Moorov* between the two possible extremes, the important point was that the jury should be properly directed so they were aware of the test which required to be applied, and since the judge's directions were not open to criticism the case was within the province of the jury to balance the similarities against the dissimilarities; and appeal refused.

REYNOLDS v. H.M. ADVOCATE, 1995 S.C.C.R. 504.

5618. Evidence—corroboration—*Moorov* doctrine

Held, on T's appeal against conviction on two charges of indecent assault occurring almost three years apart where the Crown relied on the *Moorov* doctrine (1930 S.L.T. 596), that while this was a borderline case, the appeal would be refused since there was no hard and fast rule regarding the time interval between the offences (*Russell v. H.M. Advocate* [1990] C.L.Y. 4842) and any concern about the element of time involved was overcome by a sufficient coherence in character and circumstance, namely, that both complainers were the nieces of T's wife, both were aged 20 at the time, both offences were of an opportunist nature and were committed in the homes of the girls, both girls were scantily clad, on each occasion there was a degree of fondling under the girls' clothing and when each girl objected, T desisted.

Held, further, that three months' imprisonment was excessive since this was not the most serious example of indecent assault, two years had elapsed since the second offence was committed, T, a first offender, had lost his job as a police officer and there had been a viable alternative to custody; and 150 hours' community service substituted.

TURNER v. SCOTT, 1995 S.C.C.R. 516.

5619. Evidence—corroboration—whether accused's admission corroborated by complainer's evidence

An accused person was charged along with another person on summary complaint with assault. The complainer stated that he had been engaged in an argument with the accused, his co-accused and another man and, when walking over a pontoon bridge with the accused in front of him, two men including the co-accused ran up behind him and pushed him into the sea. He said that the accused did not lay hands on him. There was also evidence that the accused admitted to the police that he and his co-accused pushed the complainer into the sea. The justice repelled a submission that there was no case for the accused to answer and convicted him. The accused appealed contending that there was no corroboration of his admission.

Held, that there was a clear conflict between the complainer's evidence and the accused's admission as to whether the accused was a party to the assault and the justice was accordingly not entitled to find corroboration in the complainer's evidence; and appeal allowed and conviction quashed.

MITCHELL v. MAGUIRE, 1994 S.L.T. 1277.

5620. Evidence—cross-examination—prior inconsistent statement

[Criminal Procedure (Scotland) Act 1975 (c.21), ss.147 and 218.]

Held, on Y's appeal against conviction of two charges of assaulting young women in their houses by presenting a knife, in one case with intent to rob and in the other with robbery of bangles and a gold charm, that the trial judge had erred, on a Crown motion for prior inconsistent statements by Y to be put to him in cross-examination under s.147 of the 1975 Act, in considering that no question of fairness arose as the section was perfectly general in its terms: the wording of s.147 did not exclude the possibility that a statement made in circumstances unfair to the accused should be excluded from being put to him; but that there had been no miscarriage of justice as the judge had in the end directed the jury that they should ignore the evidence.

Held, further, that Y's not guilty plea and the jury's verdict was insufficient as a reason for refusing to backdate a *cumulo* sentence of seven years' imprisonment (*Grummer v. H.M. Advocate* [1991] C.L.Y. 4815, especially as Y had been acquitted of one charge; and sentence backdated to when Y was taken into custody.)

YOUNG v. H.M. ADVOCATE, 1995 S.C.C.R. 418.

5621. Evidence—forensic report—service

[Criminal Justice (Scotland) Act 1980 (c. 62), s.26(4).]

Section 26(4) of the Criminal Justice (Scotland) Act 1980 provides, *inter alia*, that a copy of a report required to be served on the accused may be either personally served on the accused or sent to him by registered post or the recorded delivery service and a written execution of service together with a post office receipt for the recorded delivery letter shall be sufficient evidence of service. Section 7 of the Interpretation Act 1978 provides that where an Act requires any document to be served by post, then unless the contrary intention appears, the service is deemed to be effected by properly addressing, prepaying and posting a letter containing the document and, unless the contrary is proved, to have been effected at the time when the letter would be delivered in the ordinary course of post. An accused person, along with his wife, was tried on summary complaint for contraventions of s.5(2) and (3) of the Misuse of Drugs Act 1971. The Crown sought, without calling witnesses, to rely on a report signed by two authorised forensic scientists as sufficient evidence of the fact that the substances found in the accused's house were cannabis resin. The accused's solicitor objected to the production of the report on the ground that a copy of it had not been served on the accused as required by the 1980 Act. He explained that the accused's wife had collected from the post office the recorded delivery letter containing the report but she had not given or shown it to the accused at any time. The sheriff repelled the objection on the ground that, applying s.26(4), there was sufficient evidence of service of the report because the Crown had lodged a certificate of execution of service by a member of the procurator fiscal's staff and a recorded delivery receipt. The accused did not lead evidence that he had never received the report. The accused was convicted and appealed, arguing that the sheriff had erred in ruling on the objection without hearing evidence to show that the accused had never received a copy of the report.

Held, that (1) the sheriff's ruling did not preclude the accused from leading evidence with a view to re-opening the argument that the Crown were not entitled to rely on the report because a copy of it had not been served on the accused; (2) in any event, it was an irresistible inference, on the information given to the sheriff, that the accused's wife had been authorised to receive the letter on the accused's behalf and her receipt of it was as good as its receipt by the accused himself; and appeal refused. *Burt v. Kirkcaldy* [1965] C.L.Y.

3492 and *Hosier v. Goodall* [1962] C.L.Y. 2699, followed. *Opinion reserved*, as to whether it was open to an alleged recipient to say, in light of s.7 of the 1978 Act, that he did not receive the document at all where the legislation required the document to be served by a certain time.

DUFFY v. NORMAND, 1995 S.L.T. 1264.

5622. Evidence—forensic report—service

[Criminal Justice (Scotland) Act 1980 (c.52), s.26(3)(a) and (4).]

D appealed against conviction for simple possession and possession with intent to supply cannabis resin, along with D's wife (K), on the grounds that the sheriff misdirected himself in repelling an objection by D to the production of a report, relied on by the Crown and signed by two forensic scientists, as to the nature of the substance found in D's house. D claimed that, though the Crown produced a signed written execution of service of the copy together with a recorded delivery receipt, a copy of the report had not been effectively served on him as required by s.26(3)(a) of the 1980 Act since K, who had found a card through the door on returning from holiday to the effect that correspondence required to be uplifted from the post office, had collected two packages from the post office, one of which was addressed to D and contained the copy report and at no time did K show the contents to D. K claimed that she had put the package in a place of safety because she had not wanted any children in the house to see such court papers. D submitted that s.26(4) of the Act, while laying down methods by which service could be effected, did not state that a document was deemed to have been served if it was sent by registered post or recorded delivery, and that the sheriff had erred in not allowing D to lead evidence to show that he had not in fact received a copy of the report.

Held, appeal refused. The sheriff had to reach a decision on admissibility based on the information before him at that stage. The sheriff's ruling had not precluded D from leading evidence with a view to reopening the argument, but D chose not to give evidence nor was K cross-examined about the circumstances surrounding the serving of the copy report. There was no dispute that a copy of the report had been sent to D's home by recorded delivery some 14 days before the trial, nor was it suggested that there had been any irregularity on the part of the post office. It could be inferred from K's collecting the package addressed to D that she had authority to do so on D's behalf. Section 26(4) did not require that a document be served on the accused personally and receipt by D's wife of the document was a receipt in law by D himself (*Burt v. Kirkcaldy* [1965] C.L.Y. 3492; *Hosier v. Goodall* [1962] C.L.Y. 2699). *Opinion reserved*, on the question of whether it could be argued that a document, sent by registered post or recorded delivery, was not served because the accused did not receive it, which had not been fully argued.

DUFFY v. NORMAND, 1995.

5623. Evidence—fresh evidence. See BEATTIE v. H.M. ADVOCATE, §5652; CHURCH v. H.M. ADVOCATE, §5653; ELLIOTT v. H.M. ADVOCATE, §5654; MACKENZIE v. H.M. ADVOCATE, §5655; REID v. H.M. ADVOCATE, §5651.

5624. Evidence—identification—child giving evidence by live television link. See BROTHERSTON v. H.M. ADVOCATE, §5716.

5625. Evidence—identification—corroboration

M appealed against his conviction and sentence for murder by shooting dead X in the street in Glasgow, arguing that there was insufficient evidence to corroborate W's positive identification of M as the perpetrator. C had made a statement to the police claiming that M had admitted the offence, but in giving evidence had denied all material parts of the statement. C had then been recalled after being charged with perjury and then indicating that he wished to tell the truth (s.148A of the 1975 Act; *Birrell v. H.M. Advocate* [1993] C.L.Y. 5036, and confirmed M's admission. In charging the jury the trial judge had warned that C's evidence had to be scrutinised carefully but if they accepted it, it was capable of corroborating W. M argued that testing the evidence by the weakest link in the chain, there was no evidence other than C's capable of providing corroboration. The remaining evidence was that of K who had picked him out as resembling the perpetrator by reason of his height and haircut. K had stated that the perpetrator was around 30 and five feet eight inches in height. M was 27 and five feet seven inches tall. There was also evidence that M had left Glasgow by car for Aberdeen shortly after the shooting, and that M's car had been identified by the witnesses as similar to that at the scene. The Crown claimed that if C's evidence had been rejected by the jury K's evidence was sufficient corroboration of M's identification (*Gracie v. Allan* [1987] C.L.Y. 4128; *Ralston v. H.M. Advocate* [1988] C.L.Y. 3890; *Nelson v. H.M. Advocate* [1989] C.L.Y. 3997).

Held, appeal refused. The Crown's argument was well founded. K's evidence was capable of corroborating M's positive identification (*Nelson, supra*), and had been strengthened by the evidence identifying M's car.

Held, further, that the trial judge had erred in making a recommendation that M serve a minimum period of 15 years without specifically stating to M's counsel that he was considering doing so, but that having regard to M's previous convictions, including a serious one involving firearms, the judge was entitled to make the recommendation.

MURPHY v. H.M. ADVOCATE, 1995 S.L.T. 725.

5626. Evidence—identification—identification of driver. See SOUTER v. LEES, §6305.

5627. Evidence—identification—no parade held prior to trial. See DUDLEY v. H.M. ADVOCATE, §5601.

5628. Evidence—previous convictions—unintended disclosure

[Criminal Procedure (Scotland) Act 1975 (c.21), s.160(1).]

Held, on R's appeal against conviction for assault and robbery and other related offences on the ground that the sheriff erred in allowing the trial to proceed after G, a Crown witness had, in the course of her evidence, made three references to the acronym SACRO (Scottish Association for the Care and Resettlement of Offenders) in the context of providing R with accommodation, the appeal would be refused since G had used only the acronym, no reference had been made as to the organisation's function, the disclosure by G had been accidental, it was by no means clear to the jurors that R had in fact previously offended and, should any jurors have recognised the reference, the judge had dealt sufficiently with the situation in his charge in that he had been careful not to mention the organisation or its function and had stated clearly that the jury should not be concerned in any way with R's character.

ROBERTSON v. H.M. ADVOCATE, 1995 S.C.C.R. 497.

Evidence—road traffic. See ROAD TRAFFIC.

5629. Evidence—sufficiency—art and part—being concerned in the supply of cannabis resin. See RODDEN v. H.M. ADVOCATE, §5723.

5630. Evidence—sufficiency—assault

Held, on M's appeal against conviction for assault to S's severe injury, that there was sufficient evidence to corroborate S's evidence from two sources which, when each was taken alone, were insufficient to corroborate S's version but when put together were sufficient, where the D brothers stated that M was involved in a scuffle with two others within five feet of S immediately after the incident in which S was slashed, and R, who was not at the scene, claimed that after he had been charged, M had told her that she or anyone else taking the stand would be sorry. It was only because of the context in which the remark had been made that it could be used in that way, but the sheriff had made it clear to the injury that the evidence of guilt in this case was on the very borderline of legal sufficiency, and there being no other reasonable conclusion to be drawn from the remark, it was open to the jury to draw an inference from the remark when taken in conjunction with the other evidence that M had been responsible.

McGRORY v. H.M. ADVOCATE, 1995 S.L.T. 829.

5631. Evidence—sufficiency—circumstantial evidence. See LEANDRO v. H.M. ADVOCATE, §5719.

5632. Evidence—sufficiency—confessions. See BEATTIE v. H.M. ADVOCATE, §5652.

5633. Evidence—sufficiency—corroboration. See McGRORY v. H.M. ADVOCATE, §5630.

5634. Evidence—sufficiency—forensic report

Held, on D's appeal against conviction for unlawful possession of drugs, that the sheriff did not err in allowing a report from forensic scientists to be admitted although the report did not mention D's name and referred to the case against "Rooney plus two", as there was a sufficient link between the report and D where: D was originally detained with Rooney (R) and another; the report referred to 24 plastic phials, the contents of which matched 24 paper wraps found in D's house, and to tablets which were identical to the description of drugs found in R's possession; the date when the items were received in the forensic laboratory matched the date that the police allegedly sent the items relating to D to the laboratory; and the scientists who signed the report also signed the labels. Contrary to an argument for D, no higher standard of evidence was necessary because the document had statutory force. *Observed*, that steps should be taken to ensure that certificates or reports were expressed more clearly and with greater specification.

DRYBURGH v. SCOTT, 1995 S.C.C.R. 371.

5635. Evidence—sufficiency—forensic report—joint minute

[Criminal Justice (Scotland) Act 1980 (c.62), s.26 and Sched. 1.]

Held, on the Crown's appeal against a sheriff's decision to dismiss a case against S of possessing amphetamines, that the sheriff erred in concluding that a certificate purporting to have been signed by two forensic scientists contained a fundamental error which was incapable of being cured, where it did not state that the signatories had carried out the analysis of the drugs, as there was sufficient evidence for a conviction where, as distinguished from *Normand v. Wotherspoon*, 1994 S.L.T. 487, the parties had accepted the certificate in a joint minute, which described it as a true and accurate report, which agreement was habile to extend to the whole terms of the report, and it was therefore unnecessary for the Crown to lead evidence or satisfy the particular requirements of s.26(1) of the 1980 Act.

DONNELLY v. SCHRIKEL, 1995 S.L.T. 537.

5636. Evidence—sufficiency—forensic report—link with substance found

[Criminal Justice (Scotland) Act 1980 (c.62), s.26(2).]

Held, on A's appeal against conviction under ss.4(3)(b) and 5(2) of the Misuse of Drugs Act 1971, that there was a sufficient link in evidence between items described by the police and spoken to as having been taken from the livingroom of A's house and items the subject of a forensic report which described them in similar terms and having been taken from the same room on the same day, although neither police officer spoke to what had been written on the labels attached to the items or said that the items had been submitted for analysis. There were sufficient facts and circumstances to permit the necessary inference to be drawn (*McLeary v. Douglas* [1978] C.L.Y. 3665, applied), having regard to the terms of s.26(2) of the 1980 Act.

ALLAN v. INGRAM, 1995 S.L.T. 1086.

5637. Evidence—sufficiency—mobbing and rioting. See KILPATRICK v. H.M. ADVOCATE, §5776.

5638. Evidence—sufficiency—possession—controlled drug

Held, on B's appeal against conviction of possession of a class A drug found under the opaque cover of the windscreen wiper motor of a car in a garage rented by B, the car being a write-off with no bonnet and one on which B was to carry out work for another person but had not yet begun to do so, and B and his father being the only people seen either working in the garage or going into it, that there was insufficient evidence to show that B knew of the presence of the drugs since it could not be determined on the evidence which of B or his father had put the drugs there; and appeal allowed.

BATH v. H.M. ADVOCATE, 1995 S.C.C.R. 323.

5639. Evidence—sufficiency—robbery—recent possession

L appealed against conviction of assault and robbery on the grounds that there was insufficient evidence. L accepted that there was sufficient evidence for a conviction of reset insofar as L was in possession of the complainer's pension book one week after the robbery. L was not identified as the robber and was not seen at the locus. The sheriff convicted under reference to Alison's *Criminal Law*, i, 247. The book had been traced to L *de recenti* and he had attempted to persuade others to encash the book. L argued that the law was more correctly stated in Hume, i, 111.

Held, appeal allowed; conviction of reset substituted. L's possession of the pension book was not apparent until seven days after the robbery and he could have obtained it otherwise than by stealing (Hume, *supra*, approved; Alison, *supra*, disapproved).

Held, further, that where L was only 14 at the time of the offence, but was now 16, three months' detention under s.413 of the Criminal Procedure (Scotland) Act 1975 would be quashed and sentence deferred for six months for L to be of good behaviour.

L. v. WILSON, 1995 S.L.T. 673.

5640. Evidence—sufficiency—theft

H appealed against conviction for theft of a boat and trailer from a builder's yard on the grounds that there were insufficient criminative circumstances. The circumstances the sheriff regarded as criminative were that (1) H claimed to have bought the boat and trailer in May whereas M, who claimed to be the owner, stated that at that time both were stored in the builder's yard and it was not until June 25 that they were taken; (2) H had attempted to alter the identity of the boat by painting it; and (3) H was unable to provide any information about P, whom H claimed had sold him the boat and trailer, other than to provide a receipt for £1,700 signed by P written on the back of a piece of paper.

Held, appeal allowed and conviction quashed. As regards (1), it had been M's recollection of H's statement as to when the boat and trailer were bought that was relied upon and not that of a police officer who said that H claimed to have purchased the boat and trailer on June 27. Similarly with (2), M's evidence had been the only evidence to the effect that the boat and trailer had been painted. On (3), the details on the receipt fitted in with the details given by H as to the date and place of purchase, and there was nothing to show that the receipt was false, despite its casual nature, or that the figure on it was unusually low. Further, the boat and trailer had been on full view in H's driveway.

HAMILTON v. FRIEL, 1994 S.C.C.R. 748.

5641. Evidence—sufficiency—theft—intent to commit

[Civic Government (Scotland) Act 1982 (c.45), s.57(1).]

Held, on F's appeal against conviction for being in a guest house without lawful authority with intention to commit theft on the grounds that the magistrate erred in rejecting a plea of no case to answer, F claiming that he had been in a corridor, not in a bedroom, and there was no clear evidence that F had entered via one of the fire doors and not through the reception area, thus the inference that F intended to commit theft could not be justified (*Cameron v. Normand* [1993] C.L.Y. 4912), that the appeal would be refused since the magistrate had been entitled to find F guilty on the basis that although there was a receptionist present, F had first been seen in the corridor in the bedroom area, F claimed to be looking for a guest but had not gone to ask at reception, and there was evidence that the fire doors to the bedroom area had been open at the time.

FULTON v. NORMAND, 1995 S.C.C.R. 629.

Fishing. See FISH AND FISHERIES.

Legal aid. See LEGAL AID.

5642. Procedure—110 days elapsing after committal—justification for extension

[Criminal Procedure (Scotland) Act 1975 (c.21), s.101(2)(b) and (4).]

Section 101(2)(b) of the Criminal Procedure, (Scotland) Act 1975 provides that an accused who is committed until liberated in due course of law shall not be detained for more than 110 days unless the trial is commenced within that period, which failing he shall be liberated forthwith and forever free from further process for that offence. Subsection (4) provides that a single judge of the High Court may extend that period if he is satisfied that the delay in the commencement of the trial is due to any other sufficient cause not attributable to any fault on the prosecutor's part. An accused person was charged along with another person on indictment with, *inter alia*, armed robbery. He had been remanded in custody and the 110th day of his detention was May 24th, 1995. The accused's case was the second case in the sitting at Inverness commencing on May 9. When the accused's case was called on May 11, the Crown moved for an adjournment to the next sitting at Inverness. The trial judge had earlier intimated that he could not sit beyond May 19, as he was required to sit as chairman of the employment appeal tribunal. It had originally been thought that the trial would not last more than five or six days but on May 9, the accused's counsel insisted that it could not take fewer than eight days and that it could require 10 to 12 days. Consideration had been given by the Crown to transferring the case to another sitting elsewhere, which was found to be impractical. The trial judge had not ascertained whether another judge could be available to replace him so that the sitting could continue beyond May 19. The trial judge adjourned the trial and, in view of the seriousness of the offences and allegations that witnesses were fearful lest the accused be at liberty, refused bail and extended the 110 day period by 58 days. The accused appealed.

Held, that (1) s.101(4) did not permit the court to extend the 110 day period in order to suit the convenience of the court or its administrators; (2) it was the trial judge's responsibility to make appropriate inquiries to enable alternative arrangements to be made and, as he had not done so, he was not entitled to conclude that there was sufficient cause to extend the 110 day period and appeal allowed and decision reversed. Dictum of Lord Justice General Hope in (*Fleming v. H.M. Advocate* [1992] C.L.Y. 5422, considered).

BEATTIE v. H.M. ADVOCATE, 1995 S.L.T. 946.

5643. Procedure—110 days elapsing after committal—"liberated in due course of law"—release on bail on condition of residence in list D school

[Criminal Procedure (Scotland) Act 1975 (c.21), s.101(2).]

Held, on an application to the *nobile officium* by C, aged 16, alleging that he had been detained in excess of 110 days in breach of s.101(2)(b) of the 1975 Act, where the Crown accepted that C had continued in custody after the expiry of the period of 80 days in breach of s.101(2)(a) since after being released on bail with a condition of residence in a list D school he had been kept in secure conditions there (*K. v. H.M. Advocate* [1991] C.L.Y. 4629), but had subsequently instructed (prior to the 110 days) that he be transferred to open accommodation within the school, that although there was a dispute between C and the Crown as to whether C was at liberty in practical terms prior to the 110th day, it was appropriate to proceed on information provided by the school which supported the Crown's position; and petition granted in terms of s.101(2)(a) but refused in respect of s.101(2)(b).

X., PETR., 1995 S.C.C.R. 407.

5644. Procedure—12 months elapsing after first appearance—justification for extension

[Criminal Procedure (Scotland) Act 1995 (c.21), s.101(1).]

Section 101(1) of the Criminal Procedure (Scotland) Act 1975 provides that an accused person shall not be tried on indictment unless his trial is commenced within 12 months of his first appearance on petition, provided that a judge may on cause shown extend that period. An accused person was charged on indictment with fraud, the trial being due to commence on October 5, 1994. The 12 month period was due to expire on October 6, 1994 but on October 2 the accused was admitted to hospital and was not discharged until the early afternoon of October 5, by which time his counsel had withdrawn from acting because he was unavailable. As a result of a clerical error the Crown believed that the 12 month period expired on October 16 and arrangements were therefore made to commence the trial on October 12. On October 11 the Crown, realising its mistake, petitioned for an extension of the period. The trial judge granted an extension on the view that the Crown's error was not excusable but that the accused's illness had prevented the trial commencing within the 12 month period and that that was a sufficient reason for the exercise of his discretion in the Crown's favour. The accused appealed.

Held, that the trial judge was entitled to exercise his discretion as he did because it was impracticable for the trial to commence within the 12 month period, having regard to the accused's illness and the change of counsel; and appeal refused.

McCULLOCH v. H.M. ADVOCATE, 1995 S.L.T. 918.

5645. Procedure—appeal—appeals by two co-accused—form of judge's reports. See McLAREN v. H.M. ADVOCATE, §5825.

5646. Procedure—appeal—bill of suspension—competency—review of order of High Court. See REILLY v. H.M. ADVOCATE, §5669.

5647. Procedure—appeal—bill of suspension—failure by sheriff to draft stated case within prescribed time

Held, on B's bill of suspension against conviction of possessing 19 "unseasonable" salmon in breach of s.20 of the Salmon Fisheries (Scotland)

Act 1868, as amended, where the temporary sheriff failed to prepare a draft stated case within the time limit pursuant to s.447(1) of the Criminal Procedure (Scotland) Act 1975, as extended on several occasions by the sheriff principal, that the bill was competent as 18 months had passed since B's conviction and it was inappropriate to grant any further extensions or to seek at this stage to obtain an explanation of his conduct from the temporary sheriff, whose appointment had since been terminated; and although B's pleadings were confused, where the legal issue could be decided on a few facts the bill would be continued for hearing on the legal meaning of the word "unseasonable".

BRADY v. BARBOUR, 1994 S.L.T. 223.

5648. Procedure—appeal—bill of suspension—whether barred by acquiescence

An accused person pled guilty to three contraventions of the Road Traffic Act 1988 and the sheriff adjourned the diet for production of the accused's driving licence and a D.V.L.A. printout to a date in excess of the 21 day period permitted under s.380(1) of the Criminal Procedure (Scotland) Act 1975. The accused was thereafter fined and disqualified on September 30, 1991. After reading of the decision of the High Court in *Wilson v. Donald*, 1993 S.L.T. 31, which held that sentences imposed in such circumstances were incompetent, the accused consulted his solicitor on July 28, 1992. During that period the accused had been paying his fines and serving the disqualification. On November 2, 1993 the accused brought a bill seeking suspension of the sentences. Before the High Court the question of the delay in seeking suspension was raised.

Held, that (1) the period between September 30, 1991 and July 28, 1992 was critical because thereafter matters were in the accused's legal advisers' hands and he could not reasonably be blamed for the subsequent delays; but (2) since the accused had acted in every respect during that period on the basis that he accepted the sentences and his delay was so long as to give rise to the implication that he was willing to accept the sentences, he had acquiesced in them; and bill refused (*Storie v. Friel* [1994] C.L.Y. 5563, followed).

CASSIDY v. FRIEL, 1995 S.L.T. 391.

5649. Procedure—appeal—circumstances not before trial judge

[Criminal Procedure (Scotland) Act 1975 (c.21), s.252(c).]

An accused was convicted of a breach of the peace, and appealed against conviction. He revealed for the first time that he had been in prison on the date libelled.

Held, that, since the accused had not been in custody throughout the period covered by the latitude of time available to the Crown and since the date was not questioned with witnesses at the trial, it could not be said that he had been wrongly convicted; and appeal refused.

TARBETT v. H.M. ADVOCATE, 1994 S.C.C.R. 867.

5650. Procedure—appeal—failure by appellant to appear

[Criminal Procedure (Scotland) Act 1975 (c.21), s.453E.]

P appealed against conviction of assault and robbery. At the appeal hearing P failed to appear. The court granted a continuation for the purposes of establishing that P had been advised of the appeal date, and an explanation of P's failure to attend. P's local agents subsequently confirmed that P had been aware of the necessity for him to appear but that he had been unable to meet the cost of the journey to court. P had not told his Glasgow agents (S) of the difficulty.

Held, appeal refused for want of insistence. (1) S had fulfilled their obligations to advise P of the need for him to attend the appeal. However, it would have been preferable if there had been a written communication with his Edinburgh agents to provide the accurate information which was necessary where there was a motion to continue the appeal. (2) P had ample notice to make arrangements to ensure compliance with the undertaking given on receipt of interim liberation. An appellant who fell in breach of that undertaking had to expect the appeal to be disposed of as if abandoned (*Manson, Petr.*, February 16, 1990, noted in *McMahon v. MacPhail* [1991] C.L.Y. 4640).

PRATT v. H.M. ADVOCATE, 1994 S.C.C.R. 881.

5651. Procedure—appeal—fresh evidence

[Criminal Procedure (Scotland) Act 1975 (c.21), s.228(2).]

R appealed against conviction and sentence of three years' imprisonment (with nine months concurrent for possession of amphetamine) for possession with intent to supply 20 paper squares impregnated with L.S.D. (a class A drug), street value £120, on the grounds that additional evidence which was not available at trial had come to light to the effect that his co-accused, K, who was convicted of possessing 65 paper squares of L.S.D. and who had not given evidence at trial, had given a statement after the trial that when he was arrested, he possessed 90 paper squares of L.S.D., not 65, and that it was possible that the 20 squares allegedly found on R were part of his additional 25 squares.

Held, appeal refused. K's evidence was not sufficiently significant, substantial, convincing or trustworthy to warrant it being heard as additional evidence since it was mere speculation on K's part that the 20 paper squares said to be in R's possession were part of K's missing 25 squares and there was nothing in the evidence to exclude the possibility that R had possessed 20 squares of which K was ignorant. Sentence was not excessive where R had a previous conviction under the Misuse of Drugs Act and the sentence was intended as a deterrent. The fact that R had obtained employment during his interim liberation since sentencing was irrelevant.

REID v. H.M. ADVOCATE, 1994 S.C.C.R. 755.

5652. Procedure—appeal—fresh evidence

[Criminal Procedure (Scotland) Act 1975 (c.21), ss.252 and 263(1).]

Section 263(1) of the 1975 Act provides, *inter alia*, that the Secretary of State on consideration of any conviction, may, if he thinks fit, at any time, and whether or not an appeal against conviction has been previously heard and determined by the High Court, "refer the whole case to the High Court". An accused person was found guilty on October 4, 1973 of murder. The evidence on which the Crown relied comprised various statements made by him to the police in which he denied responsibility for the attack but gave detailed information as to the circumstances of the attack, the accused's actions in indicating to the police the location of the deceased's possessions and a knife which could have caused her injuries, the accused's presence at the locus at about the time of the deceased's death and the fact that the accused was found in possession five days after the murder of two paper tissues which were stained with blood. The blood was analysed by use of two systems and found not to be the accused's blood group but the deceased's blood group. The making and accuracy of the statements by the accused were not challenged at the trial and the accused did not give evidence. Unknown to the accused's representatives at the time of the trial, a letter dated July 11, 1973 was in the Crown's possession which referred to the possibility of another blood analysis, the MN system, which would, if it had been successful, have been more precise than the two analyses which were carried out and could have excluded the accused by establishing that the blood on the two paper tissues was his blood. An appeal on the ground that there was insufficient evidence was refused in December 1973. In 1993 the Secretary of State, under s.263(1), referred the accused's case to the appeal court on the basis of the non-production of the letter dated July 11, 1973. The accused lodged grounds of appeal contending, *inter alia*, that (1) the non-production of the letter resulted in a miscarriage of justice, (2) the decision of the appeal court in 1973 was incorrect and (3) there was insufficient evidence for conviction.

Held, that (1) as the power under s.263(1) was to refer "the whole case" to the appeal court, the court was not restricted by the ground on which the Secretary of State decided to order the review and the court could examine any alleged miscarriage of justice in the proceedings so long as it had been referred to in the grounds of appeal (*Kilpatrick v. H.M. Advocate*, 1992 J.C. 120, followed), but the court could not conduct an inquiry into the proceedings at its own hand; (2) as the accused at no stage confessed to having committed the crime, the statements were not self-corroborating special knowledge confessions and it was therefore necessary for the jury to find some other piece of independent evidence; (3) there was sufficient evidence to corroborate the accused's admission of his presence at the locus and, as no competing account was offered for the presence of the paper tissues in the accused's possession, it was open to the jury to find that the bloodstains got on the tissue at that time and this was sufficient to corroborate the inference of guilt which the jury were entitled to draw from the other evidence having rejected the accused's explanation, being the only other reasonable explanation for his knowledge, that he was merely a spectator; (4) the evidence of the grouping of the deceased's blood on the MN system described in the letter dated July 11, 1973 would not on its own have had a material part to play in the jury's determination of the question whether the bloodstains on the tissues could have come from the deceased as there was no evidence as to what the result of the testing on the MN system would have been, and it could not be said that there had been a miscarriage of justice; and appeal refused. *Observed*, that in view of the transitional provisions in Sched. 6, para. 6 to the Criminal Justice (Scotland) Act 1980, the court required to hear the appeal under the 1975 Act as originally enacted and not as amended by the 1980 Act, but that the result would have been the same even applying the test under the amended provisions.

BEATTIE v. H.M. ADVOCATE, 1995 S.L.T. 275.

5653. Procedure—appeal—fresh evidence

[Criminal Procedure (Scotland) Act 1975 (c.21), ss.228(2) and 252(*b*) and (*c*).]

Section 228(2) of the Criminal Procedure (Scotland) Act 1975 provides that a person convicted on indictment may bring under review of the High Court "any alleged miscarriage of justice in the proceedings in which he was convicted, including any alleged miscarriage of justice on the basis of the existence and significance of additional evidence which was not heard at the trial and which was not available and could not reasonably have been made available at the trial". Section 252(*b*) provides that for the purposes of an appeal the High Court may hear any additional evidence relevant to any miscarriage of justice and s.252(*c*) provides that the High Court may "take account of any circumstances relevant to the case which were not before the trial judge". An accused person was tried on indictment for assault and robbery. The accused pled alibi. The Crown's case against the accused relied upon the evidence of four witnesses who identified the accused as the robber. The robbery had been recorded on video tape by means of security cameras. Prior to the trial the accused's solicitor, on the advice of counsel, had instructed a consultant medical physicist to carry out a comparison of a photograph of the accused with the video film which the Crown had lodged as a production. The results of the comparison and analysis were inconclusive. Further comparisons were recommended but were not prepared because the accused's solicitor considered that no further funds would be made available for that purpose by the Scottish Legal Aid Board. After the accused had been convicted he was able, by means which were open to him prior to his trial, to raise sufficient funds for a further report to be prepared. The further report found significant inexplicable differences between the robber's face and the accused's face and concluded that the accused was not the person whose face had been captured on the video tape. The accused appealed on the basis of the existence of additional evidence. The Crown opposed the appeal, arguing that the additional evidence could reasonably have been made available at the trial.

Held, that (1) the function of the second part of s.228(2), introduced by the word "including", was to enlarge the preceding part of the subsection for the avoidance of doubt and was not used to limit the scope of the preceding words; (2) s.228(2) was accordingly wide enough to enable the appeal court to entertain an appeal on the ground of the existence of fresh evidence if a reasonable explanation could be given for the failure to adduce the evidence at the trial and the court could say, if it heard that evidence, that there was a miscarriage of justice in the proceedings in which the accused was convicted; (3) as the accused was on legal aid he was not acting unreasonably in not attempting to raise funds from other sources, and since he was entitled to rely on his solicitor's view that no further funds could be obtained by means of legal aid, he had a reasonable explanation for not adducing the evidence at his trial; and appeal continued to hear the additional evidence. *Observed,* that s.252 was concerned only with the powers which the appeal court could exercise and in order for an accused to reach s.252 the court had first to be satisfied that the appeal was brought on a ground which was open to an accused under s.228(2). *Opinion,* that the power in s.252(*c*) was not restricted to appeals against sentence. (Dicta in *Rubin v. H.M. Advocate* [1984] C.L.Y. 3897, not followed.)

CHURCH v. H.M. ADVOCATE, 1995 S.L.T. 604.

5654. Procedure—appeal—fresh evidence

[Criminal Procedure (Scotland) Act 1975 (c.21), ss.228(2) and 252(b).]

Section 228(2) of the Criminal Procedure (Scotland) Act 1975 provides that a person convicted on indictment may bring under review of the High Court "any alleged miscarriage of justice in the proceedings in which he was convicted, including any alleged miscarriage of justice on the basis of the existence and significance of additional evidence which was not heard at the trial and which was not available and could not reasonably have been made available at the trial". Section 252(*b*) provides that for the purposes of an appeal the High Court may hear any additional evidence relevant to any miscarriage of justice. An accused person was tried on indictment for murder. His defence was provocation. Prior to his trial the accused's solicitor had obtained reports from the accused's general medical practitioner concerning his mental state and from a consultant psychiatrist to the effect that the accused suffered from no mental disorder, illness or handicap, but that he had been chronically taunted for several months by the deceased and that that might have had some relevance to provocation. After the accused's conviction another consultant psychiatrist found that the accused was not suffering from any major mental illness, but that the death of the deceased had occurred against a background of great emotional stress for the accused and that, for that reason, the accused's state of mind was bordering on, although not amounting to, insanity. The accused appealed, contending that there was additional evidence available only after the trial that at the time of the offence he was suffering from diminished responsibility. The Crown opposed the appeal, arguing that the fresh evidence did not satisfy the requirements of admissible additional evidence prescribed by s.228(2) and that, in any event, the proposed evidence was not of such significance that a verdict reached in ignorance of it could have resulted in a miscarriage of justice.

Held, (by a bench of five judges), that (1) Parliament had made it clear in the second part of s.228(2) of the 1975 Act that if additional evidence which was not heard at the trial was to be adduced it could be adduced only if it was evidence which was not available and could not reasonably have been made available at the trial; (2) s.252(*b*) conferred upon the High Court power to hear additional evidence only in any appeal which had been brought within the terms of s.228(2); (3) since the possible defence of diminished responsibility was considered prior to the trial, the tendered evidence was not evidence which was not available and could not reasonably have been made available at the trial; (4) in any event, the proposed evidence fell far short of what was required to support a plea of diminished responsibility; and appeal refused. *Church v. H.M. Advocate*, [1995] C.L.Y. 5653, overruled; *Salusbury-Hughes v. H.M. Advocate* [1987] C.L.Y. 4144; approved; *Connelly v. H.M. Advocate* [1990] C.L.Y. 4945; and *Martindale v. H.M. Advocate* [1992] C.L.Y. 5510, applied. *Observed*, per the Lord Justice Clerk (Ross), that the court, having regard to the view which they held in *Church v. H.M. Advocate*, should not have proceeded to decide the case but should have remitted the case to be decided by a court of five judges. *Observed*, per Lord McCluskey, that the second part of s.228(2) was intended to provide the only route by which the High Court could take note of an alleged miscarriage of justice said to derive from circumstances arising outwith the proceedings in which the accused was convicted, including the existence of evidence not heard at the trial.

ELLIOTT v. H.M. ADVOCATE, 1995 S.L.T. 612.

5655. Procedure—appeal—fresh evidence

[Criminal Procedure (Scotland) Act 1975 (c.21), s.228(2).]

M and his co-accused R, O and T were charged with murdering E and burying his body in an attempt to defeat the ends of justice. The evidence showed that all the accused had repeatedly punched and kicked E over several hours and that R had stamped on E's throat, although no single injury could be blamed for his death. M did not give evidence at trial and was convicted, with R, of murder, while O and T were convicted only of assault, and M appealed. M claimed that additional evidence, which was not available and could not reasonably have been made available at his trial, was now available. M stated on affidavit that before trial, M and his co-accused (other than R) agreed to say falsely that R was responsible for the murder and that the others played lesser parts, but in actuality T had initiated the assault and although the others had joined in, T and eventually R had been the principal assailants in E's final moments. M had tried to resuscitate E and was prevented by T from telephoning for an ambulance. He was prevented from giving this evidence at trial because of threats from T and T's family. Affidavits from M's legal advisers stated that he had made it clear prior to trial that he did not want to incriminate anyone, although none of his advisers recalled M stating that he was being threatened or that he was too frightened to give evidence. Other affidavits suggested that M was scared of T and R.

Held, appeal refused. M had chosen not to provide the evidence at trial or disclose it to his advisers and therefore such evidence did not constitute evidence which was unavailable at trial (*McCormack v. H.M. Advocate* [1993] C.L.Y. 5028). Where an accused was threatened, he had to decide whether to disclose the threats to his advisers, and if he did, whether to accept their advice about giving such evidence at trial. But since M did not report that he had been threatened, his explanation could not now be regarded as acceptable. Moreover, it was unlikely in light of all the evidence that his account would have helped him at trial. There was little substance in the affidavits that he was in immediate danger because of threats he received from T. Until the trial, he was in collusion with his co-accused to five a false story, and it was unclear whether he would have been advised to testify if he had given his account of the murder to his advisers. Although M's account might have persuaded the jury that T was responsible for E's murder and not just assault, it was unlikely that it would have exculpated M. *Observed*, that if it could have been said from the affidavits that M had been prevented from giving evidence which would have been likely to have been of material assistance to the jury in their consideration of his guilt of murder, the court would have wished to hear those witnesses before deciding the appeal.

MACKENZIE v. H.M. ADVOCATE, 1995 S.L.T. 743.

5656. Procedure—appeal—referral of accused's whole case by Secretary of State to appeal court—whether appeal court restricted to sole ground of referral. See BEATTIE v. H.M. ADVOCATE, §5652.

5657. Procedure—appeal—retrial. See McDADE v. H.M. ADVOCATE, §5726.

5658. Procedure—bail

Held, where the Crown opposed bail on the basis that there were similarities between the offence with which the accused was charged and murders of prostitutes elsewhere in the United Kingdom and that they were making inquiries into those matters, but it was not asserted that the evidence being examined in relation to those other matters would be evidence bearing on the charge in the petition, that the sheriff had been entitled to grant bail.

NORMAND v. L., 1995 S.C.C.R. 130.

5659. Procedure—bail—breach of bail condition—proof

[Bail etc. (Scotland) Act 1980 (c.40), s.3(1)(b).]

Held, on a Crown appeal, that a sheriff was entitled to find not proven a charge that R was in breach of bail conditions that he would not approach or enter the matrimonial home or contact his wife (W), where it was found that R had arranged to have access to their children at W's sister's house near the matrimonial home, that W had previously asked him to let her know when he was leaving and that it was in these circumstances that he went to her house and spoke to her: contrary to the Crown's submission, they had to establish that R had acted without reasonable excuse and as he had acted on W's invitation the sheriff was entitled to hold as he did.

ANNAN v. ROBERTS, 1995 S.C.C.R. 361

5660. Procedure—bail—Crown opposing bail when committing accused for further examination—whether sheriff entitled to go behind reason given by Crown

Two accused persons appeared on petition charged with contraventions of the Misuse of Drugs Act 1971. The Crown moved for the accused to be committed to custody for further examination and stated that it was necessary that the accused remain in custody to allow these further inquiries to be prosecuted. The sheriff was not prepared to accept that assertion and invited the Crown to provide details of these inquiries. The Crown refused to do so and the sheriff admitted the accused to bail. The Crown appealed.

Held, that the sheriff misdirected himself as he should not have sought to go behind the Crown's assertion that it was necessary that the accused be kept in custody; and appeal allowed and bail refused.

ADVOCATE, H.M. v. BOYLE, 1995 S.L.T. 162.

5661. Procedure—bail—Crown seeking refusal of bail to investigate allegations of serious crimes committed in England—no further inquiries necessary into crime charged in petition

An accused person was charged on petition with assaulting a prostitute. The Crown moved for the accused to be committed for further examination in custody so that crimes of the utmost gravity committed in similar circumstances could be investigated. The sheriff granted bail and the Crown appealed.

Held, that the sheriff did not misdirect himself since the Crown did not assert that it was necessary to keep the accused in custody in order that further inquiries might be pursued to obtain evidence which would bear directly upon his guilt or innocence of the charge in the petition; and appeal refused. *Boyle v. H.M. Advocate*, 1995 S.L.T. 162, distinguished.

LEECH v. H.M. ADVOCATE, 1995 S.L.T. 289.

5662. Procedure—bail—further examination—Crown opposing bail on assertion that further inquiries into charge would be impeded if accused released

Held, in a Crown appeal against bail being granted, that where the procurator fiscal made a motion to commit the accused for further examination and stated that the Crown were continuing to make inquiries and that it was necessary for the proper pursuit of those inquiries in the public interest that the accused should remain in custody, the court should not seek to go behind that statement, but should accept that the procurator fiscal was acting for the public interest in his role as a minister of justice and his judgment should be respected; and appeal allowed.

NORMAND v. B., 1995 S.C.C.R. 128.

5663. Procedure—bill for criminal letters—competency

[Criminal Procedure (Scotland) Act 1975 (c.21), s.101(1).]

Section 101(1) of the Criminal Procedure (Scotland) Act 1975 provides, *inter alia*, that an accused person shall not be tried on indictment for any offence unless the trial is commenced within 12 months of his first appearance on petition and, failing such commencement, he shall be discharged and forever free from all question or process for that offence. Three accused persons were served with an indictment charging them with rape. Two accused had first appeared on petition on September 29, 1992 and the third accused had appeared on petition on October 2, 1992. All three were admitted to bail. They were indicted for trial at a sitting commencing on September 27, 1993, when the Crown could not proceed because a *socius*, who was an essential Crown witness, was absent and his whereabouts were unknown. The trial judge refused the Crown's motion to extend the 12 month period and the advocate depute thereupon moved the court to desert the diet *simpliciter*. The whereabouts of the witness subsequently became known and on November 23, 1994 the complainer presented a bill for criminal letters. The accused opposed the bill as being incompetent in respect that, the 12 month period having expired, they were free from further process for the crime, and on the basis that there were no exceptional circumstances justifying a private prosecution and there had been unreasonable delay in bringing the bill. The Lord Advocate withheld his concurrence but did not oppose the bill if the High Court considered the bill to be competent.

Held, that (1) s.101(1) applied only to trial on indictment and not criminal letters and the bill was accordingly competent; (2) it was nonetheless a relevant consideration that Parliament had enacted s.101(1) which conferred a very important right on accused persons; (3) the period of 18 months after desertion of the diet, whether or not it amounted to oppression, was a factor to be taken into account when determining whether to pass the bill; (4) there were no very special circumstances justifying the grant of criminal letters; and bill refused. *H. v. Sweeney* [1982] C.L.Y. 3596, distinguished.

C. v. FORSYTH, 1995 S.L.T. 905.

5664. Procedure—consolidation—supervised release order

ACT OF ADJOURNAL (CONSOLIDATION AMENDMENT) (SUPERVISED RELEASE ORDERS) 1995 (No. 1875) [£1·10], made under the Criminal Procedure (Scotland) Act 1975 (c.21), s.212A (as inserted by the Prisoners and Criminal Proceedings (Scotland) Act 1993 (c.9), s.14(1) and amended by the Criminal Justice and Public Order Act 1994 (c.33), s.132) and ss.282 and 457 (as amended by the Criminal Justice (Scotland) Act 1980 (c.62), s.65, Sched. 7); operative on September 1, 1995; substitutes a new form for a supervised release order.

[S.I. 1998 No. 110 amended.]

5665. Procedure—contempt of court. See ROBB v. CALEDONIAN NEWSPAPERS, §5757.

5666. Procedure—delay—oppression

Held, on S and R's appeal on the grounds that the sheriff erred in repelling a plea in bar of trial on the ground of delay of approximately 2½ years after the case had been reported to the fiscal, the alleged offences being carried out in the late 1980s, that the appeals would be refused since, even though S and R claimed that the documents which could have supported their defence were no longer available as various companies referred to in the indictment were no longer in existence and the accountants had destroyed some of the relevant papers, the risk of prejudice from delay was not so great that it could not be removed by a direction from the trial judge (*McFadyen v. Annan* [1992] C.L.Y. 5466), any prejudice resulting from the loss of documentation being possible rather than factual.

SKILLING v. H.M. ADVOCATE, 1994 S.C.C.R. 826.

5667. Procedure—detention—suspect to be taken to police station—whether requirement of nearest police station

[Criminal Justice (Scotland) Act 1980 (c.62), s.2.]

Held, on M's appeal against conviction for wilful fireraising on the grounds that a statement made by him while being detained under the Criminal Justice (Scotland) Act 1980 was inadmissible as the requirements of s.2 had not properly been carried out, M claiming that, as he had been detained close to Airdrie police station, he should have been interviewed there and not driven for one hour to Dunfermline police station, and that the only fair interpretation of s.2 was that the detainee should be taken to the nearest police station, that the appeal would be refused since s.2(1) and (2) required to be read together and provided only that he be taken to a police station or other premises as quickly as reasonably practicable, the whole procedure was governed by a strict timetable, evidence suggested that interviewing facilities at Airdrie were under considerable pressure that morning and all the relevant documentation was to be found at Dunfermline.

MENZIES v. H.M. ADVOCATE, 1995 S.C.C.R. 550.

5668. Procedure—indictment—discrepancy between service copy and record copy—whether proceedings incompetent

[Criminal Procedure (Scotland) Act 1995 (c.21), ss.70 and 108(1).]

Section 70 of the Criminal Procedure (Scotland) Act 1975 provides that the accused shall be served with a full copy of the indictment and of the list of the names and addresses of the witnesses to be adduced by the prosecution. Section 108(1) provides *inter alia* that no objection by the accused to the validity of the citation against him on the ground of any discrepancy between the record copy of the indictment and the copy served on him shall be competent except by leave of the court on cause shown and no such discrepancy shall entitle the accused to object to plead to such indictment unless the court shall be satisfied that the discrepancy tended substantially to mislead and prejudice the accused. An accused person was charged along with four other persons on an indictment which was served on him but omitted seven charges which did not relate to him. At a preliminary diet it was argued that the proceedings were incompetent because there had been a failure to comply with s.70. The trial judge repelled the objection on the basis that the breach was not of such a fundamental nature as to render the proceedings incompetent. The accused appealed.

Held, that the discrepancy did not tend substantially to mislead the accused and accordingly the trial judge was right to repel the objection; and appeal refused.

BENNETT v. H.M. ADVOCATE, 1995 S.L.T. 761.

5669. Procedure—indictment—service of—indictment served at address in bail order—address not accused's normal residence as disclosed at judicial examination

[Bail etc. (Scotland) Act 1980 (c.4), s.2.]

R sought suspension of a warrant for his apprehension after his failure to appear at the High Court for trial. At trial R was instructed by his counsel not to appear and proceedings were challenged on the ground that the Crown had failed to comply with s.70 of the Criminal Procedure (Scotland) Act 1975. The trial judge granted warrant as he did not accept that the Crown had failed. The indictment and intimation of the date of trial was served by a police officer at the address specified in R's bail order, being his domicile of citation. This was the address given in the petition warrant. R averred that his normal address was elsewhere, and that he had made this clear at the time of his judicial examination before he was released on bail. It was for the Crown to ensure that that address was specified in the bail order. The failure to serve the indictment at that address was fatal.

Held, appeal refused. Bail was granted subject to those conditions thought necessary to ensure an accused's attendance at every diet (s.2 of the 1980 Act). R was given a copy of the bail order and the address specified therein to be the accused's proper domicile of citation. Service at that address was sufficient (*Bryson v. H.M. Advocate* [1961] C.L.Y. 9764). The wording of s.2 (1) (b) which referred to the accused's normal place of residence was a direction to the court, not a mandatory provision, otherwise the Crown would be forced to carry out an inquiry in order to make a finding as to what was the accused's normal place of residence before granting bail. R had the option to advise the Crown of an alteration to the address (s.2 (2)). R was in no doubt about the address at which he was to be cited to appear. *Held*, further, that it was incompetent to challenge the warrant by bill of suspension given that the warrant was granted in the High Court, and that relief could only be granted on petition to the *nobile officium*.

REILLY v. H.M. ADVOCATE, 1995 S.L.T. 670.

5670. Procedure—indictment—special capacity—using wireless telegraphy apparatus

[Criminal Procedure (Scotland) Act 1975 (c.21), s.67.]

Held, of consent, on Y's appeal against conviction for unauthorised use of wireless telegraphy apparatus in breach of s.5(*b*)(i) of the Wireless Telegraphy Act 1949, that the conviction would be quashed where the sheriff directed the jury that, since the offence was alleged to have been committed in a special capacity in terms of s.67 of the Criminal Procedure (Scotland) Act 1975 and that had not been challenged by preliminary objection, they could assume that Y was an unauthorised person receiving an unauthorised message in breach of s.5(*b*)(i), if they were satisfied that the apparatus was being used in the way the Crown said, since while the allegations that Y was unauthorised and that he was using the apparatus fell within the phrase "special capacity" it did not extend to the equipment Y was using and the Crown still required to prove that it fell within the definition in s.19(1) of the Act.

YOUNG v. H.M. ADVOCATE, 1995 S.L.T. 683.

5671. Procedure—*nobile officium*—competency

Held, that an application to the *nobile officium* was not a competent means of bringing the granting of an unruly certificate under review by the court; but that it was appropriate to grant bail to Y, charged with theft by housebreaking, under condition that he reside in the secure unit of a list D school.

Y., PETR., 1995 S.C.C.R. 457.

5672. Procedure—*nobile officium*—competency—accused abandoning appeal against conviction and sentence on incomplete and inaccurate advice on prospects from solicitor

[Criminal Procedure (Scotland) Act 1975 (c.21), ss.244(1) and 262.]

Section 244(1) of the Criminal Procedure (Scotland) Act 1975 provides that an accused person may abandon his appeal by lodging a notice of abandonment and on such notice being lodged, the appeal shall have been deemed to have been dismissed. Section 262 provides *inter alia* that, subject to the exercise of the prerogative of mercy, all interlocutors of the high court shall be final and conclusive and not subject to review by any court whatsoever. An accused person was convicted after trial on indictment of conspiracy and was sentenced on December 22, 1993 to 12 years' imprisonment. He appealed against conviction and sentence and a hearing in the criminal appeal court was set for May 25, 1994. On May 22, senior counsel who had represented the accused at his trial advised that the appeal against sentence should be abandoned and that two of the three grounds of appeal against conviction were unstatable. The accused's solicitor telephoned the accused and, purportedly in light of senior counsel's opinion, advised the accused to abandon his appeal against both conviction and sentence. The accused was not advised that he was entitled to obtain a second opinion or that he could appear personally and present his own appeal if he was dissatisfied with the advice he had been given. The accused accepted the solicitor's advice and signed a notice of abandonment with the result that his appeal was deemed to be abandoned on May 25, 1994. On January 25, 1995 the accused petitioned the *nobile officium* to reinstate his appeal so that both conviction and sentence could be challenged.

Held, (the Crown not opposing), that (1) it would not be in conflict with the provisions of s.262 for the appeal court to exercise the *nobile officium* where an appeal had been deemed to be dismissed upon the lodging of a notice of abandonment; (2) the accused could not be blamed for having acted upon the inaccurate and incomplete advice which he was given and accordingly the circumstances were sufficiently exceptional and unforeseen for exercise of the *nobile officium*; and prayer granted and appeal restored. *Young, Petr.*, 1994 S.L.T. 269, considered.

McINTOSH, PETR., 1995 S.L.T. 796.

5673. Procedure—*nobile officium*—competency—restoration of legal aid

[Act of Adjournal (Consolidation) 1988 (S.I. 1988 No. 110), r. 164(2).]

Held, on M's petition to the *nobile officium* seeking restoration of his legal aid certificate, which was discharged under r. 164(1)(b) of the Act of Adjournal after M's solicitor was allowed to withdraw in the course of his trial, that although M subsequently obtained another solicitor who conducted the adjourned diet in ignorance of the withdrawal order, securing an acquittal on one of two charges, the court was precluded by r. 164(2) from granting the order sought since to do so would be in conflict with a statutory provision.

McGETTIGAN, PETR., 1995 S.C.C.R. 480.

5674. Procedure—judicial declaration—failure properly to record and execute—whether proceedings null

[Criminal Procedure (Scotland) Act 1975 (c.21), ss.20B and 78(2).]

Following his indictment on a number of charges, R lodged a notice in terms of s.76 of the 1975 Act on the grounds that the judicial declaration referred to as production 16 in the list of productions had not been properly recorded or served on him in breach of ss.20B and 78(2), thereby rendering the proceedings incompetent. At a preliminary diet, the sheriff principal accepted that the statutory provisions had not been complied with, but held that the error was not fatal to the Crown, there being no material prejudice to R. R appealed, arguing that the provisions of s.20B regarding the conduct of examinations and the recording of declarations were mandatory and that failure to observe them rendered all subsequent proceedings incompetent.

Held, appeal refused (the Lord Justice Clerk (Ross) dissenting). *Per* Lord Morison: Although the provisions of s.20B were mandatory not directory, non-compliance with a mandatory provision did not necessarily invalidate subsequent proceedings (*Brayhead (Ascot) v. Berkshire County Council* [1964] C.L.Y. 3577). Despite dicta in certain cases indicating a contrary approach in Scottish criminal proceedings, the word should not be given a different meaning in that class of case from that which it received elsewhere, and it was for the court to determine the consequences of non-compliance since s.20B was silent on this matter (*Howard v. Bodington* (1877) 2 P.D. 203). Since the purpose of s.20B was not to confer upon R the right to make a declaration but to specify the method of recording and correcting it, Parliament could not have intended that non-compliance with the statute would nullify the entire proceedings on the indictment and such a result would be contrary to the public interest. *Per* Lord Kirkwood: The meaning which the Scottish courts had given to the word "mandatory" in the context of criminal proceedings, that non-compliance resulted in nullity, was clearly established. However as the provisions related not to a right to emit a declaration but to the method of recording it, and situations could arise in which what was said required to be proved by other means, Parliament could not have intended that failure to follow them would result in the whole proceedings becoming null, and the provisions fell to be regarded as directory only. As R did not maintain that it would be oppressive to permit a trial to proceed, the appeal failed. *Per* Lords Morison and Kirkwood: If R maintained lesser prejudice, he could found on that at trial. *Per* the Lord Justice Clerk (Ross) (dissenting): It was in the interests of both prosecutor and accused that s.20B was complied with and that the record was a full and accurate one. The provisions related not merely to pre-trial procedures but to the possible giving of evidence at the trial, and s.20B should therefore be regarded as at least to some extent conceived in favour of the accused and as mandatory rather than directory. Failure to comply with such a provision resulted in nullity of the proceedings (*H.M. Advocate v. Graham* [1985] C.L.Y. 3912; *Carruthers v. H.M. Advocate* [1994] C.L.Y 5623).

ROBERTSON v. H.M. ADVOCATE, 1995 S.C.C.R. 152.

5675. Procedure—new prosecution. See B. v. H.M. ADVOCATE, §5721.

5676. Procedure—*nobile officium*. See McNAB, PETR.; ADVOCATE, H.M. v. McNAB, §5682.

5677. Procedure—oppression—abuse of process—warrant for arrest. See BENNETT v. H.M. ADVOCATE, §5744.

5678. Procedure—oppression—accused not tried with co-accused—accused subsequently indicted alone

E, charged with murder, appealed against the trial judge's decision to refuse a plea in bar of trial. E claimed that the Crown had acted oppressively in failing to indict him along with S and G, who had stood trial charged with the same crime while acting with another, now said to be E. The principal Crown witnesses would be S and G (who had been acquitted), although at their trial the Crown had attacked the credibility of their defence. E sought to incriminate S and G but would be unable to lead evidence of statements made by them, as he could have if he had been tried with them (*McLay v. H.M. Advocate* [1994] C.L.Y. 5568). Although the Crown's position was that there was insufficient evidence against E at the time of the earlier trial, it was apparent from the speech to the jury that they considered E was the third person.

Held, appeal refused. The change in the Crown's position resulted directly from the circumstance that different and additional evidence was now available, and that could not be described as oppressive behaviour (*H.M. Advocate v. O'Neill* [1992] C.L.Y. 5440), nor was it an unusual occurrence (*cf.* the position under s.141(3) of the Criminal Procedure (Scotland) Act 1975). Where the Crown had chosen to explain to the court the reasons for not proceeding against E at the earlier stage, it was not for the court to examine all the evidence in order to reassess the judgment made then.

ELDER v. H.M. ADVOCATE, 1995 S.L.T. 579.

5679. Procedure—oppression—other charge brought on summary complaint—whether that charge should be added to indictment

Held, on B's appeal from a sheriff's decision at preliminary diet to repel a submission that the Crown had acted oppressively by including on an indictment which contained two other charges, a charge of theft by house-breaking which had featured on a summary complaint, the trial for which had been adjourned, that although B claimed that if convicted of the third charge only he would be liable to be sentenced on the solemn and not the summary scale, the Crown was master of the instance and could take the view that it was in B's interest that all charges against him be taken together and tried at the same time.

BAIRD v. H.M. ADVOCATE, 1994 S.C.C.R. 678.

5680. Procedure—oppression—successive indictments and trials

J appealed against the sheriff's decision at a preliminary diet to repel a plea that it was oppressive to proceed to trial on an indictment alleging seven crimes of dishonesty. The evidence against J was a taped police interview disclosing special knowledge of a series of offences. The interview had formed the basis of some of the charges on a previous indictment, two offences of housebreaking. J maintained that when discussing what pleas on the first indictment would be acceptable, no mention had been made of the Crown's intention to prosecute for the offences on the second indictment; that the anxiety and distress involved in facing successive trials was a reason for combining charges in one indictment (Hume, ii, 172); and that the test of oppression in *McFadyen v. Annan* [1992] C.L.Y. 5466, related only to the question of undue delay.

Held, appeal refused. The Crown had a discretion and there was no risk of prejudice in regard to delay or the state of the evidence. The *McFadyen* test was a general one and required oppression which could not otherwise be dealt with by direction by the trial judge. What was complained of here was a circumstance which a sentencing judge could take into account. *Observed,* that the fact that the police were in a position to charge J with all the offences in question did not necessarily mean that the Crown were in a position to go to trial on all of them without further evidence.

JUSTICE v. H.M. ADVOCATE, 1995 S.L.T. 1011.

5681. Procedure—reporting restrictions—powers of court—publication of photograph of person related to child witness

[Criminal Procedure (Scotland) Act 1975 (c.21), s.169(1)(ii).]

C, publishers of a national newspaper, petitioned the *nobile officium* for review of an order made by a trial judge in terms of proviso (ii) to s.169(1) of the 1975 Act. The trial concerned the poisoning of a supermarket tonic water which affected a number of people including the accused's wife and 11-year-old daughter. Before the trial the judge had raised with counsel whether it was appropriate to dispense with the reporting restrictions in respect of the child which would otherwise apply under s.169. The advocate depute was of the view that there was a legitimate public interest in the case, that reports had already included particulars of the child and that the restrictions would make it difficult for the trial proceedings to be reported properly. Counsel for the accused (A) argued that some of the pre-trial publicity had already caused distress to the wife (W) and child (X) and that dispensation with the restrictions could result in further distress. The advocate depute subsequently reported that W had expressed extreme concern as the prospect of more reports identifying X given the effect on X's wellbeing following previous publicity. The judge dispensed with the requirements but only on condition that X's name and her relation to A was not revealed, and that there be no publication of photographs of either W or X. C argued that the order was incompetent in respect of W's photograph, since she was over the age of 16 and was therefore not a person referred to in s.169.

Held, that the order was incompetent to the extent that it prohibited, in absolute terms, the publication of W's photograph, and would be recalled. The only absolute prohibition on the publication of pictures contained in s.169

related to pictures of or including children. The publication of pictures of other persons, however closely related to X, was not absolutely prohibited. The court could not impose prohibitions or conditions which had the effect of enlarging the statutory restrictions. The proper approach was to leave the requirements of s.169 in place except to the extent that the judge was satisfied that they could be dispensed with. The order granted was unclear in its effect. *Observed*, in respect of an averment (not insisted in) that the judge erred in granting the order without limit of time, that the restrictions in s.169 were not expressed under reference to any time limit other than the age of the child, so that the order had to continue to apply until the child was 16 unless dispensed with under proviso (iii).

CALEDONIAN NEWSPAPERS, PETRS., 1995 S.L.T. 1335.

5682. Procedure—*res judicata*

An accused was charged on indictment. At a preliminary diet the indictment was dismissed on the ground that the accused had suffered prejudice because of undue delay on the part of the Crown. The Crown appealed but the appeal was not intimated to the accused. Counsel appeared before the High Court and purported to consent to the appeal being allowed, but without proper authority to do so. The High Court accordingly allowed the appeal. The accused then presented a petition to the *nobile officium* to set aside the allowance of the appeal. That petition was granted. The accused was indicted again on the same charges.

Held, that the question of the competency of the indictment was *res judicata*; and indictment dismissed.

McNAB, PETR.; ADVOCATE, H.M. v. McNAB (Sh.Ct.), 1994 S.C.C.R. 633.

5683. Procedure—separation of charges—whether material risk of real prejudice if charges not reported

An accused person was charged on indictment with eight offences. At a preliminary diet the accused sought separation of charges 3 to 6 from the other charges on the ground that he proposed to advance a defence of non-insane automatism in respect of charges 3 to 6, whereas the other charges related to a Crown witness whose character the accused proposed to attack and that attack was likely to result in the Crown seeking to attack the accused's character by revealing that he had a criminal record including convictions under the Misuse of Drugs Act 1971. The sheriff refused the motion on the basis that the accused would not suffer such prejudice as would constitute a palpable injustice or be oppressive to him. The accused appealed, contending that the sheriff had applied the wrong test.

Held, that (1) the sheriff had approached the matter wrongly by applying the test which would fall to be applied by the appeal court when reviewing a sheriff's decision and accordingly the matter was at large for the appeal court; (2) the question for the sheriff was whether there was a material risk of real prejudice to the accused if the charges were tried together, and that could not be affirmed; and appeal refused. (*Brown v. H.M. Advocate*, [1992] C.L.Y. 5446, applied.)

TONER v. H.M. ADVOCATE, 1996 S.L.T. 24.

5684. Procedure—summary—adjournment—whether refusal oppressive

An accused person was charged on summary complaint with assault. Prior to the commencement of the trial the court officer mistakenly informed the procurator fiscal depute that all the Crown witnesses were present although one essential witness was not present. After the evidence of two Crown witnesses had been led the Crown sought an adjournment so that the witness's evidence could be taken. The sheriff refused the motion and treated the Crown case as closed. No evidence was led for the accused. The sheriff was then informed that the witness had then been contacted and would be available to give evidence at 2 pm. The sheriff was then moved to adjourn the trial from 11.15 am to 2 pm but refused to do so and found the accused not guilty. The Crown sought advocation of the sheriff's decision.

Held, that the sheriff failed to have proper regard to the interests which would suffer or had suffered prejudice by the refusal of an adjournment and accordingly the decisions could not stand; and bill passed and decisions recalled. *Tudhope v. Lawrie* [1979] C.L.Y. 2937 followed.

McGLENNAN v. HASTIE, 1995 S.L.T. 1069.

5685. Procedure—summary—adjournment after conviction for proof of previous convictions—competency

[Criminal Procedure (Scotland) Act 1975 (c.21), s.380(1).]

Held, on B's appeal against conviction for incurring a taxi fare of £11 without paying or intending to pay for it, that (1) the justice did not err in refusing B's motion for an adjournment under s.350 of the 1975 Act to allow him to cite two witnesses as B knew of the existence of the witnesses at the time of the trial and had ample notice to bring them to trial and it was within the justice's discretion to refuse the adjournment; (2) there was no miscarriage of justice amounting to prejudice and oppression where B alleged that there was a conspiracy between the procurator fiscal and the police witnesses to secure a pretended conviction based on the police giving perjured evidence as the justice was satisfied beyond reasonable doubt that the police were telling the truth and that B was neither a credible nor a reliable witness; and (3) the justice did not err in adjourning the case prior to sentence on two occasions for more than three weeks where the adjournments were minuted as having been made at common law and not under s.380(1) of the 1975 Act, as the purpose of the adjournments was to enable evidence to be led regarding the accuracy of B's list of previous convictions and therefore represented a further stage in the proceedings before the court was in a position to proceed to sentence (*Johnstone v. Lees* [1994] C.L.Y. 5591, applied).

BURNS v. LEES, 1994 S.C.C.R. 780.

5686. Procedure—summary—appeal—bill of advocation—competency

An accused person was tried on summary complaint. In the course of the Crown case objections were taken to the admissibility of various evidence which was then heard under reservation. At the close of the Crown case the sheriff was invited to rule on the objections so that the accused would know what admissible evidence had been led against him in order to decide whether to argue that there was no case to answer. The sheriff held that it was not competent to rule on the objections until all evidence had been led and thereafter repelled a submission of no case to answer. The accused sought advocation of the sheriff's decision not to rule on the objections. Before the High Court the Crown conceded that it was competent to rule on the objections because it was unnecessary to have recourse to further evidence in order to determine the admissibility of the evidence objected to, but objected to the bill as incompetent.

Held, that since the sheriff's decision deprived the accused of the right conferred on him by s.345A of the Criminal Procedure (Scotland) Act 1975, the accused had suffered prejudice which could not necessarily be rectified at a later stage and the bill was accordingly sufficiently unusual and exceptional as to be competent; and bill passed.

RUNHAM v. WESTWATER, 1995 S.L.T. 835.

5687. Procedure—summary—appeal—bill of suspension—conviction following guilty plea

D sought suspension of a conviction under s.3.(1) of the Dangerous Dogs Act 1991 on the grounds that the case of *Tierney v. Valentine* [1995] C.L.Y. 5475, which was reported subsequent to her plea of guilty, indicated that a defence might have been available, since she had no grounds reasonably to apprehend that her dog would injure anybody.

Held, bill refused. Although the court was entitled in special circumstances to pass a bill of suspension even though a conviction had followed on a plea of guilty, D had not put forward such special circumstances since *Tierney v. Valentine* merely applied s.10(3) of the 1991 Act and the decision was not required to make D aware that in appropriate circumstances a defence might have been available to her.

DIROM v. HOWDLE, 1995 S.L.T. 1016.

5688. Procedure—summary—appeal—Crown appealing on ground not contained in application for stated case

[Criminal Procedure (Scotland) Act 1975 (c.21), ss.441(1)(b) and 452(3).]

Section 441(1)(b) of the 1975 Act provides, *inter alia*, that in an appeal against an acquittal in summary proceedings the appeal shall be by application for a stated case which shall contain a full statement of all the matters which the appellant desires to bring under review. Section 452(3) provides that except by leave of the High Court, on cause shown, it shall not be competent for an appellant to found any aspect of his appeal on a matter not contained in his application for a stated case. An accused person was tried on a summary complaint for, *inter alia*, a contravention of s.1(1) of the Carrying of Knives etc. (Scotland) Act 1993. Evidence was given by two Crown witnesses that the accused was found in possession of a folding pocket knife. The blade of the knife, when measured in court by means of a ruler, was found by one of the witnesses to be 3¼ inches in length and by the other witness to be 3½ inches long. At the close of the Crown case it was submitted that there was no case for the accused to answer because there was no evidence establishing the accuracy of the ruler used to measure the blade. The sheriff sustained the submission and acquitted the accused. The Crown appealed by stated case and argued principally that the length of the blade was an exception which in terms of s.312(v) of the 1975 Act was not for the Crown to negative although no notice of such argument had been given in the application for a stated case.

Held, that (1) as the appellant had not shown cause why he should be allowed to found his appeal on a ground not contained in his application for the stated case, the principal submission would not be entertained; (2) where use was made of an everyday object such as a ruler such evidence was admissible without further evidence that the ruler had been in some way certified as accurate; (3) the question at the close of the Crown case was not whether there was evidence which satisfied the sheriff but whether there was evidence which would establish, if accepted, that the blade exceeded 3 inches in length, and as there was such evidence the sheriff was not justified in sustaining the submission and Crown appeal allowed and case remitted to sheriff to proceed as accords. *Observed*, that the Practice Note of the High Court of Justiciary dated March 29, 1985 related to appeals in solemn procedure and appeals against sentence in summary procedure and accordingly had no application to appeals by stated case.

NORMAND v. WALKER, 1995 S.L.T. 94.

5689. Procedure—summary—appeal—stated case—ground of appeal not stated

[Criminal Procedure (Scotland) Act 1975 (c.21), s.452(3).]

Held, on A's appeal against conviction of dangerous driving, that A should not be allowed to argue that the sheriff erred in applying the test in *Allan v. Patterson*, 1980 C.L.Y. 3540, where references to the case appeared in the draft stated case and A had failed to propose a suitable question by amendment, so that the case did not contain the sheriff's response, and since the issue had been whether the facts libelled were established by the evidence and not whether they constituted dangerous driving; and appeal refused.

ANDERSON v. MACLEOD, 1995 S.C.C.R. 395.

5690. Procedure—summary—appeal—stated case—refusal to state case

[Criminal Procedure (Scotland) Act 1975 (c.21), s.444(1).]

Held, on C's application to the *nobile officium*, the Crown not opposing the petition, that a sheriff had erred in refusing to state a case on the basis that the matters sought to be raised were inadequately stated and so did not satisfy s.444(1)(b) of the 1975 Act; and that the prayer would be granted since the question of sufficiency of evidence raised was directed to particular elements of the charge (*Galloway v. Hillary* [1983] C.L.Y. 4177 and *Durrant v. Lockhart* [1985] C.L.Y. 3930, distinguished), and it was immaterial whether the matters raised appeared in the form of a statement or a question.

CROWE, PETR., 1994 S.C.C.R. 784.

5691. Procedure—summary—appeal—stated case—refusal to state case

[Criminal Procedure (Scotland) Act 1975 (c.21), ss.444(1) and 447.]

L petitioned the *nobile officium* for an order directing a justice to prepare a draft stated case. L had applied for a stated case under s.444(1) of the Criminal Procedure (Scotland) Act 1975 on the grounds that there was contradicting evidence in material respects and therefore that the court "could not reach the view it did in convicting". The justice had refused to state a case, arguing that the grounds of appeal were not sufficiently specific to identify the point L was challenging.

Held, order granted. Although the ground of appeal was not well worded, it was sufficiently specific to alert the justice to the point to be stated, and it was not for the justice to determine the relevancy of the ground on which an application was made (*McTaggart, Petr.* [1988] C.L.Y. 3951).

LEONARD, PETR., 1995 S.C.C.R. 39.

5692. Procedure—summary—complaint—competency—specification of locus

Held, the Crown not opposing the appeal, that a complaint which libelled a health and safety at work offence "on Unit 5, Ship 1047" was fundamentally null for failing to make clear that the unit referred to lay within the jurisdiction of the appropriate sheriff court, and that the sheriff erred in allowing it to be amended to provide further specification.

YARROW SHIPBUILDERS v. NORMAND, 1995 S.L.T. 1215.

5693. Procedure—summary—complaint—discrepancy between principal and service copy—evidence led without objection

[Criminal Procedure (Scotland) Act 1975 (c.21) ss.334 and 454(1).]

Held, on S seeking suspension of his conviction for driving with excess breath alcohol, on the ground that he had been misled by the terms of the service copy complaint which libelled an excess of blood alcohol, that where evidence had been led by the Crown in accordance with the principal complaint, which libelled excess breath alcohol, without objection from S, the essential point of the libel remained the same (*Fenwick v. Valentine* [1993] C.L.Y. 4989), and the question would have arisen whether amendment should be allowed had objection been taken timeously, there was no reason to consider that there had been a miscarriage of justice; and bill refused.

SUTTERFIELD v. O'BRIEN, 1995 S.C.C.R. 483.

5694. Procedure—summary—complaint—power of court to refuse to have complaint called

[Criminal Procedure (Scotland) Act 1975 (c.21), ss.288(5) and 334(1).]

B was charged with committing theft in the sheriff court district of Dumfries and a warrant was issued for his arrest. When he was arrested in Kirkcudbright, he gave a false name and address to the police and a separate complaint was raised against him for attempting to pervert the course of justice. The sheriff at Dumfries only allowed the complaint relating to the theft to be called and refused to hear the second complaint on the grounds that the Crown did not have the power to call the case without reference to the court as administrative matters were to be determined by the court. The Crown raised a bill of advocation arguing that the sheriff having jurisdiction under s.288(5) of the 1975 Act, he was bound to deal with the complaint under ss.324, 336 or 337.

Held, of consent, bill passed and case remitted to allow the complaint to call. It was for the prosecutor to determine whether a case would be called in court at any diet and the sheriff was not entitled to decline to allow him to exercise that power. Any issue of competency or relevancy could be raised thereafter in terms of s.334(1) of the 1975 Act. *Opinion reserved*, no objection having been tabled, as to the competency of the bill, having regard to the fact that the complaint had not called.

HOWDLE v. BEATTIE, 1995 S.L.T. 934.

5695. Procedure—summary—complaint—signature and warrant on separate page

W appealed against the sheriff's decision to repel a plea to the competency of a complaint which consisted of five pages. W had argued that the complaint was incompetent as the fifth page, which contained the warrant and signature of the procurator fiscal, made no reference to W other than the warrant relating to "the said accused". There was a number 5 at the top of the page but no other identification, such as serial number. W argued that as there was nothing on the fifth page to show that it related to W, it could not be relied upon by the Crown.

Held, appeal refused. As it was stapled to the rest of the complaint, and there was nothing to indicate it had been attached in error, the sheriff was entitled to conclude that the warrant related to the complaint. The warrant was clearly part of the process of which the complaint formed part.

WELSH v. NORMAND, 1995 S.C.C.R. 81.

5696. Procedure—summary—delay—oppression

Two accused persons were charged on summary complaint with a number of charges of dishonesty in connection with motor vehicles covering a period from September 1990 to January 1992. The accused were first interviewed by police in February 1992 but the complaint did not call in court until March 1994. At the calling of the complaint a plea in bar of trial was taken by both accused on the ground that there had been undue delay in bringing the case to court. The sheriff repelled the plea, taking the view that if there was any prejudice to the accused it was not so grave that the sheriff at the trial could not be expected to remove it from his mind and reach a fair verdict in the circumstances. The accused appealed to the High Court.

Held, that the sheriff had applied the correct test: the Crown's explanation for the delay had not been questioned and the sheriff had properly balanced the questions of fairness to the accused, and the risk of prejudice to the accused, against the public interest, and had taken account of the position of the trial sheriff; and appeal refused. *Normand v. Rooney* [1992] C.L.Y. 5467, followed. *Observed*, that the lapse of time was a question which the trial judge would have to weigh up carefully when he looked at the evidence.

GULDBERG v. CARDLE, 1995 S.L.T. 1001.

5697. Procedure—summary—desertion *simpliciter* by court

The Crown sought advocation of a sheriff's decision to desert a diet against G and S *simpliciter*. In July 1994 G and S tendered pleas of not guilty to charges of theft by housebreaking and a trial was fixed for November 24, 1994. At the call over on November 24, G's solicitor informed the sheriff that G was present in the building and requested that the case be recalled later so that he could locate his client. Although the depute fiscal (F) did not object to this motion, the sheriff stated that unless F was seeking a warrant for G's arrest, then she should call her first witness in the trial. F moved the court to allow the complaint against G and S to be called later, which the sheriff refused; no further motion being made, he deserted the diet *simpliciter*. The Crown argued that as the procurator fiscal was the master of the instance, he was in a position to determine the priority to be given to the cases down for trial and therefore it was inappropriate for the sheriff to desert the diet *simpliciter*.

Held, bill passed and case remitted to the sheriff to call upon G and S to plead to the charge and proceed accordingly. F's attitude in not seeking a warrant for G was entirely reasonable in the circumstances, particularly where G's solicitor had advised that G was present in the building.

CARMICHAEL v. GILMOUR, 1995 S.L.T. 1224.

5698. Procedure—summary—legal aid—withdrawal of legal aid—competency. See LAMONT, PETR., §6097.

5699. Procedure—summary—notice of penalties—service—incorrect notice

[Criminal Procedure (Scotland) Act 1975 (c.21), s.311(5).]

Held, on T seeking suspension of penalties imposed for contravention of s.5(1)(a) of the Road Traffic Act 1988 on the ground that no notice of penalties appropriate to that section had been served on him before he was called on to plead, that where on T initially being called on to plead the Crown had not accepted the pleas on realising that the notice was incorrect, and prepared and served a new notice then had the case called later the same day, at which point pleas were accepted, there had been a failure to comply with s.311(5) (*Hutchison v. Normand* [1994] C.L.Y. 5612, distinguished), but that no miscarriage of justice had been demonstrated since it had been open to T to seek further advice following service of the notice and change his plea if so advised, and it would not be appropriate to interfere with the sentence imposed; and bill refused.

TURNER v. RUSSELL, 1995 S.C.C.R. 488.

5700. Procedure—summary—oppression—conduct of prosecutor—complaint against police officers investigated along with their complaint against complainant

Two accused persons, A and B, who were police officers, were charged on summary complaint with, *inter alia*, breach of the peace. A member of the public, R, had complained about the police officer's conduct and the next day A made a complaint alleging an offence by R. Separate inquiries were carried out by two officers at different police stations. One investigating officer took statements from A and B. Another officer interviewed R and later interviewed and cautioned B who was subsequently charged by him. R was charged by the other investigating officer two days later. When, for the first time both investigating officers discovered the activities of the other, the two files were amalgamated and sent to police headquarters and subsequently passed to the procurator fiscal. The sheriff sustained pleas by A and B in bar of trial and dismissed the complaint on the ground that the procurator fiscal had gained an unfair advantage by having access to A and B's statements. The procurator fiscal sought advocation of the sheriff's decision.

Held, that the fact that the procurator fiscal had access to the statements given by the accused in relation to the complaint which they had made against R did not by itself give the procurator fiscal such an advantage as to make the prosecution oppressive and bar the trial; and bill passed and decision recalled. (*McLeod v. Tiffney* [1994] C.L.Y. 5613, distinguished.)

BOTT v. ANDERSON, 1995 S.L.T. 1308.

5701. Procedure—summary—oppression—Crown precognoscing accused on separate complaint by accused. See BOTT v. ANDERSON, §5700.

5702. Procedure—summary—oppression—police interviewing accused concerning complaint against police

Four accused persons were charged on a summary complaint with breach of the peace and one of the accused, S, was also charged with a contravention of s.41(1)(a) of the Police (Scotland) Act 1967 by resisting, obstructing, molesting and hindering two police officers in the execution of their duty. Thereafter a relative of three of the accused complained about the alleged behaviour of one of the police officers at the time of the incident giving rise to the charges. She and a witness were interviewed by a chief inspector from the complaints and discipline branch on June 30, 1993 but were neither cautioned nor advised that they could have a solicitor present. On July 2 the police officer complained against was interviewed by the same chief inspector and informed of the general nature of the complaint. On July 7 S and her co-accused, R, were interviewed by the chief inspector though the other accused were never interviewed nor did they give statements or precognitions. The Crown were not involved in the investigation of the complaint against the police officer. The accused stated pleas in bar of trial, and after hearing evidence the sheriff sustained the plea in respect of S and R and dismissed the charges against them, but repelled the plea in respect of the other accused who, along with the procurator fiscal, appealed to the High Court.

Held, that (1) there was no basis for concluding that justice had not been seen to be done since S and R were interviewed five days after the police officer had been interviewed by the chief inspector and, in any event, the police officer was told no more than the general tenor of the complaint; (2) since the other two accused did not give statements or precognitions and the information was kept entirely separate by the chief inspector, the sheriff was correct in concluding that they could not have thought what happened to them was contrary to natural justice or unfair; and Crown appeals allowed and accused's appeals refused. *McLeod v. Tiffney* [1994] 5 C.L. 517 applied. *Observed*, that fairness to the officer complained against justified his being told the general nature of the complaint and not to do so might well have prejudiced any defence that he might have had to the complaint being made against him.

NORMAND v. RAMAGE; McINTOSH v. NORMAND, 1995 S.L.T. 130.

5703. Procedure—summary—plea—plea of guilty tendered before service of complaint—whether sheriff entitled to refuse to record

[Criminal Procedure (Scotland) Act 1975 (c.21), ss.334(1) and 336.]

A sought an order by way of bill of advocation ordaining the sheriff to record his plea of guilty. A had appeared on petition for three charges under the Misuse of Drugs Act 1971. The case was then reduced to summary. Difficulties followed in serving A and when the case called by arrangement, A tendered a plea of guilty. A's agent then advised the court that as the plea was based on a courtesy copy complaint sent to her by the procurator fiscal and the service copy of the complaint with notice of penalties had not been served on A, the sheriff could not proceed to sentencing. Following an adjournment, A was properly served. When the case resumed, the sheriff insisted that A tender a plea on the existing complaint and refused to record A's initial plea, which had been tendered before formal citation. A argued that there was an inference that the Crown had accepted his original plea of guilty and therefore in terms of s.336 of the 1975 Act it should have been recorded.

Held, bill refused. The case was originally called on the assumption that the complaint had been served on A. Since the parties had proceeded upon a false basis, the sheriff was entitled to refuse to record the plea and to continue the case to allow further inquiries. In view of the information which the sheriff later received, he was correct in refusing to record A's earlier plea of guilty on the ground that A had not been properly served at that stage.

ALLAN v. McKAY, 1995 S.L.T. 92.

5704. Procedure—summary—special capacity. See ROSS v. SIMPSON, §5898.

5705. Procedure—summary—time bar—oppression

[Road Traffic Offenders Act 1988 (c.53), s.6.]

G appealed a sheriff's decision to repel his plea in bar of trial on two road traffic offences. The offences were allegedly committed on June 16, 1993. The complaint was served on G on February 18, 1994 with a certificate in terms of s.6 of the 1988 Act that sufficient evidence to warrant proceedings did not come to the prosecutor's attention until August 31, 1993. A previous complaint served on G on December 29, 1993 did not contain such a certificate; G objected on the ground of time bar and the complaint was not called. G argued that by failing to serve a certificate with the first complaint, the Crown was barred from proceeding with the present complaint and that by not calling the case in respect of the first complaint, the Crown accepted that those proceedings were time barred under s.33(1) of the Criminal Procedure (Scotland) Act 1975.

Held, appeal refused. The certificate established that evidence sufficient to warrant proceedings did not come to the prosecutor's attention until August 31, 1993 and in terms of s.6(1) of the 1988 Act, summary proceedings could be brought within six months from that date. The Crown had a choice under s.6 of the 1988 Act where objection was being taken under s.331(1) to lead evidence from the prosecutor in the course of trial to establish when evidence sufficient to warrant proceedings came to his knowledge or to proceed by means of a certificate, and where all that was done was to substitute one complaint for another so that the prosecutor would have the benefit of the provisions permitting a certificate, his decision to proceed in that way did not cause G any prejudice, and could not be said to amount to oppression.

GRAY v. NORMAND, 1995 S.L.T. 769.

5706. Procedure—summary—time bar—statutory offence—control of pollution. See McDONALD v. H. L. FRIEL & SON, §5914.

5707. Procedure—summary—trial—adjournment—failure of cited defence witness to appear

Held, on S's appeal against conviction on counterfeiting charges on the ground that the sheriff erred in refusing to adjourn the trial owing to the absence of W, a duly cited incriminee, with whom the defence wished to test the Crown witnesses' evidence of identification by having them view him, that (1) the sheriff erred in considering that there would have been something improper, because of W's privilege against self-incrimination, in conducting such a procedure in court and the matter was at large for the appeal court; (2) although it would have been a second adjournment, S having failed to appear at an earlier diet, and W had in fact been led at a later date after the trial had been adjourned for lack of time to complete, since having the Crown witnesses view W was critical to the defence case the interests of justice would have required that the motion be granted; and appeal allowed and conviction quashed.

SCOUGALL v. LEES, 1995 S.L.T. 1008.

5708. Procedure—summary—trial—conduct of sheriff—fairness

C sought suspension of a conviction on summary complaint of assault and breach of the peace. C claimed that during cross examination of the complainer (R), who was led for the defence, the sheriff warned R not to prevaricate or answer contemptuously, and appeared to lose his temper in a prolonged outburst, thumping the bench with his hand and shouting "This is a witness for the defence", and "I recognise this type of witness"; and argued that this was oppressive conduct prejudicial to the ends of justice, the sheriff's actings and comments giving the impression that he had prematurely formed a concluded view before hearing all of the evidence.

Held, bill refused. While the sheriff had made certain comments, this would plainly suggest to anyone observing that the sheriff was commenting on the fact that he had before him a witness who had been insolent and truculent and was not prepared to give a straight answer.

CORNER v. LEES, 1994 S.C.C.R. 717.

5709. Procedure—summary—trial—incriminee cited as defence witness—whether proper to ask Crown witnesses if they could identify him. See SCOUGALL v. LEES, §5707.

5710. Procedure—summary—trial—objection to evidence—whether properly stated

[Criminal Procedure (Scotland) Act 1975 (c.21), ss.359 and 454(1); Road Traffic Offenders Act 1988 (c.53), s.16.]

M appealed against conviction of drink driving. At trial M had sought to lead evidence that, notwithstanding a certificate of execution of service produced by the Crown, no copy of the analyst's certificate had been served on him. The sheriff had upheld a Crown objection that such evidence was inadmissible because no timeous objection had been taken to the lodging of the Crown productions. At that point M's solicitor had said, referring to the certificate of execution, "I cannot object to its production but will be leading contrary evidence" (according to the sheriff), or "I will be contradicting the evidence" (according to the Crown). The Crown argued that this did not amount to a formal objection for the purposes of s.454(1) of the 1975 Act. M argued that what was essential was that the Crown were put on notice that the service of the certificate was to be challenged.

Held, appeal refused. It had not been clear what M's solicitor was proposing to contradict and there had been no indication that he was intending to object to the analyst's certificate. It was important that the sheriff had not understood or noted him as having made a formal objection: there could be no objection if the court was not aware of it. In terms of s.16 of the Road Traffic Offenders Act 1988, the analyst's certificate was sufficient evidence of the facts stated in it, and unless timeous objection was taken to its production, then by s.454(1) no contrary evidence could be led to the effect that no copy of it had been served. Observed, that a party making an objection would be well advised to intimate his desire to have his objection noted (*cf.* s.359 of the 1975 Act).

MACAULAY v. WILSON, 1995 S.L.T. 1070.

5711. Procedure—summary—trial—questions asked by sheriff of accused during cross examination—whether oppression

An accused person, who was a solicitor, was charged on summary complaint with defrauding H.M. Inspector of Taxes of the tax revenue due in respect of £28,000 received by the accused on the sale of a plot of land. The accused agreed with the purchaser that £18,000 would be paid in cash and that the purchaser's solicitor would be told that the purchase price was £10,000, which was ultimately the price which was declared to the Inland Revenue by the accused. The accused's defence was that when he declared that figure he had no fraudulent intent although it was established that the only legitimate cost which he could set against the taxable amount was £200 as representing the cost of a survey. The accused was the last witness to give evidence and in the course of cross examination the sheriff asked him whether he thought it was "honourable, ethical and decent" to be a party to deceiving the purchaser's solicitor. The sheriff again interrupted the accused's answer by asking: "Did it ever occur to you that you were a party to a deceit and a lie and a party to defrauding the revenue?" The sheriff again interrupted the accused's answer by asking: "Why did you think he [the purchaser] did not want his solicitor to know that you were getting money in cash that it was not for an honest reason?" At another point during cross examination when the accused was explaining that the cash would cover his costs, the sheriff asked whether it was coincidence or "magic" that the costs exactly equalled the figure of £18,000. The accused was convicted and sought suspension on the ground that the questions indicated that the sheriff had prejudged the accused's guilt.

Held, that (1) the sheriff was entitled to ask fairly pointed questions, partly to enable him to understand precisely what the defence was and partly to concentrate the accused's mind on relevant issues; (2) it was unsurprising that the sheriff had difficulty in understanding the defence when the accused knew the purchaser was intent on defrauding the revenue, and his questions did not indicate that he had already made up his mind as to the accused's guilt and were not of such an oppressive nature as to lead to a miscarriage of justice; and bill refused.

DI CIACCA v. NORMAND, 1995 S.L.T. 482.

5712. Procedure—tholed assize—original proceedings incompetent

[Road Traffic Act 1988 (c.52), s.103(1); Criminal Procedure (Scotland) Act 1975 (c.21), s.123.]

M, charged on indictment with driving while disqualified, appealed against the sheriff's decision to repel a plea that he had tholed his assize. M had earlier pled guilty to another indictment charging him with (1) obtaining a driving licence while disqualified, contrary to s.103(1)(b) of the 1988 Act, and (2) using a vehicle without insurance, contrary to s.143. The Crown failed to notice that there was no reference to driving a vehicle and the sheriff refused a motion to amend, having pointed this out after the Crown moved for sentence. The sheriff who repelled M's plea considered that it was necessary to compare not only the statutory provisions concerned but the substance of the charges, which were not identical. M argued that the sheriff should not have refused the original motion to amend, the charge having been irrelevant; that the sheriff should have compared only the statutory provisions concerned; and that the error in the charges did not amount to a fatal irregularity so that he was entitled to take the benefit of the former trial such as it was (Alison, ii, 618–619). The Crown argued that (1) the original proceedings were incompetent, as the charge described a contravention of s.103(1)(a) which could only be prosecuted summarily, and not simply irrelevant within the description in Renton and Brown, para. 9–21(f); and (2) in any event the substance of the charges had to be compared.

Held, appeal refused. The Crown's first argument was sound and the earlier purported conviction was of no effect. *Observed*, that the Crown undertook not to oppose a bill of suspension or other proceedings to set matters right. *Opinion*, that the Crown's further submission was also correct and that the wording of the two charges had to be compared. *Observed*, further, that it would have been appropriate for the sheriff to have allowed the original charge to be amended.

McGLYNN v. H.M. ADVOCATE, 1995 S.C.C.R. 677.

5713. Procedure—trial—improper remark by Crown—correction by judge

R appealed against conviction of being concerned in the supply of drugs on the ground that the advocate-depute, in addressing the jury, had improperly referred to his co-accused (J) having pled guilty to possession with intent to supply, in commenting how J was stopped by the police and the drugs were found in his van. The judge had given an emphatic direction to the jury that

that was improper and not evidence against R, but R argued that the comment was so objectionable that no direction could have cured the matter.

Held, appeal refused. No motion to desert had been made, the matter had not been emphasised or repeated, the judge had given the direction on his own initiative clearly something which was capable of being cured by direction (*Dudgeon v. H.M. Advocate* [1988] C.L.Y. 3973, followed). *Observed*, that it was improper for R's agents to have stated in the ground of appeal that the advocate depute had commented "at length", which had caused the appeal to be continued for a transcript to be obtained.

ROSS v. H.M. ADVOCATE, 1994 S.C.C.R. 932.

5714. Procedure—trial—joint motion to adjourn to locus so that jury might view it—refusal—whether miscarriage of justice. See RODDEN v. H.M. ADVOCATE, §5723.

5715. Procedure—trial—judge's charge—identification evidence

Held, on C's appeal against conviction of armed robbery at a shop, C arguing under reference to *McAvoy v. H.M. Advocate* [1991] C.L.Y. 4584, that the only issue at trial had been identification but that the judge had not directed the jury to treat such evidence with care or indicated the approach to such evidence, that no miscarriage of justice had occurred as there was no fixed formula to be adopted and where the difficulties which could arise had been dealt with fully in both closing speeches, the judge was within his discretion in emphasising in a balanced way the substance of the points for and against each side and telling the jury in conclusion to give consideration to all the evidence relied on and the submissions made to them; and appeal refused.

Held, further, that two years' imprisonment under s.17(2) of the Firearms Act 1968 for having a shotgun with him was not excessive although made consecutive to eight years for the charge of assault and robbery, despite the fact that the same weapon was the subject of both charges, since the Act required that the punishment for that offence be additional to any other punishment imposed, and no discount should be made for that reason from the sentence which would otherwise be appropriate.

CHALMERS v. H.M. ADVOCATE, 1994 S.C.C.R. 651.

5716. Procedure—trial—judge's charge—identification evidence

[Law Reform (Miscellaneous Provisions) (Scotland) Act 1990 (c.40), ss.56 and 58.]

B appealed against conviction for murder, the offence occurring at night when a group of youths including B and L, his co-accused, chased W and his two brothers, W receiving a fatal stab wound to the neck. The grounds of appeal were: that (1) the judge had given inadequate directions to the jury on the need for care to be taken over identification evidence as the incident had occurred at night and much of the identification evidence came from child witnesses, and further, that the judge impliedly suggested that the need for care in the scrutiny of such evidence was lesser for B, who unlike L, had not lodged a special defence of alibi; (2) the judge misdirected the jury insofar as he told them that less importance should be attached to evidence given via television link than direct evidence, counsel for B claiming that this defeated the intention behind s.56 of the 1990 Act and was prejudicial to B since H, a child witness who had previously identified B at a parade, was unable to identify him in the course of his evidence; (3) the judge acted unfairly and incompetently in allowing, on general principle, D, a child witness, to make a dock identification by means of a television camera: neither s.56 nor s.58 of the 1990 Act authorised a child to see, by means of a camera panning around the courtroom, a television broadcast of what was in that courtroom and a warrant should have been sought under s.58 to enable an identification parade to be organised; in any case, a camera placed in the witness box was not equivalent to the eye of a witness.

Held, appeal refused. (1) The judge, in the course of general directions relating to the jury's approach, had explained to the jury the need for care in scrutiny and for corroboration. There was no lack of balance regarding evidence about L, the judge emphasising the need for proof that L was indeed at the locus in view of the special defence. (2) The judge's comment as to the relative value of evidence given by television link had to be taken in context of the directions as a whole and continuing criticism in the course of the trial, by B's counsel among others, of the quality of the television link. Further, it was unlikely that the jury would have been influenced in their approach merely because evidence was by means of a television link since the judge, in his directions, had reiterated the fact that H had apparently excluded both B and L from being present when the murder weapon was hidden. (3) The judge had acted correctly in not permitting D to be brought into court in order to identify B since once a child had started to give evidence via a television link, fairness required that the whole of her evidence be given in that way. In the present case the procedure adopted had been competent as s.56 of the 1990 Act was enabling in character, allowing visual images to be transmitted from the courtroom to the child and vice versa. In that a child might require to see objects and similar, the logical conclusion of this was that the child should be allowed to see what was in the courtroom. Although s.58 provided for one method of giving identification evidence, it did not imply that other methods were incompetent. *Observed*, that the use of this method of giving identification evidence required fairness to both the witnesses and the accused and the question of fairness depended on the circumstances. A child would not be asked to identify using the television link if it was clear that this would cause distress.

BROTHERSTON v. H.M. ADVOCATE, 1995 S.C.C.R. 613.

5717. Procedure—trial—judge's charge—misdirection

F appealed against conviction for robbery of V, acting with others, for which he received 12 months' imprisonment, on the grounds: (1) relying upon *Larkin v. H.M. Advocate* [1988] C.L.Y. 3978, that the sheriff misdirected the jury by telling them that V had stated in his evidence that there must have been two people involved in the offence as V had felt more than one pocket being rifled simultaneously, when V had not stated this; and (2) that, as the jury had deleted all reference to violence in the libel, they could not then return a verdict of guilty of robbery (Gordon, *Criminal Law* (2nd ed.), para. 16–02).

Held, appeal allowed in part. (1) No miscarriage of justice had occurred since at an earlier part of his charge the sheriff had correctly summarised V's evidence and had also told the jury that counsel for F had pointed out that there was only one person involved. He then went on to remind the jury of the inference which V himself appeared to draw that several pockets were being gone through at the same time. In any event there was evidence from police witnesses that two men, one of whom had been identified as F, had been seen at the locus of the offence. (2) An amended verdict of guilty of theft would be substituted since, even though a charge of robbery was possible without specifying the violence used (Criminal Procedure (Scotland) Act 1887, Sched. A), the Crown had specified the violence and the jury had negatived the use of any such violence in their verdict, thus the essential element of robbery was not present.

FLYNN v. H.M. ADVOCATE, 1995 S.C.C.R. 590.

5718. Procedure—trial—judge's charge—misdirection

Held, on A's appeal against conviction for robbery by jumping over the counter and removing money from the till at a newsagent's shop and robbing an employee (B) of money and her handbag, that (1) although the sheriff inappropriately instructed the jury that they could consider how the police would have been placed if B had said at the identification parade that A was definitely not the man, since that did not properly reflect what happened at parades, there was no substantial risk that the jury would be misled or that there would be any unfairness in their approach to the police evidence; and (2) the sheriff did not err in failing to advise the jury that they could find A guilty of theft or robbery as the issue of theft was not raised at trail, the Crown's case was specifically based on robbery and the introduction of an issue not raised at trial could have prejudiced A (*Steele v. H.M. Advocate* [1992] C.L.Y. 5502, distinguished).

ALLAN v. H.M. ADVOCATE, 1995 S.C.C.R. 234.

5719. Procedure—trial—judge's charge—misdirection

L appealed against conviction of assault and attempted robbery concerning a gun being presented to an employee of a nightclub in Aberdeen, and to two passers by during his escape. (1) L argued that there had been insufficient evidence. The only significant identification evidence had come from an identity parade at which a passer by to the incident had indicated L, saying: "I am unsure, but the features of number 1 is very similar". In addition, the fibres of the balaclava worn by the assailant were found to be of the same type and dye as those found in a sports bag, similar to that carried by the assailant, recovered from the house occupied by L's brother, who worked at the nightclub in question. This evidence was supplemented by that of A, who resided with L and who, the day before the incdient, had driven L to the station to catch the Aberdeen train. A few days later, on L's return, L gave A an account consistent with the incident telling A that he had done an armed robbery but had been chased off. He also stated, inconsistently with the other evidence, that he had fired the gun over peoples's heads. (2) L further argued that, assuming there was sufficient evidence, there was a miscarriage of justice in that the judge did not direct the jury specifically that if they did not accept A as being credible and reliable in the essentials of his evidence, or if they had a reasonable doubt about his evidence, then they would not be entitled to convict.

Held, appeal refused. (1) A's evidence on its own would not have been enough to provide a sufficiency, nor would the forensic evidence. The proper approach here was that adopted by the Crown, and that was that taking all the evidence together, the essential points were the subject of corroborated evidence and there was sufficient evidence for a conviction. (2) The direction sought would not have been appropriate since the jury had to be satisfied upon looking at the evidence as a whole, and the jury might otherwise have been given a distorted picture. The judge had left the jury in no doubt about the importance of the task which they faced in assessing A's credibility and reliability, L having spoken to a defence of alibi.

LEANDRO v. H.M. ADVOCATE, 1994 S.C.C.R. 703.

5720. Procedure—trial—judge's charge—misdirection. See SMITH v. H.M. ADVOCATE, §5616; KILPATRICK v. H.M. ADVOCATE, §5776.

5721. Procedure—trial—judge's charge—misdirection

[Criminal Procedure (Scotland) Act 1975 (c.21), s.254(1)(c).

An accused person, who suffered from impaired mental capacity, was tried on indictment for seriously assaulting her nine-month-old daughter. In the course of the trial objections were taken to the admissibility of statements allegedly made by the accused confessing to the assault. Expert witnesses gave evidence both as to the effect of the accused's mental capacity in regard to the fairness of the interviews in which she made the alleged statements and as to whether the accused was highly suggestible. The sheriff repelled the objections and in charging the jury directed that they had to consider, first, whether the accused had made the statements, and secondly, whether the admission of the evidence was fair to the accused or not. He also stated that fairness was not a one sided matter to be looked at from the accused's point of view alone and that they had to have regard to the public interest in the suppression of crime. The accused was convicted and appealed on the ground of misdirection. The Crown concluded that there had been a misdirection but sought a retrial.

Held (the Crown not opposing) that (1) the sheriff had misdirected the jury by referring to the public interest, as the only question for the jury was whether what was done was or was not fair in regard to the particular issues which had been raised in the evidence, and by not focusing the issues relating to fairness; (2) in view of the difficult issues involved the appropriate course was to allow the Lord Advocate to decide whether a new prosecution should be brought having regard to the accused's mental state and the interests of her children; and conviction set aside and retrial authorised.

B. v. H.M. ADVOCATE, 1995 S.L.T. 961.

5722. Procedure—trial—judge's charge—misdirection—comment on accused's silence at judicial examination

[Criminal Procedure (Scotland) Act 1975 (c.21), ss.20A(5) and 141(1)(b).]

Held, on D's appeal against conviction for two charges of assault where (1) the Crown stated, in breach of s.141(1)(b), that the evidence cried out for an explanation and that the jury were entitled to draw an adverse inference from D's failure to provide one, and (2) the sheriff, in breach of s.20A(5), implied that D had held something back at his judicial examination by stating that D had failed to raise the issue of self defence at his examination in contrast to his co-accused, N, who had been consistent in indicating at his examination and trial that he had acted in self defence, that the combined comments by the Crown and the sheriff were so prejudicial as to constitute a miscarriage of justice; and conviction quashed. *Opinion*, that, standing alone, the prejudicial effects of the Crown's comments would have otherwise been removed as a result of the sheriff's directions that D was entitled not to give evidence and that the jury should not draw any adverse inference from his failure to do so (*Upton v. H.M. Advocate* [1986] C.L.Y. 3875).

DEMPSEY v. H.M. ADVOCATE, 1995 S.C.C.R. 431.

5723. Procedure—trial—judge's charge—misdirection—concert

Held, on R's appeal against conviction of being concerned in the supply of cannabis resin with his co-accused (B), that (1) there had been no miscarriage of justice in the sheriff failing to direct the jury that they could not convict R unless they were satisfied that he knew B had possession of controlled drugs, where the evidence showed (a) that the police had stopped a car driven by R and asked R and B to step out of the vehicle and in doing so, B appeared to lose his footing; (b) that R and B were searched but nothing was found on them; (c) that after R and B left, the police searched the area and found a number of pieces of cannabis resin which they suspected had been dropped by B; (d) that on watching the locus, the police saw R and B return about 20 minutes later, looking anxious and agitated and crawling on their hands and knees in the place where the cannabis resin had been found; and (e) that on again being stopped by the police, two pieces of the cannabis resin which had been observed by the police at the locus were found on B. Though his directions were somewhat confusing, the jury must have appreciated that the Crown's case was based on concert and there was sufficient evidence to entitle the jury to draw the inference that R knew what they were looking for and had engaged together with B in the necessary common criminal purpose; and (2) it was within the sheriffs discretion to refuse a Crown motion, concurred in by the defence, to adjourn to inspect the locus to determine

what the visibility was like, where he determined that the risks and pitfalls attendant with the procedure outweighed any possible advantage.
RODDEN v. H.M. ADVOCATE, 1994 S.L.T. 185.

5724. Procedure—trial—judge's charge—misdirection—evidence relating to charges withdrawn

M appealed against his conviction for murder of his wife (W). M had also been charged with a prior incident of assault against W and breach of the peace. The issue was whether M should have been convicted of murder or culpable homicide. The Crown withdrew the two ancillary charges after evidence had been led. M claimed the jury were misdirected by the judge in that (a) he advised the jury they were entitled to consider the evidence on the other two charges in relation to the charge of murder, although they were directed to delete the words "and you did previously evince malice and ill will towards her" but did not say how they were to use that evidence: the only use which they were entitled to make of it was to assess the quality of M's conduct; and (b) he stated that it was for the jury to determine the relevance of the evidence on the two charges insofar as it had a bearing on the murder charge. The reference by the judge to the allegations of malice and ill will as being "an evidential matter" was confusing and should have explained more clearly the requirement of fair notice in leading such evidence (*H.M. Advocate v. Flanders* [1961] C.L.Y. 9721). The verdict was by majority and there was a serious risk that the jury had misunderstood and erred in their approach (*Paterson v. H.M. Advocate*, 1974 S.L.T. 53).

Held, appeal refused. (1) The judge had sufficiently explained the reference to malice and ill will as a matter of fair notice and had correctly left the evidence to the jury to take into account in considering the murder charge, having described murder and culpable homicide and defined the issue in terms of the inference to be drawn from the whole evidence. (2) Where the judge had invited the jury to consider "what was relevant" about the evidence on charges 1 and 2 to the murder charge, it was clear that this word was used in a general sense and not in the sense of what was relevant evidence in law, which had not been an issue. The evidence was available for the jury to give such weight to it as they thought fit, and it was not necessary for the judge to go into the way in which the jury might use the evidence.
McDONALD v. H.M. ADVOCATE, 1995 S.L.T. 1101.

5725. Procedure—trial—judges' charge—misdirection—fraud

M, who had set up a company which was engaged in the maintenance and repair of track jacks used by British Rail and later Scotrail, appealed against conviction for fraud. The Crown claimed that during a 15 month period, M had charged for categories of work in excess of what he had carried out and that during the subsequent period M had charged for parts which had not in fact been used. M's appeal was on the grounds that there had been a miscarriage of justice as a result of various misdirections of the jury by the sheriff, namely: that (1) the jury were wrongly directed that the charge was one of conspiracy and not directed adequately regarding the meaning of and requirements of proof for fraud, in particular, that there required to be corroborated evidence of false pretence; (2) the jury were not properly directed that there could be no false pretence if Scotrail knew what the charging system was which they were being asked to pay; (3) the jury were not told that crucial facts required to be corroborated; (4) the sheriff failed to give adequate directions regarding the defence case; (5) the sheriff misdirected the jury regarding the not proven verdict; (6) the sheriff misdirected the jury in defining "reasonable doubt" by stating that a reasonable doubt would stop a person from acting rather than hesitating before acting.

Held, appeal allowed. The serious nature of the misdirections in the present case had resulted in a miscarriage of justice. Regarding (1), the directions were wholly inadequate as nothing had been said about the requirements for fraud and, although some reference had been made to the necessity for a practical result, no mention was made of false pretences. As a result the jury were left in ignorance as to the significance of the relevant parts of the libel. (2) This part of the charge was defective in that the sheriff at no point made it plain to the jury that they could infer Scotrail's knowledge from the evidence of correspondence and from M which had been led before them and thus it would not be speculation to infer such knowledge. (3) In that the sheriff failed to direct the jury adequately on the definition of fraud, it was more than likely that the jury were left uncertain as to what matters required to be corroborated. (4) Although the sheriff had reminded the jury of the special defence of incrimination against K, a co-accused, that they should reject M's statement if they believed he had been coerced into making it and that they could not convict if they believed that the offence had not been M's doing, he failed to remind the jury that the evidence relied upon by the Crown had been challenged by the defence and that they could only proceed upon evidence if they accepted it. Further, the general tenor of the charge was that the sheriff had done more to criticise the defence counsel than to put the defence case properly to the jury. (5) In view of the observations in *Macdonald v. H.M. Advocate* [1989] C.L.Y. 4076 and *Fay v. H.M. Advocate* [1989] C.L.Y. 4077, the sheriff erred in attempting to explain the not proven verdict in relation to the not guilty verdict. As a result the jury were left believing that there was a restriction upon the circumstances in which they could return either of the acquittal verdicts. (6) The sheriff in failing to adhere to the well established rules laid down had indeed set too high a test and this amounted to a serious misdirection (*McKenzie v. H.M. Advocate* [1960] C.L.Y. 3486).

McDONALD v. H.M. ADVOCATE, 1995 S.C.C.R. 663.

5726. Procedure—trial—judge's charge—misdirection—judge expressing own view on matter of fact

Held, where the judge in his charge described a concession by the Crown as perhaps being "overgenerous", that he had been expressing his own view on a matter of fact and had effectively undermined an alibi defence, and that a misdirection of this kind could not in the circumstances be cured by other directions.

McDADE v. H.M. ADVOCATE, 1994 S.C.C.R. 627.

5727. Procedure—trial—judge's charge—misdirection—rape

W appealed against conviction for rape on the grounds that the trial judge's directions to the jury regarding the significance of C, the complainer's intoxication were confusing and inadequate. There was clear evidence that C was under the influence of drink at the material time. The trial judge indicated that the jury should consider whether C was inclined to indulge in intercourse which she very quickly regretted; or whether she was incapable of exercising resistance because of drink. W argued that he erred in failing to explain that if the former situation applied, then no rape would have occurred because of C's consent, while reduced ability to resist because of drink might make it easier to establish rape.

Held, appeal refused. *Per* Lords Murray and Morison: The trial judge correctly defined rape as including elements of absence of consent and overcoming opposition, and had expanded upon the issue of resistance by C. On the issue of consent, a jury of ordinary intelligence would understand that if they accepted the first possible situation outlined above, rape would not be established. While the trial judge could have better explained the contrasting effects for proof of rape on the two aspects of intoxication, as in the case of *Sweeney v. X* [1983] C.L.Y. 4202, his direction was adequate in the circumstances. *Per* the Lord Justice Clerk (Ross): Although the trial judge's directions were inadequate and the jury might have had difficulty in understanding the legal significance of a conclusion that C was incapable of resisting because of

the consumption of alcohol, the judge was attempting to tell the jury that this would amount to rape and thus any confusion would not have prejudiced W.
W. v. H.M. ADVOCATE, 1995 S.L.T. 685.

5728. Procedure—trial—judge's charge—misdirection—shameless indecency. See BATTY v. H.M. ADVOCATE, §5788.

5729. Procedure—trial—judge's charge—misdirection—statement by accused containing qualified admission

H and R both appealed against conviction for theft by housebreaking. (1) Both argued that the sheriff had failed to give the jury any direction on the question of how to deal with a mixed statement in accordance with *Morrison v. H.M. Advocate* [1991] C.L.Y. 4552 and, in particular, that he had failed to remind the jury that part of the statement was exculpatory. While it was not necessary to use the precise language recommended in *Morrison* the sheriff's direction had been insufficient as he had not told them to determine whether the whole or any part of the statement was accepted by them as the truth. (2) R further argued that the sheriff erred in allowing a taped interview to be heard by the jury, R claiming that the incriminating answers given by him to police were as a result of inducements and pressure since the police had made it plain to R that if he did not confess to the offence they would go to the home of the woman with whom R was associating and through whom R had allegedly learnt about the house which was broken into, saying that her husband was at home and probably did not know about the relationship. Such evidence, R maintained, should have been excluded on the basis of unfairness and it was not a question for the jury to decide whether the alleged confessions were extracted by unfair means as this would render the fairness test meaningless. The Crown submitted that there had been neither physical violence nor flagrant unfairness and the sheriff had given the jury adequate directions on the matter of unfairness.

Held, H's appeal refused; R's appeal allowed on ground (2) and his conviction quashed. (1) As the sheriff did give adequate instructions to the jury on the statement, although not in the recommended language, by telling them more than once to go over the whole statement with care and read everything in its context, the jury could have been in no doubt that it was for them to determine which parts of the statement they believed. (2) There had been a flagrant breach of the rules of fairness, as no reasonable jury could hold that R's statements were voluntary and had not been extracted by unfair and improper means, the police having offered an inducement. That being so, the sheriff ought to have excluded the evidence from the jury's consideration (*Balloch v. H.M. Advocate* [1977] C.L.Y. 3304; *Advocate's (Lord) Reference No. 1 of 1983* [1984] C.L.Y. 3850).

HARLEY v. H.M. ADVOCATE, 1995 S.C.C.R. 595.

5730. Procedure—trial—judge's charge—misdirection—taking part in management of company

[Company Directors Disqualification Act 1986 (c.46), s.11(1).]

D appealed against conviction of (i) fraudulently obtaining credit in respect of goods and services valued in total at £38,257, (ii) contravention of s.11(1) of the Company Directors Disqualification Act 1986 in that he had taken part in the management of a company (I) while an undischarged bankrupt and (iii) contravention of s.67(9) of the Bankruptcy (Scotland) Act 1985 by obtaining credit without intimating that he was an undischarged bankrupt. D, whose defence was that he had been merely an employee of I and not a manager, argued that the sheriff had misdirected the jury in relation to charges (i) and (iii) as to how an employee of a company could become liable for the company's debts such as to incur criminal liability for the matters charged; and that he had misdirected them in relation to charge (ii) by saying that being involved in the "management of a limited company" within s.11(1) of the 1986 Act meant someone being involved in the business affairs of the company who was neither a director nor company secretary nor shareholder but only an employee. D sought to distinguish between an individual responsible for the central direction of a company's affairs and one only responsible for some part, such as production or sales. No direction had been given relating to his being part of the management and central direction.

Held, refusing the appeal, that (1) the charge had to be read in the context of the evidence led at the trial. There was ample evidence that I was no more than a device to conceal the true state of affairs that it was D's own business, in which case he was responsible for any actings purportedly carried on in its name (*Gilford Motor Co. v. Horne* [1933] Ch. 935). The sheriff had directed the jury to decide whether D was making the day-to-day decisions, effectively managing I's affairs, in effect in day-to-day control and whether I was a device to enable him to obtain credit for goods he did not intend to pay for. It was plain from the evidence as to the scale of I's business that the management and central direction could not be distinguished from the making of the day-to-day decisions; (2) The narrow interpretation of s.11(1) contended for by D was not well founded. The sheriff had directed the jury to consider whether D was directly concerned with the management of I's affairs and that was entirely apt in its context, when he had already said that if D had only been given a genuine job with specified duties, he would not commit the s.11(1) offence.

Held, further that concurrent sentences of, respectively, two years, 18 months and 12 months' imprisonment were not excessive given the amounts obtained and that D had simply ignored the consequences of his sequestration, so that a substantial deterrent was required, although D fell to be treated as a first offender, he had obtained employment while on interim liberation, his wife had been diagnosed as suffering from a serious blood disorder and he had to play a substantial part in caring for their three children.

DREW v. H.M. ADVOCATE, 1995 S.C.C.R. 647.

5731. Procedure—trial—judge's charge—misdirection—whether miscarriage of justice

An accused person was tried along with others on charges of *inter alia* attempted murder by struggling with the complainer, knocking him to the ground, repeatedly punching and kicking him on the face and body and stabbing him on the body. The complainer gave evidence that the assault took place in two stages with the accused first struggling with the complainer when no knife was used but the complainer sustained bleeding facial injuries, and later, on the other side of the street, when the accused alone was involved and the complainer was stabbed on the leg. A co-accused, E, stated that another co-accused, M, used the knife but said that neither he nor M was involved in the later stage of the assault. M said the he did not see a knife and did not use one and that the complainer and the accused alone were involved in the later stage of the assault. In charging the jury the trial judge said that corroboration of the complainer's evidence that the accused had stabbed him was available in the complainer's blood being found on the back of the accused's trousers, but he stated that there was a little difficulty in seeing how the complainer's blood would get there if it only came from a facial injury. The accused was convicted and appealed on the ground of misdirection.

Held, that (1) it was a matter of circumstances as to whether, and to what extent, a trial judge should go into the evidence in any detail but that if he did so he should not unduly impress his own views of the evidence on the jury; (2) (the Crown not opposing) the trial judge's comment about the blood ought not to have been made; but (3) before the court could determine whether what was said constituted a misdirection producing a miscarriage of justice it was necessary to know what the defence had represented to the jury regarding the presence of the blood on the accused's trousers, and, as no reliance had been placed on the alternative explanation, there had been no miscarriage of justice; and appeal refused.

JONES v. H.M. ADVOCATE, 1995 S.L.T. 787.

5732. Procedure—trial—judge's charge—misdirection—whether miscarriage of justice

Two accused persons were tried on indictment for, *inter alia*, fraud, attempted fraud and corruptly giving and receiving an inducement contrary to s.1 of the Prevention of Corruption Act 1906. The Crown case included evidence of interviews with each accused outwith the other's presence in the course of which each accused made statements which were both incriminating and exculpatory. The statement of one accused on certain points was inconsistent with the other accused's statement. Neither accused gave evidence. The sheriff told the jury that where the statement was contrary to each accused's interests they could take it into account but that when it was also exculpatory they had to consider both sides of the statement and that they could accept parts of the statement and reject other parts. The sheriff also told the jury that they could only have regard to what the accused said as evidence against himself but on two subsequent occasions he drew attention to mutual inconsistencies between the two accused's statements and described the accused as being at odds with each other. The accused were convicted and appealed, contending that the sheriff had failed to give the directions desiderated in *Morrison v. H.M. Advocate*, [1991] C.L.Y. 4552 and that the jury might have considered that they could judge the accused's credibility by reference to what the other accused had said at his interview.

Held, that (1) slavish adherence to the formula in *Morrison v. H.M. Advocate* was not an absolute requirement and the directions amounted to a sufficient compliance with the directions prescribed in *Morrison v. H.M. Advocate*; but (2) the directions comparing the statements of each accused were at variance with the general rule that statements made by one accused outwith the presence of another accused were not evidence against the co-accused, and were a material misdirection amounting to a miscarriage of justice; and appeals allowed and convictions quashed. (*MacLeod v. H.M. Advocate* [1994] C.L.Y. 5634, applied.) *Observed*, that the sheriff might have gone further by pointing out that the answers to the questions were not tested by cross-examination as they could have been if the accused had elected to give evidence. *Opinion reserved*, whether an accused could discharge the burden of proof resting on him by relying solely on exculpatory answers given in a "mixed" statement.

RIDLER v. H.M. ADVOCATE, 1995 S.L.T. 1270.

5733/4. Procedure—trial—judge's charge—misdirection—withdrawal of defence of self-defence

Held, on E's appeal against conviction of assaulting Y to severe injury by punching, kicking and stabbing, that the sheriff was entitled to withdraw a special defence of self-defence from the jury where although in a statement on which the Crown relied for corroboration he said that he and his wife had been threatened by Y who had a knife, he also said that he had used the knife after Y had dropped it, so that the crisis was over by that point; and where in addition E had in evidence denied making the statement and had given an exculpatory account.

EARLEY v. H.M. ADVOCATE, 1995 S.C.C.R. 267.

5735. Procedure—trial—judge's charge—reckless fireraising—whether misdirection. See THOMSON v. H.M. ADVOCATE, §5766.

5736. Procedure—trial—judge's charge—whether misdirection

An accused person was tried along with two other persons on an indictment libelling, *inter alia*, assault and robbery by seizing the complainer by the throat, repeatedly punching him, knocking him to the ground and robbing him of a watch and wallet. There was evidence that the accused had been crouching or leaning over the complainer with a co-accused when property was being removed from his clothing. There was also evidence from the complainer that he felt more than one person going through his pockets but in cross-examination he said that he could not say how many people were rifling his pockets although he had the impression that there was more than one person. In re-examination he said that he experienced several of his pockets being rifled, some at the same time, like two side pockets at once, although he could not be certain if there was more than one person. The sheriff told the jury that the complainer had stated that there must have been two persons because more than one pocket was being gone through at the same time but the sheriff added that they would remember the evidence more accurately than he did. The jury found the accused guilty of robbery under deletion of all specification of acts of assault. The accused appealed contending that the sheriff had misdirected the jury and that the verdict was perverse.

Held, that (1) the sheriff was reminding the jury of the inference which the complainer had at one stage in his evidence drawn from the fact that several of his pockets were being rifled and there was no risk that the jury may have proceeded in the mistaken belief that the evidence was as the sheriff had represented it to be; (2) for robbery the article had to be taken from the custodier by use or threat of violence and since the jury had negatived any violence, they were not entitled to convict of robbery; and appeal allowed and conviction for theft substituted. (*Larkin v. H.M. Advocate* [1988] C.L.Y. 3978, distinguished.)

FLYNN v. H.M. ADVOCATE 1995 S.L.T. 1267.

5737. Procedure—trial—jury—alleged prejudice of jurors discovered after conviction

An accused person was tried on indictment with contravening s.4(3)(a) and (b) of the Misuse of Drugs Act 1971. At the outset of the trial the sheriff inquired whether any of the empanelled jurors had personal knowledge of the accused. Five jurors came forward and the sheriff excused three of them but did not excuse a D.S.S. employee, who stated that he knew the accused because he was responsible for payment of social security benefit to him, and a teacher who, along with her husband, had taught the accused. No representation was made by either the Crown or the accused's solicitor that they should be excused. The sheriff considered that their knowledge was not such as to be likely to affect their judgment. The accused was convicted and appealed, contending that the presence of these jurors and of a third juror, who was said to have seen the accused on many occasions with a person who was one of the accused's best friends and had been convicted of stealing a substantial sum of money from the juror, led to a miscarriage of justice. At the appeal the accused maintained that the D.S.S. employee had been told by the accused that he smoked cannabis and that the teacher's sons were drug users and so she would have known that he was a cannabis user.

Held, that (1) that if there was a reason for a juror to be excused, it was important that it should be made known to the presiding judge and, the matters now relied on not having been drawn to his attention, the sheriff could not be criticised for not removing the jurors; (2) the sheriff was perfectly entitled to assume that the two jurors he did not remove would decide the case on the evidence and in light of the sheriff's directions; and appeal refused. (*Pullar v. H.M. Advocate*, [1993] C.L.Y. 5034, applied.)

HAY v. H.M. ADVOCATE, 1995 S.L.T. 1236.

5738. Procedure—trial—jury—letters written by juror to court—attitude of juror—whether diet should be deserted

Held, on M's appeal against conviction for assaulting the police by presenting a shotgun at them, that the trial judge did not err in twice refusing to desert the trial *pro loco et tempore* after receiving from a sitting juror two letters requesting an expansion of the evidence, as the communications disclosed that the juror was perhaps over zealous and had an inquiring mind, not that he had a closed mind or an inability or unwillingness to obtemper the directions of the trial judge, and there had been no miscarriage of justice where the trial judge took appropriate steps, both following receipt of the letters and in his charge, to advise the jury as to how they should approach their task and to charge them that they had to decide the case on the evidence which had been led.

MILLER v. H.M. ADVOCATE, 1995 S.L.T. 347.

5739. Procedure—trial—seclusion of jury—arrangements for accommodation

[Criminal Procedure (Scotland) Act 1975 (c.21), s.153(3A).]

Held, on L's appeal against conviction for assault to injury on the grounds that a miscarriage of justice had occurred when the sheriff, having told the jury at 3.15 pm that they could return a verdict at any time, then proceeded to tell them three hours later that if they were still a long way from reaching a verdict then they would have to be put up in a hotel for the night and this would be "an awful hassle" both for them and for the court officials, the jury returning half an hour later with a majority guilty verdict, that the appeal would be allowed and a new prosecution authorised since no heed had been taken by the sheriff of the guidelines set out in *McKenzie v. H.M. Advocate* [1986] C.L.Y. 3837, 3882, and even if the sheriff did not so intend, his observations had the effect of indicating to the jury it was a matter of some urgency that they reach a verdict.

LOVE v. H.M. ADVOCATE, 1995 S.C.C.R. 501.

5740. Procedure—trust—judge's charge—misdirection

An accused person was charged on indictment with assault by, *inter alia*, striking the complainer on the head and body with a walking stick and machete, repeatedly striking him about the head and body with a piece of concrete, a stone, a wooden baton, a stick and other instruments to his severe injury, danger of life and permanent disfigurement. The accused pled self defence and argued that he had broken off once he thought that the danger had passed. There was evidence that the complainer sustained serious injuries in the course of the assault and that a spade and piece of slate could have inflicted some but not all of the injuries. There was also corroborative evidence that a machete was there although there was conflicting evidence as to how it was used and there was evidence that the accused had struck the complainer with a concrete slab. The jury found the accused guilty while acting under provocation, under deletion of the reference to the machete and piece of concrete. The accused appealed, contending that the sheriff had failed to direct the jury to consider whether each element of the assault constituted cruel excess and that they should consider what effect any deletions they made had upon the aggravations. It was also argued that the verdict was contrary to the evidence as there was no evidence to support the aggravations.

Held, that (1) it was unnecessary in this case to attempt to break down the accused's conduct into its different constituent parts and to determine whether each element on its own constituted an excessive response; (2) despite the deletions there was evidence that some of the serious injuries must have been caused by a sharp instrument and on that evidence it was open to the jury to hold that the complainer had sustained serious injuries at the accused's hands in the course of the assault described in those parts of the indictment which they affirmed; and appeal refused.

GINNITY v. H.M. ADVOCATE, 1995 S.L.T. 1080.

5741. Procedure—verdict—competency—deletions from libel. See FLYNN v. H.M. ADVOCATE, §5717.

5742. Procedure—verdict—competency—guilty of robbery under deletion of all reference to violent acts. See FLYNN v. H.M. ADVOCATE, §5736.

5743. Procedure—verdict—whether verdict perverse and contrary to evidence. See GINNITY v. H.M. ADVOCATE, §5740.

5744. Procedure—warrant—arrest of person abroad

B petitioned the *nobile officium* for suspension of a warrant for his arrest on two charges of fraud, on the grounds that its execution in England would require to be effected in reliance upon illegal actings which had resulted in B's presence there. B, a New Zealand citizen, averred that he had been arrested in South Africa in connection with English charges of deception, that arrangements had been made for him to be deported to New Zealand, but that, as a result of collusion with the Metropolitan Police, demonstrated by an internal Crown Prosecution Service memorandum, the South African authorities had put B on a flight which had stopped over at Heathrow, where he could be arrested without the need for extradition proceedings, and that, as a result of the collusion, and following a House of Lords appeal (*R. v. Horseferry Road Justices, ex p. Bennett* [1993] C.L.Y. 809), a divisional court had quashed his committal for trial in the Crown court. The Lord Advocate averred that B had been arrested in South Africa as an illegal immigrant, that he was originally to be flown to New Zealand via Taiwan, but B had destroyed his passport en route and had been sent back to South Africa on his arrival in Taiwan; that, after it had been decided to send B to London, it had been necessary for security reasons to inform the Metropolitan Police; that the Crown had intended to seek B's extradition from South Africa or from whichever country he was to be deported to; that the Lord Advocate had been advised of B's arrival in the U.K. by the Crown Prosecution Service; and that the Lord Advocate had had no direct contact with the South African authorities. B argued that the collusion between the English and South African authorities tainted the whole procedure; that B had been deprived of the safeguards of the extradition procedure; that following *ex p. Bennett*, the decision in *Sinclair v. H.M. Advocate* (1890) 17 R. 38 should be reviewed by a larger court; and that as there was a dispute as to fact evidence should be heard.

Held, petition refused. While the decision in *Sinclair*, that the Scottish courts could not inquire into a foreign government's actions which had resulted in the arrest and delivery of an accused, could be regarded as out of line with the reasoning in *ex p. Bennett*, that the maintenance of the rule of law ought to prevail over the public interest in prosecution, the House of Lords decision had proceeded on an assumption as to the occurrence of collusion, and the court was not bound by the subsequent divisional court decision that, on the evidence, there had been collusion. The Lord Advocate's own investigations had shown no such illegality, which was consistent with B having been sent first via Taiwan and only later via London, which was not extraordinary given the sanctions then operating against South Africa. B's only criticism of the legality of the South African authorities' actions, which was something into which the court could not inquire, was that he had been put on the plane in defiance of an order of the Supreme Court of South Africa, but this was not admitted by the Lord Advocate and it was not suggested he could not otherwise have been deported or that the English authorities were aware of the decision, and the memorandum relied on by B was written prior to the first flight and, read in context, merely reported on a decision of the South African police that the English authorities saw as being to their advantage. The Lord Advocate was therefore entitled to conclude that the South Africans had taken an independent decision as to the method of deportation and that there had been no illegality, and there was no basis for suspending the warrant, as it would be unreasonable to insist that the police refrain from arresting a person simply because he was in transit from another country from which he could be extradited.

BENNETT v. H.M. ADVOCATE, 1995 S.L.T. 510.

5745. Procedure—warrant—precognition on oath

[Criminal Justice (Scotland) Act 1980 (c.62), s.9.]

Held, where a person convicted of murder and rape applied to the Secretary of State to refer the case to the High Court in terms of s.263 of the Criminal Procedure (Scotland) Act 1975, that he was not an "accused" within the meaning of s.9 of the 1980 Act and accordingly that a warrant could not be granted under that provision to cite for precognition on oath an alleged witness.

GILMOUR, PETR., 1994 S.C.C.R. 872.

5746. Procedure—warrant—search—validity

[Misuse of Drugs Act 1971 (c.38). s.23(2) and (3).]

Held, on G's appeal against conviction for carrying an offensive weapon, that evidence that a knife was found on G during a search was admissible where the police were searching premises under a warrant obtained in terms of s.23 of the Misuse of Drugs Act 1971 and G knocked at the door and advised a plain clothes police officer that he wished to obtain cannabis resin: the police were entitled to conclude that G was associated with dealing in drugs or might be in possession of drugs, since he had admitted he was in some way connected with drugs, despite an argument for G that possession could not be inferred from his statement and that *Guthrie v. Hamilton* [1988] C.L.Y. 3985, paid insufficient regard to the requirement for reasonable grounds for suspicion.

GAVIN v. NORMAND, 1995 S.L.T. 741.

5747. Procedure—warrant to place accused on identification parade

M sought suspension of a warrant for him to be arrested and taken to a police station for an identification parade to be held. M was arrested in February 1994 in connection with an armed robbery in April 1993. The police were unable to hold a parade at that stage. M appeared on the petition warrant and was committed for further examination. The Crown did not oppose bail, an employee at the fiscal's office having misunderstood information from the police as to whether a parade had yet been held and the fiscal in charge of the case having been unavailable through illness. The sheriff considered that there had been a breakdown in communications and that the facts were comparable to *Lees v. Weston* [1989] C.L.Y. 4092. M argued that the trainee fiscal who appeared before the sheriff was at fault, having been told that a parade had been held, in not asking what the result was. The charge was a serious one and bail should not in any event have been unopposed.

Held, bill refused. Each case had to be looked at on its own facts and circumstances to see whether the test in *Morris v. MacNeill* [1991] C.L.Y. 4741, had been satisfied. Where the question was finely balanced as in this case, much depended on the view the sheriff took and he was entitled to hold that what happened here was an isolated occurrence which could readily be understood, and was unlikely to be repeated. The sheriff had properly balanced M's interests against the public interest in view of the limited invasion of freedom involved, having required the police to hold the parade on the day M would be arrested.

McMURTRIE v. ANNAN, 1995 S.L.T. 642.

5748. Procedure—warrant to take bodily samples—relevant considerations

A procurator fiscal applied to the sheriff to grant warrant to detain a person suspected of theft but who had been neither arrested nor charged and to convey him to a police station for a blood sample to be taken from him. The Crown averred that a motor car had been forced open and a bag and documents stolen from it. The bag was found nearby and had traces of blood on it. At approximately the same time as the theft the suspect had been seen in another car being driven at high speed in the street where the first car had been parked. The car carrying the suspect was found on the following day. A screwdriver bearing traces of blood was found inside the car. Four days later the suspect was noted to have a recent cut on one of his fingers. The sheriff, considering that the circumstances were special because of the nature of the crime, taken along with the fact that the Crown had undertaken to take no proceedings against the suspect if the comparison of blood did not implicate him, granted the warrant as craved because the taking of blood would not involve any great invasion of the person. The suspect sought suspension of the warrant.

Held, that (1) the Crown's undertaking either by itself or with other factors was not sufficient to constitute special circumstances for granting the warrant; (2) the sheriff failed to take account of the fact that the warrant also involved some degree of loss of liberty; (3) the sheriff had accordingly erred in the exercise of his discretion and it was for the High Court to consider *de novo* whether the warrant should be granted; (4) the circumstances were special because the crime was serious and the sample sought was necessary for a complete analysis and comparison of the bloodstrains, and since the taking of blood involved a fairly minor invasion of the person, the balance favoured granting the warrant provided that it was modified to exclude detention of the suspect; and bill refused. (*Morris v. MacNeill* [1991] C.L.Y. 4741, applied; *Hughes v. Normand* [1993] C.L.Y. 5045 and *Smith v. Cardle* [1993] C.L.Y. 5043, followed.) *Observed*, that the preferable view was that the liberty of the subject favoured leaving it to the individual, unless he had been arrested, to decide for himself whether or not it would be to his advantage to submit to such a procedure. (*Archibald v. Lees* [1994] C.L.Y. 5645, followed.)

WALKER v. LEES, 1995 S.L.T. 757.

5749. Procedure—warrant to take bodily samples

B, who was charged with his two co-accused of murder, sought suspension of a warrant which allowed the procurator fiscal to obtain a sample of his blood, on the grounds that there were no averments that he was injured or that any blood could have come from B either at the site of the murder or on the deceased and therefore that the petition was speculative and premature.

Held, bill refused. There was sufficient material to justify the sheriff in concluding that the warrant should be granted where a bloodstained jacket had been recovered from the bedroom of one of the co-accused, and blood samples which had already been taken from the deceased and the two co-accused revealed that that blood could not have come from any of them, but could have had a common origin with the bloodstains found at the locus of the murder, and that it was necessary in the interests of justice and for a complete analysis and comparison of bloodstains in this case, to ascertain whether any of the bloodstains could have come from B (*Hughes v. Normand* [1993] C.L.Y. 5044, followed).

BRODIE v. NORMAND, 1995 S.L.T. 739.

5750. Procedure—warrant to take bodily samples

M sought suspension of a warrant to remove him to a police office for the taking of a blood sample by the police casualty surgeon. The blood was wanted to compare with staining discovered in two vehicles, one of which M was alleged to have stolen and both of which featured in road traffic offences charged. All these charges were originally brought on complaint but were then incorporated in a petition which also alleged, *inter alia*, breach of the peace by threatening to kill A in one of the vehicles and forcing him to drive to a named location. A had since gone into hiding to avoid "repurcussions", and the Crown were in difficulty obtaining evidence on this charge. M argued that the offences for which the warrant was sought were not sufficiently serious to satisfy the test in *Morris v. MacNeill* [1991] C.L.Y. 4741.

Held, bill refused. The sheriff had applied the correct test, and while it was unlikely that the circumstances would ever be sufficiently special to justify such a warrant where the charge was to be brought summarily, the breach of the peace had first been charged on petition and was a serious one, and the circumstances were made special by the difficulty in obtaining evidence.

MELLORS v. NORMAND, 1995 S.C.C.R. 313.

5751. Procedure—warrant to take fingerprints—warrant sought after plea of not guilty tendered

W sought suspension of a sheriff's decision to grant a warrant allowing officers to obtain his fingerprints on the grounds that it was incompetent to grant the warrant since he had pled not guilty to a summary complaint of uttering, and since it would be contrary to principle that he be required to do anything which assisted the Crown in their case against him (*Smith v. Innes* [1984] C.L.Y. 3921.

Held, bill refused. The test under summary procedure should be the same as that under solemn procedure and accordingly, it was competent for the sheriff to grant a warrant to take W's fingerprints until the case came to trial, as long as W's interests had been balanced against the public interest in accordance with (*Lees v. Weston* [1989] C.L.Y. 4092, and *Frame v. Houston* [1992] C.L.Y. 4742 (*Smith, supra*, overruled).

WILLIAMSON v. FRASER, 1995 S.L.T. 777.

5752. Procedure—witness—precognition on oath. See GILMOUR, PETR., §5745.

Sentencing. See CRIMINAL SENTENCING.

CRIMINAL LAW

5753. Assault—indecent—medical practitioner—consent to examination

A medical practitioner went to trial on three charges of indecent assault involving different young women. Evidence was led that during the course of his medical examination the accused had "examined" the private parts of each complainer although each had attended with differing complaints unconnected with their genitalia. It was submitted for the accused that each complainer had presented herself at hospital for medical treatment and that nothing the accused did during the course of his medical examination went beyond what was necessary from a medical point of view and that he acted in a bona fide manner. It was also submitted that each complainer had consented to a medical examination and to what had occurred and therefore there had been no assault or, alternatively, that if consent to that part of the examination involving the complainers private parts had been obtained by fraud, then the charge should not have been one of indecent assault but one of fraud. The accused was found guilty of each charge and appealed to the High Court.

Held, that (1) any consent which had been given was consent for a proper medical examination of the particular part of the body which was concerned and there was no question of consent which went beyond that; (2) a question of fraud would have arisen only if consent had been given and the view was then taken that consent to examine the private parts had been obtained by fraud; and appeal refused.

HUSSAIN v. HOUSTON, 1995 S.L.T. 1060.

5754. Contempt of court—delay. See ROBB v. CALEDONIAN NEWSPAPERS, §5757.

5755. Contempt of court—lateness in attending court

An accused person was charged on summary complaint and was ordained to appear at an intermediate diet at 10 am. The diet was called at 10.50 am when the accused was not present. The accused was found in the court building at 11.10 am. When the case was recalled the accused explained that he had been delayed because he had been looking for a suitable jacket to wear. The accused had never been in court before and wished to be properly dressed. The sheriff, considering that the accused's lateness was wilful, found the accused in contempt of court and fined him. The accused sought suspension of the finding of contempt.

Held, that the sheriff had erred in respect that the lateness was not sufficient: what the sheriff should have asked himself was whether the accused was wilfully defying or intending disrespect to the court; and bill passed and finding suspended. (*Caldwell v. Normand* [1993] C.L.Y. 5064, applied.)

CAMERON v. ORR, 1995 S.L.T. 589.

5756. Contempt of court—newspaper articles—possible prejudice to accused

[Contempt of Court Act 1981 (c.49) ss.1 and 2.]

The Crown brought a complaint of contempt of court against C, the publishers respectively of newspapers E and R, and their editors and the reporters concerned, for contempt of court under ss.1 and 2 of the 1981 Act for publishing articles and a photograph regarding an untried prisoner, B, following his escape from custody. B had been detained until trial on various charges including assault and robbery, and was apprehended and returned to custody five days after his escape. B had previously been tried twice and ultimately acquitted in connection with a highly publicised murder. The article in E, which was headed "Danger Man on the run", contained B's photograph, and specified that B was awaiting trial for armed robbery and that the Scottish Prison Service had warned that B could present a danger to the public. The articles in R, which were headed "Alert as Killers Go on the Run", included B's photograph and described him as a killer, alleging that he had been found guilty of culpable homicide and jailed for 10 years, but did not refer to the charges outstanding against B or the fact that he was an untried prisoner. The Crown argued that in implying that B was dangerous, the article in E could have seriously impeded or prejudiced the minds of the jury regarding issues of fact which might be raised at trial, while the photograph of B could prejudice the witnesses' identification of B at trial. The article in R gave the impression that B had already been convicted and had escaped from custody while serving a prison sentence and as such could seriously impede or prejudice the minds of the jury. Sections 1 and 2 created strict liability for conduct which interfered with the course of justice, and therefore, intent was irrelevant. C submitted that as the risk of prejudice to B had to be substantial, the Crown had failed to satisfy the very high test for determining strict liability. Because of the delay between the appearance of the article and B's trial and because the article did not refer to any facts relating to the charges pending against B, there was no realistic possibility that a member of the jury would recall or be influenced by the article by the trial date. D submitted that in terms of the Act, the strict liability rule applied to a publication only if the proceedings in question were active at the time of publication, and since both its articles were written on the mistaken view that B was a convicted prisoner, there was nothing in either of its articles which indicated that proceedings were active against B, or that he was an untried prisoner. There was no substantial risk that any member of the jury at B's trial would link him with anything in the article, or that the proceedings would be otherwise prejudiced.

Held, petition granted against C and the editor of E. (1) There was nothing in the articles or the photograph published in R which indicated that B was, at the date of their publication, the subject of any active criminal proceedings within the meaning of s.2 of the Act, and therefore there was no risk that the proceedings which were then active against him would be seriously impeded or prejudiced. The strict liability rule did not impose a very high test since the public policy underlining the rule was deterrence and only remote or minimal risks would be excluded in determining whether a publication created a substantial risk of prejudice (*Att.-Gen. v. English* [1982] C.L.Y. 2436 and *H.M. Advocate v. News Group Newspapers* [1989] C.L.Y. 4117). (2) Although the article in E described B as an untried prisoner, because of the lack of detail in the article and the lapse of time between its publication and B's trial, the single, brief and unspecified reference to B's charge of armed robbery did not create any substantial risk that the minds of the jury would be prejudiced against B. However, as the publication of B's photograph 20 days after the date libelled in the charge might have affected the evidence of witnesses regarding the question of identification, there had been a contempt, though not by the reporter who was not responsible for publication of the photograph. (3) As respects penalty, it was accepted that the primary concern had been the public interest, that legal advice had been followed and that there had been no intention to break the rule, but no authority had been sought from the Lord Advocate and a substantial fine was inevitable. C and their editor were fined £2,500 and £250 respectively, to be paid within 14 days of the date of the opinion.

ADVOCATE, H.M. v. CALEDONIAN NEWSPAPERS, 1995 S.L.T. 926.

5757. Contempt of court—prejudicial publication—complaint by accused—whether consent of Lord Advocate required

R, arrested and charged in August 1993 with lewd, indecent and libidinous practices, petitioned the court to make a finding of contempt against a newspaper company (C) and its editor in respect of an allegedly prejudicial article published that month. The Crown took no action following an approach by R and the petition was not presented until March 1994. The Lord Advocate declined to concur in the application and adopted a neutral attitude. C argued, *inter alia*, that the petition was incompetent without such concurrence: the complaint was penal in character and in the nature of a prosecution, and it was the practice for the Lord Advocate to support any such averments.

Held, that the application was competent but should be dismissed on the ground of delay. (1) There was no requirement for Scotland in the Contempt of Court Act 1981 similar to s.7, which required the consent of the Attorney-General for proceedings in England, and the common law had never imposed such a requirement. If the matter also constituted a crime and was prosecuted as such, the court would not deal with it as contempt, but if it was dealt with as contempt it was under the authority of the court in exercise of its power to maintain its authority and secure the advancement of justice. It was an offence *sui generis* and not a crime. Petitions for breach of interdict were in a special category in requiring the Lord Advocate's concurrence (*Gribben v. Gribben* [1976] C.L.Y. 3341). (2) There was no fixed time limit for the bringing of proceedings such as the present. However the emphasis was on the summary nature of the proceedings, to enable the alleged contempt to be dealt with in the interests of the administration of justice as speedily and efficiently as possible. If the facts were not immediately known to the interested party a delay might be justifiable, but where there was an alleged breach of the strict liability rule in s.1 of the 1981 Act the publication should be drawn to the court's attention as soon as possible, both to prevent any further breach and in fairness to those responsible to enable them to investigate the circumstances fully. The court was not satisfied that there was a good reason for the delay in the present case, and since the Lord Advocate had not thought fit to intervene, there was no threat of further publication and C would be at a disadvantage in investigating after the delay, it would not be appropriate to take further action.

ROBB v. CALEDONIAN NEWSPAPERS, 1995 S.L.T. 631.

5758. Criminal Law (Consolidation) (Scotland) Act 1995 (c.39)

This Act seeks to consolidate several Scottish enactments relating to criminal law.

The Act received Royal Assent on November 8, 1995.

5759. Culpable homicide—supply of drugs

X was charged with supplying amphetamine, a controlled and potentially lethal drug to E, H, W and C to the danger of their health, safety and lives and to K, who died as a result of ingesting the drug, and with culpable homicide of K. Following the Crown case, X submitted in terms of s.140A of the Criminal Procedure (Scotland) Act 1975 that although he supplied the amphetamine to persons including K, and the purpose of the supply was abuse, he did not cause K's death in the sense necessary to establish culpable homicide because he did not instigate or encourage her to ingest the drug. As K had sought the supply of the drug and selected the dose she would take, the trial judge concluded that the chain of causation had been broken and acquitted X of that part of the charge. The Lord Advocate referred the case under s.263A(1) of the Criminal Procedure (Scotland) Act 1975, submitting that the trial judge erred in acquitting X as the actions of K neither broke nor interrupted the chain of causation (*Khaliq v. H.M. Advocate* [1984] C.L.Y. 3842; *Ulhaq v. H.M. Advocate* [1990] C.L.Y. 4968).

Held, that the trial judge erred in acquitting X. The principles in *Khaliq* and *Ulhaq* applied. In order to establish culpable homicide, it was not necessary to prove that K's death was the direct result of X's supply of the amphetamine. Nor was it necessary that the Crown averred that X acted recklessly as his conduct in supplying a controlled and potentially lethal drug in a lethal quantity to a number of persons, including K, knowing that their purpose was to ingest doses of the drug, was equivalent to culpable and reckless conduct. The causal link was not broken merely because a voluntary act on the part of K was required in order to produce the injurious consequences (*Khaliq*). The supply of the amphetamine was illegal and in the circumstances amounted to culpable and reckless conduct which caused not only a real risk of injury but death, and there was sufficient evidence to entitle the jury to convict X of culpable homicide. As X knew that the purchasers intended to abuse the drug, his supply was the equivalent of administration.

ADVOCATE'S (LORD) REFERENCE NO. 1 OF 1994, 1995 S.L.T. 248.

5760. Dangerous drugs—being concerned in supply. See ALLAN v. INGRAM, §5636.

5761. Dangerous drugs—being concerned in supply—art and part. See RODDEN v. H.M. ADVOCATE, §5723.

5762. Dangerous drugs—possession. See LOCKHART v. HARDIE, §5773.

5763. Dangerous drugs—possession—sufficiency of evidence. See DRYBURGH v. SCOTT, §5634; DONNELLY v. SCHRIKEL, §5635; BATH v. H.M. ADVOCATE, §5638.

5764. Dangerous drugs—possession with intent to supply. See PATERSON v. McGLENNAN, §5772; LOCKHART v. HARDIE, §5773.

5765. Embezzlement

Held, on G's appeal against conviction of embezzling £149·24 from his employer, F, that (1) where G, who was authorised to draw and sign cheques on behalf of F, had drawn a cheque on F's account in payment of his own domestic electricity bill and G had admitted this at a special meeting of the executive committee of F and stated that he was strapped for cash at the time, there was sufficient evidence for the sheriff to conclude that the cheque was drawn without the authority or consent of F, that if G had not been short of money he would not have drawn on this account and that G had therefore acted dishonestly; (2) the case did not fall because all of the evidence emanated from G as that argument confused the actings alleged to constitute the crime with the evidence required to prove that a crime had been committed: there was sufficient corroborated evidence to link G with the transaction both through his own admission and the evidence of T, an accounts assistant who identified G as the signatory and who was suspicious of the cheque, which led to the holding of the meeting and the discussion against the background that the money had not been refunded; and (3), contrary to an argument for G that he had not taken money but incorporeal property which was incapable of being embezzled, the transaction concerned money in a bank account which was capable of being embezzled and G's unauthorised actings fell clearly within the scope of embezzlement as described in Macdonald, *Criminal Law*, pp. 45–47.

GUILD v. LEES, 1995 S.L.T. 68.

5766. Fireraising—reckless fireraising

An accused person was tried on indictment with *inter alia* reckless fireraising by setting fire to papers in an office whereby the fire took effect on a desk and chair, destroying them and damaging the office. In charging the jury the sheriff directed that recklessness was conduct which fell far below the standard to be expected of a competent and careful citizen in the face of obvious and material dangers which were or should have been observed, appreciated and guarded against or in circumstances which showed a complete disregard for any potential danger which might result from the conduct. The sheriff also gave the jury an example of a man lighting his pipe and without thinking throwing the match over his shoulder. The match landed in a field and burned the growing crop there. The sheriff mistakenly told the jury that such conduct was held to be reckless. The accused was convicted and appealed on the ground of misdirection.

Held, that the example was not a good one and might itself have been misleading, but read as a whole, including the direction that recklessness involved a complete disregard of any potential danger which might result, the directions were adequate and appeal refused. (Dictum of Lord Justice-General Hope in *Carr v. H.M. Advocate* [1994] C.L.Y. 5673, applied.)

THOMSON v. H.M. ADVOCATE, 1995 S.L.T. 56.

5767. Fraud—false statement. See BUCHMANN v. NORMAND, §5792.

5768. High Court of Justiciary—practice note

This practice note sets out procedures which will apply to an appeal where the person was, on or after September 26, 1995, convicted of or, as the case may be, found to have committed the offence. The purpose of such procedures is to give effect to the introduction, on that date, of the statutory requirement of leave to appeal. This statutory requirement can be found in ss.230A, 442ZA and 453AA which have, from that date, been inserted in the Criminal Procedure (Scotland) Act 1975 by s.42 of the Criminal Justice (Scotland) Act 1995.

1. *Leave to appeal*

Any person wishing to appeal to the High Court against conviction and/or sentence under solemn or summary procedure should do so in accordance with current practice.

The appeal will be placed by the Clerk of Justiciary before a single judge of the High Court in chambers without the parties being present. The decision of the judge will be intimated by the Clerk of Justiciary to the appellant or to the solicitor who lodged the appeal in Justiciary Office on his behalf, and to the Crown Agent.

If the judge grants leave to appeal, the intimation of his decision will set out any comments which the judge has considered appropriate to make. The appellant or his solicitor need take no further action on receipt of the intimation, as the Clerk of Justiciary will assign the appeal to a court roll in accordance with current practice.

If leave to appeal is refused, the intimation will set out the reasons given by the judge for the refusal.

If the appellant accepts the refusal, he and his solicitor need take no further action.

If the appellant wishes to appeal against the refusal, he must apply to the High Court for leave to appeal *within 14 days of intimation* of the refusal of leave. Application must be made in a letter from the appellant or his solicitor addressed to the Deputy Principal Clerk of Justiciary, Parliament House, Edinburgh EH1 1RQ.

2. *Appeal after refusal of leave*

An appeal to the High Court after refusal of leave will be placed by the Clerk of Justiciary before the High Court in chambers without the parties being present. The decision of the High Court will be intimated by the Clerk of Justiciary to the appellant or to the solicitor who lodged the appeal in Justiciary Office on his behalf, and to the Crown Agent.

If the High Court grants leave to appeal, the intimation of its decision will set out any comments which the court has considered appropriate to make. The appellant or his solicitor need take no further action on receipt of the intimation, as the Clerk of Justiciary will assign the appeal to a court roll in accordance with current practice.

If leave to appeal is refused, the intimation will set out the reasons given by the court for the refusal.

5769. Misuse of drugs—being concerned in supply—art and part. See RODDEN v. H.M. ADVOCATE, §5723.

5770. Misuse of drugs—possession. See LOCKHART v. HARDIE, §5773.

5771. Misuse of drugs—possession—sufficiency of evidence. See BATH v. H.M. ADVOCATE, §5638.

5772. Misuse of drugs—possession with intent to supply

Hold, that two concurrent sentences of four months' detention were excessive for P, who had one minor non-analogous conviction, for selling a package containing herbal cannabis and for being in possession of £60 and six packets of cannabis ready for sale, since there had been an 18 month delay between the offence and the sentence, during which he had kept out of trouble, the social inquiry report indicated that P had recognised his stupidity, was no longer keeping unsuitable company and had the support of his family, and had been in employment since May 1993; and 240 hours' community service substituted.

PATERSON v. McGLENNAN, 1995 S.C.C.R. 42.

5773. Misuse of drugs—possession with intent to supply

[Misuse of Drugs Act 1971 (c.38), s.5(3).]

Held, on an unopposed Crown appeal, that the sheriff erred in acquitting H, who was found in possession of a controlled drug wrapped into recognisable deals, of possession of the drug with intent to supply on the basis that there could be no conviction under s.5(3) of the 1971 Act unless there was some present or immediate intent to supply another: intent to supply simply denoted supply taking place at some time in the future. *Observed*, that there was no ground for deleting a reference to one locus in the charge where H had been detained there and taken to the police station where a search revealed the drugs.

LOCKHART v. HARDIE, 1994 S.C.C.R. 722.

5774. Misuse of drugs—supply of cannabis. See ALLAN v. INGRAM, §5636.

5775. Misuse of drugs—supply of controlled drugs—sufficiency of evidence. See DRYBURGH v. SCOTT, §5634.

5776. Mobbing and rioting—common criminal purpose

Two accusers were charged on an indictment which libelled mobbing and rioting and then a number of specific charges to which the general charge related. At trial both accused were found guilty of a majority of the specific charges and of the general charge, but under deletion of the words "acting of common purpose". The Secretary of State referred both cases to the High Court under s.263(1) of the Criminal Procedure (Scotland) Act 1975, having concluded that a question of law had been raised which merited full legal argument, namely, whether a person charged only with mobbing and rioting could still be convicted if the jury held that the mob had no common purpose. The two accused also argued that there had been insufficient evidence, in the absence of proof of a common purpose, to convict them of the specific charges as individuals, and that, in any event, the jury had convicted them as members of a mob.

Held, that (1) the words "acting of common purpose" were an essential part of the general charge so that in their absence the convictions on that general charge could not be allowed to stand, (2) the jury's verdict on the individual crimes had not been invalidated because the charges were so structured as to admit the alternative verdicts that they were committed by the accused either as part of the mob or as individual participants, and (3) there had been sufficient evidence of direct participation by the accused to enable the jury to convict them of the specific crimes charged with the exception only of two charges against one of the accused.

KILPATRICK v. H.M. ADVOCATE, 1992 J.C. 120.

5777. Murder—self defence—accused starting trouble—whether plea barred

B appealed against conviction of murdering H on the ground that the trial judge had misdirected the jury in stating that it was a condition of the availability of the defence of self defence that the accused must not have started the trouble. B had initially been acting in an aggressive manner in a public house, and then in a disco, where he had been in an altercation with H and H's cousin (S). B had been ejected from the disco; once outside he had assaulted S and the two had fought. B had then crossed the street, S had turned again towards him and H had apparently approached B to lead S out of the way. B had then wrenched a metal bar off the side of the hamburger stall and struck H on the head with it. B's evidence was that he thought S and H were chasing him and he was scared. When he grabbed the bar S was facing him and H had his back to him; he had hit H because he "could not stop swinging the bar". The trial judge relied for his direction on Macdonald, *Criminal Law* (5th ed.), p. 106 (which followed Hume, i, 232), while recognising that there might be circumstances where it was not appropriate.

Held, appeal refused. It was clear from more recent authority (*H.M. Advocate v. Kizileviczius*, 1938 S.L.T. 245; *H.M. Advocate v. Robertson and Donoghue*, October 17, 1945, unreported; *Boyle v. H.M. Advocate* [1993] C.L.Y. 5078) that the propositions in Hume and Macdonald were stated too broadly. Where the accused had started the trouble, by provoking it or entering willingly into it, whether the defence was available depended on whether the retaliation was such that the accused was entitled then to defend himself; this depended in turn on whether the violence offered by the victim was so out of proportion to the accused's own actings as to give rise to reasonable apprehension of immediate danger from which he had no other means of escape, and whether the violence which he then used was no more than necessary to protect himself. In any event the proposition was too broadly stated for the circumstances of the present case and constituted a misdirection. However, there was no basis in the evidence led for the judge to hold that B had the apprehension necessary to establish that he was acting in self defence, and the judge could reasonably have removed the issue from the judge. There had been no miscarriage of justice.

BURNS v. H.M. ADVOCATE, 1995 S.L.T. 1090.

5778. Murder—self defence—reasonable apprehension of danger. See BURNS v. H.M. ADVOCATE, §5777.

5779. Offensive weapons—carrying knives. See STEWART v. FRIEL, §5789.

5780. Offensive weapons—reasonable excuse. See McKEE v. MacDONALD, §5781.

5781. Offensive weapons—whether offensive *per se*

[Prevention of Crime Act 1953 (c.14), s.1(4).]

Held, on M's appeal against conviction for possession of an offensive weapon, a truncheon, that the appeal would be allowed since, though it was recognised that a police truncheon was an offensive weapon *per se* (*Houghton v. Chief Constable of Greater Manchester* [1987] C.L.Y. 811) the present object, which was in general the same shape as an old fashioned police baton, was extremely light in weight, bore the legend "View sun from Spain", had a coloured cord through the handle, was not made of a solid piece of material which could cause injury if used and appeared to be in the form of a souvenir. *Doubted*, whether, had the object been considered an offensive weapon *per se*, M's claim that he had received the object from a friend returning from holiday and had put it in his car and forgotten about it could have been sufficient to constitute reasonable excuse.

McKEE v. MacDONALD, 1995 S.C.C.R. 513.

5782. Perverting the course of justice—attempt

An accused person was charged on indictment with attempting to pervert the course of justice by intimidating Crown witnesses from giving true evidence against his friend. The accused was a defence witness at a trial but entered the prosecution witness room, sat down where everyone could see him and looked at them. He did not say anything but the witnesses recognised him and were frightened. The sheriff directed the jury that it was not sufficient that the accused's presence induced fear in the witnesses and that the accused had to have acted deliberately for the purpose of intimidating the witnesses. The accused was convicted and appealed on the ground, *inter alia*, of misdirection in that the sheriff had confused the jury by giving examples of someone's behaviour being affected by the presence of another.

Held, that the jury could have been left in no doubt that mere presence was not sufficient to make the accused a participant in the crime and that they could not convict unless they were satisfied that he had deliberately behaved in a way designed to intimidate the witnesses and so pervert the course of justice; and appeal refused.

CARNEY v. H.M. ADVOCATE, 1995 S.L.T. 1208.

5783. Perverting the course of justice—attempt

J appealed against the sheriff's decision to repel a plea to the relevancy of a complaint which libelled that a complaint having been served on him with a charge of driving without insurance, he submitted a reply form in which he said that he knew nothing about the offence, with intent to induce the fiscal to discontinue the proceedings and did attempt to pervert the course of justice. J argued that he had in effect done no more than state that he was not guilty.

Held, appeal refused. While some latitude had to be given to people in completing the form without legal advice, it was untenable to assert that what was libelled could not amount to an attempt to pervert the course of justice. It all depended on J's intention, which had to be determined from what precisely was said and what implication the prosecutor was entitled to take in the circumstances.

JOHNSTONE v. LEES, 1995 S.L.T. 1174.

Procedure. See CRIMINAL EVIDENCE AND PROCEDURE.

5784. Proceeds of Crime (Scotland) Act 1995 (c.43)

This Act allows courts to confiscate the proceeds of indictable offences (except in the case of drug trafficking and certain terrorist offences) and the proceeds of certain summary offences.

The Act received Royal Assent on November 8, 1995.

5785. Rape—complainer intoxicated. See W. v. H.M. ADVOCATE, §5727.

5786. Rape—offender under 16. See W. v. H.M. ADVOCATE, §5727.

Road traffic. See ROAD TRAFFIC.

Sentence. See CRIMINAL SENTENCING.

5787. Sexual offences—lewd, indecent and libidinous conduct—scope of crime—complainers above age of puberty. See BATTY v. H.M. ADVOCATE, §5788.

5788. Shameless indecency—shamelessness—relationship of house parent to pupil

B appealed against conviction of five charges of lewd, indecent and libidinous conduct towards girls, aged over 12 but under 16, at a boarding school at which he was a house parent. B argued that the sheriff had misdirected the jury as to what was required for proof of such charges at common law: the crime could only be committed against persons under the age of puberty, as was confirmed by the passing of s.5 of the Sexual Offences (Scotland) Act 1976, and while there was sufficient evidence of acts amounting to shameless indecency, the sheriff had given insufficient directions on the question of shamelessness in that the fact of the relationship of house parent to pupil was not of itself enough to enable that quality to be inferred, the proper question being whether the relationship was of such a kind that B must have known that it would be shameless for him to commit acts of indecency with the complainers.

Held, appeal refused. The age of the complainer was not a critical factor so long as the conduct fell within the scope of shameless indecency. The statement in Macdonald, that all shamelessly indecent conduct was criminal, had been criticised as too broadly stated, but had been approved in *McLaughlan v. Boyd*, 1938 J.C. 19, and in *Watt v. Annan* [1978] C.L.Y. 3235; the question in each case was whether the requirement of shamelessness had been demonstrated. Where the complainer was at or above puberty, something more than the nature of the conduct and the age of the child was needed, but each case would depend on its own facts. In the present case the relationship between B and the pupils, one of trust with them under his care and authority, was such that indecent conduct by him towards them could undoubtedly be held to be shameless. The sheriff's directions, that the jury should decide whether the relationship existed at the relevant time, and whether the conduct described was deliberate and not accidental, and if so that they were entitled to find B guilty, were appropriate to the facts. *Opinion*, that while it was not necessary to express a firm view whether the common law crime of lewd, indecent and libidinous conduct was confined to cases where the complainer was under the age of puberty, the balance of authority was that it was not. The introduction of the statutory offence was not necessarily inconsistent with that.

BATTY v. H.M. ADVOCATE, 1995 S.L.T. 1047.

5789. Statutory offence—carrying knives—"folding pocket knife"

[Carrying of Knives etc. (Scotland) Act 1993 (c.13), s.1(3).]

S appealed against the sheriff's repelling of S's submission of no case to answer an offence under s.1 of the 1993 Act. S had been found with a lockable knife of which the sheriff was satisfied that the blade was less than three inches long. S argued there had been no evidence that the knife was not exempt as a "folding pocket knife" within s.1(3). The Crown argued it was clear the knife was not a penknife in the ordinary sense and that S had failed to discharge the onus of proof that the knife fell into the exception. The sheriff considered that arguments on onus of proof were misconceived: it was for the court to decide what description to apply to the knife in light of the evidence. On appeal S argued that "folding pocket knife" should be given its ordinary meaning and that all the necessary elements were present. Although *Harris v. D.P.P.* [1993] C.L.Y. 970 had decided that a lockable knife was not a folding pocket knife, the case should be held as wrongly decided. A knife was not dangerous just because it could be locked in the open position.

Held, appeal refused. (1) The sheriff's approach on onus was correct. (2) A knife with a blade fixable in an open position by a locking device was not a "folding pocket knife" within s.1(3). In view of the decision in *Harris* (which was applied), concerning a similar provision, if a lock knife was to have been included in the exception it would have been specifically stated.

STEWART v. FRIEL, 1995 S.C.C.R. 492.

5790. Statutory offence—child neglect—"likely to cause unnecessary suffering"—abandonment

[Children and Young Persons (Scotland) Act 1937 (c.37), s.12(1).]

M, who was separated from his wife and had sole custody of their five children, appealed against conviction of wilfully abandoning four of his children, in contravention of s.12(1) of the 1937 Act. The evidence revealed that around 11.30 am, M left the four children aged 12, 11, nine and six at a busy road close to their home in Culloden with instructions that they should go to their grandmother's house (15–20 minutes' walk away) or to school while he went to Inverness with the eldest child, O. After M and O left, the children decided not to go to their grandmother's house and two of them went to school while the other two stayed at home. They had not been fed and there was no food for them in the house. M was found by the police, drunk at a pub in Inverness around 7 pm. M accepted that there was potential for unnecessary suffering or distress but argued that the sheriff had erred in concluding that he had wilfully abandoned the children, as he had taken steps to ensure that they went somewhere safe and he had assumed that they would do as they were told.

Held, appeal refused. In view of the ages of the children, the length of time they were left alone, the place where M was found and the fact that no arrangements had been made to ensure that the children were properly cared for, the sheriff was entitled to conclude on the whole circumstances that M had acted without regard for their wellbeing and with no real concern for their welfare, having left them to their own devices for a prolonged and indeterminate period.

Held, further, that 100 hours' community service was not excessive for what was a serious offence as it was necessary to bring home to M the gravity of what he had done, although M had an insignificant record, had since co-operated with the social work department and his relationship with his children had improved.

M. v. ORR, 1995 S.L.T. 26.

5791. Statutory offence—child neglect—"likely to cause unnecessary suffering"—whether speculative events relevant

Section 12(1) of the Children and Young Persons (Scotland) Act 1937 provides inter alia that any person aged 16 years or over who has custody, charge or care of any child under 16 years of age and wilfully neglects that child in a manner likely to cause him unnecessary suffering or injury to health, shall be guilty of an offence. An accused person, the father of a 20 month old child, was charged on summary complaint with wilful neglect of his son contrary to s.12(1) of the 1937 Act. The accused had left his son unattended in a locked motor car in the street. The child was seen by a traffic warden approximately 45 minutes before the accused returned to the car during which time the child showed no sign of distress and was unharmed. The sheriff convicted the accused on the ground that during the period the child had been exposed to the risk of sudden illness, a break in to the car or its theft, a traffic accident or kidnapping and that the child had accordingly been neglected in a manner likely to cause him unneccesary suffering or injury to his health. The accused appealed.

Held, that the risks referred to by the sheriff were speculative and were not related to any particular time when the child was left unattended and accordingly the sheriff misdirected himself by taking them into account and was not entitled to convict the accused; and appeal allowed and conviction quashed. (*H v. Lees; D v. Orr,* applied.) [1993] C.L.Y. 5089.

Observed, that where a child was likely to become distressed by being left alone, that was a circumstance which might cause the child unnecessary suffering and the longer the period, the greater the distress and possible injury to health.

M. v. NORMAND, 1995 S.L.T. 1284.

5792. Statutory offence—recklessly making false statement

[Civic Government (Scotland) Act 1982 (c.45), s.7(4).]

Held, on B's appeal against conviction for breach of s.7(4) of the 1982 Act in respect of his application for a private hire car driver's licence, that the justice did not err in convicting B where the application form specified that every question should be answered, and although B had previous convictions, he left paragraph 11 (which requested the details of any convictions) blank, and there was sufficient evidence that B had recklessly made a false statement to the effect that he had no previous convictions.

BUCHMANN v. NORMAND, 1994 S.C.C.R. 929.

5793. Statutory offence—school attendance—failure to attend. See ROSS v. SIMPSON, §5898.

5794. Statutory offence—wages—failure to pay prescribed minimum. See TEVIOT SCIENTIFIC PUBLICATIONS v. McLEOD, §5468.

5795. Theft—possession of tools with intent to commit

[Civic Government (Scotland) Act 1982 (c.45), s.58(1).]

P appealed against conviction of possessing tools from which it might reasonably be inferred that he intended to commit a theft and from which he was unable to demonstrate satisfactorily that his possession of the tools was not for the purposes of committing theft, contrary to s.58(1) of the 1982 Act. The police had followed P after observing him around midnight carrying a holdall with a suspicious implement protruding from it and which appeared from its weight to contain tools. They lost sight of P temporarily, but observed him in another street without the holdall about 12.45 a.m. and thereafter detained him under s.2 of the Criminal Justice (Scotland) Act 1980. P was interviewed about his possession of the tools around 3.45 am and denied all knowledge of them. The tools were later found a quarter mile from the locus where the police had lost sight of P. P argued that the police were required to ask about the tools when they first observed him so that he had an opportunity to explain his possession of them (*Mathieson v. Crowe* [1994] C.L.Y. 5671), and since the inquiries were not made until after he was detained, they came too late and there was insufficient evidence for a conviction.

Held, appeal refused. Although the time as at which it had to be shown that P's possession of the tools was not for the purpose of committing theft was the time when P was seen in possession of them, the explanation could be required of him at any time thereafter before he was charged. *Mathieson, supra*, could be distinguished as the police there had taken no steps to raise the issue until after the appellant was charged.

PHILLIPS v. MacLEOD, 1995 S.C.C.R. 319.

Wireless telegraphy. See TELECOMMUNICATIONS.

CRIMINAL SENTENCING

5796. Appeal—unduly lenient sentence. See ADVOCATE, H.M. v. McALLISTER, §5819; ADVOCATE, H.M. v. MAY, §5822.

5797. Appeal—unduly lenient sentence—whether longer custodial sentence should be imposed after sentence served

Section 228A of the Criminal Procedure (Scotland) Act 1975 provides that where a person has been convicted on indictment the Lord Advocate may appeal against, *inter alia*, the sentence if it appears to the Lord Advocate that the sentence is unduly lenient. Section 254(3) provides that the High Court may quash the sentence and impose a more or less severe sentence in substitution therefor. An accused person pled guilty to assault to severe injury and permanent disfigurement. He had punched the complainer who he mistakenly thought was making fun of him and then struck him on the face with a bottle which broke. They both fell to the ground and the accused stabbed the complainer on the stomach with the bottle. The accused was sentenced to 60 days' imprisonment. The sheriff recognised that a sentence of not less than six months' imprisonment would be appropriate, but considered that a shorter period could be imposed because of the accused's personal circumstances and that a longer period would not perform any more corrective function. The Crown appealed against the sentence as being unduly lenient because it did not adequately reflect the gravity of the offence.

Held, that (1) the sentence was unduly lenient as it fell well below the range of sentences normally regarded as appropriate for an offence of its kind; but

(2) the public interest did not require that the accused be returned to prison to serve a longer sentence which would be measured only in months and not years; and sentence affirmed and appeal refused. (*H.M. Advocate v. McPhee* [1994] C.L.Y. 5675, commented on.)
ADVOCATE, H.M. v. BELL, 1995 S.L.T. 350.

5798. Assault—indecent. See TURNER v. SCOTT, §5618.

5799. Assault—on police

Held, where F received consecutive sentences of 18 months' detention for five charges of housebreaking, three months for reset, 12 months for dangerous driving, 15 months for assaulting a police officer by biting him, three months for failing to supply a breath sample and three months for a bail offence (4½ years in total), the 12 and 15 month sentences were not excessive since F's driving while being pursued by a police car had been thoroughly appalling, F *inter alia* crashing the car into another car while a police officer was still hanging through the passenger door, and F had twice bitten an officer in the course of a violent struggle, later commenting that he should have run them down; nor should any of the sentences be made concurrent since, even though several arose out of the same incident, they were entirely separate offences and would be treated as such.
FERGUSON v. H.M. ADVOCATE, 1995 S.C.C.R. 241.

5800. Assault—severe injury—player in rugby match

Held, that 60 days' imprisonment was not excessive where H, who had two convictions for breach of the peace but a favourable social inquiry report and was in employment, in the course of a rugby match, head butted an opponent (X), causing a fractured nose, after an incident between X and H's team mate, since H's offence was removed from the original trouble and the sheriff was entitled to consider this a serious matter.
HENDERSON v. CARMICHAEL, 1995 S.C.C.R. 126.

5801. Assault—severe injury—unduly lenient sentence. See ADVOCATE, H.M. v. BELL, §5797.

5802. Attempting to pervert the course of justice—false accusation

Held, that 60 days' imprisonment was not excessive where L, a first offender, aged 18 at the time with two young children and who had already served seven days, falsely represented to the police that her husband had assaulted her by presenting a gun at her since the false accusation had persisted for almost six months, L's husband, from whom she was now divorced, had spent a longer time in prison than that merited by the minor assault to which he pleaded (and for which he was subsequently admonished), and L had wasted the time of police, witnesses and jurors.
LEIPER v. McGLENNAN, 1995 S.C.C.R. 465.

5803. Backdating

Held, that sentences imposed on M which had been ordered to run from the date on which s.102 letters were submitted, the letters having been delayed because M's advisers had sought to have the charges reduced to summary, should be backdated a further seven weeks to the date on which M made it known that he intended to plead guilty to the charges.
MURPHY v. H.M. ADVOCATE, 1994 S.C.C.R. 767.

5804. Backdating—relevant considerations. See YOUNG v. H.M. ADVOCATE, §5620.

5805. Breach of bail—failure by accused to appear during jury trial

Held, that a sentence of 18 months to run consecutively with a sentence of two years' imprisonment on drugs charges was not excessive for breach of bail when the accused had failed to appear during his jury trial; and that he had been the author of his own misfortune in failing to report to the police the threats which, it was alleged, had caused him to breach bail.

LOGAN v. H.M. ADVOCATE, 1994 S.C.C.R. 884.

5806. Breach of the peace—absolute discharge

Held, where K, a first offender aged 42, was fined £350 for brandishing a knife in front of boys who had been harassing him for some time by kicking footballs against his garage door and tramping through his garden, that both the conviction and sentence would be set aside and an order made to discharge K absolutely (K being given leave to appeal against conviction though he had previously pleaded guilty), since this was a highly unusual situation and not enough weight had been attached to the fact that K was of good character and a conviction might have unfortunate repercussions on his career as a registered nurse.

KHEDA v. LEES, 1994 S.C.C.R. 63.

5807. Child—detention without limit of time—charges of theft by housebreaking—whether appropriate—whether excessive

[Criminal Procedure (Scotland) Act 1975 (c.21), s.206; Prisoners and Criminal Proceedings (Scotland) Act 1993 (c.9), ss.2 and 7.]

Held, where F, aged 14, who pled guilty along with co-accused (X) to nine charges by theft by housebreaking, was detained without limit of time under s.206 of the 1975 Act, X's case being remitted to the reporter for disposal by the children's hearing system, that the sentence imposed on F, who was the ringleader and planner of the offences and who had a difficult family history and had in the past shown contempt for the authorities, was excessive since, although the sheriff had decided that an indeterminate sentence would be more appropriate in that it would allow the authorities to determine in accordance with F's progress the necessary and reasonable time which F should spend in residential training, he had failed to follow the procedures set out in s.2 of the 1993 Act since he did not specify a part of the sentence which F had to spend in custody before he might be released on licence, nor did he give reasons for his decision not to make such a specification, nor did he recognise that s.7 of the 1993 Act allowed for a child detained for a fixed period under s.206 to be released on licence by the Secretary of State on the recommendation of the Parole Board; and, where F could remain in his current place of detention for another two years, and in the light of the whole background circumstances, a fixed period of two years' detention substituted, subject to s.7(2) of the 1993 Act.

F. v. H.M. ADVOCATE, 1995 S.L.T. 767.

5808. Consecutive sentences—offences committed on one occasion. See FERGUSON v. H.M. ADVOCATE, §5799; McEWAN v. H.M. ADVOCATE, §6279.

5809. Consecutive sentences—whether appropriate. See STEVEN v. LEES, §6280.

5810. Contempt of court—exemplary sentence

Held, that three months' imprisonment imposed on each of G and R, nephew and uncle, the accused and complainer in a trial, was not excessive where both men committed a contempt of court by appearing for trial under the influence of drink having spent the previous evening and the morning of the trial drinking heavily, despite the fact that both admitted and apologised

for the offence, since appearing drunk in court was not a new problem for this area and the sentences imposed, in addition to punishing G and R, were intended to act as a deterrent to others.
GILLIES v. McCLORY, 1994 S.C.C.R. 886.

5811. Custodial sentence—relevance of accused being on remand on another charge

Held, where R, whose record included convictions for theft and fraud, received five months' imprisonment, a first custodial sentence, for obtaining by fraud board and lodgings valued at £155, with one month consecutive for a bail offence, that the magistrate had erred by considering that since R was presently on remand and would be for the next two months, the equivalent of a four-month sentence with remission, it was necessary to impose a longer sentence to make the penalty effective; and three months on the first charge substituted.
ROSS v. NORMAND, 1994 S.C.C.R. 798.

5812. Dangerous drugs—possession with intent to supply. See CLARK v. H.M. ADVOCATE, §5823.

5813. Deferred sentence. See BURNS v. LEES, §5685.

5814. Fine—competency—fine in addition to imprisonment—common law offence

Held, that the imposition of a £500 fine at £5 per week and prison sentence of 21 days (backdated 21 days) for C for the same common law charge (shoplifting) was incompetent and since the period in prison had been served, the fine would be quashed (*McGunnigal v. Copeland* [1972] C.L.Y. 3678, followed, but *observed*, that it was difficult to understand what the reasons for the decision were).
COMPTON v. O'BRIEN, 1994 S.C.C.R. 657.

5815. Fine—default—imprisonment—accused subject to hospital order

Held, on M seeking suspension of an order for imprisonment for non-payment of a fine for £100 imposed for vandalism, where M, who was wholly incapable of managing his own affairs, had been made the subject of a hospital order some two months after the imposition of the fine and claimed that his regime of treatment would be damaged were he to be removed from hospital and put into prison, that the bill would be passed and the case remitted to the district court so that a supervisor could be appointed in accordance with s.400(1) of the Criminal Procedure (Scotland) Act 1975 to assist and advise M, whose state benefits had been reduced to £10 per week while he was in hospital, regarding repayment of the fine.
MUIRHEAD v. NORMAND, 1995 S.C.C.R. 632.

5816. Fine—instalments. See TONNER v. HAMILTON, §6303.

5817. Fine—unpaid fixed penalties totalling £1,800 registered for enforcement as fines on 26 different dates—45 days' imprisonment in default—competency

[Road Traffic Offenders Act 1988 (c.53), ss.55(3) and 71(7); Criminal Procedure (Scotland) Act 1975 (c.21), s.407(1)(b) and (1B).]

Section 55(3) of the Road Traffic Offenders Act 1988 provides that a fixed penalty which has not been paid can be registered for enforcement as a fine against the defaulter and s.71(7) provides that the registration of the sum shall have effect as if the sum were a fine imposed by the court on conviction of the defaulter on the date of registration. Section 407(1)(b) of the Criminal Procedure (Scotland) Act 1975 provides that where a person fails to pay a fine by a fixed date the court may impose a period of imprisonment for such failure, and subs. (1B) provides that when an offender is fined on the same day before the same court for offences charged in the same complaint or in separate complaints, the amount of the fine shall be taken to be the total of the fines imposed. An accused person was sentenced in the district court to 45 days' imprisonment for default in paying a total amount of £1,800 of fixed penalties which had been imposed under Pt. III of the Road Traffic Offenders Act 1988. Fixed penalties had been registered for enforcement against him on 26 separate dates which sums on 25 occasions would have attracted seven days' imprisonment each and on the other occasion 14 days' imprisonment. The accused sought suspension of the sentence, contending that as the largest number of fixed penalties registered on one day was seven, totalling £250, the maximum sentence available was 14 days' imprisonment.

Held, that (1) the justice had erred in basing the sentence on the total amount which was unpaid and should have applied s.407(1B) and considered whether he should impose consecutive sentences in respect of each of the days on which the fixed penalties were registered for enforcement, up to the maximum sentence of 60 days' imprisonment competent in the district court; (2) the appropriate course was to quash the sentence and remit to the justice to consider again the appropriate sentence to be imposed; and bill *passed*, sentence quashed and case remitted to the justice. (*Russell v. MacPhail* [1990] C.L.Y. 5025, considered.)

SHAW v. VALENTINE, 1995 S.L.T. 1345.

5818. Forfeiture—drink driving—car. See CARRON v. RUSSELL, §6292.

5819. Fraud—elderly persons—unduly lenient sentence

[Criminal Procedure (Scotland) Act 1975 (c.21), s.228A.]

Held, where the Crown appealed against a sentence of 240 hours' community service imposed on M for fraud and a bail offence on the ground that the sentence was unduly lenient and outside the range of appropriate sentences in view of the fact that it was M's fourth conviction for fraud since 1990, the amount involved was some £2,000 and the offence had involved an 87 year old woman who lived alone, that the sentence could not be so described since the offence had occurred in October 1993, M had since repaid the sum defrauded, he had given up his itinerant lifestyle and now had a job, a custodial sentence would have adverse effects on his wife and two children, the social inquiry report suggested that M had departed from his pattern of offending and applied his mind to changing his way of life, and M had been warned of the serious consequences should he breach the present order.

ADVOCATE, H.M. v. McALLISTER, 1995 S.C.C.R. 545.

5820. Imprisonment—competency of fine in addition—common law offence. See COMPTON v. O'BRIEN, §5814.

5821. Increase of sentence—Crown appeal. See ADVOCATE, H.M. v. BELL, §5797; ADVOCATE, H.M. v. McALLISTER, §5819; ADVOCATE, H.M. v. MAY, §5822.

5822. Lewd, libidinous and indecent practices—unduly lenient sentence

An accused person was found guilty after trial on eight charges of lewd, libidinous and indecent behaviour towards boys aged between eight and 11 years. The behaviour involved touching or fondling the boys' private parts on numerous occasions between August 1989 and December 1992 in the changing rooms of a boys' club of which the accused was leader, and in his home. The accused, who was aged 47, had no previous convictions and was in ill health, was sentenced to nine months' imprisonment. The Lord Advocate appealed against the sentence, arguing that it did not reflect the gravity of the offences and that the only appropriate sentence was between 18 months and three years. The Crown also invited the High Court to provide guidance on the appropriate level of sentence for a crime of this nature.

Held, that (1) the sheriff was exercising a discretion and had had regard to all relevant considerations, and that although the sentence was lenient it was not unduly lenient; (2) it was inappropriate in a case of this kind for the court to give guidance as to the appropriate level of sentence as circumstances varied infinitely; and appeal refused.

ADVOCATE, H.M. v. MAY, 1995 S.L.T. 753.

5823. Misuse of drugs—possession with intent to supply

Held, that four years' imprisonment for two charges of possession of class A and B drugs with intent to supply was not excessive for C, a somewhat weak person who claimed to have received drugs for his own use in return for holding the drugs for a third party, since C's refusal to name the person(s) for whom he was holding the drugs deprived his explanation of any real mitigatory significance. *Isdale v. Scott* [1991] C.L.Y. 4842, could be distinguished as the judge had not followed the approach criticised there.

CLARK v. H.M. ADVOCATE, 1995 S.C.C.R. 521.

5824. Misuse of drugs—possession with intent to supply—amphetamines

Held, that one year's imprisonment *in cumulo*, a first custodial sentence, was not excessive in view of the quantity involved where C, who had several minor convictions, was in possession of amphetamine with intent to supply it and concerned in its supply though it was accepted that C, who had since given up drugs and had a favourable social inquiry report, stable background and good work record, and four friends had clubbed together to buy the drug more cheaply in bulk, the drugs were for their own use and there was no intention to sell them for profit.

CARLIN v. H.M. ADVOCATE, 1994 S.C.C.R. 763.

5825. Murder—attempted murder—art and part

Held, that 15 years' imprisonment for assault and serious assault to severe injury, permanent impairment and danger to life amounting to an attempted murder, was not excessive where M and his co-accused, H, assaulted B by striking him in the face with a knife or similar instrument, and later seriously assaulted him, which ended with B being shot by H, and the trial judge did not err in failing to distinguish between M, who was treated as a first offender, and H in view of the whole course of events, although M was found guilty art and part on the attempted murder charge. *Observed*, that in cases where more than one accused appealed against either conviction or sentence, the trial judge should prepare self contained reports for each appellant, without reference to other reports, lest points relevant to an appeal be not observed by an appellant's advisers, either then or in subsequent proceedings.

McLAREN v. H.M. ADVOCATE, 1994 S.C.C.R. 855.

5826. Murder—recommendation as to minimum period. See MURPHY v. H.M. ADVOCATE, §5625.

5827. Obtaining credit without intimating status as undischarged bankrupt. See DREW v. H.M. ADVOCATE, §5730.

5828. Obtaining goods without paying and intending not to pay. See DREW v. H.M. ADVOCATE, §5730.

5829. Procedure—adjournment—period in excess of four weeks—competency—reason not minuted or expressed in court

[Criminal Procedure (Scotland) Act 1975 (c.21), s.380(1)(b).]

Section 380(1) of the Criminal Procedure (Scotland) Act 1975, as amended by the Prisoners and Criminal Proceedings (Scotland) Act 1993, provides that a summary court shall have power at any time before sentence to adjourn a case "providing that a court shall not for the purpose aforesaid adjourn the hearing of the case for any single period exceeding ... (b) where [the accused] is remanded on bail or is ordained to appear, eight weeks but only on cause shown and otherwise four weeks". An accused person was found guilty after trial of, *inter alia*, a contravention of s.78(1) of the Criminal Justice (Scotland) Act 1980. The justice wished to know the value of the damaged property but because the accused's solicitor objected to the witnesses then present being asked, the justice adjourned the case for a period in excess of four weeks, until the date when he was next due to sit in that court. The adjournment was recorded in the minutes of proceedings as being "for the damage to be assessed". The justice did not state in court that the adjournment was for more than four weeks because he wished to take the case and that reason was not minuted. The accused was sentenced and thereafter sought suspension on the ground that the adjournment was incompetent.

Held, that (1) there was no statutory requirement necessitating minuting the reason which the justice had for the adjournment beyond four weeks; (2) it was appropriate that, since there required to be an adjournment to allow the damage to be assessed, the adjournment should be to a date when the justice would next be sitting; and bill refused. Observed, that it was desirable that any reason for an adjournment exceeding four weeks should be stated in open court.

HUNTER v. CARMICHAEL, 1995 S.L.T. 449.

5830. Procedure—return of released prisoner. See ADVOCATE, H.M. v. DONNACHIE, §5832.

5831. Released prisoner—return to prison

[Prisoners and Criminal Proceedings (Scotland) Act 1993 (c.9), s.16.]

Held, where L, who had appeared before the court some 52 times since 1984, mostly for shoplifting and who had, within a few days of her release from prison under s.1(1) of the Prisoners and Criminal Proceedings (Scotland) Act 1991, committed a breach of the peace for which she received 30 days' imprisonment, that the magistrate was entitled to require L to serve the balance of the 56 days from the previous sentence prior to the 30 days, and that the fact that the respective offences were not analogous was of no importance.

LYNCH v. NORMAND, 1995 S.C.C.R. 404.

5832. Return of released prisoner—procedure—imposition of further sentence of imprisonment

[Prisoners and Criminal Proceedings (Scotland) Act 1993 (c.9), s.16.]

A prisoner was released under the provisions of the 1993 Act and committed a further offence during the balance of the period of his sentence. He pleaded guilty to the new offence on a summary complaint. The sheriff sentenced him to six months' detention with immediate effect and referred him to the High Court under s.16 of the Act for consideration of returning him to prison for the balance of the original sentence.

Held, that the sheriff should have referred the accused to the High Court under s.16 before imposing sentence, that the High Court had no power to vary the sentence imposed by the sheriff and that, since the new sentence had begun to run, the High Court could not order the period of his return to

prison to run prior to the new sentence; and order made for his return to prison to run concurrently with the sentence imposed by the sheriff.
ADVOCATE, H.M. v. DONNACHIE, 1994 S.C.C.R. 937.

Road traffic offences. See ROAD TRAFFIC.

Sea fishing—illegal fishing. See FISH AND FISHERIES.

5833. Statutory offence—false trade description

[Trade Description Act 1968 (c.29), s.1.(1).]

Held, where P, a company, were fined £2,500, the maximum being £5,000, for each of two offences in which they supplied Christmas tree lights which they falsely claimed were guaranteed and complied with British Standard 4647, the fines were not excessive since P had a substantial turnover and had sold 7,500,000 sets of the lights, despite claims by P that the offence was purely technical as the lights complied with the standard at the time of manufacture and the E.C. directive revising the standard related to dimension and not to safety.
PIFCO v. LEES, 1994 S.C.C.R. 775.

5834. Statutory offence—false trade description

[Trade Description Act 1968 (c.29), ss.1(1) and 14(1).]

Held, that fines totalling £1,200 at £8 per fortnight for three charges under ss.1 and 14 of the 1968 Act were excessive where R, who had been declared bankrupt in 1992, received income support and family allowance: the sheriff had failed to give due regard to R's means in terms of s.395(1) of the Criminal Procedure (Scotland) Act 1975 where the fines would take nearly six years to pay; and a total of £300 substituted.
REYNOLDS v. HAMILTON, 1994 S.C.C.R. 760.

5835. Statutory offence—taking eggs of protected birds

[Wildlife and Countryside Act 1981 (c.69), s.1.]

Held, where F, who lived with a woman and three children and received income support of £80 per fortnight, was fined £2,000, £12,500 and £1,500 with three months to pay, for three offences which concerned taking the eggs of protected birds, the fines were wholly excessive despite the cynical and blatant nature of F's conduct (which however did not involve taking for commercial purposes). The court, however, having taken account of F's means, was entitled to impose substantial fines even if this meant that payment would take several years (*Seiga v. Walkingshaw* [1994] C.L.Y. 5395); and fines of £500, £1,000 and £500 at £5 per week substituted. *Observed*, that it was most unsatisfactory that imprisonment was not available as a penalty given the likelihood of an offender not having the means to pay a fine.
FORSYTH v. CARDLE, 1994 S.C.C.R. 769.

5836. Taking part in management of company when undischarged bankrupt. See DREW v. H.M. ADVOCATE, §5730.

5837. Theft—housebreaking—child. See F. v. H.M. ADVOCATE, §5807.

5838. Theft—postal packets by post office employee

Held, where S, a postman, stole 246 packets and their contents over a period of seven months, S acquiring £20 to £30 per day, that four months' imprisonment was incompetent as S was a first offender, but that a custodial sentence would normally be imposed and that three months was appropriate in view of the public interest aspects, despite a favourable social inquiry report.

SANDERSON v. LEES, 1995 S.C.C.R. 347.

DAMAGES

5839. Breach of contract—interest on borrowing—relevancy. See NELSON (W.M.) CLADDING v. MURRAY WILLIAMSON (BUILDERS), §5486.

5840. Funeral expenses—stillborn child. See McMARTIN v. GINDHA, §6220.

5841. Heritable property—wrongful occupation

S sued W for payment and loss of profits following their refusal to vacate certain shop premises which had been run by S's husband, H, prior to his death. Although S acquired a lease of the subjects dated October 9, 1989 and November 2, 1989, W had refused to leave until February 1991 when S was granted decree for recovery of possession. W challenged S's averments regarding their occupancy and her requests that they vacate as lacking in specification. W further argued that there was no legal basis for S's claim in delict, being directed at negligent actions while the factual basis on which she relied inferred deliberate or intentional actions. The only remedy available to S as the dispossessed owner or tenant was an action for ordinary or violent profits. In addition, S's claim for loss of profit was irrelevant as it did not fall within one of the permitted categories for recovery of economic loss and the trend was to limit enlargements in the scope of negligence particularly in cases of purely economic loss. Following debate, the sheriff allowed a proof before answer and W appealed. In respect of her claim for loss of profits, S submitted that there had not been a trend away from allowing claims for economic loss, but that there had been a reformulation of the duty of care and in determining whether a duty of care existed, the court should consider whether (1) the damage was of the kind reasonably foreseeable by W; (2) S and W were in a relationship of proximity or neighbourhood such to give rise to a duty of care not to cause economic damage; and (3) the imposition of such duty was fair and reasonable. Since such a relationship of proximity existed between S and W, and it was reasonably foreseeable that W's refusal to vacate would cause economic loss to S, then holding that W owed a duty of care not to cause such loss to S was fair and reasonable.

Held, appeal dismissed and proof before answer allowed. (1) Although S's averments could have been stated more clearly, an averment that W refused to leave the premises on S assuming the tenancy was sufficient to establish that W were in occupation of the premises without right or title and without S's permission from October 1989 to February 1991. (2) With some hesitation, the sheriff's conclusion that S's averments of duty were appropriate for an action based on delict, whether the harm was negligent or intentional, would not be interfered with, as although they were expressed in terms appropriate to an action in negligence, they were introduced by the phrase "fault or negligence", and it was probable that the duties incumbent on W would be the same whether they acted negligently or intentionally. (3) The sheriff correctly concluded that the possibility of a claim for ordinary or violent profits did not preclude other remedies, as a person from whom possession had been unlawfully withheld could have a claim in delict in respect of consequential loss (*Stair Memorial Encyclopaedia*, Vol. 18, para. 170). (4) Although S's claim for loss of profits did not fall into the traditional categories of special relationship giving rise to a duty of care not to cause economic loss (*Hedley*

Byrne & Co. v. Heller and Partners [1963] C.L.Y. 2416; *Caparo Industries v. Dickman* [1990] C.L.Y. 3266 and *White v. Jones* [1995] C.L.Y. 3701, there was a relationship of proximity between the parties of a kind giving rise to some duties of care (to take reasonable care of the property and not cause physical damage) under the law of delict. In considering whether the duties argued for S also arose, the criteria posed by S were correct, and were satisfied by averments that S had right to the subjects but W had none, that W had refused to vacate when asked, that S had to pursue an action for recovery of possession, and that S had wished to run the supermarket on her own account. S had sufficiently averred that W had knowledge of her intentions; it was at least likely that S would be able to establish at proof beyond any doubt that W knew that she wished to run the supermarket business herself and therefore it was reasonably foreseeable that their failure to vacate would cause S economic loss. Since the elements of proximity or neighbourhood required to establish a duty of care existed and it was readily foreseeable that S would suffer economic loss, there was no injustice in concluding that W as the wrongful occupier had a duty of care not to cause S the economic loss.

SAEED v. WAHEED (Sh. Ct.), 1995 S.C.L.R. 504.

5842. Interest—cost of borrowing—relevancy. See NELSON (W.M.) CLADDING v. MURRAY WILLIAMSON (BUILDERS), §5486.

5843. Interest—payments to Compensation Recovery Unit. See CAVANAGH v. B.P. CHEMICALS, §5853.

5844. Interim payments—competency

[Rules of Court 1965, r. 89A(1)(c).]

A reclaimed a Lord Ordinary's decision to grant C's motion for interim damages of £15,000 in C's action for damages in respect of personal injuries sustained while employed by A on their oil rig, when a suspended reel used in the drilling process came out of its frame and rolled towards C, trapping and fracturing his right leg. C estimated his claim on the basis of full liability at £200,000 while A estimated it at £65,000. A argued that (1) as it was for C to prove that the equipment in question was not of good construction and free from patent defects and that the accident was reasonably foreseeable, the court could not be satisfied that C would succeed on the question of liability to any extent; and (2) if contributory negligency might be as much as a third, as the Lord Ordinary had estimated, then this amounted to a substantial finding and accordingly an award was not competent.

Held, reclaiming motion refused. (1) Given that the accident itself was admitted, that the regulations founded on by C imposed an absolute duty on A to ensure that all the equipment was of good construction, and a duty to take all reasonably practicable steps to ensure the safety of C, and that A had not averred that it was not reasonably practicable for them so to do, it was almost certain that C would establish that A were in breach of at least one of those regulations (*Douglas's C.B. v. Douglas* [1974] C.L.Y. 4150; *Walker v. Infabco Diving Services* [1983] C.L.Y. 4253, applied). (2) The qualification in r. 89A (1)(c)(ii) that there should be no "substantial finding of contributory negligence" was intended to prevent C receiving more in interim damages than he was finally awarded and, considering the initial hurdle C had to overcome with regard to liability, the word "substantial" was to mean something which would have a material effect on the assessment of the amount of damages (*McNeill v. Roche Products Ltd* [1988] C.L.Y. 4097, and *Duguid v. Wilh Wilhelmsen Enterprises A/S* [1988] C.L.Y. 4095, approved). There was no good reason for adopting a more restrictive interpretation of "substantial" as only large enough not to be *de minimis* (*Nelson v. Duraplex Industries* [1975] C.L.Y. 3729, *Noble v. Noble*, 1974 S.L.T. (Notes) 75, and *Herron v. Kennon* [1986] C.L.Y. 3939, disapproved). Given that it was disputed whether or not C had been instructed to stand where he was standing and whether or not it was standard practice to stand clear of the reel when in operation, it was no possible to reach any clear view in terms of a percentage as to the maximum extent to which C was likely to be held to be to blame. However, as there was no real risk that the finding of contributory negligence would be so substantial as to have a material effect on the assessment of damages, it had not been unreasonable to make the award.

COWIE v. ATLANTIC DRILLING CO., S.L.T. 1151.

5845. Interim payments—competency—whether defender insured

[Rules of Court of Session 1994, r.43.9(5).]

W sought an award of interim damages of £350,000 from D. D claimed that the award was incompetent as D had to be insured or of means to meet such an award (r.43.9(5)). D's insurers had had provisional liquidators appointed and the power of the Policyholders Protection Board to meet claims was discretionary. D earned only £104 per week. Further, as the total benefits certificate had expired on December 16, 1994 an interim award was incompetent (*Cunningham v. City of Edinburgh District Council*, 1994 G.W.D. 21–1299). W argued that the appointment of provisional liquidators was merely a holding operation and did not mean D had no valid insurance. The board were obliged to meet W's claim in full where the insurers were in liquidation (Policyholders Protection Act 1975, s.7), D's policy had been effective at the time of the accident and there were no averments that D was not insured. *Cunningham* could be distinguished as having been decided on the basis of fairness and not competency; the Social Security Administration Act 1992 did not affect the latter issue. An interim award could be restricted or suspended until an up-to-date certificate was available.

Held, motion granted. It was contended that D had not been or that she was not still insured. The discretion of the board did not preclude the making of an interim award. Presumably the board would regard any payment as being on D's behalf and one which would require to be met anyway if D's insurers were into liquidation. W's argument on *Cunningham* was sound. On the merits, W had been a rear seat passenger in D's car where D had driven carelessly. W had not been wearing a seat belt (not then compulsory) which involved 10 to 15 per cent contributory negligence. Any such contributory factor would not be so substantial as materially to affect the assessment (*Cowie v. Atlantic Drilling Co.* [1995] C.L.Y. 5844). W's claim was probably worth at least £1 million and although £40,000 had already been paid to account to enable W to adapt her parents' home for W's needs, a further award of £350,000, which was the amount required to build and equip suitable home care accommodation, did not exceed a reasonable proportion of the damages likely to be received.

WALKER v. DUNN (O.H.), 1995 S.C.L.R. 588.

5846. Interim payments—contributory negligence. See STONE v. MOUNTFORD, §5847.

5847. Interim payments—likelihood of success on question of liability

[Rules of the Court of Session 1994, r.43.9.]

Rule 43.9(3) of the Rules of the Court of Session 1994 entitles the court to order interim payment damages "if satisfied that . . . (b) if the action proceeded to proof, the pursuer would succeed in the action on the question of liability without any substantial finding of contributory negligence on his part". A mother raised an action of reparation on behalf of her child in respect of injuries sustained by the child as a result of an accident when the child fell into a quarry. The pursuer averred that the quarry was concealed by thick undergrowth and that a wall on the boundary of the defenders' property was of insufficient height to keep children out. The defenders averred that the wall was higher than stated by the pursuer and that there was in addition a barbed wire fence. The means by which the child came to fall were also in dispute. The defenders pled contributory negligence. The pursuer sought interim payment of damages. She accepted that the word "satisfied" required the court to be of the view that she would almost certainly succeed, both on liability and on contributory negligence. She argued that in assessing whether she would succeed on liability it was open to the court to look at production, including photographs. The defender argued that at this stage the court was restricted to considering the pleadings alone.

Held, that (1) that in considering a motion for interim payment of damages the discretion available to the court was such as to enable it to look at the material before it, including photographs, provided that the material in question supported a conclusion in favour of the pursuer such that it would be appropriate to make an award; (2) as there was a dispute as to essential matters of fact, including the nature of the barrier round the quarry and the mechanism of the accident itself, the court could not be satisfied to the required standard that the pursuer would succeed; and motion for interim payment damages refused. Dicta in *McCann v. Miller Insulation and Engineering* [1985] C.L.Y. 4006, not followed. *Opinion*, that a broad approach should be made to the question of contributory negligence and that it was almost certain that a substantial finding of contributory negligence would not be made.

STONE v. MOUNTFORD (O.H.), 1995 S.L.T. 1279.

5848. Lease—breach of obligation to provide house reasonably fit for human habitation—measure of damages

[Housing (Scotland) Act 1987 (c.26), Sched. 10, para. 1(2).]

Held, that the tenant of a flat who suffered inconvenience and depression, which included symptoms of low mood, poor self-esteem, hair loss and thoughts of suicide, as a result of the flat being unfit for human habitation by reason of condensation producing mould, was entitled to agreed damages of £520 in respect of items damaged by dampness and solatium of £2,500.

QUINN v. MONKLANDS DISTRICT COUNCIL (Sh. Ct.), 1995 S.C.L.R. 393.

5849. Personal injuries or death—measure of damages

A diner in her mid 20s suffered from salmonella poisoning after eating a meal at a restaurant. She was in pain for a week before admission to hospital for a week. She was unfit for work for two months.

Held, that solatium of £3,000 was appropriate together with £594 for loss of earnings and £200 for services performed by the pursuer's husband; and decree pronounced accordingly.

McINULTY v. ALAM, 1995 S.L.T. (Sh.Ct.) 56.

5850. The former employers of a joiner reclaimed against an award of damages for asbestosis suffered by the joiner who was 52 years old at the time of the proof. He suffered from pleural plaques, pleural thickening and sub-pleural fibrotic changes associated with exposure to asbestos. He also suffered a degree of airways obstruction caused by late onset asthma. His main disability was breathlessness to which the early asbestosis and unrelated asthma contributed equally. The breathlessness inhibited his ability to work but did not amount to a material incapacity. There was a risk of developing mesothelioma or lung cancer and his fibrosis would increase. The Lord Ordinary had awarded £25,000 in respect of solatium, a lump sum figure of £15,000 for loss of future earnings and sums of £1,500 each in respect of loss of services and necessary services. The reclaimers argued that each of the elements of the award was excessive.

Held, that each element of the award was within the range of what a Lord Ordinary could award; and reclaiming motion refused except in relation to the deduction of benefits from the award for future loss of wages.

McKENZIE v. CAPE BUILDING PRODUCTS, 1995 S.L.T. 701.

5851. A 38-year old woman sustained severe and irreversible brain damage with resulting speech and gait impediments, an inability to form human relationships, disorientated eating habits and personal hygiene problems. She was likely to remain a patient at a hospital for life.

Held, that solatium was properly valued at £65,000, that the values of necessary services provided by the patient's husband and daughter were £5,000 and £2,500 respectively; that the loss of services claim amounted, after a discount for likely future nervous illnesses, to £20,000 to date and £31,770 for the future; and that the curatory expenses should be assessed at 2.5 per cent of the whole fund for the first year and thereafter at the rate of 1.2 per cent of the fund, using a multiplier of 15 years, the figure derived from the Ogden tables; and decree pronounced accordingly.

G.'s CURATOR BONIS v. GRAMPIAN HEALTH BOARD (O.H.), 1995 S.L.T. 652.

See also §6159.

5852. M, aged 55 at proof, sought damages from C, in the course of his employment with whom between 1968 and 1990 he had been exposed to asbestos. M had developed the early stages of asbestosis. C admitted liability but disputed the extent to which M's loss, injury and damage were due to exposure to asbestos dust. M, a widower, was already overweight, hypertensive and developing the late onset of asthma or wheeziness from smoking which was contributing to increased breathlessness. M retired on February 2, 1990 having been invited to retire early as he was increasingly off work through chest and respiratory infections. He had not worked since, his leisure activities had been severely restricted and the slightest activity now made him breathless. For benefit purposes M had provisionally been assessed at 15 per cent disabled on account of breathlessness and loss of lung function.

Held, that M was 50 per cent disabled as a result of breathlessness but 10 per cent was attributed to obesity and 15 per cent to asthma, therefore 25 per cent was attributed to his exposure to asbestos dust. Solatium should be assessed at £27,000, one third to the past. M had a 2 per cent risk of developing mesothelioma and a 5 per cent risk of developing lung cancer. Otherwise his life expectancy was not affected. Patrimonial loss to the date of proof was agreed at £25,000 which after agreed benefit reductions, amounted to £9,360 with interest of £2,750. Future wage loss was agreed at a multiplicand of £6,922; an appropriate multiplier was 4½ years. Pension rights were agreed at £5,144. An award of £7,800, including transport costs, for past services in terms of s.8 of the Administration of Justice Act 1982 was made, where M had to have considerable help from his son and daughter in law. A lump sum of £25,000 for future services was appropriate. M needed a shower to be installed as he could not get in and out of the bath and £2,000 was awarded to meet this cost. Total award £114,153 including interest.

MYLES v. CITY OF GLASGOW DISTRICT COUNCIL (O.H.), 1994 S.C.L.R. 1112.

5853. M claimed damages from L after, during the course of biopsy of part of M's maxillary sinus on April 25, 1989, L suffered permanent nerve damage to the infra-orbital nerve which enters through the roof of the sinus cavity. M was permanently deprived of feeling below her right eye, cheek, side of nose, right handed side mouth, gum and roof of her mouth. As a result M was self conscious and had a tendency to dribble. There was no prospect of betterment and M was left with a real affliction causing her to withdraw from socialising.

Held, decree granted. Solatium assessed at £10,000, one third to the past.

McDONALD v. LOTHIAN HEALTH BOARD (O.H.), 1995 S.L.T. 1033.

5854. [Social Security Administration Act 1992 (c.5), s.103.]

A 48 year old self-employed shuttering joiner was injured in a fall in which he broke one leg and one arm badly.

Held, that solatium was properly valued at £22,500, that the pursuer was entitled to loss of wages to date and, using a multiplier of three and a half years, for the future and that his wife's services were reasonably valued at £1,000; and decree pronounced accordingly. *Observed*, that in view of the terms of s.103 of the Social Security Administration Act 1992 the court required, when assessing interest on past wage loss, to reduce the award by the amount payable to the Compensation Recovery Unit. (*Morrison v. Laidlaw* [1994] C.L.Y. 5726, not followed.)

CAVANAGH v. B.P. CHEMICALS (O.H.), 1995 S.L.T. 1287.

5855. H, an industrial radiographer aged 48 at proof, sued his employer S when he allegedly developed lateral epicondylitis (tennis elbow) from moving castings mainly of between one and five tonnes on a turntable at work. Although H first complained of pain in his right arm in late 1990, he was left to operate the turntable alone from March 1991 until he ceased work and consulted a doctor for pains in his arm in June 1991. He was made redundant in December 1991. As a result of operations to his left arm in October 1992 and his right arm in March 1993, H was left with weakness and pain on squeezing and gripping in both arms. His ability to garden, drive and write were impeded and he was unable to assist his wife with lifting and shopping. His ability to play darts and bowl were also restricted. C, a hand surgeon, stated for S that it was not scientific to assert that H's tennis elbow was work related as the condition arose constitutionally but could be aggravated externally.

Held, decree granted. Solatium was awarded at £8,000, five eighths to the past with interest at half the judicial rate from June 1, 1991.

HUNTER v. CLYDE SHAW (O.H.), 1995 S.L.T. 474.

5856. A 39-year-old man died leaving a wife, two daughters aged 19 and 16 and a son aged 13. The daughters had left home but the son lived with his father. The husband and wife, although they had separated some months before the husband's death because of the husband's behaviour, spent three or four nights a week together. The husband had done much of the cooking for his wife and for his son. *Opinion*, that loss of society for the widow, discounted for the separation, would have been valued at £10,000, that loss of society awards for the children would have been £2,000, £2,500 and £4,000 and that the widow and the son would have been entitled to nominal loss of services awards of £500 and £250 respectively.

MORRISON v. FORSYTH (O.H.), 1995 S.L.T. 539.

5857. A 52-year-old teacher, who injured his back in a road accident, sought damages including an award for future loss of earnings and for extra expenditure to be incurred in the future. The evidence was that he had a 50:50 chance of working until normal retiral age and that ordinary household tasks were difficult for him.

Held, that future loss of earnings should be recognised by an award of about one year's net earnings and that an award of £500 a year with a multiplier of 10 years was appropriate in respect of extra food costs; and decree pronounced accordingly.

DUFFY v. SHAW (O.H.), 1995 S.L.T. 602.

5858. A 60-year-old supervisor was injured in a fall. She sustained bruising of her right hip and a dislocation of her shoulder but the main enduring disability resulted from injury to her cervical spine which exacerbated pre-existing degenerative charges.

Held, that solatium was properly valued at £6,000, that wage loss should be awarded but restricted to a period of three and a half years to take account of the possibility that the pre-existing changes would have rendered the pursuer unfit for work before her normal retirement age and that the award for necessary services rendered to and for the loss of personal services of the pursuer should be valued at £1,750 for the past and £500 for the future; and decree pronounced accordingly.

REID v. EDINBURGH ACOUSTICS (O.H.), 1995 S.L.T. 659.

5859. A 63 year old former employee of builders' merchants suffered lung fibrosis. He was breathless and had a life expectancy of about five years. *Opinion*, that solatium was properly valued at £30,000.

STANNERS v. GRAHAM BUILDERS MERCHANTS (O.H.), 1995 S.L.T. 728.

5860. A 33 year old prisoner sought damages for injury to his health sustained during the course of a lengthy prison riot. The injuries complained of were said to be the result of stress and depression inducing weight loss, headaches, throat infections and nausea. *Opinion*, that, had the prisoner established fault, (1) he would have been entitled to an award of damages for significant and prolonged physical discomfort short of actual injury, and (2) the injury to his health suffered in this case in the form of intermittent stomach pain, nausea, headaches and back pain accompanied by the significant physical discomfort and mental suffering would have merited an award of solatium of £2,500.

MOFFAT v. SECRETARY OF STATE FOR SCOTLAND (O.H.), 1995 S.L.T. 729.

5861. A 29 year old janitor suffered severe lacerations of his right forearm. Treatment included skin grafting. He returned to work after three months. His right, dominant hand was permanently affected by the injury. *Opinion*, that solatium was properly valued at £6,500, that there was a slight loss of earning capacity which would have attracted an award of £500 and that the services provided by the pursuer's wife while his arm was in a splint would have attracted an award of £500.

McCUTCHEON v. LOTHIAN REGIONAL COUNCIL (O.H.), 1995 S.L.T. 917.

5862. Personal injuries or death—measure of damages. See QUINN v. MONKLANDS DISTRICT COUNCIL, §5848.

5863. Personal injuries or death—measure of damages—cost of funeral and headstone for stillborn child. See McMARTIN v. GINDHA, §6220.

5864. Personal injuries or death—measure of damages—necessary services rendered by relative. See CAVANAGH v. B.P. CHEMICALS, §5853; G.'s CURATOR BONIS v. GRAMPIAN HEALTH BOARD, §5857; McKENZIE v. CAPE BUILDING PRODUCTS, §5850; REID v. EDINBURGH ACOUSTICS, §5858.

5865. Personal injuries or death—measure of damages—personal services rendered to relative. See McKENZIE v. CAPE BUILDING PRODUCTS, §5850.

5866. Photographic negatives—measure of damages

A professional photographer who conducted his business from his tenement flat, in which there was a darkroom, sought damages from builders carrying out work to the roof and chimneys of the tenement when they caused a heavy fall of soot into an unblocked fireplace in the darkroom. Negatives left to hang in the darkroom were ruined. After a proof the sheriff assessed the value of the lost negatives at £2,025. The method of assessment used by the sheriff was not one which had been proposed by either party. The pursuer appealed to the Court of Session.

Held, that (1) the sheriff's assessment of loss could not stand where it was based on a figure which the sheriff acknowledged to be unreliable, used a multiplier when there was bound to be very great uncertainty as to the appropriate multiplier and was not based on a method of calculation proposed by either of the parties; (2) if the sheriff wished to develop an alternative method of calculating damages he should have disclosed this to the parties and invited comment; (3) in the circumstances it was appropriate for the court to make its own assessment; and appeal allowed and damages assessed at £3,500. (*Britton v. Central Regional Council* [1986] C.L.Y. 3641 applied.)

MARNIE v. ORBIT BUILDERS, 1995 S.L.T. 707.

5867. Solatium

See under **Personal injuries or death—measure of damages,** or the Quantum of damages Table near the front of this volume

5868. Solicitor—negligence—measure of damages

As a result of her solicitor's negligence, a divorced woman suffered anxiety, worry and distress over several years about the possibility of losing occupation of the former matrimonial home.

Held, that damages for the anxiety, worry and distress were appropriately valued at £3,000; and decree pronounced accordingly.

CURRAN v. DOCHERTY (O.H.), 1995 S.L.T. 716.

5869. Solicitor—negligence—measure of damages—purchase of residential property

Purchasers of a dwellinghouse sued their solicitors for negligence in allowing them to take entry on payment of a substantial deposit, the seller eventually proving to have no title. The solicitors argued that damages should be restricted to the amount paid and not recovered and that the purchasers' averments of loss, other than those related to the price, were irrelevant. The Lord Ordinary allowed proof before answer on the whole averments. The defenders reclaimed.

Held, that it would not necessarily be unreasonable to take into account the particular matters of which notice had been given in the averments; and reclaiming motion refused.

DI CIACCA v. ARCHIBALD SHARP & SONS, 1995 S.L.T. 380.

DIVORCE AND CONSISTORIAL CAUSES

Access. See CHILDREN AND YOUNG PERSONS.

Aliment—children. See CHILDREN AND YOUNG PERSONS.

5870. Aliment—"resources"—whether company car and payment to pension fund "resources" of defender

[Family Law (Scotland) Act 1985 (c.37), ss.4(1)(a), 27(1).]

Held, in an action at the instance of a wife seeking, *inter alia*, aliment for herself, that the car provided for her husband by his employers and their payment of what would normally have been the employee's contribution to a pension fund fell properly to be treated as his "resources" within the meaning

of s.4(1) of the 1985 Act but that their value did not form part of the funds available to the husband from which payment of aliment could be made.
SEMPLE v. SEMPLE (Sh.Ct.), 1995 S.C.L.R. 569.

5871. Aliment—variation of agreement—competency

[Family (Scotland) Act 1985 (c.37), ss.1 and 7.]

W reclaimed against a Lord Ordinary's decision to allow a proof before answer in H's action for variation of a minute of agreement executed on August 26, 1983 prior to H and W's divorce in 1985. The agreement provided that H would pay to W "in name of aliment" an index linked sum. W argued that there was no provision in the agreement enabling the court to vary the agreement under s.16(1) of the 1985 Act and, as H no longer owed W an obligation of aliment, variation under s.7(2) was not competent. H argued that at the time of execution H had owed W an obligation of aliment and that parties outside the relationships specified in s.1(1) were entitled to enter into a contractual obligation of aliment.

Held, reclaiming motion allowed and action dismissed. Section 1(1) exhaustively defined the relationships within which an obligation of aliment could be owed, and, as ss.1 to 7 provided for the working out of that obligation where a claim for aliment was made, "obligation to aliment" in s.7(2) clearly meant the obligations in s.1(1). Given that s.7(2) was in the present tense and that s.7(4) gave jurisdiction to consider an application under subs. (2) to a court competent to hear an action for aliment between the parties, the obligation had to be owed at the time of the application. Section 7(2) could not be invoked by a couple who cohabited or were divorced, regardless of the terms of the agreement.

DRUMMOND v. DRUMMOND, *The Scotsman*, March 1, 1995.

Custody. See CHILDREN AND YOUNG PERSONS.

5871a Expenses. See EXPENSES; ADAMS v. ADAMS (NO. 2), §5937.

5872. Jurisdiction—divorce—domicile—acquisition of domicile of choice

[Domicile and Matrimonial Proceedings Act 1973 (c.45), s.7(2) and (3).]

A wife sought divorce, founding jurisdiction on her husband's domicile. The husband argued that he had acquired a domicile of choice in Spain, thereby losing his Scottish domicile. He had been born and brought up in Scotland and had entered his father's business in Glasgow in 1972. The parties had been married in a Jewish ceremony in Spain in January 1982 and in a civil ceremony in Scotland in March 1982 and had then lived in Scotland until April 1984 when they moved to Spain, where in 1984 and 1986 their two children were born. In 1989 the husband had raised separation proceedings in Spain but although a separation agreement had been entered into, the Spanish courts had refused to give effect to it. In 1992 the husband had again raised proceedings in the Spanish courts but these were delayed by a strike. The present action was begun by the wife in June 1993, by which time the husband claimed that he was no longer domiciled in Scotland. He gave evidence that he had left Scotland for "a fresh start" in Spain after the sale of a Scottish company of which he had been the director and part owner, that he had resigned membership of his synagogue and the Jewish burial society in Glasgow on leaving Scotland and that the parties' house in Glasgow had been sold in 1989. He maintained some connection with Scotland in that he had retained a third of the shares in another company which owned property in Glasgow and he had, since leaving Scotland, continued to return for business reasons and on family occasions although the frequency of these visits was decreasing. In the three and a half years prior to the raising of the action he had been living with a girlfriend, by whom he had a child, in Spain. In Spain his social circle was British and in particular Scottish; he had not registered with the Spanish authorities as a resident; he earned no income in Spain and paid no tax but he had engaged in certain business ventures in Spain, Gibraltar and elsewhere.

Held, that (1) the dominant reason for the departure of the parties from Scotland had been to avoid a tax liability on the proceeds of the sale of the husband's shares in the company; (2) although the mere fact that the husband had moved from one country to another to avoid a tax liability in his country of origin did not mean that he could not acquire a domicile of choice in Spain, the evidence of the husband's failure to register officially as resident in Spain, the lack of direction to and continuity of his business activities in Spain and his business links with a number of other countries indicated a lack of settled intention to regard Spain as his permanent home; (3) the husband had accordingly failed to establish that he had acquired a new domicile of choice to displace his domicile of origin; and plea of no jurisdiction repelled. (*Udny v. Udny* (1869) 7 M. (H.L.) 89, applied.)

SPENCE v. SPENCE (O.H.), 1995 S.L.T. 335.

5873. Orders for financial provision on divorce—arrestment on the dependence. See MATHESON v. MATHESON, §6193.

5874. Orders for financial provision on divorce—capital sum

[Family Law (Scotland) Act 1985 (c.37), s.18(1).]

A wife raised an action of divorce against her husband on the ground as amended, that the marriage had broken down irretrievably by reason of non-cohabitation for a period in excess of five years, the parties having separated in 1983. The action was raised in May 1986. The wife sought payment of a periodical allowance and a capital sum. She lived in a council house and was dependent on state benefits. She had no capital assets of consequence and savings of £1,000. The husband, in addition to liquid funds of £3,252, owned the premises of the family business which parties were agreed was worth £65,000. The parties were in dispute as regards the value of the husband's interest in the business and also in connection with premises used by the business for storage purposes and the house in which the husband resided, both of which properties the husband had transferred into the name of his mother, who had since died. The wife argued that these properties had been put into the mother's name to defeat the wife's claim for financial provision on divorce and that, accordingly, both should be regarded as within the husband's ownership. Alternatively, she argued that both properties belonged to the husband as sole beneficiary under his mother's will and led evidence as to the terms thereof. The husband defended the merits of the action on the basis that the parties had gone through a ceremony of reconciliation and denied knowledge or the existence of any will.

Held, that (1) on the evidence the parties had been estranged since 1983 and the pursuer was entitled to divorce; (2) the capital account could not be viewed in isolation from the balance sheet and on the unchallenged evidence as to valuations the husband's interest in the business was worth £4,358; (3) it was impossible to regard the disputed properties as having been throughout within the ownership of the husband in the absence of any declarator of trust or any order of court reducing the deeds in question under s.18(1) of the Family Law (Scotland) Act 1985 or the earlier provisions of s.6(1) of the Divorce (Scotland) Act 1976; (4) as the husband could not have given marketable title to the disputed properties, they had to be regarded as part of the husband's mother's intestate estate, of which the husband would have been entitled to £31,000; (5) the husband's total capital assets were accordingly £103,610 and although one should hesitate long and hard before ordaining the disposal of an income producing asset, it was unavoidable that the business premises be sold in order to do justice between the parties, and in all the circumstances of the case a capital sum of £50,000 was reasonable with extract superseded for six months in that the business and premises were not immediately realisable; (6) no periodical allowance was justified in the circumstances; and decree pronounced accordingly. *Doubted*, that evidence as to the contents of the will was competent or admissible.

MAYOR v. MAYOR (O.H.), 1995 S.L.T. 1097.

5875. Orders for financial provision on divorce—capital sum—interest claimed for period prior to decree. See TAHIR v. TAHIR (NO. 2), §5885.

5876. Orders for financial provision on divorce—incidental orders

[Family Law (Scotland) Act 1985 (c.37), ss.3(1)(b) and 14(2)(a) and (b) and (3).]

Following a lengthy proof in a divorce case the Lord Ordinary issued an opinion indicating his intentions. The case came out by order after a delay of some months to enable effect to be given to his Lordship's opinion. By that time the circumstances of one of the children's schooling had materially altered. The wife pursuer sought divorce and custody in accordance with his Lordship's opinion and an order for educational expenses, modified to take account of the change in the child's schooling, and an order for payment out of a capital sum. She also sought incidental orders for security of the order for educational expenses and of the order for payment of a capital sum. She had no conclusions specifically directed towards security. She also sought expenses.

Held, that (1) as the order for educational expenses was alimentary, it was competent to make an order varied to take account of the change of circumstances; (2) it was incompetent to order the defender to provide security for what were alimentary payments; (3) it was competent to order the defender to provide security for payment of the capital sum without a specific conclusion seeking such security; (4) it was incompetent to grant an incidental order relating to payments of mortgage instalments already paid; (5) although expenses were not to be determined as they would be in a reparation action, nevertheless the pursuer had achieved substantial success and should be found entitled to an award of expenses modified to 60 per cent; and decree pronounced accordingly.

MACDONALD v. MACDONALD (O.H.), 1995 S.L.T. 72.

5877. Orders for financial provision on divorce—incidental orders—competency

[Family Law (Scotland) Act 1985 (c.37), ss.8 and 14(2).]

Held, that only a party seeking an order for financial provision on divorce was entitled to apply for an incidental order within the meaning of s.14(2) and accordingly that an application for an incidental order by a party who was opposing an order for financial provision but who was not seeking such an order was incompetent.

MacCLUE v. MacCLUE (Sh. Ct.), 1994 S.C.L.R. 933.

5878. Orders for financial provision on divorce—matrimonial property—joint property

[Family Law (Scotland) Act 1985 (c.37) ss.8(2), 10(6)(b) and (d) and 14(2).]

The title to a matrimonial home was held in the joint names of parties to an action of divorce raised by a wife against her husband. The property had been acquired with the proceeds of sale of a property which had been in the husband's sole name. The husband occupied the property after the separation of the parties and conducted a business therefrom, but was in receipt of income support. The wife sought an order to declare the property to be owned equally between the parties, an order for its sale and ancillary orders. The husband sought an order for transfer of the wife's share to him on the ground that it was fair and reasonable to do so having regard to the circumstances of the case, and offered a sum of money in exchange for the transfer. Having found that there were no circumstances which would justify a departure from the principle that the net value of matrimonial property at the date of separation should be shared equally between the parties, the sheriff, in order to avoid the difficulty which he thought would arise as perceived in *Wallis v. Wallis*, [1993] C.L.Y. 5221, refrained from making any order at all. He took the view that this left the parties still vested in assets of equal value, including their respective equal shares in the matrimonial home, and that they could realise those subjects in accordance with the normal law of property and thus obtain the joint benefit of any increase in the value of the house since the date of separation. Both parties appealed against the sheriff's decision.

Held, that (1) there were no grounds for interfering with the sheriff's decision that the circumstances did not justify a departure from the principle that the net value of matrimonial property should be shared equally between the parties; but (2) as the house was to be sold, the difficulty which arose in *Wallis v. Wallis* was absent, and it was competent and appropriate for the sheriff to make the orders sought by the pursuer rather than following the course which he did, of not granting decree; and wife's appeal allowed.

JACQUES v. JACQUES, 1995 S.L.T. 963.

5879. Orders for financial provision on divorce—matrimonial property—pension

[Family Law (Scotland) Act 1985 (c.37), ss.9 and 10.]

Held, where the transfer value of the husband's occupational pension was £98,526·47, that the sheriff had been entitled to conclude that the wife should receive one-third of that value, £32,840, payment of £15,000 of which should be postponed until the husband's death or retirement.

STEPHEN v. STEPHEN (Sh.Ct.), 1995 S.C.L.R. 175.

5880. Orders for financial provision on divorce—matrimonial property—pension rights—whether value of husband's pension rights relating to widow's pension to be excluded

[Family Law (Scotland) Act 1985 (c.37), s.10(5).]

One of the assets to be taken into account in assessing the matrimonial property was a husband's interest in a pension fund. The husband argued that its value should exclude the part of the total value attributable to a widow's pension rights.

Held, that the widow's benefit formed no part of the matrimonial property; and capital sum awarded on the basis that the value of pension fund excluded the part attributable to a widow's rights. (*Bannon v. Bannon* [1993] C.L.Y. 5226; *Brooks v. Brooks* [1993] C.L.Y. 5227; *Crosbie v. Crosbie* [1995] 7 C.L. 633; *Gribb v. Gribb* [1994] C.L.Y. 5786; and *Welsh v. Welsh* [1994] C.L.Y. 5782, considered.)

DIBLE v. DIBLE (O.H.), 1995 S.L.T. 1364.

5881. Orders for financial provision on divorce—matrimonial property—unequal division. See CROSBIE v. CROSBIE, §5883.

5882. Orders for financial provision on divorce—pension rights

H appealed a sheriff principal's refusal of his appeal against a sheriff's decision in May 1994, in H's action of divorce, to find W entitled to a capital sum of £29,780, of which £2,780 was to be paid at date of decree and the balance in instalments of £500 per month from July 1995 together with the interest at 8 per cent on the outstanding balance from time to time. If an instalment remained unpaid for 14 days, the whole outstanding balance was to become due. The only assets relevant to calculation of the capital sum were H's police pension, valued at £58,000, and H's car, valued at £1,560, the total value having been divided equally between H and W. As at the date of proof H also owned two houses, one purchased after H and W separated for £27,500 with a mortgage of £25,000, which was let, and another purchased in May

1993 for £79,250 with a mortgage of about £75,000 and a deposit of £4,000 borrowed from B, with whom H now lived. H argued that instead of payment by instalments, W should have been awarded a lump sum of £40,000 payable on November 29, 2001, when H would retire on completing 30 years' service, that sum being quantified in line with *Bannon v. Bannon* [1993] C.L.Y. 5226; and that H had neither capital nor free income from which to pay the instalments together with interest.

Held, appeal refused. The approach in *Bannon* might be the fairest and best solution in most cases where the only asset was a pension scheme which had a significant value but could not be used to meet an immediate liability on divorce. However, the sheriff had not been bound to adopt that approach, and given that other contingencies, such as ill health, or actions by H, such as assigning benefits, might affect the amount and date of payment of any lump sum benefits under the pension and risk frustrating the purpose of the decree, the sheriff was entitled to adopt another method for securing W's benefits, notwithstanding that some contingencies might result in a lack of alternative sources of funds. In any event, given that H, who had incurred a substantially larger mortgage with his move in May 1993, could return to his less costly home, relieving himself of added burdens, and that the outlays, which H claimed were equal to his income, were in fact those of H and B, and could, in the absence of contrary evidence, be assumed to be incurred equally by them, there could be freed from H's pattern of expenditure a sum from which the instalments could be paid. While H would in addition have to pay the outstanding interest, the principal would be paid off in four and a half years and the amount of interest would be exceeded by the growth, expected at 9 per cent per annum, in the retained funds, and, while this growth, would not be available to H either, the interest was not sufficient to change the overall picture.

McEWAN v. McEWAN, *The Scotsman*, September 27, 1995.

5883. Orders for financial provision on divorce—pension rights

Held, where parties had been married for 30 years, the husband received an army pension of £1,169, his pension rights were valued at £76,000, the wife's only income was interim aliment of £65 per week and she was taking a one year course in office technology, that she should receive a capital sum of £15,000 payable at the rate of £250 per month and a periodical allowance of £100 per month for a period of one year.

BUCKLE v. BUCKLE (Sh.Ct.), 1995 S.C.L.R. 590.

5884. Orders for financial provision on divorce—pension rights—whether value of husband's pension rights relating to widow's pension to be excluded

[Family Law (Scotland) Act 1985 (c.37), ss.8 and 10]

In an action of divorce between H and W, W appealed against the sheriff's decision not to take into account as part of the matrimonial property the widow's pension element in H's pension scheme. W argued that she had an interest in H's pension which should have been valued and formed part of the assets (*Gribb v. Gribb* [1994] C.L.Y. 5786). H had paid premiums which would provide his "spouse" with benefits and the value should be included.

Held, appeal refused. It would be unjust to put a value on the spouse's benefit in an occupational pension scheme (*Gribb*, *supra*, not followed). H might remarry and his new spouse's interest re-emerge. The position might have been different in a private pension scheme. On divorce such rights as W had were extinguished and should not be treated as an asset of H.

CROSBIE v. CROSBIE (Sh. Ct.), 1995 S.C.L.R. 399.

5885. Orders for financial provision on divorce—procedure—alleged loan acknowledged by letter and followed by decree and inhibition—whether competent to set aside letter, reduce decree and recall inhibition

[Family Proceedings Act 1984 (c.42), ss.28 and 29; Family Law (Scotland) Act 1985 (c.37), ss.8, 9 and 18.]

A woman, who had been divorced by her former husband in Pakistan, had previously raised an action of divorce in Scotland. The action continued after the grant of divorce in Pakistan in relation to the claim for a capital sum and certain ancillary orders. In the course of considering the claim for a capital sum in the divorce process it was established that (1) a decree pronounced in the sheriff court against the former husband for repayment of a loan was unjustified in that there never had been a loan, and (2) the former husband had dispossessed his wife of jewellery which had belonged to her, which was not matrimonial property, and which had a replacement value at the date of separation of £10,360 and a saleable value of £5,675.

Held, that (1) the court had power to reduce the decree following on the purported loan; and (2) the taking by the husband of the jewellery amounted to an economic advantage to him and an economic disadvantage to the former wife; and decree of reduction and decree for payment of a capital sum pronounced, excluding consideration of the sum due under the decree but adding to the figure resulting from an equal division of the matrimonial property a sum equal to the saleable value of the jewellery taken by the former husband, and with interest from the date of the foreign decree of divorce.

TAHIR v. TAHIR (NO. 2) (O.H.), 1995 S.L.T. 451.

5886. Orders for financial provision on divorce—variation of agreement—whether "fair and reasonable" at the time it was entered into

[Family Law (Scotland) Act 1985 (c.37), s.16(1)(b).]

The Family Law (Scotland) Act 1985 provides that the court may set aside or vary an agreement as to financial provision to be made on divorce if it was not fair and reasonable at the time it was entered into.

In divorce proceedings raised by a wife, she sought variations of a minute of agreement entered into following separation. In return for accepting no aliment and giving up her claim to the husband's assets except insofar as dealt with in the minute, the wife had obtained the right to purchase the husband's interest in the matrimonial home at an advantageous price. The husband's assets had included his pension rights. When later assessed, they were found to have a substantial value. The husband and wife had each received separate and independent legal advice from their solicitors before entering into the agreement. The case came to a preliminary proof on the conclusion for variation of the minute of agreement insofar as it bore to discharge the wife's right to seek payment of a capital sum by the husband.

The wife contended that the exclusion in the minute of her right to a capital sum was not fair and reasonable at the time the agreement had been entered into because, although the existence of the husband's pension rights had been known about, their full value had not then been ascertained.

Held, that (1) the mere fact that there was proved to have been an unequal division of assets between the parties did not give rise to an inference of unfairness or unreasonableness; (2) the wife, by entering into the agreement, had obtained certainty and the benefit of an appreciating asset at a discounted price in the full knowledge of the existence of the claim based on the value of the pension rights even although those rights had not by then been valued; and accordingly (3) the minute of agreement was fair and reasonable at the time of its execution and plea for variation repelled. *Observed*, that, in dealing with such issues, the following principles were to be applied: (*a*) the agreement had to be examined from the point of view of both fairness and reasonableness; (*b*) the examination had to relate to all the relevant circumstances leading up to and prevailing at the time of the execution of the agreement including amongst other things, the nature and quality of the legal advice given to either party; (*c*) evidence that some advantage had been taken by one party of the other by reason of circumstances prevailing at the time of negotiations might have a cogent bearing on the determination of the issue; (*d*) the court should not be unduly ready to overturn agreements validly entered into; and (*e*) the fact that it transpired that an agreement had led to an

unequal and possibly very unequal division of assets did not by itself necessarily give rise to any inference of unfairness or unreasonableness.
GILLON v. GILLON (No. 3) (O.H.), 1995 S.L.T. 678.

5887. Procedure—sheriff court—options hearing—failure of party to attend hearing personally

[Sheriff Courts (Scotland) Act 1907 (c.51), Sched., rr. 33.36 and 33.37(1)(c).]
Held, in an action of divorce which was defended only on the question of a capital sum claimed by the wife, that the husband who was not present but was represented by his solicitor at the options hearing, was not in default.
GRIMES v. GRIMES (Sh. Ct.), 1995 S.C.L.R. 268.

5888. Procedure—sheriff court—undefended decree of divorce—appeal

On December 14, 1994 H raised an action of divorce and on January 16, 1995 the sheriff granted an undefended decree. On March 29, 1995, W lodged a motion to allow an appeal against the decree to be marked, on the grounds that as a matter of justice the judgment should be set aside. Following H's intimation of the action, W's agents had written to H's solicitors advising of their intention to enter the process and to lodge a notice of intention to defend late so that she could apply for legal aid. However, on January 9 H lodged a minute for decree with relevant affidavits. A notice of intention to defend was sent to the sheriff clerk on January 12, along with motions to allow the notice to be received late and to sist the cause for legal aid, although no cheque was enclosed. The sheriff clerk's office advised W's agents that the cheque could be sent; it was received in their office on January 16, the same day that the sheriff granted the undefended decree. W's agents subsequently intimated the date for a hearing on the motions, which H opposed, although H later dropped his opposition. Although W's motions to sist the cause and allow the notice of intention to defend to be received late were granted on February 2, her agents were informed by the clerk's office first that the process had been lost and, later on February 18, that the motion had been dropped. When W's agents attempted to re-enrol the motions, the sheriff clerk's office informed them initially that the motions had not been accompanied by the appropriate fees, latterly that the notice of intention to defend had never been lodged and, finally on March 15, that decree had been granted in January. W's solicitors thereafter informally applied to the sheriff who granted the decree to hold it as *pro non scripto*, but she considered that she had no power to do so, and W thereafter lodged her motion to allow an appeal to be marked. W argued that as neither W nor her agents were to blame for the administrative errors and since the divorce process was W's only opportunity to make a financial claim against H, the decree should be set aside as a matter of justice (Macphail, *Sheriff Court Practice*, para. 18–02). H submitted that there was no utility in granting W's motion as the sheriff had not erred in granting the decree and therefore W could not succeed in an appeal

Held, motion refused. The only form of appeal available to W was an ordinary appeal against a final judgment under s.27 of the 1907 Act, which required W to establish that the sheriff erred in law or misunderstood the evidence, and she could not appeal on the ground that there was an acceptable explanation for allowing the decree to pass, as in support of a reponing note, since r. 8.1 of the Ordinary Cause Rules 1993, which permitted reponing in the sheriff courts, expressly excluded divorce actions. There was no practical utility in granting the motion and continuing the case to a full appeal as W had no chance of succeeding since the sheriff had not erred in a material way. *Observed*, that although H had been personally advised by the sheriff clerk's office that the computer showed that the decree had been extracted on January 31, since there was no record in the process of extract having been issued the court should proceed on that basis.
McFARLANE v. McFARLANE (Sh.Ct.), 1995 S.C.L.R. 794.

ECCLESIASTICAL LAW

5889. Church of Scotland—decision of church courts—whether subject to review

[Church of Scotland Act 1921 (c.29), Sched., Declaratory Art. IV.]

The minister of a parish church sought judicial review of deliverances of the presbytery which were of a disciplinary nature in terms of the Acts of the General Assembly Act Anent Trials by Libel. The Lord Ordinary granted the petitioner's application for interim suspension of the respondents' decision to enjoin him to abstain from exercising the functions of his office, which decision had immediate effect, and interim interdict to stop the implementation of that decision. The respondents sought recall of the interim orders, arguing that in terms of the Church of Scotland Act 1921 the matters raised by the petitioner fell within the exclusive jurisdiction of the Church of Scotland courts and outwith the jurisdiction of the Court of Session. The petitioner argued that at this stage it was not necessary for the court to make a final decision on its own jurisdiction but that the petitioner had to show only that he had a prima facie case. If the Church's exercise of its jurisdiction was not properly carried on, an aggrieved person had the right to resort to the civil courts. In any event, where Parliament had conferred powers on the Church by statute, the proceedings of the Church were subject to judicial review in line with the decision in *West v. Secretary of State for Scotland* [1992] C.L.Y. 5191.

Held, that (1) it being conceded that the petition was concerned with a "matter of discipline", and involved "questions concerning. . . office in the Church", the subject matter of the petition fell within the exclusive jurisdiction of the Church of Scotland in terms of art. IV of the Articles Declaratory of the Church of Scotland in Matters Spiritual; (2) by the Act of 1921, Parliament had recognised certain pre-existing inherent powers in the Church of Scotland, rather than conferred rights upon it, so that the courts of the Church of Scotland could not be equiparated with any tribunal created or upon which a power had been conferred by Parliament, and did not fall within the scope of the ruling in *West*; and interim orders recalled. *Opinion*, that the Court of Session had the power to determine the meaning and effect of the Church of Scotland Act 1921 and the Declaratory Articles and that the judicial review might be available in relation to certain Church matters. (*Ballantyne v. Presbytery of Wigtown*, 1936 S.L.T. 436, considered.) *Observed*, that the duty of counsel to bring all relevant authorities to the notice of the court must be assiduously observed in presenting *ex parte* applications.

LOGAN v. PRESBYTERY OF DUMBARTON (O.H.), 1995 S.L.T. 1228.

EDUCATION

5890. Assisted places

EDUCATION (ASSISTED PLACES) (SCOTLAND) REGULATIONS 1995 (No. 1713) [£4·15], made under the Education (Scotland) Act 1980 (c.44) ss.75A and 75B (both as inserted by s.5 of the Education (Scotland) Act 1981 (c.58)); operative on August 1, 1995; revoke the Education (Assisted Places) (Scotland) Regulations 1989 and the regulations which amend them.

[S.I. 1989 No. 1133, 1990 No. 1346, 1991 No. 1495, 1992 No. 1589, 1993 No. 1659, 1994 No. 1827 revoked.]

ST. MARY'S MUSIC SCHOOL (AIDED PLACES) REGULATIONS 1995 (No. 1712) [£3·70], made under the Education (Scotland) Act 1980 (c.44) ss.73(f), 74(1) (as amended by the Self Governing Schools etc. (Scotland) Act 1989 (c.39), Sched. 10); operative on August 1, 1995; consolidate and revoke the St. Mary's Music School (Aided Places) Regulations 1989 and the regulations which amended them.

[S.I. 1989 No. 1134, 1990 No. 1345, 1991 No. 1494, 1992 No. 1590, 1993 No. 1660, 1994 No. 1826 revoked.]

5891. Central institutions

ROYAL SCOTTISH ACADEMY OF MUSIC AND DRAMA (SCOTLAND) ORDER OF COUNCIL 1995 (No. 2261) [£2·80], made under the Further and Higher Education (Scotland) Act 1992 (c.37) ss.45 and 60; operative on September 21, 1995; amends the constitution, functions and powers of the Governors of the Royal Scottish Academy of Music and Drama and the arrangements to be adopted by them in the discharge of their functions and substantially replaces the Central Institutions (Scotland) Regulations 1988.

[S.I. 1988 No. 1715 partially revoked.]

5892. Educational endowments—approval of amendments to scheme for future government and management of endowment

[Trusts (Scotland) Act 1921 (c.58), s.32(1); Education (Scotland) Act 1980 (c.44), s.105(2) and (4A).]

The Education (Scotland) Act 1980, as amended, s.105(4A) provides *inter alia* that the Court of Session has the power to give effect to draft schemes for the future government and management of applicable educational endowments. In doing so the court "shall have special regard to the matters specified in paras. (*a*) to (*d*) of subsection (2)", which includes "the spirit of the intention of the founders". An application under s.105(4A) was made by the governors of a trust, being an applicable educational endowment, for an order amending the scheme under which the trust was constituted and administered. The amendment was sought to enable indemnity insurance to be provided for each governor out of the income of the trust fund. The governors were unpaid and came from a cross section of society. They averred that in certain circumstances they could incur personal liability and therefore the absence of indemnity insurance would be a disincentive for people to act as governors. The insurance cover sought was for liability in respect of any negligence, default, breach of duty or breach of trust in their capacity as governors but excluding liability for knowing or reckless disregard of breach of trust or breach of duty. The Lord Advocate sought dismissal of the petition, arguing that none of the matters specified in paras. (*a*) to (*d*) of s.105(2) gave any support to the amendments proposed: in particular, the governors had failed to show that it was in accordance with the spirit of the intention of the founders that indemnity insurance should be provided at the expense of the trust. The Lord Advocate further submitted that the governors had failed to explain what justification there might be for the proposed insurance. In particular their liability as trustees for breach of trust was not in need of indemnity insurance in view of the relief provided by s.32 of the Trusts (Scotland) Act 1921. Alternatively, if power was to be given to purchase and maintain insurance it should be restricted so that cover could be provided only for governors who had acted honestly and reasonably, being the criteria for relief under said s.32.

Held, that (1) to "have special regard to" the matters specified in paras. (*a*) to (*d*) of s.105(2) did not require a finding that the draft scheme was supported by those paragraphs, it being sufficient that the proposed amendment was not in conflict with any of the matters which were there set out; (2) the spirit of the intention of the founders would always be relevant to an application under s.105(4A) but that it would be sufficient if the court found that what was proposed was consistent with the spirit of that intention; (3) it was consistent with the spirit of the intention of the founders of the scheme in question that the wide cross section of interests represented on the governing body should not be put at risk by an unwillingness on the part of elected governors to serve or to continue to serve as governors because of a lack of insurance cover; (4) the nature and scale of the activities for which the governing body was responsible in the discharge of its duty to exercise a general supervision and control over the school justified the averment that the governors might incur personal liability for their acts and omissions as governors, and accordingly a power to provide insurance was appropriate; (5) the statutory relief at the discretion of the court in terms of s.32 of the Trusts (Scotland) Act 1921 did not provide a satisfactory alternative to contractual insurance cover in the circumstances of this case; (6) the amendment proposed by the Lord Advocate restricting the availability of insurance cover was unnecessary and inappropriate, the wording of the governors' amendment being subject to an exclusion clause appropriate to their circumstances; and prayer of the petition, as amended, granted. *Opinion*, that the governors' position was indistinguishable for present purposes from that of a charitable company.

GOVERNORS OF DOLLAR ACADEMY TRUST v. LORD ADVOCATE (O.H.), 1995 S.L.T. 596.

5893. Fees

EDUCATION (FEES AND AWARDS) (SCOTLAND) AMENDMENT REGULATIONS 1995 (No. 1271) [65p], made under the Education (Fees and Awards) Act 1983 (c.40), ss.1 and 2 (as amended by the Education Reform Act 1988 (c.40), Sched. 12, and the Further and Higher Education (Scotland) Act 1992 (c.37), Sched. 9); operative on June 1, 1995; extend the existing power to charge higher relevant fees in the case of students with no relevant connection with the United Kingdom and Islands, to cover students undertaking part-time courses begun on or after September 1, 1995.

[S.I. 1983 No. 1215 amended.]

5894. Grants

EDUCATION AUTHORITY BURSARIES (SCOTLAND) REGULATIONS 1995 (No. 1739) [£1·95], made under the Education (Scotland) Act 1980 (c.44), s.49(3); operative on August 1, 1995; consolidate with minor amendment the Education Authority Bursaries (Scotland) Regulations 1988 and regulate the exercise by education authorities of their powers to pay bursaries to students, prescribing eligibility criteria and the requirements subject to which allowances may be paid.

[S.I. 1988 No. 1042, S.I. 1988 No. 1423, S.I. 1989 No. 1113, S.I. 1990 No. 1347 revoked; S.I. 1991 No. 834, S.I. 1993 No. 3184 and S.I. 1994 No. 3148 partially revoked.]

5895. Higher education—Edinburgh College of Art

EDINBURGH COLLEGE OF ART (SCOTLAND) ORDER OF COUNCIL 1995 (No. 471) [£3·20], made under the Further and Higher Education (Scotland) Act 1992 (c.37), ss.45 and 60; operative on March 21, 1995; makes new provisions regarding the constitution, functions and powers of the Board of Governors of the Edinburgh College of Art, as a governing body of that College and the arrangements to be adopted by it in discharging its functions.

[Edinburgh College of Art Order 1959 (c.xxxiv) and S.I. 1988 No. 1715 partially revoked, S.I. 1990 No. 2202 revoked.]

5896. Higher education—universities—refusal of admission

R sought judicial review of a decision of a university (G) to refuse his application for admission to the Faculty of Medicine. G's prospectus stated in the section on the faculty under "Selection of Students" that "You will be called for interview and evidence will be sought that you have seriously considered the implications of a career in medicine and that you are sufficiently motivated as well as having the necessary intellectual ability". G also published a leaflet, of which R was unaware, which stated that "It is expected that applicants will have made some personal effort to acquaint themselves with the way of life a medical career offers. . . . We encourage potential students . . . if possible, to arrange a period of observation in a clinical setting". R, who had obtained six Highers at A grade, had submitted his application form together with a reference and a personal statement giving his reasons for choosing medicine as a career and stating that he had some experience in community care. R had been interviewed for five minutes by M and S, who completed a proforma, writing "none" after the headings "GP contact", "Hospital contact" and "Voluntary work". G wrote to R that "The specific reason for rejection was your failure to express a strong personal enthusiasm for and a commitment to medicine . . . This was reinforced by the fact that you had not made any independent effort to acquaint yourself with the way of life a medical career offers. This should have involved working in a general practice or a hospital or voluntary work in a caring environment." R argued that G had acted contrary to natural justice by making the obtaining of work experience a prerequisite of entry without advising R of this within the prospectus. G's evidence was that, while work experience was seen as evidence of a commitment to medicine as a career and students were advised, if they inquired, to undertake such experience, it was not a prerequisite, and that R had been rejected because he had failed to express any enthusiasm for medicine.

Held, petition refused. G's evidence was accepted. The fact that work experience was or might be an important factor was sufficient to explain the make up of the proforma, and the terms of the leaflet and the letter of rejection were not inconsistent with G's evidence as to their approach, which was supported by the fact that G had admitted a small number of Scottish students in 1994 who did not have any work experience.

REILLY v. UNIVERSITY OF GLASGOW, *The Times*, September 28, 1995.

5897. Local Government. See LOCAL GOVERNMENT, §6126.

5898. School attendance—failure to attend—"reasonable excuse"—onus of proof

[Education (Scotland) Act 1980 (c.44), ss.35(1) and 36; Criminal Procedure (Scotland) Act 1975 (c.21), s.312(x).]

The Crown appealed a justice's decision to uphold S's submission of no case to answer a charge that "[C], a child of school age . . . of whom you are the parent", had failed without reasonable excuse to attend school, contrary to s.35 of the 1980 Act. At the trial the Crown had lodged a certificate of attendance relating to C, but led no further evidence. S argued (1) that the special capacity, in which S was being prosecuted, was not set out in the complaint and that it had not been demonstrated S was the person named in the complaint; and (2) that the minute of proceedings under s.36(1), which provided S with an opportunity to say whether or not there was a reasonable excuse, had not been lodged and there was insufficient evidence for a conviction.

Held, appeal allowed and case remitted to the justice. While the special capacity might have been more clearly worded, there was sufficient to bring into effect s.312(x) of the 1975 Act. The minute of proceedings was not required and, given that the certificate of attendance was sufficient proof that C had failed to attend school regularly and of the number of such occasions and the onus of establishing a reasonable excuse was on S (*Buchanan v. Price* [1983] C.L.Y. 4318, *Neeson v. Lunn* [1985] C.L.Y. 4077), the justice had misdirected himself in upholding S's submission of no case to answer.

ROSS v. SIMPSON, 1995 S.L.T. 956.

5899. Teachers—superannuation. See PENSIONS AND SUPERANNUATION, §6173.

ELECTION LAW

5900. Ballot papers—failure to make official mark—whether election valid

[Representation of the People Act 1983 (c.2), ss.48(1) and 145(1).]

At a local government election four ballot papers were rejected at the count because polling officials at the polling station had inadvertently omitted to stamp them with the official mark when issuing them to voters. The candidate declared duly elected had a majority of one. If the votes on the four unstamped papers had been counted in, the nearest rival candidate would have been elected by a majority of one. That candidate petitioned the court for a declaration, as against the person "duly elected", the other candidates and the returning officer, that she had been duly elected. The petitioner alternatively sought a declaration that the election was void, by virtue of s.48(1) of the Representation of the People Act 1983, as the election was so conducted as not to be substantially in accordance with the laws as to elections or as the breach of the officials' duty had affected the result. She maintained ultimately that a further election should be held. The candidate who had been successful argued that it was only if the successful candidate was disqualified that the court could declare another person elected.

Held, that (1) the election should be declared void; (2) the petitioner would not be declared elected, but a new election should be held; and determinations made accordingly. (*Morgan v. Simpson* [1974] C.L.Y. 1109, followed.)

FITZPATRICK v. HODGE, 1995 S.L.T. (Sh.Ct.) 118.

5901. Ballot papers—failure to make official mark—whether election valid

[Representation of the People Act 1983 (c.2), ss.48(1) and 145(1).]

At a local government election two ballot papers were rejected at the count because polling officials at the polling stations had inadvertently omitted to stamp them with the official mark when issuing them to voters. After several recounts the candidate declared duly elected had a majority of one. If the votes on the two unstamped papers had been counted in, the nearest rival candidate would have been elected by a majority of one. That candidate petitioned the court for a declaration, as against the person "duly elected" and the returning officer, that the other candidate was not duly elected, by virtue of s.48(1) of the Representation of the People Act 1983, as the breach of the officials' duty had affected the result. The petitioner also sought a declaration under s.145(1) that she had been duly elected, or alternatively that the election was invalid and that a further election should be held.

Held, that (1) the election had to be declared invalid for though it had been conducted so as to be substantially in accordance with the law as to elections, the omission by the polling officials had affected the result; (2) it was not then open to the court under s.145(1) to determine that another person had been duly elected and the returning officer should instead be ordained to arrange for a further election to be held; and determination made accordingly. (*Morgan v. Simpson* [1974] C.L.Y. 1109, followed.)

MILLER v. DOBSON, 1995 S.L.T. (Sh.Ct.) 114.

5902. Election expenses—expenses not authorised by election agent—display of posters hostile to one party

[Representation of the People Act 1983 (c.2), s.75(1).]

W and D, Conservative candidates in local elections being held throughout Scotland, sought interdict and interim interdict against a trade union (U) from carrying on an advertising campaign against the Conservative Government and its policies with a view to persuading people not to vote Conservative in the elections, and an order in terms of s.46 of the Court of Session Act 1988 for removal of such advertisements as had already been posted. W and D argued that the campaign contravened s.75(1) of the 1983 Act since it was not authorised by any election agent; if one of its purposes was to secure the election (or non-election) of candidates of a particular party generally, that fell within s.75(1) as much as if it was directed towards a particular candidate in a particular ward.

Held, interim interdict refused. *R. v. Tronoh Mines* [1952] C.L.Y. 1167, approved in *D.P.P. v. Luft* [1976] C.L.Y. 848, established that on a proper construction, advertisements in the form of a generalised attack on one or more of the policies of a political party, at least at the time of a general election, would not contravene s.75(1). The present case was indistinguishable in principle from *Tronoh*. Since the elections were to take place throughout Scotland, they were national elections, albeit for local as opposed to central government, and the national political parties were deeply involved. *Meek v. Lothian Regional Council* [1983] C.L.Y. 4326, founded on by W and D, could be distinguished since the advertisements did not refer to any particular candidate or group of candidates. W and D had failed to make out a prima facie case.

WALKER v. UNISON (O.H.), 1995 S.C.L.R. 786.

5903. European elections. See EUROPEAN UNION, §2254.

5904. Redistribution of seats

PARLIAMENTARY CONSTITUENCIES (SCOTLAND) ORDER 1995 (No. 1037) [£2·40], made under the Parliamentary Constituencies Act 1986 (c.56), s.4; operative in accordance with art. 1(2); gives effect to the recommendations contained in the report of the Boundary Commission for Scotland and, *inter alia*, describes the constituencies into which Scotland will be divided and prescribes that every electoral registration officer shall be required to amend the registers of parliamentary electors to give effect to the Order.

[S.I. 1983 No. 422, 1987 No. 469, 1988 No. 1992 and 1990 No. 2298 revoked.]

5905. Redistribution of seats—Boundary Commission recommendations—relevant considerations

G sought judicial review of the Boundary Commission for Scotland's (B) recommendations in respect of the proposed constituencies of Ayr; Carrick, Cumnock and Doon Valley; and Port Glasgow and Kilmacolm. Having commenced their review in February 1992, B's provisional recommendations affecting Strathclyde were published in November 1993 and were based upon the new regional electoral boundaries produced by the Local Government Boundary Commission for Scotland. A local inquiry had been held and a report submitted by the assistant commissioner, in which he recommended that B consider departing from the regional boundaries in the case of the three constituencies. However, B decided to adhere to their recommendations. G argued that (1) by adopting a rigid policy of using only the regional boundaries in constructing constituencies B had fettered their discretion, and had failed properly to apply the rules in Sched. 2 to the Parliamentary Constituencies Act 1986: division of regional wards, as had been done previously, would have enabled local ties to be better reflected and created constituencies that would have been closer to the electoral quota; and (2) B had acted unreasonably in not using old district as well as the new regional boundaries and in failing to take account of the fact that Strathclyde Region had unusually large electoral divisions.

Held, petition dismissed. (1) Given that B had to adopt a method for constructing constituencies, that B had been required to complete their report by December 31, 1994, and that the new district ward boundaries had not then been available, it had been reasonable for B to use in the regional boundaries. B had been entitled to seek consistency throughout the entire country, although this might have led to a breaking of local ties in some cases, as B had a discretion whether or not to take account of such ties. B had not fettered their discretion, as they had reappraised their method in the light of local inquiries and the recommendations of the assistant commissioners but had concluded that achieving consistency outweighed the alleged breaking of local ties, which was in itself an exercise of their discretion. (2) The court could only intervene on the merits of an issue if B's recommendations showed such a degree of irrationality as to be in defiance of logic (*Council of Civil Service Unions v. Minister for Civil Service* [1985] C.L.Y. 12) and G's criticisms did not begin to approach that test. *Opinion reserved*, as the point was not argued, whether, given that B's recommendations were not decisions and were not binding on the Secretary of State or Parliament, the court had jurisdiction to review them.

GALLIE v. BOUNDARY COMMISSION FOR SCOTLAND (O.H.), *The Times*, February 3, 1995.

EMPLOYMENT

5906. Contracts of employment—breach by employer—failure to pay weekly wages—prescription. See REID v. BEATON, §6232.

5907. Contracts of employment—restrictive covenant. See ARAMARK v. SOMMERVILLE, §5590.

Factories. See HEALTH AND SAFETY AT WORK.

Health and safety at work. See HEALTH AND SAFETY AT WORK.

Master and servant—master's liability to servant. See NEGLIGENCE.

5908. Redundancy payments—dismissal—agreement on early retirement package

R appealed against the decision of an industrial tribunal, affirmed by the employment appeal tribunal, that their employee (L) had been dismissed for the purposes of entitlement to a redundancy payment. In pursuance of a proposed restructuring L had been approached as to his willingness to accept early retirement. L had stated that "if presented with a reasonable package" he would be "happy to leave". Agreement in principle was reached with L; R then adopted a restructuring involving the termination of his post. L signed a form indicating that he had read the letter setting out the proposed terms and wished to take early retirement. The tribunal found that it was at R's instigation that L's employment ended; and that although this was achieved through an early retirement formula, this only arose through L's position being redundant.

Held, appeal allowed. The only issue was whether L had been dismissed by R, which had to be determined by reference to s.83(2), of which only para. (a) might apply. The tribunal had not properly addressed the issue whether L's employment had been terminated by R, and the appeal tribunal were in error in understanding their decision as having done so. The issue was therefore at large for the court. In any event no reasonable tribunal could have concluded that L's contract was terminated by R, since before the decision to restructure had been taken L had indicated willingness to accept the terms proposed and there was nothing to suggest any pressure or persuasion by R. The choice had lain with L and the fact that it had been exercised in the context of the proposal and decision to abolish his post could not be regarded as itself justifying the view that it was R who really terminated the contract.

RENFREW DISTRICT COUNCIL v. LORNIE, *The Scotsman*, July 19, 1995.

5909. Unfair dismissal—procedure—new matters coming to light at appeal hearing

Employers (F) appealed against the industrial tribunal's decision, affirmed by the employment appeal tribunal, that the dismissal of an employee (L) had been procedurally unfair. L had returned late from lunch one day having been drinking; he was then unfit to work in a dock area. A disciplinary hearing was held before one S, at which L admitted a drink problem which might require treatment, and to having been under pressure in recent months. S decided to dismiss L. L exercised his right of appeal to one M. At the hearing L stated that since the earlier hearing he had consulted his doctor, who had advised that his problem was depression and not alcohol, and had prescribed pills. M accepted a suggestion that he adjourn to contact the doctor, who confirmed the advice given. On resuming M stated the result of his inquiry, and that he had gone over all the papers and was satisfied that L had been under the influence of alcohol and unfit for his work, and that the dismissal should stand. The nature of the offence was the main consideration. The industrial tribunal considered that the procedure before S was unexceptionable, but that it was unfair for M not to pursue a further medical inquiry, a condition having been disclosed for which L was receiving treatment. This vitiated the dismissal itself. The E.A.T. held that the tribunal were entitled to take the view that it would have been appropriate for M to have obtained a proper report from the doctor or for F to have had L medically examined. On appeal F argued that the tribunal had substituted its judgment without considering whether the course followed was one a reasonable employer might have taken. L argued that it was for the tribunal to apply their own view as to the scope of fairness and reasonableness, and that procedural unfairness meant that the dismissal was unfair unless the employer could reasonably have taken the view that no explanation or mitigating circumstances could alter the decision to dismiss. L however stated in addition that there was evidence before the tribunal of matters relating to his state of health and the circumstances of the misconduct having been raised at the original hearing and inadequately dealt with, and of inconsistent treatment of other employees found under the influence of drink. He sought a remit back to the tribunal to reconsider these matters if the appeal should succeed.

Held, appeal allowed and (Lord McCluskey dissenting) no remit made. L's general propositions were correct, but M had been entitled to hold that the nature of the offence was the main consideration and a reasonable employer could regard the change in background as a broad issue of no material significance in assessing the seriousness of the conduct. There could not be many situations in which, particularly at the appeal stage, an employer would have a positive duty as a matter of fairness to institute at his own instance, further investigation on a matter the essence of which was undisputed. The tribunal had also substituted its own view for F's and failed to consider whether their conduct fell within the reasonable range. There was no need for a remit where the original decision to dismiss was not open to criticism; the tribunal were not obliged to refer to every item of evidence and there was no basis for thinking that they had failed to consider what were very inspecific allegations. *Per* Lord McCluskey (dissenting on this point): The procedural position was analogous to (*Gordon v. I.R.C.* [1991] C.L.Y. 5147) in that it was open to L to seek to uphold the tribunal's decision on any ground competently before them and it was not clear that the tribunal had taken any decision at all in respect of the further matters raised. The only way to obtain such a decision was to remit to a differently constituted tribunal.

FORTH PORTS AUTHORITY v. LORIMER, 1992 S.C. 512.

5910. Unfair dismissal—procedure—new matters coming to light at appeal hearing. See FORTH PORTS AUTHORITY v. LORIMER, §5909.

5911. Unfair dismissal—transfer of trade or business—employment immediately before transfer

[Transfer of Undertakings (Protection of Employment) Regulations 1981 (S.I. 1981 No. 1794), reg. 5; Council Directive 77/187/EEC, art. 3(1).]

Regulation 8(1) of the Transfer of Undertakings (Protection of Employment) Regulations 1981 provides that a dismissal is unfair "if the transfer or a reason connected with it is the reason or principal reason for [the] dismissal". Regulation 5 provides: "(1). . . [any] contract of employment of any person employed by the transferor in the undertaking. . . which would otherwise have been terminated by the transfer shall have effect after the transfer as if originally made between the person so employed and the transferee. (2) Without prejudice to paragraph (1) above. . . on the completion of a relevant transfer—(a) all the transferor's. . . duties and liabilities under or in connection with any such contract shall be transferred by virtue of this Regulation to the transferee; and (b) anything done before the transfer is completed by or in relation to the transferor in respect of that contract or a person employed in that undertaking. . . shall be deemed to have been done by or in relation to the transferee. (3) Any reference in paragraph (1) or (2) above to a person employed in an undertaking. . . transferred by a relevant transfer is a reference to a person so employed immediately before the transfer." A local authority submitted the work of its direct services organisation to competitive tender under the Local Government Act 1988. An in-house tender was made, and a private contractor submitted a tender. The authority delivered notices of dismissal to certain employees in the direct services organisation, on the ground of redundancy, with effect from December 31, 1992. The notices referred to the failure of the in-house tender. Later the same day the authority accepted the private contractor's tender. The private contractor took over the work on January 1, 1993. The employees sought reinstatement by the authority on the ground that their dismissal had been unfair by virtue of reg. 8(1) of the 1981 Regulations. The industrial tribunal found that the dismissals had been unfair. The authority argued, however, that any obligations owed by them to the employees had been transferred to the contractor by virtue of reg. 5, and it followed that their obligations had been extinguished on January 1, 1993. The industrial tribunal dismissed the applications. The employees appealed, arguing that in reg. 5(2) the word "transfer" did not mean that the transferor's obligations were extinguished, but only that the same obligations were also imposed on the transferee. The employment appeal tribunal allowed the appeal. The authority appealed to the Court of Session. Before the Inner House, the employees also argued, in the alternative, that they had not been employed by the authority at or immediately before the transfer in terms of reg. 5(3), because the notices of dismissal had taken effect on December 31, and that accordingly the regulation did not apply.

Held, that (1) the liability of an employer for the dismissal of an employee could only be excluded by express provision of necessary implication in a statute; (2) reg. 5(2)(a) provided unambiguously that the transferor's obligations were extinguished upon the transfer; (3) in any event it followed from reg. 5(2)(b) that the liability of a transferor for an unfair dismissal was discharged upon the transfer; (4) even if the terms of the notices of dismissal meant that there had been an interval of time between the dismissal and the transfer, on a proper construction of reg. 5(3), reg. 5 applied to persons who would have been employed immediately before the transfer if they had not previously been unfairly dismissed for a reason connected with it; and appealed allowed, and order of the industrial tribunal restored. (Dictum of Morison J. in *Ibex Trading Co. v. Walton* [1994] I.C.R. 907 at p. 916, followed; [1994] C.L.Y. 2018; *Litster v. Forth Dry Dock & Engineering Co.* [1989] C.L.Y. 4304, followed; dictum of Balcombe L.J. in *Secretary of State for Employment v. Spence* [1986] I.R.L.R. 248 at p. 251, distinguished.) *Opinion*, that (1) the court's construction of the 1981 Regulations was consistent with the terms of EEC Council Directive 77/187, which the regulations had been enacted to implement; and (2) that, because Art. 3(1) of the directive provided that member states might (but did not have to) provide that transferors should continue to be liable for their obligations to the transferred employees, it was clear that it had been intend that, if no such provision was made, then there should be no such continuation, and accordingly the terms of the directive were inconsistent with the respondents' argument; and (3) if, contrary to the court's opinion, there were any ambiguity as to whether the United Kingdom had chosen not to exercise the power to provide for joint liability, it could be resolved by reference to the statement to Parliament by the Under-Secretary of State for Employment of December 7, 1981 when seeking approval for the regulations. *Berg and Busschers* [1989] I.R.L.R. 447, approved. *Observed*, that the interpretation of regulations enacted to implement an EEC directive could only be affected by the directive if there was an ambiguity in the former which could be resolved by reference to the latter.

STIRLING DISTRICT COUNCIL v. ALLAN, 1995 S.L.T. 1255.

ENVIRONMENTAL LAW

5912. Environment Act 1995 (c.25)—commencement

ENVIRONMENT ACT 1995 (COMMENCEMENT NO. 2) ORDER 1995 (C.52) (No. 2649) [65p], provides for the coming into force of the following provisions as from October 12, 1995: ss.20, 21, 22, 23, 30, 31, 32, 36, 59 and 120(1). These are principally concerned with the establishment of the Scottish Environment Protection Agency.

5913. Noise pollution—abatement notice—defence of "best practicable means"—delay after service of notice

[Control of Pollution Act 1974 (c.40), s.58(1); Control of Noise (Appeals) (Scotland) Regulations 1983 (S.I. 1983 No. 1455), reg. 4(2).]

Held, in an appeal against an abatement notice under s.58(1) where over two years had elapsed between the date of service of the notice and the appeal, during which time steps had been taken both to prevent, and to counteract the effect of, the noise complained of, that the purpose of the notice had been achieved and that the appeal should be allowed.

MERI MATE v. CITY OF DUNDEE DISTRICT COUNCIL (Sh.Ct.), 1994 S.C.L.R. 960.

5914. Pollution control—failure to comply with statutory notice—time limit—effect of suspension of notice pending appeal

[Control of Pollution Act 1974 (c.40), ss.16(3) and 85(3); Criminal Procedure (Scotland) Act 1975 (c.21) s.331.]

Held, where there was an unsuccessful appeal against a pollution notice under s.16(1) of the 1974 Act, that the time both before and after the appeal suspension of the notice counted in computing the notice's time limit and the date of the commission of the subsequent offence under s.16(4).

McDONALD v. H. L. FRIEL & SON, 1995 S.C.C.R. 461.

5915. Waste—disposal—"deposit"—"land"

[Health and Safety at Work etc. Act 1974 (c.37), s.3(1); Control of Pollution Act 1974 (c.40), ss.3(1), 4(5), 30(1) and 91(1); Control of Pollution (Licensing of Waste Disposal) (Scotland) Regulations 1977 (S.I. 1977 No. 2006), reg. 4; Control of Pollution (Special Waste) Regulations 1980 (S.I. 1980 No. 1709), reg. 4(1); Interpretation Act 1978 (c.30), Sched. 1.]

Held, on the appeal against conviction by G, a company, and D, one of its directors, under *inter alia* the 1974 Acts in respect of the handling of asbestos waste, that (1) a boilerhouse on G's premises, to which the waste was removed, was "land" within s.91(1) of the Control of Pollution Act and could be entered by enforcement officers, despite an argument for G that "land" referred to open land and not premises on the land; (2) similarly the deposit there was a deposit on land within s.3(1) of that Act; (3) plastic sacks containing the asbestos were not being used as "receptacles" within reg. 4(1)(i) of the 1977 Regulations and the deposit was therefore not exempt from s.3(1), nor did it fail to qualify as an environmental hazard within reg. 4(2) and (3); the exemptions related to the reception of waste with a view to that waste "being disposed of elsewhere", *i.e.* at a properly licensed site, and on the findings the deposit at G's premises was not with such a view; (4) the sheriff was entitled to find that there was a "material risk of . . . impairment to health" within s.4(5) although an expert stated that the risk, if the bags were unpunctured, was very small, since that did not mean there was no risk and since the degree of risk fell to be assessed with particular regard to any minimising measures taken whereas G had taken only minimal measures; (5) G were the "producers" of the waste within reg. 4(1) of the 1980 Regulations, where they had been subcontracted as specialists in the removal of asbestos waste and had done the stripping out themselves, despite an argument that either the main contractors or the owners of the premises were the producers; (6) there was sufficient evidence that persons outside G's premises were exposed to risks to their health and safety within s.3(1) of the Health and Safety Act from ruptured sacks within the premises where three witnesses each spoke to such risk and no contrary evidence was led, and it was unnecessary to prove actual discharge of asbestos dust into the atmosphere; (7) the sheriff was entitled to hold in the absence of contrary evidence that the main activity carried on at G's premises was "office activities" despite the presence of a storage warehouse, and therefore that the local authority was the appropriate enforcing authority; and appeals refused.

GOTECH INDUSTRIAL AND ENVIRONMENTAL SERVICES v. FRIEL, 1995 S.C.C.R. 22.

EUROPEAN UNION

5916. Treaties—Agreement on Social Policy—legality of administrative expenditure

[European Communities Act 1972 (c.68), s.1(2).]

The Protocol on Social Policy to the Treaty on European Union narrates that the governments of 11 member states of the EEC, excluding the United Kingdom, have adopted an Agreement on Social Policy and authorises "those 11 member states to have recourse to the institutions, procedures and mechanisms of the Treaty [of Rome] for the purposes of taking among themselves and applying so far as they are concerned the acts and decisions required for giving effect to the . . . Agreement". The Protocol further provides that "Acts adopted by the Council and any financial consequences other than administrative costs entailed for the institutions shall not be applicable to the United Kingdom". Section 2(3) of the European Communities Act 1972 provides authority for the payment by the Crown of "the amounts required to meet any Community obligation to make payments to any of the Communities". Pt. II of Sched. 1 to the Act provides that " 'Community obligation' means any obligation created or arising by or under the Treaties, whether an enforceable Community obligation or not". Section 1(2) of the 1972 Act, as amended by s.1(1) of the European Communities (Amendment) Act 1993, provides that "the Treaties" include "(k) Titles II, III and IV of the Treaty on European Union signed at Maastricht on February 7, 1992, together with the other provisions of the Treaty so far as they relate to those Titles, and the Protocols adopted at Maastricht on that date and annexed to the Treaty establishing the European Community with the exception of the Protocol on Social Policy". The Crown paid money out of the Consolidated Fund to the Commission, an indeterminate amount of which was applied to meet administrative costs entailed by the Agreement on Social Policy. An individual sought declarator that the payment of such money was *ultra vires* the Crown. It was common ground that in the absence of parliamentary authority the payment of money by the Crown was unlawful. The petitioner argued that, since the authority provided by s.2(3) extended only to amounts required to meet "Community obligations", and s.1(2) provided that "the Treaties" did not include the Protocol, any obligation arising out of the Protocol to contribute to "administrative costs" was neither created by nor arose under a Treaty, and therefore was not "Community obligation" in terms of Sched. 1. The Crown argued that the necessary parliamentary authority was to be found in s.1(2)(e) of the 1972 Act, which provides that "the Treaties" include "the decision of . . . 24th June 1988, of the Council on the Communities' system of own resources", Art. 2 of which defines certain revenues payable by member states as "own resources . . . of the Communities". Article 6 provides that "The revenue referred to in Article 2 shall be used without distinction to finance all expenditure entered in the budget of the Communities". The parties were agreed that the "administrative costs" being incurred fell to be treated as being paid out of the budget of the Communities. The Crown also argued that if there was any ambiguity in the 1972 Act, as amended, there should be taken into account a statement made by the Attorney General in the House of Commons in the course of consideration of the then European Communities (Amendment) Bill of 1993, that the authority for the Crown's contribution to the administrative costs was to be found in s.1(2)(e). The petitioner responded that it was not appropriate to do so, because in making the statement the Attorney General had not been promoting the Bill, but had been advancing objections to an opposition amendment which had ultimately been enacted as s.1(2)(k). In addition, the Crown argued that the petition was premature because no decision had been made by the EEC as to whether or not to call upon the member states to make separate contributions, independent of the budget of the Communities, to meet the administrative costs, in which case there would be no authority under s.1(2)(e) and it would be necessary to obtain an Appropriation Act from Parliament.

Held, that the incorporation of the decision of June 24, 1988 as one of the "the Treaties" within the meaning of the 1972 Act provided authority for the payment by the Crown of money towards expenditure payable out of the Community budget, and that since the "administrative costs" comprised expenditure properly paid out of the Community budget, the payment by the Crown was lawful; and petition dismissed. *Opinion,* that (1) the petition was not premature; and (2) notwithstanding the context in which the Attorney General had been speaking, his statement could have been relevant to the construction of the 1993 Act. However, it was unnecessary to take it into account because the legislation was neither unclear nor ambiguous.

MONCKTON v. LORD ADVOCATE (O.H.), 1995 S.L.T. 1201.

EVIDENCE (CIVIL)

5917. Admissibility—admission of liability—admission made in pre-litigation correspondence

A workman claimed damages against his employers for injuries sustained in an accident at work in which his finger had been trapped in a lawnmower. Prior to the commencement of the action there had been an exchange of correspondence between the pursuer's agents and the defenders' insurers, some of which had been marked "without prejudice" and in the course of which the insurers had admitted liability for the accident. The insurers had also made one payment of interim damages to the pursuer. In their defences the defenders denied liability for the accident and also pled a case of contributory negligence against the pursuer. On procedure roll the pursuer contended that the admission of liability in the correspondence constituted a unilateral obligation binding on the defenders and that in any event the defenders had waived their right to dispute liability and were also personally barred from insisting on their defence, and that proof should be restricted to quantum of damages. The defenders argued that the admission of liability had been made by the insurers in the course of discussions carried out with a view to settlement which had not been achieved and therefore could not be founded on. They argued that the pursuer's averments of unilateral obligation and personal bar should be excluded from probation.

Held, that (1), while the law of Scotland allowed, in the public interest, a measure of confidentiality to admissions or concessions made in the course of negotiation prior to litigation, the admission in the present case had been made gratuitously by the insurers, and was not conditional upon settlement being reached and was therefore not part of the negotiation process; but (2) the admission had not been contractual, did not constitute a unilateral obligation and was not a waiver of the defenders' right to dispute liability but was a representation of their position which, by operation of personal bar, they might be barred from departing from; and proof before answer allowed.

GORDON v. EAST KILBRIDE DEVELOPMENT CORPORATION (O.H.), 1995 S.L.T. 62.

5918. Admissibility—contents of document not produced—best evidence rule. See MAYOR v. MAYOR, §5874.

5919. Admissibility—documents—copy document not authenticated by person responsible for making copy

[Civil Evidence (Scotland) Act 1988 (c.32), s.6(1).]

Held, that copy documents which had not been authenticated by the person responsible for making the copies were inadmissible as evidence in a proof, even although some of them had purportedly been authenticated during the proof.

McILVENEY v. DONALD (Sh.Ct.), 1995 S.C.L.R. 802.

5920. Admissibility—fairness—whether statements made to immigration office fairly obtained. See OGHONOGHOR v. SECRETARY OF STATE FOR THE HOME DEPARTMENT, §5923.

5921. Affidavits

[Civil Evidence (Scotland) Act 1988 (c.32), s.2; Sheriff Courts (Scotland) Act 1907 (c.51), Sched. r. 72A.]

In an action of divorce by W against H, W sought a capital sum. W claimed she had made substantial financial contributions to the family from the proceeds of property sold in Australia. W's sister, S, in Australia, had sworn an affidavit on the details surrounding the various sales by W and S jointly. Due to cost and distance, S was unable to travel to give evidence in person. H and W were both assisted persons. W moved for the affidavit to be received in terms of r. 72A. H argued that such evidence required to be non-controversial and the more critical the evidence, the less appropriate was such a procedure (*Ebrahem v. Ebrahem* [1989] C.L.Y. 4237). H disputed information in the affidavit, claiming it was hearsay. H claimed its introduction would be prejudicial.

Held, motion granted. The test of appropriateness lay in s.2 of the 1988 Act. The court did not have discretion to exclude hearsay evidence otherwise admissible. Such discretion to exclude would require to be expressly conferred by statute, otherwise there would be a discretion to exclude documentary hearsay but not oral (*Smith v. Alexander Baird* [1993] C.L.Y. 5277). Where the statement was a matter of which direct oral evidence by the maker of the statement would be admissible then such documentary evidence could not be excluded. The words "may be received in evidence" in r. 72A(1) did not qualify the admissibility of a statement which passed that test. The question of relevancy and competency of particular statements in the affidavit would be reserved and the granting of W's motion did not imply that evidence was credible or reliable. W was more likely to suffer prejudice as the affidavit would be considered with caution and weighed accordingly. *Opinion*, that the fact that receiving such an affidavit would save the legal aid fund expense was not a matter bound to be taken into account.

McVINNIE v. McVINNIE, 1995 S.L.T. (Sh.Ct.) 81.

5922. Civil Evidence (Family Mediation) (Scotland) Act 1995 (c.6)

This Act makes provision for the inadmissibility as evidence in civil proceedings in Scotland of information as to what occurred during family mediation. The Act received Royal Assent on May 1, 1995.

5923. Competency—fairness—whether statements made to immigration officer fairly obtained

A Nigerian woman entered the United Kingdom on a visitor's visa. She then started a course of study and stayed beyond the expiry date of her visa, having sought permission to remain and study, which permission was refused. An immigration officer instructed to inquire into the circumstances interviewed the woman under caution in relation to her overstaying. During the interview the officer formed the view that the woman might not be merely an "overstayer" but might be an illegal immigrant, having obtained her visitor's visa at a time when she had already formed the intention of studying in the United Kingdom, but continued to question her without issuing a further caution. *Opinion*, that information obtained about the illegality of entry was unfairly obtained, the immigration officer not having made it clear to the woman that his questions were related to the issue of illegal entry.

OGHONOGHOR v. SECRETARY OF STATE FOR THE HOME DEPARTMENT (O.H.), 1995 S.L.T. 733.

5924. Competency—hearsay. See DAVIES v. McGUIRE, §5926.

5925. Confidentiality—school records

Held, that confidential records held by an education authority, relating to a pupil's behaviourial problems, might be required to be produced in a court action if necessary in the interests of justice.

M. v. BRITISH RAILWAYS BOARD, *The Scotsman*, September 13, 1995.

Evidence (Criminal). See CRIMINAL EVIDENCE AND PROCEDURE.

5926. Hearsay—evidence of earlier statements sought to be led to discredit witness in advance—competency

[Civil Evidence (Scotland) Act 1988 (c.32), ss.2, 3 and 4.]

The Civil Evidence (Scotland) Act 1988 provides for the general admission of hearsay evidence (s.2) and for its use in reflecting favourably or unfavourably on the credibility of a witness (s.3). Provision is also made in s.4 for a witness to be recalled or called as an extra witness for the purposes of ss.2 and 3. At a proof in an action relating to the death of a boy in a road accident, the defender sought to adduce evidence, in advance of the evidence to be given by eyewitnesses, of statements made by such eyewitnesses to the police investigating the accident.

Held, that neither s.2 nor s.3 of the 1988 Act warranted the leading of such evidence in advance of the evidence of such eyewitnesses, but that it was competent to recall a witness to give such evidence after the eyewitnesses had given evidence. *Observations*, on the weight to be attached to such hearsay evidence.

DAVIES v. McGUIRE (O.H.), 1995 S.L.T. 755.

5927. Hearsay—precognition—solicitor who prepared precognition giving evidence of statements made by witness

[Civil Evidence (Scotland) Act 1988 (c.32), ss.2, 3 and 4.]

The Civil Evidence (Scotland) Act 1988 provides for the general admission of hearsay evidence. At a proof in an action of damages for personal injuries a party adduced the evidence of a solicitor who had taken a precognition from a witness.

Held, that without a precise record of what was asked and what was answered, the evidence of the statements made by the witness was of little weight compared with what he said on oath in the witness box.

CAVANAGH v. B.P. CHEMICALS (O.H.), 1995 S.L.T. 1287.

EVIDENCE (CRIMINAL)

See CRIMINAL EVIDENCE AND PROCEDURE.

EXECUTORS AND ADMINISTRATORS

5928. Executor—executor-dative—liability for debts of estate on which deceased had been executrix-nominate

[Executors (Scotland) Act 1900 (c.55), ss.6 and 7.]

A widow was confirmed as executrix-nominate on the estate of her late husband. Approximately six weeks later she died and JS was appointed executrix-dative to her and confirmed to her estate. A nephew of the deceased husband claimed remuneration for services allegedly carried out for his deceased uncle and in due course raised an action against JS as executrix-dative.

Held, that the executrix of a person who was executrix-nominate of a deceased debtor was under no obligation to account for the latter's intromissions, as executrix or as universal legatory, and that in the absence of averments that the defender had intromitted with the estate of the deceased husband, the action fell to be dismissed.

DALGLEISH v. SWANSTON (Sh. Ct.), 1994 S.C.L.R. 920.

EXPENSES

5929. Caution for expenses—limited company as pursuers—consequence of failure to find caution

[Companies Act 1985 (c.6), s.726(2).]

M raised an action for payment against L for claims arising out of a building contract and L counterclaimed for the cost of remedial works resulting from

M's breach of contract. Diets of proof were fixed for November 21, 22 and 24, 1994. On October 27, 1994 the sheriff ordained M to lodge caution in the sum of £6,000 and sisted the action until caution was found. On the view that this was required by s.726(2) of the Companies Act 1985, the interlocutor did not specify a time limit within which caution had to be found. M did not lodge caution and following L's motion for decree of absolvitor with expenses and for dismissal of the counterclaim with no expenses due to or by either party, the sheriff assoilzied L although he did not deal with the counterclaim. M appealed. The sheriff stated in his note that it was implicit in the interlocutor of October 27 that the order should be complied with within a reasonable time and M's failure to obtemper it brought into play r. 59 of the Ordinary Cause Rules, enabling him to grant absolvitor in the exercise of his discretion. M argued that (1) it was not open to the court under s.726(2) to impose any time limit for the finding of caution; Macphail, *Sheriff Court Practice*, para. 11–62 was incorrect in stating that a court was entitled to grant absolvitor for failure to lodge caution and *Augustinus v. Anglia Building Society* [1990] C.L.Y. 5187 was wrongly decided; (2) a party could not be in default under s.726(2) and there was no room for the operation of r. 59(1); (3) it was incompetent for the sheriff who dealt with L's motion to purport to introduce a time limit since only an appellate court could vary an earlier interlocutor; (4) L were personally barred from seeking to impose a time limit for finding caution since their own motion did not specify a time limit; and (5) as M were now in a position to lodge caution, their failure to find caution should be excused, the appeal should be allowed and the case remitted to the sheriff.

Held, appeal refused and counterclaim dismissed. Section 726(2) did not have the narrow and restricted meaning contended for by M and allowed a court to impose a time limit at the time that it found caution. It was inconceivable that Parliament, after authorising a court to make an order for caution, intended that a party could flout that order with impunity and no possible consequence, and therefore Parliament must have intended that a court's normal powers to deal with a failure to obey an order would apply. In addition, the court was not obliged to sist the proceedings until caution was found as the provision was permissive, not mandatory. It was therefore an inevitable inference that s.726(2) implicitly allowed the court all the normal powers to secure compliance with the order, which included the imposition of a time limit or coming to an *ex post facto* view that the pursuer had defaulted in complying with the order where a reasonable time had passed (*Augustinus*, and *Pearson v. Naydler* [1977] C.L.Y. 2393, followed). It was open to the sheriff to impose a time limit for finding caution and the fact that he did not do so did not preclude the second sheriff from concluding that M had not found caution within a reasonable time, that M were therefore in default and to grant absolvitor. The appeal had to be decided on the basis of whether the sheriff was right or wrong and not on the basis that M could now lodge caution.

METRIC MODULES INTERNATIONAL v. LAUGHTON CONSTRUCTION CO (Sh.Ct.), 1995 S.C.L.R. 676.

5930. Caution for expenses—limited company as pursuers—time limit. See METRIC MODULES INTERNATIONAL v. LAUGHTON CONSTRUCTION CO, §5929.

5931. Caution for expenses—sequestrated person attempting to have reduced decree for payment on which sequestration proceeded

A sequestrated person raised an action of reduction of the decree for payment the non-payment of which had led to her sequestration. Her trustee intimated that he did not wish to be sisted to the action. The holder of the decree enrolled for the pursuer to be ordained to find caution for the expenses of the action, founding on the general rule that an undischarged bankrupt was not entitled to sue an action without finding caution. In opposing the motion the pursuer founded on the special circumstances that (1) she had been made bankrupt on the application of the holder of the decree and should accordingly be regarded as a defender rather than a pursuer; (2) issues were raised regarding the conduct of the holder of the decree; and (3) the holder of the decree was in effect her only creditor.

Held, that there were no sufficient exceptional circumstances for the pursuer to avoid the requirement for caution, especially since the holder of the decree was not the only creditor, the pursuer had already been ordained to find caution in another action and she could have raised the issue raised in the present action in the action in which decree had been pronounced against her; and decree ordaining caution in sum of £4,000 to be found pronounced.

MARSH v. BAXENDALE (O.H.), 1995 S.L.T. 196.

5932. Court of Session—fees

ACT OF SEDERUNT (RULES OF THE COURT OF SESSION 1994) (AMENDMENT No. 2) (FEES OF SOLICITORS) 1995 (No. 1396) [£1·55], made under the Court of Session Act 1988 (c.36), s.5 (as amended by the Civil Evidence (Scotland) Act 1988 (c.32) s.2(3)); operative on June 22, 1995; amends the Rules of the Court of Session 1994, Pt II of Chap. 42 by providing for a fee for an expert witness giving evidence by affidavit, clarifies the rules on lodging accounts and charges for the precognition of witnesses and increases the fees payable to solicitors and increases the maximum outlays in undefended causes.

[S.I. 1994 No. 1443 amended.]

5933. Court of Session—fees of messengers-at-arms

ACT OF SEDERUNT (FEES OF MESSENGERS-AT-ARMS) (NO. 2) 1994 (No. 3268) [£1·10], made under the Execution of Diligence (Scotland) Act 1926 (c.16), s.6 and the Court of Session Act 1988 (c.36), s.5; operative on January 9, 1995; amends the Act of Sederunt (Fees of Messengers-at-Arms) 1994 by increasing fees payable to messengers-at-arms by about 3 per cent.

[S.I. 1994 No. 391 amended.]

5934. Court of Session—scale—sheriff court ordinary scale without sanction of counsel

An action was raised in the Court of Session, not under the optional procedure, for reparation for injuries sustained in an accident at work on October 20, 1992. The sum concluded for was £10,000. The action was settled by way of minutes of tender and acceptance for the sum of £1,450. On the pursuer's motion for expenses from the date of the tender the defenders moved for expenses to be modified to the sheriff court summary cause scale without sanction for the employment of counsel.

Held, that (1) the facts of the case were simple and not unusual and that there were no difficulties in the pleadings which would require the assistance of counsel; (2) the sum sued for was grossly exaggerated; and expenses awarded to the pursuer but modified to the sheriff court ordinary cause scale without certification for the employment of counsel.

GORDON v. STRATHCLYDE BUSES (O.H.), 1995 S.L.T. 1019.

5935. Court of Session—skilled witnesses—certification—motion enrolled after award of expenses granted

[Rules of the Court of Session 1994, rr. 2.1 and 42.13(3).]

Rule 42.13 of the Rules of the Court of Session 1994 provides that the Auditor of Court may not allow any additional remuneration for a skilled witness unless the court has granted a motion, not later than the time at which it awards expenses, certifying that the witness was a skilled witness, and recording the name of the witness in the interlocutor pronounced by the court. After proof in an action of damages the Lord Ordinary granted decree of absolvitor in favour of the defenders and found the pursuer liable to the defenders in expenses. The pursuer reclaimed and the Inner House sustained the reclaiming motion. When the case called for advising before the Inner House, the pursuer moved for expenses but omitted to move for certification of certain witnesses as skilled witnesses. The Inner House pronounced an interlocutor finding the defenders liable to the pursuer in the expenses of the Outer House and of the reclaiming motion, and decerned against the defenders for payment of these expenses as taxed by the Auditor of Court. The pursuer subsequently enrolled a motion in which he sought late certification of the expert witnesses, and asked the court to exercise its dispensing power under r. 2.1 in respect of the late enrolment. The motion was unopposed but the pursuer's counsel drew the court's attention to the case of *Hodge v. British Coal Corporation (No. 3)* [1992] C.L.Y. 5779 where it had been held, in similar circumstances, that the court had no power to exercise its dispensing power, being *functus officio*.

Held, that (1) certification of the witnesses as expert witnesses would not imply any alteration or recall of the decerniture for expenses, and would not change the basis of taxation, its only effect being to enable something to be done which was consequential on the award of expenses, and the motion was therefore competent; (2) it was appropriate to exercise the dispensing power where the need for certification only arose because of the pursuer's success in the reclaiming motion, and the motion had been enrolled at the earliest opportunity after the matter had come to the notice of the pursuer's solicitor; and motion granted. (*U.C.B. Bank v. Dundas & Wilson C.S.* [1991] C.L.Y. 4997 followed; *Hodge v. British Coal Corporation*, O.H., February 18, 1992, unreported (1992 G.W.D. 15–890), overruled.)

MAINS v. UNIROYAL ENGLEBERT TYRES (NO. 2), 1995 S.L.T. 1127.

5936. Crown—award of expenses against Crown—Crown not party to litigation—whether competent

[Exchequer Court (Scotland) Act 1856 (c.56), s.24]

The Secretary of State for Scotland (S) appealed a sheriff's interlocutor in M's action for damages against U finding the Scottish Courts Administration (C) liable for the expenses occasioned by the discharge of a diet of continued proof on October 17, 1994. Following three days of proof in March and June, a further diet had been fixed for October 17. About two weeks prior to that date the sheriff had advised the sheriff clerk that he would then be on leave, but this had not been communicated to M and U, who had attended on October 17. A further hearing had been fixed for November 7, but the sheriff had been absent due to illness and another sheriff had granted a joint motion for an award of expenses against C. M and U argued that (1) at common law, the underlying principle was that expenses could be recovered from any person who had caused the expenses, and that, while awards were normally made against parties, with the exceptions of *domini litis* and law agents, the categories of exception were not closed; and (2) the 1856 Act authorised the award, as the words "in any Cause" in the second part of s.24 showed that an award against the Crown was not restricted to actions in which it was a party.

Held, appeal allowed. (1) As C had no legal persona, being merely a department of the Scottish Office, the interlocutor was incompetent. However, had M and U otherwise succeeded, the interlocutor would have been corrected by substituting S for C. (2) Apart from the above exceptions, there had not been any instance in the last 150 years of a court making an award against a person who was not a party to the litigation and it had not been open to the sheriff to depart from that policy, as otherwise it would be impossible to define the limits of any such extension. (3) Clear and unambiguous statutory authority would be required before any award could be made against the Crown, as otherwise Crown prerogative and the constitutional convention which gave Parliament sole power to control the expenditure of public revenues would be breached (*Steele Ford & Newton (a firm) v. Crown*

Prosecution Service [1993] C.L.Y. 3175). It was clear that the words "in any Cause" in s.24 related to a cause in which one of the parties was the Crown. Even considering the second part of the section alone, it required a motion for expenses to be preceded by a decree which could give rise to such a motion, which could only be a decree between the Crown and a subject. As there was no other enactment providing authority for the award, the interlocutor was incompetent. *Opinion reserved*, on S's argument that, as the basis of the award was fault and negligence by court staff, the award would in effect circumvent the immunity provided in s.2(5) of the Crown Proceedings Act 1947 and the rule that the Crown was only liable for its servants if they had acted maliciously, and accordingly had to be incompetent. *Observed*, that it was most undesirable that parties to a litigation should have to bear considerable expense simply on account of an administrative error, but that any solution to that problem would be a matter of complexity.

MEEKISON v. UNIROYAL ENGLEBERT TYRES, 1995 S.L.T. (Sh.Ct.) 63.

5937. Divorce—contested financial claims—successful defender

H sought the expenses of a divorce action following the Lord Ordinary's decision to find in H's favour on the two central questions in the proof, that the matrimonial home should be sold rather than transferred to W, and that the matrimonial property should be divided equally. W argued that, as a result of the judgment, she would be under financial stress in respect of the children's school fees, that an adverse award of expenses would seriously deplete the sums recovered by her; and that she had behaved responsibly in the litigation.

Held, H awarded the expenses of the proof and the procedure following thereon; *quoad ultra* no expenses due to or by either party. While the court's approach to expenses in cases under the Family Law (Scotland) Act 1985 had to be more flexible than in a simple petitory action (*Little v. Little*, 1990 S.L.T. 785 at p. 790; [1989] C.L.Y. 4249, [1990] C.L.Y. 5111), it was plain that W's insistence on two points of principle had necessitated the proof, and, as H had succeeded on these two points, he was entitled to an award. Given that W had not regarded these points as negotiable, it was not relevant that H had not lodged a tender or submitted an extrajudicial offer. However, an award of the whole expenses would be unjustified, as both parties' personal and financial affairs had been subject to uncertainty and neither party could adopt a final position until full and up to date information had been exchanged shortly before proof. The award made was a realistic reflection of the avoidable expense occasioned by W. The award would not be effective until the date of sale of the matrimonial home.

ADAMS v. ADAMS (NO. 2) (O.H.), *The Scotsman*, June 8, 1995.

5938. Divorce—modified award of expenses. See MACDONALD v. MACDONALD, §5876.

Factories. See HEALTH AND SAFETY AT WORK.

5939. High Court of Justiciary—fees

HIGH COURT OF JUSTICIARY FEES AMENDMENT ORDER 1994 (No. 3266) [£1·10], made under the Courts of Law Fees (Scotland) Act 1895 (c.14), s.2 (as amended by the Divorce Jurisdiction, Court Fees and Legal Aid (Scotland) Act 1983 (c.12), s.4); operative on February 1, 1995; amends the High Court of Justiciary Fees Order 1984 by substituting a new art. 3 which restricts the Crown fee exemption to matters relating to the enforcement of the criminal law and increases most fees payable to the Principal Clerk of Justiciary in relation to proceedings in the High Court of Justiciary.

[S.I. 1984 No. 252 amended.]

5940. Land Court—award of expenses—request for stated case on question of expenses

The Land Court dismissed an application by landlords for consent to the operation of a notice to quit. The landlords were found liable for the expenses incurred by the tenant. The Court stated a special case for the opinion of the Court of Session on a number of questions of law arising from the decision to dismiss. The landlords then requested the Court to state a special case for the opinion of the Court of Session on the question of expenses.

Held, that the determination on expenses was made in the exercise of the Court's discretion and did not raise separate questions of law which would properly be the subject of a special case; and requisition refused.

FANE v. MURRAY, 1994 S.L.C.R. 148.

5941. Land Court—fees

SCOTTISH LAND COURT (FEES) ORDER 1995 (No. 307) [£1·10], made under the Courts of Law Fees (Scotland) Act 1895 (c.14), s.2 (as substituted by the Divorce Jurisdiction, Court Fees and Legal Aid (Scotland) Act 1983 (c.12), s.4); operative on April 1, 1995; in most cases increases the fees payable in respect of proceedings before the Scottish Land Court.

[S.I. 1994 No. 498 revoked.]

5942. Lands Tribunal—fees

LANDS TRIBUNAL FOR SCOTLAND (AMENDMENT) (FEES) RULES 1995 (No. 308) [£1·10], made under the Lands Tribunal Act 1949 (c.42), s.3(6)(12)(e) (as inserted by the Conveyancing and Feudal Reform (Scotland) Act 1970 (c.35), s.50(2), and amended by S.I. 1972 No. 2002); operative on April 1, 1995; amend the Lands Tribunal for Scotland Rules 1971 so as to increase some of the fees payable to the tribunal.

[S.I. 1971 No. 218 amended; S.I. 1994 No. 497 revoked.]

Legal aid. See LEGAL AID.

5943. Licensing board—separate representation—whether justified. See ROBERTSON v. CITY OF EDINBURGH DISTRICT LICENSING BOARD, §6042.

5944. Sheriff court—award of expenses against Crown—Crown not party to litigation—competency. See MEEKISON v. UNIROYAL ENGLEBERT TYRES, §5936.

5945. Sheriff court—fees

ACT OF SEDERUNT (FEES OF SOLICITORS IN THE SHERIFF COURT) (AMENDMENT) 1995 (No. 1395) [£1·95], made under the Sheriff Courts (Scotland) Act 1907 (c.51), s.4 (as amended by the Secretaries of State Act 1926 (c.18), s.1(3), the Administration of Justice (Scotland) Act 1933 (c.41), schedule to and the Divorce Jurisdiction, Court fees and Legal Aid (Scotland) Act 1983 (c.12), Scheds. 1 and 2); operative on June 22, 1995; makes amendments to the General Regulations in the Act of Sederunt (Fees of Solicitors in the Sheriff Court) (Amendment and Further Provisions) 1993, increases the fees payable to solicitors and increases the maximum additional fee for a report.

[S.I. 1993 No. 3080 amended.]

5946. Sheriff court—fees. See MELLOR v. TOWLE, §6360.

5947. Sheriff court—fees—minute for decree in absence—minute including crave to amend defender's address

[Sheriff Court Fees Amendment (No. 2) Order 1993 (S.I. 1993 No. 2957). Sched., Pt. V, para. 39.]

Held, where pursuers endorsed a minute for decree in absence against two defenders on the initial writ and included in their crave for decree a crave to amend the writ by substituting the address where service had been effected for the address originally stated in the instance, that the minute fell to be treated as a minute for decree in absence for which no fee was payable, notwithstanding the fact that it included a crave to amend the writ and that a fee of £21 would have been payable for a minute of amendment.

SLEAFORD TRADING CO. v. NORMAN (Sh.Ct.), 1994 S.C.L.R. 1093.

5948. Sheriff court—fees of senior counsel

C objected to a report by an auditor of court, in which the auditor had allowed in respect of senior counsel's fees only £450 "for the first day of the eight day proof" and £225 for each of the remaining seven days, which were not required. At the commencement of the hearing, C sought to amend his note of objection to substitute for the proposed daily rate of £1,250, the actual sum charged of £1,500 per day, inclusive of preparation. F argued that C was bound by his original proposal (Macphail, *Sheriff Court Practice*, para. 19–38).

Held, amendment and objection allowed, and £1,200 per day allowed. (1) The note gave adequate notice of the matters to be reviewed and it was a matter of discretion whether to allow the precise figure to be amended. (2) The auditor had erred, first as to the nature and history of the action, in that five days of evidence had already been heard and the case set down for a further eight days when it settled, and secondly in applying the criminal legal aid scale, albeit with a 20 per cent enhancement, as this was irrelevant and when applied meant that senior counsel received less than C's solicitor for attending the first day of the continued diet of proof (*Farquhar v. Ramsay*, Dundee sheriff court, 1979/80, unreported, not followed). The action had been complex and difficult, it had concerned C's dismissal as chief executive of F and involved a large pecuniary claim, and the employment of senior counsel had been appropriate. The test of counsel's fee was essentially a market one, and unless a fee was plainly extravagant, it was to be allowed (*Caledonian Railway Co. v. Greenock Corporation*, 1922 S.L.T. 25; *Elas v. SMT Co.* [1950] C.L.Y. 4802). Considering the fee actually charged, and that F's senior counsel had charged £1,000 per day plus three days' preparation at half rate, there appeared to be an element of premium in the fee, which was confirmed by C's assessment put in the original note, and £1,200 per day would be allowed for the five days of proof, the first day of the continued diet and for two days in addition.

CASSIDY v. CELTIC FOOTBALL AND ATHLETIC CO. (Sh. Ct.), 1995 S.C.L.R. 395.

5949. Sheriff court—fees of sheriff officers

ACT OF SEDERUNT (FEES OF SHERIFF OFFICERS) (NO. 2) 1994 (No. 3267) [£1·55], made under the Sheriff Courts (Scotland) Act 1907 (c.51), s.40 (as amended by the Secretaries of State Act 1926 (c.18), s.1(3), the Administration of Justice (Scotland) Act 1933 (c.41), Sched., and the Divorce Jurisdiction, Court Fees and Legal Aid (Scotland) Act 1983 (c.12), Scheds. 1 and 2), and the Execution of Diligence (Scotland) Act 1926 (c.16), s.6; operative on January 9, 1995; amends the Act of Sederunt (Fees of Sheriff Officers) 1994 by increasing the fees payable to sheriff officers by about 3 per cent.

[S.I. 1994 No. 392 amended.]

5950. Sheriff court—fees of sheriff officers—poinding—personal liability of instructing solicitors. See STIRLING PARK & CO. v. DIGBY, BROWN & CO., §6346.

5951. Sheriff court—minute of amendment allowed to be received—award of expenses of cause to date

[Sheriff Courts (Scotland) Act 1907 (c.51), Sched. r.64(1) and (2).]

A appealed against a sheriff's interlocutor of June 23, 1994 when, after granting A's motion to allow a minute of amendment to be received and to discharge a diet of proof fixed for July 1, 1994, he awarded C the whole expenses of the cause on the basis that the amendments amounted to a total rewriting of A's case. A, who had not sought leave to appeal from the sheriff in terms of s.27(b) of the Sheriff Courts (Scotland) Act 1907, argued that the award was incompetent and that the sheriff had acted *ultra vires* of r.64(2) of the (1983) Ordinary Cause Rules which only permitted an award of expenses where an amendment was allowed, not merely when it had been allowed to be received.

Held, appeal refused. It had always been within a court's general common law powers to make an order for expenses and since a sheriff normally had complete discretion to award or withhold expenses, an award at the stage when a minute of amendment was allowed to be received could not possibly be said to be incompetent. Rule 64(2) applied only where an amendment had been allowed and did not prohibit a sheriff from dealing with questions of expenses as he saw fit at any other stage in an amendment procedure. By failing to seek leave from the sheriff, A had perilled their appeal on being able to show that what the sheriff did was incompetent.

AMPLIFLAIRE v. THE CHISHOLME INSTITUTE (Sh.Ct.), 1995 S.C.L.R. 11.

5952. Sheriff court—summary cause—three pursuers receiving a total of £1,000 but less than £750 each—appropriate scale

Held, in an action of damages by three pursuers which was settled on the basis of a total payment by the defenders of £1,000 with each pursuer receiving less than £750, that the pursuers were entitled to expenses on the summary cause scale rather than on the small claim scale.

WALKER v. J.G. MARTIN PLANT HIRE (Sh. Ct.), 1995 S.C.L.R. 398.

5953. Skilled witnesses—certification. See MAINS v. UNIROYAL ENGLEBERT TYRES (NO. 2), §5935.

5954. Solicitors—personal liability—solicitors acting on counsel's advice

A legally aided woman raised an action against three defenders in respect of an accident in which she sustained injuries. On the last day of a four day proof the pursuer advised the court she was not insisting on her case against the first defenders, no evidence having been led against those defenders. The third defenders were subsequently also assoilzied and the second defenders were found liable to the pursuer in damages. The first defenders sought expenses against the pursuer's local agents and Edinburgh agents personally on the basis that it ought to have been plain before the proof that no evidence against them existed. The solicitors had acted on the advice of counsel in maintaining the case against the first defenders.

Held, that since it was not competent to make an award against counsel personally, it would be unfair to find personally liable a solicitor who had acted on counsel's advice; and motion refused. *Observed*, that it was for consideration whether, as in England, there should be a statutory power to make an award against counsel.

REID v. EDINBURGH ACOUSTICS (No. 2) (O.H.), 1995 S.L.T. 982.

FACTORIES

See HEALTH AND SAFETY AT WORK.

FAMILY LAW

Family law. See CHILDREN AND YOUNG PERSONS; DIVORCE AND CONSISTORIAL CAUSES; HUSBAND AND WIFE; PARENT AND CHILD.

FIRE SERVICE

5955. Administration schemes

NORTH EASTERN COMBINED FIRE SERVICES AREA ADMINISTRATION SCHEME ORDER 1995 (No. 2632) [£1·55], made under the Local Government. (Scotland) Act 1973 (c.65), s.147 (as substituted by the Local Government etc. (Scotland) Act 1994 (c.39), s.36); operative on October 31, 1995; makes an administration scheme in relation to the combined fire services area, known as North Eastern, comprising the new local government areas of Aberdeenshire, Aberdeen City and Moray, the fire brigade for the existing Grampian Region being the fire brigade for the new combined area, and creates a new joint fire board; providing that the said scheme shall have effect from April 1, 1996, but that in relation to the board's constitution and the carrying out of necessary functions to bring the scheme into operation, the scheme shall have effect from the operative date of the order, October 31, 1995.

NORTHERN COMBINED FIRE SERVICES AREA ADMINISTRATION SCHEME ORDER 1995 (No. 2633) [£1·55], made under the Local Government (Scotland) Act 1973 (c.65), s.147 (as substituted by the Local Government etc. (Scotland) Act 1994 (c.39), s.36); operative on October 31, 1995; makes an administration scheme in relation to the combined fire services area, known as Northern, comprising the new local government areas of Highland, Orkney Islands, Shetland Islands and the Western Isles, the fire brigade for the existing Highland Region being the fire brigade for the new combined area, and creates a new joint fire board; providing that the said scheme shall have effect from April 1, 1996, but that in relation to the board's constitution and the carrying out of necessary functions to bring the scheme into operation, the scheme shall have effect from the operative date of the order, October 31, 1995.

SOUTH EASTERN COMBINED FIRE SERVICES AREA ADMINISTRATION SCHEME ORDER 1995 (No. 2634) [£1·55], made under the Local Government (Scotland) Act 1973 (c.65), s.147 (as substituted by the Local Government etc. (Scotland) Act 1994 (c.39), s.36); operative on October 31, 1995; makes an administration scheme in relation to the combined fire services area, known as South Eastern, comprising the new local government areas of East Lothian, Midlothian, West Lothian, the Scottish Borders and City of Edinburgh, the fire brigade for the existing Lothian and Borders Region being the fire brigade for the new combined area, and creates a new joint fire board; providing that the said scheme shall have effect from April 1, 1996, but that in relation to the board's constitution and the carrying out of necessary functions to bring the scheme into operation, the scheme shall have effect from the operative date of the order October 31, 1995.

CENTRAL COMBINED FIRE SERVICES AREA ADMINISTRATION SCHEME ORDER 1995 (No. 2635) [£1·55], made under the Local Government (Scotland) Act 1973 (c.65), s.147 (as substituted by the Local Government etc. (Scotland) Act 1994 (c.39), s.36); operative on October 31, 1995; makes an administration scheme in relation to the combined fire services area, known as Central, comprising the new local government areas of Clackmannanshire, Falkirk and Stirling, the fire brigade for the existing Central Region being the fire brigade for the new combined area, and creates a new joint fire board; providing that the said scheme shall have effect from April 1, 1996, but that in relation to the board's constitution and the carrying out of necessary functions to bring the scheme into operation, the scheme shall have effect from the operative date of the order, October 31, 1995.

MID AND SOUTH WESTERN COMBINED FIRE SERVICES AREA ADMINISTRATION SCHEME ORDER 1995 (No. 2636) [£1·55], made under the Local Government (Scotland) Act 1973 (c.65), s.147 (as substituted by the Local Government etc. (Scotland) Act 1994 (c.39), s.36); operative on October 31, 1995; makes an administration scheme in relation to the combined fire services area, known as Mid and South Western, comprising the new local government areas of Argyll and Bute, City of Glasgow, Dumbarton and Clydebank, East Dunbartonshire, Inverclyde, East Renfrewshire, East Ayrshire, North Ayrshire, South Ayrshire, North Lanarkshire, South Lanarkshire, and Renfrewshire, the fire brigade for the existing Strathclyde Region being the fire brigade for the new combined area, and creates a new joint fire board; providing that the said scheme shall have effect from April 1, 1996, but that in relation to the board's constitution and the carrying out of necessary functions to bring the scheme into operation, the scheme shall have effect from the operative date of the order, October 31, 1995.

MID EASTERN COMBINED FIRE SERVICES AREA ADMINISTRATION SCHEME ORDER 1995 (No. 2637) [£1·55], made under the Local Government (Scotland) Act 1973 (c.65), s.147 (as substituted by the Local Government etc. (Scotland) Act 1994 (c.39), s.36); operative on October 31, 1995; makes an administration scheme in relation to the combined fire services area, known as Mid Eastern, comprising the new local government areas of Angus Dundee City and Perth and Kinross, the fire brigade for the existing Tayside Region being the fire brigade for the new combined area, and creates a new joint fire board; providing that the said scheme shall have effect from April 1, 1996, but that in relation to the board's constitution and the carrying out of necessary functions to bring the scheme into operation, the scheme shall have effect from the operative date of the order, October 31, 1995.

5956. Appointments and promotion

FIRE SERVICES (APPOINTMENTS AND PROMOTION) (SCOTLAND) AMENDMENT REGULATIONS 1995 (No. 2110) [65p]; made under the Fire Services Act 1947 (c.41), s.18(1) (as amended by the Fire Services Act 1959 (c.44), s.6 and Sched.); operative on September 1, 1995; replaces references to Fire Services Drill Book with the Fire Service Training Manual.

[S.I. 1978 No. 1727 amended.]

5957. Negligence—duty of care—firefighter—whether owed to owner of property. See DUFF v. HIGHLAND AND ISLANDS FIRE BOARD (O.H.), §6156.

FIREARMS AND EXPLOSIVES

5958. Certificates

FIREARMS (SCOTLAND) AMENDMENT RULES 1994 (No. 3198) [65p], made under the Firearms Act 1968 (c.27), ss.27 (2) (as amended by the Firearms (Amendment) Act 1988 (c.45), s.23(5)) (3), 53(a) and 57(4); operative on January 1, 1995; amend the form of firearm certificate prescribed by the Firearms (Scotland) Rules 1989 by substituting five years for three years in the references to the period for which the certificate is granted or renewed.

[S.I. 1989 No. 889 amended.]

FISH AND FISHERIES

5959. Inshore fishing—prohibition

RIVER ARKAIG, LOCH ARKAIG AND ASSOCIATED WATERS PROTECTION ORDER 1995 (No. 2683) [£1·10], made under the Freshwater and Salmon

Fisheries (Scotland) Act 1976 (c.22), s.1, Sched. 1; operative on January 1, 1996; prohibits the fishing for or taking of freshwater fish in the inland waters in the prescribed areas delineated blue on the map annexed to the order, without legal right or written permission.

RIVER NITH SALMON FISHERY DISTRICT (BAITS AND LURES) REGULATIONS 1995 (No. 2682) [65p], made under the Salmon Act 1986 (c.62), s.8(5), Sched. 1; operative on January 1, 1995; prohibits the use of natural prawns and shrimp (or any part of them), for the whole of each year, as bait when fishing by rod and line for salmon and sea trout, in relation, *inter alia*, to the River Nith and its tributaries.

5960. Inshore fishing—prohibition—cockles

INSHORE FISHING (PROHIBITION OF FISHING FOR COCKLES) (SCOTLAND) ORDER 1995 (No. 1373) [65p], made under the Inshore Fishing (Scotland) Act 1984 (c.26), s.1 (as amended by the Inshore Fishing (Scotland) Act 1994 (c.27), s.1); operative on June 15, 1995; prohibits, subject to an exception, fishing for cockles from or by means of any vehicle in Scottish inshore waters and by any British fishing boat in the area described in art. 2.

[S.I. 1994 No. 2613 revoked.]

5961. Salmon and freshwater fisheries

ALNESS SALMON FISHERY DISTRICT DESIGNATION ORDER 1995 (No. 2194) [£1·10], made under the Salmon Act 1986 (c.62) Sched. 1; operative on September 22, 1995; designates the salmon fishery district to be known as the Alness Salmon Fishery District, abolishing the existing district, applies the regulations made under the said Salmon Act 1986 as set out in Sched. 2 of the Order and provides details of the permitted fishing times.

CONON SALMON FISHERY DISTRICT DESIGNATION ORDER 1995 (No. 2193) [£1·10], made under the Salmon Act 1986 (c.62), Sched. 1; operation on September 22, 1995; designates the salmon fishery district to be known as the Conon Salmon Fishery District, abolishing the existing district, applies the regulations made under the said Salmon Act 1986 as set out in the Sched. 2 of the Order and provides details of the permitted fishing times.

NORTH WEST SUTHERLAND PROTECTION ORDER 1994 (No. 3302) [£1·10], made under Freshwater and Salmon Fisheries (Scotland) Act 1976 (c.22), s.1; operative on March 15, 1995; prohibits the fishing for or taking of freshwater fish in inland waters in a prescribed area of Highland Region without legal right or written permission.

5962. Salmon and freshwater fisheries—obstructing water bailiffs—bailiffs unable to show warrant

[Salmon and Freshwater Fisheries Protection (Scotland) Act 1951 (14 & 15 Geo. VI, c.26) s.10.]

M and H appealed by means of stated case against their convictions for obstructing water bailiffs (B) who were attempting to stop and search their boat on the ground that B were not acting in the exercise of their powers in terms of s.10(3) and therefore there was no obstruction. M and H were sailing a creel boat which B believed was being used to take salmon illegally. B put to sea with the intention of stopping and examining the net being used by the crew and when they were approximately 25 to 50 feet from M and H, they advised that they had reasonable cause to suspect that the creel boat contained salmon illegally taken, although it was impossible for them to show M and H the instruments of their appointment because of the distance between the boats. While B were ingathering the net to examine it, M and H caused the net to pull into the propellers of B's boat, forcing them to stop the engine. M and H then hauled B's boat through rough waters, forcing them to cut the net free to avoid being swamped and sinking. B thereafter remained immobilised until the fouled propellor was cleared. M and H argued that in terms of s.10(3), since B were unable to produce the instruments of their appointment, they could not have been acting in the exercise of their powers and, accordingly, M and H could not have obstructed them (*Barnacott v. Passmore* (1887) 19 Q.B.D. 75).

Held, appeals refused. While by s.10(3) the production of the instruments of appointment was sufficient warrant for the exercising by a water bailiff of his powers, it was not said to be the only such warrant. B were unable to draw up alongside the creel boat because of the actions of M and H and it would be farcical to allow them to behave as they did and contend that B were not acting in the exercise of their powers because it was impossible for them to produce the instruments of their appointment. *Barnacott v. Passmore* did not concern such a case.

MACKAY v. WESTWATER, High Court of Justiciary, *The Scotsman*, November 16, 1995.

5963. Salmon and freshwater fisheries—salmon fishing—"unclean or unseasonable" fish

[Salmon Fisheries (Scotland) Act 1868 (c.123), s.20.]

B sought suspension of his conviction for possession of unclean or unseasonable salmon, contrary to s.20 of the 1868 Act. After the bill was held to be competent (see [1995] 2 C.L. 619) a hearing was arranged on the question whether "unseasonable" meant taken out of season, or related to the condition of the fish and not to the date of taking. At the hearing B did not support the former construction but submitted that "unseasonable" as used in s.20 was synonymous with "unclean", and meant a fish which has spawned or was about to spawn. The Crown argued that "unseasonable" referred to the condition of the fish just before spawning, and "unclean" to the fish returning to the sea after spawning (kelts).

Held, that the Crown's construction was correct, but bill passed on the concession that the fish in B's possession were not on the eve of spawning. It was clear from the history of the Salmon Fisheries Acts from 1828 onwards that "unseasonable" was a description which could be applied to fish irrespective of the time of year at which they were taken. In determining at what stage in its development a fish became unseasonable, as s.20 was a penal provision it had to be given a meaning which would enable a fish in that condition to be readily identified so that could be returned to the river without serious injury. A fish would be unseasonable if it had begun to spawn and also if it had reached the condition of being ready to spawn. There was then a physical condition which could be identified by gently pressing the belly towards the vent with the result that milt or spawn emerged. *Per* Lord Cowie: In most cases it would not be necessary to apply that test since at that stage in its life a fish would be showing other signs such a redness which would indicate to the discerning and responsible fisherman that it should be returned.

BRADY v. BARBOUR (No. 2), 1995 S.L.T. 920.

5964. Sea fishing—fishing methods—possession of illegal net—sentencing—competency of additional fine

[Sea Fishing (Enforcement of Community Conservation Measures) Order 1986 (S.I. 1986 No. 2090), art. 3(1)(b).]

G, the master of a German registered fishing vessel, pled guilty to contravening art. 3(1) of the 1986 Order and s.30 of the Fisheries Act 1981 by having on board a net with an illegal mesh size, and was fined £2,500 in respect of the offence and £8,215 in respect of the value of the catch on board at the time he was stopped. He was also ordered to forfeit a cod end. G sought suspension of the additional fine as incompetent as art. 3(1)(b) only allowed such a fine where the offence related to an unlawful catching of fish as opposed to having on board a prohibited net.

Held, of consent, bill passed. Article 3(1)(b) referred to fish "in respect of which the offence was committed", and the sheriff was not entitled to impose the additional fine. *Opinion reserved*, whether such a power would exist where the charge did not in terms relate to a provision which was directly concerned with fish.

GNEWUCH v. ADAM, 1995 S.C.C.R. 400.

5965. Shellfish. See FISH AND FISHERIES, §5960.

FOOD AND DRUGS

5966. Contamination

FOOD PROTECTION (EMERGENCY PROHIBITIONS) (PARALYTIC SHELLFISH POISONING) (No. 2) ORDER 1995 (No. 1422) [£1·10], made under the Food and Environment Protection Act 1985 (c.48), ss.1(1) (as amended by the Food Safety Act 1990 (c.16), s.51(2)(a) and (b)), 1(2) (as amended by the Food and Safety Act 1990 (c.16), s.51(2)(a) and (b)), 24(1) (as amended by the Food Safety Act 1990 (c.16), Sched. 3) and 24(3)); operative on June 19, 1995; contains emergency prohibitions restricting various activities in order to prevent human consumption of shellfish and designates an area of sea in the Moray Firth within which the taking of scallops is prohibited.

FOOD PROTECTION (EMERGENCY PROHIBITIONS) (PARALYTIC SHELLFISH POISONING) (No. 3) ORDER 1995 (No. 1560) [£1·10], made under the Food and Environment Protection Act 1985 (c.48), ss.1(1) (as amended by the Food Safety Act 1990 (c.16), s.51(2)(a) and (b)), 1(2) (as amended by the Food Safety Act 1990 (c.16), s.24(1) (as amended by the Food Safety Act 1990 (c.16), Sched. 3) and 24(3)); operative on June 19, 1995; contains emergency prohibitions restricting various activities in order to prevent human consumption of shellfish and designates an area within which the taking of mussels, scallops, razor clams is prohibited.

FOOD PROTECTION (EMERGENCY PROHIBITIONS) (PARALYTIC SHELLFISH POISONING) ORDER 1995 (No. 1388) [£1·10], made under the Food and Environment Protection Act 1985 (c.48), ss.1(1) (as amended by the Food Safety Act 1990 (c.16), s.51(2)(a) and (b)), 1(2) (as amended by the Food Safety Act 1990 (c.16), s.51(2)(a) and (b)), 24(1) (as amended by the Food Safety Act 1990, (c.16) Sched. 3) and 24(3)); operative on May 25, 1995; contains emergency prohibitions restricting various activities in order to prevent human consumption of shellfish and designates an area within which the taking scallops is prohibited.

5967. Dairy products—hygiene

DAIRY PRODUCTS (HYGIENE) (SCOTLAND) REGULATIONS 1995 (No. 1372) [£6·75], made under Food Safety Act 1990 (c.16), ss.6(4), 16(1), (2) and (3), 17(1) and (2), 19, 31, 48(1) and Sched. 1 paras. 2(1), (5), 6(1)(a) and 7(1); operative on June 15, 1995; give effect to the provisions of Council Directive 92/46 EEC, laying down the health rules for the production and placing on the market of raw milk, heat-treated milk and milk-based products. Also amend the Drinking Milk (Scotland) Regulations 1976 to make it an offence to described a food in breach of Art. 3(2) of Council Regulation (EEC) No. 1411/71.

[S.I. 1976 No. 1888. S.I. 1948 No. 960, 1959 No. 413 amended. S.I. 1967 No. 81, 1976 No. 875, 1983 No. 1514 and 1515, 1985 No. 1068 (partial) and 1222, 1986 No. 789 and 790, 1988 No. 1814, 2190 and 2191, 1990 No. 2392, 2463 (partial), 2507 (partial) and 2625 (partial) and 1992 No. 3136 (partial) revoked.]

Dangerous drugs. See CRIMINAL LAW.

Dangerous drugs—sentencing. See CRIMINAL SENTENCING.

5968. Food safety—prohibition order—appeal to sheriff—competency of further appeal. See EAST KILBRIDE DISTRICT COUNCIL v. KING, §6327.

Misuse of drugs. See CRIMINAL LAW.

5969. Offal

BOVINE OFFAL (PROHIBITION) (SCOTLAND) AMENDMENT REGULATIONS 1995 (No. 537) [£1·10], made under the Food Safety Act 1990 (c.16), ss.6(4) (as amended by the Deregulation and Contracting Out Act 1994 (c.40), Sched. 9), 16(1)(f)(3) and 48(1); operative on April 1, 1995; amend the Bovine Offal (Prohibition) (Scotland) Regulations 1990 by requiring a different colour stain for certain offal and transferring enforcement powers in relation to slaughterhouses and specialised bovine plants to the Secretary of State.

[S.I. 1990 No. 112 amended.]

5970. Spirit drinks

SPIRIT DRINKS (SCOTLAND) AMENDMENT REGULATIONS 1995 (No. 484) [£1·55], made under the Food Safety Act 1990 (c.16), the European Communities Act 1972 (c.68), s.2(2), and S.I. 1989 No. 1327; operative on April 3, 1995; amend the Spirit Drinks (Scotland) Regulations 1990 in relation to the definition, description and presentation of spirit drinks.

[S.I. 1990 No. 1196 amended.]

FRAUD, MISREPRESENTATION AND UNDUE INFLUENCE

5971. Misrepresentation—fraudulent—effect on enforceability of contract between others induced by misrepresentation. See UNIVERSAL IMPORT EXPORT v. BANK OF SCOTLAND, §5579.

GAMING AND WAGERING

5972. Amusements with prizes—permit—provision in public house—policy of licensing board

[Gaming Act 1968 (c.65), Sched. 9, paras. 8(2) and 15.]

T appealed against G's refusal, upheld on appeal to the sheriff, of a permit for amusement machines within T's licensed premises. T originally had separate public and lounge bars, each with one machine. After being upgraded T was granted a permit for one machine only after the dividing wall between the bars had been removed. T argued that (1) G had failed to state adequate reasons in their decision letter; and (2) G had failed to take into account the history of the bar having had two permits in the past and that the application merely sought to maintain the status quo. G had applied their policy of not granting a permit for more than one machine in each bar with a maximum of two machines in the whole premises, without regard for the merits of the application. In applying a policy decision the policy must not be destructive of the purpose of the statutory provisions or so rigid as to disable G from exercising discretion. Further, individual applications should be considered and not refused just on account of the conflict with G's policy (*Elder v. Ross and Cromarty District Licensing Board* [1990] C.L.Y. 5341).

Held, appeal refused. It was clear that T had been given an opportunity of submitting reasons for G's policy not to be applied. G had not refused to listen. The history of the premises was irrelevant. G required to consider the premises in their current form. G had given sufficiently clear reasons for their decision in outlining the three reasons for their policy and stating that they considered that two of them (adverse effect on the traditional atmosphere of public houses and protection of the rights of those who regard public houses as a place to drink in a pleasant and well regulated social environment) applied in the present case. These were matters of fact for G to determine.

BASS INNS & TAVERNS v. GLASGOW DISTRICT LICENSING BOARD (I.H.), 1995 S.C.L.R. 415.

5973. Amusements with prizes—permit—refusal—overprovision—relevant considerations

[Lotteries and Amusements Act 1976 (c. 32), s.16 and Sched. 3, para. 7(2).]

A company applied to the licensing committee for an amusement with prizes licence under s.16 of the Lotteries and Amusements Act 1976 for "prize bingo". In exercise of their general discretion under Sched. 7, para. 7(2) of the 1976 Act the licensing committee refused the application on the grounds of over provision. In their reasons for refusal the licensing committee, *inter alia*, took into account that a licensee under s.16 of the 1976 Act holding a licence for "prize bingo" could also operate amusement with prizes machines and that a licensee under s.34 of the Gaming Act 1968 holding a licence for amusement with prizes machines could also operate prize bingo. There were two s.34 licences in the area and accordingly the grant of s.16 licence would amount to overprovision. The applicants appealed to the sheriff, who refused the appeal, and to the Court of Session, arguing that as there was a distinction between s.16 and a s.34 licence and as there were no other s.16 licences in the burgh, the licensing committee erred in law in deciding that there could be overprovision.

Held, that (1) in view of the width of the discretion conferred on a licensing committee by para. 7(2) of Sched. 3 to the 1976 Act, a licensing committee could properly refuse to grant a permit on the basis that granting it would result in overprovision of the type of facility that the premises would be used for; (2) the committee entitled to look at the general character of the activity which could be carried out on the application premises under the permit and look at the same time at the general character of the activities which were being carried out at the nearby premises under the authority of permits granted under Pt. III of the 1968 Act, and to conclude that each type of activity involved low cost gaming, providing some form of amusement and relatively low value prizes; (3) it was legitimate for the committee to have regard to the developments that could take place in premises which permits without there being any further opportunity for the committee to intervene and impose any limitation for restriction; and appeal refused.

MATCHURBAN v. KYLE AND CARRICK DISTRICT COUNCIL (NO. 2), 1995 S.L.T. 1211.

5974. Betting—betting office licence application—refused—subsequent grant of second application by same applicant—whether second decision irrational

[Betting, Gaming and Lotteries Act 1963 (c.2), Sched. 1, para. 19.]

A company applied to a licensing board for the grant of a betting shop licence under the 1963 Act, to operate a betting shop in Stranraer. Operators of two of the existing betting shops in Stranraer objected to the application on the basis that existing facilities in the area were sufficient to serve the area adequately. The initial application having been refused by the board, the applicant appealed to the sheriff who directed the board to reconsider the application. At the subsequent board meeting the original application was heard together with a further application by the same applicants. The board refused the original application but granted the further application. The objectors raised a petition for judicial review seeking reduction of the board's decision to grant the second application on the grounds that the board, having refused the first application, had proceeded without interruption, additional information or further discussion of the matter to grant the second application and thereby must have acted in an irrational and unreasonable manner.

Held, that (1) it not being competent to grant both applications, there was no inherent irrationality in the board electing to grant the second rather than the first of the two applications; (2) there was no logical reason why the first application should be treated as indicative of rationality any more than the second; and (3) it was impossible to characterise the decision of the body as a whole as irrational upon speculation as to reasons that may have underlain the exercise of a particular member's vote; and petition dismissed. *Observed*, that if the petitioners had sought to challenge the rationality of both decisions of the board in order to impugn the proceedings as whole, the situation might have been different.

LADBROKE RACING (STRATHCLYDE) v. WILLIAM HILL (SCOTLAND) (O.H.), 1995 S.L.T. 134.

5975. Betting—licensed betting offices

LICENSED BETTING OFFICES (SCOTLAND) AMENDMENT REGULATIONS 1995 (No. 802) [£1·10], made under the Betting, Gaming and Lotteries Act 1963 (c.2), ss.10(6) (as inserted by the Betting, Gaming and Lotteries (Amendment) Act 1984 (c.25), s.2), 55(1) and Sched. 4, para. 3; operative on April 6, 1995; amend the Licensed Betting Offices (Scotland) Regulations 1986 and remove the prohibition of moving displays or images, being advertised outside or inside such offices.

[S.I. 1986 No. 120 amended.]

5976. Charges

GAMING (SMALL CHARGES) (SCOTLAND) VARIATION ORDER 1995 (No. 1750) [65p], made under the Gaming Act 1968 (c.65) ss.40(2) and 51(4) (as amended by s.1(3) of the Gaming (Amendment) Act 1975 (c.12); operative on August 1, 1995; prescribes the maximum daily charge which may be made in clubs and miners' welfare institutes in respect of a person taking part in games of whist and bridge.

[S.I. 1992 No. 2755 amended.]

5977. Gaming—permit—refusal—appeal sustained on ground of breach of natural justice—whether appropriate to remit to board for reconsideration. See MATCHURBAN v. KYLE AND CARRICK DISTRICT COUNCIL, §6242.

5978. Hours and charges

GAMING CLUBS (HOURS AND CHARGES) (SCOTLAND) AMENDMENT REGULATIONS 1995 (No. 1022) [65p], made under the Gaming Act 1968 (c.65), ss.14(2) and (3) and 51; operative on May 1, 1995; increase the maximum charges for admission to gaming on bingo club premises in respect of charging periods other than the shorter permitted period on a Sunday to £6·80 and in respect of the shorter permitted period to £5·12.

[S.I. 1994 No. 1042 revoked.]

5979. Variation of monetary limits and fees

AMUSEMENTS WITH PRIZES (VARIATION OF MONETARY LIMITS) (SCOTLAND) ORDER 1995 (No. 1021) [65p], made under the Lotteries and Amusements Act 1976 (c.32), ss.18(1) and 24(2); operative on May 1, 1995; increases to £30 the maximum amount permitted to be taken by way of the sale of chances under the 1976 Act.

[S.I. 1992 No. 749 revoked.]

GAMING ACT (VARIATION OF FEES) (SCOTLAND) ORDER 1995 (No. 571) [£1·10], made under the Gaming Act 1968 (c.65), ss.48(5) (as amended by the

Gaming (Amendment) Act 1990 (c.26), s.1 and Sched.) and 51(4); operative on April 1, 1995; increases the fees to be charged in Scotland under the Gaming Act 1968, s.48.

[Gaming Act 1968 (c.65), s.48 amended; S.I. 1992 No. 410 revoked.]

GAMING ACT (VARIATION OF MONETARY LIMITS) (SCOTLAND) ORDER 1995 (No. 1020) [65p], made under the Gaming Act 1968 (c.65), ss.20(3) (as amended by the Gaming (Amendment) Act 1980 (c.8), s.1) 20(8), 21(8) and 51; operative on May 1, 1995; increases to £25,000 the maximum aggregate sum permitted to be paid to players as winnings in respect of all linked games of bingo and increases to £5,000 the maximum amount by which weekly winnings in bingo clubs may exceed the stakes hazarded.

[S.I. 1993 No. 1037 and 1994 No. 1043 revoked.]

GAMING ACT (VARIATION OF MONETARY LIMITS) (SCOTLAND) (NO. 2) ORDER 1995 (No. 2360) [£1·10], made under the Gaming Act 1968 (c.65) ss.31(3), 34(9) and 51(4); operative on October 1, 1995; increases, *inter alia*, the maximum amount which, may be charged for playing a game once and, which may be offered as prizes in amusements by machines at certain fairs, licensed club premises and other commercial entertainments.

[S.I. 1985 No. 641, S.I. 1989 No. 2249 and S.I. 1992 No. 3022 revoked.]

GUARANTEE AND INDEMNITY

5980. Cautionary obligation—construction—"top slice guarantee"—entitlement to interest

[Law Reform (Miscellaneous Provisions) (Scotland) Act 1985 (c.3), s.8.]

A company granted a guarantee to a bank in relation to sums due to the bank by two other companies. The guarantee related to sums due in excess of the sum of £800,000 and the cautioners' liability was not to exceed £1,000,000 "and interest thereon". Payment having been requested under the guarantee, payment of the sum required (£1,040,589·13) was made on a "without prejudice" basis. The cautioners assigned their right to another company which raised an action against the bank, seeking, *inter alia*; (i) declarator that the guarantee was void; (ii) an accounting by the bank in respect of its realisation of securities in support of the guaranteed debt; and (iii) (as an alternative to the previous conclusions) rectification of the guarantee in terms of s.8 of the Law Reform (Miscellaneous Provisions) (Scotland) Act 1985 to the effect of providing that any securities realised by the bank were in the first place to be set against the excess over £800,000. The assignees argued that the guarantee was void because of the uncertainty as to whether interest was due on the total indebtedness or only on the excess guaranteed. They also argued that the guarantee was void since the bank had increased the risk to the cautioners by increasing the original debtor's liability under it, the bank having previously agreed that the overdraft facilities of the original debtors were to be £1,800,000 but having thereafter advanced £2,302,669. In support of the alternative conclusion for rectification the assignees argued that the chairman of the cautioners had agreed with the bank's chief executive that any sums realised from the securities over the original debtors' assets would be applied first to reduce the liability under the guarantee. The bank pleaded that the action was irrelevant.

Held, that (1) the guarantee was not ambiguous and it was clear that the liability for interest was only on the excess above £800,000; (2) the guarantee did not expressly limit the overdraft, which it secured, to £1,800,000 and such a limit could not be implied and thus making advances in excess of £1,800,000 did not increase the liability of the cautioners; (3) the assignees of the cautioners had failed to aver any legal grounds for an accounting, particularly since the guarantee provided that the cautioners had no right to any security

until the bank had been paid in full; but (4) s.8 of the 1985 Act made no distinction between patent and latent defects; that it modified the rule excluding parole evidence; that to obtain rectification a pursuer had to aver and prove that the parties had reached an agreement, that the document was intended to give effect to it but had failed to do so but it was unnecessary for the party to make all these averments together or to specify the details of the alteration sought; the assignees' averments, particularly those of the meeting between the representatives of the original cautioners and the bank were sufficient; and proof before answer allowed only on the issue of rectification.
HUEWIND v. CLYDESDALE BANK (O.H.), 1995 S.L.T. 392.

5981. Cautionary obligation—discharge—rights of cautioner—whether material alteration to contract between lender and principal debtor discharging guarantor. See HUEWIND v. CLYDESDALE BANK, §5980.

5982. Guarantee—misrepresentation by debtor against guarantor—whether constructive knowledge of creditor

M and S reclaimed against the Lord Ordinary's decision to dismiss as irrelevant actions brought by them seeking reduction of deeds granted by them to the prejudice of their rights in their respective matrimonial homes, the deeds being granted in favour of a bank (B) which was seeking security for loans to their businessmen husbands and which M and S averred had acted in bad faith since the deeds had been obtained as a result of the husbands' misrepresentations and B had failed to inquire whether M and S had been properly advised. M and S argued that *Barclays Bank v. O'Brien* [1994] 1 A.C. 180, could, contrary to the Lord Ordinary's view, be reconciled with the principles of Scots law: an analogy could be drawn with *Rodger (Builders) v. Fawdry* [1950] C.L.Y. 4871, as to failure to make appropriate inquiries giving rise to bad faith, and the cases relied on by the Lord Ordinary concerned different facts, were obiter and out of date, and in any event indicated an overriding principle of fairness.

Held, reclaiming motion refused. There was no doubt that before the *O'Brien* decision the position in Scots law was that a creditor was not liable for representations by the principal debtor made to induce a cautioner to undertake an obligation, unless it has proved that he was privy to the fact that the cautioner was being deceived (Gloag and Irvine, *Rights in Security*, p. 712, supported by *Young v. Clydesdale Bank* (1889) 17 R. 231 and *Royal Bank of Scotland v. Greenshields*, 1914 S.C. 259). A duty to make inquiry arose only where circumstances were known to the creditor which might reasonably create a suspicion of fraud: Bell, *Principles*, para. 251, and not simply because the creditor knew that the transaction was not to the cautioner's financial advantage and that the cautioner would be likely to rely on his or her principal. While the doctrine of constructive notice as explained in *O'Brien* was simply another way of expressing the same principle, the facts which were held to be sufficient to put the creditor on his inquiry were markedly different from the approach of Scots law. The tendency in English law to deal with cases of undue influence by reference to presumptions arising from the fact that the parties were related to each other differed significantly from Scots law, which recognised no presumptions and looked at the effect of the relationship in each case on its own facts, the question being whether the circumstances were such, and the influence exercised by one party so dominant, as to deprive the other of the power of apprehending the considerations applicable to the case (Gloag, *Contract* (2nd ed.), p. 527). The consequences of accepting *O'Brien* as part of Scots law would be very significant (*cf. Massey v. Midland Bank plc* [1995] C.L.Y. 2446 for the whole structure of the law in regard to undue influence, and it could not be confined to cases where financial institutions were creditors. If the duties of creditors were thought to be in need of extension, this should be by Parliament after detailed consideration by the Scottish Law Commission. *Observed*, that banks and building societies had now adopted a recommendation of the Jack committee that they issue appropriate warnings to private individuals proposing to give a guarantee or other security for another's liabilities, but that could not be said to be a matter of legal obligation.

MUMFORD v. BANK OF SCOTLAND; SMITH v. BANK OF SCOTLAND (I.H.), *The Times*, September 29, 1995.

5983. Indemnity—negligence. See NELSON v. ATLANTIC POWER AND GAS, §5571.

HEALTH AND SAFETY AT WORK

Compulsory purchase. See COMPULSORY PURCHASE.

Leases. See LANDLORD AND TENANT.

Master and servant—master's liability to servant. See NEGLIGENCE.

Matrimonial homes—occupancy rights. See DIVORCE AND CONSISTORIAL CAUSES.

Prescription. See PRESCRIPTION.

5984. Safe means of access—ladder giving access to scaffold—scaffold not yet inspected or passed fit for use

[Factories Act 1961 (c.34), s.29(1).]

An employee was injured in a fall from a ladder when gaining access to a scaffold in circumstances amounting to a breach of s.29(1) of the 1961 Act and of reg. 6(1) of the Construction (Working Places) Regulations 1966, if they applied. The scaffold had not been inspected and passed fit for use, a prerequisite of its use being allowed. The injured person had wrongly believed that it had been inspected and approved.

Held, that s.29(1) applied since, although use of the scaffolding had not been approved, its use had not been effectively forbidden; and decree pronounced in favour of the pursuer.

SCOTT v. E.D.C. PIPEWORK SERVICES (O.H.), 1995 S.L.T. 561.

5985. Safe place of work—whether foreseeability required for liability

[Factories Act 1961 (c.34) s.29(1).]

M reclaimed against a Lord Ordinary's decision to assoilzie his employers (U) in M's action for damages in respect of injuries sustained when M's fingers became trapped in a tyre making machine, the Lord Ordinary having held that, as the accident was not foreseeable, M's case alleging breach of s.29(1) of the 1961 Act failed. U argued that reasonable foreseeability was an essential ingredient in considering whether or not a place of work was safe; that "safe" meant not "dangerous", which in relation to s.14 of the 1961 Act meant giving rise to a reasonably foreseeable risk of danger; that the mere occurrence of an accident was not sufficient; and that M had to show both that the state of the workplace was a reasonably foreseeable source of injury and that the danger manifested itself in a reasonably foreseeable way in respect of M.

Held, reclaiming motion allowed. The duty under s.14 to fence dangerous machinery was absolute whereas s.29(1) contained a qualification relating to reasonable practicability and, given the different contexts, it was inappropriate to link the definition "dangerous" in s.14 to that of "safe" in s.29(1) simply because the words were antonyms (*Taylor v. Coalite Oils & Chemicals* [1967] C.L.Y. 1605, disapproved). The construction of s.29(1) had to depend on the wording of the section itself and it was clear that the obligation imposed upon U was to prevent any risk of injury arising from the state or condition of the working place, not just risks which were reasonably foreseeable, because if that had been the intention of Parliament it would have been simple for it to have said so and it would not have added anything of substance to the common law (*Robertson v. Cowe (R. B.) & Co.* [1970] C.L.Y. 3192, *Larner v. British Steel* [1993] C.L.Y. 2021; and *Neil v. Greater Glasgow Health Board* [1994] C.L.Y. 5888, followed; *Taylor* and *Morrow v. Enterprise Sheet Metal Works (Aberdeen)* [1985] C.L.Y. 3704; [1986] C.L.Y. 3618, not followed). As the statute was designed to protect the safety of workmen by heightening the obligation imposed upon U by the common law, it was not appropriate to read into it qualifications which derogated from that purpose. Such a reading did not impose an intolerable or impossible burden upon U, however, as reasonable foreseeability was relevant to whether or not it was reasonably practicable to prevent a breach of s.29(1) since it was impossible to assess the degree of risk without taking account of the element of reasonable foreseeability (*Gillies v. Glynwed Foundries* [1977] C.L.Y. 3434). Accordingly, in order to succeed under s.29(1) M required only to prove that an accident had occurred during the normal course of his work and that it was causatively related to the state of his working place, and, as U had not invoked the reasonable practicability defence, they had no defence to the action. *Per* Lord Johnston: It was questionable whether, when Parliament legislated in relation to dangerous machinery, it really also intended that issue to be covered by a general section relating to the place of work.

MAINS v. UNIROYAL ENGLEBERT TYRES, 1995 S.L.T. 1115.

HERITABLE PROPERTY AND CONVEYANCING

5986. Attestation—witness signing at different time from testator. See LINDSAY v. MILNE, §6478.

5987. Common property—division and sale—counterclaim by defender on proceeds—competency

A woman raised an action of division and sale of a cottage purchased in which title had been taken in joint names with the defender. The defender counterclaimed, seeking to recover the money which he had paid towards the purchase of the house. He had sold his house and the proceeds, along with a building society loan in joint names, were applied in the purchase of the cottage. The sheriff held that the defender had a relevant claim, but that it was inappropriate to be put forward as a counterclaim. The defender appealed to the sheriff principal.

Held, that the counterclaim was competent as it would be capable of ascertainment once the sale had taken place, and would avoid a multiplicity of actions and appeal allowed, sale of subjects allowed, and proof *prout de jure* of the counterclaim allowed.

JOHNSTON v. ROBSON, 1995 S.L.T. (Sh.Ct.) 26.

Compulsory purchase. See COMPULSORY PURCHASE.

5988. Disposition—construction—whether disposition included road to middle line—whether implied right of access

The proprietor of subjects which were described as "bounded by a road", which road was a private road, sought reduction of a disposition of the road by the proprietors of other subjects bounded by the said road to themselves. The pursuer averred that his title extended to the *medium filum* of the road. After an initial procedure roll hearing the Lord Ordinary held that the question of ownership fell to be determined by the usual presumption that subjects bounded by a road prima facie did not include the road, and that the mere fact that property on both sides of the road had been disponed was not capable of supporting a different presumption. The case was then put out by order to determine whether there was sufficient in the pursuer's pleadings to displace the presumption, or in any event to establish a right of vehicular access over the road. The pursuer argued that no separate title had ever been granted by the defenders' predecessors in title in respect of the road and that since those predecessors had subsequently disponed all their remaining property interests in the estate to a third party, by a disposition which did not include the road, the presumption had been displaced. On access the defenders argued that a plan founded on by the pursuer could not supply a right where the deed was silent on the matter and that for a prescriptive right of vehicular access to arise the pursuer required to aver dates when the right of access was asserted.

Held, that (1) the defenders' predecessors' belief at the time of disposing of their remaining interests in the estate that they did not then have title to the road could not be treated as a contemporary actings shedding light on the meaning of an earlier disposition, and the pursuer's claim to ownership of the road was accordingly irrelevant; (2) while it was doubtful whether a plan by itself could provide a sufficient foundation for a right of access, the fact that the road was part of the bounding description together with the surrounding circumstances warranted inquiry on the question of vehicular access. In any event there were sufficient averments for proof on the question of the constitution of an implied right of access, and also on prescription; and proof before answer allowed.

HARRIS v. WISHART (O.H.), 1996 S.L.T. 12.

5989. Disposition—*a non domino*—rights of disponee in possession against holder of *ex facie* valid title

Held, in an action of declarator and interdict at the instance of disponees under a disposition granted by themselves as uninfeft proprietors who had been in possession of the subjects for about 40 years, that the disposition gave them no title to possess for the purpose of interdicting interference with their possession by a person holding an *ex facie* valid title and that since the defender held such a title the pursuers were not entitled to declarator or interdict against the defender.

WATSON v. SHIELDS (Sh.Ct.), 1994 S.C.L.R. 819.

5990. Disposition—rectification

[Law Reform (Miscellaneous Provisions) (Scotland) Act 1985 (c.73), ss.8(1)(a) and 9.]

The Law Reform (Miscellaneous Provisions) (Scotland) Act 1985, s.8 provides that where the court is satisfied that a document fails accurately to express the common intention of the parties it may order the documents to be rectified in order to give effect to the common intention of the parties. Section 9(1) provides that the court shall order rectification of the document only if it is satisfied that the interests of third parties would not be affected to a material extent, but makes no provision for calling those third parties as additional defenders. The granters of a disposition raised an action seeking rectification of the disposition. They averred that they were the heritable proprietors of a piece of ground, the eastern part of which they verbally agreed to sell to the defenders. They averred that the missives which were subsequently concluded were vague and uncertain and did not reflect the terms of the prior verbal agreement reached between the parties as to the boundaries of the ground to be sold, and that the plan annexed to the disposition did not reflect the common intention of the parties arrived at in the prior verbal agreement. At debate the sheriff dismissed the action, holding that it was not competent to go behind the missives to correct the disposition. The pursuers appealed to the Court of Session.

Held, that (1) where the missives did not contain all the matters agreed between the parties, which the parties needed to agree upon in relation to the sale of heritage, it was competent to prove that agreement had been reached between the parties on vital matters which were not included in the missives; (2) the pursuers' averments were sufficient to instruct a case that agreement was reached by stages, namely in the oral agreement and later by the bargain concluded in the missives, and that the agreement embraced the common intention, which the pursuers were entitled to prove; and appeal allowed and proof before answer allowed. (*Anderson v. Lambie*, 1954 S.L.T. 73, commented upon.) *Observed*, (per Lord Murray) that it was at first sight startling that a deed affecting the rights of third parties could be rectified under s.8 without those third parties being called as additional defenders, but that was what s.9(1) provided along with the safeguards for the interests of third parties therein enacted.

McCLYMONT v. McCUBBIN, 1995 S.L.T. 1995.

5991. Disposition—reduction—deed conveying more than agreed in missives. See ABERDEEN RUBBER v. KNOWLES & SONS (FRUITERERS), §5992.

5992. Disposition—reduction—whether signed in error—burden of proof

Sellers of land received an offer for the property, which was made up of four areas. The offer was not accepted within the specified time limit. Thereafter informal correspondence was entered into by the parties' solicitors during which the sellers' solicitors indicated that their clients intended to include a fifth area in the sale. Later a qualified acceptance of the offer was sent by the sellers' solicitors to the purchasers' solicitors. This was accepted and the bargain thus concluded. A disposition prepared by the purchasers' solicitors and revised by the sellers' agents, which included the fifth area of ground, was granted by the sellers and delivered to the purchasers in exchange for the price. The sellers then raised an action seeking declarator that the missives did not include the fifth piece of land; declarator that the disposition failed to implement the agreement contained in the missives; partial reduction of the disposition insofar as it related to the fifth area of ground; and, failing such reduction, rectification of the disposition by deletion of reference to the fifth area of ground. The purchasers argued, *inter alia*, that, having regard to the informal correspondence, it could be established that the common intention of the parties had been that all five pieces of land be included in the disposition. The sellers submitted that the defences were irrelevant. They argued that the court should not have regard to the informal correspondence where the missives were unambiguous and that a clause in the missives which provided that the missives were not superseded by the disposition except insofar as fully implemented thereby, rendered the missives over the disposition as the measure of the parties' rights. After procedure roll debate the Lord Ordinary allowed a proof before answer, holding that the onus of proving that an *ex facie* unambiguous disposition did not accurately reflect the common intention of the parties lay on the sellers and was not a light one; that the purchasers were entitled to lead evidence of the informal correspondence in support of their contention that the disposition reflected the common intention of parties; and that the provision that the missives remained in force did not prevent the sellers disponing an area larger than that specified in the missives if there was agreement to do so. The sellers reclaimed, arguing that an inference could be drawn from the admitted facts which established that the common intention of the parties was not what was contained in the disposition but what was shown in the missives, and that the disposition must be taken to have been granted in error. In these circumstances, where the non-supersession clause referred to the missives alone, the purchasers could only make a relevant case if they were to aver essential error in respect of the missives and seek to reduce them *ope exceptionis*. The purchasers countered that the non-supersession clause had been entirely exhausted by the disposition in respect of the conveyance of the land and that they were entitled to prove by evidence extrinsic to the missives their averment that it was the common intention of parties that all five areas be included. If it was necessary to aver that the missives did not represent the common intention then that was implicit in the pleadings. The First Division, by a majority, allowed he reclaiming motion and pronounced decree *de plano* in favour of the sellers. The purchasers appealed to the House of Lords.

Held, that the natural inference to be drawn from the non-supersession clause was that the disposition was intended to implement the missives as regards the subjects thereby agreed to be conveyed to the purchasers, but that the only plausible explanation of why it bore to convey an additional area of ground was that the additional area had by mistake been included in the draft disposition which had been drawn and revised at an earlier time when there was no binding contract between the parties, and that the facts admitted on the pleadings satisfied the onus of proof which rested upon the sellers and established that the disposition which was ultimately executed proceeded mistakenly upon informal communings which were themselves founded on a mistake, formed no part of the contract between the parties and had been superseded; and appeal dismissed.

ABERDEEN RUBBER v. KNOWLES & SONS (FRUITERERS) (H.L.), 1995 S.L.T. 870.

5993. Disposition—title to grant—trustees for partnership

C reclaimed against a Lord Ordinary's decision to dismiss her action for reduction of a disposition granted in 1983 by L in favour of C's husband (H) and of a disposition granted in 1984 by H in favour of X. Title to the subjects had originally been granted in 1979 to C and L as trustees for a firm of which C and L were the partners. C averred that the 1983 disposition had been granted without her consent. The 1979 disposition had included a proviso that L and C and their successors in office "shall be entitled to . . . sell the said subjects . . . and . . . without limitation of anything herein contained or otherwise . . . dispose of the said subjects in whole or in part, and that all by themselves or herself alone, as if they or she were absolute beneficial owners or owner, and without the consent of any other partner . . . and all the said powers . . . may be exercised notwithstanding any changes in, or the dissolution of, the said firm". The partnership had been dissolved in 1982. L, H and X argued that (1) the proviso clearly entitled L to dispose of the subjects "herself alone" without C's consent; given that partnerships often granted powers to one of the partners to deal with firm property, such a clause would not be surprising; and that H was entitled to rely on s.2(1) of the Trusts (Scotland) Act 1961; and (2) there was no requirement on L, H and X to show that C had an alternative remedy before the court could decline to grant reduction, and the Lord Ordinary had been entitled to exercise his equitable power to refuse reduction. C argued that the action had an intelligible purpose in that, if the property were restored to the partnership, she would be entitled to a share in the winding up of the partnership, which had not yet happened; and that, as the success of an action of accounting against L would depend largely on L's means, it was impossible to say that she had an alternative remedy.

Held, reclaiming motion refused. (1) The only purpose of the words in the proviso, which derived from an old style (*Encyclopaedia of Scottish Legal Styles*, no. 261) was to provide for the foreseeable situation in which the number of trustees was reduced to one and to ensure that the remaining infeft trustee could grant a valid title without the need for inquiry by a third party (Burns, *Conveyancing Law and Practice*, Vol. II, para. 18.40). Given the nature of joint property and the practical problems which could arise if trustees wanted to do different things in relation to trust property, a clause which granted a power to any trustee alone to dispose of trust property would be highly unusual and would have to be expressed in absolutely unambiguous words and the Lord Ordinary had erred in holding that the proviso gave such a power. (2) *Per* Lords McCluskey and Sutherland: While it could not be said that the action of reduction would achieve nothing, in that title to the subjects would be restored to C and L as trustees, C, as an individual, pursuing a claim for a share in the assets of the dissolved partnership, would not be entitled to claim against the subjects themselves. Given that there were no averments as to why reduction would be conducive to the success of her claim; that C had taken no interest in running the firm since 1980; that, accordingly, it was not obvious that C had a right to challenge L's actions after 1980 or what her claim against the partnership was; that there was nothing to show that C could not have been compelled to sign the 1983 disposition or have her consent dispensed with due to her lack of interest; and that C had failed to take any steps to establish any claim against the partnership assets, she had not averred a sufficient interest to pursue the action. *Per* Lord Coulsfield: C's concessions regarding the dissolution of the partnership and her disinterest after 1980 meant that she had given no reason for thinking that any agreements made by L thereafter were open to challenge; she had not attempted to explain her position in relation to what was done with the partnership assets, and in the unusual circumstances of this case no sufficient basis had been averred that reduction would have any practical consequence. *Opinion, per* Lord McCluskey, that sufficient material did not exist in parties' pleadings to enable the court to make a judgment on the equities, and a proof before answer would have been allowed on this aspect as well. *Per* Lord Sutherland: The discretion to refuse reduction was only available in certain exceptional cases (*Grahame v. Kirkcaldy Magistrates* (1882) 9 R.(H.L.) 91), and given that X's financial loss and inconvenience would have been a consequence of accepting an invalid title, for which they might have a remedy against H or their solicitors, and X's failure to offer C any recompense, it was doubtful that X had made out a relevant case for refusing reduction. The existence of another remedy, which might or might not be more advantageous to C, did not mean that reduction had to be refused.

CAMERON v. LIGHTHEART, 1995 S.C.L.R. 443.

5994. Land obligations—variation and discharge—benefited proprietors

[Conveyancing and Feudal Reform (Scotland) Act 1970 (c.35), s.2(6).]

By s.1(3) of the Conveyancing and Feudal Reform (Scotland) Act 1970 the Lands Tribunal for Scotland may vary or discharge a land obligation on the application of any person who, in relation to the obligation, is a burdened proprietor. By s.2(6) "burdened proprietor" means a proprietor of an interest in land upon whom, by virtue of his being such proprietor, the obligation is binding, and "benefited proprietor", in relation to such an obligation, means a proprietor of an interest in land who is entitled, by virtue of his being such proprietor, to enforce the obligation. Property developers applied under s.1(3) of the Act for the discharge of alleged land obligations which they claimed prevented a proposed development of certain subjects of which they were the feuars. The obligations had been created by a feu contract by which the superiors were taken bound to impose similar obligations on neighbouring co-feuars as servitudes in favour of the feuars *inter alios*. Subsequently the *dominium utile* and *dominium directum* of the feuars' subjects were consolidated. Notwithstanding the consolidation, the alleged obligations were shown as subsisting burdens in the land certificate for the subjects, and in the proceedings before the tribunal it was common ground between the applicants and the co-feuars who appeared as objectors that the obligations subsisted by virtue of the feu contract having created a *ius quaesitum tertio* in favour of the co-feuars. That was questioned by the tribunal *ex proprio motu*.

Held, that (1) the feu contract had not created a *ius quaesitum tertio* in favour of the co-feuars, and accordingly they were not benefited proprietors in terms of s.2(6); (2) there being no other person who could enforce the obligations, the obligations were not subsisting burdens, and the applicants were not therefore burdened proprietors within the meaning of s.2(6); and application dismissed as incompetent. *Opinion*, that (1) insofar as the obligations were properly treated as servitudes, the applicants, being proprietors of the dominant tenement, could not be regarded as burdened proprietors, nor the objectors as benefited proprietors, within the meaning of s.2(6); (2) it was at least doubtful whether the tribunal had declaratory powers in an application such as this, but that it was obliged to adjudicate on any preliminary issue, including the question whether applicants were burdened proprietors within the meaning of s.2(6).

McCARTHY & STONE (DEVELOPMENTS) v. SMITH, 1995 S.L.T. (Lands Tr.) 19.

5995. Land Registers (Scotland) Act 1995 (c.14)

This Act provides that prepayment of the appropriate statutory fees, payable under s.25 of the Land Registers (Scotland) Act 1868 (c.64), as a condition of acceptance of writs for recording in the Register of Sasines and of applications for registration in the Land Register of Scotland.

The Act received Royal Assent on June 28, 1995.

5996. Land registration

LAND REGISTRATION (SCOTLAND) AMENDMENT RULES 1995 (No. 248) [£6·10], made under the Land Registration (Scotland) Act 1979 (c.33), s.27(1); operative on April 1, 1995; substitutes for the Land Registration (Scotland) Rules 1980, Sched. A, a new Schedule setting out amended forms to be used in connection with registration.

[S.I. 1980 No. 1413 amended; S.I. 1988 No. 1143 revoked.]

5997. Land Registration (Scotland) Act 1979 (c.33)—commencement

LAND REGISTRATION (SCOTLAND) ACT 1979 (COMMENCEMENT No. 9) ORDER 1995 (No. 2547) (c.50) [65p], made under the Land Registration (Scotland) Act 1979 (c.33) (2); brings into force on April 1, 1996, ss.2(1) and (2) and 3(3) for the purpose of registration of writs in the County of Aberdeen and the County of Kincardine.

Leases. See LANDLORD AND TENANT.

Matrimonial Homes—Occupying rights. See DIVORCE AND CONSISTORIAL CAUSES.

Prescription. See PRESCRIPTION.

5998. Public right of way—way no longer linking two public places—whether rights of access to intermediate points lost

A proprietor of an estate raised an action against the proprietors of neighbouring land seeking interdict against the defenders from using the line of an old road as a vehicle access to part of their land where they intended to build two houses and from laying a road surface thereon. The neighbours claimed that there was a public, or alternatively a private, right of way over the road and that they were accordingly entitled to use and maintain it. The old road no longer communicated between a public place at either end of it.

Held, that since, once a public right of way had been established between two public places, proprietors along its route were entitled to use it for access to their own properties, the fact that the road had ceased to give access between two public places did not lead to the adjacent proprietors losing their rights of access; and interdict refused in respect of the line of the old road. *Opinion reserved*, on whether the right in the proprietors adjacent to the old road was a public or a private right.

LORD BURTON v. MACKAY (O.H.), 1995 S.L.T. 507.

5999. Sale—letter of obligation—liability of solicitor. See DIGBY BROWN & CO v. LYALL, §6434.

6000. Sale—missives—breach—effect of subsequent disposition

The purchasers of a property found faults in the property which they averred were covered by the missives, and claimed damages. They had had work carried out at their own expense on alterations and extensions which they claimed had not been in conformity with building warrants or in respect of which planning permission had not been applied for. They founded upon a clause in the missives that where there had been alterations or additions the appropriate grant of planning permission, building authority warrant and completion certificate would be exhibited prior to settlement and delivered with the titles. The sellers claimed that the obligation was not a collateral one and denied liability. After debate the sheriff accepted the purchasers' argument and allowed them to lodge a minute of amendment. The sellers appealed to the sheriff principal.

Held, that there was an obligation that various documents be produced by the time of settlement and delivered with the titles but the obligation did not persist after the date of settlement and did not carry on beyond the disposition and appeal allowed and action dismissed.

RAE v. MIDDLETON, 1995 S.L.T. (Sh. Ct.) 60.

6001. Sale—missives—construction—implied term—whether purchaser had to act reasonably in resiling

H sought damages in respect of B's failure to implement missives concluded on September 7, 1990 under which B agreed to purchase a dwellinghouse and other buildings together with 13 acres of ground. B had offered to purchase the subjects on condition, *inter alia*, that the price was to include the benefit of outline planning permission for the conversion of the traditional farm buildings into a dwellinghouse. H's qualified acceptance dated August 23 provided in cl. 9 that the title granted would vary from H's existing title in accordance with boundary alterations agreed between H and N, which were specified in a covering letter and draft deed plan. Paragraph 3 of B's further formal letter provided that B would have five working days from receipt of the final version of the deed carrying through the boundary changes in which to satisfy themselves as to the position, and if not so satisfied B were entitled to resile without penalty, which H accepted. On January 18, 1991 H wrote enclosing a certified copy of the contract of excambion and deed of conditions, which disclosed that H's one-half share in the courtyard was to be subjected to a new servitude right of access in favour of N and a prohibition against parking any vehicles or other equipment there. B then intimated that they were not satisfied with the position as disclosed in the deeds and were resiling. B averred that the new burdens materially diminished the value of the subjects and that the prohibition prevented parking on the central parking area required for the new buildings, rendering the planning permission granted nugatory. H argued that (1) the missives envisaged that the final deeds might contain certain additional derogations from H's original title, that B's right to resile was subject to an implied term that B would act reasonably, and that B had no reasonable grounds for being dissatisfied with the position disclosed in the letter of January 18; and (2) in any event, B were required to prove that any derogation from the title was material and a proof should be allowed.

Held, action dismissed. Clause 9 showed that H had been offering to deliver a title which conformed to the existing title in all respects other than the alterations detailed in the letter of August 23 and which would contain no substantive real burdens not apparent from the existing title. Paragraph 3 enabled H to tender a draft document which gave effect to those alterations and provided the deed matched or threw up only *de minimis* changes then there would be no ground for B to be dissatisfied and there was no requirement to imply a term preventing B from resiling capriciously. However, the new burdens were clearly material and did not necessarily follow from the boundary changes, as H argued. B was not bound by the bargain if *ex facie* of the deed the subjects would be burdened by such additional burdens and there was no room for any implied term that B were required to act reasonably (*Gordon District Council v. Wimpey Homes Holdings* [1988] C.L.Y. 5012, and *Rockcliffe Estates v. Cooperative Wholesale Society* [1993] C.L.Y. 5385, distinguished). It was clear that H could not perform his obligations under the missives, which, in those circumstances, gave B a right to resile which B had exercised within the time limit. B were under no obligation to give reasons for resiling and questions of the materiality of any derogation were irrelevant.

HUTTON v. BARRETT (O.H.), *The Times*, December 16, 1994.

6002. Sale—missives—construction—obtaining of planning permission stated to be material condition—whether suspensive condition

By missives of sale, a purchaser agreed to buy from a proprietor certain heritable subjects. The offer letter of February 14, 1994 stated that it was a material condition of the offer that the purchaser obtain planning permission in principle for a proposed conversion of the subjects and that "such application shall be lodged within two weeks of conclusion of any bargain to follow hereon". It was further provided that in the event of planning permission not being forthcoming or on being granted on terms unacceptable to the purchaser, he might either appeal the decision or resile from the contract without penalty or resile after any appeal was refused or granted subject to unacceptable conditions. Further letters were exchanged, altering the time period within which the purchaser was to make application, and the period finally decided upon was that of four weeks following conclusion of missives. Missives were concluded on June 27, 1994 and a planning application was made outwith the four week period on July 27. No issue was raised at the time regarding this and the parties amended the missives following this. The local authority refused to entertain the application for outline planning permission. The purchaser's solicitors amended the period for application for detailed planning permission to four weeks from August 10, 1994 and this was agreed by the seller's agents. The period thus expired on September 7. An application was posted on September 9, and received by the authority on September 13, 1994. On September 14, the seller's agents intimated that, as a detailed planning permission application had not been lodged timeously in terms of the missives, the purchaser was in breach of the missives and the seller had resiled. The purchaser sought decree of declarator that the contract remained in full force and effect and for implement of it. The seller argued that the clause was suspensive of obligation. Planning permission was essential to the bargain, and failing satisfaction of the stipulation for planning permission in cl. 3 there was no date of entry. This indicated that the condition was suspensive. That being so, the time limit was a mandatory requirement of the contract and since it had not been complied with the seller was entitled to resile.

Held, that (1) the successive stipulations and counter stipulations fell properly to be read as modifying the original cl. 3; (2) it was a material condition of the offer that the purchaser obtain planning permission in principle, but that the provision that such application should be lodged within four weeks of conclusion of missives had not been expressly made a material condition of the offer; (3) while the relevant conditions in the missives could not be regarded as conceived solely in favour of the purchaser, it did not follow that, if the condition concerning the obtaining of planning permission was to be regarded as suspensive of the contract, the time limit for lodging the application had also to be so regarded, and on a construction of the missives as a whole, strict compliance with the time specified was not of the essence; and decree of declarator granted *de plano*. *Observed*, that for a condition in missives to be suspensive of all obligation, it had to contain within its terms the language necessary to indicate that. (*Zebmoon v. Akinbrook Investment Developments*, 1988 S.L.T. 146, followed; *Ford Sellar Morris Properties v. E. W. Hutchison* [1990] C.L.Y. 5366 considered.)

KHAZAKA v. DRYSDALE (O.H.), 1995 S.L.T. 1108.

6003. Sale—missives—construction—warranty

An offer to purchase land provided in condition 4: "There are no existing, and the seller has no knowledge of any intended, applications, orders, notices or the like issued by a Local or other Public Authority . . . affecting the subjects either directly or indirectly. A Certificate from the Local Authority confirming this shall be delivered prior to settlement." The seller accepted the offer subject to the modification with regard to condition 4 that "the usual Local Authority letter will be exhibited prior to the date of entry. Should said Local Authority letter disclose any matter materially prejudicial to [the purchaser's] full enjoyment of the subjects as a private residential dwellinghouse [he] will be entitled to resile". A letter from the local authority was duly delivered. The purchaser took no exception to its terms. After the conveyance of the subjects in implement of the missives, the purchaser sought reparation from the seller. He averred that the regional council had applied for planning permission for, and intended to build, a road which would directly affect the subjects; that the defender had been aware of both the application and the intention at the time of the missives; and that he was therefore in breach of contract *et separatim* had induced the pursuer to enter it by fraudulent or negligent misrepresentation. The sheriff having allowed proof before answer, the defender appealed to the sheriff principal, who dismissed the action. The pursuer appealed.

Held, that while in its original form condition 4 might not have detracted from the sellers independent warranty that he was unaware of any intended applications, *etc.*, the qualification meant that, on a proper construction of the missives, the whole of the seller's obligations under condition 4 would be met by the delivery of a satisfactory letter, and, such a letter having been exhibited, there was no independent representation by the seller of his knowledge of the facts, and the pursuer's case was accordingly irrelevant; and appeal refused.

HOOD v. CLARKSON, 1995 S.L.T. 98.

6004. Sale—missives—disposition—partial reduction. See ABERDEEN RUBBER v. KNOWLES & SONS (FRUITERERS), §5992.

6005. Sale—missives—implied terms—dwellinghouse "to be erected" on plot

Held, where purchasers had concluded missives for the purchase of a dwellinghouse "to be erected" on a specified plot, that the contract was subject to implied terms as to the quality of the dwellinghouse subsequently erected, and proof before answer allowed in an action at the instance of the purchasers against the sellers seeking damages for alleged breaches of those implied terms.

ADAMS v. WHATLINGS (Sh.Ct.), 1995 S.C.L.R. 185.

6006. Sale—passing of property—disposition delivered but not yet recorded. See SHARP v. THOMSON, §5549.

6007. Servitude—access—alteration of right. See ROBERTSON v. HOSSACK, §6008.

6008. Servitude—access—constitution—express grant or undisputed exercise—whether personal or real right created

In 1944 the middle of three plots of land forming an *unum quid* was disponed. The successor to the two flanking plots sought two interdicts against the successors to the middle plot. The first was to prevent the owners of the middle plot from entering on the western plot. The defenders maintained that a servitude right of way had been constituted either by the disposition of 1944 or by undisputed exercise since that date. The second was to prevent the owners of the middle plot from carrying out work which would have obstructed a right of access to the eastern plot reserved in the 1944 disposition. The defenders maintained that the route of the line of access was no longer that stated in the 1944 disposition but along some other path and that the works which they intended to carry out would not obstruct that path. After debate the sheriff held that the right of access contained in the 1944 disposition transmitted to successors. The pursuer appealed to the sheriff principal, who held that (1) in the absence of words indicating expressly that the right of access over the western plot was to pass to singular successors or of indications in the disposition that the parties had agreed to such a provision, the right conferred on the grantee was personal to him and did not transmit to successors; (2) the defenders had no relevant averments of prescriptive use since original disponee ceased to use the property; and (3) in the absence of averments as to the present line of access to the eastern plot, or how the right of way was varied, or how there had been acquiescence, the defences relating thereto were irrelevant; and allowed the appeal and granted interdict. The defender appealed to the Court of Session.

Held, that the sheriff principal was correct for the reasons he gave; and appeal refused.

ROBERTSON v. HOSSACK, 1995 S.L.T. 291.

6009. Standard security—default—calling-up notice—request for statement of amount due

[Conveyancing and Feudal Reform (Scotland) Act 1970 (c.35) s.19(9).]

F appealed against decree in B's favour, as holder of a standard security, for repossession of H and F's house. F had defended the action which was based on default. A calling-up notice had been served on April 15, 1993 specifying sums of principal and interest which was subject to adjustment at the stage of final determination. F argued that by letter dated April 29, 1993 she requested B to give a statement of debt and that B failed to respond. F claimed that this failure breached s.19(9) of the 1970 Act and rendered the calling-up notice ineffectual. B denied receiving F's letter. F's solicitors (S) had also written to B on April 16, 1993 requesting a statement of sums due which B complied with on April 29, 1993. F denied receiving that letter. F argued on appeal that (1) the sheriff was wrong to find sufficient averments of agency by B thus imputing F with S's knowledge: S had written in the context of F and H's divorce proof, which was the extent of their authority, and not s.19(9); and (2) as F had not admitted the sending or receipt of S's letter and B's letter, decree had been inappropriate. B argued that F's letter was not a request under s.19(9). If it was, *a fortiori* S's letter had also to be a request which B had answered.

Held, appeal refused. F's letter was not a request under s.19(9). F's letter requested an updated account of all outstanding money relating to three accounts, only two of which related to the subject of the calling-up notice, as F required the details for proof. F's letter was not in response to the calling-up notice. As such a request might have fatal consequences for a calling-up notice, a request had to be clearly invoking s.19(9) so as properly to alert a creditor to the importance of compliance. In any event F was not prejudiced as

the statement was not sought so as to clear the debt and B would be able to serve another notice to which F would have no defence.
BANK OF SCOTLAND v. FLETT (Sh.Ct.), 1995 S.C.L.R. 591.

6010. Standard security—description of subjects—particular description—whether mandatory

[Conveyancing and Feudal Reform (Scotland) Act 1970 (c.35), ss.9(2) and 53(1) and Sched. 2.]

B, owners of a flat at 2F2, 1 Roseneath Terrace, purchased from C in July 1992, sought reduction of a standard security granted by C to a bank (F) in March over "All and Whole the subjects known as 1 Roseneath Terrace". B averred that, when the standard security had been granted, C had only owned one flat, that the security had not been disclosed to B, that F were threatening to call up the security as a result of C's failure to pay money owed to F and that the security was null and void because the description of the property did not comply with the requirements of Sched. 2 to the 1970 Act. F argued that (1) a postal address was a "particular description" as referred to in Sched. 2, note 1; and (2) in any event the reference to a particular description was directory or permissive and not mandatory, as the purpose of the reference was to ensure a property was adequately identified; a postal description was sufficient for a disposition, and the keeper had accepted the security.

Held, decree of reduction granted. (1) The distinction between a general and a particular description was well understood and, considering also that Sched. D, note 2 to the Conveyancing (Scotland) Act 1924 described a postal address as a short description as opposed to a particular description, the address given clearly constituted a general description (Cusine, "Descriptions in Standard Securities" (1990) 35 J.L.S. 98, approved). (2) Given the importance of knowing what subjects were affected by a security, that F had no possession by which a general description could be further defined, and that a security might have been over only part of C's property and therefore not defined by his possession either, it was not absurd that the requirements for a description in a standard security should be greater than those for a disposition. Given further that a standard security had to be "expressed in conformity" with one of the forms in Sched. 2 (s.9(2)), the language of the forms was prima facie prescriptive and, as a general description did not "conform as closely as may be" (s.51(3)) to that requirement, the security was invalid.
BENNETT v. BENEFICIAL BANK (O.H.), 1995 S.L.T. 1105.

6011. Standard security—discharge—reduction—error—relevancy

S sought reduction of their discharge of a standard security granted by F. S had granted a secured loan in substitution of one granted by Security Pacific Trust (T). S averred that although T's standard security had been discharged three months before, T had written to solicitors (D) instructing them to arrange a discharge of their security. D had interpreted the instructions as coming from S, and after receiving confirmation, given in error, that S's loan had been repaid, D prepared a discharge, which was executed and delivered to F's new solicitors, who recorded it. F's trustee in bankruptcy (G) argued that (1) as the discharge was probative and narrated that it had been granted in consideration of all sums due and that might become due, it was incompetent to lead evidence that it had been granted gratuitously; and (2) S had not averred the reasons for the error, and, as S knew the nature and content of the document, it could not be said that the error was "reasonably entertained" (*Hunter v. Bradford Property Trust* [1970] C.L.Y. 3055).

Held, proof before answer allowed. (1) Whether the discharge had been granted gratuitously went to the proof of the error and, as S was seeking to reduce the deed and not just alter it, this could be proved by parole evidence (*Steuart's Trs. v. Hart* (1875) 3 R. 192). (2) S had signed the discharge because of their misapprehension that F had paid their debt, which was an understandable mistake and there was no reason in law or equity why G should be entitled to found upon the deed (*Dickson v. Halbert* (1854) 16 D. 586). Although S had only explained the situation by averring that mistakes had been made, this was sufficient to allow inquiry and, if necessary, to show that the error had been reasonably entertained. It could not be said that the error had not been essential as defined in *Hunter*. *Opinion*, that it was doubtful that the ratio of *Hunter* was that a material error required to be reasonably entertained.

SECURITY PACIFIC FINANCE v. T. & I. FILSHIE'S TR. (O.H.), 1994 S.C.L.R. 1100.

6012. Standard security—heritable creditor in possession of security subjects—rights of judicial factor over security subjects. See DUNLOP (G.) & SONS' JUDICIAL FACTOR v. ARMSTRONG, §6206.

6013. Standard security—obligations of heritable creditor exercising power to eject debtor. See THOMSON v. YORKSHIRE BUILDING SOCIETY, §5485.

6014. Standard security—ranking—delay in recording earlier standard security

[Titles to Land Consolidation (Scotland) Act 1868 (c.101), s.120; Conveyancing and Feudal Reform (Scotland) Act 1970 (c.35), s.11(1).]

Solicitors delayed in recording a standard security in favour of their clients, so that a second, later standard security was recorded ahead of it. In due course the clients exercised their remedy of sale under the standard security and accounted to the holders of the second standard security for their share of the sale proceeds before applying the remaining balance towards their own debt. The clients then sued their solicitors for the difference between the full amount of the debt, which should have been secured, and the balance remaining after the other, secured debt had been satisfied. The solicitors argued that their clients had been under no obligation to account to the other security holders, who had been aware of the existence of the earlier security and who had intended to be second ranking creditors.

Held, that the other security holders had acted perfectly properly, that the clients had been obliged to account to the other security holders as they had done, and that the solicitors' defence was irrelevant.

SCOTLIFE HOME LOANS (NO. 2) v. MUIR (Sh.Ct.), 1994 S.C.L.R. 791.

6015. Standard security—remedies of heritable creditor where tenant in possession

[Conveyancing and Feudal Reform (Scotland) Act 1970 (c.35), Sched. 3, condition 10.]

Held, where heritable creditors had obtained a decree against the owners of certain heritable property entitling them to enter into possession of the property and to receive the rents and thereafter had entered into unsuccessful negotiations for the sale of the subjects to the tenants, that the heritable creditors' actings did not amount to possession, they were to be deemed to have abandoned the property as an asset and that the property had thereafter reverted to the owners who were entitled to receive the rents.

ASCOT INNS (IN RECEIVERSHIP) v. BRAIDWOOD ESTATES (Sh. Ct.), 1995 S.C.L.R. 390.

6016. Subsidence—coal mining subsidence. See BRITISH COAL CORPORATION v. NETHERLEE TRUST TRS., §6139.

6017. Superior and vassal—feuing conditions—variation and discharge. See McCARTHY & STONE (DEVELOPMENTS) v. SMITH, §5994.

HIGHWAYS AND BRIDGES

Negligence. See NEGLIGENCE.

6018. Public right of way. See LORD BURTON v. MACKAY, §5998.

6019. Special roads

MOTORWAYS TRAFFIC (SCOTLAND) REGULATIONS 1995 (No. 2507) [£1·55], made under the Road Traffic Regulation Act 1984 (c.27) s.17(2) (as amended by the New Roads and Street Works Act 1991 (c.22) Sched. 8 and by the Road Traffic Act 1991 (c.40) Scheds. 4 and 8) and s.17(3); operative on October 23, 1995; re-enact the Motorways Traffic (Scotland) Regulations 1964 and the Motorways Traffic (Scotland) (Amendment) Regulations 1968 with amendments and provide for the regulation of traffic using special roads provided under the 1984 Act.

[S.I. 1964 No. 1002 and S.I. 1968 No. 960 revoked.]

Order made under the Road Traffic Regulation Act 1984 (c.27) s.17: S.I. 1995 No. 1984 (A87 Extension (Skye Bridge Crossing) Special Road Regulations.

[S.I. 1992 No. 1499 amended.]

HOUSING

6020. Homeless persons—duty of local authority—priority need—local connection

[Housing (Scotland) Act 1987 (c.26), ss.27(c), 31(1) and (2), 33 and 83.]

M sought judicial review of a district council's (K) decision to refuse her application for housing on the grounds that although she had a priority need, she did not have a local connection in terms of s.27(1) of the 1987 Act, and to refer her application to another council. M was born in 1973 in Ayr and had lived there until 1989 when she and her parents moved to Tyne and Wear. On March 4, 1994, following the birth of her daughter (D), M had been told to leave and had returned to Ayr with D and D's father and stayed with M's sister (S). In her application M stated that she wished to return to Ayr because she had grown up there, she was not accepted in Sunderland, and she wished to be near S, who also had a young child, and her grandfather and aunt, who had lived in the district all their lives, and that she did not wish to be referred to another local authority. K argued that in applying s.33 of the 1987 Act they had given due regard to the COSLA agreement on referrals issued in December 1986 as recommended by the Scottish Office code of guidance; that M had no parents children or collaterals who had been resident in the district for more than five years, and there were no exceptional circumstances which would allow her grandfather's or aunt's residence to establish a local connection; that "family associations" in s.27(1)(c) had to be more than just blood relationships, and merely wishing to be with relatives was not sufficient; that there had been no special reasons justifying a departure from the COSLA agreement; that the onus was on M to establish a local connection; and that, as the matters raised by M related solely to s.27(1)(c), there was no requirement for K to consider if there were special circumstances in terms of subs. (1)(d).

Held, petition granted. Even if M had no local connection, K retained a discretion as to whether or not to notify another authority. However, K's decision letter suggested that they had not consciously exercised their discretion, although the COSLA agreement provided that applicants should not be referred because of family associations if they objected. The COSLA agreement had been designed for the Housing (Homeless Persons) Act 1977, which had been repealed by the 1987 Act; the 1987 Act contained a wider definition of "family" (s.83(1)), and the suggestion that the residence of M's aunt or grandfather would only in exceptional circumstances establish a local connection was wrong and the demand for a five year period of continuous residence before S's residence could be taken into account involved the adoption of too rigid a rule. Section 27(1)(c) required only that there be a connection between the family and the area and there was no need to examine the nature or quality of the relationships within the family, as to do so would involve an excessively arduous investigation by K. Each and all of the factors cited by M demonstrated real and enduring links with the area and to hold that M had no connection would be unreasonable. Section 28(2), which entitled K to make investigations into whether M had a local connection, suggested that there was no onus on M to establish a local connection; s.33 was neutral on the question. K were obliged to consider all four heads in s.27(1), and their failure to consider subhead (d), when M's desire to return to the area in which she had been brought up provided at least one reason for applying it, was in itself fatal to the decision. The decision would be reduced and declarator granted that K were bound in terms of s.31(2) to secure accommodation for M.

McMILLAN v. KYLE AND CARRICK DISTRICT COUNCIL (O.H.), 1995 S.C.L.R. 365.

6021. Housing revenue account

HOUSING REVENUE ACCOUNT GENERAL FUND CONTRIBUTION LIMITS (SCOTLAND) ORDER 1995 (No. 188) [65p], made under the Housing (Scotland) Act 1987 (c.26), s.204; operative on March 1, 1995; provides that local authorities may not include in their estimates for 1995–96 any contribution from their general fund to their housing revenue account.

Local authority houses—tenants' rights. See LANDLORD AND TENANT.

Public sector houses—tenants' rights. See LANDLORD AND TENANT.

6022. Support grants

HOUSING SUPPORT GRANT (SCOTLAND) VARIATION ORDER 1995 (No. 469) [65p], made under the Housing (Scotland) Act 1987 (c.26), s.193(4) and (5); operative on February 23, 1995; reduces the aggregate amount of housing support grant originally fixed for the year 1994–95 and both its general and hostel portions.

[S.I. 1994 No. 430 amended.]

HOUSING SUPPORT GRANT (SCOTLAND) ORDER 1995 (No. 470) [£1·55], made under the Housing (Scotland) Act 1987 (c.26), ss.191 and 192 (both as amended by the Housing (Scotland) Act 1988 (c.43), Sched. 8); operative on April 1, 1995; fixes the aggregate amount payable to some local authorities, lists the authorities among whom the grants will be apportioned, and prescribes the method of apportionment among those authorities of the general and hostel portions of the aggregate amount for the year 1995–96.

HUSBAND AND WIFE

Divorce. See DIVORCE AND CONSISTORIAL CAUSES.

6023. Marriage—constitution—habit and repute

A woman raised an action for declarator of marriage and for aliment contending that the marriage was established by cohabitation with habit and repute. The parties met in 1973 at the age of 21 and 19. They had their first child about a year later and moved to live together a further year after that. Thereafter they lived together at three addresses in succession until 1983 when they separated. They had had a second child in 1979 whose birth was registered with the father's surname, which the mother also used, and the birth notice in the newspaper read as if the parents were married. The mother was generally known by the father's name. The father referred to the mother as his wife and introduced her as his wife. Their first child only learned that his parents had not undergone a marriage ceremony when he was 16. The mother's family took them to be husband and wife but the father's family disapproved of the relationship and never accepted that they were husband and wife. Neighbours and all others who dealt with them, apart from some acquaintances of the father, considered them to be husband and wife, even although some of them later became aware that there had been no marriage ceremony. The reason that there had been no formal ceremony was partly because they considered themselves to be married following the gift of a ring by the father to the mother before the first child was born and partly because, when they did discuss it, they felt that they would have to go elsewhere to get married, which was not convenient because the first child was then still a baby. The mother's maiden surname was used in taking title to properties bought for investment and resale during the cohabitation, although the fee note from the solicitor was addressed to her using the father's surname. It was argued for the father that the repute was not general enough in that the father's family did not consider them to be husband and wife, nor did some of the father's business and social associates who knew that there had not been a marriage ceremony.

Held, that (1) where there had been cohabitation at bed and board for many years and strong evidence of repute, confirmed by the terms of the second child's birth certificate, the fact that, on occasions, the father had made it plain that he was against the idea of marriage could not outweigh his actions in holding out himself and the mother as husband and wife, nor did the fact that the father's own relatives did not consider him to be married since that belief was based on a disapproval of the relationship and little knowledge of the facts; (2) the marriage could be taken as beginning when the mother and father had moved to live together with their first child; and decree of declarator pronounced.

DEWAR v. DEWAR (O.H.), 1995 S.L.T. 467.

Orders for financial provision on divorce. See DIVORCE AND CONSISTORIAL CAUSES.

IMMIGRATION

6024. Entry clearance—child "sole responsibility" of parent in United Kingdom—proper test to apply

[Immigration Rules (H.C. 169), r. 50(e) and (f).]

Paragraph 50 of the Immigration Rules provides for admission to settlement in the United Kingdom of a child if one of its parents already settled in the United Kingdom has had the sole responsibility for the child's upbringing (para. 50(3)) or if there are serious and compelling family or other considerations which make exclusion undesirable (para. 50(f)). The Immigration Appeals (Procedure) Rules 1984 apply to appeals against refusal of entry clearance, which appeals are made in the first place to an adjudicator, with provision for further appeal to the immigration appeal tribunal with leave either of the adjudicator or of the tribunal. Leave from the adjudicator has to be sought "forthwith" after the adjudicator's determination. Leave from the tribunal must be sought within 42 days after the adjudicator's determination. A 17-year-old resident in the Philippines applied under the Immigration Rules to be admitted to the United Kingdom for settlement as a relative of her mother who was already lawfully resident there. Clearance having been refused, the applicant appealed to an adjudicator against the refusal but this appeal also was unsuccessful. Leave to appeal to the immigration appeal tribunal was not sought either from the adjudicator or from the tribunal. The applicant then sought judicial review and reduction of the decision and declarator that she had a right to entry clearance for settlement in the United Kingdom, arguing that the adjudicator's decision revealed (1) a failure to consider serious and compelling family considerations which made her exclusion from the United Kingdom undesirable within para. 50(f); (2) that the adjudicator had misdirected himself when considering whether the mother had had "sole responsibility" for her upbringing within the meaning of para. 50(e), since that could never be established in a strict sense by a parent living in the United Kingdom in relation to a child living abroad and therefore the expression had a wider meaning which, rather than the strict meaning, was the correct one; and (3) that the failure to apply for leave to appeal against the decision of the adjudicator did not preclude her from seeking to obtain justice by judicial review.

Held, that (1) the adjudicator had been entitled, when considering para. 50(f), to disregard evidence of the poor behaviour of the child's father as outdated and irrelevant and, in any event, since he did not require specifically to discuss in his decision the possible inferences to be drawn from the evidence regarding the situation as at the date of the application, it could not be demonstrated that he had not considered this issue; but (2) since there was clear authority that a strict interpretation of the rules was not appropriate, the adjudicator's silence as to the proper legal interpretation of para. 50(e) and the supporting case law suggested that there might have been a failure to apply the correct interpretation; the absence of day to day care could not be determinative of the question of "sole responsibility" and the adjudicator had therefore applied the wrong test; (3) upon the full findings made by the adjudicator, the only reasonable conclusion was that the applicant did satisfy the requirements of para. 50(e); (4) judicial review was available notwithstanding the failure to use the statutory appeal process, since there were both a demonstrable miscarriage of justice and exceptional circumstances in that the adjudicator's decision had deprived the applicant of entry clearance to which it was now known she had been entitled, she had no statutory means of renewing her application since she was now over age and there had been a recommendation by the adjudicator that she be admitted notwithstanding his own refusal; and reduction and declarator pronounced. (*Bain v. Hugh L. S. McConnell* [1991] C.L.Y. 5448/9, applied.)

ALAGON v. SECRETARY OF STATE FOR THE HOME DEPARTMENT (O.H.), 1995 S.L.T. 381.

6025. Entry clearance—refusal of—appeal—judicial review. See ALAGON v. SECRETARY OF STATE FOR THE HOME DEPARTMENT, §6024.

6026. Illegal immigrant—gaining entry by deception—evidence—competency—fairness. See OGHONOGHOR v. SECRETARY OF STATE FOR THE HOME DEPARTMENT, §5923.

Matrimonial homes—occupancy rights. See DIVORCE AND CONSISTORIAL CAUSES.

Matrimonial interdicts. See DIVORCE AND CONSISTORIAL CAUSES.

INCOME TAX

6027. Charities—income—exemption—whether income applicable to charitable purposes only

[Income and Corporation Taxes Act 1988 (c.1), s.505(1)(c).]

A company established a scheme to encourage employees to purchase shares in the company. As part of the scheme a trust fund was set up, and was given a loan by the company to allow the fund to acquire shares in the company which it would then sell to employees. On the sale of shares by the fund, the fund was obliged to remit the price of the shares to the company in order to reduce the loan. Another company sought to buy the company by acquiring its shares. The offer by the purchaser required the company to buy back the shares held by the trust fund. The company accordingly bought back the shares held by the trust, and the fund was then wound up. After meeting the liabilities of the scheme, including the repayment to the company of the loan, the trust fund held a balance of money which, in terms of the trust deed setting up the trust fund, it was obliged to pay to a charitable organisation. The trustees took the view that the money given to the charitable organisation was income applicable, and applied, to charitable purposes only in terms of s.505(1)(c) of the Income and Corporation Taxes Act 1988, and sought payment of a tax credit from the Inland Revenue. The case came before a special commissioner who decided that none of the proceeds of the sale of the shares were income of a charity, none were applied to charitable purposes only, and rejected the claim for a tax credit. The trustees required the special commissioner to state a case for the opinion of the Court of Session on the question whether he was entitled so to hold. The trustees argued that as soon as the trustees determined to wind up the scheme, the charity immediately became entitled to the assets of the scheme, subject only to its liabilities. The charity was from that moment the sole beneficiary of the property. There was only one dispositive purpose which the trustees had to fulfil, which was to pay the balance of the funds in their hands after paying off the debts. The repayment of the loan was an application for charitable purposes only, and the duties of the trustees were to be seen as administrative only. The charity had acquired the whole assets of the trust subject only to its liabilities.

Held, that (1) the trust fund was not applying the funds for a charitable purpose only, if, at the time the proceeds of the shares were received by it, the trust was obliged to hold the funds for non-charitable purposes before making payment of the balance to charity; (2) the duties of the trustees could not be described as being of an administrative nature only, as they were purely for the benefit of the company: the obligation to repay the loan to the company was dispositive, not administrative in character and the charity's position could be described as being analogous to that of a residuary beneficiary; (3) the charity therefore only had an interest in the balance of the sale proceeds after payment of the loan and other expenses, and the charitable purpose arose only when the trustees had fulfilled these antecedent duties; and question answered in the affirmative.

MUIR (WILLIAM) (BOND 9) EMPLOYEES' SHARE SCHEME TRS. v. I.R.C., 1995 S.L.T. 225.

6028. Emoluments—redundancy payments—supplementary redundancy payments payable whether or not employees lost employment

[Income and Corporation Taxes Act 1970 (c.10), ss.181, 183, 187 and 188.]

Section 181 of the Income and Corporation Taxes Act 1970 provides that tax shall be payable under Sched. E on any emoluments from employment. Section 187 further provides that any payments on "termination of the holding of the office or employment or any change in its functions or emoluments" shall be taxed under Sched. E, with the exception (under s.188) that no tax is due where the payment is less than £25,000.

In 1982 a company ("company A") wished to terminate its business. It accordingly sold its share capital to another company ("company B"). On the shares being sold, company A made redundancy payments to its employees, who were to receive the redundancy payments whether or not their employment was to continue with the new owners. The payments were over and above the statutory level, but were below £25,000, and therefore not subject to tax if they fell within ss.187 and 188. After the sale company A continued in business under the control of company B. Certain employees then continued to work for company A until it ceased business in 1986. The General Commissioners decided that the sums paid to those employees were emoluments of their employment in terms of ss.181 and 183 of the Taxes Act 1970, and were thus assessable to income tax under Sched E. An employee and the husband of a second employee appealed to the Court of Session.

Held, that (1) payments made as supplementary redundancy payments to employees whose services had been terminated were different in character from payments to all employees irrespective of whether or not they were made redundant, and the payments to the appellants could not be regarded as compensation for anticipated loss of employment; (2) applying the various tests identified in the authorities, the payments to the appellants were emoluments from employment; and appeals dismissed. *Observations* on the nature of appeal by way of stated case.

ALLAN v. I.R.C., 1995 S.L.T. 771.

6029. Schedule E—benefits in kind—car available for private use—employee required to pay cost of insurance—whether deductible

[Income and Corporation Taxes Act 1988 (c.1), s.157 and Sched. 6, Pt. II, para. 4.]

Paragraph 4 of Pt. II of Sched. 6 to the Income and Corporation Taxes Act 1988 provides that if an employee was required, as a condition of a car being available for his private use, to pay any amount of money for that use. The cash equivalent treated as chargeable to tax is to be reduced by the amount so paid. A motor car had been made available to a taxpayer by his employers for his private use. The taxpayer paid "contract user payments" to his employers and it was admitted that the tax payable by him in respect of the benefit of the car fell to be reduced by these payments. The taxpayer contended that, in addition to these payments, he had to pay various other costs, including the cost of insuring the car, which represented amounts of money which he was required to pay as a condition of the car being available to him for his private use, and that these payments came within para. 4 of Pt. II of Sched. 6 to the 1988 Act. The general commissioners held that the payments made by the taxpayer for insurance fell within para. 4 and that he was entitled to a reduction from the taxable benefit under s.157 in respect of this expenditure. The revenue appealed.

Held, that (1) on a construction of para. 4 it was clear that only those payments which were made for the private use of the car were to be brought into account; (2) two tests had to be satisfied, namely that the payments had to be payments which the employee was required to make as a condition of the car being available for his private use, and that they had also to be made by the employee for the use of the car for his private use; (3) the payments in question were in respect of the insurance of the car and not the use of it, and the taxpayer was not entitled to bring the payments into account by way of reduction of the cash equivalent of the benefit of the car for his private use; and appeal allowed.

I.R.C. v. QUIGLEY, 1995 S.L.T. 1052.

6030. Schedule E—emoluments. See ALLAN v. I.R.C., §6028.

INNKEEPERS

See INTOXICATING LIQUORS

Insolvency. See BANKRUPTCY; COMPANY LAW.

INSURANCE

6031. Fire insurance—insurable interest—building damaged by fraud of insured—rights of heritable creditor

A bank raised an action against an insurance company for payment under a policy of fire insurance in respect of a building which had burned down. The bank averred that policy had been entered into by the owners of the building and that the policy had contained an endorsement in the bank's favour as heritable creditors. The endorsement stated expressly that the interest was vested in the bank as heritable creditors *primo loco* and in the proprietors in reversion. The endorsement went on to state that the bank's interest was not to be affected by any increase in the insured risk, that the policy would not lapse without notice to the bank and that no payment would be made without the bank's consent. The insurers had refused to pay under the policy on the grounds that the principal shareholder in the owners had been a party to the burning of the building and that the bank had no independent rights under the policy.

Held, that (1) the nature of the bank's rights under the endorsement depended on a proper construction of its terms; (2) the terms of the endorsement, particularly the exemption of the bank's interest from the consequences of increased risk, implied that the bank had an original interest in the policy rather than one depending on the owner's rights; and pursuers' plea to the relevancy sustained, defenders' plea repelled and proof restricted to quantum allowed.

BANK OF SCOTLAND v. GUARDIAN ROYAL EXCHANGE (O.H.), 1995 S.L.T. 763.

6032. Lease—construction. See HARRIS (VICTOR) (GENTSWEAR) v. THE WOOL WAREHOUSE (PERTH), §6060.

6033. Life assurance company—approval of proposed chief executive—procedure—fairness

The Secretary of State for Trade and Industry (S) issued a notice of objection under s.60(1) of the Insurance Companies Act 1982, on the ground that an individual (B), who had agreed to take up the position of chief executive of a life assurance company, was not a fit and proper person to be appointed to the post. B challenged the notice on the ground that the procedures adopted were irregular and contrary to natural justice. Although in the letter accompanying the written preliminary notice S had given particular reasons for his objection, consideration had been given to evidence of a senior employee at B's former company, without B having been given the opportunity to challenge that evidence; and the nature of B's proposed duties in the new position had been raised at the oral hearing without any advance notice. B argued that under s.60(4) of the Act S had a duty to disclose the evidence of primary fact so that both sides of the story might be heard; and that S had a duty to act fairly.

Held, that S could not be criticised for his approach to these matters. He was under no obligation to disclose any detailed information relating to the ground of service of the notice: the material on which S relied was put to B, at least in outline, for his response, and no material had been relied upon which had not in one way or another been canvassed with B. Further, the nature of the whole inquiry was to reach a conclusion as to whether B was a fit and proper person to be chief executive of the company, and it should have been obvious to him that S would wish to satisfy himself as to the nature of the new office.

BUCHANAN v. SECRETARY OF STATE FOR TRADE AND INDUSTRY, *The Times*, March 1, 1995.

6034. Policy—construction—endorsement—building damaged by fraud of insured—rights of heritable creditor. See BANK OF SCOTLAND v. GUARDIAN ROYAL EXCHANGE, §6031.

INTOXICATING LIQUORS

6035. Licensing—application for grant of licence—refusal—over-provision. See GLASGOW DISTRICT LICENSING BOARD v. DIN, §6039.

6036. Licensing—application for grant of licence—refusal—over-provision—"locality". See CALEDONIAN NIGHTCLUBS v. GLASGOW DISTRICT LICENSING BOARD, §6037.

6037. Licensing—application for grant of licence—refusal—over-provision—relevant considerations—nature of facilities to be provided

C appealed a sheriff's refusal of their appeal against a licensing authority's (G) refusal of C's application for a provisional entertainment licence for "a high class nightclub, providing dancing on two floors with restaurant and associated bars". A similar application in respect of the same premises by C had been granted in 1989 but C had not proceeded with the venture and the licence had lapsed in 1992. Following a submission by the chief constable that within 200 m. of the premises there were 14 other licensed premises, including one entertainment licence, six public house licences and one provisional public house licence, G had rejected the application on the ground that, considering the scale of the venture, the grant would result in overprovision of licensed premises in the locality, which for the purposes of s.17(1)(d) of the 1976 Act, G determined as a radius of 200 m from the premises. C argued that (1) G had erred in rejecting C's proposal as to the relevant locality—Glasgow city centre—on the arbitrary ground that that was "impractical and unrealistic"; and (2) G should have considered the nature of the entertainment proposed by C and that provided by the holder of the existing entertainment licence, as each licence was related to the particular entertainment specified in an application and G's consent would have been required for reconstruction or alteration of the premises. G argued that the types of entertainment proposed or carried on were irrelevant (*Chung v. Wigtown District Licensing Board* [1993] C.L.Y. 5432), as once a licence was granted, C would be entitled to carry on any of the types of entertainment specified in Sched. 1 to the 1976 Act, and that, although no information had been placed before G regarding the entertainment provided under the existing licence, G had to be taken to know their own area.

Held, appeal allowed and case remitted to the sheriff with a direction to grant the application. (1) On the basis of the information supplied by the chief constable, G had been entitled to adopt a radius of 200 m as a practical way of defining the locality (*Lazerdale v. City of Glasgow District Licensing Board*, 1988 G.W.D. 36–1485). G's reason for rejecting C's proposed locality was sufficient and was reasonable given the very large number of licensed premises in the city centre and therefore the difficulty in deciding whether one more licence constituted over-provision. (2) Given the various places of public entertainment which might be covered by an entertainment licence and that a licence was to be regarded as granted for a particular form of entertainment, G were entitled to ascertain which form was proposed by C and what was provided by the holder of the existing licence and the approach described in *Chung* had to be modified to that extent. As G had attached importance to the existing entertainment licence without knowing what type of entertainment the licence was authorised to provide, and there was nothing in their reasons given to suggest that G had relied on their local knowledge, G were not entitled to conclude that granting C's application would result in overprovision. Accordingly G had no sound reason for refusal of the licence and in terms of s.17(1) had to grant it.

CALEDONIAN NIGHTCLUBS v. GLASGOW DISTRICT LICENSING BOARD, 1995 S.C.L.R. 252.

6038. Licensing—application for grant of licence—refusal—over-provision—requirement to define "locality"

[Licensing (Scotland) Act 1976 (c.66), s.17(1)(d).]

Section 17(1)(d) of the Licensing (Scotland) Act 1976 provides, *inter alia*, that a licensing board shall refuse an application if it is satisfied that a grant would result in "over-provision of licensed premises in the locality". A licensing board granted a public house licence to applicants. An objector appealed to the sheriff, who remitted the application back to the board for reconsideration. The sheriff directed that the board required to deal with the question of locality when reconsidering the application. The board did so and granted the licence. The objector appealed to the sheriff and from the sheriff's refusal of the appeal to the Court of Session. At the rehearing the board adopted a different and larger area as being the locality which had to be considered, from that which parties had agreed to be applicable at the first hearing. The objector argued on appeal that it was not open to the board to adopt a different or larger area as being the locality, and that the sheriff had erred in holding that the defenders required to deal with "locality" at the rehearing.

Held, that (1) a board, in considering the question of over-provision, required to define with some precision what was the locality (*Chung v. Wigtown District Licensing Board* [1993] C.L.Y. 5432, followed); (2) it was necessary for the board to do so at the rehearing as they had not considered the question of locality at the first hearing in the manner required by s.17(1)(d) of the 1976 Act; and appeal refused.

ROSS v. MORAY DISTRICT LICENSING BOARD, 1995 S.L.T. 447.

6039. Licensing—application for grant of licence—refusal—reasons—adequacy of reasons

[Licensing (Scotland) Act 1976 (c.66), ss.5(2) and (7) and 17(1).]

G, a licensing board, appealed the sheriff's decision to allow an appeal by D against G's refusal to grant a new offsales licence. G had refused the licence on the basis that D was not a fit and proper person to hold a licence by reason of insufficient experience, that the premises were not suitable and that the grant of the licence would result in overprovision (s.17(1)(a), (b) and (d) of the 1976 Act). D had been a grocer for 30 years but claimed that he had also assisted a friend in an offsales two days per week for two years. A police statement produced was to the effect that D had claimed only to have done this on isolated and limited occasions. D argued that as a grocer with his experience, he was bound to have experience in handling similar goods such as cigarettes. G departed from an argument that there was an onus on D under s.17(1)(a) and (b) of the 1976 Act to satisfy them of his fitness and as to the premises, but argued that (1) they were entitled to conclude that he had insufficient experience; (2) they were entitled to find that the premises were unsuitable on the basis of a report which inferred that the shop was too small as the storeroom was already full; (3) G's decision that the grant would result in overprovision could not be assailed in light of *Chung v. Wigtown District Licensing Board* [1993] C.L.Y. 5432; G were entitled to make their decision on the basis of material before them, general knowledge and expertise (*Latif v. Motherwell District Licensing Board* [1994] C.L.Y. 5936), and while evidence on comparable areas and densities of provision was acknowledged as relevant G was not bound by this; and (4) the sheriff had erred in not remitting the application back to G for a rehearing instead of ordaining G to grant a licence.

Held, appeal refused. (1) Where it did not appear that G had rejected the information supplied by D, or why the experience narrated was deemed to be so insufficient as to render D not a fit and proper person, G had no material upon which to hold that D's experience was insufficient. Further, the error by G at first instance as to onus was fatal. (2) G's approach to the suitability of the premises was similarly flawed. The building control department had had no adverse comment to make on size. (3) The reasoning for G's decision on over-provision did not explain anything. It did not necessarily follow that because present facilities were "sufficient", to permit one more would result in overprovision. Although G were not obliged to respond in detail to issues of comparison, their failure to challenge the comparison at the time or to explain subsequently why it was invalid highlighted the inadequacy of the reasons given. (4) Neither D nor G had suggested to the sheriff that the case should be remitted back to G and in light of *Caledonian Nightclubs v. Glasgow District Licensing Board* [1995] C.L.Y. 6037, it was not appropriate to require G to reconsider the case given the lapse of time and insupportable reasons. *Observed*, that the kind of bland, standard *pro forma* reason offered by G in respect of the overprovision was to be disapproved. *Opinion*, that where more than one ground of refusal was relied on, G were obliged to vote in public on each ground of refusal and not just on the granting or refusing of the licence, since G were obliged to make a positive finding upon one or more grounds for refusal if a licence was to be refused and an adverse decision on a ground was in effect a decision on the granting of a licence and had therefore to be in public.

GLASGOW DISTRICT LICENSING BOARD v. DIN, 1995 S.C.L.R. 290.

6040. Licensing—application for grant of licence—whether onus on applicant. See GLASGOW DISTRICT LICENSING BOARD v. DIN, §6039.

6041. Licensing—application for provisional grant of licence—entertainment licence—refusal—actings of board. See PAGLIOCCA v. CITY OF GLASGOW DISTRICT LICENSING BOARD, §6048.

6042. Licensing—application for renewal of licence—refusal—reasons—sufficiency of specification of reasons

[Licensing (Scotland) Act 1976 (c.66), s.18.]

An application for renewal of an entertainment licence was refused on the ground that the licensee was no longer a fit and proper person to hold a licence. On a number of occasions over a period of months the licensee had let the premises to another individual for dances. The police had raided the premises and seized a significant amount of controlled drugs found on persons, including attendants, who were within the premises and also in various places concealed about the premises. The board's statement of reasons provided under s.18 of the 1976 Act stated: "The board considered that the lack of supervision exercised meant that the partnership was no longer a fit and proper person to hold a licence. The board expects high standards from licensees. In view of the events described in the Chief Constable's letter the Board concluded that [the applicant] no longer matches up to those standards." On appeal to the Court of Session, at which the licensing board and chief constable were separately represented, the applicant maintained that the statement of reasons was inadequate, *inter alia*, because it did not deal with certain matter put before the board.

Held, that (1) in a case of this kind it was necessary that the informed reader should be able to understand from the statement of reasons what the reasoning was that led to the decision and in the present case it was plain from the statement why the application was being refused; (2) the matters not dealt with in the statement of reasons were not important in the circumstances; and appeal refused.

Held, further, that where the attack was on the reasoning and statement of reasons of the licensing board, who had intimated that they intended to defend their decision, there was no requirement for the chief constable to be separately represented; and motion for expenses in his favour refused. *Observed*, that it could not be right that persons who had a licence to operate licensed premises ceded control to others whose fitness had never been proved or tested before the licensing board.

ROBERTSON v. CITY OF EDINBURGH DISTRICT LICENSING BOARD, 1995 S.L.T. 107.

6043. Licensing—application for transfer of licence—temporary transfer granted—competency of further temporary transfer

[Licensing (Scotland) Act 1976) (c.66), s.25(1A).]

C sought judicial review of a decision by E, a licensing board. C was the father of W, the holder of a public house licence formerly held by C. The licence had been transferred by E to W on a temporary basis under s.25(1A) of the 1976 Act. W was to apply for a permanent licence but did not apply timeously, so that a permanent transfer could not take effect when the temporary licence ceased. C applied to have the licence transferred back on a temporary basis but E refused this as incompetent. C argued that where the initial transfer had not been made permanent a further temporary transfer was competent and that to rule otherwise would lead to absurdity. E argued that there was no mention of any possibility of an application for a second temporary transfer before the first had been converted into a permanent transfer. The section only envisaged a permanent licence being transferred, subject only to the exceptions in s.25(2) and (3).

Held, petition granted. The section was badly worded but the words "at any time" in the section should be given their ordinary meaning. There was no reason in principle why a further transfer on a temporary basis could not be made. There was no need to consider *Hansard* as contended by E; in any event it did not shed any light on the problem.

CHAUDHRY v. EDINBURGH DISTRICT LICENSING BOARD (O.H.), 1995 S.C.L.R. 423.

6044. Licensing—renewal—objectors—late notice of objection—legality of continuation of application

[Licensing (Scotland) Act 1976 (c.66), ss.13(2) and 16(2).]

L sought reduction of P's decision to postpone consideration of L's application for renewal of a public house licence. Six letters, in identical terms, were received by the clerk outwith the statutory seven-day time limit before the meeting of the board (s.16(2)). The letters claimed that the application had not been advertised and sought P's consent to late objections being received, but did not give details of the objections. L's application was continued to allow the objectors to lodge details of their objections. L argued that as none of the letters specified the grounds the continuation was illegal.

Held, petition dismissed. Section 16 distinguished between competency and relevancy of objections; the power given to a board in s.13(2)(a) to postpone consideration where there had been a failure to comply with any preliminary requirements, should be read as referring to any of the requirements in s.16(2), including a failure to specify grounds. The substance of a proposed objection was not an essential matter for reaching a valid decision to postpone, either in point of general principle or the particular circumstances. P had acted legally and within their discretion. *Observed*, that P had declined to take a plea to the competency of the petition on the basis that the point was one which could be raised on appeal to the sheriff.

LOWTHER v. PERTH AND KINROSS DISTRICT LICENSING BOARD (O.H.), 1995 S.L.T. 241.

6045. Licensing—renewal of licence—whether new licence or continuation of existing licence. See BASRA v. CUNNINGHAME DISTRICT LICENSING BOARD, §6040.

6046. Licensing—suspension of licence—calculation of unexpired period of licence—days of appeal

[Licensing (Scotland) Act 1976 (c.66), s.31(6) and (7).]

The Licensing (Scotland) Act 1976, s.31(6) and (7) provides, that suspension of a licence shall not take effect until the expiry of the time within which the licence holder may appeal, or until the appeal has been determined in favour of the suspension or has been abandoned, and that the period of suspension shall be a fixed period not exceeding one year or the unexpired portion of the licence, whichever is the less, the effect of the suspension being that the licence shall cease to have effect during the period of suspension. On February 14, 1994 a licensing board suspended a licence, which was due for renewal on March 15, 1994, for one month. The licensee appealed to the sheriff. The licence was renewed at a licensing board meeting on March 15, 1994. Before the sheriff, the appellant argued that it was not competent for the board to impose a suspension of more than 14 days as the suspension could not take effect until after at least 14 days, which were allowed for appealing. The sheriff was informed that the appellant had voluntarily closed for 14 days and this should be taken into account. The sheriff refused the appeal. The appellant appealed to the Court of Session, arguing that the period of suspension was incompetent as the board could, in the circumstances, impose no more than 14 days' suspension; that, in any event, the suspension could not take effect after renewal of the licence, because the renewed licence was a new licence; and that, if the court refused the appeal, the 14 days' voluntary closure should in any event be taken into account.

Held, that (1) s.31(6) and (7) should be read separately and independently of each other and that s.31(7) fixed the period of suspension available to the board while s.31(6) provided for the time at which the suspension would then take effect; (2) the period of 14 days was not to be subtracted from the period permitted by s.31(7) to take account of the provisions of s.31(6) and the suspension of the appellant's licence for a period of one month was therefore competent; (3) a renewed licence was not a new licence but a continuation of the previous one; (4) a voluntary closure was not a closure in terms of the suspension order; and appeal refused.

BASRA v. CUNNINGHAME DISTRICT LICENSING BOARD, 1995 S.L.T. 1013.

6047. Licensing—suspension of licence—effect of voluntary closure pending appeal. See BASRA v. CUNNINGHAME DISTRICT LICENSING BOARD, §6046.

6048. Licensing board—application for provisional grant of licence—entertainment licence—refusal—actings of board

[Licensing (Scotland) Act 1976 (c.66), ss.16(1)(f), 16A and 17(1)(b) and (c).]

An application was made for the grant of a provisional entertainment licence for premises at which it was intended to play loud music and attract large numbers of young people. The premises then held an entertainment licence for use as snooker premises. The licensing board refused the licence relying on their general knowledge of the premises and the fact that the premises were to be used as a venue for live music to which large gatherings of young people would listen and dance. They took into account crime statistics for the locality provided by the chief constable. They had regard to advice given by their officials in attendance on the submissions made by the applicant about noise tests held at the venue. The licensing board refused the licence on grounds that (i) the premises were not suitable or convenient for the sale of alcoholic liquor and (ii) the use of the premises for the sale of alcoholic liquor was likely to cause undue public nuisance or threat to public order or safety (s.17(1)(b) and (c) of the 1976 Act. The applicant appealed to the sheriff who allowed the appeal, holding that there was no material before the licensing board to justify either ground of refusal. He expressed doubt that the licensing board were entitled to take into account the crime statistics provided by the chief constable because he had not made "an observation" in terms of s.16A of the 1976 Act, and that the licensing board were entitled to have regard to observations made by their officials at the hearing as the local authority now had a right to object under s.16(1)(f) of the 1976 Act. The board appealed to the Court of Session.

Held, that (1) a licensing board, unlike a court, was entitled and expected to bring to bear on applications made before it its own local knowledge and licensing experience, subsisting in the members of the board and in the board's officials who advised it; (2) where a board had specific knowledge or had private information which was not available to the parties the rules of natural justice required disclosure to the parties, but where a board considered material submitted to it on behalf of the applicant and the responses of officials and others to the submissions, it might make use of its own local knowledge and experience of licensing in drawing inferences from such material in reaching its decision (*Crofton Investment Trust v. Greater London Rent Assessment Committee* [1967] C.L.Y. 3410, referred to); (3) the sheriff had erred in failing to take into account the knowledge and licensing experience which were properly part of the Board's decision making in the latter sense; (4) on the material before it the licensing board was not entitled to find that the use of the premises for the sale of alcoholic liquor was likely to cause undue public nuisance or threat to public order or safety since the crime statistics did not bear to be causally related to the presence of licensed premises in the locality; but, the board was entitled to reach a conclusion that the premises were not suitable or convenient for the sale of alcoholic liquor, having applied the proper test of likelihood of undue noise and disturbance and appeal allowed. *Opinion reserved*, on the soundness of the doubts expressed by the sheriff in relation to the crime statistics, but *observed*, that the supply of crime statistics by the chief constable would appear to be a neutral factor on which it was desirable that the board should be properly informed.

PAGLIOCCA v. CITY OF GLASGOW DISTRICT LICENSING BOARD, 1995 S.L.T. 180.

6049. Licensing board—application for renewal of licence—refusal—appeal—separate representation of board and chief constable—whether justified. See ROBERTSON v. CITY OF EDINBURGH DISTRICT LICENSING BOARD, §6042.

6050. Licensing board—continuation of application—late notice of objection—grounds of objection not specified. See LOWTHER v. PERTH AND KINROSS DISTRICT LICENSING BOARD, §6044.

6051. Licensing board—procedure—requirement of voting in public—separate grounds for refusal. See GLASGOW DISTRICT LICENSING BOARD v. DIN, §6039.

JURIES

Jury trial. See PRACTICE (CIVIL); CRIMINAL EVIDENCE AND PROCEDURE.

JURISDICTION

6052. Court of Session—interdict—interim interdict—restraint of foreign proceedings

A helicopter, on a flight from an oil platform in the North Sea within the jurisdiction of the Scottish courts, crashed just after take-off killing one of the two pilots and 10 of the 15 passengers on board. The helicopter, of French origin, was operated by a company domiciled in Scotland and flown by a crew who lived and worked in Scotland. The passengers, most domiciled in Scotland and the remainder in England or Wales, were acting in the course of their employment on the platform which was operated by a company with a Scottish domicile, which company had requisitioned the flight. The circumstances of the accident were investigated at a fatal accident inquiry held in Scotland. The survivors, their families and the families of the deceased raised proceedings against the helicopter company in Scotland, averring that the accident had been caused by the fault and negligence of the pilot. In addition those parties instituted proceedings in Texas seeking damages against a number of defendants including the operators of the platform. The majority of the defendants in the Texan actions sought to challenge the jurisdiction of the Texas courts but until a hearing was arranged the plaintiffs were able to exercise unrestricted powers of discovery which the defendants could not comply with effectively without prejudicing their plea to jurisdiction. The defendants in the Texas proceedings sought interdict and interim interdict in the Court of Session against the plaintiffs in the Texan proceedings from *inter alia*: "(a) taking any step . . . to restrain the petitioners . . . from continuing or taking any steps . . . in the petition; (b) continuing, or taking any other step . . . in the proceedings in Texas; and (c) instituting or taking any other step . . . in fresh proceedings in Texas or elsewhere furth of the United Kingdom, in respect of any claim arising out of the crash". Interim interdict was granted in respect of (a), and subsequently in respect of (b) following an indication by the Texas court that it intended to consider what steps it could take to preserve its jurisdiction. Although the Texas court subsequently purported to take such steps by way of a "*sua sponte*" ruling, that ruling was suspended on appeal and was to be withdrawn. The respondents sought recall of the latter interim interdict. They argued that the petitioners had failed to establish a prima facie case that Scotland was the natural or appropriate forum rather than Texas. They submitted that the flavour of the accident was not Scottish. Their grounds for so contending were that two of the defendants to the proceedings in Texas were domiciled in Texas and the others had sufficient contact with Texas to make them subject to that jurisdiction; one of the non-Texan defendant companies in particular, although registered in the United Kingdom and a separate and distinct corporate entity, was the alter ego of a Texan defendant company by virtue of the latter's 100 per cent shareholding in the former; and thus the policy and direction of that activity was made in Texas. The respondent further argued that it would be unjust for them to be deprived of the legitimate, personal or judicial advantages of proceeding in Texas. These included the contingency fee system which allowed for full preparation of a case for impecunious plaintiffs, higher awards of damages and wider claims by relatives than in Scotland, punitive damages, damages in respect of injury and damage between the take-off of the helicopter and the crash, the right to a jury trial, the loss of costs already incurred if interdict were granted and the imminence of the trial diet. This latter fact was also argued in respect of the balance of convenience favouring recall of the interim interdict, in which additional respect the respondents mounted a detailed attack on the petitioners' case and made reference to the doctrine of comity.

Held, that (1) any connection between the action and Texas was fragile in the extreme and that a prima facie case had been established that the natural or appropriate forum was Scotland, being the place with which the action had the most real and substantial connection; (2) there was a prima facie case of oppression or injustice to the petitioners if the respondents were allowed to pursue the Texan proceedings, since there was a prima facie case of bad faith on the part of Texan attorneys, the petitioners could not seek the assistance of the Texan court, *inter alia*, in compelling discovery without risking being held to have accepted the jurisdiction of the court whereas the respondents might obtain an illegitimate advantage by proceeding with discovery and other preparations, and the petitioners would be deprived of the opportunity of bringing in the helicopter company as third party; (3) most if not all of the advantages claimed by the respondents of litigating in Texas were bound up with the question of the natural forum, and since the natural forum was Scotland the respondents could have no reasonable expectation of having those advantages; (4) any benefit which the respondent would derive from the contingency fee system in the United States was not a juridical advantage when the natural forum was not in the United States (*Smith Kline and French Laboratories v. Bloch* [1985] C.L.Y. 1328, followed); (5) prima facie there were no legitimate juridical advantages in Texas of which it would be unjust to deprive the respondents, but there was nothing to outweigh the prima facie oppression or injustice to the petitioners if proceedings were allowed to continue in Texas; (6) the balance of convenience would have clearly lain in favour of maintaining the interim interdict in terms of part (b) but for the doctrine of comity which in this case required that the Texan court be given the opportunity to stay the proceedings on the ground that they had not been brought in the natural or appropriate forum; and interim interdict in terms of part (b) recalled and motion to pronounce interim interdict in terms of part (c) refused. (*Société Nationale Industrielle Aérospatiale v. Lee Kui Jak* [1987] C.L.Y. 3024, and *Spiliada Maritime Corporation v. Cansulex* [1987] C.L.Y. 3135, followed.) *Opinion*, that the respondents' approach in attacking the strength of the petitioners' case in detail was misconceived at an interlocutory hearing which would not effectively dispose of the action. (*N.W.L. v. Woods* [1979] C.L.Y. 2716, distinguished.)

SHELL U.K. EXPLORATION AND PRODUCTION v. INNES, 1995 S.L.T. 807.

6053. Court of Session—statutory jurisdiction of Lands Tribunal—whether exclusive. See OSBORNE v. BRITISH COAL PROPERTY (O.H.), §6137.

6054. Domicile—acquisition of domicile of choice. See SPENCE v. SPENCE, §5872.

6055. Sheriff court—action of declarator and damages—whether judicial review

Held, that an action of declarator and damages in which a prisoner or former prisoner claimed that various searches of him while a prisoner had been carried out without authority from the Secretary of State was not one seeking judicial review and accordingly that the sheriff court had jurisdiction to hear it.

McDONALD v. SECRETARY OF STATE FOR SCOTLAND (Sh.Ct.), 1995 S.C.L.R. 598.

6056. Sheriff court—custody—habitual residence of child—divorce proceedings raised in England and after custody proceedings raised but before motion for interim custody

[Family Law Act 1986 (c.55), ss.8, 9, 10 and 11(1).]

The father of three children raised an action in the sheriff court against his wife seeking custody of his children. Jurisdiction was based on the habitual residence of the children within the sheriffdom. The father obtained interim interdict against his wife from removal of the children, but before his motion for interim custody was heard, his wife raised divorce proceedings in England. The sheriff took the view that his jurisdiction to consider the motion was excluded by the divorce proceedings in England and the effect of s.11 of the 1986 Act. The pursuer appealed to the sheriff principal.

Held, that the date of the pursuer's application was the date of citation of the defender and that, since that pre-dated the divorce proceedings in England, the sheriff had jurisdiction to consider the motion; and appeal allowed.

DORWARD v. DORWARD (Sh. Ct.), 1994 S.C.C.R. 928.

LANDLORD AND TENANT

Agricultural holdings. See AGRICULTURE.

Crofts. See SMALL LANDHOLDER.

Housing. See HOUSING.

6057. Lease—breach of contract—interim order—specific implement. See OVERGATE CENTRE v. WILLIAM LOW SUPERMARKETS, §6204.

6058. Lease—breach of contract by landlord—tenant entitled to withhold rent—expiry of lease without breach having been remedied

M, the tenant of a fish and chip shop, appealed a sheriff's decision to award P decree for £1,375 in respect of rent arrears for the period from May to June 1990, and £4,521 in damages in respect of repairs required to the premises and damage to fixtures and items of equipment, in breach of M's obligation under cl.9 of the lease to leave the shop and the fixtures and fittings in "good condition and repair" at the expiry of the lease. M argued that (1) as P had been in material breach of an implied term of the contract, in that he had cut off the water supply to the shop in May, and as he had not rectified this before the expiry of the lease in June, P was not entitled to recover rent for that period; and (2), as P had not led any evidence as to the condition of the premises at the commencement of the lease, he had not established that the premises were not in "like" good condition and repair at its expiry. P argued that he was entitled to damages in respect of the moveables because "fixtures and fittings" in cl.9 included moveable items of equipment associated with running a fish and chip shop, such equipment having been included in the definition of that term in cl.5 in relation to M's obligation to pay for all repairs to the interior and exterior of the subjects, and in the inventory of equipment which had set out the parties' understanding of what were the "fixtures and fittings"; and that, in any event, there was an implied letting to hire of the moveables (Paton and Cameron, *Landlord and Tenant*, p.72).

Held, appeal allowed only as regards the damages in respect of moveables. (1) As M had no continuing interest in persuading P to perform his obligations under the lease, and M had not formulated a counterclaim, P was entitled to decree for the arrears (*Fingland and Mitchell v. Howie*, 1926 S.L.T. 283, followed). (2) The inventory could not be looked at as representing an understanding as to the meaning of "fixtures and fittings", as the parties' rights and obligations had to be discovered from the terms of the lease alone. There was no general definition of "fittings and fixtures" in the lease and, as the definition in cl.5, which in any event only covered items which were "screwed, glued, nailed or otherwise affixed to the subjects" and therefore not wholly moveable, had to be regarded as applying only for the purpose for which it was used in that clause, "fittings and fixtures" could not include moveables. P had founded his claim for damages solely on cl.9 and there were no averments concerning a letting to hire and no such case had been put forward at proof. Accordingly, the sheriff had erred in following this line on his own initiative and had erred further in failing to give parties an opportunity to comment on his approach before he gave his judgment, and the appeal would be allowed in respect of the award of £1,159·34 for damage to moveables. (3) P had not put forward any basis for his argument that there was no evidence entitling the sheriff to hold that a water heater and an illuminated sign were fixtures, and, although it was curious that a mural had been included in the inventory of equipment along with obviously moveable items, the sheriff could not be faulted for categorising it as a fixture. (4) M's obligation in cl.9 was not to leave the subjects in the same condition as at the commencement of the lease, but to leave them in the condition which they ought to have achieved as a consequence of M fulfilling his various duties of repair and maintenance. In any event, M had accepted in the lease that the subjects had been in good tenantable condition at the commencement and he could not now argue that it was for P to prove this. Given the evidence of the unsatisfactory condition of the subjects, the sheriff had been entitled to award damages under this head.

PACITTI v. MANGANIELLO (Sh. Ct.), 1995 S.C.L.R. 557.

6059. Lease—constitution—*rei interventus* and homologation

N sought recovery of possession of subjects from G on the basis that G had no right or title to occupy. N had let the subjects to S in 1978. G was S's cohabitee. Rent was paid by a cheque drawn on a bank account in the names of G and S. A new lease was drafted in 1989 and sent to S for approval. G and

S responded by a letter which raised a number of questions concerning amendment to the draft, including a request to have the lease in their joint names. N did not respond. Rent continued to be paid until March 1992 whereafter it was paid by G alone. When rent fell in to arrears N wrote to G and S jointly for payment and threatened legal action against both. G subsequently settled all of the rent arrears. S left G around October 1992. G argued that she had a lease with N established by *rei interventus* and homologation. The sheriff refused decree. N appealed, arguing that (1) for *rei interventus* or homologation to be considered there had to be an antecedent agreement which in this case was not there; and (2) there were no circumstances amounting to homologation and *rei interventus*.

Held, appeal refused. (1) A binding contract, including one of lease, could be constituted by actings without the necessity of any prior incomplete negotiations, far less antecedent agreement (*Morrison-Low v. Paterson* [1985] C.L.Y. 3660; Gloag, *Contract*, pp. 46–47). Even though the only suggestion by N of there being a joint lease was dependent on a letter addressed to G and S, the subsequent actings of the parties could be taken as establishing a joint tenancy. The letter by G and S could reasonably be taken as a contra-offer to take on a new lease subject to certain alterations even though it consisted of a series of questions, the letter not having been prepared by legal advisers. (2) N knew that after March 1992 G was settling rent alone and that G paid the arrears. If G was not a tenant she had no obligations to make such a payment and N should not have accepted it. Repairs and redecoration carried out by G and within N's knowledge were consistent with the proposed amendments to the 1989 draft lease. It followed that N's actions could properly be looked at as homologation (*Law v. Thomson* [1978] C.L.Y. 3399, distinguished). The threat of legal action against both S and G was also an acceptance by N that S and G were joint tenants.

NELSON v. GERARD (Sh.Ct.), 1994 S.C.L.R. 1052.

6060. Lease—construction—tenant liable to pay insurance at rate to be determined by landlord—whether implication of reasonableness

Tenants were bound in terms of their lease to pay to their landlords insurance premiums in respect of certain risks affecting the premises "at such rate as the landlords from time to time consider appropriate." The landlords raised an action of payment against the tenants seeking insurance premiums which the tenants had failed to pay. The tenants pleaded an arbitration provision on the basis that there was a dispute between the parties as to the amount of the premiums because of an implication that the level of premium should be reasonable.

Held, that there was no basis for any question of dispute between the parties and that accordingly there could be no arbitration; and decree granted *de plano*.

HARRIS (VICTOR) (GENTSWEAR) v. THE WOOL WAREHOUSE (PERTH) (Sh.Ct.), 1995 S.C.L.R. 577.

6061. Lease—implied term—business efficacy

The proprietor of a farm leased part of the farm to a tenant company to use for the tipping of waste. The lease provided that the tenant was entitled to use the subjects to tip or authorise others to tip such categories of waste as were approved by the local authority. An annual rent was agreed together with a royalty payment representing one half of the gross income of the tenant in excess of a particular figure in each year. The tenant was required to submit statements detailing the number of loads and the gross income per annum. The landlord averred that throughout the duration of the lease the tenant had permitted material to be tipped for no charge or for a minimal charge only and that as a result only minimal royalties had become payable to the landlord. The landlord sued the tenant for payment of the sum estimated as the amount of royalties which would have been payable to the landlord had normal charges by the tenant been made on those who had tipped. The basis for the action was an implied condition which the landlord claimed was required for business efficacy. The tenants pled that the action was irrelevant. The landlord averred that he had entered into the lease with a view to the tenants operating the site as a commercial landfill dump site, it being clearly intended that it was to be operated with a view to maximising the income to be obtained therefrom by both parties. At procedure roll the landlord contended that it was an implied term of the contract that it would be operated in good faith as a commercial venture since without that implied term the contract would, in commercial if not in strict legal terms, be unworkable.

Held, that (1) for a term to be incorporated by implication into a contract it was not enough that it be reasonable; it had also to be necessary for the purpose of giving business efficacy to the contract; (2) in the present case this test was not met since without the implied term, the contract was not rendered unworkable and it was not obvious that the parties would have agreed to the implied term being incorporated into the contract; and action dismissed. *Opinion*, that the requirement to operate the tip "in good faith as a commercial venture with a view to income maximisation" was not so uncertain as to be irrelevant.

THOMSON v. THOMAS MUIR (WASTE MANAGEMENT) (O.H.), 1995 S.L.T. 403.

6062. Lease—implied term—whether sufficiently specific. See THOMSON v. THOMAS MUIR (WASTE MANAGEMENT), §6061.

6063. Lease—irritancy—conventional irritancy—company tenants going into receivership—whether irritancy enforceable—fair and reasonable landlord

[Law Reform (Miscellaneous Provisions) (Scotland) Act 1985 (c.73), s.5.]

The 1985 Act, s.5, provides that a landlord shall not be entitled to terminate a lease by relying on a provision of the lease purporting to allow termination in the event of, *inter alia*, a change in the tenant's circumstances, if in all the circumstances of the case a fair and reasonable landlord would not seek so to reply. The landlords of two properties on an industrial estate sought to irritate the leases after the tenant company went into receivership, relying on a clause in each lease which provided that appointment of a receiver was a ground of irritancy. In an action brought by the landlords against the tenants and the receivers for declarator of irritancy, the defenders sought to challenge the relevancy and specification of certain of the landlords' averments which related to advantages which the landlords would be able to attain by exercising the irritancy and reorganising the way in which the two properties were let as part of the industrial estate. It was argued for the defenders that these averments related to the actual landlords, instead of the hypothetical fair and reasonable landlord referred to in the Act and contemplated by the Scottish Law Commission in their report which had preceded the enactment of the provision in the 1985 Act.

Held, that (1) on a proper construction, s.5 involved the consideration of a fair and reasonable landlord in the position of the actual landlord; and (2) the averments of the landlords fell within "all the circumstances of the case" and should be allowed probation; and proof before answer allowed. *Observed*, that the width of language used in s.5 provided a result which was possibly not in the contemplation of the Scottish Law Commission and could lead to practical difficulties in assessing the evidence.

BLYTHSWOOD INVESTMENTS (SCOTLAND) v. CLYDESDALE ELECTRICAL STORES (IN RECEIVERSHIP) (O.H.), 1995 S.L.T. 150.

6064. Lease—irritancy—conventional irritancy—notice—validity. See BLYTHSWOOD INVESTMENTS (SCOTLAND) v. CLYDESDALE ELECTRICAL STORES (IN RECEIVERSHIP), §6063.

6065. Lease—obligation of tenant—obligation to keep property open for business clearing non-business leases—enforcement. See RETAIL PARKS INVESTMENTS v. THE ROYAL BANK OF SCOTLAND, §6069.

6066. Lease—obligations of landlord—tenantable or habitable condition. See FYFE v. SCOTTISH HOMES, §6077.

6067. Lease—obligations of landlord—tenantable or habitable condition—measure of damages. See QUINN v. MONKLANDS DISTRICT COUNCIL, §5848.

6068. Lease—obligations of tenant—obligation to occupy business premises—enforcement

The tenants of a shop unit under a lease which contained an obligation on them to occupy the premises notified the landlords, by letter dated February 7, 1995, of their intention to vacate the premises and sought the landlords' consent. On February 23, 1995 the landlords were granted interim interdict preventing the tenants from removing stock, fittings, sales equipment and advertising material from the premises or in any way vacating or removing or taking steps to vacate or remove therefrom. The tenants sought recall of the interim interdict. They conceded that it was competent for the landlords to enforce the obligation contained in the lease by interdicting them from vacating the premises, but argued that in its present form the terms of the interim interdict went beyond that concession.

Held, that (1) there being important questions to try as to the extent of the tenants' obligation under the lease, the balance of convenience pointed against a complete recall of the interim interdict as it served a useful purpose in preventing the occurrence of a dead shop frontage within the shopping centre; (2) the part of the interdict which prevented the removal of items from the premises was inappropriate as it related to actings which could be consistent with the normal management of a retail unit; (3) the part of the interdict which prevented the tenants from taking any steps to vacate or remove from the premises was both excessive and unnecessary; (4) interdict against the defenders "vacating or removing" from the subjects was competent and sufficiently specific; and interim interdict recalled to that extent.

RETAIL PARKS INVESTMENTS v. OUR PRICE MUSIC (O.H.), 1995 S.L.T. 1161.

6069. Lease—obligations of tenant—obligation to occupy business premises—enforcement

The tenants under a lease of premises in a shopping centre, which contained an obligation on them to use and occupy the premises as bank offices and to keep the premises open for business during specified times, notified the landlords by letter dated March 21, 1995 of their intention to cease operating part of their business from the premises as from March 24. The tenants proposed to close the branch but to maintain cash dispensing machines there, which would require servicing two to three times a day, and to make regular security checks. The landlords moved the court to grant interim orders in terms of their third to fifth conclusions. The third conclusion was to interdict the tenants from vacating or removing or taking steps to vacate or remove from the premises. The fourth conclusion was to ordain the tenants to use and occupy the premises as bank offices, to keep the premises open for business during specified times, and to permit the public to have access to the premises for the purpose of transacting business during those times. The fifth conclusion was to interdict the tenants from removing certain moveable property which would have the effect of displenishing the premises. Parties were in dispute as to whether the tenants' obligations as to use of the premises required them to keep open a branch operation within the usual hours of business, as contended by the landlords.

Held, that (1) interim interdict could not properly be pronounced in terms of the fifth conclusion in the absence of averments justifying a reasonable apprehension that the pursuers were at risk of loss of rent due; (2) having regard to the initial impact of closure on a shopping development, and there being a live issue as to whether the residual activities intended by the defenders could satisfy their obligations under the lease, the landlords were entitled to interim interdict in terms of the third conclusion but restricted by excluding references to steps in contemplation of future action, which might strike at legitimate activities under the lease; (3) as regards the fourth conclusion the landlords were entitled to protection from the prejudice which would result from the tenants' intended actions pending the resolution of the dispute on the terms of the lease; that the balance of convenience favoured the landlords; but that the order to be granted would be modified so as not to pre-empt in the landlords' favour the resolution of the contractual dispute; and pursuers' motion granted in restricted terms. *Observed*, that where one was concerned with orders for the protection or enforcement of contractual provisions, the measure of the court's power had to take account of and generally be qualified by what the parties had agreed in their contract.

RETAIL PARKS INVESTMENTS v. THE ROYAL BANK OF SCOTLAND (O.H.), 1995 S.L.T. 1156.

6070. Lease—rent review—assessment of "fair rent"

[Rent (Scotland) Act 1984 (c.58), s.48.]

Landlords (W) appealed against decisions of the rent assessment committee assessing fair rents in respect of a substantial number of regulated tenancies under the 1984 Act. The committee had reached their decision on a comparison with registered rents for comparable regulated tenancies, rejecting W's argument that a comparison should be made with statutory assured tenancies with an adjustment for scarcity in light of the terms of s.18(2) of the 1984 Act, and W's evidence that there was no longer a substantial level of scarcity and that the comparable rents for regulated tenancies were no longer valid in view of the changes made by the Housing (Scotland) Act 1988. W argued that given the terms of the 1984 Act compared with the 1988 Act, a regulated tenancy was more valuable to a tenant than an assured tenancy particularly as regards security of tenure, and the rent should reflect that; that on any view open market rents for assured tenancies were a relevant consideration and the committee erred in law in disregarding evidence of lets post-1989; and that they had failed properly to assess scarcity in the light of changing circumstances and had instead decided the matter on the basis of consistency with the register, which was improper.

Held, appeals refused. It was not disputed that the committee had applied their minds to the correct statutory test, and to the general approach described in *Western Heritable Investment Co. v. Husband* [1983] C.L.Y. 4859. The decision on scarcity was one of fact for the committee and there was evidence to support it. On comparable rentals the committee had not held themselves barred from considering post-1989 rents and their decision that these were not relevant was one of fact and not of law. While it was not correct, as argued for the tenants, that if the committee gave flawed reasons they should be in no worse position than if they had given no reasons at all, the criticisms made of their decision were not justified. They were entitled under the 1984 Act to have regard to their own knowledge and experience; they were entitled to have regard to the fact that the limited number of decisions in relation to assured tenancies had proceeded on the basis of landlord's evidence alone (which was particularly important having regard to s.25 of the 1988 Act): the fact that a tenant might be prepared to pay what might otherwise be regarded as an excessive rent, did not necessarily make that rent a proper open market rent; and they were entitled to conclude that no assistance could be obtained from the few decisions on assured tenancies then available. Similarly, evidence of concluded agreements under the 1988

Act with W's own tenants was not necessarily of weight where W had stipulated the rent on a "take it or leave it" basis; neither was evidence of lets of properties in similar locations by another company where the properties had been improved and the tenancies were mostly short term. Even if the rentals of assured tenancies were to be taken into account, this would necessarily involve substantial adjustments being made for a variety of reasons in order to arrive at a fair rent within s.18, and it was difficult to see why a committee should be compelled to embark on that exercise when there was available a directly comparable registered rent of only one year previously.

WESTERN HERITABLE INVESTMENT CO. v. JOHNSON, *The Scotsman*, August 16, 1995.

6071. Lease—rent review—notice by tenant—validity of notice

A rent review clause in a commercial lease provided that the tenants could give to the landlords notice in writing containing a proposal as to the amount of the revised rent where the landlords had not made any application to the chairman of the Scottish Branch of the Royal Institution of Chartered Surveyors before the quinquennium which began on October 26, 1991. The tenants' proposal would be the new rent unless the landlords made such application within three months after the service of such notice. In terms of cl. sixth the notice would be sufficiently served if sent by recorded delivery post to the landlords' head or registered office. By letter dated December 3, 1991 the landlords proposed an increased rent of £176,000. On December 9, 1991 the tenants' agents sent a letter to the landlords, enclosing a formal counter notice objecting to the proposed rent and outlining a counter proposal at a rent of £110,000, of which the landlords acknowledged receipt. The landlords sought declaration that they were entitled to require the appointment of a valuer, arguing that the letter of December 9, did not constitute a notice as it was not sent by the tenants but on behalf of "Smiths Food Group", the tenants' former name, and was not served by recorded delivery post at the landlords' head or registered office.

Held, that (1) for an error to invalidate a notice there had to be something which might mislead the other party, and that the landlords could not have been under any misapprehension by any formal misdescription of the tenants' name; (2) cl. sixth required any notice to be in writing but was permissive as to the method of service (*Yates Building Co. v. R. J. Pulleyn & Sons (York)* [1975] C.L.Y. 388, followed); (3) a reasonable and neutral person would have regarded the tenants' letter as a "notice in writing containing a proposal as to the amount of such revised rent" (*Yates, Petr.* [1986] C.L.Y. 4205, distinguished), and as such starting the three-month period within which it was open to the landlords to insist on the appointment of a valuer; and action dismissed.

PRUDENTIAL ASSURANCE CO. v. SMITHS FOODS (O.H.), 1995 S.L.T. 369.

6072. Lease—termination—notice—service to registered office

S, the tenant of property owned by C, reclaimed against a Lord Ordinary's decision that S had not validly served a notice of termination of the lease, for which 12 months' notice in writing was required by cl.2 of the lease, because the notice had not been sent to C's registered office as required by cl.7, S having sent notices instead to C's business address and C's agents (A). Another Lord Ordinary held after proof that A did not have authority to receive service on C's behalf. S argued that, while the requirement for 12 months' notice in writing was mandatory, cl.7 was only a procedural provision dealing with methods of service, and was directory rather than mandatory; that the words "shall be sent" were not necessarily mandatory (*Howard v. Secretary of State for the Environment* [1974] C.L.Y. 3731); that cl.7 was primarily for the benefit of the giver of a notice, as it provided that a notice sent by recorded delivery would be deemed sufficiently served 48 hours after posting and that notice could be served at an individual's last known address, in both of which cases the notice might never be received; and that cl.7 could not be mandatory because if C had been an individual living abroad the clause could not have been complied with.

Held, reclaiming motion refused. Clause 2, which was plainly mandatory, had to read as qualified by cl.7. Accordingly "notice in writing" meant a notice served on C at their registered office. Clause 7 was clearly conceived in favour of the recipient of a notice, so that the recipient knew where to look for any notices, and the language of the provisions regarding place of service was plainly intended to be mandatory (*Yates Building Co. v. Pulleyn (R.J.) & Sons (York)* [1975] C.L.Y. 388 distinguished, even though cl.7 contained other deeming provisions. Different considerations applied to the interpretation of statutes as opposed to arms length contracts (*Howard*, distinguished, and the parties, having made specific provision for the places to which notice had to be sent, were entitled to hold each other to them.

CAPITAL LAND HOLDINGS v. SECRETARY OF STATE FOR THE ENVIRONMENT, *The Times*, September 28, 1995.

6073. Nuisance—interests of tenant—title of landlord to sue. See DUNDEE DISTRICT COUNCIL (CITY OF) v. COOK, §6355.

6074. Rent—rent withheld while property unfit for use—expiry of lease without breach of contract having been remedied. See PACITTI v. MANGANIELLO, §6058.

6075. Rent—whether owed to landlord or to heritable creditor. See ASCOT INNS (IN RECEIVERSHIP) v. BRAIDWOOD ESTATES, §6015.

6076. Rent officers

RENT OFFICERS (ADDITIONAL FUNCTIONS) (SCOTLAND) AMENDMENT ORDER 1995 (No. 2361) [£1·10], made under the Housing (Scotland) Act 1988 (c.43) s.70(1) and (2); amendments to the 1990 Order are operative on October 2, 1995; those to the 1995 Order are operative on January 2, 1996; amends the Rent Officers (Additional Functions) (Scotland) Order 1990 to remove an exclusion for assured tenancies with rents determined under the 1988 Act, and amends the Rent Officers (Additional Function) Scotland Order 1995 to add a further requirement for rent officers; both the 1990 and 1995 Orders are amended to add further requirements for rent officers where rent under a tenancy has been determined unreasonably high.

[S.I. 1990 No. 396 and S.I. 1995 No. 1443 amended.]

RENT OFFICERS (ADDITIONAL FUNCTIONS) (SCOTLAND) ORDER 1995 (No. 1643) [£2·80], made under the Housing (Scotland) Act 1988 (c.43), s.70(1); operative on January 2, 1996; revokes and re-enacts with modifications, the Rent Officers (Additional Functions) (Scotland) Order 1990, together with the regulations which amended them, which conferred functions on rent officers in connection with housing benefit and rent allowance subsidy.

[S.I. 1990 No. 396, 1991 No. 533, 1993 No. 646, 1994 No. 582, 1994 No. 3108 revoked.]

Small landholder. See SMALL LANDHOLDER.

6077. Tenants' rights—house to be kept reasonably fit for human habitation

[Housing (Scotland) Act 1987 (c.26), Sched. 10, para. 1(2) and (4).]

The tenant of a house sought damages for breach of contract from her public sector landlords. She claimed that the house was not fit for habitation, that it was damp, that it could not be heated at reasonable cost, that it suffered from condensation and mould and that the house did not comply with the provisions of the Building Regulations 1981. The landlords challenged the relevancy of her complaints.

Held, that (1) the landlords' obligation to provide a habitable house was not restricted to protecting the tenant from physical danger, (2) both the comfort and the status of the tenant were relevant in determining whether the house was habitable, (3) the meaning of "habitable" had to be related to the realities of life and a house which was uninhabitable by reason of being excessively cold or damp could not be said to be habitable simply because by applying a large amount of heat and incurring inordinate heating bills it might be rendered habitable, and (4) that in terms of para. 1(4) of Sched. 10 to the 1987 Act it was relevant to have regard to the regulations which were in force for the construction of new buildings at the commencement of the tenancy, notwithstanding that those regulations were not in force when the house was built; and proof before answer allowed.

FYFE v. SCOTTISH HOMES (Sh. Ct.), 1995 S.C.L.R. 209.

6078. Tenants' rights—house to be kept reasonably fit for human habitation—measure of damages. See QUINN v. MONKLANDS DISTRICT COUNCIL, §5848.

6079. Tenants' rights—right to change landlords—sale to approved landlord—conditions annexed to offer to sell—right of pre-emption

[Housing (Scotland) Act 1988 (c.43), ss.58 and 63.]

Waverley Housing Trust applied to purchase two houses owned by Roxburgh District Council, with no change of tenancy. They received offers to sell containing a condition that, subject to any right of the tenants to purchase the properties, they should not be sold with vacant possession without being first offered to the council at the then equivalent value of a tenanted property. The applicants submitted that they would not thereby receive a "good and marketable title" in terms of s.58(10)(b) of the 1988 Act, and that the condition was in any case not reasonable in terms of that section. They also submitted that the condition was in direct conflict with the statutory assumptions contained in s.58(7) of the Act and that the prices to be paid had been wrongly assessed, no regard having been paid to the effect of the condition. The council submitted *inter alia* that the condition was reasonable given their duties under s.1 of the Housing (Scotland) Act 1987, and that the condition, as a means of retaining property available for renting, was consistent with the intentions of the 1988 Act.

Held, that (1) in the absence of positive evidence that the pre-emption clauses depressed the values placed on the two houses, the tribunal could not assume that such an effect existed (observed that the determination of price by the district valuer under the Act was final); (2) that the condition did not prevent a good and marketable title being given; but (3) a right of pre-emption would be against the specific provisions of s.63 of the 1988 Act requiring the approval of Scottish Homes to the disposal of houses transferred out of the public sector and; (4) that the condition was unreasonable and should be struck out from both offers to sell.

WAVERLEY HOUSING TRUST v. ROXBURGH DISTRICT COUNCIL, 1995 S.L.T. (Lands Tr.) 2.

6080. Tenants' rights—right to purchase—landlords' title subject to right of pre-emption

[Housing (Scotland) Act 1987 (c.26), ss.61(2) and 64.]

R, a public housing authority holding title to certain subjects, sought declarator that B, the feudal superiors to the property, were not entitled to exercise their right of pre-emption to prevent a statutory sale of the subjects to secure tenants who had an unqualified right to purchase the house in terms of s.62 of the 1987 Act as any conditions which stood in the way of that purchase held no effect. The Lord Ordinary dismissed R's action [1994] C.L.Y. 5981. R reclaimed, arguing that (1) there was nothing in s.61 which implied any exclusion of the tenants' right to purchase by B's right of pre-emption; (2) although s.64(1)(c) provided for the insertion of conditions in an offer to sell, this did not include a right of pre-emption, which was inimical to the tenants' absolute entitlement to purchase the subjects; and (3) the right of pre-emption contained in the feu charter was only relevant to voluntary transactions on the part of the feuar and therefore could not prevent a statutory sale.

Held, reclaiming motion refused (Lord Murray dissenting). *Per* the Lord Justice Clerk (Ross): (1) A secure tenant exercising his right to purchase heritable property under s.61 could only take that property subject to any burdens in the title and there was no authority that a secure tenant had an absolute right to have certain subjects sold to him (*Cooper's Exrs. v. City of Edinburgh District Council*, [1991] C.L.Y. 5189). If Parliament had intended pre-emption clauses to cease in the event of a statutory sale to a secure tenant, then it would have so provided as it had done in respect of other statutes (Halliday, *Conveyancing Law and Practice*, para. 17–77; Crofters (Scotland) Act 1993, s.17(3)), R's second argument would have been accepted (dicta in *Henderson v. City of Glasgow District Council*, 1994 S.L.T. 263 at, p.267 were unsound); while there was considerable force in the third, R did not insist on it if their primary submission failed. *Per* Lord Morison: If Parliament had intended to interfere with a superior's right of pre-emption as a consequence of legislation designed to regulate the relationship between landlord and tenant, it would have done so by express provision, not implication. The extent and nature of heritable property in Scotland which could be transferred on sale was exclusively governed by the owner's heritable title, and the heritable proprietor was not entitled to sell anything beyond or different from that contained in his title. R's title did not give them an unrestricted right to sell, since it was burdened by a pre-emptive clause which had not been waived or discharged. The conditions referred to in s.64 were those intended to regulate a sale. There was no justification for restricting the pre-emption clause to voluntary sales. *Per* Lord Murray (dissenting): There was a necessary inference under ss.61 and 64 that Parliament intended to give a purchasing tenant full and unencumbered marketable proprietory rights in its house. Parliament might occasionally annul private rights without compensation, particularly where the statute created an irresistible inference (*Westminster Bank v. Minister of Housing and Local Government* [1970] C.L.Y. 2780), and it was an irresistible inference under Pt.III of the 1987 Act that B's right of pre-emption was wholly contradictory of the primary purpose of the legislation as a tenant's statutory right to purchase was completely irreconcilable with a pre-emptive restriction on the seller's title to sell. On this view the ratio in *Henderson v. City of Glasgow District Council* [1994] C.L.Y. 5982, would be superseded.

ROSS AND CROMARTY DISTRICT COUNCIL v. PATIENCE, 1995 S.L.T. 1292.

6081. Tenants' rights—right to purchase—notice of refusal—dwellinghouse specially designed for the disabled

[Housing (Scotland) Act 1987 (c.26), s.61(4)(a).]

Section 61 of the Housing (Scotland) Act 1987 confers on a secure tenant of a public sector house a right to purchase that house. By subs. (4)(*a*) of that section it is provided that the section does not apply to a house that is one of a group which has been provided with facilities (including a call system and the services of a warden) specially designed or adapted for the needs of persons of pensionable age or disabled persons. A resident warden in a sheltered housing complex applied to purchase the house of which she was the tenant. Her tenancy was secure. The house was within a group of houses which had been designed and built as sheltered housing and which were provided with the facilities specified in subs. (4)(*a*), but it was not itself provided with those facilities, although it had been designed and built specifically to accommodate a resident warden. It contained receiving equipment connected to the call system and there was a communicating door between it and an adjoining house which was occupied by the other resident warden.

Held, that for a house to be excluded from the tenant's right to purchase, it was not enough that it was designed and equipped to accommodate a warden resident within a group of houses which had been provided with the facilities specified in s.61(4)(*a*), but that it must itself have been provided with those facilities, and that the tenant accordingly had a right to purchase the house. (*City of Dundee District Council v. Anderson* [1993] C.L.Y. 5470, applied.)

HOUSTON v. EAST KILBRIDE DEVELOPMENT CORPORATION, 1995 S.L.T. (Lands Tr.) 12.

6082. Tenants' rights—right to purchase—whether tenant "in occupation"—prisoner serving sentence

[Housing (Scotland) Act 1987 (c.26), s.61(2)(c).]

B appealed against a decision of the Lands Tribunal for Scotland to refuse his application for a finding that he had the right under s.61 of the 1987 Act to purchase a house, of which he had been the tenant under a secure tenancy from K since April 7, 1990, the tribunal having held that B had not been "in occupation" of the house for two years immediately prior to his application on November 9, 1992 as required by s.61(2)(c). In July 1991 B had been taken into custody in connection with criminal proceedings and in September had been sentenced to six years' imprisonment. His furniture and personal possessions had remained in the house. He continued to pay the rent and contents insurance and to receive housing benefit from K for a year. B's parents had stayed at the house from time to time and attended to household repairs and redecoration. B's aunt had lived in the house from August until October 1992, when K had asked her to remove. On his release from prison on July 14, 1994 B had returned to the house. B argued that, although he had been temporarily absent, he could still be "in occupation" of the house, as what mattered were the physical signs of occupation and his intention to return, and that, while if his prospective return was unreasonably distant in time B could not be regarded as in occupation, a reasonable time limit was between two and 10 years (*Brown v. Brash* [1948] C.L.Y. 3229). K argued that B's right to buy depended on him having a secure tenancy, which required that the house be his "only or principal home" (s.44(1)(b)); that s.61(2)(c) was intended to add a further constraint, as "occupation" of a house required daily enjoyment of it; that this approach fitted with s.61(10)(b), which provided for interruptions in occupation of up to two years to be disregarded, and s.61(10)(a) and (c), which provided for occupation by other persons to be taken into account.

Held, appeal allowed and case remitted to the Lands Tribunal. While s.61(2)(c) introduced an additional requirement of two years' occupation, the expression "occupation" did not add a new factor, as the requirement in s.44(1)(b) plainly implied that B was in occupation of the house. If the house ceased to be B's only or principal home, K might be able to recover possession on the ground set out in Sched. 3, Pt. I, para. 5, which distinguished ceasing to occupy from absence from the house. If there were no signs of occupation by B or his family and no intention to return, K would be entitled to treat the tenancy as abandoned under s.49. Section 61(10)(b)(i) and (ii) did not relate to periods of temporary absence, but rather to the fact that qualifying occupation in s.61(2)(c) could be in a succession of houses and that gaps could occur between occupation of one house and the next. In any event, subparas. (i) and (ii) had now been repealed, which, on K's interpretation, would have created considerable practical problems for a tenant who was temporarily absent, for however short a time. B's interpretation was supported by the statutory context and was sensible and workable in application. However, it was not appropriate that B should be found entitled to purchase the house merely on the strength of his success over interpretation, and given that K had made no explicit concession as to the result in the event of B's interpretation being accepted, the case would be remitted for consideration.

BEGGS v. KILMARNOCK AND LOUDOUN DISTRICT COUNCIL, *The Scotsman*, March 15, 1995.

6083. Tenants' rights—secure tenancies—recovery of possession—reasonableness—sufficiency of information

[Housing (Scotland) Act 1987 (c.26), s.48(2)(a); Act of Sederunt (Summary Cause Rules, Sheriff Court) 1976 (S.I. 1976 No. 476), r.18(9).]

S appealed against decree being granted for E's recovery of heritable property as local authority landlords. S had been in arrears of rent since 1989 and had defaulted on a repayment arrangement. S did not dispute that E had a valid ground for recovery or that they had properly followed the statutory procedure. E had argued that in terms of rule 18(9) the facts were sufficiently admitted to decide the cause on the merits at the stage of first calling. Further in terms of s.48(2)(a) of the 1987 Act it was reasonable to order recovery. S argued that as there had been no admission as to the amount of arrears and there had been no findings as to the history of payment between a decree previously granted and later recalled, and S's default, these factors would have an effect on the reasonableness of granting such an order and the sheriff had failed adequately to consider S's possible defence. E might have been seeking decree in order to acquire a "sword of Damocles" with which to enforce payment (*Edinburgh District Council v. Stirling and Lamb* [1993] C.L.Y. 5474).

Held, appeal refused. The question whether the sheriff was entitled to proceed under rule 18(9) was one of mixed fact and law, and the sheriff's decision would have had to be fundamentally flawed for the appeal court to interfere. All that was said for S was that the amount of arrears was disputed, but there was no suggestion as to the correct amount. The sheriff was not obliged to speculate as to factors bearing on reasonableness, nor was he obliged to continue a case to proof just in case S could bring forward these factors. Since he was not invited to adjourn the hearing he was entitled to proceed as he did. Doubted, whether E's argument on the basis of *City of Glasgow District Council v. Erhaiganoma* [1993] C.L.Y. 5473, that the test under s.48(2)(a) related only to the particular ground founded on by a landlord and could not take into account extraneous matters such as put forward by S, was sound; but opinion reserved on the point.

EDINBURGH DISTRICT COUNCIL, CITY OF v. SINCLAIR (Sh.Ct.), 1995 S.C.L.R. 194.

6084. Tenants' rights—secure tenancies—secure tenancy with housing association terminated and tenancy of different subjects entered into

[Housing (Scotland) Act 1988 (c.43), ss.12 and 43 and Sched. 4, para. 13.]

Section 12(1)(c) of the 1988 Act provides that a house is let as an assured tenancy if and so long as the tenancy is not one which cannot be an assured tenancy. Section 12(2) provides that if and so long as a tenancy falls within Sched. 4 it cannot be an assured tenancy. The exceptions in para. 13 of Sched. 4, headed "Transitional cases", include a housing association tenancy and a secure tenancy. A housing association sought a determination that a tenancy agreement was an assured tenancy and accordingly that the rent officer had no jurisdiction to register a fair rent. A secure tenancy was terminated on April 14, 1992 when the tenants entered into a lease with the housing association for a different property. The housing association contended that the subsequent agreement was an assured tenancy and that s.12 of and Sched. 4 to the 1988 Act as well as s.43 relating to persons who, immediately before a tenancy was entered into, were the secure tenant of the same landlord, were permissive provisions only. The tenants argued that it was not possible to contract out of statutory provisions designed to safeguard the interests of tenants.

Held, that (1) the tenancy could not be an assured tenancy if and so long as it was a housing association tenancy or a secure tenancy, in terms of s.12(2) of the 1988 Act; (2) the current let fell within both meanings, should be treated as a transitional case and could not be an assured tenancy; and application dismissed.

MILNBANK HOUSING ASSOCIATION v. MURDOCH, 1995 S.L.T. (Sh.Ct.) 11.

LAW REFORM

6085. Scottish Law Commission

Report on hearsay evidence in criminal proceedings (Scot. Law Com. No. 149) [H.M.S.O., £12·65].

Report on mentally incapable adults (Scot. Law Com. No. 151) [H.M.S.O., £19·65].

Report on statute law revision (Scot. Law Com. No. 150; Law Com. No. 233) [H.M.S.O., £11·65].

Scottish Law Commission twenty ninth annual report (Scot. Law Com. No. 148) [H.M.S.O., £7·40].

LEGAL AID

6086. Advice and assistance

ADVICE AND ASSISTANCE (FINANCIAL CONDITIONS) (SCOTLAND) REGULATIONS 1995 (No. 1220) [65p], made under the Legal Aid (Scotland) Act 1986 (c.47), ss.11(2) (as amended by the Social Security Act 1986 (c.50), Sched. 10), 36(1) and (2)(b) (as amended by the Legal Aid Act 1988 (c.34), Sched. 4) and s.37(1), operative on May 5, 1995; increase the disposable income limit for eligibility under the 1986 Act from £153 a week to £156 a week; increase the weekly disposable income above which a person must pay a contribution from £63 to £64 and prescribe the scale of contributions to be paid where weekly disposable income exceeds £64 but does not exceed £156.

[Legal Aid (Scotland) Act 1986 (c.47), ss.8(a) and 11(2)(a) amended; S.I. 1994 No. 997 revoked.]

ADVICE AND ASSISTANCE (SCOTLAND) AMENDMENT REGULATIONS 1995 (No. 1066) [65p], made under the Legal Aid (Scotland) Act 1986 (c.47), ss.36(1) and (2)(*a*), 37(1) and 42(3); operative on May 5, 1995; amend the Advice and Assistance (Scotland) Regulations 1987 to provide for the aggregation of the resources of a man and a woman living together as husband and wife who are not married to each other and correct a defect in S.I. 1994 No. 1061, reg. 4.

[S.I. 1987 No. 382 amended.]

6087. Assessment of liability—onus on party seeking modification

[Legal Aid (Scotland) Act 1986 (c.47), s.18(2).]

Held, that a legally-aided party who sought to have his liability for expenses before the Land Court modified to nil had failed to discharge the onus on him to prove to the Court's satisfaction that he was still in a financial position which would qualify him for a grant of legal aid; and motion refused.

MACDONALD v. TARN, 1994 S.L.C.R. 150.

6088. Civil legal aid

CIVIL LEGAL AID (FINANCIAL CONDITIONS) (SCOTLAND) REGULATIONS

1995 (No. 1221) [65p], made under the Legal Aid (Scotland) Act 1986 (c.47), s.36(1) and (2)(b) (as amended by the Legal Aid Act 1988 (c.34), Sched. 4); operative on May 5, 1995; increase the disposable income limit for eligibility for civil legal aid to £7,920 and the eligibility without payment of a contribution to £2,425.

[Legal Aid (Scotland) Act 1986 (c.47), ss.15(1) and 17(2)(a) amended; S.I. 1994 No. 998 revoked.]

CIVIL LEGAL AID (SCOTLAND) AMENDMENT REGULATIONS 1995 (No. 1065) [65p], made under the Legal Aid (Scotland) Act 1986 (c.47), ss.36(1) and (2)(*a*) and (*g*), 37(1) and 42(3); operative on May 5, 1995; amend the Civil Legal Aid (Scotland) Regulations 1987 to provide for the aggregation of the resources of a man and woman living together as husband and wife who are not married to each other and place on a regulatory footing the payment of interest earned or money held by the Scottish Legal Aid Board as property recovered or preserved for an assisted person pending determination of that person's net liability to the Scottish Legal Aid fund.

[S.I. 1987 No. 381 amended.]

6089. Civil legal aid—assessment of liability—conduct of assisted party

[Legal Aid (Scotland) Act 1986 (c.49). s.18(2).]

M sued the police (P) after M was run over by P's car. The action was settled but during the action P had obtained four awards of expenses, taxed at £2,250, against M, who was on legal aid with a nil contribution, M sought modification of liability under s.18(2) of the 1986 Act which P opposed. M had suffered serious injuries and accepted a settlement of £20,000 after he was persuaded that a stroke subsequently suffered was not as a result of the accident. M had twice amended his pleadings, twice obtempered orders of court late and had had adjustment periods extended three times. Further, three procedure roll hearings had been discharged on the day. M argued that his settlement would be spent on living expenses and house repairs. M also intended to move house to accommodate his family properly. Any award to P would require to be deducted from the settlement, on which M's present solicitors (S) already had a claim of £5,000 for expenses not allowed on taxation. M's former solicitors might also have a claim. S claimed M was a difficult client as a result of his stroke and head injury. The first of the discharges had, however, been obtained a year after the stroke and the difficulty in obtaining instructions, the reason for that discharge, was not explained. P argued that modification should be refused as a result of M's conduct and that M's award should be taken into account.

Held, M's liability modified to £1,000. The question was discretionary and M's award could be taken into account (*McInally v. Clackmannan District Council* [1993] C.L.Y. 5478; *Hanley v. James Bowen & Sons*, [1976] C.L.Y. 3133). M would not be left without means as M's net recovery would still be £12,000. On any view M's conduct was unsatisfactory. This should be judged objectively (*Burns v. McHaffie (James) & Sons* [1953] C.L.Y. 4160). In any event, M's medical condition did not properly explain the procedural steps for which M had been found liable. However since M was, and was likely to remain, on state benefits and since a significant part of the settlement had already been spent, a part exemption was appropriate.

MACKENZIE v. LOTHIAN AND BORDERS POLICE (O.H.), 1995 S.C.L.R. 737.

6090. Civil legal aid—fees

CIVIL LEGAL AID (SCOTLAND) (FEES) AMENDMENT REGULATIONS 1995 (No. 1044) [£4·70], made under the Legal Aid (Scotland) Act 1986 (c.47), ss.33(2)(*a*) and (3)(*a*), (*b*) and (*f*) and 36(1); operative on May 5, 1995; amend the Civil Legal Aid (Scotland) (Fees) Regulations 1989 so as to increase the fees allowed to solicitors and counsel for work done on or after May 5, 1995 by 3 per cent.

[S.I. 1990 No. 473, 1991 No. 565, 1992 No. 372 and 1994 No. 1015 partially revoked.]

6091. Civil legal aid—proceeding against the Board—refusal to grant legal aid—reference to sheriff

[Legal Aid (Scotland) Act 1986 (c.47), s.14(4) and (5).]

Held, in a reference to the sheriff under s.14(4) of the 1986 Act, that the applicant for legal aid for judicial review proceedings in respect of a decision of the Scottish Legal Aid Board refusing him legal aid for proceeding's against the Board had failed to demonstrate that he had a *probabiles causa litigandi*.

SCOTTISH LEGAL AID BOARD'S REFERENCE (No. 1 of 1995) (Sh.Ct.) (Notes), 1995 S.C.L.R. 760.

6092. Civil legal aid—refusal—"reasonable in the particulars circumstances of the case"—relevant considerations

[Legal Aid (Scotland) Act 1986 (c.47), s.14(1).]

M sought judicial review of the Scottish Legal Aid Board's (S) decision to refuse M legal aid in respect of her action of damages, originally raised by her husband (H) prior to his death from lung cancer in 1993, against I, a tobacco company, on the grounds that it was not reasonable in the circumstances to grant legal aid (s.14(1)(b)). In the action of damages, M averred that H had smoked I's cigarettes from 1964 until 1992; that prior to starting smoking he had been unaware that it could cause fatal diseases; that once health warnings began to appear on packets in 1971 he had attempted to give up, but due to his addiction was unable to do so and his consumption increased; that prior to 1964 I ought to have known that regular smoking could cause lung cancer; and that it was their duty to warn persons of that. I denied that smoking caused cancer; averred that by 1960 the public were well aware of the claimed risks of smoking; and pled *volenti non fit injuria* and contributory negligence. M argued that S had acted unreasonably; that, as S had accepted M had *probabilis causa litigandi* in terms of s.14(1)(a), they had to be taken to have rejected I's plea of *volenti*, and had erred in considering it in relation to s.14(1)(b); that, in stating that it could not be satisfied that all issues relating to liability and quantum would be resolved in M's favour, S had applied an unreasonably high standard, and had inverted the onus with respect to *volenti*, as it would be for I to establish that H was *volens*; that, as I had continued to advertise extensively, despite knowing of the health risks, H could not be at fault to a greater extent than I; that S should have considered what was likely to be I's ultimate liability, as there was likely to be an award of expenses in M's favour, even if there was a finding of contributory negligence; that cost could not be the sole or prime reason for refusing an application; and that, given M's evidence would be in relatively short compass, it was unfair to penalise M because of the concern that I's evidence would range far and wide increasing the cost of the litigation, as this would enable any multinational company to frustrate a valid claim by protracting litigation (*R. v. Legal Aid Area Committee No. 10 (East Midlands Area), ex p. McKenna* [1990] 1 Med. L.R. 375).

Held, petition dismissed. S's decision and its reasons were to be found in a letter dated October 19, 1993 and M could not found on a letter dated May 25 written by S's director of legal aid, expressing his opinion on M's application and the opinion of senior counsel submitted by M, as that letter had been written before M's application was formally before S. As S had considered whether or not a grant of legal aid would be reasonable, it could be inferred that S had accepted that M had *probabilis causa litigandi*. However, this did not necessarily mean that S thought that M was bound or even likely to succeed, and, in considering whether a grant was reasonable, S was entitled to take into account the prospects of success, the issues of *volenti* and contributory negligence, and the facts that in evidence given on commission H had been vague about his knowledge of the dangers of smoking and about his response to the health warnings, and that as H's cross-examination had not been completed prior to his death, these matters had not been fully elucidated. While cost could not be the sole reason for S's decision, it was relevant, given that S had a limited amount of public funds, and could be the deciding factor when balanced against the possible benefit, which, as this was not a test case, could only be the benefit to M. Given that all issues, including the causal link between smoking and lung cancer, were in issue and that M's case was the first such case in Scotland against a tobacco company, the litigation was likely to be long, complex, expensive and difficult and, although some expenses might be recovered, S's decision that it was not appropriate to hazard substantial sums of public money on a case with such limited prospects of success could not be categorised as unreasonable.

McTEAR v. SCOTTISH LEGAL AID BOARD (O.H.), 1995 S.C.L.R. 611

6093. Civil legal aid—Unassisted party seeking award out of the Fund—whether proceedings "finally decided" in her favour

[Legal Aid (Scotland) Act 1983 (c.47), s.19(1).]

Held, in an action of divorce where the wife, who was not legally aided, was generally successful and obtained an award of expenses against her former husband, who was in receipt of legal aid and whose personal liability for those expenses was modified to nil, that an award out of the Legal Aid Fund in favour of the wife under s.19 of the 1986 Act would be competent and that the case should be remitted to the sheriff to decide whether such an award was justified on its merits.

LEARMONTH v. LEARMONTH (Sh.Ct.), 1995 S.C.L.R. 768.

6094. Contempt of court proceedings

LEGAL AID IN CONTEMPT OF COURT PROCEEDINGS (SCOTLAND) AMENDMENT REGULATIONS 1995 (No. 2319) [65p], made under the Legal Aid (Scotland) Act 1986 (c.47), ss.36(1) and (2)(a), (d) and (e); operative on September 1995; provide that an application for legal aid regarding an appeal against a court decision in contempt of court proceedings shall include a statement of grounds of appeal and any other relevant circumstances to support the legal aid application.

[S.I. 1992 No. 1227 amended.]

6095. Criminal legal aid

ADVICE AND ASSISTANCE (ASSISTANCE BY WAY OF REPRESENTATION) (SCOTLAND) AMENDMENT REGULATIONS 1995 (No. 1219) [65p]; made under the Legal Aid (Scotland) Act 1986 (c.47), ss.9(1) and (2)(a), 36(1) and 37(1); operative on May 5, 1995; amend the Advice and Assistance (Assistance by Way of Representation) (Scotland) Regulations 1988 by providing for assistance by way of representation to be made available in any proceedings for the return of sound equipment under s.66(6) of the Criminal Justice and Public Order Act 1994 which gives the court power to forfeit sound equipment.

[S.I. 1988 No. 2290 amended.]

CRIMINAL LEGAL AID (SCOTLAND) AMENDMENT REGULATIONS 1995 (No. 2320) [£1·10], made under the Legal Aid (Scotland) Act (c.47) ss.36(1) and (2)(a), (c), (d) and (e); operative September 26, 1995; *inter alia*, extend the list of proceedings treated as distinct for the purposes of criminal legal aid to include appeals to the High Court of Justiciary against disposals and provide in relation to criminal legal aid applications regarding appeals, where the person was convicted or found to have committed the offence before September 26, 1995; these amendments take into account changes brought into force by the Legal Aid (Scotland) Act 1986 (c.47), s.25 and the Criminal Justice (Scotland) Act 1995 (c.30) s.65.

[S.I. 1987 No. 307 amended.]

CRIMINAL LEGAL AID (SCOTLAND) (PRESCRIBED PROCEEDINGS) AMENDMENT REGULATIONS 1995 (No. 1222) [65p], made under the Legal Aid (Scotland) Act 1986 (c.47), ss.21(2) and 36(1); operative on May 5, 1995;

amend the Criminal Legal Aid (Scotland) (Prescribed Proceedings) Regulations 1994, by adding to the proceedings where criminal legal aid is not available, proceedings to which assistance by way of representation is made available by reg. 3 of the Advice and Assistance (Assistance by way of Representation) (Scotland) Amendment Regulations 1995.

[S.I. 1994 No. 1001 amended.]

6096. Criminal legal aid—legal aid certificate withdrawn by sheriff—whether *nobile officium* can be invoked to have it restored. See McGETTIGAN, PETR., §5673; LAMONT, PETR., §6097.

6097. Criminal legal aid—summary procedure—withdrawal of legal aid—competency of procedure

[Act of Adjournal (Consolidation) 1988 (S.I. 1988 No. 110), r. 164(1).]

Rule 164(1) of the Act of Adjournal (Consolidation) 1988 provides *inter alia* that where the court, before which there are proceedings in which an assisted person is an accused person, after hearing that person, is satisfied that that person *inter alia* has without reasonable excuse failed to attend at a diet of the court at which he has been required to attend, the court may direct that the assisted person shall cease to be entitled to criminal legal aid. An accused person was charged on summary complaint. He was granted legal aid but failed to appear for an intermediate diet and the sheriff withdrew legal aid. The accused petitioned the *nobile officium* to hold that the sheriff's purported withdrawal of legal aid was incompetent because he had not allowed the accused an opportunity to be heard. A question arose as to the competency of the petition.

Held, that (1) proceedings by petition to the *nobile officium* were competent; (2) it was not competent for the sheriff to withdraw legal aid without hearing the accused; and petition granted and legal aid restored. (*J. P. Hartley, Petr.* (1968) 32 J.C.L. 191, applied.)

LAMONT, PETR., 1995 S.L.T. 566.

LICENSING

See INTOXICATING LIQUORS; LOCAL GOVERNMENT.

LIMITATION OF ACTIONS

6098. Action raised after expiry of limitation period—equitable power of court to override time limits

F sued K in respect of an accident in K's factory on August 15, 1988. The action was raised on January 13, 1992. F sought the exercise of the court's discretion under s.19A of the 1973 Act. F had been an employee of A at K's premises under instruction of K's foreman. F had been run over by a forklift truck. F had consulted his solicitors (L) within five months of the accident and a claim was then intimated to A. A's insurers (I) acknowledged receipt of the claim and advised L that at the relevant time F was subcontracted to K who were responsible for supervision. On May 15, 1989 L intimated a claim to K. K did not reply but a company (H), having the same address as K, acknowledged receipt. H's insurers who were also I then acknowledged receipt of F's claim on behalf of H/K. Further correspondence about the details of the accident were exchanged between L and I in which it was clear I had had a full account of the accident. Following further inquiries L raised an action against H. L were advised in September 1991 that they had sued the wrong defender and by January 1992 had raised the current action. K argued that s.19A was applicable where one action was raised timeously but with the wrong defender and a second action was raised outwith the triennium.

Held, preliminary proof allowed. K's argument was unsound. *Walkley v. Precision Forgings* [1979] C.L.Y. 1663, founded on by K, could be distinguished as the action there had been raised against the defender within the triennium but subsequently aborted. The court's discretion under s.19A was unfettered (*McCabe v. McLellan*, 1994 S.L.T. 346) and was not to be inhibited merely by other contrary decisions (such as *Anderson v. John Cotton (Colne)*, [1991] C.L.Y. 5201, founded on by K). A court should be reluctant to dismiss on relevancy where material facts relied on by a pursuer were not admitted. There was no clear prima facie case for F against L, and F would be put to considerable trouble. It was possible that the confusion had been caused by K. K would suffer no material prejudice having the same insurers (I) who had already carried out a thorough investigation. K had not suggested any specific disadvantage to them and even had the same solicitors as H. Since the question depended to a considerable extent on L's actings, preliminary inquiry was appropriate.

FARMER v. JAMES KEILLER & SONS (O.H.), 1995 S.C.L.R. 589.

6099. Action raised after expiry of limitation period—equitable power of court to override time limits

[Prescription and Limitation (Scotland) Act 1973 (c.52), ss.17(2)(b) and 19A.]

Section 17 of the Prescription and Limitation (Scotland) Act 1973 provides that any action of damages in respect of personal injuries must be brought within three years of the date when the injuries were sustained, or, if later, the date on which the pursuer became, or it would have been reasonably practicable for him to have become, aware *inter alia* that the injuries in question were sufficiently serious to justify his bringing an action of damages. Section 19A(1) enables the court to allow an action to proceed which would otherwise be time barred under s.17, if it seems equitable to do so. On March 8, 1988 a prison works officer injured his shoulder and back following a disturbance at work. He immediately attended hospital and was off work for some three months, then returning to lighter work. He subsequently attended various general practitioners regarding his back pain and, following advice from his union and a solicitor, he submitted a claim to the Criminal Injuries Compensation Board in June 1989, resulting in his acceptance, in November 1990, of a compensation award of £2,000. Meanwhile he continued to suffer back pain, undergoing traction and physiotherapy, and was off work between September and December 1990. He was eventually referred to hospital in April 1991 and operated on in June of that year to alleviate a protruding disc, returning to work in September 1991. Towards the end of 1991 he again contacted his union and sought advice from the union's solicitors who intimated a claim in March 1992, an action then being raised on June 3, 1992. At a proof on the defender's preliminary plea of time bar, the pursuer argued that until he became aware of his disc problems, resulting in his operation in June 1991, the injuries did not appear serious enough to justify raising an action which would only recover sums which would have to be repaid to the C.I.C.B. Additionally it was argued that, in any event, it was equitable to apply s.19A(1) because the pursuer was not apprised of the disc problem until the spring of 1991; his union officials had only advised him that he had a remedy through the C.I.C.B. and the defender could not and did not insist that the conduct of his defence was prejudiced in any way by the delay. The defender argued that the initial symptoms of the pursuer's injuries had existed well before June 1991 and were sufficiently serious to warrant the making of the

C.I.C.B. claims which merited an award not indicative of a trivial injury. Additionally the defender argued that, despite the s.19A remedy, he was still entitled to the statutory protection from state claims, despite conceding that he had not been prejudiced, because the pursuer had, by deliberately choosing to claim damages by way of the C.I.C.B. claim, lost his right to prove another now; and the pursuer had acted in an unreasonable and dilatory manner in investigating his injury and claim for damages.

Held, that (1) it was not material to the application of the s.17(2)(*b*) test that the pursuer was not aware of the whole history or subsequent development of his condition, the determining factor being how serious the situation was when it required to be considered and, given that the C.I.C.B. settlement procedure was achieved within the triennium, the pursuer had been aware that his injuries were sufficiently serious to warrant raising an action, and accordingly the s.17(2)(*b*) test was not satisfied; but (2) as the defender could not offer to prove prejudice in the conduct of his defence, being able to proceed on a fully defended basis, and given the fact that the pursuer had received unfortunate medical and legal advice, the refusal to grant relief to the pursuer by way of s.19A would cause greater prejudice to him than to allow the action to proceed would to the defender and proof before answered allowed.

FERLA v. SECRETARY OF STATE FOR SCOTLAND (O.H.), 1995 S.L.T. 662.

6100. Action raised after expiry of limitation period—equitable power of court to override time limits

[Prescription and Limitation (Scotland) Act 1973 (c.52), s.19A.]

J, who was injured in a road accident on January 6, 1989, raised an action against T for damages on May 21, 1992 and argued on procedure roll that the court should exercise its discretion in terms of s.19A and allow the case to proceed. J's mother had consulted solicitors timeously and neither J nor her mother had contributed to the delay or knew that the action had to be raised before the expiry of the triennium. T was insured and would suffer nothing as a result of the delay, while her insurers would likely have a windfall benefit if the action were dismissed. J, however, was in a state of permanent stress, almost helpless and totally dependent on her parents due to the extensive, active and crippling psoriasis which she allegedly suffered as a result of the accident and any substantial delay in the resolution of her claim would be detrimental to her health. T contended that the fact that liability was not in issue and that the sum involved was likely to be large should be considered in assessing the amount of prejudice to T.

Held, proof allowed. The delay which elapsed after the expiry of the triennium was not so large as significantly to prejudice T where the only prejudice suggested by T's insurers was the loss of their statutory defence. It was equitable that J be allowed to proceed with her action as she had taken all necessary steps to prosecute her claim and the inevitable delay in pursuing another action against her solicitors would be likely to be detrimental to her health in view of the medical evidence that her condition was deteriorating.

JOHNSTON v. THOMSON (O.H.), 1995 S.C.L.R. 554.

6101. Action raised after expiry of limitation period—equitable power of court to override time limits

[Prescription and Limitation (Scotland) Act 1973 (c.52), s.19A.]

T sued B in respect of two separate injuries to T's ankle sustained whilst T was in B's employment, on April 14, and June 4, 1990 respectively. A preliminary proof was held on time bar. T had consulted solicitors (A) in July 1990 and a claim had been intimated to B's insurers. After completing their inquiries B had sought a "detailed schedule of special damages" from A. A had attempted to supply the information but B had continued to renew the request. A subsequently failed to raise an action by April 14, 1993, admitting an error in their office in a letter to T, and another firm raised the action on

April 30. T argued that it was equitable for the court to exercise its discretion in terms of s.19A of the 1973 Act as regards the first incident.

Held, proof before answer allowed. B would suffer no prejudice beyond that of any defender. B had been involved in settlement negotiations, the stumbling block having proved to be the schedule of special damages. If T was required to pursue A for negligence in respect of the first injury but to proceed with a claim against B for the second, separate inquiries would potentially be of great prejudice to T. Both incidents were so inter-related, given that the second incident was said to have aggravated the first injury, that it was equitable that the court's discretion should be exercised.

TOMKINSON v. BROUGHTON BREWERY (Sh. Ct.), 1995 S.C.L.R. 570.

6102. **Negligence—date from which time runs—pursuer originally thinking he suffered less serious injury—whether original injuries sufficiently serious to justify raising an action.** See FERLA v. SECRETARY OF STATE FOR SCOTLAND, §6099.

6103. **Negligence—equitable power of court to override time limits.** See FARMER v. JAMES KEILLER & SONS, §6098; FERLA v. SECRETARY OF STATE FOR SCOTLAND, §6099; TOMKINSON v. BROUGHTON BREWERY, §6101.

LOCAL GOVERNMENT

Adoption. See CHILDREN AND YOUNG PERSONS.

6104. **Application of enactments**

LOCAL GOVERNMENT (APPLICATION OF ENACTMENTS) (SCOTLAND) (NO. 2) ORDER 1995 (No. 2766) [65p], made under the Local Government etc. (Scotland) Act 1994 (c.39), ss.181(1) and (2)(b); operative on November 14, 1995; provides that, in the period prior to April 1, 1995, the Public Works Loans Act 1965 (c.63), s.2 and the National Loans Act 1968 (c.13), s.3(11) and Sched. 4, shall apply to new local authorities in Scotland as they apply to the existing Scottish local authorities.

6105. **Boundaries—alteration of areas—local government reorganisation pending—judicial review**

[Local Government (Scotland) Act 1973 (c.65) s.17(2) amended; Eastwood and East Kilbride Districts (Busby) Amendment Order (S.I. 1993 No. 1312).]

Part II of the Local Government (Scotland) Act 1973 provided for the establishment of a Local Government Boundary Commission for Scotland, empowered it to make proposals to the Secretary of State for Scotland for, *inter alia*, the alteration of any local government area desirable in the interests of effective and convenient local government and obliged it to review, between 1985 and 1990, all local government areas for the purpose of considering what such proposals, if any, to make. Sections 17(2) and 233(1) of the Act empowered the Secretary of State, by order exercised by statutory instrument, to give effect to any such proposals made to him by the Boundary Commission. Section 17(4) provided that any such order, together with the report, should be laid before Parliament by the Secretary of State, and that any statutory instrument containing such an order was to be subject to annulment in pursuance of a resolution of either house of Parliament. A village was divided, along the course of a river, between two local government areas, Eastwood and East Kilbride Districts. The division had existed before local government reorganisation in 1974. Review of the boundary had been considered between 1966 and 1969 and 1974 and 1975, but no formal review in terms of the Act of 1973 was undertaken until 1987. On March 10, 1992, following inquiry, the Boundary Commission submitted proposals to the Secretary of State for the transfer of the part of the village in East Kilbride District to Eastwood District. On October 23 the Secretary of State intimated his agreement with the proposals to the respective councils and invited them to agree a transfer date. No agreement having been reached, the Secretary of State resolved to implement the change with effect from October 1, 1993. The necessary order was laid before Parliament without subsequent resolution for annulment. In June 1991 and October 1992 the Secretary of State had published consultation papers concerning the structure of local government in Scotland. Subsequently a white paper had been published with proposals for new unitary local authorities. These proposals incorporated the Boundary Commission's proposals for the village and were intended to be effective from spring 1995. East Kilbride District Council sought reduction of the transfer order, arguing first, that the Secretary of State, in determining upon the order, had failed to take into account a material consideration, the intended review of local government in Scotland, and, secondly, that the transfer to be effected by the order would involve the petitioners in substantial uncompensated loss of revenue and administrative and financing expense, that given the imminence of such review, such expense might prove unnecessary in whole or in part, and that, were such a transfer undertaken as an element of general reorganisation of local government, benefits correlative to and compensation for loss of revenue and expense arising from the transfer would be anticipated, and accordingly that the changes to be effected by the order would not aid the effective operation of local government and that the Secretary of State's determination was unreasonable in law and manifestly absurd. The Secretary of State argued, *inter alia*, that, the Secretary of State's decision to effect the proposals of the Boundary Commission having been implemented by statutory instrument approved by Parliament, considerations of *Wednesbury* unreasonableness or irrationality were irrelevant to its control by judicial reviews.

Held, that (1) the court had jurisdiction to review the making of a statutory instrument which had become final upon the expiry of the statutory time limits for a negative resolution in Parliament (*Hoffman-La Roche & Co. AG v. Secretary of State for Trade and Industry* [1974] C.L.Y. 3801, followed); (2) according to the Scottish authorities such a statutory instrument could only be held to be *ultra vires* on the grounds that it had not been authorised by the enabling statute or that the procedure required by the statute had not been followed, and while subsequent English authority was in favour of challenges on the additional grounds of bad faith, improper motive or manifest absurdity, the first two of these arose only rarely and the third could be satisfied only in the most extreme and extraordinary circumstances, so that it could not be said that the Scottish authorities had omitted anything of practical importance; (3) the order fell squarely within the terms of the enabling Act and was made in pursuance of procedures envisaged in that Act, and given that there was no challenge to the Boundary Commission's decision, but only the timing of its implementation, that the petitioners had been given the opportunity to co-operative in selecting a date that would best fit their budgeting, and that if the change were delayed until wider local government reorganisation the same costs would still be incurred, albeit that they might be less noticeable, the petitioners had failed to make out any ground of challenge whether the narrower or the wider test was applied; and petition dismissed. (*City of Edinburgh District Council v. Secretary of State for Scotland* [1985] C.L.Y. 4861, *Nottinghamshire County Council v. Secretary of State for the Environment* [1986] C.L.Y. 27, *R. v. Secretary of State for the Environment, ex p. Ham-*

mersmith and Fulham London Borough [1991] C.L.Y. 67, and *Leech v. Secretary of State for Scotland*, [1992] C.L.Y. 6216, considered.)

EAST KILBRIDE DISTRICT COUNCIL v. SECRETARY OF STATE FOR SCOTLAND (O.H.), 1995 S.L.T. 1238.

Building. See BUILDING AND CONSTRUCTION.

6106. Buildings—police

LOCAL GOVERNMENT ACT 1988 (DEFINED ACTIVITIES) (COMPETITION) (SCOTLAND) AMENDMENT REGULATIONS 1995 (No. 1972) [65p], made under the Local Government Act 1988 (c.9), s.6(3) (as amended by the Local Government Act 1992 (c.19) Sched. 1, para. (2) and s.15(6)); operative on August 20, 1995; make clear that the Local Government Act 1988 (Defined Activities) (Competition) (Scotland) Regulations do not extend to the cleaning of police buildings.

[S.I. 1988 No. 1413 amended.]

6107. Children in care of local authority—custody—interim custody sought by foster parents

[Social Work (Scotland) Act 1968 (c.49), ss.15, 16 and 20; Law Reform (Parent and Child) (Scotland) Act 1986 (c.9), s.3(1) and (2); Children Act 1975 (c.72), s.49(1) and (2); Sheriff Courts (Scotland) Act 1907 (c.51), Sched., r. 37.20(3).]

The foster parents of a child in the care of the local authority under s.15 of the 1968 Act applied for his custody. The application was approved by the local authority who considered that the child's long term interests lay in adoption by different adoptive parents. The sheriff granted the foster parents motion for interim custody without the benefit of a report under s.49(2) of the 1975 Act. In so doing the sheriff expressed the view that the effect of the interim custody order was to prevent the local authority from placing the child with prospective adoptive parents. The local authority appealed and the child's natural mother supported the sheriff's decision as she wished her son to remain with the foster parents meantime.

Held, that (1) even if the sheriff had overlooked the fact that the local authority could remove the child from the care of the foster parents after they had been granted interim custody, that did not vitiate his decision on interim custody, (2) the sheriff was not bound to give effect to the intention of the local authority with regard to the proposed adoption, and (3) there was no obligation on a court to obtain a report from a local authority under s.49(2) and r. 33.20(3) at the stage of a motion for interim custody as at that stage the application was not being "determined"; and appeal refused. *Opinion*, that a report under r. 33.20(3) was unnecessary where the local authority was a party to the proceedings.

R. v. R. (Sh.Ct.), 1994 S.C.L.R. 849.

6108. Competition

LOCAL GOVERNMENT (EXEMPTION FROM COMPETITION) (SCOTLAND) ORDER 1995 (No. 678) [£1·95], made under the Local Government Act 1988 (c.9), ss.2(10) (as inserted by the Local Government etc. (Scotland) Act 1994 (c.39), Sched. 13) and 15(5) (as amended by the 1994 Act, Sched. 13) and (7); operative on March 31, 1995; modifies the application of compulsory competitive tendering under Pt. I of the Local Government Act 1988 to local authorities in Scotland.

LOCAL GOVERNMENT, PLANNING AND LAND ACT 1980 (COMPETITION) (SCOTLAND) REGULATIONS 1995 (No. 677) [£1·10], made under the Local Government, Planning and Land Act 1980 (c.65), ss.7(1) (as amended by the Local Government Act 1988 (c.9), Sched. 6), (2), (4)(*a*)(*b*), (5) and (6), 9(3) and 23(1) (as amended by the Local Government Act 1992 (c.19), Sched. 1);

operative on March 31, 1995; replaces the Local Government (Direct Labour Organisations) (Competition) (Scotland) Regulations 1990, by raising the level above which certain services provided by local authorities and development corporations require to be exposed to competitive tender.

[S.I. 1990 No. 1782 and 1991 No. 243 revoked.]

6109. Competition—consideration of tenders

[Local Government Act 1988 (c.9, ss.7(7), 13(1)(b) and 14(2)(d).]

A district council sought judicial review of a direction by the Secretary of State under s.14(2) of the Local Government Act 1988. The council had exposed to compulsory competitive tendering the 60 per cent of the ground maintenance work within its area not already subject to such tendering. Two tenders were received. One was from a private contractor ("Brophy") and the other was from the council's own direct services organisation (D.S.O.). The bill of quantities in the tender documents set out 13 separate items. Brophy submitted a tender for the whole works which was some £13,640 less than that of the D.S.O. When individually costed, item 1 of Brophy's tender was found to be lower. For items 2–13 the D.S.O.'s tender was lower. The lower tender in each case was accepted, as the council claimed the right, disputed by Brophy, to accept a tender in whole or in part. The council refused to allow Brophy to adjust the price for item 1. Brophy then sent a letter, a few days before the commencement date for the contract, stating their opinion that no contract existed. The council immediately accepted the D.S.O. tender in respect of item 1 as well. Brophy complained to the Secretary of State for Scotland who served a notice under s.13 of the 1988 Act on the council. The Secretary of State considered that the council had acted in a manner having the effect, or intended or likely to have the effect, of restricting, distorting or preventing competition, and had thereby failed to comply with the fifth condition, set out in s.7(7) of the Act, in terms of s.13(1)(b). He considered that the council had, without adequate reason, awarded the work to the D.S.O., and that it was unreasonable to require Brophy to accept the division of the tender without adjustment as regards item 1. Although the council issued a response under s.13(3)(b) of the Act stating that it had fulfilled the s.7(7) condition, and in any event that it was inappropriate and unreasonable to give a direction, the Secretary of State gave a direction under s.14(2)(d) of the Act to the effect that the council had the power to carry out the ground maintenance works only if they were to put out to tender anew, and that if its D.S.O. intended to submit a written bid for the works, the council had to put out the works for tender in accordance with the requirements of s.7 of the Act. The council contended that the Secretary of State had misdirected himself.

Held, that (1) given the terms of the tender documents the district council had the right to accept the tender in respect of some items, but not others; (2) there was a binding contract between the district council and Brophy notwithstanding Brophy's misunderstanding of the effect of the tender documents; (3) the Secretary of State therefore misdirected in law in issuing a s.13 notice predicated upon there not being a binding contract; (4) the direction was flawed by the same misdirection and, further, no one in the position of the Secretary of State, acting reasonably, could properly have reached the view that the district council had not fulfilled the condition in s.7(7) of the Act; and Secretary of State's direction reduced. *Opinion*, that the Secretary of State had not directed his attention to the separate question of whether, even if the district council had failed to fulfil the fifth condition, it was inappropriate and unreasonable in all the circumstances to issue a direction; and that had the conclusion on the direction been different, the application would have been continued to another hearing to allow the Secretary of State to explain why a direction was made in the circumstances.

ETTRICK AND LAUDERDALE DISTRICT COUNCIL v. SECRETARY OF STATE FOR SCOTLAND (O.H.), 1995 S.L.T. 996.

6110. Competition—defined activities

LOCAL GOVERNMENT ACT 1988 (DEFINED ACTIVITIES) (EXEMPTION OF

DEVELOPMENT CORPORATIONS) (SCOTLAND) ORDER 1995 (No. 517) [65p], made under the Local Government Act 1988 (c.9), ss.2(9) and 15(5) (as amended by the Local Government etc. (Scotland) Act 1994 (c.39), Sched. 13); operative on March 31, 1995; exempts from the requirements of the 1988 Act, Pt. I, ground maintenance by four development corporations in Scotland so long as it is undertaken in the respective areas of those authorities in the period prior to their wind-up.

6111. Contracts for sale of land—relevant dates

LOCAL GOVERNMENT (RELEVANT DATE) (SCOTLAND) ORDER 1995 (No. 1894) [65p], made under the Local Government etc. (Scotland) Act 1994 (c.39), s.55(3); operative on July 31, 1995; provides that September 1, 1995 is the date on and after which certain disposals of land and contracts, specified in s.55 of the 1994 Act, cannot be entered into by an existing authority without consent of the appropriate successor or, in some cases, the Secretary of State.

6112. Council tax—appeals

[Local Government Finance Act 1992 (c.14), s.86; Council Tax (Valuation of Dwellings) (Scotland) Regulations 1992 (S.I. 1992 No. 1329, reg. 2.]

A, an assessor, appealed against a valuation appeal committee's decision upholding R's appeal and placing his property in band A instead of band B. The house had been bought from the local authority in August 1991 on a valuation within band A. Between then and April 1, 1993 R had had double glazing and extra radiators installed, which A considered took the valuation into band B. The committee considered on a construction of the Act and the regulations that these alterations fell to be left out of account. A argued that the effect of the legislation was that he was required to value the dwelling as it stood as at April 1, 1993 but to apply the levels of value which existed as at April 1, 1991. If the committee were correct in reading reg. 2(2)(c) of the 1992 Regulations as requiring that alterations carried out between those dates, which did not affect the size or layout of a dwelling, be left out of account, there would be an anomaly in that such alterations carried out after April 1, 1993 might lead to a band being altered if the subjects had been sold (s.87). The provisions of reg. 2(2)(c) were explanatory only.

Held, appeal refused. The effect of s.86(2) of the Act read with reg. 2(1) of the regulations was that the value was to be taken as the open market value as at April 1, 1991, and that was the starting point. But for reg. 2(2) A's approach would probably have been correct, but effect had to be given to the terms of the regulations and there was no justification for applying any further assumptions than were contained therein. This did not result in anomalies because A was not required to carry out an individual valuation of each dwelling but to determine which valuation band applied, and the regulations in requiring alterations to the size or layout of a dwelling between two dates to be taken into account, would cover any siginficant alteration for that purpose.

STRATHCLYDE, ASSESSOR FOR v. REA, *The Scotsman*, August 30, 1995.

6113. Council tax—discounts

COUNCIL TAX (DISCOUNTS) (SCOTLAND) AMENDMENT ORDER 1995 (No. 599) [65p], made under the Local Government Finance Act 1992 (c.14), s.113(1) and Sched. 1, para. 2; operative on April 13, 1995; amends the Council Tax (Discounts) (Scotland) Order 1992 by providing that the amount of council tax or council water charge payable under the Local Government Finance Act 1992 may be reduced where a person resident in a dwelling falls to be disregarded for the purposes of discount; and amends article 4 of the 1992 Order so that a person may qualify if he is entitled to an incapacity benefit under the Social Security Contributions and Benefits Act 1992, s.30A.

[S.I. 1992 No. 1408 amended.]

6114. Council tax—discounts—disregarded persons

COUNCIL TAX (DISCOUNTS) (SCOTLAND) AMENDMENT REGULATIONS 1995 (No. 597) [65p], made under the Local Government Finance Act 1992 (c.14), ss.113(1), 116(1) and Sched. 1, paras. 11; operative on April 1, 1995; prescribe as persons to be disregarded for the purposes of discount in relation to council tax and council water charge, certain spouses and dependants of students where not British citizens.

[S.I. 1992 No. 1409 amended.]

6115. Council tax—dwelling occupied in connection with agricultural lands and heritages—croft house—croft land not worked by occupier

[Council Tax (Valuation of Dwellings) (Scotland) Regulations 1992 (S.I. 1992 No. 1329), reg. 3(1).]

The Council Tax (Valuation of Dwellings) (Scotland) Regulations 1992 lay down certain assumptions which must be made by the assessor in valuing a house for the purposes of council tax. By reg. 3(1) if a dwelling is, *inter alia*, "occupied in connection with agricultural lands and heritages", then the assumption is to be made that it could not be used otherwise than as living accommodation by a person engaged in carrying on or directing agricultural operations on those lands or heritages. A crofter who did not work his croft himself but permitted a neighbour to graze stock on the croft without payment, appealed against the assessor's valuation of his house without reference to the assumptions in reg. 3(1). The valuation appeal committee allowed the appeal and reduced the valuation. The assessor appealed.

Held, that the crofter's occupation could not be said to be connected with the use of the croft land for agricultural purposes, and appeal allowed.

HIGHLAND REGION AND WESTERN ISLES, ASSESSOR FOR v. CAMPBELL, 1995 S.L.T. 1290.

6116. Council tax—exempt dwellings

COUNCIL TAX (EXEMPT DWELLINGS) (SCOTLAND) AMENDMENT ORDER 1995 (No. 598) [65p], made under the Local Government Finance Act 1992 (c.14), s.72(6) and (7) and Sched. 11, para. 7(2) and (3); operative on April 1, 1995; amends the schedule to the Council Tax (Exempt Dwellings) (Scotland) Order 1992 so that the presence in a dwelling of a student's spouse or dependent will not exclude that dwelling from being exempt if the spouse or dependent is not a British citizen and cannot seek employment or claim benefits, and makes exempt any dwelling occupied only by persons who are severely mentally impaired.

[S.I. 1992 No. 1333 amended.]

Education. See EDUCATION.

6117. Finance

LOCAL GOVERNMENT FINANCE (SCOTLAND) ORDER 1995 (No. 391) [£1·55], made under the Local Government Finance Act 1992 (c.14), Sched. 12, paras. 1 and 9(4); operative February 10, 1995, determines the amount of revenue support grant payable to each local authority in Scotland in respect of the financial year 1995–96, determines the amount of non-domestic rate income to be distributed to each regional and islands council in respect of that year, redetermines the amount of revenue support grant payable to two councils in respect of the financial year 1994–95 and redetermines the amount of revenue support grant payable to each local authority in Scotland in respect of the financial year 1993–94.

[S.I. 1994 No. 528 amended.]

6118. Finance—interest rate swap agreement—whether *ultra vires*

M reclaimed against a Lord Ordinary's decision that M were not entitled to repetition of £368,104·52 paid to L, a regional council, under an interest rate and currency exchange agreement which the Lord Ordinary had held to be *ultra vires* of L and void *ab initio*. L argued that (1) as the sum had been paid in error of law, M were not entitled to the remedy of repetition or recompense (*Glasgow Corporation v. Inland Revenue* [1959] C.L.Y. 3974); and (2) protection of the public finances, M's failure to ascertain the *vires* of L to enter the agreement, the absence of any coercion by L, the fact that s.69(1) of the Local Government (Scotland) Act 1973, under which the agreement was invalid, was not intended for M's protection, and the terms of the agreement, which provided that in the event of early termination any loss was to lie where it fell, all showed that it was not equitable to order repayment.

Held, reclaiming motion allowed, decree *de plano* granted and case remitted to the Lord Ordinary for discussion of interest on the sum awarded. (1) As the payments had been made in implement of an obligation under a supposed contract, M's remedy was an action of repetition under the *condictio indebiti* and not recompense (*Magistrates of Stonehaven v. Kincardine County Council*, 1939 S.L.T. 528, distinguished). (2) From a consideration of the petition and answers in *Stirling v. Earl of Lauderdale* (1733) Mor. 2930, it was clear that the court had had before it all the relevant arguments and had decided that a *condictio indebiti* was available, although there had been an error of law. This decision had been regarded in subsequent decisions (*Carrick v. Carse* (1778) Mor. 2931) and by institutional writers (Bankton, *Institute*, I. viii. 23 and 24; Erskine, *Institute*, III. iii. 54; Hume, *Lectures*, Vol. III, p. 174) as settling the point and the court in *Glasgow Corporation* had been in error in departing from this line of authority in favour of obiter remarks by Lord Brougham in *Wilson & McLellan v. Sinclair* (1830) 4 W. & S. 398 and *Dixon v. Monkland Canal Co.* (1831) 5 W. & S. 445, which had been based on English authority and which, when critically examined, did not justify the respect they had been given. The application of the maxim *ignorantia juris neminem excusat* was misconceived and, if it was to be applied at all, was to be applied equally between the parties. The absolute nature of the rule left no room for considerations of equity, and was out of place in a discussion about private rights, where a party was not seeking to be excused from his ignorance but merely showing that a payment was made in error. Accordingly the error of law rule had no sound foundation in principle (*Stirling v. Earl of Lauderdale*, Dickson J. (dissenting) in *Hydro Electric Commission of the Township of Nepean v. Ontario Hydro* (1982) 1 S.C.R. 347 and *Willis Faber Enthoven (Pty.) v. Receiver of Revenue*, 1992 (4) S.A. 202, followed; *Glasgow Corporation* and *Taylor v. Wilson's Trs.* [1979] C.L.Y. 2881, overruled). (3) M had averred that the sum was not due and that it had been paid in error, which prima facie entitled them to a remedy and, as an error did not require to be excusable, the onus lay on L to show that it was inequitable to order repayment (*Air Canada v. British Columbia*, 59 D.L.R. (4th) 161 and *David Securities Pty. v. Commonwealth Bank of Australia* [1991–92] 175 C.L.R. 353, followed). (4) It was not required for the protection of the public finances that L should be enriched by the retention of sums to which they were not entitled. L had been unaware that they were acting *ultra vires* and M could not be criticised for the error they were under at the time of the transaction. The absence of coercion was irrelevant to a claim under the *condictio*. There were no equitable considerations arising from the terms of the 1973 Act and, as the agreement was void *ab initio*, L were not entitled to rely on any of its terms. As L's averments had not established that it would be inequitable for M to recover the sums, repayment would be ordered. *Observed*, that removing the error of law rule meant that a remedy would prima facie be available where money had been paid over in response to an unlawful demand for the payment of tax, which was satisfactory, because it would have been inequitable for the remedy to be available in England, following the decision in *Woolwich Equitable Building Society v. Inland Revenue Commissioners* [1992] C.L.Y. 2508, but not in Scotland. *Per* Lord Clyde: While one essential for a claim of recompense was that there had been no intent of donation and considerations of error might come into that, error itself was not a necessary ingredient.

MORGAN GUARANTY TRUST CO. OF NEW YORK v. LOTHIAN REGIONAL COUNCIL, 1995 S.L.T. 299.

6119. Finance—revenue support grant

REVENUE SUPPORT GRANT (SCOTLAND) ORDER 1995 (No. 392) [£1·55], made under the Abolition of Domestic Rates Etc. (Scotland) Act 1987 (c.47), Sched. 4, para. 1 (as substituted by the Local Government and Housing Act 1989 (c.42), Sched. 6); operative on February 16, 1995; redetermines the amount of the revenue support grant payable to each local authority in respect of the financial years 1990–91, 1991–92 and 1992–93.

[S.I. 1994 No. 529 revoked.]

Homeless persons. See HOUSING.

Housing. See HOUSING.

Licensing—intoxicating liquors. See INTOXICATING LIQUORS.

6120. Licensing—market operator's licence. See SPOOK ERECTION v. CITY OF EDINBURGH DISTRICT COUNCIL, §6412.

6121. Licensing—taxicabs. See GLASGOW DISTRICT COUNCIL, CITY OF v. DOYLE, §6130; MONKLANDS DISTRICT COUNCIL v. McGHEE, §6129.

6122. Local Government—reorganisation—Property Commission

LOCAL GOVERNMENT PROPERTY COMMISSION (SCOTLAND) ORDER 1995 (No. 2500) [£1·10], made under the Local Government etc. (Scotland) Act 1994 (c.39) s.19(1) and (2); operative on October 17, 1995; establishes a local government Property Commission under s.19 of the 1994 Act, in connection with the reorganisation of Scottish local government taking effect on April 1, 1996, for the purpose of advising authorities on matters related to property to be transferred in terms of the Local Authorities (Property Transfer) (Scotland) Order 1995 (No. 2499) and provides for its constitution, membership and remuneration of members and staff.

6123. Local Government—reorganisation—property transfer

LOCAL AUTHORITIES (PROPERTY TRANSFER) (SCOTLAND) ORDER 1995 (No. 2499) [£2·80], made under ss.15 and 181(1) and 2(a) of the Local Government etc. (Scotland) Act (c.39) 1994 (and s.15 as applied by s.138 of the 1994 Act); operative on October 17, 1995; provides for the transfer of certain property and rights, obligations and liabilities related thereto, from existing local authorities to new unitary councils, police, fire or valuation joint boards or the Scottish Children's Reporter Administration, as a result of local government re-organisation in Scotland as at April 1, 1996 by virtue of the 1994 Act, and provides for transfer of property held by an authority as part of its common good to transfer to the authority within whose area was situated the borough of whose common good that property formed part on May 15, 1975.

6124. Local Government etc. (Scotland) Act 1994 (c.39)—commencement

LOCAL GOVERNMENT ETC. (SCOTLAND) ACT 1994 (COMMENCEMENT NO. 3) ORDER 1995 (No. 702) [£1·55], made under the Local Government etc. (Scotland) Act 1994 (c.39), s.184; provides for commencement of provisions in the Act as follows: ss.91–96 and Sched. 11 on March 10, 1995; ss.164(1)–(2), 168, 180 (part) and Scheds. 13–14 (part) on April 1, 1995; Sched. 2, subject to para. 4(2), on April 6, 1995; s.58, subject to para. 5(2), on August 1, 1995; ss.20, 33, 52 and Sched. 6 on April 1, 1996.

LOCAL GOVERNMENT etc. (SCOTLAND) ACT 1994 (COMMENCEMENT NO. 4) Order 1995 (No. 1898 (c.36)), [£1·10]; made under the Local Government etc. (Scotland) Act 1994 (c.39), s.184(2); brings into force on July 17, 1995 ss.62–64, 65(2), 66, 73 and 74, 76 and 77, s.79(1)–(3) and (5), 81, 83–90, 98, 116, 118(1), 120(1), 122 and 123 and Scheds. 7 and 8; s.177(1) and (2); s.180 and Sched. 13, para. 75(25)(b).

LOCAL GOVERNMENT ETC. (SCOTLAND) ACT 1994 (COMMENCEMENT NO. 5) ORDER 1995 (C.60) (No. 2866) [£1·10], made under the Local Government etc. (Scotland) Act 1994 (c.39), s.184(2); brings into force ss. 67, 68(1), (4) and (5), 69, 70, 71, 171, 177 and Sched, 9 on October 30, 1995 and ss.171 and 176 on April 1, 1996.

6125. Members—allowances

LOCAL AUTHORITIES ETC. (ALLOWANCES) (SCOTLAND) AMENDMENT REGULATIONS 1995 (No. 701) [£1·10], made under the Local Government (Scotland) Act 1973 (c.65), ss.45 (as amended) by the Local Government and Planning (Scotland) Act 1982 (c.43), s.60(1)(a) and repealed by the Local Government and Housing Act 1989 (c.42), Sched. 12, but saved for certain purposes by S.I. 1991 No. 344), 47 (as amended by the Local Government, Planning and Land Act 1980 (c.65), s.25(5) and the 1989 Act, Sched. 11), 49A (as inserted by the 1980 Act, s.26(3) and repealed by the 1989 Act, Sched. 12, but saved in relation to members of licensing boards by S.I. 1991 No. 344) and 235(1), and the Local Government and Housing Act 1989 (c.42), ss.18 and 190(1); operative on April 1, 1995; amend the Local Authorities Etc. (Allowances) (Scotland) Regulations 1991 by increasing various financial limits and rates in respect of payment of allowances to members of local authorities, joint boards and certain related bodies. They do not apply to the new unitary councils to be elected on April 6, 1995.

[S.I. 1991 No. 397 amended; S.I. 1994 No. 630 revoked.]

LOCAL AUTHORITIES ETC. (ALLOWANCES) (SCOTLAND) REGULATIONS 1995 (No. 912) [£3·70], made under the Local Government (Scotland) Act 1973 (c.65), ss.45(4) (as repealed by the Local Government and Housing Act 1989 (c.42), Sched. 12 but saved by S.I. 1991 No. 344), 47 (as amended by the Local Government, Planning and Land Act 1980 (c.65), s.25(5) and the 1989 Act, Sched. 11), 49A (as added by the 1980 Act, s.26(3) repealed by the 1989 Act, Sched. 12 but saved in relation to members of licensing boards by S.I. 1991 No. 344) and 235(1) and the Local Government and Housing Act 1989 (c.42), ss.18 (as amended by the Police and Magistrates' Courts Act 1994 (c.29), Sched. 4) and 190(1); operative on April 6, 1995; provide for the payment of allowances to members of new Scottish unitary councils elected on April 6, 1995, islands councils and their successors and new joint boards, require, *inter alia*, the local authorities to make schemes for payment of members' allowances, impose certain financial restrictions on the schemes and other allowances, empower joint boards to make schemes for the payment of special responsibility allowances to members, and sets out administrative arrangements and transitional provisions.

[S.I. 1991 No. 397 amended; 1992 No. 505 revoked; 1993 No. 644, 1994 No. 630, 1995 No. 701 partially revoked, all with effect from April 1, 1996.]

Rating. See RATING AND VALUATION.

6126. Reorganisation

LOCAL GOVERNMENT (APPLICATION OF ENACTMENTS) (SCOTLAND) ORDER 1995 (No. 789) [£1·95], made under the Local Government etc.

(Scotland) Act 1994 (c.39), s.181(1) and (2); operative on April 6, 1995; applies certain general and procedural provisions of the Local Government (Scotland) Act 1973 (c.65), and certain other enactments relating to local authorities, which would not otherwise apply, in the period prior to April 1, 1996, to those new councils, as they apply to existing councils.

LOCAL GOVERNMENT (COMPENSATION FOR REDUNDANCY OR PREMATURE ON REORGANISATION) (SCOTLAND) REGULATIONS 1995 (No. 340) [£1·55], made under the Superannuation Act 1972 (c.11), s.24; operative on April 6, 1995; allow a lump sum payment to be made to certain employees who cease to hold employment with a relevant body by reason of redundancy or in the interests of efficiency of their employer during a specified period in consequence of local government reorganisations.

LOCAL GOVERNMENT (COMPENSATION FOR REDUCTION OF REMUNERATION ON REORGANISATION) (SCOTLAND) REGULATIONS 1995 (No. 2865) [£1·95], made under the Superannuation Act 1972 (c.11), ss.7 (as extended by the Pensions (Increase) Act 1974 (c.9), s.2(2)), 9 (as amended by the Pensions (Miscellaneous Provisions) Act 1990 (c.7), ss.4, 8 and 11) and 24; operative on December 1, 1995; provide for payment of compensation to certain staff of local authorities and other bodies affected by local government reorganisation in Scotland who satisfy the criteria for such payment, and for rights of appeal.

[S.I. 1987 No. 1850 and S.I. 1992 No. 280 amended.]

LOCAL GOVERNMENT (EDUCATION ADMINISTRATION) (COMPENSATION FOR REDUNDANCY OR PREMATURE RETIREMENT ON REORGANISATION) (SCOTLAND) REGULATIONS 1995 (No. 840) [£1·55], made under the Superannuation Act 1972 (c.11), s.24; operative on April 6, 1995; allows a lump sum payment to be made to certain local authority employees, who cease to hold employment with a relevant body by reason of redundancy or in the interests of efficiency of their employer during a specified period in consequence of local government reorganisation in Scotland.

LOCAL AUTHORITIES (STAFF TRANSFER) (SCOTLAND) ORDER 1995 (No. 1340) [£1·55], made under the Local Government etc. (Scotland) Act 1994 (c.39), ss.97(1) and 137(1): operative on June 15, 1995; makes provision for transfer of staff to new unitary local authorities as a result of local government reorganisation.

LOCAL GOVERNMENT (TRANSITIONAL PROVISIONS) (SCOTLAND) ORDER 1995 (No. 1878) [£1·10]; made under the Local Government etc. (Scotland) Act 1994 (c.39), s.181(1) and (2); operative on August 15, 1995; makes transitional provisions in relation to the period prior to April 1, 1996, in respect of the reorganisation of local government, regarding area tourist boards, licensing and value added tax.

[Civic Government (Scotland) Act 1982 (c.45), s.9 and Value Added Tax 1994 (c.23) s.33, amended.]

6127. Social work—registered establishments

REGISTERED ESTABLISHMENTS (FEES) (SCOTLAND) ORDER 1995 (No. 749) [£1·10], made under the Social Work (Scotland) Act 1968 (c.49), ss.64A(3) (as inserted by the Registered Establishments (Scotland) Act 1987 (c.40), s.6(1)), s.90(3) and 94(1); operative on April 1, 1995; revokes the Registered Establishments (Fees) (Scotland) Order 1993 and re-enacts its provisions with amendments, which increase the maximum levels for the fees chargeable by local authorities to applicants for registration, continuation of registration and variation of conditions of registration.

[S.I. 1993 No. 768 revoked.]

6128. Taxicabs—licensing of

[Civil Government (Scotland) Act 1982 (c.45), s.3 and Sched. 1, para. 4(2).]

G, five applicants for taxi licences, sought recall of interim interdict granted on June 30, 1994 against D, a district council, from issuing licences to G in

M's action for judicial review. D had arranged a meeting for April 29 to consider applications lodged by G on November 2, 1993, to which M had objected. Following objections from G that they had not received the required seven days' notice of the meeting, D had decided not to make a final decision on April 29, and had applied to a sheriff for an extension of the six month period within which a final decision had to be made in terms of s.3(4) of the Civic Government (Scotland) Act 1982. On June 30, M had presented a petition for judicial review seeking declarator that D had failed in their duty to consider M's objections, reduction of the decision not to hold the hearing on April 29, interim interdict, and an order requiring D to fix a hearing to consider G's applications. The sheriff subsequently refused D's application, a decision confirmed by the sheriff principal. M argued that (1) as there had been no material change of circumstances since June 30, the prima facie case established then still applied, that M were entitled to have their objections heard, and that G had not been prejudiced by the short notice of the meeting of April 29; and (2) the balance of convenience favoured M, as G all had other sources of income and it was unlikely that the taxis would be operational before the second hearing of the petition. G argued that, given that seven months of the one year period covered by the licences which would have been granted following the lapse of the six month period in May had already passed, that each of them had been losing about £150 per week by reason of the non-issue and stood to lose more over the Christmas and New Year period, and that four of them were unemployed or not in permanent employment, the balance of convenience lay with G.

Held, interim interdict recalled. Given the short notice of the meeting, that D had been entitled not to reach a decision at the meeting on April 29, that as D had failed to reach a decision within six months and no extension had been granted, s.3(5) of the 1982 Act required D to issue a licence, that M would be able to make their objections if a renewal was sought, and that s.3(4) was intended to provide G with a remedy in just such circumstances, it was very likely G would succeed in establishing that they were entitled to the licences, and M had failed to aver a prima facie case. *Opinion*, that, if M had made out a prima facie case it would have been a very weak one and the balance of convenience would have favoured G.

MONKLANDS DISTRICT INDEPENDENT TAXI OWNERS ASSOCIATION v. MONKLANDS DISTRICT COUNCIL (O.H.), 1995 S.C.L.R. 547.

6129. Taxicabs—licensing of—procedure—final decision to be reached by licensing authority "within six months" of application being made—computation of time

[Civic Government (Scotland) Act 1982 (c.45), s.3(1), (4) and (5).]

Section 3(1) of the Civic Government (Scotland) Act 1982 provides that a licensing authority shall reach a final decision on an application within six months of its being made. Subject to the period being extended by the sheriff on summary application by the licensing authority under s.3(2), in terms of s.3(4) and (5) where the licensing authority have failed to reach a final decision within the period allowed, the licence shall be deemed to have been granted and remain in force for one year. On November 2, 1993 five applications were made for taxi licences and on November 3, 1993 a further six applications were made. On May 3, 1994, Monday, May 2, 1994 being a court holiday, the licensing authority applied for a two month extension of the six month period to consider these applications. The sheriff held that summary applications required to be lodged by midnight on May 1–2, and 2–3, 1994 respectively in relation to the two batches of applications and dismissed the authority's summary application as being out of time. The licensing authority appealed to the sheriff principal, contending that the day on which the applications were made should be omitted from the computation and, in respect of those who lodged their applications on November 2, 1993, that an extra day was permitted as the last day was a holiday.

Held, that (1) in computing the six month period the day from which the period ran, namely the lodging of the taxi licence applications, fell to be excluded; (2) an application was made when it was presented to court staff and not when a warrant was granted thereon (*Secretary of State for Trade and Industry v. Josolyne* [1990] C.L.Y. 447, followed); (3) it was of no consequence that the last day of the six month period was a court holiday (*McNiven v. Glasgow Corporation*, 1920 S.L.T. 57, followed); (4) in terms of s.3(4) and (5) of the 1982 Act, those five applicants who applied for licences on November 2, 1993 were deemed to have been granted licences for one year at midnight on May 2, 1994 but the summary application for the six applicants who lodged their applications on November 3, 1993 should be remitted back to the sheriff to proceed; and appeal allowed in part.

MONKLANDS DISTRICT COUNCIL v. McGHEE, 1995 S.L.T. (Sh.Ct.) 52.

6130. Taxicabs—licensing of—refusal to grant licence—natural justice

[Civic Government (Scotland) Act 1982 (c.45), Sched. 1, para. 18(9).]

Three holders of taxi (operators') licences had their applications for renewal refused by the licensing sub-committee. The committee had previously determined the number of taxi licences it considered necessary to meet local demand. All but three of this quota had been allocated at the time that the applicants' cases, together with seven further applications, were considered by the committee. The committee granted one licence on the basis that the application had special merit. It did not give consideration to the fact that the applicants were previously holders of taxi licences, but in its reasons stated that regard had been had to experience that the various applicants had had as holders of taxi drivers' licences. On this basis it awarded the two remaining licences to two of the other applicants. The three appealed to the sheriff, who held that in granting the one application on its special merit the committee had failed to specify the reasons for its success and consequently the reasons for failure of the others. He also held that in having regard to the experience of the various applicants as taxi drivers, without giving previous notice of this criterion, the committee had acted in breach of natural justice. In allowing the applicants' appeals he declined to grant the licence applications but remitted the appeals back to the committee for further consideration. The licensing authority appealed to the Court of Session, arguing that the sheriff had erred in holding that experience as a taxi driver was irrelevant, and that there was no duty on an administrative body to tell applicants what facts to put forward in support of their applications. The applicants lodged cross-appeals, arguing that the sheriff had interpreted the grounds for reversing the committee's decision too narrowly and that he had been wrong to remit the cases for reconsideration.

Held, that (1) experience as a taxi driver was not necessarily irrelevant in considering the grant of taxi operators' licences; (2) in circumstances where there was a competition between applications, the failure to give notice of the criteria to be applied and the selection of one application on the basis of undisclosed criteria amounted to a departure from the rules of natural justice; (3) as it would now be impossible to recreate the situation which had existed when the applications were initially being considered, substantial justice required that the respondents had their licences granted; and appeals refused and cross-appeals allowed to the extent of remitting the causes to the sheriff to grant the applications.

GLASGOW DISTRICT COUNCIL, CITY OF v. DOYLE, 1995 S.L.T. 327.

Town and country planning. See TOWN AND COUNTRY PLANNING.

MEDICINE

Dangerous drugs. See CRIMINAL LAW.

Dangerous drugs—sentencing. See CRIMINAL SENTENCING.

Misuse of drugs. See CRIMINAL LAW.

Misuse of drugs—sentencing. See CRIMINAL SENTENCING.

MENTAL HEALTH

6131/3. Negligence—duty of care—health board for suicidal patient. See G.'s CURATOR BONIS v. GRAMPIAN HEALTH BOARD, §6159; HAY v. GRAMPIAN HEALTH BOARD, §6159a.

6134. State hospital

MENTAL HEALTH (STATE HOSPITAL MANAGEMENT COMMITTEE, STATE HOSPITAL, CARSTAIRS) (SCOTLAND) TRANSFER AND DISSOLUTION ORDER 1995 (No. 575) [65p], made under the Mental Health (Scotland) Act 1984 (c.36), s.91(3); operative on April 1, 1995; provides for the transfer of property rights and liabilities of the State Hospital Management Committee, Carstairs to the State Hospitals Board for Scotland, and for the dissolution of the committee.

STATE HOSPITALS BOARD FOR SCOTLAND ORDER 1995 (No. 574) [£2·80], made under the National Health Service (Scotland) Act 1978 (c.29), ss.2(1) (as amended by the Health and Social Services and Social Security Adjudications Act 1983 (c.41), Sched. 7 and the National Health Service and Community Care Act 1990 (c.19), s.28) and 105(7) (as amended by the Health Services Act 1980 (c.53), Scheds. 6 and 7 and the 1983 Act, Sched. 9); operative on April 1, 1995; constitutes a special Health Board for the whole of Scotland to be known as the State Hospitals Board for Scotland with the duty to provide state hospitals for the mentally disordered who require treatment under conditions of special security.

6135. State Hospitals (Scotland) Act 1994 (c.16)—commencement

STATE HOSPITALS (SCOTLAND) ACT 1994 COMMENCEMENT ORDER 1995 (No. 576) (C.14) [65p], made under the State Hospitals (Scotland) Act 1994 (c.16), s.3(2); brings into force the provisions of the State Hospitals (Scotland) Act 1994, on April 1, 1995.

MINING LAW

6136. Coal mine—subsidence—compensation—dwellinghouse demolished prior to claim. See OSBORNE v. BRITISH COAL PROPERTY (O.H.), §6137.

6137. Coal mine—subsidence—compensation—jurisdiction to determine

[Coal Mining Subsidence Act 1991 (c.45), ss.3(1), 11(1), 40(1).]

The Coal Mining Subsidence Act 1991 makes provision in certain circumstances for payment of compensation to owners of property which has been damaged by subsidence. Section 40(1) of the Act, read with s.52(1), provides that "any question arising under this Act shall, in default of agreement, be referred to and determined by the Lands Tribunal for Scotland". Some owners of properties allegedly damaged by subsidence gave the notice required under the Act to the relevant authority only after their dwellinghouses had been demolished. They later raised an action of damages in the Court of Session, basing jurisdiction on the defenders' domicile. The defences admitted that the court had jurisdiction, but included pleas in law challenging the competency and relevancy of the action. There was no extrajudicial agreement between the parties that their dispute should be determined by the Court of Session. The defenders argued at procedure roll that it was not competent under the Act for the parties to agree that their dispute could be determined by the Court of Session, and that "in default of agreement" did not include default of agreement on the method and forum for resolving any question between them. In any event there had been no such agreement between the parties. They also argued that the action was incompetent or irrelevant because there were no averments that the pursuers were the owners of dwellinghouses existing at the time when the notices were intimated. The pursuers argued that the action was competent, and that the defenders must be deemed to have agreed to the resolution of the dispute by the Court of Session on the basis of their pleadings which did not challenge jurisdiction.

Held, that (1) "in default of agreement" in s.40(1) of the 1991 Act included default of agreement on the forum for resolution of the disputed question; (2) as the decision on the question had not been confided to the Lands Tribunal in unqualified terms, it was not incompetent to raise the action at common law; (3) the defenders' admissions related only to the territorial jurisdiction of the court and could not be construed to represent an implied agreement that the Court of Session should be the forum to resolve the question between the parties in terms of s.40(1); and (4) in the absence of any such agreement the Lands Tribunal for Scotland had exclusive jurisdiction to resolve the question; and action dismissed with no pleas sustained. (*Brodie v. Ker* [1952] C.L.Y. 4161, followed.) *Opinion*, that it was sufficient qualification for the giving of notices under the 1991 Act that the persons giving notice were then the owners of the relative heritable interest in the properties, and it did not matter that their dwellinghouses had already been demolished.

OSBORNE v. BRITISH COAL PROPERTY (O.H.), 1995 S.L.T. 1349

6138. Coal mining subsidence—shaft sunk for ironstone mining subsequently used in connection with coal mining operations. See BRITISH COAL CORPORATION v. NETHERLEE TRUST TRS., §6139.

6139. Coal mining subsidence—whether subsidence of infill material withdrawal of support from land

[Coal Mining Subsidence Act 1991 (c.45), ss.1(1) and 2(1).]

Section 2(1) of the Coal Mining Subsidence Act 1991 provides that it shall be the duty of the British Coal Corporation to take remedial action in respect of subsidence damage to any property. Section 1(1) provides: "In this Act 'subsidence damage' means any damage—(a) to land; or (b) to any buildings, structures or works on, in or over land, caused by the withdrawal of support from land in connection with lawful coal-mining operations." In 1991 part of the surface of a car park subsided over the area where a mine shaft had been sunk for the purpose of extracting ironstone. After the working of ironstone ceased the shaft was disused for some years but subsequently used by a coal company in connection with their coal mining operations. Those operations ceased late in the 19th century and the shaft was infilled and abandoned. Sometime between 1936 and 1957 the shaft was covered over and lost to view until the subsidence occurred. The Lands Tribunal for Scotland found that the damage was subsidence damage and that it had been caused by withdrawal of support from the land on which the car park was situated. The withdrawal of support had involved the movement of infill placed in the shaft in connection with lawful coal mining operations and the tribunal concluded that the withdrawal of support from the land also fell to be regarded as having been in connection with lawful coal mining operations. On appeal by the British Coal Corporation it was submitted that what had happened was that support had been lost through the collapse of infill, which was passive, and was accordingly not "withdrawal" of support, which was active. Nor was it "in connection with" coal mining operations where the surface had been created after mining operations had ceased.

Held, that (1) "withdrawal of support" could cover passive as well as active loss of support and in the circumstances there had been withdrawal of support from the car park; (2) the withdrawal had been in connection with lawful coal mining operations; and appeal refused.

BRITISH COAL CORPORATION v. NETHERLEE TRUST TRS., 1995 S.L.T. 1038.

MONEY

6140. Interest—capital sum on divorce. See TAHIR v. TAHIR (NO. 2), §5885.

Interest—damages. See DAMAGES.

NATIONAL HEALTH

6141. Charges

NATIONAL HEALTH SERVICE (CHARGES FOR DRUGS AND APPLIANCES) (SCOTLAND) AMENDMENT (NO. 2) REGULATIONS 1995 (No. 2739) [65p], made under the National Health Service (Scotland) Act 1978 (c.29) ss.69, 75A(1)(a) (as inserted by the Social Security Act 1988 (c.7) s.14 and amended by the Health and Medicines Act 1988 (c.49), Sched. 2 and the National Health Service and Community Care Act 1990 (c.19), Sched. 9), 105(7) (as amended by the Health Services Act 1980 (c.53), Scheds. 6 and 7 and by the Health and Social Services and Social Security Adjudications Act 1983 (c.41). Sched. 9) and 108(1); operative on October 20, 1995; amend the National Health Service (Charges for Drugs and Appliances) (Scotland) Regulations 1989 so that all persons (male or female) who have attained the age of 60 years shall be exempt from paying charges for drugs or appliances (other than dental or optical).

NATIONAL HEALTH SERVICE (CHARGES FOR DRUGS AND APPLIANCES) (SCOTLAND) AMENDMENT REGULATIONS 1995 (No. 699) [£1·10], made under the National Health Service (Scotland) Act 1978 (c.29), ss.19 (as amended by the Health Services Act 1980 (c.53), s.7, the Health and Social Services and Social Security Adjudications Act 1983 (c.41), Sched. 7, the Medical Act 1983 (c.54), Sched. 5 and the National Health Service and Community Care Act 1990 (c.19), s.37, and extended by the Health and Medicines Act 1988 (c.49), s.17), 27 (as amended by the 1980 Act, s.20(2), the National Health Service (Amendment) Act 1986 (c.66), s.3(3), S.I. 1987 No. 2202 and the 1990 Act, Sched. 9, and extended by the 1988 Act, s.17), 69, 75(2), 105(7) (as amended by the 1980 Act, Scheds. 6 and 7 and the 1983 Act, Sched. 9); operative on April 1, 1995; further amends the National Health Service (Charges for Drugs and Appliances) (Scotland) Regulations 1989 to increase the charges for items supplied on prescription and certain other items.

[S.I. 1989 No. 326 amended.]

NATIONAL HEALTH SERVICE (DENTAL CHARGES) (SCOTLAND) AMENDMENT REGULATIONS 1995 (No. 703) [65p], made under the National Health Service (Scotland) Act 1978 (c.29), ss.70(1A) (as inserted by the Health and Medicines Act 1988 (c.49), s.11), 71(1) (as amended by the 1988 Act (c.49), s.11), 71A (as inserted by the 1988 Act (c.49), s.11), 105(7) (as amended by the Health Services Act 1980 (c.53), Scheds. 6 and 7 and by the Health and Social Services and Security Adjudications Act 1983 (c.41), Sched. 9) and 108(1); operative on April 1, 1995; amend the National Health Service (Dental Charges) (Scotland) Regulations 1989 by increasing the maximum contribution which a patient may be required to make towards the aggregate cost of dental treatment and appliances.

[S.I. 1989 No. 363 amended.]

NATIONAL HEALTH SERVICE (OPTICAL CHARGES AND PAYMENTS) (SCOTLAND) AMENDMENT (NO. 2) REGULATIONS 1995 (No. 705) [£1·55], made under the National Health Service (Scotland) Act 1978 (c.29), ss.26 (as amended by the Health and Social Security Act 1984 (c.48), s.1(5), Scheds. 1 and 8 and Health and Medicines Act 1988 (c.49), s.13(4)), 70(1) (as amended by the 1988 Act, Sched. 3), 73(*a*), 73(*c*) (as inserted by National Health Service and Community Care Act 1990 (c.19), Sched. 9), 74(*a*) and 74(*c*) (as inserted by the 1990 Act (c.19), Sched. 9), 105(7) (as amended by the Health Services Act 1980 (c.53), Scheds. 6 and 7 and Health and Social Services and Social Security Adjudications Act 1983 (c.41), Sched. 9), 108(1), Sched. 11 para. 2 (as substituted by the 1988 Act, Sched. 2) and para. 2A (as inserted by the Health and Social Security Act 1984 (c.48), Sched. 1 and amended by the 1988 Act, s.13(2) and (5)); operative on April 1, 1995; further amend the National Health Service (Optical Charges and Payments) (Scotland) Regulations 1989.

[S.I. 1989 No. 392 amended.]

NATIONAL HEALTH SERVICE (TRAVELLING EXPENSES AND REMISSION OF CHARGES) (SCOTLAND) AMENDMENT (No. 2) REGULATIONS 1995 (No. 2381) [£1·10], made under the National Health Service (Scotland) Act 1978 s.75A (as inserted by the Social Security Act 1988 (c.7), s.14(2) and as amended by the National Health Service and Community Care Act 1990 (c.19) Sched. 9), s.105 (as amended by the Health Services Act 1980 (c.53), Scheds. 6 and 7 and by the Social Services and Social Services and Social Security Adjudications Act 1983 (c.41) Sched. 9) and s.108(1); operative on October 2, 1995; provide for remission and payment of certain charges and for payment of travelling expenses incurred in hospital attendance.

[S.I. 1988 No. 546 amended.]

NATIONAL HEALTH SERVICE (TRAVELLING EXPENSES AND REMISSION OF CHARGES) (SCOTLAND) AMENDMENT REGULATIONS 1995 (No. 700) [£1·10], made under the National Health Service (Scotland) Act 1978 (c.29), ss.75A (as inserted by the Social Security Act 1988 (c.7), s.14(2), and amended by the National Health Service and Community Care Act 1990 (c.19), Sched. 9) 105 (amended by the Health Services Act 1980 (c.53), Scheds. 6 and 7 and the Health and Social Services and Social Security Adjudications Act 1983 (c.41), Sched. 9) and 108(1); operative on April 1, 1995; further amend the National Health Service (Travelling Expenses and Remission of Charges) (Scotland) Regulations 1988 in relation, *inter alia*, to disability working allowance.

[S.I. 1988 No. 546 amended.]

6142. Fund-holding practices

NATIONAL HEALTH SERVICE (FUND-HOLDING PRACTICES) (SCOTLAND) AMENDMENT REGULATIONS 1995 (No. 1571) [£1·55], made under the National Health Service (Scotland) Act 1978 (c.29), ss.2(5) (as amended by the National Health Service and Community Care Act 1990 (c.19), Sched. 9), 87A(4) (as inserted by the National Health Service and Community Care Act 1990 (c.19), s.34), 87B(5) (as inserted by the National Health Service and Community Care Act 1990 (c.19), s.34), 105(7) (as amended by the Health Services Act 1980 (c.53), Scheds. 6 and 7 and the Health and Social Security Adjudications Act 1983 (c.41), Sched. 9) and 108(1); operative on July 21, 1995; amend the National Health Service (Fund-Holding Practices) (Scotland) Regulations 1993, creates two types of fund-holding practice, namely the standard fund-holding practice and primary care purchasing practice. A practice with at least 4,000 patients will be able to apply for recognition as a standard fund-holding practice. Existing fund-holders will automatically become standard fund-holding practices. One type of fund-holding practice can apply to become a fund-holding practice of the other type.

[S.I. 1993 No. 488 amended.]

6143. General medical services

NATIONAL HEALTH SERVICE (GENERAL MEDICAL SERVICES) (SCOTLAND) REGULATIONS 1995 (No. 416) [£9·40], made under the National Health Service (Scotland) Act 1978 (c.29), ss.2(5) (as amended by the National Health Service and Community Care Act 1990 (c.19) Sched. 9), 19 (as amended by the Health Services Act 1980 (c.53), s.7, the Health and Social Services and Social Security Adjudications Act 1983 (c.41), Sched. 7, the Medical Act 1983 (c.54), Sched. 5 and the 1990 Act, s.37), 20(1) (as amended by the 1980 Act, Sched. 6), 23(2A) and (4) (as inserted and amended by the 1990 Act, s.39(2) and (3) respectively), 24 (as amended by the 1990 Act, s.39(7)), 28(1) (as amended by the National Health Service (Amendment) Act 1986 (c.66), s.3(4)), 28(A) (as inserted by the Health and Social Security Act 1984 (c.48), s.7(2) and amended by the Health and Medicines Act 1988 (c.49), s.15), 34, 105(7) (as amended by the 1980 Act, Scheds. 6 and 7 and the 1983 Act, Sched. 9), 106(*a*), 108(1), Sched. 2, para. 3, and Sched. 9, para. 1(3) and the Health and Medicines Act 1988 (c.49), s.8(1)(*a*) and (5); operative on March 31, 1995; consolidate the National Health Service (General Medical and Pharmaceutical Services) (Scotland) Regulations 1974 provisions relating to the general medical services and regulate the terms on which general medical services are provided under the National Health Service (Scotland) Act 1978.

6144. Health service bodies—accounts and audit

NATIONAL HEALTH SERVICE (EXPENSES OF AUDIT) (SCOTLAND) REGULATIONS 1995 (No. 698) [£1·10], made under the Local Government (Scotland) Act 1973 (c.65), s.98(1)(c) (as inserted by the National Health Service and Community Care Act 1990 (c.19), Sched. 7); operative on April 1, 1995; makes provision as to how the expenses of the Accounts Commission for Scotland, in relation to their functions with respect to health service bodies, are to be met by those bodies whose accounts will be audited by the commission.

6145. Health service trusts

LAW HOSPITAL NATIONAL HEALTH SERVICE TRUST (ESTABLISHMENT) AMENDMENT ORDER 1995 (No. 741) [65p], made under the National Health Service (Scotland) Act 1978 (c.29), s.12A(1) (as inserted by the National Health Service and Community Care Act 1990 (c.19), s.31), and Sched. 7A paras. 1 and 3(1)(*b*) (as inserted by the 1990 Act Sched. 6); operative on March 31, 1995; substitutes a new article 3 in the Law Hospital National Health Service Trust (Establishment) Order 1993, allowing the trust to build a new hospital to replace Law Hospital, Carluke.

NATIONAL HEALTH SERVICE TRUSTS (ORIGINATING CAPITAL DEBT) (SCOTLAND) ORDER 1995 (No. 577) [£1·10], made under the National Health Service (Scotland) Act 1978 (c.29), s.12E(1) and (4) (as inserted by the National Health Service and Community Care Act 1990 (c.19), s.31); operative on March 14, 1995; determines the amount of the originating capital debt provided for in

12E of the National Health Service (Scotland) Act 1978 of certain NHS trusts established under that Act.

ROYAL INFIRMARY OF EDINBURGH NATIONAL HEALTH SERVICE TRUST (ESTABLISHMENT) AMENDMENT ORDER 1995 (No. 742) [65p], made under the National Health Service (Scotland) Act 1978 (c.29), s.12A(1) (as inserted by the National Health Service and Community Care Act 1990 (c.19), s.31) and Sched. 7A paras. 1 and 3(1)(*b*) (as inserted by the 1990 Act, Sched. 6); operative on March 31, 1995; substitutes a new article 3 in the Royal Infirmary of Edinburgh National Health Service Trust (Establishment) Order 1993 to allow the trust to build a new hospital to replace the Royal Infirmary of Edinburgh.

6146. Medical and pharmaceutical services

NATIONAL HEALTH SERVICE (GENERAL MEDICAL AND PHARMACEUTICAL SERVICES) (SCOTLAND) AMENDMENT REGULATIONS 1995 (No. 165) [£1·55], made under the National Health Service (Scotland) Act 1978 (c.29) ss.19 (as amended by the Health Services Act 1980 (c.53), s.7, the Health and Social Services and Social Security Adjudications Act 1983 (c.41), Sched. 7, the Medical Act 1983 (c.54), Sched. 5 and the National Health Service and Community Care Act 1990 (c.19), s.37) 27 (as amended by the 1980 Act, s.20(2), the National Health Service (Amendment) Act 1986 (c.66), s.3(3) and the 1990 Act, Sched. 9), 105(7) (as amended by the 1983 Act, Sched. 9) and 108(1); operative on February 28, 1995; amend the National Health Service (General Medical and Pharmaceutical Services) (Scotland) Regulations 1974, to enable doctors to treat patients at premises other than their practice premises outwith their normal hours of availability, provide that where a doctor engages as a deputy another doctor, the deputy alone will be responsible for his acts and omissions and those of any person employed by him or acting on his behalf and add providing or prescribing drugs against developing malaria to the list of services for which a doctor may charge a fee.

[S.I. 1974 No. 506 amended.]

6147. Medical and pharmaceutical services—application for relocation of pharmacy—whether minor relocation

[National Health Service (General Medical and Pharmaceutical Services) (Scotland) Regulations 1974 (S.I. 1974/506), reg. 281.]

S, two pharmaceutical firms carrying on business on Main Street, Barrhead, sought reduction of a decision of G, a pharmaceutical committee, which approved P's application under reg. 28(3) of the 1974 Regulations, as amended, to relocate its pharmaceutical business from Cross Arthurlie Street to Main Street. P had submitted applications to the area health board on form A(MR), which was designed for minor relocations, and form A, notice of the latter being given to S, who lodged objections. The area pharmaceutical committee (A) decided that P's proposal did not constitute a minor relocation as the population served in the new location would not be the same as that served at their existing premises, while the chief administrative pharmaceutical officer (C) concluded that the relocation was minor, being within the same neighbourhood. After considering the views of both A and C, their knowledge of the area and the terms of the 1990 Regulations, G determined (a) that the relocation was minor as the central area of Barrhead was one neighbourhood, (b) that there would be no significant change in the population which P would service and (c) that the move would have no appreciable effect on the pharmaceutical services provided by P or S. S argued (1) that the decision was *ultra vires* as there was no material other than the views expressed by C entitling G to reach its conclusions since A had opposed the application and neither S's objections nor the area and its needs were taken into account; (2) that in any event no reasonable health board, having regard to the nature of the area, S's objections and the duties incumbent upon the board regarding the provision of pharmaceutical services in terms of s.27 of the 1978 Act, would have held this a minor relocation; (3) that Barrhead consisted of two or three shopping areas which should be considered separate neighbourhoods for the purposes of reg. 28; and (4) that under regs. 28 (3E) and (3F), G should have considered P's application under form A rather than form A(MR), which was a closed procedure with no provision for objection or consultation and G had acted irrationally in failing to consider S's objections.

Held, petition dismissed. In terms of reg. 28(3A), G were bound to grant an application under the form A(MR) procedure if they were satisfied that the relocation was a minor one and in considering that issue, G were only required to take into account the views of A and C. The purpose of reg. 28 was to enable G to dispose of applications which did not merit the fuller procedure under form A; to conclude that G had to have regard to any objections would defeat the object of the regulations and, in effect, require every application to proceed under form A. In the circumstances, there was no substance in S's contention that G acted *ultra vires.* G's decision could not be said to be unreasonable where there were clear factors including the relatively short distance between P's existing and proposed premises and G's view that the areas did not form mutually exclusive shopping centres, and the questions of neighbourhood and minor relocation were matters of fact and degree to be determined by G (*R. v. Yorkshire Health Authority, ex p. Suri* [1994] 9 C.L. 271).

STRATHCLYDE PHARMACEUTICALS v. ARGYLL AND CLYDE HEALTH BOARD (O.H.), *The Times*, March 6, 1995.

6148. Medical and pharmaceutical services—inclusion in pharmaceutical list—scope of appeal from pharmacy practices committee

A company applied to a health board to be included in the board's pharmaceutical list for the provision of pharmaceutical services, from supermarket premises operated by the company. Its application was granted by the board's pharmacy practices committee. A number of the objectors to its granting appealed against this decision to the national appeal panel. In addition to the company and the objectors, other "interested persons" were heard by the panel. The appeal was upheld and the panel wrote to the company, advising of the panel's decision and that, having taken into account all the factors, including demand and supply in the area, the granting of the application was not justified at that time. The company applied for judicial review on the grounds that the panel had reached its decision on the basis of matters beyond the limited grounds of appeal, had allowed people who were not objectors to make representations, and had failed to give any reason or sufficient reasons to justify its decision.

Held, that (1) apart from the general common law constrictions of fairness and lawfulness, the panel was unfettered as to both procedure and substance provided it gave a reason for its decision, and was free to reach a decision upon all material before it, including material going beyond the grounds of appeal and submissions from persons other than objectors; (2) the letter intimating the decision to allow the appeal, setting out that an extra pharmacy was not justified in the relevant area of the particular time, when read in the context of the record of the proceedings before the panel, gave sufficient reason for allowing the appeal; and petition dismissed. *Monachan (Ian) (Central) Petrs.* [1991] C.L.Y. 4379, followed. *Opinion*, that had the petition been granted, it would have been appropriate to remit the matter back to the panel for further consideration rather than to quash or reduce its decision.

SAFEWAY STORES v. NATIONAL APPEAL PANEL (O.H.), 1995 S.L.T. 1083.

6149. Ophthalmic services

NATIONAL HEALTH SERVICE (GENERAL OPHTHALMIC SERVICES) (SCOTLAND) AMENDMENT REGULATIONS 1995 (No. 704) [£1·10], made under the National Health Service (Scotland) Act 1978 (c.29), ss.26 (as amended by the Health and Social Security Act 1984 (c.48), s.1(5) and (7) and Scheds. 1 and 8 and the Health and Medicines Act 1988 (c.49), s.13(4)), 105(7) (as amended by the Health Services Act 1980 (c.53), Scheds. 6 and 7 and the Health and Social Services and Social Security Adjudication Act 1983 (c.41), Sched. 9) and 108(1); operative on April 1, 1995; further amend the National Health Service (General Ophthalmic Services) (Scotland) Regulations 1986, to include a definition of disability working allowance and extending the categories of eligibility for free sight tests to people in receipt of disability working allowance.

[S.I. 1986 No. 965 amended.]

NATIONAL HEALTH SERVICE (OPTICAL CHARGES AND PAYMENTS) (SCOTLAND) AMENDMENT REGULATIONS 1995 (No. 1) [65p], made under the National Health Service (Scotland) Act 1978 (c.29), ss.70(1) (as amended by the Health and Medicines Act (c.49), Sched. 3) 105(7) (as amended by the Health Services Act 1980 (c.53) Scheds. 6 and 7 and the Health and Social Services and Social Security Adjudications Act 1983 (c.41), Sched. 9) and 108(1) and Sched. 11, paras. 2 (as amended by the 1988 Act, Sched. 2) and 2A (as inserted by the Health and Social Security Act 1984 (c.48), Sched. 1 and amended by the 1988 Act, s.13(2)(5)); operative on February 1, 1995; amend the National Health Service (Optical Charges and Payments) (Scotland) Regulations 1989 to increase the NHS sight test fee by about 3 per cent to £35·09.

[S.I. 1989 No. 392 amended.]

6150. Optical charges and payments

NATIONAL HEALTH SERVICE (OPTICAL CHARGES AND PAYMENTS) (SCOTLAND) AMENDMENT (No. 3) REGULATIONS 1995 (No.2369) [65p], made under the National Health Service (Scotland) Act 1978 (c.29) s.70(1) (as amended by the Health and Medicines Act 1988 (c.49) Sched. 3), s.105(7) (as amended by the Health Services Act 1980 (c.53) Scheds. 6 and 7 and by the Health and Social Services and Social Security Adjudications Act 1983 (c.41) Sched. 9) and s.108(1); operative on October 1, 1995; further amend S.I. 1989 No. 392 so as to increase the sight test fee at two levels, from £35·09 to £36·65 for home tests and from £13·15 to £13·41 in all other cases.

[S.I. 1989 No. 392 amended.]

6151. Pharmaceutical services

NATIONAL HEALTH SERVICE (PHARMACEUTICAL SERVICES) (SCOTLAND) REGULATIONS 1995 (No. 414) [£6·10], made under the National Health Service (Scotland) Act 1978 (c.29), ss.2(5) (as amended by the National Health Service and Community Care Act 1990 (c.19), Sched. 9), 19 (as amended by the Health Services Act 1980 (c.53), s.7, the Health and Social Services and Social Security Adjudications Act 1983 (c.41), Sched. 7, the Medical Act 1983 (c.54), Sched. 5, and the 1990 Act s.37), 20(1) (as amended by the 1980 Act, Sched. 6), 23(2A) and (4) as inserted and amended by the 1990 Act, s.39(2) and (3) respectively), 24 (as amended by the 1990, s.39(7)), 27 (as amended by the 1980 Act, s.20(2), the National Health Service (Amendment) Act 1986 (c.66), s.3(3) and the 1990 Act, Sched. 9), 28(1) (as amended by the 1986 Act s.3(4)), 28A (as inserted by the Health and Social Security Act 1984 (c.48), s.7(2) and amended by the 1988 Act, s.15) s.105(7) (as amended by the 1980 Act, Sched. 6 and 7 and by the 1983 Act, Sched. 9) 106(a), 108(1), Sched. 1, para. 11(b) and (c) (as amended by the 1990 Act Sched. 5), Sched. 2, para. 3 and Sched. 9, para. 1(3) and the Health and Medicines Act 1988 (c.49), s.8(1)(*a*) and (5); operative on March 31, 1995; consolidate the National Health Service (General Medical and Pharmaceutical Services) (Scotland) Regulations 1974 which relate to pharmaceutical services.

[S.I. 1974 No. 506, 1975 No. 696, 1976 No. 733, 1976 No. 1574, 1978 No. 1762, 1981 No. 56, 1981 No. 965, 1982 No. 1279, 1985 No. 296, 1985 No. 534, 1985 No. 804, 1985 No. 1625, 1985 No. 1713, 1986 No. 303, 1986 No. 925, 1986 No. 1507, 1986 No. 2310, 1987 No. 385, 1987 No. 386, 1987 No. 1382, 1988 No. 1454, 1988 No. 2259, 1989 No. 1883, 1989 No. 1990, 1990 No. 883, 1990 No. 2509, 1991 No. 572, 1991 No. 2241, 1992 No. 191, 1992 No. 2401,

1992 No. 2933, 1993 No. 521, 1993 No. 2449, 1994 No. 884, 1994 No. 2624 and 1995 No. 165 revoked; S.I. 1988 No. 1073 and 1994 No. 3130 partially revoked.]

NEGLIGENCE

6152. Contributory negligence—defenders found liable for breach of common law and statutory duties—effect of subsequent absolvitor on statutory case on apportionment of liability

An equipment test engineer on an oil rig sought damages from the installation managers and operators of the rig after his hand was caught in a winch he was working on. The sheriff found that in failing to provide an assistant for the pursuer the defenders had been in breach of both a common law and a statutory duty, but that the pursuer had also been in breach of common law and statutory duties, and that one third of the responsibility for causing the accident should be apportioned to the defenders. On appeal, the sheriff principal assoilzied the defenders of the statutory case, but did not alter the sheriffs apportionment of responsibility. The defenders appealed, arguing that once the sheriff principal had found that the pursuer's statutory case had failed, he should have reconsidered the apportionment of liability, and in particular, whether the accident had been caused by the sole fault of the pursuer.

Held, that the sheriff had done what the defenders desired, and that where it had been the same state of facts which had led the sheriff to find the defenders in breach of both common law and statutory duties, the fact that on appeal the statutory case was held to have failed had in the circumstances no bearing on the apportionment of liability, this depending on the question whose fault had caused the accident, which was a question of fact for the sheriff; and appeal refused.

OATES v. ATLANTIC DRILLING CO., 1995 S.L.T. 71.

6153. Contributory negligence—liability of chartered surveyors to building society for erroneous valuation of property for mortgage purposes—actings of building society

A building society raised an action against a firm of chartered surveyors, averring that the defenders' valuation of a property on the basis of which the pursuers had agreed to provide a secured loan had been negligent as a result of which the pursuers had sustained loss and damage on the borrowers' default. The defenders argued that the loss was due to the fault of the building society, or at least that there was contributory negligence on the part of the building society by failing to address itself adequately to the financial circumstances of the borrowers.

Held, that (1) the duty of the building society to act prudently in making loans to borrowers did not affect any issue between the lenders and the surveyors instructed to give a mortgage valuation of property; (2) any loss resulting from lending more to the borrowers due to a negligent over-valuation was relevantly laid at the door of the surveyors; and pursuers' preliminary pleas sustained and proof before answer allowed.

LEEDS PERMANENT BUILDING SOCIETY v. WALKER FRASER & STEELE, 1995 S.L.T. (Sh. Ct.) 72.

6154. Crown proceedings—sheriff clerk as servant of Crown. See WOOD v. LORD ADVOCATE, §6386.

Damages. See DAMAGES.

6155. Dangerous substance—inference of negligence—firework at public display exploding prematurely. See McQUEEN v. THE GLASGOW GARDEN FESTIVAL (1988), §6162.

6156. Duty of care—firefighter—whether owed to owner of property

A fire in a chimney was attended to by the fire brigade but restarted after they had left, causing the destruction of the house. In an action against the fire brigade the owners failed on the lack of proof of negligence. It had also been argued on behalf of the fire brigade that considerations of public policy prevented there being any duty of care owed by the brigade towards owners of property, and that in any event the only loss which could be recovered would be loss beyond the loss which would have been sustained had the fire brigade never attended at all. *Opinion*, distinguishing the position of firefighters from that of the police, that firefighters did owe a duty of care as there was a statutory duty imposed on fire authorities to make provision for firefighting purposes; and that damages for breach of the duty extended to all the loss resulting from the negligence. (*East Suffolk Rivers Catchment Board v. Kent* [1941] A.C. 74, considered.)

DUFF v. HIGHLAND AND ISLANDS FIRE BOARD (O.H.), 1995 S.L.T. 1362.

6157. Duty of care—nervous shock—fellow employee

Two employees (R and D) reclaimed against a Lord Ordinary's decision to assoilzie their employer in conjoined actions of damages in respect of nervous shock sustained by R and D as a result of witnessing the death of a colleague, who had been blown off the Forth road bridge. R and the deceased had spent the greater part of their working lives together, both as coopers in a local distillery and as bridge workmen, and often walked to and from work together and went for a drink once a week. D had known the deceased simply as a colleague. R and D argued that, as they were engaged with the deceased on the same task, they were so involved in the accident as to be within the ambit of the employer's duty of care; that they were in an analogous position to a rescuer; and that R and D were not required to establish that they were bound to the deceased by close ties of love and affection.

Held, reclaiming motion refused. The employer did not owe R and D a duty of care simply as employees and there had to exist the requisite relationship of proximity. R and D could not establish that there were such close ties of love and affection between them and the deceased, they had done nothing which could bring them within the category of a rescuer, and it could not be said that they were "involuntary cause of another's injury" (*Alcock v. Chief Constable of South Yorkshire Police* [1992] C.L.Y. 3250). Claims of ordinary bystanders were denied in cases of nervous shock either on the basis that such persons had to be assumed to be possessed of fortitude sufficient to enable them to endure the calamities of life or because defenders could not be expected to compensate the world at large (*McLoughlin v. O'Brian* [1982] C.L.Y. 2153), and while the existence of a relationship between employer and employee did to some extent restrict the number of persons who could claim, they might still be considerable in a substantial undertaking and there was no logical reason for admitting the claim of one bystander who was an employee but not the claim of another who was not. Accordingly the ordinary rule fell to be applied and, as R and D could not bring themselves within one of the recognised categories, their claim had to be rejected.

ROBERTSON v. FORTH ROAD BRIDGE JOINT BOARD, 1996 S.L.T. 263.

6158. Duty of care—sheriff clerk—servant of Crown. See WOOD v. LORD ADVOCATE, §6386.

6159. Duty of care—staff of mental hospital towards suicidal patient

A woman with a history of depressive illness, including a suicide attempt, was admitted to a psychiatric hospital for treatment. She was being kept under "close observation" but not under "special observation". Special observation involved the necessity for visual contact by staff at close range at all times. Close observation required that staff knew at all times where the patient was. The patient was seen to be going towards the toilets and showers and was assumed to be going to the toilets, although no one accompanied here there. On checking shortly afterwards, a nurse found her hanging from a shower fitment. She was rescued and resuscitated but had suffered severe brain damage as a result of hypoxia. Her curator sought damages for her injuries and argued that the nursing staff were at fault for not having known, at all times, where the patient was.

Held, that, the nurse not having known but only assumed where the patient was, negligence was established; and decree pronounced in favour of the pursuer.

G.'s CURATOR BONIS v. GRAMPIAN HEALTH BOARD (O.H.), 1995 S.L.T. 652.

See also §5851.

6159a. Duty of care—staff of mental hospital towards suicidal patient

Held, that a health authority was liable in damages to a patient who attempted suicide while under a close observation regime designed to prevent her attempting suicide, where the attempt had occurred when as a result of the regime breaking down.

HAY v. GRAMPIAN HEALTH BOARD, *The Scotsman*, December 21, 1994.

Factories. See HEALTH AND SAFETY AT WORK.

6160. Highway—bus driver opening door while vehicle in motion

M sought damages in respect of injuries sustained while attempting to board a bus operated by G. M averred that he had seen a bus pulling away from a bus stop; that he had run after it, signalling that he wished to catch it; that the driver (D) had opened the doors while the bus was still moving at a slow rate; that, as he had attempted to board, M had slipped and his foot had been injured by the bus's rear wheel; and that D had been negligent in inviting M to board the bus. G sought dismissal, arguing that merely to open the doors did not constitute an invitation to M to board the bus while it was still moving (*Fraser v. W. Alexander Northern* [1964] C.L.Y. 4247).

Held, proof before answer allowed. The averment that the bus did not accelerate but continued moving slowly, taken together with the opening of the doors, could indicate that D was giving M the opportunity to enter the bus, which was enough to raise a question of negligence and it could not be said M's action was bound to fail (*Fraser*, distinguished).

McCORRISTON v. GRAMPIAN REGIONAL COUNCIL (O.H.), 1995 S.C.L.R. 170.

6161. Highway—collision with pedestrian—driver under attack

M, curator bonis of S, sued W after S was injured and suffered brain injuries and was permanently incapacitated. W disputed liability. W had driven in to an unfamiliar area whilst with friends and was attacked by a number of youths throwing missiles and pelting W's car with stones, wood and bricks. The car bodywork was damaged and the windscreen damaged. W was in fear of being dragged from his car and drove zigzag to avoid the missiles. S had been standing on the road to W's left and was poised to strike W's windscreen with a piece of wood. W was unable, because of the zigzagging, to avoid hitting S. W left the scene but reported the incident. W was initially locked up and charged with attempted murder but after investigation the police were satisfied that the accident was not W's fault. M led evidence that W had gone to the area looking for trouble and had deliberately driven at S.

Held, absolvitor granted. M's evidence was rejected. All of W's difficulties arose from the concerted attack on him. It should have been obvious to S that W was driving under stress and not fully in control, and S should not have been standing on the road. S had disregarded his own safety and was the author of his own misfortune.

GILMOUR'S C.B. v. WYNN, *The Times*, September 28, 1995.

Limitation of actions. See LIMITATION OF ACTIONS.

6162. *Res ipsa loquitur*—firework at public display exploding prematurely

A spectator at a firework display was injured when she was struck by part of a steel launching tube which fragmented when a firework exploded inside it. In an action of damages she raised, which was in the end only insisted in against the company responsible for managing the display, it was agreed that the explosion had been caused by a defect within the firework which had caused it to explode on the ground rather than while airborne. It was further agreed that the defect had either been a flaw in, or absence of, the fuse to the lifting device within the firework, or a flaw in, or absence of, the delay device which ought to have prevented the explosion of the main bursting charge before activation of the lifting device. The pursuer sought to establish liability on three grounds: first, that the company were occupiers of the display area and as such were responsible for the consequences of detonation of dangerous articles such as fireworks in that area; secondly, that fault on the part of the company was established by the doctrine of *res ipsa loquitur*, the explosion of the firework under the management of the company being the *res* demonstrating fault; and, thirdly, that the firework was inherently dangerous and that the company had failed to take reasonable care to check its safety and control its detonation.

Held, that to succeed on the basis of any of her grounds of argument the pursuer required to establish fault on the part of the company because (1) as respects the first ground, the law of Scotland did not recognise absolute liability for such an event (*R.H.M. Bakeries (Scotland) v. Strathclyde Regional Council* [1985] C.L.Y. 4458 followed; dictum by Lord Patrick in *Western Silver Fox Ranch v. Ross and Cromarty County Council*, 1940 S.L.T. 144, not applied); (2) as respects the second ground, the defect was known to be a latent defect in the firework and accordingly the fact of the explosion was not indicative of a fault or omission on the part of the company: rather it was indicative of fault by the manufacturer (*Devine v. Colvilles* [1969] C.L.Y. 4136, distinguished); and (3) as respects the third ground, the immediately foregoing reasons applied and there was no evidence that any precautions of the sort suggested on behalf of the pursuer were normal practice or obviously required; and defenders assoilzied.

McQUEEN v. THE GLASGOW GARDEN FESTIVAL (1988) (O.H.), 1995 S.L.T. 211.

6163. Solicitor—failure to carry out instructions—scope of instructions given

A construction company engaged in works on an industrial estate sought funding to complete the project when the employers indicated that they had insufficient funds to make payment and required to postpone payment. The company's bankers, who held a floating charge over its assets, declined to advance further sums. The company applied to a foreign bank for a loan and it agreed to lend. The company's own solicitors were instructed by fax by the bank to act on its behalf and to draw up an assignation of sums due under the construction contract by the employers to the company. An assignation was duly drawn up and intimated, giving the bank the full benefit of all sums due under the building contract, and the bank advanced the money. By that time various sums had been certified under the building contract as due to the company. Within a few days of execution of the assignation the company entered into a minute of agreement with the employers agreeing further deferral of payments. Later that year the company went into receivership. The bank sought payment from the employers in terms of the assignation and raised an action against them in England. The employers argued that they were entitled to deduct from the sums due losses incurred due to bad workmanship of the company and delay resulting from its withdrawal from the contract. The bank then raised an action of damages against the solicitors, claiming that its loss and damage was due to the solicitors' breach of their implied duty of care, that they had failed to ensure that the sums due would be paid without deduction, and that had the bank been properly advised it would not have advanced the company the moneys it had on the security given. After sundry procedure the solicitors challenged the relevancy of the bank's case at procedure roll. Proof before answer was allowed by the Lord Ordinary and the solicitors reclaimed. It was argued on their behalf that the instructions given were simply to complete the mechanics of a loan the terms of which had already been agreed; that the bank's pleadings contained no averment of a contractual term involving a duty to advise on the value of the security; that there was no averment as to how a security exempt from claims of retention or set off could have been obtained as there were risks attached to any form of security; that averments alleging a conflict of interest ought to be deleted, being irrelevant to the bank's case which was based on breach of contract; and that, given that it appeared that all relevant matters were within the knowledge of all parties including the bank, there was no duty incumbent upon the solicitors to advise on matters already within the bank's knowledge.

Held, that (1) if a solicitor acting for a potential lender was in possession of information of which the potential lender was ignorant, which tended to show that the proposed security was worth significantly less than the lender seemed to believe, the solicitor might well require to advise the lender of the risk prior to acting upon instructions, and the duty was no less incumbent on the solicitor by virtue of the fact that he was already acting for the borrower; (2) while it was not difficult to read the bank's pleadings as indicating that all parties were aware of all the material facts bearing upon the value of the security, including the potential of rights of retention, which were commonplace in building contracts, its pleadings could not be read as excluding a case that the bank's knowledge was imperfect in relation to material details of which the solicitors were aware, and the court would be reluctant to reach a conclusion solely on an over critical reading of the bank's averments, particularly as Scots law was a foreign law to it; and (3) applying the test of relevancy that an action would not be dismissed as irrelevant unless it had necessarily to fail even if all the pursuer's averments were proved, the case should proceed to proof before answer; and reclaiming motion refused. (*Jamieson v. Jamieson* [1952] C.L.Y. 4378, applied.)

BANK OF EAST ASIA v. SHEPHERD & WEDDERBURN, W.S., 1995 S.L.T. 1074.

NUISANCE

6164. *Culpa*—whether equivalent to negligence

K, the owners and tenants of various flats within a tenement, sought damages from G, the tenants of the basement flat, and H, consulting engineers engaged by G, in respect of damage sustained to the upper flats on the grounds of nuisance. K averred that H had been engaged by G to advise on, design a scheme for, and direct and supervise the removal of a section of a wall in G's flat which was a load-bearing wall and which contributed to the support of the spine wall immediately above it in each of the upper flats, and that H knew or ought to have known that the removal of a section of the wall was likely to cause cracking and settlement of the spine wall and would cause damage to K's flats. H argued that K had failed to set out the breaches of duties of care incumbent on H which gave rise to the nuisance, which had to be the same as those in a case of negligence against a professional person.

Held, proof before answer allowed. (1) Although *R.H.M. Bakeries (Scotland) v. Strathclyde Regional Council* [1985] C.L.Y. 4458 had decided that the law of nuisance was based on *culpa*, this was not to be equiparated with negligence as that would overlook the fact that the modern law of nuisance was derived from the civil law maxim *sic utere tuo ut alienum non laedas*, subject to the qualification that the only injury a neighbouring occupier could complain of was one which was *plus quam tolerabile* (*Lord Advocate v. Reo Stakis Organisation* [1982] C.L.Y. 4075 and that the law was to be viewed from the standpoint of the victim rather than the alleged offender (*Watt v. Jamieson* [1954] C.L.Y. 4051). *Culpa* did not require a deliberate act or negligence but some form of personal responsibility (*Sedleigh-Denfield v. O'Callaghan* [1940] A.C. 880) and it was sufficient for K to have averred that, while in control of the premises, H had used the premises in a way in which they knew or ought to have known was likely to result in more than minimal damage to K's premises.

KENNEDY v. GLENBELLE (O.H.), *The Scotsman*, February 15, 1995.

6165. Title and interest to sue—landlord. See DUNDEE DISTRICT COUNCIL (CITY OF) v. COOK, §6355.

PARENT AND CHILD

Abduction. See CHILDREN AND YOUNG PERSONS.

Access. See CHILDREN AND YOUNG PERSONS.

Adoption. See CHILDREN AND YOUNG PERSONS.

Aliment. See CHILDREN AND YOUNG PERSONS.

Children's learnings. See CHILDREN AND YOUNG PERSONS.

Custody. See CHILDREN AND YOUNG PERSONS.

Parental rights. See CHILDREN AND YOUNG PERSONS.

Paternity, evidence of. See CHILDREN AND YOUNG PERSONS.

PARLIAMENT

Private legislation. See PRIVATE LEGISLATION PROCEDURE.

PARTNERSHIP

6166. Constitution—whether partnership or joint venture

Although there was no one provision or feature which was absolutely necessary for the existence of a partnership or joint venture, a sharing of profits and losses and mutual agency were typical of partnerships and *delectus personae* might be a further feature. In the present case, none of these features existed, which was irreconcilable with the existence of a joint venture or partnership. There was no *delectus personae* since consent to the assignation of an interest in the lease could not be reasonably refused. There was no sharing of profits or losses and no trace of mutual agency. The provision for sharing the fruits of the development was a payment which represented a return on their capital investment. There was no specific feature in any of the agreements which pointed to the existence of a partnership, and a common economic interest itself could not be regarded as a sufficient indication of partnership or joint venture as some degree of common interest was involved in any commercial contractual venture. There was nothing in the documents which inferred the existence of a partnership in order to make the scheme capable of operating effectively, and to infer the existence of a joint venture in every commercial lease would in effect place a limitation upon the operation of an irritancy in all such leases.

DOLLAR LAND (CUMBERNAULD) v. C.I.N. PROPERTIES (O.H.), 1996 S.L.T. 186.

6167. Judicial factor—personal liability. See SCOTTISH BREWERS v. J. DOUGLAS PEARSON & CO., §6465.

6168. Property—title to grant disposition. See CAMERON v. LIGHTHEART, §5993.

PEERAGES AND DIGNITIES

6169. Lyon Court and office—fees

LYON COURT AND OFFICE FEES (VARIATION) ORDER 1995 (No. 132) [£1·10], made under the Public Expenditure and Receipts Act 1968 (c.14) s.5; operative on April 1, 1995; varies certain fees for specified matters listed in Sched. B to the Lyon King of Arms Act 1867, which are exclusive of stamp duty when stamp duty is exigible.

[S.I. 1994 No. 201 revoked.]

PENSIONS AND SUPERANNUATION

6170. Local Government. See LOCAL GOVERNMENT, §6126.

6171. Local government

LOCAL GOVERNMENT (SUPERANNUATION AND COMPENSATION FOR PREMATURE RETIREMENT) (SCOTLAND) AMENDMENT REGULATIONS 1995 (No. 750) [£1·10], made under the Superannuation Act 1972 (c.11), ss.7 (as extended by the Pensions (Increase) Act 1974 (c.9), s.2(2)) and 24; operative on April 6, 1995; extend the scope of Local Government (Compensation for Premature Retirement) (Scotland) Regulations 1979 and the Local Government Superannuation (Scotland) Regulations 1987, so that they will apply to staff of new councils, new water and sewerage authorities and the Scottish Children's

Reporter Administration, which are all constituted under the Local Government etc. (Scotland) Act 1994.

[S.I. 1979 No. 785 and 1987 No. 1850 amended.]

LOCAL GOVERNMENT SUPERANNUATION (SCOTLAND) AMENDMENT REGULATIONS 1995 (No. 214) [£1·10], made under the Superannuation Act 1972 (c.11), s.7 (as extended by the Pensions (Increase) Act 1974 (c.9), s.2(2)); operative on March 1, 1995; amend reg. P6 of the Local Government Superannuation (Scotland) Regulations 1987 in relation to powers of investment conferred on local authorities.

[S.I. 1987 No. 1850 amended.]

6172. National Health Service

NATIONAL HEALTH SERVICE SUPERANNUATION SCHEME (SCOTLAND) REGULATIONS 1995 (No. 365) [£8·70], made under the Superannuation Act 1972 (c.11), ss.10 (as amended by the National Health Service (Scotland) Act 1972 (c.58), Sched. 7 and inserted by the Pensions (Miscellaneous Provisions) Act 1990 (c.7), ss.4(2), 8(5) and 10), and 12 (as inserted by the 1990 Act ss.4(2), 8(5) and 10) and Sched. 3; operative on April 1, 1995; consolidate, with amendments, the National Health Service (Superannuation) (Scotland) Regulations 1980–1992 which provide for the superannuation of persons engaged in the National Health Service in Scotland.

[S.I. 1980 No. 1177, 1981 No. 1680, 1983 No. 272, 1988 No. 1956, 1989 No. 807, 1989 No. 1749 and 1990 No. 382 revoked; S.I. 1992 No. 3046 partially revoked.]

6173. Teachers

TEACHERS' SUPERANNUATION (ADDITIONAL VOLUNTARY CONTRIBUTIONS) (SCOTLAND) REGULATIONS 1995 (No. 2814) [£3·70], made under the Superannuation Act 1972 (c.11), ss.9 (as amended by the Pensions (Miscellaneous Provisions) Act 1990 (c.7), ss.4(1), 8(3) and (4) and 1), and 12 (as amended by the said 1972 Act, s.10) and Sched. 3; operative December 1, 1995, and having effect retrospectively, from February 15, 1994; revoke and re-enact the Teaching Superannuation (Additional Voluntary Contributions) (Scotland) Regulations 1992 with amendments providing for the making of elections of various kinds.

[S.I. 1992 No. 2649 revoked.]

TEACHERS' SUPERANNUATION (SCOTLAND) AMENDMENT REGULATIONS 1995 (No. 1670) [£1·10], made under the Superannuation Act 1972 (c.11), ss.9 (as amended by ss.4(1), 8(3) and (4) and 11 of the Pensions (Miscellaneous Provisions) Act 1990 (c.7) and 12 (as amended by the 1990 Act, s.10); operative on July 31, 1995; amend the Teachers' Superannuation (Scotland) Regulations 1992, to make changes regarding, *inter alia*, eligibility for compensation for redundancy or premature retirement on reorganisation; these regulations are retrospective in their effect in terms of the Superannuation Act 1972, s.12(1).

[S.I. 1992 No. 280 amended.]

POLICE

6174. Common police services

COMMON POLICE SERVICES (SCOTLAND) ORDER 1995 (No. 707) [£1·10], made under the Police (Scotland) Act 1967 (c.77), s.36 (as substituted by the Police and Magistrates' Courts Act 1994 (c.29), s.59), (3) and (6); operative on April 1, 1995; provides for the recovery of 50 per cent of the expenses incurred by the Secretary of State in providing facilities and services under the Police (Scotland) Act 1967.

POLICE (COMMON POLICE SERVICES) (SCOTLAND) REVOCATION ORDER 1995 (No. 706) [65p], made under the Police (Scotland) Act 1967 (c.77), ss.36(5) and 48(3); operative on April 1, 1995; revokes the Police (Common Police Services) (Scotland) Order 1993.

[S.I. 1993 No. 720 revoked.]

6175. Discipline

POLICE (DISCIPLINE) (MISCELLANEOUS AMENDMENTS) (SCOTLAND) REGULATIONS 1995 (No. 647) [£1·10], made under the Police (Scotland) Act 1967 (c.77), s.26 (as amended by the Police Negotiating Board Act 1980 (c.10), s.2(4), the Police and Criminal Evidence Act 1984 (c.60), s.111(1) and Sched. 6, and the Police and Magistrates' Courts Act 1994 (c.29), ss.52(3) and 53(1)); operative on April 1, 1995; further amend the Police (Discipline) (Scotland) Regulations 1967 in relation to discipline of police constables.

[S.I. 1967 No. 1021 and 1990 No. 1017 amended.]

6176. Police areas

CENTRAL SCOTLAND COMBINED POLICE AREA AMALGAMATION SCHEME AMENDMENT ORDER 1995 (No. 2638) [£1·55], made under the Police (Scotland) Act 1967 (c.77), s.21B (inserted by the Local Government etc. (Scotland) Act 1994 (c.39), s.34); operative on October 31, 1995; amalgamates the police areas for the local government areas of Stirling, Clackmannanshire and Falkirk into the combined area to be known as Central Scotland, and the existing police force for the existing Central Scotland area will continue and be the police force for the new area; the scheme provides for the constitution of a new joint police board, its members and officers and its procedure, powers and duties; providing that the said scheme shall have effect from April 1, 1996, but that in relation to the board's constitution and the carrying out of necessary functions to bring the scheme into operation, the scheme shall have effect from the operative date of the order, October 31, 1995.

GRAMPIAN COMBINED POLICE AREA AMALGAMATION SCHEME AMENDMENT ORDER 1995 (No. 2639) [£1·55], made under the Police (Scotland) Act 1967 (c.77), s.21B (inserted by the Local Government etc. (Scotland) Act 1994 (c.39), s.34); operative on October 31, 1995; amalgamates the police areas for the local government areas of Aberdeenshire, Moray and Aberdeen City into the combined area to be known as Grampian, and the existing police force for the existing Grampian area will continue and be the police force for the new area; the scheme provides for the constitution of a new joint police board, its members and officers and its procedure, powers and duties; providing that the said scheme shall have effect from April 1, 1996, but that in relation to the board's constitution and the carrying out of necessary functions to bring the scheme into operation, the scheme shall have effect from the operative date of the order, October 31, 1995.

LOTHIAN AND BORDERS COMBINED POLICE AREA AMALGAMATION SCHEME AMENDMENT ORDER 1995 (No. 2640) [£1·55], made under the Police (Scotland) Act 1967 (c.77), s.21B (inserted by the Local Government etc. (Scotland) Act 1994 (c.39), s.34); operative on October 31, 1995; amalgamates the police areas for the local government areas of City of Edinburgh, East Lothian, Midlothian, West Lothian and Scottish Borders into the combined area to be known as Lothian and Borders, and the existing police force for the existing Lothian and Borders area will continue and be the police force for the new area; the scheme provides for the constitution of a new joint police board, its members and officers and its procedure, powers and duties; providing that the said scheme shall have effect from April 1, 1996, but that in relation to the board's constitution and the carrying out of necessary functions to bring the scheme into operation, the scheme shall have effect from the operative date of the order, October 31, 1995.

NORTHERN COMBINED POLICE AREA AMALGAMATION SCHEME AMENDMENT ORDER 1995 (No. 2641) [£1·55], made under the Police (Scotland) Act 1967 (c.77), s.21B (inserted by the Local Government etc. (Scotland) Act 1994 (c.39), s.34); operative on October 31, 1995; amalgamates the police areas for the local government areas of Highland, Western Isles, Orkney Islands and Shetland Islands into the combined area to be known as Northern, and the existing police force for the existing Northern area will continue and be the police force for the new area; the scheme provides for the constitution of a new joint police board, its members and officers and its procedure, powers and duties; providing that the said scheme shall have effect from April 1, 1996, but that in relation to the board's constitution and the carrying out of necessary functions to bring the scheme into operation, the scheme shall have effect from the operative date of the order, October 31, 1995.

STRATHCLYDE COMBINED POLICE AREA AMALGAMATION SCHEME AMENDMENT ORDER 1995 (No. 2642) [£1·55], made under the Police (Scotland) Act 1967 (c.77), s.21B (inserted by the Local Government etc. (Scotland) Act 1994 (c.39), s.34); operative on October 31, 1995; amalgamates the police areas for the local government areas of Argyll and Bute, Dumbarton and Clydebank, City of Glasgow, East Dunbartonshire, Inverclyde, North Lanarkshire, South Lanarkshire, Renfrewshire, East Renfrewshire, East Ayrshire, North Ayrshire and South Ayrshire into the combined area to be known as Strathclyde, and the existing police force for the existing Strathclyde area will continue and be the police force for the new area; the scheme provides for the constitution of a new joint police board, its members and officers and its procedure, powers and duties; providing that the said scheme shall have effect from April 1, 1996, but that in relation to the board's constitution and the carrying out of necessary functions to bring the scheme into operation, the scheme shall have effect from the operative date of the order, October 31, 1995.

TAYSIDE COMBINED POLICE AREA AMALGAMATION SCHEME AMENDMENT ORDER 1995 (No. 2643) [£1·55], made under the Police (Scotland) Act 1967 (c.77), s.21B (inserted by the Local Government etc. (Scotland) Act 1994 (c.39), s.34); operative on October 31, 1995; amalgamates the police areas for the local government areas of Perthshire and Kinross, Angus and Dundee City into the combined area to be known as Tayside, and the existing police force for the existing Tayside area will continue and be the police force for the new area; the scheme provides for the constitution of a new joint police board, its members and officers and its procedure, powers and duties; providing that the said scheme shall have effect from April 1, 1996, but that in relation to the board's constitution and the carrying out of necessary functions to bring the scheme into operation, the scheme shall have effect from the operative date of the order, October 31, 1995.

6177. Police cadets

POLICE CADETS (SCOTLAND) AMENDMENT REGULATIONS 1995 (No. 1057) [65p], made under the Police (Scotland) Act 1967 (c.77), s.27 (as amended by the Police and Criminal Evidence Act 1984 (c.60), s.111(2)); operative on May 5, 1995; amend the Police Cadets (Scotland) Regulations 1968 to increase the pay of police cadets retrospectively and to increase the charges payable by cadets for board and lodging provided by police authorities.

[S.I. 1994 No. 2096 revoked.]

6178. Police regulations

POLICE (SCOTLAND) AMENDMENT REGULATIONS 1995 (No. 137) [£1·95], made under the Police (Scotland) Act 1967 (c.77), s.26 (as amended by the Police Negotiating Board Act 1980 (c.10), s.2(4), the Police and Criminal Evidence Act 1984 (c.60), s.111 and Sched. 6, and the Police and Magistrates'

Courts Act 1994 (c.29), ss.52(3) and 53(1)) and the Police Negotiating Board Act 1980 (c.10), s.2(1); operative on February 27, 1995 but with effect in part from September 1, 1994; further amend the Police (Scotland) Regulations 1976 by introducing new pay arrangements for constables of police forces in Scotland.

[S.I. 1976 No. 1073 amended; S.I. 1979 No. 767 revoked; S.I. 1977 No. 2008, 1978 No. 1170, 1979 No. 1263, 1980 No. 1050, 1981 No. 67 and 1994 No. 2095 partially revoked.]

POLICE (SCOTLAND) AMENDMENT (No. 2) REGULATIONS 1995 (No. 596) [£1·95], made under the Police (Scotland) Act 1967 (c.77), s.26 (as amended by the Police Negotiating Board Act 1980 (c.10), s.2(4), the Police and Criminal Evidence Act 1984 (c.60), s.111 and Sched. 6, and the Police and Magistrates' Courts Act 1994 (c.29), ss.52(3) and 53(1)); operative (except reg. 10) on April 1, 1995, and (reg. 10) April 13, 1995; amend the Police (Scotland) Regulations 1976 by replacing the qualifications for appointment as chief constable, stipulating a fixed term appointment for the ranks of chief and assistant chief constable and that any vacancy in such a rank must be advertised and making other amendments, some in consequence, of the Police and Magistrates' Courts Act 1994.

[S.I. 1976 No. 1073 amended.]

POLICE (SCOTLAND) AMENDMENT (NO. 3) REGULATIONS 1995 (No. 2131) [£1·55], made under the Police (Scotland) Act 1967 (c.77) s.26; operative on September 7, 1995; amend the Police (Scotland) Regulations 1976, make minor amendments to shifts for constables below the rank of superintendent and to holidays for inspectors, increase certain allowances and make provision for pay of chief constables and assistant chief constables, retrospectively.

[S.I. 1976 No. 1073 amended; S.I. 1994 No. 2095 reg. 5(c) revoked.]

PRACTICE (CIVIL)

6179. Appeals—House of Lords, to—leave to appeal—argument not presented to Inner House

[Tribunals and Inquiries Act 1992 (c.53), s.11(7)(d).]

Held, on G's motion for leave under s.11(7)(d) to appeal to the House of Lords against the decision that he was not entitled to buy his public sector house, that leave should be refused since the decision had turned substantially if not entirely on issues of fact rather than of law; and although G referred to *Hughes v. Greenwich London Borough Council* [1993] C.L.Y. 2110, which had not been cited at the previous hearing, arguing that it appeared to be inconsistent with *De Fontenay v. Strathclyde Regional Council* [1990] C.L.Y. 5382, which the court had applied, it was inappropriate to enable G to present to the House arguments for which they had not hitherto contended and on which the House would not have the benefit of the opinion of the Court of Session. *Observed*, that it was highly unsatisfactory that the court had not been given the opportunity to consider these matters properly when it heard the appeal.

STRATHCLYDE REGIONAL COUNCIL v. GALLAGHER, 1995 S.L.T. 747.

6180. Appeals—House of Lords, to—leave to appeal—whether appropriate to grant

[Court of Session Act 1988 (c.36), s.40(1)(b).]

The BBC proposed to broadcast a television interview with the Prime Minister three days before local government elections. Two candidates standing in the elections brought an action seeking interdict against their doing so, arguing that the broadcast would be in breach of the duty, imposed on the defenders by their licence, to treat controversial subjects with due impartiality. On the day of the proposed broadcast, the Lord Ordinary granted interim interdict prohibiting it from being made before the close of the poll. A reclaiming motion by the defenders was heard on the same evening, shortly before the interview was due to be broadcast. They argued that the pursuers had not made out a prima facie case of title and interest to sue. The Inner House held that the pursuers had such a prima facie case, and refused the reclaiming motion. The following day, the defenders sought leave to appeal to the House of Lords.

Held, that (1) a question of law could not be definitively resolved at the interlocutory stage of proceedings; (2) that was particularly true in the present case, where time did not permit full arguments and the *de quo* for the House of Lords would merely be whether the Inner House had reached a tenable view of the matter; (3) as the defenders were unable to identify what it was that made it a matter of urgency that the programme be broadcast, or the case was not one of extreme urgency and importance and accordingly the necessary steps for prosecuting and giving effect to an appeal to the House of Lords could not be completed before the eve of the elections; and (4) that, although the defenders had raised an important and unresolved question of law, the foregoing considerations outweighed any advantage which the defenders were likely to achieve by showing the programme a day earlier than they could lawfully do in terms of the interim interdict; and motion for leave to appeal refused.

HOUSTON v. BRITISH BROADCASTING CORPORATION, 1995 S.L.T. 1305.

6181. Appeals—motion for early disposal of appeal—form of motion

[Rules of the Court of Session 1994 (S.I. 1994 No. 1443), rr. 38.13 and 40.11.]

Pursuers appealing against an interlocutor of the sheriff enrolled in the single bills a motion in terms of r. 40.11 seeking early disposal of the appeal in terms of that rule. *Observed*, that (1) where such a motion has been enrolled, the Keeper of the Rolls is required to put the cause out in the single bills before a division of the Inner House on the earliest available day and to have given written intimation of the diet to each party; (2) when a motion for early disposal comes before the Inner House, if the court decides to grant the motion, it may determine the appeal there and then on the single bills, or it may arrange with the Keeper of the Rolls for the case to be put out for hearing at an early date; and (3) if a party who seeks early disposal of an appeal wishes to invite the court to determine the appeal on the single bills, this intention should be made clear in the motion which is enrolled by wording the motion as "for early disposal of the appeal and for its determination in terms of r. 40.11", and that the same course would be appropriate where a motion is enrolled for early disposal of a reclaiming motion in terms of r. 38.13.

WINTER (DAVID) & SON v. GEORGE CRAIG & SONS, 1995 S.L.T. 1331.

6182. Appeals—sheriff court, from—motion for early disposal of appeal—appropriate form of motion. See WINTER (DAVID) & SONS v. GEORGE CRAIG & SONS, §6363.

6183. Appeals—sheriff court, from—without leave—competency

[Debtors (Scotland) Act 1987 (c.18), s.103(1); Rules of the Court of Session 1984, r. 40.2.]

Held, where the sheriff had granted warrant to sell poinded goods despite objection by the person in possession of them and had refused to grant leave to appeal, that a subsequent application to the Court of Session for leave to appeal in terms of r. 40.2(2) was incompetent as the sheriff's decision to refuse leave was final.

FROST v. BULMAN, 1995 S.C.L.R. 579.

6184. Arrestment—on dependence—financial provision on divorce. See MATHESON v. MATHESON, §6193.

6185. Arrestment—on dependence—recall—whether claim contingent. See RIPPIN GROUP v. I.T.P. INTERPIPE SA, §6195.

6186. Commission and diligence—evidence sought for proceedings in England—whether order premature

[Administration of Justice (Scotland) Act 1972 (c.51), s.1; Civil Jurisdiction and Judgments Act 1982 (c.27), s.28.]

Section 1 of the Administration of Justice (Scotland) Act 1972 empowers the court to order the inspection, photographing, preservation, custody and detention of documents and other property which appear to the court to be property as to which any question may relevantly arise in any existing civil proceedings before that court or in civil proceedings which are likely to be brought. By s.28 of the Civil Jurisdiction and Judgments Act 1982, s.1 is applied to cases in which proceedings have been brought or are likely to be brought in *inter alia* England and Wales. The proprietors of two European patents commenced proceedings in England against a company which they alleged was infringing the patents at their place of business in Scotland. The English proceedings were governed by Order 104, r.5(2) of the Rule of the Supreme Court in accordance with which certain detailed particulars relating to the alleged infringements required to be specified in the pleadings. In order to comply fully with this requirement, the proprietors petitioned the Court of Session for an order for the recovery and inspection of certain documents and other property in the hands of the respondents or anyone on their behalf relating to the industrial processes used by them. It was not disputed that it was competent for the Lord Ordinary to grant such an order and parties had agreed the terms of the proposed order. The question was whether, in the exercise of his discretion, an order for recovery of documents was justified. On December 9, 1994 he issued an opinion in which he found in principle that an order was justified and on December 16 he made an order in the agreed terms. The respondents reclaimed and argued *inter alia* that the Lord Ordinary had left out of account the potential for the issues between the parties to be narrowed by the process of admissions in the English proceedings, which would have identified the precise points in dispute to which discovery would thereafter be directed. Accordingly, the Lord Ordinary should have taken the view that at the time of the hearing there was no basis for making any order for recovery of documents. The petitioners argued that if the petition were dismissed they would suffer injustice in that until the stage of normal discovery in the English proceedings had been reached they would not be able to plead their case properly.

Held, that (1) it was open to the Lord Ordinary to hold that all that the petitioners could do in the current state of their knowledge was to serve pleadings which reflected the letter of r.5(2) without satisfying its spirit: on the evidence and decisions which were relied upon by the parties it was certainly debatable whether the English court would have refused to make an order for early discovery to enable a fully adequate statement of claim and particulars of infringement to be prepared and served, and in the circumstances he had not exercised his discretion in a manner which justified interference with it, whether in relation to the principle that an order should be granted or to the granting of the order in the terms which were agreed; (2) notwithstanding the service of further pleadings between December 16 and the date of the hearing of the reclaiming motion it was still correct to say that unless and until the petitioners obtained the recovery sought, they were unable to give adequate definition of their case to satisfy the spirit of r.5(2); and reclaiming motion refused and interlocutor of the Lord Ordinary adhered to subject to the condition that the court be satisfied that, so far as practicable, suitable arrangements had been made between the parties as to the persons to whom and the purposes for which the documents sought to be recovered were to be made available. *Opinion* (*per* the Lord President (Hope) and Lord Cullen that (1) there was a distinction between cases where the party against whom an order under s.28 was sought was the same party as that against whom the proceedings in the other jurisdiction had been brought, and cases where proceedings had not yet been brought or the party was a stranger to those proceedings. Where the party was the same, the Scottish court should be especially careful not to be drawn into a situation where it was persuaded to grant a discretionary remedy which the other court, possessed of a similar power, would not provide in the same circumstances; and (2) where a party to proceedings in another country claimed that an order should be made under s.28 of the 1982 Act to enable that party to satisfy a rule which applied in those proceedings, it was plain that for the purposes of deciding whether the order was reasonably necessary, it was the rules and practice of that other country and not those of Scotland to which the court required to direct its attention.

UNION CARBIDE CORPORATION v. B.P. CHEMICALS, 1995 S.L.T. 972.

6187. Counterclaim—division and sale—competency. See JOHNSTON v. ROBSON, §5987.

6188. Court of Session—practice note

Early Disposal of Reclaiming Motions and Appeals

1. Where a motion for early disposal under R.C.S. 1994, 38.13 or 40.11 is appropriate, the rule is available for the purpose of obtaining (a) an order for an early date for the hearing of the reclaiming motion or appeal on the Summar Roll or (b) determination of the reclaiming motion or appeal in the Single Bills.

2. Where the party seeking early disposal wishes to obtain an order for an early date for the hearing of the reclaiming motion or appeal on the Summar Roll, he should make this clear in his motion by enrolling for early disposal of the reclaiming motion or appeal *and* for an order for an early date for the hearing on the Summar Roll.

3. Where the party seeking early disposal wishes to have the cause determined in the Single Bills, he should make this clear in his motion by enrolling for early disposal of the reclaiming motion or appeal *and* for its determination in the Single Bills.

4. A motion under paragraph 2 or 3 will be starred and will require the appearance of counsel or other person having a right of audience. The court will wish to know parties' estimate of the duration of the hearing to determine the reclaiming motion or appeal, as the case may be.

(No. 1 of 1995: January 19, 1995.)

6189. Court of Session—practice note

Court of Session etc. Fees Amendment Order 1994

The Court of Session Etc. Fees Amendment Order 1994 which comes into effect on February 1, 1995 introduces at items B14, B15, B16, B17, B18, C16, C17, C18 and C19, fees in respect of certain "hearings".

Solicitors who currently hold a Supreme Courts' account will have the fees invoiced to them at the end of the hearing under the existing procedure for these accounts.

For solicitors who do not have a Supreme Courts' account, an account will be opened in their name for the purposes of levying hearing fees. They will be invoiced each month for the fees incurred in all actions where a hearing has taken place during the preceding month. Payment will be required within 14 days of receipt of the invoice.

In order that solicitors can monitor the fee which is charged, a copy of the Court calculation will be transmitted to solicitors at the conclusion of each hearing along with the requisite debit slip when the fee is debited to their account.

Party litigants who incur a fee for a hearing will require to pay the appropriate fee to the Clerk of Court, in the case of a hearing of up to one day's duration, at the end of the hearing. In the case of hearings lasting more than one day they will require to pay the fee at the end of each day of the hearing. The exact amount payable should be ascertained from the Clerk of Court. Details of the appropriate fees can be obtained from the Office of Court.

(No. 2 of 1995: January 26, 1995.)

6190. Court of Session—practice note

Applications for Additional Fee Remitted to the Auditor

Where an application for an additional fee has been remitted to the auditor in terms of R.C.S. 1994, 42.14(2)(b), there shall be lodged with the account of expenses a full statement of reasons in support of the particular factors which are considered to justify the allowance of an additional fee.

A copy of the statement must accompany the intimation copy of account of expenses under R.C.S. 1994, 42.1(2)(b).

(No. 3 of 1995: February 23, 1995.)

Criminal causes. See CRIMINAL EVIDENCE AND PROCEDURE.

Damages—interim payments. See DAMAGES.

6191. Decree—failure to enter defence

Rule 28 of the Schedule to the Sheriff Courts (Scotland) Act 1907 provides, as amended prior to 1993, that a defender may apply to be reponed by a note setting forth the proposed defence and an explanation of his failure to appear. The sheriff may recall the decree against the defender following consideration of the note. The permanent trustee of a firm of solicitors raised an action seeking (1) payment for services rendered by the firm and (2) damages for loss caused by misrepresentations made to the pursuer which he had had to investigate. Decree in the absence was pronounced against the first and second defenders and was extracted but not implemented. The second defender lodged a reponing note setting forth a proposed defence and explaining the failure to appear. The sheriff refused the reponing note because, although a stable defence had been set forth, he considered himself bound by authority to reject it as he was not satisfied that the second defender had a reasonable excuse for non-appearance. The second defender appealed.

Held, (1) that it was not a requirement of the rules that the sheriff had to be satisfied that there was a reasonable excuse for non-appearance; (2) as it was a matter for the sheriff's discretion he was entitled to take account of all the circumstances and to balance one consideration against another in deciding whether to allow a reponing note; and appeal allowed and case remitted to the sheriff to proceed as records. (*Dicta* in *McDonough v. Focus DIY* [1993] C.L.Y. 5848, disapproved; *Mullen v. Harmac* [1994] C.L.Y. 6309, overruled.)

FORBES v. JOHNSTONE, 1995 S.L.T. 158.

6192. Decree—summary—whether defence to action disclosed in defences

[Rules of Court 1965, r. 89B.]

Rule 89B entitled the court to grant summary decree on a pursuer's motion if satisfied that there was no defence to the action. A furnaceman raised an action against his employers in which he claimed damages for personal injuries sustained in an accident at work. He made detailed averments about the cause of an explosion which had resulted in him being struck by molten metal and alleged that his employers were liable both directly and also vicariously for the actions of a fellow employee. The employers admitted the circumstances of the accident but denied the employee's averments of the cause of the explosion and his averments of fault. The employee's averments of fault were base on the terms of the employers' report into the explosion, lodged in process by the employee. The vacation judge having allowed the parties a proof before answer, the employee sought summary decree to the extent of restricting the proof to a proof on quantum of damages, arguing that, by admitting that the accident had occurred and had caused injury although denying the causes of the accident, the employers had disclosed no defence. The employers contended that, not knowing what the cause of the explosion was, despite their investigation, they were entitled to rely on their denials and put the employee to proof, especially since the employee did not plead *res ipsa loquitur*.

Held, that having regard to the terms of the report, there was an indication of fault on the part of the employers, and since the employers offered nothing in the way of contrary proof, there was no defence to the action on the merits; and summary decree granted; and proof restricted to quantum of damages.

STRUTHERS v. BRITISH ALCAN ROLLED PRODUCTS (O.H.), 1995 S.L.T. 142.

6193. Diligence—arrestment—on dependence—financial provision on divorce

A wife raised divorce proceedings against her husband and, believing that he was seeking to dissipate his farming assets, she obtained interim interdict against such disposal and arrested sums due to him by an auction mart. The husband sought recall and satisfied the court that the disposals had been carried out under a planned alteration to the farming business in furtherance of an expert's report and were not intended to prejudice the wife's claims.

Held, that arrestments which unduly interfered with ordinary trading activities without legitimate advantage to a pursuer should be recalled where the defender made full disclosure of the transactions and the application of the proceeds; and warrant to arrest on the dependence recalled.

MATHESON v. MATHESON (O.H.), 1995 S.L.T. 765.

6194. Diligence—arrestment—on dependence—obligation to account—arrestee not in funds—validity of arrestment

R appealed a sheriff's decision to dismiss R's action of furthcoming on the ground that the arrestment placed on the dependence of R's action for payment against L, on L's solicitor (S) on April 20, 1993, was ineffective. S had acted for L in the sale of his house. Missives had been concluded on February 15, and on April 23 the purchase price had been paid to S, who that day distributed the proceeds to the secured creditors and L. R argued that, as L could have assigned the free proceeds of the sale, those proceeds were arrestable in the hands of S, that once missives had been concluded S was under an obligation to L to account for the free proceeds of sale, that the relationship of L and S was nearer that of trustee than agent, and that, accordingly, the arrestment had attached the obligation to account.

Held, appeal refused. There was a clear distinction between an arrestee who was a trustee, who was under a general obligation of accounting, and one who was an agent, who was under no obligation to account until he had received funds, and, as no debt had existed until S, who was clearly an agent, had received the funds from the sale, the arrestment was ineffectual (Stewart, *Diligence*, pp. 71–72 and 74, *Johnston v. Dundas's Trs.* (1837) 15 S. 904, *Adam v. Anderson* (1837) 15 S. 1225 and *Pearson v. Brock* (1842) 4 D. 1509, followed; *Marshall v. Nimmo & Co.* (1847) 10 D. 328, distinguished). *Per* Lord MacLean: Had the arrestment been placed on the purchaser after the conclusion of missives, it would have attached to the purchase price, although it was not due until April 23 and was conditional upon delivery of a valid disposition (*Marshall*).

ROYAL BANK OF SCOTLAND v. LAW, 1996 S.L.T. 83.

6195. Diligence—arrestment—on dependence—recall—whether claim contingent

R appealed the decision to recall arrestments on the dependence of R's action of payment against T. The contract between R and T contained an arbitration clause and applied French law to the contract. T argued that the use of arrestments was incompetent, since it would not be known if T owed R money until arbitration was determined. R argued that T was under an obligation to pay R for all sums due and that this was not contingent on the decision of the arbiter.

Held, appeal allowed. Whether R's claims were contingent had to be determined in the light of R's averments. Unlike in *Costain Building and Civil Engineering v. Scottish Rugby Union* [1994] C.L.Y. 6112, no architect or engineer's certificate was necessary before payment was due. A debt was due for payment immediately *ex hypothesi* of R's case and this was precisely averred by R. There was no necessary implication that no amount was due to be paid until arbitration had been decided. Indeed R and T were not bound to go to arbitration. Arbitration was an alternative to court and it had never been suggested that the involvement of a court to determine the merits of a claim made that claim contingent (Graham Stewart on *Diligence*, p.81).

RIPPIN GROUP v. I.T.P. INTERPIPE SA, 1995 S.L.T. 831.

6196. Division and sale—counterclaim—competency. See JOHNSTON v. ROBSON, §5987.

Divorce. See DIVORCE AND CONSISTORIAL CAUSES.

Evidence. See EVIDENCE (CIVIL).

Expenses. See EXPENSES.

Fees. See EXPENSES.

Industrial Tribunals. See EMPLOYMENT.

6197. Interdict—interim interdict—balance of convenience. See SHELL U.K. EXPLORATION AND PRODUCTION v. INNES, §6052.

6198. Interdict—interim interdict—balance of convenience—restrictive covenant. See ARAMARK v. SOMMERVILLE, §5590.

6199. Interdict—interim interdict—enforcement of tenant's obligation to occupy business premises. See RETAIL PARKS INVESTMENTS v. OUR PRICE MUSIC, §6068.

6200. Interdict—interim interdict—recall—hearing—whether appropriate to attack strength of petitioners' case in detail at interlocutory hearing. See SHELL U.K. EXPLORATION AND PRODUCTION v. INNES, §6052.

6201. Interdict—interim interdict—restraint of foreign proceedings. See SHELL U.K. EXPLORATION AND PRODUCTION v. INNES, §6052.

Interdict—matrimonial interdicts. See DIVORCE AND CONSISTORIAL CAUSES.

6202. Interdict—passing off—exporting—whether double actionability rule applied. See GRANT (WILLIAM) & SONS v. GLEN CATRINE BONDED WAREHOUSE, §6459.

6203. Interim order—provisional and protective measures—injunction obtained in England on basis not available under Scots law

[Civil Jurisdiction and Judgments Act 1982 (c.27), s.27(1)(*c*).]

Under s.27(1)(*c*) of the Civil Jurisdiction and Judgments Act 1982 the Court of Session may grant interim interdict where proceedings have been commenced or are to be commenced in various jurisdictions including England. Two individuals who had sought and obtained a general injunction in the High Court of Justice in England against disclosure of their identity and the identity of their children sought interim interdict in the same terms in Scotland under s.27(1)(*c*). It was agreed that an order similar to the English one could not have been granted in the Court of Session had the proceedings been raised in Scotland. The respondents argued that it was incompetent or at least inappropriate to pronounce an interdict under s.27(1)(*c*) if there was no comparable remedy or ground of action under the law of Scotland, especially when any final award in the English courts might not be registrable and enforceable in Scotland because of the different terms of paras. 5(5) and 6 of Sched. 7 to the 1982 Act.

Held, that (1) in the exercise of comity, the Court of Session could lend its aid by granting an order similar to the English one even although there would have been no ground of action under the law of Scotland, provided that *prima facie* there was a case according to the jurisprudence of the originating jurisdiction; (2) it was too early to determine the issue of registrability of any final English order, an issue which was uncertain; and prayer of the petition granted.

G. v. CALEDONIAN NEWSPAPERS (O.H.), 1995 S.L.T. 559.

6204. Interim order—specific implement

[Court of Session Act 1988 (c.36), ss.46 and 47(2).]

O, landlords of a shopping centre, sought an interim order under ss.46 and 47(2) of the 1988 Act ordaining W to take possession of, use, occupy and trade from certain shop units as a shop within class 1 of the Town and Country Planning (Use Classes) (Scotland) Order 1989 in terms of two leases, the tenant's interest in which had been assigned to W in August 1990, in O's action for declarator that W were the tenants of the units and for an order that W implement the lease. On February 25, 1994 O had consented to W's assignation of the leases to S, subject to O receiving draft assignations within two months (of March 14) and within three months of their return, engrossments thereof, if O elected to be parties thereto, or formal intimation thereof, if they did not. On March 28 W forwarded a draft assignation in which the date of entry was March 30 and which contained a consent by O *in gremio*, which O revised on March 29 and which, O averred and W denied, O returned on March 30 to W. By fax on June 10 W had requested the urgent return of the draft assignation, a copy of which O forwarded on the same date. On June 14 O had become aware that W had removed themselves from the units and that the subjects were boarded up with S's name showing. On June 23 W intimated that they had assigned their interest as tenants to S and that W regarded the letter of February 25 as showing O's consent. On June 28 O replied stating that they had the right to be a party to the assignation, that they had not approved the assignation which had not included their consent, and that, as W had failed to return the engrossment within three months, the letter of consent had fallen. On September 6 an engrossed assignation in terms of the revised draft was sent to O. W argued that there was nothing W had done which the court could have prohibited by interdict, and that, accordingly, the order was not competent in terms of s.46.

Held, motion refused *in hoc statu*. (1) At least up until March 30 it would have been open to O to seek interim interdict against W from vacating the premises and, although W's breach was not admitted or proved and the order might not be in the same terms as the order for specific implement ultimately granted, it was competent for the court to grant an appropriate interim order

(*Church Commissioners for England v. Abbey National* [1994] C.L.Y. 5971. (2) However, as there was a fundamental dispute as to when the revised draft assignation had been returned, upon which turned the question of whether there had been an effective assignation, it was inappropriate to make an interim order (*Maersk Co. v. National Union of Seamen* [1988] C.L.Y. 4664, followed). Further, even if W admitted breaching the lease, the order sought went too far in requiring W to use, occupy and trade from the shop as this was far too wide and inspecific (*Grosvenor Developments (Scotland) v. Argyll Stores* [1987] C.L.Y. 4846; *Postel Properties v. Miller and Santhouse* [1992] C.L.Y. 5944; *Church Commissioners for England v. Nationwide Anglia Building Society* [1994] C.L.Y. 5970, followed). *Opinion*, that considering the substantial nature of the factual dispute, that O had to be held to be aware that from March 30 W regarded S as in occupation, that O had received sums from S which represented the rent under the lease, and that on June 15 O had sought undertakings as to when S would commence trading from the unit, and notwithstanding O's argument that the continued closure of the unit affected the profitability of the other units and the centre as a whole, the balance of convenience lay with W.

OVERGATE CENTRE v. WILLIAM LOW SUPERMARKETS (O.H.), 1995 S.L.T. 1181.

6205. Interlocutor—correction—motion to correct interlocutor under appeal one year after pronouncement

[Rules of the Court of Session 1994 (S.I. 1994 No. 1443), r.4.16(7).]

The sheriff assoilzied the defenders in an action of reparation. On appeal by the pursuer, the sheriff principal allowed the appeal and awarded damages. The defenders appealed to the Court of Session. The court reversed the decision of the sheriff principal and restored that of the sheriff. In so doing, the court altered certain findings in fact made by the sheriff principal. The pursuers appealed to the House of Lords. While the appeal was pending, the defenders formed the view that one alteration to the findings in fact was inconsistent with the opinion delivered by the Court of Session. They enrolled a motion for the alteration of the interlocutor, arguing that a correction was necessary in order to convey the intention which the court had expressed in its opinion. The motion was enrolled more than one year after the interlocutor had been pronounced. The pursuer argued that the opinion and the interlocutor were not inconsistent, and that in any event, the motion was incompetent because it had not been made *de recenti*.

Held, that (1) the wording of the interlocutor was erroneous and should have been in the terms now proposed by the defenders; (2) standing the fact that the defenders had only become aware of the error 10 months after the interlocutor had been pronounced and that there had been discussion between the parties before the disagreement had become irreconcilable, the defenders' delay alone was not a sufficient reason for refusing the motion; but (3) since the court had not seen the pursuer's House of Lords pleadings, it could not assess what prejudice the motion might cause him, and because it was inappropriate for a court whose decision was under review to adjudicate upon possible prejudice to a party in the conduct of that appeal, it would not be proper to grant the motion; and motion refused. *Opinion reserved*, as to whether the rule that a motion to alter an interlocutor had to be made *de recenti* had been qualified by r. 4.16(7) of the Rules of the Court of Session 1994 and its predecessors, because the rule in any event gave the court a discretion in the exercise of which it would inevitably take into account any undue delay or prejudice to the other party.

MARTINEZ v. GRAMPIAN HEALTH BOARD, 1995 S.L.T. 1261.

6206. Judicial factor—powers—right to sell subjects burdened by standard security—holder of standard security in possession

In 1972 and 1975 a firm granted standard securities to a bank. The bank's interest in these securities was subsequently assigned, before the appointment of a judicial factor to the sequestrated estates of the firm, to the father of one of the partners. The father then assigned his interest to his son who entered into possession as heritable creditor. The judicial factor, after having paid off third party creditors, sought to realise the assets of the firm to satisfy the reversionary interests of its partners who were the daughter of the original assignee and her former husband. Various orders were sought by the judicial factor to facilitate the sale of the subjects. The son to whom the interest had been assigned argued that he, as heritable creditor, was entitled to enter into and remain in possession of the subjects and have his interests protected from the acts of any person until such time as the sum secured had first been ascertained and then paid in full. He argued further that since the judicial factor was not proposing to sell the whole of the security subjects there was a risk of prejudice to him as heritable creditor in that the full market value of the subjects might not be achieved.

Held, that, although the court would normally protect a creditor's rights against debtors whose financial affairs might be precarious, the heritable creditor's interests, which were purely financial, were sufficiently protected by an undertaking from the judicial factor, an officer of the court, to set aside funds from the proceeds of the sale to meet the heritable creditor's claim; and heritable creditor's motion for interim interdict refused and judicial factor's motion for orders and interim interdict refused as unnecessary in view of undertakings from the heritable creditor.

DUNLOP (G.) & SON'S JUDICIAL FACTOR v. ARMSTRONG (O.H.), 1995 S.L.T. 645.

6207. Judicial factor—solicitor's estate—whether entitled to deduct remuneration from estate. See LAW SOCIETY OF SCOTLAND, COUNCIL OF THE v. McKINNIE (NO. 2), §6431.

6208. Judicial factor—solicitor's estate—whether entitled to deduct remuneration from interest on clients' account. See LAW SOCIETY OF SCOTLAND, COUNCIL OF THE v. ANDREW, §6432.

Jurisdiction. See JURISDICTION.

Legal aid. See LEGAL AID.

Limitation of actions. See LIMITATION OF ACTIONS.

6209. *Nobile officium*—children's hearings—grounds for referral accepted—parents subsequently denying that grounds accepted—procedure. See M. v. KENNEDY, §5517.

6210. *Nobile officium*—children's hearings—grounds for referral not established on re-hearing—order regulating return of children to families after long absence. See L. PETRS., §5518.

6211. Pleadings—amendment—insertion of conclusions—competency

[Rules of the Court of Session, 1994, rr. 2.1(1) and (2), 13.2(1) and (2) and 24.1(1) and (2) and Forms 13.2–A and 13.2–B.]

The pursuer in an action of damages moved to amend the summons by inserting a conclusion for payment, the summons having previously contained no conclusion at all. The defenders argued that the action was a nullity and that accordingly it was incompetent for the pursuer to seek to amend the action so as to incorporate a conclusion. Rule 13.2 of the Rules of the Court of

Session required the insertion of conclusions in a summons and was a mandatory rule. If the court had a discretion to allow amendment, that discretion ought not to be exercised in the pursuer's favour since the defenders had tabled a plea to the competency of the action from the outset and the pursuer had not sought to insert conclusions prior to the record closing.

Held, that (1) the absence of a conclusion did not make the action a fundamental nullity; (2) the power to allow amendment in r. 24.1(2)(a) and in any event the power in r. 2.1, was wide enough to permit the amendment to be made; (3) the defenders would suffer no prejudice and as the omission was the result of a clerical oversight, the court's discretion should be exercised in favour of the pursuer; and motion to amend granted. *Doubted*, whether there was any basis for describing a particular rule as "mandatory" as opposed to "directory".

WILSON v. LOTHIAN REGIONAL COUNCIL (O.H.), 1995 S.L.T. 991.

6212. Pleadings—competent and omitted

A financial services agent and his sub-agent had an agreement whereby the sub-agent would receive a share of commission received by the agent in respect of insurance and pension contracts which had been arranged by him and procured by the sub-agent. One such contract lapsed and the commission became repayable. The agent brought a summary cause action for payment of £828·15 against the sub-agent, who defended the action on quantum, alleging that only £638·22 was repayable. That action was settled extrajudicially, and was disposed of by decree of dismissal with no expenses due to or by either party. The sub-agent then raised an action of count, reckoning and payment against the agent for his intromissions with commission due to her for a period which included the lapsed policy which led to the summary cause action. In his defences, the agent included a plea of law of "competent and omitted". It was argued for him that the sub-agent could, and should, have defended the summary cause action on the basis of retention or compensation, should have counterclaimed for count, reckoning and payment and that the present action was accordingly unnecessary.

Held, that (1) the proper scope of the defence of competent and omitted was that a defender who had put forward an unsuccessful defence could not in a subsequent process challenge the prior judgment on grounds which it was competent to plead but which he omitted to do (Maclaren, *Court of Session Practice*, p. 401, approved; *Dickson v. United Dominions Trust*, 1988 S.L.T. 19 and Second Division, December 19, 1986, unreported, and Beaumont, 1985 S.L.T. (News) 345, discussed); (2) the only issue before the court in the summary cause action was whether the agent was entitled to claw back the relevant commission payment, and although this issue involved the contract between the parties it was not necessary for the sub-agent to plead every other live issue arising from the contract under pain of extinction of her rights (*Cantors Properties (Scotland) v. Swears & Wells* [1980] C.L.Y. 3296 followed); (3) claims based upon retention or compensation were elective as, although a previous failure to plead compensation could prevent a party from challenging a decree, such a failure did not extinguish the right upon which compensation was based; (4) although a counterclaim for a sum greater than the financial limit in a summary cause was competent, it was for the defender in the summary cause to decide whether to submit to the constraints of that form of procedure in order to dispose of his claim, but that a pursuer could not, by choosing summary procedure, compel a defender to submit to that form of process for the disposal of a potentially substantial and complex counterclaim (Macphail, *Sheriff Court Practice*, para. 25–73, approved); and plea of competent and omitted repelled. *Opinion*, provisionally, that the plea of competent and omitted could apply even where the prior action was settled extrajudicially with decree of dismissal or absolvitor.

DICKIE v. GOLDIE (O.H.), 1995 S.L.T. 780.

6213. Pleadings—relevancy and specification. See ROBERTSON v. HOSSACK, §6008.

6214. Pleadings—relevancy and specification—admission by defenders in correspondence prior to action being raised. See GORDON v. EAST KILBRIDE DEVELOPMENT CORPORATION, §5917.

6215. Pleadings—relevancy and specification—alternative and inconsistent averments of fact. See SAFDAR v. DEVLIN, §6234.

6216. Pleadings—relevancy and specification—counterclaim—reference to defences incorporating report. See McILWRAITH v. LOCHMADDY HOTEL, §6380.

6217. Pleadings—relevancy and specification—duty to supervise employees—breach different from that averred

An action of damages was raised by an employee following an accident in which he had been hit while operating a machine by a ball which was being used in a game played by two other employees within the defenders' premises. The pursuer had pled a breach of the duties to "devise, maintain and enforce proper supervision" of employees and to "provide proper, adequate and fully qualified supervision at all times". At proof the only factual issue seriously in dispute was whether the acting foreman had turned a blind eye to the employees playing with the ball. The Lord Ordinary preferred the evidence of the acting foreman that he had not seen other employees playing with the ball but had been absent for extended periods in order to perform duties elsewhere, but found the defenders to be in breach of their duties to provide adequate supervision. The defenders reclaimed, arguing that they had been held to be in breach of duty on a ground not averred on record.

Held, that (1) the pursuer's case of fault was in essence a failure to provide adequate supervision, and although the breach of that duty took a different form from that which appeared from the averments, it was nevertheless within the case pled against the defenders; (2) as the pursuer had averred a duty of constant supervision it was not necessary to aver the intervals at which that duty was to be performed; and reclaiming motion refused.

GIBSON v. BRITISH RAIL MAINTENANCE, 1995 S.L.T. 953.

6218. Pleadings—relevancy and specification—passing off. See GRANT (WILLIAM) & SONS v. GLEN CATRINE BONDED WAREHOUSE, §6459.

Practice (Criminal). See CRIMINAL EVIDENCE AND PROCEDURE.

Prescription. See PRESCRIPTION.

6219. Proof—conclusions on disputed matters—assistance for appeal court

In an action of damages against two defenders arising out of an accident to a cyclist the Lord Ordinary assoilzied the defenders. In his opinion the Lord Ordinary did not deal with any question of apportionment of liability, or with contributory negligence, upon which full arguments had been made to him, nor did he record any of the submissions made or indicate how he would have determined those issues if it had been necessary for him to do so. Observations (*per* the Lord Justice Clerk (Ross)), on the duty of the Lord Ordinary to record the arguments and submissions made to him and to express his views on those arguments and submissions, even if they were matters which were not necessary for his opinion. (*Morrow v. Enterprise Sheet Metal Works (Aberdeen)* [1986] C.L.Y. 3618, followed.)

HOGAN v. HIGHLAND REGIONAL COUNCIL, 1995 S.L.T. 466.

6220. Proof or jury trial—special cause

[Court of Session Act 1988 (c.36), s.9.]

A husband and wife were injured in a road traffic accident. The wife, who was eight months pregnant, suffered serious injuries to her pelvis which resulted in intra-uterine foetal death and the birth of a stillborn child. They raised an action for damages against the other driver, averring, *inter alia*, that the accident and the death of the child had resulted in psychological trauma to the wife. At procedure roll the issue for consideration was the proper mode of inquiry. The defender argued that special cause terms of s.9 of the Court of Session Act 1988 existed for proof rather than jury trial to be allowed because of difficulties which were likely to arise from having to give directions to a jury upon the wife's entitlement to damages for her trauma but not for loss of society in respect of the unborn child. The defender further maintained that a claim for the expenses of the dead child's funeral and headstone was of doubtful relevance.

Held, that (1) special cause had not been shown why proof rather than jury trial should be allowed as it would be possible to explain effectively to a jury the proper limits of the pursuer's case by reference to the necessity for any award of damages being confined to psychological trauma consequent upon the accident and the stillbirth; (2) funeral expenses for a stillborn child could be seen as an item of loss arising naturally and directly from the actings of the defender; and issues allowed. (*Morris v. Drysdale* [1991] C.L.Y. 4874, considered.)

McMARTIN v. GINDHA (O.H.), 1995 S.L.T. 523.

6221. Proof or jury trial—special cause—*mora*

[Court of Session Act 1988 (c.36), s.9(b).]

The Court of Session Act 1988 provides that an action for damages for personal injuries shall be tried by jury unless the parties' consent to a proof or special cause is shown rendering the case unsuitable for jury trial. The mother and former cohabitee of a man who had committed suicide, raised an action together seeking damages from the chief constable of the relevant police authority for a failure, on the part of his officers, in their duty to care towards the deceased, the man having committed suicide while in police custody. Issues for a jury trial were allowed. Thereafter the pursuers amended, the chief constable then adding averments relating to the unsuitability of the action for trial by jury. The pursuers continued to seek a jury trial. At procedure roll the chief constable sought withdrawal of the previous allowance of issues, arguing, on the basis of his new averments, that special cause existed rendering the cause unsuitable for jury trial. He averred that the action had been delayed throughout by the pursuers who had raised the action just before the expiry of the triennium and then discharged the previous diet set down for jury trial. Four and a half years had elapsed since the original incident. The recollection of essential police witnesses to the event was now likely to be dimmed as a result of the lapse of time and likely to be confused by the holding of a fatal accident inquiry into the matter, necessitating reliance on the transcript as an aide memoire.

Held, that (1) whereas the chief constable's averments as to prejudice claimed only that the witnesses' memories were "likely" to be dimmed rather than that they had been dimmed, taking into account the nature of the case it was more likely that it would be memorable to the police witnesses; (2) in any event the detailed pleadings of both parties indicated that full inquiries, including the fatal accident inquiry, had taken place which would overcome the effect of any delay; (3) the transcript of the fatal accident inquiry, involving the same essential witnesses as the present case, would be a valuable aide memoire to witnesses in the present cause; (4) accordingly the chief constable had not shown special cause as to why the action should be withheld from a jury; and defender's plea in law to that effect repelled.

DAVIDSON v. MOODIE (O.H.), 1995 S.L.T. 545.

6222. Proof or jury trial—special cause—necessary services claim

A woman sustained serious injuries when, as a driver, she was involved in a road accident. She raised an action of damages against the two other drivers involved and sought allowance of issues. Her injuries rendered her severely and permanently disabled and dependent on services provided to her by her parents. At procedure roll the defenders both submitted that the averments in support of the pursuer's services claim were such as to justify withholding the action from trial by jury.

Held, that (1) averments in support of a claim for services had to be clear, precise and defined to an obvious basis if a case was to be heard by a jury; (2) the averments relating to services were more of the nature of a claim for compensation to the carers than a claim for services and would cause difficulty to a jury in deciding quantification, and that they accordingly amounted to special cause for withholding the action from trial by jury; and proof before answer allowed.

STARK v. FORD (O.H.), 1995 S.L.T. 69.

6223. Reduction—partial—disposition—burden of proof. See ABERDEEN RUBBER v. KNOWLES & SONS (FRUITERERS), §5992.

6224. Reduction—sheriff court decree—mode of review

Decree in absence was granted against a company, then the second defenders, in an action of damages raised against them and another company by an individual in Dumfries sheriff court, it having been intimated to the first company that the main thrust of the sheriff court action was directed against the other company. The first company had immediately forwarded the initial writ to its insurers who in turn had purported to instruct solicitors to lodge a notice of intention to defend. That letter of instruction was never in fact received and no notice of intention to defend was lodged on behalf of either company. Decree in absence passed against both companies. Although the other company was successfully reponed the first company was unaware of the existence of the decree against it until the decree had been extracted for a period in excess of six months and its attempt thereafter to repone was refused as incompetent. The company sought reduction of the decree, they maintaining that, as it had a substantial defence to the action as to both liability and quantum, and the granting of the decree amounted to a substantial miscarriage of justice, its only remedy was to reduce the decree. The defender argued that the pursuers' averments did not show that the circumstances were exceptional or that substantial justice demanded reduction of the decree. The pursuers would not suffer any loss as they would have a remedy against their insurers and a right of indemnity against the other defenders in the original action.

Held, that (1) it was necessary to examine the circumstances of each case and to reach a conclusion as to whether there existed exceptional circumstances and whether reduction was necessary to achieve substantial justice; (2) the pursuers' averments of the circumstances which led to the failure to defend the action could properly be described as exceptional; (3) substantial justice demanded that the remedy sought by the pursuers be made available to them since otherwise the pursuers' defence to the sheriff court action would never be investigated, the pursuer in that action would be overcompensated and the other defenders in that action would be likely to obtain a windfall benefit; and proof before answer allowed (*Bain v. Hugh L. S. McConnell* [1991] C.L.Y. 5448, followed). *Observed*, that it was proper to recognise the distinction between the pursuers, who were free from criticism, and their insurers (*J. & C. Black (Haulage) v. Alltransport International Group* [1980] C.L.Y. 3489, followed; *Kirkwood v. City of Glasgow District Council* [1988] C.L.Y. 4717, distinguished).

JOHNSTONE & CLARK (ENGINEERS) v. LOCKHART (O.H.), 1995 S.L.T. 440.

6225. *Res judicata*—determination by industrial tribunal

C sued her former employer, S, for breach of contract on the grounds that she was dismissed as a director without notice. At procedure roll, S argued that C's claim was *res judicata*, as C had claimed unfair dismissal before an industrial tribunal which had determined that C had not been dismissed but had left S's employment voluntarily; alternatively, that the court should apply the principle of "issue estoppel" which could preclude a court from considering an issue which had been incidental to the main decision in an earlier case between the same parties (*Carl Zeiss Stiftung v. Rayner & Keeler* [1966] C.L.Y. 1665). In addition, C's case fell because it was based upon benefits contained in a minute of agreement which was never executed by the parties and therefore no contract existed. C submitted that although the contract had not been signed, the pleading were sufficient for the action to proceed on the basis of *rei interventus* or homologation where C averred that (1) she had attended at least three board meetings in the belief that she was a director of S, (2) she had held herself out as a director and was knowingly permitted to do so by S, and (3) S's managing director had congratulated her on her appointment and had intimated to several clients that she had been appointed a director of S.

Held, proof before answer allowed. (1) The present action was based on breach of contract and the issues to be decided were not the same subject matter as whether C had been unfairly dismissed (*Turner v. London Transport Executive* [1977] I.C.R. 952). (2) There was no authority for extending the English principle of issue estoppel to Scotland, particularly where previous courts had declined to sanction an extension of the principles governing *res judicata* in the law of Scotland (*Anderson v. Wilson* [1972] C.L.Y. 4012). C's averments justified inquiry into the proposition that S's actings constituted *rei interventus* or homologation which created a binding and valid contract in terms of the draft minute of agreement.

CLINK v. SPEYSIDE DISTILLERY CO. (O.H.), 1995 S.L.T. 1344.

6226. Restrictive Practices Court. See MACKIE & DEWAR v. DIRECTOR GENERAL OF FAIR TRADING, §6456.

Sheriff court. See SHERIFF COURT PRACTICE.

6227. Title to sue—recompense. See NORWICH UNION FIRE INSURANCE SOCIETY v. ROSS, §5584.

6228. Title to sue—trade marks and names—passing off—assignation of goodwill in name. See GRANT (WILLIAM) & SONS v. GLEN CATRINE BONDED WAREHOUSE, §6459.

6229. Witnesses—skilled witnesses—certification. See MAINS v. UNIROYAL ENGLEBERT TYRES (NO. 2), §5935.

PRACTICE (CRIMINAL)

See CRIMINAL EVIDENCE AND PROCEDURE.

PRESCRIPTION

6230. Amendment of pleadings after expiry of prescriptive period—amendment seeking to add new factual averments. See SAFDAR v. DEVLIN, §6234.

6231. Negative—right to be served as heir to an ancestor—whether prescribed before becoming imprescriptible

[Prescription and Limitation (Scotland) Act 1973 (c.52), ss.8 and 14(1)(a) and Sched. 2, para. (h).]

The Prescription and Limitation (Scotland) Act 1973, s.8 and Sched. 3, para. (h) declares that any right to be served as heir to an ancestor is imprescriptible. Under the law as it stood before the coming into force of that Act, the right was subject to a 20 year negative prescriptive period. Section 14(1)(*a*) provides that time occurring before the commencement of the Act shall be reckonable towards the prescriptive period in like manner as time occurring thereafter, subject to the restriction that any time reckoned under para. (*a*) shall be less than the prescriptive period. A mother died on April 17, 1952 leaving a will naming her daughter as her sole executrix and universal legatory. Included in the estate was said to be a specified piece of land. On August 5, 1992 there was recorded in the Register of Sasines a notice of title in favour of the daughter in respect of the piece of land. The daughter died on March 7, 1993. On January 14, 1992 an individual had granted to himself an *a non domino* disposition of the same piece of land, which disposition was recorded on January 17, 1992. The daughter's executors sought reduction of the disposition, declarator that the daughter had been infeft in the land on recording of the notice of title, decree ordaining the defender to remove himself from the land and declarator that the executors were entitled to enter into possession. The defender maintained that the right to make up title to the heritable property had been extinguished by operation of prescription prior to the recording of the notice of title. The executors submitted that the right was imprescriptible by virtue of s.8 of and Sched. 3, para. (*h*) to the 1973 Act, the effect of which was retrospective by the operation of s.14(1)(*a*).

Held, that the effect of s.14(1)(*a*) of the 1973 Act was not to revive rights which had prescribed prior to the passing of the Act, and that the right to make up title to the disputed property had been extinguished by operation of prescription in 1972, prior to the passing of the Act; and action dismissed. (*Pettigrew v. Harton* [1956] C.L.Y. 12456, and *Dunlop v. McGowans* [1980] C.L.Y. 3479, applied; *Macdonald v. Scott* [1981] C.L.Y. 3522, not followed.)

PORTEOUS'S EXRS. v. FERGUSON (O.H.), 1995 S.L.T. 649.

6232. Negative—short—contract—date from which time runs—weekly wage

[Prescription and Limitation (Scotland) Act 1973 (c.52), s.6 and Sched. 1, para. 1(g) and Sched. 2, para. 1(1).]

Held, in a counterclaim made in September 1993 for arrears of wages for the period from March 1987 until October 1991, that the obligation to pay the wages became enforceable week by week, that the obligation was not covered by para. 1 of Sched. 2 to the 1973 Act and accordingly the obligation to pay wages prescribed week by week and not five years after the termination of employment.

REID v. BEATON (Sh. Ct.), 1995 S.C.L.R. 382.

6233. Negative—short—interruption—relevant claim. See DUCTFORM VENTILATION (FIFE) v. ANDREWS-WEATHERFOIL, §5490.

6234. Negative—short—interruption—relevant claim—response to new averments replacing previous admissions

[Prescription and Limitation (Scotland) Act 1973 (c.52), s.6(1) and (4)(a)(ii).]

The Prescription and Limitation (Scotland) Act 1973 provides for the prescription of certain obligations after five years. In the computation of that period there is to be ignored any period during which a creditor is induced to refrain from making a claim as a result of fraud by or error induced by the debtor in the obligation. A woman, through her husband, instructed a solicitor in the purchase of shop premises. The offer submitted on her behalf had annexed to it a schedule of conditions inappropriate for such premises in that there were no stipulations for appropriate planning permission and consents for its use as a takeaway food shop. After the purchaser took entry, stop and enforcement notices were served which required the purchaser to cease trading. She eventually had to sell the premises as an empty shop at a loss and sought damages from the solicitor. The prescriptive period began to run on January 1, 1988 and the action was raised in October 1991. The solicitor's original defences admitted having been instructed and having prepared the offer but averred that the purchaser's husband had satisfied himself with regard to planning permission. After the expiry of the prescriptive period the solicitor's averments were radically amended. She averred that the instructions had been given not to herself, but to her secretary who had prepared the offer at the husband's insistence; that the husband had been advised that the secretary was unsure which schedule to attach; that the husband had indicated that whatever was attached would be suitable; and that the offer had been signed at the husband's insistence by the solicitor's husband after he had advised the offerer's husband that he was unqualified and that legal advice should be taken before proceeding with the offer. Whilst not departing from her primary case, the pursuer proposed an alternative case in response to and based entirely on the facts as averred in the solicitor's amendments. The solicitor argued that the pursuer's case was thus irrelevant because she was pleading two alternative and inconsistent cases without asserting that she was justifiably in ignorance of the facts, and that any obligation to make reparation in respect of breaches of duty introduced in the alternative case had prescribed in terms of s.6 of the 1973 Act.

Held, that (1) there was no reason why the pursuer should not be allowed to aver the alternative case to cover the eventuality of the solicitor's revised version of what happened being preferred to her primary case, albeit that the respective cases were inconsistent on the facts and required different averments of fault as to the details of the alleged professional negligence, and that it would be unjust not to allow the pursuer to do so in the circumstances; (2) the alternative case had not prescribed since it was based on breach of the same obligation, namely the attachment of the wrong schedule to the offer; (3) the alternative case would not, in any event, have prescribed in that the period during which the solicitor had admitted how the wrong schedule had come to be attached to the offer and before the new version of events was averred, was not to be reckoned as part of the prescriptive period; and proof before answer allowed. *Observed*, that the purchaser's responsibility for the actings of her husband as her agent was no sound reason for ignoring the fact that she had not been personally involved in the events concerned when considering what cases should have been allowed to plead and that, having regard to the agency factor, she could justifiably have asserted that she was excusably in personal ignorance of the precise facts, not having been personally present at the material times, and would in any event have been entitled to aver her alternative case.

SAFDAR v. DEVLIN (O.H.), 1995 S.L.T. 530.

6235. Positive—servitude right of access. See ROBERTSON v. HOSSACK, §6008.

PRISONS

6236. Local review committees

LOCAL REVIEW COMMITTEE (SCOTLAND) REVOCATION RULES 1995 (No. 1272) [65p], made under the Prisons (Scotland) Act 1989 (c.45), s.18(5); operative on June 1, 1995; revoke the Local Review Committee (Scotland)

Rules 1967, rule 8 on June 1, 1995 and the remaining rules with effect from September 1, 1995.

[S.I. 1967 No. 1699, 1969 No. 1256, 1975 No. 1528, 1976 No. 237, 1978 No. 1325, 1983 No. 1694, 1989 No. 1761 revoked.]

6237. Parole Board

PAROLE BOARD (SCOTLAND) RULES 1995 (No. 1273) [£1·95], made under the Prisons (Scotland) Act 1989 (c.45), s.18(3A) (as inserted by the Criminal Justice and Public Order Act 1994 (c.33), s.134(3)); operative on June 1, 1995; make general provision with respect to the proceedings of the Parole Board in considering recommendations for release, or conditions in, or revocation of, licences.

6238. Release on licence

PRISONERS AND CRIMINAL PROCEEDINGS (SCOTLAND) ACT 1993 (RELEASE OF PRISONERS ETC.) ORDER 1995 (No. 911) [65p], made under the Prisoners and Criminal Proceedings (Scotland) Act 1993 (c.9), s.20(3); operative on April 1, 1995; provides that any prisoner sentenced on or after October 1, 1993 and serving a sentence of imprisonment of less than 10 years, shall be released on licence under the Prisons (Scotland) Act 1989, s.22 by the Secretary of State where the Parole Board so recommends and that the Secretary of State will be required to revoke his licence and recall him to prison if the Parole Board so recommends.

PRISONS (SCOTLAND) ACT 1989 (RELEASE OF PRISONERS ETC.) ORDER 1995 (No. 910) [65p], made under the Prisons (Scotland) Act 1989 (c.45), ss.22(1A) (as amended by the Criminal Justice and Public Order Act 1994 (c.33), s.134) and 28(1A) (as amended by the Criminal Justice and Public Order Act 1994 (c.33), s.134); operative on April 1, 1995; provides that any prisoner sentenced on or after October 1, 1993 and serving a sentence of imprisonment for four years or more but less than 10, shall be released on licence where the Parole Board for Scotland so recommends, that the Parole Board must be consulted about any changes of any condition in any licence and that if the Parole Board so recommends the Secretary of State will be required to revoke the licence of any prisoner who has been released and recall him to prison.

PRIVATE LEGISLATION PROCEDURE

6239. Provisional orders

BELL'S BRIDGE ORDER CONFIRMATION ACT 1995 (c.iv) [£2·85], made under the Private Legislation Procedure (Scotland) Act 1936 (c.52); operative on July 19, 1995; confirms a provisional order to empower Scottish Enterprise to construct works to make Bell's Bridge a permanent footbridge over the river Clyde and for related purposes.

PUBLIC ENTERTAINMENTS AND RECREATION

Amusements with prizes permit. See GAMING AND WAGERING.

6240. Public entertainment licence—application—refusal—written reasons for decision

Held, that a licensing authority's written reasons for their decision on an application did not require to canvass each piece of evidence on each assertion put to the authority, and that if an authority stated that they had had regard to the evidence and productions, it was not possible for the court to go behind such a statement, unless something else made it clear that the authority had not had regard to such material.

NOBLE v. CITY OF GLASGOW DISTRICT COUNCIL, 1995 S.L.T. 1315.

6241. Public entertainment licence—grant for reduced period—appeal by objected—health studio alleged to be front for prostitution—discretion of licensing committee

[Civic Government (Scotland) Act 1982 (c. 45), ss.9 and 41(1).]

An application for a public entertainment licence for a health studio was made to the local authority's licensing committee in terms of s.41 of the Civic Government (Scotland) Act 1982. Objection was made to the grant of a licence on the ground that the premises would be a front for a brothel. The committee by a majority granted a licence for a period of five months instead of the usual three years. In its statement of reasons the committee stated that the applicant was a fit and proper person to hold a public entertainment licence, that a petition, newspaper article and letters had been placed before the committee, that the applicant's counsel had not addressed the issue of prostitution on the basis that the police and council views on this subject were well known and that no evidence had been placed before it to suggest that the premises would be used as a place of prostitution. The objector appealed to the sheriff. After submissions on preliminary pleas had been disposed of, the objector argued that in arriving at their decision the committee had erred in law and that they had exercised their discretion in an unreasonable manner.

Held, that (1) it being impossible to say that there was no evidence to suggest that the premises would be used as a place of prostitution, the committee had erred in law; (2) no reasonable committee would have exercised its discretion in the way that the committee did; and appeal allowed, decision of the licensing committee reversed and licence revoked.

SCANLAN v. CITY OF EDINBURGH DISTRICT COUNCIL, 1995 S.L.T. (Sh.Ct.) 89.

6242. Public entertainment licence—refusal—appeal sustained on ground of breach of natural justice—whether appropriate to remit to board for reconsideration

Applicants for an entertainment licence and a permit for gaming machines appealed to the sheriff against the refusal of the applications on the ground that there had been a breach of natural justice. The sheriff upheld the appeal and remitted the applications to the committee for reconsideration. The applicants appealed to the Court of Session, arguing that there was a risk in the circumstances of the case that the committee's attitude might have hardened so that they would be unable to close their minds to their previous decision, and that the sheriff should have directed that the applications be granted.

Held, that as Parliament had decided that decisions on licensing matters should be taken by the local licensing authority, there should be compelling reasons for removing from such an authority the responsibility for taking such decisions, and it was not clear that the breach which had taken place had affected the votes cast by a majority of the committee members; and appeal refused and applications remitted to board for reconsideration. (*William Hill (Scotland) v. Kyle and Carrick District Licensing Board* [1992] C.L.Y. 5809 followed.)

MATCHURBAN v. KYLE AND CARRICK DISTRICT COUNCIL, 1995 S.L.T. 505.

6243. Tourism—boards. See TRADE AND INDUSTRY, §6458.

PUBLIC HEALTH

Food. See FOOD AND DRUGS.

Sewerage. See ENVIRONMENTAL LAW.

6244. Sewerage—application to connect drains to public sewer—refusal—appeal

A building company asked for permission to connect a private sewer onto the existing public sewer. Tayside Regional Council refused the application on the grounds that the public sewer was already overused. The building company appealed under s.12(3) and (5) of the Sewerage (Scotland) Act 1968.

Held, that the existing sewer overload did not constitute a valid reason for refusal.

TAYSIDE REGIONAL COUNCIL v. SECRETARY OF STATE FOR SCOTLAND, *The Times*, January 28, 1995.

RATING AND VALUATION

6245. Abolition of domestic rates—domestic subjects—"pertinent"—community facility owned in common by proprietors of development who had sole rights to hire it. See CENTRAL REGION, ASSESSOR FOR v. SPRINGBANK GARDENS RESIDENTS' ASSOCIATION, §6253.

6246. Agricultural lands and heritages—agricultural buildings—indoor arena and horseboxes used in livery stable business

[Valuation and Rating (Scotland) Act 1956 (c.60), s.7(2).]

B appealed against the decision of the valuation appeal committee to uphold the inclusion in the roll of a "riding establishment", from which B conducted a business advertised as "livery stables", which subjects B claimed fell to be deleted as "agricultural buildings" within s.7(2) of the 1956 Act. The buildings comprised (A) a former indoor cattle court mainly used for exercising and schooling horses, with some use also for storage of implements and sheltering sheep when lambing, (B) seven loose horse boxes also occasionally used for lambing, and (C) a building containing an office from which the livery business was run and further horse boxes used as above. The committee excluded a further building (D), part of a former byre used as a tack room. B argued that his business was not that of a riding establishment and that the stables were run as part of the farm: land had been set aside for grazing and haymaking for the horses, and there was a long practice of farmers permitting others to stable horses on their land. The assessor cross-appealed against the exclusion of building D, a reduction in valuation of the loose boxes by 50 per cent in respect of the element of agricultural use and a reduction in the rate per square metre for the indoor arena allowed by the committee.

Held, appeal refused; cross-appeal allowed in part. While it was the purpose to which subjects were put which mattered and not the description applied to them and while agricultural buildings should not lose that status simply because an informal arrangement existed for the accommodation of horses, in the present case on the evidence of the way in which the livery business was run (with its own manageress, and with several horses stabled there at any one time), the committee were entitled to find that the subjects were used at least partly in connection with a distinguishable enterprise. It followed from their decision that their treatment of building D was wrong. Further, although the assessor appeared to have conceded the point before the committee, it was wrong to apportion the degree of use for agricultural purposes and discount the value accordingly. However, this error did not appear to have influenced the committee's reduction in valuation of the arena and this part of the cross-appeal failed.

BALLANTYNE v. ASSESSOR FOR TAYSIDE REGION, 1995 S.L.T. 804.

6247. Assessors—qualifications

LOCAL GOVERNMENT (QUALIFICATIONS OF ASSESSORS) (SCOTLAND) ORDER 1995 (No. 1515) [65p]; made under the Local Government etc. (Scotland) Act 1994 (c.39), s.27(3); operative on July 13, 1993; provides that any assessor or depute assessor appointed, under the Local Government etc. (Scotland) Act 1994, s.27, must be a Fellow or Professional Associate of the Royal Institute of Chartered Surveyors.

6248. Local Government etc. (Scotland) Act 1994 (c.39)—commencement

LOCAL GOVERNMENT ETC. (SCOTLAND) ACT 1994 (COMMENCEMENT No. 2) ORDER 1994 (No. 3150 (C.74)) [£1·55], made under the Local Government etc. (Scotland) Act 1994 (c.39), s.184; appoints December 31, 1994 as the day for the coming into force of s.180(1) and Sched. 13 para. 176(1)(19)(b) of the 1994 Act, January 4, 1995 as the day for coming into force of ss.153, 160, 161 and 180(2) (in part), and April 1, 1995 as the day for coming into force of ss.152, 154, 155, 156, 158, 159, 162(1) and 180 (in part).

[S.I. 1994 No. 2850 amended.]

6249. Non-domestic rates

NON-DOMESTIC RATES (LEVYING) (SCOTLAND) REGULATIONS 1995 (No. 548) [£3·70], made under the Local Government (Scotland) Act 1994 (c.39), s.153; operative on April 1, 1995; prescribe the non-domestic rates for the financial year 1995–96 of property in Scotland.

NON-DOMESTIC RATES (SCOTLAND) ORDER 1995 (No. 312) [65p], made under the Local Government (Scotland) Act 1975 (c.30), ss.7B(1) (as inserted by the Local Government Finance Act 1992 (c.14), s.110(2) and amended by the Local Government etc. (Scotland) Act 1994 (c.39) Sched. 13) and 37(1) (as amended by the 1992 Act, Sched. 13); operative on April 1, 1995; prescribes a rate of 43·2 pence in the pound as the non-domestic rate to be levied throughout Scotland in respect of the financial year 1995–96.

NON-DOMESTIC RATING CONTRIBUTIONS (SCOTLAND) AMENDMENT REGULATIONS 1994 (No. 3146) [£1·10], made under the Local Government Finance Act 1992 (c.14), ss.113(2) and 116(1) and Sched. 12, paras. 10, 11(5)(*a*) and 12; operative on December 31, 1994; amend the rules for the calculation of payments in the Non-Domestic Rating Contributions (Scotland) Regulations 1992, to reflect the fact that from 1995–96 onwards provisional payments will be calculated by authorities rather than the Secretary of State, to reflect amendments made by the Local Government etc. (Scotland) Act 1994 (c.39) and to take account of financial year 1995–96 being a year of revaluation.

[S.I. 1992 No. 3061 amended.]

NON-DOMESTIC RATING (UNOCCUPIED PROPERTY) (SCOTLAND) AMENDMENT REGULATIONS 1995 (No. 518) [65p], made under Local Government (Scotland) Act 1966 (c.51), ss.24(2) (as substituted by the Local Government etc. (Scotland) Act 1994 (c.39), ss.154 and 155, with effect from April 1, 1995) and 24A(4) (as inserted by the 1994 Act, ss.154 and 155, with effect from April 1, 1995); operative on April 1, 1995; amend the Non-Domestic (Unoccupied Property) (Scotland) Regulations 1994 to provide that unoccupied lands and heritages with a rateable value of less than £1500 are now exempt from non-domestic rates.

[S.I. 1994 No. 3200 amended.]

6250. Non-domestic rates—telecommunications and canals

NON-DOMESTIC RATING (TELECOMMUNICATIONS AND CANALS) (SCOTLAND) ORDER 1995 (No. 239) [65p], made under the Valuation and

Rating (Scotland) Act 1956 (c.60), s.6A (as inserted by the Local Government etc. (Scotland) Act 1994 (c.39) s.161), operative on April 1, 1995; makes provision for the treatment as a single valuation unit, for non-domestic rating purposes, of certain property in Scotland which would otherwise be treated as several such units.

6251. Rates—relief—charitable purposes—social club with bar facilities

[Local Government (Financial Provisions etc.) (Scotland) Act 1962 (c.9), s.4(2).]

C, a charitable organisation, petitioned for judicial review of S's refusal to grant mandatory rating relief in terms of s.4(2) of the 1962 Act, S having determined that the charitable activities conducted on C's premises were incidental to the main activities which related to the operation of social clubs, accompanied by substantial bar facilities. C argued that while the scale of bar activities operating within their premises was significant, the bar facilities only comprised one quarter of the premises, and as their predominant purpose was the provision of social, leisure and recreational activities, no reasonable authority could conclude that C's charitable activities were merely ancillary to its non-charitable ones. S's decision was unreasonable as they had failed properly to examine C's whole activities and had accordingly misdirected themselves.

Held, petition dismissed. The test for the purposes of rating relief, which S had applied, was whether the premises were used primarily for charitable purposes (*Oxfam v. Birmingham City Council* [1985] C.L.Y. 2763). Where C's main income came from the profits on the sale of alcohol and their bars were open every evening, most lunchtimes and all day at weekends, it was reasonable for S to conclude that alcohol was essentially continuously available on C's premises to provide a social club for adult members and not as incidental or ancillary to the provision of charitable, sporting or leisure activities. S were therefore entitled to conclude that the premises were mainly used as a social club and to refuse to grant C rating relief.

COALBURN MINERS' WELFARE AND CHARITABLE SOCIETY v. STRATHCLYDE REGIONAL COUNCIL (O.H.), 1995 S.L.T. 950.

6252. Subjects—car park associated with covered shopping mall

[Valuation and Rating (Scotland) Act 1956 (c.60), S.8A.]

Section 8A of the Valuation and Rating (Scotland) Act 1956 provides: "There shall not be entered separately in the valuation roll any part of a covered shopping mall, being a part the sole or main purpose of which is to serve two or more of the lands and heritages comprised in the mall." The owners of a shopping centre appealed against the inclusion in the valuation roll of a car park serving the centre. The centre contained a covered shopping mall in which there were a large number of retail premises and various leisure facilities. The car park was on three levels adjacent to the building which contained the mall, the topmost level being on the roof of part of the building. Some of the ground on which the centre and its car park were built had previously been used as a car park, but much of the car park as it now existed was built at the same time as the centre and mainly in order to provide car parking space for those using the shops and other facilities contained in it. Although the car park was also used by people going to other shopping developments in the town centre, and was available for use by anyone regardless of his destination, most of those who used it went to shops in the centre. The cost of the maintenance and repair of the car park was covered by a service charge levied on the tenants of the premises in the centre. No charges were made for its use, but the owners were entitled to introduce such charges if they wished.

Held, that the car park did not form part of the covered shopping mall, although its main purpose was to serve two or more of the lands and heritages comprised in the mall, and that it was not therefore exempted by s.8A from being entered separately in the valuation roll.

EAST KILBRIDE DEVELOPMENT CORPORATION v. ASSESSOR FOR STRATHCLYDE REGION, 1995 S.L.T. (Lands Tr.) 27.

6253. Subjects—community centre owned in common by proprietors of dwellinghouses in development—whether "pertinent" of dwellinghouses

[Abolition of Domestic Rates Etc. (Scotland) Act 1987 (c.47), s.2(3).]

Section 2(3) of the Abolition of Domestic Rates Etc (Scotland) Act 1987 defines "domestic subjects" as including "any lands and heritages consisting of one or more dwelling-houses with any . . . pertinent belonging to and occupied along with such dwellinghouse or dwelling-houses." An assessor appealed against a decision of a valuation appeal committee deleting an entry in the roll in respect of a community centre constructed as part of a scheme of residential development and as a condition of the planning consent therefor. The committee had accepted the contention of the ratepayers that the centre was a pertinent of the various dwellings forming part of the development. The committee made a number of findings in fact, in particular that in terms of the titles of the various dwellings each proprietor had a right in common along with the other proprietors in the estate to the centre and an obligation to contribute to its upkeep. They found further that no person other than the proprietor of a dwelling forming part of the estate had a right to use the centre and that it could not be let to third parties. The assessor argued that there were no grounds on which that latter finding could be made and there was insufficient evidence in relation to the position under the ratepayers' titles. It was further argued that as the centre was plainly geographically separate, to varying degrees, from the dwellinghouses it should not be treated as forming part of a single *unum quid* on the basis of a functional test.

Held, that (1) the true question in this appeal was whether the subjects of appeal, or more precisely the rights in them enjoyed by the ratepayers, fell to be regarded as pertinents "belonging to and occupied along with" the respective dwellings occupied by them; (2) the test whether a subject was a pertinent of a dwellinghouse or houses might not be governed by the same considerations as applied to the question whether two subjects should form part of the one unit of valuation; (3) an extract from the title deed of one of the dwellings and the assessor's concession that the planning permission had the effect of preventing the centre being let in any way inconsistent with its continued use as a community facility, together with the hearsay evidence of the ratepayers' surveyor on these matters, entitled the committee to hold that the centre formed a pertinent of the dwellinghouses in the estate; and appeal dismissed. *Opinion*, that (1) in some cases tests similar to those used to determine the extent of a unit of valuation might have to be applied to determine whether a subject did fall to be regarded as a pertinent for the purposes of s.2(3) but the very special circumstances in this case made it an unsuitable case in which to do so; (2) even if these tests were applied in the present case the same result would be reached.

CENTRAL REGION, ASSESSOR FOR v. SPRINGBANK GARDENS RESIDENTS' ASSOCIATION, 1995 S.L.T. 698.

6254. Valuation appeal committee

VALUATION APPEAL COMMITTEE (PROCEDURE IN APPEALS UNDER THE VALUATION ACTS) (SCOTLAND) REGULATIONS 1995 (No. 572) [£2·80], made under the Local Government (Financial Provisions) (Scotland) Act 1963 (c.12), ss.15(2) (as amended by the Local Government (Scotland) Act 1975 (c.30), Sched. 6 and prospectively amended by the Local Government etc. (Scotland) Act 1994 (c.39), Sched. 13), (2AA) (as inserted by the Local Government and Housing Act 1989 (c.42), Sched. 6) and (2A) (as inserted by the Rating and Valuation (Amendment) (Scotland) Act 1984 (c.31), s.12(2) and amended by the 1989 Act (c.42), Sched. 6); operative on April 1, 1995; govern the procedure to be followed with respect to appeals and complaints made under the Valuation Acts to valuation appeal committees established under the Local Government (Scotland) Act 1975, s.4.

[S.I. 1984 No. 1506 partially revoked.]

6255. Valuation appeal committee—timetable

VALUATION TIMETABLE (SCOTLAND) AMENDMENT ORDER 1995 (No. 2455) [65p], made under the Valuation and Rating (Scotland) Act 1956 (c.60) ss.13(1) (as extended by the Local Government (Financial Provisions) (Scotland) Act 1963 (c.12) s.22(d) and amended by the Local Government (Scotland) Act 1975 (c.30) Sched. 6) and 42(1); operative on September 15, 1995; substitutes December 15 as the last date by which appeals and complaints with a valuation appeal committee must be lodged.

[S.I. 1995 No. 164 amended.]

VALUATION TIMETABLE (SCOTLAND) ORDER 1995 (No. 164) [£1·10], made under the Valuation and Rating (Scotland) Act 1956 (c.60), ss.13(1) (as extended by the Local Government (Financial Provisions) (Scotland) Act 1963 (c.12), s.22(d) and amended by the Local Government (Scotland) Act 1975 (c.30), Sched. 6) and 42; operative on January 27, 1995; prescribes a new timetable for things requiring to be done in connection with the making up of a valuation roll at the time of revaluation and applications for redress to the assessor, lodging of appeals and complaints and the disposal by the valuation appeal committee.

[S.I. 1989 No. 2386 and S.I. 1993 No. 2242 revoked.]

6256. Valuation joint boards

VALUATION JOINT BOARDS (SCOTLAND) ORDER 1995 (No. 2589) [£1·95], made under the Local Government etc. (Scotland) Act 1994 (c.39), ss.27(7)–(9); operative on October 27, 1995; provides for the establishment of 10 valuation boards to discharge jointly the functions of certain valuation authorities and for the constitution and proceedings of each board.

6257. Valuation rolls

VALUATION ROLL AND VALUATION NOTICE (SCOTLAND) AMENDMENT ORDER 1995 (No. 573) [65p], made under the Local Government (Scotland) Act 1975 (c.30), ss.3(2), 35(2) and 37(1); operative on March 7, 1995; amends the Valuation Roll and Valuation Notice (Scotland) Order 1989 amending the prescribed form for valuation notices.

[S.I. 1989 No. 2385 amended.]

6258. Value—Alcan Aluminium (UK) Ltd

ELECTRICITY GENERATORS (ALUMINIUM) (RATEABLE VALUE) (SCOTLAND) ORDER (No. 372) [£1·10], made under the Local Government (Scotland) Act 1975 (c.30), ss.6 (as amended by the Local Government (Scotland) Act 1978 (c.4), s.1, the Local Government Finance Act 1988 (c.41), Sched. 12, the Local Government and Housing Act 1989 (c.42), Sched. 6, the Local Government Finance Act 1992 (c.14), Sched. 13 and the Local Government etc. (Scotland) Act 1994 (c.39), ss.157 and 160), 35 and 37(1) (as amended by the 1992 Act, Sched. 13); operative on April 1, 1995; makes provision for the valuation for the financial year 1995–96 to 1999–2000 of certain lands and heritages occupied by Alcan Aluminium U.K. or the Lochaber Power Co.

[S.I. 1994 No. 2068 and 2074 revoked.]

6259. Value—British Gas

BRITISH GAS PLC (RATEABLE VALUE) (SCOTLAND) ORDER (No. 368)

[£1·95], made under the Local Government (Scotland) Act 1975 (c.30), ss.6 (as amended by the Local Government (Scotland) Act 1978 (c.4), s.1, the Local Government Finance Act 1988 (c.41), Sched. 12, the Local Government and Housing Act 1989 (c.42), Sched. 6, the Local Government Finance Act 1992 (c.14), Sched. 13 and the Local Government etc. (Scotland) Act 1994 (c.39), ss.157 and 160), 35 and 37(1) (as amended by the 1992 Act, Sched. 13); operative on April 1, 1995; makes provision for the valuation for the financial year 1995–96 to 1999–2000 of certain lands and heritages occupied by British Gas.

[S.I. 1994 No. 2069 revoked.]

6260. Value—British Railways Board

BRITISH RAILWAYS BOARD (RATEABLE VALUES) (SCOTLAND) ORDER 1995 (No. 930) [£1·95], made under the Local Government (Scotland) Act 1975 (c.30), ss.6 (as substituted by the Local Government (Scotland) Act 1978 (c.4), s.1, the Local Government Finance Act 1988 (c.41), Sched. 12, amended by the Local Government Finance Act 1992 (c.14), Sched. 13 and inserted by the Local Government and Housing Act 1989 (c.42), Sched. 6 and the Local Government etc. (Scotland) Act 1994 (c.39), ss.157 and 160) 35 and 37(1); operative on April 1, 1995; makes provision for the valuation for the financial years 1995–96 to 1999–2000 of certain lands and heritages occupied by the British Railways Board, prescribes the aggregate amount of rateable values, provides a formula for the calculation of the aggregate amount, apportions those amounts among local authorities and provides that the non-domestic water rate shall not be leviable in respect of those lands and heritages for financial year 1995–96.

[Valuation and Rating (Scotland) Act 1956, s.6(1) and the Local Government (Scotland) Act 1975, ss.2(1)(*c*), (*d*) and (*g*) and 3(4) amended.]

6261. Value—docks and harbours

DOCKS AND HARBOURS (RATEABLE VALUE) (SCOTLAND) ORDER (No. 375) [£1·10], made under the Local Government (Scotland) Act 1975 (c.30), ss.6 (as amended by the Local Government (Scotland) Act 1978 (c.4), s.1, the Local Government Finance Act 1988 (c.41), Sched. 12, the Local Government and Housing Act 1989 (c.42), Sched. 6, the Local Government Finance Act 1992 (c.14), Sched. 13 and the Local Government etc. (Scotland) Act 1994 (c.39), ss.157 and 160), 35 and 37(1) (as amended by the 1992 Act, Sched. 13); operative on April 1, 1995; amends the Docks and Harbours (Rateable Values) (Scotland) Order 1990 so that it covers certain lands and heritages occupied by the British Waterways Board, Forth Ports or Caledonian MacBrayne but excludes lands and heritages occupied by undertakings with relevant income of less than £1,000,000 and to take account of local government reorganisation.

[S.I. 1994 No. 2080 and 2081 revoked, S.I. 1990 No. 817 amended.]

6262. Value—electricity distribution

ELECTRICITY DISTRIBUTION LANDS (RATEABLE VALUE) (SCOTLAND) ORDER (No. 373) [£1·95], made under the Local Government (Scotland) Act 1975 (c.30), ss.6 (as amended by the Local Government (Scotland) Act 1978 (c.4), s.1, the Local Government Finance Act 1988 (c.41), Sched. 12, the Local Government and Housing Act 1989 (c.42), Sched. 6, the Local Government Finance Act 1992 (c.14), Sched. 13 and the Local Government etc. (Scotland) Act 1994 (c.39), ss.157 and 160), 35 and 37(1) (as amended by the 1992 Act, Sched. 13); operative on April 1, 1995; makes provision for the valuation for the financial year 1995–96 to 1999–2000 of certain lands and heritages occupied by Scottish Power and Scottish Hydro-Electric and used for the purposes of the distribution of electricity.

6263. Value—electricity generators

ELECTRICITY GENERATION LANDS (RATEABLE VALUE) (SCOTLAND) ORDER (No. 369) [£1·95], made under the Local Government (Scotland) Act

1975 (c.30), ss.6 (as amended by the Local Government (Scotland) Act 1978 (c.4), s.1, the Local Government Finance Act 1988 (c.41), Sched. 12, the Local Government and Housing Act 1989 (c.42), Sched. 6, the Local Government Finance Act 1992 (c.14), Sched. 13 and the Local Government etc. (Scotland) Act 1994 (c.39), ss.157 and 160), 35 and 37(1) (as amended by the 1992 Act, Sched. 13); operative on April 1, 1995; makes provision for the valuation for the financial year 1995–96 to 1999–2000 of certain lands and heritages occupied by Scottish Power, Scottish Hydro-Electric and Scottish Nuclear and used for the purposes of the generation of electricity.

[S.I. 1994 No. 2076, 2077 and 2078 revoked.]

ELECTRICITY GENERATORS (RATEABLE VALUE) (SCOTLAND) ORDER (No. 371) [£1·55], made under the Local Government (Scotland) Act 1975 (c.30), ss.6 (as amended by the Local Government (Scotland) Act 1978 (c.4), s.1, the Local Government Finance Act 1988 (c.41), Sched. 12, the Local Government and Housing Act 1989 (c.42), Sched. 6, the Local Government Finance Act 1992 (c.14), Sched. 13 and the Local Government etc. (Scotland) Act 1994 (c.39), ss.157 and 160), 35 and 37(1) (as amended by the 1992 Act, Sched. 13); operative on April 1, 1995; makes provision for the valuation for the financial year 1995–96 to 1999–2000 of certain lands and heritages occupied for the sole or principal purpose of generating electricity from wind, wave tidal, water power or the burning of refuse or for use in connection with the sale of both electrical power and heat.

[S.I. 1994 No. 2072 revoked.]

6264. Value—electricity transmission

ELECTRICITY TRANSMISSION LANDS (RATEABLE VALUE) (SCOTLAND) ORDER (No. 370) [£1·95], made under the Local Government (Scotland) Act 1975 (c.30), ss.6 (as amended by the Local Government (Scotland) Act 1978 (c.4), s.1, the Local Government Finance Act 1988 (c.41), Sched. 12, the Local Government and Housing Act 1989 (c.42), Sched. 6, the Local Government Finance Act 1992 (c.14), Sched. 13 and the Local Government etc. (Scotland) Act 1994 (c.39), ss.157 and 160), 35 and 37(1) (as amended by the 1992 Act, Sched. 13); operative on April 1, 1995; makes provision for the valuation for the financial year 1995–96 to 1999–2000 of certain lands and heritages occupied by Scottish Power and Scottish Hydro-Electric and used for the purposes of the transmission of electricity.

6265. Value—formula—revocations

FORMULA VALUATION (REVOCATIONS) (SCOTLAND) ORDER 1995 (No. 374) [£1·10], made under the Local Government (Scotland) Act 1975 (c.30), ss.6 (as amended by the Local Government (Scotland) Act 1978 (c.4), s.1, the Local Government Finance Act 1988 (c.41), Sched. 12, the Local Government and Housing Act 1989 (c.42), Sched. 6, the Local Government Finance Act 1992 (c.14), Sched. 13 and the Local Government etc. (Scotland) Act 1994 (c.39), ss.157 and 160) and 35; operative on April 1, 1995, revokes various orders made under s.6 of the 1975 Act.

[S.I. 1990 No. 855, S.I. 1991 No. 915, S.I. 1992 No. 1796, S.I. 1993 No. 873 and S.I. 1994 Nos. 911, 913, 2071, 2073 and 2075 revoked.]

6266. Value—mines and quarries

MINES AND QUARRIES (RATEABLE VALUE) (SCOTLAND) ORDER (No. 366) [£1·10], made under the Local Government (Scotland) Act 1975 (c.30), ss.6 (as amended by the Local Government (Scotland) Act 1978 (c.4), s.1, the Local Government Finance Act 1988 (c.41), Sched. 12, the Local Government and Housing Act 1989 (c.42), Sched. 6, the Local Government Finance Act 1992 (c.14), Sched. 13 and the Local Government etc. (Scotland) Act 1994 (c.39), ss.157 and 160), 35 and 37(1) (as amended by the 1992 Act, Sched. 13); operative on April 1, 1995; makes provision for the valuation for the financial year 1995–96 and subsequent financial years of certain mines and quarries.

[S.I. 1994 No. 912 revoked.]

6267. Value—Railtrack plc.

RAILTRACK PLC. (RATEABLE VALUES) (SCOTLAND) ORDER 1995 (No. 929) [£1·95], made under the Local Government (Scotland) Act 1975 (c.30), ss.6 (as substituted by the Local Government (Scotland) Act 1978 (c.4), s.1, the Local Government Finance Act 1988 (c.41), Sched. 12, amended by the Local Government Finance Act 1992 (c.14), Sched. 13 and inserted by the Local Government and Housing Act 1989 (c.42), Sched. 6 and the Local Government etc. (Scotland) Act 1994 (c.39), ss.157 and 160) 35 and 37(1); operative on April 1, 1995; makes provision for the valuation for the financial years 1995–96 to 1999–2000 of certain prescribed lands and heritages occupied by Railtrack, prescribes the aggregate amount of rateable values, provides a formula for the calculation of the aggregate amount, apportions these amounts among local authorities and provides that the non-domestic water rate in respect of those lands and heritages for financial year 1995–96 shall not be leviable.

[Valuation and Rating (Scotland) Act 1956, s.6(1) and the Local Government (Scotland) Act 1975, ss.2(1)(*c*), (*d*) and (*g*) and 3(4) amended; S.I. 1994 No. 2070 revoked.]

6268. Value—revenue principle—ski lifts

Subjects consisting of various chairlifts and ski tows in the Scottish Highlands were valued by apportioning the average net revenue for the five years prior to the valuation date between the hypothetical landlord as rent and the hypothetical tenant as profit. The ratepayers contended that as the enterprise was totally dependent on the uncertain weather conditions of the Highlands it was attended by more than a normal commercial risk, and to induce a tenant to undertake that risk he would have to be offered two thirds of the net revenue, leaving only one third to the landlord as rent. For the purpose of assessing the risk the ratepayers contended that it was proper to have regard to the financial results of the undertaking both prior to the five years immediately preceding the valuation date and between that date and the later date at which the physical circumstances of the subjects had to be looked at. It was argued that physical circumstances included weather and snow conditions. The assessor contended that the assessment of future risk had to be based strictly on the results of the appropriate five year period, and that in order to allow for inflation the revenue for each of the earlier years in that period should be converted to money values in the final year by the use of the retail price index.

Held, that (1) the assessment of future risk should be based only on information available to the hypothetical tenant at the valuation date; (2) that assessment might be based not only on the results of the previous five years but on all that was then known of the factors affecting the undertaking; (3) an adjustment of the figures for revenue in order to allow for inflation during the five year period was not appropriate; and (4) the average net revenue should be apportioned as to approximately 53 per cent as tenant's profit and 47 per cent as rent.

CAIRNGORM CHAIRLIFT CO. v. ASSESSOR FOR HIGHLAND REGION, 1995 S.L.T. (Lands Tr.) 35.

6269. Value—water undertakings

WATER UNDERTAKINGS (RATEABLE VALUE) (SCOTLAND) ORDER (No. 367) [£1·95], made under the Local Government (Scotland) Act 1975 (c.30), ss.6 (as amended by the Local Government (Scotland) Act 1978 (c.4), s.1, the Local Government Finance Act 1988 (c.41), Sched. 12, the Local Government and Housing Act 1989 (c.42), Sched. 6, the Local Government Finance Act 1992 (c.14), Sched. 13 and the Local Government etc. (Scotland) Act 1994 (c.39), ss.157 and 160), 35 and 37(1) (as amended by the 1992 Act, Sched. 13); operative on April 1, 1995; makes provision for the valuation for the financial

year 1995–96 of certain lands and heritages occupied by specified water authorities and used wholly or mainly for the purposes of water undertakings.
[S.I. 1994 No. 2079 revoked.]

6270. Value formula—prescribed class—"ancillary purposes"—visitor centre at nuclear power station

[Scottish Nuclear Limited (Rateable Values) (Scotland) (No. 2) Order 1991 (S.I. 1991 No. 914), art. 3.]

The occupiers of a nuclear power station sought the exclusion of a visitor centre from the valuation roll having regard to the terms of the Scottish Nuclear Limited (Rateable Values) (Scotland) (No. 2) Order 1991. The visitor centre was administered from the main administration building which was within the security fence, and its employees were under the supervision of the appellants' personnel. Only approximately 5 per cent of visitors visited only the visitor centre. The valuation appeal committee by a majority accepted the assessor's argument that the visitor centre was not used for a purpose ancillary to generation, transmission or supply of electricity, and hence was correctly entered by the assessor in the valuation roll. The ratepayers appealed, contending that the committee should have started by determining what was the unit of valuation in accordance with the general law of valuation; the next question was whether the lands and heritages satisfied the test of being "occupied by the Company and wholly or mainly used for the purposes of the generation, transmission or supply of electricity or for ancillary purposes". The committee had ignored the unit of valuation and considered the latter test exclusively by reference to the visitor centre. It was clear that the whole subjects met the test as to occupation and use which was set out in art. 3(1). The assessor submitted that for the purposes of art. 3 the correct approach, in determining what were the relevant lands and heritages, was to ascertain to what extent the subjects occupied by the company at Torness satisfied the test in art. 3(1). On that approach, in contrast to the remainder of the subjects occupied by the ratepayers, the visitor centre fell outside the scope of the class.

Held, that (1) in the absence of any indication of a contrary intention it was correct to construe "lands and heritages" in the context of the order as referring to the relevant unit of valuation; (2) accordingly the correct starting point was the determination of the unit of valuation, which in the present case consisted of the whole subjects occupied by the appellants at Torness; (3) the assessor had failed to demonstrate any convincing reason why the question whether the visitor centre in itself satisfied the test as to occupation and use in art. 3(1) should not have been posed in regard to the subjects as a whole; and appeal allowed.

SCOTTISH NUCLEAR v. ASSESSOR FOR LOTHIAN REGION (L.V.A.C.), 1995 S.L.T. 1026.

REGISTRATION OF BIRTHS, DEATHS AND MARRIAGES

6271. Fees

REGISTRATION OF BIRTHS, DEATHS, MARRIAGES AND DIVORCES (FEES) (SCOTLAND) AMENDMENT REGULATIONS 1995 (No. 646) [£1·10], made under the Registration of Births, Deaths and Marriages (Scotland) Act 1965 (c.49), ss.28(A)(4) (as inserted by the Law Reform (Miscellaneous Provisions) (Scotland) Act 1985 (c.73), s.50(1)), 38(2) and (3), 47, 54(1) (as amended by the Children Act 1975 (c.72), Sched. 4 and by the Marriage (Scotland) Act 1977 (c.15), Sched. 3) and 56; operative on April 1, 1995; amends the Registration of Births, Deaths, Marriages and Divorces (Fees) (Scotland) Regulations 1993

so as to introduce fees for certain new services and to increase certain fees with effect from April 1, 1995.
[S.I. 1993 No. 3153 amended.]

REPARATION

6272. Coal mining subsidence. See BRITISH COAL CORPORATION v. NETHERLEE TRUST TRS., §6139.

Damages. See DAMAGES.

6273. Detention—whether unlawful

[Prevention and Suppression of Terrorism (Supplemental) Temporary Provisions) Order 1984 (S.I. 1984 No. 418, arts. 4 and 9).]

B sued C, a chief constable, for damages arising from his detention between September 29 and October 4, 1988 which B claimed was wrongful and illegal. B was returning to Ireland from Scotland when apprehended and detained. B claimed that C's officers (P) had no reasonable grounds for believing B to be a person guilty of an offence under the Prevention of Terrorism (Temporary Provisions) Act 1984 or a person concerned with acts of terrorism, and that they had detained B without probable cause. B argued that he required to aver the circumstances of the detention, that it was unlawful and that it was prima facie unjustified (*Dahl v. Chief Constable, Central Scotland Police* [1983] C.L.Y. 4871; *Shields v. Shearer*, 1913 S.C. 1012; 1914 S.C. (H.L.) 33). Detention beyond the initial 12 hour period would have only been lawful pending consideration of the making of an exclusion order, but C had not averred that this had been taking place.

Held, action dismissed, B had failed to satisfy the test of wrongful detention, which was the same as that for wrongful arrest (set out in *Dahl, supra*). B required to aver that P's actions, although purportedly in exercise of a statutory power, fell out with the scope of the statutory power. There was a presumption that P acted in pursuance of their duty (*Shields, supra*). Where the power to detain did not depend on the existence of a reasonable ground for suspicion, an averment of no reasonable grounds was not *per se* enough to make the detention unlawful. B should have averred the factors necessary to make detention lawful and which of these were absent. In contrast to the position regarding extended detention under art. 4 (being concerned in acts of terrorism), reasonable ground for suspicion was not part of the foundation for detention under art. 9 (consideration of exclusion order). Clearly the Secretary of State rather than the police might have the relevant information. B did not aver his detention was not genuinely pending consideration of whether an exclusion order should be made.

BREEN *v.* CHIEF CONSTABLE OF DUMFRIES AND GALLOWAY, *The Scotsman*, May 24, 1995.

Fraud. See FRAUD, MISREPRESENTATION AND UNDUE INFLUENCE.

Limitation of actions. See LIMITATION OF ACTIONS.

Negligence. See NEGLIGENCE.

Nuisance. See NUISANCE.

Prescription. See PRESCRIPTION.

Solatium. See DAMAGES.

6274. Wrongful occupation of heritable property. See SAEED v. WAHEED, §5841.

REVENUE AND FINANCE

Income tax. See INCOME TAX.

Local government finance. See LOCAL GOVERNMENT.

RIGHTS IN SECURITY

Standard security. See HERITABLE PROPERTY AND CONVEYANCING.

ROAD TRAFFIC

6275. Careless driving—"road or other public place"—school playground. See RODGER v. NORMAND, §6277.

6276. Dangerous driving—causing death—imprisonment

Held, that seven years' imprisonment and disqualification for life for causing death by dangerous driving, with six months concurrent for driving with excess blood alcohol, was not excessive where M, whose record included non-analogous road traffic offences, drove at 65 mph, was unable to negotiate a bend and collided with oncoming traffic causing the death of one of his passengers and injury to the other and the occupant of another car, though M, an alcoholic who had unsuccessfully tried to reform, was on medication, suffered from hallucinations and had, while previously on remand, attempted suicide.

MURRAY v. H.M. ADVOCATE, 1994 S.C.C.R. 674.

6277. Dangerous driving—"road or other public place"—school playground

[Road Traffic Act 1988 (c.52), ss.2 and 3.]

R appealed against his conviction for driving a motorcycle carelessly in the grounds of a secondary school, on the grounds that the sheriff had erred in repelling R's motion of no case to answer against the original charge of dangerous driving. R argued that the grounds were not a "road or other public place" within the meaning of ss.2 or 3, as there was no public right of passage across the grounds, the grounds were not used by the public in general, and it was the policy of the owners, the regional council, not to admit people after school hours. The Crown conceded that the grounds were not a "road" within the meaning of the Act.

Held, appeal refused. As the purpose of the statute was to secure the safety of the public in places where they might be expected to be, a "public place" was to be defined as one on which members of the public might be expected to be found and over which they might be expected to pass or to which they had access, and not necessarily one to which they had a legal right of access (*Cheyne v. MacNeill* [1972] C.L.Y. 4062; *Brown v. Braid* [1985] C.L.Y. 4715; *Thomson v. MacPhail* [1992] C.L.Y. 6310). As the children and older persons, who regularly used the grounds as a leisure park outwith school hours, did so as members of the public generally and not by invitation or permission and the owners acquiesced in or tolerated such use, the grounds were a public place within the meaning of ss.2 and 3.

RODGER v. NORMAND, 1995 S.L.T. 411.

6278. Dangerous driving—speeding

Held, although the Crown had not originally supported the conviction, that a sheriff had not erred in convicting T of dangerous driving where T was speeding at 114 mph on a dual carriageway part of the A9: although the sheriff noted that there was nothing inherently dangerous about T's driving apart from his speed as the road was dry, weather conditions were good, visibility was excellent and T's car was in excellent condition, where the sheriff had also taken into account the potential hazards of a driver in T's position such as the possibility of a tyre blowing or traffic entering or leaving the road at either of two road junctions and consequent difficulties associated with control exacerbated by travelling at 114 mph, the sheriff was entitled to be satisfied that there were potential hazards on this stretch of the road which should have been taken into account by a careful and competent driver, and the significance of which had to be assessed in the light of the grossly excessive speed, and that the tests in s.2 of the Road Traffic Act 1988, as amended, had been satisfied. This was not a case where the findings negatived all the potential dangers (*Brown v. Orr*, 1994 S.C.C.R. 668 distinguished).

TRIPPICK v. ORR, 1995 S.L.T. 272.

6279. Disqualification—driving while disqualified—imprisonment

Held, where M received nine months' imprisonment for driving while disqualified (M having been disqualified for 15 months the day before), with nine months consecutive for taking and driving a vehicle and six months concurrent to that for failing to stop after an accident, that the sentences would be considered anew since the sheriff had not given reasons for making them consecutive, but were appropriate having regard to the time scale and the differing nature of the offences, despite claims by M that all the offences were committed on the same occasion and that it was normal that such sentences be concurrent (*Steven v. Lees*, 1993 S.C.C.R. 778; *Grierson v. H.M. Advocate* [1993] C.L.Y. 5760; *Hunt v. Wilson* [1991] C.L.Y. 5567 and *McGrory v. Jessop* [1990] C.L.Y. 5017).

McEWAN v. H.M. ADVOCATE, 1995 S.C.C.R. 509.

6280. Disqualification—driving while disqualified—imprisonment—consecutive sentence—whether appropriate

Held, that two months' imprisonment for driving while disqualified, one month for failing to stop and give his details and one month for failing to supply a blood specimen was not excessive for S, who had a bad record which included two road traffic offences, these offences occurring only three months after S was disqualified for one year, but that it was excessive to make the sentences consecutive, since all the offences had taken place on the same occasion; and sentences made concurrent.

STEVEN v. LEES, 1994 S.C.C.R. 778.

6281. Disqualification—driving while disqualified—proof of driving

[Road Traffic Act 1988 (c.52), ss.103(1)(b) and 143(1) and (2).]

H appealed against conviction for breach of ss.103(1)(b) and 143(1) and (2) of the Road Traffic Act 1988 on the grounds that there was insufficient evidence for the sheriff to infer that he was driving the motor vehicle prior to the arrival of the police. Two police officers had observed a motor van stationary on the roadway at about 11.45 pm, with H lying across the passenger seat. No one else was in the van or near the vicinity and the ignition keys were found on the floor under the passenger seat. The van was secured and H taken to the police station; when the officers returned approximately 15 minutes later, the engine was warm. H argued that as there was no direct evidence of any movement of the van by him, the sheriff was not entitled to infer that he had been driving the vehicle prior to the police arriving.

Held, appeal refused (the Lord Justice Clerk (Ross) dissenting). *Per* Lords McCluskey and Morison: The most obvious explanation for the van, which was apparently in working order, being in a public road just before midnight with a warm engine, a driver in the driving seat and the ignition key in the vehicle was that the van had been driven there by H and as no competing explanation was given, the sheriff was entitled to infer that H had driven the van to the locus (*Ames v. McLeod* [1971] C.L.Y. 14161 and *McArthur v. Valentine* [1990] C.L.Y. 5752, distinguished). *Per* the Lord Justice Clerk (dissenting): There was nothing in the facts to justify the inference that the van had moved while H was in it. The evidence was consistent with H having started the engine, attempting to drive and subsequently turning the engine off without moving the vehicle, and the fact that the engine was warm did not infer that the van had been recently moved. At the stage of a submission of no case to answer no weight could be attached to the absence of an alternative explanation.

HENDERSON v. HAMILTON, 1995 S.L.T. 968.

6282. Disqualification—driving without insurance. See DOCHERTY v. NORMAND, §6308.

6283. Disqualification—for life—whether excessive. See HOLLAND v. HOWDLE, §6291.

6284. Disqualification—less than minimum period of disqualification imposed—Crown appeal—appropriate disposal

Held, where H was, *inter alia*, disqualified for 60 days for dangerous driving, which H had served, that the sheriff had failed to give effect to the mandatory minimum period of disqualification of one year and until the test of competence had been passed in such cases; and that the case should be remitted to the sheriff to decide whether the minimum or a longer period should be served and to take account of the period already served in making his further order.

BARBOUR v. HAY, 1994 S.C.C.R. 685.

6285. Disqualification—speeding. See BROWN v. ORR, §6318.

6286. Disqualification—totting up—grounds for mitigating normal consequences of conviction—exceptional hardship

[Road Traffic Offenders Act 1988 (c.53), s.35(1) and (4).]

Held, on the Crown's appeal against the sheriff's decision not to disqualify D under the totting up procedure on the grounds of exceptional hardship, the Crown arguing that loss of D's licence would affect no one other than D, his wife and their immediate family and that did not amount to exceptional hardship (*Ewen v. Orr* [1994] C.L.Y. 6228), that the appeal would be refused since the question of exceptional hardship was one of fact and degree and no invariable rule existed to define it (*Allan v. Barclay* [1986] C.L.Y. 4617); the sheriff was entitled to take the view he did where D, aged 41 and married with three children under 10, had shown considerable initiative in developing new sources of income for his family since his sequestration in 1991. D, who was employed as a regional manager of a company set up in his wife's name, effectively did 90 per cent. of the required work and the effect on D and his family which would result from disqualification could in the circumstances be regarded as exceptional.

HOWDLE v. DAVIDSON, 1994 S.C.C.R. 751.

6287. Drink or drugs—analyst's certificate—objection to. See MACAULAY v. WILSON, §5710.

6288. Drink or drugs—being in charge of a motor vehicle—supervisor of learner driver

[Road Traffic Act 1988 (c.52), s.5(1)(b) and (2).]

Section 5(2) of the Road Traffic Act 1988 provides that it is a defence to a charge under s.5(1)(b) for the accused to prove that at the time of the offence "the circumstances were such that there was no likelihood of his driving the vehicle whilst the proportion of alcohol in his breath, blood or urine remained likely to exceed the prescribed limit". An accused person was charged on summary complaint with being in charge of a motor vehicle after having consumed alcohol in excess of the prescribed limit, contrary to s.5(1)(b) of the 1988 Act. The only issue at the trial was whether the defence under s.5(2) had been established. The accused was in the passenger seat of his vehicle when his wife, who was a learner driver, was driving. She accepted that her driving was imperfect and that the accused would straighten the steering wheel when she was heading in the wrong direction. The accused accepted that he would do so. The sheriff convicted the accused on the basis that it was likely that he would have to take control of the steering wheel at some point while the vehicle was being driven by the accused's wife. The accused appealed.

Held, that (1) the question raised by the defence was not whether the accused was likely to drive but whether it had been established that there was no likelihood of his driving; (2) since the accused accepted that he might take control of the vehicle as a last resort, the sheriff was entitled to conclude that the defence had not been made out and appeal refused.

WILLIAMSON v. CROWE, 1995 S.L.T. 959.

6289. Drink or drugs—blood or urine specimen—conflicting results from analyses by Crown and defence

J appealed against conviction of driving with an excess of alcohol in his blood in breach of s.5(1)(a) of the Road Traffic Act 1988. Following his arrest on March 17, 1994, J elected to supply a specimen of blood, which was divided into two parts, sealed and labelled. J chose one of the parts and the other was sent by the police for analysis in Dundee by Q and three other analysts in terms of ss.15 and 16 of the Road Traffic Offenders Act 1988. The results of the four tests were aggregated and averaged to produce the figure of 93, from which the safety factor of six was deducted resulting in Q's certified figure of 87, which was in excess of the permitted level. J took his specimen to the Department of Forensic Medicine and Science at Glasgow University on March 25, and following analysis on March 27, a certificate was issued that the proportion of alcohol in terms of the specimen was equal to, not in excess of, the prescribed limit. Following a hearing, the sheriff concluded that the police analysis truly reflected J's alcohol level as the tests had been confirmed by four analysts and there was a question whether the alcohol content in respect of J's part of the specimen had reduced because of maltreatment. J appealed arguing that the sheriff had applied the wrong test by concluding that the Glasgow analysis did not create a reasonable doubt regarding the reliability of the Dundee results, as it was for the Crown to establish beyond a reasonable doubt that the Dundee analysis was reliable.

Held, appeal refused. Since the results of the Glasgow and Dundee tests were so far apart that they could not both be accurate, the sheriff was entitled to conclude that the Dundee analysis truly reflected J's blood alcohol level, having regard to the fact that no confirmatory tests were performed in Glasgow and that although the alcohol content of a sample could be reduced by maltreatment (such as inadequate refrigeration) it could not be increased, and therefore the higher results at Dundee could not be attributed to the possibility of maltreatment.

JORDAN v. RUSSELL, 1995 S.L.T. 1301.

6290. Drink or drugs—breath tests—right to require—police on private property

[Road Traffic Act 1988 (c.52), s.6(1)(c).]

Held, that it was open to a sheriff to conclude that police officers who observed M's vehicle being driven apparently in a condition in contravention of the Construction and Use Regulations and pursued him to a harbour where he ran on to his fishing boat, were entitled to pursue him on to the boat and, having detected a smell of alcohol, to require him to take a breath test, despite M's argument that they were then on private property without right to be there, since, having ascertained from examining M's vehicle that a moving traffic offence had been committed, the police were already entitled to require him to take a test and, in the circumstances, to pursue him on to the boat as a matter of urgency for the purpose of making the requirement (*Cairns v. Keane* [1984] C.L.Y. 4535, followed).

MACKENZIE v. HINGSTON, 1995 S.L.T. 966.

6291. Drink or drugs—sentence—disqualification for life—whether excessive

Held, where H received probation with the condition that he attend a drink-impaired driver's course and was disqualified for life for driving with an excess of blood alcohol, the disqualification was excessive since H, aged 30 with two analogous convictions, was performing satisfactorily on the course; and six years substituted.

HOLLAND v. HOWDLE, 1994 S.C.C.R. 772.

6292. Drink or drugs—sentence—forfeiture

Held, where C, aged 37 and married with a child, received 120 hours' community service, was disqualified for four years and had his D registered car forfeited, for driving with a breath alcohol count of 108, his second such offence in the last 18 months, that a continuation for a valuation to be produced would be refused since this should have been available at that hearing, and that the forfeiture, the first such exercise of this new statutory power, was not excessive given the foregoing circumstances, since C's car was not essential for his work as a manager, and since no fine was imposed.

CARRON v. RUSSELL, 1994 S.C.C.R. 681.

6293. Drivers' records—exemption—breakdown vehicle

[Council Regulation (E.E.C.) No. 3821/85, art. 4.]

Held, On F's appeal against conviction of failing to use a record sheet in recording equipment in his vehicle, of consent of the Crown, that the justice erred in concluding that F's vehicle was a motor recovery vehicle but not a specialised breakdown vehicle in terms of art. 4 of Reg. 3820/85, since by the definition given in *Hamilton v. Whitelock* (79/86) [1988] R.T.R. 23, the test was a general one and could be applied to differently equipped vehicles; the fact that in this case, unlike *Hamilton*, the vehicle did not have a demountable crane for lifting or towing a broken down vehicle was not significant where F had a specially adapted flat Ford truck equipped to carry a vehicle on its back, which equipment included ramps, winch and a pulley enabling it to pull a broken down or damaged vehicle on to its ramps; and conviction quashed.

FORGAN v. HAMILTON, 1994 S.C.C.R. 733.

6294. Driving licences—disqualification—disqualification for life—whether excessive. See HOLLAND v. HOWDLE, §6291.

6295. Driving licences—disqualification—driving while disqualified—imprisonment. See McEWAN v. H.M. ADVOCATE, §6279.

6296. Driving licences—disqualification—driving while disqualified—imprisonment—consecutive sentence. See STEVEN v. LEES, §6280.

6297. Driving licences—disqualification—driving while disqualified—proof of driving. See HENDERSON v. HAMILTON, §6281.

6298. Driving licences—disqualification—driving without insurance. See DOCHERTY v. NORMAND, §6308.

6299. Driving licences—disqualification—less than minimum period of disqualification imposed—Crown appeal—appropriate disposal. See BARBOUR v. HAY, §6284.

6300. Driving licences—disqualification—speeding. See BROWN v. ORR, §6318.

6301. Driving licences—disqualification—totting up—grounds for mitigating normal consequences of conviction—exceptional hardship. See HOWDLE v. DAVIDSON, §6286.

6302. Driving without insurance—fine

Held, that fines of £400, £200 and £200 at £5 per week for driving without insurance, having no test certificate and no licence were excessive for B, who had a very bad record, since repayment would take 160 weeks and in view of the fact that B was single, unemployed and receiving benefits of £72 per fortnight this was unreasonable; and all fines halved.

BROWN v. McGLENNAN, 1995 S.C.C.R. 627.

6303. Driving without insurance—fine

[Criminal Procedure (Scotland) Act 1975 (c.21, s.395(1).]

Held, where T, aged 18 with a record and other outstanding fines, was fined £150 for driving without insurance, £100 for driving without a licence and £50 on each of two bail offences all at £5 per fortnight, that although T received only £72 per fortnight and so the fines would take almost three years to pay, a lesser fine was not appropriate given the deliberate nature of the offences.

TONNER v. HAMILTON, 1995 S.C.C.R. 469.

6304. Identification of driver. See WINTER v. HEYWOOD, §5614.

6305. Identification of driver—requirement to identify driver

[Road Traffic Act 1988 (c.52), s.172(2)a).]

S appealed against conviction for careless driving, failing to stop after and failing to report an accident, and failing to identify the driver of his vehicle, on the grounds that there was insufficient evidence for the sheriff to conclude that S was the driver of the vehicle which caused the accident. M gave evidence that after hearing a noise she saw a car (later identified as S's vehicle) drive away having made contact with another car, and that its rear light broke as it pulled away. The police later matched glass found at the locus with the broken rear light of S's car, as well as the description and registration number which M gave them.

Held, appeal refused. S was the registered owner and keeper, and although he disputed that the car was at the locus of the accident, he clearly stated to the police that no one else had the car and that he had the keys, and the sheriff was entitled to draw the inference that S had driven the car at the material time, particularly where there was no suggestion that the car had been broken into or otherwise interfered with. There was no indication in the sheriff's note that he had proceeded upon the basis that S's reply constituted an unequivocal admission, hence he was entitled to convict of the last charge.

SOUTER v. LEES, 1995 S.C.C.R. 33.

6306. Insurance—failure to insure—causing or permitting—whether strict liability

[Road Traffic Act 1988 (c.52), s.143(1).]

M appealed against conviction of permitting J to drive her car without insurance cover. J had offered to take the car for a replacement part. M's policy did not cover J's use of the car but on her inquiry J assured her, wrongly, that his own policy did. M would not have allowed J to drive had she known the true position. The fiscal argued, and the sheriff accepted, that the offence was one of strict liability, relying on *Lyons v. May* [1948] C.L.Y. 9065 and *Smith of Maddiston v. Macnab* [1975] C.L.Y. 4103.

Held, appeal allowed. The correct approach, as the Crown conceded on appeal, was that in *Newbury v. Davis* [1974] C.L.Y. 3351: no permission was given unless J had insurance to cover his use. Permission subject to an unfulfilled condition was no permission at all.

MacDONALD v. HOWDLE, 1995 S.L.T. 779.

6307. Insurance—failure to insure—certificate issued with retrospective effect

[Road Traffic Act 1988 (c.52), ss.143(1) and 147(1).]

Held, on M seeking suspension of his conviction for driving without insurance on the basis that he had pled guilty on incorrect information, that although M had telephoned his brokers the previous day and had been advised that he would be covered from midnight if he paid the premium the next day, since at the time he was stopped by the police that next day he had not yet paid the premium, he was using his vehicle "when there [was] not in force in relation to its use" the relevant insurance in terms of s.143(1)(*a*), and it did not matter that the certificate subsequently issued stated that it took effect from 0001 hours on that day; and bill refused.

McCULLOCH v. HEYWOOD, 1995 S.L.T. 1009.

6308. Insurance—failure to insure—sentence—disqualification

Held, that six months' disqualification, with a £75 fine, for driving without insurance was not excessive although D argued on the basis of *Gibb v. McGlennan* [1991] C.L.Y. 5598 that this was inappropriate for a first offender. The magistrate was entitled to consider the prevalence of the offence and the cost to law abiding motorists of uninsured claims; it had become more and more apparent recently that such offences had to be treated seriously unless there were mitigating factors present and there was nothing to prevent a disqualification being imposed even on a first offence.

DOCHERTY v. NORMAND, 1995 S.C.C.R. 20.

6309. Insurance—liability of insurer

Held, that it was an essential condition of the avoidance by an insurer of his liability to an injured party under s.151 of the Road Traffic Act 1988, on the ground that he was entitled to avoid the insured's policy, that he obtained a judicial declaration to that effect in terms of s.152 of the Act.

McBLAIN v. DOLAN, *The Times*, September 28 1995.

6310. Insurance—third party claim not covered by policy—intimation of proceedings to insurers—notice by telephone

[Road Traffic Act 1988 (c.53), S. 152(1).]

E, insurers, appealed a sheriff's decision to allow O a proof on his averments that he had given notice to E in terms of s.152(1) of the 1988 Act within seven days of the bringing of an action of damages against E's insured (F) in respect of personal injuries sustained in a road traffic accident in February 1991, in which O's motorbike had collided with F's vehicle. E averred that the circumstances of the accident did not fall within F's insurance cover. O averred that in terms of s.151 of the 1988 Act E were liable to meet any judgment against F, that following prolonged correspondence with E, O's solicitors (S) had advised E in a telephone conversation on February 9, 1994 that a court action had been raised in order to avoid time bar, that E had advised that it be served on F rather than E's solicitors, and that S had confirmed the bringing of proceedings in a fax dated February 10, which had been acknowledged by E on February 16. E argued that the notice given did not satisfy the terms of s.152(1), as giving notice by telephone was too casual, and the notice had been factually wrong as proceedings had been raised on February 10, when warrant for intimation had been granted, and not February 9 as stated.

Held, appeal refused. Section 152(1) specified only the timing of the notice to E and that it had to be "notice of the bringing of proceedings", and it was unnecessary to read into it any further requirements as to the source, manner or form of the notice, as the purpose of the section was to ensure E were aware of the proceedings in case they should wish to take over control of the litigation and to avoid the risk of decree passing by default. Given that E had already been dealing with S and had been fully apprised of O's accident and the details of his claim, the telephone conversation was significant enough to have alerted E to the matter of liability in terms of s.151 of the 1988 Act. While inaccuracy might vitiate a notice, the inaccuracy as to the date of raising proceedings had been relatively slight, had caused no prejudice to E and, in alerting E sufficiently clearly and in sufficient time to the bringing of proceedings, as confirmed by E's acknowledgment, the notice satisfied the letter and purpose of s.152(1).

ORME v. FERGUSON (Sh.Ct.), 1995 S.C.L.R. 752.

6311. Lighting—emergency lamp—whether "fitted" to vehicle

[Road Vehicles Lighting Regulations 1989 (S.I. 1989 No. 1794, reg. 16.]

Held, on B's appeal against conviction for using a motor vehicle fitted with a special warning lamp in breach of reg. 16 of the Road Vehicles Lighting Regulations 1989, that where the police found an operational blue magnetic mounted roof lamp on the rear parcel shelf of B's vehicle similar to that used by police and fire brigade personnel, the sheriff did not err in concluding that the lamp was "fitted" to B's vehicle, as the word "fitted" in reg. 16 meant "equipped" and it was irrelevant that the lamp was moveable where it was positioned in the vehicle in such a way as to give the impression that the vehicle was fitted with a warning lamp.

BROWN v. McGLENNAN, High Court of Justiciary, *The Scotsman*, November 22, 1995.

Negligence. See NEGLIGENCE.

6312. Road—"road or other public place"—car deck of ferry with loading ramp in position

[Roads (Scotland) Act 1986 (c.54), s.151.]

Held, on D's appeal against conviction for driving without insurance on the grounds that the place where D was using the vehicle, namely the car deck of a ferry which was berthed at the time (D having got in and released the handbrake after the driver had left it), was not a road within s.151 of the 1984 Act, that the appeal would be refused since, though it was accepted that while at sea the car deck would not be a "way", in the present case it was as the ramp connecting the ferry and the quay was in place to allow for the disembarkation of vehicles, and a right of passage could be exercised by paying passengers and those who worked on board even though it was restricted to the times when the ferry was berthed, the ramp was in place and vehicles were driving on or off.

DICK v. WALKINGSHAW, 1995 S.L.T. 1254.

6313. Road—"road or other public place"—school playground. See RODGER v. NORMAND, §6277.

6314. Roadside check—whether illegal

[Road Traffic Act 1988 (c.52), s.163(1).]

Section 163(1) of the Road Traffic Act 1988 provides that a person driving a mechanically propelled vehicle on a road must stop the vehicle on being required to do so by a constable in uniform. An accused person was charged on summary complaint with using or keeping on a public road a vehicle for which a licence was not then in force, contrary to s.8 of the Vehicles (Excise) Act 1971. The police gave evidence that they were carrying out a routine road check when they stopped the accused's vehicle and observed that no vehicle excise disc was displayed on it. Objection was taken to the admissibility of that evidence on the ground that the police had been carrying out an illegal road stop at the time. The magistrate heard the evidence under reservation of its admissibility and at the close of the Crown case sustained the objection and acquitted the accused. The procurator fiscal appealed by stated case.

Held, that the magistrate was wrong to sustain the objection because s.163(1) was very general in its terms and the scope of the police officers' power was to be implied from the wide terms in which the duty was expressed; and appeal allowed and case remitted to magistrate to proceed as accords. (*Beard v. Wood* [1980] C.L.Y. 2372, followed.) *Observed*, that where an offence was patent to be seen because something was not being displayed which ought to have been displayed, there was nothing which could be described as an invasion of liberty or an excess of police powers.

NORMAND v. McKELLAR, 1995 S.L.T. 798.

6315. Speeding. See TRIPPICK v. ORR, §6278.

6316. Speeding—approved radar device—proof of approval

[Road Traffic Offences Act 1988 (c.53), s.20.]

P appealed against conviction of speeding. During the trial P had made a submission of no case to answer claiming that the Crown had failed to establish that the "Gatso" mini radar device was approved by the Secretary of State for the purpose of evidence of speed measurement. The Crown had led evidence that the police had checked the accuracy before and after the reading was taken. A worksheet compiled at the time was produced and spoken to in evidence. The justice had convicted on the basis that the Secretary of State's approval was an inference to be taken from the facts and circumstances of the use of the device and regularity of the proceedings (*Mackie v. Scott* [1992] C.L.Y. 6327). The Crown could have produced a document confirming that the device was approved or led evidence to that effect but had not done so.

Held, appeal allowed. P's submission of no case to answer should have been upheld. No evidence had been led that the police had received special training in operating the device and there was no evidence that the device was in regular use (*Mackie*, supra, distinguished). The justice had, in the circumstances, not been entitled to draw the inference that he did.

PICKARD v. CARMICHAEL, 1995 S.L.T. 675.

6317. Speeding—sentence

[Road Traffic Offenders Act 1988 (c.53), ss.28(1) and 31(1).]

Held, that six penalty points, with a £150 fine, for speeding at 55 m.p.h. in a 30 m.p.h. limit was not excessive and that, despite an argument for N that previous convictions were taken into account under the totting up procedure and should not also be considered in determining the number of points, the provisions of ss.28(1) and 31(1) of the 1988 Act were entirely general so that the sheriff was entitled to consider N's three previous convictions, two in the last two years, as well as the gravity of the offence, particularly where N was speeding at nearly twice the permitted limit.

NICHOLSON v. WESTWATER, 1995 S.L.T. 1018.

6318. Speeding—sentence—disqualification

Held, on B's appeal against conviction for dangerous driving as a result of speeding at 104 mph on the A9, that where it was found that it was daylight, road conditions were good with good visibility, there was no other traffic in the vicinity and none of the field entrances, laybys, road junctions, etc., to be found on that road was sufficiently close to the points between which B's speed was measured for there to be a potential danger, there were no findings to support a further finding that the tests in s.2 of the Road Traffic Act 1988, as amended, had been satisfied (*Jansch v. Orr* [1995] 1 C.L. 543, distinguished); and conviction substituted of the alternative charge of speeding and B, who had a clean licence and used his car in his employment, fined £250 with six penalty points.

BROWN v. ORR, 1994 S.C.C.R. 668.

Taxicabs—licensing. See LOCAL GOVERNMENT.

SALE OF GOODS

6319. Acceptance of goods—reasonable opportunity to examine

[Sale of Goods Act 1979 (c.54), ss.34(1) and 35(1).]

C sought payment of the price of a number of cast aluminium panels manufactured and supplied by C to A, who alleged that the panels were defective and counterclaimed for damages. The contract provided that the panels had to be manufactured to the standard of a sample panel which had been inspected by one of A's directors, that the panels were to be "flat and true" and, in cl.11, that C would "replace without charge any of the goods or work which, under proper use, are found to be defective as to materials design or workmanship". Following manufacture, the panels had been delivered to A's subcontractors (L) for painting and then transported to other subcontractors for mounting in metal frames, which involved boring the panels to receive fixings. Thereafter, they were delivered to the site where the panels were immediately incorporated in a building by A. A averred that, after the scaffolding had been removed, the panels were found to be defective in their surface finish, that they were then removed and had been rejected by A in terms of s.11(5) of the 1979 Act. A argued that (1) A had only had a reasonable opportunity to inspect the panels after they had been installed and the whole pattern on each elevation of the building could be seen from the ground, that A had rejected the panels within a reasonable time, and that A's actings were not inconsistent with C's continued ownership of the panels, given that the panels had no value independently of the contract; (2) as the "proper use" for the panels was their incorporation in the building, A had a right to reject the panels in terms of cl.11; and (3) that, as A had written to C stating that the panels might be rejected by the architect in charge of the building work, C had, by continuing to supply the panels, impliedly consented to a variation of the contract to allow a later date of testing (*D. Allen & Son (Butcher) v. Grampian Country Pork*, C.A. January 23, 1990, unreported).

Held, A's averments anent rejection of the panels excluded from probation; case put out by order. (1) The panels had been delivered to A either at C's premises, in terms of the contract, or at the latest, at L's premises and, given that there were no averments as to why an inspection similar to that of the sample panel would not be sufficient for determining whether the panels conformed to the sample, or as to why inspection during the two weeks allowed for painting and assembly would not have been practical, there had been actual inspection in L's hands of 26 other panels leading to the rejection of those panels, and at least some panels had lain on site for considerable periods, A had had a sufficiently long time in which to decide whether to reject the panels in terms of ss.11(5) and 35(1). While the complexity of the intended function of goods was clearly a prime consideration in assessing a reasonable time in which to reject goods (*Bernstein v. Pamson Motors (Golders Green)* [1987] C.L.Y. 3335), the period between delivery and rejection had clearly not been reasonable as the panels had no mechanical properties and required examination only for their surface characteristics. Further, the work carried out to the panels was inconsistent with C's reversionary right in the panels in terms of s.35(1), as incorporation of moveable property into the structure of a building would on normal principles be wholly destructive of C's right. The diminution of value of the panels caused by A's operations was not relevant. Given that the panels were to be incorporated into another structure and would be changed by A's operations, it was common sense to apply the general rule that examination should take place on delivery, or at the time of the operations, as otherwise the policy of finality of commercial transactions would be prejudiced. Accordingly, A's reasonable opportunity to examine the goods in terms of s.34(1) was, at the latest, at L's premises and, as the only possible inference was that A had accepted the panels, they had lost their right to reject them at the stage. (2) As there were no allegations that the individual panels departed from the standard of the sample, cl.11 had no application, since if the clause related to other defects it would be inconsistent with the typewritten specification in the order form, which would have to prevail. (3) A's letter had not resulted in any agreement in relation to the panels and the subsequent deliveries did not imply any variation of the contract.

HENSHAW (CHARLES) & SONS v. ANTLERPORT, *The Scotsman*, June 28, 1995

6320. Conditions and warranties—standard form—whether condition fair and reasonable—whether practicable to give notice of defect within prescribed time limit

[Unfair Contract Terms Act 1977 (c.50), s.20(2) and Sched. 2, paras. (c) and (d).]

Section 20(2) of the 1977 Act, as amended, provides that any term of a contract which purports to exclude or restrict liability for breach of the obligations arising, *inter alia*, from s.14 of the Sale of Goods Act 1979 shall have no effect if it was not fair and reasonable to incorporate the term in the contract. Schedule 2 to the Act provides guidelines for the application of the reasonableness test, including by para. (c) whether the customer knew or ought reasonably to have known of the existence and extent of the term having regard, *inter alia*, to any previous course of dealing, and by para. (d) where the term excludes or restricts liability on non-compliance with a condition, whether it was reasonable to expect that compliance would be practicable. The seller of a printing machine raised an action for payment of the unpaid balance of the price. The buyer denied liability on the ground that the seller was in breach of contract due to a defect in the machine and counterclaimed for reimbursement of the part of the price paid and for damages for loss caused by the breach of contract. After proof, the sheriff found that the machine was not of merchantable quality and was not fit for the purpose for which it was to be put, but that the buyer's defence and counterclaim were excluded by cl. 5(c) of the conditions of sale. Clause 5(c) provided that unless the buyer gave notice to the seller within seven days of receipt of the goods, he should be deemed to have accepted them and the goods would be presumed to be in good order and fit for the purpose for which they were acquired. No notice had been given within the period. The buyer appealed to the sheriff principal, founding on paras. (c) and (d) of Sched. 2 in arguing that it was not fair and reasonable to incorporate the term in the contract. The sheriff principal, in allowing the appeal, held that having regard to the value of the machine, the defender's business experience and the fact that in each of five previous transactions with the pursuers the conditions had been used, the defender ought reasonably to have been aware of the term's existence and extent; but that since the defect was one which might not be recognised as such until some time had passed, it was not practicable to give notice of the defect within the seven-day period and it was not fair and reasonable to incorporate cl. 5(c) in the contract, so that the buyer was entitled to reject the machine and to decree in the counterclaim. The pursuers appealed to the Court of Session, arguing that cl. 5(c) required the defender to do no more than intimate in good faith that he was having problems with the machine, and was accordingly fair and reasonable.

Held, that (1) the intention of s.20(2) of the 1977 Act was to prevent a party to a contract from contracting out of liability for breach of obligations arising from certain terms and undertakings implied by statute, unless he was able to establish that when the contract was entered into it was fair and reasonable to incorporate in the contract the term limiting his liability for such breach, and that the onus rested upon the party who sought to found upon such a term; (2) the test of reasonableness was one to be applied objectively by the court, having regard to the circumstances of the particular case and to the guidelines prescribed by s.24(2) of and Sched. 2 to the Act; (3) the least that could be expected of such a term before it could pass the reasonableness test was that its meaning should be clear and unambiguous; (4) the clause had to be construed in order to define the obligation it sought to lay upon the buyer, and in the present case the clause had no clear business sense, it not being possible for the businessman buying such a machine to tell from the clause what the notice was to contain, on what it was to be based, or whether or not he should send it when he encountered what appeared to be fairly typical, apparently minor, possibly temporary, probably remedial problems; (5) prima facie it would therefore not be reasonable at the time of the contract to expect that it would be practicable for the buyer to send a written notice to the sellers within seven days of delivery of the machine in circumstances such as could reasonably be expected to obtain in this type of contract in relation to this type of machine, and the sheriff principal was entitled to reach the conclusion he did; and appeal refused.

KNIGHT MACHINERY (HOLDINGS) v. RENNIE, 1995 S.L.T. 166.

Consumer credit. See CONSUMER CREDIT.

6321. Unfair contract terms—standard form contract—whether condition fair and reasonable. See KNIGHT MACHINERY (HOLDINGS) v. RENNIE, §6320.

SEA AND SEASHORE

Fishing. See FISH AND FISHERIES.

SHERIFF COURT PRACTICE

6322. Abandonment—procedure

Held, in an action of payment, where the pursuer had lodged a minute of abandonment at common law but no accompanying motion, that the sheriff had erred in pronouncing decree of absolvitor with taxed expenses in favour of the defender without first hearing the pursuer's motion.

WALKER v. WALKER (Sh. Ct.), 1995 S.C.L.R. 387.

Adoption. See CHILDREN AND YOUNG PERSONS.

6323. Affidavits. See McVINNIE v. McVINNIE, §5921.

6324. Appeals—Court of Session, to—leave required—failure to seek leave timeously—dispensing power

[Sheriff Courts (Scotland) Act 1907 (c.51), Sched., rr. 1, 91 and 92(1).]

Held, that an application for leave to appeal to the Court of Session could not competently be made more than seven days after the date of the interlocutor against which it was desired to appeal, and that the general dispensing power under r. 1 could not be invoked to render competent an application which had ceased to be competent.

SCOTLIFE HOME LOANS (NO. 2) v. MUIR (Sh.Ct.), 1994 S.C.L.R. 967.

6325. Appeals—Court of Session, to—without leave—competency. See FROST v. BULMAN, §6183.

6326. Appeals—sheriff principal to—competency—order the bankrupt provider trustee with list of assets and liabilities. See INGLE'S TR. v. INGLE, §5484.

6327. Appeals—sheriff principal, to—competency

[Food Safety Act 1990 (c.16), s.12; Sheriff Courts (Scotland) Act 1907 (c.51), ss.27 and 28.]

The Food Safety Act 1990 provides, by s.12(1) that an authorised officer of an enforcement authority may serve an emergency prohibition notice on the proprietor of a business, the effect of which is to prohibit immediately the use of a process or treatment for the purposes of a food business for a period of three days, if he is satisfied that there is a risk of injury to health. Section 12(2) further provides that a sheriff may thereafter issue an emergency prohibition order prohibiting the continuing use of the process or treatment. An environmental health officer served an emergency prohibition notice in terms of s.12(1) of the 1990 Act on the owners of a dairy farm prohibiting the use of certain equipment said to constitute a health hazard. Two days later the officer sought an emergency prohibition order from the sheriff prohibiting the use of the equipment. The sheriff, after hearing evidence, refused to grant the prohibition order, but declared, in terms of s.12(10) of the Act, that he was satisfied that the health risk was fulfilled when the emergency prohibition order was served, with the effect that the owners of the farm were not entitled to any compensation under the Act from the local authority as a result of the service of the notice. The owners of the farm appealed to the sheriff principal against the declaration by the sheriff that the health risk had been satisfied. The sheriff principal dismissed the appeal as incompetent. The owners of the farm appealed to the Court of Session against the sheriff principal's decision.

Held, that (1) the question of whether there was any right of appeal against a decision given in terms of the provisions of a statute where appeal was not specifically excluded by the statute had to be determined by a consideration of the particular legislation concerned; (2) an examination of the scheme of the Act showed that the determination of the sheriff that he considered that the health risk had been fulfilled was intended to be final and not subject to appeal; and appeal refused. *Opinion*, *per* the Lord President (Hope), that a determination that an emergency prohibition order should be made would be a judicial decision for which the sheriff would be required to issue a written judgment in accordance with the provisions relating to summary applications, which would then be subject to the ordinary methods of appeal. *Opinion reserved*, on this point, *per* Lords Clyde and Abernethy. *Observed*, *per* the Lord President (Hope), that it was not necessary to describe the function which the sheriff was exercising under this legislation as administrative or judicial as to attempt to draw such a distinction could lead to difficulty.

EAST KILBRIDE DISTRICT COUNCIL v. KING, 1996 S.L.T. 30.

6328. Appeals—sheriff principal, to—competency—interlocutor prior to award of sequestration. See PAGANELLI PROPERTES (GLASGOW) v. BIBA, §5483.

6329. Appeals—sheriff principal, to—competency—refusal of recall of summary cause decree in absence

[Sheriff Courts (Scotland) Act 1907 (c.51), s.3(h); Sheriff Courts (Scotland) Act 1971 (c.58), ss.38 and 45(3); Act of Sederunt (Summary Cause Rules, Sheriff Court) 1976 (S.I. 1976 No. 476), rr. 13 and 19.]

Held, that (1) the sheriff's refusal to recall a summary cause decree in absence amounted to a final judgment and accordingly was appealable, and (2) where there had been a failure in the attempted service of the minute for recall of the decree on the pursuer, that that failure was caused by the pursuer's subsequent appearance at the hearing.

THOMSON v. PROCTOR (Sh.Ct.), 1995 S.C.L.R. 648.

6330. Appeals—sheriff principal, to—decree by default—decree extracted—competency

[Sheriff Courts (Scotland) Act 1907 (c.51), Sched., rr.24.1, 24.2, 24.3 and 31.1]

Decree by default was pronounced in an action after the defender's agents had withdrawn from acting. The defender had been warned of the possible consequences of his failure to lodge defences and to put his agents in funds, but no interlocutor under r. 24.2(1) ordaining the defender to appear at a "peremptory diet" was pronounced. The decree was extracted. The defender then sought leave "to allow the appeal to be heard although marked late".

Held, that the rule that there could be no appeal against an interlocutor which had been extracted was absolute and such an interlocutor could not be challenged, and appeal refused as incompetent.

WAGON FINANCE v. O'LONE (Sh.Ct.), 1995 S.C.L.R. 149.

6331. Appeals—sheriff principal, to—divorce—undefended decree of divorce. See McFARLANE v. McFARLANE, §5888.

6332. Appeals—sheriff principal, to—effect of partially successful appeal on finding of contributory negligence. See OATES v. ATLANTIC DRILLING CO., §6152.

6333. Appeals—sheriff principal, to—without leave—competency. See AMPLI-FLAIRE v. THE CHISHOLME INSTITUTE, §5951.

6334. Appeals—sheriff principal, to—without leave—competency

Held, that an order ordaining defenders to appear at the bar of the court to explain their failure to obtemper an earlier order of the court amounted to a decree *ad factum praestandum* and that an appeal to the sheriff principal was competent without leave.

BOYD v. DRUMMOND, ROBBIE & GIBSON (Sh.Ct.), 1995 S.C.L.R. 178.

6335. Arrestment—earnings arrestment—part of pension commuted into lump sum. See G.U.D. PENSION TRUSTEE v. QUINN, §6345.

Bankruptcy. See BANKRUPTCY.

6336. Caveat—failure of sheriff clerk to act on. See WOOD v. LORD ADVOCATE, §6386.

6337. Caveat—specification

[Sheriff Courts (Scotland) Act 1907 (c.51), Sched., r. 4.1 and Form G.2.]

Held, where a caveat was lodged requesting intimation of any application "for interim interdict or any other interim order" relating to a particular partnership, that "any other interim order" was not sufficiently specific and caveat restricted to interim interdict.

NICOLSON (Sh. Ct.), 1995 S.C.L.R. 389.

6338. Count, reckoning and payment—competency—employee seeking payment of commission

C, a financial consultant, raised an action of count, reckoning and payment against her former employer, E, in respect of certain commission payments allegedly due. E challenged C's action as incompetent on the ground that such an action was only appropriate where C had a right to demand and E had a liability to account, such liability being owed if E had intromitted with money truly belonging in whole or in part to C. Such an action was generally not competent by an employee against an employer. E had had neither possession of nor had intromitted with funds belonging to C and C should have raised an ordinary action for payment. C submitted that a liability to account was owed by a person who intromitted with another's money as an agent and that E had acted as her agent in receiving commission which included money E was obliged to remit to her. There was no absolute rule that employers could never have a duty to account to their employees.

Held, action dismissed. It was not appropriate for C to raise an action of count, reckoning and payment merely because she could not quantify precisely the sum due to her. For such an action to be competent, it was necessary that C had a right to demand, and E a duty to render, an account of E's intromissions with assets belonging to C. It was unrealistic to suggest that E, having received the commission due to them, thereafter intromitted with assets belonging to C. The extent or value of C's claim was to be determined not by any such intromissions but by the terms of her contract of employment, which entitled her to remuneration calculated by reference to the amount of the commission E received. *Observed*, that it should not be understood as a matter of law that an employee could never bring an action of count, reckoning and payment against an employer and there were relationships other than that of principal and agent in which such actions were commonly allowed (*Coxall v. Stewart* [1976] C.L.Y. 3326).

COLLINS v. E.I.S FINANCIAL SERVICES (Sh.Ct.), 1995 S.C.L.R. 628.

6339. Counterclaim—omitted from certified copy record—motion for decree

[Sheriff Courts (Scotland) Act 1907 (c.51), Sched., rr.9.8(2), 9.10 and 19.1(2)(a).]

H raised an action against B. B counterclaimed during the period of adjustment in terms of r. 19.1(2)(a). H's solicitors thereafter withdrew from acting and a peremptory diet was fixed. No one appeared for H at the peremptory diet and B moved for decree of absolvitor in terms of r. 16.2 and for decree in terms of the counterclaim. The sheriff granted absolvitor but refused decree in terms of the counterclaim on the grounds that, although a certified copy record had been lodged, the record did not contain the counterclaim and therefore there was nothing in the process from which the clerk could prepare the decree. The sheriff then granted B leave to appeal *ex proprio motu*.

Held, appeal allowed and case remitted to the sheriff. The sheriff erred in refusing to grant decree in terms of B's counterclaim as he had discretion under r. 19.4 to regulate the procedure in relation to a counterclaim. In addition, under r. 9.10, the sheriff was entitled to order B to lodge an open record containing all adjustments and amendments, which would have included a record containing the counterclaim omitted from the record in process. *Observed*, that if the sheriff proceeded under r. 9.10, he would have to decide whether B could simply amend the record in process to incorporate

the counterclaim, or whether in terms of r. 9.12(5) the abortive continued options hearing should be continued and B required to lodge a fresh record.
HERITAGE HOUSE v. BROWN, 1995 S.L.T.(Sh.Ct.) 101.

Criminal causes. See CRIMINAL EVIDENCE AND PROCEDURE.

6340. Declinature of jurisdiction

Held, that a sheriff who had started to hear a proof in 1987 was not entitled to decline jurisdiction to hear the remainder of the proof in 1994 on the ground that by then he knew solicitors whose evidence would have to be critically assessed in the proof.
McDONALD v. KELLY (Sh.Ct.), 1995 S.C.L.R. 187.

6341. Decree—by default

[Sheriff Courts (Scotland) Act 1907 (c.51), Sched., rr.2.1 and 16.2(1)(c), (2) and (4)(a).]

M sought damages from C following a road traffic accident. At the options hearing M was represented but C was not. The sheriff allowed M to lodge the record at the bar by exercising his dispensing power (rr.2.1(1) and 9.11(2)). Thereafter M moved for decree by default under r.16.2(1)(c) and (4). The sheriff granted decree without making further inquiry and on the basis that there was "nothing else to be done". Parties agreed on appeal that the sheriff had misdirected himself and that it was for the court to decide whether or not to recall the decree having heard C's explanation.

Held, appeal allowed and case remitted to the sheriff to fix of new an options hearing. (1) Rule 16.2(2) was discretionary and it had not been established before the sheriff whether C had a reasonable excuse for non-appearance. The sheriff should have continued the motion and ordered service on C and his representative. (2) C had not wilfully failed to obtemper the rules. A local agent was to be instructed but the letter had not been typed in time. This was an oversight which would reasonably be expected to occur at least once in the lifetime of a busy practitioner and was the very kind of situation which r.2.1 was designed to meet. It would be a complete denial of justice to grant M decree for the sums craved without C being given an opportunity of substantiating his defence either on merits or quantum (*McKelvie v. Scottish Steel Scaffolding Co.*, 1938 S.C. 278).
McGOWAN v. CARTNER (Sh. Ct.), 1995 S.C.L.R. 312.

6342. Decree—by default—solicitor withdrawing from acting—decree extracted—competency of appeal. See WAGON FINANCE v. O'LONE, §6330.

6343. Decree—summary—whether statable defence

[Sheriff Courts (Scotland) Act 1907 (c.51), Sched., r.17.2(1).]

M raised an action of furthcoming against S, the Scottish Legal Aid Board and against H, with whom she had entered into a minute of agreement providing for the custody, aliment and education of their child. M had arrested sums due by S to H. M sought payment of (1) the sum of £290 which was due and unpaid in terms of the minute of agreement (which H did not contest), and (2) the sum of £28,789·96 which represented the sum due under a decree of December 1993 less sums attached by arrestments elsewhere. H pled personal bar, averring that although he had signed a mandate enabling M to uplift the sums arrested, this was part of an agreement between them and was on the understanding that it would be implemented by the release to M of £1,700. M sought summary decree, which the sheriff granted, and H appealed. H argued that (1) the sheriff had a duty to determine, as a matter of relevancy, not only whether a statable defence had been put forward, but whether a statable defence actually existed, and (2) he had erred in concluding on the authority of *Gatty v. Maclaine*, 1921 1 S.L.T. 51, that personal bar could only arise where there was no explicit agreement between the parties. M had agreed that arrested funds to the extent of £1,700 should be released by S, and H had acted on that to his prejudice.

Held, appeal refused. (1) Where the issue was whether there was a basis in law for defending an action, and the sheriff concluded that H had not pled a statable defence, he was not under a duty to examine all the possible defences which might be available to H. (2) Questions of personal bar could arise whether or not there was an antecedent agreement. H did not suggest that M, by her words or actings had barred herself from enforcing the decree, and the alleged agreement was said to relate to H's obligations under the minute of agreement and not under the decree.

MATTHEWS v. SCOTTISH LEGAL AID BOARD (Sh.Ct.), 1995 S.C.L.R. 184.

6344. Diligence—charge—whether necessary following decree of removing in summary cause action for recovery of possession of heritable property. See MAIN v. REID, §6398.

6345. Diligence—earnings arrestment—part of pension connected into lump sum

[Debtors (Scotland) Act 1987 (c.18), s.73(2).]

Held, that an earnings arrestment did not apply to any part of a lump sum payable to the debtor where the sum was a commuted pension payment.

G.U.D. PENSION TRUSTEE v. QUINN (Sh.Ct.), 1994 S.C.L.R. 1105.

6346. Diligence—poinding—fees of sheriff officers—personal liability of instructing solicitors

Sheriff officers (S) sued solicitors (D) for payment of S's poinding fees. D had been instructed by their client (C) to enforce a decree against X. On D's instructions S had served a charge and carried out a poinding. D had paid S's fee for the charge but not that for the poinding. S were admittedly aware that D was acting on behalf of C but claimed it was a long established custom that an instructing solicitor incurred personal liability for a sheriff officer's fees and outlays. D argued that as agents for a disclosed principal they did not incur personal liability. After proof the sheriff found established by custom and usage of their respective professions an implied term that D pledged their credit to S and were personally liable. D appealed arguing that the custom was not so certain, uniform, notorious and reasonable as to give rise to a contractually binding obligation (*"Strathlorne" Steamship Co. v. Baird & Sons*, 1916 1 S.L.T. 221), as opposed to a matter of professional etiquette. The onus on S to establish the binding nature of the practice was substantial and the authorities did not recognise such an obligation.

Held, appeal refused. An agent was liable for all the ordinary expenses of conducting a cause in court (*A.B. v. C.D.* (1843) 6 D. 95). In Shand's *Practice*, pp.406–409 there was mention of a solicitor's primary liability for the fees of an officer of court; sheriff officers were officers of the court. There had been evidence in support of B's position and no contrary evidence. A sheriff officer needed to be able to rely on a solicitor's personal credit as diligence had to be done within time limits which rendered credit checks on clients impractical. A solicitor knew his client's circumstances and ought not to instruct if he knew his client could not pay.

STIRLING PARK & CO. v. DIGBY, BROWN & CO., 1996 S.L.T.(Sh.Ct.) 17.

6347. Diligence—procedure

ACT OF SEDERUNT (PROCEEDINGS IN THE SHERIFF COURT UNDER THE DEBTORS (SCOTLAND) ACT 1987) AMENDMENT) 1995 (No. 1876) [65p], made under the Sheriff Courts (Scotland) Act 1971 (c.58), s.32 (as amended by the Law Reform (Miscellaneous Provisions) (Scotland) Act 1985 (c.73), Sched.

2 and by the Civil Evidence (Scotland) Act 1988 (c.32), s.2(4)) and the Finance Act 1994 (c.9) Sched. 7 (as substituted by the Finance Act 1995 (c.4), Sched. 9); operative on August 7, 1995; amends the Act of Sederunt (Proceedings in the Sheriff Court under the Debtors (Scotland) Act 1987) 1988 regarding recovery of insurance premiums tax by summary warrant procedure and provides for diligence by way of earnings arrestment and arrestment and action of forthcoming and sale, as well as poinding and sale.

[S.I. 1988 No. 2013 amended.]

6348. Dispensing power of sheriff. See McGOWAN v. CARTNER, §6341; DE MELO v. BAZAZI, §6362; GROUP 4 TOTAL SECURITY v. JAYMARKE DEVELOPMENTS, §6365; COLVIN v. MONTGOMERY PRESERVATIONS, §6371.

6349. Dispensing power of sheriff—failure to lodge defences timeously

[Sheriff Courts (Scotland) Act 1907 (c.51), Sched., rr. 2.1(1) and 9.6(1).]

Held, in an action of damages for breach of contract, where notice of intention to defend had been lodged, the defender had timeously instructed her solicitor to lodge defences but he had failed to do so, that the dispensing power should be exercised to permit the defences to be received late and the defender's solicitors should be found personally liable in expenses.

MUIR v. STEWART (Sh.Ct.), 1994 S.C.L.R. 935.

6350. Dispensing power of sheriff—failure to lodge record timeously. See D.T.Z. DEBENHAM THORPE v. I. HENDERSON TRANSPORT SERVICES, §6364; WELSH (ANDREW) v. THORNHOME SERVICES, §6366; PRICE v. FERNANDO, §6367; MORRAN v. GLASGOW COUNCIL OF TENANTS' ASSOCIATIONS, §6368; MAHONEY v. OFFICER, §6369; RITCHIE v. MAERSK CO., §6370.

Divorce. See DIVORCE AND CONSISTORIAL CAUSES.

Evidence. See EVIDENCE (CIVIL).

Expenses. See EXPENSES.

6351. Fatal accidents and sudden deaths inquiry—appeal by way of judicial review—competency—partial reduction

[Fatal Accidents and Sudden Deaths Inquiry (Scotland) Act 1976 (c.14), s.6(1).]

Parties involved in a fatal accident inquiry held under the Fatal Accidents and Sudden Deaths Inquiry (Scotland) Act 1976 sought to bring under review, by a petition for judicial review, the determination by the sheriff in the fatal accident inquiry.

Held, that in some respects the sheriff's determination was not supported by the evidence, nor were his criticisms of, in particular, the evidence of one of the petitioners; but that it was incompetent to reduce parts of the sheriff's determination except insofar as they related to matters falling within the specific findings listed in s.6(1) of the Act; and partial reduction pronounced.

SMITH v. LORD ADVOCATE (O.H.), 1995 S.L.T. 379.

6352. Initial writ—service—whether service by leaving documents with person at place of business of firm amounted to "personal service"

[Sheriff Courts (Scotland) Act 1907 (c.51), Sched., rr. 10(1)(a) and (b), 26 and 111.]

The Schedule to the Sheriff Courts (Scotland) Act 1907, as amended prior to 1993, provides by r.10(1) that service of an initial writ or other writ may be effected "(a) personally, or (b) by being left in the hands of an inmate of or employee at the person's dwelling place or place of business. By r.26(a), a decree in absence becomes final and entitled to all the privileges of a decree *in foro* on the expiry of six months from its date "where the service of the initial writ . . . has been personal". Rule 111 provides further procedure where a schedule of arrestment "has not been personally served" on an arrestee. In January 1991, four actions of damages were raised against the suppliers of a mobile gas heater, as first defenders, and their local agents and distributors as second defenders, in respect of an accident allegedly caused by the mobile heater in January 1987. The second defenders were a partnership and were sued in their trading name. The executions of service in respect of the second defenders stated that sheriff officers had cited them to answer the writ by leaving a full copy of the writ and warrant in each case "in the hands of their servant (manager) within their office and place of business at . . . for their use and behoof". The first defenders were granted absolvitor but decrees in absence were granted against the second defenders for the sums sued for. The second defenders sought to be reponed. The sheriff found that the method of service was personal service and that the decrees had become final in terms of r. 26, and accordingly the reponing notes were in-competent. The second defenders appealed to the Court of Session and argued that the mode of service used did not amount to personal service on the second defenders as personal service could only take place where the defender was an individual; the decrees were accordingly not entitled to the privileges of decrees *in foro* and could be reponed against. The pursuers argued that the alternative provided by r. 10(1)(b) was the equivalent of personal service.

Held, that (1) the word "personally" in r. 10(1)(a) had the same meaning as it did in rule 111 and that the word "personal" in r. 26(a) also had the same meaning; (2) such service could be effected only in the case of an individual, and then only by placing the writ into the hands of the defender or arrestee personally; (3) the decrees in absence against the second defenders were therefore not entitled to the privileges of a decree *in foro* and the reponing notes were accordingly competent; and appeals allowed. (Macphail, *Sheriff Court Practice*, at paras. 6–25 and 6–26, approved; *Stair Memorial Encyclopaedia*, Vol. 17, para. 1016, disapproved.)

RAE v. CALOR GAS, 1995 S.L.T. 244.

Interdict. See DIVORCE AND CONSISTORIAL CAUSES.

6353. Interdict—interim interdict—competency. See THOMSON v. YORKSHIRE BUILDING SOCIETY, §5485.

6354. Interdict—interim interdict—effect of subsequent perpetual interdict

Held, that a decree of perpetual interdict superseded an earlier interim interdict in identical terms.

STEWART v. STALLARD (Sh.Ct.), 1995 S.C.L.R. 167.

6355. Interdict—interim interdict—title and interest to sue

Held, that a local authority had neither title nor interest to obtain interim interdict against the proprietor of a house who was allegedly abusing and frightening their tenants in nearby premises owned by them.

DUNDEE DISTRICT COUNCIL, CITY OF v. COOK (Sh.Ct.), 1995 S.C.L.R. 559.

Interdict—matrimonial interdict. See DIVORCE AND CONSISTORIAL CAUSES.

6356. Interest to sue. See DUNDEE DISTRICT COUNCIL (CITY OF) v. COOK, §6355.

6357. Interlocutor—warrant to search for and take possession of documents—specification

Held, that a warrant to open shut and lockfast places and to search for and the possession of certain, specified documents was too wide and that it should have referred to specific premises.

BOYD v. DRUMMOND, ROBBIE GIBSON (Sh.Ct.), 1995 S.C.L.R. 178.

Jurisdiction. See JURISDICTION.

Matrimonial homes—occupancy rights. See DIVORCE AND CONSISTORIAL CAUSES.

6358. Medical examination of party—whether party should be ordained to be medically examined

Held, in proceedings for access at the instance of the father where the mother alleged that he suffered from incurable manic depression, that he drank to excess which prevented his medication controlling his illness and that he had recently been detained in hospital under the Mental Health (Scotland) Act 1984, that a motion by the mother seeking recovery of his medical records and that he be ordained to be medically examined should be referred on the grounds that the averments were insufficient to justify such action and that the motion was in any event premature.

M. v. M. (Sh.Ct.), 1995 S.C.L.R. 770.

6359. Options hearing—continuation on cause shown. See WELSH (ANDREW) v. THORNHOME SERVICES, §6366.

6360. Options hearing—continued options hearing—record producer—whether further fee payable

[Sheriff Courts (Scotland) Act 1907 (c.51), Sched., rr. 9.8(1), 9.11 and 9.12; Sheriff Court Fees Amendment (No. 2) Order 1993 (S.I. 1993 No. 2957), Sched., Pt. V, para. 35.]

Held, in a case under the standard procedure, where an up-to-date copy of the record had been produced for a continued options hearing, that no fee was payable under para. 35 in respect of its lodging, and appeal allowed.

MELLOR v. TOWLE (Sh.Ct.), 1995 S.C.L.R. 76.

6361. Options hearing—dismissal by sheriff *ex proprio motu*—competency

[Sheriff Courts (Scotland) Act 1907 (c.51), Sched. rr. 9.12 and 21(2).]

At an options hearing, the pursuers in an action of interdict sought a continuation. The defender concurred and, in the event that that was not granted, sought a debate on her preliminary plea. No notice having been lodged, the sheriff noted that the defender's preliminary plea would be dismissed in terms of r. 22.1(2) of the Ordinary Cause Rules 1993. The sheriff refused the motion for a continuation and *ex proprio motu* dismissed the cause. The pursuers appealed to the sheriff principal, arguing that r. 9.12, regulating the conduct of an options hearing, did not empower the sheriff to dismiss the cause *ex proprio motu*.

Held, that there was nothing in r. 9.12 entitling the sheriff at his own hand to dismiss the action and appeal allowed. *Observed*, that although the 1993 Rules were designed to secure the expeditious progress of the cause, "they were never intended to be a snakes and ladders board from which all the ladders had been removed".

STRATHCLYDE BUSINESS PARK (MANAGEMENT) v. COCHRANE, 1995 S.L.T. (Sh. Ct.) 69.

6362. Options hearing—failure to lodge copy of record timeously—failure to appear or be represented at options hearing

[Sheriff Courts (Scotland) Act 1907 (c.51), Sched. rr. 2.1(1), 9.11 and 16.2(1)(c) and (4)(a).]

A pursuer having failed to lodge answers to a defender's counterclaim, adjust the initial writ, lodge the record as required by r. 9.11 of the Ordinary Cause Rules, or appear or be represented at the options hearing, the sheriff dismissed the pursuer's action and granted decree in terms of the counterclaim. The pursuer appealed to the sheriff principal.

Held, that the collective catalogue of errors, albeit by the pursuer's solicitor, along with the prejudice suffered by the defender, displaced the court's reluctance to allow a decree to stand where there was prima facie a substantial defence which had never been heard; and appeal refused.

DE MELO v. BAZAZI, 1995 S.L.T. (Sh.Ct.) 57.

6363. Options hearing—failure to lodge copy of record timeously—minute of acceptance of tender lodged

[Sheriff Courts (Scotland) Act 1907 (c.51), Sched., ss.9.11(2) and 9.12(5); Rules of Court 1994, r.40.11(1) and (4).]

Held, in D's appeal against a sheriff's dismissal of D's action of payment on the grounds that D had been in default in not lodging a record prior to the options hearing, but that, as a minute of acceptance of tender had been lodged by D prior to the hearing and the action had in effect been settled, the sheriff should have either prorogated the time for lodging or dispensed with it having to be lodged or continued the hearing in order to allow settlement to be completed; and appeal allowed and case remitted to sheriff. *Observed*, that a motion "for early disposal of the appeal in terms of r. 40.11" was appropriate if all a party sought was the fixing of an early diet, but, where a party was seeking to have an appeal determined on the single bills the words "and for its determination" should be added after "appeal".

WINTER (DAVID) & SON v. GEORGE CRAIG & SONS, 1995 S.L.T. 1331.

6364. Options hearing—failure to lodge copy of record timeously

[Sheriff Courts (Scotland) Act 1907 (c.51), Sched., rr. 2.1(1), 9.11 and 16.2.]

An action of payment in respect of a fee rendered was raised in the sheriff court. Defences were lodged and a date for an options hearing appointed. The record was not lodged until the day before the options hearing, in breach of r. 9.11(2) of the Ordinary Cause Rules. The sheriff, having heard the pursuers' solicitor, was not satisfied with the explanation for the late lodging, which was to the effect that the case had been wrongly entered in the pursuers' solicitors' diary, and found the pursuers to be in default and dismissed the cause in terms of r. 16.2. The pursuers appealed to the Court of Session arguing *inter alia* that the sheriff had exercised her discretion wrongly in not granting relief under the dispensing power in r. 2.1(1).

Held, that (1) the efficient operation of the rule requiring the sheriff at the options hearing to seek to secure the expeditious progress of the cause was essential if the purpose of introducing the 1993 Rules was to be achieved, it was crucial to the performance by the sheriff of his functions at the options hearing that he should have the record in his hands when he had time to prepare for the hearing by reading it; (2) the sheriff had not misdirected herself as to the relevant law or the factors to be taken into account and given the reasons for the failure and that there were no compelling reasons in the interests of justice for granting relief, the sheriff was entitled to exercise her discretion in terms of r. 16.2(2) by dismissing the action; and appeal refused and sheriff's interlocutor affirmed. Dicta in *Morran v. Glasgow District Council of Tenants' Association* [1995] 3 C.L. 736, and *Mahoney v. Officer* [1995] C.L.Y. 6369, approved.) *Observed*, that the phrase "mistake, oversight or other excusable cause" in r. 2.1(1) was wide enough to cover cases of common office error, but that the dispensing power was not available to be used to frustrate the object of the rule.

D.T.Z. DEBENHAM THORPE v. I. HENDERSON TRANSPORT SERVICES, 1995 S.L.T. 553.

6365. Options hearing—failure to lodge copy of record timeously

[Sheriff Courts (Scotland) Act 1907 (c.51), Sched., rr.2.1(1), 9.11(2); 16.2, 16.3 and 22.1.]

G appealed against the sheriff's decision to assoilzie J in G's action of payment, following G's failure to lodge a certified copy record prior to the options hearing. G's solicitor (S) had been on holiday and his deputy had not realised that the record had to be lodged. S was alerted to the problem the day before the hearing and instructed that a fax be sent to his correspondents, which was tendered at the hearing. The sheriff held that this explanation did not amount to sufficient cause in terms of r.16.3 and granted absolvitor on J's motion. G argued on appeal that while r.16.3 might not be satisfied, its terms indicated that a wider interpretation should be given to r.2.1(1). In any event the sheriff erred in granting absolvitor.

Held, decree of dismissal substituted. The relationship between rr.2.1(1) and 16.3 was unclear, but as the sheriff had failed to exercise his discretion as between dismissal and absolvitor his decision was open to review. G's explanation for the default was not persuasive, disclosing a gap in the office diary system. The mistakes disclosed would not justify the exercise of the dispensing powers unless failure to exercise it would lead to substantial injustice. Such injustice would result from absolvitor, since the fault was not G's, but not from dismissal. In line with earlier decisions of the court upholding the purpose of the new rules to achieve expeditious disposal of cases, that was the correct approach. *Observed*, that entries in *Greens Weekly Digest* were intended for reference and not as authorities for citation in court.

GROUP 4 TOTAL SECURITY v. JAYMARKE DEVELOPMENTS (Sh. Ct.), 1995 S.C.L.R. 303.

6366. Options hearing—failure to lodge copy of record timeously

[Sheriff Courts (Scotland) Act 1907 (c.51). Sched., rr. 2.1(1), 9.11, 9.12(5) and 16.2.]

Held, where the solicitor who appeared for the pursuers at an options hearing was unable to give any explanation for the late lodging of the record and was unable to provide the sheriff with any information about the facts relating to a counterclaim, that the sheriff had no information upon which he might have been able to exercise his discretion and that he had been entitled to dismiss the principal action and to grant decree in terms of the counterclaim.

WELSH (ANDREW) v. THORNHOME SERVICES (Sh.Ct.), 1994 S.C.L.R. 1021.

6367. Options hearing—failure to lodge copy of record timeously

[Sheriffs Courts (Scotland) Act 1907 (c.51), Sched., rr. 2.1(1), 9, 11(2) and 16.2.]

Held, in an action of damages for personal injuries where the copy record had been lodged less than 24 hours late for the options hearing, where the defender has been neither present nor represented at the options hearing and where the action became *prima facie* time-barred as a result of dismissal, that it was not in the interests of justice that the action should be dismissed in respect of the failure to lodge a copy of the record timeously, and appeal against dismissal allowed.

PRICE v. FERNANDO (Sh.Ct.), 1995 S.C.L.R. 23.

6368. Options hearing—failure to lodge copy of record timeously

[Sheriff Courts (Scotland) Act 1907 (c.51), Sched., r. 2.1(1).]

M appealed a sheriff's refusal to exercise the dispensing power to excuse M's failure to lodge a certified copy of the record timeously in terms of rule 9.11(2). M argued that his default had not been wilful non-observance but a genuine oversight; that there was no discernible prejudice to G, or, if there were, then it could be compensated by an award of expenses; and that the sheriff's refusal (and consequent dismissal of the cause under r. 16.2) had been unreasonable.

Held, appeal refused. Although M's oversight might be excusable in terms of r. 2.1(1), it did not follow that it was unreasonable for the sheriff not to excuse, given the serious consequences, which were that without the record the court would be unable to prepare for the options hearing and to secure the expeditious progress of the case, which was central to the philosophy underlying the new rules. The sheriff was entitled to regard M's failure to respond to G's repeated requests for adjustments as prejudicial to G, G having brought this matter to the sheriff's attention, and it could not be said that the refusal to exercise the dispensing power was unreasonable.

MORRAN v. GLASGOW COUNCIL OF TENANTS' ASSOCIATIONS, 1995 S.L.T. (Sh.Ct.) 46.

6369. Options hearing—failure to lodge copy of record timeously

[Sheriff Courts (Scotland) Act 1907 (c.51), Sched., rr. 2.1(1) and 16.2.]

M appealed against the sheriff's decision to dismiss an action of ejection against O on the ground that M had failed to lodge a record within the time limit in ordinary cause rule 9.11(2). The options hearing had been fixed for a Wednesday. The Monday of that week was a court holiday. An attempt to lodge the record the preceding Friday had failed because it was not accompanied by the requisite cheque. The record had been lodged on the Tuesday but had not been placed before the sheriff by the time of the options hearing. M argued that the sheriff's comment "Dismissal was in terms of r. 16.2(1)(a) [*sic*] as I could do nothing else in the absence of a record", indicated that he thought he had no discretion in the matter; and in any event that he had failed to exercise his discretion reasonably in having failed to give proper weight to the explanation tendered of pressure of work on M's agent's typist, taken with simple error in failing to tender a cheque on the Friday (albeit that the record was already late then) and the intervention of the holiday. Parties had agreed to seek a continuation for further adjustment. Without having the record, the sheriff could not decide whether dismissal was in the interests of justice. O, who had not opposed the motion, neither consented to nor opposed the appeal being allowed.

Held, appeal refused. (1) The sheriff had exercised his discretion; he had simply intended to convey that he had dismissed the action because M were guilty of default within r. 16.2(1)(a). (2) The new Ordinary Cause Rules had changed some of the underlying assumptions on which litigation was conducted. The sheriff was expected to take an active part in the progress of a case and particularly at the options hearing. Without a record he could not perform those functions at all, and without a timeously lodged record he could not do the preparatory reading which was necessary to a proper performance of those functions. Failure to lodge a record timeously was therefore a serious default and not lightly to be excused. The sheriff was justified in referring to the frequency of late records; some casualties would have to be accepted if the new procedure was to effect any improvement on previous practice. A sheriff would not be expected to excuse the late lodging of a record unless there was a persuasive explanation and refusal to do so would result in serious injustice. In the present case there were two errors by M's agents. Dismissal would not result in injustice since the sheriff would not have been bound to grant a continuation even on joint motion except on some substantial ground, on M's pleadings as they stood O would have been bound to succeed at debate and it was open to M to bring a fresh action with proper averments. The sheriff had been within his discretion.

Held, further, that the case should not be certified for the employment of counsel.

MAHONEY v. OFFICER, 1995 S.L.T. (Sh.Ct.) 49.

6370. Options hearing—failure to lodge copy of record timeously

[Sheriff Courts (Scotland) Act 1907 (c.51), Sched., rr. 9.11(2) and 15.2(6).]

Held, that a certified copy record lodged on the Monday before an options hearing on the Wednesday was late, because the phrase "Not later than two days before the Options Hearing" in r. 9.11(2) meant two clear court days

(*Main v. City of Glasgow District Licensing Board* [1987] C.L.Y. 4592) which time was clearly necessary if a sheriff was to be able to familiarise himself with the papers or, given that the same time limit applied under r. 15.2(6) for lodging opposition to motions, to deal with unopposed motions in chambers; but that the dispensing power would be used to allow the record to be received late.

RITCHIE v. MAERSK CO. (Sh.Ct.), 1994 S.C.L.R. 1038.

6371. Options hearing—failure to lodge note of basis of preliminary plea timeously before options hearing—dispensing power

[Sheriff Courts (Scotland) Act 1907 (c.51), Sched., rr. 2.1(1) and 22.1.]

Having failed to observe rule 22.1(1) of the Ordinary Cause Rules 1993, requiring a note of the basis of the preliminary pleas to be lodged and intimated not later than three days before the options hearing, the second defender in an action tendered the note at the options hearing and moved the sheriff, in terms of r. 2.1(1), to relieve him from the consequences of the failure. The explanation tendered was that instructions had been given for a note to be typed and lodged but that had not been done while the solicitor had been on holiday. Taking the view that the oversight amounted to professional negligence, the sheriff did not regard it as falling within the ambit of r. 2.1(1) and repelled the second defender's preliminary pleas. *Ex proprio motu* the sheriff ordered the case to proceed under the additional procedure in Chap. 10 of the Ordinary Cause Rules 1993. The second defender appealed to the sheriff principal, contending that the sheriff had taken an over critical view and that the repulsion of the preliminary pleas was nugatory when the case was to proceed under the additional procedure since the pleas repelled could simply be re-inserted.

Held, that in categorising the failure to obtemper r. 22.1(1) as professional negligence, so that it fell outwith the ambit of r. 2.1(1), the sheriff had misdirected himself and it would be appropriate to relieve the second defender from the consequences of that failure; and appeal allowed. *Opinion,* that a note under r. 22.1 ought to be lodged prior to the options hearing even where it was likely that the case might be ordered to proceed under the additional procedure.

COLVIN v. MONTGOMERY PRESERVATIONS, 1995 S.L.T. (Sh.Ct.) 15.

6372. Options hearing—family action—failure of party to attend personally. See GRIMES v. GRIMES, §5887.

6373. Options hearing—motion to adjust pleadings after prescribed period

[Sheriff Courts (Scotland) Act 1907 (c.51), Sched., rr. 9.8(4), 9.11(2) and 9.12(5).]

Rule 9.8(4) of the Ordinary Cause Rules 1993 provides that no adjustments shall be permitted within 14 days before the options hearing except with leave of the sheriff. In accordance with r. 9.11(2), the pursuers lodged a certified copy of the record. They later intimated a note of further adjustments, which added a preliminary plea, lodged a note of the basis of the plea and enrolled a motion for leave to adjust after the permitted period. When the motion was heard at the options hearing the sheriff refused it and appointed a proof. The pursuers appealed to the sheriff principal, contending that the sheriff had erred in requiring that the proposed adjustments should have been entered on the record.

Held, that, in terms of r. 9.8(4), the pursuers were not free to enter the adjustments on the record without the leave of the sheriff, who had erred in refusing the motion on the basis that they did not so appear; and appeal allowed and options hearing continued in terms of r. 9.12(5) for 28 days to allow parties to make further adjustments.

TAYLOR v. STAKIS, 1995 S.L.T. (Sh.Ct.) 14.

6374. Options hearing—preliminary matter of law—whether debate justified

[Sheriff Courts (Scotland) Act 1907 (c.51), Sched., r.9.12(3)(c).]

A appealed against the sheriff's decision to allow proof before answer in an action by B for repayment of a loan. A had sought a debate and had lodged a note on preliminary pleas under r.22.1. A's local agent had failed to satisfy the sheriff in oral submissions that there was a debate point. A argued that there was no presumption against debate, and if a responsible agent said there was a point to be debated, and referred to a r.22.1 note properly lodged, that could be taken as sufficient. The proper time to develop the argument in support of the preliminary plea was at the debate. Here A's pleas included one of prescription, and while more information could have been given to the sheriff, there was sufficient basis for it in the note lodged.

Held, appeal refused. A's approach would be equivalent to the position under the pre-1993 rules and would defeat the purpose of r.9.12(3)(c). The sheriff had to be satisfied that there was a preliminary point of law which justified a debate, and in most cases this would be on the basis of both written and oral material before him. It was therefore essential that the agent moving for the debate be fully instructed and in a position to satisfy the sheriff that this would be justified. This had not happened in the present case and the sheriff had not erred in his approach. An appellate court should be tentative in considering whether a sheriff had erred where the question was the likelihood of there being a substantial matter to be debated (*Gracey v. Sykes* [1994] C.L.Y. 6290, followed).

BLAIR BRYDEN PARTNERSHIP (THE) v. ADAIR, 1995 S.L.T. (Sh.Ct.) 98.

6375. Options hearing—preliminary matters of law—plea to relevancy of defences

[Sheriff Courts (Scotland) Act 1907 (c.51). Sched., rr. 9.12 and 17.2.]

Held, at an options hearing where the pursuers had a preliminary plea directed to the relevancy of the defences, which the sheriff considered to be well founded, that he was not entitled to sustain the plea and to grant decree as craved and that he should have sent the case to debate.

RITCHIE v. CLEARY (Sh.Ct.), 1995 S.C.L.R. 561.

6376. Options hearing—preliminary plea not supported by note lodged before options hearing—plea not repelled at options hearing—future procedure

[Sheriff Courts (Scotland) Act 1907 (c.51), Scheds., r. 22.1(1) (2) (3).]

Rule 22.1(1) of the Ordinary Cause Rules 1993 provides that a party insisting on a preliminary plea shall, prior to the options or procedural hearings, lodge a note of the basis for the plea and intimate same to any other party. Rule 22.1(2) provides that if a party fails to comply with this, he shall be deemed to be no longer insisting on the preliminary plea, which shall be repelled. Rule 22.1(3) permits parties to raise at any proof before answer or debate matters in addition to those set out in the note. In an action of reparation the defenders lodged defences stating preliminary pleas to jurisdiction and to relevancy and lodged a note under r. 22.1(1). The note dealt only with the plea to jurisdiction. At the options hearing the sheriff appointed a diet of debate. After a debate relating to jurisdiction, the sheriff repelled all of the defenders' preliminary pleas. The defenders appealed and submitted a list of authorities in support of their challenge on the matter of jurisdiction. At the appeal hearing the defenders intimated that they did not seek to challenge the sheriff's decision on jurisdiction but argued that the sheriff had not been entitled to repel their pleas to relevancy at the debate and that r. 22.1(3) enabled them to raise questions of relevancy at a later stage although not mentioned in their original note.

Held, that (1) since a preliminary plea not supported by a note under r. 22.1(1) was deemed by r. 22.1(2) to be no longer insisted in, the sheriff had been correct to repel the pleas, albeit belatedly, at the debate; (2) r. 22.1(3) did not permit the introduction of wholly new matter at a proof before answer or debate, or the resurrection of a plea which had fallen under r. 22.1(2); and appeal refused. *Opinion*, that in any event it was not open to the defenders to

present arguments on appeal in support of their pleas to relevancy when no such arguments were presented to the sheriff. *Observed*, that the Ordinary Cause Rules should be speedily amended to require appellants to state their grounds of appeal at the time of marking an appeal.
BELL v. JOHN DAVIDSON (PIPES), 1995 S.L.T. (Sh.Ct.) 18.

6377. Options hearing—preparation for hearing

[Sheriff Courts (Scotland) Act 1907 (c.51), Sched., r. 9.12(1), (2) and (3)(a).]
Opinion, that proper preparation for an options hearing would, in many cases, require agents for the parties to communicate with their clients and each other in advance of the options hearing if that hearing was to take place in accordance with the rules.
WEATHERALL v. JACK (Sh.Ct.), 1995 S.C.L.R. 189.

6378. Pleadings—adjustment. See TAYLOR v. STAKIS, §6373.

6379. Pleadings—amendment—discretion to allow

[Sheriff Court (Scotland) Act 1907 (c.51), Sched., r. 64(1)(d).]
Held, in an action to which the ordinary cause rules applied, that a minute of amendment seeking to withdraw certain admissions of fact contained in the closed record was competent.
NAPIER CO. (ARBROATH) v. FRANGOS (Sh.Ct.), 1995 S.C.L.R. 804.

6380. Pleadings—relevancy and specification—counterclaim—reference to defences incorporating report

[Sheriff Courts (Scotland) Act 1907 (c.51), Sched., r. 52.]
Held, refusing M's appeal against the grant of decree to L in a counterclaim against M, that where L referred in their defences to a report and incorporated it *brevitatis causa*, it was sufficient for them in their counterclaim to refer to the answer which incorporated the report, without again formally incorporating it in the counterclaim. The issue was one of fair notice, and reference to another part of the pleadings within the same record was not analogous to reference to an extraneous document.
McILWRAITH v. LOCHMADDY HOTEL, 1995 S.C.L.R. 595.

Prescription. See PRESCRIPTION.

6381. Procedural hearing—preliminary plea—note of basis for plea—note lodged before options hearing—whether further note required for procedural hearing

[Sheriff Courts (Scotland) Act 1907 (c.5.), Sched., rr. 2.1, 9.12(3) and (4), 10.6(3) and 22.1.]
Held, in an action of damages where the defenders had timeously lodged a note of the basis for their preliminary plea prior to the options hearing at which the sheriff appointed the court to a procedural hearing under chap. 10 of the ordinary court rules, that the defenders did not require to lodge a further note of the basis for their plea prior to the procedural hearing, and that the case should be sent to debate on that plea.
HART v. THORNTONS, W.S. (Sh.Ct.), 1995 S.C.L.R. 642.

6382. Procedure—consumer credit

ACT OF SEDERUNT (CONSUMER CREDIT ACT 1974) 1985 (AMENDMENT) 1995 (No. 1877) [£1·55], made under the Sheriff Courts (Scotland) Act 1971 (c.58), s.32 (as amended by the Law Reform (Miscellaneous Provisions) (Scotland) Act 1985 (c.73), Sched. 2 and by the Civil Evidence (Scotland) Act

1988 (c.32), s.2(4); operative on August 7, 1995; amends the Act of Sederunt (Consumer Credit Act 1974) 1985 by providing a form of application for certain orders under the Consumer Credit Act 1974.

[S.I. 1995 No. 705 amended.]

6383. Removing and ejections—summary cause—action for recovery of possession of heritable property—whether charge necessary following decree of removing. See MAIN v. REID, §6398.

6384. Reponing—test for determining whether reponing note should be allowed

[Sheriff Courts (Scotland) Act 1907 (c.51), Sched., r. 28.]

Rule 28 of the Sched. to the 1907 Act provides, as amended prior to 1993, that a defender may apply to be reponed by a note setting forth the proposed defence and an explanation of his failure to appear. The sheriff may recall the decree against the defender following consideration of the note. The permanent trustee of a firm of solicitors raised an action seeking (1) payment for services rendered by the firm and (2) damages for loss caused by misrepresentations made to the pursuer which he had to investigate. Decree in absence was pronounced against the first and second defenders and was extracted but not implemented. The second defender lodged a reponing note setting forth a proposed defence and explaining the failure to appear. The sheriff refused the reponing note because, although a statable defence had been set forth, he considered himself bound by authority to reject it as he was not satisfied that the second defender had a reasonable excuse for non-appearance. The second defender appealed.

Held, that (1) it was not a requirement of the rules that the sheriff had to be satisfied that there was a reasonable excuse for non-appearance; (2) as it was a matter for the sheriff's discretion he was entitled to take account of all the circumstances and to balance one consideration against another in deciding whether to allow a reponing note; and appeal allowed and case remitted to the sheriff to proceed as accords. (Dicta in *McDonough v. Focus DIY,* [1993] C.L.Y. 5848, disapproved; *Mullen v. Harmac* [1994] C.L.Y. 6309, overruled.)

FORBES v. JOHNSTONE, 1995 S.L.T. 158.

6385. Reponing–decree in absence—competency. See RAE v. CALOR GAS, §6352.

6386. Sheriff clerk—failure to act on caveat—whether discharging responsibilities which he has in connection with the execution of judicial process

[Crown Proceedings Act 1947 (c.44), ss.2(1)(a) and (5) and 43(b).]

Held, that a sheriff clerk who had failed to act on a duly lodged caveat in respect of any application for confirmation to an estate was discharging responsibilities which he had in connection with the execution of judicial process, and that in terms of s.2(5) of the 1847 Act no proceedings lay against the Crown in respect of his failure to act on the caveat.

WOOD v. LORD ADVOCATE (Sh.Ct.), 1994 S.C.L.R. 1034.

6387. Sheriffdoms—Glasgow and Strathkelvin

Sessions and vacation courts to be held during 1996 for the disposal of civil business will be as follows: Spring session: January 8 to March 29; vacation courts, April 3, 10, 17, 24, 1996. Summer session: April 29 to June 28; vacation courts, July 3, 10, 17, 24, 31 and August 7, 14, 21, 1996. Winter session: August 26 to December 20, 1996.

6388. Sheriffdoms—Grampian, Highland and Islands

The Sheriff Principal of Grampian, Highland and Islands has ordered that courts for the disposal of ordinary civil, summary cause and small claims business at Inverness at 10 a.m. shall be held on Friday (instead of Thursday) from the week commencing Monday, May 1, 1995.

Sessions for the disposal of civil business during 1996 will be as follows:

Aberdeen and Stonehaven: January 8 to March 29; April 29 to July 5; September 2 to December 20.

Peterhead and Banff: January 8 to March 29; April 29 to June 28; August 26 to December 20.

Elgin: January 3 to March 29; April 29 to July 1; August 26 to December 20.

Kirkwall and Lerwick: January 8 to March 29; April 29 to July 5; September 2 to December 20.

Inverness, Stornoway, Fort William, Portree, Lochmaddy, Dingwall, Tain, Dornoch and Wick: January 4 to March 29; April 29 to July 5; August 26 to December 20.

6389. Sheriffdoms—Lothian and Borders

Sessions for the disposal of civil business during 1996 will be as follows: Spring; January 4 to March 29; Summer: April 29 to June 28; Winter: August 26 to December 18.

The sheriff principal has made acts of court prescribing court holidays in the sheriff and district courts for 1996. Details have been inserted in the appropriate act books of court.

6390. Sheriffdoms—North Strathclyde

The Sheriff Principal of North Strathclyde has prescribed the following sessions for the disposal of business in 1995 (all courts): January 9 to April 6; April 14 to June 29; July 31 to December 22.

Ordinary and summary cause and small claims courts in Campbeltown are now held every fourth Friday at 10 a.m. Other court days remain as previously published.

Sessions for the disposal of civil business during 1996 will be as follows: Spring: January 3 to April 4; Summer: April 10 to July 12; Winter: July 18 to December 20. Vacation courts will be held on April 9 and July 16 and 17.

6391. Sheriffdoms—South Strathclyde, Dumfries and Galloway

The Sheriff Principal of South Strathclyde, Dumfries and Galloway has made an act of court (no. 4 of 1995) revoking no. 4 of 1982 which provided that solicitors suing for recovery of professional fees, unless challenged, need not have their accounts taxed by the auditor of court before decree.

The Sheriff Principal of South Strathclyde, Dumfries and Galloway has made an act of court prescribing court holidays in the sheriff and district courts for 1996. Details have been inserted in the appropriate act books of court.

6392. Sheriffdoms—Tayside, Central and Fife

Sessions for the disposal of civil business in all sheriff courts in this sheriffdom during 1996 will be as follows: Spring session: January 3 to March 29; Summer session: April 29 to June 28; Winter session: August 26 to December 20.

Ordinary, summary cause and small claim courts will be held during vacation on the same days as during session.

6393. Sheriffs—removal—"inability". See STEWART v. SECRETARY OF STATE FOR SCOTLAND, §5446.

Small claims—expenses. See EXPENSES.

6394. Small claims—procedure at preliminary hearing

[Act of Sederunt (Small Claim Rules) 1988 (S.I. 1988 No. 1976), rr. 12(4) and 13(5) and (6).]

Held, in a small claim where, by the date of the preliminary hearing, the principal sum had been paid without admission of liability and the sheriff, without deciding the claim on the merits, had fixed a hearing on expenses, that (1) the sheriff had erred at the preliminary hearing by neither deciding the small claim on its merits in terms of r. 13(6) nor identifying the disputed issues in terms of r. 13(5) and fixing a full hearing and (2) no award of expenses should have been made until the merits of the case had been decided.

CATTO v. LINDSAY & KIRK (Sh.Ct.), 1995 S.C.L.R. 541.

6395. Summary application—adjustment—lateness—discretion of sheriff to refuse

In a summary application where P appealed R's refusal of a gaming licence, P adjusted the pleadings one week before debate. At debate R objected, claiming that the adjustments should be refused as they constituted amendment rather than adjustment and a marked change of ground to R's prejudice as they changed a case based essentially on exercise of discretion to one of error of law. P argued that summary procedure allowed adjustment at any point up until a hearing and that to rule otherwise was against the spirit of flexibility in such applications. The questions at issue related to what had happened in open forum at R's meeting.

Held, adjustments excluded. There was a discretion in the sheriff to refuse adjustments to retain some control over procedure in the interests of fairness to the parties and compliance with the originating statutory provisions. Where there was a material change of ground, substantial or late adjustment, this should always be regulated by the sheriff. Although prompt disposal was important, preliminary pleas were still to be resolved before the facts (*Sutherland v. City of Edinburgh District Licensing Board* [1984] C.L.Y. 4216). The present case was similar to *Cambridge Street Properties v. City of Glasgow District Licensing Board*, March 3, 1993, unreported (on appeal at [1994] C.L.Y. 6255), which was followed. The more significant the adjustment the more effort should be made to intimate the adjustment early. The recollection of those involved could have been affected by the delay in intimating the case now sought to be made.

PARAMOUNT CLUBS v. RENFREW DISTRICT LICENSING BOARD (Sh. Ct.), 1995 S.C.L.R. 781.

6396. Summary causes—action for recovery of heritable property—obtaining possession of property following compulsory purchase order

[Lands Clauses Consolidation (Scotland) Act 1845 (c.19), s.89; Sheriff Courts (Scotland) Act 1971 (c.58), s.35(1)(c).]

Section 35(1)(c) of the Sheriff Courts (Scotland) Act 1971 provides that the summary cause process shall be used for the purposes of all civil proceedings brought in the sheriff court being proceedings including actions for the recovery of possession of heritable property. An airport company raised a summary cause action for recovery of possession of a dwelling, ownership of which had become vested in it by virtue of a general vesting declaration following upon a compulsory purchase order. The occupier of the property accepted that the airport had the right to enter into possession of the dwelling but challenged the competency of the procedure, arguing that the statutory procedure was prescribed by s.89 of the Lands Clauses Consolidation (Scotland) Act 1845 as by "petition" which was now by way of summary application. The sheriff repelled the occupier's plea to the competency and found the pursuers entitled to decree. The occupier appealed to the sheriff principal.

Held, that (1) the summary cause procedure was mandatory for the purposes of all civil proceedings described in s.35(1) of the 1971 Act, including actions for the recovery of heritable property, subject to the stated exceptions; (2) the summary form of procedure provided by s.89 of the 1845 Act was embraced in the definition of "summary cause" in s.35(1) of the 1971 Act; and appeal refused.

GLASGOW AIRPORT v. CHALK, 1995 S.L.T. (Sh.Ct.) 111.

6397. Summary causes—action for recovery of possession of heritable property. See EDINBURGH DISTRICT COUNCIL, CITY OF v. SINCLAIR, §6083.

6398. Summary causes—action for recovery of possession of heritable property—whether charge necessary following decree of removing

[Sheriff Courts (Scotland) Extracts Act 1892 (c.17), s.7(4); Act of Sederunt (Summary Cause Rules, Sheriff Court) 1976 (S.I. 1976 No. 476), rr. 69 and 91(2) and Form V3.)

Held, in a summary cause action for recovery of possession of heritable property, that a charge was necessary following a decree of removing. *Opinion reserved*, on the question of whether the period of charge should be 48 hours or 14 days.

MAIN v. REID (Sh. Ct.), 1994 S.C.L.R. 948.

6399. Summary causes—counterclaim—whether financial limit on summary cause procedure applicable to counterclaim. See DICKIE v. GOLDIE, §6212.

6400. Summary causes—decree in absence—minute for recall of decree—failure in service on pursuer—effect of pursuer's appearance at hearing. See THOMSON v. PROCTOR, §6329.

6401. Summary causes—decree in absence—minute for recall of decree—refusal—whether "final judgment". See THOMSON v. PROCTOR, §6329.

Summary causes—expenses. See EXPENSES.

6402. Summary causes—procedure—proof diet—decree by default—competency

[Act of Sederunt (Summary Cause Rules, Sheriff Court) 1976 (S.I. 1976 No. 476), rr. 18(7), 20 and 28(1).]

Held, where the only defence stated in a summary cause was "debt denied", a diet of proof was fixed, the defenders were neither present nor represented at that diet and the sheriff pronounced decree by default in respect of the defenders' failure to state any defence, that (1) once a proof had been fixed in a summary cause, a sheriff was not entitled to review the decision to fix such a proof, (2) at a proof diet a sheriff was not entitled to consider a question of law (such as the adequacy of a defence) until the facts had been ascertained, and (3) if a party failed to appear or to be represented at a proof diet, the sheriff had no option but to fix a peremptory diet in terms of r. 28(1).

ESCO COMPUTERS & SYSTEMS MAINTENANCE v. MORRIS AMUSEMENTS (Sh.Ct.), 1995 S.C.L.R. 551.

6403. Title to sue. See DUNDEE DISTRICT COUNCIL (CITY OF) v. COOK, §6355.

6404. Title to sue—undischarged bankrupt. See THOMSON v. YORKSHIRE BUILDING SOCIETY, §5485.

SHIPPING AND MARINE INSURANCE

Fishing. See FISH AND FISHERIES.

6405. Fraserburgh harbour

FRASERBURGH HARBOUR REVISION ORDER 1995 (No. 1527) [£2·80], made under the Harbours Act 1964 (c.40), s.14 (as amended by the Transport

Act 1981 (c.56), s.18 and Sched. 6 and Transport and Works Act 1992 (c.42), Sched. 3); operative on June 19, 1995; empowers the Fraserburgh Harbour Commissioners to underpin parts of Fraserburgh Harbour, to reface the quay walls, dredge the entrance channel to the harbour and close the harbour temporarily if deemed necessary for the purpose of carrying out the works and also enlarges the Commissioners' borrowing powers.

6406. Harbours and docks—harbour authority—power to sell land—whether *ultra vires*

[Montrose Harbour Revision Order 1974 (S.I. 1974 No. 348), arts. 2 and 21.]

A port authority acquired by statute the property, powers and responsibilities formerly vested in statutory trustees appointed to manage the harbour of Montrose. The property included lands on both banks of the River South Esk. Section 51 of the Montrose Harbour Act 1837 expressly gave the authority power to sell, feu or lease the lands on the north bank. Article 21 of the Montrose Harbour Revision Order 1974 provided express power, in respect of the lands on the south bank, to lease or grant to others the use of or servitudes over the land. Article 2 of the 1974 Order and s.20 of the Harbours, Docks and Piers Clauses Act 1847 provided an express power to buy adjoining lands for use for certain purposes. The authority, having let the lands on the south bank to tenants, agreed to accept a surrender of the lease in return for the payment by them of a sum which was to be raised partly by the sale of a part of the south bank for which the authority had no need. The authority and the purchasers presented a special case for the opinion of the Court of Session on the question whether the authority had power to sell the subjects. The purchasers argued that a statutory corporation had, in addition to their express powers, such powers as could reasonably be implied from the wording of the statutory provisions conferring express powers. In any event, such a corporation had such powers as could be implied as being reasonably incidental to the corporation's objects, which in this case were to operate the harbour, to provide lands and facilities for its users, and from time to time to improve it.

Held, that (1) the reasonable inference from Parliament's omission to include a power of sale among the specific powers which it had granted to the authority in respect of the south bank, was that the authority had not been intended to have such a power; (2) such a power could not then be regarded as reasonably incidental to or consequent upon any of the express powers; (3) the powers of a statutory corporation included those which were reasonably incidental to or consequential upon the main purposes of the corporation, but that that did not entail an implied power to do whatever appeared to be sensible, convenient and profitable, nor to do whatever was consistent with or conducive to the achievement of these purposes; (4) accordingly, the fact that the sale would raise money to achieve an object which lay within the purposes of the authority could not imply the existence of a power of sale, and, since almost anything that the authority could want to do with the land in relation to the harbour's purposes could be done by using its express powers, a power of sale was not necessary; and question answered in the negative. (*Ashbury Railway Carriage and Iron Co. v. Riche* (1875) L.R. 7 H.L. 653; *Att.-Gen. v. Great Eastern Railway Co.* (1880) 5 App.Cas. 473; *Shiell's Trs. v. Scottish Property Investment Building Society* (*in liquidation*) (1884) 12 R. (H.L.) 14; *D. & J. Nicol v. Dundee Harbour Trs., 1914 2 S.L.T. 418;* and *Hazell v. Hammersmith and Fulham London Borough Council* [1992] 2 A.C. 1, applied; *Re Kingsbury Collieries and Moore's Contract* [1907] 2 Ch. 259, distinguished.)

PIGGINS & RIX v. MONTROSE PORT AUTHORITY, 1995 S.L.T. 418.

6407. Montrose harbour. See PIGGINS & RIX v. MONTROSE PORT AUTHORITY, §6406.

6408. Shipping law—detention of ship unfit for sea—powers of Secretary of State—harbour master's authority

[Merchant Shipping Act 1988 (c.12) s.30A.]

U, trustees for Ullapool harbour, sought judicial review of a decision by S's Marine Safety Agency to detain ships within the port of Ullapool (hereinafter referred to as "S's line" as unfit to go to sea). The parties agreed that the ships in question were unfit in terms of s.30A of the 1988 Act, and that there was a lacuna in the legislation regarding the area of waters to which S's authority extended. U considered that the unfit vessels would be more safely anchored in another bay which was within the Ullapool harbour limits but several miles beyond S's line, while S directed that the ships be detained within S's line. U argued that ss.1, 2, 52, 53 and 58 of the Harbours, Docks and Piers Clauses Act 1847 gave the harbourmaster wide powers to regulate the movement of vessels within the harbour limits and to control the movements of particular vessels when they were within the port (*The Guelder Rose* (1927) 136 L.T.R. 226). Since there was nothing within s.30A conferring on S a power to restrict the movement of vessels within S's line, the restrictions imposed by S were invalid. S's power was to prohibit detained ships from going to sea until released by a competent authority and was accordingly aimed at preventing a ship "going to sea", which suggested going on a journey. If Parliament had intended to impinge on the harbourmaster's powers it would have specifically so provided in s.30A. Detention orders under s.30A should not prevent the harbourmaster from directing the movement of vessels anywhere within the harbour limits as safety considerations in his judgment so required. The existing provisions should be interpreted as empowering S to detain a ship under s.30A within harbour limits but not within only a part of the area of waters within those limits.

Held, petition dismissed. The powers of the harbour authority were displaced to some extent by the statutory powers granted to S. Having regard to the apparent intent of the legislation concerning safety, "going to sea" including going into waters properly to be regarded as the "sea" for the purposes of the legislation and "going to sea" was not necessarily restricted to going on a journey by sea to another port. The mischief which the Act was concerned with preventing was stopping unsafe ships going to waters properly classified as "sea", and accordingly S's line, being based on safety considerations, was a more appropriate sea than the harbour limit line. Since a Marine Safety Agency officer could determine that a ship was unsafe to go to sea, it must have been intended that he should have the power to prohibit that vessel from going into "sea" waters whatever the master's intentions.

ULLAPOOL HARBOUR TRUSTEES v. SECRETARY OF STATE FOR TRANSPORT (O.H.), *The Scotsman*, April 13, 1995.

6409. Stornoway harbour

STORNOWAY (FERRY TERMINAL) HARBOUR REVISION ORDER 1995 (No. 964) [£1·55], made under the Harbours Act 1964 (c.40), s.14 (as amended by the Transport Act 1981 (c.56), s.18 and Sched. 6); operative on March 31, 1995; authorises Stornoway Pier and Harbour Commission to carry out certain works connected with the construction of a ferry terminal at Stornoway harbour and the removal of part of the existing terminal.

STORNOWAY HARBOUR REVISION ORDER 1995 (No. 740) [65p], made under the Harbours Act 1964 (c.40), s.14 (as amended by the Transport Act 1981 (c.56), Scheds. 6 and 12 and the Transport and Works Act 1992 (c.42), Sched. 3); operative on March 14, 1995; provides that in place of the restriction to ratepayers, the qualification that only persons who are proprietors of business properties are qualified to be nominated or elected by the Stornoway Trust, is extended so that all those who are resident within the burgh shall be entitled to be so nominated or elected.

[Stornoway Harbour Order 1976 (c.xxi) amended.]

6410. West Burrafirth harbour

SHETLAND ISLANDS COUNCIL (WEST BURRAFIRTH) HARBOUR REVISION ORDER 1995 (No. 2380) [65p], made under the Harbours Act 1964 (c.40) s.14

(as amended by the Transport Act 1981 (c.56) s.18 and Sched. 6 and by the Transport and Works Act 1992 (c.42) s.63 and Sched. 3); operative on September 8, 1995; establishes a new harbour area at West Burrafirth.

6411. Western Isles harbours

WESTERN ISLES ISLANDS COUNCIL (VARIOUS HARBOURS JURISDICTION AND BYELAWS) HARBOUR REVISION ORDER 1995 (No. 2007) [£1·95], made under the Harbours Act 1964 (c.40), s.14 (as amended by the Transport Act 1981 (c.56) s.18, Sched. 6 and by the Transport and Works Act 1992 (c.42), Sched. 3); establishes harbour limits and provides for the making of bye-laws in respect of certain harbour areas.

[1980 c.i. and 1980 c.xxvii amended and partially revoked, 1978 c.cxv, 1982 c.ii, 1984 c.ii, 1984 c.xxx, c.xix, S.I. 1992 No. 1975, S.I. 1992 No. 1976, S.I. 1993 No. 2908, partially revoked.]

SHOPS, MARKETS AND FAIRS

6412. Licensing—market operator's licence—conditions—whether lawful

New conditions were attached to the renewal of a market operator's licence at the insistence of the Office of Trading Standards in order to address the alleged sale of counterfeit goods by some traders using the market. The licensees appealed to the sheriff. The new conditions, *inter alia*, would have allowed free access to the whole market by trading standards officers and would necessitate all their reasonable directions and requirements being complied with, which the licensees argued was *ultra vires* since trading standards officers were not included amongst those officials given a right of entry into a property such as the market by virtue of s.40 of and Sched. 1, para. 5 to the Civic Government (Scotland) Act 1982. The conditions would also have banned "fly-pitches" and required proof of identity from those requesting stalls or pitches at the market, which conditions the licensees argued were unlawful by virtue of uncertainty. It was contended that the licensing authority and the trading standards department attached different meanings to "fly-pitch". The licensees also challenged the adequacy of the written reasons given for rejecting their submissions at the hearing.

Held, that (1) it was not for a licensing authority to add to the powers of a statutory creation such as the trading standards officer where such powers had not been granted to the officer by the legislature; (2) the condition relating to "fly-pitches" was void from uncertainty since it could not be seen by anyone reading it precisely what was being struck at; (3) a condition relating to proof of identity of those requesting stalls or pitches was void from uncertainty since it was not clear what the condition meant; (4) a condition imposing an absolute duty on the licensee to ensure that other people did, and continued to do, something, went too far when a criminal sanction might be invoked for failure; (5) there was no explanation given of why the objections made by the licensees at the hearing were rejected by the authority; and appeal allowed and conditions deleted from licence.

SPOOK ERECTION v. CITY OF EDINBURGH DISTRICT COUNCIL, 1995 S.L.T. (Sh.Ct.) 107.

SMALL LANDHOLDER

6413. Croft—acquisition by crofter—apportioned common grazing—sole area sought to be acquired. See MacMILLAN v. MacKENZIE, §6416.

6414. Croft—acquisition by crofter—apportionment lying 1200m from inbye croft land—whether "adjacent or contiguous"

[Crofters (Scotland) Act 1993 (c.44), s.12(3).]

A crofter sought to purchase his croft consisting of three separate plots of inbye land and also an apportionment lying 1200m away by road, and separated from the remaining parts of the croft by a non-crofting fen, by part of a loch and by a stream.

Held, that the apportionment was adjacent or contiguous to the remainder of the croft and therefore purchasable under s.12(3) of the 1993 Act; the apportionment was only 400m in a direct line from the croft, parts of which were separated from each other by as much as 500m, the crofting activity was sufficiently diversified to include mussel farming immediately opposite the apportionment, and the apportionment formed the main working part of the croft containing the main agricultural building.

ROSS v. BARR'S TRS., 1994 S.L.C.R. 60.

6415. Croft—acquisition by crofter—objection by landlord—substantial degree of hardship

[Crofters (Scotland) Act 1993 (c.44), s.13.]

The tenant of a croft sought to acquire her croft from her landlord. The tenant had become the crofter following the death of her mother and her brother had acquired the landlord's interest in the croft at approximately the same time. The brother had purchased the land, in an attempt to retain some control over it. He objected to the application on the ground that if the court granted an order authorising acquisition this would cause him a substantial degree of hardship, in that the croft had been in his family since the 17th century, he had worked on it from the age of 11 until his mother's death and still worked a neighbouring croft, and his sister had no agricultural expertise and had failed to work the croft.

Held, that any hardship suffered by the landlord respondent was due to the severance of his connection with the land on the transfer of the tenancy to his sister, which would affect him whether or not an order was made, and accordingly the making of an order authorising acquisition would not cause him a substantial degree of hardship.

FRASER v. MACKINTOSH, 1995 S.L.T. (Land Ct.) 45.

6416. Croft—common grazings—apportionment—acquisition by crofter—sole area sought to be acquired

[Crofting Reform (Scotland) Act 1976 (c.21), s.1(3).]

Section 1(3) of the 1976 Act provided that "croft land" which a crofter might apply to be authorised to acquire, did not include "(b) any land, comprising any part of a common grazing, unless the land has been apportioned under section 27(4) of the Act of 1955 and is . . . (i) adjacent or contiguous to any other part of the croft". The tenant of certain shares in a common grazing to whom an area of the grazing had been apportioned applied to the Land Court for an order authorising him to acquire the apportioned area by virtue of the terms of the 1976 Act. The area constituted the entire croft which the applicant sought to purchase although he retained rights in the remainder of the common grazing land. The divisional court granted the application, holding that the apportioned area of common grazing formed part of the croft land which the applicant could acquire. The landlord appealed.

Held, that the apportioned land required to be adjacent or contiguous to another substantive area of land which formed part of the croft before it could be the subject of acquisition under the 1976 Act and appeal allowed. *Macdonald v. Hilleary* [1993] C.L.Y. 5891 not followed.

MacMILLAN v. MacKENZIE, 1995 S.L.T. (Land Ct.) 7.

6417. Croft—common grazings—determination of ownership of grazings share—whether owner of share entitled to membership of sheep stock club

A crofter became tenant by formal assignation from the previous tenant.

The assumption included any share in the common grazings pertaining to the croft, these being run as a sheep stock club. The crofter applied to the clerk to the common grazings to buy a share in the club. The clerk refused the application on the grounds that the share pertaining to the croft concerned had already been sold and that accordingly no share was available to the crofter. The crofter applied to the Land Court for an order (a) determining the ownership of the grazing share pertaining to, or formerly pertaining to the croft, and (b) determining that the crofter was entitled by virtue of owning the said grazing share to membership of the sheep stock club and determining the price for such membership.

Held, that on a proper interpretation of the grazings regulations a share of the sheep stock club could only be detached from the tenancy or ownership of a croft on a temporary basis with the permission of the grazings committee, and that the crofter was entitled to a one quarter share in the club on payment of a sum equal to one quarter of the value of the club stock.

WATSON v. CAMPBELL, 1994 S.L.C.R. 100.

6418. Croft—common grazings—determination of shares in the common grazings

A crofter applied to the Land Court to determine who the shareholders in the common grazings were and their respective rights in the grazings. Parties were agreed that there were four shareholders but put forward different methods by which the rights available to each crofter should be determined. The applicant favoured all the rights being determined by reference to a rental formula whereas one of the respondents submitted that the rights should be determined on the basis of the wintering capacity of the four holdings.

Held, that the shares in the common grazings should be determined on the basis of the proportion of the inbye land of each croft to the total inbye land of the crofts.

CAMPBELL v. CAMPBELL, 1994 S.L.C.R. 124.

6419. Croft—common grazings—liability for maintenance and repair of township fences

A crofter obtained an order from the Land Court finding that the liability for the maintenance, repair and, where necessary, replacement of township fences of a common grazings fell on the committee of the common grazings. The crofter then complained to the court that the groupings committee had failed to implement the order by not renewing a particular fence. He undertook to pay his share of the cost of the fence to the grazings committee.

Held, that the grazings committee should be ordered to produce various documents in order to establish the probable total cost of the fence and the amount of the crofter's share thereof.

MACASKILL v. MACLEOD, 1994 S.L.C.R. 95.

6420. Croft—common grazings—resumption by landlord—regularising the position—whether a reasonable purpose

[Crofters (Scotland) Act 1993 (c.44), s.20.]

The landlords of a common grazing applied to the Land Court for an order authorising them to resume some 28 acres for the purpose of conveying the area to the executors of a deceased tenant who had used the area as part of his agricultural holding for a considerable number of years.

Held, that, although the court would not authorise resumption for agricultural purposes, the real purpose of this application was to regularise the position which was in the interests of the estate and in the public interest; and resumption authorised.

DUNBAR'S (SIR G.C.D.S.) TRS. v. CROFTERS SHARING IN WINLESS COMMON GRAZINGS, 1994 S.L.C.R. 89.

6421. Croft—common grazings—resumption of part by landlord—site for golf clubhouse—part of common grazings used as a golf course

[Crofters (Scotland) Act 1993 (c.44), s.5(3).]

The landlords of a common grazing applied to the court to resume a small area of ground for the purpose of conveying it to the golf club for the construction of a new clubhouse. The application was sisted to enable parties to give consideration to the competency of the arrangement under which golf was played on the common grazings, and a further application was subsequently lodged by the landlords seeking the court's approval of the agreement entered into between the golf club and the shareholders in the common grazings whereby the club were allowed to play golf on part of the grazings.

Held, that (1) the agreement between the golf club and the shareholders should be approved by the court; (2) the use of the resumption site for a golf clubhouse was reasonable; and resumption authorised.

TRUSTEES OF THE TENTH DUKE OF ARGYLL v. CROFTERS SHARING IN VAUL COMMON GRAZINGS, 1995 S.L.T. (Land Ct.) 51.

6422. Croft—resumption by landlord—reasonable purpose—natural woodland regeneration scheme

[Crofters (Scotland) Act 1993 (c.44), ss.20 and 21.]

The landlord of a large croft applied to the court for authority to resume a substantial part of the croft for the purpose of selling it to a third party for a natural woodland regeneration scheme. The crofter consented to the application and as there was no contradictor the Crofters Commission were requested by the court to provide evidence on the use of croft land as woodland in the light of the relevant statutory provisions. No evidence was given as to whether resumption was sought for a reasonable purpose having regard to the good of the croft or the good of the estate. A large part of the area sought to be resumed was protected by a conservation agreement with the National Trust for Scotland and by its designation as a site of special scientific interest by Scottish Natural Heritage.

Held, that there was no justification in the circumstances of the case for the depletion of the pool of croft land simply in order to enable a potential purchaser to raise funds to finance a conservation project when the valuable features of the land were already the subject of adequate protection measurements; and resumption refused.

SHIELDAIG FARM (GAIRLOCH) v. MACRAE, 1995 S.L.T. (Land Ct.) 47.

6423. Crofter resumption by landlord—resumption subject to conditions—whether conditions *ultra vires*

In 1978 the Land Court authorised the resumption of an area of ground subject to certain conditions purporting to order the re-establishment of the common grazings after a lease of the area resumed had terminated. One of the crofters applied to the court for enforcement of the conditions.

Held, that, (1) since the effect of resumption was to remove from the court's jurisdiction land which had been surrendered by the crofter, it was not open to the Court to improve conditions which purported to have the effect of continuing the court's jurisdiction over land once it had been resumed and accordingly that the order of 1978 was *ultra vires*, and (2) special cause had been shown for leave to be granted for a motion for a rehearing, but the motion should be refused, *inter alia*, as a rehearing could serve no useful purpose.

NICOLSON v. HOSEASON-BROWN, 1994 S.L.C.R. 74.

6424. Land Court—rehearing—motion for leave to move for a rehearing on special cause. See NICOLSON v. HOSEASON-BROWN, §6423.

6425. Landholder's holding—rent—fair rent

In an application by the landlords of a landholder's holding for an order fixing a fair rent the landholder submitted that consideration should be given to the possible effect of the inclusion of his holding in an EC designated nitrate vulnerable zone. The proposed scheme was only at a consultation stage and the closing date for representations had only recently passed.

Held, that, as the court could not reasonably foresee when such a scheme was likely to be implemented, no consideration of the consequences of the imposition of the scheme should be taken into account in fixing the fair rent.

HEPBURN BOOTH TRS. v. ELDER, 1994 S.C.L.R. 139.

SOCIAL SECURITY

Housing Benefit. See HOUSING.

6426. Housing benefit—higher pensioner premium—eligibility

A appealed a decision of a housing benefit review board (B) to confirm the decision of a director of housing to refuse A's application for higher pensioner premium made on November 27, 1991. A, who had been in receipt of invalidity benefit, had opted to retire on July 12, 1986 when aged 65, and to receive retirement pension thereafter. G conceded that B had erred in holding that an amendment to the eligibility rules in para. 12(1)(a)(ii) of the Housing Benefit (General) Regulations 1987, which made those who elected to receive retirement pension before reaching the age of 70 eligible for higher pensioner premium, was not intended to apply to persons who had retired before October 9, 1989, when the amendment had been made, but G argued that, as housing benefit had only been introduced on April 1, 1988, A did not meet the requirement in para. 12(1)(a)(ii) that he had remained continuously entitled to housing benefit since retirement and that B had reached the right decision. A argued that the term "housing benefit" referred to any benefit created by Parliament to subsidise housing costs and included the benefits under the Social Security and Housing Benefits Act 1982, which A had received between retirement and April 1, 1988.

Held, petition refused. (1) Although G's argument had not been put to B and B had made a finding in fact that A "had been in receipt of housing benefit continuously from July 12, 1986", the point was properly one of law and, as the errors B were agreed or alleged to have made went to the heart of the decision, judicial review was competent to determine what was a pure question of statutory interpretation. (2) Although the term "housing benefit" was not defined in the 1987 Regulations, considering that terms in subordinate legislation were to be given the same meaning as in the legislation under which they were made (s.11, Interpretation Act 1978), the term clearly referred to the new benefit created by the Social Security Act 1986. Where in s.29(4) of the 1986 Act the term had been intended to include other benefits express provision had been made. While quite different terminology had been used with other new benefits created by the Act, the change from the plural used in the 1982 Act, referring to three benefits, to the singular used in the 1986 Act for the new benefit which had been created by merging the previous three, was small but significant. Although this produced an anomaly that persons who had opted to retire prior to April 1, 1988, would have to wait until age 80 to qualify for higher pensioner premium, some anomalies might occur as a result of conscious changes in policy. (3) Although the board had erred in reaching their decision, there were no issues of fact left uncertain or undetermined, and there was nothing to justify a convening of B for a formal restatement of the earlier result (*City of Glasgow District Council v. Secretary of State for Scotland*, 1982 S.L.T. 28, applied).

ANDREW v. CITY OF GLASGOW DISTRICT COUNCIL (O.H.), *The Scotsman*, February 9, 1995.

6427. Income support—payments for housing costs—building insurance premium

[Income Support (General) Regulations 1987 (S.I. 1987 No. 1967), reg. 17(1)(e) and Sched. 3, para. 1.]

Regulation 17(1) of the Income Support (General) Regulations 1987 provides that in calculating a claimant's weekly payment, specified housing costs are to be included. Paragraph 1 of Sched. 3 specifies which housing costs are to be taken into consideration and also provides that "(h) payments analogous to those mentioned in this paragraph" are to be included. A claimant who was the owner occupier of her house sought payment of a building insurance premium as a housing cost within the meaning of reg. 17(1). Her claim was refused by the adjudication officer but she was successful on appeal to the social security appeal tribunal. The Secretary of State appealed to the social security commissioners, who upheld the decision of the tribunal but for different reasons. The commissioner considered that although payment of a building insurance premium was not analogous to any of the individual payments listed in para. 1 of Sched. 3, the listed payments constituted a genus and the payment claimed could be regarded as analogous to those payments as a genus. The Secretary of State appealed to the Court of Session, arguing that the commissioner's reasoning was unsound in finding a common thread to the specific payments allowed, and that none of these payments were analogous to building insurance.

Held, that (1) there was no genus to be found in the payments allowed which would entitle any other claim to be brought under subpara. (h) *ejusdem generis*; (2) the intention to select certain specific housing costs as allowable to the exclusion of others would be defeated if a wide range of other costs were to be allowed, and there was no analogy between an insurance premium and any of the specified costs; and appeal allowed.

SECRETARY OF STATE FOR SOCIAL SECURITY v. McSHERRY, 1995 S.L.T. 371.

6428. Social fund—repayment of loans from—power to deduct repayments from benefit—effect of sequestration

[Bankruptcy (Scotland) Act 1985 (c.66), s.32; Social Security Administration Act 1992 (c.5) s.78(2).]

The Secretary of State (S) reclaimed against a Lord Ordinary's decision that S had acted *ultra vires* in deducting from income support received by a bankrupt (M) after her sequestration, sums in repayment of a loan from the social fund taken out by M prior to sequestration. M argued that S's power under s.78(2) of the 1992 Act to recover the loan by making deductions from benefits received by her was subject to the general rule of bankruptcy that post-sequestration income could not be set off against a pre-sequestration debt; and that S was prohibited by s.32(5) of the 1985 Act from exercising diligence against M's post-sequestration income.

Held, reclaiming motion allowed and petition dismissed. While s.78(2) had to be construed against the background of the law relating to bankruptcy, the general rule, properly stated, prohibited setting off debts acquired by M after sequestration but which vested in M's trustee (T) under s.32(6) of the 1985 Act, against claims against M which existed prior to sequestration (Goudy, *Bankruptcy* (4th ed.), pp. 554–555). However, this rule had no application to M's case, because in terms of s.187(1) of the 1992 Act her entitlement to income support did not pass to T, the bankruptcy provisions only taking effect at the stage of payment of the benefit when the net amount payable vested in M (s.32(1) of the 1985 Act), subject to T's right to apply under s.32(2) for any excess over the amount required for aliment to be paid to him (*Re Garrett* [1930] 2 Ch. 137; *Macdonald v. Macdonald's Tr.*, 1938 S.L.T. 445). T was not entitled to seek an order against S for payment of the benefit and had no right to intervene in the working out of M's entitlement to benefit. Accordingly, S was not seeking to withhold any sums payable to T, nor was he seeking to exercise diligence against M's income, as S had not sought to attach the income in M's hands. Section 78(2) authorised S to make deductions from M's benefit in order to obtain repayment of the loan. This was not an unfair preference to the prejudice of M's other creditors, and it would be contrary to the scheme of the Social Security Acts if such loans were to cease to be repayable in full so as to enable T to obtain a benefit for M's other creditors. *Per* Lord Clyde: s.78(2) merely provided one element in the calculation of the amount of income support to which M was entitled and this was not a situation in which questions of compensation arose.

MULVEY v. SECRETARY OF STATE FOR SOCIAL SECURITY, *The Times*, November 24, 1995.

SOLICITORS

6429. Expenses of action—personal liability for. See REID v. EDINBURGH ACOUSTICS (No. 2), §5954.

6430. Fees—sheriff officers' fees—personal liability of instructing solicitors. See STIRLING PARK & CO. v. DIGBY, BROWN & CO., §6346.

6431. Judicial factor on solicitor's estate—whether entitled to deduct remuneration from estate

[Solicitors (Scotland) Act 1980 (c.46), ss.41 and 42; Bankruptcy (Scotland) Act 1985 (c.66), ss.31, 33 and 51.]

In a petition of L under s.41 of the 1980 Act a judicial factor (J) was appointed to the estate of M, a solicitor, on June 23, 1988. M was subsequently sequestrated and on October 28, a permanent trustee (T) was appointed. Following an Inner House decision ([1992] C.L.Y. 6463) that sums held in M's client account did not vest in T but remained under J's administration, the Accountant of Court again reported the case to the Inner House in a note in which he took the view that J had no title to take administration expenses from client funds and had only a claim to an ordinary creditor's ranking against M's estate. The accountant argued that the client account was protected by s.42 of the 1980 Act, and that M's estate remained primarily liable for J's remuneration. T argued that J's active role terminated on the appointment of the interim trustee as the interim trustee was obliged to take up the safeguarding of M's estate; that, while J was entitled to deduct his fees and outlays from the sums realised and held by him, J had no preferential claim against the sequestrated estate; and that J had to look to L if there was a shortfall in his remuneration.

Held, note reversed. In terms of the 1980 Act J was appointed on M's "estate" and, while the Act did not define J's powers, as his appointment was inextricably bound up with the need to protect client and third party funds from M's intromissions and given the terms of s.42(1), it followed that the client funds fell within the meaning of "estate", although other funds held by M in trust would not, as M's involvement in the administration of those funds arose from a private appointment and not from his professional practice. As a general rule of law J was entitled to reimbursement of his fees and outlays from the funds subject to his management, and there was nothing in the 1980 Act implying any departure from that rule. In particular s.42 did not ring fence the client accounts, but rather the sum remaining for distribution in terms of s.42 would reflect the deduction of the appropriate proportion of J's outlays and remuneration. The distinction between M's personal estate and the client funds existed throughout the factory and, from general principles, J's fees were to be apportioned to each fund, although M's estate was liable for any deficiency in the client accounts created by the apportionment. As M's estate was insolvent, the apportionment might increase the amount which fell to be met by the guarantee fund, but this could not justify any departure from the general principle and, in any event, L would have a remedy against M's estate. The exact nature and extent of J's duties and the scope of his powers had to be determined from the circumstances of his appointment. While sequestration, in the sense of judicial assumption of the possession of property (Bell, *Commentaries*, ii, 244, para. 263), was an essential preliminary for appointment of a judicial factor to a partnership estate or trust in order to avoid the risk of two powers acting at the same time, it was not thought necessary for a sole practitioner. However, considering that J's appointment was intended to ensure the proper application of client funds and that realisation of M's estate would be required in order to settle M's liability to clients and others, it followed that on J's appointment M's estate was transferred to J with title to intromit therewith and to realise the estate and to apply the proceeds, and that what remained with M was a right to an accounting and a reversionary right to the assets comprised in the balance at the end of the factory. It was these rights which passed to T on sequestration. In an accounting J was entitled to take credit for his remuneration and outlays (*Miln's J.F. v. Spence's Trs.*, 1927 S.L.T. 425; *Jackson v. Welch* (1876) 4 M. 177), and, although as a practical solution the active administration of the estate had been passed to T before a full accounting was possible, it followed that J had a priority as against all competing claimants for reimbursement of his remuneration from T. The cash balances held by J could not be regarded as representing the whole estate for which he was liable, as J was entitled to bring any unrealised assets including work in progress into the accounting, as they were factory assets and M could not be said to have any rights of property in assets which had been totally at J's disposal. Accordingly T had taken the net indebtedness of J on an accounting and, although J had accounted to T for the gross sum because certain assets were unrealised, that had to be under an obligation on T to account to J for unpaid remuneration and outlays up to the amount subsequently realised. Observed, that, while a solicitor's sequestration or the appointment of a trust deed for creditors were events triggering the operation of s.42(1) of the 1980 Act, in the light of the earlier decision there might be questions as to the application of that provision in relation to those events and to the interaction between a judicial factor and other administrators of a solicitor's funds.

LAW SOCIETY OF SCOTLAND, COUNCIL OF THE v. McKINNIE (NO. 2), 1995 S.L.T. 880.

6432. Judicial factor on solicitor's estate—whether entitled to deduct remuneration from interest on clients' accounts

[Solicitors (Scotland) Act 1980 (c.46), ss.41 and 42; Judicial Factors Act 1849 (c.51), s.5; Judicial Factors (Scotland) Act 1889 (c.39), s.13.]

Held, in regard to a report by the Accountant of Court in a petition for the appointment of a judicial factor (J) to the estate of a firm of solicitors (W) in terms of s.41 of the Solicitors (Scotland) Act 1980, that J was entitled to have recourse to interest earned on clients' funds under his management for reimbursement of his expenses and for his remuneration for work done on behalf of the clients, as, although the interest accruing on the accounts belonged to the clients, J, who was in the same position as a trustee under a private trust deed, was entitled to be reimbursed out of the estate in respect of all expenses properly incurred in his administration of it (*Thomson v. Tough's Trs.* (1880) 7 R. 1035; *Salaman v. Rosslyn's Trs.* (1900) 3 F. 298); and accountant's note reversed. *Opinion*, that, on the same principle, if the interest was insufficient to meet J's remuneration, then J would be entitled to have recourse to the principal sums in the accounts. *Observed*, that where J had also done work for W, an apportionment would be appropriate, as the charge for the work should fall upon those on whose behalf it had been done.

LAW SOCIETY OF SCOTLAND, COUNCIL OF THE v. ANDREW, 1995 S.L.T. 877.

6433. Negligence—failure to carry out instructions—scope of instructions given. See BANK OF EAST ASIA v. SHEPHERD & WEDDERBURN, W.S., §6163.

Negligence—measure of damages. See DAMAGES.

6434. Undertaking—whether personal liability

A firm of solicitors sought to enforce a letter of obligation granted by another firm at settlement of a conveyancing transaction, so far as relating to delivery of a discharge of a standard security. The letter of obligation was signed by the firm without qualification but the obligations therein were undertaken "on behalf of our above named clients".

Held, that the obligation was not personally binding on the solicitors and action dismissed.

DIGBY BROWN & CO. v. LYALL (O.H.), 1995 S.L.T. 932.

STATUTES AND ORDERS

6435. Construction—powers of statutory corporation—power to sell land—whether reasonably incidental to or consequential upon statutory purposes. See PIGGINS & RIX v. MONTROSE PORT AUTHORITY, §6406.

6436. Construction—reference to EEC directive. See STIRLING DISTRICT COUNCIL v. ALLAN, §5911.

6437. Construction—reference to parliamentary materials. See STIRLING DISTRICT COUNCIL v. ALLAN, §5911.

6438. Construction—reference to parliamentary materials. See MONCKTON v. LORD ADVOCATE, §5916.

SUCCESSION

Services of heirs. See HERITABLE PROPERTY AND CONVEYANCING.

Wills. See WILLS.

TELECOMMUNICATIONS

6439. Wireless telegraphy—use—intention to obtain information not authorised to receive. See YOUNG v. H.M. ADVOCATE, §5670.

TIME

6440. Day at which period ends—"within six months" of application being made. See MONKLANDS DISTRICT COUNCIL v. McGHEE, §6129.

6441. Delay—contempt of court. See ROBB v. CALEDONIAN NEWSPAPERS, §5757.

6442. Delay—criminal prosecution—whether oppression. See SKILLING v. H.M. ADVOCATE, §5666.

Limitation of actions. See LIMITATION OF ACTIONS.

6443. Prescribed time—criminal prosecution—110 days elapsing after committal. See BEATTIE v. H.M. ADVOCATE, §5642; X., PETR., §5643.

6444. Prescribed time—criminal prosecution—12 months elapsing after first appearance. See McCULLOCH v. H.M. ADVOCATE, §5644.

6445. Prescribed time—criminal prosecution—summary proceedings. See GRAY v. NORMAND, §5705; McDONALD v. H. L. FRIEL & SON, §5914.

6446. Prescribed time—directors disqualification—requirement for notice—whether mandatory or directory. See SECRETARY OF STATE FOR TRADE AND INDUSTRY v. LOVAT, §5545.

Prescription. See PRESCRIPTION.

6447. Time limit—statutory notice—effect of suspension pending appeal—computation of time limit. See McDONALD v. H. L. FRIEL & SON, §5914.

TOWN AND COUNTRY PLANNING

Compulsory purchase. See COMPULSORY PURCHASE.

6448. Enforcement notice—error—incompetent requirement—whether capable of correction. See BARN PROPERTIES v. SECRETARY OF STATE FOR SCOTLAND, §6449.

6449. Enforcement notice—whether timeously served—second notice in different terms from notice served timeously

[Town and Country Planning (Scotland) Act 1972 (c.52), ss.83B, 84AA(3) and 85(1)(f).]

B, the owners of certain property, appealed against a decision by S's reporter (R) dated April 20, 1994, dismissing B's appeal against an enforcement notice served by D, a district council, subject to deleting from the notice the words "restore the use of the premises to single family occupation". B argued that the notice was time barred under s.83B of the 1972 Act, which required D to take action without four years of the purported breach. B had been served an initial notice in 1992 which alleged a breach of planning control consisting of a material change of use "namely the occupation of a single family dwellinghouse as two or more separate dwellinghouses". This notice was withdrawn and a second notice dated January 15, 1993, which was the notice appealed against, had been served allegeging the breach of planning control as "without planning permission the occupation of a single family dwellinghouse as a house in multiple occupation". B contended that the notices were directed at two different breaches and therefore the second notice should fail. In addition, R erred in law by deleting from the enforcement notice the requirement to restore the property to single family occupation. The parties agreed that it was incompetent for the planning authority to require B to use the property as it had been before the breach, and therefore the requirement was *ultra vires.* However, B contended that as s.84AA(3) required the notice to specify the steps to be taken to remedy the breach, it was essential that the steps be accurately specified and by eliminating these, the notice became a nullity. S submitted, in terms of para. P171B.10 of the *Encyclopaedia of Planning Law and Practice*, that as D had issued an enforcement notice within the four year time period, they were allowed a further four years to supplement or rectify a fault in the initial enforcement attempt. Moreover, S was entitled in terms of s.85(1)(f) to deal with any challenge to the validity of the notice and R was correct in deleting the excessive part of the requirement. The error in the second notice did not go to the root of the matter as the essential step to be taken to B was discontinuance of the non-permitted use. There was no injustice to B as the deletion reduced the requirements placed upon them by the amended notice.

Held, appeal refused. R had correctly concluded that the two notices purported to relate to the same breach in respect of multiple occupation of the premises. Reference in s.83B(4)(b) to the planning authority having "purported to take enforcement action" clearly included the possibility that the first notice contained some defect. "Purported" in this context implied intention or purpose. R was fully entitled to find that the purpose of serving both the original and the second notices was to take action against multiple occupation of the premises and accordingly s.83B(4)(b) prevented the second notice from being served out of time. In addition, R did not err in law by deleting the defective part of the notice as amendment of the requirements was permissible under s.85(1)(f) provided no injustice was caused to B or D by the variation. The enforcement notice was not fundamentally or irremediably flawed because it contained and admitted error. It was clear that the first part of the notice of January 15, 1993 which required B to discontinue the present multiple occupation was precisely what was necessary to remedy the breach, and that being so, the surplus requirement for the restoration of the house to a single family occupation was clearly separable.

BARN PROPERTIES v. SECRETARY OF STATE FOR SCOTLAND, 1995 S.C.L.R. 113.

6450. Environmental assessment—simplified planning zones. See TOWN AND COUNTRY PLANNING, §6454.

6451. Environmental protection

ENVIRONMENTAL PROTECTION (DETERMINATION OF ENFORCING AUTHORITY ETC.) (SCOTLAND) AMENDMENT REGULATIONS 1995. (No. 2742) [65p], made under the Environmental Protection Act 1990 (c.43), s.5; operative on November 10, 1995; provides that when the enforcing authority in respect of a particular prescribed process is not identified, the enforcing authority shall be the chief inspector.

[S.I. 1992 No. 530 amended.]

6452. Planning permission—grant of—judicial review—whether objections to local plan unfairly pre-empted by grant of planning permission—legitimate expectations

A planning authority granted planning permission for development. Adjoining proprietors had objected to the application on the ground that the proposed development was contrary to existing and proposed greenbelt policy. They sought judicial review of the decision to grant permission on the ground that their legitimate expectation of being able to object to the proposed new boundary line for the greenbelt area at the forthcoming local plan inquiry had been frustrated.

Held, that the planning authority had taken into account all relevant material, and that the application for judicial review could not succeed simply because the result of the grant of planning permission affected the position of the petitioners with regard to the draft local plan, its objections and the proposed inquiry, and petition dismissed.

WATSON v. RENFREW DISTRICT COUNCIL (O.H.), 1995 S.C.L.R. 82.

6453. Simplified planning zones

PLANNING AND COMPENSATION ACT 1991 (COMMENCEMENT NO. 18 AND TRANSITIONAL PROVISION) (SCOTLAND) ORDER 1995 (No. 2045) (C.42) [£1·95], made under the Planning and Compensation Act 1991 (c.34), s.84(2) and (3); brings into force on August 30, 1995, s.59 of and Sched. 11 to the Planning and Compensation Act 1991 (simplified planning zones), together with s.61 so far as relating to Sched. 13, para. 40(2), s.80 (part) and Sched. 18 (part), and s.84(6) (part) and Sched. 19 (part), the only Scottish provisions not now in force being para. 44 of Sched. 13 and the repeals in Pt. IV of Sched. 19 regarding s.101(1) and (2) of the Town and Country Planning (Scotland) Act 1972 (c.52).

TOWN AND COUNTRY PLANNING (SIMPLIFIED PLANNING ZONES) (SCOTLAND) REGULATIONS 1995 (No. 2043) [£3·70], made under the European Communities Act 1972 (c.68), s.2(2) and the Town and Country Planning (Scotland) Act 1972 (c.52) ss.273(1) (as amended by the Planning and Compensation Act 1991 (c.34) Sched. 17), 275(1) and Sched. 6A, paras. 5(2), 6 (both substituted by the Planning and Compensation Act 1991 (c.34), Sched. 11) and 12 (as amended by the 1991 Act, Sched. 11); operative on August 30, 1995; supersede the Town and Country Planning (Simplified Planning Zones) Regulations 1987 and provide the procedure for making and altering simplified planning zone schemes; and further implement Council Directive 85/337/EEC.

[S.I. 1987 No. 1532 revoked.]

6454. Simplified planning zones—developments requiring environmental assessment

TOWN AND COUNTRY PLANNING (SIMPLIFIED PLANNING ZONES) (SCOTLAND) ORDER 1995 (No. 2044) [65p], made under the Town and Country Planning (Scotland) Act 1972 (c.52), s.21E(3) (as inserted by the Housing and Planning Act 1986 (c.63) s.26); operative August 30, 1995; further implements Council Directive 85/337/EEC by providing that no simplified planning zone scheme has effect to grant planning permission for development requiring environmental assessment.

6455. Structure and local plans—approval of Secretary of State—failure to adjudicate on disputed issue—whether *ultra vires*

H sought reduction under ss.231 and 232 of the Town and Country Planning (Scotland) Act 1972 of the Secretary of State's (S) decision to approve without modification the Strathclyde Structure Plan Update 1992, which reviewed and revised the housing policies in the structure plan. In the update the regional council (R) calculated that there was an effective land supply as at March 31, 1992 of 60,822 dwellings and that there was accordingly a surplus of supply over demand for private housing. In his decision letter dated May 26, 1994 S stated that "[H]. . . have disputed the Regional Council's assessment of the effective land supply. . . [S] does not consider it appropriate for him to adjudicate on the land supply figures. Accordingly, it falls to be handled at a more local level." H argued that applying national planning policy guidelines issued by S in July 1993 the effective land supply was 44,218 dwellings indicating a shortage of supply, and that, although the guidelines had been issued after R submitted the update to S, S was bound to have regard to them, but that no reference had been made to them in the decision letter nor any reason given for preferring R's criteria. S argued that he was not bound to have regard to the guidelines, and that, as a comprehensive review of R's structure plan was promised for 1994, S had been entitled to decide that it was premature for him to determine the criteria to apply. R argued that, esto S's approval was *ultra vires*, the update should remain in force, as quashing it would be unfair on those whose planning applications or appeals had already been determined on the basis of the update, and would mean that the 1990 update, which was based on the same old criteria, would remain in force; it was unlikely that R would put the 1992 update forward again, as the 1994 review was almost ready for submission to S; there was no inequity to H, as when the update was submitted to S in June 1993 the guidelines had not been issued and had S's decision been taken within a month, S's argument as to prematurity would have prevailed; and the existence of the 1992 update would not prevent developers entering into conditional missives or putting in planning applications, which if appealed would not be decided until the new structure plan came into operation.

Held, application granted and update quashed. S was not bound to follow his own guidelines, but they had to be a material consideration. While S had clearly decided that other objections about R's estimate of housing demand and its failure to reappraise land supply against targets and to provide for a long term settlement strategy were premature and would be covered by the 1994 review, it was not clear that prematurity could be read into his reasons for failing to adjudicate on the criteria for effective land supply. In any event, the matter had been an ongoing dispute between H and R, and S could not have arrived at an informed decision on whether or not to approve the effective land supply figures without applying his mind to the appropriate criteria and without obtaining revised figures based on the new guidelines. Given that S's guidelines confirmed H's methodology and conflicted directly with R's criteria, that the dispute was plainly of considerable importance to H, as all planning decisions for at least the next two years would be based on the figures in the update, and that the decision on the appropriate criteria was clearly one for S to make and was not to be decided locally, it was an abdication of responsibility by S to defer a decision on the appropriate criteria. Accordingly his decision was *ultra vires* and could not stand. Only very recent decisions would be called into question if the update was quashed, and in any event persons would be entitled to reapply in the light of changed circumstances. While the update was not necessarily wrong and R might be able to justify their criteria, it would be chaotic for decisions to be taken on the basis of an update which should not have been approved, and for developers to have to go to the expense of appealing decisions in the hope that the 1994 review would alter the criteria. Developers were entitled to rely on the integrity of the structure plan and the plan should not remain in force any period longer than was necessary.

SCOTTISH HOUSE-BUILDERS ASSOCIATION v. SECRETARY OF STATE FOR SCOTLAND, *The Scotsman*, August 23, 1995.

TRADE AND INDUSTRY

6456. Restrictive practices—reference to Restrictive Practices Court—nomination of representative respondent—objection of nominee

[Restrictive Trade Practices Act 1976 (c.34), ss.1 and 26; Restrictive Practices Court Rules 1976 (S.I. 1976 No. 1897), rr. 3(1) and (3), 5(1) and 6(1).]

Rule 3 of the Restrictive Practices Court Rules 1976 provides that proceedings under the Restrictive Trade Practices Act 1976 shall be instituted by a notice of reference which shall sufficiently identify the agreement or agreements to which it applies. Rule 5(1) provides that the Director General of Fair Trading may nominate a "representative respondent" in such proceedings, where "several persons have a common interest . . . by reason that they are all parties to the same agreement or have entered into substantially similar agreements". Under r. 6(1) any party who objects to being made a representative respondent may apply to the court for an order revoking the nomination. A solicitors' property centre submitted an agreement consisting of a number of documents to the Director General of Fair Trading for registration under the Restrictive Trade Practices Act 1976. The Director General referred the agreement under s.1(3) of the Act by notice of reference to the Restrictive Practices Court. In those proceedings the Director General nominated a member firm of solicitors as the representative respondents. The nomination was limited to (i) the members of the centre identified as such by reference to the centre's property bulletin for a particular date, and (ii) the occasional users of the centre, "being any solicitor or firm of solicitors other than a member" whose property particulars were listed in said bulletin. The nominee firm applied to the court for an order revoking the nomination in respect of both the members and the occasional users. The nominee firm argued that the notice of reference was defective in that it did not sufficiently identify the agreement to which it purported to apply; that it was impossible to understand from the notice what the alleged agreement was supposed to be and who were the parties to it; and that that amounted to non-compliance with r. 3(3) the result that the notice of reference could not proceed and therefore it was not possible to nominate a representative respondent. The firm further argued that the Director General had failed to identify the common interest between members and occasional users, which would make it difficult for the nominee firm to represent the class of occasional users since there might be a conflict of interest between members and occasional users. To allow the nomination would mean that the court was pre-judging the issue of whether there was such a common interest.

Held, that (1) until steps were taken to rectify the register under s.26 of the 1976 Act the agreement as registered was the one to which the court had to have regard and any question as to interpretation of the agreement was a matter to be dealt with at a subsequent stage of the proceedings; (2) it was sufficient compliance with r. 3(3) that the documentation filed as constituting the agreement on the register of agreements was referred to in the notice of reference and it was unnecessary for the Director General to specify the precise interpretation he put on the agreement; (3) prima facie there was sufficient to establish a common interest in the present proceedings by reason of the fact that both members and occasional users had the same rights and were bound by the rules of the centre and expected each other to obtemper those rules; (4) it was desirable that there should be a representative respondent in such proceedings and that the hypothetical difficulties that might arise were not sufficiently cogent to warrant revocation of the nomination in relation to the class of occasional users where none of them had objected to being represented by the nominee firm; and application refused and nomination of representative respondent sustained. *Observed,* that the position might have been different if the class of occasional users had included non-solicitors.

MACKIE & DEWAR v. DIRECTOR GENERAL OF FAIR TRADING (R.P.C.), 1995 S.L.T. 1028.

6457. Restrictive practices—reference to Restrictive Practices Court—sufficient identification of agreement. See MACKIE & DEWAR v. DIRECTOR GENERAL OF FAIR TRADING, §6456.

6458. Tourism—boards

ABERDEEN AND GRAMPIAN TOURIST BOARD SCHEME ORDER 1995 (No. 1879) [£1·95], made under the Local Government etc. (Scotland) Act 1994 (c.39), s.172(1), (3) and (4); operative on August 31, 1995; makes a scheme for the establishment, for the local government areas of Aberdeenshire, City of Aberdeen and Moray, of an area tourist board to be known as the Aberdeen and Grampian Tourist Board; providing that said scheme shall have effect from April 1, 1996, but that in relation to the Board's constitution, the carrying out of necessary functions to bring the scheme into operation on that date and the winding up of an existing board, the scheme shall have effect from the operative date of the order, August 31, 1995.

ANGUS AND CITY OF DUNDEE TOURIST BOARD SCHEME ORDER 1995 (No. 1880) [£1·95], made under the Local Government etc. (Scotland) Act 1994 (c.39), s.172(1), (3) and (4); operative on August 31, 1995; makes a scheme for the establishment, for the local government areas of Angus and City of Dundee, of an area tourist board to be known as the Angus and City of Dundee Tourist Board; providing that said scheme shall have effect from April 1, 1996, but that in relation to the Board's constitution, the carrying out of necessary functions to bring the scheme into operation on that date and the winding up of an existing board, the scheme shall have effect from the operative date of the order, August 31, 1995.

ARGYLL, THE ISLES, LOCH LOMOND, STIRLING AND TROSSACHS TOURIST BOARD SCHEME ORDER 1995 (No. 1881) [£1·95], made under the Local Government etc. (Scotland) Act 1994 (c.39), s.172(1), (3) and (4); operative on August 31, 1995; makes a scheme for the establishment, for the local government areas of Argyll and Bute, Clackmannan, Dumbarton and Clydebank, Falkirk and Stirling of an area tourist board to be known as the Argyll, the Isles, Lock Lomond, Stirling and Trossachs Tourist Board; providing that said scheme shall have effect from April 1, 1996, but that in relation to the Board's constitution, the carrying out of necessary functions to bring the scheme into operation on that date and the winding up of an existing board, the scheme shall have effect from the operative date of the order, August 31, 1995.

AYRSHIRE AND ARRAN TOURIST BOARD SCHEME ORDER 1995 (No. 1882) [£1·95], made under the Local Government etc. (Scotland) Act 1994 (c.39), s.172(1), (3) and (4); operative on August 31, 1995; makes a scheme for the establishment, for the local government areas of East Ayrshire, North Ayrshire and South Ayrshire, of an area tourist board to be known as the Ayrshire and Arran Tourist Board; providing that said scheme shall have effect from April 1, 1996, but that in relation to the Board's constitution, the carrying out of necessary functions to bring the scheme into operation on that date and the winding up of an existing board, the scheme shall have effect from the operative date of the order, August 31, 1995.

DUMFRIES AND GALLOWAY TOURIST BOARD SCHEME ORDER 1995 (No. 1883) [£1·95], made under the Local Government etc. (Scotland) Act 1994 (c.39), s.172(1), (3) and (4); operative on August 31, 1995; makes a scheme for the establishment, for the local government areas of Dumfries and Galloway, of an area tourist board to be known as the Dumfries and Galloway Tourist Board; providing that said scheme shall have effect from April 1, 1996, but that in relation to the Board's constitution, the carrying out of necessary functions to bring the scheme into operation on that date and the winding up of an existing board, the scheme shall have effect from the operative date of the order, August 31, 1995.

EDINBURGH AND LOTHIANS TOURIST BOARD SCHEME ORDER 1995 (No. 1884) [£1·95], made under the Local Government etc. (Scotland) Act 1994 (c.39), s.172(1), (3) and (4); operative on August 31, 1995; makes a scheme for the establishment, for the local government areas of City of Edinburgh, East Lothian, Midlothian and West Lothian, of an area tourist board to be known as the Edinburgh and Lothians Tourist Board; providing that said scheme shall have effect from April 1, 1996, but that in relation to the Board's constitution, the carrying out of necessary functions to bring the scheme into operation on that date and the winding up of an existing board, the scheme shall have effect from the operative date of the order, August 31, 1995.

GREATER GLASGOW AND CLYDE VALLEY TOURIST BOARD SCHEME ORDER 1995 (No. 1885) [£1·95], made under the Local Government etc. (Scotland) Act 1994 (c.39), s.172(1), (3) and (4); operative on August 31, 1995; makes a scheme for the establishment, for the local government areas of the City of Glasgow, East Dunbartonshire, East Renfrewshire, Inverclyde, North Lanarkshire, Renfrewshire and South Lanarkshire, of an area tourist board to be known as the Greater Glasgow and Clyde Valley Tourist Board; providing that said scheme shall have effect from April 1, 1996, but that in relation to the Board's constitution, the carrying out of necessary functions to bring the scheme into operation on that date and the winding up of an existing board, the scheme shall have effect from the operative date of the order, August 31, 1995.

HIGHLANDS OF SCOTLAND TOURIST BOARD SCHEME ORDER 1995 (No. 1886) [£1·95], made under the Local Government etc. (Scotland) Act 1994 (c.39), s.172(1), (3) and (4); operative on August 31, 1995; makes a scheme for the establishment, for the local government area of, Highland, of an area tourist board to be known as the Highlands of Scotland Tourist Board; providing that said scheme shall have effect from April 1, 1996, but that in relation to the Board's constitution, the carrying out of necessary functions to bring the scheme into operation on that date and the winding up of an existing board, the scheme shall have effect from the operative date of the order, August 31, 1995.

KINGDOM OF FIFE TOURIST BOARD SCHEME ORDER 1995 (No. 1887) [£1·95], made under the Local Government etc. (Scotland) Act 1994 (c.39), s.172(1), (3) and (4); operative on August 31, 1995; makes a scheme for the establishment, for the local government area of Fife, of an area tourist board to be known as the Kingdom of Fife Tourist Board; providing that said scheme shall have effect from April 1, 1996, but that in relation to the Board's constitution, the carrying out of necessary functions to bring the scheme into operation on that date and the winding up of an existing board, the scheme shall have effect from the operative date of the order, August 31, 1995.

ORKNEY TOURIST BOARD SCHEME ORDER 1995 (No. 1888) [£1·95], made under the Local Government etc. (Scotland) Act 1994 (c.39), s.172(1), (3) and (4); operative on August 31, 1995; makes a scheme for the establishment, for the Orkney Islands, of an area tourist board to be known as the Orkney Tourist Board; providing that said scheme shall have effect from April 1, 1996, but that in relation to the Board's constitution, the carrying out of necessary functions to bring the scheme into operation on that date and the winding up of an existing board, the scheme shall have effect from the operative date of the order, August 31, 1995.

PERTHSHIRE TOURIST BOARD SCHEME ORDER 1995 (No. 1889) [£1·95], made under the Local Government etc. (Scotland) Act 1994 (c.39), s.172(1), (3) and (4); operative on August 31, 1995; makes a scheme for the establishment, for the local government area of Perthshire and Kinross, of an area tourist board to be known as the Perthshire Tourist Board; providing that said scheme shall have effect from April 1, 1996, but that in relation to the Board's constitution, the carrying out of necessary functions to bring the scheme into operation on that date and the winding up of an existing board, the scheme shall have effect from the operative date of the order, August 31, 1995.

SCOTTISH BORDERS TOURIST BOARD SCHEME ORDER 1995 (No. 1890) [£1·95], made under the Local Government etc. (Scotland) Act 1994 (c.39), s.172(1), (3) and (4); operative on August 31, 1995; makes a scheme for the establishment, for the local government area of The Borders, of an area tourist board to be known as the Scottish Borders Tourist Board; providing that said scheme shall have effect from April 1, 1996, but that in relation to the Board's constitution, the carrying out of necessary functions to bring the scheme into operation on that date and the winding up of an existing board, the scheme shall have effect from the operative date of the order, August 31, 1995.

SHETLAND TOURIST BOARD SCHEME ORDER 1995 (No. 1891) [£1·95], made under the Local Government etc. (Scotland) Act 1994 (c.39), s.172(1), (3) and (4); operative on August 31, 1995; makes a scheme for the establishment, for the Shetland Islands of an area tourist board to be known as the Shetland Tourist Board; providing that said scheme shall have effect from April 1, 1996, but that in relation to the Board's constitution, the carrying out of necessary functions to bring the scheme into operation on that date and the winding up of an existing board, the scheme shall have effect from the operative date of the order, August 31, 1995.

WESTERN ISLES TOURIST BOARD SCHEME ORDER 1995 (No. 1892) [£1·95], made under the Local Government etc. (Scotland) Act 1994 (c.39), s.172(1), (3) and (4); operative on August 31, 1995; makes a scheme for the establishment, for the Western Islands of an area tourist board to be known as the Western Isles Tourist Board; providing that said scheme shall have effect from April 1, 1996, but that in relation to the Board's constitution, the carrying out of necessary functions to bring the scheme into operation on that date and the winding up of an existing board, the scheme shall have effect from the operative date of the order, August 31, 1995.

ABERDEEN AND GRAMPIAN TOURIST BOARD SCHEME AMENDMENT ORDER 1995 (No. 2211) [£1·10], made under the Local Government etc. (Scotland) Act 1994 (c.39) ss.172(1) and 173(1) and (2)(e); operative on August 31, 1995; substitutes for references in the principal order and scheme to the local government area of "City of Aberdeen", that of "Aberdeen City"; provides that persons, not exceeding six in number, be nominated by the council for the local government areas of, respectively, Aberdeenshire, Aberdeen City and Moray, to be representatives of those councils on the board and provides for voting procedures in relation to the board or controlling authority of the board.

[S.I. 1995 No. 1879 amended.]

ANGUS AND CITY OF DUNDEE TOURIST BOARD SCHEME AMENDMENT ORDER 1995 (No. 2212) [£1·10], made under the Local Government etc. (Scotland) Act 1994 (c.39) ss.172(1) and 173(1) and (2)(e); operative on August 31, 1995; substitutes for references in the principal order and scheme to the local government area of "City of Dundee", that of "Dundee City"; provides that persons, not exceeding five in number, be nominated by the council for the local government areas of, respectively, Angus and Dundee City, to be representatives of those councils on the board and provides for voting procedures in relation to the board or controlling authority of the board.

[S.I. 1995 No. 1880 amended.]

ARGYLL, THE ISLES, LOCH LOMOND, STIRLING AND TROSSACHS TOURIST BOARD SCHEME AMENDMENT ORDER 1995 (No. 2213) [£1·10], made under the Local Government etc. (Scotland) Act 1994 (c.39) ss.172(1) and 173(1) and (2)(e); operative on August 31, 1995; substitutes for references in the principal order and scheme to the local government area of "Clackmannan", that of "Clackmannanshire"; provides that persons, not exceeding five in number, be nominated by the council for the local government areas of, respectively, Argyll and Bute, Clackmannanshire, Dumbarton and Clydebank, Falkirk and Stirling, to be representatives of those councils on the board and provides for voting procedures in relation to the board or controlling authority of the board.

[S.I. 1995 No. 1881 amended.]

AYRSHIRE AND ARRAN TOURIST BOARD SCHEME AMENDMENT ORDER 1995 (No. 2232) [£1·10], made under the Local Government etc. (Scotland) Act 1994 (c.39) ss.172(1) and 173(1) and (2)(e); operative on August 31, 1995; provides that persons, not exceeding five in number, be nominated by the council for the local government areas of, respectively, East Ayrshire, North Ayrshire, and South Ayrshire, to be representatives of those councils on the board and provides for voting procedures in relation to the board or controlling authority of the board.

[S.I. 1995 No. 1882 amended.]

DUMFRIES AND GALLOWAY TOURIST BOARD SCHEME AMENDMENT ORDER 1995 (No. 2233) [£1·10], made under the Local Government etc.

(Scotland) Act 1994 (c.39) ss.172(1) and 173(1) and (2)(e); operative on August 31, 1995; provides that persons, not exceeding seven in number, be nominated by the council for the local government areas of the board, and to be representatives of those councils on the board and provides for voting procedures in relation to the board or controlling authority of the board.

[S.I. 1995 No. 1883 amended.]

EDINBURGH AND LOTHIANS TOURIST BOARD SCHEME AMENDMENT ORDER 1995 (No. 2234) [£1·10], made under the Local Government etc. (Scotland) Act 1994 (c.39) ss.172(1) and 173(1) and (2)(e); operative on August 31, 1995; provides that persons, not exceeding five in number, be nominated by the council for the local government areas of the board, and to be representatives of those councils on the board and provides for voting procedures in relation to the board or controlling authority of the board.

[S.I. 1995 No. 1884 amended.]

GREATER GLASGOW AND CLYDE VALLEY TOURIST BOARD SCHEME AMENDMENT ORDER 1995 (No. 2235) [£1·10], made under the Local Government etc. (Scotland) Act 1994 (c.39) ss.172(1) and 173(1) and (2)(e); operative on August 31, 1995; provides that persons, not exceeding five in number, be nominated by the council for the local government areas of the board, and to be representatives of those councils on the board and provides for voting procedures in relation to the board or controlling authority of the board.

[S.I. 1995 No. 1885 amended.]

HIGHLANDS OF SCOTLAND TOURIST BOARD SCHEME AMENDMENT ORDER 1995 (No. 2236) [£1·10], made under the Local Government etc. (Scotland) Act 1994 (c.39) ss.172(1) and 173(1) and (2)(e); operative on August 31, 1995; provides that persons, not exceeding ten in number, be nominated by the council for the local government area of Highland, to be representatives of that council on the board and provides for voting procedures in relation to the board or controlling authority of the board.

[S.I. 1995 No. 1886 amended.]

KINGDOM OF FIFE TOURIST BOARD SCHEME AMENDMENT ORDER 1995 (No. 2237) [£1·10], made under the Local Government etc. (Scotland) Act 1994 (c.39) ss.172(1) and 173(1) and (2)(e); operative on August 31, 1995; provides that persons, not exceeding ten in number, be nominated by the council for the local government area of Fife, to be representatives of that council on the board and provides for voting procedures in relation to the board or controlling authority of the board.

[S.I. 1995 No. 1887 amended.]

ORKNEY TOURIST BOARD SCHEME AMENDMENT ORDER 1995 (No. 2238) [£1·10], made under the Local Government etc. (Scotland) Act 1994 (c.39) ss.172(1) and 173(1) and (2)(e); operative on August 31, 1995; provides that persons, not exceeding five in number, be nominated by the council for the local government area of the Orkney Islands, to be representatives of that council on the board and provides for voting procedures in relation to the board or controlling authority of the board.

[S.I. 1995 No. 1888 amended.]

PERTHSHIRE TOURIST BOARD SCHEME AMENDMENT ORDER 1995 (No. 2239) [£1·10], made under the Local Government etc. (Scotland) Act 1994 (c.39) ss.172(1) and 173(1) and (2)(e); operative on August 31, 1995; provides that persons, not exceeding five in number, be nominated by the council for the local government areas of Perthshire and Kinross, to be representatives of those councils on the board and provides for voting procedures in relation to the board or controlling authority of the board.

[S.I. 1995 No. 1889 amended.]

SCOTTISH BORDERS TOURIST BOARD SCHEME AMENDMENT ORDER 1995 (No. 2214) [£1·10], made under the Local Government etc. (Scotland) Act 1994 (c.39) ss.172(1) and 173(1) and (2)(e); operative on August 31, 1995; substitutes for references in the principal order and scheme to the local government area of "The Borders", that of "Scottish Borders"; provides that persons, not exceeding seven in number, be nominated by the council for the local government area of Scottish Borders, to be representatives of that council on the board and provides for voting procedures in relation to the board or controlling authority of the board.

[S.I. 1995 No. 1890 amended.]

SHETLAND TOURIST BOARD SCHEME AMENDMENT ORDER 1995 (No. 2240) [£1·10], made under the Local Government etc. (Scotland) Act 1994 (c.39) ss.172(1) and 173(1) and (2)(e); operative on August 31, 1995; provides that persons, not exceeding five in number, be nominated by the council for the local government area of the Shetland Islands, to be representatives of that council on the board and provides for voting procedures in relation to the board or controlling authority of the board.

[S.I. 1995 No. 1891 amended.]

WESTERN ISLES TOURIST BOARD SCHEME AMENDMENT ORDER 1995 (No. 2241) [£1·10], made under the Local Government etc. (Scotland) Act 1994 (c.39) ss.172(1) and 173(1) and (2)(e); operative on August 31, 1995; provides that persons, not exceeding nine in number, be nominated by the council for the local government area of the Western Isles, to be representatives of that council on the board and provides for voting procedures in relation to the board or controlling authority of the board.

[S.I. 1995 No. 1892 amended.]

TRADE MARKS AND TRADE NAMES

6459. Passing off—exporting—interdict—whether double actionability rule applied

A holding company and its two subsidiaries sought interdict against a competitor from passing off their business and products by, *inter alia*, "carrying on or attempting to carry on business in Scotland in connection with" various activities, including exporting gin, vodka or any other alcoholic beverage under the name "Grants" or other name colourably similar thereto, or otherwise calculated to deceive the public or to induce the belief that the competitor's business was associated with their own. Following a group reorganisation, the goodwill attached to the name "Grants" had been assigned to the holding company to be held "for its own use and for the use of . . . its subsidiary companies". The competitor argued that the company had failed to make out a prima facia relevant case in respect that they did not aver in which countries around the world the goodwill attached to the name "Grants" existed nor to which products it attached. Neither, it was argued, were there the necessary averments to the effect that the alleged passing off was actionable abroad. It was also submitted that the pleadings lacked relevant averments of damage. The competitor further argued that the subsidiaries, as separate legal entities, had no title or interest to sue, as an assignation of goodwill without assigning the business underlying it was of no effect and moreover the averments of damage resulting from the alleged passing off did not differentiate between the pursuers.

Held, that (1) the issue of double actionability did not arise as all the activities for which interdicts were sought, including exporting, were carried on in Scotland and not abroad; (2) having regard to those activities and applying the tests set out in *Warnink v. Townend & Sons (Hull)* [1979] C.L.Y. 2690 the pursuers' averments gave sufficient specification to constitute fair notice of a prima facie case and accordingly satisfied the test of relevancy; (3) the goodwill attaching to the name "Grants" was goodwill which belonged to every part of the group business and accordingly the subsidiary companies, having a stake in the goodwill, had a clear title and interest to sue; and proof before answer allowed.

GRANT (WILLIAM) & SONS v. GLEN CATRINE BONDED WAREHOUSE (O.H.), 1995 S.L.T. 936.

TRANSPORT

6460. Railways—closure—token service—whether "railway passenger service"

[Railways Act 1993 (c. 43), s.37(1)]

B, the railways board, reclaimed against the Lord Ordinary's decision to interdict them from discontinuing the London-Fort William sleeper service pending their carrying out the full closure consultation procedure in s.37 of the 1993 Act in respect of three short sections of line used only by that service. B argued that (1) the Lord Ordinary erred in excluding B's substitute services from the category of "railway passenger services" within s.37: having regard to the definitions of "railway services" in s.82(1), "services for the carriage of passengers by railway" in s.82(2) and "goods" in s.83(1), these services could only be "railway passenger services" for the purposes of s.37(1) and it did not matter that B's only reason for introducing them was to avoid the closure procedure in regard to the proposed withdrawal of the sleeper service; and (2) in any event the Lord Ordinary erred in concluding that no other railway passenger service over these sections of line could satisfy the definition in s.37. H, who had sought the interdict, challenged the Lord Ordinary's view that had he found that B had acted legally, he would not have held their decision in bad faith and unreasonable, H arguing that B's intention to defeat the legitimate interests of the public demonstrated bad faith and that no reason had been given for introducing the substitute services other than the unreasonable one that it had been to get round the s.37 procedures.

Held, reclaiming motion refused. B's approach to the construction of s.37(1) led to an absurdity, in that services which were admittedly of no benefit to the travelling public would fall within the definition of "railway passenger services". Such a result could not have been intended by Parliament in passing ss.37–50 of the 1993 Act. The admitted facts pointed clearly to the conclusion that the substitute services were a device and not railway passenger services within s.37(1), this being a question of fact and not of degree as contended for B. B had accordingly acted outwith their powers. *Opinion*, that had the opposite been held, B's decision could not have been described as irrational or unreasonable as they were entitled to have regard to financial considerations, the weight to be given to which was not a matter for the court. Nor would it have been invalidated on the ground of improper motive (*Cottle's (Gerry) Circus v. City of Edinburgh District Council*) [1990] C.L.Y. 5646.

Held, further, that the grant of interdict was appropriate and that its terms were not too wide, as the only way to protect H's right to be heard on the closure question was to pronounce interdict against the withdrawal of the sleeper service until the question had been answered by following the statutory procedure.

HIGHLAND REGIONAL COUNCIL v. BRITISH RAILWAYS BOARD, *The Times*, November 6, 1995.

6461. Special roads

ROADS (TRANSITIONAL POWERS) (SCOTLAND) ORDER 1995 (No. 1476) [£1·95], made under the Roads (Scotland) Act 1984 (c.54), ss.12A (as inserted by the Local Governments etc. (Scotland) Act 1994 (c.39), s.38(2)), 12B (as inserted by the Local Government etc. (Scotland) Act 1994 (c.39), s.38(2)), 12C (as inserted by the Local Government etc. (Scotland) Act 1994 (c.39), s.38(2)) and 143(1); operative on April 1, 1996; provides for the change in status of roads considered necessary or expedient as a result or in connection with the establishment of new local government areas on April 1, 1996, that certain roads shall become or cease to be trunk roads and makes similar provision for proposed roads which are in the course of construction or proposed to be built at June 8, 1995 and for special roads contained within special road schemes.

6462. Strathclyde Passenger Transport Authority

STRATHCLYDE PASSENGER TRANSPORT AREA (DESIGNATION) ORDER 1995 (No. 1971) [£1·10], made under the Local Government etc. (Scotland) Act

1994 (c.39), s.40(4); operative on April 1, 1996; establishes a new Strathclyde Passenger Transport Authority and designates the area of the new authority.

TRUSTS

Charitable trusts. See CHARITIES.

6463. Constructive trust—disposition of heritage delivered but not yet recorded when receiver appointed to disponer. See SHARP v. THOMSON, §5549.

6464. Curator bonis—special powers—power to take steps to mitigate effect of inheritance tax on ward's estate

C, the curator bonis for W, appealed against a sheriff's decision refusing his application seeking special powers to vary the testamentary provisions of B, W's late husband, who nominated W as the sole residuary beneficiary of his estate. As at November 10, 1994, the estimated value of W's estate, including her inheritance from B, was £385,380·41. Under her testamentary settlement, W's estate would fall on her death to I and J, the only children of W and B. C sought a variation to allow the sum of £150,000 to be redirected now to I and J, which would reduce the potential liability to inheritance tax by approximately £60,000. C argued that although W was unable to manage her own affairs and therefore had been unable to instruct the deed of variation, she would have done so if her mental capacity were unimpaired. There was no foreseeable need to encroach on capital since W's income currently exceeded her accommodation expenses and if the variation were granted, W would still have approximately £250,000 of capital, which if invested, would provide a further £11,000 per annum assuming an average rate of interest at 5 per cent. The Accountant of Court opined that in seeking the variation, C was acting in the best interests of W and her beneficiaries, but noted that there was no precedent for special powers being granted in circumstances such as the instant case. The sheriff stated in his note that in his view, the special power sought was totally at variance with the preservation and administration of W's estate. C was merely trying ultroneously to avoid tax and it was unclear whether W, if capax, would have agreed to such a donation.

Held, appeal allowed. There was no precedent for the application but it was one which could competently be entertained. The sheriff had misdirected himself in not taking the circumstances fully into account. W was aged 91 and of unsound mind; her testamentary provisions, made while still capax, were indicative of her wishes while she was of sound mind and would not now be altered during her lifetime. In exercising his power of management, C had to ask himself what W would have done if she had retained her full mental capacity and since she did not require more money for her maintenance, it was very likely that, in view of her age and means, she would have considered the advantages of reducing the amount of the estate that would pass on her death (*cf. Burns' C.B. v. Burns' Trs.*, [1961] C.L.Y. 10904). It was highly probable that W would have agreed to the variation legitimately to mitigate the incidence of inheritance tax.

B.'s CURATOR BONIS (Sh.Ct.), 1995 S.C.L.R. 671.

6465. Judicial factor—personal liability

S sought payment from D, the judicial factor on a partnership (R), of sums due in respect of beer supplied to R. On July 1, 1993 D had intimated his appointment to S, stating that he was "responsible for the business". On March 25, 1994 D and one of R's partners had completed a "request to open a credit account" with S. S argued that D was in the same position as a trustee (*Craig v. Hogg* (1896) 24 R. 6; Irons, *Judicial Factors*, p. 94), and that, as he had not explicitly excluded personal liability in either letter to S, he was personally liable for R's debts incurred during his factory.

Held, action dismissed. D was not vested in R's estate but was only an administrator and, while he might incur personal liability if he acted negligently or inconsistently with his general duties of care towards third parties, he did not incur such liability merely by carrying out business on R's behalf, whether or not he had explicitly excluded liability (Gloag, *Contract* (2nd ed.), p. 135, approved; *Craig*, distinguished).

SCOTTISH BREWERS v. J. DOUGLAS PEARSON & CO. (Sh.Ct.), 1995 S.C.L.R. 799.

Public trusts. See CHARITIES.

6466. Trustees—curator bonis—special powers. See B.'s CURATOR BONIS, §6464.

6467. Trustees—duties—whether dispositive or administrative in character. See MUIR (WILLIAM) (BOND 9) EMPLOYEES' SHARE SCHEME TRS. v. I.R.C., §6027.

6468. Trustees—judicial factor—personal liability. See SCOTTISH BREWERS v. J. DOUGLAS PEARSON & CO., §6465.

6469. Trustees—partnership property—title to grant disposition. See CAMERON v. LIGHTHEART, §5993.

6470. Variation of trusts—endowment fund—approval of amendments to scheme for future government and management of endowment. See GOVERNORS OF DOLLAR ACADEMY TRUST v. LORD ADVOCATE, §5892.

VALUE ADDED TAX

6471. Supply—offer inviting subscriptions in return for benefits—part of subscription a donation

[Value Added Tax Act 1983 (c.55) s.10.]

Section 10(2) of the Value Added Tax Act 1983 provided that if the supply is for a consideration in money its value shall be taken to be such amount as, with the addition of the tax chargeable, is equal to the consideration. By s.10(4), where a supply is not the only matter to which a money consideration relates the supply shall be deemed to be for such part of the consideration as is properly attributable to it. In order to raise funds a theatre company offered certain benefits to members of the public in return for payment of a minimum subscription. The Commissioners of Customs and Excise decided that the proceeds of the company's fundraising were liable to VAT at the standard rate. The company appealed to the VAT tribunal which rejected its argument that subscribers were making a donation of the whole subscription but held that the subscription included an extremely large element of donation and that the value of the supply was to be determined under s.10(4) of the Act by reference to only a small part of the subscription. The commissioners appealed, arguing that there was a single package of benefits supplied for a consideration and by s.10(2) the value of the supply had to be taken as equal to the subscription.

The company submitted that the tribunal were entitled and bound to hold that the benefits were supplied for a consideration amounting to less than the subscription. Section 10(2) applied only where the whole consideration was attributable to the supply.

Held, that in view of the terms of s.10(2) it was not possible, if the money paid was regarded as a consideration for the supply, to treat part of the payment as not a consideration at all, the purpose of s.10(4) being to enable an apportionment to be made when part of a consideration in money was attributable to another supply; and appeal allowed.

CUSTOMS AND EXCISE COMMISSIONERS v. TRON THEATRE, 1995 S.L.T. 1021.

6472. Supply—zero rated or exempt supply—"person constructing a building"

[Value Added Tax Act 1983 (c.55), ss.16 and 17 and Sched. 5, group 8, item no. 1.]

The commissioners (C) appealed against a decision of the VAT tribunal allowing an appeal by L, a housing association, against C's decision that the sale by L under the tenants' rights legislation of houses built by them some years earlier, was an exempt supply under s.17 of the 1983 Act and not a zero rated supply under s.16. L argued that the sale was a "grant by a person constructing a building . . . designed as a dwelling . . . of a major interest in" the building, within item 1 of Group 8 of Sched. 5 to the Act. Before the tribunal C contended that the use of the present participle meant that item 1 was limited to a grant while the building was under construction or the first grant of a major interest in a recently constructed building which had previously been unoccupied. In this case the first grant had fallen within item 1 of Group 1 of Sched. 6. On appeal C argued that item 1 was limited to the stage when the building was still under construction.

Held, appeal refused. There was no obvious reason why Parliament should have made the relief available where minor work remained to be done and not where all work was completed) perhaps only days before. Where a continuing activity was intended this was made clear, as in item 2 of Group 8. C had not argued for such a restriction in other cases; L's construction was consistent with the way in which words were used elsewhere in the Act (*e.g.* s.2(2) and (3); Sched. 7, para. 4(1) and (4)), was grammatically acceptable and produced a reasonable result.

CUSTOMS AND EXCISE COMMISSIONERS v. LINK HOUSING ASSOCIATION, 1992 S.C. 508.

6473. Transitional measures—European Community. See VALUE ADDED TAX, §5110.

WATER AND WATERWORKS

6474. Local Government. See LOCAL GOVERNMENT, §6124.

6475. River purification boards

TAY RIVER PURIFICATION BOARD (ORDIE BURN) CONTROL ORDER 1995 (No. 2382) [£1·10], made under the Natural Heritage (Scotland) Act 1991 (c.28) ss.15 and 17(2); operative on September 11, 1995; specifies the control area and the closing date by which a licence application should be made as being October 31.

6476. Water orders

Order made under the Water (Scotland) Act 1980 (c.45), s.72(4): S.I. 1995 Nos. 538 (Central Regional Council (Prohibition of Swimming, Bathing etc. in

Reservoirs) Byelaws Extension); 992 (Strathclyde Regional Council (Mill Glen, Busbie Muir, Munnoch, Caaf, Knockendon, Crosbie, Glenburn, Pundeavon, Cuffhill, Kirkleegreen) Byelaws Extension); and 1994 (Strathclyde Regional Council (Skelmorlie Lower, Skelmorlie Upper, Skelmorlie Intakes, Outerwards, Greeto Intake, Haylie, Millport Lower, Millport Upper) Byelaws Extension).

WILLS

6477. Attestation—discrepancy in name of witness

[Conveyancing (Scotland) Act 1874 (c.94), s.39.]

W sought reduction of a will signed by his late mother (R) on the ground that it had been improperly executed. The document bore to be attested by two witnesses, one of whom signed as "D C R Williamson", although the testing clause stated that it had been signed by "David Carment Reid Wilson". E, the other children and a grandchild of R, averred that the will had been signed by Wilson but that he had inadvertently written "Williamson". E argued that (1) the discrepancy in the surnames was so minor that it should be disregarded; and (2) as the document *ex facie* had been signed by R and two witnesses, s.39 of the 1874 Act, which was to be given a liberal interpretation, applied, and that, if the document had been witnessed by the person who signed as "D C R Williamson" then reduction should be refused.

Held, decree *de plano* granted. (1) The discrepancy in the surnames was not so minor that it could be disregarded and, as the signature of a witness with a surname which was not his own was not a "subscription" in terms of the authentication. (2) While the discrepancy might not be fatal if it was due to an error in the testing clause, s.39 required E to prove that the document had been subscribed "by the witness by whom such deed, instrument or writing bears to be attested", who was D C R Williamson. E were not offering to prove this and a failure to satisfy the express terms of s.39 could not be disregarded on the basis of an argument based on the policy of the section.

WILLIAMSON v. WILLIAMSON (O.H.), *The Scotsman*, August 10, 1995.

6478. Attestation—witness signing at different time from testator

A mother died leaving eight children. Her only significant asset was a house, over which she had granted a standard security in favour of her eldest son and his wife. By an apparently valid will, the mother named her eldest son executor and the house was left to him and his wife. Five of the other children raised an action for production and reduction of the will. The pursuers contended that the will was invalid because it had been inadequately witnessed by the second witness. The parties, however, disputed the circumstances in which the second witness had signed the will. The defenders contended that he had signed the will in the presence of the deceased in circumstances from which the deceased's tacit acknowledgment of her subscription to the second witness could be inferred. In particular, the defenders contended that, in the presence of the deceased, the deceased's eldest son had acted as "master of ceremonies", and asked the second witness to read the will and sign it as a witness; and that thereafter, and all in the presence of the deceased, the second witness had borrowed his wife's spectacles, read the will, discussed the acquisition of the house by the deceased's eldest son and duly signed the will. The pursuers contended that the deceased had not been present when the second witness signed the will and, *esto* the deceased had been present, she had not acknowledged her subscription to the second witness. The second witness gave evidence in support of the pursuers' contention.

Held, that the deceased had not been present when the second witness signed the will; and decree of reduction granted. Opinion, that even if the second witness's signature of the will had been added in the circumstances contended for by the defenders decree would still have been pronounced because an unambiguous acknowledgment by the deceased of her subscription to the second witness was required and such could not be inferred from the defenders' account of events. (*Cumming v. Skeoch's Trs.* (1879) 6 R. 963, applied.) Observed, that where someone admitted to having signed a document as a witness, the court should be slow to believe his evidence that he had not in fact seen the subscription by the grantor of the deed nor heard the grantor's acknowledgment of the subscription.

LINDSAY v. MILNE (O.H.), 1995 S.L.T. 487.

6479. Construction—uncertainty—validity

A testator died leaving a holograph document described as a trust disposition and settlement which appointed his sister as his executrix and thereafter contained a passage reading "and I give everything I have to her to share out as she knows I would wish it". The deceased's brother sought reduction of the deed and argued at procedure roll that it was void from uncertainty and that the estate should be distributed according to the rules of intestate succession.

Held, that the deed being silent as to who the beneficiaries were and there being no suggestion by the executrix that she was aware of the deceased's testamentary intentions, the deed, save for the provision appointing the sister as executrix, was void from uncertainty; and decree of partial reduction pronounced. (*Blair v. Duncan* (1901) 9 S.L.T. 390; (1901) 4 F.(H.L.) 1, followed.)

WOOD v. WOOD'S EXRX. (O.H.), 1995 S.L.T. 563.

6480. Executors. See EXECUTORS AND ADMINISTRATORS.

Trusts. See TRUSTS.

6481. Validity—uncertainty. See WOOD v. WOOD'S EXRX., §6479.

WORDS AND PHRASES

The table below is a cumulative guide to words and phrases judicially considered in 1995:

BOOKS AND ARTICLES

INDEX OF BOOKS

The following books were published in 1995. They are listed under the appropriate Current Law headings, following the division of the Yearbook text into U.K., England and Wales and European Union; Northern Ireland; and Scotland.

ADMINISTRATIVE LAW

Abraham, Henry J.; Perry, Barbara—Freedom and the Court. Paperback: £18·99. ISBN 0–19–508264–8. Oxford University Press Inc., USA.

Barnett, Hilaire—Constitutional and Administrative Law. Paperback: £16·95. ISBN 1–85941–114–2. Cavendish Publishing Ltd.

Bibby, Peter—Effective Use of Judicial Review. Hardback: £39·95. ISBN 0–85459–761–1. Tolley Publishing.

Cooker, Chris de—International Administration. Hardback: £125·50. ISBN 0–7923–0465–9. Martinus Nijhoff Publishers.

Fenwick, Helen—Constitutional and Administrative Law. Question and Answer Series. Paperback: £8·95. ISBN 1–85941–260–2. Cavendish Publishing Ltd.

Galligan, Denis—Administrative Law. Hardback: £35·00. ISBN 0–19–876408–1. Paperback: £10·99. ISBN 0–19–876409–X. Oxford University Press.

Herling, David—Briefcase on Constitutional and Administrative Law. Briefcase Series. Paperback: £9·95. ISBN 1–85941–247–5. Cavendish Publishing Ltd.

Lee, Robert G.—SWOT: Constitutional and Administrative Law. Paperback: £8·95. ISBN 1–85431–337–1. Blackstone Press.

Lewisch, P.—Punishment, Public Law Enforcement and the Protective State. Paperback. ISBN 3–211–82645–9. Springer-Verlag, Vienna.

Manning, Jonathan—Judicial Review Proceedings: A Practitioner's Guide. Paperback: £22·50. ISBN 0–905099–53–2. Legal Action Group.

Molan, Michael T.—Administrative Law: Textbook 1995–1996. Bachelor of Laws. Paperback: £18·95. ISBN 0–7510–0541–X. HLT Publications.

Thompson, Brian—Textbook on Constitutional and Administrative Law. Paperback: £16·95. ISBN 1–85431–445–9. Blackstone Press.

Wallington, Peter—Blackstone's Statutes on Public Law 1995–1996. Paperback: £11·95. Blackstone Press.

Yarbrough, Tinsley—Harlan I: Judicial Enigma. Hardback: £22·50. ISBN 0–19–507464–5. Oxford University Press Inc., USA.

AGENCY

Kelly, Patrick R.N.—Agency and Distribution Agreements in Europe. Hardback: £90·00. ISBN 0–85308–210–3. Jordans.

Saleh, Samir—Commercial Agency and Distributorship in the Arab Middle East. Unbound/looseleaf: £325·00. ISBN 1–85333–227–5. Graham & Trotman Publishers.

Salinger—Factoring Law and Practice. Second Edition. Hardback: £55·00. ISBN 0–421–52680–7. Sweet & Maxwell.

AGRICULTURE

Evans, Della—Agricultural Tenancies Act 1995. Paperback: £14·50. ISBN 0–421–43590–9. Sweet & Maxwell.

ANIMALS

Francione, Gary L.—Animals, Property and the Law. Ethics and Action Series. Hardback: £53·95. ISBN 1–56639–283–7. Paperback: £25·50. ISBN 1–56639–284–5. Temple State University Press.

ARBITRATION

Freeman, Michael—Alternative Dispute Resolution. The International Library of Essays in Law and Legal Theory: Areas. Hardback: £90·00. ISBN 1–85521–425–3. Dartmouth.

Matyas, Robert M.; Mathews, A. A.; Smith, Robert J.; Sperry, P.E.—Dispute Resolution Board Manual. Hardback: £36·95. ISBN 0–07–041060–7. McGraw-Hill Book Company.

Moody, Susan: Mackay, Robert—Alternative Dispute Resolution in Scotland. Paperback: £36·00. ISBN 0–414–01115–5. W. Green & Son.

AVIATION

Chance, Clifford—Cross-border Aircraft Leasing. Paperback: £225·00. ISBN 1–85044–839–6. Lloyd's of London Press.

Underdown, R.B.; Palmer, T.—Aviation Law for Pilots. Paperback: £19·99. ISBN 0–632–04064–5. Blackwell Science.

BANKING

Fuller, Geoffrey—Corporate Borrowing. Hardback: £60·00. ISBN 0–85308–232–4. Jordans.

Newton, Alan—The Law and Regulation of Derivatives. Hardback: £85·00. ISBN 0–406–04965–3. Butterworth Law.

Norton, Joseph J.—Devising International Bank Supervisory Standards. International Banking and Finance Law. Hardback: £82·00. ISBN 1–85966–185–8. Martinus Nijhoff Publishers.

Rawnsley, Judith—Going for Broke. Hardback: £14·99. ISBN 0–00–255659–6. HarperCollins.

Wood, Philip R.—Comparative Law of Security and Guarantees. Law and Practice of International Finance Series. Hardback: £65·00. ISBN 0–421–54320–5. Sweet & Maxwell.

Wood, Philip R.—Finance, Derivatives, Securitizations, Set-off and Netting. Law and Practice of International Finance Series. Hardback: £65·00. ISBN 0–421–54270–5. Sweet & Maxwell.

Wood, Philip R.—International Loans, Bonds and Securities Regulation. Law and Practice of International Finance Series. Hardback: £65·00. ISBN 0–421–54310–8. Sweet & Maxwell.

BRITISH COMMONWEALTH

Armstrong, Mark; Lindsay, David; Watterson, Ray—Media Law in Australia. Paperback: £15·99. ISBN 0–19–553603–7. O.U.P., Australia.

Kodilinye, Gilbert—Commonwealth Caribbean Law of Trusts. Paperback: £20·00. ISBN 1–85941–046–4. Cavendish Publishing Ltd.

Kodilinye, Gilbert—Commonwealth Caribbean Tort Law: Text, Cases and Materials. Legal Skills Series. Paperback: £20·00. ISBN 1–85941–118–5. Cavendish Publishing Ltd.

Walker, Gordon; Fisse, Brent—Securities Regulation in Australia and New Zealand. Hardback: £45·00. ISBN 0–19–558290–X. Oxford University Press Inc., New Zealand.

BUILDING AND CONSTRUCTION

Atkinson, G.A.—Construction Quality and Quality Standards. Hardback: £55·00. ISBN 0–419–18490–2. E & FN Spon.

Attewell, P.—Tunnelling Contracts and Site Investigation. Hardback: £59·00. ISBN 0–419–19140–2. E & FN Spon.

Barritt, C.M.H.—The Building Acts and Regulations Applied. Paperback: £15·99. ISBN 0–582–27449–4. Longman Scientific & Technical.

Connell, Lee; Callahan, Michael T.—Construction Defect Claims and Litigation. Hardback: £76·95. ISBN 0–471–11873–7. John Wiley and Sons.

Edwards, Brian—Towards Sustainable Architecture. Butterworth Architecture Legal Series. Paperback: £29·95. ISBN 0–7506–2492–2. Butterworth Architecture: an imprint of Butterworth-Heinemann.

Garner, J.F.—The Law of Sewers and Drains. Paperback: £24·95. ISBN 0–7219–0583–8. Shaw & Sons.

Keating—Building Contracts. Sixth Edition. Hardback: £150·00. ISBN 0–421–52560–6. Sweet & Maxwell.

Lavers, A.—Professional Negligence in the Construction Industry. Hardback: £27·00. ISBN 0–419–17900–3. E & FN Spon.

Lloyd, H.; Baatz, N.; Streatfeild-James, D.; Fraser, P.—Building Law Reports: Vol. 71. Hardback. ISBN 0–582–27465–6. Longman.

Lloyd, H.; Baatz, N.; Streatfeild-James, D.; Fraser, P.—Building Law Reports: Vol. 72. Hardback: £41·00. ISBN 0–582–27466–4. Longman.

Lloyd, H.; Baatz, N.; Streatfeild-James, D.; Fraser, P.—Building Law Reports: Vol. 73. Hardback: £41·00. ISBN 0–582–27467–2. Longman.

Stephenson, John—Building Regulations Explained. Builders' Bookshelf Series. Hardback: £49·50. ISBN 0–419–19690–0. E & FN Spon.

Uff, John—Construction Law Year Book: 1995. Hardback: £50·00. ISBN 0–471–95305–9. Chancery Wiley Law Publications.

CHARITIES

Cracknell, Douglas—Cracknell on Charities. Practitioner Series. Hardback: £35·00. ISBN 0–85121–638–2. FT Law & Tax.

Derwent, R.J.—Charities. Paperback: £55·00. ISBN 1–85355–408–1. Accountancy Books.

Perri; Randon, Anita—Liberty, Charity and Politics: Non-Profit Law and Freedom of Speech. Hardback: £37·50. ISBN 1–85521–507–1. Dartmouth.

Pianca, Andrew—Charity Accounts and SORP 2: The New Law. Paperback: £30·00. ISBN 0–85308–235–9. Jordans.

Richens, N.J.; Fletcher, M.J.G.—Charity Land and Premises. Paperback. ISBN 0–85308–326–6. Jordan.

CHARITIES—*cont.*

Warburton, Jean; Morris, Debra—Tudor on Charities. Hardback: £170·00. ISBN 0–421–44480–0. Sweet & Maxwell.

COMPANY LAW

Aldis—Companies Act 1985/89. Paperback: £45·00. ISBN 1–85355–558–4. Accountancy Books.

Andrews, J.; White, B.—Taxation of Directors and Employees: the Law under Schedule E. Paperback: £45·00. ISBN 1–85355–566–5. Accountancy Books.

Blake, Allan—SWOT: Company Law. Paperback: £8·95. ISBN 1–85431–478–5. Blackstone Press.

Boros, Elizabeth Jane—Minority Shareholders' Remedies. Hardback: £45·00. ISBN 0–19–825975–1. Clarendon Press.

Boyle, Alan; Marshall, Philip; Jones, Philip; Kosmin, Leslie; Richards, David; Gillyon, Philip—The Practice and Procedure of the Companies Court. Lloyd's Commercial Law Library. Hardback: £95·00. ISBN 1–85044–502–8. Lloyd's of London Press.

Bradgate, R.—Legal Practice Course Guides: Commercial Law 1994/1995. Paperback: £14·95. ISBN 1–85431–394–0. Blackstone Press.

Bryant, Roger—Developments in Group Accounts. Unbound/looseleaf: £22·00. ISBN 1–85355–570–3. Accountancy Books Digests.

Colman, Anthony—The Practice and Procedure of the Commercial Court. Hardback: £95·00. ISBN 1–85044–859–0. Lloyd's of London Press.

Companies Act Handbook and Index. Third Edition. Paperback: £16·95. ISBN 0–9505745–5–4. Ernst & Young.

Dine, Janet—Criminal Law in the Company Context. Hardback: £37·50. ISBN 1–85521–342–7. Dartmouth.

Floyd, Richard; Grier, Ian—Corporate Recovery. Paperback: £50·00. ISBN 0–7520–0105–1. FT Law & Tax.

Fox, Dennis; Bowen, Michael—Fox and Bowen on the Law of Private Companies. Hardback: £65·00. ISBN 0–421–50940–6. Sweet & Maxwell.

Freedman, Warren—Malpractice Liability in the Business Professions. Hardback: £67·50. ISBN 0–89930–874–0. Quorum Books.

Freeman, Michael—Alternative Dispute Resolution. The International Library of Essays in Law and Legal Theory: Areas. Hardback: £90·00. ISBN 1–85521–425–3. Dartmouth.

Fuller, Geoffrey—Corporate Borrowing. Hardback: £60·00. ISBN 0–85308–232–4. Jordans.

Goulding, Simon—Company Law. Paperback: £14·95. ISBN 1–874241–83–X. Cavendish Publishing Ltd.

Herzfeld, Edgar; Wilson, Adam—Joint Ventures. Hardback: £45·00. ISBN 0–85308–242–1. Jordans.

Jordans Company Law Materials: 1995. Paperback: £20·00. ISBN 0–85308–317–7. Jordans.

Kelly, David; Holmes, Ann—Business Law. Question and Answer Series. Paperback: £8·95. ISBN 1–85941–140–1. Cavendish Publishing Ltd.

King, R.—Legal Practice Course Guides -Corporate Finance 1994/1995. Paperback: £14·95. ISBN 1–85431–393–2. Blackstone Press.

Lane, David—Law Relating to Unincorporated Associations. Paperback: £15·95. ISBN 1–85941–028–6. Cavendish Publishing Ltd.

MacIntyre, Ewan—Advanced GNVQ Business Law: Lecturer's Manual. Paperback. ISBN 0–273–61240–9. Pitman Publishing.

Marsh, S.; Soulsby, J.—Business Law. Paperback: £13·99. ISBN 0–7487–1985–7. Stanley Thornes.

Mayson, Stephen—Mayson, French and Ryan on Company Law 1995/1996. Paperback: £24·95. ISBN 1–85431–438–6. Blackstone Press.

McCahery, Joseph; Picciotto, Sol; Scott, Colin—Corporate Control and Accountability. Paperback: £19·95. ISBN 0–19–825990–5. Clarendon Press.

McGee, Andrew; Williams, Christina—The Business of Company Law. Hardback: £30·00. ISBN 0–19–870304–2. Paperback: £12·00. ISBN 0 19 876305 0. Clarendon Press.

Mendelsohn, M.—Franchising Law and Practice. Commercial Series. Hardback: £69·00. ISBN 0–85121–747–8. FT Law & Tax.

Muchlinski, Peter—Multinational Enterprises and the Law. Paperback. ISBN 0–631–19818–0. Blackwell Publishers.

Parkinson, J.E.—Corporate Power and Responsibility. Paperback: £19·95. ISBN 0–19–825989–1. Clarendon Press.

Rajak, Harry—A Sourcebook of Company Law. Paperback: £27·50. ISBN 0–85308–266–9. Jordans.

Rayney, Peter—Transactions: Group Company Structures. TRNS. Paperback. ISBN 0–85121–962–4. FT Law & Tax.

Rich, Tony—Briefcase on Company Law. Briefcase Series. Paperback: £9·95. ISBN 1–85941–242–4. Cavendish Publishing Ltd.

Rose, E.—Company Law in a Nutshell. Nutshells. Paperback: £4·95. ISBN 0–421–53330–7. Sweet & Maxwell.

Shepherd, Chris—Company Law: Textbook 1995–1996. Bachelor of Laws. Paperback: £18·95. ISBN 0–7510–0540–1. HLT Publications.

COMPANY LAW—*cont.*

Simpson, Struan; Carless, Jacqueline—Business, Pollution and Regulation in the 90s. Key Resource Series. Paperback. ISBN 0–7123–0820–2. The British Library.

Slorach, Scott—Legal Practice Course Guides: Business Law 1995/1996. Paperback: £14·95. ISBN 1–85431–416–5. Blackstone Press.

Spencer, Margaret P.; Sims, Ronald R.—Corporate Misconduct. Hardback: £53·95. ISBN 0–89930–879–1. Quorum Books.

Stamp, Mark—International Insider Dealing. Hardback: £95·00. ISBN 0–7520–0179–5. FT Law & Tax.

Wainman, David—Company Structures. Hardback: £48·00. ISBN 0–421–50730–6. Sweet & Maxwell.

Wishart, David—Company Law in Context. Paperback: £27·50. ISBN 0–19–558310–8. Oxford University Press Inc., New Zealand.

Wyatt, Michael—Single Shareholder Company Manual. Paperback: £39·00. ISBN 0–7520–0187–6. FT Law & Tax.

COMPETITION

Beier, F.-K.; Schricker, G.; Fikentscher, W.—German Industrial Property, Copyright and Antitrust Laws. Unbound/looseleaf. ISBN 3–527–28730–2. VCH.

Davison, Leigh; Fitzpatrick, Edmund; Johnson, Debra—The European Competitive Environment. Paperback: £15·99. ISBN 0–7506–2278–4. Butterworth-Heinemann.

Hankey, Susan—Business Guide to Competition Law. Paperback: £24·95. ISBN 0–471–95704–6. Chancery Wiley Law Publications.

Herzfeld, Edgar; Wilson, Adam—Joint Ventures. Hardback: £45·00. ISBN 0–85308–242–1. Jordans.

Keenan, Denis; Riches, Sarah—Business Law. Paperback: £16·99. ISBN 0–273–61408–8. Pitman Publishing.

Livingston, Dorothy—Competition Law and Practice. Hardback: £85·00. ISBN 0–85121–718–4. FT Law & Tax.

Maitland-Walker, Julian—Competition Laws of Europe. Paperback: £85·00. ISBN 0–406–03325–0. Butterworth Law.

Ortiz-Blanco, Luis—E.C. Competition Procedure. Hardback: £95·00. ISBN 0–19–825967–0. Clarendon Press.

COMPULSORY PURCHASE

Hayward, Richard—Handbook of Land Compensation. Ringbinder: £128·00. ISBN 0–421–41850–8. Sweet & Maxwell.

COMPUTER LAW

Bainbridge, D.I.; Hassett, Patricia—Knowledge-based Systems in Law. Paperback: £29·95. ISBN 0–273–03787–0. Pitman Publishing.

Bott, Frank; Coleman, Allison; Eaton, Jack; Rowland, Diane—Professional Issues in Software Engineering. Paperback: £16·95. ISBN 1–85728–450–X. UCL Press.

Carr, Indira; Williams, Katherine—Computers and Law. Paperback: £19·95. ISBN 1–871516–35–8. Intellect Books.

Christie, Andrew—Integrated Circuits and Their Contents: International Protection. Hardback: £85·00. ISBN 0–421–48380–6. Sweet & Maxwell.

Galbraith, Anne; Heather, Michael; Stockdale, Michael—Law for Business Technology and Computing. Paperback: £17·95. ISBN 0–7506–2151–6. Butterworth-Heinemann.

Galler, Bernard A.—Software and Intellectual Property Protection. Hardback: £49·50. ISBN 0–89930–974–7. Quorum Books.

Gross, Michael—A Pocket Tour of Law on the Internet. Paperback: £11·99. ISBN 0–7821–1792–9. Sybex.

Lloyd, Ian J.; Simpson, Moira J.—Law on the Electronic Frontier. Hume Papers on Public Policy. Paperback: £9·95. ISBN 0–7486–0594–0. Edinburgh University Press.

Morgan, Richard; Stedman, Graham—Computer Contracts. Commercial Series. Hardback: £80·00. ISBN 0–7520–0161–2. FT Law & Tax.

Rose, Lance—NetLaw: Your Rights in the Online World. Paperback: £14·95. ISBN 0–07–882077–4. Osborne McGraw-Hill.

CONFLICT OF LAWS

Dicey & Morris on the Conflict of Laws: Second Supplement to the Twelfth Edition. Paperback: £24·00. ISBN 0–421–54180–6. Sweet & Maxwell.

Forsyth, C.F.—Conflict of Laws: Textbook 1995–1996. Bachelor of Laws. Paperback: £18·95. ISBN 0–7510–0545–2. HLT Publications.

Forsyth, C.F.—Conflict of Laws: Textbook 1995–1996. Bar Examinations. Paperback: £18·95. ISBN 0–7510–0560–6. HLT Publications.

Holt, Richard—Conflict of Laws. Question and Answer Series. Paperback: £8·95. ISBN 1–85941–142–8. Cavendish Publishing Ltd.

CONSTITUTIONAL LAW

Abraham, Henry J.; Perry, Barbara—Freedom and the Court. Paperback: £18·99. ISBN 0–19–508264–8. Oxford University Press Inc., USA.

Barnett, Hilaire—Constitutional and Administrative Law. Paperback: £16·95. ISBN 1–85941–114–2. Cavendish Publishing Ltd.

Bibby, Peter—Effective Use of Judicial Review. Hardback: £39·95. ISBN 0–85459–761–1. Tolley Publishing.

Birkinshaw, P.—Grievances, Remedies and the State. Modern Legal Studies. Paperback: £19·00. ISBN 0–421–48510–8. Sweet & Maxwell.

Caenegem, R.C. van—An Historical Introduction to Western Constitutional Law. Hardback: £40·00. ISBN 0–521–47115–X. Paperback: £15·95. ISBN 0–521–47693–3. Cambridge University Press.

Cooker, Chris de—International Administration. Hardback: £125·50. ISBN 0–7923–0465–9. Martinus Nijhoff Publishers.

Faille, Christopher C.—The Decline and Fall of the Supreme Court. Hardback: £47·95. ISBN 0–275–94826–9. Praeger Publishers.

Fenwick, Helen—Constitutional and Administrative Law. Question and Answer Series. Paperback: £8·95. ISBN 1–85941–260–2. Cavendish Publishing Ltd.

Fenwick, Helen—Sourcebook on Constitutional and Administrative Law. Paperback: £17·95. ISBN 1–85941–182–7. Cavendish Publishing Ltd.

Finer, S.E.; Bognador, Vernon; Rudden, Bernard—Comparing Constitutions. Hardback: £25·00. ISBN 0–19–876345–X. Paperback: £12·95. ISBN 0–19–876344–1. Clarendon Press.

Goldstein, Joseph—The Intelligible Constitution. Paperback: £9·99. ISBN 0–19–509375–5. Oxford University Press Inc., USA.

Herling, David—Briefcase on Constitutional and Administrative Law. Briefcase Series. Paperback: £9·95. ISBN 1–85941–247–5. Cavendish Publishing Ltd.

Hesse, Joachim Jens; Johnson Nevil, Nevil—Constitutional Policy and Change in Europe. Nuffield European Studies. Hardback: £35·00. ISBN 0–19–827991–4. Clarendon Press.

Kahn, Ronald—The Supreme Court and Constitutional Theory, 1953–1993. Paperback: £16·50. ISBN 0–7006–0711–0. University Press of Kansas.

LaRue, L.H.—Constitutional Law as Fiction. Hardback: £25·95. ISBN 0–271–01406–7. Paperback: £12·50. ISBN 0–271–01407–5. Penn State Press.

Lee, Robert G.—SWOT Constitutional and Administrative Law. Paperback: £8·95. ISBN 1–85431–337–1. Blackstone Press.

Molan, Michael T.—Constitutional and Administrative Law: Textbook 1995–1996. Bachelor of Laws. Paperback: £16·95. ISBN 0–7510–0530–4. HLT Publications.

Molan, Michael T.—Constitutional Law: Textbook 1995–1996. Common Professional Examinations. Paperback: £16·95. ISBN 0–7510–0546–0. HLT Publications.

Plescia, Joseph—The Bill of Rights and Roman Law. Hardback: £62·95. ISBN 1–57292–005–X. Paperback: £44·95. ISBN 1–57292–004–1. Austin and Winfield.

Pyper, Robert—Accountability in the British System of Government. Paperback: £16·99. ISBN 1–872–80766–6. Hodder & Stoughton Educational.

Redish, Martin H.—The Constitution as Political Structure. Hardback: £30·00. ISBN 0–19–507060–7. Oxford University Press Inc., USA.

Schlam, Lawrence—State Constitutional Amendment and Interpretation in the American System. Hardback: £58·50. ISBN 1–880921–73–1. Paperback: £39·95. ISBN 1–880921–72–3. Austin and Winfield.

Schoenbrod, David—Power Without Responsibility. Paperback: £9·50. ISBN 0–300–06518–3. Yale University Press.

Schwartz, Bernard—A History of the Supreme Court. Paperback: £11·99. ISBN 0–19–509387–9. Oxford University Press Inc, USA.

Thompson, Brian—Textbook on Constitutional and Administrative Law. Paperback: £16·95. ISBN 1–85431–445–9. Blackstone Press.

Yarbrough, Tinsley—Harlan I: Judicial Enigma. Hardback: £22·50. ISBN 0–19–507464–5. Oxford University Press Inc., USA.

CONSUMER CREDIT

Harding, Geoff—Consumer Credit and Consumer Hire. Hardback: £45·00. ISBN 0–421–48340–7. Sweet & Maxwell.

CONSUMER PROTECTION

Bowen, Alan—The Implementation of the European Directive on Package Travel. Hardback: £35·00. ISBN 0–273–60389–2. Pitman Publishing.

Howells, G.—Consumer Contract Legislation. Understanding the New Law. Paperback: £15·95. ISBN 1–85431–470–X. Blackstone Press.

Howells, Geraint G.; Weatherill, Stephen—Consumer Protection Law. Hardback: £45·00. ISBN 1–85521–729–5. Paperback: £29·50. ISBN 1–85521–733–3. Dartmouth.

Leder, Malcolm; Shears, Peter—Consumer Law. M&E Handbooks. Paperback: £12·99. ISBN 0–7121–0870–X. Macdonald and Evans.

CONSUMER PROTECTION—*cont.*

Lowe, R.; Woodroffe, G.—Consumer Law and Practice. Paperback: £24·00. ISBN 0–421–52720–X. Sweet & Maxwell.

Panford, Hilary—Consumer Law. Lecture Notes. Paperback: £13·95. ISBN 1–85941–044–8. Cavendish Publishing Ltd.

Rose, Francis—Blackstone's Statutes on Commercial Law and Consumer Law 1995/1996. Paperback: £12·95. ISBN 1–85431–473–4. Blackstone Press.

Walker, Peter M.—Consumer Law. Practice Notes. Paperback: £15·95. ISBN 0–7520–0145–0. FT Law & Tax.

CONTRACT

Atiyah, P.S.; Adams, J.N.—Sale of Goods. Paperback: £24·95. ISBN 0–273–60301–9. Pitman Publishing.

Atiyah, Patrick S.—An Introduction to the Law of Contract. Clarendon Law Series. Hardback: £45·00. ISBN 0–19–825952–2. Paperback: £18·99. ISBN 0–19–825953–0. Clarendon Press.

Bean, Gerard M.D.—Fiduciary Obligations and Joint Operating Agreements. Hardback: £50·00. ISBN 0–19–825928–X. Clarendon Press.

Beatson, Jack; Friedman, Daniel—Good Faith and Fault in Contract Law. Hardback: £55·00. ISBN 0–19–825923–9. Clarendon Press.

Downs, Anthony—Textbook on Contract. Paperback: £16·00. ISBN 1–85431–543–X. Blackstone Press.

Fitton, Peter—Contract Monitoring Manual. 125·00. ISBN 0–582–22864–6. Longman Information & Reference.

Forbes, Duncan; Shirtcliff, Clare—Debt Lawyer's Transaction Pack Transaction Packs. Unbound/looseleaf: £14·95. ISBN 0–85308–305–3. Jordans.

Gilmore, Grant—The Death of Contract. Paperback: £13·50. ISBN 0–8142–0676–X. Ohio State University Press.

Howells, G.—Consumer Contract Legislation. Understanding the New Law. Paperback: £15·95. ISBN 1–85431–470–X. Blackstone Press.

Lake, Ralph B.; Draetta, Ugo—Letters of Intent. Hardback: £85·00. ISBN 0–406–05047–3. Butterworth Law.

Lawson, Richard—Exclusion Clauses and Unfair Contract Terms. Longman Practitioner Series. Paperback: £35·00. ISBN 0–7520–0129–9. FT Law & Tax.

Leighton, Patricia; O'Donnell, Aidan—The New Employment Contract. Law at Work. Paperback: £14·99. ISBN 1–85788–021–8. Nicholas Brealey Publishing.

Mendelsohn, M.—Franchising Law and Practice. Commercial Series. Hardback: £55·00. ISBN 0–85121–747–8. Longman Law, Tax & Finance.

Poole, Jill—Casebook on Contract. Paperback: £18·95. ISBN 1–85431–441–6. Blackstone Press.

Reynolds, Michael P.—The JCT Management Contract. Hardback: £30·00. ISBN 0–632–02259–0. Blackwell Science.

Richards, Paul—Law of Contract. Pitman Law Textbook Series. Paperback: £19·99. ISBN 0–273–61412–6. Pitman Publishing.

Rose, Francis—Blackstone's Statutes on Contract, Tort and Restitution 1995/1996. Paperback: £8·95. Blackstone Press.

Stewart, B.—Restitution in Scotland: A Supplement. Paperback: £19·95. ISBN 0–414–01118–X. Sweet & Maxwell.

Stone, Richard—Contract Law. Question and Answer Series. Paperback: £8·95. ISBN 1–85941–261–0. Cavendish Publishing Ltd.

Taylor, Richard—SWOT Law of Contract. Paperback: £8·95. ISBN 1–85431–338–X. Blackstone Press.

Treital—Law of Contract. Ninth Edition. Hardback: £45·00. ISBN 0–421–51960–6. Paperback: £28·00. ISBN 0–421–51970–3. Sweet & Maxwell.

Turner, Mark; Williams, Alan—Multimedia Contracts Rights and Licensing. Special Report. Hardback: £125·00. ISBN 0–7520–0177–9. FT Law & Tax.

Upex, R.—Davies on Contract. Concise Course Texts. Paperback: £12·50. ISBN 0–421–52280–1. Sweet & Maxwell.

Wagner, William Joseph—The Contractual Reallocation of Procreative Resources and Parental Rights. Medico-Legal Series. Hardback: £39·50. ISBN 1–85521–653–1. Dartmouth.

Wilhelmsson, Thomas—Social Contract Law and European Integration. Hardback: £40·00. ISBN 1–85521–623–X. Dartmouth.

CONVEYANCING AND REAL PROPERTY

Abbey, R.—Law Questions and Answers: Conveyancing. Paperback: £7·95. ISBN 1–85431–407–6. Blackstone Press.

Artis, Denise—SWOT Land Law. Paperback: £8·95. ISBN 1–85431–383–5. Blackstone Press.

Bell, C.—Land Law: Revision Workbook. Bachelor of Laws. Paperback: £9·95. ISBN 0–7510–0605–X. HLT Publications.

Bell, Cedric D.; Henry, G.—Land Law: Textbook 1995–1996. Bachelor of Laws. Paperback: £16·95. ISBN 0–7510–0531–2. HLT Publications.

CONVEYANCING AND REAL PROPERTY—*cont.*

Bell, Cedric D.; Henry, G.—Land Law: Textbook 1995–1996. Common Professional Examinations. Paperback: £16·95. ISBN 0–7510–0550–9. HLT Publications.

Brand, Clive M.; Williams, Delyth W.—Planning Law for Conveyancers. Paperback: £35·00. ISBN 0–7520–0155–8. FT Law & Tax.

Chappelle, Diane—Land Law. Pitman Law Textbook Series. Paperback: £19·99. ISBN 0–273–61409–6. Pitman Publishing.

Coates, Ross M.—Practical Conveyancing. Practitioner Series. Paperback: £38·00. ISBN 0–7520–0209–0. FT Law & Tax.

Coveney, Stephen; Pain, R.; Andrew, J.—Interests in Land: A Practical Guide to Effective Protection at the Land Registry. Second Edition. £29·95. ISBN 0–85459–949–5. Tolley Publishing.

Dixon, Martin—Land Law. Question and Answer Series. Paperback: £8·95. ISBN 1–85941–265–3. Cavendish Publishing Ltd.

Domel, August—Legal Manual for Residential Construction. Paperback: £32·95. ISBN 0–07–017979–4. McGraw-Hill Book Company.

Dyson, Henry—Noter-up: French Real Property and Succession Law. Paperback: £4·99. ISBN 0–7090–5680–X. Robert Hale.

Farrand, Julian; Mitchell, Caroline—Insurance in Domestic Conveyancing. Longman Practitioner Series. Paperback: £23·50. ISBN 0–85121–707–9. FT Law & Tax.

Fitzgerald, Brendan—Land Registry Practice. Second Edition. Hardback: £55·00. ISBN 1–85800–046–7. Round Hall Press, Dublin.

Francione, Gary L.—Animals, Property and the Law. Ethics and Action Series. Hardback: £53·95. ISBN 1–56639–283–7. Paperback: £25·50. ISBN 1–56639–284–5. Temple State University Press.

Gravells, N.P.—Land Law: Texts and Materials. Paperback: £28·00. ISBN 0–421–37810–7. Sweet & Maxwell.

Harcup, F.J.—Green and Henderson on Land Law. Concise Course Texts. Paperback: £13·95. ISBN 0–421–52300–X. Sweet & Maxwell.

Healey, Patsy; Purdue, Michael; Ennis, Frank—Negotiating Development. Hardback: £29·95. ISBN 0–419–19410–X. E & FN Spon.

Kenny, Phillip—Blackstone's Guide to Covenants for Title: Understanding the New Law. Paperback: £12·95. ISBN 1–85431–471–8. Blackstone Press.

Kenny, Phillip—Legal Practice Course Guides: Conveyancing 1995/1996. Paperback: £14·95. ISBN 1–85431–418–1. Blackstone Press.

Lim, Hilary—Cases and Materials in Land Law. Paperback: £21·95. ISBN 0–273–61425–8. Pitman Publishing.

Martin, Jill—Residential Security. Second Edition. Hardback: £42·00. ISBN 0–421–54150–4. Sweet & Maxwell.

Philpott, Gary; Hicks, Garry—Lending on Commercial Property. Paperback: £55·00. ISBN 0–7520–0183–3. FT Law & Tax.

Reynolds, Michael P.—The JCT Management Contract. Hardback: £30·00. ISBN 0–632–02259–0. Blackwell Science.

Royle, Richard—Briefcase on Land Law. Briefcase Series. Paperback: £9·95. ISBN 1–85941–248–3. Cavendish Publishing Ltd.

Stephenson, John—Building Regulations Explained. Builders' Bookshelf Series. Hardback: £49·50. ISBN 0–419–19690–0. E & FN Spon.

Thomas, Meryl—Blackstone's Statutes on Property Law 1995/1996. Paperback: £11·95. ISBN 1–85431–433–5. Blackstone Press.

Thompson, M.P.—Land Law. Paperback: £10·95. ISBN 0–421–52710–2. Sweet & Maxwell.

Timothy, Patrick—Wontner's Guide to Land Registry Practice. Practitioner Series. Paperback: £256·00. ISBN 0–7520–0171–X. FT Law & Tax.

Walker, Bridget—SWOT Conveyancing. Paperback: £8·95. ISBN 1–85431–413–0. Blackstone Press.

Wilkie, Margaret—Law Questions and Answers: Land Law. Paperback: £7·95 ISBN 1–85431–372–X. Blackstone Press.

COPYRIGHT

Balkwill, R.—Multilingual Dictionary of Copyright, Rights and Contracts. Hardback: £55·00. ISBN 0–948905–88–3. Blueprint Publishing.

Beier, F.-K.; Schricker, G.; Fikentscher, W.—German Industrial Property, Copyright and Antitrust Laws. Unbound/looseleaf. ISBN 3–527–28730–2. VCH.

CORPORATION TAX

Dolton, Alan; Saunders, Glyn—Tolley's Tax Cases 1995. £32·95. ISBN 0–85459–972–X. Tolley.

Foreman, A.; Taylor, D.—Allied Dunbar Business Tax and Law Handbook. Hardback: £23·00. ISBN 0–7520–0073–X. FT Law & Tax.

Lovell, White & Durrant—Corporation Tax Guide. Paperback: £16·95. ISBN 1–85941–037–5. Cavendish Publishing Ltd.

CRIMINAL EVIDENCE AND PROCEDURE

Andrews, J.A.; Hirst, Michael—Andrews and Hirst on Criminal Evidence: First Supplement to the Second Edition. Criminal Law Library. Paperback: £22·00. ISBN 0–421–53340–4. Sweet & Maxwell.

Bing—Criminal Procedure and Sentencing in the Magistrates' Court: First Supplement to the Third Edition. Criminal Practice Library. Paperback: £18·00. ISBN 0–421–51300–4. Sweet & Maxwell.

Bojczuk, William; Cracknell, D.G.—Evidence: Textbook 1995–1996. Bachelor of Laws. Paperback: £18·95. ISBN 0–7510–0535–5. HLT Publications.

Bojczuk, William; Cracknell, D.G.—Evidence: Textbook 1995–1996. Bar Examinations. Paperback: £19·95. ISBN 0–7510–0553–3. HLT Publications.

Brayne, Hugh—Legal Practice Course Case Study: Criminal Litigation 1995–1996. Paperback: £9·95. ISBN 1–85431–477–7. Blackstone Press.

Ceci, Stephen J.; Bruck, Maggie—Jeopardy in the Courtroom: A Scientific Analysis of Children's Testimony. Hardback: £26·95. ISBN 1–55798–282–1. American Psychological Association.

Cheetham, Simon—Civil and Criminal Procedure: Textbook 1995–1996. Bar Examinations. Paperback: £21·95. ISBN 0–7510–0552–5. HLT Publications.

Cripps—The Legal Implications of Disclosure in the Public Interest. Hardback: £58·00. ISBN 421–50200–2. Sweet & Maxwell.

Evans, K.—Advocacy in Court. Paperback: £11·95. ISBN 1–85431–458–0. Blackstone Press.

Evidence: Revision Workbook. Bachelor of Laws. Paperback: £9·95. ISBN 0–7510–0594–0. HLT Publications.

Fionda, Julia—Public Prosecutors and Discretion. Oxford Monographs on Criminal Law and Justice. Hardback: £30·00. ISBN 0–19–825915–8. Clarendon Press.

Friedmann, Robert R.—Criminal Justice in Israel. Research and Bibliographical Guides in Criminal Justice, No. 4. Hardback: £67·50. ISBN 0–313–29439–9. Greenwood Press.

Gilmore, William C.—Mutual Assistance in Criminal and Business Regulatory Matters. Cambridge International Documents Series. Hardback: £55·00. ISBN 0–521–47297–0. Cambridge University Press.

Greer, Steven—Supergrasses: Anti-terrorist Law Enforcement in Northern Ireland. Hardback: £35·00. ISBN 0–19–825766–X. Clarendon Press.

Harding, Christopher—Criminal Justice in Europe. Hardback: £45·00. ISBN 0–19–825807–0. Clarendon Press.

Hastie, Reid—Inside the Juror. Paperback: £13·95. ISBN 0–521–47755–7. Cambridge University Press.

Helme, W.—Handbook of Procedures in Magistrates' Courts. Spiralbound: £15·50. ISBN 0–7219–0474–2. Shaw & Sons.

Hutton, Stuart—Criminal Lawyer's Transaction Pack. Transaction Packs. Unbound/looseleaf: £14·95. ISBN 0–85308–302–9. Jordans.

Huxley, Phil—Blacktone's Statutes on Evidence. Paperback: £8·95. ISBN 1–85431–436–X. Blackstone Press.

Jacob, Sir Jack; Adams, J.D.R.; Turner, R.L.; Jones, C.F.—Chitty and Jacob's Queen's Bench Forms: Eighth Cumulative Supplement to the Twenty-first Edition. Common Law Library. Paperback: £28·00. ISBN 0–421–54170–9. Sweet & Maxwell.

Jones, Alison; Kroll, Brynna; Pitts, John; Taylor, Andy—Key Issues in Probation Practice. Paperback: £14·95. ISBN 0–273–61634–X. Pitman Publishing.

Lane, P.—Inns of Court Bar Manuals: Criminal Litigation and Sentencing 1995/1996. Paperback: £21·95. ISBN 1–85431–424–6. Blackstone Press.

Murphy, Peter—Murphy on Evidence. Paperback: £19·95. ISBN 1–85431–373–8. Blackstone Press.

Murphy, Peter—Blackstone's Criminal Practice 1995. Hardback: £99·00. ISBN 1–85431–402–5. Blackstone Press.

Osborne, Craig—Legal Practice Course Guides: Criminal Litigation 1995/1996. Paperback: £14·95. ISBN 1–85431–419–X. Blackstone Press.

Pattenden, Rosemary—Criminal Appeals in English Courts. Oxford Monographs on Criminal Law and Justice. Hardback: £45·00. ISBN 0–19–825405–9. Clarendon Press.

Radevsky, Anthony—Drafting Pleadings. Second Edition. £34·95. ISBN 0–85459–948–7. Tolley.

Robertshaw, Paul—Jury and Judge. The Crown Court in Action. Hardback: £39·50. ISBN 1–85521–430–X. Dartmouth.

Robertson, Bernard; Vignaux, G.A.—Interpreting Evidence. Hardback: £24·95. ISBN 0–471–96026–8. Chancery Wiley Law Publications.

Seabrooke, Stephen—Criminal Evidence and Procedure: the Statutory Framework. Paperback: £20·00. ISBN 1–85431–415–7. Blackstone Press.

Slovenko, Ralph—Psychiatry and Criminal Culpability. Hardback: £34·95. ISBN 0–471–05425–9. John Wiley and Sons.

Smith—Criminal Evidence. Paperback: £14·95. ISBN 0–421–53580–6. Sweet & Maxwell.

Sprack, John—Emmins on Criminal Procedure. Paperback: £19·95. ISBN 1–85431–330–4. Blackstone Press.

Stone, Marcus—Stone: Cross-examination in Criminal Trials. Paperback: £18·95. ISBN 0–406–00622–9. Butterworth Law.

CRIMINAL LAW

Allard, Amanda—Child Abuse Briefing Paper. Paperback: £2·50. The Children's Society.

Allen, Michael J.—Textbook on Criminal Law. Paperback: £16·95. ISBN 1–85431–447–5. Blackstone Press.

Andrews, J.A.; Hirst, Michael—Andrews and Hirst on Criminal Evidence: First Supplement to the Second Edition. Criminal Law Library. Paperback: £22·00. ISBN 0–421–53340–4. Sweet & Maxwell.

Ashworth, Andrew—Principles of Criminal Law. Clarendon Law Series. Hardback: £50·00. ISBN 0–19–876367–0. Paperback: £14·95. ISBN 0–19–876368–9. Clarendon Press.

Baird, Norman—Criminal Law. Question and Answer Series. Paperback: £8·95. ISBN 1–85941–262–9. Cavendish Publishing Ltd.

Bing—Criminal Procedure and Sentencing in the Magistrates' Court: First Supplement to the Third Edition. Criminal Practice Library. Paperback: £18·00. ISBN 0–421–51300–4. Sweet & Maxwell.

Davies, Malcolm; Croall, Hazel; Tryer, Jane—Criminal Justice. Hardback: £45·00. ISBN 0–582–24769–1. Paperback: £14·99. ISBN 0–582–24768–3. Longman.

Dennis—Sweet & Maxwell's Criminal Law Statutes. Third Edition. Paperback: £9·95. ISBN 0–421–53370–6. Sweet & Maxwell.

Dine, Janet—Criminal Law in the Company Context. Hardback: £37·50. ISBN 1–85521–342–7. Dartmouth.

Fionda, Julia—Public Prosecutors and Discretion. Oxford Monographs on Criminal Law and Justice. Hardback: £30·00. ISBN 0–19–825915–8. Clarendon Press.

Fionda, Julia; Bryant, Michael—Briefcase on Criminal Law. Briefcase Series. Paperback: £9·95. ISBN 1–85941–243–2. Cavendish Publishing Ltd.

Gilmore, William C.—Mutual Assistance in Criminal and Business Regulatory Matters. Cambridge International Documents Series. Hardback: £50·00. ISBN 0–521–47297–0. Cambridge University Press.

Glazebrook, Peter—Blackstone's Statutes on Criminal Law 1995/1996. Paperback: £8·95. ISBN 1–85431–430–0. Blackstone Press.

Goodman, Andrew; Wasik, M.; Taylor, R.—Guide to the Criminal Justice and Public Order Act 1994. Hardback: £19·95. ISBN 1–85431–401–7. Blackstone Press.

Green's Criminal Law Statutes 1995. Paperback: £26·00. ISBN 0–414–01125–2. W.Green & Son.

Griew—The Theft Acts. Seventh Edition. Paperback: £21·95. ISBN 0–421–52270–4. Sweet & Maxwell.

Hagan, John; Peterson, Ruth—Crime and Inequality. Hardback: £35·00. ISBN 0–8047–2477–6. Paperback: £12·95. ISBN 0–8047–2404–0. Stanford University Press.

Hirschel, J. David; Wakefield, William—Criminal Justice in England and the United States. Praeger Series in Criminology and Crime Control Policy. Hardback: £58·50. ISBN 0–275–94133–7. Praeger Publishers.

Hollick, Peter—Criminal Law. Cracknell's Law Students' Companions. Paperback: £9·95. ISBN 1–85836–048–X. Old Bailey Press.

Hollick, Peter—Criminal Law. Paperback: £7·95. ISBN 1–85836–049–8. HLT Publications.

Hutton, Stuart—Criminal Lawyer's Transaction Pack. Transaction Packs. Unbound/looseleaf: £14·95. ISBN 0–85308–302–9. Jordans.

Jamieson, George—Child Custody and Abduction. Paperback: £30·00. ISBN 0–414–01093–0. W.Green & Son.

Jefferson, Michael—Criminal Law. Pitman Law Textbook Series. Paperback: £19·99. ISBN 0–273–61410–X. Pitman Publishing.

Jones, A.; Kroll, B.; Pitts, J.; Taylor, A.—Key Issues in Probation Practice. Paperback: £14·95. ISBN 0–582–23821–8. Longman Information & Reference.

Jones, Alison; Kroll, Brynna; Pitts, John; Taylor, Andy—Key Issues in Probation Practice. Paperback: £14·95. ISBN 0–273–61634–X. Pitman Publishing.

Loveland, Ian—Frontiers of Criminality. Modern Legal Studies. Paperback: £18·95. ISBN 0–421–52630–0. Sweet & Maxwell.

Mackay, R.D.—Mental Condition Defences in the Criminal Law. Oxford Monographs on Criminal Law and Justice. Hardback. £35·00. ISBN 0–19–825005–6. Clarendon Press.

Mitchell, Andrew; Hinton, Martin; Taylor, Susan—Mitchell Hinton and Taylor on Confiscation: First Supplement to the First Edition. Criminal Law Library. Paperback: £29·00. ISBN 0–421–49350–X. Sweet & Maxwell.

Molan, Michael T.—Criminal Law: Textbook 1995–1996. Bachelor of Laws. Paperback: £16·95. ISBN 0–7510–0527–4. HLT Publications.

Molan, Michael T.—Criminal Law: Textbook 1995–1996. Common Professional Examinations. Paperback: £16·95. ISBN 0–7510–0548–7. HLT Publications.

Mothersole, Brenda; Ridley, Ann—A Level Law in Action. Paperback: £12·99. ISBN 0–333–58237–3. Macmillan Press.

Newburn, Tim—Crime and Criminal Justice Policy. Longman Social Policy in Modern Britain. Paperback: £13·99. ISBN 0–582–23433–6. Longman.

Peterson, Marilyn B.—Applications in Criminal Analysis. Hardback: £71·95. ISBN 0–313–28577–2. Greenwood Press.

Plotnikoff, J.—Prosecuting Child Abuse: The Government's Speedy Progress Policy. Paperback: £14·50. ISBN 1–85431–404–1. Blackstone Press.

CRIMINAL LAW—*cont.*

Robertshaw, Paul—Jury and Judge. Hardback: £37·50. ISBN 1–85521–430–X. Dartmouth.

Ryan, Christopher—SWOT Criminal Law. Paperback: £8·95. ISBN 1–85431–339–8. Blackstone Press.

Shute, Stephen; Gardner, John; Horder, Jeremy—Action and Value in Criminal Law. Paperback: £15·99. ISBN 0–19–826079–2. Clarendon Press.

Stone, Richard—Offences against the Person. Paperback: £18·95. ISBN 1–874241–13–9. Cavendish Publishing Ltd.

Temkin, Jennifer—Rape and the Criminal Justice System. The International Library of Criminology, Criminal Justice and Penology. Hardback: £80·00. ISBN 1–85521–670–1. Dartmouth.

Tonry, Michael—Malign Neglect: Race, Crime, and Punishment in America. Hardback: £35·00. ISBN 0–19–507720–2. Oxford University Press Inc., USA.

Uglow, Stephen—Criminal Justice. Paperback: £21·95. ISBN 0–421–50510–9. Sweet & Maxwell.

Young, Alison—Imagining Crime. Hardback: £35·00. ISBN 0–8039–8622–X. Paperback: £11·95. ISBN 0–8039–8623–8. Sage Publications.

Young, Peter—Punishment, Money and Legal Order. Edinburgh Law and Society Series. Hardback: £35·00. ISBN 0–7486–0534–7. Edinburgh University Press.

CRIMINAL SENTENCING

Clarkson, C.M.V.; Morgan, Rod—The Politics of Sentencing Reform. Hardback: £35·00. ISBN 0–19–825872–0. Clarendon Press.

Jones, A.; Kroll, B.; Pitts, J.; Taylor, A.—Key Issues in Probation Practice. Paperback: £14·95. ISBN 0–582–23821–8. Longman Information & Reference.

Simmons, A. John; Cohen, Marshall; Cohen, Joshua; Beitz, Charles R.—Punishment: a Philosophy and Public Affairs Reader. Hardback: £40·00. ISBN 0–691–02956–3. Paperback: £11·95. ISBN 0–691–02955–5. Princeton University Press.

Tonry, Michael—Malign Neglect: Race, Crime, and Punishment in America. Hardback: £35·00. ISBN 0–19–507720–2. Oxford University Press Inc., USA.

Young, Peter—Punishment, Money and Legal Order. Edinburgh Law and Society Series. Hardback: £35·00. ISBN 0–7486–0534–7. Edinburgh University Press.

CUSTOMS AND EXCISE

Hawkes, Leonard; Snyder, Francis G.—Customs and Commercial Policy in Europe. Hardback: £60·00. ISBN 0–406–16701–X. Butterworth Law.

DAMAGES

Body, David; Davis, John—Personal Injury Lawyer's Transaction Pack. Transaction Packs. Unbound/looseleaf: £14·95. ISBN 0–85308–301–0. Jordans.

McLean, Sheila A.M.—Law Reform and Medical Injury Litigation. Medico-Legal Series. Hardback: £37·50. ISBN 1–85521–534–9. Dartmouth.

Carey, D.—Legal Practice Course Guides: Personal Injury Litigation 1994/1995. Paperback: 14·95. ISBN 1–85431–463–7. Blackstone Press.

Jones, Michael—Limitation Periods in Personal Injury Actions. Paperback: £24·95. ISBN 1–85431–286–3. Blackstone Press.

McLean, Sheila A.M.—Law Reform and Medical Injury Litigation. Hardback: £37·50. ISBN 1–85521–534–9. Dartmouth.

Napier, Michael—Recovering Damages for Psychiatric Injury. Paperback: £19·95. ISBN 1–85431–352–5. Blackstone Press.

Porter, R.W.—Back Injury and Litigation. Paperback: £15·95. ISBN 1–85996–110–X. Bios Scientific Publishers.

Pritchard, John; Solomon, Nicola—Personal Injury Litigation Practitioner. Paperback: £39·00. ISBN 0–7520–0128–0. FT Law & Tax.

Wells, Celia—Negotiating Tragedy: How the Law Deals with Disasters. Hardback: £18·95. ISBN 0–421–47380–0. Sweet & Maxwell.

ECCLESIASTICAL LAW

Bellomo, Manlio—The Common Legal Past of Europe, 1000–1800. Studies in Medieval and Early Modern Canon Law, Vol. 4. Hardback: £34·95. ISBN 0–8132–0813–0. Paperback: £16·95. ISBN 0–8132–0814–9. Catholic University of America Press.

Buzzard, Lynn R.; Edwards, Susan M.—Church Hiring and Volunteer Selection. Paperback: £22·50. ISBN 1–886569–00–2. University Press of America.

Home, Henry—Essays on the Principles of Morality and Natural Religion. Hardback: £50·00. ISBN 1–85506–416–2. Thoemmes Press.

EDUCATION

Boucher, Edward—GCSE Law Casebook. Paperback: £9·95. ISBN 1–85431–464–5. Blackstone Press.

EDUCATION—*cont.*

Davie, Ron; Galloway, David—Listening to Children in Education. Paperback: £12·99. ISBN 1–85346–314–0. David Fulton Publishers.

Edwards, Martin—Careers in the Law. Kogan Page Careers. Paperback: £6·99. ISBN 0–7494–1566–5. Kogan Page.

Harris, Neville—Law Relating to Schools. £29·95. ISBN 0–85459–765–4. Tolley.

Imber, Michael; Van Geel, Tyll—A Teacher's Guide to Education Law. Paperback: £22·95. ISBN 0–07–031525–6. McGraw-Hill Book Company.

Macintyre, Ewan—Advanced GNVQ Business Law. Paperback: £14·99. ISBN 0–273–61239–5. Pitman Publishing.

McMahon, Joseph A.—Education and Culture in European Community Law. European Community Law Series, Vol. 8. Hardback: £45·00. ISBN 0–485–70013–1. The Athlone Press.

Smith, Michael Clay; Fossey, Richard—Crime on Campus. Series on Higher Education. Hardback: £37·95. ISBN 0–89774–846–8. The Oryx Press.

Stewart, W.J.; Burgess, Robert—Collins Dictionary of Law. £8·99. ISBN 0–00–470009–0. HarperCollins.

EMPLOYMENT

Andrews, J.; White, B.—Taxation of Directors and Employees: The Law under Schedule E. Paperback: £45·00. ISBN 1–85355–566–5. Accountancy Books.

Barrow, C.A.—Industrial Relations Law. Paperback: £17·95. ISBN 1–85941–115–0. Cavendish Publishing Ltd.

Block, Benjamin; Wolkinson, Richard—Employment Law. Human Resource Management US. Paperback: £19·99. ISBN 1–55786–832–8. Blackwell Publishers.

Bowers, John—Bowers on Employment Law. Paperback: £25·00. ISBN 1–85431–289–8. Blackstone Press.

Bowers, John—Termination of Employment. Practice Notes. Paperback: £14·95. ISBN 0–7520–0080–2. FT Law & Tax.

Brontein, A.; Thomas, C.—European Labour Courts: International and European Labour Standards in Labour Court Decisions, and Jurisprudence on Sex Discrimination. Labour-Management Relations Series, No. 82. Paperback: £9·60. ISBN 92–2–108012–9. International Labour Office.

Chandler, Peter—An A–Z of Employment Law. Hardback: £35·00. ISBN 0–7494–1220–8. Kogan Page.

Curtis, Simpson; McMullen, John—Redundancy Law and Practice. Practitioner Series. Paperback: £35·00. ISBN 0–85121–763–X. FT Law & Tax.

Davies, Paul; Lyon-Caen, Antoine; Simitis, Spiros; Sciarra, Silvana—Principles and Perspectives on European Community Labour Law. Hardback: £35·00. ISBN 0–19–826010–5. Clarendon Press.

Doyle, Brian—Disability, Discrimination and Equal Opportunities. Studies in Labour and Social Law. Hardback: £55·00. ISBN 0–7201–2242–2. Paperback: £20·00. ISBN 0–7201–2244–9. Mansell.

Du-Feu, Viv; Warnock, Owen—Employment Law in the NHS. Medico-Legal Series. Paperback: £20·00. ISBN 1–85941–016–2. Cavendish Publishing Ltd.

Edward, Martin; Levinson, Stephen; Cockburn, David—Know-How for Employment Lawyers. Know-How Series. Paperback: £43·00. ISBN 0–7520–0008–X. FT Law & Tax.

Edwards, Martin—Careers in the Law. Kogan Page Careers. Paperback: £6·99. ISBN 0–7494–1566–5. Kogan Page.

Fitzpatrick, Peter—Nationalism, Racism and the Rule of Law Socio-legal Studies. Hardback: £35·00. ISBN 1–85521–554–3. Dartmouth.

Forbes, Duncan—Action against Racial Harassment. Paperback: £24·00. ISBN 0–905099–41–9. The Legal Action Group.

Greenhalgh, Roger—Industrial Tribunals. Law and Employment Series. Paperback: £15·95. ISBN 0–85292–592–1. Institute of Personnel and Development.

Hitchcock, Theresa—Health and Safety. Law and Employment. Paperback: £15·95. ISBN 0–85292–560–3. Institute of Personnel and Development.

Holland, J.—Legal Practice Course Guides—Employment Law 1994/1995. Paperback: £14·95. ISBN 1–85431–395–9. Blackstone Press.

Holmes, Ann E.M.—SWOT Employment Law. Paperback: £8·95. ISBN 1–85431–340–1. Blackstone Press.

Houghton-James, Hazel—Sexual Harassment. Paperback: £16·95. ISBN 1–85941–040–5. Cavendish Publishing Ltd.

Julyan, Alan—Key Employees: Drafting Service Agreements. Practitioner Series. Paperback: £50·00. ISBN 0–7520–0181–7. FT Law & Tax.

Learmond-Criqui, Jessica; Marks, David; McCarthy, Paul—Profit-related Pay. Longman Special Report. Hardback: £95·00. ISBN 0–7520–0163–9. FT Law & Tax.

Leighton, Patricia; O'Donnell, Aidan—The New Employment Contract. Law at Work. Paperback: £14·99. ISBN 1–85788–021–8. Nicholas Brealey Publishing.

Lewis, Tamara—Employment Lawyer's Transaction Pack. Transaction Packs. Unbound/looseleaf: £14·95. ISBN 0–85308–300–2. Jordans.

Lockton, Deborah—Employment Law. Question and Answer Series. Paperback: £8·95. ISBN 1–85941–143–6. Cavendish Publishing Ltd.

EMPLOYMENT—*cont.*

MacDonald, Lynda A.C.—Hired, Fired or Sick & Tired? Hardback: £20·00. ISBN 1–85788–105–2. Paperback: £9·99. ISBN 1–85788–106–0. Nicholas Brealey Publishing.

McMullen, Jeremy; Eady, Jennifer—Industrial Tribunal Procedure. Paperback: £20·00. ISBN 0–905099–47–8. The Legal Action Group.

Miller Kenneth; Craig Victor—Health and Safety at Work in Scotland. Green's Concise Scots Law Series. Paperback. £28·50. ISBN 0–414–01057–4. W. Green & Son.

Nicholls, Doug—Employment Policies and Practice in Youth and Community Work. Paperback: £14·95. ISBN 1–898924–20–1. Russell House Publishing Ltd.

Painter, R.; Cases and Materials on Employment Law. Paperback: £20·00. ISBN 1–85431–197–2. Blackstone Press.

Pitt, G.—Employment Law. Paperback: £22·00. ISBN 0–421–53090–1. Sweet & Maxwell.

Radford, Anne—Managing People in Professional Practices. Paperback: £15·95. ISBN 0–85292–571–9. Institute of Personnel and Development.

Veres III, John G.; Sims, Ronald R.—Human Resource Management and the Americans With Disabilities Act. Hardback: £49·50. ISBN 0–89930–857–0. Quorum Books.

Wedderburn, Lord—Labour Law and Freedom. Further Essays in Labour Law. Paperback: £24·95. ISBN 0–85313–810–X. Lawrence & Wishart.

Whincup, Michael—Modern Employment Law. Paperback: £19·99. ISBN 0–7506–2386–1. Butterworth-Heinemann.

Wolkinson, Richard; Block, Benjamin—Employment Law. Human Resource Management US. Hardback: £50·00. ISBN 1–55786–913–8. Blackwell Publishers.

ENVIRONMENTAL LAW

Ball, Simon—Environmental Law. Paperback: £22·00. ISBN 1–85431–443–2. Blackstone Press.

Bassett, W.H.—Environmental Health Procedures. Paperback: £39·00. ISBN 0–412–56190–5. Chapman and Hall.

Burnett-Hall, Richard—U.K. Environmental Law. Hardback: £125·00. ISBN 0–421–47090–9. Sweet & Maxwell.

Cameron, James; Werksman, Jacob; Roderick, Peter—Improving Compliance with International Environmental Law. Law and Sustainable Development, No. 2. Paperback: £19·95. ISBN 1–85383–261–8. Earthscan.

Campbell, Dennis—International Environmental Laws. Hardback: £75·00. ISBN 0–471–95229–X. Chancery Wiley Law Publications.

Chakravorty, Sumit; Krishnamurthy, Ananth; Takhar, Ravi—Environmental Protection and Finance. Longman Special Report. Hardback: £95·00. ISBN 0–7520–0055–1. FT Law & Tax.

Environmental Regulation in the Independent States. Legislative Texts. Paperback: £45·00. ISBN 1–873461–53–4. Interlist.

Feates, Frank; Barratt, Rod—Integrated Pollution Management. Hardback: £26·95. ISBN 0–07–707867–5. McGraw-Hill Book Company Europe.

Franklyn, Denise Lowe, Mark—Pollution in the U.K. Hardbardk: £42·00. ISBN 0–421045690. Sweet & Maxwell.

Fry, Michael—A Manual of Nature Conservation Law. Hardback: £55·00. ISBN 0–19–825958–1. Paperback: £25·00. ISBN 0–19–826048–2. Clarendon Press.

Graham, Tom; Wanamaker, Jessica—Contaminated Land. Paperback: £35·00. ISBN 0–85308–267–7. Jordans.

Hawke—Environmental Health Law. Hardback: £60·00. ISBN 0–421–46550–6. Sweet & Maxwell.

Keating—Building Contracts. Sixth Edition. Hardback: £150·00. ISBN 0–421–52560–6. Sweet & Maxwell.

Kummer, Katharina—International Management of Hazardous Wastes. Oxford Monographs in International Law. Hardback: £60·00. ISBN 0–19–825994–8. Clarendon Press.

Macrory, Richard; Hollins, Steve—A Source Book of European Community Environmental Law. Hardback: £25·00. ISBN 0–19–825937–9. Oxford University Press.

Mumma, Albert—Environmental Law. Paperback: £24·95. ISBN 0–07–707952–3. McGraw-Hill Book Company Europe.

Payne, Simon; Balchin, Daphne—Environmental Law. Paperback: £16·99. ISBN 0–273–60496–1. Pitman Publishing.

Reynolds, Michael P.—The JCT Management Contract. Hardback: £30·00. ISBN 0–632–02259–0. Blackwell Science.

Royal Commission on Environmental Pollution, U.K. Transport and the Environment. Paperback: £9·99. ISBN 0–19–826065–2. Oxford University Press.

Sands, Philippe—Principles of International Environmental Law: Vol. I. Frameworks, Standards and Implementation. Studies in International Law. Hardback: £60·00. ISBN 0–7190–3483–3. Paperback: £25·00. ISBN 0–7190–3484–1. Manchester University Press.

Scannell, Yvonne—Environmental and Planning Law. Hardback: £65·00. ISBN 1–858000–022–5. The Round Hall Press.

Simpson, Struan; Carless, Jacqueline—Business, Pollution and Regulation in the 90s. Key Resource Series. Paperback. ISBN 0–7123–0820–2. The British Library.

Skillern, Frank F.—Environmental Protection Deskbook. Hardback: £81·95. ISBN 0–07–172521–0. McGraw-Hill Book Company.

ENVIRONMENTAL LAW—*cont.*

Stephenson, John—Building Regulations Explained. Builders' Bookshelf Series. Hardback: £49·50. ISBN 0–419–19690–0. E & FN Spon.

Wolf, Susan; White, Anna Helen—Environmental Law. Lecture Notes Series. Paperback: £15·95. ISBN 1–85941–160–6. Cavendish Publishing Ltd.

EQUITY AND TRUSTS

Doonan, Elmer; Cutler, Andrew J.—Equity and Trusts: Textbook 1995–1996. Bachelor of Laws. Paperback: £16·95. ISBN 0–7510–0533–9. HLT Publications.

Doonan, Elmer; Cutler, Andrew J.—Equity and Trusts: Textbook 1995–1996. Common Professional Examinations. Paperback: £16·95. ISBN 0–7510–0549–5. HLT Publications.

Edwards, Richard; Stockwell, Nigel—Trust and Equity. Pitman Law Textbook Series. Paperback: £19·99. ISBN 0–273–61411–8. Pitman Publishing.

Hartley, William—Declarations of Trust. Longman Practitioner Series. Paperback: £30·00. ISBN 0–85121–991–8. FT Law & Tax.

Hudson, A.—Equity and Trusts: Revision Workbook. Bachelor of Laws. Paperback: £9·95. ISBN 0–7510–0593–2. HLT Publications.

Taylor, Anthony; Steward, Clive—The Equitable Life Tax Guide: 99th Edition. Paperback: £19·99. ISBN 0–631–19842–3. Blackwell Publishers.

EUROPEAN UNION

Anderson, David—References to the European Court of Justice. Litigation Library. Hardback: £110·00. ISBN 0–421–48300–8. Sweet & Maxwell.

Barav, Ami; Wyatt, Derrick—Yearbook of European Law: Vol. 13. 1993. Hardback: £95·00. ISBN 0–19–825781–3. Clarendon Press.

Bowen, Alan—The Implementation of the European Directive on Package Travel. Hardback: £35·00. ISBN 0–273–60389–2. Pitman Publishing.

Burrows—Green's Guide to European Law. Paperback: £28·00. ISBN 0–414–0111–2. W.Green & Son.

Craig, Paul; Burca, Grainne de—E.C. Law: Text, Cases and Materials. Hardback: £55·00. ISBN 0–19–876272–0. Paperback: £25·00. ISBN 0–19–876273–9. Clarendon Press.

Cross, Eugene—Electricity Utilities Regulation in the European Union. Hardback: £95·00. ISBN 0–471–95793–3. John Wiley and Sons.

Cuthbert, Mike—European Community Law. Question and Answer Series. Paperback: £8·95. ISBN 1–85941–264–5. Cavendish Publishing Ltd.

Davison, Leigh; Fitzpatrick, Edmund; Johnson, Debra—The European Competitive Environment. Paperback: £15·99. ISBN 0–7506–2278–4. Butterworth-Heinemann.

Dorn, Nicholas; Jepsen, Jorgen; Savona, Ernesto—European Drugs Policies and Enforcement. Hardback: £40·00. ISBN 0–333–63334–2 Paperback: £14·99. ISBN 0–333–65221–5. Macmillan Press.

European Law Students' Association—Guide to Legal Studies in Europe: 1995. Paperback: £24·28. ISBN 0–421–45350–7. Sweet & Maxwell.

Foster, Nigel—SWOT: EC Law. Paperback: £8·95. ISBN 1–85431–480–7. Blackstone Press.

Foster, Nigel—Blackstone's E.C. Legislation. 1995–96. Paperback: £11·95. ISBN 1–85431–435–1. Blackstone Press.

Gulmann, Claus; Hagel-Sorensen, Karsten—European Law. Paperback. ISBN 87–574–1896–9. Djof Publishing.

Harding, Christopher; Sherlock, Ann—European Community Law. Longman Law. Hardback: £45·00. ISBN 0–582–08976–X. Paperback: £23·99. ISBN 0–582–08975–1. Longman.

Kenner, Jeff—Trends in European Social Policy. Hardback: £40·00. ISBN 1–85521–704–X. Dartmouth.

MacLean, Robert M.—European Community Law and Human Rights: Textbook 1995–1996. Bar Examinations. Paperback: £17·95. ISBN 0–7510–0556–8. HLT Publications.

MacLean, Robert M.—European Union Law: Revision Workbook. Bachelor of Laws. Paperback: £9·95. ISBN 0–7510–0591–6. HLT Publications.

MacLean, Robert M.—European Union Law. Textbook 1995–1996. Commercial Professional Examinations. Paperback: £16·95. ISBN 0–7510–0648–3. HLT Publications.

MacLean, Robert M.—European Union Law: Textbook 1995–1996. Bachelor of Laws. Paperback: £16·95. ISBN 0–7510–0538–X. HLT Publications.

MacLeod, Iain; Hendry, Ian D.; Hyatt, Stephen—European Community External Relations. Hardback: £50·00. ISBN 0–19–825929–8. Paperback: £25·00. ISBN 0–19–825930–1. Clarendon Press.

Meinel, Wulf—Frontiers of European Broadcasting Legislation. European Media Mongraphs. Paperback: £7·95. ISBN 0–85170–413–1. BFI Publishing.

Neal, A.C.; Wright, F.B.—European Communities' Health and Safety Legislation: Vol. 2. £45·00. ISBN 0–412–57760–7. Chapman and Hall.

Prechal, Sacha—Directives in European Community Law. Hardback: £45·00. ISBN 0–19–826016–4. Clarendon Press.

Ross, Malcolm—Supervision of State Aids and Public Undertakings under EEC Law. Monographs on European International Trade Law. Hardback: £45·00. ISBN 1–85567–298–7. Pinter Publishers.

EUROPEAN UNION—*cont.*

Steiner, Josephine—Enforcing E.C. Law. Paperback: £18·95. ISBN 1–85431–320–7. Blackstone Press.

Steyger, Elies—Europe and its Members: A Constitutional Approach. Hardback: £35·00. ISBN 1–85521–655–8. Dartmouth.

Trebilcock, A.—European Labour Courts: Remedies and Sanctions in Industrial Action, Preliminary Relief. Labour-management Relations Series, No. 81. Hardback: £9·60. ISBN 92–2–109185–6. International Labour Office.

Weatherill, Stephen—Law and Economic Integration in the European Community. Clarendon Law Series. Hardback: £35·00. ISBN 0–19–876311–5. Paperback: £14·99. ISBN 0–19–876312–3. Clarendon Press.

EVIDENCE (CIVIL)

Bojczuk, William; Cracknell, D.G.—Evidence: Textbook 1995–1996. Bachelor of Laws. Paperback: £18·95. ISBN 0–7510–0535–5. HLT Publications.

Bojczuk, William; Cracknell, D.G.—Evidence: Textbook 1995–1996. Bar Examinations. Paperback: £19·95. ISBN 0–7510–0553–3. HLT Publications.

Carr, C.J.—SWOT: Law of Evidence. Paperback: £8·95. ISBN 1–85431–486–6. Blackstone Press.

Cheetham, Simon—Civil and Criminal Procedure: Textbook 1995–1996. Bar Examinations. Paperback: £21·95. ISBN 0–7510–0552–5. HLT Publications.

Cripps—The Legal Implications of Disclosure in the Public Interest. Hardback: £58·00. ISBN 421–50200–2. Sweet & Maxwell.

Evidence: Revision Workbook. Bachelor of Laws. Paperback: £9·95. ISBN 0–7510–0594–0. HLT Publications.

Murphy, Peter—Murphy on Evidence. Paperback: £19·95. ISBN 1–85431–373–8. Blackstone Press.

Phillips, Edward—Briefcase on Law of Evidence. Briefcase Series. Paperback: £9·95. ISBN 1–85941–244–0. Cavendish Publishing Ltd.

Wacks, Raymond—SWOT: Law of Evidence. Paperback: £8·95. ISBN 1–85431–475–0. Blackstone Press.

EXTRADITION

Jones—Extradition Law and Practice. Hardback: £85·00. ISBN 0–421–46030–X. Sweet & Maxwell.

FAMILY

Allard, Amanda—Child Abuse Briefing Paper. Paperback: £2·50. The Children's Society.

Bloy, Duncan—Child Law. Lecture Notes Series. Paperback: £14·95. ISBN 1–874241–59–7. Cavendish Publishing Ltd.

Bloy, Duncan J.—SWOT Family Law. Paperback: £8·95. ISBN 1–85431–341–X. Blackstone Press.

Bond, Tina—Legal Practice Course Guides: Family Law. Paperback: £14·95. ISBN 1–85431–396–7. Blackstone Press.

Centre for Family Law and Family Policy, University of East Anglia. Frontiers of Family Law: Vols. 1 & 2. Hardback: £25·00. ISBN 0–471–95730–5. Chancery Wiley Law Publications.

Collier, Richard—Masculinity, Law and Family. Hardback: £45·00. ISBN 0–415–09194–2. Paperback: £14·99. ISBN 0–415–09195–0. Routledge.

Colton, Matthew; Drury, Charlotte; Williams, Margaret—Children in Need. Hardback: £32·50. ISBN 1–85628–932–X. Avebury.

Colton, Matthew; Drury, Charlotte; Williams, Margaret—Staying Together. Hardback: £32·50. ISBN 1–85742–264–3. Paperback: £12·95. ISBN 1–85742–265–1. Arena.

Dodds, Malcolm—Family Law: Textbook 1995–1996. Bachelor of Laws. Paperback: £18·95. ISBN 0–7510–0539–8. HLT Publications.

Dodds, Malcolm—Family Law: Textbook 1995–1996. Bar Examinations. Paperback: £18·95. ISBN 0–7510–0557–6. HLT Publications.

Duckworth, Peter—Matrimonial Property and Finance. Paperback: £33·00. ISBN 0–7520–0224–4. FT Law & Tax.

Duckworth, Peter—Matrimonial Property and Finance: Set and Second Supplement. Paperback: £95·00. ISBN 0–7520–0241–4. Pearson Law Tax and Finance.

Finch, Janet; Masson, Judith; Mason, Jennifer; Hayes, Lynn; Wallis, Lorraine—Wills, Inheritance and the Family. Oxford Socio-legal Studies. Hardback: £25·00. ISBN 0–19–825834–8. Clarendon Press.

Hamilton, Carolyn—Family, Law and Religion. Modern Legal Studies. Hardback: £18·95. ISBN 0–421–45860–7. Sweet & Maxwell.

Hartley, David—Briefcase on Family Law. Briefcase Series. Paperback: £9·95. ISBN 1–85941–246–7. Cavendish Publishing Ltd.

Hughes, R.; Migdal, S.—Family Law: Revision Workbook. Bachelor of Laws. Paperback: £9·95. ISBN 0–7510–0603–3. HLT Publications.

Levy, Allan—Custody and Access. Longman Practitioner Series. Paperback: £15·00. ISBN 0–85121–316–2. FT Law & Tax.

Monro, Pat; Forrester, Liz—The Guardian *ad litem*. Family Law Guide and Practice Series. Paperback: £22·50. ISBN 0–85308–141–7. Family Law.

FAMILY—*cont.*

Oldham, Mika—Blackstone's Statutes on Family Law 1995–1996. Paperback: £11·95. ISBN 1–85431–434–7. Blackstone Press.

Pace, Peter J.—Family Law. Paperback: £12·99. ISBN 0–7121–1056–9. Macdonald and Evans.

Parker, Stephen; Dewar, John—Cohabitants. Paperback: £15·95. ISBN 0–7520–0086–1. FT Law & Tax.

Salter, David—Matrimonial Consent Orders and Agreements. Longman Practitioner Series. Paperback: £24·25. ISBN 0–85121–971–3. FT Law & Tax.

Sarat, Austin; Felstiner, William—Divorce Lawyers and their Clients. Hardback: £19·99. ISBN 0–19–506387–2. Oxford University Press, USA.

Wagner, William Joseph—The Contractual Reallocation of Procreative Resources and Parental Rights. Medico-Legal Series. Hardback: £39·50. ISBN 1–85521–653–1. Dartmouth.

Wragg, T.—Family Law in a Nutshell. Nutshells. Paperback: £4·95. ISBN 0–421–53310–2. Sweet & Maxwell.

Yarnold, Barbara M.—Abortion Politics in the Federal Courts. Hardback: £44·95. ISBN 0–275–95291–6. Praeger Publishers.

FIREARMS AND EXPLOSIVES

Bradley, Iain—Firearms. Paperback: £32·00. ISBN 0–414–01089–2. W.Green & Son.

FOOD AND DRUGS

Dorn, Nicholas; Jepsen, Jorgen; Savona, Ernesto—European Drugs Policies and Enforcement. Hardback: £40·00. ISBN 0–333–63334–2 Paperback: £14·99. ISBN 0–333–65221–5. Macmillan Press.

Shapiro, Ralph—Nutrition Labelling Handbook. Food Science and Technology Series, 69. Hardback: £0–8247–9285–8. Marcel Dekker.

Stranks, Jeremy—Food Safety Law and Practice. Practitioner. Paperback: £35·00. ISBN 0–7520–0102–7. FT Law & Tax.

FOREIGN JURISDICTIONS

Abraham, Henry J.; Perry, Barbara—Freedom and the Court. Paperback: £18·99. ISBN 0–19–508264–8. Oxford University Press Inc., USA.

Alford, William P.—To Steal a Book is an Elegant Offense. Hardback: £27·95. ISBN 0–8047–2270–6. Stanford University Press.

Allee, Mark A.—Law and Local Society in Late Imperial China. Law, Society and Culture in China. Hardback: £35·00. ISBN 0–8047–2272–2. Stanford University Press.

Beier, F.-K.; Schricker, G.; Fikentscher, W.—German Industrial Property, Copyright and Antitrust Laws. Unbound/looseleaf. ISBN 3–527–28730–2. VCH.

Burton, Jeffrey—Indian Territory and the United States, 1866–1906. Legal History of North America, Vol. 1. Hardback: £26·50. ISBN 0–8061–2754–6. University of Oklahoma Press.

Cairns, Walter; McKeon, Robert—Introduction to French Law. Paperback: £15·95. ISBN 1–85941–112–6. Cavendish Publishing Ltd.

Ceci, Stephen J.; Bruck, Maggie—Jeopardy in the Courtroom: A Scientific Analysis of Children's Testimony. Hardback: £26·95. ISBN 1–55798–282–1. American Psychological Association.

Ciambella, Franca—Investment in South East Asia. Hardback: £35·00. ISBN 981–00–6798–4. Butterworth-Heinemann.

Clayton, Cornell W.—Government Lawyers. Studies in Government and Public Policy. Hardback: £31·50. ISBN 0–7006–0706–4. University Press of Kansas.

Corne, Peter—Law and Administrative Regulation in China. Paperback: £24·95. ISBN 962–209–394–9. Hong Kong University Press.

Dadamo, Christian; Farran, Susan—The French Legal System. Paperback. ISBN 0–421–53970–4. Sweet & Maxwell.

Dooley, Frank J.; Thoms, William E. Railroad Law a Decade after Deregulation. Hardback: £49·50. ISBN 0–89930–631–4. Quorum Books.

Duxbury, Neil—Patterns of American Jurisprudence. Hardback: £40·00. ISBN 0–19–825850–X. Clarendon Press.

Dyson, Henry—Noter-up: French Real Property and Succession Law. Paperback: £4·99. ISBN 0–7090–5680–X. Robert Hale.

Edge, Ian D.—Islamic Law and Legal Theory. International Library of Essays on Law and Legal Theory. Hardback: £105·00. ISBN 1–85521–140–8. Dartmouth.

Eskridge Jr, William N.—Dynamic Statutory Interpretation. Hardback: £39·95. ISBN 0–674–21878–7. Harvard University Press.

Fernandes, Edesio—Law and Urban Change in Brazil. Hardback: £32·50. ISBN 1–85972–125–7. Avebury.

Finer, S.E.; Bognador, Vernon; Rudden, Bernard—Comparing Constitutions. Hardback: £25·00. ISBN 0–19–876345–X. Paperback: £12·95. ISBN 0–19–876344–1. Clarendon Press.

Forbes, Vivian Louis—The Maritime Boundaries of the Indian Ocean Region. Hardback: £49·95. ISBN 9971–69–192–2. Paperback: £33·95. ISBN 9971–69–189–2. Singapore University Press.

FOREIGN JURISDICTIONS—*cont.*

Frandsen, Arne Hojris—Business Law in the New South Africa. Paperback. ISBN 87–574–6471–5. Djof Publishing.

Friedmann, Robert R.—Criminal Justice in Israel. Research and Bibliographical Guides in Criminal Justice, No. 4. Hardback: £67·50. ISBN 0–313–29439–9. Greenwood Press.

Fujikura, Koichiro—Japanese Law and Legal Theory. The International Library of Essays in Law and Legal Theory. Hardback: £100·00. ISBN 1–85521–164–5. Dartmouth.

Hagan, John; Peterson, Ruth—Crime and Inequality. Hardback: £35·00. ISBN 0–8047–2477–6. Paperback: £12·95. ISBN 0–8047–2404–0. Stanford University Press.

Hallaq, Wael B.—Law and Legal Theory in Classical and Medieval Islam. Collected Studies Series, 474. Hardback: £49·50. ISBN 0–86078–456–8. Variorum.

Harding, Christopher—Criminal Justice in Europe. Hardback: £45·00. ISBN 0–19–825807–0. Clarendon Press.

Hazard Jr, Geoffrey C.; Taruffo, Michele—American Civil Procedure. Yale Contemporary Law Series. Paperback: £8·95. ISBN 0–300–06504–3. Yale University Press.

Holzman W.; Richard T.—Infringement of the United States Patent Right. Hardback: £53·95. ISBN 0–89930–864–3. Quorum Books.

Horwitz, Morton J.—The Transformation of American Law 1780–1860. Paperback: £9·99. ISBN 0–19–509259–7. Oxford University Press Inc., USA.

Hsu, Barry—Hong Kong becoming China: The Transition to 1997. Vol. 3. The Common Law in Chinese Context. Paperback: £24·95. ISBN 962–209–301–9. Hong Kong University Press.

Hutchinson, Dennis J.; Strauss, David A.; Stone, Geoffrey R.—The Supreme Court Review: 1994. Hardback: £43·25. ISBN 0–226–36311–2. The University of Chicago.

Huxley, Andrew—New Light on Old Thai Law Texts. Kiscadale Asia Research Series. Paperback: £17·50. ISBN 1–870838–41–6. Kiscadale.

Jordan, Emma Coleman; Hill, Anita F.—Race, Gender and Power in America. Hardback: £16·99. ISBN 0–19–508774–7. Oxford University Press Inc., USA.

Kellogg, Susan—Law and the Transformation of Aztec Culture, 1500–1700. Hardback: £31·50. ISBN 0–8061–2702–3. University of Oklahoma Press.

LaFont, Suzanne—The Emergence of an Afro-Caribbean Legal Tradition. Paperback: £39·95. ISBN 1–880921–91–X. Austin and Winfield.

Laiou, Angeliki E.; Simon, Dieter—Law and Society in Byzantium. Hardback: £27·95. ISBN 0–88402–222–6. Harvard University Press.

Leuchtenburg, William E.—The Supreme Court in the Age of Roosevelt. Hardback: £22·50. ISBN 0–19–508613–9. Oxford University Press Inc., USA.

Majer, Diemut—Non-Germans in the Third Reich. Hardback: £96·50. ISBN 0–8133–2359–2. Westview Press.

Marcus, Maeva—The Documentary History of the Supreme Court of the United States, 1789–1800: Vol. 5. Suits Against States. Hardback: £100·00. ISBN 0–231–08872–8. Columbia University Press.

Markovits, Inga—Imperfect Justice. Hardback: £25·00. ISBN 0–19–825814–3. Clarendon Press.

McKeever, Robert J.—Raw Judicial Power? The Supreme Court and American Society. Paperback: £14·99. ISBN 0–7190–4873–7. Manchester University Press.

Ming K. Chan; Clark, David J.—Hong Kong becoming China: The Transition to 1997. Vol. 1. Paperback: £24·95. ISBN 962–209–296–9. Hong Kong University Press.

Muchlinski, Peter—Multinational Enterprises and the Law. Paperback: ISBN 0–631–19818–0. Blackwell Publishers.

Muneer Goolamareed—Legal Reform in the Muslim World. Hardback: £53·95. ISBN 1–57292–003–3. Paperback: £35·95. ISBN 1–57292–002–5. Austin and Winfield.

Plescia, Joseph—The Bill of Rights and Roman Law. Hardback: £62·95. ISBN 1–57292–005–X. Paperback: £44·95. ISBN 1–57292–004–1. Austin and Winfield.

Saleh, Samir—Commercial Agency and Distributorship in the Arab Middle East. Unbound/looseleaf: £325·00. ISBN 1–85333–227–5. Graham & Trotman Publishers.

Samuels, Suzanne—Fetal Rights, Women's Rights. Hardback: £29·50. ISBN 0–299–14540–9. Paperback: £11·95. ISBN 0–299–14544–1. University of Wisconsin Press.

Scannell, Yvonne—Environmental and Planning Law. Hardback: £65·00. ISBN 1–858000–022–5. The Round Hall Press.

Schlam, Lawrence—State Constitutional Amendment and Interpretation in the American System. Hardback: £58·50. ISBN 1–880921–73–1. Paperback: £39·95. ISBN 1–880921–72–3. Austin and Winfield.

Schwartz, Bernard—A History of the Supreme Court. Paperback: £11·99. ISBN 0–19–509387–9. Oxford University Press Inc, USA.

Smitherman, Geneva—African American Women Speak Out on Anita Hill and Clarence Thomas. African American Life Series. Paperback: £16·95. ISBN 0–8143–2530–0. Wayne State University Press.

Takenaka, T.—Patent Claim in the U.S., Germany and Japan. IIC Studies. Paperback. ISBN 3–527–28725–6. VCH.

Tate, C. Neal; Vallinder, Torbjorn—The Global Expansion of Judicial Power. Hardback: £39·95. ISBN 0–8147–8209–4. New York University Press.

Tomkin, David; Hanafin, Patrick—Irish Medical Law. Hardback: £37·50. ISBN 1–85800–051–3. Round Hall Press.

FOREIGN JURISDICTIONS—*cont.*

Tonry, Michael—Malign Neglect: Race, Crime, and Punishment in America. Hardback: £35·00. ISBN 0–19–507720–2. Oxford University Press Inc., USA.

U.S. National Technical Information Service (NTIS)—Federal Certification Authority Liability and Policy: Law and Policy of Certificate-Based Public Key and Digital Signatures. Price: £103·70 plus £5·60 P&P. Order No. PB94–191202. Microinfo Ltd.

Urheberrecht et al—GRUR CD-ROM: Edition '95. ISBN 3–527–28731–0. VCH.

Wallace, R. Jay—Responsibility and the Moral Sentiments. Hardback: £31·95. ISBN 0–674–76622–9. Harvard University Press.

Washington, Linn—Black Judges on Justice. Hardback: £18·95. ISBN 1–56584–104–2. The New Press.

Watson, Alan—The Spirit of Roman Law. Spirit of the Laws Series, No. 1. Hardback: £39·95. ISBN 0–8203–1669–5. University of Georgia Press.

Woodman, Gordon; Obilade, Akintunde—African Law and Legal Theory. The International Library of Essays in Law and Legal Theory. Hardback: £95·00. ISBN 1–85521–572–1. Dartmouth.

GAS

Bradley Jr, Robert L.—Oil, Gas and Government. Hardback: £112·50. ISBN 0–8476–8109–2. Littlefield Adams Quality Paperbacks.

HEALTH AND SAFETY AT WORK

Asfahl, Ray C.—Industrial Safety and Health Management. Hardback: £50·50. ISBN 0–13–140881–X. Prentice Hall U.S.

Barrett, Brenda; Howells, Richard—Health and Safety Law. Paperback: £13·99. ISBN 0–7121–1057–7. Macdonald and Evans.

Brimson, Terry—The Health and Safety Survival Guide. Hardback: £39·95. ISBN 0–07–709049–7. McGraw-Hill Book Company Europe.

Centre for Hazards and Risk Management, Loughborough University—Tolley's Office Health and Safety Handbook. Paperback: £34·95. ISBN 0–85459–998–3. Tolley Publishing.

Chandler, Peter—An A–Z of Health and Safety Law. Hardback: £35·00. ISBN 0–7494–1221–6. Kogan Page.

Craig, Victor; Miller, Kenneth—Health and Safety at Work in Scotland. Green's Concise Scots Law Series. Paperback: £28·50. ISBN 0–414–01057–4. W.Green & Son.

Fingret, Ann; Smith, Alan—Occupational Health. Hardback: £37·50. ISBN 0–415–10628–1. Paperback: £13·99. ISBN 0–415–10629–X. Routledge.

Hitchcock, Theresa—Health and Safety. Law and Employment. Paperback: £15·95. ISBN 0–85292–560–3. Institute of Personnel and Development.

Leigh, J. Paul—Causes of Death in the Workplace. Hardback: £53·95. ISBN 0–89930–951–8. Quorum Books.

Neal, A.C.; Wright, F.B.—European Communities' Health and Safety Legislation: Vol. 2. £45·00. ISBN 0–412–57760–7. Chapman and Hall.

Peters, Roger. Gill, Tess—Health and Safety Liability and Litigation. Unbound/looseleaf: £139·00. ISBN 0–7520–0097–7. FT Law & Tax.

HOUSING

Forbes, Duncan; Shirtcliff, Clare—Housing Lawyer's Transaction Pack. Transaction Packs. Unbound/looseleaf: £14·95. ISBN 0–85308–304–5. Jordans.

Loveland, Ian—Housing the Homeless. Oxford Socio-legal Studies. Hardback: £35·00. ISBN 0–19–825876–3. Clarendon Press.

Luba, Jan—Repairs: Tenants' Rights. Paperback. ISBN 0–905099–49–4. The Legal Action Group.

HUMAN RIGHTS

Abraham, Henry J.; Perry, Barbara—Freedom and the Court. Paperback: £18·99. ISBN 0 10 508264 8. Oxford University Press Inc., USA.

Acton, Richard Lord; Acton, Patricia Nassif—To Go Free. Hardback: £35·95. ISBN 0–8138–2178–9. Iowa State University Press.

Beetham, David—Politics and Human Rights. Political Studies Special Issues. Paperback: £12·99. ISBN 0–631–19666–8. Blackwell Publishers.

Cassese, A.—Self-determination of Peoples. Hersch Lauterpacht Memorial Lectures, 12. Hardback: £60·00. ISBN 0–521–48187–2. Cambridge University Press.

Craven, Matthew—The International Covenant on Economic, Social and Cultural Rights. Hardback: £50·00. ISBN 0–19–825874–7. Clarendon Press.

Dornbach, Alajos—The Secret Trial of Imre Nagy. Hardback: £53·95. ISBN 0–275–94332–1. Praeger Publishers.

Doyle, Brian—Disability, Discrimination and Equal Opportunities. Studies in Labour and Social Law. Hardback: £55·00. ISBN 0–7201–2242–2. Paperback: £20·00. ISBN 0–7201–2244–9. Mansell.

Fenwick, Helen—Civil Liberties. Question and Answer Series. Paperback: £8·95. ISBN 1–85941–141–X. Cavendish Publishing Ltd.

HUMAN RIGHTS—*cont.*

Fish, Stanley—There's No Such Thing as Free Speech. Paperback: £9·99. ISBN 0–19–509383–6. Oxford University Press Inc., USA.

Forbes, Duncan—Action against Racial Harassment. Paperback: £24·00. ISBN 0–905099–41–9. The Legal Action Group.

Freedman, Monroe H.; Freedman, Eric M.—Group Defamation and Freedom of Speech. Contributions in Legal Studies, No. 78. Hardback: £58·50. ISBN 0–313–29297–3. Greenwood Press.

Ghandi, P.R.—International Human Rights Documents. Paperback: £12·95. ISBN 1–85431–409–2. Blackstone Press.

Guitton, Stephanie; Irons, Peter—Arguments on Abortion. ISBN 1–56584–223–5. The New Press.

Gutierrez-Jones, Carl—Rethinking the Borderlands. Latinos in American Society and Culture, No. 4. Hardback: £32·00. ISBN 0–520–08578–7. Paperback: £11·95. ISBN 0–520–08579–5. University of California Press.

Harris, David; Joseph, Sarah—The International Covenant on Civil and Political Rights. Hardback: £50·00. ISBN 0–19–825933–6. Clarendon Press.

Houghton-James, Hazel—Sexual Harassment. Paperback: £16·95. ISBN 1–85941–040–5. Cavendish Publishing Ltd.

Janis, Mark; Kay, Richard; Bradley, Anthony—European Human Rights Law. Hardback: £50·00. ISBN 0–19–876275–5. Paperback: £21·99. ISBN 0–19–876396–4. Clarendon Press.

Kalin—Human Rights in Times of Occupation (The Case of Kuwait). Paperback: £28·00. ISBN 372–729–3551. Sweet & Maxwell.

Kallen, Evelyn—Ethnicity and Human Rights in Canada. Paperback: £11·99. ISBN 0–19–541079–3. O.U.P., Canada.

Kent, Ann—China and Human Rights. Hardback: £10·99. ISBN 0–19–585521–3. O.U.P., Hong Kong.

McCrudden, Christopher; Chambers, Gerald—Individual Rights And the Law in Britain. Hardback: £22·50. ISBN 0–19–826022–9. Clarendon Press.

Merrills, J.G.—The Development of International Law by the European Court of Human Rights. The Melland Schill Monographs in International Law. Paperback: £14·99. ISBN 0–7190–4560–6. Manchester University Press.

Roht-Arriaza, Naomi—Impunity and Human Rights in International Law and Practice. Hardback: £40·00. ISBN 0–19–508136–6. Oxford University Press Inc., USA.

Saari, David J.—Too Much Liberty? Hardback: £49·50. ISBN 0–275–94879–X. Paperback: £14·95. ISBN 0–275–94880–3. Praeger Publishers.

Samuels, Suzanne—Fetal Rights, Women's Rights. Hardback: £29·50. ISBN 0–299–14540–9. Paperback: £11·95. ISBN 0–299–14544–1. University of Wisconsin Press.

Thomas, Terry—Privacy and Social Services. Hardback: £32·50. ISBN 1–85742–246–5. Arena.

Tucker, D.F.B.—The Rehn Quist Court and Civil Rights. Hardback: £35·00. ISBN 1–85521–310–9. Dartmouth.

Washburn, Wilcomb E.—Red Man's Land/White Man's Law. Paperback: £13·50. ISBN 0–8061–2740–6. University of Oklahoma Press.

IMMIGRATION

Goodwin-Gill, Guy S.—The Refugee in International Law. Hardback: £18·95. ISBN 0–19–826020–2. Paperback: £40·00. ISBN 0–19–826019–9. Clarendon Press.

Grant, Lawrence—Immigration Lawyer's Transaction Pack. Transaction Packs. Unbound/looseleaf: £14·95. ISBN 0–85308–303–7. Jordans.

Hing, Bill Ong—Handling Immigration Cases: Vols. 1 & 2. Hardback: £184·95. ISBN 0–471–04668–X. John Wiley and Sons.

Webb, David; Grant, Larry—Immigration and Asylum. Emergency Procedures. Second Edition. Paperback: £19·95. ISBN 0–905099–40–0. Legal Action Group.

INCOME TAX

Andrews, J.; White, B.—Taxation of Directors and Employees: The Law under Schedule E. Paperback: £45·00. ISBN 1–85355–566–5. Accountancy Books.

Saunders, G.; Smailes, D.—Tolley's Income Tax: 1995/96. Paperback: £32·95. ISBN 1–86012–008–3. Tolley Publishing.

INHERITANCE TAX

Foreman, Tony—Don't Pay Too Much Inheritance Tax. Allied Dunbar Personal Finance Guides. Paperback: £7·99. ISBN 1–85788–093–5. Nicholas Brealey Publishing.

INSOLVENCY

Doyle, Louis—Administrative Receivers. Hardback: £55·00. ISBN 0–7520–0152–3. FT Law & Tax.

Loose, Peter; Griffiths, Michael—Loose on Liquidators. Hardback: £55·00. ISBN 0–85308–234–0. Jordans.

McCormack—Reservation of Title. Second Edition. Hardback: £60·00. ISBN 0–421–51130–3. Sweet & Maxwell.

INSOLVENCY—*cont.*

Otter, Keith—Cork Gully on Insolvency Judgments 1991–1994. Hardback: £75·00. ISBN 0–7520–0081–0. FT Law & Tax.

Portwood, Timothy—Joint Ventures under EEC Competition Law. Hardback: £45·00. ISBN 0–485–70012–3. The Athlone Press.

Rajani, Shashi—Tolley's Corporate Insolvency. Second Edition. Hardback: £55·00. ISBN 0–85459–748–4. Tolley Publishing.

Wood—Principles of International Insolvency. Hardback: £65·00. ISBN 0–421–52450–2. Sweet & Maxwell.

INSURANCE

Cooper, Neil; Hand, Sean—Pension Schemes and Liquidation. Hardback: £60·00. ISBN 0–85308–233–2. Jordans.

De Wit, Ralph—Multimodal Transport. Lloyd's Shipping Law Library. Hardback: £78·00. ISBN 1–85044–894–9. Lloyd's of London Press.

Farrand, Julian; Mitchell, Caroline—Insurance in Domestic Conveyancing. Longman Practitioner Series. Paperback: £23·50. ISBN 0–85121–707–9. FT Law & Tax.

Hamilton, Peter—Life Assurance Law and Practice. Unbound/looseleaf: £195·00. ISBN 0–85121–946–2. FT Law & Tax.

Hudson, Geoffrey—The Institute Clauses. Hardback: £50·00. ISBN 1–85044–879–5. Lloyd's of London Press.

Lloyd's Market Handbook. Unbound/looseleaf: £225·00. ISBN 1–85044–878–7. Lloyd's of London Press.

McGee, Andrew—The Law and Practice of Life Assurance Contracts. Hardback: £65·00. ISBN 0–421–48080–7. Sweet & Maxwell.

Taylor, Anthony; Steward, Clive—The Equitable Life Tax Guide: 99th Edition. Paperback: £19·99. ISBN 0–631–19842–3. Blackwell Publishers.

INTELLECTUAL PROPERTY

Alford, William P.—To Steal a Book is an Elegant Offense. Hardback: £27·95. ISBN 0–8047–2270–6. Stanford University Press.

Carr, Indira; Williams, Katherine—Computers and Law. Paperback: £19·95. ISBN 1–871516–35–8. Intellect Books.

Christie, A.—Intellectual Property Statutes. Paperback. Paperback: £13·00. ISBN 0–85431–386–X. Blackstone Press.

Galler, Bernard A.—Software and Intellectual Property Protection. Hardback: £49·50. ISBN 0–89930–974–7. Quorum Books.

Hearle, Liz—World Guide to Intellectual Property Organisations. Key Resources Series. Paperback. ISBN 0–7123–0819–9. The British Library.

Higgins, Rosalyn—Problems and Process. Paperback: £15·99. ISBN 0–19–876410–3. Clarendon Press.

Legat, Michael—The Writer's Rights. Paperback: £8·99. ISBN 0–7136–4018–9. A & C Black.

Phillips, J.—The Inventor's Guide. Paperback. ISBN 0–7123–0793–1. The British Library.

Spence, Michael—Intellectual Property. Paperback: £18·95. ISBN 1–874241–86–4. Cavendish Publishing Ltd.

Turner, Mark; Williams, Alan—Multimedia Contracts Rights and Licensing. Special Report. Hardback: £125·00. ISBN 0–7520–0177–9. FT Law & Tax.

Urheberrecht et al—GRUR CD-ROM: Edition '95. ISBN 3–527–28731–0. VCH.

INTERNATIONAL LAW

Akehurst, Michael—A Modern Introduction to International Law. Paperback: £14·99. ISBN 0–415–11120–X. Routledge.

Bethlehem, Daniel; Weller, Marc—The "Yugoslav" Crisis in International Law: Part I, General Issues. Cambridge International Documents Series. Paperback: £75·00. ISBN 0–521–46304–1. Cambridge University Press.

Bodie, Thomas J.—Politics and the Emergence of an Activist. International Court of Justice. Hardback: £40·50. ISBN 0–275–95014–X. Praeger Publishers.

Boyle, Alan; Birnie, Patricia—Basic Documents on International Law and the Environment. Hardback: £55·00. ISBN 0–19–876320–4. Paperback: £19·99. ISBN 0–19–876321–2. Clarendon Press.

Brownlie, Ian—Basic Documents in International Law. Hardback: £40·00. ISBN 0–19–876380–8. Paperback: £12·95. ISBN 0–19–876381–6. Oxford University Press.

Butler, W.E.; Braginskii, M.I.; Rubanov, A.A.—The Law on Pledge in the Republics of the Former Soviet Union. The Butler Commentaries. Hardback: £85·00. ISBN 1–873461–26–7. Interlist.

Byrnes, Andrew; Chan, Johannes; Edwards, George—Hong Kong Law Reports, Vol. 1, 1991. Hardback: £79·95. ISBN 962–209–332–9. Hong Kong University Press.

Byrnes, Andrew; Chan, Johannes; Edwards, George—Hong Kong Law Reports, Vol. 2, 1992. Hardback: £112·00. ISBN 962–209–351–5. Hong Kong University Press.

INTERNATIONAL LAW—*cont.*

Byrnes, Andrew; Chan, Johannes; Edwards, George—Hong Kong Law Reports, Vol. 3, Pt. 1, 1993. Paperback: £32·00. ISBN 962–209–346–9. Hong Kong University Press.

Byrnes, Andrew; Chan, Johannes; Edwards, George—Hong Kong Law Reports, Vol. 3, Pt. 2, 1993. Paperback: £32·00. ISBN 962–209–347–7. Hong Kong University Press.

Byrnes, Andrew; Chan, Johannes; Edwards, George—Hong Kong Law Reports, Vol. 3, Pt. 3, 1993. Paperback: £32·00. ISBN 962–209–349–3. Hong Kong University Press.

Byrnes, Andrew; Chan, Johannes; Edwards, George—Hong Kong Law Reports, Vol. 3, Pt. 4, 1993. Paperback: £32·00. ISBN 962–209–350–7. Hong Kong University Press.

Cameron, James; Werksman, Jacob; Roderick, Peter—Improving Compliance with International Environmental Law. Law and Sustainable Development, No. 2. Paperback: £19·95. ISBN 1–85383–261–8. Earthscan.

Campbell, Christian; Campbell, Dennis—International Civil Procedures. Hardback: £95·00. ISBN 1–85044–863–9. Lloyd's of London Press.

Campbell, Dennis—International Personal Injury Compensation: Sourcebook. Hardback. ISBN 0–421–53040–5. Sweet & Maxwell.

Casna, Richard—International Joint Ventures: The Legal and Tax Issues. Money Manager's Library. Paperback: £125·00. ISBN 1–85271–330–5. IBC Publishing.

Charlery, Janette—International Trade Law. M&E Handbooks. Paperback: £11·99. ISBN 0–7121–0984–6. Macdonald and Evans.

Cooker, Chris de—International Administration. Hardback: £125·50. ISBN 0–7923–0465–9. Martinus Nijhoff Publishers.

Craven, Matthew—The International Covenant on Economic, Social and Cultural Rights. Hardback: £50·00. ISBN 0–19–825874–7. Clarendon Press.

Davies, Denzil—GATT: A Practical Guide. Hardback. ISBN 0–7520–0106–X. FT Law & Tax.

Dixon, Martin—Cases and Materials on International Law. Paperback: £23·00. ISBN 1–85431–408–4. Blackstone Press.

Doswald-Beck, Louise—San Remo Manual on International Law Applicable to Armed Conflicts at Sea. Hardback: £40·00. ISBN 0–521–55188–9. Paperback: £14·95. ISBN 0–521–55864–6. Cambridge University Press.

Faille, Christopher C.—The Decline and Fall of the Supreme Court. Hardback: £47·95. ISBN 0–275–94826–9. Praeger Publishers.

Fawcett, James J.—Declining Jurisdiction in Private International Law. Hardback: £50·00. ISBN 0–19–825959–X. Clarendon Press.

Franck, T.M.—Fairness in International Law. Hardback: £25·00. ISBN 0–19–825901–8. Clarendon Press.

Frankel, Francine—The Nonproliferation Treaty. Hardback: £44·95. ISBN 0–8191–9943–5. Paperback: £31·50. ISBN 0–8191–9944–3. University Press of America.

Ghandi, P.R.—International Human Rights Documents. Paperback: £12·95. ISBN 1–85431–409–2. Blackstone Press.

Gilmore, William C.—Mutual Assistance in Criminal and Business Regulatory Matters. Cambridge International Documents Series. Hardback: £50·00. ISBN 0–521–47297–0. Cambridge University Press.

Goodwin-Gill, Guy S.—The Refugee in International Law. Hardback: £18·95. ISBN 0–19–826020–2. Paperback: £40·00. ISBN 0–19–826019–9. Clarendon Press.

Gutierrez-Jones, Carl—Rethinking the Borderlands. Latinos in American Society and Culture, No. 4. Hardback: £32·00. ISBN 0–520–08578–7. Paperback: £11·95. ISBN 0–520–08579–5. University of California Press.

Harris, David; Joseph, Sarah—The International Covenant on Civil and Political Rights. Hardback: £50·00. ISBN 0–19–825933–6. Clarendon Press.

Hearle, Liz—World Guide to Intellectual Property Organisations. Key Resources Series. Paperback. ISBN 0–7123–0819–9. The British Library.

Higgins, Rosalyn—Problems and Process. Paperback: £15·99. ISBN 0–19–876410–3. Clarendon Press.

Hillier, Tim—Sourcebook on Public International Law. Sourcebook Series. Paperback: £20·95. ISBN 1–85941–050–2. Cavendish Publishing Ltd.

Jordan, Emma Coleman; Hill, Anita F.—Race, Gender and Power in America. Hardback: £16·99. ISBN 0–19–508774–7. Oxford University Press Inc., USA.

Kaczorowska, Alina—International Trade Conventions and Their Effectiveness. Nijhoff Law Specials. Paperback: £51·75. 0–7923–3362–4. Martinus Nijhoff Publishers.

Kadar, Abby; Whitehead, Geoffrey—Export Law. Paperback: £15·95. ISBN 0–13–434218–6. Prentice Hall/Woodhead-Faulkner.

Kummer, Katharina—International Management of Hazardous Wastes. Oxford Monographs in International Law. Hardback: £60·00. ISBN 0–19–825994–8. Clarendon Press.

Lauterpacht, E.J.; Greenwood, C.J.—International Law Reports: Vol. 100. International Law Reports. Hardback: £85·00. ISBN 0–521–49647–0. Cambridge University Press.

Lauterpacht, E.J.; Greenwood, C.J.—International Law Reports: Vol. 101. International Law Reports. Hardback: £85·00. ISBN 0–521–49648–9. Cambridge University Press.

Levine, Martin Lyon—Law and Psychology. The International Library of Essays in Law and Legal Theory. Hardback: £90·00. ISBN 1–85521–220–X. Dartmouth.

INTERNATIONAL LAW—*cont.*

MacLean, Robert M.—Public International Law: Revision Workbook. Bachelor of Laws. Paperback: £9·95. ISBN 0–7510–0595–9. HLT Publications.

MacLean, Robert M.—Public International Law: Textbook 1995–1996. Bachelor of Laws. Paperback: £18·95. ISBN 0–7510–0542–8. HLT Publications.

McCoubrey, Hilaire; White, Nigel—International Organizations and Civil Wars. Hardback: £40·00. ISBN 1–85521–468–7. Dartmouth.

Merrills, J.G.—The Development of International Law by the European Court of Human Rights. The Melland Schill Monographs in International Law. Paperback: £14·99. ISBN 0–7190–4560–6. Manchester University Press.

Miller, Richard Lawrence—Nazi Justiz. Hardback: £35·95. ISBN 0–275–94912–5. Praeger Publishers.

Norton, Joseph J.—Devising International Bank Supervisory Standards. International Banking and Finance Law. Hardback: £82·00. ISBN 1–85966–185–8. Martinus Nijhoff Publishers.

Pease, William H.; Pease, Jane H.; James Louis Petigru—Studies in the Legal History of the South. Hardback: £31·50. ISBN 0–8203–1680–6. University of Georgia Press.

Rayfuse, R.—ICSID Reports: Vol. 3. ICSID Reports, 3.00. Hardback: £120·00. ISBN 0–521–47512–0. Cambridge University Press.

Reuter, Paul—Introduction to the Law of Treaties. Hardback: £45·00. ISBN 0–7103–0502–8. Kegan Paul International.

Roht-Arriaza, Naomi—Impunity and Human Rights in International Law and Practice. Hardback: £40·00. ISBN 0–19–508136–6. Oxford University Press Inc., USA.

Rosenblatt—International Adoption. Paperback: £38·00. ISBN 0–421–52770–6. Sweet & Maxwell.

Sands, Philippe—Principles of International Environmental Law: Vol. I. Frameworks, Standards and Implementation. Studies in International Law. Hardback: £60·00. ISBN 0–7190–3483–3. Paperback: £25·00. ISBN 0–7190–3484–1. Manchester University Press.

Sellman, Pamela—Law of International Trade: Textbook 1995–1996. Bachelor of Laws. Paperback: £18·95. ISBN 0–7510–0537–1. HLT Publications.

Sellman, Pamela—Law of International Trade: Textbook 1995–1996. Bar Examinations. Paperback: £17·95. ISBN 0–7510–0558–4. HLT Publications.

Simma, Bruno—The Charter of the United Nations. Hardback: £140·00. ISBN 0–19–825703–1. Clarendon Press.

Suratgar, D.; MacDonald, G.—International Project Finance: Law and Practice. Hardback: £85·00. ISBN 0–85121–836–9. FT Law & Tax.

van Houtte, Hans; Schrans—International Trade and Finance Law. Hardback: £130·00. ISBN 0–421–48090–4. Sweet & Maxwell.

Williams, Philip—International Trade Law. Questions and Answers Series. Paperback: £8·95. ISBN 1–874241–31–7. Cavendish Publishing Ltd.

Wood—Principles of International Insolvency. Hardback: £65·00. ISBN 0–421–52450–2. Sweet & Maxwell.

Yarnold, Barbara M.—Abortion Politics in the Federal Courts. Hardback: £44·95. ISBN 0–275–95291–6. Praeger Publishers.

JURISPRUDENCE

Arnold, Barbara M.—Abortion Politics in the Federal Courts. Hardback: £44·95. ISBN 0–275–95291–6. Praeger Publishers.

Baird, Douglas G.; Gertner, Robert H.; Picker, Randal C.—Game Theory and the Law. Hardback: £35·95. ISBN 0–674–34119–8. Harvard University Press.

Bix, Brian—Law, Language and Legal Determinacy. Paperback: £15·99. ISBN 0–19–826050–4. Clarendon Press.

Burton, Steven J.—Judging in Good Faith. Cambridge Studies in Philosophy and Law. Paperback: £12·95. ISBN 0–521–47740–9. Cambridge University Press.

Caplan, Pat—Understanding Disputes. Explorations in Anthropology. Hardback: £29·95. ISBN 0–85496–924–1. Paperback: £12·95. ISBN 0–85496–925–X. Berg Publishers.

Cassese, A.—Self-determination of Peoples. Hersch Lauterpacht Memorial Lectures, 12. Hardback: £60·00. ISBN 0–521–48187–2. Cambridge University Press.

Cotterrell, Roger—Law's Community. Oxford Socio-legal Studies. Hardback: £35·00. ISBN 0–19–825890–9. Clarendon Press.

Cranston, Ross—Legal Ethics and Professional Responsibility. Hardback: £30·00. ISBN 0–19–825931–X. Clarendon Press.

Degroot, M.H.; Fienberg, S.E.; Kadane, J.B.—Statistics and the Law. Wiley Classics Library. Paperback: £27·50. ISBN 0–471–05538–7. John Wiley and Sons.

Duxbury, Neil—Patterns of American Jurisprudence. Hardback: £40·00. ISBN 0–19–825850–X. Clarendon Press.

Edge, Ian D.—Islamic Law and Legal Theory. International Library of Essays on Law and Legal Theory. Hardback: £105·00. ISBN 1–85521–140–8. Dartmouth.

Eskridge Jr, William N.—Dynamic Statutory Interpretation. Hardback: £39·95. ISBN 0–674–21878–7. Harvard University Press.

Fitzpatrick, Peter—Nationalism, Racism and the Rule of Law Socio-legal Studies. Hardback: £35·00. ISBN 1–85521–554–3. Dartmouth.

JURISPRUDENCE—*cont.*

Franck, T.M.—Fairness in International Law. Hardback: £25·00. ISBN 0–19–825901–8. Clarendon Press.

Freeman, Michael D.A.—Current Legal Problems 1995: Vol. 48, Part 2. Collected Papers. Hardback: £40·00. ISBN 0–19–826085–7. Clarendon Press.

Galligan, Denis—Socio-legal Studies in Context. Paperback: £12·99. ISBN 0–631–19681–1. Blackwell Publishers.

George, Robert P.—Making Men Moral. Paperback: £14·99. ISBN 0–19–826024–5. Clarendon Press.

George, Robert P.—The Autonomy of Law. Hardback: £35·00. ISBN 0–19–825786–4. Clarendon Press.

Goodin, Robert E.—Utilitarianism as a Public Philosophy. Cambridge Studies in Philosophy and Public Policy. Hardback: £40·00. ISBN 0–521–46263–0. Paperback: £13·95. ISBN 0–521–46806–X. Cambridge University Press.

Greenawalt, Kent—Law and Objectivity. Paperback: £12·99. ISBN 0–19–509833–1. Oxford University Press Inc., USA.

Hagan, John; Kay, Fiona—Gender in Practice. Hardback: £22·50. ISBN 0–19–509282–1. Oxford University Press Inc., USA.

Hagan, John; Peterson, Ruth—Crime and Inequality. Hardback: £35·00. ISBN 0–8047–2477–6. Paperback: £12·95. ISBN 0–8047–2404–0. Stanford University Press.

Hallaq, Wael B.—Law and Legal Theory in Classical and Medieval Islam. Collected Studies Series, 474. Hardback: £49·50. ISBN 0–86078–456–8. Variorum.

Halpern, Stephen C.—On the Limits of the Law. Hardback: £45·50. ISBN 0–8018–4896–2. Paperback: £15·50. ISBN 0–8018–4897–0. The Johns Hopkins University Press.

Hazlehurst, Kayleen M.—Legal Pluralism and the Colonial Legacy. Hardback: £37·50. ISBN 1–85972–078–1. Avebury.

Hirschel, J. David; Wakefield, William—Criminal Justice in England and the United States. Praeger Series in Criminology and Crime Control Policy. Hardback: £58·50. ISBN 0–275–94133–7. Praeger Publishers.

Home, Henry—Elucidations Respecting the Common and Statute Law of Scotland. Hardback: £55·00. ISBN 1–85506–421–9. Thoemmes Press.

Home, Henry—Essays on the Principles of Morality and Natural Religion. Hardback: £50·00. ISBN 1–85506–416–2. Thoemmes Press.

Jackson, Bernard S.—Making Sense in Law. Legal Semiotics Monographs, Vol. V. Hardback: £45·00. ISBN 0–9513793–6–4. Paperback: £19·95. ISBN 0–9513793–7–2. Deborah Charles Publications.

Jordan, Emma Coleman; Hill, Anita F.—Race, Gender and Power in America. Hardback: £16·99. ISBN 0–19–508774–7. Oxford University Press Inc., USA.

Jurisprudence and Legal Theory: Textbook 1995–1996. Bachelor of Laws. Paperback: £16·95. ISBN 0–7510–0534–7. HLT Publications.

Jurisprudence: Revision Workbook. Bachelor of Laws. Paperback: £9·95. ISBN 0–7510–0604–1. HLT Publications.

Kaganas, Felicity; King, Michael; Piper, Christine—Legislating for Harmony. Hardback: £14·95. ISBN 1–85302–328–0. Jessica Kingsley Publishers.

Kapur, Ratna—Feminist Terrains in Legal Domains. Hardback. ISBN 81–85107–83–1. Kali for Women.

Karst, Kenneth L.—Law's Promise, Law's Expression. Paperback: £10·95. ISBN 0–300–06507–8. Yale University Press.

Levine, Martin Lyon—Law and Psychology. The International Library of Essays in Law and Legal Theory. Hardback: £90·00. ISBN 1–85521–220–X. Dartmouth.

Lewis, A.—Current Legal Problems 1995: Vol. 48. Part 1: Annual Review. Current Legal Problems Series, Vol. 48, Part 1. Paperback: £21·95. ISBN 0–19–826041–5. Clarendon Press.

Lewisch, P.—Punishment, Public Law Enforcement and the Protective State. Paperback: £27·50. ISBN 3–211–82645–9. Springer-Verlag Vienna.

Linde, Justice Hans; Nagel, Robert F.—Intellect and Craft. New Perspectives on Law, Culture, & Society. Hardback: £37·00. ISBN 0–8133–8576–8. Westview Press.

Loveland, Ian—Frontiers of Criminality. Modern Legal Studies. Paperback: £18·95. ISBN 0–421–52630–0. Sweet & Maxwell.

Malloy, Robin Paul; Jerry Evensky—Adam Smith and the Philosophy of Law and Economics. Law and Philosophy Library. Paperback: £29·00. ISBN 0–7923–3425–6. Kluwer Academic Publishers.

Montague, Phillip—Punishment as Societal Defense. Studies in Social and Political Philosophy. Hardback: £49·95. ISBN 0–8476–8071–1. Paperback: £19·95. ISBN 0–8476–8072–X. Rowman & Littlefield.

Nair, Janaki—Women and Law in Colonial India. Hardback. ISBN 81–85107–82–3. Kali for Women.

Olsen, Frances E.—Feminist Legal Theory: Vol. I. Paperback: £25·00. ISBN 1–85521–736–8. Dartmouth.

Olsen, Frances E.—Feminist Legal Theory: Vol. II. Paperback: £25·00. ISBN 1–85521–745–7. Dartmouth.

Parker, Stephen; Sampford, Charles—Legal Ethics and Legal Practice. Hardback: £35·00. ISBN 0–19–825945–X. Clarendon Press.

JURISPRUDENCE—*cont.*

Posner, Richard A.—Overcoming Law. Hardback: £29·95. ISBN 0–674–64925–7. Harvard University Press.

Raz, Joseph—Ethics in the Public Domain. Paperback: £14·95. ISBN 0–19–826069–5. Clarendon Press.

Robert E. Goodin—Utilitarianism as a Public Philosophy. Cambridge Studies in Philosophy and Public Policy. Hardback: £40·00. ISBN 0–521–46263–0. Paperback: £13·95. ISBN 0–521–46806–X. Cambridge University Press.

Rumble, Wilfrid E.—John Austin: The Province of Jurisprudence Determined. Cambridge Texts in the History of Political Thought. Hardback: £40·00. ISBN 0–521–44244–3. Paperback: £14·95. ISBN 0–521–44756–9. Cambridge University Press.

Samuels, Suzanne—Fetal Rights, Women's Rights. Hardback: £29·50. ISBN 0–299–14540–9. Paperback: £11·95. ISBN 0–299–14544–1. University of Wisconsin Press.

Sanderson, John—Criminology: Textbook 1995–1996. Bachelor of Laws. Paperback: £17·95. ISBN 0–7510–0544–4. HLT Publications.

Simmons, A. John; Cohen, Marshall; Cohen, Joshua; Beitz, Charles R.—Punishment: a Philosophy and Public Affairs Reader. Hardback: £40·00. ISBN 0–691–02956–3. Paperback: £11·95. ISBN 0–691–02955–5. Princeton University Press.

Smith, Christopher E.—Judicial Self-interest. Hardback: £44·95. ISBN 0–275–95216–9. Praeger Publishers.

Strum, Philippa—Brandeis. American Political Thought. Paperback: £16·50. ISBN 0–7006–0687–4. University Press of Kansas.

Wacks, Raymond—Privacy and Free Speech. Paperback: £15·00. ISBN 1–85431–454–8. Blackstone Press.

Wallace, R. Jay—Responsibility and the Moral Sentiments. Hardback: £31·95. ISBN 0–674–76622–9. Harvard University Press.

Weinrib, Ernest J.—The Idea of Private Law. Hardback: £27·95. ISBN 0–674–44212–1. Harvard University Press.

Williams, Jeffrey—Manipulation on Trial. Hardback: £30·00. ISBN 0–521–44028–9. Cambridge University Press.

Wilson, G.—Frontiers of Legal Scholarship. Hardback: £45·00. ISBN 0–471–96123–X. John Wiley and Sons.

Winfield, Richard Dien—Law in Civil Society. Hardback: £26·95. ISBN 0–7006–0698–X. Paperback: £16·50. ISBN 0–7006–0699–8. University Press of Kansas.

LANDLORD AND TENANT

Bright, Susan; Gilbert, Geoff—Landlord and Tenant Law. Hardback: £50·00. ISBN 0–19–876348–4. Paperback: £22·99. ISBN 0–19–876349–2. Clarendon Press.

Evans, Della—Agricultural Tenancies Act 1994. Paperback: £14·50. ISBN 0–421–54590–9. Sweet & Maxwell.

Lloyd Holt, Suzanne; Thompson, Sarah—Landlord and Tenant (Covenants) Act 1995. Sweet & Maxwell's Legislation Handbook. Paperback: £12·50. ISBN 0–421–55410–X. Sweet & Maxwell.

Luba, Jan—Repairs: Tenants' Rights. Paperback. ISBN 0–905099–49–4. The Legal Action Group.

Male, J.M.—Landlord and Tenant. Paperback: £14·99. ISBN 0–7121–0863–7. Pitman Publishing.

Morris, John Rhys—Landlord and Tenant. Lecture Notes. Paperback: £17·95. ISBN 1–85941–045–6. Cavendish Publishing Ltd.

Pawlowski, M.—Law Questions and Answers: Landlord and Tenant. Paperback: £7·95. ISBN 1–85431–398–3. Blackstone Press.

Pawlowski, Mark; Brown, James—The Casebook on the Law of Landlord and Tenant. Paperback: £28·00. ISBN 0–421–50500–1. Sweet & Maxwell.

Sweet, Robert—Commercial Leases: Tenants' Amendments. Paperback: £35·00. ISBN 0–7520–0198–1. FT Law & Tax.

LAW REFORM

Clarkson, C.M.V.; Morgan, Rod—The Politics of Sentencing Reform. Hardback: £35·00. ISBN 0–19–825872–0. Clarendon Press.

McLean, Sheila A.M.—Law Reform and Medical Injury Litigation. Hardback: £37·50. ISBN 1–85521–534–9. Dartmouth.

Wice, Paul B.—Court Reform and Judicial Leadership. Hardback: £51·95. ISBN 0–275–95038–7. Praeger Publishers.

LEGAL AID

Hutton, Stuart—Criminal Lawyer's Transaction Pack. Transaction Packs. Unbound/looseleaf: £14·95. ISBN 0–85308–302–9. Jordans.

Pembridge, Eileen Meredith—Legal Aid Practice Manual. Unbound/looseleaf: £139·00. ISBN 0–7520–0098–5. FT Law & Tax.

LEGAL HISTORY

Cohen, David—Law, Violence, and Community in Classical Athens. Key Themes in Ancient History. Hardback: £35·00. ISBN 0–521–38167–3. Paperback: £12·95. ISBN 0–521–38837–6. Cambridge University Press.

LIBEL AND SLANDER

Braithwaite, Nick—International Libel Handbook. Hardback: £25·00. ISBN 0–7506–2488–4. Butterworth-Heinemann.

Scott-Bayfield, Julie—Defamation. Longman Practitioner Series. Paperback: £35·00. ISBN 0–85121–719–2. FT Law & Tax.

LICENSING

Stevens, Lawrence; Mehigan, Simon—Underhill's Licensing Guide. Practitioner Series. Paperback: £38·50. ISBN 0–7520–0212–0. FT Law & Tax.

Wilkof—Trade Mark Licensing. Hardback: £55·00. ISBN 0–421–44510–6. Sweet & Maxwell.

LIMITATION OF ACTIONS

Jones, Michael—Limitation Periods in Personal Injury Actions. Paperback: £24·95. ISBN 1–85431–286–3. Blackstone Press.

McNicol, Iain—Time Limits: The Index. Paperback: £30·00. ISBN 0–7520–0175–2. FT Law & Tax.

LOCAL GOVERNMENT

Himsworth, C.M.G.—Local Government etc. (Scotland) Act 1994. Paperback: £28·00. ISBN 0–414–01117–1. W. Green & Son.

MEDICINE

Barron, S. Leonard; Roberts, D.F.—Issues in Fetal Medicine. Studies in Biology, Economy and Society. Hardback: £45·00. ISBN 0–333–61552–2. Macmillan Press.

Bull, Ray H.C.; Carson, David—Handbook of Psychiatry in Legal Contexts. Hardback: £59·95. ISBN 0–471–94182–4. John Wiley and Sons.

Dimond, Brigit—Legal Aspects of Nursing. Paperback: £18·95. ISBN 0–13–190901–0. Prentice Hall US.

Guitton, Stephanie; Irons, Peter—Arguments on Abortion. ISBN 1–56584–223–5. The New Press.

Gunn, John; Taylor, Pamela J.—Forensic Psychiatry. Paperback: £65·00. ISBN 0–7506–2317–9. Butterworth-Heinemann.

Hurwitz, Brian—Clinical Guidelines and the Law. Paperback: £16·50. ISBN 1–85775–044–6. Radcliffe Medical Press.

Irwin, Stephen; Fazan, Claire; Allfrey, Richard—Medical Negligence Litigation: A Practitioner's Guide. Paperback: £35·00. ISBN 0–905099–55–9. Legal Action Group.

Jenkins, Rosemary—The Law and the Midwife. Paperback: £12·99. ISBN 0–632–03629–X. Blackwell Science.

Lewis, Charles—Medical Negligence: A Practical Guide Third Edition. £60·00. ISBN 1–86012–073–3. Blackstone Press.

McLean, Sheila—A Patient's Right to Know. Information Disclosure, the Doctor and the Law. Medico-Legal Series. Paperback: £16·95. ISBN 1–85521–021–5. Dartmouth.

McLean, Sheila A.M.—Law Reform and Medical Injury Litigation. Hardback: £37·50. ISBN 1–85521–534–9. Dartmouth.

Minns, Tracy—Quantum in Medical Negligence. Paperback: £20·00. ISBN 0–7520–0048–9. FT Law & Tax.

Newdick, Christopher—Who Should We Treat? Hardback: £40·00. ISBN 0–19–825924–7. Paperback: £15·99. ISBN 0–19–825925–5. Clarendon Press.

Obergfell, Ann M.—Law and Ethics in Diagnostic Imaging and Therapeutic Radiology. Paperback: £22·00. ISBN 0–7216–5062–7. WB Saunders.

Skone, John—AIDS and the Law. Medico-Legal Series. Paperback: £20·00. ISBN 1–85941–010–3. Cavendish Publishing Ltd.

Slovenko, Ralph—Psychiatry and Criminal Culpability. Hardback: £34·95. ISBN 0–471–05425–9. John Wiley and Sons.

Tingle, John; Cribb, A.—Nursing Law and Ethics. Paperback: £12·99. ISBN 0–632–03617–6. Blackwell Science.

Tingle, John; McHale, Jean—Law and Nursing. Paperback: £12·95. ISBN 0–7506–1594–X. Butterworth-Heinemann.

Tomkin, David; Hanafin, Patrick—Irish Medical Law. Hardback: £37·50. ISBN 1–85800–051–3. Round Hall Press.

Wagner, William Joseph—The Contractual Reallocation of Procreative Resources and Parental Rights. Medico-Legal Series. Hardback: £39·50. ISBN 1–85521–653–1. Dartmouth.

MENTAL HEALTH

Bull, Ray H.C.; Carson, David—Handbook of Psychiatry in Legal Contexts. Hardback: £59·95. ISBN 0–471–94182–4. John Wiley and Sons.

Donnelly, Anthony—Court of Protection Handbook. Practitioner Series. Paperback: £27·00. ISBN 0–7520–0231–7. Pearson Law Tax and Finance.

Gordon, Richard—Community Care Assessments. Paperback: £32·00. ISBN 0–7520–0222–8. FT Law & Tax.

Mackay, R.D.—Mental Condition Defences in the Criminal Law. Oxford Monographs on Criminal Law and Justice. Hardback: £35·00. ISBN 0–19–825995–6. Clarendon Press.

Veres III, John G.; Sims, Ronald R.—Human Resource Management and the Americans With Disabilities Act. Hardback: £49·50. ISBN 0–89930–857–0. Quorum Books.

MINORS

Allard, Amanda—Child Abuse Briefing Paper. Paperback: £2·50. The Children's Society.

Bloy, Duncan—Child Law. Lecture Notes Series. Paperback: £15·95. ISBN 1–874241–59–7. Cavendish Publishing Ltd.

Ceci, Stephen J.; Bruck, Maggie—Jeopardy in the Courtroom: A Scientific Analysis of Children's Testimony. Hardback: £26·95. ISBN 1–55798–282–1. American Psychological Association.

Colton, Matthew; Drury, Charlotte; Williams, Margaret—Children in Need. Hardback: £32·50. ISBN 1–85628–932–X. Avebury.

Donnelly, Anthony—Court of Protection Handbook. Practitioner Series. Paperback: £27·00. ISBN 0–7520–0231–7. Pearson Law Tax and Finance.

Jamieson, George—Child Custody and Abduction. Paperback: £30·00. ISBN 0–414–01093–0. W.Green & Son.

Kilbrandon, Lord—The Centre for the Study of the Child in Society. Kilbrandon Report. Children in Society. Hardback: £19·95. ISBN 0–11–495737–1. HMSO Books.

Levy, Allan—Custody and Access. Longman Practitioner Series. Paperback: £15·00. ISBN 0–85121–316–2. FT Law & Tax.

Plotnikoff, J.—Prosecuting Child Abuse: The Government's Speedy Progress Policy. Paperback: £14·50. ISBN 1–85431–404–1. Blackstone Press.

Timms, Judith—Children's Representation: A Practitioner's Guide. Paperback: £27·00. ISBN 0–421–49720–3. Sweet & Maxwell.

NATIONAL HEALTH

Du-Feu, Viv; Warnock, Owen—Employment Law in the NHS. Medico-Legal Series. Paperback: £20·00. ISBN 1–85941–016–2. Cavendish Publishing Ltd.

Harpwood, Vivienne—NHS Complaints: Litigation and Professional Discipline. Medico-Legal Series. Paperback: £20·00. ISBN 1–85941–012–X. Cavendish Publishing Ltd.

Longley, Diane—Health Care Constitutions. Medico-Legal Series. Paperback: £20·00. ISBN 1–85941–020–0. Cavendish Publishing Ltd.

NEGLIGENCE

Campbell, Dennis; Campbell, Christian—Professional Liability of Lawyers. Hardback: £95·00. ISBN 1–85044–869–8. Lloyd's of London Press.

Hurwitz, Brian—Clinical Guidelines and the Law. Paperback: £16·50. ISBN 1–85775–044–6. Radcliffe Medical Press.

Irwin, Stephen; Fazan, Claire; Allfrey, Richard—Medical Negligence Litigation: A Practitioner's Guide. Paperback: £35·00. ISBN 0–905099–55–9. Legal Action Group.

Jackson, Rupert; Powell, John—Jackson and Powell on Professional Negligence: Third Cumulative Supplement to the Third Edition. Common Law Library. Paperback: £22·00. ISBN 0–421–52180–5. Sweet & Maxwell.

Lavers, A.—Professional Negligence in the Construction Industry. Hardback: £27·00. ISBN 0–419–17900–3. E & FN Spon.

Lomas, Mark—Professional Negligence. Practitioner Series. Paperback: £38·00. ISBN 0–85121–087–2. FT Law & Tax.

Minns, Tracy—*Quantum* in Medical Negligence. Paperback: £20·00. ISBN 0–7520–0048–9. FT Law & Tax.

Scott, Walter—The General Practitioner and the Law of Negligence. Paperback: £19·95. ISBN 1–85941–023–5. Cavendish Publishing Ltd.

PARLIAMENT

Baldwin, Robert—Rules and Government. Oxford Socio-legal Studies. Hardback: £35·00. ISBN 0–19–825909–3. Clarendon Press.

Politics by Other Means. Hardback: £45·00. ISBN 0–415–90816–7. Paperback: £14·99. ISBN 0–415–90817–5. Routledge.

PARTNERSHIP

Floyd, Richard; Grier, Ian—Corporate Recovery. Paperback: £50·00. ISBN 0–7520–0105–1. FT Law & Tax.

Lindley; Banks—Lindley and Banks on Partnership. Hardback: £145·00. ISBN 0–421–48260–5. Sweet & Maxwell.

Sacker, Tony—Drafting Partnership Agreements. Paperback: £50·00. ISBN 0–85308–212–X. Jordans.

PARTNERSHIPS

Morse, Geoffrey—Partnership Law. Paperback: £11·95. ISBN 1–85431–439–4. Blackstone Press.

PATENTS AND DESIGNS

Dulken, S. van—British Patents of Invention, 1617–1977. Key Resources Series. Paperback. ISBN 0–7123–0817–2. The British Library.

Gilat, David—The Experimental Use Exemption from Patent Infringement Liability. Studies in Industrial Property and Copyright Law, 16. £60·00. ISBN 3–527–28660–8. VCH.

Holzman W., Richard T.—Infringement of the United States Patent Right. Hardback: £53·95. ISBN 0–89930–864–3. Quorum Books.

Paterson—A Concise Guide to European Patents: Law and Procedure. Paperback: £28·95. ISBN 0–421–53550–1. Sweet & Maxwell.

Singer, Romauld; Lunzer, Raph—The European Patent Convention. Hardback: £130·00. ISBN 0–421–52540–1. Sweet & Maxwell.

Takenaka, T.—Patent Claim in the U.S., Germany and Japan. IIC Studies. Paperback. ISBN 3–527–28725–6. VCH.

Vossius—European Patent Materials and Index. Paperback: £28·95. ISBN 0–421–53560–1. Sweet & Maxwell.

Wherry, Timothy Lee—Patent Searching for Librarians and Inventors. Paperback: £16·50. ISBN 0–8389–0641–9. ALA Books.

PENSIONS AND SUPERANNUATION

Calvert, Michael—Winding up of Pension Schemes. Pensions Reports. Hardback: £95·00. ISBN 0–7520–0141–8. FT Law & Tax.

Cooper, Neil; Hand, Sean—Pension Schemes and Liquidation. Hardback: £60·00. ISBN 0–85308–233–2. Jordans.

Dawes, Harriet; Samsworth, Jane—Guide to the Pensions Scheme Act. Paperback: £40·00. ISBN 0–7520–0031–4. FT Law & Tax.

Ellison, Robin—Pensions Disputes: Law, Practice and Alternatives. Paperback: £75·00. ISBN 0–7520–0059–4. Longman Law, Tax & Finance.

POLICE

Cape, Ed; Juqmani, Jawaid—Defending Suspects at Police Stations. Paperback: £30·00. ISBN 0–905099–63–X. Legal Action Group.

Harrison, John; Cragg, Stephen—Police Misconduct. Paperback: £25·00. ISBN 0–905099–58–3. The Legal Action Group.

Spiro, Brian; Bird, Steven—Police Station Adviser's Index. Hardback: £30·00. ISBN 0–7520–0130–2. FT Law & Tax.

PRACTICE (CIVIL)

Annual Practice 1995 (SCP). Paperback: £25·00. ISBN 421–53400–1. Sweet & Maxwell.

Benson, Stuart; Mayson, Stephen—Know-How for Litigation Lawyers. Know-How Series. Paperback. ISBN 0–7520–0050–0. FT Law & Tax

Biggs, A.K.; Rogers, A.P.—Probate Practice and Procedure. Paperback: £39·95. ISBN 0–85459–891–X. Tolley Publishing.

Bogle, Andrew; Fuller, John—Successful Debt Collecting. Paperback: £17·50. ISBN 0–85308–323–1. Jordans.

Boyle, Alan; Marshall, Philip; Jones, Philip; Kosmin, Leslie; Richards, David; Gillyon, Philip—The Practice and Procedure of the Companies Court. Lloyd's Commercial Law Library. Hardback. ISBN 1–85044–502–8. Lloyd's of London Press.

Campbell, Christian; Campbell, Dennis—International Civil Procedures. Hardback: £95·00. ISBN 1–85044–863–9. Lloyd's of London Press.

Cripps—The Legal Implications of Disclosure in the Public Interest. Hardback: £58·00. ISBN 421–50200–2. Sweet & Maxwell.

Darbyshire, P.—English Legal System in a Nutshell. Nutshells. Paperback: £4·95. ISBN 0–421–53320–X. Sweet & Maxwell.

Edwards, Alicia Betsy—The Practice of Court Interpreting. Benjamins Translation Library, 6. Hardback. ISBN 90–272–1602–9. Paperback. ISBN 90–272–1603–7. John Benjamins Publishing Company.

PRACTICE (CIVIL)—*cont.*

Gerlis, S.; Blackford, R.—County Court Practice Handbook: 1995–96. Practitioner Series. Paperback: £28·00. ISBN 0–7520–0191–4. FT Law & Tax.

Goodman, Andrew—The Court Guide 1995. Paperback: £10·95. ISBN 1–85431–406–8. Blackstone Press.

Greens Annotated Rules of Court 1995. Paperback: £35·00. ISBN 0–414–01123–6. W.Green & Son.

Helme, W.—Handbook of Procedures in Magistrates' Courts. Spiralbound: £15·50. ISBN 0–7219–0474–2. Shaw & Sons.

Hurst, Peter—Civil Costs. Litigation Library. Hardback: £100·00. ISBN 0–421–50710–1. Sweet & Maxwell.

Inns of Court School of Law: Bar Exam Material. Chancery Practice 1994/95. Paperback: £21·95. ISBN 1–85431–392–4. Blackstone Press.

Inns of Court School of Law: Bar Exam Material. Commercial Practice 1994/95. Paperback: £21·95. ISBN 1–85431–391–6. Blackstone Press.

Inns of Court School of Law: Bar Exam Material. General Practice 1994/95. Paperback: £21·95. ISBN 1–85431–390–8. Blackstone Press.

Jacob, Sir Jack; Adams, J.D.R.; Turner, R.L.; Jones, C.F.—Chitty and Jacob's Queen's Bench Forms: Eighth Cumulative Supplement to the 21st Edition. Common Law Library. Paperback: £26·00. ISBN 0–421–54170–9. Sweet & Maxwell.

Lane, P.—Inns of Court Bar Manuals: Advocacy, Negotiation and Conference Skills 1995/1996. Paperback: £21·95. ISBN 1–85431–422–X. Blackstone Press.

Lane, P.—Inns of Court Bar Manuals: Civil Litigation 1995/1996. Paperback: £21·95. ISBN 1–85431–426–2. Blackstone Press.

Lane, P.—Inns of Court Bar Manuals: Evidence and Casework Skills 1995/1996. Paperback: £21·95. ISBN 1–85431–423–8. Blackstone Press.

Lane, P.—Inns of Court Bar Manuals: Opinion Writing and Drafting 1995/1996. Paperback: £21·95. ISBN 1–85431–425–4. Blackstone Press.

Lane, P.—Inns of Court Bar Manuals: Remedies and Practical Background 1995/1996. Paperback: £21·95. ISBN 1–85431–427–0. Blackstone Press.

Matthews, Paul; Malek, Hodge—Discovery: Second Supplement to the First Edition. Litigation Library. Paperback: £21·00. ISBN 0–421–53680–2. Sweet & Maxwell.

McEwan—Practical Pleading. Paperback: £19·95. Sweet & Maxwell.

Morris, Gordon—Shaw's Directory of Courts in the United Kingdom: 1995/96. Paperback: £32·00. ISBN 0–7219–1402–0. Shaw & Sons.

Osborne, Craig—Legal Practice Course Guides: Civil Litigation 1995/1996. Paperback: £14·95. ISBN 1–85431–417–3. Blackstone Press.

Perry, Gren; Wright, Sue; Ballard, Joanna—Civil Litigation: 1995/96. Legal Practice Course Resource books. Paperback: £15·00. ISBN 0–85308–284–7. Jordans.

Robson, Michelle—Legal Practice Course Case Studies: Civil Litigation 1995–1996. Paperback: £9·95. ISBN 1–85431–476–9. Blackstone Press.

Silverstein, Mark—Judicious Choices. Hardback: £17·50. ISBN 0–393–03692–8. W.W. Norton.

Sime, Stuart—A Practical Approach to Civil Procedure. Paperback: £21·00. ISBN 1–85431–481–5. Blackstone Press.

Simon, Robert I.—Post-Traumatic Stress Disorder in Litigation. Hardback: £25·95. ISBN 0–88048–687–2. American Psychiatric Press.

Weinstein, Jack—Individual Justice in Mass Tort Litigations. Hardback: £28·00. ISBN 0–8101–1188–8. Northwestern University Press.

Williams, Crispin—Shaw's Directory of Tribunals and Regulatory Bodies: 1995. Paperback: £15·00. ISBN 0–7219–1410–1. Shaw & Sons.

PRESS

Crone, Tom—Law and the Media. Paperback: £16·99. ISBN 0–7506–2008–0. Butterworth-Heinemann.

McKain, Bruce; Bonnington Alistair Scots Law for Journalists. Paperback: £19·95. ISBN 0–414–01005–1. W. Green & Son.

Mecklermedia—Business and Legal CD-ROMs in Print: 1995. Paperback: £39·95. ISBN 0–88736–990–1. Mecklermedia.

Wacks, Raymond—Privacy and Press Freedom. Paperback: £16·95. ISBN 1–85431–454–8. Blackstone Press.

PRISONS

McManus, J.—Prisons, Prisoners and the Law. Paperback: £24·00. ISBN 0–414–01019–1. W. Green.

PUBLIC ENTERTAINMENTS AND RECREATION

Armstrong, Mark; Lindsay, David; Watterson, Ray—Media Law in Australia. Paperback: £15·99. ISBN 0–19–553603–7. O.U.P., Australia.

Bate, Stephen; Barendt, Eric; Dickens, Julian; Michael, James—The Yearbook of Media and Entertainment Law: Vol. 1. 1995. Hardback: £125·00. ISBN 0–19–825927–1. Clarendon Press.

PUBLIC ENTERTAINMENTS AND RECREATION—*cont.*

Crone, Tom—Law and the Media. Paperback: £16·95. ISBN 0–7506–2008–0. Butterworth-Heinemann.

Grant and Mason—Holiday Law. Paperback: £21·95. ISBN 0–421–51340–3. Sweet & Maxwell.

Meinel, Wulf—Frontiers of European Broadcasting Legislation. European Media Mongraphs. Paperback: £7·95. ISBN 0–85170–413–1. BFI Publishing.

Nelson, Vincent—The Law of Entertainment and Broadcasting. Hardback: £87·00. ISBN 0–421–50150–2. Sweet & Maxwell.

RATING AND VALUATION

Mackmin, David; Askham, Philip—Rating Law: The Uniform Business Rate. Hardback: £50·00. ISBN 0–421–52570–3. Sweet & Maxwell.

RESTITUTION

Rose, Francis—Blackstone's Statutes on Contract, Tort and Restitution 1995/1996. Paperback: £8·95. Blackstone Press.

Stewart, B.—Restitution in Scotland. First Supplement to the First Edition. Paperback: £19·95. ISBN 0–414–01118–X. Sweet & Maxwell.

REVENUE AND FINANCE

Arrowsmith, Peter; Thornton, Grant—A Practical Guide to Social Security Contributions: 1995/1996. Unbound/looseleaf: £22·00. ISBN 1–85355–584–3. Accountancy Books Digests.

Bartlett, Joseph W.—Venture Capital and Equity Finance. Hardback: £266·95. ISBN 0–471–01464–8. John Wiley.

Bean, Gerard M.D.—Fiduciary Obligations and Joint Operating Agreements. Hardback: £50·00. ISBN 0–19–825928–X. Clarendon Press.

Bryant, Roger—Developments in Group Accounts. Unbound/looseleaf: £22·00. ISBN 1–85355–570–3. Accountancy Books Digests.

Casna, Richard—International Joint Ventures: The Legal and Tax Issues. Money Manager's Library. Paperback: £125·00. ISBN 1–85271–330–5. IBC Publishing.

Derwent, R.J.—Charities. Paperback: £55·00. ISBN 1–85355–408–1. Accountancy Books.

Farmer, Paul; Lyal, Richard—E.C. Tax Law. Oxford European Community Law Series. Hardback: £55·00. ISBN 0–19–825764–3. Clarendon Press.

Foreman, A.; Taylor, D.—Allied Dunbar Business Tax and Law Handbook. Hardback: £23·00. ISBN 0–7520–0073–X. FT Law & Tax.

Foreman, Tony—Don't Pay Too Much Inheritance Tax. Allied Dunbar Personal Finance Guides. Paperback: £7·99. ISBN 1–85788–093–5. Nicholas Brealey Publishing.

Gammie, Malcolm—Tax Effective Remuneration. Tax Strategy. Paperback: £75·00. ISBN 0–85121–645–5. FT Law & Tax.

Hancock, P.J.—Taxation. Chapman & Hall Series in Accounting and Finance. Paperback: £19·99. ISBN 0–412–63940–8. Chapman and Hall.

Homer, Arnold; Burrows, Rita—Tolley's Tax Guide: 1995–96. Tolley's Tax Annual. Hardback: £24·95. ISBN 1–86012–014–8. Tolley Publishing.

Littlefair, H.—Allied Dunbar Investment and Savings Handbook: 1995–96. Hardback: £21·00. ISBN 0–7520–0075–6. FT Law & Tax.

Maas, Robert; Scott, Jacqueline—Property Taxes: 1995–96. Tax. Paperback: £36·95. ISBN 1–86012–036–9. Tolley Publishing.

Matthews, Jan; Eastaway, Nigel—Tolley's Self-Assessment. £35·95. ISBN 1–86012–038–5. Tolley.

McBurnie, R.—A Guide to the Finance Act 1995. Unbound/looseleaf: £22·00. ISBN 1–85355–598–3. Accountancy Books Digests.

Morris, Simon—Financial Services: Regulating Investment Business. Hardback: £55·00. ISBN 0–7520–0041–1. FT Law & Tax.

Noakes, Patrick; Mackley-Smith, Gary B.—Tolley's Capital Gains Tax: 1995/96. Paperback: £29·95. ISBN 1–86012–010–5. Tolley Publishing.

Norton, Joseph J.—Devising International Bank Supervisory Standards. International Banking and Finance Law. Hardback: £82·00. ISBN 1–85966–185–8. Martinus Nijhoff Publishers.

Phillips, D.; Eastaway, N.—Allied Dunbar Expatriate Tax and Investment Handbook. Hardback: £21·00. ISBN 0–7520–0166–3. FT Law & Tax.

Rawnsley, Judith—Going for Broke. Hardback: £14·99. ISBN 0–00–255659–6. HarperCollins.

Rayfuse, R.—ICSID Reports: Vol. 3. ICSID Reports, 3.00. Hardback: £120·00. ISBN 0–521–47512–0. Cambridge University Press.

Revesz, Richard L.; Stewart, Richard B.—Analyzing Superfund. Hardback: £33·00. ISBN 0–915707–75–6. Resources for the Future.

Rowes, Peter—Taxation: 1995/1996. Complete Course Texts. Paperback: £11·95. ISBN 1–85805–126–6. DP Publications.

Saunders, Glyn; Dolton, Alan—Corporation Tax: 1995/96. Tolley's Tax Annual. Paperback: £28·95. ISBN 1–86012–011–3. Tolley Publishing.

Saunders, Ian—Remedies in Taxation. Hardback: £25·00. ISBN 0–471–96080–2. John Wiley and Sons.

REVENUE AND FINANCE—*cont.*

Scott, Jacqueline—Tolley's Official Tax Statements: 1995–96. Paperback: £39·95. ISBN 1–86012–035–0. Tolley Publishing.

St. John Webster, Rory—Short and Medium Term Securities Markets. Finance and Capital Markets Series. Paperback: £85·00. ISBN 0–333–57546–6. Macmillan Press.

Stary, Erica—Transactions: High Net Worth Individuals. Transactions. Paperback: £65·00. ISBN 0–85121–958–6. FT Law & Tax.

Suratgar, D.; MacDonald, G.—International Project Finance: Law and Practice. Hardback: £85·00. ISBN 0–85121–836–9. FT Law & Tax.

Taylor, Anthony; Steward, Clive—The Equitable Life Tax Guide: 99th Edition. Paperback: £19·99. ISBN 0–631–19842–3. Blackwell Publishers.

Tingley, K.R.—Roll-over, Hold-over and Retirement Reliefs. Paperback: £39·95. ISBN 1–86012–037–7. Tolley Publishing.

Tolley's Official Tax Statements 1995–96. Paperback: £39.95. ISBN 1–86012–035–0. Tolley Publishing.

Tolley's Tax Planning 1995–96. Paperback: £69.50. ISBN 1–86012–021–0. Tolley Publishing.

Tolley's Taxation of Foreign Exchange Gains and Losses. £49·95. ISBN 0–85459–851–0. Tolley Publishing.

van Houtte, Hans; Schrans—International Trade and Finance Law. Hardback: £130·00. ISBN 0–421–48090–4. Sweet & Maxwell.

Wareham, Robert—Tolley's Value Added Tax: 1995–96. Paperback: £28·95. ISBN 1–86012–012–1. Tolley Publishing.

Wood—Comparative Financial Law. Hardback: £75·00. ISBN 0–421–54280–2. Sweet & Maxwell.

ROAD TRAFFIC

Wallis, Peter—Wilkinson's Road Traffic Offences: Vols. 1 and 2. Paperback: £215·00. ISBN 0–7520–0184–1. FT Law & Tax.

SALE OF GOODS

Atiyah, P.S.; Adams, J.N.—Sale of Goods. Paperback: £24·95. ISBN 0–273–60301–9. Pitman Publishing.

Ervine, W. Cowan, H.—Consumer Law in Scotland. Paperback: £19,95. ISBN 0–414–01064–7. W. Green & Son.

Furmston, Michael P.—Sale and Supply of Goods. Paperback: £14·95. ISBN 1–85941–281–5. Cavendish Publishing Ltd.

Harvey, Brian; Meisel, Franklin—The Law and Practice of Auctions. Hardback: £45·00. ISBN 0–19–825908–5. Oxford University Press.

McRobb, Max; Dole, Robert—The Product Liability Risk Minimisation Book. Paperback: £18·00. ISBN 0–951–20786–5. Sydney Jary Ltd.

Read, P.A.—Commercial Law: Sale of Goods, Consumer Credit and Agency: Textbook 1995–1996. Bachelor of Laws. Paperback: £18·95. ISBN 0–7510–0536–3. HLT Publications.

Read, P.A.—Sale of Goods and Credit: Textbook 1995–1996. Bar Examinations. Paperback: £18·95. ISBN 0–7510–0559–2. HLT Publications.

Sassoon, D.; Merren, H.O.—CIF and FOB Contracts. Hardback: £130·00. ISBN 0–421–51320–9. Sweet & Maxwell.

Sellar, David—Sale of Goods. ICAS. Paperback: £15·00. ISB 0–414–01106–6. W.Green & Son.

SHIPPING AND MARINE INSURANCE

Brice, Geoffrey—Maritime Law of Salvage: First Supplement to the Second Edition. Paperback: £10·00. ISBN 0–421–54620–4. Sweet & Maxwell.

Bundock, Michael—Shipping Law Handbook. Unbound/looseleaf: £60·00. ISBN 1–85044–889–2. Lloyd's of London Press.

De Wit, Ralph—Multimodal Transport. Lloyd's Shipping Law Library. Hardback: £78·00. ISBN 1–85044–894–9. Lloyd's of London Press.

Forbes, Vivian Louis—The Maritime Boundaries of the Indian Ocean Region. Hardback: £49·95. ISBN 9971–69–192–2. Paperback: £33·95. ISBN 9971–69–189–2. Singapore University Press.

Gaskell, Nicholas; Debattista, Charles—Chorley and Giles' Shipping Law. Paperback: £35·99. ISBN 0–273–03789–7. Pitman Publishing.

Packard, William—Shipping Pools. Hardback: £45·00. ISBN 1–85044–512–5. Lloyd's of London Press.

Rose, Francis—Lloyd's Maritime and Commercial Law Quarterly Index 1974–1994. Hardback: £75·00. ISBN 1–85044–804–3. Lloyd's of London Press.

SOCIAL SECURITY

Arrowsmith, Peter; Thornton, Grant—A Practical Guide to Social Security Contributions: 1995/1996. Unbound/looseleaf: £22·00. ISBN 1–85355–584–3. Accountancy Books Digests.

Bonner, D.; Hooker, I.; White, Robin—Non-Means Tested Benefits: The Legislation 1995. Paperback: £30·00. ISBN 0–421–53980–1. Sweet & Maxwell.

SOCIAL SECURITY—*cont.*

Boyd, Philip; Howard, Hugh—Social Welfare Benefits. Paperback: £26·00. ISBN 0–7520–0167–1. FT Law & Tax.

Brayne, Hugh—Law for Social Workers. Paperback: £14·95. ISBN 1–85431–442–4. Blackstone Press.

Dalrymple, Jane; Burke, Beverley—Anti-oppressive Practice: Social Care and the Law. Paperback: £12·99. ISBN 0–335–19193–2. Open University Press.

Doyle, Brian—Disability, Discrimination and Equal Opportunities. Studies in Labour and Social Law. Hardback: £55·00. ISBN 0–7201–2242–2. Paperback: £20·00. ISBN 0–7201–2244–9. Mansell.

Taylor; McDonald—The Law and the Elderly. Hardback: £45·00. ISBN 0–421–49850–1. Sweet & Maxwell.

Williams, John—Social Services Law. Paperback: £29·95. ISBN 0–85459–824–3. Tolley Publishing.

SOLICITORS

Campbell, Dennis; Campbell, Christian—Professional Liability of Lawyers. Hardback: £95·00. ISBN 1–85044–869–8. Lloyd's of London Press.

Clayton, Cornell W.—Government Lawyers. Studies in Government and Public Policy. Hardback: £31·50. ISBN 0–7006–0706–4. University Press of Kansas.

COMBAR—COMBAR: The Commercial Bar Association Directory 1995. Hardback: £20·00. ISBN 1–85431–403–3. Blackstone Press.

Cranston, Ross—Legal Ethics and Professional Responsibility. Hardback: £30·00. ISBN 0–19–825931–X. Clarendon Press.

Cross, Ian; Gibson, Andrew; Hawes, Rachel; Holtom, John; Mott, Peter; Petley, Michael; Thomas, Allun; Tonge, Victor—Skills for Lawyers: 1995/96. Legal Practice Course Resource books. Paperback: £15·00. ISBN 0–85308–283–9. Jordans.

Davies, M.—Legal Marketing. Paperback: £10·95. ISBN 1–85431–376–2. Blackstone Press.

Dezalay, Yves; Sugarman, David—Professional Competition and Professional Power. Hardback: £45·00. ISBN 0–415–09362–7. Routledge.

Freedman, Warren—A Guide to Malpractice Liability for Legal and Law-related Professions. Hardback: £62·95. ISBN 0–89930–909–7. Quorum Books.

Gill, Brian—An Advocate's Tale. Paperback: £9·95. ISBN 1–898218–08–0. Scottish Cultural Press.

Halberstadt—Accounts for Solicitors. Paperback: £15·95. ISBN 421–52970–9. Sweet & Maxwell.

Hyam, Michael—Advocacy Skills. Paperback: £9·95. ISBN 1–85431–414–9. Blackstone Press.

Jones, Philip—Legal Practice Course Guides: Lawyers' Skills 1995/1996. Paperback: £14·95. ISBN 1–85431–421–1. Blackstone Press.

Klafter, Craig—Legal Practice Management and Quality Standards. Paperback: £16·95. ISBN 1–85431–323–1. Blackstone Press.

Lentz, Bernard F.; Laband, David N.—Sex Discrimination in the Legal Profession. Hardback: £44·95. ISBN 0–89930–928–3. Quorum Books.

Maynard P.—Financial Awareness for Lawyers. Lawyers Handbook Series. Paperback: £16·95. ISBN 1–874241–03–1. Cavendish Publishing Ltd.

Pannett, Alan—Managing the Law Firm. Paperback: £10·95. ISBN 1–85431–457–2. Blackstone Press.

Weisbord, Ellen; Charnov, Bruce H.; Lindsey, Jonathan—Managing People in Today's Law firm. Hardback: £53·95. ISBN 0–89930–834–1. Quorum Books.

STAMP DUTIES

Gregory, Roger—Stamp Duties for Conveyancers. Practitioner Series. Paperback: £35·00. ISBN 0–7520–0168–X. FT Law & Tax.

Gregory, Roger—Stamp Duties for Conveyancers. Practitioner Series. Paperback: £35·00. ISBN 0–7520–0168–X. FT Law & Tax.

STATUTES AND ORDERS

Christie, A.—Intellectual Property Statutes. Paperback. Paperback: £13·00. ISBN 0–85431–386–X. Blackstone Press.

Companies Act Handbook and Index. Third Edition. Paperback: £16·95. ISBN 0–9505745–5–4. Ernst & Young.

Evans, Della—Agricultural Tenancies Act 1995. Paperback: £14·50. ISBN 0–421–54590–0. Sweet & Maxwell.

Glazebrook, Peter—Blackstone's Statutes on Criminal Law 1995/1996. Paperback: £8·95. ISBN 1–85431–430–0. Blackstone Press.

Goodman, Andrew; Wasik, M.; Taylor, R.—Guide to the Criminal Justice and Public Order Act 1994. Hardback: £19·95. ISBN 1–85431–401–7. Blackstone Press.

Home, Henry—Elucidations Respecting the Common and Statute Law of Scotland. Hardback: £55·00. ISBN 1–85506–421–9. Thoemmes Press.

Huxley, Phil—Blacktone's Statutes on Evidence. Paperback: £8·95. ISBN 1–85431–436–X. Blackstone Press.

STATUTES AND ORDERS—*cont.*

Kerr, Tony—Termination of Employment Statutes. Paperback: £35·00. ISBN 0–421–53080–4. Sweet & Maxwell.

Kidner, Richard—Blackstone's Statutes on Employment Law 1995–1996. Paperback: £10·95. ISBN 1–85431–431–9. Blackstone Press.

Marmor, Andrei—Law and Interpretation. Hardback: £35·00. ISBN 0–19–825875–5. Clarendon Press.

Moore, Victor—Statutes on Planning Law. Paperback: £12·00. ISBN 1–85431–125–5. Blackstone Press.

Oldham, Mika—Blackstone's Statutes on Family Law 1995–1996. Paperback: £11·95. ISBN 1–85431–434–7. Blackstone Press.

Reid—Requirements of Writing (Scotland Act 1995). Paperback: £16·00. ISBN 0–414–01131–7. W.Green & Son.

Rose, Francis—Blackstone's Statutes on Commercial Law and Consumer Law 1995/1996. Paperback: £12·95. ISBN 1–85431–473–4. Blackstone Press.

Rose, Francis—Blackstone's Statutes on Contract, Tort and Restitution 1995/1996. Paperback: £8·95. Blackstone Press.

Thomas, Meryl—Blackstone's Statutes on Property Law 1995/1996. Paperback: £11·95. ISBN 1–85431–433–5. Blackstone Press.

Wallington, Peter—Blackstone's Statutes on Public Law 1995–1996. Paperback: £11·95. Blackstone Press.

TAXATION

Andrews, J.; White, B.—Taxation of Directors and Employees: The Law under Schedule E. Paperback: £45·00. ISBN 1–85355–566–5. Accountancy Books.

Homer, Arnold; Burrows, Rita—Tolley's Tax Guide: 1995–96. Tolley's Tax Annual. Hardback: £24·95. ISBN 1–86012–014–8. Tolley Publishing.

TELECOMMUNICATIONS

Armstrong, Mark; Lindsay, David; Watterson, Ray—Media Law in Australia. Paperback: £15·99. ISBN 0–19–553603–7. O.U.P., Australia.

Barendt, Eric M.—Broadcasting Law. Paperback: £17·95. ISBN 0–19–826021–0. Clarendon Press.

Nelson, Vincent—The Law of Entertainment and Broadcasting. Hardback: £87·00. ISBN 0–421–50150–2. Sweet & Maxwell.

TORT

Clark, Peter—SWOT Law of Torts. Paperback: £8·95. ISBN 1–85431–343–6. Blackstone Press.

Connell, Lee; Callahan, Michael T.—Construction Defect Claims and Litigation. Hardback: £76·95. ISBN 0–471–11873–7. John Wiley and Sons.

Cooke, John—Law of Tort. Pitman Law Textbook Series. Paperback: £19·99. ISBN 0–273–61413–4. Pitman Publishing.

Green, David—Tort. Question and Answer Series. Paperback: £8·95. ISBN 1–85941–266–1. Cavendish Publishing Ltd.

Harlow, Carol—Understanding Tort Law. Understanding Law. Paperback: £7·99. ISBN 0–00–686338–8. Fontana.

Logan, John—Briefcase on Tort Law. Briefcase Series. Paperback: £9·95. ISBN 1–85941–245–9. Cavendish Publishing Ltd.

McLachlan, Campbell; Nygh, Peter—Transnational Tort Litigation. Hardback: £50·00. ISBN 0–19–825919–0. Clarendon Press.

Pannett, Alan—Law of Torts. Paperback: £12·99. ISBN 0–7121–1055–0. Pitman Publishing.

Pitchfork, E.D.—Tort: Revision Workbook. Bachelor of Laws. Paperback: £9·95. ISBN 0–7510–0607–6. HLT Publications.

Pitchfork, E.D.—Tort: Textbook 1995–1996. Bachelor of Laws. Paperback: £16·95. ISBN 0–7510–0532–0. HLT Publications.

Pitchfork, E.D.—Tort: Textbook 1995–1996. Common Professional Examinations. Paperback: £16·95. ISBN 0–7510–0551–7. HLT Publications.

Rose, Francis—Blackstone's Statutes on Contract, Tort and Restitution 1995/1996. Paperback: £8·95. Blackstone Press.

Simon, Robert I.—Post-Traumatic Stress Disorder in Litigation. Hardback: £25·95. ISBN 0–88048–687–2. American Psychiatric Press.

Tayfoor—Tort Law Cartoons. Paperback: £6·95. ISBN 1–421–53810–4. Sweet & Maxwell.

Weinstein, Jack—Individual Justice in Mass Tort Litigations. Hardback: £28·00. ISBN 0–8101–1188–8. Northwestern University Press.

TOWN AND COUNTRY PLANNING

Banks, Sandra; Casely-Hayford, Margaret—Practical Planning: Applications and Permissions. Longman Practitioner Series. Paperback: £45·00. ISBN 0–7520–0063–2. FT Law & Tax.

TOWN AND COUNTRY PLANNING—*cont.*

Blanning, John—Practical Planning. Practitioner Series Planning Library. Hardback: £45·00. ISBN 0–7520–0144–2. FT Law & Tax.

Cockram, Richard—Drafting Construction Agreements. Paperback: £60·00. ISBN 0–85308–228–6. Jordans.

Moore, Victor—Statutes on Planning Law. Paperback: £12·00. ISBN 1–85431–125–5. Blackstone Press.

Mynors, Charles—Listed Buildings and Conservation Areas. Longman Practitioner Series. Paperback: £45·00. ISBN 0–85121–902–0. FT Law & Tax.

Scannell, Yvonne—Environmental and Planning Law. Hardback: £65·00. ISBN 1–858000–022–5. The Round Hall Press.

Soares, Patrick C.—VAT Planning for Property Transactions. Hardback: £65·00. ISBN 0–7520–0045–4. FT Law & Tax.

TRADE AND INDUSTRY

Bond, Helen—Business Law. Paperback: £15·95. ISBN 1–85431–437–8. Blackstone Press.

Connolly, Michael—Briefcase on Commercial Law. Briefcase Series. Paperback: £9·95. ISBN 1–85941–241–6. Cavendish Publishing Ltd.

Cooke, Darryl—Venture Capital: Law and Practice. Commercial Series. Hardback: £65·00. ISBN 0–7520–0143–4. FT Law & Tax.

Dunfee, Thomas W. et al—Modern Business Law. Hardback: £42·95. ISBN 0–07–018212–4. McGraw-Hill Book Company.

Gilmore, William C.—Mutual Assistance in Criminal and Business Regulatory Matters. Cambridge International Documents Series. Hardback: £55·00. ISBN 0–521–47297–0. Cambridge University Press.

Harvey, Alison; Harvey, Andrew; Longshaw, Alexis; Sewell, Tim—Business Law and Practice: 1995/96. Legal Practice Course Resource Books. Paperback: £17·50. ISBN 0–85308–286–3. Jordans.

Harvey, Andrew—Business Law and Practice: Legislation Handbook 1995/96. Legal Practice Course Resource books. Paperback: £15·00. ISBN 0–85308–287–1. Jordans.

Hawkes, Leonard; Snyder, Francis G.—Customs and Commercial Policy in Europe. Hardback: £60·00. ISBN 0–406–16701–X. Butterworth Law.

Kadar, A.; Hoyle, K.; Whitehead, Geoffrey—Business Law Made Simple. Paperback: £9·99. ISBN 0–7506–2551–1. Made Simple (an imprint of Butterworth-Heinemann).

Kadar, Abby; Whitehead, Geoffrey—Export Law. Paperback: £15·95. ISBN 0–13–434218–6. Prentice Hall/Woodhead-Faulkner.

Macintyre, Ewan—Advanced GNVQ Business Law. Paperback: £16·99. ISBN 0–273–61239–5. Pitman Publishing.

Podesta, Mary—Business Law. Paperback: £12·99. ISBN 0–340–63162–7. Hodder & Stoughton Educational.

Pope, Colin; Ellis, Peter—Working with the Unions. Law and Employment. Paperback: £15·95. ISBN 0–85292–608–1. Institute of Personnel and Development.

Quality Law Group—Business Client Handbook. Ringbinder: £99·00. ISBN 0–7520–0189–2. FT Law & Tax.

Read, P.A.—Commercial Law: Revision Workbook. Bachelor of Laws. Paperback: £9·95. ISBN 0–7510–0592–4. HLT Publications.

Read, P.A.—Commercial Law: Sale of Goods, Consumer Credit and Agency: Textbook 1995–1996. Bachelor of Laws. Paperback: £18·95. ISBN 0–7510–0536–3. HLT Publications.

van Houtte, Hans; Schrans—International Trade and Finance Law. Hardback: £130·00. ISBN 0–421–48090–4. Sweet & Maxwell.

TRADE MARKS AND TRADE NAMES

Kitchin, David; Mellor, James—The Trade Marks Act 1994. Current Law Statutes Reprint. Paperback: £25·00. ISBN 0–421–53300–5. Sweet & Maxwell.

The Trade Mark Register of the United States. Hardback. ISBN 0–911522–67–0. The Trademark Register.

Wilkof—Trade Mark Licensing. Hardback: £55·00. ISBN 0–421–44510–6. Sweet & Maxwell.

Zaichowsky, Judith Lynne—Defending Your Brand against Imitation. Hardback: £44·95. ISBN 0–89930–829–5. Quorum Books.

TRADE UNIONS

Pope, Colin; Ellis, Peter—Working with the Unions. Law and Employment. Paperback: £15·95. ISBN 0–85292–608–1. Institute of Personnel and Development.

TRANSPORT

De Wit, Ralph—Multimodal Transport. Lloyd's Shipping Law Library. Hardback: £78·00. ISBN 1–85044–894–9. Lloyd's of London Press.

Dobbs; Lucraft—Road Traffic Law and Practice. Third Edition. Hardback: £58·00. ISBN 0–421–54220–9. Sweet & Maxwell.

Dooley, Frank J.; Thoms, William E.—Railroad Law a Decade after Deregulation. Hardback: £49·50. ISBN 0–89930–631–4. Quorum Books.

VALUE ADDED TAX

Hamilton, Penny; Dolton, Alan—VAT and Duties Appeals. Paperback: £29·95. ISBN 1–86012–174–8. Tolley Publishing.

Slater, Brian—Essential VAT for Property Practitioners. Paperback: £35·00. ISBN 0–7520–0157–4. FT Law & Tax.

WILLS AND SUCCESSION

Biggs, A.K.; Rogers, A.P.—Probate Practice and Procedure. Paperback: £39·95. ISBN 0–85459–891–X. Tolley Publishing.

Blake-Roberts, Philippa; Prettejohn, Philip—Know-how for Trust and Estate Practitioners. Know-how Series. Paperback: £43·00. ISBN 0–7520–0091–8. FT Law & Tax.

Dyson, Henry—Noter-up: French Real Property and Succession Law. Paperback: £4·99. ISBN 0–7090–5680–X. Robert Hale.

Finch, Janet; Masson, Judith; Mason, Jennifer; Hayes, Lynn; Wallis, Lorraine—Wills, Inheritance and the Family. Oxford Socio-legal Studies. Hardback: £25·00. ISBN 0–19–825834–8. Clarendon Press.

Miles, George—Legal Practice Course Guides: Wills, Probate and Administration 1995/1996. Paperback: £14·95. ISBN 1–85431–420–3. Blackstone Press.

Pettit, D.M.; Riddett, R.E.—The Will Draftsman's Handbook. Paperback: £45·00. ISBN 0–7520–0140–X. FT Law & Tax.

Ryan, Michael—Executorship and Administration. Lawyers' Practice and Procedure. Paperback: £34·95. ISBN 1–86012–049–0. Tolley Publishing.

Scobbie, Eilidh—Currie on Confirmation. Green's Practice Library. Hardback: £75·00. ISBN 0–414–01006–X. W.Green & Son.

Spedding, Linda S.—Succession: Textbook 1995–1996. Bachelor of Laws. Paperback: £18·95. ISBN 0–7510–0543–6. HLT Publications.

NORTHERN IRELAND

CRIMINAL EVIDENCE AND PROCEDURE

Greer, Steven—Supergrasses: Anti-terrorist Law Enforcement in Northern Ireland. Hardback: £35·00. ISBN 0–19–825766–X. Clarendon Press.

SCOTLAND

BANKRUPTCY

Adie—Bankruptcy. Paperback: £17·50. ISBN 0–414–01108–2. W.Green & Son.

McBryde—Bankruptcy. Hardback: £98. ISBN 0–414–01063–9. W.Green & Son.

CHILDREN AND YOUNG PERSONS

Jamieson—Parental Responsibilities. Paperback: £40. ISBN 0 414 01093–0. W.Green & Son

CONSUMER PROTECTION

Ervine, W.C.H.—Consumer Law in Scotland. Paperback: £19·95. ISBN 0–414–01064–7. W.Green & Son.

CONTRACT

Reid—Requirements of Writing (Scotland) Act 1995. Paperback: £16·00. ISBN 0–414–01131–7. W.Green & Son.

Wilson *et al.*—Gloag & Henderson (10th ed.). Hardback: £98·00 ISBN 0–414–01068–X. W.Green & Son.

CRIMINAL LAW

Greens Criminal Statutes 1995. Paperback: £26·00. ISBN 0–414–01125–2. W.Green & Son.

EDUCATION

Marr, Robert; Marr, Catherine—Education Law. Paperback: £28·00. ISBN 0–414–01040–X. W.Green & Son.

EUROPEAN UNION

Burrows—Greens Guide to European Law. Paperback: £28·00. ISBN 0–414–01111–2. W.Green & Son.

FIREARMS AND EXPLOSIVES

Bradley, J.—Firearms. Paperback: £32·00. ISBN 0–414–01089–2. W.Green & Son.

JURISDICTION

Beaumont, P.—Civil Jurisdiction in Scotland. Second edition. Hardback: £95·00. ISBN 0–414–01017–5. W.Green & Son.

LEGAL HISTORY

Marshall, Enid—General Principles of Scots Law. Paperback: £21·00. ISBN 0–414–01127–9. W.Green & Son.

LOCAL GOVERNMENT

Himsworth, C.—The Local Government (Scotland) Act 1994. Greens Annotated Act. Paperback: £28·00. ISBN 0–414–01117–1. W.Green & Son.

PARTNERSHIP

Bennetts—Partnership. Paperback: £17·50. ISBN 0–414–01107–4. W.Green & Son.

PRACTICE (CIVIL)

McEwan, R.—Pleading in Court. Second edition. Paperback: £19·95. ISBN 0–414–01065–5. W.Green & Son.

McKain, B; Bonnington, A.J.; Watt, G.A.—Scots Law for Journalists. Sixth edition. Paperback: £19·95. ISBN 0–414–01005–1. W.Green & Son.

Moody, Susan; Mackay, Robert—Alternative Dispute Resolution in Scotland. Paperback: £34·00. ISBN 0–414–01115–5. W.Green & Son.

PRISONS

McManus J.J.—Prisons, Prisoners and the Law. Paperback: £24·00. ISBN 0–414–01019–1. W.Green & Son.

REVENUE AND FINANCE

Muirhead and Gemmil—Scottish Financial Services. Looseleaf: £175·00. ISBN 0–414–01128–7. W.Green & Son.

SALE OF GOODS

Sellar—Sale of Goods. Paperback: £15·00. ISBN 0–414–01106–6. W.Green & Son.

SOLICITORS

Cusine et al.—Green's Practice Styles. Looseleaf/disk: £235·00 (+ £20·56 VAT). ISBN 0–414–01039–6. W.Green & Son.

TRUSTS

Addison—Judicial Factors. Paperback: £15·00. ISBN 0–414–01120–1. W.Green & Son.

WILLS

Scobbie, Eilidh—Currie on Confirmation. Green's Practice Library. Hardback: £75·00. ISBN 0–414–01006–X. W.Green & Son.

INDEX OF ARTICLES

The following articles were published in 1995. They are listed under the appropriate Current Law headings.

ADMINISTRATIVE LAW

An introduction to Scottish public law *(Tom Mullen* and *Tony Prosser)*: [1995] 1 E.P.L. 46–51.
Audit, accounting officers and accountability: the Pergau Dam affair *(F. White, I. Harden* and *K. Donelly)*: [1994] P.L. 526.
Aviation: controlling night flights at London's airports *(Richard H. Burnett-Hall)*: (1995) 2 Trans. L. & P. 78–80.
Droit public—English style *(Lord Woolf of Barnes)*: [1995] P.L. 57.
Ethics and the public service *(N. Lewis* and *D. Longley)*: [1994] P.L. 596.
Further *West*? More geometry of judicial review (*C.M.G. Himsworth*): 1995 S.L.T. (News) 127.
Interdict and the Crown in Scotland *(D. Edwards)*: (1995) 111 L.Q.R. 34.
Judicial review and the intricacies of the tripartite relationship (*Gordon Junor*): (1995) 226 SCOLAG 126.
Judicial review in the company and commercial context *(A. Leadbetter)*: 10 I.B.F.L. 62.
Judicial review of refusal to fund treatment: [1995] 63 Med. Leg. J. 80–82.
Judicial review: applying for leave—the practice and the future *(L. Bridges* and *S. Cragg)*: [1994] L.A. Dec. 19.
Law and democracy *(Sir J. Laws)*: [1995] P.L. 72.
Pergau be damned *(S. Grosz)*: (1994) 144 New L.J. 1708.
Public authorities, political protest and judicial review (*Ian Cram*): 1995 S.L.T. (News) 213.
Public interest challenges: new directions? *(C. Harlow)*: [1995] L.A. Feb. 7.
Public interest immunity *(Lord Justice Simon Brown)*: [1994] P.L. 579.
Public law and the public interest *(Richard Gordon)*: [1995] 145 New L.J. 1303.
Reinventing British Government *(F.F. Ridley)*: [1995] 48 Parl. Aff. 387–400.
Standing in judicial review (*Colin R. Munro*): 1995 S.L.T. (News) 279.
Standing room only . . . *(R. Gordon)*: (1995) 145 New L.J. 116.
The Adams exclusion order case: new enforceable civil rights in the post-Maastricht European Union? *(S. Douglas-Scott* and *J. Kimbell)*: [1994] P.L. 516.
The Advertising Standards Authority, the Committee of Advertising Practice and judicial review *(A. Lidbetter)*: (1994) 15 JML&P 113.
The Annual Report of the Pensions Ombudsman 1994–95 *(Paul Smith)*: [1995] 65 B.P.L. 5–6.
The changing face of *locus standi (David Pollitt)*: (1995) 1 C.J.R.B. 23–25.
The Council on Tribunals: visits policy and practice *(D. Foulkes)*: [1994] P.L. 564.
The duty to give reasons for decisions (*Colin R. Munro*): 1994 S.L.T. (News) 5.
The Law Commission and judicial review: managing the tensions between case management and public interest challenges *(R. Gordon)*: [1995] P.L. 11.
The Law Commission and judicial review: principle versus pragmatism *(Ivan Hare)*: (1995) 54 C.L.J. 268–279.
The Law Commission Report on Judicial Review *(H. Hodge)*: (1995) 14 C.J.Q. 97.
The principles of fairness *(A. Owen)*: (1994) 144 New L.J. 1656.
The purported ministerial revocation of the Criminal Injuries Compensation Scheme *(Ian S. Dickinson)*: [1995] 40 J.L.S.S. 280–281.
The Quantock hounds and the Trojan horse *(G. Nardell)*: [1995] P.L. 27.
Towards good administration—the reform of standing in Scots public law (*Ian Cram*): 1995 J.R. 332.
Transfer of cases between public and private law procedures: the English Law Commission's proposals *(Carl Emery)*: [1995] 14 C.J.Q. 163–175.
Trends in judicial review in Scotland *(T. Mullen, K. Pick* and *T. Prosser)*: [1995] P.L. 52.

AGENCY

Accessory to breach of trust *(Allen & Overy)*: (1995) 6 P.L.C. 71–72.
Agency and distribution in Sweden *(C. Svernlov)*: [1994] 11 ICCLR 374.
Agents and compensation *(J. Roberts)*: (1995) 145 New L.J. 453.
Compensating a commercial agent in the U.K.: Have equitable principles been displaced by political pragmatism? *(Olivier Bremon)*: (1995) 6 E.B.L.R. 123–125.
Finance Act notes: the general commission agent RIP: [1995] 3 B.T.R. 260–262.
Judge ducks agency hot potato: *Legal Times*, May 30, 1995, p.1.
Legal pitfalls in doing business in the Gulf States and Saudi Arabia *(Richard Price)*: [1995] 1 MECLR 18–22.
Right of access to books and records survives termination of underwriting agency agreement *(Jonathan Wright)*: (1995) 3 Int. ILR 178–179.

AGENCY—*cont.*

The agent's apparent authority: paradigm or paradox? *(Ian Brown)*: (1995) J.B.L. (July) 360–372.
The rights of commercial agents *(Richard Taylor* and *Helen Smith)*: [1995] McK. Law Let. Sum 17–18.
United Kingdom agents of non-residents *(Jonathan S. Schwarz)*: [1995] 20 W.T.R. 142–144.
When is an agent's knowledge to be imputed to his principal? *(Christopher Galyer)*: (1995) 3 Int. ILR 174–177.

AGRICULTURE

A farmyard revolution *(William Barr)*: (1995) 139 S.J. 650–652.
Agricultural property relief for let farms *(Jeremy De Souza)*: (1995) 4 P.C.B. 255–256.
Agricultural trade agreements with third countries *(M. Cornwall-Kelly)*: [1994] 5 E.B.L.R. 234.
Conveyancing implications of "set aside" *(A. Sydenham)*: (1994) 138 S.J. 1294.
Cowed but unbowed: Pt. 1 *(Michael Harwood)*: (1995) 139 S.J. 610–611.
Farming companies and farmhouses: (1995) 10 Farm T.B. 51–52.
Farming companies: a one way street: Pt. 1: (1995) 10 Farm T.B. 56–58.
Farming taxation (Pts. I and II) *(J. Greenwood)*: 134 Tax. 477, 538.
Of carelessness, carousels and casinos *(M. Cornwell-Kelly)* [1995] 6 E.B.L.R. 3.
Raging bull: Pt. 2 *(Michael Harwood)*: (1995) 139 S.J. 628.
State aids and agriculture *(Malachy Cornwell-Kelly)*: [1995] 6 E.B.L.R. 150–152.
The end of the grazing licence?: (1995) 10 Farm T.B. 53–54.
Veal, ideals and Europe: (1995) H.S. Brief., May, 1–2.
Views of the countryside *(R. Yates)*: [1995] *Gazette*, Apr. 5, 16.

ANIMALS

Animal nuisance complaints: the dos and don'ts *(Barry F. Peachey)*: (1995) 139 S.J. 784–785.
Blood sports and public law *(A. Lindsay)*: (1995) 145 New L.J. 412.
Cowed but unbowed: Pt. 1 *(Michael Harwood)*: (1995) 139 S.J. 610–611.
Dangerous dogs—or just innocent victims? *(J. Felthouse)* (1994) 144 New L.J. Charities Supp. 34.
Export of livestock: recent judgments in respect of Dover Harbour, Millbay Docks and Coventry Airport: moral and practical issues in the exercise of discretion *(Sandra Banks)*: (1995) 2 Trans. L. & P. 75–77.
It shouldn't happen to a vet *(C. Foster)*: (1995) 139 S.J. 186.
Raging bull: Pt. 2 *(Michael Harwood)*: (1995) 139 S.J. 628.

ARBITRATION

Arbitration law and practice within the European Union: contrasts and solutions *(Nael G. Bunni)*: (1995) 61 Arbitration 176–188.
Arbitration: change in the offing? *(Michael Lee)*: (1995) I.H.L. Jul/Aug, 32–33.
Culture change *(Alan Shilston)*: (1995) 61 Arbitration 153–156.
Egypt: a new law on arbitration: (1995) 10 A.L.Q. 31–51.
Enforcement of arbitral awards in the Arab countries *(Abdul Hamid El-Ahdab)*: (1995) 11 Arbitration Int. 169–181.
International commercial arbitration in Hong Kong *(Christopher J. Wilson* and *Graeme R. Halford)*: (1995) I.C. Lit. Jul/Aug, 15–17.
Principal regulations of the Chartered Institute of Arbitrators: made pursuant to Bye-Law 62: (1995) 61 Arbitration 212–219.
Rent review: mishap or misconduct?: (1995) 9 Comm. Leases 1–3.
Resolving disputes in worldwide infrastructure projects *(James J. Myers)*: [1995] 12 I.C.L.R. 429–439.
Settlement of law of the sea disputes *(Louis B. Sohn)*: (1995) 10 I.J.M.C.L. 205–217.
Singapore: International Arbitration Act *(Leslie Chew)*: (1995) I.C. Lit. Jul/Aug, 27–28.
Singapore's adoption of the UNCITRAL Model Law on International Commercial Arbitration *(Benny S. Tabalujan)*: (1995) 12 J. Int. Arb. 51–64.
The new arbitration rules of the China International Economic Trade and Arbitration Commission *(Rong R. Yan* and *Christopher Kuner)*: (1995) 11 Arbitration Int. 183–196.
The new Egyptian Arbitration Act in civil and commercial matters *(Abdul Hamid El-Ahdab)*: (1995) 12 J. Int. Arb. 65–101.
The new Lex Mercatoria: reality or academic fantasy? *(Vanessa L.D. Wilkinson)*: (1995) 12 J. Int. Arb. 103–117.
The politics of arbitration reform *(A. Marriot)*: (1995) 14 C.J.Q. 125.
The problems facing arbitration in the European Union *(Karl-Heinz Bockstiegel)*: (1995) 61 Arbitration 191–195.
The U.S./U.K. arbitration concerning Heathrow Airport user charges *(J. Skilbeck)*: (1995) 44 I.C.L.Q. 171.
Use of arbitration in financial services disputes *(M. Lee* and *S. Nappert)*: 10 I.B.F.L. 76.

ARMED FORCES

The external use of German armed forces—the 1994 judgment of the Bundesverfassungsgericht *(C. Kress)*: (1995) 44 I.C.L.Q. 414.

The plea of self-defence in murder: soldiers or police officers, no special case *(Rob R. Jerrard)*: (1995) 68 Pol. J. 267–269.

We want you as a new recruit *(Martin Bowley)*: (1995) 9 *Lawyer* 10.

AVIATION

A consideration of GATS and of its compatibility with the existing regime for air transport *(R. Ebdon)*: (1995) XX A. & S.L. 71.

Aeronautical charges: the need for a more specific legislative context *(Gary N. Heilbronn* and *Christopher J. Bonsall)*: (1995) XX A. & S.L. 125–136.

Air finance for Africa, legal issues—the airline perspective *(T. Garabga)*: (1995) XX A. & S.L. 18.

Airline mergers and marketing alliances: legal constraints *(John Balfour)*: (1995) XX A. & S.L. 112–117.

Aviation: controlling night flights at London's airports *(Richard H. Burnett-Hall)*: (1995) 2 Trans. L. & P. 78–80.

Carriage of goods by air: cargo of diamonds allegedly damaged by carrier's wilful misconduct: (1995) 406 L.M.L.N. 1–2.

Competition by sea and air *(Vincent Smith)*: (1995) 7 E.C.L. 43–44.

Developments in U.S. bilateral launch service agreements *(D. Burnett* and *F. Schroeder)*: (1994) XIX A. & S.L. 326.

Dispute resolution in the new Hong Kong international airport core programme projects—Pt. 3 *(D. Lewis)*: [1995] ICLR 131.

Dispute resolution in trade in civil aircraft and related services: a comparative study with other aviation issues *(R.I.R. Abeyratne)*: [1995] 14 Tr. Law 284–299.

European collaboration in civil aerospace: success or failure? *(Stephen Martin* and *Keith Hartley)*: (1995) 33 J. Com. Mar. St. 275–291.

Flying the Euro-skies (*T. Schmid*): (1994) 39 J.L.S.S. 465.

Future regulation to allow multi-national arrangements between air carriers (cross-border alliances), putting an end to air carrier nationalism *(Henri A. Wassenbergh)*: (1995) XX A. & S.L. 164–168.

Harvey Crush *(Hugh Howard)*: (1995) 139 S.J. 616.

IATA tariff co-ordination and competition law *(P. Haanappel)*: (1995) XX A. & S.L. 82.

Inter-airline co-operation in Africa *(A. Makonnen)*: (1995) XX A. & S.L. 92.

Investigation of civil aviation accidents and incidents in Europe *(Nicholas Hughes)*: (1995) 3 Trans. L. & P. 87–88.

Legal activities of the International Air Transport Association (IATA) 1993–1994 *(L. Weber)*: (1995) XX A. & S.L. 32.

Modern trends in the antitrust/competition law governing the aviation industry *(L. Weber)*: (1995) XX A. & S.L. 101.

New E.C. Directive on the investigation of air accidents and incidents *(Nicholas Grief)*: (1995) J.B.L. (July) 422–429.

News from international organizations *(H. Wassenbergh* and *P. Mendes de Leon)*: (1995) XX A. & S.L. 22.

Open skies: storms clearing, brighter weather ahead *(Elizabeth Weightman)*: (1995) 1 Int. T.L.R. 35–36.

Open skies: the battle for Community competence *(John Balfour)*: (1995) 2 Trans. L. & P. 68–69.

Recent developments in taxation of air transport—the ICAO-IATA symbiosis *(R. Abeyratne)*: (1995) XX A. & S.L. 48.

Recent developments in the aviation industry of the People's Republic of China *(C.-J. Cheng)*: (1995) XX A. & S.L. 68.

The current development of civil aviation in Russia *(V. Kasyanonko)*: (1995) XX A. & S.L. 87.

The E.C. Commission's policy on State aids for airline restructuring: is the bonfire alight? (1995) XX A. & S.L. 60.

The future Taiwan-Mainland China air links and the Cabotage concept under current international air law *(M. Sheng-ti Gau)*: (1994) XIX A. & S.L. 317.

The legal status and liability of the co-pilot, Pt. 1 *(R. Kane* and *T. Pyne)*: (1994) XIX A. & S.L. 291.

The legal status and liability of the co-pilot, Pt. 2 *(R. Kane* and *T. Pyne)*: (1995) XX A. & S.L. 2.

The Montreal Protocols and the Japanese Initiative: can the Warsaw System survive? *(A. Mercer)*: (1994) XIX A. & S.L. 301.

The recovery of route charges and the exercise of the right of detention in the United Kingdom *(Jean Mousse)*: (1995) 20 A. & S.L. 137–145.

The U.S./U.K. arbitration concerning Heathrow Airport user charges *(J. Skilbeck)*: (1995) 44 I.C.L.Q. 171.

Turbulence ahead: completing the Single Market in air transport *(Leigh Davison* and *Debra Johnson)*: (1995) 3 Eur. Access 10–12.

What can be done against bogus aircraft parts? *(S. Kaiser)*: (1994) XIX A. & S.L. 298.

BAILMENT

In Norfolk, they "dew diffrunt . . . " *(Bill Thomas)*: (1995) L. Ex. Aug. 28–29.
New Law Journal Precedent No. 8/1995: Notice to bailor regarding uncollected goods: (1995) 145 New L.J. 1261.

BANKING

A perspective from an international bank lawyer *(Mario Giovanoli)*: [1995] 4 (Supp) I.I.R. 9–15.
Ascertainability in transfer and tracing of title *(D. Hayton)*: [1994] LMCLQ 449.
"Bancassurance" and community law: current status and expected developments *(P. Woolfson)*: [1994] 11 Int. ILR 404.
Bank crises management: the case of the United Kingdom *(Richard Dale)*: (1995) 10 J.I.B.L. 326–333.
Bank notes *(P. Alexander)*: [1995] *Gazette* Feb. 1, 20.
Bank of England supervision of capital adequacy and subordinated loan capital issued by U.K. incorporated authorised institutions *(Karen Cadenhead)*: (1995) 7 C. & F.L. 137–141.
Banker-customer confidentiality in the 1990s *(R. Obank)*: 10 I.B.F.L. 113.
Banks' duty of confidentiality in the wake of computerised banking *(F. Alqudah)*: [1995] 2 JIBL 50.
Banks' liabilities relating to foreign currency loans: the Australasian experience *(P. Wensley* and *J. Walsh)*: [1995] 4 JIBL 119.
Between domestic democracy and an alien rule of law? Some thoughts on the "independence" of the Bank of England *(T. Daintith)*: [1995] P.L. 118.
Chinese corporate governance and finance in Taiwan *(Dr B. Wallace Semkow)*: 9 I.B.F.L. 528.
Connected lender liability *(P. Dobson)*: (1994) 138 S.J. 1212.
Consumer electronic banking *(C. Reed)*: [1994] 11 JIBL 451.
Creditors and collateral purposes *(N. Hopkins)*: (1995) 111 L.Q.R. 72.
Data security and document image processing: legal security for cross-border electronic banking *(I. Walden)*: [1994] 12 JIBL 507.
Derivatives: the new regulatory challenge *(R. Dale)*: 10 I.B.F.L. 11.
Electronic securities transfer and registration in Australia: issues for lenders *(J. Lipton)*: [1994] 12 JIBL 526.
Essential elements of the second German financial market promotion law *(German Federal Ministry of Finance)*: 10 I.B.F.L. 184.
Foreign investment and company laws of selected central Eastern European and central Asian republics *(G. Campbell)*: [1994] 11 ICCLR 366.
Formalism of anti-formalism: regulation and the Bank of England *(Ian Robinson* and *Roger Hussey)*: (1995) 3 J.F.R. & C. 129–134.
Implementation of the Capital Adequacy Directive *(Herbert Smith)*: (1995) 6 P.L.C. 52–55.
International banking, competitive advantage, and global marketing strategy *(Charles W. Hultman)*: [1995] 18 W. Comp. 131–154.
Jersey as a centre for international private banking *(Kevin Marshall)*: (1995) 16 *Eagle* 21–22.
Judicial review in the company and commercial context *(A. Leadbetter)*: 10 I.B.F.L. 62.
Judicial review of the Bank of England *(Michael Fordham)*: (1995) 1 C.J.R.B. 32–33.
Lazarus arisen? *(J. Jeremie)*: (1995) 139 S.J. 99.
Letters of credit and the Rome Convention *(C. Morse)*: [1994] LMCLQ 560.
Liability of credit institutions towards creditors of their clients in financial difficulty under Belgian law *(D. Van Gerven)*: [1994] 12 JIBL 532.
Listing debt securities in Hong Kong *(I. Hardee* and *L. Rita Theil)*: [1995] 1 JIBL 7.
Merchant bank takeovers *(Lovell White Durrant)*: [1995] I.H.L., Jul/Aug 44–45.
Monetary union—a cooler look *(J. Chown)*: 10 I.B.F.L. 107.
Money laundering methodology *(C. Hill)*: 10 I.B.F.L. 161.
Netting at risk? Implications for the validity of netting agreements for the E.C. draft Bankruptcy Convention and of the E.C. draft Directive on the winding-up of credit institutions *(M. Dassesse)*: 10 I.B.F.L. 18.
Netting: developments in 1994 affecting banks *(D. Turing)*: 10 I.B.F.L. 71.
New capital adequacy rules for banks *(Mark Furman* and *Martin Reynolds)*: [1995] 8 C.M. 4–6.
Private banking in London *(Heather Maizels)*: *Eagle*, June 1995, p.20.
Revisions to the United States uniform commercial code governing transactions in securities and other investment property *(S. Rocks)*: 10 I.B.F.L. 25.
Sales practices in over-the-counter derivatives transactions *(N. Jacklin)*: 10 I.B.F.L. 181.
Taking financial services to the cleaners *(M. Levi)*: (1995) 145 New L.J. 26.
The bank/customer relationship in German and European law *(Dr N. Horn)*: 10 I.B.F.L. 116.
The duties and liabilities of lead managers in syndicated loans *(G. Bhattacharyya)*: 10 I.B.F.L. 172.
The evolution of letters of credit transactions *(A. Davidson)*: 10 I.B.F.L. 128.
The fiduciary duty of the mutual fund investment adviser and portfolio manager in the United States *(G. Scagliarini)*: [1995] 2 JIBL 42.
The Guernsey law on taking security over intangible personal property *(S. Howitt)*: [1995] 1 JIBL 16.
The impact of U.S. foreign asset control regulations on international money transfer systems *(J. Flynn)*: 10 I.B.F.L. 134.

BANKING—*cont.*

The independence of the Banque de France: constitutional and European aspects *(J.-P. Duprat)*: [1995] P.L. 133.

The legal effect of the exclusive jurisdiction clause in the Brussels Convention in relation to banking matters *(Charles Chatterjee)*: (1995) 10 J.I.B.L. 334–340.

The new supervisory regime for foreign banks in the U.S.: the ROCA, Combined and SOSA rating systems *(Gary M. Welsh)*: 10 I.B.F.L. 267–271.

The path to paying gross *(J. Fernandez)*: 134 Tax. 243.

The proper law of letters of credit *(D. Petkovic)*: [1995] 4 JIBL 141.

The regulation of investment firms in the European Union (Pt. 2) *(R. Dale)*: [1994] 11 JIBL 464.

The taxation of savings in Europe and the single market: a temporary problem? *(M. Dassesse)*: 10 I.B.F.L. 176.

The Ukrainian banking system *(Sergei Tretyak* and *Arnold Vahrenwald)*: (1995) 10 JIBL 341–345.

The use of derivatives by public companies: disclosure and supervision in the United States *(Mayer, Brown and Platt Derivatives Group)*: [1995] 1 JIBL 11.

The World Bank Inspection Panel: court or quango? *(Kathigamar V.S.K. Nathan)*: [1995] 12 J. Int. Arb. 135–148.

Tortious liability of an advising bank in the letter of credit transaction *(A. Ward* and *R. Wight)*: [1995] 4 JIBL 136.

Towards a European law of investment services and institutions *(G. Ferrarini)*: [1994] 31 C.M.L.Rev. 1283.

U.K. implementation of European investment services directives *(A. Alcock)*: (1994) 15 Co Law. 291.

United States: new Federal Reserve reporting requirements may alter U.S. merchant banking investments *(Isaac B. Lustgarten)*: (1995) 14 I.B.F.L. 24–25.

Use of arbitration in financial services disputes *(M. Lee* and *S. Nappert)*: 10 I.B.F.L. 76.

What do you tell your clients? (1995) 139 S.J. 320.

When is a fixed charge not a fixed charge? [1994] 123 Comp. Acct. 31.

Which electronic purse framework for Europe? *(P. Jones)*: 10 I.B.F.L. 56.

BANKRUPTCY

Delaying tactics in bankruptcy proceedings *(Steven A. Frieze)*: (1995) L. Ex. Aug, 40–41.

Disclosure in bankruptcy *(A. Mithani)*: *Gazette* Jan. 11, 20.

"Forthwith" and avoiding sequestration (*W. J. Stewart*): 1995 S.L.T. (News) 19.

"Forthwith" and avoiding sequestration: some observations (*Donna W. McKenzie*): 1995 S.L.T. (News) 151.

House of Lords clarifies liquidation netting *(Alan Berg)*: [1995] 14 I.F.L. Rev. 20–21.

Insolvency: set off *(Dermot Turing)*: (1995) 10 JIBL N170.

Insolvency: statutory demand *(Trevor Wood)*: (1995) 10 JIBL N133–134.

Scottish Power and recovery of pre-sequestration arrears (*Anthony J. C. Kelly*): (1995) 224 SCOLAG 87.

Secured financing in the United States: developments in 1994 *(A. Bruce Schimberg)*: [1995] 10 JIBL 210–222.

Set-off and assignment of claims on bankruptcy *(Allen & Overy)*: 10 I.B.F.L. 287.

Setting aside a statutory demand *(M. Griffiths)*: (1995) 139 S.J. 248.

The implications of the Singapore Bankruptcy Act for lenders and takers of security *(Joanna R. Jeremiah)*: (1995) 10 JIBL 357–360.

The new Singapore Bankruptcy Act *(Joanna R. Jeremiah)*: [1995] 6 ICCLR 259–261.

U.S. bankruptcy reform: Chapter 11 – in balance or in the balance: Pt. 1 *(Marvin E. Jacob)*: [1995] 4 I.I.R. 54–93.

BRITISH COMMONWEALTH

Anton Pillers and Marevas in Hong Kong *(R. Morris)*: [1994] 11 JIBL 480.

Decisions of the Privy Council in other jurisdictions: limits of *stare decisis* in Commonwealth jurisdictions *(P. Edge)*: (1994) 20 CLB 720.

Developing a law reform programme: (1994) 20 CLB 688.

Dispute resolution in the new Hong Kong international airport core programme projects—Pt. 3 *(D. Lewis)*: [1995] ICLR 131.

Fair trial *(Sir Anthony Mason)*: [1995] Crim.L.J. 7.

International commercial arbitration in Hong Kong *(Christopher J. Wilson* and *Graeme R. Halford)*: [1995] I.C. Lit. Jul/Aug, 15–17.

New developments for Canadian IP litigation *(J. Kokonis)*: [1995] M.I.P. Lit. Ybk. 7.

Ostensible ownership and motor vehicle financing in England: Antipodean insights *(I. Davies)*: [1994] 11 JIBL 474.

Protection of free speech in Australia *(M. Hall)*: [1995] 13 I.M.L. 11.

Stalking: crime of the nineties? *(M. Goode)*: [1995] Crim.L.J. 21.

Tenure, allodialism and indigenous rights at common law: English, United States and Australian land law compared after *Mabo v. Queensland (B. Edgeworth)*: (1994) 23 Anglo-Am. 397.

The relationship between international law and municipal law in the light of the interim South African Constitution 1993 *(D. Devine)*: (1995) 44 I.C.L.Q. 1.

BRITISH COMMONWEALTH—*cont.*

Trade and environment: some lessons from *Castlemaine Tooheys* (Australia) and *Danish Bottles* (European Community) *(D. Geradin* and *R. Stewardson)*: (1995) 44 I.C.L.Q. 41.

BUILDING AND CONSTRUCTION

An overview of major issues on ENAA model form international contract for process plant construction, 1992 edition—a drafter's view *(N. Wakame)*: [1995] ICLR 98.

Analytical techniques for assigning responsibility *(J. Grove III)*: [1995] ICLR 84.

Appendix IV to the Latham report: the JCT and the CCSJC: [1995] 11 Const. L.J. 198–200.

Architects' certificates—are they worth the paper they are written on? (*S. Tombs*): (1995) 40 J.L.S. 66.

Bonus clauses in construction contracts *(McKenna & Co)*: [1995] I.H.L., Jun, 35.

Building a safer world? *(Kevin J. Greene)*: *Legal Times*, May 30, 1995, p.12.

CDM – what does it mean to you? *(George Markland)*: [1995] 9529 E.G. 107–109.

Construction and engineering projects: some key insurance issues for promoters and financiers *(Alan Elias* and *Nicholas Munday)*: (1995) 3 Int. ILR 161–165.

Construction products and European technical approval *(J. Dalby)*: 11 Const.L.J. 2.

Damages for rebuilding *(H. Beale)*: (1995) 111 L.Q.R. 54.

Dispute resolution in the new Hong Kong international airport core programme projects—Pt. 3 *(D. Lewis)*: [1995] ICLR 131.

Force majeure in the region—law and practice *(R. Singam)*: [1995] ICLR 156.

Global claims at the crossroads *(M. Wilson)*: 11 Const.L.J. 15.

Green Paper on fair construction contracts *(McKenna & Co)*: (1995) I.H.L. Jul/Aug, 43.

Is near enough good enough? *(Isaac E. Jacob)*: (1995) 139 S.J. 676–677.

Negligent valuations *(T. Grant* and *H. Tomlinson)*: (1995) 139 S.J. 237.

New Engineering Contract – the jury is still out *(Mike Wharton)*: [1995] 6 Cons. Law 43–46.

Partnership: a common sense approach to preventing and managing claims *(A. H. "Nick" Gaede Jr.)*: [1995] ICLR 72.

Pay when paid clauses *(G. Hevey)*: 11 Const.L.J. 79.

Resolving disputes in worldwide infrastructure projects *(James J. Myers)*: [1995] 12 ICLR 429–439.

Risk identification and allocation: saving money by improving contracts and contracting practices *(R. Smith)*: [1995] ICLR 40.

Some considerations for foreign contractors entering the Far East construction market *(P. Balachandran)*: [1995] ICLR 137.

Some contractual aspects of the major tunnelling projects in Japan *(Kenji Aoki)*: (1995) 12 ICLR 466–478.

The anchor tenant and the "keep open" clause *(G. Dale)*: (1995) 139 S.J. 94.

The Construction (Design and Management) Regulations 1994: [1995] Feb. B.L.R.A. 37.

The Construction Design and Management Regulations 1995 *(Eversheds)*: [1995] I.H.L., Jul/Aug, 61–62.

The EIC (European International Contractors) turnkey contract (conditions for design and construct projects) *(Dr. J. Goudsmit)*: [1995] ICLR 23.

The Eichleay formula: computing and recovering unabsorbed head office overheads incurred by contractors as a result of employer-caused delay *(H. Kirsh)*: 11 Const.L.J. 90.

The Latham report and post-construction liability: some danger signs from an Australian model *(Paul Bick)*: (1995) 12 ICLR 451–465.

The new CCDC 2: facilitating dispute resolution of construction projects *(D. Bristow* and *R. Vasilopolous)*: 11 Const.L.J. 95.

The new FIDIC international civil engineering subcontract *(C. Seppala)*: [1995] ICLR 5.

The value judgment *(M. Badge)*: [1995] *Gazette* Mar. 22, 16.

To what extent has the decision in *Ruxley Electronics* changed the law of damages in building disputes? *(N. Brooke* and *M. Curtis)*: 11 Const.L.J. 29.

Unification of liabilities in the European construction industry *(Christian E. Jansen)*: (1995) 12 ICLR 440–450.

Use of collateral warranties in development finance: chimera not panacea: Pt. 1 *(Anthony Lavers* and *Miles Keeping)*: (1995) 5 P.R. 151–155.

Whither the standard form? *(Douglas S. Jones)*: (1995) 12 ICLR 392–420.

BUILDING SOCIETIES

Building society benefits *(Alec Samuels)*: (1995) 139 S.J. 631.

Firms build up society work: [1995] 9 *Lawyer* 6.

Ombudsman services: consumer's view of the office of the Building Societies Ombudsmen and the Insurance Ombudsman Bureau *(Cowan Ervine)*: [1994] 2 Consum. CS12.

Share acquisitions by building societies *(Martin Saywell* and *Paul Burke)*: (1995) 10 S.J. 272–274.

The merger move *(Seema Siddiqi)*: (1995) *Legal Times* 23, Supp TE, 12.

CAPITAL GAINS TAX

A disturbing series? *(Tim Palmer)*: [1995] Tax. P., Jul, 19–20.
Capital gains tax: 134 Tax. 209.
Capital gains tax: new and revised extra-statutory concessions: (1995) 10 Farm T.B. 45.
Capital losses – making them pay *(Daron Gunson)*: (1995) 16 T.P.T. 121–123.
Definitely capital—now? *(A. Sellwood)*: 134 Tax. 404.
Enterprise investment scheme: capital gains reliefs: Inland Revenue Tax Bulletin 17 of 1995, 217–218.
Less variety please! *(Nigel Thompson)*: 135 Tax. 295–297.
No gain no loss – a capital gains tax worry revisited *(Michael D. Wood)*: (1995) 14 C.T.P. 117–118.
Non-resident settlements: a planning update *(Frank Haskew)*: (1995) 14 C.T.P. 114–117.
Not a total loss *(A. Beardsworth)*: 134 Tax. 432.
Out of the frying pan *(R. Argles)*: 134 Tax. 292.
Refused clearances – what next? *(Bradley Phillips)*: (1995) 321 Tax J. 10–12.
Small can be beautiful *(E. Manisty)*: 134 Tax. 179.
Taxation update *(R. McBurnie)*: (1995) 139 S.J. 15.

CAPITAL TAXATION

An "issue" with the capital taxes office (*Hugh J. Stevens*): (1995) 40 J.L.S. 233.

CARRIERS

Carriage of goods by air: cargo of diamonds allegedly damaged by carrier's wilful misconduct: (1995) 406 L.M.L.N. 1–2.
Law applicable in Greece on the contracts of carriage of goods by sea *(George Economou)*: (1995) 2 Int. M.L. 155–157.
No more Mr Nice Guy?: (1995) 9 P & I Int. 124–125.
Price-fixing (shipping): the Far Eastern Freight Conference case: (1995) 18 Comp. Law E.C. 151–157.

CHARITIES

Another eventful year *(H. Picarda)*: (1994) 144 New L.J. Charities Supp. 14.
Charities and sales promotion *(R. Lawson)*: 159 J.P.N. 265.
Charities, value added tax and business *(Jean Warburton)*: (1995–96) 3 C.L. & P.R. 37–46.
Charity law in Northern Ireland *(Geraldine Scullion)*: (1995) 58 Writ 4, 17.
Charity proceedings: proper parties *(A. Samuels)*: 14 Lit. 65.
Charity trustees *(A. Longley)*: (1994) 138 S.J. (Charities Supp.) 32.
Charity update *(D. Cracknell)*: (1994) 138 S.J. (Charities Supp.) 24.
Commercial reporter *(R. Lawson)*: (1995) 139 S.J. 146.
Enter the commercial participator *(Judith Hill)*: (1995–96) 3 C.L. & P.R. 17–28.
Free show: 135 Tax. 371–372.
Investing charitable funds *(F. Quint)*: (1994) 138 S.J. (Charities Supp.) 36.
Liability insurances for charities *(M. Wilson)*: (1994) 138 S.J. (Charities Supp.) 30.
Mr Pemsel: 104 years old and still going strong *(David Tweedie)*:[1995] 4 P.C.B. 309–312.
The spirit of the gift *(Jean Warburton)*: (1995–96) 3 C.L. & P.R. 1–10.
The trust versus the company under the Charities Acts 1992 and 1993 (1994) 144 New L.J. Charities Supp. 23.

CHILDREN AND YOUNG PERSONS

A new language for lawyers: Pt. I of the Children (Scotland) Bill (*J. Scott*): Fam.L.B. 14–2.
Assault and reasonable chastisement (*Elaine Ness*): 1995 S.L.T. (News) 185.
Caring for the offspring of surrogacy (*I.D. Willock*): 1995 S.L.T. (News) 41.
Children (Scotland) Bill—implications for the children's hearing system (*M. Schaffer*): Fam.L.B. 14–3.
Children (Scotland) Bill: a critical look (*D. Watson*): Fam.L.B. 14–5.
Consent to Treatment and the Children (Scotland) Bill (*B. Simon Collins*): Fam.L.B. 15–3.
D. *v.* Grampian Regional Council (*Lillian Edwards*): Fam.L.B. 15–2.
Financial support for the child in disputed parentage cases (*M. Ross and D. McKenzie*): 1995 J.R. 166.
New rules for family actions in the sheriff court: some observations (*D. Kelbie*): Civ.P.B. 2–3.
Parental responsibilities and parental rights (*Kenneth Morris*): (1995) 40 J.L.S. 340.
Representing children in court: recent changes to the Children (Scotland) Bill (*Rosemary Gallagher*): Fam.L.B. 16–3.

CIVIL LIBERTIES

Photos on driving licences—identity cards by the back door? (*C. Ewart*): (1994) 218 SCOLAG 180.
Secret hangings on Japan's death row (*Alan McMillan*): (1995) 225 SCOLAG 111.
The enforcement agency in anti-discrimination law (*Martin MacEwan*): (1995) 225 SCOLAG 113.

BOOKS AND ARTICLES

CLUBS AND ASSOCIATIONS

A problem in the construction of gifts to unincorporated associations *(Paul Matthews)*: [1995] Conv., Jul/Aug, 302–308.

It's a team of two halves: (1995) 9 Lawyer 11.

Trustees' remuneration and expenses: (1995) 9 Tr. & Est. 75–76.

COMMONS

Common land: (1995) 7 E.L.M. 93–95.

Indulging in lawful sports *(H.W. Wilkinson)*: (1995) Conv. Jul/Aug, 286–288.

Protecting our commons *(Alec Samuels)*: [1995] 139 S.J. 764.

COMPANY LAW

Amending a resolution: preventing a crisis: [1995] 6 P.L.C. 12–13.

Articles of association for partnership companies *(Colin Mercer* and *Helen Shilling)*: (1995) 9 Corp. Brief. 4–5.

Audit, accounting officers and accountability: the Pergau Dam affair *(F. White, I. Harden* and *K. Donelly)*: [1994] P.L. 526.

Barnes v. Addy: the requirements of knowledge *(M. Lodge)*: (1995) 23 A.B.L.R. 25.

Caltex and Abbco ice works—the end of the road for corporations? *(A. Bruce)*: (1995) 23 A.B.L.R. 7.

Chinese corporate governance and finance in Taiwan *(Dr B. Wallace Semkow)*: 9 I.B.F.L. 528.

Commercial law update: company law *(David P. Sellar)*: (1995) 40 J.L.S.S. 267.

Company law developments at European Union level—the European Cooperative Society, the European Mutual Society and the European Association *(C. Bovis)*: (1995) 16 Co Law. 85.

Connected undertakings and groups of undertakings under German law *(Frank Wooldridge)*: [1995] 24 Anglo-Am. 57.

Controlling directors' remuneration *(F. Le Grys)*: (1995) 139 S.J. 96.

Conveyancers and the director as purchaser *(N. Le Poidevin)*: (1995) 139 S.J. 21.

Corporate criminality: four models of fault *(J. Gobert)*: (1994) 14 L.S. 393.

CPS charging standards: a cynic's view *(F. Davies)* 159 J.P.N. 203.

Departure from the one-share one-vote rule: an overview and some lessons for New Zealand *(A. Mandelbaum)*: [1995] 2 JIBL 56.

European and American company law: a comparison after 25 years of E.C. harmonisation *(Harm-Jan de Kluiver)*: [1994] 1 M.J. 139–165.

Foreign investment and company laws of selected central Eastern European and central Asian republics *(G. Campbell)*: [1994] 11 ICCLR 366.

How far art thou? *(A. Mosawi)*: [1995] *Gazette* Jan. 25, 20.

Insolvency Act 1988 and cross-border winding up (*D. P. Sellar*): (1995) 40 J.L.S. 104.

Judicial review in the company and commercial context *(A. Leadbetter)*: 10 I.B.F.L. 62.

Legal aspects of management buyouts *(M. Dwyer)*: [1995] 4 ICCLR 129.

Let purchasers beware! *(M. Hannay)*: [1994] 123 Comp. Acct. 20.

Multinationals and the export of hazard *(S. Baughen)*: (1995) 58 M.L.R. 54.

Oman: commercial companies law: (1995) 1 M.E.C.L.R. A7–10.

Personal accountability and corporate control: the role of directors' and officers' liability insurance *(V. Finch)*: (1994) 57 M.L.R. 880.

Power to draw up conduct of business rules after the Investment Services Directive *(T. Thorkildsen)*: (1995) 139 S.J. 102.

Problems of share valuation under s.260 of the corporations law *(S. Sirianos)*: [1995] 13 C. & S.L.J. 88.

Proceedings concerning dissolved companies (*W. Holligan*): 1995 S.L.T. (News) 11.

Reforming the law of private companies *(Andrew Hicks)*: [1995] 16 Co. Law. 171–177.

Reporting on internal control *(Martyn E. Jones* and *Clive Goodhead)*: (1995) 18 C.S.R. 161–162.

Sharp v. Thomson—What now? (*Professor A. J. McDonald*): (1995) 40 J.L.S. 256.

Shelf companies and audit exemption (*David A. Bennett*): (1995) 40 J.L.S. 236.

Sick and tiered: (1995) 18 C.S.R. 166–167.

Spain: Single European Market: survey of Spanish companies *(Joaquin Munoz)*: (1995) 1 Int. T.L.R. S30–31.

Statutory liability of shadow directors (*Dr Stephen Girvan*): 1995 J.R. 414.

Statutory procedures: reduction of capital *(Claire Cranidge)*: [1995] 19 C.S.R. 32.

Super-voting shares: what's all the fuss about? *(S. Fridman)*: [1995] 13 C. & S.L.J. 31.

Tax-friendly investment in business enterprises (*Sandra Eden*): (1995) 40 J.L.S. 185.

The alter ego dilemma: recent developments (*Brian Pillans*): Bus.L.B. 15–2.

The constitution of the company: mandatory statutory provisions *v.* private agreements *(C. McGlynn)*: (1994) 15 Co Law. 301.

The corporate body *(G. Slapper)*: [1995] *Gazette* Feb. 15, 18.

The evolving standard of security applied to directors' decisions *(M. Kearney)*: 10 I.B.F.L. 30.

The nature of goodwill *(A. Slater)*: [1995] A.T.R. 31.

The problems of insider dealing (*Alastair N. Brown*): (1995) 40 J.L.S. 153.

The proposed framework for open-ended investment companies in the United Kingdom *(Tim Herrington)*: [1995] 10 I.B.F.L. 316–321.

COMPANY LAW—*cont.*

The Requirements of Writing (Scotland) Act 1995 (*Professor Robert Rennie*): 1995 J.R. 445.

The Requirements of Writing (Scotland) Act 1995 (*Professors Cusine and Rennie*): (1995) 40 J.L.S. 221.

The structure of the corporation: proposal for new provisions to the Swedish Companies Act *(Rolf Skog)*: (1995) 6 ICCLR 269–271.

The U.K.'s new strength as a holding company location *(H. McCrossan)*: [1995] 6 E.B.L.R. 5.

The use of derivatives by public companies: disclosure and supervision in the United States *(Mayer, Brown and Platt Derivatives Group)*: [1995] 1 JIBL 11.

Trading under the wrong name, personal liability or printers' error? *(P. Cuthbertson)*: (1994) 10 I.L. & P. 158.

Ultra vires actions of the managing director of a German limited liability company *(D. Weber-Rey)*: [1995] 1 ICCLR 22.

Understanding and regulating the corporation *(Christopher A. Riley)*: [1995] 58 M.L.R. 595–612.

Underwriting flotations: the safety net *(Simon Jay* and *Spencer Summerfield)*: (1995) 6 P.L.C. 31–42.

Valuation of shares: a legal and accounting conundrum *(A. Gregory* and *A. Hicks)*: [1995] J.B.L. 56.

"Voluntary dissolution" of companies (*D. A. Bennett*): (1995) 40 J.L.S. 20.

Weeding out the errors in a private allotment *(Ronald Severn)*: (1995) 18 C.S.R. 169–170.

Why be limited? (*Stuart R. Cross*): (1995) 40 J.L.S. 195.

COMPETITION

A Community right in damages for breach of E.C. competition rules? *(A. Winterstein)*: [1995] 16 ECLR 49.

A comparative analysis of the decision-taking process in competition matters in Member States of the European Union, the European Commission and the United States *(A. Haslam-Jones)*: (1995) 16 E.C.L.Rev. 154.

Ancillary restrictions in the Commission's decisions under the Merger Regulations: non-competition clauses *(J. Modrall)*: [1995] 16 ECLR 40.

Barriers to utility competition *(Philip Cullum* and *Colin Meek)*: (1995) 5 C.P.R. 127–130.

Competition law and effective penalties *(Mark Furse)*: [1995] 16 Bus. L.R. 134–136.

Competition law in the E.U.: should there be a Convention? (1995) 16 Co Law. 75.

Competition law update *(E. Singleton)*: (1995) 139 S.J. 141.

Competition policy and central Europe: (1995) 18 Comp. Law E.C. 207–208.

Competition policy in deregulated industries *(Henry Ergas)*: (1995) 23 I.B.L. 305–306, 308–310.

Competition policy: recent developments *(Nabarro Nathanson)*: [1995] 9 Corp. Brief. 6–10.

Competitive tendering in the energy sector: the E.C. Utilities Directive *(C. Mehta)*: [1995] 2 OGLTR 78.

Connected undertakings and groups of undertakings under German law *(Frank Wooldridge)*: [1995] 24 Anglo-Am. 57.

Deregulation: how does the new Act affect competition law? *(M. Furse)*: (1995) 139 S.J. 86.

Direct advertising by telephone, fax and telex: the German law on unfair competition *(B. Steckler)*: [1995] 1 ENT.LR 13.

Disarming the Commission: the debate over a European Cartel Office *(Stephen Wilks* and *Lee McGowan)*: (1995) 33 J. Com. Mar. St. 259–273.

European briefing *(P. Duffy)*: (1995) 139 S.J. 191.

E.C. competition law compliance programmes—an introduction and update *(E. S. Singleton)*: (1994) 13 Tr.L. 508.

European Community rules on public enterprise *(R. Friel)*: [1994] 12 ILT 280.

Fining a la carte: the lottery of EU competition law *(Ivo Van Bael)*: [1995] 16 E.C.L.R. 237–243.

International dimension of competition policy *(Brona Carton)*: (1995) 1 EC C.P.N. 54–55.

Joint venture analysis: the latest chapter *(A. Burnside)*: (1995) 16 E.C.L.Rev. 138.

Modern trends in the antitrust/competition law governing the aviation industry *(L. Weber)*: (1995) XX A. & S.L. 101.

Oligopolistic market failure: collective dominance versus complex monopoly *(B. Rodger)*: [1995] 16 ECLR 21.

Open skies: the battle for Community competence *(John Balfour)*: (1995) 2 Trans. L. & P. 68–69.

Predatory pricing: E.C. and U.K. competition rules *(John Boyce)*: [1995] 6 P.L.C. 17–24.

Reflections on a European Cartel office *(C. Ehlermann)*: (1995) 32 C.M.L.Rev. 471.

Rules on State Aids with Hungary in the Europe Agreement *(O. Heinz)*: [1995] 2 ECLR 116.

Surveys of Member States' powers to investigate and sanction violations of national competition law *(Laraine L. Laudati)*: (1995) 1 EC C.P.N. 13–20.

The arbitrability of competition issues *(J.H. Dalhuisen)*: (1995) 11 Arbitration Int. 151–167.

The binding of Leviathan?—The changing role of the European Commission in competition cases *(R. Brent)* (1995) 44 I.C.L.Q. 255.

The concept of third party access in the energy sector in Belgian law *(J. Périlleux* and *Frédéric Meessen)*: [1995] 1 OGLTR 11.

The concept of third party access in the gas sector in the Czech Republic *(J. De Keijzer* and *A. Musil)*: [1995] 1 OGLTR 38.

COMPETITION—*cont.*

The delimitation of jurisdiction with regard to concentration control under the E.E.A. Agreement *(M. Broberg)*: [1995] 16 ECLR 31.

The international telecommunication union: co-operation or cartel? *(J. Naftel)*: [1995] 1 C.T.L.R. 18.

The need for reform of U.K. competition policy *(Michael B. Hutchings)*: [1995] 16 E.C.L.R. 211–214.

The relationship between State regulation and E.C. competition law: two proposals for a coherent approach *(C.-M. Chung)*: [1995] 2 ECLR 87.

The Swedish block exemption for chains in the retail trade *(P. Hellstrom* and *P. Remmnelid)*: [1995] 2 ECLR 125.

The Velvet Revolution: Article 90 and the triumph of the free market in Europe's regulated sectors *(A. Gardner)*: [1995] 2 ECLR 78.

U.K. competition law: the call for reform: (1995) 6 P.L.C. 11–12.

COMPULSORY PURCHASE

Betterment: better for whom? *(Simon Purcell)*: (1995) 139 S.J. 659.

Common land: (1995) 7 E.L.M. 94–95.

Compensation for compulsory acquisition of land *(Dibb Lupton Broomhead)*: [1995] 16 Bus. L.R. 121–122.

Compulsory purchase: [1995] 5 P.E.L.B. 21.

Rail-road schemes: business relocation *(Robert Turrall-Clarke* and *Nigel Laing)*: (1995) 9534 E.G. 68–72.

COMPUTER LAW

A jurisprudence for information technology law *(S. Saxby)*: (1995) 2 IJLIT 1.

A question of liability *(R. Brent)*: [1995] *Gazette* Jan. 5, 15.

An American view on the E.U. Database Directive *(H. Fogt* and *L. Smith)*: [1995] Feb. M.I.P. 33.

Changes to the U.K. law relating to contracts for the sale and supply of goods *(D. Bainbridge)*: [1995] 11 CLSR 95.

Computer software protection in the commonwealth of independent states *(W. Butler)*: [1995] 11 CLSR 80.

Criminal law aspects of computer crime: general theory of computer crimes and the proposed Bill to modify the Brazilian Penal Code *(O. Banho Licks* and *J. Marcello de Araujo Junior)*: (1995) 2 IJLIT 64.

Database detection methods in criminal investigation *(V. Collins)*: (1995) 11 CLSR 2.

E.D.I. evidence and the Vienna Convention *(C. Nicoll)*: (1995) 2 IJLIT 21.

E.C. developments in IT law *(D. Jerrard* and *H. Small)*: (1995) 11 CLSR 27.

I am the law *(Sian Kelly)*: (1995) 9 *Lawyer* 18.

Impact of online computer services on copyright law *(A. Taebi)*: (1995) 11 CLSR 37.

IT security—the legal challenges *(J. Worthy)*: [1995] 11 CLSR 62.

Legal measures under Bulgarian law in cases of copyright infringement of software *(V. Dimitrova)*: (1995) 11 CLSR 25.

Litigation and remedies in software infringement cases in the Czech Republic *(Z. Loebl)*: (1995) 11 CLSR 23.

Local authorities: information for decision making by database *(T. Corbitt)*: 158 J.P.N. 800.

Mapping the E.C. route to the information age *(A. Scott* and *R. Durie)*: [1995] 1 C.T.L.R. 5.

New Polish copyright law *(Dr. T. Drozdowska)*: (1995) 11 CLSR 18.

Obscene material on the Internet *(Stephen Dooley)*: (1995) 139 S.J. 868–870.

Patenting algorithms: the Gordian Knot retwisted (Pt. 1) *(R. Stern)*: [1995] 1 C.T.L.R. 12.

Patenting software in the United States *(S. Glazer* and *S. Kahn)*: [1995] Feb. M.I.P. 19.

Privacy protection principles for electronic mail systems *(T. Wright)*: [1995] 11 CLSR 66.

Proposed directive for the legal protection of databases in the E.U. *(L. Kaye* and *V. Ward)*: (1994) 12 I.M.L. 95.

"Scope of use" provisions in software licence agreements *(S. Davidson)*: [1995] 11 CLSR 74.

Software escrow—providing peace of mind, but does it really work? *(R. Sheffield* and *A. Leveen)*: (1994) 10 CL&P 181.

Software patents—where next? *(Dr I. Lloyd)*: [1995] 11 CLSR 91.

Software protection in Germany—recent court decisions in copyright law *(A. Gunther* and *U. Wuermeling)*: (1995) 11 CLSR 12.

The Baltic Republics and their legal information systems *(J. Bing)*: (1995) 2 IJLIT 32.

The current status of the EC Database Directive *(Trevor M. Cook)*: (1995) 52 C.W. 27–34.

The impact of the 1984 Data Protection Act on marketing by banks and financial institutions *(R. Jay)*: 10 I.B.F.L. 109.

The Internet and bulletin board defamations *(Nick Braithwaite)*: (1995) 145 New L.J. 1216.

Theory of property rights and copyright protection of computer programs in Europe *(M. Lehmann)*: (1995) 2 IJLIT 86.

What is meant by consequential loss in relation to computer contracts? *(M. Webster)*: (1994) 10 CL&P 175.

CONFLICT OF LAWS

Choice of law in tort: a missed opportunity? *(Pippa Rogerson)*: (1995) 44 I.C.L.Q. 650–658.
Decisions of the Privy Council in other jurisdictions: limits of *stare decisis* in Commonwealth jurisdictions *(P. Edge)*: (1994) 20 CLB 720.
Doe v. Amour—forum non conveniens or a political decision? *(M. Cole* and *D. Tomkin)*: [1994] 12 ILT 267.
Enforcement of foreign judgments in Spain *(M. Martin)*: 14 L.J. 194.
English money judgments *(M. McParland)*: (1994) 144 New L.J. 1703.
Further thoughts on foreign torts: *Boys v. Chaplin* explained *(A. Dickinson)*: [1994] L.M.C.L.Q. 463.
How soon is an English court seised (revisited)? *(A. Briggs)*: [1994] L.M.C.L.Q. 471.
Implementation of Hague Conventions in domestic law: the United Kingdom approach *(G. Maher)*: (1995) 14 C.J.Q. 21.
Is international law justiciable in English courts?: (1995) 54 C.L.J. 230–232.
Jurisdiction in matters relating to a contract under the Brussels Convention *(Jonathan Hill)*: (1995) 44 I.C.L.Q. 591–619.
Law and jurisdiction in insurance contracts: limited freedom of choice in the E.C. *(Elisabeth Ruiz* and *Christopher Henin)*: (1995) 3 Int. ILR 156–160.
Letters of credit and the Rome Convention *(C. Morse)*: [1994] L.M.C.L.Q. 560.
Mandatory extraterritorial application of national law *(Serge Lazareff)*: (1995) 11 Arbitration Int. 137–150.
Provisional and protective measures in England and Ireland at common law and under the conventions: a comparative survey *(Paul Matthews)*: (1995) 14 C.J.Q. 190–202.
Tactical declarations and the Brussels Convention *(Richard Fentiman)*: (1995) 54 C.L.J. 261–263.
The Halley: holed, but shall still afloat? *(A. Briggs)*: (1995) 111 L.Q.R. 18.
The new Lex Mercatoria: reality or academic fantasy? *(Vanessa L.D. Wilkinson)*: (1995) 12 J. Int. Arb. 103–117.
The proper law of letters of credit *(D. Petkovic)*: [1995] 4 JIBL 141.
Title to sue on a contract of carriage in Anglo-American law *(C. Cashmore)*: (1994) 23 Anglo-Am. 488.
Towards a European private law?: a review essay *(Ton Hartlief)*: [1994] 1 M.J. 166–178.
Virgin/British Airways: the attractions of U.S. anti-trust law *(Susan May)*: [1995] 6 P.L.C. 10–11.
Workers of the world *(Michael James)*: [1995] 139 S.J. 768–769.

CONSTITUTIONAL LAW

A human rights bill *(Lord Lester)*: (1995) 145 New L.J. 141.
Constitutional reform moves up the political agenda *(Dawn Oliver)*: [1995] Sum, P.L., 193–197.
Current developments: European Community law: constitutional aspects *(Andrew Bell)*: (1995) 44 I.C.L.Q. 700–705.
David, Goliath and supremacy: the Isle of Man and the sovereignty of the United Kingdom Parliament *(P. Edge)*: [1995] 24 Anglo-Am. 1.
Democratic socialism and labour law *(K.D. Ewing)*: (1995) 24 I.L.J. 103–132.
Governing Scotland: the new powers of the Scottish Grand Committee (*B. K. Winetrobe*): (1994) 39 J.L.S.S. 459.
Interdict and the Crown in Scotland *(D. Edwards)*: (1995) 111 L.Q.R. 34.
Moving freely in the U.K. *(B. Andonian)*: (1995) 139 S.J. 214.
Nullity—a constitutional solution to Royal marital breakdown *(Dr M. Welstead)*: (1994) 144 New L.J. 1765.
One territory—three systems? The Hong Kong Bill of rights *(R. Swede)*: (1995) 44 I.C.L.Q. 359.
Protection of free speech in Australia *(M. Hall)*: [1995] 13 I.M.L. 11.
Public interest immunity *(Lord Justice Simon Brown)*: [1994] P.L. 579.
Renunciation of war as a universal principle of mankind—a look at the Gulf War and the Japanese Constitution *(S. Hamura* and *E. Shiu)*: (1995) 44 I.C.L.R. 426.
Royal taxation *(D. Pearce-Crump)*: [1994] B.T.R. 635.
South Africa's constitutional court *(B. Dickson)*: (1995) 145 New L.J. 246.
Stemming the flood of constitutional complaints in Germany? [1994] P.L. 553.
The British Constitution in 1994–95 *(Donald Shell)*: (1995) 48 Parl. Aff. 369–386.
The constitution of the European Union *(I. Harden)*: [1994] P.L. 609.
The delegated powers scrutiny committee *(C. Himsworth)*: [1995] P.L. 34.
The E.C. in the WTO and Advisory Opinion 1/94: an Echternach procession *(Jacques H.J. Bourgeois)*: (1995) 32 C.M.L.Rev. 763–787.
The relationship between international law and municipal law in the light of the interim South African Constitution 1993 *(D. Devine)*: (1995) 44 I.C.L.Q. 1.
The role of English courts in the determination of the place of the European Convention on Human Rights in English law *(Michael K. Addo)*: (1995) 46 N.I.L.Q. 1–17.
Towards a European Constitution? Problems of political integration *(J.-L. Seurin)*: [1994] P.L. 625.
Vive la difference? Gender discrimination and the U.S. Supreme Court (*Dr A. Campbell*): 1995 J.R. 54.

CONSUMER CREDIT

Commercial reporter *(Richard G. Lawson)*: (1995) 139 S.J. 826–827.

Data protection, confidentiality, unfair contract terms, consumer protection and credit reference agencies *(Geraint Howells)*: [1995] J.B.L., 343–359.

Time order and other orders under Consumer Credit Act 1974 (*Derek O'Carroll*): (1995) 224 SCOLAG 86.

Who gets the credit? *(John Whisson)*: [1995] 14 Tr. Law 304–306.

CONSUMER PROTECTION

Comparative advertising *(V. Hall-Smith)*: 12 I.M.L. 85.

Connected lender liability *(P. Dobson)*: (1994) 138 S.J. 1212.

Consumer protection and its integration in Community policy on food: general approach, principles and evaluation *(Nadine Fraselle)*: [1994] 2 Consum. L.J. 17–26.

Consumer protection: ticket touts' charter *(Christine Clayson)*: [1995] 14 Tr. 321–323.

Consumerism and the Citizen's Charter *(Philip Rawlings* and *Chris Willett)*: [1994] 2 Consum. L.J. 3–8.

Consumers and Europe *(D. Roberts)*: (1995) 14 Tr.L. 113.

Consuming passions: implementing the E.C. Directive on unfair terms in consumer contracts *(Colin Mercer)*: [1995] 16 Bus. L.R. 102–105.

Faulty goods, faulty law *(Alan Wilson)*: (1995) 5 C.P.R. 135–143.

Ostensible ownership and motor vehicle financing in England: Antipodean insights *(I. Davies)*: [1994] 11 JIBL 474.

Protecting the European consumer *(Emma Bonino)*: (1995) 6 ULR 95–98.

Safe products *(E. S. Singleton)*: 144 New L.J. 1634.

Suppliers beware: implementation of the Unfair Contract Terms Directive in Europe *(Richard Kemp* and *Chris Coulter)*: [1995] 11 C.L.S.R. 194–198.

The consumer credit counselling service *(M. D'Ingeo)*: (1995) 145 New L.J. 190.

The general duty to market safe products in United Kingdom law *(G. Howells)*: [1994] L.M.C.L.Q. 479.

The Swedish block exemption for chains in the retail trade *(P. Hellstrom* and *P. Remmnelid)*: [1995] 2 ECLR 125.

The time and place *(Tim Bourne)*: (1995) 92 Gazette 18–19.

The time of payment in the mail order trade – a call for reform *(Joan Lunn* and *Lilian Miles)*: [1995] 14 Tr. Law 300–303.

Three seconds to decide *(Robert Mackmurdo)*: [1995] 19 C.S.R. 9–10.

UCTA: contracts set fair for consumers *(Charlotte Brownlie)*: (1995) 22 *Legal Times* 2.

Wrongful dispositions of motor vehicles in England: a U.S. certificate of title solution? *(I. Davis)*: (1994) 23 Anglo-Am. 460.

CONTRACT

A case for awarding punitive damages in response to deliberate breaches of contract *(Nicholas J. McBride)*: [1995] 24 Anglo-Am. 369–390.

Appointment of an architect – pitfalls of the standard form *(Julian Critchlow)*: [1995] 6 Cons. Law 47–50.

Bailment with authority to mix—and substitute *(L. Smith)*: (1995) 111 L.Q.R. 10.

Caveat vendor! *(Brian Clapham)*: 14 Lit. 271–274.

Collateralisation and the ISDA Credit Support Annex *(David Suetens)*: [1995] 14 I.F.L. Rev. 15–16.

Consensus in dissensus (*Gordon D.L. Cameron*): 1995 S.L.T. (News) 132.

Consuming passions: implementing the E.C. Directive on unfair terms in consumer contracts *(Colin Mercer)*: [1995] 16 Bus. L.R. 102–105.

Effects of illegality: a comparative study in French and English law *(N. Enonchong)*: (1995) 44 I.C.L.Q. 196.

European briefing *(P. Duffy)*: (1995) 139 S.J. 88.

European law and unfair terms in consumer contracts *(J. Beatson)*: (1995) 54 C.L.J. 235–238.

Fair enough? *(Rex Newman* and *Clive Halperin)*: (1995) 139 S.J. 632–634.

Finance leases and implied terms of quality and fitness: a retrospective and prospective review (*A. Forte*): 1995 J.R. 119.

Force majeure in the region—law and practice *(R. Singam)*: [1995] ICLR 156.

Frustration of contracts for the sale of land in Singapore *(A. Phang)*: (1995) 44 ICLR 443.

Good faith and the control of contract terms: the E.C. Directive on Unfair Terms in Consumer Contracts (*I. MacNeil*): 1995 J.R. 147.

Information technology: a highway code *(Nigel Swycher* and *Michael Rebeiro)*: (1995) 6 P.L.C. 27–34.

"No deduction or set-off" clauses *(J. Adams)*: (1994) 57 M.L.R. 960.

Plain language in consumer contracts (*C. Willett*): 91995) SCOLAG 28.

Practical legal points for purchasers of goods and services *(E. Susan Singleton)*: (1995) 14 Tr.L. 118.

Recovery of benefits conferred pursuant to failed anticipated contracts—unjust enrichment, equitable estoppel or unjust sacrifice? 23 A.B.L.R. 117.

CONTRACT—*cont.*

Remoteness of loss in contract (*G.C. Borland*): 1995 S.L.T. (News) 239.
Research and development contracts *(Noel Byrne)*: (1995) 6 ICCLR 272–277.
Suppliers beware: implementation of the Unfair Contract Terms Directive in Europe *(Richard Kemp* and *Chris Coulter)*: [1995] 11 CLSR 194–198.
Sympathy for the devil? Contractual constraint and artistic autonomy in the entertainment industry *(S. Greenfield* and *G. Osborn)*: (1994) 15 JML&P 117.
The dark side of *Connelly v. Simpson* (1994 S.L.T. 1096) (*J. A. Dieckmann and R. Evans-Jones*): 1995 J.R. 90.
The Landlord and Tenant (Covenants) Act 1995. What are the changes? *(Denton Hall)*: [1995] 9 Corp. Brief. 27–29.
The limits of contractual order in public sector transacting *(P. Vincent-Jones)*: (1994) 14 LS 364.
The Requirements of Writing (Scotland) Act 1995 (*Professor Robert Rennie*): 1995 J.R. 445.
The Requirements of Writing (Scotland) Act 1995 (*Professors Cusine and Rennie*): (1995) 40 J.L.S. 221.
The right to cure defective performance *(A. Apps)*: [1994] LMCLQ 525.
Title claims and illegal transactions *(N. Enonchong)*: (1995) 111 L.Q.R. 135.
Title to sue on a contract of carriage in Anglo-American law *(C. Cashmore)*: (1994) 23 Anglo-Am. 488.
Unfair contracts—builders' missives and plain terms (*Joe Thomson*): (1995) 40 J.L.S. 273.

CONVEYANCING AND REAL PROPERTY

A lack of authority *(Daniel Worsley)*: [1994] *Gazette*, 24, 23–24.
Asset valuations: do they produce a market value? *(Roger Sewell)*: [1995] 139 S.J. 799.
Attorneys as trustees *(R. Oerton)*: [1995] *Gazette* Mar. 22, 18.
Clean-up Act *(Alex Catalano)*: (1995) E.G. 9533, 43.
Conveyancers and the director as purchaser *(N. Le Poidevin)*: (1995) 139 S.J. 21.
Conveyancing – a reasonable return: (1995) 145 New L.J. 1249.
Conveyancing implications of "set aside" *(A. Sydenham)*: (1994) 138 S.J. 1294.
Conveyancing: a new act (Pt. 1) *(T. Aldridge)*: (1994) 138 S.J. 1230.
Covenants for title *(Angela Sydenham)*: (1995) 10 Farm T.B. 54–55.
Execution of a mortgage deed *(C. Howells)*: (1995) 145 New L.J. 286.
French property: recent developments *(Ronald Austin)*: (1995) 9533 E.G. 80–81.
Henry Stewart 16th annual rent review conference: review of valuation papers *(G. Dale)*: (1995) 1 R.R.L.R. 31.
Land charges *(J. Manthorpe)*: [1995] *Gazette*, March 29, 22.
Leasehold enfranchisement: limits to a loophole *(D. Clarke)*: (1995) 139 S.J. 314.
Lenders' instructions to solicitors in domestic conveyancing transactions and legal fees in relation to mortgage related work *(Christopher Hadfield)*: [1995] *Gazette*, 24, 30–31.
Mind-boggling Act *(Edward Burroughs)*: [1995] 146 New L.J. 1130.
Negative reactions *(Kerry Stephenson)*: (1995) 139 S.J. 877.
New covenants for title *(Peta Dollar* and *Virginia Bryant)*: (1995) 5 P.R. 141–144.
Precedent editor's notes *(J. Adams)*: [1995] Conv. 102.
"Prolix and obscure" *(H. Wilkinson)*: [1995] Conv. 96.
Property possibilities *(Philip Shirley)*: (1995) 135 Tax. 521–522.
Property rights, injunctions and damages in lieu—Pt. 1 *(R. Wakefield)*: (1995) 139 S.J. 390.
Property, aristocracy and the reform of the land law in early nineteenth century England *(A.R. Buck)*: [1995] 16 J. Leg. Hist. 63–83.
Selling leaseholds *(T. Aldridge)*: (1994) 138 S.J. 1296.
Tenure, allodialism and indigenous rights at common law: English, United States and Australian land law compared after *Mabo v. Queensland (B. Edgeworth)*: (1994) 23 Anglo-Am. 397.
The home: excuses and contributions *(P. Milne)*: (1995) 145 New L.J. 423.
Truth, half-truths and the law *(John Chart)*: (1995) 9533 E.G. 63.
Under-value transactions and third party purchasers—impact of the new Act *(J.E. Adams)*: [1994] Conv. 434.

COPYRIGHT

An upheaval in film and television law in England *(A. Mosawi)*: (1994) 144 New L.J. 1654.
Cable and satellite transmissions: (1995) 6 P.L.C. 72–73.
Consent forms: can they be simpler? *(A. Mosawi)*: [1995] 13 I.M.L. 18.
Copyright law in the United Arab Emirates *(K. El Shalakany)*: [1995] 1 MECLR 7.
Fair dealing in the United Kingdom: A Clockwork Orange *(Christopher Benson)*: [1995] 17 EIPR 304–306.
GATT ratification means big changes to U.S. IP law *(B. McDonald)*: [1995] March M.I.P. 13.
Harmonisation of copyright duration in the European Economic Area (EEA) *(Bristows Cooke & Carpmael)*: (1995) 9 Corp. Brief. 17–19.
Impact of online computer services on copyright law *(A. Taebi)*: (1995) 11 CLSR 37.
Implementation of the E.C. Rental and Lending and Cable and Satellite Directives *(Keith Northrop)*: [1995] 17 E.I.P.R. D168–169.

COPYRIGHT—*cont.*

Introduction to multimedia: [1994] 1 C.C.M.L.R. 3–4.
IP and the convergence of technology and media *(C. Keck)*: [1995] March M.I.P. 26.
Legal measures under Bulgarian law in cases of copyright infringement of software *(V. Dimitrova)*: (1995) 11 CLSR 25.
Legal protection of databases: the legislative long haul: [1994] 1 C.C.M.L.R. 3.
Licensing music copyrights in relation to new technologies *(Gerald Orakwusi* and *Martine Alan)*: (1995) 51 C.W. 39–43.
Multimedia—licensing of music *(R. Taylor)*: [1995] 13 I.M.L. 22.
Multimedia: does Anacon provide a route to future protection? *(S. Hall)*: [1994] 6 ENT.LR 191.
New Polish copyright law *(Dr T. Drozdowska)*: (1995) 11 CLSR 18.
Nimmer on copyright *(D. Nimmer)*: [1995] Feb. M.I.P. 17.
Patenting software Humpty Dumpty rules (*Ian Lloyd*): 1995 S.L.T. (News) 163.
Performance protection in Australia—Pt. 2: recent developments *(S. McVicar)*: [1995] 1 ENT.LR 21.
Planning and copyright: copyright and planning *(A. Samuels)*: 159 J.P.N. 212.
Protection of results of genetic research by copyright or design rights? *(Gunnar W.G. Karnell)*: (1995) 17 E.I.P.R. 355–358.
Protection of software fonts in U.K. law *(J. Watts* and *F. Blakemore)*: [1995] 17 E.I.P.R. 133.
Publish and be damned? *(S. Gallant)*: [1995] *Gazette* Feb. 15, 20.
Software protection in Germany—recent court decisions in copyright law *(A. Gunther* and *U. Wuermeling)*: (1995) 11 CLSR 12.
Sole rights equals soul rights?: the new battleground for journalists and newspaper publishers *(Alistair Kelman)*: (1995) 53 C.W. 23–28.
Spare parts, articles and design rights (*Hector L. MacQueen*): 1995 S.L.T. (News) 155.
The issues of copyright piracy, the impact for developing countries, and ways/means to fight back *(Hasan Irfan Khan)*: [1995] 53 C.W. 39–42.
The publisher in the electronic age: caught in the area of conflict of copyright and competition law *(H. Heker)*: [1995] 17 E.I.P.R. 75.
Theory of property rights and copyright protection of computer programs in Europe *(M. Lehmann)*: (1995) 2 IJLIT 86.
Valuing intellectual property *(N. Bertolotti)*: [1995] Feb. M.I.P. 28.

CORONERS

Appearing at an inquest *(Mark Mullins)*: (1994) 138 S.J. 336.
Inquests: redressing the balance *(Kevin Grealis* and *Deborah Coles)*: (1994) 138 S.J. 321.
The coroner and the quantum of proof *(Paul Matthews)*: (1993) 12 C.J.Q. 279–289.
The medical inquest: Pt. 1 *(Stephen Irwin)*: [1995] L.A. Apr, 10–12.
What is the coroner for? *(Paul Matthews)*: (1994) 110 L.Q.R. 536–541.

CORPORATION TAX

A reappraisal of UK holding companies following the Finance Act 1994 *(David Hinds)*: (1995) 1 EC T.J. 53–77.
ACTually, no. *(Christopher Daws)*: (1995) Tax. P. Aug, 7–8.
Corporation tax: 134 Tax. 221.
Deferred tax revisited *(David Chopping)*: [1995] L. Ex., Jul, 21.
Foreign exchange and financial instruments: Inland Revenue Tax Bulletin 17 of 1995, 222–223.
Intra-group interest and similar sums treated as distributions: Inland Revenue Tax Bulletin 17 of 1995, 218–220.
It's official! Pt. 2: 135 Tax. 325–326.
Key points for companies *(John T. Newth)*: 135 Tax. 312–313.
Taxation *(Neal P. Todd)*: [1994] 3 E.C.L. 39–40.
The end of the road *(Daron Gunson)*: (1995) 321 Tax J. 13–17.
Will we ever get there? *(Sylvia Elwes)*: (1995) 135 Tax. 497–498.

CRIMINAL EVIDENCE AND PROCEDURE

"Access to Justice": Lord Woolf's Interim Report: [1995] 7 SCP News 6.
Admission of evidence of previous convictions: (1995) 59 J. Crim. L. 276–278.
Advising at the police station: Pt. 1 *(Neil O'May)*: (1995) L. Ex., Apr, 12–13.
Animal nuisance complaints: the dos and don'ts *(Barry F. Peachey)*: (1995) 139 S.J. 784–785.
Anne Rafferty *(Max Findlay)*: (1995) 139 S.J. 664.
Anton Piller orders: [1995] 18, I.P. News. 2–3.
Applications for pre-legal aid certificate costs—a lawful order: *(J.N. Parry)*: 159 J.P.N. 104.
Balance of interests *(Jeffrey Wilner)*: [1995] *Gazette*, 23, 24.
Beyond the limits of assault: a duty of care (*Andrew F. Phillips*): 1995 S.L.T. (News) 115.
Blaming the lawyer—part two (*Robert S. Shiels*): Crim.L.B. 14–3.
Can lies be evidence of guilt?: (1995) 59 J. Crim. L. 278–279.
Challenging DNA evidence *(A. Samuels)*: 159 J.P.N. 156.
Changes to rules on the use of computers in evidence *(Masons)*: [1995] I.H.L., Jun, 46.

CRIMINAL EVIDENCE AND PROCEDURE—*cont.*

Children and young persons before the adult magistrates' court—where are they tried? *(E. Franey)*: 159 J.P.N. 21.

Children in the crossfire *(Paul Collins)*: [1995] 25 Fam. Law 378–379.

Children: no order restricting disclosure: [1995] 5 L.G. & L. 5–6.

Church, Elliott and fresh evidence *(N.W. Orr)*: (1995) 15 Crim.Law 2–3.

Closed-circuit television in Scottish courts *(Kathleen Murray)*: (1995) 40 J.L.S.S. 314–316.

Committal for non-payment of local taxes *(P. Russell)*: 159 J.P.N. 228.

Consecutive sentences revisited: (1995) 15 Crim.Law 4–5.

Constitution – extradition – fair procedures – re-arrest – validity of order *(Linda Coughlan)*: [1995] 2 I.L.R.M. 1–16.

Corroboration: goodbye to all that? *(Diane Birch)*: [1995] Crim. L.R. 524–539.

Cowed but unbowed: Pt. 1 *(Michael Harwood)*: (1995) 139 S.J. 610.

Cracking the codes *(M. Cousens)*: [1995] *Gazette* Feb. 1, 18.

Crime commissions and the criminal trial *(M. Rozenes Q.C.)*: [1995] Crim. L.J. 65.

Crime reporter *(S. Gilchrist)*: (1995) 139 S.J. 18.

Criminal Justice and Public Order Act 1994—the Bail Act provisions *(F. Davies)*: 159 J.P.N. 259, 279.

Criminal Justice and Public Order Act 1994—the transfer provisions *(F. Davies)*: 159 J.P.N. 239.

Criminal Justice and Public Order Act 1994: police powers, bail sentencing *(N. O'May)*: [1995] L.A. Feb. 10.

Criminal justice and public order: an introduction to the 1994 Act *(Philip Brown)*: (1995) L. Ex., Mar, 14–18.

Criminal justice reform (*M. Dailly*): (1994) 218 SCOLAG 177.

Criminal law update *(T.V. Edwards)*: [1995] *Gazette* Mar. 22, 32.

Current topic: hospital orders without conviction *(A. Samuels)*: [1995] Crim.L.R. 220.

Curtailing the right to silence, access to legal advice and section 78 *(H. Fenwick)*: [1995] Crim.L.R. 132.

Custodial sentences: [1995] 2, S. News 2–3.

Database detection methods in criminal investigation *(V. Collins)*: (1995) 11 CLSR 2.

Direction – evidence of complainant of sexual offence or of accomplice: [1995] 6 Arch. News 3–4.

Disclosing unused material to the defence: [1995] 159 J.P. 515.

Dissimilar views of similar facts *(Colin F.H. Tapper)*: [1995] 111 (Jul), L.Q.R. 381–385.

Documents order was too wide: [1995] 159 J.P. 465.

Doubts and burdens: DNA evidence, probability and the courts *(Mike Redmayne)*: [1995] Crim.L.R. 464.

Early views of CJA 1991: [1995] 42 Probat. J. 119–120.

European co-operation in telephone tapping *(Susan Nash)*: [1995] 145 New L.J. 954.

Evidence in care order application: [1995] 5 L.G. & L. 7–8.

Exclusion of unfair evidence on summary trial: [1995] 159 J.P. 465.

Exculpatory statements and confessions *(J. Smith)*: [1995] Crim.L.R. 280.

Expensive disasters for justice *(Rinita Sarker)*: [1995] 16 Co. Law. 181–183.

Fair trial *(Sir Anthony Mason)*: [1995] Crim.L.J. 7.

Fresh evidence appeals (*Peter Ferguson*): (1995) 40 J.L.S. 264.

From committal proceedings to transfer for trial (*Robert Girvan*): (1995) 159 J.P. 379.

Genuine public interest *(Stephen Gilchrist)*: (1995) 139 S.J. 686.

Handling convictions admissible under s.27(3) of the Theft Act 1968 *(R. Munday)*: 159 J.P.N. 223, 261.

Improving custodial legal advice *(L. Bridges* and *J. Hodgson)*: [1995] Crim.L.R. 101.

Insanity, automatism, and the burden of proof on the accused *(Timothy H. Jones)*: [1995] 111 L.Q.R. 475–516.

Juries: a dinosaur bound for extinction?: [1995] 21 *Legal Times* 7.

Law Reform: hearsay and related topics: [1995] 7 Arch. News 4.

Lord Woolf's interim report: [1995] Jul/Aug Counsel 15, 16, 18.

Mental disorder and criminal proceedings (*D. Kelly*): Crim L.B. 13–6.

Mode of trial: [1995] 7 Arch. News 4–5.

New improved PACE *(R. Ede)*: (1995) 139 S.J. 298.

Non-police station interviews? (1995) 139 S.J. 299.

Not completely appealing *(A. Owers)*: (1995) 145 New L.J. 353.

Notices *(David Wurtzel)*: [1995] Jul/Aug, Counsel 30.

Offenders subject to existing sentences or orders: [1995] 2 S. News 4–5.

Piecemeal reform threatens the rights of accused persons (*T. Ross*): (1995) 218 SCOLAG 4.

Practice direction: direction by the Lord Chief Justice for the allocation of business within the Crown Court: [1995] *Gazette*, 25, 40–41.

Prejudicial evidence relied on by co-defendant – exculpatory part of "mixed statement" adduced by prosecution: [1995] 6 Arch. News 4–5.

Procedural problems in representing children *(P. Harris)*: (1995) 7 JCL 49.

Proof of wilful casting away *(Nicholas Legh-Jones)*: (1995) 3 (Aug) L.M.C.L.Q. 305–308.

CRIMINAL EVIDENCE AND PROCEDURE—*cont.*

Psychology and legal practice: fairness and accuracy in identification parades *(I. McKenzie)*: [1995] Crim.L.R. 200.
Racism, impartiality and juries *(Peter Herbert)*: [1995] 146 New L.J. 1138–1140.
Reasons to be cheerful *(A. Lindsay)*: (1994) 57 M.L.R. 954.
Restrictions on reporting proceedings: (1995) 59 J. Crim. L. 270–271.
Rigid rules keep innocent in jail? *(Thomas Ross)*: (1995) 223 SCOLAG 73–74.
Science in the criminal process *(P. Roberts)*: (1994) 14 O.J.L.S. 469.
Taxation of costs: 159 J.P.N. 155.
The all-white American jury *(Albert W. Alschuler)*: (1995) 145 New L.J. 1005–1006.
The Criminal Justice Act *(B. George)*: [1994] *Gazette* Dec. 16, 19 [1995] *Gazette* Jan. 5, 24.
The Criminal Justice and Public Order Act 1994—the effect on young offenders *(L. Jason-Lloyd)*: 159 J.P.N. 89.
The Criminal Justice and Public Order Act 1994—the evidence provisions *(I. Dennis)*: [1995] Crim.L.R. 4.
The Criminal Justice and Public Order Act 1994: Pt. 3: Evidence and the right to silence *(Neil O'May)*: [1995] Jul, Legal Action 10–13.
The erosion of *Boardman v. DPP*: Pt. 1 *(Colin Tapper)*: (1995) 145 New L.J. 1223–1225.
The form of indictments: comments on the Law Commission's consultation paper *(M. Bowes)*: [1995] Crim.L.R. 114.
The interface between crime and child protection *(Barbara Mitchels)*: [1995] L. Ex., Jul, 14–15.
The meaning of "jointly charged": [1995] 159 J.P. 529.
The Misuse of Drugs Act 1971 (*Keith S. Bovey*): (1995) 40 J.L.S. 355.
The new code for Crown prosecutors: (1) Prosecution, accountability and the public interest *(A. Ashworth* and *J. Fionda)*: [1994] Crim.L.R. 894.
The new code for Crown prosecutors: (2) A response *(R. Daw)*: [1994] Crim.L.R. 904.
The O.J. Simpson trial and the American legal system *(William T. Pizzi)*: (1995) 145 New L.J. 990.
The principles to be followed when forfeiture under consideration—the re-establishment of Venetian mercantile law?: 159 J.P.N. 124.
The prosecutor fine *(P. Duff)*: (1994) O.J.L.S. 563.
The right to silence *(A. Murdie)*: (1995) 139 S.J. 148.
The right to silence, the Bill and European human rights (*C.H.W. Gane*): Crim L.B. 13–2.
The study tour of Denmark March 1995 *(Lynne Ravenscroft)*: [1995] 51 Magistrate 136, 150.
Undercover police operations and what the suspects said (or didn't say) *(Andrew L-T. Choo* and *Manda Mellors)*: (1995) 2 Web J.C.L.I. 22–33.
Victory for criminal solicitors over standard fees: [1995] 139 S.J. 755.
What is the criminal justice system for? *(Brian P. Block)*: [1995] 159 J.P. 485–486.

CRIMINAL LAW

A judicial step too far *(A. Jack)*: (1995) 145 New I.J. 315.
After *R. v. Kingston*: is there scope for a new defence of involuntary intoxication? *(L.M. Clements)*: [1995] 59 J. Crim. L. 305–309.
All the blue bonnets are over the border: cross-border policing under the Criminal Justice and Public Order Act (*A. N. Brown*): (1994) 62 S.L.G. 135.
An analysis of fraud vitiating consent in rape cases *(Alan Reed)*: (1995) 59(3) J. Crim. L. 310–315.
Assault and reasonable chastisement (*Elaine Ness*): 1995 S.L.T. (News) 185.
Assault and s.47 of the Offences Against the Person Act 1861 *(Morayo Atoki)*: [1995] 59 J. Crim. L. 299–304.
Automatism and insanity in the laws of England and Scotland (*G. T. Laurie*): 1995 J.R. 253.
Beta-blockers and asthmatics: some lessons from the case of *R. v. Dr A.K. Sinha (R. Collins)*: 159 J.P.N. 3.
Breathalyser procedure and the hospital patient *(J. Black)*: (1994) 138 S.J. 1287.
Causing the death of an unborn child: Crim.L.B. 12–3.
Changes in the newspaper reporting of rape trials since the Second World War *(Keith Soothill* and *Chris Grover)*: (1995) 37 Res. B. 45–49.
Changes to confiscation procedures in drugs cases *(T. Millington)*: (1995) 139 S.J. 210.
Child sex tourism *(Jessica Holroyd)*: (1995) 145 New L.J. 1199–1200.
Child sexual abuse, access and the wishes of children *(E. Jones* and *P. Parkinson)*: (1995) 9 IJFL 54.
Collective trespass and related issues (*I.S. Dickson*): (1995) 40 J.L.S. 63.
Consent and offences against the person: Law Commission Consultation Paper No. 134 *(D. Ormerod)*: (1994) 57 M.L.R. 928.
Conspiracy to defraud; some comments on the Law Commission's report *(J. Smith)*: [1995] Crim.L.R. 209.
Contra bonos mores: fraud affecting consent in rape *(A. Reed)*: (1995) 145 New L.J. 174.
Corporate criminality: four models of fault *(J. Gobert)*: (1994) 14 L.S. 393.
Counterfeiting – possessing materials with intent: (1995) 59(3) J. Crim. L. 279–280.
Cowed but unbowed: Pt. 1 *(Michael Harwood)*: (1995) 139 S.J. 610–611.
Crime reporter *(S. Gilchrist)*: (1994) 138 S.J. 1254.

CRIMINAL LAW—*cont.*

Crime reporter *(S. Gilchrist)*: (1995) 139 S.J. 18.

Criminal Justice and Public Order Act 1994: obscenity, pornography and videos *(C. Manchester)*: [1995] Crim.L.R. 123.

Criminal Justice and Public Order Act 1994: the public order provisions *(N. O'May)*: [1994] L.A. Dec. 10.

Criminal law aspects of computer crime: general theory of computer crimes and the proposed bill to modify the Brazilian Penal Code *(O. Banho Licks* and *J. Marcello de Araujo Junior)*: (1995) 2 IJLIT 64.

Criminal liability in relation to tax *(Michael Jump)*: (1995–96) 4 P.T.P.R. 39–50.

Disqualification for not telling the police who the driver was *(A. Samuels)*: 158 J.P.N. 796.

Drinking and causing death by dangerous driving: [1995] 59 J. Crim. L. 271–273.

Drugs in the cells *(Linda Goldman)*: (1995) L. Ex. Aug, 43.

Excessive use of force in self-defence: [1995] 59 J. Crim. L. 281–282.

Forfeiture of property used in crime *(Alastair Brown)*: 1995 S.L.T. (News) 287.

Form and function in the law of involuntary manslaughter *(M. Wasik)*: [1994] Crim.L.R. 883.

Getting away with it *(Stephen Gilchrist)*: (1995) 139 S.J. 875.

Gypsies: the criminalisation of a way of life? *(S. Campbell)*: [1995] Crim.L.R. 28.

Hard time for soft drugs? *(P. Edge)*: (1995) 145 New L.J. 501.

Homicide of children *(D. Power)*: 159 J.P.N. 209.

International initiatives in the field of money laundering *(William C. Gilmore)*: 10 I.B.F.L. 258–264.

Manslaughter by gross negligence *(S. Gardner)*: (1995) 111 L.Q.R. 22.

Manslaughter: the dilemma facing the law reformer *(Nicola Padfield)*: [1995] 59 J. Crim. L. 291–298.

Money laundering—the complete guide—Pt. 1 *(L. Jason-Lloyd)*: (1995) 145 New L.J. 149.

Money laundering (Pt. 4) *(L. Jason-Lloyd)*: (1995) 145 New L.J. 278.

New rules for juvenile offenders *(T. Wilkinson)*: (1995) 139 S.J. 110.

Offending in breach of bail conditions *(J. Ross)*: 1995 S.L.T. (News) 85.

Professional and legal policy: police station advice in indictable-only cases: guidance from the criminal law committee of the Law Society: (1995) 92 *Gazette* 27.

Provocation and the reasonable person *(Leonard Herschel Leigh)*: (1995) 145 New L.J. 1308–1309.

Psychiatric injury and the bodily harm criterion *(D. Kell)*: (1995) 111 L.Q.R. 27.

Public order review *(J. Cooper)*: [1995] L.A. Feb. 16.

Putting joint enterprise in its place *(John Smith)*: (1995) 5 Arch. News 4–6.

Rape, fraud and consent: the correct approach *(A. Reed)*: (1995) 139 S.J. 44.

Reparation and mediation within the criminal justice system *(Bryan Clarke)*: 1995 S.L.T. (News) 225.

Restitution's uncertain progress *(Joanna Bird)*: (1995) 3(Aug) L.M.C.L.Q. 308–313.

Restraint orders and drug trafficking *(S. Whitehead)*: (1994) 145 New L.J. 446.

Rethinking corporate crime and individual responsibility *(Mark Stallworthy)*: (1995) 55 Crim.Law 5–7.

Ritual magic *(P. Edge)*: (1994) 144 New L.J. 1601.

Russia: strict penalties proposed for pirates: (1995) 53 C.W. 10–11.

Sex, public order and criminal justice *(P. Tain)*: (1994) 138 S.J. 1178.

Sexual harassment—opening up a Pandora's Box? *(P. Townsend* and *A. Baker)*: 159 J.P.N. 39.

Stalking: crime of the nineties? *(M. Goode)*: [1995] Crim.L.J. 21.

Taking the strait-jacket off: persistence and the distribution of punishment in England and Wales *(I. Brownlee)*: (1994) 14 L.S. 295.

The corporate body *(G. Slapper)*: [1995] *Gazette* Feb. 15, 18.

The Criminal Justice and Public Order Act 1994—the effect on young offenders *(L. Jason-Lloyd)*: 159 J.P.N. 71.

The Criminal Justice and Public Order Act 1994—the evidence provisions *(I. Dennis)*: [1995] Crim.L.R. 4.

The development of the law of fire raising *(M.T. Morrow)*: 1995 S.L.T. 51.

The globalization of criminology: the new frontier is the frontier *(William F. McDonald)*: (1995) 1 T.O.C. 1–22.

The hearsay provisions of the Criminal Justice (Scotland) Act 1995 *(Alastair N. Brown)*: 1995 S.L.G. 109.

The interface between crime and child protection *(Barbara Mitchels)*: (1995) L. Ex. Jul, 14–15.

The internationalization of business crime *(Dick Thornburgh)*: (1995) 1 T.O.C. 23–32.

The Metropolitan Police assault: charging offences—are they based on law? *(J. Woods)*: 159 J.P.N. 42.

The Misuse of Drugs Act 1971: Part 1: Duplication in charges *(Keith S. Bovey)*: (1995) 40 J.L.S.S. 306–308.

The police station advisers' accreditation scheme *(Michael McGhie)*: (1995) L. Ex. Aug, 44–45.

The prosecutions of war crimes in the former Yugoslavia *(C. Greenwood)*: (1994) 26 Bracton L.J. 13.

The public order elements *(A. Smith)*: [1995] Crim.L.R. 19.

The rights of the accused in Islam: Pt. 1 *(Taha J. Al Alwani)*: (1995) 10 A.L.Q. 3–16.

The saviour of many a motorist *(N. Ley* and *F. Warren)*: (1994) 144 New L.J. 1669.

CRIMINAL LAW—*cont.*

Trading standards—searches by power or consent *(V. Smith)*: 159 J.P.N. 76.
United States foreign narcopolicy: shifting focus to international crime? *(Raphael F. Perl)*: (1995) 1 T.O.C. 33–46.
Victims, mediation and criminal justice *(M. Wright)*: [1995] Crim.L.R. 187.
Watch out for the Indians! The new endorsable offences under the Traffic Signs and General Directions 1994—green arrows and barred entries: 159 J.P.N. 55.
What do you tell your clients? (1995) 139 S.J. 320.
Who cares about traffic offences? *(B. Block)*: 159 J.P.N. 19.
Who has jurisdiction for cross-frontier financial crimes? *(Geoff Gilbert)*: (1995) 2 Web J.C.L.I. 34–48.
Wild bird crime (*contributed*): Crim.L.B. 14–2.
Wounding/assault offences: from prosecution to conviction *(Patrick Collier)*: (1995) 37 Res. B. 65–70.

CRIMINAL SENTENCING

Against violence *(James Pirrie)*: (1995) 25 (Aug) Fam. Law 395–396.
An early face-lift for pre-sentence reports *(N. Stone)*: 159 J.P.N. 140.
Comment: [1995] 1 S. News 12.
Committal for non-payment of local taxes *(P. Russell)*: 159 J.P.N. 228.
Consecutive sentences revisited (*Contributed*): Crim.L.B. 15–5.
Consecutive sentences revisited: (1995) 15 Crim.Law 4–5.
Criminal Justice and Public Order Act 1994: the Bail Act provisions *(F. Davies)*: 159 J.P.N. 279.
Criminal Justice and Public Order Act 1994: police powers, bail sentencing *(N. O'May)*: [1995] L.A. Feb. 10.
Criminal justice and the trial and sentencing of white collar offenders *(R. Henham)*: 59 JCL 83.
Detention of juveniles: (1995) 4 (Aug) S. News 10–12.
Diversion from prosecution into psychiatric care (*Peter Duff*): 1995 S.L.T. (News) 159.
Effectiveness and the probation service *(P. Whitehead)*: 159 J.P.N. 226.
Melting pot mentality *(Patricia Rogers)*: (1995) 99 Prison Serv. J. 47–49.
Race and sentencing: a reply *(R. Hood)*: [1995] Crim.L.R. 272.
Racial discrimination in sentencing? A study with dubious conclusions *(T. Halevy)*: [1995] Crim.L.R. 267.
Reasons to be cheerful *(A. Lindsay)*: (1994) 57 M.L.R. 954.
Road traffic update *(Paul Niekirk)*: (1995) 92(3) Gazette 31–32.
Sentencing and justice (*Thomas Ross*): (1995) 226 SCOLAG 126.
Sentencing drink-drive offenders: (1995) 159 J.P. 565–566
Sentencing policy and the role of the Court of Appeal *(Ralph Henlam)*: (1995) 34 Howard Journal 218–227.
Taking the strait-jacket off: persistence and the distribution of punishment in England and Wales *(I. Brownlee)*: (1994) 14 LS 295.
The Criminal Justice and Public Order Act 1994—the effect on young offenders *(L. Jason-Lloyd)*: 159 J.P.N. 89.
The Misuse of Drugs Act 1971 (*Keith Bovey*): (1995) 40 J.L.S. 306.
The unacceptable face of sentencing *(Henry Fletcher)*: [1995] 9 *Lawyer* 12.
Transitional problems: [1995] 3 S. News 8–10.
Viewpoint: time to consolidate: [1995] 3 S. News 10–12.
White-haired offenders *(H. Codd)*: (1994) 144 New L.J. 1582.

CUSTOMS AND EXCISE

Customs update *(Andrew Hart)*: (1995) 47 VAT Plan. 7–8.
External adjudication of complaints against Customs & Excise *(David Cheyne)*: (1995) 45 VAT Plan. 6–7.
Generalised system of preferences: a new look for 1995: [1995] 1 B. News 9–10.
Programme of change in Customs and Excise *(Mike Rickwood)*: (1995) 1 (Spr) B. News 5.
VAT enforcement *(Adrian Shryane)*: [1995] 50 Adviser 40–42.
VAT planning: Keith – the first ten years *(Peter Trevett)*: (1995) 13 VAT Int. 1235–1237.

DAMAGES

A case for awarding punitive damages in response to deliberate breaches of contract *(Nicholas J. McBride)*: [1995] 24 Anglo-Am. 369–390.
Approaching future wage loss (*Robert Milligan*): 1995 S.L.T. (News) 173.
Assessment of pension rights in personal injuries claims (*J. Blaikie*): 1995 J.R. 40.
Avoiding the benefits trap *(P. Lucioli)*: [1995] *Gazette* Jan. 18, 18.
Civil juries on trial *(Robert Milligan)*: (1995) 4 (Jul) Reparation 6.
Claims that cannot be pensioned off *(T. Levitt* and *J. Stanbury)*: (1994) 138 S.J. (Dec. Supp.) 26.
Compensation recovery (*F. Maguire*): (1994) 39 J.L.S.S. 455.
Criminal injuries compensation: the symbolic dimension (*P. Duff*): 1995 J.R. 102.
Damages for breach of the equitable duty of confidence *(D. Capper)*: (1994) 14 L.S. 313.

DAMAGES—*cont.*

Damages for nervous shock: a developing area? *(Philip Noble)*: [1995] 139 S.J. 720–721.
Damages for psychiatric injuries *(A. Ritchie)*: (1994) 144 New L.J. 1690.
Damages for rebuilding *(H. Beale)*: (1995) 111 L.Q.R. 54.
Damages for the birth of a child *(Angus Stewart Q.C.)*: (1995) 40 J.L.S. 298.
Enforcement of cross-undertaking in damages *(I. Scott)*: (1995) 14 C.J.Q. 85.
European briefing *(Peter Duffy)*: (1995) 139 S.J. 655.
Harassment and eviction: Pt. 1 *(Nic Madge)*: (1995) 145 New L.J. 937–938.
High valuations versus bad lending *(Paul F.J. Wade)*: (1995) 4 (Jul) Reparation 2–4.
Industrial dust diseases and a forgotten compensation scheme *(Tony Fitzgerald)*: (1995) 224 SCOLAG 88.
Interdict proceedings in Scotland to prevent or restrain court actions in the United States *(Eric Brown)*: 1995 S.L.T. (News) 253.
Late payment of commercial debt—a statutory right to interest—the arguments *(A. Samuels)*: (1995) 14 Tr.L. 132.
Lending trends *(Stephen Bickford-Smith)*: *Eagle*, June 1995, 9–10.
Life is priceless *(T. Aldridge)*: (1994) 138 S.J. 1174.
Medical negligence claims *(David Sandison)*: (1995) 40 J.L.S. 309.
Multi-party actions *(W.C.H. Ervine)*: 1995 S.L.T. (News) 207.
Nervous shock *(Maurice O'Carroll)*: (1995) 40 J.L.S. 231.
Nervous shock: bystander witnessing a catastrophe *(T. Keng Feng)*: (1995) 111 L.Q.R. 48.
Overstating the case *(Michael Taub)*: *Legal Times*, May 30, 1995, pp.6, 14.
Pollution and damages – two important judicial pronouncements *(Paul Sheridan)*: (1995) Env. L.B. Jul, 6–8.
Property rights, injunctions and damages in lieu—Pt. 1 *(R. Wakefield)*: (1995) 139 S.J. 390.
Quantum of damages *(Halsbury's Monthly Bulletin)*: (1995) 145 New L.J. 307.
Suing the police *(Sailesh Mehta* and *Steven Allen)*: (1995) L. Ex. Jul, 16–18.
The assessment of damages in actions against valuers: recent U.K. decisions *(J. Biggart)*: [1994] 11 Int. ILR 401.
The calculation of damages for patent infringement *(Richard Boulton* and *Mark Bezant)*: (1995) 50 M.I.P. 32–38.
The Eichleay formula: computing and recovering unabsorbed head office overheads incurred by contractors as a result of employer-caused delay *(H. Kirsh)*: 11 Const.L.J. 90.
To deduct or not? *(Ian Cruse)*: (1995) 4 Revenue 1–2.
To what extent has the decision in *Ruxley Electronics* changed the law of damages in building disputes? *(N. Brooke* and *M. Curtis)*: 11 Const.L.J. 29.
Traumatised Hillsborough police officers fail proximity damages test: [1995] 235 H. & S.B. 13–15.
What is meant by consequential loss in relation to computer contracts? *(M. Webster)*: (1994) 10 CL&P 175.

DIVORCE AND CONSISTORIAL CAUSES

Cases under the Family Law (Scotland) Act 1985 *(I. L. S. Balfour)*: (1994) 39 J.L.S.S. 437.
Financial provision on divorce—the extent of judicial discretion *(J. Thomson)*: (1994) 62 S.L.G. 141.
Options hearings in family actions *(A. McTaggart)*: Fam.L.B. 13–10.
Proprietary rights of cohabitants *(K. McK. Norrie)*: 1995 J.R. 209.
Resistance, tolerance and impatience: an inquiry into lawyers' attitudes to cohabitation contracts *(E. Kingdom)*: 1995 S.L.G. 12.
Valuing business for matrimonial property *(Joe Thomson)*: 1995 S.L.G. 113.

EASEMENTS AND PRESCRIPTION

Abandonment of an easement: is it a question of intention only? *(Christine J. Davis)*: (1995) Conv. Jul/Aug, 291–301.
Crime and the right of prescription: (1993) 137 S.J. 1161–1163.
Easements: a review of some recent cases *(George Chesman)*: (1993) J.P.L., Nov, 1012–1017.
Limitation, prescription and unsolicited permission *(Herbert Wallace)*: [1994] Conv., May/Jun, 196–210.
Water easements *(Angela Sydenham)*: (1995) 10 Farm T.B. 48–49.
Wheeldon v. Burrows revisited *(John West)*: (1995) Conv. Jul/Aug, 346–349.

ECCLESIASTICAL LAW

Ecclesiastical lawyers and the English reformation *(R.H. Helmholz)*: (1995) 3 Ecc. L.J. 360–370.
Report of Working Party on the legal preliminaries to marriage *(M.G. Smith)*: (1995) 3 Ecc. L.J. 323–336.
The governing body of the Church in Wales: recent legislation *(Thomas Glyn Watkin)*: (1995) 3 Ecc. L.J. 341–342.
What is a peculiar? *(Paul Barber)*: (1995) 3 Ecc. L.J. 299–312.

EDUCATION

A new year and a new tribunal *(J. Robinson)*: (1995) 145 New L.J. 15.
Education and profit: (1995) 2 Revenue 7–8.
Enforcing students' rights in Irish and English law *(A. Carroll)*: [1994] 12 ILT 259.
Government and education news: FE colleges: the employment contract drama goes on *(Patricia Leighton)*: [1995] 29 Law Teach. 215–216.
Legal education and training in Europe: United Kingdom *(Richard De Friend)*: [1995] 2 I.J.L.P. 119–146.
Legislation by leaflet? *(Nick Richens)*: (1995) 22 Legal Times 4, 14.
New structures in education *(S. Simblet)*: (1995) 139 S.J. 296.
The future of local education authorities as strategic planners *(Paul Meredith)*: [1995] Sum, P.L. 234–243.

ELECTION LAW

Election advertising (*Colin r. Munro*): 1995 S.L.T. (News) 145.
Election petitions and their outcome (*Gavin D. Anderson*): (1995) 40 J.L.S. 305.
Election petitions and their outcome: when the vote counts *(Gavin D. Anderson)*: (1995) 40 J.L.S.S. 305–306.

ELECTRICITY

Electricity: the distribution price control *(Kenneth Bailey)*: (1995) 6 ULR 57–58.
Restructuring the electricity and gas power industries in Poland *(K. Oldziej)*: [1995] 1 OGLTR 26.
Third party access in the electricity industry in Spain *(Dr L. Pastor Ridruejo)*: [1995] 1 OGLTR 30.
Third party access in the energy sector in E.C. law *(S. Beeston)*: [1995] 1 OGLTR 5.
Third party access to electricity and natural gas networks in Sweden *(M. Borresen* and *J. Laver)*: [1995] 1 OGLTR 34.

EMERGENCY LAWS

Warnings for mainland U.K. from Northern Ireland *(B. McGrory)*: [1994] L.A. Dec. 9.

EMPLOYMENT

A question of liability *(R. Brent)*: [1995] *Gazette* Jan. 5, 15.
A step in the dark? *(J. Nazerali* and *K. Plumbley-Jones)*: (1995) 139 S.J. 144.
Boys wear blue: dress codes as a form of sex discrimination *(L. Flynn)*: [1994] 12 ILT 286.
Changes on the way in employment rights: domestic employment rights: E.C. driven changes: [1994] 1 CCMLR 6–7.
Changing employment practices *(Kathy Saunders)*: (1995) 1(2) T.E.L. & P. 14–15.
Creating a policy to deal with racial harassment: (1995) 19(8) C.S.R. 62–63.
Deciding when jobs of equal value can be paid unequally: an examination of s.1(3) of the Equal Pay Act 1970 *(C. Kilpatrick)*: 23 I.L.J. 311.
Developments in the U.K. law on transfer of undertakings *(M. Haworth)*: [1994] 5 E.B.L.R. 236.
Directive on the establishment of European works councils: effect of U.K. and non-E.U. companies *(R. D'Sa)*: [1994] 5 B.L.R. 295.
Disability Discrimination Bill *(Edward Myers)*: [1995] 145 New L.J. 1156.
Employment in the prison service; whither public service regulation? *(G. Morris)*: [1994] P.L. 535.
Employment law update *(M. Edwards)*: (1995) 139 S.J. 165, 605.
Employment law update (*Malcolm Mackay and Shona Simon*): (1995) 40 J.L.S. 230.
Employment update *(M. Edwards)*: [1995] *Gazette* Jan. 25, 31.
Equality—but what is the cost? (*Fergus Muirhead*): (1995) 224 SCOLAG 92.
European briefing *(P. Duffy)*: (1994) 138 S.J. 1232.
From discrimination to obstacles to free movement: recent developments concerning the free movement of workers 1989–1994 *(E. Johnson* and *D. O'Keefe)*: [1994] 31 C.M.L.Rev. 1313.
Groundwater pollution in the United States: the mess left behind *(A. Crane)*: [1994] 12 OGLTR 383.
Indirect employment *(G. Axe)*: 134 Tax. 266.
Irish fiscal incentives for film and TV production *(K. Hoy* and *S. Curran)*: (1994) 12 I.M.L. 91.
Joint liability for unfair dismissal on transfers *(T. Bettany)*: (1995) 139 S.J. 43.
"Justice doesn't mean a free lunch": the application of the principle of equal pay to occupational pension schemes *(S. Moore)*: [1995] E.L.Rev. 159.
Maternity changes—implications for employers (*Sue Morris*): (1995) 40 J.L.S. 150.
New draft acquired rights Directive—a step in the dark? *(J. Nazerali* and *K. Plumbley-Jones)*: [1995] 6 E.B.L.R. 31.
Pregnancy and dismissal: rejecting the "sick male" comparison *(L. Flynn)*: [1994] 12 ILT 257.
Pregnant pause for employers *(A. Burnside)*: [1994] 15 B.L.R. 323.
Privatisation, the rail strike and the law (*K. Miller*): Emp.L.B. 4–7.
Recent developments in U.S. environmental litigation *(C. Kline)*: [1995] 1 Int. ILR 7.
Remedies for breach of employment contracts *(D. Brown)*: 23 I.L.J. 331.

EMPLOYMENT—*cont.*

Rights vs Efficiency? The economic case for transnational labour standards *(S. Deakin* and *F. Wilkinson)*: 23 I.L.J. 289.

Rights, duties and the end of *Marshall (J. Coppel)*: (1994) 57 M.L.R. 859.

Skirting around sexual harassment *(I. Mackay* and *J. Earnshaw)*: (1995) 145 New L.J. 338.

Special briefing—Green Paper on employment law (*S. Briggs*): (1995) 218 SCOLAG 11.

Stress injuries at work *(B. McKenna)*: (1994) 144 New L.J. 1652.

Terms of employment—managing change within the law *(C. Wynn-Evans)*: [1994] 15 B.L.R. 326.

The definition of discrimination in European Community sex equality law *(E. Ellis)*: [1994] 19 E.L.Rev. 563.

The full picture *(F. Lagerberg)*: 134 Tax. 450.

The judge's pen – blue pencil or drafting tool? *(Paul Newdick)*: [1995] 21 Supp Emp *Legal Times* 16.

The legal issues of occupational stress (*V. Craig*): Emp.L.B. 4–9.

Transfer of Undertakings (Protection of Employment) Regulations 1981 (as amended)—update *(M. Ahmad)*: 158 J.P.N. 764.

Tress sense *(P. Bibby)*: (1994) 144 New L.J. 1769.

TUPE or NUPE *(S. Miller)*: (1994) 13 Tr.L. 518.

Unfair dismissal: practitioners' update *(Martin Edwards)*: (1995) L. Ex., Apr, 16–17.

Unilateral variation of contract and recovery of wages (*K. Miller*): (1994) 62 S.L.G. 137.

Whistleblowing—time for a change? *(N. Rose)*: (1995) 145 New L.J. 113.

Whistleblowing and freedom of speech in the NHS *(Lucy Vickers)*: (1995) 145 New L.J. 1257–1258.

Working overseas: (1995) 548 IDS Brief 7–12.

ENVIRONMENTAL LAW

Access to environmental information: implementation and experience with Directive 90/313/EEC *(Torsten Wasch)*: (1995) 25 (1/2) E.P. & L. 41–42.

Broadcast regulation in Italy: debating new rules to join the European audio-visual market *(E. Andreatta* and *G. Pedde)*: [1995] 1 ENT.LR 7.

Child performers in film and television productions *(I. Steel)*: [1995] 13 I.M.L. 13.

Clean-up and control: outcome of government review (*C. Smith*): Environ.L.B. 4–8.

Environmental law update *(Angela Hayes)*: (1995) 139 S.J. 629–630.

Environmental litigation and the international legal system *(Michael Bowman)*: [1995] 3 Env. Liability 70–76.

Environmental protection: "causing or knowingly permitting" pollution: recent case law *(G. Holgate)*: 158 J.P.N. 797.

Environmental protection: "causing" pollution—the final word? *(G. Holgate)*: 159 J.P.N. 127.

European update and outlook for 1995 (*D. Reid*): Environ.L.B. 4–9.

Judicial review in the UK – a new environmental weapon? *(Louise Moore)*: [1995] 13 OGLTR, 262–266.

Limitations and chemical poisoning *(A. Care)*: (1995) 139 S.J. 17.

Noise: common law controls (*Francis McManus*): 1995 49 SPEL 48.

Performance protection in Australia—Pt. 2: recent developments *(S. McVicar)*: [1995] 1 ENT.LR 21.

Planning and environmental law offences *(R. Jackson)*: (1994) 158 J.P.N. 784.

Planning and pollution control (*G. Bruce Smith*): 1995 49 SPEL 46.

Planning, pollution and noise control *(R. Stein* and *S. Humber)*: (1995) 139 S.J. 12.

Private international law of the environment (*P. R. Beaumont*): 1995 J.R. 28.

Proposals for air quality control *(Linklaters & Paines)*: (1995) 6(7) P.L.C. 62–63.

Sites of special scientific interest (*Neil Collar*): (1995) 40 J.L.S. 139.

The Braer and the admissibility of claims for pollution damage under the 1992 Protocols to the Civil Liability Convention and the Fund Convention *(Edward H.P. Brans)*: [1995] 3 Env. Liability 61–69.

The Environment Bill: provisions on contaminated land (*C. Smith*): Env. L.B. 5–4.

The importance of environmental due-diligence in corporate transactions *(D. Lawrence)*: (1994) 26 Bracton L.J. 23.

Transport and the environment *(N. Branton)*: [1995] 13 C. & S.L.J. 13.

Voluntary Eco-Management and Audit Scheme for Local Government: Department of the Environment Circular 2/95: (1995) 7 E.L.M. 111–112.

EQUITY AND TRUSTS

Ascertainability in transfer and tracing of title *(D. Hayton)*: [1994] LMCLQ 449.

Attorneys as trustees *(R. Oerton)*: [1995] *Gazette* Mar. 22, 18.

Barnes v. Addy: the requirements of knowledge *(M. Lodge)*: (1995) 23 A.B.L.R. 25.

Clarifying the benefit settlor rules *(C. Cook* and *R. Tunnicliffe)*: (1994) 138 S.J. 1286.

Creditors and collateral purposes *(N. Hopkins)*: (1995) 111 L.Q.R. 72.

Damages for breach of the equitable duty of confidence *(D. Capper)*: (1994) 14 L.S. 313.

EQUITY AND TRUSTS—*cont.*

Discretionary trusts in wills *(R. Ray)*: 135 Tax. 13.

Estoppel by convention—an old doctrine with new potential *(M. Harvey)*: (1995) 23 A.B.L.R. 45.

In rem or *in personam*? *Webb v. Webb (P. Birks)*: (1994) 8 TruLI 99.

Member trustees and augmentations of pension scheme benefits *(D. Griffiths)*: (1994) 8 TruLI 109.

New court protection rules *(S. Hutcheson)*: (1995) 139 S.J. 170.

Powers of investment – a gap between the law and practice? *(Angela Latham)*: (1995) 3 Nott. L.J. 95–105.

The benefit and burden of covenants – now where are we? *(John Snape)*: (1995) 3 Nott. L.J. 68–94.

The home: excuses and contributions *(P. Milne)*: (1995) 145 New L.J. 423.

The qualifying settlement *(C. Sokol)*: 134 Tax. 480.

The trust versus the company under the Charities Act 1992 and 1993 (1994) 144 New L.J. Charities Supp. 23.

Trustees' liability *(R. Ham)*: (1995) 9 TruLI 21.

Vendor placings: financing acquisitions with equity *(Noel Hutton* and *Patrick Rawnsley)*: (1995) 6 P.L.C. 17–25.

ESTOPPEL

Abandonment of an easement: is it a question of intention only? *(Christine J. Davis)*: (1995) Conv. Jul/Aug, 291–301.

Estoppel by convention—an old doctrine with new potential *(M. Harvey)*: (1995) 23 A.B.L.R. 45.

Matharu v. Matharu: a hard case certainly, but does it make bad law? *(Graham Battersby)*: (1995) 7 C.F.L.Q. 59–65.

Recovery of benefits conferred pursuant to failed anticipated contracts—unjust enrichment, equitable estoppel or unjust sacrifice? 23 A.B.L.R. 117.

EUROPEAN UNION

A European Union of fifteen: and more to come? Time to take stock: (1995) 13 ILT 1.

Agents and compensation *(J. Roberts)*: (1995) 145 New L.J. 453.

An American view on the E.U. Database Directive *(H. Fogt* and *L. Smith)*: [1995] Feb. M.I.P. 33.

An ever closer waiting room?: the case for eastern European accession to the European Economic Area *(S. Peers)*: (1995) 32 C.M.L.Rev. 187.

Austria in the EU: [1995] 259 E.I.R.R. 23–25.

"Bancassurance" and Community law: current status and expected developments *(P. Woolfson)*: [1994] 12 JIBL 519.

Best intentions but empty words: the European Ombudsman *(Konstantinos D. Magliveras)*: (1995) 20 E.L.R. 401–408.

Between domestic democracy and an alien rule of law? Some thoughts on the "independence" of the Bank of England *(T. Daintith)*: [1995] P.L. 118.

Broadcast regulation in Italy: debating new rules to join the European audio-visual market *(E. Andreatta* and *G. Pedde)*: [1995] 1 ENT.LR 7.

Citizenship of the Union and nationality of Member States *(C. Closa)*: (1995) 32 C.M.L.Rev. 487.

Civil jurisdiction: Anglo-Scottish conflicts (*Paul Beaumont*): 1995 S.L.G. 111.

Company law developments at European Union level—the European Cooperative Society, the European Mutual Society and the European Association *(C. Bovis)*: (1995) 16 Co Law. 85.

Competition law in the E.U.: should there be a Convention? (1995) 16 Co Law. 75.

Competition law update *(E. Singleton)*: (1995) 139 S.J. 141.

Competitive tendering in the energy sector: the E.C. Utilities Directive *(C. Mehta)*: [1995] 2 OGLTR 78.

Consumers and Europe *(D. Roberts)*: (1995) 14 Tr.L. 113.

Current developments: European Community law: constitutional aspects *(Andrew Bell)*: (1995) 44 I.C.L.Q. 700–705.

Database detection methods in criminal investigation *(V. Collins)*: (1995) 11 CLSR 2.

Democracy and the EU: legal perspectives on the political debate *(Michael O'Neill)*: [1995] 4 I.J.E.L. 48–67.

Direct advertising by telephone, fax and telex: the German law on unfair competition *(B. Steckler)*: [1995] 1 ENT.LR 13.

Direct effect of directives revisited (*P. Beaumont*): (1994) 62 S.L.G. 139.

Direct effect of Directives: stuck on vertical hold *(David Kinley)*: (1995) 1 E.P.L. 79–83.

Discrimination against individuals and enterprises on grounds of nationality: direct taxation and the European Court of Justice *(T. Lyons)*: [1994] B.T.R. 554.

Discrimination against individuals and enterprises on grounds of nationality: direct taxation and the European Court of Justice *(Timothy Lyons)*: (1995) 1 EC T.J. 27–51.

Does the E.C. have a single market insurance? *(Dr I. MacNeil)*: 10 I.B.F.L. 122.

E.U. separation of powers—a balancing act (*G. T. Lyon*): (1994) 62 S.L.G. 130.

E.U.–Slovenia relations: the legal framework *(K. Pollet)*: [1995] 6 E.B.L.R. 93.

EUROPEAN UNION—*cont.*

Enlargement: legal and procedural aspects *(E. Booss* and *J. Forman)*: (1995) 32 C.M.L.Rev. 95.
EU builds bridges in Eastern Europe: [1995] 95 E.E.B.L. 8–9.
European briefing *(P. Duffy)*: (1995) 139 S.J. 88, 191, 316.
E.C. brief: the codification of Community law *(M. Cornwell-Kelly* and *G. McFarlane)*: (1995) 145 New L.J. 144.
E.C. competition law compliance programmes—an introduction and update *(E. S. Singleton)*: (1994) 13 Tr.L. 508.
E.C. developments in IT law *(D. Jerrard* and *H. Small)*: (1995) 11 CLSR 27.
E.C. State Aids and energy *(L. Hancher)*: [1995] 2 OGLTR 62.
European Community rules on public enterprise *(R. Friel)*: [1994] 12 ILT 280.
European law *(L. Flynn)*: (1995) 13 ILT 16.
European Union Deregulation: [1995] Feb. B.L.R.A. 18.
Free movement of persons, recognition of qualifications, and working conditions *(Julian Lonbay)*: (1995) 44(3) I.C.L.Q. 705–712.
Health and safety review: Pt. II *(G. Holgate)*: (1995) 16 B.L.R. 9.
How English judges get European law wrong *(John Hodgson)*: (1995) 3 Nott. L.J. 34–55.
How far art thou? *(A. Mosawi)*: [1995] *Gazette* Jan. 25, 20.
International agreements and the European Community legal system *(I. Cheyne)*: [1994] E.L.Rev. 581.
Jurisdiction within the U.K. *(J. Tecks)*: (1995) 145 New L.J. 425.
Jurisprudence of the European Court of Human Rights in 1994 (*Wilson Finnie*): 1995 J.R. 423.
Legality, standing and substantive review in Community law *(P. Craig)*: (1994) 14 O.J.L.S. 507.
Luck of the draw? *(M. Joseph)*: (1994) 138 S.J. 1264.
Making the most of trade law opportunities *(Craig Pouncey* and *James Robinson)*: [1995] Jul/Aug G.L. & B. 22–23.
Mapping the E.C. route to the information age *(A. Scott* and *R. Durie)*: [1995] 1 C.T.L.R. 5.
Methods of interpretation in E.C. law *(J. Rinze)*: (1994) 26 Bracton L.J. 57.
Modern trends in the antitrust/competition law governing the aviation industry *(L. Weber)*: (1995) XX A. & S.L. 101.
Monetary union—a cooler look *(J. Chown)*: 10 I.B.F.L. 107.
Moving freely in the U.K. *(B. Andonian)*: (1995) 139 S.J. 214.
National tax laws reign supreme over capital freedom in the European Union *(Sideek Mohamed)*: [1995] 2 E.F.S.L. 180–185.
Netting at risk? Implications for the validity of netting agreements for the E.C. draft Bankruptcy Convention and the of the E.C. draft Directive on the winding-up of credit institutions *(M. Dassesse)*: 10 I.B.F.L. 18.
Norway: European Union *(Liv Monica Bargem)*: [1995] 5 E.C.L. 53–54.
Pregnant pause for employers *(A. Burnside)*: [1994] 15 B.L.R. 323.
Private applicants and the action for annulment under Article 173 of the E.C. Treaty *(A. Arnull)*: (1995) 32 C.M.L.Rev. 7.
Proposed directive for the legal protection of databases in the E.U. *(L. Kaye* and *V. Ward)*: (1994) 12 I.M.L. 95.
Protecting the European consumer *(Emma Bonino)*: (1995) 6 U.L.R. 95–98.
Public works procurement in Europe *(M. Frilet* and *A. Baelen)*: [1995] ICLR 123.
Religious feelings and the European Court *(D. Pannick)*: [1995] P.L. 7.
Rules on State Aids with Hungary in the Europe Agreement *(O. Heinz)*: [1995] 2 ECLR 116.
Securing a smooth shift between the two E.E.A. pillars: prolonged competence of EFTA institutions with respect to former EFTA states after their accession to the European Union *(H. Tichy* and *L. Dedichen)*: (1995) 32 C.M.L.Rev. 131.
State aid in Community law: a broad or narrow definition? *(M. Slotboom)*: [1995] E.L.Rev. 289.
Subsidiarity: principle and practice (*Tom Burns*): 1995 S.L.T. 67.
The 1996 Intergovernmental Conference *(J. Lipsius)*: [1995] E.L.Rev. 235.
The accession negotiations with Austria, Sweden, Finland and Norway: a guided tour *(M. Jorna)*: [1005] E.L.Rev. 131.
The Adams exclusion order case: new enforceable civil rights in the post-Maastricht European Union? *(S. Douglas-Scott* and *J. Kimbell)*: [1994] P.L. 516.
The avenues to the European Court *(P. Circus)*: (1995) 16 B.L.R. 7.
The bank/customer relationship in German and European law *(Dr N. Horn)*: 10 I.B.F.L. 116.
The binding of Leviathan?—The changing role of the European Commission in competition cases *(R. Brent)* (1995) 44 I.C.L.Q. 255.
The Community trade mark office *(G. de Ulloa)*: [1995] M.I.P. Ybk. 17.
The concept of "safe third country" in contemporary European refugee law *(E. Kjaegaard)*: (1995) 6 IJRL 649.
The constitution of the European Union *(I. Harden)*: [1994] P.L. 609.
The current status of the EC Database Directive *(Trevor M. Cook)*: (1995) 52 C.W. 27–34.
The direct effect of Community Directives: the Court of Justice defines the boundaries *(M. O'Neill)*: [1994] 12 ILT 283.
The ECJ rejects horizontal direct effect of Directives: judgment in *Paola Faccini Dori (E. Turnbull)*: [1994] 5 E.B.L.R. 230.

EUROPEAN UNION—*cont.*

The EEA Agreement and Norwegian law *(H. Bull)*: [1994] 5 E.B.L.R. 291.
The effects of the E.E.A. Agreement in Finland *(P. Timonen)*: [1994] 5 E.B.L.R. 251.
The extension of the scope of breach of statutory duty for accidents at work: Pt. 1 *(W. Binchy* and *R. Byrne)*: (1995) 13 ILT 4.
The Immigration (European Economic Area) Order 1994 *(S. Gondal)*: (1995) 9 I. & N.L. & P. 21.
The implications of the Europe Agreements for an expanded European Union *(P. O'Keefe)*: (1995) 44 I.C.L.Q. 161.
The independence of the Banque de France: constitutional and European aspects *(J.-P. Duprat)*: [1995] P.L. 133.
The legal framework in the United Kingdom for insurance policies sold by E.C. insurers under freedom for services *(I. MacNeil)*: (1995) 44 I.C.L.Q. 19.
The new structural funds, state aids and interventions on the single market *(T. Frazer)*: [1995] 20 E.L.Rev. 3.
The principle of open government in Schengen and the European Union: democratic retrogression? *(D. Curtin* and *H. Meijers)*: (1995) 32 C.M.L.Rev. 391.
The principle of subsidiarity: (a guide for lawyers with a particular community orientation) *(Jose Palacio Gonzalez)*: (1995) 20 E.L.R. 355–370.
The starting point *(G. Bindman)*: (1995) 145 New L.J. 62.
The taxation of savings in Europe and the single market: a temporary problem? *(M. Dassesse)*: 10 I.B.F.L. 176.
The Velvet Revolution: Article 90 and the triumph of the free market in Europe's regulated sectors *(A. Gardner)*: [1995] 2 ECLR 78.
Third party access in the electricity industry in Spain *(Dr L. Pastor Ridruejo)*: [1995] 1 OGLTR 30.
Third party access in the energy sector in E.C. law *(S. Beeston)*: [1995] 1 OGLTR 5.
Towards a European Constitution? Problems of political integration *(J.-L. Seurin)*: [1994] P.L. 625.
Trade and environment: some lessons from *Castlemaine Tooheys* (Australia) and *Danish Bottles* (European Community) *(D. Geradin* and *R. Stewardson)*: (1995) 44 I.C.L.Q. 41.
Ultra vires actions of the managing director of a German limited liability company *(D. Weber-Rey)*: [1995] 1 ICCLR 22.
Unification of liabilities in the European construction industry *(Christian E. Jansen)*: (1995) 12 I.C.L.R. 440–450.
VAT in the European Union *(H. Macnair)*: [1995] 124 Comp. Acct. 17.
Victory for common sense? *(J. Cooper)*: [1995] *Gazette* Feb. 15, 11.
What powers should the European Community have? *(John Temple Lang)*: (1995) 1 E.P.L. 97–116.

EVIDENCE (CIVIL)

Admissibility in evidence of plans etc: (1995) 14 (Jul) C.J.Q. 154–157.
Civil Evidence Act notices and non-compellable witnesses *(Timothy Lawson-Cruttenden* and *Adetutu Odutola)*: 14 Lit. 275–279.
Computerised evidence: finding the right approach *(Valerie Collins)*: (1995) 3 Nott. L.J. 11–33.
Discovery against third parties or evidence before trial? *(J.A. Jolowicz)*: (1995) 54 C.L.J. 263–265.
Discovery, or the time bomb of Peruvian guano *(Robert Turner)*: (1995) 4 (Jul) Civ. P. 2–3.
Expert evidence in family proceedings *(David Burrows)*: [1995] 139 S.J. 740–741.
Guidelines beyond reproach *(Michael Breen)*: (1995) 9 *Lawyer* 9.
Intercepted evidence: now you hear me, now you don't *(A. Tomkins)*: (1994) 57 M.L.R. 941.
Presentation of evidence at public inquiries: (1995) 5 P.E.L.B. 22–23.
Proving comparables *(Jim Cotter)*: [1995] 9531 E.G. 66.
Statements and affidavits as evidence (*Sheriff Graham Johnston*): Civ.P.B. 3–2.
The Civil Evidence (Family Mediation) Scotland Act 1995 (*Ann H. Dick*): Fam.L.B. 16–2.
The civil standard of proof uncertainty: probability, belief and justice *(D. Hamer)*: (1994) 16 SydLR 506.
The role of the investigator in civil litigation *(David Wheeler)*: (1995) L. Ex. Jul, 38–39.

EXTRADITION

Barings – cover up or lesson for the future? *(Stephen Pollard)*: (1995) 145 New L.J. 1088–1089.
Extradition and expulsion orders and the European Convention on Human Rights: the *Soering* decision and beyond *(J. Kidd)*: (1994) 26 Bracton L.J. 67.
Who has jurisdiction for cross-frontier financial crimes? *(Geoff Gilbert)*: (1995) 2 Web J.C.L.I. 34–48.

FAMILY

A jurisdiction in search of a mission: family proceedings in England and Wales *(J. Eekelaar)*: (1994) 57 M.L.R. 839.
A lifeline for the agency *(M. Rae)*: (1995) 145 New L.J. 140.
A short history of cohabitation and marriage *(V. Chauveau* and *A.-M. Hutchinson)*: (1995) 145 New L.J. 304.
Acting for children *(J. Leigh)*: (1995) 139 S.J. 40.
Agreements and marriage breakdown *(D. Burrows)*: (1995) 139 S.J. 294.

FAMILY—*cont.*

Allocating family law cases *(P. Tain)*: (1995) 139 S.J. 192.
Brussels Convention II: a new private law instrument in family matters for the European Union or the European Community? *(P. Beaumont* and *G. Moir)*: [1995] E.L.Rev. 268.
Child sexaul abuse, access and the wishes of children *(E. Jones* and *P. Parkinson)*: (1995) 9 IJFL 54.
Combating the organised sexual exploitation of Asian children: recent developments and prospects *(D. Hodgson)*: (1995) 9 IJLF 23.
Contact: a compendium *(V. Smith)*: 159 J.P.N. 188.
Delay *(Richard White)*: [1995] 145 New L.J. 1192–1193.
Disputes over mentally incapacitated adults *(F. Morris* and *M. Mullins)*: (1994) 138 S.J. 1184.
Divorce law reform and mediation: (1995) 25 (Aug) Fam. Law 454–455.
Divorce reform—do we need fault? *(P. Townsend* and *A. Baker)*: 159 J.P.N. 206.
Duress, family law and the coherent legal system *(A. Bradney)*: (1994) 57 M.L.R. 963.
Expert evidence in family proceedings *(David Burrows)*: [1995] 139 S.J. 740–741.
Family law forum *(A. Prince* and *B. Mitchels)*: (1995) 139 S.J. 62.
Family law: recent financial developments *(L. Ayrton)*: (1995) 139 S.J. 241.
Family proceedings: case management *(D. Burrows)*: (1995) 139 S.J. 168.
Gifts, inheritances and the allocation of property on divorce *(G. Miller)*: [1995] 24 Anglo-Am. 31.
Intercountry adoption of refugee children: the Hague Recommendation *(K. Beevers)*: (1995) 7 JCL 10.
Pensions and divorce: time for change *(M. Rae)*: (1995) 145 New L.J. 310.
Play-groups and child-minders: the effect of the Children Act 1989; registration and rights of appeal to the family courts *(J. Spencer)*: 159 J.P.N. 157.
Prenuptial contracts *(Helen L. Conway)*: (1995) 145 New L.J. 1290–1292.
Privilege in the family mediation process *(T. Ingman)*: (1995) 111 L.Q.R. 68.
Protection of family life: positive approaches and the ECHR *(Kath O'Donnell)*: (1995) 17 J.S.W.L. 261–279.
Provision for adult children under the Inheritance (Provision for Family and Dependants) Act 1975 *(Prof. G. Miller)*: [1995] Conv. 22.
State and family: back to basics? *(S. Cretney)*: (1995) 111 L.Q.R. 65.
Taking multiculturalism seriously: marriage law and the rights of minorities *(P. Parkinson)*: (1994) 16 SydLR 473.
The effect of divorce on wills *(R. Kerridge)*: [1995] Conv. 12.
The ideological attack on transracial adoption in the USA and Britain *(P. Hayes)*: (1995) 9 IJLF 1.
The impact of culture, society, and history on the legal process; an analysis of the legal status of same-sex relationships in the U.S. and Denmark *(M. Dupuis)*: (1995) 9 IJFL 86.
The impact of the Child Support Act on lone mothers and their children *(C. Glendinning, K. Clarke* and *G. Craig)*: (1995) 7 JCL 18.
The status of the Family Division *(Justice Wall)*: [1995] 25 Fam. Law 374–377.

FISH AND FISHERIES

Appreciating the precautionary principle as an ethical evolution in ocean management *(John M. MacDonald)*: [1995] 26 O.D. & I.L. 255–286.
Fisheries agreement between Canada and the European Union *(D. Clarke)*: (1995) 2(7) Int. M.L. 173–175.
Modifying the 1982 Law of the Sea Convention: new initiatives on governance of high seas fisheries resources: the straddling stocks negotiations *(Jon M. Van Dyke)*: [1995] 10 I.J.M.C.L. 219–227.
Policing environmental offences in international waters *(Alastair N. Brown)*: [1995] 7 Env. Law. 3–5.
Unseasonable salmon: (considering *Brady v. Barbour*, 1995 G.W.D. 11–593) (*D. R. Macleod*): (1995) 40 J.L.S. 106.

FOOD AND DRUGS

Consumer protection and its integration in Community policy on food: general approach, principles and evaluation *(Nadine Fraselle)*: [1994] 2 Consum. L.J. 17–26.
Food and the law *(Linda Goldman)*: (1995) L. Ex., May, 14.
Food law: Regulations – December 1994 to March 1995: [1995] 14 Tr. Law 328.
Food safety law and Lanark Blue *(Katharine Thompson)*: (1995) 225 SCOLAG 109–111.
Health and safety: reasonable precautions: [1995] 5 L.G. & L. 8.
Keep it clean *(Jeremy Stranks)*: (1995) 139 S.J. 624–625.

FOREIGN JURISDICTIONS

A disturbing picture *(G. Bindman)*: (1994) 144 New L.J. 1599.
Agency and distribution in Sweden *(C. Svernlov)*: [1994] 11 ICCLR 374.
An introduction to Irish public law *(Gerard Hogan)*: [1995] 1 E.P.L. 37–42.

FOREIGN JURISDICTIONS—*cont.*

Anglo-French estates *(A. Stanyer)*: (1994) 138 S.J. 1209.

Appellate patent practice in the United States *(J. Monroe)*: [1995] M.I.P. Lit. Ybk. 52.

Brussels Convention: defamation action: place where "harmful event" occurs *(Jessica Simor)*: (1995) 6 ICCLR C115–116.

Defence lawyers in Turkey *(Alan McMillan)*: (1995) 223 SCOLAG 74.

Enforcement of arbitral awards in the Arab countries *(Abdul Hamid El-Ahdab)*: (1995) 11 Arbitration Int. 169–181.

Enforcement of copyright of foreign works in Panama *(A. Aguilar Alfu)*: [1995] M.I.P. Lit. Ybk. 29.

Enforcing foreign arbitration awards: [1995] 325 Fairplay 23.

Enforcing students' rights in Irish and English law *(A. Carroll)*: [1994] 12 ILT 259.

First steps for China *(M. Abell)*: [1994] Dec. M.I.P. 42.

Foreign investment and company laws of selected central Eastern European and central Asian republics *(G. Campbell)*: [1994] 11 ICCLR 366.

Forum – shopping in personal injury cases – how to choose the right store, the right assistant and pay the right price *(Geraldine McCool)*: [1995] May Litigator 222–228.

France: current developments *(John Bell)*: [1995] 1 E.P.L. 16–22.

French IP in 1994 *(X. Buffet Delmas)*: [1994] Dec. M.I.P. 32.

French property: recent developments *(Ronald Austin)*: (1995) E.G. 9533, 80–81.

From Dingwall to the South Pacific *(Mary Morrissey)*: (1995) 40 J.L.S. 240.

History and interpretation in American jurisprudence *(N. Duxbury)*: (1994) 23 Anglo-Am. 501.

Indian shipping in the House of Lords (again) – Republic of India v India Steamship Co. Ltd *(Jon Boaden)*: (1995) 2(7) Int. M.L. 181–184.

International commercial arbitration in Hong Kong *(Christopher J. Wilson* and *Graeme R. Halford)*: (1995) I.C. Lit. Jul/Aug, 15–17.

IP and industrial property litigation in Greece *(A. Delicostopoulou)*: [1995] M.I.P. Lit. Ybk. 19.

IP in greater China *(T. Hope)*: [1994] Dec. M.I.P. 36.

IP in the U.S. courts: 1994 *(V. Cooper)*: [1994] Dec. M.I.P. 28.

IP litigation in India *(D. Mehta* and *S. Abhyanker)*: [1995] M.I.P. Lit. Ybk. 21.

IP litigation in Italy *(A. Guglielmetti* and *Dr D. de Simone)*: [1995] M.I.P. Lit. Ybk. 23.

IP litigation in the Arab Republic of Egypt *(Dr M. Alamedin)*: [1995] M.I.P. Lit. Ybk. 15.

IP litigation in the Dominican Republic *(O. Jorge Mera)*: [1995] M.I.P. Lit. Ybk. 13.

IP litigation in the Kingdom of Saudi Arabia *(Dr M. Nader)*: [1995] M.I.P. Lit. Ybk. 41.

IP litigation in the Philippines *(L. Llanillo* and *V. Amador)*: [1995] M.I.P. Lit. Ybk. 32.

IP litigation in the United States *(D. Lee* and *V. Palladino)*: [1995] M.I.P. Lit. Ybk. 49.

Irish fiscal incentives for film and TV production *(K. Hoy* and *S. Curran)*: (1994) 12 I.M.L. 91.

Italy: jurisdiction: conflict of laws *(Andrea Valli)*: (1995) 6 ICCLR C168–169.

Judicial review in Germany *(Georg Nolte* and *Peter Radler)*: [1995] 1 E.P.L. 26–32.

Law and jurisdiction in insurance contracts: limited freedom of choice in the E.C. *(Elisabeth Ruiz* and *Christopher Henin)*: (1995) 3 Int. ILR 156–160.

Legal measures under Bulgarian law in cases of copyright infringement of software *(V. Dimitrova)*: (1995) 11 CLSR 25.

Liability of credit institutions towards creditors of their clients in financial difficulty under Belgian law *(D. Van Gerven)*: [1994] 12 JIBL 532.

Litigation and remedies in software infringement cases in the Czech Republic *(Z. Loebl)*: (1995) 11 CLSR 23.

Litigation in Spain *(S. Ferrandis)*: [1995] M.I.P. Lit. Ybk. 43.

Mission to Latvia *(J. H. Webster)*: 1995 S.L.G. 14.

New Polish copyright law *(Dr T. Drozdowska)*: (1995) 11 CLSR 18.

Oman: commercial companies law: (1995) 1 MECLR A7–10.

Patent proceedings in the Czech Republic *(Z. Pradna)*: [1995] M.I.P. Lit. Ybk. 9.

People's Republic of China: IP litigation *(C. Borg-Marks)*: [1995] M.I.P. Lit. Ybk. 34.

Protection of famous trade marks in Korea *(T. Hee Lee)*: [1995] M.I.P. Lit. Ybk. 26.

Romanian IP litigation *(Dr M. Opriou)*: [1995] M.I.P. Lit. Ybk. 39.

Silicone litigation *(R. Levy)*: (1994) 138 S.J. 1214.

Singapore's adoption of the UNCITRAL Model Law on International Commercial Arbitration *(Benny S. Tabalujan)*: (1995) 12 J. Int. Arb. 51–64.

Software protection in Germany—recent court decisions in copyright law *(A. Gunther* and *U. Wuermeling)*: (1995) 11 CLSR 12.

Spain: Single European Market: survey of Spanish companies *(Joaquin Munoz)*: (1995) 1 Int. T.L.R. S30–31.

Stemming the flood of constitutional complaints in Germany? [1994] P.L. 553.

The application of foreign rules of pleading in Scotland *(James Taylor)*: (1995) I.C. Lit. Jul/Aug, 47.

The implications of the Singapore Bankruptcy Act for lenders and takers of security *(Joanna R. Jeremiah)*: (1995) 10(2) J.I.B.L. 357–360.

The new arbitration rules of the China International Economic Trade and Arbitration Commission *(Rong R. Yan* and *Christopher Kuner)*: (1995) 11(2) Arbitration Int. 183–196.

The new Egyptian Arbitration Act in civil and commercial matters *(Abdul Hamid El-Ahdab)*: (1995) 12(2) J. Int. Arb. 65–101.

FOREIGN JURISDICTIONS—*cont.*

The new German Act on marks: E.C. harmonisation and comprehensive reform *(M. Fammler)*: [1995] 17 EIPR 22.

The problems facing arbitration in the European Union *(Karl-Heinz Bockstiegel)*: (1995) 61 Arbitration 191–195.

The "rule of law" in Indonesia *(Alan McMillan)*: (1995) 224 SCOLAG 88.

The structure of the corporation: proposal for new provisions to the Swedish Companies Act *(Rolf Skog)*: (1995) 6(8) ICCLR 269–271.

The U.S. International Trade Commission *(M. Blakeslee* and *R. Zelnick)*: [1995] M.I.P. Lit. Ybk. 55.

The Ukrainian banking system *(Sergei Tretyak* and *Arnold Vahrenwald)*: (1995) 10 JIBL 341–345.

Title to sue on a contract of carriage in Anglo-American law *(C. Cashmore)*: (1994) 23 Anglo-Am. 488.

United States: new Federal Reserve reporting requirements may alter US merchant banking investments *(Isaac B. Lustgarten)*: (1995) 14(3) I.B.F.L. 24–25.

Wrongful dispositions of motor vehicles in England: a U.S. certificate of title solution? *(I. Davis)*: (1994) 23 Anglo-Am. 460.

FRAUD, MISREPRESENTATION AND UNDUE INFLUENCE

Adjusting the scales? Independent advice and partial mortgage enforcement *(Alison Dunn)*: [1995] Conv., Jul/Aug, 325–332.

Community budget – combating fraud: (1995) 6 E.B.L.R. 164–165.

Damages in lieu of rescission for misrepresentation *(H. Beale)*: (1995) 111 L.Q.R. 60.

Expensive disasters for justice *(Rinita Sarker)*: [1995] 16 Co. Law. 181–183.

Fraud in public sector contracting *(S. Cirell* and *J. Bennett)*: (1995) 139 S.J. 238.

Investigating fraud *(Tony Levitt)*: (1995) 16 *Eagle* 9–11.

New lease of life for the SFO *(Rinita Sarker)*: (1995) 16 Co. Law. 213–215.

O'Brien and its legacy: principle, equity and certainty? *(Anna Lawson)*: (1995) 54 C.L.J. 280–289.

Serious fraud office reprieved *(Rosalind Webster)*: [1995] Jun I.C. Lit. 37–39.

The duties and liabilities of lead managers in syndicated loans *(G. Bhattacharyya)*: 10 I.B.F.L. 172.

Undue influence and the function of independent advice *(A. Chandler)*: (1995) 111 L.Q.R. 51.

White collar crime isn't paying *(Grania Langdon-Down)*: (1995) 9 *Lawyer* 15.

GAMING AND WAGERING

Luck of the draw? *(M. Joseph)*: (1994) 138 S.J. 1264.

GAS

DTI forced to extend environmental assessment offshore: [1995] 245 ENDS 29–30.

Gas safety *(Elizabeth Weil)*: [1995] 50 Adviser 9–11.

Gas safety *(R. Peters)*: (1994) 138 S.J. 1256.

Gas supply in Britain—the next 10 years *(C. Atkins)*: [1994] 12 OGLTR 367.

Gas: some issues in statutory third-party access (TPA) *(Stephen R. Dow)*: (1995) 6 U.L.R. 62–65.

Industrial bypass of local gas distribution companies: the American experience (Pt. 1) *(K. Carretta, J. Cohen, P. Keeley* and *J. White)*: [1994] 11 OGLTR 331.

Industrial bypass of local gas distribution companies: the American experience (Pt. II) *(K. Carretta, J. Cohen, P. Keeley* and *J. White)*: [1994] 12 OGLTR 376.

Natural gas pricing issues: Transco and the future *(Lawrence G. Acker)*: (1995) 6 U.L.R. 65–67.

Regulation – Gas Bill – new regulatory framework expands competition *(Charles Robson)*: [1995] 13 OGLTR, D70.

Restructuring the electricity and gas power industries in Poland *(K. Oldziej)*: [1995] 1 OGLTR 26.

Texaco v. State of Louisiana: an analysis of and solution to market value litigation *(A. Thomas* and *E. Belton)*: [1995] 3 OGLTR 99.

The concept of third party access in the energy sector in Belgian law *(I. Périlleux* and *Frédéric Meessen)*: [1995] 1 OGLTR 11.

The independence of contracts of guarantee and counter-guarantee from the underlying contract *(C. Chatterjee)*: [1995] 4 JIBL 131.

The Maghreb-Europe gas pipeline: its juridicial structure *(R. Piqueras)*: [1995] 3 OGLTR 95.

Third party access in the electricity and natural gas sectors in the Netherlands *(E. Pijnacker Hordijk)*: [1995] 1 OGLTR 21.

Third party access in the energy sector in E.C. law *(S. Beeston)*: [1995] 1 OGLTR 5.

Third party access in the energy sector in France *(I. Damay* and *P. Agboyibor)*: [1995] 1 OGLTR 13.

Third party access to electricity and natural gas networks in Sweden *(M. Borresen* and *J. Laver)*: [1995] 1 OGLTR 34.

GUARANTEE AND INDEMNITY

A skeleton in the cupboard *(P. Judkins* and *H. Meek)*: [1995] *Gazette*, Apr. 12, 16.

Bank notes *(P. Alexander)*: [1995] *Gazette* Feb. 1, 20.

HEALTH AND SAFETY AT WORK

A flood of claims? *(John Messkam)*: [1995] 139 S.J. 732, 738.
Bootlegging: excise goods and the Single Market *(Christopher Burke)*: (1995) 159 J.P. 383–385.
Deregulating occupational health and safety *(Kevin Williams)*: (1995) 24 I.L.J. 133–140.
Employer's liability: reconstructing section 3(1) of the Health and Safety at Work etc. Act 1974: Pt. 2 *(Geoffrey H. Holgate)*: (1995) 159 J.P. 385–387.
Gas safety *(R. Peters)*: (1994) 138 S.J. 1256.
Health and safety protection for pregnant workers *(Kenneth Miller)*: [1995] 63 S.L.G. 74–76.
Health and safety review: Pts. I and II *(G. Holgate)*: [1994] 15 B.L.R. 331, [1995] 16 B.L.R. 9.
How much is enough? *(G. McCool* and *M. Bennett)*: (1995) 139 S.J. 284.
Recent health and safety cases *(Geoff Holgate)*: (1994) 138 S.J. 1233.
Stress at work: Part 1: Statutory and common law duties of care: (1995) 527 IRLB 2–10.
The Construction (Design and Management) Regulations 1994: [1995] Feb. B.L.R.A. 37.
The Construction Design and Management Regulations 1995 *(Eversheds)*: (1995) I.H.L. Jul/Aug, 61–62.
The extension of the scope of breach of statutory duty for accidents at work: Pt. 1 *(W. Binchy* and *R. Byrne)*: (1995) 13 ILT 4.
Unfair dismissal: health and safety dismissals: [1995] 544, IDS Brief 4–6.
Warning: work can damage your health *(David Conn)*: (1995) 139 S.J. 576.
Workplace accidents and occurrences and psychiatric injury *(G. Holgate)*: 14 Lit. 179.
Workplace health and safety: the deregulatory riddle (Pt. I) *(G. Holgate)*: 16 B.L.R. 57.

HERITABLE PROPERTY AND CONVEYANCING

Bennett v. Beneficial Bank (*Richard Leggett*): 1995 S.L.G. 107.
Coal mining inquiries (*Stewart Brymer*): (1995) 40 J.L.S. 238.
Conflict of interest in conveyancing (*B. Ritchie*): Prop.L.B. 12–7.
Conveyancing—what's coming? (*R. Rennie*): (1994) 39 J.L.S.S. 450.
Descriptions in Standard Securities (*A. J. McDonald*): (1995) 40 J.L.S. 357.
Discharge of servitudes by prescription (*D. Cusine*): 1995 J.R. 82.
High valuations versus bad lending (*Paul F. J. Wade*): Rep. B 4–2.
Holiday lettings (*W. Burns Shearar*): Prop.L.B. 14–2.
Land registration update (*A. Rennie*): (1995) 40 J.L.S. 15.
Letters of obligation: time-limits and the times we live in (*David O'Donnell*): (1994) 62 S.L.G. 127.
Mortgages explained (*F. Muirhead*): (1995) 221 SCOLAG 41.
Purchase and sale of country cottages (*Alistair H. Anderson*): Prop.L.B. 14–6.
Register of inhibitions and adjudications—a guide to indexing practice (*Ian Burdon*): Prop.L.B. 14–11.
Sharp v. Thomson—What now? (*Professor A. J. McDonald*): (1995) 40 J.L.S. 256.
Sharp v. Thomson: A civilian perspective (considering 1994 S.L.T. 1068) (*K. G. C. Reid*): 1995 S.L.T. (News) 75.
Sharp v. Thomson: Feudal purism—but is it justice? (considering 1994 S.L.T. 1068) (*A. J. McDonald*): (1995) 40 J.L.S. 7.
Sharp v. Thomson: Identifying the mischief (*N. R. Whitty*): 1995 S.L.T. (News) 79.
Solicitors and the mortgage market: (*Graham Gibson*): (1995) 40 J.L.S. 137.
Standard missives (*Colin T. Graham*): (1995) 40 J.L.S. 142.
The extinction of servitudes through confusion (*Paul O'Brien*): 1995 S.L.T. (News) 228.
The Requirements of Writing Act—A re-learning experience for conveyancers (*John McNeil*): Prop.L.B. 15–4.
The Requirements of Writing (Scotland) Act 1995 (*Professor Robert Rennie*): 1995 J.R. 445.
The Requirements of Writing (Scotland) Act 1995 (*Professors Cusine and Rennie*): (1995) 40 J.L.S. 221.
Timeshare contracts (*David S. Anderson*): Prop.L.B. 14–4.
Transactions with limited companies—*caveat emptor*? (*A.J. McDonald and S. Brymer*): Prop. L.B. 13–2.

HOUSING

Coming up to scratch *(J. Driscoll)*: [1994] *Gazette* Dec. 7, 26.
Homelessness update *(S. Knafler)*: (1994) 138 S.J. 1207.
Homelessness: duty to give reasons: [1995] 4 F.L.T. 8–9.
Housing benefit overpayments *(Angus McIntosh)*: (1995) 223 SCOLAG 67–71.
Improved rights for public sector tenants (*J. Hyslop*): (1995) 221 SCOLAG 35.
Improvement and repairs grants—time for change? (*J. Hyslop*): (1995) SCOLAG 22.
Intentional homelessness—a practitioner's guide to judicial review (*Mike Dailly*): (1995) 225 SCOLAG 103.
Negative reactions *(Kerry Stephenson)*: (1995) 139 S.J. 877.
Private bids for a public problem *(Philip Smith)*: [1995] 9532 E.G. 51–52.
Recent developments in housing law *(N. Madge* and *J. Luba)*: [1994] L.A. Dec. 10.
The effect of death on the right to buy under Part V of the Housing Act 1985 (Pt. 1) *(A. Brierley)*: [1995] Conv. 114.

HOUSING—*cont.*

Turmoil on the transfer market *(James Tickell)*: [1995] Jun 30 L.G.C. 10–11.
Unsettled on the homeless *(Andrew Arden)*: [1995] Jul 28 L.G.C. 14–15.

HUMAN RIGHTS

A disturbing picture *(G. Bindman)*: (1994) 144 New L.J. 1599.
A human rights bill *(Lord Lester)*: (1995) 145 New L.J. 141.
A new European Court of Human Rights *(A. Mowbray)*: [1994] P.L. 540.
A reform of civil procedure: rationing procedure rather than access to justice *(A.A.S. Zuckerman)*: (1995) 22 J. Law & Soc. 155–188.
Access to justice: the recommendations: (1995) 139 S.J. (L.B.) 135–139.
Balance of interests *(Jeffrey Wilner)*: [1995] *Gazette*, 23, 24.
Ban on gays in military upheld: [1995] 62 E.O.R. 46–47.
Charitable status for the advancement of religion: an abolitionist's view *(Peter Edge)*: [1995/96] 3 C.L. & P.R. 29–35.
Civil Evidence Act notices and non-compellable witnesses *(Timothy Lawson-Cruttenden* and *Adetutu Odutola)*: 14 Lit. 275–279.
Ethics and the public service *(N. Lewis* and *D. Longley)*: [1994] P.L. 596.
European briefing *(P. Duffy)*: (1994) 138 S.J. 1232, (1995) 139 S.J. 880.
Extradition and expulsion orders and the European Convention on Human Rights: the *Soering* decision and beyond *(J. Kidd)*: (1994) 26 Bracton L.J. 67.
Extradition and human rights *(S. Nash)*: (1995) 145 New L.J. 429.
Freedom from wardship or a judicial cry for freedom *(J. McCue)*: (1994) 15 JML&P 111.
Here we go again: [1995] 146 New L.J. 1117.
Human rights theory and Bill of Rights debate *(C. Adjei)*: (1995) 58 M.L.R. 17.
Intercepted evidence: now you hear me, now you don't *(A. Tomkins)*: (1994) 57 M.L.R. 941.
INTERIGHTS—an international human rights law centre *(E. Playfair)*: [1994] P.L. 573.
Is there a policy behind the decisions and judgments relating to Article 3 of the European Convention on Human Rights? *(M. Addo* and *N. Grief)*: [1995] E.L.Rev. 178.
Issues and challenges in international protection in Africa *(Office of the United Nations High Commissioner for Refugees)*: (1995) 7 I.J.R.L. 55–73.
Jurisprudence of the European court of human rights in 1994 (*Wilson Finnie*): 1995 J.R. 423.
Litigation on the run *(Shane Sayers)*: *Eagle*, June 1995, p.23.
Photographs and privacy in Germany *(A. Vahrenwald)*: [1994] 6 ENT.LR 205.
Prior restraint and Article 10 of the European Human Rights Convention *(P. Milmo)*: [1994] 6 ENT.LR 194.
Protection of family life: positive approaches and the ECHR *(Kath O'Donnell)*: (1995) 17 J.S.W.L. 261–279.
Questioning temporary protection *(D. Luca)*: (1995) 6 IJRL 535.
Remedies for violations of the American Convention on Human Rights *(S. Davidson)*: (1995) 44 I.C.L.Q. 405.
Secret hangings on Japan's death row (*Alan McMillan*): (1995) 225 SCOLAG 111.
Sex equality in the single market: new directions for the European Court of Justice *(H. Fenwick* and *T. Hervey)*: (1995) 32 C.M.L.Rev. 443.
Taking human rights seriously *(A. Lester)*: (1994–1995) K.C.L.J. 5.
"Taking rights seriously": the European Court and its fundamental rights jurisprudence—Pt. 1 *(J. Weiler* and *N. Lockhart)*: (1995) 32 C.M.L.Rev. 51.
"Taking rights seriously": the European Court and its fundamental rights jurisprudence—Pt. II *(J. Weiler* and *N. Lockhart)*: (1995) 32 C.M.L.Rev. 579.
The European Court of Human Rights and criminal legal aid in Scotland (*Wilson Finnie*): 1995 S.L.T. (News) 271.
The European Court of Human Rights and the right of the accused person to remain silent: can it be invoked by taxpayers? *(S. Frommel)*: [1994] B.T.R. 598.
The international protection of the internally displaced *(Francis M. Deng)*: (1995) 7 I.J.R.L. 74–86.
The relationship between Community citizenship and the protection of fundamental rights in Community law *(S. O'Leary)*: (1995) 32 C.M.L.Rev. 519.
The starting point *(G. Bindman)*: (1995) 145 New L.J. 62.
The United Nations and freedom of religion *(B. Dickson)*: (1995) 44 I.C.L.Q. 327.
Victory for common sense? *(J. Cooper)*: [1995] *Gazette* Feb. 15, 11.
What is the meaning and effect of the principle of "margin of appreciation" within the jurisprudence of the European Convention in Human Rights? Is this principle compatible with the concept of effective protection of rights? *(A.-M. Von Luttichau)*: (1994) 26 Bracton L.J. 99.
Will Woolf work? *(Steven Gee)*: (1995) 139 S.J. 674–675.

HUSBAND AND WIFE

Exclusion orders for cohabitees (*Brian Mohan*): (1995) 40 J.L.S. 191.

IMMIGRATION

A burden on the taxpayer? Some developments in the role of "public funds" in immigration law *(R. McKee)*: (1995) 9 I. & N.L. & P. 29.
Aliens and refugee law in Poland—recent developments *(W. Czaplinski)*: (1995) 6 IJRL 636.
Appeals from the Immigration Appeal Tribunal to the Court of Appeal: a short guide for the practitioner *(Jim Gillespie)*: (1995) 9 I. & N.L. & P. 92–94.
Border controls revisited *(R. Shah)*: (1995) 145 New L.J. 283.
British immigration controls: (1995) 20 E.C.R. 353–354.
Faultlines of nationality conflict: refugees and displaced persons from Armenia to Azerbaijan *(B. Frelick)*: (1995) 6 IJRL 581.
From migrants to refugees: Russian, Soviet and post-Soviet migration *(C. Messina)*: (1995) 6 IJRL 620.
Guidelines for women's asylum claims *(N. Kelly)*: (1995) 6 IJRL 517.
Immigrant and ethnic minorities and the EU's "democratic deficit" *(Andrew Geddes)*: (1995) 33 J. Com. Mar. St. 197–217.
Immigration for investors *(Jacqueline Thompson)*: [1995] 139 S.J. 714–715.
Immigration snapshots *(Bernard Andonian)*: (1995) 139 S.J. 626–627.
Recent developments in immigration law *(Rick Scannell)*: [1995] Legal Action, Jul,19–23.
Refugees and safe third countries *(P. Shah)*: (1995) 9 I. & N.L. & P. 3.
Testing time for asylum-seekers *(R. McKee)*: (1995) 145 New L.J. 321.
The asylum and refugee procedure in the Argentine legal system *(A. Iza)*: (1995) 6 IJRL 643.
The concept of "safe third country" in contemporary European refugee law *(E. Kjaegaard)*: (1995) 6 IJRL 649.
The emergence of a European immigration policy *(D. O'Keefe)*: [1995] 20 E.L. Rev. 20.
The Immigration (European Economic Area) Order 1994 *(S. Gondal)*: (1995) 9 I. & N.L. & P. 21.
The new immigration rules and business *(B. Andonian)*: (1995) 9 I. & N.L. & P. 14.
The refugee crisis in Africa as a crisis of the institution of the state *(A. Abdullah)*: (1995) 6 IJRL 563.
To what purpose? *(R. Mckee)*: (1994) 144 New L.J. 1701.
Work permits: the new regime under the Immigration Rules *(Bernard Andonian)*: (1995) L. Ex., Apr, 10–11.

INCOME TAX

A matter of persistence *(A. Pink)*: 134 Tax. 434.
A one-way bet? *(Philip Fisher)*: [1995] 135 Tax. 467–470.
All things being equal *(M. McLellan)*: 134 Tax. 184.
An example of simplification?—II *(J. Labrum)*: 134 Tax. 157.
An unworkable regime *(David Whiscombe)*: (1995) 135 Tax. 487–489.
Facelift for Schedule A *(Anita Monteith)*: [1995] 135 Tax. 411–414.
Home alone *(Mike Evans)*: [1995] 16 T.P.T. 113–115.
Income from property: Pt. 1 *(David Williams)*: (1995) 313 Tax J. 12–15.
Income from property: Pt. 2 *(David Williams)*: (1995) 314 Tax J. 25–27.
Income from property: Pt. 3 *(David Williams)*: (1995) 315 Tax J. 10–11.
It's official (Pt. II): 134 Tax. 532.
Schedule A transitional proposals: 134 Tax. 474.
Self-assessment: transitional arrangements – submission of accounts: (1995) 17 I.R.T.B. 225–226.
Self-assessment for income tax: another view *(C. Sandford)*: [1994] B.T.R. 674.
Self-assessment: 134 Tax. 212.
The new income tax settlement provisions *(Colin Masters)*: (1995–96) 4 P.T.P.R. 11–23.
The tax-free carrot *(Karen Munnings* and *Radha Startin)*: [1995] 135 Tax. 437–440.

INHERITANCE TAX

Delayed reaction *(R. Grierson)*: 134 Tax. 399.
Gifts, inheritances and the allocation of property on divorce *(G. Miller)*: [1995] 24 Anglo-Am. 31.
Tax efficient wills—Pt. 1 *(R. Ray)*: 134 Tax. 610.
Wrinkles and foibles (Pts. I and 2) *(R. Ray)*: 134 Tax. 238, 274.

INSOLVENCY

A perspective from a UK insolvency practitioner *(Neil Cooper)*: [1995] 4 I.I.R. 30–35.
Administration: the Insolvency Act 1986, Pt. II *(D. Prentice, F. Oditah* and *N. Segal)*: [1994] L.M.C.L.Q. 487.
Adopted employees in insolvency orphans no more *(David Pollard)*: (1995) 24 I.L.J. 141–151.
At last, partnership voluntary arrangements—but was it worth the wait? *(A. Bacon)*: (1994) 10 I.L. & P. 166.
Bankruptcy set-off *(Allen & Overy)*: (1995) 6 P.L.C. 78.
Barnes v. Addy: the requirements of knowledge *(M. Lodge)*: (1995) 23 A.B.L.R. 25.
Close-out netting in English law: comfort at last *(J. Walter)*: 10 I.B.F.L. 167.

INSOLVENCY—*cont.*

Company voluntary arrangements (*Donna McKenzie*): Bus.L.B. 16–4.
Dangerous loopholes *(R. Breckman)*: (1995) 145 New L.J. 117.
Distraint and the insolvent tenant *(Katie Bradford)*: (1995) 5 P.R. 163–164.
French insolvency law reform: same scales, different balance *(A. Sorensoen* and *B. Mills)*: [1995] 1 ICCLR 6.
Insolvency focus *(H. Anderson)*: [1995] *Gazette*, Apr. 5, 53.
Insolvency focus *(H. Anderson)*: [1995] *Gazette*, Dec. 7, 18.
Insolvency reform in the UK: a revised proposal *(Philippe Aghion)*: (1995) 11 I.L. & P. 67–74.
Insolvency set-off: a review of current issues *(C. Lynch)*: (1994) 10 I.L. & P. 161.
Insolvent partnerships *(G. Levy* and *M. Goldberg)*: (1994) 138 S.J. 1262.
Intelligent support for individual voluntary arrangements *(N. Doherty* and *K. Pond)*: (1994) 10 I.L. & P. 169.
Mexican insolvency law *(J. Barrett)*: [1994] 11 ICCLR 378.
Netting at risk? Implications for the validity of netting agreements for the E.C. draft Bankruptcy Convention and the of the E.C. draft Directive on the winding-up of credit institutions *(M. Dassesse)*: 10 I.B.F.L. 18.
Original tenant liability *(G. Webber)*: (1995) 139 S.J. 196.
Principles of international insolvency: Pt. 1 *(Philip R. Wood)*: [1995] 4 I.I.R. 94–103.
Re Arrows Limited (No. 4) (R. Reston and *C. Rapinet)*: (1994) 10 I.L. & P. 173.
Revised proposals for a new company voluntary arrangement procedure *(Cameron Markby Hewitt)*: [1995] 9 Corp. Brief. 20–23.
Revised proposals for CVAs *(Andrew Campbell)*: (1995) 139 S.J. 656–657.
Schemes of arrangement for insolvent insurance companies in the United Kingdom: current developments *(P. Fidler)*: [1995] 1 Int. ILR 18.
Taking advantage of the new rescue culture *(Helen Kavanagh)*: [1995] 13 P.P.M. 92–93.
The distributional question in insolvency: comparative aspects *(Jose M. Garrido)*: [1995] 4 I.I.R. 25–53.
The European Union *(Manfred Balz)*: [1995] 4 I.I.R. 60–71.
The Insolvent Partnerships Order 1994 *(S. Frith* and *B. Jones)*: [1995] 11 CLSR 14.
The powers of the administrator *(Michael Griffiths)*: (1995) L. Ex. Jul, 19.
The validity of debt subordination arrangements *(David Capper)*: [1995] 14 Insolv. L. 3–6.
Trading under the wrong name, personal liability or printers' error? *(P. Cuthbertson)*: (1994) 10 I.L. & P. 158.
Transactions defrauding creditors *(Richard Gregorian)*: (1995) I.H.L. Jul/Aug, 29–31.
Voluntary arrangements . . . an endangered species? *(Stephen Baister)*: (1995) L. Ex., Mar, 20–21.
When is a fixed charge not a fixed charge? [1994] 123 Comp. Acct. 31.

INSURANCE

A matter of persistence *(A. Pink)*: 134 Tax. 434.
"Bancassurance" and community law: current status and expected developments *(P. Woolfson)*: [1994] 11 Int. ILR 404.
"Bancassurance" and Community law: current status and expected developments *(P. Woolfson)*: [1994] 12 JIBL 519.
Critical illness cover (*Fergus Muirhead*): (1995) 223 SCOLAG 71.
Finance Act notes: the insurance taxation provisions – sections 51–57 *(James Macleod)*: (1995) 3 B.T.R. 217–222.
Fraud and insurance claims *(R. Hodgin)*: (1995) 145 New L.J. 136.
Green grass with hidden potholes *(J. Woolley)*: 134 Tax. 153.
Insurance cover for redundancy, accident and sickness *(Michael J. Wilson)*: [1995] 139 S.J. 722.
Insurance intermediaries: liability to third parties *(Malcolm Clarke)*: (1995) 3 I.J.I.L. 162–174.
Insurance *(K. Sutton)*: (1995) 23 A.B.L.R. 64.
Insurance regulation in Singapore *(L. Bang Tat* and *K. Anandarajah)*: [1994] 11 Int. ILR 410
Insurers—influenced but not yet induced *(M. Clarke)*: [1994] LMCLQ 473.
Jabberwocky: recent decisions on the meaning of "event" and "occurrence" in the English courts *(D. Tompkinson)*: [1995] 3 Int.ILR 82.
Liability insurance and payments to meet uninsured liabilities: an analysis of the new tax regime *(Colin R. Baxter* and *David M. MacLean)*: (1995) 3 B.T.R. 293–305.
Offshore insurance centres: Bermuda *(G. Clark* and *A. Martin)*: [1995] 4 Int. ILR 123.
Opinions by "eminent English counsel" (*Angelo Forte*): 1995 J.R. 345.
Private insurance and ageing society in France *(F. Sorin* and *B. Teze)*: [1995] 4 Int. ILR 117.
Proposals for dealing with insolvent non-life insurance companies in the United Kingdom: the Department of Trade and Industry consultative document of December 1994 *(Paul Evans)*: (1995) 3(7) Int. ILR 236–240.
Recent developments in U.S. environmental litigation *(C. Kline)*: [1995] 1 Int. ILR 7.
Reinsurance law: recent themes and trends *(R. Lee* and *R. Merkin)*: [1994] 12 Int. ILR 439.
Schemes of arrangement for insolvent insurance companies in the United Kingdom: current developments (*P. Fidler*): [1995] 1 Int. ILR 18.

INSURANCE—*cont.*

Tax deductibility of insurance premiums: a case of state aid for insurance companies? *(Marc Dassesse)*: (1995) 1 EC T.J. 15–25.

The Halley: holed, but shall still afloat? *(A. Briggs)*: (1995) 111 L.Q.R. 18.

The legal framework in the United Kingdom for insurance policies sold by E.C. insurers under freedom for services *(I. MacNeil)*: (1995) 44 I.C.L.Q. 19.

The non-disclosure/misrepresentation defence: U.K. and California law regarding the "materiality" requirement *(J. Feeley)*: [1995] 3 Int. ILR 79.

The validity of compromise agreements *(Barry Mordsley)*: [1995] 2 Emp. L.B. 87–88.

Transfer of life insurance portfolios in the United Kingdom *(H. Everett)*: [1995] 1 Int. ILR 13.

Trusts for preferred beneficiaries of life policies under statute *(Stanley Jeremiah* and *Joanna R. Jeremiah)*: (1995) 3 I.J.I.L. 175–184.

UK insurers and derivatives – are you in control? *(Michael J. Barker)*: [1995] 3 Int. ILR 226–229.

Unauthorised insured: is "illegality" still a defence? *(S. Carter)*: [1995] 4 Int. ILR 111.

What constitutes carrying on insurance business in the United Kingdom? A review of section 2 of the Insurance Companies Act 1982 *(John Young)*: [1995] 3 Int. ILR 193–198.

When is a "defence" not a "defense"? The other side of *D.R. Insurance Co. v. Seguros American Banamex (D. Hargraves)*: [1994] 12 Int. ILR 447.

Who should assume the uncovered liabilities of liquidated or bankrupt life insurance companies? *(Jukka Luukkanen)*: [1995] 3 Int. ILR 203–207.

INTELLECTUAL PROPERTY

A plea to rejuvenate the Apostille Convention *(A. David Cohen)*: (1995) 50 M.I.P. 47.

An introduction to TRIPs *(Russell H. Falconer)*: [1995] 51 M.I.P. Supp PDY 14–15.

Francovich and beyond: a German perspective *(R. Uecker)*: (1994) 5 E.B.L.R. 285.

French IP in 1994 *(X. Buffet Delmas)*: [1994] Dec. M.I.P. 32.

Harmonising intellectual property laws in the European Union: past, present and future *(Thomas C. Vinje)*: (1995) 17 EIPR 361–377.

IP in greater China *(T. Hope)*: [1994] Dec. M.I.P. 36.

IP in the U.S. courts: 1994 *(V. Cooper)*: [1994] Dec. M.I.P. 28.

IP's role in major pharmaceutical deals *(Alice Macandrew)*: (1995) 50 M.I.P. 12–16.

Licensing overview and guidelines for royalty rates *(Jeffrey A. Schwab)*: [1995] 51 M.I.P. Supp PDY 20–21.

On-line services: a direct link to liability? *(Michael Hart* and *Harry Small)*: (1995) 6 P.L.C. 15–21.

Suing for patent infringement (*K. Wotherspoon*): (1995) 40 J.L.S. 26.

The tension between national intellectual property rights and certain provisions of E.C. law *(N. Macfarlane, C. Wardle* and *J. Wilkinson)*: (1994) 16 EIPR 525.

TRIPs and plant variety protection in developing countries *(S.K. Verma)*: [1995] 17 EIPR 281–289.

U.S. antitrust guidelines *(M. Bednarek)*: [1994] Dec. M.I.P. 18.

INTERNATIONAL LAW

A perspective from a UK insolvency practitioner *(Neil Cooper)*: [1995] 4 I.I.R. 30–35.

A short history of cohabitation and marriage *(V. Chauveau* and *A.-M. Hutchinson)*: (1995) 145 New L.J. 304.

Aliens and refugee law in Poland—recent developments *(W. Czaplinski)*: (1995) 6 IJRL 636.

Children's access to adoption records—state discretion or an enforceable international right? *(G. Van Bueren)*: (1995) 58 M.L.R. 37.

Developments in U.S. bilateral launch service agreements *(D. Burnett* and *F. Schroeder)*: (1994) XIX A. & S.L. 326.

English money judgments *(M. McParland)*: (1994) 144 New L.J. 1703.

Faultlines of nationality conflict: refugees and displaced persons from Armenia to Azerbaijan *(B. Frelick)*: (1995) 6 IJRL 581.

Foreign investment and company laws of selected central Eastern European and central Asian republics *(G. Campbell)*: [1994] 11 ICCLR 366.

French insolvency law reform: same scales, different balance *(A. Sorensoen* and *B. Mills)*: [1995] 1 ICCLR 6.

From migrants to refugees: Russian, Soviet and post-Soviet migration *(C. Messina)*: (1995) 6 IJRL 620.

Future regulation to allow multi-national arrangements between air carriers (cross-border alliances), putting an end to air carrier nationalism *(Henri A. Wassenbergh)*: (1995) 20 A. & S.L. 164–168.

Implementation of Hague Conventions in domestic law: the United Kingdom approach *(G. Maher)*: (1995) 14 C.J.Q. 21.

Intercountry adoption of refugee children: the Hague Recommendation *(K. Beevers)*: (1995) 7 JCL 10.

Interim measures of protection in the recent jurisprudence of the International Court of Justice *(J. Merrills)*: (1995) 44 I.C.L.Q. 90.

International law and the protection of the Arctic environment *(D. Rothwell)*: (1995) 44 I.C.L.Q. 280.

INTERNATIONAL LAW—*cont.*

Mandatory extraterritorial application of national law *(Serge Lazareff)*: (1995) 11(2) Arbitration Int. 137–150.

NAFTA—a legal and economic analysis *(R. Abeyratne)*: (1994) 13 Tr.L. 472.

One territory—three systems? The Hong Kong Bill of rights *(R. Swede)*: (1995) 44 I.C.L.Q. 359.

Private international law, characterisation and *Wright's Trustees v. Callender* (*R. D. Leslie*): 1995 S.L.T. (News) 264.

Questioning temporary protection *(D. Luca)*: (1995) 6 IJRL 535.

Renunciation of war as a universal principle of manking—a look at the Gulf War and the Japanese Constitution *(S. Hamura* and *E. Shiu)*: (1995) 44 I.C.L.R. 426.

Secret hangings on Japan's death row (*Alan McMillan*): (1995) 225 SCOLAG 111.

Slicing the shadow—the continuing debate over unitary taxation and worldwide combined reporting *(D. Sandler)*: [1994] B.T.R. 572.

State responsibility for the prevention and resolution of forced population displacements in international law *(Chaloka Beyani)*: (1995) 7(2) IJRL 130–147.

The asylum and refugee procedure in the Argentine legal system *(A. Iza)*: (1995) 6 IJRL 643.

The concept of "safe third country" in contemporary European refugee law *(E. Kjaegaard)*: (1995) 6 IJRL 649.

The dilemma of international law in civil conflicts *(Andy Darkoh)*: [1995] 11 Com. Jud. J. 14–20.

The external use of German armed forces—the 1994 judgment of the Bundesverfassungsgericht *(C. Kress)*: (1995) 44 I.C.L.Q. 414.

The impact of U.S. foreign asset control regulations on international money transfer systems *(J. Flynn)*: 10 I.B.F.L. 134.

The multilateral treaty amendment process – a case study *(M.J. Bowman)*: (1995) 44 I.C.L.Q. 540–559.

The nature of the subjective element in customary international law *(Olufemi Elias)*: (1995) 44(3) I.C.L.Q. 501–520.

The non-disclosure/misrepresentation defence: U.K. and California law regarding the "materiality" requirement *(J. Feeley)*: [1995] 3 Int.ILR 79.

The reform of the United Nations system in the context of the law of the sea and the United Nations Conference on the Environment and Development *(Joseph S. Warioba)*: (1995) 7 R.A.D.I.C. 426–444.

The refugee crisis in Africa as a crisis of the institution of the state *(A. Abdullah)*: (1995) 6 IJRL 563.

The registration of foreign letters rogatory in the English High Court *(T. Lawson-Cruttenden)*: 14 Lit. 48.

The relationship between international law and municipal law in the light of the interim South African Constitution 1993 *(D. Devine)*: (1995) 44 I.C.L.Q. 1.

The United Nations and freedom of religion *(B. Dickson)*: (1995) 44 I.C.L.Q. 327.

Treaty interpretation in the English courts since *Fothergill v. Monarch Airlines* (1980) *(Richard Gardiner)*: (1995) 44(3) I.C.L.Q. 620–628.

UN decade of international law: (1995) 25 E.P. & L. 125–127.

JURIES

Civil juries on trial *(Robert Milligan)*: (1995) 4 (Jul) Reparation 6.

Trial by jury: a force for change in Japan *(M. Dean)*: (1995) 44 I.C.L.Q. 379.

JURISPRUDENCE

A matter of life and death *(Robert Goff)*: (1995) 3 MLR 1–21.

Crime reporter *(S. Gilchrist)*: (1995) 139 S.J. 18.

History and interpretation in American jurisprudence *(N. Duxbury)*: (1994) 23 Anglo-Am. 501.

Jurisprudence of the European Court of Human Rights in 1994 (*Wilson Finnie*): 1995 J.R. 423.

Legal security from the point of view of the philosophy of law *(Gregorio Peces-Barba Martinez)*: (1995) 8 Ratio Juris 127–141.

Odysseus and the binding directive: only a cautionary tale? *(D. Morgan)*. (1994) 14 LS 411.

Rethinking the common law *(W. Lucy)*: (1994) 14 O.J.L.S. 539.

Suum cuique tribuere. Some reflections on law, freedom and justice *(Aulis Aarnio* and *Aleksander Peczenik)*: (1995) 8 Ratio Juris 142–179.

The nature of the subjective element in customary international law *(Olufemi Elias)*: (1995) 44 I.C.L.Q. 501–520.

The role of State consent in the customary process *(I.M. Lobo De Souza)*: (1995) 44 I.C.L.Q. 521–539.

"Which arrow?": rule type and regulatory policy *(J. Black)*: [1995] P.L. 94.

LANDLORD AND TENANT

Assignment, consent and a novel proposition *(M. Haley)*: (1995) 139 S.J. 68.

Break clauses in leases *(H. Wilkinson)*: 144 New L.J. 1636.

Coming up to scratch *(J. Driscoll)*: [1994] *Gazette* Dec. 7, 26.

Commercial leases *(Nabarro Nathanson)*: (1995) 6 P.L.C. 61.

LANDLORD AND TENANT—*cont.*

Consultation Paper on privity of contract between landlords and tenants *(Andrew Watson)*: 14 Lit. 290.
Distraint and the insolvent tenant *(Katie Bradford)*: (1995) 5 P.R. 63–164.
Effect of lease termination on sub-tenancies *(K. Stepien)*: (1995) 139 S.J. 222.
Enfranchisement under the Leasehold Reform Act 1993: a note on the nominee purchaser *(J. Hicks)*: [1995] Conv. 46.
Fair rents or unfair rents? *(P. Willan)*: (1995) 145 New L.J. 348.
Harassment and eviction: Pt. 1 *(Nic Madge)*: (1995) 145 New L.J. 937–938.
Harassment and eviction: Pt. 2 *(Nic Madge)*: (1995) 145 New L.J. 1060–1061.
Henry Stewart 16th annual rent review conference: review of valuation papers *(G. Dale)*: (1995) 1 R.R.L.R. 31.
Holiday Lettings (*W. Burns Shearar*): Prop.L.B. 14–2.
IHT: leases and reservation of benefit: (1995) 10 Farm T.B. 47.
Income from property: Pt. 1 *(David Williams)*: (1995) 313 Tax J. 12–15.
Ingram: the elixir of inheritance? *(Michael Hayes)*: *Legal Times*, May 30, 1995, p. 2.
Keep-Open Clauses (*Stewart Brymer*): Prop.L.B. 15–3.
Land charges *(J. Manthorpe)*: [1995] *Gazette*, March 29, 22.
Landlord and Tenant (Covenants) Act 1995 *(Bryan Emden* and *Terry Green)*: (1995) 9533 E.G. 83.
Landlord, help yourself *(L. Wise)*: (1994) 138 S.J. 1186.
Leasehold enfranchisement: limits to a loophole *(D. Clarke)*: (1995) 139 S.J. 314.
Leasehold reform: time to abandon implied surrender *(N. Hopkins)*: [1995] 58 M.L.R. 547–552.
Leaseholds, freeholds and reservation of benefit: (1995) 10 Farm T.B. 43–44.
Local authority sales and pre-emption rights (*Douglas J. Cusine*): (1995) 40 J.L.S. 234.
Mortgage interest relief: letting a private residence – new rules from 6 April 1995: Inland Revenue Tax Bulletin, 17 of 1995, 221–222.
Original tenant liability *(G. Webber)*: (1995) 139 S.J. 196.
Original tenant liability redefined *(Kaz Stepien)*: (1995) 139 S.J. 878–879.
Possession and clearance of land for development—Pt. II *(G. Parsons)*: (1995) 1 R.R.L.R. 22.
Possession: nine tenths of the law? *(E. Bannister* and *K. Stepien)*: (1994) 138 S.J. 1266.
Precedent editor's notes *(J. Adams)*: [1995] Conv. 102.
Privity of estate and the unwary tenant *(Richard Snape)*: (1995) L. Ex., Mar, 40–41.
Probationary period for all new tenants—Dundee conference (*Contributed*): (1995) 224 SCOLAG 83.
Recent developments in housing law *(N. Madge* and *J. Luba)*: [1994] L.A. Dec. 10.
Rent review clauses: hacking through the thickets *(D. Clarke)*: (1995) 139 S.J. 36.
Rent review update *(D. Clarke)*: (1995) 139 S.J. 215.
Rent Review: headline rents v. open market rents (*Iain Doran*): (1995) 40 J.L.S. 349.
Rent-free periods and rent review—the case so far (*S. Brymer*): Prop. L.B. 13–10.
Retirement annuities: Pt. 2 *(John Hayward)*: (1995) 310 Tax J. 10–11.
Service charge *(Nabarro Nathanson)*: (1995) 6 P.L.C. 61.
Severance revisited *(L. Tee)*: [1995] Conv. 105.
Stay healthy, stay safe – and stay out of jail *(Nigel Wheeler* and *Steven Lawrie)*: (1995) 9533 E.G. 78–79.
Tax avoidance decision could cost millions: *Legal Times*, May 30, 1995, p. 2.
Tenants' break options *(Jennifer Rickard)*: (1995) 5 P.R. 165–166.
Tenants on trial (*June Hyslop*): (1995) 224 SCOLAG. 84.
The effect of death on the right to buy under Part V of the Housing Act 1985 (Pt. 1) *(A. Brierley)*: [1995] Conv. 114.
The Feudal System—going, going, gone? (*Robert Rennie*): 1995 J.R. 321.
The Landlord and Tenant Act 1954 applies to a lease even after a tenant vacates *(Simmons & Simmons)*: (1995) I.H.L. Jul/Aug, 38–39.
The Landlord and Tenant (Covenants) Act 1995. What are the changes? *(Denton Hall)*: [1995] 9 Corp. Brief. 27–29.
The need to consult sureties when rent is reviewed *(R. Colbey)*: (1995) 1 R.R.L.R. 7.
The three month shorthold assured tenancy *(Adrian Jack)*: (1995) 145 New L.J. 925–926.
Under the volcano: tenants, sureties and disclaimer *(Stuart Bridge)*: (1995) 54 C.L.J. 253–255.
Variation of lease or new tenancy? *(Dr A. Dowling)* [1995] Conv. 124.
Vietnam report: new developments *(Paul K. Wood* and *Ian Lewis)*: 10 I.B.F.L. 283–284.
Views of the countryside *(R. Yates)*: [1995] *Gazette*, Apr. 5, 16.
When a shorthold tenancy goes wrong *(Charles Ward)*: (1995) L. Ex., Apr, 14–15.
When does a repair become an extraordinary repair? (*Stewart Brymer*): Prop.L.B. 15–8.
Withdrawing notices to quit *(A. Dowling)*: [1994] Conv. 437.

LAW REFORM

Consent and offences against the person: Law Commission Consultation Paper No. 134 *(D. Ormerod)*: (1994) 57 M.L.R. 928.
Conspiracy to defraud; some comments on the Law Commission's report *(J. Smith)*: [1995] Crim.L.R. 209.

LAW REFORM—*cont.*

Criminal justice and the trial and sentencing of white collar offenders *(R. Henham)*: 59 JCL 83.
Developing a law reform programme: (1994) 20 CLB 688.
Divorce reform—do we need fault? *(P. Townsend* and *A. Baker)*: 159 J.P.N. 206.
Land reform *(J.F. Garner)*: [1995] 145 New L.J. 1026.
Law Reform: hearsay and related topics: [1995] 7 Arch. News 4.
Manslaughter: the dilemma facing the law reformer *(Nicola Padfield)*: J. (1995) 59 Crim. L. 291–298.
Medical treatment and mental incapacity *(J. Stone)*: (1995) 139 S.J. 267.
Not completely appealing *(A. Owers)*: (1995) 145 New L.J. 353.
On mental incapacity *(D. Morgan)*: (1995) 145 New L.J. 352.
Paying the bill *(R. Ellison)*: (1995) 139 S.J. 162.
Pensions and divorce: time for change *(M. Rae)*: (1995) 145 New L.J. 310.
"Prolix and obscure" *(H. Wilkinson)*: [1995] Conv. 96.
Reform of intestacy: the best we can do? *(S. Cretney)*: (1995) 111 L.Q.R. 77.
Reform of the law and procedures of divorce: the White Paper *(Andrew Watson)*: [1995] 14 Lit. 336–337.
The emergence of a statutory right to privacy tort in England *(C. Hartmann)*: (1995) 16 JML&P 10.
The Environmental Bill (*Charles Smith*): Env.L.B. 7–5.
The Finance Bill process: scope for reform? *(L. Beighton)*: [1995] B.T.R. 33.
The form of indictments: comments on the Law Commission's consultation paper *(M. Bowes)*: [1995] Crim.L.R. 114.
The Law Commission and judicial review: principle versus pragmatism *(Ivan Hare)*: (1995) 54 C.L.J. 268–279.
The Law Commission Report on Judicial Review *(H. Hodge)*: (1995) 14 C.J.Q. 97.
The Pensions Act 1995 (*Iain J. S. Talman*): (1995) 40 J.L.S. 353.
The politics of arbitration reform *(A. Marriot)*: (1995) 14 C.J.Q. 125.
The Requirements of Writing (Scotland) Act 1995 (*Professor Robert Rennie*): 1995 J.R. 445.
Towards negotiated divorce *(Simon Roberts)*: (1995) 5 Fam M. 9–11.
U.K. competition law: the call for reform: (1995) 6 P.L.C. 11–12.
Who's afraid of Lord Woolf? *(Eileen Brennan)*: (1995) 5 C.P.R. 131–134.

LEGAL AID

A climate of change *(John Hayes)*: [1995] *Gazette* 25, 17.
Access, Legal aid and rural Scotland (*Alan A. Paterson*): 1995 J.R. 266.
Applications for pre-legal aid certificate costs—a lawful order *(J.N. Parry)*: 159 J.P.N. 104.
Bashing the lawyers *(Martin Mears)*: (1995) 145 New L.J. 1220.
Costs against the Legal Aid Board *(A. Logan)*: (1995) 145 New L.J. 59.
For richer, for poorer *(R. Smith)*: [1995] *Gazette* Jan. 5, 11.
Franchising small legal aid firms and the Green Paper *(Sarah Angell)*: [1995] 7 Fam. M. 6.
Improving custodial legal advice *(L. Bridges* and *J. Hodgson)*: [1995] Crim.L.R. 101.
Legal aid—problems and possibilities (*Ian Willock*): (1995) 223 SCOLAG 75.
Legal aid and the Law Society: (1995) 25 Fam. Law 445–446.
Mediation and divorce *(Maggie Rae)*: (1995) 5 Fam M. 8.
Paying for legal aid *(J. Bezzano)*: [1995] Jan. L.A. 9.
Professional and legal policy: police station advice in indictable-only cases: guidance from the criminal law committee of the Law Society: (1995) 92 (31) *Gazette* 27.
The administration of legal aid: 159 J.P.N. 123.
The European Court of Human Rights and criminal legal aid in Scotland (*Wilson Finnie*): 1995 S.L.T. (News) 271.
The practical points *(Stephen Orchard)*: [1995] *Gazette* 24, 18–19.
Twelve reasons for rejecting the Legal Aid Green Paper *(Michael Zander)*: [1995] 145 New L.J. 1098–1099.

LEGAL HISTORY

Claverhouse and the Dalrymples (*A.G. Stevenson*): 1995 J.R. 227.
Local Commissary courts in the eighteenth century (*Michael Meston*): 1995 J.R. 377.
Lord Haldane's fee books (*R. S. Shiels*): (1994) 62 S.L.G. 133.
Lorimer, Inglis and R.L.S.: Law and the railyard lockup (*Dr Paul Mahony*): 1995 J.R. 280.
Scots law in the colonies (*Hon. McPherson J.*) 1995 J.R. 191.
Stair's property: a Romanist system? (*D. L. Carey Miller*): 1995 J.R. 70.
The case of the Ross and Cromarty Rangers (The Aberdeen riot) (*F. Lyall*): 1995 J.R. 134.
The Civilists of Aberdeen: 1495–1995 (*M. C. Meston*): 1995 J.R. 153.
The evolving criminal trial jury, in myth and reality *(Gregory Durston)*: (1995) 57 Crim. Law. 2–3.
The study of law and politics *(J.A.G. Griffith)*: (1995) 1 J.L.S. 3–15.
The Universities of Aberdeen and the Court of Session in Edinburgh (*Rt. Hon. Lord Hope*): 1995 J.R. 5.

LIBEL AND SLANDER

Cross-border libel: Pt. 1 *(E. Simpson)*: 12 I.M.L. 83.
Defamation update *(J. Scott-Bayfield)*: (1995) 139 S.J. 189.
Defaming politicians and public officials *(D. Pannick)*: [1995] P.L. 1.
English libel in the US: [1995] Spr, C.C.M.L.R. 4.
Libel over the Internet *(Heather Rowe)*: [1995] 11 C.L.S.R. 201.
MP's discover the unwelcome face of parliamentary privilege *(Penelope Gorman)*: [1995] 139 S.J. 772–723.
Protection of free speech in Australia *(M. Hall)*: [1995] 13 I.M.L. 11.

LICENSING

Building on past mistakes *(K. Pain)*: (1994) 19 Lic.Rev. 9.
Can you review a "no beer " condition? *(C. Hepher)*: (1994) 19 Lic.Rev. 8.
Children's certificates for the bar areas of licensed premises—conditions for the availability of meals *(J. Spencer)*: 159 J.P.N. 242.
Effluent treatment plants caught by waste licensing, says DoE: [1995] 245 ENDS 31–32.
European Union Deregulation: [1995] Feb. B.L.R.A. 18.
Licensed to . . . *(K. Stephenson)*: (1995) 139 S.J. 223.
Multimedia—licensing of music *(R. Taylor)*: [1995] 13 I.M.L. 22.
New street controls in London: (1995) 20 Lic.Rev. 7.
"Scope of use" provisions in software licence agreements *(S. Davidson)*: [1995] 11 CLSR 74.
Sex establishments: if at first you don't succeed. *(Christine Clayson)*: [1995] 159 J.P. 521–523.
The Waste Management Licensing Regulations 1994 – effluent treatment plants: (1995) Env. L.B. Jul, 4–5.
Waste treatment plants: (1995) nv. 4(8) L.M. 8–9.

LIMITATION OF ACTIONS

Arriving late *(Philip Tsamados)*: [1995] 50 Adviser 33–36.
Automatic strike out: [1995] 2(6) Med. L. Mon. 4.
Automatic striking out of case transferred from High Court: [1995] 6 S.C.P. News 6.
Avoiding pitfalls in personal injury claims *(Gordon Exall)*: (1995) L. Ex., Mar, 12–13.
Challenging EC law before a national court: a further restriction of the rights of natural and legal persons? *(Sharon Turner)*: [1995] 4 I.J.E.L. 68–87.
English time limitations *(Clyde & Co)*: [1995] 9 P & I Int. 130–132.
Limitation pitfalls *(R. Nelson-Jones)*: [1994] *Gazette* Nov. 16, 27.
Limitations and chemical poisoning *(A. Care)*: (1995) 139 S.J. 17.
New claims and limitations periods *(R. James)*: (1995) 14 C.J.Q. 42.
Practice – plaintiff company disappearing in corporate restructuring and being replaced by different entity after the commencement of proceedings: (1995) 411 L.M.L.N. 2–3.
Section 14(1) Limitation Act 1980 and date of knowledge: Pt. I – the problem *(Sarah Brennan)*: [1995] 11 P. & M.I.L.L. 48–50.
The difference between latent damage and latent negligence *(C. Boxer)*: (1995) 139 S.J. 217.
Time limitation in the UK: deliberate concealment after the cause of action has accrued *(Nicholas Edgell)*: (1995) 3 Int. ILR 245–247.

LOCAL GOVERNMENT

All powers have their limits *(Charles Cross)*: (1995) L.G.C. Aug 18, 16–17.
Change and challenge in Scottish local government (*June Hyslop*): (1995) 225 SCOLAG 99.
Changing the rules of the game (considering *Scotland v. Grampian Regional Council* (1994) S.L.T. 1120 (*G. Junor*): 1995 S.L.T. (News) 95.
Chill waters of change *(Arthur Price-Jones)*: [1995] 92 *Gazette* 10.
Community care—rights to service (*Simon Collins*): (1995) 226 SCOLAG 123.
Community care update *(L. Clements)*: [1994] L.A. Dec. 21.
Compulsory purchase: recent developments *(N. Osborn)*: (1995) 139 S.J. 115.
Councils await outcome of "glass wars" *(B. Davies)*: (1995) 20 Lic.Rev. 9.
Fraud in public sector contracting *(S. Cirell* and *J. Bennett)*: (1995) 139 S.J. 238.
It's the quality that counts *(Leonie Cowen)*: (1995) 9 *Lawyer* 16.
Local authorities: information for decision making by database *(T. Corbitt)*: 158 J.P.N. 800.
Local government reorganization *(J. Garner)*: 159 J.P.N. 7.
Local government update *(Andrew Arden* and *Christopher Baker)*: (1994) 138 S.J. 1181, (1995) 139 S.J. 681–682.
New street controls in London: (1995) 20 Lic.Rev. 7.
Powers to splash out *(C. Cross)*: [1994] L.G.C. Dec. 16, 16.
Probationary period for all new tenants—Dundee conference (*Contributed*): (1995) 224 SCOLAG 83.
Sex shops *(A. Samuels)*: 159 J.P.N. 91.
Taking exceptions *(C. Cross)*: [1994] L.G.C. Nov. 18, 21.
Tenants on trial (*June Hyslop*): (1995) 224 SCOLAG 84.

LOCAL GOVERNMENT—*cont.*

The limits of contractual order in public sector transacting *(P. Vincent-Jones)*: (1994) 14 LS 364.
The Local Government etc. (Scotland) Act 1994 (*Jean McFadden*): (1995) 40 J.L.S. 48.
Tweaking the volume *(Stephen Cirell* and *John Bennett)*: [1995] Jun 30 L.G.C. 20–21.

MEDICINE

A matter of life and death *(Robert Goff)*: [1995] 3 MLR 1–21.
A pain in the WRULD *(K. Nicholas* and *E. Roth)*: (1995) 139 S.J. 64.
Assessment and rehabilitation in brain injury *(C. Hedley)*: (1995) 145 New L.J. 186.
Beta-blockers and asthmatics: some lessons from the case of *R. v. Dr A.K. Sinha (R. Collins)*: 159 J.P.N. 3.
Challenging DNA evidence *(A. Samuels)*: 159 J.P.N. 156.
Civil commitment of the mentally ill: compelling arguments for reform *(D. Price)*: [1994] MLR 321.
Civil liability of physicians for new methods of treatment and experimentation: a comparative examination *(Dieter Giesen)*: [1995] 3 MLR 22–52.
Damages for psychiatric injuries *(A. Ritchie)*: (1994) 144 New L.J. 1690.
Filius Cuius: Pt. II. Further information about human fertilisation and embryology *(R. Stevens)*: 158 J.P.N. 757, 781.
Force-feeding and the Mental Health Act 1983 *(P. Fennell)*: (1995) 145 New L.J. 319.
Head injury and compensation *(M. Weller)*: (1994) 144 New L.J. 1667.
Healthcare systems *(M. Evans)*: (1995) 139 S.J. 286.
Living wills: a panacea for all ills? *(Julia Abrey)*: (1995) Legal Times 23, Supp TE, 7.
Medical consent legislation in Ontario *(B. Dickens)*: [1994] MLR 283.
Medical treatment and mental incapacity *(J. Stone)*: (1995) 139 S.J. 267.
Nervous shock: bystander witnessing a catastrophe *(T. Keng Feng)*: (1995) 111 L.Q.R. 48.
NHS trusts and the Mental Health Act 1983 (*B. Dimond*): (1994) 144 New L.J. 1662.
On mental incapacity *(D. Morgan)*: (1995) 145 New L.J. 352.
Psychiatric injury and the bodily harm criterion *(D. Kell)*: (1995) 111 L.Q.R. 27.
Reasons for decisions *(D. Morgan)*: (1995) 145 New L.J. 428.
Reconciling the irreconcilable? Recent developments in the German law on abortion *(D. Van Zyl Smit)*: [1994] MLR 302.
Silicone litigation *(R. Levy)*: (1994) 138 S.J. 1214.
Stress injuries at work *(B. McKenna)*: (1994) 144 New L.J. 1652.
Strict liability and the supply of donated gametes *(K. Stern)*: [1994] MLR 261.
The legal status of advance directives: [1995] 2 Med. L. Mon. 6–10.
The patentability of human genes in France *(X. Buffet Delmas D'Autane)*: [1995] March M.I.P. 35.
The pathologist and the civil law *(J. Brennan)*: (1994) 138 S.J. (Dec. Supp.) 36.
The role of the tort of battery in medical law *(Gwen Seabourne)*: [1995] 24 Anglo-Am. 265–298.
Withholding life-sustaining treatment *(J. Stone)*: (1995) 145 New L.J. 354.

MENTAL HEALTH

Changes needed to law on mental incapacity: [1995] 62 Med. Leg. J. 79–80.
Civil commitment of the mentally ill: compelling arguments for reform *(D. Price)*: [1994] MLR 321.
Current topic: hospital orders without conviction *(A. Samuels)*: [1995] Crim.L.R. 220.
Disputes over mentally incapacitated adults *(F. Morris* and *M. Mullins)*: (1994) 138 S.J. 1184.
Force-feeding and the Mental Health Act 1983 *(P. Fennell)*: (1995) 145 New L.J. 319.
Mental incapacity: Report by the Law Commission *(Jill Manthorpe)*: (1995) 17 J. Soc. Wel. & Fam. L. 383–386.
NHS trusts and the Mental Health Act 1983 *(B. Dimond)*: (1994) 144 New L.J. 1662.
On mental incapacity *(D. Morgan)*: (1995) 145 New L.J. 352.
Patients in the community *(K. Harrison)*: (1995) 145 New L.J. 276.
Protecting the mentally disordered defendant against herself *(J.R. Spencer)*: (1995) 54 C.L.J. 232–235.
Stress at work: publishers beware: [1995] Spr C.C.M.L.R. 7 8.
The Law Commission proposals on mental incapacity *(Philip W.H. Fennell)*: (1995) Fam. Law 25 (Aug), 420–423.

MINING LAW

Minerals and their exploitation: (1995) 10 Farm T.B. 49–50.
Planning regulation and environmental consciousness: some lessons from minerals? *(Tim Jewell)*: (1995) J.P.L., Jun, 482–498.
The reform of old mineral permissions 1948–1981 *(A.R. Everton)*: (1995) 7 E.L.M. 115–120.

MINORS

Acting for children *(J. Leigh)*: (1995) 139 S.J. 40.
Alternative remedies to care proceedings *(David Burrows)*: (1995) 139 S.J. 636–637.
Care orders case – law: threatening the policy of the Children Act? *(Stephen Gilmore)*: (1995) *Legal Action* Aug, 16–19.

MINORS—*cont.*

Child performers in film and television productions *(I. Steel)*: [1995] 13 I.M.L. 20.
Child sexual abuse, access and the wishes of children *(E. Jones* and *P. Parkinson)*: (1995) 9 IJFL 54.
Children and young persons before the adult magistrates' court: where are they tried? *(E. Franey)*: 159 J.P.N. 21.
Children in armed conflict—new moves for an old problem *(C. Hamilton)*: (1995) 7 JCL 38.
Children seeking leave to apply under the Children Act 1989 *(D. Burrows)*: (1995) 139 S.J. 396.
Children's access to adoption records: state discretion or an enforceable international right? *(G. Van Bueren)*: (1995) 58 M.L.R. 37.
Children's certificates for the bar areas of licensed premises—conditions for the availability of meals *(J. Spencer)*: 159 J.P.N. 242.
Children's wishes, children's burdens *(Brian Cantwell* and *Sue Scott)*: (1995) 17(3) J. Soc. Wel. & Fam. L. 337–353.
Combatting the organized sexual exploitation of Asian children: recent developments and prospects *(D. Hodgson)*: (1995) 9 IJLF 23.
Community care update *(L. Clements)*: [1994] L.A. Dec. 21.
Confidentiality in children cases *(David Ormerod)*: (1995) 7 C.F.L.Q. 1–14.
Contact with children in care *(L. Mendoza)*: [1995] L.A. Feb. 13.
Contact: a compendium *(V. Smith)*: 159 J.P.N. 159, 188.
Covert video surveillance – a question of children's rights? *(Terry Thomas)*: [1995] 118 Childright 2.
Criminal responsibility of children: social policy and the courts *(Peter De Cruz)*: [1995] 8 P.C.L.B. 78–81.
Discovery and disclosure in children cases *(D. Burrows)*: (1995) 139 S.J. 60.
Filius cuius: Pt. II—further information about human fertilisation and embryology: (1994) 158 J.P.N. 781.
Homicide of children *(D. Power)*: 159 J.P.N. 209.
Intercountry adoption of refugee children: the Hague Recommendation *(K. Beevers)*: (1995) 7 JCL 10.
Major flaw fails minors *(J. Coker)*: [1995] *Gazette* Jan. 25, 12.
New rules for juvenile offenders *(T. Wilkinson)*: (1995) 139 S.J. 110.
Play-groups and child-minders: the effect of the Children Act 1989; registration and rights of appeal to the family courts *(J. Spencer)*: 159 J.P.N. 144, 157.
Procedural problems in representing children *(P. Harris)*: (1995) 7 JCL 49.
State and family: back to basics? *(S. Cretney)*: (1995) 111 L.Q.R. 65.
Suffer the little children – the Government's proposals on child pornography *(Susan M. Edwards)*: (1995) 7 C.F.L.Q. 49–58.
The Criminal Justice and Public Order Act 1994—the effect on young offenders *(L. Jason-Lloyd)*: 159 J.P.N. 71.
The ideological attack on transracial adoption in the USA and Britain *(P. Hayes)*: (1995) 9 IJLF 1.
The impact of the Child Support Act on lone mothers and their children *(C. Glendinning, K. Clarke* and *G. Craig)*: (1995) 7 JCL 18.
The interface between crime and child protection *(Barbara Mitchels)*: (1995) L. Ex. Jul, 14–15.
The legal abuse of homosexual children? *(C. Lind* and *C. Butler)*: (1995) 7 JCL 3.

MORTGAGES

A skeleton in the cupboard *(P. Judkins* and *H. Meek)*: [1995] 4 ICCLR 16.
Adjusting the scales? Independent advice and partial mortgage enforcement *(Alison Dunn)*: (1995) Conv. Jul/Aug, 325–332.
Dial M for mortgage *(Kerry Stephenson)*: (1995) 139 S.J. 689.
Execution of a mortgage deed *(C. Howells)*: (1995) 145 New L.J. 286.
It's official! (Pts. 1 and 2): 134 Tax. 290, 318.
Lenders' instructions to solicitors in domestic conveyancing transactions and legal fees in relation to mortgage-related work *(Christopher Hadfield)*: [1995] *Gazette*, 24, 30–31.
Mortgage interest relief: letting a private residence – new rules from 6 April 1995: Inland Revenue Tax Bulletin, 17 of 1995, 221–222.
Mortgage possession actions: identifying and preparing an appeal *(John Martin)*: [1995] 36 (Sum) Q.A. 10–12.
Sale by mortgagees *(Simon Miller* and *Jonathan Klein)*: (1995) 139 S.J. 607.
Welfare regulations to curb housing costs: (1995) 225 SCOLAG 119–120.
Who is entitled to the benefit of MIG policies? *(Paul Murrells)*: (1995) EG 9528, 101–102.

NATIONAL HEALTH

Codes of conduct and accountability for NHS boards *(Alice Belcher)*: [1995] Sum, P.L. 288–297.
NHS trusts and the Mental Health Act 1983 *(B. Dimond)*: (1994) 144 New L.J. 1662.
Whistleblowing and freedom of speech in the NHS *(Lucy Vickers)*: (1995) 145 New L.J. 1257–1258.

NEGLIGENCE

A plea for a lost chance: *Hotson* reconsidered *(C. Foster)*: (1995) 145 New L.J. 248.

Cerebral palsy, paralysis and brain injury – some current issues in medical negligence *(Howard Hatton)*: (1995) Litigator July, 304–306.

Delictual Liability for pure economic loss: recent developments (*Joe Thomson*): 1995 S.L.T. (News) 139.

Disappointed beneficiaries, the House of Lords and Scots Law (*Kenneth McK. Norrie*): Rep. B. 3–2.

Failed Sterilisation (*Lauren Sutherland*): Rep.B. 3–4.

Foreign torts and choice of law flexibility (considering *Red Sea Insurance Co. v. Bouygues SA* [1994] 3 All E.R. 749) (*J. Blackie*): 1995 S.L.T. (News) 23.

Healthcare systems *(M. Evans)*: (1995) 139 S.J. 286.

It shouldn't happen to a vet *(C. Foster)*: (1995) 139 S.J. 186.

Lack of good will *(A. Paton)*: [1995] *Gazette* March 1, 15.

Lenders and valuers: still at war: (1995) EG 9525, 156.

Lost chances in delict (*Dr Andrew Phillips*): 1995 J.R. 401.

Medical negligence claims: the paucity of funding *(David Sandison)*: (1995) 40 J.L.S.S. 309–310.

More thoughts on the auditor's liability in negligence in respect of the audit report *(Suzanne Chua)*: (1995) 16 Co. Law. 195–201.

Negligence, securities and the expanding duty of care (*R. Rennie*): (1995) 40 J.L.S. 58.

Negligent valuations *(T. Grant* and *H. Tomlinson)*: (1995) 139 S.J. 237.

Neighbour noise working party report (*Frances McManus*): Env.L.B. 7–2.

Solicitors' professional negligence *(C. Kessel)*: (1995) 145 New L.J. 498.

Strict liability and the supply of donated gametes *(K. Stern)*: [1994] MLR 261.

The anchor tenant and the "keep open" clause *(G. Dale)*: (1995) 139 S.J. 94.

The assessment of damages in actions against valuers: recent U.K. decisions *(J. Biggart)*: [1994] 11 Int. ILR 401.

The best ten *(Philip Vaughan)*: (1995) 23 *Legal Times* 13–14. (Cases on liability for professional negligence).

The brain-damaged baby (*L. Sutherland*): Rep.B. 2–3.

The difference between latent damage and latent negligence *(C. Boxer)*: (1995) 139 S.J. 217.

The legal status and liability of the copilot, Pt. 1 *(R. Kane* and *T. Pyne)*: (1994) XIX A. & S.L. 291.

The legal status and liability of the copilot, Pt. 2 *(R. Kane* and *T. Pyne)*: (1995) XX A. & S.L. 2.

The liability of the good Samaritan (*Hon. Lord Cullen*): 1995 J.R. 20.

The negligent fiduciary *(J. Heydon)*: (1995) 111 L.Q.R. 1.

The pathologist and the civil law *(J. Brennan)*: (1994) 138 S.J. (Dec. Supp.) 36.

The value judgment *(M. Badge)*: [1995] *Gazette* Mar. 22, 16.

To be sued or not to be? *(R.A. Percy)*: *Eagle*, June 1995, 13–14.

Valuing within the "Bracket" *(H.W. Wilkinson)*: (1995) 145 New L.J. 1267–1268.

When it all goes wrong *(P. Moss)*: [1995] 134 Tax. 455.

Witholding life-sustaining treatment *(J. Stone)*: (1995) 145 New L.J. 354.

NUISANCE

Animal nuisance complaints: the dos and don'ts *(Barry F. Peachey)*: [1995] 139 S.J. 784–785.

Clocks, bells and cockerels *(R.H. Bloor)*: (1995) 3 Ecc. L.J. 393–397.

Does only the careless polluter pay? A fresh examination of the nature of private nuisance *(Gerry Cross)*: [1995] 111 L.Q.R. 445–474.

Neighbour noise working party report *(Francis McManus)*: [1995] 7 Env. Law. 2–3.

Pollution and damages – two important judicial pronouncements *(Paul Sheridan)*: (1995) Env. L.B. Jul. 6–8.

Private rights and planning consent *(Jenny Steele)*: (1995) 2 Web J.C.L.I. 145–154.

Quiet, please! *(Simon Jackson)*: (1995) 139 S.J. 578–579.

Statutory nuisance *(J. Dunkley* and *A. Murdie)*: [1995] L.A. Feb. 19.

Tree preservation orders *(Gordon Wignall* and *Barry Stanton)*: (1995) 139 S.J. 814–815.

PARLIAMENT

All-women shortlists in the Labour Party *(Howard Davis)*: [1995] Sum, P.L. 207–214.

Audit, accounting officers and accountability: the Pergau Dam affair *(F. White, I. Harden* and *K. Donelly)*: [1994] P.L. 526.

Auditing the auditors: responses to the Select Committee's review of the United Kingdom ombudsman system 1993 *(P. Giddings* and *R. Gregory)*: [1995] P.L. 45.

David, Goliath and supremacy: the Isle of Man and the sovereignty of the United Kingdom Parliament *(P. Edge)*: [1995] 24 Anglo-Am. 1.

Parliament and the poll tax: a case study in parliamentary pressure *(Philip Cowley)*: (1995) 1 J.L.S. 94–114.

The debate begins *(F. Lagerberg)*: 134 Tax. 398.

The delegated powers scrutiny committee *(C. Himsworth)*: [1995] P.L. 34.

The emergence of a statutory right to privacy tort in England *(C. Hartmann)*: (1995) 16 JML&P 10.

The Scottish Constitutional Convention *(Jean McFadden)*: [1995] Sum, P.L. 215–223.

PARTNERSHIP

Articles of association for partnership companies *(Colin Mercer* and *Helen Shilling)*: (1995) 9 Corp. Brief. 4–5.
Company law: articles of association *(Saleem Sheikh)*: [1995] 6 ICCLR C152–153.
Finance Act notes: changes for facilitating self-assessment – sections 117–123 and Schedule 22 *(Adrian J. Shipwright)*: (1995) 3 B.T.R. 236–241.
Income from property: Pt. 2 *(David Williams)*: (1995) 314 Tax J. 25–27.
Insolvency focus *(H. Anderson)*: [1994] *Gazette* Dec. 7, 18.
Insolvent partnerships *(G. Levy* and *M. Goldberg)*: (1994) 138 S.J. 1262.
Jersey offers new limited partnerships *(Moz Scott)*: (1995) 6 I.T.R. 15–16.
Partners seek company *(Julie Watterston)*: [1995] 16 T.P.T. 105–107.
Partnerships and the new regime *(David Collinson)*: 135 Tax. 328–332.
Taking advantage of the new rescue culture *(Helen Kavanagh)*: [1995] 13 P.P.M. 92–93.
The importance of partnership culture *(David Maitland)*: [1995] 13 P.P.M. 103–105.
The tax-free carrot *(Karen Munnings* and *Radha Startin)*: [1995] 135 Tax. 437–440.
"With all my profits I thee endow": the tax risks of business marriage *(Sheena Grattan)*: (1995) 46 N.I.L.Q. 72–85.

PATENTS AND DESIGNS

Appellate patent practice in the United States *(J. Monroe)*: [1995] M.I.P. Lit. Ybk. 52.
Counterfeits—E.U. acts *(K. Hull)*: [1994] Dec. M.I.P. 24.
Cumulation of protection in E.C. design proposals *(H. Cohen Jehoram)*: (1994) 16 E.I.P.R. 514.
Enforcement of copyright of foreign works in Panama *(A. Aguilar Alfu)*: [1995] M.I.P. Lit. Ybk. 29.
GATT ratification means big changes to U.S. IP law *(B. McDonald)*: [1995] March M.I.P. 13.
IP and industrial property litigation in Greece *(A. Delicostopoulou)*: [1995] M.I.P. Lit. Ybk. 19.
IP and the convergence of technology and media *(C. Keck)*: [1995] March M.I.P. 26.
IP litigation in Italy *(A. Guglielmetti* and *Dr D. de Simone)*: [1995] M.I.P. Lit. Ybk. 23.
IP litigation in the Arab Republic of Egypt *(Dr M. Alamedin)*: [1995] M.I.P. Lit. Ybk. 15.
IP litigation in the Dominican Republic *(O. Jorge Mera)*: [1995] M.I.P. Lit. Ybk. 13.
IP litigation in the Kingdom of Saudi Arabia *(Dr M. Nader)*: [1995] M.I.P. Lit. Ybk. 41.
IP litigation in the Philippines *(L. Llanillo* and *V. Amador)*: [1995] M.I.P. Lit. Ybk. 32.
IP litigation in the United States *(D. Lee* and *V. Palladino)*: [1995] M.I.P. Lit. Ybk. 49.
Litigation in Spain *(S. Ferrandis)*: [1995] M.I.P. Lit. Ybk. 43.
Managing international patent litigation *(J. Forstner)*: [1995] M.I.P. Lit. Ybk. 3.
N.B.: copying designs of spare and component parts *(A.W. Pluckrose)*: (1995) 18 C.S.R. 168.
New developments for Canadian IP litigation *(J. Kokonis)*: [1995] M.I.P. Lit. Ybk. 7.
Patent practitioners—don't let GATT get you *(M. Voet, R. Berman* and *M. Gerardi)*: [1995] March M.I.P. 20.
Patent proceedings in the Czech Republic *(Z. Pradna)*: [1995] M.I.P. Lit. Ybk. 9.
Patenting algorithms: the Gordian Knot retwisted (Pt. 1) *(R. Stern)*: [1995] 1 C.T.L.R. 12.
Patenting software in the United States *(S. Glazer* and *S. Kahn)*: [1995] Feb. M.I.P. 19.
People's Republic of China: IP litigation *(C. Borg-Marks)*: [1995] M.I.P. Lit. Ybk. 34.
Practical aspects of patent litigation in Japan *(A. Ikeda)*: [1995] Feb. M.I.P. 38.
Protecting industrial designs: an EU overview *(Freshfields)*: [1995] 51 M.I.P. 37–38.
Romanian IP litigation *(Dr M. Opriou)*: [1995] M.I.P. Lit. Ybk. 39.
Software patents—where next? *(Dr I. Lloyd)*: [1995] 11 CLSR 91.
The calculation of damages for patent infringement *(Richard Boulton* and *Mark Bezant)*: (1995) 50 M.I.P. 32–38.
The patentability of human genes in France *(X. Buffet Delmas D'Autane)*: [1995] March M.I.P. 35.
The patentability of the second therapeutic application – why must the law be changed? *(J. Savina)*: (1995) 74 P.W. 32–35.
The performance of biotech patents in the national courts of Europe (England, Germany and the Netherlands) *(Richard Ebbink)*: (1995) 75 P.W. 25–28.
The right of nationals of non-Madrid Union countries to own international registrations *(George R.F. Souter)*: [1995] 17 EIPR 333–336.
The U.S. International Trade Commission *(M. Blakeslee* and *R. Zelnick)*: [1995] M.I.P. Lit. Ybk. 55.
The UK Trade Marks Act 1994 and comparative advertising *(Dirk Meyer-Harport)*: [1995] 6 Ent. L.R. 195–197.
U.K.—major developments for 1995 *(I. Karet)*: [1995] M.I.P. Lit. Ybk. 46.
Utility models: (1995) 18 I.P. News. 2–4.
Valuing intellectual property *(N. Bertolotti)*: [1995] Feb. M.I.P. 28.

PENSIONS AND SUPERANNUATION

A market base for pension cost measurement *(Jonathan Fisher)*: [1995] 116 Accountancy 111–112.
A new era *(Stephanie Hawthorne)*: (1995) 24 Pen. World 3.
Are you opting out of the pensions review? *(Karen Nokes)*: [1995] 92 *Gazette* 22–23.
Caught in the act *(Adrian Lamb)*: (1995) 24 Pen. World 30–31.
Cheese and chalk *(Robin Ellison)*: (1995) 24 Pen. World 67–68.

PENSIONS AND SUPERANNUATION—*cont.*

Claims that cannot be pensioned off *(T. Levitt* and *J. Stanbury)*: (1994) 138 S.J. (Dec. Supp.) 26.
Coloroll decided: equalisation of pensions (*I. J. S. Tolman*): (1994) 39 J.L.S.S. 462.
Employment and pensions legislation: (1995) 6 Revenue 5–6.
"Equal access": yesterday, if not sooner *(Peter Woodhouse)*: (1995) 22 *Legal Times* 12.
Equality—but what is the cost? (*Fergus Muirhead*): (1995) 224 SCOLAG 92.
Into the twilight zone: the future of pensions in the United Kingdom *(J. Learmond* and *C. Bouch)*: [1994] 12 Int. ILR 452.
Looking after the children *(Pauline Sibbit)*: [1995] 24 Pen. World 48–49.
Member trustees and augmentations of pension scheme benefits *(D. Griffiths)*: (1994) 8 TruLI 109.
New time limits for pension claims by part-timers *(Freshfields)*: (1995) I.H.L. Jul/Aug, 58.
Part-timers *(Rowe & Maw)*: (1995) 6 P.L.C. 75.
Paying the bill *(R. Ellison)*: (1995) 139 S.J. 162.
Pension scheme trusts and Article 119: a complex relationship *(P. Docking)*: (1994) 8 TruLI 106.
Pension schemes: the legal effect of booklets, announcements and benefit statements *(D. Pollard)*: (1995) 9 TruLI 2.
Pensions after Brooks *(Maggie Rae)*: (1995) 145 New L.J. 1009–1010.
Pensions and divorce: time for change *(M. Rae)*: (1995) 145 New L.J. 310.
Pensions as property *(R. Nobles)*: (1994) 14 LS 345.
Security at a price *(Nick Sykes)*: [1995] 24 Pen. World 37–38.
Sex equality and occupational pension schemes *(Melanie Tether)*: (1995) 24 I.L.J. 194–203.
The 1995 Pensions Bill—Juvenal revisited: (*Iain J. S. Talman*): (1995) 40 J.L.S. 276.
The "survivor's" and "homemaker's" social welfare pensions *(M. Cousins)*: [1994] 12 ILT 263.
The ten commandments *(Jane Kola* and *Ian Pittaway)*: [1995] 24 Pen. World 39–40.

PETROLEUM

E.C. State Aids and energy *(L. Hancher)*: [1995] 2 OGLTR 62.
Oil and gas development in the Falklands *(E. Brown)*: [1994] 11 OGLTR 337.
Prospects for the UKCS under low oil prices after the 1993 Finance Act *(A. Kemp)*: [1994] 11 OGLTR 343.
Texaco v. State of Louisiana: an analysis of and solution to market value litigation *(A. Thomas* and *E. Belton)*: [1995] 3 OGLTR 99.
The legal and fiscal regulation of research and exploitation of hydrocarbons in Senegal following law 86-13 of 14 April 1986 (Constituting the new oil code) *(I. Ba)*: [1995] 3 OGLTR 106.
The Maghreb-Europe gas pipeline: its juridicial structure *(R. Piqueras)*: [1995] 3 OGLTR 95.

POLICE

Advising at the police station: Pt. 1 *(Neil O'May)*: (1995) L. Ex., Apr, 12–13.
Advising at the police station: Pt. 2 *(Neil O'May)*: (1995) L. Ex., May, 15.
All in the mind? *(Neil Corre)*: (1995) 139 S.J. 658.
Cracking the codes *(M. Cousens)*: [1995] *Gazette* Feb. 1, 18.
Criminal Justice and Public Order Act 1994—the Bail Act provisions *(F. Davies)*: 159 J.P.N. 279.
Criminal Justice and Public Order Act 1994: police powers, bail sentencing *(N. O'May)*: [1995] L.A. Feb. 10.
Criminal update *(A. Edwards)*: [1995] *Gazette*, Apr. 12, 36.
Curtailing the right to silence, access to legal advice and section 78 *(H. Fenwick)*: [1995] Crim.L.R. 132.
Disclosing unused material to the defence: [1995] 159 J.P. 515.
Evidence – conversation containing admissions about offence charged, but including future plans: (1995) Crim.L.R. 493–494.
Fair trial *(Sir Anthony Mason)*: [1995] Crim.L.J. 7.
Genuine public interest *(Stephen Gilchrist)*: (1995) 139 S.J. 686–687.
Improving custodial legal advice *(L. Bridges* and *J. Hodgson)*: [1995] Crim.L.R. 101.
New improved PACE *(R. Ede)*: (1995) 139 S.J. 298.
Non-police station interviews? (1995) 139 S.J. 299.
PACE update *(David Bentley)*: (1995) 139 S.J. 819–820.
Partners against drugs: the view from the police *(Keith Hellawell)*: (1995) 99 Prison Serv. J. 21–23.
PII and the police *(S. McNamara)*: (1995) 139 S.J. 262.
Police and government in Scotland (*Neil Walker*): 1995 S.L.T. (News) 199.
Police co-operation in the TEU: tiger in a Trojan horse? *(M. den Boer)*: (1995) C.M.L.Rev. 555.
Police news: (1995) 34 Howard Journal 276–277.
Privatisation without consultation *(H. Kitchen)*: [1995] Jan. L.A. 8.
Psychology and legal practice: fairness and accuracy in identification parades (*I. McKenzie)*: [1995] Crim.L.R. 200.
Pursuing the police (*Douglas Brodie*): 1995 J.R. 292.
Suing the police *(Sailesh Mehta* and *Steven Allen)*: (1995) L. Ex. Jul, 16–18.

POLICE—*cont.*

The Metropolitan Police assault: charging offences—are they based on law? *(J. Woods)*: 159 J.P.N. 42.

Traumatised Hillsborough police officers fail proximity damages test: [1995] 235 H. & S.B. 13–15.

Undercover police operations and what the suspects said (or didn't say) *(Andrew L-T. Choo* and *Manda Mellors)*: (1995) 2 Web J.C.L.I. 22–33.

Who pays the bill when the police get it wrong? *(Alan Beckley)*: [1995] 68 Pol. J. 202–206.

PRACTICE (CIVIL)

A pain in the WRULD *(K. Nicholas* and *E. Roth)*: (1995) 139 S.J. 64.

Access to justice – the interim report of Lord Woolf: [1995] Jun C.I.L.L. 1059–1062.

Allocating family law cases *(P. Tain)*: (1995) 139 S.J. 192.

Anton Pillers and Marevas in Hong Kong *(R. Morris)*: [1994] 11 JIBL 480.

Approximation of judiciary law in the European Union (*Nigel Morrison*): 1995 S.L.T. (News) 183.

Are you fully insured? *(H.H. Clapham)*: 14 L.J. 189.

Automatic striking out: another trap *(K. Browne)*: (1995) 139 S.J. 120.

Beware the forgotten order *(P. Smith)*: (1995) 145 New L.J. 346.

Cards on the table—the exchange of experts' reports and witness statements in civil litigation in England and Wales (*Robert Turner*): Civ.P.B. 3–2.

Charity proceedings: proper parties *(A. Samuels)*: 14 Lit. 65.

Civil litigation brief *(G. Exall)*: (1994) 138 S.J. 1204, (1995) 139 S.J. 272.

Civil procedure: will Woolf work? (*Robert C. Elliot*): 1995 S.L.T. (News) 263.

Commercial actions—first thoughts (*Lord Penrose*): Civ.P.B. 1–3.

Corporate clients and civil justice *(Paul Mitchard)*: (1995) Litigator July, 279–284.

Costs against the Legal Aid Board *(A. Logan)*: (1995) 145 New L.J. 59.

Decisions of the Privy Council in other jurisdictions: limits of *stare decisis* in Commonwealth jurisdictions *(P. Edge)*: (1994) 20 CLB 720.

Discovery and disclosure in children cases *(D. Burrows)*: (1995) 139 S.J. 60.

Discovery, or the time bomb of Peruvian guano *(Robert Turner)*: (1995) 4 (Jul) Civ.P.B. 2–3.

Discovery: redaction in action *(J. Goodliffe)*: (1995) 145 New L.J. 313.

Dismissal for want of prosecution *(Craig Osborne)*: (1995) L. Ex. Aug, 16–17.

European harmonisation of court procedure (*Michael Upton*) (1995) 40 J.L.S. 197.

Family proceedings: case management *(D. Burrows)*: (1995) 139 S.J. 168.

Foreign currency judgments: the Scottish experience *(G. Maher)*: (1995) 44 I.C.L.Q. 72.

How much is enough? *(G. McCool* and *M. Bennett)*: (1995) 139 S.J. 284.

Indemnity costs *(Mark Watson-Gandy)*: (1995) 159 J.P. 574.

Interim measures of protection in the recent jurisprudence of the International Court of Justice *(J. Merrills)*: (1995) 44 I.C.L.Q. 90.

Law Society proposals to improve civil justice system *(Andrew Watson)*: [1995] 14 Lit. 330–331.

Legal measures under Bulgarian law in cases of copyright infringement of software *(V. Dimitrova)*: (1995) 11 CLSR 25.

Limitation pitfalls *(R. Nelson-Jones)*: [1994] *Gazette* Nov. 16, 27.

Litigation and remedies in software infringement cases in the Czech Republic *(Z. Loebl)*: (1995) 11 CLSR 23.

New claims and limitations periods *(R. James)*: (1995) 14 C.J.Q. 42.

No fishing: recovery of medical records pre-litigation (*L. Sutherland*): Rep. L.B. 1–3.

Non-compliance with rules of court *(I. Scott)*: (1995) 14 C.J.Q. 88.

Orders for interim possession in the Sheriff Court (*Angela Grahame*): (1995) Civ.P.B. 4–5.

PII and the police *(S. McNamara)*: (1995) 139 S.J. 262.

Practice statement: procedural changes: (1995) 92 *Gazette* 35–36.

Privilege in the family mediation process *(T. Ingman)*: (1995) 111 L.Q.R. 68.

Procedural fairness (*Douglas Brodie*): 1995 S.L.T. (News) 105.

Procedural problems in representing children *(P. Harris)*: (1995) 7 JCL 49.

Procedural reform in United States courts *(M. Aspen)*: (1995) 14 C.J.Q. 107.

Procedural reform of the Court of Session (*Lord Morton of Shuna*): (1995) Civ.P.B. 1–2.

Representing children in court: recent changes to the Children (Scotland) Bill (*Rosemary Gallagher*): Fam.L.B. 16–3.

Security for costs and European law *(P. Matthews)*: [1994] LMCLQ 454.

Service by fax: betrayed by your headed notepaper? *(M. Watson-Gandy)*: 14 Lit. 47.

Slowing down the gravy train *(Paul Newman)*: [1995] 6 Cons. Law 55–59.

Some serious thoughts from Essex on civil justice *(H.H.J. Brandt)*: (1995) 145 New L.J. 350.

Stop whipping the delay boy! *(R. Williams)*: (1995) 139 S.J. 14.

Striking out appeals *(I. Scott)*: (1995) 14 C.J.Q. 90.

"Tayloring" case management to Woolf's litigation super-highway *(Iain Goldrein)*: (1995) Litigator July, 297–303.

The appropriate venue: "small personal injury claims and automatic arbitration" *(G. Holgate)*: 14 Lit. 52.

The best ten *(David Jones)*: (1995) 22 *Legal Times* 13.

The case for a civil justice review (*Lord Gill*): (1995) 40 J.L.S. 129.

The civil standard of proof uncertainty: probability, belief and justice *(D. Hamer)*: (1994) 16 SydLR 506.

PRACTICE (CIVIL)—*cont.*

The expert report (*Lauren Sutherland*): (1995) Civ.P.B. 3–7.

The registration of foreign letters rogatory in the English High Court *(T. Lawson-Cruttenden)*: 14 Lit. 48.

The use of comparative law by common law judges *(T. Allen* and *B. Anderson)*: (1994) 23 Anglo-Am. 435.

PRESS

Case points to new start for contempt law: (1994) 1 C.C.M.L.R. 5–6.

Changes in the newspaper reporting of rape trials since the Second World War *(Keith Soothill* and *Chris Grover)*: (1995) 37 Res. B. 45–49.

The accused, the jury and the media *(D. Cairney)*: (1995) 145 New L.J. 12.

The emergence of a statutory right to privacy tort in England *(C. Hartmann)*: (1995) 16 JML&P 10.

PRISONS

Calculating days in default for non-payment of fines *(F.G. Davies)*: [1995] 159 J.P. 499–501.

Do you receive me?: (1995) 9 *Lawyer* 19.

Employment in the prison service; whither public service regulation? *(G. Morris)*: [1994] P.L. 535.

Inspections: (1995) 34 Howard Journal 279–280.

Mandatory drug testing for prisoners: the initial phase of implementation *(Pat Kelly)*: (1995) 99 Prison Serv. J. 38–40.

More children held in prison: [1995] 118 Childright 3.

Pressure groups, penal policy and the gaols *(Roy Light)*: (1995) 100 Prison Serv. J. 27–38.

Prison: shield from threat, or threat to survival? *(Michael Ross)*: (1995) 99 Prison Serv. J. 23–28.

The new legal regime for prison officers *(G. Morris)*: 23 I.L.J. 326.

Time on remand: [1995] 4 (Aug) S. News 8–10.

White-haired offenders *(H. Codd)*: (1994) 144 New L.J. 1582.

PUBLIC ENTERTAINMENTS AND RECREATION

Blood sports and public law *(A. Lindsay)*: (1995) 145 New L.J. 412.

Child performers in film and television productions *(I. Steel)*: [1995] 13 I.M.L. 20.

Clubs and societies: VAT free sport and recreation – illusion or reality? *(John B. Arnold* and *David Ratcliffe)*: (1993) 26 VAT Plan. 2–3.

Consent forms: can they be simpler? *(A. Mosawi)*: [1995] 13 I.M.L. 18.

Drugs in sport—chains of custody *(E. Grayson)*: (1995) 145 New L.J. 44.

Exclusive gallery and publishing agreements: U.S. precedent and commentary *(G. Victoroff)*: [1995] 11 CLSR 53.

Multimedia—licensing of music *(R. Taylor)*: [1995] 13 I.M.L. 22.

Newspapers and U.K. media ownership controls *(L. Ainsworth* and *D. Weston)*: (1995) 16 JML&P 2.

Section 35: a guide to Ireland's film tax shelter *(F. Mannon)*: [1995] 2 ENT. LR 43.

Sympathy for the devil? Contractual constraint and artistic autonomy in the entertainment industry *(S. Greenfield* and *G. Osborn)*: (1994) 15 JML&P 117.

Synthetic movie stars—a test case for intellectual property law *(G. Poll)*: 13 I.M.L. 5.

Theatre: grand rights and theme musicals *(L. Harrison)*: 13 I.M.L. 3.

PUBLIC HEALTH

Contaminated land *(R. Stein* and *S. Humber)*: (1995) 139 S.J. 270.

Does only the careless polluter pay? A fresh examination of the nature of private nuisance *(Gerry Cross)*: [1995] 111 L.Q.R. 445–474.

Environmental protection: clarity of abatement notices: [1995] 5 L.G. & L. 13.

Neighbour noise working party report *(Francis McManus)*: [1995] 7 Env. Law. 2–3.

Residential property with adjoining holiday cottages – pig farm on adjacent land: [1995] J.P.L. 619–633.

Water pollution and the causing offence *(N. Parpworth)*: 159 J.P.N. 244.

RATING AND VALUATION

Fair rents or unfair rents? *(P. Willan)*: (1995) 145 New L.J. 348.

Rating revaluation: is the outcome appealing? *(P. Redman)*: (1995) 139 S.J. 194.

Rent review update *(D. Clarke)*: (1995) 139 S.J. 215.

REPARATION

High valuations versus bad lending (*Paul F. J. Wade*): Rep.B. 4–2.

Sheriff court reparation—a nightmare (*P. F. J. Wade*): Rep.B. 2–2.

RESTITUTION

Anticipatory contracts: restitution restrained *(Graham Virgo)*: (1995) 54 C.L.J. 243–246.
Breach of trust: accessory liability: (1995) 9 Comm. Leases 8–10.
Does a subcontractor have restitutionary rights against the employer? *(Peter Watts)*: (1995) 3 (Aug) L.M.C.L.Q. 398–403.
Striking the balance in the law of restitution *(Graham Virgo)*: (1995) 3 (Aug) L.M.C.L.Q. 362–371.

REVENUE AND FINANCE

Accounting information and company size *(David Chopping)*: (1995) L. Ex., Mar, 46.
Accounting rules! The role of accounts in establishing taxable income *(L. Cane)*: [1994] 5 B.L.R. 293.
Accounts recognition of tax *(M. Hannay)*: [1995] 124 Comp. Acct. 25.
Air finance for Africa, legal issues—the airline perspective *(T. Garabga)*: (1995) XX A. & S.L. 18.
Bringing in the money *(F. Lagerberg)*: 134 Tax. 326.
Budget 1994 *(J. Simpson)*: (1995) 40 J.L.S. 17.
Budget 1995 – representations on the form and administration of the tax system: (1995) Tax. P., Aug, 26–28.
Chinese corporate governance and finance in Taiwan *(Dr B. Wallace Semkow)*: 9 I.B.F.L. 528.
Dangerous liaisons: (1995) 16 T.P.T. 89–90.
Delayed reaction *(R. Grierson)*: 134 Tax. 399.
Dependent on revenue goodwill *(S. McKie)*: 134 Tax. 426.
Derivatives: the new regulatory challenge *(R. Dale)*: 10 I.B.F.L. 11.
Discrimination against individuals and enterprises on grounds of nationality: direct taxation and the European Court of Justice *(T. Lyons)*: [1994] B.T.R. 554.
Examine the contract! *(R. Taylor)*: 134 Tax. 346.
Farming taxation (Pts. I and II) *(J. Greenwood)*: 134 Tax. 477, 538.
Fight to finish *(C. Lintott* and *M. Bennett)*: 134 Tax. 380.
Foreign currency judgments: the Scottish experience *(G. Maher)*: (1995) 44 I.C.L.Q. 72.
Foreign exchange practices: 134 Tax. 316.
From the east, bearing gifts *(D. Southern)*: 134 Tax. 320.
Green grass with hidden potholes *(J. Woolley)*: 134 Tax. 153.
Impenetrable drafting *(A. Rowland)*: 135 Tax. 9.
Indirect employment *(G. Axe)*: 134 Tax. 266.
Investment managers' rules sharpened: 134 Tax. 502.
Is there a need for general anti-avoidance legislation in the United Kingdom? *(C. Masters)*: [1994] B.T.R. 647.
It's official (Pt. II): 134 Tax. 532.
It's official! (Pts 1 and 2): 134 Tax. 290, 318.
Let purchasers beware! *(M. Hannay)*: [1994] 123 Comp. Acct. 20.
Matching elections: Pt. 1 *(Roger Muray* and *David Small)*: (1995) 312 Tax J. 7–9.
Matching elections: Pt. 2 *(Roger Muray* and *David Small)*: (1995) 313 Tax J. 16–17.
Monetary union—a cooler look *(J. Chown)*: 10 I.B.F.L. 107.
More complex legislation *(A. Sellwood)*: 134 Tax. 534.
National tax laws reign supreme over capital freedom in the European Union *(Sideek Mohamed)*: (1995) 2 E.F.S.L. 180–185.
"No taxation without restitution"—the Law Commission's proposals on recovery of overpaid taxes *(L. Flynn)*: [1995] B.T.R. 15.
Opportunities and weaknesses of the multilateral arbitration convention *(Dirk Schelpe)*: [1995] 2 I.T.P.J. 119–129.
Power to draw up conduct of business rules after the Investment Services Directive *(T. Thorkildsen)*: (1995) 139 S.J. 102.
Recent developments in taxation of air transport—the ICAO-IATA symbiosis *(R. Abeyratne)*: (1995) XX A. & S.L. 48.
Recent trend in United Kingdom double tax treaties: [1994] B.T.R. 546.
Royal taxation *(D. Pearce-Crump)*: [1994] B.T.R. 635.
Self-assessment for income tax—another view *(C. Sandford)*: [1994] B.T.R. 674.
Self-assessment: the beasts of burden *(Russell Cockburn)*: (1995) 16 T.P.T. 137–139.
Settlement negotiations *(Gerry Jackson)*: (1995) 135 Tax. 472–473.
Slicing the shadow—the continuing debate over unitary taxation and worldwide combined reporting *(D. Sandler)*: [1994] B.T.R. 572.
Standard accounting *(David Marks)*: (1995) 316 Tax J. 6–7.
Taking financial services to the cleaners *(M. Levi)*: (1995) 145 New L.J. 26.
Taxation update *(R. McBurnie)*: (1995) 139 S.J. 15.
The debate begins *(F. Lagerberg)*: [1994] 134 Tax. 398.
The end of an era? *(Malcolm Gunn)*: [1995] 135 Tax. 383–387.
The European Court of Human Rights and the right of the accused person to remain silent: can it be invoked by taxpayers? *(S. Frommel)*: [1994] B.T.R. 598.
The Finance Bill process: scope for reform? *(L. Beighton)*: [1995] B.T.R. 33.
The full picture *(F. Lagerberg)*: [1995] 134 Tax. 450.
The international headquarters companies legislation—law and practice *(G. Richards)*: [1995] B.T.R. 7.

REVENUE AND FINANCE—*cont.*

The new regime—Pts. I and II *(T. Cohen)*: 134 Tax. 370, 402.

The OECD issues: Pt. 2 of its transfer pricing rules *(Marc M. Levey* and *Lawrence W. Shapiro)*: [1995] 6 ICCLR 237–245.

The path to paying gross (*J. Fernandez*): 134 Tax. 243.

The powers that be *(G. Axe)*: 134 Tax. 508.

The private finance initiative and local authorities: opportunities and problems *(Graham Reid)*: (1995) 10 JIBL 237–242.

The qualifying settlement *(C. Sokol)*: 134 Tax. 480.

The use of derivatives by public companies: disclosure and supervision in the United States *(Mayer, Brown and Platt Derivatives Group)*: [1995] 1 JIBL 11.

Unbalanced power *(David Williams* and *Gary Morris)*: [1995] 135 Tax. 403–406.

Vendor placings: financing acquisitions with equity *(Noel Hutton* and *Patrick Rawnsley)*: (1995) 6 P.L.C. 17–25.

Weathering the transition *(Sarah E. Deeks)*: (1995) 16 T.P.T. 97–99.

When it all goes wrong *(P. Moss)*: [1995] 134 Tax. 455.

Wrongful dispositions of motorvehicles—a legal quagmire *(I. Davies)*: [1995] J.B.L. 36.

RIGHTS IN SECURITY

A refit for the floating charge? (*David A. Bennett*): Bus.L.B. 16–2.

Reform of security over moveable property (*Andrew J.M. Steven*): 1995 S.L.T. (News) 120.

Reform of security over moveable property (*Hamish Patrick*): 1995 S.L.T. (News) 42.

Security over moveable property (*J. Murray*): 1995 S.L.T. (News) 31.

ROAD TRAFFIC

Breathalyser procedure and the hospital patient *(J. Black)*: (1994) 138 S.J. 1287.

Disqualification for not telling the police who the driver was *(A. Samuels)*: 158 J.P.N. 796.

Disqualification from driving under Road Traffic Offenders Act 1988: [1995] 2 S. News 8–11.

Magistrates – procedure – conviction following s.9 of Criminal Justice Act 1967 statements: (1995) 159 J.P. 396.

Mitigation effective and ineffective: (1995) 59(3) J. Crim. L. 258–261.

On the road to success *(Nick Lester)*: [1995] 14 L.G.C. 12–13.

Perverting the course of justice: failure to administer a breath test: [1995] 12 W.R.T.L.B. 42–43.

Road traffic update *(P. Niekirk)*: [1995] *Gazette* Feb. 1, 36.

Statutory nuisance: traffic noise: (1995) 4 E.L.M. 9–10.

The SACTRA report: its long term impact on the development of road management policy *(Derek Wood)*: (1995) 2 Trans. L. & P. 69–72.

The saviour of many a motorist *(N. Ley* and *F. Warren)*: (1994) 144 New L.J. 1669.

Totting-up driving disqualification and "Exceptional Hardship" (*Alexandra Macrae*): (1995) 224 SCOLAG 94.

Watch out for the Indians! The new endorsable offences under the Traffic Signs and General Directions 1994—green arrows and barred entries: 159 J.P.N. 55.

Who cares about traffic offences? *(B. Block)*: 159 J.P.N. 19.

SALE OF GOODS

Bulk revisited *(K.J. Brinkworth* and *D.P. Powell)*: [1995] 16 Bus. L.R. 106–109.

Buying from a friend of a friend (*Chris Willett*): (1995) 225 SCOLAG 102.

Caveat vendor! *(Brian Clapham)*: 14 Lit. 271–274.

Changes to the U.K. law relating to contracts for the sale and supply of goods *(D. Bainbridge)*: [1995] 11 CLSR 95.

Consumer protection: trading standards officer, enforcement and the Police and Criminal Evidence Act 1984 *(G. Holgate)*: 159 J.P.N. 284.

Debtor to creditor sales and the Sale of Goods Act 1979 (*Scott Crichton Styles*): 1995 J.R. 365.

Faulty goods, faulty law *(Alan Wilson)*: (1995) 5 C.P.R. 135–140.

Getting what you pay for (*Stuart Garvie*): (1995) 223 SCOLAG 78.

Lazarus arisen? *(J. Jeremie)*: (1995) 139 S.J. 99.

Misleading pricing and the 28 day rule: (1995) 18(9) Cons. L. Today 3–4.

NAFTA—a legal and economic analysis *(R. Abeyratne)*: (1994) 13 Tr.L. 472.

New Law Journal Precedent No. 8/1995: Notice to bailor regarding uncollected goods: (1995) 145 New L.J. 1261.

New sale of goods law *(E. Susan Singleton)*: (1995) 18 C.S.R. 145–146.

On the receiving end *(R. Lawson)*: [1995] *Gazette* Jan. 5, 20.

One small step for judicial man, one giant step for consumer kind? *(J. Whisson)*: (1995) 14 Tr.L. 129.

Practical legal points for purchasers of goods and services *(E. Susan Singleton)*: (1995) 14 Tr.L. 118.

Quality of Goods re-examined (*Chris Willett*): Bus.L.B. 15–4.

Romalpa theory and practice under retention of title in the sale of goods *(John De Lacy)*: [1995] 24 Anglo-Am. 327–368.

SALE OF GOODS—*cont.*

Safe products *(E. S. Singleton)*: 144 New L.J. 1634.
Sale and Supply of Goods Act 1994 (*H. L. MacQueen*): (1995) S.L.G. 5.
Sale and Supply of Goods Act 1994 (*K. R. Wotherspoon*): (1995) 40 J.L.S. 88.
Sale in the course of Business (*Chris Willett*): Bus.L.B. 16–3.
Sale of goods: changes to the transfer of ownership rules *(Sheil Bone* and *Leslie Rutherford)*: (1995) 139 S.J. 866–867.
The general duty to market safe products in United Kingdom law *(G. Howells)*: [1994] LMCLQ 479.
The Sale and Supply of Goods Act 1994 *(Michael G. Bridge)*: [1995] Jul J.B.L. 398–408.
The Sale and Supply of Goods Act 1994 (*W. C. H. Ervine*): 1995 S.L.T. (News) 1.
The Sale of Goods and Supply Act 1994 *(P. Groves)*: [1995] 16 B.L.R. 55.
Title to sue on a contract of carriage in Anglo-American law *(C. Cashmore)*: (1994) 23 Anglo-Am. 488.
Wrongful dispositions of motor vehicles in England: a U.S. certificate of title solution? *(I. Davis)*: (1994) 23 Anglo-Am. 460.
Wrongful dispositions of motorvehicles—a legal quagmire *(I. Davies)*: [1995] J.B.L. 36.

SEA AND SEASHORE

Legal implications of the entry into force of the UN Convention on the Law of the Sea (1995) 44 I.C.L.Q. 313.
Policing environmental offences in international waters (*Alastair N. Brown*): Env.L.B. 7–3.

SENTENCING

Totting-up driving disqualification and "Exceptional Hardship" (*Alexandra Macrae*): (1995) 224 SCOLAG 94.

SHERIFF COURT PRACTICE

New rules for family actions in the sheriff court: some observations (*D. Kelbie*): Civ.P.B. 2–3.
Options hearings—a view from Aberdeen (*Sheriff D. Kelbie*): Civ. P.B. 1–7.
Options hearings—a view from Glasgow (*Sheriff A. G. Johnston*): Civ.P.B. 1–5.
Orders for interim possession in the sheriff court (*Angela Grahame*): Civ.P.B. 4–5.
Reponing notes in the Sheriff Court (considering *McDonough v. Focus D.I.Y.*, 1993 S.C.L.R. 683) (*A. Grahame*): 1995 S.L.G. 10.
Some reflections on motions and counterclaims in the sheriff court (*G. Johnson*): Civ.P.B. 2–5.

SHIPPING AND MARINE INSURANCE

Australian maritime law decisions 1994 *(Martin Davies)*: (1995) 3 (Aug) L.M.C.L.Q. 385–397.
Bailment on terms *(F. Reynolds)*: (1995) 111 L.Q.R. 8.
Implementation of the LOS Convention at regional level: European Community competence in regulating safety and environmental aspects of shipping *(Andre Nollkaemper* and *Ellen Hey)*: [1995] 10 I.J.M.C.L. 281–300.
Insurance—non-disclosure—appropriate test of materiality: (1995) 407 L.M.L.N. 2–3.
Insured bills of lading – has their time come? *(William Tetley)*: (1995) 325 Fairplay 26.
Insurers heave sigh of relief on inducement: *Legal Times*, May 30, 1995, p. 3.
Limitation of shipowner's liability in Korea – interpretation of "shipowner's personal act or omission" in the 1976 Convention *(Byung-Suk Chung* and *T.H. Kim)*: (1995) 2 Int. M.L. 175–178.
New EC Consortium Regulation (Regulation 870/95) *(Philip Wareham)*: (1995) 2 Int. M.L. 178–181.
Right of access to books and records survives termination of underwriting agency agreement *(Jonathan Wright)*: (1995) 3 Int. ILR 178–179.
"Safer ships, cleaner seas": the report of the Donaldson Inquiry into the prevention of pollution from merchant shipping *(Mark W. Wallace)*: (1995) 3 (Aug) L.M.C.L.Q. 404–415.

SHOPS, MARKETS AND FAIRS

Open for business *(S. Deakin)*: 23 I.L.J. 333.
Removing bad apples: enforcing street trading rules *(B. Hough)*: (1994) 138 S.J. 1240.
Sex shops *(A. Samuels)*: 159 J.P.N. 91.
The new Sunday: reregulating Sunday trading *(I. Maher)*: (1995) 58 M.L.R. 72.
The Sunday trading episode: in defence of the Euro-defence *(M. Jarvis)*: (1995) 44 I.C.L.R. 451.
Where next in street trading? *(B. Hough)*: (1994) 138 S.J. 1210.

SOCIAL SECURITY

Appealing for simplicity *(David R. Harris)*: [1995] 317 Tax J. 11–13.
Avoiding the benefits trap *(P. Lucioli)*: [1995] *Gazette* Jan. 18, 18.
Community care update *(L. Clements)*: [1994] L.A. Dec. 21.

SOCIAL SECURITY—*cont.*

Damages for personal injuries and recoupment of social security benefit *(Geoffrey H. Holgate)*: 14 Lit. 280–289.
Due care and diligence *(David Williams)*: [1995] 50 Adviser 15–16.
Housing benefit overpayments (*Angus McIntosh*): (1995) 223 SCOLAG 67.
Incapacity benefit—what practitioners need to know (*Alan J. Gamble*): (1995) 40 J.L.S. 270.
Incapacity benefit *(M. Howard)*: 23 I.L.J. 364.
IVB and discrimination (*Stuart Allardyce*): (1995) 226 SCOLAG 129.
Recent developments in social security law *(S. Robertson* and *D. Thomas)*: [1995] Jan. L.A. 10.
Recent developments in social security law *(Sally Robertson* and *David Thomas)*: (1995) Legal Action Aug. 10–11, 14–15.
Reclaiming Social Fund loans from bankrupts (*A. Walker*): (1994) 218 SCOLAG 184.
Regression sets in at the Commission for Social Justice (*S. Allardyce*): (1994) 218 SCOLAG 175.
Representation before welfare benefit tribunals *(Marcus Branson)*: (1995) L. Ex. Aug. 32–33.
Social security update *(D. Thomas)*: [1995] *Gazette*, March 29, 28.
Unemployed? On yer bike (*S. Allardyle and A. Emsting*): (1995) SCOLAG 19.

SOLICITORS

A changing role for family lawyers *(Maggie Rae)*: [1995] Jul, Legal Action 6–7.
Blaming the lawyer—Pt. 2 (*Robert S. Shiels*): Crim.L.B. 14–3.
Come to terms with law's new face *(Tony Holland)*: (1995) 9 *Lawyer* 17.
Conditional fees: investing in the future *(Paul Balen)*: (1995) 139 S.J. 678–680.
Curtailing the right to silence, access to legal advice and section 78 *(H. Fenwick)*: [1995] Crim.L.R. 132.
Disappointed beneficiaries, the House of Lords and Scots Law (*Kenneth McK. Norrie*): Rep. B. 3–2.
Donning the advocate's gown *(Paul Hampton)*: [1995] 9 *Lawyer* 18.
Fees for speculative actions (*A. G. McCulloch*): 1994 S.L.T. (News) 401.
Improving custodial legal advice *(L. Bridges* and *J. Hodgson)*: [1995] Crim.L.R. 101.
Installing a networked computer system (*N. H. Mackay*): (1994) 62 S.L.G. 126.
Introducing quality (*S. I. Galt*): (1995) 63 S.L.G. 13.
Lack of good will *(A. Paton)*: [1995] *Gazette* March 1, 15.
Legal squad for 1995: (1995) 9 *Lawyer* 11.
Looking at . . . standard fees of solicitors *(Maggie Elliott)*: [1995] May, Litigator 218–221.
Making money work for you and your clients (*L. D. Crerar*): (1995) 40 J.L.S. 108.
Mediation as a form of alternative dispute resolution (*Fiona E. Raitt*): (1995) 40 J.L.S. 182.
PSC or LSD *(Stella Abrahams)*: (1995) 139 S.J. 688.
Society threatens advocacy review: [1995] *Gazette*, 25, 5.
Solicitors' professional negligence *(C. Kessel)*: (1995) 145 New L.J. 498.
Speech recognition sets lawyers free at Masons (*Chris Field*): 1995 S.L.G. 105.
The importance of keeping proper entries in solicitors' files (*Terence Rafferty*): Civ.P.B. 3–6.
The inevitable decline of the solicitor advocate (*R. Shiels*): (1995) 221 SCOLAG 37.
The Legal Practice Course: some reflections on the present and future *(David A. Chatterton)*: (1995) L. Ex., May, 26–27.
The National Vocational Qualification: a watershed for the legal profession? *(Rupert Kendrick)*: (1995) L. Ex., Jun, 20–21.
The Requirements of Writing (Scotland) Act 1995 (*Professors Cusine and Rennie*): (1995) 40 J.L.S. 221.
The Solicitors Indemnity Fund *(Andrew Kennedy)*: (1995) L. Ex. Jul, 45–46.
Training contracts and the LPC *(Andy Unger)*: (1995) 145 New L.J. 931–932.
Warnings for mainland U.K. from Northern Ireland *(B. McGrory)*: [1994] L.A. Dec. 9.
When a grant of representation should be renounced *(P. Rossdale)*: (1995) 139 S.J. 10.
Who judges solicitors? (1995) 145 New L.J. 285.

STAMP DUTIES

Stamping new ground *(Richard Pincher)*: (1995) 314 Tax J. 10–13.

STATUTES AND ORDERS

Administration: the Insolvency Act 1986, Pt. II *(D. Prentice, F. Oditah* and *N. Segal)*: [1994] LMCLQ 487.
Changes to confiscation procedures in drugs cases *(T. Millington)*: (1995) 139 S.J. 210.
Changes to the U.K. law relating to contracts for the sale and supply of goods *(D. Bainbridge)*: [1995] 11 CLSR 95.
Children seeking leave to apply under the Children Act 1989 *(D. Burrows)*: (1995) 139 S.J. 396.
Coming up to scratch *(J. Driscoll)*: [1994] *Gazette* Dec. 7, 26.
Commercial reporter *(R. Lawson)*: (1995) 139 S.J. 146.

STATUTES AND ORDERS—*cont.*

Consumer protection: trading standards officer, enforcement and the Police and Criminal Evidence Act 1984 *(G. Holgate)*: 159 J.P.N. 284.

Contact: a compendium *(V. Smith)*: 159 J.P.N. 159.

Conveyancers and the director as purchaser *(N. Le Poidevin)*: (1995) 139 S.J. 21.

Conveyancing: a new Act (Pts. 1 and 2) *(T. Aldridge)*: (1994) 138 S.J. 1230, 1261.

Criminal Justice and Public Order Act 1994—the Bail Act provisions *(F. Davies)*: 159 J.P.N. 259, 279.

Criminal Justice and Public Order Act 1994—the transfer provisions *(F. Davies)*: 159 J.P.N. 239.

Criminal Justice and Public Order Act 1994 (1994) 3 B.J.S.B. 2.

Criminal Justice and Public Order Act 1994: obscenity, pornography and videos *(C. Manchester)*: [1995] Crim.L.R. 123.

Criminal Justice and Public Order Act 1994: police powers, bail sentencing *(N. O'May)*: [1995] L.A. Feb. 10.

Criminal Justice and Public Order Act 1994: the public order provisions *(N. O'May)*: [1994] L.A. Dec. 10.

Curtailing the right to silence, access to legal advice and section 78 *(H. Fenwick)*: [1995] Crim.L.R. 132.

Deciding when jobs of equal value can be paid unequally: an examination of s.1(3) of the Equal Pay Act 1970 *(C. Kilpatrick)*: 23 I.L.J. 311.

Enfranchisement under the Leasehold Reform Act 1993: a note on the nominee purchaser *(J. Hicks)*: [1995] Conv. 46.

Environmental protection: "causing" pollution—the final word? *(G. Holgate)*: 159 J.P.N. 127.

Filius Cuius: Pt. II. Further information about human fertilisation and embryology *(R. Stevens)*: 158

Force feeding and the Mental Health Act 1983 *(P. Fennell)*: (1995) 145 New L.J. 319.

Gas safety *(R. Peters)*: (1994) 138 S.J. 1256.

Handling convictions admissible under s.27(3) of the Theft Act 1968 *(R. Munday)*: 159 J.P.N. 223, 261.

How they all got it wrong in Pepper v. Hart *(Francis Bennion)*: (1995) 3 B.T.R. 325–331.

Insolvency focus *(H. Anderson)*: [1994] *Gazette* Dec. 7, 18.

Insolvent partnerships *(G. Levy* and *M. Goldberg)*: (1994) 138 S.J. 1262.

Joint liability for unfair dismissal on transfers *(T. Bettany)*: (1995) 139 S.J. 43.

Leasehold enfranchisement: limits to a loophole *(D. Clarke)*: (1995) 139 S.J. 314.

Money laundering (Pt. 4) *(L. Jason-Lloyd)*: (1995) 145 New L.J. 278.

New rules for juvenile offenders *(T. Wilkinson)*: (1995) 139 S.J. 110.

New structures in education *(S. Simblet)*: (1995) 139 S.J. 296.

NHS trusts and the Mental Health Act 1983 *(B. Dimond)*: (1994) 144 New L.J. 1662.

Non-police station interviews? (1995) 139 S.J. 299.

One small step for judicial man, one giant step for consumer kind? *(J. Whisson)*: (1995) 14 Tr.L. 129.

Open for business *(S. Deakin)*: 23 I.L.J. 333.

Play-groups and child-minders: the effect of the Children Act 1989; registration and rights of appeal to the family courts *(J. Spencer)*: 159 J.P.N. 157.

Practical legal points for purchasers of goods and services *(E. Susan Singleton)*: (1995) 14 Tr.L. 118.

Procedural problems in representing children *(P. Harris)*: (1995) 7 JCL 49.

Prospects for the UKCS under low oil prices after the 1993 Finance Act *(A. Kemp)*: [1994] 11 OGLTR 343.

Provision for adult children under the Inheritance (Provision for Family and Dependants) Act 1975 *(Prof. G. Miller)*: [1995] Conv. 22.

Remedies for breach of employment contracts *(D. Brown)*: 23 I.L.J. 331.

Sex discrimination law *(A. Samuels)*: 14 L.J. 196.

Skirting around sexual harassment *(I. Mackay* and *J. Earnshaw)*: (1995) 145 New L.J. 338.

Statutory nuisance *(J. Dunkley* and *A. Murdie)*: [1995] L.A. Feb. 19.

The Construction (Design and Management) Regulations 1994: [1995] Feb. B.L.R.A. 37.

The Criminal Justice Act (Pts. 1 and 2) *(B. George)*: [1994] *Gazette* Dec. 16, 19, Jan. 5, 24.

The Criminal Justice and Public Order Act 1994: the effect on young offenders *(L. Jason-Lloyd)*: 159 J.P.N. 71, 89.

The Criminal Justice and Public Order Act 1994: the evidence provisions *(I. Dennis)*: [1995] Crim.L.R. 4.

The effect of death on the right to buy under Part V of the Housing Act 1985 (Pt. 1) *(A. Brierley)*: [1995] Conv. 114.

The fine line between trade names *(A. Mosawi)*: (1995) 145 New L.J. 410.

The Immigration (European Economic Area) Order 1994 *(S. Gondal)*: (1995) 9 I. & N.L. & P. 21.

The impact of the 1984 Data Protection Act on marketing by banks and financial institutions *(R. Jay)*: 10 I.B.F.L. 109.

The impact of the Child Support Act on lone mothers and their children *(C. Glendinning, K. Clarke* and *G. Craig)*: (1995) 7 JCL 18.

The insolvent Partnerships Order 1994 *(S. Frith* and *B. Jones)*: [1995] 11 CLSR 14.

STATUTES AND ORDERS—*cont.*

The Intelligence Services Act 1994 *(J. Wadham)*: (1994) 57 M.L.R. 916.
The nature of Royal contracts *(M. Nash)*: (1995) 145 New L.J. 282.
The new legal regime for prison officers *(G. Morris)*: 23 I.L.J. 326.
The new Sunday: reregulating Sunday trading *(I. Maher)*: (1995) 58 M.L.R. 72.
The new Trade Marks Act and the registration imperative *(P. Groves)*: (1995) 16 B.L.R. 5.
The new Trade Marks Act *(P. Groves)*: [1994] 5 B.L.R. 291.
The presumption against retrospective legislation *(D. Feldman)*: (1995) 111 L.Q.R. 32.
The right to silence *(A. Murdie)*: (1995) 139 S.J. 148.
The role of passing off under the Trade Marks Act 1994 *(D. Young)*: (1994) 138 S.J. 1258.
The Sale of Goods and Supply Act 1994 *(P. Groves)*: [1995] 16 B.L.R. 55.
The trust versus the company under the Charities Act 1992 and 1993: (1994) 144 New L.J. Charities Supp. 23.
Trade marks—good news for business *(J. Gyngell)*: (1994) 144 New L.J. 1590.
Transfer of Undertakings (Protection of Employment) Regulations 1981 (as amended)—update *(M. Ahmad)*: 158 J.P.N. 764.
TUPE or NUPE *(S. Miller)*: (1994) 13 Tr.L. 518.
Under-value transactions and third party purchasers—impact of the new act *(J.E. Adams)*: [1994] Conv. 434.
Views of the countryside *(R. Yates)*: [1995] *Gazette*, Apr. 5, 16.
Water pollution and the causing offence *(N. Parpworth)*: 159 J.P.N. 244.

STOCK EXCHANGE

Company securities—misinformation and litigation *(A. Hofler)*: (1995) 16 Co Law. 67.
CREST gets regulated *(Colin Mercer)*: (1995) 18 C.S.R. 174–175.
Electronic securities transfer and registration in Australia: issues for lenders *(J. Lipton)*: [1994] 12 JIBL 526.
Enforcement of the listing rules of the ASX *(D. Magarey)*: [1995] 13 C. & S.L.J. 6.
Essential elements of the second German financial market promotion law *(German Federal Ministry of Finance)*: 10 I.B.F.L. 184.
Listing debt securities in Hong Kong *(I. Hardee* and *L. Rita Theil)*: [1995] 1 JIBL 7.
Problems of share valuation under s.260 of the corporations law *(S. Sirianos)*: [1995] 13 C. & S.L.J. 88.
Revisions to the United States uniform commercial code governing transactions in securities and other investment property *(S. Rocks)*: 10 I.B.F.L. 25.
The Guernsey law on taking security over intangible personal property *(S. Howitt)*: [1995] 1 JIBL 16.
The use of derivatives by public companies: disclosure and supervision in the United States *(Mayer, Brown and Platt Derivatives Group)*: [1995] 1 JIBL 11.
The world view *(Anthony Hilton)*: (1995) 24 Pen. World 13.
Underwriting flotations: the safety net *(Simon Jay* and *Spencer Summerfield)*: (1995) 6 P.L.C. 31–42.
Valuation of shares: a legal and accounting conundrum *(A. Gregory* and *A. Hicks)*: [1995] J.B.L. 56.

SUCCESSION

Some of the problems of equitable compensation (*John Murray, Q.C.*): 1995 S.L.T. (News) 59.
Who is the heir of provision in trust? (*A. D. Ward*): (1995) 40 J.L.S. 30.

TELECOMMUNICATIONS

An upheaval in film and television law in England *(A. Mosawi)*: (1994) 144 New L.J. 1654.
Anti-competitive restrictions: B Sky B/Telewest/Nynex: [1995] 6 P.L.C. 11–12.
Battles in New Zealand's deregulated telecommunications industry *(R. Ahdar)*: 23 A.B.L.R. 77.
Broadcast regulation in Italy: debating new rules to join the European audio-visual market *(E. Andreatta* and *G. Pedde)*: [1995] 1 ENT.LR 7.
Competition policy in deregulated industries *(Henry Ergas)*: (1995) 23 I.B.L. 305–306, 308–310.
Direct advertising by telephone, fax and telex: the German law on unfair competition *(B. Steckler)*: [1995] 1 ENT.LR 13.
Drafting review and dispute resolution clauses *(Bird & Bird)*: [1995] Jul/Aug I.H.L. 65.
Financing the superhighway: Nynex CableComm's share offering *(Christopher Mort)*: [1995] 6 P.L.C. 23–28.
Format rights in television shows: your starter for 10: the department of trade and industry consults *(S. Lane* and *R. McD. Bridge)*: [1994] 6 ENT.LR 198.
Irish fiscal incentives for film and TV production *(K. Hoy* and *S. Curran)*: (1994) 12 I.M.L. 91.
Mapping the E.C. route to the information age *(A. Scott* and *R. Durie)*: [1995] 1 C.T.L.R. 5.
Newspapers and U.K. media ownership controls *(L. Ainsworth* and *D. Weston)*: (1995) 16 JML&P 2.
Prior restraint and Article 10 of the European Human Rights Convention *(P. Milmo)*: [1994] 6 ENT.LR 194.
Reforming telecoms competition rules *(Michael Bryan-Brown)*: (1995) 5 C.P.R. 121–126.

TELECOMMUNICATIONS—*cont.*

The courts' treatment of the broadcasting bans in Britain and the Republic of Ireland *(C. Banwell)*: (1995) 16 JML&P 21.

The Green Paper on the liberalisation of telecommunications infrastructure and cable television networks: Part 2: A common approach to the provision of infrastructure for telecommunications in the European Union *(Wolf Sauter)*: (1995) 6 U.L.R. 78–81.

The international telecommunication union: co-operation or cartel? *(J. Naftel)*: [1995] 1 C.T.L.R. 18.

Who can complain against the BBC? *(P. Robertshaw)*: (1995) 111 L.Q.R. 40.

TORT

Anthropomorphic justice: the reasonable man and his friends *(Lord Justice Hoffman)*: [1995] 29 Law Teach. 127–141.

Applying foreign law in English courts: liability for publication abroad *(James Young)*: [1995] 16 J.M.L. & P. 72–73.

Beaudesert bounces back *(N. Mullany)*: (1995) 111 L.Q.R. 44.

Choice of law in tort: a missed opportunity? *(Pippa Rogerson)*: (1995) 44(3) I.C.L.Q. 650–658.

Force majeure in the region—law and practice *(R. Singam)*: [1995] ICLR 156.

Further thoughts on foreign torts: *Boys v.* Chaplin explained *(A. Dickinson)*: [1994] LMCLQ 463.

Harassment as a tort in English and American law: the boundaries of *Wilkinson v. Downton* *(Richard Townshend-Smith)*: [1995] 24 Anglo-Am. 299–326.

Law Commission Consultation Paper No. 137 – Liability for psychiatric illness *(Kay Wheat)*: (1995) 2 Web J.C.L.I. 95–105.

Liability for psychiatric illness *(Teresa Sutton)*: (1995) 14 (Jul) C.J.Q. 158–162.

Skirting around sexual harassment *(I. Mackay* and *J. Earnshaw)*: (1995) 145 New L.J. 338.

Slippery substances *(Douglas Kinloch)*: (1995) 4 (Jul) Reparation 7.

The dividing line between goodwill and international reputation: a comparison of the law relating to passing off in the United Kingdom, Australia and other jurisdictions *(F. Martin)*: [1995] J.B.L. 70.

The duties and liabilities of lead managers in syndicated loans *(G. Bhattacharyya)*: 10 I.B.F.L. 172.

The emergence of a statutory right to privacy tort in England *(C. Hartmann)*: (1995) 16 JML&P 10.

The extension of the scope of breach of statutory duty for accidents at work: Pt. 1 *(W. Binchy* and *R. Byrne)*: (1995) 13 ILT 4.

The negligent fiduciary *(J. Heydon)*: (1995) 111 L.Q.R. 1.

The statutory prohibition of misleading or deceptive conduct in Australia and its impact on the law of contract *(D. Harland)*: (1995) 111 L.Q.R. 100.

To be sued or not to be? *(R.A. Percy)*: *Eagle*, June 1995, pp.13–14.

Tortious liability of an advising bank in the letter of credit transaction *(A. Ward* and *R. Wight)*: [1995] 4 JIBL 136.

Traffic accidents and nervous shock *(Barbara Harvey* and *Andy Robinson)*: (1995) 145 New L.J. 1100–1101.

Unsound practice: the epidemiology of medical negligence *(Patrick Hoyte)*: (1995) 3 MLR 53–73.

Who will protect the security guards? *(M. Bolger)*: [1994] 12 ILT 265.

TOWN AND COUNTRY PLANNING

A privileged position? Gypsies, land and planning law *(H. Barnett)*: [1994] Conv. 454.

A2 or not A2: that is the question *(M. Edwards* and *J. Martin)*: (1994) 138 S.J. 1228.

Compulsory purchase: recent developments *(N. Osborn)*: (1995) 139 S.J. 115.

Enforcement notices *(A. Samuels)*: (1995) 139 S.J. 138.

Golf courses and planning law *(H. Wilkinson)*: (1995) 145 New L.J. 121.

Historic parks and gardens: a review of legislation, policy guidance and significant court and appeal decisions *(David Lambert* and *Vincent Shacklock)*: [1995] Jul. J.P.L. 563–573.

Permitted Development and Environmental Assessment: Department of the Environment Circular 3/95: (1995) 7 E.L.M. 112–113.

Planning and conservation areas – where do we stand following PPG 15, and whatever happened to Steinberg? *(D.J. Hughes)*: [1995] Aug. J.P.L. 679–691.

Planning and copyright: copyright and planning *(A. Samuels)*: (1995) 159 J.P.N. 212.

Planning and environmental law offences *(R. Jackson)*: (1994) 158 J.P.N. 784.

Planning and pollution control (*G. Bruce Smith*): 1995 49 S.P.E.L. 46.

Planning and pollution control *(Neil Collar)*: (1995) 15 Prop. L. 9–11.

Planning appeals: conduct guidance: [1995] Aug. J.P.L. 698–699.

Planning policy: retailing (*Neil Collar*): Prop.L.B. 14–7.

Planning regulation and environmental consciousness: some lessons from minerals? *(Tim Jewell)*: (1995) J.P.L., Jun, 482–498.

Planning, pollution and noise control *(R. Stein* and *S. Humber)*: (1995) 139 S.J. 12.

Presentation of evidence at public inquiries: (1995) 5 P.E.L.B. 22–23.

PPG 9 "nature conservation" – a new initiative? *(Lynda M. Warren* and *Victoria Murray)*: [1995] Jul. J.P.L. 574–579.

Review of planning appeal procedures: [1995] Jul. J.P.L. 561–562.

TOWN AND COUNTRY PLANNING—*cont.*

Sounding some early warnings: (1995) 9533 E.G. 86–87.
"Structures" in planning law *(H. Wilkinson)*: (1995) 145 New L.J. 465.
Taking exceptions *(C. Cross)*: [1994] L.G.C. Nov. 18, 21.
The limits of planning agreements *(Jeremy Rowan-Robinson)*: (1995) 50 S.P.E.L. 60–63.
The power of consent *(A. Harrison)*: (1995) 139 S.J. 212.
The role and status of supplementary planning guidance *(Sean White* and *Mark Tewdwr-Jones)*: (1995) J.P.L., Jun, 471–481.
Tree preservation orders *(Gordon Wignall* and *Barry Stanton)*: (1995) 139 S.J. 814–815.
Use Classes Order: review and solicitors' offices (*N. Collar*): Prop. L.B. 13–8.

TRADE AND INDUSTRY

Alterations and remote trading *(Chris Tailby)*: (1995) 312 Tax J. 4–5.
An introduction to TRIPs *(Russell H. Falconer)*: [1995] 51 M.I.P. Supp PDY 14–15.
Australia: contract: duties of disclosure *(Irene Trethowan)*: (1995) 6 ICCLR C95–96.
Companies: disclosure of interests *(Steven M. Turnbull)*: [1995] 5 E.C.L. 38.
Comparative advertising *(V. Hall-Smith)*: 12 I.M.L. 85.
Competition: Netherlands building market *(Jessica Simor)*: (1995) 6 ICCLR C114–115.
Consumers and Europe *(D. Roberts)*: (1995) 14 Tr.L. 113.
Directive on the establishment of European works councils: effect of U.K. and non-E.U. companies *(R. D'Sa)*: [1994] 5 B.L.R. 295.
GATT ratification means big changes to U.S. IP law *(B. McDonald)*: [1995] March M.I.P. 13.
GATT: the U.S. signs away its freedom to act in IP disputes *(A. Macandrew)*: [1995] Feb. M.I.P. 5.
International credit transfers: the proposed E.C. Directive compared with the UNCITRAL Model Law *(Lotte Bojer)*: (1995) 10 JIBL 223–228.
International trade and development: (1995) 25 E.P. & L. 119–120.
Introducing the new rule of law in international trade *(Keith Steele)*: (1995) 23 I.B.L. 290–291.
Legal aspects of management buyouts *(M. Dwyer)*: [1995] 4 ICCLR 129.
Legal pitfalls in doing business in the Gulf States and Saudi Arabia *(R. Price)*: [1995] 1 MECLR 18.
Making the most of trade law opportunities *(Craig Pouncey* and *James Robinson)*: [1995] Jul/Aug G.L. & B. 22–23.
NAFTA—a legal and economic analysis *(R. Abeyratne)*: (1994) 13 Tr.L. 472.
Patent practitioners—don't let GATT get you *(M. Voet, R. Berman* and *M. Gerardi)*: [1995] March M.I.P. 20.
Principles of law relating to overseas trade: 1994 *(Reviewed by J. Mark Naftel)*: 1995) 6 ICCLR 189.
Procedural anomalies in State aid *(E. Fruithof)*: [1994] 5 E.B.L.R. 227.
Rights vs Efficiency? The economic case for transnational labour standards *(S. Deakin* and *F. Wilkinson)*: 23 I.L.J. 289.
Services join GATT: an analysis of the General Agreement on Trade in Services *(Matthew Kennedy)*: (1995) 1 Int. T.L.R. 11–20.
South Africa: trade finance – letters of credit *(A. Nico Oelofse)*: (1995) 10 JIBL N128–130.
The dividing line between goodwill and international reputation: a comparison of the law relating to passing off in the United Kingdom, Australia and other jurisdictions *(F. Martin)*: [1995] J.B.L. 70.
The origins of the World Trade Organisation *(Michael Blakeney)*: (1995) 1 Int. T.L.R. 49–53.
Trade and environment: some lessons from *Castlemaine Tooheys* (Australia) and *Danish Bottles* (European Community) *(D. Geradin* and *R. Stewardson)*: (1995) 44 I.C.L.Q. 41.
Trading law update *(R. Lawson)*: 159 J.P.N. 24.
U.K. competition law: the call for reform: (1995) 6 P.L.C. 11–12.

TRADE MARKS AND TRADE NAMES

First steps for China *(M. Abell)*: [1994] Dec. M.I.P. 42.
GATT ratification means big changes to U.S. IP law *(B. McDonald)*: [1995] March M.I.P. 13.
Intellectual property litigation in India *(D. Mehta* and *S. Abhyanker)*: [1995] M.I.P. Lit. Ybk. 21.
MIP and the convergence of technology and media *(C. Keck)*: [1995] March M.I.P. 26.
Protection of famous trade marks in Korea *(T. Hee Lee)*: [1995] M.I.P. Lit. Ybk. 26.
Registered trade mark could infringe copyright *(Denton Hall)*: (1995) 6 P.L.C. 69.
The Community trade mark office *(G. de Ulloa)*: [1995] M.I.P. Ybk. 17.
The fine line between trade names *(A. Mosawi)*: (1995) 145 New L.J. 410.
The new German Act on marks: E.C. harmonisation and comprehensive reform *(M. Fammler)*: [1995] 17 EIPR 22.
The new Trade Marks Act and the registration imperative *(P. Groves)*: [1995] 16 B.L.R. 5.
The new Trade Marks Act *(P. Groves)*: [1994] 5 B.L.R. 291.
The principle of exhaustion of track marks rights pursuant to Directive 89/104 (and Regulation 40/94) *(J. Rasmussen)*: [1995] 17 EIPR 174.
The protection of geographical indications in the European Economic Community *(B. Schwab)*: [1995] 5 EIPR 242.
The right of nationals of non-Madrid Union countries to own international registrations *(George R.F. Souter)*: [1995] 17 EIPR 333–336.

TRADE MARKS AND TRADE NAMES—*cont.*

The role of passing off under the Trade Marks Act 1994 *(D. Young)*: (1994) 138 S.J. 1258.
The "threats" section in the U.K. Trade Marks Act 1994: can a person still wound without striking? *(L. Gee)*: [1995] 17 EIPR 138.
The trademark law treaty *(G. Kunze)*: [1995] Feb. M.I.P. 23.
The UK Trade Marks Act 1994 and comparative advertising *(Dirk Meyer-Harport)*: [1995] 6 Ent. L.R. 195–197.
The UK Trade Marks Act 1994: an invitation to an olfactory occasion? *(Helen Burton)*: (1995) 17 EIPR 378–384.
Trade marks—good news for business *(J. Gyngell)*: (1994) 144 New L.J. 1590.
Trademarks in the E.C.: recent developments *(P. Groves)*: [1994] 5 E.B.L.R. 283.
Valuing intellectual property *(N. Bertolotti)*: [1995] Feb. M.I.P. 28.

TRADE UNIONS

Busy year for Certification Officer: (1995) Inland Revenue Law Bulletin No. 523, 13–14.
Employment law review 1995: Part 4: Trade union laws *(David Newell)*: (1995) 145 New L.J. 1230–1231.

TRANSPORT

A new maintenance condition?: [1995] 11 Road Law 239–240.
A new track *(S. Cromie)*: [1995] *Gazette* Feb. 8, 24.
English time limitations *(Clyde & Co)*: [1995] 9 P & I Int. 130–132.
Going off the rails? (*Gordon Junor*): 1995 S.L.G. 102.
Ostensible ownership and motor vehicle financing in England: Antipodean insights *(I. Davies)*: [1994] 11 JIBL 474.
Ro-ro ferry safety: [1995] 9(6) P & I Int. 114–118.
The SACTRA report: its long term impact on the development of road management policy *(Derek Wood)*: (1995) 2 Trans. L. & P. 69–72.
Transport and the environment *(N. Branton)*: [1995] 13 C. & S.L.J. 13.
VAT on transport? *(Andrew Pawley)*: (1995) 3 Trans. L. & P. 86–87.
Wrongful dispositions of motor vehicles in England: a U.S. certificate of title solution? *(I. Davis)*: (1994) 23 Anglo-Am. 460.

VALUE ADDED TAX

A problem only for the poorly advised *(Mark Stapleton)*: (1995) 319 Tax J. 14–15.
A thorn in customs' side *(P. Jenkins)*: 134 Tax. 374.
Arrangements have been made *(Michael Conlon)*: (1995) 13 VAT Int. 1233–1235.
Cars issue hots up *(Peter Sheppard)*: (1995) 46 VAT Plan. 2–4.
Contractual arrangements vital *(J. Price)*: 134 Tax. 626.
Distress for VAT: beating the Vatman *(A. Shryane)*: (1994) 138 S.J. 1202.
Is there a link? *(Richard Pincher)*: (1995) 3 B.T.R. 306–316.
Is there a positive side to VAT?: (1995) 6 Revenue 6–8.
Out of the frying pan *(R. Argles)*: 134 Tax. 292.
Overseas business *(Robert Killington)*: (1995) 5 Revenue 6–7.
Sledghammer to crack a nut? *(R. Nattrass)*: 134 Tax. 271.
The future VAT regime in the European Union: the opinion of the tax consultants *(Christian Amand)*: [1995] 35 Euro. Tax. 219–222.
The small business—the afterthought? *(Jill Gowtage)*: (1995) 45 VAT Plan. 2–3.
Ultimately funded training: Pt. 1 *(Ian Fleming)*: (1995) 315 Tax J. 8–9.
Ultimately funded training: Pt. 2 *(Ian Fleming)*: (1995) 316 Tax J. 14–15.
Value added tax: 134 Tax. 218.
VAT and land, and the changes *(Patrick C. Soares)*: [1995] 16 P.L.B. 22–23.
VAT and the Single Market *(David Ratcliffe)*: (1995) 45 VAT Plan. 4–6.
VAT in the European Union *(H. Macnair)*: [1995] 124 Comp. Acct. 17.
VAT issues for pension funds *(Peter Hewitt)*: (1995) 314 Tax J. 22–24.
VAT on property: recent developments *(Amanda K. Rowland)*: (1995) 139 S.J. 581–582.
Where are we now? *(Peter S. Jenkins)*: [1995] 135 Tax. 416–418.
Windfall or not? (*Alistair Duff*): 1995 S.L.T. (News) 216.

WATER AND WATERWORKS

After the periodic review – is it time for a re-evaluation of rate of return versus price-control regulation? *(Debbie Legge)*: (1995) 6 U.L.R. 74–77.
First conviction for drinking water inspectorate *(Eversheds)*: (1995) I.H.L. Jul/Aug, 59–60.
Flooding: why Scotland is out of its depth (*J. Riddell*): (1995) 40 J.L.S. 101.
Groundwater pollution in the United States: the mess left behind *(A. Crane)*: [1994] 12 OGLTR 383.

WATER AND WATERWORKS—*cont.*

OFWAT 1993–94 report on the cost of water delivered and sewage collected *(Debbie Legge)*: (1995) 6 U.L.R. 72–73.
Water easements *(Angela Sydenham)*: (1995) 10 Farm T.B. 48–49.
Water pollution and the causing offence *(N. Parpworth)*: 159 J.P.N. 244.
Water undertakings *(Dibb Lupton Broomhead)*: [1995] 16 Bus. L.R. 145.

WILLS

Disappointed beneficiaries, the House of Lords and Scots Law (*Kenneth McK. Norrie*): Rep. B. 3–2.
The Requirements of Writing (Scotland) Act 1995 (*Professor Robert Rennie*): 1995 J.R. 445.
The Requirements of Writing (Scotland) Act 1995 (*Professors Cusine and Rennie*): (1995) 40 J.L.S. 221.

WILLS AND SUCCESSION

Anglo-French estates *(A. Stanyer)*: (1994) 138 S.J. 1209.
Changes needed to law on mental incapacity: [1995] 63 Med. Leg. J. 79–80.
Discretionary trusts in wills *(R. Ray)*: 135 Tax. 13.
Frustration of testamentary intentions: a remedy for the disappointed beneficiary *(Alec Haydon)*: (1995) 54 C.L.J. 238–240.
It's a funny old world *(George Duncan)*: (1995) Legal Times 23, Supp TE, 19, 26.
Lack of good will *(A. Paton)*: [1995] *Gazette* March 1, 15.
Lady Bountiful to the Inland Revenue? *(Robert Grierson)*: [1995/96] 3 C.L. & P.R. 11–16.
New succession rules *(Jenny Higgins* and *Emma Chamberlain)*: (1995) 135 Tax. 500.
Odysseus and the binding directive: only a cautionary tale? *(D. Morgan)*: (1994) 14 L.S. 411.
Probate and tax update *(D. Chatterton)*: [1995] *Gazette*, March 29, 30.
Provision for adult children under the Inheritance (Provision for Family and Dependants) Act 1975 *(Prof. G. Miller)*: [1995] Conv. 22.
Reform of intestacy: the best we can do? *(S. Cretney)*: (1995) 111 L.Q.R. 77.
Tax efficient wills: Pt. 1 *(R. Ray)*: 134 Tax. 610.
Tax efficient wills: Pt. 4: Survivorship clauses in wills *(Ralph P. Ray)*: 135 Tax. 361–362.
The effect of divorce on wills *(R. Kerridge)*: [1995] Conv. 12.
Trustee dealings and remuneration: [1995] 9 Tr. & Est. 73–75.
Trustees' accounting responsibilities: [1995] 10 Tr. & Est. 7–8.
Variation of wills *(J. Ross-Martyn)*: [1994] Conv. 446.
When a grant of representation should be renounced *(P. Rossdale)*: (1995) 139 S.J. 10.

INDEX 1995

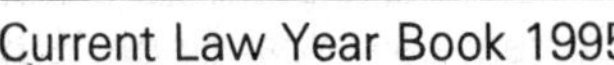